Pearson New International Edition

Abnormal Psychology
James N. Butcher   Susan M Mineka
Jill M. Hooley
Fifteenth Edition

PEARSON

Pearson Education Limited
Edinburgh Gate
Harlow
Essex CM20 2JE
England and Associated Companies throughout the world

Visit us on the World Wide Web at: www.pearsoned.co.uk

© Pearson Education Limited 2014

 ISBN 10: 1-292-02497-6
ISBN 13: 978-1-292-02497-4

British Library Cataloguing-in-Publication Data
A catalogue record for this book is available from the British Library

Printed in the United States of America

Table of Contents

Abnormal Psychology: An Overview

What Do We Mean by Abnormality?
The *DSM-5* and the Definition of Mental Disorder
Why Do We Need to Classify Mental Disorders?
What Are the Disadvantages of Classification?
How Can We Reduce Prejudicial Attitudes Toward the Mentally Ill?
How Does Culture Affect What Is Considered Abnormal?
Culture-Specific Disorders

How Common Are Mental Disorders?
Prevalence and Incidence
Prevalence Estimates for Mental Disorders
Treatment
Mental Health Professionals

Research Approaches in Abnormal Psychology

Sources of Information
Case Studies
Self-Report Data
Observational Approaches

Forming and Testing Hypotheses
Sampling and Generalization
Internal and External Validity
Criterion and Comparison Groups

Research Designs
Studying the World as It Is: Correlational Research Designs
Measuring Correlation
Statistical Significance
Effect Size
Meta-Analysis
Correlations and Causality
Retrospective Versus Prospective Strategies
Manipulating Variables: The Experimental Method in Abnormal Psychology
Studying the Efficacy of Therapy
Single-Case Experimental Designs
Animal Research

Unresolved Issues:
Are We All Becoming Mentally Ill? The Expanding Horizons
    of Mental Disorder

From Chapter 1 of *Abnormal Psychology*, Fifteenth Edition. James N. Butcher, Susan Mineka, Jill M. Hooley. Copyright © 2013 by Pearson Education, Inc. All rights reserved.

Abnormal psychology is concerned with understanding the nature, causes, and treatment of mental disorders. The topics and problems within the field of abnormal psychology surround us every day. You have only to pick up a newspaper, flip through a magazine, surf the Internet, or sit through a movie to be exposed to some of the issues that clinicians and researchers deal with on a day-to-day basis. Almost weekly some celebrity is in the news because of a drug or alcohol problem, an eating disorder, or some other psychological difficulty. Bookstores are full of personal accounts of struggles with schizophrenia, depression, phobias, and panic attacks. Films such as *A Beautiful Mind* portray aspects of abnormal behavior with varying degrees of accuracy. And then there are the tragic news stories of mothers who kill their children, in which problems with depression, schizophrenia, or postpartum difficulties seem to be implicated.

Abnormal psychology can also be found much closer to home. Walk around any college campus, and you will see flyers about peer support groups for people with eating disorders, depression, and a variety of other disturbances. You may even know someone who has experienced a clinical problem. It may be a cousin with a cocaine habit, a roommate with bulimia, or a grandparent who is developing Alzheimer's disease. It may be a coworker of your mother's who is hospitalized for depression, a neighbor who is afraid to leave the house, or someone at your gym who works out intensely despite being worrisomely thin. It may even be the disheveled street person in the aluminum foil hat who shouts, "Leave me alone!" to voices only he can hear.

The issues of abnormal psychology capture our interest, demand our attention, and trigger our concern. They also compel us to ask questions. To illustrate further, let's consider two clinical cases.

case study · Monique

Monique is a 24-year-old law student. She is attractive, neatly dressed, and clearly very bright. If you were to meet her, you would think that she had few problems in her life; but Monique has been drinking alcohol since she was 14, and she smokes marijuana every day. Although she describes herself as "just a social drinker," she drinks four or five glasses of wine when she goes out with friends and also drinks a couple of glasses of wine a night when she is alone in her apartment in the evening. She frequently misses early-morning classes because she feels too hung over to get out of bed. On several occasions her drinking has caused her to black out. Although she denies having any problems with alcohol, Monique admits that her friends and family have become very concerned about her and have suggested that she seek help. Monique, however, says, "I don't think I am an alcoholic because I never drink in the mornings." The previous week she decided to stop smoking marijuana entirely because she was concerned that she might have a drug problem. However, she found it impossible to stop and is now smoking regularly again.

case study · John

John comes from a family with no history of mental illness. He had a normal birth and seemed to develop normally when he was a child. However, when he was 21 John began to hear voices and started to believe that there was a conspiracy against him. Since that time, he has been on various different antipsychotic medications. Although these have helped a little, he still has symptoms of psychosis. Now aged 46, John has been unable to work since he became ill. He has also been hospitalized many times. John lives in sheltered accommodation, although he maintains contact with his parents and his older brother.

Perhaps you found yourself asking questions as you read about Monique and John. For example, because Monique doesn't drink in the mornings, you might have wondered whether she could really have a serious alcohol problem. She does. This is a question that concerns the criteria that must be met before someone receives a particular diagnosis. Or perhaps you wondered whether other people in Monique's family likewise have drinking problems. They do. This is a question about what we call **family aggregation**— that is, whether a disorder runs in families.

You may also have been curious about what is wrong with John and why he is hearing voices. Questions about the age of onset of his symptoms as well as predisposing factors may also have occurred to you. John has schizophrenia, a disorder that often strikes in late adolescence or early adulthood. Also, as John's case illustrates, it is not unusual for someone who develops schizophrenia to develop perfectly normally before suddenly becoming ill. You can read more about John's case and treatment in Valmaggia and colleagues (2008).

These cases, which describe real people, give some indication of just how profoundly lives can be derailed because of mental disorders. It is hard to read about difficulties such as these without feeling compassion for the people who are struggling. Still, in addition to compassion, clinicians and researchers who want to help people like Monique and John must have other attributes and skills. If we are to understand mental disorders, we must learn to ask the kinds of questions that will enable us to help the patients and families who have mental disorders. These questions are at the very heart of a research-based approach that looks

Fergie has spoken about her past struggles with substance abuse, specifically crystal meth.

to use scientific inquiry and careful observation to understand abnormal psychology.

Asking questions is an important aspect of being a psychologist. Psychology is a fascinating field, and abnormal psychology is one of the most interesting areas of psychology (although we are undoubtedly biased). Psychologists are trained to ask questions and to conduct research. Though not all people who are trained in abnormal psychology (this field is sometimes called psychopathology) conduct research, they still rely heavily on their scientific skills and ability both to ask questions and to put information together in coherent and logical ways. For example, when a clinician first sees a new client or patient, he or she asks many questions to try and understand the issues or problems related to that person. The clinician will also rely on current research to choose the most effective treatment. The best treatments of 20, 10, or even 5 years ago are not invariably the best treatments of today. Knowledge accumulates and advances are made. And research is the engine that drives all of these developments.

In this chapter, we will outline the field of abnormal psychology and the varied training and activities of the people who work within its demands. First we describe the ways in which abnormal behavior is defined and classified so that researchers and mental health professionals can communicate with each other about the people they see. Some of the issues here are probably more complex and controversial than you might expect. We also outline basic information about the extent of behavioral abnormalities in the population at large.

You will notice that a large section of this chapter is devoted to research. We make every effort to convey how abnormal behavior is studied. Research is at the heart of progress and knowledge in abnormal psychology. The more you know and understand about how research is conducted, the more educated and aware you will be about what research findings do and do not mean.

What Do We Mean by Abnormality?

It may come as a surprise to you that there is still no universal agreement about what is meant by *abnormality* or *disorder*. This is not to say we do not have definitions; we do. However, a truly satisfactory definition will probably always remain elusive (Lilienfeld & Landfield, 2008; Stein et al., 2010) even though there is a great deal of general agreement about which conditions are disorders and which are not (Spitzer, 1999).

Why does the definition of a mental disorder present so many challenges? A major problem is that there is no one behavior that makes someone abnormal. However, there are

some clear elements or indicators of abnormality (Lilienfeld & Marino, 1999; Stein et al., 2010). No single indicator is sufficient in and of itself to define or determine abnormality. Nonetheless, the more that someone has difficulties in the following areas, the more likely he or she is to have some form of mental disorder.

1. **Suffering:** If people suffer or experience psychological pain we are inclined to consider this as indicative of abnormality. Depressed people clearly suffer, as do people with anxiety disorders. But what of the patient who is manic and whose mood is one of elation? He or she may not be suffering. In fact, many such patients dislike taking medications because they do not want to lose their manic "highs." You may have a test tomorrow and be suffering with worry. But we would hardly label your suffering abnormal. Although suffering is an element of abnormality in many cases, it is neither a sufficient condition (all that is needed) nor even a necessary condition (a feature that all cases of abnormality must show) for us to consider something as abnormal.

2. **Maladaptiveness:** Maladaptive behavior is often an indicator of abnormality. The person with anorexia may restrict her intake of food to the point where she becomes so emaciated that she needs to be hospitalized. The person with depression may withdraw from friends and family and may be unable to work for weeks or months. Maladaptive behavior interferes with our well-being and with our ability to enjoy our work and our relationships. However, not all disorders involve maladaptive behavior. Consider the con artist and the contract killer, both of whom have antisocial personality disorder. The first may be able glibly to talk people out of their life savings, the second to take someone's life in return for payment. Is this behavior maladaptive? Not for them, because it is the way in which they make their respective livings. We consider them abnormal, however, because their behavior is maladaptive for and toward society.

3. **Statistical Deviancy:** The word *abnormal* literally means "away from the normal." But simply considering statistically rare behavior to be abnormal does not provide us with a solution to our problem of defining abnormality. Genius is statistically rare, as is perfect pitch. However, we do not consider people with such uncommon talents to be abnormal in any way. Also, just because something is statistically common doesn't make it normal. The common cold is certainly very common, but it is regarded as an illness nonetheless.

On the other hand, mental retardation (which is statistically rare and represents a deviation from normal) is considered to reflect abnormality. This tells us that in defining abnormality we make value judgments. If something is statistically rare and undesirable (as is severely diminished intellectual functioning), we are more likely to

As with most accomplished athletes, Venus and Serena Williams' physical ability is abnormal in a literal and statistical sense. Their behavior, however, would not be labeled as being abnormal by psychologists. Why not?

consider it abnormal than something that is statistically rare and highly desirable (such as genius) or something that is undesirable but statistically common (such as rudeness).

4. *Violation of the Standards of Society:* All cultures have rules. Some of these are formalized as laws. Others form the norms and moral standards that we are taught to follow. Although many social rules are arbitrary to some extent, when people fail to follow the conventional social and moral rules of their cultural group we may consider their behavior abnormal. For example, driving a car or watching television would be considered highly abnormal for the Amish of Pennsylvania. However, both of these activities reflect normal everyday behavior for most other Pennsylvania residents.

Of course, much depends on the magnitude of the violation and on how commonly the rule is violated by others. As illustrated in the example above, a behavior is most likely to be viewed as abnormal when it violates the standards of society and is statistically deviant or rare. In contrast, most of us have parked illegally at some point. This failure to follow the rules is so statistically common that we tend not to think of it as abnormal. Yet when a mother drowns her children there is instant recognition that this is abnormal behavior.

5. *Social Discomfort:* When someone violates a social rule, those around him or her may experience a sense of discomfort or unease. Imagine that you are sitting in an almost empty movie theater. There are rows and rows of unoccupied seats. Then someone comes in and sits down right next to you. How do you feel? In a similar vein, how do you feel when someone you met only 4 minutes ago begins to chat about her suicide attempt? Unless you are a therapist working in a crisis intervention center, you would probably consider this an example of abnormal behavior.

6. *Irrationality and Unpredictability:* As we have already noted, we expect people to behave in certain ways. Although a little unconventionality may add some spice to life, there is a point at which we are likely to consider a given unorthodox behavior abnormal. If a person sitting next to you suddenly began to scream and yell obscenities at nothing, you would probably regard that behavior as abnormal. It would be unpredictable, and it would make no sense to you. The disordered speech and the disorganized behavior of patients with schizophrenia are often irrational. Such behaviors are also a hallmark of the manic phases of bipolar disorder. Perhaps the most important factor, however, is our evaluation of whether the person can control his or her behavior. Few of us would consider a roommate who began to recite speeches from *King Lear* to be abnormal if we knew that he was playing Lear in the next campus Shakespeare production—or even if he was a dramatic person given to extravagant outbursts. On the other hand, if we discovered our roommate lying on the floor, flailing wildly, and reciting Shakespeare, we might consider calling for assistance if this was entirely out of character and we knew of no reason why he should be behaving in such a manner.

7. *Dangerousness:* It seems quite reasonable to think that someone who is a danger to him- or herself or to another person must be psychologically abnormal. Indeed, therapists are required to hospitalize suicidal clients or contact the police (as well as the person who is the target of the threat) if they have a client who makes an explicit threat to harm another person. But, as with all of the other elements of abnormality, if we rely only on dangerousness as our sole feature of abnormality, we will run into problems. Is a soldier in combat mentally ill? What about someone who is an extremely bad driver? Both of these people may be a danger to others. Yet we would not consider them to be mentally ill. Why not? And why is someone who engages in extreme sports or who has a dangerous hobby (such as free diving, race car driving or keeping poisonous snakes as pets) not immediately regarded as mentally ill? Just because we may be a danger to ourselves or to others does not mean we are mentally ill. Conversely, we cannot assume that someone diagnosed with a mental disorder must be dangerous. Although mentally ill people do commit serious crimes, serious crimes are also committed every day by people who have no signs of mental disorder. Indeed, research suggests that in people with mental illness, dangerousness is more the exception than it is the rule (Corrigan & Watson, 2005).

How important is dangerousness to the definition of mental illness? If we are a risk to ourselves or to others, does this mean we are mentally ill?

One final point bears repeating. Decisions about abnormal behavior always involve social judgments and are based on the values and expectations of society at large. This means that culture plays a role in determining what is and is not abnormal. For example, in the United States, people do not believe that it is acceptable to murder a woman who has a premarital or an extramarital relationship. However, *karokari* (a form of honor killing where a woman is murdered by a male relative because she is considered to have brought disgrace onto her family) is considered justifiable by many people in Pakistan (Patel & Gadit, 2008).

In addition, because society is constantly shifting and becoming more or less tolerant of certain behaviors, what is considered abnormal or deviant in one decade may not be considered abnormal or deviant a decade or two later. At one time, homosexuality was classified as a mental disorder. But this is no longer the case. A generation ago, pierced noses and navels were regarded as highly deviant and prompted questions about a person's mental health. Now, however, such adornments are quite commonplace, are considered fashionable by many, and generally attract little attention. What other behaviors can you think of that are now considered normal but were regarded as deviant in the past?

As you think about these issues, consider the person described in Box 1. Is he a courageous man of profound moral commitment? Or is his behavior abnormal and indicative of a mental disorder? Do others share your view about him?

The *DSM-5* and the Definition of Mental Disorder

In the United States, the accepted standard for defining various types of mental disorders is the American Psychiatric Association's *Diagnostic and Statistical Manual of Mental*

Tattoos, which were once regarded as highly deviant, are now quite commonplace and considered fashionable by many. Angelina Jolie has several.

Disorders. This manual is currently in its fourth edition and so is commonly referred to as the *DSM-IV*. However, a revision of the *DSM* is now underway, and *DSM-5* is expected in May 2013. Arabic numerals are being used instead of Roman numerals (5 versus V) to facilitate updating (e.g., DSM-5.1, DSM-5.2, etc.) in the future.

The pending revision of the *DSM* is already a subject of much debate and controversy. Many quite radical changes are being proposed, although nothing is finalized yet. We cannot therefore be certain about what changes will eventually find their way into *DSM-5*. To give you a sense of what changes might be on the horizon, however, we are including a new feature called Anticipating *DSM-5*. These brief highlights are designed to help you stay informed and to give you some sneak previews about what may be coming.

In our first Anticipating *DSM-5* highlight, we feature the proposed new *DSM-5* definition of mental illness. This definition is based on input from various *DSM-5* workgroups as well as other sources (Broome & Bortolotti, 2010; First & Wakefield, 2010; Stein et al., 2010). Although this definition will still not satisfy everyone, it brings us ever closer to a good working description. Always remember that any definition of abnormality or mental disorder must be somewhat arbitrary. Rather than thinking of the *DSM* as a finished product, it should always be regarded as a work in progress.

Within *DSM-5*, mental disorders will likely be defined as a behavioral or psychological syndrome (or pattern) that is present in an individual and that reflects some kind of underlying psychobiological dysfunction. Importantly, this behavioral syndrome should result in clinically significant distress, disability, or impairment in key areas of functioning. Predictable responses to common stressors or losses (such as death of a loved one) are excluded. It is also important that this dysfunctional pattern of behavior not stem from social deviance or conflicts that the person has with society as a whole.

Extreme Generosity or Pathological Behavior?

Zell Kravinsky was a brilliant student who grew up in a working-class neighborhood in Philadelphia. He won numerous prizes in school. At the age of 12, he began investing in the stock market. Despite his abilities, his Russian immigrant parents were, in the words of a family friend, "steadfast in denying him any praise." Kravinsky eventually completed two Ph.D. degrees and indulged his growing interest in real estate. By the time he was 45 years old, he was married with children. His assets amounted to almost $45 million.

Although Kravinsky had a talent for making money, he found it difficult to spend it. He drove an old car, did not give his children pocket money, and lived with his family in a modest home. As his fortune grew, however, he began to talk to his friends about his plans to give all of his assets to charity. His philanthropy began in earnest when he and his wife gave two gifts, totaling $6.2 million, to the Centers for Disease Control Foundation. They also donated an apartment building to a school for the disabled in Philadelphia. The following year the Kravinskys gave real estate gifts worth approximately $30 million to Ohio State University.

Kravinsky's motivation for his donations was to help others. According to one of his friends, "He gave away the money because he had it and there were people who needed it. But it changed his way of looking at himself. He decided the purpose of his life was to give away things." After he had put some money aside in trust for his wife and his

children, Kravinsky's personal assets were reduced to a house (on which he had a substantial mortgage), two minivans, and around $80,000 in stocks and cash. He had essentially given away his entire fortune.

Kravinsky's donations did not end when his financial assets became depleted. He began to be preoccupied with the idea of nondirected organ donations, in which an altruistic person gives an organ to a total stranger. When he learned that he could live quite normally with only one kidney, Kravinsky decided that the personal costs of giving away one of his kidneys were minimal compared to the benefits received by the kidney recipient. His wife, however, did not share his view. Although she had consented to bequeathing substantial sums of money to worthwhile charities, when it came to her husband offering his kidney, she could not support him.

For Kravinsky, however, the burden of refusing to help alleviate the suffering of someone in need was almost unbearable, even if it meant sacrificing his very own organs. He called the Albert Einstein Medical Center and spoke to a transplant coordinator. He met with a surgeon and then with a psychiatrist. Kravinsky told the psychiatrist that his wife did not support his desire to donate one of his kidneys. When the psychiatrist told him that he was doing something he did not have to do, Kravinsky's response was that he did need to make this sacrifice: "You're missing the whole point. It's as much a necessity as food, water, and air."

Three months later, Kravinsky left his home in the early hours of the morning, drove to the hospital, and donated his right kidney. He informed his wife after the surgery was over. In spite of the turmoil that his kidney donation created within his family, Kravinsky's mind turned back to philanthropy almost immediately. "I lay there in the hospital, and I thought about all my other good organs. When I do something good, I feel that I can do more. I burn to do more. It's a heady feeling." By the time he was discharged, he was wondering about giving away his one remaining kidney.

After the operation, Kravinsky experienced a loss of direction. He had come to view his life as a continuing donation. However, now that his financial assets and his kidney were gone, what could he provide to the less fortunate? Sometimes he imagines offering his entire body for donation. "My organs could save several people if I gave my whole body away." He acknowledges that he feels unable to hurt his family through the sacrifice of his life.

Several years after the kidney donation, Kravinsky still remains committed to giving away as much as possible. However, his actions have caused a tremendous strain in his marriage. In an effort to maintain a harmonious relationship with his wife, he is now involved in real estate and has recently bought his family a larger home. (Taken from Parker, 2004.)

Is Zell Kravinsky's behavior abnormal, or is he a man with profound moral conviction and courage?

Why Do We Need to Classify Mental Disorders?

If defining abnormality is so contentious and so difficult, why do we try to do it? One simple reason is that most sciences rely on classification (e.g., the periodic table in chemistry and the classification of living organisms into kingdoms, phyla, classes, and so on in biology). At the most fundamental level, classification systems provide us with a **nomenclature** (a naming system) and enable us to *structure information* in a more helpful manner.

Organizing information within a classification system also allows us to study the different disorders that we classify and therefore to learn more not only about what causes them but also how they might best be treated. For example, thinking back to the cases you read about, Monique has alcohol and drug dependence, and John has schizophrenia. Knowing what disorder each of them has is clearly very helpful, as John's treatment would likely not work for Monique.

A final effect of classification system usage is somewhat more mundane. As others have pointed out, the classification of mental disorders has social and political implications (see Blashfield & Livesley, 1999; Kirk & Kutchins, 1992). Simply put, defining the domain of what is considered to be pathological establishes the range of problems that the mental health profession can address. As a consequence, on a purely pragmatic level, it furthermore delineates which types of psychological difficulties warrant insurance reimbursement and the extent of such reimbursement.

What Are the Disadvantages of Classification?

Of course, there are a number of disadvantages in the usage of a discrete classification system. Classification, by its very nature, provides information in a shorthand form. However, using any form of shorthand inevitably leads to a *loss of information*. If we know the specific history, personality traits, idiosyncrasies, and familial relations of a person with a particular type of disorder (e.g., from reading a case summary) we naturally have much more information than if we were simply told the individual's diagnosis (e.g., schizophrenia). In other words, as we simplify through classification, we inevitably lose an array of personal details about the actual person who has the disorder.

Moreover, although things are improving, there can still be some **stigma** (or disgrace) associated with having a psychiatric diagnosis. Even today, people are generally far more comfortable disclosing that they have a physical illness such as diabetes than they are in admitting to any mental disorder. This is in part due to the fear (real or imagined) that speaking candidly about having a psychological disorder will result in unwanted social or occupational consequences or frank discrimination. Be honest. Have you ever described someone as "nuts," "crazy," or "a psycho"? Now think of the hurt that people with mental disorders experience when they hear such words. In a recent study, 96 percent of patients with schizophrenia reported that stigma was a routine part of their lives (Jenkins & Carpenter-Song, 2008). In spite of the large amount of information that is now available about mental health issues, the level of knowledge about mental illness (sometimes referred to as mental health literacy) is often very poor (Thornicroft et al., 2007).

This excerpt is intentionally omitted from this text.

Related to stigma is the problem of **stereotyping**. Stereotypes are automatic beliefs concerning other people that are based on minimal (often trivial) information (e.g., people who wear glasses are more intelligent; New Yorkers are rude; everyone in the South has a gun). Because we may have heard about certain behaviors that can accompany mental disorders, we may automatically and incorrectly infer that these behaviors will also be present in any person we meet who has a psychiatric diagnosis. This is reflected in the comment, "People like you don't go back to work," in the case example of James McNulty.

Take a moment to consider honestly your own attitudes toward people with mental disorders. What assumptions do you tend to make? Do you view people with mental illness as less competent, more irresponsible, more dangerous,

case study James McNulty

I have lived with bipolar disorder for more than 35 years—all of my adult life. The first 15 years were relatively conventional, at least on the surface. I graduated from an Ivy League university, started my own business, and began a career in local politics. I was married, the father of two sons. I experienced mood swings during these years, and as I got older the swings worsened. Eventually, I became so ill that I was unable to work, my marriage ended, I lost my business, and I became homeless.

At this point I had my most powerful experience with stigma. I was 38 years old. I had recently been discharged after a psychiatric hospitalization for a suicide attempt, I had no place to live, my savings were exhausted, and my only possession was a 4-year-old car. I contacted the mental health authorities in the state where I then lived and asked for assistance in dealing with my mental illness. I was told that to qualify for assistance I would need to sell my car and spend down the proceeds. I asked how I was supposed to get to work when I recovered enough to find a job. I was told, "Don't worry about going back to work. People like you don't go back to work" (McNulty, 2004).

people have. When we note that someone has an illness, we should take care not to define him or her by that illness. Respectful and appropriate language should instead be used. At one time, it was quite common for mental health professionals to describe a given patient as "a schizophrenic" or "a manic-depressive." Now, however, it is widely acknowledged that it is more accurate (not to mention more considerate) to say, "a person with schizophrenia," or "a person with manic depression." Simply put, the person is not the diagnosis.

How Can We Reduce Prejudicial Attitudes Toward the Mentally Ill?

For a long time, it was thought that educating people that mental illnesses were "real" brain disorders might be the solution. Sadly, however, this does not seem to be the case. Although there have been impressive increases in the proportion of people who now understand that mental disorders have neurobiological causes, this increased awareness has not resulted in decreases in stigma. In a recent study Pescosolido and colleagues (2010) asked people in the community to read a vignette (brief description) about a person who showed symptoms of mental illness. Some people read a vignette about a person who had schizophrenia. Others read a vignette about someone with clinical depression or alcohol dependence. Importantly, no diagnostic labels were used to describe these people. The vignettes simply provided descriptive information. Nonetheless, the majority of the people who were surveyed in this study expressed an unwillingness to work with the person described in the vignette. They also did not want to have to socialize with them and did not want them to marry into their family. Moreover, the level of rejection that was shown was just as high as it was in a similar survey that was done 10 years earlier. Over that same 10-year period, however, many more people embraced a neurobiological understanding about the causes of mental illness. So what this study tells us is that just because people understand that mental illness is caused by problems in the brain doesn't mean that they are any less prejudiced toward those with mental illness. This is a disappointing conclusion for everyone who hoped that more scientific research into the biology of mental illness would lead to the elimination of stigma.

and more unpredictable? Research has shown that such attitudes are not uncommon (see A. C. Watson et al., 2004). Can you recall movies, novels, or advertisements that maintain such stereotypes? What are some ways in which you can challenge the false assumptions that are so common in the media? Do you think reality TV shows such as *Hoarders*, *Obsessed*, or *My Strange Addiction* have a helpful or harmful impact on societal attitudes?

Finally, stigma can be perpetuated by the problem of **labeling**. A person's self-concept may be directly affected by being given a diagnosis of schizophrenia, depression, or some other form of mental illness. How might you react if you were told something like this? Furthermore, once a group of symptoms is given a name and identified by means of a diagnosis, this "diagnostic label" can be hard to shake even if the person later makes a full recovery.

It is important to keep in mind, however, that diagnostic classification systems do not classify people. Rather, they classify *the disorders that*

In the movie *Fatal Attraction*, Glenn Close plays Alex Forrest, an emotionally disturbed and self-destructive woman. In the original film ending Alex committed suicide. But that did not test well with audiences who wanted to see Alex punished. So the ending was changed. In the famous bathroom scene, a knife-wielding Alex was blown away by the wife, who shot her in self-defense. What does this say about our attitudes to the mentally ill? Does this ending give a misleading message about mental illness?

Stigma does seem to be reduced by having more contact with people in the stigmatized group (Couture & Penn, 2003). However, there may be barriers to this. Simply imagining interacting with a person who has a mental disorder can lead to distress and also to unpleasant physical reactions. In an interesting study, Graves and colleagues (2005) asked college students enrolled in a psychology course to imagine interacting with a person whose image was shown to them on a slide. As the slide was being presented, subjects were given some scripted biographical information that described the person. In some scripts, the target person was described as having been diagnosed with schizophrenia, although it was also mentioned that he or she was "doing much better now." In other trials, the biographical description made no mention of any mental illness when the person on the slide was being described. Students who took part in the study reported more distress and had more muscle tension in their brows when they imagined interacting with a person with schizophrenia than when they imagined interacting with a person who did not have schizophrenia. Heart rate changes also suggested they were experiencing the imagined interactions with the patients as being more unpleasant than the interactions with the nonpatients. Finally, research participants who had more psychophysiological reactivity to the slides of the patients reported higher levels of stigma toward these patients. These findings suggest that people may tend to avoid those with mental illness because the psychophysiological arousal these encounters create is experienced as unpleasant.

How Does Culture Affect What Is Considered Abnormal?

Just as we must consider changing societal values and expectations in defining abnormality, so too must we consider differences across cultures. In fact, this is explicitly acknowledged in the *DSM* definition of *disorder*. Within a given culture, there exist many shared beliefs and behaviors that are widely accepted and that may constitute one or more customary practices. For instance, many people in Christian countries believe that the number 13 is unlucky. The origins of this may be linked to the Last Supper, at which 13 people were present. Many of us try to be especially cautious on Friday the 13th. Some hotels and apartment buildings avoid having a 13th floor altogether.

There is no word for "depressed" in the languages of certain Native American tribes. Members of these communities tend to describe their symptoms of depression in physical rather than emotional terms.

Similarly, there is frequently no bed numbered 13 in hospital wards.

The Japanese, in contrast, are not worried about the number 13. Rather, they attempt to avoid the number 4. This is because in Japanese the sound of the word for "four" is similar to the sound of the word for "death" (see Tseng, 2001, pp. 105–6).

There is also considerable variation in the way different cultures describe psychological distress. For example, there is no word for "depressed" in the languages of certain Native Americans, Alaska Natives, and Southeast Asian cultures (Manson, 1995). Of course, this does not mean that members from such cultural groups do not experience clinically significant depression. As the accompanying case illustrates, however, the way some disorders present themselves may depend on culturally sanctioned ways of articulating distress.

case study | Depression in a Native American Elder

JGH is a 71-year-old member of a Southwestern tribe who has been brought to a local Indian Health Service hospital by one of his granddaughters and is seen in the general medical outpatient clinic for multiple complaints. Most of Mr. GH's complaints involve nonlocalized pain. When asked to point to where he hurts, Mr. GH indicates his chest, then his abdomen, his knees, and finally moves his hands "all over." Barely whispering, he mentions a phrase in his native language that translates as "whole body sickness." His granddaughter notes that he "has not been himself" recently. Specifically, Mr. GH, during the past 3 or 4 months, has stopped attending or participating in many events previously important to him and central to his role in a large extended family and clan. He is reluctant to discuss this change in behavior as well as his feelings. When questioned more directly, Mr. GH acknowledges that he has had difficulty falling asleep, sleeps intermittently through the night, and almost always awakens at dawn's first light. He admits that he has not felt like eating in recent months but denies weight loss, although his clothes hang loosely in many folds. Trouble concentrating and remembering are eventually disclosed as well. Asked why he has not participated in family and clan events in the last several months, Mr. GH describes himself as "too tired and full of pain" and "afraid of disappointing people." Further pressing by the clinician is met with silence. Suddenly the patient states, "You know, my sheep haven't been doing well lately. Their coats are ragged; they're thinner. They just wander aimlessly; even the ewes don't seem to care about the little ones." Physical examination and laboratory tests are normal. Mr. GH continues to take two tablets of acetaminophen daily for mild arthritic pain. Although he describes himself as a "recovering alcoholic," Mr. GH reports not having consumed alcohol during the last 23 years. He denies any prior episodes of depression or other psychiatric problems (Manson, 1995, p. 488).

As is apparent in the case of JGH, culture can shape the clinical presentation of disorders like depression, which are present across cultures around the world (see Draguns & Tanaka-Matsumi, 2003). In China, for instance, individuals with depression frequently focus on physical concerns (fatigue, dizziness, headaches) rather than verbalizing their feelings of melancholy or hopelessness (Kleinman, 1986; Parker et al., 2001). This focus on physical pain rather than emotional pain is also noteworthy in Mr. GH's case.

Despite progressively increasing cultural awareness, we still know relatively little concerning cultural interpretation and expression of abnormal psychology (Arrindell, 2003). The vast majority of the psychiatric literature originates from Euro-American countries—that is, Western Europe, North America, and Australia/New Zealand (Patel & Sumathipala, 2001; Patel & Kim, 2007). To exacerbate this underrepresentation, research published in languages other than English tends to be disregarded (Draguns, 2001).

Some African tribe members inflict painful and permanent scars (a process called scarification) on their faces and torsos in an effort to beautify themselves. Such a practice might be viewed as abnormal by Western European cultures, yet it is quite common among African tribes.

may become physically or verbally aggressive. Alternately, the person may faint or experience a seizure-like fit. Once the *ataque* is over, the person may promptly resume his or her normal manner, with little or no memory of the incident.

As noted earlier, abnormal behavior is behavior that deviates from the norms of the society in which the person lives. Experiences such as hearing the voice of a dead relative might be regarded as normative in one culture (e.g., in many Native American tribes) yet abnormal in another cultural milieu. Nonetheless, certain unconventional actions and behaviors arc almost universally considered to be the product of mental disorder.

Many years ago, the anthropologist Jane Murphy (1976) studied abnormal behavior by the Yoruba of Africa and the Yupik-speaking Eskimos living on an island in the Bering Sea. Both societies had words that were used to denote abnormality or "craziness." In addition, the clusters of behaviors that were considered to reflect abnormality in these cultures were behaviors that most of us would also regard as abnormal. These included hearing voices, laughing at nothing, defecating in public, drinking urine, and believing things that no one else believes. Why do you think these behaviors are universally considered to be abnormal?

Culture-Specific Disorders

Prejudice toward the mentally ill seems to be found worldwide (see Box 2). However, some types of psychopathology appear to be highly specific to certain cultures: They are found only in certain areas of the world and seem to be highly linked to culturally bound concerns. A case in point is *taijin kyofusho*. This syndrome, which is an anxiety disorder, is quite prevalent in Japan. It involves a marked fear that one's body, body parts, or body functions may offend, embarrass, or otherwise make others feel uncomfortable. Often, people with this disorder are afraid of blushing or upsetting others by their gaze, facial expression, or body odor (Levine & Gaw, 1995).

Another culturally rooted expression of distress, found in Latino and Latina individuals, especially those from the Caribbean, is *ataque de nervios* (Lizardi et al., 2009; Lopez & Guarnaccia, 2005). This is a clinical syndrome that does not seem to correspond to any specific diagnosis within the *DSM*. The symptoms of an *ataque de nervios*, which is often triggered by a stressful event such as divorce or bereavement, include crying, trembling, uncontrollable screaming, and a general feeling of loss of control. Sometimes the person

Some disorders are highly culture specific. For example, *taijin kyofusho* is a disorder that is prevalent in Japan. It is characterized by the fear that one may upset others by one's gaze, facial expression, or body odor.

2 THE WORLD AROUND US

Mad, Sick, Head Nuh Good: Mental Illness and Stigma in Jamaica

Evidence suggests that negative reactions to the mentally ill may be a fairly widespread phenomenon. Using focus groups, Arthur and colleagues (2010) asked community residents in Jamaica about the concept of stigma. Some participants came from rural communities, others from more urban areas. Regardless of their gender, level of education, or where they lived, most participants described highly prejudicial attitudes toward the mentally ill. One middle-class male participant said, "We treat them as in a sense second class citizens, we stay far away from them, ostracize them, we just treat them bad" (see Arthur et al., 2010, p. 263). Fear of the mentally ill was also commonly expressed. A rural-dwelling middle-class man described a specific situation in the following way, "There is a mad lady on the road named [...]. Even the police are afraid of her because she throws stones at them. She is very, very terrible" (p. 261). Moreover, even when more kindly attitudes were expressed, fear was still a common response. One person put it simply, "You are fearful even though you may be sympathetic" (p. 262).

The Jamaicans in this study also made a distinction between mental illness (a term used to denote less severe conditions) and madness, which was used to describe more severe problems. Madness was invariably regarded as being a permanent condition ("once yuh mad yuh mad" or "once yuh gone yuh gone"). Moreover, homelessness was almost always taken to indicate madness. In short, the results of this study suggest that stereotyping, labeling, and stigma toward the mentally ill are not restricted to industrialized countries. Although we might wish that it were otherwise, prejudicial attitudes are common. This highlights the need for antistigma campaigns in Jamaica, as well as everywhere else in the world.

Are attitudes toward the mentally ill in Jamaica more benign than they are in more industrialized countries?

In Review

● Why is abnormality so difficult to define? What characteristics help us recognize abnormality?

● What is stigma? How common is it? What are the challenges in reducing stigma toward the mentally ill?

● In what ways can culture shape the clinical presentation of mental disorders?

How Common Are Mental Disorders?

How many and what sort of people have diagnosable psychological disorders today? This is a significant question for a number of reasons. First, such information is essential when planning and establishing mental health services. Mental health planners require a precise understanding of the nature and extent of the psychological difficulties within a given area, state, or country because they are responsible for determining how resources such as funding of research projects or services provided by community mental health centers may be most effectively allocated. It would obviously be imprudent to have a treatment center filled with clinicians skilled in the treatment of anorexia nervosa (a very severe but rare clinical problem) if there were few clinicians skilled in treating anxiety or depression, which are much more prevalent disorders.

Second, estimates of the frequency of mental disorders in different groups of people may provide valuable clues as to the causes of these disorders. For example, data from the United Kingdom have shown that schizophrenia is about three times more likely to develop in ethnic minorities than in the white population (Kirkbridge et al., 2006). Rates of schizophrenia in southeast London are also high relative to other parts of the country. This is prompting researchers to explore why this might be. Possible factors may be social class, neighborhood deprivation, as well as diet or exposure to infections or environmental contaminants.

Prevalence and Incidence

Before we can further discuss the impact of mental disorders upon society, we must clarify the way in which psychological problems are counted. **Epidemiology** is the study of the distribution of diseases, disorders, or health-related behaviors in a given population. Mental health epidemiology is the study of the distribution of mental disorders. A key component of an epidemiological survey is determining the frequencies of mental disorders. There are several ways of doing this. The term **prevalence** refers to the number of active cases in a population during any given period of time. Prevalence figures are typically expressed as percentages (i.e., the percentage of the population that has the disorder). Furthermore, there are several different types of prevalence estimates that can be made.

Point prevalence refers to the estimated proportion of actual, active cases of the disorder in a given population at a given point in time. For example, if we were to conduct a study and count the number of people who have major depressive disorder (that is, clinical depression) on January 1st of next year, this would provide us with a point prevalence estimate of active cases of depression. A person who experienced depression during the months of November and December but who managed to recover by January 1st would not be included in our point prevalence calculation. The same is true of someone whose depression did not begin until January 2nd.

If, on the other hand, we wanted to calculate a **1-year prevalence** figure, we would count everyone who experienced depression at any point in time throughout the entire year. As you might imagine, this prevalence figure would be higher than the point prevalence figure because it would cover a much longer time. It would moreover include those people who had recovered before the point prevalence assessment as well as those whose disorders did not begin until after the point prevalence estimate was made.

Finally, we may also wish to obtain an estimate of the number of people who have had a particular disorder at any time in their lives (even if they are now recovered). This would provide us with a **lifetime prevalence** estimate. Because they extend over an entire lifetime and include both currently ill and recovered individuals, lifetime prevalence estimates tend to be higher than other kinds of prevalence estimates.

An additional term with which you should be familiar is **incidence**. This refers to the number of new cases that occur over a given period of time (typically 1 year). Incidence figures tend to be lower than prevalence figures because they exclude preexisting cases. In other words, if we were assessing the 1-year incidence of schizophrenia, we would not count people whose schizophrenia began before our given starting date (even if they were still ill) because they are not "new"

cases of schizophrenia. On the other hand, someone who was quite well previously but then developed schizophrenia during our 1-year window would be included in our incidence estimate.

Prevalence Estimates for Mental Disorders

Now that you have an understanding of some basic terms, let's turn to the 1-year prevalence rates for several important disorders. Three major national mental health epidemiology studies, with direct and formal diagnostic assessment of participants, have been carried out in the United States. One, the Epidemiologic Catchment Area (ECA) study, focused on sampling citizens of five communities: Baltimore, New Haven, St. Louis, Durham (NC), and Los Angeles (Myers et al., 1984; Regier et al., 1988; Regier et al., 1993).

The second, the National Comorbidity Survey (NCS), was more extensive. It sampled the entire American population using a number of sophisticated methodological improvements (Kessler et al., 1994). A replication of the NCS (the NCS-R) was completed about a decade later (Kessler et al., 2004; Kessler, Berglund, Borges, et al., 2005a; Kessler & Merikangas, 2004). The most current 1-year and lifetime prevalence estimates of the *DSM-IV* mental disorders assessed from the NCS-R study are shown in Table 1.

The lifetime prevalence of having any *DSM-IV* disorder is 46.4 percent. This means that almost half of the Americans who were questioned had been affected by mental illness at some point in their lives (Kessler, Berglund, Demler, et al., 2005b). Although this figure may seem high, it may actually be an underestimate, as the NCS study did not assess for eating disorders, schizophrenia, or autism, for example. Neither did it include measures of most personality disorders. As you can see from Table 1, the most prevalent category of psychological disorders is anxiety disorders. The most common individual disorders are major depressive disorder, alcohol abuse, and specific phobias (e.g., fear of small animals, insects, flying, heights, etc.). Social phobias (e.g., fear of public speaking) are similarly very common (see Table 2).

Although lifetime rates of mental disorders appear to be quite high, it is important to remember that, in some cases, the duration of the disorder may be relatively brief (e.g., depression that lasts for a few weeks after the breakup of a romantic relationship). Furthermore, many people who meet criteria for a given disorder will not be seriously affected by it. For instance, in the NCS-R study, almost half (48 percent) of the people diagnosed with a specific phobia had disorders that were rated as mild in severity, and only 22 percent of phobias were regarded as severe (Kessler, Chiu, et al., 2005c). Meeting diagnostic criteria for a particular disorder and being seriously impaired by that disorder are not necessarily synonymous.

table 1 Prevalence of *DSM-IV* Disorders in Adults in the United States

	1-Year (%)	Lifetime (%)
Any anxiety disorder	18.1	28.8
Any mood disorder	9.5	20.8
Any substance-abuse disorder	3.8	14.6
Any disorder	26.2	46.4

Sources: Kessler, et al. (2005a); Kessler, et al. (2005c).

table 2 Most Common Individual *DSM-IV* Disorders in the United States

Disorder	1-Year Prevalence (%)	Lifetime Prevalence (%)
Major depressive disorder	6.7	16.6
Alcohol abuse	3.1	13.2
Specific phobia	8.7	12.5
Social phobia	6.8	12.1
Conduct disorder	1.0	9.5

Sources: Kessler, et al. (2005a); Kessler, et al. (2005c).

A final finding from the NCS-R study was the widespread occurrence of comorbidity among diagnosed disorders (Kessler, Chiu, et al., 2005c). **Comorbidity** is the term used to describe the presence of two or more disorders in the same person. Comorbidity is especially high in people who have severe forms of mental disorders. In the NCS-R study, half of the individuals with a disorder rated as serious on a scale of severity (mild, moderate, serious) had two or more additional disorders. An illustration of this would be a person who drinks excessively and who is simultaneously depressed and suffering from an anxiety disorder. In contrast, only 7 percent of the people who had a mild form of a disorder also had two or more other diagnosable conditions. What this indicates is that comorbidity is much more likely to occur in people who have the most serious forms of mental disorders. When the condition is mild, comorbidity is the exception rather than the rule.

Disorders do not always occur in isolation. A person who abuses alcohol may also be depressed or pathologically anxious.

Treatment

Many treatments for psychological disorders are now available. These include medications as well as different forms of psychotherapy. However, it is important to emphasize that not all people with psychological disorders receive treatment. In some cases, people deny or minimize their suffering. Others try to cope on their own and may manage to recover without ever seeking aid from a mental health professional. Even when they recognize that they have a problem, it is typical for individuals to wait a long time before deciding to seek help. Half of individuals with depression delay seeking treatment for more than 6 to 8 years. For anxiety disorders, the delay ranges from 9 to 23 years (Wang, Berglund, et al., 2005)!

When people with mental disorders do seek help, they are often treated by their family physician rather than by a mental health specialist (Wang, et al., 2005). It is also

13

the case that the vast majority of mental health treatment is now administered on an outpatient (as opposed to an inpatient) basis (Narrow et al., 1993; O'Donnell et al., 2000). Outpatient treatment requires that a patient visit a mental health facility practitioner; however, the patient does not have to be admitted to the hospital or stay there overnight. A patient may attend a community mental health center, see a private therapist, or receive treatment through the outpatient department of a hospital.

Hospitalization and inpatient care are the preferred options for people who need more intensive treatment than can be provided on an outpatient basis. Various surveys indicate that admission to mental hospitals has decreased substantially over the past 45 years. The development of medications that control the symptoms of the most severe disorders is one reason for this change. Budget cuts have also forced many large state or county facilities to close. The limitations that insurance companies place on hospital admissions is another relevant factor here. If a hospital stay is not authorized by the insurance company, patients must seek treatment elsewhere.

Patients who need inpatient care are usually admitted to the psychiatric units of general hospitals (Narrow et al., 1993) or to private psychiatric hospitals specializing in particular mental disorders (Kiesler & Simpkins, 1993). Stays in inpatient facilities tend to be much shorter than they were in the past (see Case et al., 2007; Lay et al., 2007). Patients receive additional treatment on an outpatient basis. This trend away from the use of traditional hospitalization began several decades ago. It is referred to as deinstitutionalization.

Mental Health Professionals

When patients receive inpatient treatment, several different mental health professionals often work as a team to provide the necessary care. A psychiatrist may prescribe medications and monitor the patient for side effects. A clinical psychologist may provide individual therapy, meeting with the patient several times a week. A clinical social worker may help the patient resolve family problems, and a psychiatric nurse may check in with the patient on a daily basis to provide support and help the patient cope better in the hospital environment. The intensity of treatment that is typical in a hospital setting is designed to help the patient get better as rapidly as possible.

Patients treated in outpatient settings may also work with a team of professionals. However, the number of mental health specialists involved is typically much smaller. In some cases a patient will receive all treatment from a psychiatrist, who will prescribe medication and also provide psychotherapy. Other patients will receive medications from a psychiatrist and see a psychologist or a clinical social worker for regular therapy sessions. In other cases, depending on the type and severity of the problem, a patient (*client* is the preferred term in some settings) may see a counseling psychologist, a psychoanalyst, or a counselor specialized in the treatment of drug and alcohol problems. Details about some of these professional roles and the training required for each of them are provided in Box 3.

3 THE WORLD AROUND US

Mental Health Professionals

Clinical Psychologist
Ph.D. in psychology (with both research and clinical skill specialization) and a one-year internship in a psychiatric facility or mental health center; or Psy.D. in psychology (a professional degree with a focus on clinical work rather than research) plus 1-year internship. Some states permit clinical psychologists (with additional training) to prescribe medications to patients as psychiatrists do.

Counseling Psychologist
Ph.D. in psychology plus internship in a marital- or student-counseling setting. Normally, a counseling psychologist deals with adjustment problems rather than severe mental disorders.

School Psychologist
Ideally, a person with doctoral training in child clinical psychology, with additional training and experience in academic and learning problems. Many school systems lack the resources to maintain an adequate school psychology program.

Psychiatrist
Trained as physicians, psychiatrists are M.D.s who have completed residency training (usually 3 years) in a psychiatric setting. Psychiatrists are able to prescribe medications.

Psychoanalyst
Typically an M.D. or Ph.D. who has received intensive and extended training in the theory and practice of psychoanalysis.

In Review

- What is epidemiology?
- What is the difference between prevalence and incidence?
- What are the most common mental disorders?
- How is illness severity associated with comorbidity?
- In what ways does the training of a psychiatrist differ from the training of a clinical psychologist?

Research Approaches in Abnormal Psychology

As is apparent from the NCS-R study, the lives of large numbers of people are affected by mental disorders. To learn all that we can about these conditions, we need to conduct research. In this way, we can study the characteristics or nature of disorders. Through research we can learn about the symptoms of the disorder, its prevalence, whether it tends to be either **acute** (short in duration) or **chronic** (long in duration), and the problems and deficits that often accompany it.

Research allows us to further understand the **etiology** (or causes) of disorders. Finally, we need research to provide the best care for the patients who are seeking assistance with their difficulties. As such, we turn to the research literature to help us provide the most effective and up-to-date care for the patients whom we see.

Students new to the field of abnormal psychology often assume that all answers may be revealed through scrutinizing past case studies. However, when we study individual cases and derive inferences from them, we are as likely to develop errors in our thinking as we are to obtain knowledge. One such error is that we often attend only to data that confirm our view of how things are. For example, Dr. Smart might believe that drinking milk causes schizophrenia. When we ask Dr. Smart why he holds this view, he might say it is because every patient he has ever treated who has schizophrenia has drunk milk at some time in his or her life. Given that Dr. Smart has treated a lot of patients with schizophrenia and clearly has a great deal of experience with the disorder, we might be persuaded that he is right. Then along comes Dr. Notsofast. Dr. Notsofast decides to conduct a research study. He studies two groups of people: One group has schizophrenia; the other group does not have schizophrenia. Dr. Notsofast asks all of them about their milk-drinking habits. He finds that everyone has drunk milk at some point in his or her life and that there are no differences between the two groups with respect to their milk-drinking histories. As this simple example illustrates, research prevents us from being misled by natural errors in thinking. In short, research protects investigators from their own biases in perception and inference (Raulin & Lilienfeld, 2009).

Abnormal psychology research can take place in clinics, hospitals, schools, prisons, and even highly unstructured contexts such as naturalistic observations of the homeless on the street. It is not the setting that determines whether a given research project may be undertaken. As Kazdin aptly points out (1998b, p. x), "methodology is not merely a compilation of practices and procedures. Rather it is an approach toward problem solving, thinking, and acquiring knowledge." As such, research methodology (that is, the scientific processes and procedures we use to conduct research) is constantly evolving.

Clinical Social Worker
M.S.W. or Ph.D. in social work with specialized clinical training in mental health settings.

Psychiatric Nurse
R.N. certification plus specialized training in the care and treatment of psychiatric clients. Nurses can attain M.A. and Ph.D. in psychiatric nursing.

Occupational Therapist
B.S. in occupational therapy plus internship training with physically or psychologically handicapped individuals, with the aim of helping them make the most of their resources.

Pastoral Counselor
Ministerial background plus training in psychology and an internship in a mental health facility as a chaplain.

Community Mental Health Worker
Person with limited professional training who works under professional direction; usually involved in crisis intervention.

Alcohol- or Drug-Abuse Counselor
Limited professional training but educated in the evaluation and management of alcohol- and drug-abuse problems.

Abnormal psychology research can be conducted in a variety of settings outside the research laboratory, including clinics, hospitals, schools, or prisons.

As new techniques become available (brain-imaging techniques and new statistical procedures, to name a few), methodology in turn evolves.

Sources of Information

Case Studies

As humans, we often direct our attention to the people around us. If you were asked to describe your best friend, your father, or even the professor teaching your abnormal psychology class, you would undoubtedly have plenty to say. As is the case in virtually all other sciences, the foundation of psychological knowledge stems from observation. Indeed, a large amount of early knowledge was distilled from case studies in which specific individuals were described in great detail.

Astute clinicians such as the German psychiatrist Emil Kraepelin (1856–1926) and the Swiss psychiatrist Eugen Bleuler (1857–1939) provided us with detailed accounts of patients whom a modern-day reader would easily recognize as suffering from disorders such as schizophrenia and manic depression. Alois Alzheimer (1864–1915) depicted a patient with an unusual clinical picture that subsequently became known as Alzheimer's disease. Sigmund Freud (1856–1939), the founder of psychoanalysis, published multiple clinical cases describing what we now recognize as phobia (the case of "Little Hans") and obsessive-compulsive disorder ("the Rat Man"). Such portrayals make for fascinating reading, even today.

Much can be learned when skilled clinicians use the **case study** method. Still, the information presented in them is subject to **bias** because the writer of the case study selects what information to include and what information to omit.

Another concern is that the material in a case study is often relevant only to the individual being described. This means that the conclusions of a case study have low **generalizability**— that is, they cannot be used to draw conclusions about other cases even when those cases involve people with a seemingly similar abnormality. When there is only one observer and one subject, and when the observations are made in a relatively uncontrolled context and are anecdotal and impressionistic in nature, the conclusions we can draw are very narrow and may be mistaken. Nonetheless, case studies are an excellent way to illustrate clinical material. They can also provide some limited support for a particular theory or provide some negative evidence that can challenge a prevailing idea or assumption. Importantly, case studies can be a valuable source of new ideas and serve as a stimulus for research, and they may provide insight into unusual clinical conditions that are too rare to be studied in a more systematic way.

Self-Report Data

If we wish to study behavior in a more rigorous manner, how do we go about doing so? One approach is to collect **self-report data** from the people we wish to learn more about. This might involve having our research participants complete questionnaires of various types. Another way of collecting self-report data is from interviews. The researcher asks a series of questions and then records what the person says.

Asking people to report on their subjective experiences might appear to be an excellent way to collect information. However, as a research approach it has some limitations. Self-report data can sometimes be misleading. One problem is that people may not be very good reporters of their own subjective states or experiences. For example, when asked in an interview, one child may report that he has 20 "best friends." Yet, when we observe him, he may always be playing alone. Because people will occasionally lie, misinterpret the question, or desire to present themselves in a particularly favorable (or unfavorable) light, self-report data cannot always be regarded as highly accurate and truthful. This is something that anyone who has ever tried online dating knows only too well! And if you still need convincing, ask three people to tell you their weight. Then ask them to step on a scale. How likely is it that the weight they self-report will be the weight that appears when they step on the scale? What reasons do you think might explain the discrepancy?

Observational Approaches

When we collect information in a way that does not involve asking people directly (self-report), we are using some form of observational approach. Exactly how we go about this depends on what it is we seek to understand. For example, if we are studying aggressive children, we may wish to have trained observers record the number of times children who are classified as being aggressive hit, bite, push, punch, or kick their playmates. This would involve **direct observation** of the children's behavior.

We may also collect information about biological variables (such as heart rate) in our sample of aggressive children. Alternatively, we could collect information about stress hormones, such as cortisol, by asking the observed children to spit into a plastic container (because cortisol is found in saliva). We would then send the saliva samples to the lab for analysis. This, too, is a form of observational data; it tells us something that we want to know using a variable that is relevant to our interests.

Technology has advanced, and we are now developing methods to study behaviors, moods, and cognitions that have long been considered inaccessible. As illustrated in Figure 1, we can now use brain-imaging techniques such as functional magnetic resonance imaging (fMRI) to study the working brain. We can study blood flow to various parts of the brain during memory tasks. We can even look at which brain areas influence imagination.

With other techniques such as transcranial magnetic stimulation (TMS; see Figure 2), which generates a magnetic field on the surface of the head, we can stimulate underlying

brain tissue (for an overview, see Fitzgerald et al., 2002). This can be done painlessly and noninvasively while the person receiving the TMS sits in an armchair. Using TMS, we can even take a particular area of the brain "off-line" for a few seconds and measure the behavioral consequences. In short, we can now collect observational data that would have been impossible to obtain a decade ago.

In practice, much clinical research involves a mix of self-report and observational methods. Also, keep in mind that when we refer to observing behavior we mean much more than simply watching people. Observing behavior, in this context, refers to careful scrutiny of the conduct and manner of specific individuals (e.g., healthy people, people with depression, people with anxiety, people with schizophrenia). We may study social behavior in a sample of patients with depression by enlisting trained observers to record the frequency with which the patients smile or make eye contact. We may also ask the patients themselves to fill out self-report questionnaires that assess social skills. If we think that sociability in patients with depression may be related to (or correlated with) their severity of depression, we may further ask patients to complete self-report measures designed to assess that severity. We may

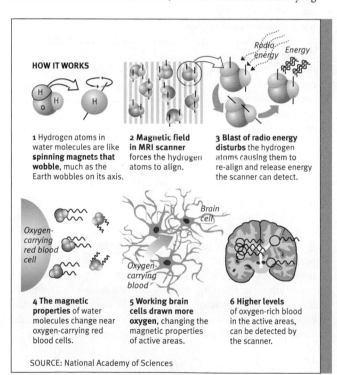

FIGURE 1

Images of the Working Brain

Functional magnetic resonance imaging, or fMRI, can pinpoint areas of the brain involved in recognizing faces, spatial reasoning, and other tasks by "reading" the millions of molecules in your brain.
Source: National Academy of Science; Globe Staff Graphic/Sean McNaughton, from *Boston Globe*, Feb. 10, 2004. Copyright 2004, Globe Newspaper Company. Republished with permission.

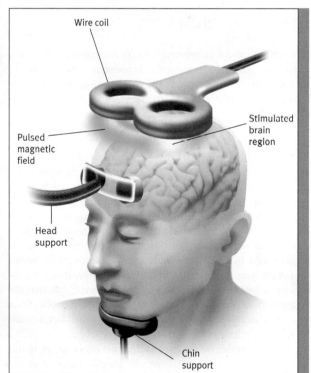

FIGURE 2

Researchers use technology, such as transcranial magnetic stimulation (TMS), to study how the brain works. This TMS technique generates a magnetic field on the surface of the head through which underlying brain tissue is stimulated. Researchers can evaluate and measure behavioral consequences of this noninvasive and painless brain stimulation.

even measure levels of certain substances in patients' blood, urine, or cerebrospinal fluid (the clear fluid that bathes the brain and that can be obtained by performing a lumbar puncture). Finally, we could possibly study the depressed patients' brains directly via brain-imaging approaches. These diverse sources of information would provide us with potentially valuable data, the basis of scientific inquiry.

In Review

- What are the strengths and limitations of case studies?
- Why is it desirable not to rely solely on self-report data as a source of information?
- What is the difference between self-report and observational data? What range of measures could be considered to reflect observational data?

Although men generally have lower rates of depression than women, the rate of depression for Jewish men and women is equal. Why would this be? A correlation between higher rates of depression and lower rates of alcohol abuse in Jewish men provides interesting ground for further study.

Forming and Testing Hypotheses

Research is all about asking questions. To make sense of behavior, researchers generate hypotheses. A **hypothesis** is an effort to explain, predict, or explore something. What distinguishes scientific hypotheses from the vague speculation that we all routinely engage in is that scientists attempt to test their hypotheses. In other words, they try to design research studies that will help them approach a fuller understanding of how and why things happen.

Anecdotal accounts such as case studies can be very valuable in helping us develop hypotheses, although case studies are not well suited for testing the hypotheses that they may have inspired. Other sources of hypotheses are unusual or unexpected research findings. One example is the higher-than-expected rate of suicide in women who have had cosmetic breast augmentation (Sarwer et al., 2007). Consider for a moment why this association might exist. Possible explanations might include higher rates of psychopathology in women who seek breast augmentation, unrealistic expectations about the positive effects that the surgery would have on their lives, postoperative complications that could lead to depressed mood, as well as other factors such as preoperative body image dissatisfaction.

Another observation in search of an explanation is the finding that, although men generally have lower rates of depression than women, this is not true of Jewish men. Why should Jewish men be more at risk for depression than non-Jewish men? One hypothesis is that there may be an interesting (and inverse) relationship between depression and alcohol use (Levav et al., 1997). Jewish men have lower rates of alcohol abuse and alcohol dependence than do non-Jewish men. Consistent with this idea, a study of members of Orthodox synagogues in London found no alcoholism and similar rates of depression in

females and males (i.e., a 1:1 gender ratio instead of the typical 2:1 ratio; Loewenthal et al., 1995). Although much more remains to be uncovered, the hypothesis that higher rates of depression in Jewish men may be related to their lower rates of alcohol abuse appears to merit further study (see Loewenthal et al., 2003).

Hypotheses are vital because they frequently determine the therapeutic approaches used to treat a particular clinical problem. The ideas we have about what might be causing a client's difficulties will naturally shape the form of intervention we use when we provide treatment. For instance, suppose we are confronted with someone who washes his or her hands 60 to 100 times a day, causing serious injury to the skin and underlying tissues (this is an example of obsessive-compulsive disorder). If we believe that this behavior is a result of subtle problems in certain neural circuits, we may try to identify which circuits are dysfunctional in the hope of ultimately finding a means of correcting them (perhaps with medication).

On the other hand, if we view the excessive hand washing as reflecting a symbolic cleansing of sinful and unacceptable thoughts, we may try to unearth and address the sources of the person's excessive guilt and concern with morality. Finally, if we regard the hand washing as merely the product of unfortunate conditioning or learning, we may devise a means to extinguish the problematic behavior. In other words, our working hypotheses regarding the causes of different disorders very much shape the approaches we use when we study and treat the disorders.

Sampling and Generalization

We can occasionally glean instructive leads from careful scrutiny of a single case. However, this strategy rarely yields enough information to allow us to reach firm conclusions. Research in abnormal psychology is concerned with gaining enhanced understanding and, where possible, control of abnormal behavior (that is, the ability to alter it in predictable ways). Edward, for instance, may accost women in supermarkets and try to lick their feet because his mother always gave him attention when, as a child, he tried on her shoes. In contrast, George may engage in the same behavior for an entirely different reason. We need to study a larger group of individuals with the same problem in order to discover which of our observations or hypotheses possess scientific credibility. The more people we study, the more confident we can be about our findings.

Whom should we include in our research study? In general, we want to study groups of individuals who have similar abnormalities of behavior. If we wanted to study people with panic disorder, a first step would be to determine criteria such as those provided in the current *DSM* for identifying people affected with this clinical disorder. We would then need to find people who fit our criteria. Ideally, we would study everyone in the world who met our criteria because these people constitute our population of interest. This, of course, is impossible to do, so instead we would try to get a representative sample of people who are drawn from this underlying population. To do this, we would use a technique called **sampling**. What this means is that we would try to select people who are representative of the much larger group of individuals with panic disorder (in the same way that jury selection involves having a representative sample of eligible voters).

Ideally, we would like our smaller sample (our study group) to mirror the larger group (the underlying population) in all important ways (e.g., in severity and duration of disorder and in demographics such as age, gender, and marital status). If we could do everything perfectly, our research sample would be randomly selected from the larger population of people with panic disorder, which is tantamount to ensuring that every person in that population would have an equal chance of being included in our study. Such a procedure would automatically adjust for potential biases in sample selection. In practice, however, this does not happen, and researchers must simply do the best they can given real-world constraints (including the fact that some people don't wish to participate in a research study!).

Because finding research participants is not always easy, researchers sometimes use "samples of convenience" in their studies. This means that they study groups of people who are easily accessible to them and who are readily available. Have

Why is so much research conducted using college students? What are the advantages and disadvantages of this?

you noticed how much research is conducted using college students? Is this because college students are intrinsically fascinating people to study? Or are other factors in play here?

Internal and External Validity

From a research perspective, the more representative our sample is, the better able we are to generalize (or extend the findings from our study) to the larger group. The extent to which we can generalize our findings beyond the study itself is called **external validity.** A research study that involves both males and females from all age groups, income levels, and education levels is more representative of the underlying population (and will have greater external validity) than research using only female college students, for example. In addition, when we study a group of people who all share a defining characteristic (e.g., a specific disorder), we may then be able to infer that additional commonalities that they share (such as a family history of depression or low levels of certain neurotransmitters) may be related to the disorder itself. Of course, this is based on the assumption that the characteristic in question is not widely shared by people who do not have the disorder.

Unlike external validity, which concerns the degree that research findings from a specific study can be generalized to other samples, contexts, or times, **internal validity** reflects how confident we can be in the results of a particular given study. In other words, internal validity is the extent to which a study is methodologically sound, free of confounds, or other sources of error, and able to be used to draw valid conclusions. For example, suppose that a researcher is interested in how heart rate changes when participants are told that they are about to be given an electric shock. Imagine also how much faith you might have in the results of the research if participants who have just completed the study are allowed to chat in the waiting area with people who are just about to participate. What if the latter learn that, in reality, no shocks are given at all? How might this information change how subjects respond? Failure to control the exchange of information in this way clearly jeopardizes the integrity of the study and is a threat to its internal validity. Some subjects (those who have not been given prior information) will expect to receive real shocks; others will not because, unbeknownst to the experimenter, information has been leaked to them beforehand.

Criterion and Comparison Groups

To test their hypotheses, researchers use a **comparison group** (sometimes called a **control group**). This may be defined as a group of people who do not exhibit the disorder being studied but who are comparable in all other major respects to the **criterion group** (i.e., the people with the disorder). By "comparable" we might mean that the two groups are similar in age, number of males and females in each group, education level, and similar demographic variables. Typically, the comparison group is psychologically healthy, or "normal," according to certain specified criteria. We can then compare the two groups on the variables of interest.

To further illustrate the idea of criterion and control groups, let us return to our example about schizophrenia and milk. Dr. Smart's hypothesis was that drinking milk causes schizophrenia. However, when a group of patients with schizophrenia (the criterion group, or group of interest) was compared with a group of patients who did not have schizophrenia (the control group), it was clear that there were no differences in milk drinking between the two groups.

Using the controlled research approaches we have just described, researchers have learned much about many different psychological disorders. We can also use extensions of this approach not only to compare one cohort of patients with healthy controls but also to compare groups of patients with different disorders.

For example, Cutting and Murphy (1990) studied how well (1) patients with schizophrenia, (2) patients with depression or mania, and (3) healthy controls performed on a questionnaire testing social knowledge. This involved a series of multiple-choice questions that presented a social problem (e.g., "How would you tell a friend politely that he had stayed too long?"). Possible answer choices included responses such as, "There's no more coffee left" and "You'd better go. I'm fed up with you staying too long." (In case you are wondering, both of these are incorrect choices; the preferred answer for this example was, "Excuse me. I've got an appointment with a friend.")

Consistent with the literature showing that social deficits are associated with schizophrenia, the patients with schizophrenia did worse on this test relative to both the healthy controls and the depressed or manic patients. The finding that the patients with schizophrenia did more poorly than the depressed or manic patients allowed the researchers to rule out the possibility that simply being a psychiatric patient is linked to poor social knowledge.

In Review

- Explain what the term *representative sample* means.

- What is a sample of convenience?

- What is the difference between internal and external validity? How can external validity be maximized?

- Why are comparison or control groups so important?

Research Designs

Studying the World as It Is: Correlational Research Designs

A major goal of researchers in abnormal psychology is to learn about the causes of different disorders. For ethical and practical reasons, however, we often cannot do this directly. Perhaps we want to learn about factors that result in depression. We may hypothesize that stress or losing a parent early in life may be important in this regard. Needless to say, we cannot create such situations and then see what unfolds!

Instead, the researcher uses what is known as a **correlational research** design. Unlike a true experimental research design (described in the next section.), correlational research does not involve any manipulation of variables. Rather, the researcher selects certain groups of interest (for example, people who have recently been exposed to a great deal of stress, or people who lost a parent when they were growing up). She would then compare the groups on a variety of different measures (including, in this example, levels of depression).

Any time we study differences between individuals who have a particular disorder and those who do not, we are utilizing this type of correlational research design. Essentially, we are capitalizing on the fact that the world works in ways that create natural groupings of people (people with specific disorders, people who have had traumatic experiences, people who win lotteries, etc.) whom we can then study. Using these types of research designs, we are able to identify factors that appear to be associated with depression, alcoholism, binge eating, or alternate psychological states of distress (for a more comprehensive description of this kind of research approach, see Kazdin, 1998b).

Measuring Correlation

Correlational research takes things as they are and determines associations among observed phenomena. Do measures vary together in a direct, corresponding manner (known as a **positive correlation**—see Figure 3) such as in the example we mentioned earlier showing that breast augmentation surgery was correlated with increased risk of suicide? Or conversely, is there an inverse correlation, or **negative correlation**, between the variables of interest (such as high socioeconomic status and decreased risk of psychopathology)? Or finally, are the variables in question entirely independent of one another, or *uncorrelated*, such that a given state or level of one variable fails to predict reliably the degree of the other variable, as was the case with our example about milk and schizophrenia?

The strength of a **correlation** is measured by a **correlation coefficient**, which is denoted by the symbol r. A correlation runs from 0 to 1, with a number closer to 1 representing a stronger association between the two variables. The + sign or − sign indicates the direction of the association between the variables. For example, a positive correlation means that higher scores on one variable are associated with higher scores on the other variable, as might be the case for hours spent studying and grade point average. A negative correlation means that, as scores on one variable go up, scores on the other variable tend to go down. An example here might be the association between hours spent partying and grade point average.

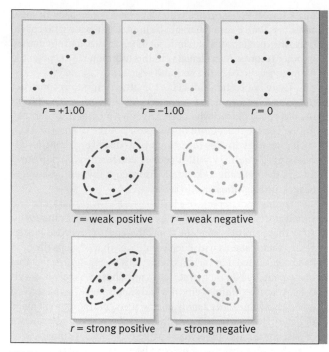

FIGURE 3

Scatterplots of data illustrating positive, negative, and no correlation between two variables. Dots indicate a given person's score on the two variables of interest. A strong positive correlation ($r = +1.0$) means that high scores on one variable are associated with high scores on the second variable, creating a forward-sloping straight line. For example, we would expect there to be a positive correlation between weight and the number of calories eaten per day. When there is a strong negative correlation ($r = -1.0$), high scores on the first variable are associated with low scores on the second variable, creating a backward-sloping straight line. A relevant example here would be the association between weight and time spent exercising per day. When there is no correlation ($r = 0$), scores on the independent variable tell us nothing about scores on the dependent variable. An example here might involve weight and astrological sign.

Statistical Significance

If you read a research article, you are likely to see correlations reported in the text. Next to the correlation you will almost certainly see a notation that reads $p < .05$. This is the level of **statistical significance**. But what does this mean? Simply put, it means that the probability that the correlation would occur purely by chance is less than 5 out of 100. Researchers adopt this conventional level of significance and consider correlations that have a $p < .05$ to be statistically significant and worthy of attention. Of course, this does not mean that the result in question could not have occurred by chance; it simply means that it is not very likely.

Statistical significance is influenced not only by the magnitude or size of the correlation between the two variables but also by the sample size. A correlation of .30 will not be significant if the sample size is 20 people but will be significant if the sample size is 50 people. Correlations based on very large samples (e.g., 1,000 people) can be very small and yet still reach statistical significance. Conversely, correlations drawn from small samples need to be very large to reach statistical significance.

Effect Size

The fact that statistical significance is influenced by sample size creates a problem when we want to compare findings across studies. Suppose that Dr. Green reports a significant association between two variables in her study. But, in a second study, Dr. Blue reports no significant correlation between these same two variables. This is not an uncommon occurrence in the scientific literature, and it often creates a lot of confusion about whose results are "correct." But if Dr. Green has a larger sample size than Dr. Blue, the same-size correlation will be significant in Dr. Green's study but not reach statistical significance in Dr. Blue's study. To avoid the problems inherent in just focusing on statistical significance, and to facilitate comparison of results across different studies (which invariably have different sample sizes), researchers often report a statistic called the **effect size**. The effect size reflects the size of the association between two variables independent of the sample size. An effect size of zero means there is no association between the variables. Because it is independent of sample size, the effect size can be used as a common metric and is very valuable when we want to compare the strength of findings across different studies. If the effect size is about the same in the studies of both Dr. Green and Dr. Blue we can conclude that they really had similar findings, regardless of the fact that the results were significant in one study but not in the other.

Meta-Analysis

When researchers want to summarize research findings in a specific area they often do a literature search and write a review. In drawing their conclusions they will rely on significance levels, noting whether more studies than not found a significant association between two variables, such as smoking and health. A far better approach, however, is to conduct a **meta-analysis**. A meta-analysis is a statistical approach that calculates and then combines the effect sizes from all of the studies. Within a meta-analysis, each separate study can be thought of as being equivalent to an individual participant in a conventional research design. Because it uses effect sizes, a meta-analysis provides a better way to summarize research findings than is possible with a literature review.

Correlations and Causality

When it comes to correlations, one thing is very important to remember: Correlation does not mean causation. Just because two variables are correlated does not tell us anything about why they are correlated. This is true regardless of the size of the correlation. Many research investigations in abnormal psychology reveal that two (or more) things regularly occur together, such as poverty and diminished intellectual development, or depression and reported prior stressors. This in no way affirms that one factor is the cause of the other.

Consider, for example, the positive correlation that exists between ice cream consumption and drowning. Does this mean that eating ice cream compromises swimming ability and so leads to drowning? Or that people who are about to drown themselves like to have one final ice cream cone before they enter the water? Both of these alternatives are clearly absurd. Much more likely is that some unknown third variable might be causing both events to happen. This is known as the **third variable problem**. What might the third variable be in this example? After a moment's reflection, you might realize that a very plausible third variable is hot summer weather. Ice cream consumption increases in the summer months. So, too, does the number of people who drown because more people swim during the summer than at any other time. The correlation between ice cream consumption and drowning is a spurious one, caused by the fact that both variables are correlated with the weather.

To use an example from abnormal psychology, even as late as the 1940s it was thought that masturbation caused insanity. This hypothesis no doubt arose from the fact that, historically, patients in mental asylums could often be seen masturbating in full view of others. Of course, we now know that masturbation and insanity were correlated not because masturbation caused insanity but because sane people are much more likely to masturbate in private than in public. In other words, the key factor linking the insanity and masturbation (and the unmeasured third variable) was that of impaired social awareness.

Even though correlational studies may not be able to pinpoint causal relationships, they can be a powerful and rich source of inference. They often suggest causal hypotheses (increased height may cause increased weight; increased weight is unlikely to cause increased height), generate questions for further research, and occasionally provide crucial data that may confirm or refute specific hypotheses. Much of what we know about mental disorders is derived from correlational studies. The fact that we cannot manipulate many of the variables we study does not mean that we cannot learn a great deal from such approaches.

Retrospective Versus Prospective Strategies

Correlational research designs can be used to study different groups of patients as they are at the time of the study (that is, concurrently). For example, if we used brain imaging to look at the size of certain brain structures in patients with schizophrenia and in healthy controls, we would be using this type of approach. But if we wanted to learn what our patients were like before they developed a specific disorder, we might adopt a **retrospective research** strategy. This involves looking back in time. In other words, we would try to collect information about how the patients behaved early in their lives with the goal of identifying factors that

might have been associated with what went wrong later. In some cases, our source material might be limited to a patient's recollections, the recollections of family members, material from diaries, or other records. A challenge with this technique is the potential for memories to be both faulty and selective.

There are certain difficulties in attempting to reconstruct the pasts of people already experiencing a disorder. Apart from the fact that a person who currently has a mental disorder may not be the most accurate or objective source of information, such a strategy invites investigators to discover what they already presume they will discover concerning background factors theoretically linked to a disorder. It invites biased procedure, unconscious or otherwise.

For instance, reports of a link between early sexual abuse and various forms of psychopathology began to emerge in the 1980s. After these reports came out, many therapists proceeded to suggest to their patients with such conditions that perhaps they too had been abused. For certain overzealous therapists, the fact that many patients had no memories of any abuse was taken as evidence that the painful memories had simply been "repressed." In other cases, a patient's simply having such common problems as difficulty sleeping or being easily startled was taken as evidence of past abuse. Over time, many patients became as convinced as their therapists that they must have been abused and that this accounted for their current difficulties. But for many patients, it simply was not the case that they had been abused. This underscores the pitfalls inherent in trying to reinterpret a person's past (or past behavior) in light of his or her present problems. Adherence to fundamental scientific principles is as crucial in the clinical domain as it is in the research laboratory.

Another approach is to use a **prospective research** strategy, which involves looking ahead in time. Here the idea is to identify individuals who have a higher-than-average likelihood of becoming psychologically disordered and to focus research attention on them before any disorder manifests. We can have much more confidence in our hypotheses about the causes of a disorder if we have been tracking influences and measuring them prior to the development of the illness in question. When our hypotheses correctly predict the behavioral problems that a group of individuals will later develop, we are much closer to establishing a causal relationship. A study that follows people over time and that tries to identify factors that predate the onset of a disorder employs a **longitudinal design**. A prototypical illustration might be a study that follows, from infancy to adulthood, the children of mothers with schizophrenia. By collecting data on the children at regular intervals, researchers can compare those who later develop schizophrenia with those who do not, with the goal of identifying important differentiating factors. In another example of a longitudinal design, researchers have shown that adolescents who report suicidal thoughts at age 15 are much more likely to have psychological problems and to have attempted suicide by age 30 than people who do not have suicidal ideas in their teens (Reinherz et al., 2006).

Manipulating Variables: The Experimental Method in Abnormal Psychology

As you have already learned, even when we find strong positive or negative associations between variables, correlational research does not allow us to draw any conclusions about directionality (i.e., does variable A cause B, or does B cause A?). This is known as the **direction of effect problem**. To draw conclusions about causality and resolve questions of directionality, an **experimental research** approach must be used. In such cases, scientists control all factors except one—the factor that could have an effect on a variable or outcome of interest. They then actively manipulate (or influence) that one factor. The factor that is manipulated is referred to as the **independent variable**. If the outcome of interest, called the **dependent variable**, is observed to change as the manipulated factor is changed, then that independent variable can be regarded as a cause of the outcome.

In Romania, children who are abandoned by their parents are traditionally raised in orphanages rather than in foster care. To study the cognitive effects of institutional versus other forms of care, researchers randomly assigned 136 children who had been institutionalized as babies to either remain in these institutions or be raised by foster families (see Nelson et al., 2007). These foster parents had been recruited for the study by the researchers. Another sample of children who lived with their birth families was also studied for comparison purposes. All the children received cognitive testing when they were 30, 42, and 54 months old. In this study, the independent variable is the living situation of the child (orphanage or foster care). The dependent variable is intellectual functioning.

This figure is intentionally omitted from this text.

Did the children assigned to foster care fare better than the children who remained in institutions? The answer is yes. At both the 42-month and the 54-month assessments, the children in foster families had significantly higher scores on the measure of cognitive functioning than the children who remained institutionalized. We can therefore conclude that there was something about being raised in a foster family that was responsible for the increased intellectual development of these children. Sadly, however, the cognitive development of both groups of children was much lower than the intellectual functioning of children who were raised in typical families. The results of this unique study therefore tell us that, although foster care helps abandoned children, these children remain at a disadvantage relative to children who are raised by their biological families. However, based at least partially on the findings from this remarkable study, Romania no longer allows children without severe disabilities to be placed in institutional care.

Studying the Efficacy of Therapy

Researchers in abnormal psychology are often interested in learning which treatments work for specific disorders. Used in the context of treatment research, the experimental method has proved to be indispensable. It is a relatively straightforward process to establish: A proposed treatment is given to a designated group of patients and withheld from a similar group of patients. Should the treated group show significantly more improvement than the untreated group, we can have confidence in the treatment's efficacy. We may

---

4 DEVELOPMENTS IN RESEARCH

Do Magnets Help with Repetitive-Stress Injury?

Magnets are often marketed to people who have chronic hand or wrist pain. This type of problem is known as repetitive-stress injury (RSI) and can be caused by extensive computer use. But do magnets really relieve the chronic pain that is associated with repetitive-stress injury? Testimonials notwithstanding, the only way to answer this question is by controlled research.

Pope and McNally (2002) randomly assigned college students with RSI to one of three groups. One group was asked to wear wristbands containing magnets for a 30-minute period (magnet group). A second group was also given seemingly identical bracelets to wear. In this case, however, and unknown both to the participants and to the assistant running the study, the magnets had been removed from the wristbands (sham group). A third group of subjects did not receive any magnets (no-treatment group).

You should note here that this study is an example of what we call a **double-blind study**. In other words, neither the subjects nor the experimenter who was working with the subjects knew who got the genuine magnets. The use of the wristbands with the magnets removed is called a **placebo treatment** condition (the word *placebo* comes from the Latin meaning "I shall please"). Placebo treatment conditions enable experimenters to control for the possibility that simply believing one is getting an effective type of treatment produces a therapeutic benefit. Finally, the no-treatment control group enables the experimenters to see what happens when they do not provide any treatment (or expectation of treatment) at all.

At the start of the study, all of the student participants completed a 4-minute typing test. This provided a measure of how many words they could type in this time period. Then, 30 minutes after wearing the magnets or fake wristbands (or, for the no-treatment subjects, after waiting 30 minutes), all participants completed another 4-minute typing test. In addition, those who had been assigned to either the genuine or the placebo magnet group were asked to rate their degree of pain relief (from no improvement to complete relief) using an 8-point scale.

What were the results? As might be expected, those people who had been assigned to the no-treatment group did not report that their level of pain changed in any appreciable way. This is hardly surprising because nothing had been done to them at all. They typed an average of about four more words on the second test (the posttest) than on the first (the pretest).

Did the people who wore the magnets do better than this? The answer is yes. Those who wore the genuine magnets reported that their pain was diminished. They also typed an average of 19 more words on the second typing test than they had on the first! In other words, with respect to both their self-report data (their pain improvement ratings) and their behavioral data (how rapidly they could type), they clearly did better than the no-treatment group.

Before you rush out to buy magnetic bracelets, however, let us look at the performance of the people who received the fake bracelets. Like the subjects who wore the genuine magnets, these participants also reported that their pain had improved. And, in fact, on the behavioral typing test, subjects in the placebo treatment group typed even more words on the second test (an average of 26 more words) than subjects who wore the real magnets did. With respect to their self-reports and their behavioral data, therefore, the group who wore the fake bracelets improved just as much as the group who wore the real magnets! On the basis of this study, then, we must conclude that magnet therapy works via the placebo effect, not because there is any genuine clinical benefit that comes from the magnets themselves. If you believe that the magnet will help your RSI, you do not actually need a magnet to bring about any clinical improvement. And this, in a nutshell, is why we need controlled research trials.

not, however, know why the treatment works, although investigators are becoming increasingly sophisticated in fine-tuning their experiments to tease out the means by which therapeutic change is induced (e.g., Hollon et al., 1987; Jacobson et al., 1996; Kazdin & Nock, 2003). Box 4 provides a nice example of a treatment research study. The findings of this study also show just how powerful placebo effects can be.

In treatment research it is important that the two groups (treated and untreated) be as equivalent as possible except for the presence or absence of the proposed active treatment. To facilitate this, patients are typically randomly assigned to the treatment condition or the no-treatment condition. **Random assignment** means that every research participant has an equal chance of being placed in the treatment or the no-treatment condition. Once a treatment has been established as effective, it can then be provided for members of the original control (untreated) group, leading to improved functioning for all those involved.

Sometimes, however, this "waiting list" control group strategy is deemed inadvisable for ethical or other reasons. Withholding a treatment that has been established as beneficial just to evaluate a new form of treatment may deprive control subjects of valuable clinical help for longer than would be considered appropriate. For this reason, there need to be stringent safeguards regarding the potential costs versus benefits of conducting the particular research project.

In certain cases, an alternative research design may be called for in which two (or more) treatments are compared in differing yet comparable groups. This method is termed a *standard treatment comparison study*. Typically, the efficacy of the control condition has been previously established; thus, patients who are assigned to this condition are not disadvantaged. Instead, the question is whether patients who receive the new treatment improve to a greater extent than those receiving the control (established) treatment. Such comparative-outcome research has much to recommend it and is being increasingly employed (Kendall et al., 2004).

Single-Case Experimental Designs

Does experimental research always involve testing hypotheses by manipulating variables across groups? The simple answer is no. We have already noted the importance of case studies as a source of ideas and hypotheses. In addition, case studies can be used to develop and test therapy techniques within a scientific framework. Such approaches are called **single-case research designs** (Hayes, 1998; Kazdin, 1998a, 1998b). A central feature of such designs is that the same individual is studied over time. Behavior or performance at one point in time can then be compared to behavior or performance at a later time, after a specific intervention or treatment has been introduced. For example, using a single-case design, Wallenstein and Nock (2007) were able to show that exercise helped a 26-year-old female patient to significantly decrease the frequency of her nonsuicidal self-injuring behaviors, which included self-hitting and head-banging.

One of the most basic experimental designs in single-case research is called the **ABAB design**. The different letters refer to different phases of the intervention. The first A phase serves as a baseline condition. Here we simply collect data on or from the participant. Then, in the first B phase, we introduce our treatment. Perhaps the person's behavior changes in some way. Even if there is a change, however, we are not justified in concluding that it was due to the introduction of our treatment. Other factors might have coincided with its introduction, so any association between the treatment and the behavior change might be spurious. To establish whether it really was the treatment that was important, we therefore withdraw the treatment and see what happens. This is the reasoning behind the second A phase (i.e., at the ABA point). Finally, to demonstrate that the behavior observed during the B phase is attainable once again, we reinstate our treatment and see if the behavioral changes we saw in the first B phase become apparent again. To further clarify the logic behind the ABAB design, let's consider the case of Kris (see Rapp et al., 2000).

case study Kris

Kris was a 19-year-old female with severe intellectual impairments. Since the age of 3 she had pulled her hair out. This disorder is called *trichotillomania* (pronounced tri-ko-til-lo-mania). Kris's hair pulling was so severe that she had a bald area on her scalp that was approximately 2.5 inches in diameter.

The researchers used an ABAB experimental design (see Figure 4) to test a treatment for reducing Kris's hair pulling. In each phase, they used a video camera to observe Kris while she was alone in her room watching television. During the baseline phase (phase A), observers measured the percentage of time that Kris spent either touching or manipulating her hair (42.5 percent of the time) as well as pulling hair (7.6 percent of the time).

In the treatment phase (B), a 2.5-lb weight was put around Kris's wrist when she settled down to watch television. When she was wearing the wrist weight, Kris's hair manipulation and hair pulling was reduced to zero. This, of course, suggested that Kris's behavior had changed because she was wearing a weight on her wrist. To verify this, the wrist weight was withdrawn in the second A phase (i.e., ABA). Kris immediately started to touch and manipulate her hair again (55.9 percent). She also showed an increase in hair pulling (4 percent of the time).

continued

case study Kris (*continued*)

When the wrist weight was reintroduced in the second B phase (ABAB), Kris's hair manipulation and pulling once again decreased, at least for a while. Although additional treatments were necessary (see Rapp et al., 2000), Kris's hair pulling was eventually eliminated entirely. Most important for our discussion, the ABAB design allowed the researchers to systematically explore, using experimental techniques and methods, the treatment approaches that might be beneficial for patients with trichotillomania.

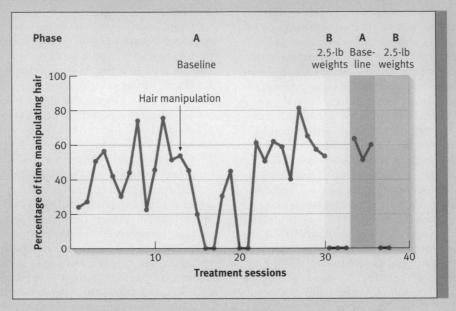

FIGURE 4

An ABAB Experimental Design: Kris's Treatment

In the A phase, baseline data are collected. In the B phase, a treatment is introduced. This treatment is then withdrawn (second A phase) and then reinstated (second B phase). In this example, hair manipulation declines with use of wrist weights, returns to pretreatment (baseline) levels when they are withdrawn, and declines again when they are reintroduced. (Data adapted from Rapp et al., 2000. Treatment of hair pulling and hair manipulation maintained by digital-tactile stimulation. *Behavior Therapy*, 31, pp. 381–93)

Animal Research

An additional way in which we can use the experimental method is by conducting research with animals. Although ethical considerations are still critical in animal research, we are able to perform studies using animal subjects that would not be possible to implement with humans (e.g., giving them experimental drugs, implanting electrodes to record brain activity, etc.).

Of course, one major assumption is that the findings from animal studies can be generalized to humans. Experiments of this kind are generally known as **analogue studies**, in which we study not the true item of interest but an approximation to it. Analogue studies may also involve humans (for example, when we try to study depression by studying healthy research participants whom we have made mildly and transiently sad).

Animal research allows behavioral scientists to manipulate and study behavior under controlled conditions that would not be possible to replicate using humans as subjects. However, results of this research may not hold up when extended to humans outside the laboratory in a real-world setting.

One current model of depression, called "hopelessness depression," has its origins in early research conducted with animals (Seligman, 1975). Laboratory experiments with dogs had demonstrated that, when subjected to repeated experiences of painful, unpredictable, and inescapable electric shock, the dogs lost their ability to learn a simple escape response to avoid further shock in a different situation later on. They just sat and endured the pain. This observation led Seligman and his colleagues to argue that human depression (which he believed was analogous to the reaction of the helpless dogs) is a reaction to uncontrollable stressful events in which one's behavior has no effect on one's environment, leading to helplessness, passivity, and depression. In other words, the findings from these animal studies provided the impetus for what first became known as the "learned helplessness theory of depression" (Abramson et al., 1978; Seligman, 1975) and is now termed "the hopelessness theory of depression" (Abramson et al., 1989). These theories of depression are not without their difficulties. Nevertheless, it is useful to remain aware of the broader message: Even though problems may arise when we generalize too readily

from animal to human models of psychopathology, the learned helplessness analogy has generated much research and has allowed us to refine and develop our understanding of depression.

In Review

- How is experimental research different from correlational research?

- What is the difference between a positive and a negative correlation? If two variables are correlated, does this mean that one variable causes the other? If so, why? If not, why not?

- In experimental research, which variable (independent or dependent) is manipulated?

- What is a placebo?

- Explain the process of performing an ABAB design. Why are such designs helpful to clinicians and researchers?

Unresolved Issues

▶ *Are We All Becoming Mentally Ill? The Expanding Horizons of Mental Disorder*

The concept of mental disorder, as we have seen, suffers from the lack of a truly objective means of determining what is disordered and what is not. It is also in the financial interests of mental health professionals to be more and more inclusive concerning the kinds of problems that might be regarded as "mentally disordered." Not surprisingly, there is often pressure to include in the *DSM* more and more kinds of socially undesirable behavior. For example, when *DSM-IV* was being developed a proposal was made to include "road rage" (anger at other drivers) as a newly discovered mental disorder (Sharkey, 1997). However, anger directed toward other drivers is so common that almost all of us would be at risk of being diagnosed with this new disorder if it had been added to the *DSM*.

There is considerable informal evidence that the committee responsible for the production of the *DSM-IV* worked hard to fend off a large number of such frivolous proposals. They largely succeeded in avoiding additional diagnoses by adopting stringent inclusion criteria. Nevertheless, this promises to be an uphill battle. Mental health professionals, like the members of other professions, tend to view the world through a lens that enhances the importance of phenomena related to their own expertise. Also, inclusion of a disorder in the *DSM* is a prerequisite for health insurers' reimbursement of services rendered.

It is thus in the interests of the public at large to keep a close eye on proposed expansions of what is considered "mentally disordered." Failure to do so could eventually lead to a situation in which much of human behavior—save for the most bland, conformist, and conventional

of conduct—would be declared a manifestation of a mental disorder. By that point, the concept of psychopathology would have become so indiscriminate as to lose most of its scientifically productive meaning. Currently proposed for addition to *DSM-5* are "apathy syndrome," "parental alienation disorder," and "Internet addiction." Do you think these warrant inclusion as new disorders? What do you think their defining features should be?

Internet addiction has been proposed as a new diagnostic category for *DSM-5*.

Summary

- A precise definition of *abnormality* remains elusive. Elements that can be helpful in considering whether something is abnormal include suffering, maladaptiveness, statistical deviancy, dangerousness, violation of societal norms, irrationality, and unpredictability.

- The *DSM* employs a category type of classification similar to that used in medicine. Disorders are regarded as discrete clinical entities, though not all clinical disorders may be best considered in this way.

- Even though it is not without problems, the *DSM* provides us with working criteria that help clinicians and researchers identify and study specific difficulties that affect the lives of many people. It is far from a "finished product." However, familiarity with the *DSM* is essential to significant study of the field.

- People with mental disorders experience a great deal of stigma. Even though it is now generally known that mental illnesses have biological causes, this does not seem to have reduced the stigma associated with being mentally ill. Negative attitudes toward the mentally ill can be found in all cultures.

- Culture shapes the presentation of clinical disorders in some cases. There are also certain disorders that appear to be highly culture specific.

- Classifying disorders provides a communication shorthand and allows us to structure information in an efficient manner. This facilitates research and treatment. However, when we classify, we lose personal information about the person with the disorder. Classification also facilitates stigma, stereotyping, and labeling.

- Epidemiology involves the study of the distribution and frequency of disorders. Just under 50 percent of people will experience some form of mental disorder over the course of their lifetimes. Mood disorders and anxiety disorders are particularly common.

- To avoid misconception and error, we must adopt a scientific approach to the study of abnormal behavior. This requires a focus on research and research methodology, including an appreciation of the distinction between what is observable and what is hypothetical or inferred.

- To produce valid results, research must be conducted on individuals who are truly representative of the diagnostic groups to which they purportedly belong.

- Research in abnormal psychology may be correlational or experimental. Correlational research examines factors as they currently are. Experimental research involves manipulating one variable (the independent variable) and observing the effect this manipulation produces with regard to another variable (the dependent variable).

- Just because two variables are correlated does not mean that there is a causal relationship between them. Always remember that correlation does not equal causation.

- Although most experiments involve the study of groups, single-case experimental designs (e.g., ABAB designs) may also be used to make causal inferences in individual instances.

- Analogue studies (e.g., animal research) are studies that provide an approximation to the human disorders of interest. Although generalizability presents an obstacle, animal research in particular has been very informative.

Key Terms

ABAB design
abnormal psychology
acute
analogue studies
bias
case study
chronic
comorbidity
comparison or control group
correlation
correlational research
correlation coefficient
criterion group
dependent variable
direct observation
direction of effect problem
double-blind study
effect size
epidemiology
etiology
experimental research
external validity
family aggregation
generalizability
hypothesis
incidence
independent variable
internal validity
labeling
lifetime prevalence
longitudinal design
meta-analysis
negative correlation
nomenclature
1-year prevalence
placebo treatment
point prevalence
positive correlation
prevalence
prospective research
random assignment
retrospective research
sampling
self-report data
single-case research design
statistical significance
stereotyping
stigma
third variable problem

Glossary

Many of the key terms listed in the glossary appear in boldface when first introduced in the text discussion. A number of other terms commonly encountered in this or other psychology texts are also included; you are encouraged to make use of this glossary both as a general reference tool and as a study aid for the course in abnormal psychology.

ABAB design. An experimental design, often involving a single subject, wherein a baseline period (A) is followed by a treatment (B). To confirm that the treatment resulted in a change in behavior, the treatment is then withdrawn (A) and reinstated (B).

Abnormal psychology. Field of psychology concerned with the study, assessment, treatment, and prevention of abnormal behavior.

Acute. Term used to describe a disorder of sudden onset, usually with intense symptoms.

Analogue studies. Studies in which a researcher attempts to emulate the conditions hypothesized as leading to abnormality.

Bias. Observer bias occurs when the researcher has preconceived ideas and expectations that influence the observations he or she makes in the research study.

Case study method. An in-depth examination of an individual or family that draws from a number of data sources, including interviews and psychological testing.

Chronic. Term used to describe a long-standing or frequently recurring disorder, often with progressing seriousness.

Comorbidity. Occurrence of two or more identified disorders in the same psychologically disordered individual.

Comparison or control group. Group of subjects who do not exhibit the disorder being studied but who are comparable in all other respects to the criterion group. Also, a comparison group of subjects who do not receive a condition or treatment the effects of which are being studied.

Correlation. The tendency of two variables to change together. With positive correlation, as one variable goes up, so does the other; with negative correlation, one variable goes up as the other goes down.

Correlational method/correlational research. A research strategy that examines whether and how variables go together (covary) without manipulating (changing) any variables.

Correlation coefficient. A statistic that ranges from $+1.0$ to -1.0 and reflects the degree of association between two variables. The magnitude of the correlation indicates the strength of the association, and the sign indicates whether the correlation is positive or negative.

Criterion group. Group of subjects who exhibit the disorder under study.

Dependent variable. In an experiment, the factor that is observed to change with changes in the manipulated (independent) variables.

Direct observation. Method of collecting research data that involves directly observing behavior in a given situation.

Direction of effect problem. Refers to the fact that, in correlational research, it cannot be concluded whether variable A causes variable B or whether variable B causes variable A.

Double-blind study. Often used in studies examining drug treatment effects, a condition where neither the subject nor the experimenter has knowledge about what specific experimental condition (or drug) the subject is receiving.

Effect size. A statistical term referring to the strength of the relationship between two variables in a statistical population.

Epidemiology. Study of the distribution of diseases, disorders, or health-related behaviors in a given population. Mental health epidemiology is the study of the distribution of mental disorders.

Etiology. Factors that are related to the development (or cause) of a particular disorder.

Experimental research. Research that involves the manipulation of a given factor or variable with everything else held constant.

External validity. The extent to which the findings from a single study are relevant to other populations, contexts, or times.

Family aggregation. The clustering of certain traits, behaviors, or disorders within a given family. Family aggregation may arise because of genetic or environmental similarities.

Generalizability. The extent to which the findings from a single study can be used to draw conclusions about other samples.

Hypothesis. Statement or proposition, usually based on observation, that is tested in an experiment; may be refuted or supported by experimental results but can never be conclusively proved.

Incidence. Occurrence (onset) rate of a given disorder in a given population.

Independent variable. Factor whose effects are being examined and which is manipulated in some way while other variables are held constant.

Internal validity. The extent to which a study is free of confounds, is methodologically sound, and allows the researcher to have confidence in the findings.

Labeling. Assigning a person to a particular diagnostic category, such as schizophrenia.

Lifetime prevalence. The proportion of living persons in a population who have ever had a disorder up to the time of the epidemiological assessment.

Longitudinal design. A research design in which people are followed over time.

Meta-analysis. A statistical method used to combine the results of a number of similar research studies. The data from each study are transformed into a common metric called the *effect size*. This allows the data from the various studies to be combined and then analyzed. You can think of a meta-analysis as being like research that you are already familiar with, except that the "participants" are individual research studies, not individual people.

Negative correlation. A relationship between two variables such that a high score on one variable is associated with a low score on another variable.

Nomenclature. A formalized naming system.

1-year prevalence. The total number of cases of a health-related state or condition in a population for a given year.

Placebo treatment. An inert pill or otherwise neutral intervention that produces desirable therapeutic effects because of the subject's expectations that it will be beneficial.

Point prevalence. The number of cases of a specific condition or disorder that can be found in a population at one given point in time.

Positive correlation. A relationship between two variables such that a high score on one variable is associated with a high score on another variable.

Prevalence. In a population, the proportion of active cases of a disorder that can be identified at a given point in time or during a given period.

Prospective research. Method that often focuses on individuals who have a higher-than-average likelihood of becoming psychologically disordered before abnormal behavior is observed.

Random assignment. A procedure used to create equivalent groups in which every research participant has an equal chance of being assigned to any group in the study.

Retrospective research. Research approach that attempts to retrace earlier events in the life of a subject.

Sampling. The process of selecting a representative subgroup from a defined population of interest.

Self-report data. Data collected directly from participants, typically by means of interviews or questionnaires.

Single-case research design. An experimental research design (e.g., an ABAB design) that involves only one subject.

Statistical significance. A measure of the probability that a research finding could have occurred by chance alone.

Stereotyping. The tendency to jump to conclusions (often negative) about what a person is like based on beliefs about that group that exist (often incorrectly) in the culture (e.g., French people are rude, homosexuals have good taste in clothes, mental patients are dangerous, etc.).

Stigma. Negative labeling.

Third variable problem. Refers to the problem of making causal inferences in correlational research where the correlation between two variables could be due to their shared correlation with an unmeasured third variable.

Photo Credits

Credits are listed in order of appearance.

Text Credits

Credits are listed in order of appearance.

Historical and Contemporary Views of Abnormal Behavior

From Chapter 2 of *Abnormal Psychology*, Fifteenth Edition. James N. Butcher, Susan Mineka, Jill M. Hooley. Copyright © 2013 by Pearson
Education, Inc. All rights reserved.

An Artist in Bedlam

The most famous patient committed to the historic Bethlem Hospital in England (better known as Bedlam) during its long existence was a well-known and talented young artist, Richard Dadd (1817–1886). Dadd was born in Chatham, England, in 1817. His father was a successful chemist. Dadd attended the Kings School in Rochester and also studied art at the Royal Academy School in London. He showed a strong aptitude for drawing and painting and was admitted to the prestigious Royal Academy of Arts at the early age of 20. When he was 25, he was invited to accompany Sir Thomas Phillips, the former mayor of Newport, on a grand tour through Europe, Greece, Turkey, Syria, and Egypt to serve as the draftsman and painter for the expedition. During the trip, Dadd produced a number of exceptional paintings of people and places he encountered on the journey, many of which are in museums today. The journey was reportedly difficult and stressful, and at one point, during a trip up the Nile River, Dadd underwent a remarkable personality change, becoming delusional and increasingly aggressive and violent towards people he met. He was reported to have expressed an urge to kill the Pope. He experienced delusional beliefs—for example, that he had come under the influence of the Egyptian god Osiris.

When he returned from the trip in 1843, he was diagnosed as being mentally unsound because of his hallucinations and his strange, delusional beliefs. In an effort to restore him to health, his family took him to recuperate in a countryside village in Kent, England. The records indicate that one day he came to the conclusion that his father was the Devil in disguise, and on a walk in the countryside Dadd killed his father with a knife. He attempted to escape by fleeing to France; however, his aggressive behavior continued, and he attempted to kill another tourist with a razor. He was arrested by the police and was eventually returned to England. He was committed to Bethlem Royal Hospital, where he was held in the criminal ward for dangerous inmates. He remained in Bethlem Hospital for almost 20 years but was transferred to Broadmoor Hospital, where he died in 1886. During his stay in both the Bethlem and Broadmoor hospitals he was allowed and encouraged to paint by the staff as part of his treatment. During this time he produced a number of paintings, many of which can be seen today in art museums.

Although he appears to have experienced symptoms of a mood disorder including acute mania it is likely that Dadd suffered from paranoid schizophrenia. Interestingly, two of his siblings appeared to suffer from the same symptom pattern; thus he may have been genetically predisposed to this condition (see Greysmith, 1979; MacGregor, 1989 for a discussion of his life and art work).

Historical Views of Abnormal Behavior

Our historical efforts to understand abnormal psychology include both humor and tragedy. In this chapter, we will highlight some views of psychopathology, and some of the treatments administered, from ancient times to the twenty-first century. In a broad sense, we will see a progression of beliefs from what we now consider superstition to those based on scientific awareness—from a focus on supernatural explanations to knowledge of natural causes. The course of this evolution has at times been marked by periods of advancement or unique, individual contributions, followed by long years of inactivity or unproductive, backward steps.

Although human life appeared on earth some 3 million or more years ago, written records extend back only a few thousand years. Thus our knowledge of our early ancestors is limited. Two Egyptian papyri dating from the sixteenth century B.C. provide some clues to the earliest treatments of diseases and behavior disorders (Okasha & Okasha, 2000). The Edwin Smith papyrus (named after its nineteenth-century discoverer) contains detailed descriptions of the treatment of wounds and other surgical operations. In it, the brain is described—possibly for the first time in history—and the writing clearly shows that the brain was recognized as the site of mental functions. The Ebers papyrus offers another perspective on treatment. It covers internal medicine and the circulatory system but relies more on incantations and magic for explaining and curing diseases that had unknown causes. Although surgical techniques may have been used, they were probably coupled with prayers and the like, which reflected the prevailing view of the origin of mental illness.

Demonology, Gods, and Magic

References to abnormal behavior in early writings show that the Chinese, Egyptians, Hebrews, and Greeks often attributed such behavior to a demon or god who had taken possession of a person. Whether the "possession" was assumed to involve good spirits or evil spirits usually depended on the affected individual's symptoms. If a person's speech or behavior appeared to have a religious or mystical significance, it was usually thought that he or she was possessed by a good spirit or god. Such people were often treated with considerable awe and respect, for people believed they had supernatural powers.

Most possessions, however, were considered to be the work of an angry god or an evil spirit, particularly when a person became excited or overactive and engaged in behavior contrary to religious teachings. Among the ancient Hebrews, for example, such possessions were thought to represent the wrath and punishment of God. Moses is quoted in the Bible as saying, "The Lord shall smite thee with madness." Apparently this punishment was thought to involve the withdrawal of God's protection and the abandonment of the person to the forces of evil. In such cases, every effort was made to rid the person of the evil spirit.

The primary type of treatment for demonic possession was exorcism, which included various techniques for casting an evil spirit out of an afflicted person. These techniques varied but typically included magic, prayer, incantation, noise-making, and the use of horrible-tasting concoctions made from sheep's dung and wine.

Hippocrates' Early Medical Concepts

The Greek temples of healing ushered in the Golden Age of Greece under the Athenian leader Pericles (461–429 B.C.). This period saw considerable progress in the understanding and treatment of mental disorders, in spite of the fact that Greeks of the time considered the human body sacred so little could be learned of human anatomy or physiology. During this period the Greek physician Hippocrates (460–377 B.C.), often referred to as the father of modern medicine, received his training and made substantial contributions to the field.

Hippocrates denied that deities and demons intervened in the development of illnesses and instead insisted that mental disorders, like other diseases, had natural causes and appropriate treatments. He believed that the brain was the central organ of intellectual activity and that mental disorders were due to brain pathology. He also emphasized the importance of heredity and predisposition and pointed out that injuries to the head could cause sensory and motor disorders.

Hippocrates classified all mental disorders into three general categories—mania, melancholia, and phrenitis (brain

Hippocrates' (460–377 B.C) belief that mental disease was the result of natural causes and brain pathology was revolutionary for its time.

fever)—and gave detailed clinical descriptions of the specific disorders included in each category. He relied heavily on clinical observation, and his descriptions, which were based on daily clinical records of his patients, were surprisingly thorough.

Maher and Maher (1994) pointed out that the best known of the earlier paradigms for explaining personality or temperament is the doctrine of the four humors, associated with the name of Hippocrates and later with the Roman physician Galen. The four elements of the material world were thought to be earth, air, fire, and water, which had attributes of heat, cold, moistness, and dryness. These elements combined to form the four essential fluids of the body—blood (sanguis), phlegm, bile (choler), and black bile (melancholer). The fluids combined in different proportions within different individuals, and a person's temperament was determined by which of the humors was dominant. From this view came one of the earliest and longest-lasting typologies of human behavior: the sanguine, the phlegmatic, the choleric, and the melancholic. Each of these "types" brought with it a set of personality attributes. For example, the person of sanguine temperament was optimistic, cheerful, and unafraid.

Hippocrates considered dreams to be important in understanding a patient's personality. On this point, he was a harbinger of a basic concept of modern psychodynamic psychotherapy. The treatments advocated by Hippocrates were far in advance of the exorcistic practices then prevalent. For the

DEVELOPMENTS IN THINKING 1

Melancholia Through the Ages

Although the modern mental health sciences have made great strides in defining, describing, classifying, determining the causes of, and treating psychological disorders, we should not ignore or minimize the contributions to understanding these conditions that were made by many individuals in antiquity. Actually, some mental health problems that are receiving a great deal of research and clinical attention today have been recognized and well described for millennia. One recent study of surviving letters from patients who were hospitalized in Edinborough Asylum between 1873 and 1906 concluded that mental health problems in the nineteenth century were very similar to those in our day (Beveridge, 1997). One such disorder is depression.

Melancholia

Perhaps no other mental disorder received so much attention from earlier scholars as depression, or (as it has been referred to in the past) melancholia. Efforts to understand melancholia have been undertaken by physicians, philosophers, writers, painters, and religious leaders in Western civilization for over 2,000 years. Moreover, conditions similar to depression are described in surviving writings from ancient Egypt (Okasha & Okasha, 2000). These disorders might have been viewed variously as medical conditions or religious states or human frailties; however, the symptom structure and behavior described were unmistakable.

Radden (2000) published an interesting compendium of important writings on melancholia that span 24 centuries, some highlights of which are provided here.

- Investigations into the nature of depression, beginning with Aristotle and Galen during the Greek and Roman eras, provide lucid descriptions of the disorder melancholia.
- Even in the Middle Ages, when scholarship and inquiry were hindered by religious persecution that included the Spanish Inquisition,

there were scholars interested in mental states such as melancholia. Hildegard (1098–1179), a nun known as the "first published woman physician," carried the Greek views of melancholia further by noting, among other things, that melancholia took different forms in men and women. Johann Weyer (1515–1588) provided astute descriptions of melancholia and examined characteristics of persons who might be so affected, even though these observations were often couched in terms of demonic possession—perhaps as a concession to leaders of the Inquisition in order to avoid persecution.

- The premodern view of melancholia as a disorder (without the taint of demonic possession or ancient Greek humors) was introduced by Philippe Pinel (1745–1826). A French physician widely recognized for his contributions to the humane treatment of people with mental disorders, Pinel also advanced our scholarly understanding of mental disorders such as melancholia by improving a classification schema and examining the causes of the disorder.
- Two early modern contributors to our understanding of depression were Wilhelm Griesinger (1817–1868) and Emil Kraepelin (1856–1926). Griesinger's views on the underlying biological basis for disorders such as melancholia focused the field of psychiatry on the need to seek biological determinants for disorders. Kraepelin is credited with preparing the way for the modern view of psychiatry. His classification schema is still cited today in contemporary writings as seminal in the evolution of diagnostic classification systems. He also identified manic depression as a major category of depression.

Even though much of our understanding of depression and our development of effective treatment methods has emerged over the past three decades, our debt to the ancients who struggled with describing and understanding this disorder needs to be recognized.

---

treatment of melancholia (see Developments in Thinking 1), for example, he prescribed a regular and tranquil life, sobriety and abstinence from all excesses, a vegetable diet, celibacy, exercise short of fatigue, and bleeding if indicated. He also recognized the importance of the environment and often removed his patients from their families.

Hippocrates' emphasis on the natural causes of diseases, on clinical observation, and on brain pathology as the root of mental disorders was truly revolutionary. Like his contemporaries, however, Hippocrates had little knowledge of physiology. He believed that hysteria (the appearance of physical illness in the absence of organic pathology) was restricted to women and was caused by the uterus wandering to various parts of the body, pining for children. For this "disease," Hippocrates recommended marriage as the best remedy.

The earliest use of the concept "delirium" to describe symptoms of mental disorders that result from fever or physical injury

or brain trauma occurred in the first century A.D. by Celsus (Adamis et al., 2007).

Early Philosophical Conceptions of Consciousness

The Greek philosopher Plato (429–347 B.C.) studied mentally disturbed individuals who had committed criminal acts and how to deal with them. He wrote that such persons were, in some "obvious" sense, not responsible for their acts and should not receive punishment in the same way as normal persons. He also made provision for mental cases to be cared for in the community (Plato, n.d.).

Plato viewed psychological phenomena as responses of the whole organism, reflecting its internal state and natural appetites. In *The Republic*, Plato emphasized the importance of individual differences in intellectual and other abilities and took into account sociocultural influences in shaping thinking and behavior. His ideas regarding treatment included a provision for "hospital" care for individuals who developed beliefs that ran counter to those of the broader social order. There they would be engaged periodically in conversations comparable to psychotherapy to promote the health of their souls (Milns, 1986). Despite these modern ideas, however, Plato shared the belief that mental disorders were in part divinely caused.

The celebrated Greek philosopher Aristotle (384–322 B.C.), who was a pupil of Plato, wrote extensively on mental disorders. Among his most lasting contributions to psychology are his descriptions of consciousness. He held the view that "thinking" as directed would eliminate pain and help to attain pleasure. On the question of whether mental disorders could be caused by psychological factors such as frustration and conflict, Aristotle discussed the possibility and rejected it; his lead on this issue was widely followed. Aristotle generally subscribed to the Hippocratic theory of disturbances in the bile. For example, he thought that very hot bile generated amorous desires, verbal fluency, and suicidal impulses.

Later Greek and Roman Thought

Hippocrates' work was continued by some of the later Greek and Roman physicians. Particularly in Alexandria, Egypt (which became a center of Greek culture after its founding in 332 B.C. by Alexander the Great), medical practices developed to a higher level, and the temples dedicated to Saturn were first-rate sanatoria. Pleasant surroundings were considered of great therapeutic value for mental patients, who were provided with constant activities including parties, dances, walks in the temple gardens, rowing along the Nile, and musical concerts. Physicians of this time also used a wide range of therapeutic measures including dieting, massage, hydrotherapy, gymnastics, and education, as well as some less desirable practices such as bleeding, purging, and mechanical restraints.

Asclepiades (c. 124–40 B.C.) was a Greek physician born at Prusa in Bithynia in Asia Minor and practiced medicine in Rome towards the end of the second century B.C. He developed a theory of disease that was based on the flow of atoms through the pores in the body and developed treatments, such as massage, special diets, bathing, exercise, listening to music, and rest and quiet, to restore to the body (Stone, 1937).

One of the most influential Greek physicians was Galen (A.D. 130–200), who practiced in Rome. Although he elaborated on the Hippocratic tradition, he did not contribute much that was new to the treatment or clinical descriptions of mental disorders. Rather, he made a number of original contributions concerning the anatomy of the nervous system. (These findings were based on dissections of animals; human autopsies were still not allowed.) Galen also took a scientific approach to the field, dividing the causes of psychological disorders into physical and mental categories. Among the causes he named were injuries to the head, excessive use of alcohol, shock, fear, adolescence, menstrual changes, economic reversals, and disappointment in love.

Galen (A.D. 130–200) believed that psychological disorders could have either physical causes, such as injuries to the head, or mental causes, such as disappointment in love.

Roman medicine reflected the characteristic pragmatism of the Roman people. Roman physicians wanted to make their patients comfortable and thus used pleasant physical therapies such as warm baths and massage. They also followed the principle of *contrariis contrarius* ("*opposite by opposite*")—for example, having their patients drink chilled wine while they were in a warm tub.

Early Views of Mental Disorders in China

China was one of the earliest developed civilizations in which medicine and attention to mental disorders were introduced (Soong, 2006). The following passage is taken from an ancient Chinese medical text supposedly written by Huang Ti (c. 2674 B.C.), the third legendary emperor.

> The person suffering from excited insanity initially feels sad, eating and sleeping less; he then becomes grandiose, feeling that he is very smart and noble, talking and scolding day and night, singing, behaving strangely, seeing strange things, hearing strange voices, believing that he can see the devil or gods. (Tseng, 1973, p. 570)

Even at this early date, Chinese medicine was based on a belief in natural rather than supernatural causes for illnesses. For example, in the concept of *yin* and *yang*, the human body, like the cosmos, is divided into positive and negative forces that both complement and contradict each other. If the two forces are balanced, the result is physical and mental health; if they are not, illness results. Thus treatments focused on restoring balance (Tseng, 1973, p. 570).

Chinese medicine reached a relatively sophisticated level during the second century, and Chung Ching, who has been called the Hippocrates of China, wrote two well-known medical works around A.D. 200. Like Hippocrates, he based his views of physical and mental disorders on clinical observations, and he implicated organ pathologies as primary causes. However, he also believed that stressful psychological conditions could cause organ pathologies, and his treatments, like those of Hippocrates, utilized both drugs and the regaining of emotional balance through appropriate activities.

As in the West, Chinese views of mental disorders regressed to a belief in supernatural forces as causal agents. From the later part of the second century through the early part of the ninth century, ghosts and devils were implicated in "ghost-evil" insanity, which presumably resulted from possession by evil spirits. The "Dark Ages" in China, however, were neither so severe (in terms of the treatment of mental patients) nor as long-lasting as in the West. A return to biological, somatic (bodily) views and an emphasis on psychosocial factors occurred in the centuries that followed. Over the past 50 years, China has been experiencing a broadening of ideas in mental health services and has been incorporating many ideas from Western psychiatry (Zhang & Lu, 2006).

Views of Abnormality During the Middle Ages

During the Middle Ages (about A.D. 500 to A.D. 1500), the more scientific aspects of Greek medicine survived in the Islamic countries of the Middle East. The first mental hospital was established in Baghdad in A.D. 792; it was soon followed by others in Damascus and Aleppo (Polvan, 1969). In these hospitals, mentally disturbed individuals received humane treatment. One outstanding figure in ancient medicine was Avicenna from Persia (c. 980–1037), called the "prince of physicians" (Campbell, 1926), and the author of *The Canon of Medicine*, perhaps the most widely studied medical work ever written. In his writings, Avicenna frequently referred to hysteria, epilepsy, manic reactions, and melancholia. The following case study illustrates Avicenna's unique approach to the treatment of a young prince suffering from mental disorder.

During the Middle Ages in Europe, scientific inquiry into abnormal behavior

Ancient Persian physician Avicenna (c. 980–1037) approached the treatment of mental disorders with humane practices unknown to Western medical practitioners of the time.

case study   An Early Treatment Case

A certain prince was afflicted with melancholia and suffered from the delusion that he was a cow. . . . He would low like a cow, causing annoyance to everyone, . . . crying, "Kill me so that a good stew may be made of my flesh." Finally . . . he would eat nothing. . . . Avicenna was persuaded to take the case. . . . First of all he sent a message to the patient bidding him be of good cheer because the butcher was coming to slaughter him, whereat . . . the sick man rejoiced. Some time afterward Avicenna, holding a knife in his hand, entered the sickroom saying, "Where is this cow that I may kill it?" The patient lowed like a cow to indicate where he was. By Avicenna's orders he was laid on the ground bound hand and foot. Avicenna then felt him all over and said, "He is too lean, and not ready to be killed; he must be fattened." Then they offered him suitable food of which he now partook eagerly, and gradually he gained strength, got rid of his delusion, and was completely cured. (Browne, 1921, pp. 88–89)

was limited, and the treatment of psychologically disturbed individuals was characterized more often by ritual or superstition than by attempts to understand an individual's condition. In contrast to Avicenna's era in the Islamic countries of the Middle East or to the period of enlightenment during the seventeenth and eighteenth centuries, the Middle Ages in Europe were largely devoid of scientific thinking and humane treatment for the mentally disturbed.

Mental disorders were quite prevalent throughout the Middle Ages in Europe, especially toward the end of the period, when medieval institutions, social structures, and beliefs began to change drastically. During this time, supernatural explanations of the causes of mental illness grew in popularity. Within this environment, it obviously was difficult to make great strides in the understanding and treatment of abnormal behavior. Although the influence of theology was growing rapidly, "sin" was not always cited as a causal factor in mental illness. For example, Kroll and Bachrach (1984) examined 57 episodes of mental illness ranging from madness and possession to alcohol abuse and epilepsy. They found sin implicated in only nine cases (16 percent). To understand better this elusive period of history, let us look at two events of the times—mass madness and exorcism—to see how they are related to views of abnormal behavior.

MASS MADNESS During the last half of the Middle Ages in Europe, a peculiar trend emerged in efforts to understand abnormal behavior. It involved **mass madness**—the widespread occurrence of group behavior disorders that were apparently cases of hysteria. Whole groups of people were affected simultaneously. Dancing manias (epidemics of raving, jumping, dancing, and convulsions) were reported as early as the tenth century. One such episode that occurred in Italy early in the thirteenth century was known as **tarantism**—a disorder that included an uncontrollable impulse to dance that was often attributed to the bite of the southern European tarantula or wolf spider. This dancing mania later spread to Germany and the rest of Europe, where it was known as **Saint Vitus's dance**.

Isolated rural areas were also afflicted with outbreaks of **lycanthropy**—a condition in which people believed themselves to be possessed by wolves and imitated their behavior. In 1541 a case was reported in which a person suffering from lycanthropy told his captors, in confidence, that he was really a wolf but that his skin was smooth on the surface because all the hairs were on the inside (Stone, 1937). To cure him of his delusions, his extremities were amputated, following which he died, still uncured.

Mass madness occurred periodically all the way into the seventeenth century but had reached its peak during the fourteenth and fifteenth centuries—a period noted for social oppression, famine, and epidemic diseases. During this time, Europe was ravaged by a plague known as the Black Death, which killed millions (according to some estimates, 50 percent of the population of Europe died) and severely disrupted social organization. Undoubtedly, many of the peculiar cases of mass madness were related to the depression, fear, and wild mysticism engendered by the terrible events of this period. People simply could not believe that frightening catastrophes such as the Black Death could have natural causes and thus could be within their power to control, prevent, or even create.

Today, so-called "mass hysteria" occurs occasionally; the affliction usually mimics some type of physical disorder such as fainting spells or convulsive movements. A case of apparent mass hysteria occurred among hundreds of West Bank Palestinian girls in April 1983. This episode threatened to have serious political repercussions because some Arab leaders initially thought that the girls had been poisoned by Israelis. Health officials later concluded that psychological factors had played a key role in most of the cases (Hefez, 1985).

Ilechukwu (1992) describes an epidemic of mass hysteria that occurred in Nigeria in 1990 in which many men feared that their genitals had simply vanished. This fear of genital retraction accompanied by a fear of death is referred to as *koro* and has been widely documented in Southeast Asia. The afflicted persons believe this genital disappearance was caused by a supernatural occurrence in which they were robbed of their genitalia in order to benefit other people magically. Ilechukwu attributes some of this panic to male resentment of women's success during a period of social strain and the symbolic equation between masculine sexuality and economic, social, and creative prowess.

EXORCISM AND WITCHCRAFT In the Middle Ages in Europe, management of the mentally disturbed was left largely to the clergy. Monasteries served as refuges and places of confinement. During the early part of the medieval period, the mentally disturbed were, for the most part, treated with considerable kindness. "Treatment" consisted of prayer, holy water, sanctified ointments, the breath or spittle of the priests, the touching of relics, visits to holy places, and mild forms of exorcism. In some monasteries and shrines, **exorcisms** were performed by the gentle "laying on of hands." Such methods were often joined with vaguely understood medical treatments derived mainly from Galen, which gave rise to prescriptions such as the following: "For a fiend-sick man: When a devil possesses a man, or controls him from within with disease, a spewdrink of lupin, bishopswort, henbane, garlic. Pound these together, add ale and holy water" (Cockayne, 1864–1866).

Interestingly, there has been a recent resurgence of superstition. For example, one can find those who believe that supernatural forces cause psychological problems and that "cures" should involve exorcism to rid people of unwanted characteristics or "spells." Fries (2001) reported on a woman tragically drowning her 4-year-old daughter in an exorcism ritual attempting to rid her of demons that the mother believed possessed her daughter. In a more recent example, CBS News reported an incident in which an autistic boy was killed in an exorcism at a church in Milwaukee (CBS News, 2003).

It had long been thought that during the Middle Ages many mentally disturbed people were accused of being witches and thus were punished and often killed (e.g., Zilboorg & Henry, 1941). But several more recent interpretations have questioned the extent to which this was so (Maher & Maher, 1985; Phillips, 2002; Schoeneman, 1984). For example, in a review of the literature, Schoeneman (1984) notes that "the typical accused witch was not a mentally ill person but an impoverished woman with a sharp tongue and a bad temper" (p. 301). He goes on to say that "witchcraft was, in fact, never considered a variety of possession either by witch hunters, the general populace, or modern historians" (p. 306). To say "never" may be overstating the case; clearly, some mentally ill people were punished as witches. Otherwise, as we will see in the next section, why did some physicians and thinkers go to great lengths to expose the fallacies of the connection? In the case of witchcraft and mental illness, the confusion may be due, in part, to confusion about demonic possession. Even Robert Burton (1576–1640), an enlightened scholar, in his classic work *The Anatomy of Melancholia* (1621), considered demonic possession a potential cause of mental disorder. There were two types of demonically possessed people: Those physically possessed were considered mad, whereas those spiritually possessed were likely to be considered witches. Over time, the distinctions between these two categories may have blurred in the eyes of historians, resulting in the perception that witchcraft and mental illness were connected more frequently in the medieval mind than was the case.

The changing view of the relationship between witchcraft and mental illness points to an even broader issue—the difficulties of interpreting historical events accurately. We will discuss this concept in more depth in the Unresolved Issues section at the end of this chapter.

In Review

- What aspects of Hippocrates' alternative approach to mental disorders were truly revolutionary?

- What were the historical views of the disorder of melancholia (known as depression today)?

- What was the role of supernatural beliefs in efforts to understand mental disorders during the Middle Ages?

- What is mass madness? Give some examples of this phenomenon.

Toward Humanitarian Approaches

During the latter part of the Middle Ages and the early Renaissance, scientific questioning reemerged and a movement emphasizing the importance of specifically human interests and concerns began—a movement (still with us today) that can be loosely referred to as humanism. Consequently, the superstitious beliefs that had hindered the understanding and therapeutic treatment of mental disorders began to be challenged.

The Resurgence of Scientific Questioning in Europe

Paracelsus (1490–1541), a Swiss physician, was an early critic of superstitious beliefs about possession. He insisted that the dancing mania was not a possession but a form of disease, and that it should be treated as such. He also postulated a conflict between the instinctual and spiritual natures of human beings, formulated the idea of psychic causes for mental illness, and advocated treatment by "bodily magnetism," later called hypnosis (Mora, 1967). Although Paracelsus rejected demonology, his view of abnormal behavior was colored by his belief in astral influences (*lunatic* is derived from the Latin word *luna*, or "moon"). He was convinced that the moon exerted a supernatural influence

VINCE TEIPSVM.

EFFIGIES IOANNIS WIERI ANNO ÆTATIS LX SALVTIS M D LXXVI

Johann Weyer, a sixteenth-century German physician, became so concerned over the torture and imprisonment of people accused of being witches that he wrote a book rebutting the church's witch-hunting handbook, the *Malleus Maleficarum*.

over the brain—an idea, incidentally, that persists among some people today.

Johann Weyer (1515–1588), a German physician and writer who wrote under the Latin name of Joannus Wierus, was so deeply disturbed by the imprisonment, torture, and burning of people accused of witchcraft that he made a careful study of the entire problem. About 1583 he published a book, *On the Deceits of the Demons*, that contains a step-by-step rebuttal of the *Malleus Maleficarum*, a witch-hunting handbook published in 1486 for use in recognizing and dealing with those suspected of being witches. In his book, Weyer argued that a considerable number, if not all, of those imprisoned, tortured, and burned for witchcraft were really sick in mind or body and that, consequently, great wrongs were being committed against innocent people. Weyer's work enjoyed the approval of a few outstanding physicians and theologians of his time. Mostly, however, it met with vehement protest and condemnation.

Weyer was one of the first physicians to specialize in mental disorders, and his wide experience and progressive views justify his reputation as the founder of modern psychopathology. Unfortunately, however, he was too far ahead of his time. He was scorned by his peers, many of whom called him "Weirus Hereticus" and "Weirus Insanus." His works were banned by the Church and remained so until the twentieth century.

The clergy, however, were beginning to question the practices of the time. For example, St. Vincent de Paul (1576–1660), at the risk of his life, declared, "Mental disease is no different than bodily disease and Christianity demands of the humane and powerful to protect, and the skillful to relieve the one as well as the other" (Castiglioni, 1924).

In the face of such persistent advocates of science, who continued their testimonies throughout the next two centuries, demonology and superstition gave ground. These advocates gradually paved the way for the return of observation and reason, which culminated in the development of modern experimental and clinical approaches.

The Establishment of Early Asylums

From the sixteenth century on, special institutions called **asylums**—sanctuaries or places of refuge meant solely for the care of the mentally ill—grew in number. The early asylums were begun as a way of removing from society troublesome individuals who could not care for themselves. Although scientific inquiry into abnormal behavior was on the increase, most early asylums, often referred to as "madhouses," were not pleasant places or "hospitals" but primarily residences or storage places for the insane.

The unfortunate residents lived and died amid conditions of incredible filth and cruelty.

The first asylum established in Europe was probably in Spain in 1409 (Villasante, 2003), although this point has been the subject of considerable discussion (Polo, 1997; Trope, 1997). Little is known about the treatment of patients in this asylum. In 1547 the monastery of St. Mary of Bethlem in London (initially founded as a monastery in 1247; see O'Donoghue, 1914) was officially made into an asylum by Henry VIII. Its name soon was contracted to "Bedlam," and it became widely known for its deplorable conditions and practices. The more violent patients were exhibited to the public for one penny a look, and the more harmless inmates were forced to seek charity on the streets of London. Tuke (1882) describes Ned Ward's account, in *History of the Insane in the British Isles*, of a visit to Bedlam:

> Accordingly we were admitted in thro' an iron gate, within which sat a brawny Cerberus, of an Idico-colour, leaning upon a money-box; we turned in through another Iron-Barricado, where we heard such a rattling of chains, drumming of doors, ranting, hollowing, singing, and running, that I could think of nothing but Don Quevedo's Vision where the lost souls broke loose and put Hell in an uproar. The first whimsey-headed wretch of this lunatic family that we observed, was a merry fellow in a straw cap, who was talking to himself, "that he had an army of Eagles at his command," then clapping his hand upon his head, swore by his crown of moonshine, he would battle all the Stars in the Skies, but he would have some claret. . . . We then moved on till we found another remarkable figure worth our observing, who was peeping through his wicket, eating of bread and cheese, talking all the while like a carrier at his supper, chewing his words with his victuals, all that he spoke being in praise of bread and cheese: "bread was good with cheese, and cheese was good with bread, and bread and cheese was good together"; and abundance of such stuff; to which my friend and I, with others stood listening; at last he counterfeits a sneeze, and shot such a mouthful of bread and cheese amongst us, that every spectator had some share of his kindness, which made us retreat. (pp. 76–77)

Such asylums for the mentally ill were gradually established in other countries, including Mexico (1566) and France (1641). An asylum was established in Moscow in 1764, and the notorious Lunatics' Tower in Vienna was constructed in 1784. This structure was a showplace in Old Vienna, an ornately

The monastery of St. Mary of Bethlem in London became an asylum for the mentally ill in the reign of King Henry the VIII during the sixteenth century. The hospital, known as "Bedlam," became infamous for its deplorable conditions and practices.

decorated round tower within which were square rooms. The doctors and "keepers" lived in the square rooms, while the patients were confined in the spaces between the walls of the rooms and the outside of the tower, where they were put on exhibit to the public for a small fee.

These early asylums were primarily modifications of penal institutions, and the inmates were treated more like beasts than like human beings.

This case study is intentionally omitted from this text.

In the United States, the Pennsylvania Hospital in Philadelphia, completed under the guidance of Benjamin Franklin in 1756, provided some cells or wards for mental patients. The Public Hospital in Williamsburg, Virginia, constructed in 1773, was the first hospital in the United States devoted exclusively to mental patients. The treatment of mental patients in the United States was no better than that offered by European institutions, however. Zwelling's 1985 review of the Public Hospital's treatment methods shows that, initially, the philosophy of treatment involved the belief that the patients needed to choose rationality over **insanity**. Thus the treatment techniques were aggressive, aimed at restoring a "physical balance in the body and brain." These techniques, though based on the scientific views of the day, were designed to intimidate patients. They included powerful drugs, water treatments, bleeding and blistering, electric shocks, and physical restraints. For example, a violent patient might be plunged into ice water or a listless patient into hot water; frenzied patients might be administered drugs to exhaust them; or patients might be bled in order to drain their system of "harmful" fluids.

Humanitarian Reform

Clearly, by the late eighteenth century, most mental hospitals in Europe and America were in great need of reform. The humanitarian treatment of patients received great impetus from the work of Philippe Pinel (1745–1826) in France.

PINEL'S EXPERIMENT In 1792, shortly after the first phase of the French Revolution, Pinel was placed in charge of La Bicêtre in Paris. In this capacity, he received the grudging permission of the Revolutionary Commune to remove the chains from some of the inmates as an experiment to test his views that mental patients should be treated with kindness and consideration—as sick people, not as vicious beasts or criminals. Had his experiment proved a failure, Pinel might have lost his head, but fortunately it was a great success. Chains were removed; sunny rooms were provided; patients were permitted to exercise on the hospital grounds; and kindness was extended to these poor beings, some of whom had been chained in dungeons for 30 or more years. The effect was almost miraculous. The previous noise, filth, and abuse were replaced by order and peace. As Pinel said, "The whole discipline was marked with regularity and kindness which had the most favorable effect on the insane themselves, rendering even the most furious more tractable" (Selling, 1943, p. 65). Interestingly, a historical document, subsequently found in the French Archives, raises some question about the date at which humanitarian reforms were begun in France. The document, provided by Jean-Baptiste Pussin (Pinel's predecessor at La Bicêtre), indicated that he had

This painting depicts Philippe Pinel supervising the unchaining of inmates at La Bicêtre hospital. Pinel's experiment represented both a great reform and a major step in devising humanitarian methods of treating mental disorders.

In contrast to the picture of Bethlem Hospital, this picture shows a male ward of the hospital under the new, more humane treatment approach. Walford (1878) pointed out that by 1815, there was no more "show for a penny" at Bethlem Hospital, and patients were afforded more humane living facilities and activities.

been the head of the hospital beginning in 1784 and had removed some of the chains from patients and employed slightly more humane straitjackets instead. He also pointed out in the document that he had issued orders forbidding the staff from beating patients (Weiner, 1979).

TUKE'S WORK IN ENGLAND At about the same time that Pinel was reforming La Bicêtre, an English Quaker named William Tuke (1732–1822) established the York Retreat, a pleasant country house where mental patients lived, worked, and rested in a kindly, religious atmosphere (Narby, 1982). This retreat represented the culmination of a noble battle against the brutality, ignorance, and indifference of Tuke's time.

The Quakers believed in treating all people, even the insane, with kindness and acceptance. Their view that kind acceptance would help mentally ill people recover sparked the growth of more humane psychiatric treatment during a period when mental patients were ignored and mistreated (Glover, 1984).

The Quaker retreat at York has continued to provide humane mental health treatment for over 200 years (Borthwick et al., 2001), even though the mental hospital movement spawned by its example evolved into large mental hospitals that became crowded and often offered less-than-humane treatment in the late nineteenth and early twentieth centuries. (See the picture of the York Retreat today.)

As word of Pinel's amazing results spread to England, Tuke's small force of Quakers gradually gained the support of English medical practitioners such as Thomas Wakley and Samuel Hitch. In 1841 Hitch introduced trained nurses into the wards at the Gloucester Asylum and put trained supervisors at the head of the nursing staffs. These innovations, quite revolutionary at the time, not only improved the care of mental patients but also changed public attitudes toward the mentally disturbed. In 1842, following Wakley's lobbying for change, the Lunacy Inquiry Act was passed, which included the requirement of effective inspection of

The historic mental health facility, the York Retreat, continues to provide services in York, England, over 200 years since it was founded by William Tuke in 1796. This mental health facility is sponsored by the Quakers and provides a broad range of services in both inpatient and outpatient care.

asylums and houses every four months (Roberts, 1981) to ensure proper diet and the elimination of the use of restraints.

In 1845, the Country Asylums Act was passed in England, which required every county to provide asylum to "paupers and lunatics" (Scull, 1996). Britain's policy of providing more humane treatment of the mentally ill was substantially expanded to the colonies (Australia, Canada, India, West Indies, South Africa, etc.) after a widely publicized incident of maltreatment of patients that occurred in Kingston, Jamaica prompted an audit of colonial facilities and practices. In Kingston, an article written by a former patient disclosed that the staff used "tanking" to control and punish mental patients. During tanking, "lunatics" were routinely held under water in a bathing tank by nurses and sometimes other patients until they were near death (Swartz, 2010).

RUSH AND MORAL MANAGEMENT IN AMERICA The success of Pinel's and Tuke's humanitarian experiments revolutionized the treatment of mental patients throughout the Western world. In the United States, this revolution was reflected in the work of Benjamin Rush (1745–1813), the founder of American psychiatry and also one of the signers of the Declaration of Independence. While he was associated with the Pennsylvania Hospital in 1783, Rush encouraged more humane treatment of the mentally ill; wrote the first systematic treatise on psychiatry in America, *Medical Inquiries and Observations upon Diseases of the Mind* (1812); and was the first American to organize a course in psychiatry (see Gentile & Miller, 2009). But even he did not escape entirely from the established beliefs of his time. His medical theory was tainted with astrology, and his principal remedies were bloodletting and purgatives. In addition, he invented and used a device called "the tranquilizing chair," which was probably more torturous than tranquil for patients. The chair was thought to lessen the force of the blood on the head while the muscles were relaxed. Despite these limitations, we can consider Rush an important transitional figure between the old era and the new.

During the early part of this period of humanitarian reform, the use of **moral management**—a wide-ranging method of treatment that focused on a patient's social, individual, and occupational needs—became relatively widespread. This approach, which stemmed largely from the work of Pinel and Tuke, began in Europe during the late eighteenth century and in America during the early nineteenth century.

Moral management in asylums emphasized the patients' moral and spiritual development and the rehabilitation of their "character" rather than their physical or mental disorders, in part because very little effective treatment was available for these conditions at the time. The treatment or rehabilitation of the physical or mental disorders was usually through manual labor and spiritual discussion, along with humane treatment.

Moral management achieved a high degree of effectiveness—which is all the more amazing because it was done without the benefit of the antipsychotic drugs used today and because many of the patients were probably suffering from syphilis, a then-incurable disease of the central nervous system. In the 20-year period between 1833 and 1853, Worcester State Hospital's discharge rate for patients who had been ill less than a year before admission was 71 percent. Even for patients with a longer preadmission disorder, the discharge rate was 59 percent (Bockhoven, 1972). In London, Walford (1878) reported that during a 100-year period ending in 1876, the "cure" rate was 45.7 percent for the famed Bedlam Hospital.

Despite its reported effectiveness in many cases, moral management was nearly abandoned by the latter part of the nineteenth century. The reasons were many and varied. Among the more obvious ones were ethnic prejudice against the rising immigrant population in hospitals, leading to tension between staff and patients; the failure of the movement's leaders to train their own replacements; and the overextension of hospital facilities, which reflected the misguided belief that bigger hospitals would differ from smaller ones only in size.

Two other reasons for the demise of moral management are, in retrospect, truly ironic. One was the rise of the **mental hygiene movement**, which advocated a method of treatment that focused almost exclusively on the physical well-being of hospitalized mental patients. Although the patients' comfort levels improved under the mental hygienists, the patients received no help for their mental problems and thus were subtly condemned to helplessness and dependency.

Advances in biomedical science also contributed to the demise of moral management and the rise of the mental hygiene movement. These advances fostered the notion that all mental disorders would eventually yield to biological explanations and biologically based treatments (Luchins, 1989). Thus the psychological and social environment of a patient was considered largely irrelevant; the best one could do was keep the patient comfortable until a biological cure was discovered. Needless to say, the anticipated biological cure-all did not arrive, and by the late 1940s and early 1950s, discharge rates were down to about 30 percent. Its negative effects on the use of moral management notwithstanding, the mental hygiene movement has accounted for many humanitarian accomplishments.

BENJAMIN FRANKLIN'S EARLY DISCOVERY OF THE POTENTIAL CURATIVE EFFECTS OF ELECTRIC SHOCK

In school, most people learn about Benjamin Franklin's early experimentation with electricity in the early eighteenth century. His kite-flying during electric storms and its influence on the physical sciences is common knowledge. However, most people (even mental health professionals) are not aware that his work with electricity was among the earliest efforts to explore electric shock to treat mental illness, an insight he gained accidentally. His proposals for using electricity to treat melancholia (depression) grew out of his observations that a severe shock he had experienced altered his memories (see the informative discussion by Finger & Zaromb, 2006). Franklin published articles describing his experience and suggested that physicians further study this method for treating melancholia. Shortly afterward, one of his friends, a physician named Ingenhousz, reported a similar incident in which he observed alterations in his thinking following a shock he had received. He too called for clinical trials to study this phenomenon as a possible treatment for psychiatric patients.

Although these early efforts pointed attention to a potentially valuable treatment approach, medical research on the procedure was slow to develop. Finger and Zaromb (2006) point out that it was not until the middle of the eighteenth century that electric shock was associated with amnesia. Moreover, it was not until the twentieth century that Cerletti and Bini (1938), at the University of Rome, initiated electric shock as a treatment for depression.

DIX AND THE MENTAL HYGIENE MOVEMENT

Dorothea Dix (1802–1887) was an energetic New Englander who became a champion of poor and "forgotten" people in prisons and mental institutions for decades during the nineteenth century. Dix, herself a child of very difficult and impoverished circumstances (Viney, 1996), later became an important driving force in humane treatment for psychiatric patients. She worked as a schoolteacher as a young adult but was later forced into early retirement because of recurring attacks of tuberculosis. In 1841 she began to teach in a women's prison. Through this contact she became acquainted with the deplorable conditions in jails, almshouses, and asylums. In a "Memorial" submitted to the U.S. Congress in 1848, she stated that she had seen

> more than 9000 idiots, epileptics and insane in the United States, destitute of appropriate care and protection . . . bound with galling chains, bowed beneath fetters

Dorothea Dix (1802–1887) was a tireless reformer who made great strides in changing public attitudes toward the mentally ill.

and heavy iron bails attached to drag-chains, lacerated with ropes, scourged with rods and terrified beneath storms of execration and cruel blows; now subject to jibes and scorn and torturing tricks; now abandoned to the most outrageous violations. (Zilboorg & Henry, 1941, pp. 583–584)

As a result of what she had seen, Dix carried on a zealous campaign between 1841 and 1881 that aroused people and legislatures to do something about the inhuman treatment accorded the mentally ill. Through her efforts, the mental hygiene movement grew in America: Millions of dollars were raised to build suitable hospitals, and 20 states responded directly to her appeals. Not only was she instrumental in improving conditions in American hospitals but she also directed the opening of two large institutions in Canada and completely reformed the asylum system in Scotland and several other countries. She is credited with establishing 32 mental hospitals, an astonishing record given the ignorance and superstition that still prevailed in the field of mental health. Dix rounded out her career by organizing the nursing forces of the Northern armies during the Civil War. A resolution presented by the U.S. Congress in 1901 characterized her as "among the noblest examples of humanity in all history" (Karnesh, with Zucker, 1945, p. 18).

Later critics have claimed that establishing hospitals for the mentally ill and increasing the number of people in them spawned overcrowded facilities and custodial care (Bockhoven, 1972; Dain, 1964). These critics have further claimed that housing patients in institutions away from society interfered with the treatment of the day (moral therapy) and deferred the search for more appropriate and effective treatments for mental disorders (Bockhoven, 1972). These criticisms, however, do not consider the context in which Dix's contributions were made (see the Unresolved Issues at the end of this chapter). Her advocacy of the humane treatment of the mentally ill stood in stark contrast to the cruel treatment common at the time (Viney & Bartsch, 1984).

THE MILITARY AND THE MENTALLY ILL

Mental health treatment was also advanced by military medicine. The first mental health facility for treating mentally disordered war casualties was opened by the Confederate Army in the American Civil War (Deutsch, 1944; Gabriel, 1987). An even more extensive and influential program of military psychiatry evolved in Germany during the late 1800s. Lengweiler (2003) reviews the evolution of military psychiatry in Germany between the Franco-Prussian War in 1870 and World War I in 1914. During this period, psychiatrists, a number of whom made great contributions to the field of abnormal psychology (e.g., Emil Kraepelin and Richard von Krafft-Ebbing), worked with the military administration, conducting research and training doctors to detect mental health problems that could interfere with performance of duty. One early research program illustrates the interplay between medicine and military administration. Kraepelin, who viewed alcohol as a key cause of psychological problems among soldiers, conducted a research project evaluating the extent to which alcohol consumption adversely affected the soldiers' ability to fire their rifles effectively.

Nineteenth-Century Views of the Causes and Treatment of Mental Disorders

In the early part of the nineteenth century, mental hospitals were controlled essentially by laypersons because of the prominence of moral management in the treatment of "lunatics." Medical professionals—or "alienists," as psychiatrists were called at this time in reference to their treating the "alienated," or insane—had a relatively inconsequential role in the care of the insane and the management of the asylums of the day. Moreover, effective treatments for mental disorders were unavailable, the only measures being such procedures as drugging, bleeding, and purging, which produced few objective results. However, during the latter part of the century, alienists gained control of the insane asylums and incorporated the traditional moral management therapy into their other rudimentary physical medical procedures.

Over time, the alienists acquired more status and influence in society and became influential as purveyors of morality, touting the benefits of Victorian morality as important to good mental health. Mental disorders were only vaguely understood, and conditions such as melancholia (depression) were considered to be the result of nervous exhaustion. That is, psychiatrists of the time thought that emotional problems were caused by the expenditure of energy or by the depletion of bodily energies as a result of excesses in living. The mental deterioration or "shattered nerves" that supposedly resulted from a person's using up precious nerve force came to be referred to as

In the first half of the twentieth century, hospital care for the mentally ill afforded very little in the way of effective treatment. In many cases, the care was considered to be harsh, punitive, and inhumane.

"neurasthenia," a condition that involved pervasive feelings of low mood, lack of energy, and physical symptoms that were thought to be related to "lifestyle" problems brought on by the demands of civilization. These vague symptoms, viewed by the alienists/psychiatrists as a definable medical condition, were then considered treatable by medical men of the times.

Changing Attitudes Toward Mental Health in the Early Twentieth Century

It is difficult to partition modern views of abnormal behavior into discrete, uniform attitudes or to trace their historical precedents without appearing arbitrary and overly simplistic. By the end of the nineteenth century, the mental hospital or asylum—"the big house on the hill"—with its fortress-like appearance, had become a familiar landmark in America (see Payne & Sacks, 2009). In it, mental patients lived under relatively harsh conditions despite the inroads made by moral management. To the general public, however, the asylum was an eerie place and its occupants a strange and frightening lot. Little was done by the resident psychiatrists to educate the public or reduce the general fear and horror of insanity. A principal reason for this silence, of course, was that early psychiatrists had little actual information to impart and in some cases employed procedures that were damaging to patients.

Gradually, however, important strides were made toward changing the general public's attitude toward mental patients.

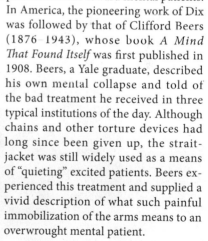

In America, the pioneering work of Dix was followed by that of Clifford Beers (1876–1943), whose book *A Mind That Found Itself* was first published in 1908. Beers, a Yale graduate, described his own mental collapse and told of the bad treatment he received in three typical institutions of the day. Although chains and other torture devices had long since been given up, the straitjacket was still widely used as a means of "quieting" excited patients. Beers experienced this treatment and supplied a vivid description of what such painful immobilization of the arms means to an overwrought mental patient.

This excerpt is intentionally omitted from this text.

After Beers recovered in the home of a kind attendant, he launched a campaign to make people realize that such treatment was no way to handle the sick. He soon won the interest and support of many public-spirited individuals, including the eminent psychologist William James and the "dean of American psychiatry," Adolf Meyer.

Mental Hospital Care in the Twenty-First Century

The twentieth century began with a continued period of growth in asylums for the mentally ill; however, the fate of mental patients during that century was neither uniform nor entirely positive (see Box 2). At the beginning of the twentieth century, with the influence of enlightened people such as Clifford Beers, mental hospitals grew substantially in number—predominantly to house persons with severe mental disorders such as schizophrenia, depression, organic mental disorders, tertiary syphilis and paresis (syphilis of the brain), and severe alcoholism. By 1940 the public mental hospitals housed over 400,000 patients, roughly 90 percent of whom resided in large state-funded hospitals; the remainder resided in private hospitals (Grob, 1994). During this period, hospital stays were typically quite lengthy, and many mentally ill individuals were destined to be hospitalized for many years. For the first half of the twentieth century, hospital care was accompanied by little in the way of effective treatment, and the care was often harsh, punitive, and inhumane. The year 1946, however, marked the beginning of an important period of

2 THE WORLD AROUND US

Chaining Mental Health Patients

Because of limited mental health treatment resources in some countries, it is not uncommon for mentally ill people to be chained. Westermeyer and Kroll (1978) conducted an epidemiologic study on the use of restraints for mentally ill people in 27 villages in Laos. They reported that mentally ill people who were aggressive toward others or who were considered to be a danger to themselves were sometimes restrained by being chained to posts. The woman from Laos in the photograph shown here suffered from a psychotic disorder and reportedly felt compelled to sweep her platform for 6 or 7 hours a day. She was restrained at a Buddhist temple in order to keep her from wandering into the jungle (Westermeyer, 2001).

of bread, a raw chili, and water each day for 21 days. Their family is charged 20 pounds a month.

Chained patients in Afghanistan

Chained patient from Laos

The men chained in the next photograph are not in prison but in mental health treatment at the Mohammad Ali Shah Shrine in eastern Afghanistan. Their treatment involves being fed only a small piece

Many temples in some countries provide homes for psychologically disturbed individuals, although the care is typically inadequate. For example, Erwady, India, near Madras, has 15 privately run homes, many of which are without electricity, tap water, toilet facilities, and beds. In 2000, six people died from waterborne disease at one of the Erwady asylums, prompting the government to direct an inquiry into the conditions of the mental health asylums. The investigation has not yet been completed. Later, fire swept through a palm-thatched shed that housed mentally ill people at one Erwady asylum, killing 25 patients and injuring 5 others, many of whom were chained to heavy stones or pillars (Associated Press, 2001). At the time of the fire, the asylum housed 46 residents; only 16 of the patients escaped uninjured.

change. In that year, Mary Jane Ward published a very influential book, *The Snake Pit*, which was popularized in a movie of the same name. This work called attention to the plight of mental patients and helped to create concern over the need to provide more humane mental health care in the community in place of the overcrowded mental hospitals. Also in 1946, the National Institutes of Mental Health was organized and provided active support for research and training through psychiatric residencies and (later) clinical psychology training programs. Moreover, the Hill-Burton Act, a program that funded community mental health hospitals, was passed during this period. This legislation, along with the Community Health Services Act of 1963, helped to create a far-reaching set of programs to develop outpatient psychiatric clinics, inpatient facilities in general hospitals, and community consultation and rehabilitation programs.

The need for reform in psychiatric hospitals was a prominent concern of many professionals and laypersons alike during the 1950s and 1960s. A great deal of professional attention was given to the need to improve conditions in mental hospitals following the publication of another influential book, *Asylums*, by the sociologist Erving Goffman (1961). This book further exposed the inhumane treatment of mental patients and provided a detailed account of neglect and maltreatment in mental hospitals. The movement to change the mental hospital environment was also enhanced significantly by scientific advances in the last half of the twentieth century, particularly the development of effective medications for many disorders—for example, the use of lithium in the treatment of manic depressive disorders (Cade, 1949) and the introduction of phenothiazines for the treatment of schizophrenia.

During the latter decades of the twentieth century, our society had seemingly reversed its position with respect to the means of providing humane care for the mentally ill in the hospital environment. Vigorous efforts were made to close down mental hospitals and return psychiatrically disturbed people to the community, ostensibly as a means of providing more integrated and humane treatment than was available in the "isolated" environment of the psychiatric hospital and because of the success of medications (chlorpromezynes) that emerged in the 1950s to alleviate psychotic symptoms (Alanen et al., 2009). Large numbers of psychiatric hospitals were closed, and there was a significant reduction in state and county mental hospital populations, from over half a million in 1950 (Lerman, 1981) to about 100,000 by the early 1990s (Narrow et al., 1993). These reductions are all the more impressive given that the U.S. population increased substantially over those years. This movement, referred to as **deinstitutionalization**, although motivated by benevolent goals, has also created great difficulties for many psychologically disturbed persons and for many communities as well.

As a phenomenon, deinstitutionalization is an international movement. For example, there has been a shift in the locus of care of patients with chronic psychiatric illnesses from psychiatric hospitals to community-based residential services in Hong Kong (Chan, 2001), in the Netherlands (Pijl et al., 2001), and in

Finland (Korkeila et al., 1998). Some countries have experienced extensive deinstitutionalization over the past 20 years. For example, in England and Wales during the last decades of the twentieth century, only 14 of 130 psychiatric institutions remained open; and Australia showed a 90 percent reduction in hospital beds over the same period (Goldney, 2003). In a follow-up study of patients from 22 hospitals in Italy, D'Avanzo and colleagues (2003) report that all were closed and 39 percent of the patients in these hospitals had been discharged to nursing homes, 29 percent to residential facilities, and 29 percent to other psychiatric hospitals; only 2 percent were returned to their families.

The original impetus behind the deinstitutionalization policy was that it was considered more humane (and cost effective) to treat disturbed people outside of large mental hospitals because doing so would prevent people from acquiring negative adaptations to hospital confinement. Many professionals were concerned that the mental hospitals were becoming permanent refuges for disturbed people who were "escaping" from the demands of everyday living and were settling into a chronic sick role with a permanent excuse for letting other people take care of them. There was great hope that new medications would promote a healthy readjustment and enable former patients to live more productive lives outside the hospital. Many former patients have not fared well in community living, however, and authorities now frequently speak of the "abandonment" of chronic patients to a cruel and harsh existence. Evidence of this failure to treat psychiatric patients successfully in the community can be readily seen in our cities: Many of the people living on the streets in large cities today are homeless and mentally ill. The problems caused by deinstitutionalization appear to be due, in no small part, to the failure of society to develop ways to fill the gaps in mental health services in the community (Grob, 1994).

Freed from the confines of institutionalized care, or abandoned by society? Many homeless people suffer from one or more mental disorders. Deinstitutionalization, though motivated by benevolent goals, has created great difficulties for many psychologically disturbed individuals who have been released to a cruel and harsh existence.

The mental institution, once thought to be the most humane way to manage the problems of the severely mentally ill, came to be seen as obsolete or as an evil alternative, more of a problem than a solution to mental health problems. By the end of the twentieth century, inpatient mental hospitals had been substantially replaced by community-based care, day treatment hospitals, and outreach.

The twentieth century closed on a note of uncertainty with respect to the best ways to manage the needs of severely disturbed psychiatric patients. It is clear that closing mental hospitals and providing treatment for severely disturbed people in the community has not proved to be the panacea it was touted to be only a few years ago (Whitaker, 2009). Deinstitutionalization has created problems for both patients and society as a whole. The role of the psychiatric hospital in helping those with severe psychiatric problems is likely to undergo further evolution as society again finds itself unable to deal effectively with the problems that severe mental illness can create if ignored or left unattended (see Grob, 1994).

In Review

- Describe the changing views toward mental illness that evolved as scientific thinking came to have greater influence in Europe in the sixteenth and seventeenth centuries.

- Discuss the development of the psychiatric hospital.

- Describe the historical development of humanitarian reform, and give some of the reasons why it occurred.

- Describe the changes in social attitudes that brought about major changes in the way persons with mental disorders have been treated.

The Emergence of Contemporary Views of Abnormal Behavior

While the mental hygiene movement was gaining ground in the United States during the latter years of the nineteenth century, great technological discoveries occurred both at home and abroad. These advances helped usher in what we know today as the scientific, or experimentally oriented, view of abnormal behavior and the application of scientific knowledge to the treatment of disturbed individuals. We will describe four major themes in abnormal psychology that spanned the nineteenth and twentieth centuries and generated powerful influences on our contemporary perspectives in abnormal behavior: (1) biological discoveries, (2) the development of a classification system for mental disorders, (3) the emergence of psychological causation views, and (4) experimental psychological research developments.

Biological Discoveries: Establishing the Link Between the Brain and Mental Disorder

Advances in the study of biological and anatomical factors as underlying both physical and mental disorders developed in this period. A major biomedical breakthrough, for example, came with the discovery of the organic factors underlying general paresis—syphilis of the brain. One of the most serious mental illnesses of the day, general paresis produced paralysis and insanity and typically caused death within 2 to 5 years as a result of brain deterioration. This scientific discovery, however, did not occur overnight; it required the combined efforts of many scientists and researchers for nearly a century.

GENERAL PARESIS AND SYPHILIS The discovery of a cure for general paresis began in 1825, when the French physician A. L. J. Bayle differentiated general paresis as a specific type of mental disorder. Bayle gave a complete and accurate description of the symptom pattern of paresis and convincingly presented his reasons for believing paresis to be a distinct disorder. Many years later, in 1897, the Viennese psychiatrist Richard von Krafft-Ebbing conducted experiments involving the inoculation of paretic patients with matter from syphilitic sores. None of the patients developed secondary symptoms of syphilis, which led to the conclusion that they must previously have been infected. This crucial experiment established the relationship between general paresis and syphilis. It was almost a decade later, in 1906, when August von Wassermann devised a blood test for syphilis. This development made it possible to check for the presence of the deadly bacteria in the bloodstream of an individual before the more serious consequences of infection appeared.

Finally, in 1917, Julius von Wagner-Jauregg, chief of the psychiatric clinic of the University of Vienna, introduced the malarial fever treatment of syphilis and paresis because he knew that the high fever associated with malaria killed off the bacteria. He infected nine paretic patients with the blood of a malaria-infected soldier and found marked improvement in paretic symptoms in three patients and apparent recovery in three others. By 1925 several hospitals in the United States were incorporating the new malarial treatment for paresis into their hospital treatments. One of the earliest controlled studies of malarial treatment for paresis was conducted by Bahr and Brutsch in Indiana in 1928. They found that out of the 100 patients studied, 37 percent of paresis patients showed significant recovery, 25 percent had been discharged, and 21 percent of those had returned to their previous or similar occupations. Today, of course, we have penicillin as an effective, simpler treatment of syphilis, but the early malarial treatment represented the first clear-cut conquest of a mental disorder by medical science. The field of abnormal psychology had come a long way—from superstitious beliefs to scientific proof of how brain pathology can cause a specific disorder. This breakthrough raised great hopes in the medical community that organic bases would be found for many other mental disorders—perhaps for all of them.

BRAIN PATHOLOGY AS A CAUSAL FACTOR With the emergence of modern experimental science in the early part of the eighteenth century, knowledge of anatomy, physiology, neurology, chemistry, and general medicine increased rapidly. Scientists began to focus on diseased body organs as the cause of physical ailments. It was the next logical step for these researchers to assume that mental disorder was an illness based on the pathology of an organ—in this case, the brain. In 1757 Albrecht von Haller (1708–1777), in his *Elementa physiologae corporis humani*, emphasized the importance of the brain in psychic functions and advocated postmortem dissection to study the brains of the insane. The first systematic presentation of this viewpoint, however, was made by the German psychiatrist Wilhelm Griesinger (1817–1868). In his textbook *The Pathology and Therapy of Psychic Disorders*, published in 1845, Griesinger insisted that all mental disorders could be explained in terms of brain pathology. Following the discovery that brain deterioration resulted in general paresis, other successes followed. Alois Alzheimer and other investigators established the brain pathology in cerebral arteriosclerosis and in the senile mental disorders. Eventually, in the twentieth century, the organic pathologies underlying the toxic mental disorders (disorders caused by toxic substances such as lead), certain types of mental retardation, and other mental illnesses were discovered.

Along with the advancements in mental health treatment in the twentieth century came some unfortunate missteps. During the early years of the twentieth century, Henry Cotton, a psychiatrist at a New Jersey hospital, developed a theory that mental health problems such as schizophrenia could be cured by removing the infections that he believed caused the condition. He used surgical procedures to remove all of a person's teeth or body parts such as tonsils, parts of the colon, testicles, or ovaries in order to reduce the infection (Scull, 2005). In the 1920s through the 1940s, an American psychiatrist, Walter Freeman, followed the strategies developed by Italian psychiatrist Egas Moniz to treat severe mental disorders using surgical procedures called *lobotomies*. Freeman modified the surgery used by Moniz, using an ice pick to sever the neural connections in the brain after entering through the patient's eye sockets (see discussion on lobotomy by El-Hai, 2005). These surgical efforts to treat mental disorder were considered to be ineffective and inappropriate by many in the profession at the time and were eventually discredited, although lobotomy is still used in some rare cases.

It is important to note here that although the discovery of the organic bases of mental disorders addressed the "how" behind causation, it did not, in most cases, address the "why." This is sometimes true even today. For example, although we know what causes certain "presenile" mental disorders—brain pathology—we do not yet know why some individuals are afflicted and others are not. Nonetheless, we can predict quite accurately the courses of these disorders. This ability is due not only to a greater understanding of the organic factors involved

but also, in large part, to the work of a follower of Griesinger, Emil Kraepelin.

The Development of a Classification System

Emil Kraepelin (1856–1926), another German psychiatrist, played a dominant role in the early development of the biological viewpoint. His textbook *Compendium der Psychiatrie*, published in 1883, not only emphasized the importance of brain pathology in mental disorders but also made several related contributions that helped establish this viewpoint. The most important of these contributions was his system of classification of mental disorders, which became the forerunner of today's *DSM-IV-TR*. Kraepelin noted that certain symptom patterns occurred together regularly enough to be regarded as specific types of mental disease. He then proceeded to describe and clarify these types of mental disorders, working out a scheme of classification that is the basis of our present system. Integrating all of the clinical material underlying this classification was a Herculean task and represented a major contribution to the field of psychopathology.

Emil Kraepelin (1856–1926) was a German psychiatrist who developed an early synthesis and classification system of the hundreds of mental disorders by grouping diseases together based on common patterns of symptoms. Kraepelin also demonstrated that mental disorders showed specific patterns in the genetics, course, and outcome of disorders.

Kraepelin saw each type of mental disorder as distinct from the others and thought that the course of each was as predetermined and predictable as the course of measles. Thus the outcome of a given type of disorder could presumably be predicted even if it could not yet be controlled. Such claims led to widespread interest in the accurate description and classification of mental disorders.

Development of the Psychological Basis of Mental Disorder

Despite the emphasis on biological research, understanding of the psychological factors in mental disorders was progressing as well. The first major steps were taken by Sigmund Freud (1856–1939), the most frequently cited psychological theorist of the twentieth century (Street, 1994). During five decades of observation, treatment, and writing, Freud developed a comprehensive theory of psychopathology that emphasized the inner dynamics of unconscious motives (often referred to as *psychodynamics*) that are at the heart of the **psychoanalytic perspective**. The methods he used to study and treat patients came to be called **psychoanalysis**. We can trace the ancestral roots of psychoanalysis to a somewhat unexpected place—the study of hypnosis, especially in its relation to hysteria (for a contemporary discussion of hysteria see Brown, 2006). Hypnosis, an induced state of relaxation in which a person is highly open to suggestion, first came into widespread use in late-eighteenth- and early-nineteenth-century France.

MESMERISM Our efforts to understand psychological causation of mental disorder start with Franz Anton Mesmer

(1734–1815), an Austrian physician who further developed the ideas of Paracelsus (the influential sixteenth-century physician and scholar; see Developments in Research 3) about the influence of the planets on the human body. Mesmer believed that the planets affected a universal magnetic fluid in the body, the distribution of which determined health or disease. In attempting to find cures for mental disorders, Mesmer concluded that all people possessed magnetic forces that could be used to influence the distribution of the magnetic fluid in other people, thus effecting cures.

Mesmer believed that the distribution of magnetic fluid in the body was responsible for determining health or disease. He further thought that all people possessed magnetic forces that could be used to influence the distribution of fluid in others, thus effecting cures. In this painting of his therapy, Mesmer stands on the far right, holding a wand. He was eventually branded a fraud by his colleagues. His theories did, however, demonstrate most of the phenomena later connected with the use of hypnosis.

3 DEVELOPMENTS IN RESEARCH

The Search for Medications to Cure Mental Disorders

For centuries physicians have sought a medicinal cure for mental disorder. One of the earliest known treatises on the use of drugs to treat mental disorders is the work of the Roman physician Galen (A.D. 130–200). His writing details both the concoction of various medications and the clinical use of drug therapy with patients experiencing mental disorders. Most of his medications were laxatives and emetics (purgatives) that were used to cleanse the body of nonhuman materials believed to be causing the person's ills. During the Middle Ages, another notable but highly controversial physician-chemist named Paracelsus (1490–1541) experimented with various chemicals as medications to treat human disorders. He even used a substance referred to as "mummy powder" (ground up particles of mummies) and various other, seemingly more potent substances such as mercury.

A more recent phase in the development of psychotropic medicine began in the 1950s. The root *Rauwolfia serpentina* had been used for centuries as an herbal folk medicine in India, where it had been prescribed for a wide array of afflictions, including insanity. In the early 1950s the

active ingredient in *Rauwolfia*, reserpine, was isolated by a Swiss drug company, and in 1953 psychiatrist R. A. Hakim wrote a prize-winning paper on using *Rauwolfia* to treat psychosis (as cited in Gupta et al., 1943). Today reserpine has been surpassed as a treatment for psychoses because of the development of other drugs and because of its side effects, and it is mostly used in the treatment of hypertension.

The second psychoactive drug to emerge in the 1950s as a treatment for severe mental disorder was chlorpromazine. A German chemist named Bernthesen, searching for compounds that would operate as dyes, first developed the drug in the latter part of the nineteenth century. He synthesized a compound that is referred to as phenothiazine. Paul Erlich, a medical researcher and father of the field of chemotherapy, thought that this compound might be effective in treating human diseases by killing nonhuman cells while preserving human tissue. The drug was first tried as a means of treating malaria, and by the 1930s it was being employed as an anesthetic. In 1951, the French surgeon Henri Labroit employed the drug as an "artificial hibernator" to prevent shock among surgical pa-

Mesmer attempted to put his views into practice in Vienna and various other cities, but it was in Paris in 1778 that he gained a broad following. There he opened a clinic in which he treated all kinds of diseases by using "animal magnetism." In a dark room, patients were seated around a tub containing various chemicals, and iron rods protruding from the tub were applied to the affected areas of the patients' bodies. Accompanied by music, Mesmer appeared in a lilac robe, passing from one patient to another and touching each one with his hands or his wand. By this means, Mesmer was reportedly able to remove hysterical anesthesias and paralyses. He also demonstrated most of the phenomena later connected with the use of hypnosis.

Mesmer was eventually branded a charlatan by his medical colleagues and an appointed body of noted scholars that included the American scientist Benjamin Franklin (Van Doren, 1938). The committee conducted what have been referred to as the first psychological experiments (Dingfelder, 2010), or tests such as tricking a woman into believing that she had been influenced by magnetism. The committee concluded that the real source of Mesmer's power was in the patients and not in "magnetism." Mesmer was forced to leave Paris and quickly faded into obscurity. His methods and results, however, were at the center of scientific controversy for many years—in fact, **mesmerism**, as his technique came to be known, was as much a source of heated discussion in the early nineteenth century as psychoanalysis became in the early twentieth century. This discussion led to renewed interest in hypnosis itself as an explanation of the "cures" that took place.

Even after mesmerism was discredited in France, this method of inducing trance and its perceived potential for treating illness had a long life in the United States. The magical powers of mesmerism were introduced in 1836 and intrigued a number of Americans, ranging from the poet Emerson to the physician Benjamin Rush, with speculations about its higher mental powers and its potential application as an anesthetic for surgical procedures (Schmit, 2005). A number of lecturers traveled the United States illustrating its medical use and giving demonstrations, including to the U.S. Congress. The early mesmerists, though considered to be "quacks" by many physicians, had an influence on medical practice until the introduction of ether as a surgical anesthetic (Schmit, 2005). In spite of its limitations, mesmerism clearly had an influence on psychology and hypnosis for many years and came to be influential in spiritual movements such as Christian Science in the nineteenth century.

THE NANCY SCHOOL Ambrose August Liébeault (1823–1904), a French physician who practiced in the town of Nancy, used hypnosis successfully in his practice. Also in Nancy at the time was a professor of medicine, Hippolyte Bernheim (1840–1919), who became interested in the relationship between hysteria and hypnosis. His interest was piqued by Liébeault's success in using hypnosis to cure a patient whom Bernheim had been treating unsuccessfully by more conventional methods for 4 years (Selling, 1943). Bernheim and Liébeault worked together to develop the hypothesis that hypnotism and hysteria were related and that both were due to suggestion (Brown & Menninger, 1940). Their hypothesis was based on two lines of evidence: (1) The phenomena observed in hysteria—such as paralysis of an arm, inability to hear, and

tients. It was not until 1952 that two French psychiatrists, Jean Delay and Pierre Deniker, finding that the drug reduced psychotic symptoms, began to use chlorpromazine to treat psychiatric patients.

The almost magical impact of antipsychotic medication was immediately felt in the psychiatric community in the United States. By 1956, the first year of widespread use of reserpine and chlorpromazine, the impact on psychiatric hospitalization had begun to show a remarkable effect. The previously increasing admission rate to psychiatric hospitals leveled off at 560,000 psychiatric inpatients in the United States. This number dropped to 490,000 by 1964 and to 300,000 by 1971. Currier (2000) reported that the number of inpatient psychiatric beds decreased sharply over the past generation, both in absolute numbers and as a percentage of total hospital beds in seven countries including the United States. The drop in available hospital beds between and 1960 and 1994 was from 4 per thousand to less than 1.3 per thousand of the population. In the United States, the available bed reductions were fostered by the movement for deinstitutionalization and the development of managed care. In Europe and other regions, the number of beds decreased largely as a result of intense government pressure to curtail health care budgets. Interestingly, the need for psychiatric inpatient care has remained despite the closing of public mental health hospitals. Hutchins and colleagues (2011) point out that the number of private mental hospitals doubled between 1976 and 1992 and that two-thirds of all psychiatric hospitals and half of all inpatient beds were in private facilities.

The effectiveness of drugs in reducing psychotic symptoms has also led researchers to develop more specific causal hypotheses for mental disorders such as schizophrenia. Researchers have noted that antipsychotic drugs such as the phenothiazines modify the levels of dopamine, a neurotransmitter associated with schizophrenia. These observations have led theoreticians to the "dopamine hypothesis"—that the metabolism of dopamine is associated with the cause of schizophrenia.

Sources: Frankenburg, 1994; Green, 1951; Moriarty et al., 1984; Pachter, 1951.

anesthetic areas in which an individual could be stuck with a pin without feeling pain (all of which occurred when there was apparently nothing organically wrong)—could be produced in normal subjects by means of hypnosis. (2) The same symptoms also could be removed by means of hypnosis. Thus it seemed likely that hysteria was a sort of self-hypnosis. The physicians who accepted this view ultimately came to be known as the **Nancy School**.

Meanwhile, Jean Charcot (1825–1893), who was head of the Salpêtrière Hospital in Paris and the leading neurologist of his time, had been experimenting with some of the phenomena described by the mesmerists. As a result of his research, Charcot disagreed with the findings of the Nancy School and insisted that degenerative brain changes led to hysteria. In this, Charcot was eventually proved wrong, but work on the problem by so outstanding a scientist did a great deal to awaken medical and scientific interest in hysteria.

The dispute between Charcot and the Nancy School was one of the major debates of medical history, and many harsh words were spoken on both sides. The adherents to the Nancy School finally triumphed. This first recognition of a psychologically caused mental disorder spurred more research on the behavior underlying hysteria and other disorders. Soon it was suggested that psychological factors were also involved in anxiety states, phobias, and other psychopathologies. Eventually, Charcot himself was won over to the new point of view and did much to promote the study of psychological factors in various mental disorders.

The debate over whether mental disorders are caused by biological or psychological factors continues to this day. The Nancy School–Charcot debate represented a major step forward for psychology, however. Toward the end of the nineteenth century, it became clear that mental disorders could have psychological bases, biological bases, or both. But a major question remained to be answered: How do the psychologically based mental disorders actually develop?

THE BEGINNINGS OF PSYCHOANALYSIS The first systematic attempt to answer this question was made by Sigmund Freud (1856–1939). Freud was a brilliant, young Viennese neurologist who received an appointment as lecturer on nervous diseases at the University of Vienna. In 1885 he went to study under Charcot and later became acquainted with the work of Liébeault and Bernheim at Nancy. He was impressed by their use of hypnosis with hysterical patients and came away convinced that powerful mental processes could remain hidden from consciousness.

On his return to Vienna, Freud worked in collaboration with another Viennese physician, Josef Breuer (1842–1925), who had incorporated an interesting innovation into the use of hypnosis with his patients. Unlike hypnotists before them, Freud and Breuer directed patients to talk freely about their problems while under hypnosis. The patients usually displayed considerable emotion and, on awakening from their hypnotic states, felt a significant emotional release, which was called a

Psychoanalysis was introduced to North America at a famous meeting at Clark University in Worcester, Massachusetts, in 1909. Among those present were (back row) A. A. Brill, Ernest Jones, and Sandor Ferenczi; (front row) Sigmund Freud, G. Stanley Hall, and Carl Jung.

catharsis. This simple innovation in the use of hypnosis proved to be of great significance: It not only helped patients discharge their emotional tensions by discussing their problems but also revealed to the therapist the nature of the difficulties that had brought about certain symptoms. The patients, on awakening, saw no relationship between their problems and their hysterical symptoms.

It was this approach that thus led to the discovery of the **unconscious**—the portion of the mind that contains experiences of which a person is unaware—and with it the belief that processes outside of a person's awareness can play an important role in determining behavior. In 1893 Freud and Breuer published their joint paper *On the Psychical Mechanisms of Hysterical Phenomena*, which was one of the great milestones in the study of the dynamics of the conscious and unconscious. Freud soon discovered, moreover, that he could dispense with hypnosis entirely. By encouraging patients to say whatever came into their minds without regard to logic or propriety, Freud found that patients would eventually overcome inner obstacles to remembering and would discuss their problems freely.

Two related methods enabled him to understand patients' conscious and unconscious thought processes. One method, **free association**, involved having patients talk freely about themselves, thereby providing information about their feelings, motives, and so forth. A second method, **dream analysis**, involved having patients record and describe their dreams. These techniques helped analysts and patients gain insights and achieve a better understanding of the patients' emotional problems. Freud devoted the rest of his long and energetic life to the development and elaboration of psychoanalytic principles. His views were formally introduced to American scientists in 1909, when he was invited to deliver a series of lectures at Clark University by the eminent psychologist G. Stanley Hall (1844–1924), who was then president of the university. These lectures created a great deal of controversy and helped popularize psychoanalytic concepts with scientists as well as with the general public.

Freud's lively and seminal views attracted a substantial following over his long career, and interest in his ideas persists today, more than 100 years after he began writing. Numerous other clinician-theorists—such as Carl Jung, Alfred Adler, and Harry Stack Sullivan—launched "spin-off" theories that have elaborated on the psychoanalytic viewpoint. Here we will examine the early development of psychological research and explore the evolution of the behavioral perspective on abnormal behavior.

The Evolution of the Psychological Research Tradition: Experimental Psychology

The origins of much of the scientific thinking in contemporary psychology lie in early rigorous efforts to study psychological processes objectively, as demonstrated by Wilhelm Wundt (1832–1920) and William James (1842–1910). Although the early work of these experimental psychologists did not bear directly on clinical practice or on our understanding of abnormal behavior, this tradition was clearly influential a few decades later in molding the thinking of the psychologists who brought these rigorous attitudes into the clinic. (For a discussion of the history of clinical psychology, see L. T. Benjamin, 2005.)

THE EARLY PSYCHOLOGY LABORATORIES In 1879 Wilhelm Wundt established the first experimental psychology laboratory at the University of Leipzig. While studying the psychological factors involved in memory and sensation, Wundt and his colleagues devised many basic experimental methods and strategies. Wundt directly influenced early contributors to the empirical study of abnormal behavior; they followed his experimental methodology and also applied some of his research strategies to study clinical problems. For example, a student of Wundt's, J. McKeen Cattell (1860–1944), brought Wundt's experimental methods to the United States and used them to assess individual differences in mental processing. He and other students of Wundt's work established research laboratories throughout the United States.

It was not until 1896, however, that another of Wundt's students, Lightner Witmer (1867–1956), combined research with application and established the first American psychological clinic at the University of Pennsylvania. Witmer's clinic focused on the problems of mentally deficient children in terms of both research and therapy. Witmer, considered to be the founder of clinical psychology (McReynolds, 1996, 1997), was influential in encouraging others to become involved in this new profession. Other clinics were soon established. One clinic of great importance was the Chicago

Juvenile Psychopathic Institute (later called the Institute of Juvenile Research), established in 1909 by William Healy (1869–1963). Healy was the first to view juvenile delinquency as a symptom of urbanization, not as a result of inner psychological problems. In so doing, he was among the first to recognize a new area of causation—environmental, or sociocultural, factors.

By the first decade of the twentieth century, psychological laboratories and clinics were burgeoning, and a great deal of research was being generated (Reisman, 1991). The rapid and objective communication of scientific findings was perhaps as important in the development of modern psychology as the collection and interpretation of research findings. This period saw the origin of many scientific journals for the propagation of research and theoretical discoveries, and as the years have passed, the number of journals has grown. The American Psychological Association now publishes 54 scientific journals, many of which focus on research into abnormal behavior and personality functioning.

THE BEHAVIORAL PERSPECTIVE Although psychoanalysis dominated thought about abnormal behavior at the end of the nineteenth century and in the early twentieth century, another school—behaviorism—emerged out of experimental psychology to challenge its supremacy. Behavioral psychologists believed that the study of subjective experience—through the techniques of free association and dream analysis—did not provide acceptable scientific data because such observations were not open to verification by other investigators. In their view, only the study of directly observable behavior—and the stimuli and reinforcing conditions that "control" it—could serve as a basis for formulating scientific principles of human behavior.

The **behavioral perspective** is organized around a central theme: the role of learning in human behavior. Although this perspective was initially developed through research in the laboratory rather than through clinical practice with disturbed individuals, its implications for explaining and treating maladaptive behavior soon became evident.

Classical Conditioning The origins of the behavioral view of abnormal behavior and its treatment are tied to experimental work on the type of learning known as **classical conditioning**—a form of learning in which a neutral stimulus is paired repeatedly with an unconditioned stimulus that naturally elicits an unconditioned behavior. After repeated pairings, the neutral stimulus becomes a conditioned stimulus that elicits a conditioned response. This work began with the discovery of the conditioned reflex by Russian physiologist Ivan Pavlov (1849–1936). Around the turn of the twentieth century, Pavlov demonstrated that dogs would gradually begin to salivate in response to a nonfood stimulus such as a bell after the stimulus had been regularly accompanied by food.

Pavlov's discoveries in classical conditioning excited a young American psychologist, John B. Watson (1878–1958), who was searching for objective ways to study human behavior.

Ivan Pavlov (1849–1936), a pioneer in demonstrating the part conditioning plays in behavior, is shown here with the staff and some of the apparatus used to condition reflexes in dogs.

B. F. Skinner (1904–1990) formulated the concept of operant conditioning, in which reinforcers can be used to make a response more or less probable and frequent.

Watson reasoned that if psychology was to become a true science, it would have to abandon the subjectivity of inner sensations and other "mental" events and limit itself to what could be objectively observed. What better way to do this than to observe systematic changes in behavior brought about simply by rearranging stimulus conditions? Watson thus changed the focus of psychology to the study of overt behavior rather than the study of theoretical mentalistic constructs, an approach he called **behaviorism**.

Watson, a man of impressive energy and demeanor, saw great possibilities in behaviorism, and he was quick to point them out to his fellow scientists and a curious public. He boasted that through conditioning he could train any healthy child to become whatever sort of adult one wished. He also challenged the psychoanalysts and the more biologically oriented psychologists of his day by suggesting that abnormal behavior was the product of unfortunate, inadvertent earlier conditioning and could be modified through reconditioning.

By the 1930s Watson had had an enormous impact on American psychology. Watson's approach placed heavy emphasis on the role of the social environment in conditioning personality development and behavior, both normal and abnormal. Today's behaviorally oriented psychologists still accept many of the basic tenets of Watson's doctrine, although they are more cautious in their claims.

Operant Conditioning While Pavlov and Watson were studying stimulus–response conditioning, E. L. Thorndike (1874–1949) and subsequently B. F. Skinner (1904–1990) were exploring a different kind of conditioning, one in which the consequences of behavior influence behavior. Behavior that operates on the environment may be instrumental in producing certain outcomes, and those outcomes, in turn, determine the likelihood that the behavior will be repeated on similar occasions. For example, Thorndike studied how cats could learn a particular response, such as pulling a chain,

if that response was followed by food reinforcement. This type of learning came to be called instrumental conditioning and was later renamed **operant conditioning** by Skinner. Both terms are still used today. In Skinner's view, behavior is "shaped" when something reinforces a particular activity of an organism—which makes it possible "to shape an animal's behavior almost as a sculptor shapes a lump of clay" (Skinner, 1951, pp. 26–27).

In this chapter we have touched on several important trends in the evolution of the field of abnormal psychology and have recounted the contributions of numerous individuals from history who have shaped our current views. The vast amount of information available can cause confusion and controversy when efforts are made to obtain an integrated view of behavior and causation. We may have left supernatural beliefs behind, but we have moved into something far more complex in trying to determine the role of natural factors—be they biological, psychological, or sociocultural—in abnormal behavior. For a recap of some of the key contributors to the field of abnormal psychology, see Table 1.

In Review

- Compare the views of the Nancy School with those of Charcot. How did this debate influence modern psychology?

- Evaluate the impact of the work of Freud and that of Watson on psychology today.

- How did early experimental science help to establish brain pathology as a causal factor in mental disorders?

- Describe the historical development of the behavioral view in psychology.

table 1 Major Figures in the Early History of Abnormal Psychology

Hippocrates

Galen

The Ancient World

Hippocrates (460–377 B.C.) A Greek physician who believed that mental disease was the result of natural causes and brain pathology rather than demonology.

Plato (429–347 B.C.) A Greek philosopher who believed that mental patients should be treated humanely and should not be held responsible for their actions.

Aristotle (384–322 B.C.) A Greek philosopher and a pupil of Plato who believed in the Hippocratic theory that various agents, or humors, within the body, when imbalanced, were responsible for mental disorders. Aristotle rejected the notion of psychological factors as causes of mental disorders.

Galen (A.D. 130–200) A Greek physician who contributed much to our understanding of the nervous system. Galen divided the causes of mental disorders into physical and mental categories.

Avicenna

The Middle Ages

Avicenna (980–1037) An ancient Persian physician who promoted principles of humane treatment for the mentally disturbed at a time when Western approaches to mental illness were inhumane.

Hildegard (1098–1179) A remarkable woman, known as the "Sybil of the Rhine," who used curative powers of natural objects for healing and wrote treatises about natural history and medicinal uses of plants.

The Sixteenth Through the Eighteenth Centuries

Paracelsus (1490–1541) A Swiss physician who rejected demonology as a cause of abnormal behavior. Paracelsus believed in psychic causes of mental illness.

Teresa of Avila (1515–1582) A Spanish nun, since canonized, who argued that mental disorder was an illness of the mind.

Johann Weyer (1515–1588) A German physician who argued against demonology and was ostracized by his peers and the Church for his progressive views.

Robert Burton (1576–1640) An Oxford scholar who wrote a classic, influential treatise on depression, *The Anatomy of Melancholia*, in 1621.

William Tuke (1732–1822) An English Quaker who established the York Retreat, where mental patients lived in humane surroundings.

Philippe Pinel (1745–1826) A French physician who pioneered the use of moral management in La Bicêtre and La Salpêtrière hospitals in France, where mental patients were treated in a humane way.

Benjamin Rush (1745–1813) An American physician and the founder of American psychiatry, who used moral management, based on Pinel's humanitarian methods, to treat the mentally disturbed.

Benjamin Rush

The Nineteenth and Early Twentieth Centuries

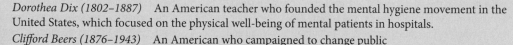

Dorothea Dix

Dorothea Dix (1802–1887) An American teacher who founded the mental hygiene movement in the United States, which focused on the physical well-being of mental patients in hospitals.

Clifford Beers (1876–1943) An American who campaigned to change public attitudes toward mental patients after his own experiences in mental institutions.

Franz Anton Mesmer (1734–1815) An Austrian physician who conducted early investigations into hypnosis as a medical treatment.

Emil Kraepelin (1856–1926) A German psychiatrist who developed the first diagnostic system.

Sigmund Freud (1856–1939) The founder of the school of psychological therapy known as psychoanalysis.

Wilhelm Wundt (1832–1920) A German scientist who established the first experimental psychology laboratory in 1879 and subsequently influenced the empirical study of abnormal behavior.

Sigmund Freud

continued

table 1 (continued)

J. McKeen Cattell (1860–1944) An American psychologist who adopted Wundt's methods and studied individual differences in mental processing.

Lightner Witmer (1867–1956) An American psychologist who established the first psychological clinic in the United States, focusing on problems of mentally deficient children. He also founded the journal *The Psychological Clinic* in 1907.

William Healy (1869–1963) An American psychologist who established the Chicago Juvenile Psychopathic Institute and advanced the idea that mental illness was due to environmental, or sociocultural, factors.

Ivan Pavlov (1849–1936) A Russian physiologist who published classical studies in the psychology of learning.

John B. Watson (1878–1958) An American psychologist who conducted early research into learning principles and came to be known as the father of behaviorism.

B. F. Skinner (1904–1990) An American learning theorist who developed the school of learning known as operant conditioning and was influential in incorporating behavioral principles into influencing behavioral change.

John B. Watson

B. F. Skinner

Unresolved Issues

▶ *Interpreting Historical Events*

Understanding current events and phenomena depends to a substantial degree on having an accurate understanding of the historical development of knowledge. Many psychologists hold the view that psychological theorizing can be advanced by greater use of historical data (McGuire, 1994). You might think that looking back in history to get a picture of events that occurred long ago would not be a difficult task—that it would be a simple matter of reviewing some history books and some publications from the time in question. However, different and conflicting views as to the importance and relevance of historical events in contemporary psychology have emerged. The traditional view maintains that historical events are stepping stones for understanding contemporary events, while a "New History" approach minimizes this cumulative and often celebratory approach and questions the cumulative knowledge aspect. Instead, this approach favors considering history as "national habits or characteristics of a culture that does not necessarily serve as cumulative force in the advancement of knowledge" (for an interesting discussion of historical approaches see Lovett, 2006). The distinction here is whether past developments in acquiring knowledge and understanding build on each other to create a more accurate picture or whether such developments should be viewed independently in their own context.

Regardless of one's view of the historical approach, those who try to understand the historical context of particular phenomena or ideas are sometimes confronted with what Burton (2001) referred to as the tenacity of historical misinformation. He pointed out that there is one discouraging theme in the history of science—the widespread acceptance of false accounts. He noted that it is not uncommon for psychological findings and theories to be exaggerated or distorted and that the exaggerations frequently spread much further through public sources than do the

authentic facts. For example, he noted the widespread acceptance, and inclusion in many textbooks, of inaccurate restatements of the widely cited study of Little Albert's fear of furry objects:

LITTLE ALBERT
Little Albert was the famous toddler who, originally unafraid of rats, exhibited such a fear when J. B. Watson and Rayner (1920) paired the presence of a rat with a loud noise. Harris (1979), Samelson (1980), and Gilovich (1991) are among the critics who have noted how frequently and consistently this case is misrepresented and exaggerated. J. B. Watson and Rayner described pairing the loud noise with the rat and later testing Albert's reaction to a rat and a rabbit, as well as to blocks, a seal coat, cotton wool, the hair of Watson and some assistants, and a Santa Claus mask. Albert never reacted to the blocks or the assistants' hair, always reacted to the rat, and reacted to the other objects with various degrees of agitation that were sometimes vividly described but sometimes merely (and vaguely) termed "negative reaction." According to Harris (1979, p. 153), secondary sources have erroneously reported the testing of "a fur pelt, . . . a man's beard, . . . a cat, a pup, a fur muff, . . . a white furry glove, . . . Albert's aunt, who supposedly wore fur, . . . either the fur coat or the fur neckpiece of Albert's mother, . . . and even a teddy bear" (pp. 228–229).

Another factor that can affect the quality of historical information is that our views of history and our understanding of events are sometimes open to reinterpretation. As Schudson (1995) points out, "Collective memory, more than individual memory, at least in liberal pluralistic societies, is provisional. It is always open to contestation" (p. 16). Any number of obstacles can stand in the way of our gaining an accurate picture of the attitudes and behaviors of people who lived hundreds of years ago. This has certainly been the case with our views of the Middle Ages (Kroll & Bachrach, 1984).

The foremost problem in retrospective psychological analysis is that we cannot rely on direct observation, a hallmark of psychological research. Instead, we must turn to written documents or historical surveys of the times. Although these sources are often full of fascinating information, they may not reveal directly the information we seek; we must therefore extrapolate "facts" from the information we have, which is not always an easy task. We are restricted in our conclusions by the documents or sources available to us. Attempting to learn about people's attitudes and subtle social perceptions hundreds of years ago by examining surviving church documents or biographical accounts is less than ideal. First, we inevitably view these documents out of the context in which they were written. Second, we do not know whether the authors had ulterior motives or what the real purposes of the documents were. For example, some historians have concluded erroneously that people of the Middle Ages considered sin to be a major causal factor in mental illness. This misconception may have been due in part to zealous authors invoking "God's punishment" against the victims of mental illnesses who happened to be their enemies. Apparently, if the victims happened to be friends, sin was typically not mentioned as a causal factor (Kroll & Bachrach, 1984). Such writings, of course, are biased, but we may have no way of knowing this. The fewer the sources surveyed, the more likely that any existing bias will go undetected.

In other cases, concepts important to historical interpretation may have quite a different meaning to us today than they had in the past, or the meaning may simply be unclear. Kroll and Bachrach (1984) point out that the concept of "possession," so critical to our views of the Middle

Ages, is a very vague and complex concept for which we have no helpful natural models. Our language fails us, except for colorful analogies and metaphors. Just as the term *nervous breakdown* means different things to different people, so too *possession* means and meant many different things and undoubtedly had a different range of meanings to medieval persons from what it has to us. This kind of uncertainty can make definitive assessments of things that happened during the Middle Ages difficult, if not impossible (Phillips, 2002).

Bias can come into play during interpretation also. Our interpretations of historical events or previously held beliefs can be colored by our own views of what is normal and what is abnormal. In fact, it is difficult to conduct a retrospective analysis without taking current perspectives and values as a starting point. For example, our modern beliefs about the Middle Ages have led, says Schoeneman (1984), to our contemporary misinterpretation that during the fifteenth and sixteenth centuries the mentally ill were typically accused of being witches. For most of us, this mistaken interpretation makes sense simply because we do not understand the medieval perspective on witchcraft.

Although reevaluations of the Middle Ages have discredited the view that demonology, sin, and witchcraft played key roles in the medieval understanding of mental illness, it is also clear that in some cases these concepts were associated with mental illness. Where does the truth lie? It appears that the last word has not been written on the Middle Ages, nor on any period of our history for that matter. At best, historical views—and, therefore, retrospective psychological studies—must be regarded as working hypotheses that are open to change as new perspectives are applied to history and as "new" historical documents are discovered.

Summary

- Understanding of abnormal behavior has not evolved smoothly or uniformly over the centuries; the steps have been uneven, with great gaps in between, and unusual—even bizarre—views or beliefs have often sidetracked researchers and theorists.

- The dominant social, economic, and religious views of the times have had a profound influence over how people have viewed abnormal behavior.

- In the ancient world, superstitious explanations for mental disorders were followed by the emergence of medical concepts in many places such as Egypt and Greece; many of these concepts were developed and refined by Roman physicians.

- After the fall of Rome near the end of the fifth century A.D., superstitious views dominated popular thinking about mental disorders for over 1,000 years. In the fifteenth and sixteenth centuries, it was still widely believed, even by scholars, that some mentally disturbed people were possessed by a devil.

- Great strides have been made in our understanding of abnormal behavior. For example, during the latter part of the Middle Ages and the early Renaissance, a spirit of scientific questioning reappeared in Europe, and several noted physicians spoke out against

inhumane treatments. There was a general movement away from superstitions and "magic" toward reasoned, scientific studies.

- With recognition of a need for the special treatment of disturbed people came the founding of various "asylums" toward the end of the sixteenth century. However, institutionalization brought the isolation and maltreatment of mental patients. Slowly this situation was recognized, and in the eighteenth century further efforts were made to help afflicted individuals by providing them with better living conditions and humane treatment, although these improvements were the exception rather than the rule.

- The nineteenth and early twentieth centuries witnessed a number of scientific and humanitarian advances. The work of Philippe Pinel in France, of William Tuke in England, and of Benjamin Rush and Dorothea Dix in the United States prepared the way for several important developments in contemporary abnormal psychology, such as moral management. Among these were the gradual acceptance of mental patients as afflicted individuals who need and deserve professional attention; the successful application of biomedical methods to disorders; and the growth of scientific research into the biological, psychological, and sociocultural roots of abnormal behavior.

- The reform of mental hospitals continued into the twentieth century, but over the last four decades of the century there was a strong movement to close mental hospitals and release people into the community. This movement remains controversial in the early part of the twenty-first century.

- In the nineteenth century, great technological discoveries and scientific advancements that were made in the biological sciences enhanced the understanding and treatment of disturbed individuals. One major biomedical breakthrough came with the discovery of the organic factors underlying general paresis—syphilis of the brain—one of the most serious mental illnesses of the day.

- Beginning in the early part of the eighteenth century, knowledge of anatomy, physiology, neurology, chemistry, and general medicine increased rapidly. These advances led to the identification of the biological, or organic, pathology underlying many physical ailments.

- The development of a psychiatric classification system by Kraepelin played a dominant role in the early development of the biological viewpoint. Kraepelin's work (a forerunner to the *DSM* system) helped to establish the importance of brain pathology in mental disorders and made several related contributions that helped establish this viewpoint.

- The first major steps toward understanding psychological factors in mental disorders occurred with mesmerism and the Nancy School, followed by the work of Sigmund Freud. During five decades of observation, treatment, and writing, he developed a theory of psychopathology, known as "psychoanalysis," that emphasized the inner dynamics of unconscious motives. Over the last half-century, other clinicians have modified and revised Freud's theory, which has thus evolved into new psychodynamic perspectives.

- Scientific investigation into psychological factors and human behavior began to make progress in the latter part of the nineteenth century. The end of the nineteenth century and the early twentieth century saw experimental psychology evolve into clinical psychology with the development of clinics to study, as well as intervene in, abnormal behavior.

- Paralleling this development was the work of Pavlov in understanding learning and conditioning. Behaviorism emerged as an explanatory model in abnormal psychology. The behavioral perspective is organized around a central theme—that learning plays an important role in human behavior. Although this perspective was initially developed through research in the laboratory (unlike psychoanalysis, which emerged out of clinical practice with disturbed individuals), it has been shown to have important implications for explaining and treating maladaptive behavior.

- Understanding the history of psychopathology—its forward steps and missteps alike—helps us understand the emergence of modern concepts of abnormal behavior.

Key Terms

asylums
behavioral perspective
behaviorism
catharsis
classical conditioning
deinstitutionalization
dream analysis
exorcisms

free association
insanity
lycanthropy
mass madness
mental hygiene movement
mesmerism
moral management
nancy School

operant conditioning
psychoanalysis
psychoanalytic perspective
saint Vitus's dance
tarantism
unconscious

Glossary

Many of the key terms listed in the glossary appear in boldface when first introduced in the text discussion. A number of other terms commonly encountered in this or other psychology texts are also included; you are encouraged to make use of this glossary both as a general reference tool and as a study aid for the course in abnormal psychology.

Asylums. Historically, these were institutions meant solely for the care of the mentally ill.

Behavioral perspective. A theoretical viewpoint organized around the theme that learning is central in determining human behavior.

Behaviorism. School of psychology that formerly restricted itself primarily to the study of overt behavior.

Catharsis. Discharge of emotional tension associated with something, such as by talking about past traumas.

Classical conditioning. A basic form of learning in which a neutral stimulus is paired repeatedly with an unconditioned stimulus (US) that naturally elicits an unconditioned response (UR). After repeated pairings, the neutral stimulus becomes a conditioned stimulus (CS) that elicits a conditioned response (CR).

Deinstitutionalization. Movement to close mental hospitals and treat people with severe mental disorder in the community.

Dream analysis. Method involving the recording, description, and interpretation of a patient's dreams.

Exorcism. Religiously inspired treatment procedure designed to drive out evil spirits or forces from a "possessed" person.

Free association. Method for probing the unconscious by having patients talk freely about themselves, their feelings, and their motives.

Insanity. Legal term for mental disorder, implying lack of responsibility for one's acts and inability to manage one's affairs.

Lycanthropy. Delusion of being a wolf.

Mass madness. Historically, widespread occurrence of group behavior disorders that were apparently cases of hysteria.

Mental hygiene movement. Movement that advocated a method of treatment focused almost exclusively on the physical well-being of hospitalized mental patients.

Mesmerism. Theory of "animal magnetism" (hypnosis) formulated by Anton Mesmer.

Moral management. Wide-ranging method of treatment that focuses on a patient's social, individual, and occupational needs.

Nancy School. Group of physicians in nineteenth-century Europe who accepted the view that hysteria was a sort of self-hypnosis.

Operant (or instrumental) conditioning. Form of learning in which if a particular response is reinforced, it becomes more likely to be repeated on similar occasions.**Psychoanalysis.** Methods Freud used to study and treat patients.

Psychoanalytic perspective. Theory of psychopathology, initially developed by Freud, that emphasizes the inner dynamics of unconscious motives.

Saint Vitus's dance. Name given to the dancing mania (and mass hysteria) that spread from Italy to Germany and the rest of Europe in the Middle Ages.

Tarantism. Dancing mania that occurred in Italy in the thirteenth century.

Unconscious. In psychoanalytic theory, a major portion of the mind, which consists of a hidden mass of instincts, impulses, and memories and is not easily available to conscious awareness yet plays an important role in behavior.

Photo Credits

Text Credits

58

Causal Factors and Viewpoints

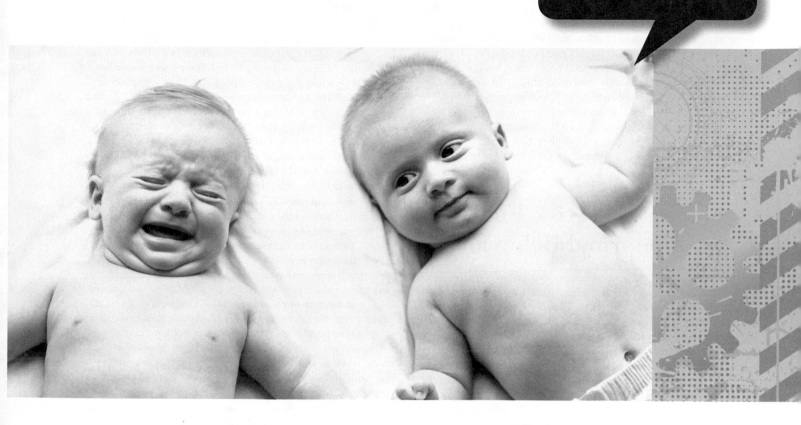

Causes and Risk Factors for Abnormal Behavior
Necessary, Sufficient, and Contributory Causes
Feedback and Bidirectionality in Abnormal Behavior
Diathesis-Stress Models

Viewpoints for Understanding the Causes of Abnormal Behavior

The Biological Viewpoint and Biological Causal Factors
Imbalances of Neurotransmitters and Hormones
Genetic Vulnerabilities
Temperament
Brain Dysfunction and Neural Plasticity
The Impact of the Biological Viewpoint

The Psychological Viewpoints
The Psychodynamic Perspectives
The Behavioral Perspective
The Cognitive-Behavioral Perspective
What the Adoption of a Perspective Does and Does Not Do

Psychological Causal Factors
Early Deprivation or Trauma
Inadequate Parenting Styles
Marital Discord and Divorce
Maladaptive Peer Relationships

The Sociocultural Viewpoint
Uncovering Sociocultural Factors Through Cross-Cultural Studies

Sociocultural Causal Factors
Low Socioeconomic Status and Unemployment
Prejudice and Discrimination in Race, Gender, and Ethnicity
Social Change and Uncertainty
Urban Stressors: Violence and Homelessness
The Impact of the Sociocultural Viewpoint

Unresolved Issues
Theoretical Viewpoints and the Causes of Abnormal Behavior

From early times, those who observed disordered behavior grappled with the question of its cause. Hippocrates, for example, had a type of disease model and suggested that an imbalance in the four bodily humors produced abnormal behavior, with each humor connected with certain kinds of behavior. To other observers, the cause was possession by demons or evil spirits. Later, bodily dysfunction was suggested as a cause.

Each attempt at identifying a cause brought with it a theory, or model, of abnormal behavior. Today we are still puzzling over the causes of abnormal behavior, and speculation about causes continues to give rise to new models of abnormality. Since about 1900, several important schools of thought have developed elaborate models to explain the origins of abnormal behavior and to suggest how it might be treated. We will discuss the most influential of these theoretical perspectives, paying special attention to the different types of causal factors that each perspective has identified. First, however, we need to address the very nature of the concept of causation as it is applied to abnormal behavior.

Causes and Risk Factors for Abnormal Behavior

Central to the field of abnormal psychology are questions about what causes people to experience mental distress and to behave maladaptively. If we knew the causes for given disorders, we might be able to prevent conditions that lead to them and perhaps reverse those that maintain them. We could also classify and diagnose disorders better if we clearly understood their causes rather than relying on clusters of symptoms, as we usually must do now.

Although understanding the causes of abnormal behavior is clearly a desirable goal, it is enormously difficult to achieve because human behavior is so complex. Even the simplest human behavior, such as speaking or writing a single word, is the product of thousands of prior events—the connections among which are not always clear. Attempting to understand a person's life in causal terms is a task of enormous magnitude, whether it be a fairly normal or adaptive life or a life characterized by severe mental disorders. As a result, many investigators now prefer to speak of *risk factors* (variables correlated with an abnormal outcome) rather than of causes (Rutter, 2006a). Nevertheless, understanding causes remains the ultimate goal.

However, this is particularly difficult to achieve when straightforward scientific approaches such as experiments using random assignment are generally not feasible for ethical reasons.

Necessary, Sufficient, and Contributory Causes

Regardless of one's theoretical perspective, several terms can be used to specify the role a factor plays in the **etiology**, or causal pattern, of abnormal behavior. A **necessary cause** (e.g., cause X) is a condition that must exist for a disorder (e.g., disorder Y) to occur. For example, general paresis (Y)—a degenerative brain disorder—cannot develop unless a person has previously contracted syphilis (X). Or more generally, if Y occurs, then X must have preceded it. Another example is Huntington's chorea—a rare degenerative brain disorder of the central nervous system—which can develop only if the person has the necessary gene (IT 15, or the Huntington's gene). To date, most mental disorders have not been found to have necessary causes, although there continues to be a search for such causes.

A **sufficient cause** (e.g., cause X) of a disorder is a condition that guarantees the occurrence of a disorder (e.g., disorder Y). For example, one current theory hypothesizes that hopelessness (X) is a sufficient cause of depression (Y) (Abramson et al., 1995; Abramson et al., 1989). Or, more generally, if X occurs, then Y will also occur. According to this theory, if you are hopeless enough about your future, then you will become depressed. However, a sufficient cause may not be a necessary cause. Continuing with the depression example, Abramson and colleagues (1989) acknowledge that hopelessness is not a necessary cause of depression; there are other causes of depression as well. Finally, what we study most often in psychopathology research are **contributory causes**. A contributory cause (e.g., cause X) is one that increases the probability of a disorder (e.g., disorder Y) developing but is neither necessary nor sufficient for the disorder to occur. Or, more generally, if X occurs, then the probability of Y occurring increases. For example, parental rejection could increase the probability that a child will later have difficulty in handling close personal relationships or could increase the probability that being rejected in a relationship in adulthood will precipitate depression. We say here that parental rejection is a contributory cause for the person's later difficulties, but it is neither necessary nor sufficient (Abramson et al., 1989; Abramson et al., 1995). See Figure 1 for a summary.

Necessary Cause	If Disorder Y occurs, then Cause X must have preceded it.
Sufficient Cause	If Cause X occurs, then Disorder Y will also occur.
Contributory Cause	If X occurs, then the probability of Disorder Y increases.

FIGURE 1

Abnormal Behavior: Types of Causes

In addition to distinguishing among necessary, sufficient, and contributory causes of abnormal behavior, we must also consider the time frame under which the different causes operate. Some causal factors occurring relatively early in life may not show their effects for many years; these would be considered *distal causal factors* that may contribute to a predisposition to develop a disorder. For example, loss of a parent early in life, or having abusive or neglectful parents as a child or adolescent, may serve as a distal contributory cause predisposing a person to depression or antisocial behaviors later in life. By contrast, other causal factors operate shortly before the occurrence of the symptoms of a disorder; these would be considered *proximal causal factors*. Sometimes a proximal causal factor may be a condition that proves too much for a child or adult and triggers the onset of a disorder. A crushing disappointment at school or work or severe difficulties with a school friend or a marital partner are examples of more proximal causal factors that could lead to depression. In other cases, proximal factors might involve biological changes such as damage to certain parts of the left hemisphere of the brain, which can lead to depression.

A *reinforcing contributory cause* is a condition that tends to maintain maladaptive behavior that is already occurring. An example is the extra attention, sympathy, and relief from unwanted responsibility that may come when a person is ill; these pleasant experiences may unintentionally discourage recovery. Another example occurs when a depressed person's behavior alienates friends and family, leading to a greater sense of rejection that reinforces the existing depression (Joiner, 2002; Joiner & Timmons, 2009).

For many forms of psychopathology, we do not yet have a clear understanding of whether there are necessary or sufficient causes, although answering this question remains the goal of much current research. We do, however, have a good understanding of many of the contributory causes for most forms of psychopathology. Some of the distal contributory causes, to be discussed later, set up vulnerability during childhood to some disorder later in life. Other more proximal contributory causes appear to bring on a disorder directly, and still others may contribute to maintenance of a disorder. This complex causal picture is further complicated by the fact that what may be a proximal cause for a problem at one stage in life may also serve as a distal contributory cause that sets up a predisposition for another disorder later in life. For example, the death of a parent can be a proximal cause of a child's subsequent grief reaction, which might last a few months or a year; however, the parent's death may also serve as a distal contributory factor that increases the probability that when the child grows up he or she will become depressed in response to certain stressors.

The loss of a parent at an early age may be a contributory cause for a child to develop depression in adulthood. Factors that may not show their effects for many years are called distal causal factors.

Feedback and Bidirectionality in Abnormal Behavior

Traditionally in the sciences, the task of determining cause-and-effect relationships has focused on isolating the condition X (cause) that can be demonstrated to lead to condition Y (effect). For example, when the alcohol content of the blood reaches a certain level, alcoholic intoxication occurs. When more than one causal factor is involved as is often the case, the term *causal pattern* is used. Here, conditions A, B, C, and so on lead to condition Y. In either case, this concept of cause follows a simple linear model in which a given variable or set of variables leads to a result either immediately or later. In the behavioral sciences, however, not only do we usually deal with a multitude of interacting causes but we also often have difficulty distinguishing between what is cause and what is effect because effects can serve as feedback that can in turn influence the causes. In other words, the effects of feedback and the existence of mutual, two-way (bidirectional) influences must be taken into account.

Consider the following example, which illustrates that our concepts of causal relationships must take into account the complex factors of bidirectionality of feedback.

case study Perceived Hostility

A boy with a history of disturbed interactions with his parents routinely misinterprets the intentions of his peers as being hostile. He develops defensive strategies to counteract the supposed hostility of those around him such as rejecting the efforts of others to be friendly, which he misinterprets as patronizing. Confronted by the boy's prickly behavior, those around him become defensive, hostile, and rejecting, thus confirming and strengthening the boy's distorted expectations. In this manner, each opportunity for new experience and new learning is in fact subverted and becomes yet another encounter with a social environment that seems perversely and persistently hostile—exactly in line with the boy's expectations.

Diathesis-Stress Models

A predisposition toward developing a disorder is termed a **diathesis**. It can derive from biological, psychological, or sociocultural causal factors, and the different viewpoints that we will be discussing tend to emphasize the importance of different kinds of diatheses. Many mental disorders are believed to develop when some kind of stressor operates on a person who has a diathesis or *vulnerability* for that disorder. Hence we will discuss what are commonly known as **diathesis-stress models** of abnormal behavior (e.g., Ingram & Luxton, 2005; Meehl, 1962; Monroe & Simons, 1991). To translate these terms into the types of causal factors described earlier, the diathesis is a relatively distal necessary or contributory cause, but it is generally not sufficient to cause the disorder. Instead, there generally must be a more proximal undesirable event or situation (the stressor), which may also be contributory or necessary but is generally not sufficient by itself to cause the disorder except in someone with the diathesis.

Stress, the response or experience of an individual to demands that he or she perceives as taxing or exceeding his or her personal resources (Folkman & Moskovitz, 2004; Monroe et al., 2009; Taylor & Stanton, 2007). It usually occurs when an individual experiences chronic or episodic events that are undesirable and lead to behavioral, physiological, and cognitive accommodations (Baum & Posluszny, 1999). It is important to note that factors contributing to the development of a diathesis are themselves sometimes highly potent stressors, as when a child experiences the death of a parent and may thereby acquire a predisposition or diathesis for becoming depressed later in life.

Researchers have proposed several different ways that a diathesis and stress may combine to produce a disorder (Ingram & Luxton, 2005; Monroe & Simons, 1991). In what is called the *additive model*, individuals who have a high level of a diathesis may need only a small amount of stress before a disorder develops, but those who have a very low level of a diathesis may need to experience a large amount of stress for a disorder to develop. In other words, the diathesis and the stress sum together, and when one is high the other can be low, and vice versa; thus, a person with no diathesis or a very low level of diathesis could still develop a disorder when faced with truly severe stress. In what is called an *interactive model*, some amount of diathesis must be present before stress will have any effect. Thus, in the interactive model, someone with no diathesis will never develop the disorder, no matter how much stress he or she experiences, whereas someone with the diathesis will show increasing likelihood of developing the disorder with increasing levels of stress. More complex models are also possible because diatheses often exist on a continuum, ranging from zero to high levels. Each of these possibilities is illustrated in Figure 2.

Since the late 1980s, attention has been focused on the concept of **protective factors**, which are influences that modify a person's response to environmental stressors, making it less likely that the person will experience the adverse consequences of the stressors (Cicchetti & Garmezy, 1993; Masten et al., 2004; Rutter, 2006a, 2011). One important protective factor in childhood is having a family environment in which at least one parent is warm and supportive, allowing the development of a good attachment relationship between the child and parent that can protect against the harmful effects of an abusive parent (Masten & Coatsworth, 1998). Ordinarily, protective

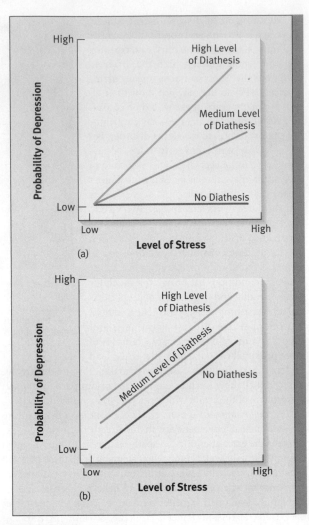

FIGURE 2

Diathesis-Stress Model

(a) Interactive model of diathesis-stress interaction. (b) Additive model of diathesis-stress interaction.

Source: Adapted from S. M. Monroe & A. D. Simons (1991). Diathesis-stress theories in the context of life stress research: Implications for the depressive disorders. *Psychological Bulletin, 110*, 406–25.

factors operate only to help resist against the effects of a risk factor rather than to provide any benefits to people without risk factors (Rutter, 2006a).

Protective factors are not necessarily positive experiences. Indeed, sometimes exposure to stressful experiences that are dealt with successfully can promote a sense of self-confidence or self-esteem and thereby serve as a protective factor; thus some stressors paradoxically promote coping. This "steeling" or "inoculation" effect is more likely to occur with moderate stressors than with mild or extreme stressors (Barlow, 2002; Hetherington, 1991; Rutter, 1987, 2009). And some protective factors have nothing to do with experiences at all but are simply some quality or attribute of a person. For example, some protective attributes include an easygoing temperament, high self-esteem, high intelligence, and school achievement, all of which can help protect against a variety of stressors (Masten, 2001; Rutter, 1987; Sapienza & Masten, 2011).

Protective factors most often, but not always, lead to **resilience**—the ability to adapt successfully to even very difficult circumstances. An example is the child who perseveres and does well in school despite his or her parent's drug addiction or physical abuse (Garmezy, 1993; Luthar, 2003; Sapienza & Masten, 2011). More generally, the term *resilience* has been used to describe the phenomenon that "some individuals have a relatively good outcome despite suffering risk experiences that would be expected to bring about serious sequelae" (Rutter, 2007, p. 205). A more everyday way of thinking of resilience is in terms of "overcoming the odds" against you. There is increasing evidence that if a child's fundamental systems of adaptation (such as intelligence and cognitive development, ability to self-regulate, motivation to achieve mastery, effective parenting, and well-functioning neurobiological systems for handling stress) are operating normally, then most threatening circumstances will have minimal impact on him or her (Masten, 2001; Sapienza & Masten, 2011). Problems tend to arise when one or more of these systems of adaptation is weak to begin with (e.g., low intelligence or poorly functioning neurobiological systems for handling stress; Lester et al., 2006) or when a serious stressor damages one or more of these systems (e.g., when a parent dies). Problems can also arise when the level of challenge far exceeds human capacity to adapt (e.g., exposure to chronic trauma in war or chronic maltreatment in abusive families; Cicchetti, 2004; Cicchetti & Toth, 2005; Masten & Coatsworth, 1998; Sapienza & Masten, 2011). We should also note, however, that resilience should not be thought of as an all-or-none capacity, and some research has shown that resilient children (that is, those who show high social competence despite high stress) may nonetheless also experience considerable self-reported emotional distress. Moreover, children who show resilience in one domain may show significant difficulties in other domains.

In sum, we can distinguish between causes of abnormal behavior that lie within and are part of the biological makeup or prior experience of a person—diatheses, vulnerabilities, or predispositions—and causes that pertain to current challenges in a person's life—stressors. Typically, neither the diathesis nor the stress is by itself sufficient to cause the disorder, but in combination they can sometimes lead the individual

to behave abnormally. In addition, we can also examine protective factors, which may derive either from particular types of experiences or from certain qualities of the person, that can promote resilience in the face of vulnerability and stress. The following hypothetical but highly plausible scenario nicely illustrates these concepts.

case study **Nature and Nurture**

Melinda and Tracy were identical twins whose parents were killed in a car accident when they were a year old. Their mother and grandmother both had histories of recurrent clinical depression. The twins were adopted into two loving middle-class families without a history of depression. Melinda's adoptive family provided a loving and supportive environment and supported her through school and college. Tracy's adoptive parents, by contrast, soon divorced, and she was raised by her adoptive mother, who developed a serious dependence on alcohol and who could not hold a job. Her mother's living circumstances deteriorated and Tracy was forced to change schools four times. Because of her adoptive mother's alcohol and other mental problems, she was unable to provide Tracy with a consistently loving and supportive environment, and when she was drunk she frequently punished Tracy for no good reason. Tracy somehow managed to graduate from high school and supported herself through a state college. Both Tracy and Melinda married after they graduated from college but, by age 27, both marriages resulted in divorce. Although Melinda developed some depressive symptoms for the first 6 weeks following the divorce, the depression was not severe and she quickly recovered. Tracy, by contrast, developed a major depressive episode that lasted for over a year.

A child growing up under conditions of adversity may be protected from problems later in life if he or she has a warm and supportive relationship with some adult—such as a grandmother. Encouraging children to ask questions, taking the time to listen to their problems and concerns, and trying to understand the conflicts and pressures they face are the important elements of such a supportive and protective relationship.

In this example, both Tracy and Melinda have identical genetic makeup and therefore the same genetic diathesis for depression. Both had experienced the same distal stressor (death of parents at an early age), and the same proximal stressor (divorce) at age 27. But Melinda had many protective factors growing up (loving and supportive family and adequate resources) that Tracy did not have (lack of a loving and supportive mother and inadequate resources). Thus Melinda showed resilience in the face of her divorce but Tracy did not.

Different models of abnormal behavior, as we shall see in the sections that follow, identify different diatheses and different stressors as the route to abnormality and different protective factors as the route to resilience in the face of adversity.

This discussion should make it very clear that diathesis-stress models need to be considered in a broad framework of *multicausal developmental models*. Specifically, in the course of development a child may acquire a variety of cumulative risk factors that may interact in determining his or her risk for psychopathology. These risk factors also interact, however, with a variety of protective processes, and sometimes with stressors, to determine whether the child develops in a normal and adaptive way—as opposed to showing signs of maladaptive behavior and psychopathology—in childhood, adolescence, or adulthood (e.g., Rutter, 2001, 2006a, 2009; Sapienza & Masten, 2011). It is also important to note, however, that to understand what is abnormal, one must always have a good understanding of normal human development at biological, psychological, and sociocultural levels of analysis. This has been the focus of the rapidly growing field of **developmental psychopathology**, which focuses on determining what is abnormal at any point in development by comparing and contrasting it with the normal and expected changes that occur in the course of development (e.g., Masten, 2006; Rutter, 2001). For example, an intense fear of the dark in a 3- to 5-year-old child may not be considered abnormal, given that most children have at least one specific fear that they bring into early adolescence (Antony et al., 1997; Barlow, 2002). However, an intense fear of the dark that causes considerable distress and avoidance behavior in a high school or college-age student would be considered a phobia.

In Review

- What is a necessary cause? a sufficient cause? a contributory cause?

- What is a diathesis-stress model of abnormal behavior?

- Define the terms *protective factors* and *resilience.* Give examples of each.

- Explain why diathesis-stress models need to be considered as multicausal developmental models.

Viewpoints for Understanding the Causes of Abnormal Behavior

Students are often perplexed by the fact that in the behavioral sciences there often are several competing explanations for the same thing. In general, the more complex the phenomenon being investigated, the greater the number of viewpoints that develop in an attempt to explain it,

although inevitably they are not all equally valid. In each case, a particular viewpoint helps researchers and theoreticians to organize the observations they have made, provides a system of thought in which to place the observed data, and suggests areas of focus for research and treatment. In a fundamental way, viewpoints also help determine the kinds of potential causes that are even examined in the first place. It is important to remember, however, that each of these viewpoints is a theoretical construction devised to orient psychologists in the study of abnormal (and normal) behavior. One potential problem is that when adherents of a particular viewpoint are overly confident about the validity of that viewpoint, they may become blind to alternative interpretations.

Sigmund Freud helped shift the focus of abnormal psychology from biological illness or moral infirmity to unconscious mental processes within the person. In recent years, three other shifts in focus seem to have been occurring in parallel in the study of abnormal behavior. First, a newer, slightly different biological viewpoint is having a significant impact; it is the dominant force in psychiatry and has become very influential in clinical science more generally. Second, the behavioral and cognitive-behavioral viewpoints have become very influential paradigms among many empirically oriented clinical psychologists and some psychiatrists. Third, a sociocultural viewpoint has also become influential among psychologists and psychiatrists interested in the effects of sociocultural factors on abnormal behavior. In the long run, however, we also know from biological, psychological, and sociocultural research that only an integrated approach is likely to provide anything close to a full understanding of the origins of various forms of psychopathology or the form that a long-lasting cure for many serious forms of psychopathology might take. Thus, in recent years, many theorists have come to recognize the need for a more integrative, **biopsychosocial viewpoint** that acknowledges that biological, psychological, and sociocultural factors all interact and play a role in psychopathology and treatment.

With this in mind, we now turn to the major different viewpoints themselves. We will present the key ideas of each perspective, along with information about attempts to evaluate its validity. We will also describe the kinds of causal factors that each model tends to emphasize.

In Review

- What are the three traditional viewpoints that have dominated the study of abnormal behavior in recent years?

- What is the central idea of the more current biopsychosocial viewpoint?

The Biological Viewpoint and Biological Causal Factors

The traditional biological viewpoint focuses on mental disorders as diseases, many of the primary symptoms of which are cognitive, emotional, or behavioral. Mental disorders are thus viewed as disorders of the central nervous system, the autonomic nervous system, and/or the endocrine system that are either inherited or caused by some pathological process. At one time, people who adopted this viewpoint hoped to find simple biological explanations. Today, however, most clinical psychologists and psychiatrists recognize that such explanations are rarely simple, and many also acknowledge that psychological and sociocultural causal factors play important roles as well.

The disorders first recognized as having biological or organic components were those associated with gross destruction of brain tissue. These disorders are neurological diseases—that is, they result from the disruption of brain functioning by physical or biochemical means and often involve psychological or behavioral aberrations. For example, damage to certain areas in the brain can cause memory loss, and damage to the left hemisphere that occurs during a stroke can cause depression.

However, most mental disorders are not caused by neurological damage per se. For example, abnormalities in neurotransmitter systems in the brain can lead to mental disorders without causing damage to the brain. Moreover, the bizarre content of delusions and other abnormal mental states like hallucinations can never be caused simply and directly by brain damage. Consider the example of a person with schizophrenia or general paresis who claims to be Napoleon. The content of such delusions must be the byproduct of some sort of functional integration of different neural structures, some of which have been "programmed" by personality and learning based on past experience (e.g., having learned who Napoleon was).

People's behavior during alcohol intoxication is one good example of how a temporary biological condition can dramatically affect functioning—in this case engaging in behavior that normally would be inhibited.

> ▶ Neurotransmitter and hormonal abnormalities in neurotransmitter systems
> ▶ Genetic vulnerabilities
> ▶ Temperament
> ▶ Brain dysfunction and neural plasticity

FIGURE 3

Biological Causal Factors

We will focus here on four categories of biological factors that seem particularly relevant to the development of maladaptive behavior: (1) neurotransmitter and hormonal abnormalities in the brain or other parts of the central nervous system, (2) genetic vulnerabilities, (3) temperament, and (4) brain dysfunction and neural plasticity. (See also Figure 3.) Each of these categories encompasses a number of conditions that influence the quality and functioning of our bodies and our behavior. They are often not independent of each other but rather interact with one another. Moreover, different factors may play more or less important roles in different people.

Imbalances of Neurotransmitters and Hormones

In order for the brain to function adequately, neurons, or nerve cells, need to be able to communicate effectively with one another. The site of communication between the axon of one neuron and the dendrites or cell body of another neuron is the **synapse**—a tiny fluid-filled space between neurons. These interneuronal transmissions are accomplished by **neurotransmitters**—chemical substances that are released into the synapse by the presynaptic neuron when a nerve impulse occurs (for details, see the figure in Developments in Research 1). There are many different kinds of neurotransmitters; some increase the likelihood that the postsynaptic neuron will "fire" (produce an impulse), and others inhibit the impulse. Whether the neural message is successfully transmitted to the postsynaptic neuron depends, among other things, on the concentration of certain neurotransmitters within the synapse.

IMBALANCES OF NEUROTRANSMITTER SYSTEMS The belief that imbalances in neurotransmitters in the brain can result in abnormal behavior is one of the basic tenets of the biological perspective today, although currently most researchers agree that this is only part of the causal pattern involved in the etiology of most disorders. Sometimes psychological stress can bring on *neurotransmitter imbalances*. These imbalances can be created in a variety of ways (see the figure in Developments in Research 1):

● There may be excessive production and release of the neurotransmitter substance into the synapses, causing a functional excess in levels of that neurotransmitter.

1 DEVELOPMENTS IN RESEARCH

Neurotransmission and Abnormal Behavior

A nerve impulse, which is electrical in nature, travels from the cell body of a neuron (nerve cell) down the axon. Although there is only one axon for each neuron, axons have branches at their ends called axon endings. These are the sites where neurotransmitter substances are released into a synapse—a tiny, fluid-filled gap between the axon endings of one neuron (the presynaptic neuron) and the dendrites or cell body of another neuron (the postsynaptic neuron). The synapse is the site of neural transmission—that is, of communication between neurons. The neurotransmitter substances are contained within synaptic vesicles near the axon endings. When a nerve impulse reaches the axon endings, the synaptic vesicles travel to the presynaptic membrane of the axon and release the neurotransmitter substance into the synapse. The neurotransmitter substances released into the synapse then act on the postsynaptic membrane of the dendrite of the receiving neuron, which has specialized receptor sites where the neurotransmitter substances pass on their message. The receptor sites then initiate the receiving cell's response. The neurotransmitters can stimulate that postsynaptic neuron to either initiate an impulse or inhibit impulse transmission. Both kinds of messages are important. Once the neurotransmitter substance is released into the synapse, it does not stay around indefinitely (otherwise, the second neuron would continue firing in the absence of a real impulse). Sometimes the neurotransmitters are quickly destroyed by an enzyme such as monoamine oxidase, and sometimes they are returned to storage vesicles in the axon endings by a reuptake mechanism—a process of reabsorption by which the neurotransmitters are reabsorbed or effectively sucked back up into the axon ending. The enzyme monoamine oxidase is also present in the presynaptic terminal and can destroy excess neurotransmitter there too.

Given that many forms of psychopathology have been associated with various abnormalities in neurotransmitter functioning and with altered sensitivities of receptor sites, it is not surprising that many of the medications used to treat various disorders have the synapse as their site of action. For example, certain medications act to increase or decrease the concentrations of pertinent neurotransmitters in the synaptic gap. They may do so by blocking the reuptake process, by altering the sensitivity of the receptor sites, or by affecting the actions of the enzymes that ordinarily break down the neurotransmitter substances. Medications that facilitate the effects of a neurotransmitter on the postsynaptic neuron are called *agonists*, and those that oppose or inhibit the effects of a neurotransmitter on a postsynaptic neuron are called *antagonists*.

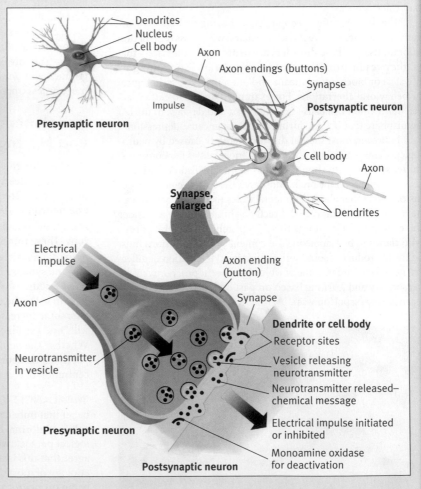

- There may be dysfunctions in the normal processes by which neurotransmitters, once released into the synapse, are deactivated. Ordinarily this deactivation occurs either through a process of reuptake of the released neurotransmitter from the synapse into the axon endings or through a process of degradation by certain enzymes that may be present in the synapse and in the presynaptic axon endings.
- Finally, there may be problems with the receptors in the postsynaptic neuron, which may be either abnormally sensitive or abnormally insensitive.

Neurons that are sensitive to a particular neurotransmitter tend to cluster together, forming neural paths between different parts of the brain known as *chemical circuits*. As we will see, different disorders are thought to stem from different patterns of neurotransmitter imbalances in various brain areas (e.g., Lambert & Kinsley, 2005; Thompson, 2000). Different medications used to treat various disorders are often believed to operate by correcting these imbalances. For example, the widely prescribed antidepressants Prozac and Zoloft appear to slow the reuptake of the neurotransmitter serotonin, thereby prolonging how long serotonin remains in the synapse.

Although over a hundred neurotransmitters have been discovered to date, five different kinds of neurotransmitters have been most extensively studied in relationship to psychopathology: (1) norepinephrine, (2) dopamine, (3) serotonin, (4) glutamate, and (5) gamma aminobutyric acid (known as GABA; Carlson, 2007; Lambert & Kinsley, 2005; Thompson, 2000). The first three belong to a class of neurotransmitters called *monoamines* because each is synthesized from a single amino acid (*monoamine* means "one amine"). Norepinephrine has been implicated as playing an important role in the emergency reactions our bodies show when we are exposed to an acutely stressful or dangerous situation, as well as in attention, orientation, and basic motives. Some of the functions of dopamine include pleasure and cognitive processing, and it has been implicated in schizophrenia as well as in addictive disorders. Serotonin has been found to have important effects on the way we think and process information from our environment as well as on behaviors and moods. Not surprisingly, then, it seems to play an important role in emotional disorders such as anxiety and depression, as well as in suicide.

HORMONAL IMBALANCES Some forms of psychopathology have also been linked to *hormonal imbalances*. **Hormones** are chemical messengers secreted by a set of endocrine glands in our bodies. Each of the endocrine glands produces and releases its own set of hormones directly into our bloodstream. The hormones then travel and directly affect target cells in various parts of our brain and body, influencing diverse events such as fight-or-flight reactions, sexual

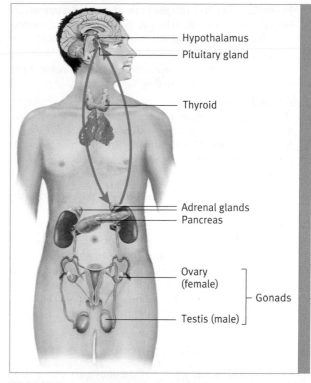

FIGURE 4

Major Glands of the Endocrine System

This figure illustrates some of the major glands of the endocrine system, which produce and release hormones into the bloodstream. The hypothalamic-pituitary-adrenal axis is also shown (blue arrows). The hypothalamus and pituitary are closely connected, and the hypothalamus periodically sends hormone signals to the pituitary (the master gland), which in turn sends another hormone to the cortical part of the adrenal glands (above the kidneys) to release epinephrine and the stress hormone cortisol.

responses, physical growth, and many other physical expressions of mental states. Our central nervous system is linked to the endocrine system (in what is known as the *neuroendocrine system*) by the effects of the hypothalamus on the **pituitary gland**, which is the master gland of the body, producing a variety of hormones that regulate or control the other endocrine glands (see Figure 4).

One particularly important set of interactions occurs in the **hypothalamic-pituitary-adrenal axis (HPA axis)**. Activation of this axis involves:

1. Messages in the form of corticotrophin-releasing hormone (CRH) travel from the hypothalamus to the pituitary.

2. In response to CRH, the pituitary releases adrenocortico-trophic hormone (ACTH), which stimulates the cortical part of the adrenal gland (located on top of the kidney) to produce epinephrine (adrenaline) and the stress hormone **cortisol**, which are released into general circulation. Cortisol mobilizes the body to deal with stress.

3. Cortisol in turn provides negative feedback to the hypothalamus and pituitary to decrease their release of CRH and ACTH, which in turn reduces the release of adrenaline and cortisol. This negative feedback system operates much as a thermostat does to regulate temperature.

As we will see, malfunctioning of this negative feedback system has been implicated in various forms of psychopathology such as depression and posttraumatic stress disorder.

Sex hormones are produced by the gonadal glands, and imbalance in these (such as the male hormones, the *androgens*) can also contribute to maladaptive behavior. Moreover, gonadal hormonal influences on the developing nervous system also seem to contribute to some of the differences between behavior in men and in women (e.g., Hayward, 2003; Hines, 2004; Money & Ehrhardt, 1972).

Genetic Vulnerabilities

The biochemical processes described above are themselves affected by **genes**, which consist of very long molecules of DNA (deoxyribonucleic acid) and are present at various locations on chromosomes. **Chromosomes** are the chain-like structures within a cell nucleus that contain the genes. Genes are the carriers of genetic information that we inherit from our parents and other ancestors, and each gene exists in two or more alternate forms called *alleles*. Although neither behavior nor mental disorders are ever determined exclusively by genes, there is substantial evidence that most mental disorders show at least some genetic influence ranging from small to large (e.g., Plomin et al., 2008; Rutter, 2006a). Some of these genetic influences, such as broad temperamental features, are first apparent in newborns and children. For example, some children are just naturally more shy or anxious, whereas others are more outgoing (e.g., Carey & DiLalla, 1994; Fox et al., 2010; Kagan & Fox, 2006). However, some genetic sources of vulnerability do not manifest themselves until adolescence or adulthood, when most mental disorders appear for the first time.

Healthy human cells have 46 chromosomes containing genetic materials that encode the hereditary plan for each individual, providing the potentialities for development and behavior of that individual throughout a lifetime. The normal inheritance consists of 23 pairs of chromosomes, one of each pair from the mother and one from the father. Twenty-two of these chromosome pairs determine, by their biochemical action, an individual's general anatomical and other physiological characteristics. The remaining pair, the *sex chromosomes*, determine the individual's sex. In a female, both of these sex chromosomes—one from each parent—are designated as X chromosomes. In a male, the sex chromosome from the mother is an X, but that from the father is a Y chromosome (see Figure 5).

Research in developmental genetics has shown that abnormalities in the structure or number of the chromosomes can be associated with major defects or disorders. For example, Down syndrome is a type of mental retardation (also associated with recognizable facial features such as a flat face and slanted eyes) in which there is a trisomy (a set of three chromosomes instead of two) in chromosome 21. Here the extra chromosome is the primary cause of the disorder. Anomalies may also occur in the sex chromosomes, producing a variety of complications, such as ambiguous sexual characteristics, that may predispose a person to develop abnormal behavior. Fortunately, advances in research have enabled us to detect chromosomal abnormalities even before birth, thus making it possible to study their effects on future development and behavior.

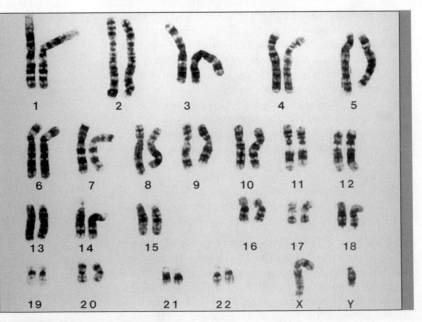

FIGURE 5

Human Chromosome Pairs

A normal human male has 23 pairs of chromosomes, including an X chromosome and a Y chromosome.

Source: "Human Chromosome Pairs," from Thomas D. Gelehrter et al. (1998). *Principles of Medical Genetics.* Reprinted with permission of Lippincott/Williams & Wilkins and Dr. Thomas D. Gelehrter.

More typically, however, personality traits and mental disorders are not affected by chromosomal abnormalities per se. Instead they are more often influenced either by abnormalities in some of the genes on the chromosomes or by naturally occurring variations of genes known as *polymorphisms*. Although you will often hear about discoveries that "the gene" for a particular disorder has been discovered, vulnerabilities to mental disorders are almost always **polygenic**, which means they are influenced by multiple genes or by multiple polymorphisms of genes, with any one gene having only very small effects (Kendler, 2005; Plomin et al., 2008). In other words, a genetically vulnerable person has usually inherited a large number of genes, or polymorphisms of genes, that operate together in some sort of additive or interactive fashion to increase vulnerability (e.g., Kendler, 2005; Plomin et al., 2008; Rutter, 2006b). Collectively these genes may, for example, lead to structural abnormalities in the central nervous system, to abnormalities in the regulation of brain chemistry and hormonal balance, or to excesses or deficiencies in the reactivity of the autonomic nervous system, which is involved in mediating many of our emotional responses.

In the field of abnormal psychology, genetic influences rarely express themselves in a simple and straightforward manner. This is because behavior, unlike some physical characteristics such as eye color, is not determined exclusively by genetic endowment; it is a product of the organism's interaction with the environment. In other words, genes can affect behavior only indirectly. Gene "expression" is normally not a simple outcome of the information encoded in DNA but is, rather, the end product of an intricate process that may be influenced by the internal (e.g., intrauterine) and external environment. Indeed, certain genes can actually be "turned on," or activated, and "turned off," or deactivated, in response to environmental influences such as stress (e.g., Plomin et al., 2008; Rutter, 2006b).

THE RELATIONSHIP OF GENOTYPES TO PHENOTYPES
A person's total genetic endowment is referred to as her or his **genotype** and, except for identical twins, no two humans ever begin life with the same endowment. The observed structural and functional characteristics that result from an interaction of the genotype and the environment are referred to as a person's **phenotype**. In some cases, the genotypic vulnerability present at birth does not exert its effect on the phenotype until much later in life. In many other cases, the genotype may shape the environmental experiences a child has, thus affecting the phenotype in yet another very important way. For example, a child who is genetically predisposed to aggressive behavior may be rejected by his or her peers in early grades because of the aggressive behavior. Such rejection may lead the child to go on to associate with similarly aggressive and delinquent peers in later grades, leading to an increased likelihood of developing a full-blown pattern of delinquency in adolescence. When the genotype shapes the environmental experiences a child has in this way, we refer to this phenomenon as a **genotype–environment correlation** (Plomin et al., 2008; Rutter, 2006, 2007).

GENOTYPE–ENVIRONMENT CORRELATIONS Researchers have found three important ways in which an individual's genotype may shape his or her environment (Jang, 2005; Plomin et al., 2008).

1. The child's genotype may have what has been termed a *passive effect* on the environment, resulting from the genetic similarity of parents and children. For example, highly intelligent parents may provide a highly stimulating environment for their child, thus creating an environment that will interact in a positive way with the child's genetic endowment for high intelligence. Conversely, parents who exhibit antisocial behavior tend to create a risky environment characterized by family dysfunction, thereby increasing the probability of certain mental disorders in their children (e.g., Rutter, 2006b).

2. The child's genotype may evoke particular kinds of reactions from the social and physical environment—a so-called *evocative effect*. For example, active, happy babies evoke more positive responses from others than do passive, unresponsive infants (Lytton, 1980). Similarly, musically talented children may be picked out at school and given special opportunities (Plomin et al., 2008).

3. The child's genotype may play a more active role in shaping the environment—a so-called *active effect*. In this case the child seeks out or builds an environment that is congenial—a phenomenon known as "niche building." For example, extraverted children may seek the company of others, for example, thereby enhancing their own tendencies to be sociable (Baumrind, 1991; Plomin et al., 2008).

GENOTYPE–ENVIRONMENT INTERACTIONS With the type of genotype–environment correlations just discussed, we see the effects that genes have on a child's exposure to the environment. But an additional, fascinating complication is that people with different genotypes may be differentially sensitive or susceptible to their environments; this is known as a **genotype–environment interaction**. One important example is illustrated by a disorder known as PKU-induced mental retardation. Children with the genetic vulnerability to PKU react very differently to many common foods with phenylalanine than do normal children because they cannot metabolize the phenylalanine (an amino acid), and as its metabolic products build up, they damage the brain (Plomin et al., 2008; Rutter, 2006b). Fortunately, this mental retardation syndrome can be prevented if the young child's diet is changed so as to eliminate foods with phenylalanine.

Another example occurs in people at genetic risk for depression, who have been shown to be more likely to respond to stressful life events by becoming depressed than are people without the genetic risk factors who experience the same stressful life events (Kendler, Kessler, et al., 1995; Moffitt, Caspi, & Rutter, 2005, 2006; Silberg, Rutter, Neale & Eaves, 2001). In one landmark study of nearly 850 young adults who had been followed since age 3, investigators found evidence for a genotype–environment interaction involving several variants on a specific gene involved in the transport of the neurotransmitter serotonin. Which of two variants of this gene a person had affected the likelihood that she or he would develop major depression in her or his 20s, but only when considered in interaction with life stress (Caspi et al., 2003). Specifically, individuals with one variant of the gene (two short alleles) who also experienced four or more major life stressors had twice the probability of developing major depression than individuals with another variant of the gene (two long alleles) who also experienced four or more major life stressors. Since then, this basic pattern of results has been replicated in many studies (and not in others), but recent evidence suggests that the effects are robust if sophisticated interview-based measures of life stress (not checklists) are used (Uher & McGuffin, 2010; see also Karg et al., 2011).

METHODS FOR STUDYING GENETIC INFLUENCES

Although advances are beginning to be made in identifying faulty genetic endowment, for the most part we are not yet able to isolate, on the genes themselves, specific defects for mental disorders. Therefore, most of the information we have on the role of genetic factors in mental disorders is based not on studies of genes but on studies of people who are related to each other. Three primary methods have traditionally been used in **behavior genetics**, the field that focuses on studying the heritability of mental disorders (as well as other aspects of psychological functioning): (1) the family history (or pedigree) method, (2) the twin method, and (3) the adoption method. More recently, two additional methods, linkage studies and association studies, have also been developed.

The **family history** (or pedigree) **method** requires that an investigator observe samples of relatives of each *proband* or *index case* (the subject, or carrier, of the trait or disorder in question) to see whether the incidence increases in proportion to the degree of hereditary relationship. In addition, the incidence of the disorder in a normal population is compared (as a control) with its incidence among the relatives of the index cases. The main limitation of this method is that people who are more closely related genetically also tend to share more similar environments, which makes it difficult to disentangle genetic and environmental effects.

The **twin method** is the second approach used to study genetic influences on abnormal behavior. *Identical (monozygotic) twins* share the same genetic endowment because they develop from a single zygote, or fertilized egg. Thus if a given disorder or trait were completely heritable, one would expect the **concordance rate**—the percentage of twins sharing the disorder or trait—to be 100 percent. That is, if one identical twin had a particular disorder, the other twin would as well. However, there are no forms of psychopathology in *DSM-IV-TR* where the concordance rates for identical twins are this high, so we can safely conclude that no mental disorders are completely heritable. Nevertheless, as we will see, there are

relatively high concordance rates for identical twins in some more severe forms of psychopathology. These concordance rates are particularly meaningful when they differ from those found for nonidentical twins. *Nonidentical (dizygotic) twins* do not share any more genes than do siblings from the same parents because they develop from two different fertilized eggs. One would therefore expect concordance rates for a disorder to be much lower for dizygotic (DZ) than for monozygotic (MZ) twins if the disorder had a strong genetic component. Thus evidence for genetic transmission of a trait or a disorder can be obtained by comparing the concordance rates between identical and nonidentical twins. For most of the disorders we will discuss, concordance rates are indeed much lower for nonidentical twins than for identical twins.

Some researchers have argued that finding higher concordance rates for a disorder in monozygotic twins than in dizygotic twins is not conclusive evidence of a genetic contribution because it is always possible that identical twins are treated more similarly by their parents and others than are nonidentical twins (Bouchard & Propping, 1993; Torgersen, 1993). However, research has provided reasonably strong evidence that the genetic similarity is more important than the similarity of the parents' behavior (e.g., Hettema, Neale, & Kendler, 1995; Plomin et al., 2008; Rutter, 2006). Nevertheless, the ideal study of genetic factors in psychopathology involves identical twins who have been reared apart in significantly different environments.

This set of identical twins from Bouchard's University of Minnesota Study of Twins Reared Apart pose here with Dr. Nancy Segal, co-director of the project. Mark Newman (left) and Gerry Levey (right) were separated at birth and raised by different parents. Both were dedicated firefighters in different New Jersey towns and met after someone mistook one of them at a firemen's convention for his twin. Both had highly similar patterns of baldness and were 6'4" tall. They both loved Budweiser beer (which they both held by placing their pinky finger under the beer can) as well as Chinese and Italian food. Both had been smokers until recently, when one had quit. They both also liked hunting and fishing and always carried knives. These eerie similarities between identical twins reared apart have been observed in many such twins as well (Segal, 2005).

Unfortunately, finding such twins is extremely difficult (there are probably only a few hundred pairs in the United States), and so only a few such small studies have been done.

The third method used to study genetic influences is the **adoption method**. This method capitalizes on the fact that adoption creates a situation in which individuals who do not share a common family environment are nonetheless genetically related (e.g., Plomin et al., 2008). In one variation on this method, the biological parents of individuals who have a given disorder (and who were adopted away shortly after birth) are compared with the biological parents of individuals without the disorder (who also were adopted away shortly after birth) to determine their rates of disorder. If there is a genetic influence, one expects to find higher rates of the disorder in the biological relatives of those with the disorder than in those without the disorder. In another variation, researchers compare the rates of disorder in the adopted-away offspring of biological parents who have a disorder with those seen in the adopted-away offspring of normal biological parents. If there is a genetic influence, then there should be higher rates of disorder in the adopted-away offspring of the biological parents who have the disorder.

Although pitfalls can arise in interpreting each of these methods, if the results from studies using all three strategies converge, one can draw reasonably strong conclusions about the genetic influence on a disorder (Plomin et al., 2008; Rutter, 1991). Developments in Thinking 2 considers various misconceptions about studies of genetics and psychopathology.

---

2 DEVELOPMENTS IN THINKING

Nature, Nurture, and Psychopathology: A New Look at an Old Topic

People have abundant misconceptions and stereotypes about studies of genetic influences on behavior, traits, and psychopathology, many stemming from outdated ideas that nature and nurture are separate rather than in constant interplay. Indeed, as we have seen in the examples of genotype-environment correlations and interactions, "In the great majority of cases, both psychological traits and mental disorders are multifactorial in origin—meaning that they involve some kind of combination, and interplay, among several genetic factors providing contributions to susceptibility or liability and several environmental factors that similarly play a part in the causal pathway" (Rutter, 2006, p. 29). Several of the more important misconceptions are presented here (Plomin et al., 2008; Rutter, 1991, 2006).

1. *Misconception:* Strong genetic effects mean that environmental influences must be unimportant. *Fact:* Even if we are discussing a trait or disorder that has a strong genetic influence, environmental factors can have a major impact on the level of that trait (Rutter, 2006). Height, for example, is strongly genetically determined, and yet nutritional factors have a very large effect on the actual height a person attains. Between 1900 and 1960 the average height of boys reared in London increased about 4 inches, thanks only to improvements in diet (Tizard, 1975).

2. *Misconception:* Genes provide a limit to potential. *Fact:* One's potential can change if one's environment changes, as the height example above illustrates. Another example comes from children born to socially disadvantaged parents but who are adopted and reared with socially advantaged parents. These children have a mean IQ about 12 points higher than those reared in the socially disadvantaged environment (Capron & Duyme, 1989; see also Duyme et al., 2004).

3. *Misconception:* Genetic strategies are of no value for studying environmental influences. *Fact:* The opposite is true because genetic research strategies provide critical tests of environmental influences on personality and psychopathology (Rutter, 2006). For example, because monozygotic twins have identical genes, concordance rates of less than 100 percent clearly illustrate the importance of environmental influences (Bouchard & Loehlin, 2001; Rutter, 2006a).

4. *Misconception:* Genetic effects diminish with age. *Fact:* Although many people assume that genetic effects should be maximal at birth, with environmental influences getting stronger with increasing age, it is now evident that this is not always true (Plomin, 1986; Rutter, 2006). For height, weight, and IQ, dizygotic twins are almost as alike as monozygotic twins in early infancy, but over time dizygotic twins show greater differences than monozygotic twins. For whatever reasons, many genetic effects on psychological characteristics increase with age up to at least middle childhood or even young adulthood. Moreover, other genetic effects do not appear until much later in life.

5. *Misconception:* Disorders that run in families must be genetic, and those that do not run in families must not be genetic. *Fact:* Many examples contradict these misconceptions. For example, teenage-onset juvenile delinquency tends to run in families, and yet this seems to be due primarily to environmental rather than genetic influences (Plomin et al., 2008; Rutter, 2006a). Conversely, autism is such a rare disorder that it doesn't appear to run in families (only about 3 percent of siblings have the disorder), and yet there seems to be a very powerful genetic effect (Plomin et al., 2008; Rutter, 2006a).

**SEPARATING GENETIC AND ENVIRONMENTAL IN-
FLUENCES** Because all of the three types of heritability studies separate heredity from environment to some extent, they
also allow for testing the influence of environmental factors
and even for differentiating "shared" and "nonshared" environmental influences (Plomin & Daniels, 1987; Plomin et al.,
2008; Rutter, 2006). *Shared environmental influences* are those
that would make children in a family more similar, whether
the influence occurs within the family (e.g., family discord and
poverty) or in the environment (e.g., two high-quality schools,
with one twin going to each). *Nonshared environmental influences* are those in which the children in a family differ. These
would include unique experiences at school and also some
unique features of upbringing in the home, such as a parent
treating one child in a qualitatively different way from another.
An example of nonshared influences occurs when parents who
are quarreling and showing hostility to one another draw some
children into the conflict while others are able to remain outside it (Plomin et al., 2008; Rutter, 2006a; Rutter et al., 1993).
For many important psychological characteristics and forms
of psychopathology, nonshared influences have appeared to
be more important—that is, experiences that are specific to a
child may do more to influence his or her behavior and adjustment than experiences shared by all children in the family
(Plomin et al., 2008; Rutter, 1991, 2006).

LINKAGE ANALYSIS AND ASSOCIATION STUDIES
More recent molecular genetic methods used to study genetic
influences on mental disorders include *linkage analysis* and *association studies*. Whereas the methods previously described
attempt to obtain quantitative estimates of the degree of genetic
influence for different disorders, linkage analysis and association studies attempt to determine the actual location of genes
responsible for mental disorders. Considerable excitement surrounds such work because identifying the location of genes for
certain disorders could provide promising leads for new forms
of treatment and even prevention of those disorders.

Linkage analysis studies of mental disorders capitalize on several currently known locations on chromosomes of
genes for other inherited physical characteristics or biological
processes (such as eye color, blood group, etc.). For example,
researchers might conduct a large family pedigree study on
schizophrenia, looking at all known relatives of a person with
schizophrenia going back several generations. At the same
time, however, they might also keep track of something like
the eye color of each individual (as well as which *DSM* diagnoses they have). Eye color might be chosen because it has a
known genetic marker located on a particular chromosome.
If the researchers found that the familial patterns for schizophrenia in one family pedigree (a sample of all relatives) were
closely linked to the familial patterns for eye color in the same
pedigree, they could infer that a gene affecting schizophrenia
must be located very nearby on the chromosome that contains the known genetic marker for eye color. In other words,
in this case one would expect all members of a particular

family pedigree with schizophrenia to have the same eye color
(e.g., blue), even though all members of a different family pedigree with schizophrenia might have brown eyes.

A number of published studies over the past 20 years using linkage analysis have provided evidence supporting, for
example, the location of a gene for bipolar disorder on chromosome 11 (e.g., Egeland et al., 1987) and the location of
genes for schizophrenia on particular parts of chromosomes
22, 6, 8, and 1 (e.g., Heinrichs, 2001). However, numerous
other studies have failed to replicate these results. Therefore,
most results are considered inconclusive at the present time
(eg., Carey, 2003; Rutter, 2006). Part of the problem in coming up with replicable results in such studies is that most of
these disorders are influenced by many different genes spread
over multiple chromosomes. To date, these linkage analysis
techniques have been most successful in locating the genes
for single-gene brain disorders such as Huntington's disease
(Plomin et al., 2008; Rutter, 2006).

Association studies start with two large groups of individuals, one group with and one group without a given disorder. Researchers then compare the frequencies in these two
groups of certain genetic markers that are known to be located
on particular chromosomes (such as eye color, blood group,
etc.). If one or more of the known genetic markers occur with
much higher frequency in the individuals with the disorder
than in the people without the disorder, the researchers infer
that one or more genes associated with the disorder are located
on the same chromosome. Ideally, the search for gene candidates for a given disorder starts with known genes for some
biological process that is disrupted in the disorder (see Moffitt
et al., 2005). For example, one study found that the genetic markers for certain aspects of dopamine functioning were present
significantly more frequently in the children with hyperactivity
than in the children without hyperactivity. This led researchers
to infer that some of the genes involved with hyperactivity are
located near the known genetic markers for dopamine functioning (Thapar et al., 2006; see also Plomin et al., 2008). For most
mental disorders that are known to be influenced polygenically,
association studies are more promising than linkage studies for
identifying small effects of any particular gene.

In summary, these molecular genetic studies using linkage
and association methodologies may hold tremendous promise
for identifying new prevention or treatment approaches. However, at present that promise has not been fulfilled because of
difficulties in producing replicable results.

Temperament

Temperament refers to a child's reactivity and characteristic
ways of self-regulation. When we say that babies differ in temperament, we mean that they show differences in their characteristic emotional and arousal responses to various stimuli
and in their tendency to approach, withdraw, or attend to various situations (Rothbart, Derryberry, & Hershey, 2000). Some
babies are startled by slight sounds or cry when sunlight hits

their faces; others are seemingly insensitive to such stimulation. These behaviors are strongly influenced by genetic factors, but prenatal and postnatal environmental factors also play a role in their development (Goldsmith, 2003; Rothbart et al., 2000).

Our early temperament is thought to be the basis from which our personality develops. Starting at about 2 to 3 months of age, approximately five dimensions of temperament can be identified: fearfulness, irritability and frustration, positive affect, activity level, and attentional persistence and effortful control, although some of these emerge later than others. These seem to be related to the three important dimensions of adult personality: (1) neuroticism or negative emotionality, (2) extraversion or positive emotionality, and (3) constraint (conscientiousness and agreeableness; Rothbart & Ahadi, 1994; Rothbart & Bates, 2006; Watson, Clark, & Harkness, 1994). The infant dimensions of fearfulness and irritability, which show few gender differences (Else-Quest et al.,

A child with a fearful and anxious temperament can become very distressed with changes in the environment, such as his mother leaving for work.

2006), correspond to the adult dimension of neuroticism—the disposition to experience negative affect. The infant dimensions of positive affect and possibly activity level seem related to the adult dimension of extraversion, and the infant dimension of attentional persistence and effortful control seem related to the adult dimension of constraint or control. One quantitative review concluded that, on average, boys show slightly higher levels of activity and intense pleasure than do girls, whereas girls, on average, seem to have greater control of their impulses and greater ability to regulate their attention (e.g., Else-Quest et al., 2006). At least some aspects of temperament show a moderate degree of stability from late in the first year of life through at least middle childhood, although temperament can also change (e.g., Fox et al., 2005; Kagan, 2003; Rothbart et al., 2000).

Just as we saw in the discussion of genotype–environment correlations, the temperament of an infant or young child has profound effects on a variety of important developmental processes (Fox et al., 2010; Rothbart et al., 2000). For example, a child with a fearful temperament has many opportunities for the classical conditioning of fear to situations in which fear is provoked; later the child may learn to avoid entering those feared situations, and evidence suggests that he or she may be especially likely to learn to fear social situations (Fox et al., 2010; Kagan, 2003). In addition, children with high levels of positive affect and activity are more likely to show high

levels of mastery motivation, whereas children with high levels of fear and sadness are less likely to show mastery motivation (Posner & Rothbart, 2007).

Finally, children with high levels of negative emotionality are more difficult for parents to be supportive of, and different parents have different styles of parenting such children. This seems to be true especially in families with lower socioeconomic status, which are, on average, less supportive of difficult children than families of mid to high socioeconomic status. The latter families seem to be more resourceful in adapting their parenting styles when faced with such high negative emotionality in a child (Paulussen-Hoogeboom et al., 2007).

Not surprisingly, temperament may also set the stage for the development of various forms of psychopathology later in life. For example, children who are fearful and hypervigilant in many novel or unfamiliar situations have been labeled *behaviorally inhibited* by Kagan, Fox, and their colleagues. This trait has a significant heritable component (Kagan, 2003) and, when it is stable, is a risk factor for the development of anxiety disorders later in childhood and probably in adulthood (e.g., Fox et al., 2005, 2010; Kagan, 2003). Conversely, 2-year-old children who are highly *uninhibited*, showing little fear of anything, may have difficulty learning moral standards for their behavior from parents or society (Frick, Cornell, Bodin, et al., 2003; Rothbart, Ahadi, & Evans, 2000), and they have been shown at age 13 to exhibit more aggressive and delinquent behavior (Schwartz, Snidman, & Kagan, 1996). If these personality ingredients are combined with high levels of hostility, the stage also might be set for the development of conduct disorder and antisocial personality disorder (Harpur et al., 1993).

Brain Dysfunction and Neural Plasticity

As noted earlier, specific brain lesions with observable defects in brain tissue are rarely a primary cause of psychiatric disorders. However, advances in understanding how more subtle deficiencies of brain structure or function are implicated in many mental disorders have been increasing at a rapid pace in the past few decades. Some of these advances come from the increased availability of sophisticated new neuroimaging techniques to study the function and structure of the brain. These and other kinds of techniques have shown that genetic programs for brain development are not so rigid and deterministic as was once believed (e.g., Gottesman & Hanson, 2005; Nelson & Bloom, 1997; Thompson & Nelson, 2001). Instead, there is considerable *neural plasticity*—flexibility of the brain in making changes in organization and function in response to pre- and postnatal experiences, stress, diet, disease, drugs, maturation, and so forth. Existing neural circuits can be modified, or new neural circuits can be generated (e.g., Fox et al., 2010; Kolb et al., 2003). The effects can be either beneficial or detrimental to the individual, depending on the circumstances.

One example of the positive effects of *prenatal experiences* comes from an experiment in which pregnant rats housed in complex, enriched environments had offspring that were less negatively affected by brain injury that occurred early in development than those without the same positive prenatal experiences (Kolb et al., 2003). One example of negative effects of prenatal experiences comes from an experiment in which pregnant monkeys exposed to unpredictable loud sounds had infants that were jittery and showed neurochemical abnormalities (specifically, elevated levels of circulating catecholamines; Schneider, 1992). Many *postnatal environmental events* also affect the brain development of the infant and child (Nelson & Bloom, 1997; Thompson & Nelson, 2001). For example, the formation of new neural connections (or synapses) after birth is dramatically affected by the experiences a young organism has (e.g., Greenough & Black, 1992; Rosenzweig et al., 2002). Rats reared in enriched environments (as opposed to in isolation) show heavier and thicker cell development in certain portions of the cortex (as well as more synapses per neuron). Similar but less extensive changes can occur in older animals exposed to enriched environments; hence neural plasticity continues to some extent throughout the life span (see Fox et al., 2010; Lambert & Kinsley, 2005).

The early implications of this kind of work were taken to suggest that human infants should be exposed to highly enriched environments. However, subsequent work has shown that normal rearing conditions with caring parents are perfectly adequate. What later work really showed is that unstimulating, deprived environments can cause retarded development (Thompson, 2000; Thompson & Nelson, 2001).

This research on neural and behavioral plasticity, in combination with the work described earlier on genotype–environment correlations, makes it clear why developmental psychopathologists have been devoting increasing attention to a **developmental systems approach** (e.g., Masten, 2006; Spencer et al., 2009). This approach acknowledges not only that genetic activity influences neural activity, which in turn influences behavior, which in turn influences the environment, but also that these influences are bidirectional. Thus Figure 6 illustrates this first direction of influence but also shows how various aspects of our environment (physical,

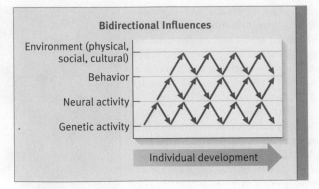

FIGURE 6

Bidirectional Influences

A systems view of psychobiological development.
Source: From Gilbert Gottlieb. 1992. *Individual Development and Evolution: The Genesis of Novel Behavior.* New York: Oxford University Press. Reprinted by permission of Lawrence Erlbaum Associates.

social, and cultural) also influence our behavior, which in turn affects our neural activity, and this in turn can even influence genetic activity (Gottlieb, 1992; Gottlieb & Halpern, 2002; see also Gottesman & Hanson, 2005; Masten, 2006).

The Impact of the Biological Viewpoint

Biological discoveries have profoundly affected the way we think about human behavior. We now recognize the important role of biochemical factors and innate characteristics, many of which are genetically determined, in both normal and abnormal behavior. In addition, since the 1950s we have witnessed many new developments in the use of drugs that can dramatically alter the severity and course of certain mental disorders—particularly the more severe ones such as schizophrenia and manic depressive illness (bipolar disorder). The host of new drugs has attracted a great deal of attention to the biological viewpoint not only in scientific circles but also in the popular media. Biological treatments seem to have more immediate results than other available therapies, and the hope is that they may in most cases lead to a "cure-all"—immediate results with seemingly little effort.

However, as Gorenstein (1992) and others argued two decades ago, there are several common errors in the way many people interpret the meaning of recent biological advances. Gorenstein points out that it is illusory to think—as some prominent biological researchers have—that establishing biological differences between, for example, individuals with schizophrenia and those without schizophrenia in and of itself substantiates that schizophrenia is an illness (e.g., Andreasen, 1984; Kety, 1974). All behavioral traits (introversion and extraversion, for example, or high and low sensation seeking) are characterized by distinctive biological characteristics, yet we do not label these traits as illnesses. Thus the decision about what constitutes a mental illness or disorder ultimately still rests on clinical judgment regarding the functional effects of the disordered behavior—specifically whether it leads to clinically significant distress or impairment in functioning. Establishing the biological substrate does not bear on this issue because all behavior—normal and abnormal—has a biological substrate.

As Gorenstein (1992) also pointed out, the effects of psychological events are always **mediated** through the activities of the central nervous system because all our behaviors, beliefs, emotions, and cognitions are ultimately reducible to a set of biological events in the brain. In actuality, then, if we find some dysfunction of the nervous system, this dysfunction could have arisen from psychological causes as well as from biological causes. In addition, psychological treatments are often as effective as drugs in producing changes in brain structure and function (e.g., Baxter et al., 2000; Linden, 2006).

At a more general level, we must remind ourselves again that few, if any, mental disorders are independent of people's personalities or of the problems they face in trying to live their lives. We will examine viewpoints that emphasize these psychological and sociocultural considerations later in the text, keeping in mind that the ultimate challenge will be to integrate these varying perspectives into a theoretically consistent biopsychosocial perspective on psychopathology.

RESEARCH CLOSE-UP

Mediate

A mediator (or mediating variable) lies between two other variables and helps explain the relationship between them. You can think of it as being like an intermediate variable, hence the name.

The Psychological Viewpoints

There are many more psychological than biological interpretations of abnormal behavior, reflecting a wider range of opinions on how best to understand humans as people with motives, desires, perceptions, thoughts, and so on rather than just as biological organisms. We will examine in some depth three perspectives on human nature and behavior that have been particularly influential: psychodynamic, behavioral, and cognitive-behavioral. (See Figure 7.) These three viewpoints represent distinct and sometimes conflicting orientations, but they are in many ways complementary. They all emphasize the importance of early experience and an awareness of psychological processes within an individual, as well as how these are influenced by social factors.

The Psychodynamic Perspectives

Sigmund Freud founded the *psychoanalytic school*, which emphasized the role of unconscious motives and thoughts and their dynamic interrelationships in the determination of both normal and abnormal behavior. A key concept here is the *unconscious*. According to Freud, the conscious part of the mind represents a relatively small area, whereas the unconscious part, like the submerged part of an iceberg, is the much larger portion. In the depths of the unconscious are the hurtful memories, forbidden desires, and other experiences that

In Review

- Describe the sequence of events involved in the transmission of nerve impulses.

- Explain how neurotransmitter and hormonal abnormalities might produce abnormal behavior.

- What is the relationship between an individual's genotype and phenotype, and how can genotypes shape and interact with the environment?

- Describe at least two methods for studying genetic influences on abnormal behavior.

- What is temperament, and why is it important for the origins of abnormal behavior?

- What do we mean by "neural plasticity"?

- ▶ The psychosocial perspectives attempt to understand humans not just as biological organisms but also as people with motives, desires, and perceptions.

- ▶ There are three major psychosocial perspectives on human nature and behavior:
  1. Psychodynamic
  2. Behavioral
  3. Cognitive-behavioral

- ▶ Also includes two other perspectives:
  1. The humanistic perspective
  2. The existential perspective

FIGURE 7

Psychosocial Perspectives

have been repressed—that is, pushed out of consciousness. However, Freud believed that unconscious material continues to seek expression and emerges in fantasies, dreams, slips of the tongue, and so forth. Until such unconscious material is brought to awareness and integrated into the conscious part of the mind—for example, through psychoanalysis (a form of psychotherapy Freud developed)—it may lead to irrational and maladaptive behavior. For our purposes, a general overview of the principles of classical psychoanalytic theory will suffice (see Alexander, 1948; Arlow, 2000; Luborsky & Barrett, 2006; or any of Freud's original works for more information). We will then discuss several of the newer *psychodynamic perspectives*, which were the second generation of theories that stemmed in some important ways out of Freud's original psychoanalytic theory and yet also departed from it in significant ways.

FUNDAMENTALS OF FREUD'S PSYCHOANALYTIC THEORY

The Structure of Personality: Id, Ego, and Superego

Freud theorized that a person's behavior results from the interaction of three key components of the personality or psyche: the id, ego, and superego (e.g., see Arlow, 2000; Engler, 2006). The **id** is the source of instinctual drives and is the first structure to appear in infancy. These drives are inherited and are considered to be of two opposing types: (1) *life instincts*, which are constructive drives primarily of a sexual nature and which constitute the **libido**, the basic emotional and psychic energy of life; and (2) *death instincts*, which are destructive drives that tend toward aggression, destruction, and eventual death. Freud used the term *sexual* in a broad sense to refer to almost anything pleasurable, from eating to painting. The id operates on the **pleasure principle**, engaging in completely selfish and pleasure-oriented behavior, concerned only with the immediate gratification of instinctual needs without reference to reality or moral considerations. Although the id can generate mental images and wish-fulfilling fantasies, referred to as **primary process thinking**, it cannot undertake the realistic actions needed to meet instinctual demands.

Consequently, after the first few months of life, a second part of the personality, as viewed by Freud, develops—the **ego**. The ego mediates between the demands of the id and the realities of the

Anxiety is almost universally experienced at some point. This woman shows her anxiety while awaiting news about the outcome of surgery on her sick child.

external world. For example, during toilet training the child learns to control a bodily function to meet parental and societal expectations, and it is the developing ego that assumes the role of mediating between the physical needs of the body/id and the need to find an appropriate place and time. One of the basic functions of the ego is to meet id demands, but in such a way as to ensure the well-being and survival of the individual. This role requires the use of reason and other intellectual resources in dealing with the external world, as well as the exercise of control over id demands. The ego's adaptive measures are referred to as **secondary process thinking**, and the ego operates on the **reality principle**.

Freud viewed id demands, especially sexual and aggressive strivings, as inherently in conflict with the rules and prohibitions imposed by society. He postulated that as a child grows and gradually learns the rules of parents and society regarding right and wrong, a third part of the personality gradually emerges from the ego—the **superego**. The superego is the outgrowth of internalizing the taboos and moral values of society concerning what is right and wrong. It is essentially what we refer to as the *conscience*. As the superego develops, it becomes an inner control system that deals with the uninhibited desires of the id. Because the ego mediates among the desires of the id, the demands of reality, and the moral constraints of the superego, it is often called the *executive branch of the personality*.

Freud believed that the interplay of id, ego, and superego is of crucial significance in determining behavior. Often inner mental conflicts arise because the three subsystems are striving for different goals. If unresolved, these **intrapsychic conflicts** lead to mental disorder.

Anxiety, Defense Mechanisms, and the Unconscious

The concept of *anxiety*—generalized feelings of fear and apprehension—is prominent in the psychoanalytic viewpoint because it is an almost universal symptom of neurotic disorders. Indeed, Freud believed that anxiety plays a key causal role in most of the forms of psychopathology. He believed that the anxiety is sometimes overtly experienced, and at other times it is repressed and then transformed into and manifested in other overt symptoms such as conversion blindness or paralysis.

Anxiety is a warning of impending real or imagined dangers as well as a painful experience, and it forces an individual to take corrective action. Often, the ego can cope with objective anxiety through rational measures. However, neurotic and moral anxiety, because they are unconscious, usually cannot be dealt with through rational measures. In these cases the ego resorts to irrational protective measures that are referred to as **ego-defense mechanisms**, some of which are described in Table 1. These defense mechanisms discharge or soothe anxiety, but they do so by helping a person push painful ideas out of consciousness (such as when we "forget" a dental appointment) rather than by dealing directly with the problem. These mechanisms result in a distorted view of reality, although some are clearly more adaptive than others.

Psychosexual Stages of Development In addition to his concept of the structure of personality, Freud also conceptualized five **psychosexual stages of development** that we all pass through from infancy through puberty. Each stage is characterized by a dominant mode of achieving libidinal (sexual) pleasure:

1. **Oral stage:** During the first 2 years of life, the mouth is the principal erogenous zone: An infant's greatest source of gratification is sucking, a process that is necessary for feeding.

2. **Anal stage:** From ages 2 to 3, the anus provides the major source of pleasurable stimulation during the time when toilet training is often going on and there are urges both for retention and for elimination.

3. **Phallic stage:** From ages 3 to 5 or 6, self-manipulation of the genitals provides the major source of pleasurable sensation.

4. **Latency period:** From ages 6 to 12, sexual motivations recede in importance as a child becomes preoccupied with developing skills and other activities.

5. **Genital stage:** After puberty, the deepest feelings of pleasure come from sexual relations.

Freud believed that appropriate gratification during each stage is important if a person is to avoid being stuck, or *fixated*, at that level. For example, he maintained that an infant who does not receive adequate oral gratification may, in adult life, be prone to excessive eating or other forms of oral stimulation, such as biting fingernails, smoking, or drinking.

The demands of the id are evident in early childhood. According to Freud, babies pass through an oral stage, in which sucking is a dominant pleasure.

table 1 Ego-Defense Mechanisms

Mechanism	Example
Displacement. Discharging pent-up feelings, often of hostility, on objects less dangerous than those arousing the feelings.	A woman harassed by her boss at work initiates an argument with her husband.
Fixation. Attaching oneself in an unreasonable or exaggerated way to some person, or arresting emotional development on a childhood or adolescent level.	An unmarried, middle-aged man still depends on his mother to provide his basic needs.
Projection. Attributing one's unacceptable motives or characteristics to others.	An expansionist-minded dictator of a totalitarian state is convinced that neighboring countries are planning to invade.
Rationalization. Using contrived explanations to conceal or disguise unworthy motives for one's behavior.	A fanatical racist uses ambiguous passages from the Scriptures to justify his hostile actions toward minorities.
Reaction formation. Preventing the awareness or expression of unacceptable desires by an exaggerated adoption of seemingly opposite behavior.	A man troubled by homosexual urges initiates a zealous community campaign to stamp out gay bars.
Regression. Retreating to an earlier developmental level involving less mature behavior and responsibility.	A man with shattered self-esteem reverts to childlike "showing off" and exhibits his genitals to young girls.
Repression. Preventing painful or dangerous thoughts from entering consciousness.	A mother's occasional murderous impulses toward her hyperactive 2-year-old are denied access to awareness.
Sublimation. Channeling frustrated sexual energy into substitutive activities.	A sexually frustrated artist paints wildly erotic pictures.

Source: Based on A. Freud (1946) and *DSM-IV-TR* (2000).

The Oedipus Complex and the Electra Complex In general, each psychosexual stage of development places demands on a child and arouses conflicts that Freud believed must be resolved in order to avoid later fixations. One of the most important conflicts occurs during the phallic stage, when the pleasures of self-stimulation and accompanying fantasies pave the way for the **Oedipus complex**. According to Greek mythology, Oedipus unknowingly killed his father and married his mother. Each young boy, Freud thought, symbolically relives the Oedipus drama. He longs for his mother sexually and views his father as a hated rival; however, each young boy also fears that his father will punish his son's lust by cutting off his penis. This **castration anxiety** forces the boy to repress his sexual desire for his mother and his hostility toward his father. Eventually, if all goes well, the boy identifies with his father and comes to have only harmless affection for his mother, channeling his sexual impulses toward another woman.

The **Electra complex** is the female counterpart of the Oedipus complex and is also drawn from a Greek tragedy. It is based on the view that each girl desires to possess her father and to replace her mother. Freud also believed that each girl at this stage experiences *penis envy*, wishing she could be more like her father and brothers. She emerges from the complex when she comes to identify with her mother and settles for a promissory note: One day she will have a man of her own who can give her a baby—which unconsciously serves as a type of penis substitute.

Resolution of this conflict is considered essential if a young adult of either sex is to develop satisfactory heterosexual relationships. The psychoanalytic perspective holds that the best we can hope for is to effect a compromise among our warring inclinations—and to realize as much instinctual gratification as possible with minimal punishment and guilt. This perspective thus presents a deterministic view of human behavior that minimizes rationality and freedom of self-determination. On a group level, it interprets violence, war, and related phenomena as the inevitable products of the aggressive and destructive instincts present in human nature.

NEWER PSYCHODYNAMIC PERSPEC-TIVES In seeking to understand his patients and develop his theories, Freud was chiefly concerned with the workings of the id, its nature as a source of energy, and the manner in which this id energy could be channeled or transformed. He also focused on the superego and the role of conscience but paid relatively little attention to the importance of the ego.

Anna Freud (1895–1982) studied the important role of the ego in normal and abnormal development and elaborated the theory of ego-defense reactions.

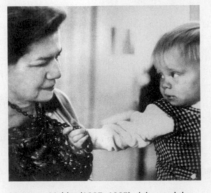

Margaret Mahler (1897–1985) elaborated the object-relations approach, which many see as the main focus of contemporary psychoanalysis.

Later theorists developed some of Freud's basic ideas in three somewhat different directions.

Ego Psychology One new direction was that taken by his daughter Anna Freud (1895–1982), who was much more concerned with how the *ego* performs its central functions as the "executive" of personality. She and some of the other influential second-generation psychodynamic theorists refined and elaborated on the ego-defense mechanisms and put the ego in the foreground, giving it an important organizing role in personality development (e.g., A. Freud, 1946). According to this view, psychopathology develops when the ego does not function adequately to control or delay impulse gratification or does not make adequate use of defense mechanisms when faced with internal conflicts. This school became known as **ego psychology**.

Object-Relations Theory A second new psychodynamic perspective was object-relations theory, developed by a number of prominent theorists including Melanie Klein, Margaret Mahler, W. R. D. Fairburn, and D. W. Winnicott, starting in the 1930s and 1940s. Although there are many variations on **object-relations theory**, they share a focus on individuals' interactions with real and imagined other people (external and internal objects) and on the relationships that people experience between their external and internal objects (Engler, 2006; Greenberg & Mitchell, 1983). *Object* in this context refers to the symbolic representation of another person in the infant's or child's environment, most often a parent. Through a process of *introjection*, a child symbolically incorporates into his or her personality (through images and memories) important people in his or her life. For example, a child might internalize images of a punishing father; that image then becomes a harsh self-critic, influencing how the child behaves. The general notion is that internalized objects could have various conflicting properties—such as exciting or attractive versus hostile, frustrating, or rejecting—and also that these objects could split off from the central ego and maintain independent existences, thus giving rise to inner conflicts. An individual experiencing such splitting among internalized objects is, so to speak, "the servant of many masters" and cannot therefore lead an integrated, orderly life.

Otto Kernberg, for example, is an influential American analyst who has a theory that people with a *borderline personality*, whose chief characteristic is instability (especially in personal relationships), are individuals who are unable to achieve a full and stable personal identity (self) because of an inability to integrate and reconcile pathological internalized objects (Kernberg 1985, 1996;

Kernberg & Caligor, 2005; Kernberg & Michels, 2009). Because of their inability to structure their internal world in such a way that the people they know (including themselves) can have a mixture of both good and bad traits, they also perceive the external world in abrupt extremes. For example, a person may be "all good" one moment and "all bad" the next (Koenigsberg et al., 2000).

The Interpersonal Perspective A third set of second-generation psychodynamic theorists focused on social determinants of behavior. We are social beings, and much of what we are is a product of our relationships with others. It is logical to expect that much of psychopathology reflects this fact—that psychopathology is rooted in the unfortunate tendencies we have developed while dealing with our interpersonal environments. This is the focus of the **interpersonal perspective**, which began with the defection in 1911 of Alfred Adler (1870–1937) from the psychoanalytic viewpoint of his teacher, Sigmund Freud, and emphasizes social and cultural forces rather than inner instincts as determinants of behavior. In Adler's view, people are inherently social beings motivated primarily by the desire to belong to and participate in a group (see Engler, 2006; Mosak, 2000, for recent reviews).

Over time, a number of other psychodynamic theorists also took issue with psychoanalytic theory for its neglect of crucial social factors. Among the best known of these theorists are Erich Fromm (1900–1980) and Karen Horney (1885–1952). Fromm focused on the orientations, or dispositions (exploitive, for example), that people adopted in their interactions with others. He believed that when these orientations to the social environment were maladaptive, they served as the bases of much psychopathology. Horney independently developed a similar view and, in particular, vigorously rejected Freud's demeaning psychoanalytic view of women (for instance, the idea that women experience penis envy).

Erik Erikson (1902–1994) also extended the interpersonal aspects of psychoanalytic theory. He elaborated and broadened Freud's psychosexual stages into more socially oriented concepts, describing crises or conflicts that occurred at eight stages, each of which could be resolved in a healthy or unhealthy way. For example, Erikson believed that during what Freud called the "oral stage," when a child is preoccupied with oral gratification, a child's real development centers on learning either "basic trust" or "basic mistrust" of her or his social world. Achieving a certain level of trust, for instance, is necessary for later competence in many areas of life.

Attachment Theory Finally, John Bowlby's **attachment theory**, which can in many ways be seen as having its roots in the interpersonal and object-relations perspectives, has become an enormously influential theory in child psychology and child psychiatry as well as in adult psychopathology. Drawing on Freud and others from these perspectives, Bowlby's theory (1969, 1973, 1980) emphasizes the importance of early experience, especially early experience with attachment relationships, as laying the foundation for later functioning throughout childhood, adolescence, and adulthood. He stresses the importance of the quality of parental care to the development of secure attachments, but he also sees the infant as playing a more active role in shaping the course of his or her own development than had most of the earlier theorists (Carlson & Sroufe, 1995; Rutter et al., 2009; Sroufe et al., 2003).

IMPACT OF THE PSYCHOANALYTIC PERSPECTIVE

Freud's psychoanalytic theory can be seen as the first systematic approach to showing how human psychological processes can result in mental disorders. Much as the biological perspective had replaced superstition with organic pathology as the suspected cause of mental disorders for many psychiatrists and psychologists, the psychoanalytic perspective replaced brain pathology with intrapsychic conflict and exaggerated ego defenses as the suspected cause of at least some mental disorders.

Freud greatly advanced our understanding of both normal and abnormal behavior. Many of his original concepts have become fundamental to our thinking about human nature and behavior and have even had an important influence on the intellectual history of Western civilization. Two of Freud's contributions stand out as particularly noteworthy:

1. He developed therapeutic techniques such as free association and dream analysis for becoming acquainted with both the conscious and the unconscious aspects of mental life. The results obtained led Freud to emphasize several points that have been incorporated (in modified forms) into current thinking: (a) the extent to which unconscious motives and defense mechanisms affect behavior, meaning that the causes

Erich Fromm (1900–1980) focused on the orientations that people adopt in their interactions with others. He believed that these basic orientations to the social environment were the bases of much psychopathology.

Erik Erikson (1902–1994) elaborated and broadened Freud's psychosexual stages into more socially oriented concepts. Erikson described conflicts that occurred at eight stages, each of which could be resolved in a healthy or unhealthy way.

of human behavior are generally not obvious or available to conscious awareness; (b) the importance of early childhood experiences in the development of both normal and abnormal personality; and (c) the importance of sexual factors in human behavior and mental disorders. Although, as we have said, Freud used the term *sexual* in a much broader sense than usual, the idea struck a common chord, and the role of sexual factors in human behavior was finally brought out into the open as an appropriate topic for scientific investigation.

2. He demonstrated that certain abnormal mental phenomena occur in the attempt to cope with difficult problems and are simply exaggerations of normal ego-defense mechanisms. This realization that the same psychological principles apply to both normal and abnormal behavior dissipated much of the mystery and fear surrounding mental disorders.

The psychoanalytic perspective came under attack, however, from many directions. Two important criticisms of traditional psychoanalytic theory center on its failure as a scientific theory to explain abnormal behavior. First, many believe that it fails to recognize sufficiently the scientific limits of personal reports of experience as the primary mode of obtaining information. Second, there is a lack of scientific evidence to support many of its explanatory assumptions or the effectiveness of traditional psychoanalysis (Erdelyi, 1992; but see also Westen, 1998). In addition, Freudian theory in particular has been criticized for an overemphasis on the sex drive, for its demeaning view of women, for pessimism about basic human nature, for exaggerating the role of unconscious processes, and for failing to consider motives toward personal growth and fulfillment.

IMPACT OF NEWER PSYCHODYNAMIC PERSPEC-TIVES The second generation of psychodynamic theorists has done much to improve scientific efforts to measure concepts such as a person's core (but unconscious) conflictual relationships (e.g., Henry et al., 1994; Horowitz et al., 1991; Luborsky & Barrett, 2006). Some progress has also been made in understanding how psychodynamic therapy works and in documenting its effectiveness for certain problems (e.g., Crits-Christoph & Barber, 2000; Crits-Christoph et al., 2004; Shedler, 2010). In addition, Bowlby's attachment theory has generated an enormous amount of research supporting many of its basic tenets about normal and abnormal child development and adult psychopathology (e.g., Carlson & Sroufe, 1995; Grossman et al., 2005; Rutter, 2006; Rutter et al., 2009).

The interpersonal perspective has also done a good deal to establish its scientific validity. In the area of diagnosis, many supporters of the interpersonal perspective believe that the reliability and validity of psychological diagnoses could be improved if a new system based on interpersonal functioning were developed, and some progress has been made toward developing such a system (e.g., Benjamin, 1993, 2005; Benjamin et al., 2006). The focus of interpersonal therapy is

on alleviating problem-causing relationships and on helping people achieve more satisfactory relationships. In recent years, major progress has been made in documenting that interpersonal psychotherapy for certain disorders such as depression, bulimia, and some personality disorders can be as effective, or nearly as effective, as cognitive-behavioral treatment—considered by many to be the treatment of choice for these disorders (Benjamin, 2004; Benjamin & Pugh, 2001; Hollon et al., 2002; Wilson & Fairburn, 2007).

Developments in Thinking 3 presents two further psychological perspectives that developed in the middle of the twentieth century in part because their founders did not believe that psychodynamic theories acknowledged a person's freedom of choice or the concept of free will.

The Behavioral Perspective

The behavioral perspective arose in the early twentieth century in part as a reaction against the unscientific methods of psychoanalysis. Behavioral psychologists believed that the study of subjective experience (e.g., free association and dream analysis) did not provide acceptable scientific data because such observations were not open to verification by other investigators. In their view, only the study of directly observable behavior and of the stimuli and reinforcing conditions that control it could serve as a basis for understanding human behavior, normal and abnormal.

Although this perspective was initially developed through laboratory research rather than clinical practice with disturbed patients, its implications for explaining and treating maladaptive behavior soon became evident. The roots of the behavioral perspective are in Pavlov's study of classical conditioning and in Thorndike's study of instrumental conditioning (later renamed operant conditioning by Skinner; today both terms are used). In the United States, where the behavioral perspective flourished, Watson did much to promote the behavioral approach to psychology with his book *Behaviorism* (1924).

Learning—the modification of behavior as a consequence of experience—is the central theme of the behavioral approach. Because most human behavior is learned, the behaviorists addressed the question of how learning occurs. Behaviorists focus on the effects of environmental conditions (stimuli) on the acquisition, modification, and possible elimination of various types of response patterns, both adaptive and maladaptive.

CLASSICAL CONDITIONING A specific stimulus may come to elicit a specific response through the process of **classical conditioning**. For example, although food naturally elicits salivation, a stimulus that reliably precedes and signals the presentation of food will also come to elicit salivation (Pavlov, 1927). In this case, food is the *unconditioned stimulus* (UCS) and salivation the *unconditioned response* (UCR). A stimulus that signals food delivery and eventually elicits salivation is

Classical Conditioning

Prior to conditioning:
Conditioned stimulus (neutral) (CS) ....Orientation response to light
(light)
Unconditioned stimulus (UCS) ....Unconditioned response (UCR)
(Painful stimulus)   (Pain and fear)

During conditioning:
Conditioned stimulus (light) (CS)
+   ....Conditioned response (fear) (CR)
Unconditioned stimulus (UCS)
(Painful stimulus)

Following conditioning:
Conditioned stimulus (alone) (CS) ....Conditioned response (fear) (CR)

FIGURE 8

Classical Conditioning

Before conditioning, the CS is neutral and has no capacity to elicit fear. However, after being repeatedly followed by a painful or frightening UCS that elicits pain, fear, or distress, the CS gradually acquires the capacity to elicit a fear CR. If there are also interspersed trials in which the UCS occurs without being preceded by the CS, conditioning does not occur because in this case the CS is not a reliable predictor of the occurrence of the UCS.

called a *conditioned stimulus* (CS). Conditioning has occurred when presentation of the conditioned stimulus alone elicits salivation—the *conditioned response* (CR). The same general process occurs when a neutral CS is paired with a painful or frightening stimulus such as a mild electric shock or loud noise, as illustrated in Figure 8, although in this case fear rather than salivation is conditioned.

The hallmark of classical conditioning is that a formerly neutral stimulus—the CS—acquires the capacity to elicit biologically adaptive responses through repeated pairings with the UCS (e.g., Bouton, 2007; Domjan, 2009). However, we also now know that this process of classical conditioning is not as blind or automatic as was once thought. Rather, it seems that animals (and people) actively acquire information about what CSs allow them to predict, expect, or prepare for an upcoming biologically significant event (the UCS). That is, they learn what is often called a *stimulus-stimulus expectancy.* Indeed, only CSs that provide reliable and nonredundant information about the occurrence of a UCS acquire the capacity to elicit CRs (Hall, 1994; Rescorla, 1988). For example, if UCSs occur as often without being preceded by a CS as they do with the CS, conditioning will not occur because the CS in this case does not provide reliable information about the occurrence of the UCS.

Classically conditioned responses are well maintained over time; that is, they are not simply forgotten (even over many years). However, if a CS is repeatedly presented without the UCS, the conditioned response gradually extinguishes. This gradual process, known as **extinction**, should not be confused with the idea of unlearning because we know that the response may return at some future point in time (a phenomenon Pavlov

called **spontaneous recovery**). Moreover, a somewhat weaker CR may also still be elicited in different environmental contexts than in the one where the extinction process took place (Bouton, 1994, 2002; Bouton et al., 2006). Thus any extinction of fear that has taken place in a therapist's office may not necessarily generalize completely and automatically to other contexts outside the therapist's office (see Craske & Mystkowski, 2006; Mystkowski & Mineka, 2007). These principles of extinction and spontaneous recovery have important implications for many forms of behavioral treatment.

Classical conditioning is important in abnormal psychology because many physiological and emotional responses can be conditioned, including those related to fear, anxiety, or sexual arousal and those stimulated by drugs of abuse. Thus, for example, one can learn a fear of the dark if fear-producing stimuli (such as frightening dreams or fantasies) occur regularly in the dark, or one can acquire a fear of snakes if bitten by a snake (e.g., Mineka & Sutton, 2006; Mineka & Zinbarg, 2006). In addition, a young man who has his first few powerful sexual experiences (UCR) with a very attractive woman (UCS) wearing some form of distinctive clothing (CS—such as black fishnet stockings) may find in the future that he becomes very sexually aroused (CR) simply upon seeing fishnet stockings.

INSTRUMENTAL CONDITIONING In **instrumental** (or **operant**) **conditioning**, an individual learns how to achieve a desired goal. The goal in question may be to obtain something that is rewarding or to escape from something that is unpleasant. Essential here is the concept of **reinforcement**, which refers either to the delivery of a reward or pleasant stimulus, or to the removal of or escape from an aversive

DEVELOPMENTS IN THINKING

3

The Humanistic and Existential Perspectives

The Humanistic Perspective

The *humanistic perspective* views human nature as basically "good." Paying less attention to unconscious processes and past causes, it emphasizes present conscious processes and places strong emphasis on people's inherent capacity for responsible self-direction. Humanistic psychologists think that much of the empirical research designed to investigate causal factors is too simplistic to uncover the complexities of human behavior. Instead, this perspective is concerned with processes such as love, hope, creativity, values, meaning, personal growth, and self-fulfillment. Although these abstract processes are not readily subject to empirical investigation, certain underlying themes and principles of humanistic psychology can be identified, including the self as a unifying theme and a focus on values and personal growth.

In using the concept of *self* as a unifying theme, humanistic psychologists emphasize the importance of individuality. Among humanistic psychologists, Carl Rogers (1902–1987) developed the most systematic formulation of the *self-concept*, based largely on his pioneering research into the nature of the psychotherapeutic process. Rogers (1951, 1959) stated his views in a series of propositions that may be summarized as follows:

- Each individual exists in a private world of experience of which the *I*, *me*, or *myself* is the center.
- The most basic striving of an individual is toward the maintenance, enhancement, and actualization of the self, and his or her inner tendencies are toward health and wholeness under normal conditions.
- A perceived threat to the self is followed by a defense, including a tightening of perception and behavior and the introduction of self-defense mechanisms.

Humanistic psychologists emphasize that values and the process of choice are key in guiding our behavior and achieving meaningful and fulfilling lives. Each of us must develop values and a sense of our own identity based on our own experiences rather than blindly accepting the values of others; otherwise, we deny our own experiences and lose touch with our own feelings. Only in this way can we become *self-actualizing*, meaning that we are achieving our full potential. According to this view, psychopathology is essentially the blocking or distortion of personal growth and the natural tendency toward physical and mental health.

The Existential Perspective

The *existential perspective* resembles the humanistic view in its emphasis on the uniqueness of each individual, the quest for values and meaning, and the existence of freedom for self-direction and self-fulfillment. However, it takes a less optimistic view of human beings and places more emphasis on their irrational tendencies and the difficulties inherent in self-fulfillment—particularly in a modern, bureaucratic, and dehumanizing mass society. In short, living is much more of a "confrontation" for the existentialists than for the humanists. Existential thinkers are especially concerned with the inner experiences of an individual in his or her attempts to understand and deal with the deepest human problems. There are several basic themes of existentialism:

- *Existence and essence.* Our existence is a given, but what we make of it—our essence—is up to us. Our essence is created by our choices because our choices reflect the values on which we base and order our lives.
- *Meaning and value.* The will-to-meaning is a basic human tendency to find satisfying values and guide one's life by them.
- *Existential anxiety and the encounter with nothingness.* Nonbeing, or nothingness, which in its final form is death, is the inescapable fate of all human beings. The awareness of our inevitable death and its implications for our living can lead to existential anxiety, a deep concern over whether we are living meaningful and fulfilling lives.

Thus existential psychologists focus on the importance of establishing values and acquiring a level of spiritual maturity worthy of the freedom and dignity bestowed by one's humanness. Avoiding such central issues creates corrupted, meaningless, and wasted lives. Much abnormal behavior, therefore, is seen as the product of a failure to deal constructively with existential despair and frustration.

---

stimulus. New responses are learned and tend to recur if they are reinforced. Although it was originally thought that instrumental conditioning consisted of simple strengthening of a stimulus–response connection every time that reinforcement occurred, it is now believed that the animal or person learns a *response–outcome expectancy* (e.g., Domjan, 2005)—that is, learns that a response will lead to a reward outcome. If sufficiently motivated for that outcome (e.g., being hungry), the person will make the response that he or she has learned produces the outcome (e.g., opening the refrigerator).

Initially a high rate of reinforcement may be necessary to establish an instrumental response, but lesser rates are usually sufficient to maintain it. In fact, an instrumental response appears to be especially persistent when reinforcement is intermittent—when the reinforcing stimulus does not invariably follow the response—as demonstrated in gambling, when occasional wins seem to maintain high rates of responding. However, when reinforcement is consistently withheld over time, the conditioned response—whether classical or instrumental—gradually extinguishes. In short, the subject eventually stops making the response.

Continuing to play blackjack after an occasional unpredictable win is an example of intermittent reinforcement. Behavior that is reinforced in this unpredictable manner occurs at high rates and is highly resistant to extinction.

A special problem arises conditioning a response in situations in which a subject has been conditioned to anticipate an aversive event and to make an instrumental response to avoid it. For example, a boy who has nearly drowned in a swimming pool may develop a fear of water and a *conditioned avoidance response* in which he consistently avoids all large bodies of water. According to one influential theory, when he sees a pond, lake, or swimming pool, he feels anxious; running away and avoiding contact lessens his anxiety and thus is reinforcing. As a result, his avoidance response is highly resistant to extinction. It also prevents him from having experiences with water that could bring about extinction of his fear. In later discussions, we will see that conditioned avoidance responses play a role in many patterns of abnormal behavior.

As we grow up, instrumental learning becomes an important mechanism for discriminating between what will prove rewarding and what will prove unrewarding—and thus for acquiring the behaviors essential for coping with our world. Unfortunately, what we learn is not always useful in the long run. We may learn to value things (such as cigarettes or alcohol) that seem attractive in the short run but that can actually hurt us in the long run, or we may learn coping patterns (such as helplessness, bullying, or other irresponsible behaviors) that are maladaptive rather than adaptive in the long run.

GENERALIZATION AND DISCRIMINATION In both classical and instrumental conditioning, when a response is conditioned to one stimulus or set of stimuli, it can be evoked by other, similar stimuli; this process is called **generalization**. A person who fears bees, for example, may generalize that fear to all flying insects. A process complementary to generalization is **discrimination**, which occurs when a person learns to distinguish between similar stimuli and to respond differently to them based on which ones are followed by reinforcement. For example, because red strawberries taste good and green ones do not, a conditioned discrimination will occur if a person has experience with both.

The concepts of generalization and discrimination have many implications for the development of maladaptive behavior. Although generalization enables us to use past experiences in sizing up new situations, the possibility of making inappropriate generalizations always exists, as when a troubled adolescent fails to discriminate between friendly and hostile teasing from peers. In some instances, an important discrimination seems to be beyond an individual's capability (as when a bigoted person deals with others on the basis of stereotypes rather than as individuals) and may lead to inappropriate and maladaptive behavior.

OBSERVATIONAL LEARNING Human and nonhuman primates are also capable of **observational learning**—that is, learning through observation alone, without directly experiencing an unconditioned stimulus (for classical conditioning) or a reinforcement (for instrumental conditioning). For instance, children can acquire new fears simply observing a parent or peer behaving fearfully with some object or situation that the child did not initially fear. In this case, they experience the fear of the parent or peer vicariously, and that fear becomes attached to the formerly neutral object (Mineka & Oehlberg, 2008; Mineka & Cook, 1993; Mineka & Sutton, 2006). For observational instrumental learning, Bandura did a classic series of experiments in the 1960s on how children observationally learned various novel, aggressive responses toward a large Bobo doll after they had observed models being reinforced for these responses (see Bandura, 1969). Although the children themselves were never directly reinforced for showing these novel aggressive responses, they nonetheless showed them when given the opportunity to interact with the Bobo doll themselves. The possibilities for observational conditioning of both classical and instrumental responses greatly expand our opportunities for learning both adaptive and maladaptive behavior.

IMPACT OF THE BEHAVIORAL PERSPECTIVE Because there was so much resistance from well-entrenched supporters of psychoanalysis, behavior therapy did not become well established as a powerful way of viewing and treating abnormal behavior until the 1960s and 1970s. By then, the behavioral assault on the prevailing psychodynamic doctrine of the time (Salter, 1949; Wolpe, 1958) was well underway and important evidence had been gathered on the power of behavior therapy techniques.

By means of relatively few basic concepts, the behavioral perspective attempts to explain the acquisition, modification, and extinction of nearly all types of behavior. Maladaptive behavior is viewed as essentially the result of (1) a failure to learn necessary adaptive behaviors or competencies, such as how to establish satisfying personal relationships, and/or (2) the learning of ineffective or maladaptive responses. Maladaptive behavior is thus the result of learning that has gone awry and is defined in terms of specific, observable, undesirable responses.

For the behavior therapist, the focus of therapy is on changing specific behaviors and emotional responses—eliminating undesirable reactions and learning desirable ones. For example, fears and phobias can be successfully treated by prolonged exposure to the feared objects or situations—an extinction procedure derived from principles of extinction of classical conditioning. Or an inappropriate sexual attraction to a deviant stimulus (such as prepubertal children) can be altered by pairing pictures of the deviant stimuli with a foul odor or another unpleasant stimulus. Classic work using the principles of instrumental conditioning also showed that chronically mentally ill people in institutions can be retaught basic living skills such as clothing and feeding themselves through the use of tokens that are earned for appropriate behavior and that can be turned in for desirable rewards (candy, time watching television, passes to go outside, etc.).

The behavioral approach is well known for its precision and objectivity, for its wealth of research, and for its demonstrated effectiveness in changing specific behaviors. A behavior therapist specifies what behavior is to be changed and how it is to be changed. Later, the effectiveness of the therapy can be evaluated objectively by the degree to which the stated goals have been achieved. Nevertheless, the behavioral perspective has been criticized for several reasons. One early criticism was that behavior therapy was concerned only with symptoms, not underlying causes. However, this criticism has been considered unfair by many contemporary behavior therapists, given that successful symptom-focused treatment often has very positive effects on other aspects of a person's life (e.g., Borkovec et al., 1995; Lenz & Demal, 2000). Still others have argued that the behavioral approach oversimplifies human behavior and is unable to explain all of its complexities. This latter criticism stems at least in part from misunderstandings about current developments in behavioral approaches (e.g., Bouton, 2007; Bouton et al., 2001; Mineka & Zinbarg, 2006; Mineka & Oehlberg, 2008). Whatever its limitations, the behavioral perspective has had a tremendous impact on contemporary views of human nature, behavior, and psychopathology.

The Cognitive-Behavioral Perspective

Since the 1950s many psychologists, including some learning theorists, have focused on cognitive processes and their impact on behavior. Cognitive psychology involves the study of basic information-processing mechanisms such as attention and memory, as well as higher mental processes such as thinking, planning, and decision making. The current emphasis within psychology as a whole on understanding all of these facets of normal human cognition originally began as a reaction against

Albert Bandura (b. 1925) stressed that people learn more by internal than external reinforcement. They can visualize the consequences of their actions rather than rely exclusively on environmental reinforcements.

the relatively mechanistic nature of the traditional, radical behavioral viewpoint (espoused by Watson and Skinner), including its failure to attend to the importance of mental processes—both in their own right and for their influence on emotions and behavior.

Albert Bandura (b. 1925), a learning theorist who developed an early cognitive-behavioral perspective, placed considerable emphasis on the cognitive aspects of learning. Bandura stressed that human beings regulate behavior by internal symbolic processes—thoughts. That is, we learn by *internal reinforcement*. According to Bandura, we prepare ourselves for difficult tasks, for example, by visualizing what the consequences would be if we did not perform them. Thus we take our automobiles to the garage in the fall and have the antifreeze checked because we can "see" ourselves stranded on a road in winter. We do not always require external reinforcement to alter our behavior patterns; our cognitive abilities allow us to solve many problems internally. Bandura (1974) went so far as to say that human beings have "a capacity for self-direction" (p. 861). Bandura later developed a theory of *self-efficacy*, the belief that one can achieve desired goals (1986, 1997). He posited that cognitive-behavioral treatments work in large part by improving self-efficacy.

Other cognitive-behavioral theorists abandoned the learning theory framework more vigorously than did Bandura and focused almost exclusively on cognitive processes and their impact on behavior. Today the cognitive or **cognitive-behavioral perspective** on abnormal behavior generally focuses on how thoughts and information processing can become distorted and lead to maladaptive emotions and behavior. One central construct for this perspective is the concept of a schema, which was adapted from cognitive psychology by Aaron Beck (b. 1921), another pioneering cognitive theorist (e.g., Beck, 1967; Neisser, 1967, 1982). A **schema** is an underlying representation of knowledge that guides the current processing of information and often leads to distortions in attention, memory, and comprehension. People develop different schemas based on their temperament, abilities, and experiences.

SCHEMAS AND COGNITIVE DISTORTIONS Our schemas about the world around us and about ourselves (self-schemas) are our guides, one might say, through the complexities of living in the world as we understand it. For example, we all have schemas about other people (for example, expectations that they are lazy or very career oriented). We also have schemas about social roles (for example, expectations about what the appropriate behaviors for a widow are) and about events (for example, what sequences of events are appropriate for a particular situation such as someone coping with a loss; Bodenhausen & Morales, in press; Clark, Beck, & Alford, 1999; Fiske & Taylor, 1991). Our **self-schemas** include our views on who we are, what we might become, and what is important to us. Other aspects of our self-schemas concern our notions of the various roles we occupy or might occupy in our social environment such as "woman," "man," "student," "parent," "physician," "American," and so on. Most people have clear ideas about at least some of their own personal attributes and less clear ideas about other attributes (Fiske & Taylor, 1991; Kunda, 1999).

Schemas about the world and self-schemas are vital to our ability to engage in effective and organized behavior because they enable us to focus on the most relevant and important bits of information among the amazingly complex array of information that is available to our senses. However, schemas are also sources of psychological vulnerabilities because some of our schemas or certain aspects of our self-schemas may be distorted and inaccurate. In addition, we often hold some schemas—even distorted ones—with conviction, making them resistant to change. This is in part because we are usually not completely conscious of our schemas. In other words, although our daily decisions and behavior are largely shaped by these frames of reference, we may be unaware of the assumptions on which they are based—or even of making assumptions at all. We think that we are simply seeing things the way they are and often do not consider the fact that other views of the "real" world might be possible or that other rules for what is "right" might exist.

We tend to work new experiences into our existing cognitive frameworks, even if the new information has to be reinterpreted or distorted to make it fit—a process known as *assimilation*. In other words, we are likely to cling to existing assumptions and to reject or distort new information that contradicts them. *Accommodation*—changing our existing frameworks to make it possible to incorporate new information that doesn't fit—is more difficult and threatening, especially when important assumptions are challenged. Accommodation is, of course, a basic goal of psychological therapies—explicitly in the case of the cognitive and cognitive-behavioral therapies, but deeply embedded in virtually all other approaches as well.

According to Beck (1967; Beck & Weishaar, 2000; Beck et al., 2004; Beck et al., 2005), different forms of psychopathology are characterized by different maladaptive schemas that have developed as a function of adverse early learning experiences. These maladaptive schemas lead to the distortions in thinking that are

Our self-schemas—our frames of reference for what we are, what we might become, and what is important to us—influence our choice of goals and our confidence in attaining them. A probable element of this older woman's self-schema was that she could accomplish her lifelong goal of obtaining a college education once her children were grown in spite of the fact she was nearly 40 years older than the average college student.

characteristic of certain disorders such as anxiety, depression, and personality disorders. In addition to studying the nature of dysfunctional schemas associated with different forms of psychopathology, researchers have also studied several different patterns of distorted information processing exhibited by people with various forms of psychopathology. This research has illuminated the cognitive mechanisms that may be involved in causing or maintaining certain disorders. For example, depressed individuals show memory biases favoring negative information over positive or neutral information. Such biases are likely to help reinforce or maintain one's current depressed state (e.g., Mathews & MacLeod, 1994, 2005; Joormann, 2009).

Another important feature of information processing is that a great deal of information is processed *nonconsciously*, or outside of our awareness. Note that the term *nonconscious* does not refer to Freud's concept of the *unconscious*, in which primitive emotional conflicts are thought to simmer. Instead, the term *nonconscious mental activity* as studied by cognitive psychologists is simply a descriptive term for mental processes that are occurring without our being aware of them. One example relevant to psychopathology is that anxious people seem to have their attention drawn to threatening information even when that information is presented subliminally (that is, without the person's awareness; e.g., Mathews & MacLeod, 1994, 2005). Another relevant example occurs in the well-known phenomenon of *implicit memory*, which is demonstrated when a person's behavior reveals that she or he remembers a previously learned word or activity even though she or he cannot consciously remember it. For example, if someone asks you for your old home phone number from about 10 years ago, you may not be able to recall it (no explicit memory for it), but if you picked up a phone you might dial it correctly (intact implicit memory for it).

ATTRIBUTIONS, ATTRIBUTIONAL STYLE, AND PSYCHOPATHOLOGY *Attribution theory* has also contributed significantly to the cognitive-behavioral approach (Anderson, Krull, & Weiner, 1996; Fiske & Taylor, 1991; Gotlib & Abramson, 1999). An **attribution** is simply the process of assigning causes to things that happen. We may attribute behavior to external events such as rewards or punishments ("He did it for the money"), or we may assume that the causes are internal and derive from traits within ourselves or others ("He did it because he is so generous"). Causal attributions help us explain our own or other people's behaviors and make it possible to predict what we or others are likely to do in the future. A student who fails a test may attribute the failure to a lack of intelligence (a personal trait) or to ambiguous test questions or unclear directions (environmental causes).

Attribution theorists have been interested in whether different forms of psychopathology are associated with distinctive and dysfunctional attributional styles. *Attributional style* is a characteristic way in which an individual tends to assign causes to bad events or good events. For example, depressed people tend to attribute bad events to internal, stable, and global causes ("I failed the test because I'm stupid" as opposed to "I failed the test because the teacher was in a bad mood and graded it unfairly"). However inaccurate our attributions may be, they become important parts of our view of the world and can have significant effects on our emotional well-being (Abramson et al., 1978; Buchanan & Seligman, 1995; Mineka et al., 2003). Interestingly, nondepressed people tend to have what is called a *self-serving bias* in which they are more likely to make internal, stable, and global attributions for positive rather than negative events (e.g., Mezulis et al., 2004).

Aaron Beck (b. 1921) pioneered the development of cognitive theories of depression, anxiety, and personality disorders. He also developed highly effective cognitive-behavioral treatments for these disorders.

COGNITIVE THERAPY Beck, who is generally considered the founder of cognitive therapy, has been enormously influential in the development of cognitive-behavioral treatment approaches to various forms of psychopathology. Following Beck's lead, cognitive-behavioral theorists and clinicians have simply shifted their focus from overt behavior itself to the underlying cognitions assumed to be producing the maladaptive emotions and behavior. Fundamental to Beck's perspective is the idea that the way we interpret events and experiences determines our emotional reactions to them. Suppose, for example, that you are sitting in your living room and hear a crash in the adjacent dining room. You remember that you left the window open in the dining room and conclude that a gust of wind must have knocked over your favorite vase, which was sitting on the table. What would your emotional reaction be? Probably you would be annoyed or angry with yourself either for having left the window open or for having left the vase out (or both!). By contrast, suppose you conclude that a burglar must have climbed in the open window. What would your emotional reaction be then? In all likelihood, you would feel frightened. Thus your interpretation of the crash you heard in the next room fundamentally determines your emotional reaction to it. Moreover, certain individuals with prominent danger schemas may be especially prone to making the burglar assumption in this example, leaving them at risk for anxiety and worry.

One central issue for cognitive therapy, then, is how best to alter distorted and maladaptive cognitions, including the underlying maladaptive schemas that lead to different disorders and their associated emotions. For example, cognitive-behavioral clinicians are concerned with their clients' self-statements—that is, with what their clients say to themselves by way of interpreting their experiences. People who interpret what happens in their lives as a negative reflection of their self-worth are likely to feel depressed; people who interpret the sensation that their heart is racing as meaning that they may have a heart attack and die are likely to have a panic attack. Cognitive-behavioral clinicians use a variety of techniques designed to alter whatever negative cognitive biases the client harbors (e.g., see Barlow, 2008; Beck et al., 2004; Hollon & Beck, 1994; Hollon et al., 2006). This is in contrast to, for example, psychodynamic practice, which assumes that diverse problems are due to a limited array of intrapsychic conflicts (such as an unresolved Oedipus complex) and tends not to focus treatment directly on a person's particular problems or complaints.

THE IMPACT OF THE COGNITIVE-BEHAVIORAL PERSPECTIVE The cognitive-behavioral viewpoint has had a powerful impact on contemporary clinical psychology. Many researchers and clinicians have found support for the

Some interpret terrifying scenes in a horror movie and the sensations of their heart pounding as a sign of excitement and having a good time; others interpret the same scenes and sensations as if something dangerous and scary is really happening. Cognitive-behavioral psychologists emphasize that the way we interpret an event can dramatically color our emotional reactions to it.

principle of altering human behavior through changing the way people think about themselves and others. Many traditional behaviorists, however, have remained skeptical of the cognitive-behavioral viewpoint. B. F. Skinner (1990), in his last major address, remained true to behaviorism. He questioned the move away from principles of operant (instrumental) conditioning. He reminded his audience that cognitions are not observable phenomena and, as such, cannot be relied on as solid empirical data. Although Skinner is gone, this debate will surely continue in some form. Indeed, Wolpe (1988, 1993), another founder of behavior therapy, also remained highly critical of the cognitive perspective until his death in 1997. However, these criticisms have seemed to be decreasing in recent years as more and more evidence accumulates for the efficacy of cognitive-behavioral treatments for various disorders ranging from schizophrenia to anxiety, depression, and personality disorders (e.g., Barlow, 2008; Butler et al., 2006; Tolin, 2010). This approach has also been greatly advanced by the accumulation of sophisticated information-processing studies of the effects of emotion on cognition and behavior (e.g., Joormann, 2009; Mathews & MacLeod, 2005). This is because such studies do not rely on the self-report techniques that were originally central to this approach, and which are especially open to the kinds of criticisms raised by Skinner and Wolpe.

What the Adoption of a Perspective Does and Does Not Do

Each of the psychological perspectives on human behavior—psychodynamic, behavioral, and cognitive-behavioral—contributes to our understanding of psychopathology, but none alone can account for the complex variety of human maladaptive behaviors. Because different causal perspectives influence which components of maladaptive behavior the observer focuses on, each perspective depends on generalizations from limited observations and research. For example, in attempting to explain a complex disorder such as alcohol dependence, the more traditional psychodynamic viewpoint focuses on intrapsychic conflict and anxiety that the person attempts to reduce through the intake of alcohol; the more recent interpersonal variant on the psychodynamic perspective focuses on difficulties in a person's past and present relationships that contribute to drinking; the behavioral viewpoint focuses on faulty learning of habits to reduce stress (drinking alcohol) and environmental conditions that may be exacerbating or maintaining the condition; and the cognitive-behavioral viewpoint focuses on maladaptive thinking including deficits in problem solving and information processing, such as irrational beliefs about the need for alcohol to reduce stress.

Thus which perspective we adopt has important consequences: It influences our *perception of maladaptive behavior*, the *types of evidence we look for*, and *the way in which we are*

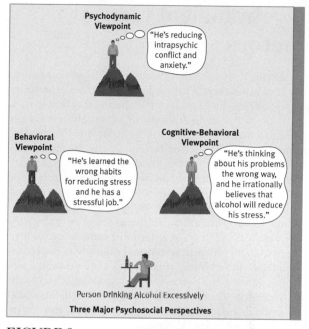

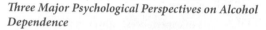

FIGURE 9

Three Major Psychological Perspectives on Alcohol Dependence

likely to interpret data. A wide range of psychological causal factors have been implicated in the origins of maladaptive behavior, and some of these different viewpoints provide contrasting (or sometimes complementary) explanations for how the causal factors exert their effects. (See Figure 9.)

In Review

- Contrast the newer psychodynamic perspectives—ego psychology, object-relations theory, and the interpersonal and attachment theory perspectives—with the earlier, Freudian perspective.

- What is the central theme of the behavioral perspective, and what has been its impact?

- How do classical and instrumental (operant) conditioning, generalization, discrimination, and observational learning contribute to the origins of abnormal behavior?

- What is the focus of the cognitive-behavioral perspective, and what has been its impact?

- Why are schemas and self-schemas so important for understanding abnormal behavior and its treatment?

- What role do cognitive distortions and attributions have in psychopathology, according to the cognitive-behavioral perspective?

Psychological Causal Factors

We begin life with few built-in patterns and a great capacity to learn from experience. What we do learn from our experiences may help us face challenges resourcefully and may lead to resilience in the face of future stressors. Unfortunately, some of our experiences may be much less helpful in our later lives, and we may be deeply influenced by factors in early childhood over which we have no control. One good example of ways in which the events in one child's life may be vastly different from those in another child's life is whether they are *predictable* or *controllable*. At one extreme are children who grow up in stable and lovingly indulgent environments, buffered to a large extent from the harsher realities of the world; at the other extreme are children whose experiences consist of constant exposure to unpredictable and uncontrollable frightening events or unspeakable cruelties. Such different experiences have corresponding effects on the adults' schemas about the world and about the self: Some suggest a world that is uniformly loving, unthreatening, and benign, which of course it is not; others suggest a jungle in which safety and perhaps even life itself are constantly in the balance. Given a preference in terms of likely outcomes, most of us would opt for the former of these sets of experiences. However, these actually may not be the best blueprint for engaging the real world, because it may be important to encounter some stressors and learn ways to deal with them in order to gain a sense of control (e.g., Barlow, 2002; Seligman, 1975) or self-efficacy (Bandura, 1986, 1997).

Exposure to multiple uncontrollable and unpredictable frightening events is likely to leave a person vulnerable to anxiety and negative affect, a central problem in a number of mental disorders such as anxiety and depression. For example, Barlow's (1988, 2002) and Mineka's (1985b; Mineka & Zinbarg, 1996, 2006) models emphasize the important role that experience with unpredictable and uncontrollable negative outcomes has in creating stress, anxiety, and depression (see also Abramson et al., 1978; Chorpita, 2001; Chorpita & Barlow, 1998; Seligman, 1975). It is important to note that a person exposed to the same frequency and intensity of negative outcomes that are predictable and/or controllable will experience less stress and be less likely to develop anxiety or depression.

In this section we will examine the types of psychological factors that make people vulnerable to disorder or that may precipitate disorder. Psychological factors are those developmental influences—often unpredictable and uncontrollable negative events—that may handicap a person psychologically, making him or her less resourceful in coping with events. (However, it is important to remember that psychological causal factors are always ultimately mediated by changes that take place in our nervous systems when emotions are activated and when new learning takes place.) We will focus on four categories of psychological causal factors that can each have important detrimental effects on a child's socioemotional development: (1) early deprivation or trauma, (2) inadequate parenting styles, (3) marital discord and divorce, and

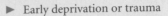

- ▶ Early deprivation or trauma
- ▶ Inadequate parenting styles
- ▶ Marital discord and divorce
- ▶ Maladaptive peer relationships

FIGURE 10

Psychological Causal Factors

(4) maladaptive peer relationships, also shown in Figure 10. Such factors typically do not operate alone. Rather, they interact with each other and with other psychological factors, as well as with particular genetic and temperamental factors and with particular sociocultural settings or environments. In other words, although psychological factors are often studied independently of genetic, temperamental, and sociocultural factors, a more comprehensive biopsychosocial understanding should be the ultimate goal.

We now turn to the four different categories of psychological causal factors.

Early Deprivation or Trauma

Children who do not have the resources that are typically supplied by parents or parental surrogates may be left with deep and sometimes irreversible psychological scars. The needed resources range from food and shelter to love and attention. Deprivation of such resources can occur in several forms. The most severe manifestations of deprivation are usually seen among abandoned or orphaned children, who may be either institutionalized or placed in a succession of unwholesome and inadequate foster homes. However, it can also occur in intact families where, for one reason or another, parents are unable (for instance, because of mental disorder) or unwilling to provide close and frequent human attention and nurturing.

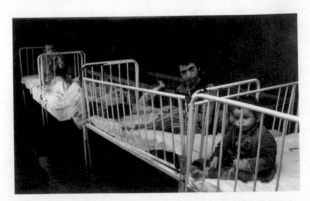

These Romanian orphans spend most of their days in playpens. The lack of physical contact and social stimulation and support causes many children who are often institutionalized starting in infancy and early childhood to show severe emotional, behavioral, and learning problems. They are also at elevated risk for psychopathology.

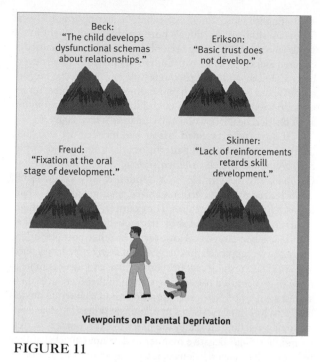

Beck:
"The child develops dysfunctional schemas about relationships."

Erikson:
"Basic trust does not develop."

Freud:
"Fixation at the oral stage of development."

Skinner:
"Lack of reinforcements retards skill development."

Viewpoints on Parental Deprivation

FIGURE 11

Viewpoints on Parental Deprivation

We can interpret the consequences of parental deprivation from several psychological viewpoints. Such deprivation might result in fixation at the oral stage of psychosexual development (Freud); it might interfere with the development of basic trust (Erikson); it might retard the attainment of needed skills because of a lack of available reinforcements (Skinner); or it might result in the child's acquiring dysfunctional schemas and self-schemas in which relationships are represented as unstable, untrustworthy, and without affection (Beck). Any of these viewpoints might be the best way of conceptualizing the problems that arise in a particular case, or some combination of them might be superior to any single one because, as we have noted, the causal pathways are usually multidimensional. (See Figure 11.)

INSTITUTIONALIZATION In some cases children are raised in an institution where, compared with an ordinary home, there is likely to be less warmth and physical contact; less intellectual, emotional, and social stimulation; and a lack of encouragement and help in positive learning. Current estimates are that worldwide up to 8 million children live in orphanages (Bos et al., 2011). Research done when institutionalization was more common in the United States and the United Kingdom makes it clear that the long-range prognosis for most children who suffer early and prolonged environmental and social deprivation through institutionalization is unfavorable, especially if the institutionalization lasts longer than 6 months (Beckett et al., 2006; Kreppner et al., 2007; Wiik et al., 2011). Many children institutionalized in infancy and early childhood show severe emotional, behavioral, and learning problems and are at risk for disturbed attachment

relationships and psychopathology (e.g., Bos et al., 2011; Ellis et al., 2004; Smyke et al., 2007). At least some of these problems may be the result of delayed maturation in brain electrical activity (McLaughlin et al., 2010).

Institutionalization later in childhood of a child who has already had good attachment experiences was not found to be so damaging (Rutter, 1987). However, even some of the children institutionalized at an early age show resilience and do well in adolescence and adulthood (Kreppner et al., 2007; Rutter et al., 2001). In some cases this is because of influential protective factors, which include having some positive experiences at school, whether in the form of social relationships or athletic or academic success, and having a supportive marital partner in adulthood; these successes probably contribute to a better sense of self-esteem or self-efficacy (Quinton & Rutter, 1988; Rutter, 1985; Rutter et al., 2001).

Fortunately, the results of this line of research have had a major impact on public policy in this and some other societies, which have recognized the need to place such children in foster or adoptive families rather than in institutions (see Johnson, 2000; Rutter, 2006). Accordingly, conducting research on the effects of institutionalization in Western societies is less urgent today—and less feasible—than it once was. Unfortunately, however, enlightened policies have not been implemented in some Eastern European countries and in some other parts of the world, where the plight of children in orphanages has often been deplorable (e.g., Johnson, 2000). We focus here on research conducted on children adopted from these Eastern European orphanages because they have been most widely studied (e.g., McLaughlin et al., 2010). Many children whose infancy was spent in these Eastern European orphanages were later adopted into homes in North America and the United Kingdom. For children who spent a significant period of time in one of these deplorable institutions in their first year or two of life, there were very significant intellectual, language, and growth deficits, and even more time spent in the institution was related to more severe deficits. Serious physiological, behavioral, psychological, and social problems also arose (e.g., Bos et al., 2011; Gunnar et al., 2001; Rutter, 2006). At least in one study the physiological changes extended to brain development, with children with severe institutional deprivation showing reduced overall brain volume, although the volumes of their amygdala which is involved in emotion regulation were enhanced (Mehta et al., 2009). When retested several years after being placed in good adoptive homes, most such children showed significant improvement in most of these areas, although they still showed deficits compared to adoptive infants who had not been institutionalized. For one of these studies, a more recent follow-up of Romanian adoptees in the United Kingdom when the children were 11 years of age has shown a wide variety of outcomes. About half of the children continued to show multiple impairments, and only about one-quarter showed fairly normal functioning across many domains (Kreppner et al., 2007; see also Wiik et al., 2011). Generally, the earlier the children were adopted (and therefore the less time they spent in the deplorable orphanages), the better they did (see Johnson, 2000, for a review; Rutter et al., 1999).

NEGLECT AND ABUSE IN THE HOME Most infants subjected to parental deprivation are not separated from their parents but, rather, suffer from maltreatment at home. In the United States, approximately 2.6 to 3.4 million reports of abuse and neglect are made annually, and about 33 to 40 percent are found to be accurate (Cicchetti & Toth, 2005; Watts-English et al., 2006). This means that about 12 out of every 1,000 children are known to be victims of abuse or neglect, with countless numbers of other unreported cases. Parents can neglect a child in various ways—by physical neglect, denial of love and affection, lack of interest in the child's activities and achievements, or failure to spend time with the child or to supervise his or her activities. Cases of parental abuse (which are less common than neglect; De Bellis, 2005) involve cruel treatment in the form of emotional, physical, or sexual abuse. Parental neglect and abuse may be partial or complete, passive or active, or subtly or overtly cruel.

Outright parental abuse (physical or sexual or both) of children has been associated with many negative effects on their emotional, intellectual, and physical development, although some studies have suggested that, at least among infants, gross neglect may be worse than having an abusive relationship. Abused children often have a tendency to be overly aggressive (both verbally and physically), even to the extent of bullying. Some even respond with anger and aggression to friendly overtures from peers (e.g., Cicchetti & Toth, 2005; Emery & Laumann-Billings, 1998). Researchers have also found that maltreated children often have difficulties in linguistic development and significant problems in behavioral, emotional, and social functioning, including conduct disorder, depression and anxiety, and impaired relationships with peers, who tend to avoid or reject them (Collishaw, Pickles, et al., 2007; Shonk & Cicchetti, 2001). Such adverse consequences are perhaps not surprising given the multitude of very long-lasting negative neurobiological effects that maltreatment has on the developing nervous system (Gunnar & Quevedo, 2007;

In February 1994, during a drug raid, Chicago police discovered 19 children living in this freezing, squalid, cockroach-infested apartment. The stove in the kitchen did not work. The children had to eat off the floor, sharing their food with dogs. The six adults in the apartment were charged with child neglect, and child abuse charges were also considered. Growing up in such a setting may predispose children to later psychological problems.

Watts-English et al., 2006). For example, an important 30-year follow-up study of individuals born on the Isle of Wight in the 1960s who reported having been physically or sexually abused as children found that about two-thirds of them had elevated rates of both adolescent and adult psychopathology compared to individuals who did not report such abuse. A recent quantitative review also reported adverse effects of childhood abuse on numerous adult physical health outcomes (Wegman & Stetler, 2009).

Abused and maltreated infants and toddlers are also quite likely to develop atypical patterns of attachment—most often a *disorganized* and *disoriented style of attachment* (Barnett, Ganiban, & Cicchetti, 1999; Crittenden & Ainsworth, 1989), characterized by insecure, disorganized, and inconsistent behavior with the primary caregiver. For example, such a child might at one point act dazed and show frozen behavior when reunited with his or her caregiver. However, at another point he or she might actually approach the caregiver but then immediately reject and avoid her. A significant portion of these children continue to show these confused patterns of relating to their caregiver up to at least age 13. Moreover, because such children's internal models of themselves in relationships to important others often generalize to new relationships, they are likely to expect others to treat them in a similar negative manner and to not expect that they will fare well in such relationships. Consequently, they may selectively avoid new experiences that could correct their expectations (Cicchetti & Toth, 1995a; Shields et al., 2001).

These effects of early abuse may endure into adolescence and adulthood. For example, previously abused or neglected children have, on average, lower levels of education, employment, and earnings (Currie & Widom, 2010). Several reviews have concluded that childhood physical abuse predicts both familial and nonfamilial violence in adolescence and adulthood, especially in abused men (Cicchetti & Toth, 1995a; Serbin & Karp, 2004). Thus, a significant proportion of parents who reject or abuse their children have themselves been the victims of parental rejection. Their early history of rejection or abuse would clearly have had damaging effects on their schemas and self-schemas, and they were probably unable to internalize good models of parenting (e.g., Serbin & Karp, 2004; Shields et al., 2001). Kaufman and Zigler (1989) estimated that there is about a 30 percent chance of this pattern of intergenerational transmission of abuse (see also Cicchetti & Toth, 1995a).

Nevertheless, it is important to remember that maltreated children—whether the maltreatment comes from abuse or from deprivation—can improve to at least some extent when the caregiving environment improves (Cicchetti & Toth, 1995a; Emery & Laumann-Billings, 1998). Moreover, there are always a range of effects, and those children who are least likely to show these negative outcomes tend to have one or more protective factors such as a good relationship with some adult during childhood, a higher IQ, positive school experiences, or physical attractiveness.

SEPARATION Bowlby (1960, 1973) first summarized the traumatic effects, for children from 2 to 5 years old, of being separated from their parents during prolonged periods of hospitalization. First, there are the short-term or acute effects of the separation, which can include significant despair during the separation as well as detachment from the parents upon reunion; Bowlby considered this to be a normal response to prolonged separation, even in infants with a *secure attachment*. However, he also found evidence that children who undergo a number of such separations may develop an *insecure attachment*. In addition, there can be longer-term effects of early separation from one or both parents. For example, such separations can cause an increased vulnerability to stressors in adulthood, making it more likely that the person will become depressed (Bowlby, 1980) or show other psychiatric symptoms (Canetti et al., 2000; Carlson et al., 2003). As with other early traumatic experiences, the long-term effects of separation depend heavily on whether support and reassurance are given a child by parents or other significant people, which is most likely if the child has a secure relationship with at least one parent (Canetti et al., 2000; Carlson & Sroufe, 1995). Interestingly, many children who experience even a parent's death do not exhibit discernible long-term effects (Brown et al., 1985; Canetti et al., 2000).

Even children who have been maltreated can improve their damaged self-schemas if one or more protective factors—for example, a positive experience at school—is present.

Inadequate Parenting Styles

Even in the absence of severe deprivation, neglect, or trauma, many kinds of deviations in parenting can have profound effects on a child's subsequent ability to cope with life's challenges and thus can create a child's vulnerability to various forms of psychopathology. Therefore, although their explanations vary considerably, the psychological viewpoints on causes of psychopathology all focus on the behavioral tendencies a child acquires in the course of early social interaction with others—chiefly parents or parental surrogates (e.g., Parke, 2004; Sroufe et al., 2000).

You should keep in mind that a parent–child relationship is always bidirectional: As in any continuing relationship, the behavior of each person affects the behavior of the other. Some children are easier to love than others; some parents are more sensitive than others to an infant's needs (e.g., Parke, 2004). For example, parents who have babies with difficult temperaments (who are very prone to negative moods) find it difficult and stressful to deal with their babies (e.g., Putnam et al., 2002; Rutter, 2006). For a second example, in an early study, Rutter and Quinton (1984) found that parents tended to react with irritability, hostility, and criticism to children who were high in negative mood and low on adaptability (see also Crouter & Booth, 2003). This in turn may set such children at risk for psychopathology because they become a "focus for discord" in the family (Rutter, 1990, p. 191).

PARENTAL PSYCHOPATHOLOGY

In general, it has been found that parents who have various forms of psychopathology (including schizophrenia, depression, antisocial personality disorder, and alcohol abuse or dependence) tend to have one or more children who are at heightened risk for a wide range of developmental difficulties (unless protective factors are also present; Brennan et al., 2003; Masten, 2007). The focus of most research in this area has been on mothers, but there is good evidence that fathers with mental disorders or others who are minimally involved in caretaking in infancy can also make significant contributions to child and adolescent psychopathology, especially to problems such as depression, conduct disorder, delinquency, and attention-deficit disorder (e.g., Boyce, et al., 2006; Hammen, 2009; Phares et al., 2002). Although some of these effects undoubtedly have a genetic component, many researchers believe that genetic influences cannot account for all of the adverse effects that parental psychopathology can have on children (e.g., Hammen, 2009; Sher et al., 2005; Speranza et al., 2006).

Consider some examples. Although many children of alcoholics do not have difficulties, others have elevated rates of truancy, substance abuse, and a greater likelihood of dropping out of school, as well as higher levels of anxiety and depression and lower levels of self-esteem (Leonard & Eiden, 2007; Marmorstein et al., 2009; Sher et al., 2005). In addition, the children of seriously depressed parents are at enhanced risk for depression and other disorders themselves (Burt et al., 2005; Cicchetti & Toth, 1998; Hammen, 2009), at least partly because depression makes

Inadequate parenting styles can have profound effects on a child's subsequent ability to cope with life's challenges and thus create vulnerability to various forms of psychopathology.

for unskillful parenting—notably including either intrusive or withdrawn behavior (Field et al., 2006), excessive criticism, and ineffectiveness in managing and disciplining the children (Cicchetti & Toth, 1998; Rogosch et al., 2004). Not surprisingly, children of depressed mothers are also more likely than children of nondepressed mothers to have insecure attachment relationships (Cicchetti & Toth, 1995b) and to live in environments with high levels of stress (e.g., Hammen, 2009).

PARENTING STYLES: WARMTH AND CONTROL Less extreme differences in parenting styles than those that may occur with various forms of parental psychopathology or parental abuse can also have a significant impact on children's development and increase their risk for psychopathology. In the past, discipline was conceived of as a method for both punishing undesirable behavior and preventing or deterring such behavior in the future. Discipline is now thought of more positively as providing needed structure and guidance for promoting a child's healthy growth. Such guidance provides a child with schemas similar to outcomes actually meted out by the world, which are contingent on a person's behavior. This allows the child a sense of control over these outcomes and her or his freedom to make deliberate choices. When punishment is deemed necessary, it is important that a parent make clear exactly what behavior is inappropriate and what behavior is expected, and that positive and consistent methods of discipline be worked out for dealing with infractions.

Researchers have been interested in how parenting styles—including their disciplinary styles—affect children's behavior over

Healthy parenting styles are those that reflect warmth and clear limits and restrictions regarding certain kinds of behaviors while allowing considerable freedom within certain boundaries. The children raised in these environments tend to be energetic and friendly and show general competencies for dealing with others.

the course of development. A parenting style reflects an attitude and values that are expressed toward a child across a wide range of settings (L. R. Williams et al., 2009). Four types of parenting styles have been identified that seem to be related to different developmental outcomes for the children: (1) authoritative, (2) authoritarian, (3) permissive/indulgent, and (4) neglectful/uninvolved. These styles vary in the degree of *parental warmth* (amount of support, encouragement, and affection versus shame, rejection, and hostility) and in the degree of *parental control* (extent of discipline and monitoring versus leaving the children largely unsupervised; Emery & Kitzmann, 1995; Manzeske & Stright, 2009; Morris, 2001). (See Figure 12.) Parental control includes both behavioral control (rewards and punishments) and psychological control (e.g., expression of approval vs disapproval, or guilt induction).

Authoritative Parenting The *authoritative style* is one in which the parents are both very warm and very careful to set clear standards and limits on certain kinds of behaviors while allowing considerable freedom within these limits. They tend to be attentive and sensitive to their needs while still enforcing their limits. This style of parenting is associated with the most positive early social development; the children tend to be energetic and friendly and to show development of general competencies for dealing with others and with their environments (Baumrind, 1993; Siegler et al., 2003; Simons et al., 2005). They also usually have secure attachment relationships (Karavasilis et al., 2003) and show high levels of overall well-being, as well as good school performance when followed into late adolescence (Berk, 2003; Slicker & Thornberry, 2002). Not surprisingly they also are less likely to exhibit either emotional disorders (e.g., anxiety and depression) or behavioural problem such as conduct problems and delinquency (L.R. Williams et al., 2009). Recent work has also shown that authoritative parenting is often effective in promoting resilience in children living in highly stressful contexts induced by war, conflict, and displacement (Salem-Pickartz & Donnelly, 2007).

Authoritarian Parenting Parents with an *authoritarian style* are high on control but low on warmth. They often appear quite cold and demanding, favoring punitive methods if their children disobey. Their children tend to be conflicted, irritable, and moody (Baumrind, 1975, 1993; Berk, 2003; Siegler et al., 2003). When followed into adolescence, these children tend to be lower in social and academic competence than children of authoritative parents, with boys doing particularly poorly in social and cognitive skills. Boys with authoritarian fathers—especially those high on hostility—are also at heightened risk of engaging in substance abuse and other delinquent activity (Bronte-Tinkew et al., 2006; Hoeve et al., 2009). If such authoritarian parents also use overly severe discipline in the form of physical punishment—as opposed to the withdrawal of approval and privileges—the result tends to be increased aggressive behavior on the part of the child (Berk, 2003; Emery & Kitzmann, 1995).

Permissive/Indulgent Parenting Parents with a *permissive/indulgent style* are high on warmth but low on discipline and control. This lenient style of parenting is associated

Authoritative	**Authoritarian**	**Permissive/ Indulgent**	**Neglectful/ Uninvolved**
Parents are high on warmth and moderate on control, very careful to set clear limits and restrictions regarding certain kinds of behaviors.	Parents are low on warmth and high on control and often cold and demanding.	Parents are high on warmth and low on control and discipline.	Parents are low on warmth and low on control.
Research Shows: Children tend to be friendly and to show development of general competencies for dealing with others and with their environments.	**Research Shows:** Children tend to be conflicted, irritable, and moody. When followed into adolescence, these children have more negative outcomes, the boys doing particularly poorly in social and cognitive skills.	**Research Shows:** Children tend to be impulsive and aggressive. Overly indulged children are characteristically spoiled, selfish, impatient, inconsiderate, and demanding.	**Research Shows:** Children tend to be moody and to have low self-esteem and conduct problems later in childhood. They also have problems with peer relations and with academic performance.

FIGURE 12

Parenting Styles

with impulsive and aggressive behavior in childhood and adolescence (Baumrind, 1967; Hetherington & Parke, 1993; Siegler et al., 2003). Overly indulged children are characteristically spoiled, selfish, impatient, inconsiderate, and demanding (Baumrind, 1971, 1975). In adolescence, they tend to do less well academically and to show more antisocial behaviors (e.g., Steinberg et al., 2006). Confusion and difficulties in adjustment may occur when "reality" forces them to reassess their assumptions about themselves and the world.

Neglectful/Uninvolved Parenting Finally, parents who are low both on warmth and on control exhibit the *neglectful/uninvolved style.* They tend to be disengaged and not supportive of their children. This style of parental uninvolvement is associated with disruptions in attachment during early childhood (Egeland & Sroufe, 1981; Karavasilis et al., 2003) and with moodiness, low self-esteem, and conduct problems later in childhood (Baumrind, 1991; Hetherington & Parke, 1993). These children of uninvolved parents also have problems with peer relations and with academic performance (Hetherington & Parke, 1993; see also Berk, 2003).

Marital Discord and Divorce

Disturbed parent–child patterns such as parental rejection are rarely found in severe form unless the total familial context is also abnormal. Thus disturbed family structure is an overarching risk factor that increases an individual's vulnerability to particular stressors. We will distinguish between intact families where there is significant marital discord and families that have been disrupted by divorce or separation.

MARITAL DISCORD Whatever the reasons for marital discord, when it is long-standing it is likely to be frustrating, hurtful, and generally damaging in its effects on both adults and their children (e.g., Amato, 2006; Amato & Booth, 2001; Parke, 2004). More severe cases of marital discord may expose children to one or more of the stressors we have already discussed: child abuse or neglect, the effects of living with a parent with a serious mental disorder, authoritarian or neglectful/uninvolved parenting, and spouse abuse. But even less severe cases of marital discord also have negative effects on many children. For example, one study showed that children of parents with high levels of overt conflict showed a greater disposition to behave aggressively toward both their peers and their parents than children from less conflictual marriages (Cummings et al., 2004; Du Rocher et al., 2004; see also Amato, 2006). Another study found that college students who reported high levels of marital conflict in their parents also showed elevated conflict in their own romantic relationships, which in turn was linked to poorer quality of their own romantic relationships (Cui & Fincham, 2010). Interestingly, one study found that children could be buffered against many of the damaging effects of marital conflict if one or both parents had the following characteristics: warmth, proneness to giving praise and approval, and ability to inhibit rejecting behavior toward their children (Katz & Gottman, 1997).

Several recent longitudinal studies have clearly documented that the damaging effects of serious marital discord on children continue into adulthood: The offspring's own marriages are more likely to be marked by discord (whether or not the parents divorced). Some of this intergenerational transmission of marital discord may be the result of the offspring having learned negative interaction styles by observing their own parents' marital interactions (Amato, 2006; Amato & Booth, 2001).

DIVORCED FAMILIES Partly as a consequence of a growing cultural acceptance of divorce, approximately a million divorces now occur yearly in the United States, according to the National Center for Health Statistics (as cited in Divorce Statistics Collection, 2005). Estimates are that about 20 percent of children under the age of 18 are living in a single-parent household—some with unwed parents and some with divorced parents. Nearly half of all marriages end in divorce, and it has been estimated that 50 to 60 percent of children born in the 1990s would live at some point in single-parent families (Amato, 2010; Hetherington et al., 1998).

Effects of Divorce on Parents Unhappy marriages are difficult, but ending a marital relationship can also be enormously stressful for the adults, both mentally and physically. The negative effects are often temporary, with most people being able to adapt constructively within 2 to 3 years, but some adults never fully recover (Amato, 2000; Hetherington, 2003a). Divorced and separated persons are overrepresented among psychiatric patients, although the ***direction of the causal relationship*** is not always clear. In their original comprehensive reviews of the effects of divorce on adults, Amato and Keith (1991a) concluded that it is a major source of psychopathology as well as of physical illness, death, suicide, and homicide. It should also be recognized, however, that divorce actually benefits some individuals (Amato, 2000, 2010)—with some evidence that women are more likely to benefit than men (Hetherington, 2003a). There is also some evidence that individuals who were in high-distress marriages before divorce are more likely to show an increase in happiness than are individuals who were in low-distress marriages before divorce (Amato & Hohmann-Marriott, 2007). In addition, favorable adjustment after divorce is positively associated with higher income, dating someone steadily, remarriage, having had relatively favorable attitudes toward divorce before it happened, and being the partner who initiated the divorce (Amato, 2000).

Effects of Divorce on Children Divorce can have traumatic effects on children, too. Feelings of insecurity and rejection may be aggravated by conflicting loyalties and,

RESEARCH CLOSE-UP

Direction of the Causal Relationship

Recall that, in a correlational or observational study, an association between two variables does not allow us to make inferences about causal direction. For example, divorce could precipitate psychological problems. Alternatively, people with psychological disorders might be more likely to have problematic marriages and end up divorced.

sometimes, by the spoiling the children may receive while staying with one of the parents. Not surprisingly, some children do develop serious maladaptive responses. Temperamentally difficult children are likely to have a more difficult time adjusting than are temperamentally easy children (Hetherington et al., 1989). Somewhat ironically, difficult children may be the ones whose parents are more likely to divorce, perhaps because having difficult children is likely to exacerbate marital problems (Block et al., 1986; Hetherington, 1999).

Delinquency and a wide range of other psychological problems such as anxiety and depression are much more frequent among children and adolescents from divorced families than among those from intact families, although it is likely that a contributing factor here is prior or continuing parental strife (Chase-Lansdale et al., 1995; Strohschein, 2005). However, findings also show that, on average, such children had shown these problems to some degree even before their parents divorced (Amato, 2010; Strohschein, 2005). In addition, a number of studies have demonstrated that the adverse effects of divorce on adaptive functioning may persist into adulthood. On average, compared to young adults from families without divorce, young adults from divorced families have somewhat lower educational attainment, lower incomes, lower life satisfaction, and an increased probability of being on welfare and having children out of wedlock (Chase-Lansdale et al., 1995; Hetherington et al., 1998). Children from divorced families are also more likely to have their own marriages end in divorce (Amato & DeBoer, 2001; Hetherington, 2003b). One particularly interesting study found that these long-lasting effects even occurred in a subsequent third generation. Specifically, in a study of nearly 700 grandparents and their grandchildren, Amato and Cheadle (2005) found that divorce in the grandparents was associated with lower education, more marital discord, and weaker parental ties in the grandchildren.

Nevertheless, many children adjust quite well to the divorce of their parents. Indeed, a quantitative review of 92 studies on parental divorce and the well-being of children, conducted on 13,000 children from 1950 to 1990, concluded that the average negative effects of divorce on children are actually quite modest (Amato, 2010; Amato & Keith, 1991b; see also Emery, 1999; Hetherington, 2003b), as are the negative effects persisting into adulthood (Amato & Keith, 1991b). Amato and Keith (1991a, 1991b) also found that the negative effects of divorce seemed to decrease from the 1950s through the 1980s (particularly since 1970), perhaps because the stigma of divorce was decreasing. However, a follow-up review of 67 such studies published in the 1990s showed no further decreases in these negative effects since 1990 (Amato, 2001).

The effects of divorce on children are often more favorable than the effects of remaining in a home torn by marital conflict and dissension (Amato, 2010; Amato & Keith, 1991b; Hetherington et al., 1998). At one time it was thought that the detrimental effects of divorce might be minimized if a successful remarriage provided an adequate environment for childrearing. Unfortunately, however, the Amato and Keith (1991b) review revealed that children living with a stepparent were often no better off than children living with a single parent, although this was more true for girls than for boys. Other studies have shown that children—especially very young children—living with a stepparent are at increased risk for physical abuse (injury and even death) by the stepparent relative to children living with two biological parents (Daly & Wilson, 1988, 1996).

Maladaptive Peer Relationships

Important peer relationships usually begin in the preschool years. Children at this stage are hardly masters of the fine points of human relationships or diplomacy. Empathy—the appreciation of another's situation, perspective, and feelings—is at best only primitively developed. We can see this in a child who rejects a current playmate when a more favored playmate arrives. The child's own immediate satisfaction tends to be the primary goal of any interaction, and there is only an uncertain recognition that cooperation and collaboration may bring even greater benefits. A substantial minority of children seem somehow ill equipped for the rigors and competition of the school years, often because of temperamental factors in the child or dysfunctional family situations. A significant number of them withdraw from their peers and become loners. A significant number of others (especially males) adopt physically intimidating and aggressive lifestyles, often becoming schoolyard or neighborhood bullies. Being either a loner or a bully does not bode well for good mental health outcomes (e.g., Dodge et al., 1997; Heilbron & Prinstein, 2010; Reijntjes et al., 2011). This is in part because both often lead to peer exclusion and peer abuse. Chronic peer

Juvenile socializing is a risky business in which a child's hard-won prestige in a group is probably perceived as being constantly in jeopardy. Actually, reputation and status in a group tend to be stable, and a child who has been rejected by peers is likely to continue to have problems in peer relationships.

exclusion is particularly likely to lead to decreased classroom participation and declining school performance, whereas peer abuse is particularly likely to lead to actual avoidance of school (Buhs et al., 2006).

Several studies have found bullies to show high levels of both proactive aggression (where they initiate the aggressive behavior) and reactive aggression (where they overreact when confronted; e.g., Salmivalli & Nieminen, 2002; Salmivalli, 2010). Although some bullies probably behave this way because of deficits in social skills, others (often the ringleader in a group of bullies) have a more sophisticated understanding of social behavior, which enables them to manipulate and organize their peers (often driven by status goals) so that they can avoid being caught while making others suffer (Salmivalli, 2010; Sutton et al., 1999). Although most children profess attitudes against bullying, when bullying actually occurs, most students do nothing to intervene or support the victim (and as many as 20 to 30 percent actually encourage the bully; Salmivalli & Voeten, 2004; Salmivalli, 2010). A small percentage (approximately 20 percent), however, do take the side of the victim and may even help defend him or her. Victims who have one or more classmates defend them show less distress and higher self-esteem.

In recent years a new form of particularly insidious bullying has emerged as an enormous problem in many North American schools. *Cyberbullying*, as it is called, includes sending offensive, harassing, or intimidating messages over the Internet, spreading ugly rumors on certain Internet sites, and spreading someone's very personal information (Willard, 2007). Some estimate that as many as one-third of teenagers who use the Internet engage in cyberbullying (Li, 2007; Scharnberg, 2007). The psychological consequences of cyberbullying on the victims can be very serious—including anxiety, school phobia, lower self-esteem, suicidal ideation, and occasional cases of suicide (Thomas, 2006).

Fortunately, there is another side to this coin. Peer relations can be difficult, but they can also be sources of key learning experiences that stand an individual in good stead for many years. For a resourceful child, the winning and losing and the successes and failures of the school years provide excellent training in coming to grips with the real world and with her or his developing self—its capabilities and limitations, its attractive and unattractive qualities. The experience of intimacy with a friend has its beginning in this period of intense social involvement. If all goes well, a child emerges into adolescence with a considerable repertoire of social knowledge and skills that add up to social competence. Such resources can be strong protective factors against parental rejection, frustration, demoralization, despair, and mental disorder (Masten, 2007; Sentse et al., 2010).

SOURCES OF POPULARITY VERSUS REJECTION What determines which children will be popular and which will be rejected? There seem to be two types of popular children—the prosocial and the antisocial types. *Prosocial* popular children communicate with their peers in friendly and assertive yet cooperative ways. They tend to be good students relative to their less popular peers (Zettergreen, 2003). *Antisocial* popular children—usually boys—tend to be "tough boys" who may be athletically skilled but who do poorly academically. They tend to be highly aggressive and defiant of authority (see Berk, 2003).

Far more attention has been devoted to determining why some children are persistently rejected by their peers and what the consequences are of such rejection. There also appear to be two types of rejected children—those who are too aggressive and those who are very withdrawn (Ladd, 2006). The rejected children who are aggressive take an excessively demanding or aggressive approach when interacting with their peers. They often take offense too readily and attribute hostile intent to the teasing of their peers, thus escalating confrontations to unintended levels (Dodge, 2006; Reijntjes et al., 2011). Indeed, the tendency to attribute hostile intent to others in grade 8 has been shown to predict levels of antisocial behavior in grade 11 (Lansford et al., 2006). Such children also tend to take a more punitive and less forgiving attitude toward such situations (Coie et al., 1991; Crick & Dodge, 1994; Reijntjes et al., 2011). This may be especially likely in children who have been maltreated by their parents and have therefore developed maladaptive mental representations of caregivers and expect maltreatment. Expecting maltreatment, they may approach social situations with hyperarousal, anxiety, and angry reactivity, which may be consistent with what they have experienced at home but is out of synch with the context they share with peers (Cicchetti & Toth, 2005; Shields et al., 2001). In addition, having a poor ability to understand a peer's emotions (such as fear and sadness) in kindergarten also predicts aggressive behavior toward peers in the third grade (Dodge et al., 2002).

Being rejected and being aggressive at one point in childhood greatly increases the probability of aggressive and delinquent behavior later on, especially in boys (Coie, 2004; Ladd, 2006; Reijntjes et al., 2011). For example, one study followed 585 children from kindergarten through the eighth grade. Results showed that those who had hostile knowledge structures (schemas) early in childhood were more likely to develop consistent aggressive behaviors over an 8-year follow-up period (Burks et al., 1999; see also Laird et al., 2001).

The second subset of children who may become chronic victims of rejection are not aggressive but, rather, are highly unassertive and quite submissive toward their peers, often because of social anxiety and fear of being scorned or attacked (Schwartz et al., 1993). Such isolation is likely to have serious consequences because it often leads to peer rejection, which in turn deprives a child of further opportunities to learn the rules of social behavior and interchange, rules that become more sophisticated and subtle with increasing age (Coie, 1990; Ladd, 2006). Repeated social failure or becoming the victim of bullies is the usual result, which has further damaging effects on self-confidence and self-esteem

and sometimes leads to loneliness, depression, and anxiety, especially during the elementary school years (Burks et al., 1995; Ladd, 2006).

In summary, both logic and research findings suggest the same conclusion: A child who fails to establish satisfactory relationships with peers during the developmental years is deprived of a crucial set of background experiences and is at higher-than-average risk for a variety of negative outcomes in adolescence and adulthood including depression, school dropout, suicidal ideation, and delinquency (Coie, 2004; Heilbron & Prinstein, 2010; Ladd, 2006). However, one should also remember that the peer social problems may also be early markers of disorders that have a heritable component but do not become full blown until later in adolescence or adulthood. What is often going on in such cases is that the peer social problems indeed reflect some heritable diathesis, but they also serve as stressors that make it more likely that the underlying vulnerability will lead to full-blown disorder later (Parker et al., 1995; see also Coie, 2004; Rutter, 2006).

In Review

- What are the most important effects of a child's being exposed to early deprivation or abuse?
- What kinds of effects does parental psychopathology have on children?
- What kinds of influences do different parenting styles tend to have on children's development? (Consider especially the variables of parental warmth and parental control.)
- What is the typical range of effects that divorce and marital discord can have on children? What about effects on adults?
- What are two different types of popular children and two different types of rejected children?

The Sociocultural Viewpoint

By the beginning of the twentieth century, sociology and anthropology had emerged as independent scientific disciplines and were making rapid strides toward understanding the role of sociocultural factors in human development and behavior. Early sociocultural theorists included such notables as Ruth Benedict, Abram Kardiner, Margaret Mead, and Franz Boas. Their investigations and writings showed that individual personality development reflects the larger society—its institutions, norms, values, and ideas—as well as the immediate family and other groups. Studies also made clear the relationship between various sociocultural conditions and mental disorders (for example, the relationship between the particular stressors in a given society and the types of mental disorders that typically occur in it). Further studies showed that the patterns of both physical and mental disorders within a given society could change over time as sociocultural conditions change. These discoveries have added important new dimensions to modern perspectives on abnormal behavior (Fabrega, 2001; Tsai et al., 2001; Westermeyer & Janca, 1997).

Uncovering Sociocultural Factors Through Cross-Cultural Studies

The sociocultural viewpoint is concerned with the impact of culture and other features of the social environment on mental disorders. The relationships are complex. It is one thing to observe that a person with a psychological disorder has come from a harsh environment. It is quite another to show empirically that these circumstances were contributory causes of the disorder as opposed to being mere correlates of the disorder. Yet people raised in different societies and exposed to very different environments have provided natural "laboratories" of sorts, and cross-cultural research can enhance our knowledge about the range of variation that is possible in human behavioral and emotional development. It can also generate ideas about what causes normal and abnormal behavior—ideas that can later be tested more rigorously in the laboratory (e.g., Rothbaum, Weisz, et al., 2000, 2001; Weisz et al., 1997).

UNIVERSAL AND CULTURE-SPECIFIC SYMPTOMS OF DISORDERS Research supports the view that many psychological disturbances—in both adults and children—are universal, appearing in most cultures studied (Butcher, 1996b, Butcher et al., 2005; Kleinman, 1988; Verhulst & Achenbach, 1995). Studying such issues is, of course, never easy because of the need to adapt psychological tests across barriers of language and culture and to validate their use in other cultures. One example of such research has shown that when some tests are translated into the language of different cultures, they need to be adapted so that they are appropriate for the new cultural context. In addition, care must be taken not to miss what may be culture-specific elements of various disorders such as anxiety and depression (e.g., Sue & Chang, 2003; Weisz et al., 2006).

The Minnesota Multiphasic Personality Inventory (MMPI) is the best validated and most widely used test that has been adapted for use in many cultures (e.g., Butcher, 2011). For example, the basic pattern of disturbed thoughts and behaviors that we call schizophrenia can be

found among nearly all peoples, although the prevalence and symptoms vary to some degree (Woo & Oei, 2007). Moreover, certain psychological symptoms, as measured, are consistently found among similarly diagnosed clinical groups in many other countries. For example, Butcher (1996a) found that psychiatric patients from Italy, Switzerland, Chile, India, Greece, and the United States who were diagnosed with paranoid schizophrenia produced similar general personality and symptom patterns on the MMPI. The same MMPI-2 pattern was also found to occur among schizophrenic patients in Japan (Hayama et al., 1999).

Nevertheless, although some universal symptoms and patterns of symptoms appear, sociocultural factors often influence which disorders develop, the forms they take, how prevalent they are, and their courses. For example, the prevalence of major depressive disorder varies widely across the cultures of the world. In one study conducted in 10 countries around the world, the prevalence ranged from 3 percent in Japan to nearly 17 percent in the United States (Andrade et al., 2004). Differences can also emerge in the prognosis or outcomes of several severe mental disorders in different countries. Several international studies have found a more favorable course of schizophrenia in developing countries than in developed countries (Kulhara & Chakrabarti, 2001).

In another example, Kleinman (1986, 1988) compared the ways in which Chinese people (in Taiwan and the People's Republic of China) and Westerners deal with stress. He found that in Western societies, depression was a frequent reaction to individual stress. In China, on the other hand, he noted a relatively low rate of reported depression (Kleinman, 2004; see also Kirmayer & Groleau, 2001). Instead, the effects of stress were more typically manifested in physical problems such as fatigue, weakness, and other complaints. Moreover, Kleinman and Good (1985) surveyed the experience of depression across cultures. Their data show that important elements of depression in Western societies—for example, the acute sense of guilt typically experienced—do not appear in many other cultures. They also point out that the symptoms of depression, such as sadness, hopelessness, unhappiness, and a lack of pleasure in the things of the world and in social relationships, have dramatically different meanings in different societies. For Buddhists, seeking pleasure from things of the world and social relationships is the basis of all suffering; a willful disengagement is thus the first step toward achieving enlightenment. For Shi'ite Muslims in Iran,

Sociocultural factors influence the form and course of certain disorders. For example, in Western societies people suffering from stress frequently will become depressed. In China, stress is not manifested as depression but in physical problems such as fatigue and weakness.

grief is a religious experience associated with recognition of the tragic consequences of living justly in an unjust world; the ability to experience grief fully is thus a marker of depth of personality and understanding. Several examples of disorders that appear only in certain cultures are given in Box 4 on culture-bound syndromes.

CULTURE AND OVER- AND UNDERCONTROLLED BEHAVIOR Studies of the prevalence of different kinds of childhood psychopathology in different cultures raise some fascinating issues. In cultures such as that of Thailand, adults are highly intolerant of *undercontrolled behavior* such as aggression, disobedience, and disrespectful acts in their children (e.g., Weisz et al., 2003). Children are explicitly taught to be polite and deferential and to inhibit any expression of anger. This raises interesting questions about whether childhood problems stemming from undercontrolled behavior are lower in Thailand than in the United States, where such behavior seems to be tolerated to a greater extent. It also raises the question of whether problems related to *overcontrolled behavior* such as shyness, anxiety, and depression would be overrepresented in Thailand relative to the United States.

4 THE WORLD AROUND US

Culture-Bound Syndromes

Name of Disorder	Culture	Description
Amok	Malaysia (also observed in Laos, the Philippines, Polynesia, Papua New Guinea, and Puerto Rico)	A disorder characterized by sudden, wild outbursts of violent aggression or homicidal behavior in which an afflicted person may kill or injure others. This rage disorder is usually found in males who are rather withdrawn, quiet, brooding, and inoffensive prior to the onset of the disorder. Episodes are often precipitated by a perceived slight or insult. Several stages have been observed, the final phase being *Amok*, in which the person jumps up, yells, grabs a knife, and stabs people or objects within reach. Exhaustion and depression usually follow, with amnesia for the rage period.
Hikikomori	Japan	A disorder of acute social withdrawal in which young people just remain in their room in their parents' house and refuse social interaction for years.
Koro	Southeast Asia and China (particularly Malaysia)	A fear reaction or anxiety state in which a man fears that his penis will withdraw into his abdomen and he may die. This reaction may appear after sexual overindulgence or excessive masturbation. The anxiety is typically very intense and of sudden onset. The condition is "treated" by having the penis held firmly by the patient or by family members or friends. Often the penis is clamped to a wooden box.
Latah	Malaysia and Indonesia (also Japan, Siberia, and the Philippines)	Hypersensitivity to sudden fright often occurring in middle-aged women of low intelligence who are subservient and self-effacing. The disorder is precipitated by the word *snake* or by tickling. It is characterized by *echolalia* (repetition of the words and sentences of others) and *echopraxia* (repetition of the acts of others). A disturbed individual may also show dissociative or trance-like behavior.
Taijin kyofusho (TKS)	Japan	A relatively common psychiatric disorder in Japan in which an individual develops a fear of offending or hurting other people through being awkward in social situations or because of an imagined physical defect or problem. The excessive concern over how a person presents himself or herself in social situations is the salient problem.
Windigo	Algonquin Indian hunters	A fear reaction in which a hunter becomes anxious and agitated, convinced that he is bewitched. Fears center on his being turned into a cannibal by the power of a monster with an insatiable craving for human flesh.
Zar	North Africa and Middle East	A person who believes he or she is possessed by a spirit may experience a dissociative episode during which shouting, laughing, singing, or weeping may occur. The person may also show apathy and withdrawal, not eating or working.

Sources: Based on American Psychiatric Association (DSM-IV-TR, 2000); Bartholomew (1997); Chowdhury (1996); Hatta (1996); Kiev (1972); Kirmayer (1991); Kirmayer et al. (1995); Lebra (1976); Lewis & Ednie (1997); Sakamoto et al. (2005); Sheung-Tak (1996); Simons & Hughes (1985).

Two cross-national studies (Weisz et al., 1987, 1993) confirmed that Thai children and adolescents do indeed have a greater prevalence of overcontrolled problems than do American children. Although there were no differences in the rate of undercontrolled behavior problems between the two countries, there were differences in the kinds of undercontrolled behavior problems reported. For example, Thai adolescents had higher scores than American adolescents on indirect and subtle forms of undercontrol not involving interpersonal aggression such as having difficulty concentrating or being cruel to animals; American adolescents, on the other hand, had higher scores than Thai adolescents on behaviors like fighting, bullying, and disobeying at school (Weisz et al., 1993). In addition, these investigators found that Thai and American parents differ a good deal in which problems they will bring for treatment. In general, Thai parents seem less likely than American parents to refer their children for psychological treatment (Weisz & Weiss, 1991; Weisz et al., 1997). This may be in part because of their Buddhist belief in the transience of problems and their optimism that their child's behavior will improve. Alternatively, Thai parents may not refer their children with undercontrolled problems for treatment simply because these problems are so unacceptable that the parents are embarrassed to go public with them (Weisz et al., 1997).

Cultural differences in psychopathology may also result from differences in what cultures consider to

In Thailand, children tend to exhibit *overcontrolled behavior* and are explicitly taught by their parents to be polite and deferential and to inhibit any expression of anger. This is in contrast to American children, whose parents tend to tolerate undercontrolled behavior to a greater extent.

be the ideal kinds of parent–child attachment relationships. Box 5 discusses research on cultural differences in what Japanese and Western cultures believe to be the nature of ideal versus disordered attachment relationships.

In Review

- Give some examples of universal and culture-specific symptoms of disorders.
- What cultural factors help account for differences in problems involving overcontrolled and undercontrolled behavior in Thai versus American children?
- Briefly describe three examples of culture-bound syndromes.

Sociocultural Causal Factors

We all receive a sociocultural inheritance that is the end product of thousands of years of social evolution, just as we receive a genetic inheritance that is the end product of millions of years of biological evolution. Because each sociocultural group fosters its own cultural patterns by systematically teaching its offspring, all its members tend to be somewhat alike. Children reared among headhunters tend to become headhunters; children reared in societies that do not sanction violence usually learn to settle their differences in nonviolent ways. The more uniform and thorough the education of the younger members of a group, the more alike they will become. Thus, in a society characterized by a limited and consistent point of view, there are not the wide individual differences that are typical in a society like ours, where children have contact with diverse, often conflicting beliefs. Even in our society, however, there are certain core values that most of us consider essential.

There are many sources of pathogenic social influences. Some of these stem from socioeconomic factors. Others stem from sociocultural factors regarding role expectations and from the destructive forces of prejudice and discrimination. We will briefly look at some of the more important ones here; see also Figure 13.

Low Socioeconomic Status and Unemployment

In our society the lower the socioeconomic class, the higher the incidence of mental and physical disorders (e.g., Caracci & Mezzich, 2001; Conger & Donnellan, 2007). The strength of

THE WORLD AROUND US

Culture and Attachment Relationships

Recently, research has shown that there are significant cross-cultural differences in views of ideal parent–child attachment relationships. Accordingly, there are different views of what constitutes disordered attachment relationships that can increase risk for psychopathology. Views on the function of good attachment relationships (and the nature of disordered attachment) in Western cultures have been found to differ rather dramatically from those seen in Japan (Rothbaum, Weisz, et al., 2000, 2001). In Western societies, secure attachment relationships are thought to occur when a mother responds in a sensitive fashion to a child's signals (e.g., signs of hunger or discomfort) yet gradually allows the child to explore the environment and develop some autonomy. In the United States one study found that teachers similarly prefer to respond to explicit expression of needs and to foster children's independence and self-expression, which would also foster secure attachments (Rothbaum et al., 2006). Importantly, securely attached children (relative to insecurely attached children) are thought to be less anxious and depressed, better able to cope with negative emotional states, and better able to form close relationships with peers.

However, in Japan, parents' goals are to anticipate all the child's needs and thereby avoid any exposure to stress such as hunger or discomfort and to foster dependency (Rothbaum, Weisz, et al., 2000,

2001). Recent findings suggest that Japanese teachers also prefer to anticipate their students' needs and to foster dependency on other tasks (Rothbaum et al., 2006). Accordingly, children who are considered securely attached in Japan are very dependent on their mothers (and teachers), and independent children are thought to have disturbed attachments. Moreover, because the Japanese value social harmony, children who are dependent and emotionally restrained and who express their feelings only indirectly are the ones viewed as competent; they also tend to be self-critical and self-effacing. This is very different from Western cultures, where children who show exploration and autonomy and are willing to express strong feelings and even disagreement openly are considered to be socially competent. Such children in Western cultures also tend to have positive self-views (Rothbaum, Weisz, et al., 2000).

Given such differences, it is not surprising that different clinical interventions are viewed as appropriate for children with behavior problems in these two cultures. For example, American therapists often help their clients to develop their own separate identities and assume that expression of negative feelings toward others (including parents) may be necessary. By contrast, Japanese therapists are more likely to encourage clients to be grateful to others (especially their parents) and encourage devotion (see Rothbaum, Weisz, et al., 2000, 2001).

▶ Low socioeconomic status and unemployment

▶ Prejudice and discrimination in race, gender, and ethnicity

▶ Social change and uncertainty

▶ Urban stressors: Violence and homelessness

FIGURE 13

Sociocultural Causal Factors

this inverse correlation varies with different types of mental disorder, however. For example, antisocial personality disorder is strongly related to socioeconomic status (SES), occurring about three times as often in the lowest income category as in the highest income category, whereas depressive disorders occur only about 1.5 times as often in the lowest income category as in the highest income category (Kessler et al., 1994; Kessler & Zhao, 1999; see also Monroe et al., 2009).

There are many reasons for this general inverse relationship (Conger & Donnellan, 2007). There is evidence that some people with mental disorders slide down to the lower rungs of the economic ladder and remain there, sometimes because they do not have the economic or personal resources to climb back up (e.g., Gottesman, 1991) and sometimes because of prejudice and stigma against those with mental illness (e.g., Caracci & Mezzich, 2001). At the same time, more affluent people are better able to get prompt help or to conceal their problems. However, it is also true that, on average, people who live in poverty encounter more—and more severe—stressors in their lives, including lower self-esteem, than do more affluent people, and they usually have fewer resources for dealing with them (e.g., Twenge & Campbell, 2002). Thus lower socioeconomic groups may show increased prevalence of mental and physical disorders due at least partly to increased stress on the people at risk (Conger & Donnellan, 2007; Eaton & Muntaner, 1999; Monroe et al., 2009).

Children and adolescents from lower-SES families also tend to have more problems (see Conger & Donnellan, 2007, for a review). A number of studies have documented a strong relationship between the parents' poverty and lower IQs in their children at least up to age 5. Persistent poverty has the most adverse effects (Duncan et al., 1994; McLoyd, 1998), including greater mental distress as well as greater risk taking and affiliating with deviant peers (Sampson et al., 2002). Children from low-SES families who were assessed when they were in preschool showed more acting-out and aggressive behaviors over the next 4 years (Dodge et al., 1994), perhaps in part because their parents are more likely to have an authoritarian parenting style and to experience marital conflict (Conger & Donnellan, 2007). Nevertheless, many inner-city children from high-risk socioeconomic backgrounds do very well, especially those with higher IQs and those with adequate relationships at home, in school, and with peers (Felsman & Valliant, 1987; Long & Valliant, 1984; Masten & Coatsworth, 1995).

Other studies have examined the effects of unemployment per se on adults and children. Since the 1970s, there have been a number of severe economic recessions experienced worldwide, and significant rates of unemployment have accompanied each. Studies have repeatedly found unemployment—with its financial hardships, self-devaluation, and emotional distress—to be associated with emotional distress and enhanced vulnerability to psychopathology (e.g., Dooley et al., 2000; Grzywacz & Dooley, 2003). Recent evidence suggests that it is the financial difficulties often resulting from unemployment that lead to the elevated levels of distress and mental disorders (Thomas et al., 2007).

In particular, rates of depression, marital problems, and somatic (bodily) complaints increase during periods of unemployment but usually normalize when employment rates recover (Dew et al., 1991; Jones, 1992; Murphy & Athanasou, 1999). It is not simply that people who are mentally unstable tend to lose their jobs. These effects occur even when mental health status before unemployment is taken into account. Not surprisingly, the wives of unemployed men are also adversely affected, exhibiting higher levels of anxiety, depression, and hostility, which seem to be at least partially caused by the distress of the unemployed husband (Dew et al., 1987). Children too can be seriously affected. In the worst cases, unemployed fathers are much more likely to engage in child abuse (Cicchetti & Lynch, 1995; Dew et al., 1991).

Finally, economic crises since 1990 have centered not only on unemployment but also on the effects that corporate restructuring and downsizing have had on upper-middle-class people, many of whom find themselves having to look for jobs requiring lower skills and paying much lower incomes than they earned in the past. In other cases people are forced to work only part time and often do not make enough to live on. In such cases of underemployment (or inadequate employment), several large studies of people who were underemployed found that rates of depression were comparable or nearly comparable to those seen in unemployed individuals (Dooley & Prause, 2004; Dooley et al., 2000; Grzywacz & Dooley, 2003).

Prejudice and Discrimination in Race, Gender, and Ethnicity

Vast numbers of people in our society have been subjected to demoralizing stereotypes as well as to both overt and covert discrimination in areas such as employment, education, and housing. We have made progress in race relations since the 1960s, but the lingering effects of mistrust and discomfort among various ethnic and racial groups can be clearly observed in many places (e.g., Eagly, 2004; Mays, Cochran, & Barnes, 2007). For example, on most college campuses, many students socialize informally only with members of their own subcultures, despite the attempts of many well-meaning college administrators to break down the barriers. These tendencies needlessly limit students' educational experiences and probably contribute to continued misinformation about, and prejudice toward, others. There are also very large health disparities between African Americans and Caucasian Americans that may at least in part be a result of various forms of discrimination (Mays et al., 2007). Perceived discrimination seems to predict lower levels of well-being for women on dimensions relating to a sense of growth, autonomy, and self-acceptance (Ryff et al., 2003). Prejudice against minority groups may also explain why these groups sometimes show increased prevalence of certain mental disorders such as depression (Cohler et al., 1995; Kessler et al., 1994). One possible reason for this is that perceived discrimination may serve as a stressor that threatens self-esteem, which in turn increases psychological distress (e.g., Cassidy et al., 2004). A recent study of Arab and Muslim Americans two years after the bombing of the World Trade Center in New York found increased psychological distress, lower levels of happiness, and increased health problems in those who had experienced personal or familial prejudice, discrimination, or violence since the World Trade Center disaster (Padela & Heisler, 2010). Finally, another study showed that African American men who experience and perceive high levels of racial discrimination are more likely to report involvement in both street violence and intimate partner violence (Reed et al., 2010).

We have made progress in recognizing the demeaning and often disabling social roles our society has historically assigned to women. Again, though, much remains to be done. Many more women than men suffer from certain emotional disorders, most notably depression and anxiety disorders, which are two of the three most common categories of disorders (Blehar, 2006). This may be at least partly a consequence of the vulnerabilities (such as passivity and dependence) intrinsic to the traditional roles assigned to women and of the sexual discrimination that still occurs in the workplace (Eagly & Carli, 2007). There are two primary types of discrimination that occur in the workplace: *access discrimination*, wherein women are not hired because they are women, and *treatment discrimination*, wherein women who have a job are paid less and receive fewer opportunities for promotion (Eagly & Carli, 2007; Eagly & Karau, 2002). Sexual harassment in the workplace is another type of stress that women may experience. In addition, the special stressors with which many modern women must cope (being full-time mothers, full-time homemakers, and full-time employees) as their traditional roles rapidly change have also been implicated in higher rates of depression, anxiety, and marital dissatisfaction in women than in the past. This is especially true if a woman works long hours (over 40 hours a week), has a higher income than her husband, and has children at home. However, it should also be noted that under at least some circumstances, working outside the home has also been shown to be a protective factor against depression and marital dissatisfaction (e.g., Brown & Harris, 1978; Helgeson, 2002).

Social Change and Uncertainty

The rate and pervasiveness of change today are different from anything our ancestors ever experienced. All aspects of our lives are affected—our education, our jobs, our families, our health, our leisure pursuits, our finances, and our beliefs and values. Constantly trying to keep up with the numerous adjustments demanded by these changes is a source of considerable stress. Simultaneously, we confront inevitable crises as the earth's consumable natural resources dwindle, as our environment becomes increasingly noxious with pollutants, and as global warming occurs. No longer are Americans confident that the future will be better than the past or that technology will solve all our problems. On the contrary, our attempts to cope with existing problems seem increasingly to create new problems that are as bad or worse. The resulting despair, demoralization, and sense of helplessness are well-established predisposing conditions for abnormal reactions to stressful events (Dohrenwend et al., 2000; Seligman, 1990, 1998). This sense of helplessness was also exacerbated for Americans by the September 11, 2001, terrorist attacks on the World Trade Center in New York and the Pentagon, with many people now living under increased worry and uncertainty over the possibility of terrorist attacks. Yet in other parts of the world, such as Israel and Palestine, people have lived with this uncertainty and worry over terrorist attacks for decades.

Today many major metropolitan areas in the United States have problems with gangs and urban violence.

Urban Stressors: Violence and Homelessness

Rapid urban growth is occurring worldwide—especially in less developed countries. Unfortunately, it is frequently unregulated and chaotic, and growing numbers of people are unemployed, homeless, or involved with illicit activities (Caracci, 2006). Perhaps not surprisingly, these areas are also plagued by a high prevalence of mental disorders. Moreover, vast numbers of people in the big cities of both developed and developing countries are direct or secondhand victims of *urban violence* (Caracci, 2006; Caracci & Mezzich, 2001). More than a decade ago it was estimated that at least 3.5 million people worldwide lose their lives to violence each year (World Health Organization, 1999), and there is no reason to think this number has declined. Domestic violence against women and children is especially widespread (e.g., Caracci, 2003). Such violence takes its toll on the victims not only in the areas of medical care and lost productivity but also in increased rates of anxiety, post-traumatic stress disorder, depression, and suicidality (e.g., Caracci, 2006; Caracci & Mezzich, 2001). One recent study of young African American mothers exposed to violence found not only increased levels of depression but also elevated levels of aggressive behavior and harsh discipline of their children (Lewin et al., 2010).

Another severe stress in urban areas worldwide is *homelessness*, which has been rapidly growing for the past few decades. Estimates are that approximately one-third of homeless people are affected by severe mental illness, but many people who are not mentally ill also become homeless because they are victims of violence or poverty (e.g., Caracci & Mezzich, 2001). Needless to say, the major stressors experienced by being homeless create mental distress including anxiety, depression, suicidality, and physical illness, even in those who started out healthy.

The Impact of the Sociocultural Viewpoint

With our increased understanding of sociocultural influences on mental health, what was previously an almost exclusive concern with individuals has broadened to include a concern with societal, communal, familial, and other group settings as factors in mental disorders. Sociocultural research has led to programs designed to improve the social conditions that foster maladaptive behavior and mental disorder, and to community facilities for the early detection, treatment, and long-range prevention of mental disorder.

There is strong evidence of cultural influences on abnormal behavior, and this area of research may yet answer many questions about the origins and courses of behavior problems as well as their treatment (Cohler et al., 1995; Miranda et al., 2005; Sue, 1999). Nevertheless, in spite of increasing research showing that patients may do better when treated by therapists from their own ethnic group (or at least by someone familiar with the patient's culture), many professionals may fail to adopt an appropriate cultural perspective when dealing with mental illness. Instead, many simply assume that the treatments that have been shown to be useful with one culture will fare as well with other cultures, when in fact this is always an empirical question (e.g., Lam & Sue, 2001; Miranda et al., 2005; Sue, 1998). In a world of instant communication with people from any country, it is crucial for our sciences and professions to take a worldview. In fact, Kleinman and Good (1985) consider cultural factors so important to our understanding of depressive disorders that they urged the psychiatric community to incorporate another axis in the *DSM* diagnostic system to reflect cultural factors in psychopathology.

Although this has not yet happened, advocates are keeping up the pressure to do so (e.g., Mezzich et al., 1999), and the authors of *DSM-IV* (APA, 1994) and *DSM-IV-TR* (APA, 2000) did take two big steps toward acknowledging the importance of cultural factors in diagnosing patients. First, they included an appendix in which they suggested ways in which cultural factors should be considered when making psychiatric diagnoses and encouraged clinicians to include cultural considerations when evaluating patients. They recommended that the clinician attend to an individual's cultural identity, to possible cultural explanations for an individual's disorder, and to cultural factors that might affect that clinician's relationship with the individual. Second, they also provided a glossary of culture-bound syndromes that usually occur only in specific societies or cultural areas and are described as "localized, folk, diagnostic categories" (APA, 2000, p. 897). Some of these are described in Box 4.

In Review

- What effects do low SES and unemployment have on adults and children?

- Describe how prejudice and discrimination, social change and uncertainty, and urban stress can have adverse effects on the development of abnormal behavior.

- In what ways did *DSM-IV* and *DSM-IV-TR* begin to acknowledge the importance of sociocultural factors in mental disorders?

Unresolved Issues

▶ *Theoretical Viewpoints and the Causes of Abnormal Behavior*

The viewpoints described here are theoretical constructions devised to orient psychologists in the study of abnormal behavior. As a set of hypothetical guidelines, each viewpoint emphasizes the importance and integrity of its own position to the exclusion of other explanations. Most psychodynamically oriented clinicians, for example, value those traditional writings and beliefs consistent with Freudian or later psychodynamic theories, and they minimize or ignore the teachings of opposing viewpoints. They usually adhere to prescribed practices of psychodynamic therapy and do not use other methods such as exposure therapy.

ADVANTAGES OF HAVING A THEORETICAL VIEWPOINT

Theoretical integrity and adherence to a systematic viewpoint have a key advantage: They ensure a consistent approach to one's practice or research efforts. Once mastered, the methodology can guide a practitioner or

researcher through the complex web of human problems. But such adherence to a theory has its disadvantages. By excluding other possible explanations, it can blind researchers to other factors that may be equally important. The fact is that none of the theories devised to date addresses the whole spectrum of abnormality—each is limited in some way in its focus.

Two general trends have occurred as a result. First, the original model or theory may be revised by expanding or modifying some elements of the system. The many examples of such modified interpretations include Adler's and Erikson's modifications of Freudian theory and the more recent cognitive-behavioral approach's modification of behavior therapy. But many of the early Freudian theorists did not accept the neo-Freudian additions, and some classical behavior therapists today still do not accept the revisions proposed by cognitive behaviorists. Therefore, the second trend has been for theoretical viewpoints to multiply and coexist—each with its own proponents—rather than being assimilated into previous views.

THE ECLECTIC APPROACH

Alternatively, aspects of two or more diverse approaches may be combined in a more general, eclectic approach. In practice, many psychologists have responded to the existence of many perspectives by adopting an eclectic stance; that is, they accept working ideas from several viewpoints and incorporate whichever they find useful. For example, a psychologist using an eclectic approach might accept causal explanations from psychodynamic theory while applying techniques of anxiety reduction from behavior therapy. Another psychologist might combine techniques from the cognitive-behavioral approach with those from the interpersonal approach. Purists in the field—those who advocate a single viewpoint—are skeptical about eclecticism, claiming that the eclectic approach tends to lack integrity and produces a "crazy quilt" of inconsistent practice with little rationale. This criticism may be true, but the approach certainly seems to work for many psychotherapists.

Typically, those who use an eclectic approach to treatment make no attempt to synthesize the theoretical perspectives. Although this approach can work in practical settings, it is not successful at a theoretical level because the underlying principles of many of the theoretical perspectives are incompatible as they now stand. Thus the eclectic approach still falls short of the final goal, which is to tackle the theoretical clutter and develop a single, comprehensive, internally consistent viewpoint that accurately reflects what we know empirically about abnormal behavior.

THE BIOPSYCHOSOCIAL UNIFIED APPROACH

At present, the only attempt at such a unified perspective that has been developing is called the *biopsychosocial viewpoint*. This viewpoint reflects the conviction that most disorders are the result of many causal factors—biological, psychological, and sociocultural—interacting with one another. Moreover, for any given person, the particular combination of causal factors may be unique, or at least not widely shared by large numbers of people with the same disorder. For example, some children may become delinquents primarily because of having a heavy genetic loading for antisocial behavior, whereas others may become delinquent primarily because of environmental influences such as living in an area with a large number of gangs. Therefore, we can still hope to achieve a scientific understanding of many of the causes of abnormal behavior even if we cannot predict such behavior with exact certainty in each individual case and are often left with some "unexplained" influences.

Summary

- In considering the causes of abnormal behavior, it is important to distinguish among necessary, sufficient, and contributory causal factors, as well as between relatively distal causal factors and those that are more proximal.

- Usually the occurrence of abnormal or maladaptive behavior is considered to be the joint product of a person's predisposition or vulnerability (diathesis) to disorder and of certain stressors that challenge his or her coping resources.

- The concept of protective factors is important for understanding why some people with both a diathesis and a stressor may remain resilient and not develop a disorder.

- Both the distal (long-ago) and proximal (immediate) risk factors for mental disorder may involve biological, psychological, and sociocultural factors. These three classes of factors can interact with each other in complicated ways during the development of mental disorders.

- This text discusses biological, psychological, and sociocultural viewpoints, each of which tends to emphasize the importance of causal factors of a characteristic type. Ultimately we strive for an integrative biopsychosocial viewpoint.

- In examining biologically based vulnerabilities, we must consider abnormalities in neurochemical and hormonal systems, genetic vulnerabilities, temperament, and brain dysfunction and neural plasticity.

- Many different neurotransmitter and hormonal abnormalities contribute to the development of mental disorders because of the effects they exert on different relevant brain and body areas for different disorders.

- Genetic vulnerabilities can affect the development of mental disorders through multiple mechanisms, including ways in which the genotype may affect the phenotype (genotype–environment correlations) and in which they affect an individual's susceptibility to environmental influences (genotype–environment interactions).

- Methods for studying the extent of genetic versus environmental influences include the family history method, the twin method, and the adoption method. More recently, linkage analysis and association studies are beginning to contribute knowledge about the exact location of genes contributing to mental disorders.

- Temperament is strongly influenced by genetic factors and refers to a baby's characteristic ways of reacting to the environment and his or her ways of self-regulation. It forms the basis of our adult personality, which in turn influences our vulnerability to different disorders.

- Studies of neural plasticity have shown that genetic programs for brain development are not as fixed as once believed and that existing neural circuits can often be modified based on experience.

- In examining psychologically based vulnerabilities, there are three primary perspectives that have developed since the end of the nineteenth century: psychodynamic, behavioral, and cognitive-behavioral.

- The oldest psychological viewpoint on abnormal behavior is Freudian psychoanalytic theory. For many years this view was preoccupied with questions about libidinal (id) energies and their containment.

- More recently, four second-generation psychodynamic theories departed in significant ways from Freud's original ideas.

- Anna Freud's ego psychology focused on the important role of the ego in normal and abnormal behavior, with special attention focused on ego-defense reactions.

- Object-relations theorists focused on the role of the quality of very early (pre-Oedipal) mother–infant relationships for normal development.

- The originators of the interpersonal perspective took exception to the Freudian emphasis on the internal determinants of motivation and behavior and instead emphasized the social and cultural forces that shape behavior.

- Attachment theory, which has roots in both the interpersonal and object-relations perspectives, emphasizes the importance of early experiences with attachment relationships for laying the foundation for later child, adolescent, and adult development.

- Psychoanalysis and closely related therapeutic approaches are termed *psychodynamic* in recognition of their attention to inner, often unconscious forces.

- The behavioral perspective focuses on the role of learning in human behavior and attributes maladaptive behavior either to a failure to learn appropriate behaviors or to the learning of maladaptive behaviors.

- The primary forms of learning studied are classical conditioning and instrumental (operant) learning. The effects of each are modified by principles of generalization and discrimination. Observational learning is also important.

- Adherents of the behavioral viewpoint attempt to alter maladaptive behavior by extinguishing it or providing training in new, more adaptive behaviors.

- The cognitive-behavioral viewpoint attempts to incorporate the complexities of human cognition, and how it can become distorted, into an understanding of the causes of psychopathology.

- People's schemas and self-schemas play a central role in the way they process information, in how they attribute outcomes to causes, and in their values. The efficiency, accuracy, and coherence of a person's schemas and self-schemas and attributions appear to provide an important protection against breakdown.

- Treatments developed from the cognitive-behavioral perspective attempt to alter maladaptive thinking and improve a person's abilities to solve problems and to achieve goals.

- Sources of psychologically determined vulnerability include early social deprivation or severe emotional trauma, inadequate parenting styles, marital discord and divorce, and maladaptive peer relationships.

- The sociocultural viewpoint is concerned with the contribution of sociocultural variables to mental disorder.

- Although many serious mental disorders are fairly universal, the form that some disorders take and their prevalence vary widely among different cultures.

- Low socioeconomic status and unemployment; being subjected to prejudice and discrimination in race, gender, and ethnicity; experiencing social change and uncertainty; and urban violence and homelessness are all associated with greater risk for various disorders.

- The biopsychosocial approach is promising, but in many ways it is merely a descriptive acknowledgment of the complex interactions among biological, psychological, and sociocultural risk factors rather than a clearly articulated theory of how they interact.

Key Terms

adoption method
association studies
attachment theory
attribution
behavior genetics
biopsychosocial viewpoint

castration anxiety
chromosomes
classical conditioning
cognitive-behavioral perspective
concordance rate
contributory cause

cortisol
developmental psychopathology
developmental systems approach
diathesis
diathesis-stress models
discrimination

ego	instrumental (operant) conditioning	psychosexual stages of development
ego psychology	interpersonal perspective	reality principle
ego-defense mechanisms	intrapsychic conflicts	reinforcement
Electra complex	learning	resilience
etiology	libido	schema
extinction	linkage analysis	secondary process thinking
family history method	necessary cause	self-schema
generalization	neurotransmitters	spontaneous recovery
genes	object-relations theory	stress
genotype	observational learning	sufficient cause
genotype–environment correlation	Oedipus complex	superego
	phenotype	synapse
genotype–environment interaction	pituitary gland	temperament
hormones	pleasure principle	twin method
hypothalamic-pituitary-adrenal axis (HPA axis)	polygenic	
	primary process thinking	
id	protective factors	

Glossary

Many of the key terms listed in the glossary appear in boldface when first introduced in the text discussion. A number of other terms commonly encountered in this or other psychology texts are also included; you are encouraged to make use of this glossary both as a general reference tool and as a study aid for the course in abnormal psychology.

Adoption method. Comparison of biological and adoptive relatives with and without a given disorder to assess genetic versus environmental influences.

Association studies. Genetic research strategy comparing frequency of certain genetic markers known to be located on particular chromosomes in people with and without a particular disorder.

Attachment theory. Contemporary developmental and psychodynamic theory emphasizing the importance of early experience with attachment relationships in laying the foundation for later functioning throughout life.

Attribution. Process of assigning causes to things that happen.

Behavior genetics. Field that studies the heritability of mental disorders and other aspects of psychological functioning such as personality and intelligence.

Biopsychosocial viewpoint. A viewpoint that acknowledges the interacting roles of biological, psychosocial, and sociocultural factors in the origins of psychopathology.

Castration anxiety. As postulated by Freud, the anxiety a young boy experiences when he desires his mother while at the same time fearing that his father may harm him by cutting off his penis; this anxiety forces the boy to repress his sexual desire for his mother and his hostility toward his father.

Chromosomes. Chain-like structures within cell nucleus that contain genes.

Classical conditioning. A basic form of learning in which a neutral stimulus is paired repeatedly with an unconditioned stimulus (US) that naturally elicits an unconditioned response (UR). After repeated pairings, the neutral stimulus becomes a conditioned stimulus (CS) that elicits a conditioned response (CR).

Cognitive-behavioral perspective. A theory of abnormal behavior that focuses on how thoughts and information processing can become distorted and lead to maladaptive emotions and behavior.

Concordance rate. The percentage of twins sharing a disorder or trait.

Contributory cause. A condition that increases the probability of developing a disorder but that is neither necessary nor sufficient for it to occur.

Cortisol. Human stress hormone released by the cortex of the adrenal glands.

Developmental psychopathology. Field of psychology that focuses on determining what is abnormal at any point in the developmental process by comparing and contrasting it with normal and expected changes that occur.

Developmental systems approach. Acknowledgment that genetic activity influences neural activity, which in turn influences behavior, which in turn influences the environment, and that these influences are bidirectional.

Diathesis. Predisposition or vulnerability to developing a given disorder.

Diathesis-stress model. View of abnormal behavior as the result of stress operating on an individual who has a biological, psychosocial, or sociocultural predisposition to developing a specific disorder.

Discrimination. Ability to interpret and respond differently to two or more similar stimuli.

Ego. In psychoanalytic theory, the rational part of the personality that mediates between the demands of the id, the constraints of the superego, and the realities of the external world.

Ego psychology. Psychodynamic theory emphasizing the importance of the ego—the "executive branch of the personality"—in organizing normal personality development.

Ego-defense mechanisms. Psychic mechanisms that discharge or soothe anxiety rather than coping directly with an anxiety-provoking situation; usually unconscious and reality distorting. Also called *defense mechanisms.*

Electra complex. Excessive emotional attachment (love) of a daughter for her father; the female counterpart of the Oedipus complex.

Etiology. Factors that are related to the development (or cause) of a particular disorder.

Extinction. Gradual disappearance of a conditioned response when it is no longer reinforced.

Family history method. Behavior genetic research strategy that examines the incidence of disorder in relatives of an index case to determine whether incidence increases in proportion to the degree of the hereditary relationship.

Generalization. Tendency of a response that has been conditioned to one stimulus to be elicited by other, similar stimuli.

Genes. Long molecules of DNA that are present at various locations on chromosomes and that are responsible for the transmission of hereditary traits.

Genotype. A person's total genetic endowment.

Genotype–environment correlation. Genotypic vulnerability that can shape a child's environmental experiences.

Genotype–environment interaction. Differential sensitivity or susceptibility to their environments by people who have different genotypes.

Hormones. Chemical messengers secreted by endocrine glands that regulate development of and activity in various parts of the body.

Hypothalamic-pituitary-adrenal axis (HPA axis). Brain endocrine system involved in responding to stress in which the hypothalamus and pituitary send messages to the adrenal gland which releases a stress hormone that feeds back on the hypothalamus.

Id. In psychoanalytic theory, the reservoir of instinctual drives and the first structure to appear in infancy.

Instrumental (operant) conditioning. Reinforcement of a subject for making a correct response that leads either to receipt of something rewarding or to escape from something unpleasant.

Interpersonal perspective. Approach to understanding abnormal behavior that views much of psychopathology as rooted in the unfortunate tendencies we develop while dealing with our interpersonal environments; it thus focuses on our relationships, past and present, with other people.

Intrapsychic conflict. Inner mental struggles resulting from the interplay of the id, ego, and superego when the three subsystems are striving for different goals.

Learning. Modification of behavior as a consequence of experience.

Libido. In psychoanalytic theory, a term used to describe the instinctual drives of the id; the basic constructive energy of life, primarily sexual in nature.

Linkage analysis. Genetic research strategy in which occurrence of a disorder in an extended family is compared with that of a genetic marker for a physical characteristic or biological process that is known to be located on a particular chromosome. A soft, silver-white metal that belongs to the alkali metal group of chemicals. It is used to treat and prevent episodes of mania and bipolar disorder. botomy. See **Prefrontal lobotomy.**

Necessary cause. A condition that must exist for a disorder to occur.

Neurotransmitters. Chemical substances that are released into a synapse by the presynaptic neuron and that transmit nerve impulses from one neuron to another.

Object-relations theory. In psychoanalytic theory, this viewpoint focuses on an infant or young child's interactions with "objects" (that is, real or imagined people), as well as how they make symbolic representations of important people in their lives.

Observational learning. Learning through observation alone without directly experiencing an unconditioned stimulus (for classical conditioning) or a reinforcement (for instrumental conditioning).

Oedipus complex. Desire for sexual relations with a parent of opposite sex; specifically, the desire of a boy for his mother, with his father a hated rival.

Phenotype. The observed structural and functional characteristics of a person that result from interaction between the genotype and the environment.

Pituitary gland. Endocrine gland associated with many regulatory functions.

Pleasure principle. Demand that an instinctual need be immediately gratified regardless of reality or moral considerations.

Polygenic. Caused by the action of many genes together in an additive or interactive fashion.

Primary process thinking. Gratification of id demands by means of imagery or fantasy without the ability to undertake the realistic actions needed to meet those instinctual demands.

Protective factors. Influences that modify a person's response to an environmental stressor, making it less likely that the person will experience the adverse effects of the stressor.

Psychosexual stages of development. According to Freudian theory, there are five stages of psychosexual development, each characterized by a dominant mode of achieving sexual pleasure: the oral stage, the anal stage, the phallic stage, the latency stage, and the genital stage.

Reality principle. Awareness of the demands of the environment and adjustment of behavior to meet these demands.

Reinforcement. The process of rewarding desired responses.

Resilience. The ability to adapt successfully to even very difficult circumstances.

Schema. An underlying representation of knowledge that guides current processing of information and often leads to distortions in attention, memory, and comprehension.

Secondary process thinking. Reality-oriented rational processes of the ego for dealing with the external world and the exercise of control over id demands.

Self-schema. Our view of what we are, what we might become, and what is important to us.

Spontaneous recovery. The return of a learned response at some time after extinction has occurred.

Stress. Effects created within an organism by the application of a stressor.

Sufficient cause. A condition that guarantees the occurrence of a disorder.

Superego. Conscience; ethical or moral dimensions (attitudes) of personality.

Synapse. Site of communication from the axon of one neuron to the dendrites or cell body of another neuron—a tiny filled space between neurons.

Temperament. Pattern of emotional and arousal responses and characteristic ways of self-regulation that are considered to be primarily hereditary or constitutional.

Twin method. The use of identical and nonidentical twins to study genetic influences on abnormal behavior.

Photo Credits

Credits are listed in order of appearance.
Stockbyte/Getty Images; Kratka Photography/Shutterstock.com; © Myrleen Ferguson Cate/PhotoEdit; © Janine Wiedel Photolibrary/Alamy; SPL/Photo Researchers, Inc.; AP Photo; David White/Alamy; Image Source Pink/Alamy; © Tongro Image Stock/AGE Fotostock; © Bettmann/CORBIS; Courtesy of the Margaret S. Mahler Psychiatric Research Foundation; Time & Life Pictures/Getty Images; Courtesy Library of Congress; Image 100/AGE Fotostock; Dr. Albert Bandura; Blend Images/Alamy; University of Pennsylvania; Image Source/Alamy; Getty Images; © Alison Wright/Corbis; Enigma/Alamy; SHOUT/Alamy; © Image Source/Alamy; Photolibrary Royalty Free; Lindsay Hebberd/Corbis; © James Marshall/CORBIS; © David R. Frazier Photolibrary, Inc./Alamy.

Text Credits

Figure 2: From S. M. Monroe & A.D. Simons. Diathesis-stress theories in the context of life stress research: Implications for the depressive disorders. *Psychological Bulletin* 110, 1991, pp. 406–25; Figure 5: From "Human Chromosome Pairs," *Principles of Medical Genetics* by Thomas D. Gelehrter et al, 1998; Figure 6: From Gilbert Gottlieb, from *Individual Development and Evolution: The Genesis of Novel behavior,* 1992; Table 1: Source: Based on Freud (1946) and *DSM-IV-TR* (2000); "Culture-Bound Syndromes" Sources: Based on American Psychiatric Association (*DSM-IV-TR,* 2000); Bartholomew (1997); Chowdhury (1996); Hatta (1996); Kiev (1972); Kirmayer (1991); Kirmayer et al (1995); Lebra (1976); Lewis & Ednie (1997); Sakamoto et al (2005); Sheung Tak (1996); Simons & Hughes (1985).

Clinical Assessment and Diagnosis

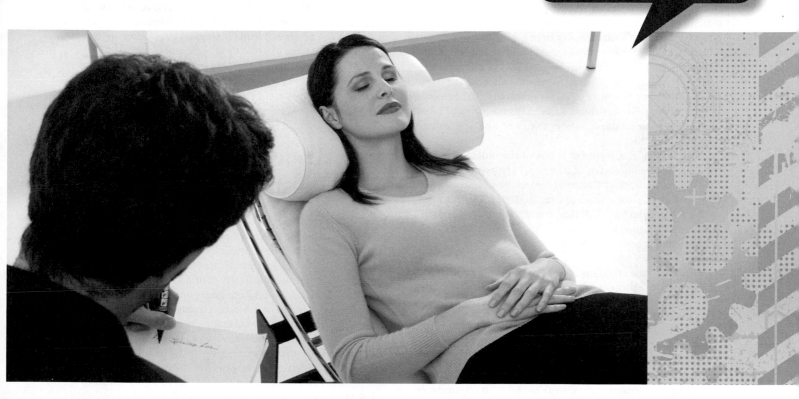

The Basic Elements in Assessment
The Relationship Between Assessment and Diagnosis
Taking a Social or Behavioral History
Ensuring Culturally Sensitive Assessment Procedures
The Influence of Professional Orientation
Reliability, Validity, and Standardization
Trust and Rapport Between the Clinician and the Client

Assessment of the Physical Organism
The General Physical Examination
The Neurological Examination
The Neuropsychological Examination

Psychosocial Assessment
Assessment Interviews
The Clinical Observation of Behavior
Psychological Tests
The Case of Andrea C.: Experiencing Violence in the Workplace

The Integration of Assessment Data
Ethical Issues in Assessment

Classifying Abnormal Behavior
Differing Models of Classification
Formal Diagnostic Classification of Mental Disorders

Unresolved Issues
The *DSM-V*: What Comes Next?

The assessment of the personality and motivation of others has been of interest to people since antiquity. Early records show that some individuals used assessment methods to evaluate potential personality problems or behaviors. There are documented attempts at understanding personality characteristics in ancient civilizations. Hathaway (1965) points out that one of the earliest descriptions of using behavioral observation in assessing personality can be found in the Old Testament. Gideon relied upon observations of his men who trembled with fear to consider them fit for duty; Gideon also observed how soldiers chose to drink water from a stream as a means of selecting effective soldiers for battle. In ancient Rome, Tacitus provided examples in which the appraisal of a person's personality entered into their leader's judgments about them. Tacitus (translated by Grant, 1956, p. 36) points out that Emperor Tiberius evaluated his subordinates in his meetings by often pretending to be hesitant in order to detect what the leading men were thinking.

Psychological assessment is one of the oldest and most widely developed branches of contemporary psychology, dating back to the work of Galton (1879) in the nineteenth century (Butcher, 2010; Weiner & Greene, 2008). We will focus in this text on the initial clinical assessment and on arriving at a clinical diagnosis according to *DSM-IV-TR*. **Psychological assessment** refers to a procedure by which clinicians, using psychological tests, observation, and interviews, develop a summary of the client's symptoms and problems. **Clinical diagnosis** is the process through which a clinician arrives at a general "summary classification" of the patient's symptoms by following a clearly defined system such as *DSM-IV-TR* or ICD-10 (International Classification of Diseases), the latter published by the World Health Organization.

Assessment is an ongoing process and may be important at various points during treatment, not just at the beginning—for example, to examine the client's progress in treatment or to evaluate outcome. In the initial clinical assessment, an attempt is usually made to identify the main dimensions of a client's problem and to predict the probable course of events under various conditions. It is at this initial stage that crucial decisions have to be made—such as what (if any) treatment approach is to be offered, whether the problem will require hospitalization, to what extent family members will need to be included as coclients, and so on. Sometimes these decisions must be made quickly, as in emergency conditions, and without critical information. As will be seen, various psychological measurement instruments are employed to maximize assessment efficiency in this type of pretreatment examination process (Harwood & Beutler, 2009).

A less obvious but equally important function of pretreatment assessment is establishing baselines for various psychological functions so that the effects of treatment can be measured. Criteria based on these measurements may be established as part of the treatment plan such that the therapy is considered successful and is terminated only when the client's behavior meets these predetermined criteria.

Comparison of posttreatment with pretreatment assessment results is an essential feature of many research projects designed to evaluate the effectiveness of various therapies.

In this text, we will review some of the more commonly used assessment procedures and show how the data obtained can be integrated into a coherent clinical picture for making decisions about referral and treatment. Our survey will include a discussion of physical, neurological, and neuropsychological assessment; the clinical interview; behavioral observation; and personality assessment through the use of projective and objective psychological tests. Later we will examine the process of arriving at a clinical diagnosis using *DSM-IV-TR*.

Let us look first at what, exactly, a clinician is trying to learn during the psychological assessment of a client.

The Basic Elements in Assessment

What does a clinician need to know? First, of course, the **presenting problem**, or major symptoms and behavior the client is experiencing, must be identified. Is it a situational problem precipitated by some environmental stressor such as divorce or unemployment, a manifestation of a more pervasive and long-term disorder, or some combination of the two? Is there any evidence of recent deterioration in cognitive functioning? What is the duration of the current complaint, and how is the person dealing with the problem? What, if any, prior help has been sought? Are there indications of self-defeating behavior and personality deterioration, or is the individual using available personal and environmental resources in a good effort to cope? How pervasively has the problem affected the person's performance of important social roles? Does the individual's symptomatic behavior fit any of the diagnostic patterns in the *DSM-IV-TR*?

The Relationship Between Assessment and Diagnosis

It is important to have an adequate classification of the presenting problem for a number of reasons. Clinically, knowledge of a person's type of disorder can help in planning and managing the appropriate treatment. Administratively, it is essential to know the range of diagnostic problems that are represented in the client population and for which treatment facilities need to be available. If most clients at a facility have been diagnosed as having personality disorders, for example, then the staffing, physical environment, and treatment facilities should be arranged accordingly, for example, with appropriate security and clearly established rules. In many cases, a formal diagnosis is necessary before insurance claims can be filed to cover the client's treatment costs. Thus the nature of the difficulty needs to be understood as clearly as possible, including a diagnostic categorization if appropriate (see the section "Classifying Abnormal Behavior" at the end).

Taking a Social or Behavioral History

For most clinical purposes, assigning a formal diagnostic classification per se is much less important than having a clear understanding of the individual's behavioral history, intellectual functioning, personality characteristics, and environmental pressures and resources. That is, an adequate assessment includes much more than the diagnostic label. For example, it should include an objective description of the person's behavior. How does the person characteristically respond to other people? Are there excesses in behavior present, such as eating or drinking too much? Are there notable deficits, for example, in social skills? How appropriate is the person's behavior? Is the person manifesting behavior that is plainly unresponsive or uncooperative? Excesses, deficits, and appropriateness are key dimensions to be noted if the clinician is to understand the particular disorder that has brought the individual to the clinic or hospital.

PERSONALITY FACTORS Assessment should include a description of any relevant long-term personality characteristics. Has the person typically responded in deviant ways to particular kinds of situations—for example, those requiring submission to legitimate authority? Are there personality traits or behavior patterns that predispose the individual to behave in maladaptive ways? Does the person tend to become enmeshed with others to the point of losing his or her identity, or is he or she so self-absorbed that intimate relationships are not possible? Is the person able to accept help from others? Is the person capable of genuine affection and of accepting appropriate responsibility for the welfare of others? Such questions are at the heart of many assessment efforts.

THE SOCIAL CONTEXT It is also important to assess the social context in which the individual functions. What kinds of environmental demands are typically placed on the person, and what supports or special stressors exist in her or his life situation? For example, being the primary caretaker for a spouse suffering from Alzheimer's disease is so challenging that relatively few people can manage the task without significant psychological impairment, especially where outside supports are lacking.

The diverse and often conflicting bits of information about the individual's personality traits, behavior patterns, environmental demands, and so on must then be integrated into a consistent and meaningful picture. Some clinicians refer to this picture as a "dynamic formulation" because it not only describes the current situation but also includes hypotheses about what is driving the person to behave in maladaptive

ways. At this point in the assessment, the clinician should have a plausible explanation for why a normally passive and mild-mannered man suddenly flew into a rage and started breaking up furniture, for example. The formulation should allow the clinician to develop hypotheses about the client's future behavior as well. What is the likelihood of improvement or deterioration if the person's problems are left untreated? Which behaviors should be the initial focus of change, and what treatment methods are likely to be most efficient in producing this change? How much change might be expected from a particular type of treatment?

Where feasible, decisions about treatment are made collaboratively with the consent and approval of the individual. In cases of severe disorder, however, they may have to be made without the client's participation or, in rare instances, even without consulting responsible family members. As has already been indicated, knowledge of the person's strengths and resources is important; in short, what qualities does the client bring to treatment that can enhance the chances of improvement? Because a wide range of factors can play important roles in causing and maintaining maladaptive behavior, assessment may involve the coordinated use of physical, psychological, and environmental assessment procedures. As we have indicated, however, the nature and comprehensiveness of clinical assessments vary with the problem and the treatment agency's facilities. Assessment by phone in a suicide prevention center (Stolberg & Bongar, 2009), for example, is quite different from assessment aimed at developing a treatment plan for a person who has come to a clinic for help (Perry, 2009).

Ensuring Culturally Sensitive Assessment Procedures

Increasingly, practitioners are being asked to conduct psychological evaluations with clients from diverse ethnic and language backgrounds. In both clinical and court settings, for

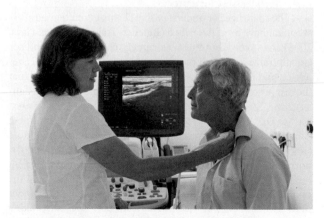

Some patients with cognitive deterioration are difficult to evaluate and to provide health care for, often requiring special facilities.

example, a psychologist might be referred a client who has limited English language skills and low exposure to American mores, values, and laws. It is critical for the psychologist to be informed of the issues involved in multicultural assessment (often referred to as **cultural competence**) and to use testing procedures that have been adapted and validated for culturally diverse clients (Hays, 2008; Hunter et al., 2009).

Psychological assessment of clients from diverse ethnic backgrounds has increased greatly in recent years. The growing number of minorities requiring a clinical or forensic evaluation comes about, in part, from the influx of immigrants or refugees, many of whom encounter adjustment difficulties. The U.S. Census Bureau (2011) reports that the Hispanic population now makes up 16 percent of the U.S. population. People of Hispanic origin are now the largest ethnic minority group in the United States. African Americans now represent 12.9 percent of the population and Asians 4.5 percent, Native Americans 1.0 percent, and Native Hawaiians/Pacific Islanders less than 0.1 percent. Many immigrants, especially those of color, become members of ethnic minorities when they relocate to North America. They may thus experience racial discrimination or may be further viewed as inferior by the nonminority community due to their lack of political power or lack of adaptive skills arising from their difficulties in acculturation (Green, 2009; Hays, 2008).

In order to fairly and successfully treat such individuals, the ethics code of the American Psychological Association (APA, 2002) recommends that psychologists consider various test factors, test-taking abilities, and other characteristics of the person being assessed, such as situational, linguistic, and cultural differences, that might affect his or her judgments or reduce the accuracy of his or her interpretations. Thus, psychologists who use tests in a culturally competent manner must bear in mind a range of issues and factors involved with culturally and linguistically diverse clients. These issues involve the importance of ensuring that the characteristics of the test being employed are appropriate across cultures and that potential biasing factors do not interfere with critical thinking in the overall assessment process.

The challenges of understanding clients in multicultural assessment have been described (Butcher, Tsai, et al., 2006; Hays, 2008) and involve both test instrument characteristics and sociocultural factors such as the relationships among culture, behavior, and psychopathology. Psychologists need to ensure that the test procedures they employ are appropriate for the particular client. For example, the psychological equivalence of the test for use with the particular population should be determined. The meaning or cultural significance of test items should be similar across cultural groups (Butcher & Han, 1996), and the norms used to compare the client should be appropriate. In using Western-developed tests, users need to take into account the dominant language, socioeconomic status, ethnicity, and gender of their clients. For example, clients from non-English-speaking countries might have insufficient English language skills, which will influence their test performance. When using a translated

version of a test, interpreters need to be aware of the possible differences that can be obtained using an adapted version. Thus it is important for psychologists to be aware of the available research on the instrument's use with the target population in order to assess whether the adapted version measures the same variables in the new cultures. Finally, test users need to be concerned with the impact and fairness of the instruments they employ with clients from diverse groups—for example, whether there are any possible performance differences on the scales between groups.

The most widely used personality measure, the Minnesota Multiphasic Personality Inventory (MMPI-2) (to be discussed later in this text), has been widely evaluated both in international applications with translated versions (Butcher & Williams, 2009) and in diverse subcultural groups in the United States (Butcher et al., 2007). There have been more than 500 publications on the MMPI and its successor, MMPI-2, and there are Spanish-language versions of the test. Recent research has provided support for the use of the MMPI-2 with minorities (Robin et al., 2003), and the analyses provided by Hall and colleagues (1999) support the use of the MMPI-2 with Hispanic clients.

The Influence of Professional Orientation

How clinicians go about the assessment process often depends on their basic treatment orientations. For example, a biologically oriented clinician—typically a psychiatrist or other medical practitioner—is likely to focus on biological assessment methods aimed at determining any underlying organic malfunctioning that may be causing the maladaptive behavior. A psychodynamic or psychoanalytically oriented clinician may choose unstructured personality assessment techniques, such as the Rorschach inkblots or the Thematic Apperception Test (TAT), to be described later, to identify intrapsychic conflicts or may simply proceed with therapy, expecting these conflicts to emerge naturally as part of the treatment process. A behaviorally oriented clinician, in an effort to determine the functional relationships between environmental events or reinforcements and the abnormal behavior, will rely on such techniques as behavioral observation and self-monitoring to identify learned maladaptive patterns; for a cognitively oriented behaviorist, the focus would shift to the dysfunctional thoughts supposedly mediating those patterns.

The preceding examples represent general trends and are in no way meant to imply that clinicians of a particular orientation limit themselves to a particular assessment method or that each assessment technique is limited to a particular theoretical orientation. Such trends are instead a matter of emphasis and point to the fact that certain types of assessments are more conducive than others to uncovering particular causal factors or for eliciting information about symptomatic behavior central to understanding and treating a disorder within a given conceptual framework.

As you will see in what follows, both physical and psychosocial data can be extremely important to understanding the patient. In the sections that follow we will discuss several assessment instruments and examine in some detail an actual psychological study of a woman who experienced a traumatic situation in the workplace that resulted in severe emotional adjustment problems.

Reliability, Validity, and Standardization

Three measurement concepts that are important in understanding clinical assessment and the utility of psychological tests are *reliability*, *validity*, and *standardization*. These concepts, illustrated throughout this text, will be briefly described. A psychological test or measurement construct needs to show reliability in order to be effective. **Reliability** is a term describing the degree to which an assessment measure produces the same result each time it is used to evaluate the same thing. If, for example, your scale showed a significantly different weight each time you stepped on it over a brief period of time, you would consider it a fairly unreliable measure of your body mass. In the context of assessment or classification, reliability is an index of the extent to which a measurement instrument can agree that a person's behavior fits a given diagnostic class. If the observations are different, it may mean that the classification criteria are not precise enough to determine whether the suspected disorder is present.

The psychological test or classification system must also be valid. **Validity** is the extent to which a measuring instrument actually measures what it is supposed to measure. In the context of testing or classification, validity is the degree to which a measure accurately conveys to us something clinically important about the person whose behavior fits the category, such as helping to predict the future course of the disorder. If, for example, a person is predicted to have or is diagnosed as having schizophrenia, we should be able to infer the presence of some fairly precise characteristics that differentiate the person from individuals who are considered normal or from those with other types of mental disorder. The classification or diagnosis of schizophrenia, for example, implies a disorder of unusually stubborn persistence, with recurrent episodes being common.

Normally, the validity of a mental health measure or classification presupposes reliability. If clinicians can't agree on the class to which a person with a disorder's behavior belongs, then the question of the validity of the diagnostic classifications under consideration becomes irrelevant. To put it another way, if we can't confidently pin down what the diagnosis is, then whatever useful information a given diagnosis might convey about the person being evaluated is lost. On the other hand, good reliability does not in itself guarantee validity. For example, handedness (left, right, ambidextrous) can be assessed with a high degree of reliability, but handedness accurately

predicts neither mental health status nor countless other behavioral qualities on which people vary; that is, it is not a valid index of these qualities (although it may be a valid index for success in certain situations involving the game of baseball, for example). In like manner, reliable assignment of a person's behavior to a given class of mental disorder will prove useful only to the extent that the validity of that class has been established through research.

Standardization is a process by which a psychological test is administered, scored, and interpreted in a consistent or "standard" manner. Standardized tests are considered to be more fair in that they are applied consistently and in the same manner to all persons taking them. Many psychological tests are standardized to allow the test user to compare a particular individual's score on the test with a reference population, often referred to as a normative sample. For example, comparing a particular individual's test score on a distribution of test scores from a large normative population can enable the user to evaluate whether the individual's score is low, average, or high along the distribution of scores (referred to as a **T score distribution**).

Trust and Rapport Between the Clinician and the Client

In order for psychological assessment to proceed effectively and to provide a clear understanding of behavior and symptoms, the client being evaluated must feel comfortable with the clinician. In a clinical assessment situation, this means that a client must feel that the testing will help the practitioner gain a clear understanding of her or his problems and must understand how the tests will be used and how the psychologist will incorporate them into the clinical evaluation. The clinician should explain what will happen during assessment and how the information gathered will help provide a clearer picture of the problems the client is facing.

Clients need to be assured that the feelings, beliefs, attitudes, and personal history that they are disclosing will be used appropriately, will be kept in strict confidence, and will be made available only to therapists or others involved in the case. An important aspect of confidentiality is that the test results are released to a third party only if the client signs an appropriate release form. In cases in which the person is being tested for a third party such as the court system, the client in effect is the referring source—the judge ordering the evaluation—not the individual being tested. In these cases the testing relationship is likely to be strained and developing rapport is likely to be difficult. Of course, in a court-ordered evaluation, the person's test-taking behavior is likely to be very different from what it would be otherwise, and interpretation of the test needs to reflect this different motivational set created by the person's unwillingness to cooperate.

People being tested in a clinical situation are usually highly motivated to be evaluated and like to know the results of the testing. They generally are eager for some definition of their discomfort. Moreover, providing test feedback in a clinical setting can be an important element in the treatment process (Harwood & Beutler, 2009). Interestingly, when patients are given appropriate feedback on test results, they tend to improve—just from gaining a perspective on their problems from the testing. The test feedback process itself can be a powerful clinical intervention (Finn & Kamphuis, 2006; Finn & Tonsager, 1997). When persons who were not provided psychological test feedback were compared with those who were provided with feedback, the latter group showed a significant decline in reported symptoms and an increase in measured self-esteem as a result of having a clearer understanding of their own resources.

In Review

- What is the difference between clinical diagnosis and psychological assessment? What components must be integrated into a dynamic formulation?

- Describe the important elements in a social or behavioral history.

- What does it mean to use culturally fair assessments?

- What is the impact of professional orientation on the structure and form of a psychological evaluation?

- Does providing test feedback to clients aid them in their adjustment?

Assessment of the Physical Organism

In some situations and with certain psychological problems, a medical evaluation is necessary to rule out the possibility that physical abnormalities may be causing or contributing to the problem. The medical evaluation may include both a general physical examination and special examinations aimed at assessing the structural (anatomical) and functional (physiological) integrity of the brain as a behaviorally significant physical system (Fatemi & Clayton, 2008).

The General Physical Examination

In cases in which physical symptoms are part of the presenting clinical picture, a referral for a medical evaluation is recommended. A physical examination consists of the kinds of procedures most of us have experienced when getting a "medical checkup." Typically, a medical history is obtained, and the major systems of the body are checked (Fatemi & Clayton, 2008;

LeBlond et al., 2004). This part of the assessment procedure is of obvious importance for disorders that entail physical problems, such as a psychologically based physical condition, addictive, and organic brain syndromes. In addition, a variety of organic conditions, including various hormonal irregularities, can produce behavioral symptoms that closely mimic those of mental disorders usually considered to have predominantly psychosocial origins. Although some long-lasting pain can be related to actual organic conditions, other such pain can result from strictly emotional factors. A case in point is chronic back pain, in which psychological factors may sometimes play an important part. A diagnostic error in this type of situation could result in costly and ineffective surgery; hence, in equivocal cases, most clinicians insist on a medical clearance before initiating psychosocially based interventions.

The Neurological Examination

Because brain pathology is sometimes involved in some mental disorders (e.g., unusual memory deficits or motor impairments), a specialized neurological examination can be administered in addition to the general medical examination. This may involve the client's getting an **electroencephalogram (EEG)** to assess brain wave patterns in awake and sleeping states. An EEG is a graphical record of the brain's electrical activity (O'Sullivan et al., 2006). It is obtained by placing electrodes on the scalp and amplifying the minute brain wave impulses from various brain areas; these amplified impulses drive oscillating pens whose deviations are traced on a strip of paper moving at a constant speed. Much is known about the normal pattern of brain impulses in waking and sleeping states and under various conditions of sensory stimulation. Significant divergences from the normal pattern can thus reflect abnormalities of brain function such as might be caused

An EEG is a graphical record of the brain's electrical activity. Electrodes are placed on the scalp, and brain wave impulses are amplified. The amplified impulses drive oscillating pens whose deviations are traced on a strip of paper moving at a constant speed. Significant differences from the normal pattern can reflect abnormalities of brain function.

by a brain tumor or other lesion. When an EEG reveals a **dysrhythmia**, or irregular pattern, in the brain's electrical activity (for example, recent research has supported a link between resting frontal EEG asymmetry and depression, see Stewart et al., 2010; and anxiety; see Thibodeau et al., 2006), other specialized techniques may be used in an attempt to arrive at a more precise diagnosis of the problem.

ANATOMICAL BRAIN SCANS Radiological technology, such as a **computerized axial tomography (CAT) scan**, is one of these specialized techniques (Mishra & Singh, 2010). Through the use of X rays, a CAT scan reveals images of parts of the brain that might be diseased. This procedure has aided neurological study in recent years by providing rapid access, without surgery, to accurate information about the localization and extent of anomalies in the brain's structural characteristics. The procedure involves the use of computer analysis applied to X-ray beams across sections of a patient's brain to produce images that a neurologist can then interpret.

CAT scans have been increasingly replaced by **magnetic resonance imaging (MRI)**. The images of the interior of the brain are frequently sharper with MRI because of its superior ability to differentiate subtle variations in soft tissue. In addition, the MRI procedure is normally far less complicated to administer, and it does not subject the patient to ionizing radiation.

Essentially, MRI involves the precise measurement of variations in magnetic fields that are caused by the varying amounts of water content of various organs and parts of organs. In this manner the anatomical structure of a cross section at any given plane through an organ such as the brain can be computed and graphically depicted with astonishing structural differentiation and clarity. MRI thus makes possible, by noninvasive means, visualization of all but the most minute abnormalities of brain structure. It has been particularly useful in confirming degenerative brain processes as shown, for example, in enlarged areas of the brain. Therefore, MRI studies have considerable potential to illuminate the contribution of brain anomalies to nonorganic psychoses such as schizophrenia, and some progress in this area has already been made (Mathalondolf et al., 2001).

Still, the MRI can be problematic. For example, some patients have a claustrophobic reaction to being placed into the narrow cylinder of the MRI machine that is necessary to contain the magnetic field and block out external radio signals. In addition, a recent evaluation and critique of the MRI approach in medicine was published by Joyce (2008), who interviewed physicians and MRI technologists and also conducted ethnographic research at imaging sites and attended radiology conferences. In her critique, she demonstrated that current beliefs about MRI draw on cultural ideas about technology and are reinforced by health care policies and insurance reimbursement practices. However, her review raises questions about the work practices of many physicians and technologists and suggests that MRI scans do not reveal the truth about the body that many medical practices often holds. For example, she concludes that MRI studies do not always lead to better outcomes for patients.

PET SCANS: A METABOLIC PORTRAIT Another scanning technique is the **positron emission tomography (PET) scan**. Whereas a CAT scan is limited to distinguishing anatomical features such as the shape of a particular internal structure, a PET scan allows for an appraisal of how an organ is functioning (Kumano et al., 2007). The PET scan provides metabolic portraits by tracking natural compounds, such as glucose, as they are metabolized by the brain or other organs. By revealing areas of differential metabolic activity, the PET scan enables a medical specialist to obtain more clear-cut diagnoses of brain pathology by, for example, pinpointing sites responsible for epileptic seizures, trauma from head injury or stroke, and brain tumors. Thus the PET scan may be able to reveal problems that are not immediately apparent anatomically. Moreover, the use of PET scans in research on brain pathology that occurs in abnormal conditions such as Alzheimer's disease may lead to important discoveries about the organic processes underlying these disorders and aid in the treatment of dementia (Saykin et al., 2006). PET scans have, however, been of somewhat limited value thus far because of the low-fidelity pictures obtained (Fletcher, 2004; Videbech et al., 2003) and their cost, since they require a very expensive instrument nearby to produce the short-lived radioactive atoms required for the procedure.

THE FUNCTIONAL MRI The technique known as **functional MRI (fMRI)** has been used in the study of psychopathology for a number of years. As originally developed and employed, the MRI could reveal brain structure but not brain activity. For the latter, clinicians and investigators remained dependent upon PET scans. Improving on these techniques, fMRI most often measures changes in local oxygenation (i.e., blood flow) of specific areas of brain tissue that in turn depend on neuronal activity in those specific regions (Bandettini, 2007). Ongoing psychological activity, such as sensations, images, and thoughts, can thus be "mapped," at least in principle, revealing the specific areas of the brain that appear to be involved in their neurophysiological processes. For example, one study (Wright & Jackson, 2007) examined the task of judgment of serve direction among tennis players and found that different patterns produce different responses in the brain.

Because the measurement of change in this context is critically time dependent, the emergence of fMRI required the development of high-speed devices for enhancing the recording process, as well as the computerized analysis of incoming data. These improvements are now widely available and will likely lead to a marked increase in studying people with disorders using functional imaging. Optimism about the ultimate value of fMRI in mapping cognitive processes in mental disorders is still strong. The fMRI is thought by some to hold more promise for depicting brain abnormalities than currently used procedures such as the neuropsychological examination (see next section).

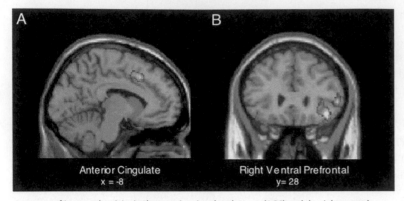

A pattern of increased activity in the anterior cingulated cortex (ACC) and the right ventral prefrontal cortex (RVPFC), shown here in persons who were excluded from participating in a game, are similar to cortical activity of persons experiencing physical pain.

A number of published studies have provided support for this optimism (MacDonald & Jones, 2009). Research using fMRI has explored the cortical functioning that underlies various psychological processes; for example, one recent study showed that psychological factors or environmental events can affect brain processes as measured by fMRI. Eisenberger, Lieberman, and Williams (2003) found that participants who were excluded from social participation showed a similar pattern of brain activation (in the right ventral prefrontal cortex) as participants experiencing physical pain. (See photo.) Longe and colleagues (2010) found that fMRI was effective at detecting neural correlates for self-critical thinking. Some researchers have pointed out that fMRI has a high potential for contributing to a treatment approach in mental health care (Schneider et al., 2009). Although some research has suggested that fMRI can be an effective procedure at detecting malingering or lying (Langleben et al., 2005), one court has recently ruled against the use of fMRI as a lie detector (Couzin-Frankel, 2010).

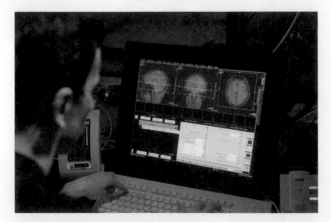

The functional MRI (fMRI), like the MRI, allows clinicians to "map" brain structure. The exciting breakthrough in fMRI technology gives clinicians the ability to measure brain activities underlying such things as sensations, images, and thoughts, revealing the specific areas of the brain involved.

Other studies have addressed problems in abnormal behavior. One study showed that the impaired time estimation found in schizophrenics might result from dysfunction in specific areas of the brain, thalamus, and prefrontal cortex (Suzuki et al., 2004), while others addressed cortical functioning in auditory hallucinations in schizophrenia (Shergill et al., 2000); effects of neuroleptic medication with schizophrenics (Braus et al., 1999); and the neuroanatomy of anxiety (Paulesu et al. 2010) and depression (Brody et al., 2001). Finally, Whalley and colleagues (2004) found that fMRI technique has the potential of adding to our understanding of the early development of psychological disorder. One study of treatment for **aphasia**, a disorder in which there is a loss of ability to communicate verbally (Meinzer et al., 2007), showed that changes in behavioral performance and the brain activation pattern were disclosed as affecting the brain's reorganization.

There are some clear methodological limitations that can influence fMRI results. For example, both MRI and fMRI are quite sensitive to instrument errors or inaccurate observations as a result of slight movements of the person being evaluated (Davidson et al., 2003). Additionally, the results of fMRI studies are often difficult to interpret. Even though group differences emerge between a cognitively impaired group and a control sample, the results usually do not provide much specific information about the processes studied. Fletcher (2004) provides a somewhat sobering analysis of the current status of fMRI in contemporary psychiatry, noting that many professionals who had hoped for intricate and unambiguous results might be disappointed with the overall lack of effective, pragmatic methodology in fMRI assessment of cognitive processes. At this point the fMRI is not considered to be a valid or useful diagnostic tool for mental disorders; however, investigators are optimistic that this procedure shows great promise for understanding brain functioning (MacDonald & Jones, 2009). The primary value of this procedure continues to be research into cortical activity and cognitive processes.

The Neuropsychological Examination

The techniques described so far have shown success in identifying brain abnormalities that are very often accompanied by gross impairments in behavior and varied psychological deficits. However, behavioral and psychological impairments due to organic brain abnormalities may become manifest before any organic brain lesion is detectable by scanning or other means. In these instances, reliable techniques are needed to measure any alteration in behavioral or psychological functioning that has occurred because of the organic brain pathology. This need is met by a growing cadre of psychologists specializing in **neuropsychological**

assessment, which involves the use of various testing devices to measure a person's cognitive, perceptual, and motor performance as clues to the extent and location of brain damage (Snyder, Nussbaum, & Robins, 2006).

In many instances of known or suspected organic brain involvement, a clinical neuropsychologist administers a test battery to a patient. The person's performance on standardized tasks, particularly perceptual-motor tasks, can give valuable clues about any cognitive and intellectual impairment following brain damage (Cullum & Lacritz, 2009; Lezak, 1995; Horton, 2008; Reitan & Wolfson, 1985). Such testing can even provide clues to the probable location of the brain damage, although PET scans, MRIs, and other physical tests may be more effective in determining the exact location of the injury

Many neuropsychologists prefer to administer a highly individualized array of tests, depending on a patient's case history and other available information. Others administer a standard set of tests that have been preselected to sample, in a systematic and comprehensive manner, a broad range of psychological competencies known to be adversely affected by various types of brain injury (Gass, 2009). The use of a constant set of tests has many research and clinical advantages, although it may compromise flexibility. Consider the components of one such standard procedure, the Halstead-Reitan neuropsychological test battery. The Halstead-Reitan battery is composed of several tests and variables from which an "index of impairment" can be computed (Horton, 2008; Reitan & Wolfson, 1985). In addition, it provides specific information about a subject's functioning in several skill areas. The Halstead-Reitan battery for adults is made up of a group of tests such as the following:

1. Halstead Category Test: Measures a subject's ability to learn and remember material and can provide clues as to his or her judgment and impulsivity. The subject is presented with a stimulus (on a screen) that suggests a number between 1 and 4. The subject presses a button indicating the number she or he believes was suggested. A correct choice is followed by the sound of a pleasant doorbell, an incorrect choice by a loud buzzer. The person is required to determine from the pattern of buzzers and bells what the underlying principle of the correct choice is.

2. Tactual Performance Test: Measures a subject's motor speed, response to the unfamiliar, and ability to learn and use tactile and kinesthetic cues. The test surface is a board that has spaces for 10 blocks of varied shapes. The subject is blindfolded (never actually seeing the board) and asked to place the blocks into the correct grooves in the board. Later, the subject is asked to draw the blocks and the board from tactile memory.

3. Rhythm Test: Measures attention and sustained concentration through an auditory perception task. It includes 30 pairs of rhythmic beats that are presented on a tape recorder. The subject is asked whether the pairs are the same or different.

4. Speech Sounds Perception Test: Determines whether an individual can identify spoken words. Nonsense words are presented on a tape recorder, and the subject is asked to identify the presented word in a list of four printed words. This task measures the subject's concentration, attention, and comprehension.

5. Finger Oscillation Task: Measures the speed at which an individual can depress a lever with the index finger. Several trials are given for each hand.

In summary, the medical and neuropsychological sciences are developing many new procedures to assess brain functioning and behavioral manifestations of organic disorder. Medical procedures to assess organic brain damage include EEGs and CAT, PET, and MRI scans. The new technology holds great promise for detecting and evaluating organic brain dysfunction and increasing our understanding of brain function. Neuropsychological testing provides a clinician with important behavioral information on how organic brain damage is affecting a person's present functioning. However, in cases where the psychological difficulty is thought to result from nonorganic causes, psychosocial assessment is used.

In Review

- Compare and contrast five important neurological procedures. What makes each one particularly valuable?
- What is the difference between a PET scan and an fMRI?
- Describe the use of neuropsychological tests in evaluating the behavioral effects of organic brain disorders.

Psychosocial Assessment

Psychosocial assessment attempts to provide a realistic picture of an individual in interaction with his or her social environment. This picture includes relevant information about the individual's personality makeup and present level of functioning, as well as information about the stressors and resources in her or his life situation. For example, early in the process, clinicians may act as puzzle solvers, absorbing as much information about the client as possible—present feelings, attitudes, memories, demographic facts—and trying to fit the pieces together into a meaningful pattern. Clinicians typically formulate hypotheses and discard or confirm them as they proceed. Starting with a global technique such as a clinical interview, clinicians may later select more specific assessment tasks or tests. The following are some of the psychosocial procedures that may be used.

Assessment Interviews

An assessment interview, often considered the central element of the assessment process, usually involves a face-to-face interaction in which a clinician obtains information about various aspects of a client's situation, behavior, and personality (Craig, 2009; Berthold & Ellinger, 2009; Meers, 2009). The interview may vary from a simple set of questions or prompts to a more extended and detailed format (Kici & Westhoff, 2004). It may be relatively open in character, with an interviewer making moment-to-moment decisions about his or her next question on the basis of responses to previous ones, or it may be more tightly controlled and structured so as to ensure that a particular set of questions is covered. In the latter case, the interviewer may choose from a number of highly structured, standardized interview formats whose reliability has been established in prior research.

STRUCTURED AND UNSTRUCTURED INTERVIEWS

Although many clinicians prefer the freedom to explore as they feel responses merit, the research data show that the more controlled and **structured assessment interview** yields far more reliable results than the flexible format. There appears to be widespread overconfidence among clinicians in the accuracy of their own methods and judgments (Taylor & Meux, 1997). Every rule has exceptions, but in most instances, an assessor is wise to conduct an interview that is carefully structured in terms of goals, comprehensive symptom review, other content to be explored, and the type of relationship the interviewer attempts to establish with the person.

Structured interviews follow a predetermined set of questions throughout the interview. For example, "Have you ever had periods in which you could not sleep lately?" and "Have you experienced feeling very nervous about being in public?" The beginning statements or introduction to the interview follow set procedures. The themes and questions are predetermined to obtain particular responses for all items. The interviewer cannot deviate from the question lists and procedures. All questions are asked of each client in a preset way. Each question is structured in a manner so as to allow responses to be quantified or clearly determined. On the negative side, structured interviews typically take longer to administer than unstructured interviews and may include some seemingly tangential questions. Clients can sometimes be frustrated by the overly detailed questions in areas that are of no concern to them.

Unstructured assessment interviews are typically subjective and do not follow a predetermined set of questions. The beginning statements in the interview are usually general, and follow-up questions are tailored for each client. The content of the interview questions is influenced by the habits or theoretical views of the interviewer. The interviewer does not ask the same questions of all clients; rather, he or she subjectively decides what to ask based on the client's response to previous questions. Because the questions are asked in an unplanned way, important criteria needed for a *DSM-IV* diagnosis might be skipped. Responses based on unstructured interviews are difficult to quantify or compare with responses of clients from other interviews. Thus, uses of unstructured interviews in mental health research are limited. On the positive side, unstructured interviews can be viewed by clients as being more sensitive to their needs or problems than more structured procedures. Moreover, the spontaneous follow-up questions that emerge in an unstructured interview can, at times, provide valuable information that would not emerge in a structured interview.

The reliability of the assessment interview may be enhanced by the use of **rating scales** that help focus inquiry and quantify the interview data. For example, the person may be rated on a 3-, 5-, or 7-point scale with respect to self-esteem, anxiety, and various other characteristics. Such a structured and preselected format is particularly effective in giving a comprehensive impression, or "profile," of the subject and her or his life situation and in revealing specific problems or crises—such as marital difficulties, drug dependence, or suicidal fantasies—that may require immediate therapeutic intervention.

Clinical interviews can be subject to error because they rely on human judgment to choose the questions and process the information. Evidence of this unreliability includes the fact that different clinicians have often arrived at different formal diagnoses on the basis of the interview data they elicited from a particular client. It is chiefly for this reason that recent versions of the *DSM* (that is, III, III-R, IV, and IV-TR) have emphasized an "operational" assessment approach, one that specifies observable criteria for diagnosis and provides specific guidelines for making diagnostic judgments. "Winging it" has limited use in this type of assessment process. The operational approach leads to more reliable psychiatric diagnoses, perhaps at some cost in reduced interviewer flexibility.

During an assessment interview, a clinician obtains information about various aspects of a patient's situation, behavior, and personality makeup. The interview is usually conducted face-to-face and may have a relatively open structure or be more tightly controlled, depending on the goals and style of the clinician.

The Clinical Observation of Behavior

One of the traditional and most useful assessment tools that a clinician has available is direct observation of a client's characteristic behavior (Hartmann et al.,

2004). The main purpose of direct observation is to learn more about the person's psychological functioning by attending to his or her appearance and behavior in various contexts. Clinical observation is the clinician's objective description of the person's appearance and behavior—her or his personal hygiene and emotional responses and any depression, anxiety, aggression, hallucinations, or delusions she or he may manifest. Ideally, clinical observation takes place in a natural environment (such as observing a child's behavior in a classroom or at home), but it is more likely to take place upon admission to a clinic or hospital (Leichtman, 2009). For example, a brief description is usually made of a subject's behavior upon hospital admission, and more detailed observations are made periodically on the ward.

Some practitioners and researchers use a more controlled, rather than a naturalistic, behavioral setting for conducting observations in contrived situations. These *analogue situations*, which are designed to yield information about the person's adaptive strategies, might involve such tasks as staged **role-playing**, event reenactment, family interaction assignments, or think-aloud procedures (Haynes et al., 2009).

In addition to making their own observations, many clinicians enlist their clients' help by providing them instruction in **self-monitoring**: self-observation and objective reporting of behavior, thoughts, and feelings as they occur in various natural settings. This method can be a valuable aid in determining the kinds of situations in which maladaptive behavior is likely to be evoked, and numerous studies also show it to have therapeutic benefits in its own right. Alternatively, a client may be asked to fill out a more or less formal self-report or a checklist concerning problematic reactions experienced in various situations. Many instruments have been published in the professional literature and are commercially available to clinicians. These approaches recognize that people are excellent sources of information about themselves. Assuming that the right questions are asked and that people are willing to disclose information about themselves, the results can have a crucial bearing on treatment planning.

RATING SCALES As in the case of interviews, the use of rating scales in clinical observation and in self-reports helps both to organize information and to encourage reliability and objectivity (Aiken, 1996; Garb, 2007). That is, the formal structure of a scale is likely to keep observer inferences to a minimum. The most useful rating scales are those that enable a rater to indicate not only the presence or absence of a trait or behavior but also its prominence or degree. The following item is an example from such a rating scale; the observer would check the most appropriate description.

Sexual Behavior

___ **1.** Sexually assaultive: aggressively approaches males or females with sexual intent.

___ **2.** Sexually soliciting: exposes genitals with sexual intent, makes overt sexual advances to other patients or staff, and masturbates openly.

___ **3.** No overt sexual behavior: not preoccupied with discussion of sexual matters.

___ **4.** Avoids sex topics: made uneasy by discussion of sex, becomes disturbed if approached sexually by others.

___ **5.** Excessive prudishness about sex: considers sex filthy, condemns sexual behavior in others, becomes panic-stricken if approached sexually.

Ratings like these may be made not only as part of an initial evaluation but also to check on the course or outcome of treatment. One of the rating scales most widely used for recording observations in clinical practice and in psychiatric research is the **Brief Psychiatric Rating Scale (BPRS)** (Overall & Hollister, 1982; Serper et al., 2004). The BPRS provides a structured and quantifiable format for rating clinical symptoms such as overconcern with physical symptoms, anxiety, emotional withdrawal, guilt feelings, hostility, suspiciousness, and unusual thought patterns. It contains 18 scales that are scored from ratings made by a clinician following an interview with a patient. The distinct patterns of behavior reflected in the BPRS ratings enable clinicians to make a standardized comparison of their patients' symptoms with the behavior of other psychiatric patients. The BPRS has been found to be an extremely useful instrument in clinical research (e.g., see Davidson et al., 2004), especially for the purpose of assigning patients to treatment groups on the basis of similarity in symptoms. However, it is not widely used for making treatment or diagnostic decisions in clinical practice. The Hamilton Rating Scale for Depression (HRSD), a similar but more specifically targeted instrument, is one of the most widely used procedures for selecting clinically depressed research subjects and also for assessing the response of such subjects to various treatments (see Beevers & Miller, 2004; Brown et al., 2007).

Psychological Tests

Interviews and behavioral observation are relatively direct attempts to determine a person's beliefs, attitudes, and problems. Psychological tests are a more indirect means of assessing psychological characteristics. Scientifically developed psychological tests (as opposed to the recreational ones sometimes appearing in magazines or on the Internet) are standardized sets of procedures or tasks for obtaining samples of behavior. A subject's responses to the standardized stimuli are compared with those of other people who have comparable demographic characteristics, usually through established test norms or test score distributions. From these comparisons, a clinician can then draw inferences about how much the person's psychological qualities differ from those of a reference group, typically a psychologically normal one. Among the characteristics that these tests can measure are coping patterns, motive patterns, personality characteristics, role behaviors, values, levels of depression or anxiety, and intellectual functioning. Impressive advances in the technology of test development have made it possible to create instruments of acceptable reliability and validity to measure almost any conceivable psychological characteristic on which people may vary. Moreover, many procedures are available in a computer-administered and computer-interpreted format (see Developments in Practice 1).

Although psychological tests are more precise and often more reliable than interviews or some observational techniques, they are far from perfect tools. Their value often depends on the competence of the clinician who interprets them. In general, they are useful diagnostic tools for psychologists in much the same way that blood tests, X-ray films, and MRI scans are useful to physicians. In all these cases, pathology may be revealed in people who appear to be normal, or a general impression of "something wrong" can be checked against more precise information. Two general

There are a wide variety of psychological tests that measure the intellectual abilities of children. The researcher in this photo is measuring this child's cognitive development by evaluating how she classifies and sorts the candy.

categories of psychological tests for use in clinical practice are intelligence tests and personality tests (projective and objective).

1

Developments in Practice
THE AUTOMATED PRACTICE: USE OF THE COMPUTER IN PSYCHOLOGICAL TESTING

Perhaps the most dramatic innovation in clinical assessment during the last 40 years has been the increasing use of computers in individual assessment. Computers are effectively used in assessment both to gather information directly from an individual and to assemble and evaluate all the information that has been gathered previously through interviews, tests, and other assessment procedures. By comparing the incoming information with data previously stored in its memory banks, a computer can perform a wide range of assessment tasks (Butcher et al., 2009; Butcher, 2009). It can supply a probable diagnosis, indicate the likelihood of certain kinds of behavior, suggest the most appropriate form of treatment, predict the outcome, and print out a summary report concerning the subject. In many of these functions, a computer is actually superior to a clinician because it is more efficient and accurate in recalling stored material (Epstein & Klinkenberg, 2001; Olson, 2001).

With the increased efficiency and reliability of the use of computers in clinical practice, one might expect a nearly unanimous welcoming of computers into the clinic. This is not always the case, however, and some practitioners we know even resist using such "modern"

techniques as e-mail, fax machines, and computerized billing in their practices (McMinn et al., 1999). Some clinicians are reluctant to use computer-based test interpretations in spite of their demonstrated utility and low cost. Even though many clinics and independent practitioners use microcomputers for record keeping and billing purposes, a smaller number incorporate computer-based clinical assessment procedures into their practice. Possible reasons for the underutilization of computer-based assessment procedures include the following: (1) Practitioners who were trained before the widespread use of computers may feel uncomfortable with them or may not have time to get acquainted with their use; (2) they may limit their practice to psychological treatment and do not use extensive pretreatment assessments in their practice; (3) they may have little interest in, or time for, the systematic evaluation of treatment efficacy that periodic formal assessments facilitate; or (4) they may feel that the impersonal and mechanized look of the booklets and answer sheets common to much computerized assessment is inconsistent with the image and style of warm and personal engagement they hope to convey to clients.

INTELLIGENCE TESTS A clinician can choose from a wide range of **intelligence tests**. The Wechsler Intelligence Scale for Children-Revised (WISC-IV) (see Weiss et al., 2006) and the current edition of the Stanford-Binet Intelligence Scale (Kamphaus & Kroncke, 2004) are widely used in clinical settings for measuring the intellectual abilities of children (Wasserman, 2003). Probably the most commonly used test for measuring adult intelligence is the Wechsler Adult Intelligence Scale-Revised (WAIS-IV) (Benson et al., 2010; Lichtenberger & Kaufman, 2009). It includes both verbal and performance material and consists of 15 subtests. A brief description of two of the subtests will serve to illustrate the types of functions the WAIS-IV measures.

David Wechsler (1896–1981) served in the military, testing army recruits during World War I. He came to believe that the ways in which psychologists viewed and measured "intelligence" was inadequate. In 1934 he began construction of the most widely used adult intelligence test battery, the Wechsler Adult Intelligence Scale (WAIS), which set the standard for practical measurement of intelligence.

- **Vocabulary (verbal):** This subtest consists of a list of words to define that are presented orally to the individual. This task is designed to evaluate knowledge of vocabulary, which has been shown to be highly related to general intelligence.

- **Digit Span (performance):** In this test of short-term memory, a sequence of numbers is administered orally. The individual is asked to repeat the digits in the order administered. Another task in this subtest involves the individual's remembering the numbers, holding them in memory, and reversing the order sequence—that is, the individual is instructed to say them backward (Lichtenberger & Kaufman, 2009).

Individually administered intelligence tests—such as the WISC-IV, the WAIS-IV, and the Stanford-Binet—typically require 2 to 3 hours to administer, score, and interpret. In many clinical situations, there is not enough time or funding to use these tests. In cases where intellectual impairment or organic brain damage is thought to be central to a patient's problem, intelligence testing may be the most crucial diagnostic procedure in the test battery. Moreover, information about cognitive functioning or deterioration can provide valuable clues to a person's intellectual resources in dealing with problems (Kihlstrom, 2002). Yet in many clinical settings and for many clinical cases, gaining a thorough understanding of a client's problems and initiating a treatment program do not require knowing the kind of detailed information about intellectual functioning that these instruments provide. In these cases, intelligence testing is not recommended.

PROJECTIVE PERSONALITY TESTS There are a great many tests designed to measure personal characteristics other than intellectual ability. It is customary to group these personality tests into projective and objective measures. **Projective personality tests** are unstructured in that they rely on various ambiguous stimuli such as inkblots or vague pictures rather than on explicit verbal questions, and in that the person's responses are not limited to the "true," "false," or "cannot say" variety. Through their interpretations of these ambiguous materials, people reveal a good deal about their personal preoccupations, conflicts, motives, coping techniques, and other personality characteristics. An assumption underlying the use of projective techniques is that in trying to make sense out of vague, unstructured stimuli, individuals "project" their own problems, motives, and wishes into the situation. Such responses are akin to the childhood pastime of seeing objects or scenes in cloud formations, with the important exception that the stimuli are in this case fixed and largely the same for all subjects. It is the latter circumstance that permits determination of the normative range of responses to the test materials, which in turn can be used to identify objectively deviant responding. Thus projective tests are aimed at discovering the ways in which an individual's past learning and personality structure may lead him or her to organize and perceive ambiguous information from the environment. Prominent among the several projective tests in common use are the Rorschach Inkblot Test, the Thematic Apperception Test (TAT), and sentence completion tests.

The Rorschach The **Rorschach Inkblot Test** is named after the Swiss psychiatrist Hermann Rorschach (1884–1922), who initiated the experimental use of inkblots in personality assessment in 1911. The test uses 10 inkblot pictures, to which a subject responds in succession after being instructed as follows (Exner, 1993):

> People may see many different things in these inkblot pictures; now tell me what you see, what it makes you think of, what it means to you.

The following excerpts are taken from a subject's responses to one of the actual blots:

> This looks like two men with genital organs exposed. They have had a terrible fight and blood has splashed up against the wall. They have knives or sharp instruments in their hands and have just cut up a body. They have already taken out the lungs and other organs. The body

is dismembered . . . nothing remains but a shell . . . the pelvic region. They were fighting as to who will complete the final dismemberment . . . like two vultures swooping down . . . .

The extremely violent content of this response was not common for this particular blot or for any other blot in the series. Although no responsible examiner would base conclusions on a single instance, such content was consistent with other data from this subject, who was diagnosed as an antisocial personality with strong hostility.

Use of the Rorschach in clinical assessment is complicated and requires considerable training (Exner & Erdberg, 2002; Weiner & Meyer, 2009). Methods of administering the test vary; some approaches can take several hours and hence must compete for time with other essential clinical services. Furthermore, the results of the Rorschach can be unreliable because of the subjective nature of test interpretations. For example, interpreters might disagree on the symbolic significance of the response "a house in flames." One person might interpret this particular response as suggesting great feelings of anxiety, whereas another interpreter might see it as suggesting a desire on the part of the patient to set fires. One reason for the diminished use of the Rorschach in projective testing today comes from the fact that many clinical treatments used in today's mental health facilities generally require specific behavioral descriptions rather than descriptions of deep-seated personality dynamics, such as those that typically result from interpretation of the Rorschach Test.

In the hands of a skilled interpreter, however, the Rorschach can be useful in uncovering certain psychodynamic issues, such as the impact of unconscious motivations on current perceptions of others. Furthermore, there have been attempts to objectify Rorschach interpretations by clearly specifying test variables and empirically exploring their relationship to external criteria such as clinical diagnoses (Exner, 1995). The Rorschach, although generally considered an open-ended, subjective instrument, has been adapted for computer interpretation (Exner, 1987). In a study of the reliability of conclusions drawn from the computer intepretation system, Meyer and colleagues (2005) found that clinicians tended to draw the same conclusions from Rorschach responses as the computer system did.

Some researchers, however, have raised questions about the norms on which the Exner Rorschach Comprehensive System, a scoring and interpretation system, is based (Shaffer et al., 1999; Wood et al., 2001). The Rorschach was shown to "overpathologize" persons taking the test—that is, the test

Hermann Rorschach (1884–1922), a Swiss psychiatrist, received his M.D. in 1912. He worked in Russia before returning to Zurich to work in mental hospitals. His interest in inkblots developed when he was a young child and enjoyed an activity called "Klecksography," the making of pictures by using inkblots. In his work with psychiatric patients he began to use their responses to inkblots as a way of understanding their personalities and motivations. In 1921 he published his major work, *Psychodiagnostics*, which described his experience with using inkblots to understand personality.

appears to show psychopathology even when the person is a "normal" person randomly drawn from the community. The extent to which the Rorschach provides valid information beyond what is available from other, more economical instruments has not been demonstrated. Although some researchers have rallied support for the Comprehensive System (Hibbard, 2003; Weiner & Meyer, 2009), the Rorschach test has also been widely criticized as an instrument with low or negligible validity (Garb et al., 1998; Hunsley & Bailey, 1999). The use of the test in clinical assessment has diminished somewhat (Piotrowski et al., 1998), in part because insurance companies do not pay for the considerable amount of time needed to administer, score, and interpret the test. However, the Rorschach remains one of the most frequently used instruments in personality assessment—even in some personnel assessment settings, as described by Del Guidice (2010)—and research today.

The Thematic Apperception Test The **Thematic Apperception Test (TAT)** was introduced in 1935 by its authors, C. D. Morgan and Henry Murray of the Harvard Psychological Clinic. It still is widely used in clinical practice (Rossini & Moretti, 1997) and personality research (Teglasi, 2010). The TAT uses a series of simple pictures, some highly representational and others quite abstract, about which a subject is instructed to make up stories. The content of the pictures, much of them depicting people in various contexts, is highly ambiguous as to actions and motives, so subjects tend to project their own conflicts and worries onto it (see Morgan, 2002, for a historical description of the test stimuli).

Several scoring and interpretation systems have been developed to focus on different aspects of a subject's stories such as expressions of needs (Atkinson, 1992), the person's perception of reality (Arnold, 1962), and the person's fantasies (Klinger, 1979). It is time-consuming to apply these systems, and there is little evidence that they make a clinically significant contribution. Hence, most often a clinician simply makes a qualitative and subjective determination of how the story content reflects the person's underlying traits, motives, and preoccupations. Such interpretations often depend as much on "art" as on "science," and there is much room for error in such an informal procedure.

An example of the way a subject's problems may be reflected in TAT stories is shown in the following case, which is based on Card 1 (a picture of a boy staring at a violin on a table in front of him). The client, David, was a 15-year-old boy who had been referred to the clinic by his parents because of their concern about his withdrawal and poor work at school.

David's TAT Response

David was generally cooperative during the testing, although he remained rather unemotional and unenthusiastic throughout. When he was given Card 1 of the TAT, he paused for over a minute, carefully scrutinizing the card.

"I think this is a . . . uh . . . machine gun . . . yeah, it's a machine gun. The guy is staring at it. Maybe he got it for his birthday or stole it or something." [Pause. The examiner reminded him that he was to make up a story about the picture.]

"OK. This boy, I'll call him Karl, found this machine gun . . . a Browning automatic rifle . . . in his garage. He kept it in his room for protection. One day he decided to take it to school to quiet down the jocks that lord it over everyone. When he walked into the locker hall, he cut loose on the top jock, Amos, and wasted him. Nobody bothered him after that because they knew he kept the BAR in his locker."

It was inferred from this story that David was experiencing a high level of frustration and anger in his life. The extent of this anger was reflected in his perception of the violin in the picture as a machine gun—an instrument of violence. The clinician concluded that David was feeling threatened not only by people at school but even in his own home, where he needed "protection."

This example shows how stories based on TAT cards may provide a clinician with information about a person's conflicts and worries as well as clues as to how the person is handling these problems.

The TAT has been criticized on several grounds (Lilienfeld et al., 2001). There is a "dated" quality to the test stimuli: The pictures, developed in the 1930s, appear quaint to many contemporary subjects, who have difficulty identifying with the characters in the pictures. Subjects often preface their stories with, "This is something from a movie I saw on the late-night movies." Additionally, the TAT can require a great deal of time to administer and interpret. As with the Rorschach, interpretation of responses to the TAT is generally subjective, which limits the reliability and validity of the test.

A review (Rossini & Moretti, 1997) pointed out an interesting paradox: Even though the TAT remains popular among practicing clinicians, clinical training programs have reduced the amount of time devoted to teaching graduate students about the TAT, and relatively few contemporary training resources (such as books and manuals) exist. Again, we must note that some examiners, notably those who have long experience in the instrument's use, are capable of making astonishingly accurate interpretations with TAT stories. Typically, however, they have difficulty teaching these skills to others. On reflection, such an observation should not be unduly surprising, but it does point to the essentially "artistic" element involved at this skill level.

Sentence Completion Test Another projective procedure that has proved useful in personality assessment is the **sentence completion test** (Fernald & Fernald, 2010). A number of such tests have been designed for children, adolescents, and adults. Such tests consist of the beginnings of sentences that a person is asked to complete, as in these examples:

1. I wish _____
2. My mother _____
3. Sex _____
4. I hate _____
5. People _____

Sentence completion tests, which are related to the free-association method, a procedure in which the client is asked to respond freely, are somewhat more structured than the Rorschach and most other projective tests. They help examiners pinpoint important clues to an individual's problems, attitudes, and symptoms through the content of her or his responses. Interpretation of the item responses, however, is generally subjective and unreliable. Despite the fact that the test stimuli (the sentence stems) are standard, interpretation is usually done in an ad hoc manner and without benefit of normative comparisons.

In sum, projective tests have an important place in many clinical settings, particularly those that attempt to obtain a comprehensive picture of a person's psychodynamic functioning and those that have the necessary trained staff to conduct extensive individual psychological evaluations. The great strengths of projective techniques—their unstructured nature and their focus on the unique aspects of personality—are at the same time their weaknesses because they make interpretation subjective, unreliable, and difficult to validate. Moreover, projective tests typically require a great deal of time to administer and advanced skill to interpret—both scarce quantities in many clinical settings.

OBJECTIVE PERSONALITY TESTS **Objective personality tests** are structured—that is, they typically use questionnaires, self-report inventories, or rating scales in which questions or items are carefully phrased and alternative responses are specified as choices. They therefore involve a far more controlled format than projective devices and thus are more amenable to objectively based quantification. One virtue of such quantification is its precision, which in turn enhances the reliability of test outcomes.

There are a large number of available personality assessment measures for use in personality and clinical assessment. For example, the NEO-PI (Neuroticism-Extroversion-Openness Personality Inventory) provides information on the major dimensions in personality and is widely used in evaluating personality factors in normal-range populations (Costa & Widiger, 2002). There are also many objective assessment instruments developed to assess focused clinical problems. For example, the Millon Clinical Multiaxial Inventory (MCMI-III;

Starke R. Hathaway (1903–1984), clinical psychologist, was a pioneer in physiological psychology and personality assessment. In 1940, he and J. C. McKinley published the Minnesota Multiphasic Personality Inventory (MMPI) for evaluating symptoms and behavior of psychiatric and medical patients. The MMPI became the most widely used personality assessment instrument in use, and its revised version (MMPI-2) is the most frequently used personality measure today.

J. C. McKinley (1891–1950), a neuropsychiatrist at the University of Minnesota Hospital, coauthored the MMPI with Starke Hathaway and conducted research on the MMPI with both medical and psychiatric populations.

The Validity and Clinical Scales of the MMPI The original MMPI, a self-report questionnaire, consisted of 550 items covering topics ranging from physical condition and psychological states to moral and social attitudes. Typically, clients are encouraged to answer all of the items either "true" or "false." The pool of items was originally administered to a large group of normal individuals (affectionately called the "Minnesota normals") and several quite homogeneous groups of patients with particular psychiatric diagnoses. Answers to all the items were then item-analyzed to see which ones differentiated the various groups. On the basis of the findings, the 10 clinical scales were constructed, each consisting of the items that were answered by one of the patient groups in the direction opposite to the predominant response of the normal group. This rather ingenious method of selecting scorable items, known as "empirical keying," originated with the MMPI and doubtless accounts for much of the instrument's power. Note that it involves no subjective prejudgment about the "meaning" of a true or false answer to any item; that meaning resides entirely in whether the answer is the same as the answer deviantly given by patients of varying diagnoses. Should an examinee's pattern of true and false responses closely approximate that of a particular pathological group, it is a reasonable inference that he or she shares other psychiatrically significant characteristics with that group—and may in fact "psychologically" be a member of that group. (See the MMPI-2 profile in Table 1.)

Each of these 10 clinical scales thus measures tendencies to respond in psychologically deviant ways. Raw scores on these scales are compared with the corresponding scores of the normal population, many of whom did (and do) answer a few items in the critical direction (suggesting psychological problems), and the results are plotted on the standard MMPI profile form. By drawing a line connecting the scores for the different scales, a clinician can construct a profile that shows how far from normal a patient's performance is on each of the scales. To reiterate the basic strategy with an example, the Schizophrenia scale is made up of the items that patients diagnosed with schizophrenia consistently answered in a way that differentiated them from normal individuals. People who score high (relative to norms) on this scale, though not necessarily schizophrenic, often show characteristics typical of that clinical population. For instance, high scorers on this scale may be socially inept, may be withdrawn, and may have peculiar thought processes; they may have diminished contact with reality and, in severe cases, may have delusions and hallucinations.

The MMPI also includes a number of validity scales to detect whether a patient has answered the questions in a

see Choca, 2004) was developed to evaluate the underlying personality dimensions among clients in psychological treatment. Here, we will focus primarily upon the most widely used personality assessment instrument, the MMPI-2.

The MMPI One of the major structured inventories for personality assessment is the **Minnesota Multiphasic Personality Inventory (MMPI)**, now called the MMPI-2 for adults after a revision in 1989 (Butcher, 2011; Greene, 2011). We focus on it here because in many ways it is the prototype and the standard of this class of instruments.

Several years in development, the MMPI was introduced for general use in 1943 by Starke Hathaway and J. C. McKinley; it is today the most widely used personality test for clinical and **forensic**—court related—assessment and in psychopathology research in the United States (Archer et al., 2006; Lally, 2003). It is also the assessment instrument most frequently taught in graduate clinical psychology programs (Piotrowski & Zalewski, 1993). Over 19,000 books and articles on the MMPI instruments have been published since the test was introduced. Moreover, translated versions of the inventory are widely used internationally (the original MMPI was translated over 150 times and used in over 46 countries; Butcher, 2010). International use of the revised inventory is increasing rapidly; over 32 translations have been made since it was published in 1989 (Butcher & Williams, 2009).

table 1 The Scales of the MMPI-2

Validity Scales

Cannot say score (?)	Measures the total number of unanswered items
Infrequency scale (F)	Measures the tendency to falsely claim or exaggerate psychological problems in the first part of the booklet; alternatively, detects random responding
Infrequency scale (FB)	Measures the tendency to falsely claim or exaggerate psychological problems on items toward the end of the booklet
Infrequency scale (Fp)	Measures the tendency to exaggerate psychological problems among psychiatric inpatients
Lie scale (L)	Measures the tendency to claim excessive virtue or to try to present an overall favorable image
Defensiveness scale (K)	Measures the tendency to see oneself in an unrealistically positive way
Superlative Self-Presentation scale (S)	Measures the tendency for some people to present themselves in a highly positive manner or superlative manner. The S scale contains 5 subscales that address ways in which the person presents in an overpositive manner.
Response Inconsistency scale (VRIN)	Measures the tendency to endorse items in an inconsistent or random manner
Response Inconsistency scale (TRIN)	Measures the tendency to endorse items in an inconsistently true or false manner

Clinical Scales

Scale 1 Hypochondriasis (Hs)	Measures excessive somatic concern and physical complaints
Scale 2 Depression (D)	Measures symptomatic depression
Scale 3 Hysteria (Hy)	Measures hysteroid personality features such as a "rose-colored glasses" view of the world and the tendency to develop physical problems under stress
Scale 4 Psychopathic deviate (Pd)	Measures antisocial tendencies
Scale 5 Masculinity-femininity (Mf)	Measures gender-role reversal
Scale 6 Paranoia (Pa)	Measures suspicious, paranoid ideation
Scale 7 Psychasthenia (Pt)	Measures anxiety and obsessive, worrying behavior
Scale 8 Schizophrenia (Sc)	Measures peculiarities in thinking, feeling, and social behavior
Scale 9 Hypomania (Ma)	Measures unrealistically elated mood state and tendencies to yield to impulses
Scale 0 Social introversion (Si)	Measures social anxiety, withdrawal, and overcontrol

Special Scales

Scale APS Addiction Proneness scale	Assesses the extent to which the person matches personality features of people in substance-use treatment
Scale AAS Addiction Acknowledgment scale	Assesses the extent to which the person has acknowledged substance-abuse problems
Scale MAC-R MacAndrew Addiction scale	An empirical scale measuring proneness to become addicted to various substances
Scale MDS Marital Distress scale	Assesses perceived marital relationship problems
Hostility scale (Ho)	Addresses hostility or anger control problems
Posttraumatic Stress scale (Pk)	Assesses a number of symptoms and attitudes that are found among people who are experiencing posttraumatic stress problems

straightforward, honest manner. For example, there is one scale that detects lying by one's claiming of extreme virtue and several scales that detect possible malingering or faking of symptoms. Extreme endorsement of the items on any of these scales may invalidate the test, whereas lesser endorsements frequently contribute important interpretive insights. In addition to the validity scales and the 10 clinical scales, a number of additional scales have been devised—for example, to detect substance abuse, marital distress, and posttraumatic stress disorder.

Clinically, the MMPI is used in several ways to evaluate a patient's personality characteristics and clinical problems. Perhaps the most typical use of the MMPI is as a diagnostic standard. As we have seen, the individual's profile pattern is compared with profiles of known patient groups. If the profile matches a group, information about patients in this group can suggest a broad descriptive diagnosis for the patient under study.

Revision of the Original MMPI The original MMPI, in spite of being the most widely used personality measure, has not been without its critics. Some psychodynamically oriented clinicians felt that the MMPI (like other structured, objective tests) was superficial and did not adequately reflect the complexities of an individual taking the test. Some behaviorally oriented critics, on the other hand, criticized the MMPI (and in fact the entire genre of personality tests) as being too oriented toward measuring unobservable "mentalistic" constructs such as traits. A more specific criticism was leveled at the datedness of the MMPI.

In response to these criticisms, the publisher of the MMPI sponsored a revision of the instrument. The scales listed on the standard original MMPI-2 profile form are described in Table 1. This revised MMPI, designated "MMPI-2" for adults, became available for general professional use in mid-1989 (Butcher, 2011; Butcher, Graham, et al., 2001), and the MMPI-A for adolescents (see Williams & Butcher, 2011) was published in 1992. The original 10 clinical scales were kept on the revised version. The revised versions of the MMPI have been validated in many clinical studies (Butcher et al., 2000; Graham, Ben-Porath, & McNulty, 1999; Greene, 2011).

Research has provided strong support for the revised versions of the MMPI (Greene et al., 2003). The clinical scales, which, apart from minimal item deletion or rewording, have been retained in their original form, seem to measure the same properties of personality organization and functioning as they always have. A comparable stability of meaning is observed for the standard validity scales (also essentially unchanged), which have been reinforced with three additional scales to detect tendencies to respond untruthfully to some items.

Advantages and Limitations of Objective Personality Tests Self-report inventories such as the MMPI have a number of advantages over other types of personality tests. They are cost effective, highly reliable, and objective; they also can be scored and interpreted (and, if desired, even administered) by computer. A number of general criticisms, however, have been leveled against the use of self-report inventories. As we have seen, some clinicians consider them too mechanistic to portray the complexity of human beings and their problems accurately. Also, because these tests require the subject to read, comprehend, and answer verbal material, patients who are illiterate or confused cannot take the tests. Furthermore, the individual's cooperation is required in self-report inventories, and it is possible that the person might distort his or her answers to create a particular impression. The validity scales of the MMPI-2 are a direct attempt to deal with this last criticism.

Because of their scoring formats and emphasis on test validation, scientifically constructed objective personality inventories lend themselves particularly well to automated interpretation. The earliest practical applications of computer technology to test scoring and interpretation involved the MMPI. Over 50 years ago, psychologists at the Mayo Clinic programmed a computer to score

and interpret clinical profiles. Computerized personality assessment has evolved substantially over the past few years, and other highly sophisticated MMPI and MMPI-2 interpretation systems have been developed (Butcher et al., 2004). Computer-based MMPI interpretation systems typically employ powerful **actuarial procedures** (Grove et al., 2000). In such systems, descriptions of the actual behavior or other established characteristics of many subjects with particular patterns of test scores have been stored in the computer. Whenever a person has one of these test score patterns, the appropriate description is printed out in the computer's evaluation. Such descriptions have been written and stored for a number of different test score patterns, most of them based on MMPI-2 scores.

The accumulation of precise actuarial data for an instrument like the MMPI-2 is difficult, time consuming, and expensive. This is in part because of the complexity of the instrument itself; the potential number of significantly different MMPI-2 profile patterns is legion. The profiles of many subjects therefore do not "fit" the profile types for which actuarial data are available. Problems of actuarial data acquisition also arise at the other end: the behaviors or problems that are to be detected or predicted by the instrument. Many conditions that are of vital clinical importance are relatively rare (for example, suicide) or are psychologically complex (for example, possible psychogenic components in a patient's physical illness). Thus it is difficult to accumulate enough cases to serve as an adequate actuarial database. In these situations, the interpretive program writer is forced to fall back on general clinical lore and wisdom to formulate clinical descriptions appropriate to the types of profiles actually obtained.

Sometimes the different paragraphs generated by the computer have inconsistencies resulting from the fact that different parts of a subject's test pattern call up different paragraphs from the computer. The computer simply prints out blindly what has been found to be typical for people making similar scores on the various clinical scales and cannot integrate the descriptions it picks up. At this point the human element comes in: In the clinical use of computers, it is always essential that a trained professional further interpret and monitor the assessment data (Atlis et al., 2006).

Computerized personality assessment is no longer a novelty but an important, dependable adjunct to clinical assessment. Computerized psychological evaluations are a quick and efficient means of providing a clinician with needed information early in the decision-making process. Examples of computer-generated descriptions for the case of Andrea C., presented in the next section, appear in the evaluations reprinted in Developments in Practice 4.2 on p.122.

The Case of Andrea C.: Experiencing Violence in the Workplace

Andrea C., a 49-year-old divorced woman, was employed as a manager in a firm whose office was located in a somewhat isolated section of the community. Her responsibilities included opening the office building at 6:00 A.M. and preparing the office activities for the day. She felt somewhat unsafe in opening up the office alone and had complained to upper management about the lack of security in the building. One morning, as she was opening the door to the building, she was accosted by a stranger who hit her on the head, knocking her unconscious, breaking her nose, and cutting her face and neck. The assailant stabbed her several times in her leg and attempted to sexually assault her but ran away with her purse as car lights came on the street.

Andrea suffered a number of physical injuries and recurring symptoms from the assault and was hospitalized for 8 days following the attack. Her symptoms included a fractured skull, fractured nose, multiple stab wounds on her body, facial injuries, dizziness, impaired balance, wrist pain, residual cognitive symptoms from being unconscious, poor memory, intense anxiety, and symptoms of posttraumatic stress. After recovery from the physical injuries she was fearful to return to work, and she applied for disability as a result of her injuries. The company for which she worked rejected her request, and she filed a lawsuit for personal injury disability.

A psychological evaluation was requested by the company's insurer to determine the legitimacy of Andrea's disability claim. As a central part of the evaluation, the MMPI-2 was administered by the psychologist hired by the defense to appraise Andrea's personality and symptoms (see the validity, clinical, and supplementary profiles shown in Figures 1 and 2). The MMPI-2 clinical scale pattern shows clear mental health problems. Her clinical scale pattern with the high scores on the D (Depression) scale, the Hs (Hypochondriasis) and Pt (Anxiety) scales, along with the high score obtained on the PTSD scale,

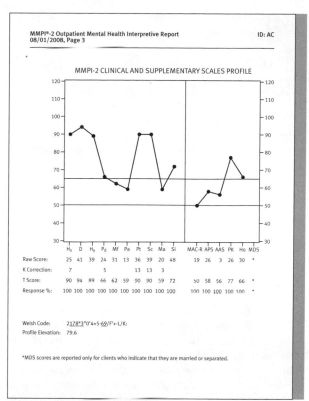

FIGURE 2

Profile of the MMPI-2 Clinical Scales and Supplementary Scales for Andrea C.

Source: Excerpted from *The Minnesota Report™: Adult Clinical System-Revised,* 4th Edition by James N. Butcher.

indicate that she is experiencing mental health symptoms related to stressful life events. A full description of this symptom picture is presented in the computer-based interpretive report shown in Developments in Practice 2.

Interestingly, the insurance company psychological expert recommended against Andrea's receiving compensation based on his interpretation of a controversial psychological scale (referred to as the Fake Bad Scale, or FBS) that was designed to assess "malingering." After an initial hearing to examine the validity and acceptability of the FBS, the judge in the case prohibited the use of the scale as a measure of effort, malingering, or overreporting of symptoms to bolster his opinion.

The case went to trial, and Andrea's attorneys relied upon the medical evidence and results of the MMPI-2 to support her claim of physical damages and posttraumatic adjustment problems. The jury awarded Andrea substantial damages as a result of the injuries and the trauma that she experienced from the assault.

EVALUATING ANDREA'S COMPUTER-GENERATED MMPI-2 REPORT The narrative report of the computer-based MMPI-2 interpretation contains technical test information to assist the assessment psychologist in interpreting the test results. The report is considered a professional-to-professional consultation and is not recommended for release to patients. The computer report for Andrea contains detailed data about the

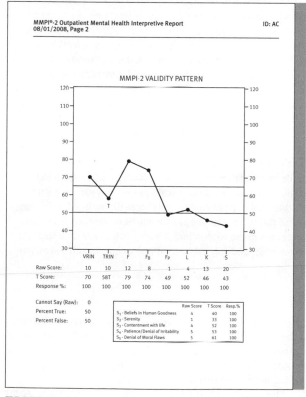

FIGURE 1

Profile of the MMPI-2 Validity Scales for Andrea C.

Source: Excerpted from *The Minnesota Report™: Adult Clinical System-Revised,* 4th Edition by James N. Butcher.

2

Developments in Practice
COMPUTER-BASED MMPI-2 REPORT FOR ANDREA C.

Profile Validity

This client endorsed a number of psychological problems, suggesting that she is experiencing a high degree of stress. Although the MMPI-2 clinical scale profile is probably valid, it may show some exaggeration of symptoms. In addition, please note that the client's approach to the MMPI-2 items was somewhat inconsistent. She endorsed items in a pattern that suggests some carelessness or inattention to content.

Symptomatic Patterns

Her profile configuration, which incorporates correlates of Hs and D, is not as clearly defined as those of many other clients from this clinical setting. In interpreting the profile, the practitioner should also consider any prominent clinical scale elevations that are close in elevation to the prototype. This client's profile presents a broad and mixed picture in which physical complaints and depressed affect are likely to be salient features. The client is exhibiting much somatic distress and may be experiencing a problem with her psychological adjustment. Her physical complaints are probably extreme, possibly reflecting a general lack of effectiveness in life. There are likely to be long-standing personality problems predisposing her to develop physical symptoms under stress. She is probably feeling quite tense and nervous, and she may be feeling that she cannot get by without help for her physical problems. She is likely to be reporting a great deal of pain, and she feels that others do not understand how sick she is feeling. She may be quite irritable and may become hostile if her symptoms are not given "proper" attention.

Many individuals with this profile have a history of psychophysiological disorders. They tend to overreact to minor problems with physical symptoms. Ulcers and gastrointestinal distress are common. The possibility of actual organic problems, therefore, should be carefully evaluated. Individuals with this profile report a great deal of tension and a depressed mood. They tend to be pessimistic and gloomy in their outlook.

In addition, the following description is suggested by the client's scores on the content scales. She endorsed a number of items suggesting that she is experiencing low morale and a depressed mood. She reports a preoccupation with feeling guilty and unworthy. She

feels that she deserves to be punished for wrongs she has committed. She feels regretful and unhappy about life, and she seems plagued by anxiety and worry about the future. She feels hopeless at times and feels that she is a condemned person. She has difficulty managing routine affairs, and the items she endorsed suggest a poor memory, concentration problems, and an inability to make decisions. She appears to be immobilized and withdrawn and has no energy for life. She views her physical health as failing and reports numerous somatic concerns. She feels that life is no longer worthwhile and that she is losing control of her thought processes.

According to her response content, there is a strong possibility that she has seriously contemplated suicide. She feels somewhat self-alienated and expresses some personal misgivings or a vague sense of remorse about past acts. She feels that life is unrewarding and dull, and she finds it hard to settle down. The client's response content suggests that she feels intensely fearful about a large number of objects and activities. This hypersensitivity and fearfulness appear to be generalized at this point and may be debilitating to her in social and work situations.

Long-term personality factors identified by other scale elevations may help provide a clinical context for the symptoms she is presently experiencing. She apparently holds some unusual beliefs that appear to be disconnected from reality. Her high score on one MMPI-2 scale, the PSYC (Psychoticism) scale, suggests that she often feels alienated from others and might experience unusual symptoms such as delusional beliefs, circumstantial and tangential thinking, and loose associations. She also shows a meager capacity to experience pleasure in life. Persons with high scores on another MMPI-2 scale, the INTR (Introversion/Low Positive Emotionality), tend to be pessimistic.

Profile Frequency

Profile interpretation can be greatly facilitated by examining the relative frequency of clinical scale patterns in various settings. The client's high-point clinical scale score (D) occurred in 7.0 percent of the MMPI-2 normative sample of women. However, only 4.4 percent of the women had D scale peak scores at or above a T score of 65, and only 2.1 percent had well-defined D spikes. Her

relative frequency of the test pattern's occurrence in relevant clinical settings and in the normative or standardized population. For example, the report provides information as to how Andrea's elevated clinical scale scores compare with persons being evaluated in an outpatient clinical setting as well as the frequency of the score in the MMPI-2 general normative sample of women. Her test results indicated that her highest score, the Depression scale score, typically occurs in 18.7 percent of

the outpatient women. Moreover, only 4.4 percent of women in the normative sample obtain this high elevation on the Depression scale. Thus, this high Depression scale elevation is considered to be a relatively common symptom among women seeking outpatient mental health services.

The reader should also note that there are some scales mentioned in the computer narrative report for Andrea that are not listed in Table 1. There are a elevated MMPI-2 profile configuration (1-2/2-1) is rare in samples of normals, occurring in 1.0 percent of the MMPI-2 normative sample of women.

This high-point MMPI-2 score is the most frequent clinical scale score in various samples of outpatient women. In the Pearson outpatient sample, the high-point clinical scale score on D occurred in 18.7 percent of the women. Moreover, 17.1 percent of the outpatient women had the D scale spike at or above a T score of 65, and 9.0 percent had well-defined D spikes. Her elevated MMPI-2 profile configuration (1-2/2-1) occurred in 2.9 percent of the women in the Pearson outpatient sample.

Profile Stability

The relative elevation of her clinical scale scores suggests that her profile is not as well defined as many other profiles. There was no difference between the profile type used to develop the present report (involving Hs and D) and the next highest scale in the profile code. Therefore, behavioral elements related to elevations on Pt should be considered as well. For example, intensification of anxiety, negative self-image, and unproductive rumination could be important in her symptom pattern.

Interpersonal Relations

She appears to be somewhat passive-dependent in relationships. She may manipulate others through her physical symptoms, and she may become hostile if sufficient attention is not paid to her complaints.

She is a very introverted person who has difficulty meeting and interacting with other people. She is shy and emotionally distant. She tends to be very uneasy, rigid, and overcontrolled in social situations. Her shyness is probably symptomatic of a broader pattern of social withdrawal. Personality characteristics related to social introversion tend to be stable over time. Her generally reclusive behavior, introverted lifestyle, and tendency toward interpersonal avoidance may be prominent in any future test results.

The client's scores on the content scales suggest the following additional information concerning her interpersonal relations. She appears to be an individual who has rather cynical views

about life. Any efforts to initiate new behaviors may be colored by her negativism. She may view relationships with others as threatening and harmful.

Diagnostic Considerations

Individuals with this profile type are often seen as neurotic and may receive a diagnosis of somatoform disorder. Actual organic problems such as ulcers or hypertension might be part of the clinical picture. Some individuals with this profile have problems with abuse of pain medication or other prescription drugs.

Treatment Considerations

Her view of herself as physically disabled needs to be considered in any treatment planning. She tends to somatize her difficulties and to seek medical solutions rather than deal with them psychologically. She seems to tolerate a high level of psychological conflict and may not be motivated to deal with her problems directly. She is probably not a strong candidate for psychotherapy treatment approaches that require self-scrutiny, insight development, and high motivation for change. Psychological treatment may progress more rapidly if her symptoms are dealt with through behavior modification techniques. However, with her generally pessimistic attitude and low energy resources, she seems to have little hope of getting better.

The client's scores on the content scales seem to indicate low potential for change. She may feel that her problems are not addressable through therapy and that she is not likely to benefit much from psychological treatment at this time. Her apparently negative treatment attitudes may need to be explored early in therapy if treatment is to be successful.

She harbors many negative work attitudes that could limit her adaptability in the workplace. Her low morale and lack of interest in work could impair future adjustment to employment, a factor that should be taken into consideration in treatment.

Source: Excerpted from *The Minnesota Report™: Adult Clinical System-Revised,* 4th Edition by James N. Butcher.

number of other MMPI-2 scales in the literature and in common use with the MMPI-2 that are not listed due to space restrictions in this book. For example, there are 15 MMPI-2 content-based scales, that is, scales that are comprised of homogeneous content themes (such as Negative Work Attitudes, Family Problems, and Type-A Behavior). These scales address specific problem themes in mental health patients.

In addition, there are five scales, referred to as the Psychopathology Five (PSY-5) scales that address the personality disorder content domains that are referred to as the "Big 5" personality dimensions. These personality dimensions include Aggressiveness, Psychoticism, Disconstraint, Negative Emotionality/Neuroticism, and Introversion/Low Positive Emotionality.

In Review

- Distinguish between structured and unstructured clinical assessment interviews.

- What are the assumptions behind the use of projective personality tests? How do they differ from objective tests?

- What advantages do objective personality tests offer over less structured tests?

- What is the Minnesota Multiphasic Personality Inventory (MMPI-2)? Describe how the scales work.

The Integration of Assessment Data

As assessment data are collected, their significance must be interpreted so that they can be integrated into a coherent working model for use in planning. Clinicians in individual private practice normally assume this complicated task on their own. In a clinic or hospital setting, assessment data are often evaluated in a staff conference attended by members of an interdisciplinary team (perhaps consisting of a clinical psychologist, a psychiatrist, a social worker, and other mental health personnel) who are concerned with the decisions to be made regarding treatment. By putting together all the information they have gathered, they can see whether the findings complement each other and form a definitive clinical picture or whether gaps or discrepancies exist that necessitate further investigation.

This integration of all the data gathered at the time of an original assessment may lead to agreement on a tentative

In a clinic or hospital setting, assessment data are usually evaluated in a staff conference attended by members of an interdisciplinary team—including, for example, a clinical psychologist, a psychiatrist, a social worker, and a psychiatric nurse. A staff decision may determine whether a severely depressed person will be hospitalized or remain with his or her family or whether an accused person will be declared competent to stand trial. Because these decisions can have such great impact on the lives of the clients, it is critical that clinicians be well aware of the limitations of assessment.

diagnostic classification for a patient. In any case, the findings of each member of the team, as well as the recommendations for treatment, are entered into the case record so that it will always be possible to check back and see why a certain course of therapy was undertaken, how accurate the clinical assessment was, and how valid the treatment decision turned out to be.

New assessment data collected during the course of therapy provide feedback on its effectiveness and serve as a basis for making needed modifications in an ongoing treatment program. As we have noted, clinical assessment data are also commonly used in evaluating the final outcome of therapy and in comparing the effectiveness of different therapeutic and preventive approaches.

Ethical Issues in Assessment

The decisions made on the basis of assessment data may have far-reaching implications for the people involved. A staff decision may determine whether a severely depressed person will be hospitalized or remain with her or his family, or whether an accused person will be declared competent to stand trial. Thus a valid decision, based on accurate assessment data, is of far more than theoretical importance. Because of the impact that assessment can have on the lives of others, it is important that those involved keep several factors in mind in evaluating test results:

1. **Potential Cultural Bias of the Instrument or the Clinician:** There is the possibility that some psychological tests may not elicit valid information for a patient from a minority group (Gray-Little, 2009; Wen-Shing & Streltzer, 2008). A clinician from one sociocultural background may have trouble assessing objectively the behavior of someone from another background. It is important to ensure—as Greene, Robin, Albaugh, Caldwell, and Goldman (2003) and Hall, Bansal, and Lopez (1999) have shown with the MMPI-2—that the instrument can be confidently used with persons from minority groups.

2. **Theoretical Orientation of the Clinician:** Assessment is inevitably influenced by a clinician's assumptions, perceptions, and theoretical orientation. For example, a psychoanalyst and a behaviorist might assess the same behaviors quite differently. The psychoanalytically oriented professional is likely to view behaviors as reflecting underlying motives, whereas the behavioral clinician is likely to view the behaviors in the context of the immediate or preceding stimulus situations. Different treatment recommendations are likely to result.

3. **Underemphasis on the External Situation:** Many clinicians overemphasize personality traits as the cause of patients' problems without paying enough attention to the possible role of stressors and other circumstances in the patients' life situations. An undue focus on a patient's personality, which some assessment techniques encourage, can divert attention from potentially critical environmental factors.

4. **Insufficient Validation:** Some psychological assessment procedures in use today have not been sufficiently validated. For example, unlike many of the personality scales, widely used procedures for behavioral observation and behavioral

self-report and the projective techniques have not been subjected to strict psychometric validation.

5. Inaccurate Data or Premature Evaluation: There is always the possibility that some assessment data—and any diagnostic label or treatment based on them—may be inaccurate or that the team leader (usually a psychiatrist) might choose to ignore test data in favor of other information. Some risk is always involved in making predictions for an individual on the basis of group data or averages. Inaccurate data or premature conclusions may not only lead to a misunderstanding of a patient's problem but also close off attempts to get further information, with possibly grave consequences for the patient.

In Review

- What are some ethical issues that clinicians should be aware of when evaluating a patient's test results?

- Are there concerns over cultural biases in some psychological tests?

- What is test validity?

Classifying Abnormal Behavior

Classification is important in any science, whether we are studying chemical elements, plants, planets, or people. With an agreed-upon classification system we can be confident that we are communicating clearly. If someone says to you, "I saw a dog running down the street," you can probably produce a mental image broadly approximating the appearance of that dog—not from seeing it but rather from your knowledge of animal classifications. There are of course many breeds of dogs, which vary widely in size, color, muzzle length, and so on, and yet we have little difficulty in recognizing the essential features of "dogness." "Dogness" is an example of what psychologists refer to as a "cognitive prototype" or "pattern."

In abnormal psychology, classification involves the attempt to delineate meaningful subvarieties of maladaptive behavior. Like defining abnormal behavior, classification of some kind is a necessary first step toward introducing order into our discussion of the nature, causes, and treatment of such behavior. Classification makes it possible to communicate about particular clusters of abnormal behavior in agreed-upon and relatively precise ways. For example, we cannot conduct research on what might cause eating disorders unless we begin with a more or less clear definition of the behavior under examination; otherwise, we would be unable to select, for intensive study, persons whose behavior displays the aberrant eating patterns we hope to understand. There are other reasons for diagnostic classifications, too, such as gathering statistics on how common the various types of disorders are and meeting the needs of medical insurance companies (which insist on having formal diagnoses before they will authorize payment of claims).

Keep in mind that, just as with the process of defining abnormality itself, all classification is the product of human invention—it is, in essence, a matter of making generalizations based on what has been observed. Even when observations are precise and carefully made, the generalizations we arrive at go beyond those observations and enable us to make inferences about underlying similarities and differences. For example, it is common for people experiencing episodes of panic to feel they are about to die. When "panic" is carefully delineated, we find that it is not in fact associated with any enhanced risk of death but, rather, that the people experiencing such episodes tend to share certain other characteristics, such as recent exposure to highly stressful events.

It is not unusual for a classification system to be an ongoing work in progress as new knowledge demonstrates an earlier generalization to be incomplete or flawed. It is important to bear in mind, too, that formal classification is successfully accomplished only through precise techniques of psychological, or clinical, assessment—techniques that have been increasingly refined over the years.

Differing Models of Classification

There are currently three basic approaches to classifying abnormal behavior: the categorical, the dimensional, and the prototypal (Widiger & Boyd, 2009). The categorical approach, like the diagnostic system of general medical diseases, assumes (1) that all human behavior can be divided into the categories of "healthy" and "disordered," and (2) that within the latter there exist discrete, nonoverlapping classes or types of disorder that have a high degree of within-class homogeneity in both symptoms displayed and the underlying organization of the disorder identified.

THE DIMENSIONAL APPROACH The dimensional and prototypal approaches differ fundamentally in the assumptions they make, particularly with respect to the requirement of discrete and internally homogeneous classes of behavior. In the dimensional approach, it is assumed that a person's typical behavior is the product of differing strengths or intensities of behavior along several definable dimensions such as mood, emotional stability, aggressiveness, gender identity, anxiousness, interpersonal trust, clarity of thinking and communication, social introversion, and so on. The important dimensions, once established, are the same for everyone. People are assumed to differ from one another in their configuration or profile of these dimensional traits (each ranging from very low to very high), not in terms of behavioral indications of a corresponding "dysfunctional" entity presumed to underlie and give rise to the disordered pattern of behavior (Miller, Reynolds, & Pilkonis, 2004; Widiger et al., 2006). "Normal" is discriminated from "abnormal," then, in terms of precise statistical criteria derived from dimensional intensities among unselected people in general, most of whom may be presumed to be close to average, or mentally "normal." We could decide, for example, that anything above the 97th normative percentile on aggressiveness and anything below the 3rd normative percentile on sociability would be considered "abnormal" findings.

Dimensionally based diagnosis has the incidental benefit of directly addressing treatment options. Because the patient's profile of psychological characteristics will normally consist of deviantly high and low points, therapies can be designed to moderate those of excessive intensity (e.g., anxiety) and to enhance those that constitute deficit status (e.g., inhibited self-assertiveness).

Of course, in taking a dimensional approach, it would be possible (perhaps even probable) to discover that such profiles tend to cluster together in types—and even that some of these types are correlated, though imperfectly, with recognizable sorts of gross behavioral malfunctions such as anxiety disorders or depression. It is highly unlikely, however, that any individual's profile will exactly fit a narrowly defined type or that the types identified will not have some overlapping features. This brings us to the prototypal approach.

THE PROTOTYPAL APPROACH A prototype (as the term is used here) is a conceptual entity (e.g., personality disorder) depicting an idealized combination of characteristics that more or less regularly occur together in a less-than-perfect or standard way at the level of actual observation. Westen, Shedler, and Bradley (2006), for example, suggest that the *DSM* should provide a narrative description of a prototypic case of each personality disorder rather than having a listing of diagnostic criteria as it now has. The diagnostician could indicate on a 5-point scale the extent to which a patient matches this description. The clinician would simply rate the overall similarity or "match" between a patient and the prototype.

As we shall see, the official diagnostic criteria defining the various recognized classes of mental disorder, although explicitly intended to create categorical entities, more often than not result in prototypal ones. The central features of the various identified disorders are often somewhat vague, as are the boundaries purporting to separate one disorder from another. Much evidence suggests that a strict categorical approach to identifying differences among types of human behavior, whether normal or abnormal, may well be an unattainable goal. Bearing this in mind as we proceed may help you avoid some confusion. For example, we commonly find that two or more identified disorders regularly occur together in the same individual—a situation known as **comorbidity**. Does this really mean that such a person has two or more entirely separate and distinct disorders? In the typical instance, probably not.

Formal Diagnostic Classification of Mental Disorders

Today, there are two major psychiatric classification systems in use: the *International Classification of Disease* (ICD-10) system, published by the World Health Organization, and the *Diagnostic and Statistical Manual of Mental Disorders* (*DSM*), published by the American Psychiatric Association. The ICD-10 system is widely used in Europe and many other countries, whereas the *DSM* system is the standard guide for the United States. Both systems are similar in many respects, such as in using symptoms as the focus of classification and in dividing problems into different facets (the multiaxial system to be described in the section that follows).

Certain differences in the way symptoms are grouped in these two systems can sometimes result in a different classification on the *DSM* than on the ICD-10. We will focus on the *DSM* system in our discussion of what is to be considered a mental disorder. This manual specifies what subtypes of mental disorders are currently officially recognized and provides, for each, a set of defining criteria in the United States and some other countries. As already noted, the system purports to be a categorical one with sharp boundaries separating the various disorders from one another, but it is in fact a prototypal one with much fuzziness of boundaries and considerable interpenetration, or overlap, of the various "categories" of disorder it identifies.

The criteria that define the recognized categories of disorder consist for the most part of symptoms and signs. The term **symptoms** generally refers to the patient's subjective description, the complaints she or he presents about what is wrong. **Signs**, on the other hand, are objective observations that the diagnostician may make either directly (such as the patient's inability to look another person in the eye) or indirectly (such as the results of pertinent tests administered by a psychological examiner). To make any given diagnosis, the diagnostician must observe the particular criteria—the symptoms and signs that the *DSM* indicates must be met.

THE EVOLUTION OF THE *DSM* The *DSM* is currently in its fourth edition (*DSM-IV*), with some more recent modifications, referred to as *DSM-IV-TR*, having been made in 2000. There are plans underway to publish *DSM-V* by 2013, but given the controversy this date might change. This system is the product of more than a five-decade evolution involving increasing refinement and precision in the identification and description of mental disorders. The first edition of the manual (*DSM-I*) appeared in 1952 and was largely an outgrowth of attempts to standardize diagnostic practices in use among military personnel in World War II. The 1968 *DSM-II* reflected the additional insights gleaned from a markedly expanded postwar research effort in mental health sponsored by the federal government. Over time, practitioners recognized a defect in both these early efforts: The various types of disorders identified were described in narrative and jargon-laden terms that proved too vague for mental health professionals to agree on their meaning. The result was a serious limitation of diagnostic reliability; that is, two professionals examining the same patient might very well come up with completely different impressions of what disorder(s) the patient had.

To address this clinical and scientific impasse, the *DSM-III* of 1980 introduced a radically different approach, one intended to remove, as much as possible, the element of subjective judgment from the diagnostic process. It did so by adopting an "operational" method of defining the various disorders that would officially be recognized. This innovation meant that the *DSM* system would now specify the exact observations that must be made for a given diagnostic label to be applied. In a typical case, a specific number of signs or symptoms from a designated list must be present before a diagnosis can properly be assigned. The new approach, continued in the *DSM-III*'s revised version of 1987 (*DSM-III-R*) and in the 1994 *DSM-IV*, clearly enhanced diagnostic reliability and made efforts to incorporate cultural and ethnic considerations. As an example of the operational approach to diagnosis, the *DSM-IV-TR* diagnostic criteria for dysthymic disorder are reproduced in the *DSM-IV-TR* box below.

The number of recognized mental disorders has increased enormously from *DSM-I* to *DSM-IV*, due both to the addition of new diagnoses and to the elaborate subdivision of older ones. Because it is unlikely that the nature of the American psyche has changed much in the interim period, it seems more reasonable to assume that mental health professionals view their field in a different light than they did 50 years ago. The *DSM* system is now both more comprehensive and more finely differentiated into subsets of disorders.

THE LIMITATIONS OF *DSM* CLASSIFICATION There are limits on the extent to which a conceptually strict categorical system can adequately represent the abnormalities of behavior to which human beings are subject (Beutler & Malik, 2002). The real problems of real patients often do not fit into the precise lists of signs and symptoms that are at the heart of the modern *DSM* effort. How should we deal, for example, with the patient who meets three of the criteria for a particular diagnosis, if four is the minimum threshold for rendering the diagnosis? The clinical reality is that the disorders people actually have are often not so finely differentiated as the *DSM* grid on which they must be mapped. Increasingly fine differentiation also produces more and more recognized types of disorder. Too often, we believe, the unintended effect is to sacrifice validity in an effort to maximize interdiagnostician agreement—reliability. This makes little sense. For example, blends of anxiety and depression are extremely common in a clinical population, and they typically show much overlap (correlation) in quantitative scientific investigations as well. Nevertheless, the *DSM* treats the two as generically distinct forms of disorder, and as a consequence, a person who is clinically both anxious and depressed may receive two diagnoses, one for each of the supposedly separate conditions.

THE FIVE AXES OF *DSM-IV-TR* *DSM-IV-TR* evaluates an individual according to five foci, or axes. The first three axes assess an individual's present clinical status or condition:

- **Axis I. The particular clinical syndromes or other conditions that may be a focus of clinical attention.** This would include schizophrenia, generalized anxiety disorder, major depression, and substance dependence. Axis I conditions are roughly analogous to the various illnesses and diseases recognized in general medicine.
- **Axis II. Personality disorders.** A very broad group of disorders that encompasses a variety of problematic ways of relating to the world, such as histrionic personality disorder, paranoid personality disorder, or antisocial personality disorder. The last of these, for example, refers to an early-developing, persistent, and pervasive pattern of disregard for accepted

DSM-IV-TR

Criteria for Dysthymic Disorder

A. Depressed mood for most of the day, for more days than not, as indicated either by subjective account or observation by others, for at least 2 years. Note: In children and adolescents, mood can be irritable and duration must be at least 1 year.

B. Presence, while depressed, of two (or more) of the following:
   1. Poor appetite or overeating
   2. Insomnia or hypersomnia
   3. Low energy or fatigue
   4. Low self-esteem
   5. Poor concentration or difficulty making decisions
   6. Feelings of hopelessness

C. During the 2-year period (1 year for children or adolescents) of the disturbance, the person has never been without the symptoms in Criteria A and B for more than 2 months at a time.

D. No Major Depressive Episode has been present during the first 2 years of the disturbance (1 year for children and adolescents); i.e., the disturbance is not better accounted for by chronic Major Depressive Disorder, or Major Depressive Disorder, In Partial Remission.

E. There has never been a Manic Episode, a Mixed Episode, or a Hypomanic Episode, and criteria have never been met for Cyclothymic Disorder.

F. The disturbance does not occur exclusively during the course of a chronic Psychotic Disorder, such as Schizophrenia or Delusional Disorder.

G. The symptoms are not due to the direct physiological effects of a substance (e.g., a drug of abuse, a medication) or a general medical condition (e.g., hypothyroidism).

H. The symptoms cause clinically significant distress or impairment in social, occupational, or other important areas of functioning.

Source: Reprinted with permission from the American Psychiatric Association. *Diagnostic and Statistical Manual of Mental Disorders*, Fourth Edition, *Text Revision* (Copyright © 2000). American Psychiatric Association.

standards of conduct, including legal strictures. Axis II provides a means of coding for long-standing maladaptive personality traits that may or may not be involved in the development and expression of an Axis I disorder. Mental retardation is also diagnosed as an Axis II condition.

- **Axis III. General medical conditions.** Listed here are any general medical conditions potentially relevant to understanding or managing the case. Axis III of *DSM-IV-TR* may be used in conjunction with an Axis I diagnosis qualified by the phrase "Due to [a specifically designated general medical condition]"—for example, where a major depressive disorder is conceived as resulting from unremitting pain associated with some chronic medical disease.

On any of these first three axes, where the pertinent criteria are met, more than one diagnosis is permissible and in fact encouraged. That is, a person may be diagnosed as having multiple psychiatric syndromes such as panic disorder and major depressive disorder; disorders of personality such as dependent or avoidant personality; or potentially relevant

medical problems such as cirrhosis (a liver disease often caused by excessive alcohol use) and overdose, cocaine.

The last two *DSM-IV-TR* axes are used to assess broader aspects of an individual's situation:

- **Axis IV. Psychosocial and environmental problems.** This group deals with the stressors that may have contributed to the current disorder, particularly those that have been present during the prior year. The diagnostician is invited to use a checklist approach for various categories of problems—family, economic, occupational, legal, and so forth. For example, the phrase "Problems with primary support group" may be included when a family disruption is judged to have contributed to the disorder.
- **Axis V. Global assessment of functioning.** This is where clinicians indicate how well the individual is coping at the present time. A 100-point Global Assessment of Functioning (GAF) Scale is provided for the examiner to assign a number summarizing a patient's overall ability to function. The GAF Scale is reproduced in the *DSM-IV-TR* box below.

DSM-IV-TR

The Global Assessment of Functioning (GAF) Scale

91–100 Superior functioning in a wide range of activities, life's problems never seem to get out of hand, is sought out by others because of his or her many positive qualities. No symptoms.

81–90 Absent or minimal symptoms (e.g., mild anxiety before an exam), good functioning in all areas, interested and involved in a wide range of activities, socially effective, generally satisfied with life, no more than everyday problems or concerns (e.g., an occasional argument with family members).

71–80 If symptoms are present, they are transient and expectable reactions to psychosocial stressors (e.g., difficulty concentrating after family argument); no more than slight impairment in social, occupational, or school functioning (e.g., temporarily falling behind in schoolwork).

61–70 Some mild symptoms (e.g., depressed mood and mild insomnia) OR some difficulty in social, occupational, or school functioning (e.g., occasional truancy or theft within the household), but generally functioning pretty well, has some meaningful interpersonal relationships.

51–60 Moderate symptoms (e.g., flat affect and circumstantial speech, occasional panic attacks) OR moderate difficulty in social, occupational, or school functioning (e.g., few friends, conflicts with peers or co-workers).

41–50 Severe symptoms (e.g., suicidal ideation, severe obsessional rituals, frequent shoplifting) OR any serious impairment in social, occupational or school functioning (e.g., no friends, unable to keep a job).

31–40 Some impairment in reality testing or communication (e.g., speech is at times illogical, obscure, or irrelevant) OR major impairment in several areas, such as work or school, family relations, judgment, thinking, or mood (e.g., depressed man avoids friends, neglects family, and is unable to work; child frequently beats up younger children, is defiant at home, and is failing at school).

21–30 Behavior is considerably influenced by delusions or hallucinations OR serious impairment in communication or judgment (e.g., sometimes incoherent, acts grossly inappropriately, suicidal preoccupation) OR inability to function in almost all areas (e.g., stays in bed all day, no job, home, or friends).

11–20 Some danger of hurting self or others (e.g., suicidal attempts without clear expectation of death; frequently violent; manic excitement) OR occasionally fails to maintain minimal personal hygiene (e.g., smears feces) OR gross impairment in communication (e.g., largely incoherent or mute).

1–10 Persistent danger of severely hurting self or others (e.g., recurrent violence) OR persistent inability to maintain minimal personal hygiene OR serious suicidal act with clear expectation of death.

0 Inadequate information.

Axes IV and V, first introduced in *DSM-III*, are significant additions. Knowing what frustrations and demands a person has been facing is important for understanding the context in which the problem behavior has developed. And someone's general level of functioning conveys important information that is not necessarily contained in the entries for the other axes and indicates how well the individual is coping with his or her problems. Some clinicians, however, object to the routine use of these axes for insurance forms and the like on the grounds that such use unnecessarily compromises a patient's right to privacy by revealing, for example, a recent divorce (Axis IV) or a suicide attempt (Axis V). Because of such concerns, Axes IV and V are now considered optional for diagnosis and in fact are rarely used in most clinical settings.

MAIN CATEGORIES OF AXIS I AND AXIS II DISORDERS

In presenting individual disorders, we will offer the *DSM-IV-TR* criteria for each. These diagnoses may be regarded as fitting into several broad etiological (major causal) groupings, each containing several subgroupings:

- Substance-use disorders, involving problems such as habitual drug or alcohol abuse.
- Disorders secondary to gross destruction or malfunctioning of brain tissue, as in Alzheimer's dementia and a wide range of other cognitive conditions based on permanent or irreversible organic brain pathology.
- Disorders of psychological or sociocultural origin having no known brain pathology as a primary causal factor. Traditionally, this group also includes severe mental disorders for which a specific organic brain pathology has not been demonstrated—such as major mood disorders and schizophrenia—although it appears increasingly likely that they may be caused at least in part by certain types of aberrant brain functioning.
- Disorders usually arising during childhood or adolescence, including a broad group of disorders featuring cognitive impairments such as mental retardation and specific learning disabilities, and a large variety of behavioral problems, such as attention-deficit/hyperactivity disorder, that constitute deviations from the expected or normal path of development.

In referring to mental disorders, several qualifying terms are commonly used. **Acute** is used to describe disorders of relatively short duration, usually under 6 months, such as transitory adjustment disorders. In some contexts, it also connotes behavioral symptoms of high intensity. **Chronic** refers to long-standing and often permanent disorders such as Alzheimer's dementia and some forms of schizophrenia. The term can also be applied generally to low-intensity disorders because long-term difficulties are often of this sort. **Mild**, **moderate**, and **severe** are terms that reflect different points on a dimension of severity or seriousness. **Episodic** and **recurrent** are used to describe unstable disorder patterns that tend to come and go, as with some mood and schizophrenic conditions.

THE PROBLEM OF LABELING The psychiatric diagnoses of the sort typified by the *DSM-IV* system are not uniformly revered among mental health professionals (e.g., MacCulloch, 2010; Sarbin, 1997). One important criticism is that a psychiatric diagnosis is little more than a label applied to a defined category of socially disapproved or otherwise problematic behavior.

The diagnostic label describes neither a person nor any underlying pathological condition ("dysfunction") the person necessarily harbors but, rather, some behavioral pattern associated with that person's current level of functioning. Yet once a label has been assigned, it may close off further inquiry. It is all too easy—even for professionals—to accept a label as an accurate and complete description of an individual rather than of that person's current behavior. When a person is labeled "depressed" or "schizophrenic," others are more likely to make certain assumptions about that person that may or may not be accurate. In fact, a diagnostic label can make it hard to look at the person's behavior objectively, without preconceptions about how he or she will act. These expectations can influence even clinically important interactions and treatment choices. For example, arrival at the diagnosis "major depressive disorder" may cut off any further inquiry about the patient's life situation and lead abruptly to a prescription for antidepressant medication (Tucker, 1998), or the application of a label such as "borderline personality" might cause the mental health treatment staff to be less optimistic about the patient's prognosis (Markham, 2003).

Once an individual is labeled, he or she may accept a redefined identity and play out the expectations of that role. ("I'm nothing but a substance abuser. I might as well do drugs—everyone expects me to anyway. Also, this is a condition deemed out of my control, so it is pointless for me to be an active participant in my treatment.") This acquisition of a new social identity can be harmful for a variety of reasons. The pejorative and stigmatizing implications of many psychiatric labels can mark people as second-class citizens with severe limitations that are often presumed to be permanent (Link, 2001; Slovenko, 2001). They can also have devastating effects on a person's morale, self-esteem, and relationships with others. The person so labeled may decide that he or she "is" the diagnosis and may thus adopt it as a life "career."

Clearly, it is in the person with the disorder's best interests for mental health professionals to be circumspect in the diagnostic process, in their use of labels, and in ensuring confidentiality with respect to both. A related change has developed over the past 50 years: For years the traditional term for a person who goes to see a mental health professional was *patient*, a term that is closely associated with medical sickness and a passive stance, waiting (patiently) for the doctor's cure. Today many mental health professionals, especially those trained in nonmedical settings, prefer the term *client* because it implies greater participation on the part of an individual and more responsibility for bringing about his or her own recovery.

LIMITED USEFULNESS OF DIAGNOSIS It should be kept in mind that a *DSM* diagnosis per se may be of limited usefulness. The *DSM-IV-TR* acknowledges this in its introduction: "Making a *DSM-IV* diagnosis is only the first step in a comprehensive evaluation. To formulate an adequate treatment plan, the clinician will invariably require considerable additional information about the person being evaluated beyond that required to make a *DSM-IV-TR* diagnosis" (American Psychiatric Association, 2000, *DSM-IV-TR*, pp. xxxiv–xxxv). Arriving at a diagnosis is usually required, at least in the form of a "diagnostic impression," before the commencement of clinical services. This is necessitated, perhaps unwisely, by medical insurance requirements and long-standing clinical administrative tradition. The additional information required for adequate clinical assessment may be extensive and extremely difficult to unearth. For the most part, in keeping with psychiatric tradition, that process is interview based. That is, the examiner engages the patient (or perhaps a family member of the patient) in a conversation designed to elicit the information necessary to place the patient in one or more *DSM* diagnostic categories. The interviewer introduces various questions and probes, typically becoming increasingly specific as she or he develops diagnostic hypotheses and checks them out with additional probes related to the criteria for particular *DSM* diagnoses. Physicians in general medical practice do something similar in the course of an examination.

UNSTRUCTURED DIAGNOSTIC INTERVIEWS Like the assessment interviews described earlier, diagnostic interviews are of two general types: unstructured and structured. In the unstructured interview, the examiner follows no preexisting plan with respect to content and sequence of the probes introduced. Unstructured interviews, as their name implies, are somewhat freewheeling. The therapist/clinician asks questions as they occur to him or her, in part on the basis of the responses to previous questions. For example, if the patient/client mentions a father who traveled a lot when he or she was a child, the clinician is free to ask, "Did you miss your father?" or (pursuing a different tack), "How did your mother handle that?" rather than being required to ask

the next question in a predetermined list. Many clinical examiners prefer this unfettered approach because it enables them to follow perhaps idiosyncratic "leads." In the above example, the clinician might have chosen to ask about the mother's reaction on the basis of a developing suspicion that the mother may have been depressed during the client's childhood years. There is one serious drawback to the freewheeling style, however: The information that an interview yields is limited to the content of that interview. Should another clinician conduct another unstructured interview of the same patient, he or she might come up with a different clinical picture.

STRUCTURED DIAGNOSTIC INTERVIEWS The structured interview probes the client in a manner that is highly controlled (Daniel & Gurczynski, 2010). Guided by a sort of master plan (sometimes to the extent of specifying the examiner's exact wording), the clinician using a structured interview typically seeks to discover whether the person's symptoms and signs "fit" diagnostic criteria that are more precise and "operational" than in the past. The use of more precise criteria and of highly structured diagnostic interviewing has substantially improved diagnostic reliability, but the structured interview format is still used only sporadically in routine clinical work. Nevertheless, the precision of clinical research, including epidemiological research to be discussed later, has profited enormously from these developments.

There are a number of structured diagnostic interviews that may be used in various contexts. In clinical and research situations, a popular instrument has been the Structured Clinical Interview for *DSM* Diagnosis (SCID), which yields, almost automatically, diagnoses carefully attuned to the *DSM* diagnostic criteria. Another structured diagnostic instrument, the Schedules for Clinical Assessment in Neuropsychiatry (SCAN), published by the World Health Organization (1994), enables the diagnostician to arrive at either an ICD-10 or a *DSM-IV* diagnosis (see Developments in Practice 3).

In Review

- Why is a classification system needed in abnormal psychology?

- What is the meaning of reliability and validity in the context of such a classification system?

- What is the difference between dimensional and prototypal classification strategies?

- Describe some factors that are likely to be considered in revising the *DSM-IV*.

Developments in Practice
SCHEDULES FOR CLINICAL ASSESSMENT IN NEUROPSYCHIATRY (SCAN)

The SCAN (Schedules for Clinical Assessment in Neuropsychiatry) is a formal system of interview questions developed by the World Health Organization (WHO) for assessing and classifying psychopathology (1994). The SCAN (formerly known as the Present State Exam) is the latest version of a long-term project undertaken by WHO to provide a systematic diagnostic schedule for classifying mental health problems. The SCAN is widely used around the world and has been translated into more than 35 languages.

The SCAN is a structured diagnostic interview in which the clinician records the patient's responses on a computer and rates the severity of the problem behavior during an interview. The clinician follows a clearly defined set of structured questions covering a broad range of information such as demographic data and physical and mental health symptoms. For example, the clinician would ask:

Some people have phobias. They feel anxious or panicky or scared in certain situations, like being afraid of heights, or open spaces, or certain animals or insects, or in some social situations. They try to avoid them or not think about them. Would that be your experience?

The interviewer then records the appropriate rating:

1 Phobias absent
0 Phobias may be present

Here is another example:

You have mentioned that in the last month you have had difficulty sleeping. Overall, how much interference has there been with your everyday activities because of this problem?

Rate interference due to sleep problems:

0 No symptoms present to a significant degree
1 Symptoms present but of little interference
2 Moderate or intermittent symptoms
3 Severe to incapacitating symptoms

Upon completion of the interview, the clinician can readily obtain clinical diagnoses by instructing the computer program to run a diagnostic algorithm. The practitioner has the option of selecting *DSM-IV* or ICD-10 or both. In addition, the practitioner can select whether the diagnosis covers the present symptoms (e.g., the past 28 days) or symptoms that have occurred at any time in the person's lifetime. Only Axis I diagnoses are provided.

The SCAN procedure has been the subject of a number of comparative research studies—for example, Babiak (2007) studied psychopaths in business. This procedure has also been widely used in other countries: for example, in a multicultural study of bipolar disorder (Di Florio et al., 2010); in Spain to study schizophrenia (Martín-Reyes, 2010), and in the United Kingdom to study substance abuse (Mazzoncini et al., 2010). Investigators have found satisfactory concordance between the SCAN procedure and clinical diagnosis. The computer administration version of the SCAN provides more reliable diagnoses than diagnostic interviews conducted by clinicians without the benefit of structured computer processing.

Unresolved Issues
▶ *The* DSM-V: *What Comes Next?*

Change is a part of life, and complex criteria such as those contained in the *DSM* diagnostic system become obsolete or inadequate as a result of new research developments or changes in clinical practice requirements. Periodic updating of the diagnostic criteria is required to make them more effective and acceptable to the professional community. In 2007, the American Psychiatric Association began the arduous task of revising the *Diagnostic and Statistical Manual*. This task has been going on for several years and involves substantial input from numerous mental health professionals, both practitioners and researchers, before it can be completed. Many aspects of the current *DSM-IV-TR* version will likely be continued into the new *DSM* generation because of their clarity and acceptance; however, some categories will no doubt be modified, moved to different locations in the system, or even dropped, and new diagnostic criteria will be added. At the time of this writing, the *DSM-5* is slated to be published in May 2013. The revision of the *DSM* has generated substantial controversy and a number of critics have expressed their concerns over various proposed changes (see discussions by Alarcón et al., 2009; Frances, 2010a, 2010b; Kornstein, 2010; Pies, 2009).

One of the most widely discussed problems with the current *DSM* is the need for classification of personality disorders, currently on Axis II.

Earlier, we described the differing views of categorizing personality disorders from the dimensional versus the prototypal perspective. The debates between the proponents of each classification approach have intensified as the *DSM* revision process proceeds (Widiger, Costa, & McCrae, 2002; Westen, Shedler, & Bradley, 2006; see also the comprehensive discussion provided by O'Donohue et al., 2007). The *DSM* revision will likely require substantial time and effort to come to terms with the issues and various viewpoints on conceptualizing personality disorders in order to produce a model that will be useful both in clinical diagnosis and in guiding research.

Personality disorders are not the only diagnostic categories requiring significant rethinking. Other categories have been found to be unclear in some respects and limited or overly narrow in others. The current *DSM-IV-TR* requires direct involvement in an experienced trauma for the PTSD diagnosis to be applied. However, as a result of experiences following the World Trade Center terrorist attack in 2001, many people who were "traumatized" by the unfolding saga through the constant media coverage of the events also experienced PTSD as a result of indirect exposure. Under the present *DSM-IV-TR*, these circumstances would not apply, and the diagnostic classification of PTSD would be considered inappropriate. This requirement has resulted in some authorities recommending a revision of the *DSM* criteria to reduce this limitation (Marshall et al., 2007), while others are concerned that doing so could result in a problematic expansion of the diagnosis of PTSD. For example, there is concern that the broadened classification would label people who might be experiencing "normal" grief as having a major depressive disorder (Frances, 2010b). This could result from a "medicalization of normal emotion" and could prompt some drug companies to "quickly and greedily" pounce upon the opportunity to mount a marketing campaign for people who are bereaved (Frances, 2010b).

Concern has also been expressed about the expansion of clinical diagnosis into potentially inappropriate areas, such as a diagnosis of "Internet addiction" (Frances, 2010a; Pies, 2009).

The diagnostic criteria for mental disorders in *DSM* are not viewed by most mental health professionals as a fixed-components system but as workable criteria that evolve and develop to accommodate new research and practical developments. The remaking of *DSM* is never a smooth transition, but the resulting system is, nevertheless, a valuable conceptual guide that provides an agreed-upon language that students, practitioners, and researchers can employ to enable clear communication about mental disorders.

Summary

- Clinical assessment is one of the most important and complex responsibilities of mental health professionals. The extent to which a person's problems are understood and appropriately treated depends largely on the adequacy of the psychological assessment.

- The goals of psychological assessment include identifying and describing the individual's symptoms; determining the chronicity and severity of the problems; evaluating the potential causal factors in the person's background; and exploring the individual's personal resources that might be an asset in his or her treatment program.

- Because many psychological problems have physical components, either as underlying causal factors or as symptom patterns, it is often important to include a medical examination in the psychological assessment.

- In cases where organic brain damage is suspected, it is important to have neurological tests—such as an EEG; a CAT, PET, or MRI scan; or an fMRI—to help determine the site and extent of organic brain disorder.

- For someone with suspected organic brain damage, a battery of neuropsychological tests might be recommended to determine whether or in what manner the underlying brain disorder is affecting her or his mental and behavioral capabilities.

- Psychosocial assessment methods are techniques for gathering psychological information relevant to clinical decisions about patients.

- The most widely used and most flexible psychosocial assessment methods are the clinical interview and behavior observation. These methods provide a wealth of clinical information.

- Psychological tests include standardized stimuli for collecting behavior samples that can be compared with other individuals' behavior via test norms. Examples include intelligence and personality tests.

- Two different personality-testing approaches have evolved: (1) projective tests, such as the Rorschach or the TAT, in which unstructured stimuli are presented to a subject, who then "projects" meaning or structure onto the stimulus, thereby revealing "hidden" motives, feelings, and so on; and (2) objective tests, or personality inventories, in which a subject is required to read and respond to itemized statements or questions.

- Objectively scored personality tests, such as the MMPI-2 and MMPI-A, provide a cost-effective means of collecting a great deal of personality information rapidly.

- Possibly the most valuable recent innovation in clinical assessment involves the widespread use of computers in the administration, scoring, and interpretation of psychological tests. It is now possible to obtain immediate interpretation of psychological test results, either through a direct computer interactive approach or through an Internet hookup.

- The formal definition of mental disorder, as offered in the fourth edition of the *Diagnostic and Statistical Manual of Mental Disorders (DSM-IV-TR)*, has certain problems that limit its clarity.

- There are problems with the category type of classification system adopted in *DSM-IV-TR*. Notably, the categories do not always result in within-class homogeneity or between-class discrimination. This can lead to high levels of comorbidity among disorders. Several possible solutions to this problem include

- dimensionalizing the phenomena of mental disorder and adopting a prototypal approach.

- For all of its problems, however, knowledge of the *DSM-IV-TR* is essential to serious study in the field of abnormal behavior.

Key Terms

actuarial procedures
acute
aphasia
Brief Psychiatric Rating Scale (BPRS)
chronic
clinical diagnosis
comorbidity
computerized axial tomography (CAT) scan
cultural competence
dysrhythmia
electroencephalogram (EEG)
episodic
forensic
functional MRI (fMRI)

intelligence test
magnetic resonance imaging (MRI)
mild
Minnesota Multiphasic Personality Inventory (MMPI)
moderate
neuropsychological assessment
objective personality tests
personality tests
positron emission tomography (PET) scan
presenting problem
projective personality tests
psychological assessment
rating scales

recurrent
reliability
role-playing
Rorschach Inkblot Test
self-monitoring
sentence completion test
severe
signs
standardization
structured assessment interview
symptoms
T score distribution
Thematic Apperception Test (TAT)
unstructured assessment interviews
validity

Glossary

Many of the key terms listed in the glossary appear in boldface when first introduced in the text discussion. A number of other terms commonly encountered in this or other psychology texts are also included; you are encouraged to make use of this glossary both as a general reference tool and as a study aid for the course in abnormal psychology.

Actuarial procedures. Methods whereby data about subjects are analyzed by objective procedures or formulas rather than by human judgments.

Acute. Term used to describe a disorder of sudden onset, usually with intense symptoms.

Aphasia. Loss or impairment of ability to communicate and understand language symbols—involving loss of power of expression by speech, writing, or signs, or loss of ability to comprehend written or spoken language—resulting from brain injury or disease.

Brief Psychiatric Rating Scale (BPRS). Objective method of rating clinical symptoms that provides scores on 18 variables (e.g., somatic concern, anxiety, withdrawal, hostility, and bizarre thinking).

Chronic. Term used to describe a long-standing or frequently recurring disorder, often with progressing seriousness.

Clinical diagnosis. The process through which a clinician arrives at a general "summary classification" of the patient's symptoms by following a clearly defined system such as *DSM-IV-TR* or ICD-10.

Comorbidity. Occurrence of two or more identified disorders in the same psychologically disordered individual.

Computerized axial tomography (CAT) scan. Radiological technique used to locate and assess the extent of organic damage to the brain without surgery.

Cultural competence. Refers to a psychologist's need to be informed of the issues involved in multicultural assessment.

Dysrhythmia. Abnormal brain wave pattern.

Electroencephalogram (EEG). Graphical record of the brain's electrical activity obtained by placing electrodes on the scalp and measuring the brain wave impulses from various brain areas.

Episodic. Term used to describe a disorder that tends to abate and recur.

Forensic. Pertaining or used in the court of law.

Functional MRI (fMRI). Internal scanning technique that measures changes in local oxygenation (blood flow) to specific areas of brain tissue that in turn depend on neuronal activity in those specific regions, allowing the mapping of psychological activity such as sensations, images, and thoughts.

Intelligence test. Test used in establishing a subject's level of intellectual capability.

Magnetic resonance imaging (MRI). Internal scanning technique involving measurement of variations in magnetic fields that allows visualization of the anatomical features of internal organs, including the central nervous system and particularly the brain.

Mild (disorder). Disorder low in severity.

Minnesota Multiphasic Personality Inventory (MMPI/MMPI-2). Widely used and empirically validated personality scales.

Moderate (disorder). Disorder intermediate in severity.

Neuropsychological assessment. Use of psychological tests that measure a person's cognitive, perceptual, and motor performance to obtain clues to the extent and locus of brain damage.

Objective personality tests. Structured tests, such as questionnaires, self-inventories, or rating scales, used in psychological assessment.

Personality test. See **Objective personality tests** and **Projective personality tests**.

Positron emission tomography (PET) scan. Scanning technique that measures metabolic processes to appraise how well an organ is functioning.

Presenting problem. Major symptoms and behavior the client is experiencing.

Projective personality tests. Techniques that use various ambiguous stimuli that a subject is encouraged to interpret and from which the subject's personality characteristics can be analyzed.

Psychological assessment. The use of psychological procedures such as behavioral observations, interview, and psychological tests to obtain a picture of a client's mental health symptoms and personality.

Rating scales. Formal structure for organizing information obtained from clinical observation and self-reports to encourage reliability and objectivity.

Recurrent. Term used to describe a disorder pattern that tends to come and go.

Reliability. Degree to which a measuring device produces the same result each time it is used to measure the same thing or when two or more different raters use it.

Role-playing. Form of assessment in which a person is instructed to play a part, enabling a clinician to observe a client's behavior directly.

Rorschach Inkblot Test. Use of 10 inkblot pictures to which a subject responds with associations that come to mind. Analysis of these responses enables a clinician to infer personality characteristics.

Self-monitoring. Observing and recording one's own behavior, thoughts, and feelings as they occur in various natural settings.

Sentence completion test. Projective technique utilizing incomplete sentences that a person is to complete, analysis of which enables a clinician to infer personality dynamics.

Severe (disorder). Disorder of a high degree of seriousness.

Signs. Objective observations that suggest to a diagnostician a patient's physical or mental disorder.

Standardization. Procedure for establishing the expected performance range on a test.

Structured assessment interview. Interview with set introduction and that follows a predetermined set of procedures and questions throughout.

Symptoms. Patient's subjective description of a physical or mental disorder.

T score distribution. A standard distribution of scores that allow for a comparison of scores on a test by comparing scores with a group of known values.

Thematic Apperception Test (TAT). Use of a series of simple pictures about which a subject is instructed to make up stories. Analysis of the stories gives a clinician clues about the person's conflicts, traits, personality dynamics, and the like.

Unstructured assessment interviews. Typically subjective interviews that do not follow a predetermined set of questions. The beginning statements in the interview are usually general, and follow-up questions are tailored for each client. The content of the interview questions is influenced by the habits or theoretical views of the interviewer.

Validity. Extent to which a measuring instrument actually measures what it purports to measure.

Photo Credits

Text Credits

Panic, Anxiety, and Their Disorders

From Chapter 6 of *Abnormal Psychology*, Fifteenth Edition. James N. Butcher, Susan Mineka, Jill M. Hooley. Copyright © 2013 by Pearson Education, Inc. All rights reserved.

Panic, Anxiety, and Their Disorders

case study Ed: A Worrier

A 27-year-old married electrician, Ed, complains of dizziness, sweating palms, heart palpitations, and ringing of the ears of more than 18 months' duration. He has also experienced dry mouth and throat, periods of extreme muscle tension, and a constant "edgy" and watchful feeling that has often interfered with his ability to concentrate. These feelings have been present most of the time during the previous 2 years . . . Because of these symptoms the patient has seen a family practitioner, a neurologist, a neurosurgeon, a chiropractor, and an ear-nose-throat specialist. . . . He also has many worries. He constantly worries about the health of his parents . . . He also worries about whether he is a "good father," whether his wife will ever leave him (there is no indication that she is dissatisfied with the marriage), and whether he is liked by coworkers on the job. Although he recognizes that his worries are often unfounded, he can't stop worrying. For the past 2 years the patient has had few social contacts because of his nervous symptoms . . . he sometimes has to leave work when the symptoms become intolerable.

The physicians that Ed consulted could not determine the cause of his physical symptoms, and one of them finally referred him for treatment at a mental health clinic, where he was diagnosed as having generalized anxiety disorder—one of seven primary anxiety disorders.

Source: Adapted with permission from the *Diagnostic and Statistical Manual of Mental Disorders*, Fourth Edition, *Text Revision*, (Copyright © 2002). American Psychiatric Association.

Sometimes even stable, well-adjusted people may develop clinical disorders such as acute stress disorder or posttraumatic stress disorder if forced to face extensive combat stress, torture, or devastating natural disaster. But when some people like Ed are faced even with the normal demands of life—concerns about being a good father, the health of one's parents, the stability of one's marriage, the seriousness of one's physical symptoms—they become seriously anxious or fearful. In the most severe cases, people with anxiety problems may be unable even to leave their homes for fear of having a panic attack or may spend many of their waking hours in maladaptive behavior such as constant hand washing.

Anxiety involves a general feeling of apprehension about possible future danger, and **fear** is an alarm reaction that occurs in response to immediate danger. Today the *DSM* has identified a group of disorders—known as the *anxiety disorders*—that share obvious symptoms of clinically significant fear or anxiety. The anxiety disorders affect approximately 25 to 29 percent of the U.S. population at some point in their lives and are the most common category of disorders for women and the second most common for men (Kessler et al., 1994; Kessler, Berglund, Delmar, et al., 2005). In any 12-month

period, about 18 percent of the adult population suffers from at least one anxiety disorder (Kessler, Chiu, et al., 2005). Anxiety disorders create enormous personal, economic, and health care problems for those affected. For example, in the late 1990s several studies estimated that the anxiety disorders cost the United States somewhere between $42.3 billion and $47 billion in direct and indirect costs (about 30 percent of the nation's total mental health bill of $148 billion in 1990; Greenberg et al., 1999; Kessler & Greenberg, 2002). Anxiety disorders are also associated with an increased prevalence of a number of medical conditions including asthma, chronic pain, hypertension, arthritis, cardiovascular disease, and irritable bowel syndrome (Roy-Byrne et al., 2008) and are very high users of medical service (e.g., Chavira et al., 2009).

Historically, cases like this and other cases of anxiety disorders were considered to be classic examples of neurotic disorders. Although individuals with **neurotic disorders** show maladaptive and self-defeating behaviors, they are not incoherent, dangerous, or out of touch with reality. To Freud, these neurotic disorders developed when intrapsychic conflict produced significant anxiety. Anxiety was, in Freud's formulation, a sign of an inner battle or conflict between some primitive desire (from the id) and prohibitions against its expression (from the ego and superego). Sometimes this anxiety was overtly expressed (as in those disorders known today as the anxiety disorders). In certain other neurotic disorders, however, he believed that the anxiety might not be obvious, either to the person involved or to others, if psychological defense mechanisms were able to deflect or mask it. In 1980 the *DSM-III* dropped the term *neurosis* and reclassified most of these disorders that did not involve obvious anxiety symptoms as either dissociative or somatoform disorders (and some neurotic disorders were absorbed into the mood disorders category as well). *DSM-III* made this change in order to group together smaller sets of disorders that share more obvious symptoms and features.

We begin by discussing the nature of fear and anxiety as emotional states and patterns of responding, both of which have an extremely important adaptive value but to which humans at times seem all too vulnerable. We will then move to a discussion of the anxiety disorders.

The Fear and Anxiety Response Patterns

There has never been complete agreement about how distinct the two emotions of fear and anxiety are from each other. Historically, the most common way of distinguishing between the fear and anxiety response patterns has been whether there is a clear and obvious source of danger that would be regarded as real by most people. When the source of danger is obvious, the experienced emotion has been called fear (e.g., "I'm afraid of snakes").

With anxiety, however, we frequently cannot specify clearly what the danger is (e.g., "I'm anxious about my parents' health").

Fear

In recent years, however, many prominent researchers have proposed a more fundamental distinction between the fear and anxiety response patterns (e.g., Barlow, 1988, 2002; Bouton, 2005; Grillon, 2008; McNaughton, 2008). According to these theorists, fear is a basic emotion (shared by many animals) that involves activation of the "fight-or-flight" response of the autonomic nervous system. This is an almost instantaneous reaction to any imminent threat such as a dangerous predator or someone pointing a loaded gun.

Its adaptive value as a primitive alarm response to imminent danger is that it allows us to escape. When the fear response occurs in the absence of any obvious external danger, we say the person has had a spontaneous or uncued **panic attack**. The symptoms of a panic attack are nearly identical to those experienced during a state of fear except that panic attacks are often accompanied by a subjective sense of impending doom, including fears of dying, going crazy, or losing control. These latter cognitive symptoms do not generally occur during fear states. Thus fear and panic have three components:

1. cognitive/subjective components ("I feel afraid/terrified"; "I'm going to die")

2. physiological components (such as increased heart rate and heavy breathing)

3. behavioral components (a strong urge to escape or flee; Lang, 1968, 1971)

These components are only "loosely coupled" (Lang, 1985), which means that someone might show, for example, physiological and behavioral indications of fear or panic without much of the subjective component, or vice versa.

Anxiety

In contrast to fear and panic, the anxiety response pattern is a complex blend of unpleasant emotions and cognitions that is both more oriented to the future and much more diffuse than fear (Barlow, 1988, 2002). But like fear, it has not only cognitive/subjective components but also physiological and behavioral components. At the cognitive/subjective level, anxiety involves negative mood, worry about possible future threats or danger, self-preoccupation, and a sense of being unable to predict the future threat or to control it if it occurs. At a physiological level, anxiety often creates a state of tension and chronic overarousal,

Fear or panic is a basic emotion that is shared by many animals, including humans, and may activate the fight-or-flight response of the sympathetic nervous system. This allows us to respond rapidly when faced with a dangerous situation, such as being threatened by a predator. In humans who are having a panic attack, there is no external threat; panic occurs because of some misfiring of this response system.

which may reflect risk assessment and readiness for dealing with danger should it occur ("Something awful may happen, and I had better be ready for it if it does"). Although there is no activation of the fight-or-flight response as there is with fear, anxiety does prepare or prime a person for the fight-or-flight response should the anticipated danger occur. At a behavioral level, anxiety may create a strong tendency to avoid situations where danger might be encountered, but there is not the immediate behavioral urge to flee with anxiety as there is with fear (Barlow, 1988, 2002). Support for the idea that anxiety is descriptively and functionally distinct from fear or panic comes both from complex statistical analyses of subjective reports of panic and anxiety and from a great deal of neurobiological evidence (e.g., Bouton, 2005; Bouton et al., 2001; Davis, 2006; Grillon, 2008).

The adaptive value of anxiety may be that it helps us plan and prepare for possible threat. In mild to moderate degrees, anxiety actually enhances learning and performance. For example, a mild amount of anxiety about how you are going to do on your next exam, or in your next tennis match, can actually be helpful. But although anxiety is often adaptive in mild or moderate degrees, it is maladaptive when it becomes chronic and severe, as we see in people diagnosed with anxiety disorders.

Although there are many threatening situations that provoke fear or anxiety unconditionally, many of our sources of fear and anxiety are learned. Years of human and nonhuman animal experimentation have established that the basic fear and anxiety response patterns are highly conditionable (e.g., Fanselow & Ponnusamy, 2008; Lipp, 2006). That is, previously neutral and novel stimuli (conditioned stimuli) that are repeatedly paired with, and reliably predict, frightening or unpleasant events such as various kinds of physical or psychological trauma (unconditioned stimulus) can acquire the capacity to elicit fear or anxiety themselves (conditioned response). Such conditioning is a completely normal and adaptive process that allows all of us to learn to anticipate upcoming frightening events if they are reliably preceded by a signal. Yet this normal and adaptive process can also lead in some cases to the development of clinically significant fears and anxieties, as we will see.

For example, a girl named Angela sometimes saw and heard her father physically abuse her mother in the evening. After this happened four or five times, Angela started to become anxious as soon as she heard her father's car arrive in the driveway at the end of the day. In such situations a wide variety of initially neutral stimuli may accidentally come to serve as cues that something threatening and unpleasant is about to happen—and thereby come to elicit fear or anxiety themselves. Our thoughts and images can also serve as conditioned stimuli capable of eliciting the fear or anxiety response pattern. For example, Angela came to feel anxious even when thinking about her father.

In Review

- Compare and contrast fear or panic with anxiety, making sure to note that both emotions involve three response systems.

- Explain the significance of the fact that both fear and anxiety can be classically conditioned.

Overview of the Anxiety Disorders and Their Commonalities

Anxiety disorders all have unrealistic, irrational fears or anxieties of disabling intensity as their principal and most obvious manifestation. *DSM-IV-TR* recognizes seven primary types of anxiety disorders:

1. specific phobia
2. social phobia
3. panic disorder with or without agoraphobia (and agoraphobia without panic)
4. generalized anxiety disorder
5. obsessive-compulsive disorder
6. acute stress disorder
7. posttraumatic stress disorder

As seen in the following brief overview, people with these varied disorders differ from one another both in terms of the relative preponderance of fear or panic versus anxiety symptoms that they experience and in the kinds of objects or situations that most concern them. For example, people with *specific* or *social* phobias exhibit many anxiety symptoms about the possibility of encountering their phobic situation, but they may also experience a fear or panic response when they actually encounter the situation. People with *panic disorder* experience both frequent panic attacks and intense anxiety focused on the possibility of having another one. By contrast, people with *generalized anxiety disorder* mostly experience a general sense of diffuse anxiety and worry about many potentially bad things that may happen; some may also experience an occasional panic attack, but it is not a focus of their anxiety. Finally, people with *obsessive-compulsive disorder* experience intense anxiety or distress in response to intrusive thoughts or images and feel compelled to engage in compulsive, ritualistic activities that temporarily help to reduce the anxiety. It is also important to note that many people with one anxiety disorder will experience at least one more anxiety disorder and/or depression either concurrently or at a different point in their lives (e.g., Brown & Barlow, 2002, 2009; Kessler, Berglund, Demler, et al., 2005).

Given these commonalities across the anxiety disorders, it should come as no surprise that there are some important similarities in the basic causes of these disorders (as well as many differences). Among biological causal factors, we will see that there are genetic contributions to each of these disorders and that at least part of the genetic vulnerability may be nonspecific, or common across the disorders (e.g., Barlow, 2002; Craske & Waters, 2005). In adults the common genetic vulnerability is manifested at a psychological level at least in part by the important personality trait called *neuroticism*—a proneness or disposition to experience negative mood states that is a common risk factor for both anxiety and mood disorders (e.g., Klein et al., 2009). The brain structures most centrally involved in most disorders are generally in the limbic system (often known as the "emotional brain") and certain parts of the cortex, and the neurotransmitter substances that are most centrally involved are gamma aminobutyric acid (GABA), norepinephrine, and serotonin.

Among common psychological causal factors, we will see that classical conditioning of fear, panic, or anxiety to a range of stimuli plays an important role in many of these disorders (Forsyth et al., 2006; Mineka & Oehlberg, 2008; Mineka & Zinbarg, 1996, 2006). In addition, people who have perceptions of a lack of control over either their environments or their own emotions (or both) seem more vulnerable to developing anxiety disorders. The development of such perceptions of uncontrollability depends heavily on the social environment people are raised in, including parenting styles (Chorpita & Barlow, 1998; Craske & Waters, 2005; Mineka & Zinbarg, 2006; Hudson & Rapee, 2009). For certain disorders, faulty or distorted patterns of cognition also may play an important role. Finally, the sociocultural environment in which people are raised also has prominent effects on the kinds of objects and experiences people become anxious about or come to fear. Ultimately what we must strive for is a good biopsychosocial understanding of how all these types of causal factors interact with one another in the development of anxiety disorders.

Finally, as we will see, there are many commonalities across the effective treatments for the various anxiety disorders (e.g., Barlow, 2004; Campbell-Sills & Barlow, 2007). For each disorder, graduated exposure to feared cues, objects, and situations—until fear or anxiety begins to habituate—constitutes the single most powerful therapeutic ingredient. Further, for certain disorders the addition of cognitive restructuring techniques can provide added benefit. What these cognitive restructuring techniques for different disorders have in common is that they help the individual understand his or her distorted patterns of thinking about anxiety-related situations and how these patterns can be changed. Medications can also be useful in treating all disorders except specific phobias, and nearly all tend to fall into two primary medication categories: antianxiety medications (anxiolytics) and antidepressant medications.

Now we will turn to a more detailed discussion of each disorder to highlight both their common and their distinct features as well as what is known about their causes. We start with the phobic disorders, which are the most common anxiety disorders. A **phobia** is a persistent and disproportionate fear of some specific object or situation that presents little or no actual danger and yet leads to a great deal of avoidance of these feared situations. As we will see in *DSM-IV-TR*, there are three main categories of phobias: (1) specific phobia, (2) social phobia, and (3) agoraphobia (now primarily considered a subcategory of panic disorder, which is where it will be discussed).

In Review

- What is the central feature of all anxiety disorders? That is, what do they have in common?
- What differentiates the anxiety disorders from one another?
- What are some common kinds of biological and psychosocial causes of the different anxiety disorders?
- What is the most important ingredient across effective psychosocial treatments for the anxiety disorders?

Specific Phobias

A person is diagnosed as having a **specific phobia** if she or he shows strong and persistent fear that s/he realizes is excessive or unreasonable and is triggered by the presence of a specific object or situation (see *DSM-IV-TR* box). When individuals with specific phobias encounter a phobic stimulus, they often show an immediate fear response that often resembles a panic attack except for the existence of a clear external trigger

(APA, *DSM-IV-TR*, 2000). Not surprisingly, such individuals also experience anxiety if they anticipate they may encounter a phobic object or situation and so go to great lengths to avoid encounters with their phobic stimulus. Indeed, they often even avoid seemingly innocent representations of it such

People with claustrophobia may find elevators so frightening that they go to great lengths to avoid them. If for some reason they have to take an elevator, they will be very frightened and have thoughts about the elevator falling, the doors never opening, or there not being enough air to breathe.

table 1 Subtypes of Specific Phobias in *DSM-IV-TR*

Phobia Type	Examples
Animal	Snakes, spiders, dogs, insects, birds
Natural Environment	Storms, heights, water
Blood-Injection-Injury	Seeing blood or an injury, receiving an injection, seeing a person in a wheelchair
Situational	Public transportation, tunnels, bridges, elevators, flying, driving, enclosed spaces
Other	Choking, vomiting, "space phobia" (fear of falling down if away from walls or other support)

Source: Adapted with permission from the *Diagnostic and Statistical Manual of Mental Disorders, Text Revision, Fourth Edition* (Copyright 2000). American Psychiatric Association.

as photographs or television images. For example, claustrophobic persons may go to great lengths to avoid entering a closet or an elevator, even if this means climbing many flights of stairs or turning down jobs that might require them to take an elevator.

This avoidance is a cardinal characteristic of phobias; it occurs both because the phobic response itself is so unpleasant and because of the phobic person's irrational appraisal of the likelihood that something terrible will happen. Table 1 lists the five subtypes of specific phobias in *DSM-IV-TR*, along with some examples.

The following case is typical of specific phobia:

case study A Pilot's Wife's Fear

Mary, a married mother of three, was 47 at the time she first sought treatment for both claustrophobia and acrophobia. She reported having been intensely afraid of enclosed spaces (claustrophobia) and of heights (acrophobia) since her teens. She remembered having been locked in closets by her older siblings when she was a child; the siblings also confined her under blankets to scare her and added to her fright by showing her pictures of spiders after releasing her from under the blankets. She traced the onset of her claustrophobia to those traumatic incidents, but she had no idea why she was afraid of heights. While her children had been growing up, she had been a housewife and had managed to live a fairly normal life in spite of her two specific phobias. However, her children were now grown, and she wanted to find a job outside her home. This was proving to be very difficult because she could not take elevators and was frightened being on anything other than the first floor of an office building. Moreover, her husband had for some years been working for an airline, which entitled him to free airline tickets. The fact that Mary could not fly (due to her phobias) had become a sore point in her marriage because they both wanted to be able to take advantage of these free tickets to see distant places. Thus, although she had had these phobias for many years, they had become truly disabling only in recent years as her life circumstances had changed and she could no longer easily avoid heights or enclosed spaces.

If people who suffer from phobias attempt to approach their phobic situation, they are overcome with fear or anxiety, which may vary from mild feelings of apprehension and distress (usually while still at some distance) to full-fledged activation of the fight-or-flight response. Regardless of how it begins, phobic behavior tends to be reinforced because every time the person with a phobia avoids a feared situation his or her anxiety decreases. In addition, the secondary benefits derived from being disabled, such as increased attention, sympathy, and some control over the behavior of others, may also sometimes reinforce a phobia.

One category of specific phobias that has a number of interesting and unique characteristics is **blood-injection-injury phobia**. It probably occurs in about 3 to 4 percent of the population (Ayala et al., 2009; Öst & Hellström, 1997). People afflicted with this phobia typically experience at least as much (if not more) disgust as fear (Schienle et al., 2005; Teachman & Saporito, 2009). They also show a unique physiological response when confronted with the sight of blood or injury. Rather than showing the simple increase in heart rate and blood pressure seen when most people with phobias encounter their phobic object, these people show an initial acceleration, followed by a dramatic drop in both heart rate and blood pressure. This is very frequently accompanied by nausea, dizziness, or fainting, which do not occur with other specific phobias (Öst & Hellström, 1997; Page & Tan, 2009).

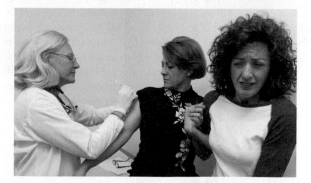

In blood-injection-injury phobia, the afflicted person experiences disgust and fear at the sight of someone receiving an injection. When confronted with the sight of blood or injury, people with this phobic disorder often experience nausea, dizziness, and fainting.

Interestingly, people with this phobia show this unique physiological response pattern only in the presence of blood and injury stimuli; they exhibit the more typical physiological response pattern characteristic of the fight-or-flight response to their other feared objects (see Dahlloef & Öst, 1998; Öst & Hugdahl, 1985). From an evolutionary and functional standpoint, this unique physiological response pattern may have evolved for a specific purpose: By fainting, the person being attacked might inhibit further attack, and if an attack did occur, the drop in blood pressure would minimize blood loss (Craske, 1999; Marks & Nesse, 1991).

Prevalence, Age of Onset, and Gender Differences

Specific phobias are quite common. Results of the National Comorbidity Survey-Replication revealed a lifetime prevalence rate of about 12 percent (Kessler, Chiu, et al., 2005). Among people with one specific phobia, over 75 percent have at least one other specific fear that is excessive (Curtis, Magee, et al., 1998). The relative gender ratios vary considerably according to the type of specific phobia, but phobias are always considerably more common in women than in men. For example, about 90 to 95 percent of people with animal phobias are women, but the gender ratio is less than 2:1 for blood-injection-injury phobia. The average age of onset for different types of specific phobias also varies widely. Animal phobias usually begin in childhood, as do blood-injection-injury phobias and dental phobias. However, other phobias such as claustrophobia and driving phobia tend to begin in adolescence or early adulthood (Barlow, 2002; Öst, 1987).

Psychological Causal Factors

A variety of psychological causal factors has been implicated in the origins of specific phobias, ranging from deep-seated psychodynamic conflicts to relatively straightforward traumatic conditioning of fear and a multitude of individual differences in who is at risk for such conditioning.

PSYCHOANALYTIC VIEWPOINT According to the psychoanalytic view, phobias represent a defense against anxiety that stems from repressed impulses from the id. Because it is too dangerous to "know" the repressed id impulse, the anxiety is displaced onto some external object or situation that has some symbolic relationship to the real object of the anxiety (Freud, 1909). However, this prototypical psychodynamic account of how phobias are acquired was long criticized as being far too speculative, and an alternative, simpler account from learning theory was first proposed by Wolpe and Rachman (1960) which has now been further refined and expanded as discussed below.

PHOBIAS AS LEARNED BEHAVIOR As an alternative to psychoanalytic accounts, Wolpe and Rachman (1960) developed an account based on learning theory, which sought to explain the development of phobic behavior through classical conditioning. Numerous other theorists in the 1960s and 1970s also agreed that the principles of classical conditioning appeared to account for the acquisition of irrational fears and phobias. The fear response can readily be conditioned to previously neutral stimuli when these stimuli are paired with traumatic or painful events. We would also expect that, once acquired, phobic fears would generalize to other, similar objects or situations. Recall, for example, that Mary's claustrophobia had probably been caused by multiple incidents as a child when her siblings locked her in closets and confined her under blankets to scare her. But as an adult Mary feared elevators and caves as well as other enclosed places. The powerful role of classical conditioning in the development of phobias was supported in a survey by Öst and Hugdahl (1981), who administered questionnaires to 106 adult phobic clients that concerned, among other things, the purported origins of their fears (see Mineka & Sutton, 2006, for a review). Fifty-eight percent cited traumatic conditioning experiences as the sources of their phobias. Some of these traumatic conditioning events were simply uncued panic attacks, which are now known to effectively condition fear (e.g., Acheson et al., 2007; Forsyth & Eifert, 1998).

Vicarious Conditioning Direct traumatic conditioning in which a person has a terrifying experience in the presence of a neutral object or situation is not the only way that people can learn irrational, phobic fears. Simply watching a phobic person behaving fearfully with his or her phobic object can be distressing to the observer and can result in fear being transmitted from one person to another through vicarious or observational classical conditioning. In addition, watching a nonfearful person undergoing a frightening experience can also lead to vicarious conditioning. For example, one man,

Monkeys who watch a model monkey (such as the one illustrated here) behaving fearfully with a live boa constrictor will rapidly acquire an intense fear of snakes themselves. Fears can thus be learned vicariously without any direct traumatic experience.

as a boy, had witnessed his grandfather vomit while dying. Shortly after this traumatic event (his grandfather's distress while dying) the boy had developed a strong and persistent vomiting phobia. Indeed, when this man was in middle age he even contemplated suicide one time when he was nauseated and feared vomiting (Mineka & Zinbarg, 2006). Related experimental findings have been observed in laboratory analogue studies of human children. For example, two studies showed that 7- to 9-year-old children who saw pictures of an unfamiliar animal (Australian marsupials) paired 10 times with fearful facial expressions showed increased fear beliefs and behavioral avoidance of this conditioned stimulus (CS) relative to children who saw the unfamiliar animal paired with happy facial expressions. These effects persisted for at least one week (Askew & Field, 2007; see Askew & Field, 2008, for a review).

Animal research using rhesus monkeys has increased our confidence that vicarious conditioning of intense fears can indeed occur. In these experiments, Mineka and Cook and their colleagues (e.g., Cook & Mineka, 1989; Mineka & Cook, 1993; Mineka, Davidson, et al., 1984) showed that laboratory-reared monkeys who were not initially afraid of snakes rapidly developed a phobic-like fear of snakes simply through observing a wild-reared monkey behaving fearfully with snakes. Significant fear was acquired after only 4 to 8 minutes of exposure to the wild-reared monkey with snakes, and there were no signs that the fear had diminished 3 months later. The monkeys could also learn the fear simply through watching a videotape of the wild-reared model monkey behaving fearfully with snakes. This suggests that the mass media also play a role in the vicarious conditioning of fears and phobias in people (Cook & Mineka, 1990; Mineka & Sutton, 2006).

Individual Differences in Learning Does the direct and vicarious conditioning model really explain the origins of most phobias? Given all the traumas that people undergo, why don't more people develop phobias (Mineka & Oehlberg, 2008; Mineka & Zinbarg, 1996, 2006; Rachman, 1990)? The answer seems to be, at least in good part, that differences in life experiences among individuals strongly affect whether or not conditioned fears or phobias actually develop. For example, years of positive experiences with friendly dogs before being bitten by one will probably keep a dog bite victim from developing a full-blown dog phobia. Thus, to understand individual differences in the development and maintenance of phobias, we need to understand the role of the different life experiences of people who undergo the same trauma.

A person who has had good experiences with a potentially phobic stimulus, such as the young woman romping here with her dog, is likely to be immunized from later acquiring a fear of dogs even if she has a traumatic encounter with one.

Some life experiences may serve as risk factors and make certain people more vulnerable to phobias than others, and other experiences may serve as protective factors for the development of phobias (Mineka & Sutton, 2006). For example, children who have had more previous nontraumatic experiences with a dentist are less likely to develop dental anxiety after a bad and painful experience than are children with fewer previous nontraumatic experiences (Ten Berge et al., 2002; Kent, 1997). This shows the importance of the individual's prior familiarity with an object or situation in determining whether a phobia develops following a fear-conditioning experience. Moreover, Mineka and Cook (1986) showed that monkeys who first simply watched nonfearful monkeys behaving nonfearfully with snakes were immunized against acquiring a fear of snakes when they later saw fearful monkeys behaving fearfully with snakes. By analogy, if a child has extensive exposure to a nonfearful parent behaving nonfearfully with the phobic object (e.g., spiders) or situation (e.g., heights) of the other, phobic parent, this may serve as a protective factor and immunize the child against the effects of later seeing the phobic parent behaving fearfully with the phobic object (Mineka & Oehlberg, 2008; Mineka & Sutton, 2006). Egliston and Rapee (2007) reported related results in an analogue study of human toddlers who either watched their mothers reacting positively to a snake or spider, or watched the snake or spider alone. Subsequently both groups of toddlers watched an experimenter reacting with fear and disgust toward the stimulus. Those in the group who had first watched their mother behaving positively acquired less fear than those who had first watched the stimulus alone.

Events that occur during a conditioning experience, as well as before it, are also important in determining the level of fear that is conditioned. For example, experiencing an inescapable and uncontrollable event, such as being attacked by a dog that one cannot escape from after being bitten, is expected to condition fear much more powerfully than experiencing the same intensity of trauma that is escapable or to some extent controllable (e.g., by running away after the attack; Mineka, 1985a; Mineka & Zinbarg, 1996, 2006). In addition, the experiences that a person has after a conditioning experience may effect the strength and maintenance of the conditioned fear (Rescorla, 1974; White & Davey, 1989). For example, the *inflation effect* suggests that a person who acquired, for example, a mild fear of driving following a minor crash might be expected to develop a full-blown phobia if he or she later were physically assaulted, even though no automobile was present during the assault (Dadds et al., 2001; Mineka, 1985b;

Mineka & Zinbarg, 1996, 2006). Even verbal information that later alters one's interpretation of the dangerousness of a previous trauma can inflate the level of fear (e.g., being told, "You're lucky to be alive because the man who crashed into your car last week had lost his license due to a record of drunk driving leading to fatal car crashes"; Dadds et al., 2001). Another way in which fear of a CS can be inflated following conditioning is if the organism later is exposed to uncontrollable stress (Baratta et al., 2007). These examples show that the factors involved in the origins and maintenance of fears and phobias are more complex than suggested by the traditional, simplistic conditioning view, although they are nevertheless consistent with contemporary views of conditioning (Mineka & Oehlberg, 2008; see also Coelho & Purkis, 2009).

It has also been shown that our cognitions, or thoughts, can help maintain our phobias once they have been acquired. For example, people with phobias are constantly on the alert for their phobic objects or situations and for other stimuli relevant to their phobia (McNally & Reese, 2009). Nonphobic persons, by contrast, tend to direct their attention away from threatening stimuli (see Mineka, Rafaeli, & Yovel, 2003). In addition, phobics also markedly overestimate the probability that feared objects have been, or will be, followed by frightening events. This cognitive bias may help maintain or strengthen phobic fears with the passage of time (Muhlberger et al., 2006; Öhman & Mineka, 2001; Tomarken, Mineka, & Cook, 1989).

Evolutionary Preparedness for Learning Certain Fears and Phobias Consider the observation that people are much more likely to have phobias of snakes, water, heights, and enclosed spaces than of motorcycles and guns, even though the latter objects may be at least as likely to be associated with trauma. This is because our evolutionary history has affected which stimuli we are most likely to come to fear. Primates and humans seem to be evolutionarily prepared to rapidly associate certain objects—such as snakes, spiders, water, and enclosed spaces—with frightening or unpleasant events (e.g., Mineka & Öhman, 2002; Öhman, 1996; Seligman, 1971). This **prepared learning** occurs because, over the course of evolution, those primates and humans who rapidly acquired fears of certain objects or situations that posed real threats to our early ancestors may have enjoyed a selective advantage. Thus "prepared" fears are not inborn or innate but rather are easily acquired or especially resistant to extinction. Guns and motorcycles, by contrast, were not present in our early evolutionary history and so did not convey any such selective advantage.

There is now a large amount of experimental evidence supporting the preparedness theory of phobias. In one important series of experiments using human subjects, Öhman and his colleagues (see Öhman, 1996; Öhman, 2009; Öhman & Mineka, 2001, for reviews) found that fear is conditioned more effectively to fear-relevant stimuli (slides of snakes and spiders) than to fear-irrelevant stimuli (slides

of flowers and mushrooms). These researchers also found that once the individuals acquired the conditioned responses to fear-relevant stimuli, these responses (including activation of the relevant brain area, the amygdala) could be elicited even when the fear-relevant stimuli (but not the fear-irrelevant stimuli) were presented subliminally (that is, presentation was so brief that the stimuli were not consciously perceived; e.g., Carlsson et al., 2004; Öhman et al., 2007). This subliminal activation of responses to phobic stimuli may help to account for certain aspects of the irrationality of phobias. That is, people with phobias may not be able to control their fear because the fear may arise from cognitive structures that are not under conscious control (Öhman & Mineka, 2001; Öhman & Soares, 1993).

Another series of experiments showed that lab-reared monkeys in a vicarious conditioning paradigm can easily acquire fears of fear-relevant stimuli such as toy snakes and toy crocodiles but not of fear-irrelevant stimuli such as flowers and a toy rabbit (Cook & Mineka, 1989, 1990). Thus both monkeys and humans seem selectively to associate certain fear-relevant stimuli with threat or danger. Moreover, these lab-reared monkeys had had no prior exposure to any of the stimuli involved (e.g., snakes or flowers) before participating in these experiments. Thus the monkey results support the evolutionarily based preparedness hypothesis even more strongly than the human experiments. For example, human subjects (unlike the lab-reared monkeys) might show superior conditioning to snakes or spiders because of preexisting negative associations to snakes or spiders rather than because of evolutionary factors (Mineka & Öhman, 2002).

Biological Causal Factors

Genetic and temperamental variables affect the speed and strength of conditioning of fear (e.g., Gray, 1987; Hettema et al., 2003; Oehlberg & Mineka, 2011). That is, depending on their genetic makeup or their temperament and personality (all of which are clearly related), people are more or less likely to acquire fears and phobias. For example, Lonsdorf and colleagues (2009) found that individuals who are carriers of one of the two variants on the serotonin-transporter gene (the *s* allele, which has been linked with heightened neuroticism) show superior fear conditioning relative to individuals who do not carry the *s* allele. However, those with one of two variants of a different gene (the COMT met/met genotype) did not show superior conditioning but did show enhanced resistance to extinction. Moreover, Kagan and his colleagues (2001) found that *behaviorally inhibited* toddlers (who are excessively timid, shy, easily distressed, etc.) at 21 months of age were at higher risk of developing multiple specific phobias by 7 to 8 years of age than were uninhibited children (32 versus 5 percent). The average number of reported fears in the inhibited group was three to four per child (Biederman et al., 1990).

Several behavior genetic studies also suggest a modest genetic contribution to the development of specific phobias. For example, a large female twin study found that monozygotic (identical) twins were more likely to share animal phobias and situational phobias (such as of heights or water) than were dizygotic (nonidentical) twins (Kendler et al., 1999b). Very similar results were also found more recently for men (Hettema et al., 2005). However, the same studies also found evidence that nonshared environmental factors (i.e., individual specific experiences not shared by twins) also played a very substantial role in the origins of specific phobias, a result that supports the idea that phobias are learned behaviors.

Treatments

A form of behavior therapy called **exposure therapy**—which is the best treatment for specific phobias—involves controlled exposure to the stimuli or situations that elicit phobic fear (Choy et al., 2007; Craske & Mystkowski, 2006). Clients are gradually placed—symbolically or increasingly under "real-life" conditions—in those situations they find most frightening.

In treatment, clients are encouraged to expose themselves (either alone or with the aid of a therapist or friend) to their feared situations for long enough periods of time so that their fear begins to subside. One variant on this procedure, known as *participant modeling,* is often more effective than exposure alone. Here the therapist calmly models ways of interacting with the phobic stimulus or situation (Bandura, 1977, 1997). These techniques enable clients to learn that these situations are not as frightening as they had thought and that their anxiety, while unpleasant, is not harmful and will gradually dissipate (Craske & Mystkowski, 2006; Craske & Rowe, 1997). For certain phobias such as small-animal phobias, flying phobia, claustrophobia, and blood-injury phobia, exposure therapy is often highly effective when administered in a single long session (of up to 3 hours) (Öst, 1997; Öst et al., 2001). This can be an advantage because some people are more likely to seek treatment if they have to go only once. This treatment has also been shown to be highly effective in youth with specific phobias (e.g., Ollendick et al., 2009).

An example of the use of exposure therapy comes from the treatment of Mary, the housewife whose acrophobia and claustrophobia we described earlier.

One variation on exposure therapy is called participant modeling. Here the therapist models how to touch and pick up a live tarantula and encourages the spider-phobic client to imitate her behavior. This treatment is graduated, with the client's first task being simply to touch the tarantula from the outside of the cage, then to touch the tarantula with a stick, then with a gloved hand, then with a bare hand, and finally to let the tarantula crawl over his hand. This is a highly effective treatment, with the most spider-phobic clients being able to reach the top of the hierarchy within 60 to 90 minutes.

case study Mary's Treatment

Treatment consisted of 13 sessions of graduated exposure exercises in which the therapist accompanied Mary first into mildly fear-provoking situations and then gradually into more and more fear-provoking situations. Mary also engaged in homework, doing these exposure exercises by herself. The prolonged in vivo ("real-life") exposure sessions lasted as long as necessary for her anxiety to subside. Initial sessions focused on Mary's claustrophobia and on getting her to be able to ride for a few floors in an elevator, first with the therapist and then alone. Later she took longer elevator rides in taller buildings. Exposure for the acrophobia consisted of walking around the periphery of the inner atrium on the top floor of a tall hotel and, later, spending time at a mountain vista overlook spot. The top of the claustrophobia hierarchy consisted of taking a tour of an underground cave. After 13 sessions, Mary successfully took a flight with her husband to Europe and climbed to the top of many tall tourist attractions there.

Recently, some therapists have begun to use virtual reality environments to simulate certain kinds of phobic situations, such as heights and airplanes, as places to conduct exposure treatment. If such techniques were highly effective and widely available, there would be no need to conduct treatment in real situations (such as real airplanes or tall buildings). About a dozen controlled studies have yielded very promising results. Moreover, although the results are not yet entirely conclusive, it appears that the relative efficacy of virtual reality versus live exposure is comparable (e.g., Choy et al., 2007; Parsons & Rizzo, 2008).

Some researchers have also tried combining cognitive restructuring techniques or medications with exposure-based techniques to see if this can produce additional gains. In general, studies using cognitive techniques alone have not produced results as good as those using exposure-based techniques, and the addition of cognitive techniques has generally not added much (Craske & Mystkowski, 2006; Wolitzky-Taylor et al., 2008). Similarly, medication treatments are ineffective by themselves, and

there is even some evidence that antianxiety medications may interfere with the beneficial effects of exposure therapy (Antony & Barlow, 2002; Choy et al., 2007). Recently, however, some studies have shown that a drug known as *d-cycloserine*, which is known to facilitate extinction of conditioned fear in animals (e.g., Davis et al., 2005; Davis et al., 2006), may enhance the effectiveness of small amounts of exposure therapy for fear of heights in a virtual reality environment (Ressler et al., 2004; Norberg et al., 2008). D-cyloserine by itself, however, has no effect. These results are very promising, but much more work is necessary before it will be known how useful this drug will be in enhancing the effects of exposure therapy for many different kinds of phobias.

In Review

- What are the five subtypes of specific phobias listed in the *DSM-IV-TR*?

- Describe the original classical conditioning explanation for the origins of specific phobias as well as how vicarious conditioning may be involved.

- Explain several sources of individual differences in learning that have improved and expanded the basic conditioning hypothesis of phobia acquisition.

- Explain how evolutionary factors have influenced which objects and situations we are most likely to learn to fear.

- Describe the most effective treatment for specific phobias.

Social Phobias

Social phobia (or social anxiety disorder), as the *DSM-IV-TR* describes it, is characterized by disabling fears of one or more specific social situations (such as public speaking, urinating in a public bathroom, or eating or writing in public; see the *DSM-IV-TR* box). In these situations, a person fears

New treatments using virtual reality environments allow therapists to simulate certain kinds of phobic situations, such as standing at heights or sitting in airplanes, in a contrived setting. Unfortunately, the equipment is currently quite costly, which makes access to this treatment somewhat limited.

that she or he may be exposed to the scrutiny and potential negative evaluation of others or that she or he may act in an embarrassing or humiliating manner. Because of their fears, people with social phobias either avoid these situations or endure them with great distress. Intense fear of public speaking is the single most common type of social phobia. *DSM-IV-TR* also identifies one subtype of social phobia known as *generalized social phobia*. People with generalized social phobia have significant fears of most social situations (rather than simply a few) and often also have a diagnosis of avoidant personality disorder (Skodol et al., 1995; Stein & Stein, 2008).

Prevalence, Age of Onset, and Gender Differences

The diagnosis of social phobia is very common and occurs even in famous performers such as Barbra Streisand and Carly Simon. The National Comorbidity Survey-Replication estimated that about 12 percent of the population will qualify for a diagnosis of social phobia at some point in their lives (Kessler, Berglund, Demler, et al., 2005; Ruscio et al., 2008). This disorder is somewhat more common among

Intense fear of public speaking is the single most common social phobia.

women than men (about 60 percent of sufferers are women). Unlike specific phobias, which most often originate in childhood, social phobias typically begin somewhat later, during early or middle adolescence or certainly by early adulthood (Bruce et al., 2005; Ruscio et al., 2008). Nearly two-thirds of people with social phobia suffer from one or more additional anxiety disorders at some point in their lives, and about 50 percent also suffer from a depressive disorder at the same time (Kessler, Chiu, et al., 2005; Ruscio et al., 2008). Approximately one-third abuse alcohol to reduce their anxiety and help them face the situations they fear (for example, drinking before going to a party; Magee et al., 1996). Moreover, because of their distress and avoidance of social situations, people with social phobia, on average, have lower employment rates and lower socioeconomic status, and approximately one-third have severe impairment in one or more domains of their life (Harvey et al., 2005; Ruscio et al., 2008). Finally, the disorder is remarkably persistent, with one study finding that only 37 percent recovered spontaneously over a 12-year period (Bruce et al., 2005).

The case of Paul is typical of social phobia (except that not all people with social phobia have full-blown panic attacks, as Paul did, in their socially phobic situations).

case study A Surgeon's Social Phobia

Paul was a single white male in his mid-30s when he first presented for treatment. He was a surgeon who reported a 13-year history of social phobia. He had very few social outlets because of his persistent concerns that people would notice how nervous he was in social situations, and he had not dated in many years. Convinced that people would perceive him as foolish or crazy, he particularly worried that people would notice how his jaw tensed up when around other people. Paul frequently chewed gum in public situations, believing that this kept his face from looking distorted. Notably, he had no particular problems talking with people in professional situations. For example, he was quite calm talking with patients before and after surgery. During surgery, when his face was covered with a mask, he also had no trouble carrying out surgical tasks or interacting with the other surgeons and nurses in the room. The trouble began when he left the operating room and had to make small talk—and eye contact—with the other doctors and nurses or with the patient's family. He frequently had panic attacks in these social situations. During the panic attacks he experienced heart palpitations, fears of "going crazy," and a sense of his mind "shutting down." Because the panic attacks occurred only in social situations, he was diagnosed as having social phobia rather than panic disorder.

Paul's social phobia and panic had begun about 13 years earlier when he was under a great deal of stress. His family's business had failed, his parents had divorced, and his mother had had a heart attack. It was in this context of multiple stressors that a personally traumatic incident probably triggered the onset of his social phobia. One day he had come home from medical school to find his best friend in bed with his fiancée. About a month later he had his first panic attack and started avoiding social situations.

Psychological Causal Factors

Social phobias generally involve learned behaviors that have been shaped by evolutionary factors. Such learning is most likely to occur in people who are genetically or temperamentally at risk.

SOCIAL PHOBIAS AS LEARNED BEHAVIOR Like specific phobias, social phobias often seem to originate from simple instances of direct or vicarious classical conditioning such as experiencing or witnessing a perceived social defeat or humiliation, or being or witnessing the target of anger or criticism (Harvey et al., 2005; Mineka & Zinbarg, 1995, 2006; Tillfors, 2004). In two studies, 56 to 58 percent of people with social phobia recalled and identified direct traumatic experiences as having been involved in the origin of their social phobias (Öst & Hugdahl, 1981; Townsley et al., 1995). Another study reported that 92 percent of an adult sample of people with social phobia reported a history of severe teasing in childhood, compared to only 35 percent in a group of people with obsessive-compulsive disorder (McCabe et al., 2003). Moreover, a recent laboratory study of people with social phobia revealed that they showed especially

robust conditioning of fear when the unconditioned stimulus was socially relevant (critical facial expressions and verbal insults) as opposed to more nonspecifically negative stimuli (such as unpleasant odors and painful pressure) (Lissek et al., 2008).

Öst and Hugdahl (1981) reported that another 13 percent of their subjects recalled vicarious conditioning experiences of some sort. One study interviewed a group of people with social phobia about their images of themselves in socially phobic situations and asked where those images had originated (Hackmann et al., 2000). Ninety-six percent of these people remembered some socially traumatic experience that was linked to their own current image of themselves in socially phobic situations. The themes of these memories included having been "criticized for having an anxiety symptom" (e.g., being red or blushing), and having felt "self-conscious and uncomfortable in public as a consequence of past criticism" such as "having previously been bullied and called a 'nothing'" (Hackmann et al., 2000, p. 606).

People with generalized social phobia also may be especially likely to have grown up with parents who were emotionally cold, socially isolated, and avoidant. Not surprisingly, such parents devalued sociability and did not encourage their children to go to social events. All these factors thus provided ample opportunity for vicarious learning of social fears (Harvey et al., 2005; Morris, 2001; Rapee & Melville, 1997). Harvey and colleagues (2005) also found that many people with social phobia reported that the onset of their social phobia had occurred during a time when they were having problems with their peers such as not fitting in. Nevertheless, as with specific phobias, it is important to recognize that not everyone who experiences direct or vicarious conditioning in social situations, or who grows up with socially avoidant parents, or who has problems with peers, develops social phobia. This is because individual differences in experiences play an important role in who develops social phobia, as is the case with specific phobias.

SOCIAL FEARS AND PHOBIAS IN AN EVOLUTIONARY CONTEXT Social fears and phobias by definition involve fears of members of one's own species. By contrast, animal fears and phobias usually involve fear of potential predators. Although animal fears probably evolved to trigger activation of the fight-or-flight response to potential predators, Öhman and colleagues proposed that social fears and phobias evolved as a byproduct of dominance hierarchies that are a common social arrangement among animals such as primates (Dimberg & Öhman, 1996; Öhman et al., 1985). Dominance hierarchies are established through aggressive encounters between members of a social group, and a defeated individual typically displays fear and submissive behavior but only rarely attempts to escape the situation completely. Thus, these investigators argued, it is not surprising that people with social phobia endure being in their feared situations rather than running away and escaping them, as people with animal phobias often do (see also Longin et al., 2010; Öhman, 2009).

If social phobias evolved as a byproduct of dominance hierarchies, it is not surprising that humans have an evolutionarily based predisposition to acquire fears of social stimuli that signal dominance and aggression from other humans. These social stimuli include facial expressions of anger or contempt, which on average all humans seem to process more quickly and readily than happy or neutral facial expressions (Öhman et al., 2001; Öhman, 2009; Schupp et al., 2004). In a series of experiments that paralleled ones for specific phobias, Öhman and colleagues demonstrated that subjects develop stronger conditioned responses when slides of angry faces are paired with mild electric shocks than when happy or neutral faces are paired with the same shocks (Dimberg & Öhman, 1996). Indeed, even very brief subliminal (not consciously perceived) presentations of the angry face that had been paired with shock were sufficient to activate the conditioned responses (e.g., Parra et al., 1997), probably because even these subliminal angry faces activate the amygdala—the central structure involved in fear learning (Öhman et al., 2007). Relatedly, recent results have also shown that people who have social phobia show greater activation of the amygdala (and other brain areas involved in emotion processing) in response to negative facial expressions (such as angry faces) than do normal controls (Goldin et al., 2009; Phan et al., 2006). Such results may help explain the seemingly irrational quality of social phobia, in that the angry faces are processed very quickly and an emotional reaction can be activated without a person's awareness of any threat. The hyperactivity to negative facial expressions is paralleled by heightened neural responses to criticism (Blair et al., 2008; see Shin & Liberzon, 2009, for a recent review).

PERCEPTIONS OF UNCONTROLLABILITY AND UNPREDICTABILITY Being exposed to uncontrollable and unpredictable stressful events (such as parental separation and divorce, family conflict, or sexual abuse) may play an important role in the development of social phobia (Mathew et al., 2001; Mineka & Zinbarg, 1995, 2006; Rapee & Spence, 2004). In the case of Paul, the precipitating event seemed to be finding his fiancée in bed with his best friend. Perceptions of uncontrollability and unpredictability often lead to submissive and unassertive behavior, which is characteristic of socially anxious or phobic people. This kind of behavior is especially likely if the perceptions of uncontrollability stem from an actual social defeat, which is known in animals to lead to both increased submissive behavior and increased fear (Mineka & Zinbarg, 1995, 2006). Consistent with this, people with social phobia have a diminished sense of personal control over events in their lives (Leung & Heimberg, 1996). This diminished expectation of personal control may develop, at least in part, as a function of having been raised in families with somewhat overprotective (and sometimes rejecting) parents (Lieb et al., 2000).

COGNITIVE BIASES Cognitive factors also play a role in the onset and maintenance of social phobia. Beck and Emery (1985) suggested that people with social phobia tend to expect that other people will reject or negatively evaluate them. They argued that this leads to a sense of vulnerability when they are around people who might pose a threat. Clark and Wells (1995; Wells & Clark, 1997) later further proposed that these danger schemas of socially anxious people lead them to expect that they will behave in an awkward and unacceptable fashion, resulting in rejection and loss of status. Such negative expectations lead to their being preoccupied with bodily responses and with stereotyped, negative self-images in social situations; to their overestimating how easily others will detect their anxiety; and to their misunderstanding how well

they come across to others (Hirsch et al., 2004). Such intense self-preoccupation during social situations, even to the point of attending to their own heart rate, interferes with their ability to interact skillfully (Hirsch et al., 2003; Pineles & Mineka, 2005). A vicious cycle may evolve: Social phobics' inward attention and somewhat awkward behavior may lead others to react to them in a less friendly fashion, confirming their expectations (D. M. Clark, 1997; Clark & McManus, 2002).

Another cognitive bias seen in social phobia is a tendency to interpret ambiguous social information in a negative rather than a benign manner (e.g., when someone smiles at you, does it mean they like you or that they think you're foolish?). Moreover, it is the negatively biased interpretations that socially anxious people make that are what is remembered (Hertel et al., 2008). It has also been suggested that these biased cognitive processes combine to maintain social phobia and possibly even contribute to its development (Hirsch, Clark, & Mathews, 2006).

Biological Causal Factors

GENETIC AND TEMPERAMENTAL FACTORS The most important temperamental variable is *behavioral inhibition*, which shares characteristics with both neuroticism and introversion (Bienvenu et al., 2007). Behaviorally inhibited infants who are easily distressed by unfamiliar stimuli and who are shy and avoidant are more likely to become fearful during childhood and, by adolescence, to show increased risk of developing social phobia (Hayward et al., 1998; Kagan, 1997). For example, one classic study was conducted on behavioral inhibition as a risk factor in a large group of children, most of whom were already known to be at risk for anxiety because their parents had an emotional disorder. Among these children, those who had been assessed as being high on behavioral inhibition between 2 and 6 years of age were nearly three times more likely to be diagnosed with social phobia (22 percent) even in middle childhood (average age of 10) than were children who were low on behavioral inhibition at 2 to

Infants and young children who are fearful and easily distressed by novel people or situations are sometimes high on the temperamental variable called behavioral inhibition. Such infants show an increased risk of developing social phobia in adolescence.

6 years (8 percent; Hirshfeld-Becker et al., 2007; see also Hayward et al., 1998). In another study, 60 children were assessed yearly for behavioral inhibition from grades 1 to 9. If they showed chronically high levels of behavioral inhibition throughout this time period, 50 percent had developed social anxiety disorder by grade 9. By contrast, none had developed social anxiety disorder in the group with chronic low behavioral inhibition (Essex et al., 2010).

Results from several studies of twins have also shown that there is a modest genetic contribution to social phobia; estimates are that about 30 percent of the variance in liability to social phobia is due to genetic factors (Hettema et al., 2005; Smoller et al., 2008). Nevertheless, these studies suggest that an even larger proportion of variance in who develops social phobia is due to nonshared environmental factors, which is consistent with a strong role for learning.

Treatments

COGNITIVE AND BEHAVIORAL THERAPIES There are very effective forms of behavior therapy and cognitive-behavior therapy for social phobia. As for specific phobias, behavioral treatments were developed first and generally involve prolonged and graduated exposure to social situations that evoke fear. More recently, as research has revealed the underlying distorted cognitions that characterize social phobia, **cognitive restructuring** techniques have been added to the behavioral techniques, generating a form of cognitive-behavioral therapy (Barlow et al., 2007). In cognitive restructuring the therapist attempts to help clients with social phobia identify their underlying negative, automatic thoughts ("I've got nothing interesting to say" or "No one is interested in me"). After helping clients understand that such automatic thoughts (which usually occur just below the surface of awareness but can be accessed) often involve cognitive distortions, the therapist helps the clients change these inner thoughts and beliefs through logical reanalysis. The process of logical reanalysis might involve asking oneself questions to challenge the automatic thoughts: "Do I know for certain that I won't have anything to say?" "Does being nervous have to lead to or equal looking stupid?"

In one highly effective version of such treatments, clients may be assigned exercises in which they manipulate their focus of attention (internally versus externally) to demonstrate to themselves the adverse effects of internal self-focus. They may also receive videotaped feedback to help them modify their distorted self-images. Such techniques have now been very successfully applied to the treatment of social phobia (Clark, Ehlers, et al., 2003, 2006; Heimberg, 2002; Mörtberg et al., 2007). Many studies over the years have shown that exposure therapy and cognitive-behavioral therapy produce comparable results. However, one study suggests that this new, very effective variant on cognitive treatment may be more effective than exposure therapy (Clark et al., 2006). Moreover, at least one study has now shown that simply training individuals with social phobia to disengage from negative social cues during a 15-minute lab task that is repeated 8 times over 4 to 6 weeks produced such remarkable reductions in social anxiety symptoms that nearly 3 out of 4 of the participants no longer met criteria for social anxiety disorder (Schmidt et al., 2009).

An example of successful combined treatment can be seen in the case of Paul, the surgeon described earlier who had social phobia.

case study   Paul's Treatment

Since the onset of his social phobia 13 years earlier, Paul had taken an antidepressant at one point. The drug had helped stop his panic attacks, but he continued to fear them intensely and still avoided social situations. Thus there was little effect on his social phobia. He had also been in supportive psychotherapy, which had helped his depression at the time but not his social phobia or his panic. When he went for treatment at an anxiety clinic, he was not on any medication or in any other form of treatment. Treatment consisted of 14 weeks of cognitive-behavioral therapy. By the end of treatment, Paul was not panicking at all and was quite comfortable in most social situations that he had previously avoided. He was seeing old friends whom he had avoided for years because of his anxiety, and he was beginning to date. Indeed, he even asked his female therapist for a date during the last treatment session! Although such a request was clearly inappropriate, it did indicate how much progress he had made.

MEDICATIONS Unlike specific phobias, social phobias can also sometimes be treated with medications. The most effective and widely used medications are several categories of antidepressants (including the monoamine oxidase inhibitors [MAOIs] and the selective serotonin reuptake inhibitors [SSRIs] Ipser et al., 2008; Roy-Byrne & Cowley, 2007). In some studies the effects of these antidepressant medications have been comparable to those seen with cognitive-behavioral treatments. However, in one study the newer version of cognitive-behavior therapy discussed earlier produced much more substantial improvement than did medication (Clark, Ehlers, et al., 2003). Moreover, the medications must be taken over a long period of time to help ensure that relapse does not occur (Blanco et al., 2002; Stein & Stein, 2008). A distinct advantage of behavioral and cognitive-behavioral therapies over medications, then, is that they generally produce more long-lasting improvement with very low relapse rates; indeed, clients often continue to improve after treatment is over. Finally, several studies have also suggested that when d-cycloserine (discussed with treatment of specific phobias) is added to exposure therapy, the treatment gains occur more quickly and are more substantial (e.g., Guastella et al., 2008).

In Review

- What are the primary diagnostic criteria for social phobia and for the subtype of generalized social phobia?
- Identify three of the psychological causal factors for social phobia and two of the biological causal factors.
- Describe the major treatment approaches used for social phobias.

Panic Disorder with and without Agoraphobia

Panic Disorder

Diagnostically, **panic disorder** is defined and characterized by the occurrence of panic attacks that often seem to come "out of the blue." According to the *DSM-IV-TR* criteria for panic disorder, the person must have experienced recurrent, unexpected attacks and must have been persistently concerned about having another attack or worried about the consequences of having an attack for at least a month (often referred to as anticipatory anxiety). For such an event to qualify as a full-blown panic attack, there must be abrupt onset of at least 4 of 13 symptoms, most of which are physical, although three are cognitive: (1) depersonalization (a feeling of being detached from one's body) or derealization (a feeling that the external world is strange or unreal); (2) fear of dying; or (3) fear of "going crazy" or "losing control" (see the *DSM-IV-TR* box below). Panic attacks are fairly brief but intense, with symptoms developing abruptly and usually reaching peak intensity within 10 minutes; the attacks usually subside in 20 to 30 minutes and rarely last more than an hour. Periods of anxiety, by contrast, do not usually have such an abrupt onset and are more long lasting.

Panic attacks are often "unexpected" or "uncued" in the sense that they do not appear to be provoked by identifiable aspects of the immediate situation. Indeed, they sometimes occur in situations in which they might be least expected, such as during relaxation or during sleep (known as *nocturnal panic*). In other cases, however, panic attacks are said to be situationally predisposed, occurring only sometimes while the person is in a particular situation such as while driving a car or being in a crowd.

Because 10 of the 13 symptoms of a panic attack are physical, it is not surprising that as many as 85 percent of people having a panic attack may show up repeatedly at emergency rooms or physicians' offices for what they are convinced is a medical problem—usually cardiac, respiratory, or neurological (White & Barlow, 2002; see also Korczak et al., 2007). Unfortunately, a correct diagnosis is often not made for years due to the normal results on numerous costly medical tests. Further complications arise because cardiac patients are at a nearly twofold elevated risk for developing panic disorder (Korczak et al., 2007). Prompt diagnosis and treatment is also important because panic disorder causes approximately as much impairment in social and occupational functioning as that caused by major depressive disorder (Roy-Byrne et al., 2008) and because panic disorder can contribute to the development or worsening of a variety of medical problems (White & Barlow, 2002).

The case of Mindy Markowitz is typical of someone who has panic disorder without agoraphobia.

DSM-IV-TR

Criteria for a Panic Attack

A discrete period of intense fear or discomfort, in which four (or more) of the following symptoms developed abruptly and reached a peak within 10 minutes:

1. Palpitations, pounding heart, or accelerated heart rate
2. Sweating
3. Trembling or shaking
4. Sensations of shortness of breath or smothering
5. Feeling of choking
6. Chest pain or discomfort
7. Nausea or abdominal distress
8. Feeling dizzy, unsteady, lightheaded, or faint
9. Derealization (feelings of unreality) or depersonalization (being detached from oneself)
10. Fear of losing control or going crazy
11. Fear of dying
12. Paresthesias (numbness or tingling sensations)
13. Chills or hot flushes

Source: Reprinted with permission from the American Psychiatric Association. *Diagnostic and Statistical Manual of Mental Disorders*, Fourth Edition, *Text Revision* (Copyright © 2000). American Psychiatric Association.

---

case study — **Art Director's Panic Attacks**

Mindy Markowitz is an attractive . . . 25-year-old art director . . . who comes to an anxiety clinic . . . seeking treatment for "panic attacks" that have occurred with increasing frequency over the past year, often two or three times a day. These attacks begin with a sudden, intense wave of "horrible fear" that seems to come out of nowhere, sometimes during the day, sometimes waking her from sleep. She begins to tremble, is nauseated, sweats profusely, feels as though she is choking, and fears that she will lose control and do something crazy, like run screaming into the street. . . .

Mindy has had panic attacks intermittently over the 8 years since her first attack, sometimes not for many months, but sometimes, as now, several times a day. There have been extreme variations in the intensity of the attacks, some being so severe and debilitating that she has had to take a day off from work.

Mindy has always functioned extremely well in school, at work, and in her social life, apart from her panic attacks. . . . She is a lively, friendly person . . . who has never limited her activities . . . She says . . . she is as likely to have an attack at home in her own bed

continued

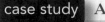 **case study**   Art Director's (*continued*)

as on the subway, so there is no point in avoiding the subway. . . . [Wherever] she has an attack . . . she says, "I just tough it out."

Source: Adapted with permission from the *Diagnostic and Statistical Manual of Mental Disorders*, Fourth Edition, *Text Revision*, (Copyright © 2002). American Psychiatric Association.

Agoraphobia

Historically, agoraphobia was thought to involve a fear of the *agora*—the Greek word for public places of assembly (Marks, 1987). In **agoraphobia** the most commonly feared and avoided situations include streets and crowded places such as shopping malls, movie theaters, and stores. Standing in line can be particularly difficult. See Table 2 for a description of situations commonly avoided by agoraphobics. What is the common theme that underlies this seemingly diverse cluster of fears? Today we think that agoraphobia usually develops as a complication of having panic attacks in one or more such situations. Concerned that they may have a panic attack or get sick, people with agoraphobia are anxious about being in places or situations from which escape would be physically difficult or psychologically embarrassing, or in which immediate help would be unavailable if something bad happened (see the *DSM-IV-TR* box). Typically people with agoraphobia are also frightened by their own bodily sensations, so they also avoid activities that will create arousal such as exercising, watching scary movies, drinking caffeine, and even engaging in sexual activity.

DSM-IV-TR

Criteria for Panic Disorder and Agoraphobia

Panic Disorder With Agoraphobia

A. Both (1) and (2):
1. Recurrent unexpected Panic Attacks
2. At least one of the attacks has been followed by 1 month (or more) of one (or more) of the following:
   a. Persistent concern about having additional attacks
   b. Worry about the implications of the attack or its consequences (e.g., losing control, having a heart attack, "going crazy")
   c. A significant change in behavior related to the attacks
B. The presence of Agoraphobia
C. The Panic Attacks are not due to the direct physiological effects of a substance (e.g., a drug of abuse, a medication) or a general medical condition (e.g., hyperthyroidism)
D. The Panic Attacks are not better accounted for by another mental disorder, such as Social Phobia (e.g., occurring on exposure to feared social situations), Specific Phobia (e.g., on exposure to a specific phobic situation), Obsessive- Compulsive Disorder (e.g., on exposure to dirt in someone with an obsession about contamination), Posttraumatic Stress Disorder (e.g., in response to stimuli associated with a severe stressor), or Separation Anxiety Disorder (e.g., in response to being away from home or close relatives).

Panic Disorder Without Agoraphobia

A. Both (1) and (2):
1. Recurrent unexpected Panic Attacks
2. At least one of the attacks has been followed by 1 month (or more) of one (or more) of the following:
   a. Persistent concern about having additional attacks
   b. Worry about the implications of the attack or its consequences (e.g., losing control, having a heart attack, "going crazy")
   c. A significant change in behavior related to the attacks
B. The absence of Agoraphobia
C. The Panic Attacks are not due to the direct physiological effects of a substance (e.g., a drug of abuse, a medication) or a general medical condition (e.g., hyperthyroidism).
D. The Panic Attacks are not better accounted for by another mental disorder, such as Social Phobia (e.g., occurring on exposure to feared social situations), Specific Phobia (e.g., on exposure to a specific phobic situation), Obsessive-Compulsive Disorder (e.g., on exposure to dirt in someone with an obsession about contamination), Posttraumatic Stress Disorder (e.g., in response to stimuli associated with a severe stressor), or Separation Anxiety Disorder (e.g., in response to being away from home or close relatives).

Agoraphobia Without History of Panic Disorder

A. The presence of Agoraphobia related to fear of developing panic-like symptoms (e.g., dizziness or diarrhea).
B. Criteria have never been met for Panic Disorder
C. The disturbance is not due to the direct physiological effects of a substance (e.g., a drug of abuse, a medication) or a general medical condition.
D. If an associated general medical condition is present, the fear described in Criterion A is clearly in excess of that usually associated with the condition.

Source: Reprinted with permission from the American Psychiatric Association. *Diagnostic and Statistical Manual of Mental Disorders*, Fourth Edition, *Text Revision* (Copyright © 2000). American Psychiatric Association.

As agoraphobia first develops, people tend to avoid situations in which attacks have occurred, but usually the avoidance gradually spreads to other situations where attacks might occur. In moderately severe cases, people with agoraphobia may be anxious even when venturing outside their homes alone. In very severe cases, agoraphobia is an utterly disabling disorder in which a person cannot go beyond the narrow confines of home—or even particular parts of the home.

The case of John D. is typical of panic disorder with agoraphobia.

case study — John D.

John D. was a 45-year-old married Caucasian man with three sons. Although well educated and successful . . . John had been experiencing difficulties with panic attacks for 15 years . . . experiencing two to five panic attacks per month. The previous week John had had a panic attack while driving with his family to a computer store. He recollected that before the panic attack he might have been "keyed up" over the kids making a lot of noise in the back seat; the attack began right after he had quickly turned around to tell the kids to "settle down." Immediately after he turned back to look at the road, John felt dizzy. As soon as he noticed this, John experienced a rapid and intense surge of other sensations including sweating, accelerated heart rate, hot flushes, and trembling. Fearing that he was going to crash the car, John quickly pulled to the side of the road. . . .

John was having only a few panic attacks per month, but he was experiencing a high level of anxiety every day, focused on the possibility that he might have another panic attack at any time. Indeed, John had developed extensive apprehension or avoidance of driving, air travel, elevators, wide-open spaces, taking long walks alone, movie theaters, and being out of town.

[His] first panic attack had occurred 15 years ago. John had fallen asleep on the living room sofa at around 1:00 A.M. after returning from a night of drinking with some of his friends. Just after awakening at 4:30, John felt stomach pains and a pulsating sensation in the back of his neck. All of a sudden, John noticed that his heart was racing, too. . . . Although he did not know what he was suffering from, John was certain that he was dying.

John remembered having a second panic attack about a month later. From then on, the panic attacks began to occur more regularly. When the panic attacks became recurrent, John started to avoid situations in which the panic attacks had occurred as well as situations in which he feared a panic attack was likely to occur. On three occasions during the first few years of his panic attacks, John went to the emergency room of his local hospital because he was sure that his symptoms were a sign of a heart attack. (Adapted from Brown & Barlow, 2001, pp. 19–22.)

table 2 Situations Frequently Avoided by People with Agoraphobia

Crowds	Standing in line
Theaters	Restaurants
Shopping malls	Sports arenas
Cars and buses	Trains and airplanes
Bridges	Tunnels
Escalators	Elevators
Being home alone	Being far away from home
Aeorbic exercise	Sauna baths
Getting angry	Sexual activity
Watching exciting or scary movies	

AGORAPHOBIA WITHOUT PANIC Although agoraphobia is a frequent complication of panic disorder, it can also occur without prior full-blown panic attacks. When this happens, there is usually a gradually spreading fearfulness in which more and more aspects of the environment outside the home become threatening. Cases of agoraphobia without panic are extremely rare in clinical settings, and over half the time when they are seen, there is a history of what are called "limited symptom attacks" (with fewer than four symptoms) or of some other unpredictable physical ailment such as epilepsy or colitis that makes the person afraid of being suddenly incapacitated (Roy-Byrne et al., 2006; White & Barlow, 2002). The most recent estimate of the lifetime prevalence of agoraphobia without panic from the National Comorbidity Survey-Replication is 1.4 percent (e.g., Kessler, Chiu, et al., 2006).

Prevalence, Age of Onset, and Gender Differences

Many people suffer from panic disorder with and without agoraphobia. The National Comorbidity Survey-Replication study found that approximately 4.7 percent of the adult population has had panic disorder with or without agoraphobia at some time in their lives, with panic disorder without agoraphobia being more common (Kessler, Chiu, et al., 2005). Panic disorder with or without agoraphobia often starts in the late teenage years, but the average age of onset is 23 to 34 years. However, it can begin, especially for women, when in a person's 30s or 40s (Hirschfeld, 1996; Kessler, Chiu, et al., 2006). Once panic disorder develops, it tends to have a chronic and disabling course, although the intensity of symptoms often waxes and wanes over time (Keller et al., 1994; White & Barlow, 2002). Indeed, one 12-year longitudinal study found that less than 50 percent of patients with panic disorder with agoraphobia had recovered in 12 years, and 58 percent of those who had recovered at some point had had a recurrence (new onset; Bruce et al., 2005). Panic disorder is about twice as prevalent in women as in men (Eaton et al., 1994; White & Barlow, 2002). Agoraphobia also occurs much more frequently in women than in men, and the percentage of women increases as the extent of agoraphobic avoidance increases. Among people with severe agoraphobia, approximately 80 to 90 percent are female (Bekker, 1996; White & Barlow, 2002). Table 3 outlines gender differences in the prevalence of all the anxiety disorders for comparison purposes.

The most common explanation of the pronounced gender difference in agoraphobia is a sociocultural one (McLean & Anderson, 2009). In our culture (and many others as well), it is more acceptable for women who experience panic to avoid the situations they fear and to need a trusted companion to accompany them when they enter feared situations. Men who experience panic are more prone to "tough it out" because of societal expectations and their more assertive, instrumental approach to life (Bekker, 1996). Although there is very little research on this topic, one study consistent with this idea was conducted by Chambless and Mason (1986), who administered a sex-role scale to both male and female agoraphobics and found that the less "masculine" one scored on the scale, the more extensive the agoraphobic avoidance, for both males and females. Another study found that cultures and societies that delineate rigid gender roles at a sociocultural level tend to have higher levels of agoraphobia. In addition, some evidence indicates that men with panic disorder may be more likely to self-medicate with nicotine or alcohol as a way of coping with and enduring panic attacks rather than developing agoraphobic avoidance (Starcevic et al., 2008).

People with severe agoraphobia are often fearful of venturing out of their homes into public places, in part because of their fear of having a panic attack in a place in which escape might prove physically difficult or psychologically embarrassing. They may even become housebound unless accompanied by a spouse or trusted companion.

table 3 Gender Differences in the Anxiety Disorders: Lifetime Prevalence Estimates

Disorder	Prevalence in Men (%)	Prevalence in Women (%)	Ratio
Specific phobias	6.7	15.7	2.34
Social phobia	11.1	15.5	1.4
Panic disorder	2.0	5.0	2.5
Generalized anxiety disorder	3.6	6.6	1.8
Obsessive-compulsive disorder	2.0	2.9	1.45
Posttraumatic stress disorder	5.0	10.4	2.08

Note: Because these figures are from different studies and may not be strictly comparable, they should be taken as approximations of current estimates of gender differences.

Sources: Eaton et al. (1994); Karno et al. (1988); Kessler et al. (1994, 1995); Magee et al. (1996).

Comorbidity with Other Disorders

The recent National Comorbidity Survey-Replication found that 83 percent of people with panic disorder have at least one comorbid disorder (Kessler, Chiu, et al., 2006). Most commonly these include generalized anxiety disorder, social phobia, specific phobia, PTSD, depression, and substance-use disorders (especially smoking and alcohol dependence; Bernstein et al., 2006; Kessler, Chiu, et al., 2006; Zvolensky & Bernstein, 2005). It is estimated that 50 to 70 percent of people with panic disorder will experience serious depression at some point in their lives (Kessler, Chiu, et al., 2006). They may also meet criteria for dependent or avoidant personality disorder. The issue of whether people with panic disorder show an increased risk of suicidal ideation and suicide attempts has been quite controversial, with a number of studies suggesting that any increased risk is due to indirect factors such as comorbid depression and substance abuse, which are known risk factors themselves (e.g., Vickers & McNally, 2004). However, two recent very large epidemiological studies (one in the United States, which had nearly 10,000 adults from the National Comorbidity Survey-Replication study, and one including over 100,000 from 21 countries) have indeed found that panic disorder is associated with increased risk for suicidal ideation and attempts independent of its relationship with comorbid disorders (Nock et al., 2009; Nock et al., 2010).

The Timing of a First Panic Attack

Although panic attacks themselves appear to come "out of the blue," the first one frequently occurs following feelings of distress or some highly stressful life circumstance such as loss of a loved one, loss of an important relationship, loss of a job, or criminal victimization (see Barlow 2002; Klauke et al., 2010, for reviews). Although not all studies have found this, some have estimated that approximately 80 to 90 percent of clients report that their first panic attack occurred after one or more negative life events.

Nevertheless, not all people who have a panic attack following a stressful event go on to develop full-blown panic disorder. Current estimates from the recent National Comorbidity Survey-Replication are that nearly 23 percent of adults have experienced at least one panic attack in their lifetimes, but most have not gone on to develop full-blown panic disorder (Kessler, Chiu, et al., 2006). People who have other anxiety disorders or major depression often experience occasional panic attacks as well (Barlow 2002; Kessler, Chiu, et al., 2006). Given that panic attacks are much more frequent than panic disorder, this leads us to an important question: What causes full-blown panic disorder to develop in only a subset of these people? Several different prominent theories about the causes of panic disorder have addressed this question.

Biological Causal Factors

GENETIC FACTORS According to family and twin studies, panic disorder has a moderate heritable component (e.g.,

Kendler et al., 1992b, 1992c; Kendler et al., 2001; Norrholm & Ressler, 2009). In a large twin study, Kendler and colleagues (2001) estimated that 33 to 43 percent of the variance in liability to panic disorder was due to genetic factors. As noted earlier, this genetic vulnerability is manifested at a psychological level at least in part by the important personality trait called neuroticism (which is in turn related to the temperamental construct of behavioral inhibition). Recently several studies have begun to identify which specific genetic polymorphisms are responsible for this moderate heritability (e.g., Strug et al., 2010), either alone or in interaction with certain types of stressful life events (e.g., Klauke et al., 2010), but this preliminary work needs to be replicated.

Some studies have suggested that this heritability is at least partly specific for panic disorder (rather than for all anxiety disorders; see Barlow, 2002, for a review), but a large female twin study suggests that there is overlap in the genetic vulnerability factors for panic disorder and phobias (Kendler, Walters, et al., 1995). This would be consistent with some preliminary evidence that people with a history of social or specific phobia are at heightened risk for developing panic disorder (Biederman et al., 2006). However, another study suggests overlap in the genetic vulnerability for panic disorder, generalized anxiety disorder, and agoraphobia (Hettema, Prescott, et al., 2005). Only further research can resolve these inconsistencies in findings (e.g., Norrholm & Ressler, 2009).

PANIC AND THE BRAIN One relatively early prominent theory about the neurobiology of panic attacks implicated the *locus coeruleus* in the brain stem (see Figure 1) and a particular neurotransmitter—norepinephrine—that is centrally involved in brain activity in this area (e.g., Goddard et al., 1996). However, today it is recognized that it is increased activity in the amygdala that plays a more central role in panic attacks than does activity in the locus coeruleus. The **amygdala** is a collection of nuclei in front of the hippocampus in the limbic system of the brain that is critically involved in the emotion of fear. Stimulation of the central nucleus of the amygdala is known to stimulate the locus coeruleus as well as the other autonomic, neuroendocrine, and behavioral responses that occur during panic attacks (e.g., Gorman et al., 2000; LeDoux, 2000). Other recent research had also implicated the periaqueductal gray area in the midbrain (e.g., Del-Ben & Graeff, 2008; Graeff & Del-Ben, 2008).

Some research has suggested that the amygdala is the central area involved in what has been called a "fear network," with connections not only to lower areas in the brain like the locus coeruleus but also to higher brain areas like the *prefrontal cortex* (e.g., Gorman et al., 2000). According to this view, panic attacks occur when the fear network is activated, either by cortical inputs or by inputs from lower brain areas. So according to this influential theory, panic disorder is likely to develop in people who have abnormally sensitive fear networks that get activated too readily to be adaptive. This theory about abnormally sensitive fear networks is also consistent with findings that individuals with panic disorder showed heightened startle responses to loud noise stimuli as well as slower habituation

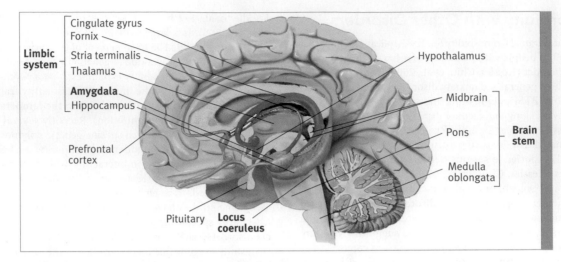

FIGURE 1

A Biological Theory of Panic, Anxiety, and Agoraphobia

According to one theory, panic attacks may arise from abnormal activity in the amygdala, a collection of nuclei in front of the hippocampus in the limbic system. The anticipatory anxiety that people develop about having another panic attack is thought to arise from activity in the hippocampus of the limbic system, which is known to be involved in the learning of emotional responses. Agoraphobic avoidance, also a learned response, may also involve activity of the hippocampus and higher cortical centers (Gorman et al., 2000).

of such responding (Ludewig et al., 2005; see also Shin & Liberzon, 2010). Sakai and colleagues (2005), using functional neuroimaging techniques, also found support for this neuroanatomical hypothesis. Abnormally sensitive fear networks may have a partially heritable basis but may also develop as a result of repeated stressful life experiences, particularly early in life (e.g., Gorman et al., 2000; Ladd et al., 2000).

But panic attacks are only one component of panic disorder. People with panic disorder also become anxious about the possibility of another attack, and those with agoraphobia also engage in phobic avoidance behavior (e.g., Gorman et al., 1989, 2000). Different brain areas are probably involved in these different aspects of panic disorder. The panic attacks themselves arise from activity in the amygdala, either by cortical inputs (e.g., evaluating a stimulus as highly threatening) or by activity coming from more downstream areas like the locus coeruleus. For people who have one or more panic attacks and who go on to develop significant conditioned anxiety about having another one in particular contexts, the *hippocampus* (also a part of the *limbic system*, below the cortex, which is very involved in the learning of emotional responses; see Figure 1) is thought to generate this conditioned anxiety (e.g., Charney et al., 1998; Gray & McNaughton, 1996, 2000), and is probably also involved in the learned avoidance associated with agoraphobia (Gorman et al., 2000). Finally, the cognitive symptoms that occur during panic attacks (fears of dying or of losing control) and overreactions to the danger posed by possibly threatening bodily sensations are likely to be mediated by higher cortical centers (see Gorman et al., 2000; Etkin, 2010).

BIOCHEMICAL ABNORMALITIES Over 30 years ago, Klein (1981) and others (Sheehan, 1982, 1983) argued that panic attacks are alarm reactions caused by biochemical dysfunctions.

This hypothesis initially appeared to be supported by numerous studies over the past 40 years, showing that people with panic disorder are much more likely to experience panic attacks when they are exposed to various biological challenge procedures than are normal people or people with other psychiatric disorders. For example, some of these laboratory tests involve infusions of sodium lactate (a substance resembling the lactate our bodies produce during exercise; e.g., Gorman et al., 1989), inhaling air with altered amounts of carbon dioxide (e.g., Woods et al., 1987), or ingesting large amounts of caffeine (e.g., Uhde, 1990). In each case, such procedures produce panic attacks in panic disorder clients at a much higher rate than in normal subjects (see Barlow, 2002, for review). There is a broad range of these so-called **panic provocation procedures**, and some of them are associated with quite different and even mutually exclusive neurobiological processes. Thus no single neurobiological mechanism could possibly be implicated (Barlow 2002; Roy-Byrne et al., 2006). However, as explained later in this section on causal factors, simpler biological and psychological explanations can account for this pattern of results. These alternative explanations stem from the observation that what all these biological challenge procedures have in common is that they put stress on certain neurobiological systems, which in turn produce intense physical symptoms of arousal (such as increased heart rate, respiration, and blood pressure).

At present, two primary neurotransmitter systems are most implicated in panic attacks—the noradrenergic and the serotonergic systems (Gorman et al., 2000; Graeff & Del-Ben, 2008; Neumeister et al., 2004). Noradrenergic activity in certain brain areas can stimulate cardiovascular symptoms associated with panic (Gorman et al., 2000). Increased serotonergic activity also decreases noradrenergic activity. This fits with results showing that the medications most widely used to treat panic disorder today (the selective serotonin reuptake inhibitors—SSRIs) seem to increase serotonergic activity in the brain but also to decrease noradrenergic activity. By decreasing noradrenergic activity, these medications decrease many of the cardiovascular symptoms associated with panic that are ordinarily stimulated by noradrenergic activity (Gorman et al., 2000).

The inhibitory neurotransmitter GABA has also been implicated in the anticipatory anxiety that many people with panic disorder have about experiencing another attack. GABA is known to inhibit anxiety and has been shown to be abnormally low in certain parts of the cortex in people with panic disorder (Goddard, Mason, et al., 2001, 2004).

Psychological Causal Factors

COMPREHENSIVE LEARNING THEORY OF PANIC DISORDER Certain investigators have proposed a comprehensive learning theory of panic disorder that accounts for most of the known findings about panic disorder (Bouton, Mineka, & Barlow, 2001; see also Barlow, 2002; Bouton, 2005; Mineka & Zinbarg, 2006). Along with advances in the study of classical conditioning, this theory builds on the earlier theory that initial internal bodily sensations of anxiety or arousal (such as heart palpitations) effectively become interoceptive conditioned stimuli associated with higher levels of anxiety or arousal (Goldstein & Chambless, 1978). According to this theory, initial panic attacks become associated with initially neutral internal (interoceptive) and external (exteroceptive) cues through an **interoceptive conditioning** (or **exteroceptive conditioning**) process (e.g., Acheson et al., 2007; Forsyth & Eifert, 1998). One primary effect of this conditioning is that anxiety becomes conditioned to these CSs, and the more intense the panic attack, the more robust the conditioning that will occur (Forsyth et al., 2000). Other types of instrumental and avoidance learning are also involved but will not be explained here.

This conditioning of anxiety to the internal or external cues associated with panic thus sets the stage for the development of two of the three components of panic disorder: anticipatory anxiety and sometimes agoraphobic fears. Specifically, when people experience their initial panic attacks (which are terrifying emotional events replete with strong internal bodily sensations), interoceptive and exeroceptive conditioning can occur to multiple different kinds of cues, ranging from heart palpitations and dizziness to shopping malls. Because anxiety becomes conditioned to these CSs, anxious apprehension about having another attack, particularly in certain contexts, may develop, as may agoraphobic avoidance of contexts in which panic attacks might occur in a subset of individuals. Moreover, a recent study demonstrated that once an individual has developed panic disorder they show greater generalization of conditioned responding to other similar cues than do controls without panic disorder (Lissek et al., 2010). In individuals who have panic disorder, a recent study showed that extinction of conditioned anxiety responses occurs more slowly than in normal controls (Michael, Blechert, et al., 2007). Because extinction involves inhibitory learning, which seems to be impaired in panic disorder, it is not surprising that individuals with panic disorder also show impaired discriminative conditioning because of their deficits in learning that a CS is a safety cue (Lissek et al., 2009).

However, another important effect is that panic attacks themselves (the third component of panic disorder) are also likely to be conditioned to certain internal cues. This leads to the occurrence of panic attacks that seemingly come out of the blue when people unconsciously experience certain internal bodily sensations (CSs). For example, one young man with panic disorder who was particularly frightened of signs that his heart was racing experienced a surprising and unexpected panic attack after hearing that his favorite presidential candidate had won. The panic attack thus occurred when he was happy and excited (which is what made it so surprising for him). However, from the standpoint of this theory, the attack was actually not surprising. Because the man was excited, his heart was racing, which probably served as an internal CS that triggered the panic (Mineka & Zinbarg, 2006). This theory also underscores why not everyone who experiences an occasional panic attack goes on to develop panic disorder. Instead, people with certain genetic, temperamental or personality, or cognitive-behavioral vulnerabilities will show stronger conditioning of both anxiety and panic (Barlow, 2002; Bouton et al., 2001; Mineka & Zinbarg, 2006). For example, the personality variable that clearly serves as a risk variable is neuroticism.

COGNITIVE THEORY OF PANIC An earlier cognitive theory of panic disorder proposed that individuals with panic disorder are hypersensitive to their bodily sensations and are very prone to giving them the direst possible interpretation (Beck & Emery, 1985; D. M. Clark, 1986, 1997). Clark referred to this as a tendency to catastrophize about the meaning of their bodily sensations. For example, a person who develops panic disorder might notice that his heart is racing and conclude that he is having a heart attack, or notice that he is dizzy, which may lead to fainting or to the thought that he may have a brain tumor. These very frightening thoughts may cause many more physical symptoms of anxiety, which further fuel the catastrophic thoughts, leading to a vicious circle culminating in a panic attack (see Figure 2). The person is not necessarily aware of making these catastrophic interpretations; rather, the thoughts are often just barely out of the realm of awareness (Rapee, 1996). These *automatic thoughts*, as Beck calls them, are in a sense the triggers of panic. Although it is not yet clear how the tendency to catastrophize develops, the cognitive model proposes that only people with this tendency to catastrophize go on to develop panic disorder (e.g., D. M. Clark, 1997).

Several lines of evidence are consistent with the cognitive theory of panic disorder. For example, people with panic disorder are much more likely to interpret their bodily sensations in a catastrophic manner (e.g., see D. M. Clark, 1997; Teachman et al., 2007), and the greater the tendency to do so, the greater the severity of panic (Casey et al., 2005). The model also predicts that changing their cognitions about their bodily symptoms should reduce or prevent panic. Evidence that cognitive therapy for panic works is consistent with this prediction (D. M. Clark et al., 1994, 1999). In addition, a brief

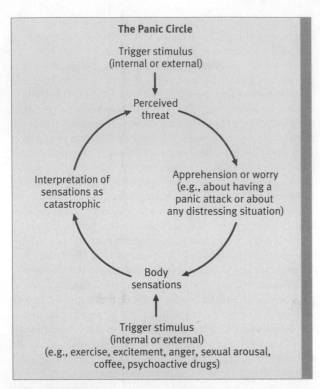

FIGURE 2

The Panic Circle

Any kind of perceived threat may lead to apprehension or worry, which is accompanied by various bodily sensations. According to the cognitive model of panic, if a person then catastrophizes about the meaning of his or her bodily sensations, this will raise the level of perceived threat, thus creating more apprehension and worry as well as more physical symptoms, which fuel further catastrophic thoughts. This vicious circle can culminate in a panic attack. The initial physical sensations need not arise from the perceived threat (as shown at the top of the circle) but may come from other sources (exercise, anger, psychoactive drugs, etc., as shown at the bottom of the circle). (Adapted from D. M. Clark, 1986, 1997.)

explanation of what to expect in a panic provocation study can apparently prevent or reduce panic symptoms (D. M. Clark, 1997). People with panic disorder either were given a brief but detailed explanation of what physical symptoms to expect from an infusion of sodium lactate and why they should not worry about these symptoms, or were given a minimal explanation. The people with the cognitive rationale about what to expect were significantly less likely to say that they had had the subjective experience of a panic attack in response to the lactate (30 percent) than were control individuals (90 percent) (see Schmidt et al., 2006, for related results).

LEARNING AND COGNITIVE EXPLANATIONS OF RESULTS FROM PANIC PROVOCATION STUDIES Earlier we noted that there are simpler psychological explanations that provide a common mechanism for understanding how so many varied panic provocation agents can all provoke panic at high rates in people with panic disorder. Because these agents

produce arousal, they mimic the physiological cues that normally precede a panic attack or may be taken as a sign of some other impending catastrophe (Barlow, 2002; Bouton et al., 2001; Margraf et al., 1986a, 1986b). People with panic disorder already start at a higher level of arousal than others and are very familiar with these early warning cues. Thus, according to the cognitive theory, people with panic attacks frequently misinterpret these symptoms as the beginning of a panic attack or a heart attack, which in turn induces the vicious circle of panic described in the previous section; this would not happen in controls who do not have the same tendency to catastrophize. Alternatively, according to the learning theory of panic disorder, it would be only those with panic disorder for whom these cues might serve as interoceptive CSs that can trigger anxiety and panic because of their prior associations with panic.

The key difference between these two theories in explaining the results of panic provocation studies lies in the great importance that the cognitive model places on the meaning that people attach to their bodily sensations; they will experience panic only if they make catastrophic interpretations of certain bodily sensations. Such catastrophic cognitions are not necessary with the interoceptive conditioning model because anxiety and panic attacks can be triggered by unconscious interoceptive (or exteroceptive) cues (Bouton et al., 2001). Thus the learning theory model is better able to explain the occurrence of the panic attacks that often occur without any preceding negative (catastrophic) automatic thoughts, as well as the occurrence of nocturnal panic attacks that occur during sleep; the occurrence of both of these kinds of attacks is difficult for the cognitive model to explain (see Developments in Research 1).

ANXIETY SENSITIVITY AND PERCEIVED CONTROL Other cognitive and learning explanations of panic and agoraphobia have looked at a number of different factors that can generally be explained within either the learning or cognitive perspective. For example, several researchers have shown that people who have high levels of anxiety sensitivity are more prone to developing panic attacks and perhaps panic disorder (McNally, 2002; Pagura et al., 2009). **Anxiety sensitivity** is a trait-like belief that certain bodily symptoms may have harmful consequences. Such a person would endorse statements such as, "When I notice that my heart is beating rapidly, I worry that I might have a heart attack." In one important study, Schmidt and colleagues (1997) followed over 1,400 young adults undergoing basic military training for 5 weeks. They found that high levels of anxiety sensitivity predicted the development of spontaneous panic attacks during this highly stressful period. Several other studies examining the same issues obtained very similar results, thus boosting confidence in the reliability of anxiety sensitivity as a predictor of panic attacks (e.g., Hayward et al., 2000; Li & Zinbarg, 2007). However, Schmidt and colleagues (2006) have reported results showing that high anxiety sensitivity also serves to predict the onset of other anxiety disorders as well as panic attacks, thus raising some questions about the specificity of its role for panic versus other anxiety disorders (see also Starcevic & Berle, 2006).

DEVELOPMENTS IN RESEARCH

1

Nocturnal Panic Attacks

Although the majority of panic attacks experienced by people with panic disorder occur during waking hours, approximately 50 to 60 percent of people report that they have experienced a panic attack during sleep at least once (Barlow, 2002; O'Mahony & Ward, 2003). Nocturnal panic refers to waking from sleep in a state of panic. It seems to occur with some regularity in about 20 to 40 percent of people with panic disorder and is frequently associated with insomnia and frequent awakenings during sleep (Craske et al., 2002; Overbeek et al., 2005; Papadimitriou & Linkowski, 2005). Although one might think that such panic attacks occur in response to nightmares, considerable research shows that this is not the case. Sleep has five stages that occur in a fairly invariant sequence multiple times throughout the night: one stage called *REM sleep* (rapid eye movement sleep) when vivid dreaming occurs, and four stages of non-REM sleep (Stages 1–4) when vivid dreams do not occur. If nocturnal panic attacks occurred in response to dreams, we would expect them to occur during REM sleep (when nightmares usually occur), but in fact they occur during Stage 2 and early Stage 3 sleep, usually a few hours after falling asleep.

It is important to note that nocturnal panic attacks are different from "sleep terrors" or "night terrors," which usually occur during Stage 4 sleep. Night terrors are usually experienced by children, who often scream and then fear that someone or something is chasing them around the room; however, they do not wake up (Barlow, 2002). Nocturnal panic attacks also differ from *isolated sleep paralysis*, which can sometimes occur during the transition from sleep to waking. It involves awareness of one's surroundings accompanied by a stark sense of terror (resembling that during a panic attack) and an inability to move, which seems to occur because the individuals are waking from REM (dream) sleep, when there is suppression of muscle activity below the neck (e.g., Hinton et al, 2005).

One reason nocturnal panic attacks have been of interest from a theoretical standpoint is that they appear to be very difficult for any strong version of the cognitive theory of panic disorder to explain, in part because it is hard to see how the catastrophic cognitions that are posited to be necessary for the occurrence of a panic attack could occur during Stage 2 or 3 sleep. On the other hand, the learning theory of panic disorder can explain their occurrence because internal bodily sensations occurring during sleep that have been previously conditioned to elicit panic can do so without the person being consciously aware of them (Bouton et al., 2001).

In addition, several important studies have shown that simply having a sense of *perceived control*—for instance, over the amount of carbon dioxide-altered air that is inhaled (a panic provocation procedure known frequently to bring on anxiety and panic)—reduces anxiety and even blocks panic (e.g., Sanderson et al., 1989; Zvolensky et al., 1998, 1999). In addition, if a person with panic disorder is accompanied by a "safe" person when undergoing a panic provocation procedure, that person is likely to show reduced distress, lowered physiological arousal, and reduced likelihood of panic relative to someone who came alone (without a "safe" person; Carter et al., 1995). Moreover, people high in anxiety sensitivity may be protected against having panic attacks during stressful periods if they have a sense of perceived control and predictability over their life situation (Schmidt & Lerew, 2002). Finally, individuals with panic disorder may also be protected against the development

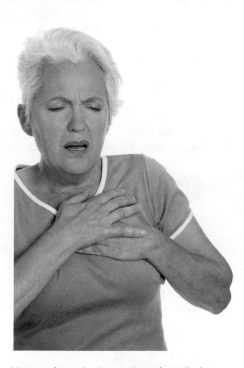

Many people experiencing a panic attack mistake their symptoms (for example, chest pain and shortness of breath) for another medical problem—most often a heart attack.

of agoraphobic avoidance if they have relatively high levels of perceived control over their emotions and threatening situations (Suarez et al., 2009; White et al., 2006).

SAFETY BEHAVIORS AND THE PERSISTENCE OF PANIC Why do people who have developed panic disorder continue to have panic attacks in spite of the fact that their direst predictions rarely, if ever, come true? Some people with panic disorder may, for example, have three or four panic attacks a week for 20 years; each time they may believe they are having a heart attack, and yet they never do. After experiencing hundreds or thousands of panic attacks without having a heart attack, one would think, from the cognitive perspective, that this catastrophic thought would have been proved wrong so many times that it would finally go away. However, evidence suggests that such disconfirmation does not occur because people with panic disorder frequently engage in safety behaviors (such as breathing slowly or carrying a bottle with anxiolytic medication) before or during an attack. They then mistakenly tend to attribute the lack of catastrophe to their having engaged in this safety behavior rather than to the idea that panic attacks actually do not lead to heart attacks. Similarly, people who think they may faint will tend to lean against solid objects (D. A. Clark, 1997; Salkovskis et al., 1996). Research suggests that it is important during treatment to identify these safety behaviors so that the person can learn to give them up and finally see that the feared catastrophe still does not occur. Indeed, a good number of studies have found that asking people to drop their safety behaviors during cognitive-behavioral treatment can increase the effectiveness of the treatment (e.g., Rachman et al., 2008).

COGNITIVE BIASES AND THE MAINTENANCE OF PANIC

Finally, many studies have shown that people with panic disorder are biased in the way they process threatening information. Such people not only interpret ambiguous bodily sensations as threatening (D. A. Clark, 1997; Teachman et al., 2006), but they also interpret other ambiguous situations as more threatening than do controls. People with panic disorder also seem to have their attention automatically drawn to threatening information in their environment such as words that represent things they fear, such as palpitations, numbness, or faint (see Lim & Kim, 2005; Mathews & MacLeod, 2005; Mineka et al., 2003, for reviews). One study using fMRI techniques demonstrated that people with panic disorder showed greater activation to threat words than did normals in brain areas involved in memory processing of threatening material (Maddock et al., 2003). Whether these information-processing biases are present before the disorder begins and help to cause it is as yet unclear, but these biases are certainly likely to help maintain the disorder once it has begun. For example, having one's attention automatically drawn to threatening cues in the environment is likely to provoke more attacks.

In summary, research into both biological and psychosocial factors involved in panic disorder has provided important insights into this disorder since it was first identified as a distinct disorder in 1980. It seems unlikely that research from either tradition alone will ever provide a complete account of this disorder, and we eagerly await more attempts at synthesizing these findings into a biopsychosocial theory.

Treatments

MEDICATIONS Many people with panic disorder (with or without agoraphobia) are prescribed *anxiolytics* (antianxiety medications) from the benzodiazepine category such as alprazolam (Xanax) or clonazepam (Klonopin). These people frequently show some symptom relief from these medications, and many can function more effectively. One major advantage of these drugs is that they act very quickly (30–60 minutes) and so can be useful in acute

situations of intense panic or anxiety. However, these anxiolytic medications can also have quite undesirable side effects such as drowsiness and sedation, which can lead to impaired cognitive and motor performance. Also, with prolonged use, most people using moderate to high doses develop physiological dependence on the drug, which results in withdrawal symptoms when the drug is discontinued (e.g., nervousness, sleep disturbance, dizziness, and further panic attacks). Withdrawal from these drugs can be very slow and difficult, and it precipitates relapse in a high percentage of cases (Pollack & Simon, 2009; Roy-Byrne & Cowley, 2007). These are the reasons why benzodiazepines are no longer considered as a first-choice treatment (Katon, 2006).

The other category of medication that is useful in the treatment of panic disorder and agoraphobia is the antidepressants (including primarily the tricyclics , the SSRIs, and most recently the serotonin-norepinephrine reuptake inhibitors—SNRIs). These medications have both advantages and disadvantages compared with anxiolytics. One major advantage is that they do not create physiological dependence in the way benzodiazepines can, and they also can alleviate any comorbid depressive symptoms or disorders (Pollack & Simon, 2009; Roy-Byrne & Cowley, 2007). However, it takes about 4 weeks before they have any beneficial effects, so they are not useful in an acute situation where a person is having a panic attack. Troublesome side effects (such as dry mouth, constipation, and blurred vision with the tricyclics, and interference with sexual arousal with the SSRIs) mean that large numbers of people refuse to take the medications or discontinue their use. Moreover, relapse rates when the drugs are discontinued are quite high (although not as high as with the benzodiazepines; Roy-Byrne & Cowley, 2007).

Today the SSRIs are more widely prescribed than the tricyclics because the SSRIs are generally better tolerated by most patients. Moreover, both are generally preferred by physicians to benzodiazepines because of the risks associated with the latter (Roy-Byrne & Cowley, 2007).

BEHAVIORAL AND COGNITIVE-BEHAVIORAL TREATMENTS

The original behavioral treatment for agoraphobia from the early 1970s involved prolonged exposure to feared situations, often with the help of a therapist or family member. Similar to what is done with specific and social phobias, the idea was to make people gradually face the situations they feared and learn that there was nothing to fear. Such exposure-based treatments were quite effective and helped about 60 to 75 percent of people with agoraphobia show clinically significant improvement (Barlow et al., 2007). These effects were generally well maintained at 2- to 4-year follow-up. But this left approximately 25 to 40 percent not improved to a *clinically significant* degree (Barlow et al., 2002).

> **RESEARCH CLOSE-UP**
>
> *Clinically Significant*
>
> Not all statistically significant changes are of sufficient magnitude to be clinically significant. Clinical significance reflects how large the effects of a particular treatment or intervention are with respect to how much meaningful change they provide in a person's level of functioning or well-being.

One limitation of these original treatments was that they did not specifically target panic attacks. In the mid-1980s, two new techniques were developed as clinical researchers increasingly recognized the importance of panic attacks to most people with agoraphobia. One technique involves the variant on exposure known as *interoceptive exposure*, meaning deliberate exposure to feared internal sensations. The idea was that fear of these internal sensations should be treated in the same way that fear of external agoraphobic situations is treated—namely, through prolonged exposure to those internal sensations so that the fear may extinguish.

The second set of techniques that were developed is cognitive restructuring techniques, in recognition that catastrophic automatic thoughts may help maintain panic attacks. Developments in Practice 2 illustrates one kind of integrative cognitive-behavioral treatment for panic disorder—*panic control treatment*. This approach targets both agoraphobic avoidance and panic attacks. Generally, this integrative treatment produces better results than the original exposure-based techniques that focused exclusively on exposure to external situations (D. M. Clark, 1997; Arch & Craske, 2009). In many of the studies conducted using one of the variants on these treatments, 70 to 90 percent of people with panic disorder were panic-free at the end of 8 to 14 weeks of treatment, and gains were well maintained at 1- to 2-year follow-up (Arch & Craske, 2008; McCabe & Gifford, 2009). Overall, the magnitude of improvement is often greater with these cognitive and behavioral treatments than with medications (Arch & Craske, 2009; Barlow et al., 2002). Moreover, these treatments have

---

2

Developments in Practice
COGNITIVE-BEHAVIORAL THERAPY FOR PANIC DISORDER

The cognitive and conditioning models of panic disorder have contributed to the formulation of new treatments that have been shown to be highly effective in dozens of different studies in many countries around the world (see Barlow et al., 2007; Mitte, 2005). Although the treatments vary somewhat, each is a form of behavioral or cognitive-behavioral therapy. In one widely used version of the Panic Control Treatment (PCT) developed by Barlow, Craske, and colleagues, several different cognitive and behavioral techniques are combined in a program that typically lasts for 12 to 15 sessions (Craske & Barlow, 2000, 2007; Craske et al., 2000).

There are several aspects to PCT. First, clients are educated about the nature of anxiety and panic and how the capacity to experience both is adaptive. By learning about the nature of the fight-or-flight response experienced during panic, clients come to understand that the sensations they experience during panic are normal and harmless. Clients are also taught to self-monitor their experiences with anxiety and panic through daily diaries.

A second part of treatment involves teaching people with panic disorder to control their breathing. First they are asked to hyperventilate, or overbreathe. Hyperventilation is known to create a variety of unpleasant physical sensations (such as lightheadedness, dizziness, and tightness of the chest) that often occur during panic attacks. (You can see this for yourself by breathing very fast and deeply for 1 to 2 minutes.) By learning how to control their breathing, they master a new coping tool that will reduce the likelihood that they themselves will create some of the symptoms they so strongly fear.

Third, clients are taught to identify the automatic thoughts they have during panic attacks as well as during anxiety-provoking situations. They are then taught about the logical errors that people who have panic are prone to making and learn to subject their own automatic thoughts to a logical reanalysis. For example, a person who fears having a heart attack at the first sign of heart palpitations is asked to examine the evidence that this might be true. (When did the doctor last tell him or her that his or her heart was perfectly healthy? What is the likelihood of having a heart attack at age 30?) In later sessions the cognitive part of the treatment is focused on teaching people how to decatastrophize—that is, to learn how to think through what the worst possible outcome might be if they did have a panic attack (e.g., if they had a panic attack while driving, they might have to pull their car over to the side of the road until the attack subsided). The entire experience of panic usually becomes less terrifying once they learn to decatastrophize.

Finally, another part of the treatment involves exposure to feared situations and feared bodily sensations. Because of the importance of *interoceptive fears* (fears of bodily sensations), clients are asked to do a variety of exercises with the therapist that bring on different bodily sensations. These include hyperventilating, breathing through a straw, shaking one's head from side to side, jogging in place, holding one's breath for a minute, and the like. After each exercise, clients describe the sensations produced, discuss how similar these sensations are to those that they experience during panic, and evaluate how scary those sensations are. Whichever exercises produce the symptoms most similar to their own during panic attacks are targeted for practice. The idea is that if clients practice inducing these sensations, their ability to tolerate discomfort will increase and their anxiety about the sensations will gradually diminish. Later, clients who also have extensive agoraphobic avoidance begin to expose themselves to their feared situations for long enough that their anxiety diminishes. This part of the treatment is delayed until clients have learned a variety of coping skills (cognitive techniques as well as breathing skills).

been extended and shown to be very useful in treating people who also have nocturnal panic (Arch & Craske, 2008).

What about the combination of medication and cognitive-behavioral therapy? In the short term, such combined treatment sometimes produces a slightly superior result compared to either type of treatment alone (Barlow et al., 2007; Mitte, 2005). In addition, one study showed that those individuals who had received combined treatment showed fewer medication side effects and fewer dropouts than those who had used medication alone (Marcus, Gorman, et al., 2007). However, in the long term, after medication has been tapered (especially benzodiazepine medications), clients who have been on medication with or without cognitive or behavioral treatment seem to show a greater likelihood of relapse (Arch & Craske, 2008; Barlow et al., 2002; Marks et al., 1993). Perhaps this is because they have attributed their gains to the medication rather than to their personal efforts (Başoğlu et al., 1994; Mitte, 2005).

In Review

- You are experiencing a panic attack. What are your symptoms?
- Describe the major diagnostic features of both panic disorder and agoraphobia, and explain how they are thought to be related.
- What biological causal factors have been implicated in panic disorder?
- Compare and contrast the learning or conditioning theory and cognitive models of panic disorder.
- Describe the major treatment approaches for panic disorder and their relative advantages and disadvantages.

Generalized Anxiety Disorder

Most of us worry and get anxious occasionally, and anxiety is an adaptive emotion that helps us plan and prepare for possible threat. But for some people, anxiety and worry about many different aspects of life (including minor events) becomes chronic, excessive, and unreasonable. In these cases, **generalized anxiety disorder (GAD)** (formerly known as free-floating anxiety) may be diagnosed. *DSM-IV-TR* criteria specify that the worry must occur more days than not for at least 6 months and that it must be experienced as difficult to control (see *DSM-IV-TR* box). The worry must be about a number of different events or activities, and its content cannot be exclusively related to the worry associated with another concurrent Axis I disorder, such as the possibility of having a panic attack. The subjective experience of excessive worry must also be accompanied by at least three of six other symptoms, as listed in the table, such as muscle tension or being easily fatigued. There is currently debate among the task force working on

revisions for *DSM-V* (to be published in 2013) as to whether this is the optimal set of criteria for GAD (e.g., the 6-month duration requirement and the excessive worry requirement; e.g., Andrews et al., 2010; Lee et al., 2008; Ruscio et al., 2005) and whether this is the optimal name for the disorder (versus generalized worry disorder or pathological worry disorder) (Andrews et al., 2010)

The general picture of people suffering from generalized anxiety disorder is that they live in a relatively constant future-oriented mood state of anxious apprehension, chronic

DSM-IV-TR

Criteria for Generalized Anxiety Disorder

Generalized Anxiety Disorder (Includes Overanxious Disorder of Childhood)

A. Excessive anxiety and worry (apprehensive expectation), occurring more days than not for at least 6 months, about a number of events or activities (such as work or school performance).
B. The person finds it difficult to control the worry.
C. The anxiety and worry are associated with three (or more) of the following six symptoms (with at least some symptoms present for more days than not for the past 6 months). Note: Only one item is required in children.
   1. Restlessness or feeling keyed up or on edge
   2. Being easily fatigued
   3. Difficulty concentrating or mind going blank
   4. Irritability
   5. Muscle tension
   6. Sleep disturbance (difficulty falling or staying asleep, or restless unsatisfying sleep)
D. The focus of the anxiety and worry is not confined to features of an Axis I disorder, e.g., the anxiety or worry is not about having a Panic Attack (as in Panic Disorder), being embarrassed in public (as in Social Phobia), being contaminated (as in Obsessive-Compulsive Disorder), being away from home or close relatives (as in Separation Anxiety Disorder), gaining weight (as in Anorexia Nervosa), having multiple physical complaints (as in Somatization Disorder), or having a serious illness (as in Hypochondriasis), and the anxiety and worry do not occur exclusively during Posttraumatic Stress Disorder.
E. The anxiety, worry, or physical symptoms cause clinically significant distress or impairment in social, occupational, or other important areas of functioning.
F. The disturbance is not due to the direct physiological effects of a substance (e.g., a drug of abuse, a medication) or a general medical condition (e.g., hyperthyroidism) and does not occur exclusively during a Mood Disorder, a Psychotic Disorder, or a Pervasive Developmental Disorder.

Source: Reprinted with permission from the American Psychiatric Association. *Diagnostic and Statistical Manual of Mental Disorders*, Fourth Edition, *Text Revision* (Copyright © 2000). American Psychiatric Association.

tension, worry, and diffuse uneasiness that they cannot control. They also frequently show marked vigilance for possible signs of threat in the environment and frequently engage in certain subtle avoidance activities such as procrastination, checking, or calling a loved one frequently to see if he or she is safe (Barlow, 2002; Barlow et al., 1996). Such anxious apprehension also occurs in other anxiety disorders (for example, the person with agoraphobia shows anticipatory anxiety about future panic attacks and about dying, and the person with social phobia is anxious about possible negative social evaluation). But this apprehension is the essence of GAD, leading Barlow and others to refer to GAD as the "basic" anxiety disorder (Roemer et al., 2002; Wells & Butler, 1997).

The nearly constant worries of people with generalized anxiety disorder leave them continually upset and discouraged. In one study, the most common spheres of worry were found to be family, work, finances, and personal illness (Roemer et al., 1997). Not only do they have difficulty making decisions, but after they have managed to make a decision they worry endlessly, even after going to bed, over possible errors and unforeseen circumstances that may prove the decision wrong and lead to disaster. They have no appreciation of the logic by which most of

Muscle tension, restlessness, and difficulty concentrating are all symptoms that people with generalized anxiety disorder may have. Such individuals also worry excessively and are hypervigilant for possible signs of threat in their environment.

us conclude that it is pointless to torment ourselves about possible outcomes over which we have no control. As two researchers in this area put it, "The result is that they fail to escape the illusory world created in their thoughts and images and rarely experience the present moment that possesses the potential to bring them joy" (Behar & Borkovec, 2006, p. 184). It is not surprising then that a recent study of the personal and economic burden of GAD found that those with GAD experienced a similar amount of role impairment and lessened quality of life to those with major depression (Hofmann et al., 2010).

The case below is fairly typical of generalized anxiety disorder.

Prevalence, Age of Onset, and Gender Differences

Generalized anxiety disorder is a relatively common condition; current estimates from the National Comorbidity Survey-Replication are that approximately 3 percent of the population suffers from it in any 1-year period and 5.7 percent at some point in their lives (Kessler et al., 1994; Kessler, Berglund, Demler, et al., 2005; Kessler, Chiu, et al., 2005). It also tends to be chronic. One 12-year follow-up study of people diagnosed with GAD found that 42 percent had not remitted 13 years

---

case study   A Graduate Student with GAD

John was a 26-year-old, single graduate student in the social sciences at a prestigious university. He reported that he had had problems with anxiety nearly all his life but they had become worse since he had left home and gone to an Ivy League college. During the past year his anxiety had seriously interfered with his functioning, and he worried about several different spheres of his life such as his own and his parents' health. During one incident a few months earlier, he had thought that his heart was beating more slowly than usual and he had experienced some tingling sensations; this led him to worry that he might die. In another incident he had heard his name spoken over a loudspeaker in an airport and had worried that someone at home must be dying. He was also very worried about his future because his anxiety had kept him from completing his master's thesis on time. John also worried excessively about getting a bad grade even though he had never had one either in college or in graduate school. In classes he worried excessively about what the professor and other students thought of him. Although he had a number of friends, he had never had a girlfriend because of his shyness about

dating. He had no problem talking or socializing with women as long as it was not defined as a dating situation. He worried that he should date a woman only if he was quite sure, from the outset, that it could be a serious relationship. He also worried excessively that if a woman did not want to date him, it meant that he was boring.

In addition to his worries, which he perceived as uncontrollable, John reported muscle tension and becoming easily fatigued. He also reported great difficulty concentrating and a considerable amount of restlessness and pacing. At times he had difficulty falling asleep if he was particularly anxious, but at other times he slept excessively, in part to escape from his worries. He frequently experienced dizziness and palpitations, and in the past he had had full-blown panic attacks.

John's mother was also quite anxious and had been treated for panic disorder. John was obviously extremely bright and had managed to do very well in school in spite of his lifelong problems with anxiety. But as the pressures of finishing graduate school and starting his career loomed before him, and as he got older and had still never dated, the anxiety became so severe that he sought treatment.

later and of those who had remitted, nearly half had had a recurrence (Bruce et al., 2005; see also Hofmann et al., 2010). However, after age 50 the disorder seems to disappear for many people (Rubio & Lopez-Ibor, 2007). If it disappears it tends to be replaced by somatization disorders, which are characterized by multiple somatic complaints with no known medical basis.

GAD is approximately twice as common in women as in men (a somewhat less dramatic difference than is seen with many specific phobias or severe agoraphobia; see Table 3 for summaries of gender differences in the different anxiety disorders). Although GAD is quite common, most people with this disorder manage to function (albeit with some role impairment) in spite of their high levels of worry and low perceived well-being (Hofmann et al., 2010; Stein et al., 2004). They are less likely to go to clinics for psychological treatment than are people with panic disorder or major depressive disorder, which are frequently more debilitating conditions. However, people with GAD do frequently show up in physicians' offices with medical complaints (such as muscle tension or gastrointestinal and/or cardiac symptoms) and are known to be overusers of health care resources (similar to people with panic disorder; Greenberg et al., 1999; Hofmann et al., 2010; Katon et al., 2002).

Age of onset is often difficult to determine because 60 to 80 percent of people with GAD remember having been anxious nearly all their lives, and many others report a slow and insidious onset (Roemer et al., 2002; Wells & Butler, 1997). However, research has also documented that GAD often develops in older adults, for whom it is the most common anxiety disorder (e.g., Roemer et al., 2002; Stein, 2004).

Comorbidity with Other Disorders

Generalized anxiety disorder often co-occurs with other Axis I disorders, especially other anxiety and mood disorders such as panic disorder, social phobia, specific phobia, PTSD, and major depressive disorder (Brown, Campbell, et al., 2001; Kessler, Chiu, et al., 2005; Tyrer & Baldwin, 2006). In addition, many people with GAD (like John) experience occasional panic attacks without qualifying for a diagnosis of panic disorder (Barlow, 1988, 2002). Even if they do not meet full diagnostic criteria for major depressive disorder (which many do), many of these people are mildly to moderately depressed as well as chronically anxious, which is not surprising given their generally gloomy outlook on the world (Beesdo et al., 2010; Hofmann et al., 2010; Stein et al., 2004). Nor is it surprising that excessive use of tranquilizing drugs, sleeping pills, and alcohol often complicates the clinical picture in generalized anxiety disorder (Tyrer & Baldwin, 2006).

Psychological Causal Factors

THE PSYCHOANALYTIC VIEWPOINT According to this viewpoint, generalized or free-floating anxiety results from an unconscious conflict between ego and id impulses that is not adequately dealt with because the person's defense mechanisms have either broken down or have never developed. Freud believed that it was primarily sexual and aggressive impulses that had been either blocked from expression or punished upon expression that led to free-floating anxiety. Defense mechanisms may become overwhelmed when a person experiences frequent and extreme levels of anxiety, as might happen if id impulses are frequently blocked from expression (e.g., under periods of prolonged sexual deprivation). According to this view, the primary difference between specific phobias and free-floating anxiety is that in phobias, the defense mechanisms of repression and displacement of an external object or situation actually work, whereas in free-floating anxiety these defense mechanisms do not work, leaving the person anxious nearly all the time. Unfortunately this viewpoint is not testable and has therefore been largely abandoned among clinical researchers.

PERCEPTIONS OF UNCONTROLLABILITY AND UNPREDICTABILITY Uncontrollable and unpredictable aversive events are much more stressful than controllable and predictable aversive events, so it is perhaps not surprising that the former create more fear and anxiety, as we discussed with specific and social phobias (Barlow, 2002; Craske & Waters, 2005; Mineka, 1985b; Mineka & Oehlberg, 2008; Mineka & Zinbarg, 1996, 2006). Conversely, experience with controlling aspects of one's life may immunize one against developing general anxiety (Chorpita, 2001; Mineka & Kelly, 1989).

This has led researchers to hypothesize that people with GAD may have a history of experiencing many important events in their lives as unpredictable or uncontrollable. For example, having a boss or spouse who has unpredictable bad moods or outbursts of temper for seemingly trivial reasons might keep a person in a chronic state of anxiety. Although the unpredictable and uncontrollable events involved in GAD are generally not as severe and traumatic as those involved in the origins of PTSD, there is some evidence that people with GAD may be more likely to have had a history of trauma in childhood than individuals with several other anxiety disorders (Borkovec et al., 2004; see also Kendler, Hettema, et al., 2003). Moreover, people with GAD clearly have far less tolerance for uncertainty than nonanxious controls and than people with panic disorder (Dugas et al., 2004, 2005; Koerner & Dugas, 2008). This low tolerance for uncertainty in people with GAD suggests that they are especially disturbed by not being able to predict the future (as none of us can; Roemer et al., 2002). Some findings also show the greater the intolerance of uncertainty, the more severe the GAD (Dugas et al., 2007). However, intolerance for uncertainty also seems to be elevated in individuals with OCD (e.g., Behar et al., 2008).

In addition, perhaps some of these people's intolerance for uncertainty, as well as their tension and hypervigilance (the sense of always looking for signs of threat), stems from their lacking safety signals in their environment. If a person mostly experiences predictable stressors (e.g., on Mondays the boss is always in a bad mood and is likely to be highly critical), he or she cannot only predict when something bad is likely to happen (e.g., Mondays at work) but can also feel safe when that signal is missing (a safety signal; e.g., Tuesdays through Fridays at work). But if another person has experienced many unpredictable or unsignaled stressors (e.g., the boss is in a bad mood and highly critical on random days of the week), she or he will not have developed safety signals for when it is appropriate to relax and feel safe, and this uncertainty may lead to chronic anxiety (Mineka, 1985a; Mineka & Zinbarg, 1996; Seligman & Binik, 1977). Thus a relative lack of safety signals may help explain why people with GAD feel constantly tense and vigilant for possible threats (Rapee, 2001).

A SENSE OF MASTERY: THE POSSIBILITY OF IMMUNIZING AGAINST ANXIETY

A person's history of control over important aspects of his or her environment is another important experiential variable strongly affecting reactions to anxiety-provoking situations. Although we cannot study this experimentally in humans, we can learn a lot from laboratory analogue studies in animals. For example, one longitudinal experiment with infant rhesus monkeys found that infant monkeys reared with a sense of mastery and control over their environments for 7 to 10 months later adapted more readily to frightening events and novel anxiety-provoking situations than did monkeys reared in environments that were identical except for the experiences with control (Mineka, Gunnar, & Champoux, 1986; see also Chorpita & Barlow, 1998; Craske & Waters, 2005; Mineka & Zinbarg, 1996, 2006). In human children, experiences with control and mastery often also occur in the context of the parent–child relationship and so parents' responsiveness to their children's needs directly influences their children's developing sense of mastery (e.g., Chorpita, 2001; Craske & Waters, 2005; Mineka & Zinbarg, 1996, 2006). Unfortunately, parents of anxious children often have an intrusive, overcontrolling parenting style, which may serve only to promote their children's anxious behaviors by making them think of the world as an unsafe place in which they require protection and have little control themselves (Craske & Waters, 2005).

THE CENTRAL ROLE OF WORRY AND ITS POSITIVE FUNCTIONS

The worry process is now considered the central feature of GAD and has been the focus of much research in recent years. Here we will first consider the nature and functions of worry. Next, we will consider why worry comes to be such a self-sustaining process in some people and why it may be perceived to be uncontrollable.

Borkovec and colleagues (Borkovec, 1994; Borkovec et al., 2004; Behar & Borkovec, 2006) investigated both what people with GAD think the benefits of worrying are and what actual functions worry serves. Several of the benefits that people with GAD most commonly think derive from worrying are:

- Superstitious avoidance of catastrophe ("Worrying makes it less likely that the feared event will occur").

It is possible that some of the chronic tension and hypervigilance that individuals with generalized anxiety disorder experience stem from their lacking safety signals in their environment. Without such safety signals, such as knowing when their boss or spouse will or will not be angry with them, they may never be able to relax and feel safe.

- Avoidance of deeper emotional topics ("Worrying about most of the things I worry about is a way to distract myself from worrying about even more emotional things, things that I don't want to think about").
- Coping and preparation ("Worrying about a predicted negative event helps me to prepare for its occurrence"; Borkovec, 1994, pp. 16–17; Borkovec et al., 2004).

There is some evidence that for a subset of people with GAD, these positive beliefs about worry play a key role in maintaining high levels of anxiety and worry, especially in early phases of the development of GAD (Dugas et al., 2007). In addition, exciting new discoveries about the functions that worry actually serves help reveal why the worry process is so self-sustaining. When people with GAD worry, their emotional and physiological responses to aversive imagery are actually suppressed. This suppression of aversive emotional physiological responding may serve to reinforce the process of worry (that is, to increase its probability; Borkovec et al., 2004; McLaughlin et al., 2007). Because worry suppresses physiological responding, it also insulates the person from fully experiencing or processing the topic that she or he is worrying about, and it is known that such full processing is necessary if extinction of that anxiety is to occur. Thus the threatening meaning of the topic being worried about is maintained (Borkovec et al., 2004; Sibrava & Borkovec, 2006).

THE NEGATIVE CONSEQUENCES OF WORRY

In spite of these positive functions that worry serves, some of its effects are clearly negative (Mineka, 2004; Mineka et al., 2002). For example, worry itself is certainly not an enjoyable activity and can actually lead to a greater sense of danger and anxiety (and lower positive mood) because of all the possible catastrophic outcomes that the worrier envisions (McLaughlin et al., 2007). In addition, people who worry about something tend subsequently to have more negative intrusive thoughts than people who do not worry. For example, Wells and Papageorgiou (1995) had people watch a gruesome film. Following the film, some were told to relax and settle down, some were told to imagine the events in the film, and some were told to worry in verbal form about the film. Over the next several days, people in the worry condition showed the most intrusive images from the film. In addition, another study showed that after engaging in worry individuals with GAD experience more intense negative emotions when reacting to a sad film (McLaughlin et al., 2007).

Finally, there is now considerable evidence that attempts to control thoughts and worry may paradoxically lead to increased experience of intrusive thoughts and enhanced perception of being unable to control them (Abramowitz et al., 2001; Wells, 1999; Wells & Butler, 1997). Somewhat paradoxically, these intrusive thoughts can serve as further trigger topics for more worry, and a sense of uncontrollability over worry may develop in people caught in this cycle that occurs in GAD. As we have noted, perceptions of uncontrollability are also known to be associated with increased anxiety, so a vicious circle of anxiety, worry, and intrusive thoughts may develop (Mineka, 2004; Mineka et al., 2002; Mineka & Zinbarg, 2006).

COGNITIVE BIASES FOR THREATENING INFORMATION Not only do people with GAD have frequent frightening thoughts, they also process threatening information in a biased way, perhaps because they have prominent danger schemas. Many studies have shown that generally anxious people tend to preferentially allocate their attention toward threatening cues when both threat and nonthreat cues are present in the environment. Nonanxious people do not show a bias except under limited circumstances, in which they actually may show the opposite bias (see Bar-Haim et al., 2007; Mathews & MacLeod, 1994, 2005; Ouimet et al., 2009). Further, this attentional vigilance for threat cues can occur at a very early stage of information processing, even before the information has entered the person's conscious awareness. If a person is already anxious, having her or his attention automatically focused on threat cues in the environment would seem only to maintain the anxiety or even make it worse. Moreover, recent evidence also strongly supports the idea that such attentional biases play a causal role in anxiety as well (e.g., MacLeod et al., 2004; Mathews, 2006; Mathews & MacLeod, 2002). For example, several studies have shown that training nonanxious individuals to show an attentional bias toward threat leads to their showing a greater increase in anxiety in stressful situations (e.g., MacLeod et al., 2002). Conversely, several other studies have shown that training anxious individuals to attend away from threat leads to an decrease in their anxiety symptom levels (e.g., Amir et al., 2009).

Generally anxious people are also more likely than nonanxious people to think that bad things are likely to happen in the future (A. K. MacLeod, 1999), and they have a much stronger tendency to interpret ambiguous information in a threatening way. For example, when clinically anxious subjects read a series of ambiguous sentences (e.g., "The doctor examined little Emma's growth" or "They discussed the priest's convictions"), they are more likely than nonanxious controls to remember the threatening interpretation of each sentence (Eysenck et al., 1991; see also MacLeod et al., 2004; Mathews & MacLeod, 2005; Ouimet et al., 2009). This tendency to interpret ambiguous information negatively has actually been shown to increase anxiety in several situations, including watching a stressful video (Wilson et al., 2006).

In summary, several psychosocial variables seem to promote the onset of generalized anxiety as well as its maintenance. Experience with unpredictable and/or uncontrollable life events may create a vulnerability to anxiety and promote current anxiety. People also believe that worry serves a number of important functions, and it may actually be reinforced because it dampens physiological arousal. But worry also has some negative consequences, including the fact that worry begets further worry and creates a sense of perceived uncontrollability over the worry process, which further enhances anxiety. Finally, anxiety is associated with an automatic attentional and interpretive bias toward threatening information.

Biological Causal Factors

GENETIC FACTORS Although evidence for genetic factors in GAD is mixed, there does seem to be a modest heritability, although perhaps smaller than that for most other anxiety disorders except phobias (Hettema, Prescott, & Kendler, et al., 2001; Kendler et al., 1992a; Plomin et al., 2001). Part of the problem for research in this area has been the evolving nature of our understanding of GAD and what its diagnostic criteria should be. Several large twin studies reveal exactly how heritability estimates vary as a function of one's definition of GAD (Hettema, Neale, & Kendler, et al., 2001; Kendler et al., 1992a). The largest and most recent of these twin studies using the *DSM-IV-TR* diagnostic criteria estimate that 15 to 20 percent of the variance in liability to GAD is due to genetic factors.

The evidence is increasingly strong that GAD and major depressive disorder have a common underlying genetic predisposition (Kendler, 1996; Kendler et al., 1992d; Kendler et al., 2007). What determines whether individuals with a genetic risk for GAD and/or major depression develop one or the other disorder seems to depend entirely on the specific environmental experiences they have (nonshared environment). At least part of this common genetic predisposition for GAD and major depression is best conceptualized as the basic personality trait commonly known as neuroticism (e.g., Clark, Watson, & Mineka, 1994; Hettema et al., 2004; Kendler et al., 2007; Mineka et al., 1998).

NEUROTRANSMITTER AND NEUROHORMONAL ABNORMALITIES

A Functional Deficiency in GABA In the 1950s the benzodiazepine category of medications was found to reduce anxiety. This discovery was followed in the 1970s by the finding that these drugs probably exert their effects by stimulating the action of GABA, a neurotransmitter now strongly implicated in generalized anxiety (Davis, 2002; LeDoux, 2002; Nutt et al., 2006). It appears that highly anxious people have a kind of functional deficiency in GABA, which ordinarily plays an important role in the way our brain inhibits anxiety in stressful situations. The benzodiazepine drugs appear to reduce anxiety by increasing GABA activity in certain parts of the brain implicated in anxiety, such as the limbic system, and by suppressing the stress hormone cortisol. Whether the functional deficiency in GABA in anxious people causes their anxiety or occurs as a consequence of it is not yet known, but it does appear that this functional deficiency promotes the maintenance of anxiety.

More recently, researchers have discovered that another neurotransmitter—serotonin—is also involved in modulating generalized anxiety (Goodman, 2004; Nutt et al., 2006). At present, it seems that GABA, serotonin, and perhaps norepinephrine all play a role in anxiety, but the ways in which they interact remain largely unknown (LeDoux, 2002).

The Corticotropin-Releasing Hormone System and Anxiety

An anxiety-producing hormone called corticotropin-releasing hormone (CRH) has also been strongly implicated as playing an important role in generalized anxiety (and depression; Leonardo & Hen, 2006; Maier & Watkins, 2005). When activated by stress or perceived threat, CRH stimulates the release of ACTH (adrenocorticotropic hormone) from the pituitary gland, which in turn causes release of the stress hormone cortisol from the adrenal gland (Leonardo & Hen, 2006); cortisol helps the body deal with stress. The CRH hormone may play an important role in generalized anxiety through its effects on the bed nucleus of the *stria terminalis* (an extension of the amygdala; see Figure 1), which is now believed to be an important brain area mediating generalized anxiety (e.g., Davis, 2006; Lang et al., 2000).

NEUROBIOLOGICAL DIFFERENCES BETWEEN ANXIETY AND PANIC

As we noted earlier, contemporary theorists are drawing several fundamental distinctions between fear, panic, and anxiety, including their neurobiological bases. Fear and panic involve activation of the fight-or-flight response, and the brain areas and neurotransmitters that seem most strongly implicated in these emotional responses are the amygdala (and locus coeruleus) and the neurotransmitters norepinephrine and serotonin. Generalized anxiety (or anxious apprehension) is a more diffuse emotional state involving arousal and a preparation for possible impending threat; and the brain area, neurotransmitters, and hormones that seem most strongly implicated are the limbic system (especially the bed nucleus of the stria terminalis, an extension of the amygdala), GABA, and CRH (Davis, 2006; Lang et al., 2000). Although serotonin may play a role in both anxiety and panic, it probably does so in somewhat different ways.

Treatments

MEDICATIONS

Many clients with generalized anxiety disorder consult family physicians, seeking relief from their "nerves" or anxieties or their various functional (psychogenic) physical problems. Most often in such cases, medications from the benzodiazepine (anxiolytic) category such as Xanax or Klonopin are used—and misused—for tension relief, reduction of other somatic symptoms, and relaxation. Their effects on worry and other psychological symptoms are not as great. Moreover, they can create physiological and psychological dependence and withdrawal and are therefore difficult to taper. A newer medication called buspirone (from a different medication category) is also effective, and it neither is sedating nor leads to physiological dependence. It also has greater effects on psychic anxiety than do the benzodiazepines. However, it may take 2 to 4 weeks to show results (Roy-Byrne & Cowley, 2002, 2007). Several categories of antidepressant medications like those used in the treatment of panic disorder are also useful in the treatment of GAD, and they also seem to have a greater effect on the psychological symptoms of GAD than do the benzodiazepines (Goodman, 2004; Roy-Byrne & Cowley, 2002, 2007). However, they also take several weeks before their effects are realized.

COGNITIVE-BEHAVIORAL TREATMENT

Cognitive-behavioral therapy (CBT) for generalized anxiety disorder has become increasingly effective as clinical researchers have refined the techniques used. It usually involves a combination of behavioral techniques, such as training in applied muscle relaxation, and cognitive restructuring techniques aimed at reducing distorted cognitions and information-processing biases associated with GAD as well as reducing catastrophizing about minor events (Barlow, Allen, & Basden, 2007; Borkovec, 2006; Borkovec et al., 2002). GAD initially appeared to be among the most difficult of the anxiety disorders to treat, and to some extent this is still true. However, advances have been made, and a quantitative review of many controlled studies showed that CBT approaches resulted in large changes on most symptoms measured (Mitte, 2005). The magnitude of the changes seen with cognitive-behavioral treatment was at least as large as those seen with benzodiazepines, and it led to fewer dropouts (i.e., it was better tolerated). Finally, CBT has also been found to be useful in helping people who have used benzodiazepines for over a year to successfully taper their medications (Gosselin et al., 2006).

case study   CBT for John's GAD

The case of John, the graduate student with GAD discussed earlier, serves as an example of the success of cognitive-behavioral therapy with this condition. Before receiving cognitive-behavioral therapy, John had seen someone at a student counseling center for several months, but he hadn't found the "talk therapy" very useful. He had heard that cognitive-behavioral therapy might be useful and had sought such treatment. He was in treatment for about 6 months, during which time he found training in deep muscle relaxation helpful in reducing his overall level of tension. Cognitive restructuring helped reduce his worry levels about all spheres of his life. He still had problems with procrastinating when he had deadlines, but this too was improving. He also began socializing more frequently and had tentatively begun dating when treatment ended for financial reasons. He could now see that if a woman didn't want to go out with him again, this did not mean that he was boring but simply that they might not be a good match.

In Review

- What are the key characteristics of GAD, and what is its typical age of onset?

- Describe the various psychosocial causal factors that may be involved in GAD, and indicate what functions worry may serve for those with GAD.

- What are the major biological causal factors in GAD?

- Compare and contrast the biological and cognitive-behavioral treatments for GAD.

Obsessive-Compulsive Disorder

Diagnostically, **obsessive-compulsive disorder (OCD)** is defined by the occurrence of unwanted and intrusive obsessive thoughts or distressing images; these are usually accompanied by compulsive behaviors performed to neutralize the obsessive thoughts or images or to prevent some dreaded event or situation (see the *DSM-IV-TR* box). More specifically, according to *DSM-IV-TR*, **obsessions** involve persistent and recurrent intrusive thoughts, images, or impulses that are experienced as disturbing, inappropriate, and uncontrollable. People who have such obsessions actively try to resist or suppress them or to neutralize them with some other thought or action. **Compulsions** can involve either overt repetitive behaviors that are performed as lengthy rituals (such as hand washing, checking, or ordering over and over again) or more covert mental rituals (such as counting, praying, or saying certain words silently over and over again). A person with OCD usually feels driven to perform this compulsive,

ritualistic behavior in response to an obsession, and there are often very rigid rules regarding how the compulsive behavior should be performed. The compulsive behaviors are performed with the goal of preventing or reducing distress or preventing some dreaded event or situation. OCD is often one of the most disabling mental disorders in that it leads to a lower quality of life and a great deal of functional impairment (Stein et al., 2009).

In addition, the person must recognize that the obsession is the product of his or her own mind rather than being imposed from without (as might occur in schizophrenia). However, there is a continuum of "insight" among persons with obsessive-compulsive disorder about exactly how senseless and excessive their obsessions and compulsions are (Mathews, 2008; Ruscio et al., 2010). In a minority of cases, this insight is absent most of the time. Most of us have experienced minor obsessive thoughts, such as whether we remembered to lock the door or turn the stove off. In addition, most of us occasionally engage in repetitive or stereotyped behavior, such as checking the stove or the lock on the door or stepping over cracks on a sidewalk

DSM-IV-TR

Criteria for Obsessive-Compulsive Disorder

A. Either obsessions or compulsions:

Obsessions as defined by (1), (2), (3), and (4):

1. Recurrent and persistent thoughts, impulses, or images that are experienced, at some time during the disturbance, as intrusive and inappropriate and that cause marked anxiety or distress
2. The thoughts, impulses, or images are not simply excessive worries about real-life problems
3. The person attempts to ignore or suppress such thoughts, impulses, or images, or to neutralize them with some other thought or action
4. The person recognizes that the obsessional thoughts, impulses, or images are a product of his or her own mind (not imposed from without as in thought insertion)

Compulsions as defined by (1) and (2):

1. Repetitive behaviors (e.g., hand washing, ordering, checking) or mental acts (e.g., praying, counting, repeating words silently) that the person feels driven to perform in response to an obsession, or according to rules that must be applied rigidly
2. The behaviors or mental acts are aimed at preventing or reducing distress or preventing some dreaded event or situation; however, these behaviors or mental acts either are not connected in a realistic way with what they are designed to neutralize or prevent or are clearly excessive

B. At some point during the course of the disorder, the person has recognized that the obsessions or compulsions are excessive or unreasonable. Note: This does not apply to children.
C. The obsessions or compulsions cause marked distress, are time consuming (take more than 1 hour a day), or significantly interfere with the person's normal routine, occupational (or academic) functioning, or usual social activities or relationships.
D. If another Axis I disorder is present, the content of the obsessions or compulsions is not restricted to it (e.g., preoccupation with food in the presence of an Eating Disorder; hair pulling in the presence of Trichotillomania; concern with appearance in the presence of Body Dysmorphic Disorder; preoccupation with drugs in the presence of a Substance Use Disorder; preoccupation with having a serious illness in the presence of Hypochondriasis; preoccupation with sexual urges or fantasies in the presence of a Paraphilia; or guilty ruminations in the presence of Major Depressive Disorder).
E. The disturbance is not due to the direct physiological effects of a substance (e.g., a drug of abuse, a medication) or a general medical condition.

Source: Reprinted with permission from the American Psychiatric Association. *Diagnostic and Statistical Manual of Mental Disorders*, Fourth Edition, *Text Revision* (Copyright © 2000). American Psychiatric Association.

People who suffer from OCD often exhibit repetitive behaviors that are structured around rigid rules for performance. For example, this person turns the key in the lock a set number of times every time she leaves the house.

thoughts involving themes of violence or aggression might include a wife being obsessed with the idea that she might poison her husband or child, or a daughter constantly imagining pushing her mother down a flight of stairs. Even though such obsessive thoughts are only very rarely carried out, they remain a source of often excruciating torment to a person plagued with them, such as Mark in the case study who had a fairly typical case of severe obsessive-compulsive disorder.

As we have noted, people with OCD feel compelled to perform acts repeatedly that often seem pointless and absurd even to them and that they in some sense do not want to perform. There are five primary types of compulsive rituals: cleaning (handwashing and showering), repeated checking, repeating, ordering or arranging, and counting (Antony et al., 1998; Mathews, 2009), and many people show multiple kinds of rituals. For a smaller number of people, the compulsions are to perform various everyday acts (such as eating or dressing) extremely slowly (primary obsessional slowness), and for others the compulsions are to have things exactly symmetrical or "evened up" (Mathews, 2009; Steketee & Barlow, 2002). Hoarding is another form of compulsive behavior that has only recently received much research attention (see "Unresolved Issues" at the end).

(e.g., Pallanti, 2009). With OCD, however, the thoughts are excessive and much more persistent and distressing, and the associated compulsive acts interfere considerably with everyday activities. Indeed, the diagnosis requires that obsessions and compulsions must take at least 1 hour in a day, and in severe cases they may take most of the person's waking hours. Nevertheless, research indicates that normal and abnormal obsessions and compulsive behaviors exist on a continuum, differing primarily in the frequency and intensity of the obsessions and in the degrees to which the obsessions and compulsions are resisted and are troubling (e.g., Steketee & Barlow, 2002). Indeed, one recent study found that more than 25 percent of people in the NCS-R comorbidity study reported experiencing obsessions or compulsions at some time in their lives (Ruscio et al., 2010).

Obsessive thoughts consist most often of contamination fears, fears of harming oneself or others, and pathological doubt. Other fairly common themes are concerns about or need for symmetry, sexual obsessions, and obsessions concerning religion or aggression. These themes are quite consistent cross-culturally and across the life span (Pallanti, 2009; Steketee & Barlow, 2002). Obsessive

Howard Stern, as with other people who have suffered from OCD, found relief in a compulsive act or ritualized series of acts to bring about a feeling of reduced tension as well as a sense of control. In his book *Miss America*, Stern describes behaviors such as turning pages in magazines only with his pinky finger, walking through doors with the right side of his body leading, and flipping through television stations in a particular order before turning the set off.

Washing or cleaning rituals vary from relatively mild ritual-like behavior such as spending 15 to 20 minutes washing one's hands after going to the bathroom, to more extreme behavior such as washing one's hands with disinfectants for hours every day to the point where the hands bleed. Checking rituals also vary in severity from relatively mild (such as checking all the lights, appliances, and locks two or three times before leaving the house) to very extreme (such as going back to an intersection where one thinks one may have run over a pedestrian and spending hours checking for any sign of the imagined accident, much as Mark does in the case study). Both cleaning and checking rituals are often performed a specific number of times and thus also involve repetitive counting. The performance of the compulsive act or the ritualized series of acts usually brings a feeling of reduced tension and satisfaction, as well as a sense of control, although this anxiety relief is typically fleeting, which is why the same rituals need to be repeated over and over (e.g., Purdon, 2009; Steketee & Barlow, 2002).

case study · Obsessions about Confessing and Compulsive Checking

Mark was a 28-year-old single male who, at the time he entered treatment, suffered from severe obsessive thoughts and images about causing harm to others such as running over pedestrians while he was driving. He also had severe obsessions that he would commit a crime such as robbing a store of a large amount of money or poisoning family members or friends. These obsessions were accompanied by lengthy and excessive checking rituals. For example, one day when he drove, he began obsessing that he had caused an accident and hit a pedestrian at an intersection, and he felt compelled to spend several hours driving and walking around all parts of that intersection to find evidence of the accident.

At the time Mark went to an anxiety disorder clinic, he was no longer able to live by himself after having lived alone for several years since college. He was a very bright young man with considerable artistic talent. He had finished college at a prestigious school for the arts and had launched a successful career as a young artist when the obsessions began in his early 20s. At first they were focused on the possibility that he would be implicated in some crime that he had not committed; later they evolved to the point where he was afraid that he might actually commit

a crime and confess to it. The checking rituals and avoidance of all places where such confessions might occur eventually led to his having to give up his career and his own apartment and move back in with his family.

At the time he presented for treatment, Mark's obsessions about harming others and confessing to crimes (whether or not he had committed them) were so severe that he had virtually confined himself to his room at his parents' house. Indeed, he could leave his room only if he had a tape recorder with him so that he would have a record of any crimes he confessed to out loud because he did not trust his own memory. The clinic was several hours' drive from his home; his mother usually had to drive because of his obsessions about causing accidents with pedestrians or moving vehicles and because the associated checking rituals could punctuate any trip with several very long stops. He also could not speak at all on the phone for fear of confessing some crime that he had (or had not) committed, and he could not mail a letter for the same reason. He also could not go into a store alone or into public bathrooms, where he feared he might write a confession on the wall and be caught and punished.

Many of us show some compulsive behavior, but people with obsessive-compulsive disorder feel compelled to perform repeatedly some action in response to an obsession, in order to reduce the anxiety or discomfort created by the obsession. Although the person may realize that the behavior is excessive or unreasonable, he or she does not feel able to control the urge. Obsessive-compulsive hand washers may spend hours a day washing and may even use abrasive cleansers to the point that their hands bleed.

Prevalence, Age of Onset, and Gender Differences

Obsessive-compulsive disorder is more prevalent than it was once thought to be, although it is still considerably less prevalent than the other anxiety disorders. Specifically, the average 1-year prevalence rate of OCD in the National Comorbidity Survey-Replication study was 1.2 percent, and the average lifetime prevalence was 2.3 percent (Ruscio et al., 2010) although lifetime prevalence in other studies has been as high as 3 percent (Kessler et al., 2009). Over 90 percent of treatment-seeking

people with OCD experience both obsessions and compulsions (Foa & Kozak, 1995; Franklin & Foa, 2007). When mental rituals and compulsions such as counting are included as compulsive behaviors, this figure jumps to 98 percent.

Divorced (or separated) and unemployed people are somewhat overrepresented among people with OCD (Karno et al., 1988; Torres et al., 2006), which is not surprising given the great difficulties this disorder creates for interpersonal and occupational functioning. Some studies showed little or no gender difference in adults, which would make OCD quite different from most of the rest of the anxiety disorders. However, one British epidemiological study found a gender ratio of 1.4 to 1 (women to men; Torres et al., 2006). Although the disorder generally begins in late adolescence or early adulthood and is most prevalent then (e.g., average age was 19.5 in the National Comorbidity Survey-Replication study), it is not uncommon in children, where its symptoms are strikingly similar to those of adults (Poulton et al., 2009; Torres et al., 2006). Childhood or early adolescent onset is more common in boys than in girls and is often associated with greater severity (Lomax et al., 2009) and greater heritability (Grisham et al., 2008, for a review). In most cases the disorder has a gradual onset, and once it becomes a serious condition, it tends to be chronic, although the severity of symptoms sometimes wax and wane over time (e.g., Mataix-Cols et al., 2002; Poulton et al., 2008).

Comorbidity with Other Disorders

Like all the anxiety disorders, obsessive-compulsive disorder frequently co-occurs with other mood and anxiety disorders. Depression is especially common, and estimates are that at least 25 to 50 percent of people with OCD may experience major depression at some time in their lives and as many as 80 percent may experience significant depressive symptoms (Steketee & Barlow, 2002; Torres et al., 2006). Given the chronic and debilitating nature of this disorder, it may not be surprising that many develop depression at least partly in response to having OCD. The anxiety disorders with which OCD most often co-occurs include social phobia, panic disorder, GAD, and PTSD (Kessler, Chiu, Demler, et al., 2005c; Mathews, 2009). The personality disorders most commonly found in people with OCD are dependent and avoidant.

Another related disorder (currently in the somatoform category) that has been studied extensively only in the past 15 years—body dysmorphic disorder (BDD)—also co-occurs rather commonly with OCD. In one large study, 12 percent of patients with OCD also had body dysmorphic disorder, which many researchers believe to be a closely related disorder (e.g., Phillips, 2000, 2005; Phillips et al., 2007; Veale & Neziroglu, 2004). Indeed researchers working on the new version of *DSM-V* are seriously considering whether to include in *DSM-V* a group of so-called OCD spectrum disorders, and BDD is considered to be perhaps the most closely related to OCD (Phillips et al., 2010).

Psychological Causal Factors

OCD AS LEARNED BEHAVIOR The dominant behavioral or learning view of obsessive-compulsive disorder is derived from Mowrer's two-process theory of avoidance learning (1947). According to this theory, neutral stimuli become associated with frightening thoughts or experiences through classical conditioning and come to elicit anxiety. For example, touching a doorknob or shaking hands might become associated with the "scary" idea of contamination. Once having made this association, the person may discover that the anxiety produced by shaking hands or touching a doorknob can be reduced by hand washing. Washing his or her hands extensively reduces the anxiety, and so the washing response is reinforced, which makes it more likely to occur again in the future when other situations evoke anxiety about contamination (Rachman & Shafran, 1998). Once learned, such avoidance responses are extremely resistant to extinction (Mineka, 2004; Mineka & Zinbarg, 1996, 2006; Salkovskis & Kirk, 1997). Moreover, any stressors that raise anxiety levels can lead to a heightened frequency of avoidance responses in animals or compulsive rituals in humans (e.g., Cromer et al., 2007).

Several classic experiments conducted by Rachman and Hodgson (1980) supported this theory. They found that for most people with OCD, exposure to a situation that provoked their obsession (e.g., a doorknob or toilet seat for someone with obsessions about contamination) did indeed produce distress, which would continue for a moderate amount of time and then gradually dissipate. If the person was allowed to engage in the compulsive ritual immediately after the provocation, however, her or his anxiety would generally decrease rapidly (although only temporarily) and therefore reinforce the compulsive ritual.

This model predicts, then, that exposure to feared objects or situations should be useful in treating OCD if the exposure is followed by prevention of the ritual, enabling the person to see that the anxiety will subside naturally in time without the ritual (see also Rachman & Shafran, 1998). This is indeed the core of the most effective form of behavior therapy for OCD, as discussed later. Thus the early behavioral model has been very useful in helping us understand what factors maintain obsessive-compulsive behavior, and it has also generated an effective form of treatment. However, it has not been so helpful in explaining why people with OCD develop obsessions in the first place and why some people never develop compulsive behaviors.

OCD AND PREPAREDNESS Just as the preparedness concept has us consider specific and social phobias in the evolutionary context of fears that may have been adaptive for our early ancestors, we have also enlarged our understanding of obsessive-compulsive disorder by looking at it in an evolutionary context (e.g., De Silva, Rachman, & Seligman, 1977; Rapoport, 1989). For example, thoughts about dirt and contamination associated with compulsive washing are so common as to make their occurrence seem nonrandom. The overall consensus seems to be that humans' obsessions about dirt and contamination and certain other potentially dangerous situations did not arise out of a vacuum but rather have deep evolutionary roots (Mineka & Zinbarg, 1996, 2006).

In addition, some theorists have argued that the displacement activities that many species of animals engage in under situations of conflict or high arousal resemble the compulsive rituals seen in obsessive-compulsive disorder (Craske, 1999; Mineka & Zinbarg, 1996; Rapoport, 1989; Winslow & Insel, 1991). Displacement activities often involve grooming (such as a bird preening its feathers) or nesting under conditions of high conflict or frustration. They may therefore be related to the distress-induced grooming (such as washing) or tidying rituals seen in people with OCD, which are often provoked by obsessive thoughts that elicit anxiety.

COGNITIVE CAUSAL FACTORS

The Effects of Attempting to Suppress Obsessive Thoughts When normal people attempt to suppress unwanted thoughts (for example, "Don't think about white bears"), they may sometimes experience a paradoxical increase in those thoughts later (Abramowitz et al., 2001; Wegner, 1994). As already noted, people with normal and abnormal obsessions differ primarily in the degree to which they resist their own thoughts and find them unacceptable. Thus one factor contributing to the frequency of obsessive thoughts, and the negative moods with which they are often associated, may be these attempts to suppress them (similar to what was discussed earlier about the effects of attempts to control worry in people with GAD). For example, when people with OCD were asked to record intrusive thoughts in a diary, both on days when they were told to try to suppress those thoughts and on days without instructions to suppress, they reported approximately twice as many intrusive thoughts on the days when they were attempting to suppress them (Salkovskis & Kirk, 1997). In addition, some other research suggests that thought suppression leads to a more general increase in obsessive-compulsive symptoms beyond just the frequency of obsessions (Purdon,

2004). Finally, using a naturalistic diary study of people with OCD, investigators found that such individuals do indeed engage in frequent, strenuous, and time-consuming attempts to control the intrusive thoughts, although they are generally not effective in doing so (Purdon et al., 2007).

Appraisals of Responsibility for Intrusive Thoughts Salkovskis (e.g., 1989), Rachman (1997), and other cognitive theorists have distinguished between obsessive or intrusive thoughts per se and the negative automatic thoughts and catastrophic appraisals that people have about experiencing such thoughts. For example, people with OCD often seem to have an inflated sense of responsibility. In turn, in some vulnerable people, this inflated sense of responsibility can be associated with beliefs that simply having a thought about doing something (e.g., attacking a patient) is morally equivalent to actually having done it (e.g., having attacked a patient), or that thinking about committing a sin increases the chances of actually doing so. This is known as *thought–action fusion* (see Berle & Starcevic, 2005; Rachman et al., 2006; Shafran & Rachman, 2004, for reviews). This inflated sense of responsibility for the harm they may cause adds to the "perceived awfulness of any harmful consequences" (Salkovskis et al., 2000, p. 348) and also may motivate compulsive behaviors such as washing and checking to try to reduce the likelihood of anything harmful happening (Rachman et al., 2006). Thus, part of what differentiates normal people who have obsessions and can ordinarily dismiss them (without a perception of responsibility) from people with OCD is this sense of responsibility that makes the thought so "awful."

Cognitive Biases and Distortions Cognitive factors have also been implicated in obsessive-compulsive disorder. Research on people with OCD has shown that their attention is drawn to disturbing material relevant to their obsessive concerns, much as occurs in the other anxiety disorders (see McNally, 2000; Mineka et al., 2003, for reviews). People with OCD also seem to have difficulty blocking out negative, irrelevant input or distracting information, so they may attempt to suppress negative thoughts stimulated by this information (Enright & Beech, 1993a, 1993b; McNally, 2000). As we have noted, trying to suppress negative thoughts may paradoxically increase their frequency. These people also have low confidence in their memory ability (especially for situations they feel responsible for), which may contribute to their repeating their ritualistic behaviors over and over again (Cougle et al., 2007; Dar et al., 2000; McNally, 2000). An additional factor contributing to their repetitive behavior is that people with OCD have deficits in their ability to inhibit both motor responses (Morein-Zamir et al., 2010) and irrelevant information (Bannon et al., 2008).

Biological Causal Factors

In the past 25 years there has been a large increase in research investigating the possible biological basis for obsessive-compulsive disorder, ranging from studies about its genetic basis to studies of abnormalities in brain function and neurotransmitter abnormalities. The evidence accumulating from all three kinds of studies suggests that biological causal factors are perhaps more strongly implicated in the causes of OCD than in any of the other anxiety disorders.

GENETIC FACTORS Most genetic studies have been twin studies or family studies. Evidence from twin studies reveals a moderately high concordance rate for monozygotic twins and a lower rate for dizygotic twins. One review of 14 published studies included 80 monozygotic pairs of twins, of whom 54 were concordant for the diagnosis of OCD, and 29 pairs of dizygotic twins, of whom 9 were concordant. This is consistent with a moderate genetic heritability, although it may be at least partially a nonspecific "neurotic" predisposition (Billett, Richter, & Kennedy, 1998; Hanna, 2000; see also van Grootheest et al., 2007). Consistent with twin studies, most family studies have found 3 to 12 times higher rates of OCD in first-degree relatives of OCD clients than would be expected from current estimates of the prevalence of OCD (Grabe et al., 2006; Hettema et al., 2001a). Finally, evidence also shows that early-onset OCD has a higher genetic loading than later-onset OCD (Grisham et al., 2008; Mundo et al., 2006).

Further compelling evidence of a genetic contribution to some forms of OCD is for one type of OCD that often starts in childhood and is characterized by chronic motor tics (Lochner & Stein, 2003). This form of tic-related OCD is linked to Tourette's syndrome, a disorder characterized by severe chronic motor and vocal tics that is known to have a substantial genetic basis. For example, one study found that 23 percent of first-degree relatives of people with Tourette's syndrome had diagnosable OCD even though Tourette's syndrome itself is very rare (Pauls et al., 1986, 1991, 1995).

Finally, in recent years a number of molecular genetic studies have begun to examine the association of OCD with specific genetic polymorphisms (naturally occurring variations of genes; e.g., Grisham et al., 2008; Mundo et al., 2006; Stewart et al., 2007). Preliminary findings suggest that different genetic polymorphisms are implicated in OCD with Tourette's syndrome and in OCD without Tourette's syndrome, suggesting that these two forms of OCD are at least partially distinguishable at a genetic level (Stewart et al., 2007).

OCD AND THE BRAIN The search for abnormalities in the brain for OCD has been intense in the past 30 years as advances have been made in brain-imaging techniques. Research has found that abnormalities occur primarily in certain cortical structures as well as in certain subcortical structures known as the *basal ganglia*. The basal ganglia are in turn linked at the amygdala to the limbic system, which controls emotional behaviors. Findings from a good number of studies using PET scans have shown that people with OCD have abnormally high levels of activity in two parts of the frontal cortex (the orbital frontal cortex and the cingulate cortex/gyrus), which are also linked to the limbic area. People with OCD also have abnormally high levels of activity in the subcortical caudate nucleus, which is part of the basal ganglia (see the three-dimensional depiction of the relevant brain parts in Figure 3). These primitive brain circuits are involved in executing primitive patterns of behavior such as those involved in sex, aggression, and hygiene concerns. Indeed, activity in some of these areas is further increased when symptoms are provoked by relevant stimuli that activate obsessive thoughts (e.g., dirt; see Evans , Lewis, & lobst, 2004; Rauch & Savage, 2000, for reviews). Some of these studies have also shown partial normalization of at least some of these abnormalities with successful

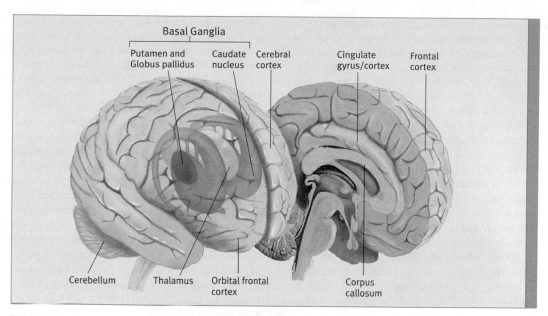

FIGURE 3

Neurophysiological Mechanisms for Obsessive-Compulsive Disorder

This three-dimensional view illustrates parts of the brain implicated in OCD. The overlying cerebral cortex has been made transparent so that the underlying areas can be seen. The orbital frontal cortex, cingulate cortex/gyrus, and basal ganglia (especially the caudate nucleus) are the brain structures most often implicated in OCD. Increased metabolic activity has been found in each of these three areas in people with OCD.

treatment through either medication or behavior therapy (Baxter et al., 2000; Saxena et al., 2002; Saxena et al., 2009).

The orbital frontal cortex seems to be where primitive urges regarding sex, aggression, hygiene, and danger come from (the "stuff of obsessions"; Baxter et al., 1991, p. 116). These urges are ordinarily filtered by the caudate nucleus as they travel through the cortico-basal-ganglionic-thalamic circuit, allowing only the strongest to pass on to the thalamus. The caudate nucleus or corpus striatum (part of the set of structures called the basal ganglia, which are involved in the execution of voluntary, goal-directed movements) is part of an important neural circuit linking the orbital frontal cortex to the thalamus. The basal ganglia also include two other structures—the globus pallidus and the substantia nigra— that are also involved in this cortico-basal-ganglionic-thalamic circuit. The thalamus is an important relay station that receives nearly all sensory input and passes it back to the cerebral cortex.

This cortico-basal-ganglionic-thalamic circuit is normally involved in the preparation of complex sets of interrelated behavioral responses used in specific situations such as those involved in territorial or social concerns. Several theories have been proposed regarding what the sources of dysfunction in this circuit are. For example, Baxter and colleagues (1991, 2000) cite evidence that when this circuit is not functioning properly, inappropriate behavioral responses may occur, including repeated sets of behaviors stemming from territorial and social concerns (e.g., checking and aggressive behavior) and from hygiene concerns (e.g., cleaning). Thus the overactivation of the orbital frontal cortex, which

stimulates "the stuff of obsessions," combined with a dysfunctional interaction among the orbital frontal cortex, the corpus striatum or caudate nucleus, and the thalamus (which is downstream from the corpus striatum) may be the central component of the brain dysfunction in OCD. According to Baxter's theory, the dysfunctions in this circuit in turn prevent people with OCD from showing the normal inhibition of sensations, thoughts, and behaviors that would occur if the circuit were functioning properly. In this case, impulses toward aggression, sex, hygiene, and danger that most people keep under control with relative ease "leak through" as obsessions and distract people with OCD from ordinary goal-directed behavior. Evidence suggests that at least part of the reason that this circuit does not function properly may be due to abnormalities in white matter in some of these brain areas; white matter is involved in connectivity between various brain structures (Szeszko et al., 2004; Yoo et al., 2007).

Considering these problems, Baxter and colleagues proposed that we can begin to understand how the prolonged and repeated bouts of obsessive-compulsive behavior in people with OCD may occur (Baxter et al., 1991, 1992, 2000). Several other slightly different theories have also been proposed as to the exact nature or source of the dysfunctions, but there seems to be general agreement about most of the brain areas involved (e.g., Friedlander & Desrocher, 2006; Harrison et al., 2009; Saxena & Rauch, 2000).

NEUROTRANSMITTER ABNORMALITIES Pharmacological studies of causal factors in obsessive-compulsive disorder intensified with the discovery in the 1970s that a tricyclic drug called Anafranil (clomipramine) is often effective in the treatment of

OCD even though other tricyclic antidepressants are generally not very effective (Dougherty et al., 2007). Research shows that this is because clomipramine has greater effects on the neurotransmitter serotonin, which is now strongly implicated in OCD (Pogarell et al., 2003; Stewart et al., 2009). Moreover, several other antidepressant drugs from the SSRI category that also have relatively selective effects on serotonin, such as fluoxetine (Prozac), have also been shown to be about equally effective in the treatment of OCD (Dougherty, Rauch, et al., 2002, 2007).

The exact nature of the dysfunction in serotonergic systems in OCD is unclear (see Gross, et al., 1998; Lambert & Kinsley, 2005). Current evidence suggests that increased serotonin activity and increased sensitivity of some brain structures to serotonin are involved in OCD symptoms. Indeed, drugs that stimulate serotonergic systems lead to a worsening of symptoms. In this view, long-term administration of clomipramine (or fluoxetine) causes a down-regulation of certain serotonin receptors, further causing a functional decrease in availability of serotonin (Dolberg et al., 1996a, 1996b). That is, although the immediate short-term effects of clomipramine or fluoxetine may be to increase serotonin levels (and exacerbate OCD symptoms too), the long-term effects are quite different. This is consistent with the finding that these drugs must be taken for at least 6 to 12 weeks before significant improvement in OCD symptoms occurs (Baxter et al., 2000; Dougherty, Rauch, et al., 2002, 2007). However, it is also becoming clear that dysfunction in serotonergic systems cannot by itself fully explain this complex disorder. Other neurotransmitter systems (such as the dopaminergic, GABA, and glutamate systems) also seem to be involved, although their role is not yet well understood (Dougherty et al., 2007; Stewart et al., 2009).

In summary, there is now a substantial body of evidence implicating biological causal factors in OCD. This evidence comes from genetic studies, from studies of abnormalities in brain function, and from studies of neurotransmitter abnormalities. Although the exact nature of these factors and how they are interrelated is not yet fully understood, major research efforts that are currently under way are sure to enhance our understanding of this very serious and disabling disorder.

Treatments

BEHAVIORAL AND COGNITIVE-BEHAVIORAL TREATMENTS

A behavioral treatment that combines **exposure and response prevention** seems be the most effective approach to treating obsessive-compulsive disorders (e.g., Franklin & Foa, 2002, 2007; Stein et al., 2009). This treatment involves having the OCD clients develop a hierarchy of upsetting stimuli and rate them on a 0 to 100 scale according to their capacity to evoke anxiety, distress, or disgust. Then the clients are asked to expose themselves repeatedly (either in guided fantasy or directly) to stimuli that will provoke their obsession (such as, for someone with compulsive washing rituals, touching the bottom of their shoe or a toilet seat in a public bathroom). Following each exposure, they are asked to not engage in the rituals that they ordinarily would engage in to reduce the anxiety or distress provoked by their obsession. Preventing the rituals is essential so that they can see that if they allow enough time to pass, the anxiety created by the obsession will dissipate naturally down to at least 40 to 50 on the 100-point scale, even if this takes several hours.

In intensive versions of this treatment, clients who, for example, are used to spending 2 to 3 hours a day showering and hand washing may be asked to not shower at all for 3 days at a time (and then only for 10 minutes). Later in treatment they are encouraged to shower for only 10 minutes a day, with no more than five 30-second hand washings at mealtimes, after bathroom use, and after touching clearly soiled objects. In addition to the exposures conducted during therapy sessions, "homework" is liberally assigned. For example, on one occasion well into treatment, a therapist drove a patient who was terrified of being contaminated by "dog dirt," bathroom germs, garbage, and dead animals in the road to a place where she had observed a dead cat on the roadside. The therapist insisted that the patient approach the "smelly" corpse, touch it with the sole of her shoe, and then touch her shoe. A pebble lying close by and a stick with which she had touched the cat were presented to the patient with the instruction that she keep them in her pocket and touch them frequently throughout the day. (See Franklin & Foa, 2008, pp. 192–205).

Although some people refuse such treatment or drop out early, it does help a majority of clients who stick with the treatment, most of whom show a 50 to 70 percent reduction in symptoms (Abramowitz et al., 2009; Steketee, 1993), as well as improvement in quality of life (Diefenbach et al., 2007). About 50 percent are much improved or very much improved, and another 25 percent are moderately improved; about 76 percent maintain their gains at several-year follow-ups. These results are considered superior to those obtained with medication (Abramowitz et al., 2009; Franklin & Foa, 2008). There is also preliminary evidence that d-cycloserine (the drug known to facilitate extinction of fear) can decrease the number of sessions of exposure and response prevention that are needed, similar to results described earlier for specific phobias (Wilhelm et al., 2009). Finally, over the past 20 years a form of cognitive-behavioral therapy has also been developed by Salkovskis and colleagues (e.g., Abramowitz et al., 2009; Salkovskis & Wahl, 2003). Some of the goals were to determine whether it might help a higher percentage of people with OCD, or help increase the degree of symptom improvement, or decrease dropout rates. Current evidence suggests that this form of treatment can also be quite effective, but unfortunately it has not been shown to be superior to exposure and response prevention therapy in any of the predicted ways (see Abramowitz et al., 2009; D. A. Clark, 2005, for reviews). Moreover, some researchers have concluded that extinction and response-prevention treatment is probably enhanced by some cognitive therapy (Abramowitz et al., 2009). Given that OCD rarely remits completely, leaving the client with some residual obsessional problems or rituals (Abramowitz et al., 2009; Franklin & Foa, 2007), there is clearly a need to improve further the efficacy of these treatments.

The successful use of this exposure and response prevention treatment in the case of Mark, the young artist with severe OCD, is described here briefly.

case study **Mark's Treatment**

Mark was initially treated with medication and with exposure and response prevention. He found the side effects of the medication (clomipramine) intolerable and gave it up within a few weeks. For the behavioral treatment, he was directed to get rid of the tape recorder and was given a series of exercises in which he exposed himself to feared situations where he might confess to a crime or cause harm to others, including making phone calls, mailing letters, and entering stores and public bathrooms (all things he had been unable to do). Checking rituals (including the tape recorder) were prevented. Although the initial round of treatment was not especially helpful, in part because of difficulty in getting to treatment, he did eventually make a commitment to more intensive treatment by moving to a small apartment closer to the clinic. Thereafter, he did quite well.

MEDICATIONS To date, medications that affect the neurotransmitter serotonin seem to be the primary class of medication that has reasonably good effects in treating persons with OCD. The other anxiety and mood disorders respond to a wider range of drugs (Bartz & Hollander, 2007; Dougherty, Baer, et al., 2002; Dougherty, et al., 2007). These medications, such as clomipramine (Anafranil) and fluoxetine (Prozac), which alter functioning of the serotonin system, appear to reduce the intensity of the symptoms of this disorder; approximately 40 to 60 percent of OCD clients show at least a 25 to 35 percent reduction in symptoms (relative to 4 to 5 percent on placebo; Dougherty et al., 2007; Iancu et al., 2000). Some clients may show greater improvement than this, but about 30 to 50 percent do not show any clinically significant improvement (e.g., Mancebo et al., 2006). In approximately one-third of people who fail to respond to these serotonergic medications, small doses of certain antipsychotic medications may produce significantly greater improvement (Bloch et al., 2006; see also Stewart et al., 2008).

A major disadvantage of medication treatment for OCD, as for other anxiety disorders, is that when the medication is discontinued relapse rates are generally very high (as high as 50 to 90 percent; Dougherty et al., 2007; Simpson & Liebowitz, 2006). Thus, many people who do not seek alternative forms of behavior therapy that have more long-lasting benefits may have to stay on these medications indefinitely. Studies in adults have generally not found that combining medication with exposure and response prevention is much more effective than behavior therapy alone (Foa et al., 2005; Franklin & Foa, 2002, 2007), although one large study showed that a combination treatment was superior in the treatment of children and adolescents with OCD (March & Franklin, 2006; Pediatric OCD Treatment Study, 2004).

Finally, because OCD in its most severe form is such a crippling and disabling disorder, psychiatrists have begun to reexamine the usefulness of certain neurosurgical techniques for the treatment of severe, intractable OCD (which may afflict as many as 10 percent of people diagnosed with OCD; Mindus, Rasmussen, & Lindquist, 1994). Before such surgery is even contemplated, the person must have had severe OCD for at least 5 years and must not have responded to any of the known treatments discussed so far (medication or behavior therapy). Several studies have shown that approximately 35 to 45 percent of these intractable cases respond quite well (at least a one-third reduction in symptoms) to neurosurgery designed to destroy brain tissue in one of the areas implicated in this condition (Dougherty, Baer, et al., 2002; Jenike, 2000; Rück et al., 2008). However, a significant number of these have adverse side effects.

In Review

- Summarize the major symptoms of obsessive-compulsive disorder.
- How have conditioning and cognitive factors been implicated in OCD?
- What are the major biological causal factors for OCD?
- Describe the major treatment approaches for OCD and their relative advantages and disadvantages.

Sociocultural Causal Factors for All Anxiety Disorders

Cross-cultural research suggests that although anxiety is a universal emotion, and anxiety disorders probably exist in all human societies, there are some differences in prevalence and in the form in which the different disorders are expressed in different cultures (Barlow, 2002; Good & Kleinman, 1985; Kirmayer et al., 1995). Within the United States, lifetime prevalence rates of several anxiety disorders vary in somewhat surprising ways across different racial and ethnic groups, including non-Hispanic whites, African Americans, and Hispanic Americans (Breslau et al., 2006). Specifically, results from the National Comorbidity Survey-Replication study showed that lifetime risk for social phobia, generalized anxiety disorder, and panic disorder is somewhat lower among the two minority groups than among the non-Hispanic whites. These differences were slightly larger for people under age 45 and from lower socioeconomic classes. However, once a disorder has developed, the disorders are equally persistent across the three groups.

Latin Americans from the Caribbean (especially those from Puerto Rico), and other people from the Caribbean, do show higher rates of a variant of panic disorder called *ataque de nervios* (Guarnaccia et al., 2010; Hinton et al., 2008; Hinton, Lewis-Fernandez, Pollack, et al., 2009) than do other groups. Most of the symptoms of ataque de nervios are the same as in a panic attack, but they may also include bursting into tears, anger, and uncontrollable shouting. Other symptoms can include shakiness, verbal or physical aggression, dissociative experiences, and seizure-like or fainting episodes. Such attacks are often associated with a stressful event relating to the family (e.g., news of a death), and the person may have amnesia for the episode (APA, *DSM-IV-TR*, 2000). At least in Puerto Rico this disorder is quite common in children and adolescents as well, affecting about 9 percent (Guarnaccia et al., 2005). Individuals who experience ataque de nervios also seem to be vulnerable to a wider range of other anxiety and mood disorders (Guarnaccia et al., 2010).

Looking at anxiety disorders from a cross-national perspective, one very large study of over 60,000 people across 14 countries (8 developed and 6 less developed) by the World Health Organization (WHO World Mental Health Survey Consortium, 2004) showed that anxiety disorders were the most common category of disorder reported in all but one country (Ukraine). However, reported prevalence rates for all the anxiety disorders combined varied from 2.4 percent (Shanghai, China) to 18.2 percent (United States). Other countries with moderately high rates of reported anxiety disorders were Colombia, France, and Lebanon, and other countries with moderately low rates were China, Japan, Nigeria, and Spain. We now turn to several examples of cultural variants on anxiety disorders that illustrate the range of expressions of anxiety that are exhibited worldwide.

Cultural Differences in Sources of Worry

In the Yoruba culture of Nigeria, there are three primary clusters of symptoms associated with generalized anxiety: worry, dreams, and bodily complaints. However, the sources of worry are very different than those in Western society; they focus on creating and maintaining a large family and on fertility. Dreams are a major source of anxiety because they are thought to indicate that one may be bewitched. The common somatic complaints are also unusual from a Western standpoint: "I have the feeling of something like water in my brain," "Things like ants keep on creeping in various parts of my brain," and "I am convinced some types of worms are in my head" (Ebigbo, 1982; Good & Kleinman, 1985). Nigerians with this syndrome often have paranoid fears of malevolent attack by witchcraft (Kirmayer et al., 1995). In India also there are many more worries about being possessed by spirits and about sexual inadequacy than are seen in generalized anxiety in Western cultures (Carstairs & Kapur, 1976; Good & Kleinman, 1985).

Another culture-related syndrome that occurs in places like China and other Southeast Asian countries is *Koro*, which for men involves intense, acute fear that the penis is retracting into the body and that when this process is complete the sufferer will die. Koro occurs less frequently in women, for whom the fear is that their nipples are retracting and their breasts shrinking. Koro tends to occur in epidemics (sometimes referred to as a form of mass hysteria; Sinha, 2011)—especially in cultural minority groups when their survival is threatened—and it is often attributed to either malicious spirits or contaminated food. A variant on this syndrome

also occurs in West African nations, where afflicted individuals report shrinking of the penis or breasts (but not retraction), which they fear will lead to loss of sexual functioning and reproductive capacity (but not death). Frequently, another person who was present at the time is blamed and often severely beaten or otherwise punished (Dzokoto & Adams, 2005). They both occur in a cultural context where there are serious concerns about male sexual potency (Barlow, 2002; Kirmayer et al., 1995).

Taijin Kyofusho

There is also some evidence that the form that certain anxiety disorders take has actually evolved to fit certain cultural patterns (e.g., Hinton et al., 2009). A good example is the Japanese disorder *taijin kyofusho*, which is related to the Western diagnosis of social phobia. Like social phobia, it is a fear of interpersonal relations or of social situations (Kim et al., 2008; Kirmayer, 1991; Kleinknecht et al., 1997). However, Westerners with social phobia are afraid of social situations where they may be the object of scrutiny or criticism. By contrast, most people with taijin kyofusho are concerned about doing something that will embarrass or offend others (Kim et al., 2008). For example, they may fear offending others by blushing, emitting an offensive odor, staring inappropriately into the eyes of another person, or through their perceived physical defects or imagined deformities (which can reach delusional levels; Kim et al., 2008). This fear of bringing shame on others or offending them is what leads to social avoidance (Kleinknecht et al., 1997). Two of the most common symptoms (phobias about eye contact and blushing) are not mentioned in the *DSM-IV-TR* description of social phobia (Kirmayer, 1991). Body dysmorphic disorder—the fear that some part of the body is defective or malformed and will disgust others—also commonly occurs in sufferers of taijin kyofusho (Nagata, van Vliet, et al., 2006).

Kirmayer (1991) and colleagues (1995) have argued that the pattern of symptoms that occurs in taijin kyofusho has clearly been shaped by cultural factors. Japanese children are raised to be highly dependent on their mothers and to have a fear of the outside world, especially strangers. As babies and young children, they are praised for being obedient and docile. There is also a great deal of emphasis on implicit communication—being able to guess another's thoughts and feelings and being sensitive to them. People who make too much eye contact are likely to be considered aggressive and insensitive, and children are taught to look at the throat of people with whom they are conversing rather than into their eyes. The society is also very hierarchical and structured, and many subtleties in language and facial communication are used to communicate one's response to social status.

At a more general level, cross-cultural researchers have noted that recognition of the cognitive component of most anxiety disorders leads one to expect many cross-cultural variations in the form that different anxiety disorders take. Anxiety disorders can be considered, at least in part, disorders of the interpretive process. Because cultures influence the categories and schemas that we use to interpret our symptoms of distress, there are bound to be significant differences in the form that anxiety disorders take in different cultures (e.g., Barlow, 2002; Good & Kleinman, 1985; Kirmayer et al., 1995).

In Review

● What are some examples of cultural differences in sources of worry?

● How is taijin kyofusho related to social phobia, and what kinds of cultural forces seem to have shaped it?

Unresolved Issues

▶ *Compulsive Hoarding: Is It a Subtype of OCD, or Is It a Separate Disorder?*

Compulsive hoarding is a fascinating condition that had received very little research attention until the past 10 to 15 years. However, as a result of recent attention it has also been brought into public awareness recently through several TV series such as A&E's *Hoarders* or TLC's *Hoarding: Buried Alive*. Traditionally, hoarding has been thought of as one particular symptom of OCD or of obsessive-compulsive personality disorder, but this categorization has been questioned in recent years, and many experts now consider it to be a separate disorder that is being seriously considered for inclusion in *DSM-V* (Mataix-Cols et al., 2010). When considered as one type of OCD symptom, compulsive hoarding occurs in approximately 10 to 40 percent of people diagnosed with OCD (Mataix-Cols, 2010; Steketee & Frost, 2004). However, as many as 4 out of 5 show only compulsive hoarding (Tolin et al., 2008), and some recent studies have estimated its prevalence at 3 to 5 percent of the adult population. Such individuals both acquire and fail to discard many possessions that seem useless or of very limited value, in part because of the emotional attachment they develop to their possessions. In addition, their living spaces are extremely cluttered and disorganized to the point of interfering with normal activities that would otherwise occur in those spaces, such as cleaning, cooking, and walking through the house. In severe cases people have literally been buried alive in their own home by their hoarded possessions.

This excerpt is intentionally omitted from this text

Part of the reason compulsive hoarding has recently been the subject of significant research is because of increasing recognition that, on average, compulsive hoarders are significantly more disabled than people with OCD without compulsive hoarding symptoms (both occupationally and socially; Mataix-Cols et al., 2010; Pertusa et al., 2010), and they may be at high risk for fire, falling, poor sanitation, and serious health risks (Mataix-Cols et al., 2010; Steketee & Frost, 2004). In addition, these individuals have a poorer prognosis for treatment than do people without hoarding symptoms (Mataix-Cols et al., 2010; Steketee & Frost, 2004). Early studies found that the medications typically used to treat OCD were generally not effective in treating people with compulsive hoarding symptoms, although more recent studies have suggested that one antidepressant can be somewhat effective (Saxena, 2007). Traditional behavioral therapy using *exposure and response prevention* (see Treatments section) is also less effective than for other forms of OCD (Saxena, 2007), although there are some promising, new intensive and prolonged behavioral treatments that include home visits, which seem to be more effective (e.g., Tolin et al., 2007, 2008).

Moreover, recent neuroimaging research has found that people diagnosed with OCD who have compulsive hoarding symptoms also show patterns of brain activation in certain areas when their symptoms are provoked that are different from those of people diagnosed with OCD who do not have hoarding symptoms (Mataix-Cols et al., 2004, 2010; Pertusa et al., 2010). This has led some to suggest that people with compulsive hoarding may be a neurologically distinct subgroup or variant of OCD (Mataix-Cols et al., 2010; Saxena, 2008). This conclusion would also be consistent with some findings of a relative lack of responsiveness to the same medications that are often successful in reducing the severity of other forms of OCD and with recent findings that different genes seem to be implicated in OCD without hoarding versus OCD with hoarding (Pertusa et al., 2010; Samuels, Shugart, et al., 2007).

Summary

- The anxiety disorders have anxiety or panic or both at their core. They were initially considered a subset of the neuroses, but beginning with the *DSM-III* this term was largely abandoned.

- Fear or panic is a basic emotion that involves activation of the fight-or-flight response of the autonomic nervous system; it occurs in response to imminent danger.

- Anxiety is a more diffuse blend of emotions that includes high levels of negative affect, worry about possible threat or danger, and the sense of being unable to predict threat or to control it if it occurs.

- Anxiety and panic are each associated with a number of distinct anxiety disorder syndromes, which have both significant commonalities and many differences.

- With *specific phobias*, there is an intense and irrational fear of specific objects or situations that leads to a great deal of avoidance behavior; when confronted with a feared object, the phobic person often shows activation of the fight-or-flight response, which is also associated with panic.

- Many sources of fear and anxiety are believed to be acquired through conditioning or other learning mechanisms. However, some people (because of either temperamental or experiential factors) are more vulnerable than others to acquiring such responses.

- We seem to have an evolutionarily based preparedness to acquire readily fears of objects or situations that posed a threat to our early ancestors.

- In *social phobia*, a person has disabling fears of one or more social situations, usually because of fears of negative evaluation by others or of acting in an embarrassing or humiliating manner; in some cases a person with social phobia may actually experience panic attacks in social situations.

- We seem to have an evolutionarily based predisposition to acquire through conditioning fears of social stimuli signaling dominance and aggression from other humans.

- People with social phobia also have prominent perceptions of unpredictability and uncontrollability and are preoccupied with negative self-evaluative thoughts that tend to interfere with their ability to interact in a socially skillful fashion.

- In *panic disorder*, a person experiences recurrent, unexpected panic attacks that often create a sense of stark terror and numerous other physical symptoms of the fight-or-flight response; panic attacks usually subside in a matter of minutes.

- Many people who experience panic attacks develop anxious apprehension about experiencing another attack; this apprehension is required for a diagnosis of panic disorder.

- Many people with panic disorder also develop agoraphobic avoidance of situations in which they fear that they might have an attack.

- Biological theories of panic disorder emphasize that the disorder may result from biochemical abnormalities in the brain as well as abnormal activity of the neurotransmitters norepinephrine and serotonin.

- Panic attacks may arise primarily from the brain area called the amygdala, although many other areas are also involved in panic disorder.

- The learning theory of panic disorder proposes that panic attacks cause the conditioning of anxiety primarily to external cues associated with the attacks and conditioning of panic itself primarily to interoceptive cues associated with the early stages of the attacks.

- The cognitive theory of panic disorder holds that this condition may develop in people who are prone to making catastrophic misinterpretations of their bodily sensations, a tendency that may be related to preexisting high levels of anxiety sensitivity.

- In *generalized anxiety disorder*, a person has chronic and excessively high levels of worry about a number of events or activities and responds to stress with high levels of psychic and muscle tension.

- Generalized anxiety disorder may occur in people who have had extensive experience with unpredictable or uncontrollable life events.

- People with generalized anxiety seem to have danger schemas about their inability to cope with strange and dangerous situations that promote worries focused on possible future threats.

- The neurobiological factor most implicated in generalized anxiety is a functional deficiency in the neurotransmitter GABA, which is involved in inhibiting anxiety in stressful situations; the limbic system is the brain area most involved.

- Thus somewhat different neurotransmitters and brain areas are involved in panic attacks and generalized anxiety.

- In *obsessive-compulsive disorder*, a person experiences unwanted and intrusive distressing thoughts or images that are usually accompanied by compulsive behaviors performed to neutralize those thoughts or images. Checking and cleaning rituals are most common.

- Biological causal factors also seem to be involved in obsessive-compulsive disorder, with evidence coming from genetic studies, studies of brain functioning, and psychopharmacological studies.

- Once this disorder begins, the anxiety-reducing qualities of the compulsive behaviors may help to maintain the disorder.

- Once a person has any of these anxiety disorders, mood-congruent information processing, such as attentional and interpretive biases, seems to help maintain it.

- Many people with anxiety disorders are treated by physicians, often with medications designed to allay anxiety or with anti-depressant medications that also have antianxiety effects when taken for at least 3 to 4 weeks.

- Such treatment focuses on suppressing the symptoms, and some anxiolytic medications have the potential to cause physiological dependence.

- Once the medications are discontinued, relapse rates tend to be high.

- Behavioral and cognitive therapies have a very good track record with regard to treatment of the anxiety disorders.

- Behavior therapies focus on prolonged exposure to feared situations; with obsessive-compulsive disorder, the rituals also must be prevented following exposure to the feared situations.

- Cognitive therapies focus on helping clients understand their underlying automatic thoughts, which often involve cognitive distortions such as unrealistic predictions of catastrophes that in reality are very unlikely to occur. Then they learn to change these inner thoughts and beliefs through a process of logical reanalysis known as cognitive restructuring.

Key Terms

agoraphobia
amygdala
anxiety
anxiety disorders
anxiety sensitivity
blood-injection-injury phobia
cognitive restructuring
compulsions
exposure and response
 prevention

exposure therapy
exteroceptive conditioning
fear
generalized anxiety disorder
 (GAD)
interoceptive conditioning
neurotic disorders
obsessions
obsessive-compulsive disorder
 (OCD)

panic attack
panic disorder
panic provocation procedures
phobia
prepared learning
social phobia
specific phobia

Glossary

Many of the key terms listed in the glossary appear in boldface when first introduced in the text discussion. A number of other terms commonly encountered in this or other psychology texts are also included; you are encouraged to make use of this glossary both as a general reference tool and as a study aid for the course in abnormal psychology.

Agoraphobia. Fear of being in places or situations where a panic attack may occur and from which escape would be physically difficult or psychologically embarrassing, or in which immediate help would be unavailable in the event that some mishap occurred.

Amygdala. A collection of nuclei that are almond shaped and that lie in front of the hippocampus in the limbic system of the brain. It is involved in regulation of emotion and is critically involved in the emotion of fear.

Anxiety. A general feeling of apprehension about possible danger.

Anxiety disorder. An unrealistic, irrational fear or anxiety of disabling intensity. *DSM-IV-TR* recognizes seven types of anxiety disorders: phobic disorders (specific or social), panic disorder (with or without agoraphobia), generalized anxiety disorder, obsessive-compulsive disorder, and posttraumatic stress disorder.

Anxiety sensitivity. A personality trait involving a high level of belief that certain bodily symptoms may have harmful consequences.

Blood–injection–injury phobia. Persistent and disproportionate fear of the sight of blood or injury, or the possibility of having an injection. Afflicted persons are likely to experience a drop in blood pressure and sometimes faint.

Cognitive restructuring. Cognitive-behavioral therapy techniques that aim to change a person's negative or unrealistic thoughts and attributions.

Compulsions. Overt repetitive behaviors (such as hand washing or checking) or more covert mental acts (such as counting, praying, saying certain words silently, or ordering) that a person feels driven to perform in response to an obsession.

Exposure and response prevention. A method of treatment for obsessive-compulsive disorder that combines intense exposure of the patient to feared conditions and then they are asked not to respond by engaging in their usual rituals to the feared stimuli.

Exposure therapy. A technique in psychological treatment of anxiety disorders that involves exposing the patient to the feared object or context without any danger in order to overcome the anxiety.

Exteroceptive conditioning. Modifying the perception of environmental stimuli acting on the body.

Fear. A basic emotion that involves the activation of the "fight-or-flight" response of the sympathetic nervous system.

Generalized anxiety disorder (GAD). Chronic excessive worry about a number of events or activities, with no specific threat present, accompanied by at least three of the following symptoms: restlessness, fatigue, difficulty concentrating, irritability, muscle tension, sleep disturbance.

Interoceptive conditioning. This term refers to a learning process that is similar to classic conditioning. There are two conditioned stimuli and one unconditioned response.

Neurotic disorders. Psychodynamic term for anxiety driven mental-health conditions that are manifest through avoidance patterns and defensive reactions.

Obsessions. Persistent and recurrent intrusive thoughts, images, or impulses that a person experiences as disturbing and inappropriate but has difficulty suppressing.

Obsessive-compulsive disorder (OCD). Anxiety disorder characterized by the persistent intrusion of unwanted and intrusive thoughts or distressing images; these are usually accompanied by compulsive behaviors designed to neutralize the obsessive thoughts or images or to prevent some dreaded event or situation.

Panic attack. A severe, intense fear response that appears to come out of the blue; it has many physical and cognitive symptoms such as fear of dying or losing control.

Panic disorder. Occurrence of repeated unexpected panic attacks, often accompanied by intense anxiety about having another one.

Panic provocation procedures. A variety of biological challenge procedures that provoke panic attacks at higher rates in people with panic disorder than in people without panic disorder.

Phobia. Persistent and disproportionate fear of some specific object or situation that presents little or no actual danger.

Prepared learning. The view that people are biologically prepared through evolution to more readily acquire fears of certain objects or situations that may once have posed a threat to our early ancestors. For example, people more readily develop fears of snakes and spiders if they are paired with aversive events, than they develop fears of knives or guns.

Social phobia. Fear of situations in which a person might be exposed to the scrutiny of others and fear of acting in a humiliating or embarrassing way.

Specific phobia. Persistent or disproportionate fears of various objects, places, or situations, such as fears of situations (airplanes or elevators), other species (snakes, spiders), or aspects of the environment (high places, water).

Photo Credits

Text Credits

References

JOURNAL ABBREVIATIONS

Acta Neurol. Scandin.—*Acta Neurologica Scandinavica*
Acta Psychiatr. Scandin.—*Acta Psychiatrica Scandinavica*
Add. Behav.—*Addictive Behaviors*
Addict. Dis. Treat.—*Addictive Disorders and Their Treatment*
Addict. Res. Theory—*Addiction Research & Theory*
Aggr. Behav.—*Aggressive Behavior*
Al. Res. Hlth.—*Alcohol Research & Health*
Al. Treat. Quart.—*Alcoholism Treatment Quarterly*
Alcoholism: Clin. Exper. Res.—*Alcoholism: Clinical and Experimental Research*
Am. J. Community Psychol.—*American Journal of Community Psychology*
Amer. J. Cardio.—*American Journal of Cardiology*
Amer. J. Clin. Nutri.—*American Journal of Clinical Nutrition*
Amer. J. Drug Alcoh. Abuse—*American Journal of Drug and Alcohol Abuse*
Amer. J. Epidemiol.—*American Journal of Epidemiology*
Amer. J. Foren. Psychol.—*American Journal of Forensic Psychology*
Amer. J. Geriatr. Psychiat.—*American Journal of Geriatric Psychiatry*
Amer. J. Hum. Gene.—*American Journal of Human Genetics*
Amer. J. Med. Genet.—*American Journal of Medical Genetics*
Amer. J. Med. Sci.—*American Journal of the Medical Sciences*
Amer. J. Ment. Def.—*American Journal of Mental Deficiency*
Amer. J. Ment. Retard.—*American Journal of Mental Retardation*
Amer. J. Nurs.—*American Journal of Nursing*
Amer. J. Occup. Ther.—*American Journal of Occupational Therapy*
Amer. J. Orthopsychiat.—*American Journal of Orthopsychiatry*
Amer. J. Psychiat.—*American Journal of Psychiatry*
Amer. J. Psychoanal.—*American Journal of Psychoanalysis*
Amer. J. Psychother.—*American Journal of Psychotherapy*
Amer. J. Pub. Hlth.—*American Journal of Public Health*
Amer. Psychol.—*American Psychologist*
Ann. Behav. Med.—*Annals of Behavioral Medicine*
Ann. Clin. Psychiat.—*Annals of Clinical Psychiatry*
Ann. Int. Med.—*Annals of Internal Medicine*
Ann. Neurol.—*Annals of Neurology*
Ann. NY Acad. Sci.—*Annals of the New York Academy of Science*
Ann. Sex Res.—*Annals of Sex Research*
Annu. Rev. Clin. Psychol.—*Annual Review of Clinical Psychology*
Annu. Rev. Med.—*Annual Review of Medicine*
Annu. Rev. Neurosci.—*Annual Review of Neuroscience*
Annu. Rev. Psychol.—*Annual Review of Psychology*

Annu. Rev. Sex Res.—*Annual Review of Sex Research*
Annu. Rev. Soc.—*Annual Review of Sociology*
App. Prev. Psychol.—*Applied and Preventive Psychology*
Arch. Clin. Neuropsychol.—*Archives of Clinical Neuropsychology*
Arch. Gen. Psychiat.—*Archives of General Psychiatry*
Arch. Gerontol. Geriatr.—*Archives of Gerontology and Geriatrics*
Arch. Int. Med.—*Archives of Internal Medicine*
Arch. Neurol.—*Archives of Neurology*
Arch. Sex. Behav.—*Archives of Sexual Behavior*
Austral. N.Z. J. Psychiat.—*Australian and New Zealand Journal of Psychiatry*
Behav. Chng.—*Behaviour Change*
Behav. Cog. Psychother.—*Behavioral & Cognitive Psychotherapy*
Behav. Gen.—*Behavior Genetics*
Behav. Mod.—*Behavior Modification*
Behav. Res. Ther.—*Behavior Research and Therapy*
Behav. Ther.—*Behavior Therapy*
Behav. Today—*Behavior Today*
Biol. Psych.—*Biological Psychology*
Biol. Psychiat.—*Biological Psychiatry*
BMJ—*British Medical Journal*
Brain—*Brain: A Journal of Neurology*
Brit. J. Addict.—*British Journal of Addiction*
Brit. J. Clin. Psychol.—*British Journal of Clinical Psychology*
Brit. J. Dev. Psychol.—*British Journal of Developmental Psychology*
Brit. J. Learn. Dis.—*British Journal of Learning Disabilities*
Brit. J. Psychiat.—*British Journal of Psychiatry*
Brit. Med. J.—*British Medical Journal*
Bull. Amer. Acad. Psychiat. Law—*Bulletin of the American Academy of Psychiatry and Law*
Canad. J. Behav. Sci.—*Canadian Journal of Behavioral Science*
Canad. J. Psychiat.—*Canadian Journal of Psychiatry*
Child Ab. Negl.—*Child Abuse and Neglect*
Child Adoles. Psychiat.—*Child and Adolescent Psychiatry*
Child Adoles. Psychiatr. Clin. N. Amer.—*Child and Adolescent Psychiatric Clinics of North America*
Child Develop.—*Child Development*
Child Psychiat. Human Devel.—*Child Psychiatry and Human Development*
Clin. Child Fam. Psych. Rev.—*Clinical Child & Family Psychology Review*
Clin. Chld. Fam. Psychol.—*Clinical Child & Family Psychology*
Clin. Exp. Res.—*Clinical and Experimental Research*
Clin. Geron.—*Clinical Gerontologis*
Clin. Neuropharmac.—*Clinical Neuropharmacology*
Clin. Neuropsych.—*The Clinical Neuropsychologist*
Clin. Pediat.—*Clinical Pediatrics*
Clin. Pharm.—*Clinical Pharmacy*

Clin. Psychol. Rev.—*Clinical Psychology Review*
Clin. Psychol. Sci. Prac.—*Clinical Psychology: Science and Practice*
Clin. Psychol.—*The Clinical Psychologist*
Cog. & Emo.—*Cognition and Emotion*
Cog. Behav. Neuro.—*Cognitive and Behavioral Neurology*
Cog. Behav. Ther.—*Cognitive Behaviour Therapy*
Cog. Ther. Res.—*Cognitive Therapy and Research*
Coll. Stud. J.—*College Student Journal*
Comm. Ment. Hlth. J.—*Community Mental Health Journal*
Compr. Psychiat.—*Comprehensive Psychiatry*
Contemp. Psychol.—*Contemporary Psychology*
Counsel. Psychol.—*Counseling Psychologist*
Crim. Just. Behav.—*Criminal Justice and Behavior*
Cult. Med. Psychiatr.—*Culture, Medicine, and Psychiatry*
Cultur. Psychiatr.—*Cultural Psychiatry*
Cur. Opin. Psychiat.—*Current Opinion in Psychiatry*
Curr. Dis. Psychol. Sci.—*Current Directions in Psychological Science*
Dev. Behav.—*Deviant Behavior*
Develop. Med. Child Neurol.—*Developmental Medicine & Child Neurology*
Develop. Psychol.—*Developmental Psychology*
Develop. Psychopath.—*Development and Psychopathology*
Dis. Nerv. Sys.—*Diseases of the Nervous System*
Drug Al. Dep.—*Drug & Alcohol Dependency*
Drug. Al. Rev.—*Drug & Alcohol Review*
Eat. Dis.—*Eating Disorders*
Eur. Arch. Psychiat. Clin. Neurosci.—*European Archives of Psychiatry and Clinical Neuroscience*
Europ. J. Neurosci.—*European Journal of Neuroscience*
Europ. J. Psychol. Assess.—*European Journal of Psychology Assessment*
Europ. Psychol.—*European Psychologist*
Except.—*Exceptionality*
Exp. Clin. Psychopharm.—*Experimental and Clinical Psychopharmacology*
Exper. Neurol.—*Experimental Neurology*
Fam. Hlth.—*Family Health*
Fam. Plann. Perspect.—*Family Planning Perspectives*
Fam. Process—*Family Process*
Fed. Proc.—*Federal Proceedings*
Gen. Hosp. Psychiat.—*General Hospital Psychiatry*
Harv. Rev. Psychiat.—*Harvard Review of Psychiatry*
Hlth. Psychol.—*Health Psychology*
Hong Kong J. Psychiatry—*Hong Kong Journal of Psychiatry*
Hosp. Comm. Psychiat.—*Hospital and Community Psychiatry*
Human Behav.—*Human Behavior*
Human Develop.—*Human Development*
Human Genet.—*Human Genetics*
Inf. Behav. Develop.—*Infant Behavior and Development*
Int. Clin. Psychopharm.—*International Clinical Psychopharmocology*

Int. J. Adol. Med. Hlth.—*International Journal of Adolescent Medicine and Health*

Int. J. Aging Hum. Dev.—*International Journal of Aging & Human Development*

Int. J. Clin. Exp. Hypn.—*International Journal of Clinical and Experimental Hypnosis*

Int. J. Eat. Dis.—*International Journal of Eating Disorders*

Int. J. Emerg. Mntl. Hlth.—*International Journal of Emergency Mental Health*

Int. J. Epidemiol.—*International Journal of Epidemiology*

Int. J. Neuropsychopharm.—*International Journal of Neuropsychopharmacology*

Int. J. Off. Ther. Comp. Crim.—*International Journal of Offender Therapy & Comparative Criminology*

Int. Rev. Psychiat.—*International Review of Psychiatry*

Integr. Psychiat.—*Integrative Psychiatry*

Inter. J. Addict.—*International Journal of Addictions*

Inter. J. Ment. Hlth.—*International Journal of Mental Health*

Inter. J. Psychiat.—*International Journal of Psychiatry*

Inter. J. Psychoanal.—*International Journal of Psychoanalysis*

Inter. J. Soc. Psychiat.—*International Journal of Social Psychiatry*

Intl. J. Clin. Hlth.—*International Journal of Clinical and Health Psychology*

J. Abn. Psychol.—*Journal of Abnormal Psychology*

J. Abnorm. Child Psychol.—*Journal of Abnormal Child Psychology*

J. Abnorm. Soc. Psychol.—*Journal of Abnormal and Social Psychology*

J. Addict. Dis.—*Journal of Addictive Diseases*

J. Adol. Hlth.—*Journal of Adolescent Health*

J. Affect. Dis.—*Journal of Affective Disorders*

J. Amer. Acad. Adoles. Psychiat.—*Journal of the American Academy of Adolescent Psychiatry*

J. Amer. Acad. Child Adoles. Psychiat.—*Journal of the American Academy of Child and Adolescent Psychiatry*

J. Amer. Acad. Child Psychiat.—*Journal of the American Academy of Child Psychiatry*

J. Amer. Acad. Psychiat. Law—*Journal of the American Academy of Psychiatry and Law*

J. Amer. Coll. Hlth.—*Journal of American College Health*

J. Amer. Geriat. Soc.—*Journal of the American Geriatrics Society*

J. Anxiety Dis.—*Journal of Anxiety Disorders*

J. Appl. Beh. Anal.—*Journal of Applied Behavior Analysis*

J. Appl. Psychol.—*Journal of Applied Psychology*

J. Atten. Dis.—*Journal of Attention Disorders*

J. Autism Devel. Dis.—*Journal of Autism and Developmental Disorders*

J. Behav. Assess.—*Journal of Behavioral Assessment*

J. Behav. Med.—*Journal of Behavioral Medicine*

J. Behav. Ther. Exper. Psychiat.—*Journal of Behavior Therapy and Experimental Psychiatry*

J. Chem. Depen. Treat.—*Journal of Chemical Dependency Treatment*

J. Child Fam. Stud.—*Journal of Child and Family Studies*

J. Child Psychol. Psychiat.—*Journal of Child Psychology and Psychiatry*

J. Child. Adol. Men. Hlth.—*Journal of Child and Adolescent Mental Health*

J. Child. Adol. Psychopharm.—*Journal of Child & Adolescent Psychopharmacology*

J. Clin. Child Psychol.—*Journal of Clinical Child Psychology*

J. Clin. Child. Adol. Psych.—*Journal of Clinical Child & Adolescent Psychology*

J. Clin. Exp. Neuropsych.—*Journal of Clinical and Experimental Neuropsychology*

J. Clin. Geropsychol.—*Journal of Clinical Geropsychology*

J. Clin. Psychiat.—*Journal of Clinical Psychiatry*

J. Clin. Psychol. Med. Set.—*Journal of Clinical Psychology in Medical Settings*

J. Clin. Psychol.—*Journal of Clinical Psychology*

J. Clin. Psychopharm.—*Journal of Clinical Psychopharmacology*

J. Cog. Neurosci.—*Journal of Cognitive Neuroscience*

J. Cog. Psychother.—*Journal of Cognitive Psychotherapy*

J. Cog. Rehab.—*Journal of Cognitive Rehabilitation*

J. Coll. Stud. Psychother.—*Journal of College Student Psychotherapy*

J. Comm. Psychol.—*Journal of Community Psychology*

J. Compar. Fam. Stud.—*Journal of Comparative Family Studies*

J. Cons. Clin. Psychol.—*Journal of Consulting and Clinical Psychology*

J. Couns. Psychol.—*Journal of Counseling Psychology*

J. Crisis Int. Suicide Prev.—*Journal of Crisis Intervention and Suicide Prevention*

J. Dev. Behav. Ped.—*Journal of Developmental & Behavioral Pediatrics*

J. Drug Al. Ed.—*Journal of Drug and Alcohol Education*

J. Drug Ed.—*Journal of Drug Education*

J. Drug Iss.—*Journal of Drug Issues*

J. Edu. Psychol.—*Journal of Educational Psychology*

J. Environ. Pschol.—*Journal of Environmental Psychology*

J. Exper. Psychol.—*Journal of Experimental Psychology*

J. Fam. Pract.—*Journal of Family Practice*

J. Fam. Psychol.—*Journal of Family Psychology*

J. Foren. Psychol. Pract.—*Journal of Forensic Psychology Practice*

J. Gen. Psychol.—*Journal of General Psychology*

J. Gerontol.—*Journal of Gerontology*

J. Head Trauma Rehab.—*Journal of Head Trauma Rehabilitation*

J. His. Behav. Sci.—*Journal of the History of the Behavioral Sciences*

J. Hlth. Soc. Behav.—*Journal of Health and Social Behavior*

J. Int. Neuropsycholog. Soc.—*Journal of the International Neuropsychological Society*

J. Intell. Develop. Dis.—*Journal of Intellectual Developmental Disability*

J. Intell. Dis. Res.—*Journal of Intellectual Disability Research*

J. Interpers. Violen.—*Journal of Interpersonal Violence*

J. Learn. Dis.—*Journal of Learning Disabilities*

J. Loss Trauma—*Journal of Loss & Trauma*

J. Marit. Fam. Ther.—*Journal of Marital and Family Therapy*

J. Marr. Fam.—*Journal of Marriage and the Family*

J. Ment. Deficien. Res.—*Journal of Mental Deficiency Research*

J. Ment. Hlth. Couns.—*Journal of Mental Health Counseling*

J. Ment. Sci.—*Journal of Mental Science*

J. Meth. Psychiat. Res.—*Journal of Methods in Psychiatric Research*

J. Nerv. Ment. Dis.—*Journal of Nervous and Mental Diseases*

J. Neurol. Neurosurg. Psychiat.—*Journal of Neurology, Neurosurgery, & Psychiatry*

J. Neuropsychiat. Clin. Neurosci.—*Journal of Neuropsychiatry and Clinical Neurosciences*

J. Neurosci.—*Journal of Neuroscience*

J. Occup. Hlth. Psych.—*Journal of Occupational Health Psychology*

J. Off. Rehab.—*Journal of Offender Rehabilitation*

J. Pediat. Psychol.—*Journal of Pediatric Psychology*

J. Pers. Assess.—*Journal of Personality Assessment*

J. Pers. Dis.—*Journal of Personality Disorders*

J. Pers. Soc. Psychol.—*Journal of Personality and Social Psychology*

J. Personal.—*Journal of Personality*

J. Psychiat. Neurosci.—*Journal of Psychiatry and Neuroscience*

J. Psychiat. Pract.—*Journal of Psychiatric Practice*

J. Psychiat. Res.—*Journal of Psychiatric Research*

J. Psychiat.—*Journal of Psychiatry*

J. Psychoact. Drugs—*Journal of Psychoactive Drugs*

J. Psychohist.—*Journal of Psychohistory*

J. Psychol.—*Journal of Psychology*

J. Psychopath. Behav. Assess.—*Journal of Psychopathology and Behavioral Assessment*

J. Psychopharm.—*Journal of Psychopharmacology*

J. Psychosom. Obst. Gyn.—*Journal of Psychosomatic Obstetrics & Gynecology*

J. Psychosom. Res.—*Journal of Psychosomatic Research*

J. Res. Person.—*Journals of Research in Personality*

J. Sex Marit. Ther.—*Journal of Sex and Marital Therapy*

J. Sex Res.—*Journal of Sex Research*

J. Speech Hear. Dis.—*Journal of Speech and Hearing Disorders*

J. Stud. Alcoh.—*Journal of Studies on Alcohol*

J. Sub. Abuse treat.—*Journal of Substance Abuse Treatment*

J. Subst. Abuse—*Journal of Substance Abuse*

J. Trauma. Stress.—*Journal of Traumatic Stress*

JAMA—*Journal of the American Medical Association*

Med. Clin. N. Amer.—*Medical Clinics of North America*

Men. Hlth. Asp. Dev. Dis.—*Mental Health Aspects of Developmental Disabilities*

Ment. Retard. Dev. Dis. Res. Rev.—*Mental Retardation & Developmental Disabilities Research Reviews*

Ment. Retard. Devel. Res. Rev—*Mental Retardation & Developmental Research Review*

Monogr. Soc. Res. Child Develop.—*Monographs of the Society for Research in Child Development*

N. Engl. J. Med.—*New England Journal of Medicine*

Neurobiol. Aging—*Neurobiology of Aging*

Neurosci. Lett.—*Neuroscience Letters*

Nord. J. Psychiat.—*Nordic Journal of Psychiatry*

Personal. Indiv. Diff.—*Personality and Individual Differences*

Personal. Soc. Psychol. Bull.—*Personality and Social Psychology Bulletin*

Personal. Soc. Psychol. Rev.—*Personality and Social Psychology Review*

Prim. Psychiat.—*Primary Psychiatry*

Prof. Psychol. Res. Pract.—*Professional Psychology: Research and Practice*

Prof. Psychol.—*Professional Psychology*

Prog. Neuropsychopharmacol. Biol. Psychiatry—*Progress in Neuropsychopharmacology & Biological Psychiatry*

Psych. Addict. Behav.—*Psychology of Addictive Behaviors*

Psych. Res. Neuroimag.—*Psychiatry Research: Neuroimaging*

Psych. Today—*Psychology Today*

Psychiat. Ann.—*Psychiatric Annals*

Psychiat. Clin. N. Amer.—*Psychiatric Clinics of North America*

Psychiat. News—*Psychiatric News*

Psychiat. Res.—*Psychiatric Research*

Psychiatr. Q.—*Psychiatric Quarterly*

Psychiatr. Serv.—*Psychiatric Services*

Psychol. Aging—*Psychology and Aging*

Psychol. Assess.—*Psychological Assessment*

Psychol. Bull.—*Psychological Bulletin*

Psychol. Inq.—*Psychological Inquiry*

Psychol. Med.—*Psychological Medicine*

Psychol. Meth.—*Psychological Methods*

Psychol. Rec.—*Psychological Record*

Psychol. Rep.—*Psychological Reports*

Psychol. Rev.—*Psychological Review*

Psychol. Sci. in the Pub. Int.—*Psychological Science in the Public Interest*

Psychol. Sci.—*Psychological Science*

Psychol. Women Quart.—*Psychology of Women Quarterly*

Psychopath.—*Psychopathology*

Psychopharm. Bull.—*Psychopharmacology Bulletin*

Psychosom. Med.—*Psychosomatic Medicine*

Psychother. Psychosom.—*Psychotherapy and Psychosomatics*

Q. J. Exp. Psych. [A]—*Quarterly Journal of Experimental Psychology: [A] Human Experimental Psychology*

Rev. Gen. Pscyhol.—*Review of General Psychology*

Roche Med. Imag. Comm.—*Roche Medical Image and Commentary*

Schiz. Res.—*Schizophrenia Research*

Schizo. Bull.—*Schizophrenia Bulletin*

School Psychol. Rev.—*School Psychology Review*

Sci. News—*Science News*

Scientif. Amer.—*Scientific American*

Soc. Develop.—*Social Development*

Soc. Psychiat. Psychiatr. Epidemiol.—*Social Psychiatry and Psychiatric Epidemiology*

Soc. Psychiat.—*Social Psychiatry*

Soc. Sci. Med.—*Social Science and Medicine*

Stress—*Stress: The International Journal on the Biology of Stress*

Trans. Cult. Psych. Res. Rev.—*Transcultural Psychiatric Research Review*

Transcult. Psychiat.—*Transcultural Psychiatry*

Aaronson, C. J., Katzman, G. P., & Gorman, J. M. (2007). Combination pharmacotherapy and psychotherapy for the treatment of depressive and anxiety disorders. In P. E. Nathan and J. M. Gorman (Eds.), *A guide to treatments that work* (pp. 681–710). New York: Oxford University Press.

Abbey, A., Zawacki, T., Buck, P. O., Clinton, A. M., & McAuslan, P. (2001). Alcohol and sexual assault. *Al. Res. Hlth.*, 25(1), 43–51.

Abel, G. G., & Rouleau, J. L. (1990). The nature and extent of sexual assault. In W. L. Marshall, D. R. Laws, & H. E. Barbaree (Eds.), *Handbook of sexual assault: Issues, theories, and treatment of the offender* (pp. 9–22). New York: Plenum.

Abela, J. R., Stolow, D., Mineka, S., Yao, S., Zhu, X. Z., & Hankin, B. L. (2011). Cognitive vulnerability to depressive symptoms in adolescents in urban and rural Hunan, China: A multiwave longitudinal study. *J. Abn. Psychol.*, 120(4), 765–78. doi: 10.1037/a0025295

Abi-Saab, D., Beauvais, J., Mehm, J., Brody, M., Gottschalk, C., & Kosten, T. R. (2005). The effect of alcohol on the neuropsychological functioning of recently abstinent cocaine-dependent subjects. *American Journal on Addictions*, 14(2), 166–78.

Abraham, H. D., & Wolf, E. (1988). Visual function in past users of LSD: Psychophysical findings. *J. Abn. Psychol.*, 97, 443–47.

Abraham, K. (1927). *Selected papers on psychoanalysis.* (International Psychoanalytical Libary, No. 13.) (Memoir by E. Jones; trans. by D. Bryan and A. Strachey.). Honolulu, HI: Hogarth Press.

Abrahamson, D. J., Barlow, D. H., Sakheim, D. K., Beck, J. G., & Athanasiou, R. (1985). Effects of distraction on sexual responding in functional and dysfunctional men. *Behav. Ther.*, 16, 503–15.

Abramowitz, C., Kosson, D., & Seidenberg, M. (2004). The relationship between childhood attention deficit hyperactivity disorder and conduct problems and adult psychopathy in male inmates. *Personal. Indiv. Diff.*, 36, 1031–47.

Abramowitz, J. S., Braddock, A. E., & Moore, E. L. (2009). Psychological treatment of obsessive-compulsive disorder. In M. M. Antony & M. B. Stein (Eds.), *Oxford handbook of anxiety and related disorders* (pp. 391–404). New York: Oxford University Press.

Abramowitz, J. S., Franklin, M. E., Street, G. P., Kozak, M. J., & Foa, E. B. (2000). Effects of comorbid depression on response to treatment for obsessive-compulsive disorder. *Behav. Ther.*, 31(3), 517–28. doi: 10.1016/s0005-7894(00)80028-3

Abramowitz, J. S., Tolin, D. F., & Street, G. P. (2001). Paradoxical effects of thought suppression: A meta-analysis of controlled studies. *Clin. Psychol. Rev.*, 21(5), 683–703.

Abrams, R. (2002). *Electroconvulsive therapy* (4th ed.). New York: Oxford University Press.

Abramson, L. Y., Alloy, L. B., Hankin, B. L., Haeffel, G. J., MacCoon, D. G., & Gibb, B. E. (2002). Cognitive vulnerability-stress models of depression in a self-regulatory and psychobiological context. In I. H. Gotlib & C. L. Hammen (Eds.), *Handbook of depression* (pp. 268–94). New York: Guilford.

Abramson, L., Alloy, L., & Metalsky, G. (1995). Hopelessness depression. In G. Buchanan & M. Seligman (Eds.), *Explanatory style* (pp. 113–34). Hillsdale, NJ: Erlbaum.

Abramson, L. Y., Metalsky, G. I., & Alloy, L. B. (1989). Hopelessness depression: A theory-based subtype of depression. *Psychol. Rev.*, 96, 358–72.

Abramson, L. Y., & Seligman, M. E. P. (1977). Modeling psychopathology in the laboratory: History and rationale. In M. Maser & M. E. P. Seligman (Eds.), *Psychopathology: Experimental models.* San Francisco: Freeman.

Abramson, L. Y., Seligman, M. E. P., & Teasdale, J. D. (1978). Learned helplessness in humans: Critique and reformulation. *J. Abn. Psychol.*, 87, 49–74.

Acheson, D. T., Forsyth, J. P., Prenovcau, J. M., & Bouton, M. E. (2007). Interoceptive fear conditioning as a learning model of panic disorder: An experimental evaluation using 20% CO-sub-2-enriched air in a non-clinical sample. *Behav. Res. Ther.*, 45(10), 2280–2294.

Ackard, D. M., Croll, J. K., & Kearney-Cooke, A. (2002). Dieting frequency among college females: Association with disordered eating, body image, and related psychological problems. *J. Psychosom. Res.*, 52, 129–36.

Ackard, D. M., Fulkerson, J. A., & Neumark-Sztainer, D. (2007). Prevalence and utility of DSM-IV eating disorder diagnostic criteria among youth. *Int. J. Eat. Dis.*, 40, 409–17.

AD2000 Collaborative Group. (2004, Jun. 26). Long-term donepezil treatment in 565 patients with Alzheimer's disease (AD2000): Randomised double blind trial. *Lancet, 363,* 2105–15.

Adamis, D., Treloar, A., Martin, F. C., & Macdonald, Alastair J. D. (2007). A brief review of the history of delirium as a mental disorder. *History of Psychiatry, 18*(4), 459–69.

Adams, M. A., & Ferraro, F. R. (1997). Acquired immunodeficiency syndrome dementia complex. *J. Clin. Psychol.*, 53(7), 767–78.

Adams, H. E., Bernat, J. A., & Luscher, K. A. (2001). Borderline personality disorder: An overview. In H. E. Adams & P. B. Sutker (Eds.), *Comprehensive handbook of psychopathology* (pp. 491–508). New York: Kluwer Academic.

Addington, J., Cadenhead, K. S., Cannon, T. D., Cornblatt, B., McGlashan, T. H., Perkins, D. O., Seidman, L. J. Tsuang, M., Walker, E. F., et al. (2007). North American Prodrome Longitudianal Study: A collaborative multisite approach to prodromal schizophrenia research. *Schizo. Bull., 33,* 665–72.

Addington, J., Cornblatt, B. A., Cadenhead, K. S., Cannon, T. D., McGlashan, T. H., Perkins, D. O., Seidman, L. J., Tsuang, M. T., Walker, E. F., Woods, S. W., & Heinssen, R. (2011). At clinical high risk for psychosis: Outcome for nonconverters. *Am. J. Psychiat., 168,* 800–13.

Addis, M. E., & Krasnow, A. D. (2000). A national survey of practicing psychologists' attitudes toward psychotherapy treatment manuals. *J. Cons. Clin. Psychol., 68,* 331–39.

Addis, M. E., & Mahalik, J. R. (2003). Men, masculinity, and the contexts of help seeking. *Amer. Psychol., 58,* 1, 5–14.

Adler, A. B., Bliese, P. D., McGurk, D., Hoge, C. W., & Castro, C. A. (2009). Battlemind debriefing and Battlemind training as early interventions with soldiers returning from Iraq: Randomization by platoon. *J Consult. Clin. Psychol., 77,* 928–940.

Adler, A. B., Litz, B. T., Castro, C. A., Suvak, M., Thomas, J. L., Burrell, L., et al. (2008). A group randomized trial of critical incident stress debriefing provided to U. S. peacekeepers. *J. Trauma. Stress., 21,* 253–263.

Adler, L. E., Olincy, A., Waldo, M., Harris, J. G., Griffith, J., Stevens, K., Flach, K., Nagamoto, H., Bickford, P., Leonard, S., & Freedman, R. (1998). Schizophrenia, sensory gating, and nicotinic receptors. *Schizo. Bull., 24*(2), 189–202.

Adler, T. (1994). Alzheimer's causes unique cell death. *Sci. News, 146*(13), 198.

Affleck, G., Tennen, H., Urrows, S., & Higgins, P. (1994). Person and contextual features of daily stress reactivity: Individual differences in relations of undesirable daily events with mood disturbance and chronic pain intensity. *J. Pers. Soc. Psychol., 66*(2), 329–40.

Afifi, T. O., Brownridge, D. A., MacMillan, H., & Sareen, J. (2010). The relationship of gambling to intimate partner violence and child maltreatment in a nationally representative sample. *J. Psychiat. Res., 44*(5), 331–37.

Agras, W. S., Walsh, T., Fairburn, C. G., Wilson, T., & Kraemer, H. C. (2000). A multicenter comparison of cognitive-behavioral therapy and interpersonal therapy for bulimia nervosa. *Arch. Gen. Psychiat., 57*(5), 459–66.

Aiken, L. R. (1996). *Rating scales and checklists.* New York: Wiley.

Akins, S., Mosher, C., Rotolo, T., & Griffin, R. (2003). Patterns and correlates of substance use among American Indians in Washington State. *J. Drug Iss., 33*(1), 45–72.

Akiskal, H. S. (1997). Overview of chronic depressions and their clinical management. In H. S Akiskal & G. B. Cassano (Eds.),*Dysthymia and the spectrum of chronic depressions* (pp. 1–34). New York: Guilford.

Akiskal, H. S. (2005). Searching for behavioral indicators of bipolar II in patients presenting with major depressive episodes: The "red sign," the "rule of three," and other biographic signs of temperamental extravagance, activation, and hypomania. *J. Affect. Dis., 84*(2–3), 279–90.

Akiskal, H. S., & Benazzi, F. (2005). Atypical depression: A variant of bipolar II or a bridge between unipolar and bipolar II. *J. Affect. Dis., 84,* 209–17.

Akiskal, H. S., & Pinto, O. (1999). The evolving bipolar spectrum: Prototypes I, II, III and IV. *Psychiat. Clin. N. Amer., 22*(3), 517–34.

Akyuz, G., Dogan, O., Sar, V., Yargic, I. L., & Tutkin, H. (1999). Frequency of dissociative identity disorder in the general population of Turkey. *Compr. Psychiat., 40(2)*, 151–59.

Alanen, Y. O., González de Chávez, M., Silver, A. S., & Martindale, B. (Eds.). (2009). *Psychotherapeutic approaches to schizophrenic psychoses.* New York: Routledge/Taylor & Francis Group.

Alarcon, M., et al. (1997). A twin study of mathematics disability. *J. Learn. Dis., 30(6)*, 617–23.

Alarcón, R. D., Becker, A. E., Lewis-Fernández, R., Like, R. C., Desai, P., Foulks, E., Gonzales, J., Hansen, H., Kopelowicz, A. , Lu, F. G., Oquendo, M. A., & Primm, A. (2009). Issues for DSM-V: The role of culture in psychiatric diagnosis. *J. Nerv. Ment. Dis., 197(8)*, 559–60.

Albano, A. M., Chorpita, B. F., & Barlow, D. H. (1996). Childhood anxiety disorders. In E. J. Mash & R. A. Barkley (Eds.),*Child psychopathology* (pp. 196–241). New York: Guilford.

Alberini, C. M. (2009). Unwind: Chronic stress exacerbates the deficits of Alzheimer's disease. *Biol. Psychiat., 65*, 916–17.

Albert, C. M., Chae, C. U., Rexrode, K. M., Manson, J. E., & Kawachi, I. (2005). Phobic anxiety and risk of coronary heart disease and sudden cardiac death among women. *Circulation, 111*, 480–87.

Albert, M. S., & Blacker, D. (2006). Mild cognitive impairment and dementia. *Annu. Rev. Clin. Psych., 2*, 379–88.

Albert, U., Maina, G., Forner, F., & Bogetto, F. (2004). DSM-IV obsessive-compulsive personality disorder: Prevalence in patients with anxiety disorders and in healthy comparison subjects. *Compr. Psychiat., 45*, 325–32.

Albright v. Abington Memorial Hospital, 696 A.2d 1159 (Pa 1997).

Alcoholics Anonymous. (2007). Membership in AA. Alcoholics Anonymous Website.

Alden, L., Laposa, J., Taylor, C., & Ryder, A. (2002). Avoidant personality disorder: Current status and future directions. *J. Pers. Dis., 16*, 1–29.

Alderson, P. (2001). Down's syndrome: Cost, quality and value of life. *Soc. Sci. Med., 53*, 627–38.

Aldwin, C. M. (2007). *Stress, coping, and development: An integrative perspective* (2nd ed.). New York: Guilford.

Alegria, M., Woo, M., Cao, Z., Torres, M., Meng, X., & Striegel-Moore, R. (2007). Prevalence and correlates of eating disorders in Latinos in the United States. *Int. J. Eat. Dis., 40(Supl.)*, S15–S21.

Aleman, A., & Larøi, F. (2008). *Hallucinations: The science of idiosyncratic perception.* Washington, DC: American Psychological Association.

Aleman, A., Kahn, R. S., & Selten, J. P. (2003). Sex differences in the risk of schizophrenia: Evidence from meta-analysis. *Arch. Gen. Psychiat., 60*, 565–71.

Alexander, F. (1948). *Fundamentals of psychoanalysis.* New York: Norton.

Alexander, G. M., & Sherwin, B. B. (1993). Sex steroids, sexual behavior, and selective attention for erotic stimuli in women using oral contraceptives. *Psychoneuroendocrinology, 18*, 91–102.

Alexander, K., Huganir, L. S., & Zigler, E. (1985). Effects of different living settings on the performance of mentally retarded individuals. *Amer. J. Ment. Def., 90*, 9–17.

Alexander, N., Kuepper, Y., Schmitz, A., Osinsky, R., Kozyra, E., & Hennig, J. (2009). Gene-environment interactions predict cortisol responses after acute stress: Implications for the etiology of depression. *Psychoneuroendocrinology, 34*, 1294–1303.

Alexopoulos, G. S., Borson, S., Cuthbert, B. N., Devanand, D. P., Mulsant, B. H., Olin, J. T., et al. (2002). Assessment of late life depression. *Biol. Psychiat., 52(3)*, 164–74.

Alison, N. G. (1994). Fetal alcohol syndrome: Implications for psychologists. *Clin. Psychol. Rev., 14*, 91–111.

Allden, K., Poole, C., Chantavanich, S., Ohmar, K., Aung, N., & Mollica, R. (1996). Burmese political dissidents in Thailand: Trauma and survival among young adults in exile. *Amer. J. Pub. Hlth., 86*(11), 1561–69.

Allen, A., & Hollander, E. (2004). Similarities and differences between body dysmorphic disorder and other disorders. *Psychiat. Ann., 34*(12), 927–33.

Allen, L. B., McHugh, R. K., & Barlow, D. H. (2008). Emotional disorders: A unified protocol. In D. H. Barlow (Ed.), *Clinical handbook of psychological disorders: A step-by-step treatment manual* (4th ed., pp. 216–49). New York: Guilford Press.

Allik, J. (2005). Personality dimensions across cultures. *J. Pers. Dis., 19*, 212–32.

Allison, K. C., Grillo, C., Masheb, R. M., & Stunkard, A. J. (2005). Binge eating disorder and night eating syndrome: A comparative study of disordered eating. *J. Cons. Clin. Psych., 73*, 1107–15.

Alloway, T., Elliott, J., & Holmes, J. (2010). The prevalence of ADHD-like symptoms in a community sample. *J. Atten. Dis., 14*(1), 52–56.

Alloy, L. B., Abramson, L. Y., Gibb, B. E., Crossfield, A. G., Pieracci, A. M., Spasojevic, J., et al. (2004). Developmental antecedents of cognitive vulnerability to depression: Review of findings from the cognitive vulnerability to depression project. *J. Cog. Psychother., 18*(2), 115–33.

Alloy, L. B., Abramson, L. Y., Keyser, J., Gerstein, R. K., & Sylvia, L.G. (2008). Negative cognitive style. In K. S. Dobson & D. J. Dozois (Eds.), *Risk factors in depression.* Oxford, U.K.: Elsevier Press.

Alloy, L. B., Abramson, L. Y., Smith, J. M., Gibb, B.E., & Neeren, A. M. (2006). Role of parenting and maltreatment histories in unipolar and bipolar mood disorders: Mediation by cognitive vulnerability to depression. *Clin. Child. Fam. Psych. Rev., 9*, 23–64.

Alloy, L. B., Abramson, L. Y., Walshaw, P. D., Gerstein, R. K., Keyser, J. D., Whitehouse, W. G., et al. (2009). Behavioral approach system (BAS)-relevant cognitive styles and bipolar spectrum disorders: Concurrent and prospective associations. *J. Abn. Psychol., 118*(3), 459–71. doi: 10.1037/a0016604

Alloy, L. B., Abramson, L. Y., Walshaw, P. D., Keyser, J., & Gerstein, R. K. (2010). Adolescent onset bipolar spectrum disorders: A cognitive vulnerability-stress perspective informed by normative brain, cognitive, and emotional/motivational development. In D. Miklowitz & D. Cicchetti (Eds.), *Bipolar disorder: A developmental psychopathology approach.*

Alloy, L. B., Abramson, L. Y., Whitehouse, W. G., Hogan, M. E., Panzarella, C., & Rose, D. T. (2006). Prospective incidence of first onsets and recurrences of depression in individuals at high and low cognitive risk for depression. *J. Abn. Psychol., 115*(1), 145–57.

Alloy, L. B., Kelly, K. A., Mineka, S., & Clements, C. M. (1990). Comorbidity of anxiety and depressive disorders: A helplessness-hopelessness perspective. In J. D. Maser & C. R. Cloninger (Eds.), *Comorbidity of mood and anxiety disorders.* (pp. 499–543): Washington, DC: American Psychiatric Association.

Almeida, D. M. (2005). Resilience and vulnerability to daily stressors assessed via diary methods. *Curr. Dis. Psychol. Sci., 14*(2), 64–68.

Alpert, J. E., Uebelacker, L. A., McLean, N. E., Nierenberg, A. A., Pava, J. A., Worthington III, J. J., Tedlow, J. R., Rosenbaum, J. F., & Fava, M. (1997). Social phobia, avoidant personality disorder and atypical depression: Co-occurrence and clinical implications. *Psychol. Med., 27*, 627–33.

Alpert, J. L., Brown, L. S., Ceci, S. J., Courtois, C. A., Loftus, E. F., & Ornstein, P. A. (1996). *Working group on investigation of memories of childhood abuse: Final report.* Washington, DC: American Psychological Association.

Alterman, A. I. (1988). Patterns of familial alcoholism, alcoholism severity, and psychopathology. *J. Nerv. Ment. Dis., 176*, 167–75.

Alterman, A. I., McDermott, P. A., Cacciola, J. S., Rutherford, M. J., Boardman, C. R., McKay, J. R., & Cook, T. G. (1998). A typology of antisociality in methadone patients. *J. Abn. Psychol., 107*(2), 412–22.

Alterman, A. I., Searles, J. S., & Hall, J. G. (1989). Failure to find differences in drinking behavior as a function of familial risk for alcoholism: A replication. *J. Cons. Clin. Psychol., 98*, 50–53.

Althof, S. E., & Schreiner-Engel, P. (2000). The sexual dysfunctions. In M. G. Gelder, J. J. Lobez-Ibor, & N. Andreasen (Eds.),*New Oxford textbook of psychiatry.* Oxford University Press.

Althof, S. E., Dean, J., Derogatis, L. R., Rosen, R. C., & Sisson, M. (2005). Current perspectives on the clinical assessment and diagnosis of female sexual dysfunction and clinical studies of potential therapies: A Statement of Concern. *J. Sex. Med., 2*, 146–53.

Altshuler, L. L., Bauer, M., Frye, M. A., Gitlin, M. J., Mintz, J., Szuba, M. P., Leight K. L., & Whybrow, P. C. (2001). Does thyroid supplementation accelerate tricyclic antidepressant response? A review and meta-analysis of the literature. *Amer. J. Psychiat., 158*, 1617–22.

Amato, P. R. (2000). The consequences of divorce for adults and children. *J. Marr. Fam., 62*, 1269–87.

Amato, P. R. (2001). Children of divorce in the 1990s: An update of the Amato and Keith (1991) meta-analysis. *J. Fam. Psychol., 15*, 355–70.

Amato, P. R. (2006). Marital discord, divorce, and children's well-being: Results from a 20-year longitudinal study of two generations. In A. Clarke-Stewart & J. Dunn (Eds.), *Families count: Effects on child and adolescent development.* (pp. 179–202). New York: Cambridge University Press.

Amato, P. R. (2010). Research on divorce: Continuing trends and new developments. *J. Marr. Fam., 72*(3), 650–66. doi: 10.1111/j.1741-3737.2010.00723.x

Amato, P. R., & Booth, A. (2001). The legacy of parents' marital discord: Consequences for children's marital quality. *J. Pers. Soc. Psychol., 81*, 627–38.

Amato, P. R., & Cheadle, J. (2005). The long reach of divorce: Divorce and child well-being across three generations. *J. Marr. Fam., 67*(1), 191–206.

Amato, P. R., & DeBoer, D. D. (2001). The transmission of marital instability across generations: Relationships skills or commitment to marriage? *J. Marr. Fam., 63*, 1038–51.

Amato, P. R., & Hohmann-Marriott, B. (2007). A comparison of high- and low-distress marriages that end in divorce. *J. Marr. Fam., 69*(3), 621–38.

Amato, P. R., & Keith, B. (1991a). Parental divorce and adult well-being: A meta-analysis. *J. Marr. Fam., 53*, 43–58.

Amato, P. R., & Keith, B. (1991b). Parental divorce and the well-being of children: A meta-analysis. *Psychol. Bull., 110*, 26–46.

Ambrogne, J. A. (2002). Reduced-risk drinking as a treatment goal: What clinicians need to know. *J. Sub. Abuse Treat., 22*(1), 45–53.

Ambruster, D., Mueller, A., Stroebel, A., Lesch, K. P., Brocke, B., & Kirschbaum, C. (2011). Predicting cortisol stress responses in older individuals: Influence of serotonin receptor 1A gene (HTR1A) and stressful life events. *Horm Behav*, March 31. [Epub ahead of print].

American Heart Association. (2001). *2001 Heart and stroke statistical update.* Dallas, TX: Author.

American Medical Association Committee on Human Sexuality. (1972). *Human sexuality* (p. 40). Chicago: American Medical Association.

American Psychiatric Association. (1968). *Diagnostic and statistical manual of mental disorders* (2nd ed.). Washington, DC: Author.

American Psychiatric Association. (1994). *Diagnostic and statistical manual of mental disorders (DSM-IV)* (4th ed.). Washington, DC: American Psychiatric Association.

American Psychiatric Association. (2000). *Diagnostic and statistical manual of mental disorders* (4th ed.). Washington, DC: Author.

American Psychological Association. (2002). Ethical principles of psychologists and code of conduct. *Amer. Psychol., 57.* 1060–73.

Amir, N., Beard, C., Taylor, C. T., Klumpp, H., Elias, J., Burns, M., & Chen, X. (2009). Attention training in individuals with generalized social phobia: A randomized controlled trial. *J. Cons. Clin. Psychol., 77*(5), 961–73. doi: 10.1037/a0016685

Ammerman, R. T., & Hersen, M. (1997). *Handbook of prevention and treatment with children and adolescents.* New York: Wiley.

Ammerman, R. T., Kane, V. R., Slomka, G. T., Reigel, D. H., Franzen, M. D., & Gadow, K. D. (1998). Psychiatric symptomatology and family functioning in children and adolescents with spina bifida. *J. Clin. Psychol. Med. Set., 5*(4), 449–65.

Anderluh, M. B., Tchanturia, K., Rabe-Hesketh, S., & Treasure, J. (2003). Childhood obsessive-compulsive personality traits in adult women with eating disorders: Defining a broader eating disorder phenotype. *Amer. J. Psychiat., 160,* 242–47.

Andersen, A. E., Bowers, W., & Evans, K. (1997). Inpatient treatment of anorexia nervosa. In D. M. Garner & P. E. Garfinkel (Eds.), *Handbook of treatment for eating disorders* (pp. 327–53). New York: Guilford.

Anderson, B., & Simpson, M. (2007). Ethical issues in online education. *Open Learning: The Journal of Open and Distance Learning, 22*(2), 129–38.

Anderson, C., Krull, D., & Weiner, B. (1996). Explanations: Processes and consequences. In E. T. Higgins & A. Kruglanski (Eds.), *Social psychology: Handbook of basic principles* (pp. 271–96). New York: Guilford.

Anderson, K., & Lehto, J. (1995). *Young people and alcohol, drugs and tobacco: European action plan.* Geneva: World Health Organization.

Anderson, N. B., & McNeilly, M. (1993). Autonomic reactivity and hypertension in blacks: Toward a contextual model. In J. C. S. Fray & J. G. Douglas (Eds.), *Pathophysiology of hypertension in blacks* (pp. 107–39). New York: Oxford.

Anderson, V. A., et al. (1997). Predicting recovery from head injury in young children: A prospective analysis. *J. Int. Neuropsychologic. Soc., 3*(6), 568–80.

Andrade, L., Caraveo-Anduaga, J. J., Berglund, P., Bijl, R. V., DeGraaf, R., Vollebergh, W., et al. (2004). The epidemiology of major depressive episodes: Results from the International Consortium of Psychiatric Epidemiology (ICPE) surveys. *Int. J. Meth. Psychiat. Res., 12*(1), 3–21.

Andreasen, N. C. (1984). *The broken brain: The biological revolution in psychiatry.* New York: Harper & Row.

Andreasen, N. C. (1985). Positive vs. negative schizophrenia: A critical evaluation. *Schizo. Bull., 11,* 380–89.

Andreasen, N. C., et al. (1995). Symptoms of schizophrenia: Methods, meanings, and mechanisms. *Arch. Gen. Psychiat., 52*(5), 341–51.

Andreasson, S., & Brandt, L. (1997). Mortality and morbidity related to alcohol. *Alcohol and Alcoholism, 32*(2), 173–78.

Andreescu, C., & Aizenstein, H. J. (2009). Amnestic disorders and mild cognitive impairment. In B. J. Sadock, A. A. Sadock, & P. Ruiz (Eds.), *Kaplan and Sadock's Comprehensive Textbook of Psychiatry* (9th ed., pp. 1198–1207). PA: Lippincott, Williams & Wilkins.

Andrews, B., Brewin, C. R., Philpott, R., & Stewart, L. (2007). Delayed-onset posttraumatic stress disorder: A systematic review of the evidence. *Amer. J. Psychiat., 164,* 1319–1326

Andrews, G., Hobbs, M. J., Borkovec, T. D., Beesdo, K., Craske, M. G., Heimberg, R. G., et al. (2010). Generalized worry disorder: A review of *DSM IV* generalized anxiety disorder and options for DSM-V. *Depression and Anxiety, 27*(2), 134–47. doi: 10.1002/da.20658

Andrews, J., & Hops, H. (2010). The influence of peers on substance use. In L. Scheier (Ed.), *Handbook of drug use etiology: Theory, methods, and empirical findings* (pp. 403–20). Washington, DC: American Psychological Association.

Angell, M. (2000). Is academic medicine for sale? *N. Engl. J. Med., 342,* 1516–18.

Angelucci, F., Ricci, V., Pompono, M., Conte, G., Mathe, A. A., Tonali, A., & Bria, P. (2007). Chronic heroin and cocaine abuse is associated with decreased serum concentrations of the nerve grown factor and brain derived neurotropic factor. *J. Psychopharm., 21,* 820–25.

Anglin, D. M., Cohen, P. R., & Chen, H. (2008). Duration of early maternal separation and prediction of schizotypal symptoms from early adolescence to midlife. *Schizo. Res., 103,* 143–50.

Angst, J., Gamma, A., Rössler, W., Ajdacic, V., & Klein, D. (2011). Childhood adversity and chronicity of mood disorders. *Eur. Arch. Psychiat. Clin. Neurosci., 261*(1), 21–27. doi: 10.1007/s00406-010-0120-3

Angst, J., & Sellaro, R. (2000). Historical perspectives and natural history of bipolar disorder. *Biol. Psychiat., 48,* 445–57.

Ansell, E. B., Pinto, A., Crosby, R. D., Becker, D. F., Añez, L. M., Paris, M., & Grilo, C. M. (2010). The prevalence and structure of obsessive-compulsive personality disorder in Hispanic psychiatric outpatients. *J Behav. Ther Exper. Psychiat., 41*(3), 275–81. Elsevier Ltd. doi:10.1016/j.jbtep.2010.02.005

Ansell, E., Pinto, A., Edelen, M., & Grilo, C. (2008). Structure of Diagnostic and Statistical Manual of Mental Disorders, Fourth Edition criteria for obsessive-compulsive personality disorder in patients with binge eating disorder. *Can. J. Psychiat., 53,* 863–67.

Antony, M. M., & Barlow, D. H. (2002). Specific phobias. In D. H. Barlow (Ed.), *Anxiety and its disorders* (2nd ed., pp. 380–417). New York: Guilford.

Antony, M. M., Brown, T. A., & Barlow, D. H. (1997). Heterogeneity among specific phobia types in DSM-IV. *Behav. Res. Ther., 35,* 1089–1100.

Antony, M., Downie, F., & Swinson, R. (1998). Diagnostic issues and epidemiology in obsessive-compulsive disorder. In R. Swinson, M. Antony, S. Rachman, & M. Richter (Eds.), *Obsessive-compulsive disorder: Theory, research, and treatments* (pp. 3–32). New York: Guilford.

APA Presidential Task Force of Evidence Based-Practice. (2006). Evidence-based practice in psychology. *Amer. Psychol., 61,* 271–85.

Appelbaum, P. S., & Greer, A. (1994). Who's on trial? Multiple personalities and the insanity defense. *Hosp. Comm. Psychiat., 45*(10), Spec. Issue 965–66.

Aragona, M., Bancheri, L, Perinelli, D., Tarsitani, L., Pizzimenti, A., Conte, A., & Inghilleri, M. (2005). Randomized double-blind comparison of serotonergic (Citalopram) versus noradrenergic (Reboxetine) reuptake inhibitors in outpatients with somatoform, DSM-IV-TR pain disorder. *European Journal of Pain, 9(1),* 33–38.

Arcelus, J., Mitchell, A. J., Wales, J., & Nielsen, S. (2011). Mortality rates in patients with anorexia nervosa and other eating disorders. *Arch. Gen. Psychiat., 68,* 724–31.

Arch, J., & Craske, M. G. (2008). Panic disorder. In W. E. Craighead, D. J. Miklowitz, & L. W. Craighead (Eds.), *Psychopathology: History, diagnosis, and empirical foundations* (pp. 115–58). Hoboken, NJ: John Wiley & Sons.

Arch, J. J., & Craske, M. G. (2009). First-line treatment: A critical appraisal of cognitive behavioral therapy developments and alternatives. *Psychiat. Clin. N. Amer., 32*(3), 525–47. doi: 10.1016/j.psc.2009.05.001

Archer, R. P., Buffington-Vollum, J. K., Stredny, R. V., & Handel, R. W. (2006). A survey of psychological test use patterns among forensic psychologists. *J. Pers. Assess., 87,* 84–94.

Arlow, J. A. (2000). Psychoanalysis. In R. J. Corsini & D. Wedding (Eds.), *Current psychotherapies* (pp. 16–53). Itasca, IL: Peacock.

Arndt, I. O., McLellan, A. T., Dorozynsky, L., Woody, G. E., & O'Brien, C. P. (1994). Desipramine treatment for cocaine dependence: Role of antisocial personality disorder. *J. Ner. Ment. Dis., 182,* 151–56.

Arnett, P. A., Howland, E. W., Smith, S. S., & Newman, J. P. (1993). Autonomic responsivity during passive avoidance in incarcerated psychopaths. *Personal. Indiv. Diff., 14*(1), 173–84.

Arnold, M. B. (1962). *Story sequence analysis: A new method of measuring motivation and predicting achievement.* New York: Columbia University Press.

Arnold, S. E. (2000). Hippocampal pathology. In P. J. Harrison & G. W. Roberts (Eds.), *The neuropathology of schizophrenia* (pp. 57–80). Oxford, UK: Oxford University Press.

Arnold, S. E., & Trojanowski, J. Q. (1996). Recent advances in defining the neuropathology of schizophrenia. *Acta Neuropathologie, 92,* 217–31.

Arntz, A., Bernstein, D., Gielen, D., Nieuwenhuyzen van, M., Penders, K., Haslam, N., & Ruscio, J. (2009). Taxometric evidence for the dimensional structure of cluster-c, paranoid, and borderline personality disorders. *J. Pers. Dis., 23*(6), 606–28.

Arntz, A., Weertman, A., & Salet, S. (2011). Behaviour research and therapy interpretation bias in cluster-c and borderline personality disorders. *Behav. Res. Ther., 49*(8), 472–81. Elsevier Ltd. doi:10.1016/j.brat.2011.05.002

Aronoff, B. (1987). *Needs assessments: What have we learned? Experiences from Refugee Assistance Programs in Hawaii.* Paper given at the Refugee

Assistance Program: Mental Health Workgroup Meeting, UCLA, February 12–13.

Arrindell, W. A. (2003). Cultural abnormal psychology. *Beh. Res. Ther., 41*, 749–53.

Arsenault, L., Cannon, M., Poulton, R., Murray, R., Caspi, A., & Moffitt, T. E. (2002). Cannabis use in adolescence and risk for adult psychosis: A longitudinal prospective study. *BMJ, 325*, 1212–13.

Arsenault, L., Cannon, M., Witton, J., & Murray, R. M. (2004). Causal association between cannabis and psychosis: Examination of the evidence. *Brit. J. Psychiat., 184*, 110–17.

Arthur, C., Hickling, F. W., Robertson-Hickling, Haynes-Robinson, T., Abel, W, & Whitley, R. (2010). "Mad, sick, head nuh good": Mental illness stigma in Jamaican communities. *Transcult. Psychiat., 47*, 252–75.

Asarnow, J. R. (2005). Childhood-onset schizotypal disorder: A follow-up study and comparison with childhood-onset schizophrenia. *J. Child Adol. Psychopharmacol., 15*, 395–402.

Ashton, A. K., Hamer, R., & Rosen, R. C. (1997). Serotonin reuptake inhibitor-induced sexual dysfunction and its treatment: A large-scale retrospective study of 596 psychiatric outpatients. *J. Sex and Marit. Ther., 23*, 165–75.

Askew, C., & Field, A. P. (2007). Vicarious learning and the development of fears in childhood. *Behav. Res. Ther., 45*(11), 2616–27.

Askew, C., & Field, A. P. (2008). The vicarious learning pathway to fear 40 years on. *Clin. Psychol. Rev., 28*(7), 1249–65. doi: 10.1016/j.cpr.2008.05.003

Askin-Edgar, S., White, K. E., & Cummings, J. L. (2002). Neuropsychiatric aspects of Alzheimer's disease and other dementing illnesses. In S. C. Yudofsky & R. E. Hales, *The American Psychiatric Publishing textbook of neuropsychiatry and clinical neurosciences* (pp. 953–88). Washington, DC: American Psychiatric Publishing.

Asmal, L., & Stein, D. J. (2009). Anxiety and culture. In M. M. Antony & M. B. Stein (Eds.), *Oxford handbook of anxiety and related disorders* (pp. 657–64). New York: Oxford University Press.

Associated Press. (2001, Aug. 7). Fire in asylum in southern India kills 25 mentally ill patients, many chained to beds. *Daily Star International News, 3*.

Associated Press. (2003, Nov. 18). Psychiatrist disputes Hinckley's recovery. .

Associated Press. (2004, Mar. 31). Doctor says mom who killed sons mentally ill. *Associated Press.*

Astley, S., Aylward, E. H., Olson, H. C., Kerns, K., Brooks, A., Coggins, T. E., Davies, J. Dorn, S., Gendler, B., Jirikowic, T., Kraegel, P., Maravilla, K., & Richards, T. (2009). Functional magnetic resonance imaging outcomes from a comprehensive magnetic resonance study of children with fetal alcohol spectrum disorders. *Journal of Neurodevelopmental Disorders, 1*(1), 61–80.

Athey, J. L., O'Malley, P., Henderson, D. P., & Ball, J. W. (1997). Emergency medical services for children: Beyond lights and sirens. *Profess. Psychol., 28*(5), 464–70.

Atkins, D. C., Berns, S. B., George, W., Doss, B., Gattis, K., & Christensen, A. (2005). Prediction of response to treatment in a randomized clinical trial of marital therapy. *J. Cons. Clin. Psychol., 73*, 893–903.

Atkinson, J. W. (1992). Motivational determinants of thematic apperception. In C. P. Smith, J. W. Atkinson, & J. Veroff (Eds.), *Motivation and personality: Handbook of thematic content analysis* (pp. 21–48). New York: Cambridge University Press.

Atlis, M. M., Hahn, J., & Butcher, J. N. (2006). Computer-based assessment with the MMPI-2. In J.

N. Butcher (Ed.), *MMPI-2: The practioner's handbook* (pp. 445–476). Washington, DC: American Psychological Association.

Attia, E., & Walsh, B. T. (2007). Anorexia nervosa. *Am. J. Psychiat., 164*, 1805–10.

Attia, E., & Roberto, C. A. (2009). Should amenorrhea be a diagnostic criterion for anorexia nervosa? *Int. J. Eat. Dis., 42*, 581–89.

Autism Genome Project (AGP). (2007). Consortium mapping autism risk loci using genetic linkage and chromosomal rearrangements. *Nature Genetics.* Published online. 18 February, 207, dai 10.1038/ng 1985.

Avants, S. K., Margolin, A., Kosten, T. R., Rounsaville, B. J., & Schottenfeld, R. S. (1998). When is less treatment better? The role of social anxiety in matching methadone patients to psychosocial treatments. *J. Cons. Clin. Psychol., 66*, 924–31.

Avenevoli, S., Knight, E., Kessler, R. C., & Merikangas, K. R. (2008). Epidemiology of depression in children and adolescents. In J. R. Z. Abela & B. L. Hankin (Eds.), *Handbook of depression in children and adolescents* (pp. 6–32). New York: Guilford Press.

Ayala, E. S., Meuret, A. E., & Ritz, T. (2009). Treatments for blood-injury-injection phobia: A critical review of current evidence. *J. Psychiat. Res., 43*(15), 1235–42. doi: 10.1016/j.jpsychires.2009.04.008

Aycicegi-Dinn, A., Caldwell-Harris, C. L., & Dinn, W. M. (2009). Obsessive-compulsive personality traits: Compensatory response to executive function deficit? *Int. J. Neurosci., 119*, 600–8.

Azar, B. (1997). Researchers debunk myth of crack baby. *Monitor, 29*(12), 14–15.

Azari, N. P., Horwitz, B., Pettigrew, K. D., & Grady, C. L. (1994). Abnormal pattern of glucose metabolic rates involving language areas in young adults with Down syndrome. *Brain & Language, 46*(1), 1–20.

Azim, H. F. (2001). Partial hospitalization programs. In W. J. Livesley (Ed.), *Handbook of personality disorders* (pp. 527–40). New York: Guilford.

Baaré, F. C., van Oel, C. J., Hulshoff Pol, H. E., Schnack, H. G., Durston, S., Sitkoorn, M. M., & Kahn, R. S. (2001). Volumes of brain structures in twins discordant for schizophrenia. *Arch. Gen. Psychiat., 58*, 33–40.

Babiak, P. (2007). From darkness into the light: Psychopathy in industrial and organizational psychology. In H. Hervé & J. C. Yuille (Eds.), *The Psychopath: Theory, Research, and Practice.* (pp. 411–28). Mahwah, NJ: Lawrence Erlbaum Associates.

Bach, A. K., Barlow, D. H., & Wincze, J. P. (2004). The enhancing effects of manualized treatment for erectile dysfunction among men using sildenafil: A preliminary investigation. *Behav. Ther., 35*, 55–73.

Bagge, C., Nickell, A., Stepp, S., Durrett, C., Jackson, K., & Trull, T. (2004). Borderline personality disorder features predict negative outcomes 2 years later. *J. Abn. Psych., 113*(2), 279–88.

Bagner, D. M., Pettit, J. W., Lewinsohn, P. M., & Seeley, J. R. (2010). Effect of maternal depression on child behavior: A sensitive period? *J. Amer. Acad. Child Adoles. Psychiat., 49*(7), 699–707.

Bailer, U. F., & Kaye, W. H. (2011). Serotonin: Imaging findings in eating disorders. *Current Topics in Behavioral Neuroscience, 6*, 59–79.

Bailey, J. M. (1999). Homosexuality and mental illness. *Arch. Gen. Psychiat., 56*, 883–84.

Bailey, J. M. (2003). *The man who would be queen.* Washington, DC: Joseph Henry Press.

Bailey, J. M., & Greenberg, A. S. (1998). The science and ethics of castration: Lessons from the Morse case. *Northwestern Law Review, 92*, 1225–45.

Bailey, J. M., & Triea, K. (2007). What many transgender activists don't want you to know and why you should know it anyway. *Persp. Biol. Med., 50*(4), 521–34.

Bailey, S. (2000). Juvenile delinquency and serious antisocial behavior. In M. G. Gelder, J. J. Lopez-Ibor, Jr., & N. C. Andreasen (Eds.), *New Oxford textbook of psychiatry* (pp. 1859–73). Oxford: Oxford University Press.

Baker, A., & Lee, N. K. (2003). A review of psychosocial interventions for amphetamine use. *Drug Al. Rev., 22*(3), 323–35.

Baker, D., Hunter, E., Lawrence, E., Medford, N., Patel, M., Senior, C., et al. (2003). Depersonalization disorder: Clinical features of 204 cases. *Brit. J. Psychiat., 182*, 428–33.

Baker, L. A., Jacobson, K. C., Raine, A., Lozano, D. I., & Bezdjian, S. (2007). Genetic and environmental bases of childhood antisocial behavior: A multi-informant twin study. *J. Abn. Psych., 116*(2), 219–23.

Bakkevig, J. F., & Karterud, S. (2010). Is the Diagnostic and Statistical Manual of Mental Disorders, Fourth Edition, histrionic personality disorder category a valid construct? *Compr. Psychiat., 51*(5), 462–70. Elsevier Inc. doi:10.1016/j.comppsych.2009.11.009

Baldessarini, R. J., & Hennen, J. (2004). Genetics of suicide. *Harv. Rev. Psychiat., 12*(1), 1–13.

Baldessarini, R. J., Salvatore, P., Khalsa, H.-M. K., & Tohen, M. (2010). Dissimilar morbidity following initial mania versus mixed-states in type-I bipolar disorder. *J. Affect. Disord., 126*(1–2), 299–302. doi: 10.1016/j.jad.2010.03.014

Baldwin, S. A., Wampold, B. E., & Imel, Z. E. (2007). Untangling the alliance-outcome correlation: Exploring the relative importance of therapist and patient variability in the alliance. *J. Consult. Clin. Psychol., 75*, 842–52.

Ball, S. A., Martino, N. C., Frankforter, T. L., Van Horn, D., Crits-Cristoph, P., & Carroll, K. M. (2007). Site matters: Multi-site randomized trial of motivational enhancement therapy in community drug abuse clinics. *J. Cons. Clin. Psychol., 75*, 556–67.

Ballard, C., Gauthier, S., Corbett, A., Brayne, C., Aarsland, D., & Jones, E. (2011). Alzheimer's Disease. *Lancet, 377*, 1019–31.

Balshem, M., Oxman, G., Van Rooyen, D., & Girod, K. (1992). Syphilis, sex and crack cocaine: Images of risk and morality. *Soc. Sci. and Med., 35*, 147–60.

Balzer, J. (2009). *Flying drunk: A Northwest Airlines Flight, three drunk pilots and one man's fight for redemption.* New York: Savas Beatie.

Bancroft, J., Carnes, L., Janssen, E., Goodrich, D., & Long, J. S. (2005). Erectile and ejaculatory problems in gay and heterosexual men. *Arch. Sex. Behav., 34*(3), 285–97.

Bancroft, J., Loftus, J., & Long, J. S. (2003). Distress about sex: A national survey of women in heterosexual relationships. *Arch. Sex. Behav., 32*, 193–208.

Bandelow, B., Krause, J., Wedekind, D., Broocks, A., Hajak, G. R., & Ruther, E. (2005). Early traumatic life events, parental attitudes, family history, and birth risk factors in patients with borderline personality disorder and healthy controls. *Psychiat. Res., 134*(2), 169–79.

Bandettini, P. (2007). Functional MRI today. *International Journal of Psychophysiology, 63*(2), 138–45.

Bandura, A. (1964). *Principles of behavior modification.* New York: Holt, Rinehart and Winston.

Bandura, A. (1969). *Principles of behavior modification.* New York: Holt, Rinehart & Winston.

Bandura, A. (1974). Behavior theory and the models of man. *Amer. Psychol., 29*(12), 859–69.

Bandura, A. (1977). Self-efficacy: Toward a unifying theory of behavioral change. *Psychol. Rev., 84*(2), 191–215.

Bandura, A. (1986). *Social foundations of thought and action: A social cognitive theory.* Englewood Cliffs, NJ: Prentice-Hall.

Bandura, A. (1997). *Self-efficacy: The exercise of control.* New York: W. H. Freeman/Times Books/Henry Holt & Co.

Banjo, O. C., Nadler, R., & Reiner, P. B. (2010). Physician attitudes towards pharmacological cognitive enhancement: Safety concerns are paramount. *PLos ONE, 5*(12): e14322. doi:10.1371/journal. pone.0014322

Bannon, S., Gonsalvez, C. J., & Croft, R. J. (2008). Processing impairments in OCD: It is more than inhibition! *Behav. Res. Ther., 46*(6), 689–700. doi: 10.1016/j.brat.2008.02.006

Baratta, M. V., Christianson, J. P., Gomez, D. M., Zarza, C. M., Amat, J., Masini, C. V., et al. (2007). Controllable versus uncontrollable stressors bi-directionally modulate but not innate fear. *Neuroscience, 146,* 1495–503.

Barbaree, H. E., & Blanchard, R. (2008). Sexual deviance over the lifespan: Reduction in deviant sexual behavior in the aging sex offender. In D. R. Laws & W. T. O'Donohue (Eds.), *Sexual Deviance: Theory, Assessment, and Treatment* (2nd ed.; pp. 37–60). New York: Guilford Press.

Barbaree, H. E., & Seto, M. C. (1997). Pedophilia: Assessment and treatment. In D. R. Laws & W. O'Donohue (Eds.), *Sexual deviance: Theory, assessment, and treatment* (pp. 175–93). New York: Guilford.

Barbee, P. W., Combs, D. C., Ekleberry, F., & Villalobos, S. (2007). Duty to warn and protect: Not in Texas. *Journal of Professional Counseling: Practice, Theory, & Research, 35*(1), 18–25.

Barch, D. M. (2005). The cognitive neuroscience of schizophrenia. *Ann. Rev. Clin. Psychol., 1,* 12.1–12.33.

Bar-Haim, Y., Lamy, D., Pergamin, L., Bakermans-Kranenburg, M. J., & van Ijzendoorn, M. H. (2007). Threat-related attentional bias in anxious and nonanxious individuals: A meta-analytic study. *Psych. Bull., 133*(1), 1–24.

Barkley, R. A. (1997). Behavioral inhibition, sustained attention, and executive function: Constructing a unified theory of ADHD. *Psychol. Bull., 121,* 65–94.

Barkley, R. A., Fischer, M., Smallish, L., & Fletcher, K. (2004). Young adult follow-up of hyperactive children: Antisocial activities and drug use. *J. Child Psychol. Psychiat., 45*(2), 195–211.

Barlow, D. H. (1988). *Anxiety and its disorders: The nature and treatment of anxiety and panic.* New York: Guilford.

Barlow, D. H. (2004). Psychological treatments. *Amer. Psychol., 59*(9), 869–78.

Barlow, D. H. (2008). *Clinical handbook of psychological disorders: A step-by-step treatment manual* (4th ed.). New York: Guilford Press.

Barlow, D. H. (Ed.). (2002). *Anxiety and its disorders: The nature and treatment of anxiety and panic* (2nd ed.). New York: Guilford.

Barlow, D. H., Allen, L. B., & Basden, S. L. (2007). Psychological treatments for panic disorder, phobias, and generalized anxiety disorder. In P. E. Nathan and J. M. Gorman (Eds.), *A guide to treatments that work.* New York: Oxford University Press, pp. 351–94.

Barlow, D. H., Chorpita, B., & Turovsky, J. (1996). Fear, panic, anxiety, and disorders of emotion. In D. Hope (Ed.), *Perspectives on anxiety, panic, and fear.* 43rd Annual Nebraska Symposium on Motivation (pp. 251–328). Lincoln: University of Nebraska Press.

Barlow, D. H., Raffa, S. D., & Cohen, E. M. (2002). Psychosocial treatments for panic disorders, phobias and generalized anxiety disorders. In P. E. Nathan & J. M. Gorman (Eds.), *A guide to treatments that work* (2nd ed., pp. 301–36). New York: Oxford University Press.

Barlow, D. H., Sakheim, D. K., & Beck, J. G. (1983). Anxiety increases sexual arousal. *J. Abn. Psychol., 92,* 49–54.

Barnett, D., Ganiban, J., & Cicchetti, D. (1999). Maltreatment, negative expressivity, and the development of Type D attachments from 12 to 24 months of age. *Monogr. Soc. Res. Child Develop., 64,* 97–118.

Baron, I. S., & Goldberger, E. (1993). Neuropsychological disturbances of hydrocephalic children with implications for special education and rehabilitation. *Neuropsychological Rehabilitation, 3*(4), 389–410.

Baron-Kuhn, & Segraves, R.T. (2007). Iatrogenic causes of female sexual disorders. In S.F. Owens and M.S. Tepper (Eds.), *Sexual health, Vol 4: State-of-the art treatments and research* (pp. 329–48). Westport, CT: Praeger.

Barringer, T. A., & Weaver, E. M. (2002). Does long-term bupropion (Zyban) use prevent smoking relapse after initial success at quitting smoking? *J. Fam. Pract., 51,* 172.

Barry, H., III. (1982). Cultural variations in alcohol abuse. In I. Al-Issa (Ed.), *Culture and psychopathology.* Baltimore: University Park Press.

Barry, R. J., Clarke, A. R., & Johnstone, S. J. (2003). A review of electrophysiology in attention deficit/ hyperactivity disorder: II. Event-related potentials. *Clinical Neurophysiology, 114*(2), 184–98.

Barsetti, I., Earls, C. M., Lalumiere, M. L., & Belanger, N. (1998). The differentiation of intrafamilial and extrafamilial heterosexual child molesters. *J. Interpers. Violen., 13*(2), 275–86.

Barsky, A. J., & Ahern, D. K. (2004). Cognitive behavior therapy for hypochondriasis: A randomized controlled trial. *JAMA, 291*(12), 1464–70.

Barsky, A. J., et al. (1998). A prospective 4- to 5-year study of DSM-III-R hypochondriasis. *Arch. Gen. Psychiat., 55*(8), 737–44.

Barsky, A. J., Orav, E. J., & Bates, D. W. (2005). Somatization increases medical utilization and costs independent of psychiatric and medical comorbidity. *Arch. Gen. Psychiat., 62*(8), 903–10.

Barsky, A. J., Wool, C., Barnett, M. C., & Cleary, P. D. (1994). Histories of childhood trauma in adult hypochondriacal patients. *Amer. J. Psychiat., 151*(3), 397–401.

Bartak, A., Andrea, H., Spreeuwenberg, M. D., Ziegler, U. M., Dekker, J., Rossum, B. V., Hamers, E. F. M., et al. (2011). Effectiveness of outpatient, day hospital, and inpatient psychotherapeutic treatment for patients with cluster B personality disorders. *Psychother. Psychosom., 80*(1), 28–38. doi:10.1159/000321999

Bartak, A., Spreeuwenberg, M. D., Andrea, H., Holleman, L., Rijnierse, P., Rossum, B. V., Hamers, E. F. M., et al. (2010). Effectiveness of different modalities of psychotherapeutic treatment for patients with cluster C personality disorders: Results of a large prospective multicentre study. *Psychother. Psychosom., 79*(1), 20–30. doi:10.1159/000254902

Bartholomew, K., Kwong, M. J., & Hart, S. D. (2001). Attachment. In W. J. Livesley (Ed.), *Handbook of personality disorders* (pp. 196–230). New York: Guilford.

Bartholomew, R. (1997). The medicalization of the exotic: Latah as a colonialism-bound "syndrome." *Dev. Behav., 18,* 47–75.

Bartholow, B. D., Sher, K. J., & Krull, J. L. (2003). Changes in heavy drinking over the third decade of life as a function of collegiate fraternity and sorority involvement: A prospective, multilevel analysis. *Hlth. Psychol., 22,* 618–26.

Barton, J., Mooney, P., & Prasad, S. (2005). Atomoxetine hydrochloride and executive function in children with attention-deficit/hyperactivity disorder. *J. Child Adol. Psychopharm., 15*(2), 147–49.

Bartz, J. A., & Hollander, E. (2007, August 28). Is Oxytocin the key to understanding? In *Mind Matters,* the *Scientific American* blog on science and mind.

Bartzokis, G., Lu, P. H., Turner, J., Mintz, J., & Saunders, C. S. (2005). Adjunctive risperidone in the treatment of chronic combat-related posttraumatic stress disorder. *Biol. Psychiat., 57*(5), 474–79.

Başoğlu, M., & Mineka, S. (1992). The role of uncontrollable and unpredictable stress in post-traumatic stress responses in torture survivors. In M. Başoğlu (Ed.), *Torture and its consequences: Current treatment approaches* (pp. 182–225). Cambridge: Cambridge University Press.

Başoğlu, M., Mineka, S., Paker, M., Aker, T., Livanou, M., & Gok, S. (1997). Psychological preparedness for trauma as a protective factor in survivors of torture. *Psychol. Med., 27,* 1421–33.

Başoğlu, M., Paker, M., Paker, O., Ozmen, E., Marks, I., Sahin, D., & Sarimurat, N. (1994). Psychological effects of torture: A comparison of tortured with nontortured political activists in Turkey. *Amer. J. Psychiat., 151,* 76–81.

Başoğlu, M., Salcioglu, E., & Livanou, M. (2007). A randomized controlled study of single-session behavioral treatment of earthquake-related post traumatic stress disorder using an earthquake simulator. *Psychol. Med., 37,* 203–213.

Bass, E., & Davis, L. (1988). *The courage to heal.* New York: Harper & Row.

Bassett, D. R., Jr., Fitzhugh, E. C., Crespo, C. J., King, G. A., & McLaughlin, J. E. (2002). Physical activity and ethnic differences in hypertension in the United States. *Preventive Medicine, 34*(2), 179–86.

Basson, R. (2003a). Biopsychosocial models of women's sexual response: Applications to management of "desire disorders." *Sexual & Relationship Therapy, 18,* 107–15.

Basson, R. (2003b). Women's difficulties with low sexual desire and sexual avoidance. In S. B. Levine, C. B. Risen, & S. E. Althof (Eds.), *Handbook of clinical sexuality for mental health professionals.* (pp. 111–30). New York: Brunner-Routledge.

Basson, R. (2005). Women's sexual dysfunction: Revised and expanded definitions. *Canadian Medical Association Journal, 172,* 1327–33.

Basson, R., Leiblum, S., Brotto, L., Derogatis, L., Fourcroy, J., Fugl-Meyer, K., et al. (2003). Definitions of women's sexual dysfunction reconsidered: Advocating expansion and revision. *J. Psychosom. Obst. Gyn., 24,* 221–29.

Basson, R., McInnes, R., Smith, M. D., Hodgson, G., & Koppiker, N. (2002). Efficacy and safety of sildenafil citrate in women with sexual dysfunction associated with female sexual arousal disorder.

Journal of Women's Health & Gender-Based Medicine, 11(4), 367–77.

Bateson, G. (1959). Cultural problems posed by a study of schizophrenic process. In A. Auerback (Ed.), *Schizophrenia: An integrated approach.* New York: Ronald Press.

Bateson, G. (1960). Minimal requirements for a theory of schizophrenia. *Arch. Gen. Psychiat., 2,* 477–91.

Bath, E. P. J., & Billick, S. B. (2010). Overview of juvenile law. In E. P. Benedek, P. Ash, & C. L. Scott (Eds.), *Principles and practice of child and adolescent forensic mental health,* (pp. 337–45). Arlington, VA: American Psychiatric Publishing, Inc.

Bath, R., Morton, R., Uing, A., & Williams, C. (1996). Nocturnal enuresis and the use of desmopressin: Is it helpful? *Child: Care, Health & Development, 22*(22), 73–84.

Battle, C. L., Shea, M. T., Johnson, D. M., Yen, S., Zlotnick, C., Zanarini, M. C., et al. (2004). Childhood maltreatment associated with adult personality disorders: Findings from the collaborative longitudinal personality disorders study. *J. Pers. Dis., 18*(2), 193–211.

Bauer, A. M., & Shea, T. M. (1986). Alzheimer's disease and Down syndrome: A review and implications for adult services. *Education and Training of the Mentally Retarded, 21,* 144–50.

Bauer, A., Rosca, P., Khawalled, R., Gruzniewski, A., & Grinshpoon, A. (2003). Dangerousness and risk assessment: The state of the art. *Israel Journal of Psychiatry & Related Sciences, 40*(3), 182–90.

Bauer, S. M., Schanda, H., Karakula, H., Olajossy-Hilkesberger, L., Rudaleviciene, P., Okribelashvili, N., Chaudhry, H., Idemudia, S. E., Gscheider, S., Ritter, K., & Stompe, T. (2011). Culture and the prevalence of hallucinations in schizophrenia. *Compr. Psychiat., 52,* 319–325.

Baum, A., & Posluszny, D. M. (1999). Health psychology: Mapping biobehavioral contributions to health and illness. *Annu. Rev. Psychol., 50,* 137–63.

Bauermeister, J. J., Canino, G., Polanczyk, G., & Rohde, L. A. (2010). ADHD across cultures: Is there evidence for a bidimensional organization of symptoms? *J. Clin. Child Adol. Psych., 39*(3), 362–72.

Baumeister, R. F., & Butler, J. L. (1997). Sexual masochism: Deviance without pathology. In D. R. Laws & W. O'Donohue (Eds.), *Sexual deviance: Theory, assessment, and treatment.* New York: Guilford.

Baumrind, D. (1967). Child care practices anteceding three patterns of preschool behavior. *Genetic Psychology Monographs, 75,* 43–88.

Baumrind, D. (1971). Current patterns of parental authority. *Develop. Psychol., 4*(1), 1–103.

Baumrind, D. (1975). *Early socialization and the discipline controversy.* Morristown, NJ: General Learning Press.

Baumrind, D. (1991). Effective parenting during the early adolescent transition. In P. A. Cowan & E. M. Hetherington (Eds.), *Family transitions* (pp. 111–64). Hillsdale, NJ: Erlbaum.

Baumrind, D. (1993). The average expectable environment is not good enough: A response to Scarr. *Child Develop., 64,* 1299–1317.

Baxter, L. R., Jr., Ackermann, R. F., Swerdlow, N. R., Brody, A., Saxena, S., Schwartz, J. M., Gregortich, J. M., Stoessel, P., & Phelps, M. E. (2000). Specific brain system mediation of obsessive-compulsive disorder responsive to either medication or behavior therapy. In W. K. Goodman, M. V. Rudorfer, et al. (Eds.), *Obsessive-compulsive disorder: Contemporary issues in treatment. Personality and clinical psychology series* (pp. 573–609). Mahwah, NJ: Erlbaum.

Baxter, L. R., Jr., Schwartz, J. M., & Guze, B. H. (1991). Brain imaging: Toward a neuroanatomy of OCD. In J. Zohar, T. Insel, & S. Rasmussen (Eds.), *The psychobiology of obsessive-compulsive disorder.* New York: Springer.

Baxter, L. R., Jr., Schwartz, J. M., Bergman, K. S., Szuba, M. P., Guze, B. H., Mazziota, J. C., Alazraki, A., Selin, C., Ferng, H. K., Munford, P., & Phelps, M. (1992). Caudate glucose metabolic rate changes with both drug and behavior therapy for obsessive-compulsive disorder. *Arch. Gen. Psychiat., 49,* 681–89.

Bayer, R. (1981). *Homosexuality and American psychiatry.* New York: Basic Books.

Bazargan, M., Bazargan, S., & Akanda, M. (2001). Gambling habits among aged African Americans. *Clin. Geron., 22*(3–4), 51–62.

Beach, S. R. H., & Jones, D. J. (2002). Marital and family therapy for depression in adults. In I. H. Gotlib & C. L. Hammen (Eds.), *Handbook of depression* (pp. 422–40). New York: Guilford.

Beal, A. L. (1995). Post-traumatic stress disorder in prisoners of war and combat veterans of the Dieppe raid: A 50 year follow-up. *Canad. J. Psychiat., 40*(4), 177–84.

Bearn, A., & Smith, C. (1998). How learning support is perceived by mainstream colleagues. *Support for Learning, 13*(1), 14–20.

Beaton, A. A. (1997). The relation of planum temporale asymmetry and morphology of the corpus callosum to handedness, gender, and dyslexia: A review of the evidence. *Brain and Language, 60*(2), 255–322.

Beaumont, P. J. V. (2002). Clinical presentation of anorexia nervosa and bulimia nervosa. In C. G. Fairburn and K. D. Brownell (Eds.), *Eating disorders and obesity: A comprehensive handbook* (2nd ed.). New York: The Guilford Press.

Beck, A. T. (1967). *Depression: Causes and treatment.* Philadelphia: University of Pennsylvania Press.

Beck, A. T. (1983). Cognitive therapy of depression: New perspectives. In P. J. Clayton & J. E. Barrett (Eds.), *Treatment of depression: Old controversies and new approaches* (pp. 265–90). New York: Raven Press.

Beck, A. T. (2005). The current state of cognitive therapy: A 40-year retrospective. *Arch. Gen. Psychiat., 62,* 953–59.

Beck, A. T., & Emery, G., (with) Greenberg, R. L. (1985). *Anxiety disorders and phobias: A cognitive perspective.* New York: Basic Books.

Beck, A. T., Emery, G., & Greenberg, R. L. (2005). *Anxiety disorders and phobias: A cognitive perspective.* New York: Basic Books.

Beck, A. T., Freeman, A., & Associates. (1990). *Cognitive therapy of personality disorders.* New York: Guilford.

Beck, A. T., Freeman, A., & Davis, D. D. (2004). *Cognitive therapy of personality disorders* (2nd ed.). New York: Guilford Press.

Beck, A. J., & Maruschak, L. M. (2001, Jul.). Mental health treatment in state prisons, 2000. *Bureau of Justice Special Report* (NCJ 188215). Washington, DC: Department of Justice.

Beck, A. T., & Rector, N. A. (2005). Cognitive approaches to schizophrenia: Theory and therapy. *Annu. Rev. Clin. Psychol., 1,* 577–606.

Beck, A. T., Rush, A. J., Shaw, B., & Emery, G. (1979). *Cognitive therapy of depression: A treatment manual.* New York: Guilford.

Beck, A. T., & Weishaar, M. (2000). Cognitive therapy. In R. J. Corsini & D. Wedding (Eds.), *Current psychotherapies* (6th ed., pp. 241–72). Itasca, IL: Peacock.

Beck, A. T., Wright, F., Newman, C., & Liese, B. (1993). *Cognitive therapy of substance abuse.* New York: Guilford.

Beck, J. G., & Barlow, D. H. (1984a). Current conceptualizations of sexual dysfunction: A review and an alternative perspective. *Clin. Psychol. Rev., 4*(4), 363–78.

Beck, J. G., & Barlow, D. H. (1984b). Unraveling the nature of sex roles. In E. A. Blechman (Ed.), *Behavior modification with women* (pp. 34–59). New York: Guilford.

Becker, A., Burwell, R. A., Gilman, S., Herzog, D. B., & Hamburg, P. (2002). Eating behaviors and attitudes following prolonged exposure to television among ethnic Fijian adolescent girls. *Brit. J. Psychiat., 180,* 509–14.

Becker, J. B., Monteggia, L. M., Perrot-Sinal, T. S., Romeo, R. D., Taylor, J. R., Yehuda, R., & Bale, T. L. (2007). Stress and disease: Is being female a predisposing factor? *J. Neurosci., 27*(44), 11851–55. doi: 10.1523/jneurosci.3565-07.2007

Becker, K. D., Stuewig, J., Herrera, V. M., & McCloskey, L. A. (2004). A study of firesetting and animal cruelty in children: Family influences and adolescent outcomes. *J. Amer. Acad. Child Adoles. Psychiat., 43,* 905–12.

Beckett, C., Maughan, B., Rutter, M., Castle, J., Colvert, E., Groothues, C., et al. (2006). Do the effects of early severe deprivation on cognition persist into early adolescence? Findings from the English and Romanian Adoptees Study. *Child Develop., 77*(3), 696–711.

Beeman, S. K., & Edleson, J. L. (2000). Collaborating on family safety: Challenges for children's and women's advocates. *Journal of Aggression, Maltreatment & Trauma, 3,* 345–58.

Beers, C. (1970). *A mind that found itself* (Rev. ed.). New York: Doubleday.

Beesdo, K., Pine, D. S., Lieb, R., & Wittchen, H.-U. (2010). Incidence and risk patterns of anxiety and depressive disorders and categorization of generalized anxiety disorder. *Arch. Gen. Psychiat., 67*(1), 47–57. doi: 10.1001/archgenpsychiatry.2009.177

Beevers, C. G., & Miller, I. W. (2004). Depression-related negative cognition: Mood-state and trait dependent properties. *Cog. Ther. Res., 28*(3), 293–307.

Beevers, C. G., Rohde, P., Stice, E., & Nolen-Hoeksema, S. (2007). Recovery from manor depressive disorder among female adolescents: A prospective test of the scar hypothesis. *J. Cons. Clin. Psychol., 75,* 888–900.

Behan, J., & Carr, A. (2000). Oppositional defiant disorder. In A. Carr (Ed.), *What works with children and adolescents? A critical review of psychological interventions with children, adolescents and their families* (pp. 102–30). Florence, KY: Taylor & Francis/Routledge.

Behar, E., & Borkovec, T. D. (2006). The nature and treatment of generalized anxiety disorder. In B. O. Rothbaum (Ed.), *Pathological anxiety: Emotional processing in etiology and treatment* (pp. 181–96). New York: Guilford Press.

Behar, E., et al. (2008). Current theoretical models of GAD: Conceptual review and treatment implications. *J. Anx. Disord., 23,* 1011–13.

Behar, L., Friedman, R., Pinto, A., Katz-Leavy, J., & Jones, W. G. (2007). Protecting youth placed in unlicensed, unregulated residential "treatment" facilities. *Family Court Review, Vol 45*(3), 399–413.

Bekker, M. H. (1996). Agoraphobia and gender: A review. *Clin. Psychol. Rev., 16*(2), 129–46.

Belanoff, J. K., Gross, K., Yager, A., & Schatzberg, A. F. (2001). Corticosteroids and cognition. *J. Psychiat. Res., 35*(3), 127–45.

Belik, S.-L., Sareen, J., & Stein, M. B. (2009). Anxiety disorders and physical comorbidity. In M. M. Antony & M. B. Stein (Eds.), *Oxford handbook of anxiety and related disorders* (pp. 596–610). New York: Oxford University Press.

Bellack, A. S., & Mueser, K. T. (1993). Psychosocial treatment for schizophrenia. *Schizo. Bull., 19*, 317–36.

Belsito, K. M., Law, P. A., Kirk, K. S., Landa, R. J., & Zimmerman, A. W. (2001). Lamotrigine therapy for autistic disorder: A randomized double-blind placebo-controlled trial. *J. Autism Devel. Dis., 31*, 175–81.

Bender, R. E., & Alloy, L. B. (2011). Life stress and kindling in bipolar disorder: Review of the evidence and integration with emerging biopsychosocial theories. *Clin. Psychol. Rev., 31*(3), 383–98. doi: 10.1016/j.cpr.2011.01.004

Benes, F. M., & Berretta, S. (2001). GABAergic interneurons: Implications for understanding schizophrenia and bipolar disorder. *Neuropsychopharmacol., 25*, 1–27.

Benjamin, L. S. (1993). *Interpersonal diagnosis and treatment of personality disorders*. New York: Guilford.

Benjamin, L. S. (2004). An interpersonal family-oriented approach to personality disorder. In M. M. MacFarlane (Ed.), *Family treatment of personality disorders: Advances in clinical practice.* (pp. 41–69). Binghampton, NY: Haworth Clinical Practice Press.

Benjamin, L. S. (2005). Interpersonal theory of personality disorders: The structural analysis of social behavior and interpersonal reconstructive therapy. In M. F. Lezenweger & J. F. Clarkin (Eds.), *Major theories of personality disorder* (2nd ed., pp. 157–230). New York: Guilford Press.

Benjamin, L. S., & Pugh, C. (2001). Using interpersonal theory to select effective treatment interventions. In W. J. Livesley (Ed.), *Handbook of personality disorders: Theory, research, and treatment* (pp. 414–36). New York: Guilford.

Benjamin, L. S., Rothweiler, J. C., & Critchfield, K. L. (2006). The use of structural analysis of social behavior (SASB) as an assessment tool. *Annu. Rev. Clin. Psychol., 2*, 83–109.

Benjamin, L. T., Jr. (2005). A history of clinical psychology as a profession in America (and a glimpse at its future). *Annu. Rev. Clin. Psychol., 1*(1), 1–30.

Bennett, D., Sharpe, M., Freeman, C., & Carson, A. (2004). Anorexia nervosa among female secondary students in Ghana. *Brit. J. Psychiat., 185*, 312–17.

Bennett, J. B., & Lehman, W. E. K. (1996). Alcohol, antagonism, and witnessing violence in the workplace: Drinking climates and social alienation-integration. In G. R. Vandenbos & E. Q. Bulatao (Eds.), *Violence in the workplace* (pp. 105–52). Washington, DC: American Psychological Association.

Bennett, T. L., Dittmar, C., & Ho, M. R. (1997). The neuropsychology of traumatic brain injury. In A. M. Horton, D. Wedding, & J. Webster (Eds.), *The neuropsychology handbook* (Vol. 2, pp. 123–72). New York: Springer.

Bennice, J. A., & Resick, P. A. (2003). Marital rape: History, research, and practice. *Trauma, Violence, & Abuse, 4*, 228–46.

Benson, N., Hulac, D. M., & Kranzler, J. H. (2010). Independent examination of the Wechsler Adult Intelligence Scale—Fourth Edition (WAIS-IV): What does the WAIS - IV measure? *Psychol. Assess., 22*(1), 121–30.

Bentovim, A., Boston, P., & Van Elburg, A. (1987). Child sexual abuse—children and families referred to a

treatment project and the effects of intervention. *Brit. Med. J., 295*, 1453–57.

Berenbaum, H., Thompson, R. J., Milanek, M. E., Boden, T. M., Bredmeier, K. (2008). Psychological trauma and schizotypal personality disorder. *J. Abn. Psych., 117*(3), 502–19.

Berenson, K. R., Downey, G., Rafaeli, E., Coifman, K. G., & Paquin, N. L. (2011). The rejection-rage contingency in borderline personality disorder. *J Abn. Psychol., 120*(3), 681–90. doi:10.1037/a0023335

Berge, M. T., Veerkamp, J. S. J., & Hoogstraten, J. (2002). The etiology of childhood dental fear: The role of dental and conditioning experiences. *J. Anx. Disord., 16*(3), 321–29. doi: 10.1016/s0887-6185(02)00103-2

Bergem, A. L. M., Engedal, K., & Kringlen, E. (1997). The role of heredity in late-onset Alzheimer disease and vascular dementia. *Arch. Gen. Psychiat., 54*(3), 264–70.

Bergeron, S., Binik, T., Khalife, S., Pagidas, K., Glazer, H. I., Meana, M., & Amsel, R. (2001). A randomized comparison of group cognitive-behavioral therapy, surface electromyographic biofeedback, and vestibulectomy in the treatment of dyspareunia resulting from vulvar vestibules. *Pain, 91*, 297–306.

Berk, L. E. (2003). *Child Develop.* (6th ed.). Boston: Allyn & Bacon.

Berk, L. S., Tan, S. A., Nehlsen-Cannarella, S., Napier, B. J., Lewis, J. E., Lee, J. W., & Eby, W. C. (1988). Humor associated laughter decreases cortisol and increases spontaneous lymphocyte blastogenesis. *Clin. Res., 36*, 435A.

Berkman, L. F., Blumenthal, J., Burg, M., Carney, R. M., Catellier, D., Cowan, M. J., Czajkowski, S. M., DeBuk, R., Hosking, J., Jaffe, A., Kaufmann, P. G., Mitchell,P., Norman, J., Powell, L. H., Raczynski, J. M., & Schneiderman, N. (2003). Effects of treating depression and low perceived social support on clinical events after myocardial infarction: The Enhancing Recovery in Coronary Heart Diseases Patients (ENRICHD) randomized trial. *JAMA, 289*, 3106–16.

Berkman, L. F., Leo-Summers, L., & Horwitz, R. I. (1992). Emotional support and survival after myocardial infarction: A prospective population-based study of the elderly. *Ann. Int. Med., 117*, 1003–9.

Berle, D., & Starcevic, V. (2005). Thought-action fusion: Review of the literature and future directions. *Clin. Psych. Rev., 25*(3), 263–84.

Berlin, F. S. (1994, May). The case for castration, part 2. *Washington Monthly, 26*, 28–29.

Berlin, F. S. (2003). Sex offender treatment and legislation. *J. Amer. Acad. Psychiat. Law, 31*(4), 510–13.

Berney, T. P. (2000). Methods of treatment. In M. G. Gelder, J. J. Lopez-Ibor, Jr., & N. C. Andreason (Eds.), *New Oxford textbook of psychiatry.* (Vol. 2, pp. 1989–94). Oxford: Oxford University Press.

Bernstein, D. P., Arntz, A., & Travaglini, L. (2009). Schizoid and avoidant personality disorders. In P. H. Blaney & T. Millon (Eds.), *Oxford textbook of psychopathology* (2nd ed., pp. 586–601). New York: Oxford University Press.

Bernstein, A., Zvolensky, M. J., Sachs-Ericsson, N., Schmidt, N. B., & Bonn-Miller, M. O. (2006). Associations between age of onset and lifetime history of panic attacks and alcohol use, abuse, and dependence in a representative sample. *Compr. Psychiat., 47*(5), 342–49.

Bernstein, D. P., & Travaglini, L. (1999). Schizoid and avoidant personality disorders. In T. Millon, P. H. Blaney, & R. D. Davis (Eds.), *Oxford textbook of psychopathology* (pp. 523–34). New York: Oxford University Press.

Bernstein, D. P., & Useda, D. J. (2007). Paranoid personality disorder. In W. O'Donohue, K. A. Fowler, & S. C. Lilienfeld (Eds.), *Personality Disorders: Toward the DSM-V* (pp. 41–62). Thousand Oaks, CA: Sage Publications, Inc.

Bernstein, G. A., & Layne, A. E. (2006). Separation anxiety disorder and generalized anxiety disorder. In M. K. Dulcan & J. M Wiener (Eds.), *Essentials of child and adolescent psychiatry* (pp. 415–39). Washington, DC: American Psychiatric Publishing.

Berrios, G. (1990). A British contribution to the history of functional brain surgery. Special Issue: History of psychopharmacology. *J. Psychopharm., 4*, 140–44.

Berthold, T., & Ellinger, M. (2009). Conducting initial client interviews. In T. Berthold, J. Miller, & A. Avila-Esparza (Eds.), *Foundations for community health workers* (pp. 197–219). San Francisco: Jossey-Bass.

Berthoud, H.-R., & Morrison, C. (2008). The brain, appetite, and obesity. *Ann. Rev. Psych., 59*, 55–92.

Bettelheim, B. (1950). *Love is not enough*. New York: The Free Press.

Beutler, L. E., & Malik, M. I. (Eds.). (2002). *Rethinking the DSM: A psychological perspective*. Washington, DC: American Psychological Association.

Beutler, L. E., Malik, M., Alimohamed, S., Harwood, T. M., Talebi, H., Noble, S., & Wong, E. (2004). In M. J. Lambert (2004). *Bergin and Garfield's handbook of Psychotherapy and behavior change* (pp. 227–306). New York: John Wiley and Sons.

Beveridge, A. (1997). Voices of the mad: Patients' letters from the Royal Edinburgh Asylum, 1873–1908. *Psychol. Med., 27*, 899–908.

Bezchlibnyk-Butler, K. Z., & Jeffries, J. J. (2003). *Clinical handbook of psychotropic drugs*. Seattle: Hogrefe & Huber.

Bickel, W. K., Amass, L., Higgins, S. T., Badger, G. J., & Esch, R. A. (1997). Effects of adding behavioral treatment to opioid detoxification with buprenorphine. *J. Cons. Clin. Psychol., 65*(5), 803–10.

Bieber, I., Dain, H. J., Dince, P. R., Drellich, M. G., Grand, H. G., Gundlach, R. H., Kremer, M. W., Rifkin, A. H., Wilbur, C. B., & Bieber, T. B. (1962). *Homosexuality: A psychoanalytic study of male homosexuals*. New York: Basic Books.

Biederman, J., Monteaux, M. C., Doyle, A. E., Seidman, L. J., Wilens, T. E., Ferraro, F., Morgan, C. L., & Farone, S. V. (2004). Impact of executive function deficits and attention deficit/hyperactivity disorder (ADHD) on academic outcomes in children. *J. Cons. Clin. Psychol., 72*, 757–76.

Biederman, J., Petty, C. R., Faraone, S. V., Hirshfeld-Becker, D. R., Henin, A., Brauer, L., et al. (2006). Antecedents to panic disorder in nonreferred adults. *J. Clin. Psychiat., 67*(8),1179–86.

Biederman, J., Petty, C. R., Monuteaux, M. C., Fried, R., Byrne, D., Mirto, T., Spencer, T., Wilens, T. E., & Faraone, S. V. (2010). Adult psychiatric outcomes of girls with attention deficit hyperactivity disorder: 11-year follow-up in a longitudinal case-control study. *Amer. J. Psychiat., 167*(4), 409–417.

Biederman, J., Rosenbaum, J. F., Hirschfeld, D. R., Faraone, S., Bolduc, E., Gersten, M., Meminger, S., Kagan, J., Snidman, N., & Reznick, J. S. (1990). Psychiatric correlates of behavioral inhibition in young children of parents with and without psychiatric disorders. *Arch. Gen. Psychiat., 47*, 21–26.

Bienvenu, O. J., Hettema, J. M., Neale, M. C., Prescott, C. A., & Kendler, K. S. (2007). Low extraversion and high neuroticism as indices of genetic and environmental risk for social phobia, agoraphobia, and animal phobia. *Amer. J. Psychiat., 164*(11), 1714–21. doi: 10.1176/appi.ajp.2007.06101667

Bijttebier, P., & Goethals, E. (2006). Parental drinking as a risk factor for children's maladjustment: The mediating role of family environment. *Psych. Addict. Behav., 20*(2), 126–30.

Billett, E., Richter, J., & Kennedy, J. (1998). Genetics of obsessive-compulsive disorder. In R. Swinson, M. Antony, S. Rachman, & M. Richter (Eds.), *Obsessive-compulsive disorder: Theory, research, and treatment* (pp. 181–206). New York: Guilford.

Binder, R. L. (1999). Are the mentally ill dangerous? *J. Amer. Acad. Psychiat. & Law, 27*(2), 189–201.

Binik, Y. M. (2005). Should dyspareunia be retained as a sexual dysfunction in *DSM-V*? A painful classification decision. *Arch. Sex. Behav., 34*(1), 11–21.

Binik, Y. M., Bergeron, S., Khalifé, S., & Leiblum, S. R. (2007). Dyspareunia and vaginismus: So-called sexual pain. In *Principles and practice of sex therapy* (4th ed.; pp. 124–156). New York: Guilford Press.

Binks, C. A., Fenton, M., McCarthy, L., Lee, T., Adams, C. E., & Duggan, C. (2006). Psychological therapies for people with borderline personality disorder. Cochrane Database Syst Rev. CD005652.

Birbaumer, N., Veit, R., Lotze, M., Erb, M., Hermann, C., Grodd, W., et al. (2005). Deficient fear conditioning in psychopathy: A functional magnetic resonance imaging study. *Arch. Gen. Psychiat., 62*(7), 799–805.

Birmaher, B., Axelson, D. A., Monk, K., Kalas, C., Clark, D. B., Ehmann, M., Bridge, J., Heo, J., & Brent, D. A. (2003). Fluoxetine for the treatment of childhood anxiety disorders. *J. Amer. Acad. Child Adoles. Psychiat., 42*(4), 415–23.

Bisson, J. I., McFarlane, A. C., Rose, S., Ruzek, J. I., & Watson, P. J. (2009). Psychological debriefing for adults. In E. B. Foa, T. M. Keane, M. J. Friedman, & J. A. Cohen (Eds.), *Effective treatments for PTSD: Practice guidelines from the International Society for Traumatic Stress Studies* (2nd ed., pp. 83–105). New York: Guilford Press.

Bittles, A. H., Bower, C., Hussain, R., & Glasson, E. J. (2007). The four ages of Down syndrome. *European Journal of Public Health, 17*(2), 121–225.

Bjorklund, D. F. (2000). *False-memory creation in children and adults: Theory, research and implications.* Mahway, NJ: Erlbaum.

Blaauw, E., Roesch, R., & Kerkhof, A. (2000). Mental disorders in European prison systems: Arrangements for mentally disordered prisoners in the prison system of 13 European countries. *International Journal of Law and Psychiatry, 23,* 649–57.

Blackburn, I. M., & Davidson, K. (1990). *Cognitive therapy for depression and anxiety.* Oxford: Blackwell Scientific.

Blader, J. C., & Carlson, G. A. (2007). Increased rates of bipolar disorder diagnoses among U.S. child, adolescent, and adult inpatients, 1996–2004. *Biol. Psychiat., 62*(2), 107–14.

Blagov, P. S., Fowler, K. A., & Lilienfeld, S. O. (2007). Histrionic personality disorder. In W. O'Donohue, K. A. Fowler, & S. O. Lilienfeld (Eds.), *Personality Disorders; Toward the DSM-V* (pp. 203–32). Thousand Oaks, CA: Sage Publications, Inc.

Blagov, P. S., & Westen, D. (2008). Questioning the coherence of histrionic personality disorder: Borderline and hysterical personality subtypes in adults and adolescents. *J. Nerv. Ment. Dis., 196*(11), 785–97. doi:10.1097/NMD.0b013e31818b502d

Blair, K., Geraci, M., Devido, J., McCaffrey, D., Chen, G., Vythilingam, M., et al. (2008). Neural response to self- and other referential praise and criticism in generalized social phobia. *Arch. Gen. Psychiat., 65*(10), 1176–84. doi: 10.1001/archpsyc.65.10.1176

Blair, K. S., Richell, R. A., Mitchell, D. G., Leonard, A., Morton, J., & Blair, R. J. (2006). They know the words, but not the music: Affective and semantic priming in individuals with psychopathy. *Biol. Psychol., 73*(2), 114–23.

Blair, R. J. (2007a). Dysfunctions of medial and lateral orbitofrontal cortex in psychopathy. In G. Schoembaum, J. A. Gottfried, E. A. Murray, & S. J. Ramus (Eds.), *Linking Affect to Action: Critical Contributions of the Orbitofrontal Cortex* (pp. 461–479). Malden, MA: Blackwell Publishing.

Blair, R. J. (2007b). The amygdala and ventromedial prefrontal cortex in morality and psychopathy. *Trends in Cognitive Sciences, 11*(9), 387–92.

Blair, R. J. R. (2006). The subcortical brain systems in psychopathy: The amygdala and associated structures. In C. J. Patrick (Ed.), *Handbook of the psychopathy.* (pp. 296–312). New York: Guilford Press.

Blair, R. J. R., Jones, L., Clark, F., & Smith, M. (1997). The psychopathic individual: A lack of responsiveness to distress cues? *Psychophysiology, 34,* 192–98.

Blanchard, J. J., Collins, L. M., Aghevli, M., Leung, W. W., & Cohen, A. S. (2011). Social anhedonia and schizotypy in a community sample: The Maryland Longitudinal Study of Schizotypy. *Schizo. Bull., 37*(3), 587. doi:10.1093/schbul/sbp107

Blanchard, R. (1985). Typology of male-to-female transsexualism. *Arch. Sex. Behav., 14,* 247–61.

Blanchard, R. (1989). The classification and labeling of nonhomosexual gender dysphorias. *Arch. Sex. Behav., 18,* 315–34.

Blanchard, R. (1991). Clinical observations and systematic study of autogynephilia. *J. Sex Marit. Ther., 17,* 235–51.

Blanchard, R. (1993). Varieties of autogynephilia and their relationship to gender dysphoria. *Arch. Sex. Behav., 22,* 241–51.

Blanchard, R. (1994). A structural equation model for age at clinical presentation in nonhomosexual male gender dysphorics. *Arch. Sex. Behav., 23,* 311–32.

Blanchard, R., & Hucker, S. J. (1991). Age, transvestitism, bondage, and concurrent paraphilic activities in 117 fatal cases of autoerotic asphyxia. *Brit. J. Psychiat., 159,* 371–77.

Blanchard, R., Barbaree, H. E., Bogaert, A. F., Dickey, R., Klassen, P., Kuban, M. E., et al. (2000). Fraternal birth order and sexual orientation in pedophiles. *Arch. Sex. Behav., 29*(5), 463–78.

Blanco, C., Anita, S. X., & Liebowitz, R. (2002). Pharmacotherapy of social anxiety disorder. *Biol. Psychiat., 51,* 109–20.

Blanco, C., Cohen, O., Luján, J. J., & Wulfert, E. (2010). Pathological gambling among patients with substance use disorders. In E. V. Nunes, J. Selzer, P. Levounis, & C. A. Davies (Eds.), *Substance dependence and co-occurring psychiatric disorders: Best practices for diagnosis and treatment* (pp. 1–15). Kingston, NJ: Civic Research Institute.

Blanco, C., Heimberg, R. G., Schneier, F. R., Fresco, D. M., Chen, H., Turk, C. L., et al. (2010). A placebo-controlled trial of phenelzine, cognitive behavioral group therapy, and their combination for social anxiety disorder. *Arch. Gen. Psychiat., 67*(3), 286–95. doi: 10.1001/archgenpsychiatry.2010.11

Blashfield, R. K., & Livesley, W. J. (1999). Classification. In T. Millon, P. H. Blaney, & R. D. Davis (Eds.), *Oxford textbook of psychopathology* (pp. 3–28). New York: Oxford University Press.

Blaszczynski, A., McConaghy, N., & Frankova, A. (1989). Crime, antisocial personality and pathological gambling. *Journal of Gambling Behavior, 5,* 137–52.

Blazer, D. G., & Hybels, C. F. (2009). Depression in later life. Epidemiology, assessment, impact, and treatment. In I. H. Gotlib & C. L. Hammen (Eds.), *Handbook of depression* (2nd ed., pp. 492–509). New York: Guilford Press.

Blehar, M. C. (2006). Women's mental health research: The emergence of a biomedical field. *Annu. Rev. Clin. Psychol., 2,* 135–60.

Bleiberg, K. L., & Markowitz, J. C. (2008). Interpersonal psychotherapy for depression. In D. H. Barlow (Ed.), *Clinical handbook of psychological disorders: A step-by-step treatment manual* (4th ed.). (pp. 306–27). New York: Guilford Press.

Bleichhardt, G., & Hiller, W. (2006). Pathological features, medical consulting behaviour and media consume in outpatients with health anxiety. *Verhaltenstherapie & Verhaltensmedizin, 21*(1), 29–41.

Bleichhardt, G., Timer, B., & Rief, W. (2004). Cognitive-behavioural therapy for patients with multiple somatoform symptoms: A randomised controlled trial in tertiary care. *J. Psychosomat. Res., 56,* 449–54.

Bleuler, E. (1950). *Dementia praecox or the group of schizophrenias.* New York: International Universities Press. (Originally published in 1911.)

Bloch, H. S. (1969). Army clinical psychiatry in the combat zone—1967-1968. *Amer. J. Psychiat., 126,* 289.

Bloch, M. H, Landeros-Weisenberger, A., Kelmendi, B., Coric, V., Bracken, M. B., & Leckman, J. F. (2006). A systematic review: Antipsychotic augmentation with treatment refractory obsessive-compulsive disorder. *Molecular Psychiatry, 11,* 622–32.

Block, J. H., Block, J., & Gjerde, P. F. (1986). The personality of children prior to divorce: A prospective study. *Child Develop., 57,* 827–40.

Blonigen, D. M., Carlson, S. R., Krueger, R. F., & Patrick, C. J. (2003). A twin study of self-reported psychopathic personality traits. *Personal. Indiv. Diff., 35*(1), 179–97.

Blonigen, D. M., Hicks, B. M., Krueger, R. F., Patrick, C. J., & Iacono, W. G. (2006). Continuity and change in psychopathic traits as measured via normal-range personality: A longitudinal-biometric study. *J. Abn. Psych., 115*(1), 85–95.

Bloom, M., & Gullotta, T. P. (2009). Primary prevention in adolescent substance abuse. In C. G. Leukefeld, T. P. Gullotta & M. Staton-Tindall (Eds.), *Adolescent substance abuse: Evidence-based approaches to prevention and treatment, Issues in children's and families' lives* (pp. 155–70). New York: Springer.

Blount, A., Schoenbaum, M., Kathol, R., Rollman, B. L., Thomas, M., O'Donohue, W., & Peek, C. J. (2007). The economics of behavioral health services in medical settings: A summary of the evidence. *Prof. Psychol. Res. Pract., 38*(3), 290–97.

Bluglass, R. (2000). Organization of services. In M. G. Gelder, J. J. Lopez-Ibor, Jr., & N. C. Andreason (Eds.), *New Oxford textbook of psychiatry* (pp. 2123–31). Oxford: Oxford University Press.

Blum, N., St. John, D., Pfohl, B., Stuart, S., McCormick, B., Allen, J., Arndt, S., & Black, D. (2008). Systems training for emotional predictability and problem solving (STEPPS) for outpatients with borderline personality disorder: A randomized controlled trial and 1-year follow-up. *Am. J. Psychiat., 165,* 468–78.

Blum, R. (1969). *Society and drugs* (Vol. 1). San Francisco: Jossey-Bass.

Blume, E. S. (1990). *Secret survivors: Uncovering incest and its aftermath in women.* New York: Wiley.

Blumenthal, J. A., Sherwood, A., Gullette, E. C. D., Georgiades, A., & Tweedy, D. (2002). Biobehavioral approaches to the treatment of essential hypertension. *J. Cons. Clin. Psychol., 70,* 569–89.

Bock, M. A. (2007). The impact of social-behavioral learning strategy training on the social interaction skills of four students with Asperger syndrome. *Focus on Autism and Other Developmental Disabilities, 22*(2), 88–95.

Bockhoven, J. S. (1972). *Moral treatment in community mental health.* New York: Springer.

Bodenhausen, G., & Morales, J. (in press). Social cognition and perception. In *Handbook of Psychology* (2nd ed.).

Bodenheimer, T. (2000). Uneasy alliance—clinical investigators and the pharmaceutical industry. *N. Engl. J. Med., 342,* 1539–44.

Boehm, G. (1968). At last—a nonaddicting substitute for morphine? *Today's Health, 46*(4), 69–72.

Boland, R. J., & Keller, M. B. (2002). Course and outcome of depression. In I. H. Gotlib & C. L. Hammen (Eds.), *Handbook of depression* (pp. 43–57). New York: Guilford.

Boland, R. J., & Keller, M. B. (2009). Course and outcome of depression. In I. H. Gotlib & C. L. Hammen (Eds.), *Handbook of depression* (2nd ed., pp. 23–43). New York: Guilford Press.

Bonanno, G. A. (2006). Is complicated grief a valid construct? *Clin. Psychol. Sci. Prac., 13*(2), 129–34.

Bonanno, G. A., & Kaltman, S. (1999). Toward an integrative perspective on bereavement. *Psychol. Bull., 125*(6), 760–76.

Bonanno, G. A., Moskowitz, J. T., Papa, A., & Folkman, S. (2005). Resilience to loss in bereaved spouses, bereaved parents, and bereaved gay men. *J. Pers. Soc. Psychol., 88*(5), 827–43.

Bonnano, G. A, Westphal, M., & Mancini, A. D. (2011). Resilience to loss and potential trauma. *Annu. Rev. Clin. Psychol., 7,* 511–35.

Bonanno, G. A., Wortman, C. B., & Nesse, R. M. (2004). Prospective patterns of resilience and maladjustment during widowhood. *Psychol. Aging, 19*(2), 260–71.

Bond, G. R, Salyers, M., Dincin, J., Drake, R. E., Becker, D. R., Graser, V. V., & Haines, M. (2007). A randomized controlled trial comparing two vocational models for persons with severe mental illness. *J. Cons. Clin. Psychol., 75,* 968–82.

Bondi, M. W., & Lange, K. L. (2001). Alzheimer's disease. In H. S. Friedman (Ed.), *The disorders: Specialty articles from the encyclopedia of mental health.* San Diego, CA: Academic Press.

Bookheimer, S. Y., Strojwas, M. H., Cohen, M. S., Saunders, A. M., Pericak-Vance, M. A., Mazziotta, J. C., & Small, G. W. (2000). Patterns of brain activation in people at risk for Alzheimer's disease. *N. Engl. J. Med., 343,* 450–56.

Bora, E., Yücel, M., & Pantelis, C. (2010). Cognitive impairment in affective psychoses: A meta-analysis. *Schizo. Bull., 36*(1), 112–25. doi: 10.1093/schbul/sbp093

Bora, E., Yücel, M., Pantelis, C., & Berk, M. (2011). Meta-analytic review of neurocognition in bipolar II disorder. *Acta Psychiatr. Scand., 123,* 165–74.

Booth-Kewley, S., Larson, G. E., Highfill-McRoy, R. M., Garland, C. F., & Gaskin, T. A. (2010). Correlates of posttraumatic stress disorder symptoms in Marines back from war. *J. Trauma. Stress., 23*(1), 69–77.

Borch-Jacobsen, M. (1997). Sybil—the making of a disease: An interview with Dr. Herbert Spiegel. *New York Review of Books, 44i,* 60–64.

Borges, G., Nock, M. K., Haro Abad, J. M., Hwang, I., Sampson, N. A., Alonso, J., Andrade, L. H., Angermeyer, M. C., Beautrais, A., Bromet, E., Bruffaerts, R., de Girolamo, G., Florescu, S., Gureje, O., Hu, C., Karam, E. G., Kovess-Masfety, V., Lee, S., Levinson, D., Medina-Mora, M. E., Ormel, J., Posada-Villa, J., Sagar, R., Tomov, T., Uda, H., Williams, D. R., & Kessler, R. C. (2010). Twelve-month prevalence of and risk factors for suicide attempts in the World Health Organization World Mental Health Surveys. *J. Clin. Psychiat., 71,* 1617–28.

Borkovec, T. D. (1985). The role of cognitive and somatic cues in anxiety and anxiety disorders. In A. Tuma & J. D. Maser (Eds.), *Anxiety and the anxiety disorders* (pp. 463–78). Hillsdale, NJ: Lawrence Erlbaum Associates.

Borkovec, T. D. (1994). The nature, functions, and origins of worry. In G. L. C. Davey & F. Tallis (Eds.), *Worrying, perspectives on theory, assessment, and treatment* (pp. 5–34). Sussex, England: Wiley.

Borkovec, T. D. (2006). Applied relaxation and cognitive therapy for pathological worry and generalized anxiety disorder. In G. C. L. Davey & A. Wells (Eds.), *Worry and its psychological disorders: Theory, assessment and treatment.* (pp. 273–87). Hoboken, NJ: John Wiley & Sons.

Borkovec, T. D., Abel, J. L., & Newman, H. (1995). Effects of psychotherapy on comorbid conditions in generalized anxiety disorder. *J. Cons. Clin. Psychol., 63*(3), 479–83.

Borkovec, T. D., Alcaine, O. M., & Behar, E. (2004). Avoidance theory of worry and generalized anxiety disorder. In Heimberg, R. G., Turk, C. L., & Mennin, D. S. (Eds.), *Generalized anxiety disorder: Advances in research and practice.* (pp. 77–108). New York: Guilford Press.

Borkovec, T. D., Newman, M. G., Pincus, A. L., & Lytle, R. (2002). A component analysis of cognitive-behavioral therapy for generalized anxiety disorder and the role of interpersonal problems. *J. Cons. Clin. Psychol., 70*(2), 288–98.

Bornovalova, M.A., Hicks, B. M., Iacono, W. G., & McGue, M. (2009). Stability, change, and heritability of borderline personality disorder traits from adolescence to adulthood: A longitudinal twin study. *Develop. Psychopath., 21*(4), 1335–53. doi:10.1017/S0954579409990186

Bornstein, R. F. (1999). Dependent and histrionic personality disorders. In T. Millon, P. H. Blaney, & R. D. Davis (Eds.), *Oxford textbook of psychopathology* (pp. 535–54). New York: Oxford University Press.

Bornstein, R. F. (2007). Dependent personality disorder. In W. O'Donohue, K. A. Fowler, & S. O. Lilienfeld (Eds.), *Personality disorders: Toward the DSM-V.* (pp. 307–24). Thousand Oaks, CA: Sage Publications.

Bornstein, R. F. (2011). Reconceptualizing personality pathology in DSM-5: Limitations in evidence for eliminating dependent personality disorder and other DSM-IV syndromes. *J. Pers. Dis., 25*(2), 235–47. doi:10.1521/pedi.2011.25.2.235

Bornstein, R. F., & Malka, I. L. (2009). Dependent and histrionic personality disorders. In P. H. Blaney & T. Millon (Eds.), *Oxford textbook of psychopathology* (2nd ed., pp. 602–21). New York: Oxford University Press.

Borthwick, A., Holman, C., Kennard, D., McFetridge, M., Messruther, K., & Wilkes, J. (2001). The relevance of moral treatment to contemporary mental health care. *J. Ment. Hlth., 10,* 427–39.

Bos, K., Zeanah, C. H., Fox, N. A., Drury, S. S., McLaughlin, K. A., & Nelson, C. A. (2011). Psychiatric outcomes in young children with a history of institutionalization. *Harv. Rev. Psychiat., 19*(1), 15–24. doi: doi:10.3109/10673229.2011.549773

Boskind-White, M., & White, W. C. (1983). *Bulimarexia: The binge-purge cycle.* New York: Norton.

Bosshard, G., Broeckaert, B., Clark, D., Materstvedt, L. J., Gordijn, B., & Muller-Busch, H. C. (2008). A role for doctors in assisted dying? An analysis of legal regulations and medical professional positions in six European countries. *J. Med. Ethics, 34*(1), 28–32.

Bostic, J. Q., Biederman, J., Spencer, T. J., Wilens, T. E., Prince, J. B., Monuteaux, M. C., Sienna, M., Polisner, D. A., & Hatch, M. (2000). Pemoline treatment of adolescents with attention deficit hyperactivity disorder: A short-term controlled trial. *J. Child. Adoles. Psychopharm., 10*(3), 205–16.

Bottlender, M., Spanagel, R., & Soyka, M. (2007). One drink, one drink—Controlled drinking by alcoholics? A 3-year outcome after intensive outpatient treatment. *Psychotherapie, Psychosomatik Medizinsche Psychologie, 57,* 32–38.

Bouchard, T. J., & Propping, P. (Eds.). (1993). *Twins as a tool of behavioral genetics.* New York: Wiley.

Bouchard, T. J., Jr., & Loehlin, J. C. (2001). Genes, evolution, and personality. *Behav. Gen., 31*(3), 243–73.

Bouma, E. M., Ormel, J., Verhulst, F. C., & Oldehinkel, A. J. (2008). Stressful life events and depressive problems in early adolescent boys and girls: the influence of parental depression, temperament and family environment. *J. Affect. Dis., 105,* 185–193.

Bouman, T. K., Eifert, G. H., & Lejeuz, C. W. (1999). Somatoform disorders. In T. Millon & P. Blaney (Eds.), *Oxford textbook of psychopathology* (pp. 444–65). New York: Oxford University Press.

Bouton, M. E. (1994). Conditioning, remembering, and forgetting. *J. Exper. Psychol.: Animal Behavior Processes, 20,* 219–31.

Bouton, M. E. (2002). Context, ambiguity, and unlearning: Sources of relapse after behavioral extinction. *Biol. Psychiat., 52*(10), 976–86.

Bouton, M. E. (2005). Behavior systems and the contextual control of anxiety, fear, and panic. In L. F. Barrett, P. M. Niedenthal, & P. Winkielman (Eds.), *Emotion and consciousness.* (pp. 205–27). New York: Guilford Press.

Bouton, M. E. (2007). *Learning and behavior: A contemporary synthesis.* Sunderland, MA: Sinauer Associates.

Bouton, M. E., Mineka, S., & Barlow, D. H. (2001). A modern learning theory perspective on the etiology of panic disorder. *Psychol. Rev., 108,* 4–32.

Bouton, M. E., Westbrook, R. F., Corcoran, K. A., & Maren, S. (2006). Contextual and temporal modulation of extinction: Behavioral and biological mechanisms. *Biol. Psychiat., 60*(4), 352–360.

Bovet, P., Perret, F., Cornuz, J., Quilindo, J., & Paccaud, F. (2002). Improved smoking cessation in smokers given ultrasound photographs of their own atherosclerotic plaques. *Preventive Medicine: An International Journal Devoted to Practice & Theory, 34*(2), 215–20.

Bowlby, J. (1960). Separation anxiety. *Inter. J. Psychounal., 41,* 89–93.

Bowlby, J. (1969). *Attachment and loss* (Vol. 1). New York: Basic Books.

Bowlby, J. (1973). Separation: Anxiety and anger. *Psychology of attachment and loss series* (Vol. 3). New York: Basic Books.

Bowlby, J. (1980). *Attachment and loss, III: Loss, sadness, and depression.* New York: Basic Books.

Bowler, J. V., et al. (1997). Comparative evolution of Alzheimer disease, vascular dementia, and mixed dementia. *Arch. Neurol., 54*(6), 697–703.

Bowman, E. S., & Markand, O. N. (2005). Diagnosis and treatment of pseudoseizures. *Psychiat. Ann., 35*(4), 306–16.

Boyce, W. T., Essex, M. J., Alkon, A., Goldsmith, H. H., Kraemer, H. C., & Kupfer, D. J. (2006). Early father involvement moderates biobehavioral susceptibility to mental health problems in middle childhood. *J. Amer. Acad. Child Adoles. Psychiat., 45*(12), 1510–20.

Boylan, K., Georgiades, K., & Szatmari, P. (2010). The longitudinal association between oppositional and depressive symptoms across childhood. *J. Amer. Acad. Child Adoles. Psychiat., 49*(2), 152–61.

Boys, A., Marsden, J., & Strang, J. (2001). Understanding reasons for drug use amongst young people: A functional perspective. *Hlth Ed. Res., 16*(4), 457–69.

Braaten, E. B. (2011). Mood disorders. In E. B. Braaten (Ed.), How to find mental health care for your child, APA LifeTools imprint (pp. 87–99). Washington, DC,: American Psychological Association.

Bradford, D., Stroup, S., & Lieberman, J. (2007). *A guide to treatments that work* (3rd Ed.). New York: Oxford University Press, p. 169–200.

Bradford, J. M. W., & Greenberg, D. M. (1996). Pharmacological treatment of deviant sexual behaviour. *Ann. Rev. Sex Res., 7*, 283–306.

Braksiek, R. J., & Roberts, D. J. (2002). Amusement park injuries and deaths. *Annals of Emergency Medicine, 39*(1), 65–72.

Brand, M., Fujiwara, E., Kalbe, E., Steingrass, H. P., Kessler, J., & Markowitsch, H. J. (2003). Cognitive estimation and affective judgments in alcoholic Korsakoff patients. *J. Clini. Exper. Neuropsych., 25*(3), 324–34.

Brandsma, J. M., Maultsby, M. C., & Welsh, R. J. (1980). *Outpatient treatment of alcoholism: A review and comparative study.* Baltimore: University Park Press.

Brans, R. G. H., Van Haren, N. E. M., van Baal, G. C., Schnack, H. G., Kahn, R. S., & Hulsoff Pol, H. E. (2008). Heritability of changes in brain volume over time in twin pairs discordant for schizophrenia. *Arch. Gen. Psychiat., 65*, 1259–68.

Branson, R., Potoczna, N., Kral, J. G., Lentes, K.-U., Hoehe, M. R., & Horber, F. F. (2003). Binge eating as a major phenotype of melanocortin 4 receptor gene mutation. *N. Engl. J. Med., 348*, 1096–103.

Braun, S. (1996). *Buzz.* (1) New York: Oxford University Press.

Braus, D., Ende, G., Weber-Fahr, W., Sartorius, A., Krier, A., Hubrich-Ungureanu, P., Ruf, M., Stuck, S., & Henn, F. A. (1999). Antipsychotic drug effects on motor activation measured by functional magnetic resonance imaging in schizophrenic patients. *Schiz. Res., 39*(1), 19–29.

Brecht, M. L., O'Brien, A., Mayrhauser, C., & Anglin, M. D. (2004). Methamphetamine use behaviors and gender differences. *Add. Behav., 29*(1), 89–106.

Brecht, M., von Mayrhauser, C., & Anglin, M. D. (2000). Predictors of relapse after treatment for methamphetamine use. *J. Psychoact. Drugs, 32*(2), 211–20.

Breier, A., Buchanan, R. W., Kirkpatrick, B., Davis, O. R., Irish, D., Summerfelt, A., & Carpenter, W. T. (1994). Effects of clozapine on positive and negative symptoms in outpatients with schizophrenia. *Amer. J. Psychiat., 151*(1), 20–26.

Breitborde, N. J. K., Srihari, V. H., Pollard, J. M., Addington, D. N., & Woods, S. W. (2010). Mediators and moderators in early intervention research. *Early Intervention in Psychiatry, 4*(2), 143–52.

Breitner, J. C. S., Gatz, M., Bergem, A. L. M., Christian, J. C., Mortimer, J. A., McClearn, G. E., Heston, L. L., Welsh, K. A., Anthony, J. C., Folstein, M. F., & Radebaugh, T. S. (1993). Use of twin cohorts for research in Alzheimer's disease. *Neurol., 43*, 261–67.

Breitner, J. C., Gau, B. A., Welsh, K. A., et al. (1994). Inverse association of anti-inflammatory treatments and Alzheimer's disease: Initial results of a co-twin control study. *Neurol., 44*, 227–32.

Brems, C. (1995). Women and depression: A comprehensive analysis. In E. E. Beckham & W. R. Leber (Eds.), *Handbook of depression* (2nd ed., pp. 539–66). New York: Guilford.

Brennan, P. A., Le Brocque, R., & Hammen, C. (2003). Maternal depression, parent-child relationships, and resilient outcomes in adolescence. *J. Amer. Acad. Child Adoles. Psychiat., 42*(12), 1469–77.

Brennan, P. A., Raine, A., Schulsinger, F., Kirkegaard-Sorensen, L., et al. (1997). Psychosociological protective factors for male subjects at high risk for criminal behavior. *Amer. J. Psychiat., 154*(6), 853–55.

Breslau, J., Aguilar-Gaxiola, S., Kendler, K. S., Su, M., Williams, D., & Kessler, R. C. (2006). Specifying race-ethnic differences in risk for psychiatric disorder in a USA national sample. *Psychol. Med., 36*(1), 57–68.

Breslau, N., & Davis, G. C. (1987). Posttraumatic stress disorder: The stressor criterion. *J. Nerv. Ment. Dis., 175*, 255–264.

Breslau, N., & Kessler, R. C. (2001). The stressor criterion in DSM-IV posttraumatic stress disorder: An empirical investigation. *Biol. Psychiat., 50*, 699–704.

Breslau, N., Davis, G. C., & Andreski, P. (1995). Risk factors for PTSD-related traumatic events: A prospective analysis. *Amer. J. Psychiat., 152*, 529–535.

Breslau, N., Davis, G. C., Andreki, P., & Peterson, E. (1991). Traumatic events and posttraumatic stress disorder in an urban population of young adults. *Arch. Gen. Psychiat., 48*, 216–222.

Breslau, N., Lucia, V. C., & Alvarado, G. F. (2006). Intelligence and other predisposing factors in exposure to trauma and posttraumatic stress disorder: A followup study at age 17 years. *Arch. Gen. Psychiat., 63*, 1238–1245.

Breslow, R. A., Faden, V. B., & Smothers, B. (2003). Alcohol consumption by elderly Americans. *J. Stud. Alcoh., 64*, 884–92.

Bretschneider, J. G., & McCoy, N. L. (1988). Sexual interest and behavior in healthy 80- to 102-year-olds. *Arch. Sex. Behav., 17*, 109–29.

Brewerton, T. D., Lydiard, R. B., Herzog, D. B., Brotman, A. W., O'Neil, P. M., & Ballenger, J. C. (1995). Comorbidity of Axis I psychiatric disorders in bulimia nervosa. *J. Clin. Psychiat., 56*, 77–80.

Brewin, C., & Holmes, E. A. (2003). Psychological theories of posttraumatic stress disorder. *Clin. Psychol. Rev., 23*(3), 339–76.

Brezo, J., Bureau, A., Merette, C., Jomphe, V., Barker, E. D., Vitaro, F., et al. (2010). Differences and similarities in the serotonergic diathesis for suicide attempts and mood disorders: A 22-year longitudinal gene-environment study. *Molec. Psychiat., 15*(8), 831–43. doi: 10.1038/mp.2009.19

Brinded, M. J., Stevens, I., Myulder, R. T., Fairley, N., Malcolm, J., & Wells, J. E. (1999). The Christchurch Prisons psychiatric epidemiology study: Methodology and prevalence rates for psychiatric disorders. *Criminal Behaviour and Mental Health, 9*, 131–43.

Brock, A. J. (1979). Galen. On the natural faculties. (English translation). Loeb Classical Library. Cambridge, MA: Harvard University Press.

Brody, A. L., Saxena, S., Mandelkern, M. A., Fairbanks, L. A., Ho, M. L., & Baxter, L. R., Jr. (2001). Brain metabolic changes associated with symptom factor improvement in major depressive disorder. *Biol. Psychiat., 50*, 171–78.

Brody, E. B. (2004). The World Federation for Mental Health: its origins and contemporary relevance to WHO and WPA policies *J. Nerv. Ment. Dis., 3*(1): 54–55.

Brokate, B., Hildebrandt, H., Eling, P., Fichtner, H., Runge, K., & Timm, C. (2003). Frontal lobe dysfunctions in Korsakoff's syndrome and chronic alcoholism: Continuity or discontinuity? *Neuropsych., 17*(3), 420–28.

Bronte-Tinkew, J., Moore, K. A., & Carrano, J. (2006). The father-child relationship, parenting styles, and adolescent risk behaviors in intact families. *Journal of Family Issues, 27*(6), 850–81.

Broome, M., & Bortolotti, L. (2010). What's wrong with mental disorders? *Psychol. Med., 40*, 1783–85.

Brown, A. S. (2011). The environment and susceptibility to schizophrenia. *Progress in Neurobiology, 11*, 23–58.

Brown, E. S., Vornik, L. A., Khan, D. A., & Rush, A. J. (2007). Bupropion in the treatment of outpatients with asthma and major depressive disorder. *International Journal of Psychiatry in Medicine, 37*(1), 23–28.

Brown, G. K., Have, T. T., Henriques, G. R., Xie, S. X., Hollander, J. E., & Beck, A. T. (2005). Cognitive therapy for the prevention of suicide attempts: A randomized controlled trial. *JAMA, 294*(5), 563–70.

Brown, G. W. (1985). The discovery of expressed emotion: Induction or deduction? In J. Leff & C. Vaughn (Eds.), *Expressed emotion in families* (pp. 7–25). New York: Guilford.

Brown, G. W., Carstairs, G. M., & Topping, G. (1958). Post hospital adjustment of chronic mental patients. *Lancet, 2*, 685–89.

Brown, G. W., & Harris, T. O. (1978). *Social origins of depression.* London: Tavistock.

Brown, G. W., & Harris, T. O. (1989). *Life events and illness.* New York: Guilford.

Brown, G. W., Harris, T. O., & Bifulco, P. M. (1985). Longterm effects of early loss of parent. In M. Rutter, C. E. Izard, & P. B. Read (Eds.), *Depression in young people: Clinical and developmental perspectives* (pp. 251–96). New York: Guilford.

Brown, J. F., & Menninger, K. A. (1940). *Psychodynamics of abnormal behavior.* New York: McGraw-Hill.

Brown, P. (1994). Toward a psychobiological model of dissociation and posttraumatic stress disorder. In S. J. Lynn & J. W. Rhue (Eds.), *Dissociation: Clinical and theoretical perspectives* (pp. 94–122). New York: Guilford.

Brown, R. D., Goldstein, E., & Bjorklund, D. F. (2000). The history and Zeitgeist of the repressed-false-memory debate: Scientific and sociological perspectives on suggestibility and childhood memory. In D. F. Bjorklund (Ed.), *False-memory creation in children and adults: Theory, research, and implications* (pp. 1–30). Mahwah, NJ: Erlbaum.

Brown, R., & Lo, R. (2000). The physical and psychosocial consequences of opioid addiction: An overview of changes in opioid treatment. *Australian & New Zealand Journal of Mental Health Nursing, 9*, 65–74.

Brown, R., Taylor, J., & Matthews, B. (2001). Quality of life: Aging and Down syndrome. *Down Syndrome: Research & Practice, 6*, 111–16.

Brown, R. J. (2006). Dissociation and conversion in psychogenic illness. In M. Hallett, S. Fahn, J. Jankovic, A. E. Lang, C. R. Cloninger, & S. C. Yudofsky (Eds.), *Psychogenic movement disorders: Neurology and neuropsychiatry* (pp. 131–43). Philadelphia: Lippincott.

Brown, T. A., & Barlow, D. H. (2001). *Casebook in abnormal psychology* (2nd ed.). Belmont, CA: Wadsworth/Thomson Learning.

Brown, T. A., & Barlow, D. H. (2002). Classification of anxiety and mood disorders. In D. H. Barlow (Ed.), *Anxiety and its disorders: The nature and treatment of anxiety and panic* (2nd ed., 292–327). New York: Guilford Press.

Brown, T. A., & Barlow, D. H. (2009). A proposal for a dimensional classification system based on the shared features of the *DSM-IV* anxiety and mood disorders: Implications for assessment and treatment. *Psychol. Assess., 21*(3), 256–71. doi: 10.1037/a0016608

Brown, T. A., Campbell, L. A., Lehman, C. L., Grisham, J. R., & Mancill, R. B. (2001). Current and lifetime comorbidity of the *DSM-IV* anxiety and mood disorders in a large clinical sample. *J. Abn. Psychol., 110*(4), 585–99.

Brown, T. L., Flory, K., Lynam, D. R., Leukefeld, C., & Clayton, R. R. (2004). Comparing the developmental trajectories of marijuana use of African American and Caucasian adolescent patterns, antecedents and consequences. *Exp. Clin. Psychopharm., 12,* 47–56.

Browne, E. G. (1921). *Arabian medicine.* New York: Macmillan.

Brownell, K. (2003). *Food fight: The inside story of the food industry.* New York: McGraw-Hill.

Brownell, K. D. (2002). Public policy and the prevention of obesity. In C. G. Fairburn & K. D. Brownell (Eds.), *Eating disorders and obesity: A comprehensive handbook* (2nd ed., pp. 619–23). New York: Guilford.

Brownmiller, S. (1975). *Against our will: Men, women, and rape.* New York: Simon & Schuster.

Bruce, L. C., & Peebles, A. M. S. (1904). Quantitative and qualitative leukocyte counts in various forms of mental illness. *J. Ment. Sci., 50,* 409–17.

Bruce, S. E., Yonkers, K. A., Otto, M. W., Eisen, J. L., Weisberg, R. B., Pagano, M., et al. (2005). Influence of psychiatric comorbidity on recovery and recurrence in generalized anxiety disorder, social phobia, and panic disorder: A 12-year prospective study. *Am. J. Psychiat, 162*(6), 1179–87.

Bruch, H. (1973). *Eating disorders: Obesity, anorexia nervosa and the person within.* New York: Basic Books.

Bruck, M., Ceci, S. J., & Hembrooke, H. (2002). The nature of children's true and false narratives. *Developmental Review, 22*(3), 520–54.

Bryant, R. A., O'Donnell, M. L., Creamer, M., McFarlane, A. C., Clark, C. R., & Silove, D. (2010). The psychiatric sequelae of traumatic injury. *Amer. J. Psychiat., 167*(3), 312–20.

Bryant-Waugh, R., & Lask, B. (2002). Childhood-onset eating disorders. In C. G. Fairburn & K. D. Brownell (Eds.), *Eating disorders and obesity: A comprehensive handbook* (2nd ed., pp. 210–14). New York: Guilford.

Buchanan, G. M., & Seligman, M. E. P. (1995). Afterword: The future of the field. In G. M. Buchanan & M. E. P. Seligman (Eds.), *Explanatory style* (pp. 247–52). Hillsdale, NJ: Erlbaum.

Buchsbaum, M. S., Haier, R. J., Potkin, S. G., Nuechterlein, K., Bracha, H. S., Katz, M., Lohr, J., Wu, J., Lottenberg, S., Jerabek, P. A., Trenary, M., Tafalla, R., Reynolds, C., & Bunney, W. E., Jr. (1992).

Frontostriatal disorder of cerebral metabolism in never-medicated schizophrenics. *Arch. Gen. Psychiat., 49*(12), 935–41.

Buckley, M. A., & Zimmermann, S. H. (2003). *Mentoring children and adolescents: A guide to the issues.* Westport, CT: Praeger Publishers.

Buckley, P. F., & Waddington, J. L. (2001). *Schizophrenia and mood disorders: The new drug therapies in clinical practice.* London: Arnold.

Budman, C. L., Braun, R. D., Park, K. S., Lesser, M., & Olson, M. (2000). Explosive outbursts in children with Tourette's disorder. *J. Amer. Acad. Child Adoles. Psychiat., 39*(10), 1270–76.

Budney, A. J., Moore, B. A., Vandrey, R. G., & Hughes, J. R. (2003). The time course and significance of cannabis withdrawal. *J. Abn. Psychol., 112,* 393–402.

Budney, A. J., Radonovich, K. J., Higgins, S. T., & Wong, C. J. (1998). Adults seeking treatment for marijuana dependence: A comparison with cocaine-dependent treatment seekers. *Exp. Clin. Psychopharm., 6*(4), 419–26.

Buhlmann, U., & Wilhelm, S. (2004). Cognitive factors in body dysmorphic disorder. *Psychiat. Ann., 34*(12), 922–26.

Buhlmann, U., Glaesmer, H., Mewes, R., Fama, J. M., Wilhelm, S., Rief, W. (2010). Updates on the prevalence of body dysmorphic disorder: a population-based survey. *Psychiatry research.* 30; 178(1):171–5.

Buhs, E. S., Ladd, G. W., & Herald, S. L. (2006). Peer exclusion and victimization: Processes that mediate the relation between peer group rejection and children's classroom engagement and achievement? *J. Edu. Psychol., 98*(1), 1–13.

Bulik, C. M., & Allison, D. B. (2002). Constitutional thinness and resistance to obesity. In C. G. Fairburn & K. D. Brownell (Eds.), *Eating disorders and obesity: A comprehensive handbook* (2nd ed., pp. 22–25). New York: Guilford.

Bulik, C. M., & Kendler, K. S. (2000). "I am what I (don't) eat": Establishing an identity independent of an eating disorder. *Amer. J. Psychiat., 157*(11), 1755–60.

Bulik, C. M., Devlin, B., Bacanu, S.-A., Thornton, L., Klump, K. L., Fichter, M., Halmi, K. A., Kaplan, A. S., Strober, M., Woodside, D. B., Bergen, A. W., Ganjei, J. K., Crow, S., Mitchell, J., Rotondo, A., Mauri, M., Cassano, G., Keel, P., Berrettini, W. H., & Kaye, W. H. (2003). Significant linkage on chromosome 10p in families with bulimia nervosa. *Amer. J. Hum. Gene., 72,* 200–07.

Bulik, C. M., Sullivan, P. F., & Kendler, K. S. (2003). Genetic and environmental contributions to obesity and binge eating. *Int. J. Eat. Dis., 33,* 293–98.

Bulik, C. M., Sullivan, P. F., Tozzi, F., Furberg, H., Lichenstieb, P., & Pedersen, N. L. (2006). Prevalence, heritability, and prospective factors for anorexia nervosa. *Arch. Gen. Psychiat., 63,* 305–12.

Bulloch, A. G., Williams, J. V., Lavorato, D. H., & Patten, S. B. (2009). The relationship between major depression and martial disruption is bidirectional. *Depression and Anxiety, 26*(12), 1172–77.

Bult, M. J. F., van Dalen, T., & Muller, A. (2008). Surgical treatment of obesity. *European Journal of En docrinology, 158,* 135–45.

Burd, L., & Christensen, T. (2009). Treatment of fetal alcohol spectrum disorders: Are we ready yet? *J. Clin. Psychopharmacol., 29*(1),1–4.

Bureau of Justice Statistics. (2004). *Monitoring the Future national results in use: Overview of key findings, 2003.* University of Michigan.

Bureau of Labor Statistics. (2011, October 7). The employment situation—September 2011. (News release). U. S. Department of Labor, USDL-11-1441.

Burke, T. (2010). Psychiatric disorder: Understanding violence. In A. Bartlett & G. McGauley (Eds.). Forensic mental health: Concepts, systems, and practice, (pp. 35–51). New York: Oxford University Press.

Burks, V. S., Dodge, K. A., & Price, J. M. (1995). Models of internalizing outcomes of early rejection. *Develop. Psychopath., 7,* 683–95.

Burks, V. S., Laird, R. D., Dodge, K. A., Pettit, G. S., & Bates, J. E. (1999). Knowledge structures, social information processing, and children's aggressive behavior. *Soc. Develop., 8,* 220–36.

Burt, K. B., Van Dulmen, M. H. M., Carlivati, J., Egeland, B., Sroufe, L. A., Forman, D. R., et al. (2005). Mediating links between maternal depression and offspring psychopathology: The importance of independent data. *J. Child Psychol. Psychiat., 46*(5), 490–99.

Burt, V. L., Whelton, P., Roccella, E. J., Brown, C., Cutler, J. A., Higgins, M., Horan, M. J., & Labarthe, D. (1995). Prevalence of hypertension in the U.S. adult population. Results from the Third National Health and Nutrition Examination Survey, 1988–1991. *Hypertension, 25,* 305–13.

Burton, G. (2001). The tenacity of historical misinformation: Titchner did not invent the Titchner illusion. *History of Psychology, 4,* 228–44.

Burton, R. (1621). *Anatomy of melancholia.* London: Oxford.

Busch, K. A., Fawcett, J., & Jacobs, D. G. (2003). Clinical correlates of inpatient suicide. *J. Clin. Psychiat., 64*(1), 14–19.

Bushman, B., Bonacci, A., Baumeister, R., & van Dijk, M. (2003). Narcissism, sexual refusal, and aggression: Testing a narcissistic model of sexual coercion. *J. Pers. Soc. Psychol., 84,* 1027–40.

Bushnell, J. A., Wells, J. E., & Oakley Browne, M. A. (1992). Long-term effects of intrafamilial sexual abuse in childhood. *Acta Psychiatr. Scandin., 85,* 136–42.

Buss, D. M. (1989). Sex differences in human mate preferences: Evolutionary hypotheses tested in 37 cultures. *Behavioral and Brain Sciences, 12,* 1–49.

Bustillo, J. R., Lauriello, J., Horan, W. P., & Keith, S. J. (2001). The psychosocial treatment of schizophrenia: An update. *Amer. J. Psychiat., 158,* 163–75.

Butcher, J. N. (1993). *User's guide for the MMPI-2 Minnesota Report: Adult Clinical System.* Minneapolis: National Computer Systems.

Butcher, J. N. (Ed.). (1996a). *International applications of the MMPI-2: A handbook of research and clinical applications.* Minneapolis, MN: University of Minnesota Press.

Butcher, J. N. (1996b). Understanding abnormal behavior across cultures: The use of objective personality assessment methods. In J. N. Butcher (Ed.), *International adaptations of the MMPI-2s* (pp. 3–25). Minneapolis: University of Minnesota Press.

Butcher, J. N. (2005). Exploring universal personality characteristics: An objective approach. *International Journal of Clinical and Health Psychology, 5,* 553–566.

Butcher, J. N. (Ed.). (2006). *MMPI-2: The practitioner's handbook.* Washington, D. C.: American Psychological Association.

Butcher, J. N. (2009). How to use computer-based reports. In J. N. Butcher (Ed.), *Oxford handbook of personality assessment* (pp. 693–706). New York: Oxford University Press.

Butcher, J. N. (2010). Personality assessment from the 19th to the early 21st century: Past achievements and contemporary challenges. *Annu. Rev. Clin. Psychol.*, 6, 1–20.

Butcher, J. N. (2011). *A beginner's guide to the MMPI-2* (3rd ed.). Washington, DC: American Psychological Association.

Butcher, J. N., Cabiya, J., Lucio, E. M., & Garrido, M. (2007). *Assessing Hispanic clients using the MMPI-2 and MMPI-A*. Washington, DC: American Psychological Association.

Butcher, J. N., Cheung, F. M., & Kim, J. (2003). Use of the MMPI-2 with Asian populations. *Psychol. Assess.*, 15(3), 248–56.

Butcher, J., Derksen, J., Sloore, H., & Sirigatti, S. (2003). Objective personality assessment of people in diverse cultures: European adaptations of the MMPI-2. *Behav. Res. Ther.*, 41(7), 819–40.

Butcher, J. N., Graham, J. R., Ben-Porath, Y. S., Tellegen, A., Dahlstrom, W. G., & Kaemmer, B. (2001). *Minnesota Multiphasic Personality Inventory-2 (MMPI-2): Manual for administration and scoring* (2nd ed.). Minneapolis: University of Minnesota Press.

Butcher, J. N., & Han, K. (1996). Methods of establishing cross-cultural equivalence. In J. N. Butcher (Ed.), *International adaptations of the MMPI-2* (pp. 44–66). Minneapolis: University of Minnesota Press.

Butcher, J. N, Mosch, S. C., Tsai, J., & Nezami, E. (2006). Cross-cultural applications of the MMPI-2. In J.N. Butcher (Ed.),*MMPI-2: A practitioner's guide* (pp. 505–37). Washington, DC: American Psychological Association.

Butcher, J. N., Perry, J., & Dean, B. L. (2009). Computer based assessment. In J. N. Butcher (Ed.), *Oxford handbook of personality assessment* (pp. 163–82). New York: Oxford University Press.

Butcher, J. N., Perry, J., & Hahn, J. (2004). Computers in clinical assessment: Historical developments, present status, and future challenges. *J. Clin. Psychol.*, 60, 331–46.

Butcher, J. N., Rouse, S. V., & Perry, J. N. (2000). Empirical description of psychopathology in therapy clients: Correlates of MMPI-2 scales. Chapter in J. N. Butcher (Ed.), *Basic sources of MMPI-2* (pp. 487–500). Minneapolis: University of Minnesota Press.

Butcher, J. N., Tsai, J., Coelho, S., & Nezami, E. (2006). Cross cultural applications of the MMPI-2. In J. N. Butcher (Ed.),*MMPI-2: The practioner's handbook* (pp. 505–37). Washington, DC: American Psychological Association.

Butcher, J. N., & Williams, C. L. (2009). Personality assessment with the MMPI-2: Historical roots, international adaptations, and current challenges. *Applied Psychology: Health and Well-Being, 2,* 105–35.

Butcher, J. N., Williams, C. L., Graham, J. R., Archer, R., Tellegen, A., Ben-Porath, Y. S., & Kaemmer, B. (1992). *MMPI-A: Manual for administration, scoring, and interpretation.* Minneapolis: University of Minnesota Press.

Butler, A. C., Chapman, J. E., Forman, E. M., & Beck, A. T. (2006). The empirical status of cognitive-behavioral therapy: A review of meta-analyses. *Clin. Psychol. Rev.*, 26(1), 17–31.

Butler, L. D., Duran, R. E., Jasiukaitis, P., Koopman, C., & Spiegel, D. (1996). Hypnotizability and traumatic experience: A diathesis–stress model of dissociative symptomatology. *Amer. J. Psychiat.*, 153, 42–63.

Butow, P., Beumont, P., & Touyz, S. (1993). Cognitive processes in dieting disorders. *Int. J. Eat. Dis.*, 14, 319–30.

Butzlaff, R. L., & Hooley, J. M. (1998). Expressed emotion and psychiatric relapse: A meta-analysis. *Arch. Gen. Psychiat.*, 55(6), 547–52.

Byrne, M., Agerbo, E., Ewald, H., Eaton, W., & Mortensen, P. B. (2003). Parental age and risk of schizophrenia. *Arch. Gen. Psychiat.*, 60, 673–78.

Cacioppo, J. T., et al. (1998). Cellular immune responses to acute stress in female caregivers of dementia patients and matched controls. *Hlth. Psychol.*, 17, 182–89.

Cacioppo, J. T., Hughes, M. E., Waite, L. J., Hawkley, L. C., & Thisted, R. A. (2006). Loneliness as a specific risk factor for depressive symptoms: Cross-sectional and longitudinal analyses. *Psychology and Aging*, 21(1), 140–51.

Cade, J. F. J. (1949). Lithium salts in the treatment of psychotic excitement. *Medical Journal of Australia, 36* (part II): 349–52.

Cadenhead, K. S., Light, G. A., Geyer, M. A., & Braff, D. L. (2000a). Sensory gating deficits assessed by the P50 event-related potential in subjects with schizotypal personality disorder. *Amer. J. Psychiat.*, 157(1), 55–59.

Cadenhead, K. S., Swerdlow, N. R., Shafer, K. M., Diaz, M., & Braff, D. L. (2000b). Modulation of the startle response and startle laterality in relatives of schizophrenic patients and in subjects with schizotypal personality disorder: Evidence of inhibitory deficits. *Amer. J. Psychiat.*, 157(10), 1660–67.

Cadoret, R. J., Yates, W. R., Troughton, E., Woodworth, G., & Stewart, M. A. (1995). Genetic-environmental interaction in the genesis of aggressivity and conduct disorders. *Arch. Gen. Psychiat.*, 52, 916–24.

Caetano, R., Clark, C. L., & Tam, T. (1998). Alcohol consumption among racial/ethnic minorities, *Alcohol World: Health and Research, 22*(4), 233–42.

Cahn, W., Hulsoff Pol, H. E., Lems, E. B. T. E., van Haren, N. E. M., Schnack, H. G., van der Linden, J. A., Schothorst, P. F., van Engeland, H., & Kahn, R. S. (2002). Brain volume changes in first-episode schizophrenia: A 1-year follow-up study.*Arch. Gen. Psychiat., 59,* 1002–10.

Cain, N. M., Pincus, A. L., & Ansell, E. B. (2008). Narcissism at the crossroads: Phenotypic description of pathological narcissism across clinical theory, social/personality psychology, and psychiatric diagnosis. *Clin. Psychol. Rev.*, 28, 638–56.

Cale, E. M., & Lilienfeld, S. O. (2002a). Histrionic personality disorder and antisocial personality disorder: Sex-differentiated manifestations of psychopathy. *J. Pers. Dis.*, 16(1), 52–72.

Cale, E. M., & Lilienfeld, S. O. (2002b). Sex differences in psychopathy and antisocial personality disorder: A review and integration. *Clin. Psychol. Rev.*, 22, 1179–1207.

Calhoun, F., & Warren, K. (2007). Fetal alcohol syndrome: Historical perspectives. *Neuroscience & Biobehavioral Reviews*, 31(2), 168–71.

Callahan, J. (2009). Emergency intervention and crisis intervention. In P. E. Kleespies (Ed.), (2009). *Behavioral emergencies: An evidence-based resource for evaluating and managing risk of suicide, violence, and victimization* (pp. 13–32). Washington, DC: American Psychological Association.

Callahan, L. A., & Silver, E. (1998). Factors associated with the conditional release of persons acquitted by reason of insanity: A decision tree approach. *Law and Human Behavior*, 22, 147–63.

Callahan, L. A., Robbins, P. C., Steadman, H., & Morrissey, J. P. (1995). The hidden effects of Montana's "abolition" of the insanity defense. *Psychiat. Q.*, 66(2), 103–17.

Calvo, R., Lazaro, L., Castro-Fornieles, J., Font, E., Moreno, E., & Toro, J. (2009). Obsessive-compulsive personality disorder traits and personality dimensions in parents of children with obsessive-compulsive disorder. *Eur. Psychiat.*, 24, 201–6.

Campbell, D. (1926). *Arabian medicine and its influence on the Middle Ages*. New York: Dutton.

Campbell, H.C., Knox, T. W., & Byrnes, T. (1892). Darkness and daylight; or, Lights and shadows of New York life. Hartford: A.D. Worthington & Co.

Campbell, M., & Cueva, J. E. (1995). Psychopharmacology in child and adolescent psychiatry: A review of the past seven years. Part 1. *J. Amer. Acad. Child Adoles. Psychiat.*, 34(9), 1124–32.

Campbell, N. D. (2010). Multiple paths to partial truths: A history of drug use etiology. In L. Scheier (Ed.), *Handbook of drug use etiology: Theory, methods, and empiriul findings* (pp. 29–50). Washington, DC: American Psychological Association.

Campbell-Sills, L., & Barlow, D. H. (2007). Incorporating emotion regulation into conceptualizations and treatments of anxiety and mood disorders. In J. J. Gross (Ed.), *Handbook of emotion regulation.* (pp. 542–59). New York: Guilford Press.

Canetti, L., Bachar, E., & Berry, E. M. (2002). Food and emotion. *Behavioural Processes*, 60, 157–64.

Canetti, L., Bachar, E., Bonne, O., Agid, O., Lerer, B., deNour, A. K., & Shalev, A. Y. (2000). The impact of parental death versus separation from parents on the mental health of Israeli adolescents. *Compr. Psychiat.*, 41, 360–68.

Canetto, S. S. (1997). Gender and suicidal behavior: Theories and evidence. In R. W. Maris, M. M. Silverman, & S. S. Canetto (Eds.), *Review of Suicidology, 1997* (pp. 138–67). New York: Guilford.

Cannon, M., Jones, P. B., & Murray, R. M. (2002). Obstetric complications and schizophrenia: Historical and meta-analytic review. *Amer. J. Psychiat.*, 159(7), 1080–92.

Cannon, T. D., Cadenhead, K., Cornblatt, B., Woods, S. W., Addington, J., Walker, E., et al. (2008). Prediction of psychosis in youth at high clinical risk: A multisite longitudinal study in North America. *Arch. Gen. Psychiat.*, 65(1), 28–37.

Cannon, T. D., Cornblatt, B., & McGorry, P. (2007). Editor's introduction: The empirical status of the ultra high-risk (prodromal) research paradigm. *Schizo. Bull.*, 33, 661–64.

Cannon, T. D., et al. (1998). The genetic epidemiology of schizophrenia in a Finnish twin cohort. *Arch. Gen. Psychiat.*, 55(1), 67–74.

Cannon, T. D., Glahn, D. C., Kim, J., Van Erp, T. G. M., Karlsgodt, K., Cohen, M. S., Nuechterlein, K. H., Bava, S., & Shirinyan, D. (2005). Dorsolateral prefrontal cortex activity during maintenance and manipulation of information in working memory in patients with schizophrenia. *Arch. Gen. Psychiat.*, 62(10), 1071–80.

Cannon, T. D., Mednick, S. A., Parnas, J., Schulsinger, F., Praestholm, J., Verstergaard, A. (1993). Developmental brain abnormalities in the offspring of schizophrenic mothers. *Arch. Gen. Psychiat.*, 50, 551–64.

Cantor, J. M., Blanchard, R., Robichaud, L. K., & Christensen, B. K. (2005). Quantitative reanalysis of aggregate data on IQ in sexual offenders. *Psych. Bull.*, 131(4), 555–68.

Cantor, J. M., Kabani, N., Christensen, B. K., Zipursky, R. B., Barbaree, H. E., Dickey, R., Kassen, P. E., Mikulis, D. J., Kuban, M. E., Blak, T., Richards, B. A., Hanratty, M. K., & Blanchard, R. (2008). Cerebral white matter deficiencies in pedophilic men. *J. Psychiat. Res., 42,* 167–83.

Cantor, J. M., Klassen, P. E., Dickey, R., Christensen, B. K., Kuban, M. E., Blak, T., et al. (2005). Handedness in pedophilia and hebephilia. *Arch. Sex. Behav., 34*(4), 447–59.

Cantor-Gracee, E., & Selten, J.-P. (2005). Schizophrenia and migration: A meta-analysis and review. *Amer. J. Psychiat., 162,* 12–24.

Cantwell, D. P., & Baker, L. (1989). Stability and natural history of DSM III childhood diagnoses. *J. Amer. Acad. Child Adoles. Psychiat., 28,* 691–700.

Capaldi, D. M., & Patterson, G. R. (1994). Interrelated influences of contextual factors on antisocial behavior in childhood and adolescence for males. In D. C. Fowles, P. Sutker, & S. H. Goodman (Eds.), *Progress in experimental personality and psychopathology research.* New York: Springer.

Capps, L., Kasari, C., Yirmiya, N., & Sigman, M. (1993). Parental perception of emotional expressiveness in children with autism. *J. Cons. Clin. Psychol., 61,* 475–84.

Capraro, R. L. (2000). Why college men drink: Alcohol, adventure, and the paradox of masculinity. *J. Amer. Coll. Hlth. 48,* 307–15.

Capron, C., & Duyme, M. (1989). Assessment of effects of socio-economic status on IQ in a full cross-fostering study. *Nature, 340,* 552–54.

Caracci, G., & Mezzich, J. E. (2001). Culture and urban mental health. *Psychiat. Clin. N. Amer., 24*(3), 581–93.

Caracci, G. (2003). Violence against women. *Inter. J. Ment. Hlth., 32*(1), 36–53.

Caracci, G. (2006). Urban mental health: An international survey. *Inter. J. Ment. Hlth, 35*(1), 39–45.

Caracci, G., & Mezzich, J. E. (2001). Culture and urban mental health. *Psychiat. Clin. N. Amer., 24*(3), 581–93.

Cardeña, E., Butler, L., & Spiegel, D. (2003). Stress disorders. In G. Stricker & T. A. Widiger (Eds.), *Handbook of psychology: Clinical psychology* (Vol. 8, pp. 229–49). New York: John Wiley & Sons, Inc.

Cardeña, E., & Carlson, E. (2011). Acute stress disorder revisited. *Annu. Rev. Clin. Psychol., 7,* 245–67.

Cardona, F., Camillo, E., Casini, M. P., Luchetti, A., & Muscetta, A. (1997). Tic disorders in childhood: A retrospective study. *Giornale di Neuropsichiatria dell'Eta Evolutiva, 17*(2), 120–26.

Carey, B. (2007). Bipolar illness soars as a diagnosis for the young. *New York Times,* September 4, 2007.

Carey, G. (2003). *Human genetics for the social sciences.* London: Sage.

Carey, G., & DiLalla, D. L. (1994). Personality and psychopathology: Genetic perspectives. *J. Abn. Psychol., 103,* 32–43.

Carey, G., & Goldman, D. (1997). The genetics of antisocial behavior. In D. M. Stoff, J. Breiling, & J. D. Maser (Eds.), *Handbook of antisocial behavior* (pp. 243–54). New York: Wiley.

Carey, K. B., Henson, J. M., Carey, M. B., & Maisto, S. A. (2007). Which heavy drinking college students benefit from Brief Motivational Intervention? *J. Cons. Clin. Psych., 75,* 663–69.

Carlat, D. J., Carmargo, C. A., & Herzog, D. B. (1997). Eating disorders in males: A report on 135 patients. *Amer. J. Psychiat., 154,* 1127–32.

Carlson R. (1997, Apr.). *Sildenafil: An effective oral drug for impotence. Inpharma, 1085: 11–12.* Annual Meeting of the American Urological Association, New Orleans.

Carlson, C. L., & Bunner, M. R. (1993). Effects of methylphenidate on the academic performance of children with Attention Deficit Hyperactivity Disorder and learning disabilities. *School Psychol. Rev., 22,* 184–98.

Carlson, E. A., & Sroufe, L. A. (1995). Contribution of attachment theory to developmental psychopathology. In D. Cicchetti & D. J. Cohen (Eds.), *Developmental psychopathology: Vol. 1 Theory and methods* (pp. 581–617). New York: Wiley.

Carlson, E. A., Sampson, M. C., & Sroufe, L. A. (2003). Implications of attachment theory and research for developmental-behavioral pediatrics. *J. Dev. Behav. Ped., 24*(5), 364–79.

Carlson, M. (2001). Child rights and mental health. *Child Adoles. Psychiatr. Clin. N. Amer., 10,* 825–39.

Carlson, N. R. (2007) *Foundations of Physiological Psychology.* Boston: Allyn & Bacon.

Carlson, S. R., Johnson, S. C., & Jacobs, P. C. (2010). Disinhibited characteristics and binge drinking among university student drinkers. *Addict. Behav., 35*(3), 242–51.

Carlsson, J. M., Olsen, D. R., Mortensen, E. L., & Kastrup, M. (2006). Mental health and health-related quality of life: A 10 year follow-up of tortured refugees. *J. Nerv. Ment. Dis., 194,* 725–731.

Carlsson, K., Petersson, K. M., Lundqvist, D., Karlsson, A., Ingvar, M., & Öhman, A. (2004). Fear and the amygdale: Manipulation of awareness generates differential cerebral responses to phobic and fear-relevant (but nonfeared) stimuli. *Emotion, 4*(4), 340–53.

Carpenter, P. K. (1989). Descriptions of schizophrenia in the psychiatry of Georgian Britain: John Haslam and James Tilly Matthews. *Compr. Psychiat., 30,* 332–38.

Carpenter, W. T., & van Os, J. (2011). Should attenuated psychosis be a DSM-5 diagnosis? *Am. J. Psychiat., 168,* 1–4.

Carpentieri, S., & Morgan, S. B. (1996). Adaptive and intellectual functioning in autistic and nonautistic retarded children. *J. Autism and Devel. Dis., 26*(6), 611–20.

Carr, A., O'Reilly, G., Walsh, P. N., & McEvoy, J. (Eds.). (2007). *The handbook of intellectual disability and clinical psychology practice.* New York: Routledge/Taylor & Francis Group.

Carr, D., & Friedman, M. A. (2005). Is obesity stigmatizing? Body weight, perceived discrimination, and psychological well-being in the United States. *J. Hlth. Soc. Behav., 46, 3,* 244–59.

Carr, L. A., Nigg, J. T., & Henderson, J. M. (2006). Attentional versus motor inhibition in adults with attention-deficit/hyperactivity disorder. *Neuropsych., 20*(4), 430–41.

Carroll, B. J. (2009). Clomipramine and glucocorticoid receptor function. *Neuropsychopharmacol., 34*(9), 2192–93.

Carroll, K. M., & Rounsaville, B. J. (1993). History and significance and childhood attention deficit disorder in treatment-seeking cocaine abusers. *Compr. Psychiat., 34,* 75–82.

Carroll, K. M., Fenton, L. R., Ball, S. A., Nich, C., Frankforter, T. L., Shi, J., & Rounsaville, B. J. (2004). Efficacy of disulfiram and cognitive behavior therapy in cocaine-dependent outpatients. *Arch. Gen. Psychiat., 61*(3), 264–72.

Carroll, K. M., Powers, M. D., Bryant, K. J., & Rounsaville, B. J. (1993). One-year follow-up status of treatmentseeking cocaine abusers: Psychopathology and dependence severity as predictors of outcome. *J. Nerv. Ment. Dis., 181*(2), 71–79.

Carstairs, G. M., & Kapur, R. L. (1976). *The great universe of Kota: Stress, change and mental disorder in an Indian village.* Berkeley: University of California Press.

Carter, A. S., Garrity-Rokous, F. E., Chazan-Cohen, R., Little, C., & Briggs-Gowan, M. J. (2001). Maternal depression and comorbidity: Predicting early parenting, attachment security, and toddler socialemotional problems and competencies. *J. Amer. Acad. Child Adoles. Psychiat., 40*(1), 18–26.

Carter, M. M., Hollon, S. D., Carson, R., & Shelton, R. C. (1995). Effects of a safe person on induced distress following a biological challenge in panic disorder with agoraphobia. *J. Abn. Psychol., 104,* 156–63.

Carter, S. A., & Wu, K. D. (2010). Relations among symptoms of social phobia subtypes, avoidant personality disorder, panic, and depression. *Behav. Ther., 41*(1), 2–13. doi:10.1016/j.beth.2008.10.002

Carter, W. P., Hudson, J. I., Lalonde, J. K., Pindyck, L., McElroy, S. L., & Pope, H. G. (2003). Pharmacologictreatment of binge eating disorder. *Int. J. Eat. Dis., 34,* S74–S88.

Cartreine, J. A., Ahern, D. K., & Locke, S. E. (2010). A roadmap to computer-based psychotherapy in the United States. *Har. Rev. Psychiat., 18*(2), 80–95.

Carver, C. S., & Sheier, M. F. (2002). Optimism. InC. R. Snyder & S. J. Lopez (Eds.), *Handbook of positivepsychology.* New York: Oxford UniversityPress, pp. 231–243.

Cartwright-Hatton, S., McNicol, K., & Doubleday, E. (2006). Anxiety in a neglected population: Prevalence of anxiety disorders in pre-adolescent children. *Clin.Psych. Rev., 26*(7), 817–33.

Case, B. G., Olfson, M., Marcus, S. C., & Siegel, C. (2007). Trends in inpatient mental health treatment of children and adolescents in US community hospitals between 1990 and 2000. *Arch. Gen. Psychiat., 64,* 89–96.

Case, R. B., Heller, S. S., & Moss, A. J. (1985). The multicenter post infarction research group: Type A behavior and survival after acute myocardial infarction. *N. Engl. J. Med., 312,* 737–41.

Casey, L. M., Newcombe, P. A., & Oei, T. P. S. (2005). Cognitive mediation of panic severity: The role of catastrophic misinterpretation of bodily sensations and panic self-efficacy. *Cognitive Therapy and Research, 29*(2), 187–200.

Caspi, A. McClay, J., Moffitt, T., Mill, J., Martin, J., Craig, I. W., et al. (2002). Role of genotype in the cycle of violence in maltreated children. *Science, 297,* 851–54.

Caspi, A., Moffitt, T. E., Cannon, M., McClay, J., Murray, R., Harrington, H., Taylor, A. et al., (2005). Moderation of the effect of adolescent-onset cannabis use on adult psychosis by a functional polymorphism in the Catechol-O-Methyltransferase gene: Longitudinal evidence of a gene x environment interaction. *Biol. Psychiat., 57,* 1117–27.

Caspi, A., Sugden, K., Moffitt, T. E., Taylor, A., Craig, I. W., Harrington, H., McClay, J., Mill, J., Martin, J., Braithwaite, A., & Poulton, R. (2003, Jul. 18). Influence of life stress on depression: Moderation by a polymorphism in the 5HTT gene.*Science, 301,* 386–89.

Cassady, J. D., Kirschke, D. L., Jones, T. F., Craig, A. S., Bermudez, O. B., & Schaffner W. (2005). Case series: Outbreak of conversion disorder among Amish adolescent girls. *J. Amer. Acad. Child Adoles. Psychiat., 44*(3), 291–97.

Cassidy, C., O'Connor, R. C., Howe, C., & Warden, D. (2004). Perceived discrimination and psychological distress: The role of personal and ethnic self-esteem. *J. Couns. Psychol., 51*(3), 329–39.

Cassidy, F., Forest, K., Murry, E., & Carroll, B. J. (1998). A factor analysis of the signs and symptoms of mania. *Arch. Gen. Psychiat., 55*(1), 27–32.

Castellini, G., Lo Sauro, C., Mannucci, E., Ravaldi, C., Rotella, C. M., Faravelli, C., & Ricca, V. (2011). Diagnostic crossover and outcome predictors in eating disorders according to *DSM-IV* and *DSM-V* proposed criteria. A 6-year follow-up study. *Psychosomat. Med., 73*, 270–79.

Castiglioni, A. (1924). *Adventures of the mind.* New York: Dutton.

Castonguay, L. G., Boswell, J. F., Constantino, M. J., Goldfried, M. R., & Hill, C. E. (2010). Training implications of harmful effects of psychological treatments. *Amer. Psychol., 65*, 34–49.

Castonguay, L. G., Reid, J. J., Halperin, G. S., & Goldfried, M. R. (2003). Psychotherapy integration. In G. Stricker, G., T. A. Widiger, & I. B. Weiner (Eds.), *Handbook of psychology: Clinical psychology* (Vol. 8, pp. 327–66). Hoboken, NJ: John Wiley & Sons.

Castro, F. G., Barrington, E. H., Walton, M. A., & Rawson, R. A. (2000). Cocaine and methamphetamine: Differential addiction rates. *Psych. Addict. Behav., 14*(4), 390–96.

Cato, C., & Rice, B. D. (1982). *Report from the study group on rehabilitation of clients with specific learning disabilities.* St. Louis: National Institute of Handicapped Research.

Cauce, A. M., Paradise, M., Ginzler, J. A., Embry, L., Morgan, C. J., Lohr, Y., & Theofelis, J. (2000). The characteristics and mental health of homeless adolescents: Age and gender differences. *Journal of Emotional & Behavioral Disorders, 8*, 230–39.

Caudill, O. B., Jr., (2009). When a mental health professional is in litigation. In S. F.Bucky, J. E. Callan, & G. Stricker (Eds.), *Ethical and legal issues for mental health professionals in forensic settings,* (pp. 127–40). New York: Routledge/Taylor & Francis Group.

Cavaco, S., Anserson, S. W., Allen, J. S., Castro-Caldas, A., & Damasio, H. (2004). The scope of preserved procedural memory in amnesia. *Brain, 127*, 1853–67.

Cavanagh, J. T., Van Beck, M., Muir, W., & Blackwood, D.H. R. (2002). Case control study of neurocognitivefunction in euthymic patients with bipolar disorder:An association with mania. *Brit. J. Psychiat., 180*,320–26.

CBS News. (2003, Aug. 5). Autistic boy dies during exorcism. New York: Columbia Broadcasting System.

CDC. (2009). Prevalence of Autism Spectrum Disorders-Autism and Pervasive Developmental Disabilities Monitoring Network, United States. MMWR Surveillance Summaries 209; 58 (SS–20).

CDC. (2010). http://www.cdc.gov/concussion/sports/stories.html

Ceci, S. J., Bruck, M., & Battin, D. B. (2000). The suggestibility of children's testimony. In D. F. Bjorklund (Ed.), *False-memory creation in children and adults: Theory, research, and implications* (pp. 169–202). Mahwah, NJ: Erlbaum.

Ceci, S. J., Kulkofsky, S., Klemfuss, J. Z., Sweeney, C. D., & Bruck, M. (2007). Unwarranted assumptions about children's testimonial accuracy. *Ann. Rev. Clin. Psych., 3*, 311–28.

Cederlund, M., Hagberg, B., Billstedt, E., Gillberg, I. C. & Gillberg, C. (2008). Asperger syndrome and autism: A comparative longitudinal follow-up study more than 5 years after original diagnosis. *Journal of Autism and Developmental Disorders, 38*(1), 72–85.

Cerletti, U., & Bini, L. (1938). Un Nuevo metodo di shockterapie "L'electroshock" (A new method of shock therapy "the electroshock"). Bolletino Academia *Medicino Roma, 64*, 136–138.

Chaffin, M., Silvosky, J. F., Funderburk, B., Valle, L. A., Brestan, E. V., Balachova, T., Jackson, S., Lensgraf, J., & Bonner, B. L. (2004). Parent-child interaction therapy with physically abusive parents: Efficacy for reducing future abuse reports. *J. Cons. Clin. Psychol., 72*, 500–10.

Chamberlin, N. L., & Saper, C. B. (2009). The agony of the ecstasy: Serotonin and obstructive sleep apnea. *Neurol., 73*(23), 1947–48.

Chambers, R. A., & Potenza, M. N. (2003). Neurodevelopment, impulsivity, and adolescent gambling. *Journal of Gambling Studies, 19*(1), 53–84.

Chambers, R. E. (1952). Discussion of "Survival factors . . ." *Amer. J. Psychiat., 109*, 247–48.

Chambless, D. L., & Mason, J. (1986). Sex, sex role stereotyping, and agoraphobia. *Behav. Res. Ther., 24*, 231–35.

Chambless, D. L., & Ollendick, T. H. (2001). Empirically supported psychological interventions: Controversies and evidence. *Annu. Rev. Psychol., 52*, 685–716.

Chambless, D. L., Frydrich, T., & Rodenabugh, T. (2008). Generalized social phobia and avoidant personality disorder: Meaningful distinction or useless duplication? *Depression and Anxiety, 25*(1), 8–19.

Champion, H. R., Holcomb, J. B., & Young, L. A. (2009). Injuries from explosions. *Journal of Trauma, 66*, 1468–76.

Chan, G. W. L. (2001). Residential services for psychiatric patients in Hong Kong. *Hong Kong J. of Psychiatry, 11*(3), 13–17.

Chan, G. W. L., Ungvari, G. S., & Leung, J. P. (2001). Residential services for psychiatric patients in Hong Kong. *Hong Kong J. Psychiatry, 11*(3), 13–17.

Chang, C-K., Hayes, R. D., Perera, G., Broadbent, M. T. M., Fernandes, A. C., Lee, W. F., Hotopf, M., & Stewart, R. (2011). Life expectancy at birth for people with serious mental illness and other major disorders from a secondary mental health care case register in London. *PLos One, 6*, e19590.

Chang, L., Alicata, D., Ernst, T., & Volkow, N. (2007). Structural and metabolic changes in the stratum associated with methamphetamine abuse. *Addiction, 102*, 16–32.

Chang, S. W., Piacentina, J., & Walkup, J. T. (2007). Behavioral treatment of Tourette Syndrome. *Clin. Psychol. Sci. Prac., 14*, 268–73.

Channon, S., German, E., Cassina, C., & Lee, P. (2004). Executive functioning, memory, and learning in phenylketonuria. *Neuropsych., 18*, 613–20.

Chapman, L. J., Chapman, J. P., & Miller, E. N. (1982). Reliabilities and intercorrelations of eight measures of proneness to psychosis. *J. Cons. Clin. Psychol., 50*, 187–95.

Chapman, L. J., Chapman, J. P., & Raulin, M. L. (1978) Body-image aberration in schizophrnia. *J. Abn. Psych., 87*, 399–407.

Chapman, L. J., Chapman, J. P., Kwapil, T. R., Eckblad, M., & Zinzer, M. (1994). Putatively psychosis-prone subjects ten years later. *J. Abn. Psychol., 103*, 171–83.

Chappel, J. N. (1993). Long-term recovery from alcoholism. *Psychiat. Clin. N. Amer., 16*, 177–87.

Chappell, D. (2010). Victimization and the insanity defense: Coping with confusion, conflict and conciliation. *Psychiatry, Psychology and Law, 17*(1), 39–51.

Chaput, J. P., Després, J. P., Bouchard, C., & Tremblay, A. (2008). The association between sleep duration and weight gain in adults: a 6-year prospective study from the Quebec Family Study. *Sleep, 31*, 517–523.

Charach, A., Ickowicz, A., & Schachar, R. (2004). Stimulant treatment over five years: Adherence, effectiveness, and adverse effects. *J. Amer. Acad. Child Adoles. Psychiat., 43*, 559–67.

Charlop-Christie, M. H., Schreibman, L., Pierce, K., & Kurtz, P. F. (1998). Childhood autism. In R. J. Morris, T. R. Kratochwill, et al. (Eds.), *The practice of child therapy* (pp. 271–302). Boston: Allyn and Bacon.

Charman, T., Swettenham, J., Baron-Cohen, S., Cox, A., Baird, G., & Drew, A. (1997). Infants with autism: An investigation of empathy, pretend play, joint attention, and imitation. *Develop, Psychol., 33*(5), 781–89.

Charney, D., Grillon, C., & Bremner, J. D. (1998). The neurobiological basis of anxiety and fear: Circuits, mechanisms, and neurochemical interactions (Part I). *The Neuroscientist, 4*, 35–44.

Chartier, M. J., Walker, J. R., & Stein, M. B. (2001). Social phobia and potential childhood risk factors in a community sample. *Psychol. Med., 31*, 307–15.

Charuvastra, A., & Cloitre, M. (2008). Social bonds and posttraumatic stress disorder. *Annu. Rev. Psychol., 59*, 301–328.

Chase-Lansdale, P. L., Cherlin, A. J., & Kieran, K. E. (1995). The long-term effects of parental divorce on the mental health of young adults: A developmental perspective. *Child Develop., 66*, 1614–34.

Chassin, L., Curran, P. J., Hussong, A. M., & Colder, C. R. (1996). The relation of parent alcoholism to adolescent substance use: A longitudinal follow-up. *J. Abn. Psychol., 105*(1), 70–80.

Chassin, L., Pillow, D. R., Curran, P. J., Molina, B. S., & Barrera, M. (1993). Relation of parental alcoholism in early adolescent substance use: A test of three mediating mechanisms. *J. Abn. Psychol., 102*, 3–19.

Chaudhuri, K. R., Odin, P., Antonini, A., & Martinez-Martin, P. (2011). Parkinson's disease: The nonmotor issues. *Parkinsonism and Related Disorders,* e pub ahead of print.

Chaturvedi, S. K., Desair, G., & Shaligram, D. (2010). Dissociative disorders in a psychiatric institute in India: A selected review and patterns over a decade. *Int'l. J. Soc. Psychiat., 56*, 533–39. doi:10.1177/0020764009347335

Chavira, D., Grilo, C., Shea, M. T., Yen, S., Gunderson, J., Morey, L., et al. (2003). Ethnicity and four personality disorders. *Compr. Psychiat., 44*, 483–91.

Chavira, D. A., Stein, M. B., & Roy-Byrne, P. (2009). Managing anxiety in primary care. In M. M. Antony & M. B. Stein (Eds.),*Oxford handbook of anxiety and related disorders* (pp. 512–22). New York: Oxford University Press.

Chen, C. C., & Yeh, E. K. (1997). Population differences in ALDH levels and flushing response. In G. Y. San (Ed.), *Molecular mechanisms of alcohol.* New York: Humana.

Chen, C. H., Suckling, J., Lennox, B. R., Ooi, C., & Bullmore, E. T. (2011). A quantitative meta-analysis of fMRI studies in bipolar disorder. *Bipolar Disord., 13*(1), 1–15. doi: 10.1111/j.1399-5618.2011.00893.x

Chen, E. Y., & Safer, D. (2010). Dialectical behavior therapy. In W. A. Agras (Ed.), *The Oxford Handbook of Eating Disorders,* New York: Oxford University Press, pp. 402–16.

Chen, M. C., Hamilton, J. P., & Gotlib, I. H. (2010). Decreased hippocampal volume in healthy girls at risk of depression. *Arch. Gen. Psychiat., 67*(3), 270–76. doi: 10.1001/archgenpsychiatry.2009.202

Chentsove-Dutton, Y. E., & Tsai, J. L. (2009). Understanding depression across cultures. In I. H. Gotlib & C. L. Hammen (Eds.), *Handbook of depression and its treatment* (2nd ed.). New York: Guilford Press.

Cherpitel, C. J. (1997). Alcohol and injuries resulting from violence: A comparison of emergency room samples from two regions of the U.S. *J. Addict. Dis., 16*(1), 25–40.

Cherpitel, C. J. (2006). Alcohol-related injury and the emergency department: Research and policy questions for the next decade. *Addiction, 101*(9), 225–1227.

Chesney, M. (1996). New behavioral risk factors for coronary heart disease: Implications for intervention. In K. Orth-Gomer & N. Schneiderman (Eds.), *Behavioral medicine approaches to cardiovascular disease prevention* (pp. 169–82). Mahwah, NJ: Erlbaum.

Chételat, G., Desgranges, B., Sayette, V., Viader, F., Berkouk, K., Landeau, B., Lalevée, C., Le, D. F., Dupuy, B., Hannequin, D., Baron, J. C., & Eustache, F. (2003). Dissociating atrophy and hypometabolism impact on episodic memory in mild cognitive impairment. *Brain, 126*, 1955–67.

Choca, J. (2004). Interpretive guide to the Millon Multiaxial Personality Inventory. Washington, DC:

Chorpita, B. F. (2001). Control and the development of negative emotion. In M. W. Vasey & M. R. Dadds (Eds.), The developmental psychopathology of anxiety (pp. 112–42). New York: Oxford University Press.

Chorpita, B. F., & Barlow, D. H. (1998). The development of anxiety: The role of control in the early environment. Psychol. Bull., 124(1), 3–21.

Chou, S. P., Dawson, D., A., Stinson, F. S., Huang, B., Pickering, R. P., Zhou, Y., & Grant, B. F. (2006). The prevalence of drinking and driving in the United States, 2001–2002: Results from the national epidemiological survey on alcohol and related conditions. *Drug Alc. Depend., 83*(2) 137–46.

Chowdhury, A. (1996) The definition and classification of Koro. *Cult. Med. Psychiat., 20,* 41–65.

Choy, Y., Fyer, A. J., & Lipsitz, J. D. (2007). Treatment of specific phobia in adults. *Clin. Psychol. Rev., 27*(3), 266–86.

Christakis, N. A., & Fowler, J. H. (2007). The spread of obesity in a large social network over 32 years. *New Eng. J. Med., 357*, 370–79.

Christensen, A., Wheeler, J. G., & Jacobson, N. S. (2007). Couple distress. In D. H. Barlow (Ed.), *Clinical handbook of psychological disorders* (4th ed.; pp. 662–89). New York: Guilford.

Christophersen, E. R., & Friman, P. C. (2010). *Elimination disorders in children and adolescents.* Cambridge, MA: Hogrefe Publishing.

Chu, B. C., & Kendall, P. C. (2004). Positive association of child involovement and treatment outcome within a manual-based cognitive-behavioral treatment for children with anxiety. *J. Cons. Clin. Psychol., 72,* 821–29.

Chu, J. A., Frey, L. M., Ganzel, B. L., & Matthews, J. A. (1999). Memories of childhood abuse: Dissociation, amnesia, and corroboration. *Amer. J. Psychiat., 156,* 749–55.

Chung, M. C., Symons, C., Gilliam, J., & Kaminski, E. R. (2010). Stress, psychiatric co-morbidity and coping in patients with chronic idiopathic urticaria. *Psychology & Health, 25*(4), 477–90.

Chutko, L. S., Yur'eva, R. G., Surushkina, S. Y., Nikishena, I. S., Yakovenko, I. S., Anisimova, T. I., &

Aitbekov, K. A. (2010). Principles of medical care for children with attention deficit hyperactivity disorder. *Neuroscience and Behavioral Physiology, 40*(3), 351–55.

Cicchetti, D. (2004). An odyssey of discovery: Lessons learned through three decades of research on child maltreatment. *Amer. Psychol.,* 731–41.

Cicchetti, D., & Garmezy, N. (1993). Prospects and promises in the study of resilience. *Develop. Psychopath., 5*(4), 497–502.

Cicchetti, D., & Lynch, M. (1995). Failures in the expectable environment and their impact on individual development: The case of child maltreatment. In D. Cicchetti & D. J. Cohen (Eds.), *Developmental psychopathology: Vol. 2. Risk, disorder, and adaptation* (pp. 32–72). New York: Wiley.

Cicchetti, D., & Toth, S. L. (1995a). Developmental psychopathology and disorders of affect. In D. Cicchetti & D. J. Cohen (Eds.), *Developmental psychopathology Vol. 2: Risk, disorder, and adaptation* (pp. 369–420). New York: Wiley.

Cicchetti, D., & Toth, S. L. (1995b). A developmental psychopathology perspective on child abuse and neglect. *J. Amer. Acad. Child Adoles. Psychiat., 34*(5), 541–65.

Cicchetti, D., & Toth, S. L. (1998). The development of depression in children and adolescents. *Amer. Psychol., 53*(2), 221–41.

Cicchetti, D., & Toth, S. L. (2005). Child maltreatment. *Annu. Rev. Clin. Psychol., 1*(1), 409–38.

Cirinclone, C., Steadman, H., & McGreevy, M. A. (1995). Rates of insanity acquittals and the factors associated with successful insanity pleas. *Bull. Amer. Acad. Psychiat. Law, 23*(3), 399–409.

Clark, D. A. (1997). Twenty years of cognitive assessment: Current status and future directions. *J. Cons. Clin. Psychol., 65*(6), 996–1000.

Clark, D. A. (2005). Focus on 'cognition' in cognitive behavior therapy for OCD: Is it really necessary? *Cognitive Behaviour Therapy, 34*(3), 131–39.

Clark, D. A., & Beck, A. T. (2010). Cognitive theory and therapy of anxiety and depression: Convergence with neurobiological findings. *Trends in Cognitive Sciences, 14*(9), 418–24. doi: 10.1016/j.tics.2010.06.007

Clark, D. A., Beck, A. T., & Alford, B. A. (1999). *Scientific foundations of cognitive theory and therapy of depression.* New York: Wiley.

Clark, D. A., Steer, R. A., & Beck, A. T. (1994). Common and specific dimensions of self-reported anxiety and depression: Implications for the cognitive and tripartite models. *Amer. J. Psychiat., 103,* 645–54.

Clark, D. C. (1995). Epidemiology, assessment, and management of suicide in depressed patients. In E. E. Beckham & W. R. Leber (Eds.), *Handbook of depression* (2nd ed., pp. 526–38). New York: Guilford.

Clark, D. M. (1986). A cognitive approach to panic. *Behav. Res. Ther., 24,* 461–70.

Clark, D. M. (1997). Panic disorder and social phobia. In C. G. Fairburn (Ed.), *Science and practice of cognitive behaviour therapy.* (pp. 119–153). New York: Oxford University Press.

Clark, D. M., & McManus, F. (2002). Information processing in social phobia. *Biol. Psychiat., 51,* 92–100.

Clark, D. M., & Wells, A. (1995). A cognitive model of social phobia. In R. G. Heimberg, M. R. Liebowitz, D. A. Hope, & F. R. Schneier (Eds.), *Social phobia: Diagnosis, assessment, and treatment* (pp. 69–93). New York: Guilford.

Clark, D. M., Ehlers, A., Hackmann, A., McManus, F., Fennell, M., Grey, N., et al. (2006). Cognitive therapy versus exposure and applied relaxation in social phobia: A randomized controlled trial. *J. Consult. Clin. Psychol., 74*(3), 568–78.

Clark, D. M., Ehlers, A., McManus, F., Hackmann, A., Fennell, M., Campbell, H., et al. (2003). Cognitive therapy versus fluoxetine in generalized social phobia: A randomized placebo-controlled trial. *J. Cons. Clin. Psychol., 71*(6), 1058–67.

Clark, D. M., Salkovskis, P. M., Hackmann, A., Middleton, H., Anastasiades, P., & Gelder, M. (1994). A comparison of cognitive therapy, applied relaxation, and imipramine in the treatment of panic disorder. *Brit. J. Psychiat., 164,* 759–69.

Clark, D. M., Salkovskis, P. M., Hackmann, A., Wells, A., Ludgate, J., & Gelder, M. (1999). Brief cognitive therapy for panic disorder: A randomized controlled trial. *J. Cons. Clin. Psychol., 67,* 583–89.

Clark, L. A. (1992). Resolving taxonomic issues in personality disorders: The value of large-scale analyses of symptom data. *J. Pers. Dis., 6,* 360–76.

Clark, L. A. (2005). Temperament as a unifying basis for personality and psychopathology. *J. Abn. Psych., 114,* 505–21.

Clark, L. A. (2007). Assessment and diagnosis of personality disorder: Perennial issues and an emerging reconceptualization. *Ann. Rev. Psych., 58,* 227–57.

Clark, L. A., & Harrison, J. A. (2001). Assessment instruments. In W. J. Livesley (Ed.), *Handbook of personality disorders* (pp. 277–306). New York: Guilford.

Clark, L. A., & Watson, D. (1991). Theoretical and empirical issues in differentiating depression from anxiety. In J. Becker & A. Kleinman (Eds.), *Psychosocial aspects of depression.* Hillsdale, NJ: Erlbaum.

Clark, L. A., Watson, D., & Mineka, S. (1994). Temperament, personality, and the mood and anxiety disorders. *J. Abn. Psychol., 103,* 103–16.

Clarke-Stewart, K. A., Vandell, D. L., McCartney, K., Owen, M. T., & Booth, C. (2000). Effects of parental separation and divorce on very young children. *J. Fam. Psychol., 14*(2), 304–26.

Clarkin, J. F., & Levy, J. N. (2004). The influence of client variables on psychotherapy. In M. J. Lambert (Ed.), *Bergin and Garfield's handbook of psychotherapy and behavior change.* (pp. 194–226.) New York: John Wiley and Sons.

Clarkin, J. F., Levy, K. N., Lenzenweger, M. F., & Kernberg, O. F. (2007). Evaluating three treatments for borderline personality disorder: A multiwave study. *Am. J. Psychiat., 164,* 922–28.

Clarkin, J., Levy, K., Lenzenweger, M., & Kernberg, O. (2004). The personality disorders institute/borderline personality disorder research foundation randomized controlled trial for borderline personality disorder: Rationale, methods, and patient characteristics. *J. Pers. Dis., 18,* 52–72.

Classen, T. J., & Dunn, R. A. (2011, Feb. 14). The effect of job loss and unemployment duration on suicide risk in the United States: A new look using mass-layoffs and unemployment duration. *Hlth. Econ.* doi: 10.1002/hec.1719. E pub ahead of print.

Cleckley, H. M. (1941). *The mask of sanity* (1st ed.). St. Louis, MO: Mosby.

Cleckley, H. M. (1982). *The mask of sanity* (Rev. ed.). New York: Plume.

Cleghorn, J. M., Franco, S., Szechtman, B., Kaplan, R. D., Szechtman, H., Brown, G. M., Nahmias, C., & Garnett, E. S. (1992). Toward a brain map of auditory hallucinations. *Amer. J. Psychiat., 149*(8), 1062–69.

Clément, F., & Belleville, S. C. (2010). Compensation and disease severity on the memory-related activations in mild cognitive impairment. *Biol. Psychiat., 68,* 894–902.

Clement, P. (1970). Elimination of sleepwalking in a seven-year-old boy. *J. Cons. Clin. Psychol., 34*(1), 22–26.

Clementz, B. A., Geyer, M. A., & Braff, D. L. (1998). Poor P50 suppression among schizophrenia patients and their first-degree biological relatives. *Amer. J. Psychiat., 155,* 1691–702.

Cloitre, M. (2009). Effective psychotherapies for post-traumatic stress disorder: A review and critique. *CNS Spectrums, 14*(1, Suppl. 1), 32–43.

Cloninger, C. R. (1987). A systematic method for clinical description and classification of personality invariants. *Arch. Gen. Psychiat., 44,* 161–67.

Cloninger, C. R., Bayon, C., & Pszybeck, T. R. (1997). Epidemiology and Axis I comorbidity of antisocial personality. In D. M. Stoff, J. Breiling, & J. D. Maser (Eds.), *Handbook of antisocial behavior* (pp. 12–21). New York: Wiley.

Cloninger, C. R., Reich, T., Sigvardsson, S., von Knorring, A. L., & Bohman, M. (1986). The effects of changes in alcohol use between generations on the inheritance of alcohol abuse. In *Alcoholism: A medical disorder.* Proceedings of the 76th Annual Meeting of the American Psychopathological Association.

Cloyes, K. G., Wong, B., Latimer, S., & Abarca, J. (2010). Time to prison return for offenders with serious mental illness released from prison: A survival analysis. *Crim. Just. Behav., 37*(2), 175–87.

Coccaro, E. F. (2001). Biological and treatment correlates. In W. J. Livesley (Ed.), *Handbook of personality disorders* (pp. 124–35). New York: Guilford.

Cockayne, T. O. (1864–1866). *Leechdoms, wort cunning, and star craft of early England.* London: Longman, Green, Longman, Roberts & Green.

Coelho, C. M., & Purkis, H. (2009). The origins of specific phobias: Influential theories and current perspectives. *Rev. Gen. Psychol., 13*(4), 335–48. doi: 10.1037/a0017759

Coffey, P., Leitenberg, H., Henning, K., Turner, T., & Bennett, R. T. (1996). The relation between methods of coping during adulthood with a history of childhood sexual abuse and current psychological adjustment. *J. Cons. Clin. Psychol., 64*(5), 1090–93.

Cohen, A. N., Hammen, C., Henry, R. M., & Daley, S. E. (2004). Effects of stress and social support on recurrence in biporal disorder. *J. Affect. Dis., 82*(1), 143–47.

Cohen, F., Kemeny, M. E., Zegans, L. S. Johnson, P., Kearney, K. A., & Stites, D. P. (2007). Immune function declines with unemployment and recovers after stressor termination. *Psychosom. Med., 69,* 225–234.

Cohen, J. A., Mannarino, A. P., & Deblinger, E. (2006). *Treating trauma and traumatic grief in children and adolescents.* New York: Guilford Press.

Cohen, L. J., & Galynker, I. I. (2002). Clinical features of pedophilia and implications for treatment. *J. Psychiat. Pract., 8*(5), 276–89.

Cohen, P., Chen, H., Gordon, K., Johnson, J., Brook, J., & Kasen, S. (2008). Socioeconomic background and the developmental course of schizotypal and borderline personality disorder symptoms. *Develop. Psychopath., 20,* 633–50.

Cohen, P., Pine, D. S., Must, A., Kasen, S., & Brook, J. (1998). Prospective associations between somatic illness and mental illness from childhood to adulthood. *Amer. J. Epidemiol., 147*(3), 232–39.

Cohen, S., Doyle, W. J., Skoner, D. P., Rabin, B. S., & Gwaltney, J. M. (1997). Social ties and susceptibility to the common cold. *JAMA, 277,* 1940–44.

Cohen, S., Tyrrell, D. A. J., & Smith, A. P. (1993). Negative life events, perceived stress, negative affect, and susceptibility to the common cold. *J. Pers. Soc. Psychol., 64*(1), 131–40.

Cohen-Kettenis, P. T., & Gooren, L. J. G. (1999). Transsexualism: A review of etiology, diagnosis, and treatment. *J. Psychosom. Res., 46,* 315–33.

Cohen-Kettenis, P. T., Dillen, C. M., & Gooren, L. J. G. (2000). [Treatment of young transsexuals in the Netherlands]. *Nederlands Tijdschrift voor Geneeskunde, 144,* 698–702.

Cohen-Kettenis, P. T., Owen, A., Kaijser, V. G., Bradley, S. J., & Zucker, K. J. (2003). Demographic characteristics, social competence, and behavior problems in children with gender identity disorder: A cross-national, cross-clinic comparative analysis. *J. Abn. Child Psych., 31*(1), 41–53.

Cohen-Kettenis, P. T., Wallien, M., Johnson, L. L., Owen-Anderson, A. F. H., Bradley, S. J., & Zucker, K. J. (2006). A parent-report gender identity questionnaire for children: A cross-national, cross-clinic comparative analysis. *Clin. Child Psych. Psychiat., 11*(3), 397–405.

Cohler, B. J., Stott, F. M., & Musick, J. S. (1995). Adversity, vulnerability, and resilience: Cultural and developmental perspectives. In D. Cicchetti & D. J. Cohen (Eds.), *Developmental psychopathology: Vol. 2. Risk, disorder, and adaptations* (pp. 753–800). New York: Wiley.

Cohn, L. D., & Adler, N. E. (1992). Female and male perceptions of ideal body shapes: Distorted views among Caucasian college students. *Psychology of Women Quarterly, 16,* 69–79.

Coid, J., Yang, M., Bebbington, P., Moran, P., Brugha, T., Jenkins, R., Farrell, M., Singleton, N., & Ulrich, S. (2009). Borderline personality disorder: Health service use and social functioning among a national household population. *Psychol. Med., 39,* 1721–31.

Coie, J. D. (1990). Toward a theory of peer rejection. In S. R. Asher & J. D. Coie (Eds.), *Peer rejection in childhood* (pp. 365–402). New York: Cambridge University Press.

Coie, J. D. (1996). Effectiveness trials: An initial evaluation of the FAST track program. Paper presented at the Fifth National Institute of Mental Health Conference on Prevention Research, Washington.

Coie, J. D. (2004). The impact of negative social experiences on the development of antisocial behavior. In J. B. Kupersmidt & K. A Dodge (Eds.). *Children's peer relations: From development to intervention* (pp. 243–67). Washington, DC: American Psychological Association.

Coie, J. D., Dodge, K. A., Terry, R., & Wright, V. (1991). The role of aggression in peer relations: An analysis of aggression episodes in boys' play groups. *Child Develop., 62,* 812–26.

Coie, J. D., Miller-Johnson, S., & Bagwell, C. (2000). Prevention science. In A. J. Sameroff & M. Lewis, et al. (Eds.), *Handbook of developmental psychopathology* (2nd ed., pp. 93–112). New York: Kluwer/Plenum.

Cole, J. O., & Bodkin, J. A. (1990). Antidepressant drug side effects. *J. Clin. Psychiat., 51,* 21–26.

Coles, M. E., Phillips, K. A., Menard, W., Pagano, M. E., Fay, C., Weisberg, R. B., & Stout, R. L. (2006). Body dysmorphic disorder and social phobia: Crosssectional and prospective data. *Depression and Anxiety 23*(1) 26–33.

Collacott, R. A., et al. (1998). Behavior phenotype for Down's syndrome. *Brit. J. Psychiat., 172,* 85–89.

Collins, N. L., Dunkel-Schetter, C., Lobel, M., & Scrimshaw, S. C. M. (2004). Social support in pregnancy: Psychosocial correlates of birth outcomes and postpartum depression. In H. T. Reis & C. E. Rusbult (Eds.), *Close relationships: Key readings* (pp. 35–55). Philadelphia: Taylor & Francis.

Collishaw, S., Dunn, J., O'Connor, T. G., & Golding, J. A. (2007). Maternal childhood abuse and offspring adjustment over time. Longitudinal Study of Parents and Children Study Team, United Kingdom. *Develop. Psychopath., 19*(2), 367–83.

Collishaw, S., Pickles, A. Messer, J., Rutter, M., Shearer, C., & Maughan, B. (2007). Resilience to adult psychopathology following childhood maltreatment: Evidence from a community sample. *Child Ab. Negl., 31,* 211–229.

Commonwealth v. Paul Shanley, 455 Mass. 752. (Superior Court, Middlesex).

Commonwealth v. Shanley, 9919 N.E.2d 1254 (Mass. 2010). Decision by the Supreme Court of Massachusets.

Compton, W. M., Thomas, Y. F., Stinson, F. S., & Grant, B. F. (2007). Prevalence, correlates, disability, and comorbidity of DSM-IV drug abuse and dependence in the United States: Results from the National Epidemiologic Survey on Alcohol and Related Conditions. *Arch. Gen. Psychiat., 64*(5), 566–76.

Conduct Problems Prevention Research Group. (2007). Fast Track randomized controlled trial to prevent eternalizing psychiatric disorders: Findings from Grades 3 or 9. *J. Amer. Acad. Child Adoles. Psychiat., 46,* 1250–62.

Conger, R. D., & Donnellan, M. B. (2007). An interactionist perspective on the socioeconomic context of human development. *Annu. Rev. Psychol., 58,* 175–99.

Conklin, H. M., & Iacono, W. G. (2002). Schizophrenia: A neurodevelopmental perspective. *Curr. Dis. Psychol. Sci., 11*(1), 33–37.

Conley, R. W. (2003). Supported employment in Maryland: Successes and issues. *Mental Retardation, 41*(4), 237–49.

Conlon, L., & Fahy, T. J. (2001). Psychological debriefing for acute trauma—a welcome demise? *International Journal of Psychological Medicine, 18*(2), 43–44.

Connell, P. (1958). *Amphetamine psychosis,* Maudsley Monographs, No. 5. London: Oxford University Press.

Connors, G. J., & Walitzer, K. S. (2001). Reducing alcohol consumption among heavily drinking women: Evaluating the contributions of life-skills training and booster sessions. *J. Cons. Clin. Psychol., 69*(3), 447–56.

Connors, G. J., Carroll, K. M., DiClemente, C. C., Longabaugh, R., & Donovan, D. M. (1997). The therapeutic alliance and its relationship to alcoholism treatment participation and outcome. *J. Cons. Clin. Psychol., 65,* 588–98.

Conrod, P. J., Pihl, R. O., & Vassileva, J. (1998). Differential sensitivity to alcohol reinforcement in groups of men at risk for distinct alcoholism subtypes. *Alcoholism: Clin. Exper. Res., 22*(3), 585–97.

Constantino, M. J., Castonguay, L. G., & Schut, A. J. (2001). The working alliance. In G. S. Tryon (Ed.), *Counseling based on process research: Applying what we know.* Boston: Allyn and Bacon.

Conte, J., Berliner, L., & Schuerman, J. (1986). *The impact of sexual abuse on children* (Final Report No. MH 37133). Rockville, MD: National Institute of Mental Health.

Conwell, Y., Duberstein, P. R., & Caine, E. D. (2002). Risk factors for suicide in later life. *Biol. Psychiat., 52*(3), 193–204.

Cook, C. R., & Blacher, J. (2007). Evidence based psychosocial treatments for tic disorders. *Clin. Psychol. Sci. Prac., 14,* 252–67.

Cook, M., & Mineka, S. (1989). Observational conditioning of fear to fear-relevant versus fear-irrelevant stimuli in rhesus monkeys. *J. Abn. Psychol., 98,* 448–59.

Cook, M., & Mineka, S. (1990). Selective associations in the observational conditioning of fear in monkeys. *J. Exper. Psychol.: Animal Behavior Processes, 16,* 372–89.

Cooke, D. J. (1996). Psychopathic personality in different cultures: What do we know? What do we need to find out? *J. Person. Dis., 10*(1), 23–40.

Cooke, D. J., & Michie, C. (1999). Psychopathy across cultures: North America and Scotland compared. *J. Abn. Psychol., 108*(1), 58–68.

Cooke, D. J., Michie, C., Hart, S. D., & Clark, D. (2005). Searching for the pan-cultural core of psychopathic personality disorder. *Personal. Indiv. Diff., 39,* 283–295,

Cooley-Quille, M., Boyd, R., Frantz, E., & Walsh, J. (2001). Emotional and behavioral impact of exposure to community violence in inner-city adolescents. *J. Clin. Child Psychol., 30,* 199–206.

Coolidge, F. L., DenBoer, J. W., & Segal, D. L. (2004). Personality and neuropsychological correlates of bullying behavior. *Personal. Indiv. Diff., 36,* 1559–69.

Coons, P. M., & Bowman, E. S. (2001). Ten-year follow-up study of patients with dissociative identity disorder. *Journal of Trauma & Dissociation, 2,* 73–89.

Cooper, C. I., & Dewe, P. (2007). In A. Monat, R. S. Lazarus & G. Reevy (Eds.), *The Praeger handbook of stress and coping.* (pp 7–31). Westport, CT.: Praeger Publishers.

Cooper, M., Todd, G., & Wells, A. (2000). *Bulimia nervosa: A cognitive therapy programme for clients.* London: Jessica Kingsley Publishers.

Cooper, S-A., & van der Speck, R. (2009). Epidemiology of mental ill health in adults with intellectual disabilities. *Cur. Opin. Psychiat., 22*(5), 431–36.

Cooper, S-A., Smiley, E., Allan, L. M., Jackson, A., Finlayson, J., Mantry, D., & Morrison, J., (2009). Adults with intellectual disabilities: Prevalence, incidence and remission of self-injurious behaviour, and related factors. *J. Intell. Dis. Res., 53*(3), 200–16.

Cooper, Z., Doll, H. A., Hawker, D. M., Byrne, S., Bonner G., Eeley, E., et al. (2010). Testing a new cognitive behavioral treatment for obesity: A randomized controlled trial with three-year follow up. *Behav. Res. Ther., 48,* 706–13.

Copeland, W. E., Miller-Johnson, S., Keeler, G., Angold, A., & Costello, E. J. (2007). Childhood psychiatric disorders and young crime: A prospective populationg-based study. *Am. J. Orthopsychiat., 164,* 1668–75.

Corcoran, J. (2011). *Mental health treatment for children and adolescents.* New York: Oxford University Press.

Cornblatt, B. A., Green, M. F., & Walker, E. F. (2008). Schizophrenia: Etiology and neurocognition. In T. Millon, P. Blaney, & R. Davis, (Eds.), *Oxford Textbook of Psychopathology* (2nd ed.). New York: Oxford University Press.

Cornblatt, B. A., Lenzenweger, M. F., & Erlenmeyer-Kimling, L. (1989). The Continuous Performance Test, identical pairs version: II. Contrasting attentional profiles in schizophrenic and depressed patients. *Psychiat. Res., 29,* 65–85.

Cornblatt, B. A., Lenzenweger, M. F., Dworkin, R. H., & Erlenmeyer-Kimling, L. (1992). Childhood attentional dysfunctions predict social deficits in unaffected adults at risk for schizophrenia. *Brit. J. Psychiat., 16* (Suppl. 18), 59–64.

Cororve, M. B., & Gleaves, D. H. (2001). Body dysmorphic disorder: A review of conceptualizations, assessment, and treatment strategies. *Clin. Psychol. Rev., 21,* 949–70.

Corrigan, P. W. (1995). Use of token economy with seriously mentally ill patients: Criticisms and misconceptions. *Psychiatr. Serv., 46*(12), 1258–63.

Corrigan, P. W. (1997). Behavior therapy empowers persons with severe mental illness. *Behav. Mod., 21*(1), 45–61.

Corrigan, P. W., & Watson, A. C. (2005). Mental illness and dangerousness: Fact or misperception and implications for stigma. In P. W. Corrigan (Ed.), *On the stigma of mental illness: Practical strategies for research and social change.* Washington, DC: American Psychological Association, 165–79.

Cortina, L. M., & Kubiak, S. P. (2006). Gender and posttraumatic stress: Sexual violence as an explanation for women's increased risk. *J. Abn. Psychol., 115,* 753–759.

Coryell, W., & Winokur, G. (1992). Course and outcome. In E. S. Paykel (Ed.), *Handbook of affective disorders* (2nd ed.). New York: Guilford.

Coryell, W., & Young, E. A. (2005). Clinical predictors of suicide in primary major depressive disorder. *J. Clin. Psychiat., 66*(4), 412–17.

Coryell, W., Endicott, J., Maser, J. D., Mueller, T., Lavori, P., & Keller, M. (1995). The likelihood of recurrence in bipolar affective disorder: The importance of episode recency. *J. Affect. Dis., 33,* 201–6.

Coryell, W., Solomon, D., Turvey, C., Keller, M., Leon, A. C., Endicott, J., et al. (2003). The long-term course of rapid-cycling bipolar disorder. *Arch. Gen. Psychiat., 60*(9), 914–20.

Costa, P. T., Jr., & Widiger, T. A. (2002). *Personality disorders and the five-factor model of personality* (2nd ed.). Washington, DC: American Psychological Association.

Costanzo, M., Krauss, D., & Pezdek, K., (Eds) (2007). *Expert psychological testimony for the courts.* Mahwah, NJ, US: Lawrence Erlbaum Associates Publishers.

Costello, E. J., Erkanli, A., & Angold, A. (2006). Is there an epidemic of child or adolescent depression? *J. Child Psychol. Psychiat., 47*(12) 1263–71.

Cota, D., Tschop, M. H., Horvath, T. L., & Levine, A. S. (2006). Cannabinoids, opiods, and eating behavior: The molecular face of hedonism? *Brain Res. Rev., 51,* 85–107.

Cote, G., O'Leary, T., Barlow, D. H., Strain, J. J., Salkovskis, P. M., Warwick, H. M. C., et al. (1996). Hypochondriasis. In T. A. Widiger, A. J. Frances, H. A. Pincus, R. Ross, M. B. First, & W. W. Davis (Eds.), *DSM-IV Sourcebook, vol. 2* (pp. 933–47). Washington, DC: American Psychiatric Association.

Cotton, N. S. (1979). The familial incidence of alcoholism. *J. Stud. Alcoh., 40,* 89–116.

Cottraux, J., & Blackburn, I. M. (2001). Cognitive therapy. In W. J. Livesley (Ed.), *Handbook of personality disorders* (pp. 377–99). New York: Guilford.

Cougle, J. R., Salkovskis, P. M., & Wahl, K. (2007). Perception of memory ability and confidence in recollections in obsessive-compulsive checking. *J. Anxiety Dis., 21*(1), 118–130.

Coulston, C. M., Perdices, M., & Tennunt, C. C. (2007). The neuropsychology of cannabis and other substance use in schizophrenia: review of the literature and critical evaluation of methodological issues. *Austral. N.Z. J. Psychiat., 41,* 869–84.

Couture, S., & Penn, D. L. (2003). Interpersonal contact and the stigma of mental illness: A review of the literature. *J. Ment. Hlth., 12,* 291–305.

Couturier, J. L. (2005). Efficacy of rapid-rate repetitive transcranial magnetic stimulation in the treatment of depression: A systematic review and meta-analysis. *J. Psychiat. Neurosci., 30*(2), 83–90.

Couzin, J. (2004). Volatile chemistry: Children and antidepressants. *Science, 305*(5683), 468–70.

Couzin-Frankel, J. (2010, Aug. 17). Brain scans not acceptable for detecting lies, says judge. *AAAS Science Insider.*

Covey, H. C. (Ed.). (2007). *The methamphetamine crisis: Strategies to save addicts, families, and communities.* Westport, CT: Praeger.

Coyne, J. C. (1976). Depression and the response of others. *J. Abn. Psychol., 55*(2), 186–93.

Coyne, J. C., Rohrbaugh, M. J., Shoham, V., Sonnega, J. S., Nicklas, J. M., & Cranford, J. A. (2001). Prognostic importance of marital quality for survival of congestive heart failure. *Amer. J. Cardio., 88,* 526–29.

Craig, R. (2009). The clinical interview. In J. N. Butcher (Ed.), *Oxford handbook of personality and clinical assessment* (pp. 201–25). New York: Oxford University Press.

Craighead, W. E., Sheets, E. S., Brosse, A. L., & Ilardi, S. S. (2007). Psychosocial treatments for major depressive disorder. In P. E. Nathan & J. M. Gorman (Eds.), *A guide to treatments that work* (3rd ed.). (pp. 289–307). New York: Oxford University Press.

Craske, M., & Barlow, D. (2007). *Mastery of your anxiety and panic: Workbook for primary care settings* (4th ed.). New York: Oxford University Press.

Craske, M. G. (1999). *Anxiety disorders: Psychological approaches to theory and treatment.* Boulder, CO: Westview.

Craske, M. G., & Barlow, D. H. (2008). Panic disorder and agoraphobia. In D. H. Barlow (Ed.), *Clinical handbook of psychological disorders* (4th ed.; pp. 1–64). New York: Guildford.

Craske, M. G., & Mystkowski, J. L. (2006). Exposure therapy and extinction: Clinical studies. In M. G. Craske, D. Hermans, & D. Vansteenwegen (Eds.), *Fear and learning: Basic Science to Clinical Application* (pp. 217–233). Washington, DC: APA Books.

Craske, M. G., & Rowe, M. K. (1997). A comparison of behavioral and cognitive treatments of phobias. In G. C. L. Davey (Ed.), *Phobias: A handbook of theory, research and treatment* (pp. 247–80). Chichester, England: Wiley.

Craske, M. G., & Waters, A. M. (2005). Panic disorders, phobias, and generalized anxiety disorder. *Annu. Rev. Clin. Psychol., 1,* 197–225.

Craske, M. G., Barlow, D. H., & Meadows, E. (2000). *Mastery of your anxiety and panic: Therapist guide for anxiety, panic, and agoraphobia (MAP-3).* San Antonio, TX: Graywind/Psychological Corporation.

Craske, M. G., Lang, A. J., Mystowski, J. L., Zucker, B. G., Bystritsky, A., & Yan-go, F. (2002). Does nocturnal panic represent a more severe form of panic disorder? *J. Nerv. & Ment. Dis., 190*(9), 611–18.

Craske, M., & Mystkowski, J. (2006). Exposure therapy and extinction: Clinical studies. In M. Craske & D. Hermans (Eds.), *Fear and learning: Contemporary perspectives.* APA Books.

Creed, F., & Barsky, A. (2004). A systematic review of the epidemiology of somatisation disorder and hypochondriasis. *J. Psychosom. Res., 56,* 391–408.

Crerand, C. E., Sarwer, D. B., Magee, L., Gibbons, L. M., Lowe, M. R., Bartlett, S. P., et al. (2004). Rate of body dysmorphic disorder among patients seeking facial plastic surgery. *Psychiat. Ann., 34*(12), 958–65.

Cretzmeyer, M., Sarrazin, M. V., Huber, D. L., Block, R. I., & Hall, J. A. (2003). Treatment of methamphetamine abuse: Research findings and clinical directions. *J. Sub. Abuse Treat., 24*(3), 267–77.

Crews, F. (1995). *The memory wards: Freud's legacy in dispute.* New York: Granta.

Crick, N. R., & Dodge, K. A. (1994). A review and reformulation of social information-processing mechanisms in children's social adjustment. *Psychol. Bull., 115*(1), 74–101.

Crisp, A. H., Douglas, J. W. B., Ross, J. M., & Stonehill, E. (1970). Some developmental aspects of disorders of weight. *J. Psychosom. Res., 14,* 313–20.

Crisp, A., et al. (2006). Death, survival and recovery in anorexia nervosa: A thirty five year study. *Eur. Eat. Dis. Rev., 14,* 168–75.

Crits-Christoph, P., & Barber, J. P. (2000). Long-term psychotherapy. In C. R. Snyder & R. E. Ingram (Eds.), *Handbook of psychological change* (pp. 455–73). New York: Wiley.

Crits-Christoph, P., & Barber, J. P. (2002). Psychosocial treatments for personality disorders. In P. E. Nathan & J. M. Gorman (Eds.), *A guide to treatments that work* (pp. 544–53). New York: Oxford University Press.

Crits-Christoph, P., & Barber, J. P. (2007). Psychological treatments for personality disorders. In P. E. Nathan & J. M. Gorman (Eds.), *A guide to treatments that work* (pp. 641–58). New York: Oxford University Press.

Crits-Christoph, P., Gibbons, M. C., & Crits-Christoph, K. (2004). Supportive-expressive psychodynamic therapy. In R. G. Heimberg, C. L. Turk, & D. S. Mennin (Eds.), *Generalized anxiety disorder: Advances in research and practice.* (pp. 293–319). New York: Guilford Press.

Crittenden, P. M., & Ainsworth, M. D. S. (1989). Child maltreatment and attachment theory. In D. Cicchetti & V. Carlson (Eds.), *Child maltreatment: Theory and research on the causes and consequences of child abuse and neglect* (pp. 432–63). Cambridge: Cambridge University Press.

Crosson-Tower, C. (2002). *Understanding child abuse and neglect* (5th ed.). New York: Longman.

Crouter, A. C., & Booth, A. (2003). *Children's influence on family dynamics: The neglected side of family relationships.* Mahwah, NJ: Lawrence Erlbaum Associates.

Crow, T. J. (2007). Genetic hypotheses for schizophrenia. *Brit. J. Psychiat., 191,* 180–81.

Crowe, S. F., Barot, J., Caldow, S., D'Aspromonte, J., Dell'Orso, J., Di Clemente, A., Hanson, K., et al. (2011). The effect of caffeine and stress on auditory hallucinations in a non-clinical sample. *Pers. Indiv. Diff., 50,* 626–30.

Crowther, J. H., Armey, M., Luce, K. H., Dalton, G. R., & Leahey, T. (2008). The point prevalence of bulimic disorders from 1990–2004. *Int. J. Eat. Dis., .*

Crowther, J. H., Kichler, J. C., Sherwood, N., & Kuhnert, M. E. (2002). The role of family factors in bulimia nervosa. *Eat. Dis., 10,* 141–51.

Cruts, M., van Duijn, C. M., Backhovens, H., van den Broeck, M., Serneels, S., Sherrington, R., Hutton, M., Hardy, J., St. George-Hyslop, P. H., & Van Broeckhoven, C. (1998). Estimations of the genetic contribution of presenilin-1 and presenilin-2 mutations in a population-based study of presenile Alzheimer disease. *Human Molecular Genetics, 7,* 43–51.

Cuellar, A. K., Johnson, S. L., & Winters, R. (2005). Distinctions between bipolar and unipolar depression. *Clin. Psychol. Rev., 25,* 307–39.

Cui, M., & Fincham, F. E. (2010). The differential effects of parental divorce and marital conflict on young

adult romantic relationships. *Personal Relationships, 17*(3), 331–43. doi:10.1111/j.1475-6811.2010.01279.x

Cullum, C. M., & Lacritz, L. H. (2009). Neuropsychological assessment in dementia. In M. F. Weiner & A. M. Lipton (Eds.), *The American Psychiatric Publishing textbook of Alzheimer disease and other dementias* (pp. 85–103). Arlington, VA: American Psychiatric Publishing.

Cummings, E. M., Goeke-Morey, M. C., & Papp, L. M. (2004). Everyday marital conflict and child aggression. *J. Abn. Psychol., 32*(2), 191–202.

Cummings, J. L. (2004). Alzheimer's disease. *N. Eng. J. Med., 351,* 56–67.

Cunningham, M. D., & Sorensen, J. R. (2007). Capital offenders in Texas prisons: Correlates, and an actuarial analysis of violent misconduct. *Law and Human Behavior, 31,* 553–71.

Currie, J., & Widom, C. S. (2010). Long-term consequences of child abuse and neglect on adult economic well-being. *Child Maltreatment, 15*(2), 111–20.

Curlin, F. A., Nwodim, C., Vance, J. L., Chin, M. H., & Lantos, J. D. (2008). To die, to sleep: US physicians' religious and other objections to physician-assisted suicide, terminal sedation, and withdrawal of life support. *American Journal of Hospice & Palliative Medicine, 25*(2), 112–20.

Currier, G. (2000). Datapoints: Psychiatric bed reductions and mortality among persons with mental disorders. *Psychiatr. Serv., 51,* p. 851.

Curtis, G. C., Magee, W. J., Eaton, W. W., Wittchen, H.-U., & Kessler, R. (1998). Specific fears and phobias: Epidemiology and classification. *Brit. J. Psychiat., 173,* 212–17.

Cutting, J. (1995). Descriptive psychopathology. In S. R. Hirsch & D. R. Weinberger, (Eds.), *Schizophrenia* (pp. 15–27). Cambridge: Cambridge University Press.

Cutting, J., & Murphy, D. (1990). Impaired ability of schizophrenics, relative to manics or depressives, to appreciate social knowledge about their culture. *Brit. J. Psychiat., 157,* 355–58.

Da Roza, Davis, J. M., & Cowen, P. J. (2001). Biochemical stress of caring. *Psychol. Med., 31,* 1475–78.

Dadds, M. R., Spence, S. H., Holland, D. E., Barren, P. M., & Laurens, K. R. (1997). Prevention and early intervention for anxiety disorders: A controlled study. *J. Cons. Clin. Psychol., 65*(4), 627–35.

Dadds, M., Davey, G. C., Graham, C., & Field, A. P. (2001). Developmental aspects of conditioning processes in anxiety disorders. In M. W. Vasey and M. R. Dadds (Eds.), *The developmental psychopathology of anxiety.* (pp. 205–30). London: Oxford University Press.

Dahl, R. E. (1992). The pharmacologic treatment of sleep disorders. *Psychiat. Clin. N. Amer., 15,* 161–78.

Dahlkamp, J., Kraske, M., von Mittelstaedt, J., Robel,S., & von Roohr, M. (2008). "How Josef Fritzl created his regime of terror. *Spiegel Online.* Retrieved 5 June 2008..

Dahllöf, O., & Öst, L.-G. (1998). The diphasic reaction in blood phobic situations: Individually or stimulus bound? *Scandinavian Journal of Behaviour Therapy, 27*(3), 97–104.

Dain, N. (1964). *Concepts of insanity in the United States: 1789–1865.* New Brunswick, NJ: Rutgers University Press.

Dallam, S. J., Gleaves, D. H., Cepeda-Benito, A., Silberg, J. L., Kraemer, H. C., & Spiegel, D. (2001). The effects of child sexual abuse: Comment on Rind, Tromovitch, and Bauserman (1998). *Psych. Bull., 127,* 715–33.

Dallman, M. F., Pecorano, N., Akana, S. F., la Fleur, S. E., Gomez, F., Houshyar, H., Bell, M. E., Bhatnagar,

S., Laugero, K. D., & Manalo, S. (2003, Sept. 30). Chronic stress and obesity: A new view of "comfort food." *Proceedings of the National Academy of Sciences, 100*(20), 11696–701.

Daly, M., & Wilson, M. (1988). *Homicide.* New York: Aldine de Gruyter.

Daly, M., & Wilson, M. I. (1996). Violence against stepchildren. *Curr. Dir. Psychol. Sci., 5*(3), 77–81.

Daniel, M., & Gurczynski, J. (2010). Mental status examination. In D. L. Segal & M. Hersen, (Eds.), *Diagnostic interviewing* (pp. 61–88). New York: Springer.

Dar, R., Rish, S., Hermesh, H., Taub, M., & Fux, M. (2000). Realsim of confidence in obsessive-compulsive checkers. *J. Abn. Psychol., 109*(4), 673–78.

Dare, C., & Eisler, I. (2002). Family therapy and eating disorders. In C. G. Fairburn & K. D. Brownell (Eds.), *Eating disorders and obesity: A comprehensive handbook* (2nd ed., pp. 314–19). New York: Guilford.

Darke, S., & Ross, J. (2001). The relationship between suicide and heroin overdose among methadone maintenance patients in Sydney, Australia. *Addiction, 96,* 1443–53.

Daskalakis, Z. J., Christensen, B. K., Chen, R., Fitzgerald, P. B., Zipursky, R. B., & Kapus, S. (2002). Evidence for impaired cortical inhibition in schizophrenia using transcranial magnetic stimulation. *Arch. Gen. Psychiat., 59,* 347–54.

Dattilio, F. M., & Freeman, A. (2007). Cognitive behavioral strategies in crisis intervention. New York: Guilford Press.

D'Avanzo, B., Barbato, A., Barbui, C., Battino, R. N., Civenti, G., & Frattura, L. (2003). Discharges of patients from public psychiatric hospitals in Italy between 1994 and 2000. *Inter. J. Soc. Psychiat., 49*(1), 27–34.

Daversa, M. T., & Knight, R. A. (2007). A structural examination of the predictors of sexual coercion against children in adolescent sexual offenders. *Crim. Just. Behav., 34*(10), 1313–33.

David, D., De Faria, L., Lapeyra, O., & Mellman, T. A. (2004). Adjunctive risperidone treatment in combat veterans with chronic PTSD. *J. Clin. Psychopharm., 24*(5), 556–58.

David, D., Szentagotai, A., Eva, K., & Macavei, B. (2005). A synopsis of rational-emotove behavior therapy (REBT): Fundamental and applied research. *Journal of Rational-Emotive and Cognitive-Behavior Therapy, 23,* 175–21.

Davidson, K., MacGregor, M. W., Stuhr, J., Dixon, K., & MacLean, D. (2000). Constructive anger verbal behavior predicts blood pressure in a population-based sample. *Hlth. Psychol., 19*(1), 55–64.

Davidson, K. W., Burg, M. M., Kronish, I. M., Shimbo, D., Dettenborn, L., Mehran, R., Vorchheimer, D., Clemow, L., Schwartz, J. E., Lespéranace, F., & Rieckman, N. (2010). *Arch. Gen. Psychiat., 67,* 480–88.

Davidson, L., Shahar, G., Stayner, et al. (2004). Supported socialization for people with psychiatric disabilities: Lessons from a randomized controlled trial. *J. Comm. Psychol., 32,* 453–77.

Davidson, M. C., Thomas, K. M., & Casey, B. J. (2003). Imaging the developing brain with fMRI. *Men. Retard. Devel. Res. Rev., 9,* 161–67.

Davidson, R. J., Pizzagalli, D., & Nitschke, J. B. (2002). The representation and regulation of emotion in depression: Perspectives from affective neuroscience. In I. H. Gotlib & C. L. Hammen (Eds.), *Handbook of depression* (pp. 219–44). New York: Guilford.

Davidson, R. J., Pizzagalli, D., & Nitschke, J. B. (2009). The representation and regulation of emotion in depression: Perspectives from affective neuroscience. In I. H. Gotlib & C. L. Hammen (Eds.), *Handbook of depression* (2nd ed., pp. 218–48). New York: Guilford Press.

Davidson, R. J., Pizzagalli, D., Nitschke, J. B., & Putnam, K. (2002b). Depression: Perspectives from affective neuroscience. *Ann. Rev. Psychol., 53*, 545–74. AnnualReviews, US.

Davis, J. O., Phelps, J. A., & Bracha, H. S. (1995). Prenatal development of monozygotic twins and concordance for schizophrenia. *Schizo. Bull., 21*(3), 357–66.

Davis, M. (2002). Role of NMDA receptors and MAP kinase in the amygdala in extinction of fear: Clinical implications for exposure therapy. *Europ. J. Neurosci., 16*(3), 395–98.

Davis, M. (2006) Neural systems involved with anxiety and fear measured with fear-potentiated startle. *Amer. Psychol., 61*, 441–756.

Davis, M. (2010). Facilitation of fear extinction and psychotherapy by D-cycloserine. *Zeitschrift für Psychologie mit Zeitschrift für angewandte Psychologie, 218*(2), 149–50. doi: 10.1027/0044-3409/a000023

Davis, M., Myers, K. M., Ressler, K. J., & Rothbaum, B. O. (2005). Facilitation of extinction of conditioned fear by d-cycloserine: Implications for psychotherapy. *Curr. Dis. Psychol. Sci., 14*(4), 214–19.

Davis, M., Ressler, K., Rothbaum, B. O., & Richardson, R. (2006). Effects of d-cycloserine on extinction: Translation from preclinical to clinical work. *Biol. Psychiat., 60*(4), 369–75.

Davison, T. E., McCabe, M. P., Mellor, D., Ski, C., George, K., & Moore, K. A. (2007). The prevalence and recognition of major depression among low-level aged

Dawkins, M. P. (1997). Drug use and violent crime among adolescents. *Adolescence, 32*, 395–405.

DAWN Report. (2006). *Opiate-related drug misuse deaths in six states:2003*. Office of Applied Statistics. Washington, DC: Substance Abuse and Mental Health Services Administration.

DAWN Report. (2007). *National estimates of drug-related emergency department visits*. DAWN Series D-28, DHHS Publication No. (SMA) 06-4143, Rockville, MD, April 2006.

DAWN Report. (2010). National estimates of drug-related emergency department visits. Drug Abuse Warning Network. U.S. Department of Health and Human Services. Substance Abuse and Mental Health Services Administration Office of Applied Studies.

Dawson, G., Panagiotides, H., Klinger, L. G., & Spieker, S. (1997). Infants of depressed and nondepressed mothers exhibit differences in frontal brain electrical activity during the expression of negative emotions. *Develop. Psychol., 33*(5), 650–56.

Day, N. (2007). Critical incident stress management and TIR. In V. R. Volkman (Ed.), *Traumatic incident reduction and critical incident stress management*. Ann Arbor, MI: Loving Healing Press.

De Bellis, M. D. (2005). The psychobiology of neglect. *Child Maltreatment, 10*(2), 150–172.

De Clercq, B., De Fruyt, F., & Widiger, T. A. (2009). Integrating a developmental perspective in dimensional models of personality disorders. *Clin. Psychol. Rev., 29*(2), 154–62. doi:10.1016/j.cpr.2008.12.002

de Jong, J. (Ed.). (2002). *Trauma, war, and violence: Public health in socio-cultural context*. New York: Kluwer Academic/Plenum, 2002.

De Kloet, C. S., Vermetten, E., Geuze, E., Kavelaars, A., Heijnen, C. J., & Westenberg, H. G. M. (2006). Assement of HPA-axis function in posttraumatic stress disorder: Pharmacological and non-pharmacological challenge tests, a review. *J. Psychiat. Res., 40*, 550–567.

De Leon, M. J., Desanti, S., Zinkowski, R., Mehta, P. D., Pratico, D., Segal, S., et al. (2004). MRI and CSF studies in the early diagnosis of Alzheimer's disease. *J.Int. Med., 256*, 205–23.

de Mello, M. F., de Jesus Mari, J., Bacaltchuk, J., Verdeli, H., & Neugebauer, R. (2005). A systematic review of research findings on the efficacy of interpersonal therapy for depressive disorders. *Eur. Arch. Psychiat. Clin. Neurosci., 255*(2), 75–82.

de Pauw, K. W., & Szulecka, T. K. (1988). Dangerous delusions: Violence and misidentification syndromes. *Brit. J. Psychiat., 152*, 91–96.

De Santi, S., de Leon, M. J., Rusinek, H., Convit, A., Tarshish, C. Y., Roche, A., Tsui, W. H., Kandil, E., Boppana, M., Daisley, K., Wang, G. J., Schlyer, D., & Fowler, J. (2001). Hippocampal formation, glucose metabolism and volume losses in MCI and AD. *Neurobiol. Aging, 22*, 529–39.

De Silva, P., Rachman, S. J., & Seligman, M. E. P. (1977). Prepared phobias and obsessions: Therapeutic outcomes. *Behav. Res. Ther., 15*, 65–78.

Deb, S., & Ahmed, Z. (2000). Specific conditions leading to mental retardation. In M. G. Gelder, J. J. Lopez-Ibor, Jr., & N. Andreason (Eds.), *New Oxford textbook of psychiatry* (pp. 1954–63). New York: Oxford University Press.

Debbané, M., Glaser, B., David, M. K., Feinstein, C., & Eliez, S. (2006). Psychotic symptoms in children and adolescents with 22q11.2 deletion syndrome: Neuropsychological and behavioral implications. *Schiz. Res., 84*, 187–93.

Declercq, F., Vanheule, S., Markey, S., & Willemsen, J. (2007). Posttraumatic distress in security guards and the various effects of social support. *Journal of Clinical Psychology, 63*, 1329–1246.

Deecher, D., Andree, T. H., Sloan, D., & Schechter, L. E. (2008). From menarche to menopause: Exploring the underlying biology of depression in women experiencing hormonal changes. *Psychoneuroendocrinology, 33*(1), 3–17. doi: 10.1016/j.psyncuen.2007.10.006

Degenhardt, L., Bruno, R., & Topp, L. (2010). Is ecstasy a drug of dependence? *Drug Alcohol Dep., 107*(1), 1–10.

Del-Ben, C. M., & Graeff, F. G. (2008). Panic disorder: Is the PAG involved? *Neural Plasticity, 2009*.

Del Boca, F. K., Darkes, J., Greenbaum, P. E., & Goldman, M. S. (2004). Up close and personal: Temporal variability in the drinking of individual college students during their first year. *J. Cons. Clin. Psychol., 72*, 155–64.

Del Guidice, M. J. (2010). What might this be? Rediscovering the Rorschach as a tool for personnel selection in organizations.*J. Pers. Assess., 92*, 78–89.

DeLuca, N. L., Moser, L. L., & Bond, G. R. (2008). Assertive community treatment. In K. T. Mueser & D. V. Jeste (Eds.), *Clinical handbook of schizophrenia* (pp. 329–338). New York: Guilford Press.

Dember, A. (2005, March 29). Mind mystery. *Boston Globe*.

den Heijer, T., Geerlings, M. I., Hoebeek, F. E., Hofman, A., Koudstaal, P. J., & Breteler, M. M. B. (2006). Use of hippocampal and amygdalar volumes on magnetic resonance imaging to predict dementia in cognitively intact elderly people. *Arch. Gen. Psychiat., 63*, 57–62.

Dennis, C. (2004). Asia's tigers get the blues. *Nature, 429*, 696–98.

Denollet, J., Vaes, J., & Brutsaert, D. L. (2000). Inadequate response to treatment in coronary heart disease: Adverse effects of Type D personality and younger age on 5-year prognosis and quality of life. *Circulation, 102*, 630–35.

Department of Defense. (2010, Aug.). The challenge and the promise: Strengthening the force, preventing suicide and saving lives. *Final report of the Department of Defense Task Force on the Prevention of Suicide by Members of the Armed Forces*.

Department of Health and Human Services (2006). Intermediate care facilities for the retarded. Centers for Medicare & Medicaid Service. U. S. Health Service.

Depue, R. A. (2009). Genetic, environmental, and epigenetic factors in the development of personality disturbance. *Develop. Psychopath., 21*(4), 1031–63. doi:10.1017/S0954579409990034

Depue, R. A., & Lenzenweger, M. F. (2001). A neurobehavioral dimensional model. In W. J. Livesley (Ed.), *Handbook of personality disorders* (pp. 136–76). New York: Guilford.

Depue, R. A., & Lenzenweger, M. F. (2005). A neurobehavioral model of personality disturbance. In M. F. Lenzenweger & J. F. Clarkin (Eds.), *Major theories of personality disorder* (2nd ed., pp. 391–453). New York: Guilford Press.

Depue, R. A., & Lenzenweger, M. F. (2006). A multidimensional neurobehavioral model of personality disturbance. In R. F. Krueger & J. L. Tackett (Eds.), *Personality and Psychopathology*. New York: Guilford Publications, Inc.

Derr, R. F., & Gutmann, H. R. (1994). Alcoholic liver disease may be prevented with adequate nutrients. *Medical Hypotheses, 42*, 1–4.

DeRubeis, R. J., Gelfand, L. A., Tang, T. Z., & Simons, A. D. (1999). Medications versus cognitive behavior therapy for severely depressed outpatients: Meta-analysis of four randomized comparisons. *Amer. J. Psychiat., 156*(7), 1007–13.

DeRubeis, R. J., Hollon, S. D., Amsterdam, J. D., Shelton, R. C., Young, P. R., Salomon, R. M., et al. (2005). Cognitive therapy vs medications in the treatment of moderate to severe depression. *Arch. Gen. Psychiat., 62*, 409–16.

Dervic, K., Brent, D. A., & Oquendo, M. A. (2008). *Psychiat. Clin. N. Amer., 31*(2), 271–91.

Deters, P. B., Novins, D. K., Fickenscher, A., & Beals, J. (2006). Trauma and posttraumatic stress disorder symptomatology: Patterns among American Indian adolescents in substance abuse treatment. *Amer. J. Orthopsychiat., 76*(3) 335–45.

Deutsch, A. (1944). Military psychiatry: The Civil War 1860–1865. In J. K. Hall (Ed.), *One hundred years of American psychiatry*. New York: Columbia University Press.

Deutsch, A. (1948). *The shame of the states*. New York: Harcourt, Brace.

Devanand, D. P., et al. (1994). Does ECT alter brain structure? *Amer. J. Psychiat., 151*, 957–70.

Devanand, D. P., Pradhanab, G., Liu, X., Khandji, A., De Santi, S., Segal, S. et al. (2007). Hippocampal and entorhinal atrophy in mild cognitive impairment. *Neurol., 68*, 828–36.

DeVane, C. L., & Sallee, F. R. (1996). Serotonin selective reuptake inhibitors in child and adolescent psychopharmacology: A review of published experience. *J. Clin. Psychiat., 57*(2), 55–66.

Deveci, A., Aydemir, O., Taskin, O., Tanelli, F., & Esen-Danaci, A. (2007). Serum brain derived neurotropic factor levels in conversion disorder: Comparative study with depression. *Psychiat. Clin. Neurosci., 61*, 571–73.

Devilly, G. J., Gist, R., & Cotton, P. (2006). Ready! Fire! Aim! The Status of Psychological Debriefing and Therapeutic Interventions: In the Work Place and After Disasters. *Rev. Gen. Psychol., 10*, 318–345.

DeVries, T. J., & Shippenberg, T. S. (2002). Neural systems underlying opiate addiction. *J. Neurosci., 22*(9), 3321–25.

Dew, M. A., Bromet, E. J., & Schulberg, H. C. (1987). A comparative analysis of two community stressors' long-term mental health effects. *Am. J. Community Psychol., 15*, 167–84.

Dew, M. A., Penkower, L., & Bromet, E. J. (1991). Effects of unemployment on mental health in the contemporary family. *Behav. Mod., 15*, 501–44.

Di Florio, A., Hamshere, M., Forty, L., Green, E. K., Grozeva, D., Jones, I., Caesar, S., Fraser, C., Gordon-Smith, K., Jones, L., Craddock, N., & Smith, D. J. (2010). Affective temperaments across the bipolar–unipolar spectrum: Examination of the TEMPS-A in 927 patients and controls. *J. Affect. Disord., 123*(1–3), 42–51.

Di Sclafani, Vi., Finn, P., & Fein, G. (2007). Psychiatric comorbidity in long-term abstinent alcoholic individuals. *Alcoholism: Clinical and Experimental Research, 31*, 795–803

Diav-Citrin, O., Shechtman, S., Wienbaum, D., Wajnberg, R., Avgil, M., Di Gianantonio, E., Clementi, M., Weber-Schoendorfer, C., Schaefer, C., & Ornoy, A. (2008). Paroxetine and fluoxetine in pregnancy: a prospective, multicentre, controlled, observational study. *Br. J. Clin. Pharmacol., 66*, 695–705.

Dickey, C. C., Morocz, I. A., Niznikiewicz, M. A., Voglmaier, M., Tone, S., Khan, U., Dreusicke, M., Yoo, S., Shenton, M. E., & McCarley, R. W. (2008). Auditory processing abnormalities in schizotypal personality disorder: An fMRI experiment using tones of deviant pitch and duration. *Schiz. Res., 103*, 26–39.

Dickey, R., Nussbaum, D., Chevolleau, K., & Davidson, H. (2002). Age as a differential characteristic of rapists, pedophiles, and sexual sadists. *J. Sex Marit. Ther., 28*, 211–18.

DiClemente, C. C. (1993). Changing addictive behaviors: A process perspective. *Curr. Dis. Psychol. Sci., 2*, 101–6.

Didie, E. R., Tortolani, C. C., Pope, C. G., Menard, W., Fay, C., & Phillips, K. A. (2006). Childhood abuse and neglect in body dysmorphic disorder. *Child Ab. Negl., 30*, 1105–15.

Diefenbach, G. J., Abramowitz, J. S., Norberg, M. M., & Tolin, D. F. (2007). Changes in quality of life following cognitive-behavioral therapy for obsessive-compulsive disorder. *Behav. Res. Ther., 45*(12), 3060–68.

Difede, J., Malta, L. S., Best, S., Henn-Haase, C., Metzler, T., Bryant, R., & Marmar, C. (2007). A randomized controlled clinical treatment trial for World Trade Center attack-related PTSD in disaster workers. *J. Nerv. Ment. Dis., 195*, 861–65.

DiGrande, L., Neria, Y., Brackbill, R. M., Pulliam, P., & Galea, S. (2011). Long-term post-traumatic stress symptoms among 3,271 civilian survivors of the September 11, 2011, terrorist attacks on the World Trade Center. *Am. J. Epidemiol, 173*, 271–281.

Dikmen, S. S., Temkin, N. R., Machamer, J. E., & Holubkov, A. L. (1994). Employment following traumatic head injuries. *Arch. Neurol., 51*(2), 177–86.

Diller, L., & Gordon, W. A. (1981). Interventions for cognitive deficits in brain-injured adults. *J. Cons. Clin. Psychol., 49*, 822–34.

Dimberg, U., & Öhman, A. (1996). Behold the wrath: Psychophysiological responses to facial stimuli. *Motivation & Emotion, 20*, 149–82.

Dimidjian, S., Barrera, M., Martel, C., Munoz, R. F., & Lewinsohn, P. M. (2011). The origins and current status of behavioral activation treatments for depression. *Annu. Rev. Clin. Psychol., 7*, 1–38. doi: 10.1146/annurev-clinpsy-032210-104535

Dimidjian, S., Hollon, S. D., Dobson, K. S., Schmaling, K. B., Kohlenberg, R. J., Addis, M. E., et al. (2006). Randomized trial of behavioral activation, cognitive therapy, and antidepressant medication in the acute treatment of adults with major depression. *J. Cons. Clin. Psych., 74*(4), 658–70.

Din-Dzietham, R., Nembhard, W. N., Collins, R., & Davis, S. K. (2004). Perceived stress following race-based discrimination at work is associated with hypertension in African-Americans. The metro Atlanta heart disease study 1999–2001. *Soc. Sci. Med., 58*, 449–61.

Dingfelder, S. F. (2010). Time capsule: The first modern psychology study. *Monitor on Psychology, 41*(7), 30–31.

DiPietro, L., Mossberg, H.-O., & Stunkard, A. J. (1994). A 40-year history of overweight children in Stockholm: Lifetime overweight, morbidity, and mortality. *International Journal of Obesity, 18*, 585–90.

Dishion, T. J., & Stormshak, E. A. (2007). *Intervening in children's lives: An ecological, family-centered approach to mental health care.* Washington, DC: American Psychological Association.

Dishion, T. J., & Kavanaugh, K. (2002). The Adolescent Transitions Program: A family-centered prevention strategy for schools. In J. B. Reid, G. R. Patterson & J. Snyder (Eds.), *Antisocial behavior in children and adolescents: A developmental analysis and model for intervention.* (pp. 257–272). Washington, DC: American Psychological Association.

Dishion, T. P., & Patterson, G. R. (1997). The timing and severity of antisocial behavior: Three hypotheses within an ecological framework. In D. M. Stoff, J. Breiling, & J. D. Maser (Eds.), *Handbook of antisocial behavior.* (pp. 205–17). New York: Wiley.

Disner, S. G., Beevers, C. G., Haigh, E. A., & Beck, A. T. (2011). Neural mechanisms of the cognitive model of depression. *Nature Reviews Neuroscience, 12*(8), 467–77. doi: 10.1038/nrn3027

Distel, M. A., Rebollo-Mesa, I., Willemsen, G., Derom, C.A., Trull, T. J., Martin, N. G., & Boomsma, D. I. (2009). Familial resemblance of borderline personality disorder features: Genetic or cultural transmission? *PLoS ONE, 4*, 4.

Divorce Statistics Collection. (2005). From http://www.divorcereform.org/stats.html

Doane, L. S., Feeny, N. C., & Zoellner, L. A. (2010). A preliminary investigation of sudden gains in exposure therapy for PTSD. *Behav. Res. Ther., 48*(6), 555–60.

Dobson, K. S., Hollon, S. D., Dimidjian, S., Schmaling, K. B., Kohlenberg, R. J., Gallop, R. J. et al., (2008). Randomized trail of behavioral activation, cognitive therapy, and antidepressant medications in the prevention of relapse and recurrence in major depression. *J. Cons. Clin. Psych., 76*, 468–77.

Docter, R. F., & Prince, V. (1997). Transvestism: A survey of 1032 cross-dressers. *Arch. Sex. Behav., 26*, 589–605.

Dodd, S., Kulkarni, J., Berk, L., Ng, F., Fitzgerald, P. B., de Castella, A. R., et al. (2010). A prospective study of the impact of subthreshold mixed states on the 24-month clinical outcomes of bipolar I disorder or schizoaffective disorder. *J. Affect. Disord., 124*(1–2), 22–28. doi: 10.1016/j.jad.2009.10.027

Dodge, K. A. (2006). Translational science in action: Hostile attributional style and the development of aggressive behavior problems. *Develop. Psychopath., 18*(3), 791–814.

Dodge, K. A., Laird, R., Lochman, J., & Zelli, A. (2002). Multidimensional latent-construct analysis of children's social information processing patterns: Correlations with aggressive behavior problems. *Psychol. Assess., 14*, 60–73.

Dodge, K. A., Lochman, J. E., Harnish, J. D., Bates, J. E., & Pettit, G. S. (1997). Reactive and proactive aggression in school children and psychiatrically impaired chronically assaultive youth. *J. Abn. Psychol., 106*(1), 37–51.

Dodge, K. A., Pettit, G. S., & Bates, J. E. (1994). Socialization mediators of the relation between socioeconomic status and child conduct problems. *Child Develop., 65*, 649–65.

Dodge, K., & Pettit, G. (2003). A biopsychosocial model of the development of chronic conduct problems in adolescence. *Develop. Psychol., 39*, 349–71.

Doering, S., Katzberger, F., Rumpold, G., Roessler, S., Hofstoeetter, B., Schatz, D. S., et al., (2000). Videotape preparation of patients before hip replacement surgery reduces stress. *Psychosom. Med., 62*, 365–73.

Dohrenwend, B. P. (2000). The role of adversity and stress in psychopathology: Some evidence and its implications for theory and research. *J. Health & Social Behavr., 41*(1), 1–19.

Dohrenwend, B. P. (2006). Inventorying stressful life events as risk factors for psychopathology: Toward resolution of the problem of intracategory variability. *Psych. Bull., 132*(3), 477–95.

Dohrenwend, B. P., Shrout, P. E., Link, B. G., Skodol, A. E., & Stueve, A. (1995). A case-control study of life events and other possible psychosocial risk factors for episodes of schizophrenia and major depression. In C. M. Mazure (Ed.), *Does stress cause psychiatric illness?* Washington, DC: American Psychiatric Press.

Dolan-Sewell, R. T., Krueger, R. F., & Shea, M. T. (2001). Co-occurrence with syndrome disorders. In W. J. Livesley (Ed.), *Handbook of personality disorders* (pp. 84–104). New York: Guilford.

Dolberg, O. T., Iancu, I., Sasson, Y., & Zohar, J. (1996a). The pathogenesis and treatment of obsessive-compulsive disorder. *Clinical Neuropharmacology, 19*(2), 129–147.

Dolberg, O. T., Sasson, Y., Marazziti, D., Kotler, M., Kendler, S., & Zohar, J. (1996b). New compounds for the treatment of obsessive-compulsive disorder. In H. G. Westenberg, J. A. Den Boer, & D. L. Murphy (Eds.), *Advances in the neurobiology of anxiety disorders* (pp. 299–311). Chichester, England: Wiley.

Domjan, M. (2005). Pavlonian conditioning: A functional perspective. *Annu. Rev. Psychol., 56*, 179–206.

Domjan, M. P. (2009). *The principles of learning and behavior: Active learning edition* (6th ed.). Stamford, CT: Wadsworth.

Donaldson, M. A., & Gardner, R., Jr. (1985). Diagnosis and treatment of traumatic stress among women after childhood incest. In C. R. Filley (Ed.), *Trauma and its wake: The study and treatment of posttraumatic stress disorder* (pp. 356–77). Newbury Park, CA: Sage.

Dooley, D., & Prause, J. (2004). *The social costs of underemployment: Inadequate employment as disguised unemployment.* New York: Cambridge University Press.

Dooley, D., & Prause, J. (2007). Predictors of early alcohol drinking onset. *Journal of Child & Adolescent Substance Abuse, 16*(2), 1–29.

Dooley, D., Prause, J., & Ham-Rowbottom, K. A. (2000). Underemployment and depression: Longitudinal relationships. *J. Hlth. Soc. Behav., 41*(4), 421–36.

Doornbos, B., Fekkes, D., Tanke, M. A. C., de Jonge, P., & Korf, J. (2008). Sequential serotonin and noradrenalin associated processes involved in postpartum blues. *Prog. Neuropsychopharmacol. Biol. Psychiatry, 32*(5), 1320–25

Dorahy, M. J. (2001). Dissociative identity disorder and memory dysfunction: The current state of experimental research and its future directions. *Clin. Psychol. Rev., 21,* 771–95.

Dorahy, M. J., & Huntjens, R. J. C. (2007). Memory and attentional processes in dissociative identity disorder. In E. Vermetten, M. Dorahy, & D. Spiegel. (Eds.), *Traumatic dissociation : Neurobiology and treatment* (pp. 55–75). Washington, DC: American Psychiatric Publishing.

Dorahy, M. J., Middleton, W., & Irwin, H. J. (2005). The effect of emotional context on cognitive inhibition and attentional processing in dissociative identity disorder. *Behav. Res. Ther., 43,* 555–68.

dos Reis, S., Zito, J. M., Safer, D. J., & Soeken, K. L. (2001). Mental health services for youths in foster care and disabled youths. *Amer. J. Pub. Hlth., 91,* 1094–99.

Dougherty, D. D., Baer, L., Cosgrove, G. R., Cassem, E. H., Price, B.H., Nierenberg, A. A., et al. (2002). Prospective long-term follow-up of 44 patients who received cingulotomy for treatment-refractory obsessivecompulsive disorder. *Amer. J. Psychiat., 159*(2), 269–75.

Dougherty, D. D., Rauch, S. L., & Jenike, M. A. (2002). Pharmacological treatments for obsessive compulsive disorder. In P. E. Nathan & J. M. Gorman (Eds.), *A guide to treatments that work* (2nd ed., pp. 387–410). New York: Oxford University Press.

Dougherty, D. D., Rausch, S. L., & Jenike, M. A. (2007). Pharmacological treatments for obsessive-compulsive disorder. In P. E. Nathan and J. M. Gorman (Eds.), *A guide to treatments that work.* New York: Oxford University Press, pp. 447–74.

Dougherty, L. R., Klein, D. N., & Davila, J. (2004). A growth curve analysis of the course of dysthymic disorder: The effects of chronic stress and moderation by adverse parent-child relationships and family history. *J. Cons. Clin. Psychol., 72*(6), 1012–21.

Douglas, K. R., Chan, G., Gelernter, J., Arias, A. J., Anton, R. F., Weiss, R. D., Brady, K., Poling, J., Farrer, L., & Kranzler, H. R. (2010). Adverse childhood events as risk factors for substance dependence: Partial mediation by mood and anxiety disorders.*Addict. Behav., 35*(1), 7–13.

Douglas, K. S., Vincent, G. M., & Edens, J. F. (2006). Risk for criminal recidivism: The role of psychopathy. In C. J. Patrick (Ed.), *Handbook of the psychopathy.* (pp. 533–54). New York: Guilford Press.

Dowlati, Y., Herrmann, N., Swardfager, W., Liu, H., Sham, L., Reim, E. K., & Lanctôt, K. L. (2010). A meta-analysis of cytokines in major depression. *Biol. Psychiat., 67*(5), 446–57. doi: 10.1016/j.biopsych.2009.09.033

Doyle, B. B. (2006). *Components of adult ADHD assessment and treatment.* Washington, DC: The American Psychiatric Association.

Dozois, D. J. A., & Dobson, K. S. (Eds.). (2004). *The prevention of anxiety and depression: Theory, research, and practice.* Washington, DC: American Psychological Association.

Draguns, J. G. (2001). Toward a truly international psychology: Beyond English only. *Amer. Psychol., 56,* 1019–30.

Draguns, J. G., & Tanaka-Matsumi, J. (2003). Assessment of psychopathology across and within cultures: Issues and findings.*Behav. Res. Ther., 41,* 755–76.

Dreyer, A. S., O'Laughlin, L., Moore, J., & Milam, Z. (2010). Parental adherence to clinical recommendations in an ADHD evaluation clinic. *J. Clin. Psychol., 66,* 1101–20.

Drtikova, I., Balastikova, B., Lemanova, H., & Zak, J. (1996). Clonazepam, clonidine and tiapride in children with tic disorder. *Homeostasis in Health & Disease, 37*(5), 216.

Drug Abuse Warning Network. (2007). *National Estimates of Drug-Related Emergency Department Visits.* U.S. Department of Health and Human Services, Substance Abuse and Mental Health Services. Administration Office of Applied Studies.

Drug Enforcement Administration, Department of Justice. (1979). *Controlled Substance Inventory List.* Washington, DC.

Drummond, K. D., Bradley, S. J., Peterson-Badali, M., & Zucker, K. J. (2008). A follow-up study of girls with gender identity disorder. *Develop. Psych., 44*(1), 34–45.

Druss, B. G. (2010). The changing face of U.S. mental health care. *Am. J. Psychiat., 167,* 1419–21.

D'Souza, D. C., Abi-Saab, W. M., Madonick, S., Forselius-Bielen, K., Doersch, A., Braley, G., et al. (2005). Delta-9-tetrahydrocannabinol effects in schizophrenia: Implications for cognition, psychosis, and addiction. *Biol. Psychiat., 57,* 594–608.

Du Rocher Schudlich, T. D, Shamir, H., & Cummings, E. M. (2004) Marital conflict, children's representations of family relationships, and children's dispositions towards peer conflict strategies. *Soc. Develop., 13,* 171–92.

Dubner, A. E., & Motta, R. W. (1999). Sexually and physically abused foster care children and posttraumatic stress disorder. *J. Cons. Clin. Psychol., 67,* 367–73.

Dugan, E. M., Snow, M. S., & Crowe, S. R. (2010). Working with children affected by Hurricane Katrina: Two case studies in play therapy. *Child and Adolescent Mental Health, 15*(1), 52–5.

Dugas, M. J., Buhr, K., & Ladouceur, R. (2004). The role of intolerance of uncertainty in etiology and maintenance. In R. G. Heimberg, C. L Turk, & D. S. Mennin. (Eds.), *Generalized anxiety disorder: Advances in research and practice.* (pp. 143–63). New York: Guilford Press.

Dugas, M. J., Marchand, A., & Ladouceur, R. (2005). Further validation of a cognitive-behavioral model of generalized anxiety disorder: Diagnostic and symptom specificity. *J. Anxiety Dis., 19*(3), 329–43.

Dugas, M. J., Savard, P., Gaudet, A., Turcotte, J., Laugesen, N., Robichaud, M., et al. (2007). Can the components of a cognitive model predict the severity of generalized anxiety disorder? *Behav. Ther., 38*(2), 169–78.

Duinkerke, A., Williams, M. A., Rigamonti, D., & Hillis, A. E. (2004). Cognitive recovery in idiopathic normal pressure hydrocephalus after shunt. *Cog. Behav. Neurol., 17*(3), 179–84.

Duncan, G. J., Brooks-Gunn, J., & Klebanov, P. K. (1994). Economic deprivation and early childhood development. *Child Develop., 65,* 296–318.

Dunlop, B. W., & Nemeroff, C. B. (2007). The role of dopamine in the pathophysiology of depression. *Arch. Gen. Psychiat., 64*(3), 327–37.

Dunmore, E., Clark, D. M., & Ehlers, A. (2001). A prospective investigation of the role of persistent Posttraumatic Stress Disorder (PTSD) after physical and sexual assault. *Behav. Res. Ther., 39,* 1063–1084.

Dunn, M. E., Burbine, T., Bowers, C. A., & Tantleff-Dunn, S. (2001). Moderators of stress in parents of children with autism.*Comm. Ment. Hlth. J., 37,* 39–52.

Dunne, E. J. (1992). Following a suicide: Postvention. In B. Bongar (Ed.), *Suicide: Guidelines for assessment, management and treatment.* New York: Oxford University Press.

DuPaul, G. J., Stoner, G., et al. (1998). *Classroom interventions for ADHD.* New York: Guilford.

Durbin, C. E., Klein, D. N., Hayden, E. P., Buckley, M. E., & Moerk, K. C. (2005). Temperamental emotionality in preschoolers and parental mood disorders. *J. Abn. Psych., 114*(1), 28–37.

During, E. H., Elahi, F. M., Taieb, O., Moro, M., & Baubet, T. (2011). A critical review of dissociative trance and possession disorders: Etiological, diagnostic, therapeutic, and nosological issues. *Can. J. Psychiat., 56,* 235–42.

Durkheim, E. (1951). *Suicide: A study in sociology* (J. A. Spaulding & G. Simpson; Trans., G. Simpson, Ed.). New York: Free Press. (Originally published in 1897.)

Durkin, K. (2010). Videogames and young people with developmental disorders. *Rev. Gen. Psychol., 14*(2), 122–40.

Durston, S. (2003). A review of the biological bases of ADHD: What have we learned from imaging studies? *Ment. Retard. Dev. Dis. Res. Rev., 9,* 184–85.

Duterte, E., Segraves, T., & Althof, S. (2007). Psychotherapy and pharmacotherapy for sexual dysfunctions. In P. E. Nathan & J. M. Gorman (Eds.), *A guide to treatments that work* (3rd ed.). (pp. 531–560). New York: Oxford University Press.

Dutta, R., Murray, R. M., Hotopf, M., Allardyce, J., Jones, P. B., & Boydell, J. (2010). Reassessing the long-term risk of suicide after a first episode of psychosis. *Arch. Gen. Psychiat., 67,* 1230–37.

Duyme, M., Arseneault, L., & Dumaret, A.-C. (2004). Environmental influences on intellectual abilities in childhood: Findings from a longitudinal adoption study. In *Human development across lives and generations: The potential for change.* (pp. 278–292). New York: Cambridge University Press.

Dworkin, R. H., Lewis, J. A., Cornblatt, B. A., & Erlenmeyer- Kimling, L. (1994). Social competence deficits in adolescents at risk for schizophrenia. *J. Nerv. Ment. Dis., 182*(2), 103 8.

Dwyer, J. (2001, Oct. 9). Fighting for life 50 floors up, with one tool and ingenuity. *New York Times,* B1.

d'Ydewalle, G., & Van Damme, I. (2007). Memory and the Korsakoff syndrome: Not remembering what is remembered. *Neuropsychologia, 45*(5) 905–20.

Dyer, C. A. (1999). Pathophysiology of phenylketonuria. *Ment. Retard. Dev. Dis. Res. Rev., 5,* 104–12.

Dzokoto, V. A., & Adams, G. (2005). Understanding genital-shrinking epidemics in West Africa: Koro, Juju, or mass psychogenic illness? *Culture, Medicine and Psychiatry, 29*(1), 53–78.

Eagly, A. H. (2004). Prejudice: Toward a more inclusive understanding. In Department of Psychology and Institute for Policy Research (Eds.), *The social psychology of group identity and social conflict: Theory, application, and practice* (pp. 45–64). Washington, DC: American Psychological Association.

Eagly, A. H., & Carli, L. L. (2007). *Through the labyrinth: The truth about how women become leaders.* Boston: Harvard Business School Press.

Eagly, A. H., & Karau, S. J. (2002). Role congruity theory of prejudice toward female leaders. *Psychol. Rev., 109,* 573–98.

Earleywine, M. (2002). *Understanding marijuana.* New York: Oxford University Press.

Earlywine, M., & Finn, P. R. (1990, Mar.). *Personality, drinking habits, and responses to cues for alcohol.* Paper presented at the 5th Congress of the International Society for Biomedical Research on Alcoholism and the Research Society on Alcoholism, Toronto, Canada.

Eaton, N. R., Krueger, R. F., Keyes, K. M., Skodol, A. E., Markon, K. E., Grant, B. F., & Hasin, D. S. (2011).

Borderline personality disorder co-morbidity: Relationship to the internalizing-externalizing structure of common mental disorders. *Psychol. Med.*, 41(5), 1041–50. doi:10.1017/S0033291710001662

Eaton, W. W., & Muntaner, C. (1999). Socioeconomic stratification and mental disorder. In A. V. Horwitz & T. L. Scheid (Eds.), *A handbook for the study of mental health: Social contexts, theories, and systems* (pp. 259–83). New York: Cambridge University Press.

Eaton, W. W., Kessler, R. C., Wittchen, H. U., & Magee, W. J. (1994). Panic and panic disorder in the United States. *Amer. J. Psychiat.*, 151(3), 413–20.

Eberle, P., & Eberle, S. (1993). *The abuse of innocence: The McMartin preschool trial.* Amherst, NY: Prometheus Books.

Ebigbo, P. O. (1982). Development of a culture specific (Nigeria) screening scale of somatic complaints indicating psychiatric disturbance. *Cult. Med. Psychiatr.*, 6, 29–43.

Ecalle, J., Magnan, A., Bouchafa, H., & Gombert, J. E. (2010). Computer-based training with ortho-phonological units in dyslexic children: New investigations. *Dyslexia: An International Journal of Research and Practice*, 15(3), 218–38.

Eckbald, M., & Chapman, L. J. (1983). Magical ideation as an indicator of schizotypy. *J. Cons. Clin. Psych.*, 51, 215–25.

Eckhardt, C. I. (2007). Effects of alcohol intoxication on anger experience and expression among partner assaultive men. *J. Cons. Clin. Psych.*, 75, 61–71.

Eddy, K. T., Dorer, K. T., Franko, D. L., Tahilani, K., Thompson-Brenner, H., & Herzog, D. B. (2008). Diagnostic cross over in anorexia nervosa and bulimia nervosa: Implications for DSM-V. *Am. J. Psychiat.*, 165, 245–50.

Eddy, K. T., Doyle, A. C., Hoste, R. R., Herzog, B. B., & le Grange, D. (2008). Eating disorder not otherwise specified in adolescents. *J. Amer. Acad. Child Adoles. Psychiat.*, 47(2), 156–64.

Edelen, M. O., Slaughter, M. E., McCaffrey, D. F., Becker, K., & Morral, A. R. (2010). Long-term effect of community - based treatment: Evidence from the adolescent outcomes project. *Drug Al. Dep.*, 107(1), 62–8.

Edens, J. F., Buffington-Vollum, J. K., Keilen, A., Roskamp, P., & Anthony, C. (2005). Predictions of future dangerousness in capital murder trials: Is it time to "disinvent the wheel"? *Law & Human Behavior*, 29(1), 55–86.

Edens, J. F., Marcus, D. K., & Morey, L. C. (2009). Paranoid personality has a dimensional latent structure: Taxometric analyses of community and clinical samples. *J. Abn. Psych.*, 118(3), 545. doi:10.1037/a0016313.Paranoid

Egan, T. (2002, Feb. 6). Meth building its Hell's Kitchen in rural America. *New York Times*, p. A14.

Egeland, B., & Sroufe, L. A. (1981). Attachment and early maltreatment. *Child Develop.*, 52, 44–52.

Egeland, J. A., Gerhard, D. S., Pauls, D. L., Sussex, J. N., Kidd, K. K., Allen, C. R., Hostetter, A. M., & Housman, D. E. (1987). Bipolar affective disorders linked to DNA markers on chromosome 11. *Nature*, 325, 783–87.

Egger, H. L., Costello, E. J., & Angold, A. (2003). School refusal and psychiatric disorders: A community study. *J. Amer. Acad. Child Adoles. Psychiat.*, 42(7), 797–807.

Egliston, K.-A., & Rapee, R. M. (2007). Inhibition of fear acquisition in toddlers following positive modelling by their mothers. *Behav. Res. Ther.*, 45(8), 1871–82.

Ehlers, A. (2000). Post-traumatic stress disorder. In M. G. Gelder, J. J. Lopez-Ibor, & N. Andreason (Eds.), *New Oxford textbook of psychiatry* (pp. 758–71). New York: Oxford University Press.

Ehlers, A., Clark, D. M., Hackman, A., McManus, F., & Fennell, M. (2005). Cognitive therapy for post-traumatic stress disorder: development and evaluation. *Behav. Res. Ther.*, 43, 413–431.

Ehlers, A., & Clark, D. M. (2008). Post-traumatic stress disorder: The development of effective psychological treatments. *Nordic Journal of Psychiatry*, 62, S47, 11–18.

Eich, E., Macaulay, D., Loewenstein, R. J., & Dihle, P. H. (1997). Implicit memory, interpersonality amnesia, and dissociative identity disorder. Comparing patients with simulators. In D. J. Read & S. D. Lindsay (Eds.), *Recollections of trauma: Scientific evidence and clinical practice* (pp. 469–74). New York: Plenum.

Eisen, J. L., Coles, M. E., Shea, M. T., Pagano, M. E., Stout, R. L., Yen, S., Grilo, C. M., & Rasmussen, S. A. (2006). Clarifying the convergence between obsessive compulsive personality disorder criteria and obsessive compulsive disorder. *J. Pers. Dis.*, 20(3), 294–305.

Eisen, J. L., Phillips, K. A., Coles, M. E., & Rasmussen, S. A. (2003). Insight in obsessive compulsive disorder and body dysmorphic disorder. *Compr. Psychiat.*, 45(1), 10–15.

Eisenberger, N. J., Lieberman, M. D., & Williams, K. D. (2003). Does rejection hurt? An fMRI study of social exclusion. *Science*, 302, 290–92.

Ekselius, L., Tillfors, M., Furmark, T., & Fredrikson, M. (2001). Personality disorders in the general population: *DSM-IV and ICD-10 defined prevalence as related to sociodemographic profile. Personal. Indiv. Diff.*, 30(2), 311–20.

El-Bassel, N., Simoni, J. M., Cooper, D. K., Gilbert, L., & Schilling, R. F. (2001). Sex trading and psychological distress among women on methadone. *Psych. Addict. Behav.*, 15, 177–84.

El-Hai, J. (2005). *The lobotomist: A maverick genius and his tragic quest to rid the world of mental illness.* New York: John Wiley and Sons, Inc.

Ellason, J. W., & Ross, C. A. (1997). Two-year follow-up of inpatients with dissociative disorder. *Amer. J. Psychiat.*, 154, 832–39.

Ellicott, A., Hammen, C., Gitlin, M., Brown, G., & Jamison, K. (1990). Life events and the course of bipolar disorder. *Amer. J. Psychiat.*, 147, 1194–98.

Elliot, R., Greenberg, L. S., & Lietaer, G. (2004). Research on experiential psychotherapies. In M. J. Lambert (Ed.), *Bergin and Garfield's handbook of psychotherapy and behavior change.* (pp. 493–539). New York: John Wiley and Sons.

Elliott, A. N., Alexander, A. A., Pierce, T. W., Aspelmeier, J. E., & Richmond, J. M. (2009). Childhood victimization, poly-victimization, and adjustment to college in women. *Child Maltreatment*, 14(4), 330–43.

Ellis, A. (1989). The history of cognition in psychotherapy. In A. Freeman, K. M. Simon, L. E. Beutler, & H. Arkowitz (Eds.), *Comprehensive handbook of cognitive therapy.* (pp. 5–19). New York: Plenum.

Ellis, A., & Dryden, W. (1997). *The practice of rational emotive behavior therapy* (2nd ed.). New York: Springer.

Ellis, B. H., Fisher, P. A., & Zaharie, S. (2004). Predictors of disruptive behavior, developmental delays, anxiety, and affective symptomology among institutionally reared romanian children. *J. Amer. Acad. Child Adoles. Psychiat.*, 43(10), 1283–92.

Else-Quest, N. M., Hyde, J. S., Goldsmith, H. H., & Van Hulle, C. A. (2006). Gender differences in temperament: A meta-analysis. *Psychol. Bull.*, 132(1), 33–72.

Elzinga, B. M., Phaf, R. H., Ardon, A. M., & van Dyck, R. (2003). Directed forgetting between, but not within, dissociative personality states. *J. Abn. Psychol.*, 112(2), 237–43.

Embury, J. E., Charron, C., E., Martynyuk, A., Zori, A. G., Liu, B., Ali, S. F., Rowland, N. E. & Laipis, P. J. (2007). PKU is a reversible neurodegenerative process within the nigrostriatum that begins as early as 4 weeks of age in Pah-super(enu2) mice. *Brain Res.*, 1127(1), 136–50.

Emerson, E. (2004). Deinstitutionalisation in England. *J. Intell. Develop. Dis.*, 29(1), 79–84.

Emery, R. E. (1999). Postdivorce family life for children: An overview of research and some implications for policy. In R. A. Thompson & P. R. Amato (Eds.), *The postdivorce family: Children, parenting, and society* (pp. 3–27). Thousand Oaks, CA: Sage.

Emery, R. E., & Kitzmann, K. M. (1995). The child in the family: Disruptions in family functions. In D. Cicchetti & D. J. Cohen (Eds.), *Developmental psychopathology: Vol. 2. Risk, disorder, and adaptation* (pp. 3–31). New York: Wiley.

Emery, R. E., & Laumann-Billings, L. (1998). An overview of the nature, causes, and consequences of abusive relationships: Toward differentiating maltreatment and violence. *Amer. Psychol.*, 53(2), 121–35.

Emmelkamp, P. M. G. (1994). Behavior therapy with adults. In A. E. Bergin & S. L. Garfield (Eds.), *Handbook of psychotherapy and behavior change* (4th ed., pp. 379–427). New York: Wiley.

Emmelkamp, P. M. G. (2004). Behavior therapy with adults. In M. J. Lambert (Ed.), *Bergin and Garfield's handbook of psychotherapy and behavior change.* (pp. 393–446). New York: John Wiley and Sons.

Emmelkamp, P. M. G., & Wessels, H. (1975). Flooding in imagination vs. flooding in vivo: A comparison with agoraphobics. *Behav. Res. Ther.*, 13(1), 7–15.

Emmers-Sommer, T. M., Allen, M., Bourhis, J., Sahlstein, E., Laskowski, K., Falato, W. L., et al. (2004). A meta-analysis of the relationship between social skills and sexual offenders. *Communication Reports*, 17, 1–10.

Emslie, G. J., Croarkin, P., & Mayes, T. L. (2010). Antidepressants. In M. K. Dulcan (Ed.), *Dulcan's textbook of child and adolescent psychiatry* (pp. 701–723). Arlington, VA: American Psychiatric Publishing.

Emslie, G. J., & Mayes, L. (2001). Mood disorders in children and adolescents: Psychopharmacological treatment. *Biol. Psychiat.*, 49(12), 1082–90.

Emslie, G. J., Rush, A. J., Weinberg, W. A., Kowatch, R. A., Hughes, C. W., Carmody, T., & Rintelmann, J. (1997). A double-blind, randomized, placebo-controlled trial of fluoxetine in children and adolescents with depression. *Arch. Gen. Psychiat.*, 54, 1031–37.

Engdahl, B. E., Harkness, A. R., Eberly, R. E., & Bielinski, J. (1993). Structural models of captivity trauma, resilience, and trauma response among former prisoners of war 20 and 40 years after release. *Soc. Psychiat. Psychiatr. Epidemiol.*, 28, 109–15.

Engelhard, I. M., Van Den Hout, M. A., Weerts, J., Arntz, A., Hox, J. C. M., & McNally, R. J. (2007). Deployment-related stress and trauma in Dutch soldiers returning from Iraq. *Brit. J. Psychiat., 191*, 140–145.

Engler, B. (2006). *Personality theories,* (7th ed.). Boston: Houghton Mifflin.

Enright, S. J., & Beech, A. R. (1993a). Further evidence of reduced cognitive inhibition in obsessive-compulsive disorder. *Personal. Indiv. Diff., 14,* 387–95.

Enright, S. J., & Beech, A. R. (1993b). Reduced cognitive inhibition in obsessive-compulsive disorder. *Brit. J. Clin. Psychol., 32,* 67–74.

Epstein, E. E. (2001). Classification of alcohol-related problems and dependence. In N. Heather & T. Peters, et al. (Eds.), *International handbook of alcohol dependence and problems* (pp. 47–70). New York: John Wiley & Sons Ltd.

Epstein, J., & Klinkenberg, W. D. (2001). From Eliza to Internet: A brief history of computerized assessment. *Computers in Human Behavior, 17,* 295–314.

Erblich, J., Earleywine, M., & Erblich, B. (2001). Positive and negative associations with alcohol and familial risk for alcoholism. *Psych. Addict. Behav., 15*(3), 204–9.

Erdelyi, M. (1992). Psychodynamics and the unconscious. *Amer. Psychol., 47*(6), 784–87.

Erickson, C. A., Posey, D. J., Stigler, K. A., & McDougle, C. J. (2007). Pharmacotherapy of autism and related disorders. *Psychiat. Ann., 37*(7), 490–500.

Erikson, K. I., Raji, C. A., Lopez, O. L., Becker, J. T., Rosano, C., Newman, A. B., Gach, H. M., Thompson, P. M., Ho, A. J., & Kuller, L. H. (2010). Physical activity predicts gray metter volume in late adulthood. *Neurol., 75,* 1415–22.

Erikson, K. I., Voss, M. W., Prakash, R. S., Basak, C., Szabo A., Chaddock, L. et al. (2011). Exercise training increases size of hippocampus and improves memory. *PNAS, 108,* 3017–22.

Erlenmeyer-Kimling, L., & Cornblatt, B. A. (1992). A summary of attentional findings in the New York High-Risk Project. *J. Psychiat. Res., 26,* 405–26.

Erlenmeyer-Kimling, L., Roberts, S. A., Rock, D., Adamo, U. H., Shapiro, B. M., & Pape, S. (1998). Prediction from longitudinal assessments of high-risk children. In M. F. Lenzenweger & R. H. Dworkin (Eds.), *Origins and development of schizophrenia.* Washington, DC: American Psychological Association.

Eronen, M., Hakola, P., & Tiihonen, J. (1996). Mental disorders and homicidal behavior in Finland. *Arch. Gen. Psychiat., 53*(6), 497–501.

ESPAD. (2000). *The 1999 ESPAD Report: Alcohol and other drug use among students in 30 European countries.* European School Survey Project on Alcohol and Other Drugs, Stockholm, Sweden.

Essex, M. J., Klein, M. H., Slattery, M. J., Goldsmith, H. H., & Kalin, N. H. (2010). Early risk factors and developmental pathways to chronic high inhibition and social anxiety disorder in adolescence. *Amer. J. Psychiat., 167*(1), 40–46. doi: 10.1176/appi.ajp.2009.07010051

Esterberg, M. L., Goulding, S. M., & Walker, E. F. (2010). Cluster A personality disorders: Schizotypal, schizoid and paranoid personality disorders in childhood and adolescence. *J. Psychopath. Behav. Assess., 32*(4), 515–28. doi:10.1007/s10862-010-9183-8

Estruch, R., Bono, G., Laine, P., Antunez, E., Petrucci, A., Morocutti, C., & Hillbom, M. (1998). Brain imaging in alcoholism. *Eur. J. Neurol., 5*(2), 119–35.

Etkin, A. (2010) Functional neuroanatomy of anxiety: A neural circuit perspective. In *Behavioral neurobiology of anxiety and its treatment.* Springer.

Ettinger, U., et al. (2001). Magnetic-resonance imaging of the thalamus in first-episode psychosis. *Amer. J. Psychiat., 158,* 116–18.

Evans, D. W., King, R. A., & Leckman, J. F. (1996). Tic disorders. In E. J. Mash & R. A. Barkley (Eds.), *Child psychopathology* (pp. 436–56). New York: Guilford.

Evans, D. W., Lewis, M. D., & Iobst, E. (2004). The role of the orbitofrontal cortex in normally developing compulsive- like behaviors and obsessive compulsive disorder. *Brain & Cognition, 55*(1), 220–34.

Evans, E., Hawton, K., & Rodham, K. (2004). Factors associated with suicidal phenomena in adolescents: A systematic review of population-based studies. *Clin. Psychol. Rev., 24,* 957–79.

Evans, G., & Stecker, R. (2004). Motivational consequences of environmental stress. *J. Environ. Psych., 24*(2), 143–65.

Evans, S., Patt, I., Giosan, C., Spielman, L., & Difede, J. (2009). Disability and posttraumatic stress disorder in disaster relief workers: Responding to September 11, 2001 World Trade Center disaster. *J. Clin. Psychol., 65,* 684–94.

Everett, C. A., & Everett, S. V. (2001). *Family therapy for ADHD.* New York: Guilford.

Evers, A. W. M., Kraaimaat, F. W., van Riel, P. L. C. M., & De Jong, A. J. L. (2002). Tailored cognitive-behavioral therapy in early rheumatoid arthritis for patients at risk: a randomized controlled trial. *Pain, 100,* 141–153.

Ewing v. Goldstein. (2004). Cal. App.4th (No. B163112. Second Dist., Div. Eight. July 16, 2004).

Exline, J. J., Baumeister, R. F., Bushman, B. J., Campbell, W. K., & Finkel, E. J. (2004). Too proud to let go: Narcissistic entitlement as a barrier to forgiveness. *J. Pers. Soc. Psych., 87*(6), 894–912.

Exner, J. E. (1987). Computer assistance in Rorschach interpretation. In J. N. Butcher (Ed.), *Computerized psychological assessment: A practitioner's guide.* New York: Basic Books.

Exner, J. E. (1993). *The Rorschach. A comprehensive system. Vol. 1: Basic Foundations.* New York: Wiley.

Exner, J. E. (1995). Why use personality tests? A brief historical view. In J. N. Butcher (Ed.), *Clinical personality assessment: Practical considerations* (10th ed., pp. 10–18). New York: Oxford University Press.

Exner, J. E., Jr., & Erdberg, P. (2002). Why use personality tests? A brief history and some comments. In J. N. Butcher (Ed.), *Clinical personality assessment: Practical approaches* (2nd ed., pp. 7–12). London: Oxford University Press.

Eysenck, M. W., Mogg, K., May, J., Richards, A., & Mathews, A. (1991). Bias in interpretation of ambiguous sentences related to threat in anxiety. *J. Abn. Psychol., 100,* 144–50.

Fabrega, H., Jr. (2001). Culture and history in psychiatric diagnosis and practice. *Cultural Psychiatry: International Perspectives, 24,* 391–405.

Fabricatore, A. N., & Wadden, T. A. (2006). Obesity. *Ann. Rev. Clin. Psych., 2,* 357–77.

Faigel, H., & Heiligenstein, E. (1996). Medication for attention deficit hyperactivity disorder: Commentary and response.*J. Amer. Coll. Hlth., 45,* 40–42.

Fairburn, C. G. (1995). *Overcoming binge eating.* New York: Guildford Press.

Fairburn, C. G., & Bohn, K. (2005). Eating disorder NOS (EDNOS): an example of the troublesome "not otherwise specified" (NOS) category in DSM-IV. *Behav. Res. Ther., 43,* 691–701.

Fairburn, C. G., & Harrison, P. J. (2003, Feb.). Eating disorders. *Lancet, 361,* 407–16.

Fairburn, C. G., Cooper, Z., Bohn, K., O'Connor, M. E., Doll, H. A., & Palmer, R. L. (2007). The severity and status of eating disorder NOS: implications for DSM-V. *Behav. Res. Ther., 45,* 1705–15.

Fairburn, C. G., Cooper, Z., Doll, H. A., O'Connor, M. E., Bohn, K., Hawker, D. M., et al. (2009). Transdiagnostic cognitive-behavioral therapy for patients with eating disorders: A two-site trial with a 60 week follow-up. *Am. J. Psychiat., 166,* 311–19.

Fairburn, C. G., Cooper, Z., Shafran, R., & Wilson, G. T. (2008). Eating disorders: A transdiagnostic protocol. In D. H. Barlow (Ed.), *Clinical handbook of psychological disorders* (4th ed.; pp. 578–614). New York: Guildford.

Fairburn, C. G., Doll, H. A., Welch, S. L., Hay, P. J., Davies, B. A., & O'Conner, M. E. (1998). Risk factors for binge eating disorder: A community-based case control study. *Arch. Gen. Psychiat., 55*(5), 425–32.

Fairburn, C. G., Jones, R., Peveler, R. C., Hope, R. A., & O'Connor, M. (1993). Psychotherapy and bulimia nervosa: Long-term effects of interpersonal psychotherapy, behavior therapy, and cognitive behavior therapy. *Arch. Gen. Psychiat., 50*(6), 419–28.

Fairburn, C. G., Marcus, M. D., & Wilson, G. T. (1993). Cognitive-behavioral treatment for binge eating and bulimia nervosa. In C. G. Fairburn & G. T. Wilson (Eds.), *Binge eating: Nature, assessment, and treatment* (pp. 361–404). New York: Guilford.

Fairburn, C. G., Welch, S. L., Doll, H. A., Davies, B. A., & O'Connor, M. E. (1997). Risk factors for bulimia nervosa: A community-based case-control study. *Arch. Gen. Psychiat., 54*(6), 509–17.

Fairweather, G. W. (1994). *Keeping the balance: A psychologist's story.* Austin, TX: Fairweather Publishing.

Falkum, E., Pedersen, G., & Karterud, S. (2009). Diagnostic and Statistical Manual of Mental Disorders, Fourth Edition, paranoid personality disorder diagnosis: A unitary or a two-dimensional construct? *Compr. Psychiat., 50*(6), 533–41. doi:10.1016/j.comppsych.2009.01.003

Fallon, A. E., & Rozin, P. (1985). Sex differences in perceptions of desirable body shape. *J. Abn. Psychol., 94,* 102–5.

Fallon, B. A. (2004). Pharmacotherapy of somatoform disorders. *J. Psychosom. Res., 56,* 455–60.

Falloon, I. R. H., Boyd, J. L., McGill, C. W., Williamson, M., & Razani, J. (1985). Family management in the prevention of morbidity of schizophrenia: Clinical outcome of a two-year longitudinal study. *Arch. Gen. Psychiat., 42,* 887–96.

Fals-Stewart, W., & Lam, W. K. K. (2010). Computer-assisted cognitive rehabilitation for the treatment of patients with substance use disorders: A randomized clinical trial. *Exper. Clin. Psychopharmacol., 18*(1), 87–98.

Fanselow, M. S., & Ponnusamy, R. (2008). The use of conditioning tasks to model fear and anxiety. In R. J. Blanchard, D. C. Blanchard, G. Griebel, & D. Nutt (Eds.), *Handbook of anxiety and fear* (pp. 29–48). San Diego, CA: Elsevier Academic Press.

Faraone, S. V., Biederman, J., Lehman, B. F., Spencer, T., Norman, T., Seidman, L. J., Kraus, I., Perrin, J., Chen, W. J., & Tsuang, M. T. (1993). Intellectual performance and school failure in children with Attention Deficit Hyperactivity Disorder and in their siblings. *J. Abn. Psychol., 102,* 616–23.

Faraone, S. V., Tsuang, M. T., & Tsuang, D. W. (1999). *Genetics of mental disorder.* New York: Guilford.

Farde, L., Wiesel, F. A., Hall, H., Halldin, C., Stone-Elander, S., & Sedvall, G. (1987). No D2 receptor increase in PET study of schizophrenia. *Arch. Gen. Psychiat., 44,* 671–72.

Farde, L., Wiesel, F. A., Stone-Elander, S., Halldin, C., Norstrom, A. L., Hall, H., & Sedvall, G. (1990). D2 dopamine receptors in neuroleptic-naïve schizophrenic patients: A positron emission tomography study with [11C] raclopride. *Arch. Gen. Psychiat., 47,* 213–19.

Farkas, M. A., & Stichman, A. (2002). Sex offender laws: Can treatment, punishment, incapacitation, and public safety be reconciled? *Crim. Just. Rev., 27*(2), 256–83.

Farmer, A., Eley, T. C., & McGuffin, P. (2005). Current strategies for investigating the genetic and environmental risk factors for affective disorders. *Brit. J. Psychiat., 186*(3), 179–81.

Farmer, C. M., O'Donnell, B. F., Niznikiewicz, M. A., Voglmaier, M. M., McCarley, R. W., & Shenton, M. E. (2000). Visual perception and working memory in schizotypal personality disorder. *Amer. J. Psychiat., 157*(5), 781–86.

Farooqi, I. S., Matarese, G., Lord, G. M., Keogh, J. M., Lawrence, E., Agwu, C., Sanna, V., Jebb, S. A., Perna, F., Fontana, S., Lechler, R. I., DePaoli, A. M., & O'Rahilly, S. (2002). Beneficial effects of leptin on obesity, T cell hyporesponsiveness, and neuroendocrine/ metabolic dysfunction of human congenital leptin deficiency. *Journal of Clinical Investigation, 110,* 1093–103.

Farrington, D. P. (2006). Family background and psychopathy. In C. J. Patrick (Ed.), *Handbook of the psychopathy.* (pp. 229–50). New York: Guilford Press.

Farrington, David P. (2010). The developmental evidence base: Prevention. In G. J. Towl & D. E. Crighton (Eds.), *Forensic psychology,* (pp. 95–112). New York: Wiley-Blackwell.

Fatemi, S., H., & Clayton, P. J. (Eds.). (2008). *The medical basis of psychiatry* (3rd ed.). Totowa, NJ: Humana Press.

Faul, M., Xu L., Wald, M. M., & Coronado, V. G. (2010). *Traumatic brain injury in the United States: emergency department visits, hospitalizations, and deaths.* Atlanta, GA: Centers for Disease Control and Prevention, National Center for Injury Prevention and Control.

Fava, M. (1997). Psychopharmacologic treatment of pathologic anger. *Psychiat. Clin. N. Amer., 20,* 427–52.

Fava, M., & Rosenbaum, J. F. (1995). Pharmacotherapy and somatic therapies. In E. E. Beckham & W. R. Leber (Eds.), *Handbook of depression* (2nd ed., pp. 280–301). New York: Guilford.

Fawcett, J. (2004). Is BDD culturally induced? *Psychiat. Ann., 34*(12), 900.

Feczer, D., & Bjorklund, P. (2009). Forever changed: Posttraumatic stress disorder in female military veterans, a case report. *Perspectives in Psychiatric Care, 45,* 278–291.

FDA. (2002). *The FDA approved Strattera.* Washington, DC: Department of Health and Human Services.

FDA. (2004). *FDA Talk paper: Warning about Strattera.* Washington, DC: Department of Health and Human Services.

Fedoroff, J. P., Fishell, A., & Federoff, B. (1999). A case series of women evaluated for paraphilic sexual disorders. *Canadian Journal of Human Sexuality, 8,* 127–40.

Feeney, L., Kelly, B. D., Whitty, P., & O'Callaghan, E. (2002). Mental illness in migrants: Diagnostic and therapeutic challenges. *Irish Journal of Psychiatric Medicine, 19*(1), 29–31.

Feldman, M. B., & Meyer, I. H. (2007). Eating disorders in diverse lesbian, gay, and bisexual populations. *Int. J. Eat. Dis., 40,* 218–26.

Feldner, M.T., Zvolensky, M. J., & Schmidt, N. B. (2004). Prevention of anxiety psychopathology: A critical review of the empirical literature. *Clin. Psychol. Sci. Prac., Vol. 11*(4), 405–24.

Felsman, J. K., & Valliant, G. E. (1987). Resilient children as adults: A 40-year study. In E. J. Anthony & B. J. Cohler (Eds.), *The invulnerable child* (pp. 289–314). New York: Guilford.

Fenna, D., et al. (1971). Ethanol metabolism in various racial groups. *Canadian Medical Association Journal, 105,* 472–75.

Fennell, M. J. V. (1989). Depression. In K. Hawton, P. M. Salkovskis, J. Kirk, & D. M. Clark (Eds.), *Cognitive behaviour therapy for psychiatric problems: A practical guide.* Oxford, UK: Oxford University Press.

Fenton, W. S., & McGlashan, T. H. (1994). Antecedents, symptom progression, and long-term outcome of the deficit syndrome in schizophrenia. *Amer. J. Psychiat., 151*(3), 351–56.

Fenton, W. S., McGlashan, T. H., Victor, B. J., & Blyler, C. R. (1997). Symptoms, subtype, and suicidality in patients with schizophrenia spectrum disorders. *Amer. J. Psychiat., 154*(2), 199–204.

Fentress et al. v. Shea Communications et al. (1990). Jefferson Circuit Court, No 90-CI-06033.

Fergusson, D. M., Horwood, L. J., & Ridder, E. M. (2007). Conduct and attentional problems in childhood and adolescence and later substance use, abuse and dependence: Results of a 25-year longitudinal study. *Drug Alc. Dep., 88,* S14–S26.

Fergusson, D. M., Horwood, L. J., & Swain-Campbell, N. R. (2003). Cannabis dependence and psychotic symptoms in young people. *Psychol. Med., 33,* 15–22.

Ferketich, A. K., Schwartzbaum, J. A., Frid, D. J., & Moeschberger, M. L. (2000). Depression as an antecedent to heart disease among women and men in the NHANES 1 Study. *Arch. Int. Med., 160*(9), 1261–68.

Fernald, P. S., & Fernald, L. D. (2010). The Sentence Completion Test: Assessing personality. In L. T. Benjamin, Jr. (Ed.), *Favorite activities for the teaching of psychology* (pp. 196–200). Washington, DC: American Psychological Association.

Fernandez, F., Ringholz, G. M., & Levy, J. K. (2002). Neuropsychiatric aspects of human immunodeficiencyvirus infection of the central nervous system. In S. Yudofsky & R. E. Hales (Eds.), *The American Psychiatric Association Publishing textbook of neuropsychiatry and clinical sciences* (4th ed., pp. 783–812). Washington, DC: American Psychiatric Publishing.

Ferri, C. P., Prince, M., Brayne, C., Brodaty, H., Fratiglioni, L., Ganguli, M., et al., (2005). Global prevalence of dementia: A Delphi consensus study. *Lancet, 366,* 2112–17.

Ferrucci, L., Harris, T., Guralnik, J., Tracy, R., Corti, M., Cohen, H., Pennix, B., Pahor, M., Wallace, R., & Havlik, R. J. (1999). Serum IL-6 level and the development of disability in older persons. *J. Amer. Geriat. Soc, 47,* 639–46.

Ferster, C. B. (1974). Behavioral approaches to depression. In R. J. Friedman & M. M. Katz (Eds.), *The psychology of depression: Contemporary theory and research.* Washington, DC: Hemisphere.

Feske, U., Tarter, R. E., Kirisci, L., & Pilkonis, P. A. (2006). Borderline personality and substance use in women. *The American Journal on Addictions, 15*(2), 131–37.

Feusner, J. D., Townsend, J., Bystritsky, A., & Bookheimer, S. (2007). Visiual information processing of faces in body dysmorphic disorder. *Arch. Gen. Psychiat., 64*(12), 1417–26.

Fichter, M. M., & Quadflieg, N. (2007). Long-term stability of eating disorder diagnoses. *Int. J. Eat. Dis., 40,* S61–S66.

Field, T., Hernandez-Reif, M., & Diego, M. (2006). Intrusive and withdrawn depressed mothers and their infants. *Developmental Review, 26,* 15–30.

Fields, J. Z., Turk, A., Durkin, M., Ravi, N. V., & Keshavarzian, A. (1994). Increased gastrointestinal symptoms in chronic alcoholics. *American Journal of Gastroenterology, 89,* 382–86.

Figueroa, E., & Silk, K. (1997). Biological implications of childhood sexual abuse in borderline personality disorder. *J. Person. Dis., 11*(1), 71–92.

Finger, S., & Zaromb, F. (2006). Benjamin Franklin and shock-induced amnesia. *Amer. Psychol., 61,* 240–248.

Fink, M. (2003). A beautiful mind and insulin coma: Social constraints on psychiatric diagnosis and treatment. *Harv. Rev. Psychiat., 11,* 284–90.

Fink, M., & Taylor, M. A. (2006). Catatonia: Subtype in DSM. *Am. J. Psychiat., 163*(11), 1875–76.

Fink, P., Ornbol, E., Toft, T., Sparle, K. C., Frostholm, L., & Olesen, F. (2004). A new empirically established hypochondriasis diagnosis. *Amer. J. Psychiat., 161*(9), 1680–91.

Fink, P., Ørnbøl, E., & Christensen, K.S. (2010). The outcome of health anxiety in primary care. a two-year follow-up study on health care costs and self-rated health. PLoS ONE 5(3): e9873. doi:10.1371/journal.pone.0009873.

Finkel, A. M., & Ryan, P. B. (2007). Risk in the workplace: Where analysis began and problems remain unsolved. In M. G. Robson & W. A. Toscano (Eds.), *Risk assessment for environmental health* (pp. 187–237). San Francisco, CA: Jossey-Bass.

Finkelhor, D. (1984). *Child sexual abuse.* New York: Free Press.

Finkenbine, R., & Miele, V. J. (2004). Globus hystericus: A brief review. *Gen. Hosp. Psychiat., 26,* 78–82.

Finn, J., Garner, M. D., & Wilson, J. (2010). Volunteer and user evaluation of the National Sexual Assault Online Hotline. *Eval. Program. Plann.* Sep 29. Epub ahead of print.

Finn, P. R., Sharkansky, E. J., Viken, R., West, T. L., Sandy, J., & Bufferd, S. (1997). Heterogeneity in the families of sons of alcoholics: The impact of familial vulnerability type on offspring characteristics. *J. Abn. Psychol., 106*(1), 26–36.

Finn, S. E., & Kamphuis, J. H. (2006). Therapeutic assessment with the MMPI-2. In J. N. Butcher (Ed.), *MMPI-2: The practioner's handbook.* (pp. 165–91). Washington, DC: American Psychological Association.

Finn, S. E., & Tonsager, M. E. (1997). Information-gathering and therapeutic models of assessment: Complementary paradigms. *Psychol. Assess., 9*(4), 374–85.

First, M. B. (2005). Desire for amputation of a limb: Paraphilia, psychosis, or a new type of identity disorder. *Psychol. Med., 35,* 919–28.

First, M. B., & Wakefield, J. C. (2010). Defining mental disorder in DSM-V. *Psychol. Med., 40,* 1779–82.

Fischer, J. L., Pidcock, B. W., Munsch, J., & Forthun, L. (2005). Parental abusive drinking and sibling role differences. *Al. Treat. Quart., 23*(1), 79–97.

Fischer, M. (1971). Psychoses in the offspring of schizophrenic monozygotic twins and their normal co-twins. *Brit. J. Psychiat., 118,* 43–52.

Fischer, M. (1973). Genetic and environmental factors in schizophrenia: A study of schizophrenic twins and their families.*Acta Psychiatr. Scandin.*, Suppl. No. 238.

Fisher, J. E., & Carstensen, L. L. (1990). Behavior management for the dementias. *Clin. Psychol. Rev., 10*, 611–30.

Fisher, P. L., & Wells, A. (2009). Psychological models of worry and generalized anxiety disorder. In M. M. Antony & M. B. Stein (Eds.), *Oxford handbook of anxiety and related disorders* (pp. 225–37). New York: Oxford University Press.

Fiske, S., & Taylor, S. (1991). *Social cognition* (2nd ed.). New York: McGraw Hill.

Fitzgerald, M. (2007). Suicide and Asperger's syndrome. *Crisis, 28*, 1–3.

Fitzgerald, P. B., Brown, T. L., & Daskalakis, Z. J. (2002). The application of transcranial magnetic stimulation in psychiatry and neurosciences research. *Acta Psychiatri. Scandi., 105*(5), 324–40.

Flegal, K. M., Carroll, M. D., Ogden, C. L., & Johnson, C. L. (2002). Prevalence and trends in obesity among US adults, 1999–2000. *JAMA, 288*, 1723–1727.

Flegal, K. M., Carroll, M. D., Ogden, C. L., & Curtin, L. R. (2010). Prevalence and trends in obesity among US adults, 1999–2008. *JAMA, 303*, 235–41.

Fleming, S. K., Blasey, C., & Schatzberg, A. F. (2004). Neuropsychological correlates of psychotic features in major depressive disorders: A review and meta-analysis. *J. Psychiat. Res., 38*, 27–35.

Fletcher, P. C. (2004). Functional neuroimaging of psychiatric disorders: Exploring hidden behavior. *Psychol. Med., 34*, 577–81.

Flier, J. S., Underhill, L. H., & Lieber, C. S. (1995). Medical disorders of alcoholism. *N. Engl. J. Med., 333*(6), 1058–65.

Flor, H., Birbaumer, N., & Turk, D. C. (1990). The psychobiology of chronic pain. *Advances in Behaviour Research & Therapy, 12*, 47–84.

Flor, H., Birbaumer, N., Hermann, C., Ziegler, S., & Patrick, C. J. (2002). Aversive Pavlovian conditioning in psychopaths: Peripheral and central correlates. *Psychophysiology, 39*(4), 505–18.

Flores, B. H., & Schatzberg, A. F. (2006). Psychotic depression. In D. J. Stein & D. J. Kupfer (Eds.), *The American Psychiatric Publishing textbook of mood disorders.* (pp. 561–571). Arlington, VA: American Psychiatric Publishing, Inc.

Foa, E. B., & Kozak, M. J. (1995). DSM-IV field trial: Obsessive-compulsive disorder. *Amer. J. Psychiat., 152*, 90–96.

Foa, E. B., Liebowitz, M. R., Kozak, M. J., Davies, S., Campeas, R., Franklin, M. E., et al. (2005). Randomized, placebo-controlled trial of exposure and ritual prevention, clomipramine, and their combination in the treatment of obsessive-compulsive disorder. *Am. J. Psychiat., 162*(1), 151–61.

Foa, E. B., & Rauch, S. A. M. (2004). Cognitive changes during prolonged exposure versus prolonged exposure plus cognitive restructuring in female assault survivors with posttraumatic stress disorder. *J. Cons. Clin. Psychol., 72*, 879–84.

Foley, D., Wormley, B., Silberg, J., Maes, H., Hewitt, J., Eaves, L., & Riley, B. (2004). Childhood adversity, MAO-A genotype, and risk for conduct disorder. *Arch. Gen. Psychiat., 61*, 738–44.

Foley, G. M., & Hochman, J. D. (2006). *Mental health in early intervention: Achieving unity in principles and practice.* Baltimore: Brookes Publishing.

Folino, J. O., & Abait, P. E. (2009). Pathological gambling and criminality. *Curr. Opin. Psychiat., 22*(5), 477–81.

Folkman, S., & Moskovitz, J. T. (2004). Coping: Pitfalls and promise. *Annu. Rev. Psychol., 55*, 745–74.

Folstein, M. F., Folstein, S., & McHugh, P. R. (1975). Minimental state: A practical method for grading the cognitive state of patients for the clinician. *J. Psychiat. Res., 12*, 189.

Foltin, R. W., & Fischman, M. W. (1997). A laboratory model of cocaine withdrawal in humans: Intravenous cocaine. *Exp. Clin. Pharm., 5*(4), 404–11.

Fombonne, E. (2005). Epidemiological Studies of Pervasive Developmental Disorders. In F. R. Volkmar, P. Rhea, A. Klin, & D. Cohen (Eds.), *Handbook of autism and pervasive developmental disorders, Vol. 1: Diagnosis, development, neurobiology, and behavior* (3rd ed.), (pp. 42–69). Hoboken, NJ: John Wiley & Sons Inc.

Fontaine, K. R., Redden, D. T., Wang, C., Westfall, A. O., & Allison, D. B. (2003). Years of life lost due to obesity. *JAMA, 289*(2), 187–93.

Forchetti, C. M. (2005). Treating patients with moderate to severe Alzheimer's disease: Implications of recent pharmacologic studies. *Primary Care Companion Journal of Clinical Psychiatry, 7*, 155–61.

Ford, D. E., Mead, L. A., Chang, P. P., Cooper-Patrick, L., Wang, N. Y., & Klag, M. J. (1998). Depression is a risk factor for coronary artery disease in men: The Precursors Study. *Arch. Int. Med., 158*, 1422–26.

Forsyth, J. P., Daleiden, E. L., & Chorpita, B. F. (2000). Response primacy in fear conditioning: Disentangling the contributions of UCS vs. UCR intensity. *Psychol. Rec., 50*(1), 17–34.

Forsyth, J. P., Eifert, G. H., & Barrios, V. (2006). Fear conditioning in an emotion regulation context: A fresh perspective on the origins of anxiety disorders. In M. G. Craske, D. Hermans, & D. Vansteenwegen (Eds.), *Fear and learning: From basic processes to clinical implications* (Vol. xiii, pp. 133–53). Washington, DC: American Psychological Association.

Forsyth, J., & Eifert, G. H. (1998). Response intensity in content-specific fear conditioning comparing 20% versus 13% CO-sub-2-enriched air as unconditioned stimuli. *J. Abn. Psychol., 107*(2), 291–304.

Forth, A. E., Kosson, D.S., & Hare, R.D. . (2003). *The Psychopathy Checklist: Youth Version manual.* Toronto, Ontario, Canada: Multi-Health Systems.

Fortune, S., Stewart, A., Yadav, V., & Hawton, K. (2007). Suicide in adolescents: Using life charts to understand the suicidal process. *J. Affect. Disord., 100*(1–3), 199–210.

Fournier, J. C., DeRubeis, R. J., Hollon, S. D., Dimidjian, S., Amsterdam, J. D., Shelton, R. C., & Fawcett, J. (2010). Antidepressant drug effects and depression severity: A patient-level meta-analysis. *JAMA, 303*(1), 47–53. doi: 10.1001/jama.2009.1943

Fowles, D. C. (1993). Electrodermal activity and antisocial behavior: Empirical findings and theoretical issues. In J.-C. Roy, W. Boucsein, D. Fowles, & J. Gruzelier (Eds.), *Progress in electrodermal research.* London: Plenum.

Fowles, D. C. (2001). Biological variables in psychopathology: A psychobiological perspective. In P. D. Sutker & H. E. Adams (Eds.), *Comprehensive handbook of psychopathology* (3rd ed., pp. 85–104). New York: Kluwer Academic.

Fowles, D. C., & Dindo, L. (2006). A dual-deficit model of psychopathy. In C. J. Patrick (Ed.), *Handbook of the psychopathy.* (pp. 14–34). New York: Guilford Press.

Fowles, D. C., & Kochanska, G. (2000). Temperament as a moderator of pathways to conscience in children: The contribution of electrodermal activity. *Psychophysiology, 37*(6), 788–95.

Fox, E. R., Young, J. H., Li, Y., Dreisbach, A. W., Keating, B. J., et al. (2011). Association of genetic variation with systolic and diastolic blood pressure among African Americans: The Candidate Gene Association Resource Study. *Human Molecular Genetics* DOI: 10.1093/hmg.ddr092

Fox, H. C., Parrott, A. C., & Turner, J. J. D. (2001). Ecstasy use: Cognitive deficits related to dosage rather than self-reported problematic use of the drug. *J. Psychopharm., 15*, 273–81.

Fox, M. J. (2002). *Lucky man.* New York: Hyperion Press.

Fox, N. A. (2010). Factors contributing to the emergence of anxiety among behaviorally inhibited children: The role of attention. *New Dir. Child Adol. Dev., 127*, 33–49. doi:10.a002/ed.261

Fox, N. A., Henderson, H. A., Marshall, P. J., Nichols, K. E., & Ghera, M. M. (2005). Behavioral inhibition: Linking biology and behavior within a developmenta framework. *Annu. Rev. Psychol., 56*, 235–62.

Fox, S. E., Levitt, P., & Nelson III, C. A. (2010). How the timing and quality of early experiences influence the development of brain architecture. *Child Dev., 81*(1), 28–40. doi:10.1111/j.1467-8624.2009.01380.x

Fraley, R. C., & Shaver, P. R. (2008). Attachment theory and its place in contemporary personality theory and research. In O. P. John, R. W. Robins, & L. A. Pervin (Eds.), *Handbook of personality: Theory and research* (3rd ed., pp. 518–41). New York: Guilford Press.

France, K. (2007). *Crisis intervention: A handbook of immediate person-to-person help* (5th ed.). Springfield, Il.: Charles C. Thomas Publisher.

Frances, A. (2010a, Feb. 11). Opening Pandora's box: The 19 worst suggestions for DSM5. *Psychiatric Times*, 1–2.

Frances, A. (2010b, Aug. 14). Good grief. *New York Times.*

Frances, A., & Ross, R. (1996). *DSM-IV Case studies: A clinical guide to differential diagnosis.* Washington, DC: American Psychiatric Press.

Francis, A. N., Bhojraj, T. S., Prasad,K. M., Kulkami, S., Montrose, D. M., Eack, S. M., & Keshavan, M. S. (2011). Abnormalities of the corpus callosum in non-psychotic high-risk offspring of schizophrenia patients. *Psychiat. Res.: Neuroimag., 191*, 9–15.

Frank, E., Kupfer, D. J., Perel, J. M., Cornes, C., Jarett, D. B., Mallinger, A. G., Thase, M. E., McEachran, A. B., & Grochocinski, V. J. (1990). Three-year outcomes for maintenance therapies in recurrent depression. *Arch. Gen. Psychiat., 47*, 1093–99.

Frank, E., Prien, R. F., Jarrett, R. B., Keller, M. B., Kupfer, D. J., Lavori, P. W., Rush, A. J., & Weissman, M. M. (1991). Conceptualization and rationale for consensus definitions of terms in major depressive disorder: Remission, recovery, relapse, and recurrence. *Arch. Gen. Psychiat., 48*, 851–55.

Frank, R. G., Conti, R. M., & Goldman, H. H. (2005). Mental health policy and psychotropic drugs. *Milbank Quarterly, 83*(2), 271–98.

Frank, R. G., McDaniel, S. H., Bray, J. H., & Heldring, M. (Eds.). (2004). *Primary care psychology.* Washington, DC: American Psychological Association.

Frankenburg, F. R. (1994). History of the development of antipsychotic medications. *Psychiat. Clin. N. Amer., 17*(3), 531–41.

Franklin, M. E., & Foa, E. B. (1998). Cognitive-behavioral treatments for obsessive-compulsive disorder. In P. E. Nathan & J. M. Gorman (Eds.), *A guide to treatments that work* (pp. 339–57). New York: Oxford University Press.

Franklin, M. E., & Foa, E. B. (2002). Cognitive behavioral treatments for obsessive compulsive disorder. In P. E. Nathan & J. M. Gorman (Eds.), *A guide to treatments that work* (2nd ed., pp. 367–86). London: Oxford University Press.

Franklin, M. E., & Foa, E. B. (2007). Cognitive behavioral treatment of obsessive compulsive disorder.

In P. E. Nathan and J. M. Gorman (Eds.). *A guide to treatments that work* (pp. 431–46). New York: Oxford University Press.

Franklin, M. E., & Foa, E. B. (2008). Obsessive-compulsive disorder. In D. H. Barlow (Ed.), *Clinical handbook of psychological disorders: A step-by-step treatment manual* (4th ed.) (pp. 164–215). New York: Guilford Press.

Franko, D. L., & Keel, P. K. (2006). Suicidality in eating disorders: Occurrence, correlates, and clinical implications. *Clin. Psych. Rev., 26,* 769–82.

Franko, D. L., Keel, P. K., Dorer, D. J., Blais, M. A., Delinsky, S. S., Eddy, K. T., Charat, V., Renn, R., & Herzog, D. B. (2004). What predicts suicide attempts in women with eating disorders? *Psychol. Med., 34,* 843–53.

Frazier, M., & Merrill, K. W. (1998). Issues in behavioral treatment of attention-deficit/hyperactivity disorder. *Education & Treatment of Children, 20*(4), 441–61.

Freedman, D., Deicken, R., Kegeles, L. S., Vinogradov, S., Bao, Y., & Brown, A. S. (2011). Maternal-fetal blood incompatibility and neuromorphic anomalies in schizophrenia: Preliminary findings. *Prog. Neuropsychopharmacol Biol. Psychiat., 35,* 1525–29.

Freeman, A., Freeman, S. M., & Rosenfield, B. (2005). Histrionic personality disorder. In G. O. Gabbard, J. S. Beck, & J. Holmes. (Eds.), *Oxford Textbook of Psychotherapy* (pp. 305–10). New York: Oxford University Press.

Freeman, W. (1959). Psychosurgery. In S. Arieti (Ed.), *American handbook of psychiatry* (Vol. 2, pp. 1521–40). New York: Basic Books

Freidenfelt, J., & Klinteberg, B. (2007). Exploring adult personality and psychopathy tendencies in former childhood hyperactive delinquent males. *J. Indiv. Diff., 28*(1), 27–36.

Freud, A. (1946). *Ego and the mechanisms of defense.* New York: International Universities Press.

Freud, S. (1909). Analysis of a phobia in a five-year-old boy. In *Standard edition, vol 10.* London: Hogarth Press (1955). First German edition 1909.

Freud, S. (1917). Mourning and melancholia. In W. Gaylin (Ed.), *The meaning of despair: Psychoanalytic contributions to the understanding of depression.* New York: Science House.

Freud, S. (1935). Letter to an American mother. Reprinted in Paul Friedman (1959), Sexual deviations, in S. Arieti (Ed.), *American Handbook of Psychiatry* (Vol. 1, pp. 606–7). New York: Basic Books.

Freund, K., & Seto, M. C. (1998). Preferential rape in the theory of courtship disorder. *Arch. Sex. Behav., 27,* 433–43.

Fricchione, G. L., Nejad, S. H., Esses, J. A., Cummings, T. J., Querques, J., Cassem, N. H., & Murray, G. B. (2008). Postoperative delirium. *Am. J. Psychiat., 165,* 803–12.

Frick, P. J. (1998). *Conduct disorders and severe antisocial behavior.* New York: Plenum.

Frick, P. J., & Marsee, M. A. (2006). Psychopathy and developmental pathways to antisocial behavior in youth. In C. J. Patrick (Ed.), *Handbook of the psychopathy.* (pp. 353–74). New York: Guilford Press.

Frick, P. J., & Morris, A. S. (2004). Temperament and developmental pathways to conduct problems. *J. Clin. Child. Adol. Psych.,* 33, 54–68.

Frick, P. J., Cornell, A. H., Barry, C. T., Bodin, S. D., & Dane, H. E. (2003). Callous-unemotional traits and conduct problems in the prediction of conduct problem severity, aggression, and self-report of delinquency. *J. Abnorm. Child Psychol., 31*(4), 457–70.

Frick, P. J., Cornell, A., Bodin, S., Dane, H., Barry, C., & Loney, B. (2003). Callous-unemotional traits and developmental pathways to severe conduct problems. *Develop. Psychol., 39,* 246–60.

Friedewald, V. E., Nesbitt, S. D., Ram, C.V. S., & Roberts, W. C. (2011). The editor's roundtable. Hypertension in African Americans and other non-Caucasian ethnic groups. *Am J. Cardiol, 106,* 1466–1472.

Friedlander, L., & Desrocher, M. (2006). Neuroimaging studies of obsessive-compulsive disorder in adults and children. *Clin. Psychol. Rev., 26*(1), 32–49.

Friedman, J. M. (2003). A war on obesity, not the obese. *Science, 299,* (5608), 856–58.

Friedman, J. M. (2004). Modern science versus the stigma of obesity. *Nature Medicine, 10*(6) 563–69.

Friedman, M., & Rosenman, R. H. (1959). Association of specific overt behavior pattern with blood and cardiovascular findings. *JAMA, 169,* 1286.

Friedman, R. M., Pinto, A., Behar, L., Bush, N., Chirolla, A., Epstein, M., Green, A., Hawkins, P., Huff, B., Huffine, C., Mohr, W., Seltzer, T., Vaughn, C., Whitehead, K., & Young, C. K. (2006). Unlicensed residential programs: The next challenge in protecting youth. *Am. J. Orthopsychiat., 76*(3), 295–303.

Friemoth, J. (2005). What is the most effective treatment for ADHD in children? *J. Fam. Pract., 54*(2), 166–68.

Fries, J. (2001, Nov. 14). Mother drowned daughter, 4, in exorcism rite. *New York Times.*

Friesen, M. D., Woodward, L. J., Horwood, L. J., & Fergusson, D. M. (2010). Childhood exposure to sexual abuse and partnership outcomes at age 30. *Psychological Medicine: A Journal of Research in Psychiatry and the Allied Sciences, 40*(4), 679–88.

Friman, P. C., Resetar, J. & DeRuyk, Kim (2008). Encopresis: Biobehavioral treatment. In W. T. O'Donohue & J. E. Fisher (2008). *Cognitive behavior therapy: Applying empirically supported techniques in your practice* (2nd ed.), (pp. 187–196). Hoboken, NJ, US: John Wiley & Sons Inc

Friman, P. C., & Warzak, W. J. (1990). Nocturnal enuresis: A prevalent, persistent, yet curable parasomnia. *Pediatrician, 17,* 38–45.

Frohlich, P. F., & Meston, C. M. (2005). Tactile sensitivity in women with sexual arousal disorder. *Arch. Sex. Behav., 34,* 207–17.

Fromm-Reichmann, F. (1948). Notes on the development of treatment of schizophrenics by psychoanalytic psychotherapy. Reprinted in D. M. Bullard (Ed.), *Psychoanalysis and psychotherapy: Selected papers of Freida Fromm-Reichmann.* Chicago: University of Chicago Press, 1959.

Frone, M. R. (2003). Predictors of overall and on-the-job substance use among young workers. *J. Occup. Hlth. Psych., 8,* 39–54.

Frone, M. R. (2006). Prevalence and distribution of illicit drug use in the workforce and in the workplace: Findings and implications from a U.S. national survey. *J. Appl. Psych., 91*(4), 856–69.

Frueh, B. C., Elhai, J. D., Grubaugh, A. L., Monnier, J., Kashdan, T. B., Sauvageot, J. A., Hamner, M. B., Burkett, B. G., & Arana, G. W. (2005). Documented combat exposure of US veterans seeking treatment for combat-related post-traumatic stress disorder. *Brit. J. Psychiat., 186,* 467–72.

Fryers, T. (2000). Epidemiology of mental retardation. In M. G. Gelder, J. J. Lopez-Ibor, Jr., & N. Andreason (Eds.), *New Oxford textbook of psychiatry* (pp. 1941–45). New York: Oxford University Press.

Fugelstad, A., Stenbacka, M., Leifman, A., Nylander, M., & Thiblin, I. (2007). Methadone

maintenance treatment: The balance between life-saving treatment and fatal poisoning. *Addiction, 102,* 406–12.

Fukutake, T., Mine, S., Yamakami, I., Yamaura, A., & Hattori, T. (2000). Rollercoaster headache and subdural hematoma. *Neurol., 54,* 264.

Fulmer, R. H., & Lapidus, L. B. (1980). A study of professed reasons for beginning and continuing heroin use. *Inter. J. Addicti., 15,* 631–45.

Fusar-Poli, Perez, J., Broome, M., Borgwardt, S., Placentino, A., Caverzasi, E., et al. (2007). Neurofunctional correlates of vulnerability to psychosis: A systematic review and meta-analysis. *Neuroscience and Biobehavioral Reviews, 31,* 465–84.

Gabbard, G. O. (1994). Inpatient services: The clinician's view. In R. K. Schreter, S. S. Sharfstein, & C. A. Schreter (Eds.), *Allies and adversaries* (pp. 22–30). Washington, DC: American Psychiatric Press.

Gabbard, G. O., & Kay, J. K. (2001). The fate of integrated treatment: Whatever happened to the biopsychosocial psychiatrist? *Amer. J. Psychiat., 158,* 1956–63.

Gabbard, G. O., Gunderson, J. G., & Fonagy, P. (2002). The place of psychoanalytic treatments within psychiatry. *Arch. Gen. Psychiat., 59,* 505–10.

Gabbard, G. O., Lazar, S. G., Hornberger, J., & Spiegel, D. (1997). The economic impact of psychotherapy: A review. *Amer. J. Psychiat., 154*(2), 147–55.

Gabriel, R. A. (1987). *No more heroes. Madness and psychiatry in war.* New York: Hill and Wang.

Gaffrey, M. S., Luby, J. L., Belden, A. C., Hirshberg, J. S., Volsch, J., & Barch, D. M. (2011). Association between depression severity and amygdala reactivity during sad face viewing in depressed preschoolers: An fMRI study. *J. Affect. Disord., 129*(1–3), 364–70.

Galanter, M., Hayden, F., Castañeda, R., & Franco, H. (2005). Group therapy, self-help groups, and network therapy. In R. J. Frances, S. I. Miller, & A. H. Mack, Avram (Eds.), *Clinical textbook of addictive disorders* (3rd ed.) (pp. 502–27). New York: Guilford Publications.

Gallop, R. J., Chris-Cristoph, P., Ten Have, T. R., Frank, A., Griffin, M. L., & Thase, M. E. (2007). Differential transitions between cocaine use and abstinence for men and women. *J. Cons. Clin. Psych., 75,* 95–103.

Galton, F. (1879). Psychometric experiments. *Brain, 2,* 179–85.

Ganju, V., & Quan, H. (1987). *Mental health service needs of refugees in Texas.* Paper given at the Refugee Assistance Program: Mental Health Workgroup Meeting, UCLA, February 12–13.

Ganzini, L., Nelson, H. D., Lee, M. A., Kraemer, D. F., Schmidt, T. A., & Delorit, M. A. (2001). Oregon physicians' attitudes about and experiences with end-of-life care since passage of the Oregon death with dignity act. *JAMA, 285*(18), 2362–69.

Garakani, A., Hirschowitz, J., & Katz, C. I. (2004). General disaster psychiatry. *Psychiat. Clin. N. Amer., 27,* 391–406.

Garb, H. N. (2007). Computer-administered interviews and rating scales. *Psychological Assessment, 19*(1), 4–13.

Garb, H. N., Florio, C. M., & Grove, W. M. (1998). The validity of the Rorschach and the Minnesota Multiphasic Personality Inventory: Results from metaanalyses. *Psychol. Sci., 9*(5), 402–4.

Garber, J., Gallerini, G. M., & Frankel, S. A. (2009). Depression in children. In I. H. Gotlib & C. L. Hammen (Eds.), *Handbook of depression and its treatment* (2nd ed.). New York: Guilford Press.

Gardner, C. D., Kiazand, A., Alhassan, S., Kim, S., Stafford, R. S., Balise, R. R., Kraemer, H. C., & King, A. C. (2007). Comparison of the Atkins, Zone,

Ornish, and LEARN diets for change in weight and related risk factors among overweight premenopausal women. *JAMA, 297*, 969–77.

Gardner, F., Shaw, D. S., Dishion, T. J., Burton, J., & Supplee, L. (2007). Randomized prevention trial for early conduct problems: Effects on proactive parenting and links to toddler disruptive behavior. *J. Fam. Psych., 21(3)*, 398–406.

Gardner, J. (2000). Living with a child with fetal alcohol syndrome. *American Journal of Maternal/Child Nursing, 25(5)*, 252–57.

Garlow, S. J., & Nemeroff, C. B. (2003). Neurobiology of depressive disorders. In R. J. Davidson, K. R. Scherer, & H. H. Goldsmith (Eds.), *Handbook of affective sciences*, pp. 1021–43. New York: Oxford Press.

Garmezy, N. (1993). Vulnerability and resilience. In D. C. Funder, R. D. Parke, et al. (Eds.), *Studying lives through time: Personality and development.* (pp. 377–98). Washington, DC: American Psychological Association.

Garner, D. (1991). *Eating disorders inventory-2. Professional manual.* Lutz, FL: Psychological Assessment Resources.

Garner, D. M. (1997). Psychoeducational principles in treatment. In D. M. Garner & P. E. Garfinkel (Eds.), *Handbook of treatment for eating disorders* (pp. 145–77). New York: Guilford.

Garner, D. M., & Garfinkel, P. E. (Eds.). (1997). *Handbook of treatment for eating disorders* (2nd ed.). New York: Guilford.

Garner, D. M., Vitousek, K. M., & Pike, K. M. (1997). Cognitive-behavioral therapy for anorexia nervosa. In D. M. Garner & P. E. Garfinkel (Eds.), *Handbook of treatment for eating disorders* (pp. 94–144). New York: Guilford.

Garratt, G., Ingram, R. E., Rand, K. L., & Sawalani, G. (2007). Cognitive processes in cognitive therapy: Evaluation of the mechanisms of change in the treatment of depression. *Clinical Psychology Science and Practice, 14*, 224–39.

Gartrell, N. (2004, Jan. 4). A doctor's toxic shock. *Boston Globe Magazine*, p. 58.

Garza, Y., Watts, R. E., & Kinsworthy, S. (2007). Filial therapy: A process for developing strong parent-child relationships. *The Family Journal, 15(3)* 277–281.

Gass, C. (2009). Use of the MMPI-2 in neuropsychological evaluations. In J. N. Butcher (Ed.), *Oxford handbook of personality and clinical assessment* (pp. 432–56). New York: Oxford University Press.

Gath, A. (2000). Families with a mentally retarded member and their needs. In M. G. Gelder, J. J. Lopez-Ibor, Jr., & N. C. Andreason (Eds.), *New Oxford textbook of psychiatry, Volume 2* (pp. 2002–5). Oxford: Oxford University Press.

Gatz, M. (2007). Genetics, dementia, and the elderly. *Curr. Dir. Psych. Sci., 16*, 123–27.

Gaudin, J. M., Jr. (1993). Effective intervention with neglectful families. *Crim. Just. Behav., 20*, 66–89.

Gawande, A. (2001, Jul. 9). The man who couldn't stop eating. *New Yorker*, 66–75.

Gawin, F. H., & Kleber, H. D. (1986). Abstinence symptomatology and psychiatric diagnosis in cocaine abusers. *Arch. Gen. Psychiat., 43*, 107–13.

Gazdzinski, S., Durazzo, T., & Meyerhoff, D. J. (2005). Temporal dynamics and determinants of whole brain tissue volume changes during recovery from alcohol dependence. *Drug Al. Dep., 78(3)*, 263–73.

Gearhardt, A. N., Grilo, C. M., DiLeone, R. J., Brownell, K. D., & Potenza, M. N. (2011). Can food be addictive? Public health and policy implications. *Addiction, 106*, 1208–12.

Gejman, P. V., Sanders, A. R., & Kendler, K. S. (2011). Genetics of schizophrenia: New findings and challenges. *Annu. Rev. Genomics Hum. Genet.*

Gelernter, J., & Stein, M. B. (2009). Heritability and genetics of anxiety disorders. In M. M. Antony & M. B. Stein (Eds.), *Oxford handbook of anxiety and related disorders* (pp. 87–96). New York: Oxford University Press.

Geller, B., & DelBello, M.P. (Eds.). (2008). *Treatment of bipolar disorder in children and adolescents.* New York: Guilford Press.

George, M. S., & Post, R. M. (2011). Daily left prefrontal repetitive transcranial magnetic stimulation for acute treatment of medication-resistant depression. *Amer. J. Psychiat., 168(4)*, 356–64. doi: 10.1176/appi.ajp.2010.10060864

Geraerts, E., Schooler, J. W., Merckelbach, H., Jelicic, M., Hauner, B., & Ambadar, Z. (2007). The reality of recovered memories. *Psychological Science, 18(7)*, 564–68.

Gerardi, M., Rothbaum, B. O., Ressler, K., Heekin, M., & Rizzo, A. (2008). Virtual reality exposure therapy using a virtual Iraq: Case Report. *J. Trauma. Stress., 21*, 209–213.

Gershuny, B. S., & Sher, K. J. (1998). The relation between personality and anxiety: Findings from a 3-year prospective study. *J. Abn. Psychol., 107(2)*, 252–62.

Gestwicki, J. E., Crabtree, G. R., & Graef, I. A. (2004). Harnessing chaperones to generate small molecule inhibitors of amyloid aggregation. *Science, 306*, 865–69.

Gettinger, M., & Koscik, R. (2001). Psychological services for children with learning disabilities. In J. N. Huges, A. W. La Greca, & J. C. Conoley (Eds.), *Handbook of psychological services for children and adolescents* (pp. 421–35). Oxford: Oxford University Press.

Ghaderi, A. (2006). Does individualization matter? A randomized trial of standard (focused) versus individualized (broader) cognitive behavior therapy for bulimia nervosa. *Behav. Res. Ther., 44*, 273–88.

Ghaemi, S. N., Hsu, D. J., Soldani, F., & Goodwin, F. K. (2003). Antidepressants in bipolar disorder: The case for caution. *Bipolar Disorders, 5*, 421–33.

Ghaziuddin, M. (2005). *Mental health aspects of autism and Asperger's syndrome.* London: Jessica Kingsley.

Chorpta, B. (2001). Control and the development of negative emotion. In M Vasey & M. Dadds (Eds). *The developmental psychopathology of anxiety.* Oxford University Press.

Gibbons, M. B. C., Crits-Christoph, P., & Hearon, B. (2008). The empirical status of psychodynamic therapies. *Annu. Rev. Clin. Psychol., 4*, 93–108.

Giesbrecht, T., Lynn, S. J., Lilienfeld, S. O., & Merckelbach, H. (2008). Cognitive processes in dissociation: An analysis of core theoretical assumptions. *Psychol. Bull., 134*, 617–47. doi:10.1037/0033-2909.134.5.617

Giesbrecht, T., Merckelbach, H., van Oorsouw, K., & Simeon, D. (2010). Skin conductance and memory fragmentation after exposure to an emotional clip in depersonalization disorder. *Psychiat. Res., 177*, 342–49. doi:10.1016/j.psychres.2010.03.010

Gilberg, C. (2002). *A guide to Asperger's syndrome.* Cambridge: Cambridge University Press.

Gilbert, D. L., Batterson, J. R., Sethuraman, G., & Sallee, F. R. (2004). Tic reduction with risperidone versus pimozide in a randomized, double-blind, crossover trial. *J. Amer. Acad. Child Adoles. Psychiat., 43(2)* 206–14.

Gilbert, J. G., & Lombardi, D. N. (1967). Personality characteristics of young male narcotic addicts. *J. Couns. Psychol., 31*, 536–38.

Gilbertson, M. W., Shenton, M. E., Ciszewski, A., Kasai, K., Lasko, N. B., Orr, S. P., & Pitman, R. K. (2002). Smaller hippocampal volume predicts pathologic vulnerability to psychological trauma. *Nature Neuroscience, 5*, 1242–47.

Gilboa, A., Winocur, G., Rosenbaum, R. S., Poreh, A., Gao, F., Black, S., Westmacott, R., & Moscovitch, M. (2006). Hippocampal contributions to recollection in retrograde and anterograde amnesia. *Hippocampus, 16*, 966–80.

Gill, K., Eagle Elk, M., Liu, Y., & Deitrich, R. A. (1999). An examination of ALDH2 genotypes, alcohol metabolism and the flushing response in Native Americans. *J. Stud. Alcoh., 60(2)*, 149–58.

Gillespie, C. F. & Nemeroff, C. B. (2007). Corticotropin releasing factor and the psychobiology of early life stress. *Curr. Dis. Psychol. Sci., 16*, 85–89.

Gilley, D. W., et al. (1997). Psychotic symptoms and physically aggressive behavior in Alzheimer's disease. *J. Amer. Geriat. Soc., 45(9)*, 1074–79.

Gillham, J. E., Reivich, K. J., Freres, D. R., Lascher, M., Litzinger, S., Shatté, A., & Seligman, M. E. P. (2006). School-based prevention of depression and anxiety symptoms in early adolescence: A pilot of a parent intervention component. *School Psychol. Quart. 21(3)*, 323–48.

Gillman, M. W., Rifas-Shiman, S. L., Kleinman, K., Oken, E., Rich-Edwards, J. W., & Taveras, E. M. (2008). Developmental origins of childhood overweight: Potential public health impact. *Obesity.*

Gilmer, W. S., Trivedi, M. H., Rush, A. J., Wisniewski, S. R., Luther, J., Howland, R. H., et al. (2005). Factors associated with chronic depressive episodes: A preliminary report from the STAR-D project. *Acta Psychiatrica Scandinavica, 112(6)*, 425–33.

Gilmore, J. H. (2010). Understanding what causes schizophrenia: A developmental perspective. *Am. J. Psychiat., 167*, 8–10.

Gilovich, T. (1991). *How do we know what isn't so: The fallibility of human reason in everyday life.* New York: Free Press.

Giotakos, O., Vaidakis, N., Markianos, M., Spandoni, P., & Christodoulou, G. N. (2004). Temperament and character dimensions of sex offenders in relation to their parental rearing. *Sexual and Relationship Therapy, 19*, 141–50.

Girgis, R. R., Minshew, N. J., Melham, N. M., Nutche, J. J., Keshavan, M. S., & Hardan, A. Y. (2007). Volumetric alterations of the orbitofrontal cortex in autism. *Progress in Neuropharmacology & Biological Psychiatry, 31*, 41–45.

Gitlin, M. J. (1996). *The psychotherapist's guide to psychopharmacology* (2nd ed.). New York: Free Press.

Gitlin, M. J. (2002). Pharmacological treatment of depression. In I. H. Gotlib & C. L. Hammen (Eds.), *Handbook of depression* (pp. 360–82). New York: Guilford.

Gjedde, A., & Wong, D. F. (1987). Positron tomographic quantification of neuroreceptors in human brain *in vivo,* with special reference to the D2 dopamine receptors in caudate nucleus. *Neurosurgical Review, 10*, 9–18.

Glaser, R., Kiecolt-Glaser, J. K., Speicher, C. E., & Holliday, J. E. (1985). Stress, loneliness, and changes in herpes virus latency. *J. Behav. Med., 8*, 249–60.

Glaser, R., Rice, J., Sheridan, J., Fertel, R., Stout, J., Speicher, C., Pinsky, R., Kotur, M., Post, A., Beck, M., & Kiecolt-Glaser, J. (1987). Stress-related immune suppression: Health implications. *Brain, Behavior, and Immunity, 1*, 7–20.

Glassman, A. H. (2005). Commentary: Does treating postmyocardial infarction depression reduce medical mortality? *Arch. Gen. Psychiat., 62*(7), 711–12.

Glassman, A. H. (2007). Depression and cardiovascular comorbidity. *Dialogues in Clinical Neuroscience, 9,* 9–17.

Gleaves, D. H. (1996). The sociocognitive model of dissociative identity disorder: A reexamination of the evidence. *Psychol. Bull., 120,* 42–59.

Gleaves, D. H., & Williams, T. L. (2005). Critical questions: Trauma, memory, and dissociation. *Psychiat. Ann., 35(8),* 649–54.

Gleaves, D. H., May, M. C., & Cardena, E. (2001). Examination of the diagnostic validity of dissociative identity disorder.*Clin. Psychol. Rev., 21,* 577–608.

Gleaves, D. H., Smith, S. M., Butler, L. D., & Spiegel, D. (2004). False and recovered memories in the laboratory and clinic: A review of experimental and clinical evidence. *Clin. Psychol. Sci. Prac., 11*(1), 3–28.

Glidden, L. M., & Schoolcraft, S. A., (2007). From diagnosis to adaptation: Optimizing family and child functioning when a genetic diagnosis is associated with mental retardation. In M. M. Mazzocco & J. L. Ross (Eds.), *Neurogenetic developmental disorders: Variation of manifestation in childhood* (pp. 391–413). Cambridge, MA: The MIT Press.

Glick, I. D., & Tandon, R. (2009). In S. S. Sharfstein, F. B. Dickerson, & J. M. Oldham (Eds.), *Textbook of hospital psychiatry* (pp. 23–35). Arlington, Va.: American Psychiatric Association.

Glisky, E. L., Ryan, L., Reminger, S., Hardt, O., Hayes, S. M., & Hupbach, A. (2004). A case of psychogenic fugue: I understand, aber ich verstehe nichts. *Neuropsychologia, 42,* 1132–47.

Glover, M. R. (1984). *The York Retreat: An early Quaker experiment in the treatment of mental illness.* York, England: William Sessions Ltd.

Goddard, A. W., Mason, G. F., Almai, A., Rothman, D. L., Behar, K. L., Petroff, O., et al. (2001). Reductions in occipital cortex GABA levels in panic disorder detected with superscript 1H-magnetic resonance spectroscopy. *Arch. Gen. Psychiat., 58*(6), 556–61.

Goddard, A. W., Mason, G. F., Rothman, D. L., Behar, K. L., Petroff, O., & Krystal, J. H. (2004). Family psychopathology and magnitude of reductions in occipital cortex GABA levels in panic disorder. *Neuropsychopharmacol., 29*(3), 639–40.

Goddard, A. W., Narayan, M., Woods, S. W., Germine, M., Gerald, L., Kramer, L. L., et al. (1996). Plasma levels of gamma-aminobutyric acid and panic disorder. *Psych. Res., 63*(2–3), 223–25.

Godleski, L. (2010). Teaching residents to recognize the impact of divorce. *Academic Psychiatry,* 34, 378–380.

Goel, M. S., McCarthy, E. P., Phillips, R. S., & Wee, C. C. (2004). Obesity among US immigrant subgroups by duration of residence.*JAMA, 292,* 2860–67.

Goff, D. C., & Coyle, J. T. (2001). The emerging role of glutamate in the pathophysiology and treatment of schizophrenia.*Amer. J. Psychiat., 158,* 1367–77.

Goffman, E. (1961). *Asylums.* New York: Doubleday.

Goin, R. P. (1998). Nocturnal enuresis in children. *Child: Care, Health, and Development, 24,* 277–88.

Goldberg, L. R. (1990). An alternative "description of personality": The big-five factor structure. *J. Pers. Soc. Psychol.,* 59(6), 1216. Retrieved from http://psycnet.apa.org/psycinfo/1991-09869-001

Golden, R. N., Gaynes, B. N., Ekstrom, R. D., Hamer, R. M., Jacobsen, F. M., Suppes, T., et al. (2005). The efficacy of light therapy in the treatment of mood disorders: A review and meta-analysis of the evidence. *Amer. J. Psychiat., 162*(4), 656–62.

Goldfein, J. A., Devlin, M. J., & Spitzer, R. L. (2000). Cognitive behavioral therapy for the treatment of binge eating disorder: What constitutes success? *Amer. J. Psychiat., 157*(7), 1051–56.

Goldin, P. R., Manber, T., Hakimi, S., Canli, T., & Gross, J. J. (2009). Neural bases of social anxiety disorder: Emotional reactivity and cognitive regulation during social and physical threat. *Arch. Gen. Psychiat., 66*(2), 170–80. doi: 10.1001/archgenpsychiatry.2008.525

Golding, S. L., Eaves, D., & Kowaz, A. M. (1989).The assessment, treatment and community outcome of insanity acquittees: Forensic history and response to treatment. *International Journal of Law and Psychiatry,* 12(2–3), 149–79.

Goldman-Rakic, P. S., & Selemon, L. D. (1997). Functional and anatomical aspects of prefrontal pathology in schizophrenia.*Schizo. Bull., 23,* 437–58.

Goldney, R. D. (2003). Deinstitutionalization and suicide. *J. Crisis Int. Suicide Prev., 24,* 39–40.

Goldsmith, D. F., & Rogoff, B. (1997). Mother's and toddler's coordinated joint focus of attention: Variations with maternal dysphoric symptoms. *Develop. Psychol., 33,* 113–19.

Goldsmith, H. H. (2003). Genetics of emotional development. In R. J. Davidson, K. R. Scherer, & H. H. Goldsmith (Eds.), *Handbook of affective sciences* (pp. 300–19). New York: Oxford University Press.

Goldsmith, R., Joanissse, D. R., Gallagher, D., Pavlovich, K., Shamoon, E., Leibel, R. L., et al. (2010). Effects of experimental weight perturbation on skeletal work efficiency, fuel utilization, and biochemistry in human subjects. *American Journal of Physiology – Regulatory, Integrative and Comparative Physiology, 298,* R79–R88.

Goldsmith, W., & Cretekos, C. (1969). Unhappy odysseys: Psychiatric hospitalization from Vietnam returnees. *Amer. J. Psychiat., 20,* 78–83.

Goldstein, A. J., & Chambless, D. (1978). A reanalysis of agoraphobia. *Behav. Ther., 9,* 47–59.

Goldstein, A., et al. (1974, Mar. 4). Researchers isolate opiate receptor. *Behav. Today, 5*(9), 1.

Goldstein, I., Lue, T. F., Padma-Nathan, H., Rosen, R. C., Steers, W. D., & Wicker, P. A. (1998). Oral sildenafil in the treatment of erectile dysfunction. *N. Engl. J. Med., 338,* 20, 1397–1404.

Goldstein, R. B. Grant, B. F., Ruan, W. J., Smith, S. M., & Saha, T. D. (2006). Antisocial personality disorder with childhood-vs adolescence-onset conduct disorder: Results from the national epidemiologic survey on alcohol and related conditions. *J. Nerv. Ment. Dis., 194*(9), 667–75.

Goldstein , S. (2009). Current literature in ADHD summarized by Sam Goldstein. *Journal of Attention Disorders,* 12(4), 386–388.

Goldstein, S., Naglieri, J. A., & Ozonoff, S. (Eds.). (2009). *Assessment of autism spectrum disorders.* New York: Guilford Press.

Golomb, M., Fava, M., Abraham, M., & Rosenbaum, J. F. (1995). Gender differences in personality disorders. *Amer. J. Psychiat., 152*(4), 579–82.

González Castro, F., Barrera, M., & Holleran Steiker, L. K., (2010). Issues and challenged in the design of culturally adapted evidence-based interventions. *Annu. Rev. Clin. Psychol., 6,* 213–39.

Good, B. J., & Kleinman, A. M. (1985). Culture and anxiety: Cross-cultural evidence for the patterning of anxiety disorders. In A. H. Tuma & J. D. Master (Eds.), *Anxiety and the anxiety disorders.* Hillsdale, NJ: Erlbaum.

Goodheart, C. D., & Rozensky, R. H. (2011). Health and medical conditions. In J. C Norcross, G. R. VandenBos, & D. K. Freedheim (Eds.), *History of psychotherapy: Continuity and change* (2nd ed., pp. 467–74). Washington, DC: American Psychological Association.

Goodman, S. H. (2007). Depression in mothers. *Ann. Rev. Clin. Psych., 3,* 107–35.

Goodman, S. H., & Brand, S. R. (2009). Depression and early adverse experiences. In I. H. Gotlib & C. L. Hammen (Eds.), *Handbook of depression and its treatment* (2nd ed.). New York: Guilford Press.

Goodman, S. H., & Gotlib, I. H. (1999). Risk for psychopathology in the children of depressed mothers: A developmental model for understanding mechanisms of transmission. *Psychol. Rev., 106,* 458–90.

Goodman, W. K. (2004). Selecting pharmacotherapy for generalized anxiety disorder. *J. Clin. Psychiat., 65*(113), 8–13.

Goodwin, D. W., Schulsinger, F., Hermansen, L., Guze, S. B., & Winokur, G. (1973). Alcohol problems in adoptees raised apart from alcoholic biological parents. *Arch. Gen. Psychiat., 28*(2), 238–43.

Goodwin, D. W., Schulsinger, F., Moller, N., Hermansen, L., Winokur, G., & Guze, S. B. (1974). Drinking problems in adopted and nonadopted sons of alcoholics. *Arch. Gen. Psychiat., 31*(2), 164–69.

Goodwin, F. K., & Jamison, K.R. (2007). *Manic-depressive illness: Bipolar disorders and recurrent depression* (2nd Ed.). New York: Oxford University Press.

Goodwin, F. K., Fireman, B., Simon, G. E., Hunkeler, E. M., Lee, J., & Revicki, D. (2003). Suicide risk in bipolar disorder during treatment with lithium and divalproex. *JAMA, 290*(11), 1467–73.

Goodwin, L. (1992). Alcohol and drug use in fraternities and sororities. *Journal of Alcohol and Drug Education, 37*(2), 52–63.

Goodwin, R. D., & Gotlib, I. H. (2004a). Gender differences in depression: The role of personality factors. *Psychiat. Res., 126,* 135–42.

Goodwin, R. D., & Gotlib, I. H. (2004b). Panic attacks and psychopathology among youth. *Acta Psychiatr. Scandin., 109*(3), 216–21.

Goodyer, I. (2000). Emotional disorders with their onset in childhood. In M. G. Gleder, J. J. Lopez-Ibor, Jr., & N. Andreason (Eds.), *New Oxford textbook of psychiatry* (pp. 1762–71). Oxford: Oxford University Press.

Goos, L. M., Ezzatian, P., & Schachar, R. (2007). Parent-of-origin effects in attention-deficit hyperactivity disorder. *Psychiat. Res., 149*(1–3), 1–9.

Gordis, E. (1997). Patient-treatment matching. *Alcohol Alert,* 36, 1–4.

Gordis, E. (2001). Cognitive impairment and recovery from alcoholism. *Alcohol Alert.* National Institute on Alcohol Abuse and Alcoholism, No. 53, U.S. Department of Health and Human Services.

Gordis, E., Dufour, M. C., Warren, K. R., Jackson, R. J., Floyd, R. L., & Hungerford, D. W. (1995). Should physicians counsel patients to drink alcohol? *JAMA, 273,* 1–12.

Gordon, R. A. (2000). *Eating disorders: Anatomy of a social epidemic* (2nd ed.). London: Blackwell.

Gorenstein, E. E. (1992). *The science of mental illness.* San Diego: Academic Press.

Gorlick, D. A. (1993). Overview of pharmacologic treatment approaches for alcohol and other drug addictions. *Psychiat. Clin. N. Amer., 16,* 141–56.

Gorman, J. M., Battista, D., Goetz, R. R., Dillon, D. J., Liebowitz, M. R., Fyer, A. J., Kahn, J. P., Sandberg, D., & Klein, D. F. (1989). A comparison of sodium bicarbonate and sodium lactate infusion in the induction of panic attacks. *Arch. Gen. Psychiat., 46,* 145–50.

Gorman, J. M., Kent, J. M., Sullivan, G. M., & Coplan, J. D. (2000). Neuroanatomical hypothesis of panic disorder, revised.*Amer. J. Psychiat., 157*, 493–505.

Gortner, E. T., Gollan, J. K., & Jacobson, N. S. (1997). Psychological aspects of perpetrators of domestic violence and their relationships with the victims. *Psychiat. Clin. N. Amer., 20*(2), 327–52.

Gosselin, P., Ladouceur, R., Morin, C. M., Dugas, M. J., & Baillargeon, L. (2006). Benzodiazepine discontinuation among adults with GAD: A randomized trial of cognitive-behavioral therapy. *J Consult. Clin. Psychol., 74*(5), 908–19.

Gothelf, D., Feinstein, C., Thompson, T., Gu, E., Penniman, L., Van Stone, E., Kwon, H., Eliez, S., & Reiss, A. L. (2007). Risk factors for the emergence of psychotic disorders in adolescents with 22q11.2 deletion syndrome. *Am. J. Psychiat.,164*, 663–69.

Gotlib, I. H., & Abramson, L. Y. (1999). Attributional theories of emotion. In T. Dalgleish & M. J. Power (Eds.), *Handbook of cognition and emotion* (pp. 613–36). Chichester, England: Wiley.

Gotlib, I. H., & Hammen, C. L. (1992). *Psychological aspects of depression: Toward a cognitive-interpersonal integration.* Chichester, UK: Wiley.

Gotlib, I. H., & Joormann, J. (2010). Cognition and depression: Current status and future directions. *Annu. Rev. Clin. Psychol., 6*, 285–312. doi: 10.1146/annurev.clinpsy.121208.131305

Gottesman, I. I. (1991). *Schizophrenia genesis: The origins of madness.* New York: Freeman.

Gottesman, I. I. (2001). Psychopathology through a life span–genetic prism. *Amer. Psychol., 56*, 867–78.

Gottesman, I. I., & Bertelson, A. (1989). Confirming unexpressed genotypes for schizophrenia: Risks in the offspring of Fischer's Danish identical and fraternal discordant twins. *Arch. Gen. Psychiat., 46*, 867–72.

Gottesman, I. I., & Gould, T. D. (2003). The endophenotype concept in psychiatry: Etymology and strategic intentions. *Am. J. Psychiat.,160*, 636–45.

Gottesman, I. I., & Hanson, D. R. (2005). Human development: Biological and genetic processes. *Annu. Rev. Psychol., 56*, 263–86.

Gottlieb, G. (1992). *Individual development and evolution: The genesis of novel behavior.* New York: Oxford University Press.

Gottlieb, G., & Halpern, C. T. (2002). A relational view of causality in normal and abnormal development. *Develop. Psychopath., 14*(3), 421–35.

Götz, J., Chen, F., van Dorpe, J., & Nitsch, R. M. (2001). Formation of neurofibrillary tangles in P301L tau transgenic mice induced by A(42) fibrils. *Science, 293*, 1491–95.

Gould, L. N. (1949). Auditory hallucinations and subvocal speech. *J. Nerv. Ment. Dis., 109*, 418–27.

Gouvier, W. D., et al. (1997). Cognitive retraining with brain-damaged patients. In A. M. Horton, D. Wedding, & J. Webster (Eds.), *The neuropsychology handbook* (Vol. 2., pp. 3–46). New York: Springer.

Grabe, H. J., Ruhrmann, S., Ettelt, S., Buhtz, F., Hochrein, A., Schulze-Rauschenbach, S., et al. (2006). Familiality of obsessive-compulsive disorder in nonclinical and clinical subjects. *Am. J. Psychiat., 163*(11), 1986–92.

Grabe, S., & Hyde, J. (2006). Ethnicity and body dissatisfaction among women in the United States: A meta-analysis. *Psych. Bull., 132*, 622–40.

Graeff, F. G., & Del-Ben, C. M. (2008). Neurobiology of panic disorder: From animal models to brain neuroimaging. *Neuroscience and Biobehavioral Reviews, 32*(7), 1326–35. doi: 10.1016/j.neubiorev.2008.05.017

Graham, J. R., Ben-Porath, Y. S., & McNulty, J. (1999). *Using the MMPI-2 in outpatient mental health settings.* Minneapolis: University of Minnesota Press.

Granato, P., Weill, S., & Revillon, J. J. (1997). Ecstasy and dementia in a young subject. *European Psychiatry, 12*(7), 369–71.

Grandin, L. D., Alloy, L. B., & Abramson, L. Y. (2006). The social Zeitgeber theory, circadian rhythms, and mood disorders: Review and evaluation. *Clin.l Psych. Rev., 26*(6), 679–94.

Granic, I., & Patterson, G. R. (2006). Toward a comprehensive model of antisocial development: A dynamic systems approach.*Psych. Rev., 113*(1), 101–131.

Grant, B. F., Chou, S. P., Goldstein, R. B., et al. (2008). Prevalence, correlates, disability, and comorbidity of DSM-IV borderline personality disorder: Results from the Wave 2 National Epidemiologic Survey on Alcohol and Related Conditions. *J. Clin. Psychiat., 69*, 533–45.

Grant, B. F., & Dawson, D. A. (1997). Age at onset of alcohol use and its association with DSM-IV alcohol abuse and dependency: Results from the National Longitudinal Alcohol Epidemiologic Survey. *J. Subst. Abuse, 9*, 103–10.

Grant, B. F., Hasin, D., Stinson, F., Dawson, D., Chou, S. P., Ruan, W. J., & Huang, B. (2005). Co-occurrence of 12-month mood and anxiety disorders and personality disorders in the US: Results from the national epidemiologic survey on alcohol and related conditions. *J. Psychiat. Res., 39*, 1–9.

Grant, B. F., Hasin, D. S., Stinson, F. S., Dawson, D. A., Chou, S. P., Ruan, W. J., & Pickering, R. P. (2004). Prevalence, correlates, and disability of personality disorders in the United States: Results From the National Epidemiologic Survey on Alcohol and Related Conditions. *J. Clin. Psychiat., 65*(7), 948–58.

Grant, B. F., Stinson, F. S., Dawson, D. A., Chou, P., Dufour, M., Compton, W., Pickering, R. P., & Kaplan, K. (2004). Prevalence and co-occurrence of substance use disorders and independent mood and anxiety disorders: Results from the national epidemiologic survey on alcohol and related conditions. *Arch. Gen. Psychiat., 61*(8), 807–16.

Grant, B. F., Stinson, F. S., Dawson, D. A., Chou, S. P., & Ruan, W. J. (2005). Co-occurrence of DSM-IV personality disorders in the United States: Results from the national epidemiologic survey on alcohol and related conditions. *Compr. Psychiat., 46*, 1–5.

Grant, J. E., & Potenza, M. N. (2010). Impulse control disorders. In J. E. Grant & M. N. Potenza (Eds.), *Young adult mental health* (pp. 335–51). New York: Oxford University Press.

Grant, M. (1956). *Tacitus: The annals of Imperial Rome* (Translated by Michael Grant). New York: Penguin Books.

Grant, S. J., & Sonti, G. (1994). Buprenorphine and morphine produce equivalent increases in extracellular single unit activity of dopamine neurons in the ventral tegmental area *in vivo. Synapse, 16*, 181–87.

Graves, R. E., Cassisi, & Penn, D. L. (2005). Pyschophysiological evaluation of stigma toward schizophrenia. *Schizo. Res., 76*, 315–27.

Gray, J. A. (1987). *The psychology of fear and stress* (2nd ed.). New York: Cambridge University Press.

Gray, J. A., & McNaughton, N. (1996). The neuropsychology of anxiety: Reprise. In D. A. Hope (Ed.), *Nebraska Symposium on Motivation, 1995: Perspectives on anxiety, panic, and fear. Current theory and research in motivation* (Vol. 43., pp. 61–134). Lincoln: University of Nebraska Press.

Gray, J. A., & McNaughton, N. (2000). *The neuropsychology of anxiety* (2nd ed.). Oxford: Oxford University Press.

Gray-Little, B. (2009). The assessment of psychopathology in racial and ethnic Minorities. In J. N. Butcher (Ed.), *Oxford handbook of personality and clinical assessment* (pp. 396–414). New York: Oxford Univesity Press.

Green, B. A. (2009). Culture and mental health assessment. In S. Eshun & R. A. Gurung, (Eds.), *Culture and mental health: Sociocultural influences, theory, and practice* (pp. 19–33). Wiley-Blackwell.

Green, B. L., Lindy, J. D., Grace, M. C., & Leonard, A. C. (1992). Chronic posttraumatic stress disorder and diagnostic comorbidity in a disaster sample. *J. Nerv. Ment. Dis., 180*, 760–66.

Green, M. F. (1997). *Schizophrenia from a neurocognitive perspective.* Needham Heights, MA: Allyn and Bacon.

Green, M. F. (2001). *Schizophrenia revealed: From neurons to social interactions.* New York: Norton.

Green, M. F. (2007). Stimulating the development of drug treatments to improve cognition in schizophrenia. *Annu. Rev. Clin. Psych., 3*, 159–80.

Green, R. (1987). *The "sissy boy syndrome" and the development of homosexuality.* New Haven: Yale University Press.

Green, R. (1992). *Sexual science and the law.* Cambridge: Harvard University Press.

Green, R. M. (1951). *Galen's hygiene.* Springfield, IL: Charles C. Thomas.

Green, R., & Fleming, D. (1990). Transsexual surgery followup: Status in the 1990's. In J. Bancroft, C. Davis, & H. Ruppel (Eds.), *Annual review of sex research.* Mt. Vernon, IA: Society for the Scientific Study of Sex.

Greenberg, J. R., & Mitchell, S. (1983). *Object relations in psychoanalytic theory.* Cambridge, MA: Harvard University Press.

Greenberg, P. E., Kessler, R. C., Birnbaum, H. G., Leong, S. A., Lowe, S. W., Berglund, P. A., et al. (2003). The economic burden of depression in the United States: How did it change between 1990 and 2000. *J. Clin. Psychiat., 64*(12), 1465–69.

Greenberg, P. E., Sisitsky, T., Kessler, R. C., Finkelstein, S. N., Berndt, E. R., Davidson, J. R. T., Ballenger, J. C., & Fyer, A. J. (1999). The economic burden of anxiety disorders in the 1990s. *J. Clin. Psychiat., 60*, 427–35.

Greene, R. L. (2011). *The MMPI-2/MMPI-2-RF: An interpretive manual.* Boston: Allyn & Bacon.

Greene, R. L., Robin, R. W., Albaugh, B., Caldwell, A., & Goldman, D. (2003). Use of the MMPI-2 in American Indians: II. Empirical correlates. *Psychol. Assess., 15*(3), 360–69.

Greenfield, S. F., Back, S. E., Lawson, K., & Brady, K. T. (2010). Substance abuse in women: Contribution of early environmental stress to alcoholism vulnerability. *Psychiat. Clin. N. Amer., 33*(2), 339–55.

Greenhill, L. L., & Waslick, B. (1997). Management of suicidal behavior in children and adolescents. *Psychiat. Clin. N. Amer., 20*(3), 641–66.

Greenough, W. T., & Black, J. E. (1992). Induction of brain structure by experience: Substrates for cognitive development. In M. R. Gunnar & C. A. Nelson (Eds.), *Minnesota Symposia on Child Psychology:Developmental Neuroscience* (Vol. 24., pp. 155–200). Hillsdale, NJ: Erlbaum.

Greenway, F. L., Fujioka, K., Plodkowski, R. A., Mudaliar, S., Guttadauria, M., Erickson, J., et al. for the COR-I Study Group. (2010, Aug. 21). Effect of naltrexone plus buproprion on weight loss in overweight and obese adults (COR-I): A multicentre, randomized, double-blind, placebo-controlled, phase 3 trial. *Lancet, 376*, 595–605.

Greenwood, T. A., Braff, D.L., Light, G. A., Cadenhead, K. S., Calkins, M. E. Dobie, D. J., Freedman, R., et al., (2007). Initial heritability analyses of endophenotypic measures for schizophrenia. *Arch. Gen. Psychiat., 64*, 1241–50.

Greeven, A., van Balkom, A. J. L. M., van Rood, Y. R., van Oppen, P., & Spinhoven, P. (2007). The boundary bewteen hypochondriasis and obsessive-compulsive disorder: A cross-sectional study from the Netherlands. *J. Clin. Psych., 67* (11), 1682–89.

Gregg, C., & Hoy, C. (1989). Coherence: The comprehension and production abilities of college writers who are normally achieving, learning disabled, and underprepared. *J. Learn. Dis., 22*, 370–72.

Gretton, H. M., Hare, R. D., & Catchpole, R. E. H. (2004). Psychopathy and offending from adolescence to adulthood: A 10-year follow-up. *J. Cons. Clin. Psych., 72*(4), 636–45.

Greysmith, D. (1979) *Richard Dadd: The rock and castle of seclusion.* London, U.K.: Tate Gallery.

Grice, D. E., Halmi, K. A., Fichter, M. M., Strober, M., Woodside, D. B., Treasure, J. T., Kaplan, A. S., Magistretti, P. J.,Goldman, D., Bulik, C. M., Jaye, W. H., & Berrettini, W. H. (2002). Evidence for a susceptibility gene for anorexia nervosa on chromosome 1. *Am. J. Human Genet., 70*(3), 787–92.

Griesinger, W. (1845). *The pathology and therapy of psychic disorders.* Stuttgart: Krabbe.

Griffifths, P., Sedefov, R., Gallegos, A., & Lopez, D. (2010). How globalization and market innovation challenge how we think about and respond to drug use: "Spice" a case study. *Addiction, 105*(6), 951–53.

Griffith, J. W., Zinbarg, R. E., Craske, M. G., Mineka, S., Rose, R. D., Waters, A. M., & Sutton, J. M. (2010). Neuroticism as a common dimension in the internalizing disorders. *Psychol. Med., 40*(07), 1125–36. doi: 10.1017/S0033291709991449.

Griffiths, M. (2003). Internet gambling: Issues, concerns, and recommendations. *Cyber Psychology & Behavior, 6*(6), 557–68.

Grillon, C. (2008). Models and mechanisms of anxiety: Evidence from startle studies. *Psychopharmacol., 199*(3), 421–37. doi: 10.1007/s00213-007-1019-1

Grilo, C. M. (2002). Binge eating disorder. In C. G. Fairburn & K. D. Brownell (Eds.), *Eating disorders and obesity: A comprehensive handbook* (2nd ed., pp. 178–82). New York: Guilford.

Grilo, C. M., Skodol, A., Gunderson, J., Sanislow, C., Stout, R., Shea, M., et al. (2004). Longitudinal diagnostic efficiency of DSM-IV criteria for obsessive-compulsive personality disorder: A 2-year prospective study. *Acta Psychiatr. Scandin., 110*, 64–68.

Grimes, K., & Walker, E. F. (1994). Childhood emotional expressions, educational attainment, and age at onset of illness in schizophrenia. *J. Abn. Psychol., 103*(4), 784–90.

Grisham, J. R., Anderson, T. M., & Perminder S, S. (2008). Genetic and environmental influences on obsessive-compulsive disorder.*Eur. Arch. Psychiat. Clin. Neurosci., 258*(2), 107–16. doi: 10.1007/s00406-007-0789-0

Grob, C. S. (2000). Deconstructing ecstasy: The politics of MDMA research. *Addiction Research, 8*(6), 549–88.

Grob, G. N. (1994). Mad, homeless, and unwanted: A history of the care of the chronically mentally ill in America. *Psychiat. Clin. N. Amer., 17*(3), 541–58.

Grob, G. N. (2008). Mental health policy in the liberal state: The example of the United States. *International Journal of Law and Psychiatry, 31*(2), 89–100.

Grodin, M., & Laurie, G. T. (2000). Susceptibility genes and neurological disorders: Learning the right lessons from the Human Genome Project. *Arch. Neurol., 57*, 1569–74.

Gross, R., Sasson, Y., Chopra, M., & Zohar, J. (1998). Biological models of obsessive-compulsive disorder: The serotonin hypothesis. In R. P. Swinson, M. M. Antony, et al. (Eds.), *Obsessive-compulsive disorder: Theory, research, and treatment.* (pp. 141–53). New York: Guilford Press.

Grossman, J. B., & Ruiz, P. (2004). Shall we make a leap-of-faith to disulfiram (Antabuse)? *Addictive Disorders & Their Treatment, 3*(3) 129–32.

Grossmann, K. E., Grossmann, K., & Waters, E. (2005). *Attachment from infancy to adulthood: The major longitudinal studies.* New York: Guilford Publications.

Grounds, A. (2000). The psychiatrist in court. In M. G. Gelder, J. J. Lopez-Ibor, Jr., & N. C. Andreason (Eds.), *New Oxford textbook of psychiatry* (pp. 2089–96). Oxford: Oxford University Press.

Grove, W. M., Zald, D. H., Lebow, B., Snitz, E., & Nelson, C. (2000). Clinical versus mechanical prediction: A meta-analysis.*Psychol. Assess., 12*, 19–30.

Grover, K. E., Carpenter, L. L., Price, L. H., Gagne, G. G., Mello, A. F., Mello, M. F., et al. (2007). The relationship between childhood abuse and adult personality disorder symptoms. *J. Pers. Disord., 21*, 442–47.

Groza, V., Maschmeier, C., Jamison, C., & Piccola, T. (2003). Siblings and out-of-home placement: Best practices. *Families in Society, 84*(4), 480–90.

Gruber, S. A., Tzilos, G. K., Silveri, M. M., Pollack, M., Renshaw, P. F., Kaufman, M. J., & Yurgelun-Todd, D. A. (2006). Methadone maintenance improves cognitive performance after two months of treatment. *Exp. Clin. Psychopharm., 14*(2), 157–64.

Grzywacz, J. G., & Dooley, D. (2003). "Good jobs" to "bad jobs": Replicated evidence of an employment continuum from two large surveys. *Soc. Sci. Med., 56*, 1749–60.

Guarnaccia, P. J., Lewis-Fernandez, R., Pincay, I. M., Shrout, P., Guo, J., Torres, M., et al. (2010). Ataque de nervios as a marker of social and psychiatric vulnerability: Results from the NLAAS. *Int'l J. Soc. Psychiat., 56*(3), 298–309. doi: 10.1177/0020764008101636

Guarnaccia, P. J., Martinez, I., Ramirez, R., & Canino, G. (2005). Are ataques de nervios in Puerto Rican children associated with psychiatric disorder? *J. Amer. Acad. Child Adoles. Psychiat., 44*(11), 1184–92.

Guastella, A. J., Richardson, R., Lovibond, P. F., Rapee, R., Gaston, J. E., Mitchell, P., & Dadds, M. R. (2008). A randomized controlled trial of D-cycloserine enhancement of exposure therapy for social anxiety disorder. *Biol. Psychiat, 63*, 544–49.

Guedeney, A. (2007). Withdrawal behavior and depression in infancy. *Infant Mental Health Journal, 28*(4), 393–408.

Guelfi, G. P., Faustman, W. O., & Csernansky, J. G. (1989). Independence of positive and negative symptoms in a population of schizophrenic patients. *J. Nerv. Ment. Dis., 177*, 285–90.

Gueorguieva, R., Wu, R., Pittman, B., Cramer, J., Rosenheck, R. A., O'Malley, S. S., & Krystal, J. H. (2007). New insights into the efficacy of naltrexone based on trajectory-based reanalyses of two negative clinical trials. *Biol. Psychiat., 61*(11), 1290–95.

Guerje, O., Simon, G. E., Ustun, T. B., & Goldberg, D. B. (1997). Somatization in cross-cultural perspective: A World Health Organization study in primary care. *Amer. J. Psychiat., 154*, 989–95.

Guerra, F. (1971). *The pre-Columbian mind.* New York: Seminar Press.

Guerrero-Pedrazza, A., McKenna, P. J., Gomar, J. J. Sarró, S., Salvador, R., Amman, B., et al., (2011). First-episode psychosis is characterized by failure of deactivation but not by hyper- or hypofrontality. *Psych. Med.*

Gull, W. (1888). Anorexia nervosa. *Lancet, i*, 516–17.

Gunderson, J. G. (2011). Borderline personality disorder. *N. Eng. J. Med., 364*, 2037–42. doi:10.1007/s11126-010-9154-y

Gunderson, J. G., Stout, R. L., McGlashan, T. H., Shea, M. T., Morey, L. C., Grilo, C. M., Zanarini, M. C., et al. (2011). Ten-year course of borderline personality disorder: Psychopathology and function from the Collaborative Longitudinal Personality Disorders Study. *Arch. Gen. Psychiat., 68*(8), 827–37. doi:10.1001/archgenpsychiatry.2011.37

Gunderson, J. G., Zanarini, M. C., & Kisiel, C. L. (1995). Borderline personality disorder. In W. J. Livesley (Ed.), *The DSM-IV personality disorders.* (pp. 141–57). New York: Guilford.

Gunn, J. (1993). Castration is not the answer. *Brit. Med. J., 307*, 790–91.

Gunnar, M. R., Morison, S. J., Chisholm, K., & Schuder, M. (2001). Salivary cortisol levels in children adopted from Romanian orphanages. *Develop. Psychopath., 13*, 611–28.

Gunnar, M., & Quevedo, K. (2007). The neurobiology of stress and development. *Annu. Rev. Psychol., 58*, 145–173.

Gunnell, D. (2005). Time trends and geographic differences in suicide: Implications for prevention. In K. Hawton (Ed.), *Prevention and treatment of suicidal behavior: From science to practice* (pp. 29–52). Oxford: Oxford University Press.

Gupta, J. C., Deb, A. K., & Kahali, B. S. (1943). Preliminary observations on the use of Rauwolfia perpentina berth in the treatment of mental disorder. *Indian Medical Gazette, 78*, 547–49.

Gupta, S., & Bonanno, G. A. (2010). Trait self-enhancement as a buffer against potentially traumatic events: A prospective study. *Psychological Trauma, 2*, 83–92.

Guskiewicz, K. M., Marshall, S. W., Bailes, McCrea, M., Cantu, R. C., Randolph, C., & Jordan, B. D. (2005). Association between recurrent concussion and late-life cognitive impairment in retired professional footballers. *Neurosurgery, 57*, 719–726.

Guskiewicz, K. M., Marshall, S. W., Bailes, McCrea, M., Harding, H. P., Matthews, A., Mihalik, J. R., & Cantu, R. C. (2007). Recurrent concussion and risk of depression in retired professional football players. *Medicine and Science in Sports and Exercise, 39*, 903–9.

Guze, S. B., Cloninger, C. R., Martin, R. L., & Clayton, P. J. (1986). A follow-up and family study of Briquet's Syndrome. *Brit. J. Psychiat., 149*, 17–23.

Haaga, D. A. F., Dyck, M. J., & Ernst, D. (1991). Empirical status of cognitive theory of depression. *Psychol. Bull., 110*(2), 215–36.

Haaga, D. A., & Davison, G. C. (1989). Outcome studies of rational-emotive therapy. In M. Bernard & R. DeGiuseppe (Eds.), *Inside rationale-motive therapy.* New York: Academic Press.

Haaga, D. A., & Davison, G. C. (1992). Disappearing differences do not always reflect healthy integration: An analysis of cognitive therapy and rational-emotive therapy. *Journal of Psychotherapy Integration, 1*, 287–303.

Haas, G. (1997). Suicidal behavior in schizophrenia. In R. W. Maris, M. M. Silverman, & S. S. Canetton (Eds.), *Review of Suicidology, 1997* (pp. 202–35). New York: Guilford.

Haber, S. N., & Knutson, B. (2010). The reward circuit: Linking primate anatomy and human imaging. *Neuropsychopharmacol., 35*(1), 4–26. doi: 10.1038/npp.2009.129

Hackmann, A., Clark, D. M., & McManus, F. (2000). Recurrent images and early memories in social phobia. *Behav. Res. Ther., 38*, 601–10.

Hackman, A., Ehlers, A., Speckens, A., & Clark, D. M. (2004). Characteristics and *Traumatic Stress, 17*, 231–40.

Hadley, S. J., Kim, S., Priday, L, & Hollander, E. (2006). Pharmacologic treatment of body dysmorphic disorder. *Primary Psychiatry, 13*(7), 61–69.

Haffner, H., et al. (1998). Causes and consequences of the gender difference in age at onset of schizophrenia. *Schizo. Bull., 24*(1), 99–114.

Hahn, R. A., Bilukha, O., Lowy, J., Crosby, A., Fullilove, M. T., Liberman, A., Moscicki, E., et al. (2005). The effectiveness of therapeutic foster care for the prevention of violence: A systematic review. *Amer. J. Prev. Med., 28*, 72–90.

Haldane, M., & Frangou, S. (2004). New insights help define the pathophysiology of bipolar affective disorder: Neuroimaging and neuropathology findings. *Prog. Neuropsychopharmacol. Biol. Psychiatry, 28*, 943–60.

Hall, D. E., Eubanks, L., Meyyazhagan, S., Kenney, R. D., & Johnson, S. C. (2000). Evaluation of covert video surveillance in the diagnosis of Munchausen syndrome by proxy: Lessons from 41 cases. *Pediatrics, 105*(6), 1305–11.

Hall, G. (1994). Pavlovian conditioning: Laws of association. In N. J. Mackintosh (Ed.), *Animal learning and cognition* (pp. 15–43). San Diego, CA: Academic Press.

Hall, G. C., Bansal, A., & Lopez, I. R. (1999). Ethnicity and psychopathology: A meta-analytic review of 31 years of comparative MMPI/MMPI-2 research. *Psychol. Assess., 11*, 186–97.

Hall, J. R., & Benning, S. D. (2006). The "successful" psychopath: Adaptive and subclinical manifestations of psychopathy in the general population. In C. J. Patrick (Ed.), *Handbook of the psychopathy.* (pp. 459–78). New York: Guilford Press.

Hallett, J. D., Zasler, N. D., Maurer, P., & Cash, S. (1994). Role change after traumatic brain injury in adults. *Amer. J. Occup. Ther., 48*(3), 241–46.

Halligan, S. L., Murray, L., Martins, C., & Cooper, P. J. (2007). Maternal depression and psychiatric outcomes in adolescent offspring: A 13-year longitudinal study. *J. Affect. Disord., 97*(1–3) 145–154.

Halmi, K. A. (2010). Psychological comorbidity of eating disorders. In W. A. Agras (Ed.), *The Oxford Handbook of Eating Disorders*, New York: Oxford University Press, pp. 292–303.

Halmi, K. A., et al. (1991). Comorbidity of psychiatric diagnoses in anorexia nervosa. *Arch. Gen. Psychiat., 48*, 712–18.

Halmi, K. A., Sunday, S., R., Strober, M., Kaplan, A., Woodside, D. B., Fichter, M., Treasure, J., Berrettini,W. H., & Kaye, W. H. (2000). Perfectionism in anorexia nervosa: Variation by clinical subtype, obsessionality, and pathological eating behavior. *Amer. J. Psychiat., 157*(11), 1799–805.

Halpern, S. (2008). Virtual Iraq. The New Yorker, May 19, 2008, pp. 32–37.

Hamilton, S. P. (2008). Schizophrenia candidate genes: Are we really coming up blank? *Am. J. Psychiat., 165*, 420–23.

Hammen, C. (1991). Generation of stress in the course of unipolar depression. *J. Abn. Psychol., 100*, 555–61.

Hammen, C. (1995). Stress and the course of unipolar disorders. In C. M. Mazure (Ed.), *Does stress cause psychiatric illness?* Washington, DC: American Psychiatric Press.

Hammen, C. (2005). Stress and depression. In *Annu. Rev. Clin. Psychol., Volume 1.* (pp. 293–319). Annual Reviews: Palo Alto, CA.

Hammen, C. (2009). Children of depressed parents. In I. H. Gotlib & C. L. Hammen (Eds.), *Handbook of depression and its treatment* (2nd ed.). New York: Guilford Press.

Hammen, C., Brennan, P. A., & Le Brocque, R. (2011). Youth depression and early childrearing: Stress generation and intergenerational transmission of depression. *J. Cons. Clin. Psychol., 79*(3), 353–63. doi: 10.1037/a0023536

Hammen, C., & Rudolph, K. D. (1996). Childhood depression. In E. J. Mash & R. A. Barkley (Eds.), *Childhood psychopathology* (pp. 153–94). New York: Guilford.

Hammen, C., Shih, J. H., & Brennan, P. A. (2004). Intergenerational transmission of depression: Test of an interpersonal stress model in a community sample. *J. Cons. Clin. Psychol., 72*, 511–22.

Hampton, T. (2011). Traumatic brain injury a growing problem among troops serving in today's wars. *JAMA, 306*, 477–79.

Hamrick, N., Cohen, S., & Rodriguez, M. S. (2002). Being popular can be healthy or unhealthy: Stress, social network diversity, and the incidence of upper respiratory infection. *Hlth. Psychol., 21*(3), 294–98.

Hance, M., Carney, R., Freedland, K., & Skala, J. (1996). Depression in patients with coronary heart disease: A 12 month follow-up.*Gen. Hosp. Psychiat., 18*, 61–65.

Handen, B. L., & Lubetsky, M. (2005). Psychopharmacotherapy in autism and related disorders. *School Psychology Quarterly, 20*, 135–71.

Haney, B., & Gold, M. (1973). The juvenile delinquent nobody knows. *Psych. Today, 7*(4), 48–52, 55.

Hankin, B. L. (2006). Adolescent depression: Description, causes, and interventions. *Epilepsy & Behavior, 8*(1), 102–114.

Hankin, B. L., & Abramson, L. Y. (2001). Development of gender differences in depression: An elaborated cognitive vulnerability-transactional stress theory. *Psychol. Bull., 127*, 773–96.

Hankin, B. L., Abramson, L. Y., Miller, N., & Haeffel, G. J. (2004). Cognitive vulnerability-stress theories of depression: Examining affective specificity in the prediction of depression versus anxiety in three prospective studies. *Cog. Ther. & Res., 28*(3), 309–45.

Hankin, B. L., Wetter, E., & Cheely, C. (2008). Sex differences in child and adolescent depression: A developmental psychopathological approach. In J. R. Z. Abela & B. L. Hankin (Eds.), *Handbook of depression in children and adolescents.* (pp. 377–414). New York: Guilford Press.

Hanna, G. L. (2000). Clinical and family-genetic studies of childhood obsessive-compulsive disorder.

In W. K. Goodman, M. V. Rudorfer, et al. (Eds.), *Obsessive-compulsive disorder: Contemporary issues in treatment. Personality and clinical psychology series* (pp. 87–103). Mahwah, NJ: Erlbaum.

Hansen, R. A., Gartlehner, G., Lohr, K. N., & Kaufer, D. I. (2007). Functional outcomes of drug treatment in Alzheimer's disease. *Drugs Aging, 24*, 155–167.

Happe, F., & Frith, U. (1996). Theory of mind and social impairment in children with conduct disorder. *Brit. J. Develop. Psychol., 14*, 385–98.

Hardy, J. (2004). Toward Alzheimer therapies based on genetic knowledge. *Annu. Rev. Med., 55*, 15–25.

Hare, E. H. (1962). Masturbatory insanity: The history of an idea. *J. Ment. Sci., 108*, 1–25.

Hare, R. D. (1970). *Psychopathy: Theory and research.* New York: Wiley.

Hare, R. D. (1980). A research scale for the assessment of psychopathy in criminal populations. *Personal. Indiv. Diff., 1*, 111–19.

Hare, R. D. (1991). *The Hare psychopathy checklist—Revised.* Toronto: Multi-Health Systems.

Hare, R. D. (1998). Psychopathy, affect and behavior. In D. J. Cooke, A. E. Forth, & R. D. Hare (Eds.), *Psychopathy: Theory, research, and implications for society* (pp. 105–37). Dordrecht, Netherlands: Kluwer Academic Publishers.

Hare, R. D. (2003). *The Hare Psychopathy Checklist Revised* (2nd ed.). Toronto, ON, Canada: Multi-Health Systems.

Hare, R. D., Cooke, D. J., & Hart, S. D. (1999). Psychopathy and sadistic personality disorder. In T. Millon, P. H. Blaney, & R. D. Davis (Eds.), *Oxford textbook of psychopathology* (pp. 555–84). New York: Oxford University Press.

Hare, R. D., McPherson, L. M., & Forth, A. E. (1988). Male psychopaths and their criminal careers. *J. Cons. Clin. Psychol. 56*, 710–14.

Harkness, K. L., & Lumley, M. N. (2008). Child abuse and neglect and the development of depression in children and adolescents. In J. R. Z. Abela & B. L. Hankin (Eds.), *Handbook of depression in children and adolescents.* (pp. 166–88). New York: Guilford Press.

Harkness, K. L., & Monroe, S. M. (2002). Childhood adversity and the endogenous versus nonendogenous distinction in women with major depression. *Am. J. Psychiat., 159*(3), 387–93.

Harkness, K. L., Washburn, D., Theriault, J. E., Lee, L., & Sabbagh, M. A. (2011). Maternal history of depression is associated with enhanced theory of mind in depressed and nondepressed adult women. *Psychiat. Res., 189*(1), 91–96. doi: 10.1016/j.psychres.2011.06.007

Harlow, J. M. (1868). Recovery from the passage of an iron bar through the head. *Publication of the Massachusetts Medical Society, 2*, 327.

Harlow, K. C. (2007). The effectiveness of a problem resolution and brief counseling EAP intervention. *Journal of Workplace Behavioral Health, 22*(1), 1–12.

Harpur, T. J., Hart, S. D., & Hare, R. D. (1993). The personality of the psychopath. In P. T. Costa & T. A. Widiger (Eds.), *Personality disorders and the five-factor model of personality* (pp. 149–73). Washington, DC: American Psychological Association.

Harrington, R., & Clark, A. (1998). Prevention and early intervention for depression in adolescence and early adult life. *Eur. Arch. Psychiat. Clin. Neurosci., 248*(1), 32–45.

Harris, B. (1979). Whatever happened to Little Albert? *Amer. Psychol., 34*, 151–60.

Harris, C. (2011, May 25). Judge: Loughner not competent to stand trial. *The Arizona Republic.*

Harris, G. T., & Rice, M. E. (2006). Treatment of psychopathy: A review of empirical findings. In C. J. Patrick (Ed.), *Handbook of the psychopathy.* (pp. 555–72). New York: Guilford Press.

Harris, J. (2005). The increased diagnosis of "Juvenile Bipolar Disorder": What are we treating? *Psyciatric Services, 56*(5), 529–31.

Harris, J. C. (2006). *Intellectual disability: Understanding its development, causes, classification, evaluation, and treatment.* New York: Oxford University Press.

Harris J. L., Bargh, J. A., & Brownell, K. D. (2009). Priming effects of television food advertising on eating behavior. *Hlth. Psych., 28,* 404–13.

Harris, T., Brown, G. W., & Bifulco, A. (1986). Loss of parent in childhood and adult psychiatric disorder: The role of lack of adequate parental care. *Psychol. Med., 16,* 641–59.

Harrison, B. J., Soriano-Mas, C., Pujol, J., Ortiz, H., López-Solà, M., Hernández-Ribas, R., et al. (2009). Altered corticostriatal functional connectivity in obsessive-compulsive disorder. *Arch. Gen. Psychiat., 66*(11), 1189–1200. doi: 10.1001/archgenpsychiatry.2009.152

Harrison, G., Amin, S., Singh, S. P., Croudace, T., & Jones, P. (1999). Outcome of psychosis in people of Afro-Caribbean family origin. *Brit. J. Psychiat., 175,* 43–49.

Harrison, G., Glazebrook, C., Brewin, J., & Cantwell, R. (1997). Increased incidence of psychotic disorders in migrants from the Caribbean to the United Kingdom. *Psychol. Med., 27*(4), 799–806.

Harrison, G., Hopper, K., Craig, T., Laska, E., Siegel, C., Wanderling, J., Dube, K. C., Ganev, K., Giel, R., An Der Heiden, W., Holmberg, S. K., Janca, A., Lee, P. W. H., León, C. A., Malhotra, S., Marsella, A. J., Nakane, Y., Sartorius, N., Shen, Y., Skoda, C., Thara, R., Tsirkin, S. J., Varma, V. K., Walsh, D., & Wiersma, D. (2001). Recovery from psychotic illness: A 15- and 25-year international follow-up study. *Brit. J. Psychiat., 178,* 506–17.

Harrop, E. N., & Marlatt, G. A. (2010). The comorbidity of substance use disorders and eating disorders in women: Prevalence, etiology, and treatment. *Addict. Behav., 35*(5), 392–98.

Harrow, M., Grossman, L. S., Herbener, E. S., & Davies, E. W. (2000). Ten-year outcome: Patients with schizoaffective disorders, schizophrenia, affective disorders and moodincongruent psychotic symptoms. *Brit. J. Psychiat., 177,* 421–26.

Hart, S. D. (1998). The role of psychopathy in assessing risk for violence: Conceptual and methodological issues. *Legal and Criminological Psychology, 3*(1), 121–37.

Hartmann, D. P., Barrios, B. A., & Wood, D. D. (2004). Principles of behavioral observation. *Comprehensive handbook of psychological assessment* (Vol. 3, pp. 108–27). New York: John Wiley & Sons.

Hartz, S. M., & Bierut, L. J. (2010). Genetics of addictions. *Psychiat. Clin. North., 33*(1), 107–24.

Harvey, A. G. (2008). Sleep and circadian rhythms in bipolar disorder: Seeking synchrony, harmony, and regulation. *Amer. J. Psychiat., 165*(7), 820–29. doi: 10.1176/appi.ajp.2008.08010098

Harvey, A. G., Schmidt, D. A., Scarna, A., Semler, C. N., & Goodwin, G. M. (2005). Sleep-related functioning in euthymic patients with bipolar disorder, patients with insomnia, and subjects without sleep problems. *Amer. J. Psychiat., 162,* 50–57.

Harvey, P. D., Reichenberg, A., & Bowie, C. R. (2006). Cognition and aging in psychopathology: Focus on schizophrenia and depression. *Ann. Rev. Clin. Psych., 2,* 389–409.

Harvey, S. T., & Taylor, J. E. (2010). A meta-analysis of the effects of psychotherapy with sexually abused children and adolescents. *Clin. Psychol. Rev., 30*(5), 517–35.

Harwood, M., & Beutler, L. (2009). Assessessment of clients in pretreatment planning. In J. N. Butcher (Ed.), *Oxford handbook of personality and clinical assessment* (pp. 643–56). New York: Oxford Univesity Press.

Harwood, D., Hawton, K., Hope, T., & Jacoby, R. (2006). Suicide in older people without psychiatric disorder. *Int. J. Ger. Psychiat., 21*(4), 363–67.

Harwood, T. M., Beutler, L. E., Fisher, D., Sandowicz, M., Albanese, A. L., & Baker, M. (1997). Clinical decision making in managed health care. In J. N. Butcher (Ed.), *Personality assessment in managed health care: Using the MMPI-2 in treatment planning* (pp. 15–41). New York: Oxford University Press.

Hasegawa, S., et al. (1997). Physical aging in persons with Down syndrome: Bases on external appearance and diseases. *Japanese Journal of Special Education, 35*(2), 43–49.

Hasin, D. S., Goodwin, R. D., Stinson, F. S., & Grant, B. F. (2005). Epidemiology of major depressive disorder: Results from the National Epidemiologic Survey on Alcoholism and Related Conditions. *Arch. Gen. Psychiat., 62*(10), 1097–1106.

Hasin, D. S., & Katz, H. (2010). Genetic and environmental factors in substance use, abuse, and dependence. In L. Scheier (Ed.), *Handbook of drug use etiology: Theory, methods, and empirical findings* (pp. 247–67). Washington, DC: American Psychological Association.

Hasler, G., Drevets, W. C., Manji, H. K., & Charney, D. S. (2004). Discovering endophenotypes for major depression. *Neuropsychopharmacol., 29*(10), 1765–81.

Hathaway, S. R. (1965). Personality inventories. In B.B. Wolman (Ed.), *Handbook of clinical psychology* (pp. 451–76). New York: McGraw Hill.

Hatta, S. M. (1996). A Malay cross cultural worldview and forensic review of amok. *Austral. NZ J. Psychiat., 30,* 505–10.

Haug Schnabel, G. (1992). Daytime and nighttime enuresis: A functional disorder and its ethological decoding. *Behaviour, 120,* 232–61.

Haugland, G., Sigel, G., Hopper, K., & Alexander, M. J. (1997). Mental illness among homeless individuals in a suburban county. *Psychiat. Serv., 48*(4), 504–9.

Haukkala, A., Konttinen, H., Laatikainen, T., Kawachi, I., & Uutela, A. (2010). Hostility, anger control, and anger expression as predictors of cardiovascular disease. *Psychosom. Med., 72,* 556–562.

Hausman, D. M. (2007). Third-party risks in research: Should IRBS address them? *IRB: Ethics & Human Research, 29*(3),1–5.

Havermans, R., Nicolson, N. A., & DeVries, M. W. (2007). Daily hassles, uplifts, and time use in individuals with bipolar disorder in remission. *J. Nerv. Ment. Dis., 195,* 861–865.

Hawkins, E. H., Cummins, L. H., & Marlatt, G. A. (2004). Preventing substance abuse in American Indian and Alaska Native youth: Promising strategies for healthier communities. *Psychol. Bull., 130,* 304–23.

Hawkins, J. D., Arthur, M. W., & Olson, J. J. (1997). Community interventions to reduce risks and enhance protection against antisocial behavior. In D. M. Stoff, J. Breiling, & J. D. Maser (Eds.), *Handbook of antisocial behavior.* (pp. 365–74). New York: Wiley.

Hawton, K. (2005) *Prevention and treatment of suicidal behavior: From science to practice.* Oxford: Oxford University Press.

Hawton, K., & Harriss, L. (2008). Deliberate self-harm by under-15-year-olds: Characteristics, trends and outcome. *J. Child Psychol. Psychiat., 49*(4), 441–48.

Hawton, K., & Williams, K. (2002). Influences of the media on suicide. *Brit. Med. J., 325,* 1374–75.

Hay, P. J., Mond, J., Buttner, P., & Darby, A. (2008). Eating disorder behaviors are increasing: Findings from two sequential community surveys in South Australia. *PLos ONE, 3*(2), e1541.

Hayama, T. (1999). Trial of the new psychological test MMPI-2 on the chronic schizophrenic patients: Investigation of the basic and content scales. *Kitasato Medicine, 29*(5), 281–97.

Hayden, M. F. (1998). Civil rights litigation for institutionalized persons with mental retardation: A summary. *Mental Retardation, 36*(1), 75–83.

Hayden, M. R. (2000). Predictive testing for Huntington's disease: the calm after the storm. *Lancet, 356,* 1944–45.

Hayes, S. C. (1998). Single case experimental design and empirical clinical practice. In A. E. Kazdin (Ed.), *Methodological issues and strategies in clinical research* (pp. 419–49). Washington, DC: American Psychological Association.

Hayes, S. C., Villatte, M., Levin, M., & Hildebrandt, M. (2011). Open, aware, and active: Contextual approaches as an emerging trend in the behavioral and cognitive therapies. *Ann. Rev. Clin. Psychol., 7,* 141–68.

Haynes, S.,Yoshioka, D. T., Kloezeman, K., & Bello, I. (2009). Behavioral assessment. In J. N. Butcher (Ed.), *Oxford handbook of personality and clinical assessment* (pp. 226–48). New York: Oxford Univesity Press.

Hays, J. T., Hurt, R. D., Rigotti, N. A., Niaura, R., Gonzales, D., Durcan, M. J., Sachs, D. P. L., Wolter, R. D., Buist, A. S., Johnston, J. A., & White, J. D. (2001). Sustained-release bupropion for pharmacologic relapse prevention after smoking cessation. *Ann. Int. Med., 135*(6), 423–33.

Hays, P. A. (2008). *Addressing cultural complexities in practice: Assessment, diagnosis, and therapy* (2nd ed.). Washington, DC: American Psychological Association.

Hayward, C. (2003). Methodological concerns in puberty-related research. In C. Hayward (Ed.), *Gender differences at puberty* (pp. 1–14). New York: Cambridge University Press.

Hayward, C., Killen, J. D., Kraemer, H. C., & Taylor, C. B. (1998). Linking self-reported childhood behavioral inhibition to adolescent social phobia. *J. Amer. Acad. Child Adoles. Psychiat., 37,* 1308–16.

Hayward, C., Killen, J. D., Kraemer, H. C., & Taylor, C. B. (2000). Predictors of panic attacks in adolescents. *J. Amer. Acad. Child Adoles. Psychiat., 39*(2), 207–14.

Hazell, P. (2007). Pharmacological management of attention-deficit hyperactivity disorder in adolescents: Special considerations. *CNS Drugs, 21*(1), 37–46.

Hazlett, E. A., Levine, J., Buchsbaum, M. S., Silverman, J. M., New, A., & Sevin, E. M. (2003). Deficient attentional modulation of the startle response in patients with schizotypal personality disorder. *Amer. J. Psychiat., 160,* 1621–26.

Heaton, R., Paulsen, J. S., McAdams, L. A., Kuck, J., Zisook, S., Braff, D., Harris, M. J., & Jesta, D. V. (1994). Neuropsychological deficits in schizophrenics: Relationship to age, chronicity, and dementia. *Arch. Gen. Psychiat., 51*(6), 469–76.

Hechinger, J., & Chaker, A.M. (2005, March 31). Boarding-school options shift for troubled teens—Shutdown of Brown schools shows challenges of selecting a 'therapeutic' program. *The Wall Street Journal.* http://online.wsj.com.

Hechtman, L. (1996). Attention-deficit hyperactivity disorder. In L. Hechtman (Ed.), *Do they grow out of it?* (pp. 17–38). Washington, DC: American Psychiatric Press.

Heck, A. M., Yanovski, J. A., & Calis, K. A. (2000). Orlistat, a new lipase inhibitor for the management of obesity. *Pharmacotherapy, 20,* 270–79.

Hefez, A. (1985). The role of the press and the medical community in the epidemic of "mysterious gas poisoning" in the Jordan West Bank. *Amer. J. Psychiat., 142,* 833–37.

Heilbrun, K. (2009). Evaluation for risk of violence in adults. New York: Oxford University Press.

Heilbron, N., & Prinstein, M. J. (2010). Adolescent peer victimization, peer status, suicidal ideation, and nonsuicidal self-injury. *Merrill-Palmer Quarterly: Journal of Developmental Psychology, 56*(3), 388–419.

Heim, C., & Nemeroff, C. B. (2001). The role of childhood trauma in the neurobiology of mood and anxiety disorders: Preclinical and clinical studies. *Biol. Psychiat., 49*(12), 1023–39.

Heim, C., Newport, J., Heit, S., Graham, Y., Wilcox, M., Bonsall, R., Miller, A., & Nemeroff, C. (2000). Pituitary- adrenal and autonomic responses to stress in women after sexual and physical abuse in childhood. *JAMA, 284,* 592–96.

Heiman, J. R. (1980). Female sexual response patterns. Interactions of physiological, affective, and contextual cues. *Arch. Gen. Psychiat., 37,* 1311–16.

Heiman, J. R. (2002). Psychologic treatments for female sexual dysfunction: Are they effective and do we need them? *Arch. Sex. Behav., 31,* 445–50.

Heimberg, R. G. (2002). Cognitive-behavioral therapy for social anxiety disorder: Current status and future directions. *Biol. Psychiat., 51,* 101–8.

Heinrichs, R. W. (2001). *In search of madness: Schizophrenia and neuroscience.* New York: Oxford University Press.

Helder, S. G., & Collier, D. A. (2010). The genetics of eating disorders. *Current Topics in Behavioral Neurosciences, 6,* DOI: 10.1007/7854_2010_79

Helfling, K. (2011, Apr. 16). Iraq, Afghan war veteran who epitomized recovery kills self. *Boston Globe.*

Helgeson, V. C. (2002). *The psychology of gender.* NJ: Pearson.

Heller, T., Miller, A. B., & Factor, A. (1997). Adults with mental retardation as supports to their parents: Effects on parental caregiving appraisal. *Mental Retardation, 35*(5), 338–46.

Helzer, J. E., Canino, G. J., Yeh, E. K., Bland, R., et al. (1990). Alcoholism—North America and Asia: A comparison of population surveys with the Diagnostic Interview Schedule. *Arch. Gen. Psychiat., 47*(4), 313–19.

Hemphill, J. F., Templeman, T., Wong, S., & Hare, R. D. (1998). Psychopathy and crime: Recidivism and criminal careers. In D. J. Cooke, A. E. Forth, & R. D. Hare (Eds.), *Psychopathy: Theory, research, and implications for society* (pp. 375–99). Dordrecht, Netherlands: Kluwer Academic Publishers.

Hendricks, P. S., & Thompson, J. K. (2005). An integration of cognitive-behavioral therapy and interpersonal therapy for bulimia nervosa: A case study using the case formulation method. *Int. J. Eat. Dis., 37,* 171–74.

Hendrie, H. C. (1998). Epidemiology of dementia and Alzheimer's disease. *Amer. J. Geriat. Psychiat., 6,* 3–18.

Henriques, J. B., & Davidson, R. J. (1990). Regional brain electrical asymmetries discriminate between previously depressed and healthy control subjects. *J. Abn. Psychol., 99,* 22–31.

Henry, W. P., Strupp, H. H., Schacht, T. E., & Gaston, L. (1994). Psychodynamic approaches. In A. E. Bergin & S. L. Garfield (Eds.), *Handbook of psychotherapy and behavior change* (4th ed., pp. 467–508). New York: Wiley.

Henshaw, C., Foreman, D., & Cox, J. (2004). Postnatal blues: A risk factor for postnatal depression. *J. Psychosom. Obst. Gyn., 25*(3–4), 267–72.

Herdt, G. (2000). Why the Sambia initiate boys before age 10. In J. Bancroft, (Ed.), *The role of theory in sex research.* pp. 82–109. Bloomington: Indiana University Press.

Herdt, G., & Stoller, R. G. (1990). *Intimate communications: Erotics and the study of a culture.* New York: Columbia University Press.

Herek, G. M., & Garnets, L. D. (2007). Sexual orientation and mental health. *Ann. Rev. Clin. Psych., 3,* 353–75.

Herman, J. L. (1993, Mar./Apr.). The abuses of memory. *Mother Jones, 18,* 3–4.

Hermann, D. H. J. (1990). Autonomy, self determination, the right of involuntarily committed persons to refuse treatment, and the use of substituted judgment in medication decisions involving incompetent persons. *International Journal of Law and Psychiatry, 13,* 361–85.

Herman-Stahl, M., & Peterson, A. C. (1999). Depressive symptoms during adolescence: Direct and stress-buffering effects of coping, control beliefs, and family relationships. *Journal of Applied Developmental Psychology, 120,* 45–62.

Heron, M. (2011). Deaths: Leading causes for 2007. *National vital statistics reports: from the Centers for Disease Control and Prevention, National Center for Health Statistics, National Vital Statistics System, 59*(8), 1–95.

Hertel, P. T., & Brozovich, F. (2010). Cognitive habits and memory distortions in anxiety and depression. *Curr. Dir. Psychol. Sci., 19*(3), 155–60. doi: 10.1177/09637214103/0137

Hertel, P. T., Brozovich, F., Joormann, J., & Gotlib, I. H. (2008). Biases in interpretation and memory in generalized social phobia. *J. Abn. Psychol., 117*(2), 278–88. doi: 10.1037/0021-843x.117.2.278

Heshka, S., Anderson, J. W., Atkinson, R. L., Greenway, F. L., & Hill, J. O., et al. (2003). Weight loss with self-help compared with a structured commercial program: A randomized trial. *JAMA, 289,*1792–98.

Heshka, S., Greenway, F., Anderson, J. W., Atkinson, R. L., Hill, J. O., Phinney, S. D., Miller-Kovach, K., & Pi-Sunyer, F. X. (2000). Self-help weight loss versus a structured commercial program after 26 weeks: A randomized controlled study. *Amer. J. Med., 109,* 282–87.

Hesketh, T., Ding, Q. J., & Jenkins, R. (2002). Suicide ideation in Chinese adolescents. *Soc. Psychiat. & Psychiatr. Epidemiol., 37*(5), 230–35.

Heston, L. (1966). Psychiatric disorders in foster home reared children of schizophrenic mothers. *Brit. J. Psychiat., 112,* 819–25.

Hetherington, E. M. (1991). The role of individual differences and family relationships in children's coping with divorce and remarriage. In P. S. Cowan & E. M. Hetherington (Eds.), *Family transitions* (pp. 165–94). Hillsdale, NJ: Erlbaum.

Hetherington, E. M. (1998). Relevant issues in developmental science: Introduction to the special series. *Amer. Psychol., 53*(2), 93–95.

Hetherington, E. M. (1999). *Coping with divorce, single parenting, and remarriage: A risk and resilience perspective.* Mahwah, NJ: Lawrence Erlbaum Associates.

Hetherington, E. M. (2003a). Intimate pathways: Changing patterns in close personal relationships across time. *Family Relations: Interdisciplinary Journal of Applied Family Studies, 52*(4), 318–31.

Hetherington, E. M. (2003b). Social support and the adjustment of children in divorced and remarried families. *Childhood: A Global Journal of Child Research, 10*(2), 217–36.

Hetherington, E. M., & Parke, R. D. (1993). *Child psychology: A contemporary viewpoint* (4th ed.). New York: McGraw Hill.

Hetherington, E. M., Bridges, M., & Insabella, G. (1998). What matters? What does not? Five perspectives on the association between marital transitions and children's adjustment. *Amer. Psychol., 53,* 167–84.

Hetherington, E. M., Stanley-Hagan, M., & Anderson, E. R. (1989). Marital transitions: A child's perspective. *Amer. Psychol., 44,* 303–12.

Hettema, J. M., Annas, P., Neale, M. C., Kendler, K. S., & Fredrikson, M. (2003). A twin study of the genetics of fear conditioning. *Arch. Gen. Psychiat., 60*(7), 702–8.

Hettema, J. M., Neale, M. C., & Kendler, K.S. (1995) Physical similarity and the equal-environment assumption in twin studies of psychiatric disorders. *Behavior Genetics, 25,* 327–35.

Hettema, J. M., Neale, M. C., & Kendler, K. S. (2001). A review and meta-analysis of the genetic epidemiology of anxiety disorders. *Amer. J. Psych., 158*(10), 1568–78.

Hettema, J. M., Prescott, C. A., & Kendler, K. S. (2001). A population-based twin study of generalized anxiety disorder in men and women. *J. Nerv. Ment. Dis., 189,* 413–20.

Hettema, J. M., Prescott, C. A., & Kendler, K. S. (2004). Genetic and environmental sources of covariation between generalized anxiety disorder and neuroticism. *Amer. J. Psych., 161*(9), 1581–87.

Hettema, J. M., Prescott, C. A., Myers, J. M., Neale, M. C., & Kendler, K. S. (2005). The structure of genetic and environmental risk factors for anxiety disorders in men and women. *Arch. Gen. Psychiat., 62*(2), 182–89.

Hettema, J., Steele, J., & Miller, W. R. (2005). Motivational interviewing. *Annu. Rev. Clin. Psychol., 1,* 91–111.

HEW. (1978). *The third report on alcohol and health.* United States Department of Public Health. Washington, DC: U.S. Government Printing Office.

Heyman, A., Wilkinson, W. E., Stafford, J. A., Helms, M. J., Sigmon, A. H., & Weinberg, T. (1984). Alzheimer's disease: A study of epidemiological aspects. *Ann. Neurol., 15,* 335–41.

Heymsfield, S. B., Allison, D. B., Heshka, S., & Pierson, R. N. (1995). Assessment of human body composition. In D. B. Allison et al. (Eds.), *Handbook of assessment methods for eating behaviors and weight-related problems: Measures, theory, research* (pp. 515–60). Thousand Oaks, CA: Sage.

Hibbard, S. (2003). A critique of Lilienfeld et al.'s "The scientific status of projective techniques." *J. Pers. Assess., 80,* 260–71.

Hibell, B., Anderson, B., Ahlstrom, S., Balakireva, O., Bjaranson, T., Kokkevi, A., & Morgan, M. (2000). *The 1999 ESPAD Report: Alcohol and other drugs among students in 30 European countries.* Stockholm: Swedish Council for Information on Alcohol and Drug Abuse.

Hicks, B., Krueger, R., Iacono, W., McGue, M., & Patrick, C. (2004). Family transmission and heritability of externalizing disorders: A twin family study. *Arch. Gen. Psychiat., 61,* 922–28.

Hiday, V. A., & Burns, P. J. (2010). Mental illness and the criminal justice system. In T. L. Scheid & T. N. Brown (Eds.), *A handbook for the study of mental health: Social contexts, theories, and systems* (2nd ed., pp. 478–98). New York: Cambridge University Press.

Higgins, J. W., Williams, R. L., & McLaughlin, T. F. (2001). The effects of a token economy employing instructional consequences for a third-grade student with learning disabilities: A data-based case study. *Education and Treatment of Children, 24,* 99–106.

Higgins, S. T., Badger, G. J., & Budney, A. J. (2000). Initial abstinence and success in achieving longer term cocaine abstinence. *Exp. Clin. Psychopharm., 8*(3), 377–86.

Higgins, S. T., Wong, C. J., Badger, G. J., Haug Ogden, D. E. H., & Dantona, R. L. (2000). Contingent reinforcement increases cocaine abstinence during outpatient treatment and 1 year of follow-up. *J. Cons. Clin. Psychol., 68*(1), 64–72.

Higuci, S. S., Matsushita, H., Imazeki, T., Kinoshita, T., Takagi, S., & Kono, H. (1994). Aldehyde dehydrogenase genotypes in Japanese alcoholics. *Lancet, 343,* 741–42.

Hijii, T. et al. (1997). Life expectancy and social adaptation in individuals with Down syndrome with and without surgery for congenital heart disease. *Clin. Pediat., 36*(6), 327–32.

Hill, A. J. (2002). Prevalence and demographics of dieting. In C. G. Fairburn & K. D. Brownell (Eds.), *Eating disorders and obesity: A comprehensive handbook* (2nd ed., pp. 80–83). New York: Guilford.

Hill, C. E., & Lambert, M. J. (2004). Methodological issues in studying psychotherapy process and outcomes. In M. J. Lambert (Ed.), *Bergin and Garfield's handbook of psychotherapy and behavior change.* (pp. 84–135). New York: John Wiley and Sons.

Hill, J. O., Wyatt, H. R., Reed, G. W., & Peters, J. C. (2003, Feb. 7). Obesity and the environment: Where do we go from here? *Science, 299,* 853–55.

Hiller, W., Fichter, M. M., & Rief, W. (2003). A controlled treatment study of somatoform disorders including analysis of health-care utilization and cost-effectiveness. *J. Psychosom. Res., 54,* 369–80.

Hiller, W., Kroymann, R., Leibbrand, R., Cebulla, M., Korn, H. J., Rief, W., et al. (2004). Effects and cost-effectiveness analysis of inpatient treatment for somatoform disorders. *Fortschritte der Neurologie, Psychiatrie, 72*(3), 136–46.

Hillman, J., Snyder, S., & Neubrander, J. (2007). *Childhood autism: A clinician's guide to early diagnosis and integrated treatment.* New York: Routledge/Taylor & Francis Group.

Hines, M. (2004). *Brain gender.* New York: Oxford University Press.

Hing, N., & Breen, H. (2001). Profiling lady luck: An empirical study of gambling and problem gambling amongst female club members. *Journal of Gambling Studies, 17*(1), 47–69.

Hinrichsen, G. A., & Niederehe, G. (1994). Dementia management strategies and adjustment of family members of older patients. *Gerontologist, 34*(1), 95–102.

Hinshaw, S. F., Zupan, B. A., Simmel, C., & Nigg, J. T. (1997). Peer status in boys with and without attentiondeficit hyperactivity disorder: Predictions from overt and covert antisocial behavior, social isolation, and authoritative parents. *Child Develop., 68*(5), 880–96.

Hinshaw, S. P. (1994). Conduct disorder in childhood: Conceptualization, diagnosis, comorbidity, and risk status for antisocial functioning in adulthood. In D. C. Fowles, P. Sutker, & S. H. Goodman (Eds.), *Progress in experimental personality and psychopathology research.* New York: Springer.

Hinshaw, S. P., Carte, E. T., Fan, C., Jassy, J. S., & Owens, E. B. (2007). Neuropsyuchological functioning of girls with attention-Deficit-Hyperactivity Disorder followed prospectively into adolescence: Evidence for continuing deficits. *Neuropsych., 21,* 263–73.

Hinton, D. E., Chong, R., Pollack, M. H., Barlow, D. H., & McNally, R. J. (2008). Ataque de nervios: Relationship to anxiety sensitivity and dissociation predisposition. *Depression and Anxiety, 25*(6), 489–95. doi: 10.1002/da.20309

Hinton, D. E., Hufford, D. J., & Kirmayer, L. J. (2005). Culture and sleep paralysis. *Transcult. Psychiat., 42*(1), 5–10.

Hinton, D. E., Lewis-Fernández, R., & Pollack, M. H. (2009). A model of the generation of ataque de nervios: The role of fear of negative affect and fear of arousal symptoms. *CNS Neuroscience & Therapeutics, 15*(3), 264–75. doi: 10.1111/j.1755-5949.2009.00101.x

Hinton, D. E., Park, L., Hsia, C., Hofmann, S., & Pollack, M. H. (2009). Anxiety disorder presentations in Asian populations: a review. *CNS Neuroscience & Therapeutics, 15*(3), 295–303. doi: 10.1111/j.1755-5949.2009.00095.x

Hiroto, D. S., & Seligman, M. E. P. (1975). Generality of learned helplessness in man. *J. Pers. Soc. Psychol., 31*(2), 311–27.

Hirsch, C. R., Clark, D. M., & Mathews, A. (2006). Imagery and interpretations in social phobia: Support for the combined cognitive biases hypothesis. *Behavior Therapy, 37*(3), 223–36.

Hirsch, C. R., Meynen, T., & Clark, D. M. (2004). Negative self-imagery in social anxiety contaminates social interactions. *Memory, 12*(4), 496–506.

Hirsch, C., Clark, D. M., Mathews, A., & Williams, R. (2003). Self-images play a causal role in social phobia. *Behav. Res. Ther., 41*(8), 909–21.

Hirsch, S. R., & Leff, J. P. (1975). *Abnormalities in parents of schizophrenics.* London: Oxford University Press.

Hirschfeld, M. (1948). *Sexual anomalies* (p. 167). New York: Emerson.

Hirschfeld, R. M. A. (1996). Panic disorder: Diagnosis, epidemiology, and clinical course. *J. Clin. Psychiat., 57*(10), 3–8.

Hirshfeld-Becker, D. R., Biederman, J., Henin, A., Faraone, S. V., Davis, S., Harrington, K., et al. (2007). Behavioral inhibition in preschool children at risk is a specific.predictor of middle childhood social anxiety: A five-year follow-up. *Journal of Developmental & Behavioral Pediatrics, 28*(3), 225–33.

Hirshfeld-Becker, D. R., Masek, B., Henin, A., Blakely, L. R., Pollock-Wurman, R.A., McQuade, J., DePetrillo, L., Briesch, J., Ollendick, T. H., Rosenbaum, J. F., & Biederman, J. (2010). Cognitive behavioral therapy for 4- to 7-year-old children with anxiety disorders: A randomized clinical trial. *J. Cons. Clin. Psychol., 78*(4), 498–510.

Hirvonen, J., van Erp, T. G., Huttunen, J., et al. (2005). Increased caudate dopamine D2 receptor availability as a genetic marker for schizophrenia. *Arch. Gen. Psychiat., 62,* 371–78.

Hlastala, S. A., Frank, E., Kowalski, J., Sherrill, J. T., Tu, X. M., Anderson, B., et al. (2000). Stressful life events, bipolar disorder, and the 'kindling model'. *J. Abn. Psych., 109*(4), 777–86.

Ho, B-C., Andreasen, N. C., Ziebell, S., Pierson, R., & Magnotta, V. (2011). Long-term antipsychotic treatment and brain volumes: A longitudinal study of first-episode schizophrenia. *Arch. Gen. Psychiat., 68,* 128–37.

Hobfoll, S., Ritter, C., Lavin, J., Hulsizer, M., et al. (1995). Depression prevalence and incidence among inner-city pregnant and postpartum women. *J. Cons. Clin. Psychol., 3,* 445–53.

Hodgins, D. C., & el-Guebaly, N. (2004). Retrospective and prospective reports of precipitants to relapse in pathological gambling. *J. Cons. Clin. Psychol., 72,* 72–80.

Hodgins, S. (1987). Men found unfit to stand trial and/or guilty by reason of insanity: Recidivism. *Canadian Journal of Criminology, 1,* 51–70.

Hodgins, S., & Lalonde, N. (1999). Major mental disorders and crime: Changes over time? In P. Cohen, C. Slomkowski, et al. (Eds.), *Historical and geographical influences on psychopathology* (pp. 57–83). Mahwah, NJ: Erlbaum.

Hoek, H. W. (2002). Distribution of eating disorders. In C. G. Fairburn & K. D. Brownell (Eds.), *Eating disorders and obesity: A comprehensive handbook* (2nd ed., pp. 233–37). New York: Guilford.

Hoek, H. W., & van Hoecken, D. (2003). Review of the prevalence and incidence of eating disorders. *Int. J. Eat. Dis., 34,* 383–96.

Hoeve, M., Dubas, J. S., Eichelsheim, V. I., van der Laan, P. H., Smeenk, W., & Gerris, J. R. M. (2009). The relationship between parenting and delinquency: A meta-analysis. *J. Abn. Child Psychol., 37*(6), 749–75. doi:10.1007/s10802-009-9310-8

Hofer, S. M., Christensen, H., Mackinnon, A., Korten, A. E., Jorm, A. F., Henderson, A. F., & Easteal, S. (2002). Change in cognitive functioning associated with ApoE genotype in a community sample of older adults. *Psychol. Aging, 17*(2), 194–208.

Hoff, A. L., Riordan, H., O'Donnell, D. W., Morris, L., & DeLisi, L. E. (1992). Neuropsychological functioning of first-episode schizphreniform patients. *Amer. J. Psychiat., 149,* 898–903.

Hoff, A. L., Sakamura, M., Razi, K., Heyderbrand, G., Csernansky, J. G., & DeLisi, L. E. (2000). Lack of association between duration of untreated illness and severity of cognitive and structural brain deficits at the first episode of schizophrenia. *Amer. J. Psychiat., 157,* 1824–28.

Hoffman, A. (1971). LSD discoverer disputes "chance" factor in finding. *Psychiat. News, 6*(8), 23–26.

Hoffman, R. E., Gueorguieva, R., Hawkins, K. A., Varanko, M., Boutros, N. N., Wu, Y.-T., Carroll, K., & Krystal, J. H. (2005). Temporoparietal transcranial magnetic stimulation for auditory hallucinations: Safety, efficacy and moderators in a fifty patient sample. *Biol. Psychiat., 58,* 97–104.

Hofman, S. G., Meuret, A. E., Smits, J. A., Simon, N. M., Pollack, M. H., Eisenmenger, K., Shiekh, M., & Otto, M. W. (2006). Augmentation of exposure therapy with D-cycloserine for social anxiety disorder. *Arch. Gen. Psychiat., 63,* 298–304.

Hogarty, G. E., Anderson, C. M., Reiss, D. J., Kornblith, S. J., Greenwald, D. P., Javna, C. D., & Madonia, M. J. (1986). Family psychoeducation, social skills training, and maintenance chemotherapy in the aftercare treatment of schizophrenia. *Arch. Gen. Psychiat., 43,* 633–42.

Hogarty, G. E., et al. (1997a). Three-year trials of personal therapy among schizophrenic patients living with or independent of family: I. Description of study and effects on relapse rate. *Amer. J. Psychiat., 154*(11), 1504–13.

Hogarty, G. E., et al. (1997b). Three-year trials of personal therapy among schizophrenic patients living with or independent of family, II: Effects on adjustment of patients. *Amer. J. Psychiat., 154*(11), 1514–24.

Hoge, C. W., Castro, C. A., Messer, S. C., McGurk, D., Cotting, D. I., & Koffman, R. L. (2004). Combat duty in Iraq and Afghanistan, mental health problems, and barriers to care. *N. Engl. J. Med., 351,* 13–32.

Hoge, C. W., McGurk, TD., Thomas, J. L., Cox, A. L., Engel, C. C., & Castro, C. A. (2008). Mild traumatic brain injury in soldiers returning from Iraq. *New England Journal of Medicine, 358,* 453–463.

Hollander, E., Buchalter, A. J., & DeCaria, C. M. (2000). Pathological gambling. *Psychiat. Clin. N. Amer., 23*(3), 626–42.

Holliday, J., Wall, E., Treasure, J., & Weinman, J. (2005). Perceptions of illness in individuals with anorexia nervosa: A comparison with lay men and women. *Int. J. Eat. Dis., 37,* 50–56.

Hollister, J. M., Laing, P., & Mednick, S. A. (1996). Rhesus incompatibility as a risk factor for schizophrenia in male adults. *Arch. Gen. Psychiat., 53,* 19–24.

Hollon, S. D., & Beck, A. T. (1994). Cognitive and cognitive-behavioral therapies. In A. E. Bergin & S. L.Garfield (Eds.), *Handbook of psychotherapy and behavior change* (4th ed., pp. 428–66). New York: Wiley.

Hollon, S. D., & Beck, A. T. (2004). Cognitive and cognitive behavioral therapies. In M. J. Lambert (Ed.), *Bergin and Garfield's handbook of psychotherapy and behavior change.* (pp. 447–52). New York: John Wiley and Sons.

Hollon, S. D., & Fawcett, J. (1995). Combined medication and psychotherapy. In G. O. Gabbard (Ed.), *Treatments of psychiatric disorders* (Vol. 1., 2nd ed., pp. 1221–36). Washington, DC: American Psychiatric Press.

Hollon, S. D., DeRubeis, R. J., & Evans, M. D. (1987). Causal mediation of change in treatment for depression: Discriminating between nonspecificity and noncausality. *Psychol. Bull., 102,* 139–49.

Hollon, S. D., DeRubeis, R. J., Shelton, R. C., Amsterdam, J. D., Salomon, R. M., O'Reardon, J. P., et al. (2005). Prevention of relapse following cognitive therapy vs medications in moderate to severe depression. *Arch. Gen. Psychiat., 62,* 417–22.

Hollon, S. D., & Dimidjian, S. (2009). Cognitive and behaviors treatment of depression. In I. H. Gotlib & C. L. Hammen (Eds.), *Handbook of depression and its treatment* (2nd ed.). New York: Guilford Press.

Hollon, S. D., Evans, M., & DeRubeis, R. (1990). Cognitive mediation of relapse prevention following treatment for depression: Implications of differential risk. In R. Ingram (Ed.), *Psychological aspects of depression.* New York: Plenum.

Hollon, S. D., Haman, K. L., & Brown, L. L. (2002). Cognitive-behavioral treatment of depression. In I. H. Gotlib & C. L. Hammen (Eds.), *Handbook of depression* (pp. 383–403). New York: Guilford.

Hollon, S. D., & Ponniah, K. (2010). A review of empirically supported psychological therapies for mood disorders in adults. *Depression and Anxiety, 27*(10), 891–32. doi: 10.1002/da.20741

Hollon, S. D., Stewart, M. O., & Strunk, D. (2006). Enduring effects for cognitive behavior therapy in the treatment of depression and anxiety. *Annu. Rev. Psychol., 57,* 285–315.

Hollon, S. D., Thase, M. E., & Markowitz, J. C. (2002). Treatment and prevention of depression. *Psychol. Sci. in the Pub. Int., 3*(2, suppl.), 39–77.

Holma, K. M., Melartin, T. K., Haukka, J., Holma, I. A., Sokero, T. P., & Isometsa, E. T. (2010). Incidence and predictors of suicide attempts in DSM-IV major depressive disorder: A five-year prospective study. *Amer. J. Psychiat., 167*(7), 801–8. doi: 10.1176/appi.ajp.2010.09050627

Holmes, D. L. (2003). *Autism through the Lifespan: The Eden Model.* New York: Woodbine House.

Holmes, E. A., James, E. L., Coode-Bate, T., & Deeprose, C. (2009). Can playing the computer game "Tetris" reduce the build-up of flashbacks for trauma? A proposal from cognitive science. PLoSONE, 4(1): e4153. doi:10.1371/journal.pone.0004153

Holmes, E. A., James, E. L., Kilford, E. J., & Deeprose, C. (2010). Key steps in developing a cognitive vaccine against traumatic flashbacks: Visuospatial Tetris versus verbal pub quiz. *PLos ONE, 5,* e13706.

Holmes, T. H., & Rahe, R. H. (1967). The social readjustment rating scale. *J. Psychosom. Res., 11*(2), 213–18.

Holroyd, K. A. (2002). Assessment and psychological management of recurrent headache disorders. *J. Cons. Clin. Psychol., 70*(3), 656–77.

Holsboer, F. (1992). The hypothalamic-pituitary-adreno-cortical system. In E. S. Paykel (Ed.), *Handbook of affective disorders* (2nd ed.). New York: Guilford.

Holsinger, T., Steffens, D. C., Helms, P. C., Havlik, R. J., Bretiner, J. C., Guralnik, J. M., & Plassman, B. L. (2002). Head injury in early adulthood and the lifetime risk of depression. *Arch. Gen. Psychiat., 59*(1), 17–22.

Holvey, D. N., & Talbott, J. H. (Eds.). (1972). *The Merck manual of diagnosis and therapy* (12th ed.). Rahway, NJ: Merck, Sharp, & Dohme Research Laboratories.

Holzbeck, E. (1996). Thiamine absorption in alcoholic delirium patients. *J. Stud. Alcoh., 57*(6), 581–84.

Holzer, C. E., Goldsmith, H. F., & Ciarlo, J. A. (1998). Effects of rural-urban county type on the availability of health and mental health care providers. In R. W. Manderscheid & M. J. Henderson (Eds.), *Mental health, United States.* Rockville, MD: Center for Mental Health Services.

Honkonen, T., Karlsson, H., Koivisto, A. M., Stengård, E., & Salokangas, R. K. R. (2003). Schizophrenic patients in different treatment settings during the era of deinstitutionalization: Three-year follow-up of three discharge cohorts in Finland. *Austral. N.Z. J. Psychiat., 37*(2), 160–68.

Hooker, E. (1957). The adjustment of the male overt homosexual. *Journal of Projective Techniques, 21,* 18–30.

Hooley, J. M. (2007). Expressed emotion and relapse of psychopathology. *Annu. Rev. Clin. Psychol., 3,* 329–352.

Hooley, J. M. (2008). Interpersonal functioning and schizophrenia. In T. Millon, P. Blaney, & R. Davis, (Eds.), *Oxford Textbook of Psychopathology* (2nd ed.). New York: Oxford University Press.

Hooley, J. M. (2010). Social factors in schizophrenia. *Curr. Dir. Psych. Sci., 19,* 238–42.

Hooley, J. M., & Campbell, C. (2002). Control and controllability: Beliefs and behavior in high and low expressed emotion relatives. *Psychol. Med., 32*(6), 1091–99.

Hooley, J. M., Cole, S. H., & Gironde, S. (in press) Borderline personality disorder. In T. Widiger (Ed.), *The Oxford handbook of personality disorders.* Oxford: Oxford University Press.

Hooley, J. M., & Gotlib, I. H. (2000). A diathesis-stress conceptualization of expressed emotion and clinical outcome. *App. Prev. Psychol., 9,* 135–51.

Hooley, J. M., Gruber, S. A., Parker, H., Guillaumot, J., Rogowska, J., & Yurgelun-Todd, D. A. (2009). Cortico-limbic response to personally-challenging emotional stimuli after complete recovery from major depression. *Psychiatry Research: Neuroimaging, 171*(2), 106–19.

Hooley, J. M., Gruber, S. A., Parker, H. A., Guillaumot, J., Rogowska, J., & Yurgelun-Todd, D. A. (2010). Neural processing of emotional overinvolvement in borderline personality disorder. *J. Clin. Psychiat., 71,* 1017–24.

Hooley, J. M., & Hiller, J. B. (2001). Family relationships and major mental disorder: Risk factors and preventive strategies. In B. R. Sarason & S. Duck (Eds.), *Personal relationships: Implications for clinical and community psychology* (pp 61–87). New York: Wiley.

Hooley, J. M., Rosen, L. R., & Richters, J. E. (1995). Expressed emotion: Toward clarification of a critical construct. In G. Miller (Ed.), *The behavioral high-risk paradigm in psychopathology* (pp. 88–120). New York: Springer.

Hopfer, C., Mendelson, B., Van Leeuwen, J. M., Kelly, S., & Hooks, S. (2006). Club drug use among youths in treatment for substance abuse. *The American Journal on Addictions, 15*(1), 94–99.

Horn, S. D. (2003). Limiting access to psychiatric services can increase total health care costs. *Drug Benefit Trends, 15*(Suppl. I), 12–18.

Horner, A. J. (2005). *Dealing with resistance in psychotherapy.* New York: Jason Aronson.

Hornish, G. G., & Leonard, K. E. (2007). The drinking partnership and marital satisfaction: The longitudinal influence of discrepant drinking. *J. Cons. Clin. Psych., 75,* 43–51.

Horowitz, J. L., & Garber, J. (2006). The prevention of depressive symptoms in children and adolescents: A meta-analytic review. *J. Cons. Clin. Psychol., 74,* 401–15.

Horowitz, J. L., Garber, J., Ciesla, J. A., Young, J. F., & Mufson, L. (2007). Prevention of depressive symptoms in adolescents: A randomized trial of cognitive-behavioral and interpersonal prevention programs. *J. Cons. Clin. Psychol., 75,* 693–706.

Horowitz, M. J., Merluzzi, R. V., Ewert, M., Ghannam, J. H., Harley, D., & Stinson, C. H. (1991). Role-relationship models of configuration (RRMC). In M. Horowitz (Ed.), *Person schemas and maladaptive interpersonal patterns* (pp. 115–54). Chicago: University of Chicago Press.

Horton, A. M. Jr. (2008). The Halstead-Reitan Neuropsychological Test Battery: Past, present, and future. In A. M. Horton, Jr., & D. Wedding (Eds.), *The neuropsychology handbook* (3rd ed., pp. 251–78). New York: Springer.

Horton, R. S., Bleau, G., & Drwecki, B. (2006). Parenting narcissus: What are the links between parenting and narcissism? *J. Pers., 74,* 345–76.

Hörz, S., Zanarini, M. C., Frankenburg, F. R., Reich, D. B., & Fitzmaurice, G. (2010). Ten-year use of mental health services by patients with borderline personality disorder and with other axis II disorders. *Psychiat. Serv., 61*(6), 612–6. doi:10.1176/appi.ps.61.6.612

Hoste, R. R., Hewell, K., & le Grange, D. (2007). Family interaction among white and ethnic minority adolescents with bulimia nervosa and their parents. *European Eating Disorders Review, 15,* 152–58.

Houtjes, W., van Meijel, B., Deeg, D. J. H., & Beekman, A. T. F. (2010). Major depressive disorder in late life: A multifocus perspective on care needs. *Aging & Mental Health, 14*(7), 874–80.

Houts, A. C., Berman, J. S., & Abramson, H. (1994). Effectiveness of psychological and pharmacological treatments for nocturnal enuresis. *J. Cons. Clin. Psychol., 62,* 737–45.

Howland, R. H., & Thase, M. E. (1999). Affective disorders: Biological aspects. In T. Millon, P. H. Blaney, et al. (Eds.), *Oxford textbook of psychopathology. Oxford textbooks in clinical psychology* (Vol. 4., pp. 166–202). New York: Oxford University Press.

Hoza, B., Mrug, S., Gerdes, A. C., Hinshaw, S. P., Bukowski, W. M., Gold, J. A., Kraemer, H. C., Pelham, W. E., Wigal, T., & Arnold, L. E. (2005). What aspects of peer relationships are impaired in children with Attention Deficit/Hyperactivity Disorder? *J. Cons. Clin. Psychol., 73,* 411–23.

Hsu, L. K., Benotti, P. N., Dwyer, J., Roberts, S. B., Saltzman, E., Shikora, S., et al. (1998). Nonsurgical factors that influence the outcome of bariatric surgery: A review. *Psychosom. Med., 60,* 338–46.

Hu, X.-Z., Rush, A. J., Charney, D., Wilson, A. F., Sorant, A. J. M., Papanicolaou, G. J., Fava, M. et al. (2007). Association between a functional serotonin transporter promoter polymorphism and citalopram treatment in adult outpatients with major depression. *Arch. Gen. Psychiat., 64,* 783–92.

Huang, P. P. (2003). Roller coaster headaches revisited. *Surg. Neurol., 60,* 398–401.

Huber, K., & Tamminga, C. A. (2007). Fragile X syndrome: Molecular mechanisms of cognitive dysfunction. *Amer. J. Psychiat., 164*(4), 556.

Hucker, S. J. (1997). Sexual sadism: Psychopathology and theory. In D. R. Laws & W. O'Donohue (Eds.), *Sexual deviance: Theory, assessment, and treatment* (pp. 210–24). New York: Guilford.

Hudson, J. I., Hiripi, E., Pope, H. G., & Kessler, R. C. (2007). The prevalence and correlates of eating disorders in the National Comorbidity Survey Replication. *Biol. Psychiat., 61*(3) 348–58.

Hudson, J. L., & Rapee, R. M. (2001). Parent-child interactions and anxiety disorders: An observational study. *Behav. Res. Ther., 39*(12), 1411–27.

Hudson, J. L., & Rapee, R. M. (2009). Familial and social environments in the etiology and maintenance of anxiety disorders. In M. M. Antony & M. B. Stein (Eds.), *Oxford handbook of anxiety and related disorders* (pp. 173–89). New York: Oxford University Press.

Hudson, S. M., & Ward, T. (1997). Rape: Psychopathology and theory. In D. R. Laws & W. O'Donohue (Eds.), *Sexual deviance: Theory, assessment and treatment* (pp. 332–55). New York: Guilford Press.

Huefner, J. C., James, S., Ringle, J., Thompson, R. W., & Daly, D. L. (2010). Patterns of movement for youth within an integrated continuum of residential services. *Children and Youth Services Review, 32*(6), 857–64.

Huey, S. J., & Henggeler, S. W. (2001). Effective community based interventions for antisocial and delinquent adolescents. In J. H. Hughes, A. M. La Greca, & J. C. Conoley (Eds.), *Handbook of psychological services for children and adolescents* (pp. 301–22). Oxford: Oxford University Press.

Hughes, A. L. (1992). The prevalence of illicit drug use in six metropolitan areas in the United States: Results from the 1991 National Household Survey on Drug Abuse. *Brit. J. Addict., 87,* 1481–85.

Hughes, J. R. (2007). Measurement of the effects of abstinence from tobacco: A qualitative review. *Psych. Addict. Behav., 21*(2), 127–37.

Hulshoff Pol, H. E., & Kahn, R. S. (2008). What happens after the first episode? A review of progressive brain changes in chronically ill patients with schizophrenia. *Schizo. Bull., 34,* 354–66.

Hummelen, B., Wilberg, T., Pedersen, G., & Karterud, S. (2007). The relationship between avoidant personality disorder and social phobia. *Compr. Psychiat., 48,* 348–56.

Humphreys, K., & Rappaport, J. (1993). From community mental health movement to the war on drugs: A study of the definition of social problems. *Amer. Psychol., 48*(8), 892–901.

Humphry, D., & Wickett, A. (1986). *The right to die: Understanding euthanasia.* New York: Harper & Row.

Hunkeler, E. M., Spector, W. D., Fireman, B., Rice, D. P., & Weisner, C. (2007). Psychiatric symptoms, impaired function, and medical care costs in an HMO setting. *Gen. Hosp. Psychiat., 25*(3), 178–84.

Hunsley, J., & Bailey, J. M. (1999). The clinical utility of the Rorschach: Unfulfilled promises and an uncertain future. *Psychol. Assess., 11*(3), 266–77.

Hunt, W. A. (1993). Are binge drinkers more at risk of developing brain damage? *Alcohol, 10,* 559–61.

Hunter, C. L., Goodie, J. L., Oordt, M. S., & Dobmeyer, A. C. (2009). *Integrated behavioral health in primary care: Step-by-step guidance for assessment and intervention.* Washington, DC: American Psychological Association.

Hunter, E. C. M., Phillips, M. L., Chalder, T., Sierra, M., & David, A. S. (2003). Depersonalization disorder: A cognitive-behavioural conceptualisation. *Behav. Res. Ther., 41,* 1451–67.

Hunter, E. J. (1978). The Vietnam POW veteran: Immediate and long-term effects. In C. R. Figley (Ed.), *Stress disorders among Vietnam veterans.* New York: Brunner/Mazel.

Huntjens, R. J. C., Peters, M. L., Postma, A., Woertman, L., Effting, M., & van der Hart, O. (2005). Transfer of newly acquired stimulus valence between identities in dissociative identity disorder (DID). *Behav. Res. Ther., 43,* 243–55.

Huntjens, R. J. C., Peters, M. L., Woertman, L, van der Hart, O., & Postma, A. (2007). Memory transfer for emotionally valenced words between identities in dissociative identity disorder. *Behav. Res. Ther., 45,* 775–789.

Huntjens, R. J. C., Postma, A., Peters, M. L., Woertma, L., & van der Hart, O. (2003). Interidentity amnesia for neutral, episodic information in dissociative identity disorder. *J. Abn. Psychol., 112*(2), 290–97.

Husain, M., & Mehta, M. A, (2011). Cognitive enhancement by drugs in health and disease. *Trends in Cognitive Sciences, 15,* 28–36.

Hussong, A. M., Hicks, R. E., Levy, S. A., & Curran, P. J. (2001). Specifying the relations between affect and heavy alcohol use among young adults. *J. Abn. Psychol., 110*(3), 449–61.

Hussong, A., Bauer, D., & Chassin, L. (2008). Telescoped trajectories from alcohol initiation to disorder in children of alcoholic parents. *J. Abn. Psych., 117,* 63–78

Hutchins, E. C., Frank, R. G., & Glied, S. A. (2011). The evolving private psychiatric inpatient market. *The Journal of Behavioral Health Services & Research, 38*(1), 122–31.

Hutter-Paier, B., Huttenen, H. J., Puglielli, L., Eckman, C. B., Kim, D. Y., Hofmeister, A., Moir, R. D., Domnitz, S. B., Frosch, M. P., Windisch, M., & Kovacs, D. M. (2004). The ACAT inhibitor CP-113,818 markedly reduces amyloid pathology in a mouse model of Alzheimer's disease. *Neuron, 44,* 227–38.

Huynen, K. B., Lutzker, J. R., Bigelow, K. B., Touchette, R. E., & Campbell, R. V. (1996). Planned activities for mothers of children with developmental disorders. *Behav. Mod., 20*(4), 406–27.

Hyman, S. E. (2011). Cognitive enhancement: Promise and perils. *Neuron, 69,* 595–98.

Iacono, W. G., Moreau, M., Beiser, M., Fleming, J. A., & Lin, T. (1992). Smooth-pursuit eye tracking in first-episode psychotic patients and their relatives. *J. Abn. Psychol., 101*(1), 104–16.

Iancu, I., Dannon, P. N., Lustig, M., Sasson, Y., & Zohar, J. (2000). Preferential efficacy of serotonergic medication in obsessive-compulsive disorder: From practice to theory. In W. K. Goodman & M. V. Rudorfer, et al. (Eds.), *Obsessive-compulsive disorder: Contemporary issues in treatment. Personality and clinical psychology series* (pp. 303–13). Mahwah, NJ: Erlbaum.

Ibarra-Rovillard, M. S., & Kuiper, N. A. (2011). Social support and social negativity findings in depression: Perceived responsiveness to basic psychological needs. *Clin. Psychol. Rev., 31*(3), 342–52. doi: 10.1016/j.cpr.2011.01.005

Iezzi, T., Duckworth, M. P., & Adams, H. E. (2001). Somatoform and factitious disorders. In P. Sutker & H. Adams (Eds.), *Comprehensive handbook of psychopathology* (pp. 211–58). New York: Kluwer Academic/Plenum.

Ilechukwu, S. T. (1992). Magical penis loss in Nigeria: Report of a recent epidemic of a koro-like syndrome. *Trans. Cult. Psych. Res. Rev., 29*(2), 91–108.

Ingenhoven, T., Lafay, P., Rinne, T., Passchier, J., & Duivenvoorden, H. (2010). Effectiveness of pharmacotherapy for severe personality disorders: meta-analyses of randomized controlled trials. *J. Clin. Psychiat., 71*(1), 14–25. Retrieved from http://www.ncbi.nlm.nih.gov/pubmed/19778496

Ilott, N., Saudino, K. J., Wood, A., & Asherson, P. (2010). A genetic study of ADHD and activity level in infancy. *Genes, Brain & Behavior, 9*(3), 296–304.

Ingram, R. E., & Luxton, D. D. (2005). Vulnerability-Stress Models. In B. J. Hankin & J. R. Z. Abela (Eds.), *Development of psychopathology: A vulnerability-stress perspective* (pp. 32–46). Thousand Oaks, CA: Sage.

Ingram, R. E., & Price, J. M. (Eds.). (2001). *Vulnerability to psychopathology: Risk across the lifespan.* New York: Guilford.

Ingram, R. E., Miranda, J., & Segal, Z. (2006). Cognitive vulnerability to depression. In L. B. Alloy & J. H. Riskind (Eds.),*Cognitive vulnerability to emotional disorders.* (pp. 63–91). Mahwah, NJ: Lawrence Erlbaum Associates Publishers.

Ingram, R. E., Scott, W., & Siegle, G. (1999). Depression: Social and cognitive aspects. In T. Millon, P. H. Blaney, et al. (Eds.), *Oxford textbook of psychopathology* (pp. 203–26). New York: Oxford University Press.

Insel, T. R. (2010). Rethinking schizophrenia. *Nature, 468* (11 November), 187–93.

Institute of Medicine. (2006). *Improving the quality of health care for mental and substance abuse conditions.* Washington, DC: National Academies Press.

in't Veld, B. A., Ruitenberg, A., Hofman, A., Launer, L. J., van Duijn, C. M., Stijnen, T., Breteler, M. M. B., & Stricker, B. H. C. (2001). Nonsteroidal anti-inflammatory drugs and the risk of Alzheimer's disease. *N. Engl. J. Med., 345,* 1515–21.

Ipser, J. C., Kariuki, C. M., & Stein, D. J. (2008). Pharmacotherapy for social anxiety disorder: a systematic review. *Expert Review of Neurotherapeutics, 8*(2), 235–57.

Irie, F., Masaki, K. H., Petrovitch, H., Abbott, R. D., Ross, G. W., Taaffe, D. R., et al. (2008). Apolipoprotein E Σ4 allele genotype and the effect of depressive symptoms on the risk of dementia in men. *Arch. Gen. Psychiat., 65*, 906–12.

Ishiwaka, S. S., Raine, A., Lencz, T., Bihrle, S., & La Casse, L. (2001). Autonomic stress reactivity and executive functions in successful and unsuccessful criminal psychopaths from the community. *J. Abn. Psychol., 110*(3), 423–32.

Isohanni, M., Jones, P., Moilanen, K., Veijola, J., Oja, H., Koiranen, M., Jokelainen, J., Croudace, T., & Järvelin, M.-R. (2001). Early developmental milestones in adult schizophrenia and other psychoses. A 31-year follow-up of the North Finland 1966 birth cohort. *Schiz. Res., 52*, 1–19.

Ivan, C. S., Seshadri, S., Beiser, A., Au, R., Kase, C., Kelly-Hayes, M., & Wolf, P. A. (2004). Dementia after stroke: The Framingham study. *Stroke, 35*, 1264–68.

Iversen, A. C., van Staden, L., Hughes, J. H., Browne, T., Hull, L., Hall, J., Greenberg, N., Rona, R. J., Hotopf, M., Wessely, S., & Fear, N. T. (2009, Oct. 30). *BMC Psychiatry, 9*, art. 68. doi:10.1186/1471-244X-9-68

Iversen, L. L. (2008). *The science of marijuana* (2nd ed.). New York: Oxford University Press.

Jablensky, A., et al. (1992). Schizophrenia: Manifestations, incidence, and course in different cultures. A World Health Organization ten-country study. *Psychological Medicine Monograph Supplement, 20*, 1–97.

Jackson, A. P., & Huang, C. C. (2000). Parenting stress and behavior among single mothers of preschoolers: The mediating role of self efficacy. *Journal of Social Service Research, 26*, 29–42.

Jacob, T., & Johnson, S. L. (2001). Sequential interactions in the parent–child communications of depressed fathers and depressed mothers. *J. Fam. Psychol., 15*(1), 38–52.

Jacobi, C., Hayward, C., de Zwaan, M., Kraemer, H. C., & Agras, W. S. (2004). Coming to terms with risk factors for eating disorders: Application of risk terminology and suggestions for a general taxonomy. *Psych. Bull., 130*(1), 19–65.

Jacobs, R. H., Becker-Weidman, E. G., Reinecke, M. A., Jordan, N., Silva, S. G., Rohde, P., & March, J. S. (2010). Treating depression and oppositional behavior in adolescents. *J. Clin. Child Adol. Psych., 39*(4), 559–67.

Jacobson, N. S., & Addis, M. E. (1993). Research on couples and couple therapy: What do we know? Where are we going? *J. Cons. Clin. Psychol., 61*, 85–93.

Jacobson, N. S., Christensen, A., Prince, S. E., Cordova, J., & Eldridge, K. (2000). Integrative behavioral couple therapy: An acceptance-based, promising new treatment for couple discord. *J. Cons. Clin. Psychol., 68*, 351–55.

Jacobson, N. S., Dobson, K. S., Truax, P. A., Addis, M. E., Koerner, K., Gollan, J. K., Gortner, E., & Prince, S. E. (1996). A component analysis of cognitive behavioral treatment for depression. *J. Cons. Clin. Psychol., 64*, 295–304.

Jacobson, N. S., Martell, C. R., & Dimidjian, S. (2001). Behavioral activation treatment for depression: Returning to contextual roots. *Clin. Psychol. Sci. Prac., 8*(3), 255–70.

Jacobson, N. S., Schmaling, K. B., & Holtzworth-Monroe, A. (1987). A component analysis of behavioral marital therapy: Two-year follow-up and prediction of relapse. *J. Marit. Fam. Ther., 13*, 187–95.

Jaffee, S., Caspi, A., Moffitt, T., Dodge, K., Rutter, M., Taylor, A., & Tully, L. (2005). Nature x nurture: Genetic vulnerabilities interact with physical maltreatment to promote conduct problems. *Develop. Psychopath., 17*, 67–84.

Jalbert, J. J., Daiello, L. A., & Lapane, K. L. (2008). Dementia of the Alzheimer type. *Epidemiol Rev. 30*, 15–34.

Jamieson, R., & Wells, C. (1979). Manic psychosis in a patient with multiple metastatic brain tumors. *J. Clin. Psychiat., 40*, 280–83.

Jamison, K. R. (1993). *Touched with fire*. New York: Free Press.

Jamison, K. R. (1995). *An unquiet mind*. New York: A. A. Knopf.

Jamison, K. R. (1999). *Night falls fast: Understanding suicide*. New York: Vintage Books.

Janet, P. (1901). *The mental state of hystericals: A study of mental stigmata and mental accidents*. New York: Putnam.

Janet, P. (1907). *The major symptoms of hysteria*. New York: Macmillan.

Jang, K. L. (2005). *The behavioral genetics of psychopathology: A clinical guide*. Mahwah, NJ: Lawrence Erlbaum Associates.

Jang, K. L., Thordarson, D.S., Stein, M. B., Cohan, S. L., & Taylor, S. (2007). Coping styles and personality: A biometric analysis. *Anxiety, Stress and Coping: An International Journal, 20*, 17–24.

Jang, K. L., Woodward, T., Lang, D., Honer, W., & Livesley, W. J. (2005). The genetic and environmental basis of the relationship between schizotypy and personality: A twin study. *J. Nerv. Ment. Dis., 193*, 153–59.

Janicak, P. G., Dowd, S. M., Strong, M. J., Alam, D., & Beedle, D. (2005). The potential role of repetitive transcranial magnetic stimulation in treating severe depression. *Psychiatr. Ann., 35*(2), 138–45.

Janicki, M. P., & Dalton, A. J. (1993). Alzheimer disease in a select population of older adults with mental retardation. *Irish Journal of Psychology: Special Issue, Psychological aspects of aging, 14*(1), 38–47.

Jankovic, J. (1997). Phenomenology and classification of tics. *Neurologic Clinics, 15*(2), 267–75.

Janofsky, J. S., Dunn, M. H., Roskes, E. J., Briskin, J. K., & Rudolph, M. S. (1996). Insanity defense pleas in Baltimore city: An analysis of outcome. *Amer. J. Psychiat., 153*(11), 1464–68.

Janowsky, D. S., Addario, D., & Risch, S. C. (1987). *Pharmacology case studies*. New York: Guilford.

Janssen, I., Hanssen, M., Bak, M., Bijl, R. V., De Graaf, R., Vollebergh, W., McKenzie, K., & van Os, J. (2003). Discrimination and delusional ideation. *Brit. J. Psychiat., 182*, 71–76.

Jaranson, J. M., & Popkin, M. K. (1998). *Caring for victims of torture*. Washington, DC: American Psychiatric Press.

Jaranson, J. M., Kinzie, J. D., Friedman, M., Ortiz, S. D., Friedman, M. J., Southwick, S., Kastrup, M., & Mollica, R. (2001). Assessment, diagnosis, and intervention. In E. Gerrity, T. M. Keane, & F. Tuma (Eds.), *The mental health consequences of torture* (pp. 249–75). New York: Kluwer/Plenum.

Jaranson, J. M., Butcher, J. N., Halcón, L., Johnson, D. R., Robertson, C., Savik, K., Spring, M., & Westermeyer, J. (2004). Somali and Oromo refugees: Correlates of torture and trauma. *Amer. J. Pub. Hlth., 94*, 591–97.

Jarvik, M. E. (1967). The psychopharmacological revolution. *Psych. Today, 1*(1), 51–58.

Javaras, K. N., Laird, N. M., Reichborn-Kjennerud, T., Bulik, C. M., Pope, H. R., & Hidson, J. I. (2008). Familiarity and heritability of binge eating disorder: Results of a case-control family study and a twin study. *Int. J. Eat. Dis., 41*, 174–79.

Javitt, D. C. (2008). Glycine transport inhibitors and the treatment of schizophrenia. *Biol. Psychiat., 63*, 6–8.

Jeffrey, R. W., Adlis, S. A., & Forster, J. L. (1991). Prevalence of dieting among working men and women: The healthy worker project. *Hlth. Psychol., 10*, 274–81.

Jenike, M. A. (2000). Neurosurgical treatment of obsessive-compulsive disorder. In W. K. Goodman, M. V. Rudorfer, et al. (Eds.),*Obsessive-compulsive disorder: Contemporary issues in treatment. Personality and clinical psychology series* (pp. 457–82). Mahwah, NJ: Erlbaum.

Jenkins, J. H., & Carpenter-Song, E. A. (2008). Awareness of stigma among persons with schizophrenia. *J. Nerv. Ment. Dis., 197*, 520–29.

Jensen, C. D., Cushing, C. C., Aylward, B. S., Craig, J. T., Sorell, D. M., & Steele, R. G. (2011). Effectiveness of motivational interviewing interventions for adolescent substance use behavior change: A metaanalytic review. *J. Cons. Clin. Psychol., 79*, 433–40.

Jensen, P. S., Arnold, L. E., Swanson, J. M., Vitiello, B., Abikoff, H. B., Greenhill, L. L. Hechtman, L., Hinshaw, S. P., Pelham, W. E., Wells, K. C., Conners, C. K., Elliott, G. R., Epstein, J. N., Hoza, B., March, J. S., Molina, B. S., Newcorn, J. H., Severe, J. B. M., Wigal, T., Gibbons, R. D., & Hur, K. (2007). 3-year follow-up of the NIMH MTA study. *J. Amer. Acad. Child Adoles. Psychiat., 46*(8), 989–1002.

Jick, H., Kaye, J. A., & Jick, S. S. (2004, Jul. 21). Antidepressants and the risk of suicidal behaviors. *JAMA, 292*(3), 338–43.

Jobe, T. H., & Harrow, M. (2010). Schizophrenia course, long-term outcome, recovery, and prognosis. *Curr. Dir. Psych. Sci., 19*, 220–25.

Johansen, M., Karterud, S., Pedersen, G., Gude, T., & Falkum, E. (2004). An investigation of the prototype validity of the borderline DSM–IV construct. *Acta Psychiat. Scand., 109*, 289–98.

Johansson, P., Høgland, P., Ulberg, R., Amlo, S., Marble, A., Bøgwald, K-P., Sørbye, O., Sjaastad, M. C., & Heyerdahl. (2010). The mediating role of insight for long-term improvements in psychodynamic therapy. *J. Cons. Clin. Psychol., 78*, 438–48.

John, O., & Naumann, L. (2008). Paradigm shift to the integrative Big-Five trait taxonomy: History, measurement, and conceptual issues. In O. P. John, R. Robins, & L. Pervin (Eds.), *Handbook of personality: Theory and Research* (3rd ed., pp. 114–58). New York: Guilford Press.

Johnson, B. A. (2010). Medication treatment of different types of alcoholism. *Amer. J. Psychiat., 167*(6), 630–39.

Johnson, C. L., Stuckey, M. K., Lewis, L. D., & Schwartz, D. M. (1982). Bulimia: A descriptive survey of 316 cases. *Int. J. Eat. Dis., 2*, 3–16.

Johnson, D. E. (2000). Medical and developmental sequelae of early childhood institutionalization in Eastern European adoptees. In C. A. Nelson (Ed.), *The Minnesota symposia on child psychology: The effects of early adversity on neurobehavioral development. Minnesota symposia on child psychology* (Vol. 31, pp. 113–62). Mahwah, NJ: Erlbaum.

Johnson, F., & Wardle, J. (2005). Dietary restraint, body dissatisfaction, and psychological distress: A prospective analysis.*J. Abn. Psychol., 114*, 119–25.

Johnson, J. D., O'Connor, K. A., Deak, T., Spencer, R. L., Watkins, L. R., & Maier, S. F. (2002). Prior stressor exposure primes the HPA axis. *Psychoneuroimmunology, 27*, 353–65.

Johnson, J. G., Cohen, P., Brown, J., Smailes, E. M., & Bernstein, D. P. (1999). Childhood maltreatment increases risk for personality disorders during early adulthood. *Arch. Gen. Psychiat., 56*, 600–6.

Johnson, J. G., Cohen, P., Kasen, S., & Brook, J. S. (2002). Childhood adversities associated with risk for eating disorders or weight problems during adolescence or early adulthood. *Amer. J. Psychiat. 159*(3), 394–400.

Johnson, J. G., Cohen, P., Kasen, S., & Brook, J. S. (2006) Dissociative disorders among adults in the community, impaired functioning, and Axis I and II comorbity. *J. Psychiat. Res., 40*, 131–40.

Johnson, J. G., Cohen, P., Smailes, E., Kasen, S., Oldham, J. M., & Skodol, A. E. (2000). Adolescent personality disorders associated with violence and criminal behavior during adolescence and early childhood. *Amer. J. Psychiat., 157*, 1406–12.

Johnson, S. L., Cuellar, A. K., & Miller, C. (2009). Bipolar and unipolar depression: A comparison of clinical phenomenology, biological vulnerability, and psychosocial predictors. In I. H. Gotlib & C. L. Hammen (Eds.), *Handbook of depression* (2nd ed., pp. 142–62). New York: Guilford Press.

Johnson, S. L., & Miller, I. (1997). Negative life events and time to recovery from episodes of bipolar disorder. *J. Abn. Psychol., 106*(3), 449–57.

Johnson, S. L., & Roberts, J. E. (1995). Life events and bipolar disorder: Implications from biological theories. *Psychol. Bull., 117*, 434–49.

Johnson, T. P. (2007). Cultural-level influences on substance use & misuse. *Substance Use & Misuse, 42*(2–3), 305–16.

Johnston, L. D., O'Malley, P. M., Bachman, J. G., & Schulenberg, J. E. (2007). Monitoring the future national results on adolescent drug use: Overview of key findings, 2006 (NIH Publication No. 07–6202). Bethesda, MD: National Institute on Drug Abuse.

Johnston, L. D., O'Malley, P. M., Bachman, J. G., & Schulenberg, J. E. (2009). *Monitoring the Future national survey results on drug use, 1975–2008: Volume I, Secondary school students* (NIH Publication No. 09-7402). Bethesda, MD: National Institute on Drug Abuse.

Joiner, T. E. (2002). Depression in its interpersonal context. In I. H. Gotlib & C. L. Hammen (Eds.), *Handbook of depression* (pp. 295–313). New York: Guilford.

Joiner, T. E., & Metalsky, G. I. (1995). A prospective test of an integrative interpersonal theory of depression: A naturalistic study of college roommates. *J. Pers. Soc. Psychol., 69*(4), 778–88.

Joiner, T. E., Jr., Brown, J. S., & Wingate, L. R. (2005). The psychology and neurobiology of suicidal behavior. *Ann. Rev. Psych., 56*, 287–314.

Joiner, T. E., Jr., & Timmons, K. A. (2009). Depression in its interpersonal context. In I. H. Gotlib & C. L. Hammen (Eds.), *Handbook of depression* (2nd ed., pp. 322–39). New York: Guilford Press.

Jones, E., & Wessely, S. (2002). Psychiatric battle casualties: An intra- and interwar comparison. *Brit. J. Psychiat., 178*, 242–47.

Jones, E., & Wessely, S. (2007). A paradigm shift in the conceptualization of trauma in the 20th century. *J. Anxiety Dis., 21*, 164–175.

Jones, E., Thomas, A., & Ironside, S. (2007). Shell shock: An outcome study of a First World War 'PIE' unit. *Psychol. Med., 37*, 215–23.

Jones, L. (1992). Specifying the temporal relationship between job loss and consequences: Implication for service delivery. *Journal of Applied Social Sciences, 16*, 37–62.

Jones, M. C. (1924). A laboratory study of fear: The case of Peter. *Pedagogical Seminary, 31*, 308–15.

Jones, P. B., Rodgers, B., Murray, R., & Marmot, M. (1994). Child developmental risk factors for adult schizophrenia in the British 1946 birth cohort. *Lancet, 344*, 1398–402.

Jones, R. S. P., Zahl, A., & Huws, J. C. (2001). First hand accounts of emotional experiences in autism: A qualitative analysis. *Disability & Society, 16*, 393–401.

Jones, S. H., Hare, D. J., & Evershed, K. (2005). Actigraphic assessment of circadian activity and sleep patterns in bipolar disorder. *Bipolar Disorders, 7*(2), 176–86.

Jones, S. R., & Fernyhough, C. (2009). Caffeine, stress, and proneness to psychosis-like experiences. *Pers. Indiv. Diff., 46*, 562–64.

Jones W. R., & Morgan, J. F. (2010). Eating disorders in men: a review of the literature. *J. Pub. Ment. Hlth., 9*, 23–31.

Joorman, J. (2009). Cognitive aspects of depression. In I. H. Gotlib & C. L. Hammen (Eds.), *Handbook of depression and its treatment* (2nd ed., pp. 298–321). New York: Guilford Press.

Jordan, B. D., Relkin, N. R., Ravdin, L. D., Jacobs, A. R., Bennett, A., & Gandy, S. (1997). Apolipoprotein E (4 associated with chronic traumatic brain injury in boxing. *JAMA, 278*, 136–40.

Joyce, K. A. (2008). *Magnetic appeal: MRI and the myth of transparency*. Ithaca, NY, and London: Cornell University Press.

Judd, L. L., Akiskal, H. S., Maser, J. D., Zeller, P. J., Endicott, J., Coryell, W., Paulus, M., et al. (1998). A prospective 12-year study of subsyndromal and syndromal depressive symptoms in unipolar major depressive disorders. *Arch. Gen. Psychiat., 55*, 694–700.

Judd, L. L., Akiskal, H. S., Schettler, P. J., Endicott, J., Maser, J., Solomon, D. A., et al. (2002). The long-term natural history of the weekly symptomatic status of bipolar I disorder. *Arch. Gen. Psychiat., 59*(6), 530–37.

Judd, L. L., Paulus, M. P., Zeller, P., Fava, G. A., Rafanelli, C., Grandi, S., et al. (1999). The role of residual subthreshold depressive symptoms in early episode relapse in unipolar major depressive disorder. *Arch. Gen. Psychiat., 56*(8), 764–65.

Judd, L. L., Schettler, P. J., Akiskal, H. S., Maser, J., Coryell, W., Solomon, D., et al. (2003). Long-term symptomatic status of bipolar I vs. bipolar II disorders. *Int. J. Neuropsychopharm., 6*(2), 127–37.

Kachigian, C., & Felthous, A. R. (2004). Court responses to Tarasoff statutes. *J. Amer. Acad. Psychiat. Law, 32*(3), 263–73.

Kaelber, C. T., Moul, D. E., & Farmer, M. E. (1995). Epidemiology of depression. In E. E. Beckham & W. R. Leber (Eds.), *Handbook of depression* (2nd ed., pp. 3–35). New York: Guilford.

Kagan, J. (1997). Temperament and the reactions to unfamiliarity. *Child Develop., 68*(1), 139–43.

Kagan, J. (2003). Biology, context and developmental inquiry. *Annu. Rev. Psychol., 54*, 1–23.

Kagan, J., & Fox, N. A. (2006). Biology, culture, and temperamental biases. In N. Eisenberg, W. Damon & R. M. Lerner (Eds.), *Handbook of child psychology: Social, emotional, and personality development.* (6 ed., Vol. 3, pp. 167–225). Hoboken, NJ: John Wiley & Sons.

Kagan, J., Snidman, N., McManis, M., & Woodward, S. (2001). Temperamental contributions to the affect family of anxiety. *Psychiat. Clin. N. Amer., 2*, 677–88.

Kahlem, P. (2006). Gene-dosage effect on chromosome 21 transcriptome in trisomy 21: Implication in Down syndrome cognitive disorders. *Behav. Genet., 36*(3), 416–28.

Kalant, O. J. (1966). *The amphetamines: Toxicity and addiction.* Brookside Monographs, No. 5. Toronto: University of Toronto Press.

Kalarchian, M. A., Wilson, G. T., Brolin, R. E., & Bradley, L. (1998). Binge eating in bariatric surgery patients. *Int. J. Eat. Dis., 23*(1), 89–92.

Kalat, J. W. (1998). *Biological psychology* (5th ed.). Belmont, CA: Wadsworth.

Kalat, J. W. (2001). *Biological psychology* (7th ed.). Belmont, CA: Wadsworth.

Kalus, O., Bernstein, D. P., & Siever, L. J. (1995). Schizoid personality disorder. In W. J. Livesley (Ed.), *The DSM-IV personality disorders.* (pp. 58–70). New York: Guilford.

Kalus, P., Senitz, D., & Beckmann, H. (1997). Cortical layer I changes in schizophrenia: A marker for impaired brain development? *Journal of Neural Transmission, 104*, 549–59.

Kamien, J. B., Mikulich, S. K., & Amass, L. (1999). Efficacy of buprenorphine: Naloxone tablet for daily vs. alternateday opioid dependency. *Drug Dependency Inc.* National Institute on Drug Abuse Monograph # 179. Washington, DC: U.S. Government Printing Office.

Kamphaus, R. W., & Kroncke, A. P. (2004). "Back to the future" of the Stanford-Binet Intelligence Scales. *Comprehensive handbook of psychological assessment* (pp. 77–86). New York: John Wiley & Sons.

Kamphuis, J. H., & Noordhof, A. (2009). On categorical diagnoses in DSM-V: Cutting dimensions at useful points? *Psychol. Assess., 21*, 294–301.

Kanapaux, W. (2004). Guilty of mental illness. *Psychiatric Times*, 21, 1–2. www.psychiatrictimes.com/risk-assessment.

Kang, H. K., Natelson, B. H., Mahan, C. M., Lee, K. Y., & Murphy, F. (2003). Post-traumatic stress disorder and chronic fatigue syndrome-like illness among Gulf War veterans: A population-based survey of 30,000 veterans. *Amer. J. Epidemiol., 157*, 141–48.

Kannel, W. B., Wolf, P. A., Garrison, R. J., Cupples, L. A., & D'Agostino, R. B. (1987). *The Framingham study: An epidemiological investigation of cardiovascular disease.* Bethesda, MD: National Heart, Lung and Blood Institute.

Kanner, L. (1943). Autistic disturbances of effective content. *Nervous Child, 2*, 217–40.

Kaplan, H. S. (1987). *The illustrated manual of sex therapy* (2nd ed.). New York: Brunner/Mazel.

Kaplan, H. S. (1979) *Disorders of sexual desire.* New York: Brunner/Mazel.

Kaplan, M. S., & Krueger, R. B. (1997). Voyeurism: Psychopathology and theory. In D. R. Laws & W. O'Donohue (Eds.), *Sexual deviance: Theory, assessment, and treatment* (pp. 297–310). New York: Guilford.

Kapner, D. A. (2003). Recreational use of Ritalin on college campuses. *Info Fact Resources.* Washington, DC: U.S. Department of Justice.

Kapur, N. (1999). Syndromes of retrograde amnesia: A conceptual and empirical synthesis. *Psychol. Bull., 125*, 800–25.

Kapur, S. (2003). Psychosis as a state of aberrant salience: A framework linking biology, phenomenology, and pharmacology in schizophrenia. *Amer. J. Psychiat., 160*, 13–23.

Kapur, S., Arenovich, T., Agid, O., Zipursky, R., Lindborg, S., & Jones, B. (2005). Evidence for the onset of antipsychotic effects within the first 24 hours of treatment. *Amer. J. Psychiat., 162*, 939–46.

Karavasilis, L., Doyle, A. B., & Markiewicz, D. (2003). Associations between parenting style and attachment to mother in middle childhood and adolescence. *International Journal of Behavioral Development, 27*(2), 153–64.

Karg, K., Burmeister, M., Shedden, K., & Sen, S. (2011). The serotonin transporter promoter variant (5-HTTLPR), stress, and depression meta-analysis revisited. *Arch. Gen. Psychiat., 68*, 444–54. doi: 10.1001/archgenpsychiatry.2010.189

Kario, K., & Ohashi, T. (1997). Increased coronary heart disease mortality after the Hanshin-Awaji earthquake among the older community on

Awaji Island. Tsuna Medical Association. *J. Amer. Geriat. Soc., 45,* 610–13.

Karlsgodt, K. H., Niendam, T. A., Bearden, C. E., & Cannon, T. D. (2009). White matter integrity and prediction of social role functioning in subjects at ultra-high risk for psychosis. *Biol. Psychiat., 66,* 562–69.

Karlsgodt, K. H., Sun, D., & Cannon, T. D. (2010). Structural and functional brain abnormalities in schizophrenia. *Curr. Dir. Psych. Sci., 19,* 226–31.

Karnesh, L. J. (with collaboration of Zucker, E. M.). (1945). *Handbook of psychiatry.* St. Louis: Mosby.

Karno, M., Golding, J. M., Sorenson, S. B., & Burnam, M. A. (1988). The epidemiology of obsessive-compulsive disorder in five U.S. communities. *Arch. Gen. Psychiat., 45,* 1094–99.

Karno, M., Jenkins, J. H., de la Selva, A., Santana, F., Telles, C., Lopez, S., & Mintz, J. (1987). Expressed emotion and schizophrenic outcome among Mexican-American families. *J. Nerv. Ment. Dis., 175*(3), 143–51.

Karon, B. P. (1995). Provision of psychotherapy under managed health care: A growing crisis and national nightmare. *Professional Psychology: Research & Practice, 26*(1), 5–9.

Karoutzou, G., Emrich, H. M., & Dietrich, D. E. (2008). The myelin-pathogenesis puzzle in schizophrenia: A literature review. *Mol. Psychiat., 13,* 245–60.

Karran, E., Mercken, M., & De Strooper, B. (2011). The amyloid cascade hypothesis for Alzheimer's disease: An appraisal for the development of therapeutics. *Nat. Rev. Drug Discov. 10,* 698–712.

Kaski, M. (2000). Aetiology of mental retardation: General issues and prevention. In M. G. Gelder, J. J. Lopez-Ibor, Jr., & N. Andreason (Eds.), *New Oxford textbook of psychiatry* (pp. 1947–52). New York: Oxford University Press.

Kaslow, N. J., Leiner, A. S., Reviere, S., Gantt, M-J., Senter, H., Jackson, E., Bethea, K., Bhaju, J., Thompson, M. P., & Rhodes, M. (2010). Suicidal, abused African-American women's response to a culturally-informed intervention. *J. Cons. Clin. Psychol., 78,* 449–58.

Kato, T., Knopman, D., & Liu, H. Y. (2001). Dissociation of regional activation in mild AD during visual encoding—a functional MRI study. *Neurol., 57,* 812–16.

Katon, W. J. (2006). Panic disorder. *New Eng. J. Med., 354*(22), 2360–67.

Katon, W. J., Roy-Byrne, P., Russo, J., & Cowley, D. (2002). Cost effectiveness and cost offset of a collaborative care intervention for primary care patients with panic disorder. *Arch. Gen. Psychiat., 59,* 1098–1104.

Katz, E. C., Brown, B. S., Schwartz, R. P., Weintraub, E., Barksdale, W., & Robinson, R. (2004). Role induction: A method for enhancing early retention in outpatient drug-free treatment. *J. Cons. Clin. Psychol., 72,* 227–34.

Katz, L. F., & Gottman, J. M. (1997). Buffering children from marital conflict and dissolution. *J. Clin. Child Psychol., 26*(2), 157–71.

Katz, R., & McGuffin, P. (1993). The genetics of affective disorders. In L. J. Chapman, J. P. Chapman, & D. C. Fowles (Eds.), *Progress in experimental personality and psychopathology research* (Vol. 16). New York: Springer.

Katz, S., Kravetz, S., & Marks, Y. (1997). Parents' and doctors' attitudes toward plastic facial surgery for persons with Down syndrome. *J. Intell. Develop. Dis., 22*(4), 265–73.

Katzmarzyk, P. T., & Davis, C. (2001). Thinness and body shape of *Playboy* centerfolds from 1978 to 1998. *International Journal of Obesity and Related Metabolic Disorders, 25*(4), 590–92.

Kaufman, J., Martin, A., King, R. A., & Charney, D. (2001). Are child-, adolescent-, and adult-onset depression one and the same disorder? *Biol. Psychiat., 49*(12), 980–1001.

Kaufman, J., Yang, B., Douglas-Palumberi, H., Crouse-Artus, M, Lipschitz, D., Krystal, J. H., & Gelernter, J. (2007). Genetic and environmental predictors of early alcohol use. *Biol. Psychiat., 61*(11) 1228–34.

Kaufman, J., & Zigler, E. (1989). The intergenerational transmission of child abuse. In D. Cicchetti & V. Carlson (Eds.), *Child maltreatment: Theory and research on the causes and consequences of child abuse and neglect* (pp. 129–50). Cambridge: Cambridge University Press.

Kaul, M., Zheng, J., Okamoto, S., Gendelman, H. E., & Lipton, S. A. (2005). HIV-1 infection and AIDS: consequences for the central nervous system. *Cell Death and Differentiation, 12,* 878–892.

Kausch, O. (2003). Patterns of substance abuse among treatment-seeking pathological gamblers. *J. Sub. Abuse Treat., 25*(4), 263–70.

Kawachi, I., Colditz, G., Ascherio, A., et al. (1994). Prospective study of phobic anxiety and risk of coronary heart disease in men. *Circulation, 89,* 1992.

Kawachi, I., Sparrow, D., Vokonas, P., et al. (1994). Symptoms of anxiety and risk of coronary heart disease: The normative aging study. *Circulation, 90,* 2225.

Kawachi, I., Sparrow, D., Vokonas, P., et al. (1995). Decreased heart rate variability in men with phobic anxiety (data from the normative aging study). *Amer. J. Cardiol., 75,* 882.

Kaye, W. (2008). Neurobiology of anorexia and bulimia nervosa. *Physiology and Behavior, 94,* 121–135.

Kaye, W. H., Bulik, C. M., Thornton, L., Barbarich, N., Masters, K., Price Foundation Collaborative Group. (2004). Comorbidity of anxiety disorders with anorexia and bulimia nervosa. *Amer. J. Psychiat., 161,* 2215–21.

Kazdin, A. E. (1995). Conduct disorder. In F. C. Verhulst & H. M. Koot (Eds.), *The epidemiology of child and adolescent psychopathology* (pp. 258–90). New York: Oxford University Press.

Kazdin, A. E. (1998a). Drawing valid inferences from case studies. In A. E. Kazdin (Ed.), *Methodological issues and strategies in clinical research* (pp. 403–17). Washington, DC: American Psychological Association.

Kazdin, A. E. (1998b). *Research design in clinical psychology.* Needham, MA: Allyn and Bacon.

Kazdin, A. E. (2007). Psychosocial treatments for conduct disorder in children and adolescents. In P. E. Nathan and J. M. Gorman (Eds.), *A guide to treatments that work* (pp. 71–104). New York: Oxford University Press. Kazdin, A. E. (2008). Evidence-based treatment and practice: New opportunities to bridge clinical research and practice, enhance the knowledge base, and improve patient care. *Amer. Psychol., 63,* 146–59.

Kazdin, A. E., & Nock, M. K. (2003). Delineating mechanisms of change in child and adolescent therapy: Methodological issues and research recommendations. *J. Child Psychol. Psychiat., 44*(8), 1116–29.

Kazdin, A. E., Holland, L., & Crowley, M. (1997). Family experience of barriers to treatment and premature termination from child therapy. *J. Cons. Clin. Psychol., 65*(3), 453–63.

Kazdin, A. E., & Weisz, J. R. (2003). *Evidence-based psychotherapies for children and adolescents.* New York: Guilford Press.

Kearney, C. A., Sims, K. E., Pursell, C. R., & Tillotson, C. A. (2003). Separation anxiety disorder in young children: A longitudinal and family analysis. *J. Clin. Child & Adol. Psych., 32*(4), 593–98.

Keck, P. E., & McElroy, S. L. (2002). Pharmacological treatments for bipolar disorder. In P. E. Nathan & J. M. Gorman (Eds.), *A guide to treatments that work* (2nd ed., pp. 277–300). New York: Oxford University Press.

Keck, P. E., Jr., & McElroy, S. L. (2007). Pharmacological treatments for bipolar disorder. In P. E. Nathan & J. M. Gorman (Eds.), *A guide to treatments that work* (3rd ed.) (pp. 323–350). New York: Oxford University Press.

Keefe, F. J., Smith, S. J., Buffington, A. L. H., Gibson, J., Studts, J. L., & Caldwell, D. S. (2002). Recent advances and future directions in the biopsychosocial assessment and treatment of arthritis. *J. Cons. Clin. Psychol., 70*(3), 640–55.

Keel, P. K. (2010). Epidemiology and the course of eating disorders.

Keel, P. K., & Klump, K. L. (2003). Are eating disorders culture-bound syndromes? Implications for conceptualizing their etiology. *Psychol. Bull., 129*(5), 747–69.

Keel, P. K., Dorer, D. J., Eddy, K. T., Franko, D., Charatan, D. L., & Herzog, D. B. (2003). Predictors of mortality in eating disorders. *Arch. Gen. Psychiat., 60,* 179–83.

Keel, P. K., Heatherton, T. F., Dorer, D. J., Joiner, T. E., & Zalta, A. K. (2006). Point prevalence of bulimia in 1982, 1992, and 2002. *Psych. Med., 36,* 119–27.

Keel, P. K., Mitchell, J. E., Miller, K. B., Davis, T. L., & Crow, S. J. (1999). Long-term outcome of bulimia nervosa. *Arch. Gen. Psychiat., 56*(1), 63–69.

Keeley, M. L., Graziano, P., & Geffken, G. R. (2009). Nocturnal enuresis and encopresis: Empirically supported approaches for refractory cases. In D. McKay & E. A. Storch (Eds.), *Cognitive-behavior therapy for children: Treating complex and refractory cases,* (pp. 445–73). New York: Springer Publishing Co.

Keller, J., Schatzberg, A. F., & Maj, M. (2007). Current issues in the classification of psychotic major depression. *Schizophrenia Bulletin, 33*(4), 877–885.

Keller, M. B. (2004). Remission versus response: The new gold standard of antidepressant care. *J. Clin. Psychiat., 65*(Suppl 4), 53–59.

Keller, M. B., Hirschfeld, R. M. A., & Hanks, D. (1997). Double depression: A distinctive subtype of unipolar depression. *J. Affect. Dis., 45*(1–2), 65–73.

Keller, M. B., McCullough, J. P., Klein, D. N., Arnow, B., Dunner, D. L., Gelenberg, A. J., Markowitz, J. C., Nemeroff, C. B., Russell, J. M., Thase, M. E., Trivedi, M. H., & Zajecka, J. (2000). A comparison of nefazodone, the cognitive behavioral-analysis system of psychotherapy, and their combination for the treatment of chronic depression. *N. Engl. J. Med., 342,* 1462–70.

Keller, M. B., Yonkers, K. A., Warshaw, M. G., Pratt, L. A., Golan, J., Mathews, A. O., et al. (1994). Remission and relapse in subjects with panic disorder and agoraphobia: A prospective short interval naturalistic follow-up. *J. Nerv. Ment. Dis., 182,* 290–96.

Keller, M. C., & Nesse, R. M. (2005). Is low mood an adaptation? Evidence for subtypes with symptoms that match precipitants. *J. Affect. Dis., 86,* 27–35.

Kelley, J. E., Lumley, M. A., & Leisen, J. C. C. (1997). Health effects of emotional disclosure in rheumatoid arthritis patients. *Hlth. Psychol., 16*(4), 331–40.

Kellner, R. (1985). Functional somatic symptoms and hypochondriasis: A survey of empirical studies. *Arch. Gen. Psychiat., 42,* 821–33.

Kelloway, E. K., Barling, J., & Hurrell, J. J. (2006). *Handbook of workplace violence.* Thousand Oaks, California: Sage.

Kelly, J. F., Dow, S. J., Yeterian, J. D., & Kahler, C. W. (2010). Can 12-step group participation strengthen and extend the benefits of adolescent addiction treatment? A prospective analysis. *Drug Alcohol Depend., 110*(1–2), 117–25.

Kelly, J. F., Stout, R. L., Magill, M., Tonigan, J. S., & Pagano, M. E. (2010). Mechanisms of behavior change in alcoholics anonymous: Does Alcoholics Anonymous lead to better alcohol use outcomes by reducing depression symptoms? *Addiction, 105*(4), 626–36.

Kelly, B. D. (2009). Criminal insanity in 19th-century Ireland, Europe and the United States: Cases, contexts and controversies. *International Journal of Law and Psychiatry, 32*(6), 362–68.

Kelsoe, J. R. (1997). The genetics of bipolar disorder. *Moskovskogo Nauchno-Issledovatel'Skogo Instituta Psikhiatrii, 27*(4), 285–92.

Kenardy, J., Arnow, B., & Agras, S. W. (1996). The aversiveness of specific emotional states associated with binge eating in obese patients. *Austral. NZ J. Psychiat., 30*(6), 839–44.

Kendall, P. C. (1990). Cognitive processes and procedures in behavior therapy. In C. M. Franks, G. T. Wilson, P. C. Kendall, & J. P. Foreyt (Eds.), *Review of behavior therapy: Theory and practice* (pp. 103–37). New York: Guilford.

Kendall, P. C., & Braswell, L. (1985). *Cognitive-behavioral therapy for impulsive children.* New York: Guilford.

Kendall, P. C., Compton, S. N., Walkup, J. T., Birmaher, B., Albano, A. M., Sherrill, J., Ginsburg, G., Rynn, M., McCracken, J., Gosch, E., Keeton, C., Bergman, L., Sakolsky, D., Suveg, C., Iyengar, S., March, J., & Piacentini, J. (2010). Clinical characteristics of anxiety disordered youth. *J. Anxiety Dis., 24*(3), 360–65.

Kendall, P. C., Holmbeck, G., & Verduin, T. (2004). Methodology, design, and evaluation in psychotherapy research. In M. J. Lambert (Ed.), *Bergin and Garfield's handbook of psychotherapy and behavior change* (5th ed., pp. 16–43). New York: John Wiley and Sons.

Kendall-Tackett, K. A., Williams, L. M., & Finkelhor, D. (1993). Impact of sexual abuse on children: A review and synthesis of recent empirical studies. *Psychol. Bull., 113*, 164–80.

Kendler, K. S. (1996). Major depression and generalised anxiety disorder: Same genes, (partly) different environments— revisited. *Brit. J. Psychiat, 168*(30), 68–75.

Kendler, K. S. (1997). The diagnostic validity of melancholic major depression in a population-based sample of female twins. *Arch. Gen. Psychiat., 54*, 299–304.

Kendler, K. S. (1999). Long-term care of an individual with schizophrenia: Pharmacological, psychological, and social factors. *Amer. J. Psychiat., 156*, 124–28.

Kendler, K. S. (2005). 'A gene for..': The nature of gene action in psychiatric disorders. *Am. J. Psychiat, 162*(7), 1243–52.

Kendler, K. S., Aggen, S. H., Czajkowski, N., Røysamb, E., Tambs, K., Torgersen, S., Neale, M. C., et al. (2008). The structure of genetic and environmental risk factors for DSM-IV personality disorders. *Arch. Gen. Psychiat., 65*(12), 1438–46. doi:10.1017/S0033291710002436

Kendler, K. S., Aggen, S. H., Knudsen, G. P., Røysamb, E., Neale, M. C., & Reichborn-Kjennerud, T. (2011). The structure of genetic and environmental risk factors for syndromal and subsyndromal common DSM-IV axis I and all axis II disorders. *Amer. J. Psychiat., 168*(1), 29–39. doi:10.1176/appi.ajp.2010.10030340

Kendler, K. S., Bulik, C. M., Silberg, J., Hettema, J. M., Myers, J., & Prescott, C. A. (2000). Childhood sexual abuse and adult psychiatric and substance use disorders in women. *Arch. Gen. Psychiat., 57*(10), 1–14.

Kendler, K. S., Czajkowski, N., Tambs, K., Torgersen, S., Aggen, S. H., Neale, M., & Reichborn-Kjennerud, T. (2006). Kendler, K. S., & Gardner, C. O. (1997). The risk for psychiatric disorders in relatives of schizophrenic and control probands: A comparison of three independent studies. *Psychol. Med., 27*, 411–19.

Kendler, K. S., Gardner, C. O., & Prescott, C. A. (2001). Panic syndromes in a population-based sample of male and female twins. *Psychol. Med., 31*, 989–1000.

Kendler, K. S., Gardner, C. O., & Prescott, C. A. (2002). Toward a comprehensive developmental model for major depression in women. *Amer. J. Psychiat., 159*(7), 1133–45.

Kendler, K. S., Gardner, C. O., & Prescott, C. A. (2003). Personality and the experience of environmental adversity. *Psychol. Med, 33*, 1193–202.

Kendler, K. S., Gardner, C. O., Gatz, M., & Pedersen, N. L. (2007). The sources of co-morbidity between major depression and generalized anxiety disorder in a Swedish national twin sample. *Psychol. Med., 37*(3), 453–62.

Kendler, K. S., & Gruenberg, A. M. (1984). An independent analysis of the Danish adoption study of schizophrenia: VI. The relationship between psychiatric disorders as defined by DSM-III in the relatives and adoptees. *Arch. Gen. Psychiat., 41*, 555–64.

Kendler, K. S., Gruenberg, A. M., & Kinney, D. K. (1994). Independent diagnoses of adoptees and relatives as defined by DSM-III in the provincial and national samples of the Danish adoption study of schizophrenia. *Arch. Gen. Psychiat., 51*(6), 456–68.

Kendler, K. S., Hettema, J. M., Butera, F., Gardner, C. O., & Prescott, C. A. (2003). Life event dimensions of loss, humiliation, entrapment, and danger in the prediction of onsets of major depression and generalized anxiety. *Arch. Gen. Psychiat., 60*, 789–96.

Kendler, K. S., Karkowski, L. M., & Prescott, C. A. (1998). Stressful life events and major depression: Risk period, long-term contextual threat and diagnostic specificity. *J. Nerv. Ment. Dis., 186*, 661–69.

Kendler, K. S., Karkowski, L. M., & Prescott, C. A. (1999a). Causal relationship between stressful life events and the onset of major depression. *Amer. J. Psychiat., 156*(6), 837–41.

Kendler, K. S., Karkowski, L. M., & Prescott, C. A. (1999b). Fears and phobias: Reliability and heritability. *Psychol. Med., 29*, 539–53.

Kendler, K. S., & Karkowski-Shuman, L. (1997). Stressful life events and genetic liability to major depression: Genetic control of exposure to the environment? *Psychol. Med., 27*, 539–47.

Kendler, K. S., Kessler, R. D., Walters, E. E., MacLean, C., et al. (1995). Stressful life events, genetic liability, and onset of an episode of major depression in women. *Amer. J. Psychiat., 152*(2), 833–42.

Kendler, K. S., Kuhn, J. W., Vittum, J., Prescott, C. A., & Riley, B. (2005). The interaction of stressful life events and a serotonin transporter polymorphism in the prediction of episodes of major depression. *Arch. Gen. Psychiat., 62*(5), 529–35.

Kendler, K. S., Kuhn, J., & Prescott, C. A. (2004). The interrelationship of neuroticism, sex, and stressful life events in the prediction of episodes of major depression. *Amer. J. Psychiat., 161*(4), 631–36.

Kendler, K. S., McGuire, M., Gruenberg, A. M., O'Hare, A., Spellman, M., & Walsh, D. (1993). The Roscommon family study: Schizophrenia-related personality disorders in relatives. *Arch. Gen. Psychiat., 50*, 781–88.

Kendler, K. S., Myers, J., Prescott, C. A., & Neale, M. C. (2001). The genetic epidemiology of irrational fears and phobias in men. *Arch. Gen. Psychiat., 58*(3), 257–65. doi: 10.1001/archpsyc.58.3.257

Kendler, K. S., Neale, M. C., Kessler, R. C., Heath, A. C., & Eaves, L. J. (1992a). Generalized anxiety disorder in women: A population-based twin study. *Arch. Gen. Psychiat., 49*, 267–72.

Kendler, K. S., Neale, M. C., Kessler, R. C., Heath, A. C., & Eaves, L. J. (1992b). The genetic epidemiology of phobias in women: The interrelationship of agoraphobia, social phobia, situational phobia, and simple phobia. *Arch. Gen. Psychiat., 49*, 273–81.

Kendler, K. S., Neale, M. C., Kessler, R. C., Heath, A. C., & Eaves, L. J. (1992c). Panic disorder in women: A population-based twin study. *Psychol. Med., 23*, 397–406.

Kendler, K. S., Neale, M. C., Kessler, R. C., Heath, A. C., & Eaves, L. J. (1992d). Major depression and generalized anxiety disorder: Same genes, (partly) different environments? *Arch. Gen. Psychiat., 49*, 716–22.

Kendler, K. S., Thornton, L. M., & Gardner, C. O. (2000). Stressful life events and previous episodes in the etiology of major depression in women: An evaluation of the "kindling" hypothesis. *Amer. J. Psychiat., 157*, 1243–51.

Kendler, K. S., Walters, E. E., Neale, M. C., Kessler, R. C., Heath, A. C., & Eaves, L. J. (1995). The structure of the genetic and environmental risk factors for six major psychiatric disorders in women: Phobia, generalized anxiety disorder, panic disorder, bulimia, major depression, and alcoholism. *Arch. Gen. Psychiat., 52*, 374–83.

Kendler. K. S., Walters, E. E., & Kessler, R. C. (1997). The prediction of length of major depressive episodes: Results from an epidemiological sample of female twins. *Psychol. Med., 27*, 107–17.

Kenis, G., & Maes, M. (2002). Effects of antidepressants on the production of cytokines. *The International Journal of Neuropharmacology, 5*, 401–12.

Kennard, D. (2004). The therapeutic community as an adaptable treatment modality across different settings. *Psychiatr. Q., 75*(3), 295–307.

Kennedy, S. H., Giacobbe, P., Rizvi, S. J., Placenza, F. M., Nishikawa, Y., Mayberg, H. S., & Lozano, A. M. (2011). Deep brain stimulation for treatment-resistant depression: Follow-up after 3 to 6 years. *Am. J. Psychiat., 168*, 502–10.

Kenrick, D. T., & Luce, C. L. (2004). *The functional mind: Readings in evolutionary psychology.* Auckland New Zealand: Pearson Education New Zealand.

Kent, G. (1997). Dental phobias. In G. C. L. Davey (Ed.), *Phobias. A handbook of theory, research and treatment* (pp. 107–27). Chichester, England: Wiley.

Kernberg, O. F. (1985). *Borderline conditions and pathological narcissism.* Northvale, NJ: Jason Aronson.

Kernberg, O. F. (1996). A psychoanalytic theory of personality disorders. In J. F. Clarkin & M. F. Lenzenweger (Eds.), *Major theories of personality disorder* (pp. 106–40). New York: Guilford.

Kernberg, O. F. (2004). Borderline personality disorder and borderline personality organization: Psychopathology and psychotherapy. In J. Magnavita (Ed.), *Handbook of Personality Disorders: Theory and Practice* (pp. 92–119). Hoboken, NJ: John Wiley & Sons.

Kernberg, O., & Caligor, E. (2005). A psychoanalytic theory of personality disorders. In

M. F. Lenzenweger & J.F. Clarkin (Eds.), *Major theories of personality disorders.* (2nd ed.) New York: Guilford Press.

Kernberg, O. F., & Michels, R. (2009). Borderline personality disorder. *Amer. J. Psychiat., 166*(5), 505–8. doi:10.1176/appi.ajp.2009.09020263

Keshavan, M., Shad, M., Soloff, P., & Schooler, N. (2004). Efficacy and tolerability of olanzapine in the treatment of schizotypal personality disorder. *Schiz. Res. 71*, 97–101.

Keshavan, M. S., Tandon, R., Boutros, N. N., & Nasrallah, H. A. (2008). Schizophrenia, "just the facts": What we know in 2008 Part 3: Neurobiology. *Schiz. Res., 106*, 89–107.

Kessing, L. V. (2007). Epidemiology of subtypes of depression. *Acta Psychiatrica Scandinavica, 115*, 85–89.

Kessler, R. C., & Zhao, S. (1999). Overview of descriptive epidemiology of mental disorders. In C. S. Aneshensel & J. C. Phelan (Eds.), *Handbook of sociology of mental health. Handbook of sociology and social research* (pp. 127–50). New York: Kluwer/Plenum.

Kessler, R. C., Adler, L. A., Barkley, R. A., Biederman, J. Conners, C. K., Demler, O., et al. (2006). The prevalence and correlates of adult ADHD in the United States. *Amer. J. Psychiat., 163*, 716–23.

Kessler, R. C., Berglund, P., Borges, G., Nock, M., & Wang, P. S. (2005a). Trends in suicide ideation, plans, gestures, and attempts in the United States. *JAMA, 293*(20), 2487–95.

Kessler, R. C., Berglund, P., Chiu, W. T., Demler, O., Heeringa, S., Hiripi, E., et al. (2004). The US National Comorbidity Survey Replication (NCS-R): Design and field procedures. *Int. J. Method. Psych. Res., 13*(2), 69–92.

Kessler, R. C., Berglund, P., Demler, O., Jin, R., & Walters, E. E. (2005b). Lifetime prevalence and age-of-onset distributions of DSM-IV disorders in the National Comorbidity Survey Replication. *Arch. Gen. Psychiat., 62*, 593–602.

Kessler, R. C., Berglund, P., Demler, O., Jin, R., Koretz, D., Merikangas, K. R., et al. (2003). The epidemiology of major depressive disorder: Results from the National Comorbidity Survey Replication. *JAMA, 289*(23), 3095–105.

Kessler, R. C., Birnbaum, H., Bromet, E., Hwang, I., Sampson, N., & Shahly, V. (2010). Age differences in major depression: Results from the National Comorbidity Survey Replication (NCS-R). *Psychol. Med., 40*(02), 225–37. doi:10.1017/S0033291709990213

Kessler, R. C., Chiu, W. T., Demler, O., & Walters, E. E. 2005c). Prevalence, severity, and comorbidity of 12-month *DSM-IV* disorders in the National Comorbidity Survey Replication. *Arch. Gen. Psychiat., 62*, 617–27.

Kessler, R. C., Chiu, W. T., Jin, R., Ruscio, A. M., Shear, K., & Walters, E. E. (2006). The epidemiology of panic attacks, panic disorder, and agoraphobia in the national comorbidity survey replication. *Arch. Gen. Psychiat., 63*(4), 415–24.

Kessler, R. C., & Greenberg, P. E. (2002). The economic burden of anxiety and stress disorders. In K. L. Davis, D. Charney, J. T. Coyle, & C. Nemeroff (Eds.), *Neuropsychopharmacology: The fifth generation of progress* (pp. 981–92). Baltimore, MD: Lippincott Williams & Wilkins.

Kessler, R. C., McGonagle, K. A., Zhao, S., Nelson, C. B., Hughes, M., Eshleman, S., Wittchen, H.-U., & Kendler, K. S. (1994). Lifetime and 12-month prevalence of DSM-III-R psychiatric disorders in the United States: Results from the National Comorbidity Survey. *Arch. Gen. Psychiat., 51*, 8–19.

Kessler, R. C., & Merikangas, K. R. (2004). The National Comorbidity Survey Replication (NCS-R). *Int. J. Method. Psych., 13*(2), 60–68.

Kessler, R. C., Merikangas, K. R., & Wang, P. S. (2007). Prevalence, comorbidity, and service utilization for mood disorders in the United States at the beginning of the twenty-first century. *Ann. Rev. Clin. Psych., 3*, 137–58.

Kessler, R. C., Rubinow, D. R., Holmes, C, Abelson, J. M. Zhao, S (1997). The epidemiology of DSM-III-R bipolar 1 disorder in a general population survey. *Psych. Med., 27*, 1079–89.

Kessler, R. C., Ruscio, A. M., Shear, K., and Wittchen, H-U. (2009) Epidemiology of anxiety disorders. In M. M. Antony & M. B. Stein (Eds.), *Oxford handbook of anxiety and related disorders* (pp. 19–33). New York: Oxford University Press.

Kessler, R. C., Sonnega, A., Bromet, E., Hughes, M., & Nelsom, C. B. (1995). Post-traumatic stress disorder in the National Comorbidity Study. *Arch. Gen. Psychiat., 52*, 1048–60.

Kessler, R. C., & Zhao, S. (1999). Overview of descriptive epidemiology of mental disorders. In C. S. Aneshensel & J. C. Phelan (Eds.), *Handbook of sociology of mental health. Handbook of sociology and social research* (pp. 127–50). New York: Kluwer/Plenum.

Kestler, L. P., Walker, E., & Vega, E. M. (2001). Dopamine receptors in the brains of schizophrenia patients: a meta-analysis of the findings. *Behav. Pharmacol., 12*, 355–71.

Kety, S. S. (1974). From rationalization to reason. *Amer. J. Psychiat., 131*, 957–63.

Kety, S. S., Rosenthal, D., Wender, P. H., Schulsinger, F., & Jacobsen, B. (1978). The biologic and adoptive families of adopted individuals who became schizophrenic: Prevalence of mental illness and other characteristics. In L. C. Wynne, R. L. Cromwell, & S. Matthyse (Eds.), *The nature of schizophrenia: New approaches to research and treatment* (pp. 25–37). New York: Wiley.

Kety, S. S., Wender, P. H., Jacobsen, B., Ingraham, L. J., Jansson, L., Faber, B., & Kinney, D. K. (1994). Mental illness in the biological and adoptive relatives of schizophrenic adoptees: Replication of the Copenhagen study in the rest of Denmark. *Arch. Gen. Psychiat., 51*(6), 442–55.

Keys, A., Brozek, J., Henschel, A., Mickelson, O., & Taylor, H. L. (1950). *The biology of human starvation.* Minneapolis: University of Minnesota Press.

Khalifa, N., & von Knorring, A. L. (2004). Prevalence of tic disorders and Tourette syndrome in a Swedish school population. *J. Amer. Acad. Child Adoles. Psychiat., 43*(2), 206–14.

Khashan, A. S., Abel, K. M., Mc. Namee, R., Pedersen, M. G., Webb, R. T., Baker, P. N., et al. (2008). Higher risk of offspring schizophrenia following antenatal maternal exposure to severe adverse life events. *Arch. Gen. Psychiat, 65*, 146–52.

Khan, A., Cowan, C., & Roy, A. (1997). Personality disorders in people with learning disabilities: A community survey. *J. Intell. Dis. Res., 41*(4), 324–30.

Khan, A., Cutler, A. J., Kajdasz, D. K., Gallipoli, S., Athanasiou, M., Robinson, D. S., Whalen, H., & Reed, C.R. (2011). A randomized, double-blind, placebo-controlled, 8-week study of vilazodone, a serotonergic agent for the treatment of major depressive disorder. *J. Clin. Psychiat., 72*, 441–47.

Khazaal, Y., Zimmerman, G., & Zullino, D. F. (2005). Depersonalization—current data. *Canad. J. Psychiat., 50*(2), 101–7.

Khouzam, H. R., El-Gabalawi, F., Pirwani, N., & Priest, F. (2004). Asperger's disorder: A review of its diagnosis and treatment. *Compr. Psychiat., 45*(3), 184–91.

Kici, G., & Westhoff, K. (2004). Evaluation of requirements for the assessment and construction of interview guides in psychological assessment. *Europ. J. Psychol. Assess., 20*, 83–98.

Kidson, M., & Jones, I. (1968). Psychiatric disorders among aborigines of the Australian Western Desert. *Arch. Gen. Psychiat., 19*, 413–22.

Kiecolt-Glaser, J. K., McGuire, L., Robles, T. F., & Glaser, R. (2002). Emotion, morbidity, and mortality: New perspectives from psychoneuroimmunology. *Ann. Rev. Psychol., 53*, 83–107.

Kiesler, C. A., & Sibulkin, A. E. (1987). *Mental hospitalization: Myths and facts about a national crisis.* Newbury Park, CA: Sage.

Kiesler, C. A., & Simpkins, C. G. (1993). *The unnoticed majority in inpatient psychiatric care.* New York: Plenum.

Kiev, A. (1972). *Transcult. Psychiat.* New York: Free Press.

Kihlstrom, J. F. (1994). One hundred years of hysteria. In S. J. Lynn & J. W. Rhue (Eds.), *Dissociation: Clinical and theoretical perspectives* (pp. 365–94). New York: Guilford.

Kihlstrom, J. F. (2001). Dissociative disorders. In P. B. Sutker & H. E. Adams (Eds.), *Comprehensive handbook of psychopathology* (3rd ed., pp. 259–76). New York: Kluwer Academic/Plenum.

Kihlstrom, J. F. (2002). To honor Kraepelin . . . : From symptoms to pathology in the diagnosis of mental illness. In L. E. Beutler & M. L. Malik (Eds.), *Rethinking the DSM: A psychological perspective* (pp. 279–303). Washington, DC: American Psychological Association.

Kihlstrom, J. F. (2005). Dissociative disorders. *Ann. Rev. Clin. Psych., 1*, 227–53.

Kihlstrom, J. F., & Schacter, D. L. (2000). Functional amnesia. In F. Boller & J. Grafman (Eds.), *Handbook of neuropsychology*, Vol 2. *Memory and its disorders* (2nd ed.), ed. L. S. Cermak (pp. 409–27). Amsterdam: Elsevier Science.

Kihlstrom, J. F., Tataryn, D. J., & Hoyt, I. P. (1993). Dissociative disorders. In P. B. Sutker & H. E. Adams (Eds.), *Comprehensive handbook of psychopathology* (pp. 203–34). New York: Plenum.

Kilpatrick, D. G., Koenan, K. C., Ruggiero, K. J., Acierno, R., Galea, S., Resnick, H. S., Roitzsch, J., Boyle, J., & Gelernter, J. (2007). The serotonin transporter genotype and social support and moderation of posttraumatic stress disorder and depression in hurricane-exposed adults. *Amer. J. Psychiat., 164*, 1693–1699.

Kilzieh, N., & Akiskal, H. S. (1999). Rapid-cycling bipolar disorder: An overview of research and clinical experience. *Psychiat. Clin. N. Amer., 22*, 585–607.

Kim, A., Galanter, M., Castaneda, R., & Lifshutz, H. (1992). Crack cocaine use and sexual behavior among psychiatric inpatients. *Amer. J. Drug Alcoh. Abuse, 18*, 235–46.

Kim, J., Rapee, R. M., & Gaston, J. E. (2008). Symptoms of offensive type Taijin-Kyofusho among Australian social phobics. *Depression and Anxiety, 25*(7), 601–8. doi: 10.1002/da.20345

Kim-Cohen, J. (2007). Resilience and developmental psychopathology. *Child Adoles. Psychiat. Clin. N. Amer., 16*(2), 271–83.

Kim-Cohen, J., Caspi, A., Taylor, A., Williams, B., Newcombe, R., Craig, I. W., et al. (2006). MAOA, maltreatment, and gene-environment interaction predicting children's mental health: New evidence and a meta-analysis. *Molecular Psychiatry, 11*(10), 903–13.

King, L. J. (1999). A brief history of psychiatry: Millennia past and present—Part II. *Ann. Clin. Psychiat., 2,* 47–54.

King, S., St-Hilaire, A., & Heidkamp, D. (2010). Prenatal factors in schizophrenia. *Curr. Dis. Psychol. Sci., 19,* 209–13.

Kinney, D. K., Holzman, P. S., Jacobsen, B., Jansson, L., Faber, B., Hildebrand, W., Kasell, E., & Zimbalist, M. E. (1997). Thought disorder in schizophrenic and control adoptees and their relatives. *Arch. Gen. Psychiat., 54*(5), 475–79.

Kinsey, A. C., Pomeroy, W. B., & Martin, C. E. (1948). *Sexual behavior in the human male.* Philadelphia: Sanders.

Kinsey, A. C., Pomeroy, W. B., Martin, C. E., & Gebhard, P. H. (1953). *Sexual behavior in the human female.* Philadelphia: Saunders.

Kinzl, J., & Biebl, W. (1992). Long-term effects of incest: Life events triggering mental disorders in female patients with sexual abuse in childhood. *Child Ab. Negl., 16,* 567–73.

Kirk, S. A., & Kutchins, H. (1992). *The selling of DSM: The rhetoric of science in psychiatry.* Hawthorne, NY: Aldine de Gruyter.

Kirkbridge, J. B., Fearon, P., Morgan, C., Dazzan, P., Morgan, K., Tarrant, J., Lloyd, T., Holloway, J., et al. (2006). Heterogeneity in incidence rates of schizophrenia and other psychotic syndromes. *Arch. Gen. Psychiat., 63,* 250–58.

Kirkland, G. (1986). *Dancing on my grave.* New York: Doubleday.

Kirmayer, L. J. (1991). The place of culture in psychiatric nosology: Taijin Kyofusho and DSM III-R. *J. Nerv. Ment. Dis., 179,* 19–28.

Kirmayer, L. J., & Groleau, D. (2001). Affective disorders in cultural context. *Cultural Psychiatry: International Perspectives, 24,* 465–78.

Kirmayer, L. J., Young, A., & Hayton, B. C. (1995). The cultural context of anxiety disorders. *Cultur. Psychiat., 18*(3), 503–21.

Kirsch, L. G., & Becker, J. V. (2007). Emotional deficits in psychopathy and sexual sadism: Implications for violent and sadistic behavior. *Clin. Psych. Rev., 27*(8), 904–22.

Kistner, J. A., Ziegert, D. I., Castro, R., & Robertson, B. (2001). Helplessness in early childhood: Prediction of symptoms associated with depression and negative self-worth. *Merrill-Palmer Quarterly, 47*(3), 336–54.

Klassen, L. J., Katzman, M. A., & Chokka, P. (2010). Adult ADHD and its comorbidities, with a focus on bipolar disorder. *J. Affect. Dis., 124*(1–2), 1–8.

Klauke, B. et al. (2010). Life events in panic disorder—an update on candidate stressors. *Depression and Anxiety,* 1–15.

Klee, H. (1998). The love of speed: An analysis of the enduring attraction of amphetamine sulphate for British youth. *J. Drug Iss., 28*(1), 33–56.

Kleespies, P. M. (Ed.). (2009). *Behavioral emergencies: An evidence-based resource for evaluating and managing risk of suicide, violence, and victimization.* Washington, DC: American Psychological Association.

Kleim, B., Ehlers, A., & Glucksman, E. (2007). Early predictors of chronic post-traumatic stress disorder in assault survivors. *Psychol. Med., 37,* 1457–1467.

Klein, D. F. (1981). Anxiety reconceptualized. In D. F. Klein & J. Rabkin (Eds.), *Anxiety: New research and changing concepts.* New York: Raven Press.

Klein, D. N. (1999). Commentary on Ryder and Bagby's "Diagnostic viability of depressive personality disorder: Theoretical and conceptual issues." *J. Pers. Dis., 13*(2), 118–27.

Klein, D. N. (2008). Dysthymia and chronic depression. In W. E. Craighead, D. J. Miklowitz, and L. W. Craighead (Eds.), *Psychopathology: History, theory, and diagnosis* (pp. 329–365). Hoboken, NJ: John Wiley & Sons.

Klein, D. N. (2010). Chronic depression: Diagnosis and classification. *Curr. Dir. Psychol. Sci., 19*(2), 96–100. doi: 10.1177/0963721410366007.

Klein, D. N., Durbin, C. E., & Shankman, S. A. (2009). Personality and mood disorders. In I. H. Gotlib & C. L. Hammen (Eds.), *Handbook of depression* (2nd ed., pp. 93–112). New York: Guilford Press.

Klein, D. N., & Shih, J. H. (1998). Depressive personality: Association with DSM-III-R mood and personality disorders and negative and positive affectivity, 30-month stability, and prediciton of course of axis I depressive disorders. *J. Abn. Psychol., 107*(2), 319–27.

Klein, D. N., Torpey, D. C. & Bufferd, S. J. (2008). *Depressive disorders. Child and adolescent psychopathology.* (pp. 477–509). Hoboken, NJ, US: John Wiley & Sons.

Klein, D. N., & Vocisano, C. (1999). Depressive and self-defeating (masochistic) personality disorders. In T. Millon, P. H. Blaney, & R. D. Davis (Eds.), *Oxford textbook of psychopathology* (pp. 653–73). New York: Oxford University Press.

Klein, D. N., Shankman, S. A., & Rose, S. (2006). Ten-year prospective follow-up study of the naturalistic course of dysthymic disorder and double depression. *Am. J. Psychiat, 163*(5), 872–80.

Kleinknecht, R. A., Dinnel, D. L., & Kleinknecht, E. E. (1997). Cultural factors in social anxiety: A comparison of social phobia symptoms and Taijin Kyofusho. *J. Anxiety Dis., 11*(2), 157–77.

Kleinman, A. (1988). *Rethinking psychiatry: From cultural category to personal experience.* New York: Free Press.

Kleinman, A. (2004). Culture and depression. *N. Engl. J. Med., 351*(10), 951–53.

Kleinman, A. M. (1986). *Social origins of distress and disease: Depression, neurasthenia and pain in modern China.* New Haven, CT: Yale University Press.

Kleinman, A. M., & Good, B. J. (1985). *Culture and depression.* Berkeley: University of California Press.

Kleinman, P. H., Kang, S., Lipton, D. S., & Woody, G. E. (1992). Retention of cocaine abusers in outpatient psychotherapy. *Amer. J. Drug Alcoh. Abuse, 18,* 29–43.

Klerman, G. L., Weissman, M. M., Markowitz, J. C., Glick, I., Wilner, P. J., Mason, B., & Shear, M. K. (1994). Medication and psychotherapy. In A. E. Bergin & S. L. Garfield (Eds.), *Handbook of psychotherapy and behavior change* (4th ed., pp. 734–82). New York: Wiley.

Klerman, G. L., Weissman, M. M., Rounsaville, B. J., & Chevron, E. S. (1984). *Interpersonal psychotherapy of depression.* New York: Basic Books.

Klinger, E. (1979). Modes of normal conscious flow. In K. S. Pope & J. L. Singer (Eds.), *The stream of consciousness: Scientific investigations into the flow of human experience.* New York: Plenum.

Klingman, A. (1993). School-based intervention following a disaster. In C. F. Saylor (Ed.), *Children and disasters* (pp. 187–210). New York: Plenum.

Kloner, R. A., Leor, J., Poole, W. K., & Perritt, R. (1997). Population-based analysis of the effect of the Northridge earthquake on cardiac death in Los Angeles County, California. *Journal of the American College of Cardiology, 30,* 1174–80.

Kloner, R. A., McDonald, S. A., Leeka, J., & Poole, W. K. (2011). Role of age, sex, and race on cardiac and total mortality associated with Super Bowl wins and losses. *Clinical Cardiology, 34,* 102–7.

Kluft, R. P. (1993). Basic principles in conducting the treatment of multiple personality disorder. In R. P. Kluft & C. G. Fine (Eds.), *Clinical perspectives on multiple personality disorder* (pp. 53–73). Washington, DC: American Psychiatric Press.

Kluft, R. P. (1999). Dissociative identity disorder. In N. Miller & K. Magruder (Eds.), *Cost-effectiveness of psychotherapy: A guide for practitioners, researchers, and policymakers* (pp. 306–13). New York: Oxford University Press.

Kluft, R. P. (2005). Diagnosing dissociative identity disorder. *Psychiat. Ann., 35*(8), 633–43.

Klump, K. L., Burt, A., McGue, M., & Iocono, W. G. (2007). Changes in genetic and environmental influences on disordered eating across adolescence. *Arch. Gen. Psychiat., 64*(12), 1409–15.

Klump, K. L., Strober, M., Bulik, C. M., Thornton, L., Johnson, C., Devlin, B., Fichter, M., Halmi, K. A.,Kaplan, A. S., Woodside, D. B., Crow, S., Mitchell, J., Rotondo, A., Keel, P., Berrettini, W. H., Plotnicov, K., Pollice, C., Lilenfeld, L. R., & Kaye, W. H. (2004). Personality characteristics of women before and after recovery from an eating disorder. *Psychol. Med., 34,* 1407–18.

Klump, K. L., Suisman, J. L., Culbert, K. M., Kashy, D. A., & Sisk, C. L. (2011). Binge eating proneness emerges during puberty in female rats: A longitudinal study. *J. Abn. Psych.*

Knapp, S. (1980). A primer on malpractice for psychologists. *Profess. Psychol., 11*(4), 606–12.

Knight, R. A. (1997). *A unified model of sexual aggression: Consistencies and differences across non-criminal and criminal samples.* Paper presented at meeting of the Association for the Treatment of Sexual Abusers, Arlington, VA.

Knight, R. A., & Guay, J.-P. (2006). The role of psychopathy in sexual coercion against women. In C. J. Patrick (Ed.), *Handbook of the psychopathy.* (pp. 512–32). New York: Guilford Press.

Knight, R., & Prentky, R. (1990). Classifying sexual offenders: The development and corroboration of taxonomic models. In W. L. Marshall, D. R. Laws, & H. E. Barbaree (Eds.), *Handbook of sexual assault: Issues, theories, and treatment of the offender* (pp. 23–52). New York: Plenum.

Knight, R., Prentky, R., & Cerce, D. (1994). The development, reliability, and validity of an inventory for the multidimensional assessment of sex and aggression. *Crim. Just. Behav., 21,* 72–94.

Kobak, K. A., Skodol, A. E., & Bender, D. S. (2008). Diagnostic measures for adults. In A. J. Rush, Jr., M. B. First, & D. Blacker, (Eds.), *Handbook of psychiatric measures* (2nd ed., pp. 35–60). Arlington, VA: American Psychiatric Publishing.

Kocsis, J. H., Zisook, S., Davidson, J., Shelton, R., Yonkers, K., Hellerstein, D. J., Rosenbaum, J., & Halbreich, U. (1997). Double-blind comparisons of sertraline, imipramine, and placebo in the treatment of dysthymia: Psychosocial outcomes. *Amer. J. Psychiat., 154*(3), 390–95.

Kodituwakku, P. W., Kalberg, W., & May, P. A. (2001). The effects of prenatal alcohol exposure on executive functioning. *Al. Res. Hlth., 25,* 198.

Koenigsberg, H. W., Kernberg, O. F., Stone, M. H., Appelbaum, A. H., Yeomans, F. E., & Diamond, D. (2000). *Borderline patients: Extending the limits of treatability.* New York: Basic Books.

Koenigsberg, H. W., Woo-Ming, A. M., & Siever, L. J. (2002). Pharmacological treatments for personality disorders. In P. E. Nathan & J. M. Gorman (Eds.), *A guide to treatments that work* (2nd ed., pp. 625–54). New York: Oxford University Press.

Koenigsberg, H. W., Woo-Ming, M., & Siever, J. (2007). Pharmacological treatments of personality disorders. In P. Nathan & J. Gorman (Eds.), *Treatments that work* (3rd ed.) (pp. 659–80). New York: Oxford. University Press.

Koerner, N., & Dugas, M. J. (2008). An investigation of appraisals in individuals vulnerable to excessive worry: The role of intolerance of uncertainty. *Cog. Ther. Res., 32*(5), 619–38. doi: 10.1007/s10608-007-9125-2

Kohut, H., & Wolff, E. (1978). The disorders of the self and their treatment: An outline. *Inter. J. Psychoanal., 59*, 413–26.

Kolata, G. B. (1981). Fetal alcohol advisory debated. *Science, 214*, 642–46.

Kolb, B., & Wishaw, I. Q. (1996). *Fundamentals of human neuropsychology* (4th ed.). New York: Freeman.

Kolb, B., Gibb, R., & Robinson, T. E. (2003). Brain plasticity and behavior. *Curr. Dis. Psychol. Sci., 12*(1), 1–5.

Koltek, M., Wilkes, T. C. R., & Atkinson, M. (1998). The prevalence of posttraumatic stress disorder in an adolescent inpatient unit. *Canad. J. Psychiat., 43*(1), 64–68.

Kominski, G. F. & Melnick, G. A. (2007). Managed care and the growth of competition. In R. M. Andersen, T. H Rice & G. F. Kominski, (Eds) *Changing the U.S. health care system: Key issues in health services policy and management* (3rd ed.). (pp. 551–568) San Francisco, CA, US: Jossey-Bass.

Komro, K., Perry, C. L., Veblen-Mortenson, S., Farbakhsh, K., Toomey, T. L., Stigler, M. H., Jones-Webb, R., Kugler, K. C., Pasch, K. E., & Williams, C. L. (2008). Outcomes from a randomized controlled trialo of a multi-component alcohol use preventive intervention for Urban Youth Project Northland Chicago. *Addiction, 103*(4), 606–18.

Komro, K. A. & Toomey, T. L. (2002). Strategies to prevent underage drinking. *Alcohol Research & Health, 26*(1), 5–14.

Konarski, J. Z., McIntyre, R. S., Kennedy, S. H., Rafi-Tari, S., Soczynska, J. K., & Ketter, T. A. (2008). Volumetric neuroimaging investigations in mood disorders: Bipolar disorder versus major depressive disorder. *Bipolar Disorders, 10*(1), 1–37. doi: 10.1111/j.1399-5618.2008.00435.x

Konrad, K., Gunther, T., Hanisch, C., & Herpertz-Dahlmann, B. (2004). Differential effects of methylphenidate on attentional functions in children with attention-deficit/hyperactivity disorder. *J. Amer. Acad. Child Adoles. Psychia., 43*(2), 191–98.

Koob, G. F., Mason, B. J., De Witte, P., Littleton, J., & Siggins, G. R. (2002). Potential neuroprotective effects of acamprosate. *Alcoholism: Clinical & Experimental Research, 26*(4), 586–92.

Koolschijn, P. C., van Haren, N. E., Lensvelt-Mulders, G. J., Hulshoff Pol, H. E., & Kahn, R. S. (2009). Brain volume abnormalities in major depressive disorder: a meta-analysis of magnetic resonance imaging studies. *Human Brain Mapping, 30*(11), 3719–35. doi: 10.1002/hbm.20801

Kopelowicz, A., Liberman, R. P., & Zarate, R. (2007). Psychosocial treatments for schizophrenia. In P. E. Nathan and J. M. Gorman (Eds.), *A guide to treatments that work* (pp. 243–270). New York: Oxford University Press.

Koponen, S., Taiminem, T., Portin, R., Himanen, L., Isoniemi, H., Heinonen, H., Hinkka, S., & Tenuvuo, O. (2002). Axis I and Axis II psychiatric disorders after traumatic brain injury: A 30-year follow up study. *Amer. J. Psychiat., 159*, 1315–21.

Korbel, J. O., Tirosh-Wagner, T., Urban, A. E., Chen, X. N., Kasowski, M., D. L., et al. (2009). *PNAS Proceedings of the National Academy of Sciences of the United States of America, 106*(29), 12031–36.

Korczak, D. J., Goldstein, B. I., & Levitt, A. J. (2007). Panic disorder, cardiac diagnosis and emergency department utilization in an epidemiologic community sample. *General Hospital Psychiatry, 29*(4), 335–39.

Korkeila, J., Lehtinen, V., Tuori, T., & Helenius, H. (1998). Patterns of psychiatric hospital service use in Finland: A national register study of hospital discharges in the early 1990's. *Soc. Psychiat. Psychiatr. Epidemiol., 33*, 218–23.

Kornstein, S. G. (2010). Gender issues and DSM-V. *Archives of Women's Mental Health, 13*(1), 11–13.

Kosten, T. R. (1997). Substance abuse and schizophrenia. *Schizo. Bull., 23*, 181–86.

Kosten, T. R. (2003). Buprenorphine for opioid detoxification: A brief review. *Addict. Dis. Treat., 2*(4), 107–12.

Kosten, T. R., & Rounsaville, B. J. (1986). Psychopathology in opioid addicts. *Psychiat. Clin. N. Amer., 9*, 515–32.

Kosten, T. R., Silverman, D. G., Fleming, J., & Kosten, T. A. (1992). Intravenous cocaine challenges during naltrexone maintenance: A preliminary study. *Biol. Psychiat., 32*, 543–48.

Kotov, R., Gamez, W., Schmidt, F., & Watson, D. (2010). Linking "big" personality traits to anxiety, depressive, and substance use disorders: A meta-analysis. *Psychol. Bull., 136*(5), 768–821. doi: 10.1037/a0020327

Kovacs, M., Devlin, B., Pollack, M., Richards, C., & Mukerji, P. (1997). A controlled family history study of childhood- onset depressive disorder. *Arch. Gen. Psychiat., 54*, 613–23.

Kovar, K. A. (1998). Chemistry and pharmacology of hallucinogens, entactogens and stimulants. *Pharmacopsychiatry, 31*(Suppl. 2), 69–72.

Kraepelin, E. (1883). *Compendium der psychiatrie.* Leipzig: Abel.

Kraepelin, E. (1896). Dementia praecox. In J. Cutting & M. Shepherd (1987), *The clinical roots of the schizophrenia concept: Translation of seminal European contributions on schizophrenia* (pp. 13–24). Cambridge: Cambridge University Press.

Kraepelin, E. (1919). *Dementia praecox and paraphrenia.* Translated by R. M. Barclay. Edinburgh, Scotland: E and S Livingstone.

Kraft, S. (2011, March). DEA Ban: Faux marijuana "Imminent threat to public safety." *Medical News Today*, 1–2.

Kramer, R. A., Warner, V., Olfson, M., Ebanks, C. M., Chaput, F., & Weissman, M. M. (1998). General medical problems among the offspring of depressed parents: A 10-year follow-up. *J. Amer. Acad. Child Adoles. Psychiat., 37*(6), 602–11.

Kramer, R. M. (1998). Paranoid cognition in social systems: Thinking and acting in the shadow of doubt. *Personal. Soc. Psychol. Rev., 2*(4), 251–75.

Kranzler, H. R., Armeli, S., Feinn, R., & Tennen, H. (2004). Targeted Naltrexone treatment moderates the relations among mood and drinking behavior among problem drinkers. *J. Cons. Clin. Psychol., 72*, 317–27.

Kranzler, H. R., Del Boca, F. K., & Rounsaville, B. (1997). Comorbid psychiatric diagnosis predicts three-year outcomes in alcoholics: A posttreatment natural history study. *J. Stud. Alcoh., 57*(6), 619–26.

Kraus, L., & Pope, K. (2010). Juvenile justice. In M. K. Dulcan (Ed.), *Dulcan's textbook of child and adolescent psychiatry*, (pp. 987–96). Arlington, VA: American Psychiatric Publishing, Inc.

Krauss, D., & Lieberman, J. (2007). Expert testimony on risk and future dangerousness. In M. Costanzo, D. Krauss & D. K. Pezdek (Eds.), *Expert psychological testimony for the courts* (pp. 227–49). Mahwah, NJ: Lawrence Erlbaum Associates.

Kreek, M. J., Borg, L., Ducat, E., & Ray, B. (2010). Pharmacotherapy in the treatment of addiction: Methadone. *J. Addict. Dis., 29*(2), 200–16.

Kremen, W. S., Koenen, K. C., Boake, C., Purcell, S., Eisen, S. A., Franz, C. E., et al. (2007). Pretrauma cognitive ability and risk for posttraumatic stress disorder: A twin study. *Arch. Gen. Psychiat., 64*, 361–68.

Kreppner, J. M., Rutter, M., Beckett, C., Castle, J., Colvert, E., Groothues, C., et al. (2007). Normality and impairment following profound early institutional deprivation: A longitudinal follow-up into early adolescence. *Developmental Psychology, 43*(4), 931–946.

Kring, A. M., & Neale, J. M. (1996). Do schizophrenic patients show a disjunctive relationship among expressive, experiential, and psychophysiological correlates of emotion? *J. Abn. Psychol., 105*, 249–57.

Krippner, S. (1994). Cross-cultural treatment perspectives on dissociative disorders. In S. J. Lynn & J. W. Rhue (Eds.), *Dissociation: Clinical and theoretical perspectives* (pp. 338–64). New York: Guilford.

Krishnan, V., & Nestler, E. J. (2010). Linking molecules to mood: New insight into the biology of depression. *Amer. J. Psychiat., 167*(11), 1305–20. doi: 10.1176/appi.ajp.2009.10030434

Kroes, M. C., Rugg, M. D., Whalley, M.G., & Brewin, C. R. (2011). Structural brain abnormalities common to posttraumatic stress disorder and depression. *J. Psychiatry Neurosci*, 256–65.

Kroll, J., & Bachrach, B. (1984). Sin and mental illness in the Middle Ages. *Psychol. Med., 14*, 507–14.

Kronfol, Z., & Remick, D. G. (2000). Cytokines and the brain: Implications for clinical psychiatry. *Amer. J. Psychiat., 157*(5), 683–94.

Krueger, R. B. (2010). The DSM diagnostic criteria for sexual masochism. *Archives of Sexual Behavior., 39, 2*, 325–45.

Krueger, R. F., & Eaton, N. R. (2010). Personality traits and the classification of mental disorders: Toward a more complete integration in DSM-5 and an empirical model of psychopathology. *Personality Disorders: Theory, Research, and Treatment, 1*(2), 97–118. doi:10.1037/a0018990

Krueger, R. F., Eaton, N. R., Clark, L. A., Watson, D., Markon, K. E., Derringer, J., Skodol, A., et al. (2011a). Deriving an empirical structure of personality pathology for DSM-5. *J. Pers. Disord., 25*(2), 170–91. doi:10.1521/pedi.2011.25.2.170

Krueger, R. F., Eaton, N. R., Derringer, J., Markon, K. E., Watson, D., & Skodol, A. E. (2011b). Personality in DSM-5: Helping delineate personality disorder content and framing the metastructure. *J. Pers. Assess., 93*(4), 325–31. doi:10.1080/00223891.2011.577478

Krueger, R. F., Hicks, B. M., Patrick, C. J., Carlson, S. R., Iacono, W. G., & McGue, M. (2002). Etiologic connections among substance dependence, antisocial behavior, and personality: Modeling the externalizing spectrum. *J. Abn. Psychol., 111*(3), 411–24.

Krueger, R. F., Markon, K. E., Patrick, C. J., Benning, S. D., & Kramer, M. D. (2007). Linking antisocial behavior, substance use, and personality: An integrative quantitative model of the adult externalizing spectrum. *J. Abn. Psych., 116*(4), 645–66.

Krueger, R. F., & South, S. C. (2009). Externalizing disorders: Cluster 5 of the proposed meta-structure for DSM-V and ICD-11.*Psychol. Med., 39*(12), 2061–70. doi: 10.1017/S0033291709990328

Krystal, J. H., Cramer, J. A., Krol, W. F., Kirk, G. F., & Rosenheck, R. A. (2001). Naltrexone in the treatment of alcohol dependence. *N. Engl. J. Med., 345*(24), 1734–39.

Krystal, J. H., Perry, E. B., Gueorguieva, R., Belger, A., Madonick, S. H., Abi-Dargham, A., Cooper, T. B., MacDougall, L., Abi-Saab W., & D'Souza, C.

(2005). Comparative and interactive psychopharmacologic effects of ketamine and amphetamine. *Arch. Gen. Psychiat., 62*, 985–95.

Kubicki, M., McCarley, R., Westin, C. F., Park, H. J., Maier, S., Kikinis, R., Jolesz, F. A., & Shenton, M. E. (2007). A review of diffusion tensor imaging studies in schizophrenia. *J. Psychiat. Res., 41*, 15–30.

Kubota, T., Ushijima, Y., Yamada, K., Okuyama, C., Kizu, O., & Nishimura, T. (2005). Diagnosis of Alzheimer's disease using brain perfusion SPECT and MRI imaging: Which modality achieves better diagnostic accuracy? *European Journal of Nuclear Medicine and Molecular Imaging, 32*, 414–21.

Kubzansky, L. D., Park, N., Peterson, C., Vokonas, P., & Sparrow, D. (2011). Healthy psychological functioning and incident coronary heart disease. *Arch. Gen. Psychiat., 68*, 400–408.

Kulhara, P., & Chakrabarti, S. (2001). Culture and schizophrenia and other psychotic disorders. *Cultural Psychiatry: International Perspectives, 24*, 449–64.

Kulkarni, J., de Castella, A., Fitzgerald, P. B., Gurvich, C. T., Bailey, M., Bartholomeusz, C., & Burger, H. (2008). Estrogen in severe mental illness: A potential new treatment approach. *Arch. Gen. Psychiat., 65*, 955–60.

Kumano, H., Ida, I., Oshima, A., Takahashi, K., Yuuki, N., Amanuma, M., Oriuchi, N., Endo, K., Matsuda, H., & Mikuni, M. (2007). Brain metabolic changes associated with predisposition to onset of major depressive disorder and adjustment disorder in cancer patients— a preliminary PET study. *J. Psychiat. Res., 41*(7), 591–99.

Kunda, Z. (1999). *Social cognition: Making sense of people.* Cambridge, MA: M.I.T. Press.

Kuperman, S., Black, D. W., & Burns, T. L. (1988). Excess mortality among formerly hospitalized child psychiatric patients. *Arch. Gen. Psychiat., 45*, 277–82.

Kupfer, D. J. (2005). The increasing medical burden in bipolar disorder. *JAMA, 293*(20), 2528–30.

Kupka, R. W., Altshuler, L. L., Nolen, W. A., Suppes, T., Luckenbaugh, D. A., Leverich, G. S., et al. (2007). Three times more days depressed than manic or hypomanic in both bipolar I and bipolar II disorder. *Bipolar Disorders, 9*(5), 531–35.

Kupka, R. W., Luckenbaugh, D. A., Post, R. M., Suppes, T., Altshuler, L. L., Keck, P. E., Jr., et al. (2005). Comparison of rapid-cycling and non-rapid-cycling bipolar disorder based on prospective mood ratings in 539 outpatients. *Amer. J. Psychiat., 162*(7), 1273–80.

Kurlan, R. (1997). Treatment of tics. *Neurologic Clinics, 15*(2), 403–9.

Kurtz, M. M., & Mueser, K. T. (2008). A meta-analysis of controlled research on social skills training for schizophrenia. *J. Cons. Clin. Psych., 76*, 491–504.

Kwapil, T. R. (1996). A longitudinal study of drug and alcohol use by psychosis-prone and impulsive-nonconforming individuals. *J. Abn. Psychol., 105*(1), 114–23.

Kwoh, L. (2010). Stress of long-term unemployment takes a toll on thousands of Jerseyans who are out of work. *Star-Ledger*, Sunday, June 13.

Laan, E., & Everaerd, W. (1995). Determinants of female sexual arousal: Psychophysiological theory and data. *Annu. Rev. Sex Res., 6*, 32–76.

LaBrie, J. W., Migliuri, S., Kenney, S. R., & Lac, A. (2010). Family history of alcohol abuse associated with problematic drinking among college students. *Addict. Behav., 35*(7), 721–25.

Ladd, C. O., Huot, R. L., Thrivikraman, K. V., Nemeroff, C. B., Meaney, M. J., & Plotsky, P. M. (2000). Longterm behavioral and neuroendocrine

adaptations to adverse early experience. In E. A. Meyer & C. B. Saper (Eds.), *Progress in brain research: Vol 122. The biological basis for mind-body interactions.* Amsterdam: Elsevier.

Ladd, G. T., & Petry, N. M. (2003). A comparison of pathological gamblers with and without substance abuse treatment histories. *Exper. Clin. Psychopharm., 11*, 202–9.

Ladd, G. W. (2006). Peer rejection, aggressive or withdrawn behavior, and psychological maladjustment from ages 5 to 12: An examination of four predictive models. *Child Develop., 77*(4), 822–46.

Lahey, B. B. (2009). Public health significance of neuroticism. *Amer. Psychol., 64*(4), 241–56. doi: 10.1037/a0015309

Lahey, B. B., Loeber, R., Burke, J. D., & Applegate, B. (2005). Predicting future antisocial personality disorder in males from a clinical assessment in childhood. *J. Cons. Clin. Psychol., 73*, 389–99.

Lahey, B. B., McBurnett, K., & Loeber, R. (2000). Are attention-deficit/hyperactivity disorder and oppositional defiant disorder developmental precursors to conduct disorder? In A. J. Sameroff, M. Lewis, et al. (Eds.), *Handbook of developmental psychopathology* (2nd ed., pp. 431–46). New York: Kluwer.

Laird, R. D., Jordan, K. Y., Dodge, K. A., Pettit, G. S., & Bates, J. E. (2001). Peer rejection in childhood, involvement with antisocial peers in early adolescence, and the development of externalizing behavior problems. *Develop. Psychopath., 13*, 337–54.

Lally, S. J. (2003). What tests are acceptable for use in forensic evaluations? A survey of experts. *Prof. Psychol: Res. Pract., 34*, 434–47.

Lalumière, M. L., Harris, G. T., Quinsey, V. L., & Rice, M. E. (2005a). Rape across cultures and time. In *The causes of rape: Understanding individual differences in male propensity for sexual aggression* (pp. 9–30). Washington, DC: American Psychological Association.

Lalumière, M. L., Harris, G. T., Quinsey, V. L., & Rice, M. E. (2005b). Sexual interest in rape. In *The causes of rape: Understanding individual differences in male propensity for sexual aggression.* (pp. 105–128). Washington, DC: American Psychological Association.

Lam, A. G., & Sue, S. (2001). Client diversity. *Psychother., 38*, 479–86.

Lam, D. H., Watkins, E. R., Hayward, P., Bright, J., Wright, K., Kerr, N., et al. (2003). A randomized controlled study of cognitive therapy for relapse prevention for bipolar affective disorder: Outcome of the first year. *Arch. Gen. Psychiat., 60*(2), 145–52.

Lam, D. H., Hayward, P., Watkins, E. R., Wright,. K., & Sham, P. (2005) Relapse prevention in patients with bipolar disorder: Cognitive therapy outcome after 2 years. *Am. J. Psychiat., 612*, 324–29.

Lamb, H. R. (1998). Deinstitutionalization at the beginning of the new millennium. *Harv. Rev. Psychiat., 6*, 1–10.

Lamberg, L. (1998). Mental illness and violent acts: Protecting the patient and the public. *JAMA, 280*, 407–8.

Lambert, K. G., & Kinsley, C. H. (2005) *Clinical neuroscience: The neurobiological foundations of mental health.* New York: Worth.

Lambert, M. J., & Ogles, B. M. (2004). The efficacy and effectiveness of psychotherapy. In M. J. Lambert (Ed.), *Bergin and Garfield's handbook of psychotherapy and behavior change* (pp. 139–93). New York: John Wiley & Sons.

Lambert, M. J., Hansen, N. B., & Finch, A. E. (2001). Patient-focused research: Using patient outcome

data to enhance treatment. *J. Cons. Clin. Psychol., 69*(2), 159–72.

Lane, H.-Y., Liu, Y.-C., Huang, C.-L., Chang, Y.-C., Liau, C.-H., Perng, C.-H., & Tsai, G. E. (2008). Sarcosine (N-Methylglycine) treatment for acute schizophrenia: A randomized, double-blind study. *Biol. Psychiat., 63*, 9–19.

Lane, S. D., Cherek, D. R., Pietras, C. J., & Steinberg, J. L. (2005). Performance of heavy marijuana-smoking adolescents on a laboratory measure of motivation. *Add. Behav., 30*(2), 815–28.

Lang, P. J. (1968). Fear reduction and fear behavior: Problems in treating a construct. In J. M. Shlien (Ed.), *Research in psychotherapy* (Vol. 3). Washington, DC: American Psychological Association.

Lang, P. J. (1971). Application of psychophysiological methods to the study of psychotherapy and behavior modification. In A. E. Bergin & S. L. Garfield (Eds.), *Handbook of psychotherapy and behavior change.* New York: Wiley.

Lang, P. J. (1985). The cognitive psychophysiology of emotion: Fear and anxiety. In A. H. Tuma & J. D. Maser (Eds.), *Anxiety and the anxiety disorders.* Hillsdale, NJ: Erlbaum.

Lang, P. J., Davis, M., & Öhman, A. (2000). Fear and anxiety: Animal modes and human cognitive psychophysiology. *J. Affec. Dis., 61*, 137–59.

Lange, W. R., Cabanilla, B. R., Moler, G., Bernacki, E. J., & Frankenfield, D. (1994). Preemployment drug screening at the Johns Hopkins Hospital, 1989 and 1991. *Amer. J. Drug Alcoh. Abuse, 20*, 35–46.

Langevin, R., Curnoe, S., Fedoroff, P., Bennett, R., Langevin, M., Peever, C., et al. (2004). Lifetime sex offender recidivism: A 25-year follow-up study. *Canadian Journal of Criminology and Criminal Justice, 46*(5), 531–52.

Langleben, D. D., Loughead, J. W., Bilker, W. B., Ruparel, K., Childress, A. R., Busch, S. I., & Gur, R. C. (2005). Telling truth from lie in individual subects with fast event-related fMRI. *Human Brain Mapping, 26*, 262–72.

Langstrom, N., & Seto, M. C. (2006). Exhibitionistic and voyeuristic behavior in a Swedish national population survey. *Arch. Sex. Behav., 35*, 427–35.

Langstrom, N., & Zucker, K. J. (2005). Tranvestic fetishism in the general population: Prevalence and correlates. *J. Sex Mar. Ther., 31*, 87–95.

Lanni, C., Lenzken, S. C., Pascale, A., Del Vecchio, I., Racchi, M., Pistoia, F., & Govoni, S. (2008). Cognition enhancers between treating and doping the mind. *Pharmacological Research, 57*, 196–213.

Lansford, J. E., Malone, P. S., Dodge, K. A., Crozier, J. C., Pettit, G. S., & Bates, J. E. (2006). A 12-year prospective study of patterns of social information processing problems and externalizing behaviors. *J. Abnorm. Child Psychol., 34*(5), 715–24.

Lapham, S. C., Smith, E., Baca, J. C., Chang, L., Skipper, B. J., Baum, G., & Hunt, W. C. (2001). Prevalence of psychiatric disorders among persons convicted of driving while impaired. *Arch. Gen. Psychiat., 58*, 943–49.

Lareau, C. R. (2007). Violence risk assessment in release decisions for NGRI aquittees: Awareness of practical realities. *J. Foren. Psychol. Pract., 7*(3), 113–24.

Large, M., Sharma, S., Compton, M. T., Slade, T., & Nielssen, O. (2011). Cannabis use and earlier onset of psychosis: A systematic meta-analysis. *Arch. Gen. Psychiat., 68*, 555–61.

Larkins, J. M., & Sher, K. J. (2006). Family history of alcoholism and the stability of personality in young adulthood. *Psych. Addict. Behav., 20*, 471–77.

Larson, S. L., Eyerman, J., Foster, M. S., & Gfroerer, J. G. (2007). Worker substance use and workplace policies and programs. Rockville, MD: Substance Abuse and Mental Health Services Administration, Office of Applied Studies.

Last, C. G., & Perrin, S. (1993). Anxiety disorders in African-American and white children. *J. Abnorm. Child Psychol., 21*, 153–64.

Latner, J. D., & Stunkard, A. (2003). Getting worse: The stigmatization of obese children. *Obesity Research, 11*(3), 452–56.

Laumann, E. O., Gagnon, J. H., Michael, R. T., & Michaels, S. (1994). *The social organization of sexuality: Sexual practices in the United States.* Chicago: The University of Chicago Press.

Laumann, E. O., Paik, A., & Rosen, R. C. (1999). Sexual dysfunction in the United States: Prevalence and predictors. *JAMA, 281*, 537–44.

Laumann, E., Paik, A., Glasser, D. B., Jeong, H. K., Wang, T., Levinson, B., et al. (2005). A cross-national study of subjective well-being among older women and men: Findings from the global study of sexual attitudes and behaviors. *Arch. Sex. Behav., 35*, 143–59.

Lawrence, A. A. (2006). Patient-reported complications and functional outcomes of male-to-female sex reassignment surgery. *Arch. of Sex. Behav., 35*, 717–27.

Lawrence, A. A. (2007). Becoming what we love: Autogynephilic transsexualism conceptualized as an expression of romantic love. *Persp. Biol. Med., 50*(4), 506–20.

Lawrence, A. A., Latty, E. M., Chivers, M. L., & Bailey, J. M. (2005). Measurement of sexual arousal in postperative male-to-female transsexuals using vaginal photoplethysmography. *Arch. Sex. Behav., 34*(2), 135–45.

Lawrence, J. G. and T. Garner v. Texas, 558 (U.S. Supreme Court 2003).

Lawrie, S. M., & Abukmeil, S. S. (1998). Brain abnormality in schizophrenia. *Brit. J. Psychiat., 172*, 110–20.

Laws, D. R., & O'Donohue, W. T. (2008). *Sexual deviance: Theory, assessment, and treatment* (2nd ed.). New York: Guilford Press.

Lawson, W. B. (2008). Schizophrenia in African Americans. In K. T. Mueser & D. V. Jeste (Eds.), *Clinical handbook of schizophrenia* (pp. 616–623). New York: Guilford.

Lay, B., Nordt, C., & Rössler, W. (2007). Trends in psychiatric hospitalization of people with schizophrenia: A register-based investigation over the last three decades. *Schizo. Res.*, 97, 68–78.

Lazarus, A. A. (1997). *Brief but comprehensive psychotherapy: The multimodal way.* New York: Springer.

Lazarus, A. A. (Ed.). (1996). *Controversies in managed mental health care.* Washington, DC: American Psychiatric Press.

Lazarus, R. S. (1993). From psychological stress to the emotions: A history of changing outlooks. *Annu. Rev. Psychol., 44*, 1–21.

Le Blanc, L. A., Hagopian, L. P., & Maglieri, K. A. (2000). Use of a token economy to eliminate excessive inappropriate social behavior in an adult with developmental disabilities. *Behavioral Interventions, 15*, 135–43.

le Grange, D., & Lock, J. (2005). The dearth of psychological treatment studies for anorexia nervosa. *Int. J. Eat. Dis., 37*, 79–91.

le Grange, D., Telch, C. F., & Tibbs, J. (1998). Eating attitudes and behaviors in 1,435 South African Caucasian and non-Caucasian college students. *Amer. J. Psychiat., 155*(2), 250–54.

Leas, L., & Mellor, D. (2000). Prediction of delinquency: The role of depression, risk-taking, and parental attachment. *Behavior Change, 17*(3), 155–66.

LeBlond, R. F., DeGowin, R. L., & Brown, D. D. (2004). *DeGowin's diagnostic examination.* New York: McGraw-Hill.

Lebra, W. (Ed.). (1976). Culture-bound syndromes, ethnopsychiatry and alternate therapies. In *Mental health research in Asia and the Pacific* (Vol. 4). Honolulu: University Press of Hawaii.

LeDoux, J. E. (2000). Emotion circuits in the brain. *Annu. Rev. Neurosci., 23*, 155–84.

LeDoux, J. E. (2002). *Synaptic self: How our brains become who we are.* Penguin, Putnam, Inc.: NewYork.

Lee, J. D., Grossman, E., DiRocco, D., Truncali, A., Hanley, K., Stevens, D., Rotrosen, J., & Gourevitch, M. N. (2010). Extended-release naltrexone for treatment of alcohol dependence in primary care. *J. Subst. Abuse Treat., 39*(1), 14–21.

Lee, J. K. P., Jackson, H. J., Pattison, P., & Ward, T. (2002). Developmental risk factors for sexual offending. *Child Ab. Negl., 26*(1), 73–92.

Lee, P. E., Gill, S. S., Freedman, M., Bronskill, S. E., Hillmer, M. P., & Rochon, P. A. (2004). Atypical antipsychotic drugs in the treatment of behavioral and psychological symptoms of dementia. *BMJ, 329*, 75–78.

Lee, S., & Katzman, M. A. (2002). Cross-cultural perspectives on eating disorders. In C. G. Fairburn & K. D. Brownell (Eds.), *Eating disorders and obesity: A comprehensive handbook* (2nd ed., pp. 260–64). New York: Guilford.

Lee, S., Ho, T. P., & Hsu, L. K. (1993). Fat-phobic and nonfat-phobic anorexia nervosa: A comparative study of 70 Chinese patients in Hong Kong. *Psychol. Med., 23*(4), 999–1017.

Lee, S., Tsang, A., Ruscio, A. M., Haro, J. M., Stein, D. J., Alonso, J., et al. (2009). Implications of modifying the duration requirement of generalized anxiety disorder in developed and developing countries. *Psychol. Med., 39*(07), 1163–76. doi: doi:10.1017/S0033291708004807

Lees-Roitman, S. E., Cornblatt, B. A., Bergman, A., Obuchowski, M., Mitropoulou, V., Keefe, R. S. E., Silverman, J. M., & Siever, L. J. (1997). Attentional functioning in schizotypal personality disorder. *Amer. J. Psychiat., 154*(5), 655–60.

Lefcourt, H. M. (2002). Humor. In C. R. Snyder & S. J. Lopez (Eds.), *Handbook of positive psychology* (pp. 619–31). New York: Oxford University Press.

Leff, J. (2001). Can we manage without the mental hospital? *Austral. N.Z. J. Psychiat., 35*(4), 421–27.

Leff, J., Kuipers, L., Berkowitz, R., Eberlein-Fries, R., & Sturgeon, D. (1982). A controlled trial of social intervention in the families of schizophrenic patients. *Brit. J. Psychiat., 141*, 121–34.

Leff, J., Wig, N. N., Ghosh, A., Bedi, H., Menon, D. K., Kuipers, L., Korten, A., Ernberg, G., Day, R., Sartorius, N., & Jablensky, A. (1987). Influence of relatives' expressed emotion in the course of schizophrenia in Chandigarh. *Brit. J. Psychiat., 151*, 166–73.

Legerstee, J. S., Tulen, J. H. M., Dierckx, B., Treffers, P. D. A., Verhulst, F. C., & Utens, E. M. (2010). CBT for childhood anxiety disorders: Differential changes in selective attention between treatment responders and non-responders. *J. Child Psychol. Psychiat., 51*(2), 162–17.

Lehman, A. F., Steinwachs, D. M., Dixon, L. B., Postrado, L., Scott, J. E., Fahey, M., Fischer, P., Hoch, J., Kasper, J. A., Lyles, A., Shore, A., & Skinner, E. A. (1998). Patterns of usual care for schizophrenia: Initial results from the Schizophrenia Patient Outcomes Research Team (PORT) Client Survey. *Schizo. Bull., 24*(1), 11–20.

Lehto, J. (1995). *Approaches to alcohol control policy: European alcohol action plan.* Geneva: World Health Organization.

Leichsenring, F. (2003). The effectiveness of psychodynamic therapy and cognitive behavior therapy in the treatment of personality disorders: A meta-analysis. *Amer. J. Psychiat., 160*(7), 1223–32. doi:10.1176/appi.ajp.160.7.1223

Leichsenring, F., Leibing, E., Kruse, J., New, A. S., & Leweke, F. (2011). Borderline personality disorder. *Lancet, 377*(9759), 74–84. doi:10.1016/S0140-6736(10)61422-5

Leichsenring, F., & Rabung, S. (2011). Long-term psychodynamic psychotherapy in complex mental disorders: Update of a meta-analysis. *Brit. J. Psychiat., 199*, 15–22.

Leichtman, M (2006). Residential treatment in children and adolescents: Past, present and future. *Am. J. Orthopsychiat., 76*, 285–94.

Leichtman, M. (2009). Behavioral observations. In J. N. Butcher (Ed.), *Oxford handbook of personality and clinical assessment* (pp. 187–99). New York: Oxford University Press.

Leit, R. A., Pope, H. G., & Gray, J. J. (2001). Cultural expectations of muscularity in men: The evolution of *Playgirl* centerfolds. *Int. J. Eat. Dis., 29*(1), 90–93.

Lemche, E., Surguladze, S., Giampietro, V. P., Anilkumar, A., Brammer, M. J., Sierria, M., Chitnis, X., Williams, S. C. R., Gasston, D., Joraschky, P., David, A. S., & Phillips, M. L. (2007). Limbic and prefrontal responses to facial emotion expressions in depersonalization. *NeuroReport, 18*(5), 473–77.

Lemmer, B. (2007). The sleep–wake cycle and sleeping pills. *Physiology & Behavior, 90*(2–3), 285–93.

LeMoult, J., Joormann, J., Sherdell, L., Wright, Y., & Gotlib, I. H. (2009). Identification of emotional facial expressions following recovery from depression. *J. Abn. Psychol., 118*(4), 828–33. doi: 10.1037/a0016944

Lengua, L. J. (2006). Growth in temperament and parenting as predictors of adjustment during children's transition to adolescence. *Develop. Psych., 42*, 819–32.

Lengweiler, M. (2003). Psychiatry beyond the asylum: The origins of German military psychiatry before World War I. *History of Psychiatry, 14*, 14–62.

Lennon, M. C., & Limonic, L. (2010). Work and unemployment as stressors. In T. L. Scheid & T. N. Brown (Eds.), *A handbook for the study of mental health: Social contexts, theories, and systems* (2nd ed, pp. 213–25). New York: Cambridge University Press.

Lenz, G., & Demal, U. (2000). Quality of life in depression and anxiety disorders: An explanatory follow-up study after intensive cognitive behaviour therapy. *Psychopath., 33*, 297–302.

Lenzenweger, M. F. (2008). Epidemiology of personality disorders. *Psychiat. Clinics N. Amer., 31*, 395–403.

Lenzenweger, M. F. (2009). Schizotypic psychopathology: Theory, evidence, and future directions. In P. H. Blaney & T. Millon (Eds.), *Oxford textbook of psychopathology* (2nd ed., pp. 692–722). New York: Oxford University Press.

Lenzenweger, M. F. (2010). *Schizotypy and schizophrenia: The view from experimental psychopathology.* New York: Guildford Press.

Lenzenweger, M. F., & Dworkin, R. H. (Ed.). (1998). *Origins and development of schizophrenia: Advances in experimental psychopathology.* Washington, DC: American Psychological Association.

Lenzenweger, M. F., Dworkin, R. H., & Wethington, E. (1991). Examining the underlying structure of schizophrenic phenomenology: Evidence for a 3-process model. *Schizo. Bull., 17,* 515–24.

Lenzenweger, M. F., Lane, M. C., Loranger, A. W., and Kessler, R. C. (2007). DSM-IV Personality disorders in the national comorbidity survey replication. *Biol. Psychiat., 62,* 553–64.

Lenzenweger, M. F., & Willett, J. B. (2009). Does change in temperament predict change in schizoid personality disorder? A methodological framework and illustration from the Longitudinal Study of Personality Disorders. *Develop. Psychopath., 21*(4), 1211–31. doi:10.1017/S0954579409990125

Leon, D. E., & McCambridge, J. (2006). Liver cirrhosis mortality rates in Britain from 1950 to 2002: an analysis of routine data. *Lancet, 367*(9504) 52–56.

Leon, G. R., Keel, P. K., Klump, K. L., & Fulkerson, J. A. (1997). The future of risk factor research in understanding the etiology of eating disorders. *Psychopharm. Bull., 33*(3), 405–11.

Leonard, K. E., & Eiden, R. D. (2007). Marital and family processes in the context of alcohol use and alcohol disorders. *Annu. Rev. Clin. Psychol., 3,* 285–310.

Leonard, L. M., & Follette, V. M. (2002). Sexual functioning in women reporting a history of child sexual abuse: Review of the empirical literature and clinical implications. *Annu. Rev. Sex Res., 13,* 346–88.

Leonardo, E. D., & Hen, R. (2006). Genetics of affective and anxiety disorders. *Ann. Rev. Psych., 57,* 117–137.

Leong, G. B., & Eth, S. (1991). Legal and ethical issues in electroconvulsive therapy. *Psychiat. Clin. N. Amer., 14,* 1007–16.

Leor, J., Poole, W. K., & Kloner, R. A. (1996). Sudden cardiac death triggered by an earthquake. *New England Journal of Medicine, 334, 7,* 413–19.

Lerman, P. (1981). *Deinstitutionalization: A cross-problem analysis.* Rockville, MD: U.S. Department of Health and Human Services.

Leserman, J., Pence, B. W., Whetten, K., Mugavero, M. J., Thielman, N. M, Schwartz, M. S., & Stangl, D. (2007). Relation of lifetime trauma and depressive symptoms to mortality in HIV. *Amer. J. Psychiat., 164,* 1707–13.

Lesperance, F., Frasure-Smith, N., Talajic, M., & Bourassa, M. G., (2002). Five-year risk of cardiac mortality in relation to initial severity and one-year changes in depression symptoms after myocardial infarction. *Circulation, 105,* 1049–53.

Lester, B. M., Masten, A., & McEwen, B. (2006). *Resilience in children.* Malden, MA: Blackwell Publishing.

Leukefeld, C. G., Logan, P. R., Clayton, C., Martin, R., Zimmerman, A., Milch, R., & Lynam, D. (1998). Adolescent drug use, delinquency, and other behaviors. In T. P. Gullotta, G. R. Adams, & R. Montemayor (Eds.), *Advances in adolescent development: An annual book series.* (Vol. 9, pp. 98–128). Thousand Oaks, CA: Sage.

Leung, A. W., & Heimberg, R. G. (1996). Homework compliance, perceptions of control, and outcome of cognitive- behavioral treatment of social phobia. *Behav. Res. Ther., 34*(5), 423–32.

Leung, A., & Chue, P. (2000). Sex differences in schizophrenia: A review of the literature. *Acta Psychiatr. Scandin., 101,* 3–38.

Levav, I., Kohn, R., Golding, J. M., & Weisman, M. M. (1997). Vulnerability of Jews to affective disorders. *Amer. J. Psychiat., 154*(7), 941–47.

LeVay, S., & Valente, S. M. (2003). *Human sexuality.* Sunderland, MA: Sinauer Associates.

LeVay, S., & Valente, S. M. (2006). *Human sexuality* (2nd ed.). Sunderland, MA US: Sinauer Associates.

Levenson, J. S., D'Amora, D. A., & Hern, A. L. (2007). Megan's Law and its impact on community re-entry for sex offenders. *Behavioral Sciences and the Law, 25,* 587–602.

Levenston, G. K., Patrick, C. J., Bradley, M. M., & Lang, P. J. (2000). The psychopath as observer: Emotion and attention in picture processing. *J. Abn. Psychol., 109*(3), 373–85.

Levin, F. R., & Hennessey, G. (2004). Bipolar disorder and substance abuse. *Biol. Psychiat., 56,* 738–48.

Levine, R. E., & Gaw, A. C. (1995). Culture-bound syndromes. *Psychiat. Clin. N. Amer.: Cultural Psychiatry, 18*(3), 523–36.

Levinson, D. F. (2006). The genetics of depression: A review. *Biol. Psychiat., 60*(2), 84–92.

Levinson, D. F. (2009). Genetics of major depression. In I. H. Gotlib & C. L. Hammen (Eds.), *Handbook of depression* (2nd cd., pp. 165–86). New York: Guilford Press.

Levor, R. M., Cohen, M. J., Naliboff, B. D., & McArthur, D. (1986). Psychosocial precursors and correlates of migraine headache. *J. Cons. Clin. Psychol., 54,* 347–53.

Levy, C., & Kershaw, S. (2001, Apr. 18). *New York Times,* p. A20.

Levy, D. L., Holzman, P. S., Matthysse, S., & Mendell, N. R. (1993). Eye tracking dysfunction and schizophrenia: A critical perspective. *Schizo. Bull., 19*(3), 461–536.

Levy, K. N., Reynoso, J. S., Wasserman, R. H., & Clarkin, J. F. (2007). Narcissistic personality disorder. In W. O'Donohue, K. A. Fowler, & S. O. Lilienfeld (Eds.), *Personality disorders: Toward the DSM-V* (pp. 233–77). Thousand Oaks, CA: Sage.

Levy, K. N., & Wasserman, R. H. (2009). Psychodynamic model of depression. In R. Ingram (Ed.), *The international encyclopedia of depression* (pp. 457–60). New York: Springer.

Levy, S. E., Mandell, D. S., & Schultz, R. T. (2009). Autism. *Lancet, 174,* Issue, 9701, 1627–38.

Lewin, L. C., Abdrbo, A., & Burant, C. J. (2010). Domestic violence in women with serious mental illness involved with child protective services. *Issues in Mental Health Nursing, 31*(2), 128–36. doi:10.3109/01612840903383984

Lewinsohn, P. M. (1974). A behavioral approach to depression. In R. J. Friedman & M. M. Katz (Eds.), *The psychology of depression: Contemporary theory and research.* New York: Halstead Press.

Lewinsohn, P. M., & Essau, C. A. (2002). Depression in adolescents. In I. H. Gotlib & C. L. Hammen (Eds.), *Handbook of depression* (pp. 541–59). New York: Guilford.

Lewinsohn, P. M., & Gotlib, I. H. (1995). Behavioral theory and treatment of depression. In E. E. Beckham & W. R. Leber (Eds.), *Handbook of depression* (2nd ed., pp. 352–75). New York: Guilford.

Lewinsohn, P. M., Gotlib, I. H., Lewinson, M., Seeley, J. R., & Allen, N. B. (1998). Gender differences in anxiety disorders and anxiety symptoms in adolescents. *J. Abn. Psychol. 107*(1), 109–17.

Lewinsohn, P. M., Hoberman, H. M., Teri, L., & Hautzinger, M. (1985). An integrative theory of depression. In S. Reiss & R. Bootzin (Eds.), *Theoretical issues in behavior therapy* (pp. 331–59). San Diego: Academic Press.

Lewinsohn, P. M., Hops, H., Roberts, R. E., Seeley, J. R., & Andrews, J. A. (1993). Adolescent psychopathology: I. Prevalence and incidence of depression and other DSM-III-R disorders in high school students. *J. Abn. Psychol., 102,* 133–44.

Lewinsohn, P. M., Joiner, T. E., & Rohde, P. (2001). Evaluation of cognitive diathesis-stress models in predicting major depressive disorder in adolescents. *J. Abn. Psychol., 110*(2), 203–15.

Lewinsohn, P. M., Rohde, P., & Seeley, J. R. (1994). Psychosocial risk factors for future adolescent suicide attempts. *J. Cons. Clin. Psychol., 62,* 297–305.

Lewinsohn, P. M., Rohde, P., Seely, J. R., Klein, D. N., & Gotlib, I. H. (2003). Psychosocial functioning of young adults who have experienced and recovered from major depressive disorder during adolescence. *J. Abn. Psychol., 112*(3), 353–63.

Lewis, C. F., & Ednie, K. (1997). Koro and homicidal behavior. *Amer. J. Psychiat., 154,* 1169.

Lewis, D. A. (2011). Antipsychotic medications and brain volume: Do we have cause for concern? *Arch. Gen. Psychiat., 68,* 126–27.

Lewis, D. O., Yeager, C. A., Swica, Y., Pincus, J. H., & Lewis, M. (1997). Objective documentation of child abuse and dissociation in 12 murderers with dissociative identity disorder. *Amer. J. Psychiat., 154*(12), 1703–10.

Lewis, J., Dickson, D. W., Lin, W.-L., Chisholm, L., Corral, A., Jones, G., Yen, S.-H., Sahara, N., Skipper, L., Yager, D., Eckman, C., Hardy, J., Hutton, M., & McGowan, E. (2001). Enhanced neurofibrillary degeneration in transgenic mice expressing mutant tau and APP. *Science, 293,* 1487–91.

Lewis, T. T., Aiello, A. E., Leurgans, S., Kelly, J., & Barnes, L. L. (2010). Self-reported experiences of everyday discrimination are associated with elevated C-reactive protein levels in older African-America adults. *Brain, Behavior, and Immunity, 24,* 438–43.

Lezak, M. D. (1995). *Neuropsychological assessment* (3rd ed.). New York: Oxford University Press.

Li, G., Wang, L. Y., Shofer, J. B., Thompson, M. L., Peskind, E. R., McCormick, W., Bowen, J. D., Crane, P. K., & Larson, E. B. (2011). Temporal relationship between depression and dementia. *Arch. Gen. Psychiat., 68,* 970–77.

Li, Q. (2007). New bottle but old wine: A research of cyberbullying in schools. *Computers in Human Behavior, 23*(4), 1777–91.

Li, W., & Zinbarg, R. E. (2007). Anxiety sensitivity and panic attacks: A 1-year longitudinal study. *Behav. Mod., 31*(2), 145–61.

Lichtenberger, E. O., & Kaufman, A. S. (2009). *Essentials of WAIS-IV assessment.* New York: John Wiley.

Lidz, T., Fleck, S., & Cornelison, A. R. (1965). *Schizophrenia and the family.* New York: International Universities Press.

Lieb, K., Zanarini, M., Schmahl, C., Linehan, M., & Bohus, M. (2004). Borderline personality disorder. *Lancet, 364,* 453–61.

Lieb, R., Schuetz, C. G., Pfister, H., von Sydow, K., & Wittchen, H. (2002). Mental disorders in ecstasy users: A prospective-longitudinal investigation. *Drug & Alcohol Dependence, 68,* 195–207.

Lieb, R., Wittchen, H.-U., Hofler, M., Fuetsch, M., Stein, M., & Merikangas, K. R. (2000). Parental psychopathology, parenting styles, and the risk of social phobia in offspring: A prospective-longitudinal community study. *JAMA, 57,* 859–66.

Lieberman, J. A., Jody, D., Alvir, J. M. J., Ashtari, M., Levy, D. L., Bogerts, B., Degreef, G., Mayerhoff, D. I., & Cooper, T. (1993). Brain morphology, dopamine, and eye-tracking abnormalities in first-episode schizophrenia: Prevalence and clinical correlates. *Arch. Gen. Psychiat., 50*(5), 357–68.

Lieberman, J. A., & Stroup, T. S. (2011). The NIMH-CATIE schizophrenia study: What did we learn? *Am. J. Psychiat.*, *168*, 770–75.

Liem, J. H. (1974). Effects of verbal communications of parents and children: A comparison of normal and schizophrenic families. *J. Cons. Clin. Psychol.*, *42*, 438–50.

Lieverse, R., Van Someren, E. J., Nielen, M. M., Uitdehaag, B. M., Smit, J. H., & Hoogendijk, W. J. (2011). Bright light treatment in elderly patients with nonseasonal major depressive disorder: A randomized placebo-controlled trial. *Arch. Gen. Psychiat.*, *68*(1), 61–70. doi: 10.1001/archgenpsychiatry.2010.183

Lilenfeld, L. R. R., Wonderlich, S., Riso, L. P., Crosby, R., & Mitchell, J. (2006). Eating disorders and personality: A methodological and empirical review. *Clin. Psych. Rev.*, *26*, 299–320.

Lilenfeld, L. R., Kaye, W. H., Greeno, C. G., Merikangas, K. R., Plotnicov, K., Pollice, C., Rao, R., Strober, M., Bulik, C. M., & Nagy, L. (1998). A controlled family study of anorexia nervosa and bulimia nervosa. *Arch. Gen. Psychiat.*, *55*, 603–10.

Lilienfeld, S. O. (1992). The association between antisocial personality and somatization disorders: A review and integration of theoretical models. *Clin. Psychol. Rev.*, *12*, 641–62.

Lilienfeld, S. O. (2002). When worlds collide: Social science, politics, and the Rind et al. (1998) child sexual abuse meta-analysis. *Amer. Psychol.*, *57*, 176–88.

Lilienfeld, S. O. (2007). Psychological treatments that cause harm. *Perspectives on Psychological Science.* *2*, 53–70.

Lilienfeld, S. O., & Landfield, K. (2008) Issues in diagnosis: Categorical vs. dimensional. In W. E. Craighead, D. J. Miklowitz, & L. W. Craighead (Eds.), *Psychopathology: History, Diagnosis, and Empirical Foundations*. Hoboken, NJ: John Wiley & Sons.

Lilienfeld, S. O., & Lynn, S. J. (2003). Dissociative identity disorder: Multiple personalities, multiple controversies. In S. O. Lilienfeld & S. J. Lynn (Eds.), *Science and pseudoscience in clinical psychology* (pp. 109–42). New York: Guilford Press.

Lilienfeld, S. O., & Marino, L. (1999). Essentialism revisited: Evolutionary theory and the concept of mental disorder. *J. Abn. Psychol.*, *108*(3), 400–11.

Lilienfeld, S. O., Lynn, S. J., Kirsch, I., Chaves, J. F., Sarbin, T. R., Ganaway, G. K., & Puwell, R. A. (1999). Dissociative identity disorder and the sociocognitive model: Recalling lessons of the past. *Psychol. Bull.*, *125*, 507–23.

Lilienfeld, S. O., Wood, J. M., & Garb, H. N. (2001, May). What's wrong in this picture? *Scientific American*, 81–87.

Lim, S.-L., & Kim, J.-H. (2005). Cognitive processing of emotional information in depression, panic, and somatoform disorder. *J. Abn. Psych.*, *114*(1), 50–61.

Lin, C. C. H., Kuo, P. H., Su, C. H., & Chen, W. J. (2006). The Taipei Adolescent Twin/Sibling Family Study I: Behavioral problems, personality features, and neuropsychological performance. *International Society for Twin Studies*, *9*, 890–94.

Lin, C. C. H., Su, C. H., Kuo, P. H., Hsiao, C. K., Soong, W. T., & Chen, W. (2007). Genetic and environmental influences on schizotypy among adolescents in Taiwan: A multivariate twin/sibling analysis. *Behav. Gen.*, *37*, 334–44.

Lin, P.-Y., & Tsai, G. (2004). Association between serotonin transporter gene promoter polymorphism and suicide: Results of a meta-analysis. *Biol. Psychiat.*, *55*(10), 1023–30.

Lincoln, A. E., Caswell, S. V., Almquist, J. L., Dunn, R. E., Norris, J. B., & Hinton, R. Y. (2011). Trends in concussion incidence in high school sports: A prospective 11-year study. *Am. J. Sports Med.*, *39*, 958–63.

Lindamer, L. A., Lohr, J. B., Harris, M. J., & Jeste, D. V. (1997). Gender, estrogen, and schizophrenia. *Psychopharm. Bull.*, *33*(2), 221–28.

Lindau, S. T., Schumm, L. P., Laumann, E. O., Levinson, W., O'Muircheartaign, C. A., & Waite, L. J. (2007). A study of sexuality and health among older adults in the United States. *N. Eng. J. Med.*, *357*(8), 762–74.

Linden, D. E. J. (2006). How psychotherapy changes the brain: The contribution of functional neuroimaging. *Molec. Psychiat.*, *11*(6), 528–38.

Lindman, R. E., & Lang, A. R. (1994). The alcohol-aggression stereotype: A cross-cultural comparison of beliefs. *Inter. J. Addict.*, *29*, 1–13.

Linehan, M. M. (1993). *Cognitive-behavioral treatment of borderline personality disorder: The dialectics of effective treatment*. New York: Guilford.

Linehan, M. M., Comtois, K. A., Murray, A. M., Brown, M. Z., Gallop, R. J., Heard, H. L., Korslund, K. E., Tutek, D. A., Reynolds, S. K., & Lindenboim, N. (2006). Two-year randomized controlled trial and follow-up of dialectical behavior therapy vs therapy by experts for suicidal behaviors and borderline personality disorder. *Arch. Gen. Psychiat.*, *63*, 757–66.

Linehan, M. M., & Dexter-Mazza, E. T. (2008). Dialectical behavior therapy for borderline personality disorder. In D. H. Barlow (Eds.), *Clinical Handbook of Psychological Disorders: A Step-by-step Treatment Manual (4th ed.)*. New York: Guilford Press.

Ling, W., Jacobs, P., Hillhouse, M., Hasson, A., Thomas, C., Freese, T., Sparenborg, S., McCarty, D., Weiss, R., Saxon, A., Cohen, A., Straus, M., Brigham, G., Liu, D., McLaughlin, P., & Tai, B. (2010). From research to the real world: Buprenorphine in the decade of the clinical trials network. *J. Subst. Abuse Treat.*, *38*(Suppl 1), S53–60.

Link, B. G. (2001). Stigma: Many mechanisms require multifaceted responses. *Epidemiologia e Psichiatria Sociale*, *10*, 8–11.

Lintzeris, N., Holgate, F., & Dunlop, A. (1996). Addressing dependent amphetamine use: A place for prescription. *Drug and Alcohol Review*, *15*(2), 189–95.

Lipp, O. V. (2006) Human fear learning: Contemporary procedures and measurement. In M. G. Craske, D. Hermans, & D. Vansteenwegen (Eds.), *Fear and learning: From basic processes to clinical implications* (pp. 37–51). Washington, DC: American Psychological Association.

Lis, E., Greenfield, B., Henry, M., Guile, J. M., & Dougherty, G. (2007). Neuroimaging and genetics of borderline personality disorder: A review. *Journal of Psychiatric Neuroscience*, *32(3)*, 162–173.

Lishman, W. A. (1990). Alcohol and the brain. *Brit. J. Psychiat.*, *156*, 635–44.

Lissek, S., Levenson, J., Biggs, A. L., Johnson, L. L., Ameli, R., Pine, D. S., & Grillon, C. (2008). Elevated fear conditioning to socially relevant unconditioned stimuli in social anxiety disorder. *Amer. J. Psychiat.*, *165*(1), 124–32. doi: 10.1176/appi.ajp.2007.06091513

Lissek, S., Rabin, S., Heller, R. E., Lukenbaugh, D., Geraci, M., Pine, D. S., & Grillon, C. (2010). "Overgeneralization of conditioned fear as a pathogenic marker of panic disorder": Correction. *Amer. J. Psychiat.*, *167*(1). doi: 10.1176/appi.ajp.2009.09030410

Lissek, S., Rabin, S. J., McDowell, D. J., Dvir, S., Bradford, D. E., Geraci, M., et al. (2009). Impaired discriminative fear-conditioning resulting from elevated fear responding to learned safety cues among individuals with panic disorder. *Behav. Res. Ther.*, *47*(2), 111–18. doi: 10.1016/j.brat.2008.10.017

Litt, M. D., Kadden, R. M., Kabele-Cormier, E., & Petry, N. (2007). Changing network support for drinking initial findings from the Nework Support Project. *J. Cons. Clin. Psych.*, *75*, 542–55.

Littrell, J. (2001). What neurobiology has to say about why people abuse alcohol and other drugs. *Journal of Social Work Practice in the Addictions*, *1*(3), 23–40.

Liu, R. T., & Alloy, L. B. (2010). Stress generation in depression: A systematic review of the empirical literature and recommendations for future study. *Clin. Psychol. Rev.*, *30*(5), 582–93. doi: 10.1016/j.cpr.2010.04.010

Liu, X., Sun, Z., Uchiyama, M., Li, Y., & Okawa, M. (2000). Attaining nocturnal urinary control, nocturnal enuresis, and behavioral problems in Chinese children aged 6 through 16 years. *J. Amer. Acad. Child Adoles. Psychiat.*, *39*, 1557–64.

Livesley, W. J. (1995). Past achievements and future directions. In W. J. Livesley (Ed.), *The DSM-IV personality disorders*. (pp. 497–506). New York: Guilford.

Livesley, W. J. (2001). Conceptual and taxonomic issues. In W. J. Livesley (Ed.), *Handbook of personality disorders* (pp. 3–38). New York: Guilford.

Livesley, W. J. (2003). Diagnostic dilemmas in classifying personality disorder. In K. A. Phillips, M. B. First, & H. A. Pincus (Eds.), *Advancing DSM: Dilemmas in psychiatric diagnosis* (pp. 153–90). Washington, DC: American Psychiatric Association.

Livesley, W. J. (2005). Behavioral and molecular genetic contributions to a dimensional classification of personality disorders. *J. Pers. Dis.*, *19*, 131–55.

Livesley, W. J. (2008) Toward a genetically-informed model of borderline personality disorder. *J. Pers. Dis.*, *22*, 42–71.

Livesley, W. J. (2011). The current state of personality disorder classification: Introduction to the special feature on the classification. *J. Pers. Disord.*, *25*(3), 269–78. doi:10.1521/pedi.2011.25.3.269

Livesley, W. J., & Jang, K. L. (2008) The behavioral genetics of personality disorder. *Ann. Rev. Clin. Psych.*, *4*, 247–74.

Lizardi, D., Oquendo, M., & Graver, R. (2009). Clinical pitfalls in the diagnosis of ataque de nervios: A case study. *Transcult. Psychiat.*, *46*, 463–86.

Lochner, C., & Stein, D. J. (2003). Heterogeneity of obsessive-compulsive disorder: A literature review. *Har. Rev. Psychiat.*, *11*(3), 113–32.

Lock, J., le Grange, D., Agras, W. S., & Dare, C. (2001). *Treatment manual for anorexia nervosa: A family-based approach*. New York: Guilford.

Lock, J., le Grange, D., Agras, S., Moye, A., Bryson, S. W., & Jo, B. (2010). Randomized clinical trial comparing family-based treatments with adolescent-focused individual therapy for adolescents with anorexia nervosa. *Arch. Gen. Psychiat.*, *67*, 1025–32.

Loeb, T. B., Williams, J. K., Carmona, J. V., Rivkin, I., Wyatt, G. E., Chin, D., & Asuan-O'Brien, A. (2002). Child sexual abuse: Associations with the sexual functioning of adolescents and adults. *Annu. Rev. Sex Res., 13,* 307–45.

Loewenthal, K. M., MacLeod, A. K., Cook, S., Lee, M., & Goldblatt, V. (2003). Beliefs about alcohol among UK Jews and Protestants: Do they fit the alcohol depression hypothesis? *Soc. Psychiat. Psychiatr. Epidemiol., 38,* 122–27.

Loewenthal, K., Goldblatt, V., Gorton, T., Lubitsch, G., Bicknell, H., Fellowes, D., & Sowden, A. (1995). Gender and depression in Anglo-Jewry. *Psychol. Med., 25,* 1051–63.

Loftus, E. F., & Bernstein, D. M. (2005). Rich false memories: The royal road to success. In A. F. Healy (Ed.), *Experimental cognitive psychology and its applications: Decade of behavior* (pp. 101–13). Washington, DC: American Psychological Association.

Loftus, E. F., & Davis, D. (2006). Recovered memories. *Ann. Rev. Clin. Psych., 2, 2006,* 469–98

Loftus, E. F., Feldman, J., & Dashiell, R. (1995). The reality of illusory memories. In D. Schacter, J. Coyle, L. Sullivan, M. Mesulam, & G. Fischbach (Eds.), *Memory distortions: Interdisciplinary perspectives.* Cambridge: Harvard University Press.

Lohr, B. A., Adams, H. E., & Davis, J. M. (1997). Sexual arousal to erotic and aggressive stimuli in sexually coercive and noncoercive men. *J. Abn. Psychol., 106,* 230–42.

Lomax, C. L., Oldfield, V. B., & Salkovskis, P. M. (2009). Clinical and treatment comparisons between adults with early- and late-onset obsessive-compulsive disorder. *Behav. Res. Ther., 47*(2), 99–104. doi: 10.1016/j.brat.2008.10.015

London, K., Bruck, M., Ceci, S. J., & Shuman, D. W. (2005). Disclosure of child sexual abuse: What does the research tell us about the ways that children tell? *Psychology, Public Policy, and Law, 11*(1), 194–226.

Long, J. V. F., & Valliant, G. E. (1984). Natural history of male psychological health, XI: Escape from the underclass. *Amer. J. Psychiat., 141,* 341–46.

Longe, O., Maratos, F. A., Gilbert, P., Evans, G., Volker, F., Rockliff, H., & Rippon, G. (2010). Having a word with yourself: Neural correlates of self-criticism and self-reassurance. *NeuroImage, 49*(2), 1849–56.

Longin, E., Chammat, M., Chapouthier, G., & Jouvent, R. (2010). Physical versus social fear: A fundamental dichotomy. *Activitas Nervosa Superior, 52*(2), 62–70.

Lonsdorf, T. B., Weike, A. I., Nikamo, P., Schalling, M., Hamm, A. O., & Öhman, A. (2009). Genetic gating of human fear learning and extinction: Possible implications for gene-environment interaction in anxiety disorder. *Psychol. Science, 20*(2), 198–206. doi: 10.1111/j.1467-9280.2009.02280.x

Looper, K. J., & Kirmayer, L. J. (2002). Behavioral medicine approaches to somatoform disorders. *J. Cons. Clin. Psychol., 70,* 810–27.

Lopez, S. R., & Guarnaccia, P. J. (2005). Cultural dimensions of psychopathology: The social world's impact on mental illness. In J. E. Maddux & B. A. Winstead (Eds.), *Psychopathology: Foundations for a contemporary understanding.* Mahwah, NJ: Lawrence Erlbaum Associates.

Lopez, S. R., Lopez, A. A., & Fong, K. T. (1991). Mexican Americans' initial preferences for counselors: The role of ethnic factors. *J. Couns. Psychol., 38,* 487–96.

López-Muñoz, F., Ucha-Udabe, R., & Alamo, C. (2005). The history of barbiturates a century after their clinical introduction. *Neuropsychiatric Disease and Treatment, 1*(4), 329–43.

Lord, C. Risi, S., DiLavore, P. S., Shulman, C., Thurm, A., & Pickles, A. (2006). Autism from 2 to 9 years of age. *Arch. Gen. Psychiat., 63*(6), 694–701.

Lord, C., & Magill-Evans, J. (1995). Peer interactions of autistic children and adolescents. *Develop. Psychopath., 7,* 611–26.

Lorenz, A. R., & Newman, J. P. (2002). Deficient response modulation and emotion processing in low-anxious Caucasian psychopathic offenders: Results from a lexical decision task. *Emotion, 2*(2), 91–104.

LoSasso, G. L., Rapport, L. J., & Axelrod, B. N. (2001). Neuropsychological symptoms associated with low-level exposure to solvents and (meth)acrylates among nail technicians. *Neuropsychiatry, Neuropsychology, & Behavioral Neurology, 14*(3), 183–89.

LoSasso, G. L., Rapport, L. J., Axelrod, B. N., & Whitman, R. D. (2002). Neurocognitive sequelae of exposure to organic solvents and (meth)acrylates among nail-studio technicians. *Neuropsychiatry, Neuropsychology & Behavioral Neurology, 15*(1), 44–55.

Lösel, F. (1998). Treatment and management of psychopaths. In D. J. Cooke, A. E. Forth, & R. D. Hare (Eds.), *Psychopathy: Theory, research, and implications for society* (pp. 303–54). Dordrecht, Netherland: Kluwer Academic Publishers.

Lovaas, O. I. (1987). Behavioral treatment of normal educational and intellectual functioning in young autistic children. *J. Cons. Clin. Psychol., 44,* 3–9.

Lovett, B. J. (2006). The New History of Psychology: A review and critique. *History of Psychology, 9*(1), 17–37.

Löwe, B., Zipfel, S., Buchholz, C., Dupont, Y., Reas, D. L., & Herzog, W. (2001). Long-term outcome of anorexia nervosa in a prospective 21-year follow-up study. *Psychol. Med., 31,* 881–90.

Lowe, J. R., Edmundson, M., & Widiger, T. A. (2009). Assessment of dependency, agreeableness, and their relationship. *Psychol. Assess., 21,* 543–53.

Lozano, B. E., & Johnson, S. L. (2001). Can personality traits predict increases in manic and depressive symptoms? *J. Affect. Dis., 63*(1-3), 103–11.

Luborsky, L., & Barrett, M. S. (2006). The history and empirical status of key psychoanalytic concepts. *Annu. Rev. Clin. Psychol., 2,* 1–19.

Lucey, M. R., Mathurin, P., & Morgan, T. R. (2009). Alcoholic hepatitis. *N. Engl. J. Med., 360*(26), 2758–69.

Luchins, A. S. (1989). Moral treatment in asylums and general hospitals in 19th-century America. *J. Psychol.: Interdisciplinary & Applied, 123*(6), 585–607.

Luckasson, R., Coulter, D. L., Polloway, E. A., Reiss, S., Schalock, R. L., Snell, M. E., Spitalnik, D. M., & Stark, J. A. (1992). *Mental retardation: Definition, classification, and systems of supports* (9th ed.). Washington, DC: American Association on Mental Retardation.

Ludascher, P., Valerius, G., Stigimayr, C., Mauchnik, J., Lanius, R. A., Bohus, M., & Schmahl, C. (2009). Pain sensitivity and neural processing during dissociative states in patients with borderline personality disorder with and without comorbid posttraumatic stress disorder: A pilot study. *J. Psychiat, Neurosci., 35,* 177–84. doi:10.1503/jpn.090022

Ludewig, S., Geyer, M. A., Ramseier, M., Vollenweider, F. X., Rechsteiner, E., & Cattapan-Ludewig, K. (2005). Information-processing deficits and cognitive dysfunction in panic disorder. *Journal of Psychiatry & Neuroscience, 30*(1), 37–43.

Ludwig, A. M., Brandsma, J. M., Wilbur, C. B., Bendfelt, F., & Jameson, D. H. (1972). The objective study of a multiple personality: Or, are four heads better than one? *Arch. Gen. Psychiat., 26,* 298–310.

Lukas, C., & Seiden, H. M. (1990). *Silent grief: Living in the wake of suicide.* New York: Bantam Books.

Lundgren, J. D., Danoff-Burg, S., & Anderson, D. A. (2004). Cognitive-behavior therapy for bulimia nervosa: An empirical analysis of clinical significance. *Int. J. Eat. Dis., 35,* 262–74.

Luntz, B. K., & Widom, C. S. (1994). Antisocial personality disorder in abused and neglected children grown-up. *Amer. J. Psychiat., 151,* 670–74.

Luo, Y., Parish, W. L., & Laumann, E. O. (2008). A population-based study of childhood sexual contact in China: Prevalence and long-term consequences. *Child Ab. Negl., 32*(7), 721–31.

Lupien, S. J., McEwen, B. S., Gunnar, M. R., & Heim, C. (2009). Effects of stress throughout the lifespan on the brain, behavior and cognition. *Nature Reviews: Neuroscience, 10,* 434–445.

Lutgendorf, S. K., Russell, D., Ullrich, P., Harris, T., & Wallace, R. (2004). Religious participation, Interleukin-6, and mortality in older adults. *Hlth. Psychol., 23, 5,* 465–75.

Lutgendorf, S., Garand, L., Buckwalter, K. C., Reimer, T. T., Hong, S., & Lubaroff, D. (1999). Life stress, mood disturbance, and elevated interleukin-6 in healthy older women. *Journals of Gerontology. Series A, Biological Sciences and Medical Sciences, 54A,* M434–39.

Luthar, S. S, Doernberger, C. H., & Zigler, E. (1993). Resilience is not a unidimensional construct: Insights from a prospective study of inner-city adolescents. *Develop. Psychopath., 5,* 703–17.

Luthar, S. S. (2003). *Resilience and vulnerability: Adaption in the context of childhood adversities.* New York: Cambridge University Press.

Lyketsos, C. G., Steinberg, M., Tschanz, J. T., Norton, M. C., Steffens, D. C., & Breitner, J. C. S. (2000). Mental and behavioral disturbances in dementia: Findings from the Cache County study on memory and aging. *Amer. J. Psychiat., 157*(5), 708–14.

Lykken, D. T. (1957). A study of anxiety in the sociopathic personality. *J. Abn. Soc. Psychol., 55*(1), 6–10.

Lykken, D. T. (1995). *The antisocial personalities.* Hillsdale, NJ: Erlbaum.

Lyman, R. D., & Campbell, N. R. (1996). *Treating children and adolescents in residential and inpatient settings.* Thousand Oaks, CA: Sage Publications.

Lymburner, J. A., & Roesch, R. (1999). The insanity defense: Five years of research (1993–1997). *International Journal of Law & Psychiatry, 22*(3–4), 213–20.

Lynam, D. R. (2002). Fledgling psychopathy. *Law & Human Behavior, 26*(2), 255–59.

Lynam, D. R., & Widiger, T. A. (2007). Using a general model of personality to understand sex differences in the personality disorders. *J. Pers. Dis., 21*(6), 583–602.

Lynam, D. R., Milich, R., Zimmerman, R., Novak, S. P., Logan, T. K., Martin, C., Leukefeld, C., & Clayton, R. (2009). Project DARE: No effects at 10-year follow-up. In G. A. Marlatt & K. Witkiewitz (Eds.), *Addictive behaviors: New readings on etiology, prevention, and treatment,* (pp. 187–96). Washington, DC: American Psychological Association.

Lynam, D. R., Moffitt, T. E., & Stouthamer-Loeber, M. (1993). Explaining the relation between IQ and delinquency: Class, race, test motivation, school failure, or self-control. *J. Abn. Psychol., 102,* 187–96.

Lynam, D. R., & Widiger, T. A. (2007). Using a general model of personality to identify basic elements of psychopathy. *J. Pers. Dis., 21(2)*, 160–78.

Lynch, D., Laws, K. R., & McKenna, P. J. (2010). Cognitive behavioral therapy for major psychiatric disorder: does it really work? A meta-analytical review of well-controlled trials. *Psychol. Med., 40*, 9–24.

Lynch, P. S., Kellow, J. T., & Willson, V. L. (1997). The impact of deinstitutionalization on the adaptive behavior of adults with mental retardation. *Education & Training in Mental Retardation & Developmental Disabilities, 32(3)*, 255–61.

Lynch, T. R., Chapman, A. L., Rosenthal, M. Z., Kuo, J. R., & Linehan, M. M. (2006). Mechanisms of change in dialectical behavior therapy: Theoretical and empirical observations. *J. Clin. Psychol., 62*, 459–80.

Lynch, T. R., Trost, W. T., Salsman, N., & Linehan, M. M. (2007). Dialectical behavior therapy for borderline personality disorder. *Ann. Rev. Clin. Psych., 3*, 181–205.

Lynn, S. J., Knox, J. A., Fassler, O., Lilienfeld, S. O., & Loftus, E. F. (2004). Memory, trauma, and dissociation. In G. M. Rosen (Ed.), *Posttraumatic stress disorder: Issues and controversies* (pp. 163–86). New York: John Wiley & Sons.

Lytton, H. (1980). *Parent–child interaction: The socialization process observed in twin and singleton families*. New York: Plenum.

Lyubomirsky, S., Caldwell, N. D., & Nolen-Hoeksema, S. (1998). Effects of ruminative and distracting responses to depressed mood on retrieval of autobiographical memories. *J. Pers. Soc. Psychol., 75*, 166–77.

Lyvers, M. (2000). "Loss of control" in alcoholism and drug addiction: A neuroscientific interpretation. *Exp. Clin. Psychopharm., 8(2)*, 225–45.

Maccoby, E. E., & Martin, J. A. (1983). Socialization in the context of the family: Parent–child interaction. In E. M. Hetherington (Ed.), *Socialization, personality, and social development; Vol. 4. Handbook of child psychology*. New York: Wiley.

MacCulloch, T. (2010). Constructions of truth, gatekeeping and the power of diagnostic labels. *Issues in Mental Health Nursing, 31(2)*, 151–52.

MacDonald, A. W., & Jones, J. A. (2009). Functional imaging in clinical assessment: The rise of neurodiagnostics with fMRI. In J. N. Butcher (Ed.), *Oxford handbook of personality assessment* (pp. 364–74). New York: Oxford University Press.

Macgowan, M., & Engle, B. (2010). Evidence for optimism: Behavior therapies and motivational interviewing in adolescent substance abuse treatment. *Child Adol. Psychiat. Clin. N. Amer., 19(3)*, 527–45.

MacGregor, J. M. (1989). *The discovery of the art of the insane*. Princeton, NJ: Princeton University Press.

Maciejewski, P. K., Zhang, B., Block, S. D., & Prigerson, H. G. (2007). An empirical examination of the stage theory of grief. *JAMA, 297(7)*, 716–23.

Mackay, L. E. (1994). Benefits of a formalized traumatic brain injury program within a trauma center. *J. Head Trauma Rehab., 9(1)*, 11–19.

MacKenzie, D. L., Wilson, D. B., Armstrong, G. S., & Glover, A. R. (2001). The impact of boot camps and traditional institutions on juvenile residents: Perceptions, adjustment, and change. *Journal of Research in Crime & Delinquency, 38(3)*, 279–313.

MacLean, H. N. (1992). *Once upon a time*. New York: HarperCollins.

Maclean, W. E., Jr. (Ed.). (1997). *Ellis' handbook of mental deficiency: Psychological theory and research*. Mahwah, NJ: Erlbaum.

MacLeod, A. K. (1999). Prospective cognitions. In T. Dalgleish & M. J. Power (Eds.), *Handbook of cognition and emotion* (pp. 267–80). Chichester, England: Wiley.

MacLeod, C., Campbell, L., Rutherford, E., & Wilson, E. (2004). The causal status of anxiety-linked attentional and interpretive bias. In J. Yiend (Ed.), *Cognition, emotion and psychopathology: Theoretical, empirical and clinical directions.* (pp. 172–89). New York: Cambridge University Press.

MacLeod, C., Rutherford, E., Campbell, L., Ebsworthy, G., & Holker, L. (2002). Selective attention and emotional vulnerability: Assessing the causal basis of their association through the experimental manipulation of attentional bias. *J. Abn. Psychol., 111(1)*, 107–23. doi: 10.1037/0021-843x.111.1.107

MacManus, D., Laurens, K. R., Walker, E. F., Brasfield, J.L., Riaz, M., & Hodgkins, S. (2011). Movement abnormalities and psychotic-like experiences in childhood: markers of developing schizophrenia. *Psych. Med.*

MacMillan, P. J., Hart, R., Martelli, M., & Zasler, N. (2002). Pre-injury status and adaptation following traumatic brain injury. *Brain Injury, 16(1)*, 41–49.

Macmillan, R. (2010). The life course consequences of abuse, neglect, and victimization: Challenges for theory, data collection, and methodology. *Child Ab. Negl., 33(10)*, 661–65.

MacMullen, J. (2007). "I don't want anyone to end up like me". *Boston Globe*, February 2.

MacNaughton, K. L., & Rodrigue, J. R. (2001). Predicting adherence to recommendations by parents of clinic-referred children. *J. Cons. Clin. Psychol., 69*, 252–70.

Maddock, R. J., Buonocore, M. H., Kile, S. J., & Garrett, A. S. (2003). Brain regions showing increased activation by threat-related words in panic disorder. *Neuroreport: For rapid communication of neuroscience research, 14(3)*, 325–28.

Maddux, J. F., Vogtsberger, K. N., Prihoda, T. J., Desmond, D. F., Watson, D. D., & Williams, M. L. (1994). Illicit drug injectors in three Texas cities. *Inter. J. Addict., 29*, 179–94.

Magee, L., Erwin, B. A., & Heimberg, R. G. (2009). Psychological treatment of social anxiety disorder and specific phobia. In M. M. Antony & M. B. Stein (Eds.), *Oxford handbook of anxiety and related disorders* (pp. 334–49). New York: Oxford University Press.

Magee, W. J., Eaton, W. W., Wittchen, H., McGonagle, K. A., & Kessler, R. C. (1996). Agoraphobia, simple phobia, and social phobia in the National Comorbidity Survey. *Arch. Gen. Psychiat., 53*, 159–68.

Magid, D. J., Houry, D., Koepsell, T. D., Ziller, A. A., Soules, M. R., & Jenny, C. (2004). The epidemiology of female rape victims who seek immediate medical care: Temporal trends in the incidence of sexual assault and acquaintance rape. *J. Interpers. Violen., 19*, 3–12.

Maguen, S., Cohen, G., Cohen, B. E., Lawhon, G. D., Marmar, C. R., & Seal, K. H. (2010a). The role of psychologists in the care of Iraq and Afghanistan veterans in primary care settings. *Prof. Psychol. Res. Pract., 41(2)*, 135–42.

Maguen, S., Lucenko, B. A., Reger, M. A., Gahm, G. A., Litz, B. T., Seal, K. H., Knight, S. J., & Marmar, C. R. (2010b). The impact of reported direct and indirect killing on mental health symptoms in Iraq War veterans. *J. Trauma. Stress., 23(1)*, 86–90.

Mahendran, R., Subramaniam, M., Cai, Y., & Chan, Y. H. (2006). Survey of sleep problems amongst Singapore children in a psychiatric setting. *Soc. Psychiat. Psychiatr. Epidemiol., 41(8)*, 669–73.

Maher, B. A., & Maher, W. R. (1985). Psychopathology: 1. From ancient times to the eighteenth century. In G. A. Kimble & K. Schlesinger (Eds.), *Topics in the history of psychology* (pp. 251–94). Hillsdale, NJ: Erlbaum.

Maher, B. A., & Maher, W. R. (1994). Personality and psychopathology: A historical perspective. *J. Abn. Psychol., 103*, 72–7.

Mahoney, M., & Arnkoff, D. (1978). Cognitive and selfcontrol therapies. In S. Garfield & A. Bergin (Eds.), *Handbook of psychotherapy and behavior change: An empirical analysis*. New York: Wiley.

Mai, F. (2004). Somatization disorder: A practical review. *Canad. J. Psychiat., 49(10)*, 652–62.

Maier, S. F., & Watkins, L. R. (1998). Cytokines for psychologists: Implications of bidirectional immune-to-brain communication for understanding behavior, mood, and cognition. *Psychol. Rev., 105(1)*, 83–107.

Maier, S. F., & Watkins, L. R. (2005). Stressor controllability and learned helplessness: The roles of the dorsal raphe nucleus, serotonin, and corticotropin-releasing factor. *Neuroscience & Biobehavioral Reviews, 29(4)*, 829–41.

Maier, S. F., Watkins, L. R., & Fleshner, M. (1994). Psychoneuroimmunology: The interface between behavior, brain, and immunity. *Amer. Psychol., 49(12)*, 1004–17.

Maier, S., Seligman, M., & Solomon, R. (1969). Pavlovian fear conditioning and learned helplessness. In B. A. Campbell & R. M. Church (Eds.), *Punishment and aversive behavior*. New York: Appleton-Century-Crofts.

Maier, W. (2008). Common risk genes for affective and schizophrenic psychoses. *Eur. Arch. Clin. Neurosci., 258*, 37–40.

Maj, M., Pirozzi, R., Formicola, A. M., Bartoli, L., & Bucci, P. (2000). Reliability and validity of the DSM-IV diagnostic category of schizoaffective disorder: Preliminary data. *J. Affect. Disord., 57(1–3)*, 95–98.

Malaspina, D., Corcoran, C., & Hamilton, S. P. (2002). Epidemiologic and genetic aspects of neuropsychiatric disorders. In S. C. Yudofsky & R. E. Hales, *The American Psychiatric Publishing textbook of neuropsychiatry and clinical neurosciences* (pp. 323–415). Washington, DC: American Psychiatric Publishing.

Malaspina, D., Harlap, S., Fennig, S., Heiman, D., Nahon, D., Feldman, D., & Susser, E. (2001). Advancing paternal age and the risk of schizophrenia. *Arch. Gen. Psychiat., 58*, 361–67.

Malcolm, R. (2003). Pharmacologic treatments manage alcohol withdrawal, relapse prevention. *Psychiat. Ann., 33(9)*, 593–601.

Maldonado, J. R., & Spiegel, D. (2001). Somatoform and factitious disorders. *Review of Psychiatry Series, 20*, 95–128.

Maldonado, J. R., & Spiegel, D. (2007). Dissociative disorders. In J. A. Bourgeois, R. H. Hales, & S. C. Yudofsky (Eds.), *The American Psychiatric Publishing board prep and review guide for psychiatry.* (pp. 251–58). Washington, DC: American Psychiatric Publishing.

Maldonado, J. R., Butler, L. D., & Spiegel, D. (2002). Treatments for dissociative disorders. In P. E. Nathan & J. M. Gorman (Eds.), *A guide to treatments that work* (2nd ed., pp. 463–96). New York: Oxford University Press.

Maletzky, B. M. (1998). The paraphilias: Research and treatment. In P. E. Nathan & J. M. Gorman (Eds.), *A guide to treatments that work* (pp. 472–500). New York: Oxford University Press.

Maletzky, B. M. (2002). The paraphilias: Research and treatment. In P. E. Nathan & J. M. Gorman (Eds.), *A guide to treatments that work* (pp. 525–58). New York: Oxford University Press.

Maletzky, B. M., & Field, G. (2003). The biological treatment of dangerous sex offenders: A review and preliminary report of the Oregon pilot depo-Provera program. *Aggression & Violent Behavior, 8*, 391–412.

Maletzky, B. M., & Steinhauser, C. (2002). A 25-year follow-up of cognitive/behavioral therapy with 7,275 sexual offenders. *Behav. Mod., 26*, 123–47.

Maletzky, B. M., Tolan, A., & McFarland, B. (2006). The Oregon Depo-Provera program: A five-year followup. *Sex Abuse, 18*, 303–16.

Malhi, G. S., Ivanovski, B., Szekeres, V., & Olley, A. (2004). Bipolar disorder: It's all in your mind: The neuropsychological profile of a biological disorder. *Can. J. Psychiat., 49*(12), 813–19.

Malhi, G. S., Lagopoulos, J., Owen, A. M., & Yatham, L. N. (2004). Bipolaroids: Functional imaging in bipolar disorder. *Acta Psychiatr. Scandin., 110*, 46–54.

Malin, D. H. (2001). Nicotine dependence: Studies with a laboratory model. *Pharmacology, Biochemistry, & Behavior, 70*(4), 551–59.

Malkoff-Schwartz, S., Frank, E., Anderson, B., Sherrill, J. T., Siegel, L., Patterson, D., & Kupfer, D. J. (1998). Stressful life events and social rhythm disruption in the onset of manic and depressive bipolar episodes: A preliminary investigation. *Arch. Gen. Psychiat., 55*(8), 702–7.

Malm, H., Artama, M., Gissler, M., & Ritvanen, A. (2011). Selective serotonin reuptake inhibitors and risk for major congenital abnormalities. *Obstet. Gynecol., 118*, 111–20.

Malnick, S. D., & Knobler, H. (2006). The medical complications of obesity. *QJM, 99*, 565–79.

Mancebo, M. C., Eisen, J. L., Pinto, A., Greenberg, B. D., Dyck, I. R., & Rasmussen, S. A. (2006). The Brown Longitudinal Obsessive Compulsive Study: Treatments received and patient impressions of improvement. *J. Clin. Psychiat., 67*(11), 1713–20.

Mangweth, B., Hudson, J. I., Pope, H. G., Hausman, A., De Col, C., Laird, N. M., Beibl, W., & Tsuang, M. T. (2003). Family study of the aggregation of eating disorders and mood disorders. *Psychol. Med., 33*, 1319–23.

Manji, H. K., & Lenox, R. H. (2000). The nature of bipolar disorder. *J. Clin. Psychiat., 61*, 42–57.

Mann, A. (2004). *Cocaine abusers' cognitive deficits compromise treatment.* Washington, DC: NIDA.

Mann, T., Tomiyama, J., Westling, E., Lew, A.-M., Samuels, B., & Chatman, J. (2007). Medicare's search for effective obesity treatments. *Amer. Psychol., 62*, 220–233.

Mannuzza, S., Klein, R. G., & Moulton, J. L., III. (2003). Persistence of attention-deficit/hyperactivity disorder into adulthood: What have we learned from the prospective follow-up studies? *J. Atten. Dis., 7*(2), 93–100.

Manson, S. M. (1995). Culture and major depression: Current challenges in the diagnosis of mood disorders. *Psychiat. Clin. N. Amer.: Cultural Psychiatry, 18*(3), 487–501.

Mantovani, A., Simeon, D., Urban, N., Bulow, P., Allart, A., & Lisanby, S. (2011). Temporo-parietal junction stimulation in the treatment of depersonalization disorder. *Psychiat. Res., 186*, 138–40. doi:10.1016/j.psychres.2010.08.022

Manzeske, D. P., & Stright, A. D. (2009). Parenting styles and emotion regulation: The role of behavioral and psychological control during

young adulthood. *J. Adult Devel., 16*(4), 223–29. doi:10.1007/s10804-009-9068-9

Mapou, R. L. (2009). Adult learning disabilities and ADHD. New York: Oxford University Press.

March, J. S., & Franklin, M. E. (2006). Cognitive-behavioral therapy for pediatric obsessive-compulsive disorder. In B. O. Rothbaum (Ed.), *Pathological anxiety: Emotional processing in etiology and treatment.* (pp. 147–65). New York: Guilford Press.

Marcotty, J. (2004). Outpatient psychiatric care is scarce: One result has been an increase in psychiatric admissions in Minnesota. *Minneapolis Star and Tribune,* Section B, pp. 1–2.

Marcus, D. K., Gurley, J. R., Marchi, M. M., & Bauer, C. (2007). Cognitive and perceptual variables in hypochondriasis and health anxiety: A systematic review. *Clin. Psych. Rev., 27*, 127–39.

Marcus, S. C., & Olfson, M. (2010). National trends in the treatment for depression from 1998 to 2007. *Arch. Gen. Psychiat., 67*(12), 1265–73. doi: 10.1001/archgenpsychiatry.2010.151

Marcus, S. M., Gorman, J., Shea, M. K., Lewin, D., Martinez, J., Ray, S., et al. (2007). A comparison of medication side effect reports by panic disorder patients with and without concomitant cognitive behavior therapy. *Amer. J. Psychiat., 164*(2), 273–75.

Margallo, L. M. L., Moore, P. B., Kay, D. W. K., Perry, R. H., Reid, B. E., Berney, T. P., & Tyrer, S. P. (2007). Fifteen-year follow-up of 92 hospitalized adults with Down's syndrome: Incidence of cognitive decline, its relationship to age and neuropathology. *Journal of Intellectual Disability Research, 51*(6), 463–77.

Margolis, A., Donkervoort, M., Kinsbourne, M., & Peterson, B. S. (2006). Interhemispheric connectivity and executive functioning in adults with Tourette syndrome. *Neuropsychol., 20*(1), 66–76.

Margolis, R. D., & Zweben, J. E. (1998). *Treating patients with alcohol and other drug problems: An integrated approach.* Washington, DC: American Psychological Association.

Margraf, J., Ehlers, A., & Roth, W. T. (1986a). Sodium lactate infusions and panic attacks: A review and critique. *Psychosom. Med., 48*, 23–51.

Margraf, J., Ehlers, A., & Roth, W. T. (1986b). Biological models of panic disorder and agoraphobia—A review. *Behav. Res. Ther., 24*, 553–67.

Mariani, J. J., & Levin, F. R. (2007). Treatment strategies for co-occurring ADHD and substance use disorders. *Am. J. Addict., 16*(Suppl 1), 45–56.

Marijuana Treatment Project Research Group. (2004). Brief treatments for cannabis dependence: Findings from a randomized multi-site trial. *J. Cons. Clin. Psychol., 72*, 455–66.

Mariotto, M. J., Paul, G. L., & Licht, M. H. (2002). Assessment in inpatient and residential settings. In J. N. Butcher (Ed.), *Clinical personality assessment* (2nd ed., pp. 466–90). New York: Oxford University Press.

Maris, R. W. (1997). Social forces in suicide: A life review, 1965–1995. In R. W. Maris, M. M. Silverman, & S. S. Canetton (Eds.), *Review of suicidology, 1997* (pp. 42–60). New York: Guilford.

Maris, R. W., Berman, A. L., & Silverman, M. M. (2000). *Comprehensive textbook of suicidology.* New York: Guilford.

Markey, E. (2002). *List of documented brain injuries on thrill rides triples.* Press release from the office of Ed Markey, United States Congress, Massachusetts Seventh District, May 7, 2002.

Markham, D. (2003). Attitudes towards patients with a diagnosis of "borderline personality disorder": Social rejection of dangerousness. *J. Ment. Hlth., 12*, 595–612.

Markon, K. E., Krueger, R. F., & Watson, D. (2005). Delineating the structure of normal and abnormal personality: An integrative hierarchical approach. *J. Pers. Soc. Psychol., 88*, 139–57.

Markon, K. E., Krueger, R. F., & Watson, D. (2005). Delineating the structure of normal and abnormal personality: An integrative hierarchical approach. *J. Pers. Soc. Psych., 88*(1), 139–57.

Markovitz, P. (2001). Pharmacotherapy. In W. J. Livesley (Ed.), *Handbook of personality disorders* (pp. 475–93). New York: Guilford.

Markovitz, P. J. (2004). Recent trends in the pharmacotherapy of personality disorders. *J. Pers. Dis., 18*(1), 90–101.

Markowitsch, H. J. (1999). Functional neuroimaging correlates of functional amnesia. *Memory, 7*, 561–83.

Markowitz, F. E. (2006). Psychiatric Hospital Capacity, Homelessness, and Crime and Arrest Rates. *Criminology, 44*, 45–72.

Markowitz, J. C., Patel, S. R., Balan, I. C., Blanco, C., Yellow Horse Brave Heart, M., Sosa, S. B., & Lewis-Fernández, R. I. (2009). Toward an adaptation of interpersonal psychotherapy for Hispanic patients with DSM-IV major depressive disorder. *J. Clin. Psychiat., 70*, 214–22.

Markowitz, J. C., Skodol, A. E., & Bleiberg, K. (2006). Interpersonal psychotherapy for borderline personality disorder: Possible mechanisms of change. *J. Cons. Clin. Psychol., 62*, 431–44.

Markowitz, J. C., Skodol, A. E., Petkova, E., Xie, H., Cheng, J., Hellerstein, D. J., et al. (2005). Longitudinal comparison of depressive personality disorder and dysthymic disorder. *Compr. Psychiat., 46*(4), 239–45.

Marks, I. M. (1987). *Fears, phobias, and rituals: Panic, anxiety, and their disorders.* New York: Oxford University Press.

Marks, I., & Nesse, R. M. (1991). Fear and fitness: An evolutionary analysis of anxiety disorders. Paper presented at the Eleventh National Conference on Anxiety Disorders. Chicago, IL.

Marks, I., Swinson, R. P., Başoğlu, M., & Kunch, K. (1993). Alprazolam and exposure alone and combined in panic disorder with agoraphobia: A controlled study in London and Toronto. *Brit. J. Psychiat., 162*, 776–87.

Marlatt, G. A. (1985). Cognitive assessment and intervention procedures for relapse prevention. In G. A. Marlatt & J. R. Gordon (Eds.), *Relapse prevention.* New York: Guilford.

Marlatt, G. A., Baer, J. S., Kivahan, D. R., Dimeoff, L. A., Larimer, M. E., Quigley, L. A., Somers, J. M., & Williams, E. (1998). Screening and brief intervention for high-risk college student drinkers: Results from a 2-year follow up assessment. *J. Cons. Clin. Psychol., 66*(4), 604–15.

Marmorstein, N. R., Iacono, W. G., & McGue, M. (2009). Alcohol and illicit drug dependence among parents: Associations with offspring externalizing disorders. *Psychol. Med., 39*(1), 149–55. doi:10.1017/s0033291708003085

Marsch, L. A., Stephens, M. A., Mudric, T., Strain, E. C., Bigelow, G. E., & Johnson, R. E. (2005). Predictors of outcome in LAAM, buprenorphine, and methadone treatment for opioid dependence. *Exp. Clin. Psychopharm., 13*(4), 293–02.

Marsella, A. J. (1980). Depressive experience and disorder across cultures. In H. C. Triandis & J. Draguns (Eds.), *Handbook of cross-cultural psychology* (Vol. 6). Boston: Allyn and Bacon.

Marsh, A. A., & Blair, R. J. R. (2008) Deficits in facial affect recognition among antisocial populations:

A meta-analysis. *Neuroscience and Biobehavioral Reviews, 32*, 454–65.

Marsh, A. A., Finger, E. C., Mitchell, D. G., Derek, G. V., Reid, M. E., Sims, C., Kosson, D. S., Towbin, K. E., Leibenluft, E. P., Pine, S. D., & Blair, R. J. (2008). Reduced amygdala response to fearful expressions in children and adolescents with callous-unemotional traits and disruptive behavior disorders. *Am. J. Psychiat., 165*(6), 712–20.

Marsh, L., & Margolis, R. L. (2009). Neuropsychiatric aspects of movement disorders. In Sadock, B. J., Sadock, A. A., & Ruiz, P. (Eds.), *Kaplan and Sadock's Comprehensive Textbook of Psychiatry* (9th ed., pp. 481–506). PA: Lippincott, Williams & Wilkins.

Marshall M., Lewis, S., Lockwood, A., Drake, R., Jones, P., & Croudace, T. (2005). Association between duration of untreated psychosis and outcome in cohorts of first-episode patients. *Arch. Gen. Psychiat., 62*, 975–83.

Marshall, R. D., Bryant, R. A., Amsel, L., Suh, E. J. Cook, J. M., & Neria, Y. (2007). The psychology of ongoing threat: Relative risk appraisal, the September 11 attacks, and terrorism-related fears. *Am. Psych., 62*(4), 304–16.

Marshall, W. L. (1998). Adult sexual offenders. In N. N. Singh (Ed.), *Comprehensive clinical psychology: Vol 9: Applications in diverse populations.* Elsevier.

Marshall, W. L., Jones, R., Ward, T., Johnston, P., & Barbaree, H. E. (1991). Treatment outcome with sex offenders. *Clin. Psychol. Rev., 11*, 465–85.

Marsman, A., van den Heuvel, M. P., Klopm, D. W. J., Kahn, R. S., Luitjen, P. R., & Hulsoff Pol, H. E. (2011). Glutamate in schizophrenia: A focused review and meta-analysis of 1H-MRS studies. *Schizo. Bull.*

Martell, D. A., & Dietz, P. E. (1992). Mentally disordered offenders who push or attempt to push victims onto subway tracks in New York City. *Arch. Gen. Psychiat., 49*(6), 472–75.

Martell, C. R. (2009). Behavioral activation for depression. In W. T. O'Donohue & J. E. Fisher (Eds.), *General principles and empirically supported techniques of cognitive behavior therapy* (pp. 138–43). Hoboken, NJ: John Wiley & Sons.

Martin, A., Buech, A., Schwenk, C., & Rief, W. (2007). Memory bias for health-related information in somatoform disorders. *J. Psychosom. Res., 63*, 663–71.

Martin, D. J., Garske, J. P., & Davis, M. K. (2000). Relation of the therapeutic alliance with outcome and other variables: A meta-analytic review. *J. Cons. Clin. Psychol., 68*, 438–50.

Martin, E. K., Taft, C. T., & Resick, P. A. (2007). A review of marital rape. *Agression and Violent Behavior, 12*(3), 329–47.

Martin, P. R., Forsyth, M. R., & Reece, J. (2007). Cognitive-behavioral therapy versus temporal pulse amplitude biofeedback training for recurrent headache. *Behav. Ther., 38*, 350–63.

Martín-Reyes, M., Quiñones, R., et al. (2010). Perceptual/attentional anomalies in schizophrenia: A family study. *Psychiat. Res., 176*(2–3), 137–42.

Martins, A., Ramalho, N., & Morin, E. (2010). A comprehensive meta-analysis of the relationship between emotional intelligence and health. *Personal. Indiv. Diff., 49*(6), 554–64.

Martins, M. P., & Harris, S. L. (2006). Teaching children with autism to respond to joint attention initiations. *Child Fam. Behav. Ther., 28*, 51–68.

Marvit, R. C. (1981). Guilty but mentally ill—an old approach to an old problem. *Clin. Psychol., 34*(4), 22–23.

Mascia, J. (August 28, 2010). Medical Use of Marijuana Costs Some a Job. *New York Times*, August 28, 2010.

Mash, E. J., & Barkley, R. A. (2006). *Treatment of childhood disorders* (3rd ed,). New York: Guilford Press.

Masi, G., Favilla, L., Mucci, M., & Millepiedi, S. (2000). Depressive comorbidity in children and adolescents with generalized anxiety disorder. *Child Psychiat. Human Devel., 30*(3), 205–15.

Mason, F. L. (1997). Fetishism: Psychopathology and theory. In D. R. Laws & W. O'Donohue (Eds.), *Sexual deviance: Theory, assessment, and treatment* (pp. 75–91). New York: Guilford.

Mason, W. A., Kosterman, R., Hawkins, J. D., Herrenkohl, T. I., Lengua, L. J., & McCauley, E. (2004). Predicting depression, social phobia, and violence in early adulthood from childhood behavior problems. *J. Amer. Acad. Child Adoles. Psychiat., 43*(3), 307–15.

Masten, A. S. (2001). Ordinary magic: Resilience processes in development. *Amer. Psychol., 56*, 227–38.

Masten, A. S. (2006). Developmental psychopathology: Pathways to the future. *International Journal of Behavioral Development, 30*(1), 47–54.

Masten, A. S. (2007). Resilience in developing systems: Progress and promise as the fourth wave rises. *Develop. Psychopath., 19*(3), 921–930.

Masten, A. S., & Coatsworth, J. D. (1995). Competence, resilience, and psychopathology. In D. Cicchetti & D. J. Cohen (Eds.),*Psychopathology: Vol. 2. Risk, disorder, and adaptation* (pp. 715–52). New York: Wiley.

Masten, A. S., & Coatsworth, J. D. (1998). The development of competence in favorable and unfavorable environments: Lessons from research on successful children. *Amer. Psychol., 53*, 205–20.

Masten, A. S., Burt, K. B., Roismon, G. I., Obradovic, J., Long, J. D., & Tellegen, A. (2004). Resources and resilience in the transition to adulthood: Continuity and change. *Develop. Psychopath, 16*, 1071–94.

Masters, W. H., & Johnson, V. E. (1966). *Human sexual response.* Boston: Little, Brown.

Masters, W. H., & Johnson, V. E. (1970). *Human sexual inadequacy.* Boston: Little, Brown.

Masters, W. H., & Johnson, V. E. (1975). *The pleasure bond: A new look at sexuality and commitment.* Boston: Little, Brown.

Masters, W. H., Johnson, V. E., & Kolodny, R. C. (1992). *Human sexuality.* New York: HarperCollins.

Mataix-Cols, D., Frost, R. O., Pertusa, A., Clark, L. A., Saxena, S., Leckman, J. F., et al. (2010). Hoarding disorder: A new diagnosis for DSM-V? *Depression and Anxiety, 27*(6), 556–72. doi: 10.1002/da.20693

Mataix-Cols, D., Rauch, S. L., Baer, L., Eisen, J. L., Shera, D. M., Goodman, W. K., et al. (2002). Symptom stability in adult obsessive-compulsive disorder: Data from a naturalistic two-year follow-up study. *Amer. J. Psychiat., 159*(2), 263–68.

Mataix-Cols, D., Wooderson, S., Lawrence, N., Brammer, M. J., Speckens, A., & Phillips, M. L. (2004). Distinct neural correlates of washing, checking, and hoarding symptom dimensions in obsessive-compulsive disorder. *Arch. Gen. Psychiat., 61*(6), 564–76.

Materro, M., Junque, C., Poca, M. A., & Sahuquillo, J. (2001). Neuropsychological findings in congenital and acquired childhood hydrocephalus. *Neuropsych., 11*, 169–78.

Mathalondolf, D. H., Sullivan, E. V., Lim, K. O., & Pfefferbaum, A. (2001). Progressive brain volume changes and the clinical course of schizophrenia in men: A longitudinal magnetic resonance imaging study. *Arch. Gen. Psychiat., 58*, 48–157.

Mathers, C. D., Lopez, A. D., & Murray, C. J. L. (2006) The burden of disease and mortality by condition: Data, methods, and results for 2001. In A. D. Lopez, C. D.

Mathew, S. J., Amiel, J. M., & Sackeim, H. A. (2005). Electroconvulsive therapy in treatment-resistant depression. *Prim. Psychiat. 12*, 52–56.

Mathew, S. J., Coplan, J. D., & Gorman, J. M. (2001). Neurobiological mechanisms of social anxiety disorder. *Amer. J. Psychiat., 158*, 1558–67.

Mathew, S. J., & Hoffman, E. J. (2009). Pharmacotherapy for generalized anxiety disorder. In M. M. Antony & M. B. Stein (Eds.), *Oxford handbook of anxiety and related disorders* (pp. 350–63). New York: Oxford University Press.

Mathews, A. (2006). Towards an experimental cognitive science of CBT. *Behav. Ther., 37*(3), 314–18.

Mathews, A. M., & MacLeod, C. (1994). Cognitive approaches to emotion and emotional disorders. *Ann. Rev. Psychol., 45*, 25–50.

Mathews, A., & MacLeod, C. (2002). Induced processing biases have causal effects on anxiety. *Cog. & Emo., 16*(3), 331–54.

Mathews, A., & MacLeod, C. (2005). Cognitive vulnerability to emotional disorders. *Annu. Rev. Clin. Psychol., 1*(1), 167–95.

Mathews, C. A. (2009). Phenomenology of obsessive-compulsive disorder. In M. M. Antony & M. B. Stein (Eds.), *Oxford handbook of anxiety and related disorders* (pp. 56–64). New York: Oxford University Press.

Matthews, K. A., & Gump, B. B. (2002). Chronic work stress and marital dissolution increase risk of post-trial mortality in men from the Multiple Risk Factor Intervention Trial. *Arch. Int. Med., 162*, 309–15.

Mattia, J. I., & Zimmerman, M. (2001). Epidemiology. In W. J. Livesley (Ed.), *Handbook of personality disorders* (pp. 107–23). New York: Guilford.

Mattila, M., Kielinen, M., Jussila, K., Linna, S. L., Bloigu, R., Ebeling, H., & Moilanen, I. (2007) An epidemiological and diagnostic study of Asperger Syndrome according to four sets of diagnostic criteria. *J. Amer. Acad. Child Adoles. Psychiat., 46*(5), 636–46.

Mattson, M. E., Allen, J. P., Longabaugh, R., Nickless, C. J., et al. (1994). A chronological review of empirical studies matching alcoholic clients to treatment *J. Stud. Alcoh. 12*, 16–29.

Matza, L. S., Revicki, D. A., Davidson, J. R., & Stewart, J. W. (2003). Depression with atypical features in the national comorbidity survey. *Arch. Gen. Psychiat., 60*, 817–26.

Maxfield, M. G., & Widom, C. S. (1996). The cycle of violence: Revisited six years later. *Archives of Pediatric and Adolescent Medicine, 150*, 390–95.

May, P. A., & Gossage, J. P. (2001). Estimating the prevalence of fetal alcohol syndrome. *Al. Res. Hlth., 25*, 159–67.

Mayberg, H. S., Lozano, A. M., Voon, V., McNeely, H. E., Seminowicz, D., Hamani, C., Schwalb, J. M., & Kennedy, S. H. (2005, Mar. 3). Deep brain stimulation for treatment-resistant depression. *Neuron, 45*, 651–60.

Mayes, R., Bagwell, C., & Erkulwater, J. (2009). *Medicating Children.* Harvard University Press.

Mays, V. M., Cochran, S. D., & Barnes, N. W. (2007). Race, race-based discrimination, and health outcomes among African Americans.*Annu. Rev. Psychol., 58*, 201–25.

Mayou, R. A., Ehlers, A., & Hobbs, M. (2000). Psychological debriefing for road traffic accident victims: Three-year follow-up of a randomised controlled trial. *Brit. J. Psychiat., 176*, 589–93.

Mazefsky, C. A., Williams, D. L., & Minshew, N. J. (2008). Variability in adaptive behavior in autism: Evidence for the importance of family history. *Journal of Abnormal Child Psychology: An official publication of the International Society for Research in Child and Adolescent Psychopathology, 36*(4), 591–99.

Mazzoncini, R., Donoghue, K., Hart, J., Morgan, C., Doody, G. A., Dazzan, P., Jones, P. B., Morgan, K., Murray, R. M., & Fearon, P. (2010). Illicit substance use and its correlates in first episode psychosis. *Acta Psychiat, Scand., 121*(5), 351–58.

Mazzucchelli, T., Kane, R., & Rees, C. (2009). Behavioral activation treatments for depression in adults: A meta-analysis. *Clinical Psychology: Science and Practice, 16*, 383–411.

McAlonan, G. M., Cheung, V., Cheung, C., Suckling, J., Lam, G. Y., Tai, K. S., Yip, L., Murphy, D. G. M., & Chua, S. E. (2005). Mapping the brain in autism. A voxel-based MRI study of volumetric differences and intercorrelations in autism. *Brain, 128*(2), 268–76.

McAnulty, R. D., Adams, H. E., & Dillon, J. (2001). Sexual disorders: The paraphilias. In P. B. Sutker & H. E. Adams (Eds.), *Comprehensive handbook of psychopathology* (pp. 749–73). New York: Kluwer/Plenum.

McCabe, M. P., & Wauchope, M. (2005). Behavioral characteristics of men accused of rape: Evidence for different types of rapists. *Arch. Sex. Behav., 34*, 241–53.

McCabe, R. E., Antony, M. M., Summerfeld, L. J., Liss, A., & Swinson, R. P. (2003). Preliminary examination of the relationship between anxiety disorders in adults and self-reported history of teasing or bullying experiences. *Cog. Behav. Ther., 32*(4), 187–93.

McCabe, R. E., & Gifford, S. (2009). Psychological treatment of panic disorder and agoraphobia. In M. M. Antony & M. B. Stein (Eds.), *Oxford handbook of anxiety and related disorders* (pp. 308–20). New York: Oxford University Press.

McCall, L. (1961). *Between us and the dark*. Originally published in 1947. Summary in W. C. Alvarez, (1961) *Minds that came back*. Philadelphia: J. B. Lippincott.

McCann, J. T. (1999). Obsessive-compulsive and negativistic personality disorders. In T. Millon, P. H. Blaney, & R. D. Davis (Eds.), *Oxford textbook of psychopathology* (pp. 585–604). New York: Oxford University Press.

McCann, U. D., Sgambati, F. P., Schwartz, A. R., & Ricaurte, G. A. (2009). Sleep apnea in young abstinent recreational MDMA ("ecstasy") consumers. *Neurol., 73*(23), 2011–17.

McCarthy, B. W. (1989). Cognitive-behavioral strategies and techniques in the treatment of early ejaculation. In S. R. Leiblum & R. C. Rosen (Eds.), *Principles and practice of sex therapy* (2nd ed., pp. 141–67). New York: Guilford.

McCarthy, J. J., & Flynn, N. (2001). Hepatitis C in methadone maintenance patients. Prevalence and public policy implications. *J. Addict. Dis., 20*, 19–31.

McClellan, J., Kowatch, R., & Findling, R. L. (2007). Work Group on Quality Issues. Practice parameter for the assessment and treatment of children and adolescents with bipolar disorder. *J. Amer. Acad. Child Adoles. Psychiat., 46*(1), 107–25.

McClellan, J., Susser, E., & King, M.-C. (2007). Schizophrenia: A common disease caused by multiple rare alleles. *Brit. J. Psychiat., 190*, 194–99.

McClelland, G. M., & Teplin, L. (2001). Alcohol intoxication and violent crime: Implications for public health policy. *American Journal on Addictions, 10*(suppl.), 70.

McClelland, L., & Crisp, A. (2001). Anorexia nervosa and social class. *Int. J. Eat. Dis., 29*, 150–56.

McCloud, A., Barnaby, B., Omu, N., Drummond, C., & Aboud, A. (2004). Relationship between alcohol use disorders and suicidality in a psychiatric population: In-patient prevalence study. *Brit. J. Psychiat., 184*, 439–45.

McComb, J. L., Lee, B. K., & Sprenkle, D. H. (2009). Conceptualizing and treating problem gambling as a family issue. *J. Marital Fam. Ther., 35*(4), 415–31.

McConaghy, N. (1998). Paedophilia: A review of the evidence. *Austral. N.Z. J. Psychiat., 32*, 252–65.

McCrae, R. R., & Costa, P. T., Jr. (2008). The five-factor theory of personality. In O. P. John, R. W. Robins, & L. A. Pervin (Eds.), *Handbook of personality: Theory and research* (3rd ed., pp. 159–81). New York: Guilford Press.

McDermut, W., Zimmerman, M., & Chelminski, I. (2003). The construct validity of depressive personality disorder. *J. Abn. Psychol., 112*, 49–60.

McDonald, L., Bellingham, S., Conrad, T., Morgan, A., et al. (1997). Families and schools together (FAST): Integrating community development with clinical strategies. *Families in Society, 78*(2), 140–55.

McElroy, S. L., Guerdjikova, A. I., O'Melia, A. M., Mori, N., & Keck, P. E. (2010). Pharmacotherapy of the eating disorders. In W. A. Agras (Ed.), *The Oxford Handbook of Eating Disorders*, New York: Oxford University Press, pp. 417–51.

McEwan, B. S. (1998). Protective and damaging effects of stress-mediators. *N. Engl. J. Med., 338*, 171–79.

McFall, R. M. (1990). The enhancement of social skills: An information-processing analysis. In W. L. Marshall, D. R. Laws, & H. E. Barbaree (Eds.), *Handbook of sexual assault: Issues, theories, and treatment of the offender* (pp. 311–30). New York: Plenum.

McFarlane, W. R., Lukens, E., Link, B., Dushay, R., Deakins, S. A., Newmark, M., Dunne, E. J., Horen, B., & Toran, J. (1995). Multiple-family groups and psychoeducation in the treatment of schizophrenia. *Arch. Gen. Psychiat., 52*, 679–87.

McGlashan, T. H., Grilo, C. M., Sanislow, C. A., Ralevski, E., Morey, L. C., et al. (2005). Two-year prevalence and stability of individual DSM-IV criteria for schizotypal, borderline, avoidant, and obsessive-compulsive personality disorders: Toward a hybrid model of axis II disorders. *Amer. J. Psychiat., 162*, 883–89.

McGrath, M., & Turvey, B. E. (2008). Sexual asphyxia. In Turvey, B. E. (Ed.), *An introduction to behavioral evidence analysis* (3rd ed.) (pp. 605–28). San Diego, CA: Elsevier Academic Press.

McGue, M. (1998). Behavioral genetic models of alcoholism and drinking. In K. E. Leonard & H. T. Blane (Eds.), *Psychological theories of drinking and alcoholism*. New York: Guilford.

McGuffin, P., Cohen, S., & Knight, J. (2007). Honing in on depression genes. *Am. J. Psychiat., 164*(2), 195–97.

McGuffin, P., Rijsdijk, F., Andrew, M., Sham, P., Katz, R., & Cardno, A. (2003). The heritability of bipolar affective disorder and the genetic relationship to unipolar depression. *Arch. Gen. Psychiat., 60*, 497–502.

McGuffin, P. Alsabban, S., & Uher, R. (2011). The truth about genetic variation in the serotonin transporter gene and response to stress and medication. *Brit. J. of Psychiat., 198*, 424–427.

McGuire, P. K., Silbersweig, D. A., Wright, I., & Murray, R. M. (1996). The neural correlates of inner speech and auditory verbal imagery in schizophrenia: Relationship to auditory verbal hallucinations. *Brit. J. Psychiat., 169*(2), 148–59.

McGuire, W. J. (1994). Uses of historical data in psychology: Comments on Munsterberg (1899). *Psychol. Rev., 101*, 243–47.

McHugh, P. F., & Kreek, M. J. (2004). In J. Brick (Ed.), *Handbook of the medical consequences of alcohol and drug abuse* (pp. 219–55). New York: Haworth Press.

McKenna, K., Gordon, C. T., & Rapoport, J. L. (1994). Childhood-onset schizophrenia: Timely neurobiological research. *J. Amer. Acad. Child Adoles. Psychiat., 33*(6), 771–81.

McKnight Investigators. (2003). Risk factors for the onset of eating disorders in adolescent girls: Results of the McKnight Longitudinal Risk Factor Study. *Amer. J. Psychiat., 160*, 248–54.

McLachlan, G. (2009, Aug. 22). Taking the spice out of legal smoking mixtures. *Lancet, 374*(9690), 600.

McLaughlin, K. A., Borkovec, T. D., & Sibrava, N. J. (2007). The effects of worry and rumination on affect states and cognitive activity. *Behavior Therapy, 38*(1), 23–38.

McLaughlin, K. A., Fox, N. A., Zeanah, C. H., Sheridan, M. A., Marshall, P., & Nelson, C. A. (2010). Delayed maturation in brain electrical activity partially explains the association between early environmental deprivation and symptoms of attention-deficit/hyperactivity disorder. *Biol. Psychiat., 68*(4), 329–36. doi:10.1016/j.biopsych.2010.04.005

McLaurin, J., Cecal, R., Kierstead, M. E., Tian, X., Phinney, A. L., Manea, M., French, J. E., Lambermon, M. H. L., Darabie, A. A., Bown, M. E., Janus, C., Chishti, M. A., Horne, P., Westaway, D., Fraser, P. E., Mount, H. T. J., Przybylski, M., & St. George-Hyslop, P. (2002). Therapeutically effective antibodies against amyloid-âpeptide target amyloid-â residues 4–10 and inhibit cytotoxicity and fibrillogenesis. *Nature Medicine, 8*(11), 1263–69.

McLean, C. P., & Anderson, E. R. (2009). Brave men and timid women? A review of the gender differences in fear and anxiety. *Clin. Psychol. Rev., 29*(6), 496–505. doi: 10.1016/j.cpr.2009.05.003

McLoyd, V. C. (1998). Socioeconomic disadvantage and child development. *Amer. Psychol., 53*(2), 185–204.

McMinn, M. R., Buchanan, T., Ellens, B. M., & Ryan, M. K. (1999). Technology, professional practice, and ethics: Survey findings and implications. *Profess. Psychol. Res. and Prac., 30*(2), 165–72.

McMurran, M., & Hollin, C. R. (1993). *Young offenders and alcohol related crime*. New York: Wiley.

McMurran, M., Huband, N., & Overton, E. (2010). Noncompletion of personality disorder treatments: A systematic review of correlates, consequences, and interventions. *Clin. Psychol. Rev., 30*(3), 277–87. doi:10.1016/j.cpr.2009.12.002

McMurray, R. G., Newbould, E., Bouloux, G. M., Besser, G. M., & Grossman, A. (1991). High-dose naloxone modifies cardiovascular and neuroendocrine function in ambulant subjects. *Psychoneuroendocrinology, 16*, 447–55.

McNally, K. (2007). Schizophrenia as split personality/Jekyll and Hyde: The origins of the informal usage in the English language. *Journal of the History of the Behavioral Sciences, 43*(1), 69–79.

McNally, R. F., & Reese, H. E. (2009). Information-processing approaches to understanding anxiety disorders. In M. M. Antony & M. B. Stein (Eds.), *Oxford handbook of anxiety and related disorders* (pp. 136–52). New York: Oxford University Press.

McNally, R. J. (2000). Information-processing abnormalities in obsessive-compulsive disorder. In

W. K. Goodman, M. V. Rudorfer, et al. (Eds.), *Obsessive-compulsive disorder: Contemporary issues in treatment. Personality and clinical psychology series* (pp. 106–16). Mahwah, NJ: Erlbaum.

McNally, R. J. (2002). Anxiety sensitivity and panic disorder. *Biol. Psychiat., 51,* 938–46.

McNally, R. J. (2004). Conceptual problems with the DSM-IV criteria for posttraumatic stress disorder. In G. M. Rosen (Ed.),*Posttraumatic Stress disorder: Issues and Controversies* (pp. 1–14). New York: Wiley.

McNally, R. J. (2008). Posttraumatic stress disorder. In P. H. Blaney, T. Millon, & S. Grossman (Eds.), *Oxford Textbook of Pyschiatry (2nd ed.).* Oxford, UK: Oxford University Press.

McNally, R. J. (2009). Can we fix PTSD in DSM-V? *Depression and Anxiety, 26,* 597–600.

McNally, R. J., Bryant, R. A., & Ehlers, A. (2003). Does early intervention promote recovery from posttraumatic stress? *Psychol. Sci. in the Pub. Int., 4,* 45–79.

McNally, R. J., Clancy, S. A., Barret, H. M., & Parker, H. A. (2005). Reality monitoring in adults reporting repressed, recovered, or continuous memories of childhood sexual abuse. *J. Abn. Psychol., 114*(1), 147–52.

McNally, R. J., & Geraerts, E. (2009). A new solution to the recovered memory debate. *Perspectives on Psychological Science, 4,* 126–34. doi:10.1111/j.1745-6924.2009.01112.x

*J. Affect. Dis.*McNaughton, N. (2008). The neurobiology of anxiety: Potential for co-morbidity of anxiety and substance use disorders. In S. H. Stewart & P. J. Conrod (Eds.), *Anxiety and substance use disorders: The vicious cycle of comorbidity* (pp. 19–33). New York: Springer Science + Business Media.

McNicholas, F., Slonims, V., & Cass, H. (2000). Exaggeration of symptoms or psychiatric Munchausen's syndrome by proxy? *Child Psych. & Psychiat. Rev., 5,* 69–75.

McNulty, J. P. (2004). Commentary: Mental illness, society, stigma, and research. *Schizo. Bull., 30*(3), 573–75.

McRae-Clark, A. L., Carter, R. E., Killeen, T. K., Carpenter, M. J., Wahlquist, A. E., Simpson, S. A., & Brady, K. T. (2009). A placebo-controlled trial of buspirone for the treatment of marijuana dependence. *Drug Alcohol Depend., 105*(1–2), 132–38.

McReynolds, P. (1996). Lightner Witmer: Little-known founder of clinical psychology. *Amer. Psychol., 51,* 237–40.

McReynolds, P. (1997). Lightner Witmer: The first clinical psychologist. In W. G. Bringmann, H. E. Luck, R. Miller, & C. E. Early (Eds.), *A pictorial history of psychology* (pp. 465–70). Chicago: Quintessence Books.

Mechanic, D. (2004). The rise and fall of managed care. *J. Hlth. Soc. Behav., 45*(Suppl.), 76–86.

Medical Council on Alcoholism. (1997). *Alcohol-related liver disease.* London: Author.

Mednick, S. A., & Schulsinger, F. (1968). Some premorbid characteristics related to breakdown in children with schizophrenic mothers. In D. Rosenthal & S. S. Kety (Eds.), *The transmission of schizophrenia* (pp. 267–91). Oxford: Pergamon.

Mednick, S. A., Machon, R. A., Huttunen, M. O., & Bonnet, D. (1988). Adult schizophrenia following prenatal exposure to an influenza epidemic. *Arch. Gen. Psychiat., 45,* 189–92.

Meehl, P. E. (1962). Schizotaxia, schizotypy, schizophrenia. *Amer. Psychol., 17,* 827–38.

Meers, G. (2009). Conducting an intake interview. In I. Marini & M. A. Stebnicki, (Eds.), *The professional counselor's desk reference* (pp. 127–34). New York: Springer.

Meewisse, M.-L., Reitsma, J. B., de Vries, G.-J., Gersons, B. P. R., & Olff, M. (2007). Cortisol and post-traumatic stress disorder in adults. *British Journal of Psychiatry, 191,* 387–392.

Megargee, E. I. (2009). Understanding and assessing aggression and violence. In J. N. Butcher (Ed.), *Oxford handbook of personality and clinical assessment* (pp. 542–66). New York: Oxford Univesity Press.

Mehta, M. A., Golembo, N. I., Nosarti, C., Colvert, E., Mota, A., Williams, S. C. R., et al. (2009). Amygdala, hippocampal and corpus callosum size following severe early institutional deprivation: The English and Romanian Adoptees Study pilot.*J. Child Psychol. Psychiat., 50*(8), 943–51. doi:10.1111/j.1469-7610.2009.02084.x

Meier, B. R., & Patkar, A. A. (2007). Buprenorphine treatment: Factors and first-hand experiences for providers to consider.*J. Addict. Dis., 26*(1) 3–14.

Meinzer, M., Obleser, J., Flaisch, T., Eulitz, C., & Rockstroh, B. (2007). Recovery from aphasia as a function of language therapy in an early bilingual patient demonstrated by fMRI. *Neuropsychologia, 45*(6), 1247–56.

Mellon, M. W., & McGrath, M. L. (2000). Empirically supported treatments in pediatric psychology: Nocturnal enuresis. *J. Pediat. Psychol., 25,* 193–214.

Meltzer, H. Y., Alphs, L., Green, A. I., Altamura, A. C., Anand, R., Bertoldi, A., Bourgeois, M., Chouinard, G., Islam, Z., Kane, J., Krishnan, R., Lindenmayer, J.-P., & Potkin, S., for the InterSePT Study Group. (2003). Clozapine treatment for suicidality in schizophrenia. *Arch. Gen. Psychiat., 60,* 82–91.

Melville, J. D., & Naimark, D. (2002). Punishing the insane: The verdict of guilty but mentally ill. *J. Amer. Acad. Psychiat. Law, 30,* 553–55.

Menaghan, E. G. (2010). Stress and distress in childhood and adolescence. In T. L. Scheid & T. N. Brown (Eds.), *A handbook for the study of mental health: Social contexts, theories, and systems (2nd ed.),* (pp. 321–33). New York: Cambridge University Press.

Mendelson, J. H., & Mello, N. (1992). Human laboratory studies of buprenorphine. In J. D. Blaine (Ed.), *Buprenorphine: An alternative treatment for opiate dependence* (pp. 38–60). Washington, DC: U.S. Department of Health and Human Services.

Mental Health Law Project. (1987, Oct.). Court decisions concerning mentally disabled people confined in institutions. *MHLP Newsletter.* Washington, DC.

Merbaum, M. (1977). Some personality characteristics of soldiers exposed to extreme war stress: A follow-up study of post-hospital adjustment. *J. Clin. Psychol., 33,* 558–62.

Merikangas, K., Jin, R., Jian-Ping-he, Kessler, R.C., Lee, S. et al. (2011). *Archives of General Psiaitry* 68 241–51.

Merikangas, K. R., & Swendsen, J. D. (1997). Genetic epidemiology of psychiatric disorders. *Epidemiological Reviews, 19*(1), 144–55.

Merikangas, K. R., Zhang, H., Avenevoli, S., Acharya, S., Neuenschwander, M., & Angst, J. (2003). Longitudinal trajectories of depression and anxiety in a prospective community study. *Arch. Gen. Psychiat., 60*(10), 993–1000.

Mervielde, I., De Clercq, B., De Fruyt, F., & Van Leeuwen, K. (2005). Temperament, personality, and developmental psychopathology as childhood antecedents of personality disorders. *J. Pers. Dis., 19,* 171–201.

Meston, C. M., & Bradford, A. (2007). Sexual dysfunctions in women. *Ann. Rev. Clin. Psych., 3,* 233–56.

Meston, C. M., & Rellini, A. (2008). Sexual dysfunction. In W. E. Craighead, D. J. Miklowitz, & L. W. Craighead (Eds.), *Psychopathology: History, diagnosis, and empirical foundations* (pp. 544–64). Hoboken, NJ: John Wiley & Sons.

Metz, M. E., Pryor, J. L., Nesvacil, L. J., Abuzzahab, F., & Koznar, J. (1997). Premature ejaculation: A psychophysiological review. *J. Sex Marit. Ther., 23,* 3–23.

Meyer, B., & Pilkonis, P. A. (2005). An attachment model of personality disorders. In M. F. Lenzenweger & J. F. Clarkin (Eds.),*Major theories of personality disorder* (2nd ed., pp. 231–81). New York: Guilford Press.

Meyer, B., Pilkonis, P. A., Krupnick, J. L., Egan, M. K., Simmens, S. J., & Sotsky, S. M. (2002). Treatment expectancies, patient alliance, and outcome: Further analyses from the National Institute of Mental Health Treatment of Depression Collaborative Research Program. *J. Cons. Clin. Psychol., 70,* 1051–55.

Meyer, G. J., Mihura, J. L., & Smith, B. L. (2005). The interclinician reliability of Rorschach interpretation in four data sets. *J. Pers. Assess., 84,* 296–314.

Meyer, G., Finn, S. E., Eyde, L. D., Kay, G. G., Moreland, K. L., Dies, R. R., Eisman, E. J., Kubiszyn, T. W., & Reed, G. M. (2001). Psychological testing and psychological assessment: A review of evidence and issues. *Amer. Psychol., 56,* 128–65.

Meyer, J. K. (1995). Paraphilias. In H. I. Kaplan & J. B. Sadock (Eds.), *Comprehensive textbook of psychiatry* (6th ed., pp. 1334–47). Baltimore: Williams and Wilkins.

Meyer, R. E., & Mirin, S. M. (1979). *The heroin stimulus: Implications for a theory of addiction.* New York: Plenum.

Mezulis, A. H., Abramson, L. Y., Hyde, J. S., & Hankin, B. L. (2004). Is there a universal positivity bias in attributions? A meta-analytic review of individual, developmental, and cultural differences in the self-serving attributional bias. *Psychol. Bull., 130*(5), 711–47.

Mezzich, J. E., Kirmayer, L. J., Kleinman, A., Fabrega, H., Jr., Parron, D. L., Good, B. J., Lin, K. M., & Manson, S. M. (1999). The place of culture in DSM-IV. *J. Nerv. Ment. Dis., 187,* 457–64.

Michael, T., Blechert, J., Vriends, N., Margraf, J. R., & Wilhelm, F. H. (2007). Fear conditioning in panic disorder: Enhanced resistance to extinction. *J.Abn. Psych., 116*(3), 612–17.

Miczek, K. A., Covington, H. E., Nikulna, E. M., & Hammer, R. P. (2004). Aggression and defeat: Persistent effects on cocaine self-administration and gene expression in peptidergic and aminergic mesocorticolimbic circuits. *Neuroscience and Biobehavioral Reviews, 27,* 787–802.

Miklowitz, D. J. (2009a). Group psychoeducation increases time to recurrence in stabilised bipolar disorders. *Evidence-Based Mental Health, 12*(4), 110. doi: 10.1136/ebmh.12.4.110

Miklowitz, D. J. (2009b). Pharmacotherapy and psychosocial treatments for bipolar disorder. In I. H. Gotlib & C. L. Hammen (Eds.), *Handbook of depression and its treatment* (2nd ed.). New York: Guilford Press.

Miklowitz, D. J., & Craighead, W. E. (2007). Psychosocial treatments for bipolar disorder. In P. E. Nathan and J. M. Gorman (Eds.), *A guide to treatments that work.* New York: Oxford University Press, pp. 309–22.

Miklowitz, D. J., & Stackman, D. (1992). Communication deviance in families of schizophrenic and other psychiatric patients: Current state of the construct. In E. F. Walker, R. H. Dworkin, & B. A. Cornblatt (Eds.), *Progress in experimental personality and psychopathology research,* (Vol. 15). New York: Springer.

Milev, P., Ho, B.-C., Arndt, S., & Andreasen, N. C. (2005). Predictive values of neurocognition and negative symptoms on functional outcome in schizophrenia: A longitudinal first-episode study with 7-year followup. *Amer. J. Psychiat., 162,* 495–506.

Millar, A., Espie, C. A., & Scott, J. (2004). The sleep of remitted bipolar outpatients: A controlled naturalistic study using actigraphy. *J. Affect. Dis., 80,* 145–53.

Miller, G. (2011). Healing the brain, healing the mind. *Science, 333,* 29 July, 514–17.

Miller, G. E., & Blackwell, E. (2006). Turning up the heat: Inflammation as a mechanism linking chronic stress, depression, and heart disease. *Curr. Dis. Psychol. Sci.,* 15, 6, 269–272.

Miller, J. D., Dir, A., Gentile, B., Wilson, L., Pryor, L. R., & Campbell, W. K. (in press). Searching for a vulnerable dark triad: Comparing Factor 2 psychopathy, vulnerable narcissism, and borderline personality disorder. *Journal of Personality.*

Miller, J. D., Reynolds, S. K., & Pilkonis, P. A. (2004). The validity of the five-factor model prototypes for personality disorders in two clinical samples. *Psychol. Assess., 16,* 310–33.

Miller, J. D., Widiger, T. A., & Campbell, W. K. (2010). Narcissistic personality disorder and the DSM-V. *J. Abn. Psychol.,* 119(4), 640–9. doi:10.1037/a0019529

Miller, L. (2007). Traumatic stress disorders. In F. M. Dattilio & A. Freeman (Eds.), *Cognitive behavioral strategies in crisis intervention.* (pp. 494–530). New York: Guilford Press.

Miller, L. J. (2002). Postpartum depression. *JAMA, 287*(6), 762–65.

Miller, M. B., Useda, J. D., Trull, T. J., Burr, R. M., & Minks-Brown, C. (2001). Paranoid, schizoid, and schizotypal personality disorders. In H. E. Adams & P. B. Sutker (Eds.), *Comprehensive handbook of psychopathology* (pp. 535–58). New York: Kluwer Academic.

Miller, N., & Lyon, D. (2003). Biology of opiates affects prevalence of addiction, options for treatment. *Psychiat. Ann., 33,* 559–64.

Miller, R. (1970). Does Down's syndrome predispose children to leukemia? *Roche Report, 7*(16), 5.

Miller, W. R. (1983). Motivational interviewing with problem drinkers. *Behav. Psychotherapy, 11,* 147–72.

Miller, W. R., Benefield, R. G., & Tonigan, J. S. (1993). Enhancing motivation for change in problem drinking: A controlled comparison of two therapist styles. *J. Cons. Clin. Psychol., 61*(3), 455–61.

Miller, W. R., Leckman, A. L., Tinkcom, M., & Rubenstein, P. B. (1986). *Longterm follow-up of controlled drinking therapies.* Paper given at the Ninety-fourth Annual Meeting of the American Psychological Association, Washington, DC.

Miller, W. R., & Rollnik, S. (2002). Motivational interviewing: Preparing people to change addictive behavior (2nd ed.). New York: Guilford Press.

Miller, W. R., & Rollnick, S. (2003). Book review of *Motivational interviewing: Peparing people for change. J. Stud. Alcoh., 63*(6), 776–77.

Miller, W. R., Walters, S. T., & Bennett, M. E. (2001). How effective is alcoholism treatment in the United States? *J. Stud. Alcoh., 62*(2), 211–20.

Miller, W. R., & Wilbourne, P. L. (2002). Mesa Grande: A methodological analysis of clinical trials of treatment for alcohol use disorders. *Addiction, 97*(3), 265–77.

Miller-Horn, J. W., Kaleyias, J., Valencia, I., Melvin, J. J., Khurana, D. S., Hardison, H. H., Marks, H., Legido, A., & Kothare, S. V. (2008). Efficacy and tolerability of ADHD medications in a clinical practice. *J. Ped. Neurol., 6*(1), 5–10.

Milliken, C. S. Aucherlonie, J. L., & Hoge, C. W. (2007). Longitudinal assessment of mental health problems among active and reserve component soldiers returning from the Iraq war. *JAMA, 298,* 2141–2148.

Millon, T. (1981). *Disorders of personality: DSM-III, Axis II.* New York: Wiley.

Millon, T., & Davis, R. D. (1995). The development of personality disorders. In D. Cicchetti & D. J. Cohen (Eds.), *Developmental psychopathology: Vol. 2. Risk, disorder, and adaptation* (pp. 633–76). New York: Wiley.

Millon, T., & Davis, R. D. (1999). Developmental pathogenesis. In T. Millon, P. H. Blaney, & R. D. Davis (Eds.), *Oxford textbook of psychopathology* (pp. 29–48). New York: Oxford University Press.

Millon, T., & Martinez, A. (1995). Avoidant personality disorder. In W. J. Livesley (Ed.), *The DSM-IV personality disorders.* (pp. 218–33). New York: Guilford.

Millon, T., & Radovanov, J. (1995). Passive-aggressive (negativistic) personality disorder. In W. J. Livesley (Ed.), *The DSM-IV personality disorders.* (pp. 312–25). New York: Guilford.

Mills, M. J., Sullivan, G., & Eth, S. (1987). Protecting third parties: A decade after Tarasoff. *Amer. J. Psychiat., 144*(1), 68–74.

Milne, J. M., Edwards, J. K., & Murchie, J. C. (2001). Family treatment of oppositional defiant disorder: Changing views and strength-based approaches. *Family Journal—Counseling & Therapy for Couples & Families, 9*(1), 17–28.

Milns, R. D. (1986). Squibb academic lecture: Attitudes towards mental illness in antiquity. *Austral. NZ J. Psychiat., 20,* 454–62.

Milos, G., Spindler, A., Ruggiero, G., Klaghofer, R., & Schnyder, U. (2002). Comorbidity of obsessive compulsive disorders and duration of eating disorders. *Int. J. Eat. Dis., 31,* 284–89.

Mindus, P., Rasmussen, S. A., & Lindquist, C. (1994). Neurosurgical treatment for refractory obsessive-compulsive disorder: Implications for understanding frontal lobe function. *J. Neuropsychiat. Clin. Neurosci., 6,* 467–77.

Mineka, S. (1985a). Animal models of anxiety-based disorders: Their usefulness and limitations. In A. H. Tuma & J. D. Maser (Eds.), *Anxiety and the anxiety disorders.* Hillsdale, NJ: Erlbaum.

Mineka, S. (1985b). The frightful complexities of the origins of fears. In F. R. Brush & J. B. Overmier (Eds.), *Affect, conditioning, and cognition: Essays on the determinants of behavior.* Hillsdale, NJ: Erlbaum.

Mineka, S. (2004). The positive and negative consequences of worry in the aetiology of generalized anxiety disorder: A learning theory perspective. In J. Yiend (Ed.), *Cognition, emotion and psychopathology: Theoretical, empirical and clinical directions.* (pp. 29–48). New York: Cambridge University Press.

Mineka, S., & Ben Hamida, S. (1998). Observational and nonconscious learning. In W. T. O'Donohue (Ed.), *Learning and behavior therapy* (pp. 421–39). Needham Heights, MA: Allyn and Bacon.

Mineka, S., & Cook, M. (1986). Immunization against the observational conditioning of snake fear in monkeys. *J. Abn. Psychol., 95,* 307–18.

Mineka, S., & Cook, M. (1993). Mechanisms underlying obervational conditioning of fear in monkeys. *J. Exper. Psychol.: General, 122,* 23–38.

Mineka, S., Davidson, M., Cook, M., & Keir, R. (1984). Observational conditioning of snake fear in rhesus monkeys. *J. Abn. Psychol., 93,* 355–72.

Mineka, S., Gunnar, M., & Champoux, M. (1986). Control and early socioemotional development: Infant rhesus monkeys reared in controllable versus uncontrollable environments. *Child Develop.* 57, 1241–56.

Mineka, S., & Kelly, K. A. (1989). The relationship between anxiety, lack of control and loss of control. In A. Steptoe & A. Appels (Eds.), *Stress, personal control and health.* Brussels-Luxembourg: J. Wiley.

Mineka, S., & Oehlberg, K. (2008). The relevance of recent developments in classical conditioning to understanding the etiology and maintenance of anxiety disorders. *Acta Psychologica, 127*(3), 567–580.

Mineka, S., & Öhman, A. (2002). Phobias and preparedness: The selective, automatic, and encapsulated nature of fear. *Biol. Psychiat., 52*(10), 927–37.

Mineka, S., Rafaeli, E., & Yovel, I. (2003). Cognitive biases in emotional disorders: Social-cognitive and information processing perspectives. In R. Davidson, H. Goldsmith & K. Scherer (Eds.), *Handbook of affective science.* Amsterdam: Elsevier.

Mineka, S., & Sutton, J. (2006). Contemporary learning theory perspectives on the etiology of fears and phobias. In M. G. Craske, D. Hermans & D. Vansteenwegen (Eds.), *Fear and learning: From basic processes to clinical implications.* (pp. 75–97). Washington, DC: American Psychological Association.

Mineka, S., Watson, D., & Clark, L. A. (1998). Comorbidity of anxiety and unipolar mood disorders. In J. T. Spence, J. M. Darley, & D. J. Foss (Eds.), *Annu. Rev. Psychol., 49,* 377–412.

Mineka, S., Yovel, I., & Pineles, S. (2002). Toward a psychological model of the etiology of generalized anxiety disorder. In D. J. Nutt, K. Rickels, & D. J. Stein (Eds.), *Generalized anxiety disorder: Symptomatology, pathogenesis and management.* London: Martin Dunitz.

Mineka, S., & Zinbarg, R. (1995). Conditioning and ethological models of social phobia. In R. Heimberg, M. Liebowitz, D. Hope, & F. Schneier (Eds.), *Social phobia: Diagnosis, assessment, and treatment.* New York: Guilford.

Mineka, S., & Zinbarg, R. (1996). Conditioning and ethological models of anxiety disorders: Stress-in-Dynamic Context anxiety models. In D. Hope (Ed.), *Perspectives on anxiety, panic, and fear: Nebraska Symposium on Motivation.* Lincoln: University of Nebraska Press.

Mineka, S., & Zinbarg, R. (2006). A contemporary learning theory perspective on the etiology of anxiety disorders: It's not what you thought it was. *Amer. Psychol.,* 61, 10–26.

Minnis, H., Everett, K., Pelosi, A. J., Dunn, J., & Knapp, M. (2006). Children in foster care: Mental health, service use and costs. *European Child & Adolescent Psychiatry, 15*(2), 63–70.

Mintzer, M. Z., Guarino, J., Kirk, T., Roache, J. D., & Griffiths, R. R. (1997). Ethanol and pentobarbital: Comparison of behavioral and subjective effects in sedative drug abusers. *Exp. Clin. Psychopharm., 5*(3), 203–15.

Minuchin, S. (1974). *Families and family therapy.* Cambridge, MA: Harvard University Press.

Minzenberg, M. J., & Siever, L. J. (2006). Neurochemistry and pharmacology of psychopathy and related disorders. In C. J. Patrick (Ed.), *Handbook of the psychopathy* (pp. 251–77). New York: Guilford Press.

Miranda, J., Bernal, G., Lau, A., Kohn, L., Hwang, W.-C, & LaFromboise, T. (2005). State of the science on psychosocial interventions for ethnic minorities. *Annu. Rev. Clin. Psychol., 1*(1), 113–42.

Mirsky, A. F., & Quinn, O. W. (1988). The Genain quadruplets. *Schizo. Bull., 14*, 595–612.

Mishara, B. L., Chagnon, F., Daigle, M., Balan, B., Raymond, S., Marcoux, I., et al. (2007). Which helper behaviors and intervention styles are related to better short-term outcomes in a telephone crisis intervention? Results from a silent monitoring study of calls to the U.S. 1-800-SUICIDE network. *Suicide Life Threat. Behav., 37*, 308–21.

Mishler, E. G., & Waxler, N. E. (1968). *Interaction in families: An experimental study of family processes and schizophrenia.* New York: Wiley.

Mishra, S. K., & Singh, P. (2010). History of neuroimaging: The legacy of William Oldendorf. *Journal of Child Neurology, 25*(4), 508–17.

Mitchell, A., & House, A. (2000). Medical and surgical conditions and treatments associated with psychiatric disorder. In Gelder et al. (Eds.), *New Oxford textbook of psychiatry* (pp. 1138–53). Oxford: Oxford University Press.

Mitchell, J. E., & Crow, S. J. (2010). Medical complications of eating disorders. In W. A. Agras (Ed.), *The Oxford Handbook of Eating Disorders* (pp. 259–66). New York: Oxford University Press.

Mitka, M. (2009). *JAMA, 302*(8), 836–37.

Mittal, V. A., Kalus, O., Bernstein, D. P., & Siever, L. J. (2007). Schizoid personality disorder. In W. O'Donohue, K. A. Fowler, & S. O. Lilienfeld (Eds.), *Personality Disorders: Toward the DSM-V* (pp. 63–79). Thousand Oaks, CA: Sage Publications, Inc.

Mittal. V. A., Neumann, C., Saczawa, M., & Walker, E. F. (2008). Longitudinal progression of movement abnormalities in relation to psychotic symptoms in adolescents at high risk of schizophrenia. *Arch. Gen. Psychiat., 65*, 165–71.

Mitte, K. (2005). A meta-analysis of the efficacy of psycho- and pharmacotherapy in panic disorder with and without agoraphobia. *J. Affect. Dis., 88*(1), 27–45.

Mittelman, M. S., Roth, D. L., Coon, D. W., & Haley, W. E. (2004). Sustained benefit of supportive intervention for depressive symptoms in the caregivers of patients with Alzheimer's disease. *Amer. J. Psychiat., 161*, 850–56.

Mizrahi, R., Rusjan, P., Agid O., Graff, A., Mamo, D. C., Zipursky, R. B., & Kapur, S. (2007). Adverse subjective experience with antipsychotics and its relationship to striatal and extrastriatal D2 receptors: A PET study in schizophrenia. *Am. J. Psychiat., 164*, 630–37.

Moeller, F. G., & Dougherty, D. M. (2001). Antisocial personality disorder, alcohol and aggression. *Alc. Res. Hlth., 25*(1), 5–11.

Moene, F. C., Spinhoven, P., Hoogduin, K., & Dyck, R. V. (2003). A randomized controlled clinical trial of a hypnosis-based treatment for patients with conversion disorder, motor type. *Int. J. Clin. Exp. Hypn., 51*(1), 29–50.

Moffatt, M. E. (1997). Nocturnal enuresis: A review of the efficacy of treatments and practical advice for clinicians. *Developmental and Behavioral Pediatrics, 18*(1), 49–56.

Moffitt, T. (1993a). Adolescence-limited and lifecourse-persistent antisocial behavior: A developmental taxonomy. *Psychol. Rev., 100*, 674–701.

Moffitt, T. E. (2005). The new look of behavioral genetics in developmental psychopathology: Gene-environment interplay in antisocial behaviors. *Psych. Bull., 131*(4), 533–54.

Moffitt, T. E. (2006). Life-course-persistent versus adolescence-limited antisocial behavior. In D. Cicchetti & D. J. Cohen (Eds.), *Developmental Psychopathology, Vol 3: Risk, disorder, and adaptation* (2nd ed.) (pp. 570–598) Hoboken, NJ: John Wiley & Sons.

Moffitt, T. E., & Caspi, A. (2001). Childhood predictors differentiate life-course-persistent and adolescencelimited antisocial pathways among males and females. *Develop. Psychopath., 13*(2), 355–75.

Moffitt, T. E., & Lynam, D. (1994). The neuropsychology of conduct disorder and delinquency: Implications for understanding antisocial behavior. In D. C. Fowles, P. Sutker, & S. H. Goodman (Eds.), *Progress in experimental personality and psychopathology research.* New York: Springer.

Moffitt, T. E., Caspi, A., & Rutter, M. (2005). Strategy for investigating interactions between measured genes and measured environments. *Arch. Gen. Psychiat. 62*(5), 473–81.

Moffitt, T. E., Caspi, A., & Rutter, M. (2006). Measured gene-environment interactions in psychopathology: Concepts, research strategies, and implications for research, intervention, and public understanding of genetics. *Perspectives on Psychological Science, 1*(1), 5–27.

Moffitt, T. E., Caspi, A., Harrington, H., & Milne, B. J. (2002). Males on the life-course-persistent and adolescence- limited antisocial pathways: Follow-up at age 26 years. *Develop. Psychopath., 14*, 179–207.

Mohler-Kuo, M., Dowdall, G. W., Koss, M. P., & Wechsler, H. (2004). Correlates of rape while intoxicated in a national sample of college women. *Journal of Studies on Alcohol, 65*(1), 37–45.

Mohr, D. C. (1995). Negative outcome in psychotherapy: A critical review. *Clin. Psychol. Sci. Prac., 2*, 1–27.

Moldin, S. O., & Rubenstein, J. L. (2006). *Understanding autism: From basic neuroscience to treatment.* Boca Raton, FL: CRC Press.

Moldovan, A. R., & David, D. (2011). Effect of obesity treatments on eating behavior: Psychosocial interventions versus surgical interventions. A systematic review. *Eating Behaviors, 12*, 161–67.

Molnar, B. E., Berkman, L. F., & Buka, S. L. (2001). Psychopathology, childhood sexual abuse and other childhood adversities: Relative links to subsequent suicidal behaviour in the US. *Psychol. Med., 31*, 965–77.

Monahan, J., & Steadman, H. J. (1997). Violent storms and violent people: How meteorology can inform risk communication in mental health law. *Amer. Psychol., 51*(9), 931–38.

Money, J. (1985). *The destroying angel* (pp. 17–31, 51–52, 61–68, 83–90, 107–20, 137–48). Buffalo, NY: Prometheus Books.

Money, J. (1986). *Lovemaps: Clinical concepts of sexual/erotic health and pathology, paraphilia, and gender transposition.* New York: Irvington.

Money, J. (1988). *Gay, straight, and in-between* (p. 77). New York: Oxford University Press.

Money, J., & Ehrhardt, A. A. (1972). *Man & woman, boy & girl: Differentiation and dimorphism of gender identity from conception to maturity.* Baltimore: Johns Hopkins University Press.

Monroe, S. M. (2008). Modern approaches to conceptualizing and measuring human life stress. *Annu. Rev. Clin. Psychol., 4*, 33–52.

Monroe, S. M., & Hadjiyannakis, K. (2002). The social environment and depression: Focusing on severe life stress. In I. H. Gotlib & C. L. Hammen (Eds.), *Handbook of depression* (pp. 314–40). New York: Guilford.

Monroe, S. M., & Harkness, K. L. (2005). Life stress, the "kindling" hypothesis, and the recurrence of depression: Considerations from a life stress perspective. *Psychol. Rev., 112*(2), 417–45.

Monroe, S. M., & Harkness, K. L. (2011). Recurrence in major depression: A conceptual analysis. *Psychol. Rev.* doi: 10.1037/a0025190.

Monroe, S. M., & Reid, M.W. (2008) Gene-environment interactions in depression research. *Psychological Science.*

Monroe, S. M., & Simons, A. D. (1991). Diathesis-stress theories in the context of life stress research: Implications for the depressive disorders. *Psychol. Bull., 110*, 406–25.

Monroe, S. M., Slavich, G. M., & Georgiades, K. (2009). The social environment and life stress in depression. In I. H. Gotlib & C. L. Hammen (Eds.), *Handbook of depression and its treatment* (2nd ed., pp. 340–60). New York: Guilford Press.

Monroe, S. M., Slavich, G. M., Torres, L. D., & Gotlib, I. H. (2007). Major life events and major chronic difficulties are differentially associated with history of major depressive episodes. *J. Abn. Psych., 116*(1), 116–24.

Monson, C. M., Gunnin, D. D., Fogel, M. H., & Kyle, L. L. (2001). Stopping (or slowing) the revolving door: Factors related to NGRI acquittees' maintenance of a conditional release. *Law and Human Behavior, 25*(3), 257–66.

Montague, C. T., Farooqi, I. S., Whitehead, J. P., Soos, M. A., Rau, H., Wareham, N. J., Sewter, C. P., Digby, J. E., Mohammed, S. N., Hurst, J. A., Cheetham, C. H., Earley, A. R., Barnett, A. H., Prins, J. B., & O'Rahilly, S. (1997, Jun. 26). Congenital leptin deficiency is associated with severe early-onset obesity in humans. *Nature, 387*, 903–8.

Monterosso, J. R., Flannery, B. A., Pettinati, H. M., et al. (2001). Predicting treatment response to naltrexone: The influence of craving and family history. *American Journal of Addictions, 10*(3), 258–68.

Moore, S. (2009). Prison term for a seller of medical marijuana. *New York Times, 158*(54), 704.

Mora, G. (1967). Paracelsus' psychiatry. *Amer. J. Psychiat., 124*, 803–14.

Moran, P., Coffey, C., Chanen, A., Mann, A., Carlin, J. B., & Patton, G. C. (2010). Childhood sexual abuse and abnormal personality: A population-based study. *Psychol. Med.,* 1–8. doi:10.1017/S0033291710001789

Morein-Zamir, S., Fineberg, N. A., Robbins, T. W., & Sahakian, B. J. (2010). Inhibition of thoughts and actions in obsessive-compulsive disorder: Extending the endophenotype? *Psychol. Med., 40*(2), 263–72. doi: 10.1017/s003329170999033x.

Moreno, C., Laje, G., Blanco, C., Jiang, H., Schmidt, A. B., & Olfson, M. (2007). National trends in the outpatient diagnosis and treatment of bipolar disorder in youth. *Arch. Gen. Psychiat., 64*, 1032–39.

Morey, L. C. (1988). Personality disorders in DSM-III and DSM-III-R: Convergence, coverage, and internal consistency. *Amer. J. Psychiat., 145*, 573–77.

Morey, L. C., Skinner, H. A., & Blashfield, R. K. (1984). A typology of alcohol abusers: Correlates and implications. *J. Abn. Psychol., 93*, 408–17.

Morgan, J. F., & Crisp, A. H. (2000). Use of leucotomy for intractable anorexia nervosa: A long-term follow-up study. *Int. J. Eat. Dis., 27*, 249–58.

Morgan, M. J. (1998). Recreational use of "ecstasy" (MDMA) is associated with elevated impulsivity. *Neuropsychopharmacol., 19*(4), 252–64.

Morgan, W. G. (2002). Origin and history of the earliest Thematic Apperception Test pictures. *J. Pers. Assess., 79*(3), 422–45.

Morganstern, J., Labouvie, E., McCrady, B. S., Kahler, C. W., & Frey, R. M. (1997). Affiliation with Alcoholics Anonymous after treatment: A study of its therapeutic effects and mechanisms of action. *J. Cons. Clin. Psychol., 65*(5), 768–77.

Morganstern, J., Langenbucher, J., Labouvie, E., & Miller, K. J. (1997). The comorbidity of alcoholism and personality disorders in a clinical population. *J. Abn. Psychol., 106*(1), 74–84.

Mori, E., et al. (1997a). Medial temporal structures relate to memory impairment in Alzheimer's disease: An MRI volumetric study. *J. Neurol. Neurosurg. Psychiat., 63*(2), 214–21.

Mori, E., et al. (1997b). Premorbid brain size as a determinant of reserve capacity against intellectual decline in Alzheimer's disease. *Amer. J. Psychiat., 154*(1), 18–24.

Moriarty, K. M., Alagna, S. W., & Lake, C. R. (1984). Psychopharmacology: An historical perspective. *Psychiat. Clin. N. Amer., 7*(3), 411–33.

Morissette, S. B., Tull, M. T., Gulliver, S. B., Kamholtz, B. W., & Zimering, R. T. (2007). Anxiety, anxiety disorders, tobacco use, and nicotine: A critical review of interrelationships. *Psychol. Bull., 133,* 245–72.

Morley, T. E., & Moran, G. (2011). The origins of cognitive vulnerability in early childhood: Mechanisms linking early attachment to later depression. *Clin. Psychol. Rev., 31*(7), 1071–82. doi: 10.1016/j.cpr.2011.06.006

Morris, D., & Turnbull, P. (2007). A survey-based exploration of the impact of dyslexia on career progression of UK registered nurses. *Journal of Nursing Management, 15*(1), 97–106.

Morris, T. L. (2001). Social phobia. In M. W. Vasey & M. R. Dadds (Eds.), *The developmental psychopathology of anxiety* (pp. 435–58). New York: Oxford University Press.

Morrison, J. (1995). *DSM-IV made easy: The clinicians guide to diagnosis.* New York: Guilford.

Mörtberg, E., Clark, D. M., Sundin, Ö., & Wistedt, A. Å. (2007). Intensive group cognitive treatment and individual cognitive therapy vs. treatment as usual in social phobia: A randomized controlled trial. *Acta Psychiat. Scand., 115*(2), 142–54. doi: 10.1111/j.1600-0447.2006.00839.x

Mosak, H. H. (2000). Adlerian psychotherapy. In R. J. Corsini & D. Wedding (Eds.), *Current psychotherapies* (pp. 54–98). Itasca, IL: Peacock.

Moscato, B. S., Russell, M., Zielezny, M., Bromet, E., Egri, G., Mudar, P., & Marshall, J. R. (1997). Gender differences in the relation between depressive symptoms and alcohol problems: A longitudinal perspective. *Amer. J. Epidemiol., 146*(11), 966–74.

Moscovitch, D. A., Antony, M. M., & Swinson, R. P. (2009). Exposure-based treatments for anxiety disorders: Theory and process. In M. M. Antony & M. B. Stein (Eds.), *Oxford handbook of anxiety and related disorders* (pp. 461–75). New York: Oxford University Press.

Moser, P. W. (1989, Jan.). Double vision: Why do we never match up to our mind's ideal? *Self,* pp. 51–52.

Mott, F. W. (1919). *War neuroses and shell shock.* Oxford: Oxford Medical Publications.

Mott, T. F., & Leach, L. (2004). Is methylphenidate useful for treating adolescents with ADHD? *J. Fam. Pract., 53*(8), 659–61.

Mowbray, R. M. (1959). Historical aspects of electric convulsant therapy. *Scott Medical Journal, 4,* 373–78.

Mowrer, O. H. (1947). On the dual nature of learning: A reinterpretation of "conditioning" and "problem solving." *Harvard Educational Review, 17,* 102–48.

Mowrer, O. H., & Mowrer, W. M. (1938). Enuresis—a method for its study and treatment. *Amer. J. Orthopsychiat., 8,* 436–59.

Mrazek, P. J., & Haggerty, R. J. (Eds.). (1994). *Reducing risks for mental disorders: Frontiers for prevention intervention research.* Washington, DC: National Academy Press.

Mueser, K. T., & Berenbaum, H. (1990). Psychodynamic treatment of schizophrenia. Is there a future? *Psychol. Med., 20,* 253–62.

Mueser, K. T., et al. (1998). Models of community care for severe mental illness: A review of research on case management. *Schizo. Bull., 24*(1), 37–74.

Mula, M., Pini, S., & Giovanni, B. C. (2007). The neurobiology and clinical significance of depersonalization in mood and anxiety disorders: A critical reappraisal. *J. Affect. Dis., 99,* 91–99.

Mulhlberger, A., Wiedemann, G., Herrmann, M. J., & Pauli, P. (2006). Phylo- and ontogenetic fears and the expectation of danger: Differences between spider- and flight-phobic subjects in cognitive and physiological responses to disorder-specific stimuli. *J. Ab. Psych., 115*(3), 580–89.

Mundo, E., Zanoni, S., & Altamura, A. C. (2006). Genetic issues in obsessive-compulsive disorder and related disorders. *Psychiat. Ann., 36*(7), 495–512.

Munoz, R. F. (2001). How shall we ensure that the prevention of onset of mental disorders becomes a national priority? *Prevention & Treatment, 4,* np.

Munoz, R. F., Mrazek, P. J., & Haggerty, R. J. (1996). Institute of Medicine report on prevention of mental disorders: Summary and commentary. *Amer. Psychol., 51*(11), 1116–22.

Munsey, C. (2007). A long road back. *Monitor on Psychology, 38,* 34–36.

Murphy, C. C., Boyle, C., Schendel, D., Decoufle, P., & Yeargin-Allsopp, M. (1998). Epidemiology of mental retardation in children. *Ment. Retard. Dev. Dis. Res. Rev., 4,* 6–13.

Murphy, G. C., & Athanasou, J. A. (1999). The effect of unemployment on mental health. *J. Occup. Org. Psychol., 72,* 83–99.

Murphy, J. M. (1976). Psychiatric labeling in cross-cultural perspective. *Science, 191,* 1019–28.

Murphy, W. D. (1997). Exhibitionism: Psychopathology and theory. In D. R. Laws & W. O'Donohue (Eds.), *Sexual deviance: Theory, assessment, and treatment* (pp. 22–39). New York: Guilford.

Murray, G. K., Leeson, V., & McKenna, P. J. (2004). Spontaneous improvement in severe, chronic schizophrenia and its neurological correlates. *Brit. J. Psychiat., 184,* 357–58.

Murray, J. B. (2001). Ecstasy is a dangerous drug. *Psychol. Rep., 88*(3), 895–902.

Murray, L., & Cooper, P. (1997). Postpartum depression and child development. *Psychol. Med., 27,* 253–60.

Murray, L., Fiori-Cowley, A., Hooper, R., & Cooper, P. (1996). The impact of postnatal depression and associated adversity on early mother-infant interactions and later infant outcomes. *Child Develop., 67*(5), 2512–26.

Musante, G. J., Costanzo, P. R., & Friedman, K. E. (1998). The comorbidity of depression and eating dysregulation processes in a diet-seeking obese population: A matter of gender specificity. *Int. J. Eat. Dis., 23*(1), 65–75.

Mussell, M. P., Mitchell, J. E., Crosby, R. D., Fulkerson, J. A., Hoberman, H. M., & Romano, J. L. (2000). Commitment to treatment goals in prediction of group cognitive-behavioral therapy treatment outcome for women with bulimia nervosa. *J. Cons. Clin. Psychol., 68,* 432–37.

Musselman, D. L., Lawson, D., Gumnick, J. F., Manatunga, A., Penna, S., Goodkin, R. S., Nemeroff, C. B., & Miller, A. H. (2001). Paroxetine for the prevention of depression induced by high dose interferon-alpha. *N. Engl. J. Med., 344,* 961–66.

Myers, J. K., Weissman, M. M., Tischler, G. L., Holzer, C. E., Leaf, P. J., & Stoltzman, R. (1984). Six-month prevalence of psychiatric disorders in three communities: 1980 to 1982. *Arch. Gen. Psychiat., 41,* 959–67.

Myers, R. H., Schaefer, E. J., Wilson, P. W., D'Agostino, R., Ordovas, J. M., Espino, A., Au, R., White, R. F., Knoefel, J. E., Cobb, J. L., McNulty, K. A., Beiser, A., & Wolf, P. A. (1996). Apolipoprotein E (4 association with dementia in a population-based study: The Framingham study. *Neurol., 46,* 673–77.

Mystkowski, J. L., & Mineka, S. (2007). Behavior therapy for specific fears and phobias: Context specificity of fear extinction. In T. A. Treat, R. R. Bootzin, & T. B. Baker (Eds.), *Psychological Clinical Science: Papers in Honor of Richard McFall* (pp. 197–222). New York: Psychology Press.

Nabeyama, M., Nakagawa, A., Yoshiura, T., Nakao, T., Nakatani, E., Togao, O., Yoshizato, C., Yoshioka, K., Tomita, M., & Kanba, S. (2008). Functional MRI study of brain activation alterations in patients with obsessive-compulsive disorder after symptom improvement. *Psychiatry Research Neuroimaging, 163,* 236–47.

Naeem, F., Ayub, M., Masood, K., Gul, H., Khalid, M., Farrukh, A., et al. (2011). Prevalence and psychosocial risk factors of PTSD; 18 months after Kashmir earthquake in Pakistan. *J. Affect. Dis., 130,* 268–74.

Nagata, T., van Vliet, I., Yamada, H., Kataoka, K., Iketani, T., & Kiriike, N. (2006). An open trial of paroxetine for the 'offensive subtype' of taijin kyofusho and social anxiety disorder. *Depression and Anxiety, 23*(3), 168–74.

Nagayama Hall, G. C. (2001). Psychotherapy research with ethnic minorities: Empirical, ethical, and conceptual issues. *J. Cons. Clin. Psychol., 69*(3), 502–10.

Najman, J. M., Dunne, M. P., Purdie, D. M., Boyle, F. M., & Coxeter, P. D. (2005). Sexual abuse in childhood and sexual dysfunction in adulthood: An Australian population–based study. *Arch. Sex. Behav., 34*(5), 517–26.

Nakamura, K., Iwabuchi, M. & Sakai, S. (2005). Use of an electronic and information technologies by Japanese children with developmental disorders. In D. W. Schwalb, J., Nukazawa & B. J. Shwalb (Eds). *Applied Developmental Psychology: Theory, practice and research from Japan.* Greenwich, Ct.: Information Age Publishing.

Nakao, T., Nakagawa, A., Yoshiura, T., Nakatani, E., Nabeyama, M., Yoshizato, C., Kudoh, A., Tada, K., Yoshioka, K., Kawamoto, M., Togao, O., & Kanba, S. (2005). Brain activation of patients with obsessive-compulsive disorder during neuropsychological and symptom provocation tasks before and after symptom improvement: A functional magnetic resonance imaging study. *Biol. Psychiat., 57,* 901–10.

Naninck, E. F. G., Lucassen, P. J., & Bakker, J. (2011). Sex differences in adolescent depression: Do sex hormones determine vulnerability? *J. Neuroendocrin., 23*(5), 383–92. doi: 10.1111/j.1365-2826.2011.02125.x

Naqvi, N. H., Rudrauf, D., Damasio, H., & Bechara, A. (2007). Damage to the insula disrupts addiction to cigarette smoking. *Science, 315*(5811), 531–34.

Naragon-Gainey, K., & Watson, D. (2011). Clarifying the dispositional basis of social anxiety: A hierarchical perspective. *Pers. Indiv. Diff., 50*(7), 926–34. doi:10.1016/j.paid.2010.07.012

Narby, J. (1982). The evolution of attitudes towards mental illness in preindustrial England. *Orthomolecular Psychiatry, 11,* 103–10.

Narrow, W. E., Regier, D. A., Rae, D. S., Manderscheld, R. W., & Locke, B. Z. (1993). Use of services by persons with mental and addictive disorders: Findings from the National Institute of Mental Health Epidemiologic Catchment Area Program. *Arch. Gen. Psychiat., 50,* 95–107.

Nasar, S. (1998). *A beautiful mind.* New York: Simon and Schuster.

Nash, M. R., Hulsey, T. L., Sexton, M. C., Harralson, T. L., & Lambert, W. (1993). Long-term sequelae of childhood sexual abuse: Perceived family environment, psychopathology, and dissociation. *J. Cons. Clin. Psychol., 61*(2), 276–83.

Nathan, P. E., & Gorman, J. M. (2007). *A guide to treatments that work.* New York: Oxford University Press.

National Advisory Mental Health Council. (2007). *Preventing child and adolescent mental disorders: Research roundtable on economic burden and cost effectiveness.* Washington, DC: National Institutes of Mental Health. http://www.nimh.nih.gov/

National Committee to Prevent Child Abuse. (1996). *Study of the national incidence and prevalence of child abuse and neglect.* Washington, DC: Author.

National Institute on Alcohol Abuse and Alcoholism (NIAAA). (1997). *Monitoring the future.* National Institutes of Mental Health. Washington, DC: Author.

National Institutes of Health. (2001). *Al. Res. Hlth., 25,* 241–306.

National Institutes of Mental Health (2007). *NIMH perspective on diagnosing and treating bipolar disorder in children.* Washington, DC: National Institutes of Mental Health.

National Mental Health Association. (1997). *Working for America's mental health.* Alexandria, VA: Author.

Natsuaki, M. N., Cicchetti, D., & Rogosch, F. A. (2009). Examining the developmental history of child maltreatment, peer relations, and externalizing problems among adolescents with symptoms of paranoid personality disorder. *Develop. Psychopath., 21*(4), 1181–93. doi:10.1017/S0954579409990101

Natsuaki, M. N., Ge, X., Leve, L. D., Neiderhiser, J. M., Shaw, D. S., Conger, R. D., & Reiss, D. (2010). Genetic liability, environment, and the development of fussiness in toddlers: The roles of maternal depression and parental responsiveness. *Devel. Psychol., 46*(5), 1147–58. doi: 10.1037/a0019659

Nattala, P., Leung, K. S., & Nagarajaiah, M. P., (2010). Family member involvement in relapse prevention improves alcohol dependence outcomes: A prospective study at an addiction treatment facility in India. *J. Stud. Alcohol Drugs, 71*(4), 581–87.

Nayani, T. H., & David, A. S. (1996). The auditory hallucination: A phenomenological survey. *Psychol. Med., 26*(1), 177–89.

Neale, J. M., & Oltmanns, T. F. (1980). *Schizophrenia.* New York: Wiley.

Neighbors, C., Larimer, M. E., & Lewis, M. A. (2004). Targeting misperceptions of descriptive drinking norms: Efficacy of a computer-delivered personalized normative feedback intervention. *J. Cons. Clin. Psychol., 72,* 202–17.

Neisser, U. (1967). *Cognitive psychology.* New York: Appleton Century Crofts.

Neisser, U. (Ed.). (1982). *Memory observed: Remembering in natural contexts.* San Francisco: Freeman.

Nelson, C. A., & Bloom, F. E. (1997). Child development and neuroscience. *Child Develop., 68*(5), 970–87.

Nelson, G., Aubry, T., & Lawrence, A. (2007). A review of the literature on the effectiveness of housing and support, assertive community treatment, and intensive case management interventions for persons with mental illness who have been homeless. *Amer. J. Orthopsychiat., 77,* 350–61.

Nemeroff, C. B. (2003). Anxiolytics: Past, present, and future agents. *J. Clin. Psychiat., 64* (Suppl. 3), 3–6.

Nemeroff, C. B., & Shatzberg, A. F. (2007). Pharmacological treatments for unipolar depression. In P. E. Nathan and J. M. Gorman (Eds.), *A guide to treatments that work* (pp. 217–88). New York: Oxford University Press.

Neria, Y., Nandi, A., & Galea, S. (2008). Post-traumatic stress disorder following disasters: A systematic review. *Psychol. Med., 38,* 467–480.

Nesse, R. M. (2000). Is depression an adaptation? *Arch. Gen. Psychiat., 57*(1), 14–20.

Nestadt, G., Grados, M., & Samuels, J. F. (2010). Genetics of obsessive-compulsive disorder. *Psychiat. Clin. N. Amer., 33*(1), 141–58.

Nestoriuc, Y., Rief, W., & Martin, A. (2008). Meta-analysis of biofeedback for tension type headache: Efficacy, specificity, and treatment moderators. *J. Consult. Clin. Psychol., 76,* 379–396.

Neumeister, A., Bain, E., Nugent, A. C., Carson, R. E., Bonne, O., Luckenbaugh, D. A., et al. (2004). Reduce serotonin type 1-sub(A) receptor binding in panic disorder. *J. Neurosci., 24*(3), 589–91.

New York Times. (1994, May 9). Multiple personality cases perplex legal system, p. A1.

Newman, J. P., & Lorenz, A. R. (2003). Response modulation and emotion processing: Implications for psychopathy and other dysregulatory psychopathology. In R. J. Davidson, K. R. Scherer, & H. H. Goldsmith (Eds.), *Handbook of affective sciences* (pp. 904–29). New York: Oxford Press.

Newsom, J. T., Mahan, T. L., Rook, K. S., & Krause, N. (2008). Stable negative social exchanges and health. *Health Psychology, 27,* 78–86.

Newton, L., Rosen, A., Tennant, C., Hobbs, C., Lapsley, H. M., & Tribe, K. (2000). Deinstitutionalisation for long-term mental illness: An ethnographic study. *Austral. NZ J. Psychiat., 34,* 484–90.

Neziroglu, F., Roberts, M., & Yaryura-Tobias, J. (2004). A behavioural model for body dysmorphic disorder. *Psychiat. Ann., 34*(12), 915–20.

Ng, B.-Y., & Chan Y.-H. (2004). Psychosocial stressors that precipitate dissociative trance disorder in Singapore. *Austral. N. Z. J. Psychol., 38*(6), 426–32.

Ng, D. M., & Jeffery, R. W. (2003). Relationships between perceived stress and health behaviors in a sample of working adults. *Hlth. Psychol., 22*(6), 638–42.

Ni, X., Chan, K., Bulgin, N., Sicad, T., Bismil, R., McMain, S. et al. (2006) Association between serotonin transporter gene and borderline personality disorder. *J. Psychiat. Res., 40,* 448–53.

Nicolson, R., & Szatmari, P. (2003). Genetic and neurodevelopmental influences in autistic disorder. *Canad. J. Psychiat., 48*(8), 526–37.

NIDA Survey. (2003). *Trends in drug related episodes. NIDA Research Report: Monitoring the Future Study.* Washington, DC: Author.

Nierenberg, A. A., Akiskal, H. S., Angst, J., Hirschfeld, R. M., Merikangas, K. R., Petukhova, M., & Kessler, R. C. (2010). Bipolar disorder with frequent mood episodes in the national comorbidity survey replication (NCS-R). *Molec. Psychiat, 15*(11), 1075–87. doi: 10.1038/mp.2009.61

Nigg, J. T. (2001). Is ADHD a disinhibitory disorder? *Psychol. Bull., 127*(5), 571–98.

Nigg, J. T., Stavro, G., Ettenhofer, M., Hambrick, D. Z., Miller, T., & Henderson, J. M. (2005). Executive functions and ADHD in adults: Evidence for selective effects on ADHD symptom domains. *J. Abn. Psych., 114*(4). 706–17.

NIMH. (2001). *Facts about the National Institute of Mental Health.* Washington, DC: U.S. Government Printing Office, 00-47-43.

NIMH. (2007). *Facts about the National Institute of Mental Health.* Washington, DC. www.nimh.nih.gov/health/publications/index.shtml.

Nisbett, R. E., & Wilson, T. D. (1977). Telling more than we can know: Verbal reports on mental processes. *Psychol. Rev., 84,* 231–59.

Nissen, M. J., Ross, J. L., Willingham, D. B., MacKenzie, T. B., & Schacter, D. L. (1988). Memory and awareness in a patient with multiple personality disorder. *Brain and Cognition, 8,* 117–34.

Nixon, R. D., & Bryant, R. A. (2005). Are negative cognitions associated with severe acute trauma responses? *Behav. Chng., 22*(1), 22–28.

Nobakht, M., & Dezhkam, M. (2000). An epidemiological study of eating disorders in Iran. *Int. J. Eat. Dis., 28,* 265–71.

Noble, E. P. (Ed.). (1979). *Alcohol and health: Technical support document.* Third special report to the U.S. Congress (DHEW Publication No. ADM79–832). Washington, DC: U.S. Government Printing Office.

Nock, M. K., Borges, G., Bromet, E. J., Alonso, J., Angermeyer, M., Beautrais, A., et al. (2008). Cross-national prevalence and risk factors for suicidal ideation, plans and attempts. *Brit. J. Psychiat., 192*(2), 98–105.

Nock, M. K., Hwang, I., Sampson, N., Kessler, R. C., Angermeyer, M., Beautrais, A., et al. (2009). Cross-national analysis of the associations among mental disorders and suicidal behavior: findings from the WHO World Mental Health Surveys. *PLoS Med, 6*(8), e1000123.

Nock, M. K., Hwang, I., Sampson, N. A., & Kessler, R. C. (2010). Mental disorders, comorbidity and suicidal behavior: Results from the National Comorbidity Survey replication. *Molec. Psychiat., 15*(8), 868–76. doi: 10.1038/mp.2009.29

Nock, M. K., Kazdin, A. E., Hiripi, E., & Kessler, R. C. (2007). Lifetime prevalence, correlates, and persistence of oppositional defiant disorder: Results from the National Comorbidity Survey Replication. *J. Child Psych. Psychiat., 48*(7), 703–13.

Nolan, E. E., & Gadow, K. D. (1997). Children with ADHD and tic disorder and their classmates: Behavioral normalization with methylphenidate. *J. Amer. Acad. Child Adoles. Psychiat., 36*(5), 597–604.

Nolen-Hoeksema, S. (1991). Responses to depression and their effects on the duration of depressive episodes. *J. Abn. Psych., 100*(4), 569–82.

Nolen-Hoeksema, S. (2000). The role of rumination in depressive disorders and mixed anxiety/depressive symptoms. *J. Abn. Psych., 109*(3), 504–11.

Nolen-Hoeksema, S. (2002). Gender differences in depression. In I. H. Gotlib & C. L. Hammen (Eds.), *Handbook of depression* (pp. 492–509). New York: Guilford.

Nolen-Hoeksema, S., & Aldao, A. (2011). Gender and age differences in emotion regulation strategies and their relationship to depressive symptoms. *Pers. Indiv. Diff., 51*(6), 704–8. doi: 10.1016/j.paid.2011.06.012

Nolen-Hoeksema, S, & Corte, C. (2004). Gender and self-regulation. In R. F. Baumeister & K. D. Vohs (Eds.), *Handbook of self-regulation: Research, theory, and applications.* (pp. 411–21). New York: Guilford Press.

Nolen-Hoeksema, S., & Hilt, L. (2009). Gender differences in depression. In I. H. Gotlib & C. L. Hammen (Eds.), *Handbook of depression and its treatment* (2 ed.). New York: Guilford Press.

Nolen-Hoeksema, S., Larson, J., & Grayson, C. (1999). Explaining the gender difference in depressive symptoms. *J. Person. Soc. Psychol., 77*(5), 1061–72.

Nolen-Hoeksema, S., Wisco, B. E; Lyubomirsky, S.. Rethinking rumination. (2008). *Perspectives on Psychological Science. 3*, 400–24.

Nopoulos, P., Flaum, M., & Andreasen, N. C. (1997). Sex differences in brain morphology in schizophrenia. *Amer. J. Psychiat., 154*(12), 1648–54.

Norberg, M. M., Krystal, J. H., & Tolin, D. F. (2008). A meta-analysis of D-cycloserine and the facilitation of fear extinction and exposure therapy. *Biol. Psychiat., 63*(12), 1118–26. doi: 10.1016/j.biopsych.2008.01.012

Nordstrom, B. R. and Levin, F. R. (2007). Treatment of cannabis use disorders: A review of the literature. *American Journal on Addictions, 16*, 331–42.

Norko, M., & Baranoski, M. V. (2005). The state of contemporary risk assessment research. *Canad. J. Psychiat., 50*(1), 18–26.

Norrholm, S. D., & Ressler, K. J. (2009). Genetics of anxiety and trauma-related disorders. *Neuroscience, 164*(1), 272–87. doi: 10.1016/j.neuroscience.2009.06.036

Norris, D. M., Gutheil, T. G., & Strasburger, L. H. (2003). This couldn't happen to me: Boundary problems and sexual misconduct in the psychotherapy relationship. *Psychiatr. Serv., 54*, 517–22.

Novak, N. L., & Brownell, K. D. (2011). Taxation as prevention and as a treatment for obesity: the case of sugar-sweetened beverages. *Curr. Pharm. Des., 17*, 1218–22.

Nuechterlein, K. H. (1977). Reaction time and attention in schizophrenia: A critical evaluation of the data and theories. *Schizo. Bull., 3*, 373–428.

Nuechterlein, K. H., Green, M. F., Kern, R. S., Baade, L. E., Barch, D. M., Cohen, J. D., et al., (2008). The MATRICS consensus cognitive battery, Part 1: Test selection, reliability, and validity. *Am. J. Psychiat., 165*, 203–13.

Nuechterlein, K. H., Snyder, K. S., & Mintz, J. M. (1992). Paths to relapse: Possible transactional processes connecting patient illness onset, expressed emotion, and psychotic relapse. *Brit. J. Psychiat., 161*(suppl. 18), 88–96.

Nukazawa & B. J. Shwalb (Eds). *Applied developmental psychology: Theory, practice and research from Japan.* Greenwich, Ct.: Information Age Publishing.

Nusslock, R., Shackman, A. J., Harmon-Jones, E., Alloy, L. B., Coan, J. A., & Abramson, L. Y. (2011). Cognitive vulnerability and frontal brain asymmetry: Common predictors of first prospective depressive episode. *J. Abn. Psychol., 120*(2), 497–503. doi: 10.1037/a0022940

Nutt, D., Argyropoulos, S., Hood, S., & Potokar, J. (2006). Generalized anxiety disorder: A comorbid disease. *European Neuropsychopharmacology, 16*(2), 109–118.

O'Brien, K. M., & Vincent, N. K. (2003). Psychiatric comorbidity in anorexia and bulimia nervosa: Nature, prevalence, and causal relationships. *Clin. Psychol. Rev., 23*, 57–74.

O'Conner, T. G., Marvin, R. S., Rutter, M., Olrick, J. T., & Britner, P. A. (2003). Child-parent attachment following early institutional deprivation. *Develop. Psychopath., 15*, 19–38.

O'Connor, B. P., McGuire, S., Reiss, D., Hetherington, E. M., & Plomin, R. (1998). Co-occurrence of depressive symptoms and antisocial behavior in adolescence: A common genetic liability. *J. Abn. Psychol., 107*(1), 27–37.

O'Connor, E. M. (2001, Dec.). Medicating ADHD: Too much? Too soon? *Monitor on Psychology*, 50–51.

O'Connor, M. J. (2001). Prenatal alcohol exposure and infant negative affect as precursors of depressive features in children.*Infant Mental Health Journal, 22*(3), 291–99.

Odell, J. D., Warren, R. P., Warren, W., Burger, R. A., & Maciulis, A. (1997). Association of genes within the major histocompatibility complex with attention-deficit hyperactivity disorder. *Neuropsychobiology, 35*(4), 181–86.

O'Donnell, C. R. (Ed.). (2004). *Culture, peers and delinquency.* Binghamton, NY: Haworth Press.

O'Donnell, I., & Farmer, R. (1995). The limitations of official suicide statistics. *Brit. J. Psychiat., 166*, 458–61.

O'Donnell, R., Rome, D., Godin, M., & Fulton, P. (2000). Changes in inpatient utilization and quality of care performance measures in a capitated HMO population, 1989–1999. *Psychiat. Clin. N. Amer., 23*(2), 319–33.

O'Donoghue, E. G. (1914). *The story of Bethlehem Hospital from its foundation in 1247.* London: Adelphi Terrace.

O'Donohue, W., Fowler, K. A., & Lilienfeld, S. O. (Eds.). (2007). *Personality disorders: Toward the DSM-V.* Thousand Oaks, CA: Sage.

O'Donovan, M. C., Craddock, N., Norton, N., Williams, H., Peirce, T., Moskvina, V. Nikolov, I. et al., (2008). Identification of loci associated with schizophrenia by genome wide association and follow-up. *Nature Genetics.*

Oetting, E. R., Deffenbacher, J. L., Taylor, M. J., Luther, N., Beauvais, F., & Edwards, R. W. (2000). Methamphetamine use by high school students: Recent trends, gender and ethnicity differences, and use of other drugs. *J. Child Adol. Subst. Abuse, 10*(1), 33–50.

Oehlberg, K. A., & Mineka, S. (2011). Fear conditioning and attention to threat: An integrative approach to understanding the etiology of anxiety disorders. In T. R. Schachtman & S. Reilly (Eds.), *Associative learning and conditioning theory: Human and non-human applications* (pp. 44–78). New York: Oxford University Press.

O'Farrell, T. J., Murphy, C. M., Stephan, S. H., Fals-Stewart, W., & Murphy, M. (2004). Partner violence before and after couples-based alcoholism treatment for male alcoholic patients: The role of treatment involvement and abstinence. *J. Cons. Clin. Psychol., 72*, 202–17.

Office of Technology Assessment. (1993). *Biological components of substance abuse and addiction.* Washington, DC: United States Congress, Office of Technology Assessment.

O'Hara, M., & Gorman, L. L. (2004). Can postpartum depression be predicted. *Prim. Psychiat., 11*(3), 42–47.

O'Hara, M., Schlecte, J., Lewis, D., & Varner, M. (1991). Controlled prospective study of postpartum mood disorders: Psychological, environmental, and hormonal variables. *J. Abn. Psychol., 100*, 63–73.

O'Hara, M. W., & Swain, A. M. (1996). Rates and risk of postpartum depression-A meta-analysis. *Intern. Rev. Psychiat., 8*(1), 37–54.

O'Hara, M., Zekoski, E., Philipps, L., & Wright, E. (1990). Controlled prospective study of postpartum mood disorders: Comparison of childbearing and non-childbearing women. *J. Abn. Psychol., 99*, 3–15.

Ohayon, M. M., & Shatzberg, A. F. (2002). Prevalence of depressive episodes with psychotic features in the general population. *Amer. J. Psychiat., 159*(11), 1855–61.

Öhman, A. (1996). Perferential preattentive processing of threat in anxiety: Preparedness and attentional biases. In R. M. Rapee (Ed.), *Current controversies in the anxiety disorders* (pp. 253–90). New York: Guilford.

Öhman, A. (2009). Of snakes and faces: An evolutionary perspective on the psychology of fear. *Scand. J. Psychol., 50*(6), 543–52. doi: 10.1111/j.1467-9450.2009.00784.x

Öhman, A., & Mineka, S. (2001). Fears, phobias, and preparedness: Toward an evolved module of fear and fear learning. *Psychol. Rev., 108*, 483–522.

Öhman, A., & Soares, J. (1993). On the automatic nature of phobic fear: Conditioned electrodermal responses to masked fear-relevant stimuli. *J. Abn. Psychol., 102*, 121–32.

Öhman, A., Carlsson, K., Lundqvist, D., & Ingvar, M. (2007). On the unconscious subcortical origin of human fear. *Physiology & Behavior, 92*(1), 180–185.

Öhman, A., Dimberg, U., & Öst, L. G. (1985). Animal and social phobias: Biological constraints on learned fear responses. In S. Reiss & R. Bootzin (Eds.), *Theoretical issues in behavior therapy* (pp. 123–75). New York: Academic Press.

Öhman, A., Lundqvist, D., & Esteves, F. (2001). The face in the crowd revisited: A threat advantage with schematic stimuli. *J. Pers. Soc. Psychol., 80*, 381–96.

Okasha, A., & Okasha, T. (2000). Notes on mental disorders in Pharaonic Egypt. *History of Psychiatry, 11*, 413–24.

Okuda, M., Balán, I., Petry, N. M., Oquendo, M., & Blanco, C. (2009). Cognitive-behavioral therapy for pathological gambling: Cultural considerations. *Amer. J. Psychiat., 166*(12), 1325–30.

O'Leary, D. S., Block, R. I., Turner, B. M., Koeppel, J., Magnotta, V. A., Ponto, B., Watkins, G. L., Hichwa, R. D., & Andreasen, N. C. (2003). Marijuana alters the human cerebellar clock. *NeuroReport: For Rapid Communication of Neuroscience Research, 14*(8), 1145–51.

Oldehinkel, A. J., Veenstra, R., Ormel, J., de Winter, A. F., & Verhulst, F. C. (2007). Temperament, parenting, and depressive symptoms in a population sample of preadolescents. *J. Child Psychol. Psychiat., 47*(7), 684–95.

Oldham, J. M. (2006). Borderline personality disorder and suicidality. *Am. J. Psychiat., 163*(1), 20–26.

Olds, D. L. (1986). Case studies of factors interfering with nurse home visitors' promotion of positive care-giving methods in high risk families. In A. S. Honig (Ed.), *Risk factors in infancy.* (pp. 149–165). Amsterdam, Netherlands: Gordon and Breach Publishers.

Olds, D. L., Henderson, C., & Tatelbaum, R. (1994). Prevention of intelletual impairment in children of women who smoke cigarettes during pregnancy. *Pediatrics, 93*, 228–33.

Olds, D. L., Henderson, C., Tatelbaum, R., & Chamberlin, R. (1986). Improving the delivery of prenatal care and outcomes of pregnancy: A randomized trial of nurse home visitation. *Pediatrics, 77*, 16–28.

Olfson, M., & Marcus, S. C. (2010). National trends in outpatient psychotherapy. *Am. J. Psychiat., 167*, 1456–63.

Olfson, M., & Marcus, S.C. (2009). National patterns in antidepressant medication treatment. *Arch. Gen. Psychiat., 66*, 848–856.

Olfson, M., Marcus, S. C., & Shaffer, D. (2006). Antidepressant drug therapy and suicide in severely depressed children and adults. *Arch. Gen. Psychiat., 63*(8), 865–72.

Olino, T. M., Klein, D. N., Dyson, M.W., Rose, S. A., & Durbin, C. E. (2010). Temperamental emotionality in preschool-aged children and depressive disorders in parents: Associations in a large community sample. *J. Abn. Psychol., 119*(3), 468–78.

Ollendick, T. H., Öst, L.-G., Reuterskiöld, L., Costa, N., Cederlund, R., Sirbu, C., et al. (2009). One-session treatment of specific phobias in youth: A randomized clinical trial in the United States and Sweden. *J. Cons. Clin. Psychol., 77*(3), 504–16. doi: 10.1037/a0015158

Ollendick, T. H., Yang, B., King, N. J., Dong, Q., et al. (1996). Fears in American, Australian, Chinese, and Nigerian children and adolescents: A crosscultural study. *Journal of Child Psychology & Psychiatry & Allied Sciences, 37*(2), 213–20.

Olney, J. W., & Farber, N. B. (1995). Glutamate receptor dysfunction and schizophrenia. *Arch. Gen. Psychiat., 52*, 998–1007.

Olson, K. R. (2001). Computerized psychological test usage in APA accredited training programs. *J. Clin. Psychol., 57*, 727–36.

Oltmanns, T. F., & Okada, M. (2006). Paranoia. In J. E. Fisher, & W. T. O'Donohue (Eds.), *Practitioner's Guide to Evidence-based Psychotherapy* (pp. 503–13). New York: Spinger Science and Business Media.

O'Mahony, J. F., & Ward, B. G. (2003). Differences between those who panic by day and those who also panic by night. *J. Behav. Ther. Exper. Psychiat., 34*, 239–49.

O'Mahony, R., Murthy, L., Akunne, A., & Young, J. (2011). Synopsis of the National Institute for Health and Clinical Excellence guideline for the prevention of dementia. *Ann. Intern. Med., 154*, 746–51.

O'Malley, S. S., Jaffe, A. J., Rode, S., & Rounsaville, B. (1996). Experience of a "slip" among alcoholics treated with naltrexone or placebo. *Amer. J. Psychiat., 153*(2), 281–83.

Ondersma, S. J., Chaffin, M., Berliner, L., Cordon, I., & Goodman, G. S. (2001). Sex with children is abuse: Comment on Rind, Tromovitch, and Bauserman (1998). *Psychol. Bull., 127*, 707–14.

O'Neil, K. A., Podell, J. L., Benjamin, C. L., & Kendall, Philip C. (2010). Comorbid depressive disorders in anxiety-disordered youth: Demographic, clinical, and family characteristics. *Child Psychiat. Human Devel., 41*(3), 330–41.

Onishi, N. (2002, Oct. 3). Globalization of beauty makes slimness trendy. *New York Times*, p. A4.

Oquendo, M. A., Galfalvy, H., Russo, S., Ellis, S. P., Grunebaum, M. F., Burke, A., et al. (2004). Prospective study of clinical predictors of suicidal acts after a major depressive episode in patients with major depressive disorder or bipolar disorder. *Amer. J. Psychiat., 161*(8), 1433–41.

Oren, D. A., & Rosenthal, N. E. (1992). Seasonal affective disorders. In E. S. Paykel (Ed.), *Handbook of affective disorders* (2nd ed., pp. 551–67). New York: Guilford.

Orne, M. T., Dinges, D. F., & Orne, E. C. (1984). On the differential diagnosis of multiple personality in the forensic context. *Int. J. Clin. Exp. Hypn., 32*, 118–69.

Orstavik, R. E., Kendler, K. S., Czajkowski, N., Tambs, K., & Reichborn-Kjennerud, T. (2007). The relationship between depressive personality disorder and major depressive disorder: A population-based twin study. *Amer. J. Psychiat., 164*, 1866–72.

Öst, L. G. (1987). Age of onset of different phobias. *J. Abn. Psychol., 96*, 223–29.

Öst, L.-G. (1997). Rapid treatment of specific phobias. In G. C. L. Davey (Ed.), *Phobias. A handbook of theory,*

research and treatment (2nd ed., pp. 227–46). Chichester, England: Wiley.

Öst, L.-G., Alm, T., Brandberg, M., & Breitholtz, E. (2001). One vs. five sessions of exposure and five sessions of cognitive therapy in the treatment of claustrophobia.

Öst, L.-G., & Hellström, K. (1997). Blood-injury-injection phobia. In G. C. L. Davey (Ed.), *Phobias. A handbook of theory, research and treatment.* (pp. 63–80). Chichester, England: Wiley.

Öst, L. G., & Hugdahl, K. (1981). Acquisition of phobias and anxiety response patterns in clinical patients. *Behav. Res. Ther., 19*, 439–47.

Öst, L. G., & Hugdahl, K. (1985). Acquisition of blood and dental phobia and anxiety response patterns in clinical patients. *Behav. Res. Ther., 23*(1), 27–34.

O'Sullivan, S. S., Mullins, G. M., Cassidy, E. M., & McNamara, B. (2006). The role of the standard EEG in clinical psychiatry. *Human Psychopharmacology: Clinical and Experimental, 21*(4), 265–71.

Otto, M. W., Teachman, B. A., Cohen, L. S., Soares, C. N., Vitonis, A. F., & Harlow, B. L. (2007). Dysfunctional attitudes and episodes of major depression: Predictive validity and temporal stability in neverdepressed, depressed, and recovered women. *J. Abn. Psych., 116*(3), 475–83.

Otto, M. W., Tolin, D. F., Simon, N. M., Pearlson, G. D., Basden, S., Meunier, S. A., et al. (2010). Efficacy of D-cycloserine for enhancing response to cognitive-behavior therapy for panic disorder. *Biol. Psychiat., 67*(4), 365–70. doi: 10.1016/j.biopsych.2009.07.036

Otway, L. J., & Vignoles, V. L. (2006). Narcissism and childhood recollections: A quantitative test of psychoanalytic predictions. *Pers. Social Psychol. Bull., 32*, 104–16.

Ouimet, A. J., Gawronski, B., & Dozois, D. J. A. (2009). Cognitive vulnerability to anxiety: A review and an integrative model. *Clin. Psychol. Rev., 29*(6), 459–70. doi: 10.1016/j.cpr.2009.05.004

Overall, J. E., & Hollister, L. E. (1982). Decision rules for phenomenological classification of psychiatric patients. *J. Cons. Clin. Psychol., 50*(4), 535–45.

Overbeek, T., van Diest, R., Schruers, K., Kruizinga, F., & Griez, E. (2005). Sleep complaints in panic disorder patients. *J. Nerv. Ment. Dis., 193*(7), 488–93.

Overmier, J. B., & Seligman, M. E. P. (1967). Effects of inescapable shock upon subsequent escape and avoidance learning. *Journal of Comparative and Physiological Psychology, 63*, 23–33.

Owen, C., Rutherford, M. J., Jones, M., Tennant, C., & Smallman, A. (1997). Noncompliance in psychiatric aftercare. *Comm. Ment. Hlth. J., 33*, 25–34.

Owen, F., & Simpson, M. D. C. (1995). The neurochemistry of schizophrenia. In S. R. Hirsch & D. R. Weinberger (Eds.), *Schizophrenia* (pp. 253–74). Cambridge: Cambridge University Press.

Owens, K., Asmundson, G., Hadjistavropoulos, T., & Owens, T. J. (2004). Attentional bias toward illness threat in individuals with elevated health anxiety. *Cog. Ther. Res., 28*(1), 57–66.

Ownby, R. L., Crocco, E., Acevedo, A., John, V., & Loewenstein, D. (2006). Depression and risk for Alzheimer disease. *Arch. Gen. Psychiat., 63*, 530–38.

Pabian, Y. L., Welfel, E., & Beebe, R. S. (2009). Psychologists' knowledge of their states' laws pertaining to Tarasoff-type situations. *Prof. Psychol. Res. Pract., 40*, 8–14.

Pachter, H. M. (1951). *Magic into science: The story of Paracelsus.* New York: Schumen.

Padela, A. I., & Heisler, M. (2010). The association of perceived abuse and discrimination after September 11, 2001, with psychological distress,

level of happiness, and health status among Arab Americans. *Amer. J. Pub. Hlth., 100*(2), 284–91. doi:10.2105/ajph.2009.164954

Padgett, D. K., Hawkins, R. L., Abrams, C., & Davis, A. (2006). In their own words: Trauma and substance abuse in the lives of formerly homeless women with serious mental illness. *Am. J. Orthopsychiat., 76*, 461–67.

Padma-Nathan, H., McMurray, J. G., Pullman, W. E., Whitaker, J. S., Saoud, J. B., Ferguson, K. M., et al. (2001). On-demand IC351 (Cialis) enhances erectile function in patients with erectile dysfunction. *International Journal of Impotence Research, 13*, 2–9.

Page, A. C., & Tan, B. J. (2009). Disgust and blood-injury-injection phobia. In B. O. Olatunji & D. McKay (Eds.), *Disgust and its disorders: Theory, assessment, and treatment implications* (pp. 191–209). Washington, DC: American Psychological Association.

Page, W. F., Engdahl, B. E., & Eberly, R. E. (1997). Persistence of PTSD in former prisoners of war. In C. S. Fullerton & R. J. Ursano (Eds.), *Posttraumatic stress disorder* (pp. 147–58). Washington, DC: American Psychiatric Press.

Pagura, J., Cox, B. J., & Enns, M. W. (2009). Personality factors in the anxiety disorders. In M. M. Antony & M. B. Stein (Eds.), *Oxford handbook of anxiety and related disorders* (pp. 190–208). New York: Oxford University Press.

Pagura, J., Stein, M. B., Bolton, J. M., Cox, B. J., Grant, B., & Sareen, J. (2010). Comorbidity of borderline personality disorder and posttraumatic stress disorder in the U.S. population. *J. Psychiat. Res., 44*, 1190–98.

Pail, G., Huf, W., Pjrek, E., Winkler, D., Willeit, M., Praschak-Rieder, N., & Kasper, S. (2011). Bright-light therapy in the treatment of mood disorders. *Neuropsychobiol., 64*(3), 152–62. doi: 10.1159/000328950

Palace, E. M., & Gorzalka, B. B. (1990). The enhancing effects of anxiety on arousal in sexually dysfunctional and functional women. *J. Abn. Psychol., 99*, 403–11.

Palermo, M. T. (2004). Pervasive developmental disorders, psychiatric comorbidities, and the law. *Int. J. Off. Ther. Comp. Crim., 48*(1), 40–48.

Pallanti, S. (2008). Transcultural observations of obsessive-compulsive disorder. *Amer. J. Psychiat., 165*(2), 169–70. doi: 10.1176/appi.ajp.2007.07111815

Palmstierno, T. (2001). A model for predicting alcohol withdrawal delirium. *Psychiatr. Serv., 52*(6), 820–23.

Palosaari, U., & Laippala, P. (1996). Parental divorce and depression in young adulthood: Adolescents' closeness to parents and self-esteem as mediating factor. *Acta Psychiat. Scandin., 93*(1), 20–36.

Pandya, M., Pozuelo, L., & Malone, D. (2007). Electroconvulsive therapy: What the internist needs to know. *Cleveland Clinic Journal of Medicine, 74*, 679–85.

Pankratz, L. (2006). Persistent problems with the Munchausen Syndrome by Proxy label. *J. Amer. Acad. Psychiat. Law, 34*, 90–95.

Panuzio, J., & DiLillo, D. (2010). Physical, psychological, and sexual intimate partner aggression among newlywed couples: Longitudinal prediction of marital satisfaction. *Journal of Family Violence, 25*(7), 689–99.

Paolucci, E. O., Genuis, M. L., & Violato, C. (2001). A meta-analysis of the published research on the effects of child sexual abuse. *J. Psychol., 135*(1), 17–36.

Papadimitriou, G. N., & Linkowski, P. (2005). Sleep disturbance in anxiety disorders. *Int. Rev. Psychiat.*, 17(4), 229–36.

Papakostas, G. I., Thase, M. E., Fava, M., Nelson, J. C., & Shelton, R. C. (2007). Are antidepressant drugs that combine serotonergic and noradrenergic mechanisms of action more effective than the selective serotonin reuptake inhibitors in treating major depressive disorder? A meta-analysis of studies of newer agents. *Biol. Psychiat.*, 62, 1217–27.

Papanicolaou, D. A., Wilder, R. I., Manolagas, S. C., & Chrousos, G. P. (1998). The pathophysiologic roles of interleukin-6 in human disease. *Ann. Int. Med.*, 128, 127–37.

Papp, L., & Gorman, J. M. (1990). Suicidal preoccupation during fluoxetine treatment. *Amer. J. Psychiat.*, 147, 1380.

Parakh, P. (2010, Jan. 16). Adverse health effects of nonmedical cannabis use. *Lancet*, 375(9710), 196–97.

Parent B. A., & Parent T. C. (2008). Anorexia, Maudsley and an impressive recovery: One family's story. *Journal of Paediatrics and Child Health*, 44, 70–73.

Paris, J. (1999). Borderline personality disorder. In T. Millon, P. H. Blaney, & R. D. Davis (Eds.), *Oxford textbook of psychopathology* (pp. 628–52). New York: Oxford University Press.

Paris, J. (2001). Psychosocial adversity. In W. J. Livesley (Ed.), *Handbook of personality disorders* (pp. 231–41). New York: Guilford.

Paris, J. (2005). Neurobiological dimensional models of personality: A review of the models of Cloninger, Depue, and Siever. *J. Pers. Dis.*, 19, 156–70.

Paris, J. (2005). Understanding self-mutilation in borderline personality disorder. *Harv. Rev. Psychiat.*, 13(3), 179–185.

Paris, J. (2007). The nature of borderline personality disorder: Multiple dimensions, multiple symptoms, but one category. *J. Pers. Dis.*, 21(5), 457–73.

Paris, J. (2009). The treatment of borderline personality disorder: Implications of research on diagnosis, etiology, and outcome. *Annu. Rev. Clin. Psychol.*, 5, 277–90. doi:10.1146/annurev.clinpsy.032408.153457

Paris, J. (2010). Estimating the prevalence of personality disorders in the community. *J. Pers. Disord.*, 24(4), 405–11. doi:10.1521/pedi.2010.24.4.405

Park, S., Holzman, P. S., & Goldman-Rakic, P. S. (1995). Spatial working memory deficits in the relatives of schizophrenic patients. *Arch. Gen. Psychiat.*, 52, 821–28.

Parke, R. D. (2004). Development in the family. *Annu. Rev. Psychol.*, 55, 365–99.

Parker, G. F. (2004). Outcomes of assertive community treatment in an NGRI conditional release program. *J. Amer. Acad. Psychiat. Law*, 32(3), 291–303.

Parker, G., Gladstone, G., & Chee, K. T. (2001). Depression in the planet's largest ethnic group: The Chinese. *Amer. J. Psychiat.*, 158(6), 857–64.

Parker, I. (2004, Aug. 2). The gift. *The New Yorker*, p. 54–63.

Parker, J. G., Rubin, K. H., Price, J. M., & DeRossier, M. E. (1995). Peer relationships, child development, and adjustment: A developmental psychopathology perspective. In D. Cicchetti & D. J. Cohen (Eds.), *Developmental psychopathology: Vol. 2. Risk, disorder, and adaptation* (pp. 96–161). New York: Wiley.

Parker, K. J., Buckmaster, C. L., Schatzberg, A. F., & Lyons, D. M. (2004). Prospective investigation of stress inoculation in young monkeys. *Arch. Gen. Psychiat.*, 61(9), 933–41.

Parra, C., Esteves, F., Flykt, A., & Öhman, A. (1997). Pavlonian conditioning to social stimuli: Backward masking and the dissociation of implicit and explicit cognitive processes. *Europ. Psychol.*, 2(2), 106–17.

Parrish, K. M., Higuchi, S., & Dufour, M. C. (1991). Alcohol consumption and the risk of developing liver cirrhosis: Implications for future research. *J. Subst. Abuse*, 3(3), 325–35.

Parrott, A. C. (2001). *Human psychopharmacology of Ecstasy (MDMA): A review of 15 years of empirical research. Human Psychopharmacology Clinical & Experimental*, 16(8), 557–77.

Parrott, A. C., & Stuart, M. (1997). Ecstasy (MDMA), amphetamine, and LSD: Comparative mood profiles in recreational polydrug users. *Human Psychopharmacology*, 12(5), 501–4.

Parrott, A. C., Lees, A., Garnham, N. J., Jones, M., & Wesnes, K. (1998). Cognitive performance in recreational users of MDMA or "ecstasy": Evidence for memory deficits. *J. Psychopharml.*, 12(1), 79–83.

Parsons, T. D., & Rizzo, A. A. (2008). Affective outcomes of virtual reality exposure therapy for anxiety and specific phobias: A meta-analysis. *J. Behav. Ther. Exper. Psychiat.*, 39(3), 250–61. doi: 10.1016/j.jbtep.2007.07.007

Pary, R. J. (2004). Behavioral and psychiatric disorders in children and adolescents with Down Syndrome. *Ment. Hlth. Asp. Dev. Dis.*, 7, 69–76.

Patel, S., & Gadit, M. (2008). Karo-Kari: A form of honor killing in Pakistan. *Transcult. Psychiat.*, 45, 683–94.

Patel, V., & Kim, Y-R. (2007). Contribution of low- and middle-income countries to research published in leading general psychiatry journals, 2002-2004. *Brit. J. Psychiat.*, 190, 77–8.

Patel, V., & Sumathipala, A. (2001). International representation in psychiatric literature: Survey of six leading journals. *Brit. J. Psychiat.*, 178, 406–9.

Patrick, C. J. (1994). Emotion and psychopathy: Startling new insights. *Psychophysiology*, 31(4), 319–30.

Patrick, C. J. (2005) Getting to the heart of psychopathy. In H. Herve & J. C. Yuille (Eds.), *Psychopathy: Theory, research, and social implications*. Hillsdale, NJ: Erlbaum

Patrick, C. J. (2006). Back to the future: Cleckley as a guide to the next generation of psychopathy research. In C. J. Patrick (Ed.), *Handbook of the psychopathy.* (pp. 605–17). New York: Guilford Press.

Patrick, C. J., Bradley, M. M., & Lang, P. J. (1993). Emotion in the criminal psychopath: Startle reflex modulation. *J. Abn. Psychol.*, 102(1), 82–92.

Patrick, C. J., Cuthbert, B. N., & Lang, P. J. (1994). Emotion in the criminal psychopath: Fear image processing. *J. Abn. Psychol.*, 103, 523–34.

Patterson, D., & Lott, I. (2008). Etiology, diagnosis, and development in Down syndrome. In J. E. Roberts, R. S. Chapman, & S. F. Warren, F. Steven (Eds.), *Speech and language development and intervention in Down syndrome and fragile X syndrome, Communication and language intervention series* (pp. 3–25). Baltimore, MD: Paul H Brookes Publishing.

Patterson, G. R., & Yoerger, K. (2002). A developmental model for early- and late-onset delinquency. In J. B. Reid, G. R. Patterson, et al. (Eds.), *Antisocial behavior in children and adolescents: A developmental analysis and model for intervention* (pp. 147–72). Washington, DC: American Psychological Association.

Patterson, G. R., Capaldi, D., & Bank, L. (1991). An early starter model for predicting delinquency. In D. Pepler & K. H. Rubin (Eds.), *The development and treatment of childhood aggression* (pp. 139–68). Hillsdale, NJ: Erlbaum.

Patterson, G. R., DeGarmo, D. S., & Knutson, N. (2000). Hyperactivity and antisocial behaviors: Comorbid or two points in the same process? *Develop. Psychopath.*, 12(1), 91–106.

Patterson, G. R., Reid, J. B., & Dishion, T. J. (1998). Antisocial boys. In J. M. Jenkins & K. Oatley (Eds.), *Human emotions: A reader* (pp. 330–36). Malden, MA: Blackwell.

Patton, G. C., Johnson-Sabine, E., Wood, K., Mann, A. H., & Wakeling, A. (1990). Abnormal eating attitudes in London schoolgirls—a prospective epidemiological study: outcome at twelve month follow-up. *Psychol. Med.*, 20(2), 383–94.

Paul, G. L. (1982). *The development of a "transportable" system of behavioral assessment for chronic patients.* Invited address. University of Minnesota, Minneapolis.

Paul, G. L., & Lentz, R. J. (1977). *Psychosocial treatment of chronic mental patients: Milieu versus social-learning programs.* Cambridge, MA: Harvard University Press.

Paul, G. L., Stuve, P., & Cross, J. V. (1997). Real-world inpatient programs: Shedding some light—A critique. *App. Prev. Psychol.*, 6(4), 193–204.

Paul, T., Schroeter, K., Dahme, B., & Nutzinger, D. O. (2002). Self-injurious behavior in women with eating disorders. *Amer. J. Psychiat.*, 159(3), 408–11.

Paulesu, E., Sambugaro, E., Torti, T., Danelli, L., Ferri, F., Scialfa, G., Sberna, M., Ruggiero, G. M., Bottini, G., & Sassaroli, S. (2010). Neural correlates of worry in generalized anxiety disorder and in normal controls: A functional MRI study. *Psychol. Med.*, 40(1), 117–24.

Pauli, P., & Alpers, G. W. (2002). Memory bias in patients with hypochondriases and somatoform pain disorder. *J. Psychom. Res.*, 52, 42–53.

Paulik, G. (2011). The role of social schema in the experience of auditory hallucinations: A systematic review and a proposal for the inclusion of social schema in a cognitive behavioral model of voice hearing. *Clin. Psych. Psychother.*, DOI: 10.1002/cpp.768

Pauls, D. L., Alsobrooke, J. P., Goodman, W., Rasmussen, S., & Leckman, J. F. (1995). A family study of obsessivecompulsive disorder. *Amer. J. Psychiat.*, 152(1), 76–84.

Pauls, D. L., Raymond, C. L., & Robertson, M. (1991). The genetics of obsessive-compulsive disorder: A review. In J. Zohar, T. Insel, & S. Rasmussen (Eds.), *The psychobiology of obsessive-compulsive disorder.* New York: Springer.

Pauls, D. L., Towbin, K. E., Leckman, J. F., Zahner, G. E., & Cohen, D. J. (1986). Gilles de la Tourette's Syndrome and obsessive-compulsive disorder. *Arch. Gen. Psychiat.*, 43, 1180–82.

Paulussen-Hoogeboom, M. C., Stams, G. J. J. M., Hermanns, J. M. A., & Peetsma, T. T. D. (2007). Child negative emotionality and parenting from infancy to preschool: A meta-analytic review. *Developmental Psychology*, 43(2), 438–453.

Pavlov, I. P. (1927). *Conditioned reflexes.* London: Oxford University Press.

Pavone, L., Meli, C., Nigro, F., & Lisi, R. (1993). Late diagnosed phenylketonuria patients: Clinical presentation and results of treatment. *Developmental Brain Dysfunction*, 6(1–3), 184–87.

Payne, C., & Sacks, O. (2009). *Asylum: Inside the closed world of the state mental hospital.* Cambridge, MA: MIT Press.

Pederson, C. B., & Mortensen, P. B. (2001). Evidence of a dose-response relationship between urbanicity during upbringing and schizophrenia risk. *Arch. Gen. Psychiat.*, 58, 1039–46.

Pedersen, E. R., LaBrie, J. W., Hummer, J. F., Larimer, M. E., & Lee, C. M. (2010). Heavier drinking American college students may self-select into study abroad programs: An examination of sex and ethnic differences within a high-risk group.

Pediatric OCD Treatment Study. (2004). Cognitive-behavior therapy, sertraline, and their combination for children and adolescents with obsessive-compulsive disorder: The pediatric OCD treatment study (POTS) randomized controlled trial. *JAMA, 292*(16), 1969–76.

Peeke, P. M., & Chrousos, G. P. (1995). Hypercortisolism and obesity. In G. P. Chrousos, R. McCarty, et al. (Eds.), *Stress: Basic mechanisms and clinical implications* (pp. 515–60). New York: New York Academy of Sciences.

Pelham, W. E., Burrows-MacLean, L., Gnagy, E. M., Fabiano, G. A., Coles, E. K., Tresco, K. E., Chacko, A., Wymbs, B. T., Wienke, A. L., Walker, K. S., & Hoffman, Martin T. (2005). Transdermal methylphenidate, behavioral, and combined treatment for children with ADHD. *Exper. Clin. Psychopharmacol., 13*(2), 111–26.

Pelham, W. E., Jr., & Fabiano, G. A. (2008). Evidence-based psychosocial treatments for attention-deficit/hyperactivity disorder. *J. Clin. Child Adol. Psych., 37*(1), 184–214.

Pelham, W. E., Jr., Hoza, B., Pillow, D. R., Gnagy, E., Kipp, H. L., Greiner, D. R., Waschbusch, D. A., Trane, S., T., Greenhouse, J., Wolfson, L., & Fitzpatrick, E. (2002). Effects of methylphenidate and expectancy on children with ADHD behavior, academic performance, and attributions in a summer treatment program and regular classroom setting. *J. Cons. Clin. Psychol., 70,* 320–25.

Pelletier, A. R., & Gilchrist, J. (2005). Roller coaster related fatalities, United States, 1994-2004. *Injury Prevention, 11,* 309–12.

Pennebaker, J. W. (1997). *Opening up: The healing power of expressing emotions.* New York: Guilford.

Penrose, L. S. (1963). *Biology of mental defect* (3rd ed.). New York: Grune & Stratton.

Perkins, D. O., Lieberman, J. A., Gu, H., Tohen, M., McEvoy, J., Green, A. I., Zipursky, R. B., Strakowski, S. M., Sharma, T., Kahn, R. S., Gur, R., & Tollefson, G. (2004). Predictors of antipsychotoic treatment response in patients with first-episode schizophrenia, schizoaffective disorder and schizophreniform disorders. *Brit. J. Psychiat., 185,* 18–24.

Perl, D. P. (1999). Abnormalities in brain structure on postmortem analysis of dementias. In D. S. Charney, E. J. Nestler, & B. S. Bunney (Eds.), *Neurobiology of mental illness.* New York: Oxford University Press.

Perlin, M. L. (1996). Myths, realities, and the political world: The anthropology of insanity defense attitudes. *Bull. Amer. Acad. Psychiat. Law, 24*(1), 5–25.

Perlis, R. P., Perlis, C. S., Wu, Y., Hwang, C., Joseph, M., & Nierenberg, A. A. (2005). Industry sponsorship and financial conflict of interest in the reporting of clinical trials in psychiatry. *Amer. J. Psychiat., 162,* 1957–60.

Perls, F. S. (1969). *Gestalt therapy verbatim.* Lafayette, CA: Real People Press.

Perreira, K. M., & Sloan, F. A. (2001). Life events and alcohol consumption among mature adults: A longitudinal analysis. *J. Stud. Alcoh., 62*(4), 501–8.

Perrin, M. A., DiGrande, L., Wheeler, K., Thorpe, L., Farfel., M., & Brackbill, R. (2007). Differences in PTSD prevalence and associated risk factors among World Trade Center disaster rescue and recovery workers. *Amer. J. Psychiat., 164,* 1385–1394.

Perrin, M. C., Opler, M. G., Harlap, S., Harkavy-Friedman, J., Kleinhaus, K., Nahon, D., Fenning, S., Susser, E. S., & Malaspina, D. (2007). Tetrachloroehtylene exposure and risk of schizophrenia: Offspring of dry cleaners in a population birth cohort, preliminary findings. *Schizo. Res., 90,* 251–54.

Perris, C. (1992). Bipolar-unipolar distinction. In E. S. Paykel (Ed.), *Handbook of affective disorders* (2nd ed.). New York: Guilford.

Perry, C., Williams, C. L., Komro, K. A., Veblen-Mortenson , S., Stigler, M. H., Munson, K. A., Farbakhsh, K., Jones, R. M. & Forster, J. L. (2002). Project Northland: Long-term outcomes of community action to reduce adolescent alcohol use. *Health Education Research, 17*(1), 117–132.

Perry, C. L., Williams, C. L., Veblen-Mortenson , S. Toomey, T. L. et al (1996). Project Northland: Outcomes of a community wide alcohol use prevention program during early adolescence. *American Journal of Public Health, 86*(7), 956–965.

Perry, J., Miller, K., & Klump, K. (2006). Treatment planning with the MMPI-2. In J. N. Butcher (Ed.), *MMPI-2: The practioner's handbook* (pp. 143–63). Washington, DC: American Psychological Association.

Perry, J. N. (2009). Assessment of treatment resistance via questionnaire. In J. N. Butcher (Ed.), *Oxford handbook of personality assessment* (pp. 667–82). New York: Oxford University Press.

Perry, L. H., & Landreth, G. L. (2001). Diagnostic assessment of children's play therapy behavior. In G. L. Landreth (Ed.), *Innovations in play therapy: Issues, process, and special population* (pp. 155–78). Philadelphia: Bruner-Routledge.

Pertusa, A., Frost, R. O., Fullana, M. A., Samuels, J., Steketee, G., Tolin, D., et al. (2010). Refining the diagnostic boundaries of compulsive hoarding: A critical review. *Clin. Psychol. Rev., 30*(4), 371–86. doi: 10.1016/j.cpr.2010.01.007

Pescosolido, B. A., Martin, J. K., Long, J. S., Medina, T. R., Phelan, J. C., & Link, B. G. (2010). "A disease like any other"? A decade of change in public reactions to schizophrenia, depression, and alcohol dependence. *Amer. J. Psychiat., 167,* 1321–30.

Peter, R., & Siegrist, J. (2000). Psychosocial work environment and the risk of coronary heart disease. *International Archives of Occupational and Environmental Health, 73,* S41–S45.

Petersen, D. J., Bilenberg, N., Hoerder, K., & Gillberg, C. (2006). The population prevalence of child psychiatric disorders in Danish 8- to 9-year-old children. *European Child & Adolescent Psychiatry, 15*(2) 71–78.

Petersen, R. C., Doody, R., Kurz, A., Mohs, R. C., Morris, J. C., Rabins, P. V., Ritchie, K., Rossor, M., Thal, L., & Winblad, B. (2001). Current concepts in mild cognitive impairment. *Arch. Neurol., 58,* 1985–92.

Peterson, P. L., Baer, J. S., Wells, E.A., Ginzler, J. A., & Garrett, S. B. (2006). Short-term effects of a brief motivational intervention to reduce alcohol and drug risk among homeless adolescents. *Psych. Addict. Behav., 20*(3), 254–64.

Petit, J. W., & Joiner, T. E. (2006) *Chronic depression: Interpersonal sources, therapeutic solutions.* Washington, DC: American Psychological Association.

Petrie, A., & Sabin, C. (2000). *Medical statistics at a glance.* Oxford, UK: Blackwell Science.

Petronis, A., Gottesman, I. I., Kan, P., Kennedy, J. L., Basile, V. S., Patterson, A. D., et al. (2003). Monozygotic twins exhibit numerous epigenetic differences: Clues to twin discordance? *Schizo. Bull., 29,* 169–78.

Petronko, M. R., Harris, S. L., & Kormann, R. J. (1994). Community-based behavioral training approaches for people with mental retardation

and mental illness. *J. Cons. Clin. Psychol., 62*(1), 49–54.

Petrovic, V. (2004). Level of psychopathology in children with war related trauma. *Psychiatry Today, 36*(1), 17–28.

Petrovich, G. (2011). Learning and motivation to eat: Forebrain circuitry. *Physiology & Behavior, 104,* 582–89.

Petry, N. (2005). *Pathological gambling: Etiology, comorbidity and treatment.* Washington, DC: .

Petry, N. M., Ammerman, Y., Bohl, J., Doersch, A., Gay, H., Kadden, R., Molina, C., & Steinberg, K. (2006). Cognitive-behavioral therapy for pathological gamblers. *J. Cons. Clin. Psych., 74*(3), 555–67.

Petry, N. M., Barry, D., Pietrzak, R. H., & Wagner, J. A. (2008). Overweight and obesity are associated with psychiatric disorders: Results from the National Epidemiologic Survey on Alcohol and Related Conditions. *Psychosom. Med., 70,* 288–97.

Petry, N. M., & Madden, G. J. (2010) Discounting and pathological gambling. In G. J. Madden & W. K. Bickel (Eds.), *Impulsivity: The behavioral and neurological science of discounting* (pp. 273–94). Washington, DC: American Psychological Association.

Petti, T. A. (2010). Milieu treatment: Inpatient, partial hospitalization, and residential programs. In M. K. Dulcan (Ed.), *Dulcan's textbook of child and adolescent psychiatry* (pp. 939–53). Arlington, VA: American Psychiatric Publishing, Inc.

Pfammatter, M., Junghan, U. M., & Brenner, H. D. (2006). Efficacy of psychological therapy in schizophrenia: Conclusions from meta-analyses. *Schizo. Bull., 32, S1,* S64–S80.

Pfeffer, C. R. (1996a). Suicidal behavior in response to stress. In C. R. Pfeffer (Ed.), *Severe stress and mental disturbance in children* (pp. 327–46). Washington, DC: American Psychiatric Association.

Pfeffer, C. R. (1996b). Suicidal behavior. In L. Hechtman (Ed.), *Do they grow out of it?* (pp. 121–38). Washington, DC: American Psychiatric Press.

Pfeffer, C. R., Hurt, S. W., Kakuma, T., Peskin, J., Siefker, C. A., & Nagbhairava, S. (1994). Suicidal children grow up: Suicidal episodes and effects of treatment during follow-up. *J. Amer. Acad. Child Adoles. Psychiat., 33,* 225–30.

Pfefferbaum, B., Call, J. A., & Sconzo, G. M. (1999). Mental health services for children in the first two years after the 1995 Oklahoma City terrorist bombing. *Psychiatr. Serv., 50*(7), 956–58.

Pfister, B. J., Chickola, L., & Smith, D. H. (2009). Head motions while riding roller coasters. *Am. J. Forensic Med. Pathol., 30,* 339–45.

Phan, K. L., Fitzgerald, D. A., Nathan, P. J., & Tancer, M. E. (2006). Association between amygdala hyperactivity to harsh faces and severity of social anxiety in generalized social phobia. *Biol. Psychiat, 59*(5), 424–29.

Phares, V., Duhig, A. M., & Watkins, M. M. (2002). Familycontext: Fathers and other supporters. In S. H. Goodman& I. H. Gotlib (Eds.), *Children of depressed parents: Mechanisms of risk and implications for treatment* (pp. 203–25). Washington DC: American Psychological Association.

Phillippi, S. W., & DePrato, D. K. (2010). Assessment and treatment of juvenile offenders. In E. P. Benedek, P. Ash, & C. L. Scott (Ed.), *Principles and practice of child and adolescent forensic mental health,* (pp. 361–88). Arlington, VA: American Psychiatric Publishing, Inc.

Phillips, K. (1996). *The broken mirror: Understanding and treating body dysmorphic disorder.* New York: Oxford University Press.

Phillips, K. (2001). Body dysmorphic disorder. In K. Phillips (Ed.), *Somatoform and factitious disorders* (pp. 67–94). Washington, DC: American Psychiatric Association.

Phillips, K. A. (2000). Body dysmorphic disorder: Diagnostic controversies and treatment challenges. *Bulletin of the Menninger Clinic, 64,* 18–35.

Phillips, K. A. (2004). Treating body dysmorphic disorder using medication. *Psychiat. Ann., 34*(12), 945–53.

Phillips, K. A. (2005). *The broken mirror: Understanding and treating body dysmorphic disorder.* (2nd ed.). New York: Oxford University Press.

Phillips, K. A., & Diaz, S. F. (1997). Gender differences in body dysmorphic disorder. *J. Nerv. Ment. Dis., 185,* 570–77.

Phillips, K. A., Grant, J., Siniscalchi, J., & Albertini, R. S. (2001). Surgical and nonpsychiatric medical treatment of patients with body dysmorphic disorder. *Psychosomatics, 42,* 504–10.

Phillips, K. A., & Menard, W. (2006). Suicidality in body dysmorphic disorder: A prospective study. *Am. J. Psychiat., 163*(7), 1280–82.

Phillips, K. A., Menard, W, & Fay, C. (2006). Gender similarities and differences in 200 individuals with body dysmorphic disorder. *Compr. Psychiat., 47*(2), 77–87.

Phillips, K. A., Pagano, M. E., & Menard, W. (2006). Pharmacotherapy for body dysmorphic disorder: Treatment received an illness severity. *Ann. Clin. Psych., 18*(4), 251–57.

Phillips, K. A., Pinto, A., Menard, W., Eisen, J. L., Manceba, M., & Rasmussen, S. A. (2007). Obsessive-comulsive disorder versus body dysmorphic disorder: A comparison study of two possibly related disorders. *Depression and Anxiety, 24,* 399–409.

Phillips, K. A., Stein, D. J., Rauch, S. L., Hollander, E., Fallon, B. A., Barsky, A., et al. (2010). Should an obsessive-compulsive spectrum grouping of disorders be included in DSM-V? *Depression and Anxiety, 27*(6), 528–55. doi: 10.1002/da.20705

Phillips, M. L., & Sierra, M. (2003). Depersonalization disorder: A functional neuroanatomical perspective. *Stress, 6*(3), 157–65.

Phillips, M. L., Drevets, W. C., Rauch, S. L., & Lane, R. (2003). Neurobiology of emotion perception II: Implications for major psychiatric disorders. *Biol. Psychiat., 54,* 515–28.

Phillips, S. (2002). Free to speak: Clarifying the legacy of witchhunts. *Journal of Psychology and Christianity, 21,* 25–37.

Phillips, W., Shannon, K. M., & Barker, R. A. (2008). The current clinical management of Huntington's disease. *Movement Disorders, 23,* 1491–504.

Pickworth, W. B., Rohrer, M. S., & Fant, R. V. (1997). Effects of abused drugs on psychomotor performance. *Exp. Clin. Psychopharm., 5*(3), 235–41.

Pies, R. (2009). Should DSM-V designate "Internet addiction" a mental disorder? *Psychiatry, 6*(2), 31–37.

Piet, J., & Hougaard, E. (2011). The effect of mindfulness-based cognitive therapy for prevention of relapse in recurrent major depressive disorder: A systematic review and meta-analysis. *Clin. Psychol. Rev., 31*(6), 1032–40. doi: 10.1016/j.cpr.2011.05.002

ietrzak, R. H., Morasco, B. J., Blanco, C., Grant, B. F., & Petry, N. M. (2007). Gambling level and psychiatric and medical disorders in older adults: Results from the National Epidemiologic Survey on Alcohol and Related Conditions. *Am. J. Ger. Psychiat., 15*(4), 301–13.

Pijl, Y., Kluiter, H., & Wiersma, D. (2001). Deinstitutionalisation in the Netherlands. *Eur. Arch. Psychiat. Clin. Neurosci., 25,* 124–29.

Pike, K. M., & Mizushima, H. (2005). The clinical presentation of Japanese women with anorexia nervosa and bulimia nervosa: A study of the Eating Disorders Inventory-2. *Int. J. Eat. Dis., 37,* 26–31.

Pike, K. M., Dohm, F., Striegel-Moore, R. H., Wilfley, D. E., & Fairburn, C. G. (2001). A comparison of black and white women with binge eating disorder. *Amer. J. Psychiat., 158*(9), 1455–60.

Pike, K. M., Walsh, B. T., Vitousek, K., Wilson, G. T., & Bauer, J. (2003). Cognitive behavioral therapy in the posthospitalization treatment of anorexia nervosa. *Amer. J. Psychiat., 160*(11), 2046–49.

Pilkonis, P. A. (2001). Treatment of personality disorders in association with symptom disorders. In W. J. Livesley (Ed.), *Handbook of personality disorders* (pp. 541–54). New York: Guilford.

Pinard, G. F., & Pagani, L. (Eds.). (2001). *Clinical assessment of dangerousness: Empirical contributions.* New York: Cambridge University Press.

Pincus, A. L., & Lukowitsky, M. R. (2010). Pathological narcissism and narcissistic personality disorder. *Annu. Rev. Clin. Psychol., 6*(8), 1–28. doi:10.1146/annurev.clinpsy.121208.131215

Pine, D. S., & Klein, R. G. (2010). Anxiety disorders. In M. Rutter, D. Bishop, D. Pine, S. Scott, J. Stevenson, E. Taylor, & A. Thapar, (Eds.), *Rutter's child and adolescent psychiatry* (5th ed.), (pp. 628–47). Wiley-Blackwell.

Pineles, S.L., & Mineka, S. (2005). Attentional biases to internal and external sources of potential threat in social anxiety. *J. Abn. Psychol., 114*(2), 314–18.

Pinto, A., Liebowitz, M. R., Foa, E. B., & Simpson, H. B. (2011). Obsessive compulsive personality disorder as a predictor of exposure and ritual prevention outcome for obsessive compulsive disorder. *Behav. Res. Ther., 49*(8), 453–8. doi:10.1016/j.brat.2011.04.004

Piotrowski, C., Belter, R. W., & Keller, J. M. (1998). The impact of "managed care" on the practice of psychological testing: Preliminary findings. *J. Pers. Assess., 70,* 441–47.

Piotrowski, C., & Zalewski, C. (1993). Training in psychodiagnostic testing in APA approved PsyD and PhD clinical psychology programs. *J. Pers. Assess., 61,* 394–405.

Piotrowski, N. A., Tusel, D. J., Sees, K. L., Reilly, P. M., Banys, P., Meek, P., & Hall, S. M. (1999). Contingency contracting with monetary reinforcers for abstinence from multiple drugs in a methadone program. *Exp. Clin. Psychopharm., 7*(4), 399–411.

Piper, A. (1998). Repressed memories from World War II: Nothing to forget. Examining Karon and Widener's (1997) claim to have discovered evidence for repression. *Profess. Psychol.: Res. Prac., 29,* 476–78.

Piper, A., & Merskey, H. (2004a). The persistence of folly: A critical examination of dissociative identity disorder. Part I. The excesses of an improbable concept. *Canad. J. Psychiat., 49*(9), 592–600.

Piper, A., & Merskey, H. (2004b). The persistence of folly: A critical examination of dissociative identity disorder. Part II. The defence and decline of multiple personality or dissociative identity disorder. *Canad. J. Psychiat., 49*(10), 678–83.

Piper, W. E., & Joyce, A. S. (2001). Psychosocial treatment outcome. In W. J. Livesley (Ed.), *Handbook of personality disorders* (pp. 323–43). New York: Guilford.

Pirelli, G., Gottdiener, W. H., & Zapf, P. A. (2011). A meta-analytic review of competency to stand trial research. *Psychology, Public Policy, and Law, 17*(1), 1–53.

Pithouse, A., & Crowley, A. (2007). National standards in children's advocacy—What do young people say? *Child Care in Practice, 13*(1), 17-32.

Pizzagalli, D. A., Nitschke, J. B., Oakes, T. R., Hendrick, A. M., Horras, K. A., Larson, C. L., et al. (2002). Brain electrical tomography in depression: The importance of symptom severity, anxiety, and melancholic features. *Biol. Psychiat., 52,* 73–85.

Platt, A. M. (1969). *The child savers: The invention of delinquency.* Chicago, IL: University of Chicago Press.

Platte, P., Zelten, J. F., & Stunkard, A. J. (2000). Body image in the Old Order Amish: A people separate from "the world." *Int. J. Eat. Dis., 28,* 408–14.

Plazzi, G., Vetrugno, R., Provini, F., & Montagna, P. (2005). Sleepwalking and other ambulatory behaviours during sleep. *Neurological Sciences, 26*(Suppl3), 193–98.

Pleis, J. R., Lucas, J. W., & Ward, B. W. (2009). Summary health statistics for U.S. adults: National Health Interview Survey, 2008. National Center for Health Statistics. *Vital Hlth. Stat. 10*(242).

Plomin, R. (1986). *Development, genetics and psychology.* Hillsdale, NJ: Erlbaum.

Plomin, R., & Daniels, D. (1987). Why are children in the same family so different from one another? *Behavioral and Brain Sciences, 10,* 1–15.

Plomin, R., & DeFries, J. C. (Eds.). (2003). *Behavioral genetics in the postgenomic era.* Washington, DC: American Psychological Association.

Plomin, R., DeFries, J. C., McClearn, G. E., & McGuffin, P. (2001). *Behavioral genetics* (4th ed.). New York: Worth.

Plomin, R., DeFries, J. C., McClearn, G. E., & McGuffin, P. (2008). *Behavioral genetics* (5th ed.). London: Worth Publishers.

Pogarell, O., Hamann, C., Popperl, G., Juckel, G., Chouker, M., Zaudig, M., et al. (2003). Elevated brain serotonin transporter availability in patients with obsessive-compulsive disorder. *Biol. Psychiat., 54*(12), 1406–13.

Pogue-Geile, M. F., & Yokley, J. L. (2010). Current research on the genetic contributors to schizophrenia. *Curr. Dis. Psychol. Sci., 19,* 214–19.

Polich, J. M., Armor, D. J., & Braiker, H. B. (1981). *The course of alcoholism: Four years after treatment.* New York: Wiley Interscience.

Poling, J., Kosten, T. R., & Sofuoglu, M. (2007). Treatment outcome predictors for cocaine dependence. *American Journal of Drug and Alcohol Abuse, 33*(2), 191–206.

Polivy, J., Herman, C. P., & Boivin, M. (2005). Eating disorders. In J. E. Maddux & B. A. Winstead (Eds.), *Psychopathology: Foundations for a contemporary understanding.* Mahwah, NJ: Lawrence Erlbaum Associates.

Pollack, M. H., & Simon, N. M. (2009). Pharmacotherapy for panic disorder and agoraphobia. In M. M. Antony & M. B. Stein (Eds.), *Oxford handbook of anxiety and related disorders* (pp. 295–307). New York: Oxford University Press.

Polo, C. (1997). *Del Padre Jofre al jofrismo. La Locura y sus instuciones.* Valencia: Disputacion de Valencia, 125–40.

Polvan, N. (1969). Historical aspects of mental ills in Middle East discussed. *Roche Reports, 6*(12), 3.

Ponce, F. Q., & Atkinson, D. R. (1989). Mexican-American acculturation, counselor ethnicity, counseling style, and perceived counselor credibility. *J. Couns. Psychol., 36,* 203–8.

Pope, H. G., Gruber, A., Choi, P., Olivardia, R., & Philips, K. (1997). Muscle dysmorphia. An underrecognized form of body dysmorphic disorder. *Psychosomatics, 38,* 548–57.

Pope, H. G., Hudson, J. I., Bodkin, J. A., & Oliva, P. (1998). Questionable validity of "dissociative amnesia" in trauma victims: Evidence from prospective studies. *Brit. J. Psychiat., 172,* 210–15.

Pope, H. G., Jr., Gruber, A. J., Hudson, J. I., Huestis, M. A., & Yurgelun-Todd, D. (2001). Neuropsychological performance in long-term cannabis users. *Arch. Gen. Psychiat., 58,* 909–15.

Pope, H. G., Oliva, P. S., Hudson, J. I., Bodkin, J. A., & Gruber, A. J. (1999). Attitudes toward DSM-IV dissociative disorder diagnoses among board-certified American psychiatrists. *Amer. J. Psychiat., 156,* 321–23.

Pope, K. W., & McNally, R. J. (2002). Nonspecific placebo effects explain the therapeutic benefits of magnets. *Scientific Review of Alternative Medicine, 6,* 10–14.

Popkin, J. (1994, Sept. 19). Sexual predators. *U.S. News and World Report,* 65–73.

Popma, A. (2007). Assessing and managing violence risk in juveniles. *J. Amer. Acad. Child Adoles. Psychiat., 46*(9), 1231–32.

Posey, D. J., & McDougle, C. J. (2003). Use of atypical antipsychotics in autism. In E. Hollander (Ed.), *Autism spectrum disorders* (pp. 247–64). New York: Marcel Dekker.

Posner, M. I., & Rothbart, M. K. (2007). Temperament and learning. In *Educating the human brain.* (pp. 121–146). Washington, DC, US: American Psychological Association.

Post, R. M. (1992). Transduction of psychosocial stress into the neurobiology of recurrent affective disorder. *Amer. J. Psychiat., 149*(8), 999–1010.

Post, R. M., Altshuler, L. L., Frye, M. A., Suppes, T., Keck, P. E., Jr., McElroy, S. L., et al. (2010). Complexity of pharmacologic treatment required for sustained improvement in outpatients with bipolar disorder. *J. Clin. Psychiat., 71*(9), 1176–86; quiz 1252–73. doi: 10.4088/JCP.08m04811yel

Post, R. M., & Frye, M. A. (2009). Carbamazepine. In B. J. Sadock, A. A. Sadock, & P. Ruiz (Eds.), *Kaplan and Sadock's comprehensive textbook of psychiatry* (9th ed., pp. 3073–89). PA: Lippincott, Williams & Wilkins.

Potash, J. B., & DePaulo, J. R. (2000). Searching high and low: A review of the genetics of bipolar disorder. *Bipolar Disorders, 2,* 8–26.

Potenza, M. N. (2002). A perspective on future directions in the prevention, treatment, and research of pathological gambling. *Psychiat. Ann., 32*(3), 203–7.

Potochnick, S. R., & Perreira, K. M. (2010). Depression and anxiety among first-generation immigrant Latino youth. *J. Nerv. Ment. Dis., 198*(7), 470–77.

Poulton, R., Milne, B. J., Craske, M. G., & Menzies, R. G. (2001). A longitudinal study of the etiology of separation anxiety. *Behav. Res. Ther., 39*(12), 1395–1410.

Powell, L. H., Calvin, J. E., & Calvin, J. E. (2007). Effective obesity treatments. *Amer. Psychol., 62,* 234–246.

Poulton, R., Grisham, J. R., & Andrews, G. (2009). Developmental approaches to understanding anxiety disorders. In M. M. Antony & M. B. Stein (Eds.), *Oxford handbook of anxiety and related disorders* (pp. 123–35). New York: Oxford University Press.

Powers, D. V., Thompson, L., Futterman, A., & Gallagher-Thompson, D. (2002). Depression in later life: Epidemiology, assessment, impact, and treatment. In I. H. Gotlib & C. L. Hammen (Eds.), *Handbook of depression.* (pp. 560–80). New York: Guilford Press.

Powers, M. B., & Emmelkamp, P. M. G. (2008). Virtual reality exposure therapy for anxiety disorders. *J. Anx. Disord., 22,* 561–69.

Powers, M. B., Halpern, J. M., Ferenschak, M. P., Gillihan, S. J., & Foa, E. B. (2010). A meta-analytic review of prolonged exposure for posttraumatic stress disorder. *Clin. Psychol. Rev.,* n.p. doi: 10.1016/j.cpr.2010.04.007

Practice guideline for the treatment of patients with Alzheimer's disease and other dementias (2007). *Am. J. Psychiat., supplement, 164,* 1–56.

Prasher, V. P., & Kirshnan, V. H. (1993). Age of onset and duration of dementia in people with Down syndrome: Integration of 98 reported cases in the literature. *Int. J. Geriat. Psychiat., 8*(11), 915–22.

Pratchett, L. C., Pelcovitz, M. R., & Yehuda, R. (2010). Trauma and violence: Are women the weaker sex? *Psychiat. Clin. N. Amer., 33*(2), 465–74.

Pratt, L., Ford, D., Crum, R., Armenian, H., Galb, J., & Eaton, W. (1996). Depression, psychotropic medication, and risk of myocardial infarction. *Circulation, 94,* 3123–29.

Prentky, R. A. (1997). Arousal reduction in sexual offenders: A review of antiandrogen interventions. *Sexual Abuse: Journal of Research and Treatment, 9,* 335–47.

Presnell, K., & Stice, E. (2003). An experimental test of the effect of weight-loss dieting on bulimic pathology: Tipping the scales in a different direction. *J. Abn. Psychol., 112,* 166–70.

Preston, K. L., Umbricht, A., Wong, C. J., & Epstein, D. H. (2001). Shaping cocaine abstinence by successive approximation. *J. Cons. Clin. Psychol., 69*(4), 643–54.

Pretzer, J. L., & Beck, A. T. (1996). A cognitive theory of personality disorders. In J. F. Clarkin & M. F. Lenzenweger (Eds.), *Major theories of personality disorder* (pp. 36–105). New York: Guilford.

Pretzer, J. L., & Beck, A.T. (2005). A cognitive theory of personality disorders. In M. F. Lenzenweger & J. F. Clarkin (Eds.), *Major theories of personality disorder* (2nd ed., pp. 43–113). New York: Guilford Press.

Price, B. H., Baral, I., Cosgrove, G. R., Rauch, S. L., Nierenberg, A. A., Jenike, M. A., & Cassem, E. H. (2001). Improvement in severe self-mutilation following limbic leucotomy: A series of 5 consecutive cases. *J. Clin. Psychiat., 62,* 925–32.

Prichard, J. C. (1835). *A treatise on insanity.* London: Sherwood, Gilbert, & Piper.

Priebe, S., & Turner, T. (2003). Reinstitutionalisation in mental health care: This largely unnoticed process requires debate and evaluation. *Brit. Med. J., 326*(7382), 175–76.

Prigatano, G. P. (1992). Personality disturbances associated with traumatic brain injury. *J. Cons. Clin. Psychol., 60*(3), 360–68.

Prince, M. (1910). *The dissociation of a personality.* New York: Longmans, Green.

Prinstein, M. J., Borelli, J. L., Cheah, C. S. L., Simon, V. A., & Aikins, J. W. (2005). Adolescent girls' interpersonal vulnerability to depressive symptoms: A longitudinal examination of reassurance-seeking and peer relationships. *J. Abn. Psych., 114*(4), 676–88.

Prizant, B. M. (1983). Language acquisition and communicative behavior in autism: Toward an understanding of the "whole" of it. *J. Speech Hear. Dis., 46,* 241–49.

Prochaska, J. O., & Norcross, J. C. (2003). *Systems of psychotherapy* (5th ed.). Pacific Grove, CA: Brooks/Cole.

Prouse, L. (2001). *Flying high: A pilot's story of alcoholism and recovery.* Minnesota: Hazelden.

Prout, H. T., & Brown, D. T. (Eds.). (2007). *Counseling and psychotherapy with children and adolescents:*

Theory and practice for school and clinical settings (4th ed.). Hoboken, NJ: John Wiley & Sons.

Prudic, J. (2009). Electroconvulsive therapy. In Sadock, B. J., Sadock, A. A., & Ruiz, P. (Eds.), *Kaplan and Sadock's comprehensive textbook of psychiatry* (9th ed., pp. 3285–301). PA: Lippincott, Williams & Wilkins.

Pulay, A. J., Stinson, F. S., Dawson, D. A., Goldstein, R. B., Chou, S. P., Huang, B., Saha, T. D., et al. (2009). Prevalence, correlates, disability, and comorbidity of DSM-IV schizotypal personality disorder: Results from the Wave 2 National Epidemiologic Survey on Alcohol and Related Conditions. *Primary Care Companion to the Journal of Clinical Psychiatry, 11*(2), 53. Physicians Postgraduate Press, Inc. Retrieved from http://www.ncbi.nlm.nih.gov/pmc/articles/PMC2707116/

Pumariega, A. J. (2007). Residential treatment for children and youth: Time for reconsideration and reform. *Am. J. Orthopsychiat., 77*(3), 343–45.

Purcell, R., Pathé, M., & Mullen, P. E. (2001). A study of women who stalk. *Amer. J. Psychiat., 158*(12), 2056–60.

Purdon, C. (2004). Empirical investigations of thought suppression in OCD. *J. Behav. Ther. Exper. Psychiat., 35*(2), 121–36.

Purdon, C. (2009). Psychological approaches to understanding obsessive-compulsive disorder. In M. M. Antony & M. B. Stein (Eds.), *Oxford handbook of anxiety and related disorders* (pp. 238–49). New York: Oxford University Press.

Purdon, C., Rowa, K., & Antony, M. M. (2007). Diary records of thought suppression by individuals with obsessive-compulsive disorder. *Behavioural and Cognitive Psychotherapy, 35*(1), 47–59.

Putnam, F. W. (1984). The psychophysiologic investigation of multiple personality disorder: A review. *Psychiat. Clin. N. Amer., 7,* 31–39.

Putnam, F. W. (1997). *Dissociation in children and adolescents: A developmental perspective.* New York: Guilford.

Putnam, S. P., Sanson, A. V., & Rothbart, M. K. (2002). Child temperament and parenting. In M. H. Bornstein (Ed.), *Handbook of parenting: Vol. 1: Children and parenting* (2nd ed., pp. 255–77). Mahwah, NJ: Lawrence Erlbaum Associates.

Puzzanchera, C. (2009). Juvenile arrests 2008. Juvenile Justice Bulletin. US Department of Justice, December 2009.

Quale, A. J., & Schanke, A-K. (2010). Resilience in the face of coping with a severe physical injury: A study of trajectories of adjustment in a rehabilitation setting. *Rehabilitation Psychology, 55,* 12–22.

Quattrocchi, M. R., & Schopp, R. F. (2005). Tarasaurus Rex: A Standard of Care That Could Not Adapt. *Psychology, Public Policy, and Law, 11*(1), 109–37.

Quilty, L. C., Sellbom, M., Tackett, J. L., & Bagby, R. M. (2009). Personality trait predictors of bipolar disorder symptoms. *Psychiat. Res., 169*(2), 159–63. doi: 10.1016/j.psychres.2008.07.004

Quinsey, V. L., & Earls, C. M. (1990). The modification of sexual preferences. In W. L. Marshall, D. R. Laws, & H. E. Barbaree (Eds.), *Handbook of sexual assault: Issues, theories, and treatment of the offender* (pp. 279–95). New York: Plenum.

Quinsey, V. L., Harris, G. T., Rice, M. E., & Cormier, C. A. (2006). *Violent offenders: Appraising and managing risk* (2nd ed.). Washington, DC:.

Quinsey, V. L., Lalumiere, M. L., Rice, M. E., & Harris, G. T. (1995). Predicting sexual-offenses. In J. C. Campbell (Ed.), *Assessing dangerousness: Violence by sexual offenders, batterers, and child abusers* (pp. 114–37). Thousand Oaks, CA: Sage.

Quinton, D., & Rutter, M. (1988). *Parenting breakdown: The making and breaking of intergenerational links.* Aldershot, Hants: Avebury.

Rabow, J., & Duncan-Schill, M. (1995). Drinking among college students. *Journal of Alcohol & Drug Education, 40*(3), 52–64.

Rachman, J. G., & Hodgson, R. (1980). *Obsessions and compulsions.* Englewood Cliffs, NJ: Prentice-Hall.

Rachman, S. J. (1990). *Fear and courage.* New York: Freeman.

Rachman, S. J. (1997). Claustrophobia. In G. C. L. Davey (Ed.), *Phobias: A handbook of theory, research and treatment* (pp. 163–81). Chichester, England: Wiley.

Rachman, S., Radomsky, A. S., & Shafran, R. (2008). Safety behaviour: A reconsideration. *Behav. Res. Ther., 46*(2), 163–73. doi: 10.1016/j.brat.2007.11.008

Rachman, S., & Shafran, R. (1998). Cognitive and behavioral features of obsessive-compulsive disorder. In R. Swinson, M. Antony, S. Rachman, & M. Richter (Eds.), *Obsessive-compulsive disorder: Theory, research, and treatment* (pp. 51–78). New York: Guilford.

Rachman, S. J., Shafran, R., & Riskind, J. (2006). Cognitive vulnerability to obsessive-compulsive disorders. In L. B. Alloy & J. H. Riskind (Eds.), *Cognitive vulnerability to emotional disorders* (pp. 235–49). Lawrence Erlbaum.

Radden, J. (Ed.). (2000). *The nature of melancholy: From Aristotle to Kristeva.* New York: Oxford University Press.

Radford, J., & Anderson, M. (2003). Encopresis in children on the autistic spectrum. *Early Child Development & Care, 173*(4), 375–82.

Rado, S. (1962). *Psychoanalysis of behavior II* (p. 96). New York: Grune & Stratton.

Rahm, C., Schulz-Juergensen, S., & Eggert, P. (2010). Effects of desmopressin on the sleep of children suffering from enuresis. *Acta Paediatrica, 99*(7), 1037–41.

Raine, A. (2006). Schizotypal personality: Neurodevelopmental and psychosocial trajectories. *Ann. Rev. Clin. Psych., 2*, 291–326.

Raine, A., Venables, P. H., & Williams, M. (1995). High autonomic arousal and electrodermal orienting at age 15 years as protective factors against criminal behavior at age 29 years. *Amer. J. Psychiat., 152*, 1595–1600.

Rais, M., Cahn, W., Van Haren, N., Schnack, H., Caspers, E., Hulshoff, H., & Kahn, R. (2008). Excessive brain volume loss over time in cannabis-using first episode patients. *Am. J. Psychiat., 165*, 490–96.

Ramchandani, P., Stein, A., Evans, J., & O'Connor, T. G. (2005). Paternal depression in the postnatal period and child development: a prospective population study. *Lancet, 365*(9478), 2201–5.

Ramey, C. H., & Weisberg, R. W. (2004). The "poetical activity" of Emily Dickinson: A further test of the hypothesis that affective disorders foster creativity. *Creativity Research Journal, 16*(2–3), 173–85.

Ramirez, J. R., Crano, W. D., Quist, R., Burgoon, M., Alvaro, E. M., & Grandpre, J. (2004). Acculturation, familism, parental monitoring, and knowledge as predictors of marijuana and inhalant use in adolescents. *Psych. Addict. Behav., 18*, 3–11.

Ramsland, K. (2005). *Inside the minds of mass murderers: Why they kill.* Westport, CT: Praeger.

Rao, V., & Lyketsos, C. (2002). Psychiatric aspects of traumatic brain injury. *Psychiat. Clin. N. Amer., 25*(1), 43–69.

Rapee, R. (2002). The development and modification of temperamental risk for anxiety disorders: Prevention of a lifetime of anxiety? *Biol. Psychiat., 52*(10), 947–57.

Rapee, R. M. (1996). Information-processing views of panic disorder. In R. M. Rapee (Ed.), *Current controversies in the anxiety disorders* (pp. 77–93). New York: Guilford.

Rapee, R. M. (2001). The development of generalized anxiety. In M. W. Vasey & M. R. Dadds (Eds.), *The developmental psychopathology of anxiety* (pp. 481–503). New York: Oxford University Press.

Rapee, R. M., & Melville, L. F. (1997). Recall of family factors in social phobia and panic disorder: Comparison of mother and offspring reports. *Depression and Anxiety, 5*, 7–11.

Rapee, R. M., & Spence, S. H. (2004). The etiology of social phobia: Empirical evidence and an initial model. *Clin. Psychol. Rev., 24*(7), 737–67.

Raphael, B., & Wooding, S. (2004). Debriefing: Its evolution and current status. *Psychiat. Clin. N. Amer., 27*, 407–23.

Raphael, B., Wooding, S., Stevens, G., & Connor, J. (2005). Comorbidity: Cannabis and complexity. *J. Psychiat. Pract., 11*(3), 161–76.

Rapoport, J. (1989). *The boy who couldn't stop washing: The experience and treatment of obsessive-compulsive disorder.* New York: Penguin.

Rapp, J. T., Miltenberger, R. G., Galensky, T. L., Ellingson, S. A., Stricker, J., Garlinghouse, M., & Long, E. S. (2000). Treatment of hair pulling and hair manipulation maintained by digital-tactile stimulation. *Behav. Ther., 31*, 381–93.

Raskin, V. D. (1993). Psychiatric aspects of substance use disorders in childbearing populations. *Psychiatr. Clin. N. Amer., 16*, 157–65.

Rasmussen, H. N., Scheier, M. F., & Greenhouse, J. B. (2009). Optimism and physical health: A meta-analytic review. *Ann. Beh. Med., 37*, 239–256.

Rasmussen, P. R. (2005). The histrionic prototype. In *Personality-guided cognitive-behavioral therapy.* (pp. 147–66). Washington, DC: American Psychological Association.

Rasmussen, P. S. (2005). *Personality-guided cognitive-behavioral therapy.* Washington, DC: American Psychological Association.

Rauch, S. L., & Savage, C. R. (2000). Investigating corticostriatal pathophysiology in obsessive-compulsive disorders: Procedural learning and imaging probes. In W. K. Goodman, M. V. Rudorfer, et al. (Eds.), *Obsessive-compulsive disorder: Contemporary issues in treatment. Personality and clinical psychology series* (pp. 133–54). Mahwah, NJ: Erlbaum.

Rauch, S. L., Phillips, K. A., Segal, E., Makris, N., Shin, L. M., Whalen, P. J., et al. (2003). A preliminary morphometric resonance imaging study of regional brain volumes in body dysmorphic disorder. *Psych. Res. Neuroimag., 122*, 13–19.

Rauktis, M. (2001). The impact of deinstitutionalization on the seriously and persistently mentally ill elderly: A one-year follow-up. *Journal of Mental Health & Aging, 7*(3), 335–48.

Raulin, M. L., & Lilienfeld, S. O. (2009). Studying psychopathology. In P. H. Blaney & T. E. Millon (Eds.), *Oxford textbook of psychopathology* (2nd ed., pp. 86–115). New York: Oxford University Press.

Ravaglia, G., Forti, P., Maioli, F., Martelli, M., Servadei, L., Brunetti, N., Porcellini, E., & Licastro, F. (2005). Homocysteine and folate as risk factors for dementia and Alzheimer disease. *Amer. J. Clin. Nutri., 82*, 636–43.

Rawson, R. A., Huber, A., McCann, M., Shoptaw, S., Farabee, D., Reiber, C., & Ling, W. (2002). A comparison of contingency management and cognitive-behavioral approaches during methadone maintenance treatment for cocaine dependence. *Arch. Gen. Psychiat., 59*(9), 817–24.

Raymaekers, L., Smeets, T., Peters, M. J. V., & Merckelbach, H. (2010). Autobiographical memory specificity among people with recovered memories of childhood sexual abuse. *J. Behav. Ther. Exper. Psychiat., 41*, 338–44. doi:10.1016/j.jbtep.2010.03.004

Read, J. (1997). Child abuse and psychosis: A literature review and implications for professional psychology. *Profess. Psychol., 28*(5), 448–56.

Read, J. P., Wood, M. D., Kahler, C. W., Maddock, J. E., & Palfai, T. P. (2003). Examining the role of drinking motives in college student alcohol use and problems. *Psych. of Addict. Beh., 17*, 13–23.

Reardon, M. L., Lang, A. R., & Patrick, C. J. (2002). An evaluation of relations among antisocial behavior, psychopathic traits, and alcohol problems in incarcerated men. *Alcoholism, 26*(8), 1188–97.

Reck, C., Stehle, E., Reinig, K., & Mundt, C. (2009). Maternity blues as a predictor of DSM-IV depression and anxiety disorders in the first three months postpartum. *J. Affect. Disord., 113*(1–2), 77–87. doi: 10.1016/j.jad.2008.05.003

Reddy, L. A., & Atamanoff, T. (2006). *From A to Z on adolescent disorder.*

Reed, E., Silverman, J. G., Ickovics, J. R., Gupta, J., Welles, S. L., Santana, M. C., & Raj A. (2010). Experiences of racial discrimination & relation to violence perpetration and gang involvement among a sample of urban African American men. *Journal of Immigrant and Minority Health, 12*(3), 319–26. doi:10.1007/s10903-008-9159-x

Reger, G., & Gahm, G. A. (2008). Virtual reality exposure therapy for active duty soldiers. *Journal of Clinical Psychology: In Session, 64*, 1–7.

Regier, D. A., Boyd, J. H., Burke, J. D., Rae, D. S., Myers, J. K., Kramer, M., Robins, L. N., George, L. K., Karno, M., & Locke, B. Z. (1988). One-month prevalence of mental disorders in the United States. *Arch. Gen. Psychiat., 45*, 877–986.

Regier, D. A., Narrow, W. E., Rae, D. S., Manderscheid, R. W., Locke, B. Z., & Goodwin, F. K. (1993). The de facto US mental and addictive disorders service system: Epidemiologic Catchment Area prospective 1-year prevalence rates of disorders and services. *Arch. Gen. Psychiat., 50*, 85–94.

Rehman, U. S., Gollan, J., & Mortimer, A. R. (2008). The marital context of depression: Research, limitations, and new directions. *Clin. Psychol. Rev., 28*(2), 179–98. doi: 10.1016/j.cpr.2007.04.007

Reich, J. (2010). *Avoidant personality disorder and its relationship to social phobia delineation of social anxiety* (2nd ed., pp. 207–22). doi:10.1016/B978-0-12-375096-9.00008-0

Reichborn-Kjennerud, T., Czajkowski, N., Neale, M. C., Orstavik, R. E., Togersen, S., Tmabs, K., Roysamb, E., Harris, J. R., & Kendler, K. (2006). Genetic and environmental influences on dimensional representations of DSM-IV cluster A personailty disorders: A population-based multivariate twin study. *Psych. Med., 37*, 645–53.

Reichborn-Kjennerud, T., Czajkowski, N., Torgersen, S., Neale, M. C., Orstavik, R. E., Tambs, K., & Kendler, K. S. (2007). The relationship between avoidant personality disorder and social phobia: A population-based twin study. *Am. J. Psychiat., 164*, 1722–28.

Reichenberg, A., Yirmiya, R., Schuld, A., Kraus, T., Haak, M., Morag, A., & Pollmacher, T. (2001). Cytokine-associated emotional and cognitive disturbances in humans. *Arch. Gen. Psychiat., 58,* 455–52.

Reid, J. B., & Eddy, J. M. (1997). The prevention of antisocial behavior: Some considerations in the search for effective interventions. In D. M. Stoff, J. Breiling, & J. D. Maser (Eds.), *Handbook of antisocial behavior* (pp. 343–56). New York: Wiley.

Reid, J. B., Patterson, G. R., & Snyder, J. (Eds.). (2002). *Antisocial behavior in children and adolescents: A developmental analysis model for intervention.* Washington, DC: American Psychological Association.

Reijntjes, A., Thomaes, S., Kamphuis, J. H., Bushman, B. J., de Castro, B. O., & Telch, M. J. (2011). Explaining the paradoxical rejection-aggression link: The mediating effects of hostile intent attributions, anger, and decreases in state self-esteem on peer rejection-induced aggression in youth. *Pers. Soc. Psychol. Bull., 37*(7), 955–63. doi:10.1177/0146167211410247

Reilly-Harrington, N. A., Alloy, L. B., Fresco, D. M., & Whitehouse, W. G. (1999). Cognitive styles and life events interact to predict bipolar and unipolar symptomatology. *J. Abn. Psychol., 108*(4), 567–78.

Reinders, A.S., Nijjenhuis, E. R., Quak, J., Korf, J., Naaksma, J., Paans, A. et al. (2006). Psychobiological characteristics of dissociative identity disorder: A symptom provocation study. *Biol. Psychiat., 60,* 730–40.

Reinecke, M. A., Washburn, J. J., & Becker-Weidman, E. (2007). Depression and suicide. In F. M. Dattilio & A. Freeman (Eds.). (2007). *Cognitive behavioral strategies in crisis intervention,* 68–92. New York: Guilford Press.

Reinharz, D., Lesage, A. D., & Contandriopoulos, A. P. (2000). II. Cost-effectiveness analysis of psychiatric deinstitutionalization. *Canad. J. Psychiat., 45,* 533–38.

Reinherz, H. Z., Tanner, J. L., Berger, S. R., Beardslee, W. R., & Fitzmaurice, G. M. (2006). Adolescent suicidal ideation as predictive of psychopthology, suicide behavior, and compromised functioning at age 30. *Amer. J. Psychiat., 163,* 1226–32.

Reisberg, B., Doody, R., Stöffler, A., Schmitt, F., Ferris, S., & Möbius, H. J. (2003). Memantine in moderate-tosevere Alzheimer's disease. *N. Engl. J. Med., 348*(14), 1333–41.

Reisman, J. M. (1991). *A history of clinical psychology.* New York: Hemisphere Press.

Reisner, A. D. (2003). The electroconvulsive therapy controversy: Evidence and ethics. *Neuropsychol. Rev., 13,* 199–219.

Reissing, E. D., Binik, Y. M., Khalife, S., Cohen, D., & Amsel, R. (2003). Etiological correlates of vaginismus: Sexual and physical abuse, Sexual knowledge sexual self-schema and relationship adjustment. *J. Sex Mar. Ther., 29*(1), 47–59.

Reissing, E. D., Binik, Y. M., Khalifé, S., Cohen, D., & Amsel, R. (2004). Vaginal spasm, pain, and behavior: An empirical investigation of the diagnosis of vaginismus. *Arch. Sex. Behav., 33,* 5–17.

Reitan, R. M., & Wolfson, D. (1985). *The Halstead-Reitan Neuropsychological Test Battery: Theory and clinical interpretation.* Tuscon, AZ: Neuropsychology Press.

Rescorla, R. A. (1974). Effect of inflation of the unconditioned stimulus value following conditioning. *Journal of Comparative and Physiological Psychology, 86,* 101–6.

Rescorla, R. A. (1988). Pavlovian conditioning: It's not what you think it is. *Amer. Psychol., 43,* 151–60.

Resnick, R. J., Bottinelli, R., Puder-York, M., Harris, H. B., & O'Keffe, B. E. (1994). Basic issues in managed mental health services. In R. L. Lowman & R. J. Resnick (Eds.), *The mental health professional's guide to managed care.* Washington, DC: American Psychological Association.

Ressler, K. J., Rothbaum, B. O., Tannenbaum, L., Anderson, P., Graap, K., et al. (2004). Cognitive enhancers as adjuncts to psychotherapy: Use of d-cycloserine in phobic individuals to facilitate extinction of fear. *Arch. Gen. Psychiat., 61,* 1136–44.

Reyes, G., & Jacobs, G. A. (Eds.). (2006). *Handbook of international disaster psychology: Interventions with special needs populations* (Vol. 4). Westport, CT: Praeger Publishers

Reynaud, M., Leleu, X., Bernoux, A., Meyer, L., Lery, J. F., & Ruch, C. (1997). Alcohol use disorders in French hospital patients. *Alcohol and Alcoholism, 32*(6), 749–55.

Ricciuti, H. N. (1993). Nutrition and mental development. *Curr. Dir. Psychol. Sci., 2*(2), 43–46.

Rice, M. E., Quinsey, V. L., & Harris, G. T. (1991). Sexual recidivism among child molesters released from a maximum security psychiatric institution. *J. Cons. Clin. Psychol., 59,* 381–86.

Richards, J., Smith, D. J., Harvey, C. A., & Pantelis, C. (1997). Characteristics of the new long-stay population in an inner Melbourne acute psychiatric hospital. *Austral. NZ J. Psychiat., 31*(4), 488–95.

Richards, S. R., & Sweet, R. A. (2009). Dementia. In Sadock, B. J., Sadock, A. A., & Ruiz, P. (Eds.), *Kaplan and Sadock's Comprehensive Textbook of Psychiatry* (9th Ed.). PA: Lippincott, Williams & Wilkins, p. 1167–98.

Richards, T., Berninger, V., Nagy, W., Parsons, A., Field, K., & Richards, A. (2005). Brain activation during language task contrasts in children with and without dyslexia: Inferring mapping processes and assessing response to spelling instruction. *Educational and Child Psychology, 22*(2), 62–80.

Rieber, R. W. (1999). Hypnosis, false memory, and multiple personality: A trinity of affinity. *Hist. Psychiatry, 10,* 3–11.

Rief, W., & Barsky, A. J. (2005). Psychobiological perspectives on somatoform disorders. *Psychoneuroendocrinology, 30,* 996–1002.

Rief, W., & Broadbent, E. (2007). Explaining medically unexplained symptoms—models and mechanisms. *Clin. Psych. Rev., 27*(7), 821–41.

Rief, W., Buhlman, U., Wilhelm, S., Borkenhagan, A., & Brahler, E. (2006). The prevalence of body dysmorphic disorder: A population-based survey. *Psych. Med., 36*(6), 877–85.

Rief, W., Hiller, W., & Margraf, J. (1998a). Cognitive aspects of hypochondriasis and the somatization syndrome. *J. Abn. Psychol., 107,* 587–95.

Rief, W., Shaw, R., & Fichter, M. M. (1998b). Elevated levels of psychophysiological arousal and cortisol in patients with somatization syndrome. *Psychosom. Med., 60,* 198–203.

Riesch, S. K., Jacobson, G., Sawdey, L., Anderson, J., & Henriques, J. (2008). Suicide ideation among later elementary school-aged youth. *Journal of Psychiatric and Mental Health Nursing, 15*(4), 263–77.

Riggins-Caspers, K. M., Cadoret, R. J., Knutson, J. F., & Langbehn, D. (2003). Biology-environment interaction and evocative biology-environment correlation: Contributions of harsh discipline and parental psychopathology to problem adolescent behaviors. *Behav. Gen., 33,* 205–20.

Rigozzi, C., Rossier, J., Dahourou, D., Adjahouisso, M., Ah-Kion, J., Amoussou-Yeye, D., Barry, O., et al. (2009). A cross-cultural study of the higher-order structures underlying personality disorders in French-speaking Africa and Switzerland. *J. Pers. Disord., 23*(2), 175–86. doi:10.1521/pedi.2009.23.2.175

Rind, B. (2003). Adolescent sexual experiences with adults: Pathological or functional? *Journal of Psychology & Human Sexuality, 15*(1), 5–22.

Rind, B. (2004). An empirical examination of sexual relations between adolescents and adults: They differ from those between children and adults and should be treated separately. *Journal of Psychology & Human Sexuality, 16*(2), 55–62.

Rind, B., & Tromovitch, P. (1997). A meta-analytic review of findings from national samples on psychological correlates of child sexual abuse. *J. Sex Res., 34,* 237–55.

Rind, B., & Tromovitch, P. (2007). National samples, sexual abuse in childhood, and adjustment in adulthood: A commentary on Najman, Dunne, Purdie, Boyle, and Coxeter (2005). *Arch. Sex. Behav., 36*(1), 101–106.

Rind, B., Bauserman, R., & Tromovitch, P. (2000). Science versus orthodoxy: Anatomy of the congressional condemnation of a scientific article and reflections on remedies for future ideological attacks. *App. Prev. Psychol., 9,* 211–26.

Rind, B., Tromovitch, P., & Bauserman, R. (1998). A meta-analytic examination of assumed properties of child sexual abuse using college samples. *Psychol. Bull., 124,* 22–53.

Rind, B., Tromovitch, P., & Bauserman, R. (2001). The validity and appropriateness of methods, analyses, and conclusions in Rind et al. (1998): A rebuttal of victimological critique from Ondersma et al. (2001) and Dallam et al. (2001). *Psychol. Bull., 127,* 734–58.

Ringwalt, C. L., Greene, J. M., Robertson, M., & McPheeters, M. (1998). The prevalence of homelessness among adolescents in the United States. *Amer. J. Pub. Hlth., 88*(9), 1325–29.

Rinne, T., van der Brink, W., Wouters, L., & van Dyck, R. (2002). SSRI treatment of borderline personality disorder: A randomized, placebo-controlled clinical trial for female patients with borderline personality disorder. *Amer. J. Psychiat., 159,* 2048–54.

Risch, N., Herrell, R., Lehner, T., Liang, K.-Y., Eaves, L., Hoh, J., et al. (2009). Interaction between the serotonin transporter gene (5-HTTLPR), stressful life events, and risk of depression: A meta-analysis. *JAMA, 301*(23), 2462–71. doi: 10.1001/jama.2009.878

Ritchie, E. C. (2007). Update on Combat Psychiatry: From the Battle Front to the Home Front and Back Again. *Military Medicine, 172,* 11–14.

Rittson, B. (1995). *Community and municipal action on alcohol: European alcohol action plan.* Geneva: World Health Organization.

Rivera, F. P., Muellar, B. A., Somes, G., Mendoza, C. T., Rushforth, N. B., & Kellerman, A. L. (1997). Alcohol and illicit drug abuse and the risk of violent death in the home. *JAMA, 278*(7), 569–75.

Rivers, I., & Noret, N. (2010). Participant roles in bullying behavior and their association with thoughts of ending one's life. *Crisis: J. Crisis Int. Suicide Prev., 31*(3), 143–48.

Rø, O., Martinsen, E. W., Hoffart, A., & Rosenvinge, J. (2005). Two-year prospective study of personality disorders in adults with longstanding eating disorders. *Int. J. Eat. Dis., 37,* 112–18.

Roberto, C. A., Larsen, P. D., Agnew, H., Baik, J., & Brownell, K. D. (2010). Evaluating the impact of menu labeling on food choices and intake. *Am. J. Pub. Hlth*, 100, 312–18.

Roberts, A. (1981) *The Lunacy Commission*. http://www.mdx.ac.uk/www/study/01.htm, Middlesex University web, London.

Roberts, G. M. P., Nestor, L., & Garavan, H. (2009). Learning and memory deficits in ecstasy users and their neural correlates during a face-learning task. *Brain Res.*, 1292, 71–81.

Roberts, R. E., Roberts, C. R., & Xing, Y. (2007). Rates of DSM-IV psychiatric disorders among adolescents in a large metropolitan area. *J. Psychiat. Res.*, 41(11), 959–67.

Roberts, R. E., Roberts, C. R., & Chen, I. G. (2000). Fatalism and risk of adolescent depression. *Psychiatry: Interpersonal & Biological Processes*, 63(3), 239–52.

Robichaud, M., & Dugas, M. J. (2009). Psychological treatment of generalized anxiety disorder. In M. M. Antony & M. B. Stein (Eds.), *Oxford handbook of anxiety and related disorders* (pp. 364–74). New York: Oxford University Press.

Robin, R. W., Greene, R. L., Albaugh, B., Caldwell, A., & Goldman, D. (2003). Use of the MMPI-2 in American Indians: I. Comparability of the MMPI-2 between two tribes and with the MMPI-2 normative group. *Psychological Assessment*, 15(3), 351–9.

Robins, C. J., Ivanoff, A. M., & Linehan, M. M. (2001). Dialectical behavior therapy. In W. J. Livesley (Ed.), *Handbook of personality disorders* (pp. 437–59). New York: Guilford.

Robins, L. N. (1978). Aetiological implications in studies of childhood histories relating to antisocial personality. In R. D. Hare & D. Schalling (Eds.), *Psychopathic behavior: Approaches to research.* (pp. 255–71). Chichester, UK: Wiley.

Robins, L. N. (1991). Conduct disorder. *J. Child Psychol. Psychiat.*, 32, 193–212.

Robins, P. M., Smith, S. M., Glutting, J. J., & Bishop, C. T. (2005). A randomized controlled trial of a cognitivebehavioral family intervention for pediatric recurrent abdominal pain. *Journal of Pediatric Psychology*, 30, 397–408.

Robinson, D. S., Kajdasz, D. K., Gallipoli, S., Whalen, H., Wamil, A., & Reed, C. R. (2011). A 1-year, open-label study assessing the safely and tolerability of vilazodone in patients with major depressive disorder. *J. Clin. Pharmacol.*, 31, 643–46.

Robinson, M. S., & Alloy, L. B. (2003). Negative cognitive styles and stress-reactive rumination interact to predict depression: A prospective study. *Cog. Ther. Res.*, 27(3), 275–92.

Robinson, N. M., & Robinson, H. B. (1976). *The mentally retarded child* (2nd ed.). New York: McGraw-Hill.

Robinson, R. G., & Downhill, J. E. (1995). Lateralization of psychopathology in response to focal brain injury. In R. J. Davidson & K. Hugdahl (Eds.), *Brain asymmetry* (pp. 693–711). Cambridge, MA: MIT Press.

Robles, T. F., Glaser, R., & Kiecolt-Glaser, J. K. (2005). Out of balance: A new look at chronic stress, depression, and immunity. *Curr. Dis. Psychol. Sci.*, 14, 2, 111–15.

Rodewald, F., Wilhelm-Gobling, C., Emrich, H. M., Reddemann, L., & Gast, U. (2011). Axis-I comorbidity in female patients with dissociative identity disorder and dissociative identity disorder not otherwise specified. *J. Nerv. Ment. Dis.*, 199, 122–31.

Rodin, J. (1993). *Body traps*. New York: Norton.

Roeleveld, N., Zielhuis, G. A., & Gabreels, F. (1997). The prevalence of mental retardation: A critical review of recent literature. *Develop. Med. Child Neurol.*, 39(2), 125–32.

Roelofs, K., Spinhoven, P., Sandijck, P., Moene, F. C., & Hoogduin, A. L. (2005). The impact of early trauma and recent life-events on symptom severity in patients with conversion disorder. *J. Nerv. Ment. Dis.*, 193, 508–14.

Roemer, L., Molina, S., & Borkovec, T. D. (1997). An investigation of worry content among generally anxious individuals. *J. Nerv. Ment. Dis.*, 185(5), 314–19.

Roemer, L., Orsillo, S. M., & Barlow, D. H. (2002). Generalized anxiety disorder. In D. H. Barlow (Ed.), *Anxiety and its disorders* (2nd ed., pp. 477–515). New York: Guilford.

Roerrig, J. L., Steffen, K. J., Mitchelle, J. E., & Zunker, C. (2010). Laxative abuse: Epidemiology, diagnosis and management. *Drugs*, 70, 1487–503.

Roesch, R., Zapf, P. A., Golding, S. L., & Skeem, J. L. (1999). Defining and assessing competency to stand trial. In A. K. Hess & I. B. Weiner (Eds.), *The handbook of forensic psychology* (2nd ed., pp. 327–49). New York: John Wiley & Sons.

Rogers, C. R. (1951). *Client-centered therapy*. Boston: Houghton Mifflin.

Rogers, C. R. (1959). A theory of therapy, personality, and interpersonal relationships as developed in the client-centered framework. In S. Koch (Ed.), *Psychology: A study of a science* (Vol. 3, pp. 184–256). New York: McGraw-Hill.

Rogers, C. R. (1961). The process equation of psychotherapy. *Amer. J. Psychother.*, 15, 27–45.

Rogers, R. (2004). Dianostic, explanatory, and detection models of Munchausen by proxy: Extrapolations from malingering and deception.*Child Ab. Negl.*, 28, 225–39.

Rogers Wood, N. A., & Petrie, T. A. (2010). Body dissatisfaction, ethnic identity and disordered eating among African American women. *J. Couns. Psychol.*, 57, 141–53.

Rogosch, F. A., Cicchetti, D., & Toth, S. L. (2004). Expressed emotion in multiple subsystems of the families of toddlers with depressed mothers. *Develop. Psychopath.*, 16(3), 689–706.

Roizen, N. J. (2007). Complementary and alternative therapies for Down syndrome. *Mental Retardation and Developmental Disabilities Research Reviews*, 11(2), 149–55.

Rolak, L. A. (2001). *Neurology secrets* (3rd ed.). Philadelphia: Hanley and Belfus.

Roma, P. G., Champoux, M., & Suomi, S. J. (2006). Environmental control, social context, and individual differences in behavioral and cortisol responses to novelty in infant rhesus monkeys. *Child Devel.*, 77(1), 118–31. doi: 10.1111/j.1467-8624.2006.00860.x

Romer, D., & Walker, E. F. (2007). *Adolescent psychopathology and the developing brain*. New York: Oxford University Press.

Ronningstam, E. F. (2005). Narcissistic personality disorder: A review. In M. Maj, H. S. Akiskal, J. E. Mezzich, A. Okasha, (Eds.), *Evidence and experience in psychiatry. Vol. 8: Personality disorders* (pp. 277–27). New York: Wiley.

Ronningstam, E. F. (2009). Narcissistic personality disorder: Facing DSM-V. *Psychiatr. Ann.*, 39, 111–21.

Rorvik, D. M. (1970, Apr. 7). Do drugs lead to violence? *Look*, 58–61.

Rosen, R. C. (1996). Erectile dysfunction: The medicalization of male sexuality. *Clin. Psychol. Rev.*, 16, 497–519.

Rosen, R. C., & Marin, H. (2003). Prevalence of antidepressant-associated erectile dysfunction. *J. Clin. Psychiat.*, 64, 5–10.

Rosenberg, J., & Rosenberg, S. (2006). *Community mental health: Challenges for the 21st Century*. New York: Routledge.

Rosenberg, L. A., Brown, J., & Singer, H. S. (1995). Behavioral problems and severity of tics. *J. Clin. Psychol.*, 51(6), 760–67.

Rosendal, M., Flemming, B., Sokolowski, I., Fink, P., Toft, T., & Olesen, F. (2005). A randomised controlled trial of brief training in assessment and treatment of somatisation: Effects on GPs' attitutes. *Family Practice*, 22, 419–27.

Rosenfarb, I. S., Goldstein, M. J., Mintz, J., & Nuechterlein, K. H. (1995). Expressed emotion and subclinical psychopathology observable within the transactions between schizophrenic patients and their family members. *J. Abn. Psychol.*, 104, 259–67.

Rosenman, R. H., Brand, R. J., Jenkins, C. D., Friedman, M., & Straus, R. (1975). Coronary heart disease in the Western Collaborative Group Study: Final follow-up experience of 8 1/2 years. *JAMA*, 233, 872–77.

Rosenstock, L., Cullen, M. R. & Fingerhut, M. (2005). Advancing worker health and safety in the developing world. *Journal of Occupational and Environmental Medicine*, 47(2), 132–136.

Rosenthal, D. (Ed.). (1963). *The Genain quadruplets*. New York: Basic Books.

Rosenzweig, M. R., Breedlove, S. M., & Leiman, A. L. (2002). *Biological psychology: An introduction to behavioral, cognitive, and clinical neuroscience* (3rd ed.). Sunderland, MA: Sinauer.

Rosler, A., & Witztum, E. (1998). Treatment of men with paraphilia with a long-acting analogue of gonadotropin-releasing hormone. *New Engl. J. Med.*, 338, 416–22.

Ross, C. A. (1997). *Dissociative identity disorder: Diagnosis, clinical features, and treatment of Multiple Personality* (2nd ed.). New York: Wiley.

Ross, C. A. (1999). Dissociative disorders. In T. Millon & P. Blaney (Eds.), *Oxford textbook of psychopathology* (pp. 466–81). New York: Oxford University Press.

Rossini, E. D., & Moretti, R. J. (1997). Thematic Apperception Test (TAT) interpretation: Practice recommendations from a survey of clinical psychology doctoral programs accredited by the American Psychological Association. *Profess. Psychol.: Res. Prac.*, 28(4), 393–98.

Rost, K., Kashner, T. M., & Smith, G. R. (1994). Effectiveness of psychiatric intervention with somatization disorder patients: Improved outcomes at reduced costs. *Gen. Hospit. Psychiat.*, 16, 381–87.

Rosten, R. A. (1961). *Some personality characteristics of compulsive gamblers*. Unpublished dissertation, UCLA.

Rotenstein, O. H., McDermut, W., Bergman, A., Young, D., Zimmerman, M., & Chelmisnki, I. (2007). The validity of DSM-IV passive-aggressive (negativistic) personality disorder. *J. Pers. Dis.*, 21(1), 28–41.

Rothbart, M. K., & Ahadi, S. A. (1994). Temperament and the development of personality. *J. Abn. Psychol.*, 103, 55–66.

Rothbart, M. K., & Bates, J. E. (2006). Temperament. In W. Damon, R. Lerner, & N. Eisenberg (Eds.), *Handbook of child psychology, Sixth edition: Social, emotional, and personality development (Vol. 3)*. 99–106. New York: Wiley.

Rothbart, M. K., Ahadi, S. A., & Evans, D. E. (2000). Temperament and personality: Origins and outcomes. *J. Pers. Soc. Psychol.*, 78, 122–35.

Rothbart, M. K., Derryberry, D., & Hershey, K. (2000). Stability of temperament in childhood: Laboratory infant assessment to parent report at seven years. In V. J. Molfese & D. L. Molfese (Eds.), *Temperament and personality development across the life span* (pp. 85–119). Mahwah, NJ: Erlbaum.

Rothbaum, B. O., & Foa, E. B. (1993). Subtypes of post-traumatic stress disorder and duration of symptoms. In J. R. T. Davidson and E. B. Foa (Eds.), *Posttraumatic stress disorder: DSM-IV and beyond* (pp., 23–35). Washington, DC: American Psychiatric Press.

Rothbaum, B. O., Anderson, P., Zimand, E., Hodges, L., Lang, D., & Wilson, J. (2006). Virtual reality exposure therapy and standard (in vivo) exposure therapy in the treatment of fear of flying. *Behav. Ther., 37*(1), 80–90.

Rothbaum, B. O., Hodges, L., Smith, S., Lee, J. H., & Price, L. (2000). A controlled study of virtual reality exposure therapy for the fear of flying. *J. Cons. Clin. Psychol., 68,* 1020–26.

Rothbaum, F., Nagaoka, R., & Ponte, I. C. (2006). Caregiver sensitivity in cultural context: Japanese and U.S. teachers' beliefs about anticipating and responding to children's needs. *Journal of Research in Childhood Education, 21*(1), 23–40.

Rothbaum, F., Weisz, J., Pott, M., Miyake, K., & Morelli, G. (2000). Attachment and culture security in the United States and Japan. *Amer. Psychol., 55,* 1093–1104.

Rothbaum, F., Weisz, J., Pott, M., Miyake, K., & Morelli, G. (2001). Deeper into attachment and culture. *Amer. Psychol., 56,* 827–29.

Rothman, R. B., Paratlla, J. S., Dersch, C. M., Carroll, F. I., Rice, K. C., & Baumann, M. H. (2000). Methamphetamine dependence: Medication development efforts based on the dual deficit model of stimulant addiction. *Ann. NY Acad. Sci., 914,* 71–81.

Rothschild, A. J., Langlais, P. J., Schatzberg, A. F., Walsh, F. X., Cole, J. O., & Bird, E. D. (1985). The effects of a single dose of dexamethasone on monoamine and metabolite levels in rat brains. *Life Sciences, 36,* 2491.

Rothschild, A. J., Williamson, D. J., Tohen, M. F., Schatzberg, A., Andersen, S. W., Van Campen, L. E., et al. (2004). A double-blind, randomized study of olanzapine and olanzapine/fluoxetine combination for major depression with psychotic features. *J. Clin. Psychopharm., 24*(4), 365–73.

Roy-Byrne, P. P., & Cowley, D. S. (2002). Pharmacological treatments for panic disorder, generalized anxiety disorder, specific phobia, and social anxiety disorder. In P. E. Nathan & J. M. Gorman (Eds.), *A guide to treatments that work* (2nd ed., pp. 337–66). New York: Oxford University Press.

Roy-Byrne, P. P., & Cowley, D. S. (2007). Pharmacological treatments for panic disorder, generalized anxiety disorder, specific phobia, and social anxiety disorder. In P. E. Nathan and J. M. Gorman (Eds.), *A guide to treatments that work.* New York: Oxford University Press, pp. 395–430.

Roy-Byrne, P. P., Craske, M. G., & Stein, M. B. (2006). Panic disorder. *Lancet, 368*(9540), 1023–32.

Roy-Byrne, P. P., Davidson, K. W., Kessler, R. C., Asmundson, G. J. G., Goodwin, R. D., Kubzansky, L., et al. (2008). Anxiety disorders and comorbid medical illness. *Gen. Hosp. Psychiat, 30*(3), 208–25. doi: 10.1016/j.genhosppsych.2007.12.006

Rozanski, A., Blumenthal, J. A., & Kaplan, J. (1999). Impact of psychological factors on the pathogenesis of cardiovascular disease and implications for therapy. *Circulation, 99,* 2192–217.

Rozin, P., Kabnick, K., Pete, E., Fischler, C., & Shields, C. (2003). The ecology of eating: Smaller portion sizes in France than in the United States help explain the French paradox. *Psychol. Sci., 14*(5), 450–54.

Rubio, R. G., & Lopez-Ibor, J. (2007). Generalized anxiety disorder: A 40-year follow-up study. *Acta Psychiat. Scand., 115,* 372–79.

Rück, C., Karlsson, A., Steele, D., Edman, G., Meyerson, B. A., Ericson, K., Nyman, H., et al. (2008). Capsulotomy for obsessive compulsive disorder. Long terms follow up of 25 patients. *Arch. Gen. Psychiat., 65,* 914–21.

Rucklidge, J. J. (2010). Gender differences in attention-deficit/hyperactivity disorder. *Psychiat. Clin. N. Amer., 33*(2), 357–73.

Rudolf, K. (2009). Adolescent depression. In I. H. Gotlib & C. L. Hammen (Eds.), *Handbook of depression and its treatment* (2nd ed.). New York: Guilford Press.

Rumbaut, R. (1985). Mental health and the refugee experience: A comparative study of Southeast Asian refugees. In T. C. Owan (Ed.), *Southeast Asian mental health: Treatment, prevention, services, training, and research* (pp. 443–86). Washington, DC: National Institute of Mental Health.

Runnheim, V. A., Frankenberger, W. R., & Hazelkorn, M. N. (1996). Medicating students with emotional and behavioral disorders and ADHD: A state survey. *Behav. Disord., 21*(4), 306–14.

Rurup, M. L., Muller, M. T., Onwuteaka-Philipsen, B. D., Van Der Heide, A., Van Der Wal, G., & Van Der Maas, P. J. (2005). Requests for euthanasia or physician- assisted suicide from older persons who do not have a severe disease: An interview study. *Psychol. Med., 35*(5), 665–71.

Ruscio, A. M., Brown, T. A., Chiu, W. T., Sareen, J., Stein, M. B., & Kessler, R. C. (2008). Social fears and social phobia in the USA: Results from the National Comorbidity Survey Replication. *Psychol. Med., 38*(1), 15–28. doi: 10.1017/s0033291707001699

Ruscio, A. M., Lane, M., Roy-Byrne, P., Stang, P. E., Stein, D. J., Wittchen, H.-U., & Kessler, R. C. (2005). Should excessive worry be required for a diagnosis of generalized anxiety disorder? Results from the US National Comorbidity Survey Replication. *Psychol. Med., 35,* 1761–72.

Ruscio, J., & Ruscio, A. M. (2000). Informing the continuity controversy: A taxometric analysis of depression. *J. Abn. Psychol., 109*(3), 473–87.

Ruscio, A. M., Stein, D. J., Chiu, W. T., & Kessler, R. C. (2010). The epidemiology of obsessive-compulsive disorder in the National Comorbidity Survey Replication. *Molec. Psychiat., 15*(1), 53–63. doi: 10.1038/mp.2008.94

Rush, B. (1812). *Medical inquiries and observations upon diseases of the mind.* Philadelphia: Grigg and Elliot.

Russell, G. F. M. (1997). The history of bulimia nervosa. In D. M. Garner & P. E. Garfinkel (Eds.), *Handbook of treatment for eating disorders* (2nd ed., pp. 11–24). New York: Guilford.

Russo, J., Vitaliano, P. P., Brewer, D. D., Katon, W., & Becker, J. (1995). Psychiatric disorders in spouse caregivers of care recipients with Alzheimer's disease and matched controls: A diathesis-stress model of psychopathology. *J. Abn. Psychol., 104,* 197–204.

Rutledge, P. C., & Sher, K. J. (2001). Heavy drinking from the freshman year into early young adulthood: The roles of stress, tension-reduction drinking motives, gender and personality. *J. Stud. Alcoh., 62*(4), 457–66.

Rutter, M. (1985). The treatment of autistic children. *Journal of Child Psychiatry, 26*(2), 193–214.

Rutter, M. (1987). Psychosocial resilience and protective mechanisms. *Amer. J. Orthopsychiat., 51,* 316–31.

Rutter, M. (1990). Psychosocial resilience and protective mechanisms. In J. Rolf, A. S. Masten, D. Cicchetti, K. H. Nuechterlein, & S. Weintraub (Eds.), *Risk and protective factors in the development of psychopathology.* New York: Cambridge University Press.

Rutter, M. (1991). Nature, nurture, and psychopathology: A new look at an old topic. *Develop. Psychopath., 3,* 125–36.

Rutter, M. (1996). Introduction: Concepts of antisocial behavior, of cause, and of genetic influences. In G. R. Bock & J. A. Goode (Eds.), *Genetics of criminal and anti-social behavior CIBA Foundation,* (Vol. 194, pp. 1–20). Chichester, England, and New York: Wiley.

Rutter, M. (2001). Resilience reconsidered: Conceptual considerations, empirical findings, and policy implications. In J. P. Shonkoff & S. J. Meisels (Eds.), *Handbook of early childhood intervention* (2nd ed., pp. 651–82). New York: Cambridge University Press.

Rutter, M. (2006a). *Genes and behavior: Nature-nurture interplay explained.* Oxford: Blackwell.

Rutter, M. (2006b). Review of attachment from infancy to adulthood. The major longitudinal studies. *Journal of Child Psychology and Psychiatry, 47*(9), 974–77.

Rutter, M. (2007). Resilience, competence, and coping. *Child Ab. Negl., 31*(3), 205–9.

Rutter, M. (2011) Gene-environment interactions in psychopathology. In K. Dodge & M. Rutter (Eds.), *Gene environment interactions in developmental psychopathology.*

Rutter, M. L., Kreppner, J. M., & O'Connor, T. G. (2001). Specificity and heterogeneity in children's responses to profound institutional privation. *Brit. J. Psychiat., 179,* 97–103.

Rutter, M., & Maughan, B. (1997). Psychosocial adversities in childhood and adult psychopathology. *J. Personal. Dis., 11,* 4–18.

Rutter, M., & Quinton, D. (1984). Parental psychiatric disorder: Effects on children. *Psychol. Med., 14,* 853–80.

Rutter, M., Andersen-Wood, L., Beckett, C., Bredenkamp, D., Castle, J., Dunn, J., Ehrich, K., Groothues, C., Harborne, A., Hay, D., Jewett, J., Keaveney, L., Kreppner, J., Messer, J., O'Connor, T., Quinton, D., & White, A. (1999). Developmental catch-up, and deficit, following adoption after severe global early privation. In S. J. Ceci & W. M. Williams (Eds.), *The nature-nurture debate: The essential readings* (pp. 107–33). Malden, MA: Blackwell.

Rutter, M., Kreppner, J., & Sonuga-Barke, E. (2009). Emanuel Miller lecture: Attachment insecurity, disinhibited attachment, and attachment disorders: Where do research findings leave the concepts? *J. Child Psychol. Psychiat., 50*(5), 529–43. doi:10.1111/j.1469-7610.2009.02042.x

Rutter, M., Silberg, J., & Simonoff, E. (1993). Whither behavioral genetics?—A developmental psychopathological perspective. In R. Plomin & G. McClearn (Eds.), *Nature, nurture, and psychology* (pp. 433–56). Washington, DC: American Psychological Association.

Rutz, W. (2001). Mental health in Europe—the World Health Organization's perspective: Diversities, possibilities, shortcomings and challenges. *Primary Care Psychiatry, 7*(3), 117–19.

Ryba, N. L., & Zapf, P. A. (2011). The influence of psychiatric symptoms and cognitive abilities on competence-related abilities. *International Journal of Forensic Mental Health, 10*(1), 29–40.

Ryan-Krause, P., Yetman, R. J., & Cromwell, P. F. (2010). Attention deficit hyperactivity disorder: Part I. *Journal of Pediatric Health Care, 24*(3), 194–98.

Ryder, A. G., & Bagby, R. M. (1999). Diagnostic viability of depressive personality disorder: Theoretical and conceptual issues. *J. Pers. Dis., 13*(2), 99–117.

Ryff, C. D., Keyes, C. L. M., & Hughes, D. L. (2003). Status inequalities, perceived discrimination, and eudiamonic well-being: Do the challenges of minority life hone purpose and growth? *J. Hlth. Soc. Beha., 44*(3), 275–91.

Sacco, P., Cunningham-Williams, R. M., Ostmann, E., & Spitznagel, E. L. (2008). The association between gambling pathology and personality disorders. *J. Psychiat. Res., 42*, 1122–30.

Sacks, F. M., Bray, G. A., Carey, V. J., Smith, S. R., Ryan, D. H., Anton, S. D., et al. (2009). Comparison of weight-loss diets with different compositions of fat, protein, and carbohydrates. *New Engl. J. Med., 360*, 9, February, 26, 859–73.

Sadock, B. J., Sadock, A. A., & Ruiz, P. (Eds.). *Kaplan and Sadock's Comprehensive Textbook of Psychiatry* (9th ed.). PA: Lippincott, Williams & Wilkins.

Sadock, B. J., & Sadock, V. A. (2003). *Kaplan and Sadock's synopsis of psychiatry*. Philadelphia: Lippincott, Williams, & Wilkins.

Safer, D. J. (1997a). Central stimulant treatment of childhood attention-deficit hyperactivity disorder: Issues and recommendations from a U.S. perspective. *CNS Drugs, 7*(4), 264–72.

Safer, D. J. (1997b). Self-reported suicide attempts by adolescents. *Ann. Clin. Psychiat., 9*(4), 263–69.

Safer, D. L., Telch, C. F., & Agras, W. S. (2001). Dialectical behavior therapy for bulimia nervosa. *Amer. J. Psychiat., 158*, 632–34.

Saha, S., Chant, D., Welham, J., & McGrath, J. (2005). A systematic review of the prevalence of schizophrenia. *PLoS Med., 2*, 413–33.

Sakai, Y., Kumano, H., Nishikawa, M., Sakano, Y., Kaiya, H., Imabayashi, E., et al. (2005). Cerebral glucose metabolism associated with a fear network in panic disorder. *Neuroreport: For Rapid Communication of Neuroscience Research, 16*(9), 927–31.

Sakamoto, N., Martin, R. G., Kumano, H., Kuboki, T., & Al-Adawi, S. (2005). Hikikomori, is it a culture-reactive or culture-bound syndrome? Nidotherapy and a clinical vignette from Oman. *International Journal of Psychiatry in Medicine, 35*(2), 191–198.

Saks, E. R. (2004). Refusing care: Forced treatment and the use of psychiatric advance directives. *J. Foren. Psychol. Pract., 4*(4), 35–50.

Salekin, R. T. (2006). Psychopathy in children and adolescents: Key issues in conceptualization and assessment. In C. J. Patrick (Ed.), *Handbook of the psychopathy*. (pp. 389–414). New York: Guilford Press.

Salekin, R., Neumann, C., Leistico, A., & Zalot, A. (2004). Psychopathy in youth and intelligence: An investigation of Cleckley's hypothesis. *J. Clin. Child. Adol. Psych., 33*, 731–42.

Salem-Pickartz, J., & Donnelly, J. (2007). The Family as a source of strength and life skill: The role of authoritative parenting in building resilience. In A. S. Loveless & T. B. Holman (Eds.), *The family in the new millennium: World voices supporting the "natural" clan* (Vol. 1, pp. 363–368). Westport, CT: Praeger Publishers/Greenwood Publishing Group.

Salkovskis, P. M. (1989). Cognitive-behavioural factors and the persistence of intrusive thoughts in obsessional problems. *Behav. Res. Ther., 27*, 677–82.

Salkovskis, P. M., & Bass, C. (1997). Hypochondriasis. In D. M. Clark & C. G. Fairburn (Eds.), *Science and practice of cognitive behaviour therapy* (pp. 313–39). Oxford: Oxford University Press.

Salkovskis, P. M., & Kirk, J. (1997). Obsessive-compulsive disorder. In D. M. Clark & C. G. Fairburn (Eds.), *Science and practice of cognitive behaviour therapy* (pp. 179–208). New York: Oxford University Press.

Salkovskis, P. M., Clark, D. M., & Gelder, M. G. (1996). Cognition-behavior links in the persistence of panic. *Behav. Res. Ther., 34*(5/6), 453–58.

Salkovskis, P. M., Wroe, A. L., Gledhill, A., Morrison, N., Forrester, E., Richards, C., Reynolds, M., & Thorpe, S. (2000). Responsibility attitudes and interpretations are characteristic of obsessive compulsive disorder. *Behav. Res. Ther., 38*, 347–72.

Salkovskis, P. M., & Wahl, K. (2003). Treating obsessional problems using cognitive behavioral therapy. In M. Reinecke & D.A. Clark (Eds.), *Cognitive therapy across the life span: Theory, research, and practice* (pp. 138–171). Cambridge, UK: Cambridge University Press.

Salkovskis, P. M., & Warwick, M. C. (2001). Meaning, misinterpretations, and medicine: A cognitive-behavioral approach to understanding health anxiety and hypochondriasis. In V. Starcevic & D. Lipsitt (Eds.), *Hypochondriasis: Modern perspectives on an ancient malady* (pp. 202–22). New York: Oxford University Press.

Salmivalli, C. (2010). Bullying and the peer group: A review. *Aggression and Violent Behavior, 15*(2), 112–20. doi:10.1016/j.avb.2009.08.007

Salmivalli, C., & Nieminen, E. (2002). Proactive and reactive aggression among school bullies, victims, and bully victims. *Aggr. Behav., 28*, 30–44.

Salmivalli, C., & Voeten, M. (2004). Connections between attitudes, group norms, and behavior in bullying situations. *International Journal of Behavioral Adjustment, 28*(3), 246–58.

Salter, A. (1949). *Conditioned reflex therapy*. New York: Creative Age Press.

Samborn, R. (1994, Jul. 4). Priests playing hardball to battle abuse charges. *National Law Journal, 16*, A1.

Samelson, F. (1980). J. B. Watson's Little Albert, Cyril Burt's twins, and the need for a critical science. *Amer. Psychol., 35*, 619–25.

Sampson, R. J., Morenoff, J. D., & Gannon-Rowley, T. (2002). Assessing "neighborhood effects": Social processes and new directions in research. *Ann. Rev. Soc., 28*, 443–78.

Samuel, D. B., & Widiger, T. A. (2006). Clinicians' judgments of clinical utility: A comparison of the DSM-IV and five-factor models. *J. Abn. Psychol., 115*(2), 298–308.

Samuel, D. B., & Widiger, T. a. (2011). Conscientiousness and obsessive-compulsive personality disorder. *Personality Disorders: Theory, Research, and Treatment, 2*(3), 161–74. doi:10.1037/a0021216

Samuels, J., Shugart, Y. Y., Grados, M. A., Willour, V. L., Bienvenu, O. J., Greenberg, B. D., et al. (2007). Significant linkage to compulsive hoarding on chromosome 14 in families with obsessive-compulsive disorder: Results from the OCD Collaborative Genetics Study. *Amer. J. Psychiat., 164*(3), 493–99.

Sanborn, K., & Hayward, C. (2003). Hormonal changes at puberty and the emergence of gender differences in internalizing disorders. In C. Hayward (Ed.), *Gender differences at puberty* (pp. 29–58). Cambridge: Cambridge University Press.

Sanchez, L., & Turner, S. M. (2003, Feb.). Practicing psychology in the era of managed care: Implications

for practice and training. *Amer. Psychol., 58*(2), 116–29.

Sanders, A. R., Duan, J., Levinson, D. F., Shi, J., He, D. Hou, C., Burrell, G. J., Rice, J. P., et al. (2008). No significant association of 14 candidate genes with schizophrenia in a large European ancestry sample: Implications for psychiatric genetics. *Amer. J. Psychiat., 165*, 497–506.

Sanderson, W. C., Rapee, R. M., & Barlow, D. H. (1989). The influence of an illusion of control on panic attacks induced via inhalation of 5.5%-carbondioxide-enriched air. *Arch. Gen. Psychiat., 46*, 157–62.

Sandfort, T. G. M., de Graaf, R., Bijl, R. V., & Schnabel, P. (2001). Same-sex sexual behavior and psychiatric disorders: Findings from the Netherlands mental health survey and incidence study (NEMESIS). *Arch. Gen. Psychiat., 58*, 85–91.

Sandnabba, N. K., Santtila, P., Alison, L., & Nordling, N. (2002). Demographics, sexual behaviour, family background and abuse experiences of practitioners of sadomasochistic sex: A review of recent research. *Sexual and Relationship Therapy, 17*(1), 39–55.

Sandweiss, D. A., Slymen, D. J., Leard-Mann, C. A., Smith, B., White, M. R., Boyko, E. J., et al. (2011). Preinjury psychiatric status, injury severity, and post-deployment posttraumatic stress disorder. *Arch. Gen. Psychiat., 68*, 496–504.

Sanislow, C. A., Little, T. D., Ansell, E. B., Grilo, C. M., Daversa, M., Markowitz, J. C., Pinto, A., et al. (2009). Ten-year stability and latent structure of the DSM-IV schizotypal, borderline, avoidant, and obsessive-compulsive personality disorders. *J. Abn. Psychol., 118*(3), 507–19. doi:10.1037/a0016478

Sansone, R., Schumacher, D., Wiederman, M., & Routsong-Weichers, L. (2008). The prevalence of binge eating disorder and borderline symptomatology among gastric surgery patients. *Eating Behaviors, 9*(2), 197–202.

Sapienza, J. K., & Masten, A. S. (2011). Understanding and promoting resilience in children and youth. *Current Opinion in Psychiatry, 24*(4), 267–73.

Sapolsky, R. M. (2000). Glucocorticoids and hippocampal atrophy in neuropsychiatric disorders. *Arch. Gen. Psychiat., 57*, 925–35.

Sar, V., Akyüz, G., Kundakçi, T., Kiziltan, E., & Dogan, O. (2004). Childhood trauma, dissociation, and psychiatric comorbidity in patients with conversion disorder. *Amer. J. Psychiat., 161*(12), 2271–76

Sarbin, T. R. (1997). On the futility of psychiatric diagnostic manuals (DSMs) and the return of personal agency. *App. Prev. Psychol., 6*(4), 233–43.

Sartorius, N., Kaelber, C. T., Cooper, J. E., Roper, M. T., Rae, D. S., Gulbinat, W., Ustun, T. B., & Regier, D. A. (1993). Progress toward achieving a common language in psychiatry: Results from the field trial of the clinical guidelines accompanying the WHO classification of mental and behavioral disorders in ICD-10. *Arch. Gen. Psychiat., 50*, 115–24.

Sarwer, D. B., Brown, G. K., & Evans, D. L. (2007). Cosmetic breast augmentation and suicide. *Amer. J. Psychiat., 164*, 1006–13.

Sarwer, D. B., Gibbons, L. M., & Crerand, C. E. (2004). Treating body dysmorphic disorder with cognitive-behavior therapy. *Psychiat. Ann., 34*, 934–41.

Sashidharan, S. P. (1993). Afro-Caribbeans and schizophrenia: The ethnic vulnerability hypothesis reexamined. *Int. Rev. Psychiat., 5*, 129–43.

Satterfield, J. H., Faller, K. J., Crinella, F. M., Schell, A. M., Swanson, J. M., & Homer, L. D. (2007). A 30-year prospective follow-up study of hyperactive boys with conduct problems: Adult criminality.

J. Amer. Acad. Child Adoles. Psychiat., Vol 46(5), 601–10.

Satz, P., et al. (1997). Mild head injury in children and adolescents: A review of studies (1970–1995). *Psychol. Bull., 122*(2), 107–31.

Sauter, S. L., Murphy, L. R., & Hurrell, J. J., Jr. (1990). Prevention of work-related psychological disorders: A national strategy proposed by the National Institute for Occupational Safety and Health (NIOSH). *Amer. Psychol., 45*(10), 1146–58.

Savin-Williams, R., C. (2006). Who's gay? Does it matter? *Curr. Dis. Psychol. Sci., 15*(1), 40–44.

Saxena, S. (2007). Is compulsive hoarding a genetically and neurobiologically discrete syndrome? Implications for diagnostic classification. *Amer. J. Psychiat., 164*(3), 380–384.

Saxena, S. (2008). Recent advances in compulsive hoarding. *Curr. Psychiat. Reports, 10*(4), 297–303. doi: 10.1007/s11920-008-0048-8

Saxena, S., & Rauch, S. L. (2000). Functional neuroimaging and the neuroanatomy of obsessive-compulsive disorder. *Psychiat. Clin. N. Amer., 23*(3), 563–586.

Saxena, S., Brody, A. L., Ho, M. L., Alborzian, S., Maidment, K. M., Zohrabi, N., et al. (2002). Differential cerebral metabolic changes with paroxetine treatment of obsessive-compulsive disorder vs major depression. *Arch. Gen. Psychiat., 59*, 250–61.

Saxena, S., & Feusner, J. D. (2006). Toward a neurobiology of body dysmorphic disorder. *Primary Psychiatry, 13*(7), 41–48.

Saxena, S., Gorbis, E., O'Neill, J., Baker, S. K., Mandelkern, M. A., Maidment, K. M., et al. (2009). Rapid effects of brief intensive cognitive-behavioral therapy on brain glucose metabolism in obsessive-compulsive disorder. *Molec. Psychiat., 14*(2), 197–205. doi: 10.1038/sj.mp.4002134

Saykin, A. J., Wishart, H. A., Rabin, L. A., Santulli, R. B., Flashman, L. A., West, J. D., McHugh, T. L., & Mamourian, A. C. (2006). Older adults with cognitive complaints show brain atrophy similar to that of amnestic MCI. *Neurology, 67*(5), 834–42.

Sbrocco, T., & Barlow, D. H. (1996). Conceptualizing the cognitive component of sexual arousal: Implications for sexuality research and treatment. In Salkovskis, P. M. (Ed.), *Frontiers of cognitive therapy* (pp. 419–49). New York: Guilford.

Scales, P. C. & Leffert, N. (1999). *Developmental assets: A synthesis of the scientific research on adolescent development.* Minneapolis, MN, US: Search Institute.

Scannell, E. D., Quirk, M. M., Smith, K., Maddern, R., & Dickerson, M. (2000). Females' coping styles and control over poker machine gambling. *Journal of Gambling Studies, 16*(4), 417–32.

Scepkowski, L. A., Wiegel, M., Bach, A. K., Weisberg, R. B., Brown, T. A., & Barlow, D. H. (2004). Attributions for sexual situations in men with and without erectile disorder: Evidence from a sex-specific attributional style measure. *Arch. Sex. Behav., 33*, 559–69.

Schacter, D. L., Norman, K. A., & Koutstaal, W. (2000). The cognitive neuroscience of constructive memory. In D. F. Bjorklund (Ed.), *False-memory creation in children and adults* (pp. 129–68). Mahwah, NJ: Erlbaum.

Schaefer, C. E. (2010). *Play therapy for preschool children.* Washington, DC: American Psychological Association.

Schafer, I., & Najavits, L. M. (2007). Clinical challenges in the treatment of patients with posttraumatic stress disorder and substance abuse. *Current Opinions in Psychiatry, 20*, 614–18.

Schapiro, M. B., & Rapoport, S. I. (1987). "Pathological similarities between Alzheimer's disease and Down's syndrome: Is there a genetic link?": Commentary. *Integr. Psychiat., 5*, 167–69.

Scharnberg, K. (2007, September 1). As bullies go online, schools crack down. *Chicago Tribune*, pp. 1.1, 1.20.

Scheid, T. L. (2010). Consequences of managed care for mental health providers. In T. L. Scheid & T. N. Brown (Eds.), *A handbook for the study of mental health: Social contexts, theories, and systems* (2nd ed., pp. 529–47). New York: Cambridge University Press.

Scher, C. D., Ingram, R. E., & Segal, Z. V. (2005). Cognitive reactivity and vulnerability: Empirical evaluation of construct activation and cognitive diatheses in unipolar depression. *Clin. Psychol. Rev., 25*, 487–510.

Scherrer, J. F., Xian, H., Kapp, J. M. K., Waterman, B., Shah, K. R., Volberg, R., & Eisen, S. A. (2007). Association between exposure to childhood and lifetime traumatic events and lifetime pathological gambling in a twin cohort. *J. Nerv. Ment. Dis., 195*(1), 72–78.

Scheurich, A. (2005). Neuropsychological functioning and alcohol dependence. *Cur. Opin. Psychiat., 18*(3), 319–23.

Schienle, A., Schafer, A., Walter, B., Stark, R., & Vaitl, D. (2005). Elevated disgust sensitivity in blood phobia. *Cognition & Emotion, 19*(8), 1229–41.

Schildkraut, J. J. (1965). The catecholamine hypothesis of affective disorders: A review of supporting evidence. *Amer. J. Psychiat., 122*, 509–22.

Schilt, T., Koeter, M. W., Smal, J. P., Gouwetor, M. N., van den Brink, W., & Schmand, B. (2010). Long-term neuropsychological effects of ecstasy in middle-aged ecstasy/polydrug users. *Psychopharmacology, 207*(4), 583–91.

Schiltz, K., Witzel, J., Northoff, G., Zierhut, K., Gubka, U., Fellmann, H., Kaufmann, J., Tempelmann, C., Wiebking, C., & Bogerts, B. (2007). Brain pathology in pedophilic offenders. *Arch. Gen. Psychiat., 64, 737–46.*

Schleifer, S. J., Keller, S. E., & Stein, M. (1985). Central nervous system mechanisms and immunity: Implications for tumor responses. In S. M. Levy (Ed.), *Behavior and cancer* (pp. 120–33). San Francisco: Jossey-Bass.

Schleifer, S. J., Keller, S. E., Bond, R. M., Cohen, J., & Stein, M. (1989). Major depressive disorder and immunity: Role of age, sex, severity, and hospitalization. *Arch. Gen. Psychiat., 46*, 81–87.

Schliebs, R., & Arendt, T. (2006). The significance of the cholinergic system in the brain during aging and Alzheimer's disease. *Journal of Neural Transmission, 113*, 1625–44.

Schmahl, C., & Bremner, J. D. (2006). Neuroimaging in borderline personality disorder. *J. Psychiat. Res., 40*(5), 419–27.

Schmahl, C., Greffrath, W., Baumgartner, U., Schlereth, T., Magerl, W., Philipsen, A., et al. (2004). Differential nociceptive deficits in patients with borderline personality disorder and self-injurious behavior: Laser-evoked potentials, spatial discrimination of noxious stimuli, and pain ratings. *Pain, 110*, 470–79.

Schmand, B., et al. (1997). The effects of intelligence and education on the development of dementia: A test of the brain reserve hypothesis. *Psychol. Med., 27*(6), 1337–44.

Schmidt, N. B., & Keough, M. E. (2010). Treatment of panic. *Annu. Rev. Clin. Psychol., 6*, 241–56. doi: 10.1146/annurev.clinpsy.121208.131317

Schmidt, N. B., & Lerew, D. R. (2002). Prospective evaluation of perceived control, predictability, and anxiety sensitivity in the pathogenesis of panic. *J. Psychopath. Behav. Assess., 24*(4), 207–14.

Schmidt, N. B., Lerew, D. R., & Jackson, R. J. (1997). The role of anxiety sensitivity in the pathogenesis of panic: Prospective evaluation of spontaneous panic attacks during acute stress. *J. Abn. Psychol., 106*, 355–65.

Schmidt, N. B., Richey, J. A., Buckner, J. D., & Timpano, K. R. (2009). Attention training for generalized social anxiety disorder. *J. Abn. Psychol., 118*(1), 5–14. doi: 10.1037/a0013643

Schmidt, N. B., Richey, J. A., Maner, J. K., & Woolaway-Bickel, K. (2006). Differential effects of safety in extinction of anxious responding to a CO-sub-2 challenge in patients with panic disorder. *J. Abn. Psych., 115*(2), 341–50.

Schmit, D. (2005). Re-visioning antebellum American psychology: The dissemination of Mesmerism, 1836–1854. *History of Psychology, 43, 403–434.*

Schmitz, J. M., Stotts, A. L., Sayre, S.L., DeLaune, K. A., & Grabowski, J. (2004). Treatment of cocaine-alcohol dependence with naltrexone and relapse prevention therapy. *Journal on Addictions, 13*(4), 333–41.

Schneider, F., Backes, V., & Mathiak, K. (2009, Nov.). Brain imaging: On the way toward a therapeutic discipline. *Eur. Arch. Psychiat. Clin. Neurosci., 259*(Suppl 2), S143–47.

Schneider, M. L. (1992). The effects of mild stress during pregnancy on birthweight and neuromotor maturation in Rhesus monkey infants *(Macaca mulatta). Inf. Behav. Develop., 15*, 389–403.

Schneider, R. H., Alexander, C. N., Staggers, F., Orme-Johnson, D. W., Rainforth, M., Salerno, J. W., Shappard, W., Castillo Richmond, A., Barnes, V. A., & Nidich, S. I. (2005). A randomized controlled trial of stress reduction in African-Americans treated for hypertension for over one year. *American Journal of Hypertension, 18*, 88–98.

Schnurr, P. P., Friedman, M. J., Engel, C. C., Foa, E. B., Shea, M. T., Chow, B. K., et al., (2007). Cognitive behavioral therapy for posttraumatic stress disorder in women. A randomized clinical trial. *JAMA, 297*, 820–830.

Schoeneman, T. J. (1984). The mentally ill witch in textbooks of abnormal psychology: Current status and implications of a fallacy. *Profess. Psychol., 15*(3), 299–314.

Schonberg, M. A., & Shaw, D. S. (2007). Risk factors for boy's conduct problems in poor and lower-middle-class neighborhoods. *Journal of Abnormal Child Psychology: An official publication of the International Society for Research in Child and Adolescent Psychopathology, 35*(5), 759–72.

Schopler, E., Yirmiya, N., Shulman, C., & Marcus, L. M. (Eds.). (2001). *The research basis for autism intervention.* Boston: Kluwer.

Schreiber, F. R. (1973). *Sybil.* New York: Warner Paperback.

Schroeder, C. S., & Gordon, B. N. (2002). *Assessment and treatment of childhood problems: A clinician's guide* (2nd ed.). New York: Cambridge University Press.

Schudson, M. (1995). Collective memory and modes of distortion. In D. Schachter, J. Coyle, L. Sullivan, M. Mesulam, & G. Fishbach (Eds.), *Memory distortion: Interdisciplinary perspectives.* Cambridge: Harvard University Press.

Schulsinger, F., Knop, J., Goodwin, D. W., Teasdale, T. W., & Mikkelsen, U. (1986). A prospective study of young men at high risk for alcoholism. *Arch. Gen. Psychiat., 43*, 755–60.

Schulte-Koerne, G. (2001). Genetics of reading and spelling disorder. *Journal of Child Psychology & Psychiatry & Allied Disciplines, 42*(8), 985–97.

Schultz, S. K. (2008). Atypical antipsychotic medications in Alzheimer's disease: Effectiveness versus expectations. *Am. J. Psychiat., 165,* 787–89.

Schulz, R., Drayer, R. A., & Rollman, B. L. (2002). Depression as a risk factor for the non-suicide mortality in the elderly. *Biol. Psychiat., 52*(3), 205–25.

Schulze-Rauschenbach, S. C., Harms, U., Schlaepfer, T. E., Maier, W., Falkai, P., & Wagner, M. (2005). Distinctive neurocognitive effects of repetitive transcranial magnetic stimulation and electroconvulsive therapy in major depression. *Brit. J. Psychiat., 186,* 410–16.

Schupf, N., Kapell, D., Lee, J. H., Ottman, R., & Mayeux, R. (1994). Increased risk of Alzheimer's disease in mothers of adults with Down's syndrome. *Lancet, 344*(8919), 353–56.

Schupf, N., Kapell, D., Nightingale, B., Lee, J. H., Mohlenhoff, J., Bewley, S., Ottman, R., & Mayeux, R. (2001). Specificity of the fivefold increase in AD in mothers with Down syndrome. *Neurology, 57*(6), 979–84.

Schupp, H. T., Öhman, A., Junghofer, M., Weike, A. I., Stockburger, J., & Hamm, A. O. (2004). The facilitated processing of threatening faces: An ERP analysis. *Emotion, 4*(2), 189–200.

Schvey, N. A., Puhl, R. M., & Brownell, K. D. (2011). The impact of weight stigma on caloric consumption. *Obesity.*

Schwarte, A. R. (2008). Fragile X syndrome. *School Psychology Quarterly, 23*(2), 290–300.

Schwartz, B. G., Mayeda, G. S., Burstein, S., Economides, C., & Kloner, R. A. (2010). When and why do heart attacks occur? Cardiovascular triggers and their potential role. *Hosp. Prac. (Minneap). 38,* 144–52.

Schwartz, C. E., Snidman, N., & Kagan, J. (1996). Early childhood temperament as a determinant of externalizing behavior in adolescence. *Develop. Psychopath., 8*(3), 527–37.

Schwartz, C. E., Snidman, N., & Kagan, J. (1999). Adolescent social anxiety as an outcome of inhibited temperament in childhood. *J. Amer. Acad. Child Adoles. Psychiat., 38,* 1008–15.

Schwartz, D., Dodge, K. A., & Coie, J. D. (1993). The emergence of chronic peer victimization in boys' play groups. *Child Develop., 64,* 1755–72.

Schwinn, T. M., Schinke, S. P., & Di Noia, J. (2010). Preventing drug abuse among adolescent girls: Outcome data from an Internet - based intervention. *Prevention Science, 11*(1), 24–32.

Scott, C. L. (Ed.). (2010). *Handbook of correctional mental health* (2nd ed.). Arlington, VA: American Psychiatric Publishing, Inc.

Scott, C. L., & Holmberg, T. (2003). Castration of sex offenders: Prisoner's rights versus public safety. *J. Amer. Acad. Psychiat. Law, 31,* 502–9.

Scott, C. L., Quanbeck, C. D., & Resnick, P. J. Assessment of dangerousness. In R. E. Hales, S. C. Yudofsky, & G. O. Gabbard (Eds.), *The American Psychiatric Publishing textbook of psychiatry* (5th ed.), (pp. 1655–72).

Scott, J., Varghese, D., & McGrath, J. (2010). As the twig is bent, the tree inclines: Adult mental health consequences of childhood adversity. *Arch. Gen. Psychiat., 67*(2), 111–12.

Scott, M. J., & Stradling, S. G. (2006). *Counseling for posttraumatic stress disorder* (3rd Ed.). Thousand Oaks, CA: Sage Publications

Scott, N., Lakin, C., & Larson, S. A. (2008). The 40th anniversary of deinstitutionalization in the United States: Decreasing state institutional populations, 1967–2007. *Trends and Milestones, 46,* 402–5.

Scull, A. (1996). *The most solitary of afflictions: Madness and society in Britain.* New Haven, CT: Yale University Press.

Scull, A. (2005). *Madhouse: A tragic tale of megalomania and modern medicine.* New Haven: Yale University Press.

Seal, K. H., Metzler, T. J., Gima, K. S., Bertenthal, D., Maguen, S., & Marmar, C. R. (2009). Trends and risk factors for mental health diagnoses among Iraq and Afghanistan veterans using Department of Veterans Affairs health care, 2002–2008.

Searles, J. S. (1991). The genetics of alcoholism: Impact on family and sociological models of addiction. *Family Dynamics of Addiction Quarterly, 1,* 8–21.

Sears, S. R., & Stanton, A. L. (2001). Physician-assisted dying: Review of issues and roles for health psychologists. *Hlth. Psychol., 20*(4), 302–10.

Seeley, M. F. (1997). The role of hotlines in the prevention of suicide. In R. W. Maris, M. M. Silverman, & S. S. Canetton (Eds.), *Review of suicidology, 1997* (pp. 251–70). New York: Guilford.

Seeman, P. (2011). All roads to schizophrenia lead to dopamine supersensitivity and elevated dopamine D2high receptors. *CNS Neuroscience and therapeutics, 17,* 118–32.

Segal, N.L. (2005). Twins reared apart design. In B. Everitt & D.C. Howell (Eds.) *Encyclopedia of statistics in behavioral science* (pp. 2072–2076). Chester, UK: John Wiley & Sons.

Segal, Z. V., Williams, J. M. G., & Teasdale, J. T. (2002). *Mindfulness-based cognitive therapy for depression: A new approach to preventing relapse.* New York: Guilford.

Segerstrom, S. C., & Miller, G. E. (2004). Psychological stress and the human immune system: A meta-analytic study of 30 years of inquiry. *Psychol. Bull., 130,* 610–30.

Segraves, R. T., Clayton, A., Croft, H., Wolf, A., & Warnock, J. (2004). Bupropion sustained release for the treatment of hypoactive sexual desire disorder in premenopausal women. *J. Clin. Psychopharm., 24,* 339–42.

Segraves, R., & Woodard, T. (2006). Female hypoactive sexual desire disorder: History and current status. *Journal of Sexual Medicine, 3,* 408–18.

Segraves, T., & Althof, S. (2002). Psychotherapy and pharmacotherapy for sexual dysfunctions. In P. E. Nathan & J. M. Gorman (Eds.), *A guide to treatments that work* (pp. 497–524). New York: Oxford University Press.

Seidman, E. (2003). Fairweather and ESID: Contemporary impact and a legacy for the twenty-first century. *Am. J. Community Psychol., 32*(3–4), 371–75.

Seifert, K. (2003). Childhood trauma: Its relationship to behavioral and psychiatric disorders. *Forensic Examiner, 12,* 27–33.

Selemon, L. D. (2004). Increased cortical neuronal density in schizophrenia. *Amer. J. Psychiat., 161,* 9.

Selemon, L. D., Rajkowska, G., & Goldman-Rakic, P. S. (1995). Abnormally high neuronal density in the schizophrenic cortex. *Arch. Gen. Psychiat., 52,* 805–18.

Seligman, M. E. P. (1971). Phobias and preparedness. *Behav. Ther., 2,* 307–20.

Seligman, M. E. P. (1974). Depression and learned helplessness. In R. J. Friedman & M. M. Katz (Eds.), *The psychology of depression: Contemporary theory and research.* Washington, DC: Hemisphere.

Seligman, M. E. P. (1975). *Helplessness: On depression, development, and death.* San Francisco: Freeman.

Seligman, M. E. P. (1990). Why is there so much depression today? The waxing of the individual and the waning of the commons. In R. E. Ingram (Ed.), *Contemporary psychological approaches to depression.* New York: Plenum.

Seligman, M. E. P. (1998). Afterword—A plea. In P. E. Nathan & J. M. Gorman (Eds.), *A guide to treatments that work* (pp. 568–71). New York: Oxford University Press.

Seligman, M. E. P., & Binik, Y. (1977). The safety signal hypothesis. In H. Davis & H. M. B. Hurwitz (Eds.), *Operant-Pavlovian interactions* (pp. 165–88). Hillsdale, NJ: Erlbaum.

Selling, L. S. (1943). *Men against madness.* New York: Garden City Books.

Selye, H. (1956). *The stress of life.* New York: McGraw-Hill.

Selye, H. (1976). *Stress in health and disease.* Woburn, MA: Butterworth.

Seminowicz, D. A., & Davis, K. D. (2006). Cortical responses to pain in healthy individuals depends on pain catastrophizing. *Pain, 120,* 297–306.

Senft, R. A., Polen, M. R., Freeborn, D. K., & Hollis, J. F. (1997). Brief intervention in a primary care setting for hazardous drinkers. *Am. J. Prev. Med., 13*(6), 464–70.

Sentse, M., Lindenberg, S., Omvlee, A., Ormel, J., & Veenstra, R. (2010). Rejection and acceptance across contexts: Parents and peers as risks and buffers for early adolescent psychopathology. The TRAILS study. *J. Abn. Child Psychol., 38*(1), 119–30. doi:10.1007/s10802-009-9351-z

Serbin, L. A., & Karp, J. (2004). The intergenerational transfer of psychosocial risk: Mediators of vulnerability and resilience. *Annu. Rev. Psychol., 55,* 333–63.

Sernyak, D. L., Leslei, D. L., Alarcon, R. D., Losonczy, M. F., & Rosenheck, R. (2002). Association of diabetes mellitus with use of atypical neuroleptics in the treatment of schizophrenia. *Amer. J. Psychiat., 159,* 561–66.

Serper, M. R., Goldberg, B. R., & Salzinger, K. (2004). Behavioral assessment of psychiatric patients in restrictive settings. *Comprehensive handbook of psychological assessment* (Vol. 3, pp. 320–45). New York: John Wiley & Sons.

Seto, M. (2004). Pedophilia and sexual offenses against children. *Ann. Rev. Sex Res., 15,* 329–69.

Seto, M. C., & Barbaree, H. E. (1995). The role of alcohol in sexual aggression. *Clin. Psychol. Rev., 15*(6), 545–66.

Seto, M. C., Cantor, J. M., & Blanchard, R. (2006). Child pornography offenses area valid diagnostic indicator of pedophilia. *J. Abn. Psych., 115*(3), 610–15.

Seto, M. C., Lalumiere, M. L., & Kuban, M. (1999). The sexual preferences of incest offenders. *J. Abn. Psychol., 108,* 267–72.

Seto, M. C., Marques, J. K., Harris, G. T., Chaffin, M., Lalumiere, M. L., Miner, M. H., et al. (2008). Good science and progress in sex offender treatment are intertwined: A response to Marshall and Marshall (2007). *Sexual Abuse: Journal of Research and Treatment, 20*(3), 247–55.

Sewell, D. W., Jeste, D. V., Atkinson, J. H., Heaton, R. K., Hesselink, J. R., Wiley, C., Thal, L., Chandler, J. L., & Grant, I. (1994). HIV-associated psychosis: A study of 20 cases. *Amer. J. Psychiat., 151*(2), 237–42.

Shadish, W. R., Matt, G. E., Navarro, A. M., & Phillips, G. (2000). The effects of psychological therapies under clinically-representative conditions: A meta-analysis. *Psychol. Bull., 126,* 512–29.

Shadish, W. R., Montgomery, L. M., Wilson, P., Wilson, M. R., Bright, I., & Okwumabua, T. (1993). Effects of family and marital psychotherapies: A meta-analysis. *J. Cons. Clin. Psychol., 61*(6), 992–1002.

Shaffer, T. W., Erdberg, P., & Haroian, J. (1999). Current nonpatient data for the Rorschach, WAIS-R and MMPI-2. *J. Pers. Assess., 73,* 305–16.

Shafran, R., & Rachman, S. (2004). Thought-action fusion. *J. Beh. Ther. & Exper. Psychiat.*, 35(2), 87–107.

Shalev, A. Y. (2009). Posttraumatic stress disorder and stress-related disorders. *Psychiat. Clin. N. Amer.*, 32(3), 687–704.

Shalev, A. Y., & Freedman, S. (2005). PTSD following terrorist attacks: a prospective evaluation. *Amer. J. Psychiat.*, 162, 1118–91.

Shapiro, F. (1996). Eye movement desensitization and reprocessing (EMDR): Evaluation of controlled PTSD research. *J. Behav. Ther. Exper. Psychiat.*, 27, 209–18.

Sharif, Z., Bradford, D., Stroup, S., & Lieberman, J. (2007). Pharmacological treatment of schizophrenia. In P. E. Nathan and J. M. Gorman (Eds.), *A guide to treatments that work* (pp. 203–242). New York: Oxford University Press.

Sharkey, J. (1997, Sept. 28). You're not bad, you're sick. It's in the book. *New York Times*, pp. 1, 5.

Sharma, V., Burt, V. K., & Ritchie, H. L. (2009). Bipolar II postpartum depression: Detection, diagnosis, and treatment. *Amer. J. Psychiat.*, 166(11), 1217–21. doi: 10.1176/appi.ajp.2009.08121902

Sharp, S. I., McQuillin, A., & Gurling, H. M. (2009). Genetics of attention-deficit hyperactivity disorder (ADHD). *Neuropharmacol.*, 57(7–8), 590–600.

Shaw, J. A. (2003). Children exposed to war/terrorism. *Clin. Child Fam. Psych. Rev.*, 6(4), 237–46.

Shedler, J. (2010). The efficacy of psychodynamic psychotherapy. *Amer. Psychol.*, 65(2), 98–109. doi:10.1037/a0018378

Sheehan, D. Z. (1982). Panic attacks and phobias. *N. Engl. J. Med.*, 307, 156–58.

Sheehan, D. Z. (1983). *The anxiety disease*. New York: Bantam Books.

Sheets, E., & Craighead, W. E. (2007). Toward an empirically based classification of personality pathology. *Clin. Psychol. Sci. Prac.*, 14(2), 77–93.

Shekelle, R. B., Hulley, S. B., Neaton, J. D., Billings, J. D., Borhani, N. O., Gerace, T. A., Jacobs, D. R., Lasser, N. L., Mittlemark, M. B., & Stamler, J. (1985). The MRFIT behavior pattern study, II: Type A behavior and incidence of coronary heart disease. *Amer. J. Epidemiol.*, 122, 559–70.

Shelton, D. (2001). Emotional disorders in young offenders. *Journal of Nursing Scholarship*, 33(3), 259–63.

Shenton, M. E., Dickey, C. C., Frumin, M., & McCarley, R. W. (2001). A review of MRI findings in schizophrenia. *Schizophrenia Research*, 49, 1–52.

Sheps, D. S., McMahon, R. P., Becker, L., Carney, R. M., Freeland, K. E., Cohen, J. D., Sheffield, D., Goldberg, A. D., Ketterer, M. W., Pepine, C. J., Raczynski, J. M., Light, K., Krantz, D. S., Stone, P. H., Knatterud, G. L., & Kaufmann, P. G. (2002). Mental stress-induced ischemia and all-cause mortality in patients with coronary artery disease. *Circulation*, 105, 1700–84.

Sher, K. J., & Rutledge, P. C. (2007). Heavy drinking across the transition to college: Predicting first-semester heavy drinking from precollege variables. *Addictive Behaviors*, 32(4), 819–35.

Sher, K. J., Bartholow, B. D., & Nanda, S. (2001). Short and long term effects of fraternity and sorority membership on heavy drinking: A social norms perspective. *Psychol. Addict. Behav.*, 15, 42–51.

Sher, K. J., Wood, M. D., Wood, P. D., & Raskin, G. (1996). Alcohol outcome expectancies and alcohol use: A latent variable cross-lagged panel study. *J. Abn. Psychol.*, 105(4), 561–74.

Sher, K., Grekin, E. R., & Williams, N. A. (2005). The development of alcohol use disorders. *Ann. Rev. Clin. Psychol.*, 1(1), 493–523.

Shergill, S. S., Brammer, M. J., Williams, S. C. R., Murray, R. M., & McGuire, P. K. (2000). Mapping auditory hallucinations in schizophrenia using functional magnetic resonance imaging. *Arch. Gen. Psychiat.*, 57, 1033–38.

Sheung-Tak, C. (1996). A critical review of Chinese koro. *Cult., Med. Psychiat.*, 20, 67–82.

Shevlin, M., Dorahy, M., & Adamson, G. (2007). Childhood traumas and hallucinations: An analysis of the National Comorbidity Survey. *J. Psychiat. Res.*, 41, 222–28.

Shields, A., Ryan, R. M., & Cicchetti, D. (2001). Narrative representations of caregivers and emotion dysregulation as predictors of maltreated children's rejection by peers. *Develop. Psychol.*, 37, 321–37.

Shif, J. I. (2006). Conditions of successful task solving in high school students with mental retardation (on the material of grammar task). *Cultural-Historical Psychology*, 3, 93–100.

Shiffman, S., Ferguson, S. G., Gwaltney, C. J., Balabanis, M. H., & Shadel, W. G. (2006). Reduction of abstinence-induced withdrawal and craving using high-dose nicotine replacement therapy. *Psychopharmacology*, 184(3–4), 637–44.

Shifrin, J. G., Proctor, B. E., & Prevatt, F. F. (2010). Work performance differences between college students with and without ADHD. *J. Atten. Dis.*, 13(5), 489–96.

Shim, Y. S., & Mossis, J. C. (2011). Biomarkers predicting Alzheimer's disease in cognitively normal aging. *J. Clin. Neurol*, 7, 60–68.

Shin, L. M., & Liberzon, I. (2009). The neurocircuitry of fear, stress, and anxiety disorders. *Neuropsychopharmacol.*, 35(1), 169–91. doi: 10.1038/npp.2009.83

Shiner, R. L. (2009). The development of personality disorders: Perspectives from normal personality development in childhood and adolescence. *Develop. Psychopath.*, 21(3), 715–34. doi: 10.1017/S0954579409000406

Shively, C. A., Clarkson, T. B., & Kaplan, J. R. (1989). Social deprivation and coronary artery atherosclerosis in female cynomolgus monkeys. *Atherosclerosis*, 77, 69–76.

Shneidman, E. S. (1997). The suicidal mind. In R. W. Maris, M. M. Silverman, & S. S. Canetton (Eds.), *Review of suicidology, 1997* (pp. 22–41). New York: Guilford.

Shonk, S. M., & Cicchetti, D. (2001). Maltreatment, competency deficits, and risk for academic and behavioral maladjustment. *Develop. Psychol.*, 37, 3–17.

Shore, D. A. (Ed.). (2007). *The trust crisis in healthcare: Causes, consequences, and cures.* New York: Oxford University Press.

Short, K. H., & Johnston, C. (1997). Stress, maternal distress, and children's adjustment following immigration: The buffering role of social support. *J. Cons. Clin. Psychol.*, 65(3), 494–503.

Shoulson, I., & Young, A. B. (2011). Milestones in Huntington disease. *Movement Disorders*, 26, 1127–33.

Shrestha, N. M., Sharma, B., Van Ommeren, M., et al. (1998). Impact of torture on refugees displaced within the developing world: Symptomatology among Bhutanese refugees in Nepal. *JAMA*, 280, 443–48.

Shwalb, D. W., Nakazawa, J., & Shwalb, B. J. (Ed.). (2005). *Applied developmental psychology: Theory, practice, and research from Japan. Advances in applied developmental psychology.* Greenwich, CT: IAP Information Age Publishing.

Sibrava, N. J., & Borkovec, T.D. (2006). The cognitive avoidance theory of worry. In G. C. L. Davey & A. Wells (Eds.), *Worry and its psychological disorders: Theory, assessment, and treatment.* West Sussex, UK: John Wiley & Sons.

Siegel, B. (1996). *The world of the autistic child.* New York: Oxford University Press.

Siegel, B. (2003). *Helping children with autism learn.* New York: Oxford University Press.

Siegel, B. (2007). *Helping Children with Autism Learn Treatment Approaches for Parents and Professionals.* New York: Oxford University Press.

Siegler, R., DeLoache, J., & Eisenberg, N. (2003). *How children develop.* New York, NY, US: Worth Publishers.

Siever, L. J., Bernstein, D. P., & Silverman, J. M. (1995). Schizotypal personality disorder. In W. J. Livesley (Ed.), *The DSM-IV personality disorders.* (pp. 71–90). New York: Guilford.

Siever, L., & Davis, K. (2004). The pathophysiology of schizophrenia disorders: Perspectives from the spectrum. *Amer. J. Psychiat.*, 161, 398–413.

Sigal, J. J., Silver, D., Rakoff, V., & Ellin, B. (1973, Apr.). Some second-generation effects of survival of the Nazi persecution. *Amer. J. Orthopsychiat.*, 43(3), 320–27.

Sigman, M. (1996). Behavioral research in childhood autism. In M. F. Lenzenweger & J. L. Haugaard (Eds.), *Frontiers of developmental psychopathology* (pp. 190–208). New York: Oxford University Press.

Signorini, A., De Filippo, E., Panico, S., De Caprio, C., Pasanisi, F., & Contaldo, F. (2007). Long-term mortality in anorexia nervosa: A report after an 8-year follow-up and review of the most recent literature. *Eur. J. Clin. Nutr.*, 61, 119–22.

Silberg, J. L., Pickles, A., Rutter, M., Hewitt, J., Simonoff, E., Maes, H., Carbonneau, R., Murrelle, L., Foley, D., & Eaves, L. (1999). The influence of genetic factors and life stress on depression among adolescent girls. *Arch. Gen. Psychiat.*, 56, 225–32.

Silberg, J. L., Rutter, M., & Eaves, L. (2001). Genetic and environmental influences on the temporal association between earlier anxiety and later depression in girls. *Biol. Psychiat.*, 49, 1040–49.

Silberg, J., Rutter, M., Neale, M., & Eaves, L. (2001). Genetic moderation of environmental risk for depression and anxiety in adolescent girls. *Brit. J. Psychiat.*, 179, 116–21.

Silk, J. S., Nath, S. R., Siegel, L. R., & Kendall, P. C. (2000). Conceptualizing mental disorders in children: Where have we been and where are we going? *Develop. Psychopathol.*, 12, 713–35.

Silove, D., Steel, Z., McGorry, P., Miles, V., & Drobny, J. (2002). The impact of torture on post-traumatic stress symptoms in war-affected Tamil refugees and immigrants. *Compr. Psychiat.*, 43, 49–55.

Silver, E. (1995). Punishment or treatment? Comparing the lengths of confinement of successful and unsuccessful insanity defendants. *Law and Human Behavior*, 19(4), 375–88.

Silver, J. M., Hales, R. E., & Yudofsky, S. C. (2002). Neuropsychiatric aspects of traumatic brain injury. In S. Yudofsky & R. E. Hales (Eds.), *The American Psychiatric Association Publishing textbook of neuropsychiatry and clinical sciences* (4th ed., pp. 625–72). Washington, DC: American Psychiatric Publishing.

Silverman, J. A. (1997). Anorexia nervosa: Historical perspective on treatment. In D. M. Garner & P. E. Garfinkel (Eds.), *Handbook of treatment for eating disorders* (2nd ed., pp. 3–10). New York: Guilford.

Silverman, K., Higgins, S. T., Brooner, R. K., & Montoya, I. D. (1996). Sustained cocaine abstinence in methadone maintenance patients through voucher-based reinforcement therapy. *Arch. Gen. Psychiat., 53*(3), 409–15.

Silverman, M. M. (1997). Current controversies in suicidology. In R. W. Maris, M. M. Silverman, & S. S. Canetton (Eds.), *Review of suicidology, 1997* (pp. 1–21). New York: Guilford.

Silverstein, A. B., Legutki, G., Friedman, S. L., & Takayama, D. L. (1982). Performance of Down's syndrome individuals on the Stanford-Binet Intelligence Scale. *Amer. J. Ment. Def., 86*, 548–85.

Simeon, D., Gross, S., Guralnik, O., & Stein, D. J. (1997). Feeling unreal: 30 cases of DSM-III-R depersonalization disorder. *Amer. J. Psychiat., 154*, 1107–13.

Simeon, D., Guralnik, O., Schmeidler, J., & Knutelska, M. (2004). Fluoxetine therapy in depersonalization disorder: Randomised controlled trial. *Brit. J. Psychiat., 185*(1), 31–36.

Simeon, D., Kozin, D. S., Segal, K., Lerch, B., Dujour, R., & Giesbrecht, T. (2008). Deconstructing depersonalization: Further evidence for symptom clusters. *Psychiat. Res., 157*, 303–6. doi: 10.1016/j.psychres.2007.07.007

Simon, C. (1997). *Mad house.* New York: Doubleday.

Simon, G. E. (2002). Management of somatoform and factitious disorders. In P. E. Nathan & J. M. Gorman (Eds.), *A guide to treatments that work* (2nd ed., pp. 447–61). New York: Oxford University Press.

Simon, R. J., & Aaronson, D. E. (1988). *The insanity defense.* New York: Praeger.

Simon, W. (2009). Follow-up psychotherapy outcome of patients with dependent, avoidant and obsessive-compulsive personality disorders: A meta-analytic review. *Int. J. Psychiat. Clin. Prac., 13*(2), 153–65. doi: 10.1080/13651500802570972

Simonoff, E. (2001). Gene-environment interplay in oppositional defiant and conduct disorder. *Child Adoles. Psychiatr. Clin. N. Amer., 10*(2), 351–74.

Simons, R. C., & Hughes, C. C. (Eds.). (1985). *The culture bound syndromes.* Boston: Reidel.

Simons, R. L., Simons, L. G., Burt, C. H., Brody, G. H., & Cutrona, C. (2005). Collective efficacy, authoritative parenting and delinquency: A longitudinal test of a model integrating community- and family-level processes. *Criminology: An Interdisciplinary Journal, 43*(4), 989–1029.

Simpson, A. I. F., McKenna, B., Moskowitz, A., Skipworth, J., & Barry-Walsh, J. (2004). Homicide and mental illness in New Zealand, 1970–2000. *Brit. J. Psychiat., 185*(5), 394–98.

Simpson, G., & Tate, R. (2002). Suicidality after traumatic brain injury: Demographic, injury and clinical correlates. *Psychol. Med., 32*, 687–97.

Simpson, H. B., & Liebowitz, M. R. (2006) Best practice in treating obsessive-compulsive disorder: What the evidence says. In B. Rothbaum (Ed.), *Pathological anxiety: Emotional processing in etiology and treatment* (Pp. 147–65). Guilford Press.

Singer, D. G., & Singer, J. L. (Eds.). (2000). *Handbook of children and the media.* Thousand Oaks, CA: Sage.

Sinha, M. (2011). Resurgence of Koro: Perception of mankind. *Asian J. Psychiat., 4*(2), 153–54. doi: 10.1016/j.ajp.2011.04.005

Sink, M. (2004, Nov. 8). Drinking deaths draw attention to old campus problem. *New York Times*, p. A14.

Siqueland, L., Crits-Christoph, P., Gallop, R., Barber, J. P., Griffin, M. L., Thase, M. E., Daley, D., Frank, A., Gastfriend, D. R., Blaine, J., Connolly, M. B., & Gladis, M. (2002). Retention in psychosocial treatment of cocaine dependence: Predictors and impact on outcome. *American Journal on Addictions, 11*(1), 24–40.

Sjogren, M., & Blennow, K. (2005). The link between cholesterol and Alzheimer's disease. *World J. Biol. Psychiat., 6*(2), 85–97.

Skaer, T. L., Robinson, L. M., Sclar, D. A., & Galin, R. S. (2000). Treatment of depressive illness among children and adolescents in the United States. *Current Therapeutic Research, 61*, 692–705.

Skinner, B. F. (1951). How to teach animals. *Scientif. Amer., 185*, 26–29.

Skinner, B. F. (1990). Can psychology be a science of mind? *Amer. Psychol., 45*, 1206–10.

Skodol, A. E. (1993). Comorbidity of DSM-III-R eating disorders and personality disorders. *Int. J. Eat. Dis., 14*, 403–16.

Skodol, A. E., Clark, L. A., Bender, D. S., Krueger, R. F., Morey, L. C., Verheul, R., Alarcon, R. D., et al. (2011). Proposed changes in personality and personality disorder assessment and diagnosis for DSM-5 Part I: Description and rationale. *Personality Disorders: Theory, Research, and Treatment, 2*(1), 4–22. doi: 10.1037/a0021891

Skodol, A. E., Oldham, J. M., Hyler, S. E., & Stein, D. J. (1995). Patterns of anxiety and personality disorder comorbidity. *J. Psychiat. Res., 29*(5), 361–74.

Skodol, A., Gunderson, J., Pfohl, B., Widiger, T., Livesely, W. J., & Siever, L. (2002). The borderline diagnosis I: Psychopathology, comorbidity, and personality structure. *Biol. Psychiat., 51*, 936–50.

Skodol, A., Siever, L., Livesley, W. J., Gunderson, J., Pfohl, B., & Widiger, T. (2002). The borderline diagnosis II: Biology, genetics, and clinical course. *Biol. Psychiat., 51*, 951–63.

Slater, E. (1986). First person account: A parent's view on enforcing medication. *Schizo. Bull., 12*, 291–92.

Slavich, G. M., Monroe, S. M., & Gotlib, I. H. (2011). Early parental loss and depression history: Associations with recent life stress in major depressive disorder. *J. Psychiat. Res., 45*(9), 1146–52.

Slavkin, M. L., & Fineman, K. (2000). What every professional who works with adolescents needs to know about firesetters. *Adolescence, 35*(140), 759–73.

Slicker, E. K., & Thornberry, I. (2002). Older adolescent well-being and authoritative parenting. *Adolescent & Family Health, 3*(1), 9–19.

Sloman, L. (1991). Use of medication in pervasive developmental disorders. *Psychiat. Clin. N. Amer., 14*, 165–82.

Slovenko, R. (2001). The stigma of psychiatric discourse. *Journal of Psychiatry & Law, 29*, 5–29.

Slutske, W. S., Heath, A. C., Dinwiddie, S. H., Madden, P. A., & Bucholz, K. K. (1998). Common genetic risk factors for conduct disorder and alcohol dependence. *J. Abn. Psychol., 107*(3), 363–74.

Slutske, W. S., Zhu, G., Meier, M. H., & Martin, N. G. (2010). Genetic and environmental influences on disordered gambling in men and women. *Arch. Gen. Psychiat., 67*(6), 624–30.

Smalley, S. L. (1991). Genetic influences in autism. *Psychiat. Clin. N. Amer., 14*, 125–39.

Smith, J. P., & Smith, G. C. (2010). Long-term economic costs of psychological problems during childhood. *Soc. Sci. Med., 71*(1), 110–15.

Smith, A. R., Hawkeswood, S. E., Bodell, L. P., & Joiner, T. E. (2011). Muscularity versus leanness: An examination of body ideals and predictors of disordered eating in heterosexual and gay college students. *Body Image, 8*, 232–36.

Smith, C. D., Andersen, A. H., Kryscio, R. J., Schmitt, F. A., Kindy, M. S., Blonder, L. X., & Avison, M. J. (2002). Women at risk for AD show increased parietal activation during a fluency task. *Neurol., 58*, 1197–202.

Smith, G. T., Goldman, M. S., Greenbaum, P. E., & Christiansen, B. A. (1995). Expectancy for social facilitation from drinking: The divergent paths of high-expectancy and low-expectancy adolescents. *J. Abn. Psychol., 104*, 32–40.

Smith, I. M., & Bryson, S. (1994). Imitation and action in autism: A critical review. *Psychol. Bull., 116*(2), 259–73.

Smith, P. M., Reilly, K. R., Miller, N. H., DeBusk, R. F., & Taylor, C. B. (2002). Application of a nurse-managed inpatient smoking cessation program. *Nicotine & Tobacco Research, 4*(2), 211–22.

Smith, R. S., & Maes, M. (1995). The macrophage-T lymphocyte theory of schizophrenia: Additional evidence. *Medical Hypotheses, 45*, 135–41.

Smith, T. W., & Ruiz, J. M. (2002). Psychosocial influences on the development and course of coronary heart disease: Current status and implications for research and practice. *J. Cons. Clin. Psychol., 70*(3), 548–68.

Smith-Spark, J. H., & Fisk, J. E. (2007). Working memory functioning in developmental dyslexia. *Memory, 15*(1), 34–56.

Smolak, L., & Murnen, S. K. (2002). A meta-analytic examination of the relationship between child sexual abuse and eating disorders. *Int. J. Eat. Dis., 31*(2), 136–50.

Smoller, J. W., Gardner-Schuster, E., & Misiaszek, M. (2008). Genetics of anxiety: Would the genome recognize the DSM? *Depression and Anxiety, 25*(4), 368–77. doi: 10.1002/da.20492

Smyke, A. T., Koga, S. F., Johnson, D. E., Fox, N. A., Marshall, P. J., Nelson, C. A., et al. (2007). The caregiving context in institution-reared and family-reared infants and toddlers in Romania. *Journal of Child Psychology and Psychiatry, 48*(2), 210–18.

Snider, W. D., Simpson, D. M., Nielsen, S., Gold, J. W., Metroka, C. E., & Posner, J. B. (1983). Neurological complications of acquired immune deficiency syndrome: Analysis of 50 patients. *Ann. Neurol., 14*(4), 403–18.

Snitz, B. E., Hellinger, A., & Daum, I. (2002). Impaired processing of affective prosody in Korsakoff's syndrome, *Cortex, 38*(5), 797–803.

Snowden, L. R., & Yamada, A.-M. (2005). Cultural differences in access to care. *Annu. Rev. Clin. Psychol., 1*, 143–66.

Snyder, C. R., & Lopez, S. J. (2002). *Handbook of positive psychology.* New York: Oxford University Press.

Snyder, D. K., Castellani, A. M., & Whisman, M. A. (2006). Current status and future directions in couple therapy. *Annu. Rev. Psychol., 57*, 317–44.

Snyder, H. N., & Sickmund, M. (2006). *Juvenile offenders and victims: 2006 national report.* Washington, DC: U. S. Department of Justice Programs, Office of Juvenile Justice and Delinquency Prevention.

Snyder, P. J., Nussbaum, P. D., & Robins, D. L. (Eds.). (2006). *Clinical neuropsychology: A pocket handbook for assessment* (2nd ed.). Washington, DC: American Psychological Association

Soar, K., Turner, J. J. D., & Parrott, A. C. (2001). Psychiatric disorders in Ecstasy (MDMA) users: A literature review focusing on personal predisposition and drug history. *Human Psychopharmacology Clinical & Experimental, 16*, 641–45.

Sobell, M. B., & Sobell, L. C. (1995). Controlled drinking after 25 years: How important was the great debate? *Addiction, 90*(9), 1149–53.

Solomon, D. A., Leon, A. C., Coryell, W. H., Endicott, J., Li, C., Fiedorowicz, J. G., et al. (2010). Longitudinal course of bipolar I disorder: Duration of mood episodes. *Arch. Gen. Psychiat., 67*(4), 339–47. doi: 10.1001/archgenpsychiatry.2010.15

Solomon, D. A., Leon, A. C., Endicott, J., Coryell, W. H., Mueller, T. I., Posternak, M. A., et al. (2003). Unipolar mania over the course of a 20-year follow-up study. *Amer. J. Psychiat., 160*(11), 2049–51.

Solomon, D. A., Leon, A. C., Endicott, J., Mueller, T. I., Coryell, W., Shea, M. T., et al. (2004). Psychosocial impairment and recurrence of major depression. *Compr. Psychiat., 45*(6), 423–30.

Solomon, D. A., Leon, A. C., Mueller, T. I., Coryell, W., Teres, J. J., Posternak, M. A., et al. (2005). Tachyphylaxes in unipolar major depressive disorder. *J. Clin. Psychiat., 66*(3), 283–90.

Solomon, Z., & Mikulincer, M. (2007). Posttraumatic intrusion, avoidance, and social functioning: A 20 year longitudinal study. *J Consult. Clin. Psychol., 75,* 336–324.

Soong, W. T. (2006). Psychiatry in Taiwan: Past, present and future. *International Medical Journal, 13,* 21–28.

Southall, A. (2010). Washington, D.C., approves medical use of marijuana. *New York Times, 159*(55), 31.

Southwick, S. M., Vythilingam, M., & Charney, D. S. (2005). The psychobiology of depression and resilience to stress: Implications for prevention and treatment. *Ann. Rev. Clin. Psych., 1*(1), 255–91.

Spadoni, A. D., McGee, C. L., Fryer, S. L., & Riley, E. P. (2007). Neuroimaging and fetal alcohol spectrum disorders. *Neuroscience & Biobehavioral Reviews.* 31(2), 239–45.

Spanos, A., Klump, K. L., Burt, S. A., McGue, M., & Iacono, W. G. (2010). A longitudinal investigation of the relationship between disordered eating attitudes and behaviors and parent-child conflict: A monozygotic twin differences design. *J. Abn. Pysch.,* 119, 293–99.

Spanos, N. P. (1994). Multiple identity enactments and multiple personality disorder: A sociocognitive perspective. *Psychol. Bull., 116,* 143–65.

Spanos, N. P. (1996). *Multiple identities and false memories: A sociocognitive perspective.* Washington, DC: American Psychological Association.

Spanos, N. P., Weekes, J. R., & Bertrand, L. D. (1985). Multiple personality: A social psychological perspective. *J. Abn. Psychol., 94,* 362–76.

Sparks, D. L., Sabbagh, M. N., Connor, D. J., Lopez, J., Launer, L. J., Browne, P., Wassar, D., Johnson-Traver, S., Lochhead, J., & Ziolkowski, C. (2005). Atorvastatin for the treatment of mild to moderate Alzheimer disease: Preliminary results. *Arch. Neurol., 62*(5), 753–57.

Spataro, J., Mullen, P. M., Burgess, P. M., Wells, D. L., & Moss, S. A. (2004). Impact of child sexual abuse on mental health: Prospective study in males and females. *Brit. J. Psychiat., 184,* 416–21.

Speck, C. E., Kukull, W. A., Brenner, D. E., Bowen, J. D., McCormick, W. C., Teri, L., Pfanschmidt, M. L., Thompson, J. D., & Larson, E. B. (1995). History of depression as a risk factor for Alzheimer's disease. *Epidemiology, 6,* 366–69.

Speed, J. (1996). Behavioral management of conversion disorder: Retrospective study. *Archives of Physical Medicine and Rehabilitation, 77,* 435–54.

Speier, P. L., Sherak, D. L., Hirsch, S., & Cantwell, D. P. (1995). Depression in children and adolescents. In E. E. Beckham & W. R. Leber (Eds.), *Handbook of depression* (2nd ed., pp. 467–93). New York: Guilford.

Spencer, J. P., Blumberg, M. S., McMurray, B., Robinson, S. R., Samuelson, L. K., & Tomblin, J. B. (2009). Short arms and talking eggs: Why we should no longer abide the nativist–empiricist debate. *Child Development Perspectives, 3*(2), 79–87. doi: 10.1111/j.1750-8606.2009.00081.x

Spencer, T. J. (2004a). ADHD treatment across the life cycle. *J. Clin. Psychiat., 65*(Suppl. 3), 22–26.

Spencer, T. J. (2004b). Non stimulant treatment of adult attention deficit hyperactivity disorder. *Psychiat. Clin. N. Amer., 27,* 373–83.

Speranza, A. M., Ammaniti, M., & Trentini, C. (2006). An overview of maternal depression, infant reactions and intervention programmes. *Clinical Neuropsychiatry: Journal of Treatment Evaluation, 3*(1), 57–68.

Sperling, R. A., Bates, J. F., Chua, E. F., Cocchiarella, A. J., Rentz, D. M., Rosen, B. R., Schacter, D. L., & Albert, M. S. (2003). FMRI studies of associative encoding in young and elderly controls and mild Alzheimer's disease. *J. Neurol. Neurosurg. Psychiat., 74,* 44–50.

Spiegel, D. (2006). Recognizing traumatic dissociation. *Am. J. Psychiat., 163*(4), 566–68.

Spiegel, D. (2010). Dissociation in the DSM5. *Journal of Trauma & Dissociation, 11,* 261–65. doi: 10.1080/15299731003780788

Spiga, R., Huang, D. B., Meisch, R. A., & Grabowski, J. (2001). Human methadone self-administration: Effects of diazepam pretreatment. *Exp. Clin. Psychopharm., 9,* 40–46.

Spirito, A., & Esposito-Smythers, C. (2006). Attempted and completed suicide in adolescence. *Ann. Rev. Clin. Psych., 2,* 237–66.

Spitzer, R. L., Skodol, A. E., Gibbon, M., & Williams, J. B. W. (1981). *DSM-III casebook.* Washington, DC: American Psychiatric Association.

Spitzer, R. L. (1999). Harmful dysfunction and the DSM definition of mental disorder. *J. Abn. Psychol., 108*(3), 430–32.

Spitzer, R. L., Gibbon, M., Skodol, A. E., Williams, J. B. W., & First, M. B. (1989). *DSM-III-R casebook.* Washington, DC: American Psychiatric Press.

Spitzer, R. L., Gibbon, M., Skodol, A. E., Williams, J. B. W., & First, M. B. (Eds.). (2002). *DSM-IV-TR casebook: A learning companion to the Diagnostic and Statistical Manual of Mental Disorders, Fourth Edition, Text Revision.* Washington, DC: American Psyciatric Press.

Sporn, A., Greenstein, D., Gogtay, N., Sailer, F., Hommer, D. W., Rawlings, R., Nicholson, R., Egan, M. F., Lenane, M., Gochman, P., Weinberger, D. R., & Rapoport, J. L. (2005). Childhood-onset schizophrenia: Smooth pursuit eye-tracking dysfunction in family members. *Schiz. Res., 73,* 243–52.

Spoth, R., Redmond, C., Shin, C., & Azevedo, K. (2004). Brief family intervention effects on adolescent substance initiation school-level growth curve analyses 6 years following baseline. *J. Cons. Clin. Psychol., 72,* 535–42.

Spunt, B., Goldstein, P., Brownstein, H., & Fendrich, M. (1994). The role of marijuana in homicide. *Inter. J. Addict., 29,* 195–213.

Squires-Wheeler, E., Friedman, D., Amminger, G. P., Skodol, A., Looser-Ott, S., Roberts, S., Pape, S., & Erlenmeyer-Kimling, L. (1997). Negative and positive dimensions of schizotypal personality disorder. *J. Personal. Dis., 11*(3), 285–300.

Srisurapanont, M., Ali, R., Marsden, J., Sunga, A., Wada, K., & Monteiro, M. (2003). Psychotic symptoms in methamphetamine psychotic in-patients. *Int. J. Neuropsychopharm., 6*(4), 347–52.

Srivareerat, M., Tran, T. T., Alzoubi, K. H., & Alkadhi, K. A. (2009). Chronic psychosocial stress exacerbates impairment of cognition and long-term potentiation in B amyloid rat model of Alzheimer's disease. *Biol. Psychiat., 65,* 918–26.

Sroufe, L. A., Carlson, E. A., Levy, A. K., & Egeland, B. (2003). Implications of attachment theory for developmental psychopathology. In M. E. Hertzig & E. A. Farber (Eds.), *Annual progress in child psychiatry and child development: 2000–2001.* (pp. 43–61). New York: Brunner-Routledge.

Sroufe, L. A., Duggal, S., Weinfeld, N., & Carlson, E. (2000). Relationships, development, and psychopathology. In A. J. Sameroff & M. Lewis (Eds.), *Handbook of developmental psychopathology* (2nd ed., pp. 75–91). New York: Kluwer/Plenum.

St. Clair, D. (2009). Copy number variation and schizophrenia. *Schiz. Bull., 35,* 9–12.

Stahl, S. M. (2000). *Essential psychopharmacology: Neuroscientific basis and practical applications* (2nd ed.). Cambridge, UK: Cambridge University Press.

Stahl, S. M. (2002). *Essential psychopharmacology of antipsychotics and mood stabilizers.* Cambridge: Cambridge University Press.

Staley, D., Wand, R., & Shady, G. (1997). Tourette Disorder: A cross-cultural review. *Compr. Psychiat., 38*(1), 6–16.

Staller, J. A. (2006). Diagnostic profiles in outpatient child psychiatry. *Am. J. Orthopsychiat., 76,* 98–102.

Stangier, U., Schramm, E., Heidenreich, T., Berger, M., & Clark, D. M. (2011). Cognitive therapy vs interpersonal psychotherapy in social anxiety disorder. *Am. J. Psychiat., 68,* 692–700.

Staniloiu, A., & Markowitsch, H. J. (2010). Searching for the anatomy of dissociative amnesia. *Zeitschrift fur Psychologie/Journal of Psychology, 218,* 96–108. doi: 10.1027/0044-3409/a000017

Stanley, B., Brodsky, B., Nelson, J., & Dulit, R. (2007). Brief dialectical behavior therapy for suicidality and self-injurious behaviors. *Arch. Suicide Res., 11,* 337–41.

Stanley, B., Brown, G., Brent, D. A., Wells, K., Poling, K., Curry, J., et al. (2009). Cognitive-behavioral therapy for suicide prevention (CBT-SP): Treatment model, feasibility, and acceptability. *J Amer. Acad. Child Adol. Psychiat., 48*(10), 1005–13. doi: 10.1097/CHI.0b013e3181b5dbfe

Starcevic, V., & Berle, D. (2006). Cognitive specificity of anxiety disorders: A review of selected key constructs. *Depression and Anxiety, 23*(2), 51–61.

Starcevic, V., Latas, M., Kolar, D., Vucinic-Latas, D., Bogojevic, G., & Milovanovic, S. (2008). Co-occurrence of Axis I and Axis II disorders in female and male patients with panic disorder with agoraphobia. *Compr. Psychiat., 49*(6), 537–43. doi: 10.1016/j.comppsych.2008.02.009

Stark, S., Sachse, R., Liedl, T., Hensen, J., Rohde, G., Wensing, G., et al. (2001). Vardenafil increases penile rigidity and tumescence in men with erectile dysfunction after a single oral dose. *European Urology, 40,* 181–88.

Stattin, H., & Klackenberg-Larsson, I. (1993). Early language and intelligence development and their relationship to future criminal behavior. *J. Abn. Psychol., 102*(3), 369–78.

Steadman, H. J., McGreevy, M. A., Morrissey, J. P., Callahan, L. A., Robbins, P. C., & Cirincione, C. (1993). *Before and after Hinckley: Evaluating insanity defense reform.* New York: Guilford.

Steadman, H. J., Mulvey, E. P., Monahan, J., Robbins, P. C., Appelbaum, P. S., Grisso, T., Roth, L. H., & Silver, E. (1998). Violence by people discharged from acute psychiatric inpatient facilities and by others in the same neighborhoods. *Arch. Gen. Psychiat., 55,* 393–401.

Steele, M., Hodges, J., Kaniuk, J., Steele, H., D'Agostino, D., Blom, I., Hillman, S., & Henderson, K. (2007). Intervening with maltreated children and their adoptive families: Identifying attachment-facilitative behaviors. In D. Oppenheim & D. F. Goldsmith (Eds.), *Attachment theory in clinical work with children bridging the gap between research and practice* (pp. 58–89). New York: Guilford Press.

Steele, R. G., & Forehand, R. (1997). The role of family processes and coping strategies in the relationship between parental chronic illness and childhood internalizing problems. *J. Abnorm. Child Psychol., 25*, 83–94.

Steen, R. G., Mull, C., McClure, R., Hamer, R. M., & Lieberman, J. A. (2006). Brain volume in first-episode schizophrenia: Systematic review and meta-analysis of magnetic resonance imaging studies. *Brit. J. Psychiat, 188*, 510–18.

Stefanoff, P., Wolanczyk, T., Gawrys, A., Swirszcz, K., Stefanoff, E., Kaminska, A., Lojewska-Bajbus, M., Mazurek, B., Majewska-Stefaniak, A., Mikulska, J., & Brynska, A. (2008). Prevalence of tic disorders among schoolchildren in Warsaw, Poland. *European Child & Adolescent Psychiatry, 17*(3) 171–78.

Stefansson, H., Rujescu, D., Cichon, S., Pietiläinen, O. P., Ingason, A., Steinberg, S., et al. (2008). Large recurrent microdeletions associated with schizophrenia. *Nature*.

Steiger, A. (2007). Neurochemical regulation of sleep. *J. Psychiat. Res., 41*(7), 537–52.

Stein, D. J., Denys, D., Gloster, A. T., Hollander, E., Leckman, J. F., Rauch, S. L., & Phillips, K. A. (2009). Obsessive-compulsive disorder: Diagnostic and treatment issues. *Psychiat. Clin. N. Amer., 32*(3), 665–85. doi: 10.1016/j.psc.2009.05.007

Stein, D. J., Phillips, K. A., Bolton, D., Fulford, K. W. M., Sadler, J. Z., & Kendler, K. S. (2010). What is a mental/psychiatric disorder? From DSM-IV to DSM-V. *Psychol. Med., 40*, 1759–1765.

Stein, D. J., & Simeon, D. (2009). Cognitive-affective neuroscience of depersonalization. *CNS Spectrums, 14*, 467–71.

Stein, G. (2008). Alcoholism in ancient Israel. *Brit. J. Psychiat., 193*(2), 113.

Stein, M. B. (2004). Public health perspectives on generalized anxiety disorder. *J. Clin. Psychiat., 65*(113), 3–7.

Stein, M. B., Heimberg, R. G., & Stein, M. B. (2004). Wellbeing and life satisfaction in generalized anxiety disorder: Comparison to major depressive disorder in a community sample. *J. Affect. Dis., 79*(1–3), 161–66.

Stein, M. B., Jang, K. L., & Livesley, W. J. (2002). Heritability of social anxiety-related concerns and personality characteristics: A twin study. *J. Nerv. Ment. Dis., 190*(4), 219–24.

Stein, M. B., & Stein, D. J. (2008). Social anxiety disorder. *Lancet, 371*(9618), 1115–25.

Steinberg, L., Blatt-Eisengart, I., & Cauffman, E. (2006). Patterns of competence and adjustment among adolescents from authoritative, authoritarian, indulgent, and neglectful homes: A replication in a sample of serious juvenile offenders. *Journal of Research on Adolescence, 16*(1), 47–58.

Steinhausen, H. C. (2002). The outcome of anorexia nervosa in the 20th century. *Amer. J. Psychiat., 159*, 1284–93.

Steketee, G. S. (1993). *Treatment of obsessive-compulsive disorder.* New York: Guilford.

Steketee, G., & Barlow, D. H. (2002). Obsessive-compulsive disorder. In D. H. Barlow (Ed.), *Anxiety and its disorders* (2nd ed., pp. 516–50). New York: Guilford.

Steketee, G., & Frost, R. (2004). Compulsive hoarding: Current status of research. *Clin. Psychol. Rev., 23*, 905–27.

Stene, J., Stene, E., Stengel-Rutkowski, S., & Murken, J. D. (1981). Paternal age and Down's syndrome,

data from prenatal diagnoses (DFG). *Human Genet., 59*, 119–24.

Stephens, R. S., Roffman, R. A., & Simpson, E. E. (1994). Treating adult marijuana dependence: A test of the relapse prevention model. *J. Cons. Clin. Psychol., 62*, 92–99.

Stermac, L. E., Segal, Z. V., & Gillis, R. (1990). Social and cultural factors in sexual assault. In W. L. Marshall, D. R. Laws, & H. E. Barbaree (Eds.), *Handbook of sexual assault* (pp. 143–60). New York: Plenum.

Stetler, C., & Miller, G. E. (2011). Depression and hypothalamic-pituitary-adrenal activation: A quantitative summary of four decades of research. *Psychosomat. Med., 73*(2), 114–26. doi: 10.1097/PSY.0b013e31820ad12b

Stevens, A. H., & Schaller, J, (2009). Short-run effects of parental job loss on children's academic achievement. National Bureau of Economic Research Working Paper 15480. http://www.nber.org/papers/w15480

Stewart, J. L., Bismark, A. W., Towers, D. N., Coan, J. A., & Allen, J. J. B. (2010). Resting frontal EEG asymmetry as an endophenotype for depression risk: Sex-specific patterns of frontal brain asymmetry. *J. Abn. Psychol., 119*(3), 502–12. doi: 10.1037/a0019196

Stewart, D., Gossop, M., & Marsden, J. (2002). Reductions in non-fatal overdose after drug misuse treatment: Results from the National Treatment Outcome Research Study (NTORS). *J. Sub. Abuse Treat., 22*(1), 1–9.

Stewart, S. E., Geller, D. A., Jenike, M., Pauls, D., Shaw, D. Mullin, B., et al. (2004). Long-term outcome of pediatric obsessive-compulsive disorder: A meta-analysis and qualitative review of the literature. *Acta Psychiatr. Scandin., 110*(1), 4–13.

Stewart, S. E., Jenike, E., & Jenike, M. A. (2009). Biological treatment for obsessive-compulsive disorder. In M. M. Antony & M. B. Stein (Eds.), *Oxford handbook of anxiety and related disorders* (pp. 375–90). New York: Oxford University Press.

Stewart, S. E., Platko, J., Fagerness, J., Birns, J., Jenike, E., Smoller, J. W., et al. (2007). A genetic family-based association study of OLIG2 in obsessive-compulsive disorder. *Arch. Gen. Psychiat., 64*(2), 209–215.

Stewart, S. H., Finn, P. R., & Pihl, R. O. (1990, Mar.). *The effects of alcohol on the cardiovascular stress response in men at high risk for alcoholism: A dose response study.* Paper presented at the annual meeting of the Canadian Psychological Association, Ottawa.

Stewart, S. M., Kennard, B. D., Lee, P. W. H., Hughes, C. W., Mayes, T., Emslie, G. J., & Lewinsohn, P. M. (2004). A cross-cultural investigation of cognitions and depressive symptoms in adolescents. *J. Abn. Psychol., 113*(2), 248–57.

Stice, E. (2001). A prospective test of the dual-pathway model of bulimic pathology: Mediating effects of dieting and negative affect. *J. Abn. Psychol., 110*(1), 124–35.

Stice, E. (2002). Risk and maintenance factors for eating pathology: A meta-analytic review. *Psychol. Bull., 128*(5), 825–48.

Stice, E., Marti, N., & Durant, S. (2011). Risk factors for onset of eating disorders: Evidence of multiple risk pathways from an 8-year prospective study. *Behav. Res. Ther.*

Stice, E., Presnell, K., & Spangler, D. (2002). Risk factors for binge eating onset in adolescent girls. A 2-year prospective study. *Hlth. Psychol., 21*(2), 131–38.

Stickle, T. R., & Blechman, E. A. (2002). Aggression and fire: Antisocial behavior in firesetting and non-firesetting juvenile offenders. *J. Psychopath. Behav. Assess., 24*, 177–93.

Stigler, M. H., Neusel, E. & Perry, C. L. (2011). School based programs to prevent and reduce alcohol use among youth. *Alcohol Research & Health Vol. 34*, 157–162.

Stolberg, R., & Bongar, B. (2009). *Oxford handbook of personality and clinical assessment.* New York: Oxford Univesity Press.

Stolberg, R. A., Clark, D. C., & Bongar, B. (2002). Epidemiology, assessment, and management of suicide in depressed patients. In I. H. Gotlib & C. L. Hammen (Eds.), *Handbook of depression* (pp. 581–601). New York: Guilford.

Stone, J., Smyth, R., Carson, A., Lewis, S., Prescott, R., Warlow, C., & Sharpe, M. (2005). Systematic review of misdiagnosis of conversion symptoms and "hysteria". *Brit. Med. J., 331*, 989.

Stone, J., Smythe, R., Carson, A., Warlow, C., & Shapre, M. (2006). La belle indifference in conversion symptoms and hysteria. *Brit. J. Psychiat., 188*, 204–9.

Stone, S. (1937). Psychiatry through the ages. *J. Abnorm. Soc. Psychol., 32*, 131–60.

Stonnington, C. M., Barry, J. J., & Fisher, R. S. (2006). Conversion disorder. *Am. J. Psychiat., 163* (9), 1510–17

Storandt, M. (2008). Cognitive deficits in the early stages of Alzheimer's disease. *Curr. Dis. Psychol. Sci.. 17*, 198–202.

Story, L. (2005, Aug. 17). A business built on the trouble of teenagers. *The New York Times.* http://www.nytimes.com.

Stossel, T. P. (2005). Regulating academic-industrial research relationships—solving problems or stifling progress? *N. Engl. J. Med., 353*, 1060–65.

Strain, J. J., & Newcorn, J. (2007). Adjustment disorder. In J. A. Bourgeois, R A. Hales, and S. C. Yudofsky (Eds.), *The American Psychiatric Publishing board prep and review guide for psychiatry.* Washington, D. C.: American Psychiatric Association.

Strange, R. E., & Brown, D. E., Jr. (1970). Home from the wars. *Amer. J. Psychiat., 127*(4), 488–92.

Strauss, R. S., & Pollack, H. A. (2003). Social marginalization of overweight children. *Archives of Pediatric and Adolescent Medicine, 157*(8), 746–53.

Strawn, J. R., Keck, P. E., & Caroff, S. N. (2007). Neuroleptic malignant syndrome. *Am. J. Psychiat., 164*, 870–76.

Street, W. (1994). *A chronology of noteworthy events in American psychology.* Washington, DC: American Psychological Association.

Striegel-Moore, R. H., & Bulik, C. M. (2007). Risk factors for eating disorders. *Amer. Psychol., 62*, 181–198.

Striegel-Moore, R. H., Dohm, F. A., Kraemer, H. C., Taylor, C. B., Daniels, S., Crawford, P. B., & Schreiber, G. B. (2003). Eating disorders in white and black women. *Amer. J. Psychiat., 160*, 1326–31.

Strober, M. (2004). Managing the chronic, treatment-resistant patient with anorexia nervosa. *Int. J. Eat. Dis., 36*, 245–55.

Strober, M., Freeman, R., Lampert, C., Diamond, J., & Kaye, W. (2000). Controlled family study of anorexia nervosa and bulimia nervosa: Evidence of shared liability and transmission of partial syndromes. *Amer. J. Psychiat., 157*(3), 393–401.

Strohschein, L. (2005). Parental divorce and child mental health trajectories. *J. Marr. Fam., 7*(5), 1286–1300.

Strote, J., Lee, J. E., & Wechsler, H. (2002). Increasing MDMA use among college students: Results of a national survey. *J. Adol. Hlth., 30*(1), 64–725.

Strug, L. J., Suresh, R., Fyer, A. J., Talati, A., Adams, P. B., Li, W., et al. (2010). Panic disorder is associated with the serotonin transporter gene (SLC6A4) but not the promoter region (5-HTTLPR). *Molec. Psychiat., 15*(2), 166–76. doi: 10.1038/mp.2008.79

Strunk, D. R., Brotman, M. A., DeRubeis, R. J., & Hollon, S. D. (2010). Therapist competence in cognitive therapy for depression: Predicting subsequent symptom change. *J. Cons. Clin. Psychol., 78*, 429–37.

Stueve, A., Dohrenwend, B. P., & Skodol, A. E. (1998). Relationships between stressful life events and episodes of major depression and nonaffective psychotic disorders: Selected results from a New York risk factor study. In B. P. Dohrenwend (Ed.), *Adversity, stress, and psychopathology* (pp. 341–57). New York: Oxford University Press.

Stuss, D. T., Gow, C. A., & Hetherington, C. R. (1992). "No longer Gage": Frontal lobe dysfunction and emotional changes. *J. Cons. Clin. Psychol., 60*(3), 349–59.

Suárez, L. M., Bennett, S. M., Goldstein, C. R., & Barlow, D. H. (2009). Understanding anxiety disorders from a "triple vulnerability" framework. In M. M. Antony & M. B. Stein (Eds.), *Oxford handbook of anxiety and related disorders* (pp. 153–72). New York: Oxford University Press.

Substance Abuse and Mental Health Services Administration, Office of Applied Studies. (2009). Results from the 2008 National Survey on Drug Use and Health: National findings. NSDUH Series H-36, HHS Publication No. SMA 09-4434. Rockville, MD.

Substance Abuse and Mental Health Services Administration, Office of Applied Studies. (2010). *Drug Abuse Warning Network, 2007: National estimates of drug related emergency department visits.* Rockville, MD.

Substance Abuse and Mental Health Services Administration. (2010). Nationwide study reveals significant differences in adult substance use rates among various Hispanic-American groups. http://www.oas.samhsa.gov/2k10/184/HispanicAdults.htm.

Sue, S. (1998). In search of cultural competence in psychotherapy and counseling. *Amer. Psychol., 53*, 440–48.

Sue, S. (1999). Science, ethnicity, and bias: Where have we gone wrong? *Amer. Psychol., 54*, 1070–77.

Sue, S., & Chang, J. (2003). The state of psychological assessment in Asia. *Psychol. Assess., 15*(3), 306–10.

Sue, S., Zane, N., & Young, K. (1994). Research on psychotherapy with culturally diverse populations. In A. E. Bergin & S. L. Garfield (Eds.), *Handbook of psychotherapy and behavior change* (pp. 783–820). New York: Wiley.

Sullivan, E. A., & Kosson, D. S. (2006). Ethnic and cultural variations in psychopathy. In C. J. Patrick (Ed.), *Handbook of the psychopathy.* (pp. 437–58). New York: Guilford Press.

Sullivan, E. V., Deshmukh, A., Desmond, J. E., Lim, K. O., & Pfefferbaum, A. (2000). Cerebellar volume decline in normal aging, alcoholism, and Korsakoff's Syndrome relation to ataxia. *Neuropsych., 14*(3), 341–52.

Sullivan, J., & Chang, P. (1999). Review: Emotional and behavioral functioning in phenylketonuria. *J. Pediat. Psychol., 24*, 281–99.

Sullivan, P. F. (1995). Mortality in anorexia nervosa. *Am. J. Psychiat., 152*, 1073–74.

Sullivan, P. F. (2002). Course and outcome of anorexia nervosa and bulimia nervosa. In C. G. Fairburn & K. D. Brownell (Eds.), *Eating disorders and*

obesity: A comprehensive handbook (2nd ed., pp. 226–30). New York: Guilford.

Sullivan, P. F., Neale, M. C., & Kendler, K. S. (2000). Genetic epidemiology of major depression: Review and meta-analysis. *Amer. J. Psychiat., 157*(10), 1552–62.

Sultzer, D. L., Davis, S. M., Tariot, P. N., Dagerman, K. S., Lebowitz, B. D., Lyketsos, C. G., Rosenheck, R. A. et al., (2008). Clinical symptom response to atypical antipsychotic medications in Alzheimer's disease: Phase 1 outcomes from the CATIE-AD effectiveness trial. *Amer. J. Psychiat., 165*, 844–54.

Sun, D., Stuart, G. W., Jenkinson, M., Wood, S. J., McGorry, P. D. Velakoulis, D., et al., (2009a). Brain surface contraction mapped in first episode schizophrenia: A longitudinal magnetic resonance imaging study. *Mol. Psychiat., 14*, 976–86.

Sun, D., Stuart, G. W., Phillips, L., Velakoulis, D., Jenkinson, M., Yung, A. et al. (2009b). Progressive brain structural changes mapped as psychosis develops in "at risk" individuals. *Schiz. Res., 108*, 85–92.

Sundin, J., Fear, N. T., Iversen, A., Rona, R. J., & Wessely, S. (2010). PTSD after deployment to Iraq: Conflicting rates, conflicting claims. *Psychol, Med., 40*(3), 367–82.

Sundquist, K., Frank, G., & Sundquist, J. (2004). Urbanisation and incidence of psychosis and depression. Follow-up study of 4.4 million women and men in Sweden. *Brit. J. Psychiat., 184*, 293–98.

Sunjic, S., & Zabor, D. (1999). Methadone syrup-related deaths in New South Wales, Australia, 1990–95. *Drug Al. Rev., 18*, 409–15.

Susser, E., Moore, R., & Link, B. (1993). Risk factors for homelessness. *Amer. J. Epidemiol., 15*, 546–66.

Sussman, N. (2009). Mental Health Parity Act becomes the law on October 3, 2009. *Prim. Psychiat., 16*(10), 10–11.

Sussman, N. (2009). Selective serotonin reuptake inhibitors. In Sadock, B. J., Sadock, A. A., & Ruiz, P. (Eds.), *Kaplan and Sadock's comprehensive textbook of psychiatry* (9th ed., pp. 3190–205). PA: Lippincott, Williams & Wilkins.

Sussman, S., Earleywine, M., Wills, T., Cody, C., Biglan, T., Dent, C. W., & Newcomb, M. D. (2004). The motivation, skills, and decision-making model of "drug abuse" prevention. *Substance Use & Misuse, 39*, 1971–2016.

Sutker, P. B. & Allain, A. N. (1995). Psychopathology in aviator prisoners of war (1995). *Clinician's Research Digest*, 13(8).

Sutker, P. B., & Allain, A. N. (2001). Antisocial personality disorder. In H. E. Adams & P. B. Sutker (Eds.), *Comprehensive handbook of psychopathology* (pp. 445–90). New York: Kluwer Academic.

Sutton, J., Smith, P. K., & Swettenham, J. (1999). Bullying and "theory of mind": A critique of the "social skills deficit" view of antisocial behaviour. *Soc. Develop., 8*, 117–27.

Sutton, S. K., Vitale, J. E., & Newman, J. P. (2002). Emotion among women with psychopathy during picture perception. *J. Abn. Psychol., 111*(4), 610–19.

Suzuki, M., Zhou, S. Y., Hagino, H., Takahashi, T., Kawasaki, Y., Nohara, S., Yamashita, I., Matsui, M., Seto, H., & Kurachi, M. (2004). Volume reduction of the right anterior limb of the internal capsule in patients with schizotypal disorder. *Psychiatry Research: Neuroimaging, 130*(3), 213–25.

Svensson, L., Larsson, A., & Oest, L.-G. (2002). How children experience brief-exposure treatment of specific phobias. *J. Comm. Psychol., 31*(1), 80–89.

Sverd, J., Sheth, R., Fuss, J., & Levine, J. (1995). Prevalence of pervasive developmental disorder in a

sample of psychiatrically hospitalized children and adolescents. *Child Psychiat. Human Devel., 25*(4), 221–40.

Swann, A. C. (2010). The strong relationship between bipolar and substance-use disorder. *Annals of the New York Academy of Sciences, 1187*(1), 276–93. doi: 10.1111/j.1749-6632.2009.05146.x

Swartz, M., Swanson, J. W., & Elbogen, E. B. (2004). Psychiatric advance directives: Practical, legal, and ethical issues. *J. Foren. Psychol. Pract., 4*(4), 97–107.

Swartz, R. (2010). Medical marijuana users in substance abuse treatment. *Harm Reduction Journal, 7*, art. 3. doi: 10.1186/1477-7517-7-3

Sylvain, C., Ladouceur, R., & Boisvert, J. M. (1997). Cognitive and behavioral treatment of pathological gambling: A controlled study. *J. Cons. Clin. Psychol., 65*(5), 727–32.

Sypeck, M. F., Gray, J. J., & Ahrens, A. H. (2004). No longer just a pretty face: Fashion magazines' depictions of ideal female beauty from 1959–1999. *Int. J. Eat. Dis., 36*, 342–47.

Sysko, R., Sha, N., Wang, Y., Duan, N., & Walsh, B. T. (2010). Early response to antidepressant treatment in bulimia nervosa. *Psych. Med., 40*, 999–1005.

Szasz, T. S. (1999). *Fatal freedom: The ethics and politics of suicide.* Westport, CT: Praeger.

Szeszko, P. R., MacMillan, S., McMeniman, M., Chen, S., Baribault, K., Lim, K. O., et al. (2004). Brain structural abnormalities in psychotropic drug-naive pediatric patients with obsessive-compulsive disorder. *Amer. J. Psychiat., 161*(6), 1049–56.

Takahashi, K., Miura, S., Mori-Abe, A., Kawagoe, J., Takata, K., Ohmichi, M., & Kurachi, H. (2005). Impact of menopause on augmentation of arterial stiffness with aging. *Gynecologic and Obstetric Investigation, 60*, 162–66.

Takei, N., Persaud, R., Woodruff, P., Brockington, I., & Murray, R. M. (1998). First episodes of psychosis in Afro-Caribbean and white people: An 18-year follow-up population-based study. *Brit. J. Psychiat., 172*, 147–54.

Takeshita, T. K., Morimoto, X., Mao, Q., Hashimoto, T., & Furuyama, J. (1993). Phenotypic differences in low Km Aldehyde de hydrogenase in Japanese workers. *Lancet, 341*, 837–38.

Tamminga, C. A., Thaker, G. K., & Medoff, D. R. (2002). Neuropsychiatric aspects of schizophrenia. In S. Yudofsky & R. E. Hales (Eds.), *The American Psychiatric Association Publishing textbook of neuropsychiatry and clinical sciences* (4th ed., pp. 989–1048). Washington, DC: American Psychiatric Publishing.

Tandon, R., Keshavan, K., & Nasrallah, H. A. (2008). Schizophrenia, "just the facts" what we know in 2008. 2. Epidemiology and etiology. *Schizophrenia Research, 102*, 1–18.

Tandon, R., Nasrallah, H. A., & Keshavan, M. S. (2010). Schizophrenia, "Just the Facts" 5. Treatment and prevention past, present, and future. *Schizophrenia Research, 122*, 1–21.

Tang, T. Z., & DeRubeis, R. J. (1999). Sudden gains and critical sessions in cognitive-behavioral therapy for depression. *J. Cons. Clin. Psychol., 67*, 894–904.

Tang, T. Z., Luborsky, L., & Andrusyna, T. (2002). Sudden gains in recovering from depression: Are they also found in psychotherapies other than cognitive-behavioral therapy? *J. Cons. Clin. Psychol., 70*, 444–47.

Tanguay, P. B. (2001). *Nonverbal learning disability at home.* Philadelphia: Jessica Kingsley.

Tareen, A., Hodes, M., & Rangel, L. (2005). Non-fat phobic anorexia nervosa in British South Asian adolescents. *Int. J. Eat. Dis., 37*, 161–65.

Tarrier, N., Kinney, C., McCarthy, E., Humphreys, L., Wittkowski, A., & Morris, J. (2000). Two-year followup of cognitive-behavioral therapy and supportive counseling in the treatment of persistent symptoms in chronic schizophrenia. *J. Cons. Clin. Psychol., 68* (5), 917–22.

Tarrier, N., Lowson, K., & Barrowclough, C. (1991). Some aspects of family interventions in schizophrenia, II: Financial considerations. *Brit. J. Psychiat., 159*, 481–84.

Tateno, A., Murata, Y., & Robinson, R. G. (2002). Comparison of cognitive impairment associated with major depression following stroke versus traumatic brain injury. *Psychosomatics, 43*(4), 295–301.

Tatetsu, S. (1964). Methamphetamine psychosis. *Folia Psychiatrica et Neurologica Japonica* (suppl. 7), 377–80.

Tavel, M. E. (1962). A new look at an old syndrome: Delirium tremens. *Arch. Int. Med., 109*, 129–34.

Taveras, E. M., Rifas-Shiman, S. L., Oken, E., Gunderson, E. P., & Gillman, M. W. (2008). Short sleep duration in infancy and risk of childhood overweight. *Archives of Pediatric and Adolescent Medicine, 162*, 305–11.

Taylor, C. B., Youngblood, M. E., Catellier, D., Veith, R. C., Carney, R. M., Burg, M. M., Kaufmann, P. G., Shuster, J., Mellman, T., Blumenthal, J. A., Krishnan, R., & Jaffe, A. S. (2005). Effects of antidepressant medication on morbidity and mortality in depressed patients after myocardial infarction. *Arch. Gen. Psychiat., 62*, 792–98.

Taylor, C., & Meux, C. (1997). Individual cases: The risk, the challenge. *Int. Rev. Psychiat., 9*(2), 285–302.

Taylor, C., Laposa, J., & Alden, L. (2004). Is avoidant personality disorder more than just social avoidance? *J. Pers. Dis., 18*, 571–94.

Taylor, H. G., & Alden, J. (1997). Age-related differences in outcomes following childhood brain insults: An introduction and overview. *J. Int. Neuropsychologic. Soc., 3*(6), 555–67.

Taylor, J., Lang, A. R., & Patrick, C. J. (2006). Psychopathy and substance use disorders. In *Handbook of the psychopathy.* (pp. 495–511). New York: Guilford Press.

Taylor, R. L. (2000). *Distinguishing psychological from organic disorders: Screening for psychological masquerade* (2nd ed.). New York: Springer.

Taylor, S. (2010). Posttraumatic stress disorder. In D. McKay, J. Abramowitz, & S. Taylor (Eds.), *Cognitive-behavioral therapy for refractory cases: Turning failure into success* (pp. 139–53). Washington, DC: American Psychological Association.

Taylor, S., & Asmundson, G. J. G. (2004). *Treating health anxiety: A cognitive-behavioural approach.* New York: Guilford Press.

Taylor, S. E., & Stanton, A. L. (2007). Coping resources, coping processes, and mental health. *Annu. Rev. Clin. Psychol., 3*, 377–401.

Taylor, W. S., & Martin, M. F. (1944). Multiple personality. *J. Abnorm. Soc. Psychol., 39*, 281–300.

Teachman, B. A., & Saporito, J. (2009). I am going to gag: Disgust cognitions in spider and blood-injury-injection fears. *Cognition and Emotion, 23*(2), 399–414. doi: 10.1080/02699930801961731

Teachman, B. A., Smith-Janik, S. B., & Saporito, J. (2007). Information processing biases and panic disorder: Relationships among cognitive and symptom measures. *Behav. Res. Ther., 45*(8), 1791–811.

Teachman, B. A., Woody, S. R., & Magee, J. C. (2006). Implicit and explicit appraisals of the importance of intrusive thoughts. *Behav. Res. Ther., 44*(6), 785–805.

Teasdale, G. M., Nicoll, J. A. R., Murray, G., et al. (1997). Association of apolipoprotein E polymorphism with outcome after head injury. *Lancet, 350*, 1069–71.

Teasdale, J. (1988). Cognitive vulnerability to persistent depression. *Cognition and Emotion, 2*, 247–74.

Teasdale, J. D. (1996). Clinically relevant therapy: Integrating clinical insight with cognitive science. In P. M. Salkovskis (Ed.), *Frontiers of cognitive therapy* (pp. 26–47). New York: Guilford.

Teasdale. J. D. (2004). Mindfulness-based cognitive therapy. In J. Yiend (Ed.), *Cognition, emotion and psychopathology: Theoretical, empirical and clinical directions* (pp. 270–89). Cambridge: Cambridge University Press.

Teasdale, J. D., Scott, J., Moore, R. G., Hayhurst, H., Pope, M., & Paykel, E. S. (2001). How does cognitive therapy prevent relapse in residual depression? Evidence from a controlled trial. *J. Cons. Clin. Psychol., 69*(3), 347–57.

Teasdale, J. D., Segal, Z. V., Williams, J. M. G., Ridgeway, V. A., Soulsby, J. M., & Lau, M. A. (2000). Prevention of relapse/recurrence in major depression by mindfulness-based cognitive therapy. *J. Cons. Clin. Psychol., 68*(4), 615–23.

Teglasi, H. (2010). *Essentials of TAT and other storytelling assessments* (2nd ed.). Hoboken, NJ: John Wiley & Sons.

Teplin, L. A., Abram, K. M., & McClelland, G. M. (1997). Mentally disordered women in jail: Who receives services? *Amer. J. Pub. Hlth., 87*(4), 604–9.

Teri, L., et al. (1997). Behavioral treatment of depression in dementia patients: A controlled clinical trial. *J. Gerontol.*, Series B, 52B, P159–P166.

Tessner, K. D., Mittal, V., & Walker, E. F. (2011). Longitudinal study of stressful life events and daily stressors among adolescents at high risk for psychotic disorders. *Schizo. Bull., 37*(2), 432–41. doi: 10.1093/schbul/sbp087

Testa, M., Livingston, J. A., Vanzile-Tamsen, C., & Frone, M. R. (2003). The role of women's substance use in vulnerability to forcible and incapacitated rape. *Journal of Studies on Alcohol, 64*(6), 756–64.

Thapar, A., Langley, K., O-Donovan, M., & Owen, M. (2006). Refining the attention-deficit hyperactivitiy disorder phenotype for molecular genetic studies. *Molec. Psychiat., 11*, 714–20.

Thase, M. E. (2009). Neurobiological aspects of depression. In Gotlib, I., & Hammen, C. (Eds.), *Handbook of depression* (2nd ed.). New York: Guilford.

Thase, M. E. (2009). Selective serotonin-norepinephrine reuptake inhibitors. In Sadock, B. J., Sadock, A. A., & Ruiz, P. (Eds.), *Kaplan and Sadock's comprehensive textbook of psychiatry* (9th ed., pp. 3184–90). PA: Lippincott, Williams & Wilkins.

Thase, M. E., & Denko, T. (2008). Pharmacotherapy of mood disorders. *Ann. Rev. Clin. Psych., 4*, 53–91.

Thase, M. E., Jindal, R., & Howland, R. H. (2002). Biological aspects of depression. In I. H. Gotlib & C. L. Hammen (Eds.), *Handbook of depression* (pp. 192–218). New York: Guilford.

Theodorou, S., & Haber, P. S. (2005). The medical complications of heroin use. *Cur. Opin. Psychiat., 18*(3), 257–63.

Thibodeau, R., Jorgensen, R. S., & Kim, S., (2006). Depression, anxiety, and resting frontal EEG asymmetry: A meta-analytic review. *J. Abn. Psychol., 115*(4), 715–29.

Thomas, A. K., & Loftus, E. F. (2002). Creating bizarre false memories through imagination. *Memory and Cognition, 30*, 423–31.

Thomas, C., Benzeval, M., & Stansfeld, S. (2007). Psychological distress after employment transitions: The role of subjective financial position as a mediator. *Journal of Epidemiology & Community Health, 61*(1), 48–52.

Thomas, C. R. (2010). Oppositional defiant disorder and conduct disorder. In M. K. Dulcan (Ed.), *Dulcan's textbook of child and adolescent psychiatry*, (pp. 223–39). Arlington, VA: American Psychiatric Publishing, Inc.

Thomas, J. D., & Riley, E. P. (1998). Fetal alcohol syndrome: Does alcohol withdrawal play a role?, *Alcohol World: Health and Research, 22*(1), 47–53.

Thomas, J. L., Wilk, J. E., Riviere, L. A., McGurk, D., Castro, C. A., & Hoge, C.W. (2011). Prevalence of mental health problems and functional impairment among Active Component and National Guard soldiers 3 and 12 months following combat in Iraq. *Arch. Gen. Psychiat., 67*, 614–23.

Thomas, S. P. (2006). From the editor—The phenomenon of cyberbullying. *Issues in Mental Health Nursing, 27*(10), 1015–16.

Thompson, P. M., Vidal, C., Giedd, J. N., Gochman, P., Blumenthal, J., Nicolson, R., Toga, A. W., & Rapoport, J. L. (2001). Mapping adolescent brain changes reveals dynamic wave of accelerated gray matter loss in very early-onset schizophrenia. *Proceedings of the National Academy of Sciences, 98, 20*, 11650–55.

Thompson, R. A., & Nelson, C. A. (2001). Developmental science and the media: Early brain development. *Amer. Psychol., 56*, 5–15.

Thompson, R. F. (2000). *The brain: A neuroscience primer* (3rd ed.). New York: Worth.

Thompson, S. B. N. (2003). Rate of decline in social and cognitive abilities in dementing individuals with Down's syndrome and other learning disabilities. *Clin. Geron., 26*(3–4), 145–53.

Thompson, W. W., Gottesman, I. I., & Zalewski, C. (2006). Reconciling disparate prevalence rates of PTSD in large samples of US male Vietnam veterans and their controls. *BMC Psychiatry, 6/19.* http://www.biomedcentral.com/1471-244X/6/19

Thornhilll, R., & Palmer, C. T. (2000). *A natural history of rape: Biological bases of sexual coercion.* Boston: MIT Press.

Thornicroft, G., Rose, D., Kassam, A., & Sartorius, N. (2007). Stigma: Ignorance, prejudice or discrimination? *Brit. J. Psychiat., 190*, 192–93.

Thornicroft, G., & Tansella, M. (2000). Planning and providing mental health services for a community. In M. G. Gelder, J. J. Lopez-Ibor, Jr., & N. C. Andreason (Eds.), *New Oxford textbook of psychiatry* (pp. 1547–58). Oxford: Oxford University Press.

Tidey, J. W., & Miczek, K. A. (1996). Social defeat stress selectively alters mesocorticolimbic dopamine release: An in vivo micro-dialysis study. *Brain Research, 721*, 140–49.

Tienari, P., Lahti, I., Sorri, A., Naarala, M., Moring, J., Wahlberg, K.-E., & Wynne, L. C. (1987). The Finnish adoptive family study of schizophrenia. *J. Psychiat. Res., 21*, 437–45.

Tienari, P., Wynne, L. C., Läksy, K., Moring, J., Nieminen, P., Sorri, A., Lahti, I., & Wahlberg, K.-E. (2003). Genetic boundaries of the schizophrenia spectrum: Evidence from the Finnish adoptive family study. *Amer. J. Psychiat., 160*, 1587–94.

Tienari, P., Wynne, L. C., Moring, J., Läksy, K., Nieminen, P., Sorri, A., Lahti, I., Wahlberg, K.-E., Naarala, M., Kurki-Suonio, K., Saarento, O., Koistinen, P., Tarvainen, T., Hakko, H., & Miettunen, J. (2000). Finnish adoptive family study: Sample selection and adoptee DSM-III-R diagnoses. *Acta Psychiatr. Scandin., 101*, 433–43.

Tienari, P., Wynne, L. C., Sorri, A., Lahti, I., Läksy, K., Moring, J., Naarala, M., Nieminen, P., & Wahlberg, K.-E. (2004). Genotype-environment interaction in schizophrenia-spectrum disorder. *Brit. J. Psychiat., 184*, 216–22.

Tignol, J., Biraben-Gotzamanis, L., Martin-Guehl, C., Grabot, D., & Aouizerate, B. (2007). Body dysmorphic disorder and cosmetic surgery: Evolution of 24 subjects with a minimal defect in appearance 5 years after their request for cosmetic surgery. *European Psychiatry, 22*(8), 520–24.

Tiihonen, J., Haukka, J., Taylor, M., Haddad, P. M., Patel, M. X., & Korhonen, P. (2011). A nationwide cohort study of oral and depot antipsychotics after first hospitalization for schizophrenia. *Am. J. Psychiat., 168*, 603–9.

Tillfors, M. (2004). Why do some individuals develop social phobia? A review with emphasis on the neurobiological influences. *Nord. J. Psychiat., 58*(4), 267–76.

Tillfors, M., Furmark, T., Ekselius, L., & Fredrikson, M. (2004). Social phobia and avoidant personality disorder: One spectrum disorder? *Nord. J. Psychiat., 58*, 147–52.

Tims, F. M., Leukefeld, C. G., & Platt, J. J. (2001). *Relapse and recovery in addictions.* New Haven, CT: Yale University Press.

Tizard, J. (1975). Race and IQ: The limits of probability. *New Behaviour, 1*, 6–9.

Tolin, D. F. (2010). Is cognitive-behavioral therapy more effective than other therapies?: A meta-analytic review. *Clin. Psychol. Rev., 30*(6), 710–20.

Tolin, D. F., Frost, R. O., Steketee, G., Gray, K. D., & Fitch, K. E. (2008). The economic and social burden of compulsive hoarding. *Psychiat. Res., 160*(2), 200–11. doi: 10.1016/j.psychres.2007.08.008

Tolin, D. F., & Foa, E. B. (2006). Sex differences in trauma and posttraumatic stress disorder: A quantitative review of 25 years of research. *Psychological Bulletin, 132*, 959–992.

Tomarken, A. J., Mineka, S., & Cook, M. (1989). Fear-relevant selective associations and covariation bias. *J. Abn. Psychol., 98*, 381–94.

Tondo, L., Isaacson, G. R., & Baldessarini, R. J. (2003). Suicidal behaviour in bipolar disorder: Risk and prevention. *CNS Drugs, 17*(7), 491–511.

Toneatto, T., Sobell, L. C., Sobell, M. B., & Rubel, E. (1999). Natural recovery from cocaine dependence. *Psychol. Addict. Behav., 13*(4), 259–68.

Tong, J., Miao, S. J., Wang, J., Zhang, J. J., Wu, H. M., Li, T., & Hsu, L. K. G. (2005). Five cases of male eating disorders in Central China. *Int. J. Eat. Dis., 37*, 72–75.

Tonigan, J. S., Toscova, R., & Miller, W. R. (1995). Meta-analysis of the literature on Alcoholics Anonymous. *J. Stud. Alcoh., 57*(1), 65–72.

Took, K. J., & Buck, B. L. (1996). Enuresis with combined risperidone and SSRI use. *J. Amer. Acad. Child Adoles. Psychiat., 35*(7), 840–41.

Torgersen, S. (1993). Genetics. In A. S. Bellack & M. Hersen (Eds.), *Psychopathology in adulthood.* Needham Heights, MA: Allyn and Bacon.

Torgersen, S., Kringlen, E., & Cramer, V. (2001). The prevalence of personality disorders in a community sample. *Arch. Gen. Psychiat., 58*(6), 590–96.

Torgersen, S., Lygren, S., Oien, P. A., Skre, I., Onstad, S., Edvardsen, J., Tambs, K., & Kringlen, E. (2000). A twin study of personality disorders. *Compr. Psychiat., 41*(6), 416–25.

Torres, A. R., Prince, M. J., Bebbington, P. E., Bhugra, D., Brugha, T. S., Farrell, M., et al. (2006). Obsessive-compulsive disorder: Prevalence, comorbidity, impact, and help-seeking in the British National Psychiatric Morbidity survey of 2000. *Amer. J. Psychiat, 163*(11), 1978–85.

Torrey, E. F. (1997). *Out of the shadows: Confronting America's mental illness crisis.* New York: Wiley.

Torrey, E. F. (2008). *The Insanity Offense: How America's Failure to Treat the Seriously Mentally Ill.* New York: W. W. Norton.

Torrey, E. F., Bower, A. E., Taylor, E. H., & Gottesman, I. I. (1994). *Schizophrenia and manic-depressive disorder: The biological roots of mental illness as revealed by the landmark study of identical twins.* New York: Basic Books.

Tortolero, S. (2010). New leadership, new directions, new format. *The Journal of Primary Prevention, 31*(3), 97–8

Toth, S. L., Manly, J. T., & Cicchetti, D. (1992). Child maltreatment and vulnerability to depression. *Develop. Psychopath., 4*, 97–112.

Toulouse, A., & Sullivan, A. M. (2008). Progress in Parkinson's disease—Where do we stand? *Progress in Neurobiology, 85*, 376–92.

Townsley, R., Turner, S., Beidel, D., & Calhoun, K. (1995). Social phobia: An analysis of possible developmental factors. *J. Abn. Psychol., 104*, 526–31.

Tozzi, F., Sullivan, P. F., Fear, J. L., McKenzie, J., & Bulik, C. M. (2003). Causes and recovery in anorexia nervosa: The patient's perspective. *Int. J. Eat. Dis., 33*, 143–54.

Trasler, G. (1978). Relations between psychopathy and persistent criminality-methodological and theoretical issues. In R. D. Hare & D. Schalling (Eds.), *Psychopathic behavior: Approaches to research.* New York: Wiley.

Treatment for Adolescents with Depression Study (TADS) Team, U.S. (2004, Aug. 18). Fluoxetine, cognitive- behavioral therapy, and their combination for adolescents with depression: Treatment for Adolescents with Depression Study (TADS) randomized controlled trial. *JAMA,* 807–20.

Treisman, G. J., Angelino, A. F., Hutton, H. E., & Hsu, J. (2009). Neuropsychiatric aspects of HIV infection and AIDS. In Sadock, B. J., Sadock, A. A., & Ruiz, P. (Eds.), *Kaplan and Sadock's Comprehensive Textbook of Psychiatry* (9th Ed.). PA: Lippincott, Williams & Wilkins, p. 506–31.

Tredget, J., Kirov, A., & Kirov, G. (2010). Effects of chronic lithium treatment on renal function. *J. Affect. Disord., 126*(3), 436–40. doi: 10.1016/j.jad.2010.04.018

Tremble, J., Padillo, A., & Bell, C. (1994). *Drug abuse among ethnic minorities, 1987.* Washington, DC: U.S. Department of Health and Human Services.

Trim, R. S., & Chassin, L. (2004). Drinking restraint, alcohol consumption and alcohol dependence among children of alcoholics. *J. Stud. Alcoh., 65*(1), 122–25.

Tronick, E. Z., & Cohn, J. F. (1989). Infant-mother face-to-face interaction: Age and gender differences in coordination and miscoordination. *Child Develop., 59*, 85–92.

Trope, H. (1997). *Locura y sociedad en la valencia de los siglos XV al XVII: Los locos del Hospital de los Inocentes sus instituciones La Locura y sus instuciones.* Valencia: Disputacion de Valencia, 141–54.

Trull, T. J., & Durrett, C. A. (2005). Categorical and dimensional models of personality disorder. *Ann. Rev. Clin. Psychol., 1*, 355–80.

Trzepacz, P. T., Meagher, D. J., & Wise, M. G. (2002). Neuropsychiatric aspects of delirium. In S. C. Yudofsky & R. E. Hales (Eds.), *The American Psychiatric Publishing textbook of neuropsychiatry and clinical neurosciences* (pp. 525–64). Washington, DC: American Psychiatric Publishing.

Tsai, A., Loftus, E., & Polage, D. (2000). Current directions in false-memory research. In D. Bjourkund (Ed.), *False-memory creation in children and adults: Theory, research, and implications* (pp. 31–44). Mahwah, NJ: Erlbaum.

Tsai, J. L., & Chentsova-Dutton, Y. (2002). Understanding depression across cultures. In I. H. Gotlib & C. L. Hammen (Eds.), *Handbook of depression* (pp. 467–91). New York: Guilford.

Tsai, J. L., Butcher, J. N., Munoz, R. F., & Vitousek, K. (2001). Culture, ethnicity, and psychopathology. In P. B. Sutker & H. E. Adams (Eds.), *Comprehensive handbook of psychopathology* (3rd ed., pp. 105–27). New York: Kluwer/Plenum.

Tseng, W. (2001). *Handbook of cultural psychiatry.* San Diego: Academic Press.

Tseng, W. S. (1973). The development of psychiatric concepts in traditional Chinese medicine. *Arch. Gen. Psychiat., 29*(4), 569–75.

Tsuang, M. T., Taylor, L., & Faraone, S. V. (2004). An overview of the genetics of psychotic mood disorders. *J. Psychiat. Res., 38*, 3–15.

Tucker, G. J. (1998). Editorial: Putting DSM-IV in perspective. *Amer. J. Psychiat., 155*(2), 159–61.

Tuerk, P. W., Grubaugh, A. I., Hammer, M. B., & Foa, E. B. (2009). Diagnosis and treatment of PTSD-related compulsive checking behaviors in veterans of the Iraq war: The influence of military context on the expression of PTSD symptoms. *Amer. J. Psychiat., 166*, 762–767.

Tuke, D. H. (1882). *History of the insane in the British Isles.* London: Kegan, Paul, Trench.

Tully, P. J., Pedersen, S. S., Winefield, H.R., Baker, R. A., Turnbull, D. A., & Denollet, J. (2011). Cardiac morbidity risk and depression and anxiety: A disorder, symptom, and trait analysis among cardiac surgery patients. *Psychol Health Med, 16*, 333–345.

Tuomisto, M. T. (1997). Intra-arterial blood pressure and heart rate reactivity to behavioral stress in normotensive, borderline, and mild hypertensive men. *Hlth. Psychol., 16*(6), 554–65.

Turan, M., & Senol, S. (2000). Tic disorders in children and adolescents. *Psikiyatri Psikoloji Psikofarmakoloji Dergisis, 8*, 215–20.

Turner, J. R. (1994). *Cardiovascular reactivity and stress: Patterns of physiological response.* New York: Plenum.

Turner, R. J., Lloyd, D. A., & Taylor, J. (2006). Physical disability and mental health: An epidemiology of psychiatric and substance disorders. *Rehabilitation Psychology, 51*(3) 214–23.

Turrisi, R. (1999). Cognitive and attitudinal factors in the analysis of alternatives to binge drinking. *Journal of Applied Social Psychology, 29*, 1510–33.

Turrisi, R., Wiersma, K. A., & Hughes, K. K. (2000). Binge-drinking-related consequences in college students: Role of drinking beliefs and mother–teen communications. *Psych. Addict. Behav., 14*(4), 342–55.

Twenge, J. M., & Campbell, W. K. (2002). Self-esteem and socioeconomic status: A meta-analytic review. *Personal. Soc. Psychol. Rev., 6*(1), 59–71.

Tyor, P. L., & Bell, L. V. (1984). *Caring for the retarded in America: A history.* Westport, CT: Greenwood Press.

Tyrer, F., Smith, L. K., & McGrother, C. W. (2007). Mortality in adults with moderate to profound intellectual disability: A population-based study. *Journal of Intellectual Disability Research, 51*(7), 520–27.

Tyrer, P., & Baldwin, D. (2006). Generalised anxiety disorder. *Lancet, 368*(9553), 2156–66.

Tyrka, A. R., Cannon, T. D., Haslam, N., Mednick, S. A., Schulsinger, F., Schulsinger, H., & Parnas, J. (1995). The latent structure of schizotypy: I. Premorbid indicators of a taxon of individuals at risk for schizophrenia-spectrum disorders. *J. Abn. Psychol., 104*(1), 173–83.

Udry, J. R. (1993). The politics of sex research. *J. Sex Res., 30*, 103–10.

Uecker, A., Mangan, P. A., Obrzut, J. E., & Nadel, L. (1993). Down syndrome in neurobiological perspective: An emphasis on spatial cognition. *J. Clin. Child Psychol., 22*(2), 266–76.

Uhde, T. W. (1990). Caffeine provocation of panic: A focus on biological mechanisms. In J. C. Ballenger (Ed.), *Neurobiology of panic disorder* (pp. 219–42). New York: Wiley-Liss.

Uher, R., & McGuffin, P. (2010). The moderation by the serotonin transporter gene of environmental adversity in the etiology of depression: 2009 update. *Molec. Psychiat., 15*(1), 18–22. doi: 10.1038/mp.2009.123

Uher, R., & Treasure, J. (2005). Brain lesions and eating disorders. *J. Neurol., Neurosurg. Psychiat., 76*, 852–57.

United States v. Batista, 483 F.3d 193 (3rd Cir. 2007).

Unützer, J., Tang, L., Oishi, S., Katon, W., Williams, J. W., Hunkeler, E., Hendrie, H., Lin, E. H. B., Levine, S., Grypma, L., Steffens, D. C., Fields, J., & Langston, C. (2006). Reducing Suicidal Ideation in Depressed Older Primary Care Patients. *J. Amer. Geriat. So., 54*(10), 1550–56.

U.S. Bureau of Labor Statistics. (2011). The employment situation–March 2011. News Release, April 1, 2011, *U. S. Department of Labor*, USDL-11-0436.

U.S. Bureau of the Census. (2010). U. S. population statistics for 2010. Washington, DC: Author. Retrieved from http://2010.census.gov.

U.S. Bureau of the Census. (2009). *Annual demographic supplement to the March 2002 Current Population Survey*. (on line). Available: www.census.gov

U.S. Bureau of the Census. (2010). *United States Census Count 2010*. Washington, DC: United States Bureau of the Census.

U.S. Census Bureau. (2011). *United States Census 2010*. Washington, DC: United States Bureau of the Census.

U.S. Department of Health and Human Services. (1994). *Preventing tobacco use among young people: A report of the Surgeon General*. U.S. Department of Health and Human Services.U.S. Department of Health and Human Services. (2001). *Mental health: Culture, race, and ethnicity—A supplement to mental health: A report of the Surgeon General*. Rockville, MD: U.S. Department of Health and Human Services, Public Health Service, Office of the Surgeon General.

U.S. Department of Health and Human Services. Public Health Service. (1997). *Survey of heroin use in the United States*. Rockville, MD: Author.

U.S. Department of Health and Human Services. (2010). *Alcohol and youth*. Rockville, MD: U.S. Department of Health and Human Services.

U.S. Department of Justice. (2006). Substance abuse and domestic violence. Washington, D. C.

U.S. Department of Justice, Office of Justice Programs. (2010). Highlights of the 2008 National Youth Gang Survey Office of Juvenile Justice and Delinquency Prevention. March 2010.

U.S. Department of Justice, Office of Justice Programs. (2010.) *National Crime Victimization Survey (NCVS)*. Bureau of Justice Statistics. Washington, D. C. http://bjs.ojp.usdoj.gov/

NIMH (2007). Facts about the National Institute of Mental Health. Washington, D. C. www.nimh.nih.gov/health/publications/index.shtml.

Üstün, T. B., Ayuso-Mateos, S., Chatterji, S., Mathers, C., & Murray, C. J. L. (2004). Global burden of depressive disorders in the year 2000. *Brit. J. Psychiat., 184*, 386–92.

Üstün, T. B., Bertelsen, A., Dilling, H., van Drimmelen, J., Pull, C., Okasha, A., Sartorius, N., and other ICD-10 Reference and Training Directors. (1996). *ICD-10 casebook. The many faces of mental disorders: Adult case histories according to ICD-10*. Washington, DC: American Psychiatric Press.

Vaillant, G. E., Gale, L., & Milofsky, E. S. (1982). Natural history of male alcoholism: II. The relationship between different diagnostic dimensions. *J. Stud. Alcoh., 43*(3), 216–32.

Valmaggia, L. R., Tabraham, P., Morris, E., & Bouman, T. K. (2008). Cognitive-behavioral therapy across stages of psychosis: Prodromal, first episode, and chronic schizophrenia. *Cognitive and Behavioral Practice, 15*, 179–93.

Van Doren, C. V. (1938). *Benjamin Franklin*. New York: Penguin.

van Hoeken, D., Veling, W., Sinke, S., Mitchell, J. E., & Hoek, H. W. (2009). The validity and utility of subtyping bulimia nervosa. *Int. J. Eat. Dis., 42*, 595–603.

Van Kampen, J., & Katz, M. (2001). Persistent psychosis after a single ingestion of "ecstasy." *Psychosomatics: Journal of Consultation Liaison Psychiatry, 42*(6), 525–27.

Van Kuyck. K., Gérard, N., Van Laere, K., Casteels, C., Pieters, G., Gabriëls, L., & Nuttin, B. (2009). Towards a neurocircuitry in anorexia nervosa: evidence from functional neuroimaging studies. *J. Psychiatr. Res., 43*, 1133–45.

van Lankveld, J. J. D. M., ter Kuile, M. M., de Groot, H. E., Melles, R., Nefs, J., & Zandbergen, M. (2006). Cognitive-behavioral therapy for women with lifelongvaginismus: A randomized waiting-list controlledtrial of efficacy. *J Consult. Clin. Psychol., 74*(1), 168–178.

Van Lier, P. A. C., Muthen, B. O., van der Sar, R. M., & Crijnen, A. A. M. (2004). Preventing disruptive behavior in elementary school children: Impact of a universal classroom-based intervention. *J. Cons. Clin. Psychol., 72*, 467–78.

van Ommeren, M., de Jong, J. T. V. M., Sharma, B., Komproe, I., Thapa, S. B., & Cardena, E. (2001). Psychiatric disorders among tortured Bhutanese refugees in Nepal. *Arch. Gen. Psychiat., 58*, 475–82.

van Orden, K. A., Witte, T. K., Selby, E. A., Bender, T. W., & Joiner, T. E., Jr. (2008). Suicidal behavior in youth. In J. R. Z. Abela & B. L. Hankin (Eds.), *Handbook of depression in children and adolescents*. (pp. 441–65). New York: Guilford Press.

van Os, J., Bak, M., Hanssen, M., Bijl, R. V., de Graaf, R., & Verdoux, H. (2002). Cannabis use and psychosis: A longitudinal population-based study. *Amer. J. Epidemiol., 156*, 319–27.

van Praag., H. M. (2005) The resistance of suicide: Why haven't antidepressants reduced suicide rates? In K. Hawton (Ed.),*Prevention and treatment of suicidal behavior: From science to practice* (pp. 239–60). Oxford: Oxford University Press.

Vandereycken, W. (2002). History of anorexia nervosa and bulimia nervosa. In C. G. Fairburn & K. D. Brownell (Eds.), *Eating disorders and obesity* (2nd ed., pp. 151–52). New York: Guilford Press.

Vanhala, M., Korpelained, R., Tapanainen, P., Kaikkonen, K., Kaikkonen, H., Saukkonen, T., & Keinänen-Kiukaanniemi, S. (2009). Lifestyle risk factors for obesity in 7-year-old children. *Obesity Research and Clinical Practice, 3*, 99–107.

Vasey, P. L., & Bartlett, N. H. (2007). What can the Samoan 'fa'afafine' teach us about the Western concept of gender identity disorder in childhood? *Persp. Biol. Med., 50*(4), 481–90.

Vasiljeva, O. A., Kornetov, N. A., Zhankov, A. I., & Reshetnikov, V. I. (1989). Immune function in psychogenic depression. *Amer. J. Psychiat., 146*, 284–85.

Veale, D. (2009). Body dysmorphic disorder. In M. M. Antony & M. B. Stein (Eds.), *Oxford handbook of anxiety and related disorders* (pp. 541–50). New York: Oxford University Press.

Veale, D., & Riley, S. (2001). Mirror, mirror on the wall, who is the ugliest of them all? The psychopathology of mirror gazing in body dysmorphic disorder. *Behav. Res. Ther., 39*, 1381–93.

Veale, J. F., Clarke, D. E., & Lomax, T. C. (2008). Sexuality of male-to-female transsexuals. *Arch. Sex. Behav., 37*, 586–97.

Velasquez, M. M., Maurer, G. G., Crouch, C., & DiClemente, C. C. (2001). *Group treatment of substance abuse*. New York: Guilford.

Velting, D. M., & Gould, M. S. (1997). Suicide contagion. In R. W. Maris, M. M. Silverman, & S. S. Canetton (Eds.), *Review of suicidology, 1997* (pp. 96–137). New York: Guilford.

Ventura, J., Nuechterlein, K. H., Hardesty, J. P., & Gitlin, M. (1992). Life events and schizophrenic relapse after withdrawal of medication. *Brit. J. Psychiat., 161*, 615–20.

Ventura, J., Nuechterlein, K. H., Lukoff, D., & Hardesty, J. P. (1989). A prospective study of stressful life events and schizophrenic relapse. *J. Abn. Psychol., 98*, 407–11.

Verdejo, A., Toribio, I., Orozco, C., Puente, K. L., & Pérez-García, M. (2005). Neuropsychological functioning in methadone maintenance patients versus abstinent heroin abusers. *Drug Al. Dep., 78*(3), 283–88.

Verghese, J., Lipton, R. B., Hall, C. B., Kuslansky, G., Katz, M. J., & Buschke, H. (2002). Abnormality of gait as a predictor of non-Alzheimer's dementia. *N. Engl. J. Med., 347*, 1761–68.

Verheul, R., & Widiger, T. (2004). A meta-analysis of the prevalence and usage of the personality disorder not otherwise specified (PDNOS) diagnosis. *J. Pers. Dis., 18*, 309–19.

Verheul, R., Bartak, A., & Widiger, T. (2007). Prevalence and construct validity of personality disorder not otherwise specified (PDNOS). *J. Pers. Dis., 21*, 359–70.

Verhulst, F. (1995). A review of community studies. In F. Verhulst & H. Koot (Eds.), *The epidemiology of child and adolescent psychiatry* (pp. 146–77). Oxford: Oxford University Press.

Verhulst, F. C., & Achenbach, T. M. (1995). Empirically based assessment and taxonomy of psychopathology: Cross cultural applications. A review. *Eur. Child Adoles. Psychiat., 4*, 61–76.

Verkerk, A. J. M. H., Pieretti, M., et al. (1991). Identification of a gene (FMR-1) containing a CGG repeat coincident with a breakpoint cluster region exhibiting length variation in fragile X syndrome. *Cell, 65*, 905–14.

Vermeiren, R., Jespers, I. & Moffit, T. (2006). Mental health problems in juvenile justice populations. *Child and Adolescent Psychiatric Clinics of North America*, 15(2), 333–351.

Vermetten, E., Schmahl, C., Lindner, S., Loewenstein, R., & Bremner, J. D. (2006). Hippocampal and amygdalar volumes in dissociative identity disorder. *Amer. J. Psychiat., 163*, 630–36.

Verona, E., Patrick, C. J., & Joiner, T. E. (2001). Psychopathy, antisocial personality, and suicide risk. *J. Abn. Psychol., 110*(3), 462–70.

Verona, E., Patrick, C., Curtin, J., Bradley, M., & Lang, P. (2004). Psychopathy and physiological response to emotionally evocative sounds. *J. Abn. Psychol., 113*, 99–108.

Vick, K. (2009). In Calif., medical marijuana laws are moving pot into the mainstream. *Washington Post, 132*(128).

Vickers, K., & McNally, R. J. (2004). Panic disorder and suicide attempt in the National Comorbidity Survey. *J. Abn. Psychol., 113*(4), 582–91.

Videbech, P., Ravnkilde, B., Kristensen, S., Egander, A., Clemmensen, K., Rasmussen, N., & Gjedde, A. (2003). The Danish/PET depression project: Poor verbal fluency performance despite normal prefrontal activation in patients with major depression. *Psychiatry Research: Neuroimaging, 123*(1), 49–63.

Viding, E., Blair, R. J., Moffitt, T. E., Plomin, R. (2005). Evidence for substantial genetic risk for psychopathy in 7-year-olds. *J. Child Psychol. Psychiat., 46*(6), 592–97.

Vidović, V., Jureša, V., Begovac, I., Mahnik, M., & Tocilj, G. (2005). Perceived family cohesion, adaptability and communication in eating disorders. *European Eating Disorders Review, 13*, 19–28.

Villanueva, M., Tonigan, J. S., & Miller, W. R. (2003). A retrospective study of client-treatment matching: Differential treatment response of Native American alcoholics in project MATCH. *Alcohol. Clin. Exp. Res., 26* (Suppl.) A 83.

Villasante, O. (2003). The unfulfilled project of the model mental hospital in Spain: Fifty years of the Santa Isabel Madhouse, Leganis (1851–1900). In T. Dening (Ed.), *Hist. Psychiat., 14*(53, Pt. 1), 3–23.

Viney, W. (1996). Dorthea Dix: An intellectual conscience for psychology. In G. A. Kimble, C. A. Boneau, & M. Wertheimer (Eds.), *Portraits of pioneers in psychology* (pp. 15–33). Washington, DC: American Psychological Association.

Viney, W., & Bartsch, K. (1984). Dorthea Lynde Dix: Positive or negative influence on the development of treatment for the mentally ill? *Social Science Journal, 21*, 71–82.

Vita, A., De Peri, L., Silenzi, C., & Dieci, M. (2006). Brain morphology in first episode schizophrenia: a meta-analysis of quantitative magnetic resonance imaging studies. *Schiz. Res., 82*, 75–88.

Vitacco, M. J., Van Rybroek, G. J., Erickson, S. K., Rogstad, J. E., Tripp, A., Harris, L., & Miller, R.(2008). Developing services for insanity acquittees conditionally released into the community: Maximizing success and minimizing recidivism. *Psychological Services, Vol 5*(2), 118–25.

Vitale, J. E., & Newman, J. P. (2008) Psychopathy as psychopathology: Key developments in etiology, assessment, and treatment. In W. E. Craighead, D. J. Miklowitz, & L. W. Craighead (Eds.), *Psychopathology: History, diagnosis, and empirical foundations.* (pp. 565–97). Hoboken, NJ: John Wiley & Sons.

Vitiello, B., & Waslick, B. (2010). Pharmacotherapy for children and adolescents with anxiety disorders. *Psychiat. Ann., 40*(4), 185–91.

Vitousek, K. B. (2002). Cognitive-behavioral therapy for anorexia nervosa. In C. G. Fairburn & K. D. Brownell (Eds.), *Eating disorders and obesity: A comprehensive handbook* (2nd ed., pp. 308–13). New York: Guilford.

Vögele, C., & Gibson, E. L. (2010). Moods, emotions, and eating disorders. In Agras, W. S. (Ed.), *The Oxford Handbook of Eating Disorders*, New York: Oxford University Press, pp. 180–205.

Vogeltanz-Holm, N. D., Wonderlich, S. A., Lewis, B. A., Wilsnack, S. C., Harris, T. R., Wilsnack, R. W., & Kristjanson, A. F. (2000). Longitudinal predictors of binge eating, intense dieting, and weight concerns in a national sample of women. *Behav. Ther., 31*, 221–35.

Voglmaier, M. M., Seidman, L. J., Niznikiewicz, M. A., Dickey, C. C., Shenton, M. E., & McCarley, R. W. (2005). A comparative profile analysis of neuropsychological function in men and women with schizotypal personality disorder. *Schiz. Res., 74*(1), 43–49.

Volk, H. E., Scherrer, J. F., Bucholz, K. K., Todorov, A., Heath, A. C., Jacob, T., & True, W. R. (2007). Evidence for specificity of transmission of alcohol and nicotine dependence in an offspring of twins design. *Drug and Alcohol Dependence, 87*(2–3) 225–32.

Volker, M. A. & Lopata, C. (2008). Autism: A review of biological bases, assessment, and intervention. *School Psychology Quarterly, 23*(2), 258–270.

Volkow, N. D., & O'Brien, C. P. (2007). Issues for DSM-V: Should obesity be included as a brain disorder? *Am. J. Psychiat., 164, 5*, 708–10.

Volkow, N. D., Ding, Y. S., Fowler, J. S., Ashby, C., Liebermann, J., Hitzemann, R., & Wolf, A. P. (1995). Is methylphenidate like cocaine? Studies on their pharmacokinetics and distribution in the human brain. *Arch. Gen. Psychiat., 52*, 456–63.

Vollmer-Larsen, A., Jacobsen, T. B., Hemmingsen, R., & Parnas, J. (2006). Schizoaffective disorder: The reliability of its clinical diagnostic use. *Acta Psych. Scand., 113*(5), 402–7.

von Haller, A. (1782) *Elementa physiologiae corporishumani.* Lausanne, Julium Henricum Pott Vreugdenhil, A., Cannell, J., Davies, A., & Razay, G. (2011). A community-based exercise programme to improve functional ability in people with Alzheimer's disease: a randomized controlled trial. *Scand. J. Caring Sci.*, epub ahead of print.

Waddington, J. L., O'Callaghan, E., Youssef, H. A., Buckley, P., Lane, A., Cotter, D., & Larkin, C. (1999). Schizophrenia: Evidence for a "cascade" process with neurodevelopmental origins. In E. Z. Susser, A. S. Brown, & J. M. Gorman (Eds.), *Prenatal exposures in schizophrenia* (pp. 3–34).Washington, DC: American Psychiatric Press.

Wade, K, Sharman, S., Garry, M., Memon, M., Garry, M., et al. (2007). False claims about false memory research. *Consciousness and Cognition, 16*, 118–28.

Wade, T. D. (2010). Genetic influences on eating and the eating disorders. In W. A. Agras (Ed.), *The Oxford Handbook of Eating Disorders*, New York: Oxford University Press, pp. 103–22.

Wade, T. D., Tiggerman, M., Bulik, C. M., Fairburn, C. G., Wray, N. R., & Martin, N. G. (2008). Shared temperament risk factors for anorexia nervosa: A twin study. *Psychosomat. Med., 70*, 239–44.

Wagner, K. D., & Ambrosini, P. J. (2001). Childhood depression: Pharmacological therapy/treatment (pharmacotherapy of childhood depression). *J. Clin. Child Psychol., 30*(1), 88–97.

Wahlberg, K.-E., Wynne, L. C., et al. (1997). Gene-environment interaction in vulnerability to schizophrenia: Findings from the Finnish adoptive family study of schizophrenia. *Amer. J. Psychiat., 154*(3), 355–62.

Wakefield, J. C. (2011). Should uncomplicated bereavement-related depression be reclassified as a disorder in the DSM-5?: Response to Kenneth S. Kendler's statement defending the proposal to eliminate the bereavement exclusion. *J. Nerv. Ment. Dis., 199*(3), 203–8. doi: 210.1097/NMD.1090b1013e31820cd31155.

Wakefield, J. C., Schmitz, M. F., First, M. B., & Horwitz, A. V. (2007). Extending the bereavement exclusion for major depression to other losses: Evidence from the National Comorbidity Survey. *Arch. Gen. Psychiat., 64*(4), 433–40.

Waldman, I. D., & Rhee, S. H., (2006) Genetic and environmental influences on psychopathy and antisocial behavior. In C. Patrick (Ed.), *Handbook of Psychopathy* (pp. 205–29). New York: Guilford Press.

Waldman, I. D., & Slutske, W. S. (2000). Antisocial behavior and alcoholism: A behavioral genetic perspective on comorbidity. *Clin. Psychol. Rev., 20*(2), 255–87.

Walford, E. (1878). *Old and new London: A narrative of its history, its people, and its places.* Vol. VI. London: Cassell, Petter, & Galpin.

Walker, E. E. (1994). Developmentally moderated expressions of the neuropathology underlying schizophrenia. *Schizo. Bull., 20*, 453–80.

Walker, E. F., & Diforio, D. (1997). Schizophrenia: A neural diathesis–stress model. *Psychol. Rev., 104*, 667–85.

Walker, E. F., & Tessner, K. (2008). Schizophrenia. *Perspectives on Psychological Science, 3*, 30–37.

Walker, E. F., Grimes, K. E., Davis, D. M., & Smith, A. J. (1993). Childhood precursors of schizophrenia: Facial expressions of emotion. *Amer. J. Psychiat., 150*(11), 1654–60.

Walker, E. F., Savoie, T., & Davis, D. (1994). Neuromotor precursors of schizophrenia. *Schizo. Bull., 20*(3), 441–51.

Walker, E., Kestler, L., Bollini, A., & Hochman, K. M. (2004). Schizophrenia: Etiology and course. *Annu. Rev. Psychol., 55*, 401–30.

Walker, E., Shapiro, D., Esterberg, M., & Trotman, H. (2010). Neurodevelopment and schizophrenia: Broadening the focus. *Curr. Dis. Psychol. Sci., 19*, 204–208.

Walker, J., Archer, J., & Davies, M. (2005). Effects of rape on men: A descriptive analysis. *Arch. Sex. Behav., 34*, 69–80.

Wallace, J., Schneider, T., & McGuffin, P. (2002). Genetics of depression. In I. H. Gotlib & C. L. Hammen (Eds.), *Handbook of depression* (pp. 169–91). New York: Guilford.

Wallenstein, M. B., & Nock, M. K. (2007). Physical exercise as a treatment for non-suicidal self injury: Evidence from a single case study. *Am. J. Psychiat., 164*, 350–51.

Waller, N. G., & Ross, C. A. (1997). The prevalence and biometric structure of pathological dissociation in the general population: Taxometric and behavior genetic findings. *J. Abn. Psychol., 106*, 499–510.

Waller, N., Putnam, F. W., & Carlson, E. B. (1996). Types of dissociation and dissociative types: A taxometric analysis of dissociative experiences. *Psychol. Meth., 1*, 300–21.

Wallin, A., & Blennow, K. (1993). Heterogeneity of vascular dementia: Mechanisms and subgroups. *Journal of Geriatric Psychiatry and Neurology, 6*(3), 177–88.

Walsh, E., Moran, P., Scott, C., McKenzie, K., Burns, T., Creed, F., Tyler, P., Murray, R. M., & Fahy, T. (2003). Prevalence of violent victimization in severe mental illness. *Brit. J. Psychiat., 183*, 233–38.

Walter, A. L., & Carter, A. S. (1997). Gilles de la Tourette's syndrome in childhood: A guide for school professionals. *School Psychol. Rev., 26*(1), 28–46.

Walters, J. (2006, Nov. 3). National Public Health official issues statement regarding South Dakota's proposed "medical" marijuana initiative. *News & Public Affairs.*

Wang, Y., Beydoun, M. A., Liang, L., Caballero, B., & Kumanyika, S. K. (2008). Will all Americans become overweight or obese? Estimating the progression and cost of the US obesity epidemic. *Obesity, 16*, 2323–30.

Wang, P. S., Berglund, P., Olfson, M., Pincus, H. A., Wells, K. B., & Kessler, R. C. (2005). Failure and delay in initial treatment contact after the first onset of mental disorders in the National Comorbidity Survey Replication. *Arch. Gen. Psychiat., 62*, 603–13.

Wang, P. S., Lane, M., Olfson, M., Pincus, H. A., Wells, K. B., & Kessler, R. C. (2005). Twelve-month use of mental health services in the United States. *Arch. Gen. Psychiat., 62*, 629–40.

Ward, C. I., & Laughlin, J. E. (2003). Social contexts, age, and juvenile delinquency: A community perspective. *J. Child Adol. Men. Hlth., 15*, 13–25.

Ward, T., McCormack, J., Hudson, S. M., & Polaschek, D. (1997). Rape: Assessment and treatment. In D. R. Laws & W. O'Donohue (Eds.), *Sexual deviance: Theory, assessment, and treatment* (pp. 356–93). New York: Guilford.

Wargo, E. (2007). Understanding the have-knots: The role of stress in just about everything. *APS Observer, 20, 11*, 18–23.

Warner, C. H., Appenzeller, G. N., Parker, J. R., Warner, C. M., & Hoge, C. W. (2011). Effectiveness of mental health screening and coordination of in-theater care prior to deployment to Iraq: A cohort study. *Am. J. Psych., 168*, 378–85.

Warner, R. (2001). The prevention of schizophrenia: What interventions are safe and effective? *Schizo. Bull., 27*, 551–62.

Warnes, H. (1973). The traumatic syndrome. *Ment. Hlth. Dig., 5*(3), 33–34.

Warren, J. I., & Hazelwood, R. R. (2002). Relational patterns associated with sexual sadism: A study of 20 wives and girlfriends. *Journal of Family Violence, 17*, 75–89.

Warren, J. I., Dietz, P. E., & Hazelwood, R. R. (1996). The sexually sadistic serial killer. *Journal of Forensic Sciences, 41*, 970–74.

Washington State Institute for Public Policy. (1995). *Boot camps: A Washington state update and overview of national findings* (#95-06-1201). Olympia, WA: Author.

Washington State Institute for Public Policy. (1998). Trends in at-risk behaviors of youth in Washington, 1998 update. (Seminar 3162). Olympia, WA: Author.

Wasserman, D. R., & Leventhal, J. M. (1993). Maltreatment of children born to cocaine-dependent mothers. *Archives of Pediatrics and Adolescent Medicine, 147*, 1324–28.

Wasserman, J. D. (2003). Assessment of intellectual functioning. *Handbook of psychology* (Vol. 10, pp. 417–42). New York: John Wiley & Sons.

Wassink, T. H., Piven, J., & Patil, S. R. (2001). Chromosomal abnormalities in a clinic sample of individuals with autistic disorder. *Psychiatric Genetics, 11*(2), 57–63.

Watanabe, H., Kawauchi, A., Kitamori, T., & Azuma, Y. (1994). Treatment system for nocturnal enuresis according to an original classification system. *European Urology, 25*, 43–50.

Waterhouse, L., & Fein, D. (1997). Genes tPA, Fyn, and FAK in autism? *J. Autism Devel. Dis., 27*(3), 220–23.

Waters, R. J., & Nicoll, A. R. (2005). Genetic influences on outcome following acute neurological insults. *Current Opinion in Critical Care, 11*, 105–10.

Watkins, S. S., Koob, G. F., & Markou, A. (2000). Neural mechanisms underlying nicotine addiction: Acute positive reinforcement and withdrawal. *Nicotine & Tobacco Research, 2*, 19–37.

Watson, A. C., Otely, E., Westbrook, A. L., Gardner, A. L., Lamb, T. A., Corrigan, P. W., & Fenton, W. S. (2004). Changing middle schoolers' attitudes about mental illness through education. *Schizo. Bull., 30*(3), 563–72.

Watson, D. (2005). Rethinking the mood and anxiety disorders: A quantitative hierarchical model for DSM-V. *J. Abn. Psych., 114*(4), 522–36.

Watson, D., Clark, L. A., & Chmielewski, M. (2008). Structures of personality and their relevance to psychopathology: II. Further articulation of a comprehensive unified trait structure. *J. Pers., 76*(6), 1545–86. doi:10.1111/j.1467-6494.2008.00531.x

Watson, D., Clark, L. A., & Harkness, A. R. (1994). Structures of personality and their relevance to psychopathology. *J. Abn. Psychol., 103*, 18–31.

Watson, D., Gamez, W., & Simms, L. J. (2005). Basic dimensions of temperament and their relation to anxiety and depression: A symptom-based perspective. *J. Res. Person., 39*(1), 46–66.

Watson, D., Kotov, R. Gamez, W. (2006) Basic dimensions of temperament in relation to personality and psychopathology. In R. F. Krueger & J. L. Tackettt (Eds.), *Personality and psychopathology.* pp. 7–38. New York: Guilford Press.

Watson, J. (1924). *Behaviorism.* New York: The People's Institute Publishing Co., Inc.

Watson, J., & Raynor, R. (1920). Conditioned emotional reactions. *Journal of Genetic Psychology, 37*, 394–419.

Watson, S., Gallagher, P., Ritchie, J. C., Ferrier, I. N., & Young, A. H. (2004). Hypothalamic-pituitary-adrenal axis function in patients with bipolar disorder. *Brit. J. Psychiat., 184*, 496–502.

Watson, S. J., Benson, J. A., Jr., & Joy, J. E. (2000). Marijuana and medicine: Assessing the science base: A summary of the 1999 Institute of Medicine Report. *Arch. Gen. Psychiat., 57*, 347–52.

Watson, T. L., Bowers, W. A., & Andersen, A. E. (2000). Involuntary treatment of eating disorders. *Amer. J. Psychiat., 157*(11), 1806–10.

Watt, N. F., Anthony, E. J., Wynne, L. C., & Rolf, J. E. (Eds.). (1984). *Children at risk for schizophrenia: A longitudinal perspective.* Cambridge: Cambridge University Press.

Watters, C., & Ingleby, D. (2004). Locations of care: Meeting the mental health and social care needs of refugees in Europe. *International Journal of Law & Psychiatry, 27*(6), 549–70.

Watts-English, T., Fortson, B. L., Gibler, N., Hooper, S. R., & DeBellis, M. D. (2006). The psychobiology of maltreatment in childhood. *Journal of Social Issues, 62*(4), 717–36.

Weatherby, N. L., Shultz, J. M., Chitwood, D. D., & McCoy, H. V. (1992). Crack cocaine use and sexual activity in Miami, Florida. *J. Psychoact. Drugs, 24*, 373–80.

Weathers, F. W., & Keane, T. M. (2007). The criterion A problem revisited: Controversies and challenges in defining and measuring psychological trauma. *J. Trauma. Stress., 20*, 101–121.

Webb, C. A., DeRubeis, R. J., & Barber, J. P. (2010). Therapist adherence/competence and treatment outcome: A meta-analytic review. *J. Cons. Clin. Psychol., 78*, 200–11.

Wechsler, H., Davenport, A., Dowdall, G., Moeykens, M. S., & Castillo, S. (1994, Dec.). Health and behavioral consequences of binge drinking in college. *JAMA*, 1672–77.

Wechsler, H., Dowdall, G. W., Maenner, G., Gledhill-Hoyt, J., & Lee, H. (1998). Changes in binge drinking and related problems among American college students between 1993 and 1997. *J. Amer. Coll. Hlth., 47*(2), 57–68.

Weggen, S., Eriksen, J. L., Das, P., Sagi, S. A., Wang, R., Pietrzik, C. U., Findlay, K. A., Smith, T. E., Murphy, M. P., Bulter, T., Kang, D. E., Marquez-Sterling, N., Golde, T. E., & Koo, E. H. (2001). A subset of NSAIDs lower amyloidogenic A(42) independently of cyclooxygenase activity. *Nature, 414*, 212–16.

Wegman, H. L., & Stetler, C. (2009). A meta-analytic review of the effects of childhood abuse on medical outcomes in adulthood. *Psychosom. Med., 71*(8), 805–12. doi: 10.1097/PSY.0b013e3181bb2b46

Wegner, D. M. (1994). Ironic processes of mental control. *Psychol. Rev., 101*(1), 34–52.

Wehman, P. (2003). Workplace inclusion: Persons with disabilities and coworkers working together. *Journal of Vocational Rehabilitation, 18*(2), 131–41.

Weinberger, D. (1997). On localizing schizophrenic neuropathology. *Schizo. Bull., 23*(3), 537–40.

Weinberger, D. R. (1987). Implications of normal brain development for the pathogenesis of schizophrenia. *Arch. Gen. Psychiat., 44*, 660–69.

Weinberger, L. E., Sreenivasan, S., Garrick, T., & Osran, H. (2005). The impact of surgical castration on sexual recidivism risk among sexually violent predatory offenders. *J. Amer. Acad. Psychiat. Law, 33*, 16–36.

Weiner, D. B. (1979). The apprenticeship of Philippe Pinel: A new document, "Observations of Citizen Pussin on the insane." *Amer. J. Psychiat., 136*(9), 1128–34.

Weiner, D. N., & Rosen, R. C. (1999). Sexual dysfunctions and disorders. In T. Millon, P. H. Blaney, & R. D. Davis (Eds.), *Oxford textbook of psychopathology* (pp. 410–43). New York: Oxford University Press.

Weiner, I. B., & Greene, R. L. (2008). *Handbook of personality assessment.* Hoboken, NJ: John Wiley & Sons.

Weiner, L. A. B., & Meyer, G. (2009). Personality assessment with the Rorschach Inkblot Method. In J. N. Butcher (Ed.), *Oxford handbook of personality and clinical assessment* (pp. 277–98). New York: Oxford University Press.

Weiner, M. F., & Lipton, A. M. (Eds.). (2009). *The American Psychiatric Publishing textbook of Alzheimer disease and other dementias.* Arlington, VA: American Psychiatric Publishing.

Weis, R., & Toolis, E. E. (2008). Military style residential treatment for disruptive adolescents: A critical review and look to the future. Advances in psychology research. In A. M. Columbus (Ed.), *Advances in psychology research* (Vol. 56, pp. 1–44). Hauppauge, NY: Nova Science Publishers.

Weiser, M. (2011). Early intervention for schizophrenia: The risk-benefit ratio of antipsychotic treatment in the prodromal phase. *Am. J. Psychiat., 168*, 761–63.

Weinstock, J., Rash, C. J., & Petry, N. M. (2010). Contingency management for cocaine use in methadone maintenance patients: When does abstinence happen? *Psych. Addict. Behav., 24*(2), 282–91.

Weisman, A., Duarte, E., Koneru, V., & Wasserman, S. (2006). The development of a culturally informed, family-focuses treatment for schizophrenia. *Fam. Process, 45*, 171–86.

Weiss, B., Weisz, J. R., & Bromfield, R. (1986). Performance of retarded and nonretarded persons on information processing tasks: Further tests of the similar structure hypothesis. *Psychol. Bull., 100*, 157–75.

Weiss, L. G., Saklofske, D. H., Prifitera, A., & Holdnack, J. A. (Eds.). (2006). *WISC-IV advanced clinical interpretation.* Burlington, MA: Elsevier Academic Press, 2006.

Weissman, M. M. (1993). The epidemiology of personality disorders: A 1990 update. *J. Pers. Dis. Supplement,* 44–62.

Weissman, M. M., & Markowitz, J. C. (2002). Interpersonal psychotherapy for depression. In I. H. Gotlib & C. L. Hammen (Eds.), *Handbook of depression* (pp. 404–21). New York: Guilford.

Weissman, M. M., Fendrich, M., Warner, V., & Wickramaratne, P. (1992). Incidence of psychiatric disorder in offspring at high and low risk for depression. *J. Amer. Acad. Child Adoles. Psychiat., 31*, 640–48.

Weisz, J. R., Donenberg, G. R., Han, S. S., & Weiss, B. (1995). Bridging the gap between laboratory and clinic in child and adolescent psychotherapy. *J. Cons. Clin. Psychol., 63*(5), 688–701.

Weisz, J. R., McCarty, C. A., Eastman, K. L., Chaiyasit, W., & Suwanlert, S. (1997). Developmental psychopathology and culture: Ten lessons from Thailand. In S. Luthar, J. Burack, D. Cicchetti, & J. Weisz (Eds.), *Developmental psychopathology: Perspectives on adjustment, risk, and disorder* (pp. 568–92). Cambridge, England: Cambridge University Press.

Weisz, J. R., Suwanlert, S., Chaiyasit, W., & Walter, B. R. (1987). Over and undercontrolled clinic-referral problems among Thai and American children and adolescents: The wat and wai of cultural differences. *J. Cons. Clin. Psychol., 55,* 719–26.

Weisz, J. R., Suwanlert, S., Chaiyasit, W., Weiss, B., Achenbach, T. M., & Eastman, K. L. (1993). Behavior and emotional problems among Thai and American adolescents: Parent reports for ages 12–16. *J. Abn. Psychol., 102,* 395–403.

Weisz, J. R., & Weiss, B. (1991). Studying the referability of child clinical problems. *J. Cons. Clin. Psychol., 59,* 266–73.

Weisz, J. R., Weiss, B., Suwanlert, S., & Chaiyasit, W. (2003). Syndromal structure of psychopathology in children of Thailand and the United States. *J. Cons. Clin. Psychol., 71*(2), 375–85.

Weisz, J. R., Weiss, B., Suwanlert, S., & Chaiyasit, W. (2006). Culture and youth psychopathology: Testing the Syndromal Sensitivity Model in Thai and American adolescents. *J Consult. Clin. Psychol., 74*(6), 1098–1107.

Welin, C., Lappas, G., & Wilhelmsen, L. (2000). Independent importance of psychological factors for prognosis after myocardial infarction. *Journal of Internal Medicine, 247,* 629–39.

Wells, A. (1999). A cognitive model of generalized anxiety disorder. *Behav. Mod., 23,* 526–55.

Wells, A., & Butler, G. (1997). Generalized anxiety disorder. In D. M. Clark & C. G. Fairburn (Eds.), *Science and practice of cognitive behaviour therapy* (pp. 155–78). New York: Oxford University Press.

Wells, A., & Clark, D. M. (1997). Social phobia: A cognitive perspective. In G. C. L. Davey (Ed.), *Phobias: A handbook of description, treatment, and theory.* Chichester, England: Wiley.

Wells, A., & Papageorgiou, C. (1995). Worry and the incubation of intrusive images following stress. *Behav. Res. Ther., 33,* 579–83.

Wells, D. L., & Ott, C. A. (2011). The "New" Marijuana (March). *Annals of Psychiatry.* Retrieved February 25, 2011, from www.theannals.com, DOI 10.1345/aph.1P580.

Welte, J. W., Barnes, G. M., Wieczorek, W. F., Tidwell, M. C., & Parker, J. C. (2004). Risk factors for pathological gambling. *Add. Behav., 29*(2), 323–35.

Wender, P. H. (2000). *ADHD: Attention deficit hyperactivity disorder in children and adults.* Oxford: Oxford University Press.

Wen-Shing, T., & Streltzer, J. (2008). Cultural competence in health care: A guide for professionals. New York: Springer.

West, J. R., Perotta, D. M., & Erickson, C. K. (1998). Fetal alcohol syndrome: A review for Texas physicians. *Medical Journal of Texas, 94,* 61–67.

Westen, D. (1998). The scientific legacy of Sigmund Freud: Toward a psychodynamically informed psychological science. *Psychol. Bull., 124*(3), 333–71.

Westen, D., Nakash, O., Thomas, C., & Bradley, R. (2006). Clinical assessment of attachment patterns and personality disorder in adolescents and adults. *J. Cons. Clin. Psychol., 74,* 1065–85.

Westen, D., Shedler, J., & Bradley, R. (2006). A prototype approach to personality disorder diagnosis. *Am. J. Psychiat., 163,* 846–56.

Westermeyer, J. (2001). Personal communication to J. N. Butcher.

Westermeyer, J., & Janca, A. (1997). Language, culture and psychopathology: Conceptual and methodological issues. *Transcult. Psychiat., 34,* 291–311.

Westermeyer, J., & Kroll, J. (1978). Violence and mental illness in a peasant society: Characteristics of violent behaviors and 'folk' use of restraints. *Brit. J. Psychiat., 133,* 529–41.

Whalley, H. C., Simonotto, E., Flett, S., et al. (2004). fMRI correlates of state and trait effects in subjects at genetically enhanced risk of schizophrenia. *Brain, 127,* 478–91.

Whang, W., Kubzansky, L. D., Kawachi, I., Rexrode, K. M., Kroenke, C. H., Glynn, R. J., et al. (2009). Depression and risk of sudden cardiac death and coronary heart disease in women: Results from the Nurses' Health Study. *J. Amer. Coll. Cardiol., 53*(11), 950–58. doi: 10.1016/j.jacc.2008.10.060

Wheeler, J. G., Christensen, A., & Jacobson, N. S. (2001). Couple distress. In D. H. Barlow (Ed.), *Clinical handbook for psychological disorders* (3rd ed., pp. 609–30). New York: Guilford.

Whiffen, V. L., & Clark, S. E. (1997). Does victimization account for sex differences in depressive symptoms? *Brit. J. Clin. Psychol., 36,* 185–93.

Whipple, J. L., & Lambert, M. J. (2011). Outcome measures for practice. *Ann. Rev. Clin. Psychol., 7,* 87–111.

Whisman, M. A. (2007). Marital distress and DSM-IV psychiatric disorders in a population-based national survey. *J. Abn. Psych., 116*(3), 63843.

Whitaker, R. (2009). Deinstitutionalization and neuroleptics: The myth and reality. In Y. O. Alanen, M. González de Chávez, A. S. Silver, & B. Martindale (Eds.), *Psychotherapeutic approaches to schizophrenic psychoses: Past, present and future (International Society for the Psychological Treatments of the Schizophrenias and Other Psychoses)* (pp. 346–56). New York, Routledge/Taylor & Francis Group.

Whitaker, R. (2010). *Anatomy of an epidemic: Magic bullets, psychiatric drugs, and the astonishing rise of mental illness in America.* New York: Crown Publishers.

Whitbeck, L. B., Johnson, K. D., Hoyt, D. R., & Walls, M. L. (2006). Prevalence and comorbidity of mental disorders among American Indian children in the northern Midwest. *J. Adol. Hlth., 39*(3), 427–34.

White, D. A., Nortz, M. J., Mandernach, T., Huntington, K., & Steiner, R. (2002). Age-related working memory impairments in children with prefrontal dysfunction associated with phenylketonuria. *J. Int. Neuropsycholog. Soc., 8,* 1–11.

White, J., Moffitt, T. E., & Silva, P. A. (1989). A prospective replication of the protective effects of IQ in subjects at high risk for juvenile delinquency. *J. Clin. Cons. Psychol., 57,* 719–24.

White, K. S., & Barlow, D. H. (2002). Panic disorder and agoraphobia. In D. H. Barlow (Ed.), *Anxiety and its disorders* (2nd ed., pp. 328–79). New York: Guilford.

White, K. S., Brown, T. A., Somers, T. J., & Barlow, D. H. (2006). Avoidance behavior in panic disorder: The moderating influence of perceived control. *Behav. Res. Ther., 44*(1), 147–57.

White, K., & Davey, G. (1989). Sensory preconditioning and UCS inflation in human "fear" conditioning. *Behav. Res. & Ther., 2,* 161–66.

Whitfield, K. E., Weidner, G., Clark, R., & Anderson, N. B. (2002). Sociodemographic diversity and behavioral medicine. *J. Cons. Clin. Psychol., 70*(3), 463–81.

Whitfield-Gabrieli, S., Thermenos, H. W., Milanovic, S., Tsuang, M. T., Faraone, S. V., McCarley, R. W., et al.,

(2009). Hyperactivity and hyperconnectivity of the default network in schizophrenia and in first-degree relatives of persons with schizophrenia. *Proceedings of the National Academy of Sciences of the United States of America, 106,* 1279–84.

Whittington C. J., Kendall, T., Fonagy, P., Cottrell, D., Cotgrove, A., & Boddington, E. (2004). Selective serotonin reuptake inhibitors in childhood depression: Systematic review of published versus unpublished data. *Lancet, 363,* 1341–45.

Whittington, C. J., Kendall, T., & Pilling, S. (2005). Are the SSRIs and atypical antidepressants safe and effective for children and adolescents? *Cur. Opin. in Psychiat., 18,* 21–25.

WHO World Mental Health Survey Consortium (2004). Prevalence, severity, and unmet need for treatment of mental disorders in the World Health Organization World Mental Health Surveys. *JAMA, 291,* 2581–90.

Whybrow, P. C. (1997). *A mood apart.* New York: Basic Books.

Widiger, R. A. (2006). Psychopathy and DSM-IV psychopathology. In C. J. Patrick (Ed.), *Handbook of the psychopathy.* (pp. 156–71). New York: Guilford Press.

Widiger, T. (2007). An empirically based classification of personality pathology: Where we are now and where do we go. *Clin. Psychol. Sci. Prac., 14*(2), 94–98.

Widiger, T. A. (2001). Official classification systems. In W. J. Livesley (Ed.), *Handbook of personality disorders: Theory, research, and treatment* (pp. 60–83). New York: Guilford.

Widiger, T. A. (2005). Five factor model of personality disorder: Integrating science and practice. *J. Res. Person., 39,* 67–83.

Widiger, T. A. (2011a). The DSM-5 dimensional model of personality disorder: Rationale and empirical support. *J. Pers. Disord., 25*(2), 222–34. doi:10.1521/pedi.2011.25.2.222

Widiger, T. A. (2011b). The comorbidity of narcissistic personality disorder with other DSM-IV personality disorders. In W. K. Campbell & J. D. Miller (Eds.), *The handbook of narcissism and narcissistic personality disorder: Theoretical approaches, empirical findings, and treatments* (pp. 248–60). John Wiley and Sons. Retrieved from http://books.google.com/books?hl=en&lr=&id=SFnMUZFqtnIC&pgis=1

Widiger, T. A., & Bornstein, R. F. (2001). Histrionic, dependent, and narcissistic personality disorders. In H. E. Adams & P. B. Sutker (Eds.), *Comprehensive handbook of psychopathology* (pp. 509–34). New York: Kluwer Academic.

Widiger, T. A., & Boyd, S. E. (2009). Personality disorder assessment instruments. In J. N. Butcher (Ed.), *Oxford handbook of personality and clinical assessment* (pp. 336–62). New York: Oxford Univesity Press.

Widiger, T. A., & Costa, P. T., Jr. (2002). Five-factor model personality disorder research. In P. T. Costa, Jr., & T. A. Widiger (Eds.), *Personality disorders and the five-factor model of personality* (2nd ed.). (pp. 59–87). Washington, DC: American Psychological Association.

Widiger, T. A., Costa, P. T., & McCrae, R. R. (2002). A proposal for Axis II. Diagnosing personality disorders using the five factor model. In P. T. Costa & T. A. Widiger (Eds.), *Personality disorders and the five factor model of personality* (2nd ed., pp. 431–456). Washington, DC: American Psychological Association.

Widiger, T. A., Costa, P. T., & Samuel, D. (2006). Assessment of maladaptive personality traits. In S. Strack & M. Lorr (Eds.), *Differentiating normal and abnormal personality* (2nd edition, pp. 311–335.). New York: Springer.

Widiger, T. A., & Frances, A. J. (1994). Toward a dimensional model for the personality disorders. In P. T. Costa, Jr., & T. A. Widiger (Eds.), *Personality disorders and the five-factor model of personality.* (pp. 19–39). Washington, DC: American Psychological Association.

Widiger, T. A., Frances, A. J., Pincus, H. A., Davis, W. W., & First, M. B. (1991). Toward an empirical classification for the DSM-IV. *J. Abn. Psychol., 100*(3), 280–88.

Widiger, T. A., Livesley, W. J., & Clark, L. A. (2009). An integrative dimensional classification of personality disorder. *Psychol. Assess., 21*(3), 243–55. doi:10.1037/a0016606

Widiger, T. A., & Mullins-Sweatt, S. (2005). Categorical and dimensional models of personality disorder. In J. Oldham, A. Skodol, & D. Bender(Eds.), *Textbook of personality disorders* (pp. 35–56). Washington, DC: American Psychiatric Press.

Widiger, T. A., & Rogers, J. (1989). Prevalence and comorbidity of personality disorders. *Psychiat. Ann., 19,* 132–36.

Widiger, T. A., & Sanderson, C. J. (1995). Toward a dimensional model of personality disorders. In W. J. Livesley (Ed.), *The DSM-IV personality disorders* (pp. 433–58). New York: Guilford.

Widiger, T. A., & Simonsen, E. (2005). Alternative dimensional models of personality disorder: Finding a common ground. *J. Pers. Dis., 19,* 110–30.

Widiger, T. A., & Trull, T. J. (1993). Borderline and narcissistic personality disorders. In P. B. Sutker & H. E. Adams (Eds.),*Comprehensive handbook of psychopathology* (2nd ed.). New York: Plenum.

Widiger, T. A., & Trull, T. J. (2007). Plate tectonics in the classification of personality disorder: Shifting to a dimensional model. *Amer. Psychol., 62*(2), 71–83.

Widiger, T. A., Trull, T. J., Clarkin, J. F., Sanderson, C. J., & Costa, P. T. (2002). A description of the DSM-IV personality disorders with the five-factor model of personality. In P. T. Costa, Jr., & T. A. Widiger (Eds.), *Personality disorders and the five-factor model of personality* (pp. 89–102). Washington, DC: American Psychological Association.

Widom, C. S. (1977). A methodology for studying non-institutionalized psychopaths. *J. Cons. Clin. Psychol., 45,* 674–83.

Widom, C. S., Czaja, S. J., & Paris, J. (2009). A prospective investigation of borderline personality disorder in abused and neglected children followed up into adulthood. *J. Pers. Disord., 23,* 433–46.

Wiederanders, M. R., Bromley, D. L., & Choate, P. A. (1997). Forensic conditional release programs and outcomes in three states. *International Journal of Law and Psychiatry, 20,* 249–57.

Wiik, K. L., Loman, M. M., Van Ryzin, M. J., Armstrong, J. M., Essex, M. J., Pollak, S. D., & Gunnar, M. R. (2011). Behavioral and emotional symptoms of post-institutionalized children in middle childhood. *J. Child Psychol. Psychiat., 52*(1), 56–63. doi: 10.1111/j.1469-7610.2010.02294.x

Wilbert-Lampen, U., Leistner, D., Greven, S., Pol, Sper, Völker, C., Güü D., Plasse, A., Knez, A., Kuchenhoff, H., & Steinbeck, G. (2008). Cardiovascular events during World Cup soccer. *N. Engl. J. Med., 358,* 475–83.

Wilbur, R. S. (1973, Jun. 2). In S. Auerbach (Ed.), POWs found to be much sicker than they looked upon release. *Los Angeles Times,* Part I, p. 4.

Wilder, D. A., et al. (1997). A simplified method of toilet training adults in residential settings. *J. Behav. Ther. Exper. Psychiat., 28*(3), 241–46.

Wildes, J. E., Emery, R. E., & Simons, A. D. (2001). The roles of ethnicity and culture in the development of eating disturbance and body dissatisfaction: A meta-analytic review. *Clin. Psychol. Rev., 21*(4), 521–51.

Wilfley, D. E., Crow, S. J., Hudson, J. I., Mitchell, J. E., Berkowitz, R. I., Blakesley, V., Walsh, B. T., et al. (2008). Efficacy of sibutramine for the treatment of binge eating disorder: A randomized multicenter placebo-controlled double-blind study. *Amer. J. Psychiat., 165,* 51–58.

Wilfley, D. E., Friedman, M. A., Dounchis, J. Z., Stein, R. I., Welch, R. R., & Ball, S. A. (2000). Comorbid psychopathology in binge eating disorder: Relation to eating disorder severity at baseline and following treatment. *J. Cons. Clin. Psychol., 68*(4), 641–49.

Wilhelm, S., Buhlmann, U., Tolin, D. F., Meunier, S. A., Pearlson, G. D., Reese, H. E., et al. (2008). Augmentation of behavior therapy with D-cycloserine for obsessive-compulsive disorder. *Amer. J. Psychiat., 165*(3), 335–41. doi: 10.1176/appi.ajp.2007.07050776

Wilk, J. E., Bliese, P. D., Kim, P. Y., Thomas, J. L., McGurk, D., & Hoge, C. W. (2010). Relationship of combat experiences to alcohol misuse among U.S. soldiers returning from the Iraq war. *Drug Alcohol Depend., 108*(1–2), 115–21.

Wilkinson, B. J., Newman, M. G., Shytle, R. D., Silver, A. A., Sandberg, P. R., & Sheehan, D. (2001). Family impact of Tourette's syndrome. *J. Child Fam. Stud., 10,* 477–83.

Willard, N. E. (2007). *Cyberbullying and cyberthreats: Responding to the challenge of online social aggression, threats, and distress.* Champaign, IL: Research Press.

Willcutt, E., & McQueen, M. (2010). Genetic and environmental vulnerability to bipolar spectrum disorders. In D. J. Miklowitz & D. Cicchetti (Eds.), *Understanding bipolar disorder: A developmental psychopathology perspective* (pp. 225–58). New York: Guilford Press.

Williams, C. J., & Weinberg, M. S. (2003). Zoophilia in men: A study of sexual interest in animals. *Arch. Sex. Behav., 32*(6), 523–35.

Williams, C. L., & Butcher, J. N. (2011). *A beginner's guide to the MMPI-A.* Washington, DC: The American Psychological Association.

Williams, D. R., Gonzalez, H. M., Neighbors, H., Nesse, R., Abelson, J. M., Sweetman, J., & Jackson, J. S. (2007). Prevalence and distribution of major depressive disorder in African Americans, Caribbean blacks, and non-Hispanic whites: results from the National Survey of American Life. *Arch. Gen. Psychiat., 64*(3), 305–15. doi: 10.1001/archpsyc.64.3.305

Williams, J. (2007, February 19). Give your head a rest. *Boston Globe.*

Williams, J. M. G., Russell, I., & Russell, D. (2008). Mindfulness- based cognitive therapy: Further issues in current evidence and future research. *J. Cons. Clin. Psych., 76*(3), 524–29.

Williams, K., Mellis, C., & Peat, J. K. (2005). Incidence and prevalence of autism. *Advances in Speech Language Pathology, 7*(1), 31–40.

Williams, L. R., Degnan, K. A., Perez-Edgar, K. E., Henderson, H. A., Rubin, K. H., Pine, D. S., et al. (2009). Impact of behavioral inhibition and parenting style on internalizing and externalizing problems from early childhood through adolescence. *J. Abn. Child Psychol., 37*(8), 1063–75. doi: 10.1007/s10802-009-9331-3

Williams, P. G., Sears, L. L., & Allard, A. (2004). Sleep problems in children with autism. *J. Sleep Res., 13*(3), 265–68.

Williams, R. B., Jr., Barefoot, J. C., Califf, R. M., Haney, T. L., Saunders, W. B., Pryor, D. B., Hlatky, M. A., Siegler, I. C., & Marks, D. B. (1992). Prognostic importance of social and economic resources among medically treated patients with angiographically documented coronary artery disease. *JAMA, 267,* 520–24.

Wilson, D. K., Kliewer, W., & Sica, D. A. (2004). The relationship between exposure to violence and blood pressure mechanisms.*Current Hypertension Reports, 6*(4), 321–26.

Wilson, E. J., MacLeod, C., Mathews, A., & Rutherford, E. M. (2006). The causal role of interpretive bias in anxiety reactivity. *J. Abn. Psych., 115*(1), 103–11.

Wilson, G. T. (1998). Manual-based treatment and clinical practice. *Clin. Psychol. Sci. Prac., 5,* 363–75.

Wilson, G. T. (2005). Psychological treatment of eating disorders. *Annu. Rev. Clin. Psychol., 1,* 439–65.

Wilson, G. T. (2010). Cognitive behavior therapy for eating disorders. In W. A. Agras (Ed.), *The Oxford Handbook of Eating Disorders,* New York: Oxford University Press, pp. 331–47.

Wilson, G. T., & Fairburn, C. G. (2007). Treatments for eating disorders. In P. E. Nathan & J. M. Gorman (Eds.), *A guide to treatments that work* (3rd ed.) (pp.579–609). New York: Oxford University Press.

Wilson, G. T., Grilo, C. M., & Vitousek, K. M. (2007). Psychological treatment of eating disorders. *Amer. Psychol., 3,* 199–216.

Wilson, G. T., Wilfley, D. E., Agras, W. S., & Bryson, S. W. (2010). Psychological treatments of binge eating disorder. *Arch. Gen. Psychiat., 67,* 94–101.

Wilson, J. A. B., Onorati, K., Mishkind, M., Reger, M. A., & Gahm (2009). Soldier attitudes about technology-based approaches to mental health care. *Cyberpsychology and Behavior, 11*(6), 767–69.

Wilson, K. G., Chochinov, H. M., McPherson, C. J., Skirko, M. G., Allard, P., Chary, S., et al. (2007). Desire for euthanasia or physician-assisted suicide in palliative cancer care. *Hlth. Psych., 26*(3), 314–23.

Wilson, K., Sinclair, I., & Gibbs, I. (2000). The trouble with foster care: The impact of stressful events on foster care. *British Journal of Social Work, 30,* 193–209.

Wilson, R. F. (2004). Recognizing the threat posed by an incestuous parent to the victim's siblings: Part I: Appraising the risk. *Journal of Child and Family Studies, 13*(2), 143–62.

Wilson, R. S., Arnold, S. E. Beck, T., Bienias, J. L., & Bennett, D. A. (2008). Changes in depressive symptoms during the prodromal phase of Alzheimer disease. *Arch. Gen. Psychiat., 65,* 439–46.

Wilson, R. S., Krueger, K. R., Arnold, S. E., Schneider, J. A., Kelly, J. F., Barnes, L. L., Tang, Y., & Bennett, D. A. (2007). Loneliness and risk of Alzheimer disease. *Arch. Gen. Psychiat., 64,* 234–40.

Winblad, B., Engedal, K., Sioininen, H., Verhey, F., Waldeman, G., Wimo, A., Wetterholm, A.-L., Zhang, R., Haglund, A., Subbiah, P., & the Donepezil Nordic Study Group. (2001). A 1-year, randomized, placebocontrolled study of donepezil in patients with mild to moderate AD. *Neurology, 57*(3), 489–95.

Wincze, J. P., Bach, A. K., & Barlow, D. H. (2008). Sexual dysfunction. In D. H. Barlow (Ed.), *Clinical handbook of psychological disorders: A step-by-step treatment manual* (4th ed.; (pp. 615–61). New York: Guilford Press.

Windhaber, J., Maierhofer, D., & Dantendorfer, K. (1998). Panic disorder induced by large doses of 3,4- methylenedioxymethamphetamine resolved by paroxetine. *J. Clin. Psychopharmacol., 18*(1), 95–96.

Wing, L. (1981). Asperger's syndrome: A clinical account. *Psychol. Med., 11*, 115–29.

Winick, B. J. (1997). *The right to refuse mental health treatment.* Washington, DC: American Psychological Association.

Wink, P. (1991). Two faces of narcissism. *J. Pers. Soc. Psychol., 61*, 590–97.

Winokur, G., & Tsuang, M. T. (1996). *The natural history of mania, depression, and schizophrenia.* Washington, DC: American Psychiatric Press.

Winslow, J. T., & Insel, T. R. (1991). Neuroethological models of obsessive-compulsive disorder. In J. Zohar, T. Insel, & S. Rasmussen (Eds.), *The psychobiology of obsessive-compulsive disorder.* New York: Springer.

Winston, A. P., Jamieson, C. P., Madira, W., Gatward, N. M., & Palmer, R. L. (2000). Prevalence of thiamin deficiency in anorexia nervosa. *Int. J. Eat. Dis., 28*, 451–54.

Winston, A., Laikin, M., Pollack, J., Samstag, L.W., McCullough, L., & Muran, C. (1994). Short-term psychotherapy of personality disorders. *Amer. J. Psychiat., 151*, 190–94.

Winton, M. A., & Mara, B. A. (2001). *Child abuse and neglect: Multidisciplinary approaches.* Boston: Allyn and Bacon.

Wirdefeldt, K., Adami, H-O., Cole, P., Trichopoulos, D., & Mandel, J. (2011). Epidemiology and etiology of Parkinson's disease: a review of the evidence. *Eur. J. Epidemiol, 26*, S1–S58.

Wise, R. A. (1996). Addictive drugs and brain stimulation reward. *Annu. Rev. Neurosci., 19*, 319–40.

Wise, R. A., & Munn, E. (1995). Withdrawal from chronic amphetamine elevates baseline intracranial self-stimulation thresholds. *Psychopharmacology, 117*(2), 130–36.

Wiseman, C. V., Gray, J. J., Mosimann, J. E., & Ahrens, A. (1992). Cultural expectations of thinness in women: An update. *Int. J. Eat. Dis., 11*, 85–89.

Wisniewski, T., Dowjat, W. K., Buxbaum, J. D., Khorkova, O., Efthimiopoulos, S., Kulczycki, J., Lojkowska, W., Wegiel, J., Wisniewski, H. M., & Frangione, B. (1998). A novel Polish presenilin-2 mutation (P117L0 is associated with familial Alzheimer's disease and leads to death as early as the age of 28 years) *Neuroreport, 9*, 217–21.

Withall, A., Harris, L. M., & Cumming, S. R. (2010). A longitudinal study of cognitive function in melancholic and non-melancholic subtypes of major depressive disorder. *J. Affect. Disord., 123*(1–3), 150–57. doi: 10.1016/j.jad.2009.07.012

Witkiewitz, K., & Marlatt, G. A. (2004). Relapse prevention for alcohol and drug problems: That was Zen, this is Tao. *Amer. Psychol., 59*(4), 224–35.

Witkiewitz, K., & Marlatt, G. A. (2007). Modeling the complexity of post-treatment drinking: It's a rocky road to relapse. *Clin. Psych. Rev., 27*(6) 724–38.

Witlox, J., Eurelings, L. S., de Jonghe, J. F., Kalisvaart, K. J., Eikelenboom, P., & van Gool, W. A. (2010). Delirium in elderly patients and the risk of post-discharge mortality, institutionalization, and dementia: A meta-analysis. *JAMA, 304*, 443–51.

Witvliet, C. V., Ludwig, T. E., & Vander Laan, K. L. (2001). Granting forgiveness or harboring grudges: Implications for emotion, physiology, and health. *Psychol. Sci., 12*(2), 117–23.

Wobrock, T., Falkai, P., Schneider-Axmann, T., Frommann, N., Wölwer, W., & Gaebel, W. (2009).

Effects of abstinence on brain morphology in alcoholism: A MRI study. *Eur. Arch. Psychiat. Clin. Neurosci., 259*(3), 143–50.

Woelwer, W., Burtscheidt, W., Redner, C., Schwarz, R., & Gaebel, W. (2001). Out-patient behaviour therapy in alcoholism: Impact of personality disorders and cognitive impairments. *Acta Psychiatr. Scandin., 103*, 30–37.

Wolf, A. J., & Guyer, M. J. (2010). Repressed memories in a controversial conviction. *J. Amer. Acad. Psychiat. Law, 38*, 607–9.

Wolff, H. G. (1960). Stressors as a cause of disease in man. In J. M. Tanner (Ed.), *Stress and psychiatric disorder.* London: Oxford University Press.

Wolff, P. H. (1972). Ethnic differences in alcohol sensitivity. *Science, 175*, 449–50.

Wolitzky-Taylor, K. B., Horowitz, J. D., Powers, M. B., & Telch, M. J. (2008). Psychological approaches in the treatment of specific phobias: A meta-analysis. *Clin. Psychol. Rev., 28*(6), 1021–37. doi: 10.1016/j.cpr.2008.02.007

Wolpe, J. (1958). *Psychotherapy by reciprocal inhibition.* Stanford, CA: Stanford University Press.

Wolpe, J. (1988). *Life without fear. Anxiety and its cure.* Oakland, CA: New Harbinger Publications, Inc.

Wolpe, J. (1993). Commentary: The cognitivist oversell and comments on symposium contributions. *J. Behav. Ther. Exper. Psychiat., 24*(2), 141–47.

Wolpe, J., & Rachman, S. J. (1960). Psychoanalytic evidence: A critique based on Freud's case of Little Hans. *J. Nerv. Ment. Dis., 131*, 135–45.

Wonderlich, S. A., Gordon, K. H., Mitchell, J. E., Crosby, R. D., & Engel, S. G. (2009). The validity and clinical utility of binge eating disorder. *Int. J. Eat. Dis., 42*, 687–705.

Wong, D. F., Wagner, H. N., Jr., Tune, L. E., Dannals, R. F., Pearlson, G. D., Links, J. M., Tamminga, C. A., Broussolle, E. P., Ravert, H. T., & Wilson, A. A. (1986). Positron emission tomography reveals elevated D2 dopamine receptors in drug-naïve schizophrenics. *Science, 234*, 1558–63.

Woo, M., & Oei, T. P. S. (2007). MMPI-2 profiles of Australian and Singaporean psychiatric patients. *Psychiat. Res., 150*(2), 153–61. doi: 10.1016/j.psychres.2006.04.007

Wood, J. M., Nezworski, M. T., Garb, H. N., & Lilienfeld, S. O. (2001). Problems with the norms of the Comprehensive System for the Rorschach: Methodological and conceptual considerations. *Clin. Psychol. Sci. Prac., 8*, 397–402.

Woodruff-Borden, J., Morrow, C., Bourland, S., & Cambron, S. (2002). The behavior of anxious parents: Examining mechanisms of transmission of anxiety from parent to child. *J. Clin. Child Adol. Psych., 31*(3), 364–74.

Woods, D. W., & Miltenberger, R. G. (2001). *Tic disorder, trichotillomania, and other repetitive disorders.* New York: Kluwer.

Woods, S. W., Charney, D. S., Goodman, W. K., & Heninger, G. R. (1987). Carbon dioxide-induced anxiety: Behavioral, physiologic, and biochemical effects of 5% CO2 in panic disorder patients and 5 and 7.5% CO2 in healthy subjects. *Arch. Gen. Psychiat., 44*, 365–75.

Woodside, D. B., Bulik, C. M., Halmi, K. A., Fichter, M. M., Kaplan, A., Berrettini, W. H., Strober, M., Treasure, J., Lilenfeld, L., Klump, K. K., & Kaye, W. H. (2002). Personality, perfectionism, and attitudes toward eating in parents of individuals with eating disorders. *Int. J. Eat. Dis., 31*(3), 290–99.

Woodside, D. B., Bulik, C. M., Thornton, L., Klump, K. L., Tozzi, F., Fichter, M., Halmi, K. A., Kaplan, A. S., Strober, M., Devlin, B., Bacanu, S.-A., Ganjei,

K., Crow, S., Mitchell, J., Rotondo, A., Mauri, M., Cassano, G., Keel, P., Berrettini, W. H., & Kaye, W. H. (2004). Personality in men with eating disorders. *J. Psychosom. Res., 57*, 273–78.

World Health Organization. (1992). *ICD-10 classification of mental and behavioral disorders: Clinical descriptions and diagnostic guidelines.* Geneva: Author.

World Health Organization. (1994). *Schedules for clinical assessment in neuropsychiatry.* Geneva: Author.

World Health Organization. (1997). *World Health Organization Report, 1997: Conquering suffering, furthering humanity.* Geneva: Author.

World Health Organization. (1999). *World Health Report.* Available at www.who.int/en/

World Health Organization. (2001). *The World Health Report 2001. Mental Health: New Understanding, New Hope.* Geneva: Author.

World Health Organization, (2003). *International and statistical classification of diseases and related health problems* (10th rev. ed,). Geneva: Author.

World Health Organization. (2110) http://www.who.int/publications/en/.

Wright, J. H., Basco, M. R., & Thase, M. E. (2006). *Learning cognitive-behavior therapy.* Washington, DC: American Psychiatric Publishing, Inc.

Wright, M. J., & Jackson, R. C. (2007). Brain regions concerned with perceptual skills in tennis: An fMRI study. *International Journal of Psychophysiology, 63*(2), 214–20.

Wright, P., Takei, N., Murray, R. M., & Sham, P. C. (1999). Seasonality, prenatal influenza exposure, and schizophrenia. In E. Z. Susser, A. S. Brown, & J. M. Gorman (Eds.), *Prenatal exposures in schizophrenia* (pp. 89–112).Washington, DC: American Psychiatric Press.

Wu, K. D., Clark. L. A., & Watson, D. (2006). Relations between obsessive-compulsive disorder and personality: Beyond Axis I-Axis II comorbidity. *Anxiety Disorders, 20*, 695–717.

Wykes, T., Reeder, C., Landau, S., Everitt, B., Knapp, M., Patel, A., & Romeo, R. (2007). Cognitive remediation therapy in schizophrenia: Randomised controlled trial. *Brit. J. Psychiat., 190*, 421–27.

Wykes, T., Huddy, V., Cellard, C., McGurk, S. R., & Czobor, P. (2011). A meta-analysis of cognitive remediation for schizophrenia: Methodology and effect sizes. *Am. J. Psychiat., 168*, 472–85.

Xia, J., Merinder, L. B., & Belgamwar, M. R. (2011). Psychoeducation for schizophrenia. *Cochran Database of Systematic Reviews, 6.*, Art. No.: CD002831. DOI: 10.1002/14651858. CD002831. pub2.

Xiao, Z., Yan, H., Wang, Z., Zou, Z., Xu, Y, Chen, J., Zhang, H., Ross, C., & Keyes, B. (2006). Trauma and dissociation in China. *Am. J. Psychiat., 163*, 1388–91.

Xiong, W., Phillips, R., Hu, X., Wang, R., Dai, Q., Kleinman, J., & Kleinman, A. (1994). Family-based intervention for schizophrenic patients in China. *Brit. J. Psychiat., 165*, 239–47.

Yang, B., & Clum, G. A. (1996). Effects of early negative life experience on cognitive functioning and risk for suicide: A review. *Clin. Psychol. Rev., 16*(3), 177–95.

Yang, M., Ullrich, S., Roberts, A., & Coid, J. (2007). Childhood institutional care and personality disorder traits in adulthood: Findings from the British National Surveys of Psychiatric Morbidity. *Am. J. Orthopsychiat., 77*(1), 67–75.

Yanovski, S. Z., & Yanovski, J. A. (2002). Obesity. *N. Engl. J. Med., 346*, 591–602.

Yapko, M. D. (1994). *Suggestions of abuse: True and false memories of childhood sexual trauma.* New York: Simon & Schuster.

Yardley, W. (2010). Violence prompts debate over medical marijuana. *New York Times, 159*(54), 982.

Yeates, K. O., et al. (1997). Preinjury family environment as a determinant of recovery from traumatic brain injuries in school-age children. *J. Int. Neuropsycholog. Soc., 3*(6), 617–30.

Yen, S., Shea, M. T., Sanislow, C. A., Skodol, A. E., Grilo, C. M., Edelen, M. O., et al. (2009). Personality traits as prospective predictors of suicide attempts. *Acta Psychiat. Scand., 120*(3), 222–29. doi: 10.1111/j.1600-0447.2009.01366.x

Yeung, A. C., Vekshtein, V. I., Krantz, D. S., Vita, J. A., Ryan, T. J., Ganz, P., & Selwyn, A. P. (1991). The effects of atherosclerosis on the vasomotor response of coronary arteries to mental stress. *N. Engl. J. Med., 325*, 1551–56.

Yoder, K. A., Whitlock, L. B., & Hoyt, D. R. (2003). Gang involvement and membership among homeless and runaway youth. *Youth and Society, 34*, 441–67.

Yoo, S. Y., Jang, J. H., Shin, Y. W., Kim, D. J., Park, H. J., Moon, W. J., et al. (2007). White matter abnormalities in drug-naïve patients with obsessive-compulsive disorder: A diffusion tensor study before and after citalopram treatment. *Acta Psychiatrica Scandinavica, 116*(3), 211–19.

Yoon, J., & Bruckner, T. A. (2009). Does deinstitutionalization increase suicide? *Health Services Research, 44*(4), 1385–405.

Yoshimoto, S., Minabe, Y., Kawai, M., Suzuki, K., Iyo, M., Isoda, H., Sakahara, H., Ashby, C. R. Jr., Takei, N., & Mori, N. (2002). Metabolite alterations in basal ganglia associated with methamphetamine-related psychiatric symptoms: A proton MRS study. *Neuropsychopharmacol., 27*(3), 453–61.

Young, E. A., & Breslau, N. (2004). Cortisol and catecholamines in posttraumatic stress disorder. An epidemiological community study. *Arch. Gen. Psychiat., 61*, 394–401.

Young, J. E., Weinberger, A. D., & Beck, A. T. (2008). Cognitive therapy for depression. In D.H. Barlow (Ed.), *Clinical Handbook of Psychological Disorders.* (4th ed.). New York: Guilford Press, pp. 250–305.

Yovel, I., Revelle, W., & Mineka, S. (2005). Who sees trees before forest: The obsessive-compulsive style of visual attention. *Psychol. Sci., 16*, 123–29.

Yung, A. R., Phillips, L. J., Yuen, H. P., & McGorry, P. D. (2004). Risk factors for psychosis in an ultra high-risk group: psychopathology and clinical features. *Schizo. Res., 67*, 131–42.

Zahl, D. L., & Hawton, K. (2004a). Media influences on suicidal behaviour: An interview study of young people. *Behav. Cog. Psychother., 32*(2), 189–98.

Zahl, D. L., & Hawton, K. (2004b). Repetition of deliberate self-harm and subsequent suicide risk: Long-term follow-up study of 11,583 patients. *Brit. J. Psychiat., 185*, 70–75.

Zammit, S., Allebeck, P., Andréasson, S., Lundberg, I., & Lewis, G. (2002). Self-reported cannabis use as a risk factor for schizophrenia: Further analysis of the 1969 Swedish conscript cohort. *BMJ, 325*, 1199–201.

Zanarini, M. C., Frankenburg, F. R., Hennen, J., Reich, D. B., & Silk, K. R. (2005). The McLean Study of Adult Development (MSAD): Overview and implications of the first six years of prospective follow-up. *J. Personal. Disord., 19*, 505–23.

Zanarini, M. C., Williams, A. A., Lewis, R. E., Reich, R. B., Vera, S. C., Marino, M. F., Levin, A., Yong, L., & Frankenburg, F. R. (1997). Reported pathological childhood experiences associated with the development of borderline personality disorder. *Amer. J. Psychiat., 154*(8), 1101–106.

Zellner, D. A., Harner, D. E., & Adler, R. L. (1989). Effects of eating abnormalities and gender on perceptions of desirable body shape. *J. Abn. Psychol., 98*, 93–96.

Zerman, P. M., & Schwartz, H. I. (1998). Hospitalization: Voluntary and involuntary. In R. Rosner (Ed.), *Principles and practice of forensic psychiatry* (pp. 111–17). London: Oxford University Press.

Zettergreen, P. (2003). School adjustment in adolescence for previously rejected, average and popular children. *British Journal of Educational Psychology, 73*(2), 207–21.

Zhang, L. D., & Lu, M. K. (2006). Psychiatry in China: Past, present and future. *International Medical Journal, 13*, 44–51.

Zhang, L., Plotkin, R. C., Wang, G., Sandel, E., & Lee, S. (2004). Cholinergic augmentation with donepezil enhances recovery in short-term memory and sustained attention after traumatic brain injury. *Archives of Physical and Medical Rehabilitation, 85*, 1050–55.

Zhou, T. X., Zhang, S. P., Jiang, Y. Q., & Wang, J. M. (2000). Epidemiology of neuroses in a Shanghai community. *Chinese Mental Health Journal, 14*, 332–34.

Zickler, P. (2002). *Study demonstrates that marijuana smokers experience significant withdrawal.* Washington, DC: NIDA.

Zilboorg, G., & Henry, G. W. (1941). *A history of medical psychology.* New York: Norton.

Zimmerman, D. P. (2004). Psychotherapy in residential treatment: Historical development and critical issues. *Child Adoles. Psychiat. Clin. N. Amer., 13*(2), 347–61.

Zimmerman, M. Rothchild, L., & Chelminski, I (2005). The prevalence of DSM-IV personality disorders in psychiatric outpatients. *Am. J. Psychiat., 162*, 1911–18.

Zimmerman, M., & Coryell, W. (1989). DSM-III personality disorder diagnoses in a nonpatient sample: Demographic correlates and comorbidity. *Arch. Gen. Psychiat., 46*, 682–89.

Zimmerman, M., & Coryell, W. (1990). Diagnosing personality disorders in the community. A comparison of self report and interview measures. *Arch. Gen. Psychiat., 47*, 527–31.

Zimmermann, P., Brückl, T., Nocon, A., Pfister, H., Lieb, R., Wittchen, H.-U., et al. (2009). Heterogeneity of DSM-IV major depressive disorder as a consequence of subthreshold bipolarity. *Arch. Gen. Psychiat., 66*(12), 1341–52. doi: 10.1001/archgenpsychiatry.2009.158

Zinbarg , R., & Mineka, S. (2007). Is emotion regulation a useful construct that adds to the explanatory power of learning models of anxiety disorders or a new label for old constructs? *Amer. Psychol., 62*(3), 259–61.

Zinbarg, R. E., Mineka, S., Craske, M., Vrshek-Schallhorn, S., et al. (2011 submitted). Prospective associations of personality traits and cognitive vulnerabilities with onsets of anxiety disorders and unipolar mood disorders over three years in adolescents.

Ziolko, H. U. (1996). Bulimia: A historical outline. *Int. J. Eat. Dis., 20*, 345–58.

Zoccolillo, M., Meyers, J., & Assiter, S. (1997). Conduct disorder, substance dependence, and adolescent motherhood. *Amer. J. Orthopsychiat., 67*(1), 152–57.

Zubin, J., & Spring, B. J. (1977). Vulnerability: A new view of schizophrenia. *J. Abn. Psychol., 86*, 103–26.

Zucker, K. J. (2005). Gender identity disorder in children and adolescents. *Ann. Rev. Clin. Psychol., 1*, 467–92.

Zucker, K. J., & Blanchard, R. (1997). Transvestic fetishism: Psychopathology and theory. In D. R. Laws & W. O'Donohue (Eds.), *Sexual deviance: Theory, assessment, and treatment.* (pp. 253–79). New York: Guilford.

Zucker, K. J., & Bradley, S. J. (1995). *Gender identity disorder and psychosexual problems in children and adolescents.* New York: Guilford.

Zucker, K. J., & Spitzer, R. L. (2005). Was the gender identity disorder of childhood diagnosis introduced into DSM-III as a backdoor maneuver to replace homosexuality? A historical note. *J. Sex Marit. Ther., 31*, 31–42.

Zucker, K. J., Bradley, S. J., Owen-Anderson, A., Kibblewhite, S. J., & Cantor, J. M. (2008). Letter to the editor: Is gender identity disorder in adolescents coming out of the closet? *J. Sex Mar. Ther., 34*, 287–90.

Zucker, K. J., Owen, A., Bradley, S. J., & Ameeriar, L. (2002). Gender-dysphoric children and adolescents: A comparative analysis of demographic characteristics and behavioral problems. *Clin. Child Psych. Psychiat., 7*, 398–411.

Zucker, K. J., Sanikhani, M., & Bradley, S. J. (1997). Sex differences in referral rates of children with gender identity disorder: Some hypotheses. *J. Abnorm. Child Psychol., 25*, 217–27.

Zuckerman, M. (2007). *Sensation seeking and risky behavior.* Washington, DC: American Psychological Association.

Zvolensky, M. J., & Bernstein, A. (2005). Cigarette smoking and panic psychopathology. *Curr. Dis. Psychol. Sci., 14*(6), 301–5.

Zvolensky, M. J., Cougle, J. R., Johnson, K. A., Bonn-Miller, M. O., & Bernstein, A. (2010). Marijuana use and panic psychopathology among a representative sample of adults. *Exper. Clin. Psychopharmacol., 18*(2), 139–34.

Zvolensky, M. J., Eiffert, G. H., Lejeuz, C. W., & McNeil, D. W. (1999). The effects of offset control over 20% carbon-dioxide-enriched air on anxious response. *J. Abn. Psychol., 108*, 624–32.

Zvolensky, M. J., Lejeuz, C. W., & Eifert, G. H. (1998). The role of offset control in anxious responding: An experimental test using repeated administrations of 20%-carbon-dioxide-enriched air. *Behav. Ther., 29*, 193–209.

Zweben, A. (2001). Integrating pharmacotherapy and psychosocial interventions in the treatment of individuals with alcohol problems. *Journal of Social Work Practice in the Addictions, 1*(3), 65–80.

Zwelling, S. S. (1985). *Quest for a cure.* Williamsburg, VA: The Colonial Williamsburg Foundation.

Mood Disorders
and Suicide

From Chapter 7 of *Abnormal Psychology*, Fifteenth Edition. James N. Butcher, Susan Mineka, Jill M. Hooley. Copyright © 2013 by Pearson Education, Inc. All rights reserved.

Mood Disorders and Suicide

case study A Successful "Total Failure"

Margaret, a prominent businesswoman in her late 40s noted for her energy and productivity, was unexpectedly deserted by her husband for a younger woman. Following her initial shock and rage, she began to have uncontrollable weeping spells and doubts about her business acumen. Decision making became an ordeal. Her spirits rapidly sank, and she began to spend more and more time in bed, refusing to deal with anyone. Her alcohol consumption increased to the point where she was seldom entirely sober. Within a period of weeks, she had suffered serious financial losses owing to her inability, or refusal, to keep her affairs in order. She felt she was a "total failure," even when reminded of her considerable personal and professional achievements; indeed, her self-criticism gradually spread to all aspects of her life and her personal history. Finally, alarmed members of her family essentially forced her to accept an appointment with a clinical psychologist.

Was something "wrong" with Margaret, or was she merely experiencing normal human emotions because of her husband's having deserted her? The psychologist concluded that she was suffering from a serious mood disorder and initiated treatment. The diagnosis, based on the severity of the symptoms and the degree of impairment, was major depressive disorder. Secondarily, she had also developed a serious drinking problem—a condition that frequently co-occurs with major depressive disorder.

Most of us feel depressed from time to time. Failing an exam, arguing with a friend, not being accepted into one's first choice of college or graduate school, and breaking up with a romantic partner are all examples of events that can precipitate a depressed mood in many people. However, **mood disorders** involve much more severe alterations in mood for much longer periods of time. In such cases the disturbances of mood are intense and persistent enough to be clearly maladaptive and often lead to serious problems in relationships and work performance. In fact, it was estimated that in 2000, depression ranked among the top five health conditions in terms of years lost to disability in all parts of the world except Africa, and it was the number-one such health condition in the United States, ranking above heart disease and stroke (Üstün et al., 2004). Overall the "disease-burden" of depression to society—that is, the total direct costs (such as for treatment) and indirect costs (such as days missed from work, disability, and premature deaths)—totaled $83.1 billion in the United States alone, with over 60 percent of the reported costs resulting from problems in the workplace (Greenberg et al., 2003).

Mood disorders are diverse in nature, as is illustrated by the many types of depression recognized in the *DSM-IV-TR* that we will discuss. Nevertheless, in all mood disorders (formerly called *affective disorders*), extremes of emotion or *affect*—soaring elation or deep depression—dominate the clinical picture. Other symptoms are also present, but the abnormal mood is the defining feature.

Mood Disorders: An Overview

The two key moods involved in mood disorders are **mania**, often characterized by intense and unrealistic feelings of excitement and euphoria, and **depression**, which usually involves feelings of extraordinary sadness and dejection. Some people with mood disorders experience only time periods or episodes characterized by depressed moods. However, other people experience manic episodes at certain time points and depressive episodes at other time points. Normal mood states can occur between both types of episodes. Manic and depressive mood states are often conceived to be at opposite ends of a mood continuum, with normal mood in the middle. Although this concept is accurate to a degree, sometimes an individual may have symptoms of mania and depression during the same time period. In these *mixed-episode* cases, the person experiences rapidly alternating moods such as sadness, euphoria, and irritability, all within the same episode of illness.

Types of Mood Disorders

We will first discuss the **unipolar depressive disorders**, in which the person experiences only depressive episodes, and then we will discuss the **bipolar disorders**, in which the person experiences both manic and depressive episodes. This distinction is prominent in *DSM-IV-TR*, and although the unipolar and bipolar forms of mood disorder may not be wholly separate and distinct, there are notable differences in symptoms, causal factors, and optimal treatments, which is why we discuss them separately. As we will see, it is also customary to differentiate among the mood disorders in terms of (1) *severity*—the number of dysfunctions experienced and the relative degree of impairment evidenced in those areas; and (2) *duration*—whether the disorder is acute, chronic, or intermittent (with periods of relatively normal functioning between the episodes of disorder).

As just noted, diagnosing unipolar or bipolar disorders first requires determining what kind of mood episode the person presently shows. The most common form of mood episode that people present with is a **major depressive episode**. As detailed in the *DSM-IV-TR* box "Criteria for Major Depressive Episode," to receive this diagnosis the person must be markedly depressed (or show a marked loss of interest in pleasurable activities) for most of every day and for most days for at least 2 weeks. In addition to these obvious emotional symptoms, he or she must show at least three or four other symptoms (for a total of five) that range from cognitive symptoms (such as feelings of worthlessness or guilt, and thoughts of suicide), to behavioral symptoms (such as fatigue or physical agitation), to physical symptoms (such as changes in appetite and sleep patterns).

The other primary kind of mood episode is a **manic episode**, in which the person shows a markedly elevated, euphoric, or expansive mood, often interrupted by occasional outbursts of intense irritability or even violence—particularly

Criteria for Major Depressive Episode

Major Depressive Disorder, Single Episode

A. Presence of a single Major Depressive Episode.

B. The Major Depressive Episode is not better accounted for by Schizoaffective Disorder and is not superimposed on Schizophrenia, Schizophreniform Disorder, Delusional Disorder, or Psychotic Disorder Not Otherwise Specified.

C. There has never been a Manic Episode, a Mixed Episode, or a Hypomanic Episode.

Major Depressive Disorder, Recurrent

A. Presence of two or more Major Depressive Episodes. Note: To be considered separate episodes, there must be an interval of at least 2 consecutive months in which criteria are not met for a Major Depressive Episode.

B. The Major Depressive Episodes are not better accounted for by Schizoaffective Disorder and are not superimposed on Schizophrenia, Schizophreniform Disorder, Delusional Disorder, or Psychotic Disorder Not Otherwise Specified.

C. There has never been a Manic Episode, a Mixed Episode, or a Hypomanic Episode.

Source: Reprinted with permission from the American Psychiatric Association. *Diagnostic and Statistical Manual of Mental Disorders,* Fourth Edition, *Text Revision* (Copyright © 2000). American Psychiatric Association.

Criteria for Manic Episode

A. A distinct period of abnormally and persistently elevated, expansive, or irritable mood, lasting at least 1 week (or any duration if hospitalization is necessary).

B. During the period of mood disturbance, three (or more) of the following symptoms have persisted (four if the mood is only irritable) and have been present to a significant degree:
   1. Iinflated self-esteem or grandiosity
   2. Decreased need for sleep (e.g., feels rested after only 3 hours of sleep)
   3. More talkative than usual or pressure to keep talking
   4. Flight of ideas or subjective experience that thoughts are racing
   5. Distractibility (i.e., attention too easily drawn to unimportant or irrelevant external stimuli)
   6. Increase in goal-directed activity (either socially, at work or school, or sexually) or psychomotor agitation
   7. Excessive involvement in pleasurable activities that have a high potential for painful consequences (e.g., engaging in unrestrained buying sprees, sexual indiscretions, or foolish business investments)

C. The symptoms do not meet criteria for a Mixed Episode.

D. The mood disturbance is sufficiently severe to cause marked impairment in occupational functioning or in usual social activities or relationships with others, or to necessitate hospitalization to prevent harm to self or others, or there are psychotic features.

E. The symptoms are not due to the direct physiological effects of a substance (e.g., a drug of abuse, a medication, or other treatment) or a general medical condition (e.g., hyperthyroidism).

Source: Reprinted with permission from the American Psychiatric Association. *Diagnostic and Statistical Manual of Mental Disorders,* Fourth Edition, *Text Revision* (Copyright © 2000). American Psychiatric Association.

when others refuse to go along with the manic person's wishes and schemes. These extreme moods must persist for at least a week for this diagnosis to be made. In addition, three or more additional symptoms must occur in the same time period, ranging from behavioral symptoms (such as a notable increase in goal-directed activity, often involving loosening of personal and cultural inhibitions as in multiple sexual, political, or religious activities), to mental symptoms where self-esteem becomes grossly inflated and mental activity may speed up (such as a "flight of ideas" or "racing thoughts"), to physical symptoms (such as a decreased need for sleep or psychomotor agitation). (See the *DSM-IV-TR* box "Criteria for Manic Episode.")

In milder forms, similar kinds of symptoms can lead to a diagnosis of **hypomanic episode**, in which a person experiences abnormally elevated, expansive, or irritable mood for at least 4 days. In addition, the person must have at least three other symptoms similar to those involved in mania but to a lesser degree (e.g., inflated self-esteem, decreased need for sleep, flights of ideas, pressured speech, etc.). Although the symptoms listed are the same for manic and hypomanic episodes, there is much less impairment in social and occupational functioning in hypomania, and hospitalization is not required.

Research suggests that mild mood disturbances are on the same continuum as the more severe disorders. That is, the differences seem to be chiefly of degree, not of kind, a conclusion supported in several large studies examining the issue (e.g.,

Kessing, 2007; Ruscio & Ruscio, 2000; South & Krueger, 2009). However, there is also considerable heterogeneity in the ways in which the mood disorders manifest themselves. Thus there are multiple subtypes of both unipolar and bipolar disorders, and somewhat different causal pathways and treatments are important for different subtypes.

It is also important to remember that suicide is a distressingly frequent outcome (and always a potential outcome) of significant depressions, both unipolar and bipolar. In fact, as discussed later, depressive episodes are clearly the most common of the predisposing causes leading to suicide.

The Prevalence of Mood Disorders

Major mood disorders occur with alarming frequency—at least 15 to 20 times more frequently than schizophrenia, for example, and at almost the same rate as all the anxiety disorders taken together. Of the two types of serious mood disorders, *unipolar major depressive disorder* (MDD), in which only major depressive episodes occur (also known as unipolar major depression), is the most common, and its occurrence has apparently increased in recent decades (Kaelber et al., 1995; Kessler et al., 2003). The most recent epidemiological results from the National Comorbidity Survey-Replication found lifetime prevalence rates of unipolar major depression at nearly 17 percent (12-month prevalence rates were nearly 7 percent; Kessler, Chiu et al., 2005).

Moreover, rates for unipolar depression are always much higher for women than for men (usually about 2:1), similar to the sex differences for most anxiety disorders (Hasin et al., 2005; Nolen-Hoeksema & Hilt, 2009). These differences occur in most countries around the world; the few exceptions are developing and rural countries such as Nigeria and Iran. In the United States, this sex difference starts in adolescence and continues until about age 65, when it seems to disappear. Yet among school children, boys are equally likely or slightly more likely to be diagnosed with depression.

The other type of major mood disorder, *bipolar disorder* (in which both manic and depressive episodes occur), is much less common. The NCS-R estimated that the lifetime risk of developing the classic form of this disorder is about 1 percent (see also Goodwin & Jamison, 2007), and there is no discernible difference in the prevalence rates between the sexes.

In Review

- What are the primary distinctions between unipolar disorders and bipolar disorders?
- How prevalent are the two types of mood disorders?
- How do the prevalence rates of unipolar and bipolar disorders differ between the sexes?

Unipolar Mood Disorders

Sadness, discouragement, pessimism, and hopelessness about matters improving are familiar feelings to most people. Feelings of depression are unpleasant when we are experiencing them, but they usually do not last long, dissipating on their own after a period of days or weeks or after they have reached a certain intensity level. Indeed, mild and brief depression may actually be "normal" and adaptive in the long run because much of the "work" of depression seems to involve facing images, thoughts, and feelings that one would normally avoid, and, at the same time, it is usually self-limiting. By slowing us down, mild depression sometimes saves us from wasting a lot of energy in the futile pursuit of unobtainable goals (Keller & Nesse, 2005; Nesse, 2000). Usually, normal depressions would be expected to occur in people undergoing painful but common life events such as significant personal, interpersonal, or economic losses.

Depressions That Are Not Mood Disorders

Normal depressions are nearly always the result of recent stress. We will consider two fairly common causes of depressive symptoms that are generally not considered mood disorders except when they are unusually severe or prolonged.

LOSS AND THE GRIEVING PROCESS We usually think of grief as the psychological process one goes through following the death of a loved one—a process that appears to be more difficult for men than for women (Bonanno & Kaltman, 1999). Grief often has certain characteristic qualities. Indeed, Bowlby's (1980) classic observations revealed that there are usually four phases of *normal response* to the loss of a spouse or close family member: (1) numbing and disbelief, (2) yearning and searching for the dead person, (3) disorganization and despair that sets in when the person accepts the loss as permanent, and (4) some reorganization as the person gradually begins to rebuild his or her life.

This has generally been considered the normal pattern, and a recent careful study of over 200 individuals who had lost a loved one due to natural causes documented that this is indeed the typical sequence (Maciejewski et al., 2007). Some people, however, become stuck somewhere in the middle of the normal response sequence. The normal nature of exhibiting a certain number of grief symptoms has led *DSM-IV-TR* to suggest that major depressive disorder usually not be diagnosed for the first 2 months following the loss, even if all the symptom criteria are met. However, results from Maciejewski and colleagues' study suggest that for most bereaved individuals, depressive symptoms actually tend to peak at 2 to 6 months following the loss,

We see here a young woman grieving at her father's grave. How do clinicians distinguish between a normal grief response and a more serious mood disorder?

suggesting that the next *DSM* should lengthen the time period between when grief symptoms start and when an individual receives a major depressive disorder diagnosis. Bonanno (2006) suggests that 10 to 20 percent of bereaved individuals have enduring and complicated grief reactions.

An additional challenge to the current *DSM* approach of not diagnosing major depressive disorder in the first 2 months following bereavement stems from recent research demonstrating that symptoms and impairment following other important losses (e.g., marital dissolution, unexpected economic misfortunes, or job loss) are virtually identical to those seen during bereavement. Such results question the *DSM-IV*'s approach of excluding only bereavement and not severe sadness responses to other kinds of losses (e.g., Wakefield et al., 2007). This issue and related ones have been hotly debated by the *DSM-5* task force and it is not yet clear how they will be resolved (Wakefield, 2011).

Ignoring for the moment the people who are eventually diagnosed as having major depressive disorder, it is easy to see uncomplicated grief as having an adaptive function (Bowlby, 1980). Traditionally, failing to exhibit grief under conditions in which it seems warranted has been a cause of concern because it was thought to suggest that the person was not fully processing the loss, at least at a psychological level. However, recent studies of bereaved individuals following the loss of a spouse, life partner, or parent have found that about 50 percent exhibit genuine resilience in the face of loss, with minimal, very short-lived symptoms of depression or bereavement. And contrary to what was previously thought, these resilient individuals are not emotionally maladjusted or unattached to their spouses (e.g., Bonanno et al., 2004; Bonanno et al., 2005).

POSTPARTUM "BLUES" Even though the birth of a child would usually seem to be a happy event, postpartum depression sometimes occurs in new mothers (and occasionally fathers) following the birth of a child, and it is known to have adverse effects on child outcomes (Ramchandani et al., 2005). In the past it was believed that postpartum major depression in mothers was relatively common, but more recent evidence suggests that only "postpartum blues" are very common. The symptoms of postpartum blues typically include changeable mood, crying easily, sadness, and irritability, often liberally intermixed with happy feelings (Miller, 2002; O'Hara et al., 1990, 1991; Reck et al., 2009). Such symptoms occur in as many as 50 to 70 percent of women within 10 days of the birth of their child and usually subside on their own (APA, *DSM-IV-TR*, 2000; Miller, 2002; Nolen-Hoeksema & Hilt, 2009). New findings show that hypomanic symptoms are also frequently observed, intermixed with the more depression-like symptoms (Sharma et al., 2009).

It appears that major depression in women occurs no more frequently in the postpartum period than would be expected in women of the same age and socioeconomic status who have not just given birth (Hobfoll et al., 1995; O'Hara & Swain, 1996). Especially rare are instances in which the major depression is accompanied by psychotic features. Thus the once firmly held notion that women are at especially high risk for major depression in the postpartum period has not been upheld. There

This new mother is experiencing postpartum blues; her mood is very labile and she cries easily.

is, however, a greater likelihood of developing major depression after the postpartum blues—especially if they are severe (Henshaw et al., 2004; Reck et al., 2009).

Hormonal readjustments (Miller, 2002; O'Hara et al., 1991) and alterations in serotonergic and noradrenergic functioning (Doornbos et al., 2008) may play a role in postpartum blues and depression, although the evidence on this issue is mixed. It is obvious that a psychological component is present as well. Postpartum blues or depression may be especially likely to occur if the new mother has a lack of social support or has difficulty adjusting to her new identity and responsibilities, or if the woman has a personal or family history of depression that leads to heightened sensitivity to the stress of childbirth (Collins et al., 2004; Miller, 2002; O'Hara & Gorman, 2004).

Dysthymic Disorder

The point at which mood disturbance becomes a diagnosable mood disorder is a matter of clinical judgment and usually concerns the degree of impairment in functioning that the individual experiences. Dysthymic disorder is generally considered to be of mild to moderate intensity, but its primary hallmark is its chronicity. To qualify for a diagnosis of **dysthymic disorder** (or dysthymia), a person must have a persistently depressed mood most of the day, for more days than not, for at least 2 years (1 year for children and adolescents). In addition, individuals with dysthymic disorder must have at least two of six additional symptoms when depressed. Periods of normal mood may occur briefly, but they usually last for only a few days to a few weeks (and for a maximum of 2 months). These intermittently normal moods are one of the most important characteristics distinguishing dysthymic disorder from major depressive disorder, which typically occurs in more discrete major depressive episodes. Nevertheless, in spite of the intermittently normal moods, because of its chronic course people with dysthymia show poorer outcomes and as much impairment as those with major depression (Klein, 2008, 2010).

Dysthymia is also quite common, with a lifetime prevalence estimated at between 2.5 and 6 percent (Kessler et al., 1994; Kessler, Berglund, Demler et al., 2005). The average duration of dysthymia is 4 to 5 years, but it can persist for 20 years or more (Keller et al., 1997; Klein et al., 2006). Chronic stress has been shown to increase the severity of symptoms over a 7.5-year follow-up period (Dougherty et al., 2004). Dysthymia often begins during the teenage years, and over 50 percent of those who present for treatment have an onset before age 21. One 10-year prospective study of 97 individuals with early-onset dysthymia found that 74 percent recovered within 10 years but that, among those who recovered, 71 percent relapsed, with most relapses occurring within approximately 3 years of follow-up (Klein et al., 2006; see also Klein, 2010).

This figure is intentionally omitted from this text.

The following case is typical of this disorder.

case study A Dysthymic Executive

A 28-year-old junior executive . . . complained of being "depressed" about everything: her job, her husband, and her prospects for the future. . . . Her complaints were of persistent feelings of depressed mood, inferiority, and pessimism, which she claims to have had since she was 16 or 17 years old. Although she did reasonably well in college, she constantly ruminated about those students who were "genuinely intelligent." She dated during college and graduate school but claimed that she would never go after a guy she thought was "special," always feeling inferior and intimidated. . . .

Just after graduation, she had married the man she was going out with at the time. She thought of him as reasonably desirable, though not "special," and married him primarily because she felt she "needed a husband" for companionship. Shortly after their marriage, the couple started to bicker. She was very critical of his clothes, his job, and his parents; and he, in turn, found her rejecting, controlling, and moody. She began to feel that she had made a mistake in marrying him.

Recently she has also been having difficulties at work. She is assigned the most menial tasks at the firm and is never given an assignment of importance or responsibility. She admits that she frequently does a "slipshod" job of what is given her, never does more than is required, and never demonstrates any assertiveness or initiative. . . . She feels that she will never go very far in her profession because she does not have the right "connections" and neither does her husband, yet she dreams of money, status, and power. Her social life with her husband involves several other couples. The man in these couples is usually a friend of her husband. She is sure that the women find her uninteresting and unimpressive and that the people who seem to like her are probably no better off than she.

Under the burden of her dissatisfaction with her marriage, her job, and her social life, feeling tired and uninterested in "life," she now enters treatment for the third time. (Adapted with permission from *Casebook: A Learning Companion to the Diagnostic and Statistical Manual of Mental Disorders*, Fourth Edition, *Text Revision*, (Copyright © 2002). American Psychiatric Association.)

Major Depressive Disorder

The diagnostic criteria for **major depressive disorder** (also known as major depression) require that the person exhibit more symptoms than are required for dysthymia and that the symptoms be more persistent (not interwoven with periods of normal mood). To receive a

A person with major depressive disorder may experience a loss of energy, too much or too little sleep, decreased appetite and weight loss, an increase or slowdown in mental and physical activity, difficulty concentrating, irrational guilt, and recurrent thoughts of death or suicide.

diagnosis of major depressive disorder, a person must be in a *major depressive episode* (*single* if initial, or *recurrent*) and never have had a manic, hypomanic, or mixed episode. An affected person must experience either markedly depressed moods or marked loss of interest in pleasurable activities most of every day, nearly every day, for at least 2 consecutive weeks. In addition to showing one or both of these symptoms, the person must experience at least three or four additional symptoms during the same period (for a total of at least five symptoms). In addition to the obvious emotional symptoms, these symptoms also include cognitive symptoms (such as feelings of worthlessness or guilt, and thoughts of suicide), behavioral symptoms (such as fatigue or physical agitation), and physical symptoms (such as changes in appetite and sleep patterns).

It should be noted that few if any depressions—including milder ones—occur in the absence of significant anxiety (e.g., Merikangas et al., 2003; Mineka et al., 1998; Watson, 2005). Indeed, there is a high degree of overlap between measures of depressive and anxious symptoms in self-reports and in clinician ratings. At the diagnostic level, there are very high levels of comorbidity between depressive and anxiety disorders (e.g., Kessler, Merikangas, & Wang, 2007; Watson, 2005). As discussed later in this text (see Developments in Thinking 2), the issues surrounding the co-occurrence of depression and anxiety, which have received a great deal of attention in recent years, are very complex.

The following account illustrates a moderately severe case of major depressive disorder.

Note that Connie's case clearly illustrates that a person with major depressive disorder shows not only mood symptoms of

case study | Connie

Connie, a 33-year-old homemaker and mother of a 4-year-old son, Robert, is referred . . . to a psychiatric outpatient program because . . . she has been depressed and unable to concentrate ever since she separated from her husband 3 months previously. Connie left her husband, Donald, after a 5-year marriage. Violent arguments between them, during which Connie was beaten by her husband, had occurred for the last 4 years of their marriage, beginning when she became pregnant with Robert. There were daily arguments during which Donald hit her hard enough to leave bruises on her face and arms. . . .

Before her marriage . . . she was close to her parents [and] had many friends who she also saw regularly. . . . In high school she had been a popular cheerleader and a good student. . . . She had no personal history of depression, and there was no family history of . . . mental illness.

During the first year of marriage, Donald became increasingly irritable and critical of Connie. He began to request that Connie stop calling and seeing her friends after work, and refused to allow them or his in-laws to visit their apartment. . . . Despite her misgivings about Donald's behavior toward her, Connie decided to become pregnant. During the seventh month of the pregnancy . . . Donald began complaining [and] began hitting her with his fists. She left him and went to live with her parents for a week. He expressed remorse . . . and . . . Connie returned to her apartment. No further violence occurred until after Robert's birth. At that time, Donald began using cocaine every weekend and often became violent when he was high.

In the 3 months since she left Donald, Connie has become increasingly depressed. Her appetite has been poor and she has lost 10 pounds. She cries a lot and often wakes up at 5:00 A.M. and is unable to get back to sleep. . . . Connie is pale and thin. . . . She speaks slowly, describing her depressed mood and lack of energy. She says that her only pleasure is in being with her son. She is able to take care of him physically but feels guilty because her preoccupation with her own bad feelings prevents her from being able to play with him. She now has no contacts other than with her parents and her son. She feels worthless and blames herself for her marital problems, saying that if she had been a better wife, maybe Donald would have been able to give up the cocaine. . . . (Adapted with permission from *DSM-IV-TR Casebook: A Learning Companion to the Diagnostic and Statistical Manual of Mental Disorders*, Fourth Edition, *Text Revision*, (Copyright © 2002). American Psychiatric Association)

sadness but also a variety of symptoms that are more severe than those in milder forms of depression. Connie shows various cognitive distortions, including feeling worthless and guilty. She complains of a lack of energy and inability to play with her child. Her physical symptoms include loss of appetite and early morning awakening. The loss of contact with friends also occurs commonly with major depression, in part because the person is unmotivated to seek contact. Connie's case also clearly illustrates the multiple complex, interacting factors that may be involved in the etiology of depression. Although she does not have a personal or a family history of depression, the experiences from 5 years of a very difficult marriage to a violent and abusive husband were sufficient to finally precipitate her major depression.

DEPRESSION AS A RECURRENT DISORDER When a diagnosis of major depressive disorder is made, it is usually also specified whether this is a first, and therefore *single* (initial), episode or a *recurrent* episode (preceded by one or more previous episodes). This reflects the fact that depressive episodes are usually time limited; the average duration of an untreated episode is about 6 to 9 months. In a large untreated sample of women with depression, certain predictors pointed to a longer time to spontaneous remission of symptoms: having financial difficulties, severe stressful life events, and high genetic risk (Kendler, Walters, & Kessler, 1997). In approximately 10 to 20 percent of people with major depression, the symptoms do not remit for over 2 years, in which case **chronic major depressive disorder** is diagnosed (Boland & Keller, 2009; Gilmer et al., 2005). Chronic major depression has been associated with serious childhood family problems and an anxious personality in childhood (Angst et al., 2011).

Although most depressive episodes remit (which is not said to occur until symptoms have largely been gone for at least 2 months), depressive episodes often recur at some future point. In recent years, **recurrence** has been distinguished from **relapse**, where the latter term refers to the return of symptoms within a fairly short period of time, a situation that probably reflects the fact that the underlying episode of depression has not yet run its course (Boland & Keller, 2002; Frank et al., 1991). For example, relapse may commonly occur when pharmacotherapy is terminated prematurely—after symptoms have remitted but before the underlying episode is really over (Hollon & Dimidjian, 2002).

Until very recently the proportion of patients who will exhibit a recurrence of major depression has been estimated as 60 percent, although the time period before a recurrence occurs is highly variable. However, a very recent careful review of the studies leading to the 60-percent estimate has shown that there were methodological flaws in the way these estimates were calculated and that a more accurate estimate is 40 or 50 percent (Monroe & Harkness, 2011). There is also evidence that the probability of recurrence increases with the number of prior episodes and when the person has comorbid disorders. Unfortunately very little is known about what the differences are between people who will only suffer a single depressive episode and those who will go on to develop more (Monroe & Harkness, 2011).

The traditional view was that between episodes a person suffering from a recurrent major mood disorder is essentially symptom free. However, as more research data on the course of depression became available (e.g., Coryell & Winokur, 1992; Judd et al., 1998), it has become clear that this is frequently not the case. For example, in a large five-site study with over 400 patients, Judd and colleagues (1998) found that patients experiencing their first episode at the time the study began showed no symptoms at all only 54 percent of the weeks during a 12-year follow-up period. Among those experiencing a second or later episode at the start of the study, this figure was only 37 percent who had any symptom-free weeks. Moreover, people with some residual symptoms, or with significant psychosocial impairment, following an episode are even more likely to have recurrences than those whose symptoms remit completely (Judd et al., 1999; Solomon et al., 2004).

DEPRESSION THROUGHOUT THE LIFE CYCLE Although the onset of unipolar depressive disorders most often occurs during late adolescence up to middle adulthood, such reactions may begin at any time from early childhood to old age. Depression was once thought not to occur in childhood, but more recent research has estimated that about 1 to 3 percent of school-age children meet the criteria for some form of unipolar depressive disorder, with a smaller percentage exhibiting dysthymic disorder than major depression (see Avenevoli et al., 2008; Garber et al., 2009). As in adults, recurrence rates are high. Even infants may experience a form of depression (formerly known as *anaclitic depression* or despair) if they are separated for a prolonged period from their attachment figure (usually their mother; Bowlby, 1973, 1980; Speier et al., 1995), although current thinking suggests this may not happen until at least 18 months of age (Guedeney, 2007).

The incidence of depression rises sharply during adolescence—a period of great turmoil for many people. Indeed, one review estimated that approximately 15 to 20 percent of adolescents experience major depressive disorder at some point and subclinical levels of depressed affect another 10 to 20 percent of the time (Avenevoli et al., 2008; Lewinsohn & Essau, 2002). It is during this time period that sex differences in rates of depression first emerge (e.g., Essau, Lewinsohn, Seeley, & Sasagawa, 2010; Hankin et al., 2008; Nolen-Hoeksema & Hilt, 2009). (See Developments in Research 1.) The long-term effects of major depressive disorder in adolescence can last at least through young adulthood, when such individuals show small but significant psychosocial impairments in many domains, including their occupational lives, their interpersonal relationships, and their general quality of life (e.g., Lewinsohn et al., 2003; Rudolph, 2009). Moreover, major depression that occurs in adolescence is very likely to recur in adulthood (Avenevoli et al., 2008; Rudolph, 2009).

The occurrence of major depression continues into later life. Although the 1-year prevalence of major depression is significantly lower in people over age 65 than in younger adults (Kessler et al., 2010), major depression and dysthymia in older adults are still considered a major public health problem today

(Blazer & Hybels, 2009; Kessler, Berglund, Demler et al., 2005). Moreover, research suggests that rates of depression among physically ill residents of nursing homes or residential care facilities are substantially higher than among older adults living at home (see Davison et al., 2007; Powers et al., 2002). Unfortunately, depression in later life can be difficult to diagnose because many of the symptoms overlap with those of several medical illnesses and dementia (Alexopoulos et al., 2002; Harvey et al., 2006). Yet it is very important to try and diagnose it reliably because depression in later life has many adverse consequences for a person's health, including doubling the risk of death in people who have had a heart attack or stroke (e.g., Schulz et al., 2002).

SPECIFIERS FOR MAJOR DEPRESSIVE EPISODES Some individuals who meet the basic criteria for diagnosis of a major depressive episode also have additional patterns of symptoms or features that are important to note when making a diagnosis because these patterns have implications for understanding more about the course of the disorder and its most effective treatment. These different patterns of symptoms or features are called **specifiers** in *DSM-IV-TR* (see Table 1 for a summary of the major specifiers). One such specifier is **major depressive episode with melancholic features**. This designation is applied when, in addition to meeting the criteria for a major depressive episode, a patient either has lost interest or pleasure in almost all activities or does not react to usually pleasurable stimuli or desired events. This severe subtype of depression is more heritable than most other forms of depression and is more often associated with a history of childhood trauma (Harkness & Monroe, 2002; Kendler, 1997). People with this subtype of depression also show greater cognitive impairment than with most other subtypes of depression (Withall et al., 2010).

Psychotic symptoms, characterized by loss of contact with reality and delusions (false beliefs) or hallucinations (false sensory perceptions), may sometimes accompany other symptoms of major depression. In such cases the specifier to the diagnosis that is noted is **severe major depressive episode with psychotic features**. Ordinarily, any delusions or hallucinations present are **mood congruent**—that is, they seem in some sense appropriate to serious depression because the content is negative in tone, such as themes of personal inadequacy, guilt, deserved punishment, death, or disease. For example, the delusional idea that one's internal organs have totally deteriorated—an idea sometimes held by people with severe depression—ties in with the mood of a person who is despondent. Feelings of guilt and worthlessness are also commonly part of the clinical picture (Keller et al., 2007; Ohayon & Shatzberg, 2002). Individuals who are psychotically depressed are likely to have longer episodes, more cognitive impairment, and a poorer long-term prognosis than those suffering from depression without psychotic features (Bora et al., 2010; Flores & Schatzberg, 2006), and any recurrent episodes are also likely to be characterized by psychotic symptoms (Fleming et al., 2004). Treatment generally involves an antipsychotic medication as well as an antidepressant (Keller et al., 2007).

table 1 Specifiers of Major Depressive Episodes

Specifier	Characteristic Symptoms
With Melancholic Features	Three of the following: Early morning awakening, depression worse in the morning, marked psychomotor agitation or retardation, loss of appetite or weight, excessive guilt, qualitatively different depressed mood.
With Psychotic Features	Delusions or hallucinations (usually mood congruent); feelings of guilt and worthlessness common.
With Atypical Features	Mood reactivity—brightens to positive events; two of the four following symptoms: weight gain or increase in appetite, hypersomnia, leaden paralysis, being acutely sensitive to interpersonal rejection.
With Catatonic Features	A range of psychomotor symptoms from motoric immobility to extensive psychomotor activity, as well as mutism and rigidity.
With Seasonal Pattern	At least two or more episodes in past 2 years that have occurred at the same time (usually fall or winter), and full remission at the same time (usually spring). No other nonseasonal episodes in same 2-year period.

A third important specifier is used when the individual shows "atypical features." **Major depressive episode with atypical features** includes a pattern of symptoms characterized by mood reactivity; that is, the person's mood brightens in response to potential positive events. In addition, the person must show two or more of the four symptoms listed in Table 1. A disproportionate number of individuals who have atypical features are females, who have an earlier-than-average age of onset and who are more likely to show suicidal thoughts (Matza et al., 2003). Research has also shown that atypical depression is linked to a mild form of bipolar disorder that is associated with hypomanic rather than manic episodes (Akiskal & Benazzi, 2005). This is also an important specifier because there are indications that individuals with atypical features may preferentially respond to a different class of antidepressants—the monoamine oxidase inhibitors—than do most other individuals with depression.

A fourth specifier is used when the individual shows marked psychomotor disturbances. **Major depressive episode with catatonic features** includes a range of psychomotor symptoms, from motoric immobility (*catalepsy*—a stuporous state) to extensive psychomotor activity, as well as mutism and rigidity. Although *DSM-IV-TR* focuses on catatonia mainly as a subtype of schizophrenia, it is actually more frequently associated with certain forms of depression and mania than with schizophrenia (Fink & Taylor, 2006).

A fifth specifier is used when individuals who experience recurrent depressive episodes show a seasonal pattern, **recurrent major depressive episode with a seasonal pattern**, also commonly known as **seasonal affective disorder**. To meet *DSM-IV-TR* criteria for this specifier, the person must have had at least two episodes of depression in the past 2 years occurring at the same time of the year (most commonly fall or winter), and full remission must also have occurred at the same time of the year (most commonly the spring). In addition, the person cannot have had other, nonseasonal depressive episodes in the same 2-year period, and most of the person's lifetime depressive episodes must have been of the seasonal variety. Prevalence rates suggest that winter seasonal affective disorder is more common in people living at higher latitudes (northern climates) and in younger people.

Although not recognized as an official specifier, it is not at all uncommon for major depression to coexist with dysthymia in some people, a condition given the designation **double depression** (Boland & Keller, 2002; Klein, 2010). People with double depression are moderately depressed on a chronic basis (meeting symptom criteria for dysthymia) but undergo increased problems from time to time, during which they also meet criteria for a major depressive episode. Among clinical samples of people with dysthymia, the experience of double depression appears to be very common, although it may be much less common in people with dysthymic disorder who never seek treatment (Akiskal, 1997). For example, one clinical sample of nearly 100 individuals with early-onset dysthymia (onset before age 21) was followed for 10 years, during which time 84 percent experienced at least one major depressive episode (Klein et al., 2006; see also Keller et al., 1997). Although nearly all individuals with double depression appear to recover from their major depressive episodes (at least for a while), recurrence is common (Boland & Keller, 2002; Klein, 2008, 2010; Klein et al., 2006).

In Review

- What are the major features that differentiate dysthymic disorder and major depressive disorder?
- Distinguish between recurrence and relapse.
- What are three common specifiers of major depressive disorder?
- What is double depression?

Causal Factors in Unipolar Mood Disorders

In considering the development of unipolar mood disorders, researchers have focused on the possible roles of biological, psychological, and sociocultural factors. Although each set of factors has usually been studied separately, ultimately the goal should be to understand how these different kinds of causal factors are interrelated in order to develop a biopsychosocial model.

Biological Causal Factors

It has long been known that a variety of diseases and drugs can affect mood, leading sometimes to depression and sometimes to elation or even mania. Indeed, this idea goes back to Hippocrates, who hypothesized that depression was caused by an excess of "black bile" in the system (c. 400 B.C.). As we will discuss, in the past half century investigators attempting to establish a biological basis for unipolar disorders have considered a wide range of factors.

GENETIC INFLUENCES *Family studies* have shown that the prevalence of mood disorders is approximately two to three times higher among blood relatives of persons with clinically diagnosed unipolar depression than in the population at large

People who live in higher latitudes (northern climates for those in the northern hemisphere) are more likely to exhibit seasonal affective disorder, in which depression occurs primarily in the fall and winter months and tends to remit in the spring or summer months.

(e.g., Levinson, 2006, 2009; Wallace et al., 2002). More importantly, however, *twin studies*, which can provide much more conclusive evidence of genetic influences on a disorder, also suggest a moderate genetic contribution to unipolar depression. Sullivan and colleagues (2000) conducted a quantitative review of numerous twin studies (the total number of twins studied was over 21,000) and found that monozygotic co-twins of a twin with unipolar major depression are about twice as likely to develop major depression as are dizygotic co-twins. Averaging across the results of these studies, this review suggested that about 31 to 42 percent of the variance in liability to major depression is due to genetic influences. The estimate is substantially higher (70 to 80 percent) for more severe, early-onset, or recurrent depressions (see also Levinson, 2009; McGuffin et al., 2007). Notably, however, Sullivan and colleagues' review concluded that even more variance in the liability to most forms of major depression is due to nonshared environmental influences (i.e., experiences that family members do not share) than to genetic factors.

Taken together, the results from family and twin studies make a strong case for a moderate genetic contribution to the causal patterns of unipolar major depression, although not as large a genetic contribution as for bipolar disorder (Farmer et al., 2005; Goodwin & Jamison, 2007). Unfortunately, the evidence for a genetic contribution to milder but chronic forms of unipolar depression such as dysthymia is very slim, probably because there has been very little research on the topic (Klein, 2008). However, it seems very probable that there is a genetic contribution to dysthymia because of its strong link to elevated levels of the personality trait neuroticism, which is moderately heritable.

Attempts to identify specific genes that may be responsible for these genetic influences have not yet been successful, although there are some promising leads (Levinson, 2006, 2009; Wallace et al., 2002). One very promising candidate for a specific gene that might be implicated is the *serotonin-transporter gene*—a gene involved in the transmission and reuptake of serotonin, one of the key neurotransmitters involved in depression. There are two different kinds of versions or alleles involved—the short allele (*s*) and the long allele (*l*), and people have two short alleles (*ss*), two long alleles (*ll*), or one of each (*sl*). Prior work with animals had suggested that having *ss* alleles might predispose a person to depression relative to a person having *ll* alleles, but human work on this issue had provided mixed results. In 2003, Caspi and colleagues published a landmark study in which they tested for the possibility of a *genotype–environment interaction* involving these two alleles of the serotonin-transporter gene. They studied 847 people in New Zealand who had been followed from birth to 26 years of age, at which time the researchers assessed diagnoses of major depressive episodes in the past year and the occur-

rence of stressful life events in the previous 5 years. Their results were very striking: Individuals who possessed the genotype with the *ss* alleles were twice as likely to develop a major depressive episode following four or more stressful life events in the past 5 years as those who possessed the genotype with the *ll* alleles and had experienced four or more stressful events (those with the *sl* alleles were intermediate). Moreover, they also found that those who had the *ss* alleles and had had severe maltreatment as children were also twice as likely to develop a major depressive episode as those with the *ll* alleles who had had severe maltreatment and as those with the *ss* alleles who had not been maltreated as children. These exciting findings strongly support a diathesis-stress model; many other (but not all) studies being conducted that have found similar results (e.g., Kendler et al., 2005; Uher & McGuffin, 2010). However, in 2009 a quantitative review by Risch and colleagues (2009) challenged these results; this led to a major controversy in the field. Fortunately by 2011 other quantitative reviews have demonstrated that the gene–environment result is robust if the studies use sensitive interview-based measures of life stress (see Psychological Causal Factors section; McGuffin, 2010; see also Karg et al., 2011). Such results suggest that the search for candidate genes that are likely to be involved in the etiology of major depression is likely to be much more fruitful if researchers also test for genotype–environment interactions (see Moffitt et al., 2005).

This figure is intentionally omitted from this text.

NEUROCHEMICAL FACTORS Ever since the 1960s, the view that depression may arise from disruptions in the delicate balance of neurotransmitter substances that regulate and mediate the activity of the brain's nerve cells has received a great deal of attention. A large body of evidence suggested that various biological therapies (discussed later in this text) that are often used to treat severe mood disorders—such as electroconvulsive therapy and antidepressant medications—affect the concentrations or the activity of neurotransmitters at the synapse. Such early findings encouraged the development of neurochemical theories of the etiology of major depression.

Early attention in the 1960s and 1970s focused primarily on two neurotransmitter substances of the monoamine class—norepinephrine and serotonin—because researchers observed that antidepressant medications seemed to have the effect of increasing these neurotransmitters' availability at synaptic junctions (e.g., Thase & Denko, 2008; Thase et al., 2002). This observation led to the once influential *monoamine theory of depression*—that depression was at least sometimes due to an absolute or relative depletion of one or both of these neurotransmitters at important receptor sites in the brain (Schildkraut, 1965). This depletion could come about through impaired synthesis of these neurotransmitters in the presynaptic neuron, through increased degradation of the neurotransmitters once they were released into the synapse, or through altered functioning of postsynaptic receptors (Thase, 2009; Thase et al., 2002). Collectively, these neurotransmitters are now known to be involved in the regulation of behavioral activity, stress, emotional expression, and vegetative functions (involving appetite, sleep, and arousal)—all of which are disturbed in mood disorders (Garlow & Nemeroff, 2003; Southwick, Vythilingam, & Charney, 2005; Thase, 2009).

However, by the 1980s it was clear that no such straightforward mechanisms could possibly be responsible for causing depression (e.g., Krishnan & Nestler, 2010; Thase, 2009). For example, some studies have found exactly the opposite of what is predicted by the monoamine hypothesis—that is, net increases in norepinephrine activity in patients with depression—especially in those with severe or melancholic depression (see Thase & Denko, 2008; Thase et al., 2002). Moreover, only a minority of patients with depression have lowered serotonin activity, and these tend to be patients with high levels of suicidal ideation and behavior. Finally, even though the immediate, short-term effects of antidepressant drugs are to increase the availability of norepinephrine and serotonin, the long-term clinical effects of these drugs do not emerge until 2 to 4 weeks later, when neurotransmitter levels may have normalized.

Other more recent research also suggests that dopamine dysfunction (especially reduced dopaminergic activity) plays a significant role in at least some forms of depression, including depression with atypical features and bipolar depression (e.g., Dunlop & Nemeroff, 2007; Krishnan & Nestler, 2010; Thase, 2009). Because the neurotransmitter dopamine is so prominently involved in the experience of pleasure and reward, such findings are in keeping with the prominence of anhedonia, the inability to experience pleasure, which is such an important symptom of depression.

Unfortunately, the early monoamine theory has not been replaced by a compelling alternative. Altered neurotransmitter activity in several systems is clearly associated with major depression, but research for the past 20 to 25 years has focused on complex interactions of neurotransmitters and how they affect cellular functioning. A number of integrative theories have been proposed that include a role for neurotransmitters, not alone but rather as they interact with other disturbed hormonal and neurophysiological patterns and biological rhythms (e.g., Garlow & Nemeroff, 2003; Thase, 2009). An interesting new focus of some of this research is on understanding how interactions among these different neurobiological systems can promote resilience in the face of major stress (a very common precipitant for depression), which in turn may help explain why only a subset of people undergoing major stressors develop depression (Southwick et al., 2005).

ABNORMALITIES OF HORMONAL REGULATORY AND IMMUNE SYSTEMS There has also been a good deal of research on possible hormonal causes or correlates of some forms of mood disorder (Southwick et al., 2005; Thase, 2009; Thase et al., 2002). The majority of attention has been focused on the *hypothalamic-pituitary-adrenal (HPA) axis*, and in particular on the hormone cortisol, which is excreted by the outermost portion of the adrenal glands and is regulated through a complex feedback loop. The human stress response is associated with elevated activity of the HPA axis, which is partly controlled by norepinephrine and serotonin. The perception of stress or threat can lead to norepinephrine activity in the hypothalamus, causing the release of corticotrophin-releasing hormone (CRH) from the hypothalamus, which in turn triggers release of adrenocorticotropic hormone (ACTH) from the pituitary. The ACTH then typically travels through the blood to the adrenal cortex of the adrenal glands, where cortisol is released. Elevated cortisol activity is highly adaptive in the short term because it promotes survival in response to life-threatening or overwhelming life circumstances. However, sustained elevations are harmful to the organism, including promoting hypertension, heart disease, and obesity (which are all elevated in depression) (Stetler & Miller, 2011; Thase, 2009). Blood plasma levels of cortisol are known to be elevated in some 20 to 40 percent of outpatients with depression and in about 60 to 80 percent of hospitalized patients with severe depression (Thase et al., 2002). Sustained elevations in cortisol—a "hallmark of mammalian stress responses"—can result from increased CRH activation (for example, during sustained stress or threat), increased secretion of ACTH, or the failure of feedback mechanisms. See Figure 1.

One line of evidence that implicates the failure of feedback mechanisms in some patients with depression comes from robust findings that in about 45 percent of patients with serious depression, a potent suppressor of plasma cortisol in normal individuals, *dexamethasone*, either fails entirely to suppress cortisol or fails to sustain its suppression (Carroll, 2009;

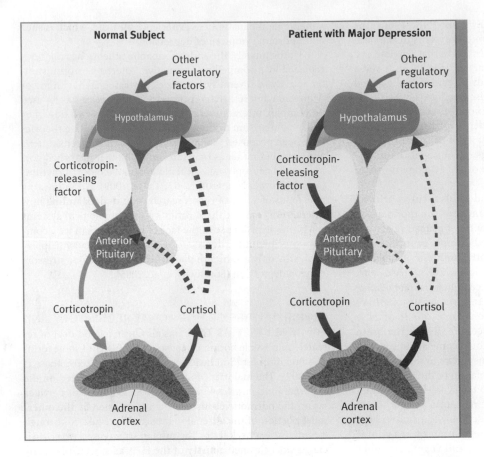

Normal Subject

Other regulatory factors

Hypothalamus

Corticotropin-releasing factor

Anterior Pituitary

Corticotropin

Cortisol

Adrenal cortex

Patient with Major Depression

Other regulatory factors

Hypothalamus

Corticotropin-releasing factor

Anterior Pituitary

Corticotropin

Cortisol

Adrenal cortex

FIGURE 1

Response to Stress in a Normal Subject and a Patient with Major Depressive Disorder

In normal subjects and in patients with major depression, periods of stress are typically associated with increased levels of both cortisol and corticotrophin-releasing factor. Corticotrophin-releasing factor stimulates the production of corticotrophin, which in turn stimulates the production of cortisol. Cortisol inhibits the release of corticotrophin from the pituitary and the release of corticotrophin-releasing factor from the hypothalamus. In patients with major depression, the sensitivity of this negative feedback system is often decreased, leading to elevated levels of cortisol.

Source: From "Rachel Yehuda. (2002, January 10). Post-traumatic stress disorder. *New England Journal of Medicine, 346*(2), 111. Reprinted with permission from Massachusetts Medical Society. Copyright © 2002 Massachusetts Medical Society. All rights reserved.

Thase et al., 2002). This means that the HPA axis is not operating properly in these "dexamethasone nonsuppressors." It was initially thought that dexamethasone nonsuppressor patients constituted a distinct subgroup of people with severe or melancholic depression (e.g., Holsboer, 1992). However, subsequent research has shown that several other groups of psychiatric patients, such as those with panic disorder, also exhibit high rates of nonsuppression. This suggests that nonsuppression may merely be a nonspecific indicator of generalized mental distress.

Research has also revealed that patients with depression with elevated cortisol also tend to show memory impairments and problems with abstract thinking and complex problem solving (Belanoff et al., 2001). Some of these cognitive problems may be related to other findings showing that prolonged elevations in cortisol, such as those seen in moderate to severe depression, result in cell death in the hippocampus—a part of the limbic system heavily involved in memory functioning (e.g., Southwick et al., 2005; Thase, 2009). Other interesting research has shown that stress in infancy and early childhood can promote long-term changes that increase the reactivity of the HPA axis, which may in turn help explain why children reared in environments with early adversity are at higher risk for developing depression later in life when they are exposed to acute stressors (e.g., Southwick et al., 2005).

The other endocrine axis that has relevance to depression is the *hypothalamic-pituitary-thyroid axis* because disturbances to this axis are also linked to mood disorders (Garlow & Nemeroff, 2003; Thase, 2009; Thase et al., 2002). For example, people with low thyroid levels (*hypothyroidism*) often become depressed. In addition, about 20 to 30 percent of patients with depression who have normal thyroid levels nevertheless show dysregulation of this axis. Moreover, preliminary findings suggest that some patients who have not responded to traditional antidepressant treatments may show improvement when administered thyrotropin-releasing hormone, which leads to increased thyroid hormone levels (Garlow & Nemeroff, 2003; Thase, 2009).

Finally, in recent years many studies have shown that depression is also accompanied by dysregulation of the *immune system*. For example, in a quantitative review Dowlati and colleagues (2010) have shown that depression is associated with activation of the inflammatory response system as evidenced by increased production of proinflammatory cytokines such as interleukin and interferon. These can both contribute directly to the development of depressive symptoms.

NEUROPHYSIOLOGICAL AND NEUROANATOMICAL INFLUENCES Exciting neurophysiological research in recent years has followed up on earlier neurological findings that

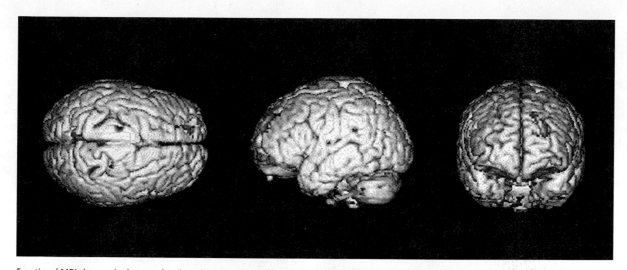

Functional MRI changes in depressed patients in response to affective stimuli from pre- to posttreatment. These red and yellow images illustrate (in three different views) the increase in left prefrontal activation that occurred in a group of depressed patients following treatment compared to their activation pattern during an acute depressive episode. Thus, the red and yellow images depict the increase in cerebral blood in the left prefrontal area in response to affective stimuli from before and after successful antidepressant treatment. The second scan was obtained 8 weeks following the first scan. Patients were treated with an antidepressant medication during those 8 weeks. (This image courtesy of Richard Davidson.)

damage (for example, from a stroke) to the left, but not the right, *anterior prefrontal cortex* often leads to depression (e.g., Davidson et al., 2009; Robinson & Downhill, 1995). This led to the idea that depression in people without brain damage may nonetheless be linked to lowered levels of brain activity in this same region (see Figure 5). A number of studies have supported this idea. When one measures the electroencephalographic (EEG) activity of both cerebral hemispheres in people who are depressed, one finds an asymmetry or imbalance in the EEG activity of the two sides of the prefrontal regions of the brain. In particular, people with depression show relatively low activity in the left hemisphere in these regions and relatively high activity in the right hemisphere (Davidson et al., 2009; Stewart et al., 2010). Similar findings have been reported using PET neuroimaging techniques (see Davidson et al., 2009; Phillips et al., 2003). Notably, patients in remission show the same pattern (Henriques & Davidson, 1990; Stewart et al., 2010), as do children at risk for depression (Bruder et al., 2007). These latter findings have seemed to hold promise as a way of identifying persons at risk both for an initial episode and for recurrent episodes. Indeed, a recent study found that left frontal asymmetry in never-depressed individuals predicted onset of major and minor depressive episodes over a 3-year period (Nusslock et al., 2011). The relatively lower activity on the left side of the prefrontal cortex in depression is thought to be related to symptoms of reduced positive affect and approach behaviors to rewarding stimuli, and increased right-side activity is thought to underlie increased anxiety symptoms and increased negative affect associated with increased vigilance for threatening information (Pizzagalli et al., 2002).

Abnormalities have also been detected in several other brain areas in patients with depression. For example, several regions of the prefrontal cortex, including the *orbital prefrontal cortex*, which is involved in responsivity to reward (e.g., Haber & Knutson, 2010), show decreased volume in individuals with recurrent depression relative to normal controls (Koolschijn et al., 2009; Phillips et al., 2003). Lower levels of activity in the *dorsolateral prefrontal cortex*, which are associated with decreased cognitive control, have also been observed in individuals with depression compared to controls (Disner et al., 2011). Another area involved is the *hippocampus*, which is critical to learning and memory and regulation of adrenocorticotropic hormone. As already noted, prolonged depression often leads to decreased hippocampal volume, at least in older people with depression (similar to what is seen in chronic PTSD), which could be due to cell atrophy or cell death (e.g., Davidson et al., 2009; Koolschijn et al., 2009). In addition, evidence of decreased hippocampal volume in never-depressed individuals who are at high (versus low) risk for depression suggests that reductions in hippocampal volume may precede the onset of depression (Chen et al., 2010).

A third such area is the *anterior cingulate cortex*, which both shows decreased volume and abnormally low levels of activation in patients with depression (Koolschijn et al., 2009). This area is involved in selective attention, which is important in prioritizing the most important information available, and therefore in self-regulation and adaptability—all important processes that are disrupted in depression.

Finally, the *amygdala*, which is involved in the perception of threat and in directing attention, tends to show increased activation in individuals with depression (and anxiety disorders), which may be related to their biased attention to negative emotional information (Davidson et al., 2009; Disner et al., 2011; Phillips et al., 2003).

This figure is intentionally omitted from this text.

SLEEP AND OTHER BIOLOGICAL RHYTHMS Although findings of sleep disturbances in patients with depression have existed as long as depression has been studied, only recently have some of these findings been linked to more general disturbances in biological rhythms.

Sleep Sleep is characterized by five stages that occur in a relatively invariant sequence throughout the night (Stages 1 to 4 of non-REM sleep and REM sleep make up a sleep cycle). REM sleep (rapid eye movement sleep) is characterized by rapid eye movements and dreaming as well as other bodily changes; the first REM period does not usually begin until near the end of the first sleep cycle, about 75 to 80 minutes into sleep. This normal sleep–wake cycle is thought to be regulated by the *suprachiasmatic nucleus* of the hypothalamus (e.g., Steiger, 2007; Thase, 2009). Patients who are depressed often show one or more of a variety of sleep problems, ranging from early morning awakening, periodic awakening during the night (poor sleep maintenance), and, for some, difficulty falling asleep. Such changes occur in about 80 percent of hospitalized patients with depression and in about 50 percent of outpatients with depression, and are particularly pronounced in patients with melancholic features.

Moreover, research using EEG recordings has found that many patients with depression enter the first period of REM sleep after only 60 minutes or less of sleep (i.e., 15 to 20 minutes sooner than patients who are not depressed do) and also show greater amounts of REM sleep during the early cycles than are seen in persons without depression. The intensity and frequency of their rapid eye movements are also greater than in patients who are not depressed (Thase et al., 2002). Because this is the period of the night when most deep sleep (Stages 3 and 4) usually occurs, the person with depression also gets a lower-than-normal amount of deep sleep. Both the reduced latency to enter REM sleep and the decreased amount of deep sleep often precede the onset of depression and persist following recovery, which suggests that they may be vulnerability markers for certain forms of major depression (Hasler et al., 2004; Thase et al., 2002).

Circadian Rhythms Humans have many circadian (24-hour, or daily) cycles other than sleep, including body temperature, propensity to REM sleep, and secretion of cortisol, thyroid-stimulating hormone, and growth hormone (Thase, 2009; Thase et al., 2002). These circadian rhythms are controlled by two related central "oscillators," which act as internal biological clocks. Research has found some abnormalities in all of these rhythms in patients with depression, though not all patients show abnormalities in all rhythms (Howland & Thase, 1999; Thase, 2009). Although the exact nature of the dysfunctions is not yet known, some kind of circadian rhythm dysfunction may play a causal role in many of the clinical features of depression. Two current theories are (1) that the size or magnitude of the circadian rhythms is blunted, and (2) that the various circadian rhythms that are normally well synchronized with each other become desynchronized or uncoupled (Howland & Thase, 1999; Thase et al., 2002).

Sunlight and Seasons Another, rather different kind of rhythm abnormality or disturbance is seen in people with *seasonal affective disorder*, in which most of those affected seem to be responsive to the total quantity of available light in the environment (Oren & Rosenthal, 1992). A majority (but not all) become depressed in the fall and winter and normalize in the spring and summer (Goodwin & Jamison, 2007; Howland & Thase, 1999). Research in animals has also documented that many seasonal variations in basic functions such as sleep, activity, and appetite are related to the amount of light in a day (which, except near the equator, is much greater in summer than in winter). Patients with depression who fit the seasonal pattern usually show increased appetite and hypersomnia rather than decreased appetite and insomnia (Howland & Thase, 1999). They also have clear disturbances in their circadian cycles, showing weaker 24-hour patterns than individuals who are not depressed (Goodwin & Jamison, 2007; Howland & Thase, 1999). A good deal of research on patients with seasonal affective disorder supports the therapeutic use of controlled exposure to light, even artificial light, which may work by reestablishing normal biological rhythms (Fava & Rosenbaum, 1995; Goodwin & Jamison, 2007).

BIOLOGICAL EXPLANATIONS FOR SEX DIFFERENCES
Before we leave the topic of possible biological causal factors for depression, we should note that it has been suggested that hormonal factors such as normal fluctuations in ovarian hormones account for sex differences in depression (Deecher et al., 2008). However, studies examining this hypothesis have yielded inconsistent results and overall are not very supportive (Nolen-Hoeksema, 2002; Nolen-Hoeksema & Hilt, 2009). It seems that for the majority of women, hormonal changes occurring at various points (e.g., at the onset of puberty, before menstruation, in the postpartum period, and at menopause) do not play a significant role in causing depression. However, it remains possible that there is a causal association that has not yet been discovered because of real methodological difficulties in conducting conclusive research on this topic (Naninck et al., 2011; Sanborn & Hayward, 2003). Moreover, for a small minority of women who are already at high risk (for example, by being at high genetic risk), hormonal fluctuations may trigger depressive episodes, possibly by causing changes in the normal processes that regulate neurotransmitter systems (Deecher

et al., 2008; Naninck et al., 2011). Some studies have suggested that women have a greater genetic vulnerability to depression than men, but many other studies have not supported this idea (e.g., Nolen-Hoeksema, 2002; Nolen-Hoeksema & Hilt, 2009; Wallace et al., 2002).

Psychological Causal Factors

The evidence for important psychological causal factors in most unipolar mood disorders is at least as strong as the evidence for biological factors. However, it is likely that the effects of at least some psychological factors such as stressful life events are mediated by a cascade of underlying biological changes that they initiate. One way in which stressors may act is through their effects on biochemical and hormonal balances and on biological rhythms (Hammen, 2005; Monroe, 2008).

STRESSFUL LIFE EVENTS AS CAUSAL FACTORS Psychological stressors are known to be involved in the onset of a variety of disorders, ranging from some of the anxiety disorders to schizophrenia, but nowhere has their role been more carefully studied than in the case of unipolar major depression. Many studies have shown that severely stressful life events often serve as precipitating factors for unipolar depression (e.g., Hammen, 2005; Monroe & Harkness, 2005; Monroe et al., 2009).

Most of the episodic stressful life events involved in precipitating depression involve loss of a loved one, serious threats to important close relationships or to one's occupation, or severe economic or serious health problems (Monroe & Hadjiyannakis, 2002; Monroe et al., 2009). For example, separations through death or divorce are strongly associated with depression, although such losses also tend to precede other disorders such as panic disorder and generalized anxiety (Kendler, Hetema et al., 2003; Kessler et al., 1997). Losses that involve an element of humiliation can be especially potent. The stress of being the caregiver to a spouse with a debilitating disease such as Alzheimer's is also known to be associated with the onset of both major depression and generalized anxiety disorder in the caregiver (e.g., Russo et al., 1995).

An important distinction has been made between stressful life events that are independent of the person's behavior and personality (*independent life events*, such as losing a job because one's company is shutting down or having one's house hit by a hurricane) and events that may have been at least partly generated by the depressed person's behavior or personality (*dependent life events*). For example, people with depression sometimes generate stressful life events through their poor interpersonal problem solving (such as being unable to resolve conflicts with a spouse), which is often associated with depression. The poor problem solving in turn leads to higher levels of interpersonal stress, which in turn leads to further symptoms of depression. Another example of a dependent life event is failing to keep up with routine tasks such as paying bills, which may lead to a variety of troubles. Evidence to date suggests that dependent life events play an even stronger role in the onset of major depression than do independent life events (Hammen, 2005; Kendler et al., 1999a).

Research on stress and the onset of depression is complicated by the fact that people with depression have a distinctly negative view of themselves and the world around them (Beck, 1967; Clark, Beck, & Alford, 1999). Thus, their own perceptions of stress may result—at least to some extent—from the cognitive symptoms of their disorder rather than cause their disorder (Dohrenwend, 2006; Monroe, 2008; Monroe & Hadjiyannakis, 2002). That is, their pessimistic outlook may lead them to evaluate events as stressful that an independent evaluator (or a friend who is not depressed) would not. Therefore, researchers have developed more sophisticated interview-based measures of life stress that do not rely on the depressed person's self-report of how stressful an event is and that take into account the biographical context of a person's life. Trained independent raters evaluate what the impact of a particular event would be expected to be for an average person who has experienced this event in these particular life circumstances; the person's subjective evaluations of stress are not recorded or taken into account in the rating of impact (Monroe, 2008). For example, the stress value of divorce for a woman who has already begun to establish a new relationship would probably not be rated as highly as the divorce of a woman whose husband left her for a younger woman (e.g., Dohrenwend et al., 1995; Monroe & Hadjiyannakis, 2002). There is widespread agreement that conclusions derived from studies using these more sophisticated interview-based techniques are more reliable and valid in predicting depressive episodes (e.g., Monroe, 2008; Monroe & Reid, 2008; Uher & McGuffin, 2010).

Several recent reviews of studies that employed these sophisticated measurements of life stress show that severely stressful episodic life events play a causal role (most often within a month or so after the event) in about 20 to 50 percent of cases (e.g., Hammen, 2005; Kendler, Karkowski, & Prescott, 1998; Monroe & Harkness, 2005). Moreover, people with depression who have experienced a stressful life event tend to show more severe depressive symptoms than those who have not experienced a stressful life event (Monroe & Hadjiyannakis, 2002). This relationship between severely stressful life events and depression is much stronger in people who are having their first onset than in those undergoing recurrent episodes (e.g., Kendler et al., 2000; Monroe & Harkness, 2005). Indeed, Monroe and Harkness (2005) estimate that about 70 percent of people with a first onset of depression have had a recent major stressful life event, whereas only about 40 percent of people with a recurrent episode have had a recent major life event.

Mildly Stressful Events and Chronic Stress Whether mildly stressful events are also associated with the onset of depression is much more controversial, with conflicting findings in the literature. However, studies applying the more sophisticated and complex strategies for assessing life stress have generally not found minor stressful events to be associated with the onset of clinically significant depression (e.g., Dohrenwend et al., 1995; Stueve et al., 1998). An interesting hypothesis has recently been raised that minor events may play more of a role in the onset of recurrent episodes than in the initial episode (Monroe & Harkness, 2005; Monroe et al., 2009). At least one recent study has confirmed this by showing that recurrent episodes are often precipitated by stressful life events of relatively mild impact, which do not tend to be involved in precipitating initial depressive episodes (Stroud et al., 2011).

Although the relationship of chronic stress to the onset of depression has not been as thoroughly studied as has the relationship with episodic life events, a number of good studies have demonstrated that chronic stress is associated with increased risk for the onset, maintenance, and recurrence of major depression (Hammen, 2005; Monroe et al., 2007). Different studies have used the term *chronic stress* (or *chronic strain* or *difficulties*) in different ways, although it usually refers to one or more forms of stress ongoing for at least several months (e.g., poverty, lasting marital discord, medical disabilities, having a disabled child). One well-validated chronic stress interview assesses chronic stress in 8 to 10 different domains (e.g., intimate relationships, close friends, family relationships, health of self and family members, etc.; Hammen, 2005).

Vulnerability and Invulnerability Factors in Responses to Stressors It is important to keep in mind that there are important individual differences in how people respond to the experiences of episodic or chronic life stress. For example, women (and perhaps men) at genetic risk for depression not only experience more stressful life events (Kendler et al., 1999a; Kendler & Karkowski-Shuman, 1997) but also are more sensitive to them (Kendler, Kessler et al., 1995). In one large study, women at genetic risk were three times more likely than those not at genetic risk to respond to severely stressful life events with depression (a good example of a genotype–environment interaction). Conversely, those at low genetic risk for depression are more invulnerable to the effects of major stressors (e.g., Caspi et al., 2003; Kendler, Kessler, et al., 1995).

In addition to genetic variables, there are a host of other psychological and social variables that may make some people more vulnerable, and other people less vulnerable, to developing depression after

If a woman living in poverty is already genetically at risk for depression, the stresses associated with living in poverty may be especially likely to precipitate a major depression in her.

experiencing one or more stressful life events (e.g., see Brown & Harris, 1978, for a classic landmark study). In the past 25 years, many researchers have been intensively focused on determining which such vulnerability and invulnerability factors are most powerful in predicting onset and maintenance of depression.

DIFFERENT TYPES OF VULNERABILITIES FOR UNIPOLAR DEPRESSION The range of psychological vulnerabilities that have been studied includes personality traits, negative styles of thinking about the world and one's experiences, early childhood adversity, and lack of social support.

Personality and Cognitive Diatheses Researchers have concluded that neuroticism is the primary personality variable that serves as a vulnerability factor for depression (and anxiety disorders as well; for reviews, see Clark, Watson, & Mineka, 1994; Klein et al., 2009; Kotov et al., 2010; see also Lahey, 2009; Zinbarg et al., 2011). Recall that *neuroticism*, or *negative affectivity*, refers to a stable and heritable personality trait that involves a temperamental sensitivity to negative stimuli. Thus, people who have high levels of this trait are prone to experiencing a broad range of negative moods, including not only sadness but also anxiety, guilt, and hostility. Moreover, several studies have also shown that neuroticism predicts the occurrence of more stressful life events, which (as already discussed) frequently lead to depression (e.g., Kendler, Gardner, & Prescott, 2003; Uliaszek et al., in press). In addition to serving as a vulnerability factor, neuroticism is associated with a worse prognosis for complete recovery from depression. Finally, some researchers attribute sex differences in depression to sex differences in neuroticism (e.g., Kendler et al., 2002; Sutin et al., 2010).

There is some more limited evidence that high levels of introversion (or low positive affectivity) may also serve as vulnerability factors for depression, either alone or when combined with neuroticism (e.g., Gershuny & Sher, 1998; Watson et al., 2005). Positive affectivity involves a disposition to feel joyful, energetic, bold, proud, enthusiastic, and confident; people low on this disposition tend to feel unenthusiastic, unenergetic, dull, flat, and bored. It is therefore not surprising that this might make them more prone to developing clinical depression, although the evidence for this is very mixed.

The cognitive diatheses that have been studied for depression generally focus on particular negative patterns of thinking that make people who are prone to depression more likely to become depressed when faced with one or more stressful life events. For example, people who attribute negative events to internal, stable, and global causes may be

Children who have lost a parent through death or permanent separation may become vulnerable to depression if they receive poor subsequent care from another parent or guardian and if their environment and routine are disrupted.

more prone to becoming depressed than people who attribute the same events to external, unstable, and specific causes (e.g., Abramson et al., 1978; Abramson et al., 1989; Abramson 2002). A pessimistic or depressive attribution for receiving a low grade on an exam might be, "I'm stupid," whereas a more optimistic attribution for the same event might be, "The teacher wrote the test when he was in a bad mood and made it especially difficult."

Early Adversity as a Diathesis A range of adversities in the early environment (such as family turmoil, parental psychopathology, physical or sexual abuse, and other forms of intrusive, harsh, and coercive parenting) can create both a short-term and a long-term vulnerability to depression. Such factors operate, at least in part, by increasing an individual's sensitivity to stressful life events in adulthood, with similar findings having been observed in animals (e.g., Gunnar & Quevedo, 2007; Harkness & Lumley, 2008; Slavich et al., 2011). The long-term effects of such early environmental adversities may be mediated by both biological variables (such as alterations in the regulation of the hypothalamic-pituitary stress response system) and psychological variables (such as lower self-esteem, insecure attachment relationships, difficulty relating to peers, and pessimistic attributions; e.g., Goodman & Brand, 2009; Harkness & Lumley, 2008). However, it is also important to realize that certain individuals who have undergone early adversity remain resilient, and if the exposure to early adversity is moderate rather than severe a form of stress inoculation may occur that makes the individual less susceptible to the effects of later stress (e.g., Parker et al., 2004). These stress-inoculation effects seem to be mediated by strengthening socioemotional and neuroendocrine resistance to subsequent stressors.

Summary As we have discussed, several different types of biological and psychological diatheses for unipolar depression have been studied, and some of these have been formulated as diathesis-stress theories, as we review in the following sections. Nevertheless it is important to keep in mind that these theories of vulnerability are not mutually exclusive, and some may simply be describing the same diathesis in different terms or at different levels of analysis. For example, there is a moderately strong genetic basis for neuroticism, and neuroticism is strongly correlated with pessimism (Clark, Watson, & Mineka, 1994; Zinbarg et al., 2010; Zinbarg et al., 2011), so these proposed diatheses are clearly somewhat interrelated. Moreover, dysfunctional early parenting, emotional abuse, and parental loss have been strongly implicated in the formation of some of the other cognitive diatheses (Alloy et al., 2004; Bowlby, 1980; Goodman & Brand, 2009). Thus, these two proposed diatheses may simply differ in whether they operate distally (poor early parenting) or proximally (negative thinking patterns) in contributing to vulnerability for depression.

We now turn to five major psychological theories of depression that have received much attention over the years.

PSYCHODYNAMIC THEORIES In his classic paper "Mourning and Melancholia" (1917), Freud noted the important similarity between the symptoms of clinical depression and the symptoms seen in people mourning the loss of a loved one. Freud and a colleague, Karl Abraham (1927), both hypothesized that when a loved one dies the mourner regresses to the oral stage of development (when the infant cannot distinguish self from others) and introjects or incorporates the lost person, feeling all the same feelings toward the self as toward the lost person. These feelings were thought to include anger and hostility because Freud believed that we unconsciously hold negative feelings toward those we love, in part because of their power over us. This is what led to the psychodynamic idea that depression is anger turned inward. Freud hypothesized that depression could also occur in response to imagined or symbolic losses. For example, a student who fails in school or who fails at a romantic relationship may experience this symbolically as a loss of his or her parents' love.

Later psychodynamic theorists proposed a number of variants on Freud and Abraham's early psychodynamic theories (see Levy & Wasserman, 2009, for a brief summary). Perhaps the most important contribution of the psychodynamic approaches to depression has been their noting the importance of loss (both real and symbolic or imagined) to the onset of depression and noting the striking similarities between the symptoms of mourning and the symptoms of depression (Bowlby, 1980). Even theorists who disagree with many of the specific details of these theories recognize that their own theories must account for these basic observations.

BEHAVIORAL THEORIES In the 1970s and 1980s, several theorists in the behavioral tradition developed behavioral theories of depression, proposing that people become depressed either when their responses no longer produce positive reinforcement or when their rate of negative reinforcements increases (such as when experiencing stressful life events; e.g., Ferster, 1974; Lewinsohn, 1974; Lewinsohn & Gotlib, 1995; Lewinsohn et al., 1985). Such theories are consistent with research showing that people with depression do indeed receive fewer positive verbal and social reinforcements from their families and friends than do people who are not depressed and also experience more negative events. Moreover, they have lower activity levels, and their moods seem to vary with both their positive and their negative reinforcement rates (see Lewinsohn & Gotlib, 1995; Martell, 2009). Nevertheless, although such findings are consistent with behavioral theories, they do not show that depression is *caused* by these factors. Instead, it may be that some of the primary symptoms of depression, such as pessimism and low levels of energy, cause the person with depression to experience these lower rates of reinforcement,

which in turn may help maintain the depression. For this and other reasons, behavioral theories of the causes of depression are no longer very influential. However, as discussed later, there is exciting new research demonstrating that a new form of behavioral treatment inspired by these behavioral theories—behavioral activation treatment—seems to be a very effective way to treat depression (Martell et al., 2009).

BECK'S COGNITIVE THEORY Since 1967 one of the most influential theories of depression has been that of Aaron Beck (b. 1921), a psychiatrist who became disenchanted with psychodynamic theories of depression early in his career and developed his own cognitive theory of depression (e.g., Beck, 1967; Clark, Beck, & Alford, 1999). Whereas the most prominent symptoms of depression have generally been considered to be the affective or mood symptoms, Beck hypothesized that the cognitive symptoms of depression often precede and cause the affective or mood symptoms rather than vice versa. For example, if you think that you are a failure or that you are ugly, it would not be surprising for those thoughts to lead to a depressed mood.

Beck's theory, a diathesis-stress theory in which negative cognitions are central, has become somewhat more elaborate over the years while still retaining its primary tenets (e.g., Beck, 1967, 1983; Clark & Beck, 2010). First, there are the underlying dysfunctional beliefs, known as **depressogenic schemas**, which are rigid, extreme, and counterproductive. An example of a dysfunctional belief (that a person is usually not consciously aware of) is, "If everyone doesn't love me, then my life is worthless." According to cognitive theory, such a belief would predispose the person holding it to develop depression if he or she perceived social rejection. Alternatively, a person with the dysfunctional belief, "If I'm not perfectly successful, then I'm a nobody" would be vulnerable to developing negative thoughts and depressed affect if she or he felt like a failure. Note that Beck did not maintain that simply having these **dysfunctional beliefs** is sufficient to make someone depressed; instead, he maintained that these dysfunctional beliefs need to be activated by the occurrence of some form of stress (e.g., perceiving social rejection or feeling like a failure).

These depression-producing beliefs or schemas are thought to develop during childhood and adolescence as a function of one's negative experiences with one's parents and significant others, and they are thought to serve as the underlying diathesis, or vulnerability, to developing depression (Beck, 1967; Ingram et al., 2006; Morley & Moran, 2011). Although they may lie dormant for years in the absence of significant stressors, when dysfunctional beliefs are activated by current stressors or depressed mood, they tend to fuel the current thinking pattern, creating a pattern of **negative automatic thoughts**—thoughts that often occur just below the surface of awareness and involve unpleasant, pessimistic predictions. These pessimistic predictions tend to center on the three themes of what Beck calls the **negative cognitive triad**: (1) negative thoughts about the self ("I'm ugly"; "I'm worthless"; "I'm a failure"); (2) negative thoughts about one's

This figure is intentionally omitted from this text.

experiences and the surrounding world ("No one loves me"; "People treat me badly"); and (3) negative thoughts about one's future ("It's hopeless because things will always be this way"; Clark, Beck, & Alford, 1999; see Figure 2).

Beck also postulated that the negative cognitive triad tends to be maintained by a variety of negative cognitive biases or errors (see also Scher et al., 2005). Each of these involves biased processing of negative self-relevant information. Examples include:

- *Dichotomous or all-or-none reasoning*, which involves a tendency to think in extremes. For example, someone might discount a less-than-perfect performance by saying, "If I can't get it 100 percent right, there's no point in doing it at all."
- *Selective abstraction*, which involves a tendency to focus on one negative detail of a situation while ignoring other elements of the situation. Someone might say, "I didn't have a moment of pleasure or fun today" not because this is true but because he or she selectively remembers only the negative things that happened.

- *Arbitrary inference*, which involves jumping to a conclusion based on minimal or no evidence. A depressed person might say, after an initial homework assignment from a cognitive therapist did not work, "This therapy will never work for me." (Examples from Fennell, 1989, p. 193)

It is easy to see how each of these cognitive distortions tends to maintain the negative cognitive triad. That is, if the content of your thoughts regarding your views of your self, your world, and your future is already negative and you tend to minimize the good things that happen to you or draw negative conclusions based on minimal evidence, those negative

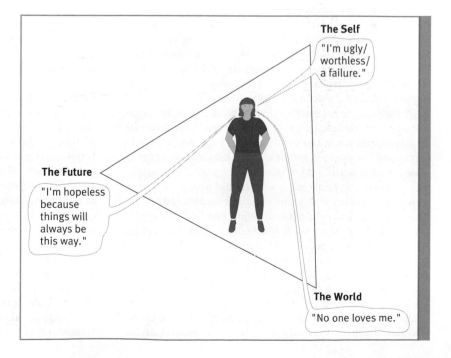

FIGURE 2

Negative Cognitive Triad

Beck's cognitive model of depression describes a pattern of negative automatic thoughts. These pessimistic predictions center on three themes: the self, the world, and the future.

thoughts are not likely to disappear. In addition, just as the underlying dysfunctional beliefs (such as, "If everybody doesn't love me, then my life is worthless") elicit the negative cognitive triad when activated, so too does the negative thinking produced by the negative triad serve to reinforce those underlying beliefs. Thus each of these components of cognitive theory serves to reinforce the others. Moreover, these negative thoughts can produce some of the other symptoms of depression such as sadness, dejection, and lack of motivation.

Evaluating Beck's Theory as a Descriptive Theory Over the past 35 years, an enormous amount of research has been conducted to test various aspects of Beck's theory. As we will see, it has generated a very effective form of treatment for depression known as cognitive therapy. In addition, it has been well supported as a descriptive theory that explains many prominent characteristics of depression (e.g., D. A. Clark, Beck, & Alford, 1999; Haaga et al., 1991). Patients with depression of all the subtypes are considerably more negative in their thinking, especially about themselves or issues highly relevant to the self, than are persons who are not depressed and are more negative than they usually are when they are not depressed. Moreover, persons with depression do think more negatively about themselves and the world around them, especially their own personal world, than do persons who are not depressed, and are quite negative about the future, especially their own future (the negative cognitive triad). By contrast, people who are not depressed show a tendency to process emotional information in an overly optimistic, self-enhancing manner, which may serve as a protective factor against depression (Mezulis et al., 2004).

Beck's theory originally proposed that stressors are necessary to activate depressogenic schemas or dysfunctional beliefs that lie dormant between episodes, but more recent research has shown that stressors are not necessary to activate the latent depressive schemas between episodes. Indeed, simply inducing a depressed mood (e.g., through listening to sad music or recalling sad memories) in an individual who was previously depressed (that is, at risk) is generally sufficient to activate latent depressogenic schemas (e.g., Ingram et al., 2006; LeMoult et al., 2009; Scher et al., 2005).

In addition to evidence for dysfunctional beliefs and negative automatic thoughts, there is also considerable evidence for certain cognitive biases for negative self-relevant information in depression. For example, people with depression show better or biased recall of negative information and negative autobiographical memories, whereas people who are not depressed tend to show biased recall of positive emotional information and positive autobiographical memories (Gotlib & Joormann, 2010; Hertel & Brozovich, 2010; Mathews & MacLeod, 2005; Mineka et al., 2003). In addition, people with depression are more likely than people who are not depressed to draw negative conclusions that go beyond the information presented in a scenario and to underestimate the positive feedback they have received (D. A. Clark, Beck, & Alford, 1999). It is easy to see how, if one is already depressed, remembering primarily the bad things that have happened is likely to maintain or exacerbate the

depression. Teasdale (1988, 1996) aptly called this the "vicious cycle of depression."

Evaluating the Causal Aspects of Beck's Theory Although research supports most of the descriptive aspects of Beck's theory, research directed toward confirming the causal hypotheses of Beck's theory has been more mixed. The causal hypotheses are usually tested with some kind of prospective study design. People who are not depressed are tested for their cognitive vulnerability (usually, dysfunctional beliefs) at Time 1 and then are followed for 1 or more months or years, after which measurements of life stress are administered. Only some studies have found that dysfunctional beliefs or attitudes at Time 1, in interaction with stressful life events, predict depression at Time 2. However, some of the studies that yielded negative results may have used inadequate study designs. Several more recent studies using more adequate designs have found results quite supportive of the causal aspects of Beck's theory (e.g., Hankin et al., 2004; Lewinsohn et al., 2001). For example, Lewinsohn and colleagues (2001) assessed about 1,500 adolescents for their dysfunctional beliefs or attitudes and then followed them for 1 year, at which point stressful life events during that year were assessed. Results indicated that those who had started with high levels of dysfunctional beliefs and who experienced high stress were more likely to develop major depression than those with low stress or than those with low dysfunctional beliefs and high stress. Another study with a large community sample of 700 women (average age was 41) also found that dysfunctional beliefs at the outset of a 3-year follow-up period predicted new onsets and recurrences of major depressive episodes over the next 3 years (Otto et al., 2007). However, unlike in the Lewinsohn, Joiner, and Rohde (2001) study, there was no evidence in the Otto and colleagues study for a diathesis-stress interaction, and dysfunctional beliefs did not have additional predictive value beyond that afforded by knowing a prior history of the person's depressive episodes. Thus, because of inconsistencies in results across studies, more research is still needed to fully assess the causal aspects of Beck's cognitive theory of depression.

THE HELPLESSNESS AND HOPELESSNESS THEORIES OF DEPRESSION Whereas Beck's theory grew out of his clinical observations and research on the pervasive patterns of negative thinking seen in depressed patients, the learned helplessness theory of depression originated out of observations in an animal research laboratory. Martin Seligman (1974, 1975) first proposed that the laboratory phenomenon known as **learned helplessness** might provide a useful animal model of depression. In the late 1960s, Seligman and his colleagues (Maier et al., 1969; Overmier & Seligman, 1967) noted that laboratory dogs who were first exposed to uncontrollable shocks later acted in a passive and helpless manner when they were in a situation where they could control the shocks. In contrast, animals first exposed to equal amounts of controllable shocks had no trouble learning to control the shocks.

Seligman and his colleagues (e.g., Maier et al., 1969; Overmier & Seligman, 1967) developed the learned helplessness

If a celebrity comes to depend on the love and adoration of her fans to feed her feelings of self-worth, she is at great risk for developing depression when that positive attention subsides.

hypothesis to explain these effects. It states that when animals or humans find that they have no control over aversive events (such as shock), they may learn that they are helpless, which makes them unmotivated to try to respond in the future. Instead they exhibit passivity and even depressive symptoms. They are also slow to learn that any response they do make is effective, which may parallel the negative cognitive set in human depression. Seligman's observations that the animals looked depressed captured his attention and ultimately led to his proposing a learned helplessness model of depression (Seligman, 1974, 1975). Subsequent research demonstrated that helpless animals also show other depressive symptoms such as lower levels of aggression, loss of appetite and weight, and changes in monoamine neurotransmitter levels. After demonstrating that learned helplessness also occurs in humans (e.g., Hiroto & Seligman, 1975), he went on to propose that learned helplessness may underlie some types of human depression. That is, people undergoing stressful life events over which they have little or no control may develop a syndrome like the helplessness syndrome seen in animals.

The Reformulated Helplessness Theory Some of the research with humans on helplessness soon led to a major reformulation of the helplessness theory, addressing some of the complexities of what humans do when faced with uncontrollable events (Abramson et al., 1978). In particular, Abramson and colleagues proposed that when people (probably unlike animals) are exposed to uncontrollable negative events, they ask themselves why, and the kinds of **attributions** that people make are, in turn, central to whether they become depressed. These investigators proposed three critical dimensions on which attributions are made: (1) internal/external, (2) global/specific, and (3) stable/unstable. They proposed that a depressogenic or pessimistic attribution for

a negative event is an internal, stable, and global one. For example, if your boyfriend treats you badly and you conclude that "It's because I'm ugly and boring," you are much more likely to become depressed than if you conclude that "It's because he's in a bad mood today after failing his exam and he is taking it out on me."

Abramson and colleagues (1978) proposed that people who have a relatively stable and consistent **pessimistic attributional style** have a vulnerability or diathesis for depression when faced with uncontrollable negative life events. This kind of cognitive style seems to develop, at least in part, through social learning (Alloy, Abramson, & Smith, 2006). For example, children may learn this cognitive style by observing and modeling inferences made by their parents. Alternatively or additionally, the parents may communicate their own inferences about negative events happening to their children, or engage in generally negative parenting practices such as high levels of negative psychological control (criticism, intrusiveness, and guilt) as well as a lack of warmth and caring.

This *reformulated helplessness theory* led to a great deal of research. Many studies demonstrated that depressed people do indeed have this kind of pessimistic attributional style, but that of course this does not mean that pessimistic attributional style plays a causal role (e.g., Abramson et al., 1995; Buchanan & Seligman, 1995). Using designs similar to those used to test the causal aspects of cognitive theory, many studies have examined the ability of a pessimistic attributional style to predict the onset of depression in interaction with negative life events (Abramson et al., 1989; Alloy et al., 2008). Some results have supported this theory and some have not.

The helplessness theory has been used to explain sex differences in depression. This theory proposes that by virtue of their roles in society, women are more prone to experiencing a sense of lack of control over negative life events. These feelings of helplessness might stem from poverty, discrimination in the workplace leading to unemployment or underemployment, the relative imbalance of power in many heterosexual relationships, high rates of sexual and physical abuse against women (either currently or in childhood), role overload (e.g., being a working wife and mother), and less perceived control over traits that men value when choosing a long-term mate, such as beauty, thinness, and youth (e.g., Heim et al., 2000; Ben Hamida et al., 1998; Nolen-Hoeksema & Hilt, 2009). There is at least some evidence that each of these conditions is associated with higher-than-expected rates of depression, although whether the effects involve a sense of helplessness has not yet been established (Brems, 1995; Nolen-Hoeksema et al., 1999; Whiffen & Clark, 1997). Combining the neuroticism theory with the helplessness theory, it is important to note that there is evidence that people who are high on neuroticism are more sensitive to the effects of adversity relative to those low on neuroticism (a genotype–environment interaction; Kendler et al., 2004; Lahey, 2009). So given that women have higher levels of neuroticism and experience more uncontrollable stress, the increased prevalence of depression in women becomes less surprising.

The Hopelessness Theory of Depression A further revision of this theory, known as the *hopelessness theory*, was later presented (Abramson et al., 1989; see Alloy et al., 2008). Abramson and colleagues (1989) propose that having a pessimistic attributional style in conjunction with one or more negative life events was not sufficient to produce depression unless one first experienced a state of hopelessness. A *hopelessness expectancy* was defined by the perception that one had no control over what was going to happen and by the absolute certainty that an important bad outcome was going to occur or that a highly desired good outcome was not going to occur. They also proposed that the internal/external dimension of attributions was not important to depression. Instead, they propose two other dimensions of pessimistic attributional style as being important components of this cognitive diathesis. Specifically, they propose that depression-prone individuals not only tend to make global and stable attributions for negative events but also tend to make negative inferences about other likely negative consequences of the event (e.g., that this means more bad things will also happen) and negative inferences about the implications of the event for the self-concept (e.g., that one is unworthy or deficient; Abramson et al., 2002).

Research over the past 20 years has been testing this theory. A major longitudinal prospective study of several hundred college students who were hypothesized to be at high risk for unipolar depression (because they had both a pessimistic attributional style and high levels of dysfunctional beliefs) has begun to yield evidence quite supportive of some of the major tenets of the hopelessness theory (e.g., Abramson et al., 2002; Alloy, Abramson. Whitehouse et al., 2006; Alloy et al., 2008). For example, in a 2.5-year follow-up period, students in the high-risk group who had never previously been depressed at the outset of the study were about four times more likely (16.2% versus 3.6%) to develop a first episode of major depression (or comorbid depression and anxiety) than those in the low-risk group. For those who had already had a previous episode of depression prior to entry into the study, the high-risk group was about three times more likely to experience a recurrent episode of major depression in the 2.5-year follow-up period.

Additional support for the hopelessness theory has been accumulating as well. Several smaller studies with similar designs to the investigation of Alloy, Abramson, and colleagues have shown evidence for the interaction of cognitive vulnerability with life stress in predicting depressive symptoms and onset of diagnosable depression (Hankin et al., 2004), although others have not (see Alloy et al., 2008). Furthermore, research has begun to integrate hopelessness theory with a motivational theory of depression that posits that depression is associated with decreased approach behavior (e.g., Nusslock et al., 2011). Specifically, some researchers have hypothesized that cognitively vulnerable individuals are at risk for decreased approach-related behavior as a result of increased hopelessness under stress, thereby contributing to depression. There is at least initial empirical support for this notion. For example, in one investigation of undergraduate students, cognitive vulnerability interacted with life stress to predict a decrease in goal-directed behavior, which was then associated with higher levels of depressive symptoms (Haeffel et al., 2008). Furthermore, this predictive relationship between cognitive vulnerability and stress with goal-directed behavior was mediated by increased feelings of hopelessness. Additional tests of the hopelessness theory and its predictions are needed, but future research on the hopelessness theory is likely to continue to provide important insights into psychosocial causes of depression.

The Ruminative Response Styles Theory of Depression Nolen-Hoeksema's ruminative response style cognitive theory of depression (e.g., 1991, 2000; Nolen-Hoeksema & Hilt, 2009) focuses on different kinds of responses that people have when they experience feelings and symptoms of sadness and distress, and how their differing response styles affect the course of their depressed feelings. Specifically, when some people have such feelings, they tend to focus intently on how they feel and why they feel that way—a process called **rumination**, which involves a pattern of repetitive and relatively passive mental activity. Other people, by contrast, have a more action-oriented or problem-solving response to such feelings and, for example, distract themselves with another activity or actually try to do something that will solve the problems that are leading to the sadness and distress. Research by Nolen-Hoeksema and colleagues has consistently shown that there are stable individual differences in the tendency to ruminate and that people who ruminate a great deal tend to have more lengthy periods of depressive symptoms. They are also more likely to develop full-blown episodes of major depressive disorder (Nolen-Hoeksema, 2000; Nolen-Hoeksema & Hilt, 2009).

Interestingly, it seems that women are more likely than men to ruminate when they become depressed (Nolen-Hoeksema & Corte, 2004; Nolen-Hoeksema & Aldao, 2011). Moreover, self-focused rumination leads to increased recall of more negative autobiographical memories, thereby feeding a vicious circle of depression (Hertel & Brozovich, 2010; Lyubomirsky et al., 1998; Nolen-Hoeksema et al., 2008). The importance of these sex differences in rumination is underscored when we consider that when gender differences in rumination are statistically controlled, gender differences in depression are no longer significant (Nolen-Hoeksema & Hilt, 2009).

Men, by contrast, are more likely to engage in a distracting activity (or consume alcohol) when they get in a depressed mood, and distraction seems to reduce depression (Nolen-Hoeksema & Corte, 2004; Nolen-Hoeksema et al., 2008). Distraction might include going to a movie, playing a sport, or avoiding thinking about why they are depressed. The origin of these sex differences in response to depression is unclear, but if further research supports this hypothesis it would certainly suggest that effective prevention efforts might include teaching girls to seek distraction rather than to ruminate as a response to depression.

The ruminative response styles theory of depression has been integrated with the two previously discussed cognitive theories of depression. For example, research reviewed recently by Alloy, Abramson, and colleagues (2008) shows that for people

DEVELOPMENTS IN RESEARCH   1

Why Do Sex Differences in Unipolar Depression Emerge During Adolescence?

It is interesting to consider why the sex difference in depression starts in adolescence (Essau et al., 2010; Hankin & Abramson, 2001; Hankin et al., 2008), beginning to emerge between ages 12 and 13 and reaching its most dramatic peak between ages 14 and 16, although it is actually more tied to pubertal status than to age per se (Becker et al., 2007; Conley & Rudolph, 2009; Sanborn & Hayward, 2003). This is a time of rapid physiological, environmental, and psychological changes known to create turmoil for many adolescents, but why are adolescent females more likely to become depressed? Hankin, Abramson, and colleagues (Hankin & Abramson, 2001; Hankin et al., 2008) have proposed an intriguing cognitive vulnerability-stress model of the development of gender differences during adolescence. Building on ideas from the reformulated helplessness and hopelessness models of depression for adults, they summarize research indicating that children and adolescents, like adults, are prone to experiencing increases in depressive symptoms if they have a pessimistic attributional style and experience stressful life events (e.g., Hankin & Abramson, 2001; Hankin, 2006). Moreover, during early adolescence, gender differences in attributional style, in rumination, and in stressful life events emerge such that girls tend to have a more pessimistic attributional style, to show more rumination, and to experience more negative life events (especially interpersonal events; Rudolph, 2009). Thus one can see how, with all three of these risk factors showing gender differences in adolescence, a synergistic effect might lead to the dramatic rise in depression in adolescent girls. Moreover, Hankin and Abramson (2001; see also Hankin et al., 2008) review evidence that the experience of negative life events

may contribute to greater cognitive vulnerability, which in turn further increases susceptibility to depressive symptoms. Furthermore, depressive symptoms in adolescent girls, as in adults, are likely to result in more dependent life stress being generated, which in turn may exacerbate depression (Liu & Alloy, 2010; Rudolph, 2009). Finally, girls not only experience more negative life events than boys but also encode them in greater detail and show better memory for emotional events (though not for nonemotional events).

Hankin and Abramson (2001) also emphasize the role of negative cognitions about attractiveness and body image in the emergence of sex differences in depression during adolescence. There is evidence that the development of secondary sexual characteristics is harder psychologically for girls than for boys. Body dissatisfaction goes up for females at this time, and down for males; moreover, body dissatisfaction is more closely related to self-esteem for girls than for boys. Much of girls' dissatisfaction with their bodies comes from their realization of the discrepancy between our society's ideal of a thin, prepubescent body shape for females and the fact that they are gaining fat as they mature sexually. Hankin and Abramson (2001) summarize evidence that girls are more likely than boys to make pessimistic attributions and other negative inferences about negative events that may occur (such as negative remarks) related to the domain of physical attractiveness. Given that physical attractiveness may be more motivationally significant for girls than for boys, it becomes plausible that this may be one important factor that makes depression especially likely in adolescent girls.

---

with high levels of dysfunctional attitudes and/or pessimistic attributional styles, their tendencies to ruminate moderated the effects of the negative cognitive styles on increasing vulnerability to depression. Specifically, those who had negative cognitive styles who also tended to ruminate a lot were most likely to develop depressive episodes. The researchers suggest that people with negative cognitive styles have a lot of negative content to their thoughts but that only if they dwell on this and brood about it (high ruminators) are they especially likely to develop clinical depression (see also Robinson & Alloy, 2003).

Developments in Thinking 2 discusses how the helplessness and hopelessness theories help explain why anxiety and depression are so often comorbid.

INTERPERSONAL EFFECTS OF MOOD DISORDERS Although there is no interpersonal theory of depression that is as clearly articulated as the cognitive theories, there has been a considerable amount of research on interpersonal factors in

depression. Interpersonal problems and social-skills deficits may well play a causal role in at least some cases of depression. In addition, depression creates many interpersonal difficulties—with strangers and friends as well as with family members (Hammen, 1995, 2005; Joiner & Timmons, 2009; Petit & Joiner, 2006).

Lack of Social Support and Social-Skills Deficits Brown and Harris (1978), in their classic study of community women in a poor area of inner London, reported that women without a close, confiding relationship were more likely than those with at least one close confidant to become depressed if they experienced a severely stressful event. Many more studies have since supported the idea that people who are lonely, socially isolated, or lacking social support are more vulnerable to becoming depressed and that individuals with depression have smaller and less supportive social networks, which tends to precede the onset of depression (e.g., Cacioppo et al., 2006; Gotlib & Hammen, 1992; Ibarra-Rovillard & Kuiper, 2011).

2 DEVELOPMENTS IN THINKING

Comorbidity of Anxiety and Mood Disorders

The issue of whether depression and anxiety can be differentiated in a reliable and valid way has received a good deal of attention over the years. Only in the past two decades, however, have researchers begun to make significant advances in understanding the real scope of the problem. The overlap between measures of depression and anxiety occurs at all levels of analysis: patient self-report, clinician ratings, diagnosis, and family and genetic factors (Barlow, 2002; Clark & Watson, 1991; Mineka et al., 1998; Watson, 2005). That is, persons who rate themselves high on symptoms of anxiety also tend to rate themselves high on symptoms of depression, and clinicians rating these same individuals do the same thing. The overlap also occurs at the diagnostic level. One review of the literature estimated that just over half of the patients who receive a diagnosis of a mood disorder also receive a diagnosis of an anxiety disorder at some point in their lives, and vice versa (e.g., Hettema, 2008; Mineka et al., 1998; Watson, 2005).

Finally, there is considerable evidence from genetic and family studies of the close relationship between anxiety and unipolar depressive disorders (Garber & Weersing, 2010; Kendler, 1996; Mineka et al., 1998). Several very large twin studies and an important review have shown that liability for unipolar depression and liability for generalized anxiety disorder come from the same genetic factors, and which disorder develops is a result of what environmental experiences occur (Barlow, 2002; Kendler, 1996; Watson, 2005). The genetic relationships between panic disorder and depression and between the other anxiety disorders and depression are more modest (Kendler, Walker et al., 1995; Mineka et al., 1998). The shared genetically based factor among these disorders seems to be the personality trait of neuroticism—a major risk factor for all of these disorders (Hettema, 2008; Watson et al., 2006; Zinbarg, Mineka et al., 2011).

At present the dominant theoretical approach to the overlap between depressive and anxiety symptoms is to assume that most of the measures used to assess both sets of symptoms tap the broad mood and personality dimension of negative affect, which includes affective states such as distress, anger, fear, guilt, and worry (Clark, Watson, & Mineka, 1994; Griffith et al., 2010; Watson et al., 2006). Depressed and anxious individuals cannot be differentiated on the basis of their high level of negative affect. But these researchers have also shown that anxiety and depression can be distinguished from one another on the basis of a second dimension of mood and personality known as positive affect, which includes affective states such as excitement, delight, interest, and pride. Depressed persons tend to be characterized by low levels of positive affect, but anxious individuals usually are not (with the exception of people with social phobia; Watson et al., 2006; Naragon-Gainey et al., 2009). That is, only depressed individuals show the signs of fatigue and lack of energy and enthusiasm characteristic of low positive affect. A number of investigators have also shown that some anxious people (especially panic patients), but not depressed people, tend to be characterized by high levels of yet another mood dimension known as anxious hyperarousal, symptoms of which include racing heart, trembling, dizziness, and shortness of breath. This tripartite model of anxiety and depression thus explains what features anxiety and depression share (high negative affect) and what features they differ on (low positive affect for depression and anxious hyperarousal for panic; Mineka et al., 1998). Each of the other anxiety disorders has its own separate and relatively unique component as well (Barlow, 2002; Mineka et al., 1998; Prenoveau et al., 2010; Watson, 2005; see also Watson et al., 2007, for another variant on this approach).

Several aspects of the comorbidity between anxiety and mood disorders at the diagnostic level raise interesting questions about what common and what distinct causal factors may exist. For example, there is usually a sequential relationship between the symptoms of anxiety and depression, both within an episode and between episodes. For example, Bowlby (1973, 1980) describes a biphasic response to separation and loss in which agitation and anxiety are followed by despair and depression. And across a lifetime, individuals are more likely to experience an anxiety disorder first and a depressive disorder later (T. A. Brown et al., 2001; Garber & Weersing, 2010; Merikangas et al., 2003).

Alloy and colleagues (1990; see also Mineka et al., 1998) proposed an expansion of the hopelessness model of depression to account for these and other features of comorbidity. In their helplessness/hopelessness model, they proposed that anxiety and anxiety disorders are characterized by prominent feelings of helplessness. People with these disorders expect that they may be helpless in controlling important outcomes, and there is indeed evidence that anxiety predicts helpless behavior in response to stress (e.g., Gazelle & Druhen, 2009). In addition, individuals with anxiety disorders believe that future control might be possible, and so they are likely to experience increased arousal and anxiety and an intense scanning of the environment in efforts to gain control. If the person becomes convinced of his or her helplessness to control important outcomes but is still uncertain about whether the bad outcome will actually occur, a mixed anxiety/depression syndrome is likely to emerge. And finally, if the person is convinced not only that he or she is helpless but also that bad outcomes will occur, helplessness becomes hopelessness and depression sets in. Alloy, Mineka, and colleagues (1990) showed how this perspective can explain certain features of comorbidity between anxiety and depressive disorders. For example, the sequential relationship is explained by the fact that one is likely to feel helpless for some time before coming to feel totally hopeless. And some anxiety disorders may be more closely associated with depression precisely because the symptoms of the disorders themselves (for example, obsessive thoughts and compulsions, panic attacks and related agoraphobic avoidance, flashbacks, and nightmares, etc.) are so distressing and seemingly uncontrollable. These symptoms may firmly convince the individual of her or his helplessness, leading to the mixed anxiety/depression diagnostic picture.

Why are people without social support networks more prone to depression when faced with major stressors?

In addition, some people with depression have social-skills deficits. For example, they seem to speak more slowly and monotonously and to maintain less eye contact; they are also less skilled than people without depression at solving interpersonal problems (e.g., Ingram et al., 1999; Joiner & Timmons, 2009).

The Effects of Depression on Others Not only do people with depression have interpersonal problems, but, unfortunately, their own behavior also seems to make these problems worse. For example, the behavior of an individual who is depressed often places others in the position of providing sympathy, support, and care. However, such positive reinforcement does not necessarily follow. Depressive behavior can, and over time frequently does, elicit negative feelings (sometimes including hostility) and rejection in other people, including strangers, roommates, and spouses (Coyne, 1976; Ingram et al., 1999; Joiner & Timmons, 2009). Although these negative feelings may initially make the person who is not depressed feel guilty, which leads to sympathy and support in the short term, ultimately a downwardly spiraling relationship usually results, making the person with depression feel worse (e.g., Joiner, 2002; Joiner & Metalsky, 1995). Social rejection may be especially likely if the person with depression engages in excessive reassurance seeking (e.g., Joiner & Timmons, 2009; Prinstein et al., 2005).

Marriage and Family Life Interpersonal aspects of depression have also been carefully studied in the context of marital and family relationships. A significant proportion of couples experiencing marital distress have at least one partner with clinical depression, and there is a high correlation between marital dissatisfaction and depression for both women and men (e.g., Beach & Jones, 2002; Rehman et al., 2008; Whisman, 2007). In addition, marital distress spells a poor prognosis for a spouse

with depression whose symptoms have remitted. That is, a person whose depression clears up is likely to relapse if he or she has an unsatisfying marriage, especially one characterized by high levels of critical and hostile comments from the spouse (Butzlaff & Hooley, 1998; Hooley, 2007).

Why should criticism be linked to relapse? One possibility is that criticism perturbs some of the neural circuitry that underlies depression. Moreover, it may be that *even after full recovery*, criticism may still be a powerful trigger for those who are vulnerable to depression. In a novel study, Hooley and colleagues (2009) exposed healthy (never depressed) controls and women with a past history of depression to critical remarks from their own mothers. While they were lying in a brain scanner, each participant heard her own mother making personally relevant critical remarks. Even though all the young women in the recovered-depressed group were completely well and had no symptoms of depression, their brains still responded differently from the healthy controls when challenged by criticism. As you can see in Figure 3, there are differences in several brain areas that, as you have already learned, have been implicated in depression. When they heard criticism from their mothers, the recovered-depressed participants showed less brain activation in the dorsolateral prefrontal cortex and anterior cingulate cortex than the never-depressed controls did. In contrast, during criticism, brain activity in the amygdala was much higher in the recovered-depressed participants than it was in the controls. What was especially interesting was that all of this occurred without the recovered-depressed subjects being aware that they were responding differently to the criticisms. Taken together, these findings suggest that criticism might be associated with relapse in depression because it is capable of activating some of the neural circuits that are thought to be involved in the disorder. They also suggest that people who are vulnerable to depression may be especially sensitive to criticism even after they have made a full recovery.

Marital distress and depression may co-occur because the depressed partner's behavior triggers negative affect in the spouse. Individuals with depression may also be so preoccupied with themselves that they are not very sensitive or responsive to the needs of their spouses. A review by Beach and Jones (2002) adapted Hammen's (1991) stress-generation model of depression to help explain the two-way relationship between marital discord and depression (that is, marital distress can lead to depression, and depression can lead to marital distress). As noted earlier, a significant amount of the stress that individuals with depression experience is somehow at least partially generated by their own behaviors, but this stress in turn also serves to exacerbate depressive symptoms. The effects of depression in one family member extend to children of all ages as well. Parental depression puts children at high risk for many problems, but especially for depression (Goodman, 2007; Hammen, 2009; Hammen et al., 2011). Although these effects occur with both fathers and mothers with depression, the effects of maternal depression are somewhat larger (Hammen, 2009). Children of parents with depression who become depressed themselves tend to become

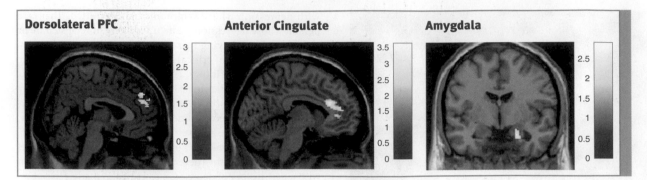

FIGURE 3

Brain Activation in Response to Maternal Criticism

When healthy (never depressed) participants hear criticism from their own mothers they show significantly greater activation in dorsolateral prefrontal cortex and anterior cingulate cortex than do people who have a history of depression but who are currently fully recovered. Amgygala activation during criticism is significantly greater in formerly depressed participants than it is in controls. (Hooley et al., 2009.)

depressed earlier and to show a more severe and persistent course than control children who become depressed who do not have a parent with depression (see Hammen, 2009).

Some of these effects probably occur because these children inherit a variety of traits such as temperament (including shyness, behavioral inhibition, and neuroticism), low levels of positive emotions, and poor ability to regulate emotions that are all known risk factors for depression (e.g., Durbin et al., 2005; see Hammen, 2009, for a review). In addition, many studies have documented the damaging effects of negative interactional patterns between mothers with depression and their children. For example, mothers with depression show more friction and have fewer playful, mutually rewarding interactions with their children (see Goodman & Gotlib, 1999; Murray & Cooper, 1997). They are also less sensitively attuned to their infants and less affirming of their infants' experiences (Goodman & Brand, 2009). Furthermore, their young children are given multiple opportunities for observational learning of negative cognitions, depressive behavior, and depressed affect. Thus, although genetically determined vulnerability is clearly involved, psychosocial influences clearly also play an important role (Hammen, 2009; Natsuaki et al., 2010), and evidence is accumulating that inadequate parenting is what mediates the association between parental depression and their children's depression (Goodman, 2007).

In Review

- Summarize the major biological causal factors for unipolar depression, including genetic, biochemical, neuroendocrinological, and neurophysiological factors.

- What is the role of stressful life events in unipolar depression, and what kinds of diatheses have been proposed to interact with them?

- Describe the following theories of depression: Beck's cognitive theory, the helplessness and hopelessness theories, ruminative response styles theory, and interpersonal theories.

Bipolar Disorders

As discussed earlier, *bipolar disorders* are distinguished from unipolar disorders by the presence of manic or hypomanic episodes, which are nearly always preceded or followed by periods of depression. A person who experiences a manic episode has a markedly elevated, euphoric, and expansive mood, often interrupted by occasional outbursts of intense irritability or even violence—particularly when others refuse to go along with the manic person's wishes and schemes. These extreme moods must persist for at least a week for this diagnosis to be made. In addition, three or more additional symptoms must occur in the same time period. There must also be significant impairment of occupational and social functioning, and hospitalization is often necessary during manic episodes. Hypomanic episodes can also occur; these involve milder versions of the same symptoms and last at least 4 days. Although the symptoms listed are the same for manic and hypomanic episodes, there is much less impairment in hypomania, and hospitalization is not required.

Cyclothymic Disorder

It has long been recognized that some people are subject to cyclical mood changes less severe than the mood swings seen in bipolar disorder. Historically these were referred to as *cyclothymic temperament* (or *personality*; Goodwin & Jamison, 2007). If such symptoms persist for at least 2 years, the person may receive a diagnosis of **cyclothymic disorder**. In *DSM-IV-TR*, cyclothymia is defined as a less serious version of full-blown bipolar disorder because it lacks certain extreme symptoms and psychotic features such as delusions and the marked impairment caused by full-blown manic or major depressive episodes.

In the depressed phase of cyclothymic disorder, a person's mood is dejected, and he or she experiences a distinct loss of interest or pleasure in customary activities and pastimes. In addition, the person may show other symptoms such as low energy, feelings of inadequacy, social withdrawal, and a pessimistic, brooding attitude. Essentially, the symptoms are similar to those in someone with dysthymia except without the duration criterion.

Symptoms of the hypomanic phase of cyclothymia are essentially the opposite of the symptoms of dysthymia. In this phase of the disorder, the person may become especially creative and productive because of increased physical and mental energy. There may be significant periods between episodes in which the person with cyclothymia functions in a relatively adaptive manner. For a diagnosis of cyclothymia, there must be at least a 2-year span during which there are numerous periods with hypomanic and depressed symptoms (1 year for adolescents and children), and the symptoms must cause clinically significant distress or impairment in functioning (although not as severe as in bipolar disorder). (See the *DSM-IV-TR* box "Criteria for Cyclothymic Disorder.") Because individuals with cyclothymia are at greatly increased risk of later developing full-blown bipolar I or II disorder (e.g., Akiskal & Pinto, 2009; Goodman & Jamison, 2007), *DSM-IV-TR* recommends that they be treated.

DSM-IV-TR

Criteria for Cyclothymic Disorder

A. For at least 2 years, the presence of numerous periods with hypomanic symptoms and numerous periods with depressive symptoms that do not meet criteria for a Major Depressive Episode. Note: In children and adolescents, the duration must be at least 1 year.

B. During the above 2-year period (1 year in children and adolescents), the person has not been without the symptoms in Criterion A for more than 2 months at a time.

C. No Major Depressive Episode, Manic Episode, or Mixed Episode has been present during the first 2 years of the disturbance. Note: After the initial 2 years (1 year in children and adolescents) of Cyclothymic Disorder, there may be superimposed Manic or Mixed Episodes (in which case both Bipolar I Disorder and Cyclothymic Disorder may be diagnosed) or Major Depressive Episodes (in which case both Bipolar II Disorder and Cyclothymic Disorder may be diagnosed).

D. The symptoms in Criterion A are not better accounted for by Schizoaffective Disorder and are not superimposed on Schizophrenia, Schizophreniform Disorder, Delusional Disorder, or Psychotic Disorder Not Otherwise Specified.

E. The symptoms are not due to the direct physiological effects of a substance (e.g., a drug of abuse, a medication) or a general medical condition (e.g., hyperthyroidism).

F. The symptoms cause clinically significant distress or impairment in social, occupational, or other important areas of functioning.

Source: Reprinted with permission from the American Psychiatric Association. *Diagnostic and Statistical Manual of Mental Disorders*, Fourth Edition, *Text Revision* (Copyright © 2000). American Psychiatric Association.

The following case illustrates cyclothymia.

case study A Cyclothymic Car Salesman

A 29-year-old car salesman was referred by his current girlfriend, a psychiatric nurse, who suspected he had a mood disorder even though the patient was reluctant to admit that he might be a "moody" person. According to him, since the age of 14 he has experienced repeated alternating cycles that he terms "good times and bad times." During a "bad" period, usually lasting 4 to 7 days, he sleeps 10 to 14 hours daily [and] lacks energy, confidence, and motivation—"just vegetating," as he puts it. Often he abruptly shifts, characteristically upon waking up in the morning, to a 3- to 4-day stretch of overconfidence, heightened social awareness, promiscuity, and sharpened thinking—"things would flash in my mind." At such times he indulges in alcohol to enhance the experience, but also to help him sleep. Occasionally the "good" periods last 7 to 10 days but culminate in irritable and hostile outbursts, which often herald the transition back to another period of "bad" days. . . .

In school, A's and B's alternated with C's and D's, with the result that the patient was considered a bright student whose performance was mediocre overall because of "unstable motivation." As a car salesman his performance has also been uneven, with "good days" canceling out the "bad days"; yet even during his "good days" he is sometimes perilously argumentative with customers and loses sales that appeared sure. Although considered a charming man in many social circles, he alienates friends when he is hostile and irritable. . . . (Spitzer et al., 2002, pp. 155–56)

Bipolar Disorders (I and II)

Although recurrent cycles of mania and melancholia were recognized as early as the sixth century, it remained for Kraepelin, in 1899, to introduce the term *manic-depressive insanity* and to clarify the clinical picture. Kraepelin described the disorder as a series of attacks of elation and depression, with periods of relative normality in between. Today *DSM-IV-TR* calls this illness bipolar disorder, although the term *manic-depressive illness* is still commonly used as well.

Bipolar I disorder is distinguished from major depressive disorder by at least one manic episode or mixed episode. A **mixed episode** is characterized by symptoms of both full-blown manic and major depressive episodes for at least 1 week, whether the symptoms are intermixed or alternate rapidly every few days. Such cases were once thought to be relatively rare but have increasingly been recognized as relatively common (e.g., Cassidy et al., 1998; Goodwin & Jamison, 2007). Indeed Goodwin & Jamison's (2007) review of 18 studies

Criteria for Bipolar I and Bipolar II Disorder

Bipolar I Disorder

There are six separate criteria sets for Bipolar I Disorder: Single Manic Episode, Most Recent Episode Hypomanic, Most Recent Episode Manic, Most Recent Episode Mixed, Most Recent Episode Depressed, and Most Recent Episode Unspecified.

Bipolar I Disorder, Single Manic Episode, is used to describe individuals who are having a first episode of mania. The remaining criteria sets are used to specify the nature of the current (or most recent) episode in individuals who have had recurrent mood episodes.

Bipolar II Disorder (Recurrent Major Depressive Episodes with Hypomanic Episodes)

A. Presence (or history) of one or more Major Depressive Episodes.

B. Presence (or history) of at least one Hypomanic Episode.

C. There has never been a Manic Episode or a Mixed Episode.

D. The mood symptoms in Criteria A and B are not better accounted for by Schizoaffective Disorder and are not superimposed on Schizophrenia, Schizophreniform Disorder, Delusional Disorder, or Psychotic Disorder Not Otherwise Specified.

E. The symptoms cause clinically significant distress or impairment in social, occupational, or other important areas of functioning.

Source: Reprinted with permission from the American Psychiatric Association. *Diagnostic and Statistical Manual of Mental Disorders*, Fourth Edition, *Text Revision* (Copyright © 2000). American Psychiatric Association.

reported that an average of 28 percent of bipolar patients at least occasionally experience mixed states. Moreover, many patients in a manic episode have some symptoms of depressed mood, anxiety, guilt, and suicidal thoughts, even if these are not severe enough to qualify as a mixed episode. See the *DSM-IV-TR* box "Criteria for Bipolar I Disorder." Recent careful longitudinal follow-up of people presenting with a full-blown mixed episode or even a subthreshold mixed episode has shown that these individuals have a worse long-term outcome than those originally presenting with a depressive or a manic episode (Baldessarini et al., 2010; Dodd et al., 2010).

Even though a client may be exhibiting only manic symptoms, it is assumed that a bipolar disorder exists and that a depressive episode will eventually occur. Thus there are no officially recognized unipolar manic or hypomanic counterparts to dysthymia or major depression. Although some researchers have noted the probable existence of a unipolar type of manic disorder (e.g., Kessler et al., 1997; Solomon et al., 2003), critics of this diagnosis argue that such patients usually have bipolar relatives and may well have had mild depressions that went unrecognized (Goodwin & Jamison, 2007; Winokur & Tsuang, 1996).

The following case illustrates both phases of Bipolar I disorder:

case study **Roller Coaster**

When Ernest Eaton's desperate wife finally got him to agree to a comprehensive inpatient evaluation, he was 37, unemployed, and had been essentially nonfunctional for several years. After a week during which he was partying all night and shopping all day, Mrs. Eaton said she would leave him if he did not check into a psychiatric hospital. The admitting psychiatrist found him to be a fast-talking, jovial, seductive man with no evidence of delusions or hallucinations.

Mr. Eaton's troubles began 7 years before when he . . . had a few months of mild, intermittent depressive symptoms, anxiety, fatigue, insomnia, and loss of appetite, [but] within a few months he was back to his usual self. A few years later . . . after removal of [an asymptomatic] mass . . . Mr. Eaton noted dramatic mood changes. Twenty-five days of remarkable energy, hyperactivity, and euphoria were followed by 5 days of depression during which he slept a lot and felt that he could hardly move. This pattern of alternating periods of elation and depression, apparently with few "normal" days, repeated itself continuously over the following years.

During his energetic periods, Mr. Eaton was optimistic and self-confident but short tempered and easily irritated. His judgment at work was erratic. He spent large sums of money on unnecessary and, for him, uncharacteristic purchases, such as a high-priced stereo system and several Doberman pinschers. He also had several impulsive sexual flings. During his depressed periods, he often stayed in bed all day because of fatigue, lack of motivation, and depressed mood. He felt guilty about the irresponsibilities and excesses of the previous several weeks. He stopped eating, bathing, and shaving. After several days of this withdrawal, Mr. Eaton would rise from bed one morning feeling better and, within 2 days, he would be back at work, often working feverishly, though ineffectively, to catch up on work he had let slide during his depressed periods. (Adapted with permission from *DSM-IV-TR Casebook: A Learning Companion to the Diagnostic and Statistical Manual of Mental Disorders*, Fourth Edition, *Text Revision*, (Copyright © 2002). American Psychiatric Association.)

DSM-IV-TR also identifies a distinct form of bipolar disorder called **bipolar II disorder**, in which the person does not experience full-blown manic (or mixed) episodes but has experienced clear-cut hypomanic episodes as well as major depressive episodes as in bipolar I disorder (Akiskal & Benazzi, 2005). Bipolar II disorder is equally or somewhat more common than bipolar 1 disorder, and, when combined, estimates are that about 2 to 3 percent of the U.S. population will suffer from one or the other disorder (e.g., Kessler et al., 2007; Kupfer, 2005). Bipolar II disorder evolves into bipolar I disorder in only about 5 to 15 percent of cases, suggesting that they are distinct forms of the disorder (Coryell et al.,

1995; Goodwin & Jamison, 2007). Recently a subthreshold form of bipolar II disorder has also been recognized as careful study has revealed that as many as 40 percent of individuals diagnosed with unipolar MDD have a similar number of hypomanic symptoms, although not with a sufficient number or duration to qualify for a full-blown hypomanic episode (Zimmerman et al., 2009). Along with related findings, such results are leading researchers and clinicians to recognize that unipolar MDD is a far more heterogeneous category than previously recognized.

Bipolar disorder occurs equally in males and females (although depressive episodes are more common in women than men) and usually starts in adolescence and young adulthood, with an average age of onset of 18 to 22 years (Goodwin & Jamison, 2007; Merikangas et al., 2007). Bipolar II disorder has an average age of onset approximately 5 years later than bipolar I disorder (Baldessarini et al., 2010). Both bipolar I and II are typically recurrent disorders, with people experiencing single episodes extremely rarely (Kessler et al., 2007). In about two-thirds of cases, the manic episodes either immediately precede or immediately follow a depressive episode; in other cases, the manic and depressive episodes are separated by intervals of relatively normal functioning. Most patients with bipolar disorder experience periods of remission during which they are relatively symptom-free, although this may occur on only about 50 percent of days (Kupka et al., 2007). Moreover, as many as 20 to 30 percent continue to experience significant impairment (occupational and/or interpersonal) and mood lability most of the time, and as many as 60 percent have chronic occupational or interpersonal problems between episodes. As with unipolar major depression, the recurrences can be seasonal in nature, in which case **bipolar disorder with a seasonal pattern** is diagnosed.

FEATURES OF BIPOLAR DISORDER The duration of manic and hypomanic episodes tends to be shorter than the duration of depressive episodes, with typically about three times as many days spent depressed as manic or hypomanic (Goodwin & Jamison, 2007). There has been controversy over whether the symptoms of the depressive episodes of bipolar disorder are clinically distinguishable from those of unipolar major depressive episodes (Cuellar et al., 2005; Perris, 1992). Although there is a high degree of overlap in symptoms, one important comprehensive review of this literature reports some significant differences. The most widely replicated differences are that, relative to people with a unipolar depressive episode, people with a bipolar depressive episode tend, on average, to show more mood lability, more psychotic features, more psychomotor retardation, and more substance abuse (Goodwin & Jamison, 2007). By contrast, individuals with unipolar depression, on average, show more anxiety, agitation, insomnia, physical complaints, and weight loss (see also Johnson et al., 2009). In spite of the high degree of similarity in symptoms, research clearly indicates that major depressive episodes in people with bipolar disorder are, on average, more severe than those seen in unipolar disorder, and, not surprisingly, they also cause more role impairment (Kessler et al., 2007).

This figure is intentionally omitted from this text.

Because a person who is depressed cannot be diagnosed with bipolar I disorder unless he or she has exhibited at least one manic or mixed episode in the past, many people with bipolar disorder whose initial episode or episodes are depressive (about 50 percent) are misdiagnosed at first and possibly throughout their lives (for instance, if no manic episodes are observed or reported, or if they die before a manic episode is experienced). Averaging across many studies, one important review estimates that somewhere between 10 and 50 percent of people who have an initial major depressive episode will later have a manic or hypomanic episode and will be diagnosed at that time as having bipolar I or II disorder (Goodwin & Jamison, 2007). Moreover, the younger the person is at the time of the first diagnosis, and the greater the number of recurrent episodes, the more likely he or she is to be diagnosed with bipolar I or II disorder. One study shows that people presenting initially with a major depressive disorder who have a history of creative achievements, professional instability, multiple marriages, and flamboyant behavior may be especially likely to be diagnosed later with bipolar II disorder (Akiskal, 2005).

Misdiagnoses are unfortunate because there are somewhat different treatments of choice for unipolar and bipolar depression. Moreover, there is evidence that some antidepressant drugs used to treat what is thought to be unipolar depression may actually precipitate manic episodes in patients who actually have as-yet-undetected bipolar disorder, thus worsening the course of the illness (Ghaemi et al., 2003; Whybrow, 1997).

On average, people with bipolar disorder suffer from more episodes during their lifetimes than do persons with unipolar disorder (although these episodes tend to be somewhat shorter, averaging 3 to 4 months; Angst & Sellaro, 2000; Solomon et al., 2010). As many as 5 to 10 percent of persons with bipolar disorder experience at least four episodes (either manic or depressive) every year, a pattern known as **rapid cycling**. In fact, those who go through periods of rapid cycling usually experience many more than four episodes a year. Our case example of Ernest Eaton ("Roller Coaster") was diagnosed with bipolar I disorder with rapid cycling. People who develop rapid cycling are slightly more likely to be women, to have a history of more episodes (especially more manic or hypomanic episodes), to have an earlier average age of onset, and to make more suicide attempts (Coryell et al., 2003; Kupka et al., 2005; Nierenberg et al., 2010). Rapid cycling is sometimes precip-

Many highly creative people are believed to have had bipolar disorder, going through periods of intense creative productivity during manic phases, and often going through unproductive periods when clinically depressed. One such individual was the British novelist Virginia Woolf (1882–1941). Woolf committed suicide by drowning herself.

itated by taking certain kinds of antidepressants (Goodman & Jamison, 2007; Kilzieh & Akiskal, 1999). Fortunately, for about 50 percent of cases, rapid cycling is a temporary phenomenon and gradually disappears within about 2 years (Coryell et al., 1995; Coryell et al., 2003).

Overall, the probabilities of "full recovery" from bipolar disorder are discouraging even with the widespread use of mood-stabilizing medications such as lithium, with one review estimating that patients with bipolar disorder spend about 20 percent of their lives in episodes (Angst & Sellaro, 2000). One 20-year prospective study in which over 200 patients were followed for an average of 17 years found that 24 percent had relapsed within 6 months of recovery; 77 percent had had at least one new episode within 4 years of recovery; and 82 percent had relapsed within 7 years (Coryell et al., 1995). Another prospective study of 146 bipolar patients found that they experienced some symptoms (mostly subsyndromal) on an average of 47 percent of the weeks during the 13-year follow-up period. During the follow-up period, depressive symptoms were three times more common than manic or hypomanic symptoms (Judd et al., 2002; see also Judd, Schettler et al., 2003). The long-term course of bipolar disorder is even more severe for patients who have comorbid substance-abuse or dependence disorders (which is even more common than with unipolar disorders; e.g., Levin & Hennessey, 2004; Swann, 2010).

In Review

- Describe the symptoms and clinical features of cyclothymia and bipolar disorder.
- Describe the typical course of bipolar I and bipolar II disorders.

Causal Factors in Bipolar Disorders

As for unipolar disorders, a host of causal factors for bipolar disorder have been posited over the past century. However, biological causal factors are clearly dominant, and the role of psychological causal factors has received significantly less attention. The majority of research has focused on bipolar I disorder, which is what we focus on here.

Biological Causal Factors

In recent years, research has increasingly highlighted the importance of a number of biological factors that are thought to play a causal role in the onset of bipolar disorder. These factors include genetic, neurochemical, hormonal, neurophysiological, neuroanatomical, and biological rhythm influences.

GENETIC INFLUENCES There is a greater genetic contribution to bipolar I disorder than to unipolar disorder. A summary of studies using refined diagnostic procedures suggests that about 8 to 10 percent of the first-degree relatives of a person with bipolar I illness can be expected to have bipolar disorder, relative to 1 percent in the general population (Katz & McGuffin, 1993; Plomin et al., 2008; Willcutt & McQueen, 2010). The first-degree relatives of a person with bipolar disorder are also at elevated risk for unipolar major depression (especially atypical depression), although the reverse is not true (Akiskal & Benazzi, 2005; Goodwin & Jamison, 2007).

Although family studies cannot by themselves establish a genetic basis for the disorder, results from twin studies dating back to the 1950s also point to a genetic basis because the concordance rates for these disorders are much higher for identical than for fraternal twins. For example, one review of numerous twin studies found that the average concordance rate was about 60 percent for monozygotic twins and about 12 percent for dizygotic twins (Kelsoe, 1997). The best study to date (McGuffin et al., 2003) found that 67 percent of monozygotic twins with bipolar disorder had a co-twin who shared the diagnosis of bipolar or unipolar disorder (60 percent of these concordant co-twins had bipolar disorder, and 40 percent had unipolar disorder). The concordance rate in dizygotic twins was 19 percent. This and other studies suggest that genes account for about 80 to 90 percent of the variance in the liability to develop bipolar I disorder (Goodwin & Jamison, 2007; McGuffin et al., 2003). This is higher than heritability estimates for unipolar disorder or any of the other major adult psychiatric disorders, including schizophrenia (Torrey et al., 1994). Moreover, genetic influences are even stronger in early- as opposed to late-onset bipolar disorder (Goodwin & Jamison, 2007).

The finding of elevated rates of both bipolar and unipolar forms of the disorder in the relatives of people with bipolar disorder may be explained in several ways. One possibility is related to the idea that bipolar disorder may be a more severe form of the same underlying disorder as unipolar disorder. If this were the case, then the increased rate of unipolar disorder in relatives of patients with bipolar disorder would occur because bipolar is the more severe disorder—and not all relatives have as severe a form of the disorder as the identified patient (Goodwin & Jamison, 2007; Plomin et al., 2008). At least one strong study, however, found no support for this hypothesis (McGuffin et al., 2003). Instead, the results suggest that about 70 percent of the genetic liability for mania is distinct from the genetic liability for depression. In other words, these results suggest that people with bipolar disorder are genetically susceptible to both depression and to mania, and that these susceptibilities are largely independent. These very important findings need to be replicated before strong conclusions can be made.

Efforts to locate the chromosomal site(s) of the implicated gene or genes in this genetic transmission of bipolar disorder suggest that it is polygenic (Willcutt & McQueen, 2010). Although a great deal of research has been directed at identifying candidate genes through linkage analysis and association studies, no consistent support yet exists for any specific mode of genetic transmission of bipolar disorder, according to several comprehensive reviews (Potash & DePaulo, 2000; Tsuang et al., 2004).

NEUROCHEMICAL FACTORS The early monoamine hypothesis for unipolar disorder was extended to bipolar disorder, the hypothesis being that if depression is caused by deficiencies of norepinephrine or serotonin, then perhaps mania is caused by excesses of these neurotransmitters. There is good evidence for increased norepinephrine activity during manic episodes and less consistent evidence for lowered norepinephrine activity during depressive episodes (Goodwin & Jamison, 2007; Manji & Lenox, 2000). However, serotonin activity appears to be low in both depressive and manic phases.

As noted earlier, norepinephrine, serotonin, and dopamine are all involved in regulating our mood states (Howland & Thase, 1999; Southwick et al., 2005). Evidence for the role of dopamine stems in part from research showing that increased dopaminergic activity in several brain areas may be related to manic symptoms of hyperactivity, grandiosity, and euphoria (Goodwin & Jamison, 2007; Howland & Thase, 1999). High doses of drugs such as cocaine and amphetamines, which are known to stimulate dopamine, also produce manic-like behavior (Cousins et al., 2009). Drugs like lithium reduce dopaminergic activity and are antimanic. In depression there appear to be decreases in both norepinephrine and dopamine functioning (Goodwin & Jamison, 2007; Manji & Lenox, 2000). Thus disturbances in the balance of these neurotransmitters seem to be one of the keys to understanding this debilitating illness, which can send its victims on an emotional roller coaster.

ABNORMALITIES OF HORMONAL REGULATORY SYSTEMS Some neurohormonal research on bipolar disorder has focused on the HPA axis. Cortisol levels are elevated in bipolar depression (as they are in unipolar depression), but they are usually not elevated during manic episodes (Goodwin & Jamison, 2007). Similarly, bipolar depressed patients show evidence of abnormalities on the dexamethasone suppression test (DST) described earlier at about the same rate as do unipolar depressed patients, and these abnormalities persist even when the patients have been fully remitted and asymptomatic for at least 4 weeks (e.g., Langan & McDonald, 2009; Watson, Gallagher et al., 2004). During a manic episode, however, their rate of DST abnormalities has generally (but not always) been found to be much lower (Goodwin & Jamison, 2007; Manji & Lenox, 2000, although see Langan & McDonald, 2009). Research has also focused on abnormalities of the hypothalamic-pituitary-thyroid axis because abnormalities of thyroid function are frequently accompanied by changes in mood. Many bipolar patients have subtle but significant abnormalities in the functioning of this axis, and administration of thyroid hormone often makes antidepressant drugs work better (Altshuler et al., 2001; Goodwin & Jamison, 2007). However, thyroid hormone can also precipitate manic episodes in patients with bipolar disorder (Goodwin & Jamison, 2007).

NEUROPHYSIOLOGICAL AND NEUROANATOMICAL INFLUENCES With positron emission tomography (PET) scans, it has even proved possible to visualize variations in brain glucose metabolic rates in depressed and manic states, although there is far less evidence regarding manic states because of the great difficulties studying patients who are actively manic. Several summaries of the evidence from studies using PET and other neuroimaging techniques show that, whereas blood flow to the left prefrontal cortex is reduced during depression, during mania it is increased in certain other parts of the prefrontal cortex (Goodwin & Jamison, 2007). Thus there are shifting patterns of brain activity during mania and during depressed and normal moods.

Other neurophysiological findings from patients with bipolar disorder have shown both similarities to and differences from patients with unipolar disorder and normal controls. For example, several recent reviews have summarized evidence that there are deficits in activity in the prefrontal cortex in bipolar disorder, which seem related to neuropsychological deficits that people with bipolar disorder have in problem solving, planning, working memory, shifting of attentional sets, and sustained attention on cognitive tasks (e.g., Chen et al., 2011; Haldane & Frangou, 2004; Malhi, Ivanovski, et al, 2004). This is similar to what is seen in unipolar depression, as are deficits in the anterior cingulate cortex (Langan & McDonald, 2009). However, structural imaging studies suggest that certain subcortical structures, including the basal ganglia and amygdala, are enlarged in bipolar disorder but reduced in size in unipolar depression. The decreases in hippocampal volume that are often observed in unipolar depression are generally not found in bipolar depression (Konarski et al., 2008). Some studies using fMRI also find increased activation in bipolar patients in subcortical brain regions involved in emotional processing, such as the thalamus and amygdala, relative to unipolar patients and normals (Chen et al., 2011; Malhi, Lagopoulos et al., 2004). Overall, it is hard to draw firm conclusions in this area yet because there are so many inconsistencies in results across studies. However, there is initial meta-analytic support for dysregulation in frontal-limbic activation in individuals with bipolar disorder compared to controls (Chen et al., 2011). Hopefully more definitive findings will follow when much-needed technological innovations unfold (Goodwin & Jamison, 2007).

SLEEP AND OTHER BIOLOGICAL RHYTHMS There is considerable evidence regarding disturbances in biological rhythms such as circadian rhythms in bipolar disorder, even when symptoms have mostly remitted (e.g., Goodwin & Jamison, 2007; Harvey, 2008; Jones et al., 2005; Murray & Harvey, 2010). During manic episodes, patients with bipolar disorder tend to sleep very little (seemingly by choice, not because of insomnia), and this is the most common symptom to occur prior to the onset of a manic episode. During depressive episodes, they tend toward hypersomnia (too much sleep). Even between episodes people with bipolar disorder show substantial sleep difficulties, including high rates of insomnia (e.g., Harvey, 2008; Harvey et al., 2005; Millar et al., 2004). Bipolar disorder also sometimes shows a seasonal pattern the way unipolar disorder does, suggesting disturbances of seasonal biological rhythms, although these may be the result of circadian abnormalities in which the onset of the sleep–wake cycle is set ahead of the onset of other circadian rhythms. Given the cyclic nature of bipolar disorder itself, this focus on disturbances in biological rhythms holds promise for future integrative theories of the biological underpinnings of bipolar disorder. This is particularly true because patients with bipolar disorder seem especially sensitive to, and easily disturbed by, any changes in their daily cycles that require a resetting of their biological clocks (Goodwin & Jamison, 2007; Jones et al., 2005; Murray & Harvey, 2010).

Psychological Causal Factors

Although biological factors play a prominent role in the onset of bipolar disorder, psychosocial factors have also been found to be involved in the etiology of the disorder. In particular, stressful life events, poor social support, and certain personality traits and cognitive styles have been identified as important psychological causal factors.

STRESSFUL LIFE EVENTS Stressful life events appear to be as important in precipitating bipolar depressive episodes as unipolar depressive episodes, and there is some evidence that stressful life events are sometimes involved in precipitating manic episodes as well (Goodwin & Jamison, 2007). The stressful life events are thought to influence the timing of an episode, perhaps by activating the underlying vulnerability. One study also found that patients who experienced severe negative events took an average of three times longer to recover from manic, depressive, or mixed episodes than those without a severe negative event (395 versus 112 days; Johnson & Miller, 1997). Even minor negative events were found to increase time to recovery.

It has long been argued that as the illness unfolds, the manic and depressive episodes become more autonomous and do not usually seem to be precipitated by stressful events (e.g., Bender & Alloy, 2011; Post, 1992). Some of these conclusions may be premature, however, given that most studies addressing this issue have relied on patients' memories of events before episodes, which may be unreliable (Johnson & Roberts, 1995). In several good prospective studies using more sophisticated stress measurement techniques, Ellicott and colleagues

(1990; see also Hammen, 1995) did not find that stress played a less important role in precipitating episodes for people who had had more episodes (see also Alloy et al., 2010; Bender & Alloy, 2011; Hlastala et al., 2000).

How might stressful life events operate to increase the chance of relapse? One hypothesized mechanism is through the destabilizing effects that stressful life events may have on critical biological rhythms. Although evidence in support of this idea is still preliminary, it appears to be a promising hypothesis, especially for manic episodes (e.g., Bender & Alloy, 2011; Malkoff-Schwartz et al., 1998; see Grandin et al., 2006, for a review).

OTHER PSYCHOLOGICAL FACTORS IN BIPOLAR DISORDER There is also some evidence that other social environmental variables may affect the course of bipolar disorder. For example, one recent study found that people with bipolar disorder who reported low social support showed more depressive recurrences over a 1-year follow-up, independent of the effects of stressful life events, which also predicted more recurrences (Cohen et al., 2004; see also Alloy et al., 2010). There is also some evidence that personality and cognitive variables may interact with stressful life events in determining the likelihood of relapse. For example, the personality variable neuroticism has been associated with symptoms of depression and mania (e.g., Quilty et al., 2009), and two studies even found that neuroticism predicts increases in depressive symptoms in people with bipolar disorder just as in unipolar disorder. Moreover, personality variables and cognitive styles that are related to goal-striving, drive, and incentive motivation have been associated with bipolar disorder (e.g., Alloy et al., 2009). For example, two personality variables associated with high levels of achievement striving and increased sensitivity to rewards in the environment predicted increases in manic symptoms—especially during periods of active goal striving or goal attainment (such as studying for an important exam and then doing very well on it; Lozano & Johnson, 2001; Meyer et al., 2001; see also Alloy et al., 2010). Another study found that students with a pessimistic attributional style who also had negative life events showed an increase in depressive symptoms whether they had bipolar or unipolar disorder. Interestingly, however, the bipolar students who had a pessimistic attributional style and experienced negative life events also showed increases in manic symptoms at other points in time (Alloy et al., 2010; Reilly-Harrington et al., 1999).

In Review

- Summarize the major biological causal factors for bipolar disorder, including genetic, biochemical, and other biological factors.

- What role do psychological factors, including stressful life events, seem to play in bipolar disorder?

Sociocultural Factors Affecting Unipolar and Bipolar Disorders

Research on the association of sociocultural factors with both unipolar and bipolar mood disorders is discussed together because much of the research conducted in this area has not made clear-cut diagnostic distinctions between the two types of disorders. Although the prevalence of mood disorders seems to vary considerably among different societies, it has been difficult to provide conclusive evidence for this because of various methodological problems, including widely differing diagnostic practices in different cultures, and because the symptoms of depression appear to vary considerably across cultures (Chentsova-Dutton & Tsai, 2009; Kaelber et al., 1995; Kleinman, 2004).

Cross-Cultural Differences in Depressive Symptoms

Although depression occurs in all cultures that have been studied, the form that it takes differs widely, as does its prevalence (e.g., Chentsova-Dutton & Tsai, 2009; Marsella, 1980). For example, in some non-Western cultures such as China and Japan where rates of depression are relatively low, many of the psychological symptoms of depression are often not present. Instead people tend to exhibit so-called somatic and vegetative manifestations such as sleep disturbance, loss of appetite, weight loss, and loss of sexual interest (Kleinman, 2004; Ryder et al., 2008; Tsai & Chentsova-Dutton, 2002). The psychological components of depression that often seem to be missing (from a Western standpoint) are the feelings of guilt, suicidal ideation, worthlessness, and self-recrimination, which are so commonly seen in the "developed" countries (Kidson & Jones, 1968; Tsai &

In some cultures the concept of depression as we know it simply does not exist. For example, Australian aborigines who are "depressed" show none of the guilt and self-abnegation commonly seen in more developed countries. They also do not show suicidal tendencies but instead are more likely to vent their hostilities onto others rather than onto themselves.

Chentsova-Dutton, 2002). Even when these "psychological" symptoms are present, in many cases the affected individuals may think that physical symptoms have more legitimacy and that it is more appropriate to reveal and discuss physical rather than psychological symptoms (Chentsova-Dutton & Tsai, 2009).

Several possible reasons for these symptom differences stem from Asian beliefs in the unity of the mind and body, a lack of expressiveness about emotions more generally, and the stigma attached to mental illness in these cultures (e.g., Chentsova-Dutton & Tsai, 2009). Another reason why guilt and negative thoughts about the self may be common in Western but not in Asian cultures is that Western cultures view the individual as independent and autonomous, so when failures occur, internal attributions are made. By contrast, in many Asian cultures individuals are viewed as inherently interdependent with others. Nevertheless, as countries like China have incorporated some Western values over the course of becoming increasingly industrialized and urbanized, the rates of depression have risen a good deal relative to several decades ago (e.g., Dennis, 2004; Hong et al., 2010; Zhou et al., 2000). Indeed, one study of adolescents from Hong Kong and the United States found levels of depressive symptoms and hopelessness to be higher in the adolescents from Hong Kong (Stewart, Kennard et al., 2004).

Cross-Cultural Differences in Prevalence

There is some similarity in the lifetime prevalence rates for bipolar spectrum disorders across many different countries ranging from India and Japan to the United States, Lebanon, and New Zealand (0.1 to 4.4 percent; Merikangas et al., 2011). Furthermore, there is remarkable similarity in the patterns of comorbidity across countries, with anxiety disorders being the most common conditions that are comorbid with bipolar disorder (Merikangas et al., 2011). Prevalence rates for depression (whether expressed primarily through somatic or psychological symptoms) vary a great deal across countries, as revealed by many epidemiological studies. For example, in Taiwan the lifetime prevalence has been estimated at 1.5 percent, whereas in the United States and Lebanon it has been estimated at 17 to 19 percent (Tsai & Chentsova-Dutton, 2002). Recurrent suicide attempts are also higher in Western cultures than in Eastern cultures (Chentsova-Dutton & Tsai, 2009). The reasons for such wide variation are undoubtedly very complex, and much work remains to be done before we fully understand them. The ideas that are being explored include different levels of important psychosocial risk variables in different cultures and different levels of stress. For example, there appear to be cross-cultural differences in hypothesized risk variables such as pessimistic attributional style, although how these differences might translate into different rates of depression is unclear because we do not yet know whether the same risk variables are operative in different cultures. However, research is beginning to explore whether psychosocial risk factors for mood disorders operate across cultures, and there is some initial evidence that factors like rumination, hopelessness, and pessimistic attributional style (Abela et al., 2011) are associated with risk for depression in other countries, such as China (Hong et al., 2010).

Demographic Differences in the United States

In our own society, the role of sociocultural factors in mood disorders is also evident. The three large epidemiological studies conducted in the United States since the early 1980s did not find any large racial or ethnic differences. However, the most recent National Comorbidity Survey-Replication (Kessler, Chiu et al., 2005)

This figure is intentionally omitted from this text.

found that the prevalence rates among African Americans were slightly lower than among European white Americans and Hispanics, which were comparable. Consistent with this result, the National Survey of American Life found that the lifetime prevalence of major depression was higher in European white Americans than in African Americans (Williams et al., 2007). However, 12-month prevalence estimates were similar across these two groups, and there was evidence that African Americans might exhibit a more chronic course of depression than European white Americans. Furthermore, Native Americans, by contrast, have significantly elevated rates compared to white Americans (e.g., Hasin et al., 2005). There are no significant differences among such groups for bipolar disorder.

Other epidemiological research indicates that rates of unipolar depression are inversely related to socioeconomic status; that is, higher rates occur in lower socioeconomic groups (e.g., Kessler, Chiu et al., 2005; Monroe et al., 2009). This may well be because low SES leads to adversity and life stress (Dohrenwend, 2000; Monroe & Hadjiyannakis, 2002). However, in spite of earlier indications that rates of bipolar disorder are *elevated* among those in higher socioeconomic groups, current evidence from carefully controlled studies has not found bipolar disorder to be related to socioeconomic class (Goodwin & Jamison, 2007).

Another group that has elevated rates of mood disorders consists of individuals who have high levels of accomplishments in the arts (see Figure 4). Indeed, a good deal of evidence has shown that both unipolar and bipolar disorder, but especially bipolar disorder,

occur with alarming frequency in poets, writers, composers, and artists (Jamison, 1993; Murray & Johnson, 2010). Jamison has also documented for a number of such famous creative individuals how their periods of productivity covary with the manic, or hypomanic, and depressive phases of their illnesses. One possible hypothesis to explain this relationship is that mania or hypomania actually facilitates the creative process, and/or that the intense negative emotional experiences of depression provide material for creative activity. A study of the eminent nineteenth-century American poet Emily Dickinson provides support for the latter part of this hypothesis—that is, evidence supports the idea that Dickinson's painful experiences with panic disorder and depression provided ideas for her especially high-quality work during those times. However, a detailed analysis of her hypomanic periods suggests that her hypomanic symptoms increased her motivation and output but not her creativity per se (Ramey & Weisberg, 2004).

In Review

- What kinds of cross-cultural differences are there in depressive symptoms, and what kinds of cross-cultural factors influence the prevalence of unipolar depression?

- What are some of the basic demographic differences in the United States influencing rates of unipolar and bipolar disorders?

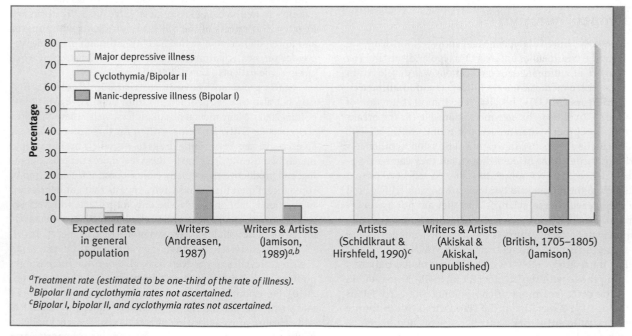

[a]Treatment rate (estimated to be one-third of the rate of illness).
[b]Bipolar II and cyclothymia rates not ascertained.
[c]Bipolar I, bipolar II, and cyclothymia rates not ascertained.

FIGURE 4

Rates of Mood Disorders in Writers and Artists

Although it is difficult to determine a reliable diagnosis of influential writers, poets, and artists (many of whom are long ago deceased), a number of psychological historians have compiled figures such as these, which clearly indicate that such individuals are far more likely than the general population to have had a unipolar or bipolar mood disorder. (Adapted from Jamison, K. R., 1993. Touched with fire. Free Press.)

Treatments and Outcomes

Many patients who suffer from mood disorders (especially unipolar disorders) never seek treatment, and even without formal treatment, the great majority of individuals with mania and depression will recover (often only temporarily) within less than a year. However, given the enormous amount of personal suffering and lost productivity that these individuals endure, and given the wide variety of treatments that are available today, more and more people who experience these disorders are seeking treatment. There was a rapid increase in the treatment of depression from 1987 to 1997, and there has been a more modest increase since 1998 (Marcus & Olfson, 2010). Interestingly, between 1998 and 2007, there was a decline in the reported use of psychotherapy, although the use of antidepressant medication remained relatively stable. These changes are happening in an era in which there is greatly increased public awareness of the availability of effective treatments and during a time in which significantly less stigma is associated with experiencing a mood disorder. Nevertheless, results from the National Comorbidity Survey-Replication showed that only about 40 percent of people with mood disorders receive minimally adequate treatment, with the other 60 percent receiving no treatment or inadequate care (Wang, Lane et al., 2005). Fortunately, the probability of receiving treatment is somewhat higher for people with severe unipolar depression and with bipolar disorder than for those with less severe depression (Kessler et al., 2007).

Pharmacotherapy

Antidepressant, mood-stabilizing, and antipsychotic drugs are all used in the treatment of unipolar and bipolar disorders. The first category of antidepressant medications was developed in the 1950s; these medications are known as **monoamine oxidase inhibitors (MAOIs)** because they inhibit the action of monoamine oxidase—the enzyme responsible for the breakdown of norepinephrine and serotonin once released. The MAOIs can be as effective in treating depression as other categories of medications discussed next, but they can have potentially dangerous, even sometimes fatal, side effects if certain foods rich in the amino acid tyramine are consumed (e.g., red wine, beer, aged cheese, salami). Thus they are not used very often today unless other classes of medication have failed. Depression with atypical features is the one subtype of depression that seems to respond preferentially to the MAOIs.

For most moderately to seriously depressed patients, including those with dysthymia (Klein, 2008; Kocsis et al., 1997), the drug treatment of choice since the early 1960s until about 1990 was one of the standard antidepressants (called **tricyclic antidepressants** because of their chemical structure) such as imipramine, which are known to increase neurotransmission of the monoamines (primarily norepinephrine and to a lesser extent serotonin; Hollon, Thase, & Markowitz, 2002; Thase & Denko, 2008). The efficacy of the tricyclics in significantly reducing depressive symptoms has been demonstrated in hundreds of studies where the response of depressed patients given these drugs has been compared with the response of patients given a placebo. Unfortunately, however, only about 50 percent show what is considered clinically significant improvement, and many of these patients still have significant residual depressive symptoms. Fortunately, about 50 percent of those who do not respond to an initial trial of medication will show a clinically significant response when switched to a different antidepressant or to a combination of medications (Hollon, Thase, & Markowitz, 2002).

Unfortunately, the tricyclics have unpleasant side effects for some people (dry mouth, constipation, sexual dysfunction, and weight gain may occur), and many patients do not continue long enough with the drug for it to have its antidepressant effects even though side effects frequently do diminish to some degree with time. In addition, because these drugs are highly toxic when taken in large doses, there is some risk in prescribing them for suicidal patients, who might use them for an overdose.

Primarily because of the side effects and toxicity of tricyclics, physicians have increasingly chosen to prescribe one of the antidepressants from the **selective serotonin reuptake inhibitor (SSRI)** category (Olfson & Marcus, 2009). These SSRI medications are generally no more effective than the tricyclics; indeed some findings suggest that the tricyclics are more effective than SSRIs for severe depression. However, the SSRIs tend to have many fewer side effects and are better tolerated by patients, as well as being less toxic in large doses. The primary negative side effects of the SSRIs are problems with orgasm and lowered interest in sexual activity, although insomnia, increased physical agitation, and gastrointestinal distress also occur in some patients (Thase, 2008).

SSRIs are used not only to treat significant depression but also to treat people with mild depressive symptoms (Gitlin, 2002). Many mental health professionals believe that prescriptions for SSRIs are being written for these milder cases at an excessive rate. Prescribing drugs to essentially healthy people merely because the drugs make them feel more energetic, outgoing, and productive raises many ethical questions. Furthermore, some recent quantitative research suggests that antidepressant medication is superior to placebo only for patients with very severe depressive symptoms, with negligible treatment effects observed for those with less severe symptoms (Fournier et al., 2010).

In the past decade, several new atypical antidepressants (neither tricyclics nor SSRIs) have also become increasingly popular, and each has its own advantages (Marcus & Olfson, 2010). For example, bupropion (Wellbutrin) does not have as many side effects (especially sexual side effects) as the SSRIs and, because of its activating effects, is particularly good for depressions with significant weight gain, loss of energy, and oversleeping. In addition, venlafaxine (Effexor) seems superior to the SSRIs in the treatment of severe or chronic depression, although the profile of side effects is similar to that for the

SSRIs. Several other atypical antidepressants that have also been shown to be effective.

THE COURSE OF TREATMENT WITH ANTIDEPRESSANT DRUGS Unfortunately, antidepressant drugs usually require at least 3 to 5 weeks to take effect. Generally, if there are no signs of improvement after about 6 weeks, physicians should try a new medication because about 50 percent of those who do not respond to the first drug prescribed do respond to a second one. Also, discontinuing the drugs when symptoms have remitted may result in relapse. Recall that the natural course of an untreated depressive episode is typically 6 to 9 months. Thus, when depressed patients take drugs for 3 to 4 months and then stop because they are feeling better, they are likely to relapse because the underlying depressive episode is actually still present, and only its symptomatic expression has been suppressed (Gitlin, 2002; Hollon, Thase, & Markowitz, 2002; Hollon et al., 2006). Because depression is often a recurrent disorder, physicians have increasingly recommended that patients continue for very long periods of time on the drugs (ideally at the same dose) in order to prevent recurrence (Nutt, 2010). Thus, these medications can often be effective in prevention, as well as treatment, for patients subject to recurrent episodes (Gitlin, 2009; Hollon et al., 2006; Thase & Denko, 2008). Nevertheless, one study found that 25 percent of patients continuing to receive medication during the maintenance phase of treatment showed recurrence of major depression even while on the drugs (e.g., Solomon et al., 2005). Other studies have indicated that patients showing even a few residual symptoms are most likely to relapse, indicating the importance of trying to treat the patient to full remission of symptoms (e.g., Keller, 2004; Thase & Denko, 2008).

LITHIUM AND OTHER MOOD-STABILIZING DRUGS Lithium therapy has now become widely used as a mood stabilizer in the treatment of both depressive and manic episodes of bipolar disorder. The term *mood stabilizer* is often used to describe lithium and related drugs because they have both antimanic and antidepressant effects—that is, they exert mood-stabilizing effects in either direction. **Lithium** has been more widely studied as a treatment of manic episodes than of depressive episodes, and estimates are that about three-quarters of manic patients show at least partial improvement. In the treatment of bipolar depression, lithium may be no more effective than traditional antidepressants (study results are inconsistent), but about three-quarters show at least partial improvement (Keck & McElroy, 2007). However, treatment with antidepressants is associated with significant risk of precipitating manic episodes or rapid cycling, although the risk of this happening is reduced if the person also takes lithium (e.g., Keck & McElroy, 2007; Thase & Denko, 2008).

Lithium is also often effective in preventing cycling between manic and depressive episodes (although not necessarily for patients with rapid cycling), and bipolar patients are frequently maintained on lithium therapy over long time periods, even when not manic or depressed, simply to prevent new episodes. Although early studies indicated that lithium was quite effective in preventing repeated bipolar attacks, more recently several large studies have found that only slightly more than one-third of patients maintained on lithium remained free of an episode over a 5-year follow-up period. Nevertheless, maintenance on lithium does clearly lead to having fewer episodes than are experienced by patients who discontinue their medication. In a quantitative study of patients discontinuing medication, the risk of having a new episode was 28 times higher per month when not on medication than when on medication (Keck & McElroy, 2007).

Lithium therapy can have some unpleasant side effects such as lethargy, cognitive slowing, weight gain, decreased motor coordination, and gastrointestinal difficulties. Long-term use of lithium is occasionally associated with kidney malfunction and sometimes permanent kidney damage, although end stage renal disease seems to be a very rare consequence of long-term lithium treatment (Goodwin & Jamison, 2007; Tredget et al., 2010). Not surprisingly, these side effects, combined with the fact that many bipolar patients seem to miss the highs and the abundance of energy associated with their hypomanic and manic episodes, sometimes create problems with compliance in taking the drug.

In the past several decades, evidence has emerged for the usefulness of another category of drugs known as the *anticonvulsants* (such as carbamazepine, divalproex, and valproate) in the treatment of bipolar disorder (Keck & McElroy, 2007). These drugs are often effective in patients who do not respond well to lithium or who develop unacceptable side effects from it (Thase & Denko, 2008), and they may also be given in combination with lithium (Post et al., 2010). However, a number of studies have indicated that risk for attempted and completed suicide was nearly two to three times higher for patients on anticonvulsant medications than for those on lithium (Goodwin et al., 2003; Thase & Denko, 2008), suggesting one major advantage of giving lithium to patients who can tolerate its side effects. Both bipolar and unipolar patients who show signs of psychosis (hallucinations and delusions) may also receive treatments with *antipsychotic medications* in conjunction with their antidepressant or mood-stabilizing drugs (Gitlin, 2009; Keck & McElroy, 2002; Rothschild et al., 2004).

Alternative Biological Treatments

In addition to the use of pharmacotherapy, there are several other biologically oriented approaches to the treatment of mood disorders. These approaches have been the subject of empirical study in recent years, and they appear to be promising treatment options.

ELECTROCONVULSIVE THERAPY Because antidepressants often take 3 to 4 weeks to produce significant improvement, **electroconvulsive therapy (ECT)** is often used with severely depressed patients (especially among the elderly) who may present an immediate and serious suicidal risk, including those with psychotic or melancholic features (Gitlin, 2009; Goodwin & Jamison, 2007). It is also used in patients who cannot take antidepressant medications or who are otherwise resistant to medications (e.g., Heijnen et al., 2010; Mathew et al., 2005). When selection criteria for this form of treatment are carefully observed, a complete remission of symptoms occurs for many patients after about 6 to 12 treatments (with treatments administered about every other day). This means that a majority of severely depressed patients can be vastly better in 2 to 4 weeks (Gitlin, 2009; Mathew et al., 2005). The treatments, which induce seizures, are delivered under general anesthesia and with muscle relaxants. The most common immediate side effect is confusion, although there is some evidence for lasting adverse effects on cognition, such as amnesia and slowed response time (Sackeim et al., 2007). Maintenance dosages of an antidepressant and a mood-stabilizing drug such as lithium are then ordinarily used to maintain the treatment gains achieved until the depression has run its course (Mathew et al., 2005; Sackeim et al., 2009). ECT is also very useful in the treatment of manic episodes; reviews of the evidence suggest that it is associated with remission or marked improvement in 80 percent of manic patients (Gitlin, 1996; Goodwin & Jamison, 2007). Maintenance on mood-stabilizing drugs following ECT is usually required to prevent relapse.

TRANSCRANIAL MAGNETIC STIMULATION (TMS)
Although *transcranial magnetic stimulation* has been available as an alternative biological treatment for some time now, only in the past decade has it begun to receive significant attention. TMS is a noninvasive technique allowing focal stimulation of the brain in patients who are awake. Brief but intense pulsating magnetic fields that induce electrical activity in certain parts of the cortex are delivered (Goodwin & Jamison, 2007; Janicak et al., 2005). The procedure is painless, and thousands of stimulations are delivered in each treatment session. Treatment usually occurs 5 days a week for 2 to 6 weeks. Although not all studies have found TMS to be effective in treating depression (see Couturier, 2005, for one review), many studies have shown it to be quite effective—indeed in some studies quite comparable to unilateral ECT and antidepressant medications (George & Post, 2011; Janicak et al., 2005; Schulze-Rauschenbach et al., 2005). In particular, research suggests that TMS is a promising approach for the treatment of unipolar depression in patients who are moderately resistant to other treatments (George & Post, 2011). Moreover, TMS has advantages over ECT in that cognitive performance and memory are not affected adversely and sometimes even improve, as opposed to to ECT, where memory-recall deficits are common (Schulze-Rauschenbach et al., 2005).

DEEP BRAIN STIMULATION
In recent years, deep brain stimulation has been explored as a treatment approach for individuals with refractory depression who have not responded to other treatment approaches, such as medication, psychotherapy, and ECT. Deep brain stimulation involves implanting an electrode in the brain and then stimulating that area with electric current (Mayberg et al., 2005). Although more research on deep brain stimulation is needed, initial results suggest that it may have potential for treatment of unrelenting depression.

BRIGHT LIGHT THERAPY
In the past decade an alternative nonpharmacological biological method has received increasing attention—*bright light therapy* (see Pail et al., 2011, for a review). This was originally used in the treatment of seasonal affective disorder, but it has now been shown to be effective in nonseasonal depressions as well (see Golden et al., 2005, for a quantitative review; see also Lieverse et al., 2011).

Psychotherapy

There are several forms of specialized psychotherapy, developed since the 1970s, that have proved effective in the treatment of unipolar depression, and the magnitude of improvement of the best of these is approximately equivalent to that observed with medications. Considerable evidence also suggests that these same specialized forms of psychotherapy for depression, alone or in combination with drugs, significantly decrease the likelihood of relapse within a 2-year follow-up period (Hollon et al., 2005; Hollon & Dimidjian, 2009). Other specialized treatments have been developed to address the problems of people (and their families) with bipolar disorder.

COGNITIVE-BEHAVIORAL THERAPY
One of the two best-known psychotherapies for unipolar depression with documented effectiveness is **cognitive-behavioral therapy (CBT)** (also known as **cognitive therapy**), originally developed by Beck and colleagues (Beck et al., 1979; Clark, Beck, & Alford, 1999). It is a relatively brief form of treatment (usually 10 to 20 sessions) that focuses on here-and-now problems rather than on the more remote causal issues that psychodynamic psychotherapy often addresses. For example, cognitive therapy consists of highly structured, systematic attempts to teach people with unipolar depression to evaluate systematically their dysfunctional beliefs and negative automatic thoughts. They are also taught to identify and correct their biases or distortions in information processing and to uncover and challenge their underlying depressogenic assumptions and beliefs. Cognitive therapy relies heavily on an empirical approach in that patients are taught to treat their beliefs as hypotheses that can be tested through the use of behavioral experiments.

One example of challenging a negative automatic thought through a behavioral experiment can be seen in the following interchange between a cognitive therapist and a depressed patient.

Therapy Session: "My Husband Doesn't Love Me Anymore"

case study

PATIENT:	My husband doesn't love me any more.
THERAPIST:	That must be a very distressing thought. What makes you think that he doesn't love you?
PATIENT:	Well, when he comes in in the evening, he never wants to talk to me. He just wants to sit and watch TV. Then he goes straight off to bed.
THERAPIST:	OK. Now, is there any evidence, anything he does, that goes against the idea that he doesn't love you?
PATIENT:	I can't think of any. Well, no, wait a minute. Actually it was my birthday a couple of weeks ago, and he gave me a watch which is really lovely. I'd seen them advertised and mentioned I liked it, and he took notice and went and got me one.
THERAPIST:	Right. Now how does that fit with the idea that he doesn't love you?
PATIENT:	Well, I suppose it doesn't really, does it? But then why is he like that in the evening?
THERAPIST:	I suppose him not loving you any more is one possible reason. Are there any other possible reasons?
PATIENT:	Well, he has been working very hard lately. I mean, he's late home most nights, and he had to go in to the office at the weekend. So I suppose it could be that.
THERAPIST:	It could, couldn't it? How could you find out if that's it?
PATIENT:	Well, I could say I've noticed how tired he looks and ask him how he's feeling and how the work's going. I haven't done that. I've just been getting annoyed because he doesn't pay any attention to me.
THERAPIST:	That sounds like an excellent idea. How would you like to make that a homework task for this week? (From Fennell, M. J. V. (1989). Depression. In K. Hawton, P. M. Salkovskis, J. Kirk, & D. M. Clark (Eds.), Cognitive behaviour therapy for psychiatric problems: A practical guide. Oxford University Press.)

The usefulness of cognitive therapy has been amply documented in dozens of studies, including several studies on unipolar depressed inpatients and on patients diagnosed with depression with melancholic features (Craighead et al., 2007; Hollon, Haman, & Brown, 2002; Hollon et al., 2006). When compared with pharmacotherapy, it is at least as effective when delivered by well-trained cognitive therapists. It also seems to have a special advantage in preventing relapse, similar to that obtained by staying on medication (Hollon & Ponniah, 2010). Moreover, evidence is beginning to accumulate that it can prevent recurrence several years following the episode when the treatment occurred (Craighead et al., 2007; Hollon & Dimidjian, 2009). Perhaps not surprisingly, some recent interesting brain-imaging studies have shown that the biological changes

in certain brain areas that occur following effective treatment with cognitive therapy versus medications are somewhat different, suggesting that the mechanisms through which they work are also different (e.g., Clark & Beck, 2010; Hollon & Dimidjian, 2009). One possibility is that medications may target the limbic system whereas cognitive therapy may have greater effects on cortical functions.

Whether cognitive therapy is as effective as medication in the treatment of *severe* unipolar depression has been the more controversial question. However, recent evidence suggests that CBT and medications are equally effective in the treatment of severe depression (DeRubeis et al., 1999; Hollon et al., 2006). For example, one important two-site study of moderate to severe depression found that 58 percent responded to either cognitive therapy or medication (DeRubeis et al., 2005). However, by the end of the 2-year follow-up, when all cognitive therapy and medications had been discontinued for 1 year, only 25 percent of patients treated with cognitive therapy had had a relapse versus 50 percent in the medication group (a highly significant difference; Hollon et al., 2005; Hollon & Dimidjian, 2009). (See Figure 5)

Another variant on cognitive therapy, called *mindfulness-based cognitive therapy*, has been developed in recent years to be used with people with highly recurrent depression who have been treated with medication in order to help prevent further recurrences (e.g., Segal, Williams, & Teasdale, 2002; Teasdale, 2004). The logic of this treatment is based on findings that people with recurrent depression are likely to have negative thinking patterns activated when they are simply in a depressed mood. Perhaps rather than trying to alter the content of their negative thinking as in traditional cognitive therapy, it might be more useful to change the way in which these people relate to their thoughts, feelings, and bodily sensations. This group treatment involves training in mindfulness meditation techniques aimed at developing patients' awareness of their unwanted thoughts, feelings, and sensations so that they no longer automatically try to avoid them but rather learn to accept them for what they are—simply thoughts occurring in the moment rather than a reflection of reality. A recent meta-analysis of findings from six randomized controlled trials of individuals in remission from depression suggests that mindfulness-based cognitive therapy is an effective treatment for reducing risk of relapse in those with a history of three or more prior depressive episodes who have been treated with antidepressant medication (Piet & Hougaard, 2011).

Although the vast majority of research on CBT has focused on unipolar depression, recently there have been indications that a modified form of CBT may be quite useful, in combination with medication, in the treatment of bipolar disorder as well (Lam et al., 2003, 2005; Miklowitz, 2009). There is also preliminary evidence that mindfulness-based cognitive therapy may be useful in treating bipolar patients between episodes (Williams et al., 2008).

BEHAVIORAL ACTIVATION TREATMENT A relatively new and promising treatment for unipolar depression is called **behavioral activation treatment**. This treatment

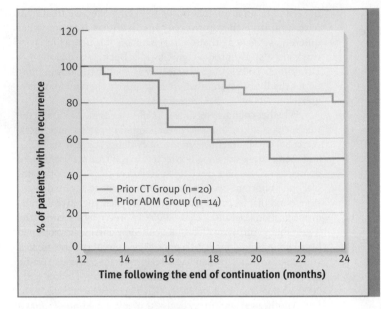

FIGURE 5

Survival curve illustrating how many months following the end of treatment it took patients from the two groups before they had another episode of depression (recurrence). One group had previously received cognitive therapy (CT) and the other group had received antidepressant medication (ADM).

Source: From Hollon, et al. (2005, April). Prevention of relapse following cognitive therapy vs. medications in moderate to severe depression. Arch. Gen. Psychiat., 62(4), 417–26. © 2005 American Medical Association. Reprinted with permission.

approach focuses intensively on getting patients to become more active and engaged with their environment and with their interpersonal relationships. These techniques include scheduling daily activities and rating pleasure and mastery while engaging in them, exploring alternative behaviors to reach goals, and role-playing to address specific deficits. Traditional cognitive therapy attends to these same issues but to a lesser extent. Behavioral activation treatment, by contrast, does not focus on implementing cognitive changes directly but rather on changing behavior. The goals are to increase levels of positive reinforcement and to reduce avoidance and withdrawal (Dimidjian et al., 2011). Early results were very promising, suggesting it may be as effective as more traditional cognitive therapies (Jacobson et al., 2001), and there is now meta-analytic support for this notion (Mazzacchelli et al., 2009). Indeed, one study found that moderately to severely depressed patients who received behavioral activation treatment did as well as those on medication and even slightly better than those who received cognitive therapy (Dimidjian et al., 2006). However, the slight superiority of behavioral activation treatment relative to cognitive therapy was not maintained, with some results indicating a trend for cognitive therapy to be slightly superior at follow-up (Dobson et al., 2008). However, because it is easier to train therapists to administer behavioral activation treatment than cognitive therapy, it seems likely that there will be increased attention paid to this relatively new treatment in the coming years.

INTERPERSONAL THERAPY The **interpersonal therapy (IPT)** approach has not yet been subjected to as extensive an evaluation as cognitive-behavioral therapy, nor is it as widely available. However, the studies that have been completed strongly support its effectiveness for treating unipolar depression (see Cuijpers et al., 2011, for a quantitative review; see also Hollon & Ponniah, 2010). Indeed, interpersonal therapy seems to be about as effective as medications or cognitive-behavioral treatment (Hollon, Thase, & Markowitz, 2002; Weissman & Markowitz, 2002). This IPT approach focuses on current relationship issues, trying to help the person understand and change maladaptive interaction patterns (Bleiberg & Markowitz, 2008). Interpersonal therapy can also be useful in long-term follow-up for individuals with severe recurrent unipolar depression (Frank et al., 1990; Weissman & Markowitz, 2002). Patients who received continued treatment with IPT once a month or who received continued medication were much less likely to have a recurrence than those maintained on a placebo over a 3-year follow-up period (although those maintained on medication were even less likely to relapse than those treated with monthly IPT). Furthermore, there is meta-analytic support for the notion that a combined maintenance treatment of IPT and medication is associated with lower recurrence rates than maintenance medication treatment alone (Cuijpers et al., 2011).

In addition, IPT has been adapted for treatment of bipolar disorder by adding a focus on stabilizing daily social rhythms that, if they become destabilized, may play a role in precipitating bipolar episodes. In this new treatment, called *interpersonal and social rhythm therapy*, patients are taught to recognize the effect of interpersonal events on their social and circadian rhythms and to regularize these rhythms. As an adjunct to medication, this treatment seems promising (Miklowitz & Craighead, 2007; Miklowitz, 2009b).

FAMILY AND MARITAL THERAPY Of course, in any treatment program, it is important to deal with unusual stressors in a patient's life because an unfavorable life situation may lead to a recurrence of the depression and may necessitate longer treatment. This point has been well established in studies indicating that relapse in unipolar and bipolar disorders, as in schizophrenia, is correlated with certain noxious elements in family life (Hooley, 2007; Hooley & Hiller, 2001). Behavior by a spouse that can be interpreted by a former patient as criticism seems especially likely to produce depression relapse. For example, for bipolar disorder, some types of family interventions directed at reducing the level of expressed emotion or hostility, and at increasing the information available to the family about how to cope with the disorder, have been found to be very useful in preventing relapse in these situations (e.g., Miklowitz, 2009; Miklowitz & Craighead, 2007). For married people who have unipolar depression and marital discord, marital therapy (focusing on the marital discord rather than on the depressed spouse alone) is as effective as cognitive therapy in reducing unipolar depression in the depressed spouse. Marital therapy has the further advantage of producing greater increases in marital satisfaction than cognitive therapy (Beach & Jones, 2002).

CONCLUSIONS Even without formal therapy, as we have noted, the great majority of patients with mania and depression recover from a given episode in less than a year. With the modern methods of treatment discussed here, the general outlook for a given episode if treatment is obtained has become increasingly favorable for many, but by no means all, afflicted individuals. However, at least half never receive even minimally adequate treatment. Although relapses and recurrences often occur, these can now often be prevented or at least reduced in frequency by maintenance therapy—through continuation of medication and/or through follow-up therapy sessions at regular intervals.

At the same time, the mortality rate for individuals with depression is significantly higher than that for the general population, partly because of the higher incidence of suicide but also because there is an excess of deaths due to natural causes (see Coryell & Winokur, 1992; Goodwin & Jamison, 2007), including coronary heart disease (e.g., Glassman, 2005; Whang et al., 2009). Patients with mania also have a high risk of death because of such circumstances as accidents (often with alcohol as a contributing factor), neglect of proper health precautions, or physical exhaustion (Goodwin & Jamison, 2007). Thus, the need for still-more-effective treatment methods, both immediate and long term, clearly remains. Also, a great need remains to study the factors that put people at risk for depressive disorders and to apply relevant findings to early intervention and prevention.

Kurt Cobain, lead vocalist of the rock band Nirvana, died from a self-inflicted gunshot wound on April 8, 1994. He left behind his wife, Courtney Love, and their daughter, Frances, to deal with the emotional burden of his suicide. Forty to sixty percent of those who successfully commit suicide are depressed.

In Review

- Evaluate the effectiveness of antidepressant medications, mood-stabilizing drugs such as lithium, and electroconvulsive therapy in the treatment of unipolar and bipolar disorders.
- Describe the three major forms of psychotherapy that have been shown to be effective for treating depression.

Suicide

The risk of **suicide**—taking one's own life—is a significant factor in all types of depression. Although it is obvious that people also commit suicide for reasons other than depression, estimates are that about 50 to 90 percent of those who complete the act do so during a depressive episode or in the recovery phase (Holma et al., 2010; van Praag, 2005). Paradoxically, the act often occurs at a point when the person appears to be emerging from the deepest phase of the depressive attack. The risk of suicide is about 1 percent during the year in which a depressive episode occurs, but the lifetime risk for someone who has recurrent depressive episodes is about 15 percent (D. C. Clark, 1995; Stolberg et al., 2002). Moreover, even when suicide is not associated with depression, it is still generally associated with some other mental disorder; estimates are that approximately 90 percent of people who either attempted or successfully committed suicide had some psychiatric disorder at the time, although only about half of those had been diagnosed prior to the suicide (Goodwin & Jamison, 2007; Kessler, Berglund, Borges et al., 2005; Nock et al., 2010). Moreover, individuals with two or more mental disorders are at even greater risk than those with only one (Nock et al., 2008, 2010).

Suicide now ranks among the 10 leading causes of death in most Western countries (Kessler et al., 2005). In the United States, it is the 10th or 11th leading cause of death, with current estimates of about 35,000 suicides each year (National Vital Statistics Report, 2011). Moreover, most experts agree that the number of actual suicides is at least several times higher than the number officially reported because many self-inflicted deaths are attributed in official records to other, more "respectable" causes (e.g., O'Donnell & Farmer, 1995; M. M. Silverman, 1997). In addition to completed suicides, estimates are that approximately half a million people attempt suicide each year and that nearly 3 percent of Americans have made a suicide attempt at some time in their lives (Goodwin & Jamison, 2007). Approximately 9 percent have experienced suicidal ideation or thoughts (Nock et al., 2008).

Statistics, however accurate, cannot begin to convey the tragedy of suicide in human terms. Most people who commit suicide are ambivalent about taking their own lives and make this irreversible choice when they are alone and in a state of severe psychological distress and anguish, unable to see their problems objectively or to evaluate alternative courses of action. Thus one tragedy is that many do not really want to die. A second tragic concern arises from the long-lasting distress among those left behind. Studies of survivors show that the loss of a loved one through suicide "is one of the greatest burdens individuals and families may endure" (Dunne, 1992, p. 222).

In the discussion that follows, we will focus on various aspects of the incidence and clinical picture of suicide, on factors that appear to be of causal significance, on degrees of intent and ways of communicating it, and on issues of treatment and prevention.

The Clinical Picture and the Causal Pattern

Who commits suicide? What are the motives for taking one's own life? What general sociocultural variables appear to be relevant to an understanding of suicide? These are the questions we will consider next.

Who Attempts and Who Commits Suicide?

Until recently, *suicide attempts* were most common in people between 25 and 44 years old (Stolberg et al., 2002), but it is now people between 18 and 24 years old who have the highest rates (Kessler, Berglund, Borges et al., 2005). In the United States, women are about three times as likely to attempt suicide as men (Goodwin & Jamison, 2007; Holma et al., 2010). Rates of suicide attempts are also about three or four times higher in people who are separated or divorced than in those with any other marital status. Most attempts occur in the context of interpersonal discord or other severe life stress. The story is different, however, for *completed suicides*, which are far less frequent than suicide attempts. In the United States, recent reports indicate that suicide was the seventh leading cause of death for men (accounting for 2.3% of total deaths), whereas it was the 15th leading cause of death for women (accounting for 0.6% of total deaths; National Vital Statistics Report, 2011). The only exception to these patterns of gender differences seems to be in people who have bipolar disorder, among whom as many, or even more, women as men actually complete suicide (Goodwin & Jamison, 2007; Tondo et al., 2003). The highest rate of completed suicides is in the elderly (aged 65 and over). Although these rates had been coming down since 1930, especially for elderly men (Stolberg et al., 2002), the 1980s and 1990s saw a trend back upward. Among elderly victims, a high proportion are divorced or widowed or suffer from a chronic physical illness that can lead to increased risk

for suicide, very often because the person is depressed (Conwell, Duberstein, & Caine, 2002). However, full-blown mental disorders are relatively rare in those elderly persons who commit suicide compared to their prevalence among people in younger age groups who commit suicide (Harwood et al., 2006). For women, the method most commonly used is drug ingestion; men tend to use methods more likely to be lethal, particularly gunshot, which may be a good part of the reason why completed suicides are higher among men.

Besides the elderly, persons with mood disorders, and separated or divorced persons, there are a number of other high-risk groups among adults. For example, people with fairly severe and recurrent mood disorders have the highest risk of suicide at some point in their lives (about a 15 percent risk), and those with less severe forms of mood disorders show only a somewhat elevated risk (Goodwin & Jamison, 2007). Some researchers have estimated that people with schizophrenia have about a 10 to 13 percent risk, and those hospitalized for alcohol dependence have about a 3 to 4 percent risk, relative to the average risk of 1.4 percent in the general population (e.g., Haas, 1997; Joiner et al., 2005; Stolberg et al., 2002). Rates of attempted and completed suicides are also elevated in individuals with borderline personality disorder and antisocial personality disorder. The depressed mood and hopelessness often seen in borderline personality disorder are often implicated. Furthermore, a history of conduct disorder has been found to be a strong predictor of suicide attempts as well (Borges et al., 2010). In addition, risk for different suicide behaviors may differ as a function of psychopathology. For example, in the National Comorbidity Survey-Replication, major depression was found to be the strongest risk factor for suicide ideation but not for suicide plans or attempts among individuals with ideation (Nock, Hwang et al., 2010). In contrast, anxiety, impulse-control, and substance use disorders were the strongest predictors of suicide plans and attempts. Finally, people living alone or with low levels of perceived social support and people from socially disorganized areas are also at heightened risk (e.g., Holma et al., 2010). Certain highly creative or successful scientists, health professionals (e.g., physicians and psychologists), business people, composers, writers, and artists are also at higher-than-average risk (Jamison, 1999).

Suicide in Children

Another disturbing trend is that rates of completed suicide among children, while still very low, have been increasing (Stolberg et al., 2002; van Orden et al., 2008). Suicide in children under age 10 is extremely rare. In children between ages 10 to 14 suicide is also rare in absolute terms (accounting for approximately 5% of deaths) but is nevertheless the fourth leading cause of death in the United States for this age group (National Vital Statistics Report, 2011). Further, the trend is by no means limited to youngsters from deprived or troubled backgrounds. Children are at increased risk for suicide if they have lost a parent or have been abused (Jamison, 1999). Several forms of psychopathology—depression, antisocial behavior, and high impulsivity—are also known to be risk factors for suicide in children.

Suicide in Adolescents and Young Adults

For persons between the ages of 15 and 24, the rate of successful suicides essentially tripled between the mid-1950s and the mid-1980s. Suicide ranks as the third most common cause of death in the United States for 15- to 19-year-olds (after accidents and homicide), accounting for approximately 11 percent of total deaths in this age range (National Vital Statistics Report, 2011). The increases in suicide rates for adolescents are not unique to this country but, rather, have been observed in most of the many countries studied (Jamison, 1999).

As for suicide attempts, one large survey of 15,000 high school students across 32 states has estimated the rates of self-reported suicide attempts within a 12-month period to be an alarming 8.5 percent, with about twice that many reporting that they have at least seriously considered it (Spiroto & Esposito-Smythers, 2006). In recent years, these have been the highest rates of suicide attempts at any point in the human life span. Most of these attempts have very low lethality and do not require medical attention, but they do need to be taken seriously. Indeed, prior suicide attempts have occurred in about 25 to 33 percent of completed suicides. Suicide rates in college students are also high, and it is the second leading cause of death in this group. One large survey found that about 10 percent of college students had seriously contemplated suicide in the past year and that most of these attempters had had some sort of plan (Jamison, 1999).

KNOWN RISK FACTORS FOR ADOLESCENT SUICIDE

Studies have found that mood disorders, conduct disorder, and substance abuse (especially alcohol) are relatively more common in both completers and nonfatal attempters. Among those with two or more of these disorders, risk for completion increases. Unfortunately, recent evidence suggests that treatment of adolescent mood disorders with antidepressant medication also seems to produce a very slightly increased risk for suicidal ideation (or thoughts) and behavior in children and adolescents, and so now pharmaceutical companies must put warnings to this effect on these medications (e.g., Whittington et al., 2005).

Why has there been such a surge in suicide attempts and completed suicides in adolescence? One obvious reason is that this is a period during which depression, anxiety, alcohol and drug use, and conduct disorder problems also show increasing prevalence, and these are all factors associated with increased risk for suicide (e.g., Evans, Hawton, & Rodham, 2004). Increased availability of firearms has also probably played a role as well. Exposure to suicides (especially those of celebrities) through the media, where they are often portrayed in dramatic terms, has probably also contributed to these aggregate increases in adolescent suicide, perhaps because adolescents are highly susceptible to suggestion and imitative behavior (Hawton & Williams, 2002; Jamison, 1999). One review estimated that between 1 and 13 percent of adolescent suicides occur as a result of contagion factors (Velting & Gould, 1997). Finally, the fact that the media rarely discuss the mental disorders suffered by the suicide victims may further increase the likelihood of imitation.

Many college students also seem very vulnerable to the development of suicidal ideation and plans. The combined stressors of academic demands, social interaction problems, and career choices—perhaps interacting with challenges to their basic values—evidently make it impossible for some students to continue making the adjustments their life situations demand. For an overview of warning signs for student suicide, see The World Around Us 3.

3 ## THE WORLD AROUND US

Warning Signs for Student Suicide

A marked change in a student's mood and behavior may be a significant warning of possible suicide. Characteristically, the student becomes depressed and withdrawn, undergoes a marked decline in self-esteem, and shows deterioration in personal hygiene. He or she may also show uncharacteristically impulsive or reckless behavior, including self-mutilating behavior. The student may also write about death or suicide. These signs are accompanied by a profound loss of interest in studies. Often he or she stops attending classes and stays at home most of the day. The student's distress is usually communicated to at least one other person, often in the form of a veiled suicide warning.

When college students attempt suicide, one of the first explanations to occur to those around them is that they may have been doing poorly in school. As a group, however, they are superior students, and although they tend to expect a great deal of themselves in terms of academic achievement, their grades and academic competition are not regarded as significant precipitating stressors. Also, although many lose interest in their studies before becoming suicidal and thus receive worse grades, this loss of interest appears to be associated with depression and withdrawal caused by other problems. Moreover, in that minority of cases where academic failure does appear to trigger suicidal behavior, the underlying cause of the behavior seems to be loss of self-esteem and failure to live up to parental expectations rather than academic failure itself.

For most suicidal students, both male and female, the major precipitating stressor appears to be either the failure to establish, or the loss of, a close interpersonal relationship. Often the breakup of a romance is the key precipitating factor. It has also been noted that significantly more suicide attempts and suicides are made by students from families that have experienced separation, divorce, or the death of a parent.

Although most colleges and universities have mental health facilities to assist distressed students, few suicidal students seek professional help. Thus it is of vital importance for those around a suicidal student to notice any warning signs and try to obtain assistance.

Other Psychosocial Factors Associated with Suicide

The most frequently discussed personality traits associated with suicide are impulsivity (especially a lack of premeditation), aggression, pessimism, and negative affectivity, which all seem to increase the risk for suicide (Hawton, 2005; Oquendo et al., 2004; Yen et al., 2009). Though the specific factors that lead a person to suicide may take many forms, suicide is often associated with negative events such as severe financial reversals, imprisonment, and interpersonal crises of various sorts. Some believe the common denominator may be that these events lead either to the loss of a sense of meaning in life or to hopelessness about the future (e.g., Beck et al., 1993), both of which can produce a mental state that looks to suicide as a possible way out. However, hopelessness about the future may be a better long-term predictor of suicide (say, 1 or 2 years later) than it is for the short term (for instance, weeks or months later; Coryell & Young, 2005; Goodwin & Jamison, 2007). There is also initial evidence that people who have a strong implicit association between the self and death or suicide is predictive of future suicide attempts, even over and above the effects of other known risk factors (Nock et al., 2010). Other symptoms that seem to predict suicide more reliably in the short term in patients with major depression include severe psychic anxiety, panic attacks, severe anhedonia (inability to experience pleasure), global insomnia, delusions, and alcohol abuse (Busch et al., 2003; Goodwin & Jamison, 2007). Indeed, in one study of 76 people who had committed suicide while being hospitalized, the hospital records revealed that 79 percent of these people had been severely anxious and agitated in the week prior to committing suicide (Busch et al., 2003).

Shneidman, a leading suicidologist for over 35 years, has written extensively about the "suicidal mind."

This figure is intentionally omitted from this text.

Research indicates that suicide is the end product of a long sequence of events that begins in childhood. People who become suicidal often come from backgrounds in which there was some combination of a good deal of family psychopathology, child maltreatment, and family instability (e.g., Borges et al., 2010; Molnar et al., 2001). These early experiences are in turn associated with the child (and later the adult) having low self-esteem, hopelessness, and poor problem-solving skills. Such experiences may affect the person's cognitive functioning in a very negative way, and these cognitive deficits may in turn mediate the link with suicidal behavior (e.g., Yang & Clum, 1996).

Biological Causal Factors

There is strong evidence that suicide sometimes runs in families and that genetic factors may play a role in the risk for suicide (Goodwin & Jamison, 2007). For example, averaging across 22 studies, the concordance rate for suicide in identical twins is about three times higher than that in fraternal twins (Baldessarini & Hennen, 2004). Moreover, this genetic vulnerability seems to be at least partly independent of the genetic vulnerability for major depression (e.g., Brezo et al., 2010).

There is also increasing evidence that this genetic vulnerability may be linked to the neurochemical correlates of suicide that have now been found in numerous studies. Specifically, suicide victims often have alterations in serotonin functioning, with reduced serotonergic activity being associated with increased suicide risk—especially for violent suicide (Goodwin & Jamison, 2007). Such studies have been conducted not only in postmortem studies of suicide victims but also in people who have made suicide attempts and survived. This association appears to be independent of psychiatric diagnosis, including suicide victims with depression, schizophrenia, and personality

Ernest Hemingway (left) committed suicide on July 2, 1961. Thirty-five years later to the day, his granddaughter Margaux (right) took her own life as well. The Hemingway family has endured five suicides over four generations—Ernest's father Clarence, Ernest and his siblings Ursula and Leicester, and granddaughter Margaux.

disorders (Goodwin & Jamison, 2007). People hospitalized for a suicide attempt who have low serotonin levels are also 10 times more likely to kill themselves in the next year than are those without low serotonin levels. Several studies have tried to document an association between suicide and the short allele serotonin-transporter gene (which controls the uptake of serotonin from the synapse), previously discussed as being implicated in the vulnerability to depression. Although not all studies have found positive results, a quantitative review of these studies did find that people with one or two copies of the short allele are at heightened risk for suicide following stressful life events (Lin & Tsai, 2004). There is also growing support for associations between additional serotonergic gene variants and suicide attempts (Brezo et al., 2010).

Sociocultural Factors

Substantial differences in suicide rates occur among different ethnic or racial groups in the United States. For example, whites have significantly higher rates of suicide than African Americans, except among young males, where rates are similar between white and African American men (see Figure 6). Only young Native American men show a suicide rate similar to that of white males.

Suicide rates also appear to vary considerably from one society to another. The United States has a rate of approximately 11 per 100,000. Countries with low rates (less than 9 per 100,000) include Greece, Italy, Spain, and the United Kingdom (Maris et al., 2000). In contrast, Hungary, with an annual incidence of more than 40 per 100,000, has the world's highest rate (almost four times that of the

United States). Other Western countries with high suicide rates—20 per 100,000 or higher—are Switzerland, Finland, Austria, Sweden, Denmark, and Germany. Rates in Japan and China are also high; indeed, in China the estimated suicide rate is three times the global average (Hesketh et al., 2002). Moreover, almost 30 percent of suicides worldwide are estimated to occur in China and India (WHO International Suicide Statistics Resource Page, 2009). Some have estimated the global mortality from suicide at 16 to 18 per 100,000 (Mathers et al., 2006; WHO International Suicide Statistics Resource Page, 2009). These estimates should, however, be considered in light of the fact that there are wide differences across countries in the criteria used for determining whether a death was due to suicide, and such differences may well contribute to the apparent differences in suicide rates.

Religious taboos concerning suicide and the attitudes of a society toward death are also apparently important determinants of suicide rates. Both Catholicism and Islam strongly condemn suicide, and suicide rates in Catholic and Islamic countries are correspondingly low. In fact, most societies have developed strong sanctions against suicide, and many still regard it as a crime as well as a sin.

Japan is one of the few societies in which suicide has been socially approved under certain circumstances—such as conditions that bring disgrace to an individual or group. During World War II, many Japanese villagers and Japanese military personnel were reported to have committed mass suicide when faced with defeat and imminent capture by Allied forces. There were also reports of group suicide by Japanese military personnel under threat of defeat. In the case of the kamikaze, approximately 1,000 young Japanese pilots deliberately crashed their

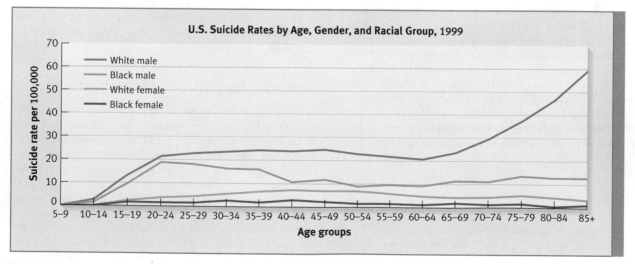

FIGURE 6

U.S. Suicide Rates by Age, Gender, and Racial Group

Suicide rates are higher in males than in females and higher in whites than in African Americans.

Source: National Institute of Mental Health, October 20, 2002. Data: Centers for Disease Control and Prevention, National Center for Health Statistics.

explosives-laden planes into American warships during the war's final stages as a way of demonstrating complete personal commitment to the national purpose. Comparable acts of self-destruction occur today in the Middle East, where Muslim extremists and terrorists all too often commit suicide in order to ensure that a bomb explodes in a designated target area. In the case of the Al Qaeda attacks on September 11, 2001, terrorists took over commercial jets and then flew them into the World Trade Center and the Pentagon, killing themselves and over 3,000 innocent people. A few years later in Iraq, after the fall of Saddam Hussein, suicide bombers formed a major part of the insurgency in Iraq against U.S. and other foreign soldiers, as well as against members of Iraq's newly formed government forces.

There are also interesting cross-cultural gender differences in whether men or women are more likely to attempt and complete suicide. Although women are more likely to attempt and men to complete suicide in the United States, in India, Poland, and Finland men are more likely than women to engage in nonfatal suicide attempts. In China, India, and Papua New Guinea, women are more likely to complete suicide than men (Canetto, 1997; Jamison, 1999).

In a pioneering study of sociocultural factors in suicide, the French sociologist Emile Durkheim (1897/1951) attempted to relate differences in suicide rates to differences in group cohesiveness. Analyzing records of suicides in different countries and during different historical periods, Durkheim concluded that the greatest deterrent to committing suicide in times of personal stress is a sense of involvement and identity with other people. More contemporary studies tend to confirm this idea, showing, for example, that being married and having children tends to protect one from suicide (Maris, 1997; Stolberg et al., 2002).

Durkheim's views also seem relevant to understanding the higher incidence of suicide among individuals subjected to conditions of uncertainty and social disorganization in the absence of strong group ties. For example, there is a well-known association between unemployment and suicide (especially for men), which may well be related to the effects that unemployment has on mental health (Gunnell, 2005; Jamison, 1999). Similarly, suicide rates have been found to be higher among groups subject to severe social pressures. For example, in 1932, at the height of the Great Depression in the United States, the suicide rate increased from less than 10 to 4 per 100,000.

In Review

- Which groups of people are most likely to attempt suicide, and which groups are most likely to complete suicide? What are some of the major precipitants of suicide?
- Summarize the psychological, biological, and sociocultural causal factors associated with suicide.

Suicidal Ambivalence

Ambivalence often accompanies thoughts of suicide. Some people (most often women) do not really wish to die but instead want to communicate a dramatic message to others concerning their distress. Their suicide attempts tend to involve nonlethal methods such as minimal drug ingestion or minor wrist slashing. They usually arrange matters so that intervention by others is almost inevitable. In stark contrast, a small minority of suicidal people are seemingly intent on dying. They give little or no warning of their intent, and they generally rely on the more violent and certain means of suicide such as shooting themselves or jumping from high places. A third subset of people are ambivalent about dying and tend to leave the question of death to fate. A person in this group may entertain and tend to use methods that are often dangerous but moderately slow acting, such as drug ingestion. The feeling during such attempts can be summed up as, "If I die, the conflict is settled, but if I am rescued that is what was meant to be."

After an unsuccessful attempt, a marked reduction in emotional turmoil usually occurs, especially if the attempt was expected to be lethal, such as jumping in front of a moving train. This reduction in turmoil is usually not stable, however, and subsequent suicidal behavior may follow (e.g., Holma et al., 2010). In the year after a suicide attempt, repetition of the behavior occurs in 15 to 25 percent (Zahl & Hawton, 2004b) of cases, and there is an increased risk that the second or third attempt will be fatal, especially if the first attempt was a serious one. Long-term follow-ups of those who have made a suicide attempt show that about 7 to 10 percent will eventually die by suicide, a risk about five times greater than the average risk of 1.4 percent (Stolberg et al., 2002). Of people who do kill themselves, about 20 to 40 percent have a history of one or more previous attempts; however, more than half of those who commit suicide have no previous attempts (Stolberg et al., 2002; Zahl & Hawton, 2004b).

Communication of Suicidal Intent

Research has clearly disproved the tragic belief that those who threaten to take their lives seldom do so. One review of many studies conducted around the world that involved interviewing friends and relatives of people who had committed suicide revealed that more than 40 percent had communicated their suicidal intent in very clear and specific terms and that another 30 percent had talked about death or dying in the months preceding their suicide. These communications were usually made to several people and occurred a few weeks or months before the suicide (D. C. Clark, 1995). Nevertheless, most of those interviewed said the suicide came as a surprise. It is also interesting that most of these communications of intent were to friends and family members and not to mental health professionals. Indeed, nearly 50 percent of people who die by suicide have never seen a mental health professional in their lifetime, and only about 20 percent are under the care of one at the time of their death (Goodwin & Jamison, 2007).

On the other hand, if a clinician knows that someone has been suicidal (for example, he or she is being hospitalized for a suicide attempt), he or she should also not take the patient's denial of suicidal intent as necessarily being valid. One fascinating study of clinical correlates of inpatients who had committed suicide revealed some sobering statistics: Among patients who were being hospitalized for having had either suicidal ideation or intent, nearly 80 percent denied suicidal ideation the last time they spoke with a clinician before actually committing suicide; moreover, over 50 percent of those who committed suicide did so while on a 15-minute suicide watch or under 1-on-1 observation (Busch et al., 2003).

Suicide Notes

Several investigators have analyzed suicide notes in an effort to understand the motives and feelings of people who take their own lives. Several large studies of completed suicides found that only about 15 to 25 percent left notes, usually addressed to relatives or friends (Jamison, 1999; Maris, 1997). The notes, usually coherent and legible, either had been mailed or were found on the person's body or near the suicide scene. Some notes included statements of love and concern, which may have been motivated by the desire to be remembered positively and to reassure the survivor of the worth of the relationship. Occasionally, though, notes contained very hostile content, such as, "I used to love you but I die hating you and my brother too" (Jamison, 1999, p. 78).

Although one might think that such notes would express deep and tragic emotions, this is typically not the case. Many notes are often quite short and straightforward: "I am tired of living" or "I could not bear it any longer" or "No one is to blame for this. It's just that I could never be reconciled with life itself. God have mercy on my soul" (Jamison, 1999, pp. 77–78).

Suicide Prevention and Intervention

Preventing suicide is extremely difficult. Most people who are depressed and contemplating suicide do not realize that their thinking is restricted and irrational and that they are in need of assistance. Rather than seeking psychological help,

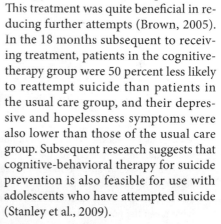

In recent years, the availability of competent assistance at the time of suicidal crisis has been expanded through the establishment of suicide prevention centers. But how successful are these interventions?

they are more likely to visit a doctor's office with multiple vague complaints of physical symptoms that the doctor often does not detect as symptoms of depression or alcoholism. Others are brought to the attention of mental health personnel by family members or friends who are concerned because the person appears depressed or has made suicide threats. The vast majority, however, do not receive the help they desperately need, which is unfortunate because if a person's cry for help can be heard in time it is often possible to intervene successfully.

Currently, there are three main thrusts of preventive efforts: treatment of the person's current mental disorder(s) as noted above, crisis intervention, and working with high-risk groups.

Treatment of Mental Disorders

One way to help prevent suicide might be through treating the underlying mental disorder(s) the potentially suicidal person has. In the case of depression, such treatment is often in the form of antidepressant medications or lithium. Lithium seems to be an especially powerful antisuicide agent over the long term (not in the acute situation; Goodwin & Jamison, 2007). Benzodiazepines can also be useful in treating the severe anxiety and panic that so often precede suicide attempts. Although there is not a great deal of work using cognitive-behavioral treatments for suicide, one important study examined adults who had already made at least one attempt and gave them 10 sessions of cognitive therapy focused on suicide prevention. This treatment was quite beneficial in reducing further attempts (Brown, 2005). In the 18 months subsequent to receiving treatment, patients in the cognitive-therapy group were 50 percent less likely to reattempt suicide than patients in the usual care group, and their depressive and hopelessness symptoms were also lower than those of the usual care group. Subsequent research suggests that cognitive-behavioral therapy for suicide prevention is also feasible for use with adolescents who have attempted suicide (Stanley et al., 2009).

Crisis Intervention

The primary objective of crisis intervention is to help a person cope with an immediate life crisis. If a serious suicide attempt has been made, the first step involves emergency medical treatment, followed by referral to inpatient or outpatient mental health facilities in order to reduce the risk for future attempts (e.g., Stolberg et al., 2002).

When people contemplating suicide are willing to discuss their problems with someone at a suicide prevention center, it is often possible to avert an actual suicide attempt. Here the primary objective is to help these people regain their ability to cope with their immediate problems as quickly as possible. Emphasis is usually placed on (1) maintaining supportive and often highly directive contact with the person over a short period of time—usually one to six contacts; (2) helping the person to realize that acute distress is impairing his or her ability to assess the situation accurately and to see that there are better ways of dealing with the problem; and (3) helping the person to see that the present distress and emotional turmoil will not be endless.

Since the 1960s, the availability of competent assistance at times of suicidal crisis has been expanded through the establishment of *suicide hotlines* for suicide prevention centers. There are now more than several thousand such hotlines in the United States, but questions have been raised about the quality of care offered by the majority of them (e.g., Seeley, 1997). These centers are geared primarily toward crisis intervention, usually via the 24-hour-a-day availability of telephone contact. Suicide hotlines are usually staffed primarily by nonprofessionals who are supervised by psychologists and psychiatrists. The worker attempts to establish the seriousness of the caller's intent and simultaneously tries to show empathy and to convince the person not to attempt suicide. Efforts are also made to mobilize support from family or friends. Unfortunately, good information on the assessment of the effects of these hotlines and suicide prevention centers has not revealed much impact on suicide rates.

Focus on High-Risk Groups and Other Measures

Many investigators have emphasized the need for broad-based prevention programs aimed at alleviating the life problems of people who are in groups at high risk for suicide (Maris et al., 2000). Few such programs have actually been initiated, but one approach has been to involve older men—a high-risk group—in social and interpersonal activities that help others. Playing such roles may lessen these men's sense of isolation and meaninglessness, which often stems from forced retirement, financial problems, the deaths of loved ones, impaired physical health, and feeling unwanted. Other programs have been targeted at young adolescents who are at higher risk because of previous suicidal ideation and behavior or mood or substance-use disorders (Zahl & Hawton, 2004a).

In Review

- What is meant by suicidal ambivalence, and how might it be related to communication of suicidal intent?
- What are the goals of suicide intervention programs, and how successful do they seem to be?

Unresolved Issues
▶ *Is There a Right to Die?*

Most of us respect the preservation of human life as a worthwhile value. Thus, in our society, suicide is generally considered not only tragic but also "wrong." Efforts to prevent suicide, however, involve ethical problems. If people wish to take their own lives, what obligation—or right—do others have to interfere? Not all societies have taken the position that others should interfere when someone wishes to commit suicide. For example, the classical Greeks believed in dignity in death, and people who were extremely ill could get permission from the state to commit suicide. Officials of the state gave out hemlock (a poison) to those who received such permission (Humphry & Wickett, 1986). Today, in certain Western European countries such as the Netherlands and Belgium the law allows terminally ill people to be given access to drugs that they can use to commit suicide (Bosshard et al., 2008; Maris et al., 2000). In 1994 the state of Oregon passed the Oregon Death with Dignity Act (ODDA) allowing physician-assisted suicide for terminally ill patients who request a prescription for lethal medications that they will ingest to end their own lives (e.g., Sears & Stanton, 2001). As of 2007 an estimated 341 people had taken their lives under the ODDA.

Passage of the ODDA was (and is) highly controversial in the United States and was challenged several times by U.S. Attorney General John Ashcroft in federal courts. So far the law remains in effect even after being reviewed by the Supreme Court, where it was upheld in January 2006. Furthermore, in 2008 Washington became the second state to pass a death with dignity act. Nevertheless, there is still very heated debate all over the country about the right of people who are terminally ill or who suffer chronic and debilitating pain to shorten their agony. One group, the Hemlock Society, supports the rights of terminally ill people to get help in ending their own lives when they wish; the society also provides support groups for people making this decision.

Several other groups press related issues at a legislative level. One late physician in Michigan, Dr. Jack Kevorkian (1928–2011), helped over 130 gravely ill people commit suicide and, in so doing, tried to get Michigan to pass laws permitting such acts. For years the state tried to block Kevorkian from assisting in any further suicides, and at several points he was even imprisoned, and his medical license revoked, because he refused to obey injunctions not to assist with any more suicides. In 1998 Kevorkian invited further attention—and prosecution—when he released a videotape to the CBS program *60 Minutes,* and millions watched him assisting in a suicide. He was later charged, and convicted in April 1999, of second-degree murder and was released and paroled for good behavior in 2007 after serving 8 years of a 10- to 25-year term in prison. In spite of Kevorkian's failure to prompt the passage of laws supporting assisted suicide for such gravely ill individuals (indeed, Michigan passed a law prohibiting assisted suicide!), substantial numbers of people, including many physicians and dying patients, have come to sympathize with this position (Curlin et al., 2008; Wilson, Chochinov et al., 2007; see also Szasz's 1999 book *Fatal Freedom: The Ethics and Politics of Suicide*).

Arguments against this position have included fears that the right to suicide might be abused. For example, people who are terminally ill and severely incapacitated might feel pressured to end their own lives rather than burden their families with their care or with the cost of their care in a medical facility or hospice. However, in places where assisted suicide is legal, such as the Netherlands and Oregon, this has not happened. Indeed, physicians in Oregon seem to have become more aware of and sensitive to the needs of terminally ill patients in terms of recommending hospice care and learning more about prescribing the high doses of pain medication needed to relieve suffering (Ganzini et al., 2001).

But what about the rights of suicidal people who are not terminally ill and who have dependent children, parents, a spouse, or other loved ones who will be adversely affected, perhaps permanently (Lukas & Seiden, 1990; Maris et al., 2000), by their death? Here a person's "right to suicide" is not immediately obvious, and physicians are very unlikely to provide assistance in such cases (Rurup et al., 2005). The right to suicide

is even less clear when we consider that, through intervention, many suicidal people regain their perspective and see alternative ways of dealing with their distress.

Rather than focusing on suicide "prevention," some have suggested suicide "intervention" both as a more appropriate term and as descriptive of a more ethically defensible professional approach to suicidal behavior. According to this perspective, suicide intervention embodies a more neutral moral stance than suicide prevention—it means interceding without the implication of preventing the act—and, in certain circumstances, such as when people are terminally ill, it may even encompass the possibility of facilitating the suicidal person's objective (e.g., M. M. Silverman, 1997).

The dilemma about the prevention concept becomes even more intense when prevention requires that a person be hospitalized involuntarily, when personal items (such as belts and sharp objects) are taken away, and when calming medication is more or less forcibly administered. Sometimes considerable restriction is needed to calm the individual. Not uncommonly, particularly in these litigious times, the responsible clinician feels trapped between threats of legal action on both sides of the issue. Moreover, preventive efforts may be fruitless; truly determined persons may find a way to commit suicide even on a "suicide watch." Indeed, about 5 percent of all completed suicides are committed by psychiatric patients while they are hospitalized in inpatient psychiatric units that are supposed to help prevent suicide (Stolberg et al., 2002).

Thus the vexing ethical problems of whether and to what extent one should intervene in cases of threatened suicide have now been complicated by no-less-vexing legal problems. As in other areas of professional practice, clinical judgment is no longer the only consideration in intervention decisions. This is a societal problem, and the solutions—if any—will have to be societal ones.

Summary

- Mood disorders are those in which extreme variations in mood—either low or high—are the predominant feature. Although some variations in mood are normal, for some people the extremity of moods in either direction becomes seriously maladaptive, even to the extent of suicide.

- Most people with mood disorders have some form of unipolar depression—dysthymia or major depression. Such individuals experience a range of affective, cognitive, motivational, and biological symptoms including persistent sadness, negative thoughts about the self and the future, lack of energy or initiative, too much or too little sleep, and gaining or losing weight.

- Among biological causal factors for unipolar disorder, there is evidence of a moderate genetic contribution to the vulnerability for major depression and probably dysthymia as well. Moreover,

  major depressions are clearly associated with multiple interacting disturbances in neurochemical, neuroendocrine, and neurophysiological systems. Disruptions in circadian and seasonal rhythms are also prominent features of depression.

- Among psychosocial theories of the causes of unipolar depression are Beck's cognitive theory and the reformulated helplessness and hopelessness theories, which are formulated as diathesis-stress models, and a tendency to ruminate about one's mood or problems exacerbates their effects. The diathesis is cognitive in nature (e.g., dysfunctional beliefs and pessimistic attributional style, respectively), and stressful life events are often important in determining when those diatheses actually lead to depression.

- Personality variables such as neuroticism may also serve as diatheses for depression.

- Psychodynamic and interpersonal theories of unipolar depression emphasize the importance of early experiences (especially early losses and the quality of the parent–child relationship) as setting up a predisposition for depression.

- In the bipolar disorders (cyclothymia and bipolar I and II disorders), the person experiences episodes of both depression and hypomania or mania. During manic or hypomanic episodes, the symptoms are essentially the opposite of those experienced during a depressive episode.

- Biological causal factors probably play an even more prominent role for bipolar disorders than for unipolar disorders. The genetic contribution to bipolar disorder is among the strongest of such contributions to the major psychiatric disorders. Neurochemical imbalances, abnormalities of the hypothalamic-pituitary-adrenal axis, and disturbances in biological rhythms all play important roles in bipolar disorders.

- Stressful life events may be involved in precipitating manic or depressive episodes, but it is unlikely that they cause the disorder.

- Biologically based treatments such as medications or electroconvulsive therapy are often used in the treatment of the more severe major disorders. Increasingly, however, specific psychosocial treatments such as cognitive therapy, behavioral activation treatment, and interpersonal therapy are also being used to good effect in many cases of these more severe disorders as well as in the milder forms of mood disorder. Considerable evidence suggests that recurrent depression is best treated by specialized forms of psychotherapy or by maintenance on medications for prolonged periods.

- Suicide is a constant danger with depressive syndromes of any type or severity. Accordingly, an assessment of suicide risk is essential in the proper management of depressive disorders.

- A small minority of suicides appear unavoidable—chiefly those where the person really wants to die and uses a highly lethal method. However, a substantial amount of suicidal behavior is performed as a means of indirect interpersonal communication.

- Somewhere between these extremes is a large group of people who are ambivalent about killing themselves and who initiate dangerous actions that they may or may not carry to completion, depending on momentary events and impulses.

- Suicide prevention (or intervention) programs generally consist of crisis intervention in the form of suicide hotlines. Although these programs undoubtedly avert fatal suicide attempts in some cases, the long-term efficacy of treatment aimed at preventing suicide in those at high risk is much less clear at the present time.

Key Terms

attributions

behavioral activation treatment

bipolar disorder with a seasonal pattern

bipolar disorders

bipolar I disorder

bipolar II disorder

chronic major depressive disorder

cognitive-behavioral therapy (CBT) (cognitive therapy))

cyclothymic disorder

depression

depressogenic schemas

double depression

dysfunctional beliefs

dysthymic disorder

electroconvulsive therapy (ECT)

hypomanic episode

interpersonal therapy (IPT)

learned helplessness

lithium

major depressive disorder

major depressive episode

major depressive episode with atypical features

major depressive episode with catatonic features

major depressive episode with melancholic features

mania

manic episode

mixed episode

monoamine oxidase inhibitors (MAOIs)

mood congruent

mood disorders

negative automatic thoughts

negative cognitive triad

pessimistic attributional style

rapid cycling

recurrence

recurrent major depressive episode with a seasonal pattern

relapse

rumination

seasonal affective disorder

selective serotonin reuptake inhibitor (SSRI)

severe major depressive episode with psychotic features

specifiers

suicide

tricyclic antidepressants

unipolar depressive disorder

Glossary

Attribution. Process of assigning causes to things that happen.

Behavioral activation treatment. Treatment for depression in which the patient and the therapist work together to help the patient find ways to become more active and engaged with life.

Bipolar disorder with a seasonal pattern. Bipolar disorder with recurrences in particular seasons of the year.

Bipolar disorders. Mood disorders in which a person experiences both manic and depressive episodes.

Bipolar I disorder. A form of bipolar disorder in which the person experiences both manic (or mixed) episodes and major depressive episodes.

Bipolar II disorder. A form of bipolar disorder in which the person experiences both hypomanic episodes and major depressive episodes.

Chronic major depressive disorder. A disorder in which a major depressive episode does not remit over a two year period.

Cognitive-behavioral therapy (CBT). Therapy based on altering dysfunctional thoughts and cognitive distortions.

Cyclothymic disorder. Mild mood disorder characterized by cyclical periods of hypomanic and depressive symptoms.

Depression. Emotional state characterized by extraordinary sadness and dejection.

Depressogenic schemas. Dysfunctional beliefs that are rigid, extreme, and counterproductive and that are thought to leave one susceptible to depression when experiencing stress.

Double depression. This condition is diagnosed when a person with dysthymia has a superimposed major depressive episode.

Dysfunctional beliefs. Negative beliefs that are rigid, extreme, and counterproductive.

Dysthymic disorder. Moderately severe mood disorder characterized by a persistently depressed mood most of the day for more days than not for at least 2 years. Additional symptoms may include poor appetite, sleep disturbance, lack of energy, low self-esteem, difficulty concentrating, and feelings of hopelessness.

Electroconvulsive therapy (ECT). Use of electricity to produce convulsions and unconsciousness; a treatment used primarily to alleviate depressive and manic episodes. Also known as *electroshock therapy*.

Hypomanic episode. A condition lasting at least 4 days in which a person experiences abnormally elevated, expansive, or irritable mood. At least 3 out of 7 other designated symptoms similar to those in a manic episode must also be present but to a lesser degree than in mania.

Interpersonal therapy (IPT). A time-limited psychotherapy approach that focuses on the interpersonal context and on building interpersonal skills.

Learned helplessness. A theory that animals and people exposed to uncontrollable aversive events learn that they have no control over these events and this causes them to behave in a passive and helpless manner when later exposed to potentially controllable events. Later extended to become a theory of depression.

Lithium. A common salt that consists of a soft, silver-white metal; it has been found to reduce the symptoms of bipolar disorder although it has a number of negative side-effects.

Major depressive disorder. Moderate to severe mood disorder in which a person experiences only major depressive episodes but no hypomanic, manic or mixed episodes. *Single episode* if only one; *recurrent episode* if more than one.

Major depressive episode. A mental condition in which a person must be markedly depressed for most of every day for most days for at least 2 weeks. In addition, a total of at least 5 out of 9 designated symptoms must also be present during the same time period.

Major depressive episode with atypical features. A type of major depressive episode which includes a pattern of symptoms characterized by marked mood reactivity, as well as at least 2 out of 4 other designated symptoms.

Major depressive episode with catatonic features. A subset of major depression disorders that is characterized by severe disturbances in motor function.

Major depressive episode with melancholic features. A type of major depressive episode which includes marked symptoms of loss of interest or pleasure in almost all activities, plus at least 3 of 6 other designated symptoms.

Mania. Emotional state characterized by intense and unrealistic feelings of excitement and euphoria.

Manic episode. A condition in which a person shows markedly elevated, euphoric, or expansive mood, often interrupted by occasional outbursts of intense irritability or even violence that lasts for at least 1 week. In addition at least 3 out of 7 other designated symptoms must also occur.

Mixed episode. A condition in which a person is characterized by symptoms of both full-blown manic and major depressive episodes for at least 1 week, whether the symptoms are intermixed or alternate rapidly every few days.

Monoamine-oxidase inhibitors (MAOIs). Class of antidepressant drugs sometimes used for treating depression.

Mood congruent. Delusions or hallucinations that are consistent with a person's mood.

Mood disorders. Disturbances of mood that are intense and persistent enough to be clearly maladaptive.

Negative automatic thoughts. Thoughts that are just below the surface of awareness and that involve unpleasant pessimistic predictions.

Negative cognitive triad. Negative thoughts about the self, the world, and the future.

Pessimistic attributional style. Cognitive style involving a tendency to make internal, stable, and global attributions for negative life events.

Rapid cycling. A pattern of bipolar disorder involving at least four manic or depressive episodes per year.

Recurrence. A new occurrence of a disorder after a remission of symptom.

Recurrent major depressive episode with a seasonal pattern. A form of major depression where the episodes of depression recur on a regular seasonal basis (fall/winter), but not at other times of the year.

Relapse. Return of the symptoms of a disorder after a fairly short period of time.

Rumination. Refers to the process of going over and over in one's mind or going over a thought repeatedly time and again.

Seasonal affective disorder. Mood disorder involving at least two episodes of depression in the past two years occurring at the same time of year (most commonly fall or winter), with remission also occurring at the same time of year (most commonly spring).

Selective serotonin reuptake inhibitors (SSRIs). A medication that inhibits serotonin that is use in the treatment of depression

Severe major depressive episode with psychotic features. Major depression involving loss of contact with reality, often in the form of delusions or hallucinations.

Specifiers (in mood disorders). Different patterns of symptoms that sometimes characterize major depressive episodes which may help predict the course and preferred treatments for the condition.

Suicide. Taking one's own life.

Tricyclic antidepressants. Medications used to treat depression, and sometimes anxiety disorders, that are thought to block the reuptake of norepinephrine and serotonin at the synapse.

Unipolar depressive disorder. Mood disorder in which a person experiences only depressive episodes, as opposed to bipolar disorder, in which both manic and depressive episodes occur.

Photo Credits

Text Credits

Somatoform and Dissociative Disorders

What Are Somatoform Disorders?

Hypochondriasis

Somatization Disorder

Pain Disorder

Conversion Disorder

Distinguishing Somatization, Pain, and Conversion Disorders
from Malingering and Factitious Disorder

Body Dysmorphic Disorder

What Are Dissociative Disorders?

Depersonalization Disorder

Dissociative Amnesia and Dissociative Fugue

Dissociative Identity Disorder (DID)

Sociocultural Factors in Dissociative Disorders

Treatment and Outcomes in Dissociative Disorders

Unresolved Issues

DID and the Reality of "Recovered Memories"

From Chapter 8 of *Abnormal Psychology*, Fifteenth Edition. James N. Butcher, Susan Mineka, Jill M. Hooley. Copyright © 2013 by Pearson Education, Inc. All rights reserved.

Have you ever had the experience, particularly during a time of serious stress, when you felt like you were walking around in a daze or like you just weren't all there? Or have you known people who constantly complained about being sure they had a serious illness even though several medical tests their doctor had performed failed to show anything wrong? Both of these are examples of mild dissociative and somatoform symptoms experienced at least occasionally by many people. However, when these symptoms become frequent and severe and lead to significant distress or impairment, a somatoform or dissociative disorder may be diagnosed. *Somatoform* and *dissociative disorders* appear to involve more complex and puzzling patterns of symptoms than those we have so far encountered. As a result, they confront the field of psychopathology with some of its most fascinating and difficult challenges. Unfortunately, however, we do not know much about them—in part because many of them are quite rare and difficult to study.

Both somatoform and dissociative disorders were once included with the various anxiety disorders (and neurotic depression) under the general rubric *neuroses*, where anxiety was thought to be the underlying cause of all neuroses whether or not the anxiety was experienced overtly. But in 1980, when *DSM-III* abandoned attempts to link disorders together on the basis of hypothesized underlying causes (as in neurotic disorders) and instead focused on grouping disorders together on the basis of overt symptomatology, the anxiety, mood, somatoform, and dissociative disorders each became separate categories.

What Are Somatoform Disorders?

The **somatoform disorders** are a group of conditions that involve physical symptoms and complaints suggesting the presence of a medical condition but without any evidence of physical pathology to account for them (APA, 2000). In other words, they involved medically unexplained physical symptoms (Witthöft & Hiller, 2010). Despite a wide range of clinical manifestations, in each case the person is preoccupied with some aspect of her or his health or appearance to the extent that she or he shows significant impairments in functioning. **Soma** means "body," and somatoform disorders involve patterns in which individuals complain of bodily symptoms or defects that suggest the presence of medical problems but for which no organic basis can be found that satisfactorily explains the symptoms such as paralysis or pain. Such individuals are typically preoccupied with their state of health and with various presumed disorders or diseases of bodily organs. Equally key to these disorders is the fact that the affected patients have no control over their symptoms. They are also not intentionally faking symptoms or attempting to deceive others. For the most part, they genuinely and sometimes passionately believe something is terribly wrong with their bodies and so they frequently

show up in the practices of primary-care physicians, who then have the difficult task of managing their complaints, which have no known medical basis.

Sometimes, of course, people do deliberately and consciously feign disability or illness. For these instances, the *DSM* distinguishes between *malingering* and *factitious disorder* on the basis of the feigning person's apparent goals. In **malingering** the person is intentionally producing or grossly exaggerating physical symptoms and is motivated by external incentives such as avoiding work or military service or evading criminal prosecution (APA, 2000; Maldonado & Spiegel, 2001). In **factitious disorder** the person also intentionally produces psychological or physical symptoms (or both), but there are no external incentives. Instead, the person's goal is simply to obtain and maintain the personal benefits that playing the "sick role" (even undergoing repeated hospitalizations) may provide, including the attention and concern of family and medical personnel.

In our discussion, we will focus on five more or less distinct somatoform patterns that have been identified: (1) hypochondriasis, (2) somatization disorder, (3) pain disorder, (4) conversion disorder, and (5) body dysmorphic disorder. However, as discussed in Box 1, there has been a great deal of debate in the literature about whether this is the optimal way to categorize and label these disorders.

Hypochondriasis

According to *DSM-IV-TR*, people with **hypochondriasis** are preoccupied either with fears of contracting a serious disease or with the idea that they actually have such a disease even though they do not. Their very distressing preoccupations are all based on a misinterpretation of one or more bodily signs or symptoms (e.g., being convinced that their slight cough is a sign of lung cancer). Of course the decision that a hypochondriacal complaint is based on a misinterpretation of bodily signs or symptoms can be made only after a thorough medical evaluation does not find a medical condition that could account for the signs or symptoms. Another defining criterion for hypochondriasis is that the person is not reassured by the results of a medical evaluation; that is, the fear or idea of having a disease persists despite medical reassurance. Indeed, these individuals are sometimes disappointed when no physical problem is found. Finally, the condition must persist for at least 6 months for the diagnosis to be made so as to not diagnose relatively transient health concerns.

Not surprisingly, people with hypochondriasis usually first go to a medical doctor with their physical complaints. Because they are never reassured for long and are inclined to suspect that their doctor has missed something, they sometimes shop for additional doctors, hoping one might discover what their problem really is. Because they repeatedly seek medical advice (e.g., Bleichart & Hiller, 2006; Fink et al., 2004), it is not surprising that their yearly medical costs are much higher than those of most of the rest of the population (e.g., Fink et al., 2010; Hiller et al., 2004). These individuals generally resist the idea that their problem is a

Criteria for Hypochondriasis

A. Preoccupation with fears of having, or the idea that one has, a serious disease based on the person's misinterpretation of bodily symptoms.

B. The preoccupation persists despite appropriate medical evaluation and reassurance.

C. The belief in Criterion A is not of delusional intensity (as in Delusional Disorder, Somatic Type) and is not restricted to a circumscribed concern about appearance (as in Body Dysmorphic Disorder).

D. The preoccupation causes clinically significant distress or impairment in social, occupational, or other important areas of functioning.

E. The duration of the disturbance is at least 6 months.

F. The preoccupation is not better accounted for by Generalized Anxiety Disorder, Obsessive-Compulsive Disorder, Panic Disorder, a Major Depressive Episode, Separation Anxiety, or another Somatoform Disorder.

Source: Reprinted with permission from the American Psychiatric Association. *Diagnostic and Statistical Manual of Mental Disorders*, Fourth Edition, *Text Revision* (Copyright © 2000). American Psychiatric Association.

psychological one that might best be treated by a psychologist or psychiatrist.

Hypochondriasis may be one of the two most commonly seen somatoform disorders with a prevalence in general medical practice officially estimated at between 2 and 7 percent (APA, 2000). It occurs about equally often in men and women and can start at almost any age, although early adulthood is the most common age of onset. Once hypochondriasis develops, it tends to be a chronic disorder if left untreated, although the severity may wax and wane over time. Individuals with hypochondriasis often also suffer from mood disorders, panic disorder, or other somatoform disorders (especially somatization disorder; Creed & Barsky, 2004).

MAJOR CHARACTERISTICS Individuals with hypochondriasis are often highly preoccupied with bodily functions (e.g., heart beats or bowel movements) or with minor physical abnormalities (e.g., a small sore or an occasional cough) or with vague and ambiguous physical sensations (such as a "tired heart" or "aching veins"; APA, 2000). They attribute these symptoms to a suspected disease and often have intrusive thoughts about it. The diagnoses they make for themselves range from tuberculosis to cancer, exotic infections, AIDS, and numerous other diseases.

Although people with hypochondriasis are usually in good physical condition, they are sincere in their conviction that the symptoms they detect represent real illness. They are not *malingering*—consciously faking symptoms to achieve specific goals such as winning a personal injury lawsuit. Not surprisingly, given their tendency to doubt the soundness of their doctors' conclusions (i.e., that they have no medical problem) and recommendations, the doctor–patient relationships are often marked by conflict and hostility.

The following case captures a typical clinical picture in hypochondriasis and incidentally demonstrates that a high level of medical sophistication does not necessarily rule out a person's developing this disorder.

case study An "Abdominal Mass"

This 38-year-old physician/radiologist initiated his first psychiatric consultation after his 9-year-old son accidentally discovered his father palpating (examining by touch) his own abdomen and said, "What do you think it is this time, Dad?" The radiologist describes the incident and his accompanying anger and shame with tears in his eyes. He also describes his recent return from a 10-day stay at a famous out-of-state medical diagnostic center to which he had been referred by an exasperated gastroenterologist colleague who had reportedly "reached the end of the line" with his radiologist patient. The extensive physical and laboratory examinations performed at the center had revealed no significant physical disease, a conclusion the patient reports with resentment and disappointment rather than relief.

The patient's history reveals a long-standing pattern of over-concern about personal health matters, beginning at age 13 and exacerbated by his medical school experience. Until fairly recently, however, he had maintained reasonable control over these concerns, in part because he was embarrassed to reveal them to other physicians. He is conscientious and successful in his profession and active in community life. His wife, like his son, has become increasingly impatient with his morbid preoccupation about life-threatening but undetectable diseases.

In describing his current symptoms, the patient refers to his becoming increasingly aware, over the past several months, of various sounds and sensations emanating from his abdomen and of his sometimes being able to feel a "firm mass" in its left lower quadrant. His tentative diagnosis is carcinoma (cancer) of the colon. He tests his stool for blood weekly and palpates his abdomen for 15 to 20 minutes every 2 to 3 days. He has performed several X-ray studies of himself in secrecy after hours at his office.

Source: Adapted with permission from *DSM-IV-TR Casebook: A Learning Companion to the Diagnostic and Statistical Manual of Mental Disorders*, Fourth Edition, *Text Revision* (pp. 88–90). Washington, DC: (Copyright © 2002). American Psychiatric Association.

Individuals with hypochondriasis are preoccupied with health matters and unrealistic fears of disease. They are convinced that they have symptoms of physical illness, but their complaints typically do not conform to any coherent symptom pattern, and they usually have trouble giving a precise description of their symptoms.

CAUSAL FACTORS IN HYPOCHONDRIASIS Knowledge of causal factors in somatoform disorders, including hypochondriasis, is quite minimal compared to that of many other Axis I disorders such as mood and anxiety disorders. Today many people think hypochondriasis is closely related to the anxiety disorders. Indeed, many researchers currently prefer the term *health anxiety* to *hypochondriasis*—even though the term *health anxiety* usually refers to a broader spectrum of dysfunctional health concerns that may not qualify for a diagnosis of hypochondriasis and yet cause clinically significant distress (e.g., Marcus, Gurley et al., 2007; Taylor & Asmundson, 2004). Currently, cognitive-behavioral views of hypochondriasis are perhaps most widely accepted and have as a central tenet that it is a disorder of cognition and perception. Misinterpretations of bodily sensations are currently a defining feature of the syndrome, but in the cognitive-behavioral view these misinterpretations also play a causal role. It is believed that an individual's past experiences with illnesses (in both him- or herself and others, and as observed in the mass media) lead to the development of a set of dysfunctional assumptions about symptoms and diseases that may predispose a person to developing hypochondriasis (Marcus, Gurley et al., 2007; Salkovskis & Warwick, 2001). These dysfunctional assumptions might include notions such as,

"Bodily changes are usually a sign of serious disease, because every symptom has to have an identifiable physical cause" or "If you don't go to the doctor as soon as you notice anything unusual, then it will be too late" (Salkovskis & Bass, 1997, p. 318; see also Marcus, Gurley, et al., 2007).

Because of these dysfunctional assumptions, individuals with hypochondriasis seem to focus excessive attention on symptoms, with experimental studies showing that these individuals do in fact have an attentional bias for illness-related information (Owens et al., 2004; see also Jasper & Witthöft, 2011). Although their physical sensations per se probably do not differ from those in normal controls (Marcus, Gurley et al., 2007), they perceive their symptoms as more dangerous than they really are and judge a particular disease to be more likely or dangerous than it really is. Once they have misinterpreted a symptom, they tend to look for confirming evidence and to discount evidence that they are in good health; in fact, they seem to believe that being healthy means being completely symptom-free (Rief, Hiller, & Margraf et al., 1998). They also perceive their probability of being able to cope with the illness as extremely low (Salkovskis & Bass, 1997) and see themselves as weak and unable to tolerate physical effort or exercise (Rief, Hiller, & Margraf et al., 1998). All this tends to create a vicious cycle in which their anxiety about illness and symptoms results in physiological symptoms of anxiety, which then provide further fuel for their convictions that they are ill.

If we also consider the secondary reinforcements that individuals with hypochondriasis obtain by virtue of their disorder, we can better understand how such patterns of thought and behavior are maintained in spite of the misery these individuals often experience. Most of us learn as children that when we are sick special comforts and attention are provided and, furthermore, that we may be excused from a number of responsibilities. Barsky and colleagues (1994) found that their patients with hypochondriasis reported much childhood sickness and missing of school. People with hypochondriasis also tend to have an excessive amount of illness in their families while growing up, which may lead to strong memories of being sick or in pain (Pauli & Alpers, 2002), and perhaps also of having observed some of the secondary benefits that sick people sometimes reap (Cote et al., 1996; Kellner, 1985).

Interestingly, one study retested patients with hypochondriasis 4 to 5 years later and found that those who had remitted at follow-up had acquired significantly more (real) major medical problems than their nonremitting counterparts (Barsky et al., 1998). In other words, it appears that hypochondriacal tendencies were reduced by the occurrence of serious medical conditions. The authors suggested that having a serious medical illness "served to legitimize the patients' complaints, sanction their assumption of the sick role, and lessen the skepticism with which they had previously been regarded . . . . As one noted, 'Now that I know Dr. X is paying attention to me, I can believe him if he says nothing serious is wrong'" (p. 744).

TREATMENT OF HYPOCHONDRIASIS More than a dozen studies on cognitive-behavioral treatment of hypochondriasis have found that it can be a very effective treatment for hypochondriasis (e.g., Barsky & Ahern, 2004; Tyrer et al., 2011; see also

Hedman et al., 2011, for an example of Internet-based CBT). The cognitive components of this treatment approach focus on assessing the patient's beliefs about illness and modifying misinterpretations of bodily sensations. The behavioral techniques include having patients induce innocuous symptoms by intentionally focusing on parts of their body so that they can learn that selective perception of bodily sensations plays a major role in their symptoms. Sometimes they are also directed to engage in response prevention by not checking their bodies as they usually do and by stopping their constant seeking of reassurance. The treatment is relatively brief (6 to 16 sessions) and can be delivered in a group format. In these studies such treatment produced large changes in hypochondriacal symptoms and beliefs as well as in levels of anxiety and depression. There is also some preliminary evidence that certain antidepressant medications (especially SSRIs) may be effective in treating hypochondriasis, although they may not be as helpful to a high percentage of afflicted individuals as is cognitive-behavior therapy (e.g., Fallon, 2004; Greeven et al., 2007).

Somatization Disorder

Somatization disorder is characterized by many different complaints of physical ailments, over at least several years beginning before age 30, that are not adequately explained by independent findings of physical illness or injury and that lead to medical treatment or to significant life impairment. Not surprisingly, therefore, somatization disorder is seen most often among patients in primary medical care settings in cultures all over the world (Guerje et al., 1997; Iezzi et al., 2001). Indeed, patients with somatization disorder are enormously costly to health care systems because they often have multiple unnecessary hospitalizations and surgeries (Barsky et al., 2005; Hiller et al., 2003).

In addition to the requirement of multiple physical complaints that are not intentionally produced or faked, *DSM-IV-TR* (APA, 2000) lists symptoms from four other symptom categories that must be met at some time during the course of the disorder before a diagnosis of somatization disorder can be made. The four other symptom categories in which symptoms must have occurred are:

1. **Four Pain Symptoms** experienced with respect to at least four different sites or functions—for example, head, abdomen, back, joints, or rectum, or during sexual intercourse or urination.

2. **Two Gastrointestinal Symptoms** other than pain, such as nausea, bloating, diarrhea, or vomiting when not pregnant.

3. **One Sexual Symptom** other than pain, such as sexual indifference or dysfunction, menstrual irregularity, or vomiting throughout pregnancy.

4. **One Pseudoneurological Symptom** suggestive of a neurological condition such as various symptoms that mimic sensory or motor impairments like loss of sensation or involuntary muscle contraction in a hand.

DSM-IV-TR

Criteria for Somatization Disorder

A. A history of many physical complaints beginning before age 30 years that occur over a period of several years and result in treatment being sought or significant impairment in social, occupational, or other important areas of functioning.

B. Each of the following criteria must have been met, with individual symptoms occurring at any time during the course of the disturbance:
  1. four pain symptoms: a history of pain related to at least four different sites or functions (e.g., head, abdomen, back, joints, extremities, chest, rectum, during menstruation, during sexual intercourse, or during urination)
  2. two gastrointestinal symptoms: a history of at least two gastrointestinal symptoms other than pain (e.g., nausea, bloating, vomiting other than during pregnancy, diarrhea, or intolerance of several different foods)
  3. one sexual symptom: a history of at least one sexual or reproductive symptom other than pain (e.g., sexual indifference, erectile or ejaculatory dysfunction, irregular menses, excessive menstrual bleeding, vomiting throughout pregnancy)
  4. one pseudoneurological symptom: a history of at least one symptom or deficit suggesting a neurological condition not limited to pain (conversion symptoms such as impaired coordination or balance, paralysis or localized weakness, difficulty swallowing or lump in throat, aphonia, urinary retention, hallucinations, loss of touch or pain sensation, double vision, blindness, deafness, seizures; dissociative symptoms such as amnesia; or loss of consciousness other than fainting)

C. Either (1) or (2):
  1. after appropriate investigation, each of the symptoms in Criterion B cannot be fully explained by a known general medical condition or the direct effects of a substance (e.g., a drug of abuse, a medication)
  2. when there is a related general medical condition, the physical complaints or resulting social or occupational impairment are in excess of what would be expected from the history, physical examination, or laboratory findings

D. The symptoms are not intentionally produced or feigned (as in Factitious Disorder or Malingering).

Source: Reprinted with permission from the American Psychiatric Association. *Diagnostic and Statistical Manual of Mental Disorders*, Fourth Edition, *Text Revision* (Copyright © 2000). American Psychiatric Association.

Thus to qualify for a diagnosis of somatization disorder, a patient must have experienced a total of at least 8 of the 33 specified symptoms (Rief & Barsky, 2005). It should be noted, however, that many researchers today also include patients with "somatization syndrome" in their studies. These constitute a larger number of individuals who do not meet these strict criteria for somatization disorder but who have at least 8 somatoform symptoms of any type (e.g., Rief & Broadbent, 2007).

If the symptoms of somatization disorder seem similar to you in some ways to those of hypochondriasis, that is because there are indeed significant similarities between the two conditions (and they sometimes co-occur; Mai, 2004), but according to *DSM-IV-TR* there are also enough distinguishing features that they are considered two separate disorders. For example, although both disorders are characterized by preoccupation with physical symptoms, only people with hypochondriasis tend to be convinced that they have an organic disease. Moreover, with hypochondriasis the person usually has only one or a few primary symptoms, but in somatization disorder, by definition, there are multiple symptoms. Nevertheless, given their similarities, some leading researchers in this area have concluded that it is as yet unclear whether they really are two separate disorders (e.g., Creed & Barsky, 2004). See Box 1.

The main features of somatization disorder are illustrated in the following case summary, which also involves a secondary diagnosis of depression.

case study   Not-Yet-Discovered Illness

This 38-year-old married woman, the mother of five children, reports to a mental health clinic with the chief complaint of depression, meeting diagnostic criteria for major depressive disorder . . . . Her marriage has been a chronically unhappy one; her husband is described as an alcoholic with an unstable work history, and there have been frequent arguments revolving around finances, her sexual indifference, and her complaints of pain during intercourse.

The history reveals that the patient . . . describes herself as nervous since childhood and as having been continuously sickly beginning in her youth. She experiences chest pain and reportedly has been told by doctors that she has a "nervous heart." She sees physicians frequently for abdominal pain, having been diagnosed on one occasion as having a "spastic colon." In addition to M.D. physicians, she has consulted chiropractors and osteopaths for backaches, pains in her extremities, and a feeling of anesthesia in her fingertips. She was recently admitted to a hospital following complaints of abdominal and chest pain and of vomiting, during which admission she received a hysterectomy. Following the surgery she has been troubled by spells of anxiety, fainting, vomiting, food intolerance, and weakness and fatigue. Physical examinations reveal completely negative findings.

Source: Adapted with permission from *DSM-IV-TR Casebook: A Learning Companion to the Diagnostic and Statistical Manual of Mental Disorders,* Fourth Edition, *Text Revision* (pp. 404–5). Washington, DC. (Copyright © 2002). American Psychiatric Association.

DEMOGRAPHICS, COMORBIDITY, AND COURSE OF ILLNESS Somatization disorder usually begins in adolescence and is believed by many to be about three to ten times more common among women than among men. It also tends to occur more among less educated individuals and in lower socioeconomic classes. The lifetime prevalence has been estimated to be between 0.2 and 2.0 percent in women and less than 0.2 percent in men (APA, 2000). Somatization disorder very commonly co-occurs with several other disorders including major depression, panic disorder, phobic disorders, and generalized anxiety disorder. It has generally been considered to be a relatively chronic condition with a poor prognosis, although sometimes the disorder remits spontaneously (e.g., Creed & Barsky, 2004).

CAUSAL FACTORS IN SOMATIZATION DISORDER Despite its significant prevalence in medical settings, we remain quite uncertain about the developmental course and specific etiology of somatization disorder. There is evidence that somatization disorder runs in families and that there is a familial linkage between antisocial personality disorder in men and somatization disorder in women. That is, one possibility is that some common, underlying predisposition, probably at least partly genetically based, leads to antisocial behavior in men and to somatization disorder in women (Cale & Lilienfeld, 2002b; Guze et al., 1986; Lilienfeld, 1992). Moreover, somatic symptoms and antisocial symptoms in women tend to co-occur (Cale & Lilienfeld, 2002b). However, we do not yet have a clear understanding of this relationship. One possibility is that the two disorders may be linked through a common trait of impulsivity, but the nature of this relationship is not yet understood.

Other possible contributory causal factors probably include an interaction of personality, cognitive, and learning variables. People high on neuroticism who come from certain kinds of family backgrounds may develop a tendency to misinterpret their bodily sensations as threatening or even disabling. This might be especially likely in families where a child is frequently exposed to models complaining of pain and vicariously learns that complaining about physical symptoms can lead to the garnering of sympathy and attention (social reinforcement) and even to avoidance of responsibilities. (This may be especially common in rather disorganized and uncohesive families with inconsistent parental care—more often from lower socioeconomic classes.)

It has also become clear that people with somatization disorder selectively attend to, and show perceptual amplification of, bodily sensations. They also tend to see bodily *sensations* as somatic *symptoms* (Martin, Buech et al., 2007). Like patients with hypochondriasis, they tend to catastrophize about minor bodily complaints (taking them as signs of serious physical illness) and to think of themselves as physically weak and unable to tolerate stress or physical activity (Martin, Buech et al., 2007; Rief et al., 1998). One possible scenario suggested by Rief, Hiller, & Margraf et al. (1998) is that a vicious cycle may develop. If one thinks of oneself as being weak, has low tolerance for pain and stress, and selectively attends to bodily sensations (while assuming that being healthy equals being without bodily sensations), one will avoid many daily activities that require much exertion, including physical activity. Ironically, however, lowered physical activity can lead to being physically unfit, which can in turn increase bodily sensations about which to catastrophize. Moreover, selectively attending to bodily sensations may actually increase the intensity of the sensations, further exacerbating the vicious cycle. Finally, Rief, Miller, and Margraf (1998) also found that patients with somatization disorder have elevated levels of cortisol (a stress hormone) and do not show normal habituation to psychological stressors. Thus the physiological arousal caused by psychological stressors may remain elevated and may further contribute to the bodily sensations that individuals suffering from this condition worry about (Rief & Barsky, 2005).

TREATMENT OF SOMATIZATION DISORDER Somatization disorder has long been considered to be extremely difficult to treat, and general practitioners experience a great deal of uncertainty and frustration in working with these patients. However, in the past decade some treatment research has begun to suggest that a certain type of medical management along with cognitive-behavioral treatments may be quite helpful and that general practitioners can be educated in how to better manage and treat somatization patients and be less frustrated by them (Rosendal et al., 2005; see also Edwards et al., 2010). One moderately effective treatment involves identifying one physician who will integrate the patient's care by seeing the patient at regular visits (thereby trying to anticipate the appearance of new problems) and by providing physical exams focused on new complaints (thereby accepting her or his

When one physician integrates a patient's care, the physical functioning of patients with somatization disorder may improve. Why is this so?

symptoms as valid). At the same time, however, the physician avoids unnecessary diagnostic testing and makes minimal use of medications or other therapies (Looper & Kirmayer, 2002; Mai, 2004). Several studies have found that these patients show substantial decreases in health care expenditures over subsequent months and sometimes an improvement in physical functioning (although not necessarily in psychological distress; e.g., Rost et al., 1994). This type of medical management

1 THE WORLD AROUND US

Somatoform Disorders: *DSM-5* Proposed Revisions

At the time this text was most recently revised, a work group examining what changes should be made for *DSM 5* for somatoform disorders had made several provisional recommendations. Among these recommendations are the following:

- The category of somatoform disorders would be renamed to "somatic symptom disorders" because it is thought that the current terminology is confusing and because other conditions besides somatoform disorders (psychological factors affecting medical conditions, factitious disorder) share their core feature—reporting physical symptoms or a concern about a physical health problem.
- Because it is difficult to reliably rule out a medical explanation for symptoms, "medically unexplained symptoms" would no longer be emphasized as a core feature of somatic symptom disorders.
- Somatization disorder, hypochondriasis, and somatoform pain disorder would be combined into a single, common disorder named complex somatic symptom disorder when present chronically (i.e., for 6 months or more) because they share features including somatic symptoms and cognitive distortions. When there are fewer cognitive distortions or when symptoms are present for less than

6 months, but more than 1 month, the diagnosis would be simple somatic symptom disorder.

- Based on available research, the work group expects that most patients previously diagnosed with hypochondriasis will be diagnosed with complex somatic symptom disorder. However, some patients with hypochondriasis have very minimal somatic symptoms and are instead preoccupied with a *worry* that they are sick. These patients would be diagnosed with illness anxiety disorder.
- Conversion disorder may be renamed functional neurological disorder; however, this decision is still actively under discussion. Diagnosing this disorder would no longer require that the clinician establish that (1) the patient is not feigning symptoms, as this is very difficult to prove, or (2) there are psychological factors present.
- Body dysmorphic disorder is being reviewed by the anxiety disorders work group and, depending upon the conclusions drawn, may be moved to that section or may instead be integrated into complex somatic symptom disorder.

Source: American Psychiatric Association. *DSM-5* development. Retrieved 27 September, 2011, from http://www.dsm5.org/ProposedRevision/Pages/SomaticSymptomDisorders.aspx

can be even more effective when combined with cognitive-behavioral therapy that focuses on promoting appropriate behavior, such as better coping and personal adjustment, and discouraging inappropriate behavior such as illness behavior and preoccupation with physical symptoms (e.g., Bleichhardt et al., 2004; Mai, 2004). As with hypochondriasis, the focus is on changing the way the patient thinks about bodily sensations, teaching a variety of coping strategies, and reducing any secondary gain the patients may receive from physicians and family members.

Pain Disorder

The symptoms of somatoform pain disorder resemble the pain symptoms seen in somatization disorder; but with pain disorder the other kinds of symptoms of somatization disorder are not present. Thus **pain disorder** is characterized by the experience of persistent and severe pain in one or more areas of the body that is not intentionally produced or feigned. Although a medical condition may contribute to the pain, psychological factors must be judged to play an important role. The pain disorder may be *acute* (duration of less than 6 months) or *chronic* (duration of over 6 months). In approaching the phenomenon of somatoform pain disorder, it is very important to remember that the pain that is experienced is very real and can hurt as much as pain with purely medical causes. It is also important to note that pain is always, in part, a subjective experience that is private and cannot be objectively identified by others.

The prevalence of pain disorder in the general population is unknown. It is definitely quite common among patients at pain clinics. It is diagnosed more frequently in women than in men and is very frequently comorbid with anxiety or mood disorders, which may occur first or may arise later as a consequence

The experience of pain is always subjective and private, making pain impossible to assess with pinpoint accuracy. Pain does not always exist in perfect correlation with observable tissue damage or irritation.

of the pain disorder (APA, 2000). People with pain disorder are often unable to work (they sometimes go on disability) or to perform some other usual daily activities. Their resulting inactivity (including an avoidance of physical activity) and social isolation may lead to depression and to a loss of physical strength and endurance. This fatigue and loss of strength can then exacerbate the pain in a kind of vicious cycle (Bouman et al., 1999; Flor et al., 1990). In addition, the behavioral component of pain is quite malleable in the sense that it can increase when it is reinforced by attention, sympathy, or avoidance of unwanted activities (Bouman et al., 1999). Finally, there is suggestive evidence that people who have a tendency to catastrophize about the meaning and effects of pain may be the ones most likely to progress to a state of chronic pain (Seminowicz & Davis, 2006).

TREATMENT OF PAIN DISORDER Perhaps because it is a less complex and multifaceted disorder than somatization disorder, pain disorder is usually easier to treat. Indeed, cognitive-behavioral techniques have been widely used in the treatment of both physical and psychogenic pain syndromes. Treatment programs using these techniques generally include relaxation training, support and validation that the pain is real, scheduling of daily activities, cognitive restructuring, and reinforcement of "no-pain" behaviors (Simon, 2002). Patients receiving such treatments tend to show substantial reductions in disability and distress, although changes in the intensity of their pain tend to be smaller in magnitude. In addition, antidepressant medications (especially the tricyclic antidepressants) and certain SSRIs have been shown to reduce pain

DSM-IV-TR

Criteria for Pain Disorder

Pain Disorder Associated With Psychological Factors: psychological factors are judged to have the major role in the onset, severity, exacerbation, or maintenance of the pain. (If a general medical condition is present, it does not have a major role in the onset, severity, exacerbation, or maintenance of the pain.) This type of Pain Disorder is not diagnosed if criteria are also met for Somatization Disorder.

Pain Disorder Associated With Both Psychological Factors and a General Medical Condition: both psychological factors and a general medical condition are judged to have important roles in the onset, severity, exacerbation, or maintenance of the pain. The associated general medical condition or anatomical site of the pain (see below) is coded on Axis III.

Source: Reprinted with permission from the American Psychiatric Association. *Diagnostic and Statistical Manual of Mental Disorders*, Fourth Edition, *Text Revision* (Copyright © 2000). American Psychiatric Association.

intensity in a manner independent of the effects the medications may have on mood (Aragona et al., 2005; Simon, 2002).

Conversion Disorder

Conversion disorder involves a pattern in which symptoms or deficits affecting sensory or voluntary motor functions lead one to think that a patient has a medical or neurological condition. However, upon a thorough medical examination, it becomes apparent that the pattern of symptoms or deficits cannot be fully explained by any known medical condition. A few typical examples include partial paralysis, blindness, deafness, and pseudoseizures. In addition, psychological factors must be judged to play an important role in the symptoms or deficits because the symptoms usually either start or are exacerbated by preceding emotional or interpersonal conflicts or stressors. Finally, the person must not be intentionally producing or faking the symptoms (APA, 2000).

Early observations dating back to Freud suggested that most people with conversion disorder showed very little of the anxiety and fear that would be expected in a person with a paralyzed arm or loss of sight. This seeming lack of concern (known as *la belle indifférence*—French for "the beautiful indifference") in the way the patient describes what is wrong was thought for a long time to be an important diagnostic criterion for conversion disorder. However, more careful research later showed that *la belle indifférence* actually occurs in only about 20 percent of

DSM-IV-TR

Criteria for Conversion Disorder

A. One or more symptoms or deficits affecting voluntary motor or sensory function that suggest a neurological or other general medical condition.

B. Psychological factors are judged to be associated with the symptom or deficit because the initiation or exacerbation of the symptom or deficit is preceded by conflicts or other stressors.

C. The symptom or deficit is not intentionally produced or feigned (as in Factitious Disorder or Malingering).

D. The symptom or deficit cannot, after appropriate investigation, be fully explained by a general medical condition, or by the direct effects of a substance, or as a culturally sanctioned behavior or experience.

E. The symptom or deficit causes clinically significant distress or impairment in social, occupational, or other important areas of functioning or warrants medical evaluation.

F. The symptom or deficit is not limited to pain or sexual dysfunction, does not occur exclusively during the course of Somatization Disorder, and is not better accounted for by another mental disorder.

Source: Reprinted with permission from the American Psychiatric Association. *Diagnostic and Statistical Manual of Mental Disorders*, Fourth Edition, *Text Revision* (Copyright © 2000). American Psychiatric Association.

patients with conversion disorder, so it has been dropped as a criterion from recent editions of the *DSM* (Stone et al., 2006). Conversion disorder is one of the most intriguing and baffling patterns in psychopathology, and we still have much to learn about it. The term *conversion disorder* is relatively recent, and historically this disorder was one of several disorders that were grouped together under the term **hysteria** (the others being somatization disorder and hysterical neurosis—dissociative type; see Developments in Thinking 3).

Freud used the term *conversion hysteria* for these disorders (which were fairly common in his practice) because he believed that the symptoms were an expression of repressed sexual energy—that is, the *unconscious conflict* that a person felt about his or her sexual desires was repressed. However, in Freud's view, the repressed anxiety threatens to become conscious, so it is unconsciously *converted* into a bodily disturbance, thereby allowing the person to avoid having to deal with the conflict. For example, a person's guilty feelings about the desire to masturbate might be solved by developing a paralyzed hand. This is not done consciously, of course, and the person is not aware of the origin or meaning of the physical symptom. Freud also thought that the reduction in anxiety and intrapsychic conflict was the "primary gain" that maintained the condition, but he noted that patients often had many sources of "secondary gain" as well, such as receiving sympathy and attention from loved ones.

PRECIPITATING CIRCUMSTANCES, ESCAPE, AND SECONDARY GAINS Freud's theory that conversion symptoms are caused by the conversion of sexual conflicts or other psychological problems into physical symptoms is no longer accepted outside psychodynamic circles. However, many of Freud's astute clinical observations about primary and secondary gain are still incorporated into contemporary views of conversion disorder. Although the condition is still called a conversion disorder, the physical symptoms are usually seen as serving the rather obvious function of providing a plausible bodily "excuse" enabling an individual to escape or avoid an intolerably stressful situation without having to take responsibility for doing so. Typically, it is thought that the person first experiences a traumatic event that motivates the desire to escape the unpleasant situation, but literal escape may not be feasible or socially acceptable. Moreover, although becoming sick or disabled is more socially acceptable, this is true only if the person's motivation to do so is unconscious.

Thus, in contemporary terms, the **primary gain** for conversion symptoms is continued escape or avoidance of a stressful situation. Because this is all unconscious (that is, the person sees no relation between the symptoms and the stressful situation), the symptoms go away only if the stressful situation has been removed or resolved. Relatedly, the term **secondary gain**, which originally referred to advantages that the symptom(s) bestow beyond the "primary gain" of neutralizing intrapsychic conflict, has also been retained. Generally, it is used to refer to any "external" circumstance, such as attention from loved ones or financial compensation, that would tend to reinforce the maintenance of disability.

Given the important role attributed to stressful life events in precipitating the onset of conversion disorder, it is unfortunate that little is actually known about the exact nature and timing of these psychological stress factors (Roelofs et al., 2005). However, one study compared the frequency of stressful life events in the recent past in patients with conversion disorder and depressed controls and did not find a difference in frequency between them (and it is well known that stressful life events often precipitate depressive episodes). Moreover, the greater the negative impact of the preceding life events, the greater the severity of the conversion disorder symptoms (Roelofs et al., 2005). Another study compared levels of a neurobiological marker of stress (lower levels of brain-derived neurotropic factor) in individuals with conversion disorder versus major depression versus no disorder. Both those with depression and those with conversion disorder showed reduced levels of this marker relative to the nondisordered controls (Deveci et al., 2007). This also provides support for the link between stress and the onset of conversion disorder.

DECREASING PREVALENCE AND DEMOGRAPHIC CHARACTERISTICS Conversion disorders were once relatively common in civilian and (especially) military life. In World War I, conversion disorder was the most frequently diagnosed psychiatric syndrome among soldiers; it was also

Conversion disorders were fairly common during World War I and World War II. The disorder typically occurred in otherwise "normal" men during stressful combat conditions. The symptoms of conversion disorder (e.g., paralysis of the legs) enabled a soldier to avoid high-anxiety combat situations without being labeled a coward or being court-martialed.

relatively common during World War II. Conversion disorder typically occurred under highly stressful combat conditions and involved men who would ordinarily be considered stable. Here, conversion symptoms—such as paralysis of the legs—enabled a soldier to avoid an anxiety-arousing combat situation without being labeled a coward or being subject to court-martial.

Today, however, conversion disorders constitute only some 1 to 3 percent of all disorders referred for mental health treatment. The prevalence in the general population is unknown, but even the highest estimates have been around only 0.005 percent (APA, 2000). Interestingly, this decreased prevalence seems to be closely related to our growing sophistication about medical and psychological disorders: A conversion disorder apparently loses its defensive function if it can be readily shown to lack an organic basis. When it does occur today, it is most likely to occur in rural people from lower socioeconomic circles who are medically unsophisticated. For example, a highly unusual "outbreak" of cases of severe conversion disorder involving serious motor weakness and wasting symptoms was reported in five 9- to 13-year-old girls living in a small, poor, rural Amish community. Each of these girls had experienced substantial psychosocial stressors including behavioral problems, dysfunctional family dynamics, and significant community stress from a serious local church crisis (see Cassady et al., 2005). Fortunately, after the caregivers of these girls were educated regarding the psychological nature of the symptoms and given advice to stick with one doctor, minimize stress, and avoid reinforcement of the "sick role," four of the five girls showed significant improvement over the next 3 months. In the fifth case the family refused to acknowledge the psychological component of the illness, holding to the belief that the symptoms were caused by parasites.

Conversion disorder occurs two to ten times more often in women than in men. It can develop at any age but most commonly occurs between early adolescence and early adulthood (Maldonado & Spiegel, 2001). It generally has a rapid onset after a significant stressor and often resolves within 2 weeks if the stressor is removed, although it commonly recurs. In many other cases, however, it has a more chronic course. Like most other somatoform disorders, conversion disorder frequently occurs along with other disorders, especially major depression, anxiety disorders, and somatization and dissociative disorders.

RANGE OF CONVERSION DISORDER SYMPTOMS The range of symptoms for conversion disorder is practically as diverse as it is for physically based ailments. In describing the clinical picture in conversion disorder, it is useful to think in terms of four categories of symptoms: (1) sensory, (2) motor, (3) seizures, and (4) mixed presentation of the first three categories (APA, 2000).

Sensory Symptoms or Deficits Conversion disorder can involve almost any sensory modality, and it can often be diagnosed as a conversion disorder because symptoms in the affected area are inconsistent with how known anatomical sensory pathways operate. Today the sensory symptoms or deficits are most often in the visual system (especially blindness and tunnel vision), in the auditory system (especially deafness), or in the sensitivity to feeling (especially the anaesthesias). In the *anaesthesias*, the person loses her or his sense of feeling in a part of the body. One of the most common is *glove anaesthesia*, in which the person cannot feel anything on the hand in the area where gloves are worn, although the loss of sensation usually makes no anatomical sense.

With conversion blindness, the person reports that he or she cannot see and yet can often navigate about a room without bumping into furniture or other objects. With conversion deafness, the person reports not being able to hear and yet orients appropriately upon "hearing" his or her own name. Such observations lead to obvious questions: In conversion blindness (and deafness), can affected persons actually not see (or hear), or is the sensory information received but screened from consciousness? In general, the evidence supports the idea that the sensory input is registered but is somehow screened from explicit conscious recognition (explicit perception). This *implicit perception* will be discussed later in Developments in Thinking 3.

Motor Symptoms or Deficits Motor conversion reactions also cover a wide range of symptoms (e.g., Maldonado & Spiegel, 2001; see also Stone et al., 2010). For example, conversion paralysis is usually confined to a single limb such as an arm or a leg, and the loss of function is usually selective for certain functions. For example, a person may not be able to write but may be able to use the same muscles for scratching, or a person may not be able to walk most of the time but may be able to walk in an emergency such as a fire where escape is important. The most common speech-related conversion disturbance is *aphonia*, in which a person is able to talk only in a whisper although he or she can usually cough in a normal manner. (In true, organic laryngeal paralysis, both the cough and the voice are affected.) Another common motor symptom, called *globus hystericus*, is difficulty swallowing or the sensation of a lump in the throat (Finkenbine & Miele, 2004).

Seizures Conversion seizures, another relatively common form of conversion symptom, involve pseudoseizures, which resemble epileptic seizures in some ways but can usually be fairly well differentiated via modern medical technology (Bowman & Markand, 2005; Stonnington et al., 2006). For example, patients with pseudoseizures do not show any EEG abnormalities and do not show confusion and loss of memory afterward, as patients with true epileptic seizures do. Moreover, patients with conversion seizures often show excessive thrashing about and writhing not seen with true seizures, and they rarely injure themselves in falls or lose control over their bowels or bladder, as patients with true seizures frequently do.

The following case of conversion disorder clearly shows how "functional" a conversion disorder may be in the overall life circumstances of a patient despite its exacting a certain cost in illness or disability.

case study A Wife with "Fits"

Mrs. Chatterjee, a 26-year-old patient, attends a clinic in New Delhi, India, with complaints of "fits" for the last 4 years. The "fits" are always sudden in onset and usually last 30 to 60 minutes. A few minutes before a fit begins, she knows that it is imminent, and she usually goes to bed. During the fits she becomes unresponsive and rigid throughout her body, with bizarre and thrashing movements of the extremities. Her eyes close and her jaw is clenched, and she froths at the mouth. She frequently cries and sometimes shouts abuses. She is never incontinent of urine or feces, nor does she bite her tongue. After a "fit" she claims to have no memory of it. These episodes recur about once or twice a month. She functions well between the episodes.

Both the patient and her family believe that her "fits" are evidence of a physical illness and are not under her control. However, they recognize that the fits often occur following some stressor such as arguments with family members or friends . . . . She is described by her family as being somewhat immature but "quite social" and good company. She is self-centered, she craves attention from others, and she often reacts with irritability and anger if her wishes are not immediately fulfilled. On physical examination, Mrs. Chatterjee was found to have mild anemia but was otherwise healthy. A mental status examination did not reveal any abnormality . . . and her memory was normal. An electroencephalogram showed no seizure activity.

Source: Adapted with permission from *DSM-IV-TR Casebook: A Learning Companion to the Diagnostic and Statistical Manual of Mental Disorders, Fourth Edition, Text Revision* (pp. 469–70). Washington, DC. (Copyright © 2002). American Psychiatric Associaion.

IMPORTANT ISSUES IN DIAGNOSING CONVERSION DISORDER Because the symptoms in conversion disorder can simulate a variety of medical conditions, accurate diagnosis can be extremely difficult. It is crucial that a person with suspected conversion symptoms receive a thorough medical and neurological examination. Unfortunately, however, misdiagnoses can still occur. Nevertheless, as medical tests (especially brain imaging) have become increasingly sophisticated, the rate of misdiagnoses has declined substantially from in the past, with estimates of misdiagnoses in the 1990s at only 4 percent down from nearly 30 percent in the 1950s (e.g., Stone et al., 2005).

Several other criteria are also commonly used for distinguishing between conversion disorders and true organic disturbances:

- The frequent failure of the dysfunction to conform clearly to the symptoms of the particular disease or disorder simulated. For example, little or no wasting away or atrophy

Virtually all the symptoms of conversion disorder can be temporarily reduced or reproduced by hypnotic suggestion.

of a "paralyzed" limb occurs in conversion paralyses, except in rare and long-standing cases.

- The selective nature of the dysfunction. As already noted, in conversion blindness the affected individual does not usually bump into people or objects, and "paralyzed" muscles can be used for some activities but not others.
- Under hypnosis or narcosis (a sleeplike state induced by drugs), the symptoms can usually be removed, shifted, or reinduced at the suggestion of the therapist. Similarly, a person abruptly awakened from a sound sleep may suddenly be able to use a "paralyzed" limb.

TREATMENT OF CONVERSION DISORDER Our knowledge of how best to treat conversion disorder is extremely limited because no well-controlled studies have yet been conducted (e.g., Bowman & Markand, 2005; Looper & Kirmayer, 2002). However, it is known that some hospitalized patients with motor conversion symptoms have been successfully treated with a behavioral approach in which specific exercises are prescribed in order to increase movement or walking, and then reinforcements (e.g., praise and gaining privileges) are provided when patients show improvements. Any reinforcements of abnormal motor behaviors are removed in order to eliminate any sources of secondary gain. In one small study using this kind of treatment for 10 patients, all had regained their ability to move or walk in an average of 12 days, and for seven of the nine patients available at approximately 2-year follow-up the improvements had been maintained (Speed, 1996). Some studies have used hypnosis combined with other problem-solving therapies, and there are some suggestions that hypnosis, or adding hypnosis

to other therapeutic techniques, can be useful (Looper & Kirmayer, 2002; Moene et al., 2003).

Distinguishing Somatization, Pain, and Conversion Disorders from Malingering and Factitious Disorder

Earlier we mentioned that the *DSM* distinguishes between *malingering* and *factitious disorder* on the basis of the feigning person's apparent goals. Malingering is diagnosed if the person is intentionally producing or grossly exaggerating physical symptoms and is motivated by external incentives such as avoiding work or obtaining financial compensation. Factitious disorder is diagnosed if the person intentionally produces psychological or physical symptoms, the person's goal being simply to obtain and maintain the personal benefits that playing the "sick role" (even undergoing repeated hospitalizations) may provide, including the attention and concern of family and medical personnel. In factitious disorder, frequently these patients surreptitiously alter their own physiology—for example, by taking drugs—in order to simulate various real illnesses. Indeed, they may be at risk for serious injury or death and may even need to be committed to an institution for their own protection. (See The World Around Us 2 for a particularly pathological variation on this.) In the past, severe and chronic forms of factitious disorder with physical symptoms were called "Munchausen's syndrome," where the general idea was that the person had some kind of "hospital addiction" or a "professional patient" syndrome.

It is sometimes possible to distinguish between a conversion (or other somatoform) disorder and malingering, or factitiously "sick-role-playing," with a fair degree of confidence, but in other cases it is more difficult to make the correct diagnosis. Persons engaged in malingering (for which there are no formal diagnostic criteria) and those who have factitious disorder are consciously perpetrating frauds by faking the symptoms of diseases or disabilities, and this fact is often reflected in their demeanor. In contrast, individuals with conversion disorders (as well as with somatization and pain disorders) are not consciously producing their symptoms, feel themselves to be the "victims of their symptoms," and are very willing to discuss them, often in excruciating detail (Maldonado & Spiegel, 2001, p. 109). When inconsistencies in their behaviors are pointed out, they are usually unperturbed. Any secondary gains they experience are byproducts of the conversion symptoms themselves and are not involved in motivating the symptoms. On the other hand, persons who are feigning symptoms are inclined to be defensive, evasive, and suspicious when asked about them; they are usually reluctant to be examined and slow to talk about their symptoms lest the pretense be discovered. Should inconsistencies in their behaviors be pointed out, deliberate deceivers as a rule immediately become more defensive. Thus conversion disorder and deliberate faking of illness are considered distinct patterns.

2 | THE WORLD AROUND US

Factitious Disorder by Proxy (Munchausen's Syndrome by Proxy)

In a somewhat bizarre variant of factitious disorder called **factitious disorder by proxy** (or *Munchausen's syndrome by proxy*), the person seeking medical help or consulting a mental health professional has intentionally produced a medical or psychiatric illness (or appearance of an illness) in another person who is under his or her care (usually a child; e.g., Pankratz, 2006). In a typical instance, a mother presents her own child for treatment of a medical condition she has deliberately caused, disclaiming any knowledge of its origin. Of course, the health of such victims is often seriously endangered by this repeated abuse, and the intervention of social service agencies or law enforcement is sometimes necessary. In as many as 10 percent of cases, this atypical form of child abuse may lead to a child's death (Hall et al., 2000).

This disorder may be indicated when the victim's clinical presentation is atypical, when lab results are inconsistent with each other or with recognized diseases, or when there are unduly frequent returns or increasingly urgent visits to the same hospital or clinic. The

Over a period of 20 months, Jennifer, 8, shown here with her mother, Kathy Bush, was taken to the hospital more than 130 times, underwent 40 surgeries, and amassed over $3 million in medical expenses. Doctors and nurses testified that Jennifer's condition always worsened after her mother visited her daughter at the hospital behind closed doors. In addition, Jennifer's health had significantly improved since being removed from her mother's care. The jury was convinced that Kathy Bush was responsible for causing Jennifer's illnesses. Bush was arrested and diagnosed with Munchausen's syndrome by proxy.

perpetrators (who often have extensive medical knowledge) tend to be highly resistant to admitting the truth (McCann, 1999), and it has been estimated that the average length of time to confirm the diagnosis is 14 months (Rogers, 2004). If the perpetrator senses that the medical staff is suspicious, he or she may abruptly terminate contact with that facility, only to show up at another one to begin the entire process anew. Compounding the problem of detection is the fact that health care professionals who realize they have been duped may be reluctant to acknowledge their fallibility for fear of legal action. Misdiagnosing the disorder when the parent is in fact innocent can also lead to legal difficulties for the health care professionals (McNicholas et al., 2000; Pankratz, 2006). One technique that has been used with considerable success is covert video surveillance of the mother and child during hospitalizations. In one study, 23 of 41 suspected cases were finally determined to have factitious disorder by proxy, and in 56 percent of those cases video surveillance was essential to the diagnosis (Hall et al., 2000).

DSM-IV-TR

Criteria for Factitious Disorder

Factitious Disorder

A. Intentional production or feigning of physical or psychological signs or symptoms.
B. The motivation for the behavior is to assume the sick role.
C. External incentives for the behavior (such as economic gain, avoiding legal responsibility, or improving physical wellbeing, as in Malingering) are absent.

Factitious Disorder by Proxy

A. Intentional production or feigning of physical or psychological signs or symptoms in another person who is under the individual's care.

B. Motivation for the perpetrator's behavior is to assume the sick role by proxy.
C. External incentives for the behavior (such as economic gain) are absent.

Source: Reprinted with permission from the American Psychiatric Association. *Diagnostic and Statistical Manual of Mental Disorders,* Fourth Edition, *Text Revision* (Copyright © 2000). American Psychiatric Association.

Body Dysmorphic Disorder

Body dysmorphic disorder (BDD) is officially classified in *DSM-IV-TR* (APA, 2000) as a somatoform disorder because it involves preoccupation with certain aspects of the body. People

with BDD are obsessed with some *perceived* or *imagined flaw* or flaws in their appearance to the point they firmly believe they are disfigured or ugly. This preoccupation is so intense that it causes clinically significant distress and impairment in social or occupational functioning. Although it is not considered necessary for the diagnosis, most people with BDD have compulsive checking behaviors (such as checking their appearance in the mirror excessively or hiding or repairing a perceived flaw). Another very common symptom is avoidance of usual activities because of fear that other people will see the imaginary defect and be repulsed. In severe cases they may become so isolated that they lock themselves up in their houses and never go out even to work, with the average employment rate estimated at only about 50 percent (Neziroglu et al., 2004). Table 1 illustrates the range of activities that BDD interferes with.

People with BDD may focus on almost any body part: Their skin has blemishes, their breasts are too small, their face is too thin (or too fat) or disfigured by visible blood vessels that others find repulsive, and so on. One large study found that some of the more common locations for perceived defects include skin (73 percent), hair (56 percent), nose (37 percent), eyes (20 percent), breasts/chest/nipples (21 percent), stomach (22 percent), and face size/shape (12 percent; Phillips, 2005). Many sufferers have perceived defects in more than one body part. It is very important to remember that these are not the ordinary concerns that most of us have about our appearance; they are far more extreme, leading in many cases to complete

People with body dysmorphic disorder are preoccupied with perceived defects in certain aspects of their body and frequently spend an inordinate amount of time obsessively checking their appearance in the mirror.

preoccupation and significant emotional pain. Some researchers estimate that about half the people with BDD have concerns about their appearance that are of delusional intensity (e.g., Allen & Hollander, 2004). It is important to remember that others do not even see the defects that the person with BDD believes she or he has, or if they do, they see only a very minor defect within the normal range.

Another common feature of BDD is that people with this condition frequently seek reassurance from friends and family about their defects, but the reassurances almost never provide more than very temporary relief. They also frequently seek reassurance for themselves by checking their appearance in the mirror countless times in a day (although some avoid mirrors completely). They are usually driven by the hope that they will look different, and sometimes they may think their perceived defect does not look as bad as it has at other times. However, much more commonly they feel worse after mirror gazing (Veale & Riley, 2001). They frequently engage in excessive grooming behavior, often trying to camouflage their perceived defect through their hairstyle, clothing, or makeup (Sarwer et al., 2004).

The case below illustrates the primary features of this disorder.

case study   The Elephant Man

Chris is a shy, anxious-looking, 31-year-old carpenter who has been hospitalized after making a suicide attempt . . . . He asks to meet with the psychiatrist in a darkened room. He is wearing a baseball cap pulled down over his forehead. Looking down at the floor, Chris says he has no friends, has just been fired from his job, and was recently rejected by his girlfriend. "It's my nose . . . these huge pockmarks on my nose. They're grotesque! I look like a monster. I'm as ugly as the Elephant Man! These marks on my nose are all that I can think about. I've thought about them every day for the past 15 years, and I think that everyone can see them and that they laugh at me because of them. That's why I wear this hat all the time. And that's why I couldn't talk to you in a bright room . . . you'd see how ugly I am."

The psychiatrist couldn't see the huge pockmarks that Chris was referring to, even in a brightly lit room. Chris is, in fact, a handsome man with normal-appearing facial pores. [Later Chris says,] "I've pretty much kept this preoccupation a secret because it's so embarrassing. I'm afraid people will think I'm vain. But I've told a few people about it, and they've tried to convince me that the pores

really aren't visible . . . . This problem has ruined my life. All I can think about is my face. I spend hours a day looking at the marks in the mirror . . . . I started missing more and more work, and I stopped going out with my friends and my girlfriend . . . staying in the house most of the time . . . ."

Chris . . . had seen a dermatologist to request dermabrasion, but was refused the procedure because "there was nothing there." He finally convinced another dermatologist to do the procedure but thought it did not help. Eventually he felt so desperate that he made two suicide attempts. His most recent attempt occurred after he looked in the mirror and was horrified by what he saw . . . "I saw how awful I looked, and I thought, I'm not sure it's worth it to go on living if I have to look like this and think about this all the time."

Source: Adapted with permission from *DSM-IV-TR Casebook: A Learning Companion to the Diagnostic and Statistical Manual of Mental Disorders,* Fourth Edition, *Text Revision* (pp. 7–9). Washington, DC. (Copyright © 2002). American Psychiatric Association.

Table 1 Interference in Functioning

Problem	% of People with BDD Who Experienced the Problem or Average Number of Days
Interference with social functioning (e.g., with friends, family, or intimate relationships) due to BDD	99%
Periods of avoidance of nearly all social interactions because of BDD	95%
Ever felt depressed because of BDD	94%
Interference with work or academic functioning because of BDD	90%
Ever thought about suicide because of BDD*	63%
Completely housebound for at least 1 week because of BDD	29%
Psychiatrically hospitalized at least once because of BDD	26%
Ever attempted suicide	25%
Ever attempted suicide because of BDD	14%
Days of work missed because of BDD*	52 days
Days of school missed because of BDD*	49 days

*Since BDD began

Source: Adapted from Katherine A. Phillips. *The Broken Mirror: Understanding and Treating Dysmorphic Disorder.* © 2005 Oxford University Press. Reprinted by permission.

DSM-IV-TR

Criteria for Body Dysmorphic Disorder

A. Preoccupation with an imagined defect in appearance. If a slight physical anomaly is present, the person's concern is markedly excessive.

B. The preoccupation causes clinically significant distress or impairment in social, occupational, or other important areas of functioning.

C. The preoccupation is not better accounted for by another mental disorder (e.g., dissatisfaction with body shape and size in Anorexia Nervosa).

Source: Reprinted with permission from the American Psychiatric Association. *Diagnostic and Statistical Manual of Mental Disorders*, Fourth Edition, *Text Revision* (Copyright © 2000). American Psychiatric Association.

PREVALENCE, GENDER, AND AGE OF ONSET There are no official estimates of the prevalence of BDD, and they might actually be difficult to obtain because of the great secrecy that usually surrounds this disorder. Some leading researchers estimate that it is not a rare disorder, affecting perhaps 1 to 2 percent of the general population and up to 8 percent of people with depression (e.g., Phillips, 2005; Rief et al., 2006; Buhlmann et al., 2010). The prevalence seems to be approximately equal in men and women, although the primary body parts that are focused on differ in men and women (Phillips, 2005; Phillips & Diaz, 1997). Men are more likely to obsess about their genitals, body build, and balding whereas women tend to obsess more about their skin, stomach, breasts, buttocks, hips, and legs (Phillips, Menard, & Fay, 2006). The age of onset is usually in adolescence, when many people start to become preoccupied with their appearance. People with BDD very commonly also have a depressive diagnosis (with most estimates being over 50 percent; Allen & Hollander, 2004), and, as in Chris's case, it often leads to suicide attempts or completed suicide (Neziroglu et al., 2004; Phillips & Menard, 2006). Indeed, of nearly 200 patients with BDD, Phillips and Menard (2006) found that 80 percent reported a history of suicidal ideation, and 28 percent had a history of a suicide attempt. Rates of comorbid social phobia and obsessive-compulsive disorder are also quite substantial, although not as high as for depression (Allen & Hollander, 2004; Coles et al., 2006; see also Fang & Hofmann, 2010).

Sufferers of BDD like Chris commonly make their way into the office of a dermatologist or plastic surgeon, one estimate being that over 75 percent seek nonpsychiatric treatment (Phillips et al., 2001). One study found that 8 percent of those seeking cosmetic medical treatments met criteria for BDD (Crerand et al., 2004), although other studies have estimated this to be as high as 20 percent (Phillips, 2005). In another study, 33 percent of patients seeking rhinoplasty (commonly referred to as a "nose job") demonstrate at least moderate levels of BDD symptoms (Picavet et al., 2011). An astute doctor will not do the requested procedures and may instead make a referral to a psychologist or psychiatrist. All too often, though, the patient, like Chris, does get what he or she requests—and unfortunately is almost never satisfied with the outcome. Even if they are satisfied with the outcome, such patients still tend to retain their diagnosis of BDD (Tignol et al., 2007).

RELATIONSHIP TO OCD AND EATING DISORDERS
Many researchers believe that BDD is closely related to obsessive-compulsive disorder and have proposed it as one of the obsessive-compulsive spectrum disorders being discussed for *DSM-5* (e.g., Allen & Hollander, 2004; Phillips et al., 2007). At this point, the similarities to OCD should be fairly obvious. Like people with OCD, those with BDD have prominent obsessions, and they engage in a variety of ritualistic behaviors such as reassurance seeking, mirror checking, comparing themselves to others, and camouflage. Moreover, they are even more convinced that their obsessive beliefs are accurate than are people with OCD (Eisen et al., 2003). But in addition to these similarities in symptoms, research is also increasingly suggesting an overlap in causes. For example, the same neurotransmitter (serotonin) and the same sets of brain structures are implicated in the two disorders (Rauch et al., 2003; Saxena & Feusner, 2006), and, as we will discuss later, the same kinds of treatments that work for OCD are also the treatments of choice for BDD (Phillips, 2005).

Other researchers have also noted significant overlapping features between BDD and eating disorders (especially anorexia nervosa), the most striking similarity being the body image distortion in both kinds of conditions. Specifically, excessive concerns and preoccupation about physical appearance, dissatisfaction with one's body, and a distorted image of certain features of one's body are central to the diagnostic criteria for each (Allen & Hollander, 2004; Cororve & Gleaves, 2001). Nevertheless, it is important to remember that people with BDD look normal and yet are terribly obsessed and distressed about some aspect of their appearance. By contrast, people with anorexia are emaciated and generally satisfied with this aspect of their appearance (Phillips, 2005).

WHY NOW? BDD has clearly existed for centuries, if not for all time. It also seems to be a universal disorder, occurring in all European countries, the Middle East, China, Japan, and Africa (Phillips, 2005). Why, then, did its examination in the literature begin only recently? One possible reason is that its prevalence may actually have increased in recent years as contemporary Western culture has become increasingly focused on "looks as everything," with billions of dollars spent each year on enhancing appearance through makeup, clothes, plastic surgery, and other means (Fawcett, 2004). A second reason BDD has been understudied is that most people with this condition never seek psychological or psychiatric treatment. Rather, they suffer silently or go to dermatologists or plastic surgeons (Crerand et al., 2004; Phillips, 1996, 2001; Tignol et al., 2007). Reasons for this secrecy and shame include worries that others will think they are superficial, silly, or vain and that if they mention their perceived defect others will notice it and focus more on it. Part of the reason why more people are now seeking treatment is that starting in the past 15 years the disorder has received a good deal of media attention. It has even been discussed on some daily talk shows, where it is sometimes

called "imaginary defect disorder." As increasing attention is focused on this disorder, the secrecy and shame often surrounding it should decrease, and more people will seek treatment. A leading researcher in this area is Katharine Phillips (1996, 2005), who carefully described the condition in *The Broken Mirror: Understanding and Treating Body Dysmorphic Disorder,* a book that was written (and later revised) for people who suffer from this disorder as well as for their families and clinicians.

CAUSAL FACTORS: A BIOPSYCHOSOCIAL APPROACH TO BDD Our understanding of what causes BDD is still at a preliminary stage, but recent research seems to suggest that a biopsychosocial approach offers some reasonable hypotheses. First, it seems likely that there is a partially genetically based personality predisposition (such as high neuroticism) that people with BDD may share in common with people who have OCD and perhaps other anxiety disorders, although evidence for this currently is minimal. Second, BDD seems to be occurring, at least today, in a sociocultural context that places great value on attractiveness and beauty, and people who develop BDD often hold attractiveness as their primary value. This means that their self-schemas are heavily focused around such ideas as, "If my appearance is defective, then I am worthless" (endorsed by 60 percent in one study; Buhlmann & Wilhelm, 2004, p. 924). One possibility why this occurs is that, in many cases, these people were reinforced as children for their overall appearance more than for their behavior (Neziroglu et al., 2004). Another possibility is that they were teased or criticized for their appearance, which caused conditioning of disgust, shame, or anxiety to their own image of some part of their body. For example, one study of individuals with BDD found that 56 to 68 percent reported a history of emotional neglect or emotional abuse, and approximately 30 percent reported a history of physical or sexual abuse or physical neglect (Didie et al., 2006).

In addition, substantial empirical evidence now demonstrates that people with BDD show biased attention and interpretation of information relating to attractiveness (e.g., Buhlmann & Wilhelm, 2004). They selectively attend to positive or negative words such as *ugly* or *beautiful* more than to other emotional words not related to appearance, and they tend to interpret ambiguous facial expressions as contemptuous or angry more than do controls. When they are shown pictures of their own face that have been manipulated to be more or less symmetrical than in reality, they show a greater discrepancy than controls between judgments of their "actual" face and their "ideal" face. Asked to choose the pictures that best matched their faces, controls' choices were more symmetrical than their real faces, while patients with BDD lacked this bias (Lambrou et al., 2011). Moreover, several studies that used fMRI technology found that patients with BDD showed fundamental differences in visually processing other people's faces relative to controls. Specifically, they showed a bias for extracting local, detailed features rather than the more global or holistic processing of faces seen in controls (Feusner et al., 2007). A second study showed that when patients with BDD are shown a picture of their own face they demonstrate greater activation than do healthy controls in brain regions associated with inhibitory processes and the rigidity of behavior and thinking (the orbitofrontal cortex and the caudate) (Feusner et al., 2010). Similarly, compared to controls, patients with BDD demonstrate performance deficits on tasks that measure executive functioning (e.g., manipulating information, planning, and organization), which is thought to be guided by prefrontal brain regions (Dunai et al., 2010). Whether or not these factors play a causal role is not yet known, but certainly having such biases and deficits in processing information would, at a minimum, serve to perpetuate the disorder once it has developed.

TREATMENT OF BODY DYSMORPHIC DISORDER As we have already noted, the treatments that are effective for BDD are closely related to those used in the effective treatment of obsessive-compulsive disorder. There is some evidence that antidepressant medications from the SSRI category often produce moderate improvement in patients with BDD, but many are not helped or show only a modest improvement (Phillips, 2004, 2005; Phillips, Pagano, & Menard, 2006). However, in some cases showing only modest improvement it is possible that inadequate doses of the medication were used, thus leading to an underestimation of their true potential effects. In general, it seems that higher doses of these medications are needed to effectively treat BDD relative to OCD (Hadley et al., 2006). In addition, a form of cognitive-behavioral treatment emphasizing exposure and response prevention has been shown to produce marked improvement in 50 to 80 percent of treated patients (Sarwer et al., 2004; Simon, 2002; Williams et al., 2006). These treatment approaches focus on getting the patient to identify and change distorted perceptions of his or her body during exposure to anxiety-provoking situations (e.g., when wearing something that highlights rather than disguises the "defect") and on prevention of checking responses (e.g., mirror checking, reassurance seeking, and repeated examining of the imaginary defect). The treatment gains are generally well maintained at follow-up (Looper & Kirmayer, 2002; Sarwer et al., 2004). Although no studies have as yet compared CBT with medications within the same study, one quantitative review of treatment studies found that substantially greater improvement was observed following CBT than SSRI medications (Williams et al., 2006).

In Review

- What are the primary characteristics of hypochondriasis, and how does the cognitive-behavioral viewpoint explain their occurrence?

- What are the symptoms of somatization disorder and of pain disorder?

- What are sources of primary and secondary gains involved in conversion disorders, and how is conversion disorder distinguished from malingering and from factitious disorder?

- What are the primary symptoms of body dysmorphic disorder, and how are they related to obsessive-compulsive disorder?

What Are Dissociative Disorders?

Whereas somatoform disorders involve physical symptoms and complaints that suggest the presence of a medical condition when there is none, **dissociative disorders** are a group of conditions involving disruptions in a person's normally integrated functions of consciousness, memory, identity, or perception (APA, 2000). Included here are some of the more dramatic phenomena in the entire domain of psychopathology: people who cannot recall who they are or where they may have come from, and people who have two or more distinct identities or personality states that alternately take control of the individual's behavior.

The term **dissociation** refers to the human mind's capacity to engage in complex mental activity in channels split off from, or independent of, conscious awareness (Kihlstrom, 1994, 2001, 2005). The concept of dissociation was first promoted over a century ago by the French neurologist Pierre Janet (1859–1947). We all dissociate to a degree some of the time. Mild dissociative symptoms occur when we daydream or lose track of what is going on around us, when we drive miles beyond our destination without realizing how we got there, or when we miss part of a conversation we are engaged in. As these everyday examples of acts performed without conscious awareness suggest, there is nothing inherently pathological about dissociation itself.

More specifically, much of the mental life of all human beings involves automatic nonconscious processes that are to a large extent autonomous with respect to deliberate, self-aware direction and monitoring. Such unaware processing extends to the areas of implicit memory and implicit perception, where it can be demonstrated that all persons routinely show indirect evidence of remembering things they cannot consciously recall (**implicit memory**) and respond to sights or sounds as if they had perceived them (as in conversion blindness or deafness) even though they cannot report that they have seen or heard them (**implicit perception**; Kihlstrom, 2001, 2005; Kihlstrom et al., 1993). The general idea of unconscious mental processes has been embraced by psychodynamically oriented clinicians for many years. But only in the past quarter-century has it also become a major research area in the field of cognitive psychology (though without any of the psychodynamic implications for why so much of our mental activity is unconscious).

In persons with dissociative disorders, however, this normally integrated and well-coordinated multichannel quality of human cognition becomes much less coordinated and integrated. When this happens, the affected person may be unable to access information that is normally in the forefront of consciousness, such as his or her own personal identity or details of an important period of time in the recent past. That is, the normally useful capacity of maintaining ongoing mental activity outside of awareness appears to be subverted, sometimes for the purpose of managing severe psychological threat. When that happens, we observe the pathological dissociative symptoms that are the cardinal characteristic of dissociative disorders. Like somatoform disorders, dissociative disorders appear mainly to be ways of avoiding anxiety and stress and of managing life problems that threaten to overwhelm the person's usual coping resources. Both types of disorders also enable the individual to deny personal responsibility for his or her "unacceptable" wishes or behavior. In the case of *DSM*-defined dissociative disorders, the person avoids the stress by pathologically dissociating—in essence, by escaping from his or her own autobiographical memory or personal identity. The *DSM-IV-TR* recognizes several types of pathological dissociation.

Depersonalization Disorder

Two of the more common kinds of dissociative symptoms are derealization and depersonalization, because they sometimes occur during panic attacks. In **derealization** one's sense of the reality of the outside world is temporarily lost, and in **depersonalization** one's sense of one's own self and one's own reality is temporarily lost. As many as half of us have such experiences in mild form at least once in our lives, usually during or after periods of severe stress, sleep deprivation, or sensory deprivation (e.g., Khazaal et al., 2005). But when episodes of depersonalization (and derealization) become persistent and recurrent and interfere with normal functioning, **depersonalization disorder** may be diagnosed.

In this disorder, people have persistent or recurrent experiences of feeling detached from (and like an outside observer of) their own bodies and mental processes. They may even feel they are, for a time, floating above their physical bodies, which may suddenly feel very different—as if drastically changed or unreal. During periods of depersonalization, unlike during psychotic states, reality testing remains intact. The related experience of derealization, in which the external world is perceived as strange and new in various ways, may also occur. As one leader in the field described it, in both states "the feeling puzzles the experiencers: the changed condition is perceived as unreal, and as discontinuous with his or her previous ego-states. The object of the experience, self (in depersonalization) or world (in derealization), is commonly described as isolated, lifeless, strange, and unfamiliar; oneself and others are perceived as 'automatons,' behaving mechanically, without initiative or self-control" (Kihlstrom, 2001, p. 267). Often sufferers also report feeling as though they are living in a dream or movie (Maldonado et al., 2002). In keeping

People with derealization symptoms experience the world as hazy and indistinct.

with such reports, recent research has shown that emotional experiences are attenuated or reduced during depersonalization—both at the subjective level and at the level of neural and autonomic activity that normally accompanies emotional responses to threatening or unpleasant emotional stimuli (Lemche et al., 2007; Phillips & Sierra, 2003; Stein & Simeon, 2009). After viewing an emotional video clip, participants with depersonalization disorder showed higher levels of subjective and objective memory fragmentation than controls (Giesbrecht et al., 2010). Memory fragmentation is marked by difficulties forming an accurate or coherent narrative sequence of events, which is consistent with earlier research suggesting that time distortion is a key element of the experience of depersonalization (Simeon et al., 2008).

A number of researchers have noted elevated rates of comorbid anxiety and mood disorders as well as avoidant, borderline, and obsessive-compulsive personality disorders (e.g., Hunter et al., 2003; Mula et al., 2007). Another study of over 200 cases found that the disorder had an average age of onset of 23. Moreover, in nearly 80 percent of cases, the disorder has a fairly chronic course (with little or no fluctuation in intensity; Baker, Hunter, et al., 2003).

The case of the foggy student on the next page is fairly typical.

A Foggy Student

A 20-year-old male college student sought psychiatric consultation because he was worried that he might be going insane. For the past 2 years he had experienced increasingly frequent episodes of feeling "outside" himself. These episodes were accompanied by a sense of deadness in his body. In addition, during these periods he was uncertain of his balance and frequently stumbled into furniture; this was more apt to occur in public, especially if he was somewhat anxious. During these episodes he felt a lack of easy, natural control of his body, and his thoughts seemed "foggy" as well. . . .

The patient's subjective sense of lack of control was especially troublesome, and he would fight it by shaking his head and saying "stop" to himself. This would momentarily clear his mind and restore his sense of autonomy, but only temporarily, as the feelings of deadness and of being outside himself would return. Gradually, over a period of several hours, the unpleasant experiences would fade. . . . At the time the patient came for treatment, he was experiencing these symptoms about twice a week, and each incident lasted from 3 to 4 hours. On several occasions the episodes had occurred while he was driving his car and was alone; worried that he might have an accident, he had stopped driving unless someone accompanied him.

Source: Adapted with permission from *DSM-IV-TR Casebook: A Learning Companion to the Diagnostic and Statistical Manual of Mental Disorders,* Fourth Edition, *Text Revision* (pp. 270–71). Washington, DC. (Copyright © 2002). American Psychiatric Association.

The lifetime prevalence of depersonalization disorder is unknown, but occasional depersonalization symptoms are not uncommon in a variety of other disorders such as schizophrenia, borderline personality disorder, panic disorder, acute stress disorder, and PTSD (Hunter et al., 2003). Although severe depersonalization symptoms can be quite frightening and may make the victim fear imminent mental collapse, such fears are usually unfounded. Sometimes, however, feelings of depersonalization are early manifestations of impending decompensation and the development of psychotic states. In either case, professional assistance in dealing with the precipitating stressors and in reducing anxiety may be helpful.

Dissociative Amnesia and Dissociative Fugue

Retrograde amnesia is the partial or total inability to recall or identify previously acquired information or past experiences; by contrast, *anterograde amnesia* is the partial or total inability to retain new information (Gilboa et al., 2006; Kapur, 1999). Persistent amnesia may occur in several Axis I disorders, such as dissociative amnesia and dissociative fugue, and in organic brain pathology including traumatic brain injury and diseases of the central nervous system. If the amnesia is caused by *brain pathology* (diagnosed as "Amnestic Disorder Due to a General Medical

Condition"), it most often involves failure to retain new information and experiences (anterograde amnesia). That is, the information contained in experience is not registered and does not enter memory storage (Kapur, 1999).

On the other hand, **dissociative amnesia** (or *psychogenic amnesia*) is usually limited to a failure to recall previously stored personal information (retrograde amnesia) when that failure cannot be accounted for by ordinary forgetting. The gaps in memory most often occur following intolerably stressful circumstances—wartime combat conditions, for example, or catastrophic events such as serious car accidents, suicide attempts, or violent outbursts (Maldonado & Spiegel, 2007). In this disorder, apparently forgotten personal information is still there beneath the level of consciousness, as sometimes becomes apparent in interviews conducted under hypnosis or narcosis (induced by sodium amytal, or so-called truth serum) and in cases where the amnesia spontaneously clears up. Several types of dissociative amnesia are recognized by *DSM-IV-TR*. One is *localized* amnesia (a person remembers nothing that happened during a specific period, most commonly the first few hours or days following some highly traumatic event). Another is *selective* amnesia (a person forgets some but not all of what happened during a given period).

Usually amnesic episodes last between a few days and a few years, and although many people experience only one such episode, some people have multiple episodes in their lifetimes (Maldonado & Spiegel, 2007). In typical dissociative amnesic reactions, individuals cannot remember certain aspects of their personal life history or important facts about their identity. Yet their basic habit patterns—such as their abilities to read, talk, perform skilled work, and so on—remain intact, and they seem normal aside from the memory deficit (Kihlstrom, 2005; Kihlstrom & Schacter, 2000). Thus the only type of memory that is affected is *episodic* (pertaining to events experienced) or *autobiographical memory* (pertaining to personal events experienced). The other recognized forms of memory—semantic (pertaining to language and concepts), procedural (how to do things), and short-term storage—seem usually to remain intact,

In the movie *Memento,* the lead character has anterograde amnesia, which makes him unable to form any short-term memories. He has to write notes to himself and refer to them constantly in order to function on a daily basis.

although there is very little research on this topic (Kihlstrom, 2005; Kihlstrom & Schacter, 2000). Usually there is no difficulty encoding new information (Maldonado & Spiegel, 2007).

In a related but very rare disorder, a person may retreat still further from real-life problems by going into an amnesic state called a **dissociative fugue**, which, as the term implies (the French word *fugue* means "flight"), is a defense by actual flight—a person is not only amnesic for some or all aspects of his or her past but also departs from home surroundings. This is accompanied by confusion about personal identity or even the assumption of a new identity (although the identities do not alternate as they do in dissociative identity disorder). During the fugue, such individuals are unaware of memory loss for prior stages of their life, but their memory for what happens during the fugue state itself is intact (Kihlstrom, 2005; Kihlstrom & Schacter, 2000). Their behavior during the fugue state is usually quite normal and unlikely to arouse suspicion that something is wrong. However, behavior during the fugue state often reflects a rather different lifestyle from the previous one (the rejection of which is sometimes fairly obvious). Days, weeks, or sometimes even years later, such people may suddenly emerge from the fugue state and find themselves in a strange place, working in a new occupation, with no idea how they got there. In other cases, recovery from the fugue state occurs only after repeated questioning and reminders of who they are. In either case, as the fugue state remits, their initial amnesia remits—but a new, apparently complete amnesia for their fugue period occurs.

The pattern in dissociative amnesia and dissociative fugue is essentially similar to that in conversion symptoms, except that instead of avoiding some unpleasant situation by becoming physically dysfunctional, a person unconsciously avoids thoughts about the situation or, in the extreme, leaves the scene (Maldonado & Spiegel, 2007; Maldonado et al., 2002). Thus people experiencing dissociative amnesia and fugue are typically faced with extremely unpleasant situations from which they see no acceptable way to escape. Eventually the stress becomes so intolerable that large segments of their personalities and all memory of the stressful situations are suppressed.

DSM-IV-TR

Criteria for Dissociative Amnesia

A. The predominant disturbance is one or more episodes of inability to recall important personal information, usually of a traumatic or stressful nature, that is too extensive to be explained by ordinary forgetfulness.
B. The disturbance does not occur exclusively during the course of Dissociative Identity Disorder, Dissociative Fugue, Posttraumatic Stress Disorder, Acute Stress Disorder, or Somatization Disorder and is not due to the direct physiological effects of a substance (e.g., a drug of abuse, a medication) or a neurological or other general medical condition (e.g., Amnestic Disorder Due to Head Trauma).
C. The symptoms cause clinically significant distress or impairment in social, occupational, or other important areas of functioning.

Criteria for Dissociative Fugue

A. The predominant disturbance is sudden, unexpected travel away from home or one's customary place of work, with inability to recall one's past.
B. Confusion about personal identity or assumption of a new identity (partial or complete).
C. The disturbance does not occur exclusively during the course of Dissociative Identity Disorder and is not due to the direct physiological effects of a substance (e.g., a drug of abuse, a medication) or a general medical condition (e.g., temporal lobe epilepsy).
D. The symptoms cause clinically significant distress or impairment in social, occupational, or other important areas of functioning.

Source: Reprinted with permission from the American Psychiatric Association. *Diagnostic and Statistical Manual of Mental Disorders*, Fourth Edition, *Text Revision* (Copyright © 2000). American Psychiatric Association.

Several of these aspects of dissociative fugue are illustrated in the following case.

case study A Middle Manager Transformed into a Short-Order Cook

Burt Tate, a 42-year-old short-order cook in a small-town diner, was brought to the attention of local police following a heated altercation with another man at the diner. He gave his name as Burt Tate and indicated that he had arrived in town several weeks earlier. However, he could produce no official identification and could not tell the officers where he had previously lived and worked. Burt was asked to accompany the officers to the emergency room of a local hospital so that he might be examined . . . .

Burt's physical examination was negative for evidence of recent head trauma or any other medical abnormality . . . . He was oriented as to current time and place, but manifested no recall of

his personal history prior to his arrival in town. He did not seem especially concerned about his total lack of a remembered past . . . .

Meanwhile, the police . . . discovered that Burt matched the description of one Gene Saunders, a resident of a city some 200 miles away who had disappeared a month earlier. The wife of Mr. Saunders . . . confirmed the real identity of Burt, who . . . stated that he did not recognize Mrs. Saunders.

Prior to his disappearance, Gene Saunders, a middle-level manager in a large manufacturing firm, had been experiencing considerable difficulties at work and at home. A number of stressful work problems, including failure to get an expected promotion, the loss of some of his key staff, failure of his section to meet production goals, and increased criticism from his superior—all occurring within a brief time frame—had upset his normal equanimity. He had become morose and withdrawn at home and had been critical of his wife and children. Two days before he had left, he had had a violent argument with his 18-year-old son, who had declared his father a failure and had stormed out of the house to go live with friends.

Source: Adapted with permission from *DSM-IV-TR Casebook: A Learning Companion to the Diagnostic and Statistical Manual of Mental Disorders,* Fourth Edition, *Text Revision* (pp. 254–55). Washington, DC. (Copyright © 2002). American Psychiatric Association.

MEMORY AND INTELLECTUAL DEFICITS IN DISSO-CIATIVE AMNESIA AND FUGUE Unfortunately, very little systematic research has been conducted on individuals with dissociative amnesia and fugue. What is known comes largely from intensive studies of the memory and intellectual functioning of isolated cases with these disorders, so any conclusions should be considered tentative pending further study of larger samples with appropriate control groups. What can be gathered from a handful of such case studies is that these individuals' semantic knowledge (assessed via the vocabulary subtest of an IQ test) seems to be generally intact. The primary deficit these individuals exhibit is their compromised episodic or autobiographical memory (Kihlstrom, 2005; Kihlstrom & Schacter, 2000). Indeed, several studies using brain-imaging techniques have confirmed that when people with dissociative amnesia are presented with autobiographical memory tasks, they show reduced activation in their right frontal and temporal brain areas relative to normal controls doing the same kinds of tasks (Kihlstrom, 2005; Markowitsch, 1999). In a recent review of nine cases of dissociative amnesia for which brain imaging data were available, the authors conclude there was evidence of significant changes in the brains of these patients, mostly centered on subtle loss of function in the right anterior hemisphere—changes similar to those seen in the brains of patients with organic memory loss (Staniloiu & Markowitsch, 2010).

However, several cases (some nearly a century old) have suggested that *implicit memory* is generally intact. For example, Jones (1909, as cited in Kihlstrom & Schacter, 2000) studied a patient with dense amnesia and found that although he could not remember his wife's or daughter's names, when asked to guess what names might fit them, he produced their names correctly. In a more contemporary case (Lyon, 1985, as cited in Kihlstrom & Schacter, 2000), a patient who could not retrieve any autobiographical information was asked to dial numbers on a phone randomly. Without realizing what he was doing, he dialed his mother's phone number, which then led to her identifying him. In one particularly fascinating contemporary case of dissociative fugue, Glisky and colleagues (2004) describe a German man who had come to work in the United States several months before he had experienced a traumatic incident in which he had been robbed and shot. After the trauma he wandered along unfamiliar streets for an unknown period of time. Finally, he stopped at a motel and asked if the police could be called because he did not know who he was (and had no

ID because he'd been robbed) and could not recall any personal details of his life. He spoke English (with a German accent) but could not speak German and did not respond to instructions in German (which he denied that he spoke). In spite of his extensive loss of autobiographical memory (and the German language), when given a variety of memory tasks, he showed intact implicit memory. Especially striking was his ability to learn German–English word pairs, which he learned much faster than did normal controls, suggesting implicit knowledge of German even though he had no conscious knowledge of it.

Some of these memory deficits in dissociative amnesia and fugue have been compared to related deficits in explicit perception that occur in conversion disorders. This has convinced a good number of current theorists that conversion disorder should be classified with dissociative disorders rather than with somatoform disorders, as discussed in Developments in Thinking 3.

Dissociative Identity Disorder (DID)

According to *DSM-IV-TR*, **dissociative identity disorder (DID)**, formerly called *multiple personality disorder* (MPD), is a dramatic dissociative disorder in which a patient manifests two or more distinct identities that alternate in some way in taking control of behavior. There is also an inability to recall important personal information that cannot be explained by ordinary forgetting. Each identity may appear to have a different personal

Chris Sizemore was the inspiration for the book and movie *Three Faces of Eve,* which explore her multiple personality disorder (now known as DID). Sizemore recovered in 1975 and then worked as an advocate for the mentally ill.

3 · DEVELOPMENTS IN THINKING

Should Conversion Disorder Be Classified as a Dissociative Disorder?

Starting with Freud and Janet, and for a large portion of the twentieth century prior to the publication of *DSM-III* in 1980, conversion disorders were classified together with dissociative disorders as subtypes of hysteria (e.g., Hysterical Neurosis, Dissociative Type rather than the Hysterical Neurosis, Conversion Type listed in *DSM-II*). When it was determined that *DSM-III* would rely heavily on overt behavioral symptoms rather than on presumed underlying etiology (namely, repressed anxiety) for classifying disorders, the decision was made to include conversion disorder with the other somatoform disorders because the symptoms always appeared to be physical ones with no demonstrable organic basis. However, as Kihlstrom (1994, 2001, 2005) and others have pointed out, this way of linking conversion disorders together with all the other somatoform disorders, by focusing on their all having baseless physical complaints, ignores several important differences between conversion disorders and other somatoform disorders. The most important overall difference is that conversion symptoms (but not those of the other somatoform disorders) are nearly always pseudoneurological in nature (blindness, paralysis, anaesthesias, deafness, seizures, etc.), mimicking some true neurological syndromes, just as most of the dissociative disorders do.

The disorders we currently classify as dissociative disorders (such as dissociative amnesia and fugue and DID) involve disruptions in explicit memory for events that have occurred, or who or what one's identity is, or both. However, it is clear that events occurring during a period of amnesia or in the presence of one identity are indeed registered in the nervous system because they influence behavior indirectly even when the person cannot consciously recollect them (i.e., *implicit memory* remains at least partially intact in dissociative disorders). Similarly, Kihlstrom and others have argued that the conversion disorders involve disruptions in *explicit perception* and *action*. That is, people with conversion disorders have no conscious recognition that they can see or hear or feel, or no conscious knowledge that they can walk or talk or feel. However, patients with conversion disorder *can* see, hear, feel, or move when tricked into doing so or when indirect physiological or behavioral measures are used (see Janet, 1901, 1907; Kihlstrom, 1994, 2001, 2005). Thus Kihlstrom (1994, 2001, 2005) makes a compelling argument that when the next edition of *DSM* appears, the term *conversion disorder* should be dropped and the sensory and motor types of the syndrome should be reclassified as forms of dissociative disorders. This way, the central feature of all dissociative disorders would be a disruption of the normally integrated functions of consciousness (memory, perception, and action). Such a proposal is also consistent with observations that dissociative symptoms and disorders are quite common in patients with conversion disorder (e.g., Sar et al., 2004).

DSM-IV-TR

Criteria for Dissociative Identity Disorder

A. The presence of two or more distinct identities or personality states (each with its own relatively enduring pattern of perceiving, relating to, and thinking about the environment and self).

B. At least two of these identities or personality states recurrently take control of the person's behavior.

C. Inability to recall important personal information that is too extensive to be explained by ordinary forgetfulness.

D. The disturbance is not due to the direct physiological effects of a substance (e.g., blackouts or chaotic behavior during Alcohol Intoxication) or a general medical condition (e.g., complex partial seizures). Note: In children, the symptoms are not attributable to imaginary playmates or other fantasy play.

history, self-image, and name, although there are some identities that are only partially distinct and independent from other identities. In most cases the one identity that is most frequently encountered and carries the person's real name is the **host identity**. Also in most cases, the host is not the original identity, and it may or may not be the best-adjusted identity. The **alter identities** may differ in striking ways involving gender, age, handedness, handwriting, sexual orientation, prescription for eyeglasses, predominant affect, foreign languages spoken, and general knowledge. For example, one alter may be carefree, fun-loving, and sexually provocative, and another alter quiet, studious, serious, and prudish. Needs and behaviors inhibited in the primary or host identity are usually liberally displayed by one or more alter identities. Certain roles such as a child and someone of the opposite sex are extremely common.

Much of the reason for abandoning the older diagnostic term *multiple personality disorder* in favor of DID was the growing recognition that it had misleading connotations, suggesting multiple occupancy of space, time, and victims' bodies by differing, but fully organized and coherent, "personalities." In fact, alters are not in any meaningful sense personalities but rather reflect a failure to integrate various aspects of a person's identity, consciousness, and memory (APA, 2000; Spiegel, 2006). The term *DID* better captures these changes in consciousness and identity than does *MPD*. Indeed Spiegel (one prominent theorist in this area) has argued that "the problem is not having more than one personality, it is having less than one" (Spiegel, 2006, p. 567).

Alter identities take control at different points in time, and the switches typically occur very quickly (in a matter of seconds), although more gradual switches can also occur (APA, 2000). When switches occur in people with DID, it is often easy to observe the gaps in memories for things that have happened—often for things that have happened to other identities. But this amnesia is not always symmetrical; that is, some identities may know more about certain alters than do other identities. Sometimes one submerged identity gains control by producing hallucinations (such as a voice inside the head giving instructions). In sum, DID is a condition in which normally integrated aspects of memory, identity, and consciousness are no longer integrated. Additional symptoms of DID include depression, self-mutilation, frequent suicidal ideation and attempts, erratic behavior, headaches, hallucinations, post-traumatic symptoms, and other amnesic and fugue symptoms (APA, 2000; Maldonado et al., 2002). Depressive disorders, PTSD, substance-use disorders, and borderline personality disorder are the most common comorbid diagnoses (Maldonado & Spiegel,

2007). One recent study found that among patients with diagnoses of DID, the average number of comorbid Axis I diagnoses (based on structured diagnostic interviews) was five, with PTSD being the most common (Rodewald et al., 2011).

DID usually starts in childhood, although most patients are in their teens, 20s, or 30s at the time of diagnosis (Maldonado & Spiegel, 2007). Approximately three to nine times more females than males are diagnosed as having the disorder, and females tend to have a larger number of alters than do males (APA, 2000; Maldonado & Spiegel, 2007). Some believe that this pronounced gender discrepancy is due to the much greater proportion of childhood sexual abuse among females than among males, but this is a highly controversial point, as discussed later.

Many of these features are illustrated in the case of Mary Kendall below.

The number of alter identities in DID varies tremendously and has increased over time (Maldonado & Spiegel, 2007). One review of 76 classic cases published in 1944 reported that two-thirds of these cases had only two personalities and most of the rest had three (Taylor & Martin, 1944). Yet more recent estimates in *DSM IV TR* are that about 50 percent now show over 10 identities (APA, 2000), with some respondents claiming as many as a hundred. This historical trend of increasing multiplicity suggests the operation of social factors, perhaps through the encouragement of therapists, as we discuss below (e.g., Kihlstrom, 2005;

case study | Mary and Marian

Mary, a 35-year-old divorced social worker, had . . . in her right forearm and hand . . . chronic pain. Medical management of this pain had proved problematic, and it was decided to teach her self-hypnosis as a means whereby she might control it. She proved an excellent hypnotic subject and quickly learned effective pain control techniques.

Her hypnotist/trainer, a psychiatrist, describes Mary's life in rather unappealing terms. She is said to be competent professionally but has an "arid" personal and social life . . . . She spends most of her free time doing volunteer work in a hospice . . .

In the course of the hypnotic training, Mary's psychiatrist discovered that she seemed to have substantial gaps in her memory. One phenomenon in particular was very puzzling: She reported that she could not account for what seemed an extraordinary depletion of the gasoline in her car's tank. She would arrive home from work with a nearly full tank, and by the following morning as she began her trip to work would notice that the tank was now only half-full. When it was advised that she keep track of her odometer readings, she discovered that on many nights on which she insisted she'd remained at home the odometer showed significant accumulations of up to 100 miles. The psychiatrist, by now strongly suspecting that Mary had a dissociative disorder, also established that there were large gaps in her memories of childhood. He shifted his focus to exploring the apparently widespread dissociative difficulties.

In the course of one of the continuing hypnotic sessions, the psychiatrist again asked about "lost time," and was greeted with a response in a wholly different voice tone that said, "It's about time you knew about me." Marian, an apparently well-established alter identity, went on to describe the trips she was fond of taking at night . . . Marian was an extraordinarily abrupt and hostile "person," the epitome in these respects of everything the compliant and self-sacrificing Mary was not. Marian regarded Mary with unmitigated contempt, and asserted that "worrying about anyone but yourself is a waste of time."

In due course some six other alter identities emerged . . . . There was notable competition among the alters for time spent "out," and Marian was often so provocative as to frighten some of the more timid others, which included a six-year-old child . . . .

Mary's history, as gradually pieced together, included memories of physical and sexual abuse by her father as well as others during her childhood . . . . Her mother was described . . . as having abdicated to a large extent the maternal role, forcing Mary from a young age to assume these duties in the family.

Four years of subsequent psychotherapy resulted in only modest success in achieving a true "integration" of these diverse trends in Mary Kendall's selfhood.

Source: Adapted with permission from DSM-IV-TR Casebook *(pp. 56–57). Washington, DC. (Copyright © 2002). American Psychiatric Association.*

DID, Schizophrenia, and Split Personality: Clearing Up the Confusion

The general public has long been confused by the distinction between DID and schizophrenia. It is not uncommon for people diagnosed with schizophrenia to be referred to as having a "split personality." We have even heard people say such things as, "I'm a bit schizophrenic on this issue" to mean that they have more than one opinion about it!

Although this misuse of the term *split personality* actually began among psychiatric professionals, today it reflects the public's general misunderstanding of schizophrenia, which does not involve a "split" or "Jekyll and Hyde" personality at all. The original confusion may have stemmed from the term *schizophrenia*, which was first coined by a Swiss psychiatrist named Bleuler. *Schizien* is German for "split," and *phren* is the Greek root for "mind." The notion that schizophrenia is characterized by a split mind or personality may have arisen this way (see McNally, 2007, for a historical review of how this confusion arose).

However, this is not at all what Bleuler intended the word *schizophrenia* to mean. Rather, Bleuler was referring to the splitting

of the normally integrated *associative threads* of the mind—links between words, thoughts, emotions, and behavior. Splits of this kind result in thinking that is not goal-directed or efficient, which in turn leads to the host of other difficulties known to be associated with schizophrenia.

It is very important to remember that people diagnosed with schizophrenia do *not* have multiple distinct identities that alternately take control over their mind and behavior. They may have a delusion and believe they are someone else, but they do not show the changes in identity accompanied by changes in tone of voice, vocabulary, and physical appearance that are often seen when identities "switch" in DID. Furthermore, people with DID (who are probably closer to the general public's notion of "split personality") do not exhibit such characteristics of schizophrenia as disorganized behavior, hallucinations coming from outside the head, and delusions, or incoherent and loose associations (e.g., Kluft, 2005).

Lilienfeld et al., 1999; Piper & Merskey, 2004a, 2004b). Another recent trend is that many of the reported cases of DID now include more unusual and even bizarre identities than in the past (such as being an animal) and more highly implausible backgrounds (for example, ritualized satanic abuse in childhood).

PREVALENCE—WHY HAS DID BEEN INCREASING?
Owing to their dramatic nature, cases of DID have received a great deal of attention and publicity in fiction, television, and motion pictures. But in fact, until relatively recently, DID was extremely rare—or at least rarely diagnosed—in clinical practice. Prior to 1979, only about 200 cases could be found in the entire psychological and psychiatric literature worldwide. By 1999, however, over 30,000 cases had been reported in North America alone (Ross, 1999), although as we will discuss later, many researchers in this area believe that this is a gross overestimate of true cases (e.g., Piper & Merskey, 2004b). Because their diagnosed occurrence in both clinical settings and in the general population has increased enormously in recent years, prevalence estimates in the general population vary. One study of 658 people in upstate New York estimated a 1.5 percent prevalence (Johnson et al., 2006), but it is possible that no such estimates are valid, given how hard it is to make this diagnosis reliably. (For example, recall that Mary's DID was uncovered only in the course of hypnotic sessions for pain management.)

Many factors probably have contributed to the drastic increase in the reported prevalence of DID (although in an absolute sense it is still very rare, and most practicing psychotherapists never see a person with DID in their entire careers).

For example, the number of cases began to rise in the 1970s after the publication of Flora Rhea Schreiber's *Sybil* (1973), which increased public awareness of the condition (ironically, however, the case was later thoroughly discredited; see Borch-Jacobsen, 1997; Rieber, 1999). At about the same time, the diagnostic criteria for DID (then called MPD) were clearly specified for the first time in 1980 with the publication of *DSM-III*. This seems to have led to increased acceptance of the diagnosis by clinicians, which may have encouraged reporting of it in the literature. Clinicians were traditionally (and often still are today) somewhat skeptical of the astonishing behavior these patients often display—such as undergoing sudden and dramatic shifts in personal identity before the clinicians' eyes.

Another reason why the diagnosis may be made more frequently since 1980 is that the diagnostic criteria for schizophrenia were tightened in *DSM-III* (1980). A good number of people who had been inappropriately diagnosed with schizophrenia before that time probably began to receive the appropriate diagnosis of MPD (now called DID). (See The World Around Us 4 above). In addition, beginning in about 1980, prior scattered reports of instances of childhood abuse in the histories of adult DID patients began building into what would become a crescendo. As we will see later, many controversies arose regarding how to interpret such findings, but it is definitely true that these reports of abuse in patients with DID drew a great deal of attention to this disorder, which in turn may have increased the rate at which it was being diagnosed.

Finally, it is almost certain that some of the increase in the prevalence of DID is *artifactual* and has occurred because some therapists looking for evidence of DID in certain patients may suggest the existence of alter identities (especially when the person is under hypnosis and very suggestible; e.g., Kihlstrom, 2005; Piper & Merskey, 2004b). The therapist may also subtly reinforce the emergence of new identities by showing great interest in these new identities, as will be discussed in more detail later. Nevertheless, such factors cannot account for all cases of diagnosed DID, which has been observed in most parts of the world, even where there is virtually no personal or professional knowledge of DID, including rural Turkey (Akyuz et al., 1999; see also Maldonado & Spiegel, 2007) and Shanghai, China (Xiao et al., 2006).

EXPERIMENTAL STUDIES OF DID The vast majority of what is known about DID comes from patients' self-reports and from therapists' or researchers' clinical observations. Indeed, only a small number of experimental studies of people with DID have been conducted to corroborate clinical observations that go back a hundred years. Moreover, most of these studies have been conducted on only one or a few cases, although very recently a few larger studies have been done that include appropriate control groups (e.g., Dorahy et al., 2005; Huntjens et al., 2003, 2007). In spite of such shortcomings, most of the findings from these studies are generally consistent with one another and reveal some very interesting features of DID.

The primary focus of these studies has been to determine the nature of the amnesia that exists between different identities. As we have already noted, most people with DID have at least some identities that seem completely unaware of the existence and experiences of certain alter identities, although other identities may be only partially amnesic of some alters (e.g., Elzinga et al., 2003; Huntjens et al., 2003). This feature of DID has been corroborated by studies showing that when one identity (Identity 1) is asked to learn a list of word pairs, and an alter identity (Identity 2) is later asked to recall the second word in each pair using the first word as a cue, there seems to be no transfer to Identity 2 of what was learned by Identity 1. This interpersonality amnesia with regard to conscious recall of the activities and experiences of at least some other identities has generally been considered a fundamental characteristic of DID (Kihlstrom, 2001, 2005; Kihlstrom & Schacter, 2000). Nevertheless, several interesting recent studies, each with about 20 DID patients, have challenged any idea that this interpersonality amnesia is complete, instead sometimes finding partial transfer of explicit memory across identities in certain tasks (Huntjens et al., 2003, 2007; see also Dorahy & Huntjens, 2007, for a review).

As noted earlier, there are kinds of memory other than simply what can be brought to awareness (*explicit memory*). As with dissociative amnesia and fugue, there is evidence that Identity 2 has some *implicit memory* of things that Identity 1 learned. That is, although Identity 2 may not be able to recall consciously the things learned by Identity 1, these apparently forgotten events may influence Identity 2's experiences, thoughts, and behaviors unconsciously (Kihlstrom, 2001, 2005). This might be reflected in a test asking Identity 2 to learn the list of words previously learned by Identity 1. Even though Identity 2 could not consciously recall the list of words,

Identity 2 would learn that list more rapidly than a brand-new list of words, an outcome that suggests the operation of implicit memory (e.g., Eich et al., 1997; Elzinga et al., 2003; see Kihlstrom, 2001, 2005, for reviews).

Related studies on implicit transfer of memories have shown that emotional reactions learned by one identity often transfer across identities, too. Thus, even though Identity 2 may not be able to recall an emotional event that happened to Identity 1, a visual or auditory reminder of the event (a conditioned stimulus) administered to Identity 2 may elicit an emotional reaction even though Identity 2 has no knowledge of why it did so (e.g., Ludwig et al., 1972; Prince, 1910). Moreover, one study by Huntjens and colleagues (2005) had 22 DID patients in Identity 1 learn to reevaluate a neutral word in a positive or negative manner through a simple evaluative conditioning procedure in which neutral words are simply paired with positive or negative words; the neutral words then come to take on positive or negative connotations. When Identity 2 was later asked to emerge, he or she also categorized the formerly neutral word in the same positive or negative manner as learned by Identity 1, showing implicit memory for the reevaluation of the word learned by Identity 1 (although complete subjective amnesia was reported by Identity 2). Nevertheless, other sophisticated studies have made it clear that implicit memory transfer across personalities does not always occur, particularly with certain kinds of implicit memory tasks where memory performance may be strongly influenced by the identity currently being tested (e.g., Dorahy, 2001; Eich et al., 1997; Nissen et al., 1988). However, the results that do show implicit memory transfer are very important because they demonstrate that explicit amnesia across identities cannot occur simply because one identity is trying actively to suppress any evidence of memory transfer. If this were possible, there would be no leakage of implicit memories across identities (Dorahy, 2001; Eich et al., 1997).

An even smaller number of experimental studies have examined differences in brain activity when individuals with DID are tested with different identities at the forefront of consciousness. For example, in an early classic study, Putnam (1984) investigated EEG activity in 11 DID patients during different identities, and in 10 control subjects who were simulating different personality states, in order to determine whether there were different patterns of brain wave activity during different identities (real or simulated), as would be found if separate individuals were assessed. The study found that there were indeed differences in brain wave activity when the patients with DID were in different personality states and that these differences were greater than those found in the simulating subjects (see Kihlstrom et al., 1993; Putnam, 1997). Lapointe and colleagues (2006) reported similar findings using a slightly different research design.

One particularly interesting study by Reinders and colleagues (2006) examined subjective and cardiovascular activation patterns to both neutral and traumatic memories in 11 people diagnosed with DID. Each patient had one alter with a neutral identity such as the one active when they were functioning in everyday life, and each had another alter with a traumatic identity who had access to traumatic memories. As expected, when exposed to a script of neutral personal memories neither identity displayed much subjective or cardiovascular reactivity. However, when exposed to a script of personal memories of traumatizing events, responding differed in the two identity states. Specifically, the traumatic identity state (but not the neutral identity state) showed subjective and cardiovascular reactivity reflecting emotional distress to the personal traumatic memory. Such results support the idea that one function of certain alters is to protect the person from traumatic memories that a traumatic identity state has access to.

CAUSAL FACTORS AND CONTROVERSIES ABOUT DID There are at least four serious, interrelated controversies surrounding DID and how it develops. First, some have been concerned with whether DID is a real disorder or is faked, and whether, even if it is real, it can be faked. The second major controversy is about how DID develops. Specifically, is DID caused by early childhood trauma, or does the development of DID involve some kind of social enactment of multiple different roles that have been inadvertently encouraged by careless clinicians? Third, those who maintain that DID is caused by childhood trauma cite mounting evidence that the vast majority of individuals diagnosed with DID report memories of an early history of abuse. But are these memories of early abuse real or false? Finally, if abuse has occurred in most individuals with DID, did the abuse play a *causal role*, or was something else correlated with the abuse actually the cause?

Is DID Real or Is It Faked? The issue of possible factitious or malingering origins of DID has dogged the diagnosis of DID for at least a century. One obvious situation in which this issue becomes critical is when it has been used by defendants and their attorneys to try to escape punishment for crimes ("My other personality did it"). For example, this defense was used, ultimately unsuccessfully, in the famous case of the Hillside Strangler, Kenneth Bianchi (Orne et al., 1984), but it has probably been used successfully in other cases that we are unaware of (unaware almost by definition because the person is not sent to prison but rather to a mental hospital in most cases). Bianchi was accused of brutally raping and murdering 10 young women in the Los Angeles area. Although there was a great deal of evidence that he had committed these crimes, he steadfastly denied it, and some lawyers thought perhaps he had DID. He was subsequently

Kenneth Bianchi, known as the "Hillside Strangler," brutally raped and murdered 10 women in the Los Angeles area. Hoping to create a plea of "not guilty by reason of insanity," Bianchi fabricated a second personality—"Steve"—who "emerged" while Kenneth was under hypnosis. A psychologist and psychiatrist specializing in DID determined he was faking the diagnosis, and Bianchi was subsequently convicted of the murders.

interviewed by a clinical psychologist, and under hypnosis a second personality, "Steve," emerged, who confessed to the crimes, thereby creating the basis for a plea of "not guilty by reason of insanity." However, Bianchi was later examined even more closely by a renowned psychologist and psychiatrist specializing in this area, the late Martin Orne. Upon closer examination, Orne determined that Bianchi was faking the condition. Orne drew this conclusion in part because when he suggested to Bianchi that most people with DID have more than two identities, Bianchi suddenly produced a third (Orne et al., 1984). Moreover, there was no evidence of multiple identities existing prior to the trial. When Bianchi's faking the disorder was discovered, he was convicted of the murders. In other words, some cases of DID may involve complete fabrication orchestrated by criminal or other unscrupulous persons seeking unfair advantages, and not all prosecutors have as clever and knowledgeable an expert witness as Martin Orne to help detect this. But most researchers think that factitious and malingering cases of DID (such as the Bianchi case or cases in which the person has a need to be a patient) are relatively rare.

If DID Is Not Faked, How Does It Develop: Posttraumatic Theory or Sociocognitive Theory? Many professionals acknowledge that, in most cases, DID is a real syndrome (not consciously faked), but there is marked disagreement about how it develops and how it is maintained. In the contemporary literature, the original major theory of how DID develops is **posttraumatic theory** (Gleaves, 1996; Maldonado & Spiegel, 2007; Ross, 1997, 1999). The vast majority of patients with DID (over 95 percent by some estimates) report memories of severe and horrific abuse as children (see Figure 1). According to this view, DID starts from the child's attempt to cope with an overwhelming sense of hopelessness and powerlessness in the face of repeated traumatic abuse. Lacking other resources or routes of escape, the child may dissociate and escape into a fantasy, becoming someone else. This escape may occur through a process like self-hypnosis (Butler et al., 1996), and if it helps to alleviate some of the pain caused by the abuse it will be reinforced and occur again in the future. This notion is consistent with recent evidence that inducing a dissociative state in research participants can lead to decreased pain sensitivity (Ludäscher et al., 2009). Sometimes the child simply imagines the abuse is happening

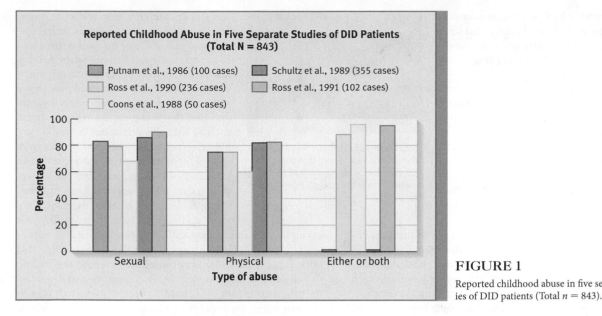

Reported Childhood Abuse in Five Separate Studies of DID Patients
(Total N = 843)

- Putnam et al., 1986 (100 cases)
- Schultz et al., 1989 (355 cases)
- Ross et al., 1990 (236 cases)
- Ross et al., 1991 (102 cases)
- Coons et al., 1988 (50 cases)

FIGURE 1

Reported childhood abuse in five separate studies of DID patients (Total *n* = 843).

to someone else. If the child is fantasy prone, and continues to stay fantasy prone over time, the child may unknowingly create different selves at different points in time, possibly laying the foundation for multiple dissociated identities.

But only a subset of children who undergo traumatic experiences are prone to fantasy or self-hypnosis, which leads to the idea that a diathesis-stress model may be appropriate here. That is, children who are prone to fantasy and those who are easily hypnotizable may have a diathesis for developing DID (or other dissociative disorders) when severe abuse occurs (e.g., Butler et al., 1996; Kihlstrom et al., 1993). However, it should also be emphasized that there is nothing inherently pathological about being prone to fantasy or readily hypnotizable (Kihlstrom et al., 1994).

Increasingly, those who view childhood abuse as playing a critical role in the development of DID are beginning to see DID as perhaps a complex and chronic variant of posttraumatic stress disorder, which by definition is caused by exposure to some kind of highly traumatic event(s), including abuse (e.g., Brown, 1994; Maldonado & Spiegel, 2007; Maldonado et al., 2002). Anxiety symptoms are more prominent in PTSD than in DID, and dissociative symptoms are more prominent in DID than in PTSD. Nevertheless, both kinds of symptoms are present in both disorders (Putnam, 1997). Moreover, some (but not all) investigators have estimated that a very high percentage of individuals diagnosed with DID have a comorbid diagnosis of PTSD, suggesting the likelihood of some important common causal factors (Vermetten et al., 2006; see also Rodewald et al., 2011).

At the other extreme from posttraumatic theory is **sociocognitive theory**, which claims that DID develops when a highly suggestible person learns to adopt and enact the roles of multiple identities, mostly because clinicians

have inadvertently suggested, legitimized, and reinforced them and because these different identities are geared to the individual's own personal goals (Lilienfeld & Lynn, 2003; Lilienfeld et al., 1999; Spanos, 1994, 1996). It is important to realize that at the present time, the sociocognitive perspective maintains that this is not done intentionally or consciously by the afflicted individual but, rather, occurs spontaneously with little or no awareness (Lilienfeld et al., 1999). The suspicion is that overzealous clinicians, through fascination with the clinical phenomenon of DID and unwise use of such techniques as hypnosis, are themselves largely responsible for eliciting this disorder in highly suggestible, fantasy-prone patients (e.g., Giesbrecht et al., 2008; Piper & Merskey, 2004a, 2004b; Spanos, 1996).

Consistent with the sociocognitive hypothesis, Spanos, Weekes, and Bertrand (1985) demonstrated that normal college students can be induced by suggestion under hypnosis to exhibit some of the phenomena seen in DID, including the adoption of a second identity with a different name that shows a different profile on a personality inventory. Thus people can enact a second identity when situational forces encourage it. Related situational forces that may affect the individual outside the therapist's office include memories of one's past behavior (e.g., as a child), observations of other people's behavior (e.g., others being assertive and independent, or sexy and flirtatious), and media portrayals of DID (Lilienfeld et al., 1999; Piper & Merskey, 2004b; Spanos, 1994).

Sociocognitive theory is also consistent with evidence that most DID patients did not show unambiguous signs of the disorder before they entered therapy and with evidence that the number of alter identities often increases (sometimes dramatically) with time in therapy (Piper & Merskey, 2004b). It is also consistent with the increased prevalence of DID since the 1970s, when the first popular accounts of DID reached the general public, and since 1980, when therapist awareness of the condition increased as well (Lilienfeld et al., 1999; Piper & Merskey, 2004a).

However, there are also many criticisms of sociocognitive theory. For example, Spanos and colleagues' demonstration of role-playing in hypnotized college students is interesting, but it does not show that this is the way DID is actually caused in real life. For example, someone might be able to give a convincing portrayal of a person with a broken leg, but this would not establish how legs are usually broken. Moreover, the hypnotized participants in this and other experiments showed only a few of the most obvious symptoms of DID (such as more than one identity) and showed them only under short-lived, contrived laboratory conditions. No such studies have shown that other symptoms such as depersonalization, memory lapses for prolonged periods, or auditory hallucinations can occur under such laboratory conditions. Thus, although some of the *symptoms* of DID could be created by social enactment, there is no evidence that the *disorder* can be created this way (e.g., Gleaves, 1996).

Are Recovered Memories of Abuse in DID Real or False? Case reports of the cruelty and torture that some DID patients suffered as children are gut-wrenching to read or hear. However, the accuracy and trustworthiness of these reports of widespread sexual and other forms of childhood abuse in DID have become a matter of major controversy in recent years. Critics (who are often proponents of sociocognitive theory) argue that many of these reports of DID patients, which generally come up in the course of therapy, may be the result of false memories, which are in turn a product of highly leading questions and suggestive techniques applied by well-meaning but inadequately skilled and careless psychotherapists (Lilienfeld et al., 1999; Loftus & Davis, 2006; Yapko, 1994). It seems quite clear to many investigators that this sort of thing has happened, often with tragic consequences. Innocent family members have been falsely accused by DID patients and have sometimes been convicted and imprisoned. But it is also true that brutal abuse of children occurs far too often and that it can have very adverse effects on development, perhaps encouraging pathological dissociation (e.g., Maldonado & Spiegel, 2007; Nash et al., 1993). In such cases, prosecution of the perpetrators of the abuse is indeed appropriate. Of course, the real difficulty here is in determining when the recovered memories of abuse are real and when they are false (or some combination of the two). This bitter controversy about the issue of false memory is more extensively considered in the Unresolved Issues section at the end of this chapter.

One way to document that particular recovered memories are real might be if some reliable physiological test could be developed to distinguish between them. Thus, some

Former Georgia football star Herschel Walker has written a book, *Breaking Free: My Life with Dissociative Identity Disorder* (2008), in which he tells about his struggle with this disorder.

researchers are currently trying to determine whether there are different neural correlates of real and false memories that could be used to make this determination reliably. Another somewhat easier way to document whether a particular recovered memory is real would be to have independent verification that the abuse had actually occurred, such as through physician, hospital, and police records. A number of studies have indeed reported that they have confirmed the reported cases of abuse, but critics have shown that the criteria used for corroborating evidence are almost invariably very loose and suspect as to their validity. For example, Chu and colleagues (1999) simply asked their subjects, "Have you had anyone confirm these events?" (p. 751) but did not specify what constituted confirmation and had no way of determining if subjects were exaggerating or distorting the information they provided as confirming evidence (Loftus & Davis, 2006; Piper & Merskey, 2004a). In another example of a flawed study, Lewis and colleagues (1997) studied 12 convicted murderers and then confirmed through medical, social service, and prison records that all 12 had been severely abused as children. Unfortunately, this study did not include a control group of otherwise comparable murderers who did not exhibit DID symptoms. Hence we cannot be certain that the childhood abuse of these subjects is not as much (or more) associated with violence or conviction for murder as with the development of DID specifically. Moreover, Lewis and colleagues should have carefully assessed for the possibility that some of the murderers might have been malingering (i.e., faking DID; Lilienfeld et al., 1999). Thus, although this study may have been one of the most impressive attempts yet to document abuse independently in people with DID, it was significantly flawed and therefore highly inconclusive.

If Abuse Has Occurred, Does It Play a Causal Role in DID? Let us put the previous controversy about the reality of recovered memories of abuse aside for a moment and assume that severe abuse has occurred in the early childhood backgrounds of many people with DID. How can we determine whether this abuse has played a critical *causal role* in the development of DID (e.g., Piper & Merskey, 2004a)? Unfortunately, many difficulties arise in answering this question. For example, child abuse usually happens in family environments plagued by many other sources of adversity and trauma (for example, various forms of psychopathology and extreme neglect and poverty). One or more of these other, correlated sources of adversity could actually be playing the causal role (e.g., Lilienfeld et al., 1999; Nash et al., 1993). Another difficulty of determining the role of abuse is that people who have experienced child abuse as well as symptoms of DID may be more likely to seek treatment than people with symptoms of DID who did not experience abuse. Thus the individuals in most studies on the prevalence of child abuse in DID may not be representative of the population of all people who suffer from DID. Finally, childhood abuse has been claimed by some to lead to many different forms of psychopathology including depression, PTSD, eating disorders, somatoform disorders, and borderline personality disorder, to name just a few. Perhaps the most we will ever be able to say is that childhood abuse may play a *nonspecific* role for many disorders, with other, more specific factors determining which disorder develops.

Comments on a Few of These Controversies About DID As we have seen, numerous studies indicate that the separate identities harbored by DID patients are somewhat physiologically and cognitively distinct. For example, EEG activity of various alters may be quite different. Because such differences cannot in any obvious way be simulated (e.g., Eich et al., 1997), it seems that DID must, in at least some cases, involve more than simply the social enactment of roles. Moreover, this should not be too surprising, given the widespread evidence of separate (dissociated) memory subsystems and nonconscious active mental processing, which indicates that much highly organized mental activity is normally carried on in all of us in the background, outside of awareness (e.g., Kihlstrom, 2005). Moreover, some people seem to be especially prone to pathological variants of these dissociative processes (Waller et al., 1996; Waller & Ross, 1997).

We should also note that each of these controversies has usually been stated in a dichotomous way: Is DID real or faked? What causes DID—spontaneous social enactment of roles or repeated childhood trauma? Are recovered memories of abuse real or false? If abuse occurs, does it play a primary causal role? Unfortunately, however, such dichotomously stated questions encourage oversimplified answers. The human mind does not seem to operate in these dichotomous ways, and we need to address the complex and multifaceted nature of the dissociated mental processes that these often miserable and severely stressed patients are experiencing. Fortunately, theorists on both sides of these controversies have begun to soften their positions just a bit and acknowledge that multiple different causal pathways are likely to be involved. For example, Ross (1997, 1999), a long-time advocate for a strong version of posttraumatic theory, later acknowledged that some cases are faked and that some may be inadvertently caused by unskilled therapists in the course of treatment. In addition, other advocates of posttraumatic theory have recently acknowledged that both real and false memories do occur in these patients, noting that it is critical that a method for determining which is which be developed (e.g., Gleaves & Williams, 2005; Gleaves et al., 2004). From the other side, Lilienfeld and colleagues (1999), who have been vocal advocates for Spanos' sociocognitive theory since his death in 1994, have acknowledged that some people with DID may have undergone real abuse, although they believe it occurs far less often, and is less likely to play a real causal role, than the trauma theorists maintain (see also Kihlstrom, 2005).

Sociocultural Factors in Dissociative Disorders

There seems little doubt that the prevalence of dissociative disorders, especially their more dramatic forms such as DID, is influenced by the degree to which such phenomena are accepted or tolerated either as normal or as legitimate mental disorders by the surrounding cultural context. Indeed, in our own society, the acceptance and tolerance of DID as a legitimate disorder have varied tremendously over time. Compared to relatively high reported rates of DID in Western cultures, a recent study of 893 patients diagnosed with some type of dissociative disorder over 10 years at a psychiatric hospital in India found no cases of DID (Chaturvedi et al., 2010). Nevertheless, although its prevalence varies, DID has now been identified in all racial groups, socioeconomic classes, and cultures where it has been studied. For example, outside North America it has been found in countries ranging from Nigeria and Ethiopia to Turkey, India, China, Australia, and the Caribbean, to name a few (Maldonado et al., 2002; Xiao et al., 2006).

Many seemingly related phenomena, such as spirit possession and dissociative trances, occur very frequently in many different parts of the world where the local culture sanctions them (Krippner, 1994). When entered into voluntarily, trance and possession states are not considered pathological and should not be construed as mental disorders. But *DSM-IV-TR* has noted that some people who enter into these states voluntarily because of cultural norms develop distress and impairment; in such cases, they might be diagnosed with *dissociative trance disorder* (a provisional diagnostic category in *DSM-IV-TR*). People receiving this provisional diagnosis must either experience trances or possession trances. A *trance* is said to occur when someone experiences a temporary marked alteration in state of consciousness or identity (but with no replacement by an alternative identity). It is usually associated with either a narrowing of awareness of the immediate surroundings, or stereotyped behaviors or movements that are experienced as beyond one's control. A *possession trance* is similar except that the alteration of consciousness or identity is replaced by a new identity that is attributed to the influence of a spirit, deity, or other power. In both cases there is typically amnesia for the trance state. One study of 58 individuals from Singapore with this diagnosis, as well as 58 individuals with a diagnosis of major depression, found that conflicts over religious or cultural issues, prior exposure to trance states, and being a spiritual healer or healer's helper were most predictive of who had dissociative trance disorder relative to major depression (Ng & Chan, 2004). A recent review of 402 cases of dissociative trance and possession disorders indicates that migration and struggles with acculturation are associated with these disorders (During et al., 2011).

There are also cross-cultural variants on dissociative disorders, such as *Amok*, which is often thought of as a rage disorder. Amok occurs when a dissociative episode leads to violent, aggressive, or homicidal behavior directed at other people and objects. It occurs mostly in men and is often precipitated by a perceived slight or insult. The person often has ideas of persecution, anger, and amnesia, often followed by a period of exhaustion and depression. Amok is found in places such as Malaysia, Laos, the Philippines, Papua New Guinea, and Puerto Rico and among Navajo Indians (APA, 2000).

Treatment and Outcomes in Dissociative Disorders

Unfortunately, virtually no systematic, controlled research has been conducted on treatment of depersonalization disorder, dissociative amnesia, and dissociative fugue, and so very little is known about how to treat them successfully. Numerous case histories, sometimes presented in small sets of cases, are available, but without control groups who are assessed at the same time or who receive nonspecific treatments it is impossible to know the effectiveness of the varied treatments that have been attempted (Kihlstrom, 2005).

Depersonalization disorder is generally thought to be resistant to treatment (e.g., Simeon et al., 1997), although treatment may be useful for associated psychopathology such as anxiety and depressive disorders. Some think that hypnosis, including training in self-hypnosis techniques, may be useful because patients with depersonalization disorder can learn to dissociate and then "reassociate," thereby gaining some sense of control over their depersonalization and derealization experiences (Maldonado & Spiegel, 2007; Maldonado et al., 2002). Many types of antidepressant, antianxiety, and antipsychotic drugs have also been tried and sometimes have modest effects. However, the only randomized controlled study showed no difference between treatment with Prozac versus with placebo (Simeon et al., 2004). One recent treatment showing some promise for the treatment of DPD involves administering rTMS to the temporo-parietal junction, an area of the brain highly involved in the experience of a unified self and body (Mantovani et al., 2011). After three weeks of treatment, half of the subjects showed significant reductions in depersonalization, with nonresponders showing symptom reduction after an additional three weeks of treatment. In dissociative amnesia and fugue, it is important for the person to be in a safe environment, and simply removing her or him from what he or she perceives as a threatening situation sometimes allows for spontaneous recovery of memory. Hypnosis, as well as drugs such as benzodiazepines, barbiturates, sodium pentobarbital, and sodium amobarbital, is often used to facilitate recall of repressed and dissociated memories (Maldonado & Spiegel, 2007; Maldonado et al., 2002). After memories are recalled, it is important for the patient to work through the memories with the therapist so that the experiences can be reframed in new ways. However, unless the memories can be independently corroborated, they should not be taken at their face value (Kihlstrom, 2005).

For DID patients, most current therapeutic approaches are based on the assumption of posttraumatic theory that the disorder was caused by abuse (Kihlstrom, 2005). Most therapists set integration of the previously separate alters, together with their collective merging into the host personality, as the ultimate goal of treatment (e.g., Maldonado & Spiegel, 2007). There is often considerable resistance to this process by the DID patients, who often consider dissociation as a protective device (e.g., "I knew my father could get some of me, but he couldn't get all of me"; Maldonado & Spiegel, 2007, p. 781). If successful integration occurs, the patient eventually develops a unified personality, although it is not uncommon for only partial integration to be achieved. But it is also very important to assess whether improvement in other symptoms of DID and associated disorders has occurred. Indeed, it seems that treatment is more likely to produce symptom improvement, as well as associated improvements in functioning, than to achieve full and stable integration of the different alter identities (Maldonado & Spiegel, 2007; Maldonado et al., 2002).

Typically the treatment for DID is psychodynamic and insight-oriented, focused on uncovering and working through the trauma and other conflicts that are thought to have led to the disorder (Kihlstrom, 2005). One of the primary techniques used in most treatments of DID is hypnosis (e.g., Kluft, 1993; Maldonado & Spiegel, 2007; Maldonado et al., 2002). Most DID patients are hypnotizable and when hypnotized are often able to recover past unconscious and frequently traumatic memories, often from childhood. Then these memories can be processed, and the patient can become aware that the dangers once present are no longer there. (But then the danger is that they are more suggestible under hypnosis, so much of what is recalled may not be accurate; see Kihlstrom, 2005; Loftus & Davis, 2006; and the Unresolved Issues section on p. 295.) Through the use of hypnosis, therapists are often able to make contact with different identities and reestablish connections between distinct, seemingly separate identity states. An important goal is to integrate the personalities into one identity that is better able to cope with current stressors. Clearly, successful negotiation of this critical phase of treatment requires therapeutic skills of the highest order; that is, the therapist must be strongly committed as well as professionally competent. Regrettably, not all therapists are.

Most reports in the literature are treatment summaries of single cases, and reports of successful cases should always be considered with caution, especially given the large bias in favor of publishing positive rather than negative results. Treatment outcome data for large groups of DID patients have been reported in only four studies we are aware of, and none of these included a control group, although it is quite clear that DID does not spontaneously remit simply with the passage of time, nor if a therapist chooses to ignore DID-related issues (Kluft, 1999; Maldonado et al., 2002). For example, Ellason and Ross (1997) reported on a 2-year postdischarge follow-up of DID patients originally treated in a specialized inpatient unit. Of the original 135 such patients, 54 were located and

THE WORLD AROUND US

5

Dissociative Disorders: Proposed Revisions for *DSM-5*

Successfully integrating dissociative disorders into the *DSM* diagnostic system has been challenging (Spiegel, 2010). In survey research, a substantial proportion of clinicians reported uncertainty regarding whether these diagnoses even belong in the psychiatric nosology (Pope et al., 1999). Nonetheless, dissociative disorders will remain in the *DSM-5*.

The criteria for depersonalization will be altered such that the diagnosis will require the primary symptom of depersonalization *or* derealization (and will now be referred to as depersonalization/derealization disorder). This change is consistent with evidence that individuals suffering only from derealization do not differ in

important ways from those experiencing depersonalization. The extremely rare dissociative fugue will become a subtype of dissociative amnesia.

The criteria for DID will be broadened to include dissociative trance and dissociative possession, which should increase the *DSM*'s ability to capture the variety of presentations of dissociative disorders seen in non-Western cultures. The language about different personality states "taking control" of a person's behavior will be removed. New specifiers for DID offer clinicians the chance to note the presence of conversion symptoms (e.g., nonepileptic seizures) that sometimes accompany DID and require clinical attention.

---

systematically assessed. All these patients, and especially those who had achieved full integration, generally showed marked improvements in various aspects of their lives. However, only 12 of the 54 had achieved full integration of their identities. Such results are promising, but we must wonder about the clinical status of the 81 "lost" patients who may likely have done less well. Another 10-year follow-up study reported similar results in a smaller sample of 25 treated DID patients. Only 12 were located 10 years later; of these, six had achieved full integration, but two of those had partially relapsed (Coons & Bowman, 2001). In general it has been found that (1) for treatment to be successful, it must be prolonged, often lasting many years, and (2) the more severe the case, the longer that treatment is needed (Maldonado & Spiegel, 2007; Maldonado et al., 2002).

In Review

- Describe the symptoms known as depersonalization and derealization, and indicate which disorder is primarily characterized by their appearance.

- Describe dissociative amnesia and dissociative fugue, and indicate what aspects of memory are affected.

- What are the primary symptoms of dissociative identity disorder (DID), and why is its prevalence thought to increasing?

- Review the four major controversies surrounding DID that were discussed in this chapter.

Unresolved Issues

▶ *DID and the Reality of "Recovered Memories"*

As we have seen in this chapter, many controversies surround the nature and origins of DID. None have been more bitter than those related to the truth value of "recovered" memories of childhood abuse, particularly sexual abuse, which posttraumatic theorists assert is the major causal factor in the development of DID. Indeed, a virtual chasm has developed between the "believers" (mostly but not exclusively private practitioners who treat people with DID) and the "disbelievers" (mostly but not exclusively the more academic and science-oriented mental health professionals). The disbelievers are very sympathetic to people suffering DID symptoms, but they have tended to doubt that the disorder is usually caused by childhood abuse and have challenged the validity or accuracy of recovered memories of abuse (see Loftus & Davis, 2006, for a review of the recovered memory debate).

For 20 years, these controversies have moved beyond professional debate and have become major public issues, leading to countless legal proceedings. DID patients who recover memories of abuse (often in therapy) have often sued their parents for having inflicted abuse. But ironically, therapists and institutions have also been sued for implanting memories of abuse that they later came to believe had not actually occurred. Some parents, asserting they had been falsely accused, formed an international support organization—the False Memory Syndrome Foundation—and have sometimes sued therapists for damages, alleging that the therapists induced false memories of parental abuse in their child. Many families have been torn apart in the fallout from this remarkable climate of suspicion, accusation, litigation, and unrelenting hostility.

Whether DID originates in childhood abuse and whether recovered memories of abuse are accurate are basically separate issues, but they have tended to become fused in the course of the debate. Hence those who doubt the validity of memories of abuse are also likely to regard the phenomenon of DID as stemming from the social enactment of roles encouraged or induced—like the memories of abuse themselves—by misguided therapy (e.g., see Bjorklund, 2000; Lilienfeld et al., 1999; Lynn et al., 2004; Piper & Merskey, 2004a, 2004b). Believers, on the other hand, have usually taken both DID and the idea that abuse is its cause to be established beyond doubt (e.g., see Gleaves, 1996; Gleaves et al., 2001; Ross, 1997, 1999).

Much of the controversy about the validity of recovered memories is rooted in disagreements about the nature, reliability, and malleability of human autobiographical memory. With some exceptions, evidence for childhood abuse as a cause of DID is restricted to the "recovered memories" (memories not originally accessible) of adults being treated for dissociative experiences. Believers argue that before treatment such memories had been "repressed" because of their traumatic nature or had been available only to certain alter identities that the host identity was generally not aware of. Treatment, according to this view of believers, dismantles the repressive defense and thus makes available to awareness an essentially accurate memory recording of the past abuse.

Disbelievers counter with several scientifically well-supported arguments. For example, scientific evidence in support of the repression concept is quite weak (e.g., Kihlstrom, 2005; Loftus & Davis, 2006; Piper, 1998). In many alleged cases of repression, the event may have been lost to memory in the course of ordinary forgetting rather than repression, or it may have occurred in the first 3 to 4 years of life, before memories can be recorded for retrieval in adulthood. In many other cases, evidence for repression has been claimed in studies where people may simply have failed to report a previously remembered event, often because they were never asked or were reluctant to disclose such very personal information (Kihlstrom, 2005; Loftus & Davis, 2006; Pope et al., 1998).

In addition, even if memories can be repressed, there are very serious questions about the accuracy of recovered memories. Human memory of past events does not operate in a computer-like manner, retrieving with perfect accuracy an unadulterated record of information previously stored and then repressed. Rather, human memory is malleable, constructive, and very much subject to modification on the basis of events happening after any original memory trace is established (Loftus & Bernstein, 2005; Loftus & Davis, 2006; Schacter et al., 2000).

Indeed, there is now good evidence that in certain circumstances, people are sometimes very prone to the development of false memories (see Wade et al., 2007, for a review). For example, a number of studies have now shown that when normal adult subjects are asked to imagine repeatedly events that they are quite sure had not happened to them before age 10, they later increase their estimate of the likelihood that these events actually had happened to them (Tsai et al., 2000). Moreover, even in a relatively short time frame, adult subjects sometimes come to believe they have performed somewhat bizarre acts (e.g., kissing a magnifying glass), as well as common acts (e.g., flipping a coin), after simply having imagined they had engaged in these acts several times 2 weeks earlier (Thomas & Loftus, 2002). These and other studies clearly show that repeated imagining of certain events

(even somewhat bizarre events) can lead people to have false memories of events that never happened (Loftus & Bernstein, 2005; Loftus & Davis, 2006). In addition, an experimental study by McNally and colleagues (2005) looked at individuals who reported either repressed or recovered memories of childhood sexual abuse and found some evidence that they had greater difficulty on at least some measures than normal controls in distinguishing between words that they had seen versus words that they had only imagined. This suggests that people with repressed or recovered memories of abuse may have greater difficulty distinguishing between what has actually happened to them and what they have imagined happened to them. However, a different study found that those who report recovered memories of childhood sexual abuse did not show increased difficulty retrieving non-abuse-related autobiographic memories compared to those who reported continuous memories of childhood sexual abuse or a control group reporting no childhood sexual abuse (Raymaekers et al., 2010).

By the early 1990s, however, many poorly trained therapists, uninformed about how the human memory system works, bought into the notion that a suitably vigorous therapeutic approach could uncover a true and accurate record of the traumatic childhood experiences of their clients. In addition, many were convinced that certain rather common adult symptoms and complaints (e.g., headaches, poor self-esteem, unexplained anxiety) were indicative of a history of childhood trauma (e.g., see Bass & Davis, 1988; Blume, 1990) and justified relentless demands that the client remember the traumatic abuse. Persuaded by the therapist's certainty and persistence, which were accompanied by liberal use of techniques such as hypnosis and age regression, techniques known to enhance suggestibility, many clients did eventually "remember" such incidents, confirming the therapist's "expert" opinion. However, the veracity of such memories has been seriously questioned. For example, one fascinating study compared a group of people who had continuous memories of childhood abuse with two groups who had recovered memories of abuse. In one of the latter groups the memories had been recovered during therapy and in the other the memories had been recovered out of therapy. The researchers then attempted to corroborate these recovered memories, and found corroborative evidence for over half of those who had recovered memories outside of therapy and for none in the group who recovered their memories during therapy (Geraerts et al., 2007).

Attempting to mediate this conflict and debate about the veracity of recovered memories and to provide both its members and the public with guidance on the issues involved, in the mid-1990s the American Psychological Association (APA) convened a bipartisan panel of experts on both sides called the Working Group on the Investigation of Memories of Childhood Abuse (Alpert et al., 1996). As one further measure of the amount of dissent and controversy raging in this field, the Working Group agreed on almost nothing, and each side wrote an independent report instead of contributing to an integrated one as originally hoped for. Unfortunately, no significant progress toward consensus has been made since the publication of that report in 1996. Thus the public and many professionals who are not directly involved remain divided and confused about what to believe about dissociative phenomena and their connection (if any) with actual childhood abuse. The conflicting viewpoints of psychologists with respect to this debate were highly visible in a recent court case (Commonwealth v. Shanley). The supreme court of the state of Massachusetts upheld the conviction of a priest, Paul Shanley, for sexual abuse of a child. In this case, the accusations by the plaintiff were made entirely on the basis of memories that were recovered after 13 years of dissociative amnesia, surfacing after the plaintiff learned that former classmates were accusing this priest of abuse (Wolf & Guyer, 2010). Prominent psychologists argued both for and against the validity of repressed memories of abuse, with memory researcher Elizabeth Loftus claiming there was "no credible scientific evidence for the idea that years of brutalization can be massively repressed" (*Commonwealth* v. *Shanley*, 2010) and James A. Chu, a psychiatrist from Harvard's medical school calling such dissociation "not at all rare" (*Commonwealth* v. *Shanley*, 2010).

Recently, McNally and Geraerts (2009) have offered a different perspective on recovered memories, one that attempts to bridge the gap between the conviction that repression underlies recovered memories and the alternate conviction that all recovered memories are false. This third perspective suggests that some recovered memories are genuine but were never actually repressed. Instead, some abuse victims may simply not have thought about their abuse for a long period of time, have been deliberately attempting to forget the abuse (suppression rather than repression), or may have forgotten prior instances when they did recall the abuse, resulting in the false impression that a recently surfaced memory had been repressed for years.

Summary

- Somatoform disorders are those in which psychological problems are manifested in physical disorders (or complaints of physical disorders) that often mimic medical conditions but for which no evidence of corresponding organic pathology can be found.

- In hypochondriasis, an anxious preoccupation with having a disease is based on a misinterpretation of bodily signs or symptoms. Medical reassurance does not help.

- Somatization disorder is characterized by many different complaints of physical ailments in four symptom categories over at least several years. The symptoms need not actually have existed as long as they were complained about.

- Pain disorder is characterized by pain severe enough to disrupt life but in the absence of enough medical pathology to explain its presence.

- Conversion disorder involves patterns of symptoms or deficits affecting sensory or voluntary motor functions leading one to think there is a medical or neurological condition, even though medical examination reveals no physical basis for the symptoms.

- Body dysmorphic disorder involves obsessive preoccupation with some perceived flaw or flaws in one's appearance. Compulsive checking behaviors (such as mirror checking) and avoidance of social activities because of fear of being rejected are also common.

- Dissociative disorders occur when the processes that normally regulate awareness and the multichannel capacities of the mind apparently become disorganized, leading to various anomalies of consciousness and personal identity.

- Depersonalization disorder occurs in people who experience persistent and recurrent episodes of derealization (losing one's sense of reality of the outside world) and depersonalization (losing one's sense of oneself and one's own reality).

- Dissociative amnesia involves an inability to recall previously stored information that cannot be accounted for by ordinary forgetting and seems to be a common initial reaction to highly stressful circumstances. The memory loss is primarily for episodic or autobiographical memory.

- In dissociative fugue, a person not only goes into an amnesic state but also leaves his or her home surroundings and becomes confused about his or her identity, sometimes assuming a new one.

- In dissociative identity disorder, the person manifests at least two or more distinct identities that alternate in some way in taking control of behavior. Alter identities may differ in many ways from the host identity. There are many controversies about DID, including whether it is real or faked; how it develops; whether memories of childhood abuse are real; and, if the memories are real, whether the abuse played a causal role.

Key Terms

alter identities	dissociative fugue	malingering
body dysmorphic disorder (BDD)	dissociative identity disorder (DID)	pain disorder
conversion disorder	factitious disorder	posttraumatic theory (of DID)
depersonalization	factitious disorder by proxy	primary gain
depersonalization disorder	host identity	secondary gain
derealization	hypochondriasis	sociocognitive theory (of DID)
dissociation	hysteria	soma
dissociative amnesia	implicit memory	somatization disorder
dissociative disorders	implicit perception	somatoform disorders

Glossary

Many of the key terms listed in the glossary appear in boldface when first introduced in the text discussion. A number of other terms commonly encountered in this or other psychology texts are also included; you are encouraged to make use of this glossary both as a general reference tool and as a study aid for the course in abnormal psychology.

Alter identities. In a person with dissociative identity disorder, personalities other than the host personality.

Body dysmorphic disorder (BDD). Obsession with some perceived flaw or flaws in one's appearance.

Conversion disorder. Pattern in which symptoms of some physical malfunction or loss of control appear without any underlying organic pathology; originally called *hysteria*.

Depersonalization. Temporary loss of sense of one's own self and one's own reality.

Depersonalization disorder. Dissociative disorder in which episodes of depersonalization and derealization become persistent and recurrent.

Derealization. Experience in which the external world is perceived as distorted and lacking a stable and palpable existence.

Dissociation. The human mind's capacity to mediate complex mental activity in channels split off from or independent of conscious awareness.

Dissociative amnesia. Psychogenically caused memory failure.

Dissociative disorders. Conditions involving a disruption in an individual's normally integrated functions of consciousness, memory, or identity.

Dissociative fugue. A dissociative amnesic state in which the person is not only amnesic for some or all aspects of his or her past but also departs from home surroundings.

Dissociative identity disorder (DID). Condition in which a person manifests at least two or more distinct identities or personality states that alternate in some way in taking control of behavior. Formerly called *multiple personality disorder*.

Factitious disorder. Feigning of symptoms to maintain the personal benefits that a sick role may provide, including the attention and concern of medical personnel or family members.

Factitious disorder by proxy. A variant of factitious disorder in which a person induces medical or psychological symptoms in another person who is under his or her care (usually a child).

Host identity (personality). The identity in dissociative identity disorder which is most frequently encountered and carries the person's real name. This is not usually the original identity and it may or may not be the best adjusted identity.

Hypochondriasis. Preoccupation, based on misinterpretations of bodily symptoms, with the fear that one has a serious disease.

Hysteria. Older term used for conversion disorders; involves the appearance of symptoms of organic illness in the absence of any related organic pathology.

Implicit memory. Memory that occurs below the conscious level.

Implicit perception. Perception that occurs below the conscious level.

Malingering. Consciously faking illness or symptoms of disability to achieve some specific nonmedical objective.

Pain disorder. Experience of pain of sufficient duration and severity to cause significant life disruption in the absence of medical pathology that would explain it.

Posttraumatic theory (of DID). The view that DID starts from the child's attempt to cope with an overwhelming sense of hopelessness and powerlessness in the face of repeated traumatic abuse.

Primary gain. In psychodynamic theory it is the goal achieved by symptoms of conversion disorder by keeping internal intrapsychic conflicts out of aware-ness. In contemporary terms it is the goal achieved by symptoms of conver-sion disorder by allowing the person to escape or avoid stressful situations.

Secondary gain. External circumstances that tend to reinforce the maintenance of disability.

Sociocognitive theory (of DID). View that DID develops when a highly suggestible person learns to adopt and enact the roles of multiple identi-ties, mostly because clinicians have inadvertently suggested, legitimized, and reinforced them and because these different identities are geared to the individual's own personal goals.

Soma. Greek word for body.

Somatization disorder. Multiple complaints, over a long period beginning before age 30, of physical ailments that are inadequately explained by inde-pendent findings of physical illness or injury and that lead to medical treat-ment or to significant life impairment.

Somatoform disorders. Conditions involving physical complaints or disabilities that occur without any evidence of physical pathology to account for them.

Photo Credits

Credits are listed in order of appearance.

Text Credits

Credits are listed in order of appearance.

Eating Disorders and Obesity

Weighing a mere 88 pounds on her 5-foot-8 frame, Brazilian model Ana Carolina Reston succumbed to a generalized infection on November 15, 2006, while battling anorexia nervosa. She was 21 years old. Having modeled for Armani and Versace and in numerous countries around the world, Carolina was initially hospitalized for kidney failure. Ana Carolina's anorexia nervosa apparently began after she was criticized for being "too fat" during a casting call in China. At the height of her illness her diet consisted only of tomatoes and apples. Her death highlights the health risks associated with eating disorders.

This model's struggles with anorexia nervosa also reveal the extent to which ideals of beauty are intertwined with thinness. Looking good often means being slim, especially for those in the public eye. Not surprisingly, many celebrities, including Nicole Richie, Mary-Kate Olsen, Victoria Beckham, and the late Princess Diana, have also struggled with eating disorders.

After the death in 2006 of Luisel Ramos, a model from Uruguay, some steps were taken by the fashion industry to try to address the situation. The organizers of the Madrid Fashion Week decided to ban models who did not have a body mass index (a measure of a person's weight relative to height) in the healthy range. In 2010, Victoria Beckham reportedly deemed 23 models "too skinny" and refused to have them be part of her New York Fashion Week runway show. And in France, legislation has been proposed to prohibit media that encourage emaciation, or extreme thinness. What do you think? Should models be required to get a certificate of health from their doctors before being allowed on the catwalks? Should we expect the fashion industry to police itself, or should legislation be involved? Are you ready to see healthier-looking models in the pages of *Vogue,* or does ultrathin still mean ultrafashionable to you?

According to the *DSM-IV-TR* (APA, 2000), **eating disorders** are characterized by a severe disturbance in eating behavior. No doubt you have heard about anorexia nervosa and bulimia nervosa. Within the *DSM* these are considered to be separate syndromes, and they reflect two types of adult eating disorders. However, disordered eating is not their most striking feature. At the heart of both disorders is an intense fear of becoming overweight and fat and an accompanying pursuit of thinness. This pursuit is relentless and sometimes deadly.

In this chapter we focus on both of these disorders. We also examine obesity. Obesity is not considered be to an eating disorder or a psychiatric condition in the *DSM*; however, its prevalence is rising at an alarming rate. Obesity also accounts for more morbidity and mortality than all other eating disorders combined. Because obesity clearly involves disordered eating patterns, and because it has been suggested that obesity be included in the next *DSM* (although we do not expect this will happen), we discuss it in detail in this chapter.

Eating Disorders

Clinical Aspects of Eating Disorders

Anorexia Nervosa

The term *anorexia nervosa* literally means "lack of appetite induced by nervousness." This definition is something of a misnomer, however, as a lack of appetite is neither the core difficulty nor necessarily even true. At the heart of **anorexia nervosa** is an intense *fear of gaining weight* or becoming fat,

Model Ana Carolina Reston weighed just 88 pounds when she died from medical complications of anorexia nervosa.

Like many other celebrities, Mary-Kate Olsen (shown here (right) with her twin sister, Ashley) has struggled with anorexia nervosa.

The late Princess Diana's courage in discussing her own struggles with bulimia nervosa helped many other individuals with the same problem to seek treatment.

Criteria for Anorexia Nervosa

A. Refusal to maintain body weight at or above a minimally normal weight for age and height (e.g., weight loss leading to maintenance of body weight less than 85% of that expected; or failure to make expected weight gain during period of growth, leading to body weight less than 85% of that expected).

B. Intense fear of gaining weight or becoming fat, even though underweight.

C. Disturbance in the way in which one's body weight or shape is experienced, undue influence of body weight or shape on self-evaluation, or denial of the seriousness of the current low body weight.

D. In postmenarcheal females, amenorrhea, i.e., the absence of at least three consecutive menstrual cycles. (A woman is considered to have amenorrhea if her periods occur only following hormone, e.g., estrogen, administration.).

Source: Reprinted with permission from the American Psychiatric Association. *Diagnostic and Statistical Manual of Mental Disorders,* Fourth Edition, *Text Revision* (Copyright © 2000). American Psychiatric Association.

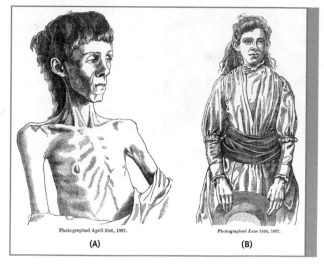

FIGURE 1

Gull's patient with anorexia nervosa. (A) Before treatment. (B) After treatment.
Source: Gull, W. (1888). Anorexia nervosa. *Lancet*, pp. i, 516–17.

combined with a *refusal to maintain even a minimally low body weight*. The *DSM-IV-TR* criteria for anorexia nervosa are shown in the *DSM* criteria box. Box 1 describes some of the changes to these diagnostic criteria that are anticipated in *DSM-5*.

Although we may think of anorexia nervosa as a modern problem, it is centuries old. Descriptions of extreme fasting that were probably signs of anorexia nervosa can be found in early religious literature (Vandereycken, 2002). The first known medical account of anorexia nervosa, however, was published in 1689 by Richard Morton (see Silverman, 1997, for a good general historical overview). Morton described two patients, an 18-year-old girl and a 16-year-old boy, who

suffered from a "nervous consumption" that resulted in wasting of body tissue. The female patient eventually died because she refused treatment.

The disorder did not receive its current name until 1873, when Charles Lasègue in Paris and Sir William Gull in London independently described the clinical syndrome. In his last publication on the condition, Gull (1888) described a 14-year-old girl who began "without apparent cause, to evince a repugnance to food; and soon afterwards declined to take any whatever, except half a cup of tea or coffee." After being prescribed to eat light food every few hours, the patient made a good recovery. Gull's illustrations of the patient before and after treatment appear in Figure 1.

Even though they may look painfully thin or even emaciated, many patients with anorexia nervosa deny having any problem. Indeed, they may come to feel fulfilled by their weight loss. Despite this quiet satisfaction, however, they may feel ambivalent

THE WORLD AROUND US

1

Anticipating *DSM-5*: Proposed Changes to the Diagnostic Criteria for Anorexia Nervosa

Although the *DSM-IV-TR* criteria for anorexia nervosa require that postmenarcheal females stop menstruating in order to be diagnosed with the disorder, this will likely not be the case in *DSM-5*. Studies have suggested that women who continue to menstruate but meet all the other diagnostic criteria for anorexia nervosa are very similar psychologically to women who have amenorrhea and have ceased menstruating (Attia & Roberto, 2009). Amenorrhea is also not a criterion

that can be used for males, nor can it be assessed in prepubescent girls or in women who use hormonal contraceptives. Current recommendations call for this criterion to be dropped in *DSM-5*. Another important change that is anticipated is that the term "significantly low body weight" (defined as a weight that is less than minimally normal) be used instead of the confusing phase about having a "body weight less that 85% of what is expected."

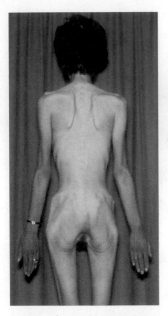

Patients with anorexia nervosa may be emaciated while still denying that they have any problems with their weight. They will go to great lengths to conceal their thinness by wearing baggy clothes, or by drinking massive amounts of water prior to being weighed (in a hospital setting, for instance).

about their weight. Efforts may be made to conceal their thinness by wearing baggy clothes or carrying hidden bulky objects so that they will weigh more when measured by others. Patients with anorexia nervosa may even resort to drinking large amounts of water to increase their weight temporarily.

There are two types of anorexia nervosa: the restricting type and the binge-eating/purging type. The central difference between these two subtypes concerns the way in which patients maintain their very low weight. In the *restricting type*, every effort is made to limit the quantity of food consumed. Caloric intake is tightly controlled. Patients often try to avoid eating in the presence of other people. When they are at the table, they may eat excessively slowly, cut their food into very small pieces, or dispose of food secretly (Beaumont, 2002).

The relentless restriction of food intake is not possible for all patients with anorexia nervosa. Patients with the *binge-eating/purging type* of anorexia nervosa differ from patients with restricting anorexia nervosa because they either binge, purge, or binge *and* purge. A **binge** involves an out-of-control consumption of an amount of food that is far greater than what most people would eat in the same amount of time and under the same circumstances. These binges may be followed by efforts to **purge**, or remove from their bodies, the food they have eaten. Methods of purging commonly include self-induced vomiting or misusing laxatives, diuretics, and enemas. Other compensatory behaviors that do not involve purging are excessive exercise or fasting. Even purging strategies, however, do not prevent the absorption of all calories from food.

Indicative of the distorted values of eating-disordered patients (see Table 1 for personal comments that provide examples of this) those with the restricting type of anorexia nervosa are often greatly admired by others with eating disorders. One patient reported that she had not been "successful" in her anorexia nervosa because of her failure to reach an

table 1 Distorted Thinking in Anorexia Nervosa

"I have a rule when I weigh myself. If I've gained then I starve the rest of the day. But if I've lost, then I starve too."
"Bones define who we really are, let them show."
"An imperfect body reflects an imperfect person."
"Anorexia is not a self-inflicted disease, it's a self-controlled lifestyle."
"It's not deprivation, it's liberation."

extremely low weight. Her belief was that the hallmark of a truly successful person with anorexia nervosa was death from starvation, and that patients who were able to accomplish this should somehow be revered (see Bulik & Kendler, 2000).

In the example that follows, we describe the case of Tim, who is suffering from the restricting type of anorexia nervosa. Tim's case reminds us that eating disorders can occur in young children as well as in boys. It further highlights the high comorbidity between eating disorders and obsessive-compulsive symptoms and personality traits, which we will subsequently discuss. In fact, Tim warrants an additional diagnosis of obsessive-compulsive disorder.

case study — Tim: Obsessed with His Weight

Tim is 8 years old. He is extremely concerned about his weight and weighs himself daily. Tim complains that he is too fat, and if he does not lose weight, he cuts back on food. He has lost 10 pounds in the past year and still feels that he is too fat. However, it is clear that he is underweight. In desperation, his parents have removed the scales from the house; as a result, Tim is keeping a record of the calories that he eats daily. He spends an excessive amount of time on these calculations, checking and rechecking that he has done it just right.

In addition, Tim is described as being obsessed with cleanliness and neatness. Currently, he has no friends because he refuses to visit them, feeling that their houses are "dirty." He becomes upset when another child touches him. He is always checking whether he is doing things the way they "should" be done. He often feels very agitated and anxious about this. Each day, he has to wake up at least 2 hours before leaving for school in order to allow himself sufficient time to get ready. Recently, he woke up at 1:30 A.M. to prepare for school.

Source: Adapted with permission from *DSM-IV-TR Casebook: A Learning Companion to the Diagnostic and Statistical Manual of Mental Disorders, Fourth Edition, Text Revision.* Washington, DC: American Psychiatric Association.

Ballet dancers are at very high risk for developing eating disorders. According to Gelsey Kirkland, once the premier ballerina at the New York City Ballet, the value placed on being thin can create a "concentration camp aesthetic" supported and encouraged by the dance company.

Because the artistic standards of their profession emphasize a slender physique, ballet dancers are at an especially high risk for eating disorders (see the case study of Ms. R.). Gelsey Kirkland, who developed an eating disorder while she was a premier ballerina with the New York City Ballet, described the existence of a "concentration camp aesthetic" within the company. This was no doubt fostered by the famous choreographer George Balanchine, who, as described by Kirkland in her autobiography, tapped her on the ribs and sternum after one event and exhorted that he "must see the bones" (Kirkland, 1986, pp. 55–56).

Bulimia Nervosa

Bulimia nervosa is characterized by uncontrollable binge eating and efforts to prevent resulting weight gain by using inappropriate behaviors such as self-induced vomiting and excessive exercise. Bulimia nervosa was recognized as a psychiatric syndrome relatively recently. The British psychiatrist G. F. M. Russell (1997) proposed the term in 1979, and it was adopted into the *DSM* in 1987. The word *bulimia* comes from the Greek *bous* (which means "ox"), and *limos* ("hunger"). It is meant to denote a hunger of such proportions that the person "could eat an ox." The *DSM-IV-TR* criteria for bulimia nervosa are shown in the *DSM* box.

The clinical picture of the binge-eating/purging type of anorexia nervosa has much in common with bulimia nervosa. Indeed, some researchers have argued that the bulimic type of anorexia nervosa should really be considered another form of bulimia nervosa. The difference between a person with bulimia nervosa and a person with the binge-eating/purging type of anorexia nervosa is weight. By definition, the person with anorexia nervosa is severely underweight. This is not true of the person with bulimia nervosa.

Consequently, if the person who binges or purges also meets criteria for anorexia nervosa, the diagnosis is anorexia nervosa (binge-eating/purging type) and not bulimia nervosa. In other words, the anorexia nervosa diagnosis "trumps" the bulimia nervosa diagnosis. This is because there is a far greater mortality rate associated with anorexia nervosa than with bulimia nervosa. Recognizing this, the *DSM* requires that the more severe form of eating pathology take precedence diagnostically.

case study · Ms. R.: Going to Extremes

Ms. R. is a very thin, 19-year-old, single ballet student who comes in at the insistence of her parents for a consultation concerning her eating behavior. Ms. R. has had a lifelong interest in ballet. She began to attend classes at age 5 and by age 8 was recognized by her teachers as having impressive talent. Since the age of 14 she has been a member of a national ballet company.

Ms. R. has had difficulties with eating since age 15 when, for reasons she is unable to explain, she began to induce vomiting after what she felt was overeating. The vomiting was preceded by many years of persistent dieting, which began with the encouragement of her ballet teacher. Over the past 3 years, Ms. R.'s binges have occurred once a day in the evening and have been routinely followed by self-induced vomiting. The binges consist of dozens of rice cakes or, more rarely, half a gallon of ice cream. Ms. R. consumes this food late at night after her parents have gone to bed. For some time, Ms. R.'s parents have been concerned that their daughter has a problem with her eating, but she consistently denied difficulties until about a month before this consultation.

Ms. R. reached her full height of 5 feet 8 inches at age 15. Her greatest weight was 120 pounds at age 16, which she describes as being fat. For the past 3 years, her weight has been reasonably stable in the range of 100 to 104 pounds. She exercises regularly as part of her profession, and she denies using laxatives, diuretics, or diet pills as a means of weight control. Except when she is binge eating, she avoids the consumption of foods high in fat or sugar.

Since age 15, she has been a strict vegetarian and consumes no meat or eggs and little cheese. For the past 3 or 4 years, Ms. R. has been uncomfortable eating in front of other people and goes to great lengths to avoid such situations. This places great limitations on her social life. Ms. R. had two spontaneous menstrual periods at age 16 when her weight hovered around 120 pounds. She has not menstruated since, however. (Adapted with permission from *DSM-IV Case Studies: A Clinical Guide to Differential Diagnosis*, Copyright 1996. American Psychiatric Association.)

Criteria for Bulimia Nervosa

A. Recurrent episodes of binge eating. An episode of binge eating is characterized by both of the following:
   1. eating, in a discrete period of time (e.g., within any 2-hour period), an amount of food that is definitely larger than most people would eat during a similar period of time and under similar circumstances
   2. a sense of lack of control over eating during the episode (e.g., a feeling that one cannot stop eating or control what or how much one is eating).

B. Recurrent inappropriate compensatory behavior in order to prevent weight gain, such as self-induced vomiting; misuse of laxatives, diuretics, enemas, or other medications; fasting; or excessive exercise.

C. The binge eating and inappropriate compensatory behaviors both occur, on average, at least twice a week for 3 months.

D. Self-evaluation is unduly influenced by body shape and weight.

E. The disturbance does not occur exclusively during episodes of Anorexia Nervosa.

Source: Reprinted with permission from the American Psychiatric Association. *Diagnostic and Statistical Manual of Mental Disorders,* Fourth Edition, *Text Revision* (Copyright © 2000). American Psychiatric Association.

People with anorexia nervosa and bulimia nervosa share a common fear of being or becoming fat. However, unlike patients with anorexia nervosa, those with bulimia nervosa are typically of normal weight or sometimes even slightly overweight. The fear of becoming fat helps explain the development of bulimia nervosa. Bulimia typically begins with restricted eating motivated by the desire to be slender. During these early stages, the person diets and eats low-calorie foods. Over time, however, the early resolve to restrict gradually erodes, and the person starts to eat "forbidden foods" such as potato chips, pizza, cake, ice cream, and chocolate. Of course, some patients binge on whatever food is available, including such things as raw cookie dough. During an average binge, someone with bulimia nervosa may consume as many as 4,800 calories (Johnson et al., 1982). After the binge, in an effort to manage the breakdown of self-control, the person begins to vomit, fast, exercise excessively, or abuse laxatives. This pattern then persists because, even though those with bulimia nervosa are disgusted by their behavior, the purging alleviates the fear of gaining weight that comes from eating.

Bulimia can be a costly disorder for many patients. High food bills can create financial difficulties, and patients sometimes resort to stealing food from others. The *DSM-IV-TR* distinguishes between *purging* and *nonpurging types* of bulimia nervosa on the basis of whether, in the current episode, the person has employed purgative methods of preventing weight gain (e.g., vomiting, use of laxatives). The purging type is by far the most common and accounts for the vast majority of cases (Eddy, Doyle, et al., 2008). The nonpurging type, which involves fasting or exercise to counteract the effects of binging but not the use vomiting, laxatives, or diuretics, will likely be dropped as a subtype in *DSM-5* (see van Hoecken et al., 2009).

People with anorexia nervosa often deny the seriousness of their disorders and are surprised by the shock and concern with which others view their emaciated conditions. In contrast, those with bulimia nervosa are often preoccupied with shame, guilt, self-deprecation, and efforts at concealment as they struggle (often unsuccessfully) to master their urges to binge. The case described below depicts a typical pattern.

case study | Nicole: Too Full to Eat

Nicole awakens in her cold, dark room and already wishes it were time to go back to bed. She dreads the thought of going through this day, which will be like so many others in the recent past. She asks herself the same question every morning: "Will I be able to make it through the day without being totally obsessed by thoughts of food, or will I blow it again and spend the day binging?" She tells herself that today she will begin a new life; today she will start to live like a normal human being. However, she is not at all convinced that the choice is hers.

She feels fat and wants to lose weight, so she decides to start a new diet: "This time it'll be for real! I know I'll feel good about myself if I'm thinner. I want to start my exercises again because I want to make my body more attractive." Nicole plans her breakfast but decides not to eat until she has worked out for a half an hour or so. She tries not to think about food because she is not really hungry. She feels anxiety about the day ahead of her. "It's this tension," she rationalizes. That is what is making her want to eat.

Nicole showers and dresses and plans her schedule for the day—classes, studying, and meals. She plans this schedule in great detail, listing where she will be at every minute and what she will eat at every meal. She does not want to leave blocks of time when she might feel tempted to binge. "It's time to exercise, but I don't really want to; I feel lazy. Why do I always feel so lazy? What happened to the will power I used to have?" Gradually, Nicole feels the binging signal coming on. Halfheartedly she tries to fight it, remembering the promises she made to herself about changing. She also knows how she is going to feel at the end of the day if she spends it binging. Ultimately, though, Nicole succumbs to her urges because, for the moment, she would rather eat.

Due to her decision to have something to eat right away, Nicole delays her trip to the gym. She even rationalizes that she might as well eat some "good" food. She makes a poached egg and toast and brews a cup of coffee, all of which goes down in about 30 seconds. She knows this is the beginning of several hours of whirlwind emotions and behavior.

After rummaging through the cupboards, Nicole realizes that she does not have any "binge" food. It is cold and snowy outside and she has to be at school fairly soon. Nevertheless, she bundles up and runs down the street. First she stops at the bakery for a bagful of sweets—cookies and doughnuts. While munching on these, she stops and buys a few bagels. Then, she makes a quick run to the grocery store for granola and milk. At the last minute, Nicole adds several candy bars. By the time she is finished, she has spent a lot of money.

Nicole can hardly believe that she is going to put all of this food, this junk, into her body. Even so, her adrenaline is flowing and all she wants to do is eat, think about eating, and anticipate getting it over with. She winces at the thought of the number of pounds represented by her purchased food, yet she knows she will throw it all up afterward. She tells herself that there is no need to worry.

At home, Nicole makes herself a few bowls of cereal and milk, which she gobbles down with some of the bagels smothered with butter, cream cheese, and jelly. All the while, she continues to munch on the goodies from the bakery and the candy bars. She drowns all of this with huge cups of coffee and milk, which help speed up the process even more. All this has taken no longer than 45 minutes. Nicole feels as though she has been racing at 90 miles an hour.

Nicole dreads reaching this stage, where she is so full that she absolutely has to stop eating. She will throw up, which she feels both compelled and loath to do. At this point she has to acknowledge that she has been binging. She wishes she were dreaming, but she knows all too well that this is real. The thought of actually digesting all of those calories, from all of that junk, terrifies her.

In her bathroom, Nicole ties her hair back, turns on the shower (so none of the neighbors can hear her), drinks a big glass of water, and proceeds to force herself to vomit. She feels sick, ashamed, and incredulous that she is actually doing this. She feels trapped—she does not know how to break out of this pattern. As her stomach empties, she steps on and off the scale to make sure she has not gained any weight.

Nicole knows she needs help, but she wishes her problem would just go away on its own. As she crashes on her bed to recuperate, her head is spinning. "I'll never do this again," she vows. "Starting tomorrow, I'm going to change. I'll go on a fast for a week and then I'll feel better." Unfortunately, deep inside, Nicole does not believe any of this. She knows this will not be the last time. Reluctantly, she leaves for school, late and unwilling to face the work and responsibilities that lie ahead. She almost feels as though she could eat again to avoid going to school. She wonders how many hours it will be until she starts her next binge. (Adapted from Boskind-White & White, 1983, pp. 29–32.)

Other Forms of Eating Disorders

In addition to anorexia nervosa and bulimia nervosa, the *DSM-IV-TR* includes the diagnosis of **eating disorder not otherwise specified (EDNOS)**. This is used for patterns of disordered eating that do not exactly fit the criteria for any of the more specific diagnoses. For example, a woman who meets all criteria for anorexia nervosa except disrupted menstrual periods would be diagnosed as having EDNOS. An EDNOS diagnosis would also be given to someone who fails to meet the full diagnostic criteria for bulimia nervosa because she binges and purges less frequently than twice a week, even though she might binge and purge between one and seven times per month over a 3-month period.

By definition, the diagnostic category of "not otherwise specified," or NOS, is a residual category. This classification appears throughout the *DSM* for many types of disorders (e.g., anxiety disorder NOS). Typically, only a minority of cases will be classified in this way. However, this is not so for the diagnosis of EDNOS, which is given to around 60 percent of adolescents and adults who seek treatment in outpatient settings (Eddy, Doyle, et al., 2008; Fairburn & Bohn, 2005). Moreover, research suggests that cases of EDNOS are not mild and, therefore, unimportant. On the contrary, the diagnosis of EDNOS tends to reflect severe and long-standing clinical problems (Fairburn et al., 2007). At the end of this chapter we discuss some of the ways in which the diagnosis of EDNOS is likely to change in *DSM-5*.

Another form of eating disorder currently classified as eating disorder NOS is called **binge-eating disorder (BED)** (see the *DSM-IV-TR* box). Binge-eating disorder has provisional status in *DSM-IV*, which encourages researchers to study it. Although BED has some clinical features in common with the nonpurging subtype of bulimia nervosa, recent research supports the idea that BED is a distinct clinical syndrome (Wonderlich et al., 2009). BED will likely lose its provisional status and become a formal diagnosis in *DSM-5*.

DSM-IV-TR

Criteria for Binge-Eating Disorder (BED)

A. Recurrent episodes of binge eating. An episode of binge eating is characterized by both of the following:
   1. eating, in a discrete period of time (e.g., within any 2-hour period), an amount of food that is definitely larger than most people would eat in a similar period of time under similar circumstances
   2. a sense of lack of control over eating during the episode (e.g., a feeling that one cannot stop eating or control what or how much one is eating).

B. The binge-eating episodes are associated with three (or more) of the following:
   1. eating much more rapidly than normal
   2. eating until feeling uncomfortably full
   3. eating large amounts of food when not feeling physically hungry
   4. eating alone because of being embarrassed by how much one is eating
   5. feeling disgusted with oneself, depressed, or very guilty after overeating.

C. Marked distress regarding binge eating is present.

D. The binge eating occurs, on average, at least 2 days a week for 6 months.

Source: Reprinted with permission from the American Psychiatric Association. *Diagnostic and Statistical Manual of Mental Disorders,* Fourth Edition, *Text Revision* (Copyright © 2000). American Psychiatric Association.

table 2 Comparing Anorexia Nervosa, Bulimia Nervosa, and Binge-Eating Disorder

Symptom	Anorexia Nervosa		Bulimia Nervosa		Binge-Eating Disorder
	Restricting	*Binge/Purge*	*Purging*	*Nonpurging*	
Body weight	Underweight by 15% or more	Underweight by 15% or more	Normal weight or slightly overweight	Normal weight or slightly overweight	Typically overweight or obese
Fear of weight gain, becoming fat	yes	yes	yes	yes	no
Body image	Distorted perception	Distorted perception	Overconcerned with weight	Overconcerned with weight	May be unhappy with body and weight
Amenorrhea in females	yes	yes	no	no	no
Binge eating	no	yes	yes	yes	yes
Purging	no	yes	yes	no	no
Use of nonpurging methods to avoid weight gain	yes	yes	yes	yes	no
Feeling of lack of control over eating	no	During binges	yes	yes	yes

BED differs from the nonpurging type of bulimia (where binges are followed by exercise or fasting) in one important way: The individual with BED binges at a level comparable to that of a patient with bulimia nervosa but does not regularly engage in any form of inappropriate "compensatory" behavior (such as purging, using laxatives, or even exercising) to limit weight gain (Table 2 summarizes the similarities and differences between different types of eating disorders). There is also much less dietary restraint in BED than is typical of either

bulimia nervosa or anorexia nervosa (Wilfley et al., 2000). Not surprisingly, binge-eating disorder is associated with being overweight or even obese (Hudson et al., 2007; Pike et al., 2001), although weight is not a factor involved in making the diagnosis. Interestingly, individuals with binge-eating disorder are more likely to have overvalued ideas about the importance of weight and shape than overweight or obese patients who do not have binge-eating disorder. In this respect they resemble people who suffer from bulimia nervosa (Allison et al., 2005).

case study **Ms. A.: Feeling Out of Control**

Ms. A. was a 38-year-old African American woman who was single, lived alone, and was employed as a personnel manager at a hotel in New York. Her height was 6 feet, and she weighed 292 pounds (BMI = 39.6; see Table 4) when she was initially seen at the eating disorders clinic. Her chief reason for going to the clinic was that she felt her eating was out of control and, as a result, she had gained approximately 80 pounds over the previous year.

Ms. A. reported a lifetime history of obesity and a history of binge eating beginning at approximately age 11. At her intake session, she described her eating. She felt out of control and ate large amounts of food nearly every day, typically in the evenings when she was on her way home from work or alone at home. She tended to feel out of control throughout the day, which contributed to her daily snacking on three or four regular candy bars or three or four medium

cookies and one ice cream bar. Ms. A. would consequently feel that a binge episode was inevitable.

A typical binge episode consisted of two pieces of chicken, one small bowl of salad, two servings of mashed potatoes, one hamburger, one large serving of french fries, one fast-food serving of apple pie, one large chocolate shake, one large bag of potato chips, and 15 to 20 small cookies—all within a 2-hour period. During her binge episodes, Ms. A. ate much more rapidly than usual until she felt uncomfortably full, ate large amounts of food when she didn't feel physically hungry, ate alone because she was embarrassed by the quantity of food she ate, and felt disgusted with herself and very guilty after eating. She was also extremely distressed about her weight. She sadly acknowledged that her weight and shape were the most important factors in determining her feelings about herself. (Adapted with permission from the *American Journal of Psychiatry,* Copyright 2000. American Psychiatric Association.)

Competitive eating contests, such as the hot dog eating contest that is held every year in Coney Island, New York, attract many spectators. During a 10 minute time span, some competitors are able to eat 60 or more hot dogs. Do you think this is a healthy sport? What messages does it send about food? In what ways is competitive eating different from binge eating disorder?

Age of Onset and Gender Differences

Eating disorders are often considered to be "modern" disorders, yet pathological patterns of eating date back several centuries (Silverman, 1997). St. Catherine of Sienna began to starve herself when she was around 16 years of age. She died in 1380 (at the age of 32 or 33) because she refused to consume either food or water (Keel & Klump, 2003). Moreover, as far back as the second century, the Greek physician Galen referred to a syndrome characterized by overeating, vomiting, and fainting, which he termed *bulimos* (see Ziolko, 1996). It was not until the 1970s and 1980s, however, that eating disorders began to attract significant attention. Clinicians began seeing more and more patients with pathological eating patterns. It soon became apparent that this was an important clinical problem.

Anorexia nervosa and bulimia nervosa do not occur in appreciable numbers before adolescence. Children as young as 7, though, have been known to develop eating disorders, especially anorexia nervosa (Bryant-Waugh & Lask, 2002). Anorexia nervosa is most likely to develop in 15- to 19-year-olds. For bulimia nervosa, the age group at highest risk is young women falling in the age range of 20 to 24 (Hoek & van Hoecken, 2003). Most patients with binge-eating disorder are older than those with anorexia nervosa or bulimia nervosa, generally between 30 and 50 years of age.

Eating disorders do occur in males, with binge-eating disorder being relatively common. However, they are more likely to be found in women. Although in the past it was thought that the gender ratio was as high as 10:1, more recent estimates suggest that there are 3 females for every male with an eating disorder (Jones & Morgan, 2010). This downward revision of the gender ratio reflects the fact that

eating disorders in men may have been underdiagnosed in the past. Some of the reasons for this are discussed in Box 2.

Prevalence of Eating Disorders

How common are eating disorders? As we mentioned earlier, the most common form of eating disorder in clinical samples is eating disorder NOS. The prevalence of ED-NOS in community studies is somewhere between 5 and 10 percent (Keel, 2010). However, because this is a residual diagnostic category, these prevalence estimates are not especially meaningful. Looking at the prevalence of specific types of disorders subsumed under the EDNOS category makes much more sense.

The most common form of eating disorder NOS for which we have prevalence estimates is binge-eating disorder. Community-based estimates from the National Comorbidity Survey indicate a lifetime prevalence of around 3.5 percent in women and 2 percent in men (Hudson et al., 2007). In obese people, the prevalence of binge-eating disorder is higher and in the range of 6.5 to 8 percent (Grilo, 2002; Sansone et al., 2008).

Data from the National Comorbidity Survey further show that the lifetime prevalence of bulimia nervosa is around 1.5 percent for women and 0.5 percent for men (Hudson et al., 2007). Somewhat less frequent is anorexia nervosa. Estimates from the United States suggest that this disorder has a lifetime prevalence of 0.9 percent in women and 0.3 percent in men (Hudson et al., 2007). These figures are comparable to prevalence estimates from Sweden, where the rate of anorexia nervosa is 1.2 percent in women and 0.29 percent in men (Bulik et al., 2006). Although anorexia nervosa is sometimes viewed as a very rare disorder, in its severe form it is about as common as schizophrenia.

The risk of developing anorexia nervosa seemed to increase during the twentieth century. In one study, lifetime rates of this disorder were higher in people born after 1945 than before this time (Klump et al., 2007). This is true for both males and females. This increase is not fully explained by increased awareness of the disorder and better detection by clinicians. There was also a rise in the number of new cases of bulimia nervosa from 1970 to 1993 (Keel & Klump, 2003). However, much of this increase may have occurred in the time period up to 1982. A more recent analysis has indicated that the prevalence of bulimia nervosa decreased from 1982 to 1992 and remained stable from 1992 to 2002 (Keel et al., 2006). Stable rates of bulima nervosa from 1990 to 2004 have also been reported (Crowther et al., 2008).

Despite the encouraging news of a decrease in the prevalence of bulimia nervosa over the last few decades, many young people, particularly girls and young women in their adolescence and early adulthood, show some evidence of disturbed eating patterns or have distorted self-perceptions about their bodies. For example, in a

Eating Disorders in Men

Eating disorders have long been regarded as occurring primarily in women. As a result of this stereotype, men with eating disorders often go undiagnosed. Another reason for the underdiagnosis of eating disorders in men is the gender bias in the *DSM* criteria. These emphasize the type of weight and shape concerns (e.g., desire to be thin) and methods of weight control (dieting) that are more typical of women. For men, body dissatisfaction often involves a wish to be more muscular. Overexercising as a means of weight control is also more common in men. As a result, men are less likely to recognize that they have an eating disorder, are more likely to be misdiagnosed when they do, and are less likely to receive specialist treatment (Jones & Morgan, 2010).

One established risk factor for eating disorders in men is homosexuality. Gay and bisexual men have higher rates of eating disorders than heterosexual men do (Feldman & Meyer, 2007). Gay men (like heterosexual men) value attractiveness and youth in their romantic partners. Because gay men (like women) are seeking to be sexually attractive to men, body dissatisfaction may therefore be more of an issue for gay men than it is for heterosexual men. In support of this idea, Smith and colleagues (2011) found that gay men were more dissatisfied with their bodies and had higher levels of disordered eating than heterosexual men did. Moreover, gay

Men are now experiencing sociocultural pressures to have toned and muscular bodies. For many men, body dissatisfaction takes the form of wanting to have a more muscular upper torso.

men tended to believe that a potential mate would want then to be leaner than they themselves wanted to be. Other specific subgroups of men who are at higher risk of eating disorders are wrestlers and jockeys, who need to "make weight" in order to compete or work (Carlat et al., 1997).

Although eating disorders generally occur less frequently in men, one disorder that is found almost exclusively in men is "reverse anorexia" or "muscle dysmorphia" (Pope et al., 1997). This condition is characterized by a preoccupation with muscularity. Males with this disorder often go to extreme efforts to "bulk up" and resort to the use of anabolic steroids to achieve their desired appearance. The growing prevalence of this phenomenon may be associated with changing cultural norms concerning the most desired body type for men. Leit, Pope, and Gray (2001) estimated the body fat content and level of muscularity of male centerfolds in *Playgirl* from 1973 to 1997. The results revealed that over time the bodies of the centerfold men had become more "dense." In other words, the level of muscularity went up while the level of body fat went down. Although muscle dysmorphia is not classified as an eating disorder, its core features of body image disturbance coupled with efforts to manipulate the appearance of the body suggest that it may have conceptual similarities to anorexia nervosa. Much more research is needed to explore this issue, however.

sample of 4,746 middle and high school students, 41.5 percent of girls and 24.9 percent of boys reported problems with body image, and more than a third of the girls and almost a quarter of the boys said they placed a lot of importance on weight and shape with regard to their self-esteem (Ackard et al., 2007). Questionnaire studies further suggest that up to 19 percent of students report some bulimic symptoms (Hoek, 2002). Also of concern are findings from a survey of adults in Australia showing a twofold increase in binge eating, purging, and strict dieting or fasting in the period from 1995 to 2005 (Hay et al., 2008). Disordered eating behaviors that do not meet criteria for an eating disorder diagnosis are of concern because, in some

cases, they may worsen over time, eventually leading to clinically significant problems. Table 3 shows some sample items from the Eating Disorders Inventory, a questionnaire measure that is often used in research.

Medical Complications of Eating Disorders

The tragic death of Ana Carolina Reston from kidney failure serves as a sad reminder of just how lethal a disorder anorexia nervosa is. In fact, anorexia nervosa has the highest mortality rate of any psychiatric disorder. The mortality rate for females

table 3 Sample Items from the Eating Disorders Inventory

Sample Statement

I am terrified of gaining weight.
I eat or drink in secrecy.
I think my hips are too big.

Source: Reproduced by special permission of the Publisher, Psychological Assessment Resources, Inc., 16204 North Florida Avenue, Lutz, Florida 33549, from the *Eating Disorder Inventory-3* by David M. Garner, PhD, Copyright 1984, 1991, 2004, by Psychological Assessment Resources, Inc. (PAR). Further reproduction is prohibited without permission of PAR.

with anorexia nervosa is more than 12 times higher than the mortality rate for females aged 15 to 24 in the general U.S. population (Sullivan, 1995, 2002). When patients with this disorder die, it is most often because of medical complications. Overall, approximately 3 percent of people with anorexia nervosa die from the consequences of their self-imposed starvation (Signorini et al., 2007).

Malnutrition also takes its toll in other ways (see Mitchell & Crow, 2010). Many patients with anorexia nervosa disorder look extremely unwell. Their hair on the scalp thins and becomes brittle, as do their nails. Their skin becomes very dry, and downy hair (called "lanugo") starts to grow on the face, neck, arms, back, and legs. Many patients also develop a yellowish tinge to their skin, especially on the palms of their hands and bottoms of their feet. Some of these problems are illustrated in Figure 2.

Because they are so undernourished, people with this disorder have a difficult time coping with cold temperatures. Their hands and feet are often cold to the touch and have a purplish-blue tinge due to problems with temperature regulation and lack

of oxygen to the extremities. As a consequence of chronically low blood pressure, patients often feel tired, weak, dizzy, and faint. Thiamin (vitamin B1) deficiency may also be present; this could account for some of the depression and cognitive changes documented in low-weight anorexia patients (Winston et al., 2000). Although many of these problems resolve when patients gain weight, anorexia nervosa may result in increased risk for osteoporosis in later life. This is because peak bone density is normally attained during the years of early adulthood. The failure to eat healthily during this time may result in more brittle and fragile bones forever (Attia & Walsh, 2007).

People with anorexia nervosa can die from heart arrhythmias (irregular heartbeats). Sometimes this is caused by major imbalances in key electrolytes such as potassium (Mitchell & Crow, 2010). Chronically low levels of potassium (hypokalemia) can also result in kidney damage and renal failure severe enough to require dialysis.

Abuse of laxatives, which occurs in 10 to 60 percent of patients with eating disorders (Roerrig et al., 2010), makes all of these problems much worse. Laxatives are used to induce

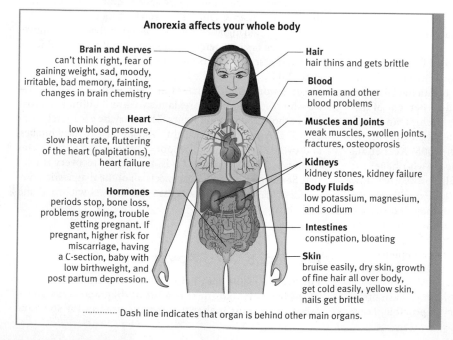

FIGURE 2

Anorexia nervosa takes its toll on the body and causes many medical problems. When starved, the body turns on itself in an effort to provide energy. Fat is burned first, then muscle. Eventually, organs are destroyed in the body's struggle to find fuel.

diarrhea so that the person feels thinner or to remove unwanted calories from the body. Laxative abuse can lead to dehydration, electrolyte imbalances, and kidney disease as well as damage to the bowels and gastrointestinal tract.

Bulimia nervosa is much less lethal than anorexia nervosa, although it is still associated with a mortality rate that is approximately twice that found in people of comparable age in the general population (Arcelus et al., 2011). Bulimia nervosa also creates a number of medical concerns (Mitchell & Crow, 2010). Purging can cause electrolyte imbalances and low potassium, which, as we have already mentioned, puts the patient at risk for heart abnormalities. Another complication is damage to the heart muscle, which may be due to using ipecac syrup (a poison that causes vomiting). More typically, however, patients develop calluses on their hands from sticking their fingers down their throats to make themselves sick. In extreme cases, where objects such as a toothbrush are used to induce vomiting, tears to the throat can occur.

Because the contents of the stomach are acidic, patients damage their teeth when they throw up repeatedly. Brushing teeth immediately after vomiting damages them even more. Mouth ulcers and dental cavities are a common consequence of repeated purging, as are small red dots around the eyes that are caused by the pressure of throwing up. Finally, patients with bulimia very often have swollen parotid (salivary) glands caused by repeatedly vomiting. These are known as "puffy cheeks" or "chipmunk cheeks" by many bulimia sufferers. Although such swellings are not painful, they are often quite noticeable to others.

Course and Outcome

We begin this section with a sobering statistic. After medical complications, the second most common cause of death in those who suffer from anorexia nervosa is suicide. Recent estimates suggest that one out of five deaths in individuals with anorexia nervosa is the result of suicide (Arcelus et al., 2011). Somewhere between 3 and 23 percent of patients with anorexia will make a suicide attempt, and rates of completed suicide are 50 times greater than they are in the general population (Franko & Keel, 2006; Keel et al., 2003). It has been suggested that patients who have lost their ability to maintain an "emotionally protective" low body weight are at particularly high risk of suicide (Crisp et al., 2006). Patients who are older when they first receive clinical attention for their disorder are also more likely to have a premature death (Arcelus et al., 2011). Bulimia nervosa is not associated with increased risk of completed suicide, although suicide attempts are made in 25 to 30 percent of cases (Franko & Keel, 2006).

Although the clinical outcome for some patients is tragic, over the very long term recovery is possible. Löwe

and colleagues (2001) examined what happened to patients with anorexia nervosa 21 years after they had first sought treatment. Reflecting the high morbidity associated with anorexia nervosa, 16 percent of the patients (all of whom were women) were no longer alive, having died primarily from complications of starvation or from suicide. Another 10 percent were still suffering from the disorder, and a further 21 percent had partially recovered. On the positive side, however, 51 percent of the individuals were fully recovered at the time of the follow-up. In another 6-year follow-up study, 52.1 percent of patients who had received outpatient cognitive behavioral therapy for their anorexia nervosa eventually recovered (Castellini et al., 2011). These findings provide grounds for optimism for those who suffer from this disorder. They indicate that even after a series of treatment failures it is still possible for women with anorexia nervosa to become well again.

With regard to bulimia nervosa, in the long term, prognosis tends to be quite good. Two outcome studies have shown that around 70 percent of women initially diagnosed with this disorder will be in remission and will no longer meet diagnostic criteria for any eating disorder by the end of an 11- to 12-year follow-up (Keel et al., 1999; Fichter & Quadflieg, 2007). The remaining 30 percent, however, will continue to experience significant difficulties with their eating. Substance-abuse problems, more frequent binges, more shape concerns, as well as a longer duration of illness predict worse outcomes over time (Castellini et al., 2011; Keel et al., 1999).

Finally, like patients with bulimia nervosa, patients with binge-eating disorder also have high rates of clinical remission. Following a period of intensive treatment, two-thirds of a sample of 60 patients no longer had any form of eating disorder (Fichter & Quadflieg, 2007). In a larger study involving 137 Italian patients who received individual cognitive-behavior therapy, 60 percent were found to be recovered when they were assessed 6 years after the end of treatment (Castellini et al., 2011).

It is worth noting that, even when well, many individuals who recover from anorexia nervosa and bulimia nervosa still harbor residual food issues. They may be excessively concerned about shape and weight, restrict their dietary intakes, and overeat and purge in response to negative mood states (Sullivan, 2002). In other words, the idea of recovery is relative. Someone who no longer meets all of the diagnostic criteria for an eating disorder may still have issues with food and body image.

Diagnostic Crossover

One way in which eating disorders differ from other types of disorders is that there is a lot of diagnostic crossover. What this means is that it is quite common for someone who is diagnosed with one form of eating disorder to be later diagnosed with another eating disorder. Many of these changes reflect transitions from anorexia nervosa or bulimia nervosa to EDNOS (Fichter & Quadflieg, 2007). This happens when minor clinical improvements mean that the person no longer meets diagnostic criteria for the original diagnosis. Other forms of diagnostic crossover also occur, however, suggesting that there may be some problems with the current classification of eating disorders within the *DSM*.

Over a 7-year period, Eddy and colleagues (2008) report that the majority of women in their study experienced diagnostic crossover. Bidirectional transitions between the two subtypes of anorexia nervosa (restricting and binge-purging) were especially common. This calls into question the current subtyping system for anorexia nervosa.

Shifts from anorexia nervosa to bulimia nervosa also occurred in about a third of patients. Interestingly, however, there were no cases of direct transition from the restricting type of anorexia nervosa directly into bulimia nervosa. Instead, the transition to bulimia nervosa seems to occur after an earlier transition to the binge-purging subtype of anorexia nervosa. You may also recall that the main difference between patients with the binge-purging subtype of anorexia nervosa and bulimia nervosa is weight (and associated amenorrhea). So if someone with anorexia nervosa (binge-purge subtype) gains weight, the diagnosis will change to bulimia nervosa to reflect this fact, even though there may not be a big clinical change in the illness itself. Moreover, even after they have crossed over into bulimia nervosa, these women remain vulnerable to relapsing back into anorexia nervosa. This suggests that clinicians should pay attention to a past history of anorexia nervosa even when patients no longer meet the low-weight criterion necessary for its diagnosis.

Only a minority of patients with bulimia nervosa transition into anorexia nervosa. In one study the figure was 14 percent (Eddy, Dorer, et al., 2008). In another it was 9.2 percent (Castellini et al., 2011). When transitions do occur it is to the binge-purging subtype rather than to the restricting subtype. Crossovers from the restricting subtype of anorexia nervosa into binge-eating disorder do not seem to occur at all. Diagnostic crossover from bulimia nervosa into binge-eating disorder occurs in about 10.9% of cases (Castellini et al., 2011).

Finally, we note that binge-eating disorder and anorexia nervosa appear to be quite distinct disorders. Over the course of a 12-year follow-up, no patient with binge-eating disorder developed anorexia nervosa and no patient with anorexia nervosa developed binge-eating disorder (Fichter & Quadflieg, 2007). In other words, there was no diagnostic crossover between these diagnoses. However, around 10 percent of patients who previously had binge-eating disorder transitioned into bulimia nervosa during this time. Figure 3 illustrates some of these trends.

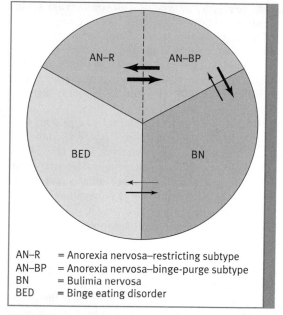

AN–R	= Anorexia nervosa–restricting subtype
AN–BP	= Anorexia nervosa–binge-purge subtype
BN	= Bulimia nervosa
BED	= Binge eating disorder

FIGURE 3

Diagnostic Crossover in Eating Disorders

Diagnostic crossover is common in eating disorders with transitions between the two subtypes of anorexia nervosa being very common. Transitions from the binge-purge subtype of anorexia nervosa to bulimia nervosa also often occur. In the figure, the width of the arrow denotes the relative likelihood of any transition. (Adapted from Fichter & Quadflieg, 2007, and Eddy, Dorer, et al., 2008.)

Association of Eating Disorders with Other Forms of Psychopathology

Eating disorder diagnoses are commonly associated with other diagnosable psychiatric conditions. In fact, comorbidity is the rule rather than the exception (Hudson et al., 2007). For instance, approximately 68 percent of patients with anorexia nervosa, 63 percent of patients with bulimia nervosa, and almost 50 percent of people with binge-eating disorder are also diagnosed with depression (Brewerton et al., 1995; Halmi et al., 1991; Hudson et al., 2007; O'Brien & Vincent, 2003). Obsessive-compulsive disorder is often found in patients with anorexia nervosa and bulimia nervosa (Kaye et al., 2004; Milos et al., 2002; O'Brien & Vincent, 2003). In addition, there is frequent co-occurrence of substance-abuse disorders in the binge-purging subtype of anorexia nervosa as well as in bulimia nervosa. The restrictive type of anorexia nervosa, however, tends not to be associated with higher rates of substance abuse (Halmi, 2010).

Comorbid personality (Axis II) disorders are frequently diagnosed in people with eating disorders (Rø et al., 2005).

Those with the restrictive type of anorexia nervosa are inclined toward personality disorders in the anxious-avoidant cluster (Cluster C; Skodol et al., 1993). In contrast, eating disorders that involve binge/purge syndromes (both anorexia nervosa and bulimia nervosa) are more likely to be associated with dramatic, emotional, or erratic (Cluster B) problems, especially borderline personality disorder (Halmi, 2010).

Consistent with this, more than a third of patients with eating disorders have engaged in the kinds of self-harming behaviors (cutting or burning themselves, for example) that are symptomatic of borderline personality disorder (Paul et al., 2002). Personality disorders are similarly reported in patients with BED, although no clear pattern has emerged (Wilfley et al., 2000). People with BED also have high rates of anxiety disorders (65 percent), mood disorders (46 percent), and substance-use disorders (23 percent; see Hudson et al., 2007).

One problem with simple examinations of personality disorders in patients with eating disorders is that some of the disturbances found in these patients could reflect the consequences of malnourishment. Starvation is known to increase both irritability and obsessionality (Keys et al., 1950). We must therefore be cautious in our conclusions.

Even though the physiological consequences of eating disorders may exacerbate personality disturbances, they may only be enhancing traits that were present prior to the development of the illness. Research suggests that some personality traits in eating-disordered patients might both predate the onset of the disorder and remain even when the eating disorder remits and the patient has recovered (Kaye et al., 2004; Klump et al., 2004). Consistent with this, around two-thirds of a sample of patients with anorexia nervosa reported that they were rigid and perfectionistic, even as children (Anderluh et al., 2003).

Eating Disorders Across Cultures

Although the majority of research on eating disorders is conducted in the United States and Europe, eating disorders are not confined to these areas. Widespread eating disorder difficulties have been reported among both Caucasian and black South African college students (le Grange et al., 1998). Anorexia nervosa and bulimia nervosa are also clinical problems in Japan, Hong Kong, Taiwan, Singapore, and Korea (Lee & Katzman, 2002).

Cases of eating disorders have also been documented in India and Africa. The prevalence of eating disorders in Iran is comparable to that in the United States (Nobakht & Dezhkam, 2000). And a few years ago, the first published report of five men in central China who were diagnosed with eating disorders appeared (Tong et al., 2005). Far from being confined to industrialized Western countries, eating disorders are becoming a problem worldwide.

Being Caucasian, however, does appear to be associated with subclinical problems that may place individuals at higher risk for developing eating disorders. Examples of such problems include body dissatisfaction, dietary restraint, and a drive for thinness. A *meta-analysis* involving a total of 17,781 participants has shown that such attitudes and behaviors are significantly more prevalent in whites than in nonwhites (Wildes et al., 2001).

Although Asian women exhibit levels of pathological eating similar to those of white women (Wildes et al., 2001), it has long been held that African Americans are less susceptible to subclinical types of eating problems and body image concerns than Caucasians are. For example, in one sample of 1,061 black women, no case of anorexia nervosa was found. In contrast, out of a sample of 985 white women, 15 (1.5 percent) met clinical criteria for this disorder. Fewer black than white women also had bulimia nervosa (0.4 percent versus 2.3 percent; see Striegel-Moore et al., 2003).

However, as minorities become more and more integrated and internalize white, middle-class societal values about the desirability of thinness, we should expect to see increases in the rates of eating disorders. As example of this, Alegria and colleagues (2007) have demonstrated that rates of eating disorders were higher in Latinos who were born in the United States compared with those who were not. In Box 3 we discuss the protective role of ethnic identity in African American women.

A select number of the clinical features of *diagnosed* forms of eating disorders may also vary according to culture. For instance, about 58 percent of anorexia nervosa patients in Hong Kong are not excessively concerned about fatness. The reason they give for refusing food is fear of stomach bloating (Lee et al., 1993). Anorexia nervosa patients who were living in Britain but who had South Asian (Indian, Pakistani, Bangladeshi) ethnic origins also were less likely than patients with English ethnic origins to show evidence of fat phobia (Tareen et al., 2005).

In yet another study, young women in Ghana who had anorexia nervosa were also not especially concerned about their weight or shape. Rather, they emphasized religious ideas of self-control and denial of hunger as the motivation for their self-starvation (Bennett et al., 2004). In a final example, Japanese women with eating disorders reported significantly lower levels

RESEARCH CLOSE-UP

Meta-analysis

A meta-analysis is a statistical method used to combine the results of a number of similar research studies. The data from each separate study are transformed into a common metric called the effect size. Doing this allows data from the various studies to be combined and then analyzed. You can think of a meta-analysis as being just like the research with which you are already familiar, except that the "participants" are individual research studies, not individual people!

THE WORLD AROUND US

3

Ethnic Identity and Disordered Eating

In contrast to young white, Asian American, and Hispanic girls, black adolescent girls seem less inclined to use weight and appearance to fuel their sense of identity and self-worth (Grabe & Hyde, 2006; Polivy et al., 2005). This may provide them with some protection from the development of eating disorders. However, any protection afforded to black women seems to be linked to how strongly they identify with their ethnic group and how much they receive culturally consistent messages that value what their bodies naturally look like and support who they are.

In a study of 322 African American female college students, Rogers and colleagues (2010) found that women who had stronger ethnic identities were less likely to have internalized U.S. societal beauty ideals about the importance of being thin and attractive. This is an important finding because, in the same study, internalization of these ideals was found to be linked to disordered eating. An important factor in the ethnic distribution and occurrence of eating disorders is therefore the extent to which minority women are both exposed to and willing to internalize the same kind of white, middle-class values that have been linked to increased risk for eating disorders. There is already some evidence that the body dissatisfaction difference between blacks and whites is getting smaller over time (Grabe & Hyde, 2006). This highlights the importance of healthy role models for young black girls. Without these, black women will no longer remain unique among American ethnic groups in their lower levels of body dissatisfaction.

African-American women who have a strong identification with their ethnicity and cultural heritage have less risk of developing eating disorders than African American women who have internalized white middle class values about the desirability of thinness.

of perfectionism and less of a drive for thinness than did American women with eating disorders (Pike & Mizushima, 2005). Findings such as these highlight the considerable role played by culture in the clinical presentation of eating disorders.

Cases of anorexia nervosa have been reported throughout history. They have furthermore been shown to occur all over the world. In light of this reality, Keel and Klump (2003) have concluded that anorexia nervosa is not a culture-bound syndrome. Of course, as we have just noted, culture may influence the disorder's clinical manifestation. The more important point, however, is that anorexia nervosa is not a disorder that occurs simply because of exposure to Western ideals and the modern emphasis on thinness. In contrast, bulimia nervosa does seem to be a culture-bound syndrome. More specifically, it seems to occur in people who have had some exposure to Western ideals about thinness, who have access to large amounts of food, and who, because of modern plumbing, can purge in private (Keel, 2010).

In Review

● What are the major clinical differences between patients with anorexia nervosa and patients with bulimia nervosa? What clinical features do these two forms of eating disorders have in common?

● How do the prevalence rates for eating disorders vary according to gender, sexual orientation, and ethnicity?

● What kinds of medical problems do patients with eating disorders suffer from?

● What is the long-term outcome for patients with anorexia nervosa? In what ways is the clinical outcome of patients with anorexia nervosa different from the clinical outcome of patients with bulimia nervosa?

● What is EDNOS? Why is this diagnostic category so problematic?

● Why is bulimia nervosa viewed as a culture-bound syndrome when anorexia nervosa is not?

Risk and Causal Factors in Eating Disorders

There is no single cause of eating disorders. In all probability, they reflect the complex interaction between genetic and environmental factors. Biological, sociocultural, family, and individual variables likely all play a role. However, it is important not to regard these areas as distinct and in competition with each other. The question of whether eating disorders are caused by biological factors or by cultural pressures is not an appropriate one. Biological and cultural explanations are interlinked. For example, being exposed to cultural attitudes that emphasize thinness is significant in the development of eating disorders. However, only a small number of people who are exposed to such attitudes actually develop eating disorders. Genetic factors may give rise to individual differences that help explain why certain people are more sensitive than others to cultural attitudes and other environmental risk factors. In other words, eating disorders are now being conceptualized in terms of the diathesis-stress model, where genes render some people more susceptible to environmental pressures and hence to the development of problematic eating attitudes and behaviors.

Biological Factors

GENETICS Much research attention is now being devoted to the study of genetic factors in eating disorders. This is because the tendency to develop an eating disorder has been shown to run in families (Wade, 2010). The biological relatives of people with anorexia nervosa or bulimia nervosa have elevated rates of anorexia nervosa and bulimia nervosa themselves. In one large family study of eating disorders, the risk of anorexia nervosa for the relatives of individuals with anorexia nervosa was 11.4 times greater than for the relatives of the healthy controls (Strober et al., 2000).

For the relatives of people with bulimia nervosa, the risk of bulimia nervosa was 3.7 times higher than it was for the relatives of the healthy controls (Strober et al., 2000). It is of additional interest that the relatives of patients with eating disorders are more likely to suffer from a variety of other disorders as well as eating disorders. For example, high rates of major depressive disorder are found in the relatives of patients with anorexia nervosa, bulimia nervosa, and binge-eating disorder (Lilenfeld et al., 1998; Lilenfeld et al., 2006; Mangweth et al., 2003). The relatives of people suffering from bulimia nervosa also have an increased likelihood of having problems with alcohol and drug dependence, while the relatives of those diagnosed with anorexia nervosa are at increased risk of obsessive-compulsive disorder and obsessive-compulsive personality disorder (Lilenfeld et al., 1998).

As you know, family studies do not allow for the untangling of the different contributions of genetic and environmental influences. These kinds of questions are best resolved by twin and adoption studies. Presently, we have none of the latter.

Fortunately, a number of twin studies do exist. Considered together, these studies suggest that both anorexia nervosa and bulimia nervosa are heritable disorders (Fairburn & Harrison, 2003; Wade, 2010). Indeed, it has been suggested that the contribution of genetic factors to the development of eating disorders may be about as strong as the contribution of genetic factors to bipolar disorder and schizophrenia (Kaye, 2008).

There is also provocative evidence for a gene (or genes) on chromosome 1 that might be linked to susceptibility to the restrictive type of anorexia nervosa (Grice et al., 2002). Recent evidence has suggested that susceptibility to bulimia nervosa, particularly self-induced vomiting, may be linked to chromosome 10 (Bulik, Devlin, et al., 2003). Of course, until these findings are widely replicated, they must be viewed as preliminary. A major international collaborative study is now underway that will explore the genetics of anorexia nervosa in 400 families who have two or more individuals affected by the disorder (Kaye, 2008). Results are expected in the near future.

Eating disorders have additionally been linked to genes that are involved in the regulation of the neurotransmitter serotonin (Wade, 2010). This makes sense, given the role that serotonin is known to play in the regulation of eating behavior. Furthermore, serotonin is known to be involved in mood. With this in mind, it is interesting to note that mood disorders and eating disorders often cluster together in families (Halmi, 2010).

At present, researchers are still some distance away from understanding the precise role genes play in the development of eating disorders. Given the high degree of overlap between anorexia nervosa and bulimia nervosa (many women with anorexia nervosa later develop bulimia nervosa and many women with bulimia nervosa report histories of anorexia nervosa), it is likely that these two eating disorders may have some genetic factors in common (Helder & Collier, 2010). There is also reason to believe that genetic factors may play more of a role after puberty than before it (Klump et al., 2007). In other words, the magnitude of genetic influences may increase over the course of development. This could be because genetic factors may determine how different individuals respond to the psychosocial risk factors (pressure to be thin, family conflict) that may develop or become more important during the adolescent years.

BRAIN ABNORMALITIES An area of the brain that plays an important role in eating is the **hypothalamus**. Animal studies have demonstrated that when the lateral hypothalamus (the side areas of the hypothalamus) is stimulated electrically the animal will start to eat, even if it has eaten very recently. During stimulation of the lateral hypothalamus, animals will also tolerate shock and other unpleasant stimuli in order to gain access to food.

There is no good evidence that abnormalities in the hypothalamus play a central role in eating disorders, however. Uher and Treasure (2005) review a series of case reports of patients with tumors in the hypothalamus. Although these were sometimes associated with an increase or loss of appetite, there was no evidence that they resulted in specific eating disorders. In contrast, damage to the frontal and the temporal cortex did seem to be linked to the development of anorexia nervosa in some cases and bulimia nervosa in others. This is interesting because the temporal cortex is known to be involved in body image perception. Parts of the frontal cortex (particularly an area called the orbitofrontal cortex) also play a role in monitoring the pleasantness of stimuli such a smell and taste (van Kuyck et al., 2009).

Although very speculative at this time, it is possible that the lateral hypothalamus acts as a site that integrates information relevant for regulating food intake. The lateral hypothalamus receives information from many parts of the brain, including the frontal cortex and the amygdala (which is a part of the brain involved in emotion and fear learning). Animal research suggests that a network involving these (and other) brain areas may be important not only for overeating in response to environmental cues but for suppressing eating in response to fear (Petrovich, 2011). As research progresses we will learn more about how the pieces of the puzzle fit together to result in different types of eating disorders.

SET POINTS There is a well-established tendency for our bodies to resist marked variation from some sort of biologically determined **set point** or weight that our individual bodies try to "defend" (Garner, 1997). Anyone intent on achieving and maintaining a significant decrease in body mass below his or her individual set point may be trying to do this in the face of internal physiologic opposition, which is aimed at trying to get the body back close to its original set-point weight.

One important kind of physiologic opposition designed to prevent us from moving far from our set point is hunger. As we lose more and more weight, hunger may rise to extreme levels, encouraging eating, weight gain, and a return to a state of equilibrium. Far from having little or no appetite, patients with anorexia nervosa may think about food constantly and make intense efforts to suppress their increasing hunger. Accordingly, chronic dieting may well enhance the likelihood that a person will encounter periods of seemingly irresistible impulses to gorge on large amounts of high-calorie food. For patients with bulimia nervosa, these hunger-driven impulses may escalate into uncontrollable binge eating.

SEROTONIN **Serotonin** is a neurotransmitter that has been implicated in obsessionality, mood disorders, and impulsivity. It also modulates appetite and feeding behavior. Because many patients with eating disorders respond well to treatment with antidepressants (which target serotonin), some researchers have concluded that eating disorders involve a disruption in the serotonergic system (Bailer & Kaye, 2011).

Serotonin is made from an essential amino acid called tryptophan. This can only be obtained from food. After tryptophan is consumed, it is converted to serotonin via

British model Twiggy was the first superthin model to achieve international fame.

a series of chemical reactions. People with anorexia nervosa have low levels of 5-HIAA, which is a major metabolite of serotonin. This may be because they are eating so little food. In contrast, levels of 5-HIAA are normal in people with bulimia nervosa. What is interesting is that, after recovery, both of these patient groups have *higher* levels of 5-HIAA than control women do; they also have higher levels of 5-HIAA than they had when they were in the ill state (Kaye, 2008). Although the finding of higher levels of 5-HIAA in recovered patients compared to controls seems counterintuitive, it has been suggested that resuming normal eating makes it possible to detect abnormalities in the serotonin system (such as higher levels of serotonin in several different brain areas) that might be involved in risk for eating disorders. Kaye and colleagues have further suggested that people with serotonin overactivity may use dieting as a way to regulate this by decreasing the amount of tryptophan that is available to make serotonin (Bailer & Kaye, 2010).

Of course, it is important to remember that neurotransmitters like serotonin do not work in isolation. A change in the serotonin system will have implications for other neurotransmitter systems too (e.g., dopamine, norepinephrine). So the situation is undoubtedly complex. Nonetheless, investigating the role of serotonin in eating disorders is still an active area of research.

Sociocultural Factors

What is the ideal body shape for women in Western culture? Next time you glance at a glossy fashion magazine, take a moment to consider the messages contained in its pages. The overall body size of the models that appear on the covers of such magazines as *Vogue* and *Cosmopolitan* has become increasingly thinner over the years (Sypeck et al., 2004). Young women are avid consumers of such magazines and are bombarded with images of unrealistically thin models. These magazines are also widely available all over the world. *British Vogue* is published in 40 or more countries and can be found in India, Argentina, and Kenya among other places (see Gordon, 2000). Moreover, social pressures toward thinness may be particularly powerful in higher socioeconomic backgrounds, from which a majority of girls and women with anorexia nervosa appear to come (McClelland & Crisp, 2001).

It is likely that thinness became deeply rooted as a cultural ideal in the 1960s, although prior to this time women had certainly been concerned with their weight and appearance. However, the type of body that was regarded as glamorous and attractive (e.g., Marilyn Monroe) was more curvaceous. One landmark event was the arrival of Twiggy on the fashion scene. Twiggy was the first superthin supermodel. Although her appearance was initially regarded as shocking, it did not take long for the fashion industry to embrace the look she exemplified.

The emphasis on thinness in the fashion industry continues. Although, as we noted earlier, some efforts are being made to exclude excessively thin models from the runways, these changes are still being resisted by many designers. In an example of the glamorization of anorexia, British supermodel Kate Moss has even made up a new word to describe herself. The word is "rexy," a hybrid term that combines "anorexic" and "sexy."

A provocative illustration of the importance of the media in creating pressures to be thin comes from a now classic study that was done by Anne Becker and her colleagues (2002). When Becker first began conducting research in Fiji in the 1990s, she was struck by the considerable percentage of Fijians (especially women) who were overweight with respect to their Western counterparts. From a cultural perspective, however, this made sense. Within Fijian culture, being fat was associated with qualities that were highly valued such as being strong, able to work, and kind and generous. Being thin, in contrast, was regarded negatively because it was thought to reflect being sickly, incompetent, or having somehow received poor treatment. Culturally, fatness was preferred over thinness, and dieting was viewed as offensive. What was also striking was the total absence of any condition that could be considered an eating disorder.

After television came to Fiji, however, the cultural climate changed. Not only were Fijians able to see programs such as *Beverly Hills 90210* and *Melrose Place* that were popular at that time, but many young women also began to express concerns about their weight and dislike of their bodies. For the first time, women in Fiji started to diet in earnest. The young Fijian women studied by Becker also made comments that suggested that their body dissatisfaction and wish to lose weight were motivated by a desire to emulate the actors they had seen on television.

Although Becker did not collect information about eating disorders themselves (she measured attitudes toward eating), this "natural experiment" provides us with some anecdotal information as to the way in which Western values about thinness may begin to infest themselves into foreign cultural environments. In another reflection of this, after 51 years of Nigeria

British supermodel Kate Moss has coined the term "rexy" (a contraction of anorexic and sexy) to describe herself.

In her home country of Nigeria, Agbani Darego was considered too thin to be beautiful. Nonetheless, she was selected to represent the country in the 2001 Miss World contest and won the coveted crown.

being unsuccessful in the Miss World beauty pageant, a 19-year-old Nigerian contestant finally won the coveted crown in 2001. Her success was later attributed to the fact that, for the first time, Nigerians had selected a contestant to represent them who was not considered to be beautiful by local standards on account of being too thin (Onishi, 2002).

Family Influences

Clinicians have long been aware that certain problems seem to regularly characterize the families of patients with anorexia nervosa, prompting many clinicians to advocate a family therapy approach to treatment intervention (Lock et al., 2001). Echoing this sentiment, more than one-third of patients with anorexia nervosa reported that family dysfunction was a factor that contributed to the development of their eating disorder (Tozzi et al., 2003). Patients with anorexia nervosa perceive their families as more rigid, less cohesive, and as having poorer communication than healthy control participants do (Vidovic et al., 2005).

In addition, many of the parents of patients with eating disorders have long-standing preoccupations regarding the desirability of thinness, dieting, and good physical appearance (Garner & Garfinkel, 1997). Like their children, they have perfectionistic tendencies (Woodside et al., 2002).

Family factors have also been studied in connection with bulimia nervosa. Both white and ethnic minority (black, Hispanic, and biracial) adolescents with bulimia nervosa perceive their families to be less cohesive than their parents do (Hoste et al., 2007). Fairburn and colleagues (1997) have also noted that women with bulimia nervosa could be differentiated from both a general psychiatric control group and a healthy control group on such risk factors as high parental expectations, other family members' dieting, and degree of critical comments from other family members about shape, weight, or eating. In a large sample of college-age women, the strongest predictor of bulimic symptoms was the extent to which family members made disparaging comments about the woman's appearance and focused on her need to diet (Crowther et al., 2002).

Still, when attempting to depict family characteristics associated with eating disorders, we must remember that having an individual with an eating disorder in the family is likely to affect family functioning in a negative way. That is, the causal connection, if any, might be in the other direction. In fact, recent longitudinal data from a twin study suggest that disordered eating attitudes may predate parent–child conflict (Spanos et al., 2010). If this finding is replicated in future studies, we may need to reconsider the role of family conflict as a risk factor for the development of eating problems.

Individual Risk Factors

Not everyone who lives in a society that places excessive emphasis on being thin goes on to develop an eating disorder. If that were the case, eating disorders would be much more prevalent than they are. There must be other factors that increase a given person's susceptibility to the development of disordered eating. As we noted earlier, some of these factors may be biological, while others may be more psychological in nature. In a further reflection of gene–environment interaction, genetic factors may actually influence some of the traits (e.g., perfectionism, obsessiveness, anxiety) that may make some people more likely to respond to cultural pressures with disturbed eating patterns.

GENDER As you have already learned, eating disorders are much more frequently found in women than in men. Being female is a strong risk factor for developing eating disorders, particularly anorexia nervosa and bulimia nervosa (Jacobi et al., 2004). Moreover, the greatest period of risk for these disorders occurs in adolescence. Binge-eating disorder does not follow this pattern, however. The onset of binge-eating disorder is typically well after adolescence. Binge-eating disorder is also much more likely to be found in males as well as in females.

INTERNALIZING THE THIN IDEAL The Duchess of Windsor once said that you could never be too rich or too thin. Clearly she had internalized the thin ideal, buying into the notion that being thin is highly desirable. Think for a moment about the extent to which you think this way. Do you regard thin people as unhealthy and weak? Or do you associate being thin with feeling attractive, being popular, and being happy?

Large Seated Bather, Pierre-Auguste Renoir. This painting by the eighteenth-century French painter Renoir depicts an idealized view of the female body. Note how ideals about feminine beauty in the 1800s differed from those of today.

The extent to which people internalize the thin ideal is associated with a range of problems that are thought to be risk factors for eating disorders. These include body dissatisfaction, dieting, and negative affect (Stice, 2002). In fact, there is empirical evidence to suggest that internalizing the thin ideal may be an early component of the causal chain that culminates in disordered eating (McKnight Investigators, 2003; Stice, 2001).

PERFECTIONISM Perfectionism (needing to have things exactly right) has long been regarded as an important risk factor for eating disorders (Bruch, 1973). This is because people who are perfectionistic may be much more likely to subscribe to the thin ideal and relentlessly pursue the "perfect body." It has also been suggested that perfectionism helps maintain bulimic pathology through the rigid adherence to dieting that then drives the binge/purge cycle (Fairburn et al., 1997).

In general, research supports the association of perfectionism and eating disorders. Halmi and colleagues (2000) studied 322 women with anorexia nervosa. They found that these women scored higher on a measure of perfectionism than did a sample of controls without an eating disorder. The women with anorexia nervosa scored higher on perfectionism regardless of whether they had the restricting subtype of anorexia nervosa or subtypes that involved either purging or binge eating and purging. In fact, a large proportion of bulimia nervosa patients demonstrate a long-standing pattern of excessive perfectionism (Anderluh et al., 2003; Garner & Garfinkel, 1997).

Of course, any personality characteristics found in eating-disordered patients could be the result of the eating disorder itself rather than contributory in a causal sense. However, a recent twin study suggests that this is not the case. Not only were high levels of perfectionism found in the twins with anorexia nervosa but high levels of perfectionism were also found in the co-twins, who did not suffer from eating disorders (Wade et al., 2008). This suggests that perfectionism may not simply be a correlate of eating problems. Rather, the data suggest that perfectionism may predate disordered eating and also have a genetic basis. Other research is also consistent with the idea that perfectionism may be an enduring personality trait of individuals that places them at higher risk for the development of eating disorders (Lilenfeld et al., 2006; Stice, 2002).

Interestingly, men with eating disorders are less perfectionistic than are women with eating disorders (Woodside et al., 2004). If men are generally less perfectionistic than women, this might help them avoid having some of the weight and shape concerns that seem to be a stepping stone to the development of eating disorders.

NEGATIVE BODY IMAGE One consequence of sociocultural pressure to be thin is that some young girls and women develop highly intrusive and pervasive perceptual biases regarding how "fat" they are (e.g., Fallon & Rozin, 1985; Rodin, 1993; Wiseman et al., 1992; Zellner et al., 1989). In sharp contrast, young Amish people (who live radically separated from the modern world) do not display such body image distortions (Platte et al., 2000). This supports the notion that sociocultural influences are implicated in the discrepancy between the way many young girls and women perceive their own bodies and the "ideal" female form as represented in the media. Such perceptual biases lead girls and women to believe that men prefer more slender shapes than they in fact do. Many women also feel evaluated by other women, believing that their female peers have even more stringent standards of weight and shape than they do themselves (see Figure 4).

It would be one thing if women had a reasonable chance of attaining their "ideal" bodies simply by not exceeding an average caloric intake or by maintaining a healthy weight. Quite simply, this is not possible for most people. In fact, as pointed out by Garner (1997), the average body weight of young American women has been increasing over the past four decades at least, probably as a consequence of general improvements in nutrition, pediatric health care, and other

table 4 Calculating Body Mass Index

$$\frac{\text{weight (lb.)}}{\text{height (in.)}^2} \times 703 = \text{BMI}$$

	BMI
Healthy	18.5–24.9
Overweight	25–29.9
Obese	30–39.9
Morbidly obese	40

factors as well (e.g., the widespread availability of high-calorie foods). Yet, as women's average weight has been increasing since the late 1950s, the weight of such cultural icons of attractiveness as *Playboy* centerfolds and Miss America contestants has decreased at a roughly comparable rate. It has been calculated that 70 percent of *Playboy* centerfolds have a body mass index (see Table 4) below 18.5 (Katzmarzyk & Davis, 2001).

Even children's toys promote unrealistically slender ideals. Consider, for instance, the size and shape of the Barbie doll. For an average woman to achieve Barbie's proportions she would have to be 7 feet 2 inches tall, lose 10 inches from her waist, and add 12 inches to her bust (Moser, 1989).

The research literature strongly implicates body dissatisfaction as an important risk factor for pathological eating (McKnight Investigators, 2003). Indeed, in a recent prospective longitudinal study, body dissatisfaction emerged as the most powerful predictor of the onset of eating disorders in a sample of almost 500 adolescent girls (Stice et al., 2011). Body dissatisfaction is

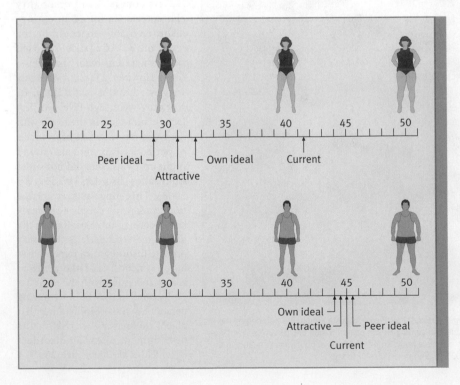

FIGURE 4

Mean body figure ratings of women (top) and men (bottom). Total scale values range from 10 to 90. Ratings reflect participants' responses to four questions: (1) "Which drawing looks most like your figure?" (current); (2) "Which figure do you most want to look like?" (own ideal); (3) "Which figure do you think most members of the opposite sex find most attractive?" (attractive); and (4) "Which figure do you think members of your own sex find most attractive?" (peer ideal).
Source: Adapted from Cohn, L. D., & Adler, N. E. (1992). Female and male perceptions of ideal body shapes: Distorted views among Caucasian college students. *Psychology of Women Quarterly*, 16, 69–79.

also associated with dieting and with negative affect. Pointedly, if we don't like how we look, we are likely to feel bad about ourselves. We may also try to lose weight in order to look better. As we'll see in the next case, Rebecca's eating disorder was triggered by the dissatisfaction she felt about her body after her boyfriend criticized her and pressured her to lose weight.

case study Disgusted by Her Body

Rebecca, a 25-year-old Hispanic female, referred herself for treatment of eating difficulties and depressed mood. At intake, she was 6 feet tall and weighed 150 pounds (body mass index = 20.3). She reported binging and inducing vomiting approximately once per week and dated the onset of this behavior at 3 months before coming to therapy. She recalled that she had never had any concerns about her physical appearance until the time of her first romantic relationship at age 21. Apparently, her first boyfriend had criticized her 175-pound (BMI = 23.7) physique and pressured her to lose weight, substantially affecting the way she viewed her body. At the end of this relationship, Rebecca felt disgusted with her appearance and decided that the only way to ensure success in future relationships was to lose weight.

An additional precipitating factor for her eating disturbance appeared to be graduation from college at age 22. Feeling that she had little control over the direction of her life, Rebecca restricted her eating behavior in an attempt to "have control over something" in her life. At one point, her body weight dropped to 135 pounds (BMI = 18.3). Alarmed at her behavior, Rebecca moved to her hometown to be closer to family and friends. She slightly increased her food intake and gradually gained weight. However, she remained unhappy and was determined to restrict her diet and modify her appearance. According to her report, Rebecca began to binge and vomit as a way to cope with her depression. To further manage her negative affect, she began drinking to intoxication two to three times per week. These binge-drinking episodes often coincided with her episodes of binging and purging. (From Hendricks & Thompson, 2005.)

DIETING When people wish to be thinner, they typically go on a diet. Nearly all instances of eating disorders begin with the "normal" dieting that is routine in our culture. Have you ever dieted? Most people have, at some point in their lives (Jeffrey et al., 1991). Estimates are that, at any one time, approximately 39 percent of women and 21 percent of men are trying to lose weight (Hill, 2002).

Dieting is a risk factor for the development or worsening of eating disorders (Jacobi et al., 2004; Striegel-Moore & Bulik, 2007). In a large sample of adolescent girls, body dissatisfaction and dieting predicted symptoms of bulimia nervosa at a 1-year follow-up (Johnson & Wardle, 2005). In another large-scale longitudinal study, it was found that the majority of adolescent girls who went on to develop anorexia nervosa had been dieters (Patton et al., 1990).

As we all know, however, not everyone who diets develops an eating disorder. And in some cases diets can be helpful. For example, when overweight women were randomly assigned to either a low-calorie diet or a waiting list control group (that did not involve a diet), those who received the diet lost weight and showed a *decrease* in bulimic symptoms (Presnell & Stice, 2003). So why has dieting been linked to eating disorders?

As Stice (2002) notes in his comprehensive review of this topic, when our efforts to diet fall short, it is almost inevitable that we will feel bad about ourselves (see also Ackard et al., 2002). Dieting itself may therefore not be the real problem (which is good news for people who are obese and who need to lose weight). Rather, it may be the case that the people who often report that they are trying to lose weight are the people who are most unhappy with their bodies and who are most inclined to feel negatively about themselves when they fail to stick to their diet plans. Other factors, such as perfectionism, may also play a role. Those who have the highest expectations of themselves may be the people who are most likely to feel bad when they fail to meet their own self-imposed high standards.

NEGATIVE EMOTIONALITY **Negative affect** (feeling bad) is a causal risk factor for body dissatisfaction (Stice, 2002). When we feel bad, we tend to become very self-critical. We may focus on our limitations and shortcomings while magnifying our flaws and defects. This seems to be especially true of individuals with eating disorders, who, like people with depression, tend to show distorted ways of thinking and of processing information received from the environment (e.g., Butow et al., 1993; Garner et al., 1997). In many cases, there is widespread negative self-evaluation (e.g., Fairburn et al., 1997). These cognitive distortions ("I'm fat; I'm a failure; I'm useless") have the potential to make people feel even worse about themselves.

Longitudinal studies have confirmed that depression and general negative affect are predictive of a high risk for later developing an eating disorder (Johnson, Cohen, et al., 2002; Leon et al., 1997). Moreover, evidence suggests that negative affect may work to maintain binge eating (see Stice, 2002). Patients often report that they engage in binges when they feel stressed, down, or bad about themselves. They further indicate that in the very short term, eating provides much needed comfort. These reports are highly consistent with affect-regulation models that view binge eating as a distraction from negative feelings (see Vögele & Gibson, 2010). Of course, a major problem is that after binges patients feel disappointed or even disgusted with themselves. In short, a difficult situation leads to behavior that makes circumstances even worse.

CHILDHOOD SEXUAL ABUSE Childhood sexual abuse has been implicated in the development of eating disorders (Jacobi et al., 2004). However, there is some debate about whether sexual abuse is truly a risk factor for eating disorders (see Stice, 2002). In one prospective study, Vogeltanz-Holm and colleagues (2000) failed to find that early sexual abuse predicted the later onset of binge eating. However, another prospective study found that children who had been sexually abused or physically neglected had higher rates of eating disorders and eating problems in adolescence and adulthood (Johnson, Cohen, et al., 2002). A meta-analysis of 53 studies also revealed a weak—but positive—association between childhood sexual abuse and eating pathology (Smolak & Murnen, 2002).

This suggests that the two variables are linked in some way, although the precise nature of the link is not yet clear. One possibility is that being sexually abused increases the risk of developing other known risk factors for eating disorders, such as having a negative body image or high levels of negative affect. In other words, the causal pathway from early abuse to later eating disorder may be an indirect one (rather than a direct one) that involves an array of other intervening variables.

In Review

- What evidence suggests that genetic factors may play a role in the development of eating disorders?

- What brain areas are implicated in eating and eating disorders?

- What neurotransmitter has been implicated (and most well studied) in eating disorders?

- What individual characteristics are associated with increased risk for eating disorders?

- How might a diathesis-stress model be used to explain the development of eating disorders?

Treatment of Eating Disorders

Patients with eating disorders are often very conflicted about getting well. Approximately 17 percent of patients with severe eating disorders have to be committed to a hospital for treatment against their will (Watson, Bowers, & Andersen, 2000). Suicide attempts are often made, and clinicians need to be mindful of this risk, even when patients have received a great deal of treatment (Franko et al., 2004).

This ambivalence toward recovery is apparent in the behavior of individuals admitted to inpatient units. Hospitalization also often means that those with anorexia nervosa will be exposed to other patients who are thinner and more experienced than they are. This can lead to competitive pressure to be the "best anorexic" patient on the unit (Wilson, Grilo, & Vitousek, 2007). Box 4 describes how patients with eating disorders now use the Internet to communicate with each other—again in ways that are very countertherapeutic.

Treatment of Anorexia Nervosa

Individuals with anorexia nervosa view the disorder as a chronic condition and are generally pessimistic about their potential for recovery (Holliday et al., 2005). They have a high dropout rate from therapy; and patients with the binge-purging subtype of anorexia nervosa are especially likely to terminate inpatient treatment prematurely (Steinhausen, 2002; Woodside et al.,

4 THE WORLD AROUND US

Eating Disorders and the Internet

The Internet is a valuable source of information and advice. People also use it to connect with like-minded individuals. For the person with anorexia nervosa, however, this may have problematic consequences. Rather than supporting people with anorexia nervosa to seek treatment, some "pro-ana" (short for "pro-anorexia") websites provide practical tips and "thinspiration" to those who feel compelled to keep starving themselves.

One website contains the "Ana Prayer," which begins, "Strict is my diet. I must not want." The same site even lists the "Thin Commandments" ("If you aren't thin, you aren't attractive" and "Being thin is more important than being healthy"). The "Ana Creed" contains even more statements that express, with chilling clarity, the distorted thinking associated with severe anorexia

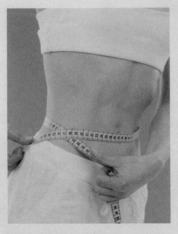

Some websites actively support anorexic or bulimic behavior, creating much concern in the treatment community.

nervosa ("I believe in bathroom scales as an indicator of my daily successes and failures" and "I believe in Control, the only force mighty enough to bring order to the chaos that is my world").

In response to pressure from the treatment community and those who run sites designed to provide genuine help for individuals with eating disorders, many large Web servers have shut down pro-ana sites. But the Internet is difficult to patrol. Many pro-ana (or *pro-mia* [pro-bulimia]) sites have simply "gone underground," thereby becoming even more difficult to find and remove.

Without question, the people who frequent these sites need help. Sadly, the individuals to whom they turn—with online names like "PerfectLeighThin" and "Neverthinenuf"—are the very people least able to offer the help they really need.

2004). Making the situation even worse, there have been surprisingly few controlled studies on which to base an informed judgment about which treatment modality will work best (le Grange & Lock, 2005; Wilson, Grilo, & Vitousek, 2007). In part, this is due to the fact that the disorder is rare. However, patients who suffer from anorexia nervosa are also often extremely reluctant to seek treatment. And when they do, taking part in research studies is unlikely to be a priority for them. These factors combine to make treatment research extremely difficult.

The most immediate concern with patients who have anorexia nervosa is to restore their weight to a level that is no longer life threatening. In severe cases, this requires hospitalization and extreme measures such as intravenous feeding. This is followed by rigorous control of the patient's caloric intake so as to progress toward a targeted range of weight gain (Andersen et al., 1997). Normally, this short-term effort is successful. However, without treatment designed to address the psychological issues that fuel the anorexic behavior, any weight gain will be temporary and the patient will soon need medical attention again. In some cases even aggressive treatment efforts can backfire. What mistakes do you think were made in the clinical management of the following case?

case study | Hospitalized Against Her Will

M., a 29-year-old woman, had been chronically ill since age 13. She had been hospitalized numerous times throughout the country and treated by exceptionally skilled therapists. Coming close to death on several occasions, she still managed to pursue a doctoral degree in mathematics and volunteered at a local community center for senior citizens despite having a BMI of 12.2. A female aide at the center eventually struck up a friendship with M., but M. declined her repeated requests to socialize after work.

This aide, increasingly worried that M.'s emaciation and ongoing resistance to eating might be a form of suicidal depression, took her concern to the center's director, who intervened by persuading M. to seek medical evaluation at a local hospital. Concerned about the gravity of her condition, the evaluating physician had M. detained involuntarily for psychiatric treatment. M. was soon judged by the psychiatric staff to be incompetent to make medical decisions despite her acknowledgment that she had anorexia nervosa, that the illness was resistant to usual care, and that she was aware of the detrimental effects of the disease. M. implored staff not to attempt any weight gain, explaining that this would only aggravate her psychological state. She proposed instead that she be allowed the alternative of supportive outpatient care.

M.'s request to be released was summarily rejected. Over the next month, there were various clumsy, at times coercive, attempts to increase her weight. M. then sought legal counsel and was ordered released into her own custody. Fearing any further contact with health professionals, her weight dropped precipitously and she died 3 months later of cardiac arrest. (From Strober, 2004.)

MEDICATIONS Antidepressants are sometimes used in the treatment of anorexia nervosa, although there is no evidence that they are especially effective (McElroy et al., 2010; Wilson, Grilo, & Vitousek, 2007). In contrast, research suggests that treatment with an antipsychotic medication called olanzapine may be beneficial (McElroy et al., 2010). Antipsychotic medications (which help with disturbed thinking) are routinely used in the treatment of schizophrenia. These medications also provide benefits in the treatment of anorexia nervosa, which is characterized by distorted beliefs about body shape and size. More importantly, one side effect of olanzapine is weight gain. Although this is a problem for patients with schizophrenia, in the treatment of anorexia nervosa weight gain is obviously much more desirable.

FAMILY THERAPY For adolescents with anorexia nervosa, family therapy is considered to be the treatment of choice. The best-studied approach, which (very importantly) blames neither the parents nor the child for the anorexia nervosa, is known as the Maudsley model (le Grange & Lock, 2005). A typical treatment program involves 10 to 20 sessions spaced over 6 to 12 months. The treatment has three phases. In the *refeeding phase*, the therapist works with the parents and supports their efforts to help their child (typically a daughter) to eat healthily once more. Family meals are observed by the therapist, and efforts are made to guide the parents as a functioning support team for their daughter's recovery. After the patient starts to gain weight, the *negotiations for a new pattern of relationships phase* begins, and family issues and problems begin to be addressed. Later, in the *termination phase* of treatment, the focus is on the development of more healthy relationships between the patient and her parents (see Lock et al., 2001). The case study of Ann describes how, after starting family-based Maudsley treatment, she was able to make a full recovery.

Family therapy is now regarded as the treatment of choice for adolescents with anorexia nervosa. The therapy is most effective for those in the earlier stages of the illness.

case study   One Family's Story

Ann was a clever, enthusiastic, and outgoing teenager. Prior to the development of her anorexia, she had shown no signs of any emotional problems. Yet after she began to train intensively for cross-country running, Ann started to eat "more healthily." She lost weight, became more withdrawn, and was short tempered with her family. Although her parents were concerned that she was not eating enough, no one suspected that Ann was developing anorexia.

Over the next 6 months, Ann's condition deteriorated still further. She lost more weight, and her joy in life ebbed away. Her parents took her to the family doctor. But her condition continued to deteriorate. She found it difficult to eat, she had no self-esteem, and she was miserable.

After her weight dropped to 34 kg (75 lbs) Ann had to be fed every night via a tube inserted into her nose. After 5 months, her weight had increased, and the tube feeding ceased. But Ann was still desperately ill. She was unable to eat unless her parents watched over her. She was also convinced that people were laughing at her because she was so "fat and disgusting."

At around this time, Ann's parents learned about the Maudsley treatment approach via a website (http://www.maudsleyparents.org) and consulted with a specialist who was trained in the treatment. With the support of a team of therapists, Ann' parents learned to accept that her angry outbursts, her destructive behaviors, and her insistence that she "didn't want to get better" were just symptoms of an illness over which she had no control. Ann's parents established a nonnegotiable program of regular meals and snacks, staying with Ann until she had eaten every scrap of food. Ann fought them tooth and nail. She tried to undermine her treatment by secretly vomiting after meals or by exercising in bed. But her parents responded by keeping her in sight for at least an hour after meals or staying with her overnight. Of course, this took its toll on the family. Ann's mother gave up work to devote herself to helping Ann recover. But the effort paid off. Six months after her family had started the refeeding program, Ann's weight was back to normal. Shortly after, her mood began to improve, and she started to engage in social activities once more. Twenty months after beginning the Maudsley treatment, Ann is now fully recovered and has shown no signs of relapse. (Adapted from Parent & Parent, 2008).

the course of a year. At the end of treatment 42 percent of patients who received family treatment were in full remission. For those who received individual therapy, the corresponding figure was 23 percent. When followed up another year later, 49 percent of the patients who had received family-based therapy were well, compared with 23 percent of those who had been treated with individual therapy (Lock et al., 2010). What is encouraging about these findings is that that overwhelming majority of adolescents completed the treatments and did not drop out. This suggests that, although individual therapy (which encouraged weight gain, the development of autonomy, and accepting responsibility for food-related issues) was slightly less efficacious overall than family treatment, it was still very acceptable to the adolescents who received it and it still provided some benefit. This is good news, especially for adolescents whose family members are unable or unwilling to participate in family treatment.

Not surprisingly, family treatment is more helpful for some patients than it is for others. Patients who develop anorexia nervosa before age 19 and have been ill for fewer than 3 years seem to do better than patients who have been ill for longer or who have bulimia nervosa (Dare & Eisler, 2002). This highlights the importance of early treatment, which may save some patients from a lifetime of suffering. For patients who are older or who have a long history of anorexia nervosa, the Maudsley approach unfortunately provides little clinical benefit (Wilson, Grilo, & Vitousek, 2007).

COGNITIVE-BEHAVIORAL THERAPY Cognitive-behavioral therapy (CBT), which involves changing behavior and maladaptive styles of thinking, has proved to be very effective in treating bulimia nervosa. Because anorexia nervosa shares many features with bulimia nervosa, CBT is often used with anorexia nervosa patients as well (Vitousek, 2002). The recommended length of treatment is 1 to 2 years. A major focus of the treatment involves modifying distorted beliefs concerning weight and food, as well as distorted beliefs about the self that may have contributed to the disorder (e.g., "People will reject me unless I am thin").

Pike and colleagues (2003) treated, after they had been discharged from the hospital, a sample of 33 women who had anorexia nervosa. Over the course of 1 year, the women received either 50 sessions of CBT or nutritional counseling. Despite this, only 17 percent of patients who received CBT showed full recovery. None of the women who received nutritional counseling was fully well (i.e., normal weight, no binge eating or purging, and with eating attitudes and concerns about weight within normal limits) at the end of treatment. These results highlight the current limitations of CBT for

Randomized controlled trials have shown that patients treated with family therapy for 1 year do better than patients who are assigned to a control treatment (where they receive supportive counseling on an individual basis). Five years after treatment, 75 to 90 percent of patients show full recovery (le Grange & Lock, 2005). In a more recent study, 121 adolescents were randomly assigned to receive either family-based treatment or individual therapy. Both treatments involved a total of 24 hours of treatment spaced over

RESEARCH CLOSE-UP

Randomized Controlled Trials

A randomized controlled trial involves a specific treatment group (which is the group the researchers are most interested in) as well as a control treatment group (against which the treatment group will be compared). Participants have an equal chance of being placed in either group because which group they go into is randomly determined.

this group of patients, as well as the pressing need for new treatment developments, particularly for older patients with more long-standing problems.

Treatment of Bulimia Nervosa

MEDICATIONS It is quite common for patients with bulimia nervosa to be treated with antidepressant medications. Researchers became interested in using these medications after it became clear that many patients with bulimia nervosa also suffer from mood disorders. Generally speaking (and in contrast to patients with anorexia nervosa), patients taking antidepressants do better than patients who are given inert, placebo medications. A positive response is usually apparent within the first three weeks. People who do not show early improvement are unlikely to benefit from further treatment with the same medication (Sysko et al., 2010). Perhaps surprisingly, antidepressants seem to decrease the frequency of binges as well as improve patients' mood and preoccupation with shape and weight (McElroy et al., 2010).

COGNITIVE-BEHAVIORAL THERAPY The leading treatment for bulimia nervosa is CBT. Most of the current treatment approaches are based on the work of Fairburn and colleagues in Oxford, England. Multiple controlled studies that include posttreatment and long-term follow-up

outcomes attest to the clinical benefits of CBT for bulimia (Fairburn, Jones et al., 1993; Wilson, 2010). Such studies have included comparisons with medication therapy (chiefly antidepressants) and with interpersonal psychotherapy (IPT; see Agras et al., 2000). They generally reveal CBT to be superior. In fact, combining CBT and medications produces only a modest increment in effectiveness over that attainable with CBT alone.

The "behavioral" component of CBT for bulimia nervosa focuses on normalizing eating patterns. This includes meal planning, nutritional education, and ending binging and purging cycles by teaching the person to eat small amounts of food more regularly. The "cognitive" element of the treatment is aimed at changing the cognitions and behaviors that initiate or perpetuate a binge cycle. This is accomplished by challenging the dysfunctional thought patterns typically present in bulimia nervosa, such as the "all-or-nothing" or dichotomous thinking described earlier. For instance, CBT challenges the tendency to divide all foods into "good" and "bad" categories. This is done by providing factual information, as well as by arranging for the patient to demonstrate to herself that ingesting "bad" food does not inevitably lead to a total loss of control over eating. Figure 5 shows a cognitive worksheet that was completed by a patient. It provides a good example of the kind of "hot thought" that can facilitate a binge.

Emma's completed worksheet: Identifying permissive thoughts

Situation	Feelings and sensations	Permissive thoughts
Friday, at college, alone, had a free period, thinking about my assignment (how difficult it was going to be). Ate a bar of chocolate, knew I was going to binge. Got on the bus to town, went to Burger King—had a burger, two portions of fries, a milkshake, one big bar of chocolate, another smaller bar of chocolate.	Anxious Heavy Blank	I might as well keep eating now I've started. *(I can make myself sick afterwards—so it doesn't matter—I can have what I want and I won't gain weight.)* I might as well carry on until my money has run out. I've got to eat more and more.
• When was it? • Where were you? • Who were you with? • What were you doing? • What were you thinking about?	• What feelings did you have? • What body sensations did you notice?	• What were you saying to yourself that made it easier to keep eating? • Identify and circle the hot thought. This is the thought that makes it most likely that you will binge.

FIGURE 5

Cognitive Worksheet

Source: Reproduced from M. Cooper, G. Todd, and A. Wells, *Bulimia Nervosa: A Cognitive Therapy Programme for Clients* with permission from Jessica Kingsley Publishers. Copyright © 2000 Myra Cooper, Gillian Todd, and Adrian Wells.

Treatment with CBT clearly helps to reduce the severity of symptoms in patients with bulimia nervosa. Still, patients with the disorder are rarely entirely well at the end of treatment (Lundgren et al., 2004). Binging and purging is eliminated in around 30 to 50 percent of cases (Wilson, 2010). Even after treatment, weight and shape concerns may remain. In an effort to improve treatment efficacy, new approaches such as dialectical behavior therapy (which is a treatment for borderline personality disorder) are now being explored, with some success (Safer et al., 2001; Chen & Safer, 2010). Another promising development involves using more individualized cognitive-behavior therapy approaches that are specifically tailored to the needs of the patient as opposed to a more standardized treatment format (Ghaderi, 2006). Finally, as we note in Box 5 one of the newest developments in the treatment of eating disorders is to adopt a transdiagnostic approach to treatment.

Treatment of Binge-Eating Disorder

Binge-eating disorder is not a disorder in *DSM-IV*, although, as we have already noted, it is likely to be added to the *DSM-5*. Even so, BED has attracted a lot of attention from researchers, and a number of different treatment approaches have been suggested. Due to the high level of comorbidity between binge-eating disorder and depression, antidepressant medications are sometimes used to treat this disorder. Other categories of medications, such as appetite suppressants and anticonvulsant

medications, have also been a focus of interest (McElroy et al., 2010). Sibutramine, a medication that inhibits the reuptake of serotonin and norepinephrine, has been shown to reduce the frequency of binges and to be associated with more weight loss than a placebo medication in a one clinical trial (Wilfley et al., 2008).

In one of the largest and most scientifically rigorous studies to date, Wilson and colleagues (2010) randomly assigned 205 overweight or obese men and women who met diagnostic criteria for BED to one of three different treatments. Some people received interpersonal psychotherapy (IPT), which is a therapy sometimes used in the treatment of depression. Others received CBT in the form of a self-help book (*Overcoming Binge Eating*, Fairburn, 1995), guided by a therapist. People in the third group were assigned to a behavioral weight loss treatment that involved exercise and moderate restriction of calories. So how did everyone do? At the end of six months of treatment, there were no significant differences between the groups with regard to remission from binge eating. However, at 2-year follow up, people who had received either IPT or guided CBT were doing better than those in the behavioral weight loss group. What is also noteworthy is that the dropout rate was much lower for people in the IPT group (7% dropped out) than it was in the guided CBT (30%) or behavioral weight loss groups (28%). This is important because, overall, the dropout rate for minorities in this study was very high (approximately one-third). The findings therefore suggest that for racial and ethnic minorities with BED, interpersonal psychotherapy might be a particularly suitable treatment approach.

---

5 THE WORLD AROUND US

Transdiagnostic Cognitive Behavioral Therapy for Eating Disorders

As we have mentioned earlier in this chapter, the majority of patients with eating disorders have a mixed clinical picture. What this means is that they show some symptoms of anorexia and some symptoms of bulimia, combined in a variety of ways. Recently, Fairburn and colleagues (2009) have reformulated cognitive behavior therapy for bulimia nervosa so that it is now a relevant treatment for pathological eating no matter what the diagnosis is. One form of the treatment is quite focused, targeting eating issues as well as concerns about shape and weight, extreme dieting, purging, and binge eating. The other form of the treatment is broader and also addresses such things as perfectionism, low self-esteem, and relationship problems.

Results from a randomized control trial show that patients who receive these treatments do much better than those assigned

to a waiting list condition. At the end of both treatments, regardless of their initial *DSM-IV* diagnosis, more than half of the sample had responded well. There were also some hints that patients who had more problems did a little better when they received the broader treatment whereas for more straightforward cases the focused form of treatment was very successful. It is important to mention that very low weight patients with anorexia were excluded from this study. Overall, however, the results suggest that the form of the treatment that a patient receives may not need to be tailored to a very specific *DSM-IV* diagnosis. Rather, "transdiagnostic" treatments may have a lot of promise for patients with eating disorders, broadly defined.

In Review

- What factors make eating disorders (especially anorexia nervosa) so difficult to treat?

- Describe the main features of the Maudsley approach for the treatment of anorexia nervosa. For what kind of patients does this approach yield better results?

- What treatment approaches have been shown to be helpful for binge eating disorder?

- Why do you think cognitive-behavioral therapy is so beneficial for patients with bulimia nervosa?

- What is a transdiagnostic treatment approach?

Obesity

case study | Battling Obesity

Vincent Caselli's battle with obesity began in his late 20s. "I always had some weight on me," he said. He was 200 pounds when he married his wife. A decade later he reached 300. He would diet and lose 75 pounds, only to put 100 back on. Eventually, he weighed 400 pounds. On one diet, he got down to 190, but he gained it all back. "I must have gained and lost a thousand pounds," he said. He developed high blood pressure, high cholesterol, and diabetes. His knees and his back ached all the time, and he had limited mobility. He used to get season tickets to the local hockey games and go out regularly to the track every summer to see auto racing. Years ago, he drove in races himself. Now he could barely walk to his pickup truck. He hadn't been on an airplane in two decades, and it had been 2 years since he had visited the second floor of his own house because he couldn't negotiate the stairs. He had to move out of the bedroom upstairs into a small room off the kitchen. Unable to lie down, he had slept in a recliner ever since. Even so, he could doze only in snatches because of sleep apnea (a breathing problem), which is common among the obese and is thought to be related to excessive fat in the tongue and soft tissues of the upper airway. Every 30 minutes his breathing would stop and he'd wake up asphyxiating. He was perpetually exhausted. (Adapted from Gawande, 2001.)

Humans have evolved to be able to store surplus energy as fat. This has obvious advantages: It serves as a hedge against periods of food shortage and makes survival more likely during times of famine. But in our modern world, access to food is no longer a problem for millions of people. The food supply is stable, and large amounts of energy-dense foods are readily available. Not surprisingly, most of us are getting heavier. For some people, the problem becomes even more extreme and results in obesity. Considered in this way, obesity can be regarded as a state of excessive, chronic fat storage (Berthoud & Morrison, 2008).

The Problem of Obesity

Worldwide, obesity is now a major public health problem. From 1980 to 2002 the prevalence of obesity almost tripled in adults in the United Kingdom. In China, rates of obesity in preschool children were 1.5 percent in 1989 and 12.6 percent just 9 years later (Flegal et al., 2002). The most recent estimates show that one-third of adults in the United States are obese (Flegal et al., 2010). Figure 6 shows how much more prevalent obesity has become in the past two decades.

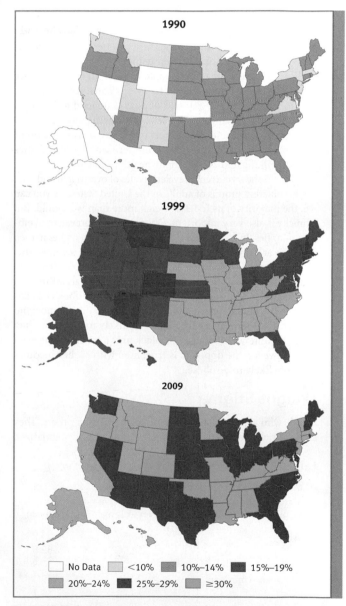

FIGURE 6

Obesity has increased dramatically in the US over the past 20 years.
Source: CDC.gov/obesity/trends.html

Medical Issues

Obesity brings with it increased risk for many health problems. These include high cholesterol, hypertension, heart disease, arthritis, diabetes, and cancer (Malnick & Knobler, 2006). It has been estimated that, by 2030, the cost of treating these problems in the United States alone will exceed 850 billion dollars annually (Wang et al., 2008). In addition, people who are obese have a reduced life expectancy of 5 to 20 years (Fontaine et al., 2003). It should therefore come as no surprise that the World Health Organization has recognized obesity as one of the top 10 global health problems.

Definition and Prevalence

Obesity is defined on the basis of a statistic called the **body mass index (BMI)**. This is a measure of a person's weight relative to height and is calculated using the formula shown in Table 4. Generally speaking, people with a BMI below 18.5 are considered underweight; 18.5 to 24.9 is considered normal; 25.0 to 29.9 is overweight; and obesity is defined as having a BMI above 30. Having a BMI above 40 or being more than 100 pounds overweight is called morbid obesity. This is the point at which excess weight begins to interfere with basic activities such as walking and creates many health problems.

Table 5 shows current prevalence rates of overweight and obesity for different groups of adults in the United States. As you can see, the majority of us (68.3%) weigh more than we should. But ethnicity is also very important. Obesity is more prevalent in ethnic minorities. In general, rates of obesity are slightly higher in men than they are in women. The notable exception here involves African Americans. One in every two black women is obese. This is the highest rate of obesity found for any group (Flegal et al., 2010).

Another demographic variable linked to obesity is social class, although again gender and ethnicity are important. Higher income women are much less likely to be obese than lower income women are. For black and Mexican American men, however, the opposite is true; men with higher incomes are more likely to be obese.

Weight Stigma

People who are obese are often judged harshly by others. They are routinely ridiculed, discriminated against, and stigmatized

table 5 Prevalence (%) of Overweight and Obesity in U.S. Adults

Group	Overweight	Obese
All	68.3	33.9
White	67.5	32.8
Hispanic	76.9	37.9
Mexican American	77.5	39.3
Black	73.7	44.1

Note: Figures based on BMI of 25 or above for overweight and 30 or above for obesity. Source: Flegal et al. (2010).

(Carr & Friedman, 2005). A powerful source of this is the media, which perpetuates weight-based stereotypes and often depicts overweight or obese people in a very negative light. Compared to thin television characters, those who are overweight or obese are more likely to be shown when eating, are less likely to be depicted as being involved in romantic relationships, and are more likely to be the target of derisive comments (see Schvey et al., 2011). Audiences also laugh more when negative comments are directed to overweight characters, especially female ones. Box 6 describes some of the consequences that stigma has on people who are overweight.

But being obese may not be the personal choice that many people believe it is. The more research progresses, the more we are learning about how important genes and other biological factors are in determining the drive to eat and the way our bodies respond when we eat less. We are also learning how powerful environmental factors can be. In short, the idea that we can simply decide to control our weight by eating less and exercising more does not always fit with the scientific facts.

Obesity and the *DSM*

From a diagnostic perspective, obesity is not an eating disorder, and it is not included in *DSM-IV-TR*. However, Volkow and O'Brien (2007) suggest that some forms of obesity are driven by an excessive motivational desire for food. They liken such symptoms as the compulsive consumption of food and the inability to restrain eating despite the wish to do so to symptoms of substance abuse and drug dependence. This parallels the view, offered by some, that obesity is a "food addiction" (see Cota et al., 2006). It has also been suggested that obesity and addiction may both concern problems in key brain regions involved in motivation, reward, and inhibitory control. Some thought is now being given to the idea of including obesity as a brain disorder in *DSM-5*. Although this idea is very controversial and we do not anticipate that it will happen, it reflects how much ideas about obesity are beginning to change.

Risk and Causal Factors in Obesity

The Role of Genes

Are you the kind of person who can eat high-calorie foods without significant weight gain? Or does it seem as though you need only to look at a piece of chocolate cake to gain a few pounds? In all probability our genetic makeup plays an important role in determining how predisposed we are to becoming obese in the modern environment of increased food availability. Some of the genes that may, in our ancestral past, have been advantageous and helped us survive in times of famine may predispose those who carry them to readily gain weight when food is plentiful. Interestingly, population groups that

Do Negative Messages About Being Overweight Encourage Overweight People to Eat More or Less?

In our society many people still consider it acceptable to make fun of those who are overweight or obese. But what effect does this have on the people who receive such stigmatizing messages? To address this question Schvey and colleagues (2011) asked overweight and normal weight women to view one of two videos. One video depicted clips from neutral scenes such as insurance commercials. The other video contained clips from televisions shows and movies that depicted overweight and obese women in negative ways (e.g., as clumsy, lazy, and loud). After watching the videos, all the women were given questionnaires to complete in private. The room also contained three different bowls of snack foods, which the women were invited to eat.

The variable that the researchers were most interested in was how much the women ate after being exposed to the different types of films. After seeing the stigmatizing videos the overweight women consumed 303 calories of snack food. This is more than three times as much as the 89 calories consumed by the overweight women who had watched the neutral film. The overweight women who had watched the stigmatizing videos also ate significantly more calories than the normal-weight women who watched either type of film.

Television is a powerful source of weight-based stereotypes. The average American watches around 150 hours of television a month. Far from motivating overweight and obese people to lose weight, the negatively biased portrayals of obesity that we routinely see on TV may actually lead people to eat more rather than less.

In Review

- Why is the increase in the prevalence of obesity such a public health concern?

- Explain the importance of the body mass index in the definition of obesity.

- How are ethnicity, gender, and social class related to rates of obesity?

- How do the media portray people who are overweight and obese? What are some of the consequences of this?

- On what grounds is the argument being made that obesity might be a brain disorder? What effect might this have on stigma?

were most susceptible to starvation throughout history (e.g., Pima Indians, Pacific Islanders) are those that are most inclined to become obese when they have a sedentary lifestyle and a Western diet (see Friedman, 2003).

Thinness seems to run in families (Bulik & Allison, 2002). Genes associated with thinness and leanness have been found in certain animals, and a special type of rat has now been bred that does not become obese even when fed a high-fat diet. Twin studies further suggest that genes play a role both in the development of obesity and in the tendency to binge (Bulik et al., 2003; Javaras et al., 2008).

Indeed, a genetic mutation has been discovered that is specifically associated with binge eating (Branson et al., 2003). Although this mutation was found only in a minority (5 percent) of the obese people in the study, all of the obese people with the gene reported problems with binge eating. In contrast, only 14 percent of obese people who did not have the genetic mutation displayed a pattern of binge eating.

Hormones Involved in Appetite and Weight Regulation

In the course of a year, the average person will consume 1 million calories or more and yet keep a reasonably stable weight. How do we accomplish this? The answers lie in the remarkable ability of our bodies to regulate the daily quantity of food consumed and to balance this with our energy output over the longer term. This is relevant to the concept of set point that we described earlier. Remarkably, we are able to regulate our energy balance with a precision of more than 99.5 percent. This is far in excess of what we could monitor in any conscious or mindful way (Friedman, 2004).

One key element of this homeostatic system is a hormone called **leptin**. Leptin is produced by fat cells, and it acts to reduce our intake of food. Increased body fat leads to increased levels of leptin, which leads to decreased food intake. When body fat levels decrease, leptin production decreases and food intake is stimulated. Rare genetic mutations that result in an inability to produce leptin cause people to have an insatiable appetite and result in morbid obesity. One 9-year-old girl in England weighed 200 pounds. She could hardly walk because of her extreme weight. When it was discovered that she was lacking leptin, she was treated with injections of the hormone, and her weight consequently returned to normal (Farooqi et al., 2002; Montague et al., 1997).

Unfortunately, when leptin is given to overweight individuals, in the majority of cases it has little effect. People who are overweight generally have high levels of leptin in their bloodstream. The problem is that they are resistant to its effects. In fact, it has been suggested that obesity may result from a person's being resistant to leptin (Friedman, 2004). Despite this complication, the leptin system is still a major focus of interest in the search for antiobesity drugs.

Why do we get hungry at regular times during the day even if we do not even see or smell food? The reason may lie in a hormone called **grehlin**. Grehlin (the name comes from a Hindu word meaning "growth") is a hormone that is produced by the stomach. It is a powerful appetite stimulator. Under normal circumstances, grehlin levels rise before a meal and fall after we have eaten. When grehlin is injected into human volunteers, it makes them very hungry. This suggests that grehlin is a key contributor to the appetite control system.

People with a rare condition called Prader-Willi syndrome have chromosomal abnormalities that create many problems, one of which is very high levels of grehlin. Sufferers are extremely obese and often die before age 30 from obesity-related causes. The food cravings experienced by Prader-Willi sufferers can be so extreme that food has to be kept locked away so that they cannot binge. Although this genetic disorder is very unusual, findings

Food portions have increased significantly over the past several decades. Today a typical hamburger weighs 6 ounces and contains 618 calories.

This woman suffers from Prader-Willi syndrome, a rare genetic disorder that makes people insatiably hungry. After a year in a group home with rigid dietary rules, she lost 80 pounds.

such as this highlight the role of genetics in the regulation of eating behavior and weight. They also illustrate how the biological drive to eat can be so powerful that willpower is no match for it.

Sociocultural Influences

The examples of Prader-Willi syndrome and mutations of the leptin gene tell us that genes alone can sometimes explain why people differ in their weight and eating patterns. However, in most cases environmental factors also play an important role. As with other disorders, a diathesis-stress perspective is most appropriate. Some of us, by virtue of our genetic makeup and personality, are likely to experiences more weight-related problems from living in a culture that provides ready access to high-fat, high-sugar (junk) foods, encourages overconsumption, and makes it easy to avoid exercise.

Consider your own lifestyle issues. How often do you eat fast food? Are you more likely to take the stairs or the elevator? Even when we have good intentions, we sometimes make poor food choices or get too little exercise. A major culprit is time pressure. Because we are so chronically short of time, we drive rather than walk. We put food into our mouths far too quickly, outpacing our natural feelings of fullness. This leads us to keep eating. Finally, as the pace of life gets faster, we have less time to prepare food. So we eat out more often or buy more prepackaged or fast food. Which of these behaviors do you recognize in yourself?

As Brownell and his colleagues (Brownell, 2003; Gearhardt et al., 2011) have pointed out, the food industry is also highly skilled at getting us to maximize our food intake. Restaurants in the United States serve large portions of foods that are engineered to be hyperpalatable (especially tasty and rewarding) because they contain so much sugar or fat. Some examples of commonly eaten foods are shown in Table 6. One comparison of the same fast-food chains and eateries in Philadelphia and Paris found that the average portion sizes in Paris were 25 percent smaller (Rozin et al., 2003). In addition, the culture of supersizing tempts us to buy more than we might choose to buy otherwise simply because it costs only a little bit more (Brownell, 2003). In several ballparks you can now buy an "all-you-can-eat" seat. The price includes unlimited hot dogs, nachos, peanuts, popcorn, and soft drinks.

Consider also the issue of accessibility. Foods with low nutritional value (high fat, high sugar) are less expensive and also much easier to find than foods with high nutritional value. Next time you go to a gas station or go out to see a movie, look at the food choices that are available. How much healthy food is on offer? Is it easier to find an apple or a candy bar? Notice how easy is it to mindlessly pick up a cheap high-calorie item that provides little nutrition.

If you like to snack in front of the TV you should also be aware of how powerful food advertising can be. Food

table 6 Sugar and Fat in Traditional and Hyperpalatable Foods

Food	Portion Size	Type	Sugar	Fat
Apple	1 medium	T	19g	0g
Tomato	1 medium	T	3g	0g
Orange	1 cup, sections	T	17g	0g
Chicken breast	3 ounces	T	0g	3g
Coca-cola	1 can	H	39g	0g
McDonalds Fries	1 medium	H	0g	19g
Dairy Queen	1 medium ice cream	H	34g	10g

Note: T = traditional food; H = hyperpalatable food. Dairy Queen ice cream cone is chocolate flavor.

Source: Gearhardt et al. (2011).

Food advertising leads us to eat more even when we are not hungry. In one study children ate 45% more when they watched a cartoon that contained food advertising.

An LA Dodgers fan carries four hot dogs, nachos, peanuts, and four sodas from the concessions area. Sitting in the popular all-you-can-eat area costs $40, in seats that used to cost $8.

advertising seems to trigger the kind of automatic and unconscious eating that is not related to being hungry. In one study, children ate 45 percent more after watching a TV cartoon that contained food advertisements than they did if the cartoon contained advertising for other products (Harris et al., 2009).

Continued exposure to a culture that provides easy access to highly palatable foods, offers large portions, and bombards people with endless food advertisements may explain why rates of obesity increase in immigrants after they have lived in the United States for a while. Although recent immigrants are less likely to be overweight and obese than people born in the United States, after they have lived in the country for 10 years or longer they have a significant increase in their body mass index (Goel et al., 2004). This suggests that sociocultural factors are likely to be playing a major role. In addition to the emphasis on food, what other aspects of American culture do you think might be exerting an influence here?

Family Influences

Family behavior patterns may also play a role in the development of excessive eating and obesity. In some families, a high-fat, high-calorie diet (or an overemphasis on food) may lead to obesity in many or all family members, including the family pet. In other families, eating (or overeating) becomes a habitual means of alleviating emotional distress or showing love (Musante et al., 1998). Children whose mothers smoked during pregnancy or whose mothers gained a lot of weight during the pregnancy are also at a higher risk of being overweight at age 3 (Gillman et al., 2008).

Family attitudes toward food are important because their consequences are likely to remain with us for a long time. Obesity is related to the number and size of fat (adipose) cells in the body (Heymsfield et al., 1995). People who are obese have markedly more adipose cells than people of normal weight (Peeke & Chrousos, 1995). When obese people lose weight, the size of the cells is reduced but not their number.

Research suggests that obesity can be socially contagious. If someone close to us becomes obese, the chance that we will later become obese can increase by as much as 57 percent.

Some evidence suggests that the total number of adipose cells stays the same from childhood onward (Crisp et al., 1970).

It is possible that overfeeding infants and young children causes them to develop more adipose cells and may thus predispose them to weight problems in adulthood. Consistent with this, DiPietro and colleagues (1994) found that, in a 40-year follow-up study, the majority of a sample of 504 overweight children became overweight adults.

Finally, there is some evidence that obesity might be "socially contagious." Provocative research findings have shown that if someone close to us (e.g., a spouse, sibling, or friend) becomes obese, the chance that we ourselves will later become obese can increase by as much as 57 percent. The effect is most marked within same-sex versus opposite-sex relationships, suggesting that social influences might be playing a key role. In contrast, weight gain in neighbors was not associated with later weight gain in those who lived close by, again suggesting that it is the closeness of the relationship, rather than exposure to common environmental factors, that might be important (Christakis & Fowler, 2007). Although the mechanisms of this social transmission are far from clear, it is possible that obesity in our close friends and family members could lead us to change our attitudes about weight or perhaps influences our eating patterns.

Stress and "Comfort Food"

Do you eat when you are stressed or unhappy? If you do, what kinds of food do you crave? Foods that are high in fat or carbohydrates are the foods that console most of us when we are feeling troubled (Canetti et al., 2002). Workers who say that they are under a lot of stress report that they eat less healthy foods, and foods that are higher in fat, relative to their less stressed counterparts (Ng & Jeffery, 2003).

Eating for comfort is found in rats too. When rats were placed under chronic stress (being subjected to cold temperatures), they selected diets that were higher in fat and sugar (Dallman et al., 2003). What is also interesting in this study is that the rats that ate the comfort food gained weight in their bellies and became calmer in the face of new acute stress. This prompted the researchers to speculate that the sugary and fatty foods helped to reduce activation in the stress response system.

Might overeating function as a means of reducing feelings of distress or depression? Certainly many people with obesity experience psychological problems such as depression. In a large community sample of more than 40,000 people, lifetime rates of mood disorders were higher in people who were obese than in people whose weight was in the normal range (Petry et al., 2008). Other research has found that a striking percentage of subjects with an eating disorder binge eat in response to aversive emotional states, such as feeling depressed or anxious (Kenardy et al., 1996).

In light of Dallman's data on the stressed rats, it is easy to grasp how weight gain (or a tendency to maintain excessive weight) may be explained quite simply in terms of learning principles (Fairburn et al., 1998). We are all conditioned to eat in response to a wide range of environmental stimuli (at parties, during movies, while watching TV). Obese individuals have been shown to be conditioned to more cues—both internal and external—than others of normal weight. Anxiety, anger, boredom, and depression may lead to overeating. Eating in response to such cues is then reinforced because the taste of good food is pleasurable and because the individual's emotional tension is reduced.

Pathways to Obesity

Understanding the causes of obesity is complex. In all probability, obesity results from a combination of genetic, environmental, and sociocultural influences. An important step along the pathway to obesity, however, may be binge eating. In a prospective study of 231 adolescent girls, Stice, Presnell, and Spangler (2002) established that binge eating is a predictor of later obesity. This suggests that we should pay close attention to the causes of binge eating.

Animal studies show that, in rats, any genetic differences that exist in the tendency to binge eat only start to emerge during puberty (Klump et al., 2011). Biological risk factors may thus become more important as we enter adolescence. Unfortunately, this is also the developmental period when sociocultural pressures may be most intense.

Relevant here is research suggesting that one pathway to binge eating may be through social pressure to conform to the thin ideal, as ironic as this may seem (Stice et al., 2002). Being heavy often leads to dieting, which may lead to binge eating when willpower wanes (see Figure 7). Another pathway to binge eating may operate through depression and low self-esteem. In Stice and colleagues' (2002)

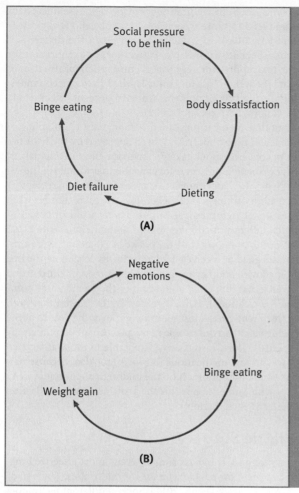

FIGURE 7

Pathways to Obesity

One pathway to obesity is through social pressures to be thin. Another pathway may operate via depression and low self-esteem.

Treatment of Obesity

There are three main treatment options for people who are overweight or obese. These are (1) lifestyle modifications (diet, exercise, and behavior therapy), (2) medications, and (3) bariatric surgery.

Lifestyle Modifications

A first step in the treatment of obesity is a clinical approach that, ideally, involves a low-calorie diet, exercise, and some form of behavioral intervention. Several research trials have now demonstrated that lifestyle modification approaches yield positive benefits for patients, although the results are far from dramatic. Sustained weight loss of around 7 pounds (3.2 kilograms) is quite typical (Powell et al., 2007). However, it is important to keep in mind that for people who are overweight even small amounts of weight loss may yield some health benefits. Using meal-replacement products (e.g., calorie-controlled shakes), continuing a relationship with a treatment provider, and maintaining a high level of physical activity all help improve efforts at long-term weight control (Fabricatore & Wadden, 2006).

What about popular diets? Gardner and colleagues (2007) compared the Atkins diet, the Zone diet, the Ornish diet, and a more traditional diet approach in a sample of overweight and obese women aged 25 to 50. At the end of a year, those who had followed the Atkins diet had lost the most weight (10.4 pounds or 4.7 kilograms) compared with a weight loss of 3.5 pounds (1.6 kilograms) for the Zone, 5.7 pounds (2.6 kilograms) for the Ornish, and 4.8 pounds (2.2 kilograms) for the traditional approach. Nonetheless, even for the

prospective study, low levels of support from peers, as well as depression, made girls more at risk for binging. We further have confirmation that when children are overweight, they are more likely to be rejected by their peers (Latner & Stunkard, 2003; Strauss & Pollack, 2003), consequently increasing their negative affect. As Figure 7 shows, a pattern of binge eating in response to negative emotions may make a bad situation much worse—increasing weight, depression, and fostering alienation from peers in a vicious cycle.

Sustained weight loss of around 7 pounds is typical for people who exercise and reduce their intake of calories. Even modest weight loss can lead to health benefits.

most successful dieters, the amount of weight loss was not especially large.

Weight Watchers is the only commercial weight-loss program with demonstrated efficacy in a randomized controlled trial. Over the course of 6 months, overweight and obese people who attended Weight Watchers lost more weight (10.5 versus 3 pounds) than did people who received self-help materials and two brief sessions with a nutritionist (Heshka et al., 2000). At a later follow-up, those who had attended Weight Watchers were still doing better than the people who had been assigned to the self-help group (Heshka et al., 2003).

"Crash" diets and extreme treatments to bring about dramatic weight loss (including starvation of patients in a hospital setting) are now considered to be outmoded and ineffective approaches. Although they lead to weight loss in the short term, the weight loss is not maintained. Indeed, at follow-up, people who have been subjected to these procedures usually weigh more than they did before the treatment started (Mann et al., 2007).

Although we may be tempted by every new diet or weight loss fad that comes along, in the long run it is the calories that matter. Recent research has shown that focusing on the proportion of fat, protein, or carbohydrates in the diet is far less important than just eating less (Sacks et al., 2009). If you are able to do this, regardless of what kind of diet you chose, you will have some success.

But the harsh reality is that losing weight is difficult for most people. And for those who are obese, losing weight and maintaining the weight loss present a truly formidable challenge. As we mentioned earlier, our bodies try to defend a set-point weight. When we try to go below this, marked metabolic and hormonal changes occur. The body goes into "starvation mode" and hunger is increased, the metabolic rate slows, and we also feel less full after eating (Goldsmith et al., 2010). It is also the case that energy expenditure decreases significantly following weight loss. This means that if an obese person loses 100 pounds, decreasing in weight from 300 pounds to 200 pounds, the person has to consume far fewer calories to maintain this new weight than a person who already weighed 200 pounds would (Friedman, 2004). It is hardly surprising, therefore, that relapse rates are so high after weight loss and that people who attempt to lose weight often feel so discouraged. Indeed, some researchers now maintain that obesity is resistant to psychological methods of treatment (Cooper et al., 2010). This makes prevention all the more important.

Medications

Drugs that are used to promote weight loss fall into two main categories. One group of medications reduces eating by suppressing appetite, typically by increasing the availability of neurotransmitters. A second group of medications works by preventing some of the nutrients in food from being absorbed.

Two medications are approved by the FDA for use in conjunction with a reduced-calorie diet. Sibutramine (Meridia) inhibits the reuptake of serotonin and norepinephrine and, to a lesser extent, dopamine. Orlistat (Xenical) works by reducing the amount of fat in the diet that can be absorbed once it enters the gut. Both medications provide modest clinical benefits and lead to more weight loss than placebo (Fabricatore & Wadden, 2006). In some cases, however, the differences are not especially impressive. Patients who take Orlistat for 1 year lose approximately 9 percent of their pretreatment weight. The weight loss for controls who take a placebo medication during this time is just under 6 percent (Heck et al., 2000; Yanovski & Yanovski, 2002).

Another medication, called Rimonabant (Acomplia), is available in Europe but has not been approved by the FDA because of concerns about its depressive side effects. Rimonabant works by blocking a receptor for cannabis that stimulates the appetite. It may be better known to some as the "munchie receptor."

In addition to specific weight loss drugs, recent research suggests that two medications routinely used in psychiatry and addiction medicine might also be helpful. The 1,742 obese participants with a BMI between 30 and 45 were randomly assigned to receive a higher or lower dose of naltrexone combined with another drug called bupropion. A third group received a placebo. Only about half of the participants completed the treatment. However, the results showed that both drug treatment groups lost more weight over the course of the following year than did people in the placebo group (Greenway et al., 2010). These results are comparable to those associated with weight loss medications like Orlistat. Also, because naltrexone and buproprion act on the midbrain dopamine system, they provide some support for the growing conceptualization of obesity as an addiction.

Bariatric Surgery

Bariatric or gastric bypass surgery is the most effective long-term treatment for people who are morbidly obese (Bult et al., 2008; Moldovan & David, 2011). Several different techniques can be used both to reduce the storage capacity of the stomach and, sometimes, to shorten the length of the intestine so that less food can be absorbed. Before the operation, the stomach might be able to hold about a quart of food and liquid. After the procedure, the stomach might be able to hold only the contents of a shot glass. Binge eating becomes virtually impossible. The operation takes only a few hours, but because it is performed on an obese patient, recovery can be difficult.

Weight loss is quite dramatic after bariatric surgery. A year and a half after his surgery, Vincent Caselli, the patient in the case study you read earlier, weighed 250 pounds and was still losing weight. His case fits well with some of the empirical research findings. Surgical treatment of obesity tends to result in substantial weight loss, averaging between 44 and 88 pounds (Bult et al., 2008). Interestingly, levels of the appetite hormone grehlin are also suppressed after particular types of surgical procedures. Of course, some patients manage to find ways to continue to binge eat after surgery (Kalarchian et al., 1998) and tend to regain their weight over an 18-month period (Hsu et al., 1998). Although bariatric surgery is not without risk (mortality rates hover around 1 percent), the risk of the surgery should be evaluated against the health risks that accompany untreated obesity.

Al Roker, the NBC weatherman on the *Today* show, had gastric bypass surgery, one form of bariatric surgery. He weighed 320 pounds at the time of his surgery. A year later, Roker had shed 100 pounds.

The Importance of Prevention

Reducing the prevalence of obesity is now a top priority. But if obesity is to be prevented, it must first be recognized. Astonishingly, in a recent study conducted in Finland, 57 percent of parents who had an overweight or obese 7-year-old child failed to recognize that their child was overweight (Vanhala et al., 2009). In this Finnish study, childhood obesity was predicted by having an obese parent, skipping breakfast, habitual overeating, and not being physically active. Because we know that childhood obesity predicts adult obesity, parental education is clearly very important.

Losing weight is difficult because it is a battle against biological mechanisms designed to keep us at our current weight. This highlights to importance of not gaining weight in the first place. Over an 8-year period, the average adult (in the 20–40 age range) will gain about 14 to 16 pounds (Hill et al., 2003). How may this be avoided? Most of the weight gain that people often regard as inevitable could be prevented through a combination of increased energy expenditure and reduced food intake. And this may be easier to do than we might imagine. Hill and colleagues (2003) have calculated that all that we need to do is cut back on our intake of calories by a mere 100 calories per day or walk an extra mile each day. Here are some simple ways to accomplish this:

- Eat three fewer bites of food when you eat a meal. Three bites of hamburger, for example, equals 100 calories.
- Take the stairs, combine a meeting with a walk, or park a little farther from your destination. A mile of walking is only 2,000 to 2,500 extra steps, and we can add these in small increments throughout the day.
- Sleep more. Research is showing that babies who sleep fewer than 12 hours a day are more likely to be overweight at age 3 (Taveras et al., 2008). And adults who sleep only 5 to 6 hours a night gain more weight over time than those who sleep 7 to 8 hours a night (Chaput et al., 2008).

By making these habits part of your daily routine, you will be able to prevent weight gain as you age, improving your overall health.

At the national level the problem of obesity is unlikely to be solved without changes in public policy. Some of the changes suggested by Brownell and colleagues (Brownell,

Although the restaurant industry lobbied hard against it, a new law now requires calorie information to be posted on menus in fast food and chain restaurants. When people select food from these menus, they consume fewer calories.

It has been estimated that increasing the tax on sugar sweetened beverages by 20% could lead to an average weight loss of almost 4 lbs a year for adults.

2002; Novak & Brownell, 2011) include (1) improving opportunities for physical activity, (2) better regulation of food advertising aimed at children, (3) prohibiting the sale of fast food and soft drinks in schools, (4) subsidizing the sale of healthful foods and (5) increasing taxes on sugar sweetened beverages like soda (Novak & Brownell, 2011). Another recent development concerns menu labeling. In 2008, much to the dismay of the restaurant industry, New York City became the first place to require chain restaurants to post calorie information on their menu boards. This is an important move because most people consistently underestimate the calories in the food they eat outside the home. A recent study also suggests that when people order from a menu that includes calorie information, they consume 14 percent fewer calories than people who order from a menu that contains no calorie information (Roberto et al,

2010). Have you seen information of this kind? Did it effect what you decided to order? What do you think needs to be done to stop the nationwide problem of obesity from escalating even further out of control?

In Review

- Why is losing weight so difficult for most people?

- What is the most effective treatment for people who are morbidly obese?

- What are the elements of a lifestyle modification treatment for obesity?

- What social policy changes might reduce or prevent obesity?

Unresolved Issues

▶ *Will* DSM-5 *Solve the Problem of Eating Disorder NOS?*

Most people who seek treatment for an eating disorder are diagnosed with eating disorder NOS (EDNOS). This is a problem because it means that the majority of patients with eating disorders are being given a residual diagnosis that conveys almost nothing about their specific pathology. To help remedy the problem of EDNOS it has been suggested that the diagnostic criteria for anorexia nervosa and bulimia nervosa should be made less stringent. This will likely happen in *DSM-5*. Changes to the diagnosis of anorexia nervosa will mean that the absence of menstruation will no longer be required. The diagnostic criteria for bulimia nervosa are also being relaxed; binge eating and purging now has to occur on average once a week (instead of twice a week) over a 3-month period. These changes to the diagnostic criteria are supported by research that shows that people with subthreshold anorexia nervosa and subthreshold bulimia nervosa are remarkably similar to those who have the full syndrome (Eddy, Doyle, et al., 2008;

Fairburn et al., 2007). They will have the effect of moving many people out of the EDNOS category.

Another proposed change that will have a marked effect concerns binge eating disorder. Many people with EDNOS actually have binge eating disorder. If, as we expect, binge eating disorder becomes a formal diagnosis in *DSM-5*, this will also remove large numbers of people from the EDNOS category.

If all of these proposed changes to the diagnostic criteria are implemented in *DSM-5* people currently diagnosed with EDNOS will instead be diagnosed with more specific disorders. In fact, it is likely that the whole diagnosis of EDNOS will not appear in *DSM-5*. Instead it is likely to be replaced by another broad category that will include clinically significant problems involving feeding and eating. Purging disorder (which involves purging in normal weight people who have not eaten large amounts of food) is one example of this.

Summary

- *DSM-IV-TR* recognizes three different eating disorders: anorexia nervosa, bulimia nervosa, and eating disorder NOS (not otherwise specified). Binge-eating disorder, which is currently listed as a form of EDNOS, has been proposed for inclusion in *DSM-5* but is not yet an official diagnosis.

- Both anorexia nervosa and bulimia nervosa are characterized by an intense fear of becoming fat and by a drive for thinness.

- Patients with anorexia nervosa are severely underweight. This is not true of patients with bulimia nervosa.

- Eating disorders are more common in women than in men (3:1 ratio). They can develop at any age, although they typically emerge in adolescence or early adulthood. Anorexia nervosa usually begins at an earlier age (15–19) than bulimia nervosa (20–24).

- Anorexia nervosa has a lifetime prevalence of approximately 0.9 percent. Bulimia nervosa is more common, with a lifetime prevalence of 1 to 3 percent. Many more people suffer from less severe forms of disturbed eating patterns.

- Genetic factors play an important role in eating disorders. Genes may make some people more susceptible to binge eating or to sociocultural influences, or may underlie personality styles (e.g., perfectionism) that increase risk for eating disorders.

- The neurotransmitter serotonin has been implicated in eating disorders. This neurotransmitter is also involved in mood disorders, which are highly comorbid with eating disorders.

- Sociocultural influences are integral in the development of eating disorders. Our society places great value on being thin. Western values concerning thinness may be spreading. This may help explain why eating disorders are now found throughout the world.

- Individual risk factors such as internalizing the thin ideal, body dissatisfaction, dieting, negative affect, and perfectionism have been implicated in the development of eating disorders.

- Anorexia nervosa is very difficult to treat. Treatment is long term, and many patients resist getting well. For younger patients, family therapy appears to be very beneficial.

- The treatment of choice for bulimia nervosa is CBT. CBT is also helpful for binge-eating disorder. Interpersonal therapy (IPT) seems to be helpful for binge eating disorder and may be especially acceptable to minorities.

- Obesity is defined as having a body mass index of 30 or above. Obesity is associated with many medical problems and increased mortality. Obesity is not currently viewed as an eating disorder or as a psychiatric condition in the *DSM*.

- A tendency toward being thin or heavy may be inherited. Our genetic makeup may make us more or less likely to gain weight in a cultural environment that promotes overconsumption of food and a sedentary lifestyle.

- Minorities are at especially high risk for obesity. Obesity rates are highest (50%) in black women. Low income is associated with obesity for women, but higher income is associated with obesity in black and Mexican American men.

- Obesity is a chronic problem. Lifestyle modifications and medications help patients to lose small amounts of weight. Drastic weight loss, however, usually requires bariatric surgery.

- Because obesity tends to be a lifelong problem and because treating obesity is so difficult, there is now a focus on trying to prevent people from becoming obese in the first place. Implementing many of the approaches that have been recommended will require changes in social policy.

Key Terms

anorexia nervosa
binge
binge-eating disorder (BED)
body mass index (BMI)
bulimia nervosa
cognitive-behavioral therapy (CBT)

eating disorder
eating disorder not otherwise specified (EDNOS)
grehlin
hypothalamus
leptin

negative affect
obesity
perfectionism
purge
serotonin
set point

Glossary

Many of the key terms listed in the glossary appear in boldface when first introduced in the text discussion. A number of other terms commonly encountered in this or other psychology texts are also included; you are encouraged to make use of this glossary both as a general reference tool and as a study aid for the course in abnormal psychology.

Anorexia nervosa. Intense fear of gaining weight or becoming "fat" coupled with refusal to maintain adequate nutrition and with severe loss of body weight.

Binge. An out-of-control consumption of an amount of food that is far greater than what most people would eat in the same amount of time and under the same circumstances.

Binge-eating disorder (BED). Distinct from nonpurging bulimia nervosa, whereby binging is not accompanied by inappropriate compensatory behavior to limit weight gain.

Body mass index (BMI). An estimation of total body fat calculated as body weight in kilograms divided by height (in meters) squared.

Bulimia nervosa. Frequent occurrence of binge-eating episodes accompanied by a sense of loss of control of overeating and recurrent inappropriate behavior such as purging or excessive exercise to prevent weight gain.

Cognitive-behavioral therapy (CBT). Therapy based on altering dysfunctional thoughts and cognitive distortions.

Eating disorders. Disorders of food ingestion, regurgitation, or attitude that affect health and well-being, such as anorexia, bulimia, or binge eating.

Eating disorder not otherwise specified (EDNOS). A diagnostic category reserved for disorders of eating that do not meet criteria for any other specific eating disorder.

Grehlin. Grehlin is a hormone that is produced by the stomach. It stimulates appetite.

Hypothalamus. Key structure at the base of the brain; important in emotion and motivation.

Leptin. Leptin is a hormone produced by fat cells that acts to reduce food intake.

Negative affect. The experience of an emotional state characterized by negative emotions. Such negative emotions might include anger, anxiety, irritability, and sadness.

Obesity. The condition of having elevated fat masses in the body. Obesity is defined as having a body mass index (BMI) of 30 or higher.

Perfectionism. The need to get things exactly right. A personality trait that may increase risk for the development of eating disorders, perhaps because perfectionistic people may be more likely to idealize thinness.

Purge. Purging refers to the removal of food from the body by such means as self-induced vomiting or misuse of laxatives, diuretics, and enemas.

Serotonin. A neurotransmitter from the indolamine class that is synthesized from the amino acid tryptophan. Also referred to as 5-HT(5-hydroxytryptamine), this neurotransmitter is thought to be involved in a wide range of psychopathological conditions.

Set point. The tendency of our bodies to resist efforts to bring about a marked change (increase or decrease) in weight.

Photo Credits

Credits are listed in order of appearance.

Sam Barnes/Alamy; DAVID GRAY/Reuters/orbis; Everett Collection Inc./Alamy; David Cooper/Alamy; NMSB/Custom Medical Stock Photo; Meeke/zefa/Corbis/Glow Images; Cal Vornberger/Alamy; Somos Images/Alamy; Push Pictures/Corbis/Glow Images; Pictorial Press Ltd/Alamy; London Entertainment/Alamy; YOAV LEMMER/AFP/Getty Images; The Art Gallery Collection/Alamy; Begsteiger/Insadco/AGE Fotostock; Fancy/Alamy; Taxi/Getty Images; Photo by Janet Knott/ *Boston Globe* via Getty Images; moodboard/Alamy; AP Photo/ Richard Lui; Benelux/zefa/Corbis/Glow Images; Stockbyte/Getty Images; Steve Azzara/Sygma/Corbis; Najlah Feanny/Corbis; CJ Burton/Corbis; Chloe Johnson/Alamy.

Text Credits

Credits are listed in order of appearance.

"Criteria for Anorexia Nervosa" Reprinted with permission from the *Diagnostic and Statistical Manual of Mental Disorders*, Fourth Edition, *Text Revision*, (Copyright © 2000). American Psychiatric Association; Figure: Gull, W. (1888). Anorexia nervosa. *Lancet*, pp. i, 516–17; "Tim: Obsessed with His Weight" adapted with permission from *DSMIV- TR Casebook: A Learning Companion to the Diagnostic and Statistical Manual of Mental Disorders*, Fourth Edition, *Text Revision*. Washington, DC: American Psychiatric Association; "Ms. R.: Going to Extremes" adapted with permission from *DSM-IV Case Studies: A Clinical Guide to Differential Diagnosis* (Copyright 1996). American Psychiatric Association; "Criteria for Bulimia Nervosa" Reprinted with permission from the *Diagnostic and Statistical Manual of Mental Disorders*, Fourth Edition, *Text Revision*, (Copyright © 2000). American Psychiatric Association; "Nicole: Too Full to Eat" from *Bulimarexia: The Binge/Purge Cycle*, 1st Edition, by Marlene Boskind-White, William C. White. Copyright © 1983 by Marlene Boskind-White and William C. White, Jr. Used by permission of W. W. Norton & Company, Inc.; "Criteria for Binge-Eating Disorder (BED)" Reprinted with permission from the *Diagnostic and Statistical Manual of Mental Disorders*, Fourth Edition, *Text Revision*, (Copyright © 2000). American Psychiatric Association; "Ms. A.: Feeling Out of Control" adapted with permission from the *American Journal of Psychiatry* (Copyright 2000). American Psychiatric Association; Table: Reproduced by special permission of the Publisher, Psychological Assessment Resources, Inc., 16204 North Florida Avenue, Lutz, Florida 33549, from the *Eating Disorder Inventory-3* by David M. Garner, PhD, Copyright 1984, 1991, 2004, by Psychological Assessment Resources, Inc. (PAR). Further reproduction is prohibited without permission of PAR.; Figure: From http://healthmad.com/conditions-and-diseases/10-shockingly-terrible-eating-related-diseases; Figure: From Fichter et al., 2007, and Eddy et al., 2008; Figure: From Cohn, L. D., & Adler, N. E. (1992). Female and male perceptions of ideal body shapes: Distorted views among Caucasian college students. *Psychology of Women Quarterly*, 16, 69–79; "Disgusted by Her Body" from Hendricks, P. S., & Thompson, J. K. (2005). An integration of cognitive-behavioral therapy and interpersonal therapy for bulimia nervosa. *International Journal of Eating Disorders*, 37, 171–74; "Hospitalized Against Her Will" from Strober, M. (2004). Managing the chronic, treatment-resistant patient with anorexia nervosa. *International Journal of Eating Disorders*, 36, 245–55; "One Family's Story" adapted from Parent B. A. & Parent T. C. (2008). Anorexia, Maudsley and an impressive recovery: One family's story. *Journal of Paediatrics and Child Health*, 44, 70–73; over 200 words/4 pages; Figure: Copyright © Myra Cooper, Gillian Todd and Adrian Wells 2000. Reproduced by permission of Jessica Kingsley Publishers; "Battling Obesity" adapted from Gawande, A. (2001, Jul. 9). "The man who couldn't stop eating." *New Yorker*, 66–75; Figure: Source: CDC.gov/obesity/trends.html.

Personality Disorders

From Chapter 10 of *Abnormal Psychology*, Fifteenth Edition. James N. Butcher, Susan Mineka, Jill M. Hooley. Copyright © 2013 by Pearson Education, Inc. All rights reserved.

Personality Disorders

A person's broadly characteristic traits, coping styles, and ways of interacting in the social environment emerge during childhood and normally crystallize into established patterns by the end of adolescence or early adulthood. These patterns constitute the individual's *personality*—the set of unique traits and behaviors that characterize the individual. Today there is reasonably broad agreement among personality researchers that about five basic personality trait dimensions can be used to characterize normal personality. This five-factor model of personality traits includes the following five trait dimensions: neuroticism, extraversion/introversion, openness to experience, agreeableness/antagonism, and conscientiousness (e.g., Goldberg, 1990; John & Naumann, 2008; McCrae & Costa, 2008).

Clinical Features of Personality Disorders

For most of us, our adult personality is attuned to the demands of society. In other words, we readily comply with most societal expectations. In contrast, there are certain people who, although they do not necessarily display obvious symptoms of an Axis I disorder, nevertheless have certain traits that are so inflexible and maladaptive that they are unable to perform adequately at least some of the varied roles expected of them by their society, in which case we may say that they have a **personality disorder** (formerly known as a *character disorder*). Two of the general features that characterize most personality disorders are chronic interpersonal difficulties and problems with one's identity or sense of self (Livesley, 2001).

In the case below, many of the varied characteristics of someone with a personality disorder are illustrated.

According to general *DSM-IV-TR* criteria for diagnosing a personality disorder, the person's enduring pattern of behavior must be *pervasive* and *inflexible*, as well as *stable* and of *long duration*. It must also cause either *clinically significant distress* or *impairment in functioning* and be manifested in at least two of the following areas: cognition, affectivity, interpersonal functioning, or impulse control. From a clinical standpoint, people with personality disorders often cause at least as much difficulty in the lives of others as in their own lives. Other people tend to find the behavior of individuals with personality disorders confusing, exasperating, unpredictable, and, to varying degrees, unacceptable. Whatever the particular trait patterns affected individuals have developed (obstinacy, covert hostility, suspiciousness, or fear of rejection, for example), these patterns color their reactions to each new situation and lead to a repetition of the same maladaptive behaviors because they do not learn from previous mistakes or troubles. For example, a dependent person may wear out a relationship with

case study — Narcissistic Personality Disorder

Bob, age 21, comes to the psychiatrist's office accompanied by his parents. He begins the interview by announcing he has no problems . . . . The psychiatrist was able to obtain the following story from Bob and his parents. Bob had apparently spread malicious and false rumors about several of the teachers who had given him poor grades, implying that they were having homosexual affairs with students. This, as well as increasingly erratic attendance at his classes over the past term, following the loss of a girlfriend, prompted the school counselor to suggest to Bob and his parents that help was urgently needed. Bob claimed that his academic problems were exaggerated, his success in theatrical productions was being overlooked, and he was in full control of the situation. He did not deny that he spread the false rumors but showed no remorse or apprehension about possible repercussions for himself.

Bob is a tall, stylishly dressed young man. His manner is distant but charming . . . . However, he assumes a condescending, cynical, and bemused manner toward the psychiatrist and the evaluation process. He conveys a sense of superiority and control over the evaluation . . . . His mother . . . described Bob as having been a beautiful, joyful baby who was gifted and brilliant. The father . . . noted that Bob had become progressively more resentful with the births of his two siblings. The father laughingly commented that Bob "would have liked to have been the only child." . . . In his early school years, Bob seemed to play and interact less with other children than most others do. In fifth grade, after a change in teachers, he become arrogant and withdrawn and refused to participate in class. Nevertheless, he maintained excellent grades . . . . It became clear that Bob had never been "one of the boys." . . . When asked, he professed to take pride in "being different" from his peers . . . . Though he was well known to classmates, the relationships he had with them were generally under circumstances in which he was looked up to for his intellectual or dramatic talents. Bob conceded that others viewed him as cold or insensitive . . . but he dismissed this as unimportant. This represented strength to him. He went on to note that when others complained about these qualities in him, it was largely because of their own weakness. In his view, they envied him and longed to have him care about them. He believed they sought to gain by having an association with him.

Source: Adapted with permission from *DSM-IV-TR Casebook: A Learning Companion to the Diagnostic and Statistical Manual of Mental Disorders*, Fourth Edition, *Text Revision* (pp. 239–41). Washington, DC. (Copyright ©2002). American Psychiatric Association.

someone such as a spouse by incessant and extraordinary demands such as never being left alone. After that partner leaves, the person may go almost immediately into another equally dependent relationship without choosing the new partner carefully.

Personality disorders typically do not stem from debilitating reactions to stress in the recent past, as do posttraumatic stress disorder or many cases of major depression. Rather, these disorders stem largely from the gradual development of inflexible and distorted personality and behavioral patterns that result in persistently maladaptive ways of perceiving, thinking about, and relating to the world. In many cases, major stressful life events early in life help set the stage for the development of these inflexible and distorted personality patterns.

The category of personality disorders is broad, encompassing behavioral problems that differ greatly in form and severity. In the milder cases we find people who generally function adequately but who would be described by their relatives, friends, or associates as troublesome, eccentric, or hard to get to know. Like Bob, they may have difficulties developing close relationships with others or getting along with those with whom they do have close relationships. One especially severe personality disorder (*antisocial*) results in extreme and often unethical "acting out" against society. Many such individuals are incarcerated in prisons, although some are able to manipulate others and keep from getting caught.

The *DSM-IV-TR* personality disorders are grouped into three clusters on the basis of what were originally thought to be important similarities of features among the disorders within a given cluster. (See Table 1.)

- **Cluster A: *Includes paranoid, schizoid, and schizotypal personality disorders.*** People with these disorders often seem odd or eccentric, with unusual behavior ranging from distrust and suspiciousness to social detachment.
- **Cluster B: *Includes histrionic, narcissistic, antisocial, and borderline personality disorders.*** Individuals with these disorders share a tendency to be dramatic, emotional, and erratic.
- **Cluster C: *Includes avoidant, dependent, and obsessive-compulsive personality disorders.*** In contrast to the other two clusters, people with these disorders often show anxiety and fearfulness.

Two additional personality disorders—depressive and passive-aggressive personality disorders—are listed in *DSM-IV-TR* in an appendix.

Although these clusters are used in *DSM-IV-TR*, substantial research since 1980—when these clusters of personality disorders were first included (in *DSM-III*)—has raised many questions about their validity. As will be discussed later in this chapter (see "Unresolved Issues"

at the end of the chapter), there are substantial limitations to the category and cluster designations of the *DSM-IV-TR*. Indeed, proposals currently under consideration by the *DSM-5* task force drop several of the personality disorder categories listed earlier and abandon the cluster organization entirely. One of the primary issues is that there are simply too many overlapping features across both categories and clusters (Krueger & Eaton, 2010; Sheets & Craighead, 2007; Widiger & Mullins-Sweatt, 2005). Nevertheless, because much of the research literature to date has used these clusters as an organizing rubric in one way or another, we still include mention of them here.

There is not as much evidence for the prevalence of personality disorders as there is for most of the other disorders, in part because there has never been a really large ***epidemiological study*** comprehensively examining all the personality disorders the way the two National Comorbidity Surveys examined the Axis I disorders (Kessler et al., 1994; Kessler, Berglund, Demler et al., 2005). Nevertheless, a handful of epidemiological studies in recent years have assessed the prevalence of the personality disorders, albeit with differing conclusions (Lenzenweger, 2008; Paris, 2010). However, prevalence estimates for one or more personality disorders have ranged from 4.4 percent to 14.8 percent (Grant et al., 2005; Lenzenweger, 2008; Paris, 2010). Such discrepancies are likely due to the problematic diagnostic criteria in the *DSM-IV*, discussed at length in this chapter. One review averaging across six relatively small epidemiological studies estimated that about 13 percent of the population meets criteria for at least one personality disorder at some point in their lives (Mattia & Zimmerman, 2001; see also Weissman, 1993). Several studies from Sweden have yielded very similar estimates (Ekselius et al., 2001; Torgersen et al., 2001). In addition, a very large subset of people in the NCS-Replication received a modified personality disorders interview that allowed assessment of the prevalence of Cluster A, B, and C personality disorders but only two specific personality disorders (Lenzenweger et al., 2007). This study estimated that about 10 percent of the population exhibits at least one personality disorder, with 5.7 percent in Cluster A, 1.5 percent in Cluster B, and 6 percent in Cluster C. Due to the high comorbidity between clusters, some individuals meet criteria for personality disorders in more than one cluster, so the percent of people in each cluster adds up to more than 10 percent.

In *DSM-IV-TR*, as in *DSM-III* and *DSM-III-R*, the personality disorders are coded on a separate axis, Axis II (along with mental retardation), because they are regarded as different enough from the standard psychiatric syndromes (which are coded on Axis I) to warrant separate classification. Although a person might be diagnosed on Axis II only, Axis I disorders are frequently also present in people with personality disorders (leading to diagnoses on

RESEARCH CLOSE-UP

Epidemiological Study

Epidemiological studies are designed to establish the prevalence (number of cases) of a particular disorder in a very large sample (usually many thousands) of people living in the community.

both Axes I and II). For example, personality disorders are often associated with anxiety disorders, mood disorders, substance-abuse and dependence, and sexual deviations. (See e.g., L. A. Clark, 2005, 2007; Grant, Hasin et al., 2005; Grant, Stinson et al., 2005; Mattia & Zimmerman, 2001). One summary of evidence estimated that about three-quarters of people diagnosed with a personality disorder also have an Axis I disorder (Dolan-Sewell et al., 2001).

In Review

- What is the definition of a personality disorder?
- What are the general *DSM* criteria for diagnosing personality disorders?

Difficulties Doing Research on Personality Disorders

Before we consider what is known about the clinical features and causes of personality disorders, we should note that several important aspects of doing research in this area have hindered progress relative to what is known about many Axis I disorders. Two major categories of difficulties are briefly described.

Difficulties in Diagnosing Personality Disorders

A special caution is in order regarding the diagnosis of personality disorders because more misdiagnoses probably occur here than in any other category of disorder. There are a number of reasons for this. One problem is that diagnostic criteria for personality disorders are not as sharply defined as they are for most Axis I diagnostic categories so they are often not very precise or easy to follow in practice. For example, it may be difficult to diagnose reliably whether someone meets a given criterion for dependent personality disorder such as "goes to excessive lengths to obtain nurturance and support from others" or "has difficulty making everyday decisions without an excessive amount of advice and reassurance from others." Because the criteria for personality disorders are defined by inferred traits or consistent patterns of behavior rather than by more objective behavioral standards (such as having a panic attack or a prolonged and persistent depressed mood), the clinician must exercise more judgment in making the diagnosis than is the case for many Axis I disorders.

With the development of semistructured interviews and self-report inventories for the diagnosis of personality disorders,

certain aspects of diagnostic reliability have increased substantially. However, because the agreement between the diagnoses made on the basis of different structured interviews or self-report inventories is often rather low, there are still substantial problems with the reliability and validity of these diagnoses (Clark & Harrison, 2001; Livesley, 2003; Trull & Durrett, 2005). This means, for example, that three different researchers using three different assessment instruments may identify groups of individuals with substantially different characteristics as having a particular diagnosis such as borderline or narcissistic personality disorder. Of course, this virtually ensures that few obtained research results will be replicated by other researchers even though the groups studied by the different researchers have the same diagnostic label (e.g., Clark & Harrison, 2001).

Given problems with the unreliability of diagnoses (e.g., Clark, 2007; Livesley, 2003; Trull & Durrett, 2005), a great deal of work over the past 20 years has been directed toward developing a more reliable and accurate way of assessing personality disorders. Several theorists have attempted to deal with the problems inherent in categorizing personality disorders by developing dimensional systems of assessment for the symptoms and traits involved in personality disorders (e.g., Clark, 2007; Krueger & Eaton, 2010; Trull & Durrett, 2005; Widiger et al., 2009). However, a unified dimensional classification of personality disorders has been slow to emerge, and some researchers are trying to develop an approach that will integrate the many different existing approaches (e.g., Markon et al., 2005; Krueger, Eaton, Clark et al., 2011; Widiger et al., 2009).

The model that has perhaps been most influential is the five-factor model, which builds on the five-factor model of normal personality mentioned earlier to help researchers understand the commonalities and distinctions among the different personality disorders by assessing how these individuals score on the five basic personality traits (e.g., Clark, 2007; Widiger & Trull, 2007; Widiger et al., 2009). In order to fully account for the myriad ways in which people with personality disorders differ, it is necessary also to measure the six different facets or subcomponents of each of the five basic personality traits. For example, the trait of neuroticism is comprised of the following six facets: anxiety, angry-hostility, depression, self-consciousness, impulsiveness, and vulnerability. Different individuals who all have high levels of neuroticism may vary widely in which facets are most prominent—e.g., some might show more prominent anxious and depressive thoughts, others might show more self-consciousness and vulnerability, and yet others might show more angry-hostility and impulsivity. And the trait of extraversion is composed of the following six facets: warmth, gregariousness, assertiveness, activity, excitement seeking, and positive emotions. (All the facets of each of the five basic trait dimensions and how they differ across people with different personality disorders are explained in Table 2) By assessing whether a person scores low, high, or somewhere in between on each of these 30 facets, it is easy to see how this system can account for an enormous range of different personality patterns—far more than the mere 10 personality disorders currently classified in *DSM-IV-TR*.

In current provisional proposals for the *DSM-5* personality disorders, these normal personality trait dimensions are recast into corresponding domains that represent more pathological extremes of these dimensions: negative affectivity (neuroticism); detachment (extreme introversion); antagonism (extremely low agreeableness) and disinhibition (extremely low conscientiousness). A fifth dimension, psychoticism, does not appear to be a pathological extreme of the final dimension of normal personality (openness)—rather, as we will discuss later in the chapter in the section on schizotypal personality disorder it reflects traits similar to the symptoms of psychotic disorders (e.g., schizophrenia) (Watson et al., 2008).

With these cautions and caveats in mind, we will look at the elusive and often exasperating clinical features of the personality disorders. It is important to bear in mind, however, that what we are describing is merely the prototype for each personality disorder. In reality, as would be expected from the standpoint of the five-factor model of personality disorders, it is rare for any individual to fit these "ideal" descriptions.

One of the problems with the diagnostic categories of personality disorders is that the exact same observable behaviors may be associated with different personality disorders and yet have different meanings with each disorder. For example, this woman's behavior and expression looking out this closed window could suggest the suspiciousness and avoidance of blame seen in paranoid personality disorder, or they could indicate the social withdrawal and absence of friends that characterize schizoid personality disorder, or they could indicate the social anxiety about interacting with others because of fear of being rejected or negatively evaluated seen in avoidant personality disorder.

Difficulties in Studying the Causes of Personality Disorders

Little is yet known about the causal factors in most personality disorders, partly because such disorders have received consistent attention by researchers only since *DSM-III* was published in 1980 and partly because they are less amenable to thorough study. One major problem in studying the causes of personality disorders stems from the high level of comorbidity among them. For example, in an early review of four studies, Widiger and colleagues found that 85 percent of patients who qualified for one personality disorder diagnosis also qualified for at least one more, and many qualified for several more (Widiger & Rogers, 1989; Widiger et al., 1991). A study of nearly 900 psychiatic outpatients reported that 45 percent qualified for at least one personality disorder diagnosis and, among those with one, 60 percent had more than one and 25 percent had two or more (Zimmerman et al., 2005). Even in a nonpatient sample, Zimmerman and Coryell (1989) found that of those with one

personality disorder, almost 25 percent had at least one more (see also Mattia & Zimmerman, 2001). This substantial comorbidity adds to the difficulty of untangling which causal factors are associated with which personality disorder.

Another problem in drawing conclusions about causes occurs because researchers have more confidence in prospective studies, in which groups of people are observed before a disorder appears and are followed over a period of time to see which individuals develop problems and what causal factors have been present. To date, relatively little prospective research has been conducted with the personality disorders. Instead, the vast majority of research is conducted on people who already have the disorders; some of it relies on retrospective recall of prior events, and some of it relies on observing current biological, cognitive, emotional, and interpersonal functioning. Thus, any conclusions about causes that are suggested must be considered very tentative.

Of possible biological factors, it has been suggested that infants' temperament (an inborn disposition to react affectively to environmental stimuli) may predispose them to the development of particular personality traits and disorders (e.g., L. A. Clark, 2005; Mervielde et al., 2005). Several of the most important dimensions of temperament that have been studied are negative emotionality, sociability versus social inhibition or shyness, and activity level. One way of thinking about temperament is that it lays the early foundation for the development of the adult personality, but it is not the sole determinant of adult personality. Given that most temperamental and personality traits have been found to be moderately heritable (e.g., Bouchard & Loehlin, 2001; Livesley, 2005), it is not surprising that there is increasing evidence for genetic contributions to certain personality disorders (e.g., Kendler et al., 2008; Kendler et al., 2011; Livesley, 2005, 2008; Livesley & Jang, 2008; Torgersen et al., 2000). However, for at least most disorders, the genetic contribution appears to be mediated by the genetic contributions to the primary trait dimensions most implicated in each disorder rather than to the disorders themselves (Livesley, 2005; Kendler et al., 2008). In addition, some progress is being made in understanding the psychobiological substrate of at least some of the traits prominently involved in the personality disorders (e.g., Depue, 2009; Depue & Lenzenweger, 2001, 2006; Livesley, 2008; Paris, 2005, 2007).

Genetic propensities and temperament may be important predisposing factors for the development of particular personality traits and disorders. Parental influences, including emotional, physical, and sexual abuse, may also play a big role in the development of personality disorders.

Among psychological factors, psychodynamic theorists originally attributed great importance in the development of character disorders to an infant's getting excessive versus insufficient gratification of his or her impulses in the first few years of life. More recently, learning-based habit patterns and maladaptive cognitive styles have received more attention as possible causal factors (e.g., Beck et al., 1990; Beck et al., 2004; Millon & Davis, 1999). Many of these maladaptive habits and cognitive styles that have been hypothesized to play important roles for certain disorders may originate in disturbed parent–child attachment relationships rather than derive simply from differences in temperament (e.g., Benjamin, 2005; Fraley & Shaver, 2008; Meyer & Pilkonis, 2005; Shiner, 2009). Parental psychopathology and ineffective parenting practices have also been implicated in certain disorders (e.g., Farrington, 2006; Paris, 2001, 2007). Many studies have also suggested that early emotional, physical, and sexual abuse may be important factors in a subset of cases for several different personality disorders (Battle et al., 2004; Grover et al., 2007).

Various kinds of social stressors, societal changes, and cultural values have also been implicated as sociocultural causal factors (De Clerq et al, 2009; Paris, 2001). Ultimately, of course, the goal is to achieve a biopsychosocial perspective on the origins of each personality disorder, but today we are far from reaching that goal.

In Review

What are three reasons for the high frequency of misdiagnoses of personality disorders?

What are two reasons why it is difficult to conduct research on personality disorders?

Cluster A Personality Disorders

As mentioned earlier, people with Cluster A personality disorders display unusual behavior such as distrust, suspiciousness, and social detachment and often come across as odd or eccentric. In the following section, we will look at paranoid, schizoid, and schizotypal personality disorders.

Paranoid Personality Disorder

Individuals with **paranoid personality disorder** have a pervasive suspiciousness and distrust of others, leading to numerous interpersonal difficulties. They tend to see themselves as blameless, instead blaming others for their own mistakes and failures—even to the point of ascribing evil motives to others. Such people are chronically tense and "on guard," constantly expecting trickery and looking for clues to validate their expectations while

DSM-IV-TR

Criteria for Paranoid Personality Disorder

A. A pervasive distrust and suspiciousness of others such that their motives are interpreted as malevolent, beginning by early adulthood and present in a variety of contexts, as indicated by four (or more) of the following:
1. suspects, without sufficient basis, that others are exploiting, harming, or deceiving him or her
2. is preoccupied with unjustified doubts about the loyalty or trustworthiness of friends or associates
3. is reluctant to confide in others because of unwarranted fear that the information will be used maliciously against him or her
4. reads hidden demeaning or threatening meanings into benign remarks or events
5. persistently bears grudges, i.e., is unforgiving of insults, injuries, or slights
6. perceives attacks on his or her character or reputation that are not apparent to others and is quick to react angrily or to counterattack
7. has recurrent suspicions, without justification, regarding fidelity of spouse or sexual partner
B. Does not occur exclusively during the course of Schizophrenia, a Mood Disorder With Psychotic Features, or another Psychotic Disorder and is not due to the direct physiological effects of a general medical condition.

Source: Reprinted with permission from the American Psychiatric Association. *Diagnostic and Statistical Manual of Mental Disorders*, Fourth Edition, *Text Revision* (Copyright © 2000). American Psychiatric Association.

disregarding all evidence to the contrary. They are often preoccupied with doubts about the loyalty of friends and hence are reluctant to confide in others. They commonly bear grudges, refuse to forgive perceived insults and slights, and are quick to react with anger and sometimes violent behavior (Bernstein & Useda, 2007; Oltmanns & Okada, 2006). Recent research has suggested that paranoid personality disorder may consist of elements of both suspiciousness and hostility (Edens et al., 2009; Falkum et al., 2009).

It is important to keep in mind that people with paranoid personalities are not usually psychotic; that is, most of the time they are in clear contact with reality, although they may experience transient psychotic symptoms during periods of stress (M. B. Miller, Useda et al., 2001). People with paranoid schizophrenia share some symptoms found in paranoid personality, but they have many additional problems including more persistent loss of contact with reality, delusions, and hallucinations. Nevertheless, individuals with paranoid personality disorder do appear to be at elevated liability for schizophrenia (Lenzenweger, 2009).

CAUSAL FACTORS Little is known about important causal factors for paranoid personality disorder at this point (Falkum et al., 2009). Some have argued for partial genetic transmission that may link the disorder to schizophrenia, but results examining this issue are inconsistent, and if there is a significant relationship it is not a strong one (Kendler et al., 2006; M. B. Miller, Useda et al., 2001). There is a modest genetic liability to paranoid personality disorder itself that may occur through the heritability of high levels of antagonism (low agreeableness) and neuroticism (angry-hostility), which are among the primary traits in paranoid personality disorder (Widiger, Trull et al., 2002; see also Kendler et al., 2006; Falkum et al., 2009). (See Table 2.) Psychosocial causal factors that are suspected to play a role include parental neglect or abuse and exposure to violent adults, although any links between early adverse experiences and adult paranoid personality disorder are clearly not specific to this one personality disorder but may play a role for other disorders as well (Battle et al., 2004; Grover et al., 2007; Natsuaki et al., 2009).

Schizoid Personality Disorder

Individuals with **schizoid personality disorder** are usually unable to form social relationships and usually lack much interest in doing so. Consequently, they typically do not have good friends, with the possible exception of a close relative.

---

case study **Paranoid Construction Worker**

A 40-year-old construction worker believes that his coworkers do not like him and fears that someone might let his scaffolding slip in order to cause him injury on the job. This concern followed a recent disagreement on the lunch line when the patient felt that a coworker was sneaking ahead and complained to him. He began noticing his new "enemy" laughing with the other men and often wondered if he were the butt of their mockery . . . .

The patient offers little spontaneous information, sits tensely in the chair, is wide-eyed, and carefully tracks all movements in the room. He reads between the lines of the interviewer's questions, feels criticized, and imagines that the interviewer is siding with his coworkers . . . .

He was a loner as a boy and felt that other children would form cliques and be mean to him. He did poorly in school but blamed his teachers—he claimed that they preferred girls or boys who were "sissies." He dropped out of school and has since been a hard and effective worker, but he feels he never gets the breaks. He believes that he has been discriminated against because of his Catholicism but can offer little convincing evidence. He gets on poorly with bosses and coworkers, is unable to appreciate joking around, and does best in situations where he can work and have lunch alone. He has switched jobs many times because he felt he was being mistreated.

The patient is distant and demanding with his family. His children call him "Sir" and know that it is wise to be "seen but not heard" when he is around . . . . He prefers not to have people visit his house and becomes restless when his wife is away visiting others.

DSM-IV-TR

Criteria for Schizoid Personality Disorder

A. A pervasive pattern of detachment from social relationships and a restricted range of expression of emotions in interpersonal settings, beginning by early adulthood and present in a variety of contexts, as indicated by four (or more) of the following:
1. neither desires nor enjoys close relationships, including being part of a family
2. almost always chooses solitary activities
3. has little, if any, interest in having sexual experiences with another person
4. takes pleasure in few, if any, activities
5. lacks close friends or confidants other than first-degree relatives
6. appears indifferent to the praise or criticism of others
7. shows emotional coldness, detachment, or flattened affectivity
B. Does not occur exclusively during the course of Schizophrenia, a Mood Disorder With Psychotic Features, another Psychotic Disorder, or a Pervasive Developmental Disorder and is not due to the direct physiological effects of a general medical condition.

Such people are unable to express their feelings and are seen by others as cold and distant. They often lack social skills and can be classified as loners or introverts, with solitary interests and occupations, although not all loners or introverts have schizoid personality disorder (Bernstein et al., 2009; M. B. Miller, Useda et al., 2001). They tend not to take pleasure in many activities, including sexual activity, and rarely marry. More generally, they are not very emotionally reactive, rarely experiencing strong positive or negative emotions, but rather show a generally apathetic mood. These deficits contribute to their appearing cold and aloof (M. B. Miller, Useda et al., 2001; Mittal et al., 2007). In terms of the five-factor model, they show high levels of introversion (especially low on warmth, gregariousness, and positive emotions). They are also low on openness to feelings (one facet of openness to experience) (Widiger, Trull et al., 2002).

CAUSAL FACTORS We know very little about the causes of schizoid personality disorder, which, like paranoid personality disorder, has not been the focus of much research attention. Early theorists considered a schizoid personality to be a likely precursor to the development of schizophrenia, but this viewpoint has been challenged, and any genetic link that may exist is very modest (Kalus et al., 1995; Kendler et al., 2006; Lenzenweger, 2010; Miller, Useda et al., 2001). Schizoid personality traits have also been shown to have only a modest heritability (Kendler et al., 2006).

Some theorists have suggested that the severe disruption in sociability seen in schizoid personality disorder may be due to severe impairment in an underlying affiliative system (Depue & Lenzenweger, 2005, 2006). Cognitive theorists propose that individuals with schizoid personality disorder exhibit cool and aloof behavior because of maladaptive underlying schemas that lead them to view themselves as self-sufficient loners and to view others as intrusive. Their core dysfunctional belief might be, "I am basically alone" (Beck et al., 1990, p. 51) or "Relationships are messy [and] undesirable" (Pretzer & Beck, 1996, p. 60; see also Beck et al., 2004). Unfortunately, we do not know why or how some people might develop such dysfunctional beliefs.

People with schizoid personality disorder are often loners interested in solitary pursuits, such as assembling odd collections of objects.

Schizotypal Personality Disorder

Individuals with **schizotypal personality disorder** are also excessively introverted and have pervasive social and interpersonal deficits (like those that occur in schizoid personality disorder), but in addition they have cognitive and perceptual distortions, as well as oddities and eccentricities in their communication and behavior (Raine, 2006; Widiger, Trull et al., 2002). Although contact with reality is usually maintained, highly personalized and superstitious thinking is characteristic of people with schizotypal personality, and under extreme stress

---

case study The Introverted Computer Analyst

Bill, a highly intelligent but quite introverted and withdrawn 33-year-old computer analyst, was referred for psychological evaluation by his physician, who was concerned that Bill might be depressed and unhappy. Bill had virtually no contact with other people. He lived alone in his apartment, worked in a small office by himself, and usually saw no one at work except his supervisor, who occasionally visited to give him new work and pick up completed projects. He ate lunch by himself, and about once a week, on nice days, went to the zoo for his lunch break.

Bill was a lifelong loner; as a child he had had few friends and had always preferred solitary activities over family outings (he was the oldest of five children). In high school he had never dated and in college had gone out with a woman only once—and that was with a

group of students after a game. He had been active in sports, however, and had played varsity football in both high school and college. In college he had spent a lot of time with one relatively close friend—mostly drinking. However, this friend now lived in another city.

Bill reported rather matter-of-factly that he had a hard time making friends; he never knew what to say in a conversation. On a number of occasions he had thought of becoming friends with other people but simply couldn't think of the right words, so "the conversation just died." He reported that he had given some thought lately to changing his life in an attempt to be more "positive," but it had never seemed worth the trouble. It was easier for him not to make the effort because he became embarrassed when someone tried to talk with him. He was happiest when he was alone.

they may experience transient psychotic symptoms (APA, 2000; Widiger & Frances, 1994). Indeed, they often believe that they have magical powers and may engage in magical rituals. Other cognitive–perceptual problems include ideas of reference (the belief that conversations or gestures of others have special meaning or personal significance), odd speech, and paranoid beliefs.

Oddities in thinking, speech, and other behaviors are the most stable characteristics of schizotypal personality disorder (McGlashan et al., 2005) and are similar to those often seen in schizophrenic patients. In fact, many researchers conceptualize schizotypal personality disorder as an attenuated form of schizophrenia (Lenzenweger, 2010; Raine, 2006). Interestingly, although some aspects of schizotypy appear related to the five-factor model of normal personality (specifically facets of introversion and neuroticism), the other aspects related to cognitive and perceptual distortions are *not* adequately explained by the five-factor model of normal personality (Watson et al., 2008). Indeed, these core symptoms of schizotypy form the basis of the only proposed trait that does not map neatly unto the five

factors of normal personality. This final pathological trait is psychoticism, which consists of three facets: unusual beliefs and experiences, eccentricity, and cognitive and perceptual dysregulation (Krueger, Eaton, Derringer et al., 2011).

CAUSAL FACTORS Unlike schizoid and paranoid personality disorders, there has been a significant amount of research on schizotypal personality disorder (Esterberg et al., 2010). In fact, in current proposals for the *DSM-5*, schizotypal personality is the only categorical disorder retained from Cluster A. Estimates of the prevalence of this disorder in the general population have varied somewhat, but one good review of such studies has estimated that the prevalence is about 2 percent in the general population (Raine, 2006). The heritability of schizotypal personality disorder is moderate (Raine, 2006; Lin et al., 2006, 2007).

The biological associations of schizotypal personality disorder with schizophrenia are remarkable (Cannon et al., 2008; Jang et al., 2005; Siever & Davis, 2004; Yung et al., 2004). For example, a number of studies on patients, as well as on college stu-

table 1 Summary of Personality Disorders

Personality Disorder	Characteristics	Prevalence	Gender Ratio Estimate
Cluster A			
Paranoid	Suspiciousness and mistrust of others; tendency to see self as blameless; on guard for perceived attacks by others	0.5–2.5%	males > females
Schizoid	Impaired social relationships; inability and lack of desire to form attachments to others	<1%	males > females
Schizotypal	Peculiar thought patterns; oddities of perception and speech that interfere with communication and social interaction	3%	males > females
Cluster B			
Histrionic	Self-dramatization; over concern with attractiveness; tendency to irritability and temper outbursts if attention seeking is frustrated	2–3%	males = females
Narcissistic	Grandiosity; preoccupation with receiving attention; self-promoting; lack of empathy	<1%	males > females
Antisocial	Lack of moral or ethical development; inability to follow approved models of behavior; deceitfulness; shameless manipulation of others; history of conduct problems as a child	1% females 3% males	males > females
Borderline	Impulsiveness; inappropriate anger; drastic mood shifts; chronic feelings of boredom; attempts at self-mutilation or suicide	2%	females > males (by 3:1)
Cluster C			
Avoidant	Hypersensitivity to rejection or social derogation; shyness; insecurity in social interaction and initiating relationships	0.5–1%	males = females
Dependent	Difficulty in separating in relationships; discomfort at being alone; subordination of needs in order to keep others involved in a relationship; indecisiveness	2%	males = females
Obsessive-Compulsive	Excessive concern with order, rules, and trivial details; perfectionistic; lack of expressiveness and warmth; difficulty in relaxing and having fun	1%	males > females (by 2:1)

Source: APA, *DSM-IV-TR* (1994); Weissman (1993); Zimmerman & Coryell (1990).

Criteria for Schizotypal Personality Disorder

A. A pervasive pattern of social and interpersonal deficits marked by acute discomfort with, and reduced capacity for, close relationships as well as by cognitive or perceptual distortions and eccentricities of behavior, beginning by early adulthood and present in a variety of contexts, as indicated by five (or more) of the following:
1. ideas of reference (excluding delusions of reference)
2. odd beliefs or magical thinking that influences behavior and is inconsistent with subcultural norms (e.g., superstitiousness, belief in clairvoyance, telepathy, or "sixth sense"; in children and adolescents, bizarre fantasies or preoccupations)
3. unusual perceptual experiences, including bodily illusions
4. odd thinking and speech (e.g., vague, circumstantial, metaphorical, overelaborate, or stereotyped)
5. suspiciousness or paranoid ideation
6. inappropriate or constricted affect
7. behavior or appearance that is odd, eccentric, or peculiar
8. lack of close friends or confidants other than first-degree relatives
9. excessive social anxiety that does not diminish with familiarity and tends to be associated with paranoid fears rather than negative judgments about self

B. Does not occur exclusively during the course of Schizophrenia, a Mood Disorder With Psychotic Features, another Psychotic Disorder, or a Pervasive Developmental Disorder.

dents, with schizotypal personality disorder (e.g., Raine, 2006; Siever et al., 1995) have shown the same deficit in the ability to track a moving target visually that is common in schizophrenia (Coccaro, 2001). They also show numerous other mild impairments in cognitive functioning (Voglmaier et al., 2005), including deficits in their ability to sustain attention (Lees-Roitman et al., 1997; Raine, 2006) and deficits in working memory (e.g., being able to remember a span of digits), both of which are common in schizophrenia (Farmer et al., 2000; Squires-Wheeler et al., 1997). In addition, individuals with schizotypal personality disorder, like patients with schizophrenia, show deficits in their ability to inhibit attention to a second stimulus that rapidly follows presentation of a first stimulus. For example, normal individuals presented with a weak auditory stimulus about 0.1 second before a loud sound that elicits a startle response show a smaller startle response than those

not presented the weak auditory stimulus first (Cadenhead, Light et al., 2000; Cadenhead, Swerdlow et al., 2000). This normal inhibitory effect is reduced in people with schizotypal personality disorder and with schizophrenia, a phenomenon that may be related to their high levels of distractibility and difficulty staying focused (see also Hazlett et al., 2003; Raine, 2006). Finally, they also show language abnormalities that may be related to abnormalities in their auditory processing (Dickey et al., 2008).

A genetic relationship to schizophrenia has also long been suspected. In fact, this disorder appears to be part of a spectrum of liability for schizophrenia that often occurs in some of the first-degree relatives of people with schizophrenia (Kendler & Gardner, 1997; Raine, 2006; Tienari et al., 2003). Moreover, teenagers who have schizotypal personality disorder have been shown to be at increased risk for developing schizophrenia and schizophrenia-spectrum disorders in adulthood (Asarnow, 2005; Cannon et al., 2008; Raine, 2006; Tyrka et al., 1995). Nevertheless, it has also been proposed that there is a second subtype of schizotypal personality disorder that is not genetically linked to schizophrenia. This subtype is characterized by cognitive and perceptual deficits and is instead linked to a history of childhood abuse and early trauma (Berenbaum et al., 2008; Raine, 2006). Schizotypal personality disorder in adolescence has been associated with elevated exposure to stressful life events (Anglin et al., 2008; Tessner et al., 2011) and low family socioeconomic status (Cohen et al., 2008).

Cluster B Personality Disorders

In the following section, we'll look closely at histrionic, narcissistic, antisocial, and borderline personality disorders. Remember that people with Cluster B personality disorders share a tendency to be dramatic, emotional, and erratic.

Histrionic Personality Disorder

Excessive attention-seeking behavior and emotionality are the key characteristics of individuals with **histrionic personality disorder**. According to *DSM-IV-TR* (APA, 2000), these individuals tend to feel unappreciated if they are not the center of attention; their lively, dramatic, and excessively extraverted styles often ensure that they can charm others into attending to them. But these qualities do not lead to stable and satisfying relationships because others tire of providing this level of attention. In craving stimulation and attention, their appearance and behavior are often quite theatrical and emotional as well as sexually provocative and seductive (Freeman et al., 2005). They may attempt to control their partners through seductive behavior and emotional manipulation, but they also show a good deal of dependence (e.g., Blagov et al., 2007; Bornstein & Malka, 2009; P. R. Rasmussen, 2005). Their speech is often vague and impressionistic, and they are

This woman could be just "clowning around" one night in a bar with friends. But if she frequently seeks opportunities to engage in seductive and attention-seeking behavior, she could have histrionic personality disorder.

usually considered self-centered, vain, and excessively concerned about the approval of others, who see them as overly reactive, shallow, and insincere.

The prevalence of this disorder in the general population is estimated at 2 to 3 percent, and some (but not all) studies suggest that this disorder occurs more often in women than in men (Lynam & Widiger, 2007; Widiger & Bornstein, 2001). Reasons for the possible sex difference have been very controversial. One review of these controversies suggested that this sex difference is not surprising, given the number of traits that occur more often in females that are involved in the diagnostic criteria. For example, many of the criteria for histrionic personality disorder (as well as for several other personality disorders such as dependent) involve maladaptive variants of female-related traits (e.g., Widiger & Bornstein, 2001) such as overdramatization, vanity, seductiveness, and overconcern with physical appearance. However, other personality traits prominent in histrionic personality disorder are actually more common in men than in women (e.g., high excitement seeking and low self-consciousness). A recent careful analysis of the issue suggests that the higher prevalence of histrionic personality in women actually would not be predicted based on known sex differences in the personality traits prominent in the disorder. This does indeed suggest the influence of some form of sex bias in the diagnosis of this disorder (Lynam & Widiger, 2007).

CAUSAL FACTORS Very little systematic research has been conducted on histrionic personality disorder, perhaps as a result of the difficulty researchers have had in differentiating it from other personality disorders (Bornstein & Malka, 2009). Histrionic personality disorder is highly comorbid with borderline, antisocial, narcissistic, and dependent personality disorder diagnoses (Bakkevig & Karterud, 2010; Blagov and Westen, 2008; Bornstein & Malka, 2009).

case study   A Histrionic Housewife

Lulu, a 24-year-old housewife, was seen in an inpatient unit several days after she had been picked up for "vagrancy" after her husband had left her at the bus station to return her to her own family because he was tired of her behavior and of taking care of her. Lulu showed up for the interview all made-up and in a very feminine robe, with her hair done in a very special way. Throughout the interview with a male psychiatrist, she showed flirtatious and somewhat childlike seductive gestures and talked in a rather vague way about her problems and her life. Her chief complaints were that her husband had deserted her and that she couldn't return to her family because two of her brothers had abused her. Moreover, she had no friends to turn to and wasn't sure how she was going to get along. Indeed, she complained that she had never had female friends, whom she felt just didn't like her, although she wasn't quite sure why, assuring the interviewer that she was a very nice and kind person.

Recently she and her husband had been out driving with a couple who were friends of her husband's. The wife had accused Lulu of being overly seductive toward the wife's husband, and Lulu had been hurt, thinking her behavior was perfectly innocent and not at all out of line. This incident led to a big argument with her own husband, one in a long series over the past 6 months in which he complained about her inappropriate behavior around other men and about how vain and needing of attention she was. These arguments and her failure to change her behavior had ultimately led her husband to desert her.

There is some evidence for a genetic link with antisocial personality disorder, the idea being that there may be some common underlying predisposition that is more likely to be manifested in women as histrionic personality disorder and in men as antisocial personality disorder (e.g., Cale & Lilienfeld, 2002a, 2002b). The suggestion of some genetic propensity to develop this disorder is also supported by findings that histrionic personality disorder may be characterized as involving extreme versions of two common, normal personality traits, extraversion and, to a lesser extent, neuroticism—two normal personality traits known to have a partial genetic basis (Widiger & Bornstein, 2001). In terms of the five-factor model (see Table 2), the very high levels of extraversion of patients with histrionic personality disorder include high levels of gregariousness, excitement seeking, and positive emotions. Their high levels of neuroticism particularly involve the depression and self-consciousness facets; they are also high on openness to fantasies (Widiger, Trull et al., 2002).

Cognitive theorists emphasize the importance of maladaptive schemas revolving around the need for attention to validate self-worth. Core dysfunctional beliefs might include, "Unless I captivate people, I am nothing" and "If I can't

Criteria for Histrionic Personality Disorder

A pervasive pattern of excessive emotionality and attention seeking, beginning by early adulthood and present in a variety of contexts, as indicated by five (or more) of the following:

1. is uncomfortable in situations in which he or she is not the center of attention
2. interaction with others is often characterized by inappropriate sexually seductive or provocative behavior
3. displays rapidly shifting and shallow expression of emotions
4. consistently uses physical appearance to draw attention to self
5. has a style of speech that is excessively impressionistic and lacking in detail
6. shows self-dramatization, theatricality, and exaggerated expression of emotion
7. is suggestible, i.e., easily influenced by others or circumstances
8. considers relationships to be more intimate than they actually are

Source: Reprinted with permission from the American Psychiatric Association. *Diagnostic and Statistical Manual of Mental Disorders,* Fourth Edition, *Text Revision* (Copyright © 2000). American Psychiatric Association.

entertain people, they will abandon me" (Beck et al., 1990, p. 50; Beck et al., 2003). No systematic research has yet explored how these dysfunctional beliefs might develop.

Narcissistic Personality Disorder

Individuals with **narcissistic personality disorder** show an exaggerated sense of self-importance, a preoccupation with being admired, and a lack of empathy for the feelings of others (Pincus & Lukowitsky, 2010; Ronningstam, 2005, 2009). Numerous studies support the notion of two subtypes of narcissism: grandiose and vulnerable narcissism (Cain et al., 2008, Ronningstam, 2005). The grandiose presentation of narcissistic patients, stressed by the *DSM-IV-TR* criteria, is manifested by traits related to grandiosity, aggression, and dominance. These are reflected in a strong tendency to overestimate their abilities and accomplishments while underestimating the abilities and accomplishments of others. Their sense of entitlement is frequently a source of astonishment to others, although they themselves seem to regard their lavish expectations as merely what they deserve. They behave in stereotypical ways (for example, with constant self-references and bragging) to gain the acclaim and recognition they crave. Because they believe they are so special, they often think they can be understood only by other high-status people or that they should associate only with such people, as was the case with Bob at the beginning of the chapter. Finally, their sense

of entitlement is also associated with their unwillingness to forgive others for perceived slights, and they easily take offense (Exline et al., 2004).

The vulnerable presentation of narcissism is not as clearly reflected in the *DSM-IV-TR* criteria but nevertheless represents a subtype long observed by researchers and clinicians. Vulnerable narcissists have a very fragile and unstable sense of self-esteem, and for these individuals, arrogance and condescension is merely a façade for intense shame and hypersensitivity to rejection and criticism (Cain et al., 2008; Miller et al., 2010; Pincus & Lukowitsky, 2010; Ronningstam, 2005). Vulnerable narcissists may become completely absorbed and preoccupied with fantasies of outstanding achievement but at the same time experience profound shame about their ambitions. They may avoid interpersonal relationships due to fear of rejection or criticism.

There is increasing evidence that the grandiose and vulnerable presentations of narcissism are related but distinct in important ways. In terms of the five-factor model, both

Criteria for Narcissistic Personality Disorder

A pervasive pattern of grandiosity (in fantasy or behavior), need for admiration, and lack of empathy, beginning by early adulthood and present in a variety of contexts, as indicated by five (or more) of the following:

1. has a grandiose sense of self-importance (e.g., exaggerates achievements and talents, expects to be recognized as superior without commensurate achievements)
2. is preoccupied with fantasies of unlimited success, power, brilliance, beauty, or ideal love
3. believes that he or she is "special" and unique and can only be understood by, or should associate with, other special or high-status people (or institutions)
4. requires excessive admiration
5. has a sense of entitlement, i.e., unreasonable expectations of especially favorable treatment or automatic compliance with his or her expectations
6. is interpersonally exploitative, i.e., takes advantage of others to achieve his or her own ends
7. lacks empathy: is unwilling to recognize or identify with the feelings and needs of others
8. is often envious of others or believes that others are envious of him or her
9. shows arrogant, haughty behaviors or attitudes

Source: Reprinted with permission from the American Psychiatric Association. *Diagnostic and Statistical Manual of Mental Disorders,* Fourth Edition, *Text Revision* (Copyright © 2000). American Psychiatric Association.

subtypes are associated with high levels of interpersonal antagonism/low agreeableness (which includes traits of low modesty, arrogance, grandiosity, and superiority), low altruism (expecting favorable treatment and exploiting others), and tough-mindedness (lack of empathy). (See Table 2.) However, the primarily grandiose narcissist is exceptionally low in certain facets of neuroticism and high in extraversion. For the grandiose narcissist, close friends and relatives may be more distressed about his or her behavior than the narcissist him- or herself! One study concluded, "The strongest impairment associated with narcissistic personality disorder is the distress of 'pain and suffering' experienced not by the narcissist but by his or her significant others" (J. D. Miller, 2007, p. 176). However, the case is quite different for the vulnerable narcissist, who has very high levels of negative affectivity/neuroticism (Cain et al., 2008; Miller et al., 2010). Thus, spouses describe patients with either grandiosity or vulnerability as being "bossy, intolerant, cruel, argumentative, dishonest, opportunistic, conceited, arrogant, and demanding," but only those high on grandiosity were additionally described as being "aggressive, hardheaded, outspoken, assertive, and determined," while those high on vulnerability were described as "worrying, emotional, defensive, anxious, bitter, tense, and complaining" (Wink, 1991, p. 595). Importantly, some narcissistic individuals may fluctuate between grandiosity and vulnerability (Pincus & Lukowitsky, 2010; Ronningstam, 2009).

Narcissistic personalities also share another central trait—they are unwilling or unable to take the perspective of others, to see things other than "through their own eyes." Moreover, if they do not receive the validation or assistance they desire, they are inclined to be hypercritical and retaliatory (P. S. Rasmussen, 2005). Indeed, one study of male students with high levels of narcissistic traits showed that they had greater tendencies toward sexual coercion when they were rejected by the target of their sexual desires than did men with lower levels of narcissistic traits. They also rated filmed depictions of rape less unfavorably and as more enjoyable and sexually arousing than did the men with low levels of narcissistic traits (Bushman et al., 2003).

According to *DSM-IV-TR*, narcissistic personality disorder may be more frequently observed in men than in women (APA, 2000; Golomb et al., 1995), and a recent quantitative review has confirmed this finding and also shown that this gender difference is to be expected, based on known sex differences in the personality traits most prominent in narcissistic personality disorder (Lynam & Widiger, 2007). Compared with some of the other personality disorders, it is thought to be relatively rare and is estimated to occur in about 1 percent of the population.

CAUSAL FACTORS Until the past decade, there was a wealth of theories (Kohut & Wolff, 1978; Millon & Davis, 1995; Widiger & Bornstein, 2001) but precious little empirical data on the environmental and genetic factors involved in the etiology of narcissistic personality disorder. Fortunately, a number of researchers are now actively trying to understand the causes of this fascinating disorder. A key finding has been that the grandiose and vulnerable forms of narcissism are associated with different causal factors. Grandiose narcissism has not generally been associated with childhood abuse, neglect, or poor parenting. Indeed, there is some evidence that grandiose narcissism is associated with parental overvaluation. By contrast, vulnerable narcissism has been associated with emotional, physical, and sexual abuse, as well parenting styles characterized as intrusive, controlling, and cold (Horton et al., 2006; Miller & Campbell, 2008; Miller et al., 2011; Otway & Vignoles, 2006).

case study ▸ A Narcissistic Student

A 25-year-old, single graduate student complains to his psychoanalyst of difficulty completing his Ph.D. in English literature and expresses concerns about his relationships with women. He believes that his thesis topic may profoundly increase the level of understanding in his discipline and make him famous, but so far he has not been able to get past the third chapter. His mentor does not seem sufficiently impressed with his ideas, and the patient is furious at him but also self-doubting and ashamed. He blames his mentor for his lack of progress and thinks that he deserves more help with his grand idea, that his mentor should help with some of the research. The patient brags about his creativity and complains that other people are "jealous" of his insight. He is very envious of students who are moving along faster than he and regards them as "dull drones and ass-kissers." He prides himself on the brilliance of his class participation and imagines someday becoming a great professor.

He becomes rapidly infatuated with women and has powerful and persistent fantasies about each new woman he meets, but after several experiences of sexual intercourse feels disappointed and finds them dumb, clinging, and physically repugnant. He has many "friends," but they turn over quickly, and no one relationship lasts very long. People get tired of his continual self-promotion and lack of consideration of them. For example, he was lonely at Christmas and insisted that his best friend stay in town rather than visit his family. The friend refused, criticizing the patient's self-centeredness; and the patient, enraged, decided never to see this friend again.

Source: Adapted with permission from the *DSM III Diagnostic and Statistical Manual of Mental Disorders*, Third Edition, *Case Book*, (Copyright © 1981). American Psychiatric Association.

Otto Kernberg (b. 1928) is an influential contemporary psychoanalytic theorist who has written a great deal about borderline and narcissistic personality disorders.

Heinz Kohut (1913–1981), another contemporary psychoanalytic thinker, theorized that poor parenting can cause narcissistic personality disorder by failing to build a child's normal self-confidence.

Antisocial Personality Disorder

Individuals with antisocial personality disorder (ASPD) continually violate and show disregard for the rights of others through deceitful, aggressive, or antisocial behavior, typically without remorse or loyalty to anyone. They tend to be impulsive, irritable, and aggressive and to show a pattern of generally irresponsible behavior. This pattern of behavior must have been occurring since the age of 15, and before age 15 the person must have had symptoms of conduct disorder, a similar disorder occurring in children and young adolescents who show persistent patterns of aggression toward people or animals, destruction of property,

deceitfulness or theft, and serious violation of rules at home or in school. Because this personality disorder and its causes have been studied far more extensively than the others, and because of its enormous costs to society, it will be examined in some detail later (see also Table 2).

Borderline Personality Disorder

According to *DSM-IV-TR* (APA, 2000), individuals with **borderline personality disorder (BPD)** show a pattern of behavior characterized by impulsivity and instability in interpersonal relationships, self-image, and moods. However, the term *borderline personality* has a long and rather confusing history (Hooley, Cole, & Gironde, in press). Originally it was most often used to refer to a condition that was thought to occupy the "border" between neurotic and psychotic disorders (as in the term *borderline schizophrenia*). Later, however, this sense of the term *borderline* became identified with schizotypal personality disorder, which (as we noted earlier) is biologically related to schizophrenia. The current diagnosis of borderline personality disorder is no longer considered to be biologically related to schizophrenia.

The central characteristic of BPD is *affective instability*, manifested by unusually intense emotional responses to environmental triggers, with delayed recovery to a baseline emotional state. Affective instability is also characterized by drastic and rapid shifts from one emotion to another (Livesley, 2008; Paris, 2007). In addition, people with borderline personality disorder have a *highly unstable self-image* or sense of self, which is sometimes described as "impoverished and/or fragmented" (Livesley, 2008, p. 44). Given their affective instability combined with unstable self-image, it is not surprising that these people have highly unstable interpersonal relationships. These relationships tend to be intense but stormy, typically involving overidealizations of friends or lovers that later end in bitter disillusionment, disappointment, and anger (Gunderson et al., 1995; Lieb et al., 2004). Nevertheless, they may make desperate efforts to avoid real or imagined abandonment, perhaps because their fears of abandonment are so intense (Lieb et al., 2004; Livesley, 2008). Recent experimental research supports a causal link between the perception of rejection and intense, uncontrollable rage in BPD (Berenson et al., 2011).

Another very important feature of borderline personality disorder is *impulsivity* characterized by rapid responding to environmental triggers without thinking (or caring) about long-term consequences (Paris, 2007). These individuals'

A Thief with Antisocial Personality Disorder

Mark, a 22-year-old, was awaiting trial for car theft and armed robbery. His case records included a long history of arrests beginning at age 9, when he had been picked up for vandalism. He had been expelled from high school for truancy and disruptive behavior. On a number of occasions he had run away from home for days or weeks at a time—always returning in a disheveled and "run-down" condition. To date he had not held a job for more than a few days at a time even though his generally charming manner enabled him to obtain work readily. He was described as a loner with few friends. Although initially charming, Mark usually soon antagonized those he met with his aggressive, self-oriented behavior. Shortly after his first therapy session, he skipped bail and presumably left town to avoid his trial.

table 2 *DSM-IV* Personality Disorders and the Five-Factor Model

NEO-PI-R domains and facets	PAR	SZD	SZT	ATS	BDL	HST	NAR	AVD	DEP	OBC
Neuroticism										
Anxiety			H		H			H	H	
Angry-hostility	H			H	H		H			
Depression					H	H		H		
Self-consciousness			H			H	H	H	H	
Impulsiveness					H					
Vulnerability					H			H	H	
Extraversion										
Warmth		L	L			H			H	
Gregariousness		L	L			H		L		
Assertiveness								L	L	H
Activity										
Excitement seeking				H		H		L		
Positive emotions		L	L			H				
Openness to Experience										
Fantasy		H			H	H				
Aesthetics										
Feelings		L				H				
Actions			H							
Ideas			H							
Values										L
Agreeableness										
Trust	L		L		L	H			H	
Straightforwardness	L			L						
Altruism				L			L		H	
Compliance	L			L	L				H	L
Modesty							L		H	
Tender mindedness				L			L			
Conscientiousness										
Competence					L					H
Order										H
Dutifulness				L						H
Achievement striving							H			H
Self-discipline				L						
Deliberation				L						

Note: NEO-PI-R = Revised NEO Personality Inventory. H, L = high, low, respectively, based on the fourth edition of the *Diagnostic and Statistical Manual of Mental Disorders* (*DSM-IV*; American Psychiatric Association, 1994) diagnostic criteria. Personality disorders: PAR = paranoid; SZD = schizoid; SZT = schizotypal; ATS = antisocial; BDL = borderline; HST = histrionic; NAR = narcissistic; AVD = avoidant; DEP = dependent; OBC = obsessive-compulsive.

Source: Adapted from Widiger, Trull et al. (2002). A description of the DSM-IV personality disorders with the five-factor model of personality. In P. T. Costa & T. A. Widiger (Eds.), *Personality disorders and the five-factor model of personality* (2nd ed.) (p. 90). Washington DC: APA Books.

high levels of impulsivity combined with their extreme affective instability often lead to erratic, self-destructive behaviors such as gambling sprees or reckless driving. Suicide attempts, often flagrantly manipulative, are frequently part of the clinical picture (Paris, 1999, 2007). However, such attempts are not always simply manipulative; prospective studies suggest that approximately 8 to 10 percent may ultimately complete suicide (Oldham, 2006; Skodol, Gunderson et al., 2002). *Self-mutilation* (such as repetitive cutting behavior) is another characteristic feature of borderline personality. In some cases the self-injurious behavior is associated with relief from anxiety or dysphoria, and it also serves to communicate the person's level of distress to others (Paris, 2007). Research has also documented that borderline personality is associated with

Criteria for Borderline Personality Disorder

A pervasive pattern of instability of interpersonal relationships, self-image, and affects, and marked impulsivity beginning by early adulthood and present in a variety of contexts, as indicated by five (or more) of the following:

1. frantic efforts to avoid real or imagined abandonment. Note: Do not include suicidal or self-mutilating behavior covered in Criterion 5.
2. a pattern of unstable and intense interpersonal relationships characterized by alternating between extremes of idealization and devaluation
3. identity disturbance: markedly and persistently unstable self image or sense of self
4. impulsivity in at least two areas that are potentially self-damaging (e.g., spending, sex, substance abuse, reckless driving, binge eating). Note: Do not include suicidal or self-mutilating behavior covered in Criterion 5.
5. recurrent suicidal behavior, gestures, or threats, or self-mutilating behavior
6. affective instability due to a marked reactivity of mood (e.g., intense episodic dysphoria, irritability, or anxiety usually lasting a few hours and only rarely more than a few days)
7. chronic feelings of emptiness
8. inappropriate, intense anger or difficulty controlling anger (e.g., frequent displays of temper, constant anger, recurrent physical fights)
9. transient, stress-related paranoid ideation or severe dissociative symptoms

Source: Reprinted with permission from the American Psychiatric Association. *Diagnostic and Statistical Manual of Mental Disorders,* Fourth Edition, *Text Revision* (Copyright © 2000). American Psychiatric Association.

analgesia in as many as 70 to 80 percent of women with BPD (analgesia is the absence of the experience of pain in the presence of a theoretically painful stimulus; Figueroa & Silk, 1997; Schmahl et al., 2004). The following prototypic case illustrates the frequent risk of suicide and self-mutilation among borderline personalities.

case study
Self-Mutilation in Borderline Personality Disorder

A 26-year-old unemployed woman was referred for admission to a hospital by her therapist because of intense suicidal preoccupation and urges to mutilate herself with a razor. The patient was apparently well until her junior year in high school, when she became preoccupied with religion and philosophy, avoided friends, and was filled with doubt about who she was. Academically she did well, but later, during college, her performance declined. In college she began to use a variety of drugs, abandoned the religion of her family, and seemed to be searching for a charismatic religious figure with whom to identify. At times, massive anxiety swept over her, and she found it would suddenly vanish if she cut her forearm with a razor blade.

Three years ago she began psychotherapy and initially rapidly idealized her therapist as being incredibly intuitive and empathic. Later she became hostile and demanding of him, requiring more and more sessions, sometimes two in one day. Her life centered on her therapist, by this time to the exclusion of everyone else. Although her hostility toward her therapist was obvious, she could neither see it nor control it. Her difficulties with her therapist culminated in many episodes of her forearm cutting and suicidal threats, which led to the referral for admission.

Source: Adapted with permission from the *DSM III Diagnostic and Statistical Manual of Mental Disorders,* Third Edition, *Case Book,* (Copyright © 1981). American Psychiatric Association.

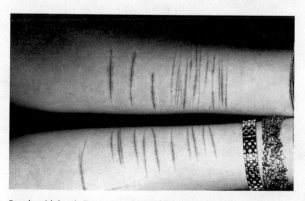

People with borderline personalities often engage in self-destructive behaviors including repetitive cutting and other forms of self-mutilation.

In addition to affective and impulsive behavioral symptoms, as many as 75 percent of people with borderline personality disorder have cognitive symptoms that include relatively short or transient episodes in which they appear to be out of contact with reality and experience delusions or other psychotic-like symptoms such as hallucinations, paranoid ideas, or severe dissociative symptoms (Lieb et al., 2004; Paris, 2007; Skodol, Gunderson et al., 2002).

Estimates are that only about 1 to 2 percent of the population may qualify for the diagnosis of BPD (Lenzenweger et al., 2007), but they represent about 10 percent of patients in outpatient and 20 percent of patients in inpatient clinical settings (Lieb et al., 2004; Torgersen et al., 2001). Although early research found that approximately 75 percent of individuals receiving this diagnosis in clinical settings are women, such findings likely arise from a gender imbalance in treatment seeking rather than prevalence of the disorder. In support of this, more recent epidemiological studies of community residents suggest an equal gender ratio (Coid et al., 2009; Grant et al., 2008; Hooley et al., in press).

COMORBIDITY WITH OTHER AXIS I AND AXIS II DISORDERS Given the many and varied symptoms of BPD, it is not surprising that this personality disorder produces significant impairment in social, academic, and occupational functioning (Bagge et al., 2004; Grant et al., 2008; Horz et al., 2010). BPD commonly co-occurs with a variety of Axis I disorders ranging from unipolar and bipolar mood and anxiety disorders (especially panic and PTSD) to substance-use and eating disorders (Hooley et al., in press; Pagura et al., 2010). In the past, many clinical researchers hypothesized that BPD had a special relationship with bipolar and recurrent unipolar mood disorders because about 50 percent of those with BPD also qualified for a mood disorder diagnosis at some point (Adams et al., 2001; Paris, 2007). However, other Axis II disorders (such as dependent, avoidant, and obsessive-compulsive personality disorders) are actually more commonly associated with depression than is borderline personality disorder. Moreover, recent neuroimaging data indicates that BPD individuals show different neural responses to emotional stimuli than do individuals with chronic depression (Hooley et al., 2010).

There is also substantial co-occurrence of BPD with other personality disorders—especially histrionic, dependent, antisocial, and schizotypal personality disorders. Nevertheless, Widiger and Trull (1993) noted the following differences in prototypic cases of these personality disorders: "The prototypic borderline's exploitative use of others is usually an angry and impulsive response to disappointment, whereas the antisocial's is a guiltless and calculated effort for personal gain. Sexuality may play a more central role in the relationships of histrionics than in [those of] borderlines, evident in the histrionic's tendency to eroticize situations . . . and to be inappropriately seductive. The prototypic schizotypal lacks the emotionality of the borderline, and tends to be more isolated, odd and peculiar" (Widiger & Trull, 1993, p. 371). These differences can also be seen using the five-factor model of personality disorders (see Table 2).

CAUSAL FACTORS Research suggests that genetic factors play a significant role in the development of BPD (Distel et al., 2009; Livesley, 2008; Skodol, Siever et al., 2002). This heritability may be partly a function of the fact that personality traits of affective instability and impulsivity, which

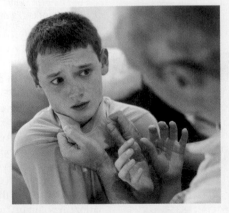

Many studies have shown that people with borderline personality disorder report a large number of negative, even traumatic, events in childhood. These include abuse and neglect, and separation and loss.

are both very prominent in borderline personality disorder, are themselves partially heritable (Hooley et al., in press; Paris, 2007). There is also some preliminary evidence that certain parts of the 5-HTT gene implicated in depression may also be associated with borderline personality disorder (e.g., Lis et al., 2007; Ni et al., 2006). Recent research also suggests a link with other genes involved in regulating dopamine transmission (Hooley et al., in press).

There has also been an intense search for the biological substrate of BPD. For example, people with BPD often appear to be characterized by lowered functioning of the neurotransmitter serotonin, which is involved in inhibiting behavioral responses. This may be why they show impulsive-aggressive behavior, as in acts of self-mutilation; that is, their serotonergic activity is too low to "put the brakes on" impulsive behavior (e.g., Figueroa & Silk, 1997; Schmal & Bremner, 2006; Skodol, Siever et al., 2002b). Patients with BPD may also show disturbances in the regulation of noradrenergic neurotransmitters that are similar to those seen in chronic stress conditions such as PTSD (Hooley, 2008). In particular, their hyperresponsive noradrenergic system may be related to their hypersensitivity to environmental changes (Figueroa & Silk, 1997; Skodol, Siever et al., 2002). Moreover, certain brain areas that ordinarily serve to inhibit aggressive behavior when activated by serotonin (such as the orbital prefrontal and medial prefrontal cortex) seem to show decreased activation in BPD (Skodol, Siever et al., 2002; see also Lieb et al., 2004). In addition, research suggests certain structural brain abnormalities in BPD, including reductions in both hippocampal and amygdalar volume, features associated with aggression and impulsivity (Hooley et al., in press).

Much theoretical and research attention has also been directed to the role of psychosocial causal factors in borderline personality disorder. Although the vast majority of this research is retrospective in nature, relying on people's memories of their past to discover the antecedents of the disorder, two prospective community-based studies have shown that childhood adversity and maltreatment is linked to adult BPD (Johnson et al., 1999; Widom et al., 2009). These studies are consistent with a wealth of retrospective research showing that people with this disorder usually report a large number of negative—even traumatic—events in childhood. These experiences include abuse and neglect, and separation and loss. For example, in one large study on abuse and neglect, Zanarini and colleagues (1997) reported on the results of detailed interviews of over 350 patients with BPD and over 100 patients with other personality disorders. Patients with BPD reported significantly higher rates of abuse than did patients with other personality disorders (which were also quite high): emotional abuse (73 versus 51 percent), physical abuse (59 versus 34 percent), and sexual abuse (61 versus 32 percent). Overall, about 90 percent of patients with borderline personality disorder reported some type of childhood abuse or neglect (emotional, physical, or sexual). (See also Bandelow et al., 2005; Battle et al., 2004.) Although these rates of abuse and neglect seem alarming, remember that the majority of children who experience early abuse and neglect do not end up with any serious personality disorders or Axis I psychopathology. (See Paris, 1999, 2007; Rutter & Maughan, 1997.)

Although this and many other related studies (see Dolan-Sewell et al., 2001; Paris, 2007) suggest that BPD (and perhaps other personality disorders as well) is often associated with early childhood trauma, most such studies have many shortcomings and unfortunately cannot tell us that such early childhood trauma plays a causal role. First, although prospective research to date supports this idea (Johnson et al., 1999; Widom et al., 2009), the majority of evidence comes from retrospective self-reports of individuals who are known for their exaggerated and distorted views of other people (Paris, 1999, 2007; Rutter & Maughan, 1997). Second, childhood abuse is certainly not a specific risk factor for borderline pathology because it is also reported at relatively high rates with some other personality disorders as well as with Axis I disorders such as dissociative identity disorder (Moran et al., 2010). Third, childhood abuse nearly always occurs in families with various other pathological dynamics, such as marital discord and family violence, that actually may be more important than the abuse per se in the development of BPD (Paris, 1999, 2007).

Paris (1999, 2007) has offered an interesting multidimensional diathesis-stress theory of BPD. He proposes that people who have high levels of two normal personality traits—impulsivity and affective instability—may have a diathesis to develop borderline personality disorder, but only in the presence of certain psychological risk factors such as trauma, loss, and parental failure (see Figure 1). When such nonspecific psychological risk factors occur in someone who is affectively unstable, he or she may become dysphoric and labile and, if he or she is also impulsive, may engage in impulsive acting out to cope with the dysphoria. Thus the dysphoria and impulsive acts fuel each other. In addition, Paris proposes that children who are impulsive and unstable tend to be "difficult" or troublesome children and therefore may be at increased risk for being rejected or abused. If the parents are personality disordered themselves, they may be especially insensitive to their difficult child, leading to a vicious cycle in which the child's problems are exacerbated by inadequate parenting, which in turn leads to increased dysphoria, and so on. Paris further suggests that borderline personality disorder may be more prevalent in our society than in many other cultures, and more prevalent today than in the past, because of the weakening of the family structure in our society.

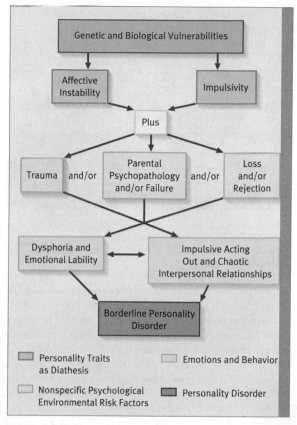

FIGURE 1

Multidimensional Diathesis-Stress Theory of Borderline Personality Disorder

Source: Paris (1999).

Cluster C Personality Disorders

People with Cluster C personality disorders often show anxiety and fearfulness, characteristics that we haven't seen in the other two clusters. In the following section, we'll examine avoidant, dependent, and obsessive compulsive personality disorders.

Avoidant Personality Disorder

Individuals with **avoidant personality disorder** show extreme social inhibition and introversion, leading to lifelong patterns of limited social relationships and reluctance to enter into social interactions. Because of their hypersensitivity to, and fear of, criticism and rebuff, they do not seek out other people, yet they desire affection and are often lonely and bored. Unlike schizoid personalities, people with avoidant personality disorder do not enjoy their aloneness; their inability to relate comfortably to other people causes acute anxiety and is accompanied by low

The key difference between the loner with schizoid personality disorder and the loner who is avoidant is that the avoidant personality is shy, insecure, and hypersensitive to criticism. The schizoid personality is cold, aloof, and indifferent to criticism.

self-esteem and excessive self-consciousness, which in turn are often associated with depression (Grant, Hasin et al., 2005). Feeling inept and socially inadequate are the two most prevalent and stable features of avoidant personality disorder (McGlashan et al., 2005). In addition, researchers have documented that individuals with this disorder also show more generalized timidity and avoidance of many novel situations and emotions (including positive emotions), and show deficits in their ability to experience pleasure as well (Taylor et al., 2004).

case study The Avoidant Librarian

Sally, a 35-year-old librarian, lived a relatively isolated life and had few acquaintances and no close personal friends. From childhood on, she had been very shy and had withdrawn from close ties with others to keep from being hurt or criticized. Two years before she entered therapy, she had had a date to go to a party with an acquaintance she had met at the library. The moment they had arrived at the party, Sally had felt extremely uncomfortable because she had not been "dressed properly." She left in a hurry and refused to see her acquaintance again.

In the early treatment sessions, she sat silently much of the time, finding it too difficult to talk about herself. After several sessions, she grew to trust the therapist, and she related numerous incidents in her early years in which she had been "devastated" by her alcoholic father's obnoxious behavior in public. Although she had tried to keep her school friends from knowing about her family problems, when this had become impossible, she instead had limited her friendships, thus protecting herself from possible embarrassment or criticism.

When Sally first began therapy, she avoided meeting people unless she could be assured that they would "like her." With therapy that focused on enhancing her assertiveness and social skills, she made some progress in her ability to approach people and talk with them.

The key difference between the loner with schizoid personality disorder and the loner who is avoidant is that the one with an avoidant personality is shy, insecure, and hypersensitive to criticism, whereas the one with a schizoid personality is aloof, cold, and relatively indifferent to criticism (Millon & Martinez, 1995). The avoidant personality also desires interpersonal contact but avoids it for fear of rejection, whereas the schizoid lacks the desire or ability to form social relationships. A less clear distinction is that between avoidant personality disorder and generalized social phobia. Numerous studies have found substantial overlap between these two disorders, leading some investigators to conclude that avoidant personality disorder may simply be a somewhat more severe manifestation of generalized social phobia (Alpert et al., 1997; Carter & Wu, 2010; Tillfors et al., 2004) that does not warrant a separate diagnosis (Chambless et al., 2008). This is consistent with the finding that there are cases of generalized social phobia without avoidant personality disorder but very few cases of avoidant personality disorder without generalized social phobia. Somewhat higher levels of dysfunction and distress are also found in the individuals with avoidant personality disorder, including more consistent feelings of low self-esteem (Millon & Martinez, 1995; Hummelen et al., 2007; Tillfors et al., 2004).

CAUSAL FACTORS Some research suggests that avoidant personality may have its origins in an innate "inhibited" temperament

DSM-IV-TR

Criteria for Avoidant Personality Disorder

A pervasive pattern of social inhibition, feelings of inadequacy, and hypersensitivity to negative evaluation, beginning by early adulthood and present in a variety of contexts, as indicated by four (or more) of the following:

1. avoids occupational activities that involve significant interpersonal contact, because of fears of criticism, disapproval, or rejection
2. is unwilling to get involved with people unless certain of being liked
3. shows restraint within intimate relationships because of the fear of being shamed or ridiculed
4. is preoccupied with being criticized or rejected in social situations
5. is inhibited in new interpersonal situations because of feelings of inadequacy
6. views self as socially inept, personally unappealing, or inferior to others
7. is unusually reluctant to take personal risks or to engage in any new activities because they may prove embarrassing

Source: Reprinted with permission from the American Psychiatric Association. *Diagnostic and Statistical Manual of Mental Disorders,* Fourth Edition, *Text Revision* (Copyright © 2000). American Psychiatric Association.

that leaves the infant and child shy and inhibited in novel and am-biguous situations. A large twin study in Norway has shown that traits prominent in avoidant personality disorder show a mod-est genetic influence (Reichborn-Kjennerud et al., 2006), and that the genetic vulnerability for avoidant personality disorder is at least partially shared with that for social phobia (Reichborn-Kjennerud et al., 2007). Moreover, there is also evidence that the fear of being negatively evaluated, which is prominent in avoid-ant personality disorder, is moderately heritable (Stein et al., 2002); introversion and neuroticism are also both elevated (see Table 2), and they too are moderately heritable. This genetically and biologically based inhibited temperament may often serve as the diathesis that leads to avoidant personality disorder in some children who experience emotional abuse, rejection, or humili-ation from parents who are not particularly affectionate (Alden et al., 2002; Bernstein & Travaglini, 1999; Kagan, 1997). Such abuse and rejection would be especially likely to lead to anxious and fearful attachment patterns in temperamentally inhibited children (Bartholomew et al., 2001).

Dependent Personality Disorder

Individuals with **dependent personality disorder** show an ex-treme need to be taken care of, which leads to clinging and sub-missive behavior. They also show acute fear at the possibility of separation or sometimes of simply having to be alone because they see themselves as inept (Bornstein, 2007, 2011; Widiger & Bornstein, 2001). These individuals usually build their lives around other people and subordinate their own needs and

case study The Dependent Wife

Sarah, a 32-year-old mother of two and a part-time tax accountant, came to a crisis center late one evening after Michael, her husband of a year and a half, had abused her physically and then left home. Although he never physically harmed the children, he frequently threatened to do so when he was drunk. Sarah appeared acutely anxious and worried about the future and "needed to be told what to do." She wanted her husband to come back and seemed rather unconcerned about his regular pattern of physical abuse. At the time, Michael was an unemployed resident in a day treatment pro-gram at a halfway house for paroled drug abusers. He was almost always in a surly mood and "ready to explode."

Although Sarah had a well-paying job, she voiced great concern about being able to make it on her own. She realized that it was foolish to be "dependent" on her husband, whom she referred to as a "real loser." (She had had a similar relation-ship with her first husband, who had left her and her oldest child when she was 18.) Several times in the past few months, Sarah had made up her mind to get out of the marriage but couldn't bring herself to break away. She would threaten to leave, but when the time came to do so, she would "freeze in the door" with a numbness in her body and a sinking feeling in her stom-ach at the thought of "not being with Michael."

views to keep these people involved with them. Accordingly, they may be indiscriminate in their selection of mates. They often fail to get appropriately angry with others because of a fear of losing their support, which means that people with de-pendent personalities may remain in psychologically or physi-cally abusive relationships. They have great difficulty making even simple, everyday decisions without a great deal of advice and reassurance because they lack self-confidence and feel helpless even when they have actually developed good work skills or other competencies. They may function well as long as they are not required to be on their own.

Estimates are that dependent personality disorder occurs in 1.5 percent of the population and is more common in women than in men. This gender difference is not due to a sex bias in mak-ing the diagnosis but rather to the higher prevalence in women of certain personality traits such as neuroticism and agreeableness, which are prominent in dependent personality disorder (Lynam & Widiger, 2007). It is quite common for people with dependent personality disorder to have a comorbid diagnosis of mood and anxiety disorders (Bornstein, 1999; Grant, Hasin et al., 2005).

Some features of dependent personality disorder overlap with those of borderline, histrionic, and avoidant personality dis-orders, but there are differences as well (see also Table 2). For ex-ample, both borderline personalities and dependent personalities fear abandonment. However, the borderline personality, who usu-ally has intense and stormy relationships, reacts with feelings of emptiness or rage if abandonment occurs, whereas the dependent personality reacts initially with submissiveness and appeasement and then finally with an urgent seeking of a new relationship. Histrionic and dependent personalities both have strong needs for reassurance and approval, but the histrionic personality is much more gregarious, flamboyant, and actively demanding of attention, whereas the dependent personality is more docile and self-effacing. It can also be hard to distinguish between depen-dent and avoidant personalities. As noted, dependent personali-ties have great difficulty separating in relationships because they feel incompetent on their own and have a need to be taken care of, whereas avoidant personalities have trouble initiating rela-tionships because they fear criticism or rejection, which will be humiliating (APA, *DSM-IV-TR*, 2000; Millon & Martinez, 1995). Even so, we should remember that avoidant personality occurs with dependent personality disorder rather frequently (Alden et al., 2002; Arntz et al., 2009; Bernstein & Travaglini, 1999; Bornstein, 2011). This fits with the observation that people with avoidant personality disorder do not avoid absolutely everyone and that their dependent personality disorder characteristics are fo-cused on the one or few individuals whom they do not avoid (Alden et al., 2002). In terms of the five-factor model, dependent person-ality disorder is associated with high levels of neuroticism and agreeableness (Lowe et al., 2009).

CAUSAL FACTORS Some evidence indicates that there is a modest genetic influence on dependent personality traits (Bornstein, 2011; Reichborn-Kjennerud et al., 2006). More-over, several other personality traits such as neuroticism and agreeableness that are also prominent in dependent personality disorder also have a genetic component (Widiger & Bornstein,

DSM-IV-TR

Criteria for Dependent Personality Disorder

A pervasive and excessive need to be taken care of that leads to submissive and clinging behavior and fears of separation, beginning by early adulthood and present in a variety of contexts, as indicated by five (or more) of the following:

1. has difficulty making everyday decisions without an excessive amount of advice and reassurance from others
2. needs others to assume responsibility for most major areas of his or her life
3. has difficulty expressing disagreement with others because of fear of loss of support or approval. Note: Do not include realistic fears of retribution.
4. has difficulty initiating projects or doing things on his or her own (because of a lack of self-confidence in judgment or abilities rather than a lack of motivation or energy)
5. goes to excessive lengths to obtain nurturance and support from others, to the point of volunteering to do things that are unpleasant
6. feels uncomfortable or helpless when alone because of exaggerated fears of being unable to care for himself or herself
7. urgently seeks another relationship as a source of care and support when a close relationship ends
8. is unrealistically preoccupied with fears of being left to take care of himself or herself

Source: Reprinted with permission from the American Psychiatric Association. *Diagnostic and Statistical Manual of Mental Disorders,* Fourth Edition, *Text Revision* (Copyright © 2000). American Psychiatric Association.

Individuals with obsessive-compulsive personality disorder are highly perfectionistic, leading to serious problems finishing various projects. They are also excessively devoted to work, inflexible about moral and ethical issues, and have difficulty delegating tasks to others. They are also inclined to be ungenerous with themselves and others.

Obsessive-Compulsive Personality Disorder

Perfectionism and an excessive concern with maintaining order and control characterize individuals with **obsessive-compulsive personality disorder (OCPD)**. Their preoccupation with maintaining mental and interpersonal control occurs in part through careful attention to rules, order, and schedules. They are very careful in what they do so as not to make mistakes, but because the details they are preoccupied with are often trivial they use their time poorly and have a difficult time seeing the larger picture (Aycicegi-Dinn et al., 2009; Yovel et al., 2005). This perfectionism is also often quite dysfunctional in that it can result in their never finishing projects. They also tend to be devoted to work to the exclusion of leisure activities and may have difficulty relaxing or doing anything just for fun (Widiger & Frances, 1994). At an interpersonal level, they have difficulty delegating tasks to others and are quite rigid, stubborn, and cold, which is how others tend to view them. Research indicates that rigidity, stubbornness, and perfectionism, as well as reluctance to delegate, are the most prevalent and stable features of OCPD (Ansell et al., 2008; Grilo et al., 2004; McGlashan et al., 2005; Samuel & Widiger, 2011).

It is important to note that people with OCPD do not have true obsessions or compulsive rituals that are the source of extreme anxiety or distress in people with Axis I obsessive-compulsive disorder (OCD). Instead, people with OCPD have

2001). It is possible that people with these partially genetically based predispositions to dependence and anxiousness may be especially prone to the adverse effects of parents who are authoritarian and overprotective (not promoting autonomy and individuation in their child but instead reinforcing dependent behavior). This might lead children to believe that they are reliant on others for their own well-being and are incompetent on their own (Widiger & Bornstein, 2001). Cognitive theorists describe the underlying maladaptive schemas for these individuals as involving core beliefs about weakness and competence and needing others to survive (P. S. Rasmussen, 2005), such as, "I am completely helpless" and "I can function only if I have access to somebody competent" (Beck et al., 1990, p. 60; Beck et al., 2003). Recent experimental evidence supports the hypothesis that these beliefs characterize those with dependent personality disorder (Arntz et al., 2011).

DSM-IV-TR

Criteria for Obsessive-Compulsive Personality Disorder

A pervasive pattern of preoccupation with orderliness, perfectionism, and mental and interpersonal control, at the expense of flexibility, openness, and efficiency, beginning by early adulthood and present in a variety of contexts, as indicated by four (or more) of the following:

1. is preoccupied with details, rules, lists, order, organization, or schedules to the extent that the major point of the activity is lost

2. shows perfectionism that interferes with task completion (e.g., is unable to complete a project because his or her own overly strict standards are not met)

3. is excessively devoted to work and productivity to the exclusion of leisure activities and friendships (not accounted for by obvious economic necessity)

4. is overconscientious, scrupulous, and inflexible about matters of morality, ethics, or values (not accounted for by cultural or religious identification)

5. is unable to discard worn-out or worthless objects even when they have no sentimental value

6. is reluctant to delegate tasks or to work with others unless they submit to exactly his or her way of doing things

7. adopts a miserly spending style toward both self and others; money is viewed as something to be hoarded for future catastrophes

8. shows rigidity and stubbornness

Source: Reprinted with permission from the American Psychiatric Association. *Diagnostic and Statistical Manual of Mental Disorders*, Fourth Edition, *Text Revision* (Copyright © 2000). American Psychiatric Association.

case study · The Perfectionist Train Dispatcher

Alan appeared to be well suited to his work as a train dispatcher. He was conscientious, perfectionistic, and attended to minute details. However, he was not close to his coworkers, and they reportedly thought him "off." He would get quite upset if even minor variations to his daily routine occurred. For example, he would become tense and irritable if coworkers did not follow exactly his elaborately constructed schedules and plans.

In short, Alan got little pleasure out of life and worried constantly about minor problems. His rigid routines were impossible to maintain, and he often developed tension headaches or stomachaches when he couldn't keep his complicated plans in order. His physician, noting the frequency of his physical complaints and his generally perfectionistic approach to life, referred him for a psychological evaluation. Psychotherapy was recommended, but he did not follow up on the treatment recommendations because he felt that he could not afford the time away from work.

distinguishing features. For example, individuals with narcissistic and antisocial personality disorders may share the lack of generosity toward others that characterizes OCPD, but the former tend to indulge themselves, whereas those with OCPD are equally unwilling to be generous with themselves. In addition, both the schizoid and the obsessive-compulsive personalities may have a certain amount of formality and social detachment, but only the schizoid personality lacks the capacity for close relationships. The person with OCPD has difficulty in interpersonal relationships because of excessive devotion to work and great difficulty expressing emotions.

CAUSAL FACTORS Theorists who take a five-factor dimensional approach to understanding obsessive-compulsive personality disorder note that these individuals have excessively high levels of conscientiousness (Samuel & Widiger, 2011), which leads to extreme devotion to work, perfectionism, and excessive controlling behavior (McCann, 1999). They are also high on assertiveness (a facet of extraversion) and low on compliance (a facet of agreeableness). (See Table 2.) Another influential biological dimensional approach—that of Cloninger (1987)—posits three primary dimensions of personality: novelty seeking, reward dependence, and harm avoidance. Individuals with obsessive-compulsive personalities have low levels of novelty seeking (i.e., they avoid change) and reward dependence (i.e., they work excessively at the expense of pleasurable pursuits) but high levels of harm avoidance (i.e., they respond strongly to aversive stimuli and try to avoid them). Recent research has also demonstrated that the OCPD traits show a modest genetic influence (Calvo et al., 2009; Reichborn-Kjennerud et al., 2006).

lifestyles characterized by overconscientiousness, inflexibility, and perfectionism but without the presence of true obsessions or compulsive rituals (Barlow, 2002). Indeed, only about 20 percent of patients with obsessive-compulsive disorder have a comorbid diagnosis of OCPD. This is not significantly different from the rate of OCPD in patients with panic disorder (Albert et al., 2004) people with OCD are more likely to be diagnosed with avoidant or dependent personality disorder than with obsessive-compulsive personality disorder (Wu et al., 2006), and there are only three symptoms of OCPD that seem to occur at elevated rates in people with OCD relative to controls: perfectionism, preoccupation with details, and hoarding (Eisen et al., 2006).

Some features of obsessive-compulsive personality disorder overlap with some features of narcissistic, antisocial, and schizoid personality disorders, although there are also

General Sociocultural Causal Factors for Personality Disorders

The sociocultural factors that contribute to personality disorders are not well understood. As with other forms of psychopathology, the incidence and particular features of personality disorders vary somewhat with time and place, although not as much as one might guess (Allik, 2005; Rigozzi et al., 2009). Indeed, there is less variance across cultures than within cultures. This may be related to findings that all cultures (both Western and non-Western, including Africa and Asia) share the same five basic personality traits discussed earlier, and their patterns of covariation also seem universal (see Allik, 2005, for a review).

Some researchers believe that certain personality disorders have increased in American society in recent years (e.g., Paris, 2001). If this claim is true, we can expect to find the increase related to changes in our culture's general priorities and activities. Is our emphasis on impulse gratification, instant solutions, and pain-free benefits leading more people to develop the self-centered lifestyles that we see in more extreme forms of the personality disorders? For example, there is some evidence that narcissistic personality disorder is more common in Western cultures, where personal ambition and success are encouraged and reinforced (e.g., Widiger & Bornstein, 2001). There is also some evidence that histrionic personality might be expected to be (and is) less common in Asian cultures, where sexual seductiveness and drawing attention to oneself are frowned on; by contrast, it may be higher in Hispanic cultures, where such tendencies are common and well tolerated (e.g., Bornstein, 1999). Within the United States, rates of borderline personality disorder are higher in Hispanic Americans than in African Americans and Caucasians, but rates of schizotypal personality disorder are higher in African Americans than in Caucasians (Chavira et al., 2003).

It has also been suggested that known increases over the 60 years since World War II in emotional dysregulation (e.g., depression, parasuicide, and suicide) and impulsive behaviors (substance abuse and criminal behavior) may be related to increases in the prevalence of borderline and antisocial personality disorders over the same time period. This could stem from increased breakdown of the family and other traditional social structures (Paris, 2001, 2007) and may vary across cultures depending on whether similar breakdowns have occurred.

In Review

- What are the general characteristics of the three clusters of personality disorders?
- Describe and differentiate among the following Cluster A personality disorders: paranoid, schizoid, and schizotypal.
- Describe and differentiate among the following Cluster B personality disorders: histrionic, narcissistic, antisocial, and borderline.
- Describe and differentiate among the following Cluster C personality disorders: avoidant, dependent, and obsessive-compulsive.

Treatments and Outcomes for Personality Disorders

Personality disorders are generally very difficult to treat, in part because they are, by definition, relatively enduring, pervasive, and inflexible patterns of behavior and inner experience. Moreover, many different goals of treatment can be formulated, and some are more difficult to achieve than others. Goals might include reducing subjective distress, changing specific dysfunctional behaviors, and changing whole patterns of behavior or the entire structure of the personality.

In many cases, people with personality disorders enter treatment only at someone else's insistence, and they often do not believe that they need to change. Moreover, those from the odd/eccentric Cluster A and the erratic/dramatic Cluster B have general difficulties in forming and maintaining good relationships, including with a therapist. For those from the erratic/dramatic Cluster B, the pattern of acting out typical in their other relationships is carried into the therapy situation, and instead of dealing with their problems at the verbal level they may become angry at their therapist and loudly disrupt the sessions. Noncompletion of treatment is a particular problem in the treatment of personality disorders; a recent review of the research reported that an average of 37 percent of personality disorder patients drop out of therapy prematurely (McMurran et al., 2010).

In addition, people who have both an Axis I and an Axis II disorder do not, on average, do as well in treatment for their Axis I disorders as patients without comorbid personality disorders (Crits-Christoph & Barber, 2002, 2007; Pilkonis, 2001). This is partly because people with personality disorders have rigid, ingrained personality traits that often lead to poor therapeutic relationships and additionally make them resist doing the things that would help improve their Axis I condition.

Adapting Therapeutic Techniques to Specific Personality Disorders

Therapeutic techniques must often be modified. For example, recognizing that traditional individual psychotherapy tends to encourage dependence in people who are already too dependent (as in dependent, histrionic, and borderline personality disorders), it is often useful to develop treatment strategies specifically aimed at altering these traits. Patients from the anxious/fearful Cluster C, such as those with dependent and avoidant personalities, may also be hypersensitive to any criticism they may perceive from the therapist, so therapists need to be extremely careful to make sure that they do not come across as critical.

For people with severe personality disorders, therapy may be more effective in situations where acting-out behavior can be constrained. For example, many patients with borderline personality disorder are hospitalized at times, for safety reasons, because of their frequent suicidal behavior. However, partial-hospitalization programs are increasingly being used as an intermediate and less expensive alternative to inpatient treatment (Azim, 2001). In these programs, patients live at home and receive extensive group treatment and rehabilitation only during weekdays. Several studies conducted in the Netherlands suggest that short-term inpatient treatment is more effective than outpatient treatment in both Cluster B and Cluster C personality disorders (Bartak et al., 2010, 2011).

Specific therapeutic techniques are a central part of the relatively new cognitive approach to personality disorders that assumes that the dysfunctional feelings and behavior associated with the personality disorders are largely the result of schemas that tend to produce consistently biased judgments, as well as tendencies to make cognitive errors (e.g., Beck et al., 2003; Cottraux & Blackburn, 2001; Pretzer & Beck, 2005). Changing these underlying dysfunctional schemas is difficult but is at the heart of cognitive therapy for personality disorders, which uses standard cognitive techniques of monitoring automatic thoughts, challenging faulty logic, and assigning behavioral tasks in an effort to challenge the patient's dysfunctional beliefs.

Treating Borderline Personality Disorder

Of all the personality disorders, the most clinical and research attention has been paid to the treatment of borderline personality disorder, partly because the treatment prognosis (probable outcome) has typically been considered to be guarded because of these patients' long-standing problems and extreme instability. Treatment often involves a judicious use of both psychological and biological treatment methods, with drugs being used as an adjunct to psychological treatment, which is considered essential.

BIOLOGICAL TREATMENTS The use of medications is controversial with this disorder because it is so frequently associated with suicidal behavior. Today, antidepressant medications (most often from the SSRI category) are considered most safe and useful for treating rapid mood shifts, anger, and anxiety (Lieb et al., 2004), as well as for impulsivity symptoms including impulsive aggression such as self-mutilation (Koenigsberg et al., 2002, 2007; Markovitz, 2004). In addition, low doses of antipsychotic medication have modest but significant effects that are broad based; that is, patients show some improvement in depression, anxiety, suicidality, impulsive aggression, rejection sensitivity, and especially transient psychotic symptoms (Koenigsberg et al., 2007; Markovitz, 2001, 2004). Finally, mood-stabilizing medications such as carbazemine may be useful in reducing irritability, suicidality, and impulsive aggressive behavior (Koenigsberg et al., 2007; Lieb et al., 2004). However, the consensus to date is that drugs are only mildly beneficial for borderline personality disorder (Paris, 2009).

PSYCHOSOCIAL TREATMENTS Clinical trials suggest that several types of psychotherapy may be effective for borderline personality disorder. As discussed below, however, these treatments share a common weakness: their relative complexity and long duration, which makes them difficult to disseminate to the broader population (Paris, 2009).

Linehan's very promising **dialectical behavior therapy** is a unique kind of cognitive and behavioral therapy specifically adapted for this disorder (Linehan, 1993; Linehan & Dexter-Mazza, 2008; Robins et al., 2001). Linehan believes that patients' inability to tolerate strong states of negative affect is central to this disorder, and one of the primary goals of treatment is to encourage patients to accept this negative affect without engaging in self-destructive or other maladaptive behaviors. Accordingly, she has developed a problem-focused treatment based on a clear hierarchy of goals, which prioritizes decreasing suicidal and self-harming behavior and increasing coping skills. The therapy combines individual and group components as well as phone coaching. In the group setting, patients learn interpersonal effectiveness, emotion regulation, and distress tolerance skills. The individual therapist, in turn, uses therapy sessions and phone coaching to help the patient identify and change problematic behavior patterns and apply newly learned skills effectively.

Dialectical behavior therapy appears to be an efficacious treatment for borderline personality disorder (Binks et al., 2006; Paris, 2009). Patients receiving dialectical behavior therapy show reductions in self-destructive and suicidal behaviors as well as in levels of anger (Linehan et al., 2006; Lynch et al., 2007). Evidence also suggests that these gains are sustainable (Zanarini et al., 2005). Such results are considered extraordinary by most therapists who work with this population, and many psychodynamic therapists are now incorporating important components of this treatment into their own treatment. However, dialectical behavior therapy is still not put into wide practice, likely because multifaceted treatment is complex and lasts several years (Paris, 2009). Accordingly, some researchers are currently working on developing briefer versions of the treatment (Stanley et al., 2007).

Other psychosocial treatments for BPD involve variants of psychodynamic psychotherapy adapted for the particular problems of persons with this disorder. For example, Kernberg (1985, 1996) and colleagues (Koenigsberg et al., 2000; see also Clarkin et al., 2004) have developed a form of psychodynamic psychotherapy that is much more directive than is typical of psychodynamic treatment. The primary goal is seen as strengthening the weak egos of these individuals, with a particular focus on their primary primitive defense mechanism of splitting, which leads them to black-and-white, all-or-none thinking, as well as to rapid shifts in their reactions to themselves and to other people (including the therapist) as "all good" or "all bad." One major goal is to help them see the shades of gray between these extremes and integrate positive and negative views of themselves and others into more nuanced views. Although this treatment is often expensive and time-consuming (often lasting a number of years), it has been shown in at least one study to be as effective as dialectical behavior therapy, which is now considered to be the most established, effective treatment (Clarkin et al., 2007). Such results will, however, need to be replicated in other treatment centers before we can place a great deal of confidence in its usefulness (Clarkin et al., 2004; Crits-Christoph & Barber, 2002, 2007).

Treating Other Personality Disorders

Treatment of Cluster A and other Cluster B personality disorders is not, so far, as promising as some of the recent advances that have been made in the treatment of borderline personality disorder. In schizotypal personality disorder, low doses of antipsychotic drugs (including the newer, atypical antipsychotics; e.g., Keshavan et al., 2004; Koenigsberg et al., 2007; Raine, 2006) may result in modest improvements, and antidepressants from the SSRI category may also be useful. However, no treatment has yet produced anything approaching a cure for most people with this disorder (Koenigsberg et al., 2002, 2007; Markovitz, 2001, 2004). Other than uncontrolled studies or single cases, no systematic, controlled studies of treating people with either medication or psychotherapy yet exist for paranoid, schizoid, narcissistic, or histrionic disorder (Beck et al., 2003; Crits-Christoph & Barber, 2007).

Treatment of some of the personality disorders from Cluster C, such as dependent and avoidant personality disorders, has not been extensively studied but appears somewhat more promising than that for the disorders from Clusters A and B. For example, Winston and colleagues (1994) found significant improvement in patients with Cluster C disorders using a form of short-term psychotherapy that is active and confrontational (see also Pretzer & Beck, 1996). Several studies using cognitive-behavioral treatment with avoidant personality disorder have also reported significant gains (see Crits-Christoph & Barber, 2007), and a recent meta-analysis concludes both cognitive-behavioral and psychodynamic therapies result in significant and lasting treatment gains in Cluster C patients (Simon, 2009). Another recent study in the Netherlands concludes that short-term inpatient treatment for Cluster C personality disorders is even more effective than long-term inpatient or outpatient therapy (Bartak et al., 2011). Moreover, antidepressants from the MAOI and SSRI categories may sometimes help in the treatment of avoidant personality disorder, just as they do in closely related social phobia (Koenigsberg et al., 2007; Markovitz, 2001).

In Review

- Why are personality disorders especially resistant to therapy?
- Under what circumstances do individuals with personality disorders generally get involved in psychotherapy?
- What is known about the effectiveness of treatments for borderline personality disorder?

Antisocial Personality Disorder and Psychopathy

The outstanding characteristic of people with **antisocial personality disorder (ASPD)** is their tendency to persistently disregard and violate the rights of others. They do this through a combination of deceitful, aggressive, and antisocial behaviors. These people have a lifelong pattern of unsocialized and irresponsible behavior with little regard for safety—either their own or that of others. These characteristics bring them into repeated conflict with society, and a high proportion become incarcerated. Only individuals 18 or over are diagnosed with antisocial personality disorder. According to *DSM-IV-TR*, this diagnosis is made if, after age 15, the person repeatedly performs acts that are grounds for arrest; shows repeated deceitfulness, impulsivity, irritability, and aggressiveness; shows disregard for safety; and shows consistent irresponsibility in work or financial matters. Moreover, the person must also have shown symptoms of conduct disorder before age 15.

DSM-IV-TR

Criteria for Antisocial Personality Disorder

A. There is a pervasive pattern of disregard for and violation of the rights of others occurring since age 15 years, as indicated by three (or more) of the following:
   1. failure to conform to social norms with respect to lawful behaviors as indicated by repeatedly performing acts that are grounds for arrest
   2. deceitfulness, as indicated by repeated lying, use of aliases, or conning others for personal profit or pleasure
   3. impulsivity or failure to plan ahead
   4. irritability and aggressiveness, as indicated by repeated physical fights or assaults
   5. reckless disregard for safety of self or others
   6. consistent irresponsibility, as indicated by repeated failure to sustain consistent work behavior or honor financial obligations
   7. lack of remorse, as indicated by being indifferent to or rationalizing having hurt, mistreated, or stolen from another

B. The individual is at least age 18 years.
C. There is evidence of Conduct Disorder with onset before age 15 years.
D. The occurrence of antisocial behavior is not exclusively during the course of Schizophrenia or a Manic Episode.

Source: Reprinted with permission from the American Psychiatric Association. *Diagnostic and Statistical Manual of Mental Disorders,* Fourth Edition, *Text Revision* (Copyright © 2000). American Psychiatric Association.

Psychopathy and Antisocial Personality Disorder

The use of the term *antisocial personality disorder* dates back only to *DSM-III* in 1980, but many of the central features of this disorder have long been labeled **psychopathy** or *sociopathy*. Although several investigators identified the syndrome in the nineteenth century under such labels as "moral insanity" (Prichard, 1835), the most comprehensive, systematic early description of psychopathy was made by Cleckley (1941, 1982) in the 1940s. In addition to the defining features of antisocial personality in *DSM-III* and *DSM-IV-TR*, psychopathy also includes such affective and interpersonal traits as lack of empathy, inflated and arrogant self-appraisal, and glib and superficial charm (see Patrick, 2006, for an analysis of Cleckley's work in light of contemporary research). In their strong emphasis on behavioral criteria that can be measured reasonably objectively, *DSM-III* and *DSM-IV-TR* broke with the tradition of psychopathy researchers in an attempt to increase the reliability of the diagnosis (i.e., the level of agreement of clinicians on the diagnosis). However, much less attention has been paid to the validity of the diagnosis—that is, whether it measures a meaningful construct and whether that construct is the same as psychopathy.

According to *DSM-IV-TR* estimates, the prevalence of ASPD in the general population is about 3 percent for males and about 1 percent for females. However, a recent, very large epidemiological study has shown that the real prevalence may be as low as 1 percent (Lenzenweger et al., 2007). There are no epidemiological studies estimating the prevalence of psychopathy, but Hare and colleagues (1999) estimated it is likely to be about 1 percent in North America.

TWO DIMENSIONS OF PSYCHOPATHY Research since 1980 by Robert Hare and colleagues suggests that ASPD and psychopathy are related but differ in significant ways. Hare (1980, 1991, 2003) developed a 20-item Psychopathy Checklist-Revised (PCL-R) as a way for clinicians and researchers to diagnose psychopathy on the basis of the Cleckley criteria following an extensive interview and careful checking of past school, police, and prison records. Extensive research with this checklist has shown that there are two related but separable dimensions of psychopathy, each predicting different types of behavior:

1. The first dimension involves the affective and interpersonal core of the disorder and reflects traits such as lack of remorse or guilt, callousness/lack of empathy, glibness/superficial charm, grandiose sense of self-worth, and pathological lying.

2. The second dimension reflects behavior—the aspects of psychopathy that involve an antisocial, impulsive, and socially deviant lifestyle such as the need for stimulation, poor behavior controls, irresponsibility, and a parasitic lifestyle.

The second dimension is much more closely related than the first to the *DSM-III* and *DSM-IV-TR* diagnosis of antisocial personality disorder (Hare et al., 1999; Widiger, 2006). Not surprisingly, therefore, when comparisons have been made in prison settings to determine what percentage of prison inmates qualify for a diagnosis of psychopathy versus antisocial personality disorder, it is typically found that about 70 to 80 percent qualify for a diagnosis of ASPD but that only about 25 to 30 percent meet the criteria for psychopathy (Patrick, 2005). Put somewhat differently, only about half of imprisoned individuals diagnosed with ASPD also meet the criteria for psychopathy, but most imprisoned individuals with a diagnosis of psychopathy also meet the criteria for ASPD (Widiger, 2006). That is, a significant number of inmates show the antisocial and aggressive behaviors necessary for a diagnosis of antisocial personality disorder but do not show enough selfish, callous, and exploitative behaviors to qualify for a diagnosis of psychopathy (Hare et al., 1999).

The issues surrounding these diagnoses remain highly controversial. Although there was considerable discussion about expanding the *DSM-IV* criteria for antisocial personality disorder to include more of the traditional affective and interpersonal features of psychopathy, a conservative approach was taken and such changes were not made (Sutker & Allain, 2001; Widiger, 2006). However, many researchers continue to use the Cleckley/Hare psychopathy diagnosis rather than the *DSM-IV-TR* ASPD diagnosis, both because of the long and rich research tradition on psychopathy and because the psychopathy diagnosis has been shown to be a better predictor of a variety of important facets of criminal behavior than the ASPD diagnosis. Overall, a diagnosis of psychopathy appears to be the single best predictor we have of violence and recidivism (offending again after imprisonment; Douglas et al., 2006; Gretton et al., 2004; Hart, 1998). For example, one review estimated that people with psychopathy are three times more likely to reoffend and four times more likely to reoffend violently following prison terms than are people without a psychopathy diagnosis (Hemphill et al., 1998). Moreover, adolescents diagnosed with psychopathy are not only more likely to show violent reoffending but are also more likely to reoffend more quickly (Gretton et al., 2004). (See Figure 2.)

An additional concern about the current conceptualization of ASPD is that it does not include what may be a substantial segment of society who show many of the features of the first, affective and interpersonal dimension of psychopathy but not as many features of the second, antisocial dimension, or at least few enough that these individuals do not generally get into trouble with the law. Cleckley clearly did not believe that aggressive behavior was central to the concept of psychopathy (Patrick, 2006). This group might include, for example, some unprincipled and predatory business professionals, manipulative lawyers, high-pressure evangelists, and crooked politicians (Hall & Benning, 2006; Hare et al., 1999). Unfortunately, because they are difficult to find to study, little research has been conducted on such psychopathic persons who manage to stay out of correctional institutions. One researcher (Widom, 1977)

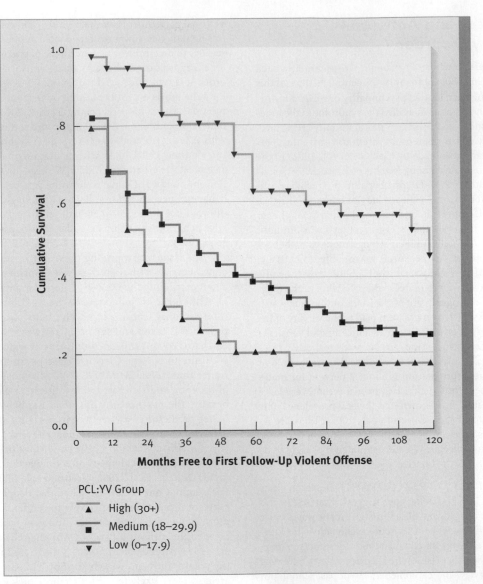

FIGURE 2

Survival curve of months free in the community until first violent reoffense by Hare Psychopathy Checklist: Youth Version (PCL:YV) group. The survival curve illustrates the percentage of individuals in each group who have not shown a violent reoffense at 12-month intervals. Those in the High-PCL-YV group are more likely to have violent reoffenses than those in the other two groups (lower probability of survival) and are more likely to have them sooner after release (indicated by the steeper slope).

Source: From Gretton et al., (2004). Psychopathy and offending from adolescence to adulthood: A ten-year follow-up. *Journal of Consulting and Clinical Psychology, 72*, 636–45. Copyright © 2004 by the American Psychological Association. Reproduced with permission.

who wanted to study these individuals ran an ingenious ad in local newspapers:

> Are you adventurous? Psychologist studying adventurous, carefree people who've led exciting, impulsive lives. If you're the kind of person who'd do almost anything for a dare and want to participate in a paid experiment, send name, address, phone, and short biography proving how interesting you are to . . . (p. 675)

When those who responded were given a battery of tests, they turned out to be similar in personality makeup to that of institutionalized psychopaths. Several further studies on people with noncriminal psychopathy confirmed this finding (Hall & Benning, 2006; Hare et al., 1999). However, some experimental research that we will discuss later suggests that these two groups may also differ biologically in some significant ways (Ishikawa et al., 2001).

These controversies over the use of a diagnosis of psychopathy versus ASPD are not likely to be resolved soon. Different researchers in this area make different choices, so interpreting the research on causal factors can be difficult. Because the causal factors are almost certainly not identical, we will attempt to make it clear which diagnostic category was used in different studies.

The Clinical Picture in Psychopathy and Antisocial Personality Disorder

Often charming, spontaneous, and likable on first acquaintance, psychopaths are deceitful and manipulative, callously using others to achieve their own ends. Many of them seem to live in a series of present moments without consideration for the past or future. But also included in this general category are hostile people who are prone to acting out impulses in remorseless and often senselessly violent ways.

We will summarize the major characteristics of psychopaths and antisocial personalities and then describe a case that illustrates the wide range of behavioral patterns that may be involved. Although all the characteristics examined in the following sections are not usually found in any one particular case, they are typical of psychopaths as first carefully described by Cleckley (1941, 1982), and a subset of these characteristics occur in ASPD as well.

INADEQUATE CONSCIENCE DEVELOPMENT Psychopaths appear unable to understand and accept ethical values except on a verbal level. They may glibly claim to adhere to high moral standards that have no apparent connection with their behavior. In short, their conscience development is severely retarded or nonexistent, and they behave as though social regulations and laws do not apply to them (Frick & Marsee, 2006; Salekin, 2006). These characteristics of psychopathy are most strongly related to the interpersonal and affective core of psychopathy (Fowles & Dindo, 2006). In spite of their retarded conscience development, their intellectual development is typically normal. Nevertheless, intelligence is one trait that has different relationships with the two dimensions of psychopathy. The first, affective and interpersonal dimension is positively related to verbal intelligence (Salekin et al., 2004), but the second, antisocial dimension is negatively related to intelligence (Frick, 1998; Hare et al., 1999).

IRRESPONSIBLE AND IMPULSIVE BEHAVIOR Psychopaths learn to take rather than earn what they want. Often prone to thrill seeking and deviant and unconventional behavior, they often break the law impulsively and without regard for the consequences. They seldom forgo immediate pleasure for future gains and long-range goals. These aspects of psychopathy are most closely related to the second, antisocial dimension of psychopathy (Patrick, 2005).

Many studies have shown that antisocial personalities and some psychopaths have high rates of alcohol abuse and dependence and other substance-abuse/dependence disorders (e.g., Taylor & Lang, 2006; Waldman & Slutske, 2000). Alcohol abuse is related only to the antisocial or deviant dimension of the PCL-R (Patrick, 2005; Reardon al., 2002). Antisocial personalities also have elevated rates of suicide attempts and completed suicides, which are also associated only with the second,

antisocial dimension of psychopathy and not with the first, affective dimension (Verona et al., 2001).

ABILITY TO IMPRESS AND EXPLOIT OTHERS Some psychopaths are often charming and likable, with a disarming manner that easily wins new friends (Cleckley, 1941, 1982; Patrick, 2006). They seem to have good insight into other people's needs and weaknesses and are adept at exploiting them. These frequent liars usually seem sincerely sorry if caught in a lie and promise to make amends—but will not do so. Not surprisingly, then, psychopaths are seldom able to keep close friends. They seemingly cannot understand love in others or give it in return. Manipulative, exploitative, and sometimes coercive in sexual relationships, psychopaths are irresponsible and unfaithful mates.

Hare, a highly influential researcher in this area, summarized the prototypic psychopath in the following manner:

> Conceptualizing psychopaths as remorseless predators helped me to make sense of what often appears to be senseless behavior. These are individuals who, lacking in conscience and feelings for others, find it easy to use charm, manipulation, intimidation, and violence to control others and to satisfy their own social needs . . . . without the slightest sense of guilt or regret . . . . they form a significant proportion of persistent criminals, drug dealers, spouse and child abusers, swindlers and con men . . . . They are well represented in the business and corporate world, particularly during chaotic restructuring, where the rules and their enforcement are lax . . . . Many psychopaths emerge as "patriots" and "saviors" in societies experiencing social, economic, and political upheaval (e.g., Rwanda, the former Yugoslavia, and the former Soviet Union) . . . . by callously exploiting ethnic, cultural, or racial tensions and grievances. (1998, pp. 128–29)

Psychopathy is well illustrated in the following classic case study published by Hare (1970).

Serial killer Ted Bundy exhibited antisocial behavior at its most extreme and dangerous. Bundy used his clean-cut image to get close to his victims—mainly young university women—whom he sexually assaulted and then savagely murdered. From all outward appearances, Bundy was a fine, upstanding citizen.

case study A Psychopath in Action

Donald, 30 years old, has just completed a 3-year prison term for fraud, bigamy, false pretenses, and escaping lawful custody. The circumstances leading up to these offenses are interesting and consistent with his past behavior. With less than a month left to serve on an earlier 18-month term for fraud, he faked illness and escaped from the prison hospital. During the 10 months of freedom that followed, he engaged in a variety of illegal enterprises; the activity that resulted in his recapture was typical of his method of operation. By passing himself off as the "field executive" of an international philanthropic foundation, he was able to enlist the aid of several religious organizations in a fund-raising campaign. The campaign moved slowly at first, and in an attempt to speed things up, he arranged an interview with the local TV station. His performance during the interview was so impressive that funds started to pour in. However, unfortunately for Donald, the interview was also carried on a national news network. He was recognized and quickly arrested. During the ensuing trial it became evident that he experienced no sense of wrongdoing for his activities . . . . At the same time, he stated that most donations to charity are made by those who feel guilty about something and who therefore deserve to be bilked.

While in prison he was used as a subject in some of the author's research. On his release he applied for admission to a university and, by way of reference, told the registrar that he had been one of the author's research colleagues! Several months later the author received a letter from him requesting a letter of recommendation on behalf of Donald's application for a job.

Background. Donald was the youngest of three boys born to middle-class parents. Both of his brothers led normal, productive lives. His father spent a great deal of time with his business; when he was home he tended to be moody and to drink heavily when things were not going right. Donald's mother was a gentle, timid woman who tried to please her husband and to maintain a semblance of family harmony . . . . However, . . . on some occasions [the father] would fly into a rage and beat the children, and on others he would administer a verbal reprimand, sometimes mild and sometimes severe.

By all accounts Donald was considered a willful and difficult child. When his desire for candy or toys was frustrated he would begin with a show of affection, and if this failed he would throw a temper tantrum; the latter was seldom necessary because his angelic appearance and artful ways usually got him what he wanted . . . . Although he was obviously very intelligent, his school years were academically undistinguished. He was restless, easily bored, and frequently truant . . . when he was on his own he generally got himself or others into trouble. Although he was often suspected of being the culprit, he was adept at talking his way out of difficulty.

Donald's misbehavior as a child took many forms including lying, cheating, petty theft, and the bullying of smaller children. As he grew older he became more and more interested in sex, gambling, and alcohol. When he was 14 he made crude sexual advances toward a younger girl, and when she threatened to tell her parents he locked her in a shed. It was about 16 hours before she was found. Donald at first denied knowledge of the incident, later stating that she had seduced him and that the door must have locked itself . . . . His parents were able to prevent charges being brought against him . . . .

When he was 17, Donald . . . forged his father's name to a large check and spent about a year traveling around the world. He apparently lived well, using a combination of charm, physical attractiveness, and false pretenses to finance his way. During subsequent years he held a succession of jobs, never . . . for more than a few months. Throughout this period he was charged with a variety of crimes, including theft, drunkenness in a public place, assault, and many traffic violations. In most cases he was either fined or given a light sentence.

A Ladies' Man. His sexual experiences were frequent, casual, and callous. When he was 22, he married a 41-year-old woman whom he had met in a bar. Several other marriages followed, all bigamous . . . . The pattern was the same: He would marry someone on impulse, let her support him for several months, and then leave. One marriage was particularly interesting. After being charged with fraud Donald was sent to a psychiatric institution for a period of observation. While there he came to the attention of a female member of the professional staff. His charm, physical attractiveness, and convincing promises to reform led her to intervene on his behalf. He was given a suspended sentence, and they were married a week later. At first things went reasonably well, but when she refused to pay some of his gambling debts he forged her name to a check and left. He was soon caught and given an 18-month prison term . . . . He escaped with less than a month left to serve.

It is interesting to note that Donald sees nothing particularly wrong with his behavior, nor does he express remorse or guilt for using others and causing them grief. Although his behavior is self-defeating in the long run, he considers it to be practical and possessed of good sense. Periodic punishments do nothing to decrease his egotism and confidence in his own abilities . . . . His behavior is entirely egocentric, and his needs are satisfied without any concern for the feelings and welfare of others. (Reprinted with permission of Robert P. Hare, University of British Columbia, rhare@interchange.ubc.ca)

The repetitive behavior pattern exhibited by Donald is common among people diagnosed as psychopathic. Some of the multitude of etiological factors that are involved in the development of this very serious personality disorder are considered next.

Causal Factors in Psychopathy and Antisocial Personality

Contemporary research has variously stressed the causal roles of genetic factors, temperamental characteristics, deficiencies in fear and anxiety, more general emotional deficits, the early learning of antisocial behavior as a coping style, and the influence of particular family and environmental patterns. Because an antisocial person's impulsiveness, acting out, and intolerance of discipline and a psychopathic person's callous interpersonal traits tend to appear early in life, many investigators have focused on the role of early biological and environmental factors as causative agents in antisocial and psychopathic behaviors.

GENETIC INFLUENCES Until recently, most behavior genetic research focused on genetic and environmental influences on antisocial behavior or criminality rather than on psychopathy per se. At least 100 studies have compared concordance rates between monozygotic and dizygotic twins, and a number of studies used the adoption method, wherein rates of criminal behavior in the adopted-away children of criminals were compared with the rates of criminal behavior in the adopted-away children of normals. The results of both kinds of studies show a moderate heritability for antisocial or criminal behavior (Carey & Goldman, 1997; Sutker & Allain, 2001) and for ASPD (Waldman & Rhee, 2006), although nonshared environmental influences play an equally important role. More recently, several strong studies have also demonstrated that psychopathy and some of its important features also show a moderate heritability (e.g., Blonigen et al., 2003, 2006; see Vitale & Newman,

2008; Waldman & Rhee, 2006, for reviews). For example, a twin study of 3,687 twin pairs at age 7 found that the early signs of callous/unemotional traits in these children were highly heritable (Viding et al., 2005).

However, researchers also note that strong environmental influences (to be discussed later) interact with genetic predispositions (a genotype–environment interaction) to determine which individuals become criminals or antisocial personalities (Carey & Goldman, 1997; Moffitt, 2005). Indeed, this must be the case, given the dramatic increases in crime that have occurred in the United States and the United Kingdom since 1960, as well as the tenfold-higher murder rate in the United States than in the United Kingdom (Rutter, 1996); such findings cannot be accounted for by genetic factors alone but must involve psychosocial or sociocultural causal factors.

One excellent study by Cadoret and colleagues (1995; see also Riggins-Caspers et al., 2003) found that adopted-away children of biological parents with ASPD were more likely to develop antisocial personalities if their adoptive parents exposed them to an adverse environment than if their adoptive parents exposed them to a more normal environment. Adverse environments were characterized by some of the following: marital conflict or divorce, legal problems, and parental psychopathology. Similar findings of a gene–environment interaction were also found in twins who were at high or low risk for conduct disorder (typically a childhood precursor of ASPD); in this study, the environmental risk factor was physical maltreatment (Jaffee et al., 2005).

The most exciting study on gene–environment interactions and ASPD identified a candidate gene that seems to be very involved (Caspi et al., 2002). This gene, known as the *monoamine oxidase-A gene (MAO-A gene)*, is involved in the breakdown of neurotransmitters like norepinephrine, dopamine, and serotonin—all neurotransmitters affected by the stress of maltreatment that can lead to aggressive behavior

This figure is intentionally omitted from this text

The relationship between antisocial behavior and substance abuse is sufficiently strong that some have questioned whether there may be a common factor leading to both alcoholism and antisocial personality. Early studies of genetic factors involved in the predisposition to antisocial personality and to alcoholism were inconsistent (Carey & Goldman, 1997), but most recent research suggests that there is significant genetic involvement in their high level of comorbidity (e.g., Krueger et al., 2002; Slutske et al., 1998; Taylor & Lang, 2006). Moreover, one study found that ASPD and other externalizing disorders (like alcohol and drug dependence and conduct disorder) all share a strong common genetic vulnerability; environmental factors were more important in determining which disorder a particular person developed (Hicks et al., 2004; Krueger et al., 2007).

THE LOW-FEAR HYPOTHESIS AND CONDITIONING

Research evidence indicates that psychopaths who are high on the egocentric, callous, and exploitative dimension have low trait anxiety and show poor conditioning of fear (Fowles & Dindo, 2006; Lykken, 1995; Patrick, 2005). In an early classic study, for example, Lykken (1957) found that psychopaths showed deficient conditioning of skin conductance responses (reflecting activation of the sympathetic nervous system) when anticipating an unpleasant or painful event and that they were slow at learning to stop responding in order to avoid punishment. As a result, psychopaths presumably fail to acquire many of the conditioned reactions essential to normal passive avoidance of punishment, to conscience development, and to socialization (Trasler, 1978; see also Fowles & Dindo, 2006; Fowles & Kochanska, 2000). Hare aptly summarized work on this issue: "It is the emotionally charged thought, images, and internal dialogue that give the 'bite' to conscience, account for its powerful control over behavior, and generate guilt and remorse for transgressions. This is something that psychopaths cannot understand. For them conscience is little more than an intellectual awareness of rules others make up—empty words" (1998, p. 112).

An impressive array of studies since the early work of Lykken has confirmed that psychopaths are deficient in the conditioning of at least subjective and certain physiological components of fear (e.g., Birbaumer et al., 2005; Flor et al., 2002; Fowles, 2001; Lykken, 1995), although they do learn at a purely cognitive level that the CS predicts the US (Birbaumer et al., 2005). Because such conditioning may underlie successful avoidance of punishment, this may also explain why their impulsive behavior goes unchecked. According to Fowles, the deficient conditioning of fear seems to stem from psychopaths' having a deficient *behavioral inhibition system* (Fowles, 1993, 2001; Fowles & Dindo, 2006; Hare et al., 1999). The be-

havioral inhibition system has been proposed by Gray (1987; Gray & McNaughton, 1996) to be the neural system underlying anxiety (Fowles & Dindo, 2006). It is also the neural system responsible for learning to inhibit responses to cues that signal punishment. In this *passive avoidance learning*, one learns to avoid punishment by not making a response (for example, by not committing robbery, one avoids punishment). Thus deficiencies in this neural system (currently identified as involving the septohippocampal system and the amygdala) are associated both with deficits in conditioning of anticipatory anxiety and, in turn, with deficits in learning to avoid punishment. Recent research suggests that "successful" psychopaths do not show these same deficits. This may be why they are successful at not getting caught, as discussed in The World Around Us 1.

Other support for the low-fear hypothesis comes from work by Patrick and colleagues on the human startle response. Both humans and animals show a larger startle response if a startle probe stimulus (such as a loud noise) is presented when the subject is already in an anxious state (e.g., Patrick et al., 1993); this is known as *fear-potentiated startle*. Comparing psychopathic and nonpsychopathic prisoners, Patrick and colleagues found that the psychopaths did not show this effect, but the nonpsychopathic prisoners did. Indeed, the psychopaths showed smaller rather than larger startle responses when viewing unpleasant and pleasant slides than when watching neutral slides (see also Patrick, 1994; Sutton et al., 2002, for related results). These deficits in fear-potentiated startle responding are related only to the first, affective dimension of psychopathy (not to the second, antisocial dimension; Patrick, 2005).

The second important neural system in Gray's model is the *behavioral activation system*. This system activates behavior in response to cues for reward (positive reinforcement) as well as to cues for active avoidance of threatened punishment (such as in lying or running away to avoid punishment that one has been threatened with). According to Fowles's theory, the behavioral activation system is thought to be normal or possibly overactive in psychopaths, which may explain why they are quite focused on obtaining reward. Moreover, if they are caught in a misdeed, they are very focused on actively avoiding threatened punishment (e.g., through deceit and lies, or running away). This hypothesis of Fowles that psychopaths have a deficient behavioral inhibition system and a normal or possibly overactive behavioral activation system seems to account for three important features of psychopathy: (1) psychopaths' deficient conditioning of anxiety to signals for punishment, (2) their difficulty learning to inhibit responses that may result in punishment (such as illegal and antisocial acts), and (3) their normal or hypernormal active avoidance of punishment (by deceit, lies,

"Successful" Psychopaths

As already noted, most research on antisocial and psychopathic personalities has been conducted on institutionalized individuals, leaving us quite ignorant about the large number who stop short of criminal activity or who never get caught. Several early studies found the personality makeup of such individuals (as solicited from ads such as Widom's) to be very similar to that of institutionalized individuals. However, Widom (1978) also speculates that the "everyday," noncriminal psychopaths (sometimes known as "successful" psychopaths because they somehow manage to avoid being incarcerated for long periods of time) she had studied might well not show the same autonomic nervous system deficits that are typically seen in criminal psychopaths. Specifically, as noted earlier, criminal psychopaths typically show smaller skin conductance (sweaty palm) responses in anticipation of punishment than criminal nonpsychopaths, and several other studies showed that criminal psychopaths also demonstrate lower cardiovascular (heart rate) reactivity during fear imagery or anticipation of punishment (e.g., Arnett et al., 1993; Patrick et al., 1994; see Hall & Benning, 2006, for a review).

Several later studies provide tentative support for Widom's hypothesis that successful psychopaths would not show these deficits. One study, for example, showed that 15-year-old antisocial boys who later managed to avoid criminal convictions through age 29 exhibited increased autonomic arousal (heart rate and skin conductance) relative to 15-year-old antisocial boys who were later convicted of crimes (Raine et al., 1995; see also Brennan et al., 1997). More direct support for Widom's hypothesis is provided by a study examining autonomic

stress reactivity in successful and unsuccessful criminal psychopaths and control subjects, all living in the community and trying to find temporary employment (Ishiwaka et al., 2001). Each subject was told to give a short speech about his personal faults and weaknesses, during which time he was observed and videotaped. While subjects were preparing for and giving the speech, their heart rate was monitored. The results indicated that successful psychopaths (who had committed approximately the same number and type of crimes as the unsuccessful psychopaths, although they had never been convicted) showed greater heart rate reactivity to this stressful task than did the controls or the unsuccessful psychopaths. Thus, just as Widom had predicted, the successful psychopaths did not show the reduced cardiovascular responsivity that the unsuccessful psychopaths exhibited when anticipating and experiencing a stressor. This is consistent with the idea that the increased cardiac reactivity of the successful psychopaths may serve them well in processing what is going on in risky situations and in making decisions that may prevent their being caught. Additional neuropsychological tests revealed that the successful psychopaths also showed superior "executive functioning" (higher-order cognitive processes such as planning, abstraction, cognitive flexibility, and decision making), which also probably enhanced their ability to elude punishment. Moreover, they also tend to come from less disadvantaged socioeconomic backgrounds than criminal psychopaths (Hall & Benning, 2006). Clearly, more research is needed on this important group of successful, nonincarcerated psychopaths, who commit a great deal of crime but somehow manage to avoid being caught.

and escape behavior) when actively threatened with punishment (Fowles, 1993, p. 9; see also Hare, 1998).

Newman and colleagues (e.g., Newman, 2008; Newman & Lorenz, 2003) have also conducted research suggesting that people with psychopathy have a dominant response set for reward. Their excessive focus on reward is thought to interfere with their ability to use punishment or other contextual cues or information to modulate (or modify) their responding when rewards are no longer forthcoming at the same rate that they once were. Moreover, Newman and colleagues believe that this response modulation deficit is more central to psychopathy than is a fear deficit (or even a general emotional deficit). A number of interesting studies they have conducted are consistent with their theory. However, there is still significant controversy over whether this response modulation deficit hypothesis can account for the wide array of findings in support of the low-fear (and other emotional deficits) hypothesis. Only future research will be able to resolve these controversies.

MORE GENERAL EMOTIONAL DEFICITS Researchers have also been interested in whether there are more general emotional deficits in psychopaths than simply deficits in the conditioning of anxiety (Fowles & Dindo, 2006; Hare et al., 1999; Patrick, 2005). Psychopaths showed less significant physiological reactivity to distress cues (slides of people crying who are obviously quite distressed) than nonpsychopaths, a result consistent with the idea that psychopaths are low on empathy (Blair, 2006; Blair et al., 1997), in addition to being low on fear. However, they were not underresponsive to unconditioned threat cues such as slides of sharks, pointed guns, or angry faces. Consistent with this, Patrick and colleagues showed that this effect of smaller (rather than larger) startle responses when viewing unpleasant slides is especially pronounced with slides depicting scenes of victims who have been mutilated or assaulted but not with slides representing threats to the self (aimed weapons or looming attackers; Levenston et al., 2000). This specific failure to show larger startle responses with victim scenes might be related to the lack of empathy common in psychopathy (e.g., Blair et al., 1997). Blair (2006) summarizes evidence showing that such emotional deficits seem to be due, at least in part, to the dysfunction in the amygdala that is commonly seen in psychopathy. For example, individuals with psychopathy show less activity in the amygdala (relative to controls) not only during fear conditioning but also when viewing sad or frightened faces (see Marsh & Blair, 2008, for a quantitative review).

Hare has hypothesized that the kinds of emotional deficits discussed so far are only a subset of more general difficulties that psychopaths have with processing and understanding the meaning of affective stimuli, including positive and negative words and sounds (e.g., Blair et al., 2006; Lorenz & Newman, 2002; Verona et al., 2004). Hare summarized work in this area as follows: "Psychopaths . . . seem to have difficulty in fully understanding and using words that for normal people refer to ordinary emotional events and feelings . . . . It is as if emotion is a second language for psychopaths, a language that requires a considerable amount of . . . cognitive effort on their part" (1998, p. 115). It has been suggested that such deficits in turn are closely linked to the deficits in moral reasoning and behavior seen in people with psychopathy because to reason about moral issues requires that an individual has concern about the rights and welfare of other people (Blair, 2007b).

EARLY PARENTAL LOSS, PARENTAL REJECTION, AND INCONSISTENCY In addition to genetic factors and emotional deficits, slow conscience development and high levels of both reactive and instrumental aggression are influenced by the damaging effects of parental rejection, abuse, and neglect accompanied by inconsistent discipline (e.g., Farrington, 2006; Luntz & Widom, 1994). However, studies of gene–environment interactions reviewed earlier clearly indicate that these kinds of disturbances are not sufficient explanations for the origins of psychopathy or antisocial personality because some people are clearly more susceptible to these effects than others. Moreover, these same conditions have been implicated in a wide range of later maladaptive behaviors. In the following section, we present an integrated developmental perspective using a biopsychosocial approach with multiple interacting causal pathways.

A Developmental Perspective on Psychopathy and Antisocial Personality

It has long been known that these disorders generally begin early in childhood, especially for boys, and that the number of antisocial behaviors exhibited in childhood is the single best predictor of who will develop an adult diagnosis of ASPD, and the younger they start, the higher the risk (Robins, 1978, 1991). These early antisocial symptoms are today

associated with a diagnosis of conduct disorder and include theft, truancy, running away from home, and associating with delinquent peers. Long-term prospective studies have now shown that the family factors that are most important in predicting which children will show the most antisocial behaviors are poor parental supervision, harsh or erratic parental discipline, physical abuse or neglect, disrupted family life, and a convicted mother (Farrington, 2006). But what causes some children to be more susceptible than others to the adverse effects of such environmental influences?

Prospective studies have shown that it is children with an early history of *oppositional defiant disorder*—characterized by a pattern of hostile and defiant behavior toward authority figures that usually begins by the age of 6 years, followed by early-onset conduct disorder around age 9—who are most likely to develop ASPD as adults (c.g., Lahey et al., 2005). For these children, the types of antisocial behaviors exhibited across the first 25 years of life change a great deal with development but are persistent in nature (Hinshaw, 1994). By contrast, children without the pathological background who develop conduct disorder in adolescence do not usually become lifelong antisocial personalities but instead have problems largely limited to the adolescent years (Frick & Marsee, 2006; Moffitt & Caspi, 2001; Patterson & Yoerger, 2002).

The second early diagnosis that is often a precursor to adult psychopathy or ASPD is *attention-deficit/hyperactivity disorder (ADHD)*. ADHD is characterized by restless, inattentive, and impulsive behavior, a short attention span, and high distractibility. When ADHD co-occurs with conduct disorder (which happens in at least 30 to 50 percent of cases), this leads to a high likelihood that the person will develop a severely aggressive form of ASPD and possibly psychopathy (Abramowitz et al., 2004; Lahey et al., 2005; Patterson et al., 2000). Indeed, Lynam (2002) has referred to children with ADHD and conduct disorder as "fledgling psychopaths," and several ways of assessing psychopathy in youth have been developed, with the Psychopathy Checklist—Youth Version (Forth et al., 2003) being perhaps the best validated (Salekin, 2006; Salekin et al., 2004).

There is increasing evidence that genetic propensities to mild neuropsychological problems such as those leading to hyperactivity or attentional difficulties, along with a difficult temperament, may be important predisposing factors for early-onset conduct disorder, which often leads to life-course-persistent adult ASPD. The behavioral problems that these predisposing factors create have a cascade of pervasive effects over time. For example, on the basis of extensive longitudinal prospective research, Moffitt, Caspi, and colleagues (2002; Moffitt, 2006) have suggested that

"Life-course-persistent" antisocial behavior originates early in life, when the difficult behavior of a high-risk young child is exacerbated by a high-risk social environment. According to the theory, the child's risk emerges from inherited or acquired neuropsychological variation, initially manifested as subtle cognitive deficits, difficult temperament, or hyperactivity. The environment's risk comprises factors such as inadequate parenting, disrupted family bonds, and poverty. The environmental risk domain expands beyond the family as the child ages, to include poor relations with people such as peers and teachers, then later with partners and employers. Over the first 2 decades of development, transactions between individual and environment gradually construct a disordered personality with hallmark features of physical aggression, and antisocial behavior persisting to midlife. (Moffit et al., 2002, p. 180)

Many other psychosocial and sociocultural contextual variables contribute to the probability that a child with the genetic or constitutional liabilities discussed above will develop conduct disorder and, later, ASPD. As discussed above, these include the parents' own antisocial behaviors, divorce and other parental transitions, poverty and crowded inner-city neighborhoods, and parental stress (e.g., Dishion & Patterson, 1997; Dodge & Pettit, 2003; Farrington, 2006; Reid et al., 2002). All of these contribute to poor and ineffective parenting skills—especially ineffective disciplining, monitoring, and supervising—which are highly predictive of antisocial behavior (e.g., Farrington, 2006; Granic &

Patterson, 2006). Moreover, antisocial behavior involving coercive interchanges trains children in these behaviors. This in turn all too often leads to association with deviant and aggressive peers and to the opportunity for further learning of antisocial behavior (Dodge & Pettit, 2003; Farrington, 2006).

Until fairly recently it was not apparent how this integrated model applied to the development of the traits and behaviors representing the affective–interpersonal core of psychopathy. In the past decade, Frick and colleagues have developed a way of assessing children's callous and unemotional traits, which seem to represent early manifestations of this first dimension of psychopathy (e.g., Frick & Marsee, 2006; Frick & Morris, 2004; Frick et al., 2003). They have noted that there are at least two different dimensions of children's difficult temperament that seem to lead to different developmental outcomes. Some children have great difficulty learning to regulate their emotions and show high levels of emotional reactivity, including aggressive and antisocial behaviors when responding to stressful demands and negative emotions like frustration and anger. Such children are at increased risk for developing ASPD and high scores on the antisocial dimension of psychopathy. But other children may

This figure is intentionally omitted from this text.

Children and adolescents who show persistent patterns of aggression toward people or animals, destruction of property, deceitfulness or theft, and serious violation of rules at home or in school may be at risk for developing conduct disorder and antisocial personality disorder.

have few problems regulating negative emotions, instead showing fearlessness and low anxiety as well as callous/unemotional traits and reduced activation of the amygdala while responding to fearful facial expressions (e.g., Marsh et al., 2008). These are the children most likely to show poor development of conscience, and their aggressive behaviors are more instrumental and premeditated rather than reactive as seen with those children who have emotional regulation difficulties. These latter children are likely to develop high scores on the first, interpersonal affective core of psychopathy, leading to the cold, remorseless psychopaths described earlier by Hare (1998), who show low fear and lack of empathy (Fowles & Dindo, 2006).

SOCIOCULTURAL CAUSAL FACTORS AND PSYCHOPATHY Cross-cultural research by Murphy (1976) on psychopathy reveals that it occurs in a wide range of cultures including nonindustrialized ones as diverse as the Inuit of northwest Alaska and the Yorubas of Nigeria. The Yorubas' concept of a psychopath is "a person who always goes his own way regardless of others, who is uncooperative, full of malice, and bullheaded," and the Inuit's concept is of someone whose "mind knows what to do but he does not do it . . . . This is an abstract term for the breaking of the many rules when awareness of the rules is not in question" (Murphy, 1976, p. 1026, as cited in Sullivan & Kosson, 2006, p. 430). Nevertheless, the exact manifestations of the disorder are influenced by cultural factors, and the prevalence of the disorder also seems to vary with sociocultural influences that encourage or discourage its development (Cooke et al., 2005; Hare et al., 1999; Sullivan & Kosson, 2006).

Regarding different cross-cultural manifestations of the disorder, one of the primary symptoms where cultural variations occur is the frequency of aggressive and violent behavior. Socialization forces have an enormous impact on the expression of aggressive impulses. Thus it is not surprising that in some cultures, such as China, psychopaths may be much less likely to engage in aggressive, especially violent, behavior than they are in most Western cultures (Cooke, 1996). By contrast, cross-cultural studies have indicated that the affective-interpersonal dimension of psychopathy is the most consistent across cultures (Cooke et al., 2005).

Moreover, cultures can be classified along a dimension distinguishing between individualistic and collectivist societies. Competitiveness, self-confidence, and independence from others are emphasized in relatively individualistic societies, whereas contributions and subservience to the social group, acceptance of authority, and stability of relationships are encouraged in relatively collectivist societies (Cooke, 1996; Cooke & Michie, 1999). Thus we would expect individualistic societies (such as in the United States) to be more likely to promote some of the behavioral characteristics that, carried to the extreme, result in psychopathy. These characteristics include "grandiosity, glibness and superficiality, promiscuity . . . as well as a lack of responsibility for others . . . . The competitiveness . . . not only produces higher rates of criminal behavior but also leads to an increased use of . . . deceptive, manipulative, and parasitic behavior" (Cooke & Michie, 1999, p. 65). Although the evidence bearing on this is minimal, it is interesting to note that estimates of the prevalence of ASPD are much lower in Taiwan, a relatively collectivist society, than they are in the United States (approximately 0.1 to 0.2 percent versus 1.5 to 4 percent).

Treatments and Outcomes in Psychopathic and Antisocial Personality

Most people with psychopathic and antisocial personalities do not suffer from much personal distress and do not believe they need treatment. Those who run afoul of the law may participate in rehabilitation programs in penal institutions, but they are rarely changed by them. Even when more and better therapeutic facilities are available, effective treatment will still be a challenging task, and many clinical researchers working with these populations have concluded that these disorders are extraordinarily difficult, if not impossible, to treat at this time, with psychopathy being even more difficult to treat than ASPD (e.g., Hare et al., 1999; Harris & Rice, 2006; Vitale & Newman, 2008). Such conclusions are not made lightly. Dozens of studies have made substantial efforts in trying to treat this disorder. Alarmingly, a few studies have found that treatments that work for other criminal offenders can actually be harmful for psychopaths in that rates of reoffending increase rather than decrease (Harris & Rice, 2006). This may be especially likely to occur if the treatment program emphasizes training in social skills or empathy because such skills may simply make them better at charming or conning future victims (Vitale & Newman, 2008).

Biological treatment approaches for antisocial and psychopathic personalities—including electroconvulsive therapy and drugs—have not been systematically studied, partly because the few results that have been reported suggest modest changes at best. Drugs such as lithium and anticonvulsants used to treat bipolar disorder have had some success in treating the aggressive/impulsive behavior of violent aggressive criminals, but evidence on this is scant (Markovitz, 2001; Minzenberg & Siever, 2006). There have also been some tentative but promising results using antidepressants from the SSRI category, which can sometimes reduce aggressive/impulsive behavior and increase interpersonal skills (Lösel, 1998; Minzenberg & Siever, 2006). However, none of these biological treatments has any substantial impact on the disorder as a whole. Moreover, even if effective pharmacological treatments were found, the problem of these individuals generally having little motivation to take their medications would remain (Markovitz, 2001).

COGNITIVE-BEHAVIORAL TREATMENTS For reasons discussed earlier, punishment by itself is generally ineffective for changing antisocial behavior. Cognitive-behavioral treatments have thus often been thought to offer the greatest promise of more effective treatment (Harris & Rice, 2006; Lösel, 1998; Piper & Joyce, 2001). Common targets of cognitive-behavioral interventions include the following: (1) increasing self-control, self-critical thinking, and social perspective taking; (2) increasing victim awareness; (3) teaching anger management; (4) changing antisocial attitudes; and (5) curing drug addiction. Such interventions require a controlled situation in which the therapist can administer or withhold reinforcement and the individual cannot leave treatment (such as an inpatient or prison setting) because when treating antisocial behavior, we are dealing

with a total lifestyle rather than a few specific, maladaptive behaviors (e.g., Piper & Joyce, 2001). Even the best of these multifaceted, cognitive-behaviorally oriented treatment programs generally produce only modest changes, although they are somewhat more effective in treating young offenders (teenagers) than older offenders, who are often hard-core, lifelong psychopaths. Moreover, although such treatments may be useful in reducing inmates' antisocial behavior while in a prison or other forensic setting, the results do not usually generalize to the real world if the person is released (Harris & Rice, 2006). Thus some experts in the area have concluded that at the present time it may be best to think about management rather than treatment of psychopathic offenders.

Fortunately, the criminal activities of many psychopathic and antisocial personalities seem to decline after the age of 40 even without treatment, possibly because of weaker biological drives, better insight into self-defeating behaviors, and the cumulative effects of social conditioning. Such individuals are often referred to as "burned-out psychopaths." Although there is not a great deal of evidence on this issue (Douglas et al., 2006), one important study that followed a group of male psychopaths over many years found a clear and dramatic reduction in levels of criminal behavior after age 40. However, over 50 percent of these people continued to be arrested after age 40 (Hare et al., 1988). Moreover, it is only the antisocial behavioral dimension of psychopathy that seems to diminish with age; the egocentric, callous, and exploitative affective and interpersonal dimension persists (Cloninger et al., 1997; Hare et al., 1999).

In view of the distress and unhappiness that psychopaths inflict on others and the social damage they cause, it seems desirable—and more economical in the long run—to put increased effort into the development of effective prevention programs. Longitudinal prevention research on children at risk for conduct disorder is discussed in Developments in Practice 2.

In Review

- List the three DSM criteria that must be met before an individual is diagnosed with antisocial personality disorder, and cite the additional personality traits that define psychopathy.

- What are several reasons why many researchers believe psychopathy is a more valid construct than antisocial personality disorder?

- What biological factors contribute to these disorders?

- What are the primary features of today's developmental perspective on these disorders?

2

Developments in Practice
PREVENTION OF PSYCHOPATHY AND ANTISOCIAL PERSONALITY DISORDER

Given the difficulties in treating conduct disorder, ASPD, and psychopathy, there is an increasing focus on prevention programs oriented toward both minimizing some of the developmental and environmental risk factors described earlier and breaking some of the vicious cycles that at-risk children seem to get into. Intelligence is one naturally occurring protective factor for some adolescents who are at risk for developing psychopathy or antisocial personality in adulthood (Hawkins et al., 1997). For example, several studies found that many adolescents with conduct disorder never get involved in criminal behavior because they are positively influenced by schooling and focus their energies on more socially accepted behaviors (e.g., White et al., 1989). Of course, not all at-risk adolescents have high intelligence, and those who do not may benefit from more structured prevention programs.

Given the life-course developmental model for the etiology of ASPD, devising prevention strategies becomes very complex because many different stages present targets for preventive interventions (e.g., Conduct Problems Prevention Research Group, 2007; Dodge & Pettit, 2003). Some interventions that have been shown to help are aimed at mothers estimated to be at high risk (poor, first-time, and single) for producing children who could be at risk and include prenatal care aimed at improving maternal nutrition, decreasing smoking and other substance use, and improving parenting skills (Olds et al., 1986, 1994; Reid & Eddy, 1997).

For young children, Patterson, Dishion, Reid, and colleagues have developed programs that target the family environment and teach effective parental discipline and supervision (e.g., Dishion & Kavanaugh, 2002; Gardner, Shaw et al., 2007; Reid et al., 2002). At-risk children whose families receive such interventions do better academically, are less likely to associate with delinquent peers, and are less likely to get involved in drug use. Such family or parent training can even be effective at reducing or preventing further antisocial behavior in children and adolescents already engaged in antisocial behavior, although conducting the intervention with pre–elementary school children was more effective and less labor intensive (see Reid & Eddy, 1997, for a review). In general, the earlier the prevention and intervention efforts are started, the greater the likelihood that they may succeed. However, it is also important to realize that any single intervention by itself is unlikely to be successful because there are so many different kinds of forces that influence at-risk children throughout their development (Conduct Problems Prevention Research Group, 2007; Dodge & Pettit, 2003).

Some significant advances have also been made in prevention programs targeting the school environment or the school and family environments concurrently. One especially promising multisite, 10-year intervention study of this sort is called the FAST Track (Families and Schools Together) intervention. In the early 1990s over 400 kindergarten students who attended schools associated with high risk (generally those that serve inner-city and poor neighborhoods) and who already showed poor peer relations and high levels of disruptive behavior were recruited for this intensive program, which included parent training and school interventions. Another group of over 400 high-risk children were assigned to a control group who received treatment as usual (i.e., no new special programs). There was a focus on improving social-cognitive and cognitive skills, friendships with peers, emotional awareness, and self-control. Teachers and parents were taught how to manage disruptive behavior, and parents were informed of what their children were being taught. Early results through the third grade were quite promising in terms of reducing later conduct problems (Conduct Problems Prevention Research Group, 1999, 2002). Parenting behavior and children's social-cognitive skills also showed significant improvement. Children in FAST Track were also less likely to be nominated by peers as aggressive, and they tended to be better liked and to show better reading skills (Coie, 1996; Reid & Eddy, 1997). Later results by grade 9 were remarkable for the children in the highest risk category (top 3 percent on risk). Among these children, the intervention group had lower rates of conduct disorder (reduced by 75 percent) and ADHD (reduced by 53 percent) relative to the control group (Conduct Problems Prevention Research Group, 2007). Although such interventions are expensive (the estimated cost per child was $58,000 over 10 years), if they can prevent (or at least dramatically reduce) the extremely costly effects on society of these children if they develop full-blown adult ASPD or psychopathy, the long-term benefits will outweigh the initial costs. And indeed, estimates are that each very high-risk youth costs society $1.2 to $2 million in rehabilitation, incarceration, and costs to victims. Thus a $58,000 intervention may be enormously cost-effective in the long run (Conduct Problems Prevention Research Group, 2007).

Unresolved Issues

▶ **DSM-5:** *Moving Toward a Dimensional System of Classification*

Proposed revisions to the personality disorders in the upcoming *DSM-5* are among the most radical of any disorders covered in this text. Although the details are currently being hotly debated among experts, the eventual revisions will almost certainly incorporate a more dimensional approach to the assessment and diagnosis of personality pathology (Livesley, 2011; Skodol et al., 2011; Widiger et al., 2009). It is worthwhile to consider the specific issues that have led researchers to this conclusion.

While reading this chapter, you may have intuitively grasped some of the difficulties with the use of an exclusively categorical diagnostic system for personality disorders. For instance, you may have had some difficulty in developing a clear, distinctive picture of each of the personality disorders. It is quite likely that as you studied the descriptions of the different disorders, the characteristics and attributes of some of them, say, the schizoid personality disorder, seemed to blend with other conditions, such as the schizotypal or the avoidant personality disorders. Although we attempted to highlight the apparent differences between prototypic cases of the different personality disorders that have the greatest potential for overlap, as noted early in the chapter, people frequently do not fit these prototypes neatly and instead qualify for a diagnosis of more than one personality disorder (e.g., Clark, 2007; Grant, Stinson et al., 2005; Widiger et al., 1991). In addition, one of the most common diagnoses is the grab-bag category of "Personality disorder not otherwise specified" (e.g., Livesley, 2007; Krueger & Eaton, 2010; Verheul & Widiger, 2004; Verheul et al., 2007); this category is reserved for persons who exhibit features from several different categories but do not cleanly fit within any of them. Such issues are much less problematic when a dimensional system is used because it is expected that across individuals there will be many different patterns of elevation of scores on different facets of different traits.

A second major difficulty with the unreliability of Axis II categorical diagnoses stems from the assumption in *DSM-IV-TR* that we can make a clear distinction between the presence and the absence of a personality disorder (Livesley, 1995, 2001; Widiger, 2005). As noted earlier, the personality traits classified on Axis II are dimensional in nature. For example, everyone is suspicious at times, but the degree to which this trait exists in someone with paranoid personality disorder is extreme. A dimensional system would diminish such problems because people are rated on the degree to which they exhibit each facet and trait dimension—not on whether they do or do not have a given personality disorder.

In the past, many studies of personality disorder categories were conducted in an effort to find discrete breaks in such personality dimensions—that is, points at which normal behavior becomes clearly distinct from pathological behavior—and none were found (Livesley, 2001; Widiger & Sanderson, 1995). Moreover, changes in the cut-points, or thresholds for diagnosis of a personality disorder, can have drastic and unacceptable effects on the apparent prevalence rates of a particular personality disorder diagnosis (Widiger & Trull, 2007). For instance, when the *DSM-III* was revised to the *DSM-III-R*, it was noted that the rate of schizoid personality disorder increased by 800 percent and narcissistic personality disorder by 350 percent (Morey, 1988).

A third problem inherent in the Axis II categorical classification system is that there are enormous differences in the kinds of symptoms that people with the same diagnosis can have (e.g., Clark, 1992; Kamphius & Noordhof, 2009; Widiger & Trull, 2007). For example, to obtain a *DSM-IV-TR* diagnosis of borderline personality disorder, a person has to meet five out of nine possible symptom criteria, a threshold with essentially no empirical support (Kamphius & Noordhof, 2009). This means that there are 256 different ways (through different combinations of symptoms) to meet the *DSM-IV-TR* criteria for borderline personality disorder (Johansen et al., 2004). Moreover, two people with the same diagnosis might share only one symptom. For example, one person might meet criteria 1–5, and a second person might meet criteria 5–9. By contrast, a third individual who meets only criteria 1–4 would obtain no borderline personality diagnosis at all, yet surely that individual would be more similar to the first person than the first two people would be to each other. This heterogeneity poses a major problem for researchers trying to understand the causes and best treatments for these disorders. With a dimensional system, many of these problems would be circumvented because each individual would be rated on numerous dimensions, and these differences would thus be expected rather than problematic.

In spite of all these problems with the Axis II categorical classification system, researchers and clinicians usually agree that the developers of *DSM-III* made a crucial theoretical leap when they recognized the importance of weighing premorbid personality factors in the clinical picture and thus developed the second axis (e.g., L. A. Clark, 2005, 2007; Widiger, 2001). Use of the Axis II concepts can lead to a better understanding of a case, particularly with regard to treatment outcomes. Strongly ingrained personality characteristics can work against treatment interventions, but the use of Axis II can help a clinician attend to these long-standing and difficult-to-change personality factors in planning treatment.

Over the past few years, there has been lively debate among psychologists and psychiatrists over the best way to design a more dimensional system in the *DSM-5* (Clark, 2007; Livesley, 2011; Skodol et al., 2011). Although it has long been clear that a more dimensional system is needed, actually implementing this has proven challenging, and there are many opportunities for disagreement. A major challenge has been creating a scientifically valid diagnostic system that is not overly complicated and does not render the substantial research on existing categories useless. For example, in February 2010, the Personality and Personality Disorders Work Group of the *DSM-5* proposed a dimensional rating system combined with a set of narrative prototypes, in which clinicians would rate how well a particular patient matched a prototypical description of the disorders. However, some researchers—particularly those working on borderline personality disorder—felt that this would undermine the great deal of research that has been conducted on existing categories. Consequently, 26 of the top researchers signed a petition to the APA raising their strong objections, and the narrative prototype approach was abandoned (APA, 2011).

At the time of writing (September, 2011), the proposed revisions reflect a *hybrid dimensional–categorical* model for personality disorders consisting of both categorical components and dimensional components (see http://www.dsm5.org for the current status). This model includes a set of general criteria for personality disorders, an overall dimensional measure of the severity of personality dysfunction, a limited set of personality disorder types, and a set of pathological personality traits that can be specified in the absence of one of the personality disorder types. The categorical component retains 6 of the original 10 specific personality disorder types (antisocial, avoidant, borderline, narcissistic, obsessive-compulsive, and schizotypal).

However, the greatest departure lies in the incorporation of dimensional components. The new personality domain is intended to describe personality characteristics of *all* patients, even those without a specific personality disorder. Current proposals allow clinicians to rate the level of impairment in personality functioning, reflecting aspects of both identity (having a stable and coherent sense of self and the ability to pursue meaningful life goals) and interpersonal functioning (the capacity for empathy and intimacy). In addition, diagnosticians can indicate the degree to which the patient shows substantial abnormality on five trait domains (negative affectivity, detachment, antagonism, disinhibition, and psychoticism), which are based primarily on the five-factor trait model discussed in this chapter.

The complexity of the proposed model speaks to the difficulty of creating a valid yet utilitarian diagnostic system that satisfies the different needs of clinicians and researchers. But it is important to keep in mind that, ultimately, researchers do not see the *DSM-5* as the final word in classification (Krueger & Eaton, 2010; Krueger, Eaton, Clark et al., 2011; Livesley, 2011). Instead, the revision is intended to serve the same role as prior versions of the *DSM*—a stepping stone that can foster greater clarity and facilitate the further development of an empirical classification system for psychopathology.

Summary

- Personality disorders appear to be rather inflexible and distorted behavioral patterns and traits that result in maladaptive ways of perceiving, thinking about, and relating to other people and the environment.

- Even with structured interviews, the reliability of diagnosing personality disorders typically is less than ideal. Most researchers today agree that a dimensional approach for assessing personality disorders would be preferable.

- It is difficult to determine the causes of personality disorders as categories because most people with one personality disorder also have at least one more and because most studies to date are retrospective.

- Three general clusters of personality disorders have been described in *DSM*, although research has increasingly questioned the validity of these clusters.

- Cluster A includes paranoid, schizoid, and schizotypal personality disorders; individuals with these disorders seem odd or eccentric. Little is known about the causes of paranoid and schizoid disorders, but genetic and other biological factors are implicated in schizotypal personality disorder.

- Cluster B includes histrionic, narcissistic, antisocial, and borderline personality disorders; individuals with these disorders share a tendency to be dramatic, emotional, and erratic. Little is known about the causes of histrionic and narcissistic disorders. Certain biological and psychosocial causal factors have been identified as increasing the likelihood of developing borderline personality disorder in those at risk because of high levels of impulsivity and affective instability.

- Cluster C includes avoidant, dependent, and obsessive-compulsive personality disorders; individuals with these disorders show fearfulness or tension, as in anxiety-based disorders. Children with an inhibited temperament may be at heightened risk for avoidant personality disorder, and individuals high on neuroticism and agreeableness, with authoritarian and overprotective parents, may be at heightened risk for dependent personality disorder.

- There is relatively little research on treatments for most personality disorders.

- Treatment of the Cluster C disorders seems most promising, and treatment of Cluster A disorders is most difficult.

- A new form of behavior therapy (dialectical behavior therapy) shows considerable promise for treating borderline personality disorder, which is in Cluster B.

- A person with psychopathy shows elevated levels of two different dimensions of traits: (1) an affective–interpersonal set of traits reflecting lack of remorse or guilt, callousness/lack of empathy, glibness/superficial charm, grandiose sense of self-worth, and pathological lying; and (2) antisocial, impulsive, and socially deviant behavior, irresponsibility, and parasitic lifestyle. A person diagnosed with ASPD is primarily characterized by traits from the second dimension of psychopathy.

- Genetic and temperamental, learning, and adverse environmental factors seem to be important in causing psychopathy and ASPD.

- Psychopaths also show deficiencies in fear and anxiety as well as more general emotional deficits.

- Treatment of individuals with ASPD psychopathy is difficult, partly because they rarely see any need to change and tend to blame other people for their problems.

Key Terms

antisocial personality disorder (ASPD)
avoidant personality disorder
borderline personality disorder (BPD)
dependent personality disorder
dialectical behavior therapy

histrionic personality disorder
narcissistic personality disorder
obsessive-compulsive personality disorder (OCPD)
paranoid personality disorder

personality disorder
psychopathy
schizoid personality disorder
schizotypal personality disorder

Glossary

Many of the key terms listed in the glossary appear in boldface when first introduced in the text discussion. A number of other terms commonly encountered in this or other psychology texts are also included; you are encouraged to make use of this glossary both as a general reference tool and as a study aid for the course in abnormal psychology.

Antisocial personality disorder (ASPD). Disorder characterized by continual violation of and disregard for the rights of others through deceitful, aggressive, or antisocial behavior, typically without remorse or loyalty to anyone.

Avoidant personality disorder. Extreme social inhibition and introversion, hypersensitivity to criticism and rejection, limited social relationships, and low self-esteem.

Borderline personality disorder (BPD). Impulsivity and instability in interpersonal relationships, self-image, and moods.

Dependent personality disorder. Extreme dependence on others, particularly the need to be taken care of, leading to clinging and submissive behavior.

Dialectical behavior therapy. A unique kind of cognitive and behavioral therapy specifically adapted for treating borderline personality disorder.

Histrionic personality disorder. Excessive attention seeking, emotional instability, and self-dramatization.

Narcissistic personality disorder. Exaggerated sense of self-importance, preoccupation with being admired, and lack of empathy for the feelings of others.

Obsessive-compulsive personality disorder (OCPD). Perfectionism and excessive concern with maintaining order, control, and adherence to rules.

Paranoid personality disorder. Pervasive suspiciousness and distrust of others.

Personality disorder. Gradual development of inflexible and distorted personality and behavioral patterns that result in persistently maladaptive ways of perceiving, thinking about, and relating to the world.

Psychopathy. A condition involving the features of antisocial personality disorder and such traits as lack of empathy, inflated and arrogant self-appraisal, and glib and superficial charm.

Schizoid personality disorder. Inability to form social relationships or express feelings and lack of interest in doing so.

Schizotypal personality disorder. Excessive introversion, pervasive social interpersonal deficits, cognitive and perceptual distortions, and eccentricities in communication and behavior.

Photo Credits

Text Credits

Credits are listed in order of appearance.

Substance-Related Disorders

From Chapter 11 of *Abnormal Psychology*, Fifteenth Edition. James N. Butcher, Susan Mineka, Jill M. Hooley. Copyright © 2013 by Pearson Education, Inc. All rights reserved.

Substance-Related Disorders

Alcohol Abuse and Dependence
The Prevalence, Comorbidity, and Demographics of Alcohol Abuse
 and Dependence
The Clinical Picture of Alcohol Abuse and Dependence
Biological Causal Factors in the Abuse of and Dependence on Alcohol
Psychosocial Causal Factors in Alcohol Abuse and Dependence
Sociocultural Causal Factors
Treatment of Alcohol-Related Disorders

Drug Abuse and Dependence
Opium and Its Derivatives (Narcotics)
Cocaine and Amphetamines (Stimulants)

Methamphetamine
Barbiturates (Sedatives)
Hallucinogens: LSD and Related Drugs
Ecstasy
Marijuana
Stimulants: Caffeine and Nicotine

Unresolved Issues
Exchanging Addictions: Is This an Effective Treatment Approach?

Remarkable Recoveries from Life-Threatening Substance Abuse

Lyle Prouse was born in Wichita, Kansas in 1938 of American Indian heritage. As a child he was very interested in aviation and won his first airplane ride by writing an essay for Beechcraft Aircraft Company. Prouse, who grew up in the Indian community in Wichita, had a serious, long-term substance abuse problem, as did his parents, both of whom died from alcohol abuse. Many of his friends and associates were heavy alcohol abusers. After he finished high school he joined the U.S. Marines, became a pilot, and served in the Vietnam War. He was awarded several air medals for his service in Vietnam. He left the military and obtained a flying position at Northwest Airlines, where he attained the rank of captain and worked for 22 years, flying Boeing 727 passenger aircraft.

In 1990, Captain Prouse and his flight crew enjoyed a night of heavy drinking while on a layover in Fargo, North Dakota. Prouse consumed a number of rum-and-Diet-Cokes, and his crew drank several pitchers of beer and apparently were very loud and belligerent. Although his crew left the bar earlier, Prouse remained longer and continued drinking. During their drinking binge the flight crew angered a customer in the pub, who later called the FAA, warning them against the problem drinking of the crew. The next morning the Northwest crew continued their flight to Minneapolis and were arrested and given substance use tests. They showed high levels of alcohol in their bloodstreams and were charged with violating a federal law, which included prison time as a result of operating a public transportation carrier under the influence of drugs or alcohol. Captain Prouse and his crewmembers served 12 months of the 16-month sentence they received. All three pilots lost their jobs and their pilot's licenses as a result of the substance use violations.

Captain Prouse felt a great deal of depression and shame at the problems that he created for himself and others following the loss of the aviation career that he loved. He also experienced a great deal of financial problems from his employment termination. On several occasions he contemplated committing suicide. Captain Prouse entered inpatient substance abuse treatment not long after the incident.

After completing his recovery in an inpatient substance abuse treatment center, Prouse began a long and difficult process of rehabilitation and effort to restore his life without using alcohol. He made many public speeches describing his substance abuse and later wrote a book detailing what he had gone through (Prouse, 2001). Throughout his recovery he was determined to regain his flying status. It was necessary for him to retrain and retake all of the FAA licensing examinations in order to have his qualifications restored because he was required to requalify for every one of his licenses and ratings.

Captain Prouse was assisted in his recovery by a number of people who were impressed by his public disclosure of wrong-doing and his high motivation to recover from his substance abuse. After he appealed to the court to allow him the opportunity to obtain recertification, the court waived the legal restrictions that had been placed upon him at the trial. A friend of his who owned a trainer aircraft allowed him to earn the necessary flying time needed to be relicensed as a pilot. The CEO of Northwest Airlines, John Dasburg, who himself had grown up in a family with alcoholic abuse problems, took personal interest in Prouse's struggle and encouraged his return to duty. He returned to flying with Northwest Airlines. Captain Prouse's efforts and success at rehabilitation were indeed impressive. In 2001 he was granted a presidential pardon by President Clinton.

Interestingly, another one of the pilots on the Northwest "drunk pilots" flight, flight engineer Joe Balzer, who also spent 12 months in federal prison, also rehabilitated himself. He became involved with Alcoholics Anonymous and, over time, requalified for the aviation certification, eventually returning to the cockpit as a pilot for American Airlines (see his autobiographical account in Balzer, 2009).

The extensive problem of substance abuse and substance dependence in our society has drawn both public and scientific attention. Although our present knowledge is far from complete, investigating these problems as maladaptive patterns of adjustment to life's demands, with no social stigma involved, has led to clear progress in understanding and treatment. Such an approach, of course, does not mean that an individual bears no personal responsibility in the development of a problem. On the contrary, individual lifestyles and personality features are thought by many to play important roles in the development of substance-related disorders and are central themes in some types of treatment.

Substance-related disorders can be seen all around us: in extremely high rates of alcohol abuse and dependence, and in tragic exposés of cocaine abuse among star athletes and entertainers. **Addictive behavior**—behavior based on the pathological need for a substance—may involve the abuse of substances such as nicotine, alcohol, Ecstasy, or cocaine.

Addictive behavior is one of the most prevalent and difficult-to-treat mental health problems facing our society today.

The most commonly used problem substances are those that affect mental functioning in the central nervous system—**psychoactive substances**: alcohol, nicotine, barbiturates, tranquilizers, amphetamines, heroin, Ecstasy, and marijuana. Some of these substances, such as alcohol and nicotine, can be purchased legally by adults; others, such as barbiturates or pain medications like OxyContin (or marijuana in some states), can be used legally under medical supervision; still others, such as heroin, Ecstasy, and methamphetamine, are illegal.

For diagnostic purposes, addictive or substance-related disorders are divided into two major categories.

1. The first category includes those conditions that involve organic impairment resulting from the prolonged and excessive ingestion of psychoactive substances—for

example, an alcohol-abuse dementia disorder involving amnesia, formerly known as Korsakoff's syndrome.

2. The other category includes substance-induced organic mental disorders and syndromes (the latter of which are within the organic mental disorders). These conditions stem from **toxicity**, the poisonous nature of the substance (leading to, for example, amphetamine delusional disorder, alcoholic intoxication, or cannabis delirium), or physiological changes in the brain due to vitamin deficiency.

The majority of substance-related disorders fall into the second category, which focuses on the maladaptive behaviors resulting from regular and consistent use of a substance and includes *substance-abuse disorders* and *substance-dependence disorders*. The system of classification for substance-related disorders that is followed by both *DSM-IV-TR* and ICD-10 (International Classification of Disease System, published by the World Health Organization) provides two major categories: substance-abuse and substance-dependence disorders. Although some researchers and clinicians disagree with the dichotomous grouping, others consider this classification approach to have both research and clinical utility (Epstein, 2001). The following distinctions are important to understanding and diagnosing substance-related disorders:

- **Substance abuse** generally involves an excessive use of a substance resulting in (1) potentially hazardous behavior such as driving while intoxicated or (2) continued use despite a persistent social, psychological, occupational, or health problem. See the *DSM-IV-TR* box Criteria for Substance-Abuse Disorders and Substance Dependence.

- **Substance dependence** includes more severe forms of substance-use disorders and usually involves a marked physiological need for increasing amounts of a substance to achieve the desired effects. Dependence in these disorders means that an individual will show a tolerance for a drug and/or experience withdrawal symptoms when the drug is unavailable.

- **Tolerance**—the need for increased amounts of a substance to achieve the desired effects—results from biochemical changes in the body that affect the rate of metabolism and elimination of the substance from the body.

- **Withdrawal** refers to physical symptoms such as sweating, tremors, and tension that accompany abstinence from the drug.

Alcohol Abuse and Dependence

The terms **alcoholic** and **alcoholism** have been subject to some controversy and have been used differently by various groups in the past. The World Health Organization no longer recommends the term *alcoholism* but prefers the term *alcohol dependence syndrome*—"a state, psychic and usually also physical, resulting from taking alcohol, characterized by behavioral and other responses that always include a compulsion to take alcohol on a continuous or periodic basis in order to experience its psychic effects, and sometimes to avoid the discomfort of its absence; tolerance may or may not be present" (1992, p. 4). However, because the terms *alcoholic* and *alcoholism* are still widely used in practice, in scientific journals, and in government agencies and publications, we will sometimes use them in this text.

People of many ancient cultures, including the Egyptians, Greeks, Romans, and Israelites, made extensive and often excessive use of alcohol. Beer was first made in Egypt around 3000 B.C. The oldest surviving wine-making formulas were recorded by Marcus Cato in Italy almost a century and a half before the birth of Christ. About A.D. 800, the process of distillation was developed by an Arabian alchemist, thus making possible an increase in both the range and the potency of alcoholic beverages. Problems with excessive use of alcohol were observed almost as early as its use began. Cambyses, King of Persia in the sixth century B.C., has the dubious distinction of being one of the early alcohol abusers on record.

The Prevalence, Comorbidity, and Demographics of Alcohol Abuse and Dependence

Alcohol abuse and alcohol dependence are major problems in the United States and are among the most destructive of the psychiatric disorders because of the impact excessive alcohol use can have upon users' lives and those of their families and friends. It is estimated that 50 percent of adults who are 18 or older are current regular drinkers and only 21 percent are lifetime abstainers (Pleis et al., 2009). In 2008, 23.3 percent of Americans aged 12 or older reported binge drinking, and 6.7 percent were found to be heavy drinkers (Substance Abuse and Mental Health Services Administration, 2010). An estimated 12.4 percent of persons 12 or older drove under the influence of alcohol at least once over the past year. An estimated 22.2 million persons (8.9 percent of the population aged 12 or older) were classified with substance dependence

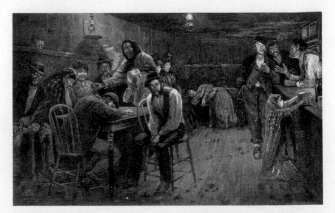

The picture shows an 1891 Stale Beer Dive on Mulberry Street Bend, New York with several drunk people from the neighborhood and includes beers being served by a young girl (Campbell et al., 1892).

DSM-IV-TR

Criteria for Substance-Abuse

A. A maladaptive pattern of substance use leading to clinically significant impairment or distress, as manifested by one (or more) of the following, occurring within a 12-month period:

1. recurrent substance use resulting in a failure to fulfill major role obligations at work, school, or home (e.g., repeated absences or poor work performance related to substance use; substance-related absences, suspensions, or expulsions from school; neglect of children or household)

2. recurrent substance use in situations in which it is physically hazardous (e.g., driving an automobile or operating a machine when impaired by substance use)

3. recurrent substance-related legal problems (e.g., arrests for substance-related disorderly conduct)

4. continued substance use despite having persistent or recurrent social or interpersonal problems caused or exacerbated by the effects of the substance (e.g., arguments with spouse about consequences of intoxication, physical fights)

B. The symptoms have never met the criteria for Substance Dependence for this class of substance.

Source: Reprinted with permission from the American Psychiatric Association. *Diagnostic and Statistical Manual of Mental Disorders*, Fourth Edition, *Text Revision* (Copyright © 2000). American Psychiatric Association.

DSM-IV-TR

Criteria for Substance-Dependence

A maladaptive pattern of substance use, leading to clinically significant impairment or distress, as manifested by three (or more) of the following, occurring at any time in the same 12-month period:

1. tolerance, as defined by either of the following:
   (a) a need for markedly increased amounts of the substance to achieve Intoxication or desired effect
   (b) markedly diminished effect with continued use of the same amount of the substance

2. Withdrawal, as manifested by either of the following:
   (a) the characteristic withdrawal syndrome for the substance (refer to Criteria A and B of the criteria sets for Withdrawal from the specific substances)
   (b) the same (or a closely related) substance is taken to relieve or avoid withdrawal symptoms

3. the substance is often taken in larger amounts or over a longer period than was intended

4. there is a persistent desire or unsuccessful efforts to cut down or control substance use

5. a great deal of time is spent in activities necessary to obtain the substance (e.g., visiting multiple doctors or driving long distances), use the substance (e.g., chainsmoking), or recover from its effects

6. important social, occupational, or recreational activities are given up or reduced because of substance use

7. the substance use is continued despite knowledge of having a persistent or recurrent physical or psychological problem that is likely to have been caused or exacerbated by the substance (e.g., current cocaine use despite recognition of cocaine-induced depression, or continued drinking despite recognition that an ulcer was made worse by alcohol consumption)

Source: Reprinted with permission from the American Psychiatric Association. *Diagnostic and Statistical Manual of Mental Disorders*, Fourth Edition, *Text Revision* (Copyright © 2000). American Psychiatric Association.

or abuse in the past year based on *DSM* diagnostic criteria. In this sample, 3.1 million people were classified with dependence on or abuse of both alcohol and illicit drugs, 3.9 million were dependent on or abused illicit drugs but not alcohol, and 15.2 million were dependent on or abused alcohol but not illicit drugs (Substance Abuse and Mental Health Services Administration, 2009).

The potentially detrimental effects of excessive alcohol use—for an individual, his or her loved ones, and society—are legion. Heavy drinking is associated with vulnerability to injury (Cherpitel et al., 1997), marital discord (Hornish & Leonard, 2007), and becoming involved in intimate partner violence (Eckhardt, 2007). The life span of the average person with alcohol dependence is about 12 years shorter than that of the average person without this disorder. Alcohol significantly lowers performance on cognitive tasks such as problem solving—and the more complex the task, the more the impairment (Pickworth et al., 1997). Organic impairment, including brain shrinkage, occurs in a high proportion of people with alcohol dependence (Gazdzinski et al., 2005), especially among binge drinkers—people who abuse alcohol following periods of sobriety (Hunt, 1993).

One study reported that of the 1.3 million emergency room visits associated with drug misuse or abuse in 2007, 7 percent involved alcohol abuse in patients under age 21 (USDHHS, 2010). Cherpitel and colleagues (2006) explored the association of alcohol use and emergency room (ER) services among injured patients in several countries. Of 9,743 injured patients surveyed in 37 ERs in 14 countries, drinking within 6 hours before injury was associated with prior visits to the ER during the last 12 months. People who were heavy drinkers or were alcohol dependent were significantly more likely to report multiple prior emergency room visits.

Alcohol is associated with over 40 percent of deaths and serious injuries suffered in automobile accidents in the United States each year (see Chou et al., 2006).

Alcohol abuse is associated with over 40 percent of the deaths suffered in automobile accidents each year (Chou et al., 2006) and with about 40 to 50 percent of all murders (Bennett & Lehman, 1996), 40 percent of all assaults, and over 50 percent of all rapes (Abbey et al., 2001). About one of every three arrests in the United States is related to alcohol abuse, and over 43 percent of violent encounters with the police involve alcohol (McClelland & Teplin, 2001). In research on substance abuse and violent crime, Dawkins (1997) found that alcohol is more frequently associated with both violent and nonviolent crime than drugs such as marijuana and that people with violence-related injuries are more likely to have a positive Breathalyzer test (Cherpitel, 1997). Of the 1 million violent crimes that were suspected to be alcohol related in 2002, 30 percent of them were determined to involve alcohol use on the part of the offender. Two-thirds of cases in which victims suffered violence from an intimate (a current or former spouse) were alcohol related (U.S. Department of Justice, 2006).

Alcohol abuse and alcohol dependence in the United States cut across all age, educational, occupational, and socio-economic boundaries. Alcohol abuse is found in priests, politicians, surgeons, law enforcement officers, and teenagers; the image of the alcohol-abusing person as an unkempt resident of skid row is clearly inaccurate. Alcohol abuse is considered a serious problem in industry, in the professions, and in the military as well. Recent research has shown that alcohol abuse has a strong presence in the workplace, with 15 percent of employees showing problem behaviors; many (1.68 percent, or 2.1 million people) actually drinking on the job; and 1.83 percent, or 2.3 million workers, drinking before they go to work (Frone, 2006). Some myths about alcoholism are noted in Table 1.

In the past, most problem drinkers—people experiencing life problems as a result of alcohol abuse—were men; for example, men become problem drinkers at about five times the frequency of women (Helzer et al., 1990). Recent epidemiological research has suggested that the traditional gap between men and women has narrowed when it comes to the development of substance abuse disorders (Greenfield et al., 2010). There do not seem to be important differences in rates of alcohol abuse between black and white Americans, although Native Americans tend to have higher rates of alcohol abuse, and Asian Americans tend to have lower usage. It appears that problem drinking may develop during any life period from early childhood through old age. About 10 percent of men over age 65 are found to be heavy drinkers (Breslow et al., 2003). Surveys of alcoholism rates across different cultural groups around the world have found varying rates of the disorder across diverse cultural samples (Caetano et al., 1998; Hibell et al., 2000).

Over 37 percent of alcohol abusers suffer from at least one coexisting mental disorder (Lapham et al., 2001). Not surprisingly, given that alcohol is a depressant, depression ranks high among the mental disorders often comorbid with alcoholism. There is a high comorbidity of substance abuse disorders and eating disorders (Harrop & Marlatt, 2009). It is also no surprise that many alcoholics commit suicide (McCloud et al., 2004). In addition to the serious problems that excessive drinkers create for themselves, they also pose serious difficulties for others (Gortner et al., 1997). Alcohol abuse also co-occurs with high frequency with personality disorder. Grant and colleagues (2004) report that among individuals with a current alcohol-use disorder, 28.6 percent have at least one personality disorder.

The Clinical Picture of Alcohol Abuse and Dependence

A great deal of progress has been made in understanding the physiological effects of alcohol on the brain. The first is a tendency toward decreased sexual inhibition but, simultaneously, lowered sexual performance. An appreciable number of alcohol abusers also experience blackouts—lapses of memory. At first these occur at high blood alcohol levels, and a drinker may carry on a rational conversation or engage in other relatively complex activities but have no trace of recall the next day. For heavy drinkers, even moderate drinking can elicit memory lapses. Another phenomenon associated with alcoholic intoxication (intoxication is defined as a state of being affected by one or more psychoactive drugs) is the hangover, which many drinkers experience at one time or another. As yet, no one has come up with a satisfactory explanation of or remedy for the symptoms of headache, nausea, and fatigue that are characteristic of the hangover.

Exessive use of alcohol can produce unexpected and often dramatic changes in behavior. The young men shown here illustrate the behavior that can occur following alcohol abuse.

table 1 Some Common Misconceptions About Alcohol and Alcohol Abuse

Fiction	Fact
Alcohol is a stimulant.	Alcohol is actually both a nervous system stimulant and a depressant.
You can always detect alcohol on the breath of a person who has been drinking.	It is not always possible to detect the presence of alcohol. Some individuals successfully cover up their alcohol use for years.
One ounce of 86-proof liquor contains more alcohol than two 12-ounce cans of beer.	Two 12-ounce cans of beer contain more than an ounce of alcohol.
Alcohol can help a person sleep more soundly.	Alcohol may interfere with sound sleep.
Impaired judgment does not occur before there are obvious signs of intoxication.	Impaired judgment can occur long before motor signs of intoxication are apparent.
An individual will get more intoxicated by mixing liquors than by taking comparable amounts of one kind—e.g., bourbon, Scotch, or vodka.	It is the actual amount of alcohol in the bloodstream rather than the mix that determines intoxication.
Drinking several cups of coffee can counteract the effects of alcohol and enable a drinker to "sober up."	Drinking coffee does not affect the level of intoxication.
Exercise or a cold shower helps speed up the metabolism of alcohol.	Exercise and cold showers are futile attempts to increase alcohol metabolism.
People with "strong wills" need not be concerned about becoming substance abusers.	Alcohol is seductive and can lower the resistance of even the "strongest will."
Alcohol cannot produce a true addiction in the same sense that heroin can.	Alcohol has strong addictive properties.
One cannot become a substance abuser by drinking just beer.	One can consume a considerable amount of alcohol by drinking beer. It is, of course, the amount of alcohol that determines whether one becomes a substance abuser.
Alcohol is far less dangerous than marijuana.	There are considerably more individuals in treatment programs for alcohol problems than for marijuana abuse.
In a heavy drinker, damage to the liver shows up long before brain damage appears.	Heavy alcohol use can be manifested in organic brain damage before liver damage is detected.
The physiological withdrawal reaction from heroin is considered more dangerous than is withdrawal from alcohol.	The physiological symptoms accompanying withdrawal from heroin are no more frightening or traumatic to an individual than alcohol withdrawal. Actually, alcohol withdrawal is potentially more lethal than opiate withdrawal.
Everybody drinks.	Actually, 28 percent of men and 50 percent of women in the United States are abstainers.

ALCOHOL'S EFFECTS ON THE BRAIN Alcohol has complex and seemingly contradictory effects on the brain. At lower levels, alcohol stimulates certain brain cells and activates the brain's "pleasure areas," which release opium-like endogenous opioids that are stored in the body (Braun, 1996). At higher levels, alcohol depresses brain functioning, inhibiting one of the brain's excitatory neurotransmitters, glutamate, which in turn slows down activity in parts of the brain (Koob et al., 2002). Inhibition of glutamate in the brain impairs the organism's ability to learn and affects the higher brain centers, impairing judgment and other rational processes and lowering self-control. As behavioral restraints decline, a drinker may indulge in the satisfaction of impulses ordinarily held in check. Some degree of motor uncoordination soon becomes apparent, and the drinker's discrimination and perception of cold, pain, and other discomforts are dulled. Typically the drinker experiences a sense of warmth, expansiveness, and well-being. In such a mood, unpleasant realities are screened out and the drinker's feelings of self-esteem and adequacy rise. Casual acquaintances become the best and most understanding of friends, and the drinker enters a generally pleasant world of unreality in which worries are temporarily left behind.

In most U.S. states, when the alcohol content of the bloodstream reaches 0.08 percent, the individual is considered intoxicated, at least with respect to driving a vehicle. Muscular coordination, speech, and vision are impaired and thought processes are confused. Even before this level of intoxication is reached, however, judgment becomes impaired to such an extent that the person misjudges his or her condition. For example, drinkers tend to express confidence in their ability to drive safely long after such actions are in fact quite unsafe. When the blood alcohol level reaches

449

approximately 0.5 percent (the level differs somewhat among individuals), the entire neural balance is upset and the individual passes out. Unconsciousness apparently acts as a safety device because concentrations above 0.55 percent are usually lethal.

In general, it is the amount of alcohol actually concentrated in the bodily fluids, not the amount consumed, that determines intoxication. The effects of alcohol vary for different drinkers, depending on their physical condition, the amount of food in their stomach, and the duration of their drinking. In addition, alcohol users may gradually build up a tolerance for the drug so that ever-increasing amounts may be needed to produce the desired effects. Women metabolize alcohol less effectively than men and thus become intoxicated on lesser amounts (Gordis et al., 1995).

DEVELOPMENT OF ALCOHOL DEPENDENCE Excessive drinking can be viewed as progressing insidiously from early- to middle- to late-stage alcohol-related disorder, although some abusers do not follow this pattern. Many investigators have maintained that alcohol is a dangerous systemic poison even in small amounts, but others believe that in moderate amounts it is not harmful to most people. For pregnant women, however, even moderate amounts are believed to be dangerous; in fact, no safe level has been established, as is discussed in Developments in Research 1. The photos show the differences between the brain of a normal teenager and those born with *fetal alcohol syndrome* (FAS), a condition that is caused by excessive alcohol consumption during pregnancy and results in birth defects such as mental retardation.

1 DEVELOPMENTS IN RESEARCH

Fetal Alcohol Syndrome: How Much Drinking Is Too Much?

Research indicates that heavy drinking by expectant mothers can affect the health of unborn babies, particularly binge drinking and heavy drinking during the early days of pregnancy (Burd & Christensen, 2009; Calhoun & Warren, 2007)—a condition known as *fetal alcohol syndrome*. Newborn infants whose mothers drank heavily during pregnancy have been found to have frequent physical and behavioral abnormalities (Alison, 1994), including aggressiveness and destructiveness (Gardner, 2000), and may experience symptoms of withdrawal (Thomas & Riley, 1998). For example, such infants have shown growth deficiencies, facial and limb irregularities, damage to the central nervous system, and impairment in cognitive functioning (Kodituwakku et al., 2001). Neuroimaging research has shown that there is an overall reduction of brain size and prominent brain shape abnormalities, with narrowing in the parietal region along with reduced brain growth in portions of the frontal lobe (Spadoni et al., 2007). Moreover, children with fetal alcohol syndrome often show significant working memory deficits and altered activations patterns in some brain regions (Astley et al., 2009).

As noted in *The Third Report on Alcohol and Health* (HEW, 1978), alcohol abuse in pregnant women is the third-leading cause of birth defects—the first two being Down syndrome and spina bifida (the incomplete formation and fusion of the spinal canal). Although data on fetal alcohol syndrome are often difficult to obtain, the prevalence has been estimated at between 0.5 and 2 cases per 1,000 births (May & Gossage, 2001).

How much drinking endangers a newborn's health? The HEW report warns against drinking more than 1 ounce of alcohol per day (one 12-ounce can of beer or one 5-ounce glass of wine, for ex-

The effects of fetal alcohol syndrome can be both dramatic and long-lasting. This young child who had been diagnosed with fetal alcohol syndrome shows some of the permanent physical abnormalities characteristic of the syndrome.

ample). The actual amount of alcohol that can safely be ingested during pregnancy is not known, but existing evidence for fetal alcohol syndrome is strongest when applied to binge drinkers or heavy alcohol users rather than to light or moderate users (Kolata, 1981). Nonetheless the surgeon general and many medical experts have concurred that pregnant women should abstain from using alcohol as the "safest course" until the safest amount of alcohol consumption can be determined (Raskin, 1993).

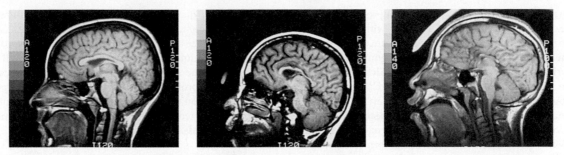

MRIs of three teenagers: (left) Normal control, 13-year-old female; (center) FAS, 13-year-old male with focal thinning of the corpus callosum; (right) FAS, 14-year-old male with complete agenesis (nondevelopment) of the corpus callosum.

THE PHYSICAL EFFECTS OF CHRONIC ALCOHOL USE

For individuals who drink to excess, the clinical picture is highly unfavorable (Turner et al., 2006). Alcohol that is taken in must be assimilated by the body, except for about the 5 to 10 percent that is eliminated through breath, urine, and perspiration. The work of alcohol metabolism is done by the liver, but when large amounts of alcohol are ingested, the liver may be seriously overworked and eventually suffer irreversible damage (Lucey et al., 2009). In fact, from 15 to 30 percent of heavy drinkers develop cirrhosis of the liver, a disorder that involves extensive stiffening of the blood vessels. About 40 to 90 percent of the 26,000 annual cirrhosis deaths every year are alcohol related (Parrish et al., 1991). Some countries, for example Britain and Scotland, have shown an increase in cirrhosis-related deaths in the last two decades because of the increased use of alcohol in their populations (Leon & McCambridge, 2006).

Alcohol is also a high-caloric drug. A pint of whiskey—enough to make about eight to ten ordinary cocktails—provides about 1,200 calories, which is approximately half the ordinary caloric requirement for a day (Flier et al., 1995). Thus consumption of alcohol reduces a drinker's appetite for other food. Because alcohol has no nutritional value, the excessive drinker can suffer from malnutrition (Derr & Gutmann, 1994). Furthermore, heavy drinking impairs the body's ability to utilize nutrients, so the nutritional deficiency cannot be made up by popping vitamins. Many alcohol abusers also experience increased gastrointestinal symptoms such as stomach pains (Fields et al., 1994).

PSYCHOSOCIAL EFFECTS OF ALCOHOL ABUSE AND DEPENDENCE

In addition to various physical problems, a heavy drinker usually suffers from chronic fatigue, oversensitivity, and depression. Initially, alcohol may seem to provide a useful crutch for dealing with the stresses of life, especially during periods of acute stress, by helping screen out intolerable realities and enhance the drinker's feelings of adequacy and worth. The excessive use of alcohol eventually becomes counterproductive, however, and can result in impaired reasoning, poor judgment, and gradual personality deterioration. Behavior typically becomes coarse and inappropriate, and the drinker assumes increasingly less responsibility, loses pride in personal appearance, neglects spouse and family, and becomes generally touchy, irritable, and unwilling to discuss the problem.

As judgment becomes impaired, an excessive drinker may be unable to hold a job and generally becomes unqualified to cope with new demands that arise (Frone, 2003). General personality disorganization and deterioration may be reflected in loss of employment and marital breakup. By this time, the drinker's general health is likely to have deteriorated, and brain and liver damage may have occurred. For example, there is some evidence that an alcoholic's brain is accumulating diffuse organic damage even when no extreme organic symptoms are present (Sullivan, Deshmukh et al., 2000), and even mild to moderate drinking can adversely affect memory and problem solving (Gordis, 2001). Other researchers have found extensive alcohol consumption to be associated with an increased amount of organic damage in later life (Lyvers, 2000), however, recent research using fMRI has shown that this damage is partially reversible if the person abstains from alcohol use (Wobrock et al., 2009).

PSYCHOSES ASSOCIATED WITH SEVERE ALCOHOL ABUSE

Excessive use of alcohol can result in severe mental health problems. Several acute psychotic reactions fit the diagnostic classification of substance-induced disorders. These reactions may develop in people who have been drinking excessively over long periods of time or who have a reduced tolerance for alcohol for other reasons—for example because of brain lesions from excessive long-term use. Such acute reactions usually last only a short time and generally consist of confusion, excitement, and delirium. There is some evidence that delirium may be associated with lower levels of thiamine in alcoholics (Holzbeck, 1996). These disorders are often called "alcoholic psychoses" because they are marked by a temporary loss of contact with reality.

Among those who drink excessively for a long time, a reaction called **alcohol withdrawal delirium** (formerly known as **delirium tremens**) may occur (Palmstierno, 2001).

This reaction usually happens following a prolonged drinking spree when the person enters a state of withdrawal. Slight noises or suddenly moving objects may cause considerable excitement and agitation. The full-blown symptoms include (1) disorientation for time and place, in which, for example, a person may mistake the hospital for a church or jail, no longer recognize friends, or identify hospital attendants as old acquaintances; (2) vivid hallucinations, particularly of small, fast-moving animals like snakes, rats, and roaches; (3) acute fear, in which these animals may change in form, size, or color in terrifying ways; (4) extreme suggestibility, in which a person can be made to see almost any animal if its presence is merely suggested; (5) marked tremors of the hands, tongue, and lips; and (6) other symptoms including perspiration, fever, a rapid and weak heartbeat, a coated tongue, and foul breath.

The delirium typically lasts from 3 to 6 days and is generally followed by a deep sleep. When a person awakens, few symptoms—except for possibly slight remorse—remain, but frequently the individual is badly scared and may not resume drinking for several weeks or months. Usually, however, drinking is eventually resumed, followed by a return to the hospital with a new attack. The death rate from withdrawal delirium as a result of convulsions, heart failure, and other complications once approximated 10 percent (Tavel, 1962). With drugs such as chlordiazepoxide, however, the current death rate during withdrawal delirium and acute alcoholic withdrawal has been markedly reduced.

A second alcohol-related psychosis is persisting alcohol disorder or alcohol amnestic disorder (formerly known as Korsakoff's syndrome). This condition was first described by the Russian psychiatrist Korsakoff in 1887 and is one of the most severe alcohol-related disorders (d'Ydewalle & Van Damme, 2007). The outstanding symptom is a memory defect (particularly with regard to recent events), which is sometimes accompanied by falsification of events (confabulation). Persons with this disorder may not recognize pictures, faces, rooms, and other objects that they have just seen, although they may feel that these people or objects are familiar. Such people increasingly tend to fill in their memory gaps with reminiscences and fanciful tales that lead to unconnected and distorted associations. These individuals may appear to be delirious, delusional, and disoriented for time and place, but ordinarily their confusion and disordered actions are closely related to their attempts to fill in memory gaps. The memory disturbance itself seems related to an inability to form new associations in a manner that renders them readily retrievable. Such a reaction usually occurs in long-time alcohol abusers after many years of excessive drinking. These patients have also been observed to show other cognitive impairments such as planning deficits (Brokate et al., 2003), intellectual decline, emotional deficits (Snitz et al., 2002), judgment deficits (Brand et al., 2003), and cortical lesions (Estruch et al., 1998).

The symptoms of alcohol amnestic disorder are now thought to be due to vitamin B (thiamine) deficiency and other dietary inadequacies. Although it had been believed that

a diet rich in vitamins and minerals generally restores such a patient to more normal physical and mental health, some research evidence suggests otherwise. Lishman (1990) reports that alcohol amnestic disorder did not respond well to thiamine replacement. Some memory functioning appears to be restored with prolonged abstinence. However, some personality deterioration usually remains in the form of memory impairment, blunted intellectual capacity, and lowered moral and ethical standards.

case study Alcohol Amnestic Disorder

Averill B. was brought into the detoxification unit of a local county hospital by the police after an incident at a crowded city park. He was arrested because of his assaultive behavior toward others (he was walking through the crowded groups of sunbathers muttering to himself, kicking at people). At admission to the hospital, Averill was disoriented (did not know where he was), incoherent, and confused. When asked his name, he paused a moment, scratched his head, and said, "George Washington." When asked about what he was doing at the park, he indicated that he was "marching in a parade in his honor."

Biological Causal Factors in the Abuse of and Dependence on Alcohol

In trying to identify the causes of problem drinking, some researchers have stressed the role of genetic and biochemical factors; others have pointed to psychosocial factors, viewing problem drinking as a maladaptive pattern of adjustment to the stress of life; and still others have emphasized sociocultural factors such as the availability of alcohol and social approval of excessive drinking. As we will see, some combination of all of these factors seems to influence risk for developing alcohol abuse or alcohol dependency. As with most other forms of maladaptive behavior, there may be several types of alcohol abuse and dependency, each with somewhat different patterns of biological, psychosocial, and sociocultural causal factors.

How do substances such as alcohol, cocaine, and opium (discussed later in the chapter) come to have such powerful effects—an overpowering hold that occurs in some people after only a few uses of the drug? Although the exact mechanisms are not fully agreed on by experts in the field, two important factors are apparently involved. The first is the ability of most, if not all, addictive substances to activate areas of the brain that produce intrinsic pleasure and sometimes immediate, powerful reward. The second factor involves the person's biological makeup, or constitution, including his or her genetic inheritance and the environmental influences (learning factors) that enter into the need to seek mind-altering substances to an increasing degree as use continues. The development of an alcohol addiction is a complex process involving many elements—constitutional vulnerability and environmental encouragement, as well as the unique biochemical properties of certain psychoactive substances. Let's examine each of these elements in more detail.

THE NEUROBIOLOGY OF ADDICTION Let's first examine the role that substances like alcohol play in the process of addiction. Psychoactive drugs differ in their biochemical properties as well as in how rapidly they enter the brain. There are several routes of administration—oral, nasal, and intravenous. Alcohol is usually drunk, the slowest route, whereas cocaine is often self-administered by injection or taken nasally. Central to the neurochemical process underlying addiction is the role the drug plays in activating the "pleasure pathway." The **mesocorticolimbic dopamine pathway (MCLP)** is the center of psychoactive drug activation in the brain. The MCLP is made up of neuronal cells in the middle portion of the brain known as the ventral tegmental area (see Figure 1) and connects to other brain centers such as the nucleus accumbens and then to the prefrontal cortex. This neuronal system is involved in such functions as control of emotions, memory, and gratification. Alcohol produces euphoria by stimulating this area in the brain. Research has shown that direct electrical stimulation of the MCLP produces great pleasure and has strong reinforcing properties (Littrell, 2001). Other psychoactive drugs also op-

erate to change the brain's normal functioning and to activate the pleasure pathway. Drug ingestion or behaviors that lead to activation of the brain reward system are reinforced, so further use is promoted. The exposure of the brain to an addictive drug alters its neurochemical structure and results in a number of behavioral effects. With continued use of the drug, neuroadaptation to or tolerance and dependence on the substance develop.

GENETIC VULNERABILITY The possibility of a genetic predisposition to developing alcohol-abuse problems has been widely researched. Many experts today agree that heredity probably plays an important role in a person's developing sensitivity to the addictive power of drugs like alcohol (Plomin & DeFries, 2003; Volk et al., 2007). Several lines of research point to the importance of genetic factors in substance-related disorders.

A review of 39 studies of the families of 6,251 alcoholics and of 4,083 nonalcoholics who had been followed over 40 years reported that almost one-third of alcoholics had at least one parent with an alcohol problem (Cotton, 1979). Likewise, a study of children of alcoholics by Cloninger and colleagues (1986) reported strong evidence for the inheritance of alcoholism. They found that for males, having one alcoholic parent increased the rate of alcoholism from 12.4 percent to 29.5 percent and having two alcoholic parents increased the rate to 41.2 percent. For females with no alcoholic parents, the rate was 5.0 percent; for those with one alcoholic parent, the rate was 9.5 percent; and for those with two alcoholic parents, it was 25.0 percent.

Alcohol abuse problems clearly tend to run in families (Hartz & Beirut, 2010; Hasin & Katz, 2010). Research has shown that some people, such as the sons of alcoholics, have a high risk for developing problems with alcohol because of an inherent motivation to drink or sensitivity to the drug (Conrod et al., 1998). Research on the children of alcoholics who were adopted by other (nonalcoholic) families has also provided useful information. Studies have been conducted of alcoholics' children who were placed for adoption early in life and so did not come under the environmental influences of their biological parents. For example, Goodwin and colleagues (1973) found that children of alcoholic parents who had been adopted by nonalcoholic foster parents were nearly twice as likely to have alcohol problems by their late 20s as a control group of adopted children whose biological parents were not alcoholics. In another study, Goodwin and colleagues (1974) compared alcoholic parents' sons who were adopted in infancy by nonalcoholic parents and sons raised by their alcoholic parents. Both adopted and nonadopted sons later evidenced high rates of alcoholism—25 percent and 17 percent, respectively. These investigators concluded that being born to an alcoholic parent, rather than being raised by one, increases the risk of a son's becoming an alcoholic.

Another approach to understanding the precursors to alcohol-related disorders is to study prealcoholic personalities—individuals who are at high risk for substance abuse but who

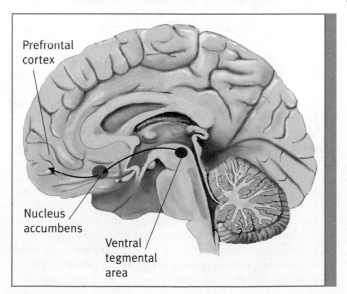

FIGURE 1

The Mesocorticolimbic Pathway

The mesocorticolimbic pathway (MCLP), running from the ventral tegmental area to the nucleus accumbens to the prefrontal cortex, is central to the release of the neurotransmitter dopamine and in mediating the rewarding properties of drugs.

Source: Office of Technology Assessment, 1993.

are not yet affected by alcohol. The heritability of personality characteristics has been widely explored (Bouchard & Loehlin, 2001). An alcohol-risk personality has been described as an individual (usually an alcoholic's child) who has an inherited predisposition toward alcohol abuse and who is impulsive, prefers taking high risks, and is emotionally unstable.

Research has shown that prealcoholic men (those who are genetically predisposed to developing drug or alcohol problems but who have not yet acquired the problem) show different physiological patterns than nonalcoholic men in several respects. Prealcoholic men tend to experience a greater lessening of feelings of stress with alcohol ingestion than do nonalcoholic men (Finn et al., 1997). Prealcoholic men also show different alpha wave patterns on EEGs (Stewart et al., 1990) and have been found to have larger conditioned physiological responses to alcohol cues than individuals who were considered at a low risk for alcoholism, according to Earleywine and Finn (1990). These results suggest that prealcoholic men may be more prone to developing tolerance for alcohol than low-risk men.

Some research suggests that certain ethnic groups, particularly Asians and Native Americans, have abnormal physiological reactions to alcohol—a phenomenon referred to as "alcohol flush reaction." Fenna and colleagues (1971) and Wolff (1972) found that Asian and Eskimo subjects showed a hypersensitive reaction including flushing of the skin, a drop in blood pressure, heart palpitations, and nausea following the ingestion of alcohol (see also Gill et al., 1999). This physiological reaction is found in roughly half of all Asians (Chen & Yeh, 1997) and results from a mutant enzyme that fails to break down alcohol molecules in the liver during the metabolic process (Takeshita et al., 1993). Although cultural factors may also play a role, the relatively lower rates of alcoholism among Asian groups might be related to the extreme discomfort associated with the alcohol flush reaction (Higuci et al., 1994).

GENETICS—THE WHOLE STORY? As with the other disorders described in this text, genetics alone is not the whole story, and the exact role it plays in the development of alcohol-related disorders remains unclear. This issue continues to be debated, and some experts are not convinced of the primary role of genetics in substance-abuse disorders. The genetic mechanism or model for the generally agreed-upon observation that alcoholism is familial is insufficient to explain the behavior fully. That is, genetic transmission in the case of alcohol-related disorders does not follow the hereditary pattern found in strictly genetic disorders. Some investigators have employed the evidence that genetics appears to play a stronger role in men than in women (Merikangas & Swendsen, 1997) to question the relative power of genetics as an explanatory factor in substance abuse. Searles (1991) points to the ambiguous evidence for the genetics of alcohol-related disorders and cautions against interpreting genetics as a causal factor in its development. Negative results have been found in both twin and adoptive studies and in studies designed to follow up the

behavior of high-risk individuals. The great majority of children who have parents with alcohol-related problems do not themselves develop substance-abuse disorders—whether or not they are raised by their biological parents. The children of substance abusers who make successful life adjustments have not been sufficiently studied. In one study of high-risk children of substance abusers, a group of young men 19 to 20 years of age who were presumably at high risk for developing substance-abuse problems were carefully studied for symptoms of psychopathology. Schulsinger and colleagues (1986) found that they did not differ in psychopathology or in alcohol-abuse behavior from a control sample similar to the general population. In another study of high-risk individuals, Alterman and colleagues (1989) failed to find differences in drinking behavior or alcohol-related symptoms between a group of high-risk subjects (those who had alcoholic fathers) and a group of non-high-risk subjects.

Although much evidence implicates genetic factors in the etiology of alcoholism, we do not know what precise role they play. At present, it appears that the genetic interpretation of alcoholism remains an attractive hypothesis; however, additional research is needed for us to hold this view with confidence. It is not likely that genetics alone will account for the full range of alcohol and drug problems. Social circumstances are still considered powerful forces in providing both the availability and the motivation to use alcohol and other drugs. McGue (1998) notes that the mechanisms of genetic influence should be viewed as compatible, rather than competitive, with psychological and social determinants of this disorder.

GENETIC INFLUENCES AND LEARNING When we talk about familial or constitutional differences, we are not strictly limiting our explanation to genetic inheritance. Rather, learning factors appear to play an important part in the development of constitutional or predetermined tendencies to behave in particular ways. Having a genetic predisposition or biological vulnerability to substance abuse, of course, is not a sufficient cause of the disorder. The person must be exposed to the substance to a sufficient degree for the addictive behavior to appear. In the case of alcohol, almost everyone in America is exposed to the drug to some extent—in most cases through peer pressure, parental example, and advertising (Andrews & Hops, 2010). The development of alcohol-related problems involves living in an environment that promotes initial as well as continuing use of the substance. People become conditioned to stimuli and tend to respond in particular ways as a result of learning. Learning appears to play an important part in the development of substance abuse and antisocial personality disorders. There clearly are numerous reinforcements for using alcohol in our social environments and everyday lives. However, research has also shown that psychoactive drugs such as alcohol contain intrinsic rewarding properties—apart from the social context or the drug's operation to diminish worry or frustration. As we saw earlier, the drug stimulates pleasure centers in the brain and develops a reward system of its own.

Psychosocial Causal Factors in Alcohol Abuse and Dependence

Not only do alcohol abusers become physiologically dependent on alcohol, they develop a powerful psychological dependence as well—they become socially dependent on the drug to help them enjoy social situations.

FAILURES IN PARENTAL GUIDANCE Stable family relationships and parental guidance are extremely important molding influences for children (Hasin & Katz, 2010), and this stability is often lacking in families of substance abusers. Children who have parents who are extensive alcohol or drug abusers are vulnerable to developing substance-abuse and related problems (Erblich et al., 2001). The experiences and lessons we learn from important figures in our early years have a significant impact on us as adults. Children who are exposed to negative role models and family dysfunction early in their lives or experience other negative circumstances because the adults around them provide limited guidance often falter on the difficult steps they must take in life (Fischer et al., 2005). These formative experiences can have a direct influence on whether a young person becomes involved in maladaptive behavior such as alcohol or drug abuse.

In one sophisticated program of research aimed at evaluating the possibility that negative socialization factors influence alcohol use, Chassin and colleagues (1993; Trim & Chassin, 2004) replicated findings that alcohol abuse in parents is associated with substance use in adolescents. They then evaluated several possible mediating factors that can affect whether adolescents start using alcohol. They found that parenting skills or parental behavior was associated with substance use in adolescents. Specifically, alcohol-abusing parents are less likely to keep track of what their children are doing, and this

Parent substance use is associated with early adolescent substance use, and negative parental models can have longer-range negative consequences once children leave home.

lack of monitoring often leads to the adolescents' affiliation with drug-using peers. In addition, Chassin and colleagues (1993) found that stress and negative affect (more prevalent in families with an alcoholic parent) are associated with alcohol use in adolescents. They reported that "parental alcoholism was associated with increases in negative uncontrollable life events which, in turn, were linked to negative affect, to associations with drug-using peers, and to substance use" (p. 16). In a follow-up study, Chassin and colleagues (1996) reported that the direct effect of fathers' alcohol abuse is strong, even after controlling for stress and negative affect. Extremely stressful childhood experiences such as physical abuse (Douglas et al., 2010; Kaufman et al., 2007) or child sexual abuse might also make a person vulnerable to later problems. Women who have a history of child sexual abuse are at risk for developing a wide range of psychological problems including substance abuse (Kendler et al., 2000).

PSYCHOLOGICAL VULNERABILITY Is there an "alcoholic personality"—a type of character organization that predisposes a person to use alcohol rather than adopt some other defensive pattern of coping with stress? Research has suggested that personality factors related to having a family history of alcoholism are associated with the development of alcohol-use disorders (Larkins & Sher, 2006). Research has shown that children of alcoholics progressed more quickly from initial alcohol use to the onset of disorder than did matched adolescents in the control sample (Hussong et al, 2008).

Do some individuals self-medicate or reduce their discomfort by excessive use of alcohol? In efforts to answer this question, investigators have found that many potential alcohol abusers tend to be emotionally immature, expect a great deal of the world, require an inordinate amount of praise and appreciation, react to failure with marked feelings of hurt and inferiority, have low frustration tolerance, and feel inadequate and unsure of their abilities to fulfill expected male or female roles. Persons at high risk for developing alcohol-related problems have been found to be significantly more impulsive and aggressive than those at low risk for abusing alcohol (Morey et al., 1984).

In recent years, substantial research has focused on the link between alcohol-related disorders and such other disorders as antisocial personality, depression, and schizophrenia to determine whether some individuals are more vulnerable to substance-abuse disorders. About half of the persons with schizophrenia have either alcohol or drug abuse or dependence as well (Kosten, 1997). By far, most of the research on comorbidity has related antisocial personality and addictive disorders, where about 75 to 80 percent of the studies have shown a strong association (Alterman, 1988), and conduct disorder (Slutske et al., 1998). Interestingly, antisocial personality disorder, alcohol, and aggression are strongly associated (Moeller & Dougherty, 2001), and in a survey of eight alcohol-treatment programs, Morganstern and colleagues (1997) found that 57.9 percent of those in treatment had a personality disorder, with 22.7 percent meeting criteria for antisocial personality disorder. One study reports that substance abusers with antisocial personality disorder had lower expectations of remaining abstinent from alcohol use (Di Sclafani et al., 2007).

Considerable research has suggested that there is a relationship between depressive disorders and alcohol abuse, and there may be gender differences in the association between these disorders (Kranzler et al., 1997). One group of researchers (Moscato et al., 1997) found the degree of association between depression and alcohol-abuse problems stronger among women.

For whatever reason they co-occur, the presence of other mental disorders in alcohol- or drug-abusing patients is a very important consideration when it comes to treatment, as will be discussed later in this chapter.

STRESS, TENSION REDUCTION, AND REINFORCEMENT Research studies on patients undergoing substance-abusing treatment have shown high levels of trauma in their prior histories—about 25 to 50 percent of PTSD patients also have substance-abuse disorders (Schafer & Najavits, 2007). In one study, Deters and colleagues (2006) found that 98 percent of the American Indian adolescents in their substance-abuse study reported having a history of trauma such as threat of personal injury, witnessing of injury, or sexual abuse. One recent controlled-treatment study of disaster workers who experienced PTSD following the World Trade Center trauma (Difede et al., 2007) found that excessive alcohol use was associated with dropout from treatment. Wilk and colleagues (2010) found that high exposure to threatening situations and atrocities (i.e., among Iraq war veterans) was associated with a positive screen for alcohol abuse.

A number of investigators have pointed out that the typical alcohol abuser is discontented with his or her life and is unable or unwilling to tolerate tension and stress (for example, Rutledge & Sher, 2001). Hussong and colleagues (2001) reported a high degree of association between alcohol consumption and negative affectivity such as anxiety and somatic complaints. In other words, alcoholics drink to relax. In this view, anyone who finds alcohol tension-reducing is in danger of abusing alcohol, even without an especially stressful life situation. However, the tension-reduction causal model is difficult to accept as a sole explanatory hypothesis. If this process were a main cause, we would expect substance-abuse disorder to be far more common than it is because alcohol tends to reduce tension for most people who use it. In addition, this model does not explain why some excessive drinkers are able to maintain control over their drinking and continue to function in society whereas others are not.

RESEARCH CLOSE-UP

Moderating

A moderating variable is a variable that influences the association between two other variables. For example, depression is common after bereavement. However, men who have lost a spouse tend to be more likely to be depressed than women who have lost a spouse. In this case, gender is a key moderating variable for the bereavement–depression relationship.

EXPECTATIONS OF SOCIAL SUCCESS Some research has explored the idea that cognitive expectation may play an important role both in the initiation of drinking and in the maintenance of drinking behavior once the person has begun to use alcohol (see, for example, Marlatt, et al., 1998). Many people, especially young adolescents, expect that alcohol use will lower tension and anxiety and increase sexual desire and pleasure in life (Seto & Barbaree, 1995). According to the reciprocal-influence model, adolescents begin drinking as a result of expectations that using alcohol will increase their popularity and acceptance by their peers.

This view gives professionals an important and potentially powerful means of deterring drinking among young people or at least delaying its onset. From this perspective, alcohol use in teenagers can be countered by providing young people with more effective social tools and with ways of altering these expectancies before drinking begins. Smith and colleagues (1995) have suggested that prevention efforts should be targeted at children before they begin to drink so that the positive feedback cycle of reciprocal reinforcement between expectancy and drinking will never be established.

Time and experience do have ***moderating*** influences on these alcohol expectancies. In a longitudinal study of college drinking, Sher and colleagues (1996) found that there was a significant decrease in outcome expectancy over time. That is, older students showed less expectation of the benefits of alcohol than beginning students (see The World Around Us 2).

MARITAL AND OTHER INTIMATE RELATIONSHIPS Adults with less intimate and supportive relationships tend to show greater drinking following sadness or hostility than those with close peers and with more positive relationships (Hussong et al., 2001). Excessive drinking often begins during crisis periods in marital or other intimate personal relationships, particularly crises that lead to hurt and self-devaluation. The marital relationship may actually serve to maintain the pattern of excessive drinking. (See the Case Study on p. 390.) Marital partners may behave toward each other in ways that promote or enable a spouse's excessive drinking. For example, a husband who lives with a wife who abuses alcohol is often unaware of the fact that, gradually and inevitably, many of the decisions he makes every day are based on the expectation that his wife will be drinking. These expectations, in turn, may make the drinking behavior more likely. Eventually an entire marriage may center on the drinking of a substance-abusing spouse. In some instances, the husband or wife may also begin to drink

Binge Drinking in College

Two alcohol-related student deaths shocked the Colorado college community in the fall of 2004. Lynn B., an entering freshman at the University of Colorado, drank so much whiskey and wine during a fraternity initiation that he became unconscious and died as a result of alcohol poisoning. This tragic incident occurred just 2 weeks after a 19-year-old sophomore at Colorado State University, Samantha S., died of alcohol poisoning after a party at which she had consumed an estimated 40 drinks (Sink, 2004).

How extensive is college binge drinking? In spite of the fact that alcohol use is illegal for most undergraduates, binge drinking on campus is widespread (Rabow & Duncan-Schill, 1995) and increased substantially between 1998 and 2005 (Mitka, 2009). Sher and Rutledge (2007) reported that college students who drank in high school are likely to continue drinking during their first year in college. According to a survey by Wechsler and colleagues (1994), 44 percent of college students in the United States are binge drinkers, and Goodwin (1992) reports that 98 percent of fraternity and sorority members drink some amount every week. Some research has suggested, however, that the pattern of drinking can vary widely, with binge drinking being more of an occasional rather than a regular event (Del Boca et al., 2004). Wechsler and colleagues (1994) conducted a nationwide survey of 140 college campuses in 40 states and obtained survey information pertaining to the drinking behavior and health consequences of drinking on 17,592 students (with approximately a 69 percent response rate). Students completed a 20-page survey of their drinking practices, including such information as recency of last drink, how many times they had five drinks or more in a row, and how many times they had four drinks in a row. They were also asked to provide information as to whether they experienced any of the following consequences after drinking: had a hangover, missed a class, got behind in schoolwork, did something they later regretted, forgot where they were or what they did, argued with friends, engaged in unplanned sexual activities, failed to use protection when having sex, damaged property, got into trouble with the campus police, got hurt, or required medical treatment for an alcohol overdose.

The colleges surveyed in the study varied widely in the extent of binge drinking among the student body. As one might expect—some colleges earn reputations as being "party schools"—some institutions had a large number of students (70 percent) heavily involved in alcohol and binge drinking, but the problem occurred to some degree across most college campuses. Recent research has suggested that heavier drinking students may self-select into certain study abroad programs with specific intentions to use alcohol (Pedersen et al. 2010).

What are the reasons for the widespread problem of binge drinking in college? Many factors can be cited, such as students'

expressing independence from parental influence (Turrisi et al., 2000); peer group and situational influences (Read et al., 2003); developing and asserting gender roles, particularly for men adopting a "macho" role (Capraro, 2000); and holding beliefs that alcohol can help make positive transformations, such as "having a few drinks to celebrate special occasions" (Turrisi, 1999). One recent study suggested that a family history of alcohol abuse was associated with problematic drinking among college students (LaBrie, et al. 2010).

The consequences of college binge drinking can be far-reaching and often involve disinhibited behavior (Carlson et al., 2010). In their survey, Wechsler and colleagues (1994) reported a strong association between the frequency of binge drinking and alcohol-related health and life problems. In fact, binge drinkers were nearly 10 times more likely than those who did not indulge in binge drinking to engage in unplanned sexual activity, not to use protection when having sex, to get into trouble with campus police, to damage property, and to get hurt after drinking. Men and women tended to report similar problems, except that men engaged in more property damage than women. Over 16 percent of the men and 9 percent of the women reported having gotten into trouble with the campus police. About 47 percent of the frequent binge drinkers, compared with 14 percent of the non–binge drinkers, indicated that they had experienced five or more of the problems surveyed. In a more recent follow-up survey of college drinking in 1997, Wechsler and colleagues (1998) reported strikingly similar results.

One recent study suggests that extensive drinking in college, even among the heaviest drinkers from sororities and fraternities, might be determined to a great extent by situational events, factors that change with graduation. In a follow-up study of drinking behavior a year after graduation, Sher and colleagues (2001) reported that being a member of a fraternity or sorority did not predict postcollege drinking. Interestingly, a long-term follow-up of over 11 years has shown that the heavy drinking during college did not translate to heavy drinking during later years (Bartholow et al., 2003). These investigators found that heavy drinking that is associated with Greek society involvement does not generally lead to sustained heavy drinking in later life.

Some institutions provide a psychological intervention in an effort to reduce the extent of drinking among college students. One recent study reported that a procedure referred to as Brief Motivational Intervention, or BMI, produced greater self-regulation among a sample of binging college students by providing skills for them to moderate their drinking behavior (Carey et al., 2007). This procedure was more effective among students who also showed, in their pretreatment assessment, a readiness to change.

excessively. Thus one important concern in many treatment programs today involves identifying the personality or lifestyle factors in a relationship that tend to foster the drinking in the alcohol-abusing person. Of course, such relationships are not restricted to marital partners but may also occur in those involved in love affairs or close friendships.

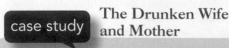

The Drunken Wife and Mother

Evelyn C., a 36-year-old homemaker and mother of two school-age children (from a previous marriage), began to drink to excess especially following intense disagreements with her husband, John, a manager of a retail business. For several months, she had been drinking during the day when her children were at school and on two occasions was inebriated when they came home. On one recent occasion, Evelyn failed to pick up her older daughter after an after-school event. Her daughter called John's cell phone (he was out of town on a business trip), and he had an assistant pick her up. When they arrived home, Evelyn (apparently unaware of the problem she had caused) created a scene and was verbally abusive toward the assistant. Her out-of-control drinking increased when her husband of 3 years began staying out all night. These emotionally charged encounters resulted in John's physically abusing her one morning when he came back home after a night away. John moved out of the house and filed for divorce.

Excessive use of alcohol is one of the most frequent causes of divorce in the United States (Perreira & Sloan, 2001) and is often a hidden factor in the two most common causes—financial and sexual problems. The deterioration in interpersonal relationships of the alcohol abuser or dependent, of course, further augments the stress and disorganization in her or his life. The breakdown of marital relationships can be a highly stressful situation for many people. The stress of divorce and the often erratic adjustment period that follows can lead to increased substance abuse.

Family relationship problems have also been found to be central to the development of alcoholism (Dooley & Prause, 2007). In a classic longitudinal study of possible etiologic factors in alcohol abuse, Vaillant and colleagues (1982) described six family relationship factors that were significantly associated with the development of alcoholism in the individuals they studied. The most important family variables that were considered to predispose an individual to substance-use problems were the presence of an alcoholic father, acute marital conflict, lax maternal supervision and inconsistent discipline, many moves during the family's early years, lack of "attachment" to the father, and lack of family cohesiveness.

Sociocultural Causal Factors

Alcohol use is a pervasive component in the social life in Western civilization. Social events often revolve around alcohol use, and alcohol use before and during meals is commonplace. Alcohol is often seen as a "social lubricant" or tension reducer that enhances social events. Thus investigators have pointed to the role of sociocultural as well as biological and psychological factors in the high rate of alcohol abuse and dependence among Americans.

The effect of cultural attitudes toward drinking is well illustrated by Muslims and Mormons, whose religious values prohibit the use of alcohol, and by orthodox Jews, who have traditionally limited its use largely to religious rituals. The incidence of alcoholism among these groups is minimal. In comparison, the incidence of alcoholism is high among Europeans. For example, one survey showed the highest alcohol-use rates among young people to be in Denmark and Malta, where one in five students reported having drunk alcohol 10 times within the past 30 days (ESPAD, 2000). Interestingly, Europe and six countries that have been influenced by European culture—Argentina, Canada, Chile, Japan, the United States, and New Zealand—make up less than 20 percent of the world's population and yet consume 80 percent of the alcohol (Barry, 1982). Alcohol abuse continues to be a problem in Europe by, for example, contributing to accidents (Lehto, 1995), crime (Rittson, 1995), liver disease (Medical Council on Alcoholism, 1997), and the extent to which young people are developing substance-use problems (Anderson & Lehto, 1995). The French appear to have the highest rate of alcoholism in the world, involving approximately 15 percent of the population. France has both the highest per capita alcohol consumption and one of the highest death rates from cirrhosis of the liver (Noble, 1979). In addition, France shows the highest prevalence rates: In a broad

The cultural influences on alcoholism are clear when one looks at the extremely low incidence of alcoholism among Muslims, Mormons, and orthodox Jews, whose religious values prohibit social drinking.

survey of hospital patients, 18 percent (25 percent for men and 7 percent for women) were reported to have alcohol-use disorders even though only 6 percent of admissions were for alcohol problems (Reynaud et al., 1997). In Sweden, another country with high rates of alcoholism, 13.2 percent of men's hospital admissions, and 1.1 percent of women's, are attributed to alcohol (Andreasson & Brandt, 1997). Thus it appears that religious sanctions and social customs can influence whether alcohol is one of the coping methods commonly used in a given group or society.

The behavior that is manifested under the influence of alcohol also seems to be influenced by cultural factors. Lindman and Lang (1994), in a study of alcohol-related behavior in eight countries, found that most people expressed the view that aggressive behavior frequently follows their drinking "many" drinks. However, the expectation that alcohol leads to aggression is related to cultural traditions and early exposure to violent or aggressive behavior.

In sum, we can identify many reasons why people drink—as well as many conditions that can predispose them to do so and reinforce their drinking behavior—but the exact combination of factors that results in a person's becoming an alcoholic is still unknown.

Treatment of Alcohol-Related Disorders

Alcohol abuse and dependence are difficult to treat because many alcohol abusers refuse to admit that they have a problem before they "hit bottom," and many who do go into treatment leave before therapy is completed. DiClemente (1993) refers to the addictions as "diseases of denial." However, in a review of several large alcohol-treatment studies, Miller, Walters, and Bennett (2001) reported that two-thirds of studies show large and significant decreases in drinking and related problems. In this section, we will examine both biological and psychosocial treatment strategies. Some treatment approaches appear to reduce drinking-related problems more effectively than others (Miller & Wilbourne, 2002; Zweben, 2001). In general, a multidisciplinary approach to the treatment of drinking problems appears to be most effective because the problems are often complex, requiring flexibility and individualization of treatment procedures (Margolis & Zweben, 1998). Also, a substance abuser's needs change as treatment progresses. Treatment objectives usually include detoxification, physical rehabilitation, control over alcohol-abuse behavior, and the individual's realizing that he or she can cope with the problems of living and lead a much more rewarding life without alcohol.

Traditional treatment programs usually have as their goal abstinence from alcohol (Ambrogne, 2002). However, some programs attempt to promote controlled drinking as a treatment goal for problem drinkers. For example, one procedure referred to as Brief Motivational Intervention attempts to modify clients' behavior through providing information and advice about the consequences of the substance use in an effort to challenge the users about their use—but leaves the responsibility to the individual (Carey et al., 2007; Miller & Rollnik, 2002; Peterson, et al., 2006). No matter what the treatment method, relapse is common, and many in the field see relapse as a factor that must be addressed in the treatment and recovery process.

USE OF MEDICATIONS IN TREATING ALCOHOL ABUSE AND DEPENDENCY Biological approaches include a variety of treatment measures such as medications to reduce cravings, to ease the detoxification process, and to treat co-occurring health (National Institutes of Health, 2001) and mental health problems that may underlie the drinking behavior.

Medications to Block the Desire to Drink Disulfiram (Antabuse), a drug that causes violent vomiting when followed by ingestion of alcohol, may be administered to prevent an immediate return to drinking (Grossman & Ruiz, 2004). However, such deterrent therapy is seldom advocated as the sole approach because pharmacological methods alone have not proved effective in treating many severe alcohol-abuse problems (Gorlick, 1993). For example, because the drug is usually self-administered, an alcohol-dependent person may simply discontinue the use of Antabuse when he or she is released from a hospital or clinic and begins to drink again. In fact, the primary value of drugs of this type seems to be their ability to interrupt the alcohol-abuse cycle for a period of time during which therapy may be undertaken. Uncomfortable side effects may accompany the use of Antabuse; for example, alcohol-based aftershave lotion can be absorbed through the skin, resulting in illness. Moreover, the cost of Antabuse treatment, which requires careful medical maintenance, is higher than that for many other, more effective treatments.

Another type of medication that has been used in a promising line of research (Kranzler et al., 2004) is naltrexone, an opiate antagonist that helps reduce the craving for alcohol by blocking the pleasure-producing effects of alcohol (Gueorguieva et al., 2007; Lee et al., 2010). O'Malley and colleagues (1996) have shown that naltrexone reduced the alcohol intake and lowered the incentive to drink for alcohol abusers compared with a control sample given a placebo. Some research has suggested that naltrexone is particularly effective with individuals who have a high level of craving (Monterosso et al., 2001) and show effects of binge drinking (Johnson, 2010). Other research, however, has failed to find naltrexone effective at reducing craving (Krystal et al., 2001), so confidence in its use for this purpose must await further research.

Medications to Reduce the Side Effects of Acute Withdrawal In cases of acute intoxication, the initial focus is on detoxification (the elimination of alcoholic substances from an individual's body), on treatment of the withdrawal symptoms described earlier, and on a medical regimen for physical rehabilitation. One of the primary goals in treatment of withdrawal symptoms is to reduce the physical symptoms characteristic of withdrawal such as insomnia, headache, gastrointestinal distress, and tremulousness. Central to the medical treatment approaches are the prevention of heart arrhythmias, seizures, delirium, and death. These steps can usually best be handled in a hospital or clinic, where drugs such as Valium have largely revolutionized the treatment of withdrawal symptoms. Such drugs overcome motor excitement, nausea, and vomiting; prevent withdrawal delirium and convulsions; and help alleviate the tension and anxiety associated with withdrawal. Pharmacological treatments with long-lasting benzodiazepines, such as diezepam, to reduce the severity of withdrawal symptoms have been shown to be effective (Malcolm, 2003).

Concern is growing, however, that the use of *tranquilizers*—drugs that depress the central nervous system (CNS), resulting in calmness, relaxation, reduction of anxiety, and sleeping—does not promote long-term recovery and may simply transfer the addiction to another substance. Accordingly, some detoxification clinics are exploring alternative approaches including a gradual weaning from alcohol instead of a sudden cutoff. Maintenance doses of mild tranquilizers are sometimes given to patients withdrawing from alcohol to reduce anxiety and help them sleep. Such use of medications may be less effective than no treatment at all, however. Usually patients must learn to abstain from tranquilizers as well as from alcohol because they tend to misuse both. Further, under the influence of medications, patients may even return to alcohol use.

PSYCHOLOGICAL TREATMENT APPROACHES Once the patient has her or his drinking under control, detoxification is optimally followed by psychological treatment, including family counseling and the use of community resources related to employment and other aspects of a person's social readjustment. Although individual psychotherapy is sometimes effective, the focus of psychosocial measures in the treatment of alcohol-related problems often involves group therapy, environmental intervention, behavior therapy, and the approach used by Alcoholics Anonymous and family groups such as Al-Anon and Alateen.

Group Therapy Group therapy has been shown to be effective for many clinical problems (Galanter et al., 2005), especially substance-related disorders (Velasquez et al., 2001). In the confrontational give-and-take of group therapy, alcohol abusers are often forced (perhaps for the first time) to face their problems and their tendencies to deny or minimize them. These group situations can be extremely difficult for those who have been engrossed in denial of their own responsibilities, but such treatment also helps them see new possibilities for coping with circumstances that have led to their difficulties. Often this paves the way for them to learn more effective ways of coping and other positive steps toward dealing with their drinking problem.

In some instances, the spouses of alcohol abusers and even their children may be invited to join in group therapy meetings. In other situations, family treatment is itself the central focus of therapeutic efforts. In that case, the alcohol abuser is seen as a member of a disturbed family in which all members have a responsibility for cooperating in treatment. Because family members are frequently the people most victimized by the alcohol abuser's addiction, they often tend to be judgmental and punitive, and the person in treatment, who has already passed harsh judgment on himself or herself, may tolerate this further source of devaluation poorly. In other instances, family members may unwittingly encourage an alcohol abuser to remain addicted—for example, a man with a need to dominate his wife may find that a continually drunken and remorseful spouse best meets his needs.

Environmental Intervention As with other serious maladaptive behaviors, a total treatment program for alcohol abuse or dependency usually requires measures to alleviate a patient's aversive life situation. Environmental support has been shown to be an important ingredient of an alcohol abuser's recovery. People often become estranged from family and friends because of their drinking and either lose or jeopardize their jobs. As a result, they are often lonely and live in impoverished neighborhoods. Typically, the reaction of those around them is not as understanding or as supportive as it would be if the alcohol abuser had a physical illness of comparable magnitude. Simply helping people with alcohol-abuse problems learn more effective coping techniques may not be enough if their social environment remains hostile and threatening. For those who have been hospitalized, halfway houses—designed to assist them in their return to family and community—are often important adjuncts to their total treatment program.

Behavioral and Cognitive-Behavioral Therapy An interesting and often effective form of treatment for alcohol-related disorders is behavioral therapy, of which several types exist. One is aversive conditioning therapy, which involves the presentation of a wide range of noxious stimuli with alcohol consumption in order to suppress drinking behavior. For example, the ingestion of alcohol might be paired with an electric shock or a drug that produces nausea. A variety of pharmacological and other deterrent measures can be used in behavioral therapy after detoxification. One approach involves an intramuscular injection of emetine hydrochloride, an emetic. Before experiencing the nausea that results from the injection, a patient is given alcohol, so that the sight, smell, and taste of the beverage become associated with severe retching and vomiting. That is, a conditioned aversion to the taste and smell of alcohol develops. With repetition, this classical conditioning procedure acts as a strong deterrent to further drinking—probably in part because it adds an immediate and unpleasant physiological consequence to the more general socially aversive consequences of excessive drinking.

One of the most effective contemporary procedures for treating alcohol abusers has been the cognitive-behavioral approach recommended by Alan Marlatt (1985) and Witkiewitz and Marlatt (2004). This approach combines cognitive-behavioral strategies of intervention with social-learning theory and modeling of behavior. The approach, often referred to as a "skills training procedure," is usually aimed at younger problem drinkers who are considered to be at risk for developing more severe drinking problems because of an alcohol-abuse history in their family or their current heavy consumption. This approach relies on such techniques as imparting specific knowledge about alcohol, developing coping skills in situations associated with increased risk of alcohol use, modifying cognitions and expectancies, acquiring stress-management skills, and providing training in life skills (Connors & Walitzer, 2001). Cognitive-behavioral treatments have been shown to be effective; for example, O'Farrell and colleagues (2004) report that partner violence was significantly reduced following cognitive-behavioral treatment.

Self-control training techniques, such as the Brief Motivational Intervention noted earlier, in which the goal of therapy is to get alcoholics to reduce alcohol intake without necessarily abstaining altogether, have a great deal of appeal for some drinkers. For example, one recent approach to improve drinking outcomes by altering the drinker's social networks was found to be successful (Litt et al., 2007) and motivational interviewing with adolescents was found to be promising (Macgowan & Engle, 2010). There is now even a computer-based self-control training program available that has been shown to reduce problem drinking in a controlled study (Fals-Stewart & Lam, 2010; Neighbors et al., 2004). It is difficult, of course, for individuals who are extremely dependent on the effects done of alcohol to abstain totally from drinking. Thus many alcoholics fail to complete traditional treatment programs.

CONTROLLED DRINKING VERSUS ABSTINENCE Other psychological techniques have also received attention in recent years, partly because they are based on the hypothesis that some problem drinkers need not give up drinking altogether but rather can learn to drink moderately (Miller, Walters, & Bennett, 2001; Sobell & Sobell, 1995). Several approaches to learning controlled drinking have been attempted (McMurran & Hollin, 1993), and research has suggested that some alcoholics can learn to control their alcohol intake (Senft et al., 1997). Miller and colleagues (1986) evaluated the results of four long-term follow-up studies of controlled-drinking treatment programs. Although they found a clear trend of increased numbers of abstainers and relapsed cases at long-term follow-up, they also found that a consistent percentage (15 percent) of subjects across the four studies controlled their drinking. The researchers concluded that controlled drinking was more likely to be successful in persons with less severe alcohol problems. The finding that some individuals are able to maintain some control over their drinking after treatment (without remaining totally abstinent) was also reported in a classic study by Polich et al. (1981). These researchers found that 18 percent of the alcoholics they studied had reportedly been able to drink socially without problems during the 6-month follow-up of treatment.

Many people in the field have rejected the idea that alcohol abusers can learn to control their drinking, and some recent research has found that controlled drinking is not effective (Bottlender et al., 2007). And some groups, such as Alcoholics Anonymous, are adamant in their opposition to programs aimed at controlled drinking for alcohol-dependent individuals.

ALCOHOLICS ANONYMOUS A practical approach to alcoholism that has reportedly met with considerable success is that of Alcoholics Anonymous (AA). This organization was started in 1935 by two men, Dr. Bob and Bill W., in Akron, Ohio. Bill W. recovered from alcoholism through a "fundamental spiritual change" and immediately sought out Dr. Bob, who, with Bill's assistance, also achieved recovery. They in turn began to help other alcoholics. Since that time, AA has grown to over 52,000 groups in the United States, with an annual growth rate of about 6 to 7 percent (Alcoholics Anonymous, 2007). In addition, there are nearly 5,000 AA groups in Canada and over 45,000 groups in many other countries.

Alcoholics Anonymous operates primarily as a self-help counseling program in which both person-to-person and group relationships are emphasized. AA accepts both teenagers and adults with drinking problems, has no dues or fees, does not keep records or case histories, does not participate in political causes, and is not affiliated with any religious sect, although spiritual development is a key aspect of its treatment approach. To ensure anonymity, only first names are used. Meetings are devoted partly to social activities, but they consist mainly of discussions of the participants' problems with alcohol, often with testimonials from those who have stopped drinking. Such members usually contrast their lives before they broke their alcohol dependence with the lives they now live without alcohol. We should point out here that the term *alcoholic* is used by AA and its affiliates to refer either to persons who currently are drinking excessively or to people who have stopped drinking but must, according to AA philosophy, continue to abstain from alcohol consumption in the future. That is, in the AA view, one is an alcoholic for life, whether or not one is drinking; one is never "cured" of alcoholism but is instead "in recovery."

An important aspect of AA's rehabilitation program is that it appears to lift the burden of personal responsibility by helping alcoholics accept that alcoholism, like many other problems, is bigger than they are. Henceforth, they can see themselves not as weak willed or lacking in moral strength but rather simply as having an affliction—they cannot drink—just as other people may not be able to tolerate certain types of medication. Through mutual help and reassurance from group members who have had similar experiences, many alcoholics acquire insight into their problems, a new sense of purpose, greater ego strength, and more effective coping techniques. Continued participation in the group, of course, can help prevent the crisis of a relapse. Affiliated movements such as Al-Anon family groups and Alateen (which has over

35,000 groups in the United States and Canada) are designed to bring family members together to share experiences and problems, to gain understanding of the nature of alcoholism, and to learn techniques for dealing with their own problems living in a family with one or more affected individuals.

The reported success of Alcoholics Anonymous is based primarily on anecdotal information rather than on objective study of treatment outcomes because AA does not directly participate in external comparative research efforts. However, several studies have found AA conditions effective in helping people avoid drinking (Kelly, Stout et al., 2010). In a classic study, Brandsma and colleagues (1980) included an AA program in their extensive comparative study of alcoholism treatments. The success of this treatment method with severe alcoholics was found to be quite limited. Another important finding was that the AA method had high dropout rates compared with other therapies. About half of the people who go to AA drop out of the program within 3 months. Chappel (1993) attributes the very high dropout rate to alcoholics' denial that they have problems, resistance to external pressure, and resistance to AA itself. Apparently many alcoholics are unable to accept the quasireligious quality of the sessions and the group-testimonial format that is so much a part of the AA program. In the Brandsma study, the participants who were assigned to the AA group subsequently encountered more life difficulties and drank more than the people in the other treatment groups. On the positive side, however, a study by Morganstern and colleagues (1997) reports that affiliation with AA after alcohol treatment was associated with better outcomes than without such involvement, and a study by Tonigan and colleagues (1995) found that AA involvement was strongly associated with success in outpatient samples.

OUTCOME STUDIES AND ISSUES IN TREATMENT The outcome of treatment for alcohol-related disorders varies considerably, depending on the population studied and on the treatment facilities and procedures employed. Results range from low rates of success for hard-core substance abusers to recovery rates of 70 to 90 percent when modern treatment and aftercare procedures are used. Substance abusers who are also diagnosed as having a personality disorder or mood disorder tend to have poorer outcomes in alcohol treatment than those for whom the diagnosis is simply alcohol-abuse problems

These people are participating in an Alcoholics Anonymous (AA) meeting. AA accepts both teenagers and adults, has no dues or fees, does not keep records or case histories, does not participate in political causes, and is not affiliated with any religious sect, although spiritual development is a key aspect of its treatment approach. To ensure anonymity, only first names are used at meetings. AA is one of the most popular alcohol-treatment programs, promoting total abstinence rather than controlled drinking.

(Woelwer et al., 2001). Treatment is most likely to be effective when an individual realizes that she or he needs help, when adequate treatment facilities are available, and when the individual attends treatment regularly. Having a positive relationship with the therapist is also associated with better treatment outcome (Connors et al., 1997). One important treatment strategy is aimed at reinforcing treatment motivation and abstinence early in the treatment process by providing "check-up" follow-ups on drinking behavior. Miller and colleagues (1993) report that "Drinking Check-Up" sessions during the early stages of therapy resulted in a reduction of drinking in the first 6 weeks of therapy compared with clients who did not have check-up sessions.

Some researchers have maintained that treatment for alcohol-use and -abuse disorders would be more effective if important patient characteristics were taken into account (Mattson et al., 1994). That is, patients with certain personality characteristics or with differing degrees of severity might do better with one specific therapeutic approach rather than with another. This view was evaluated in a study of patient–treatment matching (referred to as "Project MATCH") that was sponsored by the National Institute on Alcohol Abuse and Alcoholism (NIAAA, 1997). This extensive study, initiated in 1989, involved 1,726 patients who were treated in 26 alcohol-treatment programs in the United States by 80 different therapists representing three treatment approaches. The research design included both inpatient and outpatient treatment components. The results of this study were unexpected: Matching the patients to particular treatments did not appear to be important to having an effective outcome because the treatments studied all had equal outcomes. Gordis (1997) concludes that patients from competently run alcoholism-treatment programs will do as well in any of the three treatments studied.

RELAPSE PREVENTION One of the greatest problems in the treatment of addictive disorders is maintaining abstinence or self-control once the behavioral excesses have been checked (Tims et al., 2001). Most alcohol-treatment programs show high success rates in "curing" the addictive problems, but many programs show lessening rates of abstinence or controlled drinking at various periods of follow-up. Many treatment programs do not pay enough attention to maintaining effective behavior and preventing relapse into previous maladaptive patterns (Miller & Rollnick, 2003).

Given that alcohol-dependent people are highly vulnerable to relapse, some researchers have focused on the need to help them remain abstinent. In one cognitive-behavioral approach, relapse behavior is a key factor in alcohol treatment (Witkiewitz & Marlatt, 2007). One recent study (Nattala et al., 2010) found that relapse prevention treatment worked most effectively when family members were involved in the treatment.

The behaviors underlying relapse are seen as "indulgent behaviors" that are based on an individual's learning history. When an individual is abstinent or has an addiction under control, she or he gains a sense of personal control over the indulgent behavior. The longer the person is able to maintain this control, the greater the sense of achievement—the self-efficacy or confidence—and the greater the chance that she or he will be able to cope with the addiction and maintain control. However, a person may violate this rule of abstinence through a gradual, perhaps unconscious, process rather than through the sudden "falling off the wagon" that constitutes the traditional view of craving and relapse. In the cognitive-behavioral view, a person may, even while maintaining abstinence, inadvertently make a series of mini-decisions that begin a chain of behaviors that render relapse inevitable. For example, an abstinent alcohol abuser who buys a quart of bourbon just in case his friends drop by is unconsciously preparing the way for relapse.

Another type of relapse behavior involves the "abstinence violation effect," in which even minor transgressions are seen by the abstainer as having drastic significance. The effect works this way: An abstinent person may hold that she or he should not, under any circumstance, transgress or give in to the old habit. Abstinence-oriented treatment programs are particularly guided by this prohibitive rule. What happens, then, when an abstinent person becomes somewhat self-indulgent and takes a drink offered by an old friend or joins in a wedding toast? He or she may lose some of the sense of self-efficacy—confidence—needed to control his or her drinking. Feeling guilty about having technically violated the vow of abstinence, the person may rationalize that he or she "has blown it and become a drunk again, so why not go all the way?"

Appealing advertisements and displays that encourage drinking can make abstinence particularly difficult and can contribute, at the very least on a subconscious level, to a relapse.

In *relapse prevention treatment*, clients are taught to recognize the apparently irrelevant decisions that serve as early warning signals of the possibility of relapse. High-risk situations such as parties or sports events are targeted, and the individuals learn to assess their own vulnerability to relapse. Clients are also trained not to become so discouraged that if they do relapse they lose their confidence. Some cognitive-behavioral therapists have even incorporated a "planned relapse" phase into the treatment. Research with relapse prevention strategies has shown them to be effective in providing continuing improvement over time (Rawson et al., 2002). In other words, when patients are taught to expect a relapse, they are better able to handle it.

In Review

- What is the difference between alcohol abuse and alcohol dependence?

- What are the major physiological effects of alcohol?

- Identify the physical, interpersonal, and social/occupational problems that can result from chronic alcohol use.

- What neurobiological processes underlie addiction?

- What are five major psychosocial causal factors that may contribute to alcohol abuse and dependence?

- Describe four psychosocial interventions used to treat alcohol dependence.

Drug Abuse and Dependence

Aside from alcohol, the psychoactive drugs most commonly associated with abuse and dependence in our society appear to be (1) narcotics such as opiates or opioids, including opium and heroin; (2) sedatives such as barbiturates; (3) stimulants such as cocaine and amphetamines; (4) antianxiety drugs such as benzodiazepines; (5) pain medications such as OxyContin; (6) hallucinogens such as LSD (the effects of these and other drugs are summarized in Table 2); and (7) caffeine and nicotine, which are also drugs of dependence (disorders associated with tobacco withdrawal and caffeine intoxication are included in the *DSM-IV-TR* diagnostic classification system).

An estimated 20.1 million Americans who are 12 years of age or older reported using an illicit drug during the month before a recent survey. This represents 8.0 percent of the population (Substance Abuse and Mental Health Services Administration, 2009). According to the Monitoring the Future Study, in 2008 the annual prevalence rate of using any illicit drug was

table 2 Psychoactive Drugs Commonly Involved in Drug Abuse

Classification	Drug	Effect
Sedatives	Alcohol (ethanol)	Reduce tension
		Facilitate social interaction
		"Blot out" feelings or events
	Barbiturates	Reduce tension
	Nembutal (pentobarbital)	
	Seconal (secobarbital)	
	Veronal (barbital)	
	Tuinal (secobarbital and amobarbital)	
Stimulants	Amphetamines	Increase feelings of alertness and confidence
	Benzedrine (amphetamine)	
	Dexedrine (dextroamphetamine)	Decrease feelings of fatigue
	Methedrine (methamphetamine)	Stay awake for long periods
	Cocaine (coca)	Increase endurance
		Stimulate sex drive
Opiates	Opium and its derivatives	Alleviate physical pain
	Opium	Induce relaxation and pleasant reverie
	Morphine	Alleviate anxiety and tension
	Codeine	
	Heroin	
	Methadone (synthetic narcotic)	Treatment of heroin dependence
Hallucinogens	Cannabis	Induce changes in mood, thought, and behavior
	Marijuana	
	Hashish	
	Mescaline (peyote)	"Expand" one's mind
	Psilocybin (psychotogenic mushrooms)	Induce stupor
	LSD (lysergic acid diethylamide-25)	
	PCP (phencyclidine)	
Anti-anxiety drugs	Librium (chlordiazepoxide)	Alleviate tension and anxiety
(minor tranquilizers)	Miltown (meprobamate)	Induce relaxation and sleep
	Valium (diazepam)	
	Xanax	

Note: This list is by no means complete; for example, it does not include drugs such as Ritalin, which are designed to produce multiple effects; it does not include the less commonly used volatile hydrocarbons such as glue, paint thinner, gasoline, cleaning fluid, and nail polish remover, which are highly dangerous when sniffed for their psychoactive effects; and it does not include the antipsychotic and antidepressant drugs, which are abused, but relatively rarely.

37 percent for 12th graders, 35 percent for college students, 34 percent for 19- to 28-year-olds, 27 percent for 10th graders, and 14 percent for 8th graders (Johnston et al., 2009). The extent of drug abuse in the population is likely to be underestimated because many abusers do not seek help (Compton et al., 2007). Although they may occur at any age, drug abuse and dependence are most common during adolescence and young adulthood (Campbell, 2010) and vary according to metropolitan area, race and ethnicity, labor force status, and other demographic characteristics (Hughes, 1992). Substance-abuse problems are relatively more prominent in economically depressed minority communities (Akins et al., 2003).

The extent to which drug abuse has become a problem for society is reflected in a study of drug involvement among applicants for employment at a large teaching hospital in Maryland (Lange et al., 1994). Beginning in 1989, and for a 2-year period, all applicants for employment were screened through a preemployment drug-screening program (individuals were not identified in the initial study). Of 593 applicants, 10.8 percent were found to have detectable amounts of illicit drugs in their systems. The most frequently detected drug was marijuana (55 percent of those who tested positively), followed by cocaine (36 percent) and opiates (28 percent).

The impact of drug use among employed people has also been reported to be significant. In an extensive survey of illegal drug use among 40,000 currently employed workers, researchers found the following rates of illicit drug use within the month prior to the survey: 19 percent for those age 18 or younger, 10.3 percent for those between 18 and 25, 7 percent for those between 26 and 34, 7 percent for those between 35 and 49, and 2.6 percent for those between 50 and 64 (Larson et al., 2007). The overall frequency of illegal drug use rate in this work sample was 8.2 percent. The high rate of drug use in this population (many reported actually using drugs on the job) is problematic. For example, among those workers who reported current illicit drug use, 12.3 percent reported that they had worked for three or more employers in the past year, compared with 5.1 percent for nonabusing workers.

Among people who abuse drugs, behavior patterns vary markedly depending on the type, amount, and duration of drug use; on the physiological and psychological makeup of the individual; and, in some instances, on the social setting in which the drug experience occurs. Thus it appears most useful to deal separately with some of the drugs that are more commonly associated with abuse and dependence in contemporary society.

Opium and Its Deriviates (Narcotics)

OPIUM People have used opium and its derivatives for centuries. Galen (A.D. 130–201) considered theriaca, whose principal ingredient was opium, to be a panacea:

> It resists poison and venomous bites, cures inveterate headache, vertigo, deafness, epilepsy, apoplexy, dimness of sight, loss of voice, asthma, coughs of all kinds, spitting of blood, tightness of breath, colic, the iliac poisons, jaundice, hardness of the spleen, stone, urinary complaints, fevers, dropsies, leprosies, the trouble to which women are subject, melancholy and all pestilences. (See Brock, 1979, for a discussion of Galen.)

Even today, opiates are still used for some of the conditions Galen mentioned.

Opium is a mixture of about 18 chemical substances known as alkaloids. In 1805 the alkaloid present in the largest amount (10 to 15 percent) was found to be a bitter-tasting powder that could serve as a powerful sedative and pain reliever; it was named **morphine** after Morpheus, the god of sleep in Greek mythology. The hypodermic needle was introduced in America around 1856, allowing morphine to be widely administered to soldiers during the Civil War—not only to those wounded in battle but also to those suffering from dysentery. As a consequence, many Civil War veterans returned to civilian life addicted to the drug, a condition euphemistically referred to as "soldier's illness."

Scientists concerned with the addictive properties of morphine hypothesized that one part of the morphine

The adolescent shown here is injecting the drug heroin—a dangerous and highly addictive substance that is widely available to adolescents today.

molecule might be responsible for its analgesic properties (that is, its ability to eliminate pain without inducing unconsciousness) and another for its addictiveness. At about the turn of the century, it was discovered that if morphine was treated with an inexpensive and readily available chemical called acetic anhydride, it would be converted into another powerful analgesic called **heroin**. Heroin was hailed enthusiastically by its discoverer, Heinrich Dreser (Boehm, 1968). Leading scientists of his time agreed on the merits of heroin, and the drug came to be widely prescribed in place of morphine for pain relief and related medicinal purposes. However, heroin was a cruel disappointment, for it proved to be an even more dangerous drug than morphine, acting more rapidly and more intensely and being equally if not more addictive. Eventually, heroin was removed from use in medical practice.

As it became apparent that opium and its derivatives—including codeine, which is used in some cough syrups—were perilously addictive, the U.S. Congress enacted the Harrison Act in 1914. Under this and later legislation, the unauthorized sale and distribution of certain drugs became a federal offense; physicians and pharmacists were held accountable for each dose they dispensed. Thus, overnight, the role of a chronic narcotic user changed from that of addict—whose addiction was considered a vice, but was tolerated—to that of criminal. Unable to obtain drugs through legal sources, many turned to illegal channels, and eventually to other criminal acts, as a means of maintaining their suddenly expensive drug supply.

In one survey, about 2.4 million Americans acknowledged having tried heroin, and almost a quarter of a million people admitted to using it within the previous 12 months (U.S. Department of Health and Human Services, 1997). In 2005, heroin overdose accounted for 10 percent of all drug-abuse-related emergency room admissions (DAWN Report, 2010).

BIOLOGICAL EFFECTS OF MORPHINE AND HEROIN

Morphine and heroin are commonly introduced into the body by smoking, snorting (inhaling the powder), eating, "skin popping," or "mainlining," the last two being methods of introducing the drug via hypodermic injection. Skin popping is injecting the liquefied drug just beneath the skin, while mainlining is injecting the drug directly into the bloodstream. In the United States, a young addict usually moves from snorting to mainlining.

Among the immediate effects of mainlined or snorted heroin is a euphoric spasm (the rush) lasting 60 seconds or so, which many addicts compare to a sexual orgasm. However, vomiting and nausea have also been known to be part of the immediate effects of heroin and morphine use. This rush is followed by a high, during which an addict typically is in a lethargic, withdrawn state in which bodily needs, including needs for food and sex, are markedly diminished; pleasant feelings of relaxation and euphoria tend to dominate. These effects last from 4 to 6 hours and are followed—in addicts—by a negative phase that produces a desire for more of the drug.

The use of opiates over a period of time generally results in a physiological craving for the drug. The time required to establish the drug habit varies, but it has been estimated that continual use over a period of 30 days is sufficient. Users then find that they have become physiologically dependent on the drug in the sense that they feel physically ill when they do not take it. In addition, users of opiates gradually build up a tolerance to the drug so increasingly larger amounts are needed to achieve the desired effects.

When people addicted to opiates do not get a dose of the drug within approximately 8 hours, they start to experience withdrawal symptoms. The character and severity of these reactions depend on many factors including the amount of the narcotic habitually used, the intervals between doses, the duration of the addiction, and especially the addict's health and personality.

Withdrawal from heroin is not always dangerous or even very painful. Many addicted people withdraw without assistance. Withdrawal can, however, be an agonizing experience for some people, with symptoms including runny nose, tearing eyes, perspiration, restlessness, increased respiration rate, and an intensified desire for the drug. As time passes, the symptoms may become more severe. Typically, a feeling of chilliness alternates with flushing and excessive sweating, vomiting, diarrhea, abdominal cramps, pains in the back and extremities, severe headache, marked tremors, and varying degrees of insomnia. Beset by these discomforts, an individual refuses food and water, and this, coupled with the vomiting, sweating, and diarrhea, results in dehydration and weight loss. Occasionally, symptoms include delirium, hallucinations, and manic activity. Cardiovascular collapse may also occur and can result in death. If morphine is administered, the subjective distress experienced by an addict temporarily ends and physiological balance is quickly restored.

Withdrawal symptoms are usually on the decline by the third or fourth day and by the seventh or eighth day have disappeared. As the symptoms subside, the person resumes normal eating and drinking and rapidly regains lost weight. After withdrawal symptoms have ceased, the individual's former tolerance for the drug is reduced; as a result, there is a risk that taking the former large dosage might result in overdose.

SOCIAL EFFECTS OF MORPHINE AND HEROIN

Typically, the life of a person addicted to opiates becomes increasingly centered on obtaining and using drugs, so the addiction usually leads to socially maladaptive behavior as the individual is eventually forced to lie, steal, and associate with undesirable contacts to maintain a supply of drugs. Many addicts resort to petty theft to support their habits, and some addicts turn to prostitution as a means of financing their addictions.

Along with the lowering of ethical and moral restraints, addiction has adverse physical effects on an individual's well-being—for example, disruption of the immune system (Theodorou & Haber, 2005). Lifestyle factors can lead to further problems; an inadequate diet, for example, may lead to ill health and increased susceptibility to a variety of physical ailments. The use of unsterile equipment may also lead to various problems including liver damage from hepatitis (Lucey et al. 2009) and transmission of the AIDS virus. In addition, the use of such a potent drug without medical supervision and government controls to ensure its strength and purity can result in fatal overdose. Injection of too much heroin can cause coma and death. In fact, heroin-related deaths have shown an increase in cities where data are collected (DAWN Report, 2006). The most common drug-related deaths in the United States involve combinations of heroin, cocaine, and alcohol. Women who use heroin during pregnancy subject their unborn children to the risk of dire consequences. One tragic outcome is premature babies who are themselves addicted to heroin and vulnerable to a number of diseases.

Addiction to opiates usually leads to a gradual deterioration of well-being (Brown & Lo, 2000). For example, some research has shown that opiates actively alter the immune system, rendering the person vulnerable to organ damage (McHugh & Kreek, 2004). The ill health and general personality degeneration often found in opiate addiction do not always result directly from the pharmacological effects of the drug, however; rather, they are often products of the sacrifices of money, proper diet, social position, and self-respect as an addict becomes more desperate to procure the required daily dosage.

CAUSAL FACTORS IN OPIATE ABUSE AND DEPENDENCE

No single causal pattern fits all addictions to opiate drugs. A study by Fulmer and Lapidus (1980) concludes that the three most frequently cited reasons for beginning to use heroin were pleasure, curiosity, and peer pressure. Pleasure was, by far, the single most widespread reason—given by 81 percent of addicts. Other reasons such as a desire to escape life stress, personal maladjustment, and sociocultural conditions also play a part. Zuckerman (2007) provided the view that substance abuse

Celebrities Lindsay Lohan, Paris Hilton, and Nicole Richie have all received jail terms for substance-related driving offenses.

such as smoking, drinking, and the use of drugs are all related to a personality characteristic he refers to as "sensation seeking." He considered this trait to be mediated through genetic and biological mechanisms as well as through peer influences.

NEURAL BASES FOR PHYSIOLOGICAL ADDICTION

Research teams have isolated and studied receptor sites for narcotic drugs in the brain (Goldstein et al., 1974). Such receptor sites are specific nerve cells into which given psychoactive drugs fit like keys into the proper locks. This interaction of drug and brain cells apparently results in a drug's action and, in the case of narcotic drugs, may lead to addiction. The repeated use of opiates results in changes in the neurotransmitter systems that regulate incentive and motivation and the ability to manage stress (DeVries & Shippenberg, 2002). Research has demonstrated that heroin users show a number of central nervous system dysfunctions including slowed reaction time, impaired learning and attention, impaired cognitive processing, and impulse control problems (Angelucci et al., 2007).

The human body produces its own opium-like substances, called **endorphins**, in the brain and pituitary gland. These substances are produced in response to stimulation and are believed to play a role in an organism's reaction to pain. Some investigators have suspected that endorphins play a role in drug addiction, speculating that chronic underproduction of endorphins leads to a craving for narcotic drugs. Research on the role of endorphins in drug addiction has generally been inconclusive, and no effective treatment has resulted from this line of research.

ADDICTION ASSOCIATED WITH PSYCHOPATHOLOGY

A high incidence of antisocial personality has been found among heroin addicts (Alterman, et al., 1998; Feske, et al.,

2006). In a comparison between a group of 45 young institutionalized male addicts and a control group of nonaddicts, Gilbert and Lombardi (1967) found that the distinguishing features were "the addict's antisocial traits, his depression, tension, insecurity, and feelings of inadequacy, and his difficulty in forming warm and lasting interpersonal relationships" (p. 536). Meyer and Mirin (1979) found that opiate addicts are highly impulsive and unable to delay gratification. Kosten and Rounsaville (1986) reported that about 68 percent of heroin abusers are also diagnosed as having a personality disorder. As in the case of alcoholism, however, it is essential to exercise caution in distinguishing between personality traits present before and those present after addiction; the high incidence of psychopathology among narcotics addicts may in part result from, rather than precede, the long-term effects of addiction.

DRUG USE ASSOCIATED WITH SOCIOCULTURAL FACTORS

In our society, a so-called narcotics subculture exists in which addicts can obtain drugs and protect themselves against society's sanctions (Johnson, 2007). The decision to join this culture has important future implications, for from that point on, addicts' activities will revolve around their drug-user role. In short, addiction becomes a way of life. In a survey of three large cities in Texas, Maddux and colleagues (1994) found that the majority of illicit drug injectors were undereducated and unemployed individuals from minority groups.

With time, most young addicts who join the drug culture become increasingly withdrawn, indifferent to their friends (except those in the drug group), and apathetic about sexual activity (Tremble et al., 1994). They are likely to abandon scholastic and athletic endeavors and to show a marked reduction in competitive and achievement strivings. Most of these addicts appear to lack clear sex-role identification and to experience feelings of inadequacy when confronted with the demands of adulthood. They feel progressively isolated from the broader culture, but their feelings of group belongingness are bolstered by continued association with the addict milieu. At the same time, they come to view drugs both as a means of revolt against authority and conventional values and as a device for alleviating personal anxieties and tensions.

TREATMENTS AND OUTCOMES Treatment for opiate addiction is initially similar to that for alcoholism in that it involves building up an addict both physically and psychologically and providing help through the withdrawal period. Addicts often dread the discomfort of withdrawal, but in a hospital setting it is less abrupt and usually involves the administration of medication that eases the distress.

After physical withdrawal has been completed, treatment focuses on helping a former addict make an adequate adjustment to his or her community and abstain from the further use of opiates. Traditionally, however, the prognosis has been unfavorable, with many clients dropping out of treatment (Katz et al., 2004). Withdrawal from heroin does not remove the craving for the drug. Thus a key target in treatment of heroin addiction must be the alleviation of this craving. One approach to dealing with the physiological craving for heroin was pioneered by a research team at Rockefeller University in New York. It involved the use of the drug **methadone** in conjunction with a rehabilitation program (counseling, group therapy, and other procedures) directed toward the "total resocialization" of addicts. Methadone hydrochloride is a synthetic narcotic that is related to heroin and is equally addictive physiologically. Its usefulness in treatment lies in the fact that it satisfies an addict's craving for heroin without producing serious psychological impairment, if only because it is administered as a "treatment" in a formal clinical context and can result in reduced drug use and improved cognitive performance (Gruber et al., 2006; Kreek et al., 2010). (See the Unresolved Issues section at the end of this chapter.)

Other medications, such as buprenorphine, have also been used to treat heroin addiction (Meier & Patkar, 2007). Buprenorphine promises to be as effective a substitute for heroin as methadone but with fewer side effects (Ling et al., 2010). It operates as a partial antagonist to heroin and produces the feelings of contentment associated with heroin use (Mendelson & Mello, 1992). Yet the drug does not produce the physical dependence that is characteristic of heroin (Grant & Sonti, 1994) and can be discontinued without severe withdrawal symptoms. Like methadone, buprenorphine appears to work best at maintaining abstinence if it is provided along with behavior therapy (Bickel et al., 1997).

Cocaine and Amphetamines (Stimulants)

In contrast to narcotics, which depress (slow down) the action of the central nervous system, cocaine and amphetamines stimulate it (speed it up).

COCAINE Like opium, **cocaine** is a plant product discovered in ancient times and used ever since. It was widely used in the pre-Columbian world of Mexico and Peru (Guerra, 1971). Because for many years it was typically very costly in the United States, cocaine was considered as the "high" for the affluent. However, with more widespread availability and lowering of prices, the drug's use increased significantly in the United States during the 1980s and 1990s—to the point where its use was considered epidemic, especially among middle- and upper-income groups. "Crack" is the street name that is applied to cocaine that has been processed from cocaine hydrochloride to a free base for smoking. The name refers to the crackling sound emitted when the mixture is heated.

In 2008, cocaine use was reported in 1.5 percent of young adults (Substance Abuse and Mental Health Services Administration, 2009). In 2005, there was a substantial increase in cocaine-related emergency room visits per 100,000 drug-related admissions (about 29 percent of drug-related emergencies). This amount is about three times greater than heroin-related admissions (DAWN Report, 2010).

Like the opiates, cocaine may be ingested by sniffing, swallowing, or injecting. Also like the opiates, it precipitates a euphoric state of 4 to 6 hours' duration, during which a user experiences feelings of confidence and contentment. However, this blissful state may be preceded by headache, dizziness, and restlessness. When cocaine is chronically abused, acute toxic psychotic symptoms may occur, including frightening visual, auditory, and tactual hallucinations similar to those in acute schizophrenia.

Unlike the opiates, cocaine stimulates the cortex of the brain, inducing sleeplessness and excitement as well as stimulating and accentuating sexual feelings. Dependence on cocaine also differs somewhat from dependence on opiates. It was formerly believed that tolerance was not increased appreciably with cocaine use. However, acute tolerance has now been demonstrated, and some chronic tolerance may occur as well. Moreover, cognitive impairment associated with cocaine abuse is likely to be an important consideration in long-term effects of the drug (Abi-Saab et al., 2005; Mann, 2004). The previous view that cocaine abusers did not develop physiological dependence on the drug also has changed. Gawin and Kleber (1986) demonstrated that chronic abusers who become abstinent develop uniform, depression-like symptoms, but the symptoms are transient. Our broadened knowledge about cocaine abuse, particularly with respect to the many health and social problems resulting from dependence on the drug, has resulted in considerable modification of professional views of cocaine over the past 20 years. For example, the modifications in the *DSM-IV-TR* diagnostic classification reflect a significant increase in our knowledge of cocaine's addictive properties. A new disorder is described—cocaine withdrawal—that involves symptoms of depression, fatigue, disturbed sleep, and increased dreaming (Foltin & Fischman, 1997). The psychological and life problems experienced by cocaine users are often great. Employment, family, psychological, and legal problems are all more likely to occur among cocaine and crack users than among nonusers. Many life problems experienced by cocaine abusers result in part from the considerable amounts of money that are required to support their habits. Increased sexual activity, often trading sex for drugs, has been associated with crack cocaine use (Weatherby et al., 1992), as has engaging in sexual activity with anonymous partners (Balshem et al., 1992). However, problems in sexual functioning have been reported to be associated with crack cocaine use. Kim and colleagues (1992) report that most users lose interest in sex and develop sexual dysfunction with prolonged usage.

Women who use cocaine when they are pregnant place their babies at risk for both health and psychological problems. Although research has suggested that there is no "fetal crack syndrome" similar to what has been shown with alcohol-abusing mothers (Azar, 1997), children of crack-using mothers are at risk of being maltreated as infants as well as of losing their mothers during infancy. Wasserman and Leventhal (1993) studied a group of cocaine-exposed children and a control sample of nonexposed children for a 24-month period following their birth. They found that children who were regularly exposed to cocaine *in utero* were more likely to be mistreated (23 percent compared with only 4 percent of controls).

TREATMENT AND OUTCOMES Treatment for dependence on cocaine does not differ appreciably from that for other drugs that involve physiological dependence (see Kosten et al., 1992; Schmitz et al., 2004). In order to reduce cravings as part of psychological therapy and to ensure treatment compliance, drugs such as naltrexone have been used to reduce cocaine use (Carroll et al., 2004). The feelings of tension and depression that accompany absence of the drug have to be dealt with during the immediate withdrawal period. One recent study reported that methadone was effective in promoting abstinence among individuals with less severe cocaine use (Weinstock et al., 2010)

Some success in the treatment of cocaine abusers has been reported. For example, Siqueland and colleagues (2002) found that patients who remained in drug treatment longer used drugs less often after treatment than those who dropped out; and Stewart and colleagues (2002) found that patients who completed therapy had lower rates of drug overdose than those who failed to complete treatment. Carroll and colleagues (1993) have shown that many cocaine abusers do well in maintaining treatment goals, and one-third are abstinent at a 12-month follow-up. They found several factors associated with poorer outcomes: severity of abuse, poorer psychiatric functioning, and presence of concurrent alcoholism. Higgins and colleagues (2000) found that people who were not able to sustain abstinence during the treatment had poorer outcomes following therapy.

One of the problems clinicians face in working with cocaine abusers is their "dropping out": Only 42 percent of those in one study remained in treatment for six or more sessions (Kleinman et al., 1992). Another problem encountered in drug treatment is that many of the cocaine-dependent patients have severe antisocial personality disorder—a situation resulting in treatment resistance (Poling et al., 2007)—or are "psychosis-prone" personalities (Kwapil, 1996). Arndt and colleagues (1994) found that cocaine-dependent patients with antisocial personality characteristics made few therapeutic gains, whereas those without antisocial features made significant progress. Gallop and colleagues (2007) report a study in which gender differences were found for being able to maintain abstinence from cocaine use; men tended to have more problems transitioning to abstinence after cocaine abuse.

Is treatment always necessary for cocaine abusers to recover? An interesting study suggests that some abusers can improve without therapy. Toneatto and colleagues (1999) describe a study of natural (nontreated) recovery among cocaine abusers. They report that abusers who resolved their dependence on cocaine were similar to those who did not resolve their cocaine problems in terms of demographic characteristics, substance abuse, and psychiatric history. The successful abstainers considered their "improved self-concept" crucial to their success.

AMPHETAMINES The earliest **amphetamine** to be introduced—Benzedrine, or amphetamine sulfate—was first synthesized in 1927 and became available in drugstores in the early 1930s as an inhalant to relieve stuffy noses. However, the manufacturers soon learned that some customers were chewing the wicks in the inhalers for "kicks." Thus the stimulating effects of amphetamine sulfate were discovered by the public before the drug was formally prescribed as a stimulant by physicians. In the late 1930s, two newer amphetamines were introduced—Dexedrine (dextroamphetamine) and Methedrine (methamphetamine hydrochloride, also known as "speed"). The latter preparation is a far more potent stimulant of the central nervous system than either Benzedrine or Dexedrine and hence is considered more dangerous. In fact, its abuse can be lethal.

Initially these preparations were considered to be "wonder pills" that helped people stay alert and awake and function temporarily at a level beyond normal. During World War II, military interest was aroused in the stimulating effects of these drugs, and they were used by both Allied and German soldiers to ward off fatigue (Jarvik, 1967). Similarly, among civilians, amphetamines came to be widely used by night workers, long-distance truck drivers, students cramming for exams, and athletes striving to improve their performances. It was also discovered that amphetamines tend to suppress appetite, and they became popular with people trying to lose weight. In addition, they were often used to counteract the effects of barbiturates or other sleeping pills that had been taken the night before. As a result of their many uses, amphetamines were widely prescribed by doctors.

Today amphetamines are occasionally used medically for curbing the appetite when weight reduction is desirable; for treating individuals suffering from narcolepsy, a disorder in which people cannot prevent themselves from continually falling asleep during the day; and for treating hyperactive children. Curiously enough, amphetamines have a calming rather than a stimulating effect on many of these young people. Amphetamines are also sometimes prescribed for alleviating mild feelings of depression, relieving fatigue, and maintaining alertness for sustained periods of time. By far, however, the most frequent use of amphetamines is for recreational purposes, the most typical user being a young person interested in the high that the drug induces (Klee, 1998).

Since the passage of the Controlled Substance Act of 1970 (Drug Enforcement Administration, 1979), amphetamines have been classified as Schedule II controlled substances—that is, drugs with high abuse potential that require a prescription for each purchase. As a result, medical use of amphetamines has declined in the United States in recent years, and they are more difficult to obtain legally. However, it is often easy to find illegal sources of amphetamines, which thus remain among the most widely abused drugs. Amphetamines are among the most widely used illicit drugs in other countries as well, for example, in Australia (Lintzeris, Holgate et al., 1996). In 2007, about 5 percent of drug-related emergency room visits involved amphetamines or methamphetamines (DAWN Report, 2010).

EFFECTS OF AMPHETAMINE ABUSE Despite their legitimate medical uses, amphetamines are not a magical source of extra mental or physical energy. Instead, they push users toward greater expenditures of their own resources—often to the point of hazardous fatigue. Amphetamines are psychologically and physically addictive, and the body rapidly builds up tolerance to them (Wise, 1996). Thus habituated abusers may use the drugs in amounts that would be lethal to nonusers. In some instances, users inject the drug to get faster and more intense results.

For a person who exceeds prescribed dosages, amphetamine consumption results in heightened blood pressure, enlarged pupils, unclear or rapid speech, profuse sweating, tremors, excitability, loss of appetite, confusion, and sleeplessness. Injected in large quantities, Methedrine can raise blood pressure enough to cause immediate death. In addition, chronic abuse of amphetamines can result in brain damage and a wide range of psychopathology, including a disorder known as "amphetamine psychosis," which appears similar to paranoid schizophrenia. Suicide, homicide, assault, and various other acts of violence are also associated with amphetamine abuse.

Methamphetamine, known as "crystal" or "ice," can be "cooked" in large quantities in makeshift laboratories. The man shown in this photo was arrested in a police raid on one such laboratory.

TREATMENTS AND OUTCOMES Research on the effectiveness of various treatments for withdrawing patients from

amphetamines is scarce (Baker & Lee, 2003). Although withdrawal from amphetamines is usually safe, some evidence suggests that physiological dependence upon the drug is an important factor to consider in treatment (Wise & Munn, 1995). In some instances, abrupt withdrawal from the chronic, excessive use of amphetamines can result in cramping, nausea, diarrhea, and even convulsions. Moreover, abrupt abstinence commonly results in feelings of weariness and depression. The depression usually peaks in 48 to 72 hours, often remains intense for a day or two, and then tends to lessen gradually over a period of several days. Mild feelings of depression and lassitude may persist for weeks or even months. If brain damage has occurred, the residual effects may include impaired ability to concentrate, learn, and remember, with resulting social, economic, and personality deterioration.

Methamphetamine

Methamphetamine, referred to on the streets as "crystal" or "ice" because of its appearance, is a highly addictive stimulant drug that can provide a quick and long-lasting "high." However, it is one of the most dangerous illegal drugs because of its treacherous properties and its unwelcome results (Covey, 2007). Methamphetamine is a form of amphetamine that can be "cooked" in large quantities in makeshift laboratories in out-of-the-way places that defy and frustrate detection. This drug is relatively cheap to manufacture and is often referred to as "poor people's cocaine." It can be manufactured, for example, in a portable cooler with ingredients that can be legally obtained from any drugstore. The drug can be ingested in a variety of ways, through smoking, snorting, swallowing, or injecting. The drug's effects can be almost instantaneous if it is smoked or injected.

Methamphetamine operates by increasing the level of dopamine in the brain, and prolonged use of the drug produces structural changes in the brain (Chang, Alicata et al., 2007). The severity of psychiatric symptoms associated with the drug is significantly related to the duration of use (Yoshimoto et al., 2002). Moreover, discontinuing the drug after the person has become habituated can result in problems with learning, memory, and cognitive dysfunction (Cretzmeyer et al., 2003; Rothman et al., 2000) and severe mental health problems such as paranoid thinking and hallucinations (Brecht et al., 2004; Srisurapanont et al., 2003). This drug is metabolized more slowly than other drugs such as cocaine and produces a high for a longer period of time. When the drug wears off or when users "come down from the high," they are likely to feel extremely weak, lethargic, sleepy, and depressed. Egan

(2002) provides the following descriptions of two meth users from the State of Washington:

> Lacy B., 26, drives around in the rain, her skin twitching, her mind racing, her nails bitten to a pulp. She has been trying to shed her addiction and is awaiting counseling. But she also carries a grocery list under the seat of her car, with all the ingredients for cooking meth.
>
> "Solvents from the paint store, lithium from batteries, Sudafed—I know a lot of this stuff could kill me," Ms. B. said in an interview. "But I also know that it gets me through. There are times when I don't feel normal without meth."
>
> Another Snohomish County woman, a Bertina P., 33, has been drug-free for two years, but she still shudders at her low point. "I took a pocket knife and tried to lance an abscess in my mouth." She said, "I was doing my own dentistry. Lucky I didn't kill myself." (33)

Use of the drug increased substantially during the 1990s; 4.9 million people in the United States (2.3 percent of the population) had tried methamphetamine by 1998 (NIDA, 2003). In one survey of almost 630,000 high school students, Oetting and colleagues (2000) report that methamphetamine use more than doubled between 1989 and 1996. The number of people starting to use methamphetamine decreased in 2008 and was significantly lower than it was in 2007 (Substance Abuse and Mental Health Services Administration, 2009). Interestingly, the use of methamphetamine in the United States has been somewhat of a regional phenomenon; most use has occurred in the Southwest, on the West Coast, and in Hawaii, with very little use in the North, South, and Midwest (DAWN, 2007). This situation results from the fact that meth labs have been concentrated in Mexico, California, and Hawaii.

There is some evidence that people become more quickly addicted to methamphetamine and require treatment sooner than those using cocaine (Castro et al., 2000). Addicted methamphetamine users are highly resistant to treatment, and post-treatment relapse is common. In one California study of 98 methamphetamine abusers, the investigators reported that over half of the participants had returned to methamphetamine use by the time they were interviewed 2 to 3 years following therapy; 36 percent reported that they had returned to methamphetamine use within 6 months of therapy (Brecht et al., 2000).

Barbiturates (Sedatives)

For over a hundred years, powerful sedatives called **barbiturates** have been available as an aid to falling asleep (Lopez-Munoz et al., 2005). Although barbiturates have legitimate medical uses, they are extremely dangerous drugs commonly associated with both physiological and psychological dependence and lethal overdoses.

EFFECTS OF BARBITURATES Barbiturates were once widely used by physicians to calm patients and induce sleep. They act as depressants—somewhat like alcohol—to slow down the action of the central nervous system (Nemeroff, 2003) and significantly reduce performance on cognitive tasks (Pickworth et al., 1997). Shortly after taking a barbiturate, or "downer," an individual experiences a feeling of relaxation in which tensions seem to disappear, followed by a physical and intellectual lassitude and a tendency toward drowsiness and sleep—the intensity of such feelings depends on the type and amount of barbiturate taken. Strong doses produce sleep almost immediately; excessive doses are lethal because they result in paralysis of the brain's respiratory centers. Impaired decision making and problem solving, sluggishness, slow speech, and sudden mood shifts are also common effects of barbiturates (Lemmer, 2007).

Excessive use of barbiturates leads to increased tolerance as well as to physiological and psychological dependence. It can also lead to brain damage and personality deterioration. Unlike tolerance for opiates, tolerance for barbiturates does not increase the amount needed to cause death. This means that users can easily ingest fatal overdoses, either intentionally or accidentally.

CAUSAL FACTORS IN BARBITURATE ABUSE AND DEPENDENCE Although many young people experiment with barbiturates, most do not become dependent. In fact, the people who do become dependent on barbiturates tend to be middle-aged and older people who often rely on them as "sleeping pills" and who do not commonly use other classes of drugs (except possibly alcohol and minor tranquilizers). These people have been referred to as "silent abusers" because they take the drugs in the privacy of their homes and ordinarily do not become public nuisances. Barbiturates are often used with alcohol. Some users claim they can achieve an intense high by combining barbiturates, amphetamines, and alcohol. However, one possible effect of combining barbiturates and alcohol is death because each drug potentiates (increases the action of) the other.

TREATMENTS AND OUTCOMES As with many other drugs, it is often essential in treatment to distinguish between barbiturate intoxication, which results from the toxic effects of overdose, and the symptoms associated with drug withdrawal, because different procedures are required. With barbiturates, withdrawal symptoms are more dangerous, severe, and long-lasting than in opiate withdrawal. A patient going through barbiturate withdrawal becomes anxious and apprehensive and manifests coarse tremors of the hands and face; additional symptoms commonly include insomnia, weakness, nausea, vomiting, abdominal cramps, rapid heart rate, elevated blood pressure, and loss of weight. An acute delirious psychosis may develop.

For persons accustomed to taking large dosages, withdrawal symptoms may last for as long as a month, but usually they tend to abate by the end of the first week. Fortunately, the withdrawal symptoms in barbiturate addiction can be minimized by administering increasingly smaller doses of the barbiturate itself or another drug that produces similar effects. The withdrawal program is still a dangerous one, however, especially if barbiturate addiction is complicated by alcoholism or dependence on other drugs.

Hallucinogens: LSD and Related Drugs

The **hallucinogens** are drugs that are thought to induce hallucinations. However, these preparations usually do not in fact "create" sensory images but distort them so that an individual sees or hears things in different and unusual ways. These drugs are often referred to as psychedelics. The major drugs in this category are LSD (lysergic acid diethylamide) or "acid," mescaline, and psilocybin.

LSD The most potent of the hallucinogens, the odorless, colorless, and tasteless drug **LSD** can produce intoxication with an amount smaller than a grain of salt. It is a chemically synthesized substance first discovered by the Swiss chemist Albert Hoffman in 1938. Hoffman was not aware of the potent hallucinatory qualities of LSD until he swallowed a small amount. This is his report of the experience:

> Last Friday, April 16, 1943, I was forced to stop my work in the laboratory in the middle of the afternoon and to go home, as I was seized by a peculiar restlessness associated with a sensation of mild dizziness. On arriving home, I lay down and sank into a kind of drunkenness which was not unpleasant and which was characterized by extreme activity of imagination. As I lay in a dazed condition with my eyes closed (I experienced daylight as disagreeably bright) there surged upon me an uninterrupted stream of fantastic images of extraordinary plasticity and vividness and accompanied by an intense kaleidoscope-like play of colors. This condition gradually passed off after about two hours. (Hoffman, 1971, p. 23)

Hoffman followed up this experience with a series of planned self-observations with LSD, some of which he described as "harrowing." Researchers thought LSD might be useful for the induction and study of hallucinogenic states or "model psychoses," which were thought to be related to schizophrenia. About 1950, LSD was introduced into the United States for purposes of such research and to ascertain whether it might have medical or therapeutic uses. Despite considerable research, however, LSD did not prove to be therapeutically useful.

After taking LSD, a person typically goes through about 8 hours of changes in sensory perception, mood swings, and feelings of depersonalization and detachment. The LSD experience is not always pleasant. It can be extremely traumatic, and the distorted objects and sounds, the illusory colors, and the new thoughts can be menacing and terrifying. For example, while under the influence of LSD, a British law student tried to continue time by using a dental drill to bore a hole in his head (Rorvik, 1970). In other instances, people undergoing bad trips have set themselves aflame, jumped from high places, and taken other drugs that proved lethal in combination with LSD.

An interesting and unusual phenomenon that may occur some time following the use of LSD is the **flashback**, an involuntary recurrence of perceptual distortions or hallucinations weeks or even months after the individual has taken the drug. Flashbacks appear to be relatively rare among people who have taken LSD only once—although they do sometimes occur. Even if no flashbacks occur, one study found that continued effects on visual function were apparent at least 2 years after LSD use. In this study, Abraham and Wolf (1988) report that individuals who had used LSD for a week had reduced visual sensitivity to light during dark adaptation and showed other visual problems compared with controls.

Although the widespread use of LSD during the 1960s and 1970s has waned in recent years with the availability of other drugs, it is still used among young people associated with the "rave culture" or club scene. One recent study reported that in a sample of 782 youths in treatment for substance abuse, 42 percent had used LSD (Hopfer et al., 2006).

MESCALINE AND PSILOCYBIN Two other hallucinogens are **mescaline**, which is derived from the small, disc-like growths (mescal buttons) at the top of the peyote cactus, and **psilocybin**, which is obtained from a variety of "sacred" Mexican mushrooms known as *Psilocybe mexicana*. These drugs have been used for centuries in the ceremonial rites of Native peoples living in Mexico, the American Southwest, and Central and South America. In fact, they were used by the Aztecs for such purposes long before the Spanish invasion. Both drugs have mind-altering and hallucinogenic properties, but their principal effect appears to be enabling an individual to see, hear, and otherwise experience events in unaccustomed ways—transporting him or her into a realm of "nonordinary reality." As with LSD, no definite evidence shows that mescaline and psilocybin actually "expand consciousness" or create new ideas; rather, they mainly alter or distort experience.

Ecstasy

The drug **Ecstasy**, or MDMA (3,4-methylenedioxymethylamphetamine), is both a hallucinogen and a stimulant that is popular as a party drug among young adults. The drug was originally patented in 1914 by the pharmaceutical company Merck, supposedly to be sold as a diet pill, but the company decided against marketing the drug because of its side effects. The drug was further evaluated and tested during the 1970s and 1980s as a potential medication for use in psychological treatment for a wide range of conditions such as posttraumatic stress, phobias, psychosomatic disorders, depression, suicidality, drug addiction, and relationship difficulties (Grob, 2000).

This photo from a rock show shows several young people intoxicated with Ecstasy.

The Ecstasy drug (MDMA—3,4-methylenedioxymethylamphetamine) is taken in pill form and is often used at "raves" or nightclubs to enhance mood. Ecstasy is an illegal substance, and manufacturers do not follow regulation and quality control.

However, its value in this capacity was not supported. At present, this drug is considered a "dangerous" drug and is listed in the most restricted category by the Drug Enforcement Administration (Murray, 2001). It is currently available in the United States only through illicit means.

Ecstasy is chemically similar to methamphetamine and to the hallucinogen mescaline and produces effects similar to those of other stimulants, although some research has suggested that the drug's hallucinogenic properties exceed those of mescaline (Kovar, 1998; Parrott & Stuart, 1997). Usually about 20 minutes after ingesting Ecstasy (typically in pill form), the person experiences a "rush" sensation followed by a feeling of calmness, energy, and well-being. The effects of Ecstasy can last for several hours. People who take the drug often report an intense experience of color and sound and mild hallucinations (Fox et al., 2001; Lieb et al., 2002; Soar et al., 2001) in addition to the high levels of energy and excitement that are produced. The drug MDMA is an addictive substance, but it is not thought to be as addictive as cocaine (Degenhardt et al., 2010). Use of the drug is accompanied by a number of adverse consequences such as nausea, sweating, clenching of teeth, muscle cramps, blurred vision, and hallucinations (Parrott, 2001).

Ecstasy has been used increasingly among college students and young adults as a party enhancement or "rave" drug at dances (Hopfer et al., 2006). In a survey of 14,000 college students, Strote and colleagues (2002) found that between 1997 and 1999, Ecstasy use increased 69 percent, from 2.8 percent to 4.7 percent. Ecstasy reportedly grew in use among 8th, 10th, and 12th graders, as noted by the Monitoring the Future study, in which nearly 5 percent of 10th and 12th graders and about 2 percent of 8th graders reportedly had used MDMA in the past year. In a recent survey of Americans over the age of 12, .02 percent of the sample reported using Ecstasy (Substance Abuse and Mental Health Services Administration, 2009).

As with many other illicit drugs, the recreational use of Ecstasy has been associated with personality characteristics of impulsivity and poor judgment (Morgan, 1998). Ecstasy users have been found to be more likely to use marijuana, engage in binge drinking, smoke cigarettes, and have multiple sexual partners (Strote et al., 2002). However, Ecstasy use is also found among naïve partygoers who are provided the drug as a means of staying awake while socializing (Boys et al., 2001).

The negative psychological and health consequences (including death) of using Ecstasy have been widely reported in the literature. One study reported on the case of a 21-year-old man who developed panic disorder after taking Ecstasy (Windhaber et al., 1998); in another case study, an 18-year-old woman reportedly developed a prolonged psychosis after a single recreational use of Ecstasy (Van Kampen & Katz, 2001). The use of Ecstasy has also been found to be associated with memory impairment (Parrott et al., 1998) and obstructive sleep apnea (Chamberlin & Saper, 2009; McCann et al. 2009). Severe organic brain problems have also been reported. Granato and colleagues (1997) describe a case in which a 20-year-old male suffered from cerebrovascular injury after taking Ecstasy. The youth went into a coma about a minute or so after taking the drug. Upon awakening, he was found to have dissociation, delirium, visual hallucinations, and poor memory for past events. Subsequent examination showed damage to his frontal lobes and his right temporal lobe. Ecstasy users have consistently shown memory deficits (Roberts et al., 2009). A recent study by Schilt and colleagues (2010) found long-term harmful neurological effects in middle-aged ecstasy users. Moderate to heavy ecstasy users showed moderate memory loss compared to controls.

Marijuana

Marijuana comes from the leaves and flowering tops of the hemp plant, *Cannabis sativa*, which grows in mild climates throughout the world. In its prepared state, marijuana consists chiefly of dried green leaves—hence the colloquial name *grass*. It is ordinarily smoked in the form of cigarettes (variously referred to as "pot," "reefers," "joints," "stash," "weed," etc.) or in pipes. In some cultures the leaves are steeped in hot water and the liquid is drunk, much as one might drink tea. Marijuana is related to a stronger drug, **hashish**, which is derived from the resin exuded by the cannabis plant and made into a gummy powder. Hashish, like marijuana, is usually smoked. Although marijuana can be considered a mild hallucinogen, there are significant differences between the nature, intensity, and duration of its effects and those induced by drugs like LSD, mescaline, and other major hallucinogens.

Both marijuana use and hashish use can be traced far back into history. Cannabis was apparently known in ancient China (Blum, 1969) and was listed in the herbal compendiums of the Chinese Emperor Shen Nung, written about 2737 B.C. Until the late 1960s, marijuana use in the United States was confined largely to members of lower-socioeconomic-status and minority groups and to people in entertainment and related fields, but marijuana use is commonplace today. Now marijuana is the most frequently used illicit drug. In 2008, 6.7 percent of the U. S. population between 12 and 17 years of age used marijuana; 16.5 percent of young adults did as well (Substance Abuse and Mental Health Services Administration, 2009), although according to the most recent Monitoring the Future study, college students have begun to show some decline in marijuana use in recent years (Johnston et al., 2009).

Minority group members and Caucasians have been shown to have comparable rates of use (Brown et al., 2004), however, one recent survey found that Hispanic American adults had lower rates of current illicit drug use (Substance Abuse and Mental Health Services Administration, 2010). Cannabis is the most commonly used drug by people with schizophrenia (Coulston et al., 2007). In a separate survey of drug-related visits to the emergency room (DAWN, 2010), 16 percent were for marijuana abuse. Many of these emergency room visits, as one might suspect, involved the use of other substances along with marijuana.

EFFECTS OF MARIJUANA The specific effects of marijuana vary greatly, depending on the quality and dosage of the drug, the personality and mood of the user, the user's past experiences with the drug, the social setting, and the user's expectations. However, considerable consensus exists among regular users that when marijuana is smoked and inhaled, a state of slight intoxication results. This state is one of mild euphoria distinguished by increased feelings of well-being, heightened perceptual acuity, and pleasant relaxation, often accompanied by a sensation

Marijuana can produce extreme euphoria, hilarity, and hypertalkativeness, but it can also produce intense anxiety and depression as well as delusions, hallucinations, and other psychotic-like behavior.

of drifting or floating away. Sensory inputs are intensified. Marijuana has the effect on the brain of altering one's internal clock (O'Leary et al., 2003). Often a person's sense of time is stretched or distorted so that an event that lasts only a few seconds may seem to cover a much longer span. Short-term memory may also be affected, as when one notices that a bite has been taken out of a sandwich but does not remember having taken it. For most users, pleasurable experiences, including sexual intercourse, are reportedly enhanced. When smoked, marijuana is rapidly absorbed, and its effects appear within seconds to minutes but seldom last more than 2 to 3 hours. Marijuana has also been used to relieve pain or nausea; see Box 3 for a discussion of the controversy over medical marijuana.

Marijuana may lead to unpleasant as well as pleasant experiences. For example, if a person uses the drug while in an unhappy, angry, suspicious and paranoid, or frightened mood, these feelings may be magnified. With higher dosages and with certain unstable or susceptible individuals, marijuana can produce extreme euphoria, hilarity, and overtalkativeness, but it can also produce intense anxiety (Zvolensky et al., 2010) and depression as well as delusions, hallucinations, and other psychotic-like experiences. Evidence suggests a strong relationship between daily marijuana use and the occurrence of psychotic symptoms (Raphael et al., 2005).

Marijuana's short-range physiological effects include a moderate increase in heart rate, a slowing of reaction time, a slight contraction of pupil size, bloodshot and itchy eyes, a dry mouth, and increased appetite. Furthermore, marijuana induces memory dysfunction and a slowing of information processing (Pope et al., 2001). Continued use of high dosages over time tends to produce lethargy and passivity along with reduced life success (Lane et al., 2005). In such cases marijuana appears to have a depressant and a hallucinogenic effect. The effects of long-term and habitual marijuana use are still under investigation, although a number of possible adverse side effects have been found to be related to the prolonged, heavy use of marijuana (Earleywine, 2002). For example, marijuana use tends to diminish self-control. One study exploring past substance-use history in incarcerated murderers reported that among men who had committed murder, marijuana was the most commonly used drug. One-third indicated that they had used the drug before the homicide, and two-thirds were experiencing some effects of the drug at the time of the murder (Spunt et al., 1994).

TREATMENT Some research has reported that many marijuana users who abstain report having uncomfortable withdrawal-like symptoms such as nervousness, tension, sleep

THE WORLD AROUND US

3

Should Marijuana Be Marketed and Sold Openly as a Medication?

Although marijuana is a Schedule 1 Drug according to the 1970 Controlled Substances Act, and U. S. Government drug control agencies have strongly opposed legalization of the drug (Walters, 2006), there have been substantial efforts to broaden its use and availability. In recent years marijuana has been distributed for pain or nausea relief from medical conditions such as cancer, AIDS, glaucoma, multiple sclerosis, migraines, and epilepsy. Proponents of medical marijuana cite its value in the treatment of these conditions, and some have pointed out that medical marijuana treatment is consistent with participation in other forms of drug treatment and may not adversely affect the outcome (Swartz, 2010). Marijuana does not cure any illness; it only reduces pain for which other medications exist (Watson, Benson et al., 2000).

Proponents of medical marijuana have made considerable inroads in securing legalization of marijuana as a treatment in 14 states and the District of Columbia. Although many professional researchers and practitioners discourage the use of marijuana because of the ill effects, others, including mental health professionals, politicians, and lay persons, press society to change the rigid control over the drug and make it legal.

States vary in how medical marijuana is made available to the public. Some locations, such as the District of Columbia, have approved medical marijuana use by a limited and controlled number of dispensaries (Southall, 2010) while others, such as California, have allowed a broad and less controlled environment to develop. A recent article by Vick (2009) points out that California's medical marijuana law (Proposition 215) has enabled the opening of more than 400 public dispensaries of medical marijuana in the Los Angeles area and resulted in marijuana becoming "mainstream." This ready access to marijuana heightens concerns over the drug serving as an "entry level" drug for more addictive and dangerous illicit substances. This problem has been a focus of the U.S. government's opposition to legalizing marijuana since it has become more widely available (Walters, 2006).

A number of problems with the use of medical marijuana have been reported, in part because of the unregulated availability of the drug; for example, one can get a "prescription" for the drug by walking into one of the many "treatment centers" and talking with a salesperson. A recent article by Moore (2009) describes the sentencing of an owner of a marijuana dispensary to a year in prison for distributing marijuana. Thus, providers of medical marijuana to the public can still face the possibility of jail time in some situations. Yardley (2010) recently pointed out a number of crimes that resulted from the medical marijuana users having had large amounts of marijuana in their homes. Mascia (2010) highlighted another problem in using medical marijuana in employment settings. A number of people have lost jobs or have not been offered a position as a result of drug screening—a requirement for employment in many positions such as security personnel, police applicants, pilots, and even some corporations such as Walmart.

Iversen (2008) makes a strong case for the research supporting the use of medical marijuana, but others continue to question the scientific basis of the medical use (Walters, 2006). Others have also pointed out that medical use of cannabis has been shown to be significantly associated with nonmedical use and could result in adverse consequences (Parakh, 2010).

Should "medical marijuana" be considered a legitimate pharmaceutical treatment? Is marijuana an effective drug based on the research, or is it without any medical value? Is marijuana being unfairly criminalized by the federal government, or does its potential as an entry drug and its medical side effects counter its value as a treatment? Should cannabis be approved for medical use by a vote of the people, as already has been done in many states, or should medical marijuana be scientifically evaluated and its use be guided by science? The controversy is likely to continue as more states vote to legalize medical marijuana and as other problems with the broadened availability of the drug emerge.

problems, and appetite change (Budney et al., 2003; Zickler, 2002). One study of substance abusers showed that marijuana users were more ambivalent and less confident about stopping use than were cocaine abusers (Budney et al., 1998).

Psychological treatment methods have been shown to be effective in reducing marijuana use in adults who are dependent on the drug (Marijuana Treatment Project Research Group, 2004). In a comparative review of psychological treatment studies of marijuana users, Nordstrom and Levin (2007) conclude that a number of therapies have been found to be effective in treating cannabis dependency, but no specific treatment approach has been found to be more effective than the others.

Some investigators have also reported that many patients do not show a positive treatment response. No pharmacotherapy treatment for cannabis dependency has been shown to be very effective (Nordstrom & Levin, 2007); however, one recent study using busiprone for treatment of marijuana dependency showed slight improvement over a placebo group (McRae et al., 2009).

As with other addictive drugs, there may be among the users many individuals with serious antisocial or "psychosis-prone" personalities (Kwapil, 1996). Treatment of marijuana use is hampered by the fact that there might be an underlying personality disorder. One study compared the effectiveness of two treatments, Relapse Prevention and Support Group, with marijuana-dependent adults (Stephens et al., 1994). Both treatment conditions resulted in substantial reduction in marijuana use in the 12 months following treatment. Relapse Prevention and Support Group discussion sessions were equally effective in bringing about changes in marijuana use.

SYNTHETIC MARIJUANA Not all discoveries or product developments today are innovations that contribute to the public good. An example of a recent chemical that is widely marketed and can result in harm for the consumers is a marijuana substitute that goes under the name of "Spice." Spice is an herbal compound that is touted as an incense blend (as are several other chemical brands such as "K2," "Blaze," and "Red X Dawn") and marketed on the Internet and in specialty shops. These products are advertised as a legal alternative to controlled substances such as marijuana. Spice is typically smoked along with tobacco; however, it tends to take longer to feel the effects than marijuana.

Many people who use Spice report that it has effects equal to or stronger than those obtained by smoking cannabis. Very little is known at this point about the make-up of Spice or its long-term effects. Reports suggest that it may contain up to 15 different herbs, of which wild dagga (*Leonotis leonurus*) and Indian warrior (*Pedicularis densiflora*) are considered to be the most likely candidates for producing a psychoactive effect. In addition, other synthetic chemicals may have been added to the drug (Griffiths et al., 2010). Although there is a limited amount of research and clinical information about synthetic marijuana, there are reports that the toxicity lasts 3 to 4 hours and often has adverse effects such as anxiety, tachycardia, hypertension, abnormally fast breathing, chest pain, heart palpitations, hallucinations, racing thoughts, and seizures (Wells & Ott, 2011).

Spice has come under the attention of drug control agencies because of the extreme and damaging side effects. A number of efforts are being made to place legal restrictions on its use and availability (McLachlan, 2009). In November 2010, the United States Drug Enforcement Administration (DEA) used its emergency scheduling authority to temporarily control five chemicals that are used to make fake marijuana products. In March of 2011, the DEA declared these chemicals to be illegal substances (Kraft, 2011).

Stimulants: Caffeine and Nicotine

The *DSM-IV-TR* includes addictions to two legally available and widely used substances: **caffeine** and **nicotine**. Al-

though these substances do not involve the extensive and self-destructive problems found in alcohol- and drug-use disorders, they can create important physical and mental health problems in our society for several reasons:

- These drugs are easy to abuse. It is easy to become addicted to them because they are widely used and most people are exposed to them early in life.
- These drugs are readily available to anyone who wants to use them; in fact, because of peer pressure, it is usually difficult to avoid using them in our society.
- Both caffeine and nicotine have clearly addictive properties; use of them promotes further use, until one craves a regular "fix" in one's daily life.
- It is difficult to quit using these drugs both because of their addictive properties and because they are so embedded in the social context. (Nicotine use, however, is falling out of favor in many settings.)
- The extreme difficulty most people have in dealing with the withdrawal symptoms when trying to "break the habit" often produces considerable frustration.
- The health problems and side effects of these drugs, particularly nicotine, have been widely noted (USDHHS, 1994). One in seven deaths in the United States is associated with cigarette consumption.

Because they are socially acceptable and readily available, caffeine and nicotine can be insidiously addictive substances. Though they do not result in the same kind of extensive, self-destructive problems as alcohol and drug disorders, caffeine and nicotine addiction can cause a myriad of health problems and are now included in the *DSM-IV-TR*.

Because of their tenacity as habits and their contributions to many major health problems, we will examine each of these addictions in more detail.

CAFFEINE The chemical compound caffeine is found in many commonly available drinks and foods. Although the consumption of caffeine is widely practiced and socially promoted in contemporary society, problems can result from excessive caffeine intake. The negative effects of caffeine involve intoxication rather than withdrawal. Unlike addiction to drugs such as alcohol or nicotine, withdrawal from caffeine does not produce severe symptoms, except for headache, which is usually mild.

As described in *DSM-IV-TR*, caffeine-induced organic mental disorder (also referred to as "caffeinism") involves symptoms of restlessness, nervousness, excitement, insomnia, muscle twitching, and gastrointestinal complaints. It follows the ingestion of caffeine-containing substances such as coffee, tea, cola, and chocolate. The amount of caffeine that results in intoxication differs among individuals.

NICOTINE The poisonous alkaloid nicotine is the chief active ingredient in tobacco; it is found in such items as cigarettes, chewing tobacco, and cigars, and it is even used as an insecticide. The use of tobacco is a significant problem in the general population. The number of Americans age 12 and older who use some form of tobacco is estimated at 70.9 million people, or about 28.4 percent of the population (Substance Abuse and Mental Health Services Administration, 2009). However, an estimated 63 percent of women and 53 percent of men have never smoked (Pleis et al. 2009).

Strong evidence exists for a nicotine-dependence syndrome (Malin, 2001; Watkins et al., 2000), which nearly always begins during the adolescent years and may continue into adult life as a difficult-to-break and health-endangering habit. Supporting the finding that nicotine may have an antianxiety property, nicotine use has been observed as being highly prevalent among those with anxiety disorders (Morissette et al., 2007). Recent evidence from stroke-related brain injury suggests that nicotine addiction might be controlled by a portion of the brain near the ear called the insula (Naqvi et al., 2007). A stroke patient with damage to that area of the brain reported that his craving for cigarettes vanished. This result suggests that the insula might be an important center for addiction to smoking, but more research is needed to support this conclusion.

The "nicotine withdrawal disorder," as it is called in *DSM-IV-TR*, results from ceasing or reducing the intake of nicotine-containing substances after an individual has developed physical dependence on them. The diagnostic criteria for nicotine withdrawal include (1) the daily use of nicotine for at least several weeks, and (2) the following symptoms after nicotine ingestion is stopped or reduced: craving for nicotine; irritability, frustration, or anger; anxiety; difficulty concentrating; restlessness; decreased heart rate; and increased appetite or weight gain. Several other physical concomitants are associated with withdrawal from nicotine including decreased metabolic rate, headaches, insomnia, tremors, increased coughing, and impairment of performance on tasks requiring attention.

These withdrawal symptoms usually continue for several days to several weeks, depending on the extent of the nicotine habit. Some individuals report a desire for nicotine continuing for several months after they quit smoking. In general, nicotine withdrawal symptoms operate in a manner similar to those of withdrawal from other addictions—they are time limited and are reduced over time as the drug intake stops, (Hughes, 2007).

TREATMENT OF NICOTINE WITHDRAWAL Over the past three decades, numerous treatment programs have been developed to help smokers quit (Hughes, 2007). Available programs use many different methods including social support groups; various pharmacologic agents that replace cigarette consumption with safer forms of nicotine such as candy, gum, or patches; self-directed change that involves giving individuals guidance in changing their own behaviors; and professional treatment using psychological procedures such as behavioral or cognitive-behavioral interventions. One recent study provided smokers with ultrasound photographs of their carotid and femoral arteries along with quit-smoking counseling. This group showed higher quit rates than controls (Bovet et al., 2002).

In general, tobacco dependence can be successfully treated, and most of the quit-smoking programs enjoy some success. They average only about a 20 to 25 percent success rate, however, although rates have been reported to be higher with treatment (Hays et al., 2001). This same level of success appears to result from the use of nicotine replacement therapy (NRT). Shiffman and colleagues (2006) point out that high-dose NRT reduces withdrawal symptoms. Treatment with active patches reduced withdrawal and craving during cessation and completely eliminated deprivation-related changes in affect or concentration. Recently, encouraging results have been reported on the use of the drug bupropion (Zyban) in preventing relapse for smokers trying to quit. The drug reduced relapse as long as the person was taking it, but relapse rates were similar to those of other treatments once the drug was discontinued (Barringer & Weaver, 2002). The highest self-reported quit rates for smokers were reportedly among patients who were hospitalized for cancer (63 percent), cardiovascular disease (57 percent), or pulmonary disease (46 percent; Smith, Reilly, et al., 2002).

Not all addictive disorders involve the use of substances with chemical properties that induce dependence. As discussed in The World Around Us 4, people can develop "addictions" to certain activities that can be just as life-threatening as severe alcoholism and just as damaging, psychologically and socially, as drug abuse. One such addiction, **pathological gambling**, is in many ways similar to substance abuse. The maladaptive behaviors involved and the treatment approaches shown to be effective suggest that these addictive disorders are quite similar to the various drug-use and drug-induced disorders.

In Review

- What are the major biological and psychological effects of using opiates such as morphine and heroin?

- What are three major causal factors in the development of opiate abuse and dependence?

- What is methamphetamine? What are the major health factors related to methamphetamine use?

- What are the physical risks of taking Ecstasy?

- Describe the effects of cannabis.

- Describe the effects of nicotine and caffeine use, and explain why these commonly available substances are included in this chapter on substance abuse.

Pathological Gambling

Although pathological gambling does not involve a chemically addictive substance (it is classified as an impulse control disorder in *DSM-IV-TR*), it is considered by many to be an addictive disorder because of the personality factors that tend to characterize compulsive gamblers (Petry & Madden, 2010). Like the substance abuse disorders, pathological gambling involves behavior maintained by short-term gains despite long-term disruption of an individual's life. There is a high comorbidity between pathological gambling and alcohol abuse disorders (Blanco, Cohen et al., 2010) and with personality disorders (Sacco et al., 2008). Pathological gambling, also known as "compulsive gambling" or disordered gambling, is a progressive disorder characterized by continuous or periodic loss of control over gambling, a preoccupation with gambling and with obtaining money for gambling, and continuation of the gambling behavior in spite of adverse consequences.

Estimates place the number of pathological gamblers worldwide at between 1 and 2 percent of the adult population (Petry, 2005). Both men and women appear to be vulnerable to pathological gambling (Hing & Breen, 2001). However, rates differ by subpopulation; for example, in some high-risk populations, such as alcoholics, the rates are higher. One study of elderly African Americans from two senior citizen centers documented the extent of gambling problems in this population; 17 percent were found to be heavy pathological gamblers (Bazargan et al., 2001). Pietrzak and colleagues (2007) found that older, disordered gamblers were significantly more likely than nongambling older adults to have alcohol-abuse problems, nicotine addiction, and health problems.

Cultural factors also appear to be important in the development of gambling problems. Pathological gambling is a particular problem among Southeast Asian refugees, especially those from Laos. Surveys of mental health problems have reported almost epidemic compulsive gambling among such groups (Aronoff, 1987; Ganju & Quan, 1987).

Gambling in our society takes many forms including casino gambling, betting on horse races or sports (legally or otherwise), Internet gaming, numbers games, lotteries, dice, bingo, and cards. Whatever an individual gambler's situation, compulsive gambling significantly affects the social, psychological, and economic well-being of the gambler's family. In fact, studies have found that a high proportion of pathological gamblers commit crimes that are related to gambling (Blaszczynski et al., 1989), family violence (Afifi et al., 2010) and other crimes of aggression (Folino & Abait, 2009).

Pathological gambling seems to be a learned pattern that is highly resistant to extinction. Some research suggests that control over gambling is related to duration and frequency of playing (Scannell et al., 2000). However, many people who become pathological gamblers won a substantial sum of money the first time they gambled; chance alone would dictate that a certain percentage of people would have such "beginner's luck." The reinforcement a person receives during this introductory phase may be a significant factor in later pathological gambling. Because everyone is likely to win from time to time, the principles of intermittent reinforcement—the most potent reinforcement schedule for operant conditioning—could explain an addict's continued gambling despite excessive losses.

Despite their awareness that the odds are against them, and despite the fact that they rarely or never repeat their early success, compulsive gamblers continue to gamble avidly. To "stake" their gambling, they often dissipate their savings, neglect their families, default on bills, and borrow money from friends and loan companies. Some resort to embezzlement, writing bad checks, or other illegal means of obtaining money. In a pioneering study of former pathological gamblers, Rosten (1961) found that they tended to be rebellious, unconventional individuals who did not seem to understand fully the ethical

Unresolved Issues

▶ *Exchanging Addictions: Is This an Effective Treatment Approach?*

Withdrawal from heroin can be extremely difficult because of the intense craving that develops for the drug. Wouldn't it be great if we had a magic bullet—a medication—that would allow people who are addicted to heroin to withdraw from it painlessly? One approach that has been used for several decades involves the administration of methadone (methadone hydrochloride, a synthetic narcotic that is as addictive as heroin), often in conjunction with a psychological or social rehabilitation program that is aimed at resocialization of the abuser. The value of this treatment comes from the fact that methadone satisfies an addict's craving for heroin without producing serious psychological impairment.

Many researchers have concluded that in addition to facilitating psychological or social rehabilitation, this drug is effective at reducing the dependence on heroin (Kreek et al., 2010). Thus, it enables many people to experience reduced craving, allowing them to alter somewhat the often desperate life circumstances they find themselves in through trying to support their expensive and all-consuming habit. In addition, opiate addicts who remain on methadone have a substantially lower death rate than those discharged from methadone maintenance programs (Fugelstad et al., 2007).

The idea that addicts may need to be maintained for life on methadone, itself a powerful and addicting drug, has been questioned both norms of society. Half of the group described themselves as "hating regulations." Often they had the unshakable feeling that "tonight is my night." Typically, they had also followed the so-called "Monte Carlo fallacy"—that after so many losses, their turn was coming up and they would hit it big. Many of the men discussed the extent to which they had "fooled themselves" by elaborate rationalizations.

Later studies also describe pathological gamblers as typically immature, rebellious, thrill-seeking, superstitious, basically antisocial, and compulsive (Hollander et al, 2000). Research has shown that pathological gambling frequently co-occurs with other disorders, particularly substance abuse such as alcohol and cocaine dependence (Kausch, 2003; Welte et al., 2004) and impulse disorders (Grant & Potenza, 2010). Those with co-occurring substance-abuse disorders typically have the most severe gambling problems (Ladd & Petry, 2003).

The causes of impulse-driven behavior in pathological gambling are complex. Some research has suggested that early trauma might contribute to the development of compulsive gambling (Scherrer et al., 2007). Although learning undoubtedly plays an important part in the development of personality factors underlying the "compulsive" gambler, recent research in brain mechanisms that are involved in motivation, reward, and decision making indicates that these mechanisms could influence the underlying impulsivity in personality (Chambers & Potenza, 2003). These investigators have suggested that important neurodevelopmental events during adolescence occur in brain regions associated with motivation and impulsive behavior. Recent research has also suggested that genetic factors might play a part in developing pathological gambling habits (Slutske et al., 2010).

Treatment of pathological gamblers has tended to parallel that of other addictive disorders. The most extensive treatment approach used with pathological gamblers is cognitive-behavioral therapy (Okude et al.,

2009). For example, Sylvain and colleagues (1997) provided cognitive-behavioral therapy for 58 pathological gamblers recruited through the media. Although 18 participants dropped out at the start and 11 quit during therapy, those who remained in treatment showed significant improvement. Of those who completed therapy, 86 percent were considered "no longer" pathological gamblers at a 1-year follow-up. However, one study (Hodgins & el-Guebaly, 2004) reports very high relapse rates among pathological gamblers—only 8 percent were free of gambling 12 months after treatment. Even studies that show improvement during treatment also report participants' difficulty remaining abstinent. In a study of 231 gamblers (Petry et al., 2006), some improved when receiving cognitive-behavioral therapy and when attending at Gambler's Anonymous (GA), an organization modeled after Alcoholics Anonymous, or when attending GA and receiving a workbook. The patients tended not to remain abstinent, although incidents were less than they usually reported. Most participants reported some gambling during the follow-up period. More positive outcomes in treating pathological gambling have been found when family relationship problems are addressed in the treatment (McComb et al., 2009).

Pathological gambling is on the increase in the United States (Potenza, 2002), particularly with the widely available gambling opportunities on the Internet (Griffiths, 2003). Liberalized gambling legislation has permitted state-operated lotteries, horse racing, and gambling casinos in an effort to increase state tax revenues. In the context of this apparent environmental support and "official" sanction for gambling, it is likely that pathological gambling will increase substantially as more and more people "try their luck." Given that pathological gamblers are resistant to treatment, future efforts to develop more effective preventive and treatment approaches will need to be increased as this problem continues to grow.

on moral and practical grounds. Methadone advocates, however, point out that addicts on methadone can function normally and hold jobs, which is not possible for most heroin addicts. In addition, methadone is available legally, and its quality is controlled by government standards. Advocates for methadone programs point out that it is not necessary to increase the dosage over time as it is with heroin use. In fact, some patients can eventually stop taking methadone without danger of relapse to heroin addiction.

However, negative consequences are sometimes associated with the use of methadone (Miller & Lyon, 2003). Methadone patients are at increased risk for health problems such as hepatitis (McCarthy & Flynn, 2001) and cognitive impairment (Scheurich, 2005; Verdejo et al., 2005). In addition, many social problems, such as trading sex for drugs, persist (El-Bassel et al., 2001); some addicts get involved with other drugs such as cocaine (Avants et al. 1998; Silverman et al., 1996);

suicide attempts are common (Darke & Ross, 2001); and violent deaths and drug overdoses are common among methadone patients (Sunjic & Zabor, 1999).

A great deal of research has shown that administering psychotherapy along with methadone increases the effectiveness of treatment (Marsch et al., 2005). However, a persistent problem of methadone maintenance programs has been the relatively high dropout rate. Several variations in methadone maintenance programs have been aimed at keeping addicts in therapy. These variations include the use of such additional drugs as clonidine (an antihypertensive drug used to treat essential hypertension and prevent headache), which aid in the detoxification process and reduce the discomfort of withdrawal symptoms. In one study, the joint use of tranquilizers such as diazepam was shown to decrease the amount of methadone consumed (Spiga et al., 2001). Another approach involves the use of behavioral shaping through contingent reinforcers (monetary vouchers) to reward abstinent patients (Preston et al., 2001).

A new approach to treating opiate dependence is one that promotes drug abstinence for addicts rather than permanent maintenance on methadone (Kosten, 2003). This program, referred to as methadone transition treatment (MTT), involves several elements over its 180-day duration. During the first 100 days, the addict is provided a stable dose of methadone to begin the withdrawal from heroin. During this period the addict also receives a psychosocial intervention that includes weekly psychoeducational classes, biweekly group therapy, and 6 months of individual therapy that continues after drug maintenance has terminated. The program ends with 80 days of phaseout in which the addict is "weaned" from methadone through systematically decreasing the doses (Piotrowski et al., 1999).

Summary

- Substance-related disorders such as alcohol or drug abuse and dependency are among the most widespread and intransigent mental health problems facing us today.

- Many problems of alcohol or drug use involve difficulties that stem solely from the intoxicating effects of the substances.

- Dependence occurs when an individual develops a tolerance for the substance or exhibits withdrawal symptoms when the substance is not available.

- Several psychoses related to alcoholism have been identified: withdrawal delirium, chronic alcoholic hallucinosis, and dementia associated with alcoholism.

- Drug-related abuse disorders may involve physiological dependence on substances such as opiates—particularly heroin—or barbiturates; however, psychological dependence may also occur with any of the drugs that are commonly used today—for example, marijuana.

- A number of factors are considered important in the etiology of substance-abuse disorders. Some substances, such as alcohol and opiates, stimulate brain centers that produce euphoria—which then becomes a desired goal.

- It is widely believed that genetic factors play some role in causing susceptibility to alcohol-abuse problems through such biological avenues as metabolic rates and sensitivity to alcohol.

- Psychological factors—such as psychological vulnerability, stress, and the desire for tension reduction—and disturbed marital relationships or failure in parental guidance are also seen as important etiologic elements in substance-use disorders.

- Although the existence of an "alcoholic personality type" has been disavowed by most theorists, a variety of personality factors apparently play an important role in the development and expression of addictive disorders.

- Sociocultural factors such as attitudes toward alcohol may predispose individuals to alcohol-related disorders.

- Possible causal factors in drug abuse include the influence of peer groups, the existence of a so-called "drug culture," and the availability of drugs as tension reducers or pain relievers.

- Some recent research has explored a possible physiological basis for drug abuse. The discovery of endorphins, opium-like substances produced by the body, has led to speculation that a biochemical basis of drug addiction may exist.

- The so-called "pleasure pathway"—the mesocorticolimbic pathway (MCLP)—has come under a great deal of study in recent years as the possible potential anatomic site underlying the addictions.

- The treatment of individuals who abuse alcohol or drugs is generally difficult and often fails. The abuse may reflect a long history of psychological difficulties; interpersonal and marital distress may be involved; and financial and legal problems may be present.

- In addition, all such problems must be dealt with by an individual who may deny that the problems exist and who may not be motivated to work on them.

- Several approaches to the treatment of chronic substance-related disorders have been developed—for example, medication to deal with withdrawal symptoms and withdrawal delirium, and dietary evaluation and treatment for malnutrition.

- Psychological therapies such as group therapy and behavioral interventions may be effective with some alcohol- or drug-abusing individuals. Another source of help for alcohol abusers is Alcoholics Anonymous; however, the extent of successful outcomes with this program has not been sufficiently studied.

- Most treatment programs require abstinence; however, some research has suggested that some alcohol abusers can learn to control their drinking while continuing to drink socially. The controversy surrounding controlled drinking continues.

- Relapse prevention strategies have proved successful in helping substance-abusing patients to deal with the challenges encountered in abstinence-based treatment approaches.

Key Terms

addictive behavior
alcohol withdrawal delirium
alcoholic
alcoholism
amphetamine
barbiturates
caffeine
cocaine
delirium tremens
Ecstasy
endorphins

flashback
hallucinogens
hashish
heroin
LSD
marijuana
mescaline
mesocorticolimbic dopamine pathway (MCLP)
methadone
morphine

nicotine
opium
pathological gambling
psilocybin
psychoactive substances
substance abuse
substance dependence
substance-related disorders
tolerance
toxicity
withdrawal

Glossary

Many of the key terms listed in the glossary appear in boldface when first introduced in the text discussion. A number of other terms commonly encountered in this or other psychology texts are also included; you are encouraged to make use of this glossary both as a general reference tool and as a study aid for the course in abnormal psychology.

Addictive behavior. Behavior based on the pathological need for a substance or activity; it may involve the abuse of substances, such as nicotine, alcohol, or cocaine, or gambling.

Alcohol withdrawal delirium. Acute delirium associated with withdrawal from alcohol after prolonged heavy consumption; characterized by intense anxiety, tremors, fever and sweating, and hallucinations.

Alcoholic. A term used to characterize a person who is addicted to alcohol.

Alcoholism. Dependence on alcohol that seriously interferes with life adjustment.

Amphetamine. Drug that produces a psychologically stimulating and energizing effect.

Barbiturates. Synthetic drugs that act as depressants to calm the individual and induce sleep.

Caffeine. A drug of dependence found in many commonly available drinks and foods.

Cocaine. Stimulating and pain-reducing psychoactive drug.

Delirium tremens. See **Alcohol withdrawal delirium**.

Ecstasy. A human manufactured drug that is taken orally and acts as both a stimulant and a hallucinogen. The drug effects include feelings of mental stimulation, emotional warmth, enhanced sensory perception, and increased physical energy.

Endorphins. Opiates produced in the brain and throughout the body that function like neurotransmitters to dampen pain sensations. They also play a role in the body's building up tolerance to certain drugs.

Flashback. Involuntary recurrence of perceptual distortions or hallucinations weeks or months after taking a drug; in post-traumatic stress disorder, a dissociative state in which the person briefly relives the traumatic experience.

Hallucinogens. Drugs known to induce hallucinations; often referred to as psychedelics.

Hashish. Strongest drug derived from the hemp plant; a relative of marijuana that is usually smoked.

Heroin. Powerful psychoactive drug, chemically derived from morphine, that relieves pain but is even more intense and addictive than morphine.

LSD (lysergic acid diethylamide). The most potent of the hallucinogens. It is odorless, colorless, and tasteless, and an amount smaller than a grain of salt can produce intoxication.

Marijuana. Mild hallucinogenic drug derived from the hemp plant, often smoked in cigarettes called reefers or joints.

Mescaline. Hallucinogenic drug derived from the peyote cactus.

Mesocorticolimbic dopamine pathway (MCLP). Center of psychoactive drug activation in the brain. This area is involved in the release of dopamine and in mediating the rewarding properties of drugs.

Methadone. Synthetic narcotic related to heroin; used in treatment of heroin addiction because it satisfies the craving for heroin without producing serious psychological impairment.

Morphine. Addictive drug derived from opium that can serve as a powerful sedative and pain reliever.

Nicotine. Addictive akaloid that is the chief active ingredient in tobacco and a drug of dependence.

Opium. Narcotic drug that leads to physiological dependence and the development of tolerance; derivatives are morphine, heroin, and codeine.

Pathological gambling. Progressive disorder characterized by loss of control over gambling, preoccupation with gambling and obtaining money for gambling, and irrational gambling behavior in spite of adverse consequences.

Psilocybin. Hallucinogenic drug derived from a variety of mushrooms.

Psychoactive substance. Drug that affects mental functioning.

Substance abuse. Maladaptive pattern of substance use manifested by recurrent and significant adverse consequences related to the use of the substance.

Substance dependence. Severe form of substance use disorder involving physiological dependence on the substance, tolerance, withdrawal, and compulsive drug taking.

Substance-related disorders. Patterns of maladaptive behavior centered on the regular use of a substance, such as a drug or alcohol.

Tolerance. Need for increased amounts of a substance to achieve the desired effects.

Toxicity. Poisonous nature of a substance.

Withdrawal. Intellectual, emotional, or physical retreat.

Photo Credits

Credits are listed in order of appearance.

Text Credits

Credits are listed in order of appearance.

Sexual Variants, Abuse, and Dysfunctions

From Chapter 12 of *Abnormal Psychology*, Fifteenth Edition. James N. Butcher, Susan Mineka, Jill M. Hooley. Copyright © 2013 by Pearson Education, Inc. All rights reserved.

Sexual Variants, Abuse, and Dysfunctions

Loving, sexually satisfying relationships contribute a great deal to our happiness, and if we are not in such relationships, we are apt to spend a great deal of time, effort, and emotional energy looking for them. Sexuality is a central concern of our lives, influencing with whom we fall in love and mate and how happy we are with our partner and with ourselves.

In this chapter we shall first look at the psychological problems that make sexual fulfillment especially difficult for some people—the vast majority of them men—who develop unusual sexual interests that are difficult to satisfy in a socially acceptable manner. For example, exhibitionists are sexually aroused by showing their genitals to strangers, who are likely to be disgusted, frightened, and potentially traumatized. Other *sexual or gender variants* may be problematic primarily to the individual: Transsexualism, for example, is a disorder involving discomfort with one's biological sex and a strong desire to be of the opposite sex. (In the current *DSM*, transsexualism is called "gender identity disorder in adolescents and adults.") Still other variants such as fetishism, in which sexual interest centers on some inanimate object or body part, involve behaviors that, although bizarre and unusual, do not clearly harm anyone. Perhaps no other area covered in this text exposes the difficulties in defining boundaries between normality and psychopathology as clearly as variant sexuality does.

The second issue we shall consider is *sexual abuse*, a pattern of pressured, forced, or inappropriate sexual contact. During the last few decades, there has been a tremendous increase in attention to the problem of sexual abuse of both children and adults. A great deal of research has addressed its causes and consequences. As we shall see, some related issues, such as the reality of recovered memories of sexual abuse, are extremely controversial.

The third category of sexual difficulties examined in this chapter is *sexual dysfunctions*, which include problems that impede satisfactory performance of sexual acts. People who have sexual dysfunctions (or their partners) typically view them as problems. Premature ejaculation, for example, causes men to reach orgasm much earlier than they and their partners find satisfying. And women with orgasmic disorder get sexually aroused and enjoy sexual activity but have a persistent delay, or absence, of orgasm following a normal sexual excitement or arousal phase.

Much less is known about sexual deviations, abuse, and dysfunctions than is known about many of the other disorders we have considered thus far in this text. There are also fewer sex researchers than researchers for many other disorders, so fewer articles related to research on sexual deviations and dysfunctions are published compared to the number of articles on anxiety and mood disorders or schizophrenia. One major reason is the sex taboo. Although sex is an important concern for most people, many have difficulty talking about it openly—especially when the relevant behavior is socially stigmatized, as homosexuality has often been historically. This makes it hard to obtain knowledge about even the most basic facts, such as the frequency of various sexual practices, feelings, and attitudes.

A second reason why sex research has progressed less rapidly is that many issues related to sexuality—including homosexuality, teenage sexuality, abortion, and childhood sexual abuse—are among our most divisive and controversial. In fact, sex research is itself controversial and not well funded. In the 1990s two large-scale sex surveys were halted because of political opposition even after the surveys had been officially approved and deemed scientifically meritorious (Udry, 1993). Conservative former senator Jesse Helms and others had argued that sex researchers tended to approve of premarital sex and homosexuality and that this would likely bias the results of the surveys. Fortunately, one of these surveys was funded privately, though on a much smaller scale, and it is still considered the definitive study although it was conducted in the 1990s (Laumann et al., 1994; see also Laumann et al., 1999). Another attack led by social conservatives occurred in 2003, when several federal grants were criticized because they focused on sex (Kempner, 2008). A legislative attempt to defund five of the grants barely failed.

Despite these significant barriers, significant progress has been made in the past half-century in understanding some important things about sexual and gender variants and dysfunctions. The contemporary era of sex research was first launched by Alfred Kinsey in the early 1950s (Kinsey et al., 1948; Kinsey et al., 1953). Kinsey and his pioneering work are portrayed in a fascinating way in the 2004 award-winning movie *Kinsey*. However, before we discuss this progress, we first examine sociocultural influences on sexual behavior and attitudes in general. We do so to provide some perspective about cross-cultural variability in standards of sexual conduct and how these perspectives have changed over time. Such examples will remind us that we must exercise special caution in classifying sexual practices as "abnormal" or "deviant."

Loving, sexually satisfying relationships contribute a great deal to our happiness, but our understanding of them has advanced slowly, largely because they are so difficult for people to talk about openly and because funding for research is often hard to come by.

Sociocultural Influences on Sexual Practices and Standards

Although some aspects of sexuality and mating, such as men's greater emphasis on their partner's attractiveness, are cross-culturally universal (Buss, 1989, 2012), others are quite variable. For example, all known cultures have taboos against sex between close relatives, but attitudes toward premarital sex have varied considerably across history and around the world. Ideas about acceptable sexual behavior also change over time. Less than 100 years ago, for example, sexual modesty in Western cultures was such that women's arms and legs were always hidden in public. Although this is by no means the case in Western cultures today, it remains true in many Muslim countries.

Despite the substantial variability in sexual attitudes and behavior in different times and places, people typically behave as though the sexual standards of their own time and place are obviously correct, and they tend to be intolerant of sexual nonconformity. Sexual nonconformists are often considered evil or sick. We do not mean to suggest that such judgments are always arbitrary. There has probably never existed a society in which Jeffrey Dahmer, who was sexually aroused by killing men, having sex with them, storing their corpses, and sometimes eating them, would be considered psychologically normal. Nevertheless, it is useful to be aware of historical and cultural influences on sexuality. When the expression or the acceptance of a certain behavior varies considerably across eras and cultures, we should at least pause to consider the possibility that our own stance is not the only appropriate one.

Because the influences of time and place are so important in shaping sexual behavior and attitudes, we begin by exploring three cases that illustrate how opinions about "acceptable" and "normal" sexual behavior may change dramatically over time and may differ dramatically from one culture to another. In the first case, America during the mid-1800s, "degeneracy theory," a set of beliefs about sexuality, led to highly conservative sexual practices and dire warnings about most kinds of sexual "indulgence." In the second case, we look briefly at the Sambia tribe in New Guinea, in which a set of beliefs about sexuality prescribe that all normal adolescent males go through a stage of homosexuality before switching rather abruptly to heterosexuality in adulthood. Finally, in the third case, we consider changes across time in the status of homosexuality in Western culture.

Case 1: Degeneracy and Abstinence Theory

During the 1750s, Swiss physician Simon Tissot developed *degeneracy theory*, the central belief of which was that semen is necessary for physical and sexual vigor in men and

for masculine characteristics such as beard growth (Money, 1985, 1986). He based this theory on observations about human eunuchs and castrated animals. We now know, of course, that loss of the male hormone testosterone, and not of semen, is responsible for the relevant characteristics of eunuchs and castrated animals. On the basis of his theory, however, Tissot asserted that two practices were especially harmful: masturbation and patronizing prostitutes. Both of these practices wasted the vital fluid, semen, as well as (in his view) overstimulating and exhausting the nervous system. Tissot also recommended that married people engage solely in procreative sex to avoid the waste of semen.

A descendant of degeneracy theory, abstinence theory, was advocated in America during the 1830s by the Reverend Sylvester Graham (Money, 1985, 1986). The three cornerstones of his crusade for public health were healthy food (graham crackers were named for him), physical fitness, and sexual abstinence. In the 1870s Graham's most famous successor, Dr. John Harvey Kellogg, published a paper in which he ardently disapproved of masturbation and urged parents to be wary of signs that their children were indulging in it. He wrote about the 39 signs of "the secret vice," which included weakness, dullness of the eyes, sleeplessness, untrustworthiness, bashfulness, love of solitude, unnatural boldness, mock piety, and round shoulders.

As a physician, Kellogg was professionally admired and publicly influential, and he earned a fortune publishing books discouraging masturbation. His recommended treatments for "the secret vice" were quite extreme. For example, he advocated that persistent masturbation in boys be treated by sewing the foreskin with silver wire or, as a last resort, by circumcision without anesthesia. Female masturbation was to be treated by burning the clitoris with carbolic acid. Kellogg, like Graham, was also very concerned with dietary health—especially with the idea that consumption of meat increased sexual desire. Thus, he urged people to eat more cereals and nuts and invented Kellogg's cornflakes "almost literally, as anti-masturbation food" (Money, 1986, p. 186).

Given the influence of physicians like Kellogg, it should come as no surprise that many people believed that masturbation caused insanity (Hare, 1962). This hypothesis had started with the anonymous publication in the early eighteenth century in London of a book entitled *Onania, or the Heinous Sin of Self-Pollution*. It asserted that masturbation was a common cause of insanity. This idea probably arose from observations that many patients in mental asylums masturbated openly (unlike sane people, who are more likely to do it in private) and that the age at which masturbation tends to begin (at puberty in adolescence) precedes by several years the age when the first signs of insanity often appear (in late adolescence and young adulthood) (Abramson & Seligman, 1977). The idea that masturbation may cause insanity appeared in some psychiatry textbooks as late as the 1940s.

Although abstinence theory and associated attitudes seem highly puritanical by today's standards, they have had a long-lasting influence on attitudes toward sex in American and other Western cultures. It was not until 1972 that the American Medical Association declared, "Masturbation is a normal part of adolescent sexual development and requires no medical management" (American Medical Association Committee on Human Sexuality, 1972, p. 40). Around the same time, the *Boy Scout Manual* dropped its antimasturbation warnings. Nonetheless, in 1994 Jocelyn Elders was fired as U.S. Surgeon General for suggesting publicly that sex education courses should include discussion of masturbation. Moreover, the Roman Catholic Church still holds that masturbation is sinful.

Case 2: Ritualized Homosexuality in Melanesia

Melanesia is a group of islands in the South Pacific that has been intensively studied by anthropologists, who have uncovered cultural influences on sexuality unlike any known in the West. During the recent past between 10 and 20 percent of Melanesian societies practice a form of homosexuality within the context of male initiation rituals, which all male members of society must experience.

The best-studied society has been the Sambia of Papua New Guinea (Herdt, 2000; Herdt & Stoller, 1990). Two beliefs reflected in Sambian sexual practices are *semen conservation* and *female pollution*. Like Tissot, the Sambians believe that semen is important for many things including physical growth, strength, and spirituality. Furthermore, they believe that it takes many inseminations (and much semen) to impregnate a woman. Finally, they believe that semen cannot easily be replenished by the body and so must be conserved or obtained elsewhere. The female pollution doctrine is the belief that the female body is unhealthy to males, primarily because of menstrual fluids. At menarche, Sambian women are secretly initiated in the menstrual hut forbidden to all males.

In order to obtain or maintain adequate amounts of semen, young Sambian males practice semen exchange with each other. Beginning as boys, they learn to practice fellatio (oral sex) in order to ingest sperm, but after puberty they can also take the penetrative role, inseminating younger boys. Ritualized homosexuality among the young Sambian men is seen as an exchange of sexual pleasure for vital semen. (It is ironic that although both the Sambians and the Victorian-era Americans believed in semen conservation, their solutions to the problem were radically different.) When Sambian males are well past puberty, they begin the transition to heterosexuality. At this time the female body is thought to be less dangerous because the males have ingested protective semen over the previous years. For a time, they may begin having sex with women and still participate in fellatio with younger boys, but homosexual behavior stops after the birth of a man's first child. Most of the Sambian men make the transition to exclusive adult heterosexuality without problems, and those who do not are viewed as misfits.

Ritualized homosexuality among the Melanesians is a striking example of the influence of culture on sexual attitudes and behavior. A Melanesian adolescent who refuses to practice homosexuality would be viewed as abnormal, and such adolescents are apparently absent or rare. In the United States ritualized homosexuality of this type would be stigmatized as homosexual pedophilia, but Melanesian boys who practice it appear neither to have strong objections nor to be derailed from eventual heterosexuality. Obviously, homosexuality among the Sambia is not the same as homosexuality in contemporary America, with the possible exception of those Sambian men who have difficulty making the transition to heterosexuality.

Case 3: Homosexuality and American Psychiatry

During the past half-century, the status of homosexuality has changed enormously, both within psychiatry and psychology and for many Western societies in general. In the not-too-distant past, homosexuality was a taboo topic. Now, movies, talk shows, and television sitcoms and dramas address the topic explicitly by including gay men and lesbians in leading roles. As we shall see, developments in psychiatry and psychology have played an important part in these changes. Homosexuality was officially removed from the *DSM* (where it had previously been classified as a sexual deviation) in 1973 and today is no longer regarded as a mental disorder. A brief survey of attitudes toward homosexuality within the mental health profession itself will again illustrate how attitudes toward various expressions of human sexuality may change over time.

HOMOSEXUALITY AS SICKNESS Reading the medical and psychological literature on homosexuality written before 1970 can be a jarring experience, especially if one subscribes to views prevalent today. Relevant articles included "Effeminate homosexuality: A disease of childhood" and "On the cure of homosexuality." It is only fair to note, however, that the view that homosexual people are mentally ill was relatively tolerant compared with some earlier views—for example, the idea that homosexual people are criminals in need of incarceration (Bayer, 1981). British and American cultures had long taken punitive approaches to homosexual behavior. In the sixteenth century, King Henry VIII of England declared "the detestable and abominable vice of buggery [anal sex]" a felony punishable by death, and it was not until 1861 that the maximum penalty was reduced to 10 years' imprisonment. Similarly, laws in the United States were very repressive until recently, with homosexual behavior continuing to be a criminal offense in some states (Eskridge, 2008) until the 2003 Supreme Court ruling that struck down a Texas state law banning sexual behavior between two people of the same sex (*Lawrence & Garner v. Texas*). For the first time, this ruling established a broad constitutional right to sexual privacy in the United States.

During the late nineteenth and early twentieth centuries, several prominent sexologists such as Havelock Ellis and Magnus Hirschfeld suggested that homosexuality is natural and consistent with psychological normality. Freud's own attitude toward homosexual people was also remarkably progressive for his time and is well expressed in his touching "Letter to an American Mother" (1935).

> Dear Mrs. . . .
>
> I gather from your letter that your son is a homosexual. I am most impressed by the fact that you do not mention this term yourself in your information about him. May I question you, why you avoid it? Homosexuality is assuredly no advantage, but it is nothing to be ashamed of, no vice, no degradation, it cannot be classified as an illness. . . . Many highly respectable individuals of ancient and modern times have been homosexuals, several of the greatest men among them (Plato, Michelangelo, Leonardo da Vinci, etc.). It is a great injustice to persecute homosexuality as a crime, and cruelty too. . . .
>
> By asking me if I can help, you mean, I suppose, if I can abolish homosexuality and make normal heterosexuality take its place. The answer is, in a general way, we cannot promise to achieve it. . . .
>
> Sincerely yours with kind wishes,
> Freud

Beginning in the 1940s, however, other psychoanalysts, led by Sandor Rado, began to take a more pessimistic view of the mental health of homosexual people—and a more optimistic view of the possible success of therapy to induce heterosexuality (Herek, 2010). Rado (1962) believed that homosexuality develops in people whose heterosexual desires are too psychologically threatening; thus, in this view, homosexuality is an escape from heterosexuality and therefore incompatible with mental health (see also Bieber et al., 1962). In the case of male homosexuality, one argument was that domineering, emotionally smothering mothers and detached, hostile fathers played a causal role. Unfortunately, these psychoanalysts based their opinions primarily on their experiences seeing gay men in therapy, who are obviously more likely than other gay men to be psychologically troubled (Herek, 2010).

HOMOSEXUALITY AS NONPATHOLOGICAL VARIATION Around 1950, the view of homosexuality as sickness began to be challenged by both scientists and homosexual people themselves (e.g., Herek, 2010). Scientific blows to the pathology position included Alfred Kinsey's finding that homosexual behavior was more common than had been previously believed (Kinsey et al., 1948; Kinsey et al., 1953). Influential studies also demonstrated that trained psychologists could not distinguish the psychological test results of homosexual subjects from those of heterosexual subjects (e.g., Hooker, 1957).

Gay men and lesbians also began to challenge the psychiatric orthodoxy that homosexuality is a mental disorder. The 1960s saw the birth of the radical gay liberation movement, which took the more uncompromising stance that "gay is good." The decade closed with the famous Stonewall riot in New York City, sparked by police mistreatment of gay men, which sent a clear signal that homosexual people would no longer tolerate

being treated as second-class citizens. By the 1970s, openly gay psychiatrists and psychologists were working from within the mental health profession to have homosexuality removed from *DSM-II* (APA, 1968).

After acrimonious debate in 1973 and 1974, the American Psychiatric Association (APA) voted in 1974 by a vote of 5,854 to 3,810 to remove homosexuality from *DSM-II*. This episode was a milestone for gay rights. We believe the APA made a correct decision here because the vast majority of evidence shows that homosexuality is compatible with psychological normality (e.g., Herek, 2010). Challenges by gay and lesbian people forced mental health professionals to confront the issue explicitly, and these professionals made the correct determination that homosexuality is not a psychological disorder.

After mental health professionals stopped merely assuming that homosexuality was pathological, research began systematically to address mental health concerns of gay men and lesbians. Several large and careful surveys have examined rates of mental problems in people with and without homosexual feelings or behavior (Chakraborty et al., 2011; Sandfort et al., 2001; see Herek & Garnets, 2007, for a review). Homosexual people do appear to have elevated risk for some mental problems. For example, compared with heterosexual men and women, gay men and lesbians have higher rates of anxiety disorders and depression, and they are more likely to contemplate and attempt suicide (Savin-Williams, 2006). Lesbians also have a higher rate of substance abuse (Herek & Garnets, 2007; Sandfort et al., 2001). Although it remains unclear why homosexual people have higher rates of certain problems (Bailey, 1999), one plausible explanation is that such problems result from stressful life events related to societal stigmatizing of homosexuality (Hatzenbeuhler et al., 2010; Herek & Garnets, 2007). Regardless, homosexuality is compatible with psychological health—most gay men and lesbians do not have mental disorders.

During the past 50 years gay men and lesbians have made momentous progress toward legal rights and social acceptance in much of the developed world. For example, in 2010 for the first time a majority of Americans viewed homosexual relations between adults as morally acceptable (Gallup, 2010). A plurality of Americans now support marriage for same-sex couples (Smith, 2011), and in many nations and several U.S. states gay men and lesbians have the legal right to marry. In some parts of the world, however, progress toward equal rights and acceptance has lagged far behind. In some countries in Africa and the Middle East, large majorities disapprove of homosexuality (Pew Research Center, 2007), and in a few of those countries homosexual people may be subject to capital punishment. The marked cross-cultural and historical variation in treatment of homosexual people should remind us to be cautious in assuming that a currently unpopular or uncommon trait is pathological without careful and persuasive analysis. Sometimes it is culture that is the problem.

In Review

- What does each of the three examples of sociocultural influences on sexual practices and standards reveal about cultural differences and historical changes in what is considered acceptable and normal sexual behavior?

- How has the psychiatric view of homosexuality changed over time? Identify a few key historical events that propelled this change.

Sexual and Gender Variants

We now turn to the problematic sexual variants included in *DSM-IV-TR*. There are two general categories: paraphilias and gender identity disorders.

The Paraphilias

People with **paraphilias** have recurrent, intense sexually arousing fantasies, sexual urges, or behaviors that generally involve (1) nonhuman objects, (2) the suffering or humiliation of oneself or one's partner, or (3) children or other nonconsenting persons. To meet *DSM-IV-TR* criteria, these patterns must last at least 6 months. According to *DSM-IV-TR* (APA, 2000), five of these conditions can be diagnosed simply if the person has acted on his fantasies or urges and has not experienced significant distress or impairment—which is otherwise a criterion for nearly all mental disorders (see also Maletzky, 2002). This practice recognizes that certain paraphilic behaviors are problematic even if the individual is not bothered by them. A useful distinction proposed for *DSM-5* is that between paraphilias and paraphilic disorders (Blanchard, 2010). Paraphilias are unusual sexual interests, but they need not cause harm either to the individual or to others. Only if they cause such harm do they become paraphilic disorders. One can imagine two paraphilic patients, both with a fetish for women's feet, but only one of them is bothered by his erotic interest. In this hypothetical example, both have paraphilias but only one has a paraphilic disorder.

Although mild forms of these conditions probably occur in the lives of many normal people, a paraphilic person is distinguished by the insistence, and in some cases the relative exclusivity, with which his sexuality focuses on the acts or objects in question—without which orgasm is sometimes impossible. Paraphilias also frequently have a compulsive quality, and some individuals with paraphilias require orgasmic release as often as 4 to 10 times per day (Money, 1986; Weiner & Rosen, 1999). Individuals with paraphilias may or may not have persistent desires to change their sexual preferences. Because nearly all such persons are male (a fact whose etiological implications we consider later), we use masculine pronouns to refer to them (see Federoff et al., 1999, for some case examples of women with paraphilias).

No one knows how common different paraphilias are. Good prevalence data do not exist, in part because people are often reluctant to disclose such deviant behavior (Maletzky, 2002). The *DSM-IV-TR* recognizes eight specific paraphilias: (1) fetishism, (2) transvestic fetishism, (3) voyeurism, (4) exhibitionism, (5) sexual sadism, (6) sexual masochism, (7) pedophilia, and (8) frotteurism (rubbing one's genital area against a nonconsenting person). An additional category, paraphilias not otherwise specified, includes several rarer disorders such as telephone scatologia (obscene phone calls), necrophilia (sexual desire for corpses), zoophilia (sexual interest in animals; Williams & Weinberg, 2003), apotemnophilia (sexual excitement and desire about having a limb amputated), and coprophilia (sexual arousal to feces). Although some of different paraphilias tend to co-occur together, we will discuss each of them separately. In addition, our discussion of pedophilia is postponed until a later section concerning sexual abuse.

FETISHISM In **fetishism**, the individual has recurrent, intense sexually arousing fantasies, urges, and behaviors involving the use of some inanimate object to obtain sexual gratification (see *DSM-IV-TR* Criteria for Several Different Paraphilias). As is generally true for the paraphilias, reported cases of female fetishists are extremely rare (Mason, 1997). Usually the fetishistic object is required or strongly preferred during sexual arousal and activity. Many men have a strong sexual fascination for paraphernalia such as bras, garter belts, hose, and high heels, but most do not typically meet diagnostic criteria for fetishism because the paraphernalia are not necessary or strongly preferred for sexual arousal. Nevertheless, they do illustrate the relatively high frequency of fetish-like preferences among men. Fetishism occurs frequently in the context of sadomasochistic activity but is relatively rare among sexual offenders (Kafka, 2010).

DSM-IV-TR states that a fetish is diagnosed only when the object is inanimate, such as lingerie or shoes, but traditionally most sex researchers have not made this distinction. Rather, an erotic preoccupation with nonsexual body parts such as feet, hair, ears, and hands—referred to as partialism—is generally included under fetishism. In rare cases, more unusual fetishes develop, as, for example, in men who are sexually fixated on people who have an amputated limb (First, 2005). The mode of using these objects to achieve sexual excitation and gratification varies considerably, but it commonly involves masturbating while kissing, fondling, tasting, or smelling the objects. In the context of consensual sexual relationships fetishism does not normally interfere with the rights of others. However, some partners who do not share an erotic fascination with

DSM-IV-TR

Criteria for Several Different Paraphilias

Fetishism

A. Over a period of at least 6 months, recurrent, intense sexually arousing fantasies, sexual urges, or behaviors involving the use of nonliving objects (e.g., female undergarments).

B. The fantasies, sexual urges, or behaviors cause clinically significant distress or impairment in social, occupational, or other important areas of functioning.

C. The fetish objects are not limited to articles of female clothing used in cross-dressing (as in Transvestic Fetishism) or devices designed for the purpose of tactile genital stimulation (e.g., a vibrator).

Transvestic Fetishism

A. Over a period of at least 6 months, in a heterosexual male, recurrent, intense sexually arousing fantasies, sexual urges, or behaviors involving cross-dressing.

B. The fantasies, sexual urges, or behaviors cause clinically significant distress or impairment in social, occupational, or other important areas of functioning.

Voyeurism

A. Over a period of at least 6 months, recurrent, intense sexually arousing fantasies, sexual urges, or behaviors involving the act of observing an unsuspecting person who is naked, in the process of disrobing, or engaging in sexual activity.

B. The person has acted on these sexual urges, or the sexual urges or fantasies cause marked distress or interpersonal difficulty.

Exhibitionism

A. Over a period of at least 6 months, recurrent, intense sexually arousing fantasies, sexual urges, or behaviors involving the exposure of one's genitals to an unsuspecting stranger.

B. The person has acted on these sexual urges, or the sexual urges or fantasies cause marked distress or interpersonal difficulty.

Sexual Sadism

A. Over a period of at least 6 months, recurrent, intense sexually arousing fantasies, sexual urges, or behaviors involving acts (real, not simulated) in which the psychological or physical suffering (including humiliation) of the victim is sexually exciting to the person.

B. The person has acted on these sexual urges with a nonconsenting person, or the sexual urges or fantasies cause marked distress or interpersonal difficulty.

Sexual Masochism

A. Over a period of at least 6 months, recurrent, intense sexually arousing fantasies, sexual urges, or behaviors involving the act (real, not simulated) of being humiliated, beaten, bound, or otherwise made to suffer.

B. The fantasies, sexual urges, or behaviors cause clinically significant distress or impairment in social, occupational, or other important areas of functioning.

Pedophilia

A. Over a period of at least 6 months, recurrent, intense sexually arousing fantasies, sexual urges, or behaviors involving sexual activity with a prepubescent child or children (generally age 13 years or younger).

B. The person has acted on these sexual urges, or the sexual urges or fantasies cause marked distress or interpersonal difficulty.

C. The person is at least age 16 years and at least 5 years older than the child or children in Criterion A.

Source: Reprinted with permission from the American Psychiatric Association. *Diagnostic and Statistical Manual of Mental Disorders*, Fourth Edition, *Text Revision* (Copyright © 2000). American Psychiatric Association.

a fetishistic object may understandably object to participating. Some paraphilic men are so ashamed of their desires that they cannot bring themselves to ask partners. Bergner (2009) relates the case of a foot fetishist who chooses chemical castration to suppress his desire rather than tell his wife.

To obtain the required object, some men with fetishes may commit burglary, theft, or even assault. The articles most commonly stolen by such individuals are probably women's undergarments. In such cases, the excitement and suspense of the criminal act itself typically reinforce the sexual stimulation and sometimes actually constitute the fetish, the stolen article itself being of little importance. One example of this pattern of fetishism is provided in the case of a man whose fetish was women's panties:

Panties

A single, 32-year-old male freelance photographer. . . . related that although he was somewhat sexually attracted by women, he was far more attracted by "their panties." . . . [His] sexual excitement began about age 7, when he came upon a porno-graphic magazine and felt stimulated by pictures of partially nude women wearing "panties." His first ejaculation occurred at 13 via masturbation to fantasies of women wearing panties. He masturbated into his older sister's panties, which he had stolen without her knowledge. Subsequently he stole panties from her friends and from other women he met socially. . . . The pattern of masturbating into women's underwear had been his preferred method of achieving sexual excitement and orgasm from adoles-cence until the present consultation.

Source: Adapted with permission from the *DSM III Diagnostic and Sta-tistical Manual of Mental Disorders,* Third Edition, *Case Book,* (Copyright ©1981). American Psychiatric Association.

One common hypothesis regarding the etiology of fetishism emphasizes the importance of classical condi-tioning and social learning (e.g., Maletzky, 2002; Mason, 1997). For example, it is not difficult to imagine how women's underwear might become eroticized via its close association with sex and the female body. But only a small number of men develop fetishes so even if the hypoth-esis has merit there must be individual differences in conditionability of sex-ual responses (just as there are differ-ences in the conditionability of fear and anxiety responses). Men high in sexual conditionability would be prone to de-veloping one or more fetishes. We will return later to the role of conditioning in the development of paraphilias more generally.

TRANSVESTIC FETISHISM Accord-ing to *DSM-IV-TR,* heterosexual men who experience recurrent, intense sexu-ally arousing fantasies, urges, or be-haviors that involve cross-dressing as a female may be diagnosed with **trans-vestic fetishism** (see *DSM-IV-TR* Crite-ria on p. 420). Although some gay men dress "in drag" on occasion, they do not typically do this for sexual pleasure and hence are not transvestic fetishists. Typically, the onset of transvestism is

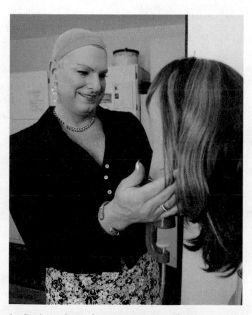

Studies have shown that transvestic men often feel sexual arousal while cross-dressing, as well as less anxiety and shyness when in their female roles. What are some of the emotional issues cross-dressing presents both for the man and for his family?

during adolescence and involves masturbation while wear-ing female clothing or undergarments. Blanchard (1989, 2010) has hypothesized that the psychological motiva-tion of many transvestites includes *autogynephilia:* para-philic sexual arousal by the thought or fantasy of being a woman (Blanchard, 1991, 1993; Lawrence, 2007; Zucker & Blanchard, 1997). The great sexologist Magnus Hirschfeld first identified a class of cross-dressing men who are sexu-ally aroused by the image of themselves as women: "They feel attracted not by the women outside them, but by the woman inside them" (Hirschfeld, 1948, p. 167). Not all men with transvestic fetishism show clear evidence of autogy-nephilia (Blanchard, 2010). The others seem quite similar to typical fetishists, focusing on specifics of their preferred female clothing and without having clear fantasies of be-coming women. Among transvestic fetishists, strength of autogynephilic fantasies strongly predicts gender dyspho-ria and desire for sex reassignment surgery (Blanchard, 2010). Like other kinds of fetishism, tranvestic fetishism causes overt harm to others only when accompanied by such an illegal act as theft or destruction of property.

One large survey of over 2,400 men and women in Swe-den estimated that almost 3 percent of the men and 0.4 per-cent of the women reporting having engaged in at least one episode of erotic cross-dressing, but the actual prevalence of the disorder is likely much lower (Langstrom & Zucker, 2005). This same study reported on various demographic and experiential differences between the men who had cross-dressed and those who had not. Among the most interesting findings were that the men who had cross-dressed had experi-enced more sexual abuse before age 10, were more easily sexu-ally aroused, had a higher fre-quency of masturbation, made greater use of pornography, and had other paraphilias. An ear-lier survey of over 1,000 men who frequently crossed-dressed reported that the vast majority (87 percent) were heterosexual, 83 percent had married, and 60 percent were married at the time of the survey (Docter & Prince, 1997). Many managed to keep their cross-dressing a secret, at least for a while. However, wives often found out and had a wide range of reactions, from accept-ing to being extremely disturbed. The following case illustrates both the typical early onset of transvestic fetishism and the dif-ficulties the condition may raise in a marriage.

case study A Transvestite's Dilemma

Mr. A., a 65-year-old security guard, formerly a fishing-boat captain, is distressed about his wife's objections to his wearing a nightgown at home in the evening now that his youngest child has left home. His appearance and demeanor, except when he is dressing in women's clothes, are always appropriately masculine, and he is exclusively heterosexual. Occasionally, over the past 5 years, he has worn an inconspicuous item of female clothing even when dressed as a man, sometimes a pair of panties. . . . He always carries a photograph of himself dressed as a woman.

His first recollection of an interest in female clothing was putting on his sister's bloomers at age 12, an act accompanied by sexual excitement. He continued periodically to put on women's underpants—an activity that invariably resulted in an erection, sometimes a spontaneous emission, sometimes masturbation. . . . He was competitive and aggressive with other boys and always acted "masculine." During his single years he was always attracted to girls. . . .

His involvement with female clothes was of the same intensity even after his marriage. Beginning at age 45, after a chance exposure to a magazine called *Transvestia*, he began to increase his cross-dressing activity. He learned there were other men like himself, and he became more and more preoccupied with female clothing in fantasy and progressed to periodically dressing completely as a woman. More recently he has become involved in a transvestite network . . . occasionally attending transvestite parties.

Although still committed to his marriage, sex with his wife has dwindled over the past 20 years as his waking thoughts and activities have become increasingly centered on cross-dressing. . . . He always has an increased urge to dress as a woman when under stress; it has a tranquilizing effect. If particular circumstances prevent him from cross-dressing, he feels extremely frustrated. . . .

Because of disruptions in his early life, the patient has always treasured the steadfastness of his wife and the order of his home. He told his wife about his cross-dressing practice when they were married, and she was accepting so long as he kept it to himself. Nevertheless, he felt guilty . . . and periodically he attempted to renounce the practice, throwing out all his female clothes and makeup. His children served as a barrier to his giving free rein to his impulses. Following his retirement from fishing, and in the absence of his children, he finds himself more drawn to cross-dressing, more in conflict with his wife, and more depressed.

Source: Adapted with permission *DSM-IV-TR Casebook: A Learning Companion to the Diagnostic and Statistical Manual of Mental Disorders*, Fourth Edition, *Text Revision* (pp. 257–59). (Copyright © 2002). American Psychiatric Association.

VOYEURISM A person is diagnosed with **voyeurism** according to *DSM-IV-TR* if he has recurrent, intense sexually arousing fantasies, urges, or behaviors involving the observation of unsuspecting females who are undressing or of couples engaging in sexual activity (see *DSM-IV-TR* Criteria on p. 420). Frequently, such individuals masturbate during their peeping activity. Peeping Toms, as they are commonly called, commit these offenses primarily as young men. Voyeurism often co-occurs with exhibitionism, and it is also associated with interest in sadomasochism and cross-dressing (Langstrom & Seto, 2006). Voyeurism is probably the most common illegal sexual activity (Langstrom, 2010).

How do some young men develop this pattern? First, viewing the body of an attractive female is sexually stimulating for many, if not most, heterosexual men. In addition, the privacy and mystery that have traditionally surrounded sexual activities tend to increase curiosity about them. Third, if a young man with such curiosity feels shy and inadequate in his relations with the opposite sex, he may accept the substitute of voyeurism, which satisfies his curiosity and to some extent meets his sexual needs without the trauma of actually approaching a female. He thus avoids the rejection and lowered self-status that such an approach might bring. In fact, voyeuristic activities often provide important compensatory feelings of power and secret domination over an unsuspecting victim, which may contribute to the maintenance of this pattern. If a voyeur manages to find a wife in spite of his interpersonal difficulties, as many do, he is rarely well adjusted sexually in his relationship with his wife, as the following case illustrates.

case study A Peeping Tom

A young, married college student had an attic apartment that was extremely hot during the summer months. To enable him to attend school, his wife worked; she came home at night tired and irritable and not in the mood for sexual relations. In addition, "the damned springs in the bed squeaked." In order "to obtain some sexual gratification," the youth would peer through his binoculars at the room next door and occasionally saw the young couple there engaged in erotic activities. This stimulated him greatly, and he decided to extend his peeping to a sorority house. During his second venture, however, he was reported and was apprehended by the police. This offender was quite immature for his age, rather puritanical in his attitude toward masturbation, and prone to indulge in rich but immature sexual fantasies.

More permissive laws concerning "adult" movies, videos, and magazines in recent years have removed some of the secrecy about sexual behavior and also have provided an alternative source of gratification for would-be voyeurs. However, for many voyeurs, these movies and magazines probably do not provide an adequate substitute for secretly watching the sexual behavior of an unsuspecting couple or the "real-life" nudity of a woman who mistakenly believes she enjoys privacy. Moreover, the actual effect of these "adult materials" on voyeurism is a matter of speculation because there never have been good epidemiological data on the prevalence of this paraphilia, although it is thought to be one of the most common paraphilias (Kaplan & Krueger, 1997; Maletzky, 2002). The large Swedish survey mentioned earlier that was conducted with over 2,400 men and women found that 11.5 percent of the men and 3.0 percent of the women had at some time engaged in voyeuristic activity (Langstrom & Seto, 2006). Among those who did report such activity, they also reported more psychological problems, less satisfaction with life, higher rates of masturbation, greater use of pornography, and greater ease of sexual arousability.

Although a voyeur may become reckless in his behavior and thus may be detected or even apprehended by the police, voyeurism does not ordinarily have any other serious criminal or antisocial behaviors associated with it. In fact, many people probably have some voyeuristic inclinations, which are checked by practical considerations such as the possibility of being caught and by ethical attitudes concerning the right to privacy.

EXHIBITIONISM Exhibitionism (*indecent exposure* in legal terms) is diagnosed in a person with recurrent, intense urges, fantasies, or behaviors that involve exposing his genitals to others (usually strangers) in inappropriate circumstances and without their consent (see *DSM-IV-TR* Criteria on p. 420). Frequently the element of shock in the victim is highly arousing to these individuals. The exposure may take place in some secluded location such as a park or in a more public place such as a department store, church, theater, or bus. In cities, an exhibitionist (also known as a flasher) often drives by schools or bus stops, exhibits himself while in the car, and then drives rapidly away. In many instances the exposure is repeated under fairly constant conditions, such as only in churches or buses or in the same general vicinity and at the same time of day. In one case, a youth exhibited himself only at the top of an escalator in a large department store. For a male offender, the typical victim is ordinarily a young or middle-aged female who is not known to the offender, although children and adolescents may also be targeted (Murphy, 1997).

Exhibitionism, which usually begins in adolescence or young adulthood, is the most common sexual offense reported to the police in the United States, Canada, and Europe, accounting for about one-third of all sexual offenses (McAnulty et al., 2001; Murphy, 1997). According to some estimates, as many as 20 percent of women have been the target of either exhibitionism or voyeurism (Kaplan & Krueger, 1997; Meyer, 1995). Although there are no good epidemiological data on the prevalence of this paraphilia, the large Swedish survey of over 2,400 people mentioned earlier reported that 4.1 percent of the men and 2.1 percent of the women had had at least one episode of exhibitionistic behavior (Langstrom & Seto, 2006). It commonly co-occurs with voyeurism and also tends to co-occur with sado-masochistic interests and cross-dressing (Langstrom, 2010). Exhibitionism is associated with greater psychological problems, lower life satisfaction, greater use of pornography, and more frequent masturbation.

In some instances, exposure of the genitals is accompanied by suggestive gestures or masturbation, but more often there is only exposure. A significant minority of exhibitionists commit aggressive acts, sometimes including coercive sex crimes against adults or children. Some men who expose themselves may do so because they have antisocial personality disorder, rather than a paraphilia (Langstrom, 2010).

Despite the rarity of aggressive or assaultive behavior in these cases, an exhibitionistic act nevertheless takes place without the viewer's consent and may be emotionally upsetting, as is indeed the perpetrator's intent. This intrusive quality of the act, together with its explicit violation of propriety norms about "private parts," ensures condemnation. Thus society considers exhibitionism a criminal offense.

FROTTEURISM Frotteurism is sexual excitement at rubbing one's genitals against, or touching, the body of a non-consenting person. As with voyeurism, frotteurism reflects inappropriate and persistent interest in something that many people enjoy in a consensual context. Frotteurism commonly co-occurs with voyeurism and exhibitionism (Langstrom, 2010). Being the victim of a frottueristic act is fairly common among regular riders of crowded buses or subway trains. Some have speculated that frotteurs' willingness to touch others sexually without their consent means that they are at risk for more serious sexual offending, but there is currently no evidence supporting this concern (Langstrom, 2010).

Men who engage in exhibitionism often cause emotional distress in the viewers because of the intrusive quality of the act, along with its explicit violation of propriety norms.

SADISM The term **sadism** is derived from the name of the Marquis de Sade (1740–1814), who for sexual purposes inflicted such cruelty on his victims that he was eventually committed as insane. In *DSM-IV-TR*, for a diagnosis of sadism, a person must have recurrent, intense sexually arousing fantasies, urges, or behaviors that involve inflicting psychological or physical pain on another individual (see *DSM-IV-TR* Criteria on p. 420). Sadistic fantasies often include themes of dominance, control, and humiliation (Kirsh & Becker, 2007). A closely related, but less severe, pattern is the practice of "bondage and discipline" (B & D), which may include tying a person up, hitting or spanking, and so on to enhance sexual excitement. The large majority of sexually sadistic acts probably occur in the context of a consensual sexual relationship without any evident harm. A small minority, though, are nonconsensual, serious, and fatal (Chang & Heide, 2009; Dietz et al., 1990; R. B. Krueger, 2010b).

In some cases, sadistic activities lead up to or terminate in actual sexual relations; in others, full sexual gratification is obtained from the sadistic practice alone. A sadist, for example, might slash a woman with a razor or stick her with a needle, experiencing an orgasm in the process. The pain inflicted by sadists may come from whipping, biting, cutting, or burning; the act may vary in intensity, from fantasy to severe mutilation and even murder. Mild degrees of sadism (and masochism, discussed below) are involved in the sexual foreplay customs of many cultures, and some couples in our own society— both heterosexual and homosexual—regularly engage in such practices, which are often quite ritualized. It is thus important to distinguish transient or occasional interest in sadomasochistic practices from sadism as a paraphilia. Surveys have found that perhaps 5 to 15 percent of men and women enjoy sadistic and/ or masochistic activities voluntarily on occasion (Baumeister & Butler, 1997; Hucker, 1997). Paraphilic sadism and masochism, in which sadomasochistic activities are the preferred or exclusive means to sexual gratification, are much rarer; not uncommonly, they co-occur in the same individual (Kirsh & Becker, 2007). The situation can range from full consent of the victim to complete lack of consent, although changes to *DSM-IV-TR* in 2000 require either that the diagnosis of sadism be reserved for cases in which the victim is nonconsenting or that the sadistic experience is marked by distress or interpersonal difficulties. Many cases of sexual sadism have comorbid Axis II disorders—especially the narcissistic, schizoid, or antisocial personality disorders (Kirsh & Becker, 2007).

Extreme sexual sadists may mentally replay their torture scenes later while masturbating. Serial killers, who tend to be sexual sadists, sometimes record or videotape their sadistic acts. One study characterized 20 sexually sadistic serial killers who were responsible for 149 murders throughout the United States and Canada (Warren et al., 1996). Most were white males in their late 20s or early 30s. Their murders were remarkably consistent over time, reflecting sexual arousal to the pain, fear, and panic of their victims. Choreographed assaults allowed them to carefully control their victims' deaths. Some of the men reported that the God-like sense of being in control of the life and death of another human being was especially exhilarating. Eighty-five percent of the sample reported consistent violent sexual fantasies, and 75 percent collected materials with a violent theme including audiotapes, videotapes, pictures, or sketches of their sadistic acts or sexually sadistic pornography.

Notorious serial killers include Ted Bundy, who was executed in 1989. Bundy confessed to the murder of over 30 young women, nearly all of whom fit a targeted type: women with long hair parted in the middle. Bundy admitted that he used his victims to re-create the covers of detective magazines or scenes from "slasher movies." Jeffrey Dahmer was convicted in 1992 of having mutilated and murdered 15 boys and young men, generally having sex with them after death. (He was subsequently murdered in prison.) Dennis Rader, the BTK Killer (for Bind, Torture, Kill), was captured in 2005 after committing 10 murders over 30 years in Wichita, Kansas. Rader exemplifies several interesting phenomena associated with homicidal sexual sadism. As a child he tortured animals and fantasized about tying up and torturing attractive children he watched on television. When he began enacting his fantasies, he stalked his victims for weeks to learn their habits before he attacked them. He enjoyed tying them up and then strangled them. Only after they were dead would he gratify himself sexually through masturbation. He often retained clothing of his victims, which he would sometimes

Dennis Rader was married with two children, an active member in his church, and a respected member of the community; he was also a serial killer known as the BTK killer.

wear. Sometimes in private he would practice bondage on himself because he found this erotic.

What causes some men to be sexually sadistic killers? Although many sadists have had chaotic childhoods, Bundy, Dahmer, and Rader all came from apparently stable and loving families. Unfortunately, we do not have a good understanding of the causal factors involved in these extreme cases of sadism.

Sexual sadism is understandably an important concern of criminologists, law enforcement officers, and forensic mental health professionals. Unfortunately, the *DSM-IV* diagnosis of sexual sadism is not very reliable (Marshall & Hucker, 2006) or valid (Kingston et al., 2010). This is concerning, given how important it is to detect dangerous sexual sadists and how stigmatizing a diagnosis of sexual sadism might be to someone whose sexual desires are harmless. One promising modification currently being considered is a dimensional approach that could distinguish sexual sadists who are dangerous from those who are not (R. B. Krueger, 2010b; Marshall & Hucker, 2006).

MASOCHISM The term **masochism** is derived from the name of the Austrian novelist Leopold V. Sacher-Masoch (1836–1895), whose fictional characters dwelt lovingly on the sexual pleasure of pain. In sexual masochism, a person experiences sexual stimulation and gratification from the experience of pain and degradation in relating to a lover. According to *DSM-IV-TR* (see *DSM-IV-TR* Criteria on p. 420), the person must have experienced recurrent, intense sexually arousing fantasies, urges, or behaviors involving the act of being humiliated, beaten, or bound, often in a ritualistic pattern of behavior (Sandnabba et al., 2002). Interpersonal masochistic activities require the participation of at least two people—one superior "disciplinarian" and one obedient "slave." In a significant minority of cases, the women who fall into such a pattern with their partners were sexually or physically abused as children (Warren & Hazelwood, 2002).

Sadomasochistic activities, including bondage and discipline, are often performed communally within "dungeons" popular in major cities.

Such arrangements in mild form are not uncommon in either heterosexual or homosexual relationships. Masochists do not usually want, or cooperate with, true sexual sadists, but with individuals willing to hurt or humiliate them within limits they set. Masochism appears to be more common than sadism and occurs in both men and women (Baumeister & Butler, 1997; Sandnabba et al., 2002). Sadomasochistic activities, including bondage and discipline, are often performed communally within "dungeons" popular in major cities. Such activities might involve men being bound and whipped by women called "dominatrixes," who wear tight leather or rubber outfits and are paid to inflict pain and humiliation in a sexually charged sense. Most members of this sadomasochistic community are high functioning and do not appear to suffer because of their sexual interests (Krueger, 2010a).

Some rare forms of masochism are more problematic, however. One particularly dangerous form of masochism, called *autoerotic asphyxia*, involves self-strangulation. Although some writers have speculated that loss of oxygen to the brain intensifies orgasm, there is little evidence that this motivates practitioners of autoerotic asphyxia. In contrast, studies of such practitioners have found that their sexual fantasies are strongly masochistic (Hucker, 2011). Coroners in most major U.S. cities are familiar with cases in which the deceased is found hanged next to masochistic pornographic literature or other sexual paraphernalia. Accidental deaths attributable to this practice have been estimated to range between 500 and 1,000 per year in the United States (LeVay & Valente, 2006). Although autoerotic asphyxia is much more common in men, it can occur in women, and it has occurred across many cultures going back hundreds of years. In some cases it occurs in a consensual or nonconsensual sadomasochistic act between two or more people (McGrath & Turvey, 2008).

The following is a case of autoerotic asphyxia with a tragic ending.

case study "I Got Tangled in the Rope"

A woman heard a man shouting for help and went to his apartment door. . . .

The woman with her two sons . . . broke into the apartment. They found the man lying on the floor, his hands tied behind him, his legs bent back, and his ankles secured to his hands. A mop handle had been placed behind his knees. He was visibly distraught, sweating, and short of breath, and his hands were turning blue. He had defecated and urinated in his trousers. In his kitchen the woman found a knife and freed him.

When police officers arrived and questioned the man, he stated that he had returned home that afternoon, fallen asleep on his couch, and awakened an hour later only to find himself hopelessly bound. The officers noted that the apartment door had been locked when the neighbors broke in . . . [and] when the

continued

case study "I Got Tangled in the Rope" (*continued*)

officers filed their report, they noted that "this could possibly be a sexual deviation act." Interviewed the next day, the man confessed to binding himself in the position in which he was found.

A month later, the police were called back to the same man's apartment. A building manager had discovered him face down on the floor in his apartment. A paper bag covered his head like a hood. When the police arrived, the man was breathing rapidly with a satin cloth stuffed in his mouth. Rope was stretched around his head and mouth and wrapped his chest and waist. Several lengths ran from his back to his crotch, and ropes at his ankles had left deep marks. A broom handle locked his elbows behind his back. Once freed, the man explained, "While doing isometric exercises, I got tangled up in the rope." . . .

Two years passed and the man moved on to another job. He failed to appear for work one Monday morning. A fellow employee found him dead in his apartment. During their investigation, police were able to reconstruct the man's final minutes. On the preceding Friday, he had bound himself in the following manner: sitting on his bed and crossing his ankles, left over right, he had bound them together with twine. Fastening a tie around his neck, he then secured the tie to an 86-inch pole behind his back. . . . [By a complicated set of maneuvers he applied] pressure to the pole, still secured to the tie around his neck, [and] strangled himself.

Source: Adapted with permission from *DSM-IV-TR Casebook: A Learning Companion to the Diagnostic and Statistical Manual of Mental Disorders,* Fourth Edition, *Text Revision* (pp. 86–88). (Copyright © 2002). American Psychiatric Association.

Men's vulnerability to paraphilias such as fetishism may be a result of their greater dependence on visual stimuli. This in turn makes them more likely to form sexual associations to nonsexual stimuli such as women's legs or high-heeled shoes, quite possibly through a process of classical conditioning.

Causal Factors and Treatments for Paraphilias

Many individuals with paraphilias have explanations for their unusual sexual preferences. For example, one amputee paraphilic (whose preference was a partner with a missing limb) recalled that his fascination with female amputees originated during adolescence. He was neglected emotionally by his cold family but heard a family member express sympathetic feelings for an amputee. He developed the wish that he would become an amputee and thus earn their sympathy (see First, 2005, for a discussion of this paraphilia, known as *apotemnophilia*). This story raises many questions. Emotionally cold families are not uncommon, and sympathy for amputees is nearly universal. Certainly not every male in a cold family who detects sympathy for amputees develops an amputee paraphilia. Such stories do not necessarily have any validity because we are often unaware of the forces that shape us (Nisbett & Wilson, 1977).

Several facts about paraphilia are likely to be important in their development. First, as we have already noted, nearly all persons with paraphilias are male; females with most paraphilias are so rare that they are found in the literature only as case reports or a series of case reports (e.g., Fedoroff et al., 1999). When occasionally found in women, the most likely ones are pedophilia (being aroused by prepubescent boys), sadomasochistic activities, and exhibitionism. Second, paraphilias usually begin around the time of puberty or early adolescence. Third, people with paraphilias often have a very strong sex drive, with affected men often masturbating many times a day. Fourth, people with paraphilias frequently have more than one. For example, the corpses of men who died accidentally in the course of autoerotic asphyxia were partially or fully cross-dressed in 25 to 33 percent of cases (Blanchard & Hucker, 1991). There is no obvious reason for the association between sexual masochism and transvestism. Why should it be so?

Money (1986) and others have suggested that male vulnerability to paraphilias is closely linked to their greater dependence on visual sexual imagery. Perhaps sexual arousal in men depends on physical stimulus features to a greater degree than in women, whose arousal may depend more on emotional context such as being in love with a partner. If so, men may be more vulnerable to forming sexual associations to nonsexual stimuli, which may be most likely to occur after puberty, when the sexual drive is high. Many believe that

1 ## DEVELOPMENTS IN RESEARCH

Hypersexual Disorder

The concept of "sexual addiction" has become part of popular culture, exemplified by men who repeatedly engage in sexual behaviour that is bad for them in various ways, including their jobs, their romantic relationships, and their health. The sex addict watches pornography incessantly, hires prostitutes after he is broke, or can't seem to stop having affairs despite ostensibly loving his wife. Scientists have been slow to embrace the concept of sexual addiction, however. This is partly because of skepticism and lack of evidence that the same processes that cause addiction to drugs and alcohol also underlie the self-destructive patterns of sexual behaviour.

Instead of "sexual addiction," hypersexual disorder has been proposed for *DSM-V* (Kafka, 2010). Hypersexual disorder is conceptualized as a nonparaphilic problem involving sexual impulsivity. Individuals with hypersexual disorder do not typically engage in sexual behaviour that is unappealing to most people, but they do so more than they should. Furthermore, excessive sexual behaviour may occur in response to negative mood states or stressful life events. An individual must continue to engage in sexual behavior despite risks to himself or others. He must make unsuccessful attempts to stop, and his hypersexuality cannot be due to substance abuse. Common sexual behaviors excessively engaged in by individuals with hypersexual disorder include watching pornography, masturbation, phone sex, prostitution, cybersex, and attending strip clubs.

these associations arise as a result of classical and instrumental conditioning and/or social learning that occurs through observation and modeling. When observing paraphilic stimuli (e.g., photographs of models in their underwear), or when fantasies about paraphilic stimuli occur, boys may masturbate, and the reinforcement by orgasm-release may serve to condition an intense attraction to paraphilic stimuli (e.g., Kaplan & Krueger, 1997; LeVay & Valente, 2006).

TREATMENTS FOR PARAPHILIAS The vast majority of studies concerning the treatment of paraphilias have been conducted with sex offenders. The literature concerning treatment of men with paraphilias who have not committed any offense, or who have victimless paraphilias (e.g., masochism), consists primarily of case reports because most people with paraphilias do not seek treatment for these conditions. Thus we defer discussion of the treatment of paraphilias until we discuss the treatment of sex offenders, many of whom have paraphilias.

Gender Identity Disorders

Gender identity refers to one's sense of maleness or femaleness, and it may be distinguished from *gender role*, which refers to the masculinity and femininity of one's overt behavior (Money, 1988). Of all behavioral traits, gender identity may have the strongest correlation with biological sex, but the correlation is not perfect. Some rare individuals feel extreme discomfort and unhappiness with their biological sex and strongly desire to change to the opposite sex. Indeed, some adults with gender identity disorders, often called *transsexuals*, opt for expensive and complicated surgery to accomplish just that. In *DSM-IV-TR*, **gender identity disorder** is characterized by two

components: (1) a strong and persistent **cross-gender identification**—that is, the desire to be, or the insistence that one is, of the opposite sex—and (2) **gender dysphoria**—persistent discomfort about one's biological sex or the sense that the gender role of that sex is inappropriate. The disorder may occur in children and adults and in males and females. One proposal for *DSM-5* is to change "gender identity disorder" to "gender dysphoria" (Cohen-Kettenis & Pfafflin, 2010). The proposed terminology is both usefully descriptive and theoretically neutral. That is, individuals who have been diagnosed with gender identity disorder certainly experience gender dysphoria, but whether or not this is always due to atypical gender identity development is less clear. Gender dysphoria can be diagnosed at two different life stages, either during adolescence or adulthood (i.e., gender dysphoria in adolescents and adults) or childhood (gender dysphoria in children).

GENDER IDENTITY DISORDER OF CHILDHOOD Boys with gender identity disorder show a marked preoccupation with traditionally feminine activities (Zucker, 2010; Zucker & Bradley, 1995). They may prefer to dress in female clothing. They enjoy stereotypical girls' activities such as playing dolls and playing house. They usually avoid rough-and-tumble play and often express the desire to be a girl. Boys with gender identity disorder are often ostracized as "sissies" by their peers.

Girls with gender identity disorder typically balk at parents' attempts to dress them in traditional feminine clothes such as dresses, preferring boys' clothing and short hair. Fantasy heroes typically include powerful male figures like Batman and Superman. They show little interest in dolls and increased interest in sports. Although mere tomboys frequently have many or most of these traits, girls with gender identity disorder are distinguished by their desire to be a boy or to grow up

DSM-IV-TR

Criteria for Gender Identity Disorder

A. A strong and persistent cross-gender identification (not merely a desire for any perceived cultural advantages of being the other sex).

In children, the disturbance is manifested by four (or more) of the following:

1. Repeatedly stated desire to be, or insistence that he or she is, the other sex
2. In boys, preference for cross-dressing or simulating female attire; in girls, insistence on wearing only stereotypical masculine clothing
3. Strong and persistent preferences for cross-sex roles in make-believe play or persistent fantasies of being the other sex
4. Intense desire to participate in the stereotypical games and pastimes of the other sex
5. Strong preference for playmates of the other sex

In adolescents and adults, the disturbance is manifested by symptoms such as a stated desire to be the other sex, frequent passing as the other sex, desire to live or be treated as the other sex, or the conviction that he or she has the typical feelings and reactions of the other sex.

B. Persistent discomfort with his or her sex or sense of inappropriateness in the gender role of that sex.

In children, the disturbance is manifested by any of the following:

In boys, assertion that his penis or testes are disgusting or will disappear or assertion that it would be better not to have a penis, or aversion toward rough-and-tumble play and rejection of male stereotypical toys, games, and activities; In girls, rejection of urinating in a sitting position, assertion that she has or will grow a penis, or assertion that she does not want to grow breasts or menstruate, or marked aversion toward normative feminine clothing.

In adolescents and adults, the disturbance is manifested by symptoms such as preoccupation with getting rid of primary and secondary sex characteristics (e.g., request for hormones, surgery, or other procedures to physically alter sexual characteristics to simulate the other sex) or belief that he or she was born the wrong sex.

C. The disturbance is not concurrent with a physical intersex condition.

D. The disturbance causes clinically significant distress or impairment in social, occupational, or other important areas of functioning.

Source: Reprinted with permission from the American Psychiatric Association. *Diagnostic and Statistical Manual of Mental Disorders,* Fourth Edition, *Text Revision* (Copyright © 2000). American Psychiatric Association.

as a man. Young girls with gender identity disorder are treated better by their peers than are boys with gender identity disorder because cross-gender behavior in girls is better tolerated (Cohen-Kettenis et al., 2003; Zucker et al., 1997). In clinic-referred gender identity disorder, boys outnumbered girls 5 to 1 in one study (Cohen-Kettenis et al., 2003) and by 3 to 1 in another study (Cohen-Kettenis et al., 2006). An appreciable percentage of that imbalance may reflect greater parental concern about femininity in boys than about masculinity in girls.

The most common adult outcome of boys with gender identity disorder appears to be homosexuality rather than transsexualism (Zucker, 2005). In Richard Green's (1987) prospective study of 44 very feminine boys from the community, only one sought sex change surgery by age 18. About three-quarters became gay or bisexual men who were evidently satisfied with their biological sex. However, several later studies of clinic-referred children have found that 10 to 20 percent of boys with gender identity disorder later were diagnosed as transsexual by age 16 or 18, and about 40 to 60 percent identified themselves as homosexual or bisexual, a percentage

that may have increased by the time they were older (Zucker, 2005). There are several smaller prospective studies of girls with gender identity disorder that have shown that 35 to 45 percent may show persistent gender identity disorder (leading to a desire for sex reassignment surgery in many), and approximately half had a homosexual orientation. However, the largest prospective study to date, which followed 25 girls with gender identity disorder (ages 3–12) into young adulthood (average age 23), found somewhat lower rates of persistent gender identity disorder and homosexuality. At follow-up three were classified as being dissatisfied with their gender, and two of these three wanted to have sex reassignment surgery. However, 32 percent had homosexual or bisexual fantasies, and 24 percent engaged in homosexual or bisexual behavior. These rates are clearly much higher than expected from base rates of gender identity disorder in the population but not as high as in boys with gender identity disorder (Drummond et al., 2008).

Given that many such children typically adjust well in adulthood, should they be considered to have a mental disorder

Boys with gender identity disorder enjoy dressing up in female clothing and makeup and enjoy stereotypical girls' activities. As a consequence, they are often ostracized as "sissies" by their peers.

as children? Some have argued that such children should not be considered "disordered" because the primary obstacle to their happiness may be a society that is intolerant of cross-gender behavior. However, many researchers who work with these children maintain that the distress and unhappiness these children and adolescents have about the discrepancy between their biological sex and their psychological gender are consistent with this being called a mental disorder (e.g., Zucker, 2005, 2010). Moreover, these children are frequently mistreated by their peers and have strained relations with their parents even though their cross-gender behavior harms no one.

Research from non-Western cultures shows that stigmatization of gender-nonconforming children is not universal (Vasey & Bartlett, 2007). In Samoa, very feminine males are often considered "Fa'afafine" (roughly meaning "in the manner of women"), a kind of third gender, neither male nor female. Fa'afafine are identified as young children by their behavior and usually are accepted by their families and culture. As adults these individuals are sexually attracted to other men and typically have sexual relations with heterosexual men. They do not in general recall that their childhood gender nonconformity was associated with distress. Because of this, some have argued

that childhood gender identity disorder should not appear in *DSM-5* (Vasey & Bartlett, 2007). Despite these objections, the diagnosis will likely be retained as gender dysphoria in children (Zucker, 2010).

Treatment Children and adolescents with gender identity disorder are often brought in by their parents for psychotherapy (Zucker et al., 2008). Specialists attempt both to treat the child's unhappiness with his or her biological sex and to ease strained relations with parents and peers. Children with gender identity disorders often have other general psychological and behavioral problems such as anxiety and mood disorders that also need therapeutic attention (Zucker et al., 2002). Therapists try to improve peer and parental relations by teaching such children how to reduce their cross-gender behavior, especially in situations where it might cause interpersonal problems. Gender dysphoria is typically treated psychodynamically—that is, by examining inner conflicts. Controlled studies evaluating such treatment remain to be conducted (Zucker, 2005). If a child will eventually transition into the other sex, it is beneficial to prevent full sexual maturity from occurring in the original, unwanted, sex. Thus, in the progressive Netherlands, under some circumstances, gender dysphoric early adolescents are given hormonal treatment to delay puberty while they decide how to proceed (Cohen-Kettenis, 2010).

Two related facts about gender dysphoria in children are especially important clinically. First, as we have noted, most gender dysphoric children do not become gender dysphoric adults. The problem generally remits during childhood (Wallien & Cohen-Kettenis, 2008). Second, individuals who are still gender dysphoric into adolescence are likely to remain so into adulthood, and they are also likely to take medical steps to transform their bodies. The crucial age period at which many gender dysphoric children desist or persist appears to be 10 to 13 (Steensma et al., 2011). Increasing numbers of parents of gender dysphoric children cooperate with their children's wishes and allow them socially to assume an identity opposite their birth sex (Rosin, 2008). On the one hand, this surely decreases the anguish that such children feel. On the other hand, it is plausible that this strategy will ultimately lead to more transsexual adolescent or adult outcomes.

TRANSSEXUALISM **Transsexualism** occurs in adults with gender identity disorder who desire to change their sex, and surgical advances have made this goal, although expensive, partially feasible. Transsexualism represents the extreme on a continuum of transgenderism, or the degree to which one identifies as the other sex (Cohen-Kettenis & Pfafflin, 2010). Transsexualism is apparently a very rare disorder. In the past, European studies suggested that approximately 1 in 30,000 adult males and 1 in 100,000 adult females seek sex reassignment surgery. However, more recent estimates suggest that about 1 in 12,000 men in Western countries has actually undergone the surgery (Lawrence, 2007). Until fairly recently, most researchers assumed that transsexualism was the adult version of childhood gender identity disorder, and indeed this is often the case. That is, many transsexuals had gender identity disorder as children (despite the fact that most children with gender identity disorder do not become transsexual), and their adult behavior is analogous. This appears to be the case for all female-to-male transsexuals (individuals born female who become male). Virtually all such individuals recall being extremely tomboyish, with masculinity persisting unabated into adulthood. Most, but not all, female-to-male transsexuals are sexually attracted to women.

This excerpt is intentionally omitted from this text.

In contrast to female-to-male transsexuals, there are two kinds of male-to-female transsexuals, with very different causes and developmental courses: *homosexual* and *autogynephilic transsexuals* (Bailey, 2003; Blanchard, 1989). Homosexual transsexual men are generally very feminine and have the same sexual orientation as gay men: They are sexually attracted to biological males (their preoperative biological sex). However, because these transsexual men experience their gender identity as female, they often define their sexual orientation as heterosexual and resent being labelled gay. Thus what is referred to in the research literature as a homosexual male-to-female transsexual is a genetic male seeking a sex change operation who describes himself as a woman trapped in a man's body and who is sexually attracted to heterosexual male partners (Bailey, 2003). In contrast, autogynephilic transsexuals are motivated by **autogynephilia**—a paraphilia in which their attraction is to thoughts, images, or fantasies of themselves as a woman (Blanchard, 1991, 1993). This diagnostic distinction has not been made in the *DSM-IV* but is briefly mentioned. Although it may not be relevant for treatment purposes (both types of transsexuals are appropriate candidates for sex reassignment surgery), this distinction is fundamental to understanding the diverse psychology of male-to-female transsexualism. Moreover, recent estimates show an increased prevalence in Western countries of male-to-female transsexualism in recent years, and most of this increase is in autogynephilic transsexualism (Lawrence, 2007).

One important finding is that homosexual transsexuals generally have had gender identity disorder since childhood, paralleling what is found in female-to-male transsexuals, as discussed above. However, because most male children with gender identity disorder do not become transsexual adults (but instead become gay or bisexual men), there must be other important determinants of transsexualism. One hypothesis is that there are some prenatal hormonal influences affecting which children who develop gender identity disorder later become transsexuals (Meyer-Bahlburg, 2011).

Mianne Bager (a Danish-born Australian resident) is a male-to-female transsexual who has golfed professionally in women's tournaments since 2003. She is the first known female professional golfer who was born male. Before she could play women's tournaments, rule changes had to be implemented in Europe, Australia, and other countries so that it was no longer required that a competitor be female at birth.

Autogynephilic (sometimes called heterosexual) transsexualism almost always occurs in genetic males who usually report a history of transvestic fetishism. However, unlike other transvestites, autogynephilic transsexuals fantasize that they have female genitalia, which can lead to acute gender dysphoria, motivating their desire for sex reassignment surgery. Autogynephilic transsexuals may report sexual attraction to women, to both men and women, or to neither. Research has shown that these subtypes of autogynephilic transsexuals (varying in sexual orientation) are very similar to each other and differ from homosexual transsexuals in other important respects (Bailey, 2003; Blanchard, 1985, 1989, 1991). For example, relative to homosexual transsexuals, the autogynephilic transsexuals have more fetishistic and masochistic tendencies, a stronger preference for younger and more attractive partners, and a stronger interest in uncommitted sex (Veale et al., 2008). Unlike homosexual transsexuals, autogynephilic transsexuals do not appear to have been especially feminine in childhood or adulthood, and they typically seek sex reassignment surgery much later in life than do homosexual transsexuals (Blanchard, 1994). The causes of autogynephilic transsexualism thus probably overlap etiologically with the causes of other paraphilias (with which they often co-occur) but are not yet well understood (Veale et al., 2008).

Autogynephilia remains a controversial concept among some transgender individuals, who object that autogynephilia is inconsistent with their experiences and that their motivation to change their sex is not sexual (Winters, 2008). Some supporters of the theory of autogynephilia attribute the denial of autogynephilia to factors including sexual shame and stigmatization (Bailey & Triea, 2007). *DSM-5* is likely to omit mention of autogynephilia because of "strong resistance" to the idea (Cohen-Kettenis & Pfafflin, 2010). Sexual orientation (i.e., the distinction between homosexual and autogynephilic) appears to be a highly valid predictor of other differences between the two types of male-to-female transsexuals (Lawrence, 2010). However, this may be a case in which a trade-off is made between scientific rigor and social acceptability.

Treatment Psychotherapy is usually not effective in helping adolescents or adults resolve their gender dysphoria (Cohen-Kettenis et al., 2000; Zucker & Bradley, 1995). The only treatment that has been shown to be effective is surgical sex reassignment. Initially, transsexuals who want and are awaiting surgery are given hormone treatment. Biological men are given estrogens to facilitate breast growth, skin softening, and shrinking of muscles. Biological women are given testosterone, which suppresses menstruation, increases facial and body hair, and deepens the voice. Before they are eligible for surgery, transsexuals typically must live for many months with hormonal therapy, and they generally must live at least a year as the gender they wish to become. If they successfully complete the trial period, they undergo surgery and continue to take hormones indefinitely. In male-to-female transsexuals, this entails removal of the penis and testes and the creation of an artificial vagina. One fascinating study by Lawrence, Bailey, and colleagues of 11 male-to-female transsexuals found that the artificial vaginal tissue created from penile tissue showed signs of sexual arousal to male erotic stimuli if the person was a homosexual male-to-female transsexual, and to female erotic stimuli if the person was an autogynephilic transsexual (Lawrence et al., 2005). Male-to-female transsexuals must also undergo extensive electrolysis to remove their beards and body hair. They also have to learn to raise the pitch of their voice.

Female-to-male transsexuals typically are given mastectomies and hysterectomies and often have other plastic surgery to alter various facial features (such as the Adam's apple). Only a subset of female-to-male transsexuals seek an artificial penis because relevant surgical techniques are still somewhat primitive and very expensive. Moreover, the artificial penis is not capable of normal erection, so those who have this surgery must rely on artificial supports to have intercourse anyway. The others function sexually without any penis.

Does sex reassignment surgery help transsexuals lead satisfying lives? In 1990 a review of the outcome literature found that 87 percent of 220 male-to-female transsexuals had satisfactory outcomes (meaning that they did not regret their decisions) and that 97 percent of 130 female-to-male transsexuals had successful outcomes (Green & Fleming, 1990). More recent studies have reported similar findings. Thus the majority of transsexuals are satisfied with the outcome of sex reassignment surgery, although there is variability in the degree of satisfaction (Cohen-Kettenis & Gooren, 1999; Lawrence, 2006). The Lawrence study (2006) of 232 male-to-female transsexuals all operated on by the same surgeon found the participants to be least satisfied with vaginal lubrication and vaginal touch sensations, although overall level of satisfaction was still high. Regarding psychological adjustment, a recent follow-up showed that transsexuals who had sex reassignment surgery were less well adjusted compared with normal controls (Dhejne et al., 2011). The optimal comparison, however, is not to normal controls but to transsexuals not given sex reassignment surgery. In spite of the reasonably good success record for transsexual patients who are carefully chosen, such surgery remains controversial because some professionals continue to maintain that it is inappropriate to treat psychological disorders through drastic anatomical changes.

In Review

● Define *paraphilia*, and cite six paraphilias recognized in the *DSM*, along with their associated features.

● What two components characterize gender identity disorder?

● Identify the two types of male-to-female transsexuals, and describe their developmental course as well as that of female-to-male transsexuals.

● What are the most effective treatments for childhood gender identity disorder and adult transsexualism?

Sexual Abuse

Sexual abuse is sexual contact that involves physical or psychological coercion or at least one individual who cannot reasonably consent to the contact (e.g., a child). Such abuse includes pedophilia, incest, and rape, and it concerns society much more than any other sexual problem. It is somewhat ironic, then, that of these three forms of abuse, only pedophilia is included in *DSM-IV-TR*. This partly reflects the seriousness with which society views these offenses and its preference for treating coercive sex offenders as criminals rather than as having a mental disorder (although obviously many criminals also have mental disorders).

Childhood Sexual Abuse

The past few decades have seen intense concern about childhood sexual abuse, with an accompanying increase in relevant research. There are at least three reasons for including some discussion of this here. First, there are possible links between childhood sexual abuse and some mental disorders, so such abuse may be important in the etiology of some disorders. Second, much evidence suggests that, broadly defined, childhood sexual abuse is more common than was once assumed, and it is important to understand some of its causes. Third, some dramatic and well-publicized cases involving allegations of childhood sexual abuse have raised very controversial issues such as the validity of children's testimony and the accuracy of recovered memories of sexual abuse. We shall consider all three of these issues in turn.

PREVALENCE OF CHILDHOOD SEXUAL ABUSE

The prevalence of childhood sexual abuse depends on its definition, which has varied substantially across studies. For example, different studies use different definitions of "childhood," with the upper age limit ranging from 12 to as high as 19 years. Some studies have counted any kind of sexual interaction, even that which does not include physical contact (e.g., exhibitionism); others have counted only physical contact; others have counted only genital contact; and still others have counted consensual sexual contact with a minor. A recent review of data from 22 countries estimated that 7.9 percent of men and 19.7 percent of women had suffered sexual abuse prior to age 18. The highest rates were from African countries, and the lowest rates were from Europe; U.S. figures were intermediate. Obviously "prior to age 18" comprises a wide range of ages, and, for example, age 17 is not always viewed as part of childhood.

CONSEQUENCES OF CHILDHOOD SEXUAL ABUSE

Childhood sexual abuse may have both short-term and long-term consequences. The most common short-term consequences are fears, posttraumatic stress disorder, sexual inappropriateness (e.g., touching others' genitals or talking about sexual acts), and poor self-esteem, but approximately one-third of sexually abused children show no symptoms (e.g., Kendall-Tackett et al., 1993; McConaghy, 1998).

Associations between reports of childhood sexual abuse and adult psychopathology have been commonly reported (Maniglio, 2009). Specific examples include borderline personality disorder (Bandelow et al., 2005; Battle et al., 2004), somatization disorder with dissociative symptoms (Sar et al., 2004), and dissociative identity disorder (Maldonado & Spiegel, 2007; Ross, 1999). A wide variety of sexual symptoms have also been alleged to result from early sexual abuse (e.g., Leonard & Follette, 2002; Loeb et al., 2002; see review in Maniglio, 2009), ranging, for example, from sexual aversion to sexual promiscuity. A similar range of negative consequences has also been reported in a sample of about 3,000 male and female adults in China, although the rate of childhood sexual abuse in China is lower than in Western countries (Luo et al., 2008). Unfortunately, knowledge about these hypothesized associations is very limited because of difficulties in establishing causal links between early experiences and adult behavior (see also Unresolved Issues at the end of this chapter).

CONTROVERSIES CONCERNING CHILDHOOD SEXUAL ABUSE

Several types of high-profile criminal trials have highlighted the limitations of our knowledge concerning questions of great scientific and practical importance. In one type of case, children have accused adults working in day-care settings of extensive, often bizarre sexual abuse, and controversial issues have been raised about the degree to which children's accusations can be trusted. In a second type of case, adults claim to have repressed and completely forgotten memories of early sexual abuse and then to have "recovered" the memories during adulthood, typically while seeing a therapist who believes that repressed memories of childhood sexual abuse are a very common cause of adult psychopathology. Many controversial issues have been raised about the validity of these "recovered" memories.

Children's Testimony Several cases of alleged sexual abuse in day-care settings shocked the country starting in the 1980s and continuing into the early 1990s. The most notorious was the McMartin Preschool case in California (Eberle & Eberle, 1993). In 1983 Judy Johnson complained to police that her son had been molested by Raymond Buckey, who helped run the McMartin Preschool, which her son attended. Johnson's complaints grew increasingly bizarre. For example, she accused Buckey of sodomizing her son while he stuck the boy's head in a toilet and of making him ride naked on a horse. Johnson was later diagnosed with acute paranoid schizophrenia, and she died of alcohol-related liver disease in 1986. By the time she died, prosecutors no longer needed her. Children at the preschool who were interviewed began to tell fantastically lurid stories—for example, that they were forced to dig up dead bodies at cemeteries, jump out of airplanes, and kill animals with bats. Nevertheless, prosecutors and many McMartin parents believed the children. Buckey and his mother (who owned the day-care facility) were tried in a trial that took 2 and a half years and cost $15 million. The jury acquitted Ms. Buckey on all counts and failed to convict Raymond Buckey on any; however, he was freed only after retrial, after having spent 5 years in jail. The jurors' principal reason for not finding the defendants guilty was their concern that interviewers had used leading questions or coercive methods of questioning. Moreover, subsequent research on children who reported satanic abuse found no evidence (including physical evidence) that such abuse had occurred, and so any such reports of satanic abuse are scientifically very doubtful (London et al., 2005). Despite these concerns, some day-care workers accused of satanic sexual abuse have served years in prison.

Obviously, investigations of possible child sexual abuse will often depend on the reports and testimony of children. We have noted the tendency in recent times of people to believe children's reports, no matter how unlikely they seem. Is the confidence in children's reports of sexual abuse well-founded? In a very important series of studies, the psychologists Stephen Ceci and Maggie Bruck have shown that children can easily be led to concoct stories of events that never occurred (Bruck

Evidence has suggested that the use of anatomically correct dolls to question young children about where they may have been touched in alleged incidents of sexual abuse does not improve the accuracy of their testimony relative to verbal interviews alone.

et al., 2002; Ceci et al., 2000; Ceci et al., 2007; London et al., 2005). The likelihood of concocting stories increases when interviewers have asked leading questions, repeated questioning, and reinforcing some kinds of answers more than others. This research shows that failure to proceed with care in interrogating children can easily lead to false accusations and injustice. In the legal case *U.S. v. Desmond Rouse* (2004) a federal appeals court (that is, a court just below the U.S. Supreme Court) established new rules for evaluating the admissibility of children's testimony based almost exclusively on the work of Ceci and Bruck.

Recovered Memories of Sexual Abuse In 1990, a young woman named Eileen Franklin testified in court that she had seen her father rape and murder an 8-year-old playmate 20 years earlier. Remarkably, despite her claim to have witnessed the murder, she had had no memory of the event until she "recovered" the memory by accident in adulthood (MacLean, 1992). Franklin's father was convicted and given a life sentence, although in 1995 the conviction was overturned because of two serious constitutional errors made during the original trial that might have affected the jury's verdict. In a different kind of case, Patricia Burgus sued her two psychiatrists in Chicago for false-memory implantation, claiming the doctors had persuaded her through hypnosis and other therapeutic techniques "to believe that she was a member of a satanic cult, that she was sexually abused by multiple men, and that she engaged in cannibalism and abused her own children" (Brown et al., 2000, p. 3). In 1997 she was awarded $10.6 million.

Whether traumatic experiences can be utterly forgotten and then somehow recovered intact years later has been heatedly debated over the past several decades. Some have argued that repressed memories are common (e.g., Herman, 1993) and are responsible for a great deal of psychopathology. In

the controversial but very popular book *The Courage to Heal*, journalists Ellen Bass and Laura Davis assert, "If you are unable to remember any specific instances [of sexual abuse] . . . but still have the feeling that something abusive happened to you, it probably did" (1988, p. 21). Yet as researchers have pointed out, there is absolutely no evidence that this statement is true. Some therapists still routinely give this book to their clients, and those clients often do report "recovering" such memories. Those skeptical about recovery of repressed memories point out that even normal, unrepressed memories can be highly inaccurate and that false memories can be induced experimentally (Davis & Loftus, 2009; Loftus et al., 1995). The debate about the validity of memories of childhood sexual abuse that arise during therapy remains extremely heated. Some researchers (the nonbelievers) maintain that the concept of repressed memory is wholly or largely invalid. In their view, virtually all "recovered memories" are false (Crews, 1995; Davis & Loftus, 2009; Thomas & Loftus, 2002). Others (the believers) maintain that false memories rarely occur and that recovered memories are typically valid. Still others believe that valid recovered memories are simply the remembering of events forgotten because, at the time, they were not traumatic (McNally & Geraerts, 2009). Psychologists equally familiar with the evidence have argued bitterly about this issue, and, a task force assembled by the American Psychological Association to study the issue in the mid-1990s failed to reach a consensus. This lack of consensus continues today. Indeed, the debate concerning recovered memories of sexual abuse is one of the most important and interesting contemporary controversies in the domains of psychopathology and mental health. Despite the continuing controversy among scientists, cases of recovered memories of sexual abuse appear to have become much rarer. A survey conducted of the False Memory Syndrome Foundation—largely parents who say they have been accused by their children of sexual abuse based on recovered memories—showed that accusations peaked in 1991 and 1992, with 579 made during that time. In 1999 and 2000 only 36 accusations were made (McHugh et al., 2004).

Pedophilia

According to *DSM-IV-TR*, **pedophilia**—a paraphilia not discussed earlier—is diagnosed when an adult has recurrent, intense sexual urges or fantasies about sexual activity with a prepubertal child; acting on these desires is not necessary for the diagnosis (see *DSM-IV-TR* Criteria on p. 420). It is important to emphasize that pedophilia is defined by the body maturity, not the age, of the preferred partner. Thus studies of childhood sexual abuse, which often define childhood in terms of an age range that may extend well into adolescence, do not necessarily concern pedophilia. A proposal for *DSM-5* is to also diagnose sexual interest in pubescent children and adolescents, that is, those beginning to show signs of puberty (Blanchard et al., 2009; Blanchard, 2010). Typical ages for pubescents are 10 to 13, but the pubescent period can extend outside that period. Men interested in pubescents are hebephilic, and so the proposed revised diagnosis in *DSM-5* encompassing both pedophilia and hebephilia is *pedohebephilia*. It is important to emphasize that sexual interest in fully sexually mature adolescents is inconsistent with a diagnosis of pedohebephilia.

Pedohebephilia frequently involves manual or oral contact with a child's genitals; penetrative anal or vaginal sex is much rarer. Although penetration and associated force are often injurious to the child, injuries are usually a byproduct rather than the goal they would be with a sadist (although a minority of men diagnosed with pedohebephilia are also sexual sadists; Cohen & Galynker, 2002).

Nearly all individuals with pedohebephilia are male, and about two-thirds of their victims are girls, typically between the ages of 8 and 11 (Cohen & Galynker, 2002). Most pedophebephiles prefer girls, but perhaps one in four prefers boys. The rate of homosexuality among pedophebephiles is much higher than the analogous rate among normal adult-attracted men (Seto, 2008). Although some social conservatives have argued that this shows that gay men tend to commit pedohebephilic acts, this is an incorrect inference. Gay men are no more interested in male children than heterosexual men are in female children. Homosexual pedohebephilia is an entirely different erotic preference from normal male homosexuality (Herek, 2009). Homosexual pedohebephiles tend to have more victims than heterosexual pedohebephiles (Blanchard et al., 2000; Cohen & Galynker, 2002). A majority also use childhood pornography (Seto, 2004).

Studies investigating the sexual responses of men with pedohebephilia have revealed several patterns of results (Barbaree & Seto, 1997; Seto et al., 2006). Such studies typically use a *penile plethysmograph* to measure erectile responses to sexual stimuli directly rather than relying on self-report. (A plethysmograph consists of an expandable band placed around the penis that is connected to a recording device.) Men with pedohebephilia typically show greater sexual arousal than matched nonoffenders in response to pictures of nude or partially clad girls—and greater arousal to such pictures than to pictures of adult women. But some men with pedophilia respond to children as well as to adolescents and/or adults (Seto, 2004; Seto et al., 1999).

Child molesters are more likely than nonoffenders to engage in self-justifying cognitive distortions, including the beliefs that children will benefit from sexual contact with adults and that children often initiate such contact (Marziano et al., 2006). Motivationally, many pedohebephiles appear to be shy and introverted yet still desire mastery or dominance over another individual. Some also idealize aspects of childhood such as innocence, unconditional love, or simplicity (Cohen & Galynker, 2002).

Pedohebephilia usually begins in adolescence and persists over a person's life. Many engage in work with children or youth so that they have extensive access to children; a subset never take advantage, but many others do. Several studies show that adolescent and adult men with pedohebephilia are much more likely than controls to have been sexually or physically abused as children than are rapists of adults (Daversa & Knight, 2007; Lee et al., 2002).

However, recent research findings also support the importance of several neurobiological influences on pedohebephilia. Compared with nonpedohebephilic sex offenders, men with pedodphilia have lower IQs (Cantor, Blanchard et al., 2005; Seto, 2004), threefold higher rates of non-right-handedness (Cantor, Klassen et al., 2005; Seto, 2004), higher rates of head injuries resulting in loss of consciousness, and differences in brain structure detected by brain-imaging techniques, at least some of which are critical for normal sexual development (Cantor et al., 2008; Schiltz et al., 2007). All these findings point to pedohebephilia involving certain perturbations of early neurodevelopment that may create a vulnerability to the disorder.

For several decades we have seen an increasing number of cases of pedohebephilia among a group long considered to be highly trustworthy: the Catholic clergy. Although the majority of priests are innocent of sexual wrongdoing, the Catholic Church has been repeatedly forced to admit that a significant minority have committed sexual abuse, including pedohebephilia. In a large study of the problem, 81 percent of complainants against Catholic clergy were male, and more than 40 percent of cases involved children aged 12 or younger when the alleged abuse began (John Jay College of Criminal Justice, 2004). At least 400 priests were charged with sexual abuse during the 1980s, and $400 million was paid in damages between 1985 and the early 1990s (Samborn, 1994). One very serious scandal involved James R. Porter, a 57-year-old father of four who was alleged to have sexually abused as many as 100 children when he was a priest in Massachusetts during the 1960s. Porter later admitted to his offenses and was convicted. The Church settled a multimillion-dollar suit with 25 men whom Porter had abused while a priest.

This scandal erupted anew in 2002, with heightened publicity regarding revelations that not only had a substantial number of priests in many cities been sexually involved with children and adolescents, but a significant number had also been protected by their superiors. Indeed, this scandal led, after a prolonged public outcry, to the resignation of Cardinal Bernard Law of the Archdiocese of Boston. Over many years, Law had protected numerous priests who were guilty of sexual misconduct, allowing them to move from one parish to another after their sexual misconduct was discovered. Thus he allowed their sexual molestation to continue with more and more girls and boys. The Conference of Bishops subsequently adopted a policy of mandatory removal of any priest from his ministerial duties if he is known to have had sexual contact with a minor. This new policy seems to be working at least to some extent. In September 2005, for example, Cardinal Francis George of the Archdiocese of Chicago permanently removed 11 priests from public ministerial duties for reasons of sexual misconduct (*Chicago Tribune*,

September 27, 2005). New cases continue to emerge, and there is no particular reason to expect they will stop anytime soon. Similar problems of priests engaging in abuse have also occurred in Ireland (LeVay & Valente, 2006).

Not all men with pedophebephilia molest children. In a confidential study of German men who sought mental health services because of their pedohebephilic feelings, 30 percent reported that they had never had sexual contact with a child. Most of those, however, had viewed child pornography (Neutze et al., 2011). The organization B4UAct (Before You Act) is intended to support law-abiding men with pedohebephilic feelings and to raise awareness that such men exist and suffer due to societal prejudice (Clark-Flory, 2011).

Incest

Culturally prohibited sexual relations (up to and including coitus) between family members such as a brother and sister or a parent and child are known as **incest**. Although a few societies have sanctioned certain incestuous relationships—at one time it was the established practice for Egyptian pharaohs to marry their sisters to prevent the royal blood from being "contaminated"—the incest taboo is virtually universal among human societies. Incest often produces children with mental and physical problems because close genetic relatives are much more likely than nonrelatives to share the same recessive genes (which often have negative biological effects) and hence to produce children with two sets of recessive genes. Presumably for this reason, many nonhuman animal species, and all known primates, have an evolved tendency to avoid matings between close relatives. The mechanism for human incest avoidance appears to be lack of sexual interest in people to whom one is continuously exposed from an early age. For example, biologically unrelated children who are raised together in Israeli kibbutzim rarely marry or have affairs with others from their rearing group when they become adults (Kenrick & Luce, 2004). Evolutionarily, this makes sense. In most cultures, children reared together are biologically related.

In our own society, the actual incidence of incest is difficult to estimate because it usually comes to light only when reported to law enforcement or other agencies. It is almost certainly more common than is generally believed, in part because many victims are reluctant to report the incest or do not consider themselves victimized. Brother–sister incest is the most common form of incest even though it is rarely reported (LeVay & Valente, 2006). The second most common pattern is father–daughter incest. It seems that girls living with stepfathers are at especially high risk for incest, perhaps because there is less of an incest taboo among nonblood relatives (Finkelhor, 1984;

Former priest John Geoghan was found guilty of sexually molesting two boys and accused of sexually molesting dozens more in several parishes in the Boston area.

Masters et al., 1992). Mother–son incest is thought to be relatively rare. Frequently, incest offenders do not stop with one child in a family (Wilson, 2004), and some incestuous fathers involve all of their daughters serially as they become pubescent.

Incestuous child molesters tend to have some pedohebephilic arousal patterns (Barsetti et al., 1998; Seto et al., 1999), suggesting that they are at least partly motivated by sexual attraction to children, although they also show arousal to adult women. However, they differ from extrafamilial child molesters in at least two respects (Quinsey et al., 1995). First, the large majority of incest offenses are against girls, whereas extrafamilial offenses show a more equal distribution between boys and girls. Second, incest offenders are more likely to offend with only one or a few children in the family, whereas pedohebephilic child molesters are likely to have more victims (LeVay & Valente, 2006).

In 2007 the world was shocked at revelations concerning the case of an Austrian incest perpetrator named Josef Fritzl. Years earlier Fritzl had kidnapped his own daughter Elisabeth when she was 18 and incarcerated her in a soundproof compartment he had built in his own basement. He forced her to write a note saying that she had joined a cult and that she wanted no further contact with the family. She lived there for 24 years without the knowledge of her mother and other family members who lived upstairs. During her long incarceration, her father repeatedly forced her to have sex. During those years she bore seven children (one of whom died in infancy). Three of the children were reared by the family upstairs, ostensibly having been left for the family by Elisabeth. The other three lived in the basement with her. It was due to a medical problem in one of the latter children that the ordeal finally ended. She begged Josef to let her take the child to the hospital, and he agreed. Hospital staff thought the Fritzls' cover story to be suspicious and alerted police, who successfully investigated (Dahlkamp et al., 2008).

Rape

The term **rape** describes sexual activity that occurs under actual or threatened forcible coercion of one person by another (see Figure 1). In most states, legal definitions restrict forcible rape to forced intercourse or penetration of a bodily orifice by a penis or other object. *Statutory rape* is sexual activity with a person who is legally defined (by statute or law) to be under the age of consent (18 in most states) even if the underage person consents. In the vast majority of cases, rape is a crime of men against women, although in prison settings it is often committed by men against men.

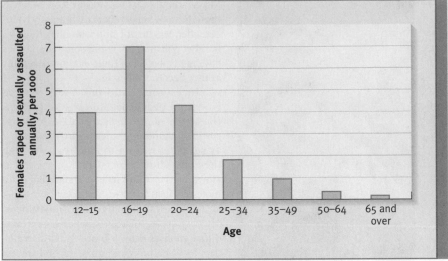

FIGURE 1

Age of Rape and Sexual Assault Victims

Young women are most at risk. (Data from U.S. Department of Justice, 2000a.)

It is important to note that forced sex is not unique to humans but rather occurs in many species in the animal kingdom, where it has often evolved as a reproductive strategy by males to produce more offspring. It has also existed in most human societies (including preliterate ones) at some time in history (Lalumiere et al., 2005a). Across history, rape is traditionally most frequent during and following wars, when it sometimes reaches epidemic proportions. This may be because during war, men perceive few costs for the offense and it is perceived as a good way to express antagonism and contempt toward the enemy (Lalumiere et al., 2005a).

PREVALENCE The results of different studies estimating the prevalence of rape have varied widely. This is, at least in part, because of differences across studies in the precise definition of rape and the way information is gathered (direct or indirect questions, for example). For instance, the U.S. Department of Justice figures from 1998 estimated that one in three women would experience rape or attempted rape at some point in their lives, with many of these being attempted but not completed rapes; but other estimates have been substantially lower. Marital rape is now illegal in all 50 states in the United States and is estimated to occur in 10 to 14 percent of married women and 40 to 50 percent of battered women (Martin, Taft, & Resick, 2007). Since the late 1970s, the prevalence of rape has diminished dramatically, from nearly 3 to fewer than 0.5 per 1,000 individuals per year (Bureau of Justice, 2011). This decline is surely related to a general decline in crime in the United States during that period (Barker, 2010).

IS RAPE MOTIVATED BY SEX OR AGGRESSION? Traditionally, rape has been classified as a sex crime, and society has assumed that a rapist is motivated by lust. However, in the 1970s some feminist scholars began to challenge this view, arguing that rape is motivated by the need to dominate, to assert power, and to humiliate a victim rather than by sexual desire for her (e.g., Brownmiller, 1975). Certainly from the perspective of the victim, rape—which is among women's greatest fears—is always an act of violence and is certainly not a sexually pleasurable experience, whatever the rapist's motivation.

In spite of the fact that feminist writers have argued that rape is primarily a violent act, there are many compelling reasons why sexual motivation is often, if not always, a very important factor too (e.g., Ellis, 1989; Thornhill & Palmer, 2000; Bryden & Grier, 2011). For example, although rape victims include females of all degrees of physical attractiveness, the age distribution of rape victims is not at all random but includes a very high proportion of women in their teens and early 20s, who are generally considered the most sexually attractive. This age distribution is quite different from the distribution of other violent crimes, in which the elderly are overrepresented because of their vulnerability. Furthermore, rapists usually cite sexual motivation as a very important cause of their actions. Finally, as we shall see, at least some rapists exhibit features associated with paraphilias and have multiple paraphilias (Abel & Rouleau, 1990; LeVay & Valente, 2006). Men with paraphilias are typically highly sexually motivated.

In the past few decades, several prominent researchers studying sex offenders have shown that all rapists actually have both aggressive and sexual motives but to varying degrees. For example, Knight and Prentky (1990) identified four subtypes of rapists, with two subtypes motivated primarily by aggression and two subtypes motivated primarily by distorted sexual motives (see also Knight et al., 1994). More recently, McCabe and Wauchope (2005) provided empirical support for a somewhat different classification system that also has four subtypes of rapists with differing amounts of sexual and aggressive motives. At present it is not clear which scheme of classification is best, and some rapists cannot readily be characterized (LeVay & Valente, 2006).

RAPE AND ITS AFTERMATH Stranger rape tends to be a repetitive activity rather than an isolated act, and most rapes are planned events. About 80 percent of rapists commit the act in the neighborhoods in which they reside; most rapes occur in an urban setting at night, in places ranging from dark, lonely streets to elevators and hallways, and apartments or homes. About a third or more of all rapes involve more than one offender. The remainder are single-offender rapes in which the victim and the offender are acquainted with each other (in about two-thirds of rapes); this includes wives (Bennice & Resick, 2003) (see Figure 2).

In addition to the physical trauma inflicted on a victim, the psychological trauma may be severe, leading in a substantial number of female victims to PTSD, which, when caused by rape, is often also associated with severe sexual problems. A rape may also have a negative impact on a victim's marriage or other intimate relationships. Although there has been little systematic study of men who have been raped, one study of 40 male rape victims revealed that nearly all experienced some long-term psychological distress following rape, including anxiety, depression, increased feelings of anger, and loss of self-image (Walker et al., 2005).

Rape, even at its least violent, is a bullying, intrusive violation of another person's integrity, selfhood, and personal boundaries that deserves to be viewed with more gravity—and its victims with more compassion and sensitivity—than has often been the case. Nevertheless, the myth of "victim-precipitated" rape, once a favorite of defense attorneys and of some police and court jurisdictions, still remains in certain circles. According to this view, a victim (especially a repeat victim), though often bruised both psychologically and physically, is regarded as the cause of the crime, often on such grounds as the alleged provocativeness of her clothing, her past sexual behavior, or her presence in a location considered risky (LeVay & Valente, 2006; Stermac et al., 1990). The attacker, on the other hand, is regarded as unable to quell his lust in the face of such irresistible provocation—and therefore is not treated as legally responsible for the act. Fortunately, *rape shield laws* began to be introduced in the 1970s. These laws protect rape victims by, for example, preventing the prosecutor from using evidence of a victim's prior sex history; however, many problems in these laws still remain (LeVay & Valente, 2006).

A recent example of the complexity inherent in the legal situation of rape prosecution is that of Dominique Strauss-Kahn (DSK), who was managing director of the International Monetary Fund and an aspiring French politician. In May 2011, he was accused by a New York City hotel worker of sexually assaulting her when she entered his hotel room to clean it. A police investigation confirmed that sexual contact had occurred, but DSK insisted that it was consensual. Subsequently another woman came forward accusing him of raping her years earlier in France. However, the 2011 case unravelled when prosecutors learned that DSK's accuser had lied about other matters, including the claim that she had been raped in her country of origin. The charges were dropped. It is possible that DSK got away with rape. It is also possible that he was falsely accused. Cases such as the accusations against DSK highlight both barriers to prosecuting rape cases and the need for adequate protections for the accused.

RAPISTS AND CAUSAL CONSIDERATIONS Information gathered by the FBI about arrested and convicted rapists suggests that rape is usually a young man's crime. According to FBI Uniform Crime Reports, about 60 percent of all rapists arrested are under 25 years old. Of the rapists who get into police records, about 30 to 50 percent are married and living with their wives at the time of the crime. As a group, they come from the low end of the socioeconomic ladder and commonly have a prior criminal record (Ward et al., 1997). They are also quite likely to have experienced sexual abuse, a violent home environment, and inconsistent caregiving in childhood (Hudson & Ward, 1997).

One subset of rapists, date rapists (a date rapist is an acquaintance who rapes a woman in the context of a date or other social interaction), have a somewhat different demographic profile in that they are often middle- to upper-class young men who rarely have criminal records. However, these men, like incarcerated rapists, are characterized by promiscuity, hostile

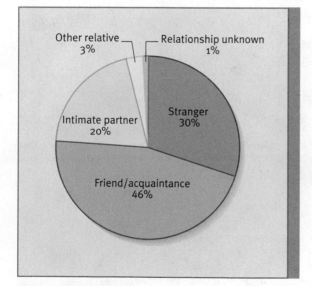

FIGURE 2

Most Rapes Are Not Committed by Strangers
The graph shows the relationships of perpetrators of rape and sexual assault to their victims. (Data from U.S. Department of Justice, 2000b.)

masculinity, and an emotionally detached, predatory personality (e.g., Knight, 1997; LeVay & Valente, 2003). Their victims are often highly intoxicated (Mohler-Keuo et al., 2004; Testa et al., 2003). What distinguishes them, primarily, is that incarcerated rapists show much higher levels of impulsive, antisocial behavior than date rapists.

As suggested earlier, there is evidence that some rapists are afflicted by a paraphilia (Abel & Rouleau, 1990; Freund & Seto, 1998). For example, rapists often report having recurrent, repetitive, and compulsive urges to rape. Although they typically try to control these urges, the urges sometimes become so strong that they act on them. Many rapists also have other paraphilias such as exhibitionism and voyeurism. They also frequently have a characteristic pattern of sexual arousal (Abel & Rouleau, 1990; Clegg & Fremouw, 2009; Lohr et al., 1997). Most rapists are similar to normal, nonoffending men in being sexually aroused by depictions of mutually satisfying, consensual intercourse, but many rapists are also sexually aroused by depictions of sexual assaults involving an unwilling victim (Clegg & Fremouw, 2009; Lalumiere et al., 2005b). A small minority of rapists are sexual sadists, characterized by very violent assaults and aroused more by assault than by sexual stimuli.

In terms of personality, rapists are very often characterized by impulsivity, quick loss of temper, lack of personally intimate relationships, and insensitivity to social cues or pressures (Giotakos et al., 2004), and a subset qualify for a diagnosis of psychopathy (e.g., Knight & Guay, 2006). Many rapists also show some deficits in social and communication skills (Emmers-Sommer et al., 2004), as well as in their cognitive appraisals of women's feelings and intentions (Ward et al., 1997). For example, they are particularly deficient in skills involved in successful conversation, which is necessary for developing consenting relationships with women. In addition, they have difficulty decoding women's negative cues during social interactions and often interpret friendly behavior as flirtatious or sexually provocative (Emmers-Sommer et al., 2004). This can lead to inappropriate behaviors that women would experience as sexually intrusive.

Estimates are that only 20 to 28 percent of rapes are ever reported, compared to 60 percent of robberies, but the proportion of rapes being reported has increased over the past several decades (Magid et al., 2004). Among men who are arrested, only about half are convicted; of these, only about two-thirds serve a jail term (LeVay & Valente, 2006). Convictions often bring light sentences, and a jail term does not dissuade a substantial number of offenders from repeating their crimes. The upshot of all this is that the large majority of rapists are not in prison but out among us.

Which scenario do you think is more likely to lead to rape? It is difficult to guess because date rape is increasingly common, and rapes by casual acquaintances usually occur in dark, lonely places.

Treatment and Recidivism of Sex Offenders

There is growing intolerance for sex offenders who repeat their crimes. Soon after his release from prison, convicted sex offender Earl Shriner forced a 7-year-old boy off his bike in the woods near Tacoma, Washington, and then raped and stabbed him before cutting off the boy's penis. Just before his release from prison, Shriner had confided to a cellmate that he still had fantasies of molesting and murdering children (Popkin, 1994). In a similar case, 7-year-old Megan Kanka was sexually molested and murdered by a convicted pedohebephile living in her neighborhood. Cases such as these have inspired a number of measures to protect society from sexual predators (see The World Around Us 2).

But are such stories representative? Are sex offenders typically incurable? Should they receive life sentences on the presumption that they are bound to offend again? Or have they been unfairly singled out by media sensationalism even though they really are responsive to treatment? The efficacy of treatment for sex offenders is controversial, and this is the topic to which we now turn (e.g., Fedoroff, 2009, 2010).

In general, sex offender recidivism is actually markedly lower than for many other kinds of crimes. Recidivism rates for some types of offenders are higher than they are for others, however (Mann et al., 2010). Specifically, sex offenders with deviant sexual preferences (e.g., exhibitionists, severe sadists, and those who are most attracted to children) have particularly high rates of sexual recidivism (Dickey et al., 2002; Langevin et al., 2004). One follow-up study of more than 300 sex offenders over 25 years found that over half were charged with at least one additional sexual offense (Langevin et al., 2004). A recent review found that sexualized violence—a preference for sadistic or coercive sex—was the strongest predictor of recidivism. Other predictors included negative social influences, poor cognitive problem-solving, and loneliness (Mann et al., 2010). The recidivism rate for rapists steadily decreases with age, as does performance of sexually deviant behavior more generally (Barbaree & Blanchard, 2008).

PSYCHOTHERAPIES AND THEIR EFFECTIVENESS

Therapies for sex offenders typically have at least one of the following four goals: to modify patterns of sexual arousal, to modify cognitions and social skills to allow more appropriate sexual interactions with adult partners, to change habits or behavior that increases the chance of reoffending, or to reduce sexual drive. Attempts to modify sexual arousal patterns usually involve *aversion therapy*, in which a paraphilic stimulus such

2 | THE WORLD AROUND US

Megan's Law

On July 29, 1994, 7-year-old Megan Kanka, from Hamilton Township, New Jersey, was walking home from her friend's house when a neighbor invited her to his house to see his new puppy. The neighbor, Jesse Timmendequas, 33, was a landscaper who had lived across the street for about a year. Unknown to Megan, to Megan's parents, or to anyone else in the neighborhood, he was also a twice-convicted child molester (who lived with two other convicted sex offenders). When Megan followed him inside, he led her to an upstairs bedroom, strangled her unconscious with his belt, raped her, and asphyxiated her with a plastic bag. Timmendequas then placed Megan's body in a toolbox, drove to a soccer field, and dumped it near a portable toilet. Timmendequas was subsequently apprehended, convicted, and sentenced to death; however, because New Jersey abolished the death penalty in 2007, he will serve a life term in prison.

Megan's murder sparked outrage at the fact that dangerous sex offenders could move into a neighborhood without notifying the community of their presence. In response, the New Jersey state legislature passed Megan's Law, which mandates that upon release, convicted sex offenders register with police and that authorities notify neighbors that convicted sex offenders have moved in by distributing fliers, alerting local organizations, and canvassing door-to-door. Similar laws have been passed in many other states, and it is now possible in several states to visit a website containing pictures and addresses of convicted sex offenders, subject to that state's Megan's Law. Although Megan's Laws have been enormously popular with state legislators and citizens, they have not been uncontroversial. Civil libertarians have objected to community notification requirements, which, they argue, endanger released offenders (who have arguably paid their debts to society) and also prevent them from integrating successfully back into society. Although the various Megan's Laws are intended to protect potential victims rather than to encourage harassment of sex offenders, the latter has occurred, with up to one-third to one-half of registered offenders in some states experiencing one or more of the following: loss of a job or home, threats, harassment, property damage, and/or harm to family members (Levenson et al., 2007). In addition, the limited amount of relevant data has brought the effectiveness of Megan's Laws into question. For example, since 1995 a number of studies have compared recidivism rates from the period before which registration as a sex offender was required to rates after these laws were passed. Unfortunately, the results have not really provided any reassuring evidence that notifying communities has enhanced community safety (Levenson et al., 2007). A recent analysis in New Jersey, where Megan Kanka lived and died, found that Megan's Law had made no difference (Zgoba et al., 2008).

as a slide of a nude prepubescent girl for a man with pedohilia is paired with an aversive event such as forced inhalation of noxious odors or a shock to the arm. An alternative to electric aversion therapy is *covert sensitization*, in which the patient imagines a highly aversive event while viewing or imagining a paraphilic stimulus, or *assisted covert sensitization*, in which a foul odor is introduced to induce nausea at the point of peak arousal (Maletzky, 2002).

Deviant arousal patterns also need to be replaced by arousal to acceptable stimuli (Maletzky, 2002; Quinsey & Earls, 1990). Most often, investigators have attempted to pair the pleasurable stimuli of orgasm with sexual fantasies involving sex between consenting adults. For example, sex offenders are asked to masturbate while thinking of deviant fantasies. At the moment of ejaculatory inevitability, the patient switches his fantasy to a more appropriate theme. Although aversion therapy has been shown to be somewhat effective in the laboratory (Maletzky, 1998; Quinsey & Earls, 1990), how well this therapeutic change generalizes to the patient's outside world is uncertain if his motivation wanes. Further, although aversion therapy is still widely used for sex offenders, it is not used anymore as a sole form of treatment (Marshall, 1998).

The remaining psychological treatments are aimed at reducing the chances of sexual reoffending. *Cognitive restructuring* attempts to eliminate sex offenders' cognitive distortions because these may play a role in sexual abuse (Maletzky, 2002). For example, an incest offender who maintained that "If my ten-year-old daughter had said no, I would have stopped" might be challenged about a number of implied distortions: that a child has the capacity to consent to have sex with an adult; that if a child does not say no, she has consented; and that it is the child's responsibility to stop sexual contact. In addition, *social-skills training* aims to help sex offenders (especially rapists) learn to process social information from women more effectively and to interact with them more appropriately (Maletzky, 2002; McFall, 1990). For example, some men read positive sexual connotations into women's neutral or negative messages or believe that women's refusals of sexual advances reflect "playing hard to get." Training typically involves interaction of perpetrators with female partners, who can give the offenders feedback on their response to the interactions.

Although some studies in the treatment literature have reached positive conclusions (see Maletzsky, 2002, for a review), other studies have found essentially no differences between treated and untreated offenders (Emmelkamp, 1994; Rice et al., 1991). A recent meta-analysis of 23 recidivism outcome studies revealed an advantage for treatment: 10.9 percent of treated sex offenders versus 19.2 percent of untreated offenders committed another sex crime (Hanson et al., 2009). The most effective treatment programs followed the Canadian "Risk-Need-Responsiveness" model, in which an offender's risk is first assessed to determine who should get the most intensive treatment. Second, there is a focus on factors that directly increase chance of reoffending such as paraphilic desire or impulsivity. Third, correctional programs should be matched to offender characteristics such as learning style, level of motivation,

and the offender's individual characteristics. Such multifaceted cognitive-behavioral techniques appear to be more effective than older techniques such as aversion therapy. There are also indications in the literature that certain paraphilias respond better to treatment than others (Laws & O'Donohue, 2008). For example, one very long-term follow-up (5 to 15 years) of over 2,000 sex offenders who had entered a cognitive-behavioral treatment program found that child molesters and exhibitionists achieved better overall success rates than pedohebephiles and rapists (Maletzky & Steinhauser, 2002).

BIOLOGICAL AND SURGICAL TREATMENTS In recent years antidepressants from the SSRI category have been found to be useful in treating a variety of paraphilias by reducing paraphilic desire and behavior; they are not, however, useful in treatment of sexual offenders. The most controversial treatment for sex offenders involves castration—either surgical removal of the testes or the hormonal treatment sometimes called "chemical castration" (e.g., Berlin, 2003; Bradford & Greenberg, 1996; Weinberger et al., 2005). Both surgical and chemical castration lower the testosterone level, which in turn lowers the sex drive, allowing the offender to resist any inappropriate impulses. Chemical castration has most often involved the administration of antiandrogen steroid hormones such as Depo-Provera and Lupron, which can both have serious side effects. One uncontrolled study of the drug Lupron yielded dramatic results: Thirty men with paraphilias reported an average of 48 deviant fantasies per week prior to therapy, and no such fantasies during treatment (Rosler & Witztum, 1998; see also Maletzky & Field, 2003). However, relapse rates upon discontinuation of the drug were very high (Maletzky, 2002).

Studies of surgical castration of repeat sex offenders with violent tendencies conducted in Europe and more recently in the United States had similar results (but without high rates of relapse; Weinberger et al., 2005). These studies have typically included diverse categories of offenders, from pedohebephiles to rapists of adult women. Follow-up has sometimes exceeded 10 years. Recidivism rates for castrated offenders are typically less than 3 percent, compared with greater than 50 percent for uncastrated offenders (e.g., Berlin, 1994; Green, 1992; Prentky, 1997). However, many feel that the treatment is brutal, unethical, and dehumanizing (Farkas & Strichman, 2002; Gunn, 1993), although this assumption has been challenged (Bailey & Greenberg, 1998).

Interestingly, some recent cases have involved a request by the sex offender himself to be castrated in exchange for a lighter sentence (LeVay & Valente, 2006). In some states such as California, a repeat offender's eligibility for probation or parole following childhood molestation is linked to his acceptance of mandated hormonal therapy (Scott & Holmberg, 2003). Oregon evaluated the success of requiring such treatment and found that those receiving chemical castration fared better in terms of committing fewer new offenses and fewer parole violations, and were less likely to return to prison (Maletzky et al., 2006). Nevertheless, civil libertarians, exemplified by the ACLU, have argued that because of potentially severe side effects, such requirements violate the Constitution's ban on cruel and unusual punishment. More research is desirable to determine whether, and under what conditions, such biological treatments should be used with some sex offenders (Rice & Harris, 2011). Such research should be a priority.

COMBINING PSYCHOLOGICAL AND BIOLOGICAL TREATMENTS Not surprisingly, many treatment programs now use a combination of hormone therapy and cognitive-behavioral treatments, the hope being that the hormone treatment can be tapered off after the offender has learned techniques for impulse control (Maletzky, 2002). However, the single most important defect of nearly all available studies is the lack of randomly assigned controls who are equally motivated for treatment. Some have argued that denying treatment to sex offenders is unethical (e.g., Marshall et al., 1991). However, this would be true only if the treatment were effective, and it is not clear at this point whether it is. Thus others have argued that randomized controlled trials are crucial for making progress in his area (e.g., Seto et al., 2008). Research in this area is further complicated by the fact that the outcome variable in most studies is whether the man is convicted for another sex offense during the follow-up period. The fact that most sex offenses go unpunished (the offender is often never even caught, let alone convicted) might exaggerate the apparent effectiveness of treatment and underestimate the dangerousness of sex offenders. Given the social importance of determining whether sex offenders can be helped and how likely they are to reoffend, it is crucial that society devote the resources necessary to answering these questions.

SUMMARY It is possible both to acknowledge that sex offenders cause immense human suffering and to feel sympathy for the plight of the many offenders who have been burdened with a deviant sexual arousal pattern that has caused them great personal and legal trouble. Consider the case of Scott Murphy, a convicted pedohebephile:

> He lives alone with a friend, works odd hours, and doesn't go out of his way to meet neighbors. Ironically, Murphy has never been prouder of his behavior. He admits he'll never be cured and will always be attracted to young boys. But he says he is now making every attempt to steer clear of them: "I went from constantly living my whole life to molest kids to now living my whole life to not molest kids." It's a 24-hour-a-day job. On the highway, Murphy keeps at a distance to guarantee he makes no eye contact with the young passengers in school buses. When the Sunday paper arrives at home, he immediately throws out the coupon section because the glossy ads often depict attractive boy models. He refuses to leave the office when kids might be walking to or from school and got rid of his television so the sit-com images of young boys wouldn't distract him. (Popkin, 1994, p. 67)

Society cannot allow Murphy to act on his sexual preference, nor can his past crimes be forgotten. Nevertheless, in deciding how to treat people like Scott Murphy, it is important and humane to remember that many of them have a tormented inner life.

In Review

● What are the short-term consequences of childhood sexual abuse, and why are we less certain about its long-term consequences?

● What are the major issues surrounding children's testimony about sexual abuse and adults' recovered memories of sexual abuse?

● Define pedohebephilia, incest, and rape, and summarize the major clinical features of the perpetrators of these crimes.

● Identify the main goals of treatment of sex offenders, and describe the different treatment approaches.

Sexual Dysfunctions

The term **sexual dysfunction** refers to impairment either in the desire for sexual gratification or in the ability to achieve it. The impairment varies markedly in degree, but regardless of which partner is alleged to be dysfunctional, the enjoyment of sex by both parties in a relationship is typically adversely affected. Sexual dysfunctions occur in both heterosexual and homosexual couples. In some cases, sexual dysfunctions are caused primarily by psychological or interpersonal factors. In others, physical factors are most important, including many cases of sexual dysfunction that are secondary consequences of medications people may be taking for other, unrelated medical conditions (Baron-Kuhn & Segraves, 2007). In recent years, both explanations and treatments of sexual dysfunction have become more biological, although some psychological treatments have been ***empirically validated***, and psychosocial factors clearly play a causal role as well (Heiman, 2002; Meston & Rellini, 2008; Segraves & Althof, 2002).

Today researchers and clinicians typically identify four different phases of the human sexual response as originally proposed by Masters and Johnson (1966, 1970, 1975) and Kaplan (1979). According to *DSM-IV-TR*, disorders can occur in any of the first three phases:

● The first phase is the **desire phase**, which consists of fantasies about sexual activity or a sense of desire to have sexual activity.

● The second phase is the **excitement (or arousal) phase**, characterized both by a subjective sense of sexual pleasure and by

RESEARCH CLOSE-UP

Empirically Validated

Empirically validated treatments are treatments that have been determined to be helpful based on well-designed, scientific research by more than just one group of researchers.

physiological changes that accompany this subjective pleasure, including penile erection in the male and vaginal lubrication and clitoral enlargement in the female.

- The third phase is **orgasm**, during which there is a release of sexual tension and a peaking of sexual pleasure.
- The final phase is **resolution**, during which the person has a sense of relaxation and well-being.

Although these four phases are described as if they were distinct, it is important to remember that they are experienced by an individual as a continuous set of feelings and biological and behavioral reactions. There are other conceivable ways to discuss and organize the sequence that occurs. For example, the *DSM* work group on sexual dysfunction has proposed that dysfunctions of desire and dysfunctions of arousal be categorized together because research has not adequately demonstrated that they are separate (Brotto, 2010a; Graham, 2010). However, we will follow the scheme that the current *DSM* has used to categorize dysfunctions. We will first describe the most common dysfunctions occurring in the first three phases and then discuss causation and treatment. In addition, *DSM* lists two disorders involving pain that are not clearly tied to these three phases.

How common are sexual dysfunctions? It is obviously difficult to do large-scale research on such a sensitive topic. Nevertheless, the National Health and Social Life Survey (Laumann et al., 1999) assessed sexual problems in 3,159 randomly selected Americans by asking them if they had experienced the symptoms of any of the different sexual dysfunctions in the past 12 months. Sexual problems were very common, with 43 percent of women and 31 percent of men reporting having experienced at least one of these problems in the previous 12 months. For women, the reported rate of sexual problems decreased with age; for men it increased. Married men and women, and those with higher educational attainment, had lower rates of problems. For women, the most common complaints were lack of sexual desire (22 percent) and sexual arousal problems (14 percent). For men, climaxing too early (21 percent), erectile dysfunction (5 percent), and lack of sexual interest (5 percent) were reported most frequently. However, this study was criticized by Bancroft and colleagues (2003), who believe that these numbers overestimate how many people have true sexual dysfunctions. Although the Laumann and colleagues' results are often referred to as being about sexual *dysfunction*, in fact, the investigators never asked people about whether the problems caused them distress or impairment in any way; yet these are necessary criteria for making a diagnosis in *DSM-IV-TR*. When Bancroft and colleagues (2003) did a related survey (although just in women), they found very similar percentages to those found by Laumann and colleagues. However, Bancroft and colleagues found that only about half as many reported that the problem caused them "severe distress." Nevertheless, this is still a relatively high percentage of people experiencing sexual dysfunction at some point in their lives.

Sexual dysfunctions can occur in the desire, excitement, or orgasm phases of the sexual response cycle. Many people, if not most, will experience some sexual dysfunction sometime during their lives. If it becomes chronic or disturbing to one or both partners, it warrants treatment.

Interestingly, a later study of 27,500 people across 29 countries all over the world revealed fairly similar results (Laumann et al., 2005). There were some differences, of course, in prevalence across countries, but the results were more similar than different. East Asian and Southeast Asian countries reported slightly higher rates of sexual problems than most other countries.

Sexual Desire Disorders

Researchers have delineated two types of sexual desire disorders. The first is **hypoactive sexual desire disorder**. It is a dysfunction in which either a man or a woman shows little or no sexual drive or interest (see *DSM-IV-TR* Criteria on p. 422). Research on the degree to which the diminished sex drive has a biological basis remains controversial, but in many (and perhaps most) cases (and especially in women), psychological factors appear to be more important than biological factors (Meston & Bradford, 2007; Segraves & Woodard, 2006). In the past, these people usually came to the attention of clinicians primarily at the request of their partners (who typically complained of insufficient sexual interaction), but as public knowledge about the frequency of this disorder has increased, more people are presenting for treatment on their own. This fact exposes one problem with the diagnosis, because it is known that preferences for frequency of sexual contact vary widely among otherwise normal individuals. Who is to decide what is "not enough"? *DSM-IV-TR* explicitly indicates that this judgment is left to the clinician, taking into account the person's age and the context of his or her life. In extreme cases, sex actually becomes psychologically aversive and warrants a diagnosis of **sexual aversion disorder**, the second type of sexual desire disorder. With this disorder, the person shows extreme aversion to, and avoidance of, all genital sexual contact with a partner.

DSM-IV-TR

Criteria for Different Sexual Dysfunctions

Sexual Desire Disorders

Hypoactive Sexual Desire Disorder

A. Persistently or recurrently deficient (or absent) sexual fantasies and desire for sexual activity. The judgment of deficiency or absence is made by the clinician, taking into account factors that affect sexual functioning, such as age and the context of the person's life.

B. The disturbance causes marked distress or interpersonal difficulty.

C. The sexual dysfunction is not better accounted for by another Axis I disorder (except another Sexual Dysfunction) and is not due exclusively to the direct physiological effects of a substance (e.g., a drug of abuse, a medication) or a general medical condition.

Sexual Aversion Disorder

A. Persistent or recurrent extreme aversion to, and avoidance of, almost (or almost all) genital sexual contact with a sexual partner.

B. The disturbance causes marked distress or interpersonal difficulty.

C. The sexual Dysfunction is not better accounted for by another Axis I disorder (except another Sexual Dysfunction).

Sexual Arousal Disorders

Female Sexual Arousal Disorder

A. Persistent or recurrent inability to attain, or to maintain until completion of the sexual activity, an adequate lubrication/swelling response of sexual excitement.

B. The disturbance causes marked distress or interpersonal difficulty.

C. The sexual dysfunction is not better accounted for by another Axis I disorder (except another Sexual Dysfunction) and is not due exclusively to the direct physiological effects of a substance (e.g., a drug of abuse, a medication) or a general medical condition.

Male Erectile Disorder

A. Persistent or recurrent inability to attain, or to maintain until completion of the sexual activity, an adequate erection.

B. The disturbance causes marked distress or interpersonal difficulty.

C. The erectile dysfunction is not better accounted for by another Axis I disorder (other than a Sexual Dysfunction) and is not due exclusively to the direct physiological effects of a substance (e.g., a drug of abuse, a medication) or a general medical condition.

Orgasmic Disorders

Female Orgasmic Disorder

A. Persistent or recurrent delay in, or absence of, orgasm following a normal sexual excitement phase. Women exhibit wide variability in the type or intensity of stimulation that triggers orgasm. The diagnosis of Female Orgasmic Disorder should be based on the clinician's judgment that the woman's orgasmic capacity is less than would be reasonable for her age, sexual experience, and the adequacy of sexual stimulation she receives.

B. The disturbance causes marked distress or interpersonal difficulty.

C. The orgasmic dysfunction is not better accounted for by another Axis I disorder (except another Sexual Dysfunction) and is not due exclusively to the direct physiological effects of a substance (e.g., a drug of abuse, a medication) or a general medical condition.

Premature Ejaculation

A. Persistent or recurrent ejaculation with minimal sexual stimulation before, on, or shortly after penetration and before the person wishes it. The clinician must take into account factors that affect duration of the excitement phase, such as age, novelty of the sexual partner or situation, and recent frequency of sexual activity.

B. The disturbance causes marked distress or interpersonal difficulty.

C. The premature ejaculation is not due exclusively to the direct effects of a substance (e.g., withdrawal from opioids).

Sexual Pain Disorders

Dyspareunia

A. Recurrent or persistent genital pain associated with sexual intercourse in either a male or a female.

B. The disturbance causes marked distress or interpersonal difficulty.

C. The disturbance is not caused exclusively by Vaginismus or lack of lubrication, is not better accounted for by another Axis I disorder (except another Sexual Dysfunction), and is not due exclusively to the direct physiological effects of a substance (e.g., a drug of abuse, a medication) or a general medical condition.

Vaginismus

A. Recurrent or persistent involuntary spasm of the musculature of the outer third of the vagina that interferes with sexual intercourse.

B. The disturbance causes marked distress or interpersonal difficulty.

C. The disturbance is not better accounted for by another Axis I disorder (e.g., Somatization Disorder) and is not due exclusively to the direct physiological effects of a general medical condition.

Subtypes

The following subtypes apply to all primary Sexual Dysfunctions. One of the following subtypes may be used to indicate the nature of the onset of the Sexual Dysfunction:

Lifelong Type. This subtype applies if the sexual dysfunction has been present since the onset of sexual functioning.

Acquired Type. This subtype applies if the sexual dysfunction develops only after a period of normal functioning.

One of the following subtypes may be used to indicate the context in which the Sexual Dysfunction occurs:

Generalized Type. This subtype applies if the sexual dysfunction is not limited to certain types of stimulation, situations, or partners.

Situational Type. This subtype applies if the sexual dysfunction is limited to certain types of stimulation, situations, or partners. The specific situational pattern of the dysfunction may aid in the differential diagnosis. For example, normal masturbatory function in the presence of impaired partner relational functioning would suggest that a chief complaint of erectile dysfunction is more likely due to an interpersonal or intrapsychic problem rather than attributable to a general medical condition or a substance.

One of the following subtypes may be used to indicate etiological factors associated with the Sexual Dysfunction:

Due to Psychological Factors. This subtype applies when psychological factors are judged to have the major role in the onset, severity, exacerbation, or maintenance of the Sexual

Dysfunction, and general medical conditions and substances play no role in the etiology of the Sexual Dysfunction.

Due to Combined Factors. This subtype applies when

1) psychological factors are judged to have a role in the onset, severity, exacerbation, or maintenance of the Sexual Dysfunction; and 2) a general medical condition or substance use is also judged to be contributory but is not sufficient to account for the Sexual Dysfunction. If a general medical condition or substance use (including medication side effects) is sufficient to account for the Sexual Dysfunction, Sexual Dysfunction Due to a General Medical Condition and/or Substance-Induced Sexual Dysfunction is diagnosed.

Source: Reprinted with permission from the American Psychiatric Association. *Diagnostic and Statistical Manual of Mental Disorders*, Fourth Edition, *Text Revision* (Copyright © 2000). American Psychiatric Association.

A leading researcher on sexual dysfunction has recently argued that sexual aversion disorder should be considered as an anxiety disorder akin to simple phobias rather than as a sexual dysfunction (Brotto, 2010b).

Prior or current depression or anxiety disorders may contribute to many cases of sexual desire disorders (Meston & Bradford, 2007). Although sexual desire disorders typically occur in the absence of obvious physical pathology, there is evidence that physical factors sometimes play a role. For example, in both men and women, sexual desire depends in part on testosterone (Alexander & Sherwin, 1993; Meston & Rellini, 2008). That sexual desire problems increase with age may be in part attributable to declining levels of testosterone, but testosterone replacement therapy is usually not beneficial, except in men and women who have very low testosterone levels (Meston & Rellini, 2008). In addition, medications from the SSRI category of antidepressants not uncommonly reduce sexual desire. Different antidepressants vary considerably in their negative effect on sexual function, and psychiatrists have not always paid close enough attention to the impact that these effects have on patients' general functioning (Serretti & Chiesa, 2009). Psychological factors thought to contribute to sexual desire disorders include low relationship satisfaction, daily hassles and worries, increased disagreements and conflicts, low levels of feelings, and reduced cues of emotional bonding (Meston & Rellini, 2008). In some cases a history of unwanted sexual experiences such as rape may also contribute.

Hypoactive sexual desire disorder appears to be the most common female sexual dysfunction in the United States and most other countries across the world (Laumann et al., 1994, 1999, 2005). Despite this fact, it has inspired far less research into its origins and treatment than have male dysfunctions, especially erectile disorder and premature ejaculation. One main reason for this disparity is doubtless the great importance that many men place on their ability to perform sexually. Until recently, there has also been a more general neglect of female sexuality and an implicit (though largely mistaken) societal attitude that women simply do not care much about sex.

Fortunately, this has been changing gradually in recent years (e.g., Althof et al., 2005; Basson, 2005; Meston & Bradford, 2007). One emerging finding is that it is uncommon for women to cite sexual desire as a reason or incentive for sexual activity. For many women, sexual desire is experienced only after sexual stimuli have led to subjective sexual arousal (Basson et al., 2003a; Meston & Bradford, 2007), and for others, motivation for sexual activity may involve a desire for increasing emotional intimacy or increasing one's sense of well-being and one's self-image as an attractive female (Basson, 2003, 2005). Thus, some research suggests that the supposedly linear sequence of desire leading to arousal, leading to orgasm that was originally posited for women as well as men by Masters and Johnson (1970) and the *DSM* is not very accurate for women (e.g., Basson, 2005; Meston & Bradford, 2007).

Treatment Although there has been interest since antiquity in the possibility that a drug to increase sexual desire might be found, no effective aphrodisiacs yet exist. As noted earlier, testosterone appears to be effective only in men and women who have very low levels of testosterone; that is, raising levels of this important sex hormone above normal levels has no beneficial effects (e.g., Meston & Rellini, 2008). Consistent with an effect of hormones, a German study showed that women using oral contraceptions, which sometimes work by raising estrogen levels, which in turn reduce testosterone levels, had somewhat lower levels of sexual desire and arousal compared with those who did not (Wallwiener et al., 2010).

Several studies have found that sustained use of bupropion (an atypical antidepressant), relative to placebo, improved sexual arousability and orgasm frequency in women who were in a committed relationship and had hypoactive sexual desire disorder (e.g., Segraves et al., 2004). Another drug, flibanserin, has been developed to increase sexual desire in women, but the Food and Drug Administration denied approval for this use in 2010, saying that there is not yet sufficient research (Wilson, 2010). Pharmaceutical companies are eager to find a treatment for low sexual desire in women, but some women have argued that the companies are more concerned about making money than about curing a legitimate illness (Segal, 2008).

There are no well-established psychotherapies for hypoactive sexual desire disorders. Typically therapists focus on education, communication training, cognitive restructuring of dysfunctional beliefs about sexuality, sexual fantasy training, and sensate focus training (Meston & Rellini, 2008). Sensate focus exercises are also used in the treatment of several other forms of sexual dysfunctions, as we will see. They involve teaching couples to focus on the pleasurable sensations brought about by touching without the goal of actually having intercourse or orgasm. Relationship problems often contribute importantly to low sexual desire, as do concerns related to body-image (Basson, 2010). Addressing these problems thus may be helpful.

Sexual Arousal Disorders

Sexual arousal disorders affect both men and women. They are not an issue of sexual desire but rather experiencing difficulty in becoming physically aroused. In the following section, we discuss **male erectile disorder**—the inability to achieve or maintain an erection—and **female sexual arousal disorder**—the absence of feelings of sexual arousal and an unresponsiveness to most or all forms of erotic stimulation.

MALE ERECTILE DISORDER Inability to achieve or maintain an erection sufficient for successful sexual intercourse was formerly called *impotence*. It is now known as male erectile disorder and can be diagnosed only when the difficulties are considered to originate from either psychogenic or a combination of psychogenic and medical factors (see *DSM-IV-TR* Criteria on p. 422). In lifelong erectile disorder, a man with adequate sexual desire has never been able to sustain an erection long enough to accomplish a satisfactory duration of penetration. In acquired or situational erectile disorder, a man with adequate sexual desire has had at least one successful experience of sexual activity requiring an erection but is presently unable to produce or maintain the required level of penile rigidity. Lifelong erectile disorder is relatively rare, but most men of all ages occasionally have difficulty obtaining or maintaining an erection. Laumann and colleagues' (1999) landmark study on the prevalence of sexual dysfunction estimates that 7 percent of 18- to 19-year-old men and 18 percent of 50- to 59-year-old men reported having erectile disorder.

Masters and Johnson (1975; Masters et al., 1992) and Kaplan (1987) hypothesized that erectile dysfunction is primarily a function of anxiety about sexual performance. In other reviews of the accumulated evidence, however, Barlow and colleagues (Beck & Barlow, 1984a; Sbrocco & Barlow, 1996) have played down the role of anxiety per se—because under some circumstances, anxiety can actually enhance sexual performance in normally functioning men and women (Barlow et al., 1983; Palace & Gorzalka, 1990; see Sbrocco & Barlow, 1996, for a review). Barlow (2002) emphasizes that it is the cognitive distractions frequently associated with anxiety in dysfunctional people that seem to interfere with their sexual

arousal. For example, one study found that nondysfunctional men who were distracted by material they were listening to on earphones while watching an erotic film showed less sexual arousal than men who were not distracted (Abrahamson et al., 1985). Barlow and colleagues hypothesize that sexually dysfunctional men and women get distracted by negative thoughts about their performance during a sexual encounter ("I'll never get aroused" or "She'll think I'm inadequate"). Their research suggests that this preoccupation with negative thoughts, rather than anxiety per se, is responsible for inhibiting sexual arousal (see also Weiner & Rosen, 1999; Wincze et al., 2008). Moreover, such self-defeating thoughts not only decrease pleasure but also can increase anxiety if the erection does not happen, and this in turn can fuel further negative, self-defeating thoughts (Sbrocco & Barlow, 1996). A related finding is that men with erectile dysfunction make more internal and stable causal attributions for hypothetical negative sexual events that do men without sexual dysfunction, much as depressed people do for more general hypothetical negative events (Nobre, 2010; Scepkowski et al., 2004). Combined with Bancroft and colleagues' (2005) findings that fear of performance failure is a strong predictor of erectile dysfunction in both gay and heterosexual men, one can see how a vicious cycle develops in which fears of failure are sometimes followed by erectile dysfunction, which is then attributed to internal and stable causes, thereby perpetuating the problem.

Erectile problems occur in as many as 90 percent of men on certain antidepressant medications (especially the SSRIs) and are one of the primary reasons men cite for discontinuing these medications (Rosen & Marin, 2003). These problems are also a common consequence of aging. One large study of over 1,400 men found that 37 percent between ages 57 and 85 reported significant erectile difficulties, with the problems gradually increasing with age (Lindau et al., 2007). However, complete and permanent erectile disorder before the age of 60 is relatively rare. Moreover, studies have indicated that men and women in their 80s and 90s are often quite capable of enjoying intercourse (Masters et al., 1992; Meston & Rellini, 2008). For example, in one study of 202 healthy men and women between the ages of 80 and 102, it was found that nearly two-thirds of the men and one-third of the women were still having sexual intercourse, although this was generally not their most common form of sexual activity (Bretschneider & McCoy, 1988).

The most frequent cause of erectile disorder in older men is vascular disease, which results in decreased blood flow to the penis or in diminished ability of the penis to hold blood to maintain an erection. Thus hardening of the arteries, high blood pressure, and other diseases such as diabetes that cause vascular problems often account for erectile disorder. Smoking, obesity, and alcohol abuse are associated lifestyle factors, and lifestyle changes can improve erectile function (Gupta et al., 2011). Diseases that affect the nervous system, such as multiple sclerosis, can also cause erectile problems. For young men, one cause of erectile problems is having had priapism—that is, an erection that will not diminish even after a couple of hours, typically unaccompanied by sexual excitement. Priapism can occur as a result of prolonged

The once taboo topic of erectile dysfunction now gets plenty of attention through the popularity of the drug Viagra, the most popular treatment for the disorder.

sexual activity, as a consequence of disease, or as a side effect of certain medications. Untreated cases of priapism are likely to result in erectile dysfunction and thus should be regarded as a medical emergency (Morrison & Burnett, 2011).

Treatment A variety of treatments—primarily medical—have been employed in recent years, often when cognitive-behavioral treatments have failed. These include: (1) medications that promote erections like Viagra, Levitra, and Cialis; (2) injections of smooth-muscle-relaxing drugs into the penile erection chambers (corpora cavernosa); and (3) even a vacuum pump (Duterte et al., 2007; Rosen, 1996). In extreme cases, for example when erections are impossible due to nerve damage that can be a consequence of surgery for prostate cancer, penile implants may still be used. These devices can be inflated to provide erection on demand. They are made of silicone rubber or polyurethane rubber. Such treatments have generally shown success in clinical trials, although they are rather extreme interventions that often evoke bothersome side effects such as decreased penis size (Duterte et al., 2007; Bettochi et al., 2010). They were used in thousands of cases in the 1960s and 1970s before current medications were available.

In 1998 the revolutionary drug Viagra (sildenalfil) was introduced on the U.S. market and was received with a great deal of attention. Viagra works by making nitric oxide, the primary neurotransmitter involved in penile erection, more available. Viagra is taken orally at least 30 to 60 minutes before sexual activity. Unlike some other biological treatments for erectile dysfunction, Viagra promotes erection only if some sexual excitation is present. Thus, contrary to some myths, Viagra does not improve libido or promote spontaneous erections (Duterte et al., 2007; Segraves & Althof, 2002). Two other related medications introduced in 2003 to treat erectile dysfunction are Levitra (vardenafil; Stark et al., 2001) and Cialis (tadalafil; Padma-Nathan et al., 2001), with the effects of Cialis being longer lasting (up to 36 hours). Clinical trials of these medications have been impressive. In one early double-blind study, over 70 percent of men receiving at least 50 mg of Viagra reported that their erections had improved, compared with fewer than 30 percent of men receiving a placebo (Carlson, 1997; see also Goldstein et al., 1998).

Results with Cialis and Levitra are similar. Overall efficacy rates in terms of ability to obtain an erection are 40 to 80 percent, but levels of satisfaction are often much lower, perhaps because these medications do not increase sexual desire or satisfaction and perhaps because sexual desire and satisfaction are more closely intertwined with psychological and relationship factors. Side effects are relatively uncommon and not serious (e.g., the most common side effects are headache and facial flushing, seen in 10 to 20 percent of men), provided that the person had no serious preexisting heart problems (Duterte et al., 2007). When heart problems do exist, these medications should be prescribed with caution because they can interact in dangerous ways with heart medications. These medications have been highly successful commercially—for example, in 2008 almost $2 billion worth of Viagra was sold. Interestingly, however, many men who fill one prescription never refill it, according to the drug companies' own statistics. The commercial success of drugs like Viagra and Cialis is an indication of both the high prevalence of sexual dysfunction in men and the importance that people attach to sexual performance. There are also a few studies showing that the usefulness of these medications may be further enhanced when used in conjunction with cognitive-behavioral treatment (e.g., Bach et al., 2004; Meston & Rellini, 2008).

FEMALE SEXUAL AROUSAL DISORDER Formerly and somewhat pejoratively known as *frigidity*, female sexual arousal disorder—the absence of feelings of sexual arousal and an unresponsiveness to most or all forms of erotic stimulation—is in many ways the female counterpart of erectile disorder (see *DSM-IV-TR* Criteria on p. 443). Its chief physical manifestation is a failure to produce the characteristic swelling and lubrication of the vulva and vaginal tissues during sexual stimulation—a condition that may make intercourse quite uncomfortable and orgasm impossible.

One reason why progress toward understanding this disorder is slow is that the correlation between subjective sexual arousal and physiological sexual arousal (genital response) is lower for women than for men (Heiman, 1980; Laan & Everaerd, 1995). That is, it is not uncommon for women to feel unaroused sexually at a subjective level (sexual excitement and pleasure) but to have some genital response; the reverse can also occur, although less frequently. This has led to a suggestion that female sexual arousal disorder be separated into two subtypes: genital and subjective (Basson et al., 2003), with many women having a combination subtype (Meston & Bradford, 2007; Meston & Rellini, 2008).

Although the causes of this disorder are not well understood, possible reasons for this inhibition of sexual feelings range from early sexual traumatization; to excessive and distorted socialization about the "evils" of sex; to dislike of, or disgust with, a current partner's sexuality; to her partner's restricted repertoire of sexual activity. One interesting study also found that women with sexual arousal disorder show lower tactile sensitivity than is seen in other women, and the lower the level of tactile sensitivity, the more severe the arousal dysfunction (Frolich & Meston, 2005). Biological causal factors include the use of SSRIs for anxiety and depression, the occurrence of certain medical illnesses (e.g., spinal cord injury, cancer treatment, diabetes, etc.), and the decreases in estrogen levels that occur during and following menopause. Some difficulties with physiological arousal and lubrication have been noted in 20 to 30 percent of sexually active women and in as many as 44 percent of postmenopausal women. Moreover, arousal disorder in women very frequently co-occurs with hypoactive sexual desire disorder. Indeed, having problems with sexual arousal may often lead to lack of desire (Meston & Bradford, 2007).

Treatment Few controlled treatment studies of female arousal disorder have been conducted (Meston & Bradford, 2007), although clinical experience suggests that psychotherapy and sex therapy may play important roles in helping women with this disorder. Typically the techniques that are used are similar to those used in hypoactive sexual desire disorder. The widespread use of vaginal lubricants may effectively mask and treat the symptoms of this disorder in many women, but lubricants do not enhance genital blood flow or genital sensations, which are often reduced with this disorder.

In addition, because female genital response depends in part on the same neurotransmitter systems as male genital response, there has been great interest in the possibility that Viagra, Levitra, or Cialis would have positive effects for women analogous to their positive effects for men (Meston & Rellini, 2008). Unfortunately, enough research has now been performed to make it clear that such drugs are not as useful for women as they are for men (Basson et al., 2002; Meston & Rellini, 2008). Although these medications may enhance genital arousal and perceptions of physical sensations in women, they do not impact women's psychological experiences of arousal, probably because these are more related to relationship satisfaction and mood in women than they are in men. One promising drug, bremelanotide, has had some success in treating female sexual arousal disorder (Jordan et al., 2011), but it has not yet been approved by the FDA.

Orgasmic Disorders

Orgasmic disorder refers to the inability for an individual to reach orgasm during sexual stimulation. In the following section, we'll discuss premature ejaculation, male orgasmic disorder, and female orgasmic disorder and their respective treatments.

PREMATURE EJACULATION Premature ejaculation is the persistent and recurrent onset of orgasm and ejaculation with minimal sexual stimulation. It may occur before, on, or shortly after penetration and before the man wants it to (see *DSM-IV-TR* Criteria on p. 442). The average duration of time to ejaculate in men with this problem is 15 seconds or 15 thrusts of intercourse. The consequences often include failure of the partner to achieve satisfaction and, often, acute embarrassment for the prematurely ejaculating man, with disruptive anxiety about recurrence on future occasions. Men who have had this problem from their first sexual encounter often try to diminish sexual excitement by avoiding stimulation, by self-distracting, and by "spectatoring," or psychologically taking the role of an observer

rather than a participant (Metz et al., 1997). Premature ejaculation decreases sexual and relationship satisfaction both in men who have it and their partners (Graziottin & Althof, 2011).

An exact definition of prematurity is necessarily somewhat arbitrary. For example, the age of a client must be considered—the alleged "quick trigger" of the younger man being more than a mere myth (McCarthy, 1989). Indeed, perhaps half of young men complain of early ejaculation. Not surprisingly, premature ejaculation is most likely after a lengthy abstinence. *DSM-IV-TR* acknowledges these many factors that may affect time to ejaculation by noting that the diagnosis is made only if ejaculation occurs before, on, or shortly after penetration and before the man wants it to. Premature ejaculation is the most common male sexual dysfunction at least up to age 59 (Meston & Rellini, 2008; Segraves & Althof, 2002).

In sexually normal men, the ejaculatory reflex is, to a considerable extent, under voluntary control. They monitor their sensations during sexual stimulation and are somehow able, perhaps by judicious use of distraction, to forestall the point of ejaculatory inevitability until they decide to "let go," with the average latency to ejaculation from penetration being 10 minutes for men with no sexual problems. Men with premature ejaculation are for some reason unable to use this technique effectively. Explanations have ranged from psychological factors such as increased anxiety, to physiological factors such as increased penile sensitivity and higher levels of arousal to sexual stimuli. Presently, however, no explanation has received much empirical support, and it is clear that none of these possible explanations alone can account for all men with the problem (Meston & Rellini, 2008).

Treatment For many years, most sex therapists considered premature ejaculation to be psychogenically caused and highly treatable via behavioral therapy such as the pause-and-squeeze technique developed by Masters and Johnson (1970). This technique requires the man to monitor his sexual arousal during sexual activity. When arousal is intense enough that the man feels that ejaculation might occur soon, he pauses, and he or his partner squeezes the head of the penis for a few moments until the feeling of pending ejaculation passes, repeating the stopping of intercourse as many times as needed to delay ejaculation. Initial reports suggested that this technique was approximately 60 to 90 percent effective; however, more recent studies have reported a much lower overall success rate (Duterte et al., 2007; Segraves & Althof, 2002). In recent years, for men for whom behavioral treatments have not worked, there has been increasing interest in the possible use of pharmacological interventions. Antidepressants such as paroxetine (Paxil), sertraline (Zoloft), fluoxetine (Prozac), and dapoxetine (Priligy), which block serotonin reuptake, have been found to significantly prolong ejaculatory latency in men with premature ejaculation (Porst, 2011). Evidence suggests, however, that the medications work only as long as they are being taken.

MALE ORGASMIC DISORDER Sometimes called *retarded ejaculation*, **male orgasmic disorder** refers to the persistent inability to ejaculate during intercourse (see *DSM-IV-TR*

Criteria on p. 443). It occurs in only about 3 to 10 percent of men. Men who are completely unable to ejaculate are rare. About 85 percent of men who have difficulty ejaculating during intercourse can nevertheless achieve orgasm by other means of stimulation, notably through solitary masturbation (Wincze et al., 2008). In milder cases a man can ejaculate in the presence of a partner but only by means of manual or oral stimulation.

In other cases, retarded ejaculation can be related to specific physical problems such as multiple sclerosis or to the use of certain medications. For example, we noted that antidepressants that block serotonin reuptake appear to be an effective treatment for premature ejaculation. However, in other men, these same medications—especially the SSRIs—sometimes delay or prevent orgasm to an unpleasant extent (Ashton et al., 1997; Meston & Rellini, 2008). These side effects are common but can sometimes be treated pharmacologically with medications like Viagra (Ashton et al., 1997).

Treatment Psychological treatments include couples therapy in which a man tries to get used to having orgasms through intercourse with a partner rather than via masturbation. Treatment may also emphasize the reduction of performance anxiety about the importance of having an orgasm versus sexual pleasure and intimacy in addition to increasing genital stimulation (Meston & Rellini, 2008; Segraves & Althof, 2002).

FEMALE ORGASMIC DISORDER The diagnosis of orgasmic dysfunction in women is complicated by the fact that the subjective quality of orgasm varies widely among women, within the same woman from time to time, and in regard to mode of stimulation (Graham, 2010). Nevertheless, according to *DSM-IV-TR*, **female orgasmic disorder** can be diagnosed in women who are readily sexually excitable and who otherwise enjoy sexual activity but who show persistent or recurrent delay in or absence of orgasm following a normal sexual excitement phase and who are distressed by this (see *DSM-IV-TR* Criteria on p. 443). Of these women, many do not routinely experience orgasm during sexual intercourse without direct supplemental stimulation of the clitoris; indeed, this pattern is so common that it is generally not considered dysfunctional (Meston & Bradford, 2007). A small percentage of women are able to achieve orgasm only through direct mechanical stimulation of the clitoris, as in vigorous digital manipulation, oral stimulation, or the use of an electric vibrator. Even fewer are unable to have the experience under any known conditions of stimulation; this condition, which is called lifelong orgasmic dysfunction, is analogous to lifelong erectile disorder in males. More commonly, women experience difficulty having an orgasm only in certain situations or were able to achieve orgasm in the past but currently can rarely do so (Meston & Bradford, 2007). Laumann and colleagues (1999) found that rates of this disorder are highest in the 21- to 24-year-old age category and decline thereafter, and other studies have estimated that about one in three or four women report having had significant orgasmic difficulties in the past year (Meston & Bradford, 2007).

What causes female orgasmic disorder is not well understood, but a multitude of contributory factors have been hypothesized. For example, some women feel fearful and inadequate in sexual relations. A woman may be uncertain whether her partner finds her sexually attractive, and this may lead to anxiety and tension, which then interfere with her sexual enjoyment. Or she may feel inadequate or experience sexual guilt (especially common in religious women) because she is unable to have an orgasm or does so infrequently. Sometimes a nonorgasmic woman will pretend to have orgasms to make her sexual partner feel fully adequate. The longer a woman maintains such a pretense, however, the more likely she is to become confused and frustrated; in addition, she is likely to resent her partner for being insensitive to her real feelings and needs. This in turn only adds to her sexual difficulties.

Possible biological causal factors sometimes contributing to orgasmic difficulties in women (as they do in men) include intake of the SSRIs as antidepressant medications. Many medical conditions already mentioned with other sexual disorders are also sometimes associated with orgasmic difficulties (Meston & Rellini, 2008). Recent evidence suggests that differences between women in their genital anatomy may allow some women to have orgasms during intercourse more easily than other women can (Wallen & Lloyd, 2011).

Treatment One important issue regarding treatment is whether women should seek it or not. Most clinicians agree that a woman with lifelong orgasmic disorder needs treatment if she is to become orgasmic. However, in the middle range of orgasmic responsiveness, our own view is that this question is best left to a woman herself to answer. If she is dissatisfied about her responsiveness, then she should seek treatment.

For those who do seek treatment, it is important to distinguish between lifelong and situational female orgasmic dysfunction. Cognitive-behavioral treatment of orgasmic dysfunction usually involves education about female sexuality and female sexual anatomy, as well as directed masturbation exercises. Later the partner may be included to explore these activities with the client. For those with lifelong orgasmic dysfunction, such programs can have nearly a 100 percent success rate in terms of the woman's ability to have an orgasm at least through masturbation, but transition to having an orgasm with a partner can be slow and difficult in some cases (Meston & Rellini, 2008). "Situational" anorgasmia (where a woman may experience orgasm in some situations, with certain kinds of stimulation, or with certain partners, but not under the precise conditions she desires) often proves more difficult to treat, perhaps in part because it is often associated with relationship problems that may also be hard to treat (Althof & Schreiner-Engel, 2000).

Sexual Pain Disorders

Sexual pain disorders are marked by pain experienced in the pelvic area during or after intercourse. This can occur in both men and women. Two such disorders, vaginismus and dyspareunia, are distinguished in *DSM-IV-TR*. The *DSM-5* work group on sexual dysfunctions has proposed that these disorders should be combined into one: genito-pelvic pain/penetration disorder (Binik, 2010a, 2010b). Vaginismus and dyspareunia and their treatments are covered in the following sections.

VAGINISMUS According to *DSM-IV-TR*, **vaginismus** involves an involuntary spasm of the muscles at the entrance to, and outer third of, the vagina (not due to a physical disorder) that prevents penetration and sexual intercourse (see *DSM-IV-TR* Criteria on p. 443). However, researchers have recently raised important questions about this diagnostic criterion, noting that most diagnosticians do not require a physical exam in order to confirm the presence of involuntary muscle spasm. Moreover, there are serious doubts about the reliability of involuntary spasm as the primary diagnostic criterion for vaginismus. For example, Reissing and colleagues (2004) found that only about a quarter of women with diagnosed vaginismus reported experiencing spasm with attempted intercourse, and less than a third experienced spasm during a gynecological exam. However, muscle *tension* (not spasm) in the vaginal and pelvic muscles was common. Moreover, they did find that women diagnosed with vaginismus frequently experienced pain upon examination, and the researchers suggest that pain upon penetration (as well as fear and avoidance of penetration) is perhaps a more reliable diagnostic criterion than involuntary spasm. Leading researchers in the field have therefore recommended that the definition be changed such that involuntary muscle spasms are not a requirement for the diagnosis but rather that the emphasis be on persistent difficulties in allowing a penis, finger, or any other object to enter the vagina in spite of the woman's expressed wish to do so (Basson et al., 2003; Meston & Bradford, 2007).

In some cases, women who suffer from vaginismus also have sexual arousal disorder, possibly as a result of conditioned fears associated with earlier traumatic sexual experiences (e.g., Reissing et al., 2003). In many cases, however, they show normal sexual arousal and can experience orgasm through clitoral stimulation but are still afflicted with vaginismus. This form of sexual dysfunction is relatively rare (estimates range from 1 to 6 percent), but when it occurs, it is likely to be extremely distressing for both an affected woman and her partner and may sometimes lead to erectile or ejaculatory dysfunction in the partner (Duterte et al., 2007).

Treatment Treatment of vaginismus typically involves a combination of banning intercourse, training of the vaginal muscles, and graduated self-insertion of vaginal dilators of increasing size, often while practicing relaxation exercises. The

little available empirical research suggests that vaginismus is not easy to treat successfully (Lahaie et al., 2010).

DYSPAREUNIA Painful coitus, or **dyspareunia**, involves persistent or recurrent genital pain associated with sexual intercourse that causes distress or interpersonal difficulty. It can occur in men but is far more common in women—especially young women (Meston & Bradford, 2007). This is the form of sexual dysfunction most likely to have an obvious physical basis. Some examples of physical causes include acute or chronic infections or inflammations of the vagina or internal reproductive organs, vaginal atrophy that occurs with aging, scars from vaginal tearing, or insufficiency of sexual arousal. Understandably, dyspareunia is often associated with vaginismus, and some have questioned whether they are indeed distinct disorders.

Recently, some prominent sex researchers have argued against classifying dyspareunia as a "sexual disorder" rather than as a "pain disorder" (e.g., Binik, 2005; Binik et al., 2007). For example, Binik and colleagues argue that the pain in "sexual pain disorders" is qualitatively similar to the pain in other, nonsexual areas of the body and that the causes of "sexual pain disorder" are more similar to the causes of other pain disorders (e.g., lower back pain) than to the causes of other sexual dysfunctions. They have thus recommended that dyspareunia be reclassified as a "pelvic pain disorder." It is also interesting to note in this regard that the pain of dyspareunia sometimes precedes any sexual experiences—for example, in some adolescent girls trying to use a tampon.

Treatment As with vaginismus, cognitive-behavioral interventions have been developed that can be effective in many cases. Treatment techniques tend to include education about sexuality, identifying and correcting maladaptive cognitions, graduated vaginal dilation exercises to facilitate vaginal penetration, and progressive muscle relaxation (e.g., Bergeron, Binik et al., 2001).

In Review

- Compare and contrast the symptoms of the dysfunctions of sexual desire, arousal, and orgasm in men and women.
- Why have common female sexual dysfunctions been studied less than male sexual dysfunctions?
- What are the most effective treatments for male erectile disorder and premature ejaculation and for female orgasmic disorder?

Unresolved Issues

▶ *How Harmful Is Childhood Sexual Abuse?*

Most contemporary Americans believe that childhood sexual abuse (CSA) is very harmful. This is reflected both in their concern for the victims of CSA and in their outrage at its perpetrators. The assumption of harmfulness is so deeply ingrained that many people find it shocking even to consider the alternative possibility that, at least sometimes, CSA is not very harmful. Surely, though, the issue of harm is answerable by empirical means. What do the results show?

In 1998 psychologist Bruce Rind of Temple University and two colleagues published, in the prestigious journal *Psychological Bulletin,* an article reviewing 49 previous studies that had asked college students about their sexual experiences during childhood (Rind et al., 1998). Furthermore, the studies assessed the students' current adjustment, enabling Rind and colleagues to examine the association between early sexual experiences and mental health in young adulthood. Here are some conclusions of this study:

- Correlations between childhood sexual abuse and later problems were of surprisingly small magnitude, suggesting that such experiences are not typically very harmful.
- After general family problems had been statistically controlled for, the small association between CSA and adult problems was reduced to essentially zero, suggesting that the negative family environment in which child sexual abuse often occurs, rather than the sexual abuse per se, might explain much of the link between CSA and later problems. Indeed, poor family environment predicted adjustment problems an average of nine times more strongly than CSA did (Rind & Tromovitch, 2007).
- Incest (sex with relatives) and forced sex were both associated with more problems than sex between nominally consenting, nonrelated individuals.
- Age at which CSA was experienced was unrelated to adult outcome.

At first, the study's provocative conclusions attracted little attention. However, after the conservative radio personality Dr. Laura Schlessinger learned of the study, she incited a firestorm of controversy. Both Dr. Laura and other critics accused Rind and his coauthors of giving comfort to child molesters and being insensitive to victims of CSA. The controversy culminated in 1999 with a resolution by the U.S. House of Representatives that condemned the study (Lilienfeld, 2002; Rind et al., 2000).

Rind's study was attacked on two general grounds: First, some argued that it is socially dangerous to make the kinds of claims that the authors make in their article (Ondersma et al., 2001). Second, some argued that the study was not strong enough, scientifically, to justify such risky conclusions. Let us examine both criticisms.

Clearly, it would be wrong to understate the harm of CSA. Victims of CSA would suffer from having their pain unappreciated, and we may well invest too little in solving problems related to CSA. But overstating the harm of CSA may also entail significant costs. For example, people who are led to believe that they have been gravely and permanently harmed by CSA may suffer unnecessarily if CSA actually does not invariably have grave and permanent consequences. If CSA is often not very harmful, we need to know that.

Assessing the validity of Rind's study is a scientific matter. *Psychological Bulletin* published a lengthy scientific critique of Rind's study (Dallam et al., 2001) along with a reply by Rind and his coauthors (2001). One criticism of the original study was that it relied on college students, who may be unrepresentative. Perhaps they were able to attend college despite CSA because they were especially resilient. However, in another study, Rind analyzed data from community samples (samples not selected on the basis of educational attainment) and got virtually identical results (Rind & Tromovitch, 1997). Some of Rind's statistical decisions and analyses have also been criticized, but he has shown that his results do not change much when he analyzes the data the way his critics would.

A later meta-analysis of a large representative group of nearly 1,800 adult Australians (ages 18 to 59) reported that CSA in women is associated with their having more symptoms of sexual dysfunction in adulthood (Najman et al., 2005). However, a later reanalysis of these data by Rind and Tromovitch (2007) showed that the magnitude of this relationship was quite small (similar to that in Rind et al.'s 1998 study). Moreover, Najman and colleagues did not statistically control for other important factors, such as poor family environment, that were shown to be even more important in the study by Rind et al.

Rind (2003, 2004) also extended his discussion to the issue of how harmful *adult–adolescent* sexual relationships are. The current American view, which has spread throughout the Western world, is that such relations are by definition also "childhood sexual abuse" even though marriages involving young teenagers were common in previous centuries. He reviewed evidence showing that current views on this topic are driven by ideology and moral panic rather than by any empirical research showing these experiences to be harmful—especially those between adolescent boys and adult females, where considerable evidence suggests that many teenage boys see perceived benefits from such relationships regarding their sexual confidence and self-acceptance. These are obviously controversial issues that deserve additional careful research in the future.

Clearly these studies do not yet definitively answer the question of "How harmful is CSA?" but future research must contend with their findings and pay close attention to the relative importance of other negative family factors that are usually highly correlated with CSA.

Summary

- Defining boundaries between normality and psychopathology in the area of variant sexuality is very difficult, in part because sociocultural influences on what have been viewed as normal or aberrant sexual practices abound.

- Degeneracy theory and abstinence theory were very influential for long periods of time in the United States and many other Western cultures and led to very conservative views on heterosexual sexuality.

- In contrast to Western cultures, in the Sambia tribe in Melanesia, homosexuality is practiced by all adolescent males in the context of male sexual initiation rites; these males transition to heterosexuality in young adulthood.

- Until rather recently in many Western cultures, homosexuality was viewed either as criminal behavior or as a form of mental illness. However, since 1974 homosexuality has been considered by mental health professionals to be a normal sexual variant.

- Sexual deviations in the form of paraphilias involve persistent and recurrent patterns of sexual behavior and arousal, lasting at least 6 months, in which unusual objects, rituals, or situations are required for full sexual satisfaction. They occur almost exclusively in males, who often have more than one of them. The paraphilias include fetishes, transvestic fetishism, voyeurism, exhibitionism, sadism, masochism, pedophilia, and frotteurism.

- Gender identity disorders occur in children and adults. Childhood gender identity disorder occurs in children who have cross-gender identification and gender dysphoria. Most boys who have this disorder grow up to have a homosexual orientation; a much smaller number become transsexuals. Prospective studies of girls who have this disorder have reported similar results.

- Transsexualism is a very rare disorder in which the person believes that he or she is trapped in the body of the wrong sex and goes through the elaborate steps necessary to change his or her sex. It is now recognized that there are two distinct types of male-to-female transsexuals: homosexual transsexuals and autogynephilic transsexuals, each with different characteristics and developmental antecedents.

- The only known effective treatment for transsexuals is a sex change operation. Although its use remains highly controversial, it does appear to have fairly high success rates when the people are carefully diagnosed before the surgery as being true transsexuals.

- There are three overlapping categories of sexual abuse: pedophilia, incest, and rape. All three kinds of abuse occur at alarming rates today.

- Active debate persists about several issues related to sexual abuse and identification of its perpetrators. These include controversies about the accuracy of children's testimony and the accuracy of recovered memories of sexual abuse that often occur in psychotherapy.

- All sexual abuse can sometimes have serious short-term and long-term consequences for its victims. What leads people to engage in sexual abuse is poorly understood at this time.

- Treatment of sex offenders has not as yet proved highly effective in most cases, although promising research in this area is being conducted.

- Sexual dysfunction involves impairment either in the desire for sexual gratification or in the ability to achieve it. Dysfunction can occur in the first three of the four phases of the human sexual response: the desire phase, the excitement phase, and orgasm.

- Both men and women can experience hypoactive sexual desire disorder, in which they have little or no interest in sex. In more extreme cases, they may develop sexual aversion disorder, which involves a strong disinclination to sexual activity.

- Dysfunctions of the arousal phase include male erectile disorder and female arousal disorder.

- Dysfunctions of orgasm for men include premature ejaculation and male orgasmic disorder (retarded ejaculation), and for women include female orgasmic disorder.

- There are also two sexual pain disorders: vaginismus, which occurs in women, and dyspareunia (painful coitus), which can occur in women and occasionally in men.

- In the past 35 years, remarkable progress has been made in the treatment of sexual dysfunctions.

Key Terms

autogynephilia
cross-gender identification
desire phase
dyspareunia
excitement (or arousal) phase
exhibitionism
female orgasmic disorder
female sexual arousal disorder
fetishism
frotteurism
gender dysphoria

gender identity disorder
hypoactive sexual desire disorder
incest
male erectile disorder
male orgasmic disorder
masochism
orgasm
paraphilias
pedophilia
premature ejaculation
rape

resolution
sadism
sexual abuse
sexual aversion disorder
sexual dysfunction
transsexualism
transvestic fetishism
vaginismus
voyeurism

Glossary

Many of the key terms listed in the glossary appear in boldface when first introduced in the text discussion. A number of other terms commonly encountered in this or other psychology texts are also included; you are encouraged to make use of this glossary both as a general reference tool and as a study aid for the course in abnormal psychology.

Autogynephilia. Paraphilia characterized by sexual arousal in men at the thought or fantasy of being a woman.

Cross-gender identification. The desire to be, or the insistence that one is, of the opposite sex.

Desire phase. First phase of the human sexual response, consisting of fantasies about sexual activity or a sense of desire to have sexual activity.

Dyspareunia. Painful coitus in a male or a female.

Excitement (arousal) phase. Second phase of the human sexual response, in which there is generally a subjective sense of sexual pleasure and physiological changes, including penile erection in the male and vaginal lubrication and enlargement in the female.

Exhibitionism. Intentional exposure of one's genitals to others under inappropriate circumstances and without their consent.

Female orgasmic disorder. Persistent or recurrent delay in, or absence of, orgasm after a normal sexual excitement phase.

Female sexual arousal disorder. Sexual dysfunction involving an absence of sexual arousal and unresponsiveness to most or all forms of erotic stimulation.

Fetishism. Sexual variant in which sexual interest centers on some inanimate object or nonsexual part of the body.

Frotteurism. A term that refers to interest in rubbing, usually one's pelvis or erect penis, against a non-consenting person for sexual gratification.

Gender dysphoria. Persistent discomfort about one's biological sex or the sense that the gender role of that sex is inappropriate.

Gender identity disorder. Identification with members of the opposite sex, persistent discomfort with one's biological sexual identity, and strong desire to change to the opposite sex.

Hypoactive sexual desire disorder. Sexual dysfunction in which either a man or a woman shows little or no sexual drive or interest.

Incest. Culturally prohibited sexual relations between family members, such as a brother and sister or a parent and child.

Male erectile disorder. Sexual dysfunction in which a male is unable to achieve or maintain an erection sufficient for successful sexual gratification; formerly known as impotence.

Male orgasmic disorder. Retarded ejaculation, or the inability to ejaculate following a normal sexual excitement phase.

Masochism. Sexual stimulation and gratification from experiencing pain or degradation in relating to a lover.

Orgasm. Third phase of the human sexual response, during which there is a release of sexual tension and a peaking of sexual pleasure.

Paraphilias. Persistent sexual behavior patterns in which unusual objects, rituals, or situations are required for full sexual satisfaction.

Pedophilia. Paraphilia in which an adult's preferred or exclusive sexual partner is a prepubertal child.

Premature ejaculation. Persistent and recurrent onset of orgasm and ejaculation with minimal sexual stimulation.

Rape. Sexual activity that occurs under actual or threatened forcible coercion of one person by another.

Resolution. Final phase of the human sexual response, during which a person has a sense of relaxation and well-being.

Sadism. Achievement of sexual gratification by inflicting physical or psychic pain or humiliation on a sexual partner.

Sexual abuse. Sexual contact that involves physical or psychological coercion or occurs when at least one individual cannot reasonably consent to the contact.

Sexual aversion disorder. Sexual dysfunction in which a person shows extreme aversion to, and avoidance of, all genital sexual contact with a partner.

Sexual dysfunction. Impairment either in the desire for sexual gratification or in the ability to achieve it.

Transsexualism. Individuals who identify with members of the opposite sex (as opposed to acceptance of their own biological sex) and who strongly desire to (and often do) change their sex. In most cases this is gender identity disorder in adults.

Transvestic fetishism. Achievement of sexual arousal and satisfaction by dressing as a member of the opposite sex.

Vaginismus. Involuntary spasm of the muscles at the entrance to the vagina that prevents penetration and sexual intercourse.

Voyeurism. Achievement of sexual pleasure through clandestine "peeping," usually watching other people disrobe and/or engage in sexual activities.

Photo Credits

Credits are listed in order of appearance.

Text Credits

Credits are listed in order of appearance.

Schizophrenia and Other Psychotic Disorders

From Chapter 13 of *Abnormal Psychology*, Fifteenth Edition. James N. Butcher, Susan Mineka, Jill M. Hooley. Copyright © 2013 by Pearson Education, Inc. All rights reserved.

Schizophrenia and Other Psychotic Disorders

case study | Emilio: "Eating Wires and Lighting Fires"

Emilio is a 40-year-old man who looks 10 years younger. He is brought to the hospital, his 12th hospitalization, by his mother because she is afraid of him. He is dressed in a ragged overcoat, bedroom slippers, and a baseball cap, and he wears several medals around his neck. His affect ranges from anger at his mother ("She feeds me shit . . . what comes out of other people's rectums") to a giggling, obsequious seductiveness toward the interviewer. His speech and manner have a childlike quality, and he walks with a mincing step and exaggerated hip movements. His mother reports that he stopped taking his medication about a month ago and has since begun to hear voices and to look and act more bizarrely. When asked what he has been doing, he says "eating wires and lighting fires." His spontaneous speech is often incoherent and marked by frequent rhyming and clang associations (where sounds, rather than meaningful relationships, govern word choice).

Emilio's first hospitalization occurred after he dropped out of school at age 16, and since that time he has never been able to attend school or hold a job. He has been treated with neuroleptics (medications used to treat schizophrenia) during his hospitalizations, but he doesn't continue to take his medications when he leaves, so he quickly becomes disorganized again. He lives with his elderly mother, but he sometimes disappears for several months at a time and is eventually picked up by the police as he wanders the streets. (Modified from Spitzer et al., 2002, pp. 189–90.)

The disorder that Emilio has is called schizophrenia. Schizophrenia is a severe disorder that is often associated with considerable impairments in functioning. This chapter describes the pieces of the schizophrenia puzzle as we currently know them. Keep in mind from the outset that not all of the pieces or their presumed interconnections have been found, so our puzzle is far from being solved. As you read through this chapter you will learn just how complex and challenging this disorder is—not only for patients who suffer from it and for their families who try to care for them, but also for the clinicians who attempt to treat it and the researchers who are determined to understand it.

Schizophrenia

Schizophrenia occurs in people from all cultures and from all walks of life. The disorder is characterized by an array of

The internal suffering of the person with schizophrenia is often readily apparent, as are bizarre behavior and unusual appearance.

diverse symptoms, including extreme oddities in perception, thinking, action, sense of self, and manner of relating to others. However, the hallmark of schizophrenia is a significant loss of contact with reality, referred to as **psychosis**. Although the clinical presentation of schizophrenia differs from one patient to another, the case of Emilio is quite typical.

Origins of the Schizophrenia Construct

The first detailed clinical description of what we now recognize to be schizophrenia was offered in 1810 by John Haslam, the apothecary at the Bethlem Hospital in London, England. Haslam described the case of a patient who appears to have suffered from a variety of symptoms—including delusions—that are typical of schizophrenia (see Carpenter, 1989). Fifty years later, the Belgian psychiatrist Benedict Morel described the case of a 13-year-old boy who had formerly been the most brilliant pupil in his school but who gradually lost interest in his studies; became increasingly withdrawn, lethargic, seclusive, and quiet; and appeared to have forgotten everything he had learned. Morel thought the boy's intellectual, moral, and physical functions had deteriorated as a result of brain degeneration of hereditary origin. He used the term term *démence précoce* (mental deterioration at an early age) to describe the condition and to distinguish it from the dementing disorders associated with old age.

It is the German psychiatrist Emil Kraepelin (1856–1926) who is best known for his careful description of what we now regard as schizophrenia. Kraepelin used the Latin version of Morel's term (*dementia praecox*) to refer to a group of conditions that all seemed to feature mental deterioration beginning early in life. Kraepelin, an astute observer of clinical phenomena, describes the patient with dementia praecox as someone who "becomes suspicious of those around him, sees poison in his food, is pursued by the police, feels his body is being influenced, or thinks that he is going to be shot or that the neighbours are jeering at him" (Kraepelin, 1896). Kraepelin also noted that the disorder was characterized by hallucinations, apathy and indifference, withdrawn behavior, and an incapacity for regular work.

It was a Swiss psychiatrist named Eugen Bleuler (1857–1939) who gave us the diagnostic term we still use today. In 1911, Bleuler used *schizophrenia* (from the Greek roots of *sxizo*, pronounced "schizo" and meaning "to split or crack," and *phren*, meaning "mind") because he believed the condition was characterized primarily by disorganization of thought processes, a lack of coherence between thought and emotion, and an inward orientation away (split off) from reality. Although the term is often thought to reflect a "Jekyll and Hyde" split personality, this is a major misconception. The splitting does not refer to multiple personalities (an entirely different form of disorder now called dissociative identity disorder). Instead, in schizophrenia there is a split within the intellect, between the intellect and emotion, and between the intellect and external reality. Interestingly, the subtitle of Bleuler's monograph (Bleuler, 1911/1950) was "The Group of Schizophrenias," indicating that he believed this disorder was not a single diagnostic entity.

Epidemiology

The risk of developing schizophrenia over the course of one's lifetime is a little under 1 percent—actually around 0.7 percent (Saha et al., 2005). What this means is that approximately 1 out of every 140 people alive today who survive until at least age 55 will develop the disorder. Of course, a statistic like this does not mean that everyone has exactly the same risk. This is an average lifetime risk estimate. As we shall see later, some people (e.g., those who have a parent with schizophrenia) have a statistically higher risk of developing the disorder than do others (e.g., people who come from families where there has never been a case of schizophrenia).

There are also other groups of people who seem to have an especially high risk of developing schizophrenia. For example, people whose fathers were older (aged 45–50 years or more) at the time of their birth have two to three times the normal risk of developing schizophrenia when they grow up (Byrne et al., 2003; Malaspina et al., 2001). Having a parent who works as a dry cleaner is also a risk factor (Perrin, Opler et al., 2007). Moreover, people of Afro-Caribbean origin living in the United Kingdom have higher-than-expected rates of schizophrenia (Harrison et al., 1997). Although the reasons for these differences are not well understood, they are of great interest to researchers.

The vast majority of cases of schizophrenia begin in late adolescence and early adulthood, with 18 to 30 years of age being the peak time for the onset of the illness (Tandon et al., 2009). Although schizophrenia is sometimes found in children, such cases are rare (Green et al., 1992; McKenna et al., 1994). Schizophrenia can also have its initial onset in middle age or later, but again, this is not typical. Interestingly,

Children whose fathers are older at the time of their birth have 2 to 3 times the normal risk of developing schizophrenia.

schizophrenia tends to begin earlier in men than in women. In men, there is a peak in new cases of schizophrenia between ages 20 and 24. The incidence of schizophrenia in women peaks during the same age period, but the peak is less marked than it is for men. After about age 35, the number of men developing schizophrenia falls markedly, whereas the number of women developing schizophrenia does not. Instead, there is a second rise in new cases that begins around age 40.

This figure is intentionally omitted from this text

In addition to having an earlier age of onset, males also tend to have a more severe form of schizophrenia (Leung & Chue, 2000). Brain-imaging studies show that schizophrenia-related anomalies of brain structure (discussed later) are more severe in male patients than they are in female patients (Nopoulos et al., 1997). Gender-related differences in illness severity may also explain why schizophrenia is more common in males than it is in females. The male-to-female sex ratio is 1.4:1. So for every three men who develop the disorder, only two women do so (Aleman et al., 2003; Kirkbridge et al., 2006). If women have a less severe form of schizophrenia, and if they also have more

In Review

- What did Kraepelin mean by the term *dementia praecox*? How accurate is this description?

- What was Bleuler's use of the term *schizophrenia* meant to convey?

- Is schizophrenia the same thing as split personality?

- What is the prevalence of schizophrenia? What groups of people show lower or higher rates of schizophrenia than expected?

- How does the age of onset and severity of schizophrenia vary by gender?

- How does gender influence the severity of schizophrenia? Why might this be?

symptoms of depression (see Leung & Chue, 2000), they may either not be diagnosed at all or else be diagnosed with other disorders, thus giving rise to the sex ratio imbalance.

What might explain the better clinical outcome of women with schizophrenia? One possibility is that female sex hormones play some protective role. When estrogen levels are low (as is true premenstrually) or are falling, psychotic symptoms in women with schizophrenia often get worse (Lindamer et al., 1997). The protective effect of estrogen may therefore help explain the delayed onset of schizophrenia in women. Declining levels of estrogen around menopause might also explain why late-onset schizophrenia is much more likely to strike women than men. And there is some evidence that this late-onset pattern in women is associated with a more severe clinical presentation (Haffner et al., 1998).

Clinical Picture

As we have mentioned earlier, the *DSM* is a work in progress. Diagnostic criteria are not fixed and immutable but instead change subtly over time as new research findings become available. We show the current *DSM-IV-TR* criteria for the diagnosis of schizophrenia in the *DSM-IV-TR* table. These are broadly similar to the diagnostic criteria in the ICD (WHO, 2003), which is the diagnostic system used in Europe and other parts of the world. One change that is expected in *DSM-5* is that the requirement (listed in parentheses in our table) that only one

DSM-IV-TR

Criteria for Schizophrenia

A. Characteristic symptoms: Two (or more) of the following, each present for a significant portion of time during a 1-month period (or less if successfully treated):
   1. delusions
   2. hallucinations
   3. disorganized speech (e.g., frequent derailment or incoherence)
   4. grossly disorganized or catatonic behavior
   5. negative symptoms, i.e., affective flattening, alogia, or avolition

   Note: Only one Criterion A symptom is required if delusions are bizarre or hallucinations consist of a voice keeping up a running commentary on the person's behavior or thoughts, or two or more voices conversing with each other.

B. Social/occupational dysfunction: For a significant portion of the time since the onset of the disturbance, one or more major areas of functioning such as work, interpersonal relations, or self-care are markedly below the level achieved prior to the onset (or when the onset is in childhood or adolescence, failure to achieve expected level of interpersonal, academic, or occupational achievement).

C. Duration: Continuous signs of the disturbance persist for at least 6 months. This 6-month period must include at least 1 month of symptoms (or less if successfully treated) that meet Criterion A (i.e., active-phase symptoms) and may include periods of prodromal or residual symptoms. During these prodromal or residual periods, the signs of the disturbance

may be manifested by only negative symptoms or two or more symptoms listed in Criterion A present in an attenuated form (e.g., odd beliefs, unusual perceptual experiences).

D. Schizoaffective and Mood Disorder exclusion: Schizoaffective Disorder and Mood Disorder With Psychotic Features have been ruled out because either (1) no Major Depressive, Manic, or Mixed Episodes have occurred concurrently with the active-phase symptoms; or (2) if mood episodes have occurred during active-phase symptoms, their total duration has been brief relative to the duration of the active and residual periods.

E. Substance/general medical condition exclusion: The disturbance is not due to the direct physiological effects of a substance (e.g., a drug of abuse, a medication) or a general medical condition.

F. Relationship to a Pervasive Developmental Disorder: If there is a history of Autistic Disorder or another Pervasive Developmental Disorder, the additional diagnosis of Schizophrenia is made only if prominent delusions or hallucinations are also present for at least a month (or less if successfully treated).

Source: Reprinted with permission from the American Psychiatric Association. *Diagnostic and Statistical Manual of Mental Disorders*, Fourth Edition, *Text Revision* (Copyright © 2000). American Psychiatric Association.

symptom needs to be present if delusions are bizarre or if the auditory hallucinations are of a certain type will be eliminated.

In isolation, however, lists of symptoms convey little about the clinical essence of schizophrenia. In the sections that follow, we elaborate on the hallmark symptoms of this major form of psychotic disorder.

Delusions

A **delusion** is essentially an erroneous belief that is fixed and firmly held despite clear contradictory evidence. The word *delusion* comes from the Latin verb *ludere*, which means "to play." In essence, tricks are played on the mind. People with delusions believe things that others who share their social, religious, and cultural backgrounds do not believe. A delusion therefore involves a disturbance in the *content* of thought. Not all people who have delusions suffer from schizophrenia. However, delusions are common in schizophrenia, occurring in more than 90 percent of patients at some time during their illness (Cutting, 1995). In schizophrenia, certain types of delusions or false beliefs are quite characteristic. Prominent among these are beliefs that one's thoughts, feelings, or actions are being controlled by external agents (made feelings or impulses), that one's private thoughts are being broadcast indiscriminately to others (thought broadcasting), that thoughts are being inserted into one's brain by some external agency (thought insertion), or that some external agency has robbed one of one's thoughts (thought withdrawal). Also common are delusions of reference, where some neutral environmental event (such as a television program or a song on the radio) is believed to have special and personal meaning intended only for the person. Other strange propositions, including delusions of bodily changes (e.g., bowels do not work) or removal of organs, are also not uncommon.

Sometimes delusions are not just isolated beliefs. Instead they become elaborated into a complex delusional system. The next case study provides an example of this. This material was printed on a flier and handed to one of the authors by a man who appeared to be in his 30s. Any errors of grammar are errors in the original flier.

case study
Are You Being Mind Controlled?

Are you being or were you mind controlled to do something very stupid? Twenty-five percent of our population have what is called electronic hearing. This twenty-five percent can hear a silent radio and do not hear it. You might be one. In hearing pitch the average person hears from zero to sixteen thousand cycles. Twenty-five percent can hear up to thirty thousand cycles. The silent radio can be heard by these high hearing frequency persons. The silent radio sounds the same as thoughts in their minds.

This silent radio tricks these persons into every crime imaginable. It tricks them into bad decisions, to quit jobs, to divorce, to run away, to be sheriff saled and any stupidity possible. The broadcasters over this silent radio are government, medical, psychiatrists, religious

and educational. This is an enormous budget used to destroy the innocent and helpless. The media is scared to cover this up.

This minority, which can be in any ethnic or race, has lost all rights under law because the Russians do it everywhere. It is shocking to discover very large corporations and all colleges have mind control departments. If you and your family constantly make bad decisions and have ruinous problems, you probably are mind controlled. Every year these mind controlled people are going down the economic ladder as they cannot be trusted. No company knows when one will be selected as a guinea pig. Who could risk a sizeable work force of persons with electronic hearing for your competitor could easily wipe you out?

Hallucinations

A **hallucination** is a sensory experience that seems real to the person having it, but occurs in the absence of any external perceptual stimulus. This is quite different from an illusion, which is a misperception of a stimulus that actually exists. The word comes from the Latin verb *hallucinere* or *allucinere*, meaning to "wander in mind" or "idle talk" (Aleman & Larøi, 2008). Hallucinations can occur in any sensory modality (auditory, visual, olfactory, tactile, or gustatory). However, auditory hallucinations (e.g., hearing voices) are by far the most common. In a sample recruited from 7 different countries, auditory hallucinations were found in 75 percent of patients with schizophrenia (Bauer et al., 2011). In contrast, visual hallucinations were reported less frequently (39 percent of patients), and olfactory, tactile, and gustatory hallucinations were even more rare (1–7 percent). Even deaf people who are diagnosed with schizophrenia sometimes report auditory hallucinations (Aleman & Larøi, 2008). As Box 1 illustrates, hallucinations can even be induced in healthy people if they are under a lot of stress and drink a lot of caffeine.

Hallucinations often have relevance for the patient at some affective, conceptual, or behavioral level. Patients can become

The inner world of people with schizophrenia is often confused, punctuated by alien voices, paranoia, and illogical thoughts.

THE WORLD AROUND US

1

Stress, Caffeine, and Hallucinations

Do you feel that you are under a lot of stress? Do you drink a lot of caffeinated beverages each day? If so, you may be interested in the findings from a recent study that was conducted using healthy volunteers who had no history of psychiatric disorders (Crowe et al., 2011). 92 participants were recruited into what they believed was a study of auditory perception. As participants entered the testing room to begin the experiment, the song "White Christmas" by Bing Crosby was playing. After the song ended, participants were given headphones and asked to listen to white noise. They were told that the White Christmas song they had just heard might be embedded in the white noise at a subthreshold level. Every time they thought they heard a fragment of the song during the 3 minutes of white noise, participants were told to note this using a hand counter.

In reality, no sound fragments of White Christmas were embedded in the sound at all. Participants only heard white noise. However, those participants who reported that they had been under a high level of stress in the past year *and* who were high caffeine users (5 or more drinks per day) reported hearing significantly more embedded song fragments than participants in the low-stress and low-caffeine group did. Moreover, it was the combination of high stress and high caffeine intake that was important. In participants who reported high stress but low caffeine intake or in participants who reported low stress but high caffeine intake, the number of false alarms or "hallucinations' (hearing a song fragment that was not there) was not elevated. The associations also remained when variables such as age, creativity, social desirability, mental imagery ability, and hallucination-proneness were taken into account.

Overall the results of this study demonstrate that, under certain conditions, the combination of high caffeine consumption

The combination of high stress levels and high caffeine intake is associated with hallucinations in psychiatrically healthy people.

and high stress can render normal people vulnerable to auditory hallucinations. Caffeine is known to increase how much cortisol is produced in response to a stressor. Caffeine consumption has also been found to correlate with hallucination proneness in other studies of healthy people (Jones & Fernyhough, 2009). It is also important to note that patients with schizophrenia typically drink a great deal of coffee. During times of high stress, this might perhaps increase their risk of having an exacerbation in hallucinatory symptoms.

emotionally involved in their hallucinations, often incorporating them into their delusions. In some cases, patients may even act on their hallucinations and do what the voices tell them to do. People who consider themselves to be socially inferior tend to perceive the voices they hear as being more powerful than they are and to behave accordingly (Paulik, 2011).

In an interesting study of the phenomenology of auditory hallucinations, Nayani and David (1996) interviewed 100 hallucinating patients and asked them a series of questions about their hallucinatory voices. The majority of patients (73 percent) reported that their voices usually spoke at a normal conversational volume. Hallucinated voices were often those of people known to the patient in real life, although sometimes unfamiliar voices or the voices of God or the Devil were heard. Most patients reported that they heard more than one voice and that their hallucinations were worse when they were alone. Most commonly, the hallucinated voices uttered rude and vulgar expletives or else were critical ("You are stupid"), bossy ("Get the

milk"), or abusive ("Ugly bitch"), although some voices were pleasant and supportive ("My darling").

Are patients who are hallucinating really hearing voices? Neuroimaging studies of hallucinating patients are providing answers to this interesting question. Several research groups have used PET and fMRI to look at activity in the brains of patients when they are actually experiencing auditory hallucinations (Cleghorn et al., 1992; McGuire et al., 1996). Although it might be expected that patients hearing voices would show an increase of activity in areas of the brain involved in speech comprehension (e.g., Wernicke's area in the temporal lobe), imaging studies reveal that hallucinating patients show increased activity in Broca's area—an area of the temporal lobe that is involved in speech production. In some cases, the pattern of brain activation that occurs when patients experience auditory hallucinations is very similar to that seen when healthy volunteers are asked to imagine that there is another person talking to them (Shergill et al., 2000). Overall, the research findings suggest that auditory hallucinations occur when patients misinterpret their own self-generated and verbally mediated thoughts (inner speech or self-talk) as coming from another source. Indeed, if transcranial magnetic stimulation (in which a magnetic field passing through the skull temporarily disrupts activity in underlying brain areas) is used to reduce activity in speech production areas, hallucinating patients actually show a reduction in their auditory hallucinations (Hoffman et al., 2005)! Modern research approaches are thus supporting a very old idea: Auditory hallucinations are really a form of misperceived subvocal speech (Gould, 1949).

Disorganized Speech and Behavior

Delusions reflect a disorder of thought *content*. Disorganized speech, on the other hand, is the external manifestation of a disorder in thought *form*. Basically, an affected person fails to make sense, despite seeming to conform to the semantic and syntactic rules governing verbal communication. The failure is not attributable to low intelligence, poor education, or cultural deprivation. Years ago, Meehl (1962) aptly referred to the process as one of "cognitive slippage"; others have referred to it as "derailment" or "loosening" of associations or, in its most extreme form, as "incoherence."

In disorganized speech, the words and word combinations sound communicative, but the listener is left with little or no understanding of the point the speaker is trying to make. In some cases, completely new, made-up words known as neologisms (literally, "new words") appear in the patient's speech. An example might be the word *detone*, which looks and sounds like a meaningful word but is a neologism. *Formal thought disorder* (a term clinicians use to refer to problems in the way that disorganized thought is expressed in disorganized speech) is well illustrated in the following example. It is taken from a letter written by a man with schizophrenia and addressed to Queen Beatrix of the Netherlands.

case study
Disorganized Speech: A Letter to Queen Beatrix

I have also "killed" my ex-wife, [name], in a 2.5 to 3.0 hours sex bout in Devon Pennsylvania in 1976, while two Pitcairns were residing in my next room closet, hearing the event. Enclosed, please find my urology report, indicating that my male genitals, specifically my penis, are within normal size and that I'm capable of normal intercourse with any woman, signed by Dr. [name], a urologist and surgeon who performed a circumcision on me in 1982. Conclusion: I cannot be a nincompoop in a physical sense (unless Society would feed me chemicals for my picture in the nincompoop book).

Disorganized behavior can show itself in a variety of ways. Goal-directed activity is almost universally disrupted in schizophrenia. The impairment occurs in areas of routine daily functioning, such as work, social relations, and self-care, to the extent that observers note that the person is not himself or herself anymore. For example, the person may no longer maintain minimal standards of personal hygiene or may exhibit a profound disregard of personal safety and health. In other cases, grossly disorganized behavior appears as silliness or unusual dress (e.g., wearing an overcoat, scarf, and gloves on a hot summer day). Many researchers attribute these disruptions of "executive" behavior to impairment in the functioning of the prefrontal region of the cerebral cortex (Lenzenweger & Dworkin, 1998).

Catatonia is an even more striking behavioral disturbance. The patient with catatonia may show a virtual absence of all movement and speech and be in what is called a *catatonic stupor*. At other times, the patient may hold an unusual posture for an extended period of time without any seeming discomfort. This was true for Anna, the patient described in the next case study.

case study
Anna, the Student with Catatonia

Anna is a 22-year-old, unmarried student of mathematics in Finland. She was brought to the psychiatric hospital by the police after she attacked a child. She had walked up to a 9-year-old girl at a bus stop and tried to strangle her. Some passersby fortunately intervened, restraining Anna, and called the police. At first she fought violently and tried to get at the child, but then suddenly she became motionless and rigid as a statue, with one arm stretched out toward the child and a wild stare on her face. When the police arrived, it was very difficult to get her into the car because she would not move and resisted attempts to move her.

At the police station she said nothing, kept standing in an awkward position, and stared straight ahead. A physician decided that immediate admission to the psychiatric hospital was appropriate. When she was brought to the ward, she remained standing just inside the entrance and resisted invitations to go further. She refused to have anything to eat and would not go into the examination room. She remained standing rigid, with her right arm stretched out in front of her, staring at her hand. She did not answer questions or respond in any way to the ward assistants. After several hours she finally had to be taken to her room and put in bed with the use of mild force. She lay in bed in the position where she had been placed, staring at the ceiling. She seemed tense, with an apprehensive and worried look on her face. She was given an injection of 10 mg of haloperidol and did not resist. Afterward she fell asleep.

During a clinical interview the next day, Anna appeared to be fully oriented. She knew she was in the hospital but would not or could not explain what had happened. At times she suddenly stiffened and stared for half a minute or so. At other times she just mechanically repeated the questions that were asked of her.

Anna's sister arrived. She said that the family had been concerned about Anna for some time. For the last 2 or 3 months she had seemed reclusive and odd, with recurrent episodes of muteness that lasted for several minutes. Several times she made peculiar statements such as, "Children are trying to destroy mathematics" and "Rational figures have a hard time." She stopped going to the university and stayed in her room, leaving it only for a walk in the evening. She seemed to be preoccupied with writing numbers on pieces of paper. (Adapted from Üstün et al., 1996.)

Positive and Negative Symptoms

Since the days of Bleuler, two general symptom patterns, or syndromes, of schizophrenia have been differentiated. These are referred to as positive- and negative-syndrome schizophrenia (e.g., Andreasen, 1985; Andreasen et al., 1995). Statistical procedures have further indicated that some symptoms like disordered speech and disorganized behavior that were previously thought to reflect positive symptoms might be better separated from "true" positive symptoms like hallucinations and delusions. A **disorganized symptom** pattern is now also recognized (Lenzenweger et al., 1991). These symptom types are illustrated in Table 1.

Positive symptoms are those that reflect an excess or distortion in a normal repertoire of behavior and experience, such as delusions and hallucinations. **Negative symptoms**, by contrast, reflect an absence or deficit of behaviors that are normally present. Important negative symptoms in schizophrenia include **flat affect**, or blunted emotional expressiveness, and **alogia**, which means very little speech. Another negative symptoms is **avolition**, or the inability to initiate or persist in goal-directed activities. For example, the patient may sit for long periods of time staring into space or watching TV with little interest in any outside work or social activities.

Although most patients exhibit both positive and negative symptoms during the course of their disorders (Breier et al.,

Positive, negative, and disorganized symptoms can co-occur in the same patient. This woman appears to exhibit marked social withdrawal (a negative symptom) in addition to showing bizarre behavior (a disorganized symptom).

1994; Guelfi et al., 1989), a preponderance of negative symptoms in the clinical picture is not a good sign for the patient's future outcome (e.g., Fenton & McGlashan, 1994; Milev et al., 2005).

Not all negative symptoms are exactly what they seem, however. Kring and Neale (1996) studied unmedicated male patients with schizophrenia while they were watching film clips. Three different types of film clips were used, the scenes in them being very positive, very negative, or neutral in terms of the emotions they were designed to elicit in the viewers. Videotapes of how the patients looked while they were watching the films were then coded by trained raters. As might be expected, the patients with schizophrenia showed less facial expressiveness than a group of healthy controls.

What *was* surprising was that when the patients were asked about their emotional experiences during the films, they reported as many emotional feelings as the controls—and sometimes slightly more. Measures of autonomic arousal also showed that when they were watching the films, the patients exhibited more physiological reactivity than the controls did. What these findings suggest, therefore, is that even though patients with schizophrenia may sometimes not look very emotionally expressive, they are nonetheless experiencing plenty of emotion.

Subtypes of Schizophrenia

What we call schizophrenia probably encompasses a variety of disordered processes of varied etiology, developmental pattern, and outcome—perhaps more so than is the case for any other psychiatric diagnosis. Reflecting this, attempts have been made to identify meaningful subtypes of schizophrenia. However, as Box 2 describes, these efforts have not been especially successful. In the sections below we describe some other disorders in the "schizophrenia family" that are thought to be related to but somewhat less severe than schizophrenia itself.

Other Psychotic Disorders

SCHIZOAFFECTIVE DISORDER The *DSM-IV-TR* recognizes a diagnostic category called **schizoaffective disorder** (see the *DSM-IV-TR* table for diagnostic criteria). This diagnosis is conceptually something of a hybrid in that it is used to describe people who have features of schizophrenia and severe mood disorder. In other words, the person has psychotic symptoms that

table 1 Positive, Negative, and Disorganized Symptoms of Schizophrenia

Positive Symptoms	Negative Symptoms	Disorganized Symptoms
Hallucinations	Emotional flattening	Bizarre behavior
Delusions	Poverty of speech	Disorganized speech
	Asociality	
	Apathy	
	Anhedonia	

THE WORLD AROUND US

Anticipating *DSM*-5: Subtypes of Schizophrenia

There is a great deal of heterogeneity in the presentation of schizophrenia, and patients with this disorder often look quite different clinically. In consideration of this, the *DSM-IV-TR* recognizes several subtypes of schizophrenia. The most clinically meaningful of these are **paranoid schizophrenia** (where the clinical picture is dominated by absurd and illogical beliefs that are often highly elaborated and organized into a coherent, though delusional, framework), **disorganized schizophrenia** (which is characterized by disorganized speech, disorganized behavior, and flat or inappropriate affect) and **catatonic schizophrenia** (which involves pronounced motor signs that reflect great excitement or stupor).

However, questions have been raised about the overall usefulness of subtyping schizophrenia in this way. For example, there is no strong evidence that this information is helpful when it comes to planning treatment. Research using the subtyping approach has also not yielded major insights into the etiology of the disorder. Reflecting this, it has been proposed that subtypes of schizophrenia not be included in *DSM-5*.

A person with catatonia may maintain an odd position for minutes or even hours.

DSM-IV-TR

Criteria for Schizoaffective Disorder

A. An uninterrupted period of illness during which, at some time, there is either a Major Depressive Episode, a Manic Episode, or a Mixed Episode concurrent with symptoms that meet Criterion A for Schizophrenia.
   Note: The Major Depressive Episode must include Criterion

A. depressed mood.

B. During the same period of illness, there have been delusions or hallucinations for at least 2 weeks in the absence of prominent mood symptoms.

C. Symptoms that meet criteria for a mood episode are present for a substantial portion of the total duration of the active and residual periods of the illness.

D. The disturbance is not due to the direct physiological effects of a substance (e.g., a drug of abuse, a medication) or a general medical condition.

Source: Reprinted with permission from the American Psychiatric Association. *Diagnostic and Statistical Manual of Mental Disorders*, Fourth Edition, *Text Revision* (Copyright © 2000). American Psychiatric Association.

meet criteria for schizophrenia but also has marked changes in mood for a substantial amount of time. Because mood disorders can be unipolar or bipolar in type, there also are two subtypes of schizoaffective disorder (bipolar and unipolar subtype).

The reliability of schizoaffective disorder tends to be quite poor, and clinicians often do not agree about who meets the criteria for the diagnosis (Maj et al., 2000; Vollmer-Larsen et al., 2006). In an effort to improve this, in *DSM-5* it will be specified that major mood symptoms have to be present for at least 30 percent of the total illness time. Clarifying what is meant by "a substantial proportion" of time should help improve the reliability of this diagnosis and possibly also decrease the number of people who receive it.

In general, the prognosis for patients diagnosed with schizoaffective disorder is somewhere between that of patients with schizophrenia and that of patients with mood disorders (Walker et al., 2004). Research suggests that the long-term (10-year) outcome is much better for patients with schizoaffective disorder than it is for patients with schizophrenia (Harrow et al., 2000).

SCHIZOPHRENIFORM DISORDER Schizophreniform disorder is a category reserved for schizophrenia-like psychoses that last at least a month but do not last for 6 months and so do not warrant a diagnosis of schizophrenia (see the *DSM-IV-TR* table for diagnostic criteria). It

DSM-IV-TR

Criteria for Schizophreniform Disorder

A. Criteria A, D, and E of Schizophrenia are met.

B. An episode of the disorder (including prodromal, active, and residual phases) lasts at least 1 month but less than 6 months. (When the diagnosis must be made without waiting for recovery, it should be qualified as "Provisional.")

may include any of the symptoms described in the preceding sections. Because of the possibility of an early and lasting remission after a first psychotic breakdown, the prognosis for schizophreniform disorder is better than that for established forms of schizophrenia.

DELUSIONAL DISORDER Patients with **delusional disorder**, like many people with schizophrenia, hold beliefs that are considered false and absurd by those around them. Unlike individuals with schizophrenia, however, people given the diagnosis of delusional disorder may otherwise behave quite normally. Their behavior does not show the gross disorganization and performance deficiencies characteristic of schizophrenia, and general behavioral deterioration is rarely observed in this disorder, even when it proves chronic (see the *DSM-IV-TR* table for criteria for delusional disorder). One interesting subtype of delusional disorder is *erotomania*. Here, the theme of the delusion involves great love for a person, usually of higher status. One study suggests that a significant proportion of women who stalk are diagnosed with erotomania (Purcell et al., 2001).

BRIEF PSYCHOTIC DISORDER **Brief psychotic disorder** is exactly what its name suggests. It involves the sudden onset of psychotic symptoms or grossly disorganized or catatonic behavior. Even though there is often great emotional turmoil, the episode usually lasts only a matter of days (too short to warrant a diagnosis of schizophreniform disorder). After this, the person returns to his or her former level of functioning and may never have another episode again (see the *DSM-IV-TR* table for

DSM-IV-TR

Criteria for Brief Psychotic Disorder

A. Presence of one (or more) of the following symptoms:
   1. delusions
   2. hallucinations
   3. disorganized speech (e.g., frequent derailment or incoherence)
   (4) grossly disorganized or catatonic behavior

   Note: Do not include a symptom if it is a culturally sanctioned response pattern.

B. Duration of an episode of the disturbance is at least 1 day but less than 1 month, with eventual full return to premorbid level of functioning.

C. The disturbance is not better accounted for by a Mood Disorder With Psychotic Features, Schizoaffective Disorder, or Schizophrenia and is not due to the direct physiological effects of a substance (e.g., a drug of abuse, a medication) or a general medical condition.

DSM-IV-TR

Criteria for Delusional Disorder

A. Nonbizarre delusions (i.e., involving situations that occur in real life, such as being followed, poisoned, infected, loved at a distance, or deceived by spouse or lover, or having a disease) of at least 1 month's duration.

B. Criterion A for Schizophrenia has never been met.
   Note: Tactile and olfactory hallucinations may be present in Delusional Disorder if they are related to the delusional theme.

C. Apart from the impact of the delusion(s) or its ramifications, functioning is not markedly impaired and behavior is not obviously odd or bizarre.

D. If mood episodes have occurred concurrently with delusions, their total duration has been brief relative to the duration of the delusional periods.

E. The disturbance is not due to the direct physiological effects of a substance (e.g., a drug of abuse, a medication) or a general medical condition.

criteria for brief psychotic disorder). Cases of brief psychotic disorder are infrequently seen in clinical settings, perhaps because they remit so quickly.

This case study is intentionally omitted from this text.

SHARED PSYCHOTIC DISORDER Finally, **shared psychotic disorder** (also known by its French name, *folie à deux*) is a delusion that develops in someone who has a very close relationship with another person who is delusional (see the *DSM-IV-TR* table for criteria for shared psychotic disorder). Over time, this second individual comes to believe in the delusions of the other person. In some cases, the contagion of thought may spread even further, and whole families may adopt the same delusional beliefs. Although this is a separate diagnosis in *DSM-IV*, in *DSM-5* it will likely be considered to be a subtype of delusional disorder.

DSM-IV-TR

Criteria for Shared Psychotic Disorder

A. A delusion develops in an individual in the context of a close relationship with another person(s), who has an already-established delusion.

B. The delusion is similar in content to that of the person who already has the established delusion.

C. The disturbance is not better accounted for by another Psychotic Disorder (e.g., Schizophrenia) or a Mood Disorder With Psychotic Features and is not due to the direct physiological effects of a substance (e.g., a drug of abuse, a medication) or a general medical condition.

Source: Reprinted with permission from the American Psychiatric Association. *Diagnostic and Statistical Manual of Mental Disorders*, Fourth Edition, *Text Revision* (Copyright © 2000). American Psychiatric Association.

In Review

● What are the major symptoms of schizophrenia?

● How is a hallucination different from a delusion?

● Explain the differences among positive, negative, and disorganized symptoms.

● Why are subtypes of schizophrenia unlikely to be included in *DSM-5*?

● In what ways are schizophrenia and schizoaffective disorder different?

● How will the planned change to the criteria for schizoaffective disorder in *DSM-5* improve the reliability of this diagnosis?

● What are the major differences between schizophreniform disorder and brief psychotic disorder?

Risk and Causal Factors

What causes schizophrenia? Despite enormous efforts by researchers, this question still defies a simple answer. In the sections that follow, we discuss what is currently known about the etiology of schizophrenia. What is clear is that no one factor can fully explain why schizophrenia develops. The old dichotomy of nature versus nurture is as misleading as it is simplistic. Psychiatric disorders are not the result of a single genetic switch being flipped. Rather, a complex interplay between genetic and environmental factors is responsible.

Genetic Factors

It has long been known that disorders of the schizophrenic type are "familial" and tend to "run in families." There is overwhelming evidence for higher-than-expected rates of schizophrenia among biological relatives of *index* cases, that is, the diagnosed group of people who provide the starting point for inquiry (also called *probands*). Figure 1 shows the percentage risk of developing schizophrenia given a specific genetic relationship with someone who has the disorder. As you can see, there is a strong association between the closeness of the blood relationship (i.e., level of gene sharing or consanguinity) and the risk for developing the disorder. For example, the prevalence of schizophrenia in the first-degree relatives (parents, siblings, and offspring) of a proband with schizophrenia is about 10 percent. For second-degree relatives who share only 25 percent of their genes with the proband (e.g., half-siblings, aunts, uncles, nieces, nephews, and grandchildren), the lifetime prevalence of schizophrenia is closer to 3 percent.

Of course, just because something runs in families does not automatically implicate genetic factors. The terms *familial* and *genetic* are not synonymous, and a disorder can run in a family for nongenetic reasons (if I am obese and my dog is also obese, the reasons for this are clearly not genetic!). As we have repeatedly emphasized, the interpretation of familial concordance patterns is never completely straightforward, in part because of the

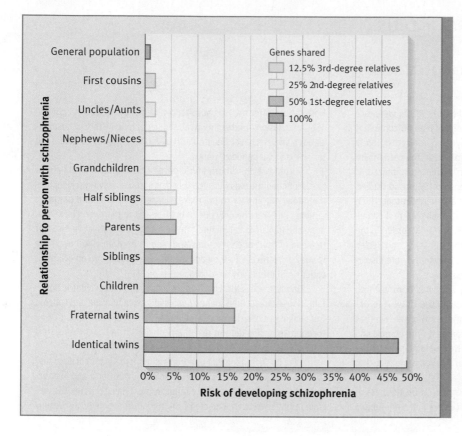

FIGURE 1

Risk of Developing Schizophrenia by Genetic Relationship

Lifetime age-adjusted, averaged risks for the development of schizophrenia-related psychoses in classes of relatives differing in their degree of genetic relatedness.

Source: Compiled from family and twin studies in European populations between 1920 and 1987. From I. I. Gottesman. (1991). *Schizophrenia Genesis: The Origins of Madness* (p. 96). Copyright © 1991 by Irving I. Gottesman. Used with permission of W.H. Freeman and Company/Worth Publishers.

strong relationship between the sharing of genes and the sharing of the environments in which those genes express themselves. Although they are indispensable in providing a starting point for researchers, family studies cannot, by themselves, tell us why a disorder runs in families. To disentangle the contributions of genes and environment, we need twin and adoption studies.

TWIN STUDIES As with the mood disorders, schizophrenia concordance rates for identical twins are routinely and consistently found to be significantly higher than those for fraternal twins or ordinary siblings. The most famous case of concordance for schizophrenia is summarized in Box 3, The Genain Quadruplets.

Although being a twin does not increase one's risk for developing schizophrenia (the incidence of schizophrenia among twins is no greater than it is for the general population), study after study has shown a higher concordance for schizophrenia among identical, or monozygotic (MZ), twins than among people related in any other way, including fraternal, or dizygotic (DZ), twins.

E. Fuller Torrey is a noted schizophrenia researcher who has a sister with the disorder. He and his colleagues (1994) have published a review of the major literature worldwide on twin studies of schizophrenia. The overall pairwise concordance rate is 28 percent in MZ twins and 6 percent in DZ twins. This suggests

that a reduction in shared genes from 100 percent to 50 percent reduces the risk of schizophrenia by nearly 80 percent. Also note that sharing 50 percent of one's genes with a co-twin with schizophrenia is associated with a lifetime risk for schizophrenia of 6 percent. Although this is low in absolute terms, it is markedly higher than the baseline risk of less than 1 percent found in the general population.

If schizophrenia were exclusively a genetic disorder, the concordance rate for identical twins would, of course, be 100 percent. Although MZ concordance rates vary from one twin study to another, and although some researchers report higher rates than the 28 percent reported by Torrey and colleagues (1994), they are never even close to 100 percent. Two conclusions can therefore be drawn: First, genes undoubtedly play a role in causing schizophrenia. Second, genes themselves are not the whole story. Twin studies provide some of the most solid evidence that the environment plays an important role in the development of schizophrenia. But why one MZ twin should develop schizophrenia when his or her co-twin does not is a fascinating question.

A great deal of research attention is now being directed at studying people with a known genetic liability for schizophrenia. Historically, the most important subjects to study in this regard have been MZ twins who are discordant for schizophrenia. This investigative strategy was pioneered by Fischer (1971, 1973) in an ingenious study. Fischer reasoned that genetic influences, if present, would be just as likely to

THE WORLD AROUND US

The Genain Quadruplets

The Genain quadruplets, born sometime in the early 1930s, were rare MZ quadruplets who each developed schizophrenia, an outcome that would be expected to occur by chance only once in approximately 1.5 billion births. The genetically identical girls, given the pseudonym *Genain* (from the Greek for "dreadful gene"), were hospitalized at the National Institute of Mental Health in the mid-1950s and studied intensively by lead researcher David Rosenthal (see Rosenthal, 1963; see also Mirsky & Quinn, 1988). Rosenthal also selected first names for the girls using the initials of the institution, NIMH. Accordingly, the women are known to us as Nora (the firstborn), Iris, Myra, and Hester. They are all concordant for schizophrenia. However, they are discordant with regard to the severity of their illnesses.

The most severely ill Genain is Hester, who was born last and had the lowest birth weight. Hester was always the slowest to develop, and she was removed from school after 11th grade. She has never held a job outside the home and has suffered from chronic and unremitting severe symptoms since age 18. Neurocognitive testing at NIMH revealed that, along with Nora, Hester showed a great deal of evidence of brain disturbance.

Nora was always considered by the family to be the best of the four girls. She had the highest IQ and was the first to get a job.

Nonetheless, after she was hospitalized at the age of 22 with hallucinations, delusions, and withdrawal, she had a long history of hospitalizations and has never been able to live independently or hold a job for an extended period of time.

In contrast, third-born Myra, despite having some problems in her 20s (when she was questionably diagnosed as having schizophrenia), does not appear to have experienced delusions and paranoia until her mid-40s. The only one of the Genains to marry and have children, she has a clinical picture that suggests schizoaffective disorder (a blend of psychotic symptoms and mood symptoms). Although she is not psychiatrically well by any means, she was able to go off medications and eventually went into remission.

Finally, there is Iris. Like Nora, Iris had her first psychiatric hospitalization at age 22. She spent 12 years in a state hospital and suffered from hallucinations, delusions, and motor abnormalities. Although neurocognitive testing did not reveal any obvious brain disturbance, it is clear that she has suffered from a severe form of schizophrenia.

Why do these identical quadruplets not have identical illnesses? We do not know. Did Nora and Hester, being born first and last, experience more traumatic birth complications? Has Iris done less well than might have been expected from her neurocognitive test results

---

show up in the offspring of the twins without schizophrenia in discordant pairs (see Figure 2) as they would be to show up in the offspring of the twins with schizophrenia (because they share all their genes in common). And, in a search of official records in Denmark, Fischer found exactly that. Subsequent to this, in a follow-up of Fischer's subjects, Gottesman and Bertelson (1989) report an **age-corrected incidence rate** for schizophrenia of 17.4 percent for the offspring of the MZ twins without schizophrenia (i.e., the well MZ twins). This rate, which far exceeds normal expectancy, was not significantly different from that for offspring of the twins with schizophrenia in discordant pairs or from that for offspring of DZ twins with schizophrenia. Assuming that exposure to an aunt or uncle with schizophrenia would have, at most, limited etiologic significance, these results lend impressive support to the genetic hypothesis. They also, as the authors note, indicate that a predisposition to schizophrenia may remain "unexpressed" (as in the twins without schizophrenia in discordant pairs) unless "released" by unknown environmental factors.

ADOPTION STUDIES One major assumption that twin studies make is that any differences found between MZ and DZ twins are attributable to genes. At the heart of this

RESEARCH CLOSE-UP

Age-Corrected Incidence Rate

Incidence is the number of new cases that develop. An age-corrected incidence rate takes into account predicted breakdowns for subjects who are not yet beyond the age of risk for succumbing to the disorder.

assumption is the idea that the environments of MZ twins are no more similar than the environments of DZ twins. But it is very reasonable to expect that, because MZ twins are identical (and always of the same gender), their environments will actually be more similar than the environments of DZ twins. To the extent that this is true, twin studies will overestimate the importance of genetic factors (because some similarities between MZ twins that actually occur for nongenetic reasons will be attributed to genetic factors). In some cases, of course, MZ twins go to a great deal of effort to try to be different from one another. The bottom line, however, is that the assumption that MZ and DZ twins have equally similar environments can create some problems when we try to interpret the findings of twin studies.

Several studies have attempted to overcome the shortcomings of the twin method in achieving a true separation of hereditary from environmental influences by using what is called the adoption strategy. Here, concordance rates for schizophrenia are compared for the biological and the adoptive relatives of persons who have been adopted out of their biological families at an early age (preferably at birth) and have subsequently developed schizophrenia. If concordance is greater among the patients' biological than adoptive relatives, a hereditary influence is strongly suggested; the reverse pattern would argue for environmental causation.

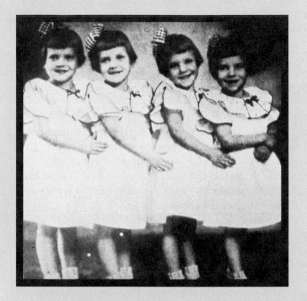

because her parents insisted on treating the quads as though they were two sets of twins—a superior and talented set consisting of Nora and Myra, and an inferior, problematic set consisting of Iris and Hester? Did being paired with Hester somehow compromise Iris's development? Has Myra done so well (relatively) because she was the most favored and because she did not sustain any brain damage?

And why did the quadruplets develop schizophrenia at all? In all probability, there was a family history of the disorder. Mr. Genain's mother (the girls' grandmother) had a nervous breakdown in her teens and appears to have had some symptoms of paranoid schizophrenia. It is also clear that the family environment was far from healthy and may have provided the stress that acted on the quadruplets' genetic predispositions to induce full-blown illness. Mr. Genain was very disturbed and spent most of his time drinking and expressing his various fears and obsessions to his family. He imposed extreme restrictions and surveillance on the girls until the time of their breakdowns. He was sexually promiscuous and was reported to have sexually molested at least two of his daughters. Mrs. Genain seems to have ignored the sexual exploitation occurring in the home. In short, nothing about the family environment can be considered to have been normal.

The first study of this kind was conducted by Heston in 1966. Heston followed up 47 children who had been born to mothers who were in a state mental hospital suffering from schizophrenia. The children had been placed with relatives or into foster homes within 72 hours of their birth. In his follow-up study, Heston found that 16.6 percent of these children were later diagnosed with schizophrenia. In contrast, none of the 50 control children (selected from among residents of the same foster homes whose biological mothers did not have schizophrenia) developed schizophrenia. In addition to the greater probability of being diagnosed with schizophrenia, the offspring whose mothers had schizophrenia were also more likely to be

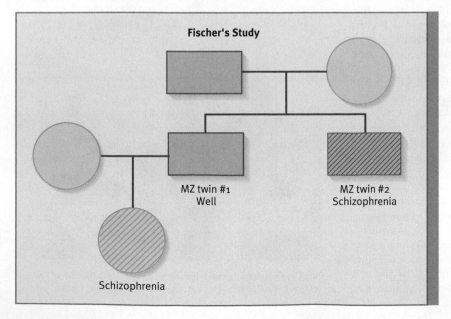

FIGURE 2

Fischer's Study

Because MZ twins have identical genes, the children of the well twin will have an elevated risk of schizophrenia even if their parent did not suffer from the disorder.

diagnosed as mentally retarded, neurotic, or psychopathic (that is, antisocial). They also had been involved more frequently in criminal activities and had spent more time in penal institutions. These findings are often taken to suggest that any genetic liability conveyed by the mothers is not specific to schizophrenia but also includes a liability for other forms of psychopathology, but we must be careful about drawing such a conclusion. Heston's study provided no information about psychopathology in the fathers of the children. We therefore cannot know to what extent some of the problems the children had were due to genetic liability conveyed by their fathers.

Heston's study began by identifying mothers with schizophrenia and then traced what had happened to their adopted-away offspring. An alternative approach involves locating adult patients with schizophrenia who were adopted early in life and then looking at rates of schizophrenia in their biological and adoptive relatives. A large-scale and multifaceted adoption study of this type was undertaken in Denmark, with Danish and American investigators working in collaboration (Kendler & Gruenberg, 1984; Kendler et al., 1994; Kety et al., 1978, 1994). As would be expected on the basis of a genetic model, the data showed a preponderance of schizophrenia and "schizophrenia-spectrum" problems (e.g., schizotypal and paranoid personality disorder) in the biological relatives of adoptees with schizophrenia. More specifically, 13.3 percent of the 105 biological relatives had schizophrenia or schizophrenia-spectrum disorders themselves. In contrast, only 1.3 percent of the 224 adoptive parents showed such problems.

THE QUALITY OF THE ADOPTIVE FAMILY The Danish adoption studies did not include independent assessments of the child-rearing adequacy of the adoptive families into which the index children (those who developed schizophrenia) and the control children (those who did not) had been placed. It remained for Tienari and colleagues (Tienari et al., 1987, 2000, 2004) to add this feature to their research design. The Finnish Adoptive Family Study of Schizophrenia, as it is known, followed up the adopted-away children of all women in Finland who were hospitalized for schizophrenia between 1960 and 1979. As they grew to adulthood, the functioning of these index children was compared with the functioning of a control sample of adoptees whose biological mothers were psychiatrically healthy. Over the course of a 21-year follow-up, the index adoptees developed more schizophrenia and schizophrenia-related disorders than did the controls (Tienari et al., 2000, 2003). What sets this study apart, however, is what it tells us about the interaction between genes and environment.

One measure of the family environment that the researchers looked at was communication deviance (Wahlberg et al., 1997). Communication deviance is a measure of how understandable and "easy to follow" the speech of a family member is. Vague, confusing, and unclear communication reflects high communication deviance. What Wahlberg and colleagues found was that it was the combination of genetic risk and high communication deviance in the adopted families that

was problematic. Children who were at genetic risk and who lived in families where there was high communication deviance showed high levels of thought disorder at the time of the follow-up. In contrast, the control adoptees who had no genetic risk for schizophrenia showed no thought disorder regardless of whether they were raised in a high- or a low-communication-deviance family. Perhaps what was most remarkable, though, was the outcome for the high-risk children who were raised by adopted families low in communication deviance. These children were healthier at follow-up than any of the other three groups! In other words, if they are raised in a benign environment, even children who are at genetic risk for schizophrenia appear to do very well.

Tienari and colleague have provided further evidence of a genotype–environment interaction in schizophrenia (Tienari et al., 2004). Using interviews, the researchers first looked at the quality of the family environment in which the adopted children were raised. They then looked at what happened to the children who were raised in healthy versus dysfunctional families. The degree of adversity in the family environment predicted later problems in the adopted children. However, only those children who were raised in dysfunctional families *and* had high genetic risk for schizophrenia went on to develop schizophrenia-related disorders themselves. Children at high genetic risk who were raised in healthy family environments did not develop problems any more frequently than did children at low genetic risk.

These findings are important because they suggest that our genetic makeup may control how sensitive we are to certain aspects of our environments. If we have no genetic risk, certain kinds of environmental influences may not affect us very much. But if we have high genetic risk, we may be much more vulnerable to certain types of environmental risks such as high communication deviance or adverse family environments. Findings such as these also raise the exciting possibility that certain kinds of environments may protect people with a genetic susceptibility to schizophrenia from ever developing the illness.

Even if children are at genetic high risk for schizophrenia they are less likely to develop the disorder if they are raised in a healthy family environment.

In summary, these findings indicate a strong interaction between genetic vulnerability and an unfavorable family environment in the causal pathway leading to schizophrenia. Of course, it could be argued that the children who went on to develop problems caused the disorganization of their adoptive families. However, there is little support for this alternative interpretation (see Tienari et al., 2004; Wahlberg et al., 1997). Some independent work reported by Kinney and colleagues (1997) also fails to show diminished mental health in adoptive parents raising children who later developed schizophrenia. Everything considered, the Finnish Adoptive Family Study has provided strong confirmation of the diathesis-stress model as it applies to the origins of schizophrenia.

MOLECULAR GENETICS Family studies tell us that schizophrenia runs in families, and twin and adoption studies help us explore the relative contributions of genes and environment. These approaches also tell us about the genetic heterogeneity of schizophrenia. For example, in addition to higher rates of schizophrenia, higher rates of schizotypal personality disorder are also found in the relatives of patients with schizophrenia (Kendler et al., 1993). This supports the idea of the schizophrenia spectrum and suggests that a genetic liability to schizophrenia can sometimes manifest itself in a form of pathology that is "schizophrenia-like" but not exactly schizophrenia itself (see Lenzenweger, 2010).

Researchers no longer believe that schizophrenia will, like Huntington's disease, be explained by one mutated gene on one specific chromosome. Rather, in most cases, schizophrenia probably involves many genes working together to confer susceptibility to the illness. The individual's "dose" of schizophrenia genes may explain why one person develops schizophrenia and another develops a milder variant within the schizophrenia spectrum, such as schizotypal personality disorder.

Researchers are now trying to locate and identify the genes that are involved in schizophrenia using the techniques of molecular genetics. In one approach, they are using known DNA markers to try to learn where aberrant genes might lie. As Faraone and colleagues (1999) aptly state, DNA markers are the "milemarkers" on our chromosomal highways. Molecular geneticists capitalize on the fact that we know the locations of some important genes that are associated with observable traits (such as genes for color blindness, for blood group, and for the human leukocyte antigen). Because genes that are close together on the same chromosome tend to stay together when genetic information is shuffled (as happens during reproduction), researchers can see whether a disorder like schizophrenia tends to co-occur with any known DNA marker traits. This is the rationale behind **linkage analysis**. Linkage analysis has been very successful in helping locate the genes associated with diseases that have well-defined models of inheritance. Even newer approaches such as *genome-wide association methods* (which may be able to detect genes that have very small effects) are also now being used to identify susceptibility genes.

In much of the research to date, failures to replicate previously reported findings have been more the rule than the exception. Nonetheless, studies are suggesting specific regions on certain chromosomes that may contribute to schizophrenia. Currently, there is a great deal of interest in regions on chromosomes 1, 2, 6, 8, 13, and 22 among others (Karoutzou et al., 2008; Maier, 2008; O'Donovan et al., 2008; Pogue-Geile & Yokley, 2010; Stefansson et al., 2008).

Why are these chromosomes of such interest? The reason is that, in some cases, they host genes that are known to be involved in processes that are believed to be aberrant in schizophrenia. These genes are known as **candidate genes**. An example is the COMT (catechol-O-methyltransferase) gene. This gene is located on chromosome 22 and is involved in dopamine metabolism. As you will soon learn, dopamine is a neurotransmitter that has long been implicated in psychosis (impaired reality testing). Interestingly, children who have a genetic syndrome (called *velocardiofacial syndrome*) that involves a deletion of genetic material on chromosome 22 are at high risk for developing schizophrenia as they move through adolescence (Gothelf et al., 2007). Prior to the onset of any disorder, they often report transient psychotic symptoms (such as auditory hallucinations) and have poor social functioning and reduced IQ (Debbané et al., 2006). Furthermore, as we shall see later, people with a particular variant of the COMT gene are much more likely to become psychotic as adults if they use cannabis during adolescence. For obvious reasons, schizophrenia researchers are very interested in chromosome 22 and in the COMT gene in their search to understand the origins of the disorder. Other genes implicated in schizophrenia are the neuregulin 1 gene (located on chromosome 8), the dysbindin gene (on chromosome 6), the DISC1

Many genes, each with a small effect, probably contribute to the development of schizophrenia. Genes that play a role in brain development may be especially implicated.

(which stands for "disrupted in schizophrenia") gene on chromosome 1, and several dopamine receptor genes (Gejman et al., 2011; Pogue-Geile & Yokley, 2010). These genes are involved in various neurobiological processes that are thought to have gone awry in schizophrenia.

ENDOPHENOTYPES Although we are certain that schizophrenia has a genetic basis, we are still a long way from understanding which genes are involved and what effects they have. Progress has been frustratingly slow because schizophrenia appears to be very complex genetically. A major collaborative study that examined 14 genes thought to be involved in schizophrenia has recently found no association between these genes and schizophrenia, disappointing many researchers (Sanders et al., 2008). However, it is possible that the genes involved may have only weak effects or else may be relevant in only certain population subgroups. A robust finding in one segment of the sample could therefore be washed out in a very large and mixed overall sample (Hamilton, 2008). Another difficulty is that researchers are still not sure exactly what phenotype (that is, measurable characteristic of interest) they should be looking for (remember Bleuler's idea of "the schizophrenias"?). Because genetic analysis requires that we know who is "affected" and who is not, this is a big problem.

To simplify things, researchers are now focusing on less complex and more homogenous phenotypes (such as specific symptom clusters) that may potentially be under the control of a smaller number of genes. They are also exploring **endophenotypes**—discrete, stable, and measurable traits that are thought to be under genetic control. By studying different endophenotypes, researchers hope to get closer to specific genes that might be important in schizophrenia (Gottesman & Gould, 2003; Lenzenweger, 2010). Accordingly, researchers are interested in people who score high on certain tests or measures that are thought to reflect a predisposition to schizophrenia. One example is subjects who score high on a self-report measure of schizotypic traits involving perceptual aberrations and magical ideation (the Per-Mag Scale; see Chapman et al., 1982; Chapman et al., 1994). Examples of items from these scales are shown in Table 2. Other endophenotypic risk markers for schizophrenia include abnormal performance on measures of cognitive functioning such as tests of working memory (see Barch, 2005; Lenzenweger, 2010). By studying these traits rather than the disorder itself, researchers hope to speed up progress in the search for the genes related to schizophrenia. Major collaborative studies designed to explore different endophenotypes are now under way, although they are still in their early stages (Greenwood et al., 2007).

Prenatal Exposures

Whether or not a genotype is expressed depends on biological and environmental triggers. We now know that a range of environmental factors, including such things as maternal exposure to stress, are capable of influencing patterns of gene expression in the developing offspring. In the sections below we highlight some environmental risk factors that might either cause schizophrenia or trigger it in a genetically vulnerable person.

VIRAL INFECTION The idea that schizophrenia might result from some kind of virus is not new. Kraepelin (1919) suggests that "infections in the years of development might have a causal significance" for schizophrenia. We also know that in the Northern Hemisphere, more people with schizophrenia are born between January and March than would be expected by chance (Waddington et al., 1999). Could some seasonal factor, such as a virus, be implicated?

In 1957 there was a major epidemic of influenza in Finland. Studying the residents of Helsinki, Mednick and colleagues (1988) found elevated rates of schizophrenia in children born to mothers who had been in their second trimester of pregnancy at the time of the influenza epidemic. The link between maternal influenza and subsequent schizophrenia in the grown offspring has now been well replicated using influenza epidemic information from other countries (see Wright et al., 1999). Risk of schizophrenia seems to be greatest when the mother gets the flu in the fourth to seventh month of gestation. Although the size of the effect is small and influenza clearly does not account for very many cases of schizophrenia, the fact that this association exists is very provocative. But how can maternal influenza set the stage

table 2 Sample Items Measuring Psychosis-Proneness

Magical Ideation

T	F	Things seem to be in different places when I get home, even though no one has been there.
T	F	I have sometimes felt that strangers were reading my mind.
T	F	At times, I have felt that a professor's lecture was meant especially for me.

Perceptual Aberration

T	F	Sometimes people whom I know well begin to look like strangers.
T	F	Ordinary colors sometimes seem much too bright for me.
T	F	Now and then, when I look in the mirror, my face seems quite different than usual.

Sources: Eckbald & Chapman, 1983; Chapman et al., 1978. Answering "true" to these items is more indicative of psychosis–proneness.

for schizophrenia in a child two or three decades later? One possibility is that the mother's antibodies to the virus cross the placenta and somehow disrupt the neurodevelopment of the fetus (Waddington et al., 1999). Other maternal infections such as rubella (German measles) and toxoplasmosis (a parasitic infection) that occur during this time have also been linked to increased risk for the later development of schizophrenia (Brown, 2011).

RHESUS INCOMPATIBILITY The idea that the mother's immune system might somehow damage the developing brain of the fetus is not as far-fetched as it might sound. Rhesus (Rh) incompatibility occurs when an Rh-negative mother carries an Rh-positive fetus. (Rhesus-positive or -negative is a way of typing a person's blood.) Incompatibility between the mother and the fetus is a major cause of blood disease in newborns. Interestingly, Rh incompatibility also seems to be associated with increased risk for schizophrenia. Hollister, Laing, and Mednick (1996) have shown that the rate of schizophrenia is about 2.1 percent in males who are Rh-incompatible with their mothers. For males who have no such incompatibility with their mothers, the rate of schizophrenia is 0.8 percent—very near the expected base rate found in the general population. Hollister is another example of a schizophrenia researcher who has a family member with the disorder, in this case a sister who was Rh-incompatible with her mother.

How might Rh incompatibility increase the risk for schizophrenia? One possibility is that the mechanism involves oxygen deprivation, or hypoxia. This suggestion is supported by studies that have linked the risk for schizophrenia to birth complications. Recent research also suggests that incompatibility between the blood of the mother and the blood of the fetus may increase the risk of brain abnormalities of the type known to be associated with schizophrenia (Freedman et al., 2011).

PREGNANCY AND BIRTH COMPLICATIONS Patients with schizophrenia are much more likely to have been born following a pregnancy or delivery that was complicated in some way (Cannon et al., 2002). Although the type of obstetric complication varies, many delivery problems (for example, breech delivery, prolonged labor, or the umbilical cord around the baby's neck) affect the oxygen supply of the newborn. Although we still have much to learn, the research again points toward damage to the brain at a critical time of development.

EARLY NUTRITIONAL DEFICIENCY Yet another piece of evidence that supports the idea that schizophrenia might be caused or triggered by environmental events that interfere with normal brain development comes from a tragedy that occurred in the Netherlands toward the end of World War II. In October 1944, a Nazi blockade resulted in a severe famine that affected people living in Amsterdam and other cities in the west of the country. The Dutch Hunger Winter (as it was known) continued until the Netherlands was liberated in May 1945. The population was severely malnourished during this time, and many died of starvation. Not surprisingly, fertility levels fell and the birth rate

dropped precipitously. However, some children were born during this time. Those who were conceived at the height of the famine had a twofold increase in their risk of later developing schizophrenia (Brown, 2011). Early prenatal nutritional deficiency appears to have been the cause. Whether the problem was general malnutrition or the lack of a specific nutrient such as folate or iron is not clear. But again, something seems to have compromised the development of the fetus during a critical stage.

MATERNAL STRESS If a mother experiences an extremely stressful event late in her first trimester of pregnancy or early in the second trimester the risk of schizophrenia in her child is increased (King et al., 2010). For example, in a large population study conducted in Denmark, the death of a close relative during the first trimester was associated with a 67 percent increase in the risk of schizophrenia in the child (Khashan et al., 2008). Currently, it is thought that the increase in stress hormones that pass to the fetus via the placenta might have negative effects on the developing brain, although the mechanisms through which maternal stress increases risk for schizophrenia are not yet well understood.

Genes and Environment in Schizophrenia: A Synthesis

Without question, schizophrenia has a strong genetic component. Current thinking is that genetic risk for schizophrenia emerges in one of two ways. The first is from large numbers (perhaps thousands) of common genes. The individual contribution of each of these genes is likely very small. However, when all of these genetic variants interact together, they set the stage for the development of the illness. The other way that schizophrenia may arise is because of very rare genetic mutations. These could be highly specific to certain people or to certain families (see Crow, 2007; McClellan, Susser, & King, 2007). These genetic events might involve microdeletions (bits of the DNA sequence that are missing in some places) or problems in the DNA sequence itself (such as repetitions of specific sections; St. Clair, 2009).

It is also possible that the focus on MZ concordance rates has caused us to overestimate the heritability of schizophrenia. This is because some MZ, and all DZ, twins do not have equally similar prenatal environments. Around two-thirds of MZ embryos are monochorionic, which means they share a placenta and blood supply. The remaining MZ twins and all DZ twins are dichorionic; they have separate placentas and separate fetal circulations. The higher concordance rate for schizophrenia in MZ than in DZ twins might therefore be a consequence, at least in part, of the greater potential for monochorionic MZ twins to share infections. Davis, Phelps, and Bracha (1995) have found that MZ twins who are monochorionic are much more likely to be concordant for schizophrenia (around 60 percent concordance) than MZ twins who are dichorionic (around 11 percent concordance). The concordance figure for dichorionic

MZ twins is very similar to that generally reported for DZ twins. Monochorionic MZ twins may therefore have inflated concordance rates in schizophrenia, which may have caused us to overattribute to genetics what might more accurately be attributed to environmental influences.

This figure is intentionally omitted from this text.

Finally, we need to keep in mind that genes get "turned on" and "turned off" in response to environmental changes. MZ twins who are discordant for schizophrenia show differences in their gene expression (Petronis et al., 2003). Perhaps some environmental "hits" turn on the genes for schizophrenia in one twin and not in the other. And perhaps some environments can keep the genes for schizophrenia from ever being turned on at all. Unfortunately, consistent with the diathesis-stress perspective, being at genetic risk does seem to make people more susceptible to environmental insults. In a study looking at the consequences of birth complications, Cannon and colleagues (1993) found that only the people who had a parent with schizophrenia and who had birth complications later showed brain abnormalities in adulthood such as enlarged ventricles (fluid-filled spaces in the brain). Moreover, for people who had two parents with schizophrenia, the problems were even worse. In contrast, people with no family history of schizophrenia did not show enlarged ventricles regardless of whether they experienced delivery complications when they were born. The message seems to be clear: A genetic liability to schizophrenia may predispose an individual to suffer more damage from environmental insults than would be the case in the absence of the genetic predisposition.

An Neurodevelopmental Perspective

Earlier in this chapter you learned that schizophrenia typically strikes people in late adolescence or early adulthood. Yet in the sections above, we saw that some of the factors thought to cause schizophrenia occur very early in life—in some cases before birth. How can this be? Current thinking is that schizophrenia is a disorder in which the development of the brain is disturbed very early on. Risk for schizophrenia may start with the pres-

ence of certain genes that, if turned on, have the potential to disrupt the normal development of the nervous system. Exposure to environmental insults in the prenatal period may turn on these genes or may create problems in other ways, independently of genotype. What this means is that the stage for schizophrenia, in the form of abnormal brain development, may be set very early in life. Nonetheless, problems may not be apparent until other triggering events take place or until the normal maturation of the brain reveals them. This may not occur until the brain is fully mature, typically late in the second decade of life (Conklin & Iacono, 2002; Weinberger, 1987).

What goes wrong? We are not yet certain. Brain development is a complex process that involves a programmed, orderly, and progressive sequence of events (Romer & Walker, 2007). Interestingly, some of the genes that have been implicated in schizophrenia are known to play a role in brain development and neural connections. And organic solvents used in the dry cleaning business might disrupt fetal neurodevelopment and so explain why having a parent who works as a dry cleaner triples the risk of schizophrenia in the offspring. If there were a disruption in cell migration some cells might fail to reach their target destinations, greatly affecting the "internal connectivity" of the brain. And neuronal migration is known to occur during the second trimester—exactly the period in development during which the consequences of maternal influenza seem to be most devastating.

If the seeds of schizophrenia are sown so early in life, can we see early indications of vulnerability to the disorder before the illness itself strikes? An ingenious series of studies reported by Walker and colleagues nicely illustrates the association between early developmental deviation and schizophrenia risk. These investigators gathered family home movies made during the childhoods of 32 persons who eventually developed schizophrenia. Trained observers made "blind" ratings (i.e., the observers were uninformed of outcomes) of certain dimensions of the emotional (Grimes & Walker, 1994) and facial expressions (Walker et al., 1993), motor skills, and neuromotor abnormalities (Walker et al., 1994) of these children and their healthy-outcome siblings from the same movie clips. The facial and emotional expressions and the motor competence of the "preschizophrenia" and the healthy-outcome children were found by the raters to differ significantly. The "preshizophrenia" children showed more motor abnormalities including unusual hand movements than their healthy siblings; they also showed less positive facial emotion and more negative facial emotion. In some instances these differences were apparent by age 2. Of course, we must keep in mind that these early problems do not characterize all children who will later develop schizophrenia. But they do tell us that subtle abnormalities can be found in children who are vulnerable to the disorder. We should also note that a major advantage of Walker's research design was that it avoided the problem of retrospective bias. Rather than asking parents or siblings what patients were like when they were growing up, the study used home movies to provide an objective behavioral record.

Another way to explore childhood indicators without the problem of retrospective bias is to use a prospective research design. Jones and colleagues (1994) and Isohanni and colleagues (2001) studied whole cohorts of children born in particular years and followed them up over time. Both groups of researchers found evidence of delayed speech and delayed motor development at age 2 in children who later went on to develop schizophrenia.

Yet another approach is to follow children who are known to be at high risk for schizophrenia by virtue of their having been born to a parent with the disorder. This strategy, pioneered by Mednick and Schulsinger (1968), has led to several other studies of high-risk children (for reviews, see Cornblatt et al., 1992; Erlenmeyer-Kimling & Cornblatt, 1992; Neale & Oltmanns, 1980; Watt et al., 1984). Obviously, research of this kind is both costly and time consuming. It also requires a great deal of patience on the part of researchers because children at risk have to be identified early in their lives and then followed into adulthood. Moreover, because the majority of people with schizophrenia do not have a parent with the disorder (in fact, 89 percent of patients have no first- or second-degree relatives

with schizophrenia [Gottesman, 2001]), high-risk samples are not particularly representative. Nonetheless, they have provided us with some valuable information about what people at risk look like prior to developing the full illness.

One of the most consistent findings from high-risk research is that children with a genetic risk for schizophrenia are more deviant than control children on research tasks that measure attention (Erlenmeyer-Kimling & Cornblatt, 1992). Adolescents at risk for schizophrenia are also rated lower in social competence than adolescents at risk for affective illness (Dworkin et al., 1994; Hooley, 2010). Some of the social problems that these high-risk children have may result from underlying attentional problems (Cornblatt et al., 1992).

Echoing the findings from Walker's home movie study is evidence that early motor abnormalities might be an especially strong predictor of later schizophrenia. Using data from the New York High-Risk Study, Erlenmeyer-Kimling and colleagues (1998) reported that, of an initial group of 51 high-risk children, 10 developed schizophrenia or schizophrenia-like psychosis as adults. Of these, 80 percent had shown unusual motor behavior when they were between 7 and 12 years of age. In another study, adolescents at high risk for schizophrenia showed more movement abnormalities (e.g., facial tics, blinking, tongue thrusts) than either nonclinical controls or adolescents with personality or behavioral problems (Mittal et al., 2008). Moreover, these movement abnormalities became more marked with time and also became more strongly correlated with psychotic symptoms as the children got older. Although we might have suspected that schizophrenia would first begin to show itself via hallucinations or delusions, it may be that the first signs of the illness can instead be found in the way that children move. This could be because movement abnormalities and psychotic symptoms share some of the same neural circuitry in the brain. Problems in this neural circuitry might show themselves first via movement abnormalities. Then, as the brain matures, problems in the same neural circuits manifest themselves in psychotic symptoms (see MacManus et al., 2011; Mittal et al., 2008).

The original high-risk studies have given us many insights into the problems that characterize people at risk for schizophrenia. But researchers have now changed their strategies. A new generation of high-risk studies is focusing on young people who are at clinical (as opposed to genetic) high risk. By focusing on those who are already showing some **prodromal**, or very early, signs of schizophrenia, researchers are hoping to improve their ability to detect, and also perhaps intervene with, people who appear to be on a pathway to developing the disorder (Addington et al., 2007; Cannon et al., 2007).

Structural and Functional Brain Abnormalities

Technological developments now allow us to study the brain in ways that used to be impossible. Positron emission tomography (PET), magnetic resonance imaging (MRI),

Ratings of clips of old home movies revealed that children who went on to develop schizophrenia showed more unusual hand movements than their healthy siblings, even when they were just 2 years old.
Source: Walker (1994).

and other even more sophisticated approaches are in wide use. They are revealing abnormalities in the structure and function of the brain as well as in neurotransmitter activity in people who suffer from schizophrenia. In the sections below we describe some of the problems in cognitive functioning that have long been known to characterize people with this disorder. We then consider what brain abnormalities in the structure of the brain might be responsible for these and other problems.

NEUROCOGNITION Schizophrenia patients experience many problems with their neurocognitive functioning (see Cornblatt et al., 2008; Green, 1997, for reviews). For example, they perform much worse than healthy controls on a broad range of neuropsychological tests (Heaton et al., 1994; Hoff et al., 1992; Hoff et al., 2000). Furthermore, patients who have only recently become ill perform about the same on neuropsychological tests as patients who have been ill for many years (and both groups obviously perform worse than controls). In other words, cognitive difficulties can be seen right from the start of the illness and so are unlikely to be due to the effects of extended hospitalizations or medications.

Other cognitive deficits are also apparent. For example, when asked to respond to a stimulus as quickly and appropriately as possible (this is a measure of reaction time) schizophrenia patients do poorly compared with controls (see Nuechterlein, 1977). In addition, they show deficits on the Continuous Performance Task (CPT; e.g., Cornblatt et al., 1989). This task requires the subject to attend to a series of letters or numbers and then to detect an intermittently presented target stimulus that appears on the screen along with the letters or numbers (e.g., "Press when you see the number 7"). There are also problems with working memory (Barch, 2005; Park et al., 1995), which can be thought of as our "mental blackboard." When they engage in tasks of working memory, patients with schizophrenia show less prefrontal brain activity compared to healthy controls (Cannon et al., 2005).

Somewhere between 54 and 86 percent of people with schizophrenia also show eye-tracking dysfunction (see Figure 3) and are deficient in their ability to track a moving target such as a pendulum (Cornblatt et al., 2008). This is a skill referred to as smooth-pursuit eye movement (Levy et al., 1993; Lieberman et al., 1993). In contrast, only about 6 to 8 percent of the general population shows problems with eye tracking. Especially interesting is that around 50 percent of the first-degree relatives of schizophrenia patients also show eye-tracking problems even though they do not have schizophrenia themselves (e.g., Iacono et al., 1992; Levy et al., 1993; Sporn et al., 2005). This suggests that disturbances in eye tracking have a genetic basis and that eye tracking may represent a viable endophenotype for genetic studies.

Perhaps the strongest finding in the area of neurocognition and schizophrenia, however, concerns a psychophysiological measure called P50 (see Heinrichs, 2001). When two clicks are heard in close succession, the brain (receiving the auditory signal) produces a positive electrical response to each click. This response is called P50 because it occurs 50 milliseconds after the click. In normal subjects, the response to the second click is less marked than the response to the first click because the normal brain dampens, or "gates," responses to repeated sensory events. If this didn't happen, habituation to a stimulus would never occur. Many patients with schizophrenia, in contrast, respond almost as strongly to the second click as to the first. This is referred to as "poor P50 suppression." First-degree family members of patients with schizophrenia are also more likely than controls to have problems with P50 suppression (Clementz et al., 1998). It has been suggested that poor P50 suppression is the result of problems with specific receptors in the hippocampus of the medial temporal lobe (Adler et al., 1998). As you will soon learn, the hippocampus is one brain region that appears to be compromised in schizophrenia. Cells in the hippocampus

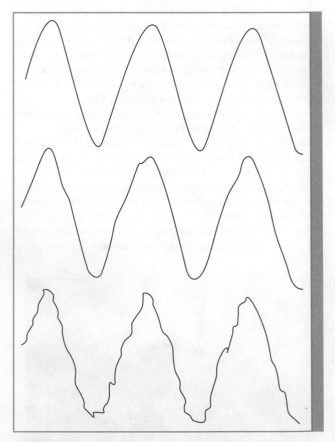

FIGURE 3

Normal and Abnormal Eye Tracking of a Sinusoidal Wave

The top pattern is the target, the middle pattern is a record of normal tracking, and the lowest pattern is the kind of abnormal record produced by some patients with schizophrenia.

Source: Figure from Levy et al. (1993). Eye tracking dysfunction and schizophrenia: A critical perspective. *Schizophrenia Bulletin, 19*(3), 461–536. Used with permission of Oxford University Press.

are also especially susceptible to damage from hypoxia during brain development.

Taken together, the weight of the evidence suggests that patients with schizophrenia have problems with the active, functional allocation of attentional resources. What this means is that they are unable to attend well on demand. Although many of the findings may not be highly specific to schizophrenia (some of the neurocognitive deficits can be found in patients with mood disorders, for example), it has long been suspected that attentional dysfunctions could be indicators of a biological susceptibility to at least some forms of schizophrenia (Cornblatt et al., 1992). In the sections below, we consider some of the reasons that this might be the case.

LOSS OF BRAIN VOLUME One of the most well-replicated findings concerns the brain ventricles. These are fluid-filled spaces that lie deep within the brain. Compared with controls, patients with schizophrenia have enlarged brain ventricles, with males possibly being more affected than females (Lawrie & Abukmeil, 1998; Shenton et al., 2001). Figure 4 illustrates enlarged ventricles in identical twins, one of whom suffers from schizophrenia. However, we must also point out that enlarged brain ventricles are apparent only in a significant minority of patients. Enlarged brain ventricles also are not specific to schizophrenia and can be seen in patients with Alzheimer's disease, Huntington's disease, and chronic alcohol dependence.

Enlarged brain ventricles are important because they are an indicator of a reduction in the amount of brain tissue. The brain normally occupies fully the rigid enclosure of the skull. Enlarged ventricles therefore imply that the brain areas that

border the ventricles have somehow shrunk or decreased in volume, the ventricular space becoming larger as a result. In fact, MRI studies of patients with schizophrenia show about a 3 percent reduction in whole brain volume relative to that in controls (Hulshoff Pol & Kahn, 2008). This decrease in brain volume is present very early in the illness. Even patients with a recent onset of schizophrenia have lower overall brain volumes than controls (Steen et al., 2006; Vita et al., 2006) or else show evidence of enlarged ventricles (Cahn et al., 2002). These findings suggest that some brain abnormalities likely predate the illness rather than develop as a result of untreated psychosis or as a consequence of taking neuroleptic medications. Consistent with this, important new research shows that brain volume changes can be seen in genetically high risk individuals as the illness is starting to develop. Indeed, it has been suggested that these changes may play a causal role in the onset of symptoms (Karlsgodt et al., 2010; Sun et al., 2009).

We also know that the brain changes that characterize people in the early stages of the illness progressively get worse with time. Cahn and colleagues (2002) measured changes in the overall volume of gray matter (which is made up of nerve cells) in patients who were experiencing their first episode of schizophrenia. Thirty-four patients and 36 matched, healthy comparison subjects received MRI brain scans at the start of the study and then again 1 year later. The results showed that the volume of gray matter declined significantly over time in the patients but not in the controls. More specifically, there was almost a 3 percent decrease in the volume of gray matter in the patients in the 1-year period between the first and the second scans. Figure 5 illustrates the progressive loss of gray matter over a 5-year period in another sample of adolescents with schizophrenia compared to healthy controls.

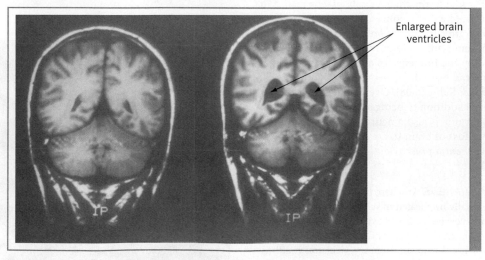

Enlarged brain ventricles

FIGURE 4

Enlarged Brain Ventricles in Schizophrenia

MRI scans of 28-year-old male identical twins, showing the enlarged brain ventricles in the twin with schizophrenia (right) compared with his well brother (left).
Source: Courtesy of E. Fuller Torry, M.D., and Daniel Weinberger, M.D.

Significant **Progressive Gray Matter** Loss **in Schizophrenia**

FIGURE 5

Progressive Gray Matter Loss in Schizophrenia

Compared with normal adolescents, young people with early-onset schizophrenia show a progressive loss of gray matter in their brains over time. MRI scans repeated over a 5-year period show a much greater loss of brain tissue in patients with schizophrenia than in healthy controls. Gray matter loss occurs in many brain areas, beginning in the parietal cortex and spreading to the temporal cortex and the frontal cortex.
Source: Thompson, R. A., & Nelson, C. A. (2001). Developmental science and the media: Early brain development. *American Psychologist, 56,* 5–15.

Studies of more chronically ill patients suggest that decreases in brain tissue and increases in the size of the brain ventricles are not limited to the early phases of this illness. Instead, progressive brain deterioration continues for many years. Moreover, these brain changes can also be found in MZ twins where one has schizophrenia and the other does not. The fact that brain changes are present in the discordant twin (the one without schizophrenia) suggests that they cannot be explained by the influence of antipsychotic medications and may instead be under genetic control (Brans et al., 2008; Hulshoff Pol & Kahn, 2008). Overall, the research findings suggest that in addition to being a neurodevelopmental disorder, schizophrenia is also a neuroprogressive disorder characterized by a loss of brain tissue over time. Kraepelin's use of the term *dementia praecox* may have been highly appropriate after all.

AFFECTED BRAIN AREAS Are there particular regions of the brain that are especially implicated in schizophrenia? Although much remains to be learned, there is evidence of reductions in the volume of regions in the frontal and temporal lobes. These brain areas play critical roles in memory, decision making, and in the processing of auditory information. More specifically, there is a reduction in the volume of such medial temporal areas as the amygdala (which is involved in emotion), the hippocampus (which plays a key role in memory), and the thalamus—a relay center that receives almost all sensory input

(Ettinger et al., 2001; Keshavan et al., 2008; Shenton et al., 2001; Tamminga et al., 2002; Weinberger, 1997). Again, however, remember that the alterations in brain structure that are found in schizophrenia are not specific only to this diagnosis.

WHITE MATTER PROBLEMS When we talk about volume loss in the brains of people with schizophrenia we are referring to the loss of brain cells or gray matter. However, evidence is growing that schizophrenia also involves problems with white matter. Nerve fibres are covered in a myelin sheath (which looks white in color in a chemically preserved brain). Myelin acts as an insulator and increases the speed and efficiency of conduction between nerve cells. White matter is therefore crucially important for the connectivity of the brain. If there are disruptions in the integrity of white matter, there will be problems in how well the cells of the nervous system can function. For example, imagine the problems you would have in a group of networked computers if the connections that linked them were damaged in some way.

Studies of patients with schizophrenia show that they have reductions in white matter volume as well as structural abnormalities in the white matter itself. Interestingly, these abnormalities can be found in first-episode patients and also in people at genetically high risk for the disorder. This suggests that they are not a result of the disease itself or the effects of treatment.

At the clinical level, white matter abnormalities have been shown to be correlated with cognitive impairments (Kubicki et al., 2007). In people at high risk of developing schizophrenia, white matter changes in the temporal areas of the brain also predict later social functioning (Karlsgodt et al., 2009).

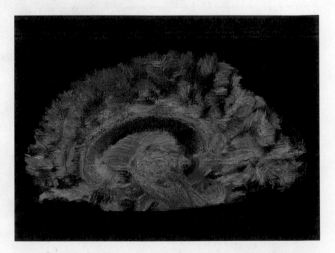

Nerve fibers are covered in by a fatty myelin sheath, which looks white in a preserved brain (hence the term white matter). Myelin improves the electrical conductivity of nerve cells. This image illustrates white matter tracts (shown here in color for better clarity) and shows how interconnected the brain is.

Another interesting recent finding is that children of people with schizophrenia, even though they are not psychotic themselves, have a reduction in the volume of the corpus callosum—a massive tract of white matter fibers that connects the two hemispheres of the brain (Francis et al., 2011). Although much remains to be learned, it is becoming increasingly clear that abnormalities in white matter, and in white matter development, may provide us with important additional insights into what goes wrong with the brain in schizophrenia.

BRAIN FUNCTIONING Studies of brain functioning tell us what is going on in the working brain, either when it is engaged in a task or at rest. You have already learned about the structural brain abnormalities associated with schizophrenia and the problems that patients with schizophrenia have on various neurocognitive tests. Given this, you will hardly be surprised to learn that neuroimaging research is showing us just how disrupted brain functioning is in patients with this disorder.

For example, some patients show abnormally low frontal lobe activation (known as "hypofrontality") when they are involved in mentally challenging tasks such as the Wisconsin Card Sorting Test (WCST) or in other tests generally thought to require substantial frontal lobe involvement. Essentially, this brain area does not seem to be able to kick into action when patients perform complex tasks (see Figure 6). In other patients, hyperactivation in frontal brain areas is found, suggesting that they are having to work harder to be successful on the task. In both sets of circumstances, however, the brain is not functioning in an optimal and efficient way (Keshavan et al., 2008).

Impaired functioning of the frontal lobes during cognitive tasks is also found in patients in the early stages of schizophrenia as well as in people at high risk for developing the disorder (Fusar-Poli et al., 2007). Again, however, it is important to remember that such alterations in functioning are not characteristic of all patients (e.g., Buchsbaum et al., 1992; Heinrichs, 2001). Nonetheless, frontal lobe dysfunction is believed to account for some of the negative symptoms of schizophrenia and perhaps to be involved in some attentional-cognitive deficits (Cannon et al., 1998; Goldman-Rakic & Selemon, 1997).

Dysfunction of the temporal lobe is also found, although here the findings are often not very consistent (Keshavan et al., 2008). However, what may be most important is that there may be a problem with the way activity in different brain regions gets *coordinated*. When we are at rest

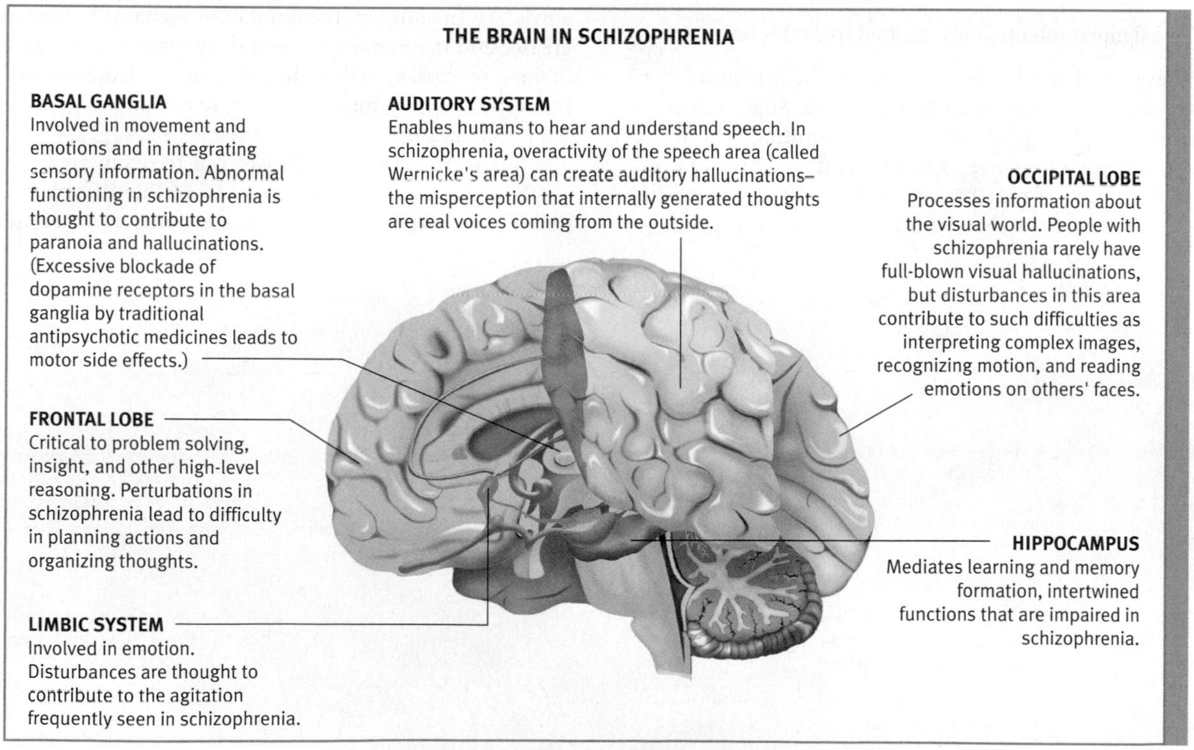

THE BRAIN IN SCHIZOPHRENIA

BASAL GANGLIA
Involved in movement and emotions and in integrating sensory information. Abnormal functioning in schizophrenia is thought to contribute to paranoia and hallucinations. (Excessive blockade of dopamine receptors in the basal ganglia by traditional antipsychotic medicines leads to motor side effects.)

FRONTAL LOBE
Critical to problem solving, insight, and other high-level reasoning. Perturbations in schizophrenia lead to difficulty in planning actions and organizing thoughts.

LIMBIC SYSTEM
Involved in emotion. Disturbances are thought to contribute to the agitation frequently seen in schizophrenia.

AUDITORY SYSTEM
Enables humans to hear and understand speech. In schizophrenia, overactivity of the speech area (called Wernicke's area) can create auditory hallucinations—the misperception that internally generated thoughts are real voices coming from the outside.

OCCIPITAL LOBE
Processes information about the visual world. People with schizophrenia rarely have full-blown visual hallucinations, but disturbances in this area contribute to such difficulties as interpreting complex images, recognizing motion, and reading emotions on others' faces.

HIPPOCAMPUS
Mediates learning and memory formation, intertwined functions that are impaired in schizophrenia.

FIGURE 6

The Brain in Schizophrenia
Many brain regions and systems operate abnormally in schizophrenia, including those highlighted here.

or relaxing there is activation in a network of brain regions that comprise the "default mode network." You can think of this as the brain on standby. Then, when we are actively engaged in a task, activity in this network of brain areas has to be suppressed in favor of activity in brain areas that are relevant to the task at hand. But imagine what might happen if it was difficult to disengage from the default mode. Performance on the task would suffer. This is what researchers now think may be happening in people with schizophrenia. Whereas healthy people find it easy to suppress activity in the default mode network (tuning their brains into the "correct station" so to speak), people with schizophrenia may not be able to do this as efficiently (Guerrero-Padrazza et al., 2011; Whitfield-Gabrieli et al., 2009). This lack of ability to disengage the default mode network may help us understand why people with schizophrenia have so many difficulties with a wide range of tasks across a broad array of areas (Karlsgodt et al., 2010).

CYTOARCHITECTURE As we have seen, one hypothesis about schizophrenia is that genetic vulnerabilities, perhaps combined with prenatal insults, can lead to disruption of the migration of neurons in the brain. If this is true, some cells will fail to arrive at their final destinations, and the overall organization of cells in the brain (the brain's *cytoarchitecture*) will be compromised.

This figure is intentionally omitted from this text.

There are also other ways in which the organization of cells in the brain appears to be disrupted. Some researchers, using complex, three-dimensional counting techniques, have reported an increase in neuronal density in some areas of the brains of patients with schizophrenia (see Selemon, 2004). There are also abnormalities in the distribution of cells in different layers of the cortex and hippocampus (Arnold, 2000; Kalus et al., 1997; Selemon et al., 1995), as well as evidence that patients with schizophrenia are missing particular types of neurons known as "inhibitory interneurons" (Benes & Berretta, 2001). These neurons are responsible for regulating the excitability of other neurons. Their absence may mean that bursts of activity by excitatory neurons in the brain go unchecked. Again, research suggests that the brains of patients with schizophrenia may be less able to regulate or dampen down overactivity in certain key neural circuits (see Daskalakis et al., 2002). As we will see shortly, patients with schizophrenia have difficulty handling even normal levels of stress. Given what we have just learned, this makes a great deal of sense.

BRAIN DEVELOPMENT IN ADOLESCENCE Although we have every reason to believe that risk genes and early prenatal experiences compromise brain development in the fetus, the story may not end so early. The brain continues to develop and mature through adolescence and into young adulthood. For example, we all have an excess of synapses well into our late teens. However, normal processes that occur during adolescence prune (or reduce) these synapses, so decreasing "neuronal redundancy." There is also a normal reduction in gray matter volume that occurs in adolescence, as well an increase both in white matter and in the volume of the hippocampus and the amygdala. In addition, the number of excitatory synapses decreases and the number of inhibitory synapses increases. All of these processes are thought to occur to enhance brain function overall and to make the brain more "adult" (Insel, 2010; Walker et al., 2010).

But what if these processes fail to occur in a normal way? We might expect to see many of the differences (reduced gray matter volume, less white matter, reduced volume

Major brain changes take place during adolescence as the brain matures. If problems occur during this critical phase of development schizophrenia may be the result.

of the hippocampus) that we do actually see in schizophrenia. Of course, we still have much to learn. The etiology of schizophrenia is very complicated. But many of the answers lie in what goes wrong in the brain at critical periods of development.

SYNTHESIS The brain is compromised in schizophrenia, although the compromise is often very subtle. Some of the brain abnormalities that are found are likely to be genetic in origin. Others may reflect environmental insults. For example, Baaré and colleagues (2001) used MRI to study the brains of MZ and DZ twins who were discordant for schizophrenia and then compared the results for these groups to results from a group of healthy twins. What these researchers found was that the patients with schizophrenia had smaller brain volumes than their well co-twins. What was interesting, however, was that these well co-twins also had smaller brains than the healthy control twins. Baaré and colleagues (2001) propose that genetic risk for schizophrenia may be associated with reduced brain development early in life. This is why the healthy twins who had a co-twin with schizophrenia had smaller brain volumes than the healthy controls. Baaré and colleagues also hypothesize that patients who develop schizophrenia suffer additional brain abnormalities that are not genetic in origin. This explains why the twins with schizophrenia had smaller brain volumes than their discordant co-twins. In people at genetic risk for schizophrenia (but not in those without genetic risk), a history of fetal oxygen deprivation has been shown to be associated with brain abnormalities in later life (Cannon et al., 2002). In other words, what we may have here is an excellent example of

how genes can create an enhanced susceptibility to potentially aversive environmental events. Moreover, even when both members of a twin pair have identical genes (as is the case for MZ twins), if only one of them experiences the environmental insult (for example, a birth cord around the neck, creating hypoxia), only one twin might be pushed across the threshold into illness while the co-twin remains healthy.

Finally, we emphasize that it is unlikely that schizophrenia is the result of any one problem in any one specific region of the brain. The brain is comprised of *functional circuits*—regions that are linked to other regions by a network of interconnections. If there is a problem at any point in the circuit, the circuit will not function properly. The focus now is on learning how the brain is wired and what regions are functionally linked. Research on the default mode network is an example of this. Subtle brain abnormalities in some key functional circuits (or deficiencies in the ability to switch from one functional circuit to another) may wreak havoc with normal functioning. As we gain more knowledge about how the brain does its job, we will understand more about how exactly the brain is compromised in schizophrenia.

NEUROCHEMISTRY After researchers discovered in 1943 that LSD could cause profound mental changes, those interested in schizophrenia began to consider the possible biochemical basis of the disorder. Now the idea that serious mental disorders are due to "chemical imbalances" in the brain is commonplace. This phrase is often used to provide a general explanation of why someone has a disorder like schizophrenia. But the notion of "chemical imbalance" is vague and imprecise. All it really conveys is the widely accepted notion that alterations in brain chemistry may be associated with abnormal mental states.

The most important neurotransmitter implicated in schizophrenia is **dopamine**. The *dopamine hypothesis* dates back to the 1960s and was derived from three important observations. The first is the pharmacological action of the drug chlorpromazine (Thorazine). Chlorpromazine was first used in the treatment of schizophrenia in 1952. It rapidly became clear that this drug was helpful to patients. Eventually, it was learned that the therapeutic benefits of chlorpromazine were linked to its ability to block dopamine receptors.

The second piece of evidence implicating dopamine in schizophrenia came from an entirely different direction. Amphetamines are drugs that produce a functional excess of dopamine (i.e., the brain acts as if there is too much dopamine in the system). In the late 1950s and early 1960s, researchers began to see that abuse of amphetamines led, in some cases, to a form of psychosis that involved paranoia and auditory hallucinations (Connell, 1958; Kalant, 1966; Tatetsu, 1964). There was thus clinical evidence that a drug that gave rise to a functional excess of dopamine also gave rise to a psychotic state that looked a lot like schizophrenia.

The third piece of indirect evidence linking dopamine to schizophrenia came from clinical studies that actually treated patients by giving them drugs that increase the availability of dopamine in the brain. An example here is Parkinson's disease, which is caused by low levels of dopamine in a specific brain area (the basal ganglia; see Figure 6) and is treated with a drug called L-DOPA. Psychotic symptoms are a significant complication of treatment with L-DOPA. Again, then, the circumstantial evidence pointed to the role of dopamine in inducing psychosis.

How could dopamine induce psychosis? Activity in the dopamine system may play a role in determining how much salience we give to internal and external stimuli. Dysregulated dopamine transmission may actually make us pay more attention to and give more significance to stimuli that are not especially relevant or important. This is called "aberrant salience" (see Kapur, 2003). If this is the case, it is quite easy to see why patients might develop delusions or experience hallucinations and why psychotic experiences might be so shaped by the patient's culture and history. In the early stages of their illnesses, patients often report heightened sensory awareness ("My senses were sharpened. I became fascinated by the little insignificant things around me") or increased meaning in events ("I felt that there was some overwhelming significance in this"). If dopamine creates aberrant salience, the person will struggle to make sense of everyday experiences that were previously in the background but that now have become inappropriately important and worthy of attention. In this way, the hum of a refrigerator could become a voice talking; or the arrival of a package could signal a threat, which then prompts the patient to look carefully at the subtle behaviors of others to see who could be a source of harm and persecution.

But how might a functional excess of dopamine in the system come about? One way is through too much dopamine available in the synapse (the gap between nerve cells that has to be "bridged" by a neurotransmitter for a nerve impulse to be carried from one neuron to another). This could come about by increasing the synthesis or production of dopamine, by releasing more of it into the synapse, by slowing down the rate at which dopamine is metabolized or broken down once it is in the synapse, or by blocking

neuronal reuptake (the "recycling" of dopamine back into the neuron). Any or all of these could increase the overall availability of dopamine. There are also ways in which a functional excess of dopamine could be produced or, more accurately, mimicked. If the receptors that dopamine acts on (i.e., those on the postsynaptic membrane) are especially dense and prolific or if they are especially sensitive (or both), the effects of a normal amount of dopamine being released into the synapse would be multiplied. In other words, the system acts as though there were more dopamine available even though there really isn't.

Before the development of highly sophisticated imaging techniques, researchers interested in learning about dopamine in the brains of people with schizophrenia could use one of two approaches. They could measure dopamine in the (postmortem) brains of decreased patients, or they could study dopamine indirectly by measuring its major metabolite (what most of it is converted into). The major metabolite of dopamine is homovanillic acid, or HVA. However, HVA is best collected in cerebrospinal fluid (CSF). This requires that the patient agree to a lumbar puncture, which involves a large needle being inserted into the spine to draw off fluid. Not only is this potentially dangerous, it also leaves the patient with a violent headache.

The early studies that examined concentrations of HVA in the CSF of patients with schizophrenia and in controls

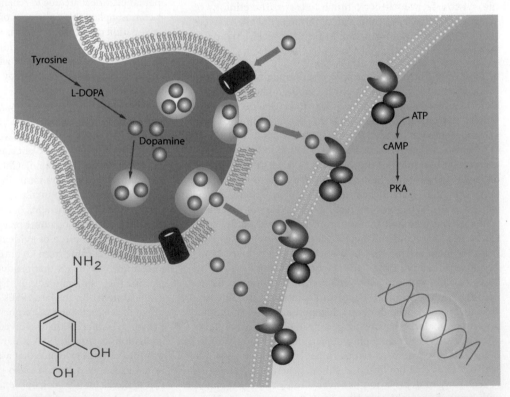

After being synthesized, dopamine is stored until it is released into the synapse. Dopamine binds to receptors on the post-synaptic neuron (shown in blue) triggering other reactions. It is then recycled back into the neuron to be used again.

yielded generally negative results (see Heinrichs, 2001; Owen & Simpson, 1995). The same was true of postmortem studies. Researchers were forced to conclude that there was no strong evidence to support the idea that patients with schizophrenia were producing more dopamine than controls were. Research efforts therefore moved toward exploring the idea that the problem lay not in overall dopamine levels (dopamine turnover) but in receptor density and receptor sensitivity. These studies were facilitated by technological developments such as PET scans, which allow us to study the working brain and to look at the density of dopamine receptors in living patients.

There are five subtypes of dopamine receptors (D1–D5). Of these, the D2 receptor is the most relevant clinically, and most of the research has focused on this. In general, postmortem studies show that there are about 1.4 times more D2 receptors in the brains of deceased patients with schizophrenia than there are in controls (Seeman, 2011). Early PET studies also found evidence for a more-than-twofold increase in D2 receptors in living patients with schizophrenia compared with controls (Wong et al., 1986; Gjedde & Wong, 1987), although some nonsignificant findings (Farde et al., 1987, 1990) led to a great deal of debate and controversy.

Subsequent research, however, has now established that the density of D2 receptors is indeed increased in patients with schizophrenia (Kestler et al., 2001; Seeman, 2011). Although some of this increase is no doubt related to medication effects (older patients, who have taken more medications over their lives, have the highest densities of D2 receptors), medication effects do not explain all the findings. Importantly, we now have evidence that D2 receptors are also elevated in the healthy co-twins of patients with schizophrenia (Hirvonen et al., 2005). Not only does this tell us that the elevation in D2 receptors is not simply attributable to taking medications, but it also tells us that having more D2 receptors doesn't necessarily mean that someone will develop psychosis.

So what else is going on? Current thinking is that people with schizophrenia are supersensitive to dopamine (Seeman, 2011). This arises because they have greater numbers of a form of D2 receptor (called a D2high receptor) that has a very high affinity for dopamine. What is also exciting is that animal studies suggest that anoxia (oxygen deprivation) at the time of birth can lead to dopamine supersensitivity. What this means is that we now have a bridge between problems with dopamine system and some of the prenatal problems (e.g., birth complications) that we discussed earlier.

But dopamine is not the only neurotransmitter implicated in schizophrenia. Before leaving our discussion of neurochemistry, we take a quick look at another key neurotransmitter that is attracting a lot of attention.

Glutamate is an excitatory neurotransmitter that is widespread in the brain. As was the case for dopamine, there are a number of reasons why researchers suspect that a dysfunction in glutamate transmission might be involved in schizophrenia. First, PCP, or angel dust, is known to block glutamate receptors. PCP also induces symptoms (both positive and negative) that are very similar to those of schizophrenia. Moreover, when people with schizophrenia take PCP, it exacerbates their symptoms.

Second, physicians had to stop using ketamine, which is an anesthetic, because when it is given intravenously to normal subjects, it produces schizophrenia-like positive and negative symptoms (see Krystal et al., 2005). When given to patients whose schizophrenia is stable and well controlled, ketamine exacerbates hallucinations, delusions, and thought disorder. But what is all the more remarkable about ketamine is that it does not cause any of these problems when it is administered to children, for whom it continues to be used as an anesthetic. This suggests that age (and brain maturity) determines whether ketamine causes psychosis.

Like PCP, ketamine blocks glutamate receptors. Researchers are now exploring concentrations of glutamate in postmortem brains of patients with schizophrenia and finding lower levels of glutamate in both the prefrontal cortex and the hippocampus compared with the levels in control subjects (Goff & Coyle, 2001). Recent results from a meta-analysis further suggest that glutamate levels are also low in the brains of living patients who have schizophrenia (Marsman et al., 2011). This is exciting because, many years ago, Olney and Farber (1995) proposed that diminished activity at certain types of glutamate receptors (known as "NMDA" receptors) may not only trigger schizophrenia-like symptoms but may also cause the degeneration of neurons in key brain areas. In other words, if the NMDA receptors are not normally active (perhaps because glutamate levels are low), subtle brain damage may result.

For all of these reasons, the *glutamate hypothesis* of schizophrenia is now attracting a lot of research attention. It is also prompting the development of new experimental drugs that might provide additional ways to treat schizophrenia. For example, amino acids such as glycine and D-serine are now being used to enhance neurotransmission at NMDA receptor sites. This research is still in its early stages; nonetheless, the initial findings look very promising (Javitt, 2008; Lane et al., 2008).

Finally, does the importance of glutamate challenge the importance of dopamine in the neurochemistry of schizophrenia? No. One action of dopamine receptors is to inhibit the release of glutamate. Simply stated, an overactive dopaminergic system could result in excessive suppression of glutamate, leading to the underactivity of the NMDA receptors. The dopamine hypothesis of schizophrenia is actually made all the more credible by discoveries about glutamate.

Psychosocial and Cultural Factors

DO BAD FAMILIES CAUSE SCHIZOPHRENIA? Years ago, parents were routinely assumed to have caused their children's disorders through hostility, deliberate rejection, or gross parental ineptitude. Many professionals blamed parents, and their feedback to them was often angry and insensitive. Mothers were particularly singled out for criticism. The idea of the "schizophrenogenic mother," whose cold and aloof behavior was the root cause of schizophrenia, was very influential in many clinical circles (Fromm-Reichman, 1948). This was very distressing for families. Not only were they faced with the difficulties of coping with a son or daughter who had a devastating illness, but they suffered all the more because of the blame that was directed toward them by mental health professionals.

Today, things are very different. Theories that were popular many decades ago—for example, the idea that schizophrenia was caused by destructive parental interactions (Lidz et al., 1965)—have foundered for lack of empirical support. Another idea that has not stood the test of time is the *double-bind hypothesis* (Bateson, 1959, 1960). A double bind occurs when the parent presents the child with ideas, feelings, and demands that are mutually incompatible (for example, a mother may complain about her son's lack of affection but freeze up or punish him when he approaches her affectionately). According to Bateson's etiologic hypothesis, such a son is continually placed in situations where he cannot win, and he becomes increasingly anxious. Presumably, over time, such disorganized and contradictory communications in the family come to be reflected in his own thinking. However, no solid support for these ideas has ever been reported.

Instead, we have learned from past research that disturbances and conflict in families that include an individual with schizophrenia may well be caused by having a person with psychosis in the family (e.g., Hirsch & Leff, 1975). In other words, rather than causing the schizophrenia, family communication problems could be the result of trying to communicate with someone who is severely ill and disorganized (Liem, 1974; Mishler & Waxler, 1968). Of course, some families do show unusual communication patterns that we now refer to as "communication deviance" and which we described earlier. These amorphous and fragmented communications may actually reflect genetic susceptibility to schizophrenia on the part of the relative (Hooley & Hiller, 2001; Miklowitz & Stackman, 1992). However, as we know from the Finnish Adoptive Study, adverse family environments and communication deviance probably have little pathological consequence if the child who is exposed has no genetic risk for schizophrenia (Tienari et al., 2004; Wahlberg et al., 1997).

FAMILIES AND RELAPSE Although schizophrenia is often a chronic disorder, its symptoms may be especially severe at some times (i.e., when there is a relapse) and less severe at other times (for example, during a period of remission). Decades ago, George Brown and his colleagues (1958) observed that the kind of living situation patients with schizophrenia had after they left the hospital predicted how well they would fare clinically. Surprisingly, patients who returned home to live with parents or with a spouse were at higher risk of relapse than patients who left the hospital to live alone or with siblings. Brown reasoned that highly emotional family environments might be stressful to patients. Unlike his counterparts across the Atlantic, he suspected that what might be important was not the presence of markedly disturbed or pathological patient–family relationships (although those certainly existed in

some families) but something much more ordinary and commonplace. Brown's hunch was that researchers should focus on "the range of feelings and emotions to be found in ordinary families" (see Brown, 1985, p. 22). This was an unusual insight at the time. But viewed today in the context of the diathesis-stress model, we see just how prescient Brown was.

In a series of studies, Brown and his colleagues went on to develop and refine the construct of **expressed emotion**, or **EE**. Expressed emotion is a measure of the family environment that is based on how a family member speaks about the patient during a private interview with a researcher (Hooley, 2007). It has three main elements: criticism, hostility, and emotional overinvolvement (EOI). The most important of these is criticism, which reflects dislike or disapproval of the patient. Hostility is a more extreme form of criticism that indicates a dislike or rejection of the patient as a person. Finally, EOI reflects a dramatic or overconcerned attitude on the part of the family member toward the patient's illness.

EE is important because it has been repeatedly shown to predict relapse in patients with schizophrenia. In a meta-analysis of 27 studies, Butzlaff and Hooley (1998) demonstrated that living in a high-EE home environment more than doubled the baseline level of relapse risk for schizophrenia patients in the 9 to 12 months after hospitalization. Moreover, even though EE predicts relapse regardless of whether the patients studied have been ill for a short, medium, or long time, EE seems to be an especially strong predictor of relapse for patients who are chronically ill.

Of course, it could be that families simply tend to be more critical of patients who are more severely ill and that this is why EE and relapse are correlated. However, a review of the literature provides no strong support for this assumption (see Hooley et al., 1995). Also, EE predicts relapse even when potentially important patient variables are controlled statistically (Nuechterlein et al., 1992). Finally, research shows that when EE levels in families are lowered (usually by clinical interventions), patients' relapse rates also decrease (Falloon et al., 1985; Hogarty et al., 1986; Leff et al., 1982; McFarlane et al., 1995). This suggests that EE may play a causal role in the relapse process.

But how might EE trigger relapse? There is a great deal of evidence that patients with schizophrenia are highly sensitive to stress. Consistent with the diathesis-stress model, environmental stress is thought to interact with preexisting biological vulnerabilities to increase the probability of relapse (Nuechterlein et al., 1992). We know, for example, that independent stressful life events occur more frequently just prior to psychotic relapse than at other times (Ventura et al., 1989, 1992) and may exert their effects over longer periods of time too. Furthermore, in a thoughtful review, Walker and Diforio (1997) note that one of the primary manifestations of the stress response in humans is the release of cortisol (a glucocorticoid) from the adrenal cortex. Animal and human studies show that cortisol release triggers dopamine activity (McMurray et al., 1991; Rothschild et al., 1985). Glucocorticoid secretion also affects glutamate release (Walker & Diforio, 1997). In other words, two of the major neurotransmitters implicated in schizophrenia (dopamine and glutamate) are affected by cortisol, which is released when we are stressed.

Along these lines, Hooley and Gotlib (2000) have suggested that, to the extent that high-EE behaviors exhibited by family members are perceived as stressful by patients, these behaviors are likely to trigger the release of cortisol. In support of this idea, high-EE relatives have been found to be more behaviorally controlling of patients than low-EE relatives are (Hooley & Campbell, 2002). When they try to help, they seem to do so in rather intrusive ways (e.g., "She wouldn't go to sleep so I held her head down onto the pillow"). Furthermore, controlling behaviors such as these predict relapse in patients with schizophrenia. Quite possibly, relatives' well-meaning attempts to get patients to function better simply backfire. If patients are stressed by what their relatives do, this could increase cortisol levels, affect important neurotransmitter systems, and perhaps eventually lead to a return of symptoms.

At the present time, we have no direct evidence that this happens. However, one study is worthy of note. A group of researchers studied the behavior of patients with schizophrenia when they were involved in interactions with high-EE and low-EE relatives (Rosenfarb et al., 1995). The researchers observed that when patients said something strange (e.g., "If that kid bites you, you'll get rabies"), high-EE relatives tended to respond by being critical of the patient. What was interesting was that when this happened, it tended to be followed by another unusual remark from the patient. In other words, an increase in patients' unusual thinking occurred immediately after the patient was criticized by a family member. Although other interpretations of the findings are possible, the results of this study are consistent with the idea that negative (stress-inducing) behaviors by relatives can trigger increases in unusual thinking in patients with schizophrenia. Although we have no way of knowing what was happening to the cortisol levels of these patients, it is intriguing to speculate that increased cortisol release might somehow be involved.

Researchers are now using functional neuroimaging techniques to learn more directly how EE affects to brain. Recent findings show that hearing criticism or being exposed to emotionally overinvolved comments leads to different patterns of brain activity in people who are vulnerable to psychopathology compared to healthy controls (Hooley et al., 2010; Hooley et al., 2009). We do not yet know if people who show this pattern of brain activation are at increased risk of relapse, although this might be expected.

URBAN LIVING Being raised in an urban environment seems to increase a person's risk of developing schizophrenia. Pederson and Mortensen (2001) studied a sample of 1.9 million people in Denmark, a country in which information about where people live is recorded in a national registry and people have to notify authorities when they change addresses in order to retain eligibility for benefits. The researchers found that

Research suggests that growing up in an urban environment increases a person's risk of developing schizophrenia in adulthood.

children who had spent the first 15 years of their lives living in an urban environment were 2.75 times more likely to develop schizophrenia in adulthood than were children who had spent their childhoods in more rural settings. Other methodologically sound studies also confirm this association (Sundquist et al., 2004). It has been estimated that if this risk factor could be removed (that is, if we all lived in relatively rural settings) the number of cases of schizophrenia could decrease by about 30 percent (see Brown, 2011).

IMMIGRATION The findings showing that urban living raises a person's risk for developing schizophrenia suggest that stress or social adversity might be important factors to consider with respect to this disorder. Supporting this idea, research is also showing that recent immigrants have much higher risks of developing schizophrenia than do people who are native to the country of immigration. Looking at the results of 40 different studies involving immigrant groups from many different parts of the world, Cantor-Graae and Selten (2005) found that

Patients with schizophrenia who live in families where there is a high level of emotional tension have more than twice the risk of relapse.

first-generation immigrants (i.e., those born in another country) had 2.7 times the risk of developing schizophrenia; for second-generation immigrants (i.e., those with one or both parents having been born abroad), the relative risk was even higher at 4.5. In other words, there is something about moving to another country that appears to be a risk factor for developing schizophrenia. The following case study illustrates this.

Immigration has been found to be a risk factor for developing schizophrenia. People who leave their native land to live in another country have almost 3 times the risk of developing schizophrenia compared to people who remain living in their home country. What factors may contribute to this increased risk?

case study | Schizophrenia in an Immigrant from China

A young Chinese woman was sent by her parents to live in Ireland after she lost her job in China and was unable to find another. She enrolled in language school and subsequently began to study for a master's degree in business administration. Initially she lived in a boarding house, moving later to live in a house with eight other young Chinese. Those who knew her described her as a private person who did not have many friends. She spent her time alone reading or playing solitary games.

After she learned of the unnatural deaths of two young Chinese nationals in Dublin, the young Chinese woman became extremely alarmed. She left the language school and moved back with her old landlady from the boarding house. She developed a belief that a "presence" was living in her abdomen. She also reported that multiple voices were coming from the "presence." The voices spoke Chinese and English, and they included the voices of her family, her landlady, and teachers in her language school. She also reported that the picture on a banknote that she had recently received from her family in China spoke to her, stating, "You are no longer welcome here." In addition, she developed the belief that the family with whom she had grown up was not her real family. She immediately cut off contact with them and expressed a wish to contact her "real" mother. She also stated that the CIA was looking for her but could provide no explanation of why this should be the case. (Adapted from Feeney et al., 2002.)

Why should immigration be associated with an elevated risk of developing schizophrenia? One possibility is that immigrants are more likely to receive this diagnosis because of cultural misunderstandings (Sashidharan, 1993). However, there is no convincing evidence that this is the case (Harrison et al., 1999; Takei et al., 1998). Another hypothesis is that people who are genetically predisposed to develop schizophrenia are more likely to move to live in another country. However, some of the impairments associated with the early stages of schizophrenia seem incompatible with this idea because negative symptoms and frontal lobe dysfunctions may make it harder to be organized enough to emigrate (see Cantor-Graae & Selten, 2005).

Perhaps the strongest clue comes from the finding that immigrants with darker skin have a much higher risk of developing schizophrenia than do immigrants with lighter skin (Cantor-Graae & Selten, 2005). This raises the possibility that experiences of being discriminated against could lead some immigrants to develop a paranoid and suspicious outlook on the world, which could set the stage for the development of schizophrenia. In support of this idea, the results of a prospective study show that healthy people who felt discriminated against were more likely to develop psychotic symptoms over time than were healthy people who did not perceive any discrimination (Janssen et al., 2003). Another possibility suggested by animal studies is that the stress that results from social disadvantage and social defeat may have an effect on dopamine release or dopamine activity in key neural circuits (Tidey & Miczek, 1996). Moreover, some of these biological changes could make people more sensitive to the effects of using illicit substances (Miczek et al., 2004). This is especially interesting in light of new evidence linking cannabis abuse to the development of schizophrenia.

CANNABIS ABUSE People with schizophrenia are twice as likely as people in the general population to smoke cannabis (van Os et al., 2002). This has prompted researchers to ask whether there is a causal link between cannabis abuse and the development of psychosis. A methodologically rigorous study of conscripts to the Swedish army shows that, compared to those who had never used cannabis, young men who were heavy cannabis users by the time they were 18 were more than six times more likely to have developed schizophrenia 27 years later (Zammit et al., 2002). This association also remained even after people who had used other kinds of drugs were removed from the statistical analysis.

Other studies have now replicated this link (Arsenault et al., 2002, 2004; Fergusson et al., 2003; van Os et al., 2002) and highlighted early cannabis use as being particularly problematic. For example, Arsenault and colleagues (2002) report that 10.3 percent of those who used cannabis by age 15 were diagnosed with signs of schizophrenia by age 26, compared with only 3 percent of the controls who did not use cannabis. Taken together, the research findings suggest that using cannabis during adolescence more than doubles a person's risk of developing schizophrenia at a later stage of life.

A major methodological concern in studies of this kind is whether people who are in the early stages of developing psychosis are more likely to use cannabis. If this were the case, cannabis use would simply be a correlate of schizophrenia and not a cause. However, even after childhood psychotic symptoms are considered and accounted for statistically, cannabis use has still been found to be a predictor of later schizophrenia (Fergusson et al., 2003). Moreover, a meta-analysis involving 8,167 patients with psychosis has shown that those who used cannabis (but not those who used alcohol) had an earlier onset of their symptoms compared to nonusers. These findings are consistent with the idea that cannabis use might trigger or bring forward the onset of psychosis (Large et al., 2011).

Of course, the vast majority of people who use cannabis do not develop schizophrenia. So can we predict who is at higher risk? Using a large population sample, Caspi and colleagues (2005) have reported that people who carry a particular form of the COMT gene (one or two copies of the valine or val allele) are at increased risk for developing psychotic symp- toms (hallucinations or delusions) in adulthood if they used cannabis during adolescence. In contrast, using cannabis has no adverse influence on those who have a different form of the COMT gene (two copies of the methionine or met allele). This is an exciting finding because it illustrates the impor- tance of gene–environment interactions in the development of schizophrenia.

This figure is intentionally omitted from this text.

Why should the val allele of the COMT gene be a risk factor? We do not know exactly. However, the finding is pro- vocative because the COMT gene (which you may recall is on chromosome 22) codes for a protein that plays a role the breakdown of dopamine. One of the active ingredients of can- nabis (called THC) is also thought to increase the synthesis of dopamine. We further know that cannabis makes symptoms worse in patients who already have schizophrenia (D'Souza et al., 2005). So again, we have evidence of the importance of dopamine in schizophrenia and of the problems associated with cannabis use, although how everything fits together re- mains to be discovered.

Finally, we note that new research is showing that canna- bis may actually accelerate the progressive brain changes that seem to go along with schizophrenia. Rais and colleagues (2008) collected brain scan data from 51 patients with recent-onset schizophrenia and 31 healthy controls. Nineteen of the patients were using cannabis (but not other illicit drugs) and 32 patients were not. When MRI scans were conducted again 5 years later, the patients who had continued to use cannabis during this time showed more marked decreases in brain volume relative to the patients who did not use cannabis. The changes in gray matter (brain cell) volume in the healthy controls, cannabis-using patients, and patients who did not use cannabis over the 5-year period are shown in Figure 7. Although both groups of patients lost more brain tissue over time than the healthy controls did, loss of brain tissue was especially pronounced in the patients who used cannabis. The conclusion is obvious. If you have schizophrenia, cannabis is probably very bad for your brain.

A Diathesis-Stress Model of Schizophrenia

Biological factors undoubtedly play a role in the etiology of schizophrenia. But genetic predispositions can be shaped by environmental factors such as prenatal exposures, infections, and stressors that occur during critical periods of brain development. Favorable environments may also reduce the chance that a genetic predisposition will result in schizophrenia. As we have discussed, children at genetic risk who are adopted into healthy family environments do very well (Tienari et al., 2004; Wahlberg et al., 1997). What you should take away from this section of the chapter therefore is an understanding that schizophrenia is a genetically influenced, not a genetically determined, disorder (Gottesman, 2001).

The diathesis-stress model, whose origins largely derive from schizophrenia research, predicts exactly these sorts of scenarios (e.g., Walker & Diforio, 1997; Zubin & Spring, 1977). Figure 8 provides a general summary of the interplay between genetic factors, prenatal events, brain maturational processes, and stress in the development of schizophrenia.

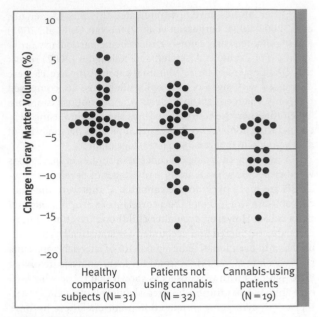

FIGURE 7

Brain Volume Changes over 5 Years in Schizophrenia Patients and Healthy Comparison Subjects

Patients with schizophrenia who also use cannabis show more loss of gray matter over the course of a 5-year follow-up than patients who do not use cannabis or healthy controls.
Source: American Journal of Psychiatry. Online by Rais. Copyright 2009 by American Psychiatric Association (Journals). Reproduced with permission of American Psychiatric Association (Journals) in the format Textbook via Copyright Clearance Center.

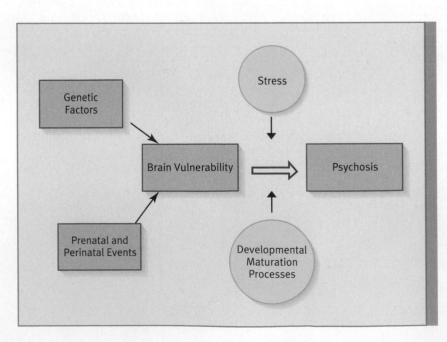

FIGURE 8

A Diathesis-Stress Model of Schizophrenia

Genetic factors and acquired constitutional factors (such as prenatal events and birth complications) combine to result in brain vulnerability. Normal maturational processes, combined with stress factors (family stress, cannabis use, urban living, immigration, etc.), may push the vulnerable person across the threshold and into schizophrenia.

The bottom line is that there is no simple answer to the question of what causes schizophrenia. The etiology of this disorder (or group of related disorders) is complicated and complex. In the case of a person who develops schizophrenia, predisposing genetic factors must have combined in additive and interactive ways with multiple environmental risk factors, some known and some still unknown, that operate prenatally, perinatally, and also postnatally (see Gottesman, 2001; Walker & Tessner, 2008). The net result of this is that brain pathways develop abnormally. It is also very likely that these same pathways can be damaged in a host of different ways (in much the same way as a car engine can be damaged by lack of oil, lack of coolant, or from using the wrong kind of fuel). In other words, lots of roads may lead to the same end point, which is schizophrenia or a schizophrenia-like illness. This helps explain why past efforts to find the single cause of schizophrenia were doomed to fail, although no one could know this at the time. How we are born and how we live makes a major contribution. As one researcher has so aptly stated, "Schizophrenia may be the uniquely human price we pay as a species for the complexity of our brain; in the end, more or less by genetic and environmental chance, some of us get wired for psychosis" (Gilmore, 2010, p. 9).

In Review

- What evidence supports a genetic contribution to schizophrenia?

- What is the dopamine hypothesis? Describe the current status of this explanation for schizophrenia.

- What neuroanatomical abnormalities differentiate people with schizophrenia from people who do not suffer from this disorder?

- What environmental factors are important in the development of schizophrenia?

- Why is avoiding cannabis so important for people with schizophrenia?

- Why do we believe that schizophrenia is both a developmental and a neuroprogressive disorder?

- Why is the diathesis-stress perspective so appropriate for understanding schizophrenia?

Treatments and Outcomes

Before the 1950s the prognosis for schizophrenia was bleak. Treatment options were very limited. Agitated patients might be put in straitjackets or treated with electroconvulsive "shock" therapy. Most lived in remote and forbidding institutions that they were expected never to leave (Deutsch, 1948).

Dramatic improvement came in the 1950s when a class of drugs known as antipsychotics were introduced. Pharmacotherapy (treatment by drugs) with these medications rapidly transformed the environment of mental hospitals by calming patients and virtually eliminating their wild, dangerous, and out-of-control behaviors. A new and more hopeful era had arrived.

Clinical Outcome

Studies of clinical outcome show that 15 to 25 years after developing schizophrenia, around 38 percent of patients have a generally favorable outcome and can be thought of as being recovered (Harrison et al., 2001). This does not mean that patients return to how they were before they became ill, however. Rather, it means that with the help of therapy and medications, patients can function quite well. Unfortunately, only around 16 percent of patients recover to the extent that they no longer need any treatment. Moreover, for a minority of patients (around 12 percent), long-term institutionalization is necessary. Finally, around a third of patients show continued signs of illness, usually with prominent negative symptoms. In other words, although things now are a great deal better than they were 50 or 60 years ago, a "cure" for schizophrenia has not materialized.

Interestingly, patients who live in less industrialized countries tend to do better overall than patients who live in more industrialized nations (Jablensky et al., 1992). This may be because levels of expressed emotion are much lower in countries such as India than in the United States and Europe. For example, in highly industrialized cultures, more than 50 percent of families are high in expressed emotion. In contrast, studies with Mexican American and Hindi-speaking Indian samples show that only 24 percent and 41 percent of families, respectively, are high in EE (see Karno et al., 1987; Leff et al., 1987). These differences may help explain why the clinical outcome of patients is different in different parts of the world.

Sometimes, patients who have been very severely impaired by schizophrenia show considerable improvement late in the course of their illness. These spontaneous improvements can occur even when there is no change in the medications that patients are taking.

MORTALITY The health risks of having schizophrenia cannot be understated. This is a disorder that reduces life expectancy. Recent data from the United Kingdom show that men with schizophrenia die 14.6 years earlier than would be expected based on national norms. For women with schizoaffective disorder the reduction in lifespan is 17.5 years (Chang et al., 2011). Some of the factors implicated in the early deaths of patients with schizophrenia and schizophrenia-related illnesses are long-term use of antipsychotic medications, obesity, smoking, poor diet, use of illicit drugs, and lack of physical activity. The risk of suicide in patients with schizophrenia is also high compared to the general population, with about 12 percent of patients

From Impairment to Improvement

`case study`

The patient is a 46-year-old man who first became ill when he was 17 years old. At the time his illness began, he was hearing voices and he had grandiose delusions. He also had delusions of being persecuted.

By the time he was 30, he was living in the hospital. He experienced continuous symptoms including delusions, hallucinations, and incoherent speech. His self-care was also very poor. His symptoms showed only minimal improvement after he was treated with clozapine.

Spontaneous clinical improvement was noted when the patient was in his forties. He became less isolated and he began to spend more time doing activities. Although he had previously been incoherent when he spoke, he began to speak rationally, although there was still some poverty in the content of his speech. His self-care also improved. However, hospital staff still needed to prompt him to bathe and change his clothes. (Adapted from Murray et al., 2004.)

ending their lives in this way (Dutta et al., 2010). In general, overall mortality is lower in patients who are treated with antipsychotic medications compared to untreated patients (Tiihonen et al., 2011). This no doubt reflects the extent to which people who are actively psychotic are a risk to themselves.

Pharmacological Approaches

Medications are widely used in the treatment of schizophrenia. Over 60 different antipsychotic drugs have been developed. The common property that they all share is their ability to block dopamine D2 receptors in the brain (Seeman, 2011).

FIRST-GENERATION ANTIPSYCHOTICS First-generation **antipsychotics** are medications like chlorpromazine (Thorazine) and haloperidol (Haldol), which were among the first to be used to treat psychotic disorders. Sometimes referred to as **neuroleptics** (literally, "seizing the neuron"), these medications revolutionized the treatment of schizophrenia when they were introduced in the 1950s and can be regarded as one of the major medical advances of the twentieth century (Sharif et al., 2007). They are called first-generation antipsychotics (or typical antipsychotics) to distinguish them from a new class of antipsychotics that was developed much more recently. These are referred to as second-generation (or atypical) antipsychotics.

There is overwhelming evidence that antipsychotic medications help patients. Large numbers of clinical trials have demonstrated the efficacy and effectiveness of these drugs (Sharif et al., 2007). Also, the earlier patients receive these medications, the better they tend to do over the longer term (Marshall et al., 2005; Perkins et al., 2004). As we discussed earlier, first-generation antipsychotics are thought to work because they are dopamine antagonists. This means that they block the action of dopamine, primarily by blocking (occupying) the D2 dopamine receptors.

Some clinical change can be seen within the first 24 hours of treatment (Kapur et al., 2005). This supports the idea that these medications work by interfering with dopamine transmission at the D2 receptors because dopamine blockade begins within hours after the patient is given the medication. However, it may take several weeks or even months for maximal clinical benefit to be achieved, although how a patient does on a particular medication in the first 2 to 4 weeks of treatment is a good predictor of how much he or she will benefit overall (Tandon et al., 2010).

First-generation antipsychotics work best for the positive symptoms of schizophrenia. In quieting the voices and diminishing delusional beliefs, these medications provide patients with significant clinical improvement (Tandon et al., 2010). This comes at a cost, however. Common side effects of these medications include drowsiness, dry mouth, and weight gain. Many patients on these antipsychotics also experience what are known as *extrapyramidal side effects* (EPS). These are involuntary movement abnormalities (muscle spasms, rigidity, shaking) that resemble Parkinson's disease.

African Americans and other ethnic minorities appear to be at increased risk of extrapyramidal side effects (Lawson, 2008). Such side effects are usually controlled by taking other medications. Some patients who have been treated with neuroleptics for long periods of time may also develop *tardive dyskinesia*. This involves marked involuntary movements of the lips and tongue (and sometimes the hands and neck). Rates of tardive dyskinesia are about 56 percent when patients have taken neuroleptics for 10 years or more, with females being especially susceptible (Bezchlibnyk-Butler & Jeffries, 2003). Finally, in very rare cases there is a toxic reaction to the medication that is called *neuroleptic malignant syndrome* (Strawn et al., 2007). This condition is characterized by high fever and extreme muscle rigidity, and if left untreated it can be fatal.

SECOND-GENERATION ANTIPSYCHOTICS In the 1980s a new class of antipsychotic medications began to appear. The first of these to be used clinically was clozapine (Clozaril). This drug was introduced in the United States in 1989, although clinicians in Europe had been using it prior to this. Although initially reserved for use with treatment-refractory patients (those who were not helped by other medications), clozapine is now used widely.

Other examples of second-generation antipsychotic medications are risperidone (Risperdal), olanzapine (Zyprexa), quetiapine (Seroquel), and ziprasidone (Geodon). More recent additions include aripiprazole (Abilify) and lurasidone (Latuda). The reason why these medications are called "second-generation antipsychotics" is that they cause fewer extrapyramidal symptoms than the earlier antipsychotic medications such as Thorazine and Haldol. Although it was initially believed that second-generation antipsychotics were more effective at treating the symptoms of schizophrenia, recent research findings provide no support for this view (Lieberman & Stroup, 2011; Tandon et al., 2010). The exception here concerns clozapine, which does seem to be more valuable than other medications for treatment refractory patients. Nonetheless, most patients are now treated with these newer (and more expensive) medications.

Although they are less likely to cause movement problems, the newer neuroleptic medications are not without other side effects. Drowsiness and considerable weight gain are very common. Diabetes is also a very serious concern (Sernyak et al., 2002). In rare cases, clozapine also causes a life-threatening drop in white blood cells known as agranulocytosis. For this reason, patients taking this medication must have regular blood tests.

The disappointing findings about the efficacy of second-generation antipsychotic treatments mean that there is an urgent need for innovative approaches and new medications that work better than the ones currently available. This is all the more important in light of new research showing that antipsychotic medications may actually contribute to the progressive brain tissue loss we see in schizophrenia (Ho et al., 2011).

In the meantime, researchers continue to seek other ways to help patients. As Box 4 shows, one interesting new approach involves estrogen.

THE PATIENT'S PERSPECTIVE Not all patients benefit from antipsychotic medications, and many who do show clinical improvement will still have problems functioning without a great deal of additional help. We must also not lose sight of what it is like for patients with schizophrenia to have to take medications every day, often for years or for a lifetime. Side effects that can sound trivial to someone on the outside can be so bad for patients that they refuse to take their medications, even when those medications give them relief from their hallucinations and delusions.

Research using PET also shows that increased blockade of D2 dopamine receptors is associated with patients reporting more negative subjective experiences such as feeling tired and depressed even when other side effects (such as movement problems) are absent (Mizrahi et al., 2007). This highlights the need for better medications and for using lower dosages wherever this is clinically feasible. We also need to remember that

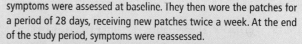

4 THE WORLD AROUND US

Using Estrogen to Help Patients with Schizophrenia

At the beginning of the chapter, you learned that women with schizophrenia tend to do better than men. They have a later age of onset and, often, seem to have a less severe form of the illness. This has prompted some researchers to explore the potentially beneficial role of estrogen in the treatment of the disorder (see Kulkarni et al., 2008).

In an interesting study, 102 young women with schizophrenia (all of whom were receiving antipsychotic medications) were randomly assigned to one of two conditions. Some were given a transdermal (skin) patch containing estrogen; the others received a similar (placebo) patch that contained no active ingredient. The women's

symptoms were assessed at baseline. They then wore the patches for a period of 28 days, receiving new patches twice a week. At the end of the study period, symptoms were reassessed.

What were the findings? Remarkably, the women who had worn the genuine (estrogen containing) patches reported significantly fewer overall symptoms at the end of the 1-month study compared to the placebo group, with the difference for positive symptoms (shown in Figure 9) being most striking. Overall, the results suggest that estrogen has antipsychotic effects and that providing supplemental estrogen to women with schizophrenia may give them additional clinical benefits.

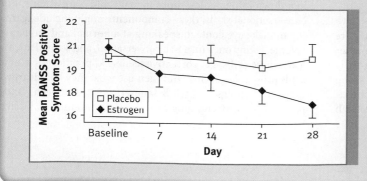

FIGURE 9

Estrogen Treatment and Positive Symptoms

Positive symptoms at baseline (day 0) and on days 7, 14, 21, and 28 for the estrogen and placebo groups.

Source: Figure 3 from Kulkarni et al. (2008). *Arch, Gen, Psychiat.,* 65(8), 958. © 2008 American Medical Association. Reprinted with permission.

Patients with schizophrenia benefit from psychosocial treatments. These include individual therapy, case management, cognitive remediation and family therapy

some patients may try to avoid taking medications because, to them, needing to take medications confirms that they are mentally ill.

This excerpt is intentionally omitted from this text.

Psychosocial Approaches

For a long time, medications were often the only form of treatment that patients with schizophrenia received. But things are now very different. Psychosocial interventions are also now available. Some of these approaches, which are typically used in conjunction with medication, are briefly described below.

FAMILY THERAPY The literature that links relapse in patients with schizophrenia to high family levels of expressed emotion (EE) inspired several investigators to develop family intervention programs. The idea was to reduce relapse in schizophrenia by changing those aspects of the patient–relative relationship that were regarded as central to the EE construct. At a practical level, this generally involves working with patients and their families to educate them about schizophrenia, to help them improve their coping and problem-solving skills, and to enhance communication skills, especially the clarity of family communication.

In general, the results of research studies in this area have shown that patients do better clinically and relapse rates are lower when families receive family treatment (see Pfammatter et al., 2006). Studies done in China indicate that these treatment approaches can also be used in other cultures (Xiong et al., 1994). Despite this, family treatment is still not a routine element in the accepted standard of care for patients with schizophrenia (Lehman et al., 1998). Given its clear benefits to patients and its considerable cost-effectiveness (Tarrier et al. [1991] calculate that family treatment results in an average cost savings of 27 percent per patient), this seems very unfortunate.

CASE MANAGEMENT Case managers are people who help patients find the services they need in order to function in the community. Essentially, the case manager acts as a broker, referring the patient to the people who will provide the needed service (e.g., help with housing, treatment, employment, and the like). Assertive community treatment programs are a specialized form of case management. Typically, they involve multidisciplinary teams with limited caseloads to ensure that discharged patients don't get overlooked and "lost in the system." The multidisciplinary team delivers all the services the patient needs (see DeLuca et al., 2008; Mueser et al., 1998).

Assertive community treatment programs reduce the time that patients spend in the hospital. They also enhance the stability of patients' housing arrangements. These approaches seem to be especially beneficial for patients who are already high utilizers of psychiatric and community services (see Bustillo et al., 2001).

SOCIAL-SKILLS TRAINING Even when their symptoms are controlled by medications, patients with schizophrenia often have trouble forming friendships, finding and keeping a job, or living independently. How well patients do in their everyday lives is referred to as *functional outcome*. (This is in contrast to *clinical outcome*, which is concerned with symptoms.) Improving the functional outcomes of patients with schizophrenia is now an active area of research.

One way to help improve the functional outcomes of patients with schizophrenia is through social-skills training. Patients with schizophrenia often have very poor interpersonal skills (for a review, see Hooley, 2008). Social-skills training is designed to help patients acquire the skills they need to function better on a day-to-day basis. These skills include employment skills, relationship skills, self-care skills, and skills in managing medications or symptoms. Social routines are broken down into smaller, more manageable components. For conversational skills, these components might include learning to make eye contact, speaking at a normal and moderate volume, taking one's turn in a conversation, and so on. Patients learn these skills, get corrective feedback, practice their new skills using role-playing, and then use what they have learned in natural settings (Bellack & Mueser, 1993). As Green (2001, p. 139) has noted, engaging in social-skills training is a bit like taking dance lessons. It does not resemble traditional "talk therapy" in any obvious manner.

Although the results of some early studies were mixed, the most recent research findings look more positive. Social-skills training does seem to help patients acquire new skills, be more assertive, and improve their overall levels of social functioning. These improvements also seem to be maintained over time. Importantly, patients who receive social-skills training are less likely to relapse and need hospital treatment (Kurtz & Mueser, 2008; Pfammatter et al., 2006).

COGNITIVE REMEDIATION Earlier we described some of the cognitive problems that go along with having schizophrenia. Researchers are now recognizing that these cognitive problems are likely to place limits on how well patients can function in the community. Because of this, the neurocognitive deficits of schizophrenia are becoming targets for treatment in their own right. The search is on to develop new medications that will enhance cognitive functioning in patients (Green, 2007; Nuechterlein et al., 2008).

A major treatment effort is also being devoted to **cognitive remediation** training. Using practice and other compensatory techniques, researchers are trying to help patients improve some of their neurocognitive deficits (e.g., problems with verbal memory, vigilance, and performance on card-sorting tasks). The hope is that these improvements will translate into better overall functioning (e.g., conversational skills, self-care, job skills, and so on). Overall, the findings give cause for optimism. Cognitive remediation training does seem to help patients improve their attention, memory, and executive functioning skills. Patients who receive cognitive remediation training also show improvements in their social functioning. Especially encouraging is that even when patients have been ill for many years, they still seem to benefit from this treatment approach (Pfammatter et al., 2006; Wykes et al., 2007). Cognitive remediation approaches may work best when they are added to other existing rehabilitation (employment skills) strategies and offered to patients who are already clinically stable (Wykes et al., 2011).

COGNITIVE-BEHAVIORAL THERAPY As you have already learned, cognitive-behavioral therapy (CBT) approaches are widely used in the treatment of mood and anxiety disorders as well as many other conditions (Beck, 2005). Until fairly recently, however, researchers did not consider using them for patients with schizophrenia, no doubt because patients with schizophrenia were considered too impaired. Pioneered by researchers and clinicians in the United Kingdom, cognitive-behavioral approaches have gained momentum in the treatment of schizophrenia. The goal of these treatments is to decrease the intensity of positive symptoms, reduce relapse, and decrease social disability. Working together, therapist and patient explore the subjective nature of the patient's delusions and hallucinations, examine evidence for and against their veracity or veridicality, and subject delusional beliefs to reality testing.

Although the results from the early research studies were encouraging, whether CBT is an effective treatment for schizophrenia is now the subject of some debate. Current data suggest that CBT is not very helpful for negative symptoms (Tandon et al., 2010). A recent meta-analysis also suggests that CBT is no better than control interventions (often supportive counselling) in the treatment of schizophrenia (Lynch et al., 2010). Nonetheless, the possibility that CBT works very well for some subgroups of patients is still a very real possibility.

INDIVIDUAL TREATMENT Before 1960 the optimal treatment for patients with schizophrenia was psychoanalytically oriented therapy based on a Freudian type of approach. This is what Nobel Prize–winning mathematician John Nash received when he was a patient at McLean Hospital in Massachusetts in 1958 (Nash's story is told in Box 5). By 1980, however, things had changed. Research began to suggest that in some cases, psychodynamic treatments made patients worse (see Mueser & Berenbaum, 1990). This form of individual treatment thus fell out of favor.

Individual treatment for schizophrenia now takes a different form. Hogarty and colleagues (1997a, 1997b) have reported on a controlled 3-year trial of what they call "personal therapy." Personal therapy is a nonpsychodynamic approach that equips patients with a broad range of coping techniques and skills. The therapy is staged, which means that it comprises different components that are administered at different points in the patient's recovery. For example, in the early stages, patients examine the relationship between their symptoms and their stress levels. They also learn relaxation and some cognitive techniques. Later, the focus is on social and vocational skills. Overall, this treatment appears to be very effective in enhancing the social adjustment and social role performance of discharged patients.

Educating patients about the illness and its treatment (this approach is called psychoeducation) is also helpful (Xia et al., 2011). Patients who receive psychoeducation in addition to standard treatment are less likely to relapse or be readmitted to the hospital compared to patients who receive standard treatment only. These patients also function better overall and are more satisfied with the treatment they receive. All of this highlights the importance of including patients in their own care and increasing their knowledge and understanding about their illness.

In summary, although rigorous psychoanalytic approaches may be too demanding and stressful for patients with schizophrenia, supportive forms of therapy that offer an opportunity to learn skills and yet are low-key and responsive to patients' individual concerns might well be

THE WORLD AROUND US

5

A Beautiful Mind

The film *A Beautiful Mind* (based on the book of the same name by Sylvia Nasar, 1998) vividly depicts the descent of Princeton mathematician John Nash into schizophrenia, his subsequent recovery, and his winning of the Nobel Prize in economics. By any measure the film is engaging, disturbing, and wonderfully uplifting. But how accurate is it? What is the real story of John Nash?

John Forbes Nash was born in West Virginia. An exceptional student from a young age, he went on to complete a Ph.D. in the prestigious mathematics department at Princeton. At Princeton Nash rarely went to classes, and he alienated some people with his odd behavior, his arrogance, and his eccentricities. Although we might now regard these as early warning signs of schizophrenia, he did not develop schizophrenia at that time. Rather, he impressed his peers and colleagues by inventing a new board game and developing his ideas about the equilibrium point (the Nash equilibrium), for which he would later win the Nobel Prize.

After graduating from Princeton, Nash took a job at M.I.T., where he was regarded as shamelessly elitist, brash, boastful, and

Princeton mathematician John Nash won the 1994 Nobel Prize for his mathematical contributions to game theory. Nash's struggle with schizophrenia is depicted in the movie *A Beautiful Mind.*

egocentric. His brilliant mind, however, meant that people tolerated his abrasive interpersonal style. In 1953, Nash met Alicia Larde, a talented physics major who was a student in one of his classes. They married in 1957, and all seemed to be well. However, a year later, when Alicia was pregnant, Nash went rapidly downhill. He told colleagues that he was getting coded messages from the *New York Times*, that he had delusions about men in red ties at M.I.T., and that he had turned down a job at the University of Chicago because he was scheduled to become Emperor of Antarctica. He painted black spots on his bedroom wall, and in February 1958 he was hospitalized at McLean Hospital in Belmont, Massachusetts, just a few miles from M.I.T. At McLean he was diagnosed with paranoid schizophrenia and given Thorazine. Contrary to the account in the movie, Nash did not experience visual hallucinations. And even when people with schizophrenia do experience visual hallucinations, the hallucinations rarely seem like real people. More typically, they are fleeting visual "fragments." No doubt the hallucinated roommate and his niece in the movie were a creative

very beneficial. Just as progress in research on schizophrenia requires a partnership between scientists across many areas, progress in the treatment of schizophrenia requires balancing pharmacology with a consideration of the specific needs of the patient. For patients who are at high risk of relapse and who live with their families, family-based interventions will be required. If patients have continuing and disturbing hallucinations and delusions, CBT may be appropriate. When patients are clinically stable, social-skills training and rehabilitation efforts may be helpful. But in all of this, we must not lose sight of the need of patients (and their families) for support, validation, and respectful care. The treatment of patients with schizophrenia is not easy, and there is no "quick fix." Although many treatment advances have occurred, we still need more effective, high-quality, and clinically sensitive care.

In Review

- What kinds of clinical outcomes are associated with schizophrenia? Is full recovery possible or typical?

- Why do patients with schizophrenia have increased rates of early mortality?

- In what ways are first- and second-generation (conventional and atypical) neuroleptic medications similar, and in what ways are they different? How effective are these treatments for patients with schizophrenia?

- Describe the major psychosocial approaches used in treating schizophrenia.

device used to sidestep the fact that delusions (i.e., beliefs) do not play well in a visual medium.

After 50 days in McLean, Nash was released with assistance from his lawyer. He resigned from M.I.T., withdrew all the money from his pension fund, and left for Europe. Fearing for his welfare, Alicia went with him, leaving their baby, Johnny, with Alicia's mother. Nash disappeared while they were in Paris and then spent the next 9 months wandering Europe trying to renounce his U.S. citizenship. He was eventually deported.

When Nash returned to the United States, he and Alicia moved back to Princeton, and Alicia worked to support the family. Nash was offered a job at Princeton but was so delusional that he refused to sign the necessary tax forms and so could not be hired. Within 2 years of leaving McLean he was hospitalized again, this time at Trenton State Hospital in New Jersey. Trenton State was a very different environment from the country-club setting of McLean. It was crowded and full of poorly treated patients. As is accurately depicted in the movie, Nash was treated with insulin coma therapy. This treatment (which had already been phased out in most other hospitals) involved an injection of insulin that led to a rapid decrease in blood sugar, coma, and convulsions. Nash received this therapy 5 days a week for 6 weeks. He was discharged 6 months later with some improvement in his symptoms.

The following year, when he was 34, Nash disappeared to Europe again. He regularly sent friends and family members postcards that were both bizarre and frightening. Later that same year, Alicia filed for divorce.

For the next several years Nash wandered around, sometimes living in Boston, and then abruptly leaving. He began to take antipsychotics and showed some improvement. Then, like many patients, he would abruptly stop taking the medications and his symptoms would come back again. Around this time, Nash also began to hear voices.

By 1970 Nash was essentially indigent. Alicia took pity on him and took him in. She promised not to rehospitalize him and provided him with a supportive home environment. Nash became a regular visitor to Princeton, roaming the campus for a decade and leaving mathematical scribblings on blackboards and windows. He was trying to prove the existence of God through mathematics. The Princeton community was extremely tolerant of him, and slowly, perhaps because he was able to remain in a low-stress environment, Nash began to get better. He later said he willed himself to get better, rejecting what the voices said and deciding not to listen to them. At age 66, remarried to Alicia, he walked in front of the King of Sweden and received the Nobel Prize, to the delight of his jubilant colleagues. His recovery was long in coming, as was the formal recognition of his genius. Sadly, however, the Nash family is not finished dealing with schizophrenia. Nash's son with Alicia, also a mathematician, suffers from the same illness as his father.

Unresolved Issues

▶ *What Is the Best Way to Prevent Schizophrenia?*

Once schizophrenia has developed, most patients are likely to experience recurring positive and negative symptoms, as well as persistent impairments in their work or social functioning for a large part of their lives (Jobe & Harrow, 2010). The idea of preventing this disorder is therefore very appealing. But is this really feasible? What should we do? What are the risks and benefits of the approaches that could be used?

At the societal level, some public health changes could be considered. Because fetal brain damage is implicated in schizophrenia, one approach might involve improving obstetric care for women with schizophrenia and first-degree relatives of schizophrenia patients (see Warner, 2001). This would result in fewer birth complications. Although such a program would not result in a major decline in the incidence of schizophrenia, it has no potential for harm. And if it prevented just a handful of new cases of schizophrenia, the savings in human suffering and money would be far from trivial. In a related vein, it has been suggested that

preventing cannabis abuse in 15-year-olds would reduce the later development of schizophrenia in the population by 8 percent (see Arsenault et al., 2004).

Most of the current efforts to prevent schizophrenia, however, center around early intervention for people who are at high clinical risk of developing the disorder. The idea here is to treat patients in the prodromal stage, before full-blown psychotic symptoms develop. But is it really appropriate and ethical to prescribe antipsychotic medications to someone who has no psychotic symptoms? And what are the risks of doing this? After several research groups published findings showing that treating people who had very-low-level psychotic symptoms with second-generation antipsychotic medications was beneficial, this practice began to be more widely accepted (see Weiser, 2011). Indeed, a new (and highly controversial) diagnostic category, called attenuated psychosis syndrome, has been proposed for *DSM-5* (see Carpenter & van Os, 2011). This would allow people thought to be in the early stages of schizophrenia to be diagnosed and treated.

But do we really want to do this? As you have learned, second-generation antipsychotic medications are not as effective as had been initially hoped. They also appear to be associated with some very undesirable changes (such as tissue loss) in the brain (Ho et al., 2011; Lewis, 2011). Given this, it is important that they only be given to people who truly are on their way to developing psychosis.

How can we accurately identify these people? Current strategies may cast too wide a net. For a period of 2.5 years, Addington and colleagues (2011) followed 303 young adults who were showing prodromal symptoms of schizophrenia. At the end of the follow-up period the majority of these young people (71 percent) had not made the transition into psychosis. Although the follow-up period was relatively short, one take-home message from this study is that the majority of people identified as being at high risk are *not* on their way to developing a psychotic disorder. Routinely prescribing antipsychotics to these people "just in case" is therefore not warranted. The findings of this study also force us to consider whether we should be adding a new diagnostic category to *DSM-5* that will contain so many false positives (people who look like they will develop psychosis but do not). Finally, it is important to recognize that many of the people who did not transition to psychosis still had some difficulties with their cognitive functioning, social functioning, and work skills. Although treatment with antipsychotic medications cannot be justified, providing other forms of psychological help for people in this group remains important.

Summary

- Schizophrenia is the most severe form of mental illness. It is characterized by impairments in many domains and affects just under 1 percent of the population.

- Most cases of schizophrenia begin in late adolescence or early adulthood. The disorder begins earlier in men than in women. Overall, the clinical symptoms of schizophrenia tend to be more severe in men than in women. Women also have a better long-term outcome.

- Characteristic symptoms of schizophrenia include hallucinations, delusions, disorganized speech, disorganized and catatonic behavior, and negative symptoms such as flat affect or social withdrawal.

- Genetic factors are clearly implicated in schizophrenia. Having a relative with the disorder significantly raises a person's risk of developing schizophrenia.

- Other factors that have been implicated in the development of schizophrenia include prenatal exposure to the influenza virus, early nutritional deficiencies, rhesus incompatibility, maternal stress, and perinatal birth complications.

- Current thinking about schizophrenia emphasizes the interplay between genetic and environmental factors.

- Even though schizophrenia first shows itself clinically in early adulthood, researchers believe that it is a neurodevelopmental disorder. Problems with brain development are implicated. Some of the genes implicated in schizophrenia play a role in brain development.

- Patients with schizophrenia have problems in many aspects of their cognitive functioning. They show a variety of attentional deficits (e.g., poor P50 suppression and deficits on the Continuous Performance Test). They also show eye-tracking dysfunctions.

- Many brain areas are abnormal in schizophrenia, although abnormalities are not found in all patients. The brain abnormalities that have been found include enlarged ventricles (which reflects decreased brain volume), frontal lobe dysfunction, reduced volume of the thalamus, and abnormalities in temporal lobe areas such as the hippocampus and amygdala.

- Major changes in the brain occur during adolescence. These include synaptic pruning, decreases in the number of excitatory neurons, and increases in the number of inhibitory neurons. There is also an increase in white matter which enhances the connectivity of the brain. Some of these changes may be abnormal in people who will later develop schizophrenia.

- Some of the brain abnormalities that are characteristic of schizophrenia get worse over time. This suggests that, in addition to being a neurodevelopmental disorder, schizophrenia is also a neuroprogressive disorder.

- The most important neurotransmitters implicated in schizophrenia are dopamine and glutamate. Research shows that the dopamine (D2) receptors of patients with schizophrenia are supersensitive to dopamine.

- Urban living, immigration, and cannabis use during adolescence have been shown to increase the risk of developing schizophrenia.

- Patients with schizophrenia are more likely to relapse if their relatives are high in expressed emotion (EE). High-EE environments may be stressful to patients and may trigger biological changes that cause dysregulations in the dopamine system. This could lead to a return of symptoms.

- For many patients, schizophrenia is a chronic disorder requiring long-term treatment or institutionalization. However, with therapy and medications, around 38 percent of patients can show a reasonable recovery. Only about 16 percent of patients recover to the extent that they no longer need treatment.

- Patients with schizophrenia are usually treated with first- or second-generation antipsychotic (neuroleptic) medications. Second-generation antipsychotics are about as effective as first-generation antipsychotics but cause fewer extrapyramidal (motor abnormality) side effects. Antipsychotic drugs work by blocking dopamine receptors.

- Psychosocial treatments for patients with schizophrenia include cognitive-behavioral therapy, social-skills training, cognitive remediation training, and other forms of individual treatment, as well as case management. Family therapy provides families with communication skills and other skills that are helpful in managing the illness. Family therapy also reduces high levels of expressed emotion.

Key Terms

alogia	disorganized schizophrenia	negative symptoms
antipsychotics (neuroleptics)	disorganized symptoms	paranoid schizophrenia
avolition	dopamine	positive symptoms
brief psychotic disorder	endophenotypes	prodromal
candidate genes	expressed emotion (EE)	psychosis
catatonic schizophrenia	flat affect	schizoaffective disorder
cognitive remediation	glutamate	schizophrenia
delusion	hallucination	schizophreniform disorder
delusional disorder	linkage analysis	shared psychotic disorder

Glossary

Many of the key terms listed in the glossary appear in boldface when first introduced in the text discussion. A number of other terms commonly encountered in this or other psychology texts are also included; you are encouraged to make use of this glossary both as a general reference tool and as a study aid for the course in abnormal psychology.

Alogia. A term referring to poverty of speech a symptom that often occurs in schizophrenia.

Antipsychotics (neuroleptics). Medications that alleviate or diminish the intensity of psychotic symptoms such as hallucinations or delusions.

Avolition. Refers to a psychological state that is characterized by a general lack of drive or motivation to pursue meaningful goals.

Brief psychotic disorder. Brief episodes (lasting a month or less) of otherwise uncomplicated delusional thinking.

Candidate genes. Genes that are of specific interest to researchers because they are thought to be involved in processes that are known to be aberrant in that disorder (e.g., serotonin transporter genes in depression, or dopamine receptor genes in schizophrenia).

Catatonic schizophrenia. See **Schizophrenia, catatonic type.**

Cognitive remediation. Training efforts designed to help patients improve their neurocognitive (e.g., memory, vigilance) skills. The hope is that this will also help improve patients' overall levels of functioning.

Delusion. False belief about reality maintained in spite of strong evidence to the contrary.

Delusional disorder. Nuturing, giving voice to, and sometimes taking action on beliefs that are considered completely false by others; formerly called *paranoia*.

Disorganized schizophrenia. See **Schizophrenia, disorganized type.**

Disorganized symptoms. Symptoms such as bizarre behavior or incomprehensible speech.

Dopamine. Neurotransmitter from the catecholamine family that is initially synthesized from tyrosine, an amino acid common in the diet. Dopamine is produced from l-dopa by the enzyme dopamine decarboxylase.

Endophenotypes. Discrete, measurable traits that are thought to be linked to specific genes that might be important in schizophrenia or other mental disorders.

Expressed emotion (EE). Type of negative communication involving excessive criticism and emotional overinvolvement directed at a patient by family members.

Flat affect. The lack of emotional expression.

Glutamate. An excitatory neurotransmitter that is widespread throughout the brain.

Hallucinations. False perceptions such as things seen or heard that are not real or present.

Linkage analysis. Genetic research strategy in which occurrence of a disorder in an extended family is compared with that of a genetic marker for a physical characteristic or biological process that is known to be located on a particular chromosome. A soft, silver-white metal that belongs to the alkali metal group of chemicals. It is used to treat and prevent episodes of mania and bipolar disorder. botomy. See **Prefrontal lobotomy**.

Negative symptoms. Symptoms that reflect an absence or deficit in normal functions (e.g., blunted affect, social withdrawal).

Paranoid schizophrenia. See **Schizophrenia, paranoid type**.

Positive symptoms. Symptoms that are characterized by something being added to normal behavior or experience. Includes delusions, hallucinations, motor agitation, and marked emotional turmoil.

Prodromal. Considered to be an early (subclinical) stage of schizophrenia, characterized by very low-level symptoms or behavioral idiosyncracies.

Psychosis. Severe impairment in the ability to tell what is real and what is not real.

Schizoaffective disorder. Form of psychotic disorder in which the symptoms of schizophrenia co-occur with symptoms of a mood disorder.

Schizophrenia. Disorder characterized by hallucinations, delusions, disorganized speech and behavior, as well as problems in self care and general functioning.

Schizophreniform disorder. Category of schizophrenic-like psychosis less than 6 months in duration.

Shared psychotic disorder. Psychosis in which two or more people develop persistent, interlocking delusional ideas. Also known as *folie à deux*.

Photo Credits

Credits are listed in order of appearance.

itanistock/Alamy; Vladimir Kirienko/Shutterstock; Phil Borden/PhotoEdit, Inc.; WoodyStock/Alamy; Danny Smythe/Alamy; Grunnitus Studio/Photo Researchers, Inc.; Grunnitus Studio/Photo Researchers, Inc.; Monte S. Buchsbaum, M.D.; Myrleen Pearson/Alamy; Science Photo Library/Alamy; Dr. Elaine F. Walker, PhD; Drs. E. Fuller Torrey and Daniel R. Weinberger; Dr. Paul Thompson; David Shattuck and Paul Thompson/UCLA Laboratory of Neuro Imaging; Kathy deWitt/Alamy; Meletios/Shutterstock; LWA-Dann Tardif/CORBIS/Glow Images; PhotoAlto/Alamy; Ellen McKnight/Alamy; Barry Lewis/Alamy; BOB STRONG/AFP/Getty Images.

Text Credits

Credits are listed in order of appearance.

Figure: From Haffner, H., et al. (1998). Causes and consequences of the gender difference in age at onset of schizophrenia. *Schizophrenia Bulletin*, 24(1), 99–114; "Criteria for Schizophrenia" Reprinted with permission from the *Diagnostic and Statistical Manual of Mental Disorders*, Fourth Edition, *Text Revision*, (Copyright © 2000). American Psychiatric Association; "Anna, the Student with Catatonia" adapted from Üstün, T. B., et al., (1996). ICD-10 casebook. The many faces of mental disorders: Adult case histories according to ICD-10. World Health Organization; "Criteria for Schizoaffective Disorder" Reprinted with permission from the *Diagnostic and Statistical Manual of Mental Disorders*, Fourth Edition, *Text Revision*, (Copyright © 2000). American Psychiatric Association; "Criteria for Schizophreniform Disorder" Reprinted with permission from the *Diagnostic and Statistical Manual of Mental Disorders*, Fourth Edition, *Text Revision*, (Copyright © 2000). American Psychiatric Association; "Criteria for Brief Psychotic Disorder" Reprinted with permission from the *Diagnostic and Statistical Manual of Mental Disorders*, Fourth Edition, *Text Revision*, (Copyright © 2000). American Psychiatric Association; "Criteria for Delusional Disorder" Reprinted with permission from the *Diagnostic and Statistical Manual of Mental Disorders*, Fourth Edition, *Text Revision*, (Copyright © 2000). American Psychiatric Association; "Four Days of Symptoms and Rapid Recovery" adapted from Janowsky, D. S., Addario, D., & Risch, S. C., Pharmacology case studies, 1987, p. 1; "Criteria for Shared Psychotic Disorder" Reprinted with permission from the *Diagnostic and Statistical Manual of Mental Disorders*, Fourth Edition, *Text Revision*, (Copyright © 2000). American Psychiatric Association; Figure: Compiled from family and twin studies in European populations between 1920 and 1987. *From Schizophrenia Genesis: The Origins of Madness* (p. 96), by I. I. Gottesman, 1991; Table: Sources: Eckblad & Chapman, 1983; Chapman et al., 1978. Figure: From Davis, J. O., Phelps, J. A., & Bracha, H. S. (1995). Prenatal development of monozygotic twins and concordance for schizophrenia. *Schizophrenia Bulletin*, 21(3), 357–66. Figure: From Eye Tracking Dysfunction and Schizophrenia: A Critical Perspective by Deborah L. Levy, et al. in *Schizophrenia Bulletin* (1993), 19(3), 461–536; Figure: Courtesy of E. Fuller Torry, M.D., and Daniel Weinberger, M.D.; Figure: Thompson, R. A., & Nelson, C. A. (2001). Developmental science and the media: Early brain development, *American Psychologist*, 56, 5–15; Figure: Figure 7.1 in *Search of Madness: Schizophrenia and Neuroscience* by Heinrichs, R. Walter (2001), Oxford University Press, p. 196, adapted from Arnold, S. E., & Trojanowski, J. Q. (1996). Recent advances in defining the neuropathology of schizophrenia. *Acta Neuropathologie*, 92, 217–231 and Kolb, B., & Wishaw, I. Q. (1996). Fundamentals of human neuropsychology (4th ed.). New York: Freeman; "Schizophrenia in an Immigrant from China" Reproduced courtesy of the *Irish Journal of Psychological Medicine*, Dublin, Ireland; Figure: From Moderation of the Effect of Adolescent-Onset Cannabis Use on Adult Psychosis by a Functional Polymorphism in the Catechol-O-Methyltransferase Gene: Longitudinal Evidence of a Gene X Environment Interaction; Figure: From *American Journal of Psychiatry Online* by Rais, 2009; "From Impairment to Improvement" adapted from Murray, G. K., et al (2004). Spontaneous improvement in severe, chronic schizophrenia and its neurological correlates. *British Journal of Psychiatry* 184, 357–58; "As a parent I also know that medication is not perfect . . ." from Slater, E. (1986). First person account: A parent's view on enforcing medication. *Schizophrenia Bulletin*, 12, 291–92.

Neurocognitive Disorders

From Chapter 14 of *Abnormal Psychology*, Fifteenth Edition. James N. Butcher, Susan Mineka, Jill M. Hooley. Copyright © 2013 by Pearson Education, Inc. All rights reserved.

Neurocognitive Disorders

A Simple Case of Mania?

A highly successful businessman, age 45, with no previous history of psychiatric disorder, began to act differently from his usual self. He seemed driven at work. His working hours gradually increased until finally he was sleeping only 2 to 3 hours a night; the rest of the time he worked. He became irritable and began to engage in uncharacteristic sprees of spending beyond his means.

Although he felt extremely productive and claimed he was doing the work of five men, the man's boss felt otherwise. He was worried about the quality of that work, having observed several recent examples of poor business decisions. Finally, when the man complained of headaches, his boss insisted that he seek help. (Adapted from Jamieson & Wells, 1979.)

The case you have just read concerns a man who, on first glance, looks as if he might be having an episode of mania. In fact, he is suffering from four tumorous masses in his brain. Clues that this man has a brain disorder rather than a mood disorder include the facts that he is experiencing headaches at the same time as a major change in behavior and that he has no prior history of psychopathology (see Taylor, 2000). Clinicians always need to be alert to the possibility that brain impairment itself may be directly responsible for their patients' symptoms. Failure to do so could result in serious diagnostic errors, as when a clinician falsely attributes a mood change to psychological causes and fails to consider a neuropsychological origin such as a brain tumor.

The brain is an astonishing organ. Weighing around 3 pounds and having the consistency of firm jelly, it is the most complex structure in the known universe (Thompson, 2000). It is also the only organ capable of studying and reading about itself. It is involved in every aspect of our lives from eating and sleeping to falling in love. The brain makes decisions, and it contains all the memories that make us who we are. Whether we are physically ill or mentally disturbed, the brain is involved.

Because it is so important, the brain is protected in an enclosed space and covered by a thick outer membrane called the dura mater (literally, "hard mother" in Latin). For further protection, the brain is encased by the skull. The skull is so strong that, if it were placed on the ground and weight were applied very slowly, it could support as much as 3 tons (Rolak, 2001, p. 403)! These anatomical facts alone indicate just how precious the brain is.

Even though it is highly protected, the brain is vulnerable to damage from many sources. When the brain is damaged, cognitive changes result, as you saw in the case study above. Although there may be other signs and symptoms (such as mood or personality changes) as well, changes in cognitive functioning are the most obvious signs of a damaged brain.

In this chapter we focus on disorders that arise because of changes in brain structure, function, or chemistry. In some cases, such as with Parkinson's disease or Alzheimer's disease, these are caused by internal changes that lead to destruction of brain tissue. In others, they result from damage caused by external influences such as trauma from accidents or from the repeated blows to the head that can occur in boxing, soccer, or football.

Why are neurocognitive disorders discussed at all in a text on abnormal psychology? There are several reasons. First, as their inclusion in the *DSM* indicates, these disorders are regarded as psychopathological conditions. Second, as you just saw in the **case study** above, some brain disorders cause symptoms that look remarkably like other abnormal psychology disorders. Third, brain damage can cause changes in behavior, mood, and personality. You will recognize this more clearly later when we describe the case of Phineas Gage (who survived a metal bar being blown through his head). Understanding what brain areas are involved when behavior, mood, and personality change after brain damage may help researchers better understand the biological underpinnings of many problems in abnormal psychology. Fourth, many people who suffer from brain disorders (for example, people who are diagnosed as having Alzheimer's disease) react to the news of their diagnosis with depression or anxiety. Prospective studies also suggest that depressive symptoms may herald the onset of disorders such as Alzheimer's disease by several years and that episodes of depression can double the risk for Alzheimer's disease even 20 years later (Speck et al., 1995). Finally, neurocognitive disorders of the type we describe in this chapter take a heavy toll on family members, who, for many patients, must shoulder the burden of care. Again, depression and anxiety in relatives of the patients themselves are not uncommon.

Brain Impairment in Adults

The causes of neurocognitive disorders are often much more specific than is the case for many of the disorders we have discussed so far in this text. In *DSM-IV* these disorders are listed in a section called "Delirium, Dementia, and Amnestic and Other Cognitive Disorders" (see APA, 2000). However, some important changes are proposed for *DSM-5*. These are described in Box 1.

Clinical Signs of Brain Damage

With a few exceptions, cell bodies and neural pathways in the brain do not appear to have the power of regeneration, which means that their destruction

RESEARCH CLOSE-UP

Case Study

Case studies are descriptions of one specific case. Case studies can be a useful source of information and can help researchers generate hypotheses. Because of their highly selective nature, however, they cannot be used to draw any scientific conclusions.

THE WORLD AROUND US

Anticipating *DSM-5*: New Category, New Diagnoses

In *DSM-5*, the disorders now known as "Delirium, Dementia, and Amnestic and Other Cognitive Disorders" will be part of a newly proposed category called Neurocognitive Disorders. Subsections of this diagnostic category will include delirium, major neurocognitive disorder (formerly dementia), and a new category of minor neurocognitive disorder. The distinction between major and minor neurocognitive disorder will basically be one of severity.

Within each broad diagnostic category the specific diagnosis will be determined by what is thought to be the cause of the problem.

For example, the diagnosis of major neurocognitive disorder associated with Alzheimer's disease will be used for patients thought to have Alzheimer's. For patients whose brain damage is caused by a traumatic brain injury the diagnosis will be major (or minor) neurocognitive disorder associated with traumatic brain injury. In this way the diagnosis provides information about both the cause of the neurocognitive disorder as well as its degree of severity.

---

is permanent. When brain injury occurs in an older child or adult, there is a loss in established functioning. Often, the person who has sustained this loss is painfully aware of what he or she is no longer able to do, adding a pronounced psychological burden to the physical burden of having the lesion. In other cases the impairment may extend to the capacity for realistic self-appraisal (a condition called anosognosia), leaving these patients relatively unaware of their losses and hence poorly motivated for rehabilitation.

The degree of mental impairment is usually related to the degree of damage to the brain. However, this is not invariably so. Much depends on the nature and location of the damage as well as the premorbid (predisorder) competence and personality of the individual. In some cases involving relatively severe brain damage, mental change is astonishingly slight. In other cases of

seemingly mild and limited damage, there may be quite marked alterations in functioning, as in the following case example.

Diffuse Versus Focal Damage

The disorders discussed in this section are characterized by neurocognitive problems, although psychopathological problems (such as psychosis or mood change for example) may also be associated with them. Some of these disorders are generally well understood, with symptoms that have relatively constant features in people whose brain injuries are comparable in location and extent. For example, attention is often impaired by mild to moderate *diffuse*—or widespread—damage, such as might occur with moderate oxygen deprivation or the ingestion of toxic substances such as mercury. Such a person may

---

case study Hit on the Head with a Rake

A 17-year-old girl was referred by her father for neuropsychiatric evaluation because of the many changes that had been observed in her personality during the past 2 years. She had been an A student and had been involved in many extracurricular activities during her sophomore year in high school. But now, as a senior, she was barely able to maintain a C average, was "hanging around with the bad kids," and was frequently using marijuana and alcohol. A careful history revealed that 2 years before, her older brother had hit her in the forehead with a rake, which stunned her but did not cause her to lose consciousness. Although she had a headache after the accident, no psychiatric or neurological follow-up was pursued.

Neuropsychological testing at the time of evaluation revealed a significant decline in intellectual functioning from her "preinjury" state. Testing revealed poor concentration, attention, memory, and reasoning abilities. Academically, she was unable to "keep up" with the friends she had had before her injury. She began to socialize with a group of students who had little interest in academics, and she began to see herself as a rebel. When the neuropsychological test results were explained to the patient and her family as a consequence of the brain injury, she and her family were able to understand the "defensive" reaction to her changed social behavior. (Adapted from Silver et al., 2002.)

complain of memory problems due to an inability to sustain focused retrieval efforts, while his or her ability to store new information remains intact.

This table is intentionally omitted from this text

In an illustration of this, LoSasso and colleagues (2001, 2002) found that nail salon technicians reported significantly more cognitive and neurological impairments than controls did. The nail salon technicians also performed more poorly than the controls on tests of attention and information processing. This is likely due to routine exposure to (meth)acrylates and a variety of organic solvents such as toluene, acetone, and formaldehyde that are known to be potentially damaging to the central nervous system. Such findings highlight the consequences of even low-level exposure to neurotoxic substances that can be found in places where many people work and where many others routinely visit.

In contrast to diffuse damage, *focal* brain lesions involve circumscribed areas of abnormal change in brain structure. This is the kind of damage that might occur with a sharply defined traumatic injury or an interruption of blood supply (a stroke) to a specific part of the brain. Figure 1 explains how a stroke occurs.

The location and extent of the damage determine what problems the patient will have. As you are aware, the brain is highly specialized. Although the two hemispheres are closely interrelated, they are involved in somewhat different types of mental processing. At the risk of oversimplifying, it is generally accepted that functions that are dependent on serial processing of familiar information, such as language and solving mathematical equations, take place mostly in the left hemisphere for nearly everyone. Conversely, the right hemisphere appears to be generally specialized for grasping overall meanings in novel situations; reasoning on a nonverbal, intuitive level; and appreciating of spatial relations. Even within hemispheres, the various lobes and regions mediate specialized functions (see Figure 2).

Although none of these relationships between brain location and behavior can be considered universally true, it is possible to make broad generalizations about the likely effects of damage to particular parts of the brain. Damage to the frontal areas, for example, is associated with one of two contrasting clinical pictures: (1) being unmotivated and passive and with limited thoughts and ideas or (2) featuring

The brain can be damaged by exposure to solvents. Nail studios frequently use a variety of organic solvents that are known to be potentially damaging to the central nervous system.

impulsiveness and distractibility. Damage to specific areas of the right parietal lobe may produce impairment of visual-motor coordination, and damage to the left parietal area may impair certain aspects of language function, including reading and writing, as well as arithmetical abilities. Damage to certain structures within the temporal lobes disrupts an early stage of memory storage. Extensive bilateral temporal damage can produce a syndrome in which remote memory remains relatively intact but nothing new can be stored for later retrieval. Damage to other structures within the temporal lobes is associated with disturbances of eating, sexuality, and emotion. Occipital damage produces a variety of visual impairments and visual association deficits, the nature of the deficit depending on the particular site of the lesion. For example, a person may be unable to recognize familiar faces. Unfortunately, many types of brain disease are general and therefore diffuse in their destructive effects, causing multiple and widespread interruptions of the brain's circuitry. Some consequences of brain disorders are described in Table 1.

The Neurocognitive/Psychopathology Interaction

Most people who have a neurocognitive disorder do not develop psychopathological symptoms such as panic attacks, dissociative episodes, or delusions. However, many show at least mild deficits in cognitive processing and self-regulation. Similarly, some people who suffer from

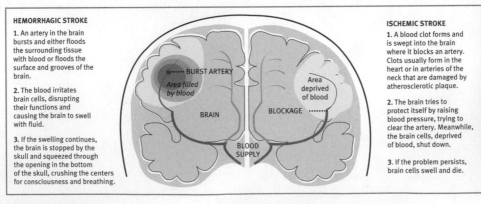

HEMORRHAGIC STROKE

1. An artery in the brain bursts and either floods the surrounding tissue with blood or floods the surface and grooves of the brain.

2. The blood irritates brain cells, disrupting their functions and causing the brain to swell with fluid.

3. If the swelling continues, the brain is stopped by the skull and squeezed through the opening in the bottom of the skull, crushing the centers for consciousness and breathing.

BURST ARTERY
Area filled by blood
BRAIN
BLOOD SUPPLY
Area deprived of blood
BLOCKAGE

ISCHEMIC STROKE

1. A blood clot forms and is swept into the brain where it blocks an artery. Clots usually form in the heart or in arteries of the neck that are damaged by atherosclerotic plaque.

2. The brain tries to protect itself by raising blood pressure, trying to clear the artery. Meanwhile, the brain cells, deprived of blood, shut down.

3. If the problem persists, brain cells swell and die.

FIGURE 1

How a Stroke Occurs

Most strokes occur when an artery in the brain is blocked by a clot. The others, about 13 percent of strokes, occur when a brain artery bursts. Both types can be disastrous.

Source: Dr. Steven Warach, National Institute of Neurological Disorders and Stroke; American Heart Association.

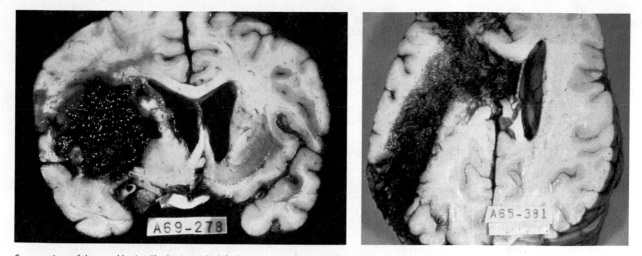

Cross sections of damaged brains. The brain on the left shows damage from a stroke. Damage from a bullet is shown on the right.

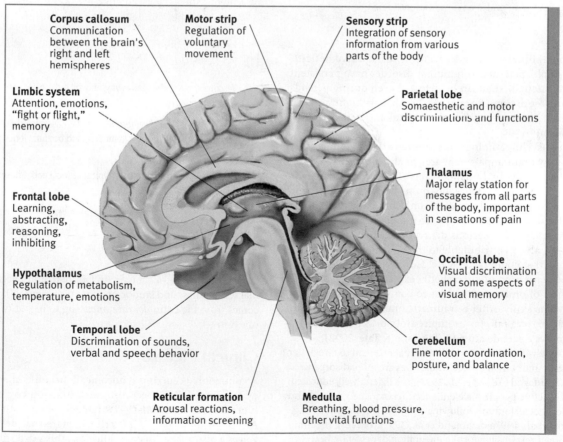

Corpus callosum
Communication between the brain's right and left hemispheres

Motor strip
Regulation of voluntary movement

Sensory strip
Integration of sensory information from various parts of the body

Limbic system
Attention, emotions, "fight or flight," memory

Parietal lobe
Somaesthetic and motor discriminations and functions

Frontal lobe
Learning, abstracting, reasoning, inhibiting

Thalamus
Major relay station for messages from all parts of the body, important in sensations of pain

Hypothalamus
Regulation of metabolism, temperature, emotions

Occipital lobe
Visual discrimination and some aspects of visual memory

Temporal lobe
Discrimination of sounds, verbal and speech behavior

Cerebellum
Fine motor coordination, posture, and balance

Reticular formation
Arousal reactions, information screening

Medulla
Breathing, blood pressure, other vital functions

FIGURE 2

Brain Structures and Associated Behaviors

table 1 Impairments Associated with Brain Disorders

The following types of difficulties are often the consequences of brain disease, disorder, or damage.

1. *Impairment of memory.* The individual has trouble remembering recent events, although memory for past events may remain more intact. Some patients with memory problems may confabulate—that is, invent memories to fill in gaps. In severe instances, no new experience can be retained for more than a few minutes.

2. *Impairment of orientation.* The individual may not know where he or she is, what the day is, or who familiar people are.

3. *Impairment of learning, comprehension, and judgment.* The individual's thinking becomes clouded, sluggish, or inaccurate. The person may lose the ability to plan with foresight or to understand abstract concepts and hence to process complex information (described as "thought impoverishment").

4. *Impairment of emotional control or modulation.* The individual is emotionally overreactive: laughing, crying, or flying into a rage with little provocation.

5. *Apathy or emotional blunting.* The individual is emotionally underreactive and seems indifferent to people or events.

6. *Impairment in the initiation of behavior.* The individual lacks self-starting capability and may have to be reminded repeatedly about what to do next, even when the behavior involved remains well within the person's range of competence. This is sometimes referred to as "loss of executive function."

7. *Impairment of controls over matters of propriety and ethical conduct.* The individual may manifest a marked lowering of personal standards in areas such as appearance, personal hygiene, sexuality, or language.

8. *Impairment of receptive and expressive communication.* The individual may be unable to comprehend written or spoken language or may be unable to express his or her own thoughts orally or in writing.

9. *Impaired visuospatial ability.* The individual has difficulty coordinating motor activity with the characteristics of the visual environment, a deficit that affects graphomotor (handwriting and drawing) and constructional (e.g., assembling things) performance.

psychopathological disorders also have cognitive deficits. For example, patients with bipolar disorder have persistent cognitive deficits that can be detected even during periods of illness remission (Bora et al., 2011). This highlights the close link between psychopathological and neuropsychological conditions.

The psychopathological symptoms that do sometimes accompany brain impairment are not always predictable and can reflect individual nuances consistent with the patient's age (see Tateno et al., 2002), her or his prior personality, and the total psychological situation confronting the patient. We should also never just assume that a psychological disorder—for example, a serious depression that follows a brain injury—is always attributable to the patient's brain damage. Certainly that could be the case. However, it is also possible that the depression might be better explained by the patient's awareness of dramatically lessened competence and the loss of previous skills. After a traumatic brain injury caused by an accident or a fall, for example, around 18 percent of patients make a suicide attempt (Simpson & Tate, 2002).

People with more favorable life situations tend to fare better after brain injury than people whose lives are more disorganized or disadvantaged (Yeates et al., 1997). Intelligent, well-educated, mentally active people have enhanced resistance to mental and behavioral deterioration following significant brain injury (e.g., see Mori et al., 1997a; Schmand et al., 1997). Because the brain is the organ responsible for the integration of behavior, however, there are limits to the amount of brain damage that anyone can tolerate or compensate for without exhibiting abnormal behavior.

In Review

- Describe some of the major ways in which the brain can become damaged.

- What kinds of clinical symptoms are often associated with damage to the frontal, parietal, temporal, and occipital lobes of the brain?

- List nine impairments that are typical of focal and diffuse brain damage.

Delirium

Delirium is a state of acute brain failure that lies between normal wakefulness and stupor or coma (see Figure 3). The word comes from the Latin *delirare*, meaning to be out of one's furrow or track.

Clinical Picture

A commonly occurring syndrome, delirium is characterized by confusion, disturbed concentration, and cognitive dysfunction (see the *DSM-IV-TR* table for diagnostic criteria). Although the *DSM-IV-TR* criteria state that delirium involves a disturbance in consciousness, this word will likely be removed in *DSM-5*. This is because the essence of delirium is better captured by the idea of a disturbance in awareness.

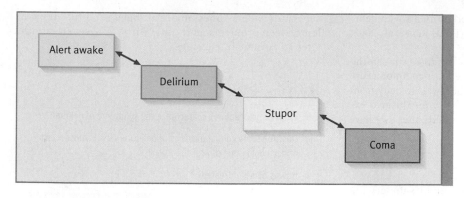

FIGURE 3

Continuum of Level of Consciousness
Source: Adapted with permission from the *American Psychiatric Publishing Textbook of Neuropsychiatry and Behavioral Neurosciences*, Fifth Edition, (Copyright © 2008). American Psychiatric Publishing.

Think of delirium as a condition with a sudden onset that involves a fluctuating state of reduced awareness.

In addition to a disturbance in level of awareness, delirium also involves impairments of memory and attention as well as disorganized thinking. Hallucinations and delusions are quite common (see Trzepacz et al., 2002). In addition, the syndrome often includes abnormal psychomotor activity such as wild thrashing about and disturbance of the sleep cycle. A delirious person is essentially unable to carry out purposeful mental activity of any kind. The intensity of the symptoms also fluctuates over the course of a 24-hour period, as described in the following case study.

Delirium can occur in a person of any age. However, the elderly are at particularly high risk, perhaps because of brain changes caused by normal aging that lead to reduced "brain

case study Delirium Following a Routine Operation

Mrs. Petersen, a 75-year-old widow, was admitted to the hospital after breaking her leg. She had a routine operation, and after this, she began to show signs of confusion. Her consciousness became clouded, with reduced attention and awareness. She could not remember what had happened to her or why she was in the hospital. During the day, she showed mild and aimless hyperactive behavior. She was unable to read or watch television and could not always recognize relatives who visited her. She was seen having conversations with imaginary persons and staring at a point on the ceiling. She was irritable and would burst out in anger. She knocked her meals onto the floor and refused to take any medications. Between outbursts Mrs. Petersen calmed down and was able to sleep for up to half an hour, but at night she seemed unable to sleep at all, and the hyperactivity increased. As other patients fell asleep for the night, Mrs. Petersen started wandering about the ward waking them up again. She went into other people's rooms and tried to climb into their beds. Several times she tried to leave the hospital in her nightdress but was stopped and brought back to her room. (Adapted from Üstün et al., 1996.)

DSM-IV-TR

Criteria for Delirium

A. Disturbance of consciousness (i.e., reduced clarity of awareness of the environment) with reduced ability to focus, sustain, or shift attention.

B. A change in cognition (such as memory deficit, disorientation, language disturbance) or the development of a perceptual disturbance that is not better accounted for by a preexisting, established, or evolving dementia.

C. The disturbance develops over a short period of time (usually hours to days) and tends to fluctuate during the course of the day.

D. There is evidence from the history, physical examination, or laboratory findings that the disturbance is caused by the direct physiological consequences of a general medical condition.

Source: Reprinted with permission from the American Psychiatric Association. *Diagnostic and Statistical Manual of Mental Disorders*, Fourth Edition, *Text Revision* (Copyright © 2000). American Psychiatric Association.

reserve." As described in the case of Mrs. Petersen, delirium is very common in the elderly after they have had surgery, with patients over 80 being particularly at risk (Trzepacz et al., 2002). At the other end of the age spectrum, children are also at high risk of delirium, perhaps because their brains are not yet fully developed. In addition to advanced age, other risk factors for delirium include dementia, depression, and tobacco use (Fricchione et al., 2008).

Estimates of the prevalence of delirium vary widely with the age of the population studied. However, somewhere between 10 and 51 percent of patients who have had surgery will experience delirium; patients who have had cardiac surgery seem to be at especially high risk. The presence of delirium is also a bad prognostic sign. Delirium is correlated with cognitive decline, longer hospital stays, more health problems, and increased mortality; 25 percent of elderly patients with delirium die within the following 6 months (Fricchione et al., 2008; Witlox et al., 2010).

Delirium may result from several conditions including head injury and infection. However, the most common cause of delirium is drug intoxication or withdrawal. Toxicity from medications also causes many cases of delirium. This may explain why delirium is so common in the elderly after they have had surgery.

Treatments and Outcomes

Delirium is a true medical emergency, and its underlying cause must be identified and managed. Most cases of delirium are reversible, except when the delirium is caused by a terminal illness or by severe brain trauma. Treatment involves medication, environmental manipulations, and family support. The medications that are used for most cases are neuroleptics (Fricchione et al., 2008; Lee et al., 2004). These are the same drugs that are used to treat schizophrenia. For delirium caused by alcohol or drug withdrawal, benzodiazepines (such as those used in the treatment of anxiety disorders) are used (Trzepacz et al., 2002). In addition, environmental manipulations that help patients stay oriented, such as good lighting, clear signage, and easily visible calendars and clocks, can be helpful. It is also important that staff members introduce themselves when they work with patients, explain what their role is, and provide reorienting prompts whenever necessary (O'Mahoney et al., 2011). Some patients, however, especially elderly ones, may still have orientation problems, sleep problems, and other difficulties even months after an episode of delirium.

In Review

- What clinical features characterize the syndrome of delirium?
- Describe some common causes of delirium. Who is most at risk of developing this clinical condition?
- How is delirium treated?

Dementia

Unlike delirium, dementia does not have a sudden onset, and its symptoms do not wax and wane. **Dementia** implies loss, and it is characterized by a decline from a previously attained level of functioning (see the table *DSM-IV-TR* Criteria for Dementia). The onset of dementia is typically quite gradual. Early on, the individual is alert and fairly well attuned to events in the environment. Even in the early stages, however, memory is affected, especially memory for recent events. As time goes on, patients with dementia show increasingly marked deficits in abstract thinking, the acquisition of new knowledge or skills, visuospatial comprehension, motor control, problem solving,

---

DSM-IV-TR

Criteria for Dementia

A. The development of multiple cognitive deficits manifested by both
1. memory impairment (impaired ability to learn new information or to recall previously learned information)
2. one (or more) of the following cognitive disturbances:
   a. aphasia (language disturbance)
   b. apraxia (impaired ability to carry out motor activities despite intact motor function)
   c. agnosia (failure to recognize or identify objects despite intact sensory function)
   d. disturbance in executive functioning (i.e., planning, organizing, sequencing, abstracting)

B. The cognitive deficits in Criteria A1 and A2 each cause significant impairment in social or occupational functioning and represent a significant decline from a previous level of functioning.

C. The course is characterized by gradual onset and continuing cognitive decline.

D. The cognitive deficits in Criteria A1 and A2 are not due to any of the following:
1. other central nervous system conditions that cause progressive deficits in memory and cognition (e.g., cerebrovascular disease, Parkinson's disease, Huntington's disease, subdural hematoma, normal-pressure hydrocephalus, brain tumor)
2. systemic conditions that are known to cause dementia (e.g., hypothyroidism, vitamin B12 or folic acid deficiency, niacin deficiency, hypercalcemia, neurosyphilis, HIV infection)
3. substance-induced conditions

E. The deficits do not occur exclusively during the course of a delirium.

F. The disturbance is not better accounted for by another Axis I disorder (e.g., Major Depressive Disorder, Schizophrenia).

Source: Reprinted with permission from the American Psychiatric Association. *Diagnostic and Statistical Manual of Mental Disorders*, Fourth Edition, *Text Revision* (Copyright © 2000). American Psychiatric Association.

and judgment. Dementia is often accompanied by impairments in emotional control and in moral and ethical sensibilities; for example, the person may engage in crude solicitations for sex. Dementia may be progressive (getting worse over time) or static, but is more often the former. Occasionally dementia is reversible if it has an underlying cause that can be removed or treated (such as vitamin deficiency). In *DSM-5* it has been recommended that the word *dementia* be replaced by the term *major neurocognitive disorder* to reduce stigma.

At least 50 different disorders are known to cause dementia (Bondi & Lange, 2001). They include degenerative diseases such as Huntington's disease and Parkinson's disease (which are described below). Other causes are strokes (see Ivan et al., 2004); certain infectious diseases such as syphilis, meningitis, and AIDS; intracranial tumors and abscesses; certain dietary deficiencies (especially of the B vitamins); severe or repeated head injury; anoxia (oxygen deprivation); and the ingestion or inhalation of toxic substances such as lead or mercury. As Figure 4 illustrates, the most common cause of dementia is degenerative brain disease, particularly Alzheimer's disease. In this chapter we will focus primarily on this greatly feared disorder. We will also briefly discuss dementia caused by HIV infection and vascular dementia.

Parkinson's Disease

Named after James Parkinson, who first described it in 1817, **Parkinson's disease** is the second most common neurodegenerative disorder (after Alzheimer's disease). It is more often found in men than in women, and it affects between 0.5 and 1 percent of people between ages 65 and 69 and 1 to 3 percent of people over 80 (Toulouse & Sullivan, 2008). However, the actor Michael J. Fox developed Parkinson's disease when he was only 30 years old. His book *Lucky Man* (2002) offers a moving personal account of his struggle with the illness and well describes some of its major symptoms.

Parkinson's disease is characterized by motor symptoms such as resting tremors or rigid movements. The underlying cause of this is loss of dopamine neurons in an area of the brain called the substantia nigra. Dopamine is a neurotransmitter that is involved in the control of movement. When dopamine neurons are lost, a person is unable to move in a controlled and fluid manner. In addition to motor symptoms, Parkinson's disease can involve psychological symptoms such as depression, anxiety, apathy, cognitive problems, and even hallucinations and delusions (Chaudhuri et al., 2011). Later on in the illness, dementia may also develop. Over time, 25 to 40 percent of patients with Parkinson's disease will show signs of dementia (Marsh & Margolis, 2009). The causes of Parkinson's disease are not clear, although both genetic and environmental factors are suspected. Genetic factors may be more important in cases where the Parkinson's disease develops earlier

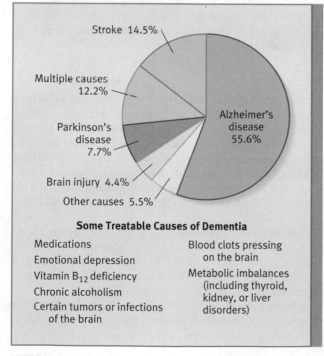

FIGURE 4

Distribution of Dementia by Probable Cause

Source: Dennis J. Selkoe. (1993). Aging brain, aging mind. In *Mind and Brain: Readings from Scientific American* (p. 111). New York: Freeman. (2003, Sept.). *Scientific American*. Copyright © 2003 by Scientific American, Inc. All rights reserved. Reprinted by permission.

Actor Michael J. Fox developed Parkinson's disease when he was only 30 years old. After the diagnosis, he started a foundation to fund research into a cure for the disorder.

in life, and environmental factors may be more relevant in later onset cases (Wirdefeldt et al., 2011). Interestingly, smoking and drinking coffee may provide some protection against the development of Parkinson's disease, although the reasons for this remain unclear (Toulouse & Sullivan, 2008; Wirdefeldt et al., 2011).

The symptoms of Parkinson's disease can be temporarily reduced by medications, such as Mirapex (pramipexole), that increase the availability of dopamine in the brain. However, once the medications wear off, the symptoms return. Another treatment approach that is now being tried is deep brain stimulation. In the future, stem cell research may also offer some hope for patients with this disease.

Huntington's Disease

Huntington's disease is a rare degenerative disorder of the central nervous system that afflicts about 1 in every 10,000 people (Phillips et al., 2008). It was first described in 1872 by the American neurologist George Huntington. The illness begins in midlife (the mean age of onset is around 40 years), and it affects men and women in equal numbers. Huntington's disease is characterized by a chronic, progressive chorea (involuntary and irregular movements that flow randomly from one area of the body to another). However, subtle cognitive problems often predate the onset of motor symptoms by many years. These cognitive problems are no doubt due to the progressive loss of brain tissue (detectable with brain imaging) that occurs as much as a decade before the formal onset of the illness (Shoulson & Young, 2011). Patients eventually develop dementia, and death usually occurs within 10 to 20 years of first developing the illness. There are currently no effective treatments that can restore functioning or slow down the course of this terrible and relentless disorder. American folk singer Woody Guthrie, whose song "This Land Is Your Land" is well known, died of the disease in 1967 when he was 55 years of age.

Huntington's disease is caused by a single dominant gene (the Huntingtin gene) on chromosome 4. This genetic mutation was discovered as a result of intense research on people living in villages around Lake Maracaibo in Venezuela, where this disease is extremely common (Marsh & Margolis, 2009). Because the Huntingtin gene is a dominant gene, anyone who has a parent with the disease has a 50 percent chance of developing the disease himself or herself. A genetic test can be given to at-risk individuals to determine whether they will eventually develop the disorder. However, in the United States, only about 10 percent of people who are eligible for testing choose to know what their genetic destiny is (Shoulson & Young, 2011). If you were in this situation, what would you do? One interesting finding here is that the majority of people who have asked to be tested are women (Hayden, 2000).

Alzheimer's Disease

Alzheimer's disease is a progressive and fatal neurodegenerative disorder. It takes its name from Alois Alzheimer (1864–1915), the German neuropathologist who first described it in 1907. It is the most common cause of dementia (Jalbert et al., 2008). In the *DSM-IV-TR* it is referred to (on Axis I) as "dementia of the Alzheimer's type." In *DSM-5* it will likely be called "major neurocognitive disorder associated with Alzheimer disease." Alzheimer's disease is associated with a characteristic dementia syndrome (see the case study below) that has an imperceptible onset and a usually slow but progressively deteriorating course, terminating in delirium and death.

case study · The Forgetful Mail Carrier

Hans is a 66-year-old man who has become so forgetful that his wife is now afraid to leave him alone, even in the house. At the age of 60, Hans took early retirement from his job in a government office because for the previous 5 years he had not been able to carry out his duties properly. He constantly made mistakes when delivering the mail to different sections of the building. At the same time, he had gradually given up his hobbies and had become more and more quiet. At first, his growing forgetfulness had not been very noticeable in his home environment. Then one day, at the age of 62, when leading a hike in an area he knew well, he could not find the way home. Since then, his memory failures became ever more pronounced. He mislaid things, forgot appointments, and could no longer find his way around the area where he had lived for more than 40 years. He failed to recognize even good friends and lost interest in newspapers and television. (Adapted from Üstün et al., 1996.)

CLINICAL PICTURE The diagnosis of Alzheimer's disease is made after a thorough clinical assessment of the patient. However, the diagnosis can only be confirmed after the patient's death. This is because an autopsy must be performed to see the brain abnormalities that are such distinctive signs of this disease. In the living patient, the diagnosis is normally given only after all other potential causes of dementia are ruled out by medical and family history, physical examination, and laboratory tests.

Alzheimer's disease usually begins after about age 45 (Malaspina et al., 2002). Contrary to what many people believe, it is characterized by multiple cognitive deficits, not just problems with memory. There is a gradual declining course that involves slow mental deterioration.

In its earliest stages Alzheimer's disease involves mild cognitive impairment. For example, the person may have difficulty recalling recent events, make more errors at work, or take

This figure is intentionally omitted from this text

longer to complete routine tasks. In the later stages, there is evidence of dementia; deficits become more severe, cover multiple domains, and result in an inability to function. For example, the person may be easily disoriented, have poor judgment, and neglect his or her personal hygiene. Because they have impaired memory for recent events, many patients have "empty" speech in which grammar and syntax remain intact but vague and seemingly pointless expressions replace meaningful conversational exchange (for example, "It's a nice day, but it might rain"). The case study below, which involves a man who had retired some 7 years prior to his hospitalization, is typical.

Perhaps because Alzheimer's disease damages the temporal lobes of the brain, delusions are also found in some patients (Lyketsos et al., 2000). Although delusions of persecution are predominant, delusional jealousy is sometimes seen. Here, the person persistently accuses his or her partner or spouse—who is often of advanced age and physically debilitated—of being sexually unfaithful. Family members may be accused of poisoning the patient's food or of plotting to steal the patient's funds. One study of physically aggressive patients with Alzheimer's disease found that 80 percent of them were delusional (Gilley et al., 1997).

With appropriate treatment, which may include medication and the maintenance of a calm, reassuring, and unprovocative social environment, many people with Alzheimer's disease show some alleviation of symptoms. In general, however, deterioration continues its downward course over a period of months or years. Eventually, patients become oblivious to their surroundings, bedridden, and reduced to a vegetative state. Resistance to disease is lowered, and death usually results from pneumonia or some other respiratory or cardiac problem. The median time to death is 5.7 years from the time of first clinical contact (Jalbert et al., 2008).

PREVALENCE Alzheimer's disease is becoming a major public health problem, straining societal and family resources. It accounts for most cases of dementia (Lyketsos et al., 2000). Although this disease is not an inevitable consequence of aging (Betty White hosted *Saturday Night Live* when she was 89) age is a major risk factor.

It has been estimated that the rate of Alzheimer's disease doubles about every 5 years after a person reaches the age of

case study   Restless and Wandering

During the past 5 years, the patient had shown a progressive loss of interest in his surroundings and during the last year had become increasingly "childish." His wife and eldest son had brought him to the hospital because they felt they could no longer care for him in their home, particularly because of the grandchildren. They stated that he had become careless in his eating and other personal habits and was restless and prone to wandering about at night. He could not seem to remember anything that had happened during the day but was garrulous concerning events of his childhood and middle years.

After admission to the hospital, the patient seemed to deteriorate rapidly. He could rarely remember what had happened a few minutes before, although his memory for remote events of his childhood remained good. When visited by his wife and children, he mistook them for old friends, and he could not recall anything about the visit a few minutes after they had departed.

The following brief conversation with the patient, which took place after he had been in the hospital for 9 months (and about 3 months before his death), shows his disorientation for time and person.

DOCTOR: How are you today, Mr. _____?
PATIENT: Oh . . . hello [looks at doctor in rather puzzled way as if trying to make out who he is].
DOCTOR: Do you know where you are now?
PATIENT: Why yes . . . I am at home. I must paint the house this summer. It has needed painting for a long time but it seems like I just keep putting it off.
DOCTOR: Can you tell me the day today?
PATIENT: Isn't today Sunday . . . why, yes, the children are coming over for dinner today. We always have dinner for the whole family on Sunday. My wife was here just a minute ago but I guess she has gone back into the kitchen.

Cognitive difficulties are not an inevitable consequence of aging. Betty White hosted *Saturday Night Live* when she was 89 years old.

40 (Hendrie, 1998). Whereas fewer than 1 percent of 60- to 64-year-olds have the disease, up to 40 percent those aged 85 and older do (Jalbert et al., 2008). Worldwide, approximately 35 million people are living with Alzheimer's disease. By 2030 it is expected that this figure will rise to a staggering 66 million (Vreugdenhil et al., 2011). The future prospects are therefore somewhat alarming. If we have not solved the problem of preventing Alzheimer's disease (or arresting it in its early stages) by around that time, society will be faced with the overwhelming problem of caring for millions of demented senior citizens.

For reasons that are not yet clear, women seem to have a slightly higher risk of developing Alzheimer's disease than men (Jalbert et al., 2008). Indeed, Alois Alzheimer's original case was a 51-year-old woman. Women tend to live longer than men, but this may not entirely explain the increased prevalence of women with Alzheimer's disease. However, a relevant factor may be loneliness. In one study of 800 elderly people (the majority of whom were female), those who reported that they felt lonely had twice the risk of developing Alzheimer's disease over the course of the 4-year follow-up. This association was independent of their scores on a measure of cognition, suggesting that loneliness is not an early sign of dementia or a consequence of impaired cognitive skill (Wilson, Krueger et al., 2007). It is reasonable to suggest that women are more likely to experience loneliness because they live longer and so outlive their husbands. This may be important when trying to understand sex differences in the risk for Alzheimer's disease.

In addition to advanced age and being female, other risk factors for Alzheimer's disease include being a current smoker, having fewer years of formal education, having lower income, and having a lower occupational status (Jalbert et al., 2008). Table 2 provides a summary of the most well researched risk factors to date.

The prevalence of Alzheimer's disease is higher in North America and Western Europe and lower in such places as Africa, India, and South East Asia (Ballard et al., 2011; Ferri et al., 2005). Such observations have led researchers to suspect that lifestyle factors such as a high-fat, high-cholesterol diet are implicated in the development of Alzheimer's disease (Sjogren & Blennow, 2005). Also implicating diet, researchers have found that high levels of an amino acid called homocysteine (which is a risk factor for heart disease) seem to increase a person's risk of developing Alzheimer's disease later in life (Ravaglia et al., 2005). Levels of homocysteine in the blood can be reduced by taking folic acid and certain B vitamins. Taking statin drugs to lower cholesterol also seems to offer some protection against Alzheimer's disease (Sparks et al., 2005).

CAUSAL FACTORS When we picture a typical Alzheimer's patient, we imagine a person of very advanced age. Sometimes, however, the disease begins much earlier and affects people in their 40s or 50s. In such cases, cognitive decline is often rapid. Considerable evidence suggests a substantial genetic contribution in early-onset Alzheimer's disease, although different genes may be involved in different families (see Gatz, 2007). Genes also play a role in late-onset Alzheimer's disease.

Cases of **early-onset Alzheimer's disease** appear to be caused by rare genetic mutations. So far, three such mutations have been identified (Ballard et al., 2011). One involves

table 2 Summary of Risk Factors for Alzheimer's Disease

Advanced age
Female
Current smoker
Fewer years of education
Lower income
Lower occupational status
Head trauma

Patients with Alzheimer's disease slowly lose their mental capacities, beginning with memory and progressing to disorientation, poor judgment, and neglect of personal hygiene.

the *APP* (amyloid precursor protein) *gene,* which is located on chromosome 21. Mutations of the APP gene are associated with an onset of Alzheimer's disease somewhere between 55 and 60 years of age (Cruts et al., 1998).

The fact that a mutation of a gene on chromosome 21 has been found to be important is interesting because it has long been known that people with Down syndrome (which is caused by a tripling, or trisomy, of chromosome 21) who survive beyond about age 40 develop an Alzheimer's-like dementia (Bauer & Shea, 1986; Janicki & Dalton, 1993). They also show similar neuropathological changes (Schapiro & Rapoport, 1987). In addition, cases of Down syndrome tend to occur more frequently in the families of patients with Alzheimer's disease (Heyman et al., 1984; Schupf et al., 1994). One study has found that mothers who gave birth to a child with Down syndrome before age 35 had a 4.8-times-greater risk of developing Alzheimer's disease when they were older compared to mothers of children with other types of mental retardation (Schupf et al., 2001).

Other cases of even earlier onset appear to be associated with mutations of a gene on chromosome 14 called *presenilin 1* (PS1) and with a mutation of the *presenilin 2* (PS2) gene on chromosome 1. These genes are associated with an onset

of Alzheimer's disease somewhere between 30 and 50 years of age (Cruts et al., 1998). One carrier of the PS1 mutation is even known to have developed the disorder at age 24 (Wisniewski et al., 1998). Remember, however, that these mutant genes, which are autosomal dominant genes and so nearly always cause disease in anyone who carries them, are extremely rare. The APP, PS1, and PS2 genetic mutations probably account, together, for no more than about 5 percent of cases of Alzheimer's disease.

A gene that plays an important role in cases of late-onset Alzheimer's disease is the APOE (apolipoprotein) gene on chromosome 19. This gene codes for a blood protein that helps carry cholesterol through the bloodstream. We know that differing forms (genetic alleles) of APOE differentially predict risk for **late-onset Alzheimer's disease**. Three such alleles have been identified, and everyone inherits two of them, one from each parent. One of these alleles, the **APOE-E4 allele**, significantly enhances risk for late-onset disease. Thus a person may inherit zero, one, or two of the APOE-E4 alleles, and his or her risk for Alzheimer's disease increases correspondingly. For example, having two APOE-E4 alleles results in a sevenfold increase in a person's chances of developing the disease (Ballard et al., 2011). Another such allele, APOE-E2, seems to convey protection against late-onset Alzheimer's disease. The remaining and most common allele form, APOE-E3, is of neutral significance. The alleles differ in how efficient they are in clearing amyloid, with APOE-E2 being most efficient and APOE-E4 least efficient (Karran et al., 2011).

APOE-E4 has been shown to be a significant predictor of memory deterioration in older individuals with or without clinical dementia (Hofer et al., 2002). The APOE-E4 allele is relatively uncommon in Chinese people compared to its frequency in people from Europe or North America. In contrast, people of African descent are especially likely to have this allele (Waters & Nicoll, 2005). Table 3 summarizes the genes that have been implicated in Alzheimer's disease.

table 3 Genes Associated with Alzheimer's Disease

Gene	Chromosome	Type
Amyloid precursor protein gene (APP)	21	mutation
Presenilin 1 (PS1)	14	mutation
Presenilin 2 (PS2)	1	mutation
Apolipoprotein E (APOE)	19	susceptibility gene

The APOE-E4 allele (which can be detected by a blood test) is overrepresented in all types of Alzheimer's disease including the early-onset and late-onset forms. Approximately 65 percent of patients have at least one copy of the APOE-E4 allele (see Malaspina et al., 2002). Exciting as they are, however, these discoveries still do not account for all cases of Alzheimer's disease, not even all late-onset cases (e.g., Bergem et al., 1997). Many people who inherit the most risky APOE pattern (two APOE-E4 alleles) do not succumb to the disorder. One study found that only 55 percent of people who had two APOE-E4 alleles had developed Alzheimer's disease by age 80 (Myers et al., 1996). And others with Alzheimer's disease have no such APOE-E4 risk factor. In addition, substantial numbers of monozygotic twins are discordant for the disease (Bergem et al., 1997; Breitner et al., 1993).

Why should this be? Current thinking is that our genetic susceptibility interacts with other genetic factors and with environmental factors to determine whether we will succumb to any particular disorder. Clearly, other genes involved in the development of Alzheimer's disease still remain to be found. However, environmental factors may also play a key role. As we have noted, the differences in the prevalence of Alzheimer's disease across different parts of the world suggest that diet may be an important mediating environmental variable. Being overweight, having Type 2 diabetes, or not being physically active have also been implicated as risk factors. The association with diabetes is interesting because researchers have found that insulin levels are abnormally low in some of the brain areas that are most affected by Alzheimer's disease. Other environmental factors under consideration include exposure to metals such as aluminum and experiencing head trauma. One prospective study has found that traumatic brain injury is associated, for up to 5 years after the injury, with a fourfold increase in risk of developing Alzheimer's disease (see Malaspina et al., 2002). And, as illustrated in Box 2, depression also elevates risk of later Alzheimer's disease). On the other hand, exposure to nonsteroidal anti-inflammatory drugs such as ibuprofen may be protective and lead to a lower risk of Alzheimer's disease (Breitner et al., 1994; in't Veld et al., 2001; Weggen et al., 2001). People with more cognitive reserve (a concept combining education, occupation, and mental engagement) also seem to be at reduced risk (Ballard et al., 2011). In other words, it may be possible to reduce or delay the occurrence of Alzheimer's disease by deliberately limiting exposure to risks and taking other preventive measures.

NEUROPATHOLOGY When Alois Alzheimer performed the first autopsy on his patient (she was known as Auguste D.), he identified a number of brain abnormalities that are now known to be characteristic of the disease. These are (1) amyloid plaques, (2) neurofibrillary tangles, and (3) atrophy (shrinkage) of the brain. Although plaques and tangles are also found in normal brains, they are present in much greater numbers in patients with Alzheimer's disease, particularly in the temporal lobes.

Current thinking is that, in Alzheimer's disease, neurons in the brain secrete a sticky protein substance called

---

2 | ## DEVELOPMENTS IN RESEARCH

Depression Increases the Risk of Alzheimer's Disease

Having a history of depression seems to put a person at higher risk for the later development of Alzheimer's disease (Ownby et al., 2006). Although we are not yet sure why this is, researchers speculate that some of the changes in the brain that are known to be associated with depression and with stress may somehow leave the brain more vulnerable to problems down the road (Wilson et al., 2008).

Depression may also be an early warning sign of the onset of dementia. In a large, community-based prospective study of people aged 65 and older, researchers found that people who had no early (before age 50) history of depression but who developed symptoms of depression later in life were about 46 percent more likely to develop dementia over the course of the (approximately 7-year) follow-up period (Li et al., 2011). What this means is that late life depression may be more than a risk factor for depression. Rather, it could be an early manifestation of the dementia itself. This raises the interesting question of whether treating depression might delay the clinical onset of dementia down the road.

People with a genetic risk for Alzheimer's disease because they carry the APOE-E4 gene may be especially vulnerable to developing Alzheimer's disease if they also have a history of depression. In one study, depressed men who had the APOE-E4 gene were more than seven times more likely to develop Alzheimer's disease over the course of a 6-year follow-up compared to men who had neither the gene nor a history of depression. For men who did not have the gene but did have a history of depression, the risk of later Alzheimer's disease was also higher (1.6-fold increase), but not nearly as high as the risk for the men who had the gene *and* the history of depression (Irie et al., 2008). Having the APOE-E4 allele does not make a person more likely to develop depression; however, when the gene and depression occur together, the risk of later Alzheimer's disease is especially high.

beta amyloid much faster than it can be broken down and cleared away. This beta amyloid then accumulates into **amyloid plaques** (see Figure 5). These are thought to interfere with synaptic functioning and to set off a cascade of events that leads to the death of brain cells. Beta amyloid has been shown to be neurotoxic (meaning it causes cell death). Amyloid plaques also trigger local chronic inflammation in the brain and release cytokines that may further exacerbate this process.

Having the APOE-E4 form of the APOE gene is associated with the more rapid buildup of amyloid in the brain (Jalbert et al., 2008). Animal studies also suggest that stress makes the neurocognitive consequences of amyloid accumulation much worse (Srivareerat al., 2009; Alberini, 2009). Insulin may also play a role in regulating amyloid. Although some scientists believe that the accumulation of beta amyloid plays a primary role in the development of Alzheimer's disease, others suspect that it may be a defensive response rather than a causal factor. Importantly, amyloid deposits can be present as many as 10 years before clinical signs of Alzheimer's disease first show themselves (Shim & Morris, 2011). It is not yet known if symptoms become apparent when the amyloid burden in the brain crosses a certain threshold or if amyloid buildup itself triggers other destructive processes that eventually culminate in symptoms (Karran et al., 2011).

Neurofibrillary tangles are webs of abnormal filaments within a nerve cell. These filaments are made up of another protein called *tau*. In a normal, healthy brain, tau acts like a scaffolding, supporting a tube inside neurons and allowing them to conduct nerve impulses. In Alzheimer's disease the tau is misshaped and tangled. This causes the neuron tube to collapse.

Although abnormal tau aggregation can occur independently, there is reason to believe that buildup of tau protein is accelerated by an increasing burden of amyloid in the brain (Shim & Morris, 2011). Animal studies of mice that have been genetically modified to be highly susceptible to developing Alzheimer's disease (so-called transgenic mice) support this idea (Götz et al., 2001; Lewis et al., 2001). If correct, it suggests that the most promising drug treatments for Alzheimer's disease may be those that can target and prevent amyloid buildup.

Another notable alteration in Alzheimer's disease concerns the neurotransmitter *acetylcholine* (ACh). This neurotransmitter is known to be important in the mediation of memory. Although there is widespread destruction of neurons in Alzheimer's disease, particularly in the area of the hippocampus (Adler, 1994; Mori et al., 1997b), evidence suggests that among the earliest and most severely affected structures are a cluster of cell bodies located in the basal forebrain and involved in the release of ACh (Schliebs & Arendt, 2006). The reduction in brain ACh activity in patients with Alzheimer's disease is correlated with the extent of neuronal damage (i.e., plaques, tangles) that they have sustained.

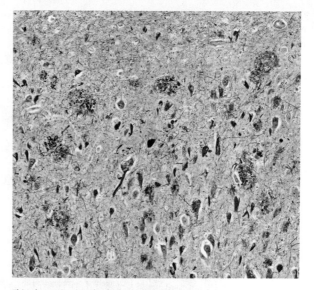

This photomicrograph of a brain tissue specimen from an Alzheimer's patient shows the characteristic plaques (dark patches) and neurofibrillary tangles (irregular pattern of strand-like fibers).

The loss of cells that produce ACh makes a bad situation much worse. Because ACh is so important in memory, its depletion contributes greatly to the cognitive and behavioral deficits that are characteristic of Alzheimer's disease. For this reason, drugs (called cholinesterase inhibitors) that inhibit the breakdown of ACh (and so increase the availability of this neurotransmitter) can be clinically beneficial for patients (Winblad et al., 2001).

TREATMENT AND OUTCOME Despite extensive research efforts, we still have no treatment for Alzheimer's disease that will restore functions once they have been destroyed or lost. Current treatments, targeting both patients and family members, aim to diminish agitation and aggression in patients and reduce distress in caregivers as much as possible (Practice Guideline, 2007).

Some common problematic behaviors associated with dementia are wandering off, incontinence, inappropriate sexual behavior, and inadequate self-care skills. These can be somewhat controlled via behavioral approaches. Behavioral treatments need not be dependent on complex cognitive and communication abilities (which tend to be lacking in patients with dementia). Because of this, they may be particularly well suited for therapeutic intervention with Alzheimer's disease. In general, reports of results are moderately encouraging in terms of reducing unnecessary frustration and embarrassment for the patient and difficulty for the caregiver (Fisher & Carstensen, 1990; Mintzer et al., 1997; Teri et al., 1997).

As we noted earlier, some patients with Alzheimer's disease develop psychotic symptoms and are very agitated. Antipsychotic medications (like those used in the treatment of schizophrenia)

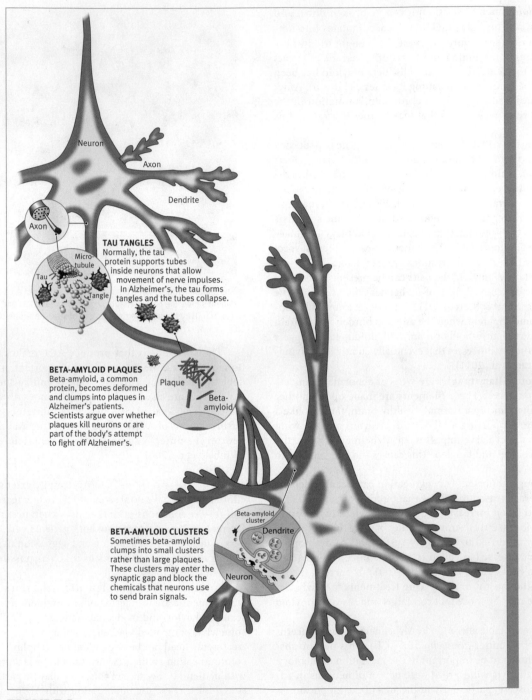

Neuron

Axon

Dendrite

Axon

TAU TANGLES
Normally, the tau protein supports tubes inside neurons that allow movement of nerve impulses. In Alzheimer's, the tau forms tangles and the tubes collapse.

Micro-tubule

Tau

Tangle

BETA-AMYLOID PLAQUES
Beta-amyloid, a common protein, becomes deformed and clumps into plaques in Alzheimer's patients. Scientists argue over whether plaques kill neurons or are part of the body's attempt to fight off Alzheimer's.

Plaque

Beta-amyloid

Beta-amyloid cluster

Dendrite

BETA-AMYLOID CLUSTERS
Sometimes beta-amyloid clumps into small clusters rather than large plaques. These clusters may enter the synaptic gap and block the chemicals that neurons use to send brain signals.

Neuron

FIGURE 5

Brain Damage in Alzheimer's Disease

Source: Dember, A. (2005, March 29). Mind mystery. *Boston Globe.*

are sometimes given to alleviate these symptoms. However, these medications must be used with great caution. The Food and Drug Administration has issued a warning that patients with dementia who receive atypical antipsychotic medications are at increased risk of death (Schultz, 2008). Moreover, although antipsychotic medications may alleviate some symptoms to a very modest degree, there is no good evidence that they are better than placebo when it comes to patients' overall daily functioning and cognition (Sultzer et al., 2008).

Treatment efforts to improve cognitive functioning have focused on the consistent findings of acetylcholine depletion in Alzheimer's disease. The reasoning here is that it might be possible to improve functioning by administering drugs that enhance the availability of brain ACh. Currently, the most effective way of doing so is by inhibiting the production of acetylcholinesterase, the principal enzyme involved in the metabolic breakdown of acetylcholine. This is the rationale for administering drugs such as tacrine (Cognex) and donepezil (Aricept). Winblad and colleagues (2001) studied 286 patients who were randomly assigned to receive either medication (donepezil) or placebo for a 1-year period. Patients' cognitive functioning and ability to perform daily activities were measured at the start of the study and again at regular intervals over the study period. Patients who received the medication did better overall than patients who received the placebo. However, all patients declined in their functioning over the course of the study. Furthermore, although donepezil does help patients a little, these gains do not mean that patients taking the drug are any less likely to avoid institutionalization than those who are not taking the medication (AD2000 Collaborative Group, 2004).

The newest medication that has been approved to treat Alzheimer's disease is memantine, which is marketed as Namenda. Unlike other approved medications, memantine is not a cholinesterase inhibitor. Instead, it appears to regulate the activity of the neurotransmitter glutamate, perhaps by protecting cells against excess glutamate by partially blocking NMDA receptors. Memantine, which can be used alone or in combination with donepezil, appears to provide patients with some cognitive benefits (Forchetti, 2005; Reisberg et al., 2003). However when it comes to day-to-day functioning, the improvements that come from taking medications are still very small (Ballard et al., 2011; Hansen et al., 2007).

Yet another line of treatment research is focused on developing vaccines that might help clear away any accumulated amyloid plaques. Although initial findings from animal research looked promising (e.g., McLaurin et al., 2002), human clinical trials of a vaccine were terminated prematurely because of dangerous side effects. Nonetheless, researchers continue to explore novel treatment approaches (Gestwicki et al., 2004; Hardy, 2004; Hutter-Paier et al., 2004). To date, however, all efforts to develop new drugs to treat Alzheimer's disease have been unsuccessful. No new medications have become available since Namenda was approved in 2003. This is very disappointing for patients and for their families, who live in hope of major breakthroughs.

Unfortunately, once most types of neuronal cells have died they are permanently lost. This means that even if some new treatment could halt a patient's progressive loss of brain tissue, he or she would still be left seriously impaired. This makes the research effort to detect Alzheimer's disease in its earliest stages all the more important.

EARLY DETECTION Most researchers believe that signs of Alzheimer's disease might be detectable long before clinical symptoms appear. To explore this, they are using a range of brain-imaging techniques to study the brains of people at high risk for developing the disease. People at high risk include those who have the APOE-E4 allele as well as people who are experiencing mild cognitive impairment, or MCI. MCI is thought to be on a continuum between healthy aging and the earliest signs of dementia (Albert & Blacker, 2006; Petersen et al., 2001). Some people with MCI report problems with memory. However, other (non-memory-related) cognitive problems are also predictive of later Alzheimer's disease (Storandt, 2008).

Brain scans of people with MCI show that, like patients with Alzheimer's disease, they have atrophy in a number of brain areas, including the hippocampus (which you may recall is involved in memory) (Chételat et al., 2003; Kubota et al., 2005; Devanand et al., 2007). Moreover, reduction in the size of the hippocampus predicts the later development of Alzheimer's disease both in people with MCI and in elderly people who do not report any memory or cognitive impairments (de Leon et al., 2004; den Heijer et al., 2006). This suggests that atrophy of this brain area is an early sign of the disease.

Functional imaging techniques also show that the hippocampus is less active when patients with Alzheimer's disease (compared to controls) are engaged in memory tasks (Kato et al., 2001; Sperling et al., 2003). Again, this is also true of people with MCI (Chételat et al., 2003; De Santi et al., 2001). These findings are in contrast to those found in people who are cognitively normal but who are at high risk because they carry the APOE-E4 allele. These people do not show a lack of activation in the hippocampus when they are involved in memory tasks. Instead, brain-imaging studies reveal the opposite. Rather than underactivity, people who are at genetic high risk show increased activity in various parts of the brain, including the hippocampus, when they engage in memory tasks (Bookheimer et al., 2000; Smith, Andersen et al., 2002).

How can we explain these rather contradictory findings? Current thinking is that the greater degree of brain activation in people who are cognitively normal but at high risk for developing Alzheimer's disease reflects the greater effort they need to make to manage cognitive tasks. Simply put, carriers of the APOE-E4 allele may have to work harder. Because their brain tissue is still healthy (unlike in people with Alzheimer's disease or MCI), we see an *increase* in brain activation in response to a cognitive challenge rather than the decrease in activation that is more typical of Alzheimer's disease patients

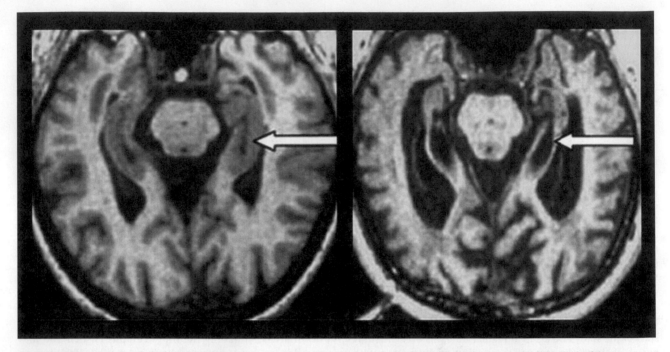

Atrophy of the hippocampus, a brain area critical for memory, is an early sign of Alzheimer' disease. In these pictures, arrows highlight the body of the hippocampus. Note the atrophy in the image on the right.

or those with mild cognitive impairment. A similar pattern of increased brain activation in certain key areas is also found in people with MCI who are able to perform better on cognitive tests compared to those who perform worse (Clément & Belleville, 2010).

Does brain-imaging research allow us to identify people who are going to develop dementia? Not yet. None of the changes found to date are specific enough to be used to make an early diagnosis. This, however, is the goal for the future. In the meantime, if you want to preserve your brain, you might consider reading Box 3. And if you think this information is just for older people, keep in mind that the brain starts to decrease in size after about age 18. By the time we reach the age of 80, our brain has lost about 15 percent of its original weight (Perl, 1999).

3 THE WORLD AROUND US

Exercising Your Way to a Healthier Brain?

If you want to preserve your brain function as you age, you may be surprised to learn that one of the best things you can do is to exercise regularly. A growing amount of research suggests that exercise has considerable neurocognitive benefits. For example, in one prospective study of 299 elderly people (average age 78 years), those who walked 6 to 9 miles per week had much less loss of gray matter over time than did those who were more sedentary (Erikson et al., 2010). In another year-long study, people aged 55 to 80 years who had no dementia were randomly assigned to a program of 40-minute walks three times a week or a program of stretching and toning that lasted the same amount of time. At the end of one year, those who had exercised by walking showed a 2 percent increase in the size of their hippocampus. In contrast, those in the stretching and toning control group showed a decline in their hippocampal volume (which is expected with normal aging). In other words, exercise seemed to reverse the age related loss whereas stretching and toning did not. What is also interesting is that increases in the volume of the hippocampus were also directly related to improvements in memory (Erikson et al., 2011).

Not surprisingly, researchers are now actively studying the effects of exercise in patients with Alzheimer's disease. Recent findings suggest that even a short program of exercise for 4 months conducted at home under the supervision of a carer or other family member can improve cognitive and physical functioning in elderly patients with Alzheimer's disease (Vreugdenhil et al., 2011). Inexpensive and easy to implement, exercise programs are now providing some much needed hope for patients and families coping with dementia.

SUPPORTING CAREGIVERS

In the past few decades there has been a sharp increase in the number of dementia special care units in nursing homes. The vast majority of patients with dementia will be institutionalized before they die. Until patients reach the stage of being severely impaired, however, most live in the community, cared for by their family members. Very often, the burden of care falls on a single person.

Any comprehensive approach to therapeutic intervention must consider the stresses experienced by caregivers. Some of the heart-breaking losses that they encounter are depicted in such movies as *Iris* and *Away from Her*. In 2008 former Supreme Court justice Sandra Day O'Connor disclosed that her husband, who suffers from Alzheimer's disease, had found new happiness by developing a romantic relationship with a fellow Alzheimer's sufferer in the facility in which he lives. Although this story garnered a great deal of media attention, it is far from a rare occurrence. Not all families are able to cope with this difficult situation with the love and grace that has characterized Sandra Day O'Connor and her family.

Not surprisingly, as a group, caregivers are at high risk for becoming socially isolated and for developing depression (Richards & Sweet, 2009). One study showed that in those caregivers who were not clinically depressed, cortisol levels were essentially similar to those in patients with major depression (Da Roza et al., 2001). Caregivers of patients with Alzheimer's disease tend to consume high quantities of psychotropic medication themselves and to report many stress symptoms and poor health (Cummings, 2004; Hinrichsen & Niederehe, 1994). Providing caregivers with counseling and supportive therapy is very beneficial and produces measurable reductions in their levels of depression (Mittelman et al., 2004).

Dementia from HIV-1 Infection

Infection with the human immunodeficiency virus (HIV) wreaks havoc on the immune system. Over time, this infection can lead to acquired immune deficiency syndrome, or AIDS. Worldwide, the HIV type 1 virus has infected more than 36 million people and resulted in approximately 20 million deaths (Kaul et al., 2005).

In addition to devastating the body, the HIV virus is also capable of inducing neurological disease that can result in dementia. This can happen in two ways. First, because the immune system is weakened, people with HIV are more susceptible to rare infections caused by parasites and fungi. However, the virus also appears capable of damaging the brain more directly, resulting in neuronal injury and destruction of brain cells (see Snider et al., 1983; Kaul et al., 2005).

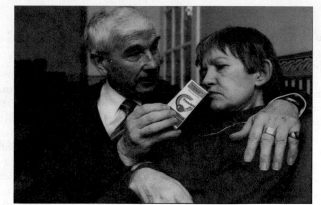

Why must therapeutic interventions also consider the caregivers of Alzheimer's patients?

The neuropathology of **HIV-associated dementia** involves various changes in the brain, among them generalized atrophy, edema (swelling), inflammation, and patches of demyelination (Adams & Ferraro, 1997; Sewell et al., 1994). No brain area may be entirely spared, but the damage appears to be concentrated in subcortical regions, notably the central white matter, the tissue surrounding the ventricles, and deeper gray matter structures such as the basal ganglia and thalamus. Ninety percent of patients with AIDS show evidence of such changes on autopsy (Adams & Ferraro, 1997).

The neuropsychological features of AIDS tend to appear as a late phase of HIV infection, although they often appear before the full development of AIDS itself. They begin with mild memory difficulties, psychomotor slowing, and diminished attention and concentration (see Fernandez et al., 2002, for a review). Progression is typically rapid after this point, with clear-cut dementia appearing in many cases within 1 year, although considerably longer periods have been reported. The later phases of AIDS dementia include behavioral regression, confusion, psychotic thinking, apathy, and marked withdrawal.

Estimates from the early 1990s suggested HIV-related dementia was present in 20 to 30 percent of people with advanced HIV disease. Fortunately, the arrival of highly active antiretroviral therapy has not only resulted in infected people living longer but has also reduced the prevalence of HIV-related dementia to around 10.5 percent (Kaul et al., 2005). However, although rates of frank dementia have decreased, around 30 percent of people who are infected with the HIV virus show some signs of mild cognitive impairment (Treisman et al., 2009). Moreover, for reasons that are not yet clear, women may be at especially high risk of HIV-related cognitive impairment.

Treatment with antiretroviral therapy does not fully prevent the HIV virus from damaging the brain (Kaul et al., 2005). This may be because HIV penetrates into the nervous system soon after a person becomes infected. What this means is that even though the new therapies have made HIV/AIDS a chronic but manageable condition (at least for those who have access to the necessary medications), prevention of infection remains the only certain strategy for avoiding the cognitive impairments associated with this disease.

Vascular Dementia

Vascular dementia is frequently confused with Alzheimer's disease because of its similar clinical picture of progressive dementia and its increasing incidence and prevalence rates with advancing age. However, it is an entirely different disease in terms of its underlying neuropathology. In this disorder, a series of circumscribed cerebral infarcts—interruptions of the blood supply to minute areas of the brain because of arterial disease, commonly known as "small strokes"—cumulatively destroy neurons over expanding brain regions. The affected regions become soft and may degenerate over time, leaving only cavities. Although vascular dementia tends to have a more varied early clinical picture than Alzheimer's disease (Wallin & Blennow, 1993), the progressive loss of cells leads to brain atrophy and behavioral impairments that ultimately mimic those of Alzheimer's disease (Bowler et al., 1997). In *DSM-5* this disorder will likely be called major neurocognitive disorder associated with vascular disease.

Vascular dementia tends to occur after the age of 50 and affects more men than women (Askin-Edgar et al., 2002). Abnormalities of gait (e.g., being unsteady on one's feet) may be an early predictor of this condition (Verghese et al., 2002). Vascular dementia is less common than Alzheimer's disease, accounting for only 19 percent of dementia cases in a community sample aged 65 years or older (Lyketsos et al., 2000). One reason for this is that these patients have a much shorter course of illness because they are vulnerable to sudden death from stroke or cardiovascular disease (Askin-Edgar et al., 2002). Accompanying mood disorders are also more common in vascular dementia than in Alzheimer's disease, perhaps because subcortical areas of the brain are more affected (Lyketsos et al., 2000).

The medical treatment of vascular dementia, though complicated, offers slightly more hope than that of Alzheimer's disease. Unlike Alzheimer's disease, the basic problem of cerebral arteriosclerosis (decreased elasticity of brain arteries) can be medically managed to some extent, perhaps decreasing the likelihood of further strokes. The daunting problems that caregivers face, however, are much the same in the two conditions, indicating the appropriateness of support groups, stress reduction techniques, and the like.

In Review

- What is dementia? How is it different from delirium?
- List five diseases or clinical disorders that can cause dementia.
- What genes are implicated in Alzheimer's disease?
- Describe some of the major environmental risk factors for Alzheimer's disease.
- What kinds of neuropathological abnormalities are typical of the Alzheimer's brain?

Amnestic Disorder

"Amnestic" is just another way of saying "amnesia," and the characteristic feature of **amnestic disorder** is strikingly disturbed memory (see table *DSM-IV-TR* Criteria for Amnestic Disorder). Immediate recall (that is, the ability to repeat what has just been heard) is not usually affected. Memory for remote past events is also usually relatively preserved. However, short-term memory is typically so impaired that the person is unable to recall events that took place only a few minutes previously. To compensate, patients sometimes confabulate, making up events to fill in the void that they have in their memories.

DSM-IV-TR

Criteria for Amnestic Disorder

A. The development of memory impairment as manifested by impairment in the ability to learn new information or the inability to recall previously learned information.

B. The memory disturbance causes significant impairment in social or occupational functioning and represents a significant decline from a previous level of functioning.

C. The memory disturbance does not occur exclusively during the course of a delirium or a dementia.

D. There is evidence from the history, physical examination, or laboratory findings that the disturbance is the direct physiological consequence of a general medical condition (including physical trauma).

Source: Reprinted with permission from the American Psychiatric Association. *Diagnostic and Statistical Manual of Mental Disorders*, Fourth Edition, *Text Revision* (Copyright © 2000). American Psychiatric Association.

In contrast to dementia, overall cognitive functioning in an amnestic disorder is often quite good. The affected person may be able to execute a complex task if it provides its own distinctive cues for each stage of the sequence.

Brain damage is the root cause of amnestic disorder. This damage might be caused by strokes, injury, tumors, or infections (Andreescu & Aizenstein, 2009). However, not all brain damage is permanent. **Korsakoff's syndrome** is an amnestic disorder that is caused by deficiency in vitamin B1 (thiamine). Because of this, the memory problems associated with Korsakoff's syndrome can sometimes be reversed if it is detected early enough and vitamin B1 is given. Korsakoff's syndrome is often found in chronic alcoholics or in other people who do not eat healthily.

This excerpt is intentionally omitted from this text.

Another common cause is head trauma. Stroke, surgery in the temporal lobe area of the brain, hypoxia (oxygen deprivation), and some forms of brain infections (such as encephalitis) can also lead to amnestic disorder. In these cases, depending on the nature and extent of damage to the affected neural structures and on the treatment undertaken, the disorder may remit with time. A wide range of techniques have been developed to assist the good-prognosis amnestic patient in remembering recent events (e.g., Gouvier et al., 1997). Moreover, because procedural memory (i.e., the ability to learn routines, skills, and actions) is often preserved in patients with amnesia, even patients without memory for specific personal experiences can still can be taught to perform tasks that might help them reenter the workforce (Cavaco et al., 2004).

In Review

- What are the most striking clinical features of amnestic syndrome?

- What are some of the major causes of amnestic syndrome?

Disorders Involving Head Injury

Traumatic brain injury (TBI) occurs frequently, affecting just under 2 million people each year in the United States. The most common cause of TBI are falls, followed by motor vehicle accidents. Other causes include assaults and sports injuries (although the vast majority of these are probably never even reported). Children aged 0 to 4, adolescents aged 5 to 19, and adults aged 65 years and older are most likely to experience a TBI. In every age group rates of TBI are higher for males than they are for females (Faul et al., 2010).

We are also now experiencing an escalation of cases of traumatic brain injury caused by explosive blasts (Champion et al., 2009). Blasts seem to damage the brain in ways that are different from the brain damage seen in civilian cases of TBI. So many veterans have been injured by improvised explosive devices that traumatic brain injury has been referred to as the signature injury of the Iraq War. Research suggests that around 15 percent of soldiers who have served in Iraq have experienced a traumatic brain injury (Hoge et al., 2008). The military is now making efforts to improve screening and to increase rehabilitation service for veterans (see Munsey, 2007). However, for many, a full recovery may never be possible.

Former Arizona Congresswoman Gabrielle Giffords is recovering from a traumatic brain injury sustained after an assailant shot her in the head. She is receiving extensive therapy and is making considerable progress.

In *DSM-IV-TR*, brain injuries that have notable, long-standing effects on adaptive functioning are coded on Axis I using the appropriate syndromal descriptive phrase, with the qualifier "due to head trauma." (Examples include "dementia due to head trauma," "amnestic disorder due to head trauma," and the like.) In *DSM-5* we expect that these diagnoses will be replaced by new diagnostic terms such as "major (or minor) neurocognitive disorder associated with head trauma."

Clinical Picture

Clinicians categorize brain injuries as resulting from either a closed-head injury (where the cranium remains intact) or a penetrating head injury (where some object such as a bullet enters the brain). In closed-head injury, the damage to the brain is indirect—caused by inertial forces that cause the brain to come into violent contact with the interior skull wall or by rotational forces that twist the brain mass relative to the brain stem. Not uncommonly, closed-head injury also causes diffuse neuron damage because of the inertial force. In other words, the rapid movement of the rigid cranium is stopped on contact with an unyielding object. However, the softer brain tissue within keeps moving, and this has a shearing effect on nerve fibers and their synaptic interconnections. This is illustrated in Figure 6.

Severe head injuries usually cause unconsciousness and disruption of circulatory, metabolic, and neurotransmitter regulation. Normally, if a head injury is severe enough to result in unconsciousness, the person experiences **retrograde amnesia**, or inability to recall events immediately *preceding* the injury. Apparently, the trauma interferes with the brain's capacity to consolidate into long-term storage the events that were still being processed at the time of the trauma. **Anterograde amnesia** (also called posttraumatic amnesia) is the inability to store effectively in memory events that happen during variable periods of time *after* the trauma. It is also frequently observed and is regarded by many as a negative prognostic sign.

A person rendered unconscious by a head injury usually passes through stages of stupor and confusion on the way to recovering clear consciousness. This recovery of consciousness may be complete in the course of minutes, or it may take hours or days. Following a severe injury and loss of consciousness, a person's pulse, temperature, blood pressure, and important aspects of brain metabolism are all affected, and survival may be uncertain. In rare cases, an individual may live for extended periods of time without regaining consciousness, a condition known as *coma*. The duration of the coma is generally related to the severity of the injury. If the patient survives, coma may be followed by delirium, marked by acute excitement and disorientation and hallucinations. Gradually the confusion may clear up and the individual may regain contact with

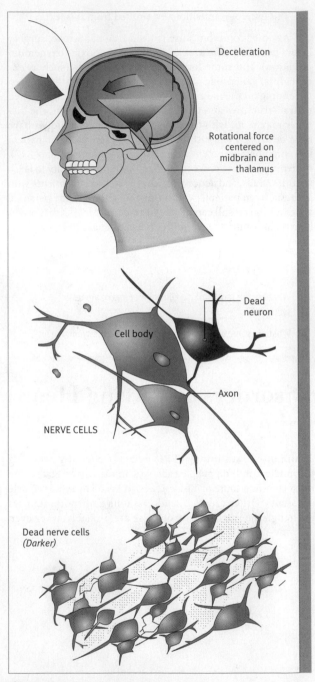

FIGURE 6

Traumatic Brain Injury

Source: Williams, J. (2007, Feb. 19). Give your head a rest. *Boston Globe*.

reality. Individual courses of recovery are highly variable and difficult to predict (Waters & Nicoll, 2005).

Large numbers of relatively mild closed-head brain concussions and contusions (bruises) occur every year as

THE WORLD AROUND US
4

Can Thrill Rides Cause Brain Damage?

A 24-year-old Japanese woman developed a headache after spending the day at the Fujikyu Highland Park in Japan. During that time, she had ridden twice on each of three different roller coasters, including the Fujiyama, which is 259 feet tall, has a drop of 230 feet, and reaches speeds of over 81 miles per hour. The young woman's headache lasted 4 days and was initially diagnosed as a tension headache. It was only 4 months later, after she had received an MRI scan, that it became clear that this young woman had something much more serious: She had subdural hematomas (areas of bleeding) on both sides of her brain (see Fukutake et al., 2000).

The thrill-ride-seeking public is always hungry for new and more extreme rides, and the amusement park industry has responded accordingly. Currently, the fastest roller coaster in the world (Formula

Exposure to high G-forces, such as those experienced on some theme park rides, can cause neurological injury in some individuals by creating small tears in delicate blood vessels in the brain.

Rossa, located in Ferrari World in Abu Dhabi, United Arab Emirates) reaches speeds of up to 150 mph. In the United States, the world's tallest roller coaster Kingda Ka at Six Flags Great Adventure in Jackson Township, New Jersey—is 456 feet high, reaches a speed of 128 miles per hour, and also has the greatest drop in the world (418 feet). But do these rides expose the body to dangerously high G-forces?

G-force is a measure of the acceleration of an object divided by the acceleration caused by gravity. In the United States, several roller coasters produce G-forces comparable to those experienced by fighter pilots. For example, the Rock 'n' Roll Coaster at Disney MGM Studios in Orlando, Florida, registers 5.0 Gs and Taz's Tornado at Six Flags AstroWorld in Houston, Texas, registers 6.5 Gs. Although these are clearly high figures, what is important is for how long the force is applied. The human body can tolerate exposure to very high G forces for very brief periods of time. Fighter pilots only lose consciousness after 40 seconds or more of exposure to forces in the range of 5 to 9 Gs (Pfister et al., 2009). Because roller coasters only expose us to high G forces for a short period of time, we experience a thrill but we do not black out.

Nonetheless, the rotational and positional changes that the body experiences may create small tears in delicate blood vessels in a very tiny minority of riders (see Braksiek & Roberts, 2002; Huang, 2003). There are at least 58 known cases of brain injuries from roller coasters (Markey, 2002). It is also estimated that 2 deaths per year can be attributed to brain haemorrhages that result from roller coaster rides (Pelletier & Gilchrist, 2005). Although these statistics are unlikely to dissuade you from heading to a theme park the next time you want to have some fun, they have prompted some calls for greater oversight of the industry.

a result of car accidents, athletic injuries, falls, and other mishaps. As Box 4 illustrates, riding roller coasters that generate high G-forces may cause brain injury in some people.

People who play certain sports are at high risk of experiencing concussions and brain injuries. For males, the greatest risk comes from playing football; for females, the greatest risk comes from playing soccer (Lincoln et al., 2011). Signs of concussion are listed in Table 4. However, the majority of concussions do not involve a loss of consciousness. It is important to know that, after a concussion, the brain is four or five times more vulnerable to a second impact and that this increased vulnerability lasts for several weeks. As described in Box 5, and as illustrated in the following case study (both), athletes at every level sometimes want to get back into the game without adequate recovery time, often with devastating consequences.

table 4 Signs of a Concussion

Loss of consciousness
Confusion
Amnesia
Nausea
Vomiting
Drowsiness
Slurred speech
Uneven pupil size
Ringing in the ears
Unusual eye movements
Not all these symptoms may be apparent immediately. Some symptoms may develop several days after the injury.

Source: Williams (2007). Give your head a rest. *Boston Globe*, February 19.

5 THE WORLD AROUND US

Brain Damage in Professional Athletes

For athletes, collisions are often part of the game. But new evidence is forcing many in collegiate and professional sports to consider the potential for long-term brain damage that may come from heading the ball or tackling another player. This issue came to the attention of sports fans when Ted Johnson, a former Super Bowl champion and linebacker for the New England Patriots, went public about the crippling depressions and headaches he now experiences (MacMullan, 2007). Johnson, who has been diagnosed with a chronic postconcussion syndrome (involving fatigue, irritability, memory loss, and depression), is also showing signs of early brain damage. He believes that his problems are a direct result of the multiple hits to the head he sustained during his playing career.

Repeat concussions are very serious. After a blow to the head, the brain remains in a vulnerable state for several weeks. A second injury during this time will cause an exponential amount of damage. Johnson's cognitive functioning declined dramatically after he was involved in a serious collision during an exhibition game and had to be pulled off the field. Four days later, he was expected to engage in full contact during practice. Although he knew this was a bad idea, his pride, combined with the pressure not to appear weak, kept him from asking to be excused from the physical drills. During the practice he took a mild hit and experienced the warm and hazy sensation that signals a concussion. For Johnson, it was the beginning of the end.

Johnson decided to go public with his story after the suicide of former NFL defensive back Andre Waters. Waters, who was known to be a tough and hard-hitting player, suffered many repeat concussions during the course of his career. After his death at age 44, a neurologist examined his brain and reported that the tissue resembled that of an 85-year-old; Waters also had some signs of Alzheimer's disease. Repeat concussions were suspected to be the cause of his brain damage.

Research supports this speculation. A study of 2,552 retired professional football players showed that the majority (61 percent) had experienced at least one concussion during their playing careers. Moreover, those players who had a history of three or more concussions were five times more likely to be diagnosed with cognitive problems and had three times more memory impairment than players with no concussion history (Guskiewicz et al., 2005). Players who had had repeat concussions were also more likely to later be diagnosed with depression (Guskiewicz et al., 2007).

The risks associated with concussions are now being taken very seriously in the NFL and also in the NHL. Several hockey players have had their careers cut short by concussions. In 2011, Sidney Crosby, captain of the Pittsburgh Penguins waited 10 months to return to the ice after experiencing two concussions only to be sidelined again shortly afterwards. After taking a hit, staying out of future games until the brain has had enough time to heal is of critical importance.

Sidney Crosby, captain of the Pittsburgh Penguins hockey team, is still experiencing concussion-like symptoms more than a year after being injured. His future remains uncertain.

case study Zack's Story

Zack, a gifted athlete who played both offense and defense on his junior high school football team, was injured at 13 when his head struck the ground after tackling an opponent. The official called a time out, and Zack was sidelined for just three plays before half-time. Despite the blow, Zack shook it off and by the start of the third quarter he was back in the game. "He always wanted to be part of the play" his father recalls.

After a hard-played second half, Zack collapsed on the field. He was airlifted to a medical facility where he underwent emergency life-saving surgery to remove the left and right side of his skull to relieve pressure from his injured and swelling brain. He experienced numerous strokes, spent seven days on a ventilator, and was in a coma for three months before he awoke to a new reality. It was 9 months before Zack spoke his first word, 13 months before he could move a leg or an arm, and he spent 20 months on a feeding tube. Confined to a wheelchair, it was nearly 3 years until Zack was able to stand, with assistance, on his own two feet.

In 2009 the state of Washington passed a new law named after Zack. It requires that any young athlete who shows signs of a concussion be examined and cleared for play by a licensed health care provider. The law protects young athletes from the kind of life-threatening and potentially life-long consequences that can be caused by shaking off an injury and returning to play. (Adapted from CDC, 2010).

We are also learning something about the factors that may increase a person's susceptibility to having problems after a brain injury. One important risk factor appears to be the presence of the APOE-E4 allele that we discussed earlier (Waters & Nicoll, 2005). In one study of boxers, the presence of the APOE-E4 genetic risk factor was associated with more chronic neurological deficits (Jordan et al., 1997). A study of patients being treated in a neurosurgical unit found that APOE-E4 predicted patients doing more poorly at 6-month follow-up. This was true even after controlling for such factors as severity of the initial injury (Teasdale et al., 1997).

Perhaps the most famous historical example of traumatic brain injury is the case of Phineas Gage (Harlow, 1868). Gage, 25 years old, was the foreman of a gang of men who were building a railroad in Cavendish, Vermont. On September 13, 1848, there was an accident, and an iron rod (3 feet 7 inches in length, about an inch in diameter, and weighing just over 13 pounds) was blown through Gage's skull, entering through his lower cheek. Gage was thrown back by the force of the explosion but started to speak a few minutes later. His men put him in an ox cart and took him to his hotel, whereupon he walked, with a little assistance, to his room, bleeding profusely. Miraculously, Gage survived the accident and eventually made a full physical recovery. However, in other respects he was a different man. What was most striking was the change in his personality. As his doctor noted, "He is fitful, irreverent, indulging at times in the grossest profanity (which was not previously his custom), manifesting but little deference for his fellows, impatient of restraint or advice when it conflicts with his desires, at times pertinaciously obstinate, yet capricious and vacillating, devising many plans of future operations, which are no sooner arranged than they are abandoned in turn for others" (Harlow, 1868, p. 327). As others have noted, changes such as this (emotional dyscontrol, personality alterations, and impairment of self-awareness) are fairly characteristic of severe damage to the frontal lobes (Stuss et al., 1992).

Treatments and Outcomes

As illustrated in the case of Zack, prompt medical treatment of a brain injury may be necessary to save the person's life and remove the pressure on the brain caused by intense swelling. Immediate medical treatment may also have to be supplemented by a long-range program of reeducation and rehabilitation involving many different professionals.

Although many TBI patients show few residual effects from their injury, particularly if they have experienced only a brief loss of consciousness, other patients sustain definite and long-lasting impairment. Common symptoms of mild TBI include headaches, memory problems, sensitivity to light and sound, dizziness, anxiety, irritability, fatigue, and impaired concentration (Miller, 2011). When the brain damage is extensive, a patient's general intellectual level may be considerably reduced, especially if there is damage to the temporal lobe or parietal lobes. Most people have significant delays in returning to their occupations, and many are unable to return at all (Dikmen et al., 1994). Other losses of adult social role functioning are also common (Hallett et al., 1994). Some 24 percent of TBI cases, overall, develop posttraumatic epilepsy, presumably because of the growth of scar tissue in the brain. Seizures usually develop within 2 years of the head injury. For decades after a head injury, there is also an elevated risk of depression as well as other disorders such as substance abuse, anxiety disorders, and personality disorders (Holsinger et al., 2002; Koponen et al., 2002).

In a minority of brain injury cases, dramatic personality changes occur such as those described in the case of Phineas Gage. Other kinds of personality changes include passivity, loss of drive and spontaneity, agitation, anxiety, depression, and paranoid suspiciousness. Like cognitive changes, the kinds of personality changes that emerge in severely damaged people depend, in large measure, on the site and extent of their injury (Prigatano, 1992). However, even though more than half the people who sustain TBI develop psychological symptoms, and even though alleviation of such symptoms can improve rehabilitation outcome, there are currently few studies of risk factors, pathogenesis, and treatment of these disturbances (Rao & Lyketsos, 2002).

Children who undergo significant traumatic brain injury are more likely to be adversely affected the younger they are at the time of injury and the less language, fine-motor, and other competencies they have. This is because brain damage makes it harder to learn new skills and because young

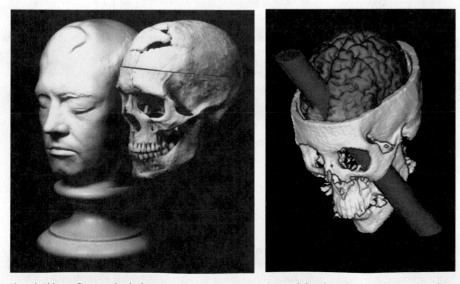

Though Phineas Gage survived when a tamping iron entered his face and shot through his head, his personality was altered such that his friends found that he was "no longer Gage."

losses that may be permanent (Bennett et al., 1997). Research is also showing that patients with TBI may sometimes benefit from treatment with donepezil, an acetylcholinesterase inhibitor widely used in the treatment of Alzheimer's disease (Zhang et al., 2004). Table 5 shows some of the variables that are associated with patients having a more favorable outcome after a traumatic brain injury.

Video games are now being used in the treatment of traumatic brain injury.

table 5 Predictors of Clinical Outcome After Traumatic Brain Injury

Outcome is more favorable when there is:

- only a short period of unconsciousness or posttraumatic anterograde amnesia
- minimal cognitive impairment
- a well-functioning preinjury personality
- higher educational attainment
- a stable preinjury work history
- motivation to recover or make the most of residual capacities
- a favorable life situation to which to return
- early intervention
- an appropriate program of rehabilitation and retraining

Sources: Bennett et al. (1997); Dikmen et al. (1994); Diller & Gordon (1981); Mackay (1994); MacMillan et al. (2002).

children have fewer developed skills to begin with. The severity of their injury and the degree to which their environment is accommodating also affect children's recovery (Anderson et al., 1997; Taylor & Alden, 1997; Yeates et al., 1997). When the injury is mild, most children emerge without lasting negative effects (Satz et al., 1997).

Treatment of traumatic brain injury beyond the purely medical phase is often long, difficult, and expensive. It requires careful and continuing assessment of neuropsychological functioning and the design of interventions intended to overcome the deficits that remain. Many different treatment approaches are used including medication, rehabilitative interventions (such as occupational, physical, and speech/language therapy, cognitive therapy, behavior therapy, social skills training, vocational and recreational therapy) as well as individual, group, and family therapy (Hampton, 2011). Often, a treatment goal is to provide patients with new techniques to compensate for

In Review

- Why is it so important to take concussions very seriously?
- What is the link between the APOE-E4 allele and problems after head injury?
- What kinds of clinical problems are associated with head injury in the short and longer term?
- What factors are associated with the degree of disability after head injury?

Unresolved Issues

▶ *Should Healthy People Use Cognitive Enhancers?*

In the search for a cognitive advantage, many healthy people, young and old, are now turning to drugs that may provide cognitive benefits. Many of us routinely use caffeine, which improves vigilance, working memory, and incidental learning. Others use nicotine, which, although clearly detrimental to health when smoked, may enhance attention, working

memory, and attention in the short term (Husein & Mehta, 2011; Lanni et al., 2008).

A more recent trend, however, involves the use of prescription stimulants. These include methylphenidate (Ritalin), which is used in the treatment of attention deficit disorder, and modafinil (Provigil), which is used as a wake-promoting agent for people with excessive daytime sleepiness. These compounds (which are not always legally prescribed) are now being used by students seeking better grades as well as by military personnel who need to remain awake during long missions.

Studies suggest that physicians are disinclined to prescribe these medications to young, cognitively healthy people (Banjo et al., 2010). In part, this reluctance stems from concerns about the safely of these compounds and beliefs that the benefits they provide are very small. Certainly, evidence suggests that the benefits of cognitive enhancers in healthy individuals are indeed very modest. But there are ethical issues,

too (Hyman, 2011; Lanni et al., 2008). Should drugs developed as treatments be used as cognitive enhancers in people who do not have the disorders the drugs were designed to help? What do you think? Would you take a drug approved for Alzheimer's disease if you thought it would help you do better on a test? Who is most likely to have access to these cognitive enhancers? And will their use lead to a "cognitive arms race" rather like that in some professional sports where athletes who do not take steroids are highly disadvantaged? Is it possible that students of the future might be required to provide a urine sample before taking a high-stakes exam?

Summary

- The *DSM-IV-TR* recognizes various neurocognitive disorders including delirium, dementia, and amnestic disorder. Typically these disorders result from transient or permanent damage to the brain. Chronic neurocognitive disorders involve the permanent loss of neural cells.

- There is no simple relationship between extent of brain damage and degree of impaired functioning. Some people who have severe damage develop no severe symptoms, whereas some with slight damage have extreme reactions.

- Although such inconsistencies are not completely understood, it appears that an individual's premorbid personality and life situation are important in determining his or her reactions to brain damage. The APOE-E4 genetic allele is also important.

- Delirium has a sudden onset. Common among the elderly, it is characterized by a state of awareness that fluctuates between wakefulness and stupor or coma. Delirium is treated with neuroleptic medications and also with benzodiazepines.

- Dementia involves a loss of function and of previously acquired skills. It has a slow onset and a deteriorating course. The most common cause of dementia is Alzheimer's disease.

- Age is a major risk factor for Alzheimer's disease as well as for other forms of dementia such as vascular dementia.

- Genes play a major role in susceptibility to and risk for Alzheimer's disease. Genetic mutations of the APP, presenilin 1,

- and presenilin 2 genes are implicated in early-onset Alzheimer's disease. The APOE-E4 allele of the APOE gene is also a risk factor for Alzheimer's disease.

- The characteristic neuropathology of Alzheimer's disease involves cell loss, plaques, and neurofibrillary tangles. Plaques contain a sticky protein called beta amyloid. Neurofibrillary tangles contain abnormal tau protein.

- Alzheimer's disease causes the destruction of cells that make acetylcholine, a neurotransmitter important for memory. Drug treatments for Alzheimer's disease include cholinesterase inhibitors such as donepezil (Aricept). These drugs help stop ACh from being broken down and so make more of it available to the brain.

- Amnestic disorders involve severe memory loss. The most common cause of amnestic disorders is chronic alcohol abuse.

- Head injuries can cause amnesia as well as other cognitive impairments. Retrograde amnesia is inability to recall events that preceded the trauma. Anterograde amnesia is inability to remember things that follow it.

- Any comprehensive treatment approach for cognitive disorders should also involve caregivers, who are often under a great deal of stress and have difficulty coping. They may benefit from medications as well as from support groups.

Key Terms

Alzheimer's disease	dementia	neurofibrillary tangles
amnestic disorder	early-onset Alzheimer's disease	Parkinson's disease
amyloid plaques	HIV-associated dementia	retrograde amnesia
anterograde amnesia	Huntington's disease	traumatic brain injury (TBI)
APOE-E4 allele	Korsakoff's syndrome	vascular dementia
delirium	late-onset Alzheimer's disease	

Glossary

Many of the key terms listed in the glossary appear in boldface when first introduced in the text discussion. A number of other terms commonly encountered in this or other psychology texts are also included; you are encouraged to make use of this glossary both as a general reference tool and as a study aid for the course in abnormal psychology.

Alzheimer's disease. A progressive and fatal neurodegenerative disorder that is characterized by deterioration in memory, cognition, and basic self-care skills.

Amnestic disorder. Striking deficit in the ability to recall ongoing events more than a few minutes after they have taken place, or the inability to recall the recent past.

Amyloid plaques. Found in the brains of people with Alzheimer's disease, these deposits of aluminum silicate and abnormal protein (beta amyloid) are believed to cause loss of neurons.

Anterograde amnesia. Loss of memory for events that occur *following* trauma or shock.

APOE-4 allele. Variant of a gene on chromosome 19 that significantly enhances risk for late-onset Alzheimer's disease.

Delirium. State of mental confusion characterized by relatively rapid onset of widespread disorganization of the higher mental processes, caused by a generalized disturbance in brain metabolism. May include impaired perception, memory, and thinking and abnormal psychomotor activity.

Dementia. Progressive deterioration of brain functioning occurring after the completion of brain maturation in adolescence. Characterized by deficits in memory, abstract thinking, acquisition of new knowledge or skills, visuospatial comprehension, motor control, problem solving, and judgment.

Early-onset Alzheimer's disease. Form of Alzheimer's disease that appears in people who are younger than approximately 60 years of age. Thought to be caused by rare genetic mutations.

HIV-associated dementia. A progressive brain deterioration that is caused by infection from the HIV virus.

Huntington's disease. A rare and fatal degenerative disorder which is manifested in jerking, twitching movements and mental deterioration. Caused by a dominant gene on chromosome 4. Formerly called *Huntington's chorea*.

Korsakoff's syndrome. This disorder, also referred to as Korsakoff's dementia, Korsakoff's psychosis, or amnesic-confabulatory syndrome, is a neurological condition resulting from chronic alcohol abuse and severe malnutrition (vitamin B).

Late-onset Alzheimer's disease. The occurrence of Alzheimer's disease in the more elderly. One gene thought to be involved in this form of Alzheimer's disease is the APOE gene.

Neurofibrillary tangles. Twisted and weblike nerve filaments that characterize the brains of patients with Alzheimer's disease.

Parkinson's disease. A neurodegenerative disease characterized by motor problems (rigidity, tremors) and caused by destruction of dopamine neurons in the brain.

Retrograde amnesia. Loss of memory for events that occurred during a cir-cumscribed period prior to brain injury or damage.

Traumatic brain injury (TBI). Brain damage resulting from motor vehicle crashes, bullets or other objects entering the brain, and other severe impacts to the head.

Vascular dementia. A brain disorder in which a series of small strokes destroy neurons, leading to brain atrophy and behavioral impairments that are similar to Alzheimer's disease.

Photo Credits

Text Credits

Disorders of Childhood and Adolescence

From Chapter 15 of *Abnormal Psychology*, Fifteenth Edition. James N. Butcher, Susan Mineka, Jill M. Hooley. Copyright © 2013 by Pearson Education, Inc. All rights reserved.

Disorders of Childhood and Adolescence

case study A Case of Adolescent Depression and Attempted Suicide

Emily is 15-year-old girl from a middle-class Caucasian background who had a history of depression during her childhood. She had periods of low mood, poor self-esteem, and social withdrawal. She also had symptoms of anxiety and was very reluctant to leave her home. During her year in the seventh grade she became so fearful of going to school that she missed so many days she had to repeat the grade. She currently is in the eighth grade and has, to this point, missed a great deal of school. Her family became very concerned over Emily's low mood and isolation, so they enrolled her in an outpatient treatment program for depression, anxiety episodes, and eating disorders. Her depression continued, and she became more isolated, lonely, and depressed and would not leave her room even for meals. One day her grandmother found her in their car in the garage with the engine running in an effort to end her life. Emily was admitted into an inpatient treatment program following her serious suicide attempt.

There is a history of psychiatric problems, particularly mood disorders, in her family. Her mother has been hospitalized on three occasions for depression. Her maternal grandfather, now deceased, was hospitalized at one time following a manic depressive episode.

In the early phases of her hospitalization, Emily underwent an extensive psychological and psychiatric evaluation. She was administered a battery of tests, including the Minnesota Multiphasic Personality Inventory for Adolescents (MMPI-A). She was cooperative with the evaluation and provided the assessment staff with sufficient information regarding her mood and attitudes to assist in developing a treatment program.

Emily showed many symptoms of a mood disorder in which both depression and anxiety were prominent features. The psychological evaluation indicated that she was depressed, anxious, and felt unable to deal with the school stress that her condition prompted. Moreover, her physical appearance and eating behavior suggested the strong likelihood of anorexia nervosa. Emily showed an extreme degree of social introversion on several measures and acknowledged her reticence at engaging in social interactions. The assessment psychologist concluded that her personality characteristics of social withdrawal, isolation, and difficult interpersonal relationships would likely result in her having problems in establishing a therapeutic relationship. Her treatment program involved supportive cognitive therapy along with antidepressant medication.

Although she endorsed a broad range of anxiety symptoms, in her testing and in the intake interview she endorsed few items regarding suicidal ideation. This was not sufficient evidence to support a conclusion that she was at less risk for suicide; however, it could simply reflect her unwillingness to openly discuss her recent attempt. Her past behavior and low mood indicated a need to consider the possibility of further suicide attempts.

She remained in inpatient treatment for three weeks and was discharged with the summary that she had shown substantial improvement. She was, however, referred for further psychological treatment on an outpatient basis. (Adapted from Williams & Butcher, 2011, pp. 151–63)

Until the twentieth century, little account was taken of the special characteristics of psychopathology in children; maladaptive patterns considered relatively specific to childhood, such as autism, received virtually no attention at all. Only since the advent of the mental health movement and the availability of child guidance facilities at the beginning of the twentieth century have marked strides been made in assessing, treating, and understanding the maladaptive behavior patterns of children and adolescents.

The problems of childhood were initially seen simply as downward extensions of adult-oriented diagnoses. The prevailing view was one of children as "miniature adults." But this view failed to recognize special problems, such as those associated with the developmental changes that normally take place in childhood or adolescence. Only relatively recently have clinicians come to realize that they cannot fully understand childhood disorders without taking these developmental processes into account. Today, even though great progress has been made in providing treatment for disturbed children, facilities are still inadequate to the task, and most children with mental health problems do not receive psychological attention.

The number of children affected by psychological problems is considerable. Research studies in several countries have provided estimates of childhood disorders. Roberts and colleagues (2007) found that 17.1 percent of adolescents in large metropolitan areas of the United States meet the criteria for one or more *DSM-IV-TR* diagnoses. Verhulst (1995) conducted an evaluation of the overall prevalence of childhood disorder based on 49 studies involving over 240,000 children across many countries and found the average rate to be 12.3 percent. In most studies, maladjustment is found more commonly among boys than among girls; however, for some diagnostic problems such as eating disorders, rates are higher for girls than for boys. The most prevalent disorders are attention-deficit/hyperactivity disorder (Ryan-Krause et al., 2010) and separation anxiety disorders (Cartwright-Hatton et al., 2006). Some subgroups of the population—for example, Native Americans—tend to have higher rates of mental disorders. One study reported that 23 percent of the Native American children rated in the sample met criteria for 1 of the 11 mental disorders in the survey and 9 percent met criteria for two or more of the disorders (Whitbeck et al., 2006).

Maladaptive Behavior in Different Life Periods

Several behaviors that characterize maladjustment or emotional disturbance are relatively common in childhood. Because of the manner in which personality develops, the various steps in growth and development, and the differing stressors people face in childhood, adolescence, and adulthood, we would expect to find some differences in maladaptive behavior in these periods. The fields of developmental science (Hetherington, 1998) and, more specifically, **developmental psychopathology** (Kim-Cohen, 2007) are devoted to studying the origins and course of individual maladaptation in the context of normal growth processes.

It is important to view a child's behavior in the context of normal childhood development (Silk et al., 2000). We cannot consider a child's behavior abnormal without determining whether the behavior in question is appropriate for the child's age. For example, temper tantrums and eating inedible objects might be viewed as abnormal behavior at age 10 but not at age 2. Despite the somewhat distinctive characteristics of childhood disturbances at different ages, there is no sharp line of demarcation between the maladaptive behavior patterns of childhood and those of adolescence, or between those of adolescence and those of adulthood. Thus, although our focus in this chapter will be on the behavior disorders of children and adolescents, we will find some inevitable carryover into later life periods.

Varying Clinical Pictures

The clinical picture of childhood disorders tends to be distinct from the clinical picture of disorders in other life periods. Some of the emotional disturbances of childhood may be relatively short lived and less specific than those occurring in adulthood. However, some childhood disorders severely affect future development. One study found that individuals who had been hospitalized as child psychiatric patients (between the ages of 5 and 17) died early in life due to unnatural causes (about twice the rate of the general population) when followed up from 4 to 15 years later (Kuperman et al., 1988). The suicide risk among some disturbed adolescents is long-lasting and requires careful follow-up and attention (Fortune et al., 2007). Suicidal thoughts are not uncommon in children. Riesch and colleagues (2008) report that 18 percent of sixth graders have thoughts of killing themselves. Two other recent studies have reported rates for children under age 15. Dervic and colleagues (2008) report that international suicide rates are 3.1 per million. Hawton and Harriss (2008) report that the long-term risk of suicide is 1.1 percent, with girls more likely than boys to commit suicide. Both studies report that difficult family relationships are the leading cause

of suicidal behavior. Being bullied by another child is another factor that has been found to be associated with risk of suicide (Rivers & Noret, 2010).

Special Psychological Vulnerabilities of Young Children

Young children are especially vulnerable to psychological problems (Ingram & Price, 2001). In evaluating the presence or extent of mental health problems in children and adolescents, one needs to consider the following:

- They do not have as complex and realistic a view of themselves and their world as they will have later; they have less self-understanding; and they have not yet developed a stable sense of identity or a clear understanding of what is expected of them and what resources they might have to deal with problems.

- Immediately perceived threats are tempered less by considerations of the past or future and thus tend to be seen as disproportionately important. As a result, children often have more difficulty than adults in coping with stressful events (Mash & Barkley, 2006). For example, children are at risk for posttraumatic stress disorder after a disaster, especially if the family atmosphere is troubled—a circumstance that adds additional stress to the problems resulting from the natural disaster (Menaghan, 2010).

- Children's limited perspectives, as might be expected, lead them to use unrealistic concepts to explain events. For young children, suicide or violence against another person may be undertaken without any real understanding of the finality of death.

- Children also are more dependent on other people than are adults. Although in some ways this dependency serves as a buffer against other dangers because the adults around him or her might "protect" a child against stressors in the environment, it also makes the child highly vulnerable to experiences of rejection, disappointment, and failure if these adults, because of their own problems, ignore the child (Lengua, 2006).

- Children's lack of experience in dealing with adversity can make manageable problems seem insurmountable (Scott et al., 2010). On the other hand, although their inexperience and lack of self-sufficiency make them easily upset by problems that seem minor to the average adult, children typically recover more rapidly from their hurts.

The Classification of Childhood and Adolescent Disorders

Until the 1950s no formal, specific system was available for classifying the emotional or behavioral problems of children and adolescents. Kraepelin's (1883) classic textbook on the classification of mental disorders did not include childhood disorders. In 1952, the first formal psychiatric nomenclature (*DSM-I*) was published, and childhood disorders were included. This system was quite limited and included only two childhood emotional disorders: childhood schizophrenia and adjustment reaction of childhood. In 1966, the Group for the Advancement of Psychiatry provided a classification system for children that was detailed and comprehensive. Thus, in the 1968 revision of the *DSM* (*DSM-II*), several additional categories were added. However, growing concern remained—both among clinicians attempting to diagnose and treat childhood problems and among researchers attempting to broaden our understanding of childhood psychopathology—that the then-current ways of viewing psychological disorders in children and adolescents were inappropriate and inaccurate for several reasons. The greatest problem was that the same classification system that had been developed for adults was used for childhood problems even though many childhood disorders (such as autism, learning disabilities, and school phobias) have no counterpart in adult psychopathology. The early systems also ignored the fact that in childhood disorders, environmental factors play an important part in the expression of symptoms—that is, symptoms are highly influenced by a family's acceptance or rejection of the behavior. In addition, symptoms were not considered with respect to a child's developmental level. Some of the problem behaviors might be considered age appropriate, and troubling behaviors might simply be behaviors that the child will eventually outgrow.

In Review

- Define developmental psychopathology.
- Discuss the special psychological vulnerabilities of children.

Common Disorders of Childhood

In *DSM-IV-TR* disorders of childhood are referred to as Disorders Usually First Diagnosed in Infancy, Childhood or Adolescence. The proposed system for classification of these disorders in *DSM-5* is Neurodevelopmental Disorders. At present the *DSM-IV-TR* provides diagnoses for a large number of childhood and adolescent disorders diagnosed on Axis I. In addition, several disorders, involving mental retardation, are diagnosed on Axis II. Space limitations do not allow us to

explore fully the mental disorders of childhood and adolescence included in the *DSM* system, so we have selected several disorders to illustrate the broad spectrum of problems that can occur in childhood and adolescence. Some of these disorders are more transient—and also perhaps more amenable to treatment.

Attention-Deficit/Hyperactivity Disorder

Attention-deficit/hyperactivity disorder (ADHD), often referred to as hyperactivity, is characterized by difficulties that interfere with effective task-oriented behavior in children—particularly impulsivity, excessive or exaggerated motor activity such as aimless or haphazard running or fidgeting, and difficulties in sustaining attention (Nigg et al., 2005; see *DSM-IV-TR* Criteria for Attention-Deficit/ Hyperactivity Disorder). There are some proposed changes to the ADHD criteria for *DSM-5*; however, many of the symptoms and behaviors shown in the criteria for *DSM-IV-TR* are maintained. The proposed modifications in the forthcoming *DSM-5* include some clarification of criteria for ADHD.

Children with ADHD are highly distractible and often fail to follow instructions or respond to demands placed on them (Wender, 2000). Perhaps as a result of their behavioral problems, children with ADHD are often lower in intelligence, usually about 7 to 15 IQ points below average (Barkley, 1997). Children with ADHD also tend to talk incessantly and to be socially intrusive and immature. Recent research has shown that many children with ADHD show deficits on neuropsychological testing that are related to poor academic functioning (Biederman et al., 2004).

Children with ADHD generally have many social problems because of their impulsivity and overactivity. Hyperactive children usually have great difficulty in getting along with their parents because they do not obey rules. Their behavior problems also result in their being viewed negatively by their peers (Hoza et al., 2005). In general, however, hyperactive children are not anxious, even though their overactivity, restlessness, and distractibility are frequently interpreted as indications of anxiety. They usually do poorly in school and often show specific learning disabilities such as difficulties in reading or in learning other basic school subjects. Hyperactive children also pose behavior problems in the elementary grades.

The symptoms of ADHD are relatively common among children seen at mental health facilities in the United States, with from 3 to 7 percent reported in *DSM-IV-TR* and 8 percent reported in a recent study in the United Kingdom (Alloway et al., 2010). In fact, hyperactivity is the most frequently diagnosed mental health condition in children in

DSM-IV-TR

Criteria for Attention-Deficit/Hyperactivity Disorder

A. Either (1) or (2):

1. six (or more) of the following symptoms of inattention have persisted for at least 6 months to a degree that is maladaptive and inconsistent with developmental level:

Inattention

a. often fails to give close attention to details or makes careless mistakes in schoolwork, work, or other activities

b. often has difficulty sustaining attention in tasks or play activities

c. often does not seem to listen when spoken to directly

d. often does not follow through on instructions and fails to finish schoolwork, chores, or duties in the workplace (not due to oppositional behavior or failure to understand instructions)

e. often has difficulty organizing tasks and activities

f. often avoids, dislikes, or is reluctant to engage in tasks that require sustained mental effort (such as schoolwork or homework)

g. often loses things necessary for tasks or activities (e.g., toys, school assignments, pencils, books, or tools)

h. is often easily distracted by extraneous stimuli

i. is often forgetful in daily activities

2. six (or more) of the following symptoms of hyperactivity/impulsivity have persisted for at least 6 months to a degree that is maladaptive and inconsistent with developmental level:

Hyperactivity

a. often fidgets with hands or feet or squirms in seat

b. often leaves seat in classroom or in other situations in which remaining seated is expected

c. often runs about or climbs excessively in situations in which it is inappropriate (in adolescents or adults, may be limited to subjective feelings of restlessness)

d. often has difficulty playing or engaging in leisure activities quietly

e. is often "on the go" or often acts as if "driven by a motor"

f. often talks excessively

Impulsivity

g. often blurts out answers before questions have been completed

h. often has difficulty awaiting turn

i. often interrupts or intrudes on others (e.g., butts into conversations or games)

B. Some hyperactive-impulsive or inattentive symptoms that caused impairment were present before age 7 years.

C. Some impairment from the symptoms is present in two or more settings (e.g., at school [or work] and at home).

D. There must be clear evidence of clinically significant impairment in social, academic, or occupational functioning.

E. The symptoms do not occur exclusively during the course of a Pervasive Developmental Disorder, Schizophrenia, or other Psychotic Disorder and are not better accounted for by another mental disorder (e.g., Mood Disorder, Anxiety Disorder, Dissociative Disorder, or a Personality Disorder).

Source: Reprinted with permission from the American Psychiatric Association. *Diagnostic and Statistical Manual of Mental Disorders,* Fourth Edition, *Text Revision* (Copyright © 2000). American Psychiatric Association.

the United States (Ryan-Krause et al., 2010). The disorder occurs most frequently among preadolescent boys—it is six to nine times more prevalent among boys than among girls. ADHD occurs with the greatest frequency before age 8 and tends to become less frequent and to involve briefer episodes thereafter. ADHD has also been found to be comorbid with other disorders such as oppositional defiant disorder (Staller, 2006), which we discuss later. Some residual effects, such as attention difficulties, may persist into adolescence or adulthood (Odell et al., 1997). ADHD is found in other cultures (Bauermeister et al., 2010)—for example, one study of 1,573

children from 10 European countries reported that ADHD symptoms are similarly recognized across all countries studied and that the children are significantly impaired across a wide range of domains.

CAUSAL FACTORS IN ATTENTION-DEFICIT/HYPERAC-TIVITY DISORDER The cause or causes of ADHD in children have been much debated. It still remains unclear to what extent the disorder results from environmental or biological factors (Carr et al., 2006; Hinshaw et al., 2007), and recent research points to both genetic (Sharp et al., 2009; Ilott et al., 2010) and

Children with ADHD are described as overactive, impulsive, and having a low tolerance for frustration and an inability to delay gratification. Incessant talkers, they tend not to obey rules and often run the risk of a multitude of problems with schoolwork, teachers, and other students.

Gina, a Student with Hyperactivity

case study

Gina was referred to a community clinic because of overactive, inattentive, and disruptive behavior. Her hyperactivity and uninhibited behavior caused problems for her teacher and for other students. She would impulsively hit other children, knock things off their desks, erase material on the blackboard, and damage books and other school property. She seemed to be in perpetual motion, talking, moving about, and darting from one area of the classroom to another. She demanded an inordinate amount of attention from her parents and her teacher, and she was intensely jealous of other children, including her own brother and sister. Despite her hyperactive behavior, inferior school performance, and other problems, she was considerably above average in intelligence. Nevertheless, she felt stupid and had a seriously devaluated self-image. Neurological tests revealed no significant organic brain disorder.

social environmental precursors (Hechtman, 1996). Many researchers believe that biological factors such as genetic inheritance will turn out to be important precursors to the development of ADHD (Durston, 2003). But firm conclusions about any biological basis for ADHD must await further research.

The search for psychological causes of ADHD has yielded similarly inconclusive results, although temperament and learning appear likely to be factors. One study suggested that family pathology, particularly parental personality, can be transmitted to children (Goos et al., 2007). Currently, ADHD is considered to have multiple causes and effects (Hinshaw et al., 1997). Whatever cause or causes are ultimately

determined to be influential in ADHD, the mechanisms underlying the disorder need to be more clearly understood and explored. There is general agreement that processes operating in the brain are disinhibiting the child's behavior (Nigg, 2001), and some research has found different EEG patterns occurring in children with ADHD than in children without ADHD (Barry et al., 2003). At this time, however, theorists do not agree what those central nervous system processes are.

TREATMENTS AND OUTCOMES Although the hyperactive syndrome was first described more than 100 years ago, disagreement over the most effective methods of treatment continues, especially regarding the use of drugs to calm a child with ADHD. Yet this approach to treating children with ADHD has great appeal in the medical community; one survey (Runnheim et al., 1996) found that 40 percent of junior high school children and 15 percent of high school children with emotional and behavioral problems and ADHD are prescribed medication, mostly **Ritalin** (methylphenidate), an amphetamine. In fact, school nurses administer more daily medication for ADHD than for any other chronic health problem.

Interestingly, research has shown that amphetamines have a quieting effect on children—just the opposite of what we would expect from their effects on adults. For children with ADHD, such stimulant medication decreases overactivity and distractibility and, at the same time, increases their alertness (Konrad et al., 2004). As a result, they are often able to function much better at school (Hazell, 2007; Pelham et al., 2002). Jensen and colleagues (2007), in a NIMH study, conclude that medication treatment of ADHD can make a long-term difference for some children if it is appropriately continued and initiated early in the child's clinical course.

Fava (1997) concludes that Ritalin can often lower the amount of aggressiveness in children with ADHD. In fact, many children whose behavior has not been acceptable in regular classes can function and progress in a relatively normal manner when they use such a drug. In a 5-year follow-up study, Charach and colleagues (2004) reported that children with ADHD on medication showed greater improvement in teacher-reported symptoms than nontreated children. The possible side effects of Ritalin, however, are numerous: decreased blood flow to the brain, which can result in impaired thinking ability and memory loss; disruption of growth hormone, leading to suppression of growth in the body and brain of the child; insomnia; psychotic symptoms; and others. Although amphetamines do not cure ADHD, they have reduced the behavioral symptoms in about one-half to two-thirds of the cases in which medication appears warranted.

Ritalin has been shown to be effective in the short-term treatment of ADHD (Goldstein, 2009; Spencer, 2004a). There are newer variants of the drug, referred to as extended-release methylphenidate (Concerta), that have similar benefits but with available doses that may better suit an adolescent's lifestyle (Mott & Leach, 2004; Spencer, 2004b).

Three other medications for treating ADHD have received attention in recent years. **Pemoline** is chemically very different from Ritalin (Faigel & Heiligenstein, 1996); it exerts beneficial effects on classroom behavior by enhancing cognitive processing but has less adverse side effects (Bostic et al., 2000; Pelham et al., 2005). **Strattera** (atomoxetine), a noncontrolled treatment option that can be obtained readily, is an FDA-approved non-stimulant medication (FDA, 2002). This medication reduces the symptoms of ADHD (Friemoth, 2005) but its mode of operation is not well understood. The side effects for the drug are decreased appetite, nausea, vomiting, and fatigue. The development of jaundice has been reported, and the FDA (2004) has warned of the possibility of liver damage from using Strattera. Although Strattera has been shown to reduce some symptoms of ADHD, further research is needed to evaluate its effectiveness and potential side effects (Barton et al., 2005). Another drug that reduces symptoms of impulsivity and hyperactivity in children with attention deficit/hyperactivity disorder is **Adderall**. This medication is a combination of amphetamine and dextroamphetamine; however, research has suggested that Adderall has no advantage or improvement in results over Ritalin or Strattera (Miller-Horn et al., 2008).

Although the short-term pharmacological effect of stimulants on the symptoms of hyperactive children is well established, their long-term effects are not well known (Safer, 1997a). Carlson and Bunner (1993) reported that studies of achievement over long periods of time failed to show that the medication has beneficial effects. The pharmacological similarity of Ritalin and cocaine, for example, has caused some investigators to be concerned about its use in the treatment of ADHD (Volkow et al., 1995). There have also been some reported recreational uses of Ritalin, particularly among college students. Kapner (2003) described several surveys in which Ritalin was reportedly abused on college campuses. In one survey, 16 percent of students at one university reported using Ritalin, and in another study 1.5 percent of the population surveyed reported using Ritalin for recreational purposes within the past 30 days. Some college students share the prescription medications of friends as a means of obtaining a "high" (Chutko et al., 2010).

Some authorities prefer using psychological interventions in conjunction with medications (Mariani & Levin, 2007). The behavioral intervention techniques that have been developed for ADHD include selective reinforcement in the classroom (DuPaul et al., 1998) and family therapy (Everett & Everett, 2001). Another effective approach to treating children with ADHD involves the use of behavior therapy techniques featuring positive reinforcement and the structuring of learning materials and tasks in a way that minimizes error and maximizes immediate feedback and success (Frazier & Merrill, 1998). An example is providing a boy with ADHD immediate praise for stopping to think through a task he has been assigned before he starts to do it. The use of behavioral treatment methods for ADHD has reportedly been quite successful, at least for short-term gains.

The use of psychosocial treatment of ADHD has also shown positive results (Pelham & Fabiano, 2008; Corcoran, 2011). Van Lier and colleagues (2004) conducted a school-based behavioral intervention program using positive reinforcement aimed at preventing disruptive behavior in elementary school children. They found this program to be effective with children with ADHD with different levels of disorder but most effective with children at lower or intermediate levels.

It is important to recognize that gender differences, as noted above, are found in ADHD, with the disorder being more prominent among boys than girls and the symptoms appraised differently. Recent concerns have been expressed over the possibility that treatment of females with symptoms of ADHD might not be provided because they are more often diagnosed as "predominantly inattentive" than boys. Rucklidge (2010) points out that females are less likely to be referred to treatment than males with ADHD although treatments appear to be equally effective for both genders. She points out that future research should be attentive to gender differences in the disorder and further examine potential differences that might occur in treatment and outcomes.

ADHD BEYOND ADOLESCENCE Some researchers have reported that many children with ADHD retain symptoms and behavior into early adulthood. Kessler, Adler, and colleagues (2006) reported a prevalence rate of 4.4 percent in adult patients. Many children with ADHD go on to have other psychological problems such as overly aggressive behavior or substance abuse in their late teens and early adulthood (Barkley et al., 2004). For example, Carroll and Rounsaville (1993) found that 34.6 percent of treatment-seeking cocaine abusers in their study had met the criteria for ADHD when they were children. In a 30-year follow-up study of hyperactive boys with conduct problems, Satterfield and colleagues (2007) reported that such boys are at substantial increased risk for adult criminality. Biederman and colleagues (2010) conducted an 11-year follow-up study of girls with ADHD and found that girls with ADHD were at high risk for antisocial, addictive, mood, anxiety, and eating disorders. In another recent study, college students with ADHD have been shown to exhibit more on-the-job difficulties than peers without ADHD (Shifrin et al., 2010).

More ***longitudinal research*** is clearly needed before we can conclude that children with ADHD go on to develop similar or other problems in adulthood. Mannuzza, Klein, & Moulton (2003) reported that estimates of the numbers of children with ADHD who will experience symptoms of ADHD in adulthood are likely to vary considerably. However, some of the research cited suggests that a significant percentage of adolescents continue to have problems in later life, and many continue to obtain treatment for ADHD (Doyle, 2006) or for other disorders such as major depression or bipolar disorder in their adult years (Klassen et al., 2010).

RESEARCH CLOSE-UP

Longitudinal Research

Longitudinal research involves studying and collecting baseline information on a specific group of interest (patients with a given disorder, high-risk children, etc.) and then following up with them at a future date (e.g., 1, 5, or even 20 years later) to determine the changes that have occurred over the intervening period.

Oppositional Defiant Disorder and Conduct Disorder

The next group of disorders involves a child's or an adolescent's relationship to social norms and rules of conduct. In both oppositional defiant disorder and conduct disorder, aggressive or antisocial behavior is the focus. As we will see, oppositional defiant disorder is usually apparent by about age 8, and conduct disorder tends to be seen by age 9. These disorders are closely linked (Thomas, 2010). However, it is important to distinguish between persistent antisocial acts—such as setting fires, where the rights of others are violated—and the less serious pranks often carried out by normal children and adolescents. Also, oppositional defiant disorder and conduct disorder involve misdeeds that may or may not be against the law; **juvenile delinquency** is the legal term used to refer to violations of the law committed by minors. (See the Unresolved Issues section at the end of this chapter.)

THE CLINICAL PICTURE IN OPPOSITIONAL DEFIANT DISORDER An important precursor of the antisocial behavior seen in children who develop conduct disorder is often what is now called **oppositional defiant disorder (ODD)**. The essential feature is a recurrent pattern of negativistic, defiant, disobedient, and hostile behavior toward authority figures that persists for at least 6 months (American Psychiatric Association, *DSM-IV-TR*, 2000). This disorder usually begins by the age of 8, whereas full-blown conduct disorders typically begin from middle childhood through adolescence. The lifetime prevalence of ODD as

reported in a national sample of adult respondents was relatively high: 11.2 percent for boys and 9.2 percent for girls (Nock et al., 2007). Prospective studies have found a developmental sequence from oppositional defiant disorder to conduct disorder, with common risk factors for both conditions (Hinshaw, 1994). That is, virtually all cases of conduct disorder are preceded developmentally by oppositional defiant disorder, but not all children with oppositional defiant disorder go on to develop conduct disorder within a 3-year period (Lahey et al., 2000). The risk factors for both include family discord, socioeconomic disadvantage, and antisocial behavior in the parents.

THE CLINICAL PICTURE IN CONDUCT DISORDER The essential symptomatic behavior in **conduct disorder** involves a persistent, repetitive violation of rules and a disregard for the rights of others. Children with conduct disorder show a deficit in social behavior (Happe & Frith, 1996; see *DSM-IV-TR* Criteria for Conduct Disorder). In general, they manifest such characteristics as overt or covert hostility, disobedience, physical and verbal aggressiveness, quarrelsomeness, vengefulness, and destructiveness. Lying, solitary stealing, and temper tantrums are common. Such children tend to be sexually uninhibited and inclined toward sexual aggressiveness. Some may engage in cruelty to animals (Becker et al., 2004), bullying (Coolidge et al., 2004), firesetting (Becker et al., 2004; Slavkin & Fineman, 2000; Stickle & Blechman, 2002), vandalism, robbery, and even homicidal acts. Children and adolescents with conduct disorder are also frequently comorbid for other disorders

DSM-IV-TR

Criteria for Conduct Disorder

A. A repetitive and persistent pattern of behavior in which the basic rights of others or major age-appropriate societal norms or rules are violated, as manifested by the presence of three (or more) of the following criteria in the past 12 months, with at least one criterion present in the past 6 months:

Aggression to people and animals

1. often bullies, threatens, or intimidates others
2. often initiates physical fights
3. has used a weapon that can cause serious physical harm to others (e.g., a bat, brick, broken bottle, knife, gun)
4. has been physically cruel to people
5. has been physically cruel to animals
6. has stolen while confronting a victim (e.g., mugging, purse snatching, extortion, armed robbery)
7. has forced someone into sexual activity

Destruction of property

8. has deliberately engaged in fire setting with the intention of causing serious damage
9. has deliberately destroyed others' property (other than by fire setting)

Deceitfulness or theft

10. has broken into someone else's house, building, or car
11. often lies to obtain goods or favors or to avoid obligations (i.e., "cons" others)
12. has stolen items of nontrivial value without confronting a victim (e.g., shoplifting, but without breaking and entering; forgery)

Serious violations of rules

13. often stays out at night despite parental prohibitions, beginning before age 13 years
14. has run away from home overnight at least twice while living in parental or parental surrogate home (or once without returning for a lengthy period)
15. is often truant from school, beginning before age 13 years

B. The disturbance in behavior causes clinically significant impairment in social, academic, or occupational functioning.

C. If the individual is age 18 years or older, criteria are not met for Antisocial Personality Disorder.

Source: Reprinted with permission from the American Psychiatric Association. *Diagnostic and Statistical Manual of Mental Disorders,* Fourth Edition, *Text Revision* (Copyright © 2000). American Psychiatric Association.

Hostility and aggressive behavior have been found to play a role in the development of conduct disorder. Children who develop this disorder early in childhood are at special risk for problems later in life.

such as substance-abuse disorder (Goldstein et al., 2006) or depressive symptoms (O'Connor et al., 1998). Zoccolillo and colleagues (1997) found that conduct disorder is a risk factor for unwed pregnancy and substance abuse in teenage girls. Goldstein and colleagues (2006) report that early-onset conduct disorder is highly associated with later development of antisocial personality disorder; Fergusson and colleagues (2007) and Yang and colleagues (2007) found that conduct disorder in childhood and adolescence is generally related to later substance use, abuse, and dependence.

CAUSAL FACTORS IN OPPOSITIONAL DISORDER AND CONDUCT DISORDER Understanding of the factors associated with the development of conduct problems in childhood has increased tremendously in the past 20 years. Several factors will be covered in the sections that follow.

A Self-Perpetuating Cycle Evidence has accumulated that a genetic predisposition (Simonoff, 2001) leading to low verbal intelligence, mild neuropsychological problems, and difficult temperament can set the stage for early-onset conduct disorder. Baker and colleagues (2007) reported strong heritable effects of conduct problems and antisocial behavior across ethnically and economically diverse samples. The child's difficult temperament may lead to an insecure attachment because parents find it hard to engage in the good parenting that would promote a secure attachment. In addition, the low verbal intelligence and mild neuropsychological deficits that have been documented in many of these children—some of which may involve deficiencies in self-control functions such as sustaining attention, planning, self-monitoring, and inhibiting unsuccessful or impulsive behaviors—may help set the stage for a lifelong course of difficulties. In attempting to explain why the relatively mild neuropsychological deficits typically seen can have such pervasive

effects, Moffitt and Lynam (1994) provided the following scenario: A preschooler has problems understanding language and tends to resist his mother's efforts to read to him. This deficit then delays the child's readiness for school. When he does enter school, the typically busy curriculum does not allow teachers to focus their attention on students at his low readiness level. Over time, and after a few years of school failure, the child will be chronologically older than his classmates, setting the stage for social rejection. At some point, the child might be placed into remedial programs that contain other pupils who have similar behavioral disorders as well as learning disabilities. This involvement with conduct-disordered peers exposes him to delinquent behaviors that he adopts in order to gain acceptance.

Age of Onset and Links to Antisocial Personality Disorder Children who develop conduct disorder at an earlier age are much more likely to develop psychopathy or antisocial personality disorder as adults than are adolescents who develop conduct disorder suddenly in adolescence (Copeland et al., 2007). The link between conduct disorder and antisocial personality is stronger among lower-socioeconomic-class children (Lahey et al., 2005). It is the pervasiveness of the problems first associated with oppositional defiant disorder and then with conduct disorder that forms the pattern associated with an adult diagnosis of psychopathy or antisocial personality. Although only about 25 to 40 percent of cases of early-onset conduct disorder go on to develop adult antisocial personality disorder, over 80 percent of boys with early-onset conduct disorder do continue to have multiple problems of social dysfunction (in friendships, intimate relationships, and vocational activities) even if they do not meet all the criteria for antisocial personality disorder. By contrast, most individuals who develop conduct disorder in adolescence do not go on to become adult psychopaths or antisocial personalities but instead have problems limited to the adolescent years. These adolescent-onset cases also do not share the same set of risk factors that the child-onset cases have, including low verbal intelligence, neuropsychological deficits, and impulsivity and attentional problems.

Psychosocial Factors In addition to the genetic or constitutional liabilities that may predispose a person to develop conduct disorder and adult psychopathy and antisocial personality, Kazdin (1995) underscored the importance of family and social context factors as causal variables. Children who are aggressive and socially unskilled are often rejected by their peers, and such rejection can lead to a spiraling sequence of social interactions with peers that exacerbates the tendency toward antisocial behavior (Freidenfelt & Klinteberg, 2007). Severe conduct problems can lead to other mental health problems as well. Mason and colleagues (2004) found that children who report higher levels of conduct problems are nearly four times more likely to experience a depressive episode in early adulthood.

This socially rejected subgroup of aggressive children is also at the highest risk for adolescent delinquency and probably for adult antisocial personality. In addition, parents and teachers may react to aggressive children with strong negative affect such as anger (Capaldi & Patterson, 1994), and they may in turn reject these aggressive children. The combination of rejection by parents, peers, and teachers leads these children to become isolated and alienated. Not surprisingly, they often turn to deviant peer groups for companionship, at which point a good deal of imitation of the antisocial behavior of their deviant peer models may occur.

Investigators generally seem to agree that the family setting of a child with conduct disorder is typically characterized by ineffective parenting, rejection, harsh and inconsistent discipline, and parental neglect (Frick, 1998). Frequently, the parents have an unstable marital relationship, are emotionally disturbed or sociopathic, and do not provide the child with consistent guidance, acceptance, or affection. Even if the family is intact, a child in a conflict-charged home feels overtly rejected. For example, Rutter and Quinton (1984) concluded that family discord and hostility are the primary factors defining the relationship between disturbed parents and disturbed children; this is particularly true with respect to the development

Ineffective parenting, harsh and inconsistent discipline, parental neglect, and marital discord can all contribute to oppositional defiant disorder (ODD) and conduct disorders. So can poverty and parental stress and depression.

of conduct disorders in children and adolescents. Such discord and hostility contribute to poor and ineffective parenting skills, especially ineffective discipline and supervision. These children are "trained" in antisocial behavior by the family—directly via coercive interchanges and indirectly via lack of monitoring and consistent discipline (Capaldi & Patterson, 1994). This all too often leads to association with deviant peers and the opportunity for further learning of antisocial behavior.

In addition to these familial factors, a number of broader psychosocial and sociocultural variables increase the probability that a child will develop conduct disorder and, later, adult psychopathy or antisocial personality disorder (Granic & Patterson, 2006) or depressive disorder (Boylan et al., 2010). Low socioeconomic status, poor neighborhoods, parental stress, and depression all appear to increase the likelihood that a child will become enmeshed in this cycle (Schonberg & Shaw, 2007).

TREATMENTS AND OUTCOMES By and large, our society tends to take a punitive, rather than a rehabilitative, attitude toward an antisocial, aggressive youth. Thus the emphasis is on punishment and on "teaching the child a lesson." Such treatment, however, seems to intensify rather than correct the behavior. Treatment for oppositional defiant disorder and conduct disorder tends to focus on the dysfunctional family patterns described above and on finding ways to alter the child's aggressive or otherwise maladaptive behaviors (Behan & Carr, 2000; Milne et al., 2001).

The Cohesive Family Model Therapy for a child with conduct disorder is likely to be ineffective unless some way can be found

to modify the child's environment. One interesting and often effective treatment strategy with conduct disorder is the cohesive family model (Granic & Patterson, 2006; Patterson et al., 1998). In this family-group-oriented approach, parents of children with conduct disorder are viewed as lacking in parenting skills and as behaving in inconsistent ways, thereby reinforcing inappropriate behavior and failing to socialize their children. Children learn to escape or avoid parental criticism by escalating their negative behavior. This tactic, in turn, increases their parents' aversive interactions and criticism. The child observes the increased anger in his or her parents and models this aggressive pattern. The parental attention to the child's negative, aggressive behavior actually serves to reinforce that behavior instead of suppressing it. Viewing conduct problems as emerging from such interactions places the treatment focus squarely on the interaction between the child and the parents (Patterson et al., 1991).

Obtaining treatment cooperation from parents who are themselves in conflict with each other is difficult. Often, an overburdened parent who is separated or divorced and working simply does not have the resources, the time, or the inclination to learn and practice a more adequate parental role (Clarke-Stewart et al., 2000). In more extreme cases, the circumstances may call for a child to be removed from the home and placed in a foster home or institution, with the expectation of a later return to the home if intervening therapy with the parent or parents appears to justify it (Hahn et al., 2005).

Unfortunately, children who are removed to new environments often interpret this removal as further rejection not only by their parents but by society as well. Unless the changed environment offers a warm, kindly, and accepting yet consistent and firm setting, such children are likely to make little progress (see Pumariega, 2007).

Behavioral and Biologically Based Treatments The effectiveness of behavior therapy techniques and biologically based treatments has made the outlook brighter for children with conduct disorder (Kazdin & Weisz, 2003). A recent study of treating depression and oppositional defiant behavior with the antidepressant medication fluoxetine (Prozac) and cognitive behavior therapy found a reduction in oppositionality over those not receiving the medication (Jacobs et al., 2010).

Teaching control techniques to the parents of such children is particularly important so that they can function as therapists in reinforcing desirable behavior and modifying the environmental conditions that have been reinforcing maladaptive behavior in their children. The changes brought about when parents consistently accept and reward their child's positive behavior and stop focusing on the negative behavior may finally change their perception of and feelings toward the child, leading to the basic acceptance that the child has so badly needed.

Although effective tactics for behavioral management can be taught to parents, they often have difficulty carrying out treatment plans. If this is the case, other techniques, such as family therapy or parental counseling, are used to ensure that the parent or person responsible for the child's discipline is sufficiently assertive to follow through on the program.

In Review

- Describe two common anxiety disorders found in children and adolescents.

- Distinguish among conduct disorder, oppositional defiant disorder, and juvenile delinquency.

Anxiety and Depression in Children and Adolescents

Anxiety Disorders of Childhood and Adolescence

In modern society, no one is totally insulated from anxiety-producing events or situations, and the experience of traumatic events can predispose children to develop anxiety disorders

(Shevlin et al., 2007). Most children are vulnerable to fears and uncertainties as a normal part of growing up, and children can get generalized panic disorder just as adults do. Children with anxiety disorders, however, are more extreme in their behavior than those experiencing "normal" anxiety. These children appear to share many of the following characteristics: oversensitivity, unrealistic fears, shyness and timidity, pervasive feelings of inadequacy, sleep disturbances, and fear of school (Goodyer, 2000). Children diagnosed as suffering from an anxiety disorder typically attempt to cope with their fears by becoming overly dependent on others for support and help. In the *DSM*, anxiety disorders of childhood and adolescence are classified similarly to anxiety disorders in adults (Albano et al., 1996). Research has shown that anxiety disorders are often comorbid with depressive disorders (Kendall et al., 2010; O'Neil et al., 2010) or may be influential in later depression (Silberg, Rutter, Neale et al., 2001); children who have these comorbid conditions often have significantly more symptoms than children who have anxiety disorders without depression (Masi et al., 2000).

Anxiety disorders are common among children. In a recent review of the epidemiological studies of anxiety in children, Pine & Klein (2010) concude that the prevalence for any anxiety disorder accompanied by impairment appears to be about 5 to 10 percent. For example, 9.7 percent of children in one community-based school sample clearly met diagnostic criteria for an anxiety-based disorder (Dadds et al., 1997). There is a greater preponderance of anxiety-based disorder in girls than in boys (Lewinsohn et al., 1998). And, among adolescents, Goodwin and Gotlib (2004b) reported that panic attacks occurred in 3.3 percent of a large community-based epidemiological study.

DSM-IV-TR

Criteria for Separation Anxiety Disorder

A. Developmentally inappropriate and excessive anxiety concerning separation from home or from those to whom the individual is attached, as evidenced by three (or more) of the following:

1. recurrent excessive distress when separation from home or major attachment figures occurs or is anticipated
2. persistent and excessive worry about losing, or about possible harm befalling, major attachment figures (e.g., health, accidents, death)
3. persistent and excessive worry that an untoward event will lead to separation from a major attachment figure (e.g., getting lost or being kidnapped)
4. persistent reluctance or refusal to go to school, work, or elsewhere because of fear of separation
5. persistent and excessive fear about or reluctance to be alone or without major attachment figures
6. persistent reluctance or refusal to go to sleep without being near a major attachment figure or to sleep away from home
7. repeated nightmares involving the theme of separation

8. repeated complaints of physical symptoms (such as headaches, stomachaches, nausea, or vomiting) when separation from major attachment figures occurs or is anticipated

B. The duration of the disturbance is at least 4 weeks.

C. The onset is before age 18 years.

D. The disturbance causes clinically significant distress or impairment in social, academic (occupational), or other important areas of functioning.

E. The separation anxiety is not restricted to the symptoms of another mental disorder, such as Autism Spectrum Disorder, Schizophrenia or another Psychotic Disorder and, in adolescents and adults, is not restricted to symptoms of Panic Disorder (e.g., anxiety about having panic attacks), Agoraphobia (e.g., avoidance of situations in which may become incapacitated), or Generalized Anxiety Disorder (e.g., worry about ill health of family members).

Source: Reprinted with permission from the American Psychiatric Association. *Diagnostic and Statistical Manual of Mental Disorders,* Fourth Edition, *Text Revision* (Copyright © 2000). American Psychiatric Association.

SEPARATION ANXIETY DISORDER **Separation anxiety disorder** is the most common of the childhood anxiety disorders, reportedly occurring in 2 to 41 percent of children in past population health studies (Cartwright-Hatton et al., 2006; see *DSM-IV-TR* Criteria for Separation Anxiety Disorder). Children with separation anxiety disorder exhibit unrealistic fears, oversensitivity, self-consciousness, nightmares, and chronic anxiety. They lack self-confidence, are apprehensive in new situations, and tend to be immature for their age. Such children are described by their parents as shy, sensitive, nervous, submissive, easily discouraged, worried, and frequently moved to tears. Typically, they are overly dependent, particularly on their parents. The essential feature in the clinical picture of this disorder is excessive anxiety about separation from major attachment figures, such as their mother, and from familiar home surroundings (Bernstein & Layne, 2006). In many cases, a clear psychosocial stressor can be identified, such as the death of a relative or a pet. The case study below illustrates the clinical picture in this disorder.

When children with separation anxiety disorder are actually separated from their attachment figures, they typically become preoccupied with morbid fears, such as the worry that their parents are going to become ill or die. They cling helplessly to adults, have difficulty sleeping, and become intensely demanding. Separation anxiety is more common in girls (Bernstein & Layne, 2006), and the disorder is not very stable over time (Poulton et al., 2001). One study, for example, reported that 44 percent of youngsters showed recovery at a 4-year follow-up (Cantwell & Baker, 1989). However, some children go on to exhibit school refusal problems (a fear of leaving home and parents to attend school) and continue to have subsequent adjustment difficulties. A disproportionate number of children with separation anxiety

case study
Johnny's Severe Separation Anxiety

Johnny was a highly sensitive 6-year-old who suffered from numerous fears, nightmares, and chronic anxiety. He was terrified of being separated from his mother, even for a brief period. When his mother tried to enroll him in kindergarten, he became so upset when she left the room that the principal arranged for her to remain in the classroom. After 2 weeks, however, this arrangement had to be discontinued, and Johnny had to be withdrawn from kindergarten because his mother could not leave him even for a few minutes. Later, when his mother attempted to enroll him in the first grade, Johnny manifested the same intense anxiety and unwillingness to be separated from her. At the suggestion of the school counselor, Johnny's mother brought him to a community clinic for assistance with the problem. The therapist who initially saw Johnny and his mother was wearing a white clinic jacket, which led to a severe panic reaction on Johnny's part. His mother had to hold him to keep him from running away, and he did not settle down until the therapist removed his jacket. Johnny's mother explained that he was terrified of doctors and that it was almost impossible to get him to a physician even when he was sick.

disorder also experience a high number of other anxiety-based disorders such as phobia and obsessive-compulsive disorder (Egger et al., 2003; Kearney et al., 2003).

CAUSAL FACTORS IN ANXIETY DISORDERS A number of causal factors have been emphasized in explanations of the childhood anxiety disorders. Although genetic factors have been thought to contribute to the development of anxiety disorders, particularly obsessive-compulsive disorder, in children (Nestadt et al., 2010), social and cultural factors are likely to be influential in resulting in anxiety disorders in children. For example, Potochnick

When children with separation anxiety disorder are actually separated from their attachment figures, they typically become preoccupied with morbid fears, such as the worry that their parents are going to become ill or die.

and Perreira (2010) found an increased risk of anxiety and depression among immigrant Latino youth. Parental behavior and family stress in minority families have been particularly noted as potential influential factors in the origin of anxiety disorders in children; however, broader cultural factors are also important considerations.

Anxious children often manifest an unusual constitutional sensitivity that makes them easily conditionable by aversive stimuli. For example, they may be readily upset by even small disappointments—a lost toy or an encounter with an overeager dog. They then have a harder time calming down, a fact that can result in a build-up and generalization of surplus fear reactions.

The child can become anxious because of early illnesses, accidents, or losses that involved pain and discomfort. The traumatic effect of experiences such as hospitalizations makes such children feel insecure and inadequate. The traumatic nature of certain life changes such as moving away from friends and into a new situation can also have an intensely negative effect on a child's adjustment.

Overanxious children often have the modeling effect of an overanxious and protective parent who sensitizes a child to the dangers and threats of the outside world. Often, the parent's overprotectiveness communicates a lack of confidence in the child's ability to cope, thus reinforcing the child's feelings of inadequacy (Woodruff-Borden et al., 2002).

Indifferent or detached parents (Chartier et al., 2001) or rejecting parents (Hudson & Rapee, 2001) also foster anxiety in their children. The child may not feel adequately supported in mastering essential competencies and in gaining a positive self-concept. Repeated experiences of failure stemming from poor learning skills may lead to subsequent patterns of anxiety or withdrawal in the face of "threatening" situations. Other children may perform adequately but may be overcritical of themselves and feel intensely anxious and devalued when they perceive themselves as failing to do well enough to earn their parents' love and respect.

The role that social-environmental factors might play in the development of anxiety-based disorders, though important, is not clearly understood. A cross-cultural study of fears (Ollendick et al., 1996) found significant differences among American, Australian, Nigerian, and Chinese children and adolescents. These authors suggest that cultures that favor inhibition, compliance, and obedience appear to increase the levels of fear reported. In another study in the United States, Last and Perrin (1993) reported that there are some differences between African American and white children with respect to types of anxiety disorders. White children are more likely to present with school refusal than are African American children, who show more PTSD symptoms. This difference might result from differing patterns of referral for African American and white families, or it might reflect differing environmental stressors placed on the children. Several studies have also reported a strong association between exposure to violence and a reduced sense of security and psychological well-being (Cooley-Quille et al., 2001). Children who experience a sense of diminished control over negative environmental factors may become more vulnerable to the development of anxiety than those children who achieve a sense of efficacy in managing stressful circumstances.

TREATMENTS AND OUTCOMES The anxiety disorders of childhood occasionally continue into adolescence and young adulthood, leading first to maladaptive avoidance behavior and later to increasingly idiosyncratic thinking and behavior or an inability to "fit in" with a peer group. Typically, however, this is not the case. As affected children grow and have wider interactions in school and in activities with peers, they often benefit from experiences such as making friends and succeeding at given tasks. Teachers who are aware of the needs of both overanxious and shy, withdrawn children are often able to ensure that they will have successful experiences that help alleviate their anxiety.

Biologically Based Treatments Psychopharmacological treatment of anxiety disorders in children and adolescents is becoming more common today (Vitiello & Waslick, 2010). Birmaher and colleagues (2003) evaluated the efficacy of using fluoxetine in the treatment of a variety of anxiety-based disorders and found the medication useful. However, the cautious use of medications with anxiety-based disorders involves obtaining diagnostic clarity since these conditions often coexist with other disorders.

Psychological Treatment Behavior therapy procedures, sometimes used in school settings, often help anxious children (Mash & Barkley, 2006). Such procedures include assertiveness training to provide help with mastering essential competencies

and desensitization to reduce anxious behavior. Kendall and colleagues have reported the successful use of manual-based cognitive-behavioral treatment (well-defined procedures using positive reinforcement to enhance coping strategies to deal with fears) for children with anxiety disorders (Chu & Kendall, 2004). Behavioral treatment approaches such as desensitization must be explicitly tailored to a child's particular problem, and in vivo methods (using real-life situations graded in terms of the anxiety they arouse) tend to be more effective than having the child "imagine" situations. Svensson and colleagues (2002) reported successful treatment of phobic children using brief exposure.

Cognitive behavioural therapy has been shown to be highly effective at reducing anxiety symptoms in young children (Legerstee et al., 2010; Hirshfield-Becker et al., 2010). An interesting and effective cognitive-behavioral anxiety prevention and treatment study was implemented in Australia. In an effort to identify and reduce anxiousness in young adolescents, Dadds and colleagues (1997) identified 314 children who met the criteria for an anxiety disorder out of a sample of 1,786 children 7 to 14 years old in a school system in Brisbane, Australia. They contacted the parents of these anxious children to engage them in the treatment intervention, and the parents of 128 of the children agreed to participate. The treatment intervention involved holding group sessions with the children in which they were taught to recognize their anxious feelings and deal with them more effectively than they otherwise would have. In addition, the parents were taught behavioral management procedures to deal more effectively with their child's behavior. Six months after therapy was completed, significant anxiety reduction was shown for the treatment group compared with an untreated control sample.

Childhood Depression and Bipolar Disorder

Childhood depression includes behaviors such as withdrawal, crying, avoidance of eye contact, physical complaints, poor appetite, and even aggressive behavior and in some

Childhood depression includes behaviors such as withdrawal, crying, avoiding eye contact, physical complaints, poor appetite, and in some extreme cases, aggressive behavior and suicide.

cases suicide (Pfeffer, 1996a, 1996b). One epidemiological study (Cohen et al., 1998) reported an association between somatic illness and childhood depressive illness, suggesting that there may be some common etiologic factors.

Currently, childhood depression is classified according to essentially the same *DSM* diagnostic criteria used for adults (American Psychiatric Association, *DSM-IV-TR*, 2000). However, research on the neurobiological correlates and treatment responses of children, adolescents, and adults has shown clear differences in hormonal levels and in the response to treatment (Kaufman et al., 2001). Gaffrey and colleagues (2011) recently reported an fMRI study indicating that depressed preschoolers exhibit a significant positive relationship between depression severity and right amygdala activity when viewing facial expressions of negative affect.

Future neuroimaging studies are needed to explore these differences further. One modification used for diagnosing depression in children is that irritability is often found as a major symptom and can be substituted for depressed mood.

This case study is intentionally omitted from this text.

Depression in children and adolescents occurs with high frequency. The overall prevalence rates are as follows: under age 13, 2.8 percent; ages 13 to 18, 5.6 percent (girls, 5.9 percent; boys, 4.6 percent). These rates have been generally consistent over the past 30 years. (Costello et al., 2006). Lewinsohn and colleagues (1993) report that 7.1 percent of the adolescents surveyed reported having attempted suicide in the past; in another epidemiological study, Lewinsohn and colleagues (1994) point out that 1.7 percent of adolescents between 14 and 18 had made a suicide attempt.

There is an increased use of bipolar diagnosis among children and adolescents in the United States (see Developments in Research 1). Moreno and colleagues (2007) reported that the estimated annual number of youth office-based visits with a diagnosis of bipolar disorder increased from 25 (1994–1995) to 1,003 (2002–2003) visits per 100,000 population, as did adult visits, with the majority of visits by males (66.5). A high percentage of these adolescents received a comorbid diagnosis, frequently ADHD.

CAUSAL FACTORS IN CHILDHOOD DEPRESSION The causal factors implicated in the childhood anxiety disorders are pertinent to the depressive disorders as well.

Biological Factors There appears to be an association between parental depression and behavioral and mood problems in children (Halligan et al., 2007; Hammen et al., 2004). Children of parents with major depression are more impaired, receive more psychological treatment, and have more psychological diagnoses than children of parents with no psychological disorders (Kramer et al., 1998). This is particularly the case when the parent's depression affects the child through less-than-optimal interactions (Carter et al., 2001). A controlled study of family history and onset of depression found that children from mood-disordered families had significantly higher rates of depression than those from nondisordered families (Kovacs et al., 1997). The suicide attempt rate has also been shown to be higher for children of depressed parents (7.8 percent) than for the offspring of control parents (Weissman et al., 1992).

Other biological factors might also make children vulnerable to psychological problems like depression. These factors include biological changes in the neonate as a result of alcohol intake by the mother during pregnancy, as prenatal exposure to alcohol is related to depression in children. M. J. O'Connor's (2001) study of children exposed to alcohol in utero reveals a continuity between alcohol use by the mother and infant negative affect and early childhood depression symptoms.

Learning Factors Learning maladaptive behaviors appears to be important in childhood depressive disorders, and there are likely to be learning or cultural factors in the expression of depression. Stewart, Kennard and colleagues (2004) reported that depression symptoms and hopelessness are higher in Hong Kong than in the United States. In addition, a number of studies have indicated that children's exposure to early traumatic events can increase their risk for the development of depression. Children who have experienced past stressful events are susceptible to states of depression that make them vulnerable to suicidal thinking under stress (Silberg et al., 1999). Intense or persistent sensitization of the central nervous system in response to severe stress might induce hyperreactivity and alteration of the neurotransmitter system, leaving these children vulnerable to later depression (Heim & Nemeroff, 2001). A recent study by Olino and colleagues (2010) found that temperamental emotionality was associated with having a depressed parent. Children who are exposed to negative parental behavior or negative emotional states may develop depressed affect themselves (Herman-Stahl & Peterson, 1999). For example,

1 DEVELOPMENTS IN RESEARCH

Bipolar Disorder in Children and Adolescents: Is There an Epidemic?

Bipolar disorder is often characterized by extreme mood swings and aggressive, irritable behavior (Braaten, 2011). Until recent years it was thought to largely be a disorder occurring in adulthood. But in the late 1990s, many psychiatrists began applying the diagnosis to children and adolescents and prescribing bipolar medication for their treatment (see Geller & DelBello, 2008). Bipolar disorder is often co-morbid with other disorders such as ADHD (Klassen et al., 2010). Is there an epidemic of depression and bipolar disorder among children and adolescents?

Bipolar disorders differ from unipolar mood disorders by the presence of manic or hypomanic symptoms. A person who experiences a manic episode has a markedly elevated, euphoric, and expansive mood that is often interrupted by occasional outbursts of intense irritability or even violence. In order to meet *DSM-IV-TR* diagnostic criteria, these extreme moods must persist for at least a week. In addition, three or more additional symptoms must occur in the same time period. There must also be significant impairment of life or social functioning. Hospitalization is often necessary during manic episodes. In about two-thirds of cases, the manic episodes either immediately precede or immediately follow a depressive episode; in other cases, the manic and depressive episodes are separated by intervals of relatively normal functioning. Bipolar disorder occurs equally in males and females and usually starts in adolescence and young adulthood. The likelihood of a full recovery from bipolar disorder is low even with the use of mood-stabilizing medications such as lithium because bipolar disorder is typically a recurrent condition that continues into adulthood.

The *DSM-IV-TR* provides criteria to define bipolar disorder in children that are based on how the disorder typically appears in adults; however, there is not a specific childhood or adolescent bipolar condition in the present *DSM* manual. The diagnostic criteria for bipolar disorder have not changed over the past decade (McClellan et al., 2007) even though there is an increased use of the diagnosis among children and adolescents in the United States, as noted by recent news media reports (Carey, 2007) as well as recent research surveys. For example, Moreno and colleagues (2007) recently reported that the estimated annual number of youth office-based visits with a diagnosis of bipolar disorder increased from 25 (1994–1995) to 1,003 (2002–2003) per 100, 000 population, as did adult visits, with the majority of visits by males (66.5). A high percentage of these adolescents received a comorbid diagnosis, frequently ADHD.

The question of overdiagnosis of bipolar disorder in children has emerged, in part, because of the increased use of antidepressant prescriptions for children and adolescents. For example, Harris (2005) points out that during a recent 3-month period in the child assessment unit at Cambridge Hospital in Massachusetts, a quarter of the children ages 3 to 13 years who were in her care had been given a diagnosis of bipolar disorder by their outpatient clinicians and were receiving mood stabilizers or antipsychotics. Another quarter were believed to have bipolar disorder by their parents, who requested that appropriate medications be started. A number of authorities, however, have questioned the extreme increase in the use of bipolar diagnoses for children and adolescents and the more extensive use of medications for treating bipolar disorder among young people.

Does the increased rate of bipolar diagnosis for young people result from changes in practice in which clinicians are using the diagnosis more? Or are younger people acquiring the disorder more commonly? Or are practitioners now recognizing more patients with the disorder that they had "missed" in the past? Many experts theorize that the increase reflects the fact that doctors are more aggressively applying the diagnosis to children, not an indication that the incidence of the disorder has increased. Blader and Carlson (2007) point out that the growth in the rate of bipolar disorder–diagnosed discharges might reflect a "progressive rebranding" of the same clinical phenomena for which hospitalized children previously received different diagnoses such as ADHD. Basing their conclusions on data from the National Hospital Discharge Survey, Blader and Carlson reported that the rate of bipolar diagnoses jumped from 10.0 percent to 34.1 percent for all pediatric psychiatric discharges during the study period, and it rose from 10.2 percent to 25.9 percent in adolescents. They concluded that the rate for discharge diagnosis of bipolar disorder in children has increased by 25 percent annually.

The reported increase in depression and bipolar disorder among children and adolescents has, however, been questioned by some studies. For example, using published rates of admission in epidemiological research in the United Kingdom, Costello and colleagues (2006) report different results. They conducted a meta-analysis of 26 epidemiological studies on children born between 1965 and 1996 that included nearly 60,000 interviews that allowed for a diagnosis of depression and concluded that there is not an increased prevalence of adolescent depression over the past 30 years.

Several authorities have advised caution in the use of bipolar diagnoses in children and adolescents. Harris (2005) points out that child and adolescent psychiatrists must demand tighter criteria and higher quality of evidence in regard to juvenile bipolar disorder in order to ensure diagnostic accuracy and also integrate these criteria into case formulations that lead to an effective treatment plan. One concern resulting from possible inaccurate diagnoses of bipolar disorder is that psychiatrists might overprescribe medications used in the treatment of bipolar disorder (NIMH, 2007).

childhood depression has been found to be more common in divorced families (Palosaari & Laippala, 1996).

One important area of research is focusing on the role of the mother–child interaction in the transmission of depressed affect. Specifically, investigators have been evaluating the possibility that mothers who are depressed transfer their low mood to their infants through their interactions with them (Jackson & Huang, 2000). Depression among mothers is not uncommon and can result from several sources, such as financial or marital problems. One study found that parenting problems and depressed mood in mothers are associated with depression in children (Oldehinkel et al., 2007).

Depressed mothers do not respond effectively to their children (Goldsmith & Rogoff, 1997), and they tend to be less sensitively attuned to, and more negative toward, their infants than nondepressed mothers. Other research has shown that negative (depressed) affect and constricted mood on the part of a mother, which shows up as unresponsive facial expressions and irritable behavior, can produce similar responses in her infant (Tronick & Cohn, 1989). Interestingly, the negative impact of depressed mothers' interaction style has also been studied at the physiological level. Infants have been reported to exhibit greater frontal brain electrical activity during the expression of negative emotionality by their mothers (Dawson et al., 1997). Although many of these studies have implicated the mother–child relationship in development of the disorder, depression in fathers has also been related to depression in children (Jacob & Johnson, 2001).

Considerable evidence has accumulated that depressive symptoms are positively correlated with the tendency to attribute positive events to external, specific, and unstable causes and negative events to internal, global, and stable causes (Klein et al., 2008); with fatalistic thinking (Roberts et al., 2000); and with feelings of helplessness (Kistner et al., 2001). For example, the child may respond to peer rejection or teasing by concluding that he or she has some internal flaw.

TREATMENTS AND OUTCOMES The view that childhood and adolescent depression is like adult depression has prompted researchers to treat children displaying mood disorders—particularly adolescents who are viewed as suicidal (Greenhill & Waslick, 1997)—with medications that have worked with adults. Research on the effectiveness of antidepressant medications with children is both limited (Emslie & Mayes, 2001) and contradictory at best, and some studies have found antidepressants to be

Mothers who are depressed may transmit their depression to their children by their lack of responsiveness to the children as a result of their own depression (Bagner et al., 2010). Unfortunately, depression among mothers is all too common. Exhaustion, marital distress as a result of the arrival of children in a couple's lives, delivery complications, and the difficulties of particular babies may all play a part.

only moderately helpful (Wagner & Ambrosini, 2001). Some studies using fluoxetine (Prozac) with depressed adolescents have shown the drug to be more effective than a placebo (DeVane & Sallee, 1996; Emslie et al., 1997), and other research has shown fluoxetine to be effective in the treatment of depression when administered as part of cognitive-behavioral therapy (Treatment for Adolescents with Depression Study [TADS] Team, U.S., 2004), although complete remission of symptoms was seldom obtained. Antidepressant medications may also have some undesirable side effects (nausea, headaches, nervousness, insomnia, and even seizures) in children and adolescents. Four accidental deaths from a drug called desipramine have been reported (Campbell & Cueva, 1995).

Emslie and colleagues (2010) recently pointed out that antidepressants are among the most widely used drugs in treating children and adolescents for a variety of disorders, with significant increases over the past 20 years. Primarily, antidepressants are used for the same disorders as in adults (i.e., depression, anxiety).

Depressed mood has come to be viewed as an important risk factor in suicide among children and adolescents. About 7 to 10 percent of adolescents report having made at least one suicide attempt (Safer, 1997b). Children who attempt suicide are at greater risk for subsequent suicidal episodes than are nonattempters, particularly within the first 2 years after their initial attempt (Pfeffer et al., 1994), and some research has suggested that antidepressant medication treatment in children and adolescents is associated with an increased risk of suicide (Olfson et al., 2006). Among the childhood disorders, depression especially merits aggressive treatment. Recent attention is being paid to the increased potential of suicidal ideation and behavior in children and adolescents who are taking SSRIs for their depression (Whittington et al., 2004), and some risk of suicide for those taking the medication has been noted (Couzin, 2004). The extent to which these medications represent an additional threat of suicide is being investigated.

An important facet of psychological therapy with children, whether for depression or anxiety or other disorders, is providing a supportive emotional environment in which they can learn more adaptive coping strategies and more effective emotional expression (see Gillham et al., 2006; Rice et al., 2007). Older children and adolescents often benefit from a positive therapeutic relationship in which they can discuss their feelings openly (Harvey & Taylor, 2010). Younger children and those with less developed verbal skills may benefit from play therapy. Play therapy has been found to be an effective psychological treatment with children

Children can often express their feelings more directly through play than in words, as shown in this play therapy session.

(Schaefer, 2010; Steele et al., 2007), particularly using a developmentally appropriate and skill-based approach (Reddy & Atamanoff, 2006). As a treatment technique, play therapy emerged out of efforts to apply psychodynamic therapy to children. Through their play, children often express their feelings, fears, and emotions in a direct and uncensored fashion, providing a clinician with a clearer picture of problems and feelings (Perry & Landreth, 2001). Research has shown that play therapy is as effective as other types of treatment such as behavior therapy at engaging children in expressing problems. In one study, in which play therapy was integrated into an 8-week intervention program to treat children with conduct disorder, the subjects showed significant gains at a 2-year follow-up (McDonald et al., 1997).

The predominant approach for treating depression in children and adolescents over the past few years has been the combined use of medication and psychotherapy (Skaer et al., 2000). Controlled studies of psychological treatment with depressed adolescents have shown significantly reduced symptoms with cognitive-behavioral therapy (Horowitz et al., 2007; Mash & Barkley, 2006). Short-term residential treatment can also be effective with depressed children (Leichtman, 2006). A recent longitudinal follow-up study of adolescents who had been treated for depression showed that effective treatment can reduce the recurrence of depression (Beevers et al., 2007).

In Review

- How do the symptoms of childhood depression compare to those seen in adult depression?

- Describe the symptoms of ADHD.

- Identify four common symptom disorders that can arise in childhood.

Symptom Disorders: Enuresis, Encopresis, Sleepwalking, and Tics

The childhood disorders we will deal with in this section—"elimination disorders" (enuresis and encopresis), sleepwalking, and tics—typically involve a single outstanding symptom rather than a pervasive maladaptive pattern.

Functional Enuresis

The term **enuresis** refers to the habitual involuntary discharge of urine, usually at night, after the age of expected continence (age 5). In *DSM-IV-TR*, functional enuresis is described as bed-wetting that is not organically caused. Children who have primary functional enuresis have never been continent; children who have secondary functional enuresis have been continent for at least a year but have regressed.

Enuresis may vary in frequency, from nightly occurrence to occasional instances when a child is under considerable stress or is unduly tired. It has been estimated that some 4 to 5 million children and adolescents in the United States suffer from the inconvenience and embarrassment of this disorder. Estimates of the prevalence of enuresis reported in *DSM-IV-TR* are 5 to 10 percent among 5-year-olds, 3 to 5 percent among 10-year-olds, and 1.1 percent of children age 15 or older. An epidemiological study in China reported a 4.3 percent prevalence, with a significantly higher percentage of boys than girls (Liu et al., 2000).

Enuresis may result from a variety of organic conditions, such as disturbed cerebral control of the bladder (Goin, 1998), neurological dysfunction, other medical factors such as medication side effects (Took & Buck, 1996), or having a small functional bladder capacity and a weak urethral sphincter (Dahl, 1992). One group of researchers reported that 11 percent of their enuretic patients had disorders of the urinary tract (Watanabe et al., 1994). However, most investigators have pointed to a number of other possible causal factors: (1) faulty learning, resulting in the failure to acquire inhibition of reflexive bladder emptying; (2) personal immaturity, associated with or stemming from emotional problems; (3) disturbed family interactions, particularly those that lead to sustained anxiety, hostility, or both; and (4) stressful events (Haug Schnabel, 1992). For example, a child may regress to bed-wetting when a new baby enters the family and becomes the center of attention.

Medical treatment of enuresis typically centers on using medications such as the antidepressant drug imipramine. The mechanism underlying the action of the drug is unclear, but it may simply lessen the deepest stages of sleep to light sleep, enabling the child to recognize bodily needs more effectively (Dahl, 1992). An intranasal desmopressin (DDAVP) has also been used to help children manage urine more effectively

(Rahm et al., 2010). This medication, a hormone replacement, apparently increases urine concentration, decreases urine volume, and therefore reduces the need to urinate. The use of this medication to treat enuretic children is no panacea, however. Disadvantages of its use include its high cost and the fact that it is effective only with a small subset of enuretic children, and then only temporarily. Bath and colleagues (1996) reported that treatment with desmopressin was disappointing but conclude that this treatment has some utility as a way to enable children to stay dry for brief periods of time—for example, at a camp or on a holiday. Moffatt (1997) suggested that DDAVP has an important place in treating nocturnal enuresis in youngsters who have not responded well to behavioral treatment methods. It is good to remember that medications by themselves do not cure enuresis and that there is frequent relapse when the drug is discontinued or the child habituates to the medication (Dahl, 1992).

Conditioning procedures have proved to be highly effective treatment for enuresis (Cristopherson et al., 2010; Friman et al., 2008). Mowrer and Mowrer (1938), in their classic research that is still relevant today, introduced a procedure in which a child sleeps on a pad that is wired to a battery-operated bell. At the first few drops of urine, the bell is set off, thus awakening the child. Through conditioning, the child comes to associate bladder tension with awakening. Some evidence suggests that a biobehavioral approach—that is, using the urine alarm along with desmopressin—is most effective (Mellon & McGrath, 2000).

With or without treatment, the incidence of enuresis tends to decrease significantly with age, but many experts still believe that enuresis should be treated in childhood because there is presently no way to identify which children will remain enuretic into adulthood (Goin, 1998). In an evaluation of research on the treatment of bed-wetting, Houts and colleagues (1994) concluded that treated children are more improved at follow-up than nontreated children. They also found that learning-based procedures are more effective than medications.

Encopresis

The term **encopresis** describes a symptom disorder of children who have not learned appropriate toileting for bowel movements after age 4. This condition is less common than enuresis; however, *DSM-IV-TR* estimates that about 1 percent of 5-year-olds have encopresis. A study of 102 cases of encopretic children yielded the following list of characteristics: The average age of children with encopresis was 7, with a range of ages 4 to 13. About one-third of encopretic children were also enuretic, and a large sex difference was found, with about six times more boys than girls in the sam-

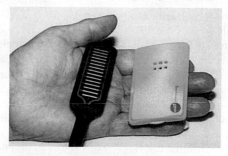

When combined with medication such as desmopressin, a urine alarm (shown here) can be very effective in treating enuresis. The child sleeps with a wetness detector, which is wired to a battery-operated alarm in his or her undergarment. Through conditioning, the child comes to associate bladder tension with awakening.

ple. Many of the children soiled their clothing when they were under stress. A common time was in the late afternoon after school; few children actually had this problem at school. Most of the children reported that they did not know when they needed to have a bowel movement or were too shy to use the bathrooms at school.

Many encopretic children suffer from constipation, so an important element in the diagnosis is a physical examination to determine whether physiological factors are contributing to the disorder. The treatment of encopresis usually involves both medical and psychological aspects. Several studies of the use of conditioning procedures with encopretic children have reported moderate treatment success; that is, no additional incidents occurred within 6 months following treatment (Friman et al., 2008). However, research has shown that a minority of children (11 to 20 percent) do not respond to learning-based treatment approaches (Keeley et al., 2009).

Sleepwalking (Somnambulism)

Although the onset of **sleepwalking disorder** is usually between the ages of 6 and 12, the disorder is classified broadly under sleep disorders in *DSM-IV-TR* rather than under disorders of infancy, childhood, and adolescence (APA, 2000). The symptoms of sleepwalking disorder involve repeated episodes in which a person leaves his or her bed and walks around without being conscious of the experience or remembering it later.

The incidence of sleepwalking reported for children in the *DSM* is high for one episode—between 10 and 30 percent is relatively common—and girls are more likely to experience sleepwalking than boys (Mahendran et al., 2006). The incidence for repeated episodes is usually low—from 1 to 5 percent. Children subject to this problem usually go to sleep in a normal manner but arise during the second or third hour of sleep. They may walk to another room of the house or even outside, and they may engage in complex activities. Finally, they return to bed and in the morning remember nothing that had taken place. While moving about, sleepwalkers' eyes are partially or fully open; they avoid obstacles, listen when spoken to, and ordinarily respond to commands, such as to return to bed. Shaking them will usually awaken sleepwalkers, and they will be surprised and perplexed at finding themselves in an unexpected place. Sleepwalking takes place during NREM (non–rapid eye movement) sleep, and sleepwalking episodes usually last only a few minutes (Plazzi et al., 2005). The causes of sleepwalking—a condition of arousal in which the subject arises from deep sleep, even displaying long, complex behavior including leaving the bed and walking, with memory impairment of the event—are not fully understood.

Little attention has been devoted to the treatment of sleepwalking. Clement (1970), however, reported on the treatment of a 7-year-old boy through behavior therapy. During treatment, the therapist learned that just before each sleepwalking episode, the boy had a nightmare about being chased by "a big black bug." After his nightmare began, he perspired freely, moaned and talked in his sleep, tossed and turned, and finally got up and walked through the house. He did not remember the sleepwalking episode when he awoke the next morning. Assessment data revealed no neurological or other medical problems and indicated that he was of normal intelligence. He was, however, found to be a very anxious, guilt-ridden little boy who avoided performing assertive and aggressive behaviors appropriate to his age and sex (p. 23). The therapist focused treatment on having the boy's mother awaken him each time he showed signs of an impending episode. After washing his face with cold water and making sure he was fully awake, the mother would return him to bed, where he was to hit and tear up a picture of the big black bug. (At the start of the treatment program, he had made several of these drawings.)

Eventually, the nightmare was associated with awakening, and he learned to wake up on most occasions when he was having a bad dream. Thus the basic behavior therapy followed in this case was the same as that used in the conditioning treatment for enuresis, where a waking response is elicited by an intense stimulus just as urination is beginning and becomes associated with, and eventually prevents, nocturnal bed-wetting.

Tic Disorders

A **tic** is a persistent, intermittent muscle twitch or spasm, usually limited to a localized muscle group. The term is used broadly to include blinking the eye, twitching the mouth, licking the lips, shrugging the shoulders, twisting the neck, clearing the throat, blowing the nose, and grimacing, among other actions. Tics occur most frequently between the ages of 2 and 14 (Evans et al., 1996). In some instances, as in clearing the throat, an individual may be aware of the tic when it occurs, but usually he or she performs the act habitually and does not notice it. In fact, many individuals do not even realize they have a tic unless someone brings it to their attention. A cross-cultural examination of tics found a similar pattern in research and clinical case reports from other countries (Staley et al., 1997). Moreover, the age of onset (average 7 to 8 years) and predominant gender (male) of cases were reported to be similar across cultures (Turan & Senol, 2000). A recent study on the prevalence of tic disorder in children and adolescents conducted by Stefanoff and colleagues (2008) reported that tic disorders are common among schoolchildren. They found that the lifetime prevalence of tic disorders (TD) is 2.6 percent for transient tic disorder (TTD), 3.7 percent for chronic tic disorder (CTD), and 0.6 percent for Tourette disorder (TD).

The psychological impact that tics can have on an adolescent is illustrated in the following case.

case study | **The Adolescent Who Wanted to Be a Teacher**

An adolescent who had wanted very much to be a teacher told the school counselor that he was thinking of giving up his plans. When asked why, he explained that several friends had told him that he had a persistent twitching of the mouth muscles when he answered questions in class. He had been unaware of this muscle twitch and, even after being told about it, could not tell when it took place. However, he became acutely self-conscious and was reluctant to answer questions or enter into class discussions. As a result, his general level of tension increased, and so did the frequency of the tic, which now became apparent even when he was talking to his friends. Thus a vicious circle had been established. Fortunately, the tic proved amenable to treatment by conditioning and assertiveness training.

Tourette's disorder is an extreme tic disorder involving multiple motor and vocal patterns. This disorder typically involves uncontrollable head movements with accompanying sounds such as grunts, clicks, yelps, sniffs, or words. Some, possibly most, tics are preceded by an urge or sensation that seems to be relieved by execution of the tic. Tics are thus often difficult to differentiate from compulsions, and they are sometimes referred to as "compulsive tics" (Jankovic, 1997). An epidemiological study in Sweden reported the prevalence of Tourette's disorder in children and adolescents to be about 0.56 percent (Khalifa & von Knorring, 2004). About one-third of individuals with Tourette's disorder manifest coprolalia, which is a complex vocal tic that involves the uttering of obscenities. Some people with Tourette's disorder also experience explosive outbursts (Budman et al., 2000). The average age of onset for Tourette's disorder is 7, and most cases have an onset before age 14. The disorder frequently persists into adulthood, and it is about three times more frequent among males than among females. Although the exact cause of Tourette's disorder is undetermined, evidence suggests an organic basis (Margolis et al., 2006). There are many types of tics, and many of them appear to be associated with the presence of other psychological disorders (Cardona et al., 1997), particularly obsessive-compulsive disorder (OCD). Most tics, however, do not have an organic basis but stem from psychological causes such as self-consciousness or tension in social situations, and they are usually associated with severe behavioral problems (Rosenberg et al., 1995). As in the case of the adolescent boy previously described, an individual's awareness of the tic often increases tension and the occurrence of the tic.

Among medications, neuroleptics are the most predictably effective tic-suppressing drugs (Kurlan, 1997). Clonazepam, clonidine, and tiapride have all shown effectiveness in reducing motor tics; however, tiapride has shown the greatest decrease in the intensity and frequency of tics (Drtikova et al.,

1996). Campbell and Cueva (1995) reported that both halo-peridol and pimozide reduced the severity of tics by about 65 percent but that haloperidol seemed the more effective of the two medications. Gilbert and colleagues (2004) reported that risperidone outperformed pimozide in tic suppression.

Most people suffering from tic disorders do not receive treatment for their symptoms (Cook & Blacher, 2007); however, behavioral intervention techniques have been used successfully in treating tics (Woods & Miltenberger, 2001). One successful program, habit reversal treatment or HRT, involves several sequential elements, beginning with awareness training, relaxation training, and the development of incompatible responses, and then progressing to cognitive therapy and modification of the individual's overall style of action (Chang, Piacentina, & Walkup, 2007). Finally, perfectionist expectations about self-image (which are often found in children and adolescents with tics) are addressed through cognitive restructuring. Because children with Tourette's disorder can have substantial family adjustment (Wilkinson et al., 2001) and school adjustment problems (Nolan & Gadow, 1997), interventions should be designed to aid their adjustment and to modify the reactions of peers to them. School psychologists can play an effective part in the social adjustment of the child with Tourette's disorder (Walter & Carter, 1997) by applying behavioral intervention strategies that help arrange the child's environment to be more accepting of such unusual behaviors.

In Review

- What is functional enuresis? Describe a traditional and highly effective treatment for enuresis.
- What is encropresis? In this condition more common among boys or girls?
- What is somnambulism?

Pervasive Developmental Disorders

The **pervasive developmental disorders (PDDs)** are a group of severely disabling conditions that are among the most difficult to understand and treat. They make up about 3.2 percent of cases seen in inpatient settings (Sverd et al., 1995). They are considered to be the result of some structural differences in the brain that are usually evident at birth or become apparent as the child begins to develop (Siegel, 1996). There is fairly good diagnostic agreement in the determination of pervasive developmental disorders in children whether one follows the *DSM-IV-TR* or the ICD-10 (the International Classification of Disease, published by the World Health Organization), which have slightly different criteria for some disorders. Several pervasive

developmental disorders are covered in *DSM-IV-TR*—for example, **autism**, one of the most severe and puzzling disorders occurring in early childhood, and **Asperger's disorder**, which is a severe and persistent impairment in social interaction that involves marked stereotypic (repetitive) behavior and inflexible adherence to routines and also appears in childhood (see Goldstein et al., 2009, for a comprehensive discussion of the assessment of pervasive developmental disorders).

Autism

One of the most disabling of the pervasive developmental disorders is autistic disorder, which is often referred to as autism, childhood autism (Schopler et al., 2001), or, in the prospective *DSM-5*, autism spectrum disorder. It is a developmental disorder that involves a wide range of problematic behaviors including deficits in language and perceptual and motor development; defective reality testing; and an inability to function in social situations. The following case illustrates some of the behaviors that may be seen in a child with autism.

case study　The Need for Routine

Mathew is 5 years old. When spoken to, he turns his head away. Sometimes he mumbles unintelligibly. He is neither toilet trained nor able to feed himself. He actively resists being touched. He dislikes sounds and is uncommunicative. He cannot relate to others and avoids looking anyone in the eye. He often engages in routine manipulative activities such as dropping an object, picking it up, and dropping it again. He shows a pathological need for sameness. While seated, he often rocks back and forth in a rhythmic motion for hours. Any change in routine is highly upsetting to him.

Autism in infancy and childhood was first described by Kanner (1943). It afflicts tens of thousands of American children from all socioeconomic levels and is seemingly on the increase—estimates range between 30 and 60 people in 10,000 (Fombonne, 2005). A recent study by the Centers for Disease Control and Prevention (CDC, 2009) reported that the rate of autism among 8 year olds is about 1 in 110. The reported increase in autism in recent years is likely due to methodological differences between studies and changes in diagnostic practice and public and professional awareness in recent years rather than an increase in prevalence (Williams et al., 2005). Autism is usually identified before a child is 30 months of age and may be suspected in the early weeks of life. Diagnostic stability over the childhood years is quite high for autism. Lord and colleagues (2006) report that children diagnosed with autism by age 2 tend to be similarly diagnosed at age 9. One study found that autistic behavior such as lack of empathy, inattention to others, and inability to imitate is shown as early as 20 months (Charman et al., 1997).

DSM-IV-TR

Criteria for Autistic Disorder

A. A total of six (or more) items from (1), (2), and (3), with at least two from (1), and one each from (2) and (3):

1. qualitative impairment in social interaction, as manifested by at least two of the following:

   a. marked impairment in the use of multiple nonverbal behaviors such as eye-to-eye gaze, facial expression, body postures, and gestures to regulate social interaction

   b. failure to develop peer relationships appropriate to developmental level

   c. a lack of spontaneous seeking to share enjoyment, interests, or achievements with other people (e.g., by a lack of showing, bringing, or pointing out objects of interest)

   d. lack of social or emotional reciprocity

2. qualitative impairments in communication as manifested by at least one of the following:

   a. delay in, or total lack of, the development of spoken language (not accompanied by an attempt to compensate through alternative modes of communication such as gesture or mime)

   b. in individuals with adequate speech, marked impairment in the ability to initiate or sustain a conversation with others

   c. stereotyped and repetitive use of language or idiosyncratic language

   d. lack of varied, spontaneous make-believe play or social imitative play appropriate to developmental level

3. restricted repetitive and stereotyped patterns of behavior, interests, and activities, as manifested by at least one of the following:

   a. encompassing preoccupation with one or more stereotyped and restricted patterns of interest that is abnormal either in intensity or focus

   b. apparently inflexible adherence to specific, nonfunctional routines or rituals

   c. stereotyped and repetitive motor mannerisms (e.g., hand or finger flapping or twisting, or complex whole body movements)

   d. persistent preoccupation with parts of objects

B. Delays or abnormal functioning in at least one of the following areas, with onset prior to age 3 years: (1) social interaction, (2) language as used in social communication, or (3) symbolic or imaginative play.

C. The disturbance is not better accounted for by Rett's Disorder or Childhood Disintegrative Disorder.

Source: Reprinted with permission from the American Psychiatric Association. *Diagnostic and Statistical Manual of Mental Disorders,* Fourth Edition, *Text Revision* (Copyright © 2000). American Psychiatric Association.

THE CLINICAL PICTURE IN AUTISTIC DISORDER Children with autism show varying degrees of impairments and capabilities. In this section, we will discuss some of the behaviors that may be evident in autism. A cardinal and typical sign is that a child seems apart or aloof from others, even in the earliest stages of life (Hillman & Snyder, 2007). Mothers often remember such babies as never being cuddly, never reaching out when being picked up, never smiling or looking at them while being fed, and never appearing to notice the comings and goings of other people.

A Social Deficit Typically, children with autism do not show any need for affection or contact with anyone, and they usually do not even seem to know or care who their parents are. Several studies, however, have questioned the traditional view that autistic children are emotionally flat. These studies (Capps et al., 1993) have shown that children with autism do express emotions and should not be considered as lacking emotional reactions (Jones et al., 2001). Instead, Sigman (1996) has characterized the seeming inability of children with autism to respond to others as a lack of social understanding—a deficit in the ability to attend to social cues from others. The child with autism is thought to have a "mind blindness," an inability to take the attitude of others or to "see" things as others do. For example, a child with autism appears limited in the ability to understand where another person is pointing. Additionally, children with autism show deficits in attention and in locating and orienting to sounds in their environment (Hillman & Snyder, 2007).

The lack of social interaction among children with autism has been well described. A behavioral observation study by Lord and Magill-Evans (1995) noted that the youngsters with autism engaged in fewer social interactions than other children; however, this study also made the important observation that the children with autism did not play—particularly, did not show spontaneous play. In fact, much of the time, nothing was going on.

Encopresis is common (Siegel, 2003) among children with autism. Radford and Anderson (2003) point out that relatively little of the clinical descriptive literature on children with autism addresses the problem of toilet training. They note that failing to cooperate in toilet training is a common problem and one that creates added difficulty for parents of children with autism, and they provide practical advice and training guidelines for dealing with this problem behavior. In addition, a high prevalence of sleep problems has been reported for children with autism (Williams et al., 2004).

Children with autism seem to actively exclude or limit intervention from other people.

An Absence of Speech Children with autism do not effectively learn by imitation (Smith & Bryson, 1994). This dysfunction might explain their characteristic absence or severely limited use of speech. If speech is present, it is almost never used to communicate except in the most rudimentary fashion, such as by saying "yes" in answer to a question or by the use of **echolalia**—the parrot-like repetition of a few words. Whereas the echoing of parents' verbal behavior is found to a small degree in normal children as they experiment with their ability to produce articulate speech, persistent echolalia is found in about 75 percent of autistic children (Prizant, 1983).

Self-Stimulation Self-stimulation is often characteristic of children with autism. It usually takes the form of such repetitive movements as head banging, spinning, and rocking, which may continue by the hour. Other bizarre repetitive behaviors are typical.

Children with autism seem to actively arrange the environment on their own terms in an effort to exclude or limit variety and intervention from other people, preferring instead a limited and solitary routine. These children often show an active aversion to auditory stimuli, crying even at the sound of a parent's voice. The pattern is not always consistent, however; children with autism may at one moment be severely agitated or panicked by a very soft sound and at another time be totally oblivious to a loud noise.

Intellectual Ability Compared with the performance of other groups of children on cognitive or intellectual tasks, children

with autism often show marked impairment. For example, children with autism are significantly impaired on memory tasks when compared with both normal children and children with mental retardation. They show a particular deficit in representing mental states—that is, they appear to have deficits in social reasoning but can manipulate objects. Carpentieri and Morgan (1996) found that the cognitive impairment in children with autism is reflected in their greater impairment in adaptive behaviors than is seen in mentally retarded children without autism.

Some children with autism are quite skilled at fitting objects together; thus their performance on puzzles or form boards may be average or above. Even in the manipulation of objects, however, difficulty with meaning is apparent. For example, when pictures are to be arranged in an order that tells a story, children with autism show a marked deficiency in performance. Moreover, adolescents with autism, even those who are functioning well, have difficulty with symbolic tasks such as pantomime—in which they are asked to recall motor actions to imitate tasks (e.g., ironing) with imagined objects—in spite of the fact that they might perform the task well with real objects (Hillman & Snyder, 2007).

Maintaining Sameness Many children with autism become preoccupied with and form strong attachments to unusual objects such as rocks, light switches, or keys. In some instances, the object is so large or bizarre that merely carrying it around interferes with other activities. When their preoccupation with the object is disturbed—for example, by its removal or by attempts to substitute something in its place—or when anything familiar in the environment is altered even slightly, these children may have a violent temper tantrum or a crying spell that continues until the familiar situation is restored. Thus children with autism are often said to be "obsessed with the maintenance of sameness."

CAUSAL FACTORS IN AUTISM The precise cause or causes of autism are unknown, although most investigators agree that a fundamental disturbance of the central nervous system is involved (Girgis et al., 2007; Volker & Lopata, 2008). Many investigators believe that autism begins with some type of inborn defect that impairs an infant's perceptual-cognitive functioning—the ability to process incoming stimuli and to relate to the world. Recent MRI research suggests that abnormalities in the brain anatomy may contribute to the brain metabolic differences and behavioral phenotype in autism (McAlonan et al., 2005). Whatever the physiological mechanisms or brain structures involved, evidence has accumulated that defective genes or damage from radiation or other conditions during prenatal development may play a significant role in the etiologic picture (Nicolson & Szatmari, 2003; Waterhouse & Fein, 1997). Evidence for a genetic contribution to autism comes from examining the risk for autism in the siblings of autistic children (Levy et al., 2009; Mazefsky et al., 2008). The best estimates are that in families with one child with autism there is a 3 to 5 percent risk of a sibling having autism as well. Although this figure may seem low in an absolute sense, it is in fact extremely high, given the frequency of autism in the population. The most extensive autism genetics research project recently reported that tiny, rare variations in genes increase the risk of autism spectrum disorder (Autism Genome Project, 2007). These results suggest that components of the brain's glutamate neurotransmitter system are involved in autism. Thus, autism seemingly results from faulty wiring in the early stages of development. That is, glutamate increases neuronal activity and plays an important role in wiring the brain during early development.

Nevertheless, the exact mode of genetic transmission is not yet understood, but it seems likely that relatives may also show an increased risk for other cognitive and social deficits that are milder in form than true autism (Smalley, 1991). In other words, just as in schizophrenia, there may be a spectrum of disorders related to autism (Gottesman & Hanson, 2005).

TREATMENTS AND OUTCOMES OF AUTISM The treatment prognosis for autistic disorder is poor, and because of the severity of their problems, those diagnosed with autism are often insufficiently treated (Moldin & Rubenstein, 2006). Moreover, because of the typically poor response to treatment, children with autism are often subjected to a range of fads and "novel" approaches that turn out to be equally ineffective.

Medical Treatment In the past, the use of medications to treat children with autism has not proved effective. The drugs most often used in the treatment of autism are antidepressants (21.7 percent), antipsychotic medication (16.8 percent), and stimulants (13.9 percent; Handen & Lubetsky, 2005); but the data on their effectiveness do not support their use unless a child's behavior is unmanageable by other means (Sloman, 1991). If irritability and aggressiveness are present, the medical management of a case might involve the use of medications to lower the level of aggression (Fava, 1997). Although there are no

Some studies show that intensive behavioral treatment of children with autism, requiring a significant investment of time and energy on the part of therapist and parents, can bring about improvement, particularly if this treatment continues at home rather than in an institution.

sure-fire medications approved for this purpose, the drug clomipramine has had some beneficial effects (see the discussion by Erickson et al., 2007). However, no currently available medication reduces the symptoms of autism enough to encourage its general use. We will thus direct our attention to a variety of psychological procedures that have been more successful in treating children with autism.

Behavioral Treatment Behavior therapy in an institutional setting has been used successfully in the elimination of self-injurious behavior, the mastery of the fundamentals of social behavior, and the development of some language skills (Charlop-Christie et al., 1998). The late Ivar Lovaas (1987), a pioneer in behavioral treatment of children with autism, reported highly positive results from a long-term experimental treatment program. The intervention developed by Lovaas and colleagues is very intensive and is usually conducted in the children's homes rather than in a clinical setting. The children are usually immersed in a one-to-one teaching situation for most of their waking hours over several years. The intervention is based on both discrimination-training strategies (reinforcement) and contingent aversive techniques (punishment). The treatment plan typically enlists parents in the process and emphasizes teaching children to learn from and interact with "normal" peers in real-world situations. Of the treated children in the study by Lovaas and colleagues, 47 percent achieved normal intellectual functioning, and another 40 percent attained the mildly retarded level. In comparison, only 2 percent of the untreated control children achieved normal functioning, and 45 percent attained mildly retarded functioning. These remarkable results did, however, require a considerable staffing effort, with well-qualified therapists working with each child at least 40 hours per week for 2 years.

Some of the other impressive results with children with autism have also been obtained in projects that involve parents, with treatment in the home (Siegel, 2003). Treatment contracts with parents specify the desired behavior changes in their child and spell out the explicit techniques for bringing about these changes. Such "contracting" acknowledges the value of the parents as potential agents of change (Huynen et al., 1996). See Developments in Practice 2 for an example of the use of technology to improve autistic behavior.

The Effectiveness of Treatment It is too early to evaluate the long-term effectiveness of the newer treatment methods or the degree of improvement they actually accomplish, although reports of effective behavioral intervention in some areas, such as attention skills, have been noted (Martins & Harris, 2006). The prognosis for children with autism, particularly for children showing symptoms before the age of 2, is poor. Commonly, the long-term results of autism treatments have been unfavorable. A great deal of attention has thus been given to high-functioning children with autism (children who meet the criteria for autism yet develop functional speech).

One important factor limiting treatment success is the difficulty that children with autism have in generalizing behavior

Developments in Practice
CAN VIRTUAL REALITY VIDEO GAMES IMPROVE TREATMENT OF CHILDREN WITH PERVASIVE DEVELOPMENTAL DISORDERS?

Many children and adolescents with learning disabilities or pervasive developmental disorders, like other children today, are readily drawn to computer video games and will spend long hours at machines. The potential value of video media and virtual reality games at engaging and training young people appears to be great. These approaches have shown considerable promise in interesting and motivating children who might have cognitive processing impairments (Ecalle et al., 2010). Even though many of these children have problems in social relationships, deficits in attention, and often volatile and disruptive behaviors they can readily become engrossed in the world of virtual reality (see informative discussion by Durkin, 2010). Recent projects in developmental psychology in Japan have incorporated the use of computer-based media technology for influencing young people, including those with disabilities, to learn and experience new ways of functioning (Shwalb et al., 2005). For example, Nakamura and colleagues (2005) report an intervention using cell phone calls to promote a qualitative change in communication behavior in a boy with autism.

Although video games as a medium for teaching life skills are recognized as having potential for the development of effective treatments (Cartreine et al., 2010), a successful treatment requires more than its value as entertainment or time consumption. It is not necessarily a productive goal for a child with autism to just sit and stare in front of a TV screen and watch the same program all day as often happens. The treatment benefit needs to be more carefully considered. Programs for treatment or education require specifically tailored strategies to

obtain the most effective results. Machines can only perform as they are programmed to do. Thus appropriate behavioral change strategies need to be developed and studied for particular applications. The effectiveness of behavior modification approaches using computer technology for children with developmental disorders has not been widely demonstrated or even explored for many problem areas. It takes considerable research and development, along with extensive programming skills, to address particular problems that can change behavior. At this time, the psychological knowledge and research base lingers behind the expanding developments in technical equipment.

The video and virtual reality game phenomena that have attracted many young people's interest have also prompted some unanswered questions. This approach to education and treatment has come under criticism and raised potential concerns over its use. For example, there is concern that this approach has a strong potential for "addiction" to virtual reality games that could potentially adversely influence a child's development (Pies, 2009). Questions have also been raised about the need for further considerations as to possible ethical issues, involving such factors as identity, equity and confidentiality, that face instructors and therapists who use online teaching or therapy (Anderson & Simpson, 2007).

Although the available and acceptable use of computer-based learning methods show promise, there are professional issues and program research limitations that need to be more fully explored before the full potential of this methodology is reached.

outside the treatment context. Children with severe developmental disabilities do not transfer skills across situations very well. Consequently, learning behavior in one situation does not appear to help them meet challenges in others.

In spite of a few remarkable cases of dramatic success, the overall prognosis for children with autism remains guarded. Less than one-fourth of the children who receive treatment attain even marginal adjustment in later life. Even with intensive, long-term care in a clinical facility, where gratifying improvements in specific behaviors may be brought about, children with autism are a long way from becoming normal.

Parenting children with autism can be trying and stressful (Dunn et al., 2001) and can be very financially stressful for families. Parents of children with autism often find themselves in the extremely frustrating situation of trying to understand their child, providing day-to-day care, and searching for possible educational resources for their child in the present health and educational environment. An informative book on the

topic of autism is *The World of the Autistic Child* (Siegel, 1996, 2007). Siegel discusses the impact that having a child with autism can have on the family—both parents and siblings—and describes ways of dealing with the problems that can arise, including the possible need of psychological treatment for other family members. The book is a particularly valuable guide to accessing the resources available for educating and treating children with autism and negotiating the confusing educational environment. Whether to seek residential placement, clearly a necessity in some situations and families, is also an important decision that parents of many children with autism must address.

Asperger's Disorder

This disorder, often referred to as an autistic spectrum disorder, was first described by Hans Asperger in 1944 (Wing, 1981). Many of the behaviors found in this disorder are similar to those found in autism. This pattern of behavior usually appears later than other pervasive developmental disorders such as autism, but it nevertheless involves substantial long-term psychological disability. Asperger's disorder shares many features of social impairment disorder, restricted interests, and repetitive behaviors with autistic disorder, but it may become manifest somewhat later than autism and in most cases is not associated with the severe delay in language development and social interactions that autism is (Khouzam et al., 2004). The prevalence rates per 1,000 are 2.5 according to the *DSM-IV* (Mattila et al., 2007).

The behavior associated with Asperger's disorder is often viewed by laypersons as odd or eccentric (Fitzgerald, 2007), including nonverbal learning disability (Tanguay, 2001), striving to maintain sameness, physical awkwardness, problems with language and social skills, and emotional instability. According to the *DSM-IV-TR*, the essential features of Asperger's disorder involve both severe and sustained impairment of interpersonal interactions, including impairment of facial expressions, body postures, and gestures, and people with Asperger's fail to develop peer relationships. Interestingly, in contrast to autism, in Asperger's disorder there are usually no clinically significant delays in early language or age-appropriate self-help skills. However, several researchers have described the high rate of suicide during adolescence among persons with Asperger's disorder (Fitzgerald, 2007; Ghaziuddin, 2005; Gilberg, 2002).

Patients with Asperger's disorder are often treated with psychotropic medication including antidepressants, antipsychotic (thioridazine and haloperidol; Posey & McDougle, 2003), and mood stabilizers such as lithium (Belsito et al., 2001). A number of behavioral treatment approaches to improve the functioning of Asperger patients have also been used. For example, Bock (2007) found that a social-behavioral learning strategy intervention was effective at reducing problem behavior and improving cooperative learning activities with peers. Cederlund and colleagues (2008) followed up 70 males with Asperger's disorder for 5 years and found that the outcome was good in 27 percent of the cases; however, 26 percent had a very restricted life, with no occupation or activity and no friends. In general, though, the outcomes for Asperger patients are better than for those with autism.

In Review

● What is known about the causes and treatments of autistic disorder?

Learning Disabilities

The inadequate development found in **learning disorders**, a term that refers to delayed development, may be manifested in language, speech, mathematical, or motor skills, and it is not due to any reliably demonstrable physical or neurological defect. Of these types of problems, the best known and most widely researched are a variety of reading/writing difficulties known collectively as **dyslexia**. In dyslexia, the individual manifests problems in word recognition and reading comprehension; often he or she is markedly deficient in spelling and memory (Smith-Spark & Fisk, 2007) as well. On assessments of reading skill, these persons routinely omit, add, and distort words, and their reading is typically painfully slow.

The diagnosis of learning disability or disorder is restricted to those cases in which there is clear impairment in school performance or (if the person is not a student) in daily living activities—impairment not due to mental retardation or to a pervasive developmental disorder such as autism. Skill deficits due to attention-deficit/hyperactivity disorder are coded under that diagnosis. This coding presents another diagnostic dilemma, however, because some investigators hold that an attention deficit is basic to many learning disorders; evidence for the latter view is equivocal (see Faraone et al., 1993). Children (and adults) with these disorders are more generally said to be learning disabled (LD). Significantly more boys than girls are diagnosed as learning disabled, but estimates of the extent

Children with learning disorders can experience deep emotional tension under normal learning circumstances.

of this gender discrepancy have varied widely from study to study. Prevalence estimates have shown that approximately 1 in 59, or 4.6 million people, in the United States (National Institutes of Mental Health, 2007) are learning disabled.

Children with learning disabilities are initially identified as such because of an apparent disparity between their expected academic achievement level and their actual academic performance in one or more school subjects such as math, spelling, writing, or reading. Typically, these children have overall IQs, family backgrounds, and exposure to cultural norms and symbols that are consistent with at least average achievement in school. They do not have obvious, crippling emotional problems, nor do they seem to be lacking in motivation, cooperativeness, or eagerness to please their teachers and parents—at least not at the outset of their formal education. Nevertheless, they fail, often abysmally and usually with a stubborn, puzzling persistence.

It is unfortunately the case that LD, despite its having been recognized as a distinct and rather common type of disorder for more than 40 years, and despite its having generated a voluminous research literature, still fails to be accorded the status it deserves in many school jurisdictions. Instead, many classroom teachers and school administrators resort to blaming the victim and attributing the affected child's problems to various character deficiencies (see Bearn & Smith, 1998). Where lock-step uniformity is the rule, as it is in most public and many alternative educational systems, a child who learns academic skills slowly or in a different way is treated as a troublemaker.

The consequences of these encounters between children with learning disabilities and rigid school systems can be disastrous to these children's self-esteem and general psychological well-being, and research indicates that these effects do not necessarily dissipate after secondary schooling ends but impact their career adjustment (Morris & Turnbull, 2007). Thus even when LD difficulties are no longer a significant impediment, an individual may bear, into maturity and beyond, the scars of many painful school-related episodes of failure.

But there is also a brighter side to this picture. High levels of general talent and of motivation to overcome the obstacle of a learning disorder sometimes produce a life of extraordinary achievement. Sir Winston Churchill, British statesman, author, and inspiring World War II leader, is said to have been dyslexic as a child. The same attribution is made to Woodrow Wilson, former university professor and president of the United States, and to Nelson Rockefeller, former governor of New York and vice president of the United States. Such examples remind us that the "bad luck" and personal adversity of having a learning disorder need not be uniformly limiting; quite the contrary.

Causal Factors in Learning Disabilities

Probably the most widely held view of the causes of specific learning disabilities is that they are the products of subtle central nervous system impairments. In particular, these disabilities are thought to result from some sort of immaturity,

deficiency, or dysregulation limited to those brain functions that supposedly mediate, for normal children, the cognitive skills that LD children cannot efficiently acquire. For example, many researchers believe that language-related LDs such as dyslexia are associated with a failure of the brain to develop in a normally asymmetrical manner with respect to the right and left hemispheres. Specifically, portions of the left hemisphere, where language function is normally mediated, for unknown reasons appear to remain relatively underdeveloped in many dyslexic individuals (Beaton, 1997). Recent work with functional magnetic resonance imaging has suggested that dyslexic individuals have a deficiency of physiological activation in the cerebellum (Richards et al., 2005).

Some investigators believe that the various forms of LD, or the vulnerability to develop them, may be genetically transmitted. This issue seems not to have been studied with the same intensity or methodological rigor as in other disorders, but identification of a gene region for dyslexia on chromosome 6 has been reported (Schulte-Koerne, 2001). Although it would be somewhat surprising if a single gene were identified as the causal factor in all cases of reading disorder, the hypothesis of a genetic contribution to at least the dyslexic form of LD seems promising. One twin study of mathematics disability has also turned up evidence of some genetic contribution to this form of LD (Alarcon et al., 1997).

Treatments and Outcomes

Because we do not yet have a confident grasp of what is "wrong" with the average LD child it is important to have a clear assessment of their problems and abilities (Mapou, 2009) so that successful treatment can be implemented. We have had limited success in treating many of these children. Many informal and single-case reports claim success with various treatment approaches, but direct instruction strategies often do not succeed in transforming these children's abilities (Gettinger & Koscik, 2001), and there are few well-designed and well-executed outcome studies on specific treatments for learning disorders.

We have only limited data on the long-term, adult adjustments of people who grew up with the personal, academic, and social problems that LD generally entails. Two studies of college students with LD (Gregg & Hoy, 1989) suggest that as a group they continue to have problems—academic, personal, and social—into the postsecondary education years. In a community survey of LD adults, Khan and colleagues (1997) found that some 50 percent of them had personality abnormalities. Cato and Rice (1982) extracted from the available literature a lengthy list of problems experienced by the typical LD adult. These include—in addition to expected difficulties with self-confidence—continuing problems with deficits in the ordinary skills such as math that these people had trouble with as children. The authors do note, however, that there are considerable individual differences in these outcomes and that some adults with LD are able to manage very well.

Mental Retardation

The American Psychiatric Association (2000) in the *DSM-IV-TR* defines **mental retardation** as "significantly subaverage general intellectual functioning . . . that is accompanied by significant limitations in adaptive functioning" (p. 41) in certain skill areas such as self-care, work, health, and safety. For the diagnosis to apply, these problems must begin before the age of 18. Mental retardation is thus defined in terms of level of performance as well as intelligence. The definition says nothing about causal factors, which may be primarily biological, psychosocial, sociocultural, or a combination of these. By definition, any functional equivalent of mental retardation that has its onset after age 17 must be considered a dementia rather than mental retardation. The distinction is an important one because the psychological situation of a person who acquires a pronounced impairment of intellectual functioning after attaining maturity is vastly different from that of a person whose intellectual resources were below normal throughout all or most of his or her development. The diagnosis of mental retardation is likely to be changed somewhat in the *DSM-5* based upon further refinement of some categories.

Mental retardation occurs among children throughout the world (Fryers, 2000). In its most severe forms, it is a source of great hardship to parents as well as an economic and social burden on a community. The point prevalence rate of diagnosed mental retardation in the United States is estimated to be about 1 percent, which would indicate a population estimate of some 2.6 million people. In fact, however, prevalence is extremely difficult to pin down because definitions of mental retardation vary considerably (Roeleveld et al., 1997). Most states have laws providing that persons with IQs below 70 who show socially incompetent or persistently problematic behavior can be classified as "mentally retarded" and, if

judged otherwise unmanageable, may be placed in an institution. Informally, IQ scores between about 70 and 90 are often referred to as "borderline" or (in the upper part of the range) as "dull-normal."

Initial diagnoses of mental retardation occur very frequently at ages 5 to 6 (around the time that schooling begins for most children), peak at age 15, and drop off sharply after that. For the most part, these patterns in age of first diagnosis reflect changes in life demands. During early childhood, individuals with only a mild degree of intellectual impairment, who constitute the vast majority of the mentally retarded, often appear to be normal. Their subaverage intellectual functioning becomes apparent only when difficulties with schoolwork lead to a diagnostic evaluation. When adequate facilities are available for their education, children in this group can usually master essential school skills and achieve a satisfactory level of socially adaptive behavior. Following the school years, they usually make a more or less acceptable adjustment in the community and thus lose the identity of being mentally retarded.

Levels of Mental Retardation

The various levels of mental retardation, as defined in *DSM-IV-TR*, are listed in Table 1 and described in greater detail in the following sections.

MILD MENTAL RETARDATION Individuals with mild mental retardation constitute by far the largest number of those diagnosed with mental retardation. Within the educational context, people in this group are considered educable, and their intellectual levels as adults are comparable to those of average 8- to 11-year-old children. Statements such as the latter, however, should not be taken too literally. An adult with mild retardation with a mental age of, say, 10 (that is, his or her intelligence test performance is at the level of the average 10-year-old) may not in fact be comparable to the average 10-year-old in information-processing ability or speed (Weiss et al., 1986). On the other hand, he or she will normally have had far more experience in living, which would tend to raise the measured intelligence scores.

The social adjustment of people with mild mental retardation often approximates that of adolescents, although they tend to lack normal adolescents' imagination, inventiveness,

Individuals with mild mental retardation constitute the largest number of those categorized as mentally retarded. With help, a great majority of these individuals can adjust socially, master simple academic and occupational skills, and become self-supporting citizens.

table 1 Retardation Severity and IQ Ranges

Diagnosed Level of Mental Retardation	Corresponding IQ Range
Mild retardation	50–55 to approximately 70
Moderate retardation	35–40 to 50–55
Severe retardation	20–25 to 35–40
Profound retardation	below 20–25

and judgment. Ordinarily, they do not show signs of brain pathology or other physical anomalies, but often they require some measure of supervision because of their limited abilities to foresee the consequences of their actions. With early diagnosis, parental assistance, and special educational programs, the great majority of borderline and individuals with mild mental retardation can adjust socially, master simple academic and occupational skills, and become self-supporting citizens (Maclean, 1997).

MODERATE MENTAL RETARDATION Individuals with moderate mental retardation are likely to fall in the educational category of trainable, which means that they are presumed able to master certain routine skills such as cooking or minor janitorial work if provided specialized instruction in these activities. In adult life, individuals with moderate mental retardation attain intellectual levels similar to those of average 4- to 7-year-old children. Although some can be taught to read and write a little and may manage to achieve a fair command of spoken language, their rate of learning is slow, and their level of conceptualizing is extremely limited. They usually appear clumsy and ungainly, and they suffer from bodily deformities and poor motor coordination. Some individuals with moderate mental retardation are hostile and aggressive; more typically, they are affable and nonthreatening. In general, with early diagnosis, parental help, and adequate opportunities for training, most individuals with moderate mental retardation can achieve partial independence in daily self-care, acceptable behavior, and economic sustenance in a family or other sheltered environment.

SEVERE MENTAL RETARDATION In individuals with severe mental retardation, motor and speech development are severely retarded and sensory defects and motor handicaps are common. They can develop limited levels of personal hygiene and self-help skills, which somewhat lessen their dependency, but they are always dependent on others for care. However, many profit to some extent from training and can perform simple occupational tasks under supervision.

PROFOUND MENTAL RETARDATION Most individuals with profound mental retardation are severely deficient in adaptive behavior and unable to master any but the simplest tasks. Useful speech, if it develops at all, is rudimentary. Severe physical deformities, central nervous system pathology, and retarded growth are typical; convulsive seizures, mutism, deafness, and other physical anomalies are also common. These individuals must remain in custodial care all their lives. They tend, however, to have poor health and low resistance to disease and thus a short life expectancy. Severe and profound cases of mental retardation can usually be readily diagnosed in infancy because of the presence of obvious physical malformations, grossly delayed development (e.g., in taking solid food), and other obvious symptoms of abnormality. These individuals show a marked impairment of overall intellectual functioning.

Causal Factors in Mental Retardation

Some cases of mental retardation occur in association with known organic brain pathology (Kaski, 2000). In these cases, retardation is virtually always at least moderate, and it is often severe. Profound retardation, which fortunately is rare, always includes obvious organic impairment. Organically caused retardation is, in essential respects, similar to dementia, except for the different history of prior functioning. In this section, we will consider five biological conditions that may lead to mental retardation, noting some of the possible interrelationships among them. Then we will review some of the major clinical types of mental retardation associated with these organic causes.

GENETIC-CHROMOSOMAL FACTORS Mental retardation, especially mild retardation, tends to run in families. Poverty and sociocultural deprivation, however, also tend to run in families, and with early and continued exposure to such conditions, even the inheritance of average intellectual potential may not prevent subaverage intellectual functioning.

Genetic-chromosomal factors play a much clearer role in the etiology of relatively infrequent but more severe types of mental retardation such as Down syndrome and a heritable condition known as fragile X (Huber & Tamminga, 2007; Schwarte, 2008). The gene responsible for fragile X syndrome (FMR-1) was identified in 1991 (Verkerk et al., 1991). In such conditions, genetic aberrations are responsible for metabolic alterations that adversely affect the brain's development. Genetic defects leading to metabolic alterations may, of course, involve many other developmental anomalies besides mental retardation—for example, autism (Wassink et al., 2001). In general, mental retardation associated with known genetic-chromosomal defects is moderate to severe.

INFECTIONS AND TOXIC AGENTS Mental retardation may be associated with a wide range of conditions due to infection such as viral encephalitis or genital herpes (Kaski, 2000). If a pregnant woman is infected with syphilis or HIV-1 or if she gets German measles, her child may suffer brain damage.

A number of toxic agents such as carbon monoxide and lead may cause brain damage during fetal development or after birth (Kaski, 2000). In rare instances, immunological agents such as antitetanus serum or typhoid vaccine may lead to brain damage. Similarly, if taken by a pregnant woman, certain drugs, including an excess of alcohol (West et al., 1998), may lead to congenital malformations. And an overdose of drugs administered to an infant may result in toxicity and cause brain damage. In rare cases, brain damage results from incompatibility in blood types between mother and fetus. Fortunately, early diagnosis and blood transfusions can minimize the effects of such incompatibility.

TRAUMA (PHYSICAL INJURY) Physical injury at birth can result in mental retardation (Kaski, 2000). Although the fetus is normally well protected by its fluid-filled placenta during gestation, and although its skull resists delivery stressors, accidents do happen during delivery and after birth. Difficulties in labor due to malposition of the fetus or other complications may irreparably damage the infant's brain. Bleeding within the brain is probably the most common result of such birth trauma. Hypoxia—lack of sufficient oxygen to the brain stemming from delayed breathing or other causes—is another type of birth trauma that may damage the brain.

IONIZING RADIATION In recent decades, a good deal of scientific attention has been focused on the damaging effects of ionizing radiation on sex cells and other bodily cells and tissues. Radiation may act directly on the fertilized ovum or may produce gene mutations in the sex cells of either or both parents, which may lead to defective offspring. Sources of harmful radiation were once limited primarily to high-energy X rays used in medicine for diagnosis and therapy, but the list has grown to include nuclear weapons testing and leakages at nuclear power plants, among others.

MALNUTRITION AND OTHER BIOLOGICAL FACTORS It was long thought that dietary deficiencies in protein and other essential nutrients during early development of the fetus could do irreversible physical and mental damage. However, it is currently believed that this assumption of a direct causal link may

have been oversimplified. Ricciuti (1993) cited growing evidence that malnutrition may affect mental development more indirectly by altering a child's responsiveness, curiosity, and motivation to learn. According to this hypothesis, these losses would then lead to a relative retardation of intellectual facility. The implication here is that at least some malnutrition-associated intellectual deficit is a special case of psychosocial deprivation, which is also involved in retardation outcomes, as described below.

A limited number of cases of mental retardation are clearly associated with organic brain pathology. In some instances—particularly of the severe and profound types—the specific causes are uncertain or unknown, although extensive brain pathology is evident.

Organic Retardation Syndromes

Mental retardation stemming primarily from biological causes can be classified into several recognizable clinical types (Murphy et al., 1998), of which Down syndrome, phenylketonuria, and cranial anomalies will be discussed here. Table 2 presents information on several other well-known forms.

DOWN SYNDROME First described by Langdon Down in 1866, **Down syndrome** is the best known of the clinical conditions associated with moderate and severe mental retardation.

table 2 Other Disorders Sometimes Associated with Mental Retardation

Clinical Type	Symptoms	Causes
No. 18 trisomy syndrome	Peculiar pattern of multiple congenital anomalies, the most common being low-set malformed ears, flexion of fingers, small jaw, and heart defects	Autosomal anomaly of chromosome 18
Tay-Sachs disease	Hypertonicity, listlessness, blindness, progressive spastic paralysis, and convulsions (death by the third year)	Disorder of lipoid metabolism, carried by a single recessive gene
Turner's syndrome	In females only; webbing of neck, increased carrying angle of forearm, and sexual infantilism; mental retardation may occur but is infrequent	Sex chromosome anomaly (XO)
Klinefelter's syndrome	In males only; features vary from case to case, the only constant finding being the presence of small testes after puberty	Sex chromosome anomaly (XXY)
Niemann-Pick's disease	Onset usually in infancy, with loss of weight, dehydration, and progressive paralysis	Disorder of lipoid metabolism
Bilirubin encephalopathy	Abnormal levels of bilirubin (a toxic substance released by red cell destruction) in the blood; motor incoordination frequent	Often, Rh (ABO) blood group incompatibility between mother and fetus
Rubella, congenital	Visual difficulties most common, with cataracts and retinal problems often occurring together, and with deafness and anomalies in the valves and septa of the heart	The mother's contraction of rubella (German measles) during the first few months of her pregnancy

Source: Based on American Psychiatric Association (2000); Harris (2006).

The prevalence of Down syndrome has been reported to be 5.9 per 10,000 of the general population (Cooper, Smiley, et al., 2009). It is a condition that creates irreversible limitations on survivability, intellectual achievement, and competence in managing life tasks (Bittles et al., 2007; Patterson et al., 2008) and is associated with health problems in later life such as pneumonia and other respiratory infections. The availability of amniocentesis and chorionic villus sampling in expectant mothers has made it possible to detect in utero the extra genetic material involved in Down syndrome, which is most often the trisomy of chromosome 21, yielding 47 rather than the normal 46 chromosomes (see Figure 1).

The Clinical Picture in Down Syndrome A number of physical features are often found among children with Down syndrome, but few of these children have all of the characteristics commonly thought to typify this group. The eyes appear almond-shaped, and the skin of the eyelids tends to be abnormally thick. The face and nose are often flat and broad, as is the back of the head. The tongue, which seems too large for the mouth, may show deep fissures. The iris of the eye is frequently speckled. The neck is often short and broad, as are the hands. The fingers are stubby, and the little finger is often more noticeably curved than the other fingers. Although facial surgery is sometimes tried to correct the more stigmatizing features,

Physical features found among children with Down syndrome include almond-shaped eyes, abnormally thick skin on the eyelids, and a face and nose that are often flat and broad. The tongue may seem too big for the mouth and may show deep fissures. The iris of the eye is frequently speckled. The neck is often short and broad, as are the hands. The fingers are stubby, and the little finger is often more noticeably curved than the other fingers.

its success is often limited (Roizen, 2007). Also, parents' acceptance of their Down syndrome child is inversely related to their support of such surgery (Katz et al., 1997).

There are special medical problems with Down syndrome children that require careful medical attention and examinations (Tyrer et al., 2007). Death rates for children with Down syndrome have, however, decreased dramatically in the past century. In 1919 the life expectancy at birth for such children was about 9 years; most of the deaths were due to gross physical problems, and a large proportion occurred in the first year of life. Thanks to antibiotics, surgical correction of lethal anatomical defects such as holes in the walls separating the heart's chambers, and better general medical care, many more of these children now live to adulthood (Hijii et al., 1997). Nevertheless, they appear as a group to experience an accelerated aging process (Hasegawa et al., 1997) and a decline in cognitive abilities (Thompson, 2003). One recent study reported that of those with Down syndrome who were age 60 and above, a little more than 50 percent had clinical evidence of dementia (Margallo et al., 2007).

Despite their problems, children with Down syndrome are usually able to learn self-help skills, acceptable social behavior, and routine manual skills that enable them to be of assistance in a family or institutional setting (Brown et al., 2001). The traditional view has been that children with Down syndrome are unusually placid and affectionate. However, research has called into question the validity of this generalization (Pary, 2004). These children may indeed be very docile, but probably in no greater proportion than normal children; they may also be equally (or more) difficult in various areas. In general, the quality of a child's social relationships depends on both IQ level and a supportive home environment (Alderson, 2001). Adults with Down syndrome may manifest less maladaptive behavior than comparable persons with other types of learning disabilities (Collacott et al., 1998).

Research has also suggested that the intellectual defect in Down syndrome may not be consistent across various abilities. Children with Down syndrome tend to remain relatively unimpaired in their appreciation of spatial relationships and in visual-motor coordination, although some evidence disputes

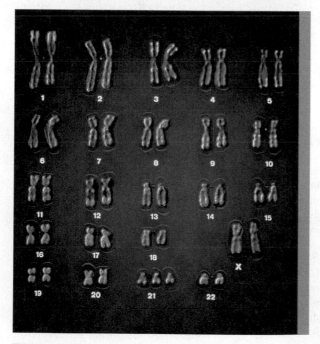

FIGURE 1

Trisomy of Chromosome 21 in Down Syndrome

This is a reproduction (karyotype) of the chromosomes of a female patient with Down syndrome. Note the triple (rather than the normal paired) representation at chromosome 21.

Source: Reproduced with permission by Custom Medical Stock Photo, Inc.

Today many more Down syndrome children are living to adulthood than in the past and are able to learn self-help, social, and manual skills. It is not unusual for Down syndrome children to be mainstreamed to some extent with unimpaired children, such as this boy (center, with glasses). Children with Down syndrome tend to remain relatively unimpaired in their appreciation of spatial relationships and visual-motor coordination; they show their greatest deficits in verbal and language-related skills.

this conclusion (Uecker et al., 1993). Research data are quite consistent in showing that their greatest deficits are in verbal and language-related skills (Azari et al., 1994; Silverstein et al., 1982). Because spatial functions are known to be partially localized in the right cerebral hemisphere, and language-related functions localized in the left cerebral hemisphere, some investigators speculate that the syndrome is especially crippling to the left hemisphere.

Chromosomal abnormalities other than the trisomy of chromosome 21 may occasionally be involved in the etiology of Down syndrome. However, the extra version of chromosome 21 is present in at least 94 percent of cases. As we noted earlier, it may be significant that this is the same chromosome that has been implicated in research on Alzheimer's disease, especially given that persons with Down syndrome are at extremely high risk for Alzheimer's as they get into and beyond their late 30s (Prasher & Kirshnan, 1993).

The reason for the trisomy of chromosome 21 is not clear, and research continues to address the potential causes (Korbel et al., 2009), but the defect seems definitely related to cognitive deficit (Kahlem, 2006) and to parental age at conception. It has been known for many years that the incidence of Down syndrome increases on an accelerating slope (from the 20s on) with increasing age of the mother. A woman in her 20s has about 1 chance in 2,000 of conceiving a Down syndrome baby, whereas the risk for a woman in her 40s is 1 in 50 (Holvey & Talbott, 1972). As in the case of all birth defects, the risk of having a Down syndrome baby is also high for very young mothers, whose reproductive systems have not yet fully matured. Research has also indicated that the father's age at conception is implicated in Down syndrome, particularly at higher ages (Stene et al., 1981).

Thus it seems that advancing age in either parent increases the risk of the trisomy 21 anomaly, although the effect of

maternal age is greater. It is not yet clear how aging produces this effect. A reasonable guess is that aging is related to cumulative exposure to varied environmental hazards such as radiation that might have adverse effects on the processes involved in zygote formation or development.

PHENYLKETONURIA In **phenylketonuria (PKU)**, a baby appears normal at birth but lacks a liver enzyme needed to break down phenylalanine, an amino acid found in many foods. The genetic error results in mental retardation only when significant quantities of phenylalanine are ingested, which is virtually certain to occur if the child's condition remains undiagnosed (Grodin & Laurie, 2000). This disorder occurs in about 1 in 12,000 births (Deb & Ahmed, 2000). This condition is reversible (Embury et al., 2007); however, if the condition is not detected and treated, the amount of phenylalanine in the blood increases and eventually produces brain damage.

The disorder usually becomes apparent between 6 and 12 months after birth, although such symptoms as vomiting, a peculiar odor, infantile eczema, and seizures may occur during the early weeks of life. Often, the first symptoms noticed are signs of mental retardation, which may be moderate to severe, depending on the degree to which the disease has progressed. Lack of motor coordination and other neurological problems caused by the brain damage are also common, and often the eyes, skin, and hair of untreated PKU patients are very pale (Dyer, 1999).

The early detection of PKU by examining urine for the presence of phenylpyruvic acid is routine in developed countries, and dietary treatment (such as the elimination of phenylalanine-containing foods such as diet soda or turkey) and related procedures can be used to prevent the disorder (Sullivan & Chang, 1999). With early detection and treatment—preferably before an infant is 6 months old—the deterioration process can usually be arrested so that levels of intellectual functioning may range from borderline to normal. A few children suffer mental retardation despite restricted phenylalanine intake and other preventive efforts, however. Dietary restriction in late-diagnosed PKU may improve the clinical picture somewhat, but there is no real substitute for early detection and prompt intervention (Pavone et al., 1993).

It appears that for a baby to inherit PKU, both parents must carry the recessive gene. Thus, when one child in a family is discovered to have PKU, it is especially critical that other children in the family be screened as well. Also, a pregnant PKU mother whose risk status has been successfully addressed by early dietary intervention may damage her at-risk fetus unless she maintains rigorous control of phenylalanine intake.

Patients with PKU are typically advised to follow a restricted diet over their life span in order to prevent cognitive impairment. Some investigators have reported mild deficits in cognitive functioning even with long-term treatment (White et al., 2002). However, other research has found little support for the hypothesis that deficits will occur even with dietary restrictions (Channon et al., 2004).

CRANIAL ANOMALIES Mental retardation is associated with a number of conditions that involve alterations in head size and shape and for which the causal factors have not been definitely established (Carr et al., 2007). In the rare condition known as **macrocephaly** (large-headedness), for example, there is an increase in the size and weight of the brain, an enlargement of the skull, visual impairment, convulsions, and other neurological symptoms resulting from the abnormal growth of glial cells that form the supporting structure for brain tissue.

Microcephaly The term **microcephaly** means "small-headedness." This condition is associated with a type of mental retardation resulting from impaired development of the brain and a consequent failure of the cranium to attain normal size.

The most obvious characteristic of microcephaly is a small head, the circumference of which rarely exceeds 17 inches, compared with the normal size of approximately 22 inches. Penrose (1963) also describes children with microcephaly as being invariably short in stature but having relatively normal musculature and sex organs. Beyond these characteristics, they differ considerably from one another in appearance, although there is a tendency for the skull to be cone-shaped, with a receding chin and forehead. Children with microcephaly fall within the moderate, severe, and profound categories of mental retardation, but most show little language development and are extremely limited in mental capacity.

Microcephaly may result from a wide range of factors that impair brain development, including intrauterine infections and pelvic irradiation during the mother's early months of pregnancy. Miller (1970) noted a number of cases of microcephaly in Hiroshima and Nagasaki that apparently resulted from the atomic bomb explosions during World War II. The role of genetic factors is not clear, although there is speculation that a single recessive gene is involved in a primary, inherited form of the disorder (Robinson & Robinson, 1976). Treatment is ineffective once faulty development has occurred; at present, preventive measures focus on the avoidance of infection and radiation during pregnancy.

Hydrocephaly The condition referred to as **hydrocephaly** is a relatively rare disorder in which the accumulation of an abnormal amount of cerebrospinal fluid within the cranium causes damage to the brain tissues and enlargement of the skull (Materro et al., 2001). In congenital cases, the head either is already enlarged at birth or begins to enlarge soon thereafter, presumably as a result of a disturbance in the formation, absorption, or circulation of the cerebrospinal fluid. The disorder can also arise in infancy or early childhood following the development of a brain tumor, subdural hematoma, meningitis, or other conditions. In these cases, the condition appears to result from a blockage of the cerebrospinal pathways and an accumulation of fluid in certain brain areas.

The clinical picture in hydrocephaly depends on the extent of neural damage, which in turn depends on the age at onset and the duration and severity of the disorder. In chronic cases, the chief symptom is the gradual enlargement of the upper part of the head out of proportion to the face and the rest of the body. While the expansion of the skull helps minimize destructive pressure on the brain, serious brain damage occurs nonetheless. This damage leads to intellectual impairment and to such other effects as convulsions and impairment or loss of sight and hearing. The degree of intellectual impairment varies, being severe or profound in advanced cases.

Hydrocephaly can be treated by a procedure in which shunting devices are inserted to drain cerebrospinal fluid. With early diagnosis and treatment, this condition can usually be arrested before severe brain damage has occurred (Duinkerke et al., 2004). Even with significant brain damage, carefully planned and early interventions that take into account both strengths and weaknesses in intellectual functioning may minimize disability (Baron & Goldberger, 1993).

Treatments, Outcomes, and Prevention

A number of programs have demonstrated that significant changes in the adaptive capacity of children with mental retardation are possible through special education and other rehabilitative measures (Berney, 2000). The degree of change that can be expected is related, of course, to the individual's particular situation and level of mental retardation.

TREATMENT FACILITIES AND METHODS Parents of children with mental retardation often find that childrearing is a very difficult challenge (Glidden & Schoolcraft, 2007). For example, recent research has shown that learning disability is associated with a higher incidence of mental health problems (Cooper & van der Speck, 2009). One decision that the parents of a mentally retarded child must make is whether to place the child in an institution (Gath, 2000). Most authorities agree that this should be considered as a last resort, in light of the unfavorable outcomes normally experienced—particularly in regard to the erosion of self-care skills (Lynch et al., 1997). In general, children who are institutionalized fall into two groups: (1) those who, in infancy and childhood, manifest severe mental retardation and associated physical impairment and who enter an institution at an early age; and (2) those who have no physical impairments but show relatively mild mental retardation and a failure to adjust socially in adolescence, eventually being institutionalized chiefly because of delinquency or other problem behavior (see Stattin & Klackenberg-Larsson, 1993). In these cases, social incompetence is the main factor in the decision. The families of patients in the first group come from all socioeconomic levels, whereas a significantly higher percentage of the families of those in the second group come from lower educational and occupational strata.

Long-term institutional care is linked with behavioral and emotional problems (Yang et al., 2007). The effect of being institutionalized in adolescence depends heavily on the institution's facilities as well as on individual factors because great care must be taken in assessing the residents' needs and in the recruitment of staff personnel (Petronko et al., 1994). For the many teenagers with mental retardation whose families are not in a position to help them achieve a satisfactory adjustment, community-oriented residential care seems a particularly effective alternative (Alexander et al., 1985). Unfortunately, many neighborhoods resist the location of such facilities within their confines and reject integration of residents into the local society (Short & Johnston, 1997).

For individuals with mental retardation who do not require institutionalization, educational and training facilities have historically been woefully inadequate. It still appears that a very substantial proportion of individuals with mental retardation in the United States never get access to services appropriate to their specific needs (Luckasson et al., 1992).

This neglect is especially tragic in view of the ways that exist to help these people. For example, classes for individuals with mild mental retardation, which usually emphasize reading and other basic school subjects, budgeting and money matters, and developing of occupational skills, have succeeded in helping many people become independent, productive community members. Classes for those with moderate and severe mental retardation usually have more limited objectives, but they emphasize the development of self-care and other skills—e.g., toilet habits (Wilder et al., 1997)—that enable individuals to function adequately and to be of assistance in either a family (e.g., Heller et al., 1997) or an institutional setting. Just mastering toilet training and learning to eat and dress properly may mean the difference between remaining at home or in a community residence and being institutionalized.

Today, there are approximately 129,000 people with mental retardation and other related conditions who receive intermediate care although many are not institutionalized. This is considerably less than the number of residents in treatment 40 years ago. These developments reflect both the new optimism that has come to prevail and, in many instances, new laws and judicial decisions upholding the rights of retarded people and their families. A notable example is Public Law 94–142, passed by Congress in 1975 and since modified several times (see Hayden, 1998). This statute, termed the Education for All Handicapped Children Act, asserts the right of mentally retarded people to be educated at public expense in the least restrictive environment possible.

During the 1970s, there was a rapid increase in alternative forms of care for individuals with mental retardation (Tyor & Bell, 1984). These included the use of decentralized regional facilities for short-term evaluation and training, small private hospitals specializing in rehabilitative techniques, group homes or halfway houses integrated into the local community, nursing homes for the elderly with mental retardation, the placement of children with severe mental retardation in more enriched foster-home environments, varied forms of support to the family for own-home care, and employment services (Conley, 2003). The past 25 years have seen a marked enhancement in alternative modes of life for individuals with mental retardation, rendering obsolete (and often leading to the closing of) many public institutions formerly devoted exclusively to this type of care.

EDUCATION AND INCLUSION PROGRAMMING Typically, educational and training procedures involve mapping out target areas of improvement such as personal grooming, social behavior, basic academic skills, and (for retarded adults) simple occupational skills (see Shif, 2006). Within each area, specific skills are divided into simple components that can be learned and reinforced before more complex behaviors are required. Behavior modification that builds on a step-by-step progression can bring retarded individuals repeated experiences of success and lead to substantial progress even in severely impaired individuals (Mash & Barkley, 2006).

For children with mild mental retardation, the question of what schooling is best is likely to challenge both parents and school officials. Many such children fare better when they attend regular classes for much of the day. Of course, this type of approach—often called **mainstreaming** or "inclusion programming"—requires careful planning, a high level of teacher skill, and facilitative teacher attitudes (Wehman, 2003).

In Review

- Compare and contrast mild, moderate, severe, and profound mental retardation.
- Describe five biological conditions that may lead to mental retardation.
- Describe some of the physical characteristics of children born with Down syndrome. What is its cause?
- What is the cause of and the preventive treatment for phenylketonuria (PKU)?
- Describe rehabilitation approaches to mental retardation.

Planning Better Programs to Help Children and Adolescents

In our earlier discussion of several disorders of childhood and adolescence, we noted the wide range of treatment procedures available as well as the marked differences in outcomes. In concluding this chapter, we will discuss certain special factors associated with the treatment of children and adolescents that can affect the success of an intervention.

Special Factors Associated with Treatment of Children and Adolescents

Mental health treatment, psychotherapy, and behavior therapy have been found to be as effective with children and adolescents as with adults (Kazdin & Weisz, 2003), but treatments conducted in laboratory-controlled studies are more effective than "real-world" treatment situations (Weisz et al., 1995). There are a number of special factors to consider in relation to treatment for children and adolescents, as follows:

THE CHILD'S INABILITY TO SEEK ASSISTANCE Most emotionally disturbed children who need assistance are not in a position to ask for help themselves or to transport themselves to and from child-treatment clinics. Thus, unlike an adult, who can usually seek help, a child is dependent, primarily on his or her parents. Adults should realize when a child needs professional help and take the initiative in obtaining it. Often, however, adults are unaware of the problems or neglect this responsibility.

The law identifies four areas in which treatment without parental consent is permitted: (1) in the case of mature minors (those considered capable of making decisions about themselves); (2) in the case of emancipated minors (those living independently, away from their parents); (3) in emergency situations; and (4) in situations in which a court orders treatment. Many children, of course, come to the attention of treatment agencies as a consequence of school referrals, delinquent acts, abuse by parents, or as a result of family custody court cases.

VULNERABILITIES THAT PLACE CHILDREN AT RISK FOR DEVELOPING EMOTIONAL PROBLEMS Children and youth who experience or are exposed to violence are at increased risk for developing psychological disorders (Seifert, 2003). In addition, many families provide an undesirable environment for their growing children (Ammerman et al., 1998). Studies have shown that up to a fourth of American children may be living in inadequate homes and that 7.6 percent of American youth have reported spending at least one night in a shelter, public place, or abandoned building (Ringwalt et al., 1998). Another epidemiological study (Susser et al., 1993) reveals that 23 percent of newly homeless men in New York City reported a history of out-of-home care as children. Parental substance abuse has also been found to be associated with the vulnerability of children to develop psychological disorders (Bijttebier & Goethals, 2006).

High-risk behaviors or difficult life conditions need to be recognized and taken into consideration (Harrington & Clark, 1998). For example, there are a number of behaviors such as engaging in sexual acts or delinquency and using alcohol or drugs that might place young people at great risk for developing later emotional problems. Moreover, physical or sexual abuse, parental divorce, family turbulence, and homelessness (Cauce et al., 2000; Spataro et al., 2004) can place young people at great risk for emotional distress and subsequent maladaptive behavior (see The World Around Us 3). Dodge and

colleagues (1997) found that children from homes with harsh discipline and physical abuse, for example, were more likely to be aggressive and conduct disordered than those from homes with less harsh discipline and from nonabusing families.

NEED FOR TREATING PARENTS AS WELL AS CHILDREN Because many of the behavior disorders specific to childhood appear to grow out of pathogenic family interactions and result from having parents with psychiatric problems themselves (Johnson et al., 2000), it is often important for the parents, as well as their child, to receive treatment (Dishion & Stormshak, 2007). In some instances, in fact, the treatment program may focus on the parents entirely, as in the case of child abuse.

Increasingly, then, the treatment of children has come to mean family therapy in which one or both parents, along with the child and siblings, may participate in all phases of the program. This is particularly important when the family situation has been identified as involving violence (Chaffin et al., 2004). Many therapists have discovered that fathers are particularly difficult to engage in the treatment process. For working parents and for parents who basically reject the affected child, such treatment may be hard to arrange (Gaudin, 1993), especially in the case of poorer families who lack transportation and money. Thus both parental and economic factors help determine which emotionally disturbed children will receive assistance.

POSSIBILITY OF USING PARENTS AS CHANGE AGENTS In essence, parents can be used as change agents by training them in techniques that enable them to help their child. Typically, such training focuses on helping the parents understand their child's behavior disorder and teaching them to reinforce adaptive behavior while withholding reinforcement for undesirable behavior. Encouraging results have been obtained with parents who care about their children and want to help them (Garza et al., 2007). Kazdin and colleagues (1997) described a number of barriers to parental involvement in treatment that result in dropout from therapy. For example, coming from a disadvantaged background, having parents who are antisocial, or having parents who are under great stress tends to result in premature termination of treatment. Research on parental adherence to clinical recommendations has shown that many of the treatment suggestions made during evaluations are not followed by caregivers. However, one recent study by Dreyer and colleagues (2010) found that 81 percent of the recommendations from an ADHD evaluation were followed up.

PROBLEM OF PLACING A CHILD OUTSIDE THE FAMILY Most communities have juvenile facilities that, day or night, will provide protective care and custody for young victims of unfit homes, abandonment, abuse, neglect, and related conditions. Depending on the home situation and the special needs of the child, he or she will later be either returned to his or her parents or placed elsewhere. In the latter instance, four types of facilities are commonly relied on: (1) foster homes, (2) private institutions for the care of children such as group homes, (3) county or state

3 THE WORLD AROUND US

The Impact of Child Abuse on Psychological Adjustment

Children who are physically or sexually abused show problems in social adjustment (Macmillan, 2010) and are particularly likely to feel that the outcomes of events are determined by external factors beyond their own control (Kinzl & Biebl, 1992; Toth et al., 1992). They are also more likely to experience depressive symptoms (Bushnell et al., 1992; Emery & Laumann-Billings, 1998). As a result, abused children are dramatically less likely to assume personal responsibility for themselves, and they generally demonstrate less interpersonal sensitivity than control children. Children who have been abused have been shown to have long-term adjustment problems, for example, in adjustment to college (Elliott, 2009) and adjustment in intimate relationships later in life (Friesen et al., 2010). Moreover, child abuse and neglect may initiate a chain of violence. Child abuse is also associated with delinquent and criminal behavior when the victim grows up. Maxfield and Widom (1996), in a follow-up study of 908 people who were abused as children, found that their arrest rate for nontraffic offenses was significantly higher than that of a control sample of people who had not been abused as children.

Child abuse is an increasing concern in the United States (Crosson-Tower, 2002). A survey of reported incidents of child abuse in this country found that such reports increased 1.7 percent in 1995, the total number of incidents exceeding 3.1 million; an estimated 1,215 children were killed in 1995 in child abuse incidents (National Committee to Prevent Child Abuse, 1996). The excessive use of alcohol or drugs in a family appears to increase the risk of violent death in the home (Rivera et al., 1997). Some evidence suggests that boys are more often physically abused than girls. It is clear that many children brought to the attention of legal agencies for abuse have been abused before. Moreover, the significantly higher rates among psychiatric inpatients of having been abused as children suggest that such maltreatment plays a causal role in the development of severe psychopathology (Read, 1997).

When the abuse involves a sexual component such as incest or rape, the long-range consequences can be profound (Paolucci et al., 2001). Adults who were sexually abused as children often show serious psychological symptoms such as a tendency to use dissociative defense mechanisms to excess, excessive preoccupation with bodily functions, lowered self-esteem (Nash et al., 1993), or a tendency to disengage as a means of handling stress (Coffey et al., 1996).

The role of sexual abuse in causing psychological problems has been the subject of several longitudinal studies. A large percentage of sexually abused children experience intense psychological symptoms following the incident (for example, the 74 percent reported by Bentovim et al., 1987). At follow-up, however, the improvement often seems dramatic (Bentovim et al., 1987; Conte et al., 1986). Several investigators have conceptualized the residual symptoms of sexual abuse as a type of posttraumatic stress disorder (PTSD) because the symptoms experienced are similar—for example, nightmares, flashbacks, sleep problems, and feelings of estrangement (Donaldson & Gardner, 1985; Koltek et al., 1998).

Child abuse all too frequently produces maladaptive social behavior in its victims (Winton & Mara, 2001). The treatment of abused children thus needs to address their problems of inadequate social adjustment, depression, and poor interpersonal skills. However, treatment can be effective if the therapy is targeted to specific needs of the child (Harvey & Taylor, 2010).

---

institutions, and (4) the homes of relatives. At any one time, more than half a million children are living in foster-care facilities, many of whom have been abused or neglected (Minnis et al., 2006).

The quality of a child's new home is, of course, a crucial determinant of whether the child's problems will be alleviated or made worse, and there is evidence to suggest that foster-home placement has more positive effects than group-home placement (Buckley & Zimmermann, 2003; Groza et al., 2003). Efforts are usually made to screen the placement facilities and maintain contact with the situation through follow-up visits, but even so, there have been cases of mistreatment in the new home (Dubner & Motta, 1999; Wilson et al., 2000). In cases of child abuse, child abandonment, or a serious childhood behavior problem that parents cannot control, it had often been assumed that the only feasible action was to take the child out of the home and find a temporary substitute. With such a child's own home so obviously inadequate, the hope was that a more stable outside placement would be better for the child. But when children are taken from their homes and placed in an institution (which promptly tries to change them) or in a series of foster homes (where they obviously do not really belong), they are likely to feel rejected by their own parents, unwanted by their new caretakers, rootless, constantly insecure, lonely, and bitter. Not surprisingly, children and adolescents in foster homes tend to require more mental health services than do other children (dos Reis et al., 2001).

Accordingly, the trend today is toward permanent planning. First, every effort is made to hold a family together and to give the parents the support and guidance they need for adequate childrearing. If this is impossible, then efforts are made to free the child legally for adoption and to find an adoptive home as soon as possible. This, of course, means that the public agencies need specially trained staffs with reasonable caseloads and access to resources that they and their clients may need.

VALUE OF INTERVENING BEFORE PROBLEMS BECOME ACUTE Over the last 25 years, a primary concern of many researchers and clinicians has been to identify and provide early help for children who are at special risk (Athey et al., 1997). Rather than waiting until these children develop acute psychological problems that may require therapy or major changes in living arrangements, psychologists are attempting to identify conditions in the children's lives that seem likely to bring about or maintain behavior problems and, where such conditions exist, to intervene before development has been seriously distorted (Schroeder & Gordon, 2002). An example of this approach is provided in the work of Steele and Forehand (1997). These investigators found that children of parents who had a chronic medical condition (the fathers were diagnosed as having hemophilia, and many were HIV positive) were vulnerable to developing internalizing problems and avoidant behavior, particularly when the parent–child relationship was weak. These symptoms in the child were associated with depression in the parent. The investigators concluded that clinicians may be able to reduce the impact of parental chronic illness by strengthening the parent–child relationship and decreasing the child's use of avoidant strategies.

Another type of early intervention has been developed in response to the special vulnerability children experience in the wake of a disaster or trauma such as a hurricane, accident, hostage-taking, or shooting (Shaw, 2003). Children and adolescents often require considerable support and attention to deal with such traumatic events, which are all too frequent in today's world. Individual and small-group psychological therapy might be implemented for victims of trauma (Cohen et al., 2006); support programs might operate through school-based interventions (Klingman, 1993); or community-based programs might be implemented to reduce the posttraumatic symptoms.

Early intervention has the double goal of reducing the stressors in a child's life and strengthening the child's coping mechanisms. It can often reduce the incidence and intensity of later maladjustment, thus averting problems for both the individuals concerned and the broader society. It is apparent that children's needs can be met only if adequate preventive and treatment facilities exist and are available to the children who need assistance.

Family Therapy as a Means of Helping Children

To address a child's problems, it is often necessary to alter pathological family interaction patterns that produce or serve to maintain the child's behavior problems (Mash & Barkley, 2006). Several family therapy approaches have been developed (Prout & Brown, 2007) that differ in some important ways—for example, in terms of how the family is defined (whether to include extended family members); what the treatment process will focus on (whether communications between the family members or the aberrant behavior of the problem family members is the focus); and what procedures are used in treatment (analyzing and interpreting hidden messages in the family communications

or altering the reward and punishment contingencies through behavioral assessment and reinforcement). But whatever their differences, all family therapies view a child's problems, at least in part, as an outgrowth of pathological interaction patterns within the family, and they attempt to bring about positive change in family members through analysis and modification of the deviant family patterns (Everett & Everett, 2001).

Treatment outcome research strongly supports the effectiveness of family therapy in improving disruptive family relationships and promoting a more positive atmosphere for children (Shadish et al., 1993).

Child Advocacy Programs

Today there are over 74 million people under age 18 in the United States (U. S. Bureau of the Census, 2009). Children who encounter mental health problems are at substantial risk for adjustment problems in later life (Smith & Smith, 2010). Unfortunately, both treatment and preventive programs for our society's children remain inadequate for dealing with the extent of psychological problems among children and adolescents. In 1989 the United Nations General Assembly adopted the U.N. Convention on the Rights of the Child, which provides a detailed definition of the rights of children in political, economic, social, and cultural areas. This international recognition of the rights of children can potentially have a great impact in promoting the humane treatment of children. However, implementing those high ideals on a practical level is difficult at best.

In the United States, one approach that has evolved in recent years is mental health child advocacy. Advocacy programs attempt to help children or others receive services that they need but often are unable to obtain for themselves. In some cases, advocacy seeks to better conditions for underserved populations by changing the system (Pithouse & Crowley, 2007). Federal programs offering services for children are fragmented in that different agencies serve different needs; thus no government agency is charged with considering the whole child and planning comprehensively for children who need help. Consequently, child advocacy is often frustrating and difficult to implement.

Outside the federal government, advocacy efforts for children have until recently been supported largely by legal and special-interest citizen's groups such as the Children's Defense Fund, a public interest organization based in Washington, DC. Mental health professionals were typically not involved. Today, however, there is greater interdisciplinary involvement in attempts to provide effective advocacy programs for children (Carlson, 2001; Singer & Singer, 2000).

Although such programs have made important local gains toward bettering conditions for children with mental disabilities, a great deal of confusion, inconsistency, and uncertainty still persist in the advocacy movement as a whole (Beeman & Edleson, 2000), and there is still a need to improve the accountability of mental health services for children. In addition, the tendency at both federal and state levels has for some time been to cut back on funds for social services. Even so, some important steps have been taken toward child advocacy, and new efforts to identify and help high-risk children have been made (National Advisory Mental Health Council, 2007). If the direction and momentum of these efforts can be maintained and if sufficient financial support for them can be procured, the psychological environment for children could substantially improve.

In Review

● What special factors must be considered in providing treatment for children and adolescents?

● Why is therapeutic intervention a more complicated process with children than with adults?

Unresolved Issues

▶ *Can Society Deal with Delinquent Behavior?*

One of the most troublesome and widespread problems in childhood and adolescence is delinquent behavior, especially that involving juvenile violence (Popma, 2007). This behavior includes such acts as destruction of property, violence against other people, and various behaviors contrary to the needs and rights of others and in violation of society's laws. The term *juvenile delinquency* is a legal one that refers to illegal acts committed by individuals between the ages of 8 and 18 (depending on state law). It is not recognized in *DSM-IV-TR* as a disorder. The actual incidence of juvenile delinquency is difficult to determine because many delinquent acts are not reported. However, some data are available:

● Of the more than 2 million young people who go through the juvenile courts each year in the United States, about a million and a half are there for delinquent acts, with the remainder there for status offenses such as running away that are not considered crimes for adults. About one in five adolescents entering the juvenile justice system suffers from a mental health condition (Phillippi & DePrato, 2010).

● In 2008, there were over 2.1 million juveniles arrested in the United States, which accounts for about 16 percent of all violent crime arrests; 1,740 juveniles were murder victims (about 11 percent of all murders) (Puzzanchera, 2009).

● A high prevalence of mental health problems has been found among adolescents in juvenile justice populations (Vermeiren et al., 2006). A significant research literature shows that adolescents detained in adult correctional facilities have a high rate of suicide or are likely to commit more crimes when they are released (Bath & Billick, 2010).

● Although most juvenile crime is committed by males, the rate has also risen for females. Female delinquents are commonly apprehended for drug use, sex offenses, running away from home, and incorrigibility, but crimes against property such as stealing have also markedly increased among this group.

● Both the incidence and the severity of delinquent behavior are disproportionately high for lower-class adolescents (Puzzanchera, 2009) with the violent crime arrest rate five times greater for African Americans than whites.

CAUSAL FACTORS

As noted in the text, only a small group of "continuous" delinquents actually evolve from oppositional defiant behavior to conduct disorder and then to adult antisocial personality; most people who engage in delinquent acts as adolescents do not follow this path (Moffitt, 1993a). The individuals who show adolescence-limited delinquency are thought to do so as a result of social

More than 2 million children a year go through the juvenile justice system for committing delinquent acts.

mimicry. As they mature, they lose their motivation for delinquency and gain rewards for more socially acceptable behavior. Several key variables seem to play a part in the genesis of delinquency. They fall into the general categories of personal pathology, pathogenic family patterns, and undesirable peer relationships.

Personal Pathology

Genetic Determinants Although the research on genetic determinants of antisocial behavior is far from conclusive, some evidence suggests possible hereditary contributions to criminality. Bailey (2000) points out that genetic factors in individual differences might operate through "an effect on hyperactivity and inattention, impulsivity, and physiological reactivity rather than through aggression" (p. 1861).

Brain Damage and Learning Disability In a distinct minority of delinquency cases (an estimated 1 percent or less), brain pathology results in lowered inhibitory controls and a tendency toward episodes of violent behavior. Such adolescents are often hyperactive, impulsive, emotionally unstable, and unable to inhibit themselves when strongly stimulated. The actual role that intellectual factors play in juvenile delinquency is still being debated (Lynam et al., 1993).

Psychological Disorders Some delinquent acts appear to be directly associated with behavior disorders such as hyperactivity (Freidenfelt & Klinteberg, 2007) or pervasive developmental disorders (Palermo, 2004). One study reported that over half of delinquents show evidence of mental disorders and 14 percent are judged to have mental disorder with substantial impairment that requires a highly restrictive environment (Shelton, 2001).

Antisocial Traits Many habitual delinquents appear to share the traits typical of antisocial personalities (Bailey, 2000). They are impulsive, defiant, resentful, devoid of feelings of remorse or guilt, incapable of establishing and maintaining close interpersonal ties, and seemingly unable to profit from experience. In essence, these individuals are unsocialized.

Drug Abuse Many delinquent acts—particularly theft, prostitution, and assault—are directly associated with alcohol or drug use (Leukefeld et al., 1998). Most adolescents who abuse hard drugs such as heroin are forced to steal to maintain their habit, which can be very expensive. In the case of female addicts, theft may be combined with or replaced by prostitution as a means of obtaining money.

Pathogenic Family Patterns

Of the various family patterns that have been implicated in contributing to juvenile delinquency, the following appear to be the most important.

Parental Absence or Family Conflict Delinquency appears to be much more common among youths from homes in which parents have separated or divorced than among those from homes in which a parent has died, suggesting that parental conflict may be a key element in causing delinquency. The effects of parental absence vary—for example, parental separation or divorce may be less troubling for children than parental conflict and dissension. It is parental disharmony and conflict in lieu of a stable home life that appears to be an important causal variable.

Parental Rejection and Faulty Discipline In many cases, one or both parents reject a child. When the father is the rejecting parent, it is difficult for a boy to identify with him and use him as a model for his own development. However, the detrimental effects of parental rejection and inconsistent discipline are by no means attributable only to fathers. Adolescents who experience alienation from both parents have been found to be more prone to delinquent behavior (Leas & Mellor, 2000).

Undesirable Peer Relationships

Delinquency tends to be an experience shared by a cultural group (O'Donnell, 2004). In a classic study, Haney and Gold (1973) found that about two-thirds of delinquent acts are committed in association with one or two other people, and most of the remainder involve three or four others. Usually the offender and the companion or companions are of the same sex. Interestingly, girls are more likely than boys to have a constant friend or companion in delinquency.

Broad social conditions may also tend to produce or support delinquency (Ward & Laughlin, 2003). An adolescent's developmental level can have a great deal of influence over how effectively he or she engages with the justice system and resolves his or her problems (Kraus & Pope, 2010). Interrelated factors that appear to be of key importance include alienation and rebellion, social rejection, and the psychological support afforded by membership in a delinquent gang. Gang activity remains a widespread problem across the United States, with prevalence rates remaining significantly elevated in 2008 compared with numbers in the early 2000s (U.S. Department of Justice, Office of Justice Programs, 2010). Every state and every large city has a gang problem, and gangs are cropping up in small rural towns across the United States as well. The problem of gang membership is most prevalent in lower-SES areas and more common among ethnic minority adolescents (48 percent are African Americans; 43 percent are Hispanic Americans) than among Caucasians. Although young people join gangs for many reasons, most members appear to feel inadequate in and rejected by the larger society. About 1 percent of youth ages 10 to 17 are gang members (Snyder & Sickmund, 2006). One study (Yoder et al., 2003) found that a significant number of homeless youth (32 percent of the sample) become gang members. Gang membership gives them a sense of belonging and a means of gaining some measure of status and approval.

DEALING WITH DELINQUENCY

If juvenile institutions have adequate facilities and personnel, they can be of great help to youth who need to be removed from aversive environments (see Scott, 2010, for a comprehensive overview). These institutions can give adolescents a chance to learn about themselves and their world, to further their education and develop needed skills, and to find purpose and meaning in their lives. In such settings, young people may also have the opportunity to receive psychological counseling and group therapy. The use of "boot camps" (juvenile facilities designed along the lines of army-style basic training) has received some support as a means of intervening in the delinquency process (Weis & Toolis, 2008), although some of the early programs were highly criticized as being both overly harsh and noneffective in bringing about positive change. One early study reported that youth in boot camps viewed their environment as more positive and therapeutic than did those enrolled in traditional programs and that they showed less antisocial behavior at the end of the training (MacKenzie et al., 2001). However, the harsh, punitive programs favored by many "law and order" politicians (as noted by the Washington State Institute for Public Policy, 1995, 1998) often fail because they do not bring about the necessary behavioral changes through reinforcing alternative behaviors (Huey & Henggeler, 2001). There are currently about 50 public and privately administered juvenile boot camp programs in the United States and other countries (Weis & Toolis, 2008), with many operating as an intervention for first time offenders and serve as a form of "intermediate sanction" that ranges between juvenile detention and probation. The value of the boot camp as a behavioral change approach for young delinquents remains to be determined by research.

Behavior therapy techniques based on the assumption that delinquent behavior is learned, maintained, and changed according to the same principles as other learned behavior have shown promise in the rehabilitation of juvenile offenders who require institutionalization (Ammerman & Hersen, 1997). Counseling with parents and related environmental changes are generally of vital importance in a total rehabilitation program (Farrington, 2010), but it is often difficult to get parents involved with incarcerated delinquents.

Summary

- Children once were viewed as "miniature adults." It was not until the second half of the twentieth century that a diagnostic classification system focused clearly on the special problems of children.

- In this chapter, the *DSM-IV-TR* classification system is followed in order to provide clinical descriptions of a wide range of childhood behavior problems.

- Attention-deficit/hyperactivity disorder is one of the more common behavior problems of childhood. In this disorder, the child shows impulsive, overactive behavior that interferes with his or her ability to accomplish tasks.

- The major approaches to treating children with ADHD have been medication and behavior therapy. Using medications such as amphetamines with children is somewhat controversial. Behavior therapy, particularly cognitive-behavioral methods, has shown a great deal of promise in modifying the behavior of children with hyperactivity.

- In conduct disorder, a child engages in persistent aggressive or antisocial acts. The possible causes of conduct disorder or delinquent behavior include biological factors, personal pathology, family patterns, and peer relationships.

- Specific learning disorders are those in which failure of mastery is limited to circumscribed areas, chiefly involving academic skills such as reading. General cognitive ability may be normal or superior.

- Affected children are commonly described as learning disabled (LD). Some localized defect in brain development is often considered the primary cause of the disorder. Learning disorders create great turmoil and frustration in victims, their families, schools, and professional helpers.

- Children who suffer from anxiety or depressive disorders typically do not cause trouble for others through their aggressive conduct. Rather, they are fearful, shy, withdrawn, and insecure and have difficulty adapting to outside demands.

- The anxiety disorders may be characterized by extreme anxiety, withdrawal, or avoidance behavior. A likely cause is early family relationships that generate anxiety and prevent the child from developing more adaptive coping skills.

- Several other disorders of childhood involve behavior problems characterized by a single outstanding symptom rather than pervasive maladaptive patterns. The symptoms may involve enuresis, encopresis, sleepwalking, or tics.

- In children with autism, extreme maladaptive behavior occurs during the early years and prevents affected children from developing psychologically.

- It has not been possible to normalize the behavior of children with autism through treatment, but newer instructional and behavior modification techniques have been helpful in improving the functioning of less severely impaired children with autism.

- When serious organic brain impairment occurs before the age of 18, the cognitive and behavioral deficits experienced are referred to as mental retardation. Relatively common forms of such mental retardation, which in these cases is normally at least moderate in severity, include Down syndrome, phenylketonuria (PKU), and certain cranial anomalies.

- This organic type of mental deficit accounts for only some 25 percent of all cases of mental retardation. Mental retardation diagnoses, regardless of the underlying origins of the deficit, are coded on Axis II of *DSM-IV-TR*.

- We reviewed a number of potential causes for the disorders of childhood and adolescence. Although genetic predisposition appears to be important in several disorders, parental psychopathology, family disruption, and stressful circumstances (such as parental death or desertion and child abuse) can also contribute.

- There are special problems, and special opportunities, involved in treating childhood disorders. The need for preventive and treatment programs for children is always growing, and in recent years child advocacy has become effective in some states. Unfortunately, the financing and resources necessary for such services are not always readily available, and the future of programs for improving psychological environments for children remains uncertain.

Key Terms

Adderall	encopresis	Pemoline
Asperger's disorder	enuresis	pervasive developmental disorders (PDDs)
attention-deficit/hyperactivity disorder (ADHD)	hydrocephaly	phenylketonuria (PKU)
	juvenile delinquency	
autism	learning disorders	Ritalin
conduct disorder	macrocephaly	separation anxiety disorder
developmental psychopathology	mainstreaming	sleepwalking disorder
Down syndrome	mental retardation	Strattera
dyslexia	microcephaly	tic
echolalia	oppositional defiant disorder (ODD)	Tourette's disorder

Glossary

Many of the key terms listed in the glossary appear in boldface when first introduced in the text discussion. A number of other terms commonly encountered in this or other psychology texts are also included; you are encouraged to make use of this glossary both as a general reference tool and as a study aid for the course in abnormal psychology.

Adderall. A habit forming drug comprised of a combination of dextroamphetamine and amphetamine.

Asperger's disorder. Severe and sustained childhood impairment in social relationships and peculiar behaviors but without the language delays seen in autism.

Attention-deficit/hyperactivity disorder (ADHD). Disorder of childhood characterized by difficulties that interfere with task-oriented behavior, such as impulsivity, excessive motor activity, and difficulties in sustaining attention.

Autism. Pervasive developmental disorder beginning in infancy and involving a wide range of problematic behaviors, including deficits in language, perception, and motor development; defective reality testing; and social withdrawal.

Conduct disorders. Childhood and adolescent disorders that can appear by age 9 and are marked by persistent acts of aggressive or antisocial behavior that may or may not be against the law.

Developmental psychopathology. Field of psychology that focuses on determining what is abnormal at any point in the developmental process by comparing and contrasting it with normal and expected changes that occur.

Down syndrome. Form of moderate to severe mental retardation associated with a chromosomal abnormality and typically accompanied by characteristic physical features.

Dyslexia. Impairment of the ability to read.

Echolalia. Parrot-like repetition of a few words or phrases.

Encopresis. Disorder in children who have not learned appropriate toileting for bowel movements after age 4.

Enuresis. Bed wetting; involuntary discharge of urine after the age of expected continence (age 5).

Hydrocephaly. Relatively rare condition in which the accumulation of an abnormal amount of cerebrospinal fluid within the cranium causes damage to the brain tissues and enlargement of the skull.

Juvenile delinquency. Legal term used to refer to illegal acts committed by minors.

Learning disorders. A set of disorders that reflect deficits in academic performance.

Macrocephaly. Rare type of mental retardation characterized by an increase in the size and weight of the brain, enlargement of the skull, visual impairment, convulsions, and other neurological symptoms resulting from abnormal growth of glial cells that form the supporting structure for brain tissue.

Mainstreaming. Placement of mentally retarded children in regular school classrooms for all or part of the day.

Mental retardation. Significantly subaverage general intellectual functioning that is accompanied by significant limitations in adaptive functioning and is obvious during the developmental period.

Microcephaly. Type of mental retardation resulting from impaired development of the brain and a consequent failure of the cranium to attain normal size.

Oppositional defiant disorder (ODD). Childhood disorder that appears by age 6 and is characterized by persistent acts of aggressive or antisocial behavior that may or may not be against the law.

Pemoline. Drug, similar to Ritalin, used to treat ADHD **Perception.** Interpretation of sensory input.

Pervasive developmental disorders (PDDs). Severely disabling conditions marked by deficits in language, perceptual, and motor development; defective reality testing; and inability to function in social situations.

Phenylketonuria (PKU). Type of mental retardation resulting from a baby's lack of a liver enzyme needed to break down phenylalanine, an amino acid found in many foods.

Ritalin. Central nervous system stimulant often used to treat ADHD.

Separation anxiety disorder. Childhood disorder characterized by unrealistic fears, oversensitivity, self-consciousness, nightmares, and chronic anxiety.

Sleepwalking disorder. Disorder of childhood that involves repeated episodes of leaving the bed and walking around without being conscious of the experience or remembering it later. Also known as *somnambulism.*

Strattera. A medication used in the treatment of ADHD.

Tic. Persistent, intermittent muscle twitch or spasm, usually limited to a localized muscle group, often of the facial muscles.

Tourette's syndrome. Extreme tic disorder involving uncontrollable multiple motor and vocal patterns.

Photo Credits

Credits are listed in order of appearance.

Text Credits

Credits are listed in order of appearance.

Therapy

From Chapter 16 of *Abnormal Psychology*, Fifteenth Edition. James N. Butcher, Susan Mineka, Jill M. Hooley. Copyright © 2013 by Pearson Education, Inc. All rights reserved.

case study

Medications and Psychotherapy

At this point in my existence, I cannot imagine leading a normal life without both taking lithium and having had the benefits of psychotherapy. Lithium prevents my seductive but disastrous highs, diminishes my depressions, clears out the wool and webbing from my disordered thinking, slows me down, gentles me out, keeps me from ruining my career and relationships, keeps me out of a hospital, alive, and makes psychotherapy possible. But ineffably, psychotherapy heals. It makes some sense of the confusion, reins in the terrifying thoughts and feelings, returns some control and hope and possibility of learning from it all. Pills cannot, do not, ease one back into reality; they only bring one back headlong, careening, and faster than can be endured at times. Psychotherapy is a sanctuary; it is a battleground; it is a place I have been psychotic, neurotic, elated, confused, and despairing beyond belief. But, always, it is where I have believed—or learned to believe—that I might someday be able to contend with all of this.

No pill can help me deal with the problem of not wanting to take pills; likewise, no amount of psychotherapy alone can prevent my manias and depressions. I need both. It is an odd thing, owing life to pills, one's own quirks and tenacities, and this unique, strange, and ultimately profound relationship called psychotherapy.

Source: From *An Unquiet Mind* by Kay Redfield Jamison (pp. 88–89), copyright © 1995 by Kay Redfield Jamison. Used by permission of Alfred A. Knopf, a division of Random House, Inc.

Most of us have experienced a time or situation when we were dramatically helped by talking things over with a relative or friend. Most therapists, like all good listeners, rely on receptiveness, warmth, and empathy and take a nonjudgmental approach to the problems their clients present.

But there is more to therapy than just giving someone an opportunity to talk. Therapists also introduce into the relationship psychological interventions that are designed to promote new understandings, behaviors, or both on the client's part. The fact that these interventions are deliberately planned and systematically guided by certain theoretical preconceptions is what distinguishes professional therapy from more informal helping relationships.

An Overview of Treatment

The belief that people with psychological problems can change—can learn more adaptive ways of perceiving, evaluating, and behaving—is the conviction underlying all **psychotherapy**. Achieving these changes is by no means easy.

Sometimes a person's view of the world and her or his self-concept are distorted because of pathological early relationships that have been reinforced by years of negative life experiences. In other instances, environmental factors such as an unsatisfying job, an unhappy relationship, or financial stresses must be the focus of attention in addition to psychotherapy. Because change can be hard, people sometimes find it easier to bear their present problems than to challenge themselves to chart a different life course. Therapy also takes time. Even a highly skilled and experienced therapist cannot undo a person's entire past history and, within a short time, prepare him or her to cope adequately with difficult life situations. Therapy offers no magical transformations. Nevertheless, it holds promise even for the most severe mental disorders. Moreover, contrary to common opinion, psychotherapy can be less expensive in the long run than alternative modes of intervention (Dobson et al., 2008; Gabbard et al., 1997).

Numerous therapeutic approaches exist, ranging from psychoanalysis to Zen meditation. However, the era of managed care has prompted new and increasingly stringent demands that the efficacy of treatments be empirically demonstrated. This chapter will explore some of the most widely accepted psychological and biological treatment approaches in use today. Although we recognize that different groups of mental health professionals often have their own preferences with respect to the use of the terms *client* and *patient*, in this chapter we use the terms interchangeably.

Why Do People Seek Therapy?

People who seek therapy vary widely in their problems and in their motivations to solve them. Below we explore a few such motivations.

STRESSFUL CURRENT LIFE CIRCUMSTANCES Perhaps the most obvious candidates for psychological treatment are people experiencing sudden and highly stressful situations such as a divorce or unemployment—people who feel so overwhelmed by a crisis that they cannot manage on their own. These people often feel quite vulnerable and tend to be open to psychological treatment because they are motivated to alter their present intolerable mental states. In such situations, clients may gain considerably—and in a brief time—from the perspective provided by their therapist.

PEOPLE WITH LONG-STANDING PROBLEMS Other people entering therapy have experienced long-term psychological distress and have lengthy histories of maladjustment. They may have had interpersonal problems such as an inability to be comfortable with intimacy, or they may have felt susceptible to low moods that are difficult for them to shake. Chronic unhappiness and the inability to feel confident and secure may finally prompt them to seek outside help. These people seek psychological assistance out of dissatisfaction and despair. They may enter treatment with a high degree of motivation, but as therapy proceeds, their persistent patterns of maladaptive behavior may generate resistance with which a therapist must contend. For example, a narcissistic client who expects to be praised by his or her therapist may become disenchanted and hostile when such ego "strokes" are not forthcoming.

RELUCTANT CLIENTS Some people enter therapy by a more indirect route. Perhaps they had consulted a physician for their headaches or stomach pains, only to be told that nothing was physically wrong with them. After they are referred to a therapist, they may at first resist the idea that their physical symptoms are emotionally based. Motivation to enter treatment differs widely among psychotherapy clients. Reluctant clients may come from many situations—for example, an alcoholic whose spouse threatens "either therapy or divorce," or a suspected felon whose attorney advises that

things will go better at trial if it can be announced that the suspect has "entered therapy." In general, males are more reluctant to enter therapy than females are (see Box 1). A substantial number of angry parents bring their children to therapists with demands that their child's "problematic behavior," which they view as independent of the family context, be "fixed." These parents may be surprised and reluctant to recognize their own role in shaping their child's behavior patterns.

PEOPLE WHO SEEK PERSONAL GROWTH A final group of people who enter therapy have problems that would be considered relatively normal. That is, they appear to have achieved success, have financial stability, have generally accepting and loving families, and have accomplished many of their life goals. They enter therapy not out of personal despair or impossible interpersonal involvements but out of a sense

1 THE WORLD AROUND US

Why Are Men So Reluctant to Enter Therapy?

Compared to women, men are much more likely to resist seeking treatment from health professionals when they are experiencing difficulties. For example, they visit their primary physicians less frequently; they also visit mental health specialists less often, and they are less likely to enter psychotherapy or counseling than women are. In the case of depression, far more men than women say that they would never consider seeing a therapist; when men are depressed they are even reluctant to seek informal help from their friends. Moreover, when men do seek professional help, they tend to ask fewer questions than women do (see Addis & Mahalik, 2003).

Why is the average man, regardless of age, social background, and ethnicity, so much more reluctant than the average woman to utilize health services? One answer is that men are less able than women to recognize and label feelings of distress and to identify these feelings as emotional problems. In addition, men who subscribe to masculine stereotypes emphasizing self-reliance and lack of emotionality also tend to experience more gender-role conflict when they consider traditional counseling, with its focus on emotions and emotional disclosure. For a man who prides himself on being emotionally stoic, seeking help for a problem like depression may present a major threat to his self-esteem. Seeking help also requires giving up some control and may run counter to the ideology that "a real man helps himself."

How can men be encouraged to seek help when they have difficulties? One basic problem is that the kinds of services that are available may not be the kinds of services that men who endorse traditional masculine roles can readily accept. In other words, for some men, there may be a mismatch between what is available and what they can psychologically tolerate. Part of the solution may be to develop treatment approaches that are based on theories of how men are socialized and

that provide a better fit for men who are constrained by gender-role expectations. Another strategy is to use more creative approaches to encourage men to seek help and support. For example, television commercials for erectile dysfunction use professional basketball players and football coaches to encourage men with similar problems to "step up to the plate" and talk to their doctors. Making men more aware of other "masculine men" who have been "man enough" to go for help when they needed it may be an important step toward educating those whose adherence to masculine gender roles makes it difficult for them to acknowledge and seek help for their problems.

that they have not lived up to their own expectations and realized their own potential. These people, partly because their problems are more manageable than the problems of others, may make substantial gains in personal growth.

Psychotherapy, however, is not just for people who have clearly defined problems, high levels of motivation, and an ability to gain insight into their behavior. Psychotherapeutic interventions have been applied to a wide variety of chronic problems. Even severely disturbed clients with psychosis may profit from a therapeutic relationship that takes into account their level of functioning and maintains therapeutic subgoals that are within their capabilities (e.g., Kendler, 1999; Valmaggia et al., 2008).

It should be clear from these brief descriptions that there is no "typical" client. Neither is there a "model" therapy. No currently used form of therapy is applicable to all types of clients, and all of the standard therapies can document some successes. Most authorities agree that client variables such as motivation to change and the severity of symptoms are exceedingly important to the outcome of therapy (Clarkin & Levy, 2004). As we will see, the various therapies have relatively greater success when a therapist takes the characteristics of a particular client into account in determining treatment approaches.

Who Provides Psychotherapeutic Services?

Members of many different professions have traditionally provided advice and counsel to individuals in emotional distress. Physicians, in addition to caring for their patients' physical problems, often become trusted advisers in emotional matters as well. Many physicians are trained to recognize psychological problems that are beyond their expertise and to refer patients to psychological specialists or to psychiatrists.

Another professional group that deals extensively with emotional problems is the clergy. A minister, priest, or rabbi is frequently the first professional to encounter a person experiencing an emotional crisis. Although some clergy are trained mental health counselors, most limit their counseling to religious matters and spiritual support and do not attempt to provide psychotherapy. Rather, like general-practice physicians, they are trained to recognize problems that require professional management and to refer seriously disturbed people to mental health specialists.

Often the first person that someone experiencing an emotional crisis will talk to is a trusted member of his or her religious community.

The three types of mental health professionals who most often administer psychological treatment in mental health settings are clinical psychologists, psychiatrists, and psychiatric social workers. In addition to their being able to provide psychotherapy, the medical training and licensure qualifications of psychiatrists enable them to prescribe psychoactive medications and also to administer other forms of medical treatment such as electroconvulsive therapy. In some states, appropriately supervised psychologists and other clinical specialists may prescribe medications if they have received additional training. Although mental health professionals differ with respect to their training and approach to treatment, generally, psychiatrists differ from psychologists insofar as they treat mental disorders using biological approaches (e.g., medications), whereas psychologists treat patients' problems by examining and in some cases changing their patients' behaviors and thought patterns.

In a clinic or hospital (as opposed to an individual practice), a wide range of treatment approaches may be used. These range from the use of medications, to individual or group psychotherapy, to home, school, or job visits aimed at modifying adverse conditions in a client's life—for example, helping a teacher become more understanding and supportive of a child-client's needs. Often the latter is as important as treatment directed toward modifying the client's personality, behavior, or both.

This willingness to use a variety of procedures is reflected in the frequent use of a team approach to assessment and treatment, particularly in group practice and institutional settings. This approach ideally involves the coordinated efforts of medical, psychological, social work, and other mental health personnel working together as the needs of each case warrant. Also of key importance is the current practice of providing treatment facilities in the community. Instead of considering maladjustment to be an individual's private misery, which in the past often required confinement in a distant mental hospital, this approach integrates family and community resources in a total treatment approach.

The Therapeutic Relationship

The therapeutic relationship evolves out of what both client and therapist bring to the therapeutic situation. The outcome of psychotherapy normally depends on whether the client and therapist are successful in achieving a productive working alliance. The client's major

What are some of the key elements of an effective therapeutic alliance between client and therapist?

contribution is his or her motivation. Clients who are pessimistic about their chances of recovery or who are ambivalent about dealing with their problems and symptoms respond less well to treatment (e.g., Mussell et al., 2000).

The establishment of an effective working alliance between client and therapist is seen by most investigators and practitioners as essential to psychotherapeutic gain. Our experiences as therapists affirm this basic observation, as does the research literature. In a very real sense, the relationship with the therapist is therapeutic in its own right. Studies of the therapeutic relationship show that how well patients do over the course of therapy is predicted by the ability of their therapist to form a strong alliance with them (Baldwin et al., 2007).

Although definitions of the therapeutic alliance vary, its key elements are (1) a sense of working collaboratively on the problem, (2) agreement between patient and therapist about the goals and tasks of therapy, and (3) an affective bond between patient and therapist (see Constantino et al., 2001; Martin et al., 2000). Clear communication is also important. This is no doubt facilitated by the degree of shared experience in the backgrounds of client and therapist.

Almost as important as motivation is a client's expectation of receiving help. This expectancy is often sufficient in itself to bring about substantial improvement, perhaps because patients who expect therapy to be effective engage more in the process (Meyer et al., 2002). Just as a placebo often lessens pain for someone who believes it will do so, a person who expects to be helped by therapy is likely to be helped, almost regardless of the particular methods used by a therapist. The downside of this fact is that if a therapy or therapist fails for whatever reason to inspire client confidence, the effectiveness of treatment is likely to be compromised.

To the art of therapy, a therapist brings a variety of professional skills and methods intended to help people see themselves and their situations more objectively—that is, to gain a different perspective. Besides helping provide a new perspective, most

therapy situations also offer a client a safe setting in which he or she is encouraged to practice new ways of feeling and acting, gradually developing both the courage and the ability to take responsibility for acting in more effective and satisfying ways.

To bring about such changes, an effective psychotherapist must help the client give up old and dysfunctional behavior patterns and replace them with new, functional ones. Because clients will present varying challenges in this regard, the therapist must be flexible enough to use a variety of interactive styles.

In Review

- Why do people seek therapy?
- What kinds of professionals provide help to people in psychological distress? In what kinds of settings does treatment occur?
- What factors are important in determining how well patients do in therapy?

Measuring Success in Psychotherapy

Evaluating treatment success is not always as easy as it might seem (Hill & Lambert, 2004). Attempts at estimating clients' gains in therapy generally depend on one or more of the following sources of information: (1) a therapist's impression of changes that have occurred, (2) a client's reports of change, (3) reports from the client's family or friends, (4) comparison of pretreatment and posttreatment scores on personality tests or other instruments designed to measure relevant facets of psychological functioning, and (5) measures of change in selected overt behaviors. Unfortunately, each of these sources has its own limitations.

A therapist may not be the best judge of a client's progress because any therapist is likely to be biased in favor of seeing himself or herself as competent and successful (after all, therapists are only human). In addition, the therapist typically has only a limited observational sample (the client's in-session behavior) from which to make judgments of overall change. Furthermore, therapists can inflate improvement averages by deliberately or subtly encouraging difficult clients to discontinue therapy. The problem of how to deal with early dropouts from treatment further complicates many studies of therapy outcomes. Should these patients be excluded from analyses of outcome? (After all, they have received little or none of the therapy being evaluated.) Or should they be included and counted as treatment failures? These issues have been at the heart of much debate and discussion.

Also, a client is not necessarily a reliable source of information on therapeutic outcomes. Not only may clients want to believe for various personal reasons that they are getting better, but in an attempt to please the therapist they may report that they are being helped. In addition, because therapy often requires a considerable investment of time, money, and sometimes emotional distress, the idea that it has been useless is a dissonant one. Relatives of the client may also be inclined to "see" the improvement they had hoped for, although they often seem to be more realistic than either the therapist or the client in their evaluations of outcome.

Clinical ratings by an outside, independent observer are sometimes used in research on psychotherapy outcomes to evaluate the progress of a client; these ratings may be more objective than ratings made by those directly involved in the therapy. Another widely used objective measure of client change is performance on various psychological tests. A client evaluated in this way takes a battery of tests before and after therapy, and the differences in scores are assumed to reflect progress, or lack of progress, or

RESEARCH CLOSE-UP

Regression to the Mean

This reflects the statistical tendency for extreme scores (e.g., very high or very low scores) on a given measure to look less extreme at a second assessment (as occurs in a repeated-measures design). Because of this statistical artifact, people whose scores are farthest away from the group mean to begin with (e.g., people who have the highest anxiety scores or the lowest scores on self-esteem) will tend to score closer to the group mean at the second assessment, even if no real clinical change has occurred.

occasionally even deterioration. However, some of the changes that such tests show may be artifactual, as with *regression to the mean*, wherein very high (or very low) scores tend on repeated measurement to drift toward the average of their own distributions, yielding a false impression that some real change has been documented. Also, the particular tests selected are likely to focus on the theoretical predictions of the therapist or researcher. Thus they are not necessarily valid predictors of the changes, if any, that the therapy actually induces or of how the client will behave in real life. And without follow-up assessment, they provide little information on how enduring any change is likely to be.

Objectifying and Quantifying Change

Generalized terms such as *recovery*, *marked improvement*, and *moderate improvement*, which were often used in outcome research in the past, are open to considerable differences in interpretation. Today the emphasis is on using

2 DEVELOPMENTS IN RESEARCH

Using Brain Activation to Measure Therapeutic Change

Functional magnetic resonance imaging (fMRI) is a technique that can be used to measure changes in activation in the human brain. When certain areas of the brain are active and in use, it is believed that they require more oxygen. By measuring the amount of blood flow and oxygen in a given region of the brain, scientists can begin to learn what is happening in the human mind.

Researchers are now using neuroimaging to explore the changes that occur in the brain in response to psychotherapy. For example, Nakao and colleagues (2005) studied 10 outpatients with obsessive-compulsive disorder (OCD). At the start of the study, all the patients received a brain scan while they were engaged in a task that required them to think about words (e.g., *sweat, urine, feces*) that triggered their obsessions and compulsions. Patients were then treated for 12 weeks either with the SSRI fluvoxamine (Luvox) or with behavior therapy. At the end of this treatment period, the brain scanning was repeated.

The results showed that, before treatment, certain areas of the brain thought to be involved in OCD (for example, a brain region in the frontal lobe called the orbitofrontal cortex) were activated during the symptom-provocation task. However, after therapy, these same regions showed much less activation when the patients were challenged to think about the provocative trigger words. In subsequent research these scientists have also shown that, after 12 weeks of

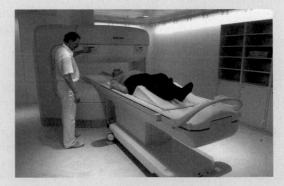

Researchers are now using functional magnetic resonance imaging (fMRI) to look at brain activity before and after treatment.

behaviour therapy, patients with OCD again show changes in several brain regions that are implicated in this disorder (Nabeyama et al., 2008). Although methodological problems (e.g., small number of subjects) limit the conclusions that can be drawn from these studies, research of this type suggests that physiological changes may accompany the clinical gains that occur in psychotherapy.

more quantitative methods of measuring change. For example, the Beck Depression Inventory (a self-report measure of depression severity) and the Hamilton Rating Scale for Depression (a set of rating scales used by clinicians to measure the same thing) both yield summary scores and have become almost standard in the pre- and posttherapy assessment of depression. Changes in preselected and specifically denoted behaviors that are systematically monitored, such as how many times a client with obsessions about contamination washes his or her hands, are often highly valid measures of outcome. Such techniques, including client self-monitoring, have been widely and effectively used, mainly by behavioral and cognitive-behavioral therapists. In research settings, functional magnetic resonance imaging (fMRI) to examine brain activity before and after treatment is sometimes used (see Box 2). It is important to keep in mind, however, that changes on rating scales (or on MRI scans) do not necessarily tell us how well the patient is functioning in everyday life (Kazdin, 2008).

Would Change Occur Anyway?

What happens to disturbed people who do not obtain formal treatment? In view of the many ways in which people can help each other, it is not surprising that improvement often occurs without professional intervention. Moreover, some forms of psychopathology such as depressive episodes or brief psychotic disorder sometimes run a fairly short course with or without treatment. In other instances, disturbed people improve over time for reasons that are not apparent.

Even if many emotionally disturbed persons tend to improve over time without psychotherapy, psychotherapy can often accelerate improvement or bring about desired behavior change that might not otherwise occur. Most researchers today would agree that psychotherapy is more effective than no treatment (see Shadish et al., 2000), and indeed the pertinent evidence, widely cited throughout this entire text, confirms this strongly. The chances of an average client benefiting significantly from psychological treatment are, overall, impressive (Lambert & Ogles, 2004). Research suggests that about 50 percent of patients show clinically significant change after 21 therapy sessions. After 40 sessions, about 75 percent of patients have improved (Lambert et al., 2001).

But *why* do patients improve? Remarkably, we know very little about the mechanisms through which therapeutic change occurs, or about the "active ingredients" of effective therapy (Kazdin, 2008; Hayes et al., 2011). We do know that progress in therapy is not always smooth and linear, however. Sudden

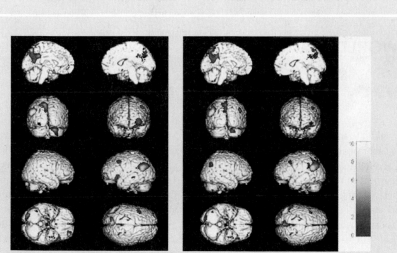

Before   After

Treatment changes the patterns of brain activation of OCD patients during an experimental task. After receiving treatment, patients' brain activation patterns look similar to those of normal controls when they perform the same task. This suggests that OCD symptoms might suppress activity in key brain areas involved in cognitive performance and that treatment may help to correct this.
Source: Nakao et al. (2005).

gains can occur between one therapy session and another (Tang & DeRubeis, 1999; Tang et al., 2002). These clinical leaps appear to be triggered by cognitive changes or by psychodynamic insights that patients experience in certain critical sessions. Researchers are now actively exploring how such factors as *therapist adherence* (how well a therapist delivers a particular type of therapy) and *therapist competence* (how skilfully the therapist administers the therapy) impact how well the patient does (see Webb et al., 2010). For patients receiving cognitive therapy for depression, therapist competence has been shown to be a predictor of better clinical outcome, as might be expected (Strunk et al., 2010).

Can Therapy Be Harmful?

The outcomes of psychotherapy are not invariably either neutral (no effect) or positive. Some clients are actually harmed by their encounters with psychotherapists (see Box 3). According to one estimate, somewhere between 5 and 10 percent of clients deteriorate during treatment (Lambert & Ogles, 2004). Patients suffering from borderline personality disorder and from obsessive-compulsive disorder typically have higher rates of negative treatment outcomes than do patients with other problems (Mohr, 1995).

Problems in the therapeutic alliance account for some instances of treatment failure. For example, a mismatch of therapist and client personality characteristics may produce deteriorating outcomes. Our impression, supported by some evidence (see Beutler et al., 2004; Castongauy et al., 2010), is that certain therapists, probably for reasons of personality or lack of interpersonal skills, just do not do well with certain types of client problems. In light of these intangible factors, it is ethically required of all therapists (1) to monitor their work with various types of clients to discover any such deficiencies, and (2) to refer to other therapists those clients with whom they may be ill-equipped to work (APA, 2002).

Unfortunately, clinicians are often quite bad at recognizing when their clients are not doing well (Whipple & Lambert, 2011). To address this problem, research-based measures to assess clinical deterioration are now being developed. If clinicians are willing to use these in their routine clinical practice they will be able to be warned when their clients are not progressing in an expected manner. A major hurdle, however, is implementation. We would not be surprised to learn that the worst therapists are the ones most reluctant to use such patient-monitoring methods.

A special case of therapeutic harm concerns what are called *boundary violations*. This is when the therapist behaves in ways that exploit the trust of the patient or engages in behavior that is highly inappropriate (e.g., taking the patient to dinner, giving the patient gifts). One case involved a patient who had been treated by a psychiatrist for 10 years. During this time the patient gave the therapist gifts of a refrigerator and a dining table and six chairs. She also sold him her Waterford crystal, her china, and a silver service. The silver had an appraised value of $1,600. However, it was purchased by the psychiatrist for only $200. The psychiatrist also sold the patient two of his boats, without her even having seen them (Norris et al., 2003).

3 THE WORLD AROUND US

When Therapy Harms

There are many ways in which therapy can be detrimental. For example, a particular therapy might make certain symptoms worse, make a person more concerned about the symptoms they do have, or make the client excessively dependent on the therapist in order to function. Encounters with some therapists or forms of therapy may also make a person less willing to seek therapy in the future.

Lilienfeld (2007) has developed a list of therapies that have potentially harmful consequences. One example is "rebirthing" therapy for children with attachment problems. This approach, which involves therapists wrapping children in blankets, sitting on them, and squeezing them in an attempt to mirror the birth process, has resulted in several children dying of suffocation.

Another problematic technique is facilitated communication, which is based on the premise that children with autism can communicate if they have the assistance of a facilitator who helps the child communicate using a computer keyboard. Facilitated communication has been linked to dozens of child sexual abuse allegations against the parents of children with autism. This has exposed these families to a great deal of needless emotional pain and suffering because studies show that the communications in facilitated communication do not come from the children themselves. Rather, they are unknowingly generated by the facilitators themselves as they guide the child's hands over the keyboard.

All practicing clinicians and therapists owe it to their clients (and to the families of their clients) to educate themselves about research on potentially harmful treatments. They should also monitor their own behavior and adhere to high ethical standards of practice. In this way they can minimize the likelihood that they will cause damage to the people who come to them seeking help.

A sexual relationship between the patient and the therapist represents perhaps the most obvious and extreme example of a serious boundary violation. This is highly unethical conduct. Given the frequently intense and intimate quality of therapeutic relationships, it is not surprising that sexual attraction arises. However, it is the therapist's professional responsibility to maintain the appropriate boundaries at all times. When exploitive and unprofessional behavior on the part of therapists does occur, it results in great harm to patients (Norris et al., 2003). Anyone seeking therapy needs to be sufficiently aware enough to determine that the therapist she or he has chosen is committed to high ethical and professional standards. For the vast majority of therapists, this is indeed the case.

In Review

- What approaches can be used to evaluate treatment success? What are the advantages and limitations of these approaches?
- Do people who receive psychological treatment always show a clinical benefit?
- What is a boundary violation? Give three examples.

What Therapeutic Approaches Should Be Used?

Before optimal treatment can be provided, a number of important decisions must be made. In the sections below we consider some of the factors that are important.

Evidence-Based Treatment

When a pharmaceutical company develops a new drug, it must obtain approval of the drug from the federal Food and Drug Administration (FDA) before that drug can be marketed. This involves, among other things, demonstrating through research on human subjects that the drug has **efficacy**—that is, that it does what it is supposed to do in curing or relieving some target condition. These tests, using voluntary and informed patients as subjects, are called **randomized clinical trials (RCTs)** or, more simply, *efficacy trials*. Although these trials may become quite elaborate, the basic design is one of randomly assigning (e.g., by the flip of a coin) half the patients to the supposedly "active" drug and the other half to a visually identical but physiologically inactive *placebo*. Usually, neither the patient nor the prescriber is informed which is to be administered; that information is recorded in code by a third party. This *double-blind* procedure is an effort to ensure that

expectations on the part of the patient and prescriber play no role in the study. After a predetermined treatment interval, the code is broken and the active or placebo status of all subjects is revealed. If subjects on the active drug have improved in health significantly more than subjects on the placebo, the investigator has evidence of the drug's efficacy. Obviously, the same design could be modified to compare the efficacy of two or more active drugs, with the option of adding a placebo condition. Thousands of such studies are in progress daily across the country. They usually take place in academic medical settings, and many are financially supported by the pharmaceutical industry.

Investigators of psychotherapy outcomes have attempted to apply this research design to their own field of inquiry, with necessary modifications (see Chambless & Ollendick, 2001). A source of persistent frustration has been the difficulty of creating a placebo condition that will appear credible to patients. Most such research has thus adopted the strategy of either comparing two or more purportedly "active" therapies or using a no-treatment ("wait list") control of the same duration as the active treatment. However, withholding treatment from patients in need (even temporarily) by placing them on a wait list sometimes raises ethical concerns. Another problem is that therapists, even those with the same theoretical orientations, often differ markedly in the manner in which they deliver therapy. (In contrast, pills of the same chemical compound and dosage do not vary.) To test a given therapy, it therefore becomes necessary to develop a treatment manual to specify just how the therapy under examination will be delivered. Therapists in the research trial are then trained (and monitored) to make sure that their therapy sessions do not deviate significantly from the procedures outlined in the manual (e.g., see Blum et al., 2008).

Efforts to "manualize" therapy represent one way that researchers have tried to minimize the variability in patients' clinical outcomes that might result from characteristics of the therapist themselves (such as personal charisma). Although **manualized therapies** originated principally to standardize psychosocial treatments to fit the RCT paradigm, some therapists recommend extending their use to routine clinical practice after efficacy for particular disorders has been established (e.g., see Wilson, 1998). Practicing clinicians, however, vary in their attitudes toward treatment manuals (Addis & Krasnow, 2000).

Efficacy, or RCT, studies of psychosocial treatments are increasingly common. These time-limited studies typically focus on patients who have a single *DSM-IV-TR* diagnosis (patients with comorbid diagnoses are sometimes excluded) and involve two or more treatment or control (e.g., wait list) conditions, where at least one of the treatment conditions is a psychosocial one (another could be some biological therapy, such as a particular drug). Client-participants are randomly assigned to these conditions, whose effects, if any, are evaluated systematically with a common battery of assessment instruments, usually administered both before and after treatment.

Efficacy studies of the outcomes of specific psychosocial treatment procedures are considered the most rigorous type of evaluation we have for establishing that a given therapy "works" for clients with a given *DSM-IV-TR* diagnosis. Treatments that meet this standard are often described as *evidence-based* or *empirically supported* (APA Presidential Task Force, 2006).

Medication or Psychotherapy?

Advances in **psychopharmacology** have allowed many people who would otherwise need hospitalization to remain with their families and function in the community. These advances have also reduced the time patients need to spend in the hospital and have made restraints and locked wards largely relics of the past. In short, medication has led to a much more favorable hospital climate for patients and staff alike.

Nevertheless, certain issues arise in the use of psychotropic drugs. Aside from possible unwanted side effects, there is the complexity of matching drug and drug dosage to the needs of the specific patient. It is also sometimes necessary for patients to change medication in the course of treatment. In addition, the use of medications in isolation from other treatment methods may not be ideal for some disorders because drugs themselves generally do not cure disorders. Nonetheless, as Box 4 illustrates, there is now a national trend toward greater use of psychiatric medications at the expense of psychotherapy. This may be problematic because, as many investigators have pointed out, drugs tend to alleviate symptoms by inducing biochemical changes, not by helping the individual understand and change the personal or situational factors that may be creating or reinforcing maladaptive behaviors. Moreover, when drugs are discontinued, patients may be at risk of

relapsing (Dobson et al., 2008). For many disorders, a variety of evidence-based forms of psychotherapy may produce more long-lasting benefits than medications alone unless the medications are continued indefinitely.

Combined Treatments

The integration of medication and psychotherapy remains common in clinical practice, particularly for disorders such as schizophrenia and bipolar disorder (Olfson & Marcus, 2010). Such integrated approaches are also appreciated and regarded as essential by the patients themselves, as you saw in the case study that opened this chapter. The integrative approach is a good example of the biopsychosocial perspective that best describes current thinking about mental disorders and that is reflected throughout this text.

Medications can be combined with a broad range of psychological approaches. In some cases, they can help patients benefit more fully from psychotherapy. For example, patients with social anxiety disorder who receive exposure therapy do much better if they are given an oral dose of D-cycloserine before each session. D-cycloserine is an antibiotic used in the treatment of tuberculosis. When taken alone, it has no effect on anxiety. However, D-cycloserine activates a receptor that is critical in facilitating extinction of anxiety. By making the receptor work better, the therapeutic benefits of exposure training are enhanced in people taking D-cycloserine versus placebo (Guastella et al., 2008; Hofman et al., 2006).

Typically, psychosocial interventions are combined with psychiatric medications. This may be especially beneficial for patients with severe disorders (see Gabbard & Kay, 2001). Keller and colleagues (2000) compared the outcomes of 519 depressed

---

4 THE WORLD AROUND US

We Have a Pill for That

Despite the benefits provided by evidence-based psychotherapies, an increasing number of mental health outpatients are now being treated solely with medications. Recent findings from a national survey show that, over the 10-year period from 1998 to 2007, the percentage of people being treated with medications and psychotherapy declined from 40 percent to 32 percent. In contrast, the number of people being treated with medications alone rose from 41 percent to 51 percent (Olfson & Marcus, 2010). This is a surprising trend because the number of people who receive therapy in a given year has remained stable at around 3 percent.

The trend may be related to the billions of dollars spent by the pharmaceutical industry to promote their products both to physicians and the general public alike. How many times have you seen a TV ad

telling you to ask your doctor whether a certain medication is right for you? Because of this, many people are now receiving their psychiatric medications from their primary care physician and are never referred for (or do not seek) psychotherapy from a mental health specialist. Managed care organizations have also had financial incentives to get patients to substitute medications for psychotherapy (Druss, 2010).

All of these changes are occurring at a time when serious concerns are being raised about psychiatric drugs and the harm that they may be causing in our society (Whitaker, 2010). Some of the drugs used in the treatment of mental disorders may actually make things worse for patients in the long run. It therefore remains essential to preserve treatment options for patients and to improve access to evidence-based psychotherapies for all who need them.

patients who were treated with an antidepressant (nefazodone), with psychotherapy (cognitive-behavioral), or with a combination of both of these treatments. In the medication-alone condition, 55 percent of patients did well. In the psychotherapy-alone condition, 52 percent of patients responded to treatment. However, patients for whom the two treatments were combined did even better, with an overall positive response rate of 85 percent. Quite possibly, combined treatment is effective because medications and psychotherapy may target different symptoms and work at different rates. As Hollon and Fawcett (1995) have noted, "Pharmacotherapy appears to provide rapid, reliable relief from acute distress, and psychotherapy appears to provide broad and enduring change, with combined treatment retaining the specific benefits of each" (p. 1232).

It is important to note that combined treatments are not always superior to single treatments. Adding psychiatric medications does not generally improve the clinical efficacy of psychosocial treatments for anxiety disorders, for example. However, for people suffering from chronic or recurrent depression, combined treatments often result in better clinical outcomes (Aaronson et al., 2007).

In Review

- What are the advantages and drawbacks of using a manualized therapy?
- What does it mean to describe a treatment as evidence-based?
- For what kinds of disorders is combination therapy superior?

Psychosocial Approaches to Treatment

People are fascinated by psychotherapy. As practicing therapists, we are often asked about the work that we do and the kinds of patients we see. In this section, we try to give you a sense of the different clinical approaches that therapists sometimes use. Our goal here is to provide you with a better sense of the different therapeutic approaches, illustrating them with case studies whenever possible.

Behavior Therapy

Behavior therapy is a direct and active treatment that recognizes the importance of behavior, acknowledges the role of learning, and includes thorough assessment and evaluation. Instead of exploring past traumatic events or inner conflicts, behavior therapists focus on the presenting problem—the problem or symptom that is causing the patient great distress. A major assumption of behavior therapy is that abnormal behavior is acquired in the same way as normal behavior—that is, by learning. A variety of behavioral techniques have therefore been developed to help patients "unlearn" maladaptive behaviors by one means or another.

EXPOSURE THERAPY As you know, a behavior therapy technique that is widely used in the treatment of anxiety disorders is exposure. If anxiety is learned, then, from the behavior therapy perspective, it can be unlearned. This is accomplished through guided exposure to anxiety-provoking stimuli. During exposure therapy, the patient or client is confronted with the fear-producing stimulus in a therapeutic manner. This can be accomplished in a very controlled, slow, and gradual way, as in **systematic desensitization**, or in a more extreme manner, as in **flooding**, in which the patient directly confronts the feared stimulus at full strength. (An example is a housebound patient with agoraphobia being accompanied outdoors by the therapist.) Moreover, the form of the exposure can be real (also known as *in vivo* **exposure**) or imaginary (**imaginal exposure**).

The rationale behind systematic desensitization is quite simple: Find a behavior that is incompatible with being anxious (such as being relaxed or experiencing something pleasant) and repeatedly pair this with the stimulus that provokes anxiety in the patient. Because it is difficult if not impossible to feel both pleasant and anxious at the same time,

Exposure therapy involves confronting anxiety-provoking situations. It can be done in vivo (in real life) or in thoughts or imagination. In vivo is preferable whenever practically possible.

systematic desensitization is aimed at teaching a person, while in the presence (real or imagined) of the anxiety-producing stimulus, to relax or behave in some other way that is inconsistent with anxiety. It may therefore be considered a type of counterconditioning procedure. The term *systematic* refers to the carefully graduated manner in which the person is exposed to the feared stimulus.

The prototype of systematic desensitization is the classic experiment of Mary Cover Jones (1924), in which she successfully eliminated a small boy's fears of a white rabbit and other furry animals. She began by bringing the rabbit just inside the door at the far end of the room while the boy, Peter, was eating. On successive days, the rabbit was gradually brought closer until Peter could pat it with one hand while eating with the other.

Joseph Wolpe (1958; Rachman & Hodgson, 1980) elaborated on the procedure developed by Jones and coined the phrase *systematic desensitization* to refer to it. On the assumption that most anxiety-based patterns are, fundamentally, conditioned responses, Wolpe worked out a way to train a client to remain calm and relaxed in situations that formerly produced anxiety. Wolpe's approach is elegant in its simplicity, and his method is equally straightforward.

A client is first taught to enter a state of relaxation, typically by progressive concentration on relaxing various muscle groups. Meanwhile, patient and therapist collaborate in constructing an anxiety hierarchy that consists of imagined scenes graded as to their capacity to elicit anxiety. For example, for a dog-phobic patient, a low-anxiety step might be imagining a small dog in the distance being walked on a leash by its owner. In contrast, a high-anxiety step might be imagining a large and exuberant dog running toward the patient. Therapy sessions consist of the patient's repeatedly imagining, under conditions of deep relaxation, the scenes in the hierarchy, beginning with low-anxiety images and gradually working toward those in the more extreme ranges. Treatment continues until all items in the hierarchy can be imagined without notable discomfort, at which point the client's real-life difficulties typically have shown substantial improvement.

Imaginal procedures have some limitations, an obvious one being that not everybody is capable of vividly imagining the required scenes. In an influential early study of clients with agoraphobia, Emmelkamp and Wessels (1975) conclude that prolonged exposure *in vivo* is superior to imaginal exposure. Since then, therapists have sought to use *in vivo* exposure whenever practical, encouraging clients to confront anxiety-provoking situations directly. As practicing clinicians, we sometimes see on listservs used by behavior therapists requests for instructions about how to make concoctions that look like vomit. In these cases the therapist is treating someone who has a vomiting phobia and has a need for something that looks realistic for an *in vivo* exposure.

Of course, *in vivo* exposure is not possible for all stimuli. In addition, occasionally a client is so fearful that he or she cannot be induced to confront the anxiety-arousing situation

directly. Imaginal procedures are therefore a vital part of the therapeutic exposure repertoire. An important development in behavior therapy is the use of virtual reality to help patients overcome their fears and phobias (Rothbaum, Hodges, et al., 2000). Such approaches are obviously needed when the source of the patient's anxiety is something that is not easily reproduced in real life, such as flying. Overall, the outcome record for exposure treatments is impressive (Barlow et al., 2007; Emmelkamp, 2004). It is also encouraging that the results from virtual reality exposure are comparable to the results obtained from *in vivo* exposure (Powers & Emmelkamp, 2008).

AVERSION THERAPY Aversion therapy involves modifying undesirable behavior by the old-fashioned method of punishment. Probably the most commonly used aversive stimuli today are drugs that have noxious effects, such as Antabuse, which induces nausea and vomiting when a person who has taken it ingests alcohol. In another variant, the client is instructed to wear a substantial elastic band on the wrist and to "snap" it when temptation arises, thus administering self-punishment.

In the past, painful electric shock was commonly employed in programs that paired it with the occurrence of the undesirable behavior, a practice that certainly contributed to aversion therapy's negative image among some segments of the public. Although aversive conditioning has been used to treat a wide range of maladaptive behaviors including smoking, drinking, overeating, drug dependence, gambling, sexual deviance, and bizarre psychotic behavior, interest in this approach has declined as other treatment options have become available (see Emmelkamp, 2004).

MODELING As the name implies, in **modeling** the client learns new skills by imitating another person, such as a parent or therapist, who performs the behavior to be acquired. A younger client may be exposed to behaviors or roles in peers who act as assistants to the therapist and then be encouraged to imitate and practice the desired new responses. For example, modeling may be used to promote the learning of simple skills such as self-feeding for a child with profound mental retardation or more complex skills such as being more effective in social situations for a shy, withdrawn adolescent. In work with children especially, effective decision making and problem solving may be modeled when the therapist "thinks out loud" about everyday choices that present themselves in the course of therapy (Kendall, 1990; Kendall & Braswell, 1985).

Modeling and imitation are adjunctive aspects of various forms of behavior therapy as well as other types of therapy. For example, in an early classic work, Bandura (1964) found that live modeling of fearlessness, combined with instruction and guided exposure, was the most effective treatment for snake phobia, resulting in the elimination of phobic reactions in over 90 percent of the cases treated. The photographs taken during the treatment of spider phobia provide a graphic example of a similar approach.

SYSTEMATIC USE OF REINFORCEMENT Systematic programs that use reinforcement to suppress (extinguish) unwanted behavior or to elicit and maintain desired behavior have achieved notable success. Often called contingency management programs, these approaches are often used in institutional settings, although this is not always the case.

Suppressing problematic behavior may be as simple as removing the reinforcements that support it, provided, of course, that they can be identified. Sometimes identification is relatively easy, as in the following case. In other instances, it may require extremely careful and detailed observation and analysis for the therapist to learn what is maintaining the maladaptive behavior.

> **case study** | Showing Off in Class
>
> Billy, a 6-year-old first grader, was brought to a psychological clinic by his parents because he hated school and because his teacher had told them that his showing off was disrupting the class and making him unpopular. It became apparent in observing Billy and his parents during the initial interview that both his mother and his father were noncritical and approving of everything Billy did. After further assessment, a three-phase program of therapy was undertaken: (1) Billy's parents were helped to discriminate between showing-off behavior and appropriate behavior on Billy's part. (2) They were instructed to ignore Billy when he engaged in showing-off behavior while continuing to show their approval of appropriate behavior. (3) Billy's teacher was also instructed to ignore Billy, insofar as it was feasible, when he engaged in showing-off behavior and to devote her attention at those times to children who were behaving more appropriately.
>
> Although Billy's showing off in class increased during the first few days of this behavior therapy program, it diminished markedly after his parents and teacher no longer reinforced it. As his maladaptive behavior diminished, he was better accepted by his classmates. This helped reinforce more appropriate behavior patterns and changed Billy's negative attitude toward school.

Billy's was a case in which unwanted behavior was eliminated by eliminating its reinforcers. On other occasions, therapy is administered to establish desired behaviors that are missing. Examples of such approaches are *response shaping* and use of *token economies*. In **response shaping**, positive reinforcement is used to establish, by gradual approximation, a response that is actively resisted or is not initially in an individual's behavioral repertoire. This technique has been used extensively in working with children's behavior problems (Kazdin, 2007). For example, a child who refuses to speak in front of others (selective mutism) may be first rewarded (with praise or a more tangible treat) for making any sound. Later, only complete words, and later again only strings of words, would be rewarded.

TOKEN ECONOMIES Years ago, when behavior therapy was in its infancy, token economies based on the principles of operant conditioning were developed for use with chronic psychiatric inpatients. When they behaved appropriately on the hospital ward, patients earned tokens that they could later use to receive rewards or privileges (Paul, 1982; Paul & Lentz, 1977).

Token economies have been used to establish adaptive behaviors ranging from elementary responses such as eating and making one's bed to the daily performance of responsible hospital jobs. In the latter instance, the **token economy** resembles the outside world, where an individual is paid for his or her work in tokens (money) that can later be exchanged for desired objects and activities. Although sometimes the subject of criticism and controversy, token economies remain a relevant treatment approach for the seriously mentally ill and those with developmental disabilities (see Higgins et al., 2001; Le Blanc et al., 2000).

Similar reinforcement-based methods are now being used to treat substance abuse. In one study, people being treated for cocaine dependence were rewarded with vouchers worth 25 cents if their urine tests came back negative (see Higgins, Wong, et al., 2000). Patients could then ask a staff member to purchase for them items from the community with the vouchers they had accumulated. Patients who received the incentive vouchers based on their abstinence from cocaine had better clinical outcomes than a comparison group of patients who also received vouchers but whose vouchers were not contingent on their abstinent behavior.

EVALUATING BEHAVIOR THERAPY Compared with some other forms of therapy, behavior therapy has some distinct advantages. Behavior therapy usually achieves results in a short period of time because it is generally directed to specific symptoms, leading to faster relief of a client's distress and to lower costs. The methods to be used are also clearly delineated, and the results can be readily evaluated. Overall, the outcomes achieved with behavior therapy compare very favorably with those of other approaches (Emmelkamp, 2004; Nathan & Gorman, 2007).

As with other approaches, behavior therapy works better with certain kinds of problems than with others. Generally, the more pervasive and vaguely defined the client's problem, the less likely behavior therapy is to be useful. For example, it appears to be only rarely employed to treat complex personality disorders, although *dialectical behavior therapy* for patients with borderline personality disorder is an exception (Crits-Christoph & Barber, 2007). On the other hand, behavioral techniques remain central to the treatment of anxiety disorders (Barlow et al., 2007; Franklin & Foa, 2007). Behavior therapy can even be used with psychotic patients (Kopelowicz et al., 2007).

A recent development in the treatment of depression is a brief and structured form of therapy called *behavioral activation*. In this treatment the patient and the therapist work together to help the patient find ways to become more active and engaged with life. The patient is encouraged to engage in activities that will help improve mood and lead to better ways of coping with specific life problems. Although this sounds quite simple, it is not always that easy to accomplish. However, evidence to date suggests that this form of therapy is very beneficial for patients and can lead to enduring change (Dimidjian et al., 2011; Dobson et al., 2008).

Cognitive and Cognitive-Behavioral Therapy

The early behavior therapists focused on observable behavior and regarded the inner thoughts of their clients as unimportant. However, starting in the 1970s, a number of behavior therapists began to reappraise the importance of "private events"—thoughts, perceptions, evaluations, and self-statements—and started to see them as processes that mediated the effects of objective stimulus conditions to determine behavior and emotions (Borkovec, 1985; Mahoney & Arnkoff, 1978).

Cognitive and *cognitive-behavioral therapy* (terms for the most part used interchangeably) stem from both cognitive psychology (with its emphasis on the effects of thoughts on behavior) and behaviorism (with its rigorous methodology and performance-oriented focus). No single set of techniques defines cognitively oriented treatment approaches. However, two main themes are important: (1) the conviction that cognitive processes influence emotion, motivation, and behavior; and (2) the use of cognitive and behavior-change techniques in a pragmatic (hypothesis-testing) manner. In the following discussion, we briefly describe the rational emotive behavior therapy of Albert Ellis and then focus in more detail on the cognitive therapy approach of Aaron Beck.

According to the cognitive model, how we think about situations is closely linked to our emotional responses to them. If this young man is having automatic thoughts such as, "I'll never get to play. I'm such a loser," he is likely to be more emotionally distressed about waiting on the sideline than if he has a thought such as, "There's a lot I can learn from watching how this game is going."

RATIONAL EMOTIVE BEHAVIOR THERAPY The first form of behaviorally oriented cognitive therapy was developed by Albert Ellis and called **rational emotive behavior therapy (REBT)** (see Ellis & Dryden, 1997). REBT attempts to change a client's maladaptive thought processes, on which maladaptive emotional responses, and thus behavior, are presumed to depend.

Ellis posited that a well-functioning individual behaves rationally and in tune with empirical reality. Unfortunately, however, many of us have learned unrealistic beliefs and perfectionistic values that cause us to expect too much of ourselves, leading us to behave irrationally and then to feel that we are worthless failures. For example, a person may continually think, "I should be able to win everyone's love and approval" or "I should be thoroughly adequate and competent in everything I do." Such unrealistic assumptions and self-demands inevitably spell problems.

The task of REBT is to restructure an individual's belief system and self-evaluation, especially with respect to the irrational "shoulds," "oughts," and "musts" that are preventing the individual from having a more positive sense of self-worth and an emotionally satisfying, fulfilling life. Several methods are used. One method is to dispute a person's false beliefs through rational confrontation ("Why should your failure to get the promotion you wanted mean that you are worthless?").

REBT therapists also use behaviorally oriented techniques. For example, homework assignments might be given to encourage clients to have new experiences and to break negative chains of behavior. Although the techniques differ dramatically, the philosophy underlying REBT has something in common with that underlying humanistic therapy (discussed later) because both take a clear stand on personal worth and human values. Rational emotive behavior therapy aims to increase an individual's feelings of self-worth and clear the way for self-actualization by removing the false beliefs that have been stumbling blocks to personal growth.

BECK'S COGNITIVE THERAPY Beck's cognitive therapy approach was originally developed for the treatment of depression and later for anxiety disorders. Now, however, this form of treatment is used for a broad range of conditions, including eating disorders and obesity, personality disorders, substance abuse, and even schizophrenia (Beck, 2005; Beck & Rector, 2005; Hollon & Beck, 2004). The cognitive model is basically an information-processing model of psychopathology. A fundamental assumption of the cognitive model is that problems result from biased processing of external events or internal stimuli. These biases distort the way that a person makes sense of the experiences that she or he has in the world, leading to cognitive errors.

But why do people make cognitive errors at all? According to Beck (2005), underlying these biases is a relatively stable set of cognitive structures or schemas that contain dysfunctional beliefs. When these schemas become activated (by external or internal triggers), they bias how people process information.

In the case of depression, people become inclined to make negatively biased interpretations of themselves, their world, and their future.

In the initial phase of cognitive therapy, clients are made aware of the connection between their patterns of thinking and their emotional responses. They are first taught simply to identify their own automatic thoughts (such as, "This event is a total disaster") and to keep records of their thought content and their emotional reactions (see Wright et al., 2006). With the therapist's help, they then identify the logical errors in their thinking and learn to challenge the validity of these automatic thoughts. The errors in the logic behind their thinking lead them (1) to perceive the world selectively as harmful while ignoring evidence to the contrary; (2) to overgeneralize on the basis of limited examples—for example, seeing themselves as totally worthless because they were laid off from work; (3) to magnify the significance of undesirable events—for example, seeing the job loss as the end of the world for them; and (4) to engage in absolutistic thinking—for example, exaggerating the importance of someone's mildly critical comment and perceiving it as proof of their instant descent from goodness to worthlessness. In the case study below, the therapist describes some of these errors in thinking to a depressed patient.

Much of the content of the therapy sessions and homework assignments is analogous to experiments in which a therapist and a client apply learning principles to alter the client's biased and dysfunctional cognitions and continuously evaluate the effects that these changes have on subsequent thoughts, feelings, and overt behavior. It is important to note, however, that in Beck's cognitive therapy, clients do not change their beliefs by debate and confrontation as is common in REBT. Rather, they are encouraged to gather information about themselves. For example, a young man who believes that he will be rejected by any attractive woman he approaches would be led to a searching analysis of the reasons why he holds this belief. The client might then be assigned the task of "testing" this dysfunctional "hypothesis" by actually approaching seemingly appropriate women whom he admires. The results of the "test" would then be discussed with the cognitive therapist, and any cognitive "errors" that may have interfered with a skillful performance would be identified and corrected.

In addition, the client is encouraged to discover the faulty assumptions or dysfunctional schemas that may be leading to problem behaviors and self-defeating tendencies (Young et al., 2008). These generally become evident over the course of therapy as the client and the therapist examine the themes of the client's automatic thoughts. Because these dysfunctional schemas are seen as making the person vulnerable (e.g., to depression), this phase of treatment is considered essential in ensuring resistance to relapse

case study   Cognitive Therapy

THERAPIST: You have described many instances today where your interpretations led to particular feelings. You remember when you were crying a little while ago and I asked you what was going through your mind? You told me that you thought that I considered you pathetic and that I wouldn't want to see you for therapy. I said you were reading my mind and putting negative thoughts in my mind that were not, in fact, correct. You were making an arbitrary inference, or jumping to conclusions without evidence. This is what often happens when one is depressed. One tends to put the most negative interpretations on things, even sometimes when the evidence is contrary, and this makes one even more depressed. Do you recognize what I mean?

PATIENT: You mean even my thoughts are wrong?

THERAPIST: No, not your thoughts in general, and I am not talking about right and wrong. As I was explaining before, interpretations are not facts. They can be more or less accurate, but they cannot be right or wrong. What I mean is that some of your interpretations, in particular those relating to yourself, are biased negatively. The thoughts you attributed to me could have been accurate. But there were also many other conclusions you could have reached that might have been less depressing for you, in that they would reflect less badly on you. For example, you could have thought that since I was spending time with you, that meant I was interested and that I wanted to try and help. If this had been your conclusion, how do you think that you would have felt? Do you think that you would have felt like crying?

PATIENT: Well, I guess I might have felt less depressed, more hopeful.

THERAPIST: Good. That's the point I was trying to make. We feel what we think. Unfortunately, these biased interpretations tend to occur automatically. They just pop into one's head and one believes them. What you and I will do in therapy is to try and catch these thoughts and examine them. Together we will look at the evidence and correct the biases to make the thoughts more realistic. Does this sound all right with you?

PATIENT: Yes.

Source: From I-M. Blackburn and K. M. Davidson. (1990). *Cognitive therapy for depression and anxiety: A practitioner's guide* (pp. 106–7). Copyright © 1995 Blackwell Science.

when the client faces stressful life events in the future. That is, if the underlying cognitive vulnerability factors are not changed, the client may show only short-term improvement and will still be subject to recurrent depression.

For disorders other than depression, the general approach is quite similar. However, the nature of the patient's automatic thoughts and underlying beliefs is obviously quite different across disorders. In panic disorder, for example, the focus is on identifying the automatic thoughts about feared bodily sensations and on teaching the client to "decatastrophize" the experience of panic (Craske & Barlow, 2008). In bulimia nervosa, the cognitive approach centers on the person's overvalued ideas about body weight and shape, which are often fueled by low self-esteem and fears of being unattractive. In addition, faulty cognitions about which foods are "safe" and which "dangerous" are explored (Fairburn et al., 2008; Wilson, 2005).

EVALUATING COGNITIVE-BEHAVIORAL THERAPIES

In spite of the widespread attention that Ellis's REBT has enjoyed, it has been less well assimilated into the mainstream than Beck's cognitive therapy (David et al., 2005). Nonetheless, REBT is still very much alive and well. In general, this approach may be most useful in helping basically healthy people to cope better with everyday stress and perhaps in preventing them from developing full-blown anxiety or depressive disorders (Haaga & Davison, 1989, 1992). With respect to controlled research studies with carefully diagnosed clinical populations, REBT appears to be inferior to exposure-based therapies in the treatment of anxiety disorders such as agoraphobia, social phobia (Haaga & Davison, 1989, 1992), and probably obsessive-compulsive disorder (Franklin & Foa, 1998).

In contrast, the efficacy of Beck's cognitive treatment methods has been well documented. Research suggests that these approaches are extremely beneficial in alleviating many different types of disorders (see Hollon & Beck, 2004). For depression, cognitive-behavioral therapy is at least comparable to drug treatment for all but the most severe cases (e.g., psychotic depression). It also offers long-term advantages, especially with regard to the prevention of relapse (Craighead et al., 2007). Cognitive therapy also produces dramatic results in the treatment of panic disorder and generalized anxiety disorder (Hollon & Beck, 2004), and cognitive-behavioral therapy is now the treatment of choice for bulimia (Wilson, 2010; Wilson & Fairburn, 2007). Finally, cognitive approaches have promise in the treatment of conduct disorder in children (Kazdin, 2007), substance abuse (Beck et al., 1993), and certain personality disorders (Beck et al., 1990; Linehan, 1993).

The combined use of cognitive and behavior therapy approaches is now quite routine. Some disagreement remains about whether the effects of cognitive treatments are actually the result of cognitive changes as the cognitive theorists propose (Hollon & Beck, 2004; Jacobson et al., 1996). At least for depression and panic disorder, it does appear that cognitive change is the best predictor of long-term outcome, just as cognitive theory maintains (Hollon et al., 1990). Exactly what the

"active ingredients" of cognitive treatments really are, however, remains a source of debate and research (e.g., Garratt et al., 2007; Teasdale et al., 2001).

Humanistic-Experiential Therapies

The humanistic-experiential therapies emerged as significant treatment approaches after World War II. In a society dominated by self-interest, mechanization, computerization, mass deception, and mindless bureaucracy, proponents of the humanistic-experiential therapies see psychopathology as stemming in many cases from problems of alienation, depersonalization, loneliness, and a failure to find meaning and genuine fulfilment. Problems of this sort, it is held, are not likely to be solved either by delving into forgotten memories or by correcting specific maladaptive behaviors.

The humanistic-experiential therapies are based on the assumption that we have both the freedom and the responsibility to control our own behavior—that we can reflect on our problems, make choices, and take positive action. Humanistic-experiential therapists feel that a client must take most of the responsibility for the direction and success of therapy, with the therapist serving merely as counselor, guide, and facilitator. Although humanistic-experiential therapies differ in their details, their central focus is always expanding a client's "awareness."

CLIENT-CENTERED THERAPY

The **client-centered** (person-centered) **therapy** of Carl Rogers (1902–1987) focuses on the natural power of the organism to heal itself (Rogers, 1951, 1961). Rogers saw therapy as a process of removing the constraints and restrictions that grow out of unrealistic demands that people tend to place on themselves when they believe, as a condition of self-worth, that they should not have certain kinds of feelings such as hostility. By denying that they do in fact have such feelings, they become unaware of their actual "gut" reactions. As they lose touch with their own genuine experience, the result is lowered integration, impaired personal relationships, and various forms of maladjustment.

The primary objective of Rogerian therapy is to resolve this incongruence—to help clients become able to accept and be themselves. To this end, client-centered therapists establish a psychological climate in which clients can feel unconditionally accepted, understood, and valued as people. Within this context, the therapist employs nondirective techniques such as empathic reflecting, or restatement of the client's descriptions of life difficulties. If all goes well, clients begin to feel free, for perhaps the first time, to explore their real feelings and thoughts and to accept hates and angers and ugly feelings as parts of themselves. As their self-concept becomes more congruent with their actual experience, they become more self-accepting and more open to new experiences and new perspectives; in short, they become better-integrated people.

In contrast to most other forms of therapy, the client-centered therapist does not give answers, interpret what a client says, probe for unconscious conflicts, or even steer the client toward certain topics. Rather, he or she simply listens attentively and acceptingly to what the client wants to talk about, interrupting only to restate in different words what the client is saying. Such restatements, devoid of any judgment or interpretation by the therapist, help the client to clarify further the feelings and ideas that he or she is exploring—really to look at them and acknowledge them. The following excerpt from a therapist's second interview with a young woman will serve to illustrate these techniques of reflection and clarification.

case study   Client-Centered Therapy

ALICE:	I was thinking about this business of standards. I somehow developed a sort of a knack, I guess, of—well—habit—of trying to make people feel at ease around me, or to make things go along smoothly. . . .
COUNSELOR:	In other words, what you did was always in the direction of trying to keep things smooth and to make other people feel better and to smooth the situation.
ALICE:	Yes. I think that's what it was. Now the reason why I did it probably was—I mean, not that I was a good little Samaritan going around making other people happy, but that was probably the role that felt easiest for me to play. I'd been doing it around home so much. I just didn't stand up for my own convictions, until I don't know whether I have any convictions to stand up for.
COUNSELOR:	You feel that for a long time you've been playing the role of kind of smoothing out the frictions or differences or what not.
ALICE:	M-hm.
COUNSELOR:	Rather than having any opinion or reaction of your own in the situation. Is that it?
ALICE:	That's it. Or that I haven't been really honestly being myself, or actually knowing what my real self is, and that I've been just playing a sort of a false role. Whatever role no one else was playing, and that needed to be played at the time, I'd try to fill it in.

(From Rogers, 1951, pp. 152–53.)

Pure client-centered psychotherapy, as originally practiced, is rarely used today in North America, although it is still relatively popular in Europe. Motivational interviewing is a new form of therapy that is based on this empathic style.

MOTIVATIONAL INTERVIEWING People tend to be ambivalent about making changes in their lives. They want to change, but they also don't want to change. **Motivational interviewing (MI**; see Hettema, Steele, & Miller, 2005) is a brief form of therapy that can be delivered in one or two sessions. It was developed as a way to help people resolve their ambivalence about change and make a commitment to treatment (Miller, 1983). At its center is a supportive and empathic style of relating to the client that has its origins in the work of Carl Rogers. However, MI differs from client-centered counseling because it also employs a more direct approach that explores the client's own reasons for wanting to change. The therapist encourages this "change talk" by asking the client to discuss his or her desire, ability, reasons, and need for change. These are reflected back by the therapist, thus exposing the client to periodic summaries of his or her own motivational statements and thoughts about change. The result is that clients can develop and strengthen their commitment to change in an active, accepting, and supportive atmosphere.

Motivational interviewing is most often used in the areas of substance abuse and addiction. When added to the beginning of a treatment program, it appears to benefit patients, perhaps because it facilitates patients' staying in treatment and following the treatment plan. Hettema and colleagues' (2005) meta-analysis of the MI literature has also shown that MI has a large effect when it is used with ethnic minorities. In one alcoholism-treatment trial, Native American participants did better if they received four sessions of MI than if they received 12 sessions of cognitive-behavior therapy or else participated in a 12-step program (Villanueva et al., 2003). Quite possibly, the supportive and nonconfrontational style of MI may be more congruent with the typical and culturally sanctioned communication style of Native Americans and thus represent a culturally appropriate intervention. The collaborative and nonconfrontational style of motivational interviewing may also make it acceptable to adolescents. Even a very small number of sessions of motivational

Motivational interviewing is a brief intervention that helps people resolve their ambivalence about making change. It is often used in the treatment of substance abuse and addiction.

interviewing can promote behavior change in adolescents who use drugs and alcohol (Jensen et al., 2011).

GESTALT THERAPY In German, the term *gestalt* means "whole," and gestalt therapy emphasizes the unity of mind and body—placing strong emphasis on the need to integrate thought, feeling, and action. **Gestalt therapy** was developed by Frederick (Fritz) Perls (1969) as a means of teaching clients to recognize the bodily processes and emotions they had been blocking off from awareness. As with the client-centered and humanistic approaches, the main goal of gestalt therapy is to increase the individual's self-awareness and self-acceptance.

Although gestalt therapy is commonly used in a group setting, the emphasis is on one person at a time, with whom a therapist works intensively, trying to help identify aspects of the individual's self or world that are not being acknowledged in awareness. The individual may be asked to act out fantasies concerning feelings and conflicts or to represent one side of a conflict while sitting in one chair and then switch chairs to take the part of the adversary. Often the therapist or other group members will ask such questions as, "What are you aware of in your body now?" and "What does it feel like in your gut when you think of that?"

In Perls's approach to therapy, a good deal of attention is also paid to dreams, but with an emphasis very different from that of classical psychoanalysis. In gestalt theory, all elements of a dream, including seemingly inconsequential, impersonal objects, are considered to be representations of unacknowledged aspects of the dreamer's self. The therapist urges the client to suspend normal critical judgment, to "be" the object in the dream, and then to report on the experience. This is illustrated in the following case study.

case study Gestalt Therapy

A college professor and therapist was preoccupied with his academic promotion and tenure and found himself unable to experience any joy. He sought the assistance of a friend who was a gestalt therapist. She asked him to conjure up a daydream rather than a dream. The daydream that emerged spontaneously was one of skiing. The therapist asked him to be the mountain, and he began to experience how warm he was when he was at his base. As he got closer to the top, what looked so beautiful was also very cold and frozen. The therapist asked the professor to be the snow, and he experienced how hard and icy he could be near the top. But near the bottom, people ran over him easily and wore him out. When the session was finished, the professor did not feel like crying or shouting; he felt like skiing. So he went, leaving articles and books behind. In the sparkle of the snow and sun, he realized that joy in living emerges through deeds and not through words. In his rush to succeed, he had committed one of the cardinal sins against himself—the sin of not being active. (Adapted from Prochaska & Norcross, 2003, p. 183.)

EVALUATING HUMANISTIC-EXPERIENTIAL THERAPIES Many of the humanistic-experiential concepts—the uniqueness of each individual, the importance of therapist genuineness, the satisfaction that comes from realizing one's potential, the importance of the search for meaning and fulfillment, and the human capacity for choice and self-direction—have had a major impact on our contemporary views of both human nature and the nature of good psychotherapy.

However, humanistic-experiential therapies have been criticized for their lack of agreed-upon therapeutic procedures and their vagueness about what is supposed to happen between client and therapist. In response, proponents of such approaches argue against reducing people to abstractions, which can diminish their perceived worth and deny their uniqueness. Because people are so different, they argue, we should expect different techniques to be appropriate for different cases.

Controlled research on the outcomes achieved by many forms of humanistic-existential therapy was lacking in the past. However, research in this area is now on the increase. There is evidence to suggest that these treatment approaches are helpful for patients with a variety of problems including depression, anxiety, trauma, and marital difficulties (Elliot et al., 2004). And, as we have already noted, motivational interviewing is now established as an effective method for promoting behaviour change in people with substance abuse problems (Ball et al., 2007; Jensen et al., 2011).

Psychodynamic Therapies

Psychodynamic therapy is a broad treatment approach that focuses on individual personality dynamics, usually from a psychoanalytic or some psychoanalytically derived perspective. Psychoanalytic therapy is the oldest form of psychological therapy and began with Sigmund Freud. The therapy is mainly practiced in two basic forms: classical psychoanalysis and psychoanalytically oriented psychotherapy. As developed by Freud and his immediate followers, classical psychoanalysis is an intensive (at least three sessions per week), long-term procedure for uncovering repressed memories, thoughts, fears, and conflicts presumably stemming from problems in early psychosexual development—and helping individuals come to terms with them in light of the realities of adult life. For example, excessive orderliness and a grim and humorless focus on rigorous self-control would probably be viewed as deriving from difficulties in early toilet training.

In psychoanalytically oriented psychotherapy, the treatment and the ideas guiding it may depart substantially from the principles and procedures laid out by orthodox Freudian theory, yet the therapy is still loosely based on psychoanalytic concepts. For example, many psychoanalytically oriented therapists schedule less frequent sessions (e.g., once per week) and sit face-to-face with the client instead of having the latter recline on a couch with the analyst out of sight behind him or her. Likewise, the relatively passive stance of the analyst (primarily listening to the client's "free associations" and rarely offering "interpretations") is replaced with an active conversational style in which the therapist attempts to clarify distortions and gaps in the client's construction of the origins and consequences of his or her problems, thus challenging client "defenses" as they present themselves. It is widely believed that this more direct approach significantly shortens total treatment time. We will first examine Freud's original treatment methods, in part because of their historical significance and enormous influence; we will then look briefly at some of the contemporary modifications of psychodynamic therapy, which for the most part focus on interpersonal processes. Before we do so, however, let's consider the case of Karen.

case study — Psychodynamic Therapy

Karen was about to be terminated from her nursing program if her problems were not resolved. She had always been a competent student who seemed to get along well with peers and patients. Now, since the beginning of her rotation on 3 South, a surgical ward, she was plagued by headaches and dizzy spells. Of more serious consequence were the two medical errors she had made when dispensing medications to patients. She realized that these errors could have proved fatal, and she was as concerned as her nursing faculty about why such problems had begun in this final year of her education. Karen knew she had many negative feelings toward the head nurse on 3 South, but she did not believe these feelings could account for her current dilemma. She entered psychotherapy.

After a few weeks of psychotherapy, the therapist realized that one of Karen's important conflicts revolved around the death of her father when she was 12 years old. Karen had just gone to live with her father after being with her mother for 7 years. She remembered how upset she was when her father had a heart attack and had to be rushed to the hospital. For a while it looked as though her father was going to pull through, and Karen began enjoying her daily visits to see him. During one of these visits, her father clutched his chest in obvious pain and told Karen to get a nurse. She remembered how helpless she felt when she could not find a nurse, although she did not recall why this was so difficult. Her search seemed endless, and by the time she finally found a nurse, her father was dead.

The therapist asked Karen the name of the ward on which her father had died. She paused and thought, and then she blurted out, "3 South." She cried at length as she told how confused she was and how angry she felt toward the nurses on the ward for not being more readily available, although she thought they might have been involved with another emergency. After weeping and shaking and expressing her resentment, Karen felt calm and relaxed for the first time in months. Her symptoms disappeared, and her problems in the nursing program were relieved. (Adapted from Prochaska & Norcross, 2003, p. 28.)

In classical (Freudian) psychoanalysis the technique of free association may be used to explore the contents of the preconscious.

FREUDIAN PSYCHOANALYSIS Psychoanalysis is a system of therapy that evolved over a period of years during Freud's long career. Psychoanalysis is not easy to describe, and the problem is complicated by the fact that many people have inaccurate conceptions of it based on cartoons and other forms of caricature. The best way to begin our discussion is to describe the four basic techniques of this form of therapy: (1) free association, (2) analysis of dreams, (3) analysis of resistance, and (4) analysis of transference. Then we will note some of the most important changes that have taken place in psychodynamic therapy since Freud's time.

Free Association The basic rule of *free association* is that an individual must say whatever comes into her or his mind regardless of how personal, painful, or seemingly irrelevant it may be. Usually a client lies in a relaxed position on a couch and gives a running account of all the thoughts, feelings, and desires that come to mind as one idea leads to another. The therapist normally takes a position behind the client so as not to disrupt the free flow of associations in any way.

Although such a running account of whatever comes into one's mind may seem random, Freud did not view it as such; rather, he believed that associations are determined just like other events. The purpose of free association is to explore thoroughly the contents of the preconscious—that part of the mind considered subject to conscious attention but largely ignored. Analytic interpretation involves a therapist's tying together a client's often disconnected ideas, beliefs, and actions into a meaningful explanation to help the client gain insight into the relationship between his or her maladaptive behavior and the repressed (unconscious) events and fantasies that drive it.

Analysis of Dreams Another important, related procedure for uncovering unconscious material is the analysis of dreams. When a person is asleep, repressive defenses are said to be lowered, and forbidden desires and feelings may find an outlet in dreams. For this reason, dreams have been referred to as the "royal road to the unconscious." Some motives, however, are so unacceptable to an individual that even in dreams they are not revealed openly but are expressed in disguised or symbolic form. Thus a dream has two kinds of content: (1) **manifest content**, which is the dream as it appears to the dreamer, and (2) **latent content**, which consists of the actual motives that are seeking expression but are so painful or unacceptable that they are disguised.

It is a therapist's task, in conjunction with the associations of the patient, to uncover these disguised meanings by studying the images that appear in the manifest content of a client's dream and in the client's associations to them. For example, a client's dream of being engulfed in a tidal wave may be interpreted by a therapist as indicating that the client feels in danger of being overwhelmed by inadequately repressed fears or hostilities.

Analysis of Resistance During the process of free association or of associating to dreams, an individual may evidence **resistance**—an unwillingness or inability to talk about certain thoughts, motives, or experiences. For example, a client may be talking about an important childhood experience and then suddenly switch topics, perhaps stating, "It really isn't that important" or "It is too absurd to discuss." Resistance may also be evidenced by the client's giving a too-glib interpretation of some association, or coming late to an appointment, or even "forgetting" an appointment altogether. Because resistance prevents painful and threatening material from entering awareness, its sources must be sought if an individual is to face the problem and learn to deal with it in a realistic manner (Horner, 2005).

Analysis of Transference As client and therapist interact, the relationship between them may become complex and emotionally involved. Often people carry over, and unconsciously apply to their therapist, attitudes and feelings that they had in their relations with a parent or other person close to them in the past, a process known as **transference**. Thus clients may react to their analyst as they did to that earlier person and feel the same love, hostility, or rejection that they felt long ago. If the analyst is operating according to the prescribed role of maintaining an impersonal stance of detached attention, the often affect-laden reactions of the client can be interpreted, it is held, as a type of projection—inappropriate to the present situation yet highly revealing of central issues in the client's life. For example, should the client vehemently (but inaccurately) condemn the therapist for a lack of caring and attention to the client's needs, this would be seen as a "transference" to the

therapist of attitudes acquired (possibly on valid grounds) in childhood interactions with parents or other key individuals.

In helping the client to understand and acknowledge the transference relationship, a therapist may provide the client with insight into the meaning of his or her reactions to others. In doing so, the therapist may also introduce a corrective emotional experience by refusing to engage the person on the basis of his or her unwarranted assumptions about the nature of the therapeutic relationship. If the client expects rejection and criticism, for example, the therapist is careful to maintain a neutral manner. Or contrarily, the therapist may express positive emotions at a point where the client feels particularly vulnerable, thereby encouraging the client to reframe and rethink her or his view of the situation. In this way it may be possible for the individual to recognize these assumptions and to "work through" the conflict in feelings about the real parent or perhaps to overcome feelings of hostility and self-devaluation that stem from the earlier parental rejection. In essence, the negative effects of an undesirable early relationship are counteracted by working through a similar emotional conflict with the therapist in a therapeutic setting. A person's reliving of a pathogenic past relationship in a sense re-creates the neurosis in real life, and therefore this experience is often referred to as a *transference neurosis*.

It is not possible here to consider at length the complexities of transference relationships, but a client's attitudes toward his or her therapist usually do not follow such simple patterns as our examples suggest. Often the client is ambivalent—distrusting the therapist and feeling hostile toward him or her as a symbol of authority, but at the same time seeking acceptance and love. In addition, the problems of transference are not confined to the client, for the therapist may also have a mixture of feelings toward the client. This **countertransference**, wherein the therapist reacts in accord with the client's transferred attributions rather than objectively, must be recognized and handled properly by the therapist. For this reason, it is considered important that therapists have a thorough understanding of their own motives, conflicts, and "weak spots"; in fact, all psychoanalysts undergo psychoanalysis themselves before they begin independent practice.

The resolution of the transference neurosis is said to be the key element in effecting a psychoanalytic "cure." Such resolution can occur only if an analyst successfully avoids the pitfalls of countertransference. That is, the analyst needs to keep track of his or her own transference or reaction to a client's behavior. Failure to do so risks merely repeating, in the therapy relationship, the typical relationship difficulties characterizing the client's adult life. Analysis of transference and the phenomenon of countertransference are also part of most psychodynamic derivatives of classical psychoanalysis, to which we now turn.

Psychodynamic Therapy Since Freud The original version of psychoanalysis is practiced only rarely today. Arduous and costly in time, money, and emotional commitment, it may take several years before all major issues in the client's life have been satisfactorily resolved. In light of these heavy demands, psychoanalytic or psychodynamic therapists have worked out modifications in procedure designed to shorten the time and expense required. A good review of some of these approaches can be found in Prochaska and Norcross (2003).

Object Relations, Attachment-Based Approaches, and Self-Psychology

The most extensive revisions of classical psychoanalytic theory undertaken within recent decades have been related to the object-relations perspective (in psychoanalytic jargon, "objects" are other people) and, to a lesser extent, the attachment and self-psychology perspectives (see Prochaska & Norcross, 2003). Whether or not psychotherapy investigators and clinicians use the term *object relations* (or *attachment* or *self-psychology*) to denote their approach, increasing numbers of them describe procedures that focus on interpersonal relationship issues, particularly as they play themselves out in the client–therapist relationship.

Interpersonally oriented psychodynamic therapists vary considerably in their time focus: whether they concentrate on remote events of the past, on current interpersonal situations and impasses (including those of the therapy itself), or on some balance of the two. Most seek to expose, bring to awareness, and modify the effects of the remote developmental sources of the difficulties the client is currently experiencing. These therapies generally retain, then, the classical psychoanalytic goal of understanding the present in terms of the past. What they ignore are the psychoanalytic notions of staged libidinal energy transformations and of entirely internal (and impersonal) drives that are channeled into psychopathological symptom formation.

EVALUATING PSYCHODYNAMIC THERAPIES

Classical psychoanalysis is routinely criticized by outsiders for being relatively time-consuming and expensive; for being based on a questionable, stultified, and sometimes cult-like approach to human nature; for neglecting a client's immediate problems in the search for unconscious conflicts in the remote past; and for there being no adequate proof of its general effectiveness. Concerning this, we note that there have been no rigorous, controlled outcome studies of classical psychoanalysis. This is understandable, given the intensive and long-term nature of the treatment and the methodological difficulties inherent in testing such an approach. Nonetheless, there are some hints that this treatment approach has some value (Gabbard et al., 2002). Psychoanalysts also argue that manualized treatments unduly limit treatment for a disorder. They note that simply because a treatment cannot be standardized does not mean that it is invalid or unhelpful. Whether the clinical benefits justify the time and expense of psychoanalysis, however, remains uncertain.

In contrast, there is much more research on some of the newer psychodynamically oriented approaches. There are signs that psychodynamic approaches may be helpful in the treatment of depression, panic disorder, PTSD, and substance-abuse disorders (Gibbons et al., 2008). Recent research also supports the idea that increases in insight ("insight" is a key construct in psychodynamic theory and involves cognitive and emotional understanding of inner conflicts) must occur before there is long-term clinical change (Johansson et al., 2010).

Psychoanalytically oriented treatments are also showing promise in the treatment of borderline personality disorder. One example is *transference-focused psychotherapy*, or TFP. Developed by Kernberg and colleagues, this treatment approach uses such techniques as clarification, confrontation, and interpretation to help the patient understand and correct the distortions that occur in his or her perception of other people, including the therapist. In a clinical trial, patients with borderline personality disorder who received TFP did as well as those who were assigned to receive dialectical behavior therapy (Clarkin et al., 2007). A recent meta-analysis provides further support for the idea that long-term psychodynamic psychotherapy (50 sessions or more) may be more beneficial than less intensive forms of treatment for patients with complex mental disorders (Leichsenring & Rabung, 2011). Findings such as these are creating renewed interest in psychodynamic forms of psychotherapy and energizing the field of treatment research.

Couple and Family Therapy

Many problems that therapists deal with concern distressed relationships. A common example is couple or marital distress. Here, the maladaptive behavior exists between the partners in the relationship. Extending the focus even further, a family systems approach reflects the assumption that the within-family behavior of any particular family member is subject to the influence of the behaviors and communication patterns of other family members. It is, in other words, the product of a "system" that may be amenable to both understanding and change. Addressing problems deriving from the in-place system thus requires therapeutic techniques that focus on relationships as much as, or more than, on individuals.

COUPLE THERAPY

Relationship problems are a major cause of emotional distress. The large numbers of couples seeking help with troubled relationships have made couple counseling

Couple therapists try to help couples improve their communication skills and develop more adaptive ways of solving their problems.

---

a growing field of therapy. Typically the couple is seen together. Improving communication skills and developing more adaptive problem-solving styles are both major foci of clinical attention. Although it is quite routine at the start of therapy for each partner secretly to harbor the idea that only the other will have to do the changing, it is nearly always necessary for both partners to alter their reactions to the other.

For many years the gold standard of **couple therapy** has been **traditional behavioral couple therapy** (TBCT; see Christensen et al., 2007). TBCT is based on a social-learning model and views marital satisfaction and marital distress in terms of reinforcement. The treatment is usually short term (10 to 26 sessions) and is guided by a manual. The goal of TBCT is to increase caring behaviors in the relationship and to teach partners to resolve their conflicts in a more constructive way through training in communication skills and adaptive problem solving.

Traditional behavioral couple therapy is an empirically supported treatment for couple distress (Snyder, Castellani, & Whisman, 2006). Early research established that two-thirds of couples tend to do well and to show improvement in relationship satisfaction (Jacobson et al., 1987). However, it rapidly became apparent that this form of treatment does not work for all couples (Jacobson & Addis, 1993). Moreover, even among couples who do show an improvement in relationship satisfaction, the improvement is not always maintained over time (Jacobson et al., 1987).

These limitations of TBCT led researchers to conclude that a change-focused treatment approach was not appropriate for all couples. This created the impetus for the development of **integrative behavioral couple therapy** (IBCT; see Jacobson et al., 2000; Wheeler et al., 2001). Instead of emphasizing change (which sometimes has the paradoxical effect of making people not want to change), IBCT focuses on acceptance and includes strategies that help each member of the couple come to terms with and accept some of the limitations of his or her partner. Of course, change is not forbidden. Rather, within IBCT, acceptance strategies are integrated with change strategies to provide a form of therapy that is more tailored to individual characteristics, relationship "themes" (long-standing patterns of conflicts), and the needs of the couple.

Although IBCT is a relative newcomer in the couple therapy field, the preliminary findings are quite promising. In one study, improvement rates were 80 percent in the couples treated with IBCT versus 64 percent in couples receiving TBCT (Jacobson et al., 2000). In another, larger study, 70 percent of couples who received IBCT showed clear improvement in their relationship compared with 61 percent of couples receiving TBCT (see Christensen et al., 2007). Although these differences are not statistically different from each, other data show that couples who stay together after receiving IBCT are significantly happier than couples who stay together following treatment with TBCT (Atkins et al., 2005).

FAMILY THERAPY Therapy for a family obviously overlaps with couple and marital therapy but has somewhat different roots. Couple therapy developed in response to the large number of clients who came seeking help for relationship problems. **Family therapy** began with the finding that many people

who had shown marked clinical improvement after individual treatment—often in institutional settings—had a relapse when they returned home. As you have already learned, family-based treatment approaches designed to reduce high levels of criticism and family tension have been successful in reducing relapse rates in patients with schizophrenia and mood disorders (Miklowitz & Craighead, 2007; Pfammatter et al., 2006).

Another approach to resolving family disturbances is called **structural family therapy** (Minuchin, 1974). This approach, which is based on systems theory, holds that if the family context can be changed, then the individual members will have altered experiences in the family and will behave differently in accordance with the changed requirements of the new family context. Thus an important goal of structural family therapy is changing the organization of the family in such a way that the family members will behave more supportively and less pathogenically toward each other.

Structural family therapy is focused on present interactions and requires an active but not directive approach on the part of a therapist. Initially, the therapist gathers information about the family—a structural map of the typical family interaction patterns—by acting like one of the family members and participating in the family interactions as an insider. In this way, the therapist discovers whether the family system has rigid or flexible boundaries, who dominates the power structure, who gets blamed when things go wrong, and so on. Armed with this understanding, the therapist then operates as an agent for altering the interaction among the members, which often has transactional characteristics of enmeshment (overinvolvement), overprotectiveness, rigidity, and poor conflict resolution skills. The "identified client" is often found to play an important role in the family's mode of conflict avoidance. Structural family therapy has quite a good record of success in the treatment of anorexia nervosa.

Eclecticism and Integration

The various "schools" of psychotherapy that we have just described once stood more in opposition to one another than they do now. Today, clinical practice is characterized by a relaxation of boundaries and a willingness on the part of therapists to explore differing ways of approaching clinical problems (see Castonguay et al., 2003, for a discussion), a process sometimes called *multimodal therapy* (Lazarus, 1997). When asked what their orientation is, most psychotherapists today reply "eclectic," which usually means that they try to borrow and combine concepts and techniques from various schools, depending on what seems best for the individual case. This inclusiveness extends to efforts to combine biological and psychosocial approaches as well as individual and family therapies.

One example of an eclectic form of therapy is *interpersonal psychotherapy*. Developed by Klerman and colleagues (1984) as a treatment for depression, IPT focuses on current relationships in the patient's life and has the goals of reducing symptoms and improving functioning. Interpersonal therapy was based on the interpersonal theory of Harry Stack Sullivan as well as on

Bowlby's attachment theory. Its central idea is that all of us, at all times, involuntarily invoke schemas acquired from our earliest interactions with others, such as our parents, in interpreting what is going on in our current relationships. Although it is sometimes considered to be a form of psychodynamic psychotherapy, IPT uses techniques from several other treatment approaches. It is also focused and time limited. In addition, the emphasis in treatment is on the present, not the past (see Bleiberg & Markowitz, 2008).

IPT has demonstrable value in the treatment of depression (de Mello et al., 2005). It has also been adapted for other disorders including bulimia nervosa (Fairburn, Jones, et al., 1993), anxiety disorders (Stangier et al., 2011) and borderline personality disorder (Markowitz et al., 2006).

In Review

- Describe the different techniques that can be used to provide anxious patients with exposure to the stimuli they fear.

- In what ways are REBT and cognitive therapy similar? In what ways are they different?

- Explain the concepts of transference and countertransference.

- What special difficulties do clinicians face when they work with couples? How have techniques of marital therapy evolved over recent years?

Sociocultural Perspectives

The criticism has been raised—from both inside and outside the mental health professions—that psychotherapy can be viewed as an attempt to get people adjusted to a "sick" society rather than to encourage them to work toward its improvement. As a consequence, psychotherapy has often been considered the guardian of the status quo. This issue is perhaps easier for us to place in perspective by looking at other cultures. For example, there had been frequent allegations that psychiatry was used as a means of political control in the former Soviet Union, an abuse that was eventually officially acknowledged (see *Schizophrenia Bulletin*, 1990, vol. 16, no. 4). Although few would claim that psychiatry in most industrialized societies is used to gain control over social critics, there is nevertheless the possibility that therapists in some ways play the role of "gatekeepers" of social values. Such charges, of course, bring us to the question: What do we mean by "abnormal"? That question can be answered only in the light of our values.

Social Values and Psychotherapy

In a broader perspective, there is the complex and controversial issue of the role of values in science. Psychotherapy is not, or at least should not be, a system of ethics; it is a set of tools to be used at the discretion of a therapist in pursuit of a client's welfare. Thus mental health professionals are confronted with the same kinds of questions that confront scientists in general: Should a physical scientist who helps develop weapons of mass destruction be morally concerned about how they are used? Similarly, should a psychologist or behavioral scientist who develops powerful techniques to influence or control how people behave be concerned about how those techniques are used?

Many psychologists and other scientists try to sidestep this issue by insisting that science is value free—that it is concerned only with gathering facts, not with how the facts are applied. Each time therapists decide that one behavior should be eliminated or substituted for another, however, they are making a value judgment. For example, is a therapist to assume that the depression of a young mother who is abused by an alcoholic husband is an internally based disorder requiring "treatment," as once would have been the routine interpretation? Or does the therapist have a larger responsibility to look beyond individual pathology and confront the abnormality of the marital relationship? Therapy takes place in a context that involves the values of the therapist, the client, and the society in which they live. There are strong pressures on a therapist—from parents, schools, courts, and other social institutions—to help people adjust to the world as it is. At the same time, there are many counter-pressures, particularly from young people who are seeking support in their (sometimes overdone) attempts to become authentic people rather than blind conformists.

The dilemma in which contemporary therapists may find themselves is illustrated by the following case study.

case study **Who Needs Therapy?**

A 15-year-old high school sophomore is sent to a therapist because her parents have discovered that she has been having sexual intercourse with her boyfriend. The girl tells the therapist that she feels no guilt or remorse over her behavior even though her parents strongly disapprove. In addition, she reports that she is quite aware of the danger of becoming pregnant and is careful to take contraceptive measures.

What is the role of the therapist here? And what is the goal of treatment? Should the girl be encouraged to conform to her parents' expectations and postpone sexual activity until she is older and more mature? Or should the parents be helped to adjust to the pattern of sexual behavior their daughter has chosen? As we noted earlier, it is not unusual for an individual to be referred for psychological treatment because her or his behavior, though not particularly destructive or disturbing, has caused concern among family members, who want the therapist to "fix" her or him.

Psychotherapy and Cultural Diversity

As we have seen, the establishment and maintenance of an effective psychotherapeutic "working alliance" between client and therapist is generally regarded as a crucial and indispensable element in determining the success of the outcome. What does this mean for a client whose background is considerably different from that of the therapist?

As yet, there is little or no solid evidence that psychotherapeutic outcomes are diminished when client and therapist differ in race or ethnicity (Beutler et al., 2004; Sue et al., 1994). However, members of minority groups are seriously underrepresented in treatment research studies, and this makes it difficult to fully assess their needs and outcomes (Miranda et al., 2005; Nagayama Hall, 2001). Moreover, racial and ethnic minorities are clearly underserved by the mental health system (Snowden & Yamada, 2005; U.S. Department of Health and Human Services, 2001). However, the factors that are behind these disparities are complex and not well understood.

Many minorities are economically disadvantaged and simply do not have the health insurance they need to seek treatment. It is also difficult for patients to find the kind of therapists they want. In general, minority patients tend to prefer ethnically similar therapists over European American therapists. Mexican Americans state a strong preference for therapists who share their ethnic background and express the view that such therapists are more "credible" than Anglo therapists would be (Lopez et al., 1991; Ponce & Atkinson, 1989). However, finding an ethnically matched therapist may present difficulties. In one survey, for example, only 2 percent of psychiatrists, 2 percent of psychologists, and 4 percent of social workers said they were African-Americans (Holzer et al., 1998). The number of mental health professionals who are representative of other minority groups is no better (U.S. Department of Health and Human Services, 2001). The lack of trained therapists familiar with the issues important to different ethnic groups is a serious drawback, given the unique problems often associated with certain groups. This is illustrated in the following case, which concerns a Southeast Asian refugee woman in her mid-40s who was relocated to the United States.

case study ▸ A Khmer Woman

"I lost my husband, I lost my country, I lost every property/fortune we owned. And coming over here, I can't learn to speak English and the way of life here is different; my mother and oldest son are very sick: I feel crippled, I can do nothing. I can't control what's going on. I don't know what I'm going to do once my public assistance expires. I may feel safe in a way—there is no war here, no Communist to kill or torture you—but deep down inside me, I still don't feel safe or secure. I get scared. I get scared so easily." (From Rumbaut, 1985, p. 475.)

When specialized, culturally adapted interventions are made available in community settings, minority clients are less likely to drop out of treatment and often do well (Gonzales-Castro et al., 2010; Snowden & Yamada, 2005). However, such programs are still lacking in many communities. Also lacking are research investigations designed to understand how culture and ethnicity affect a person's ability to access and receive psychiatric and psychological treatments. Nonetheless, there are encouraging developments. For example, Weisman and colleagues are developing culturally informed treatments for the families of patients with schizophrenia (Weisman et al., 2006). This approach considers the role of family cohesiveness as well as spirituality and religion in the therapy process. Researchers are also developing culturally informed psychotherapy for Hispanic patients with major depression (Markowitz et al., 2009), as well as for African American women who are suicidal and in abusive relationships (Kaslow et al., 2010).

In Review

- Can psychotherapy ever be value free? Why or why not?
- What special issues do racial and ethnic minorities face when they seek therapy?

Biological Approaches to Treatment

The field of psychopharmacology is characterized by rapid and exciting progress. Clinical breakthroughs are occurring on a regular basis, and there is now real hope for patients previously considered to be beyond help. In the following sections we discuss some of the major classes of medications that are now routinely used to help patients with a variety of mental disorders, as well as some additional treatment approaches (such as electroconvulsive therapy) that are less widely used but highly effective, especially for patients who fail to show a good clinical response to other treatments.

These drugs are sometimes referred to as psychoactive (literally, "mind-altering") medications, indicating that their major effects are on the brain. As we examine these medications, it is important to remember that people differ in how rapidly they metabolize drugs—that is, in how quickly their bodies break down the drugs once ingested. For example, many African Americans metabolize antidepressant and antipsychotic medications more slowly than whites do. What this means is that African Americans sometimes show a more rapid and greater response to these medications but also experience more side effects (see U.S. Department of Health and Human Services, 2001, p. 67). Determining the correct dosage is critical because too little of a drug can be ineffective; on the other hand, too much medication can cause toxicity that may be life-threatening, depending on the individual and the medication concerned.

Antipsychotic Drugs

As their name suggests, *antipsychotic drugs* (also called neuroleptics) are used to treat psychotic disorders such as schizophrenia and psychotic mood disorders. The key therapeutic benefit of antipsychotics derives from their ability to alleviate or reduce the intensity of delusions and hallucinations. They do this by blocking dopamine receptors. Table 1 lists some of the more commonly used neuroleptic drugs as well as information about typical dose ranges.

Studies have found that approximately 60 percent of patients with schizophrenia who are treated with traditional antipsychotic medications have a resolution of their positive symptoms within 6 weeks, compared to only about 20 percent of those treated with placebo (see Sharif et al., 2007). These drugs are also useful in treating other disorders with psychotic symptoms such as mania, psychotic depression, and schizoaffective disorder, and they are occasionally used to treat transient psychotic symptoms when these occur in people with borderline personality disorder and schizotypal personality disorder (Koenigsberg et al., 2007). Finally, antipsychotic medications are sometimes used to treat the delusions, hallucinations, paranoia, and agitation that can occur with Alzheimer's disease. However, antipsychotic medications pose great risks to patients with dementia because they are associated with increased rates of death (Sultzer et al.,

2008). Because of this, there is now a "black box warning" about using these medications with dementia patients.

Antipsychotic medications are usually administered daily by mouth. However, some patients, like the patient with chronic schizophrenia described in the case study below, are often not able to remember to take their medications each day. In such cases, depot neuroleptics can be very helpful. These are neuroleptics that can be administered in a long-acting, injectable form. The clinical benefits of one injection can last for up to 4 weeks, which makes depot neuroleptics very valuable for patients who need medication but are unwilling or unable to take drugs every day. Research suggests that patients with schizophrenia who take depot medications do better than those who use oral compounds (Tiihonen et al., 2011).

case study — **He Forgets to Take His Medications**

A 45-year-old male patient with chronic schizophrenia has a history of recurrent delusions of persecution and ideas of reference as well as auditory persecutory hallucinations. He has a history of 19 inpatient psychiatric admissions. He will generally keep outpatient appointments, but he forgets to take his antipsychotic medications and usually relapses within 2 weeks of discontinuing them. While in the hospital, he has an alleviation of his psychotic symptoms when he is given 20 mg per day of fluphenazine hydrochloride (Prolixin) orally. Because he responds well to medication but is not compliant, his psychiatrist decides to treat him with a biweekly injection of a depot neuroleptic. (Adapted from Janowsky et al., 1987.)

table 1 Commonly Prescribed Antipsychotic Medications

Drug Class	Generic Name	Trade Name	Dose Range (mg)
Second-Generation (Atypical)	clozapine	Clozaril	300–900
	risperidone	Risperdal	1–8
	olanzapine	Zyprexa	5–20
	quetiapine	Seroquel	100–750
	ziprasidone	Geodon	80–160
	aripiprazole	Abilify	15–30
	lurasidone	Latuda	40–120
First-Generation (Conventional)	chlorpromazine	Thorazine	75–900
	perphenazine	Trilafon	12–64
	molindone	Moban	50–200
	thiothixene	Navane	15–60
	trifluroperazine	Stelazine	6–40
	haloperidol	Haldol	2–100
	fluphenazine	Prolixin	2–20

Sources: Bezchlibnyk-Butler & Jeffries (2003); Buckley & Waddington (2001); and Sadock et al. (2009).

One very problematic side effect that can result from treatment with conventional antipsychotic medications such as chlorpromazine is **tardive dyskinesia**. Tardive (from *tardy*) dyskinesia is a movement abnormality that is a delayed result of taking antipsychotic medications. The problem of tardive dyskinesia is well illustrated in the following case. Because movement-related side effects are a little less common with atypical antipsychotic medications such as clozapine (Clozaril) and olanzapine (Zyprexa), these medications are often preferred in the clinical management of schizophrenia. Clozapine also seems to be especially beneficial for psychotic patients at high risk of suicide (Meltzer et al., 2003).

case study
Suffering from Tardive Dyskinesia

A 62-year-old woman with chronic schizophrenia who has been a 20-year inpatient in a state mental hospital is noted to manifest bizarre repetitive movements of her mouth, tongue, hands, and feet. Her mouth involuntarily grimaces, and her tongue intermittently protrudes. Her fingers repetitively flex and she is often noted to rock back and forth. Her hand and feet movements appear choreiform (pronounced chor-ray-if-form; means "jerky and flowing"). The patient has a history of paranoid delusions and hallucinations, beginning 25 years previously. She has not manifested these symptoms of schizophrenia for 6 years. She has been treated with a progression of antipsychotic drugs in moderate doses for the past 18 years. (Adapted from Janowsky et al., 1987.)

Even the atypical neuroleptics have side effects, however. Weight gain and diabetes are a major source of clinical concern (Sernyak et al., 2002). You may recall that an even more serious side effect of clozapine is a potentially life-threatening drop in white blood cells called agranulocytosis, which occurs in 1 percent of patients (Sharif et al., 2007). Accordingly, patients must have their blood tested every week for the first 6 months of treatment and then every 2 weeks thereafter for as long as they are on the medication. Because of this, clozapine is best regarded as a medication to consider after other medications (e.g., some of the other atypical antipsychotic medications) have proved ineffective. Current thinking is that the atypical antipsychotics described above (with the exception of clozapine) are the first-choice treatments for psychosis and that clozapine and conventional antipsychotics (e.g., Haldol) are best considered as second-line therapies.

Antidepressant Drugs

Antidepressants are the most commonly prescribed psychiatric medications. More than 90 percent of patients being treated for depressive disorders will be given these medications. (Olfson & Marcus, 2010).

SELECTIVE SEROTONIN REUPTAKE INHIBITORS (SSRIS)
As is the case for antipsychotic medications, the drugs that were discovered first (so-called classical antidepressants such as monoamine oxidase inhibitors and tricyclic antidepressants) have now been replaced in routine clinical practice by "second-generation" treatments such as the SSRIs. In 1988 fluoxetine (Prozac) became the first SSRI to be released in the United States. Its pharmacological cousins include sertraline (Zoloft) and paroxetine (Paxil). More recent additions to the SSRI family are fluvoxamine (Luvox), which is used in the treatment of obsessive-compulsive disorder; citalopram (Celexa); and escitalopram (Lexapro). All are equally effective. Table 2 lists some of the most widely used antidepressant medications.

SSRIs are chemically unrelated to the older, tricyclic antidepressants and to the monoamine oxidase inhibitors. However, most antidepressants work by increasing the availability of serotonin, norepinephrine, or both. As their name implies, the SSRIs serve to inhibit the reuptake of the neurotransmitter serotonin following its release into the synapse. Unlike the tricyclics (which inhibit the reuptake of both serotonin and norepinephrine), the SSRIs selectively inhibit the reuptake of serotonin (see Figure 1). They have become the preferred **antidepressant drugs**, in large part due to very aggressive advertising by the pharmaceutical companies. SSRIs are also easier to use, have fewer side effects, and are generally not found to be fatal in overdose, as the tricyclics can be. However, there is no compelling evidence that they are more effective than other types of antidepressants (Sussman, 2009b).

More recently, another class of medications has been introduced. These are called serotonin and norepinephrine reuptake inhibitors (SNRIs); (see Thase, 2009). Examples of antidepressants in this drug family are venlafaxine (Effexor) and duloxetine (Cymbalta). SNRIs block reuptake of both norepinephrine and serotonin. They have similar side effects to the SSRIs, and they are relatively safe in overdose. SNRIs seem to help a significant number of patients who have not responded well to other antidepressants, and they are slightly more effective than SSRIs in the treatment of major depression (Papakostas et al., 2007).

The actress Brooke Shields is one of many public figures who have been open with the public about their experiences with depression.

table 2 Commonly Prescribed Antidepressant Medications

Drug Class	Generic Name	Trade Name	Dose Range (mg)
SSRI	fluoxetine	Prozac	10–80
	sertraline	Zoloft	50–200
	paroxetine	Paxil	10–60
	fluvoxamine	Luvox	50–300
	citalopram	Celexa	10–60
	escitalopram	Lexapro	10–20
SNRI	venlafaxine	Effexor	75–375
	duloxetine	Cymbalta	40–60
Tricyclic	amitriptyline	Elavil	75–300
	clomipramine	Anafranil	75–300
	desipramine	Norpramin	75–300
	doxepin	Sinequan	75–300
	imipramine	Tofranil	75–300
	nortriptyline	Aventyl	40–200
	trimipramine	Surmontil	75–300
MAOI	phenelzine	Nardil	45–90
	tranylcypromine	Parnate	20–60
	isocarboxazid	Marplan	30–50
Atypical	bupropion	Wellbutrin	225–450
	trazodone	Desyrel	150–600

Sources: Bezchlibnyk-Butler & Jeffries (2003); Buckley & Waddington (2001); and Sadock et al. (2009).

The newest antidepressant, which received FDA approval in 2011, is called Viibryd (vilazodone). It is a novel combination of an SSRI and a serotonin receptor agonist. Early reports suggest that vilazodone is safe and well tolerated by patients (Robinson et al., 2011) and that it works better than placebo for patients who are depressed (Khan et al., 2011). However, it remains to be learned how efficacious this medication is compared to other antidepressants in widespread use.

Clinical trials with the SSRIs indicate that patients tend to improve after about 3 to 5 weeks of treatment. Patients who show at least a 50 percent improvement in their symptoms are considered to have had a positive response to treatment (see Figure 2). However, although considerably better, such patients are not fully well. When treatment removes all of a patient's symptoms, patients are considered to be in a period of remission (see Figure 3). If this remission is sustained for 6 to 12 months or more, the patient is

FIGURE 1

SSRIs

Serotonin is synthesised from the amino acid tryptophan. After being released into the synaptic cleft it binds to receptors on the post-synaptic neuron. A serotonin reuptake transporter then returns it back to the presynaptic neuron. SSRI medications block this reuptake process, leaving more serotonin available in the synapse.

Source: Ciccarelli, S.K., and White, J.N. Reprinted from *Psychology*, Second Edition, © 2008, Pearson Education Inc., Upper Saddle River, NJ.

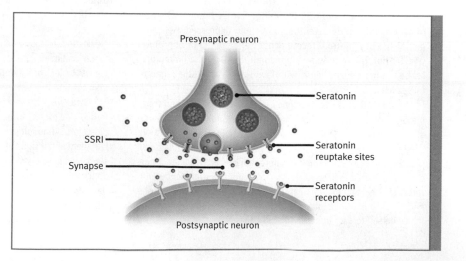

665

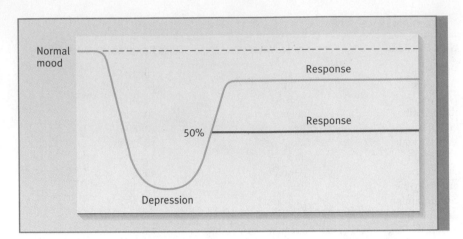

FIGURE 2

Defining a Positive Response

When treatment of depression results in at least 50 percent improvement in symptoms, it is called a response. Such patients are better, but not well.

Source: From S. M. Stahl. (2000). *Essential psychopharmacology: Neuroscientific basis and practical applications* (2nd ed.), p. 143. Copyright © Cambridge University Press, 2000. Reprinted with the permission of Cambridge University Press.

considered to have recovered. In other words, he or she is fully well again.

Side effects of the SSRIs include nausea, diarrhea, nervousness, insomnia, and sexual problems such as diminished sexual interest and difficulty with orgasm (Nemeroff & Schatzberg, 2007). After early reports linking Prozac with increased risk of suicide (e.g., Cole & Bodkin, 1990; Papp & Gorman, 1990) there was a decline in its use. However, Prozac is no more associated with suicide than other antidepressants are (Jick et al., 2004). Recently there has also been concern that, when used during pregnancy, fluoxetine (Prozac) and paroxetine (Paxil) may increase the risk of heart abnormalities in the baby (Diav-Citrin et al.,

2008; Malm et al., 2011). For this reason these medications are not recommended as a first option for women planning to become pregnant. It is important to keep in mind, however that all the risks we have just described are small when weighed against the risks associated with leaving depressed people without adequate treatment.

Although SSRIs help many people, as the following case study illustrates, some people have side effects that are so extreme that they are unable to continue to take their medication as prescribed. Researchers are now exploring the role that genes play in making some people especially susceptible to the adverse effects of specific medications (Hu et al., 2007).

case study   A Psychiatrist Gets a Taste of Her Own Medicine

Dr. G. had been a psychiatrist for many years when, during a consultation with a patient, she broke into a sweat, started to shake, and felt as if she were disintegrating. A close friend was dying of cancer and she felt weighed down and depressed. Her partner, also a psychiatrist, recommended that she take bupropion (Wellbutrin). This was an antidepressant that Dr. G. had often prescribed to her own patients, with favorable results. She began to take it herself.

Within 10 days she developed insomnia, agitation, and tremors. She lost the ability to distinguish between sadness and the side effects of the drug. She began to develop panic attacks and could barely function at work. Even so, she was terrified that she might feel worse if she stopped taking the bupropion or started taking a new drug. Determined to keep taking the medication despite her deteriorating physical and mental health, she tried to follow the advice she had given to hundreds of her own patients to stick things out. She forced herself to eat but lost 10 pounds. Sometimes she felt paranoid

and wondered if she was delusional. When she wasn't working, she curled up in a fetal position and wondered if she should hospitalize herself.

After 4 weeks she had had enough. She began to taper the medication, although her symptoms, insomnia, lack of appetite, agitation, and panic attacks continued for 3 weeks after she had taken the last tablet. For a month she felt weak, as if she had just recovered from the flu.

After her experiences with bupropion, Dr. G. now describes potential side effects to her patients in much greater detail than she did before. Although she continues to prescribe the medication, she is vigilant about signs of distress in her patients. Whereas in the past she would have encouraged patients with side effects to stick it out, anticipating that these would eventually pass, she now switches her patients to a new medication at the first sign of problems. A taste of her own medicine has made her a more attentive and aware physician. (Adapted from Gartrell, 2004.)

MONOAMINE OXIDASE (MAO) INHIBITORS Although they are used infrequently now, these were the first antidepressant medications to be developed, in the 1950s. These drugs were being studied for the treatment of tuberculosis when they were found to elevate the mood of patients (Stahl, 2000). They were later shown to be effective in treating depression. Monoamine oxidase (MAO) inhibitors include isocarboxazid (Marplan), phenelzine (Nardil), tranylcypromine (Parnate), and selegiline (Eldepryl). They inhibit the activity of monoamine oxidase, an enzyme present in the synaptic cleft that helps break down the monoamine neurotransmitters (such as serotonin and norepinephrine) that have been released into the cleft. Patients taking MAO inhibitors must avoid foods rich in the amino acid tyramine (such as salami and Stilton cheese). This limits the drugs' clinical usefulness. Nevertheless, they are used in certain cases of atypical depression that are characterized by hypersomnia and overeating and do not respond well to other classes of antidepressant medication (Nemeroff & Schatzberg, 2007).

TRICYCLIC ANTIDEPRESSANTS The tricyclic antidepressants (TCAs) operate to inhibit the reuptake of norepinephrine and (to a lesser extent) serotonin once these have been released into the synapse. Their discovery was also serendipitous in that the first TCA—imipramine—was being studied as a possible treatment for schizophrenia when it was found to elevate mood. The theory that these drugs work by increasing norepinephrine activity is now known to be oversimplified. It is also known that when the tricyclics are taken for several weeks, they alter a number of other aspects of cellular functioning including how receptors function and how cells respond to the activation of receptors and the synthesis of neurotransmitters. Because these alterations in cellular functioning parallel the time course for these drugs to exert their antidepressant effects, one or more of these changes are likely to be involved in mediating their antidepressant effects (see Figure 3).

OTHER ANTIDEPRESSANTS Trazodone (Desyrel) was the first antidepressant to be introduced in the United States that was not lethal when taken in overdose. It specifically inhibits the reuptake of serotonin. Trazodone has heavy sedating properties that limit its usefulness. It is sometimes used in combination with SSRIs and taken at night to help counter the adverse effects the SSRIs often have on sleep. In rare cases, it can produce a condition in men called priapism (Nemeroff & Schatzberg, 2007). Priapism is prolonged erection in the absence of any sexual stimulation.

Bupropion (Wellbutrin) is an antidepressant that is not structurally related to other antidepressants. It inhibits the reuptake of both norepinephrine and dopamine. In addition to being an antidepressant medication, bupropion also reduces nicotine cravings and symptoms of withdrawal in people who want to stop smoking. One clinical advantage of bupropion is that, unlike some of the SSRIs, it does not inhibit sexual functioning (Nemeroff & Schatzberg, 2007).

USING ANTIDEPRESSANTS TO TREAT ANXIETY DISORDERS, BULIMIA NERVOSA, AND PERSONALITY DISORDERS In addition to their usefulness in treating depression, the antidepressant drugs are also widely used in the treatment of various other disorders. For example, SSRIs are often used in the treatment of panic disorder, social phobia, and generalized anxiety disorder, as well as obsessive-compulsive disorder (Dougherty et al., 2007; Roy-Byrne & Cowley, 2007). However, some people with panic disorder are greatly bothered by the side effects of these drugs (which create some of the symptoms to which panic patients are hypersensitive), so they quickly discontinue the medication. SSRIs and tricyclic antidepressants are also used in the treatment of bulimia nervosa. Many studies have shown that these antidepressants are useful in reducing binge eating and purging (Wilson & Fairburn, 2007). Patients with Cluster B personality disorders such as borderline personality disorder may show a decrease in certain symptoms, most notably mood lability, if they take SSRIs (Rinne et al., 2002).

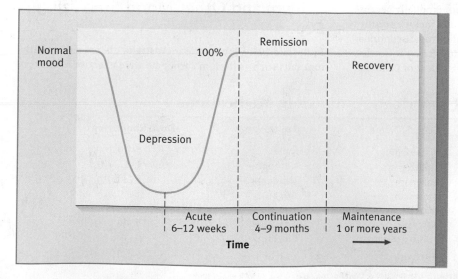

FIGURE 3

Defining Recovery

When treatment of depression results in removal of essentially all symptoms, it is called remission for the first several months, and then recovery if it is sustained for longer than 6 to 12 months. Such patients are not just better—they are well.

Source: From S. M. Stahl. (2000). *Essential psychopharmacology: Neuroscientific basis and practical applications* (2nd ed.), p. 143. Copyright © Cambridge University Press, 2000. Reprinted with the permission of Cambridge University Press.

Antianxiety Drugs

Antianxiety drugs are used for conditions in which tension and anxiety are significant components. They do not provide a cure. However, these medications can keep symptoms under control until patients are able to receive other forms of effective psychological treatments. The fact that they are so widely prescribed has caused concern among some leaders in the medical and psychiatric fields because of these drugs' addictive potential and sedating effects. Antianxiety medications have little place in the treatment of psychosis. However, they are often used as supplementary treatments in certain neurological disorders to control such symptoms as convulsive seizures.

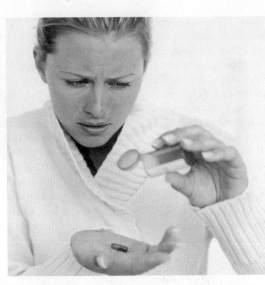

Antianxiety medications are widely prescribed. Why has this caused concern among some leaders in the medical and psychiatric fields?

BENZODIAZEPINES The most important and widely used class of antianxiety (or anxiolytic) drugs are the benzodiazepines. (Another class of drugs, the barbiturates (e.g., phenobarbitol), are seldom used today except to control seizures or as anesthetics during electroconvulsive therapy.) The first benzodiazepines were released in the early 1960s. They are now the drugs of choice for the treatment of acute anxiety and agitation. They are rapidly absorbed from the digestive tract and start to work very quickly. At low doses they help quell anxiety; at higher doses they act as sleep-inducing agents and can be used to treat insomnia. For this reason, people taking these medications are cautioned about driving or operating machinery.

One problem with benzodiazepines is that patients can become psychologically and physiologically dependent on them (Roy-Byrne & Cowley, 2007). Patients taking these medications must be "weaned" from them gradually because of the risk of withdrawal symptoms, which include seizures in some cases. Moreover, relapse rates following discontinuation of these drugs are extremely high (Roy-Byrne & Cowley, 2007). For example, as many as 60 to 80 percent of panic patients relapse following discontinuation of Xanax. Table 3 lists some commonly prescribed antianxiety medications.

Benzodiazepines and related anxiolytic medications are believed to work by enhancing the activity of GABA receptors (Stahl, 2000). GABA (gamma aminobutyric acid) is an inhibitory neurotransmitter that plays an important role in the way our brain inhibits anxiety in stressful situations. The benzodiazepines appear to enhance GABA activity in certain parts of the brain known to be implicated in anxiety such as the limbic system.

OTHER ANTIANXIETY MEDICATIONS The only new class of antianxiety medication that has been released since the early 1960s is buspirone (Buspar), which is completely unrelated to the benzodiazepines and is thought to act in complex ways on serotonergic functioning rather than on GABA. It has been shown to be as effective as the benzodiazepines in treating generalized anxiety disorder (Roy-Byrne & Cowley, 2007), although patients who have previously taken benzodiazepines tend not to respond as well as patients who have never taken them. Buspar has a low potential for abuse, probably because it has no sedative or muscle-relaxing properties and so is less pleasurable for patients. It also does not cause any withdrawal effects. The primary drawback to the use of buspirone is that it takes 2 to 4 weeks to exert any anxiolytic effects. It is therefore not useful in acute situations. Because it is nonsedating, it cannot be used to treat insomnia.

Lithium and Other Mood-Stabilizing Drugs

In the late 1940s John Cade in Australia discovered that lithium salts such as lithium carbonate were effective in treating

table 3 Commonly Prescribed Antianxiety Medications

Drug Class	Generic Name	Trade Name	Dose Range (mg)
Benzodiazepines	alprazolam	Xanax	0.5–10
	clonazepam	Klonopin	1–6
	diazepam	Valium	4–40
	lorazepam	Ativan	1–6
	oxazepam	Serax	30–120
	clorazepate	Tranxene	15–60
	chlordiazepoxide	Librium	10–150
Other	buspirone	Buspar	5–30

Sources: Bezchlibnyk-Butler & Jeffries (2003); Buckley & Waddington (2001); and Sadock et al. (2009).

manic disorders. One of Cade's (1949) own cases serves well as an illustration of the effects of lithium treatment.

case study · Lithium Helps a Difficult Patient

Mr. W. B. was a 51-year-old man who had been in a state of chronic manic excitement for 5 years. So obnoxious and destructive was his behavior that he had long been regarded as the most difficult patient on his ward in the hospital.

He was started on treatment with a lithium compound, and within 3 weeks his behavior had improved so much that transfer to the convalescent ward was deemed appropriate. He remained in the hospital for another 2 months, during which time his behavior continued to be essentially normal. Prior to discharge, he was switched to another form of lithium salts because the one he had been taking had caused stomach upset.

He was soon back at his job and living a happy and productive life. In fact, he felt so good that, contrary to instructions, he stopped taking his lithium. Thereafter he steadily became more irritable and erratic; some 6 months following his discharge, he had to cease work. In another 5 weeks he was back at the hospital in an acute manic state.

Lithium therapy was immediately reestablished, with prompt positive results. In another month Mr. W. B. was pronounced ready to return to home and work, provided that he not fail to continue taking a prescribed dosage of lithium.

It was about 20 years until lithium treatment was introduced, around 1970, in the United States. There were at least two reasons for this delay. First, lithium had been used in the 1940s and 1950s as a salt substitute for patients with hypertension before its toxic side effects were known. Some tragic deaths resulted, making the medical community very wary of using it for any reason. Second, because it is a naturally occurring compound, it is unpatentable. This meant that drug companies did not find it profitable to investigate its effects. Nevertheless, lithium is still widely used for the treatment of bipolar disorder and is marketed as Eskalith and Lithobid. Although lithium has been used for many years, exactly how it brings about its therapeutic effect is still not certain (Stahl, 2000).

Even though we still do not know exactly how it works, there is no doubt about the effectiveness of lithium. As many as 70 to 80 percent of patients in a clear manic state show marked improvement after 2 to 3 weeks of taking lithium (Keck & McElroy, 2002). In addition, lithium sometimes relieves depression, although probably mainly in patients with bipolar depression (Stahl, 2000). There is increasing evidence that lithium maintenance treatment may be less reliable at preventing future episodes of mania than was once thought. For example, several studies of bipolar patients maintained on lithium for 5 years or more found that only just over one-third remained in remission. Nevertheless, discontinuation of lithium is also very risky. The

probability of relapse is estimated to be 28 times higher after withdrawal than when the patient is on lithium, with about 50 percent relapsing within 6 months (Keck & McElroy, 2007).

Side effects of lithium include increased thirst, gastrointestinal difficulties, weight gain, tremor, and fatigue. In addition, lithium can be toxic if the recommended dose is exceeded or if the kidneys fail to excrete it from the body at a normal rate. Lithium toxicity is a serious medical condition. If not treated swiftly and appropriately, it can cause neuronal damage or even death.

Despite the clinical benefits of lithium, not all patients with bipolar disorder take it exactly as prescribed. Many seem to miss the "highs" and the abundance of energy associated with their hypomanic episodes, so when faced with unpleasant side effects and the loss of these highs they may stop taking the drug. This is illustrated in the following case study.

case study · I'd Rather Not Take It

Even though I was a clinician and a scientist, and even though I could read the research literature and see the inevitable, bleak consequences of not taking lithium, for many years after my initial diagnosis I was reluctant to take my medications as prescribed. Why was I so unwilling? Why did I have to go through more episodes of mania, followed by long suicidal depressions, before I would take lithium in a medically sensible way?

Some of my reluctance, no doubt, stemmed from a fundamental denial that what I had was a real disease. This is a common reaction that follows, rather counterintuitively, in the wake of early episodes of manic-depressive illness. Moods are such an essential part of the substance of life, of one's notion of oneself, that even psychotic extremes in mood and behavior somehow can be seen as temporary, even understandable reactions to what life has dealt. . . . It was difficult to give up the high flights of mind and mood, even though the depressions that inevitably followed nearly cost me my life.

My family and friends expected that I would welcome being "normal," be appreciative of lithium, and take in stride having normal energy and sleep. But if you have had stars at your feet and rings of planets through your hands, are used to sleeping only 4 or 5 hours a night and now sleep 8, are used to staying up all night for days and weeks in a row and now cannot, it is a very real adjustment to blend into a three-piece-suit schedule, which, though comfortable to many, is new, restrictive, seemingly less productive, and maddeningly less intoxicating. People say, when I complain of being less lively, less energetic, less high-spirited, "Well, now you're just like the rest of us," intending, among other things, to be reassuring. But I compare myself with my former self, not with others. Not only that, I tend to compare my current self with the best I have been, which is when I have been mildly manic.

Source: From K. F. Jamison. (1995). *An Unquiet Mind* by Kay Redfield Jamison (pp. 91–95). Copyright © 1995 by Kay Redfield Jamison. Used by permission of Alfred A. Knopf, a division of Random House, Inc.

table 4 Commonly Prescribed Mood-Stabilizing Medications

Drug Class	Generic Name	Trade Name	Dose Range (mg)
Lithium	lithium	Eskalith	400–1200
Anticonvulsants	carbamazepine	Tegretol	300–1600
	divalproex	Depakote	750–3000
	lamotrigine	Lamictal	100–500
	gabapentin	Neurontin	900–3600
	topiramate	Topamax	50–1300

Sources: Bezchlibnyk-Butler & Jeffries (2003); Buckley & Waddington (2001); and Sadock et al. (2009).

Although lithium is still widely used, other drugs are also considered first-line treatments for bipolar disorder (see Table 4). These include divalproic acid (Depakote) and carbamazepine (Tegretol). Other drugs that are currently being researched and used clinically as treatments for rapid cycling bipolar disorders are gabapentin (Neurontin), lamotrigine (Lamictal), and topiramate (Topamax). Many of these drugs are also used in the treatment of epilepsy and are anticonvulsant agents (Keck & McElroy, 2007). Carbamazepine has been associated with significant side effects including blood problems, hepatitis, and serious skin conditions (Post & Frye, 2009). As with lithium, careful blood monitoring of patients is required. Valproate probably has the fewest and mildest side effects, which can include nausea, diarrhea, sedation, tremor, and weight gain. Abilify, an antipsychotic medication, is also now being marketed as a treatment for bipolar disorder.

Carrie Fisher, who played Princess Leia in the *Star Wars* films, has been helped by ECT.

Electroconvulsive Therapy

Using convulsions to treat mental disorders dates back to the Swiss physician and alchemist Paracelsus (1493–1541), who induced a patient with "lunacy" to drink camphor until he experienced convulsions (Abrams, 2002; Mowbray, 1959). However, Ladislas von Meduna, a Hungarian physician, is generally regarded as the modern originator of this treatment approach. Von Meduna noted—erroneously, as it turned out—that schizophrenia rarely occurred in people with epilepsy. This observation caused him to infer that schizophrenia and epilepsy were somehow incompatible and to speculate that one might be able to cure schizophrenia by inducing convulsions. In an early treatment effort, von Meduna used camphor to induce convulsions in a patient with schizophrenia, who relatively quickly regained lucidity after the convulsive therapy. Later, von Meduna began to use a drug called Metrazol to induce convulsions because it operated more rapidly.

Another early approach, adopted by Sakel in the 1930s, was to cause convulsions by injecting patients with insulin (see Fink, 2003). However, these chemical methods gave physicians no control over the induction and timing of the seizures. Then, in 1938, the Italian physicians Ugo Cerletti and Lucio Bini tried the simplest method of all—passing an electric current through a patient's head. This method, which became known as *electroconvulsive therapy (ECT)*, is still used today. In the United States, about 100,000 patients are treated with ECT each year (Prudic, 2009).

The general public often views ECT as a horrific and primitive form of treatment, influenced no doubt by its depiction in movies such as *One Flew over the Cuckoo's Nest*. Indeed, a number of malpractice lawsuits have been brought against psychiatrists who use ECT, primarily over the failure to obtain appropriate patient consent, which can be very difficult when patients may not be legally competent to give such consent due to their illness (Abrams, 2002; Leong & Eth, 1991). However, despite the distaste with which some people regard ECT, it is a safe, effective, and important form of treatment. In fact, it is the only way of dealing with some severely depressed and suicidal patients—patients who may have failed to respond to other forms of treatment. In addition, it is often the treatment of choice for severely depressed women who are pregnant, for whom taking antidepressants may be problematic, as well as for the elderly, who may have medical conditions that make taking antidepressant drugs dangerous (Pandya et al., 2007).

Reviews evaluating research on ECT have concluded that it is an effective treatment for patients with severe or psychotic-level depression, as well as for some patients with mania (Prudic, 2009). Properly administered, ECT is not thought to cause structural damage to the brain (Devanand et al., 1994), although this issue remains controversial (Reisner, 2003). Every neurotransmitter system is affected by ECT, and ECT is known to downregulate the receptors for norepinephrine, increasing the functional availability of this neurotransmitter. However, exactly how ECT works is still not fully clear (Abrams, 2002).

ECT can be administered in one of two ways. In bilateral ECT, electrodes are placed on either side of the patient's head (see Figure 4), and brief constant-current electrical pulses of either high or low intensity are passed from one side of the head to the other for up to about 1.5 seconds. In contrast, unilateral ECT (see Figure 4) involves limiting current flow to one side of the brain, typically the nondominant side (right side, for most people). A general anesthetic allows the patient to sleep through the procedure, and muscle relaxants are used to prevent the violent contractions that, in the early days of ECT,

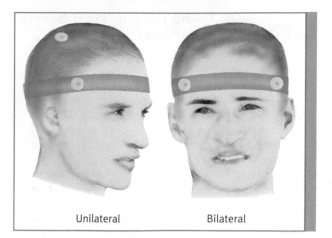

| Unilateral | Bilateral |

FIGURE 4

Electrode Placement for ECT

In unilateral ECT, current is limited to one side of the brain. In bilateral ECT, electrodes are placed on each side of the head. Bilateral ECT is more effective but is also associated with more cognitive side effects and memory problems. Adapted from Sadock & Sadock (2003, p. 1142).

could be so severe as to cause the patient to fracture bones. A bite block is also used to avoid injury to the teeth. Today, if you were to observe someone receiving ECT, all you might see would be a small twitch of the hand, perhaps, as the convulsions occurred.

After the ECT is over, the patient has amnesia for the period immediately preceding the therapy and is usually somewhat confused for the next hour or so. Normally, a treatment series consists of fewer than a dozen sessions, although occasionally more are needed. Treatments are usually administered two or three times per week (Pandya et al., 2007).

Empirical evidence suggests that bilateral ECT is more effective than unilateral ECT. Unfortunately, bilateral ECT is also associated with more severe cognitive side effects and memory problems (Reisner, 2003). For instance, patients often have difficulty forming new memories (anterograde amnesia) for about 3 months after ECT ends. Physicians must therefore weigh the greater clinical benefits of bilateral ECT against its tendency to cause greater cognitive side effects. Some clinicians recommend starting with unilateral ECT and switching to bilateral after five or six treatments if no improvement is seen (Abrams, 2002).

A dramatic early example of successful ECT treatments is provided in the autobiographical account of Lenore McCall (1947/1961), who suffered a severe depressive disorder in her middle years.

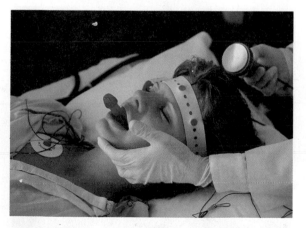

A patient who receives electroconvulsive therapy (ECT) today is given sedative and muscle-relaxant medications prior to the procedure to prevent violent contractions. In the days before such medication was available, the initial seizure was sometimes so violent as to fracture vertebrae.

case study — Using ECT to Treat Severe Depression

Ms. McCall, a well-educated woman of affluent circumstances and the mother of three children, noticed a feeling of persistent fatigue as the first sign of her impending descent into depression. Too fearful to seek help, she at first attempted to fight off her increasingly profound apathy by engaging in excessive activity, a defensive strategy that accomplished little but the depletion of her remaining strength and emotional reserves.

In due course, she noticed that her mental processes seemed to be deteriorating—her memory appeared impaired and she could concentrate only with great difficulty. Emotionally, she felt an enormous loneliness, bleakness of experience, and increasingly intense fear about what was happening to her mind. She came to view her past small errors of commission and omission as the most heinous of crimes and increasingly withdrew from contact with her husband and children. Eventually, at her husband's and her physician's insistence, she was hospitalized despite her own vigorous resistance. She felt betrayed and shortly thereafter attempted suicide by shattering a drinking glass and ingesting its fragments. To her great disappointment, she survived.

Ms. McCall then spent nearly 4 years continuously in two separate mental hospitals, during which time she deteriorated further. She was silent and withdrawn, behaved in a mechanical fashion, lost an alarming amount of weight, and underwent a seemingly premature aging process. She felt that she emitted an offensive odor. At this time, ECT was introduced into the therapeutic procedures in use at her hospital.

A series of ECT treatments was given to Ms. McCall over about a 3-month period. Then one day, she woke up in the morning with a totally changed outlook: "I sat up suddenly, my heart pounding. I looked around the room and a sweep of wonder surged over me. God in heaven, I'm well. I'm myself. . . . " After a brief period of convalescence, she went home to her husband and children.

Neurosurgery

Although **neurosurgery** was used occasionally in the nineteenth century to treat mental disorders by relieving pressure in the brain (Berrios, 1990), it was not considered a treatment for psychological problems until the twentieth century. In 1935 in Portugal, Antonio Moniz introduced a neurosurgical procedure in which the frontal lobes of the brain were severed from the deeper centers underlying them. This technique eventually evolved into an operation known as prefrontal lobotomy, which stands as a dubious tribute to the extremes to which professionals have sometimes been driven in their search for effective treatments for the psychoses. In retrospect, it is ironic that this procedure—which results in permanent structural changes in the brain of the patient and has been highly criticized by many within the profession—won Moniz the 1949 Nobel Prize in medicine (although he was later shot by a former patient who was, presumedly, less than grateful).

From 1935 to 1955 (when antipsychotic drugs became available), tens of thousands of mental patients in this country and abroad were subjected to prefrontal lobotomies and related neurosurgical procedures. In some settings, as many as 50 patients were treated in a single day (Freeman, 1959). Initial reports of results tended to be enthusiastic, downplaying complications (which included a 1 to 4 percent death rate) and undesirable side effects. It was eventually recognized, however, that the side effects of psychosurgery could be very undesirable indeed. In some instances they included a permanent inability to inhibit impulses, in others an unnatural "tranquility" with undesirable shallowness or absence of feeling

The introduction of the major antipsychotic drugs caused an immediate decrease in the widespread use of psychosurgery, especially prefrontal lobotomy. Such operations are rare today and are used only as a last resort for patients who have not responded to any other form of treatment for a period of 5 years and who are experiencing extreme and disabling symptoms.

Modern surgical techniques involve the selective destruction of minute areas of the brain. Psychosurgery is sometimes used for patients with debilitating obsessive-compulsive disorder (Dougherty et al., 2007), treatment-resistant severe self-mutilation (Price et al., 2001), or even intractable anorexia nervosa (Morgan & Crisp, 2000). However, such approaches carry serious risks. In one study, 25 patients who had received brain lesions to treat severe obsessive-compulsive disorder were followed up an average of 11 years later. Twelve of the 25 patients experienced significant relief from their OCD symptoms after the surgery. They also showed

Rosemary Kennedy, sister of former President John F. Kennedy, had developmental delays and behavioral problems. When she was 21, medical professionals recommended a prefrontal lobotomy. The surgery was a tragic failure, wiping out all her accomplishments and leaving little of her former personality. Rosemary is shown here on the right with her sister Kathleen (left) and mother Rose (center) before the surgery.

reductions in depression. However, 10 of the patients who showed clinical improvement also showed evidence of frontal lobe dysfunction at follow-up, including impaired executive functioning on cognitive tests, problems with apathy, and disinhibited behavior (Rück et al., 2008). These results highlight the risks of brain surgery even when it is effective in treating the symptoms of OCD.

Deep brain stimulation is a treatment approach that involves surgery but does not result in a permanent lesion being made in the brain. As Box 5 describes, this innovative form of therapy is now being used to help patients get some relief from their unrelenting symptoms of depression.

In Review

- What kinds of disorders can be treated with antipsychotic drugs? How do these drugs help patients? What are their drawbacks?

- Why have the SSRIs largely replaced MAO inhibitors and tricyclic antidepressants in routine clinical practice? What kinds of conditions can be treated with antidepressants?

- What kinds of medications can be used to treat acute anxiety and agitation? How are these medications believed to work?

- Do the clinical advantages of ECT outweigh its disadvantages?

5 THE WORLD AROUND US

Deep Brain Stimulation for Treatment-Resistant Depression

An important development in the treatment of patients with severe and chronic mental health problems is deep brain stimulation. This involves stimulating patients' brains electrically over a period of several months. First, surgeons drill holes into the brain and implant small electrodes. Because this procedure is done under local anaesthetic, patients can talk to the doctors about what is happening to them and tell the doctors about the changes they experience. In an early study involving 6 patients, all reported a response to the electrical stimulation even though they had no cues to tell them when current was being passed through the electrodes or when the current was off (Mayberg et al., 2005). When current was flowing into an area of the brain that is thought to be metabolically overactive in depression (the cingulate region), patients reported that they felt better and had experiences of "sudden calmness or lightness," "connectedness," or "disappearance of the void" (p. 652).

After the electrodes have been implanted, patients receive short sessions of deep brain stimulation in which current is passed through the implanted electrodes. Using the reports of the patients as a guide, the researchers can select the settings that will be used to provide stimulation through an implanted pulse device after the patients leave the hospital.

How effective is deep brain stimulation as a treatment for unrelenting depression? A total of 20 people who have received this treatment have now been followed up for an average of 3.5 years (Kennedy et al., 2011). The results suggest that this treatment is beneficial for approximately half of the patients. Many of those who responded also returned to work or began to volunteer in their communities. Although a 50 percent response rate may not strike you as very high, keep in mind that only the most chronically ill people are eligible to receive this treatment. Although it is invasive, deep brain stimulation may be able to help a small majority of patients who have failed to show improvement with any other methods.

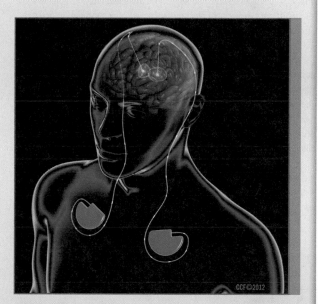

FIGURE 5

Deep Brain Stimulation

In deep brain stimulation, electrodes are implanted into the brain. These are stimulated by pulse generators implanted into the chest region.

Source: Reprinted with permission, Cleveland Clinic Center for Medical Art & Photography © 2012. All Rights Reserved.

Unresolved Issues

▶ *Is There Bias in the Reporting of Drug Trials?*

Many researchers, especially those who conduct clinical trials of drugs, receive money directly from the pharmaceutical industry to conduct their studies. Some academic researchers in medical schools and universities receive grants from drug companies. Other clinical investigators are actually employed by the drug companies themselves. Clinical investigators often also have other links to the pharmaceutical industry. For example, they may own stock in the company whose drug they are studying. They may also serve as consultants for drug companies or receive speaking fees from them.

Do such financial conflicts of interest have any implications for the results of the clinical trials that these researchers conduct? Interest in this issue escalated after Jesse Gelsinger, a teenager, died after participating in a University of Pennsylvania study led by a researcher with a financial interest in the company that was sponsoring the research (see Bodenheimer, 2000). Although some argue that researchers with financial ties to drug companies remain independent and objective collectors of data, others believe that such ties may subtly influence scientific judgment, leading to bias in the findings that are reported (Angell, 2000; Stossel, 2005).

In an examination of this issue, Perlis and colleagues (2005) looked at all the clinical drug trials that were reported in four of the most prestigious psychiatry journals between January 2001 and December 2003. They noted who funded the study and also determined whether authors reported financial conflicts of interest such as being employed by the drug company or owning stock in it. They then looked at the results of the clinical trials that were published.

It is noteworthy that the majority (60 percent) of the clinical trials were funded by the pharmaceutical industry. Financial conflicts of interest were also quite common (47 percent of studies). The central question, however, is whether either of these factors was associated with the likelihood that the authors reported a positive finding (i.e., drug better than placebo) for their study.

Perlis and colleagues' findings (2005) show that the chances of a positive finding are not associated with who funded the clinical trial. In other words, receiving financial support from a drug company to do the study did not make it more likely that the drug would be reported as performing better than the placebo. However, there was an association between author conflict of interest and positive results. Specifically, when at least one author had a financial interest in the company, the odds of positive findings being reported were 4.9 times greater than when there was no conflict of interest.

How can the link between author conflict of interest and the outcome of the clinical trial be explained? One possibility is that the most senior and experienced investigators were also those who served as consultants for the drug companies, and perhaps these senior investigators also designed better clinical trials that yielded positive findings. But then again, perhaps authors with an interest in the company might have been more inclined to use research designs that could have favored the drug produced by their sponsors. Authors with financial conflicts of interest might also have been less inclined to publish negative findings that did not show the drug of their sponsors to be superior to placebo.

To prevent selective reporting, all clinical trials must now be registered in a public registry prior to the enrollment of any patients. What this means is that no study can remain hidden if it yields negative results. Perlis and colleagues' findings also validate the current practice of journals' requiring authors to disclose any financial links they have with industry. They also raise the possibility that there may be subtle factors operating to undermine the objectivity of scientific researchers, perhaps even without them being fully aware of this.

Summary

- Psychological treatment is aimed at reducing abnormal behavior through psychological means. The goals of psychotherapy include changing maladaptive behavior, minimizing or eliminating stressful environmental conditions, reducing negative affect, improving interpersonal competencies, resolving personal conflicts, modifying people's inaccurate assumptions about themselves, and fostering a more positive self-image.

- Although these goals are by no means easy to achieve, psychological treatment methods have been shown to be generally effective in promoting adaptive psychological functioning in many troubled people.

- A key element in all therapies is the development of an effective "working alliance." A principal social issue in psychotherapy is ensuring the development of a good therapeutic working alliance between client and therapist, even when they differ widely in cultural, ethnic, and/or socioeconomic backgrounds.

- Evaluation of the success of psychotherapy in producing desired changes in clients is difficult. Treatments that have been demonstrated to result in therapeutic change in controlled trials are referred to as evidence-based treatments.

- Behavior therapy is extensively used to treat many clinical problems. Behavior therapy approaches include exposure, aversion therapy, modeling, and reinforcement approaches.

- Cognitive or cognitive-behavioral therapy attempts to modify a person's self-statements and construal of events in order to change his or her behavior. Cognitive-behavioral methods have been used for a wide variety of clinical problems—from depression to anger control—and with a range of clinical populations. Much research attests to the efficacy of these approaches.

- Other psychological treatment approaches include humanistic-experiential therapies and gestalt therapy.

- Classical psychoanalysis dates back to Sigmund Freud. It is rarely practiced today, and there is little empirical support for its efficacy.

- Several variants of therapy have developed out of the psychoanalytic tradition. These diverge from classical psychoanalysis on matters such as the duration of therapy and the role of primitive psychosexual drives in personality dynamics. Many of the newer psychodynamic forms of treatment emphasize the way interpersonal processes are affected by early interactions with parents and other family members.

- In addition to their use in treating individuals, some psychological treatment methods are applied to problematic relationships through couple or family therapy. These approaches typically assume that a person's problems lie partly in his or her interactions with others. Consequently, the focus of treatment is on changing the ways in which members of the social or family unit interact.

- Medications are important in the treatment of many disorders. It is now common in clinical practice to combine medication and psychological treatments.

- The most commonly used antipsychotic medications are the atypical neuroleptics. These improve both positive and negative symptoms and have fewer extrapyramidal symptoms (unwanted side effects involving movement) than conventional (first-generation) antipsychotics.

- Some of the earlier antidepressant medications (e.g., tricyclics and monoamine oxidase inhibitors) have now been replaced by SSRIs and SNRIs. Although more widely used, there is no compelling evidence that these newer medications are more effective than the older antidepressants. In general, antidepressants work through their influence on the serotonin and norepinephrine neurotransmitter systems.

- Anxiolytic (antianxiety) medications work via their effect on the GABA system. They are widely prescribed.

- Lithium is an important medication in the treatment of mania. However, some of the newer mood-stabilizing drugs (which are also used to treat epilepsy) are now more frequently prescribed.

- Although not frequently used, ECT is a safe and effective treatment for depression and other disorders. It causes some short-term cognitive side effects, especially when administered bilaterally.

- Neurosurgery is used as a treatment of last resort. Even when patients improve clinically, they may have permanent, adverse side effects.

Key Terms

antianxiety drugs

antidepressant drugs

behavior therapy

client-centered therapy

countertransference

couple therapy

efficacy

family therapy

flooding

gestalt therapy

imaginal exposure

in vivo exposure

integrative behavioral couple therapy

latent content

manifest content

manualized therapy

modeling

motivational interviewing

neurosurgery

psychodynamic therapy

psychopharmacology

psychotherapy

randomized clinical trials (RCTs)

rational emotive behavior therapy (REBT)

resistance

response shaping

structural family therapy

systematic desensitization

tardive dyskinesia

token economy

traditional behavioral couple therapy

transference

Glossary

Many of the key terms listed in the glossary appear in boldface when first introduced in the text discussion. A number of other terms commonly encountered in this or other psychology texts are also included; you are encouraged to make use of this glossary both as a general reference tool and as a study aid for the course in abnormal psychology.

Antianxiety drugs. Drugs that are used primarily for alleviating anxiety.

Antidepressant drugs. Drugs that are used primarily to elevate mood and relieve depression. Often also used in the treatment of certain anxiety disorders, bulimia, and certain personality disorders.

Behavior therapy. Use of therapeutic procedures based primarily on principles of classical and operant conditioning.

Client-centered (person-centered) therapy. Nondirective approach to psychotherapy, developed chiefly by Carl Rogers, that focuses on the natural power of the organism to heal itself; a key goal is to help clients accept and be themselves.

Countertransference. Psychodynamic concept that the therapist brings personal issues, based on his or her own vulnerabilities and conflicts, to the therapeutic relationship.

Couple therapy. Treatment for disordered interpersonal relationships involving sessions with both members of the relationship present and emphasizing mutual need gratification, social role expectations, communication patterns, and similar interpersonal factors.

Efficacy. In a situation where treatment is tested under ideal conditions (usually in a controlled clinical trial) efficacy is how well a given treatment improves clinical outcome compared to a control or comparison condition.

Family therapy. A treatment approach that includes all family members, not just the identified patient.

Flooding. Anxiety-eliciting therapeutic technique involving having a client repeatedly experience the actual internal or external stimuli that had been identified as producing anxiety reactions.

Gestalt therapy. Therapy designed to increase the integration of thoughts, feelings, and actions and to promote self-awareness and self-acceptance).

Imaginal exposure. Form of exposure therapy that does not involve a real stimulus. Instead, the patient is asked to imagine the feared stimulus or situation.

In vivo **exposure.** Exposure that takes place in a real-life situation as opposed to the therapeutic or laboratory setting.

Integrative behavioral couple therapy. Modification of traditional behavioral couple therapy that has a focus on acceptance of the partner rather than being solely change oriented.

Latent content. In psychoanalytic theory, repressed actual motives of a dream that are seeking expression but are so painful or unacceptable that they are disguised by the manifest content of the dream.

Manifest content. In psychoanalytic theory, the apparent (or obvious) meaning of a dream; masks the latent (or hidden) content.

Manualized therapy. Standardization of psychosocial treatments (as in development of a manual) to fit the randomized clinical paradigm.

Modeling. Learning of skills by imitating another person who performs the behavior to be acquired.

Motivational interviewing. A brief form of therapy, often used in areas of substance abuse and addiction, that allows clients to explore their desires, reasons, ability, and need for change.

Neurosurgery. Surgery on the nervous system, especially the brain.

Psychodynamic therapy. Psychological treatment that focuses on individual personality dynamics, usually from a psychodynamic or psychodynamically derived perspective.

Psychopharmacology. Science of determining which drugs alleviate which disorders and why they do so.

Psychotherapy. Treatment of mental disorders by psychological methods.

Randomized clinical trials (RCTs). A clinical trial in which participants are randomly assigned to different treatments.

Rational emotive behavior therapy (REBT). Form of psychotherapy focusing on changing a client's maladaptive thought processes, on which maladaptive emotional responses and thus behavior are presumed to depend.

Resistance. Selye's second stage of responding to continuing trauma, involving finding some means to deal with the trauma and adjust to it. In psychodynamic treatment, the person's unwillingness or inability to talk about certain thoughts, motives, or experiences.

Response shaping. Positive reinforcement technique used in therapy to establish, by gradual approximation, a response not initially in a person's behavioral repertoire.

Structural family therapy. Treatment of an entire family by analysis of interaction among family members.

Systematic desensitization. Behavior therapy technique for extinguishing maladaptive anxiety responses by teaching a person to relax or behave, while in the presence of the anxiety-producing stimulus, in some other way that is inconsistent with anxiety.

Tardive dyskinesia. Neurological disorder resulting from excessive use of antipsychotic drugs. Side effects can occur months to years after treatment has been initiated or has stopped. The symptoms involve involuntary movements of the tongue, lips, jaw, and extremities.

Token economies. Reinforcement techniques often used in hospital or institutional settings in which patients are rewarded for socially constructive behaviors with tokens that can then be exchanged for desired objects or activities.

Traditional behavioral couple therapy. Widely used form of therapy that uses behavioral approaches to bring about changes in the marital relationship.

Transference. In psychodynamic therapy, a process whereby clients project onto the therapist attitudes and feelings that they have had for a parent or others close to them.

Photo Credits

Credits are listed in order of appearance.

Text Credits

Credits are listed in order of appearance.

"Medications and Psychotherapy" from *An Unquiet Mind* by Kay Redfield Jamison, 1995, pp. 88–89; "Cognitive Therapy" adapted from *Cognitive Therapy for Depression and Anxiety: A Practitioner's Guide* by Ivy-Marie Blackburn and Kate M. Davidson, 1995, pp. 106–107; "Client-Centered Therapy" from Rogers, C. R. (1951). *Client-Centered Therapy*, pp. 152–53; "Gestalt Therapy" adapted from Prochaska, J. O. & Norcross, J. C. (2003). *Systems of Psychotherapy* (5th ed.). p. 183; "Psychodynamic Therapy" adapted from Prochaska, J. O. & Norcross, J. C. (2003). *Systems of Psychotherapy* (5th ed.), p. 28; "A Khmer Woman" Source: Rumbaut, R. (1985). Mental health and the refugee experience: A comparative study of Southeast Asian refugees. In T. C. Owan (Ed.), Southeast Asian mental health: Treatment, prevention, services, training, and research (pp. 443–86). Washington, DC: National Institute of Mental Health; "He Forgets to Take His Medications" adapted from Janowsky, D. S., Addario, D., & Risch, S. C. (1987). Pharmacology case studies; Table: Sources: Bezchlibnyk-Butler & Jeffries (2003); Buckley & Waddington (2001); and Sadock et al., (2009). "Suffering from Tardive Dyskinesia" adapted from Janowsky, D. S., Addario, D., & Risch, S. C. (1987). Pharmacology case studies; Sources: Table: Bezchlibnyk-Butler & Jeffries (2003); Buckley & Waddington (2001); and Sadock et al., (2009). Figure: Ciccarelli, S.K., and White, J.N. Reprinted from *Psychology*, Second Edition, © 2008, Pearson Education Inc., Upper Saddle River, NJ.; Figure: From *Essential Psychopharmacology: Neuroscientific Basis and Practical Applications*, 2E, p. 143, by Stephen M. Stahl, 2000; "A Psychiatrist Gets a Taste of Her Own Medicine" adapted from Gartrell, N. (2004, Jan. 4). "A doctor's toxic shock." *Boston Globe Magazine*, p. 58; Figure: From *Essential Psychopharmacology: Neuroscientific Basis and Practical Applications*, 2E, p. 143, by Stephen M. Stahl, 2000; Table: Sources: Bezchlibnyk-Butler & Jeffries (2003); Buckley & Waddington (2001); and Sadock et al., (2009). "I'd Rather Not Take It" adapted from Gartrell, N. (2004, Jan. 4). "A doctor's toxic shock." *Boston Globe Magazine*, p. 58; Table: Sources: Bezchlibnyk-Butler & Jeffries (2003); Buckley & Waddington (2001); and Sadock et al., (2009); Figure: Adapted from Sadock, B. J., & Sadock, V. A., (2003). Kaplan and Sadock's synopsis of psychiatry, p. 1142; Figure: Reprinted with permission, Cleveland Clinic Center for Medical Art & Photography © 2012. All Rights Reserved.

Contemporary and Legal Issues in Abnormal Psychology

From Chapter 17 of *Abnormal Psychology*, Fifteenth Edition. James N. Butcher, Susan Mineka, Jill M. Hooley. Copyright © 2013 by Pearson Education, Inc. All rights reserved.

Contemporary and Legal Issues in Abnormal Psychology

case study **A Tragic Case of Murder as an Outcome of Severe Mental Illness**

On Mother's Day weekend in 2003, Deanna Laney, a very religious 39-year-old housewife and mother from Texas, began to see "signs from God" that she was supposed to do something drastic about her children. The first sign indicated to her that she was supposed to destroy her children when she saw her fourteen-month-old son, Aaron, playing with a spear. She hesitated because she was uncertain of exactly what the sign from God meant. Then she received another sign when Aaron handed her a rock that he was playing with. She then saw him squeezing a frog and began to conclude that she was supposed to kill her children, either by stoning them, strangling them, or stabbing them. She believed that God had given her three ways to kill them but concluded that killing them with rocks would be better than strangulation.

She killed two of her sons by beating them with a rock; her third son, Aaron, was severely injured but survived her attack. She called 911 and reported that she had killed her sons.

After she was arrested she was very puzzled and behaved in an extreme manner, for example, lying in a fetal position and crying in the cell, walking around the cell singing gospel songs, and often praying and crying. The sheriff in the prison reported that "when she suddenly realizes what she's done she goes an extreme blank stare and withdrawal." She was placed on a suicide watch because of her intense and psychotic behavior.

Laney had a history of serious mental illness including a prior psychotic experience in which she was hospitalized. During this episode, she reported that she had smelled sulfur and concluded that this was God's way of warning her that the devil was close. She was diagnosed with schizophrenia.

At her murder trial, Laney pleaded Not Gulty by Reason of Insanity (NGRI) (to be discussed later in the chapter). Her defense was based on her belief that God had told her the world was going to end and "she had to get her house in order," which included killing her children. The psychiatric evaluations of her mental health status prior to the trial reflected a strong consensus as to her condition. Psychiatrists who served as experts from both the defense and the prosecution in this case testified that Laney was psychotic at the time of the crime and met the criteria for NGRI. The evaluating psychiatrists concluded that Laney had crushed her sons' skulls with rocks because she was suffering from delusions and did not know right from wrong.

The jury acquitted her of all charges on grounds that she was insane at the time of the crime. Apparently, there was no premeditation, and Laney did not believe that she was doing wrong; thus she was found not guilty by reason of insanity (Associated Press, 2004; Ramsland, 2005).

This chapter has traditionally been somewhat of a highlight for several important topics in abnormal psychology. These issues are very important to understanding the field of abnormal psychology and will give the reader a broader perspective on ways our society deals with, or in some cases fails to deal with, abnormal behavior or its consequences. We begin with the topic of prevention of mental disorders. Over the years, most mental health efforts have been geared toward helping people after they have already developed serious problems. If the goal is to reduce or eliminate emotional problems in our country or the world, then a major alteration in thinking is required. We need to expand efforts at prevention through early intervention (Breitborde et al., 2010; Tortolero, 2010).

Next, we will describe inpatient mental health treatment and the state of mental hospitals in contemporary society, including a discussion of the prison system where many mental health patients end up. We will discuss changes that have taken place and some of the forces that have affected inpatient psychiatric care today. Following this, several legal issues pertinent to psychiatric care and the hospitalization of people with severe psychological problems will be addressed. We will then briefly survey the scope of organized efforts for mental health both in the United States and throughout the world. Finally, we will consider what each of us can do to foster mental health.

Perspectives on Prevention

In the early 1990s, the U.S. Congress directed the National Institute of Mental Health (NIMH) to work with the Institute of Medicine (IOM) to develop a report detailing a long-term prevention research program. Among other things, the IOM report focused attention on the distinction between prevention and treatment efforts (Dozois & Dobson, 2004; Munoz, 2001; Munoz et al., 1996). Prevention efforts are classified into three subcategories:

1. **Universal interventions**: Efforts that are aimed at influencing the general population.

2. **Selective interventions**: Efforts that are aimed at a specific subgroup of the population considered at risk for developing mental health problems—for example, adolescents or ethnic minorities (Coie et al., 2000).

3. **Indicated interventions**: Efforts that are directed toward high-risk individuals who are identified as having minimal but detectable symptoms of mental disorder but who do not meet criteria for clinical diagnosis—for example, individuals forced from their homes by a flood or some other disaster (see Reyes & Jacobs, 2006).

As shown in Figure 1, preventive efforts are clearly differentiated from treatment and maintenance interventions.

Universal Interventions

Universal interventions perform two key tasks: (1) altering conditions that can cause or contribute to mental disorders (risk factors) and (2) establishing conditions that foster positive mental health (protective factors). Epidemiological studies help investigators obtain information about the incidence and distribution of various maladaptive behaviors (Dozois & Dobson, 2004) such as those seen in anxiety-based disorders (Feldner et al., 2004). These findings can then be used to suggest what preventive efforts might be most appropriate. For example, various epidemiological studies and reviews have shown that certain groups are at high risk for mental disorders: recently divorced people (Bulloch et al., 2009), the physically disabled (Goodheart & Rozensky, 2011), elderly people (Houtjes et al., 2010), the physically abused (Panuzio & DiLillo, 2010), people who have been uprooted from their homes (Caracci & Mezzich, 2001), and victims of severe trauma (Jaranson et al., 2004). Although findings such as these may be the basis for immediate selective or indicated prevention, they may also aid in universal prevention by telling us what to look for and where to look—in essence, by focusing our efforts in the right direction. Universal prevention is very broad and includes biological, psychosocial, and sociocultural efforts. Virtually any effort that is aimed at improving the human condition would be considered a part of universal prevention of mental disorder.

BIOLOGICAL STRATEGIES Biologically based universal strategies for prevention begin with promoting adaptive lifestyles. Many of the goals of health psychology can be viewed as universal prevention strategies. Efforts geared toward improving diet, establishing a routine of physical exercise, and developing overall good health habits can do much to improve physical well-being (Martins et al., 2010). Physical illness always produces some sort of psychological stress that can result in such problems as depression, so with respect to good mental health, maintaining good physical health is prevention.

PSYCHOSOCIAL STRATEGIES In viewing normality as optimal development and viewing high functioning (rather than the mere absence of pathology) as the goal, we imply that people need opportunities to learn physical, intellectual, emotional, and social competencies.

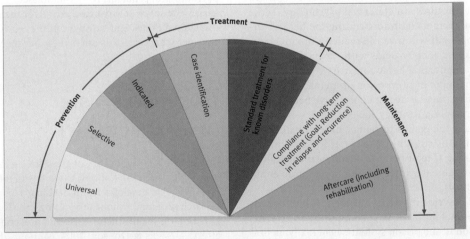

FIGURE 1

Classification of Prevention Strategies, Treatment, and Maintenance

The traditional terminology for describing general strategies of disease prevention in the field of public health has been revised to provide a more useful perspective on prevention efforts. The new classification system for prevention (universal, selective, and indicated strategies) is shown in this context as distinct from treatment interventions and maintenance approaches to mental health problems.

Source: From P. J. Mrazek & R. J. Haggerty (Eds.). (1994). *Reducing risks for mental disorders: Frontiers for preventive intervention research.* Copyright © 1994 by the National Academy of Sciences. Courtesy of the National Academy Press, Washington, DC.

Preventing mental disorders and maintaining psychosocial health require that a person be prepared for the types of problems likely to be encountered during given life stages. For example, how might young people who want to marry and have children prepare themselves for the tasks of building a mutually satisfying relationship and helping children develop their abilities?

1. The first requirement for psychosocial health is that a person develop the skills needed for effective problem solving, for expressing emotions constructively, and for engaging in satisfying relationships with others. Failure to develop these protective skills places the individual at a serious disadvantage in coping with stresses and the unavoidable risk factors for mental disorder.

2. The second requirement for psychosocial health is that a person acquires an accurate frame of reference on which to build his or her identity. We have seen repeatedly that when people's assumptions about themselves or their world are inaccurate, their behavior is likely to be maladaptive. Consider, for example, the young woman who believes that being thin can bring happiness and so becomes anorexic.

3. The third requirement for psychosocial health is that a person be prepared for the types of problems likely to be encountered during given life stages. For example, young people who want to marry and have children must be prepared for the tasks of building a mutually satisfying relationship and helping children develop their abilities. Similarly, a middle-aged adult needs to be prepared for problems that are likely to arise during retirement and old age.

In recent years, psychosocial measures aimed at prevention have received a great deal of attention. The field of behavioral medicine has been influential (Hunter et al., 2009), with efforts being made to change the psychological factors underlying unhealthy habits such as smoking, excessive drinking, and poor eating habits.

SOCIOCULTURAL STRATEGIES Individual development is stifled without a supportive community. At the same time, without responsible, psychologically healthy individuals, the community will not thrive and, in turn, cannot be supportive.

The psychosocially impaired victims of disorganized communities lack the wherewithal to create better communities to protect and sustain the psychological health of those who come after them, and a persistently unprotective environment results. Sociocultural efforts toward universal prevention are focused on making the community as safe and attractive as possible for the individuals within it.

With our growing recognition of the role that pathological social conditions play in producing maladaptive behavior (in socially impoverished communities), increased attention must be devoted to creating social conditions that will foster healthy development and functioning in individuals. Efforts to create these conditions include a broad spectrum of measures—ranging from public education and Social Security to economic planning and social legislation directed at ensuring adequate health care for all.

Selective Interventions

Preventing mental health problems through social change in the community is difficult. Although the whole psychological climate can ultimately be changed by a social movement such as the civil rights movement of the 1960s, the payoff of such efforts is generally far in the future and may be difficult or impossible to predict or measure. Attempts to effect psychologically desirable social change are also likely to involve ideological and political issues that may inspire powerful opposition, including opposition from government itself. Efforts to bring about change through targeting a smaller segment of the population can have more effective results. For example, a recent review of the research in reducing depression in children concludes that selective intervention programs are more effective than universal programs (Horowitz & Garber, 2006) in reducing the extent of depressive disorders.

AN ILLUSTRATION OF SELECTIVE PREVENTION STRATEGIES Though difficult to formulate, mobilize, and carry out, selective intervention can bring about major improvements. In this section, we will look at the mobilization of prevention resources aimed at curtailing or reducing the problem of teenage alcohol and drug abuse. Prominent social forces such as advertising and marketing campaigns that are attractive to youth, the influence of peer groups, and the ready availability of alcohol, tobacco, and even many illicit drugs are instrumental in promoting the early use of alcohol in young people.

Although recent years have witnessed a decrease in the rate of adolescent substance use in the United States (Johnston et al., 2007), alcohol, tobacco, and other drug use by teenagers remains a persistent public health problem. Alcohol is the most commonly used drug among adolescents (Komro et al. 2008). Alcohol use among youth is related to many social, emotional, and behavioral problems (e.g., using illegal drugs, fighting, stealing, driving under the influence, having unplanned sex, and having school problems).

In fact, early alcohol use is a strong predictor of lifetime alcohol abuse or dependence (Grant & Dawson, 1997).

Because the factors that entice adolescents to begin using alcohol and drugs are influenced by social factors, it is tempting to think that if these forces could be counterbalanced with equally powerful alternative influences, the rate of substance abuse might radically decline. But this is easier said than done. The U.S. government has approached the drug-abuse problem with three broad strategies for dealing with adolescent substance use, all of which have proved insufficient:

Efforts to teach schoolchildren about the dangers of drugs before they reach the age of maximum risk are based on the premise that if children are made aware of the dangers of drugs and alcohol, they will choose not to use them. However, evaluative studies have cast doubt on the effectiveness of programs such as D.A.R.E. What do you think might account for D.A.R.E.'s lack of success?

1. *Intercepting and/or Reducing the Supply of Drugs Available.* The reduction of supply by policing our borders has had minimal impact on the availability of drugs. These programs do little to affect the supply of the two drugs most abused by adolescents—alcohol and tobacco—which are, of course, available in corner stores and even in the adolescent's home. Reducing the supply of these drugs to adolescents is especially challenging given mass-media messages and other societal signals that these legal products can bring about social acceptance, are essential for celebrations, and can mark a young person's passage into adulthood, with limited cautions about their potential to damage health.

2. *Providing Treatment Services for Those who Develop Drug Problems.* Although much money is spent each year on treatment, treating substance abuse is perhaps the least effective way to reduce the problem. Addictive disorders are very difficult to overcome, and treatment failure or relapse are the rule rather than the exception. Therapeutic programs for those addicted to drugs or alcohol, though necessary, are not the answer to eliminating or even significantly reducing the problems in our society.

3. *Encouraging Prevention.* By far the most desirable—and potentially the most effective—means of reducing the drug problem in our country is through prevention methods aimed at alerting citizens to the problems that surround drugs and teaching young people ways to avoid using them (Bloom et al., 2009). Although past efforts have had some limited success in discouraging adolescent drug use, many initially promising prevention efforts have failed to bring about the desired reduction in substance use. There are a number of reasons for this: The intervention typically has not been conducted for a long enough period to show the desired effect; the intervention efforts have not been powerful enough to make a sufficient impact on the participants; or the strategy may not have been well implemented.

In recent years prevention specialists have taken a more proactive position and have attempted to establish programs that prevent the development of abuse disorders before young people become so involved with drugs or alcohol that future adjustment becomes difficult, if not impossible. These recent prevention strategies have taken some diverse and promising directions. We will examine several such efforts and then discuss the limitations of these prevention approaches.

School-Based Interventions The most promising alcohol- and drug-prevention curricula are based on behavioral theory; target the risk (e.g., peer pressure, mass-media messages) and protective (e.g., alcohol-free activities, messages supporting "no use" norms) factors associated with adolescent use; include developmentally appropriate information about alcohol and other drugs; are skill-based and interactive; and emphasize normative education that increases the awareness that most students do not use alcohol, tobacco, or other drugs (Komro & Toomey, 2002). While several such programs exist, some have been evaluated more extensively than others; for example, the Drug Abuse Resistance Program, or D.A.R.E. (a program that uses local police officers who are invited by the local school districts to speak and work with students after undergoing special training), recently underwent an extensive number of evaluative studies that have generally concluded that the program has limited success at deterring substance use. In fact, a 10-year follow-up study reported no success of the D.A.R.E. program (Lynam et al., 2009).

Intervention Programs for High-Risk Teens Intervention programs identify high-risk teenagers and take special measures to circumvent their further use of alcohol or other potentially dangerous drugs (Hawkins et al., 2004). Programs such as these are often school-based efforts and are not strictly prevention programs because they intervene with young people who have already developed problems. Programs for early intervention can be effective in identifying adolescents before their alcohol or drug problems become entrenched (Foley & Hochman, 2006).

RESEARCH CLOSE-UP

Intervention Programs of High-Risk Populations

This research strategy involves identifying high-risk individuals and providing special approaches to circumvent their problems; for example, identifying adolescents at risk for abusing alcohol and implementing a program to prevent the problem behavior.

Parent Education and Family-Based Intervention Programs Through their own drinking or positive verbalizations about alcohol, parents may encourage or sanction alcohol use among teens. Some research has shown that parental involvement and monitoring reduces substance use among adolescents (Ramirez et al., 2004). Thus, many prevention programs focus upon family interventions (Spoth et al., 2004) with good success.

Extracurricular Strategies Various extracurricular activities and youth programs have the potential to reduce problem behaviors like alcohol and drug use, school dropouts, violence, and juvenile delinquency (Scales & Leffert, 1999). These programs may be especially beneficial for high-risk teens who are unsupervised outside of school or who, because of poverty, may not have access to opportunities like sports, music, or other programs available to middle-class youth.

Why do you think peer programs, like those offered at the Boys and Girls Clubs, tend to be more successful than adult-driven programs in getting children and adolescents to avoid drug and alcohol abuse?

Internet-based Intervention Programs One recent study (Schwinn et al., 2010) examined adolescent girls (seventh through ninth grade) who were given an online test battery and 12 sessions of gender-specific drug prevention strategies. At follow-up, girls receiving the Internet intervention program reported lower rates of use for alcohol and drugs compared with the control sample.

Comprehensive Prevention Strategies A consensus seems to be developing in the field that the most effective way to prevent complex problems like adolescent alcohol and other drug use is through the use of multicomponent programs that combine aspects of the various strategies described previously (Stigler, Neusel, and Perry, 2011). Typically, classroom curricula are used as the core component to which other strategies (e.g., parent programs, mass media, extracurricular activities, and community strategies to reduce access to alcohol via enforcement of age of drinking laws) are added.

Partly because of this lack of positive results for alcohol use, a team of University of Minnesota researchers developed Project Northland—an exemplary research-based set of interventions that aims to delay the onset of drinking in young adolescents, reduce alcohol use among those already drinking, and limit the number of alcohol-related problems during adolescence . Project Northland included multiple years of behavioral curricula, parental involvement and education, peer leadership opportunities, community task forces, and community-wide media campaigns (e.g., Perry et al., 1996, 2002). Interventions started with students in the sixth grade and continued until high school graduation. The program included peer-led and activity-driven learning strategies that involved students, parents, teachers, and community members in support of "no use" messages, while at the same time promoting alcohol-free norms for youth, providing fun alternatives to alcohol use, and reducing youth access to alcohol. Innovative activities and games were used to ensure

Recognizing the huge market potential of teenagers, advertisers exploit the tremendous value that the appearance of sophistication has for this age group. Some efforts have been aimed at deglamorizing these messages by showing ads that graphically depict the negative aspects alcohol and drug use, like the antismoking ad on the right.

high participation rates in the program, and comprehensive teacher and peer-leader trainings were core features (go to http://www.hazelden.org/web/go/projectnorthland for descriptions of the program).

The success of prevention programs has come to the attention of educators, and a number of efforts are under way to "export" these laboratory programs for broader use in America's schools. Perhaps the most noteworthy is the National Registry of Effective Prevention Programs (NREPP), a program of the U.S. Department of Health and Human Services Substance Abuse and Mental Health Services Administration (http://www.samhsa.gov). However, the jury is still out on the relative success of the various substance-abuse prevention programs at reducing alcohol and drug problems in adolescents. For example, an effort to implement the Northland project in a large Midwestern inner city where problems with gangs, violence, drug dealing, and housing were perceived as more pressing than underage drinking did not have the positive outcomes that were obtained in the more rural environment of northern Minnesota (Komro et al., 2008). It will take time and further research efforts to determine which of the strategies are superior to others in reducing alcohol and drug problems in adolescents, and in which settings.

Indicated Interventions

Indicated intervention emphasizes the early detection and prompt treatment of maladaptive behavior in a person's family and community setting. In some cases—for example, in a crisis or after a disaster (Garakani et al., 2004)—indicated prevention involves immediate and relatively brief intervention to prevent any long-term behavioral consequences of the traumatic events (Raphael & Wooding, 2004).

Inpatient Mental Health Treatment in Contemporary Society

Mental disorders are common in the United States. An estimated 26.2 percent of Americans ages 18 and older, or about one in four adults, suffer from a diagnosable mental disorder in a given year (Kessler, Chiu et al., 2005). Over 57.7 million people ages 18 and older suffer from one or more psychiatric disorders. Of these, approximately 2.4 million American adults, or about 1.1 percent of the population ages 18 and older in a given year, are diagnosed as having schizophrenia. While most people experiencing mental health problems seek or obtain help in an outpatient program, some individuals require admission to an inpatient treatment program because of perceived danger they experience in their daily lives. Inpatient admission to a psychiatric hospital can be a significant step that is taken as a means of protecting the individual or those close to him or her from harm by providing a secure environment to allow the patient to recover from his or her extreme symptoms.

The Mental Hospital as a Therapeutic Community

In cases where individuals might be considered dangerous to themselves or others (Richards et al., 1997) or where their symptoms are so severe that they are unable to care for themselves in the community, psychiatric hospitalization may be necessary in order to prevent the development of further problems and the individual's further psychological deterioration. Most of the traditional forms of therapy may, of course, be used in a residential or inpatient hospital setting. In addition, in many mental hospitals, these techniques are supplemented by efforts to make the hospital environment itself a "therapeutic community" (Kennard, 2004). That is, the social environment is manipulated to provide the patient with the greatest benefit. All the ongoing activities of the hospital are brought into the total treatment program, and the environment, or milieu, is a crucial aspect of the therapy. This approach is thus often referred to as **milieu therapy** (Petti, 2010; Zimmerman, 2004). Three general therapeutic principles guide this approach to treatment:

1. Staff expectations are clearly communicated to patients. Both positive and negative feedback are used to encourage appropriate verbalizations and actions by patients.

2. Patients are encouraged to become involved in all decisions made, and in all actions taken, concerning them. A self-care, do-it-yourself attitude prevails.

3. All patients belong to social groups on the ward. The group cohesiveness that results gives the patients support and encouragement, and the related process of group pressure helps shape their behavior in positive ways.

In a therapeutic community, as few restraints as possible are placed on patients' freedom, and patients are encouraged to take responsibility for their behavior and participate actively in their treatment programs. Open wards permit patients to use the grounds and premises. Self-government programs give patients responsibility for managing their own affairs and those of the ward. All hospital personnel are expected to treat the patients as human beings who merit consideration and courtesy. The interaction among patients—whether in group therapy sessions, social events, or other activities—is planned in such a way as to be of therapeutic benefit. In fact, it is becoming apparent that often the most beneficial aspect of a therapeutic community is the interaction among the patients themselves. Differences in social roles and backgrounds may make empathy between staff and patients difficult, but fellow patients have been there—they have had similar problems and breakdowns and have experienced the anxiety and humiliation of being labeled "mentally ill" and being hospitalized. Constructive relationships frequently develop among patients in a supportive, encouraging milieu. However, although **residential treatment** has improved over time, such treatment for children and adolescents continues to face challenges (see Box 1 describing residential care for children and adolescents).

Another successful method for helping patients take increased responsibility for their own behavior is the use of **social-learning programs**. Such programs normally make use of learning principles and techniques such as token economies to shape more socially acceptable behavior (Corrigan, 1995, 1997; Mariotto et al., 2002; Paul et al., 1997).

Although a strong case can be made for the use of psychiatric hospitalization in stabilizing adjustment of people living with psychiatric disorders (Glick & Tandon, 2009), a persistent concern about hospitalization is that the mental hospital may become a permanent refuge from the world. Over the past four decades, considerable effort has been devoted to reducing the population of inpatients by closing hospitals and treating patients who have mental disorders as outpatients. This effort, which is often referred to as **deinstitutionalization**, was initiated to prevent the negative effects, for many psychiatric patients, of being confined to a mental hospital for long periods of time as well as to lower health care costs. To keep the focus on returning patients to the community and on preventing their return to the institution, contemporary hospital staffs try to establish close ties with patients' families and communities and to provide them with positive expectations about the patients' recovery.

The rise of the biological therapies has meant that between 70 and 90 percent of patients diagnosed with psychosis and admitted to mental hospitals can now be discharged within a few weeks, or at most a few months. Even where disorders have become chronic, effective treatment methods have been developed. In one of the most extensive and well-controlled studies of chronic hospitalized patients, Paul and Lentz (1977) compared the relative effectiveness of three treatment approaches:

1. Milieu therapy focuses on structuring a patient's environment to provide clear communication of expectations and to get the patient involved in the treatment. One major goal is to encourage the patient to participate in the therapeutic community through the group process.

2. A social-learning treatment program, organized around learning principles and using a rigorously programmed token economy system, with ward staff as reinforcing agents. Undesirable behavior was not reinforced, whereas the accumulation of many tokens through effective functioning made a patient eligible for attractive amenities not normally available in public mental hospitals.

3. Traditional mental hospital treatments including pharmacotherapy, occupational therapy, recreational therapy, activity therapy, and individual or group therapy. No systematic application of milieu therapy or the social-learning program was given to this group.

The treatment project covered a period of 6 years: an initial phase of staff training, patient assessment, and baseline recording; a treatment phase; an aftercare phase; and a long (year and a half) follow-up. The changes targeted included resocialization, learning new roles, and reducing or eliminating bizarre behavior. There were 28 chronic schizophrenic patients in each treatment group matched for age, sex, socioeconomic level, symptoms, and duration of hospitalization. The results of the study were impressive. Both milieu therapy and the social-learning program produced significant improvement in overall functioning and resulted in more successful hospital releases than the traditional hospital care. The behaviorally based social-learning program, however, was clearly superior to the more diffuse program of milieu therapy, as evidenced by the fact that over 90 percent of the released patients from the social-learning program remained continuously in the community, compared with 70 percent of the released patients who had had milieu therapy. The figure for the traditional treatment program was less than 50 percent.

Despite the promise of the token economy approach, emulating as it does certain "real-world" principles of exchange that the patient will face outside the institution, it has not enjoyed wide public acceptance (Mariotto et al., 2002). Many feel that it is cruel and inhumane to expect mental health patients to govern their behavior in accordance with a prescribed schedule of reinforcements. One might ask, however, whether it is more humane to consign the patient to the status of a passive and helpless recipient of whatever the environment has to offer, which in many institutional settings is not very much. Is that truly the message we want to convey about the patient's relationship to his or her environment? Probably not, especially in light of the considerable evidence that most chronic mental health patients are surprisingly adept at making successful adaptations that are within their range of control.

Aftercare Programs

Even where hospitalization has successfully modified maladaptive behavior and a patient has learned needed occupational and interpersonal skills, readjustment in the community following release may still be difficult (Seidman, 2003; Thornicraft & Tansella, 2000). Many studies have shown that in the past, up to 45 percent of individuals with schizophrenia have been readmitted within the first year after

1 DEVELOPMENTS IN THINKING

Residential Treatment Programs: Do They Help Troubled Children and Adolescents?

Out-of-home placements for children and adolescents with mental health problems have a checkered history and questionable future. In times past, families and the professionals assisting them often addressed the problems of disturbed children and adolescents whose behavior was of concern to others by removing them from their homes and placing them in such places as almshouses, hospitals, or religious homes in order to, they hoped, restore or establish more stable functioning. Although residential care has from the beginning been considered a humane alternative to neglect and maltreatment of children with severe problems, many of these efforts have proved to be ineffective and sometimes harmful to the child (Leichtman, 2006; Platt, 1969).

Types of Residential Programs

There are several types of residential programs for children and adolescents, depending upon the problems presented, the family resources, and accessibility. Some of the existing programs are nonprofit (e.g., church-related) whereas others are for-profit programs including large treatment facility chains (Hechinger & Chaker, 2005; Story, 2005). A variety of settings are available, such as campus-based group homes or wilderness-based "camps" as well as schools, programs, or treatment centers. However, residential treatment has been considered by many experts to be an often inappropriate and overused placement choice (Leichtman, 2006; Lyman & Campbell, 1996).

Problems with Residential Treatment Programs

The basic view underlying residential mental health programs is that they can provide psychological treatment in the context of an environment that enables the child to learn effective adaptive skills in the "other

Many residential treatment facilities, such as the one shown here, have proved to be ineffective and sometimes harmful to children. What types of changes do most experts agree are needed to improve the quality of such treatment facilities?

23 hours" (Leichtman, 2006), or the time the child is not being seen by the therapist. The placement of children or adolescents in residential treatment may be only a temporary solution for the family's problems, however; in many cases, either the child or the family members fail to make appropriate changes to allow the youngster to reenter the family environment at a more functional level. Pumariega (2007) points out that "exiling" a child in this way might make it impossible for him or her to return to the family because doing so may not solve the dysfunctional situation that led up to and likely contributed to the child's problems.

The Alliance for Safe, Therapeutic and Appropriate Use of Residential Treatment (START) has called attention to a number of problems

their discharge. Community-based treatment programs, now referred to as "aftercare programs," are live-in facilities that serve as a home base for former patients as they make the transition back to adequate functioning in the community. Typically, community-based facilities are run not by professional mental health personnel but by the residents themselves. Aftercare programs can help smooth the transition from institutional to community life and reduce the number of relapses. However, some individuals do not function well in aftercare programs. Owen and colleagues (1997) found that clients who were likely to hold unskilled employment, to have nonpsychotic symptoms, to have committed a crime, or to be more transient tended to be noncompliant in aftercare programs. The investigators conclude that many of the discharged patients did not "fit" the services typically offered to released psychiatric inpatients. Those with less severe

symptoms may fail because they appear to aftercare staff as not needing much help; most services are geared to those patients who exhibit more extreme symptoms.

Sometimes aftercare includes a "halfway" period in which a released patient makes a gradual return to the outside world in what were formerly termed "halfway houses." Aftercare programs do not always live up to their name, however. Levy and Kershaw (2001) disclose a number of problems in which relevant treatment was not made available and staff did not provide a secure environment.

Although some patients continue to have mental health problems including suicide attempts (Fenton et al., 1997), and many have trouble gaining the acceptance and support of the community (Fairweather, 1994; Seidman, 2003), efforts to treat severely disturbed patients in the community are often very successful.

in current residential care such as mistreatment and abuse, including harsh discipline, inappropriate seclusion and restraint, substandard psychological interventions, medical neglect, and rights violations including deaths, usually from use of restraints, excessive physical demands, or suicide. Friedman and colleagues (2006) highlighted a number of reports that have been published in recent years regarding the mistreatment, abuse, and death of young people in residential programs. Leichtman (2006) also pointed out that many contemporary facilities overuse medications to manage problem children, a treatment that actually limits the child's or adolescent's adaptive capacity further.

Moreover, many residential treatment facilities have not provided the positive life-changing capacity that was initially hoped for or resulted in positive long-term effects (Edelen et al., 2010). In addition, the child may not fit into that environment or, worse, may become less adaptable. Leichtman (2006) pointed out that the "other 23 hours" thought to aid the child or adolescent in making a more successful adaptation are often not effectively used to help the child accomplish normal development tasks because the facilities tend to be staffed with untrained or unqualified ward staff.

Behar and colleagues (2007) and Friedman and colleagues (2006) described many of the problems with ensuring quality of the residential care facilities, noting that there is great variability in licensing requirements among the states. For example, Montana, which has more residential programs than most other states, currently has no licensing requirement for private behavioral health care programs. And Utah, which is believed to have the most residential programs of any state, also has no licensing requirement for residential facilities, although recent problems led to a 2005 law amending regulations for programs and facilities.

Recommendations for Improving Residential Care in the United States

Recent evidence suggests that there is a continuum of intensive residential services that can serve the needs of youth with significant emotional and behavioral needs (Huefner et al. 2010). Friedman and colleagues (2007) make several recommendations to ensure more effective and safe treatment environments in residential care facilities. They consider it important that all states have laws and policies that promote licensing and procedures for monitoring programs to ensure that quality services are provided and to decrease the possibility of abusive or harmful behavior to children and adolescents. In cases of harm, they state that there should be a program for reporting and correcting the situations underlying incidents of abuse. Friedman and colleagues also think that this protective effort should be part of an overall child-protection program monitored by an agency of the federal government. In addition, they recommended that professionals in the mental health field actively respond to the growing evidence of mistreatment and abuse of youth in the unregulated program environment in the country today.

Although residential care is a necessary decision in some cases because of the severity of a child's problems and the family's inability to cope with her or him, the out-of-home placement can be problematic. In addition, the child can be placed at unnecessary risk. Most experts agree that the government and professional community need to more actively pursue more appropriate guidance for structuring and maintaining quality treatment and security for children at these facilities.

Deinstitutionalization

The population of psychiatric patients in the United States has shrunk considerably over the past 40 years. Between 1967 and 2007, the number of people in state mental hospitals dropped 81 percent (Scott et al., 2008). The deinstitutionalization movement, which involves closing down mental hospitals and treating persons with severe mental disorders in community programs, has not been limited to the United States. On the contrary, there has been a worldwide trend to shift the care of mental patients from inpatient hospitals to community-based programs (Emerson, 2004; Honkonen et al., 2003).

Deinstitutionalization has been a source of considerable controversy. Some authorities consider the emptying of mental hospitals a positive expression of society's desire to free previously confined persons, maintaining that deinstitutionalized patients show significant improvement compared with those who remain hospitalized (Newton et al., 2000; Reinharz et al., 2000). Others, however, speak of the "abandonment" of chronic patients to a cruel and harsh existence (Grob, 2008), which for many includes homelessness, violent victimization (Walsh et al., 2003), or suicide (Goldney, 2003). Many citizens, too, complain of being harassed, intimidated, and frightened by obviously disturbed persons wandering the streets of their neighborhoods. In an effort to address concerns of patients, some professionals and community members alike have lobbied to call attention to mental health challenges brought about by deinstitutionalization (Rosenberg & Rosenberg, 2006).

Some of the reduction in mental health services in recent years has come about because of changes in the health care system. (See the Unresolved Issues section at the end of this chapter.) The planned community efforts to fill the gaps in service never really materialized at effective levels (Lamb, 1998).

A number of factors have interacted to alter the pattern of mental hospital admissions and discharges in recent years. Antipsychotic drugs have made it possible for many patients who would otherwise have required confinement to live in the community, but not all mental health problems can be managed with medication. In addition, changing treatment philosophy and the desire to eliminate mental institutions were bolstered by the assumption that society wanted and could afford to provide better community-based care for chronic patients outside of large mental hospitals.

In theory, closing the public mental hospitals seemed workable. The plan was to open many community-based mental health centers that would provide continuing care to the residents of hospitals after discharge. Residents would be given welfare funds (supposedly at less cost to the government than maintaining large mental hospitals) and would be administered medication to keep them stabilized until they could obtain continuing care. Many patients would be discharged to home and family; others would be placed in smaller, home-like board-and-care facilities or nursing homes.

Unforeseen problems arose, however, and in many cases, homeless shelters in metropolitan communities have become a "makeshift alternative" to inpatient mental health care (Haugland et al., 1997). Many residents of mental institutions have no families or homes to go to; board-and-care facilities are often substandard; and the community mental health centers have often been ill prepared and insufficiently funded to provide needed services for chronic patients, particularly as national funding priorities shifted during the 1980s (Humphreys & Rappaport, 1993). Many patients are not carefully selected for discharge and are not ready for community living, and many of those who are discharged are not followed up sufficiently or often enough to ensure their successful adaptation outside the hospital. In addition, some research has suggested that deinstitutionalization has increased the rates of suicide among people with mental illness (Yoon & Bruckner, 2009).

One important court case (*Albright* v. *Abington Memorial Hospital*, 1997) involved charges that the hospital failed to provide sufficient care for a seriously disturbed woman who later killed herself. Countless patients have been discharged to fates harsher than the conditions in any of the hospitals. The following case illustrates the situation.

Aftercare facilities do not always provide the safe refuge promised. Homeless people often live in large cities under austere conditions, as noted in this photograph, that resemble those seen in mental institutions several decades ago.

case study — **From Institution to Homelessness**

Dave B., 49 years old, had been hospitalized for 25 years in a state mental hospital. When the hospital was scheduled for phaseout, many of the patients, particularly those who were regressed or aggressive, were transferred to another state hospital. Dave was a borderline mentally retarded man who had periodic episodes of psychosis. At the time of the hospital closing, however, he was not hallucinating and was "reasonably intact." Dave was considered to be one of the "less disturbed" residents because his psychotic behavior was less pronounced and he presented no dangerous problems. He was discharged to a board-and-care facility (actually an old hotel where most of the residents were former inpatients). At first, Dave seemed to fit in well at the facility; mostly he sat in his room or in the outside hallway, and he caused no trouble for the caretakers. Two weeks after he had arrived, however, he wandered off the hotel grounds and was missing for several days. The police eventually found him living in the city dump. He had apparently stopped taking his medication, and when he was discovered he was regressed and catatonic. He was readmitted to a state hospital.

Research on the effects of deinstitutionalization has been mixed. Some reports have noted positive benefits of briefer hospitalization (Honkonen et al., 2003; Rauktis, 2001), and some data suggest that deinstitutionalization appears not to be associated with an increased risk of homicide by people who are mentally ill (Simpson et al., 2004). However, others have reported problems with discharged patients and point to failures in programs to deinstitutionalize mental patients (Chan et al., 2001; Leff, 2001).

There is some recent indication that inpatient psychiatric hospitalization may be increasing because of the failures to provide adequate mental health care for patients in need of mental health services in the community (Marcotty, 2004). A similar increase in the number of people being hospitalized has been reported in the United Kingdom (Priebe & Turner, 2003).

The full extent of problems created by deinstitutionalization is not precisely known, partly because there has been little rigorous follow-up on patients discharged from mental hospitals. Such research investigations are difficult to conduct because the patients are transient and hard to track over time. Certainly, not all homeless people are former mental patients, but deinstitutionalization has contributed substantially to the number of homeless people (Whitaker, 2009) and to the number of mentally ill people in prison (Markowitz, 2006), as described in Box 2. On the positive side, a study by Nelson and colleagues (2007) concluded that there has been a significant reduction in homelessness and significant improvements in "well-being" outcomes resulting from recent programs that provide permanent housing and support for the homeless. For example, Padgett, and colleagues (2006) showed that assertive community treatment and programs to reduce harm can be successful in producing housing stability and reduction in the trauma of homelessness.

In Review

- What are some strategies for biological, psychosocial, and sociocultural universal interventions?
- Define the term *selective intervention*. What selective intervention programs have shown promise in helping prevent teenage alcohol and drug abuse?
- What is indicated intervention?
- What is milieu therapy?
- What problems have resulted from deinstitutionalization?

2 THE WORLD AROUND US

Jails and Prisons: Serving as Mental Hospitals Again

The number of people with mental disorders in prison populations is alarming (Markowitz, 2006). Kanapaux (2004) estimated that about 70,000 inmates in U.S. prisons are psychotic and that from 200,000 to 300,000 male and female prison inmates suffer from mental disorders such as schizophrenia, bipolar disorder, or major depression. Mentally ill persons who are evaluated in jails or prisons are twice as likely to have been homeless before their arrest. Moreover, mentally ill inmates tend to have more incarcerations than other prisoners, and more than three-quarters of them have been sentenced to jail or prison in the past.

As a result of deinstitutionalization over recent years and the subsequent closing of so many psychiatric facilities, there are fewer

In the United States and Canada, jails and prisons are extremely overcrowded and unable to implement rehabilitation efforts for those imprisoned. Inmates are typically at great risk of developing further problems such as aggression, illness, mental health problems, higher suicide rates, and increased likelihood of recidivism.

places where mentally ill patients can receive inpatient treatment (Torrey, 2008). Moreover, there has been insufficient development of community-based services to provide outpatient care for people who need it. Consequently, many people become homeless because they cannot take care of themselves or because they commit crimes as a result of their uncontrolled behavior.

The high rates of psychiatrically disturbed persons in prisons and jails are a problem not only in the United States but in other countries as well (Bluglass, 2000). One study of prison inmates in 13 European countries reported similar high rates of mental disorder in the inmate population and indicated that countries differ widely in how they deal with mentally disordered inmates (Blaauw et al., 2000). Comparably high rates of mental disorder in prisons have also been reported in New Zealand (Brinded et al., 1999).

Do mentally ill men and women who are incarcerated actually receive mental health treatment? One survey by the U.S. Department of Justice reports that 1,394 of the nation's public and private adult correctional facilities provide mental health services to inmates. Almost 70 percent of the facilities that responded screen inmates when they are incarcerated, and 65 percent conduct some type of psychiatric examination. In addition, 51 percent of these facilities provide around-the-clock mental health services, but only 2 percent of the prison population live in a 24-hour treatment unit. The survey also shows that 71 percent of the facilities provide counseling and 73 percent distribute medications to inmates (Beck & Maruschak, 2001). However, many authorities have reported that mental health services are typically not provided for the majority of inmates who require them. Teplin and colleagues (1997) reported that only 23.5 percent of the women who needed mental health services received them while they were in jail, despite the fact that 80 percent of the sample met criteria for a lifetime mental disorder.

Controversial Legal Issues and the Mentally Ill

A number of important issues are related to the legal status of mentally ill people—the subject matter of **forensic psychology** or **forensic psychiatry**—and they center on the rights of patients and the rights of members of society to be protected from disturbed individuals. For a survey of some of the legal rights that mentally ill people have gained over the years, see Box 3.

Civil Commitment

Persons with psychological problems or behaviors that are so extreme and severe as to pose a threat to themselves or others may require protective confinement. Those who commit crimes, whether or not they have a psychological disorder, are dealt with primarily through the judicial system—arrest, court trial, and, if convicted, possible confinement in a penal institution. People who are judged to be potentially dangerous because of their psychological state may, after **civil commitment** procedures, be confined in a mental institution. The steps in the commitment process vary slightly depending on state law, the locally available community mental health resources, and the nature of the problem. For example, commitment procedures for a person with mental retardation are different from those for a person whose problem is alcohol abuse.

There is a distinction between voluntary hospitalization and involuntary commitment. In most cases, people accept voluntary commitment or hospitalization. In these cases, they can, with sufficient notice, leave the hospital if they wish. But in cases where a person may be considered dangerous or is unable to provide for his or her own care, the need for involuntary commitment may arise (Zerman & Schwartz, 1998).

---

3 THE WORLD AROUND US

Important Court Decisions for Patient Rights

Several important court decisions have helped establish certain basic rights for individuals suffering from mental disorders. But they have also curtailed these rights, amid continuing controversy.

- **Right to Treatment.** In 1972 a U.S. district court in Alabama rendered a landmark decision in the case of *Wyatt v. Stickney.* It ruled that a mentally ill person or a person with mental retardation had a right to receive treatment. Since that decision, the state of Alabama has increased its budget for the treatment of mental illness and mental retardation by 300 percent (see Winick, 1997).
- **Freedom from Custodial Confinement.** In 1975 the U.S. Supreme Court upheld the principle that patients have a right to freedom from custodial confinement if they are not dangerous to themselves or others and if they can safely survive outside of custody. In *Donaldson v. O'Connor,* the defendants were required to pay Donaldson $10,000 for having kept him in custody without providing treatment.
- **Right to Compensation for Work.** In 1973 a U.S. district court ruled in the case of *Souder v. Brennan* (the secretary of labor) that a patient in a nonfederal mental institution who performed work must be paid according to the Fair Labor Standards Act. Although a 1978 Supreme Court ruling nullified the part of the lower court's decision dealing with state hospitals, the ruling still applies to mentally ill persons and patients with mental retardation in private facilities.
- **Right to Live in a Community.** In 1974 a U.S. district court decided, in the case of *Staff v. Miller,* that released state mental hospital patients have a right to live in "adult homes" in the community.

- **Right to Less Restrictive Treatment.** In 1975 a U.S. district court issued a landmark decision in the case of *Dixon v. Weinberger.* The ruling established the right of individuals to receive treatment in less restrictive facilities than mental institutions.
- **Right to Legal Counsel at Commitment Hearings.** The Wisconsin State Supreme Court decided in 1976, in the case of *Memmel v. Mundy,* that an individual has the right to legal counsel during the commitment process.
- **Right to Refuse Treatment.** Several court decisions have provided rulings, and some states have enacted legislation, permitting patients to refuse certain treatments such as electroconvulsive therapy and psychosurgery.
- **The Need for Confinement Must Be Shown by Clear, Convincing Evidence.** In 1979 the U.S. Supreme Court ruled, in the case of *Addington v. Texas,* that a person's need to be kept in an institution must be based on demonstrable evidence.
- **Limitation on Patients' Rights to Refuse Psychotropic Medication.** In 1990 the U.S. Supreme Court ruled, in *Washington v. Harper,* that a Washington State prison could override a disturbed prisoner's refusal of psychotropic medications. This decision was based on a finding that the prison's review process adequately protected the patient's rights. We see in this instance that changes in the national political climate can reverse prior trends that favored patients' rights.

Source: Grounds (2000), Hermann (1990), Mental Health Law Project (1987), Saks (2004), and Swartz, Swanson, & Elbogen (2004).

Being mentally ill is not sufficient grounds for placing a person in a mental institution against his or her will. Although procedures vary somewhat from state to state, several conditions beyond mental illness usually must be met before formal involuntary commitment can occur (Simon & Aaronson, 1988). In brief, such individuals must be judged to be

- Dangerous to themselves or to others *and/or*
- Incapable of providing for their basic physical needs *and/or*
- Unable to make responsible decisions about hospitalization *and*
- In need of treatment or care in a hospital

Typically, filing a petition for a commitment hearing is the first step in the process of committing a person involuntarily. This petition is usually filed by a concerned individual such as a relative, physician, or mental health professional. When such a petition is filed, a judge appoints two examiners to evaluate the proposed patient. In Minnesota, for example, one examiner must be a physician (not necessarily a psychiatrist); the other can be a psychiatrist or a psychologist. The patient is asked to appear voluntarily for psychiatric examination before the commitment hearing. The hearing must be held within 14 days, which can be extended to 30 more days if good cause for the extension can be shown. The law requires that the court-appointed examiners interview the patient before the hearing.

When a person is committed to a mental hospital for treatment, the hospital must report to the court within 60 days on whether the person needs to be confined even longer. If the hospital gives no report, the patient must be released. If the hospital indicates that the person needs further treatment, then the commitment period becomes indeterminate, subject to periodic reevaluations.

Because the decision to commit a person is based on the conclusions of others about the person's capabilities and his or her potential for dangerous behavior, the civil commitment process leaves open the possibility of the unwarranted violation of a person's civil rights. As a consequence, most states have stringent safeguards to ensure that any person who is the subject of a petition for commitment is granted due process, including rights to formal hearings with representation by legal counsel. If there is not time to get a court order for commitment or if there is imminent danger, however, the law allows emergency hospitalization without a formal commitment hearing. In such cases, a physician must sign a statement saying that an imminent danger exists. The patient can then be picked up (usually by the police) and detained under a "hold order," usually not to exceed 72 hours, unless a petition for commitment is filed within that period.

Involuntary commitment in a psychiatric facility is largely contingent on a determination that a person is dangerous and requires confinement out of a need to protect herself or himself or society. Once committed, a patient may refuse treatment—a situation that mental health professionals working in psychiatric facilities often face. We will now turn to the important issue of evaluating patients in terms of potential dangerousness. (For a discussion of prisoners who are released from prison and then returned because of other offenses see Box 4).

Assessment of "Dangerousness"

Although most psychiatric patients are not considered dangerous, some are violent and require close supervision—perhaps confinement until they are no longer dangerous. Rates of assaultiveness vary from setting to setting, but in all reported studies the overall number of assaultive patients is relatively low. An increasing number of clinical researchers in recent years have discovered that a history of violent behavior and some classes of mental disorder appear to be associated with violence (Pinard & Pagani, 2001). Although most disordered people reportedly show no tendency toward violence (Lamberg, 1998), an increased risk of violence appears more likely among some who are experiencing symptoms of psychosis (Hodgins & Lalonde, 1999). The disorders that have an increased risk for violent behavior include schizophrenia, mania, personality disorder, substance abuse, and the rarer conditions of organic brain injury and Huntington's disease. One study from Finland (Eronen et al., 1996) reported that homicidal behavior among former patients was considerably more frequent among patients with schizophrenia and even more common among patients with antisocial personality or alcoholism. In another study, psychiatric patients who abused alcohol (Steadman et al., 1998) were found to be notably violent.

Practitioners are often called upon to evaluate the possibility that a patient might be dangerous, and there is some evidence that mental health professionals can contribute to such an assessment (Cunningham & Sorensen, 2007;

Prediction of aggressive behavior is an important but not necessarily an easy task to accomplish in our society.

THE WORLD AROUND US

Controversial Not Guilty Pleas: Can Altered Mind States or Personality Disorder Limit Responsibility for a Criminal Act?

If a person commits a capital offense when his or her consciousness (and reason) is impaired, as in an altered state, should he or she be held responsible for the crime? Can using psychotropic medicine such as Prozac or Zoloft "poison" a person's mind to such an extreme degree that she or he commits murder? If a murder is committed while someone is heavily "sedated"—for example, with Xanax or Halcion—should that person be released from criminal responsibility because he or she was involuntarily intoxicated with medications prescribed by a health professional? If a person experiences "multiple personalities" and a crime is committed by one personality, should all of the personalities suffer the consequences? These defense strategies are interesting and controversial challenges to today's legal system.

Altered States of Consciousness

In a civil trial, the jury failed to find the manufacturer of Prozac (Eli Lilly) liable in court action that resulted from a 1989 mass murder allegedly committed "under the influence" of Prozac. The murderer (Joseph Wesbecker), in a rage against his employer, killed 8 people and wounded 12 others before killing himself. Survivors and family members of several people who were killed in the incident filed a suit against Eli Lilly because the killer was taking the drug Prozac at the time of the murders and because the drug was alleged to be responsible for "intoxicating" the assassin and lowering his inhibitions. After a long trial, the jury found in favor of the manufacturer (*Fentress et al. v. Shea Communications et al.*, 1990).

Courts have generally not considered altered states of consciousness such as being intoxicated on drugs or alcohol sufficient grounds for an insanity defense because of the issue of volition—that is, that the perpetrator of the crime consciously chose to become intoxicated in the first place. However, the question of intoxication by drugs that were taken for the purpose of medication has added a new dimension to the defense. This issue has not been fully resolved in the court system.

Altered Personality States

Possibly the most fascinating of controversial insanity pleas are those raised by the phenomenon of dissociative identity disorder (DID), formerly known as multiple personality disorder, which has become a more common diagnosis in recent years. Although some professionals dispute even the existence of such a condition, others find it a plausible argument for a plea of not guilty by reason of insanity (NGRI).

The general nature of the problem can be stated quite succinctly: Within a legal system strongly oriented to the precise identification of individual responsibility for acts, what, if any, are the limits of the assignment of responsibility and sanctions for infractions of the law where the same physical space and body are occupied at different times by more than one distinct and legally recognizable person? Consider the following legal dilemmas:

- Who, among various copersonalities, is empowered to sign for withdrawals from a bank account?
- Are the provisions and obligations of a contract entered into by one constituent personality binding on all others regardless of their particular desires in the matter?
- Does the swearing of an oath, as in court, apply to the entire collection of personalities, or must each be sworn individually if he or she is to testify?
- In the case of a guilty verdict for the criminal act of a given personality, where other personalities did not acquiesce to the crime, how should punishment be fairly meted out?
- If no constituent personality meets a test of insanity, is it reasonable and lawful to declare DID itself an instance of insanity?
- Has rape occurred if the copersonalities of a 26-year-old woman who had acquiesced to intercourse included one or more personalities who had vehemently objected to it? (Such a case was prosecuted in Wisconsin in 1990.)
- And, of course, the most common real-life legal dilemma: Should an individual, as the primary personality, be held legally accountable for, say, a capital crime that evidence suggests may have actually been committed surreptitiously, so to speak, by an alter personality?

The scenario just mentioned has rather often been the contention underlying a plea of not guilty by reason of insanity. Usually, as in the case of the "Hillside Strangler," Kenneth Bianchi (convicted of 12 rapes and murders in California and Washington State), and in the case of a woman who kidnapped a newborn from a hospital and later claimed that an alter personality had actually committed the crime (Appelbaum & Greer, 1994), the plea has failed. On a very few occasions, however, the NGRI plea has worked, as in the well-publicized 1978 case of Ohio resident Billy Milligan, who claimed to be host to 10 personalities and was accused of raping four women (*New York Times*, 1994). The legal maneuvers inspired by the DID construct admittedly have a quality of whimsy about them. It is consequently difficult to convince most juries that the defendant was so taken over by an alter personality who perpetrated the crime that he or she should be absolved of guilt and responsibility.

Quinsey et al., 2006), at least on a short-term basis (Binder, 1999). The determination that a patient is potentially dangerous can be difficult to make (Bauer et al., 2003), yet this is one of the most important responsibilities of professionals working in the fields of law and psychology (Burke, 2010). Scott and colleagues (2010) point out that the accuracy of a clinician's assessment of future violence is determined by many factors, such as the circumstances of the evaluation and the length of time over which violence is predicted. When asked to perform an evaluation of dangerousness in a client, a clinician has a clear responsibility to try to protect the public from potential violence or other uncontrolled behavior of dangerous patients.

ATTEMPTS TO PREDICT DANGEROUSNESS It is very difficult—for professionals and laypersons alike—to accurately appraise "dangerousness" in some individuals (Heilbrun, 2009). The complex problem of risk assessment or prediction of dangerousness can be likened to predicting the weather. "Ultimately, the goal of a warning system in mental health law is the same as the goal of a warning system in meteorology: to maximize the number of people who take appropriate and timely actions for the safety of life and property" (Monahan & Steadman, 1997, p. 937).

It is usually easy to determine, after the fact, that a person has demonstrated dangerous behavior, but how well do mental health professionals do in predicting the occurrence of dangerous acts? Not as well as we would like (Edens et al., 2005). Violent acts are particularly difficult to predict because they are apparently determined as much by situational circumstances (for example, whether a person is under the influence of alcohol) as by an individual's personality traits or violent predispositions. One obvious and significantly predictive risk factor is a past history of violence (Burke, 2010; Megargee,

2009), but clinicians are not always able to unearth this type of background information.

As already noted, some types of patients, particularly individuals with active schizophrenia and mania (Hodgins & Lalonde, 1999) and patients with well-entrenched delusions (de Pauw & Szulecka, 1988), are far more likely than others to commit violent acts. Martell and Dietz (1992) reported a study of persons convicted of pushing or attempting to push unsuspecting victims in front of New York City subway trains and found that most were both psychotic and homeless at the time of the act. Norko and Baranoski (2005) noted that although many studies point to a modest increased risk of violence associated with mental illness, particularly psychosis, other studies have not confirmed these findings.

Expert testimony to establish dangerousness or future violence in offenders has become an important part of the U.S. legal system. However, the prediction of dangerousness is often questionable (Krauss & Lieberman, 2007). Mental health professionals typically overpredict violence and consider felons to be more dangerous than they actually are, and usually predict a greater percentage of clients to be dangerous than actually become involved in violent acts (Megargee, 2009). Such a tendency is of course understandable from the perspective of the practitioner, considering the potentially serious consequences of releasing a violent individual. It is likely, however, that many innocent patients thereby experience a violation of their civil rights. Given a certain irreducible level of uncertainty in the prediction of violence, it is not obvious how this dilemma can be completely resolved.

THE DUTY TO PROTECT: IMPLICATIONS OF THE TARASOFF DECISION What should a therapist do upon learning that a patient is planning to harm another person? Can the therapist violate the legally sanctioned confidence of the therapy contract and take action to prevent the patient from committing the act? Today, in most states, the therapist not only can violate confidentiality with impunity but also may be required by law to take action to protect people from the threat of imminent violence against them. In its original form, this requirement was conceived as a duty to warn the prospective victim.

The duty-to-warn legal doctrine was given great impetus in a 1976 California court ruling in the case of *Tarasoff v. Regents of the University of California et al.* (Mills et al., 1987). In this case, Prosenjit Poddar was being seen in outpatient psychotherapy by a psychologist at the university mental health facility. During his treatment, Mr. Poddar indicated that he intended to kill his former girlfriend, Tatiana Tarasoff, when

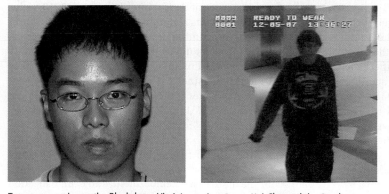

Two mass murderers, the Blacksburg, Virginia, student Seung Hui-Cho, and the Omaha, Nebraska, mall killer Robert Hawkins, were known to have severe mental health problems and were considered to be potentially dangerous.

she returned from vacation. Concerned about the threat, the psychologist discussed the case with his supervisors, and they agreed that Poddar was dangerous and should be committed for further observation and treatment. They informed the campus police, who picked up Poddar for questioning, subsequently judged him to be rational, and released him after he promised to leave Ms. Tarasoff alone. Poddar then terminated treatment with the psychologist. About 2 months thereafter, he stabbed Ms. Tarasoff to death. Her parents later sued the University of California and staff members involved in the case for their failure to hospitalize Poddar and their failure to warn Tarasoff about the threat to her life. In due course, the California Supreme Court in 1974 ruled that the defendants were not liable for failing to hospitalize Poddar; it did, however, find them liable for failing to warn the victim. Ironically, Prosenjit Poddar, the criminal, was released on a trial technicality and returned home to India. In a later analysis of the case, Knapp (1980) says that the court ruled that difficulty in determining dangerousness does not exempt a psychotherapist from attempting to protect others when a determination of dangerousness exists. The court acknowledged that confidentiality was important to the psychotherapeutic relationship but stated that the protection privilege ends where public peril begins.

The duty-to-warn ruling—which has come to be known as the **Tarasoff decision**—spelled out a therapist's responsibility in situations where there has been an explicit threat on a specific person's life, but it left other areas of application unclear. For example, does this ruling apply in cases where a patient threatens to commit suicide, and how might the therapist's responsibility be met in such a case? What, if anything, should a therapist do when the target of violence is not clearly named—for example, when global threats are made? Would the duty-to-warn ruling hold up in other states? Or might deleterious effects on patient–therapist relationships outweigh any public benefit to be derived from the duty to warn? Responding to mounting pressures for clarification, chiefly from professional mental health organizations, the California Supreme Court in 1976 issued a revised opinion called the "duty to warn doctrine." In this decision the court ruled that the duty was to protect, rather than specifically to warn, the prospective victim, but it left vague the question of how this duty might be discharged—presumably in order to give practitioners latitude in dealing with danger to third parties. Meanwhile, however, numerous other lawsuits in other jurisdictions have been filed and adjudicated in inconsistent and confusing ways (Mills et al., 1987).

The many perplexing issues for practitioners left in the wake of Tarasoff were partly resolved, at least in California, by the legislature's adoption in 1985 of a new state law essentially establishing that the duty to protect is discharged if the therapist makes "reasonable efforts" to inform potential victims and an appropriate law enforcement agency of the pending threat. The Tarasoff ruling was extended in 2004 (*Ewing v. Goldstein*,

2004) when the California Court of Appeals ruled that a communication from a patient's family member constitutes a "patient communication" that can trigger the therapist's duty to protect.

In other court jurisdictions, however, the inconsistent judicial fallout from Tarasoff has continued and has been a source of much anxiety and confusion among mental health professionals, many of whom continue to believe, on ethical and clinical grounds, that strict confidentiality is an absolute and inviolable trust. Some states—for example, Maryland, Texas, and Pennsylvania—have explicitly affirmed that position, abandoning Tarasoff altogether, while 23 states impose a duty to warn, although the criteria for this typically vary (Barbee et al., 2007). There has been considerable debate over the need and utility of the Tarasoff ruling, and some authorities have raised questions about its survivability as a law (Quattrocchi & Schopp, 2005).

Official professional ethics codes, such as that of the American Psychological Association (2002), normally compel compliance with relevant laws regardless of one's personal predilections. Where the law is itself vague or equivocal, however, as it often is in this area, there is much room for individual interpretation (Kachigian & Felthous, 2004). Today there is considerable confusion among practitioners about their responsibility with regard to rules of their state with respect to Tarasoff ruling. A recent survey of clinicians found that 76 percent of clinicians failed to correctly identify their state's duty-to-protect law from a multiple-choice list (Pabian et al., 2009). Therapists are at greater risk of a lawsuit for failing to deal with risk of danger posed by some clients (Caudill, 2009).

The Insanity Defense

Some people who are being tried for murder use the **insanity defense**—also known as the **NGRI plea** ("not guilty by reason of insanity")—in an attempt to escape the legally prescribed consequences of their crimes (Chappell, 2010; Kelly, 2009). These defendants claim that they were not legally responsible for their criminal acts. In technical legal terms, they invoke the ancient doctrine that their acts, while guilty ones (*actus rea*), lacked moral blameworthiness because they were not intentional since the defendants did not possess their full mental faculties at the time of the crime and did not "know what they were doing" (*mens rea*)—the underlying assumption being that "insanity" somehow precludes or absolves the harboring of a guilty intent. (See Box 5) One of the most notorious uses of the not guilty by reason of insanity plea in American history was in the case of Jeffrey Dahmer, on trial for the murder, dismemberment, and cannibalization of 15 men in Milwaukee. In the Dahmer case, the planned insanity defense proved unsuccessful, which is the usual outcome (Steadman et al., 1993).

By contrast, attorneys for John Hinckley, who shot President Reagan and his press secretary, James Brady, in

5 THE WORLD AROUND US

Does Having Mental Health Problems Result in Convicted Felons Being Returned to Prison After Being Released?

Given that many individuals with severe mental health problems are sentenced to prison terms and receive no mental health treatment while in prison, are they able to adjust to society once they are released? Are psychologically disturbed people who receive prison terms more vulnerable to maladjustment when they are freed from prison? Questions have been raised about the impact of mental health problems on the ability of convicted prisoners to successfully return to society if they are paroled, serve out their terms, or are released because they are believed to no longer be a threat to themselves or others in the case of a successful NGRI decision. Cloyes and colleagues (2010) evaluated parole violation rates among inmates who had significant mental health problems versus those who did not and found that there was a significant difference in return rates and community tenure for offenders with significant mental illness compared to inmates without mental health problems. They found that 23 percent of their sample of inmates with significant mental health problems returned to prison sooner than those without mental health problems.

Persons who have been charged with a crime but found not guilty by reason of insanity can be released from confinement if or when they are no longer judged to be of a danger to themselves or others. Although return to the community is not guaranteed for persons who are incarcerated after an NGRI plea, they can be released, and the state can determine explicit conditions for release, for example, follow-up mental health treatment, substance abuse treatment, frequent monitoring, and so forth. Some research has suggested that with conditional treatment and careful monitoring many people are able to return to society. However, the efficacy of treatment or careful monitoring has shown mixed results with many people being returned to confinement. Vitacco and colleagues (2008) found that 33.8 percent of inmates were returned to prison, with the majority of these being returned for failure to comply with treatment. When the amount of monitoring was taken into consideration they found that those who were placed on higher restrictions and received closer monitoring had lower rates of return to confinement. Hiday and Burns (2010), in their evaluation of the role of mental illness in the criminal justice system, concluded although the arrest rates and incarceration rates were higher for mentally ill persons than the general population, most people with mental illness are not violent and only a small percentage of the population become violent.

early 1981, successfully pleaded NGRI. (See the case study on p. 616.) The outcome of the Hinckley case was different in a number of important respects because the jury in this instance considered the defendant to be acting "outside of reason" and found him not guilty by reason of insanity. At trial in June 1982, Hinckley was acquitted on those grounds. This verdict immediately unleashed a storm of public protest and generated widespread, often hasty attempts to reform the law to make the NGRI defense a less attractive option to defendants and their attorneys. Hinckley himself was committed to the care of a federally operated, high-security mental hospital, to be involuntarily detained there until such time as his disorder remits sufficiently that his release would not constitute a danger to himself or others. He remains incarcerated; however, under a 1999 federal appeals court ruling, Hinckley has been able to take supervised day trips off hospital grounds, and most recently was allowed to spend several weeks at his mother's home. However, his "recovery" continues to be questioned. Psychiatric testimony (Associated Press, 2003) has indicated that Hinckley still suffers from the same narcissistic personality disorder that drove him to shoot Reagan and three others in 1981.

Jeffrey Dahmer was torturing and drowning cats and dogs by age 7. He never heard voices or broke with reality. He tricked his victims into being handcuffed (they thought it was part of a sexual game) and then dripped acid into their flesh and skulls, rendering them zombies. Then he would engage them sexually and would occasionally cannibalize them. Dahmer was charged with and later convicted of murder after body parts of several young men were found in his apartment. While serving his time in prison, he was bludgeoned to death by a psychotic killer in 1994.

case study
Hinckley's Successful Insanity Plea

On March 30, 1981, in an apparent scheme to attract the attention of actress Jodie Foster, with whom he was obsessed, John Hinckley, Jr., shot six bullets at President Ronald Reagan in an assassination attempt. President Reagan was seriously injured, as was Press Secretary James Brady. At the end of his trial in 1982, Hinckley was found not guilty by reason of insanity. Since his trial, Hinckley has been confined to St. Elizabeth's Hospital in Washington, DC. After what seemed to be significant improvement in his mental health, Hinckley was allowed unsupervised visits in April 2000, but these visits were revoked when guards discovered a smuggled book on Jodie Foster in his room.

Releasing Hinckley from custody would almost certainly bring forth another public outcry demanding abolition or limitation of the insanity defense. This unfortunate public outrage at all insanity defense pleas results from a persistent failure of legal scholars to examine critically and rigorously the guilt-absolving insanity construct and the *mens rea* doctrine from which it derives.

In recent years the use of the NGRI defense in trials where the defendant's life is at stake has been surrounded by controversy, largely owing to the uproar created by the outcome of the Hinckley trial (Steadman et al., 1993). Some have contended that the objection to the insanity defense in capital crimes might reflect negative social attitudes toward the insane (Perlin, 1996). There has been some concern, especially in cases of high visibility, that guilty defendants may feign mental disorder and hence avoid criminal responsibility. Good defense attorneys are of course aware of this public cynicism, which is likely to be shared by juries. They attempt to counteract it in various ways, often by portraying their purportedly "insane at the time of the act" clients as having been themselves victims of heinous and traumatic acts at an earlier time in their lives. Some of them undoubtedly were victimized, but the strategy of creating sympathy while

offering a plausible explanation for the "insane" act would have a compelling attraction in any case. On the other hand, the insanity defense is often not employed where it is appropriate, as it would have been, for example, in two high-visibility cases: those of John Salvi (the abortion clinic assassin) and Theodore Kaczynski (the Unabomber). Apparently neither defendant wanted his mental state to be a part of the proceedings. Severe delusional disorder is likely to have played a significant role in both of their crimes. (There have been notable efforts to fake the insanity defense to avoid punishment; see the following case study).

case study
Detected Faking of the Insanity Defense

Michael McDermott testified that Michael the Archangel had sent him on a mission to prevent the Holocaust when he gunned down seven coworkers on December 26, 2000. McDermott also stated that he believed he was soulless and that by killing he would earn a soul. McDermott claimed to have been raped by a neighbor when he was a young boy and had a history of paranoia and suicide attempts. Despite this claim of insanity, a jury found McDermott guilty in the shooting deaths of his seven coworkers. The prosecution argued that McDermott was motivated to kill because his employer was about to deduct from his wages back taxes owed to the IRS. Evidence seized from his computer showed that McDermott had researched how to fake being mentally ill. McDermott is currently serving seven consecutive life sentences for his crimes.

In some cases in some states, individuals with psychosis who fail to meet the standards set for the NGRI plea and are convicted of murder can receive the death sentence even though they were actually psychologically disturbed at the time of the crime and remain so as the execution approaches. An appeals process can be effective at showing that there may be extenuating circumstances that warrant softening the sentence on grounds that the death penalty would be cruel and unusual punishment because of the person's severe mental health problems or mental retardation. Pirelli and colleagues (2011) conducted an analysis of the results of 68 studies that had been published between 1967 and 2008 that compared competent and incompetent defendants on a number of variables. The most robust findings were that defendants who were diagnosed with a psychotic disorder were about eight times more likely to be found incompetent than defendants without a psychotic disorder diagnosis. The likelihood of being found incompetent was approximately double for unemployed defendants as compared to employed defendants. Defendants who had a previous psychiatric hospitalization were about twice more likely to be found not guilty by reason of insanity than those without a hospitalization history.

There have been cases in which a failed use of the NGRI plea led to greater punishment. In one recent case (*United States v. Batista*, 2007) a defendant in a murder trial intentionally feigned mental illness in an effort to avoid prison. His charade was discovered and he actually received an enhanced sentence after the trial because of his abuse of mental health protections in the legal system.

Despite some features that make it an appealing option to consider, especially when the undisputed facts are strongly aligned against the defendant, the NGRI defense has actually been employed quite rarely—in less than 2 percent of capital cases in the United States over time (Lymburner & Roesch, 1999; Steadman et al., 1993). Studies have confirmed, however, that in some jurisdictions, persons acquitted of crimes by reason of insanity spend less time, on the whole, in a psychiatric hospital than persons who are convicted of crimes spend in prison (Lymburner & Roesch, 1999) even though the determination that they are no longer dangerous might be difficult to ascertain. In addition, states differ widely in the amount of time that persons found not guilty by reason of insanity are actually confined. For example, one study by Callahan and Silver (1998) reported that in the states of Ohio and Maryland nearly all persons acquitted as NGRI have been released within 5 years, whereas in Connecticut and New York conditional release has been much more difficult to obtain. The rearrest rates for freed NGRI claimants vary, with some studies reporting rates as high as 50 percent (Callahan & Silver, 1998; Wiederanders et al., 1997). Monson and colleagues (2001) conducted a follow-up of 125 NGRI acquittees and found a similarly high rearrest rate. These investigators reported that persons discharged to live with their family of origin or to alone or semi-independent living were more likely to maintain their conditional release and not reoffend. These investigators also reported that such factors as minority status, comorbid substance abuse, and prior criminal history were associated with return to custody after release. One recent study in which an active community treatment program was implemented reported low rearrest rates (1.4 percent) and moderate rehospitalization rates (14 percent) (Parker, 2004).

Up to this point in the discussion, we have used the term *insanity defense* loosely. We must now become more attentive to the many precise legal nuances involved. Established precedents that define the insanity defense are as follows:

1. The M'Naghten Rule (1843). Under this ruling, which is often referred to as the "knowing right from wrong" rule, people are assumed to be sane unless it can be proved that at the time of committing the act they were laboring under such a defect of reason (from a disease of the mind) that they did not know the nature and quality of the act they were doing—or, if they did know they were committing the act, they did not know that what they were doing was wrong.

2. The Irresistible Impulse Rule (1887). A second precedent in the NGRI defense is the doctrine of the "irresistible impulse." This view holds that accused persons might not be responsible for their acts—even when they knew that what they were doing was wrong (according to the M'Naghten rule)—if they had lost the power to choose between right and wrong. That is, they could not avoid doing the act in question because they were compelled beyond their will to commit the act.

3. The Durham Rule. In 1954, Judge David Bazelon, in a decision of the U.S. Court of Appeals, broadened the insanity defense further. Bazelon did not believe that the previous precedents allowed for a sufficient application of established scientific knowledge of mental illness and proposed a test that would be based on this knowledge. Under this rule, which is often referred to as the "product test," the accused is not criminally responsible if her or his unlawful act was the product of mental disease or mental defect.

4. The American Law Institute (ALI) Standard (1962). Often referred to as the "substantial capacity test" for insanity, this test combines the cognitive aspect of M'Naghten with the volitional focus of irresistible impulse in holding that the perpetrator is not legally responsible if at the time of the act she or he, owing to mental disease or defect, lacked "substantial capacity" either to appreciate the act's criminal character or to conform her or his behavior to the law's requirements.

5. The Federal Insanity Defense Reform ACT (IDRA). Adopted by Congress in 1984 as the standard for the insanity defense to be applied in all federal jurisdictions, this act abolished the volitional element of the ALI standard and modified the cognitive standard to read "unable to appreciate," thus bringing the definition quite close to M'Naghten. IDRA also specified that the mental disorder involved must be a severe one and shifted the burden of proof from the prosecution to the defense. That is, the defense must clearly and convincingly establish the defendant's insanity, in contrast to the prior requirement that the prosecution clearly and convincingly demonstrate the defendant to have been sane when the prohibited act was committed.

This shifting of the burden of proof for the insanity defense, by the way, had been instituted by many states in the wake of the Hinckley acquittal. The intent of this reform was to discourage use of the insanity defense, and it proved quite effective in altering litigation practices in the intended direction (Steadman et al., 1993).

At the present time, most states and the District of Columbia subscribe to a version of either the ALI or the more restrictive M'Naghten standard. New York is a special case. It uses a version of M'Naghten to define insanity, with the burden of proof on the defense, but an elaborate procedural code has been enacted to promote fairness in outcomes while ensuring lengthy and restrictive hospital commitment for defendants judged to be dangerous; this approach appears to have worked well (Steadman et al., 1993). In some jurisdictions, when an insanity plea is filed, the case is submitted for pretrial screening, which includes a psychiatric evaluation, review of records, and appraisal of criminal responsibility. In one study of 190 defendants who entered a plea of not criminally responsible, the following outcomes were obtained: 105 were judged to be criminally responsible, charges against 34 were dropped, and 8 defendants were agreed by both the prosecution and the defense to be insane and not responsible. A total of 134 withdrew their insanity pleas (Janofsky et al., 1996). The insanity defense was noted in this study to be somewhat of a "rich man's defense" in that such cases involved private attorneys rather than public defenders.

Silver (1995) found that the successful use of the NGRI defense varied widely among states. In addition, Silver reports that the length of confinement was related more to the judged seriousness of the crime than to whether the person was employing the NGRI defense. One study (Cirinclone et al., 1995) found that an NGRI plea was most likely to be successful if one or more of the following factors were present:

- A diagnosed mental disorder, particularly a major mental disorder
- A female defendant
- The violent crime was other than murder
- There had been prior mental hospitalizations

Three states—Idaho, Montana, and Utah—have entirely abolished the attribution of insanity as an acceptable defense for wrongdoing—a somewhat more harsh or severe solution that compensates in clarity for what some feel it lacks in compassion. As expected, with the disappearance of the insanity acquittals in Montana, there was a corresponding rise in the use of the "incompetent to stand trial" plea (see the following section), in which the charges were actually dismissed, largely negating the desired result (more effective prosecution) of doing away with the insanity defense (Callahan et al., 1995).

How, then, is guilt or innocence determined? Many authorities believe that the insanity defense sets the courts an impossible task—determining guilt or innocence by reason of insanity on the basis of psychiatric testimony. In some cases, conflicting testimony has resulted because both the prosecution and the defense have their own panel of expert psychiatric witnesses, who are in complete disagreement (see discussion by Lareau, 2007).

Finally, states have adopted the optional plea and verdict of **guilty but mentally ill (GBMI)**. In these cases, a defendant may be sentenced but placed in a treatment facility rather than in a prison. This two-part judgment serves to prevent the type of situation in which a person commits a murder, is found not guilty by reason of insanity, is turned over to a mental health facility, is found to be rational and in no further need of treatment by the hospital staff, and is unconditionally released to the community after only a minimal period of confinement. Under the two-part decision, such a person would remain in the custody of the correctional department until the full sentence has been served. Marvit (1981) has suggested that this approach might "realistically balance the interest of the mentally ill offender's rights and the community's need to control criminal behavior" (p. 23). However, others have argued that the GBMI defense is confusing to jurors and should be eliminated (Melville & Naimark, 2002). Interestingly, in Georgia, one of the states adopting this option, GBMI defendants receive longer sentences and longer periods of confinement than those who plead NGRI and lose. Overall, outcomes from the use of the GBMI standard, which is often employed in a plea-bargaining strategy, have been disappointing (Steadman et al., 1993).

Competence to Stand Trial

There is, in English common law, a principle that a person charged with a crime must be **competent to stand trial** (Roesch et al., 1999). If someone is charged with a crime and is considered to be unable to understand the trial proceedings as a result of intellectual deficit or mental health problems, they can be hospitalized until their mental state is judged to be improved sufficiently for them to be competent to stand trial. Several factors can influence a court decision that the defendant in the case is not competent to stand trial. Both cognitive abilities (such as capability in making decisions, having a working memory, being able to attend to proceedings, and being able to process events successfully) and psychiatric symptoms (psychoticism, withdrawal, depression, hostility) can be crucial factors in a person being able to stand trial.

In May 2011, a federal court judge ruled that Jared Loughner was not competent to stand trial for shooting Congresswoman Gabrielle Giffords and killing six others (Harris, 2011). This court decision was based upon the opinion of expert witness psychiatrists from both the defense and prosecution who examined Loughner. The defendant will be held in a federal hospital for prisoners in Springfield, Illinois, until such time that he has demonstrated that he is able to stand trial.

Research has underscored the role of cognitive deficits or mental health problems in determining a defendant's competence to stand trial. Ryba and Zapf (2011) recently reported that cognitive abilities accounted for higher scores for all three competence-related abilities than did the psychiatric symptoms, although there was an additive effect when these groups of variables were considered collectively. In a recent evaluation of the published literature on competence to stand trial, Pirelli and colleagues (2011) concluded that defendants who had been diagnosed as having a psychotic disorder were approximately eight times more likely to be found incompetent than defendants without a psychotic disorder diagnosis. In addition, they found that defendants who had a previous psychiatric hospitalization, as compared with those never hospitalized, or had been unemployed, as compared to employed defendants, were more likely to be determined as incompetent to stand trial.

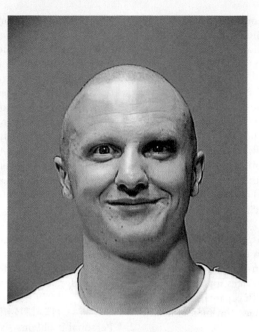

Jared Loughner, who killed six people and severely wounded congresswoman Gabriel Giffords in May 2011, was determined to be not competent to stand trial as a result of his mental disorder.

In Review

- What conditions must be met before an individual can be involuntarily committed to a mental institution? Describe the legal process that follows.

- What are the implications of the Tarasoff decision for practicing clinicians?

- What is the insanity (NGRI) defense in criminal cases?

- What is the Federal Insanity Defense Reform Act? How does it differ from the M'Naghten rule?

Organized Efforts for Mental Health

Public awareness of the magnitude of contemporary mental health problems and the interest of government, professional, and lay organizations have stimulated the development of programs directed at better understanding, more effective treatment, and long-range prevention. Efforts to improve mental health are apparent not only in our society but also in many other countries, and they involve international as well as national and local organizations and approaches.

U.S. Efforts for Mental Health

In the United States in the eighteenth and nineteenth centuries, dealing with mental disorders was primarily the responsibility of state and local agencies. During World War II, however, the extent of mental disorders in the United States was brought to public attention when a large number of young men—two out of every seven recruits—were rejected for military service for psychiatric reasons. This discovery led to a variety of organized measures for taking care of people with mental illness.

THE FEDERAL GOVERNMENT AND MENTAL HEALTH
In 1946, aware of the need for more research, training, and services in the field of mental health, Congress passed its first comprehensive mental health bill, the National Mental Health Act. In that same year, the NIMH was formed in Washington, DC. The agency was to serve as a central research and training center and as headquarters for the administration of a grant-in-aid program designed to foster research and training elsewhere in the nation and to help state and local communities expand and improve their own mental health services. Congress authorized the Institute to provide mental health project grants for experimental studies, pilot projects, surveys, and general research. Today the NIMH is a separate institute under the National Institutes of Health within the Department of Health and Human Services (NIMH, 2001).

The NIMH (1) conducts and supports research on the biological, psychosocial, and sociocultural aspects of mental disorders; (2) supports the training of professional and paraprofessional personnel in the mental health field; (3) helps communities plan, establish, and maintain more effective mental health programs; and (4) provides information on mental health to the public and the scientific community. Two companion institutes—the National Institute on Alcohol Abuse and Alcoholism (NIAAA) and the National Institute on Drug Abuse (NIDA)—perform comparable functions in these more specialized fields.

Although the federal government provides leadership and financial aid, the states and local organizations actually plan and run most NIMH programs. Most state and local governments, however, have not been able to fund programs and facilities because of cuts in federal support. As a result, many programs devoted to mental health training, research, and services have been greatly reduced or abandoned even as the need for them has increased. There is considerable uncertainty about the extent to which mental health problems will be included in forthcoming revisions of national health care policy and about the forms any such inclusion might take.

PROFESSIONAL ORGANIZATIONS AND MENTAL HEALTH A number of national professional organizations exist in the mental health field. These include the American Psychological Association (APA), the American Psychological Society (APS), the American Psychiatric Association (APA), the American Medical Association (AMA), the Association for the Advancement of Behavior Therapy (AABT), the American Association for Correctional and Forensic Psychology (AACFP), and the National Association for Social Work (NASW).

A key function of professional organizations is the application of insights and methods to contemporary social problems—for example, in lobbying national and local government agencies to provide more services for underserved populations. Professional mental health organizations are in a unique position to serve as consultants on mental health problems and programs.

Another important function of these organizations is to set and maintain high professional and ethical standards within their specific areas. This function may include (1) establishing and reviewing training qualifications for professional and paraprofessional personnel; (2) setting standards and procedures for the accreditation of undergraduate and graduate training programs; (3) setting standards for the accreditation of clinics, hospitals, or other service operations and carrying out inspections to see that the standards are followed; and (4) investigating reported cases of unethical or unprofessional conduct and taking disciplinary action when necessary.

THE ROLE OF VOLUNTEER ORGANIZATIONS AND AGENCIES Although professional mental health personnel and organizations can give expert technical advice with regard to mental health needs and programs, informed citizens are essential in planning and implementing these programs. In fact, it is primarily concerned nonprofessionals who have blazed the trails in the mental health field.

Prominent among the many volunteer mental health agencies is the National Mental Health Association (NMHA). This organization was founded in 1909 by Clifford Beers as the National Association for Mental Health and has subsequently expanded through various mergers. The NMHA works for the improvement of services in community clinics and mental hospitals; it helps recruit, train, and place volunteers for service in treatment and aftercare programs; and it works for enlightened mental health legislation and for the provision of needed facilities and personnel. It also offers special educational programs aimed at fostering positive mental health and helping people understand mental disorders. In addition, the National Mental Health Association has been actively involved in many court decisions affecting patient rights (1997).

In several cases, the organization has sponsored litigation or served as *amicus curiae* (friend of the court) in efforts to establish the rights of mental patients to treatment, to freedom from custodial confinement, to freedom to live in the community, and to protection of their confidentiality.

The ARC the largest national community-based organization advocating for people with intellectual and developmental disabilities, works to reduce the incidence of mental retardation, to seek community and residential treatment centers and services for people with mental retardation, and to carry on a program of education aimed at better public understanding of mental retardation and greater support for legislation. The ARC also fosters scientific research into mental retardation, recruitment and training of volunteer workers, and programs of community action.

These and other volunteer health organizations such as Alcoholics Anonymous and the National Alliance for the Mentally Ill (NAMI) need the backing of a wide constituency of knowledgeable and involved citizens in order to succeed.

MENTAL HEALTH RESOURCES IN PRIVATE INDUSTRY Personal problems—such as marital distress or other family problems, alcohol or drug abuse, financial difficulties, and job-related stress—can adversely affect employee morale and performance. Sheid (2010) pointed out that employees' disagreement with organizational priorities can also lead to employee burnout, emotional exhaustion, and depersonalization, which can contribute to adjustment problems that require mental health services. Moreover, violence in the workplace has grown to be a common occurrence in our society (Kelloway et al., 2006) and often requires that employers take special steps to limit mental-health-related aggression.

Psychological difficulties among employees may result in numerous problems such as absenteeism, accident proneness, poor productivity, and high job turnover. The National Institute for Occupational Safety and Health (NIOSH) recognizes psychological disorders as one of the 10 leading work-related health problems, and work-related mental health risk factors may be increasing with changes in the economy, in technology, and in demographic factors in the workforce (Sauter et al., 1990). Research has shown, however, that persons with severe mental health problems can be integrated into the workplace if a supportive employment model is used to assist their involvement (Bond et al., 2007). Since the passage of the Americans with Disabilities Act, people with psychiatric problems cannot be discriminated against in the workplace. Employers are encouraged to alter the workplace as needed to accommodate the needs of persons with mental illness. Although employers often object that it is too costly to hire psychiatrically impaired persons, great benefits for society can result from integrating into productive jobs people who have disabilities but who also have appropriate skills (Kramer, 1998).

A great deal more research is needed to identify specific mental health risk factors in work situations. We already know (e.g., Rosenstock et al., 2005) that serious, unrecognized problems may exist in the many areas of job design and conditions of work:

- **Workload and Pace.** The critical factor here appears to be the degree of control the worker has over the pace of work rather than output demand. Machine-paced assembly work may be particularly hazardous to mental health.
- **Work Schedule.** Rotating shifts and night work have been associated with elevated risk for psychological difficulties.
- **Role Stressors.** Role ambiguity (such as uncertainty about who has responsibility for what), said to be common in many work situations, has a negative impact on mental and physical health, as does role conflict (incompatible role demands).
- **Career Security Factors.** Feelings of insecurity related to issues such as job future or obsolescence, career development, and encouragement of early retirement adversely affect mental and physical health.
- **Interpersonal Relations.** Poor or unsupportive relationships among work colleagues significantly increase the risk of untoward psychological reactions.
- **Job Content.** Poor mental health has been associated with work assignments involving fragmented, narrow, unvarying tasks that allow for little creativity and give the worker little sense of having contributed to the ultimate product.

Many corporations have long recognized the importance of worker mental health and of enhancing mental health–promoting factors in the workplace, yet only recently have many of them acted on this knowledge. Today many companies have expanded their "obligations" to employees to include numerous psychological services. Employee assistance programs (EAPs) are means through which larger corporations can actively provide mental health services to employees and their family members (Finkel & Ryan, 2007; Harlow, 2007).

International Efforts for Mental Health

Mental health is a major issue not only in the United States but also in the rest of the world. Indeed, many of the problems in this country with regard to the treatment of mental disorders are greatly magnified in poorer countries and countries with repressive governments. The severity of the world mental health problem is reflected in the World Health Organization's estimate that mental disorders affect more than 200 million people worldwide, partly because of the significant world refugee crisis (de Jong, 2002; Watters & Ingleby, 2004). Recognition of this great problem served to bring about the formation of several international organizations at the end of World War II. Here we will briefly discuss the World Health Organization (WHO) (2010) and the World Federation for Mental Health (WFMH).

THE WORLD HEALTH ORGANIZATION The World Health Organization (2001) has always been keenly aware of the close interrelationships among biological, psychosocial, and sociocultural factors. Examples include the influence of rapid change and social disruption on both physical and mental health; the impossibility of major progress toward mental health in societies where a large proportion of the population suffers from malnutrition, parasites, and disease; and the frequent psychological and cultural barriers to successful programs in family planning and public health (Rutz, 2001).

Formed after World War II as part of the United Nations system, WHO's earliest focus was on physical diseases; it has helped make dramatic progress toward the conquest of such ancient scourges as smallpox and malaria. Over the years, mental health, too, has become an increasing concern among the member countries. WHO's goals are to integrate mental health resources to deal with the broad problems of overall health and socioeconomic development that many member countries face (World Health Organization, 2010).

Another important contribution of WHO has been its International Classification of Diseases (ICD), which enables clinicians and researchers in different countries to use a uniform set of diagnostic categories. The American Psychiatric Association's *DSM-IV* classification has been coordinated with the WHO's ICD-10 classification (Sartorius et al., 1993). Currently both *DSM-IV* and ICD-10 are undergoing revision.

THE WORLD FEDERATION FOR MENTAL HEALTH The World Federation for Mental Health was established in 1948 as an international congress of nongovernmental organizations and individuals concerned with mental health. Its purpose is to promote international cooperation among governmental and nongovernmental mental health agencies, and its membership now extends to more than 50 countries (Brody, 2004). The federation has been granted consultative status by WHO, and it assists the UN agencies by collecting information on mental health conditions all over the world (World Health Organization, 2007).

The last century witnessed an amazing openness and a lowering of previously impassable barriers between nations. Along with this increased interchange of ideas and cooperation, we expect to see a broader mental health collaboration. It is vital that greater international cooperation in the sciences and in health planning continue, along with more sharing of information and views on mental health.

In Review

- What is the role of the National Institute of Mental Health in providing care for the mentally ill?
- What is the NMHA, and how does it contribute to improvement in mental health services?
- What have been the major contributions of WHO in improving services in mental health?

Challenges for the Future

Even though international cooperation in efforts to understand and enhance mental health is encouraging, the media confront us daily with the stark truth that we have a long way to go before our dreams of a better world are realized. Many people question whether the United States or any other technologically advanced nation can achieve improvements in mental health for the majority of its citizens in our time. Racism, poverty, youth violence, terrorism, the uprooting of developing world populations, and other social problems that contribute to mental disorder sometimes seem insurmountable.

Other events in the rest of the world affect us also, both directly and indirectly. Worldwide economic instability and shortages and the possibility of the destruction of our planet's life ecology breed widespread anxiety about the future. The vast resources we have spent on military programs over the past half century to protect against perceived threats have absorbed funds and energy that otherwise might have been devoted to meeting human and social needs here and elsewhere in the world. The limited resources we are now willing to allocate to mental health problems prevent our solving major problems resulting from drug and alcohol abuse, homelessness, broken families, and squalid living conditions.

The Need for Planning

The Institute of Medicine (2006) recently reported that sweeping quality improvements are needed in the U.S. mental health care system. The report noted that only 20 percent of people with substance abuse or dependency and only 40 percent of people with serious mental illness actually receive treatment for their problems. If mental health problems are going to be reduced or eliminated, it is imperative that more effective planning be done at community, national, and international levels. Many challenges must be met if we are to create a better world for ourselves and future generations. Without slackening our efforts to meet needs at home, we will probably find it essential to participate more broadly in international measures aimed at reducing group tensions and promoting mental health and a better world for people everywhere. At the same time, we can expect that the measures we undertake to reduce international conflict and improve the general condition of humankind will make a significant contribution to our own nation's social progress and mental health. Both kinds of measures will require understanding and moral commitment from concerned citizens.

Within our own country and the rest of the industrialized world, progress in prolonging life has brought with it burgeoning problems in the prevalence of disorders associated with advanced age, particularly in the area of conditions such as Alzheimer's disease. Judging by the numbers of people already affected, it is not certain at this time that we will find the means of eradicating or arresting this threat before it has overwhelmed us. Planning and preparation would seem our only rational hope of forestalling a potential disaster of unprecedented magnitude; we need to make a beginning.

The Individual's Contribution

History provides clear examples of individuals whose efforts were instrumental in changing the way we think about mental health problems. Recall that Pinel took off the chains, Dorothea Dix initiated a movement to improve the conditions of asylums, and Clifford Beers inspired the modern mental health movement with his autobiographical account of his own experience with mental illness. Who will lead the next revolution in mental health is anyone's guess. What is clear is that a great deal can be accomplished by individual effort.

When students become aware of the tremendous scope of the mental health problem both nationally and internationally and of the woefully inadequate facilities for coping with it, they often ask, "What can I do?" Thus it seems appropriate to suggest a few of the lines of action that interested students can take.

Many opportunities in mental health work are open to trained personnel, both professional and paraprofessional. Social work, clinical psychology, psychiatry, and other mental health occupations are personally fulfilling. In addition, many occupations, ranging from law enforcement to teaching and the ministry, can and do play key roles in the mental health and well-being of many people. Training in all these fields usually offers individuals opportunities to work in community clinics and related facilities, to gain experience in understanding the needs and problems of people in distress, and to become familiar with community resources.

Citizens can find many ways to be of direct service if they are familiar with national and international resources and programs and if they invest the effort necessary to learn about their community's special needs and problems. Whatever their roles in life—student, teacher, police officer, lawyer, homemaker, business executive, or trade unionist—their interests are directly at stake, for although the mental health of a nation may be manifested in many ways—in its purposes, courage, moral responsibility, scientific and cultural achievements, and quality of daily life—its health and resources derive ultimately from the individuals within it. In a participatory democracy, it is they who plan and implement the nation's goals.

Besides accepting some measure of responsibility for the mental health of others through the quality of one's own interpersonal relationships, there are several other constructive courses of action open to each citizen. These include (1) serving as a volunteer in a mental hospital, community mental health center, or service organization; (2) supporting realistic measures for ensuring comprehensive health services for all age groups; and (3) working toward improved public education, responsible government, the alleviation of prejudice, and the establishment of a more sane and harmonious world.

All of us are concerned with mental health for personal as well as altruistic reasons, for we want to overcome the nagging problems of contemporary living and find our share of happiness in a meaningful and fulfilling life. To do so, we may sometimes need the courage to admit that our problems are too much for us. When existence seems futile or the going becomes too difficult, it may help to remind ourselves of the following basic facts, which have been emphasized throughout this text: From time to time, each of us has serious difficulties in coping with the problems of living. During such crises, we may need psychological and related assistance. Such difficulties are not a disgrace; they can happen to anyone if the stress is severe enough. The early detection and treatment of maladaptive behavior are of great importance in preventing the development of more severe or chronic conditions. Preventive measures—universal, selected, and indicated—are the most effective long-range approach to the solution of both individual and group mental health problems.

In Review

- What are national and international programs aimed at providing solutions to mental health problems?
- Describe several ways in which individuals can contribute to the advancement of mental health.
- After reading the Unresolved Issues feature, discuss the controversy over the effects of managed health care on the treatment and prevention of mental illness.

Unresolved Issues

▶ *The HMOs and Mental Health Care*

A **health maintenance organization (HMO)** is a business or management corporation that provides a form of health care coverage in the United States that is fulfilled through contracts with hospitals, doctors, and other health providers. Unlike traditional health insurance, the health care is made available through agreements with health professionals to treat more patients and in return usually to provide services at a discount. This business arrangement allows the HMO to charge a lower monthly premium, which is an advantage over indemnity insurance, provided that its members are willing to abide by the additional restrictions (Frank et al., 2004). The HMO serves as a "gatekeeper" between the patient and the health provider. This arrangement has clearly affected access to mental health care in the United States in that business decisions often take precedence over treatment need. Treatment, when it is allowed by the HMO, tends to be limited in both duration and quality. The disillusionment with HMOs in the 1990s led to the development of alternative health funding or **managed health care** products. Several programs emerged that were less restrictive, giving patients more options in treatment choices. However, this has done little to reduce the anger toward managed care, and there is still a need for an alternative approach to providing more effective health care (Kominski & Melnick, 2007).

Mental health treatment is valuable for preventing as well as easing mental disorders. Yet mental health treatment has been less readily available than physical health treatment, and its cost has been less often reimbursed. HMO programs establish a treatment staff through systems of professionals, referred to as "panels," who are considered to have efficacy and efficiency in providing a wide range of services. Some HMOs—referred to as "open-panel systems"—have allowed patients some choice of health providers and allow any qualified professional in the community to participate. However, most are closed-panel systems, which limit the selection of available providers. The benefits vary from plan to plan and usually include limits on the problems covered or on the maximum amount of care provided or services available. To keep costs low, some HMOs have operated according to a system of "capitation," a method of payment in which a health care provider contracts to deliver all the health care services required by a population for a fixed cost or flat fee per enrolled member or employee (Sanchez & Turner, 2003). The HMO thus assumes some risk, but capitation allows for great profit if the subscriber's fees can be set higher than the cost of health services.

The need for comprehensive and effective mental health treatment is great. About one in four adults, or about 26.2 percent of Americans ages 18 and older, suffer from a diagnosable mental disorder in a given year (Kessler, Chiu et al., 2005). It has also been estimated that 70 percent of adults and 80 percent of children who require mental health services do not receive treatment, primarily because of discriminatory insurance practices (Sussman, 2009). Many people with mental health problems seek medical treatment for their psychological symptoms, thereby increasing the cost of medical care. In one study, Hunkeler and colleagues (2003) point out a strong association between psychiatric symptoms, impaired functioning, and general medical care costs. About 75 percent of patients with depression seek treatment for physical symptoms (Unutzer et al., 2006). Moreover, patients with other psychiatric conditions such as PTSD also present with physical symptoms. Health care costs in general are reportedly rising, and the presence of any psychiatric diagnosis increases the health care cost.

In response to these mental health needs, health care administrators have created a diverse array of programs in an attempt to provide services at a cost that the system can afford.

MENTAL HEALTH TREATMENT—WHO DECIDES WHAT KIND AND HOW LONG?

In one common approach to reducing health care costs, the managed care agency negotiates a reduced price directly with the health service provider. The provider then bills the health service organization for the time spent, and the HMO can obtain "low-bid" services from the health professional. This approach poses little financial risk to the provider. As might be apparent even to the casual observer of managed care systems, the procedures for determining the amount of money paid to providers have frequently been a problem for mental health professionals—psychologists and psychiatrists (Resnick et al., 1994). The HMO representative or "gatekeeper" to reimbursement, often a medical generalist untrained in either psychiatric disorders or psychosocial interventions, controls access to therapy and sometimes the type of treatment to be provided (Resnick et al., 1994). In some systems of managed care, the gatekeeper might be a business professional who, in the view of the health service provider, is determining treatment by requiring that the clinician periodically justify treatment decisions to someone who has little or no background in mental health. Conflicts can develop in such situations, and patients may be deprived of appropriate and necessary care (Resnick et al., 1994). HMOs that are overly cost conscious have come to be viewed by some practitioners as simply tending to business and neglecting patients' needs (Karon, 1995).

TIME-LIMITED THERAPY

The mental health services typically covered by HMOs have favored less expensive and less labor-intensive approaches. As might be expected, pharmacotherapy is the most frequent mental health treatment provided by HMOs (Frank et al., 2005)—a situation that some research suggests actually reduces health care costs. Other research has shown that cost-containment measures that are intended to reduce drug costs by restricting access to medications can—and often do—wind up increasing total health care costs (Horn, 2003). Further, psychosocial interventions such as individual psychotherapy are discouraged or limited to relatively few sessions. Long-term psychotherapy has been substantially reduced for all but a small number of wealthy private clients (Lazarus, 1996). On the other hand, group psychotherapy is often promoted and encouraged because it is often thought of as cost effective. Many managed care corporations have adopted the model of providing focused, brief, intermittent mental health treatment for most problems. Many forms of behavioral health services such as counseling programs to teach patients how to manage their illness, how to use relaxation response methods, or how to reduce unhealthy behaviors such as smoking or drinking have been implemented to improve health care while reducing costs (Blount et al., 2007).

Patients who require longer treatments or need inpatient hospitalization are typically not well served in managed care organizations. In fact, long-term mental health treatment is usually discouraged by managed health care organizations. For example, most managed care groups approve only short inpatient stays (less than 10 days) and four to six sessions of outpatient mental health treatment at a time. Few if any of the decisions regarding the amount and type of services provided are directly guided by empirical criteria. Decisions whether to cover 8 or 20 sessions of psychotherapy, for example, are arbitrary and often seem capricious to both practitioner and patient (Harwood et al., 1997).

A clear divide has developed between health service providers and managers. Available services are often governed more by financial concerns than by a mental health professional's judgment. Critics of managed care argue that there is no convincing evidence that current efforts are actually controlling costs (Harwood et al., 1997) and that there is no scientific support for the limited-benefit options being exercised. Some researchers have pointed out that the administrative costs for managed care centers (including high salaries for HMO executives) are exorbitant. Gabbard (1994), for example, estimated that about one-fourth of the health care expenditures in the United States go for managed care administration.

The general lack of mental health care support has clearly created controversy in the field of psychotherapy, and the mental health field is being altered by economic considerations. Sanchez and Turner (2003) provide an overview of the impact of managed care on psychological practice and the provision of mental health services to clients in need. They point out that the economics of the mental health care system have greatly impacted the practice of behavioral health care by limiting treatment to time-limited and symptom-focused services. The most frequently cited problems include the remarkable shift of treatment decision-making power from the behavioral health care provider to policymakers. In addition, practitioners have experienced a reduction in income, which has likely impacted quality of care because less-well-trained (non-doctoral-level) therapists have taken on more responsibility and offer short-term therapeutic approaches instead of needed long-term therapy. The nature of the mental health professions is changing, and there is a growing discontent with health maintenance organizations in society today (Mechanic, 2004). Both clients and mental health professionals have long experienced a breakdown in trust of the managed care system (Shore, 2007).

Although discrimination against mental health care compared with medical or surgical treatment has long affected the provision of mental health treatment in the United States, recent attempts to provide parity for mental health care might bring about some much needed changes. A new law, referred to as the Mental Health Parity Act (MHPA) of 2008, or the *Paul Wellstone, Pete Domenici Parity Act Prohibits Discrimination*, requires that the annual or lifetime dollar caps on mental health benefits be no lower than the dollar limits for medical and surgical benefits (Sussman, 2009). The parity act prohibits group health insurance plans, typically provided by employers, from restricting access to care by limiting benefits and requiring higher patient costs than those that apply to general medical or surgical benefits.

It is difficult at this point to venture as to what the impact the new health care plan and the parity bill will have on improving the quality and availability of mental health care in the United States. Any solutions to the long-standing problems are likely to be complex and require substantial change to the present system.

Summary

- Many mental health professionals are trying not only to cure mental health problems but also to prevent them, or at least to reduce their effects.

- Prevention can be viewed as focusing on three levels: (1) universal interventions, which attempt to reduce the long-term consequences of having had a disorder; (2) selective interventions, which are aimed at reducing the possibility of disorder and fostering positive mental health efforts in subpopulations that are considered at special risk; and (3) indicated interventions, which attempt to reduce the impact or duration of a problem that has already occurred.

- With the advent of many new psychotropic medications and changing treatment philosophies, there has been a major effort to discharge psychiatric patients into the community.

- There has been a great deal of controversy over deinstitutionalization and the failure to provide prompt and adequate follow-up of these patients in the community as soon as possible.

- Being mentally ill is not considered sufficient grounds for involuntary commitment. There must be, in addition, evidence that the individual either is dangerous to himself or herself or represents a danger to society.

- It is not an easy matter, even for trained professionals, to determine in advance whether a person is dangerous and likely to harm others. Nevertheless, professionals must sometimes make such judgments.

- Recent court rulings have found professionals liable when patients they were treating caused harm to others. The Tarasoff decision held that a therapist has a duty to protect potential victims if her or his patient has threatened to kill them.

- The insanity plea for capital crimes is an important issue in forensic psychology. Many mental health and legal professionals, journalists, and laypersons have questioned the present use of the not guilty by reason of insanity (NGRI) defense.

- The original legal precedent, the M'Naghten rule, held that at the time of committing the act the accused must have been laboring under such a defect of reason as not to know the nature and quality of the act or not to know that what he or she was doing was wrong.

- More recent broadenings of the insanity plea, as in the American Law Institute standard, leave open the possibility of valid NGRI pleas by persons who are not diagnosed to be psychotic.

- The successful use of the NGRI defense by John Hinckley, attempted assassin of President Reagan, set off a storm of protest. One effective and widely adopted reform was to shift the burden of proof (of insanity) to the defense.

- Federal agencies such as the National Institute of Mental Health (NIMH), the National Institute on Drug Abuse (NIDA), and the National Institute on Alcohol Abuse and Alcoholism (NIAAA) are devoted to promoting research, training, and services to the mental health community.

- Several professional and mental health organizations, many corporations, and a number of volunteer associations are also active in programs to promote mental health.

- International organizations such as the World Health Organization (WHO) and the World Federation for Mental Health have contributed to mental health programs worldwide.

Key Terms

civil commitment
competent to stand trial
deinstitutionalization
forensic psychology (forensic psychiatry)
guilty but mentally ill (GBMI)

health maintenance organization (HMO)
indicated interventions
insanity defense
managed health care
milieu therapy

NGRI plea
residential treatment
selective interventions
social-learning programs
Tarasoff decision
universal interventions

Glossary

Many of the key terms listed in the glossary appear in boldface when first introduced in the text discussion. A number of other terms commonly encountered in this or other psychology texts are also included; you are encouraged to make use of this glossary both as a general reference tool and as a study aid for the course in abnormal psychology.

Civil commitment. Procedure whereby a person certified as mentally disordered can be hospitalized, either voluntarily or against his or her will.

Competent to stand trial. The determination that a person that is charged with a crime has the mental health capability to participate in the proceedings.

Deinstitutionalization. Movement to close mental hospitals and treat people with severe mental disorder in the community.

Forensic psychology and psychiatry. Branches of psychology and psychiatry dealing with legal problems related to mental disorders and the legal rights and protection of mental patients and members of society at large.

Guilty but mentally ill (GBMI). Plea and possible verdict that would provide an alternative to pleading not guilty by reason of insanity (NGRI) and would allow for placing a defendant in a treatment facility rather than in a prison.

Health maintenance organization (HMO). Health plan that provides services to employers and individuals for a fixed, prepaid fee.

Indicated intervention. Early detection and prompt treatment of maladaptive behavior in a person's family and community setting.

Insanity defense (NGRI). The not guilty by reason of insanity plea used as a legal defense in criminal trials.

Managed health care. System of corporations that secures services from hospitals, physicians, and other providers for treating a designated population, with the goal of holding down health care cost.

Milieu therapy. General approach to treatment for hospitalized patients that focuses on making the hospital environment itself a therapeutic community.

NGRI plea. The not guilty by reason of insanity plea, or NGRI, is a legal defense a defendant might use to claim that he or she was not guilty of a crime because of insanity.

Residential treatment. Out-of-home placements for children and adolescents with mental health problems.

Selective intervention. Mobilization of prevention resources to eliminate or reduce a particular type of problem (such as teenage pregnancy or alcohol or drug abuse).

Social-learning programs. Behavioral programs using learning techniques, especially token economies, to help patients assume more responsibility for their own behavior.

Tarasoff decision. Ruling by a California court (1974) that a therapist has a duty to warn a prospective victim of an explicit threat expressed by a client in therapy.

Universal intervention. The tasks of altering conditions that cause or contribute to mental disorders (risk factors) and establishing conditions that foster positive mental health (protective factors).

Photo Credits

Credits are listed in order of appearance.

Text Credits

Credits are listed in order of appearance.

Index

711